West A

THE ROUGH GUIDE

There are more than two hundred Rough Guide titles
covering destinations from Alaska to Zimbabwe and subjects from
Acoustic Guitar to Travel Health

Forthcoming travel guides include

Dordogne & the Lot • Menorca • Tenerife • Vancouver • Malta & Gozo

Forthcoming reference guides include

100 Essential Latin CDs • Videogaming • Personal Computers
Pregnancy & Birth • Trumpet & Trombone

Rough Guides online
www.roughguides.com

ROUGH GUIDE CREDITS

Text editors: Claire Saunders, Amanda Tomlin and James McConnachie
Series editor: Mark Ellingham
Editorial: Martin Dunford, Jonathan Buckley, Jo Mead, Kate Berens, Ann-Marie Shaw, Paul Gray, Helena Smith, Judith Bamber, Kieran Falconer, Orla Duane, Olivia Eccleshall, Ruth Blackmore, Sophie Martin, Geoff Howard, Gavin Thomas, Alexander Mark Rogers, Polly Thomas, Joe Staines, Lisa Nellis, Andrew Tomičić (UK); Andrew Rosenberg, Mary Beth Maioli (US)
Production: Susanne Hillen, Andy Hilliard, Link Hall, Helen Ostick, Julia Bovis, Michelle Draycott, Anna Wray, Katie Pringle, Robert Evers

Cartography: Melissa Baker, Maxine Repath, Nichola Goodliffe, Ed Wright
Picture research: Louise Boulton
Online editors: Alan Spicer, Kate Hands (UK); Kelly Cross (US)
Finance: John Fisher, Gary Singh, Ed Downey
Marketing & Publicity: Richard Trillo, Niki Smith, David Wearn, Jemima Broadbridge (UK); Jean-Marie Kelly, Myra Campolo, Simon Carloss (US)
Administration: Tania Hummel, Charlotte Marriott, Demelza Dallow

PUBLISHING INFORMATION

This third edition published November 1999 by Rough Guides Ltd, 62–70 Shorts Gardens, London, WC2H 9AH. Reprinted July 2001. Previous editions published 1990, 1995.
Distributed by the Penguin Group:
Penguin Books Ltd, 27 Wrights Lane, London W8 5TZ
Penguin Putnam Inc. 375 Hudson Street, New York 10014, USA
Penguin Books Australia Ltd, 487 Maroondah Highway, PO Box 257, Ringwood, Victoria 3134, Australia
Penguin Books Canada Ltd, 10 Alcorn Avenue, Toronto, Ontario, Canada M4V 1E4
Penguin Books (NZ) Ltd, 182–190 Wairau Road, Auckland 10, New Zealand
Typeset in Linotron Univers and Century Old Style to an original design by Andrew Oliver.
Printed in England by Clays Ltd, St Ives PLC.
Illustrations in Part One and Part Three by Edward Briant.

Illustrations for Basics, Contexts and the country title pages are by Henry Iles; incidental illustrations in "Basics" and "Contexts" by Edward Briant.
© Jim Hudgens and Richard Trillo 1999
No part of this book may be reproduced in any form without permission from the publisher except for the quotation of brief passages in reviews.
1232p – Includes index
A catalogue record for this book is available from the British Library
ISBN 1-85828-468-6

The publishers and authors have done their best to ensure the accuracy and currency of all the information in *The Rough Guide to West Africa*, however, they can accept no responsibility for any loss, injury, or inconvenience sustained by any traveller as a result of information or advice contained in the guide.

AUTHORS' ACKNOWLEDGEMENTS

The authors jointly want to thank: all our contributors who travelled in West Africa and delivered the goods magnificently; James McConnachie for editing assistance; Lone Mouritsen for stepping into the breach to update Basics; Paul Whitfield for extra Basics research; Stratigraphics and Maxine Repath's ever-unfazed team for cartography; Anna Wray for typesetting; Russell Walton for proofreading; Louise Boulton and Catherine Marshall for picture research; Helena Smith for a fine new index; and most of all our wonderful editors Mandy Tomlin, who got the project off the ground, and Claire Saunders, who piloted it with great skill and humour for many months and made a perfect landing.

Richard: Ron Hughes and staff at Cape Verde Travel; Chris Frean; Christian Hyde and Dominique Hyde; Peter Moszynski; Emma Gregg for unexpected filming duties; Teresa, David and Phoebe for putting up with my absence even though I was at home; and especially Alex Trillo, for coming to Cape Verde with me on his first research trip, getting to the top of Mount Fogo at the daunting pace set by our guide, and accompanying me on the roughest sea crossing either of us ever wants to experience.

Jim: In gratitude and love to Arba and Sallee for their support and encouragement and to Lindsey, Carie, Ryan, Marisa, Brittany, Katie, William and Gregory.

West Africa

THE ROUGH GUIDE

written and researched by

Jim Hudgens and Richard Trillo

This edition was researched and updated by

Jack Barker, Anne Barrett, Paolo Cortini, Emma Gregg, Morten
Hagen, Lone Mouritsen, Greg Pilley, Judith Ravin, Noo Saro-Wiwa
and Jennifer Scott

THE ROUGH GUIDES

THE ROUGH GUIDES

TRAVEL GUIDES • PHRASEBOOKS • MUSIC AND REFERENCE GUIDES

 We set out to do something different when the first Rough Guide was published in 1982. Mark Ellingham, just out of university, was traveling in Greece. He brought along the popular guides of the day, but found they were all lacking in some way. They were either strong on ruins and museums but went on for pages without mentioning a beach or taverna. Or they were so conscious of the need to save money that they lost sight of Greece's cultural and historical significance. Also, none of the books told him anything about Greece's contemporary life – its politics, its culture, its people, and how they lived.

So with no job in prospect, Mark decided to write his own guidebook, one which aimed to provide practical information that was second to none, detailing the best beaches and the hottest clubs and restaurants, while also giving hard-hitting accounts of every sight, both famous and obscure, and providing up-to-the-minute information on contemporary culture. It was a guide that encouraged independent travelers to find the best of Greece, and was a great success, getting shortlisted for the Thomas Cook travel guide award, and encouraging Mark, along with three friends, to expand the series.

The Rough Guide list grew rapidly and the letters flooded in, indicating a much broader readership than had been anticipated, but one which uniformly appreciated the Rough Guide mix of practical detail and humor, irreverence and enthusiasm. Things haven't changed. The same four friends who began the series are still the caretakers of the Rough Guide mission today: to provide the most reliable, up-to-date and entertaining information to independent-minded travelers of all ages, on all budgets.

We now publish more than 150 titles and have offices in London and New York. The travel guides are written and researched by a dedicated team of more than 100 authors, based in Britain, Europe, the USA and Australia. We have also created a unique series of phrasebooks to accompany the travel series, along with an acclaimed series of music guides, and a best-selling pocket guide to the Internet and World Wide Web. We also publish comprehensive travel information on our web site:

www.roughguides.com

THE AUTHORS

Richard Trillo was conceived in Canada in 1956 and born in England. He spent most of his youth dreaming about travelling and plotting his big escape. There were several attempts, and then a hitchhiking trip to Timbuktu with a friend and $100 cash between them. They had to be helped home. Since then he has travelled extensively in Africa, writing and co-writing the Rough Guides to Kenya and West Africa along the way. He is Rough Guides' director of marketing, publicity and rights, and is married, with three children.

Born in Oakland, California, **Jim Hudgens** received B.A. degrees from UC Berkeley in Political Economics and German before moving between Paris, France and Lomé, Togo, where he worked as a freelance editor, writer and translator. In 1992, he received an M.A. degree in African Area Studies with a concentration in Film and Television from UCLA. He currently works as an editor at UCLA Academic Publications.

HELP US UPDATE

We've done our best to make sure that this third edition of *The Rough Guide to West Africa* is as useful, accurate and up-to-the-minute as possible, credit for which is due in large part to the fantastic response to our request in the last edition to keep us posted as you travel. Events move fast in West Africa and we can only keep it all current in future editions by hearing from readers. We are conscious of the fact that, while we have had some African contributors, the book has been largely put together on the basis of the research and opinions of white travellers, and we are therefore particularly keen to have feedback from black readers.

If we've got it wrong, or you feel there are places we've overrated or under-praised, or find we've missed something good or covered something which has gone, then please write and tell us. Letters about obscure routes off the beaten track are as welcome as a postcard about your favourite club or hotel, and we are always trying to

improve our maps. It is always a great help if information about different countries comes on different pages.

Since the first edition was published we have established more or less permanent correspondents in several countries. We would welcome hearing from anyone – either nationals or expatriates – who would like to pass on their knowledge and experience. Please write a letter updating and commenting upon the book. Please mark the letters West Africa Ed 3 Update and send to: Rough Guides, 62–70 Shorts Gardens, London WC2H 9AH or Rough Guides, 375 Hudson St, 4th Floor, New York, NY 10014 Alternatively, you can send email to mail@roughguides.co.uk To read our latest online updates visit Rough Guides' Web site at *www.roughguides.com*

We will acknowledge all information used in the next edition and will send a free of this or any other Rough Guide for the best (and most legible!) letters.

ACKNOWLEDGEMENTS TO READERS AND CONTRIBUTORS

Anne Barrett thanks Ann Slind & Mr Sidibeh, Shawna O'Hearn, Kebba Nasso & others at the National Environment Agency, Yusupha Jawara, Rowan Stewart, Liz Hughes, Kath & Sol Adetunji, Ian Whinnet, Manuel Huertas, Louie Rosencrens, Henriette Brummer, Eogman O'Suilleabháin, Clare Levi, Lynne Benson & VSO The Gambia, Ruth Hunter (VSO London), Adama Bah (Gambia Tourism Concern), Jimmy Reid, Lesley & Andrew Dornan, Tricia Wall, Nula Mahon, Paul Doyle, Stephen Humphries, Anne-Marie McCarthy & Wissam Wazni, Idris Bengeloune (St-Louis Tourist Office), Ibrahima Sagna (*Asta Kebe* – Tambacounda), Momadou Bâ (*Chez Diao* – Kedougou), Khady in Mbour, Patrick Sothern (West African Tours in The Gambia), James English & Lawrence Williams (Makasutu Culture Forest in The Gambia), Derek Smith, Esther Beattie, Claire Messenger, Linda Swain, Carla de Jesus, Tone Nystrom, Bryan Savage, Nelvina Barreto-Gomes and David Makepeace.

Paolo Cortini thanks Koffi Afagnibo, Yao Yao Hounjago, Sophie, Emmanuelle, Lisa, Brooke and Severine.

Emma Gregg would like to thank in London: Richard, for everything, and Piers, for everything else; in Paris: Koumba Traoré at Espace Mali; in

Bamako: Ibrahim and Hamma Barry for helping out, Andrew Innerari for spoiling me, and Momo; in Ségou: Modibou Ballo, Aguibou at Balanzan and Ziad at *L'Auberge* for his generosity; in Mopti: Anja & Belco Ba at Ashraf Voyages; in Bandiagara: Aly Tembely for a staggering motorbike trek and a memorable *trente-et-un*, Momodou for the concert, Daniela Curioso, and Mamadou Traoré; in Sikasso: Maggie Chartier for her video skills, Issa Cissé at Galerie Kéné Arts, and Sarah, Kathy, Stephanie, John and the other PCVs for all their help and hospitality; in Kita: Baye Diabaté the *maître batteur*, Abdoulaye Diabaté the kora player, Ibrahim Diakité of PLAN International, Fousseni & Lassi Diara the twins and assistant *djembé*-makers, Bimba Amara Diabaté (Tos), all the actors and musicians of *Sabougnouman*, the staff at *Le Relais*, and, of course, Funky the silversmith.

Morten Hagen thanks Bayo, Tomi, Ayomide and Bayo jr (the Adekanye family) for their hospitality.

Jim Hudgens thanks Apou Gata Djima, Lisa Washington, Babacar So, Matthew Christensen, Kairn Kleiman, "Buster" Boahen, Vijitha and Ndede Eyango, Duke Agunente, Tony Adedze, Anthony Mainer, Dr Teshome H. Gabriel, Jolia Brombead, Gotzon Zaratiegi, Doghe K. Mensah, Conerly Casey, Kendahl Radcliffe, Shirley Radcliffe, Bruce Bailey,

Luc and Fati Denesle, Luca and Sara Guiliani, Pauline Ava, Fay Sueltz, Belinda Sunnu, Wendy Belcher, Senen Garcia, Kimberly Kato and Terrell Patterson, Richard L. Adkins, Francis Behnke, Lawrence Mack, Eric Knox, Doug and Diana Pray, Tim and Lara Sexton, Christine Rasmussen, Lisa Kelley, Kone Nicolas and June Spector.

Lone Mouritsen and Greg Pilley thank Chris Freer (Guinness Cameroun SA), Sherry Hornung, Genevieve Faure (British Consulate), Daan Gerretsen and Judith Henderson (VSO), Maureen Roëll and Gilles Nicolet, Peace Corp Cameroon, Fiona (Boo) Maisels (Kilum Mountain Forest Project), Francis Esong, Abdou Allotey (Foumban Museum), WWW Yokadouma, and special thanks to James Acworth and Florence Akame.

Judith Ravin would like to thank Raymond Paré, whose linguistic skills were invaluable.

Noo Saro-Wiwa would like to thank Dominique Hyde, Claude Dunn and Deekontee for all the help they gave in Côte d'Ivoire.

Jennifer Scott would like to thank, in Ghana: Valery Sackey, Humphrey Quaye, Charles Duwor, Abigail Tagoe, Mr and Mrs Wiredu, Nick Ankudey, Kwame Sarpong, Inusah Mohammed, Akwesi Owusu and Akwesi Owusu Sekyere; in Burkina: Beatrice Bado, Eleonore Tapsoba, Hien Gervais, Pierette Bayala, Moussa Drame, Sore Daouda, Kabou Sansan Aboubacar and Jean Louis Richard.

Continuing thanks from both authors must go to the following people who helped shape the first and second editions: Kabba Camara, Teresa Driver, Paul Everett, Samba M Fye, Jonathan Graepne, Barry Hanson, Paul Hayward, Simon Heap, Henry Iles, Bill Jackson, Daniel Jacobs, David Lawrence, Monica Mackaness, Kevin Malone, Dave Muddyman, Manfred Prinz, Rexford Quaye, George Senger, Chris Scott, Chris Seward, Caroline Shaw, Hamidou Soumah, Jim Taylor, David Warne, Robert Walker, Paul Whitfield and Tony Zurbrugg.

READERS' LETTERS

All our thanks to the following **readers** whose letters and emails were, as ever, immensely useful in pointing us in the right direction this time around. Keep them coming!

Edward Acquah, Doug Adams, Abi Allanson, Axel Arft, Katy Aros, Alby Ball, Thomas Banks, Viviana Barnett, Michèle Beasley, Jerry van Beers, Ruud Bläcker, Dirk Bogaert, Lynette Bouchie, Norman Brett, Bill Brodie, Jessica Broome and class, Bacar Camara, Tony Chafer, Tomasz Cienkus, Abbie Challenger, Robert Clark, Peter Coles, Charlotte Cook, Graeme Counsel, Colleen Davenport-Adiyia, Lode Delbar, Sarah Dodds, Javier Gómez Duaso, Ben Edwards, Henry Epino, Robert Evans, Cathy Farnworth, Ferdinand Fellinger, JH Fieldëg, Amanda Galton, John Garratt, Tony & Elly van Gastel, Suzy Gillett, Valerie Godsalve, Sabine Graton, Amber Grove, Lisa Growcott, Simon Hancock, LP Hardy, Paul Hardy, Ruth Harvey, Bryn Haworth, Carole Hayward, Simon Heap, Zoe Hoida, Nicole C Holmes, Sherry Hornung, Christian Hyde, Tim Jacoby, Claire Jones, Stephen Jones, Brett and Helen Keillor, Fran King, André Kreft, Olivier Leenhardt, Simon Longshaw, Wendy Lubin, Kenneth Mack, NP Mann, Jeannine Marchand, Susan K Matheson, Boo Matthews, Beth Mellor, Andy McMullen, Monica Mackaness, Geerdt Magiels, Amy Marsh, Phil Michaels, Peter Moorhouse, LF Morgan, Pat Morgan, Charles Nilon, Craig Norman, Lucy Paterson, Harry Pearson, Anne Marie Pogorelc, Janet Preedy, Emile Benoit Quenum, Marc Reinhardt, Peter Riddelsdell, Clare Ridout, Michael Rogerson, Christof Romahn, Latif Sanyang, Johan Schepkens, Rachel Schneller, Mark Schulman, Benny Nalin Shah, Peter Shinnie, Ann Slind, David Stanley, James Tartaglia, Melissa Thackway, Peter Theuwissen, Lucette Thoma, Peter Ton, Tami Toroyan, Beate Uschkoreit, Richard Vergaelen, Diane Vickers, Keith Woodruff, Kate Wyche, Jacob Zoethout, Hendrijk Jan Zonnenveld.

CONTENTS

Introduction x

LIST OF MAPS

MAP SYMBOLS

▬▬▬▪	International boundary		◆	Point of interest
▬▬▬	Railway		🕌	Mosque
═══	Paved road (regional maps)		✈	Airport
▬▬▬	Unpaved road (regional maps)		🕴	Lighthouse
-----	Footpath		⛽	Petrol station
⌇⌇⌇	River		⚠	Campground
- - - -	Seasonal river		◉	Accommodation
— —	Ferry route		⊠	Post office
▪▪▪▪	Wall		⊞	Hospital
⌐⌐	Escarpment		⌑	Salt pan
⌂⌂	Mountains		◧	Sand dunes
▲	Peak		■	Building
⌇⌇	Rocks		⊞	Church
) (	Bridge		▦	Beach
⃫	Waterfall		▨	National Park
⌇	Marshland		▨	Park
⌕	Swamp		⊞	Cemetery

INTRODUCTION

The physical and cultural diversity of **West Africa** would be hard to exaggerate. This is perhaps the world's most complex region – seventeen countries, from the tiny Cape Verde Islands to giant Nigeria – with a total area and population comparable to that of the continental United States. And behind this mosaic of modern territories lies a different, more organic pattern – the West Africa of old nations built over centuries: the Yoruba city states and Hausa emirates of Nigeria; the Mossi kingdoms of Burkina Faso and Ghana; the Asante empire; the Wolof states of Senegal; the Muslim theocracy of Fouta Djalon in Guinea; the Bamiléké chiefdoms of Cameroon; the Mali empire, and many more. From this older perspective, the countries of today are imposters, fixed in place by the colonial powers of Britain, France, Germany and Portugal. Although the national borders are established and nationalism is a part of each country's social fabric, the richness and variety of West Africa only comes into focus with some understanding of its ancient past. One of the aims of this book is to bring that to the fore.

Some of the biggest pleasures of West Africa, however, are the small things. You'll encounter a degree of good humour, vitality and openness which can make the hard insularity of Western cultures seem absurd. Entering a shop or starting a conversation with a stranger without proper greetings and hand-shaking becomes inconceivable. If you stumble in the street, passers-by will tell you "sorry" or some similar expression of condolence for which no adequate translation exists in English. You're never ignored; you say hello a hundred times a day. This intimacy – a sense of barriers coming down – sharpens the most everyday events and eases the more mundane hardships. Travel, without a doubt, is rarely easy. Going by bus, shared taxi or pick-up van, you'll be crushed for hours, subjected to mysterious delays and endless halts at police road-blocks, jolted over potholes, and left in strange towns in the middle of the night. The sheer physicality never lets up. Comfort becomes something you seek, find, leave behind, and then long for again. Cold water, dry skin and clean clothes take on the status of unattainable luxuries.

But the material hardships provide a background against which experiences stand out with clarity. Africa's sensuousness is undeniable: the brilliance of red earth and emerald vegetation in the forest areas; the intricate smells of cooking, wood smoke and damp soil; towering cloud-scaped skies over the savannah at the start of the rains; villages of sun-baked mud houses, smoothed and moulded together like pottery; the singing rhythm of voices speaking tonal languages; the cool half-hour before dawn on the banks of the Niger when the soft clunk of cowbells rises on a haze of dust from the watering herds…

The physical picture

Physically, West Africa is predominantly flat or gently undulating. Although most countries have their **"highlands"**, these are generally rugged hills rather than mountain ranges. The most mountainous parts of the region are Guinea's Fouta Djalon and the highlands of Cameroon and eastern Nigeria (where Mount Cameroon peaks at a respectable 4000 metres and gets a little frost). The big river of West Africa is the **Niger**, which flows in a huge arc from the border of Sierra Leone, northeast through Guinea, into Mali and to the very fringes of the Sahara (where sand dunes rise on the bank behind snorting hippos) before turning south through Nigeria and into the Atlantic. The Niger is highly seasonal and river traffic depends on the annual rains.

As for the scenic environment, expectations of tropical forest are usually disappointed, at least to begin with. While the natural vegetation across the whole southern coastal belt is **rainforest** – with a gap in the Ghana–Togo area where grasslands come nearly to the coast – by far the commonest scene in the densely populated parts is of a desolate, bush-stripped landscape where dust and bare earth figure heavily. True rainforest, however, is still present in parts of Guinea, Sierra Leone, Liberia, Côte d'Ivoire, in southeast Nigeria and Cameroon. Guinea also features beautiful **savannah** lands, as does Burkina Faso. Along the coast, creeks and mangroves make many parts inaccessible. The best **beaches** are in Sierra Leone and Côte d'Ivoire, with Ghana, Senegal, The Gambia and Cameroon creditable runners-up. The currents tend to be strong, though, making many shorelines unsuitable for swimming – take care.

Where to go

If you have the time, by far the most satisfying way of visiting West Africa is **overland**, traversing the yawning expanse of the **Sahara**, arriving in the dry northern reaches of the Sahel – these days most likely in Mauritania – to the ravishing shock of an alien culture, and then adapting to a new landscape, a new climate and new ways of behaving.

Choosing **where to go** is no easy task: the region offers so much and Africa repeatedly confounds all expectations and assumptions. In the main section of the guide, the individual country introductions give an idea of what to look forward to. However, at the risk of reinforcing stereotypes, it's possible to make a few generalizations about the feel of the countries.

Of the eleven Francophone, **ex-French colonies**, the three nations most dominated by French culture and language are Cameroon, Senegal and Côte d'Ivoire; these can also be the more expensive countries to travel in, and their relatively Westernized cities are inclined to be hustly. **Senegal** is an obvious choice as a base from which to launch travels: facilities are much better than in many parts of the region and the verdant **Basse Casamance** district has a remarkable network of village-based accommodation (but see the boxed warning, p.xiv). **Côte d'Ivoire** provides a melange of the traditional and modern, African and French. **Cameroon** – which is English-speaking in the west – blends magnificent scenery and national parks with an extraordinary richness of culture, running the whole African gamut from "Pygmy" hunting camps to Arabic-speaking trading towns and taking in the colourful kingdoms of the western highlands.

Vast, land-locked **Mali** is blessed with the great inland delta of the Niger River and, again, striking cultural contrasts – the old **Islamic cities** of Gao, Timbuktu and Djenné (on, or near the river), and the traditionally non-Muslim **Dogon country** along the rocky cliff of the Bandiagara escarpment. Other Francophone countries include the narrow strips of **Togo** and **Benin**, the latter being especially easy-going and fairly undeveloped as far as tourism is concerned; the laid-back, former revolutionary republic of **Burkina Faso**; and the remote and dramatic expanses of **Mauritania** and **Niger**. Perhaps the most impressive of the *pays francophones*, however, is the republic of **Guinea**, with only a thin overlay of European culture and an extraordinary vitality released by the end of dictatorship.

Four of the West African countries are **former British colonies**, divided from each other by the speed of the French invasion in the nineteenth century. **The Gambia** is an easy place to set out from, a winter holiday destination that's small and personable enough to feel accessible for the least adventurous visitor. The distinctive personality of **Ghana** provides flamboyant cultural experiences and its splendid, palm-lined coast, dotted with old European forts, a handful of good wildlife sanctuaries and official encouragements to the tourist industry, make it one of West Africa's most promising countries to travel in. **Sierra Leone**, at one time hugely likeable, has always been a more demanding destination. It has some of the best beaches in the world – only minutes away from the raffish tumble of Freetown – but the devastating civil strife of recent years rules out any recommendation to visit for the present. **Nigeria**, despite its new, ostensibly democratic government,

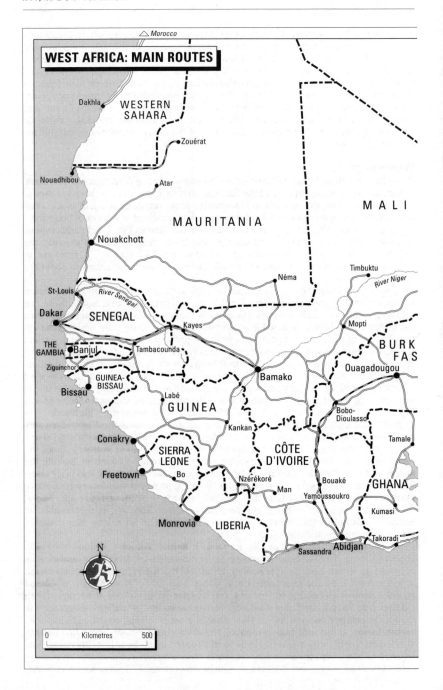

WEST AFRICA: MAIN ROUTES

Morocco

Dakhla

WESTERN
SAHARA

Zouérat

Nouadhibou

Atar

MAURITANIA

MALI

Nouakchott

Néma

Timbuktu

River Niger

St-Louis

River Senegal

Kayes

Mopti

Dakar

SENEGAL

BURK
FAS

THE
GAMBIA

Banjul

Tambacounda

Bamako

Ouagadougou

Ziguinchor

GUINEA-
BISSAU

Bissau

Labé

GUINEA

Bobo-
Dioulasso

Kankan

Tamale

Conakry

SIERRA
LEONE

CÔTE
D'IVOIRE

GHANA

Freetown

Bo

Nzérékoré

Bouaké

Man

Yamoussoukro

Kumasi

Monrovia

LIBERIA

Takoradi

Sassandra

Abidjan

N

0   Kilometres   500

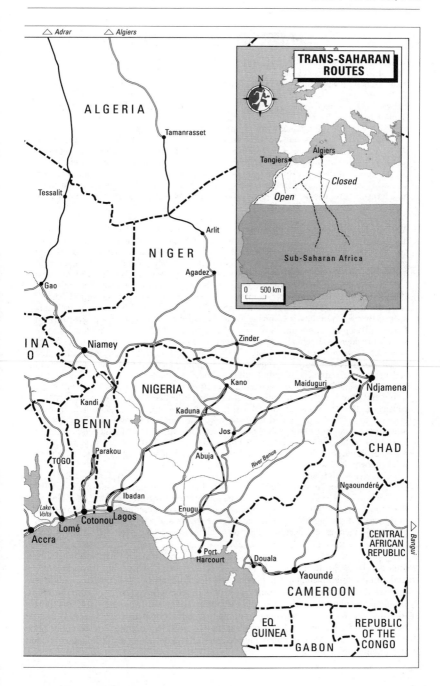

NO-GO ZONES

At the time of writing, August 1999, travel to several parts of West Africa is highly inadvisable. Only urgent business should take you to war-torn **Sierra Leone**, while **Liberia**, though technically peaceful, is too ragged after its decade of brutalization for tourism. None of the thousands of pages of readers' letters we received before researching this edition included any first-hand experience in either country more recently than April 1997. Rough Guide researchers have not visited Sierra Leone or Liberia for this edition, though we have gleaned some recent information from returning journalists, which is outlined below.

The other danger zones you should be very wary of entering are **Guinea-Bissau** and the neighbouring **Basse Casamance** region of southern Senegal. Further details about the situation in these two areas are included in the respective chapters. In particular, mines are a persistent risk, as they are in Sierra Leone and Liberia. More minor localized conflicts in various other countries could potentially limit your travels, but they don't normally warrant a high level of apprehension: again, these problem areas are detailed in the relevant chapters.

SIERRA LEONE

After the Liberian civil war spilled over into Sierra Leone in the early 1990s, the country descended into virtual anarchy as various groups fought over control of the country's principal resource – diamonds. The main rebel group, the Liberian-backed **RUF**, was repeatedly aided by underpaid government troops, or *sobels* (soldiers turned rebel) who had themselves overthrown the corrupt government of Joseph Momoh. In 1996, a new civilian government, under **Ahmed Tejan Kabbah**, was democratically elected, but in 1997, Kabbah was overthrown by another section of the military together with RUF fighters, and the capital, Freetown, was thrown into bloody chaos. In 1998, with the tacit support of Britain, the military company, Sandline, assisted the Nigerian-led West African **Ecomog** (Economic Community of West African States Monitoring Group) force in reinstating President Kabbah, an operation greeted with jubilation by the majority of Sierra Leonians. However, in January 1999, the RUF launched a carefully planned and savage assault on Freetown, only just repulsed by Ecomog, which left up to 8000 people dead and razed hundreds of buildings to the ground. Nearly every major building east of Congo Cross Bridge was badly damaged or destroyed and almost everyone in Freetown who could afford to leave the city, did so. Kabbah effectively rules over a country that consists of the battle-scarred capital and a scattering of upcountry bases held by government forces and surrounded by ravaged countryside, much of it abandoned by its inhabitants, hundreds of thousands of whom have fled to Guinea, Liberia and beyond. In June 1999, Kabbah signed a pact with Foday Sankoh, the leader of the RUF, giving the rebels a significant role in government, but it is not clear whether all the RUF fighters will lay down their weapons.

If you have to **visit** Sierra Leone, you can fly to Lungi airport from Banjul on Bellview airlines. Lungi is an oasis of Nigerian-protected officialdom and semi-normality where your visa will be checked. Ferries from the airport to **Freetown** are out of operation as the open sea is still a battle zone, and helicopters are currently making the connection to the city. Of the big hotels, only the *Cape Sierra* is still functioning, but it's hard to get a room as most are occupied long-term by military trainers and aid workers. You

seems barely awake to its tourism potential. There are, however, big travel incentives inland – in the fine uplands of the plateau and the old cities of the north, to mention just two areas. It's a hard country to come to terms with, but once you're away from the slightly psychotic manifestation of Lagos, and the hubbub of one or two other big cities, there's no denying the overall ease and even tranquillity which accompany travels here. The same cannot be said for **Liberia** – a former vassal state of the USA, nominally independent since 1847 – which is struggling to make any recovery after a decade of civil conflict, confusion and economic breakdown.

could try *Ben's* near Aberdeen bridge. Electricity and water are sporadically functional, and the phone system works to a limited extent. Most banks have been destroyed: credit cards are no use. Small groceries and chop houses are open. The British, Guinean and German embassies are open, but the American embassy was closed at the time of writing. To get about the city, battered blue-and-yellow taxis are still running. Apart from a couple of beach bars at the top of Lumley Beach, beach life has ceased. The remains of bodies can still be seen by the shore quite close to the city and the famously beautiful River No.2 Beach, a few kilometres down the Freetown peninsula, is currently the frontline. To leave the city you would need official permission both of the government and of Ecomog (in practice such travel is impossible except by special helicopter charter). A curfew operates from 7pm or sometimes earlier.

LIBERIA

Charles Taylor's invasion of Liberia in 1989 led to the execution of President Doe, the first upcountry president of West Africa's oldest independent state. Previous incumbents had been Americo-Liberians, descendants of the freed slaves shipped here by the United States. Liberia became the battleground of rival groups claiming to be fighting for the country's salvation while fulfilling their own purely mercenary, or survival-based, agendas. In 1996, there was serious fighting in Monrovia – the headquarters of the Nigerian-led West African Ecomog force – which destroyed much of the capital. More than a dozen failed peace agreements eventually came to fruition with the help of talks in Nigeria, and Taylor got his presidency after a disputed election in 1997, following which the peace-keepers left the country. Since then, the Liberian diaspora, especially in the US, has campaigned unevenly for the emergence of real democracy in Liberia and the removal of the increasingly tyrannical Taylor.

Visits to Liberia are becoming easier as the less dramatic grind of poverty and economic failure replaces the misery of civil conflict, but the country is not ready for tourists of even the hardiest and most independent streak. White visitors face the uncomfortable fact that the West supported the democratically elected government in Sierra Leone against the Liberian-backed rebels of the RUF and, outside the immediate environs of Monrovia, they may thus be misidentified by Liberian police and military as mercenaries, spies or other undesirables. Flights to Robertsfield airport, an hour's drive south of Monrovia, come in from Conakry and Abidjan (there are no flights from Europe). Overland travel is possible from Côte d'Ivoire. **Monrovia** has been slowly progressing towards a semblance of West African normality in recent years, with services, banks and other businesses more or less functioning. Accommodation and other needs tend to be expensive but there is some variety. Telecommunications, and even Internet access, are usually possible in the city. The US embassy is open, but most European missions have yet to return. Most of Liberia's coastal and upcountry towns have been comprehensively destroyed over the last decade and in many areas the population is now hugely reduced, too. Nevertheless, it is possible to travel to most parts by bush taxi and, while road conditions and roadblocks can make journeys slow and hazardous, recent travellers report relatively uneventful journeys.

The **former Portuguese colonies** are West Africa's least-known destinations. The **Cape Verde Islands** are immediately beguiling: volcanic outcrops and desert islands in the mid-Atlantic, with a scenery and lifestyle that make them hard to leave. **Guinea-Bissau** has its own island highlights – the Bijagos – luxuriant green forests in the warm, inshore sea, as different from the Cape Verdes as it's possible to imagine. At the time of writing, however – August 1999 – the army's mutiny, the widescale destruction of Bissau city and the installation of a new government, make it hard to predict travel conditions in the new millennium.

Guidelines for travel

The first recommendation in all this, is to give yourself **time**. It's tempting to try to cover as much of this fascinating region as possible. But the rewards become thinner the faster you go and, beyond a certain pace, the point of being there is lost in the pursuit of the next goal. While it may be hard to stop completely, or just to limit yourself to a small corner, that is precisely the way to get the most out of your trip – and, incidentally, also how to put the most in. In such a poor region, the idea of some kind of reciprocity is one worth keeping: everything comes back to you in the end. Patience and generosity always pay off; haste and intolerance tend to lead to disaster.

If you're travelling alone – and it's really the best way if you want to get to know West Africa rather than your travelling companion(s) – it may be useful to know about the main **travellers' crossroads** in the region, where you might team up for a while or swap experiences: Nouadhibou at the edge of the desert, Bamako or Mopti in Mali, Bobo-Dioulasso in Burkina Faso, Cotonou in Benin, and Busua or Accra on the Ghanaian coast.

More than ever, with so many countries undergoing tumultuous change, it's important to keep your ear to the ground before travelling on to the next country on your itinerary.

When to travel

Individual climate details are given for each country. The big consideration is not the heat – temperatures, in fact, only occasionally climb very much higher than you might experience in Europe – but the humidity and particularly the timing of the rainy seasons. Broadly the rains come in the "summer" months, some time between April and October. Although travel is rarely out of the question during the rains, it's obviously not an ideal time. You can be pretty sure of dry weather everywhere from mid-November to the end of January. Where the rainy seasons are very marked, the very end of the dry season is best avoided as it can be stiflingly humid. The best time to leave on an overland trip planned to last several months is September.

GETTING TO WEST AFRICA: GENERAL INFORMATION

The most straightforward – and usually the least expensive – way to get to West Africa is by air. If you have the time, though, making your way partly overland, either with your own vehicle or using any available transport along the way, gives rewards of its own – and an unbeatable introduction to the region.

You can travel in a similar style, with most of your needs looked after, by going on an organized overland tour. These, like inclusive package holidays to West Africa, are fairly limited in choice.

There's detailed information over the following pages for travel from Britain, Ireland, North America, Australia, New Zealand and the rest of Africa. There are also plenty of options for getting to West Africa if you're starting from France, Switzerland, Germany or the Benelux countries. To get started, contact the following: in France, Air Afrique (☎01/43.23.81.81; *www.airfrance.fr*), Nouvelles Frontières (☎01/41.41.58.58; *www.nouvelles-frontiers.com*), Point Afrique (☎01/47.73.62.64) or the club Aventures du Bout du Monde (☎01/45.38.66.36); in Belgium, Sabena (☎02/723 23 23; *www.sabena.com*) or Nouvelles Frontières (☎022/799 31 11); in Switzerland, Swissair (☎022/799 31 11; *www.swissair.com*); in the Netherlands, KLM (☎20/649 9123; *www.klm.nl*); and in Germany, Lufthansa (☎0221/8260; *www.lufthansa.com*) or an adventure travel specialist like Travel Overland (☎089/272760; *www.travel-overland.de*).

DISCOUNT FLIGHT TICKETS

In the main, travel agents offer tickets for scheduled flights at substantially **discounted rates** – well below the official fares agreed by IATA, the association to which most airlines belong. Airlines prepared to sell off their tickets through these agents have in the past been generally the less reputable ones left with the most unsold seats, but more and more major carriers are cashing in to maintain full flights. Note, however, that discounts are sometimes subject to **restrictions**: check if you have to be a student, for example, or under a certain age for them to apply.

BOOKING AND BUYING

Discount agencies are, almost without exception, respectable travel agents, even if first impressions might suggest otherwise. When **booking**, note whether the agent reserves seats directly with the airline by telephone or on a computer system, or has to go through another agent. While many agents have ticketing agreements with certain airlines and can write tickets on the premises, they may have to order some from the nominated "consolidator" of the airline concerned – usually another agent. Don't expect to see your ticket until you've paid in full.

Always get receipts and ask if your deposit is refundable, and what **refund** you can expect if anything goes wrong after the ticket is issued (it's wise to be insured from this point on). Also check how easy it will be to **change your reservation dates** once you've got your ticket. You can sometimes leave a round-trip ticket "open-dated" on its return portion, but in that case you'll have to make a seat reservation yourself with the airline. It's just as easy, and safer, to have a confirmed seat and change the date if necessary (and if seats are available). Note that if you book through a discount agency, you cannot deal direct with the airline on your booking until you have your ticket, though you can always quote them the details and ask them to check the reservation is held under your name. If it's not, don't panic. It will probably be held under the agent's block allocation of seats.

Airline "seasons" for West Africa vary considerably but many discounted fares are non-seasonal: they don't vary. Most student and youth fares, however, do have a seasonal structure to tie in with summer and Christmas holiday periods.

Book as far in advance as you can. Some routes are full to capacity at peak periods, especially Christmas, and discounted seat availability is often snapped up quickly.

TICKETS AND FARES

Round-trip fares are generally of three types – short excursions (usually one month, sometimes requiring advance purchase – Apex), three-month excursions and one year (never more). A **one-way fare** (valid a year) is normally half the "yearly" fare. You may be able to fly out to one destination and back from another (an "**open jaw**"), depending on the airline and the agent's contract. In rare cases, you may also be able to purchase a ticket *back* from West Africa, before you leave – useful if you're travelling out overland. Point Afrique (see overleaf) currently offers charter flight connections between Atar in Mauritania, and Paris or Marseilles, for just £130 single (£140 round-trip). However, offers change constantly, so it's best to keep your eyes and ears open.

Once you have your ticket, check the status boxes are what you've been told: a confirmed seat on the flight will be marked "OK", a place on the waiting list "WL". If your ticket says "RQ" you're not even waitlisted, merely "requested". Note that a ticket has to be "OK" before you can actually fly.

GETTING THERE FROM BRITAIN AND IRELAND

The airline with the busiest West Africa schedule is the Belgian airline Sabena, which routes all flights through its home airport of Amsterdam. British Airways only flies to Abidjan, Accra and Lagos. Other useful airlines include the Dutch airline KLM, Air France, Swissair and Air Afrique.

When booking in Britain, it's a good idea to check your agent is an ATOL (Air Travel Operator's Licence) holder. If not, they should be an authorized agent of an ATOL holder and thus by extension offer the same protection. An ATOL ensures that in the event of the airline going bust, your money is safe.

You can pay anything from under £350 to nearly £700 for a return flight from London to West Africa. Most discounted return fares fall somewhere between £350 and £500. One-ways are rarely less than £200. In the **peak season**, the cheapest fares to many destinations are often on the Russian airline, Aeroflot, and on Balkan Bulgarian Airlines. The Aeroflot timetable has, however, been diminishing in recent years and the few remaining flights all require a stopover in Moscow (basic hotel at their expense); most of the better agents are unwilling to deal with them. Balkan Bulgarian's weekly flight to Accra and Lagos via Sofia, though not a pleasant journey, is reliable enough.

For an idea of the saving over the airlines' own fares, make a few calls to their fares departments

NEW TELEPHONE NUMBERS

On April 22, 2000, the UK's telephone-numbering system will change.

All **London** numbers will have a new area code, ☎020. The old ☎0171 numbers will be prefixed with a 7, while ☎0181 numbers will be prefixed with an 8, thus making all London telephone numbers 8 digits.

The area code for the whole of **Northern Ireland** will become ☎028. Existing Belfast numbers will be prefixed with 90, thus becoming 8 digits long.

AIRLINES IN THE UK

Check with the airlines for schedules and full fares. Airlines prefer to avoid being officially associated with particular agents and do not as a rule quote discounted fares. However they may refer you to their consolidator agents, for whom various addresses are given in the "Discount Agents" box on p.7.

Aeroflot Russian International Airlines (SU), 70 Piccadilly, London W1 9HH (☎0171/355 2233). Heavily discounted one-year fares available on most of their routes through many discount agencies.

Air Afrique (RK), 4th Floor, 86 Hatton Garden, London EC1N (☎0171/430 0284). Flights via Paris to most West African capitals. No UK discounts.

Air France (AF), 1st Floor, 10 Warwick St, London W1R 5RA (☎0181/742 6600; *www.airfrance.fr*). Flights via Paris. Discounted seats available.

Balkan Bulgarian Airlines (LZ), 322 Regent St, London W1R 5AB (☎0171/637 7637). Overnight flights to Accra and Lagos via Sofia. Among the cheapest during peak seasons.

British Airways (BA), 156 Regent St, London W1R 5TA (☎0181/897 4000; *www.british-airways.com*). Connections to Accra and Lagos out of Dublin, Edinburgh, Manchester and Newcastle (via London). Student fares available through selected agents. Some specially discounted (and unrestricted) fares.

Cameroon Airlines (UY), 2nd Floor, Clifford St, London W1X (☎0171/734 7676). Non-stop flight London–Douala on Tuesday, arrives Douala Wednesday morning. Own fares.

Egyptair (MS), 31 Piccadilly, London W1V OPT (☎0171/734 2395). Flights to Abidjan, Accra, Lagos and Kano via Cairo (with an overnight at the airline's expense). Extended stopovers in Cairo are possible, which makes this an interesting alternative. Discounted fares are widely available; especially good deals on one-year tickets.

Ghana Airways (GH), 3 Princes St, London W1R (☎0171/499 0201). Three flights a week to Accra. Economical fares direct from the airline or through agents.

Iberia (IB), 29 Glasshouse St, London W1R 6JU (☎0171/830 0011; *www.iberia.com*). Flights via

Madrid to Dakar, and via Las Palmas to Nouakchott and Nouadhibou.

KLM Royal Dutch Airlines (KL), Terminal 4, Heathrow (☎0990/750 9000; *www.klm.nl*). A good and reliable airline. Flights via Amsterdam (out of Belfast, Cardiff and Southampton as well as London) to a number of West African cities. Many agents offer discounted fares and one or two have longer validities and "open jaw" deals available at very competitive prices.

Lufthansa German Airlines (LH), 10 Old Bond St, London W1X 4EN (☎0345/737747; *www.lufthansa.co.uk*). Flights to Accra, Dakar and Lagos via Frankfurt. Rarely discounted.

Nigeria Airways (WT), 43 Davies St, London W1Y (☎0171/493-9726). Overnight flights direct to Kano and Lagos, but can be unreliable. Occasionally good discounted fares.

Sabena Belgian Airlines (SN), Gemini House, 10/18 Putney Hill, London SW15 6AA (☎0181/780 1444; *www.sabena.com*). Reliable airline. Flights via Brussels (and ex Belfast, Birmingham, Bristol, Dublin, Edinburgh, Glasgow, Leeds, Manchester and Newcastle), include some less common destinations (Bamako, Niamey and Yaoundé, for example). Discounted fares available.

Swissair (SR), Swiss Centre, 1 Swiss Court, London W1V 4BJ (☎0171/434 7200; *www. swissair.co.uk*). Flights via Zurich to Abidjan, Accra, Douala, Lagos and Yaoundé. Some discounts available.

TACV (VR). No London Office. Flights from Lisbon, Amsterdam, Munich and Paris to Sal, Cape Verde. Through-bookings from London can be made with most discount agents in London.

TAP Air Portugal (TP), 38–44 Gillingham St, London SW1V 1JW (☎0171/828 2092). Via Lisbon to Abidjan, Bissau, Dakar and Sal. No discounts.

(see above). Current IATA one-month excursion fares in the region go from around £750 to £1000. If you want to try some detective work, ask the airline for their consolidators' details. Some are only too happy, others refuse.

There are no non-stop flights from **Ireland** to West Africa: the best routings are via Brussels on Sabena or via Amsterdam on KLM (overnight stay sometimes required). For other destina-

tions, or more price choices, talk to a clued-up travel agent and expect to route through London or Paris – though not without incurring some delay.

The only regular **charter flights** from Britain to West Africa are to The Gambia from London Gatwick and Manchester. Flight prices range from around £270–450, depending on the season and the length of stay. Special promotions are

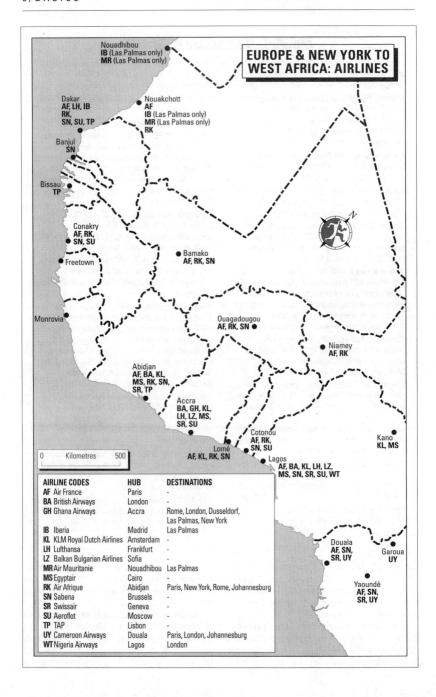

EUROPE & NEW YORK TO WEST AFRICA: AIRLINES

Nouadhibou
IB (Las Palmas only)
MR (Las Palmas only)

Nouakchott
AF
IB (Las Palmas only)
MR (Las Palmas only)
RK

Dakar
AF, LH, IB
RK,
SN, SU, TP

Banjul
SN

Bissau
TP

Conakry
AF, RK,
SN, SU

Freetown

Bamako
AF, RK, SN

Monrovia

Ouagadougou
AF, RK, SN

Niamey
AF, RK

Abidjan
AF, BA, KL,
MS, RK, SN,
SR, TP

Accra
BA, GH, KL,
LH, LZ, MS,
SR, SU

Cotonou
AF, RK,
SN, SU

Kano
KL, MS

Lomé
AF, KL, RK, SN

Lagos
AF, BA, KL, LH, LZ,
MS, SN, SR, SU, WT

Douala
AF, SN,
SR, UY

Garoua
UY

Yaoundé
AF, SN,
SR, UY

0   Kilometres   500

AIRLINE CODES	HUB	DESTINATIONS
AF Air France	Paris	-
BA British Airways	London	-
GH Ghana Airways	Accra	Rome, London, Dusseldorf, Las Palmas, New York
IB Iberia	Madrid	Las Palmas
KL KLM Royal Dutch Airlines	Amsterdam	-
LH Lufthansa	Frankfurt	-
LZ Balkan Bulgarian Airlines	Sofia	-
MR Air Mauritanie	Nouadhibou	Las Palmas
MS Egyptair	Cairo	-
RK Air Afrique	Abidjan	Paris, New York, Rome, Johannesburg
SN Sabena	Brussels	-
SR Swissair	Geneva	-
SU Aeroflot	Moscow	-
TP TAP	Lisbon	-
UY Cameroon Airways	Douala	Paris, London, Johannesburg
WT Nigeria Airways	Lagos	London

sometimes introduced to fill seats, and these can be really excellent value.

One off-beat route to West Africa from the UK is **via the Canary Islands**. You can pick up exceptionally cheap last-minute package holidays to Las Palmas, Gran Canaria, then cancel, or possibly sell off, your seat back. Going on from Las Palmas, the shortest (and cheapest) flight to West Africa is to Nouadhibou in Mauritania; both Air Mauritanie (£270 one-way) and charter operator Air Atlantique (£100 one-way) fly twice a week. Iberia flies three times a week to Dakar (around £360).

PACKAGE HOLIDAYS FROM THE UK

The Gambia is the best-known West African package destination from Britain. Most travel agents will have a choice of brochures which include it, and it is a good place to go if you're looking for a short winter holiday, with guaranteed sun and a low-key African atmosphere that is not too over-exploited. Read the brochures carefully, ask for the full details of the hotel from the agent's manual, and look carefully through the listings in our chapter on the country. Most operators also offer summer departures (during the rainy season), which are much cheaper, and there are often good, last-minute offers available.

In the past, other mainstream package alternatives have included the Cap Skiring coast in **Senegal**, and **Sierra Leone**, though at the time of writing, neither was available through a high street operator. Caravela, the holiday arm of the Portuguese

---

DISCOUNT AGENTS IN BRITAIN

Africa Travel Centre, 21 Leigh St, London WC1H 9QX (☎0171/387 1211; *www. africatravel.co.uk*). Helpful and resourceful Africa specialists offering packages, overland tours, books, maps and advice. Particularly good deals on British Airways flights.

African Travel Specialists, 7 Glen House, Stag Place, London SW1E 5JL (☎0171/630 5434; *africatravel@compuserve.com*). Africa specialists with good deals on KLM flights to Accra and Lagos.

Bridge the World, 47 Chalk Farm Rd, Camden Town, London NW1 8AN (☎0171/911 0900; 24hr ☎0171/813 3350; *www.b-t-w.co.uk*). Competitive independent travel firm.

Holiday Planners, 111 Bell St, London NW1 (☎0171/7242255); Manchester (☎0161/8323167). A good range of cheap deals.

North-South Travel, Moulsham Mill Centre, Parkway, Chelmsford, Essex CM2 7PX (☎01245/492882). Small agency with good deals to most major cities whose modest profits are devoted to developing-world charities.

Nouvelles Frontieres, 2–3 Woodstock St, London W1R 1HE (☎0171/629 7772; *www. nouvelles-frontieres.com*). French-owned tour operator specializing in scheduled and charter flights, and package tours.

Quest Worldwide, 10 Richmond Rd, Kingston, Surrey KT2 5HL (☎0181/5473322). Good deals with all major airlines.

Redcoat Express, Global House, Manor Court, Manor Royal, Crawley, West Sussex RH10 2PI (☎01293/552440). Good selection of cheap fares.

Soliman Travel, 113 Earl's Court Rd, London SW5 (☎0171/3706446). Egyptair specialists.

STA Travel, 86 Old Brompton Rd, London SW7 (☎0171/3616262; *www.statravel.co.uk*). Full range of cities and airlines for West Africa, from 20 UK offices and 120 worldwide. Special fares for students and young people.

Student Travel Centre, 24 Rupert St, London W1V 7FN (☎0171/4376370; *www.student-travel-centre.com*) Student discounts on flights and travel insurance. Good deals also available to non-students.

Trailfinders, 42–50 Earl's Court Rd, London W8 6FT (☎0171/9383366; *www.trailfinders.com*). Respected discount flights agency with a range of other services and several regional branches.

Usit Campus, 52 Grosvenor Gardens, London SW1W 0AG (☎0171/7308111; *www. campustravel.co.uk*). Nationwide student/youth specialist with over thirty branches.

DISCOUNT AGENTS IN IRELAND

Joe Walsh Tours, 8–11 Baggot St, Dublin 2 (☎01/676 3053). General discount agent.

Thomas Cook, 118 Grafton St, Dublin 2 (☎01/677 0469) and 11 Donegall Place, Belfast (☎01232/550232 or 554455). Reasonable range of mainstream discount fares.

Usit, O'Connell Bridge, 19/21 Aston Quay, Dublin 2 (☎01/602 1700) and Fountain Centre, College St, Belfast BT1 6ET (☎01232/324073). Ireland's foremost student and youth specialists.

PLANNING AHEAD

AIRPORTS

If you're uncertain where to fly in, this rundown of West Africa's airports might help to narrow down your choice. Another factor to consider before you buy an air ticket is whether you need a visa for that country and how easy that will be to obtain (see p.19).

• Some airports are simply best avoided. **Lagos** (Nigeria) and **Douala** (Cameroon) do not make promising first impressions. Both are likely to be swelteringly hot and they have in the past been notoriously corrupt. Lagos, after dark, is downright unsafe and the journey to the city by taxi can be unnerving (Kano, in northern Nigeria is a much less nerve-wracking international airport).

• Smaller capitals, naturally enough, have the most agreeable airports. Good candidates include **Banjul** (The Gambia), **Sal** (Cape Verde), **Bamako** (Mali), **Ouagadougou** (Burkina Faso) and **Niamey** (Niger).

• Among medium-sized capitals, **Abidjan** (Côte d'Ivoire) is well-organized and convenient and **Accra** (Ghana), **Dakar** (Senegal) and **Conakry** (Guinea) aren't bad.

• **Cotonou** (Benin) is probably the best all-round choice – small and well-run, pretty much unaffected by hassles and chaos and very close to the city centre.

OVERNIGHT FLIGHTS

An additional factor is the time you will arrive. It's obviously preferable to **arrive by day**, especially in a large city – but, unfortunately, overnight flights to West Africa are in the minority. Most flights arrive in the evening, or at best the late afternoon.

These airlines operate at least some flights from Europe by night, to arrive in West Africa the next morning:

Accra (ex London and ex Sofia)
Ghana Airways and Bulkan Bulgarian Airlines
Cotonou (ex Paris)
Air Afrique
Douala (ex London and Paris)
Cameroon Airlines
Garoua (ex Paris)
Cameroon Airlines
Lagos (ex London and ex Sofia)
Balkan Bulgarian Airlines and British Airways/Nigeria Airways

DIRECT LONDON–WEST AFRICA

The following services operate direct flights from London to:
Abidjan British Airways (Thurs & Sun)
Accra British Airways (Mon, Wed–Fri & Sun) and Ghana Airways (Tues, Thurs, Sat & Sun)
Banjul Charter operators
Douala Cameroon Airlines (Tues)
Lagos British Airways/Nigeria Airways (daily)
Yaoundé Cameroon Airlines (Wed)

airline TAP, offers holidays in **Cape Verde**, and you can find a number of interesting trips through **French operators** and agents if you visit Paris.

An excellent option from Britain is the highly recommended **Ghana homestay programme** operated by Insight Travel, 6 Norton Rd, Garstang, Preston, Lancs PR3 1JY (☎01995/606095; *insight@provider.co.uk*), in which you stay as a guest near Kumasi and participate in local life.

WEST AFRICA BY FREIGHTER

Surprisingly perhaps, going by **cargo ship** from Europe to "the Coast" is not quite history. At the bottom end of the scale, this is an unusual and price-competitive way of travelling to West Africa. While conditions vary from adequate to luxurious depending on the ship and your choice of cabin, fares include all meals. Stays in port will vary from a few hours to a couple of days or more. You may need to embark from a north European port. Suitable insurance cover is required, which for over-65s can be expensive.

Gdynia American Shipping Lines, 18 Banner St, London EC1Y (☎0171/253 9561 or 251 3389), are agents for Polish Ocean Lines, which depart every two weeks or so from Szczecin to Hamburg, Rotterdam, Las Palmas, Dakar, Banjul, Freetown, Monrovia, Abidjan, Tema, Lomé, Cotonou, Lagos, Port Harcourt, Douala and then back again (total round-trip voyage around 50–70 days). Not every port is visited on every voyage. At a round-trip fare of £1360, sharing a twin cabin, this is the cheapest line, but it can be difficult to get one-way tickets. These are small ships, around 7000 tonnes.

UK PACKAGE OPERATORS

THE GAMBIA
The main operators to The Gambia include Thompson, Kuoni, Going Places, Airtours and Hayes and Jarvis.
The Gambia Experience, Kingfisher House, Rownhams Lane, North Baddesley, Hampshire SO52 9LP (☎01703/730888; *www.serenity.co.uk/gambia*). Gambia specialists with a strong commitment to the country. Includes some offbeat hotels and good offers.

OTHER COUNTRIES
Caravela Tours, 38–44 Gillingham St, London SW1V 1HU (☎0171/630 9223). One- or two-week packages to Cape Verde. Expensive.
Club Med, 106–110 Brompton Rd, London SW3 1LJ (☎0171/581 1161). All-inclusive stays at holiday villages in Senegal and Côte d'Ivoire. Fun, if you speak reasonable French, and good for families, but very insulated from anything local or West African.

The Grimaldi Line, 103–105 Jermyn St, London SW1Y 6ES (☎0171/930 5683), operates new Italian container ships (much bigger and designed with passengers in mind, even with swimming pools) from Tilbury to Antwerp, Le Havre, Dakar, Abidjan, Tema, Lomé, Cotonou, Lagos, Douala and Abidjan, then back to Tilbury via Amsterdam and Hamburg. A round-trip is estimated to take 44 days and fares start at £1930 per person sharing a twin-berth cabin. One-way fares (Europe to West Africa or back) start at £850. Car tariffs start at £416 and motorbikes £240. Ships depart about every three weeks.

Various German lines offer a regular West African service from Felixstowe, via Le Havre, Nouackchott, Dakar, Banjul, Conakry, Freetown, Monrovia, Abidjan, San Pedro, Lomé, Tema, Cotonou, Lagos and Douala, then back via Abidjan. Fares for the 64-day round-trip, in very comfortable cabins, start at £2055 (one-way Felixstowe–Dakar from £765).

Strand Voyages, Charing Cross Shopping Concourse, London WC2N 4HZ (☎0171/836 6363; *www.strandtravel.co.uk*), has been in the business a long time and can supply full details and make **bookings** on all the above routes.

GETTING THERE FROM NORTH AMERICA

Currently the only direct flights from the US to West Africa are Air Afrique's service from New York to Dakar (continuing to Abidjan) and Ghana Airways' flights to Accra – also from New York. Although Ghana Airways

has come up with some good promotions in recent years (under $900 round-trip), fares for direct flights are typically twice as expensive as alternatives via Paris, Amsterdam or Brussels – where Air France, Air Afrique, KLM and Sabena connect to most Francophone capitals – or via London.

Discount fares are available by booking through one of the discount agencies (consolidators) listed on p.10. Air **courier services** rarely offer West African destinations. You might save money on air tickets by flying to a **European city** like London (from about $400–600), stopping over for a few days and picking up a discounted flight there, for example to Accra ($750-plus), but it's probably cheaper to buy your ticket in the US – unless, that is, you find an exceptional deal and don't mind spending some time in Europe.

AIRLINES IN NORTH AMERICA

Air Afrique (☎1-800/456-9192 or 212/586-5908; *www.airafrique-airlines.com*). Weekly flights from New York to Abidjan, via Dakar.

Air Canada (US: ☎1-800/776-3000; Canada: ☎1-888/247-2262; *www.cdnair.ca*). From many Canadian cities to European cities.

Air France (US: ☎1-800/237-2747; Canada: ☎1-800/667-2747; *www.airfrance.fr*). Several flights daily to Paris from New York, plus Chicago, Houston, LA, Miami, San Francisco and Washington, all non-stop.

British Airways (US: ☎1-800/247-9297; Canada: ☎1-800/668-1059; *www.british-airways.com*). From many North American cities to London.

Canadian Airlines (☎1-800/426-7000; Canada ☎1-800/665-1177; *www.cdnair.com*). From major Canadian cities to major European cities.

Ghana Airways (☎1-800/404-4262; *www.ghana-airways.com*) Six flights a week from New York to Accra, two via Dakar.

Northwest/KLM Airlines (☎1-800/447-4747; *www.nwa.com*). From LA (3 times a week) and New York (daily) to Amsterdam and on to Accra.

Sabena (☎1-800/955-2000; *www.sabena-usa.com*). Eastern US cities to Brussels, with connections on to West Africa.

South African Airways (☎1-800/722-9675 or 954/769-5000; *www.saa.co.za*). One flight a week from New York to Jo'burg, via Sal, Cape Verde.

TACV 535 Boylston St, 3rd floor, Boston, MA 02116 (☎617/578-8940). Flights from Boston to Sal, Cape Verde, summer and Christmas only.

Tower Air (☎1-800/221-2500 or 718/553-8500; *www.towerair.com*). Often the cheapest fare between LA–New York and New York–Paris.

Virgin (☎1-800/862-8261; *www.fly.virgin.com*). From many US cities to London.

DISCOUNT AGENTS IN NORTH AMERICA

All of the companies listed below offer reduced-rate tickets. Most book flights all the way to Africa, while others are included because they have special fares to Europe if you need to break up your trip.

Adventure Travel Service, 18 E Third, Grove, OK, (☎1-800/488-7901; *www.greencis.net/~ats/*).

Air Hitch, 1434 Second St, Santa Monica, CA (☎1-800/326-2009 or 212/864-2000; *www.airhitch.org*). Offices in New York, San Francisco and Paris.

Air Travel Discounts, 370 Lexington Ave, Ste 500, New York (☎1-800/888-2621; *www.airdisc.com*). Branches in LA and West Palm Beach. Consolidator with offices on both coasts; request fares online and they will fax you back within 24 hours.

Around the World, 2241 Polk St, San Francisco, CA 94109 (☎415/673-9950).

Council Travel, 205 E 42nd St, New York, NY 10017 (☎1-800/2-COUNCIL or 212/822-2700; *www.counciltravel.com*), and branches in many other US cities. Student/budget travel agency.

Farebeater (*www.flifo.com*). A good online resource for budget airline travel.

Fly Cheap (☎1-800/FLY-CHEAP). San Diego-based consolidator. Ask for the international department when booking to West Africa, or they may quote a price from their domestic service, without access to bargain fares worldwide.

Flytime, 45 W 34th St, Suite 305, New York, NY 10001 (☎212/760-3737).

Interworld, 3400 Coral Way, Miami, FL 33145 (☎305/443-4929).

New Coast Travel, 440 Lincoln Blvd, Venice, CA 90291 (☎310/452-1990).

Nomad Travel Bazaar, 243 E Seventh St, New York, NY 10009 (☎1-888/466-6623 or 212/228-5240; *www.travelbazaar.com*).

Pan-Express Travel, 209 Mail St, San Francisco, CA 94108 (☎415/989-8282).

Spector Travel, 2 Park Plaza, Boston, MA 02116 (☎1-800/879-2374 or 617/338-0111; *www.spectortravel.com*). Well-connected travel agency and regional flight broker, dealing only with Africa.

STA Travel, Head Office: 48 E 11th St, New York, NY 10003 (☎1-800/777-0112 or 212/627-3111; *www.sta-travel.com*). Branches across the country.

Swan Travel, 400 Madison Ave, New York, NY 10017 (☎212/421-1010).

Tickets for Less, 1801 JFK Blvd, Philadelphia, PA (☎1-888/LOFARE-1; *www.ticketsforless.com*). Low fares on Air Afrique flights and on Northwest flights connecting to Accra.

Travac Tours, 989 Ave, Sixth 16th Floor, New York, NY 10018 (☎1-800/872-8800 or 212/563-3303; *www.travac.com*). Consolidator and charter broker. They will fax current fares from their fax line: 1-888/872-8327 or quote seasonal fares from their Web site.

Travel Cuts, Head Office: 187 College St, Toronto, ON M5T 1P7 (☎416/979-2406; *www.travelcuts.com*). Branches all over Canada, plus an office in San Francisco (☎415/247-1800). Specializes in student fares, IDs and other travel services.

If you do break your journey in Europe, remember that the "two pieces" luggage limit that applies on transatlantic flights becomes a "20kg" (44lb) limit for the rest of the world.

FLIGHTS FROM THE EAST COAST

If you're a **student**, **youth** or **teacher**, Council Travel should be your first call. They offer New York–Abidjan flights from around $1000 round-trip in the off-season ($1050 to Dakar). Compare their fares with those of STA Travel, who have a large international network of offices. They offer roughly $1200–1500 return to West Africa, on the basis of restricted eligibility, destination and season.

Classified advertisers in the **Sunday travel sections** of the *New York Times* or *Village Voice* offer various discounted fares open to all, including occasional last-minute specials to West Africa. Non-students should also check the **budget agencies**, some of whose fares are only slightly higher than those of Council and STA (sometimes as low as $900 return to Accra). Good one-way deals are very rare.

FLIGHTS FROM THE WEST COAST

Again, it's a good idea to give Council and STA Travel a call first. Off-season, their fares for LA–**Abidjan**, with a stopover in Europe, start at around $1600 ($1350 to **Dakar**) and sometimes they have bargain deals open to all. Also, and especially if you're not a student, check the agents listed opposite (Spector Travel, for example, offers some very attractive rates, and some of the online consolidators like Travac or Farebeater quote off-season prices as low as $1550 from LA, San Francisco, or Seattle to Abidjan). Finally, make a search of the Sunday travel pages of the *Los Angeles Times* or the *San Francisco Examiner/Chronicle*. Offers for low-fare travel to Africa are still rare, but you can often find really good deals on **flights to Europe**.

FLIGHTS FROM CANADA

There are **no direct flights** to West Africa from any Canadian city. You have two main options for getting there. First you could fly to New York and connect with an Africa-bound flight there. Or you could fly to London or another European capital, either connecting on to West Africa, or stopping over long enough to make onward arrangements.

If you fly to London, Paris, Amsterdam or another capital in northern Europe, you're looking at anything from a rock-bottom CAN$600 round-trip out-of-season fare from Toronto, or CAN$800 from Vancouver, to perhaps CAN$1000 or CAN$1200 high season. If you are a student or under 26, try Travel Cuts, the college agents, with offices all over the country.

GETTING THERE FROM AUSTRALIA AND NEW ZEALAND

From Australia and New Zealand, you'll have the most options if you fly first to Europe, and then connect with a flight to West Africa, though you could fly via Kuala Lumpur or Singapore to Cairo, then on to Kano, Lagos, Accra or Abidjan with Egyptair. There are more frequent connections if you route through Bangkok, where you can either pick up an Egyptair flight to Cairo or fly Ethiopian Airlines (*www. ethiopianairlines.com*) to Addis Ababa, with conections on to Abidjan, Accra, Douala, Lagos and Lomo.

The only **direct flights** to Africa from Australia or New Zealand currently on offer are the four flights a week that go from Sydney and

AIRLINES IN AUSTRALIA AND NEW ZEALAND

Air New Zealand (*www.airnz.co.nz*) Quay House, 29 Customs St W, Auckland (☎09/357 3000); in Australia free call ☎13 2476. Daily flights from Auckland to London, Singapore and Europe with connections to Australian state capitals.

British Airways (*www.british-airways.com*) Melbourne (☎03/9603 1133); Chifley Square, 70 Hunter St, Sydney (☎02/8904 8800). Elsewhere in Australia free call ☎1800/113 722. In Auckland ☎09/356 8690. Frequent flights from New Zealand and Australian state capitals via Asia to Europe, often in conjunction with Qantas.

Malaysia Airlines (*www.malaysia-airlines.com*) 16 Spring St, Sydney (☎13 2627); 12–26 Swanson St, Auckland (☎09/373 2741 or 0800/657 472). Often competitively priced routes to Europe through Kuala Lumpur.

Qantas (*www.qantas.com.au*) Chifley Square, 70 Hunter St, Sydney and 233 Collins St, Melbourne (☎13 1313); and Qantas House, 199 Queen St, Auckland (☎09/357 8900). Daily flights to Singapore and Europe from major cities in Australia and New Zealand, and four weekly flights from Sydney to Johannesburg and Harare via Perth.

Singapore Airlines (*www.singaporeair.com*) 17–19 Bridge St, Sydney 2000 (☎02/9350 0100; *info_syd@singaporeair.com.au*); and West Plaza Building, corner Customs St and Albert St, Auckland (☎09/379 3209). Daily flights to Europe from all major Australian and New Zealand cities and three weekly connections from Singapore to Cairo. Also near-daily non-stop flights from Singapore to Johannesburg.

DISCOUNT AGENTS IN AUSTRALIA

Anywhere Travel, 345 Anzac Parade, Kingsford, Sydney (☎02/9663 0411; *anywhere@aussiemail.com.au*). Local agency specializing in cheap airfares.

Flight Centres (*www.flightcenter.com*) 1 Macquarie Place, Sydney (☎02/9241 2422); 19 Bourke St, Melbourne (☎03/9650 2899), plus dozens of branches nationwide. Call ☎13 1600 to find your closest branch. Near ubiquitous High Street agency frequently offering some of the lowest fares around.

Harvey World Travel. Franchised organization with agencies all over Australia. Call ☎13 2757 to find your closest branch.

Northern Gateway, 22 Cavenagh St, Darwin (☎08/8941 1394; *oztravel@norgate.com.au*). Local discount agent.

STA Travel (*www.statravel.com.au*) Shop 6, 127–139 Macleay St, Kings Cross, Sydney 2011 (☎02/9368 1111; *traveller@statravel.com.au*); 273 Little Collins St, Melbourne 3000 (☎03/9654 8722); plus other offices (nearest branch ☎13 1776). Major player in student, youth and budget travel.

Topdeck Travel, 65 Grenfell St, Adelaide (☎08/8232 7222). Locally owned and efficient agency.

Trailfinders (*www.trailfinders.com/australia*) 91 Elizabeth St, Brisbane 4000 (☎07/3229 0887); 3 Hides Corner, Lake St, Cairns 4870 (☎07/4041 1199); 8 Spring St, Sydney 2000 (☎02/9247 7666). Knowledgeable staff skilled at turning up odd itineraries and good prices.

Travel.com.au (*www.travel.com.au*) 80 Clarence St, Sydney 2000 (☎02/9290 1500). Youth-oriented centre with an efficient travel agency.

DISCOUNT AGENTS IN NEW ZEALAND

Budget Travel (*www.budgettravel.co.nz*). Major countrywide flight discounter. Call ☎0800/808 040 to find your nearest agency.

Flight Centres, National Bank Towers, cnr Queen and Darby streets, Auckland (☎09/309 6171); Shop 1M, National Mutual Arcade, 418 Colombo St, Christchurch (☎03/379 6396); 50–52 Willis St, Wellington (☎04/472 8101); plus other branches countrywide.

STA Travel (*www.statravel.com.au*) 10 High St, Auckland (☎09/309 9995); 130 Cuba St,

Wellington (☎04/385 0561); 90 Cashel St, Christchurch (☎03/379 6372); plus other branches. Major player in student, youth and budget travel.

Usit Beyond (*www.usitbeyond.co.nz*), cnr Shortland St and Jean Batten Place, Auckland (☎09/379 4224); cnr Courtenay Place and Taranaki St, Wellington (☎04/801 7238) and other branches. Youth-oriented travel agency. Nationwide freephone ☎0800/788336.

Perth to southern Africa courtesy of Qantas/Air Zimbabwe and South African Airways. Two of these flights take you direct to Johannesburg, the other two go via Harare. From Johannesburg or Harare you can pick up connections to West Africa – see the next section.

GETTING THERE FROM THE REST OF AFRICA

From South Africa, Air Afrique and South African Airways share the Johannesburg to Abidjan route, connecting with Air Afrique flights across West Africa; Ghana Airways flies via Harare to Accra with onward connections; and Cameroon Airlines flies weekly from Jo'burg to Douala via Harare and Kinshasa. South African Airways has daily flights from Jo'burg to Sal, Cape Verde, en route to New York, and twice-weekly direct flights to Lagos.

From **Harare**, the only direct connections are these Ghana Airways flights, plus flights from Harare to Douala on Cameroon Airlines. There are also flights from Harare to Nairobi five times a week on Air Zimbabwe and Kenya Airways, with connections west from Nairobi.

From East Africa to West Africa, **Nairobi** is the natural hub for flights, though even here, where discount ticket agents thrive, special fares to West Africa, apart from the odd Apex, are unknown. Kenya Airways has direct flights to Abidjan, Douala and Lagos, and there is also a weekly direct flight on Ethiopian Airlines to Accra

and – with a change of planes in Addis Ababa – connections to Abidjan, Bamako and Dakar, Lagos and Lomé. Cameroon Airlines runs flights twice a week between Douala and Nairobi via Bujumbura, Kinshasa and Kigali.

From North Africa, Royal Air Maroc connects **Casablanca** to Abidjan, Bamako, Conakry, Dakar and Nouakchott; Air Algerie connects **Algiers** to Bamako, Dakar, Nouakchott and Ouagadougou; and from **Tunis**, Balkan Bulgarian Airlines has a weekly flight to Accra, and Tunis Air a weekly flight to Dakar and Nouakchott.

OVERLAND AND ADVENTURE TRAVEL

Despite the troubles which have effectively closed the route through Algeria to West Africa, overlanding from Europe – via Morocco and into Mauritania – is still feasible. It's the best way to get to the region if you want to become fully immersed in the identities and landscapes of West Africa: as you finally arrive on the far side of the sea of sand and rock, the first sensations of another world are ones that endure. If you don't have the time or the inclination to do the trip alone, a number of companies will take you, or meet you from a flight for an escorted overland trip through one or more countries.

If you're setting off on extensive travels, the best time to leave is at the end of the European summer. Especially if you plan to hitch and use public transport, you should aim to be in North Africa in September and across the Sahara in October. Throughout most of the region, this gives you at least six months before you can realistically expect to be rained upon.

TRANS-SAHARAN ROUTES

If you're planning to cross the desert you should be careful to obtain the most up-to-date information. Talk to returning travellers and read the African news magazines. Since the early 1990s there have been sporadic clashes between **Tuareg nomads** and the governments of Mali and Niger. Incidents of banditry on trans-Saharan tourists led to armed escorts for convoys and eventually to border closures.

Meanwhile, in **Algeria**, the fundamentalist GI (Groupe Islamique Armée) has murdered dozens of foreigners (mostly expatriate workers) who ignored their September 1993 deadline to leave the country. As a result of the dangers of travel in Algeria, the traditional trans-Saharan routes were still effectively closed to foreigners as this book

went to press, with no prospects of conditions improving sufficiently to make either of them safe – though the Hoggar route (see box, opposite) does now see some tourist traffic. A brief description is given below for information in the event of their reopening.

Mauritania has conceded to pressure from overlanders seeking an alternative route, effectively opening its northern border to southbound traffic using the **Atlantic route** that hugs the coast through southern Morocco to **Nouadhibou**, the mineral port just inside Mauritania. It's a safe enough route, though convoys lead vehicles past minefields near the Mauritanian border. Apart from a difficult section from Nouadhibou to Nouakchott along the coast (guide essential) – which can be avoided by putting your vehicle on the **ore train** heading inland – this route is relatively easy on vehicles, although scenically less impressive than the old Algerian routes.

DRIVING YOURSELF

Driving to West Africa isn't a difficult feat in itself, and many people complete the journey with unmodified road vehicles. Obviously, high ground clearance is important, as is good structural and mechanical condition. Local mechanics are much more familiar with French models, and spares for these are also far more likely to be available. All motorized travellers (whether on two, four or six wheels) agree that the comfort and independence of their **own vehicle** is a mixed blessing. It insulates you from the life of Africa; it's a permanent security headache, especially in towns; and it says one thing – money – to everyone you meet along the way. You can feel like a travelling circus after a few weeks of this. Taking account of fuel, maintenance and insurance, it is a fairly expensive business, too. And unless you have someone aboard who knows the vehicle inside out (and even then), any serious breakdown can be immensely tedious and costly.

The outstanding **advantages** of taking your own vehicle are that you can get off the beaten track (assuming the vehicle is sturdy enough) and visit areas that see a local vehicle only once in a toddler's lifetime. To a great extent, you can actually avoid towns and cities, or at least avoid staying overnight in them by driving out into the wilderness and camping.

One consideration can't be stressed enough – give yourself **time**. Rushing around in Africa is a

> The practical information at the beginning of each country chapter has details on overland arrival from that country's neighbours, including transport availability, road conditions and the kind of treatment you might expect from border officials. As a general rule, borders close at dusk and often on public holidays. Very few are open 24 hours.

THE CLOSED ROUTES AND THE TUAREG

Until the early 1990s, the main trans-Saharan routes were through **Algeria**, now a country whose north is effectively closed to foreigners because of attacks by Muslim fundamentalists. Even before the civil war, the Algerian routes were becoming risky due to Tuareg banditry. What follows summarizes the routes as they were in the late 1980s. When overlanders start using them again, the tracks are likely to be hard to follow and what facilities that existed along the way will have fallen into disrepair.

From the Mediterranean coast, the Sahara is just a day's drive to the south – and a couple of days will see you well into the heart of it. The great majority of travellers (in their own vehicles or otherwise) used the **Hoggar**, a route with long portions of asphalt, stunning variety of scenery, and more towns to break the drive. These include historic settlements like **In Salah** and **El Goléa** and administrative outposts like **Tamanrasset**, a gathering point for desert nomads. The Hoggar mountains peak at 2908m near **Assekrem**, while around Djanet, in the east, the **Tassili** plateau reaches heights of 2154m in the remote **Tassili National Park**, the site of prehistoric cave paintings from an age when the Sahara was bursting with life. The last Algerian post is at **In Guezzam**, from where a 25km stretch of sandy, track-scrawled no-man's-land fills the space before godforsaken **Assamakka**, the Nigérien border post. The drive from Assamakka to the start of the tarmac at **Arlit** takes around six hours. Follow the markers.

Though less scenically compelling, the **Tanezrouft** route would be the one to choose for the most dramatic introduction to sub-Saharan Africa. It's a bigger adventure – and a more personal experience, as fewer people use it. This stretch of desert is almost completely flat and barren and distances between settlements can seem endless. Picturesque oases like **Taghit**, **Beni-Abbès** and **Timimoun** dot the route in its early stages, well to the north of the Tropic of Cancer. By the time you reach the end of the tarmac at **Reggane**, roughly a third of the way across, there still remains over 1300km of uninterrupted *piste* before arrival at the next town, **Gao**, in Mali, on the almost lush banks of the Niger River.

There are two main **Tuareg groups** living in the Algerian Sahara: the **Kel Ahaggar**, who occupy the Hoggar near Tamanrasset, and the **Kel Ajjer**, who live in the Tassili near Djanet. Further afield, other groups are scattered throughout the desert. Among them are the Kel Aïr and Kel Gress in Niger, and the Kel Tademaket in the Timbuktu region of Mali.

The Tuareg speak **Tamashek** (or *Tamahaq*, or numerous other spellings), a Berber dialect that's one of the few African languages with its own script. Traditionally, they controlled trans-Saharan trade, offering protection to caravans or raiding those that refused their services. Their society was highly stratified, with classes ranging from nobles to slaves, and the **Harratin**, blacks who formerly worked as indentured servants, still live in virtual chatteldom in many of the desert oases. The Algerian Tuareg have become increasingly sedentary, due in part to a government plan to settle them, and in part to the crippling effects of the drought of the mid-1980s.

---

bad enough idea using local transport. But to try to drive in your own vehicle with a fixed number of days and weeks is to court disaster. Allow a month, at the very least, to get from the Mediterranean to sub-Saharan Africa. It's simply not worth the work, in any case, to rush through at a breakneck pace.

Good **books** for drivers heading to West Africa include: *Through Africa: the Overlanders' Guide*, Bob Swain and Paula Snyder (Bradt, 1991), and *Sahara Overland* by Chris Scott (Trailblazer Guides, due to be published January 2000). Chris Scott's related Web site (*www.sahara-overland.com*) is also a good source of up-to-date information.

SELLING YOUR VEHICLE

A good way to cut the cost of overland travel to West Africa is to take a vehicle along with you for sale; all sorts are worth more in Africa. The profit

you can expect depends on the price you pay for the car in the first place; the UK, unfortunately, is not the best place to buy (prices are high and the steering wheel is on the wrong side).

If you intend to sell your vehicle in West Africa, your **best investment** would be a three-year-old left-hand-drive **Peugeot 505** *familiale* station wagon or a **Mercedes saloon**. Most end up in service as *taxis brousse*. **Mercedes commercial vans** are also much in demand. **Twin-cab pick-ups** sell like hot cakes and **4WDs**, preferably Toyota, are also very popular.

Where you sell the vehicle can depend on how well it is still working. Selling the car earlier than planned and hitching a lift with other travellers is always an option. In **Mauritania** the car's details are entered into your passport; if you sell the vehicle, it is vital to go with the buyer to the customs office to fill in the paperwork and pay the import duty that will allow you to leave the country without the vehicle. Some purchasers will suggest driving down to the Senegalese border at Rosso to evade Mauritanian duty: be suspicious. Rosso is a confusing border at the best of times and it is easy to get ripped off here; you'd be better off just driving across yourself and selling the vehicle without any customs hassle in **Senegal**. In Senegal, **Mali**, **Burkina Faso** and most West African countries there is no problem selling cars; any problems will be faced by the buyer when he registers it locally. The **worst countries** to sell a car in are **Ghana** and **Nigeria**, which require a carnet (see below), and **Côte d'Ivoire**, where the bureaucracy makes any car sale time-consuming and expensive. Bear in mind that as you near the coast you will start to compete with imports that arrive, rather less depreciated, by boat.

VEHICLE DOCUMENTS

Travelling by private vehicle drastically increases the red tape you'll have to deal with. First and foremost, you must be able to produce the vehicle's **carte grise**, an international registration certificate issued, in Britain, by the AA or RAC on production of the vehicle's log book and the payment of a £4 fee. Effectively making your car's log book obsolete once in Africa, the carte grise states ownership, country of registration and the registration, chassis and engine numbers – all of which can be checked thoroughly at borders. It is useful to carry a few photocopies of it as well. If you're not the owner of the car you're driving, you'll require a **notified document** (*attestation du propriétaire* in French) stating permission to use the car.

You'll also need an **international driving licence** – issued in Britain by the AA and other motoring organizations for a £4 fee. Spare copies can be useful, as it's the first thing police will confiscate in the event of a traffic offence and you won't get far without one.

A **carnet** is also taken by many motorists. These documents allow you to take your car into a country without paying import duties or a deposit. They're expensive, however, at £55 (RAC) or £65 (AA) and you'll have to place a bank guarantee (usually 150 percent of the value of your car) or cash deposit before a carnet will be issued (though it's possible to take out insurance to cover this deposit). Most West African countries will issue a document that will allow **temporary importation** – in Senegal a *passavant*, in Mali a *laissez-passer*, Côte d'Ivoire a *carte touristique*, while Mauritania just writes

the car details in your passport. However there is almost always a fee to be paid for these documents, and a carnet also speeds your passage through borders. In West Africa only **Nigeria** and **Ghana** absolutely require a carnet. If you plan to **sell your car**, of course, a carnet is the last thing you need: if the vehicle isn't correctly stamped in and out of each country you'll lose your deposit.

Motor **insurance** is obligatory and varies in cost. Motorbike insurance is approximately half the cost of cars, and commercial vehicles (including minibuses with eight seats plus driver) twice as much. **Morocco** is now covered by the European "Green Card" (often free; ask your insurance company), without which you will have to buy insurance at the border (about £30 for ten days). Both **Mauritania** and **Senegal** require drivers to buy into their national insurance scheme, but most other countries in West Africa are covered by a **carte brune**, an insurance policy that can be taken out in any ECOWAS (Economic Community of West Africa) country.

HITCHING AND USING LOCAL TRANSPORT

If you're going to travel **under your own steam**, it's worth considering a cheap, one-way flight to Morocco or the Canary Isles to get started. Bearing in mind the possible cost of even a minimum number of days of travel through Europe this can be a positive saving.

Of course, you can do it the hard way. Not a few Timbuktu-bound travellers have begun the trip hitching to a British channel port for the crossing to France and the unpredictable haul through Spain to North Africa. Of the Mediterranean ferry ports, Algeciras is the cheapest and easiest embarkation point for Morocco with several ferries a day to Tangier and to the Spanish enclave of Ceuta on the Moroccan coast.

If you camp, and have the stamina to keep hitching, there's no reason you shouldn't get to the Mauritanian side of the Sahara at remarkably little cost. The ease of hitching in Morocco compensates for the common misery of the roadside in southern Europe, though as you venture into the far southern regions of Morocco, you will simply need to be lucky: there's no public transport to the Mauritanian border and travellers without their own transport will have to find lifts with overlanders (free and often fun) or the occasional truck, which will usually charge. The final section of the **Western Sahara** will usually cost you to

OVERLAND OPERATORS AND AGENTS IN BRITAIN

Africa Travel Centre, 4 Medway Court, Leigh St, London WC1H 9QX (☎0171/387 1211). The best specialist Africa agent in London, with good expertise and lots of trips to offer through many operators.

Burkima, 55 Huddlestone Rd, Willesden Green, London NW2 5DL (☎0181/451 2446; *burkima@ compuserve.com*). Twice-yearly departures from London to Accra – via Mauritania and Mali – where connections are made with Ghana–Mombassa tours.

Dragoman, 99 Camp Green, Debenham, Suffolk IP14 6LA (☎01728/861133; *www.dragoman.co.uk*). Personal and creative operators with notably good trucks. Twice-yearly trans-African departures via Mauritania include Mali, Côte d'Ivoire and Ghana.

Encounter Overland, 267 Old Brompton Rd, London SW5 9JA (☎0171/370 6845; *www. encounter-overland.com*). Specialists in long trips; their London–Nairobi tour passes through Mauritania and Mali, and then either flies or drives from Nigeria/Cameroon across to Uganda.

Explore Worldwide, 1 Frederick St, Aldershot, Hampshire GU11 1LQ (☎01252/760000; *info@explore.co.uk*). Highly respected small-groups operator with an excellent reputation. Trips include a 16-day "Foot Safari" in Mali from £1295.

Guerba Expeditions, Wessex House, 40 Station Rd, Westbury, Wiltshire BA13 3JN (☎01373/826611 or 856956; *www.guerba.co.uk*). One of the best African specialist operators. Trips include 7 weeks Dakar to Lomé (as part of a trans-Africa trip), and 3 weeks Lomé to Bamako via the Dogon country.

Nomadic Expeditions, 263 Barkham Rd, Wokingham, Berkshire RG41 4BY (☎0118/978 0800; *info@nomadic.co.uk*). Small company specializing in West Africa; offers comprehensive trans-West Africa tours of up to 15 weeks.

Oasis Overland, 33 Travellers Way, Hounslow, Middx TW4 7QB (☎0181/759 5597; *oasisoverland @travellersway.demon.co.uk*). Budget expeditions from UK–Ghana and Ghana–Kenya, with only a few departures.

OVERLAND OPERATORS AND AGENTS IN THE US

Adventure Center, 1311 63rd St, Suite 200, Emoryville, CA 94608 (☎1-800/227-8747 or 510/654-1879). Wide range of tours and safaris, including trans-African and trans-Saharan treks.

Africa Desk, 329 Danbury Rd, New Milford, CT 06776 (☎1-800/284-8796; *www.africadesk.com*). Cultural tours to Ghana, Côte d'Ivoire, and Senegal.

Africa Travel Centre, 499 Ernston Rd, Parlin, NJ 08859 (☎1-800/631-5650 or 908/721-2929). Sister company of London-based Africa Travel Centre.

Born Free Safaris & Tours, 12504 Riverside Drive, North Hollywood, CA 91607. (☎1-800/372-3274). Culture-focused tours.

Global Safaris, 2601 Chapman Ave, Fullerton, CA 92631 (☎1-800/548-3140 or 714/738-7979). Wide range of safaris.

International Bicycle Fund, 4887 Columbia Drive S, Seattle, WA 98108-1919 (☎ & Fax 206/767-0848; *www.ibike.org*). Campaigning bicycle outfit offers several 2-week tours covering two or more countries including Mali, Senegal, Gambia, Guinea, Ghana, Togo, Burkina and Benin.

ITC, 4134 Atlantic Ave, #205, Long Beach, CA 90807. (☎1-800/257-4981 or 562/595-6905). Safaris and special interest tours in West African

destinations including Senegal, Côte d'Ivoire and Ghana. Some flexibility to organize your own tours.

Journeys, 1536 NW 23rd Ave, Portland, OR 97210 (☎503/226-7200); and at Powell's Travel Store, Pioneer Courthouse Square, Portland (☎503/226-4849). Tailor-made trips for individuals and groups. To receive their quarterly newsletter, *The African Traveler*, send $10 annual subscription.

Safari Centre, 3201 N Sepulveda Blvd, Manhattan Beach, CA 90266 (☎1-800/223-6046 or 310/546-4411; *www.safaricentre.com*). West African package includes stops in Côte d'Ivoire, Ghana, Togo and Benin.

Spector Travel, 31 St James Ave, Boston, MA 02116 (☎1-800/TRY-AFRICA; *www.spectortravel.com*). All-round Africa specialists with good West Africa knowledge.

Turtle Tours, Box 1147, Carefree, AZ 85377 (☎1-888/299-1439; *www.turtletours.com*). Sahelian destinations with focus on cultural events. Trips are flexible and may be customized.

Wilderness Travel, 1102 Ninth St, Berkeley, CA 94710 (☎1-800/368-2794 or 510/558-2488; *www.wildernesstravel.com*). Various excursions including a package to the Dogon country in Mali.

OVERLAND OPERATORS AND AGENTS IN CANADA

Adventures Abroad, 2148, 20800 Westminster Highway, Richmond, BC V6V 2W3. (☎1-800/665-3998 or 604/303-1099). Packages to Sahelian towns with stops in Timbuktu, Mopti and surrounding areas.

Carlton Travel, 1600 Merivale Rd Ottawa, ON K2G 5J8 (☎613/226-1730). Overland tours from London, including some shorter jaunts within West Africa.

Fresh Tracks (☎1-800/627-7492 or 604/737-7880; *www.freshtracks.com*). British Columbia-based

wilderness and adventure travel specialist, offering cultural excursions to Mali and Burkina Faso.

G.A.P. Adventures, 266 Dupont St, Toronto, ON M5R 1V7 (☎1-800/465-5600 or 416/922-8899). Overland and packaged excursions to the Sahel.

World Expeditions, 78 George St, Ottawa, ON K1N 5W1 (☎613/230-8676; *www.worldexpeditions.com*) Wide range of adventure treks, including a tour of the Dogon country.

OVERLAND OPERATORS AND AGENTS IN AUSTRALIA

Adventure World, 11/343 Little Collins St, Melbourne (☎03/9670 0125); 73 Walker St, North Sydney (☎02/9956-7766); and other branches. Mainly deal directly with travel agents.

Africa Bound Holidays, 8/87 Canning Hwy, Victoria Park, Perth (☎08/9361 2047; *safaris@ons.com.au*). A small team of Africa experts dealing in everything from independent travel to swanky safaris.

Africa Travel Centre, 4/182 Victoria Parade, East Melbourne (☎03/9663 9709; *classicmel@africatravel.com.au*); 11/456 Kent St, Sydney (free call ☎1800/622 984 or 02/9267 3048; *africa@africatravel.com.au*). Overlanding and truck safaris right through to upmarket lodge packages.

Journeys Worldwide, 7/333 Adelaide St, 2nd Floor, Brisbane (☎07/3221 4788). Offers overland tours in Africa.

Peregrine Adventures, 258 Lonsdale St, Melbourne (☎03/9662 2700); 5/38 York St, Sydney (☎02/9290 2758; *charlotte@syd.peregrine.net.au*). Worldwide adventure travel with a subsidiary – African Adventure Tours – specializing in overland tours.

Sydney Adventure Centre, 7/428 George St, Sydney (☎02/9221-8555; *sydney@travellers.com.au*). Not Africa specific, but deal in overland tours.

Thor Adventure Travel, 228 Rundel St, Adelaide (☎08/8232 3155; *tashi@olis.net.au*). Some Africa experts at this general travel agency.

OVERLAND OPERATORS AND AGENTS IN NEW ZEALAND

Adventure Travel Company, 164 Parnell Rd, Parnell, PO Box 37334, Auckland (☎09/379 9755; *advakl@hot.co.nz*). Large agency dealing in all manner of adventure travel worldwide with plenty of African packages, with a few pitched at West Africa.

Adventure World, 101 Great South Rd, Remuera, PO Box 74008, Auckland (☎09/524 5118;

discover@adventureworld.co.nz; www.adventureworld.co.nz). New Zealand branch of the Australian organization.

Africa Travel Centre, 21 Remuera Rd, Newmarket, Auckland 3 (☎09/520 2000). From the same stable as the Australian company, and the only agent specializing solely in Africa.

---

cross. Car sellers may have room for hitchers, but tourist vehicles are generally packed to the gills.

INCLUSIVE OVERLAND TOURS

The "**overland tour**" catch-all covers most of the organized holidays that don't feel like packages. Not all of them are *overland* the entire way. The "fly out, tour around by truck, fly back" option is increasingly popular. Note that operators sometimes run trips "in association" with each other, and the number of trips offered each year is actually quite small.

If you're interested in one of the more inexpensive (sometimes regrettably one-off) expedition

companies that advertise in the travel pages of UK and European papers, it's worth paying them a visit. They're often just a private trip hoping to minimize costs by taking others. Scrutinizing their literature gives a good indication of their probable preparedness and real know-how. If their prospectus looks cheap or hasty, forget it.

As a destination for specialist **American Africa operators**, West Africa is little known in comparison with East and southern Africa. Hence the all-inclusive tours that are available are mainly **adventure treks** targeting younger travellers, similar to what's on offer in Europe. You won't find Princess

Cruises to this part of the world and even Club Med has only conquered a few isolated beaches.

CYCLING

If you have enough **time** (the most precious commodity), energy and stamina, it's quite feasible to consider mountain biking through Europe in the summer, down through Morocco in the autumn, loading your machine aboard a lorry for the hardest part of the Sahara crossing and then cycling where your fancy takes you through the dry season.

It is of course possible to take a sturdy touring bike, or even use a locally bought roadster. A tourer is much faster on the main roads and a fit cyclist could expect to cover 120km a day or more. But you're likely to suffer more from broken spokes and punctures at unexpected potholes and you're much less free to leave the highways. Some routes and regions for which a mountain-bike is ideal are beyond the scope of other bikes.

More cycling practicalities are detailed in "Getting Around" on p.46. If you still need convincing, write to International Bicycle Fund or visit their Web site (see box, p.17) for details of their **escorted cycle tours**.

BIKES BY AIR

If time is limited, you can **fly your bike** to West Africa. To avoid paying excess baggage charges, you should write in advance to the ground operations manager of the airline, pack as many heavy items into your hand luggage as possible and arrive several hours before the flight to get to know the check-in staff. It's rare that you'll be obliged to pay.

It's much harder, as a rule, to avoid excess fees on charter flights. Let them know in advance and plead your case. The 20kg weight allowance, which your bike and luggage is likely to exceed, is a notional figure with no bearing on air safety, used to extract more profit from the passengers.

Few airlines will insist your bike be boxed or bagged. But it's best to turn the handlebars into the frame and tie them down, invert the pedals and deflate the tyres.

RED TAPE AND VISAS

All visitors to West Africa require a full ten-year passport, which should remain valid for at least six months beyond the end of the trip. Some West African countries will not allow you in with less. Allow at least one blank page per country to be visited.

If your passport gives an **occupation**, student, teacher or business person is best. Try to avoid declaring yourself a journalist, photographer or anything similar that might be misconstrued.

Further kinds of red tape which may entangle you on your travels include currency declaration forms, photography permits and international vaccination certificates – all dealt with in detail further on. Other pieces of paper are mentioned in the introductory Practical Information at the beginning of relevant country chapters.

GETTING VISAS BEFORE DEPARTURE

If you're flying out to a limited number of countries on a short trip, you should get **visas** in advance. If you'll be away for longer, note that few visas remain valid beyond three months, and that certain countries, notably Nigeria and Cameroon, will generally only issue visas in the passport holder's country of residence, or nearest embassy representing that country. Although costly, it may make sense to obtain visas for these countries before you leave, let them expire, and then have them renewed later on, quite easily, at the relevant embassies in West Africa.

Visa regulations in West Africa are notoriously fickle and hard to pin down. While there are few rules that can't be broken in an emergency, cases do occur – too often – of people sent back hundreds of kilometres for want of a stamp. It pays to plan ahead.

DIPLOMATIC MISSIONS IN BRITAIN AND IRELAND

All the following offices are open Mon–Fri, unless otherwise stated.

Benin, 16 The Broadway, Stanmore, Middlesex HA8 4DW (☎0181/954 8800). Open 10am–12.30pm & 2–4.30pm. Visas £30 on the spot; single entry for a maximum of 30 days, easily extended in the country.

Burkina Faso, 5 Cinnamon Row, Plantation Wharf, London SW11 3TW (☎0171/738 1800). Open 10am–12.30pm & 2.30–4.30pm. Multiple entry visa, immediate issue, £25.

Cameroon, 84 Holland Park, London W11 3SB (☎0171/727 0771). Open 10.30am–12.30pm. 3-month multiple entry visas in 24hr, £40.

Côte d'Ivoire, 2 Upper Belgrave St, London SW1X 8BJ (☎0171/2356991). Open 10am–1pm. Visa costs £40 for UK nationals, £20 for Irish. A return ticket is demanded.

The Gambia, 57 Kensington Court, London W8 5DG (☎0171/937 6316). Open 9.30am–5pm (closes 1pm Fri). 3-month single-entry visa in 48hr costs £20.

Ghana, 104 Highgate Hill, London N6 5HE (☎0171/235 4142). Open 9.30am–5pm. Three working days to issue visas. 3-month single entry £15, multiple entry £35.

Guinea, 20 Upper St, London W1X 9PB (☎0171/333 0044). Visa in 24hr for £45.

Guinea-Bissau, 8 Palace Gate, London W8 4RP (☎0171/589 5253). One month visas in 24hr for £30.

Liberia, 2 Pembridge Place, London W2 4XB (☎0171/221 1036).

Morocco, 49 Queen's Gate Gardens, London SW7 5NE (☎0171/724 0719).

Nigeria, Nigeria House, 9 Northumberland Ave, London WC2N 5BX (☎0171/839 1244). Open 9.30am–6pm (1pm Fri). Also at 56 Leeson Park, Dublin 6 (☎01/660 4366 or 660 4051). Return ticket or covering documentation required, as well as evidence of sufficient funds. Visas take five working days to issue and cost £40 for UK nationals, £20 for Irish.

Senegal, 39 Marioes Rd, London W8 6LA (☎0171/938 4048).

Sierra Leone, 33 Portland Place, London W1N 3AG (☎0171/636 6483 or 636 6485).

To obtain visas for **Mauritania**, **Cape Verde**, **Mali** and **Niger** contact the appropriate embassies in Europe: Mauritania, 89 rue Cherche-Midi, 75006 Paris (☎01.40.49.00.63); Cape Verde, 33 Avda Restelo, 1400 Lisbon (☎01/301 5271); Mali, 89 rue Cherche-Midi, 75006 Paris (☎01.45.48.58.43); Niger, 154 rue de Longchamp, 75116 Paris (☎01/45.04.80.60) or use a visa service. The French consulate in London (6a Cromwell Place, SW7; ☎0171/838 2050) may be able to help with a Togolese visa.

DIPLOMATIC MISSIONS IN NORTH AMERICA

Benin, 2737 Cathedral Ave NW, Washington, DC 20008 (☎202/232-6656); 58 Glebe Ave, Ottawa K1S 2C3 (☎613/233-4429).

Burkina Faso, 2340 Massachusetts Ave NW, Washington, DC 20008 (☎202/332-5577); 115 E 73rd St, New York, NY 10021 (☎212/288-7575); 48 Range Rd, Ottawa K1N 8J4 (☎613/238-3812).

Cameroon, 2349 Massachusetts Ave NW, Washington, DC 20008; 22 E 73rd St, New York,

NY 10021 (☎212/794-2295); 170 Clemow Ave, Ottawa K1S 2B4 (☎613/236-3885).

Cape Verde, 3415 Massachusetts Ave NW, Washington, DC 20007 (☎202/965-6820); 535 Boylston St, Boston, MA 02116 (☎617/353-0014).

Côte d'Ivoire, 46 E 74th St, New York, NY 10021 (☎212/717-5555); 2424 Massachusetts Ave NW, Washington, DC 20008 (☎202/797-0300); 9 Marlborough Ave, Ottawa K1N 8E6 (☎613/236-9919).

Bear in mind also that a visa only constitutes "permission to apply to enter". This isn't mere pedantry. You can be turned away despite having a visa (for arriving on a one-way ticket, for example, in the case of Cameroon) and the length of **validity** of a visa may bear no relation to how long you're allowed to stay in the country when you arrive. It's almost always possible to **extend** a first stay, but in several countries it can be a serious matter if you overstay without extending.

There seems to be little sense to the who-does and who-doesn't of visa requirements. Ten of the

countries covered in this book – Niger, Burkina Faso, Cape Verde, Guinea-Bissau, Guinea, Ghana, Togo, Benin, Nigeria and Cameroon – require all non-West Africans to have visas. Visa requirements do change, however, and it's always advisable to check the current situation before leaving home.

To get a visa in your home country you'll fairly often be asked to provide evidence of a return air ticket and occasionally have to show an invitation or a covering letter stating the purpose of your trip. Tourist visas and business visas are always distinct. The latter usually require a letter

The Gambia, 1115 15th St NW, Washington, DC 20005 (☎202/842-1356); 820 Second Ave, Suite 900C, New York, NY 10017 (☎212/949-6640).

Ghana, 3512 International Drive NW, Washington, DC 20008 (☎202/686-4500); 19 E 47th St, New York, NY 10017 (☎212/832-1300); 1 Clemow Ave, Ottawa K1S 2A9 (☎613/236-0871).

Guinea, 2112 Leroy Place NW, Washington, DC 20008 (☎202/483-9420); 140 E 39th St, New York, NY 10016 (☎212/687-8115); 483 Wilbrod St, Ottawa K1N 6N1 (☎613/789-8444).

Guinea-Bissau, 918 16th St NW, Mezzanine Suite, Washington, DC 20006 (☎202/872-4222); 211 E 43rd St, Suite 604, New York, NY 10017 (☎212/661-3977).

Liberia, 5201 16th St NW, Washington, DC 20011 (☎202/291-0761).

Mali, 111 E 69th St, New York, NY 10021 (☎212/737-4150); 2130 R St NW, Washington, DC 20008 (☎202/332-2249); 50 Goulburn Ave, Ottawa K1N 8C8 (☎613/232-7429).

Mauritania, 2129 Leroy Place NW, Washington, DC 20008 (☎202/232-5700); 211 E 43rd St, New York, NY 10017 (☎212/986-7963).

Morocco, 1601 21st St NW, Washington, DC 20009 (☎202/462-7979); 10 E 40th St, New York, NY 10016 (☎212/758-2625); 38 Range Rd, Ottawa K1N 8J4 (☎613/236-7391).

Niger, 2204 R St NW, Washington, DC 20008, (☎202/483-4224); 417 E 50th St, New York, NY 10022 (☎212/421-3260); 38 Blackburn Ave, Ottawa K1N 8A2 (☎613/232-4291).

Nigeria, 2201 M St NW, Washington, DC 20037 (☎202/822-1500); 828 Second Ave, New York, NY 10017 (☎212/953-9130); 295 Metcalfe St, Ottawa K2P 1R9 (☎613/236-0521).

Senegal, 2112 Wyoming Ave NW, Washington, DC 20008 (☎202/234-0540); 238 E 68th St, New York, NY 10021 (☎212/517-9030); 57 Marlborough Ave, Ottawa K1N 8E8 (☎613/238-6392).

Sierra Leone, 1701 19th St NW, Washington, DC 20009 (☎202/939-9261); 245 E 49th St, New York, NY 10017 (☎212/688-1656).

Togo, 2208 Massachusetts Ave NW, Washington, DC 20008 (☎202/234-4212); 12 Range Rd, Ottawa K1N 8J3 (☎613/238-5916).

DIPLOMATIC MISSIONS IN AUSTRALIA

Cameroon 65 Bingara Rd, Beecroft, NSW 2119 (☎02/9876 4544).

Morocco 11 West St, North Sydney, NSW 2060 (☎02/9922 4999).

Nigeria 7 Terrigal Crescent, O'Malley, Canberra, ACT 2606 (☎02/6286 1322).

For **Burkina Faso**, **Côte d'Ivoire**, **Mauritania**, **Senegal** and **Togo**, contact the French Consulate General (*www.france.net.au*): in WA, NT, QLD, NSW & ACT apply to 31 Market St, Sydney (☎02/9261 5779; *cgsydney@france.net.au*); in Vic, Tas & SA apply to 492 St Kilda Rd, Melbourne 3004 (☎03/9820 0921; *cgmelb@france.net.au*).

DIPLOMATIC MISSIONS IN SOUTH AFRICA

Côte d'Ivoire, 795 Government Ave, POB 13510, Hatfield, Pretoria 0083 (☎012/342-6913).

Ghana, 1038 Arcadia St, POB 12537, Hatfield, Pretoria 0001 (☎012/342-5847).

Guinea, 336 Orient St, POB 13523, Arcadia, Pretoria 0083 (☎012/342-8465).

Mali, 106 Infotech Bldg, Suite 106, 1090 Arcadia St, Pretoria 0083 (☎012/342-7464).

Nigeria, 138 Beckett St, Arcadia, POB 27332, Pretoria 0083 (☎012/343-2021).

from your company and often a letter from an African contact. It's always worth asking for a **multiple entry visa** (which often costs more). Should you need to go back from a neighbouring country it saves a lot of hassle.

VISA SERVICES

If you're in a hurry, need a visa for a country which doesn't have a representative in your home country, or anticipate some kind of hassle getting it, it may be worth considering a commercial **visa service**, whereby, for a set fee, you sign the application forms and mail them your passport and they do all the legwork. If you're flying straight into a country you may have little choice, since personal applications abroad by mail can take several months to process. In that specific instance, however, it is sometimes permitted to organize your visa at the airport on arrival (check that the airline won't refuse you boarding if you don't have the required visa).

A visa service can be extremely practical, if not essential, in the **US** – where West African embassies are almost exclusively based in Washington DC (although many have permanent

VISA SERVICES IN THE UK

The Visa Service, 2 Northdown St, King's Cross, London N1 9BG (☎0171/833 2709). The largest and most efficient agency. They charge £47 per visa, plus the visa price and courier fees for overseas applications.

VISA SERVICES IN THE US

AAT Visa Services, 3417 Haines Way, Falls Church, VA 22041 (☎703/820-5612).
Embassy Visa Service, 1519 Connecticut Ave NW, Suite 300, Washington, DC 20036 (☎202/387-0300).
International Passports and Visas, 205 Beverly Drive, Suite 204, Beverly Hills, CA (☎310/274-2020).

Travel Agenda, 119 W 57th St, Suite 1008, New York NY 10019 (☎212/265-7887).
Travisa (☎1-800/222-2589; *www.travisa.com*). Offices in Washington DC, Chicago, San Francisco, Detroit, New York and San Juan, PR.

VISA SERVICES IN AUSTRALIA AND NEW ZEALAND

DX Travcour, 65 New North Rd, Eden Terrace, Auckland (☎09/366-0635); Store 2, 477 Plummer St, Port Melbourne (☎03/9646 3822); 112–120 Euston Rd, Alexandria, Sydney (☎02/9557 7180).

---

missions that issue visas in New York) and where each one can take six weeks (if you're lucky) or many months to process by mail. With an agency, you still need to plan ahead, but they can generally get visas in about a week; count on another two to three weeks to send the applications back and forth through the mail and have your passport returned. Given the expense ($15–30 per visa plus the visa fee), if you're planning on covering a lot of territory, you might just get visas for the first couple of countries to be visited and pick up the rest in Africa, checking the map on p.24 to make sure onward destinations are represented in the country you arrive in.

GETTING VISAS ALONG THE WAY

On an **overland trip**, it would seem to be simplest to pick up the visas you need along the way – were it not for the fact that some West African embassies in the region may occasionally refuse to issue visas to passport holders who could have obtained them in their own country. A further obstacle – though one that's steadily diminishing – is the lack of representation for a number of countries which have very few embassies. Plan ahead to see where you should be getting your next visa. The visa map of West Africa on p.24 indicates in which cities you *should* be able to obtain which visas. Certain nationalities will have hassles getting some of these, so it's worth trying at the first opportunity. Often an **expired visa** can be a help in getting another for the same country, though reckless applications can be an expensive hobby. Take plenty of passport **photos** – allow three or four for each visa you expect to need.

In the country chapters of this guide, addresses have been given in as much detail as possible in the "Listings" section at the end of each capital city. Once you've located the embassy in question – where you've any choice it's the *consulate* you need to go to – **obtaining visas** should be fairly straightforward in most cases and is often a good deal easier than sorting things out at home. Nevertheless, you ought to be prepared for an average 2–3 days' wait from application to delivery, and have a handy hotel address to use as your intended address in the country (nothing too slummy).

A **letter of introduction** from your own embassy is sometimes required (this can usually be provided on the spot, for a fee). Countries for which a letter of introduction is either helpful or mandatory include Mauritania, Guinea, Cameroon and Nigeria, but it's hard to generalize as rules and norms vary greatly from embassy to embassy. Ask about this in advance if you're unsure.

The person whose signature is required for the visa is invariably the **consul**. If you're being delayed or messed around, ask to see him or her in person. Never give up. If you get stonewalled, or you're in a hurry and told to come back next week, try putting in an hour or two in the waiting room. This often has miraculous effects, especially combined with persistent whining.

Visa fees can be high (up to £40/$64 equivalent or more) and they sometimes vary mysteriously from one applicant to the next, not always depending on different nationalities.

BRITISH DIPLOMATIC MISSIONS IN NORTH AND WEST AFRICA

For general enquiries, the Travel Advice Unit at the Consular Division of the Foreign and Commonwealth Office, 1 Palace St, London SW1E 5HE (☎0171/238 4503) can be helpful, or try their Web site: *www.fco.gov.uk*. In the following listing, where there is only an honorary consul, cities in brackets indicate the location of the embassy or high commission in authority.

Benin (LAGOS) C.M. Barnes, Honorary Consul, Lot 24, Patte d'Oie, Cotonou (☎30.11.20).

Burkina Faso (ABIDJAN) A.C. Bessey, Honorary Consul, Tobacco Marketing Consultants Ltd, BP 3769, Ouagadougou (☎31.11.37; Fax 31.05.03).

Cameroon British Embassy, av Winston Churchill, Yaoundé (BP 547, Yaoundé; ☎22.05.45; Fax 22.01.48).

Cape Verde (DAKAR) A. Canuto, Honorary Consul, Shell Cabo Verde, Avda Amilcar Cabral CP4, Mindelo, Sao Vincente (☎31.41.32; Fax 31.47.55).

Côte d'Ivoire British Embassy, Immeuble "Les Harmonies", 3rd Floor, corner bd Carde and av Dr Jamot, Plateau, Abidjan (01 BP 2581 01, Abidjan; ☎22.68.50; Fax 22.32.21).

The Gambia British High Commission, 48 Atlantic Rd, Fajara (PO Box 507, Banjul; ☎495133; Fax 496134).

Ghana British High Commission, Osu Link, off Abdul Nasser Ave, Accra (PO Box 296, Accra; ☎021/22.16.65; Fax 021/66.46.52).

Guinea (DAKAR) Mrs V.A. Treitlein, Honorary Consul, BP 834, Conakry (☎44.69.82; Fax 46.16.80).

Guinea-Bissau (DAKAR) J. Van Maanen, Honorary Consul, Mavegro Int, Bissau (CP 100, Bissau; ☎20.12.24; Fax 20.12.65).

Mali (DAKAR) J. Chaloner, Honorary Consul, American International School of Bamako, (BP 34, Bamako; ☎22.47.38; Fax 22.08.53).

Mauritania (RABAT) Mrs N Abeiderrahmane, Unofficial British Representative, BP 2069 Nouakchott (☎252337).

Morocco British Embassy, 17 bd de la Tour Hassan, Rabat (BP 45, Rabat; ☎7/72.09.05; Fax 7/70.45.31).

Niger (ABIDJAN) B. Niandou, Honorary Vice-Consul, BP 11168, Niamey (☎73.20.51 or 73.25.39; Fax 73.36.92).

Nigeria British High Commission, 11 Eleke Crescent, Victoria Island, (PMB 12136, Lagos; ☎1/266 7061 or 1/266 6413; Fax 1/266 6909).

Senegal British Embassy, 20 rue du Docteur Guillet (BP 6025, Dakar; ☎823 73 92; Fax 823 27 66).

Togo (ACCRA) Mrs J.A. Sayer, Honorary Consul, British School of Lomé (BP 20050, Lomé; ☎21.46.06; Fax 21.49.89).

US EMBASSIES IN NORTH AND WEST AFRICA

Algeria 4 Chemin Cheikh Brahimi, Alger-Gare 16000 Algiers (☎2/60.11.86).

Benin rue Caporal Anani Bernard, Cotonou (BP 2012, Cotonou; ☎30.17.92 or 30.06.50; Fax 30.19.74).

Burkina Faso rue Raoul Folereau, Ouagadougou, 01 (BP 34; ☎31.26.60 or 30.67.23; Fax 31.23.68).

Cameroon rue Nachtigal, Yaoundé (BP 817, Yaoundé; ☎23.40.14; Fax 23.07.53).

Cape Verde rua Abilio M. Macedo 81, Praia (CP 201, Praia; ☎61.56.16; Fax 61.13.55).

Côte d'Ivoire 5 rue Jesse Owens, Abidjan (01 BP 1712, Abidjan; ☎21.09.79; Fax 22.32.59).

The Gambia Kairaba Ave, Fajara (PO Box 19, Banjul; ☎392856 or 392858; Fax 392475).

Ghana Ring Road East, Accra (PO Box 194, Accra; ☎021/77.53.47; Fax 021/77.60.08).

Guinea corner of 2nd Blvd and 9th Ave, Conakry (BP 603, Conakry; ☎44.15.20; Fax 44.15.22).

Guinea Bissau Bairro de Penha, Bissau (CP 297 Bissau; ☎25.22.73; Fax 25.22.82).

Mali rue Rochester NY, Bamako (BP 34, Bamako; ☎22.54.70; Fax 22.37.12).

Mauritania rue Abadallaye, Nouakchott (BP 232, Nouakchott; ☎252660; Fax 252589).

Morocco 2 Charia Marrakech, Rabat (☎7/76.22.65).

Niger bd des Ambassades, Niamey (BP 11201, Niamey; ☎72.26.61; Fax 73.31.67).

Nigeria 2 Louis Farrakhan Crescent, Victoria Island, Lagos (PO Box 554; ☎1/261 0097; Fax 1/261 2218).

Senegal av Jean XXIII, Dakar (BP 49, Dakar; ☎823 34 24; Fax 822 29 91).

Togo rue Vauban, Lomé (BP 852, Lomé; ☎21.29.91 or 21.77.17; Fax 21.79.52).

Visas are often issued with fiscal stamps stuck in your passport, or a handwritten sum of money. The value should be what you paid. If it differs, it's worth complaining and asking for a receipt. There may have been an accidental overpayment...

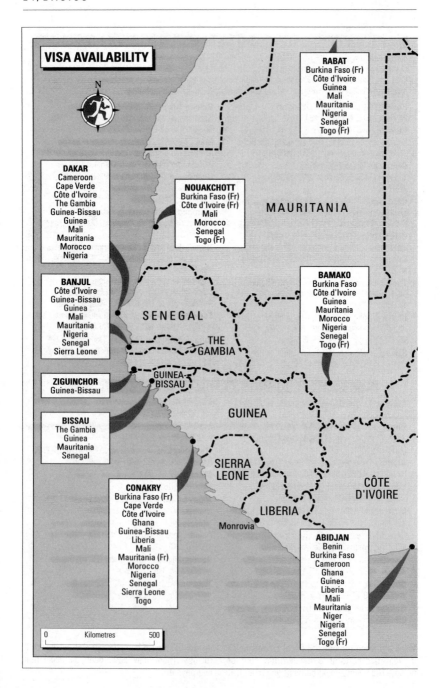

VISA AVAILABILITY

N

RABAT
Burkina Faso (Fr)
Côte d'Ivoire
Guinea
Mali
Mauritania
Nigeria
Senegal
Togo (Fr)

DAKAR
Cameroon
Cape Verde
Côte d'Ivoire
The Gambia
Guinea-Bissau
Guinea
Mali
Mauritania
Morocco
Nigeria

NOUAKCHOTT
Burkina Faso (Fr)
Côte d'Ivoire (Fr)
Mali
Morocco
Senegal
Togo (Fr)

MAURITANIA

BANJUL
Côte d'Ivoire
Guinea-Bissau
Guinea
Mali
Mauritania
Nigeria
Senegal
Sierra Leone

BAMAKO
Burkina Faso
Côte d'Ivoire
Guinea
Mauritania
Morocco
Nigeria
Senegal
Togo (Fr)

SENEGAL

THE
GAMBIA

ZIGUINCHOR
Guinea-Bissau

GUINEA-
BISSAU

BISSAU
The Gambia
Guinea
Mauritania
Senegal

GUINEA

CONAKRY
Burkina Faso (Fr)
Cape Verde
Côte d'Ivoire
Ghana
Guinea-Bissau
Liberia
Mali
Mauritania (Fr)
Morocco
Nigeria
Senegal
Sierra Leone
Togo

SIERRA
LEONE

CÔTE
D'IVOIRE

LIBERIA

Monrovia

ABIDJAN
Benin
Burkina Faso
Cameroon
Ghana
Guinea
Liberia
Mali
Mauritania
Niger
Nigeria
Senegal
Togo (Fr)

0   Kilometres   500

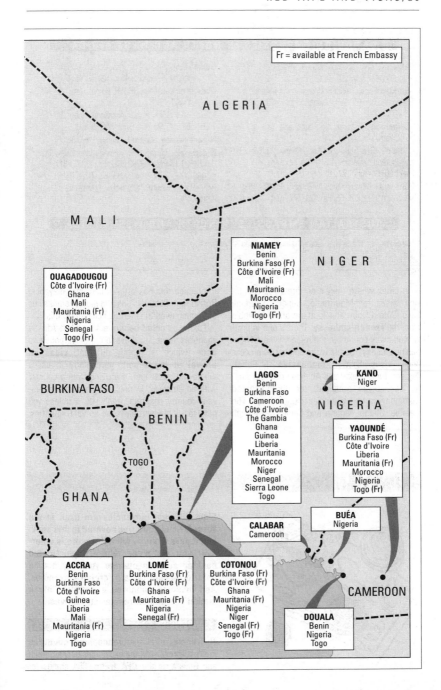

Fr = available at French Embassy

ALGERIA

MALI

NIGER

NIAMEY
Benin
Burkina Faso (Fr)
Côte d'Ivoire (Fr)
Mali
Mauritania
Morocco
Nigeria
Togo (Fr)

OUAGADOUGOU
Côte d'Ivoire (Fr)
Ghana
Mali
Mauritania (Fr)
Nigeria
Senegal
Togo (Fr)

BURKINA FASO

BENIN

TOGO

GHANA

LAGOS
Benin
Burkina Faso
Cameroon
Côte d'Ivoire
The Gambia
Ghana
Guinea
Liberia
Mauritania
Morocco
Niger
Senegal
Sierra Leone
Togo

KANO
Niger

NIGERIA

YAOUNDÉ
Burkina Faso (Fr)
Côte d'Ivoire
Liberia
Mauritania (Fr)
Morocco
Nigeria
Togo (Fr)

BUÉA
Nigeria

CALABAR
Cameroon

CAMEROON

ACCRA
Benin
Burkina Faso
Côte d'Ivoire
Guinea
Liberia
Mali
Mauritania (Fr)
Nigeria
Togo

LOMÉ
Burkina Faso (Fr)
Côte d'Ivoire (Fr)
Ghana
Mauritania (Fr)
Nigeria
Senegal (Fr)

COTONOU
Burkina Faso (Fr)
Côte d'Ivoire (Fr)
Ghana
Mauritania (Fr)
Nigeria
Niger
Senegal (Fr)
Togo (Fr)

DOUALA
Benin
Nigeria
Togo

CANADIAN EMBASSIES IN NORTH AND WEST AFRICA

Algeria 27 bis rue Ali Massoudi, Alger-Gare 16000 Algiers (☎2/60.59.20).

Burkina Faso Canadian Development Centre, Ouagadougou (BP 548, Ouagadougou) ☎31.18.94; Fax 31.19.00).

Cameroon 572 Immeuble Stamatiade, Yaoundé (BP 572, Yaoundé; ☎23.02.03).

Côte d'Ivoire Immeuble Trade Centre, 23 Nogues av, Plateau, Abidjan (01 BP 4104, Abidjan; ☎21.20.09; Fax 21.77.28).

Ghana 42 Independence Ave, Accra (PO Box 1639, Accra; ☎021/22.85.55; Fax 021/77.37.92).

Guinea Corniche Sud, Quartier Coléah, Conakry (BP 99, Coléah; ☎46.44.48 or 46.23.95; Fax 46.42.35).

Mali rte de Koulikoro, BP 198, Bamako (☎21.22.36; Fax 21.43.62).

Morocco 13 bis rue Jaafar as-Sadik, Rabat (BP 709, Rabat; ☎7/77.28.80; Fax 7/77.28.87).

Niger Immeuble Sonara 1, Niamey (☎73.36.86).

Nigeria 4 Idowu Taylor St, Victoria Island, Lagos (PO Box 54506, Lagos; ☎1/262 2512; Fax 1/262 2517).

Senegal Immeuble Daniel Sorano, 45 bd de la République, Dakar (BP 3373, Dakar; ☎823 92 90; Fax 823 87 49).

AUSTRALIAN EMBASSIES IN NORTH AND WEST AFRICA

Nigeria Australian High Commission, 2 Ozumba Mbadiwe Ave, Victoria Island, Lagos (☎261.8875; Fax 261.8703).

In cities where there's no direct representation, visas for Mauritania, Senegal, Burkina Faso, Côte d'Ivoire and Togo are often available from the **French embassy**. There's one in pretty well every country in the region. Where Niger has no embassy, Côte d'Ivoire embassies process Niger visas. **British embassies** in Rabat, Algiers, Tunis, Dakar and Abidjan provide a similar service, in principle, for unrepresented Commonwealth countries (including The Gambia, Ghana, Nigeria and Cameroon) though in practice this has often fallen into abeyance. British High Commissions (the mutual embassies of Commonwealth countries) cannot do this.

Lastly, as noted before, a few West African countries issue, or have an official policy to issue (which is slightly different) **visas on arrival** at the airport, particularly in cases where the passenger is arriving from a country with no embassy. Details are given in the relevant country chapters. Don't risk it unless you have to – it always delays the arrival formalities.

MONEY AND COSTS

Eight different currencies are used in the West African countries covered in this book, and it pays to know what the score is wherever you are. Even where sophisticated banking systems operate you may not be able to change certain foreign currencies. And in some countries a parallel "black market" in hard currencies still thrives.

CURRENCIES

The currency of all the **Francophone countries** in West Africa, with the exceptions of Mauritania and Guinea, is the **CFA franc**. CFA stands for

Communauté Financière Africaine. Recently Guinea-Bissau, though not Francophone, joined the CFA club. Cameroon's currency is also CFA, but of a different regional grouping – the Coopération Financière en Afrique Centrale – which includes Chad, Central African Republic, Gabon, Equatorial Guinea and Republic of the Congo. CFA francs are guaranteed by the French treasury and, since devaluation in early 1994, have a fixed value of 100:1 against the French franc (FF, now part of the single European currency, the euro).

Although of equal value, these two types of CFA can't be spent outside their own region, and cannot be interchanged in any bank in the region either. In Europe, major banks will sometimes exchange CFA francs at their French franc equivalent. Because of the French backing, the CFA (commonly pronounced "Sefa") is a relatively hard currency and currency laws in the countries which use it are generally relaxed. In theory there are limits to the value of CFA you can export, even from one CFA state to another, but in practice these limits are very rarely enforced. CFA comes in 1, 5, 10, 25, 50, 100 and 250 coins and notes of 500, 1000, 2500, 5000 and 10,000, making it easily the most convenient African currency.

The countries outside the franc zone have their own, usually weaker ("soft") currencies. Mauritania uses the **ouguiya**; Cape Verde the Cape Verdean **escudo**; The Gambia the **dalasi**; Guinea the **Guinean franc**; Ghana the **cedi**; and Nigeria the **naira**.

MONEY

If you're travelling widely in West Africa, you're best off carrying a large part of your funds in **French franc travellers' cheques**. Apart from any commission on exchanging them for cash, if you're using them in CFA countries, you've already effectively made the exchange when you bought them. In the CFA zone you'll always know how much you've got in local currency and your funds won't vary in value as you travel.

You generally end up better off if you have French francs to convert to CFA, rather than going straight from, say, US$ or £ sterling to CFA, because the national banks of the CFA zone normally set their own rates for exchanges with non-franc currencies. Indeed, in some towns in the CFA zone, banks will not deal in non-franc currencies – frustrating in a business-minded place like

Côte d'Ivoire. Hotels and some shops and traders will take French franc travellers' cheques but it's essential to have some **French francs in cash** as a stand-by.

Where CFA countries border non-CFA countries, your surplus CFA cash can't be changed in the banks but it can generally be changed with ease on the black market as it's commonly used by people crossing the borders to buy goods (though note the details overleaf on declaring your currency). If you're heading directly for one of the **soft currency countries**, or intending to spend most of your time there, then either **US dollars** or **pounds sterling** is probably the best currency to take. Again, carry some in cash – you'll often need it at borders and airports for your first food or transport.

Denominations of travellers' cheques and cash should be as small as you can manage, bearing in mind the bulk that a large sum of exchange will amount to. If you take mostly US$50 or FF500 denominations for convenience, make sure you have plenty of US$10 and 20 or FF100 and 200 as well. A small stash of really low value hard currency notes (US$1 and 2) is always useful.

Travelling through the CFA zone, the issuing authority of your travellers' cheques isn't of much consequence. Outside the CFA countries, however, **American Express** is by far the most widely recognized brand and, should the need arise, also the fastest to supply replacements for lost cheques.

Always keep the original **receipt** when you buy travellers cheques. Most banks outside the major cities won't cash your cheque without it.

CARRYING AND KEEPING MONEY

How you carry your funds around is something to which you should give serious consideration, especially if you're travelling for a long time. In certain cities, travellers are vulnerable and it only takes one piece of bad luck (or simple carelessness) to terminate your trip prematurely.

It's wise to carry valuable hard currency cash (as opposed to local soft currency) in a very safe place, ideally in a soft **leather pouch** under your waistband, hanging from a loop around your belt. This is comfortable and virtually impregnable to ordinary theft – even in the unlikely event it's noticed. It's probably worth wearing shorts, skirts or jeans with strong waistbands and a belt just for this purpose. Larger, strong, leather **belt-pouches** worn on the outside are good for passport, local money,

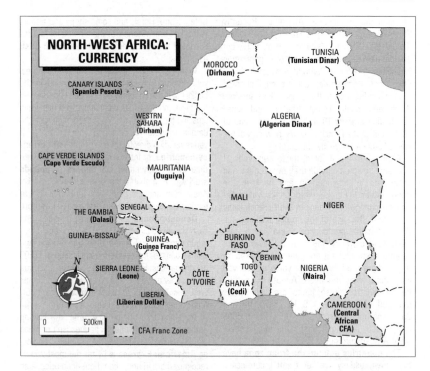

NORTH-WEST AFRICA: CURRENCY

CANARY ISLANDS
(Spanish Peseta)

MOROCCO
(Dirham)

TUNISIA
(Tunisian Dinar)

WESTRN
SAHARA
(Dirham)

ALGERIA
(Algerian Dinar)

CAPE VERDE ISLANDS
(Cape Verde Escudo)

MAURITANIA
(Ouguiya)

MALI

NIGER

THE GAMBIA
(Dalasi)

SENEGAL

GUINEA-BISSAU

GUINEA
(Guinea Franc)

BURKINO
FASO

BENIN

NIGERIA
(Naira)

SIERRA LEONE
(Leone)

CÔTE
D'IVOIRE

TOGO

GHANA
(Cedi)

LIBERIA
(Liberian Dollar)

CAMEROON
(Central
African
CFA)

N

0   500km

CFA Franc Zone

travellers' cheques and anything replaceable. Hanging **neck pouches** worn beneath a shirt are vulnerable, but fairly safe if the loop is strong. Nylon **money belts** are painfully hot and bulky.

Bank notes and travellers cheques (and airline tickets) need protecting from sweat in small plastic bags. Defaced, they can become worthless.

DECLARATIONS

On arrival in many soft currency countries you'll have to make a **declaration** of the money you're carrying in cash and travellers' cheques. This may be accompanied by a search, varying from the cursory to the intimate. Mostly, you simply say what you've got and then show some of it.

You may also be issued with a **currency declaration** or **exchange control form**, which you retain until departure. This shows the money you imported and is supposed to be stamped and amended every time you change money at an authorized bank, hotel or bureau de change. In theory, when you leave any country, your currency declaration form is checked against the money you

have on you and any discrepancy (which must have been exchanged unofficially, or lost, or given away . . .) has to be accounted for. In practice, forms are taken much more seriously on arrival than on departure. It's wise to assume, however, that your experience will turn out to be the exception.

None of this applies if you're travelling to, or within, **CFA zone countries** only. Here the fiscal arrangements commonly leave you feeling you're merely in an overseas French *departement* and there's rarely any interest in the money you have on you, nor any currency declaration forms or concern about where you change your money.

BANKS

West African **banking systems** are generally slow and limited. The capital cities are by far the best, if not the only, place to change money. Always try to arrive early in the day and remember your passport. Never start the transaction without checking the rate of exchange, the commission and any other charges. It's best to establish how much you'll receive in advance, before the paperwork starts. In the **CFA zone** there can be marked differences in the rates offered by different banks: their scales of commission and rates are often well behind the latest American and European swings. In **non-CFA countries** it is also a good idea to check out the rate at the bureau de change, which may be quicker than the banks, give you much less bureaucratic hassle and often even offer a better rate.

WIRING

Try to avoid **sending home for money**. It's expensive and even faxed or telexed draft orders can take weeks to reach you at the counter – though the normal delay should be only four or five working days. **Western Union** – the cheapest and fastest service – now has links to banks in most countries in the region, but although it should in principle offer a swift service, unfortunately some of the handling banks in West Africa are not as efficient.

When receiving money you should make sure that you have the money transfer **control number**; you'll be told in Europe that this isn't necessary, but you risk being refused your money by West African banks without it. Note also that money is only paid out in the local currency and you probably won't be able to receive hard currency except in the CFA zone, and not necessarily even then.

Basically, it's far better to bring with you on your trip all you'll need, and more, in travellers' cheques.

CREDIT CARDS

Visa, American Express, Access-MasterCard and Diners' Club are of some use in cities and large towns for tourist services such as upmarket hotels and restaurants, flights, tours and car rental. **American Express** has offices or agents in Morocco, Mauritania, Senegal, The Gambia, Mali, Côte d'Ivoire, Ghana, Togo and Nigeria. You can buy hard currency travellers' cheques with an Amex card – very useful. **Visa** and **MasterCard** have offices or agents in Morocco, Senegal and Ghana.

Don't count on **cash advances** against credit cards outside the CFA zone, though it is possible in a few rare cases. Even in Francophone capitals you'll have to find the right local bank.

BLACK MARKETS

An unofficial, **parallel exchange rate** (the "black market") exists wherever there's a local demand for hard, foreign currency that can't be met through official channels.

Out of the CFA zone, you can't usually walk into a bank and buy dollars, sterling, or other hard currency over the counter. Hard currency is kept in state control and sold to private citizens only reluctantly and with all sorts of conditions. Local currencies are worthless beyond these countries' borders and local people have enormous difficulty in obtaining hard currency to travel abroad, conduct business or support relatives. In most of the non-CFA countries, you can exchange your hard currency for local money at higher-than-bank rates. **Black market rates** can vary from a few percentage points to several *hundred* percent better than the bank rate.

In the CFA zone, a parallel market of cross-border traders and businessmen flourishes in the main commercial centres, useful for those unwilling to pay the banks' commission rates (generally much higher than in non-CFA countries) and – since it is impossible to buy any of the softer currencies in the banks – for those crossing over into a non-CFA zone.

It may seem unfair on strangled economies to squeeze even harder for the sake of cheap local currency by depriving the banks of foreign exchange. But on the other hand it's naive to hold exaggerated views of the importance of your hard currency to the national development of the country you're in, or of the net benefit to local people of putting your money into a bank rather than private hands. Sometimes the official exchange rate is simply set at an unrealistically high level that makes the place swingingly expensive. It's worth noting that most prices tend to adjust to black market levels and that some services (especially hotels) may, in any case, be payable only in hard currency at the official rate of exchange. Questions of altruism and morality apart, it needs to be said, whatever else you do on your travels, *never change money on the street*. You run a high risk of being skilfully ripped off in public, even if the police informer scenario rarely comes to pass. Always take five minutes out to sit down in a shop or somewhere similar and count everything before handing over your cash.

COSTS AND BARGAINING

It's perhaps surprising to find that, in general, West Africa is an expensive part of the world. Mere survival can be dirt cheap, but anything like a Euro-American lifestyle costs as much, if not more, than in Europe or America. In between these extremes you can use the cheapest transport, eat market food and spend nights either camping in the bush, staying with people or in budget hotels. Travelling like this it's possible to get by on **£300/$480 a month** (though £600/$960 split between two gets

EXCHANGE RATES

As we go to press the following official exchange rates (approximate) apply:

	£1	$1		£1	$1
BENIN *CFA franc*	900	560	GUINEA *Guinean franc*	2100	1300
BURKINA FASO *CFA franc*	900	560	GUINEA-BISSAU *CFA franc*	900	560
CAMEROON *Central African CFA franc*		900	MALI *CFA franc*	900	560
560			MAURITANIA *ouguiya*	300	180
CAPE VERDE *escudo*	160	100	NIGER *CFA franc*	900	560
CÔTE D'IVOIRE *CFA franc*	900	560	NIGERIA *naira*	130	80
THE GAMBIA *dalasi*	17	10	SENEGAL *CFA franc*	900	560
GHANA *cedi*	4300	2700	TOGO *CFA franc*	900	560

you more value for money). It's clearly much harder to keep costs down in cities such as Dakar and Abidjan, where a panoply of tempting comforts and consumables is available in every direction and where it's hard to avoid staying in **hotels** – likely to be your biggest single expense.

The best way to keep costs *really* low is to **cycle**, which not only gives you free transport but also enables you to seek out inexpensive or free accommodation or tent space. A cycle tour of West Africa need not cost more than £5/$8 a day.

As a very general guideline to budget planning, a twin room in a **cheap hotel** can usually be had for under £10/$16, often under £7/$11 but rarely under £5/$8. Long-distance road **transport** works out, on average, at about £2–3 ($3–5) per 100km, though it varies with the quality and speed of the vehicle. Train travel, if it's an option where you are, tends to be cheaper, river trips more expensive. As for **food**, you can always fill yourself with calories for under £1 ($1.50) if you eat street food or sit at a market or lorry park chop house.

Travelling on a different budget, **car rental** rates are some of the highest in the world (in a number of countries it's not difficult to work up bills of £130/$210 a day or more *without* taking the air-conditioned Range Rover). In most cities, too, top flight **international standard hotels** are very expensive.

BARGAINING

You'll need to get into **bargaining** quickly. It's expected and is the normal way of conducting business. Moreover every time you pay an unreasonable price for goods or services you contribute to local inflation. In **markets** there's generally a "fixed price" which the seller has in mind. You can assume the one you're quoted is more, but a few good natured offers will establish the fact. Try

offering a bulk price for several items at once, or add some "presents" to the thing you're negotiating over. Loads of good humour counts for much.

General stores, groceries and supermarkets invariably have **fixed prices**. Transport costs are usually subject to state control and almost always fixed, but baggage can be haggled over. Pretty well every other service (including budget hotel rooms in some countries) can and should be bargained for. This is often just a case of showing reluctance to pay what you're told is the going rate and getting some sort of "**discount**".

It's in **buying major items** – particularly **crafts** – that you'll have the most fun bargaining. There's enormous flexibility around a few immutable rules. The most important is never to engage in bargaining if you've no intention of buying the item at any price. To offer what you thought was a silly price and then refuse to pay can cause grave offence. Nor should you embark on negotiations when you're in a hurry, or if you are feeling less than one hundred percent – it's an exhausting business.

When negotiating, don't automatically assume you're in the clutches of a rip-off artist. Concepts of **honour** are very important, and stalls are often minded by friends and relatives with whom, if you're quick and convincing, you can sometimes strike real bargains. Don't forget, from the trader's point of view, you're selling *money*.

Most importantly, men should make **physical contact** – hand-clasping is usually enough to emphasize a point. Be as jocular as possible and don't be shy of making a big scene – the bluffing and mock outrage on both sides is part of the fun. Women can't pursue these negotiating tactics in quite the same way, except when buying from women – invariably much tougher anyway.

Getting down to figures, try to delay the moment when you have to name your price. When you hear

"One hundred how much you pay?", say nothing. It's amazing how often the seller's price drops way below your expectation before you've made any offer, so forget the standard "offer-a-third-come-up-to-a-half" formulae. If you do arrive at an unbridgeable gap you can always drop the matter and come by later. With stalemates, a disinterested companion tugging your sleeve is always a help.

HEALTH

There's no reason to expect to get ill in West Africa, but plenty of opportunities to do so if you're unlucky or careless. The most likely hazards are stomach problems and malaria. Health details for each country, with a brief rundown on local problems and issues, are given in each chapter.

The only officially required International Vaccination Certificates are yellow fever and cholera. A **yellow fever certificate** is *always* a requirement, even if you're flying in direct from Europe, in Benin, Burkina Faso, Cameroon, Côte d'Ivoire, Ghana, Guinea, Niger, Nigeria, Senegal and Togo. Several others require to see the yellow fever certificate if you're staying for longer than two weeks. All West African countries require the certificate if you've arrived by way of an infected area – in practice *any other sub-Saharan country*.

The **cholera certificate** is a bureaucratic, rather than a health issue. These days, many doctors who keep up with tropical medicine advances don't recommend the cholera jab for the reasons given below and some will quite willingly provide a cholera certificate discreetly indicating you *haven't* had the jab. It seems to do the job at borders and airports.

If you lose a vaccination certificate, you can buy blank ones in many stationery stores. Explain your situation at a hospital or clinic and have it stamped and signed by someone (there'll probably be a small charge).

VACCINATIONS

Plan ahead. A first-time cholera inoculation needs at least two weeks between the two injections of the course, while a yellow fever certificate only becomes valid ten days after you've had the shot.

The validity of a **cholera inoculation** is a nominal six months, and it doesn't provide a great deal of protection against the disease. In fact the risks of contracting cholera are negligible unless you're living in the middle of an epidemic. The most recent epidemics have been in Conakry, parts of Guinea-Bissau, in Mindelo in the Cape Verde islands and in refugee camps around Liberia and Sierra Leone.

Yellow fever jabs are good for ten years and confer high immunity. Yellow fever is a monkey disease but it can be spread by mosquitoes to humans. Once contracted, there are no specific drugs to cure the illness, which takes a few days to develop into liver failure and kills about fifty percent of its victims. Outbreaks are very rare, but the jab is nonetheless essential.

You shouldn't consider major travels without a **typhoid vaccination** (which lasts three years) or **polio** and **tetanus** boosters. Nor is there any reason not to get Havrix shots which protect you for up to ten years against the common form of **hepatitis** ("A") spread by contaminated food and water. It's a lot nicer having the jabs than catching the disease, which seriously damages your liver and can leave it permanently scarred. The only problem with Havrix is its cost and the fact that you need to have the first shot at least four weeks before departure. Hepatitis "B", like HIV, is caught through the transfer of blood products, usually from dirty needles.

Whether you have the hepatitis "A" shots or not, be extra careful about cleanliness and in particular about contamination of water – a serious problem where, for example, a single water tank or barrel holds the whole water supply in a cockroach-infested toilet-cum-bathroom.

MALARIA

Protection against **malaria** (*le paludisme* or *"palu"* in French) is absolutely essential. The disease, caused by a parasite carried in the saliva of *Anopheles* mosquitoes, is endemic in tropical Africa: many people carry it in their bloodstream and get occasional bouts of fever. It has a variable

IF YOU GO DOWN WITH MALARIA

Don't compare yourself with local people who may have considerable immunity. The priority, if you think you might be getting a fever, is **treatment**. Delay is potentially risky. Overly casual travellers die of the disease every year.

Ideally, confirm your diagnosis by getting to a doctor and having a blood test to identify the strain (a new, but very costly, self-test kit – Malapac Travel Kit – is now available in a few selected stores in the UK, Australia and New Zealand). If this isn't possible take 2 **quinine** tablets (600mg) twice daily for 5 days and then 3 Fansidar tablets. This should clear up any strain. If you don't have quinine tablets, then take ordinary **chloroquine** tablets at the rate of 10mg per kilo body weight up to a maximum of 600mg (usually 4 tablets) immediately, then half as much (usually 2 tablets) 8 hours later.

Assuming you feel an improvement, take this second dose again on the second and third days. If you notice no improvement after the *initial* dose, try again to see a doctor or take 3 Fansidar tablets if you have them – *your malaria is chloroquine resistant*. The Fansidar should clear it up within a few hours.

incubation period of a few days to several weeks so you can become ill long after being bitten. If you go down with malaria, you'll probably know. The fever, shivering and headaches are something like severe flu and come in waves, usually beginning in the early evening. Malaria is not infectious but it can be dangerous and even fatal if not treated quickly.

Female *Anopheles* mosquitoes – the aggressors – prefer to bite in the evening. They can be distinguished by their rather eager head-down position. As well as a few common-sense measures – covering up after dark and using repellant (on your skin and clothes) – it's vital to be prepared with a course of tablets.

TABLETS

When taking **preventive tablets** it's important to keep a routine and cover the period before and after your trip with doses. Doctors can advise on which kind to take, but you can buy most of them at a pharmacy without a prescription.

Once in West Africa, the **chloroquine**-based tablets (such as Nivaquin, Aralen and Resochin), **proguanil**-based Paludrin and **pyrimethamine**-based Daraprim can be bought in small shops and from street drug stalls all over, but the newer drugs to which falciparum malaria – the common African strain – is less often resistant, are only available in big towns. Chloroquine-resistant malaria has now been reported all over West Africa, so complacency isn't in order, although even moderately resistant malaria is held at bay by proguanil and chloroquine.

Common preventive combinations are a small daily dose of proguanil and a weekly dose of chloroquine, or chloroquine alone with a supply of Fansidar to be used immediately if chloroquine-resistant malaria is suspected and you can't get to a doctor. **Mefloquine** (sold as Lariam), taken once a week only, is worth asking your doctor about but, because of the risk of neuro-psychiatric side-effects, it is recommended that you start taking the tablets two weeks before you start your trip, so you can shift to the less effective chloroquine-proguanil combination if they affect you badly.

Chloroquine is safe **during pregnancy** but Fansidar sometimes has side-effects and isn't recommended (whether you're pregnant or not) as a prophylaxis. Some pills give some people mouth ulcers – you might want to be prepared with a suitable remedy.

In various parts of West Africa, the local or seasonal malaria risk is low but you shouldn't break your course of pills as it's vital to keep your parasite-fighting level as high as possible.

NETS AND REPELLANTS

Sleep under a **mosquito net** when possible – they're not expensive to buy locally – and burn **mosquito coils** (which you can buy everywhere) for a peaceful night. Don't use Cock Brand or Lion Brand, however, which are said to contain DDT and are banned in many countries. Whenever the mosquitoes are particularly bad (and that's not often) cover your exposed parts with something strong. So-called **"Neat Deet"** (the insecticide diethyltoluamide) works well, and you could try soaking wrist and ankle bands in the stuff, diluted 1:9 with water. Beware: Deet is very corrosive and will chew through plastics and artificial fibres. **Electric mosquito destroyers**, which you fit with a pad every night, are less pungent than mosquito coils but more expensive – and you need electricity.

Strangely, the best mosquito repellant of all is said to be Avon bath oil (not that they sell it as such). Lastly, some people swear by the effects of vitamin B in deterring mosquitoes.

OTHER DISEASES

BILHARZIA

Bilharzia – also known as schistosomiasis – is potentially very nasty, though easily curable. The usual recommendation is never to swim in, wash with, drink or even touch lake or river water that's not been vouched for. On a long trip out in the bush, this isn't always possible, particularly if you're drinking with local people. Snail-free water that's stood for two days, or has been boiled or chlorinated, is safe, as is salt or brackish water.

Bilharzia comes from tiny flukes that live in freshwater snails and which, as part of their life cycle, leave their hosts and burrow into animal (or human) skin to multiply in the bloodstream. The snails themselves favour only stagnant water, though the flukes can be swept downstream. While it's possible to pick it up from one brief contact, the risk of contracting bilharzia is fairly low unless you repeatedly come into contact with infected water. If infected, you'll get a slightly itchy rash an hour or two later where the flukes have entered the skin.

Bilharzia is most prevalent in the Sahelian regions and particularly in artificial lakes and dams. If you have severe abdominal pains and pass blood – the first symptoms after 4–6 weeks – see a doctor.

SLEEPING SICKNESS

Sleeping sickness – trypanosomiasis – is mainly a disease of wild animals, but it also affects cattle and horses and to a much lesser extent people. It's carried by tse-tse ("setsy") flies that crowd streams and riverbanks in deep bush areas. They're determined, brutish insects with a painful bite, attracted to large moving objects such as elephants or Land Rovers. They tend to fly in the windows of vehicles driving through game parks.

Infection is extremely uncommon among travellers – fortunately, because the drugs used to treat it aren't very sophisticated. But a boil which suddenly appears, several *days* after a tse-tse fly bite, *might* indicate an infection you should get examined. Untreated, sleeping sickness results in infections of the central nervous system and drowsiness. Not amusing.

RIVER BLINDNESS

Though it's alarmingly common among West Africans, travellers virtually never pick up **river**

MEDICINE BAG

There's no need to take a mass of drugs and remedies you'll probably never use. Various items, however, are immensely useful, especially on a long trip, and well worth buying in advance. On a local level, if you're interested in herbal and other natural remedies, you'll find a wealth of natural cures in markets. Intuition, common sense and persistent enquiries are all you need to judge whether they're worth trying.

Paracetamol Safer than aspirin for pain and fever relief.

Water purifying (chlorine) tablets or iodine tincture Both taste foul but do the trick, iodine more efficiently than chlorine. Ascorbic acid (vitamin C) can be used to neutralize the taste of iodine.

Anti-malaria tablets Enough for prophylactic use, plus several courses of Fansidar and/or quinine tablets in case of attack.

Codeine phosphate This is the preferred emergency anti-diarrhoeal pill but is on prescription only. Some GPs may oblige. Lomotil (Co-phenotrope) is second best.

Antibiotics Amoxil (amoxycillin) is a broad spectrum antibacterial drug useful against many infections. Ciproxin (ciprofloxacin) can feel like a lifesaver in a bowel crisis. Both should only be used as a last resort when you cannot see a doctor. Again these are normally prescription drugs only.

Zinc oxide powder Useful anti-fungal powder (Canestan) for sweaty crevices.

Antiseptic Cicatrin is good, but creams in metal tubes invariably squeeze out messily sooner or later. Bright red or purple *mercurochrome* liquid dries wounds.

Alcohol swabs Paper Medi-swabs are invaluable for cleaning wounds, insect bites and infections.

Sticking plaster, steri-strip wound closures, sterile gauze dressing, micropore tape You don't need much of this stuff, and you can buy it in most capital cities.

Lip balm Invaluable.

Thermometer Very useful. Ideally you'll be 37.5°C. A Feverscan forehead thermometer is unbreakable and gives a ready reckoning (from pharmacies).

Lens solution If you wear contact lenses you'll need a good supply of solution.

blindness – onchocerciasis – a disease common along several river systems. It's spread by tiny blackflies, which have a vicious bite and pass on minute worms, which in turn move to the eyes and can eventually cause blindness. If you find yourself suffering from impaired vision, it may well be caused by long-term use of chloroquine against malaria – nothing to do with onchocerciasis.

SEXUALLY TRANSMITTED DISEASES AND AIDS

The only other real likelihood of your encountering a serious disease in West Africa is if it's **sexually transmitted**. Assorted venereal diseases are widespread, particularly in the larger towns, and the HIV virus which causes AIDS – known as SIDA in Francophone countries – is alarmingly prevalent and spreading all the time. It's very easily passed between people suffering relatively minor, but ulcerous, sexually transmitted diseases, and the very high prevalence of these is thought to account for the high incidence of heterosexually transmitted HIV. So there you have it: not exactly an incitement to throw caution to the winds.

On the associated topic of receiving **blood transfusions** or injections in an emergency, you might want to carry a sterile emergency kit to be used by a doctor if you get into trouble. Usually, however, such treatment can only be offered in a hospital environment where most staff are familiar with the need for sterile equipment and fresh needles.

WATER AND BUGS

In many places in West Africa, the **water** you drink will have come from a tap and is likely to be clean. Since bad water is the most likely cause of **diarrhoea**, you should be cautious of drinking rain-or well-water.

In truth, **stomach upsets** don't plague many travellers badly. If you're visiting for a **short time** only, it makes sense to be scrupulous – purifying tablets and/or boiling kills most things. If you want to be absolutely safe, **purification**, a two-stage process involving both filtration and sterilization, gives the most complete treatment. Portable water purifiers range from pocket-size units weighing 60 grams, up to 800 grams.

For **longer stays**, and especially if you're travelling widely, think of re-educating your stomach rather than fortifying it. It's virtually impossible to travel around the region without exposing yourself to strange bugs from time to time. Take it easy at first, don't overdo the fruit (and wash it in clean, safe water before peeling), don't keep food too

---

GENERAL HEALTH TIPS

Some people sweat heavily and lose a lot of salt. Salt tablets, however, are unnecessary. Sprinkle extra **salt** on your food. Even if you're not a great perspirer it's important to keep a healthy salt balance. The body can't function without it and it's not uncommon to experience sudden exhaustion and collapse a few days after arrival in a hot climate.

Pawpaws (papaya), and their seeds – which taste like watercress – can be eaten as a kind of tonic. They contain excellent supplies of invigorating minerals and vitamins and are reckoned to help the healing process and to aid digestion. The smaller and more fragrant mountain varieties are delicious but in many parts of West Africa, pawpaws aren't even regarded as worth selling. They grow as giant weeds, left for the children, and not relished as proper fruit at all. If you don't see them for sale, approach the people of a house where they're growing in the compound and ask to buy one.

MEDICAL TREATMENT

If you need **medical treatment** in West Africa, you'll discover a frightening lack of well-equipped hospitals. In each country, we've tried to indicate which are the best and to give general practitioners and dentists in city "Listings". For serious treatment you're almost certain to want to come home. Blood and urine tests can be performed locally but needles and other instruments may not be fresh from a sealed package. If in doubt, insist on paying for new ones.

Moderate injuries can be treated locally. In remote areas, **missions** are usually the first recourse. If you require treatment, it's normally proficient and the charges low, though comforts fairly rudimentary.

CONTRACEPTIVES

Condoms are available from most pharmacies, or alternatively from some clinics and dispensaries, but they tend to be expensive or of dubious manufacture. Take some with you. If you use **oral contraceptives**, get your doctor to prescribe a supply. And don't forget an alternative method to fall back on if you have a stomach upset or take a course of antibiotics, as either can leave you unprotected for the rest of the month.

IMMUNIZATIONS AND ADVICE IN BRITAIN AND IRELAND

For **British travellers**, the first source of advice and probable supplier of jabs and prescriptions is your GP. Family doctors are often well-informed and some won't charge you for routine injections. For yellow fever and other exotic shots you'll normally have to visit a specialist clinic, often in a county town health authority headquarters.

In London, advice and low-cost **inoculations** are available at the **Travel Clinic of the Hospital for Tropical Diseases**, St Pancras Hospital, 4 St Pancras Way, London NW1 0PE (☎0171/338 9600; Mon–Fri 9am–5pm by appointment only). A consultation here costs £15 (waived if you have your injections here too). A recorded **Healthline** (☎0839/337733 premium rate) gives hints on hygiene and illness prevention as well as listing appropriate immunizations. With a referral from your GP, the Hospital for Tropical Diseases will also give you a complete check-up on your return if you think it may be worth it.

Also in London, the **British Airways Travel Clinic**, 156 Regent St, London W1 (☎0171/439 9584 or 439 9585; Mon–Fri 9am–5.15pm, Sat 10am–4pm; no appointment necessary) can provide a wide variety of inoculations. British Airways also operate around forty **regional clinics** throughout the country (call ☎01276/685040 to find the one nearest to you.

Trailfinders, 194 Kensington High St, London (☎0171/938 3999) also run a no-appointment-necessary immunization clinic (Mon–Fri 9am–5pm,

Thurs to 6pm, Sat 9.30am–4pm). Its Glasgow branch, 254–284 Sauchiehall St (☎0141/353 0066), is open Wed and Thurs 2–5.30pm.

Call **MASTA** (Medical Advisory Services for Travellers Abroad; ☎0891/224100, premium rate) based at the London School of Hygiene and Tropical Diseases, Keppel Street, London WC1E 7HT, for the latest information by post. They offer very detailed, personalized "Health Briefs" for whichever countries you're visiting, advise on inoculations and give run-downs on all the diseases you're likely (or not) to fall victim to. MASTA also sell sterile emergency packs and other items.

A helpful resource is the **Malaria Helpline** (☎0891/600350, premium rate), giving 24hr up-to-date recorded information.

Other centres in Britain and Ireland include:

Communicable Diseases Unit, Ruchill Hospital, Glasgow G20 9NB (☎0141/946 7120).

Department of Communicable and Tropical Diseases, Birmingham Heartland Hospital, Bordesley Green Rd, Birmingham B9 5ST (☎0121/766 6611).

Gravel Medicine Services, 16 College St, Belfast (☎01232/315220).

Liverpool School of Tropical Medicine, Pembroke Place, Liverpool L3 5QA (☎0151/708 9393).

Tropical Medicine Bureau, Grafton St Medical Centre, 34 Grafton St, Dublin 2 (☎01/671-9200; *www.tmb.ie*).

IMMUNIZATIONS AND ADVICE IN NORTH AMERICA

North American travellers should not immediately head for expensive specialist travel clinics, where the cost of various jabs can easily run into hundreds of dollars. Local county or city health departments across the country offer inoculations at a far lower rate. A helpful resource is the West African country information put out by the **Center for Disease Control and Prevention**, 1600 Clifton Rd NE, Atlanta, GA (☎1-800/311-3435; *www.cdc.gov/travel/wafrica.htm*).

In Canada, immunizations and advice can be had from your local travel medicine clinic; listings are available from the **Canadian Society for International Health**, 1 Nicholas St, Suite 1105, Ottawa, ON K1N 7B7 (☎613/241-5785; *www.csih.org/trav_inf.html*). Information on disease outbreaks and immunizations is available 24 hours a day from the **Health Protection Branch – Laboratory Centre for Disease Control** (Fax: 613/941-3900; *www.hc-sc.gc.ca/hpb/lcdc/osh/tmp_ e.html*).

IMMUNIZATIONS AND ADVICE IN AUSTRALIA AND NEW ZEALAND

In **Australia** and **New Zealand** you can usually get vaccinations at your GP or local health centre but you're likely to find more specialized information from the privately run centres below.

Travellers' Medical and Vaccination Centres (*www.tmvc.com.au*) 2nd Floor, 393 Little Bourke St, Melbourne (☎03/9602 5788; *melb@tmvc.com.au*); 7th Floor Dymocks Building, 428 George St, Sydney (☎02/9221 7133; *syd@tmvc.com.au*) and offices in all the

main cities and, increasingly, in smaller towns too. To find your nearest call ☎1300/658 844. In **New Zealand**: Level 1 Canterbury Arcade, 170 Queen St, Auckland (☎09/373 3531; *auck@tmvc.com.au*); Shop 15 Grand Arcade, 16–18 Willis St, Wellington (☎04/473 0991; *wellington@tmvc.com.au*); 147 Armagh St, Christchurch (☎03/479 4000; *chch@tmvc.com.au*); and in Hamilton and Tauranga.

long and be very wary of salads. If you travel across the desert, particularly if you hitch or use public transport, gradually acclimatizing, you'll probably find you can survive without ill effect most of the bugs you must be consuming. Ironically, perhaps, if you're travelling on a shoestring budget and rarely eat restaurant meals, your chances of picking up stomach bugs are considerably reduced.

If you do have a **serious attack**, 24 hours of nothing but plain tea (or just boiled water) may rinse it out. The important thing is to replace lost fluids. If you feel in need you can make up a **rehydration mix** with four heaped teaspoons of sugar or honey and half a teaspoon of salt in a litre of water, but most upsets resolve themselves. If the diarrhoea seems to be getting worse – or, horrifically, you have to travel a long distance while stricken – any pharmacy should have name brand anti-diarrhoea remedies. These (Lomotil, codeine phosphate, etc) shouldn't be overused. A day's worth of doses is about the most you should take.

Avoid jumping for **antibiotics** at the first sign of trouble. They annihilate what's nicely known as your gut flora (most of which you want to keep) and will not work on viruses. By the time you're considering their use, you should really seek a doctor. If you've definitely got blood in your diarrhoea and it's impossible to see a doctor, then this is the time to take a course of metronidazole (Flagyl). You'd have to arrange this on prescription with your physician or GP before your trip. Antibiotics and anti-diarrhoeal drugs shouldn't be used as preventives – this is potentially very dangerous.

Lastly, two common gynaecological problems. **Cystitis** can be relieved, if not eradicated, with acidy fruit juice: oranges and pineapples are available in abundance over much of the region. Don't fail to get medical treatment as soon as possible however, as cystitis can be very dangerous in a hot climate. **Thrush** responds well to a good dose of yogurt (both eaten and applied).

INJURIES, RASHES AND ATTACKS

Take more care than usual over minor **cuts and scrapes** – the most trivial scratch can become a throbbing infection if you ignore it. Otherwise, there are all sorts of potential **bites**, **stings** and **rashes** that rarely, if ever materialize.

Many people get a bout of **prickly heat** rash at first, before they've acclimatized. It's an infection of the sweat ducts caused by excessive perspiration which doesn't dry off. A cool shower, **zinc oxide powder** and cotton clothes should help. On the subject of heat, it's important not to overdose

> For a book on your health in tropical countries, you couldn't do better than Dr Richard Dawood's *Traveller's Health* (Oxford University Press, 1992). Exceptionally sane, detailed and well-written, it covers just about every imaginable symptom. If you're living in West Africa, especially if you need to treat yourself or others, get hold of the brilliant classic *Where There is No Doctor* by David Werner (Macmillan UK/Hesperian Foundation US, 1993).

on **sunshine** – at least in the first week or two. The powerful heat and bright light can mess up your system. A hat and sunglasses are necessities.

As for animal attacks, West African **dogs** are usually sad and skulking and pose little threat, though like captive **monkeys** they may carry rabies. **Scorpions** and **spiders** abound but are hardly ever seen unless you go turning over rocks or logs. Scorpion stings are painful but almost never fatal – and scorpions usually need considerable goading before they'll bring their tail into attack. Spiders are mostly quite harmless. The large, terrifyingly fast and active **solifugids** (also known as camel spiders or wind scorpions) do sometimes have a painful bite, but you're not likely to sit around and find out. **Snakes** are common but, again, the vast majority are harmless and to see one at all you'll need to search stealthily – walk heavily and they obligingly disappear. For reassurance about larger beasts, see p.73.

TEETH

Make sure that you have a thorough **dental check-up** before leaving and take extra care of your teeth while in West Africa. Stringy meat, acid fruit and too many soft drinks are some of the hazards. Floss and brush at least once in the middle of each day. You could, too, get into the habit of using a fresh "toothbrush stick" cut from a branch, as many locals do. Some varieties (for sale at markets) contain a plaque-destroying enzyme. Get into the habit of chewing gum after eating – even sweet varieties quickly lose their sugar and are soon performing a useful function on your teeth.

If you lose a filling and aren't inclined to see a dentist locally, try and get hold of some *gutta percha* – a natural, rubbery substance – which is available from some pharmacies. You heat it and then pack it in the hole as a temporary filling. Your dentist could get you some to take with you. **Emergency dental packs** are available from many vaccination centres.

INSURANCE

Insurance, in the light of the potential health risks, is too important to ignore. In addition to covering medical expenses and emergency repatriation, it also insures your money and belongings against loss and theft.

In **Britain**, good-value policies are issued by Columbus Travel Insurance, 17 Devonshire Square, London EC2 (☎0171/375 0011; *www.columbusdirect.co.uk*); Endsleigh Insurance, 97–107 Southampton Row, London WC1B 4AG (☎0171/436 4451); and Worldwide, The Business Centre, 1–7 Commercial Rd, Tonbridge, Kent TN12 6YT (☎01892/833338; *www.wwtis.co.uk*). In **Ireland**, travel insurance is best obtained through a travel specialist such as Usit, which has branches at Fountain Centre, College Street, Belfast BT1 6ET (☎01232/324073), and at 19 Aston Quay, Dublin 2 (☎01/6021777 or 6778117).

An outlay of around £50 per month will cover you against all sorts of calamities as well as lost baggage, flight cancellations and hospital charges. Some activities (climbing for example) are usually specifically excluded but can often be included as a supplement; ask your insurers for advice. Ask them to include bicycle and motorbike travel, as you may well find yourself a passenger, if not the "driver".

Whatever insurance you decide on, make sure you're not paying a high premium for cover you don't need – too much baggage cover, or a huge sum for personal liability – and make sure you *are* covered for what you intend to do. **If you need to claim**, you must have a police report in the case of theft or loss, and supporting evidence in the case of hospital and medication bills. Keep photocopies of everything before you send it to the insurer and write immediately to tell them what's happened. You can usually claim later.

NORTH AMERICAN INSURANCE

In the **US** and **Canada**, insurance tends to be much more expensive, and may be medical cover only. Before buying a policy, check that you're not already covered by existing insurance plans. Canadians are usually covered by their provincial health plans; holders of ISIC cards and some other student/teacher/youth cards are entitled to $3000 worth of accident coverage and sixty days ($100 per diem) of hospital inpatient benefits for the period during which the card is valid. Students will often find that their student health coverage extends during the vacations and for one term beyond the date of last enrolment. Bank and credit cards (particularly American Express) often have certain levels of medical or other insurance included, and travel insurance may also be included if you use a major credit or charge card to pay for your trip. Homeowners' or renters' insurance often covers theft or loss of documents, money and valuables while overseas, though conditions and maximum amounts vary from company to company.

Only after exhausting the possibilities above might you want to contact a **specialist travel insurance company**. Try Access America (☎1-800/284-8300; *www.accessamerica.com*); Europ Assistance Worldwide Services, 1331 F St NW, Washington, DC 20004 (☎1-800/821-2828; *www.champion-ins.com*); International SOS Assistance, 8 Neshaminy Interplex, Suite 207, Trevose, PA 19053 (☎215/245-4707; *www.intsos.com/*); Travel Assistance International, Suite 400, 1133 15th St NW, Washington, DC 20008 (☎1-800/821-2828; *www.1travel.com/protect/why.htm*); or TravelSafe Insurance, P.O. Box 7050, Wyomissing, PA 19610-6050 (☎1-800/523-8020; *www.travelsafe.com*).

Premiums vary widely, from the very reasonable ones offered primarily through student/youth agencies (STA's policies range from about $55 for 15 days to $180 for two months), to those so expensive that the cost for anything more than two months will probably equal the cost of the worst possible combination of disasters. If you're engaging in any high-risk outdoor activity while in

West Africa, you'll need to take out an additional rider – this will add an extra 30–50 percent to the premium.

Most of these American policies do not insure against **theft** while overseas. North American travel policies apply only to items **lost** from, or **damaged** in, the custody of an identifiable, responsible third party – hotel porter, airline, luggage consignment, etc. Even in these cases you will have to contact the local police to have a complete report made out so that your insurer can process the claim.

One thing to check: if you enter a country against the official advice of your government (see p.41), your policy may become invalid.

AUSTRALIAN AND NEW ZEALAND

Australians and **New Zealanders** may find that if they pay for their travel with a credit card (especially American Express) then a certain amount of travel insurance is included. For the majority of people though it makes sense to get separate travel insurance, most easily done through the major travel and discount flight agents (see p.12 for contact details). Unless you've got unusual requirements, you are likely to find there is little to choose in price between those on offer. You can expect to pay around A$130/NZ$145 for two weeks, A$190/NZ$210 for a month and A$280/NZ$310 for two months.

In **New Zealand**, one of the best deals is with Covermore (available through Budget Travel and Flight Centre) who have a low-cost policy which covers you for West Africa and the UK, but not the rest of Europe (except for a maximum of six days in transit). If you are planning to spend a week or more on the European continent you're better off with one of the policies offered by STA Travel.

In **Australia**, one of the best is Readyplan (available through Africa Travel Centres). Covermore (through Flight Centres) and AFTA (through STA and others) are also good.

MAPS AND INFORMATION

Although you will find maps of individual countries, and even certain cities, when you get to West Africa, they're almost always expensive and hard to obtain. Buy those you need in advance. As for tourist offices, those few that exist are usually attached to embassies or airlines and rarely offer more than vague and outdated leaflets.

MAPS

The single most useful item to take is the **Michelin map #953** *Africa North and West*. It covers all of northwest Africa with the exception of southern Cameroon (which appears on the #955 *Africa Central and South*). The latest (1996) edition of the #953 takes account of most new roads, showing water and fuel sources, roads liable to flood, ferry crossings and a mass of other details at a scale of 40km:1cm (63 miles:1inch). The only serious competition is Kummerly & Frey's *Africa North & West* map – on the same scale but less detailed and altogether less user-friendly.

For individual countries, the **French Institut Géographique National** (IGN, 107 rue La-Boétie, 8ieme, Paris; ☎01.43.98.85.00) has maps for a number of Francophone countries (plus Guinea-Bissau), many of which were updated in the early 1990s. There's also a good **Michelin** map of Côte d'Ivoire, a number of road maps of Nigeria, and a good one of Cameroon by **Macmillan**. Other maps, where they exist, are hard to obtain abroad.

MAP RETAILERS AND TRAVEL BOOKSHOPS IN BRITAIN

LONDON

Africa Bookcentre, 38 King St, WC2E 8JT
(☎0171/240 6649). Located in the Africa Centre.
A very wide selection of books from and about
the continent, with an emphasis on African writers and academic works. Mon–Fri 10am–6pm,
Sat 10am–7pm.

Daunt Books for Travellers, 83 Marylebone
High St, W1M 4AL (☎0171/224 2295) and 193
Haverstock Hill, NW3 4QL (☎0171/794 4006).
Superb place to browse, with both indigenous
fiction and travel literature.

Stanfords, 12–14 Long Acre, WC2E 9LP
(☎0171/8361321). The best travel book and map

store in the world, with wide coverage. IGN
agent. Mail and phone order available, plus
email order via *sales@standfords.co.uk*.

The Travel Bookshop, 13–15 Blenheim
Crescent, W11 2EE (☎0171/229 5260; *www.
thetravelbookshop.co.uk*). Very good new and
secondhand section on Africa, with some
French-language guides. Mon–Sat 10am–6pm.

GLASGOW

John Smith & Sons, 57–61 St Vincent St, G2
5TB (☎0141/221 7472; *www.johnsmith.co.uk*).
Specialist map department, mail order service.

MAP RETAILERS AND TRAVEL BOOKSHOPS IN IRELAND

BELFAST

Waterstone's, Queens Building, 8 Royal Ave,
BT1 1DA (☎01232/247355).

DUBLIN

Eason's Bookshop, 40 O'Connell St, Dublin 1
(☎01/8733811).

Hodges Figgis Bookshop, 56–58 Dawson St,
Dublin 2 (☎01/6774754).

MAP RETAILERS AND TRAVEL BOOKSHOPS IN PARIS

Astrolabe, 46 rue de Provence, 75009
(☎01.42.85.42.95). Paris's largest travel books
and map store.

Ulysse, 26 rue St-Louis-en-l'Île, 75004
(☎01.43.25.17.35). Crammed full of guides, old
books and maps.

MAP RETAILERS AND TRAVEL BOOKSHOPS IN NORTH AMERICA

BOSTON

The Globe Corner Bookstore, 500 Boylston
St, MA 02116 (☎617/859-8008;
www.globecorner.com). A broad selection of
books and maps, with a second location on
Harvard Square.

CHICAGO

Savvy Traveller, 310 South Michigan Ave, IL
60602 (☎1-888/666-6200; *www.
thesavvytraveller.com*).

LOS ANGELES

The Literate Traveller, 8306 Wilshire Blvd,
Suite 591, Beverly Hills, CA 90211 (☎1-800/850-
2665 or 310/398-8781;
www.literatetraveller.com). Independent bookseller specializing in travel literature and guides.

Travel Bookcase, 8375 W Third St, CA
(☎213/655-0575).

The Travel Gallery, 1007 Manhattan Ave,
Manhattan Beach, CA (☎310/379-9199).

MONTRÉAL

Aux Quatre Points Cardinaux, 551 Ontario E
(☎514/843-8116).

Ulysses Travel Bookshop, 4176 St-Denis
(☎514/289-0993).

NEW YORK

The Complete Traveler Bookstore, 199
Madison Ave, NY 10016 (☎212/685-9007).

Traveler's Bookstore, 22 W 52nd St, NY 10019
(☎212/664-0995).

SAN FRANCISCO

Get Lost, 1825 Market St, CA (☎415/437-0529)

Travel Market, 130 Pacific Ave Mall, Golden
Gateway Commons, San Francisco, CA (☎415/421-
4080).

SANTA BARBARA

Map Link, 30 S La Patera Lane, Unit #5, CA
93117 (☎805/692-6777; *www.maplink.com*).
Mail order supply, including some hard-to-find
maps of Africa.

Pacific Travellers' Supply, 12 W Anapamu St
(☎1-888/PAC-TRAV). Map Link's shop.

SEATTLE

Elliot Bay Book Company, 101 S Main St, WA
98104 (☎1-800/962-5311; *www.
seattlesquare.com/elliotbaybooks/*).

Wide World Books and Maps, 1911 N 45th,
WA 98103 (☎1-888/534-3453; *www.
travelbooksandmaps.com/*).

TORONTO
Open Air Books and Maps, 25 Toronto St, ON M5R 2C1 (☎416/363-0719).
Ulysses Travel Bookshop, 101 Yorkville Ave, ON M5R 1C1 (☎1-800/268-4395; *www.curioustraveller.com*).
VANCOUVER
The Travel Bug, 2667 W Broadway, BC V6K 2G2 (☎604/737-1122; *www.swifty.com/tbug/*).

WASHINGTON DC
ADC Map & Travel Centre, 1636 I St NW (☎202/628-2608).
Travel Books & Language Centre, 4437 Wisconsin Ave, NW 20016 (☎1-800/220-2665; *www.ambook.org/bookstore/travelbks*).
Note: **Rand McNally** now has more than 20 stores across the US; call ☎1-800333-0136 (ext 2111) for your nearest store or for mail order.

MAP RETAILERS AND TRAVEL BOOKSHOPS IN AUSTRALIA AND NEW ZEALAND

ADELAIDE
The Map Shop, 6–10 Peel St, SA 5000 (☎08/8231 2033; *mercator@mapshop.net.au*; *http://mapshop.net.au*).
AUCKLAND
Speciality Maps, 58 Albert St (☎09/307 2217).
BRISBANE
Worldwide Maps and Guides, 187 George St (☎07/3221 4330; *wwmaps@powerup.com.au*).

MELBOURNE
Melbourne Map Centre, 738–740 Waverley Rd, Chadstone, VIC and PO Box 55, Holmesglen, VIC, 3148 (☎03/9569 5472; *info@melbmap.com.au*; *http://melbmap.com.au*).
SYDNEY
Travel Bookshop, 6 Bridge Street, NSW 2000 (☎ 02/92413554).

LIBRARIES AND RESOURCE CENTRES IN NORTH AMERICA

Black Studies Library, Ohio State University, 1858 Neil Avenue Mall, Room 226, Columbus, OH 43210-1286 (☎614/688-8676; *http://aaas.ohio-state.edu/Library.html*).
Boston University African Studies Center, 270 Bay State Rd, Boston, MA 02215 (☎617/353-7303).
Carleton University African Studies Committee, Ottawa, ON K1S 5B6 (☎613/564-3816).
Center for African Studies, University of Florida, 427 Grinter Hall, Gainesville, FL 32611 (☎352/392-2183; *http://web.africa.ufl.edu/*).
Centre for African Studies, Dalhousie University, Halifax, NS B3H 4H6 (☎902/424-3814).
Herskovits Library of African Studies, Northwestern University, Evanston, IL 60181-2300 (☎847/467-3084). One of the largest libraries for the study of Africa.
Howard University African Studies, Sixth St, Howard Place NW, Washington, DC 20059 (☎202/636-7115).
Indiana University African Studies Program, 300 North Jordan Ave, Bloomington, I–47405-7700 (*www.indiana.edu/~afrist/*).

Institute of African Affairs, Columbia University, 1103 School of International Affairs, 420 W 118th St, New York NY 10027 (☎212/280-4633; *www.columbia.edu/cu/sipa/REGIONAL/IAS/*).
Michigan State University Africa Studies Center, 100 International Center, East Lansing, MI 48823 (☎517/353-1700; *www.isp.msu.edu/AfricanStudies/*).
Schomburg Center for Research in Black Culture, New York Public Library, 515 Malcolm X Boulevard, New York, NY 10037-1801 (☎212/491-2200; *www.nypl.org/research/sc/sc.html*).
University of Illinois African Studies Center, 910 S Fifth St, Room 210, Champaign, IL 61820 (☎217/333-6335; *http://wsi.cso.uiuc.edu/CAS/*).
University of Wisconsin African Studies, 1454 Van Hise Hall, 1220 Linden Drive Madison, WI 53706 (☎608/262-2380).
Yale University Council on African Studies, 89 Trumbull St, New Haven, CT 06520 (☎203/432-3436).

LIBRARIES AND RESOURCE CENTRES IN BRITAIN

Africa Centre, 38 King St, London WC2E 8JT (☎0171/836 1973). Office and reading room open Mon–Fri 9.30am–6pm. The UK's best independent charity institute for African affairs, open to all – reading room with magazines and newspapers, exhibitions, music, theatre, cinema, language teaching. Bar and restaurant open seven days. A good place to meet people.

Commonwealth Institute, Kensington High St, London W8 6NQ (☎0171/603 4535). Large centre offering library and resource services, shop, exhibitions, workshops and a performance venue.

Royal Geographical Society, 1 Kensington Gore, London SW7 2AR. Helpful Expedition Advisory Service (☎0171/591 3030) provides a wealth of information, including maps and technical guides.

School of Oriental and African Studies Library, Thornhaugh St, Russell Square, London WC1H 0XG (☎0171/637 2388). Open Mon–Thurs 9am–8.45pm, Fri 9am–7pm, Sat 9.30am–5pm; summer vacation Mon–Sat 9am–5pm. If you are a non-student a day-pass costs £6, and you must arrive before 1pm. A vast collection of books, journals and maps – probably the world's foremost African studies library.

Again, details for each country are given in their individual Practical Information sections at the beginning of each chapter.

TRAVEL AND TOURIST INFORMATION

Few countries in West Africa have money to promote tourism abroad. Those that have tourist offices can offer little more than uninspiring leaflets and brochures. Specialist **bookshops** and **libraries** are the best sources of information about West Africa. For general pre-departure reading have a look at the "Books" section in Contexts. For the official line from the UK Foreign and Commonwealth Office Travel Advice Unit, call them on ☎0171/270 4129, look up their Web site (*www.fco.gov.uk*), or tune to Ceefax pp.564–568 and trawl through the notices. For the same thing in the US, contact the Department of State Travel Advisory Dept, 2201 C St NW, Washington, DC, 20520 (☎202/647-5225; *http://travel.state.gov/*).

One of the best sources of up-to-the-minute news about conditions in West Africa are the various **Africa-centred Web sites** – try *www.africanews.org*, *www.africaonline.com* or *www.usafricaonline.com* – and **magazines**.

The latter are patchily available in major West African cities, and include:

Africa Confidential (73 Farringdon Rd, London EC1M 3JB; ☎0171/831-3511; *www.africa-confidential.com*). Fortnightly 8-page newsletter with solid inside info. Subscription only (£150, £50 students).

African Business (7 Coldbath Square, London EC1R 4LQ; ☎0171/713-7711; *icpub @dial.pipex.com*). Good general coverage.

Focus on Africa (Bush House, PO Box 76, Strand, London WC2B 4PH; ☎0171/257-2906). The BBC World Service's colour quarterly retrospective of news and reportage.

Jeune Afrique (Groupe Jeune Afrique, 57 bis d'Auteuil, 75016 Paris; ☎01.44.30.19.60; *www.jeuneafrique.com*). Influential weekly in the style of *Newsweek*, with African and international news.

New African (IC Publications, 7 Coldbath Square, London EC1R 4LQ; ☎0171/713-7711; *icpub@dial.pipex.com*). Well-edited news magazine with good sports coverage.

West Africa (321 City Rd, London EC1). Widely available and long-established weekly news magazine.

GETTING AROUND

Information about local route and transport conditions in each country is given under "Arrival" and "Getting Around" in the practical information at the beginning of each chapter. Specific transport practicalities are also detailed in the coverage of each capital city and in "Moving On" details throughout. What follows here is a general user's guide to West African transport.

BUSH TAXIS

The classic form of West African public transport is the **bush taxi** (*taxi brousse* in French, plus numerous local terms). This can vary from a reasonably comfortable Peugeot **station wagon** seating five or six plus driver, to the same thing seating nine or ten in discomfort, to a converted **Japanese pick-up** with slat-wood benches and a canvas awning jammed with fifteen people or more. A basket of chickens stuffed under the bench, and maybe a goat or two tied to the roof are regular fare-paying additions. Larger French **box vans**, increasingly replaced by Japanese and Korean **minibuses**, are no less zoo-like, though padded benches or seats help, as does the extra ventilation. Most vehicles have roof-rack luggage carriers and a more expensive seat or two at the front, next to the driver.

The chaos that seems to accompany bush taxi journeys is an illusion. They are nearly all licensed passenger vehicles, serving approved routes at fixed rates. Many even have notional schedules, though these are never published and rarely adhered to.

Peugeot taxis generally sell their places and drive straight from A to B, if possible without stopping. They often do the trip in half the time it

takes a more beat-up bush taxi, which may drop people off and take fares en route. But the converted pick-ups (*bâchés* in French, after their tarpaulins) are often the only way to get to more obscure destinations, or to travel on the roughest roads. Not surprisingly they're cheaper.

Beware of inadvertently **chartering** a bush taxi for private rental (a *déplacement* in French). Once you've done it, there's no way of avoiding paying for all the seats.

TAXI PARKS

Most towns have a **taxi park** ("motor park", "station", "stand", *gare routière*, *autogare*) where vehicles assemble to fill with passengers. Larger towns may have several, each serving different routes and usually located on the relevant road out, at the edge of town.

Practice varies slightly from country to country, but generally when you go to the taxi park, you'll find you're quickly surrounded by **taxi scouts** trying to get you into their vehicle. This can be trying and sometimes unnerving – when there's lots of competition and you're physically mobbed. It pays to behave robustly and to know exactly where you're going, and the names of any towns en route or beyond. It's often the case that your destination is not where all the vehicles are headed. You may have to change, or get out earlier. The ideal **time to travel** is early in the morning. By a couple of hours after sunrise the best vehicles have gone. In many parts there won't be another until the next day.

Before long on your travels, you'll run into a situation where you seem to be the only passenger in a vehicle you were assured was about to leave.

BUSH TAXI SURVIVAL

Bush taxis are probably the most dangerous vehicles on the roads so don't be afraid to make a very big fuss if the driver appears to have lost all sense. Ask and then shout at him to **"Slow down!"** (*"Ralenti!"* in French) and try to enlist the support of fellow travellers – though this is rarely forthcoming. In Peugeots it's nice to have a couple of **cassettes** for the stereo. In any vehicle, and in most parts of West Africa, sharing some **kola nuts** goes down well (see p.60). Lastly, if you're in a van with an engine mounted behind the front cab, be sure not to sit near it – you'll melt.

Beware of this. It's true your presence will encourage others to join you – which is why they wanted you there in the first place. But sometimes it's better to forget over-ambitious travel plans (especially any time after noon) or to take a shorter journey with a vehicle that's nearly ready to go. Taxi parks are full of interest for up to an hour or so. But a half-day spent in one acting as passenger bait is a waste of time.

As for **fares**: in order to guarantee you'll stay and attract others, drivers, owners and scouts will often try to get you to pay up front. Again, practice varies from country to country. Your luggage tied on the roof generally ought to be sufficient sign of your good faith and, unless you see others paying, it's always best to delay. Make sure you pay the right person when you do.

Over-charging is almost unheard of. It's your **luggage** that will cost you if you don't argue fiercely about how small, light and streamlined it is. Fellow passengers are just as likely to suffer but aren't in such a good position to create a scene. Shout, compare and contrast; tell the crowd how he's trying to kill you with his grasping ways. Make them laugh; make him happy to give you a good price. If you get nowhere, go to one side with him and be conspiratorial – this sometimes works because people like to show off business acumen and it draws attention again. You shouldn't have to pay more than **one-third** of your fare for a backpack or large bag. It's normally much less. Remember, you can argue forever about what you're *going* to pay, but once you've paid it, the argument is over.

During long waits it's a good idea to keep an eye on your luggage. Anything tied on the roof is safe, but taxi parks are notorious haunts for **thieves**, and bags sometimes get grabbed through open windows. Keep valuables round your neck. Don't worry unduly, however, if the vehicle, while waiting to fill, and with booked passengers scattered around, suddenly takes off with all your gear on top. While it's obviously a good idea to make a discreet mental note of the vehicle registration, you should avoid offence by appearing suspicious. Make friends with other passengers and relax. Maybe nobody knows where they've gone (probably to fill up with fuel), but they'll be back.

BUSES

Bus travel, when you've the option, is usually more comfortable and less expensive, though certain manifestations are little better than gigantic bush taxis and not always much faster. Niger, Burkina Faso, The Gambia, Mali, Côte d'Ivoire, Ghana, Nigeria and Cameroon all have quite well-developed bus services. Ghana's state-run service is particularly good, and not expensive.

The big advantage of most buses is having your own seat (even Peugeot bush taxis usually sell more places than there are seats) and being able to buy tickets in advance for a departure at a set time. There's still some room for discussion over the cost of transporting your luggage, but it's rarely a big issue.

Whether travelling by bus or bush taxi, it's worth considering your general direction through the trip and **which side to sit on** for the shadiest ride. This is especially important on dirt roads when the combination of slow, bumpy ride, dust and fierce sun can be horrible. If you're travelling on a *busy* dirt road with lots of other traffic, you don't want to be seated on the left of the vehicle in any case.

TRUCKS

Although it's usually against the law, on all main routes – and in the remotest regions too – you'll be able to travel by **lorry**. Pick up a lift in small villages or along the road: because of its illegality, you'll rarely find a truck ride in a large town. Once aboard, you can expect the lorry to stop at every checkpoint to pay bribes – slow progress.

There's sometimes a spare seat or two in the cab, but more often space in the back. **Travelling in the back** of panelled vehicles is pretty miserable, but many older trucks are open at the back with wood-frame sides. When loaded with suitable cargo, these can be a delight to travel in. You get great views and even, on occasions, a comfortable ride in a recumbent position. Do bear in mind your safety however (look out for low branches) and avoid getting the driver in trouble with the police by being conspicuous or foolhardy.

Travelling in an empty goods lorry on bad roads can be close to intolerable. They go much faster unladen and you're typically forced to stand and clasp the sides as the vehicle smashes through the potholes, causing severe discomfort to loose parts of the anatomy. For truck travel, you need to know the equivalent bush taxi or bus fares and distances or you'll find yourself **paying** over the odds. Lorries often drive late into the night too – if you're being carried outside, be sure to have **something warm to wear** for later.

HITCHING

The majority of rural people in West Africa get around by **waving down a vehicle**, but they invariably pay, whether on public transport, a truck or in a private car with a spare place. Private vehicles are still comparatively rare and usually full. **Travelling for free** is often considered to be rather improper and most people will assume your car has broken down. There's some sense, however, in hitching in and out of large cities, especially if you're stuck for money or can't find a bus or taxi. The kinds of drivers who respond positively are usually foreign-educated business types or expats.

Hitching **techniques** need to be exuberant. A modest thumb-in-the-air is more likely to be interpreted as a friendly, or rude, gesture than a request. Beckon the driver to stop with your palm. You'll feel like a policeman but that doesn't matter. Always explain first if you can't – or won't – pay, and don't be surprised if you're left at the side of the road.

Best chances for conventional hitching are in Senegal, Côte d'Ivoire, Niger and Nigeria. Hitching with overland tourists can be a good change of pace, and – more calculatingly – if you're in the right vicinity it can throw you in with people visiting game parks, which tend otherwise to be inaccessible to those without their own transport.

TRAINS

For many (colonial) years there was a French plan to push a **railway** across the Sahara, linking Algiers with Dakar. Had it succeeded, it might have altered today's network, in which only two of the eight West African railway systems cross borders. And of those systems most are no more than single lines running from the coast to the interior.

POLICE AND ARMY CHECKPOINTS

You should pay some attention to the condition of driver and vehicle before deciding to give him your custom. It's rare to undertake any journey over 20km in West Africa without encountering a posse of uniforms at the side of the road. A neatly turned-out Peugeot with a well-tied load and quite possibly some persons of influence inside is likely to pause for a greeting and move on. Conversely, a bruised and shaken *camion bâché* with 19 passengers, no lights and the contents of someone's house on the roof may be detained for some hours.

In practice only three lines are much used by travellers: in Cameroon between **Yaoundé and Ngaoundéré**; the Océan-Niger line between **Bamako and Dakar**; and the line between **Abidjan and Ouagadougou**. Timed right, you could do a trip as short as two or three weeks, substantially by train, through Senegal, Mali, Burkina Faso and Côte d'Ivoire.

Details are given on all these railways through the relevant parts. Although **other railway lines** exist, not all of them are running and some are freight only. The ones marked on our map of the region on pp.viii-ix currently operate passenger services. Some offer student discounts, though these are usually intended for nationals.

Travelling by train in West Africa is usually slower than road and while you can always get street food through the windows at stations, you should take your own drinking water for the duration. Toilets are rarely useable by the time you've left the city.

FERRIES

There are still hundreds of small, hand-hauled or spluttering diesel ferries pulling people and vehicles across the rivers of West Africa. But river transport upstream or down is very limited. The most attractive **ferry services** run on the Niger River in Mali, from the height of the rainy season to a couple of months after it finishes. Apart from the Ghanaian services on Lake Volta, there are few other significant car ferries operating in the region.

On the Niger, more or less anywhere between Kouroussa in Guinea and Niamey in the Republic of Niger, you can usually negotiate a passage in a **pirogue** (a dug-out/plank canoe) or a **pinasse** (a larger, motorized freight-carrying vessel) at any time of year, but in parts of Mali this has now become prohibitively expensive.

There's virtually no scheduled regional **sea transport**. Ferries connect the Cape Verde islands with each other and Dakar, and there's minor shipping on the coasts of Senegal, Guinea-Bissau, Nigeria and Cameroon.

REGIONAL & DOMESTIC FLIGHTS

West African inter-state **flights** are expensive, and travel by air not automatically the quickest option. On several coast connections the combination of flying time, formalities and transfers to and from the airports are enough to counteract any advantage over fast road transport. Abidjan–Accra can be done in a day, and Dakar–Banjul, and hops between Accra–Cotonou–Lagos, in a few hours. In most cases, however, flying is the best way to go if you're in a hurry.

Aviation in West Africa is in financial trouble and changes happen often. Currently the big West African inter-state **airlines** are Air Afrique – owned by a consortium of Francophone governments – and Cameroon Airlines. Together they more or less cover the region. Others (the larger of which operate inter-state services) include Nigeria Airways, Ghana Airways, Air Burkina, Air Ivoire, Air Sénégal, Air Mauritanie and TACV of Cape Verde. Airlines in a less certain state of repair include TAGB of Guinea-Bissau and Air Guinée. Several "national airlines" are virtually defunct and everywhere, with the new market-economic thrust of recent years, private entrepreneurs are setting up small airlines of light and medium-size planes. Most flights on the private airlines are operated on a charter basis, though sometimes with regularity, so you can buy a seat, in effect, from the charterer.

You can expect domestic flights to **cost** in the order of twice the surface transport rate. Also, beware of lower-than-expected baggage allowances on some internal flights.

AIR TICKET TACTICS

The air ticket set-up in West Africa is quite different from that in Europe or North America. There's little unofficial discounting of **fares**. Most tickets get sold at the approved rate, though some airlines operate anomalously, in which case you'll find it hard to discover what those fares are. If you possess an ISIC student card it's always worth requesting a **student reduction**.

You can expect some problems in **getting a reservation**, further problems at the airport getting a boarding pass and (occasionally) problems yet again in exchanging the boarding pass for a seat. Many domestic and regional flights in West Africa are heavily and permanently block-booked by government and not-so-government departments. Only when the actual number of required seats is notified to the airline can they open normal reservations to the public. In many cases notification comes, if at all, on the day of departure, in the airport.

There's little you can do about all this. Obviously, book as soon as you can and rebook if

plans change, rather than wait until you're certain. This anyway gives you leverage in terms of personal recognition at the airline office, and airline bookings don't require a deposit as a rule. Be utterly sceptical of a "confirmed seat" until you're sitting in it. Arrive at the airport long before the flight if you've any doubt about your status, and use every angle and pull every string you can to improve your chances. Clearly this is a worst-case scenario, but even when there appears to be no problem and no question of not getting on, always **reconfirm your seat** in person two days before the flight.

CAR RENTAL

Car rental is available in nearly every capital city, at most of the larger airports and in one or two provincial towns in a number of countries. Hertz and Avis have a fair network, enabling you to pre-book. Countries covered by **Hertz** (UK international reservations on ☎0990/996699) include Senegal, Mali, Cameroon, Côte d'Ivoire and Ghana. **Avis** (UK International reservations on ☎0990/900500) is found in Senegal, Mali, Guinea, Côte d'Ivoire, Burkina Faso, Ghana, Togo, Benin, Nigeria and Cameroon. Outlets are local licensed firms and, apart from being more expensive, not necessarily much different from others which don't have the international trademark.

There are several general points to bear in mind. First, rented cars cannot as a rule, be driven into **neighbouring countries**. In a number of countries, private self-drive car rental is a novelty and authorities feel uneasy about it beyond the **city limits**. You may be obliged to take a **driver** with the car and this inevitably puts the price up, though it isn't always a bad arrangement in itself – and can work out brilliantly. Some firms insist on **four-wheel-drive** (4WD) if you'll be departing from surfaced highways. The **costs** can be astronomical and you may spend in a day what would pay for a week's self-drive in Europe or North America.

An alternative is to consider simply renting a **taxi** on a daily basis. Buy the fuel separately or you'll never get anywhere and settle every other question – the driver's bed, board, cigarettes – in advance too. However good the price, don't take on a vehicle that's unsafe, or a driver you don't like and can't communicate with.

Whether you're driving or being driven, you should have an **international driving licence** with you. At delicate moments, some American, and all British, driving licences count for little as they lack the important identity photo. Minimum age for renting a car varies from 21 to 25 (18 for Nigeria) with one or two year's experience.

DRIVING

Don't automatically assume the vehicle is roadworthy. **Before setting off**, have a look at the engine and tyres and don't leave without checking water, battery and spare tyre (preferably two and the means to change them) and making sure you've a few tools. Except on certain main highways, it's important to keep jerry cans of water and fuel on board. As for breakdowns, local mechanics are usually excellent and can apply creative ingenuity to the most disastrous situations. But spare parts, tools and proper equipment are rare away from the Michelin map's red highways – and not really common along them.

When driving, beware of unexpected rocks and ditches – not to mention animals and people – on the road. It's accepted practice to honk your horn stridently to warn pedestrians, though be cautious of doing so in built-up areas which may have local laws you'd quickly fall foul of.

All of West Africa **drives on the right**, though in reality vehicles keep to the best part of the road until they have to pass each other (fatefully positioned potholes account for many head-on collisions). Right- and left-hand **signals** are conventionally used to say "Please overtake" or "Don't overtake!", but you shouldn't assume the driver in front can see. In fact, never assume anything about the behaviour of other drivers. Road death statistics are horrifying – Nigeria, famously, taking the lead in this respect.

You're unlikely to be kept for long by **police** or other security forces at the roadside, but you should *never* pass a checkpoint or barrier without stopping and waiting to be waved on. Nor should you ever drive anywhere without all your **documents**.

MOTORBIKING

Motorcycle rental is less common than car rental, but available in some cities. However, if you have some experience, it is well worth considering buying a machine in West Africa, avoiding the expense and paperwork of riding or shipping a bike all the way from Europe: in Mali, for example, reliable and economical Honda CG 125s are widely available, and make ideal machines, if not overloaded.

CYCLING

In many ways **cycling** is the ideal form of transport in West Africa, giving you total independence. You can camp out all the time if you wish, or take your bike into hotel rooms with you. When in rural areas you can often leave the bike unattended for a while if you're eating in a chop house or visiting a market – a crowd of onlookers will make sure no one touches it. If you get tired of pedalling you've the simple option of transporting your bike on top of a bush taxi or bus (reckon on paying about half-fare) or even "cycle-hitching".

A bike gives scope for exploring off the beaten track and getting round cities. Routes that can't be used by motor vehicles – even motorbikes – because they're too rough, or involve crossing rivers, are all accessible. With a tough bike, you can explore off the roads altogether, using bush paths – though remember to give ample verbal warning to people walking in your direction ahead of you, who may otherwise be seriously frightened by your sudden arrival behind them.

On busy roads a rear-view mirror is close to essential.

BIKE PRACTICALITIES

Apart from the commonest parts, **spares for mountain bikes** are rare in West Africa. But take only what you're sure to need – spare tubes, spare spokes and a good tool kit. If you need to do anything major, you can always borrow large spanners and other heavy equipment. Don't bother with spare tyres if you're going for under six months. On a long trip, it's worth depositing some money with a reputable dealer before you leave so that, in an emergency, you could fax from a public fax office and have a part sent out by a courier service like DHL.

You can forgo these hassles by buying one of the heavyweight **roadsters** on sale locally. There are bike shops and market areas devoted to cycling in most large towns. Ouagadougou in Burkina Faso has long been one of the cheapest places to buy, with a vast area devoted to bikes and good secondhand possibilities from about £60 ($90). You should be able to get a new bike for under £140 ($210). Bikes with three-speed hub gears (usually Raleighs or Peugeots) come somewhat more expensive. If you go for the gearless mount, console yourself with the fact that hub gears are fiddly to adjust and almost impossible to mend if anything packs up inside.

BIKE RENTAL

You can **rent bicycles and mopeds** in a number of places, including The Gambia, Basse Casamance (Senegal) and Ouagadougou (Burkina Faso). But they're not usually well-adapted for touring, although they often have carriers. Anywhere you fancy cycling, however, you can often make informal arrangements to lease a bike for a few days.

If you're taking a bike with you, then you'll probably want to **carry your gear** in panniers. These are fiendishly inconvenient when not attached to the bike, however, and you might consider sacrificing ideal load-bearing and streamlining technology for a backpack you can lash down on the rear carrier; you'll probably have to do this anyway if you buy a bike locally having travelled out to West Africa by more conventional means. Using the kind of cane that is used for cane furniture, plus lashings of inner tube rubber strips, you can create your own highly un-aerodynamic carrier, with room for a box of food and a gallon of water underneath.

With a bike from home, remember to take a battery **lighting system** (dynamo lighting is a pain) – it's surprising how often you'll need it. The front light doubles as a torch and getting batteries is no problem.

Take a U-bolt **cycle lock**. In situations where you have to lock the bike, you'll always find something to lock it to. Out in the bush it's less important. Local bikes can be locked with a padlock and chain in a hose which you can buy and fix up in any market.

Finding and carrying **water** is a daily chore on a long cycle trip. You'll need at least one five-litre container per person (more if you're camping out and want to wash) but you shouldn't often need to carry it full. Empty plastic oil jars and jerry cans, available all over North and West Africa, are convenient.

Lastly, **distances**: depending on your fitness and enthusiasm, expect to cycle around 1000km a month, including at least two days off for every three on the road. During periods when you're basically cycling from A to B (often on a paved road, which is somewhat slow on a mountain bike), you'll find 40–50km in the early morning and 20–30km more in the afternoon is plenty.

OTHER FORMS OF LOCOMOTION

Clearly, if you're hardy and not tied to any schedule, you can simply **walk**. All over the region, you'll come across local people walking vast distances because they have no money at all to pay for transport. If you're hiking for a few days you can fall in with them (if you manage to keep up), but they'll rarely speak any French or English. From a more recreational angle, we've covered a number of **hiking possibilities** throughout West Africa, mostly in upland and mountainous regions.

Using a **beast of burden** for your travels is an attractive idea. Unfortunately, **horses** succumb quickly in the more southern tse-tse fly regions and a horse in good shape is expensive. If you know what to look for and how to look after a horse, the most promising districts are sub-Sahelian – most of southern Mali, Burkina Faso, southern Niger, northern Nigeria and further south into highland Cameroon. If you ride south towards the coast, however, and sell your animal, it's likely to end up in a pot.

Donkeys are a lot tougher, cheaper and will happily go further south in the dry season. They're used to long treks. You'd need three donkeys between two with luggage, however. Then there are **camels** (dromedaries: *méharis* or *chameaux* in French). It's not impossible to join a caravan in the desert or northern Sahel, though fewer and fewer such journeys are made these days. But buying, equipping and travelling with your own animals is not to be undertaken lightly even by the most qualified romantic.

ACCOMMODATION

There's not a huge diversity of accommodation options in West Africa. A good
range of hotels is found only in the cities,
and in several countries even hotels are
rather uncommon outside the capital.
Hostels of various kinds are usually an
urban phenomenon, often permanently full
and not to be relied upon, and there are no
IYHA youth hostels. In some countries
you'll find government rest houses and in
remote parts where tourists are rare you
may be able to stay in volunteer rest houses and missions.

Campsites, too, are very rare. Campements
(not the same), in several of the French-speaking
countries, are more typical: these are basically
rustic motels, usually in the bush. The options of
staying with local people or camping in the
bush are usually there depending on how you
travel.

HOTELS

In large towns, and specifically capitals, you'll
want and probably have to stay in hotels. There
tends to be a gap between the expensive places
and the dives and you sometimes need to look
hard to find something good at a reasonable
price. If you're splurging there's usually a clutch of
international establishments bookable from
abroad. Local star ratings are not much used and
in any case about as hopeless an indication of
value for money as anywhere.

There's not much local market for Western-
style hotels (with reception, bars, restaurant)
except in countries with a mobile, salaried middle
class. The few mid-range hotels are usually
well-run and nice enough places to stay. But
small town hotels – and of course the cheapest
joints in the cities – are usually equated with
drinking and prostitution. Rooms are often taken

ACCOMMODATION PRICE CODES

All accommodation prices in this book are coded according to the following scales. Prices refer to the rate
you can expect to pay for a room with two beds. Single rooms, or single occupancy, will normally cost at least
two-thirds of the twin-occupancy rate. Bear in mind that only the most expensive establishments have a set
rate for every room and there's often a chance to negotiate a better deal. In most countries, for a simple but
decent twin room with clean sheets, air conditioning and bathroom, expect to pay upwards of £10–15
($16–24). You can often get a fairly mediocre place, usually without AC and certainly without hot water, for
about £5–10 ($8–16). The CFA countries generally have the cheapest hotels. Mauritania and Cape Verde are
expensive and you'll find little below the ③ bracket in those countries. The Gambia, Ghana and Nigeria fall
somewhere in between. The range of facilities you can expect across the seven price bands is given separately for each country in the Practical Information section at the beginning of each chapter.

① under £5/under $8   ④ £20–30/$32–48   ⑥ £40–50/$64–80
② £5–10/$8–16   ⑤ £30–40/$48–64   ⑦ over £50/over $80
③ £10–20/$16–32

ACCOMMODATION ABBREVIATIONS

AC Airconditioning, air-conditioned
S/C Self-contained, with private shower or bath,
and toilet

B&B Bed and breakfast
HB Half board, meaning dinner, bed and breakfast
FB Full board, meaning all meals included

CHEAP HOTEL PRACTICALITIES

- Always ask to **see the room first** and don't be surprised if it looks like a tornado's passed through, especially in the morning before it's been cleaned.

- Unless there's a proper tariff sheet, it's always worth haggling over the **price** of a room. If there's air conditioning or a fan but no electricity, ask for a discount. Check there'll be no **tax** on top.

- In highland regions or during the *Harmattan* it's normally expected you'll ask for a bucket of **hot water** to supplement the cold tap – but it may not be offered.

- You usually **pay** on taking the room and may have to leave your **passport** with the person in charge if there's no registration card to fill out.

- Always ask for fresh clean sheets and towel if you're not happy with them.

- Use discretion about leaving your **keys** with the management and, if your door locks by padlock, use your own and check the fixture.

- If you suspect **bedbugs** may lurk behind the plaster, pull the beds away from the wall. Keeping the light on deters them.

for a few hours only, and there may well be a gang of women and toddlers permanently in residence. Don't be put off unduly. These can be fun places to stay – and by no means all are intimidating places for female travellers – though you may have to pick a room carefully (not easy) for anything like a quiet night.

HOSTELS

Although there are no internationally affiliated youth hostels in West Africa, you'll find **YMCA** and **YWCA** hostels in several Anglophone cities (notably Accra and Lagos) which are usually permanently full of students and single professionals. If you can get in they're great places to meet people and, though they're generally run by slightly pious types, there are few limiting restrictions on what you do and when.

CAMPEMENTS AND REST HOUSES

For non-camping travellers, alternative types of "hotel" accommodation are popular options in the rural areas. **Campements**, in French-speaking countries, have a fairly loose definition. They're certainly not camping sites, though you can sometimes camp at them, but they represent more the modern equivalent of a colonial caravanserai or "encampment" in the bush, often associated with game parks and areas of natural beauty. They tend to consist of huts or small room blocks made of local materials (often mud bricks and thatch) with shared washing and toilet facilities – at the top end they're effectively hotels. But at their most innovative, in Senegal, where some are known as CTRIs – *campements touristiques rurals integrés* ("rurally integrated") – they are

built with government loans by the people of a village in order to host independent travellers.

In the English-speaking countries a network of **government rest houses**, for the use of officials on tour, is theoretically at the disposal of travellers when rooms aren't occupied. There's a similar *réseau* of government *villas* in Guinea. In fact, these places are very often unused for long periods and need a good airing. Water and electricity are often turned off or disconnected. First, in any case, you have to find the caretaker to open up.

And lastly there are the **aid and development organization rest houses** and rest houses of voluntary organizations like the United States Peace Corps (some 1400 of whose graduate volunteers are on placements in thirteen West African countries at any one time) and, somewhat thinly these days, **missions**. If you're travelling extensively, you may find these alternatives helpful and generous. In some cases – a few of the Peace Corps rest houses for example – there's a special tariff for "outsiders". But in general you'll be staying explicitly as a guest, using facilities intended for others. Where such arrangements are based on informal invitations and strictly word-of-mouth, we've usually kept them that way and not included them in this book. It would be unfair to suggest that such accommodation is universally open to all, and it's sometimes abused.

CAMPING

The few **campsites** that exist in West Africa are covered in the main country chapters. There are some in Mali, Mauritania, Côte d'Ivoire, Burkina Faso and Niger, one or two on the coast in Togo and virtually no others.

Bring the lightest **tent** you can afford; there are lots of good geodesic models around these days with snap-together aluminium frames. Or, if the prices put you off, consider making your own with ripstop nylon and fine nylon netting.

Camping rough depends much on your style of travel. Clearly, if you're driving your own vehicle it's only necessary to find a good spot for the night. Don't assume you can always do this anonymously. A vehicle in the deep bush is unusual and noisy and people will flock round to watch you.

Bush-camping is easier if you're **cycling** or **walking**. For safety's sake, always get right away from the main road to avoid being accidentally run over or exciting the interest of occasional motorized pirates. You may still be visited by delegations of machete-wielding villagers, especially if you light a fire, but satisfaction that you're harmless is usually their first concern. Some cigarettes or a cup of tea breaks any ice.

If you're travelling by **public transport**, it's a lot harder to camp effectively night after night. Vehicles go from town to town and it's rare to be dropped off at just the right spot in between, all ready and supplied for a night under the stars. Walking out of town in search of a place to camp is an exercise which soon palls, and it can be miles.

STAYING WITH PEOPLE

In this context there's not much to be said. Experiences vary enormously and depend as much on the guest as the host. But all over the region you'll run into people who want to put you up for the night. A warm, but more noticeably, a *dutiful* hospitality characterizes most of these contacts. The visitors most open to them are sin-

CAMPING MATTERS

In more **heavily populated** or farmed districts it's usually best to ask someone before pitching a tent. Out in **the wilds**, hard or thorny ground is likely to be the only obstacle. Fill your water bottles from a village before looking for a site. During the dry seasons, you'll rarely have trouble finding wood for a small fire so a **stove** isn't absolutely necessary. But it's very useful for wet or barren conditions. You can find *camping gaz* butane cartridges in most capital cities. Petrol stoves are more convenient once you've shelled out for them. If you're cycle-camping, a small kerosene lamp is perfectly feasible. Be sure to buy kerosene (*pétrole* in French) however, and not petrol/gasoline (*essence*). **Wild animals** pose little threat (see p.73). Night-time noises, especially in forest regions – some spectacularly eerie and sinister shrieks and calls – merely add to the atmosphere.

gle travellers who get into conversation on public transport. Your hosts are typically a low-income family with ambitions whose son has been away and has brought you home. You'll be expected to correspond later and send photographs.

It's sometimes difficult to know how to repay such hospitality, particularly since it often seems so disruptive of family life, with you set up in the master bedroom and kids sent running for special things for the guest. While it's impossible to generalize, for female guests a trip to the market with the woman/women of the household is an opportunity to pay for everything. Men can't do this, but buying a sack of rice or a big bundle of yams (get it delivered by barrow or porter) makes a generous gift.

EATING AND DRINKING

While West Africa has little in the way of well-defined cuisines this is in large part because supplies are erratic, recipes aren't written down, and no two meals ever taste quite the same. Nevertheless, there's a considerable variety of culinary pleasures and an infinite range of intoxicating drinks. Describing it all is complicated by the variety of terms used for common ingredients. Indigenous food and drink was one area in which colonial interests were limited. As far as possible, "Eating and Drinking" sections in the practical information section for each country chapter give an indication of what you can expect, and describe the local specialities.

FOOD

The great thing about West African food is its massive calorific value. Although less bulky alternatives are usually available, most meals consist of a pile of the staple diet plus a sauce or stew often called "soup".

The **staple** varies geographically. **Rice** predominates everywhere from Mauritania to Liberia and across the Sahel and is expanding as a commercial staple. **Root crops** (varieties of yam and cassava) and **plantains** figure heavily along the coast from Côte d'Ivoire through Nigeria to Cameroon. In the Sahara, **couscous**, tiny grains of durum wheat flour, is common.

Sauces can be based on **palm oil** (thick and copper-coloured, all along the coast from The Gambia south and eastwards), on **groundnut paste** (peanut butter, found mostly in Sahelian regions), **okra** ("gumbo" or "ladies' fingers" – five-sided, green pods with a high slime content which is much appreciated), various **beans** and the **leaves** of sweet potatoes and cassava among others. All of them are usually heavily spiced, often with **chillies** – "hot pepper" – though the emphasis on this ingredient tends to be exaggerated. It's rarely too much and only southern Nigeria is really dangerous territory for tender mouths. Whatever else they consist of, sauces are made with *bouillon* cubes – invariably Maggi cubes. Maggi sauce, too, is ubiquitous in every cheap restaurant.

The more expensive, or festive, "sauces" have an emphasis on their animal protein content. **Fish** and **mutton** are probably the most common. **Eggs** are rarely very popular (they're sometimes attributed with contraceptive powers) but they're always available. **Beef** tends to be reserved for special occasions. **Chicken** is pricey, but a favourite meat for guests. **Pork** is very localized and hogs foraging at the roadside are a sure sign you're in a non-Islamic district. Various kinds of **"bush meat"** are widely eaten except in the most devoutly Muslim regions, and often bought and sold. Large, herbivorous rodents ("bush rat", "cutting grass", "agouti") are the commonest and usually delicious, but antelopes, monkeys, even cats, dogs and giant snails are eaten in various parts of West Africa.

WHERE TO EAT

If you're lucky enough to be staying **with a family**, you're likely to experience consistently well-prepared and tasty food – though according to their means this may depend on how much you contribute. In homes, or when travelling on long-distance trucks, or by trading canoe, people eat around a **communal dish** (in strictly Islamic regions always males at one, females at another – you generally finish in order of age, the eldest first). Because of this, restaurants, where someone goes and buys a meal for themselves, are not all that common.

But it's wrong to assume you can't eat well at the cheapest **street food stalls** and roadside or market **restaurants**. The secret is to eat early – this means late morning (11am–noon) and dusk (5–6pm), when most people eat and food is fresh. Street food isn't usually a takeaway – there's often a table and benches, plastic bowls, spoons and cold water. Anything extra you want –

WEST AFRICAN FOOD PLANTS

There's a multitude of names in different languages for the same few food plants. Some of the names appear in the "Eating and Drinking" sections in the practical information at the beginning of each chapter. This section is an attempt to clarify things a little (botanical and French names in brackets).

Aubergine/Eggplant (*Solanum*). Grown on garden plots all over and come in many shapes and colours (round, white, yellow, red) but rarely in the familiar large, purple variety. Known variously as garden eggs or bitter balls, they can be identified as aubergines by the star-shaped, leathery, leafy bits at the stalk end.

Cassava (*Manihot; Manioc* in French). Spindly 2-metre shrub from South America, with hand-like leaves, seen growing all over. The tubers, which tend to have a bitter taste, are large and coarse and have to be boiled and then usually pounded in a mortar to reduce them to an edible glob of nearly pure starch (*fufu/foufou/eba*). Cassava leaves taste much nicer and are full of vitamins. They're finely shredded and used like spinach. *Gari* is cassava flour (from which tapioca is made), but the word gets used quite broadly.

Cocoyam (*Colocasia*). Tastier than yams or cassava, but easily confused. Grown mostly in wet forest regions, the plants have unmistakeably huge, heart-shaped, edible leaves. Tubers are rounded with a fleshy stalk and commonly known as "koko", "mankani", "taro", "eddo" or "dasheen". Similar names are often given to the introduced **Tannia** (*Xanthosoma*). This "new cocoyam" has giant arrow-shaped leaves and tasty, smaller, dark, hairy tubers.

Cowpeas (*Vigna*). The commonest type of bean ("black-eye beans"), cowpeas come in many varieties and are grown throughout the region. They're usually dried and stored for use, or made into flour, but you often see them freshly harvested in their long, pale pods. Mashed cowpeas are used for *akara* – "deep-fried balls" sold nearly everywhere. Common names include *wake* and *niebe*.

Groundnut (*Arachis; Arachide* or *cacahouètes* in French). Groundnuts (peanuts, monkey nuts) are grown widely to be used as the basis of sauces, and you'll see little dollops of peanut butter on leaves, for sale in markets everywhere.

Maize (*Zea; Maïs* in French). Grown a lot in forest region clearings, this is exactly the same as "corn" and "sweetcorn" and used widely on the cob as a stop-gap and a roasted or boiled snack. Maize flour is used quite extensively in some parts as a staple – in Ghana for fermented corn dough (*kenkey*) for example.

Melon seeds (*Cucumeropsis*). Certain types of melon are good only for their large, oily seeds, commonly known by the Yoruba name, *egusi*, and widely used when crushed to flavour soups.

Millet (*Pennisetum*). Looks like bullrushes, with a maize-like stalk, grown mostly in the Sahel. *Gero* in Hausa. Used for porridge, gruel and making beer.

Plantain (*Musa*). These mega-bananas are found all over the rainier southern part of West Africa. They're not eaten raw, but cooked (fried when ripe, boiled and sometimes pounded to a tasty *fufu* when hard).

Potatoes (*Ipomoea; Patate* in French). Unless specified as "Irish", these are always the *sweet* variety with pink skins, known in America, confusingly, as "yams". They're grown in mounds and ridges and have a mass of creeping vines. They tend to be something of a luxury, used to add flavour to stews and sauces. The leaves are good and widely used. Regular, Irish potatoes (*Solanum*) only grow in West Africa above an altitude of about 1200 metres.

Sorghum (*Sorghum; Sorgho* in French). Tall plants (2 to 4 metres) similar to maize but with feathery, white- or red-grained flower heads. Also known as "guinea corn" and "giant millet", sorghum is grown mainly in the savannah zone, and is made into porridge and pap. Sorghum beer – known as *bilibili, burukutu* and *pito* – is widespread.

Yam (*Dioscorea; Ignames* in French). Massive tubers that grow singly beneath a climbing, vine-like plant with spade-shaped leaves, commonly seen in southern parts of the region, especially in Nigeria. They come in white (which is preferred) and yellow varieties and are used like cassava to make pounded yam *fufu*, but they have a better flavour.

Other common food plants include **onions** and **tomatoes** (available everywhere, even in the driest districts, but often tiny and sold in piles of four), **lettuces** (wash very carefully), short but tasty **cucumbers**, **avocados** (wonderful, huge specimens in Cameroon), **tiger nuts** (*chufa* – tiny coconut-flavoured tubers like shrivelled beans), **pigeon peas** (small, round, brown and white beans), **white haricot**, **lima** and **butter beans**, and various kinds of **gourd**, **pumpkin** and **squash**.

soft drinks, instant coffee – can be fetched for you from nearby.

If you want to eat in more privacy, most towns, even the smallest, have at least one or two **basic**

restaurants. Much of the menu or blackboard is likely to be unavailable, however, and there's probably more cause for hesitation over what you eat in small restaurants where you can't be certain of the freshness or provenance of your food, than there is from street stalls where it all has to be cooked – or has just been cooked – before your eyes.

Large towns have more restaurants and, in general, less street food options. Eating chop house cooking at inflated prices in a silver service restaurant seems odd at first, but can be a real treat. The eating out alternative to African food, in cities, is usually **French** or vaguely **European**, **Chinese**, or **Middle Eastern**. **Lebanese fast-food joints**, providing snacks and sandwiches, especially **chawarma** (sometimes *shawarma*) – mutton in French or pita bread – are as common as burger franchises in the US.

STREET FOOD

Street food varies widely from country to country and regionally too, and is covered in more detail for each country. One snack that's pretty well universal is the **brochette** (*suya* in Hausa) – a tiny stick of kebabed meat. This is often eaten as a sandwich in a piece of French bread.

Although common, bread isn't a staple food in West Africa, but more of a luxury, often something to eat on long journeys. Different kinds tend to conform to the colonial recipes. In the Francophone countries it's a *baguette* – a French stick – though rarely as long or as crunchy as the real thing. In the Anglophone countries you have to search hard to find good bread. Mostly it's spongey white stuff, far worse than anything pumped out of supermarkets, sometimes very sweet, and often dyed a horrid yellow, or pink.

In the French-speaking countries you're likely to adopt the habit of eating **breakfast** in the street. Practice and adroitness vary, but in several countries you'll get excellent hot, whipped Nescafé with *pain beurre* (and real butter) for a set price of about 60p/$1. But be ready with appropriate French if you want your coffee black or – big shock to local people – without sugar. As it's sometimes made with sweetened condensed milk, white-no-sugar can be a problem.

DRINKING

Probably the most widely consumed beverage in the region – after water – is **green tea** (in reality yellow). In the Sahel, from Senegal to northern Cameroon, it's an essential part of every day and no long journey is completed without it. It's common further south, too, in all regions where Islam predominates. Rock sugar in huge lumps, China tea leaves and water are brought to the boil in a little kettle on a handful of coals, then poured out repeatedly to infuse and froth the brew. It's traditional to drink three glasses – strong and bitter, sweet and full-bodied, and sweet and mild – and considered rude to refuse. But like everything, form isn't always followed. The tea has to be Green Gunpowder, however – a tin of which makes a very good little gift.

Apart from Nescafé, **coffee** is less popular, and real coffee rare except in big hotels. Various **infusions** are locally common. One which has wide popularity in the western part of West Africa (as a base for mixing in a lot of *lait concentré sucré*) is *kenkeliba* (also spelled "quinceliba" and various other ways). It's reasonable on its own straight from the hot bucket or kettle, but don't mistake it for water and have Nescafé added.

VEGETARIAN WEST AFRICA

West Africa makes no concessions to vegetarians. Eating ready-prepared food, whether on the street, or in any category of restaurant, is unrewarding: animal protein is the focus of most dishes, and even where it's apparently absent there's likely to be some stock somewhere (rice is often cooked in it, or fat is added to the vegetables). This means, if you're strictly vegetarian, you're mostly going to have to stick to market fruit and veg and any food you cook for yourself. Peanuts and locally ground **peanut butter** are a good source of vegetable protein. Groundnuts can be found boiled as well as roasted.

Milk in various forms (and milk powder) and **hard-boiled eggs** are usually obtainable. Cheese is largely unheard of, except in its processed and E-supplemented, foil-packaged variety. **Bread** and canned margarine are available everywhere. Vegetarians who are the guests of African families have a hard time – with such status attached to meat, vegetarianism is regarded as an untenable philosophy. Avoiding meat is particularly trying if you consent to have eggs with every meal instead, as you can find yourself presented with six or more, specially prepared for you, every day.

COMMON WEST AFRICAN FRUIT AND NUTS

The most satisfying eating in West Africa is **fruit**. There's a magnificent variety in the markets south of the Sahel, though even in the drier regions you'll find citrus most of the year, mangoes in season and the odd pawpaw. The main ones to watch out for are:

Banana. If you spend long in West Africa, you may never be able to face a banana again. But local varieties are often wonderfully flavoured compared to the imported, white-fleshed supermarket type. Look out for very thin-skinned dwarf bananas in huge bunches, and for very fat, squat varieties with pale orange flesh and sometimes red skins.

Cashew. Not just a nut, the cashew also has a fruit attached. The arrangement of the nut at the apex of the cashew "apple" is hard to believe when you first see it. You can't eat the apple because the fibrous flesh is bitter, but curiously you can *chew* it to extract the delicious, light juice. In some parts this stuff is made into a potent hooch. Beware of feasting off cashew trees. They only have a small number of valuable nuts each and owners get very upset.

Coconut. The familiar brown "nuts" of coconut shies are contained within a thick husk and the whole thing is green and about the size of a football. Coconuts are very hard to open without a machete, but all along the coast (they won't grow easily above 500 metres) you'll have the opportunity to try them in several, satisfying conditions as the flesh changes from a thin jelly to a thick layer of coconut. They're not seasonal.

Grapefruit. African varieties are often exceptionally sweet and really big. Leave the segments to dry for a while and peel off the inner skins to reveal hundreds of little packets of grapefruit juice. A fine pleasure.

Guava. Don't buy unripe ones. They should have a very strongly perfumed scent. The best ones have pink flesh.

Mango. A royal fruit this; available and rightly esteemed everywhere, it comes in hundreds of varieties. The mango season coincides with the end of the dry season and the first rains (roughly March–June depending on where you are).

They're expensive at first and rapidly drop in price until they're two a penny (sometimes literally). Whole villages devote themselves to eating and selling the fruit. The very best, found in southern Cameroon, are long and narrow with bright green skins and very firm, orange, stringless flesh.

Oranges and tangerines. These – often bright green, even when prefectly ripe – are the main juicy fruits of West Africa. Oranges are always available for a few pence from girls and women with trays and sharp knives. The peel is shaved off, leaving the orange in its pith, then the top is lopped off and you squeeze the juice into your mouth and discard the emptied orange. You can easily go through a dozen or twenty in a day like this – diabolical on the front teeth.

Pawpaw. Not much eaten but widely obtainable. Very good (and good for you) with lime juice. Non-seasonal. See "Health".

Pineapple. Pineapples grow on the ground, with a spiky fringe of long sisal-like leaves around them. Commonest in coastal districts of Côte d'Ivoire and eastwards to Cameroon. Available throughout the dry season.

Sugar cane. Sometimes sold in markets, you simply strip off the shiny outside and chomp on the pith, which oozes sucrose. Another dental nightmare.

You'll also come across **starfruit** (attractively shaped but tasteless), **custard apples** or **soursops** (lovely pear-drop flavour in the roughly heart-shaped, green fruit) and **mangosteens** (amazing taste inside the small, round, brownish fruit with very thick skin). Towards the Sahara you get **dates** in all their different grades and, lastly, at certain times and places, quite a variety of **wild-collected fruit**, some of which (like the *ditak* in Senegal) is particularly good.

When you can't get cold water, **soft drinks** – especially fizzy orange and lemonade and Coke – are permanent standbys and in remote areas any establishment with electricity is almost bound to have a fridge of battered bottles (bottles are always returned to the wholesaler: *never* take the bottle away – this is serious theft!). **Soda water** (*eau gazeuse*), however, is rare. In the Francophone

countries, supermarkets and some general stores carry large bottles of French-style **mineral water** but, like soda water, you'll rarely find this in roadside fridges. On the street, however, you'll often see locally made **fruit juices**, cold water and ices, in plastic bags, sold by children from buckets of ice. Ginger is refreshing, as too is the white sherbet made from baobab fruits. Don't assume the soft drinks bottling plant necessarily applies any more hygienic methods of manufacture than local outlets. The water they use is almost certainly the same as what comes out of the village pump.

BEER AND SPIRITS

The most obvious drink in the region is **beer**, and almost every country has at least one brewery. Nigeria has many, and a whole host of competing brands. Only the Islamic Republic of Mauritania is dry. Beer, usually in half-litre bottles, is mostly strong, gassy, sometimes quite bitter in flavour and, most of the time, cold – including Guinness, brewed by local branches of European breweries. However, this European-style beer is extremely expensive to the majority of local people and it can therefore sometimes be difficult to find in smaller villages. As a convenient alternative the local traditional brews are well worth experiencing.

You can sample **home-made beer** under many different names. It's as varied in taste and colour as its ingredients – basically a fermented mash of sugar and cereal, usually sorghum, maize or millet, sometimes with herbs and roots for flavouring. The results are cloudy, frothy and deceptively strong.

Home-made beer is usually drunk in the round, each person taking their turn with the dipper, from a central calabash. It's always made by women.

In coastal parts, **palm wine** is produced from palm sap which, after tapping, ferments in a day from a pleasant, mildly intoxicating juice to a ripe and pungent brew with seriously destabilizing qualities. The flavour is aromatic and slightly acidic. The most common palms tapped are oil palms, which also produce palm nuts for palm oil, and the short and tall raphia palms. Taller *borassus* and coconut palms can also be tapped, but rarely are.

Spirits distilled from beer, palm wine or sugar cane are locally much in evidence across the continent (in Ghana, Cameroon, Burkina Faso, Nigeria and Cape Verde for example) and normally only alcoholically dangerous, rather than actually denatured with unknown toxic additives, as in other parts of Africa. But nevertheless, beware.

Imported spirits are excessively expensive. **Imported beer**, too, is rarely worth the price. Cheap French **wine**, on the other hand, is fairly affordable in Senegal and Côte d'Ivoire (unless you're French when it'll seem extortionate) where you can often buy it from ordinary general stores.

MEDIA

Local press and broadcasting in West Africa isn't likely to give you much of an idea of what's going on in the rest of world – though we've tried to uncover the best and most intrepid of the output in the "Communications" details in the practical information at the beginning of each country chapter. The availability of imported English-language newspapers and magazines is slowly improving. If you're travelling for any length of time, it's a good idea to invest in a pocket-size shortwave radio in order to listen to the BBC World Service – quite an institution in West Africa.

THE PRESS

There has been a rebirth of the **press** in West Africa since the advent of "democracy" in the early 1990s. Countries which formerly had almost no newspapers, now have a thriving press,

though critical and independent editors can still find themselves in serious trouble with governments – or government figures – uncomfortable with the results of their own policies. At the time of writing, several governments are actively engaged in trying to muffle freedom of speech.

If you want a more international view of events, assuming you're in a big city, some **British and European newspapers**, plus the *Herald Tribune* and *USA Today*, are often available in the more expensive hotel lobbies together with *Time*, *Newsweek* and *Jeune Afrique*. You'll find some of them, too, for sale, a few days later, from street vendors.

RADIO AND TV

Apart from general BBC World Service coverage several excellent Africa Service programmes to listen out for include the morning magazine

Network Africa (4–7am GMT) and the vital **Focus on Africa** repeated two times every afternoon Monday to Friday. You can also listen to the BBC in French, Hausa and Portuguese. Write to BBC World Service, Bush House, London WC2B 4PH, for full schedules, or check out their Web site (*www.bbc.co.uk/worldservice*).

The best frequencies for the BBC are 6.005MHz (49m), 11.765MHz (25m) and 15.400MHz (19m) in the morning, and 17.830MHz (16m) in the afternoon and evening. Generally, you'll get the best signal on a lower frequency (higher wavelength) early and late, and on a higher frequency (lower wavelength) during the middle of the day.

Voice of America broadcasts for shorter hours. It has a less interesting output and not such good reception.

National and local radio stations have blossomed in recent years, along with the print media. It's now common to have a local FM station or two, though, as with the press, they're frequently subject to all sorts of harassment.

Most West African countries have **TV stations**, usually with a rather uninspired mix of deeds and words from government ministers and imported soaps and movies. Video rental and satellite television have swept across the region.

MAIL, TELEPHONE AND EMAIL

Mail and telecommunications have improved enormously over the last ten years. Ordinary letters sent from main post offices rarely go astray if they're carefully addressed, though receiving mail is a little more variable. As for phoning, all the West African countries are now theoretically on International Direct Dialling, and for mobile phone users, Vodaphone and Cellnet have roaming agreements with Senegal and Ghana. Specifics for each country are covered in each case under the practical information at the start of each chapter.

MAIL

In French-speaking countries the post office is called the **PTT** (Postes, Télécommunications et Télédiffusion), in English-speaking ones, the **GPO**

and in Portuguese-speaking territories the Correio or **CTT**. Post offices in Francophone countries usually have separate counters (*guichets*) for different services, so make sure you're in the right line.

SENDING MAIL

It's easiest and most secure to use **aerograms** for writing home. Although these are often in high demand and forever going out of stock, they're usually postage pre-paid, so you don't have to worry about weighing and handing over letters.

If you have **urgent mail** to send, the best place is usually not the main post office, but the airport, from where mail is often sent on the next flight out. There may not be much of a post office, just a mail box. For similar reasons, if you're sending slightly heavy, or valuable items, it's worth doing so with a friend or contact who's flying. A lot of ordinary mail is sent this way too. It's always quicker. Leave it unsealed for customs.

If you're travelling widely, look ahead to the next country before sending your mail. **Postal rates** vary widely, especially between CFA and non-CFA countries – the latter are often cheaper.

POSTE RESTANTE

It's not wise to have mail sent anywhere except **capital cities**, not just in order to maximize your chances of getting it, but to speed up the delivery (Kano, Nigeria is an exception). Note, too, that some post offices only hold mail for a few weeks before returning it to the sender. From Europe, allow two weeks for post to be received and one week, or at most ten days, to mail out. For the rest of the world allow three days longer.

Post office staff are often remarkably uncivil, even rude, so be prepared to smile and plead. To collect mail, write your name on a piece of paper as you'd expect it to appear on the letter, and go armed with your passport, without which you'll rarely be allowed to receive mail.

For clarity's sake, ask people to write your address in this form:

DRIVER, Teresa
Poste Restante
PTT
Ouagadougou
BURKINA FASO,

and to put their own address on the back.

Alternatives to public Poste Restante are your **embassy** or **high commission** (some of which will hold mail for up to three months) or **American Express** offices, all of which will hold mail for customers, even if you only have their travellers' cheques. Local addresses are given throughout the book.

TELEPHONES

Despite IDD, most international phone calls from West Africa take a while to fix up. There always seems to be someone "occupying" the line, or an operator in the ether somewhere. If you have to go through an **operator**, always insist on "station to station" (number to number) rather than a personal call. The latter costs more and will only connect you if the person you name is available. Increasingly, **phonecards** are replacing cumbersome counter procedures for making international calls and the phone booths are set up in many cities. Unfortunately, the cards, manufactured

outside of West Africa, are often unavailable for months on end.

Reverse charge or collect calls ("PCV" – pay say vay – in French) are possible from most countries, but not easy to make. In principle, there should be no problem, but you may have some pleading to do. It's often easier, if you want to have a phone conversation, but aren't up to the very high likely cost, to arrange in advance to *receive* a call at a certain time and number.

To **call home** from West Africa, you dial the international access code, which is usually 00, followed by your country code, then the area code (without the initial "0" if there is one) and then the number:

UK: 00+44+area code+number
Ireland: 00+353+area code+number
US and Canada: 00+1+area code+number
Australia: 00+61+area code+number
New Zealand: 00+64+area code+number
South Africa: 00+27+area code+number

It's very useful to have access to a **fax** number at home through which urgent messages can be relayed to friends or family. Fax is more flexible than telephone – and usually works out cheaper. You might contact a local fax bureau before you leave home to establish you can fax through them. Every large town in West Africa has public fax offices at which you can send and receive messages (the cost of receiving a fax is nominal). Most large hotels have fax services, too, at slightly more expensive rates.

EMAIL

In countries with a reasonably stable telephone service, most major towns have at least one **cybercafé** or email service. Details are given in the "Listings" sections of the country chapters.

WEST AFRICAN IDD COUNTRY CODES

Benin 229 plus six-digit number
Burkina Faso 226 plus six-digit number
Cameroon 237 plus six-digit number
Cape Verde 238 plus six-digit number
Côte d'Ivoire 225 plus six-digit number
The Gambia 220 plus five-digit number
Ghana 233 plus area code plus number
Guinea 224 plus six-digit number

Guinea-Bissau 245 plus six-digit number
Mali 223 plus area code and number totalling six-digits
Mauritania 222 plus area code and number totalling six digits
Niger 227 plus six-digit number
Nigeria 234 plus area code plus number
Senegal 221 plus six-digit number
Togo 228 plus six-digit number

HOLIDAYS, FESTIVALS AND TIME

In addition to the main Christian and Islamic religious festivals, each country in West Africa has its own national holidays, listed in the practical information at the start of each country chapter. These are rarely as established as you would find, for example, in Europe. Some, commemorating no longer respected events, are quietly ignored. In one or two countries, the practice of mounting national celebrations for the president's birthday and similar anniversaries adds a bizarre and unfamiliar quality. Traditional, community festivals, connected either to annual agricultural cycles or to life cycle events, are more attractive but less accessible. Details are given chapter by chapter wherever possible.

ISLAMIC HOLIDAYS

Each West African country, with the exception of Cape Verde, has a significant Muslim population. Islam is the dominant religion in most, but Mauritania is the only nation to dub itself an Islamic Republic. In other countries, Muslim holy days are variably observed – devoutly in strictly Muslim districts, perhaps only vaguely in the capital city.

The **principal events** of which to be aware are the ten days of the Muslim New Year which starts with the month of Moharem (**Ashoura** on the 10th of Moharem celebrates, among other events, Adam and Eve's first meeting after leaving Paradise), the **Prophet Muhammad's birthday** (known as *Mouloud*, or *Maulidi*), the month-long fast of **Ramadan** and the feast of relief which follows immediately after (known as *Id al-Fitr* or *Id al-Sighir*), and the **Feast of the Sacrifice** or *Tabaski*, which coincides with the annual *Hajj* pilgrimage to Mecca, when every Muslim family with the means to do so slaughters a sheep.

The last of these festivals (known as the *fête des moutons* in French) can be a lot of fun. **Ramadan** isn't an entirely miserable time either. Fasting applies throughout the daylight hours, and covers every pleasure (food, drink, tobacco and sex); while non-Muslims are not expected to observe the fast, it's highly affronting in strict Muslim areas to contravene publicly. Instead, switch to the night shift, as everyone else does, with special soup to break the fast at dusk, and applied eating and entertainment through the night.

The **Islamic calendar** is lunar, divided into twelve months of 29 or 30 days (totalling 354 days). The twelfth month has 29 days and a thirtieth day 11 times every thirty years. The calendar dates from 622 AD, the "Year of the *Hijra*" (AH), when the prophet fled from Mecca to Medina. The Islamic year 1416 AH began on May 30, 1995.

CHRISTIAN HOLIDAYS

Christmas, and to a much lesser extent, **Easter** are observed as religious ceremonies in Christian areas and, on a more or less secular, national

NATIONAL INDEPENDENCE DAYS

Benin Aug 1, 1960	**Ghana** March 20, 1956	**Morocco** March 2, 1956
Burkina Faso Aug 5, 1960	**Guinea** March 6, 1957	**Niger** Aug 3, 1960
Cameroon Jan 1, 1960	**Guinea-Bissau** Sept 10, 1974	**Nigeria** Oct 1, 1960
Cape Verde July 5, 1975	**Mali** June 20, 1960	**Senegal** June 20, 1960
Côte d'Ivoire Aug 7, 1960	**Mauritania** Nov 28, 1960	**Togo** April 27, 1960
The Gambia Feb 18, 1965		

ISLAMIC FESTIVALS – APPROXIMATE DATES

Beginning of Ramadan (1st Ramadan)	Dec 10 1999	Nov 28 2000	Nov 17 2001
Id al-Fitr/Id al-Sighir (1st Shawwal)	Jan 8 2000	Dec 27 2000	Dec 15 2001
Tabaski/Id al-Kabir (10th Dhu'l Hijja)	March 17 2000	March 5 2001	Feb 22 2002
New Year's Day (1st Moharem)	April 15 2000	March 24 2001	March 13 2002
Ashoura (10th Moharem)	April 15 2000	April 3 2001	April 23 2002
Mouloud/Maulidi (12th Rabia)	June 15 2000	June 3 2001	May 23 2002

Islamic dates in parentheses. Also see www.moonsighting.com/calendar.html

basis, in every country. But if you can't find a bank or post office open, you'll have no trouble finding street food and some transport.

Christmas and **New Year** are the occasion of street parades and carnival festivities in a number of cities. On the downside, Christmas is a time to avoid contact, as far as possible, with people in uniform. This most applies to the police in the English-speaking countries, where a misappropriated tradition of "Christmas Boxes" survives and is relentlessly cultivated from mid-December to the middle of January.

Lastly, both Guinea-Bissau and Cape Verde have inherited and elaborated upon the Portuguese-Brazilian institution of **Carnaval** and host float parades and street festivals in February or March.

TIME IN WEST AFRICA

Most of West Africa is on Greenwich Mean Time (**GMT**). Cape Verde is one hour earlier (11am when it's noon GMT) while Benin, Niger, Nigeria and Cameroon are all one hour later (1pm). The 24-hour clock is widely used in the French and Portuguese-speaking countries. The 12-hour system is usual in the English-speaking countries.

Although all of West Africa lies north of the equator, the coastal region from Monrovia to Douala, just a few degrees north, has roughly the equatorial twelve hours of **daylight** – a little more in summer, a little less in winter. Sunrise comes earlier in the west (about 05.00 GMT) and later in the east (about 07.00 GMT). Latitudes further north experience greater seasonal variation, with slightly longer summer days, though it's almost always going to be light by the time you wake, and dusk still comes before 20.00 GMT.

The notion that the **tropical dusk** is extraordinarily brief is true. With the sun tracing a nearly perfect arc through ninety degrees most of the year, it plunges vertically below the horizon and is lost in minutes. In more extreme latitudes it slides obliquely into night leaving the long period of twilight familiar in Europe and North America.

TIME-KEEPING

People and things in West Africa are usually late. That said, if you try to anticipate **delays** you'll be caught out. Scheduled transport does leave on time at least some of the time. More importantly, transport may leave *early* if it's full. Even planes have been known to take off before schedule.

Although many people wear digital watches – which have flooded the region in the last twenty years – they're essentially jewellery. Notions of time and duration are pretty hazy. Outside the cities, dusk and dawn are the significant markers. You'll soon find you, too, are judging time by the sun, and reckoning how long before dark.

Note that in remote areas, if a driver tells you he's going somewhere "today", it doesn't necessarily mean he expects to *reach* there today. Always allow extra time. There's no better way to ruin West African travel than to attempt to rush it.

WARRI, WOLE, OURIL – THE GAME OF HOLES AND SEEDS

There's an ancient game for two people played all over Africa with two opposing rows of holes and a handful each of seeds, cowries or pebbles. It goes under dozens of different names and the rules vary locally. But the principle is always the same. Seeds are deposited in each hole and then the players take turns to pick up a pile from one of their holes and "sow" them, usually one by one, around the board. Depending on the rules, the hole the last seed is sown into determines the continuation of play, and, if it makes up a certain number of seeds in that hole, then they're captured. The player with the most seeds at the end, wins. It's a game that's devastatingly simple and, at the same time, mathematically highly complex in its endless chain of cause and effect – financial analysts love it.

GREETINGS, BODY LANGUAGE AND SOCIAL NORMS

You can't hope to avoid social gaffes on a West African stay, but humour and tolerance aren't lacking, so you won't be left to stew in embarrassment. Getting it right really takes an upbringing, but people are delighted when you make the effort.

GREETINGS

Greetings are fundamental. No conversation starts without one. This means a handshake followed by polite enquiries, even as you enter a shop. Traditionally, such exchanges can last a minute or two, and you'll often hear them, performed in a formal, incantatory manner between two men. Long greetings help subsequent negotiations. In French or English you can swap something like "How are you?" "Fine, How's the day?" "Fine, How's business?" "Fine, How's the family?", "Fine, Thank God". It's usually considered polite, while someone is speaking to you at length, to grunt in the affirmative, or say thank you at short intervals. Breaks in conversation are filled with more greetings.

Shaking hands is normal between all men present, on arrival and departure. Women shake hands with each other, but with men only in more sophisticated milieux. Soul brother handshakes and variations on the finger snap are popular among young males. Less natural for Westerners (certainly for men) is an unconscious ease in physical contact. Male visitors need to get used to holding hands with strangers as they're shown around the house, or guided down the street, and,

on public transport, to hands and limbs draped naturally wherever's most comfortable.

SOCIAL NORMS

Be aware of the **left hand rule**. Traditionally the left hand is reserved for unhygienic acts and the right for eating and touching, or passing things to others. Like many "rules" it's very often broken. Don't think about it then.

Unless you want a serious confrontation, never **point** with your finger. It's equivalent to an obscene gesture. For similar reasons, beckoning is done with the palm down, not up.

Don't be put off by apparent shiftiness in **eye contact**, especially if you're talking to someone much younger than you. It's fairly normal for those deferring to others to avoid direct looks.

Hissing ("Tsss!") is an ordinary way to attract a stranger's attention. You'll get a fair bit of it, and it's quite in order to hiss at the waiter in a restaurant.

Answering anything in the negative is often considered impolite. If you're asking questions, don't ask yes-no ones. And try not to phrase things in the negative ("Isn't the lorry leaving?") because the answer will often be "Yes..." ("...it isn't leaving").

Be on the look out too, for a host of **unexpected turns of phrase** which often pop up in West African English. "I am coming", for example, is often said by someone just as they leave your company – which means they're going, but coming back.

KOLA NUTS

Giving and receiving **kola nuts** is a traditional exchange of friendship. Kola nuts are the chestnut-sized fruit from the pods of an indigenous tree, cultivated widely all over the forest belt and traded on a grand scale throughout West Africa. Before the arrival of tobacco, cannabis, tea and coffee, kola was the main non-alcoholic drug of the region, an appetite depressant and a mild stimulant. It comes in dark red, pink and white varieties, of which the latter are the best and more expensive. Kola should be fresh and hard, not old and rubbery, and you chew it – don't swallow – for the bitter juice. Buy a handful for long journeys, as much to share among fellow passengers as to stay awake.

TROUBLE AND PERSONAL SAFETY

It's easy to exaggerate the potential hassles and disasters of travel in West Africa. Keep in mind while reading this section that bad experiences are unusual. True, there is a scattering of urban locations, easily enough pinpointed, where snatch robberies and muggings are common. But most of the region carries minimal risk to personal safety compared with Europe and North America. The main problems are sneak thieving and corrupt people in uniforms. The first can be avoided. And dealing with the second can become a game once you know the rules.

AVOIDING TROUBLE

Obviously, if you flaunt the trappings of wealth where there's **urban poverty**, somebody will want to remove them. There's always less risk in leaving your valuables in a securely locked hotel room or, judiciously, with the management. If you clearly have nothing on you (this means not wearing jewellery or a wristwatch), you're unlikely to feel, or be, threatened.

Public transport rarely produces scare stories. Apart from the standard of driving, which is another matter, you haven't much to worry about on the roads – except in Lagos, which is acquiring a certain notoriety for hold-ups (exaggerated, even so). Trains provide thieves with more opportunities, however. People fall asleep and robbers have been known to climb aboard and steam through the carriages. Establish a rapport with your fellow passengers as soon as possible.

If you're flying into West Africa, or arriving overland in your **first big city**, it's obviously wise to be particularly cautious for the first day or two. There's always a lot going on and it's important to distinguish harmlessly robust, up-front interaction (commonly part of the public transport scene) from more dangerous preludes. At the risk of sensationalism, the box overleaf outlines some good strategies for big city survival in Dakar, Abidjan, Lagos or Douala – the most difficult to deal with. Praia, Nouakchott, Banjul and Ouagadougou are more relaxed, while Lomé, Bamako and Niamey fall somewhere in between.

Don't feel unnecessarily victimized, but be rationally suspicious of everyone until you've caught your breath. It doesn't take long. Every rural immigrant coming to the city for the first time goes through exactly the same process, and many are considerably less streetwise than you, easier pickings for never having been in a big town before.

In one or two cities, **scams** which play on your conscience have begun to appear: a favourite is the "student agitator" routine, in which you get chatting to a friendly young person and either give him a little money, or exchange addresses. As soon as they have gone, a group of heavies arrives, claiming to be undercover police and informing you that you have been observed planning seditious activities. You could be arrested, or pay a fine now . . . Make a big fuss and insist on going to the police station with someone in uniform. They will disappear.

Lastly, don't forget that impoverished fellow travellers are as likely – or as unlikely – to rip you off as anyone else. None of this is meant to induce paranoia. But a controlled rise in your adrenalin level is a good thing. New York, London, Paris, Rome – if you can cope with any of them, you can handle a West African city.

THEFT

Hotel room **burglaries** and car break-ins do occur. If you get **mugged**, it will be over in an instant and you're not likely to be hurt. But the hassles, and worse, that gather as soon as you try to do something about it, make it doubly imperative not to let it happen in the first place. Robbers and pickpockets caught red-handed are usually dealt with summarily by the crowd – often killed – so when you shout "Thief!" (or "Voleur!" in French), be swift to intercede once you've retrieved your belongings.

Usually you'll have no chance, or desire, to catch your assailant(s), and the first reaction is to go to the **police**. Unless, however, you've lost a lot of money (and cash is virtually irretrievable) or irreplaceable property, think twice about doing this. The police rarely do something for nothing – even stamping an insurance form may cost you – and you should consider the ramifications if you and they set off to try to catch the culprits. If you're not certain of their identities, pointing the finger of suspicion at people is the worst possible thing to do. If they're arrested, as they probably will be, a night in the cells usually means a beating and confiscation of possessions.

In smaller towns, or where you have some contacts, a workable alternative to police involvement is to enlist **traditional help** in searching for your stolen belongings. Various diviners and traditional doctors operate nearly everywhere. If the culprits get to hear of what you're doing you're likely to get some of your stuff back. Or you could offer a reward. Local people will often go out of their way to help.

DEALING WITH THE POLICE

Police in West Africa are probably no worse than most around the world. But badly paid and poorly educated as they often are, it's wise to avoid them as far as possible. You will inevitably come into a fair amount of **contact**. Even in the vast majority of countries where you're no longer obliged to check in at the local police station in every town, the notion of "control" remains highly developed. Checks on the movement of people (police and security services) and goods (customs, *douanes*) take place at junctions and along highways in most countries. Many capital cities have major checkpoints on their access roads.

Police forces vary considerably from one country to the next. For example, in Côte d'Ivoire they're not excessively corrupt but can be unnervingly conscientious and pedantic, while in Guinea they're outrageously on the make and seemingly unfazed by the question of upholding actual laws. Most police forces constitute a separate entity from the rest of the people: they have their own

compounds and staff villages and receive – or procure – subsidized rations and services.

In **unofficial dealings**, the police, especially in remote outposts, can sometimes go out of their way to help you with food, transportation and accommodation. Try to reciprocate. Police salaries are always low and often months overdue and they rely on unofficial income to get by. Only brand new police forces and realistic salaries could alter the entrenched situation which now exists in most countries.

If you have **official business** with the police, smiles and handshakes always help, as do terms of address like "Sir", "Officer" or (in a French-speaking country) "*Mon Commandant*". If you're expected to give a bribe – as you often are – wait for it to be hinted at and haggle over it as you would any payment. A pound or two (say $2 or $3) is often enough to oil small wheels. If you're **driving**, you'll rarely be forced to pay sweeteners, except sometimes on entry to and exit from the country. If you're travelling by lorry or bush taxi, it's the driver who pays. If you're singled out, *remind them* it's the driver who pays. Avoid any show of temper. Aggressive travellers always have the worst police stories.

Having said all that, note that currency smuggling or drug possession can easily land you a large fine or worse, and possibly deportation. Don't expect to buy yourself easily out of this kind of trouble.

BRIBERY AND CORRUPTION

Bribery is indeed a way of life. But probably not yours. If you find yourself confronting an implaca-

---

BIG CITY SURVIVAL

Pickpocketing can happen anywhere – usually the work of pocket-high thieves, hanging around in markets or other crowded places. Make sure your valuables are secure.

Heavier attacks usually take place in specific areas of the city – downtown shopping streets, docks and waterfront, city centre parks and central markets. Less threatening districts include transport parks (full of tough young men with jobs who tend to be on the lookout for threats to their passengers) and, surprisingly perhaps, the lower income suburbs and slums away from the city centre, where people just aren't used to travellers.

When walking – assuming you have money or valuables on you – have a destination in mind

and stay alert. Be aware of what's going on around you. Scan ahead. Don't dawdle or dream. Keep your hands to yourself. Loose hands are likely to be caught: in heavy places, a handshake from a stranger in the street, or a knick-knack pressed into your hand, or some murmured offer or suggestion can foreshadow a more aggressive act. If you want to give off strong defensive vibes, hands in pockets or round the straps of a backpack are effective.

Steer clear of creepy-looking street sharks in jeans and running shoes (every robbery ends in a sprint). And never allow yourself to be steered down an alley or between parked cars.

DRUGS

Grass (marijuana, cannabis) is the biggest illegal drug in the region, much cultivated (clandestinely) and as much an object of confused opprobrium and fascination as anywhere else in the world. Many social problems are routinely attributed to smoking the "grass that kills" and it's widely believed to cause insanity. In practice, if you indulge discreetly, it's not likely to get you into trouble. The usual result of a fortuitous bust is on-the-spot fines all round.

An altogether different state of affairs exists with **heroin** and **cocaine**, which are smuggled though West African airports en route to Europe (often inside hapless female "swallowers"). Some of the consignments get on to the streets of capitals like Accra and Lagos, together with the associated tensions and paranoia. Stay well clear. Very long prison sentences and the death penalty are not unknown for those involved.

ble person in uniform, you don't have to give in to tacit demands for gifts or money. The golden rule is to **keep talking**. Most laws, including imaginary ones about the importation of backpacks, the possession of two cameras or the writing of diaries, are there to be discussed rather than enforced. If you haven't got all day, a *dash* or **"small present"** – couched in exactly those terms – is all it usually takes. If you can't, or won't give gifts to officials, give words. On extensive West African travels, you have literally hundreds

of police, army, customs, immigration and security checkpoints to cross and you'll sail through ninety percent of them. With patience and good humour, the other ten percent can be negotiated relatively painlessly too. When you know they know your "infraction" is bogus, keep joking, keep pleading and hang on. If you think you may be in breach of a law (or someone's interpretation of it) you might suggest paying the "fine" (*amende*) immediately, or "coming to an agreement" (*faire arrangement* or *s'arranger* in French).

BEHAVIOUR

- Never go out without **identification**. You don't have to carry a passport at all times, but a photocopy of the first few pages in a plastic wallet is very useful. Not carrying an ID (*carte d'identité*, *papiers* or *pièces* in French) is usually against the law.
- If you're heading for remote regions, to hike for example, it's worth leaving some details behind with your embassy or the honorary consul.
- Be warned that failure to observe the following points of **public etiquette** can get you arrested or force you to pay a bribe:

    Stand still on any occasion a national anthem is played or a flag raised or lowered. If you see others suddenly cease all activity, do the same.

    Pull off the road completely if motorcycle outriders and limos appear, or stand still.

    Never destroy banknotes, no matter how worthless they may be.

    And don't urinate in public.

TRAVELLERS' FRENCH

Apart from some specialized vocabulary, there's little that non-fluent speakers will find characteristic about West African French beyond the accent. It's generally a lot easier to understand than French as spoken in France, because it's more vigorously pronounced. And the French colonists encouraged the use of French far more than the British, so that, assuming you have at least some French, there are fewer language problems in the *pays francophones*.

As with English spoken as a second language, West African French will have the rhythmic and tonal colouring of the speaker's mother tongue.

WEST AFRICAN FRENCH: A TRAVELLER'S GLOSSARY

This is a mix of pertinent words and expressions together with some French and West African street slang and a few historical terms that have found their way into West African French.

amende	fine, penalty
atelier	workshop, studio
bâché	pick-up van, (lit. "tarpaulined")
balise	beacon or cairn, usually in the desert
banco	mud and straw mixture for building
barrage	road block, barrier
barraquer	to stop, rest awhile, camp
berline	saloon car
bic	disposable pen
biche	doe, gazelle, pet
bidonville	slum, shanty town
bonne arrivée	favoured greeting in Francophone Africa
bord	fortress (Arabic)
bordelle	prostitute, pick-up
borne	kilometre marker, "kilometre"
bouffer	to eat
break	estate car, station wagon
bricolage	the art of preserving equipment or making something out of nothing
brousse	countryside, the bush
buvette	outside bar, refreshments stall
cadeauter	to give a present; children may tell you, "*il faut me cadeauter*"
caféman	coffee, bread and omelette man
campement	budget motel or country guest-house
canari	clay pot for storing cool water
carte d'identité	identity card
carte routière	road map
case	hut, small house
chef	boss, chief
chômer	to be unemployed
cinq cent quatre	Peugeot 504
climatisée	air-conditioned (room)
colon	a colonial
commander	ask someone to do something
contrôle	checkpoint
coupe-coupe	machete
coupers de route	roadside bandits
dancing	dance floor, disco
dépannage	breakdown service
depuis	a long time
devises	money or (hard) currency
discuter	to discuss, negotiate
doux	good (even a hot pepper soup, far from mild, can be *doux*)
eau potable	drinking water
en panne	out of order, broken down
escalier	washboard road surface
escroc	swindler, con-man
exigé	required, demanded
faisable	feasible, do-able
féticheur	religious man with a knowledge of the ways of the spirits
fiche	form, document to fill in
flic	cop, policeman
fréquenter	to go to school
fric	cash, dosh
fromager	silk-cotton (kapok) tree
garé	parked, not in use

BASIC FRENCH WORDS AND PHRASES

today	*aujourd'hui*	this one	*ceci*
yesterday	*hier*	that one	*cela*
tomorrow	*demain*	open	*ouvert*
in the morning	*le matin*	closed	*fermé*
in the afternoon	*l'après-midi*	big	*grand*
in the evening	*le soir*	small	*petit*
now	*maintenant*	more	*plus*
later	*plus tard*	less	*moins*
at one o'clock	*à une heure*	a little	*un peu*
at three o'clock	*à trois heures*	a lot	*beaucoup*
at ten-thirty	*à dix heures et*	cheap	*bon marché*
	demie	expensive	*cher*
at midday	*à midi*	good	*bon*
man	*un homme*	bad	*mauvais*
woman	*une femme*	hot	*chaud*
here	*ici*	cold	*froid*
there	*là*		

gare routière	motor transport station	*pièces*	identity papers
gare ferroviaire	railway station	*pirogue*	dugout canoe
gargote	cheap restaurant or chop-house	*piste*	track, trail
gaté	spoiled, broken, needing repair	*préfet/sous-préfet*	administrative prefect/assistant
gênant	bothersome, a hassle		prefect (equivalent of District
gîte (d'étape)	boarding house, inn (staging		Commissioner and assistant)
	post)	*quatre-quatre*	four-wheel-drive
goudron	tar, tarmac	*récolte*	harvest
gri-gri	charm, amulet, juju	*régler*	to sort out, settle up, pay up
griot	traditional musician, storyteller,	*renseignements*	information, details
	court minstrel	*route bitumée*	surfaced road
hivernage	rainy season	*sapeur*	one who is well dressed-up,
HLM	"low rent housing" (council flats)		usually for discos and
Immeuble (Imm.)	Building		hanging out; from Sape, the
insh'allah	if Allah wills it (hopefully)		fictitious Société des
intéressant	good, enjoyable; eg a film or the		ambianceurs et persons
	food you're eating		élégants
lampe tempête	hurricane lamp, kerosene lamp	*sofa*	Nineteenth-century Muslim
livres sterling	pounds sterling		cavalry
machin	thingamajig, whatsitsname	*source (d'eau)*	spring, water source
mairie	town hall, city hall	*sous*	money
maison de	boarding house used as	*sucrerie*	mineral or soft drink
passage	a brothel	*sympa/sympathique*	nice, friendly
marigot	creek	*tampon*	rubber stamp
marque	make or brand (eg vehicle or	*tata*	fortress (Mande)
	spare part)	*tôle ondulée*	corrugated iron, washboard
mec	guy, fellow	*tourner*	to go out, go dancing, hang out
moustiquaire	mosquito net/mosquito screen	*triptyque*	triptych; a document in three
occasion	a seat or place in a bush taxi		folds
ornières	wheel ruts	*trop*	more often means "very" than
paillote	straw hut, sunshade, thatched		"too much"
	awning	*truc*	thing, whatsit
palétuviers	mangroves	*ventilée*	"ventilated" – a room with a
palu/paludisme	malaria		fan
patron	boss, chief, mister		
phacochère	warthog		

TALKING TO PEOPLE

Excuse me	*Pardon*	OK/agreed	*d'accord*
Do you speak English ?	*Vous parlez anglais?*	please	*s'il vous plaît*
How do you say it in French ?	*Comment ça se dit en Français?*	thank you	*merci*
		hello	*bonjour*
What's your name ?	*Comment vous appelez-vous?*	goodbye	*au revoir*
		good morning/afternoon	*bonjour*
My name is . . .	*Je m'appelle . . .*	good evening	*bonsoir*
I'm English/	*Je suis anglais[e]*	good night	*bonne nuit*
Irish/	*irlandais[e]*	How are you ?	*Comment allez-*
Scottish/	*écossais[e]*		*vous?/*
Welsh/	*gallois[e]*		*Ça va?*
American/	*américain[e]*	Fine, thanks	*Très bien, merci*
Australian/	*australien[ne]*	I don't know	*Je ne sais pas*
Canadian/	*canadien[ne]*	Let's go	*Allons-y*
a New Zealander	*néo-zélandais[e]*	See you tomorrow	*à demain*
yes	*oui*	See you soon	*à bientôt*
no	*non*	Sorry	*Pardon, Madame/ je*
I understand	*Je comprends*		*m'excuse*
I don't understand	*Je ne comprends pas*	Leave me alone (aggressive)	*Fichez-moi la paix!*
Can you speak slower ?	*s'il vous plaît, parlez moins vite?*	Please help me	*Aidez-moi, s'il vous plaît*

FINDING THE WAY

bus	*autobus, bus, car*		*descendre à . . .*
car	*voiture*	the road to . . .	*la route pour . . .*
boat	*bâteau*	near	*près/pas loin*
plane	*avion*	far	*loin*
What time does it leave ?	*Il part à quelle heure?*	left	*à gauche*
		right	*à droite*
What time does it arrive ?	*Il arrive à quelle heure?*	straight on	*tout droit*
		on the other side of	*l'autre côté de*
a ticket to . . .	*un billet pour . . .*	on the corner of	*à l'angle de*
ticket office	*vente de billets*	next to	*à côté de*
how many kilometres ?	*combien de kilomètres?*	behind	*derrière*
		in front of	*devant*
how many hours ?	*combien d'heures?*	before	*avant*
on foot	*à pied*	after	*après*
Where are you going ?	*Vous allez où?*	under	*sous*
I'm going to . . .	*Je vais à . . .*	to cross	*traverser*
I want to get off at . . .	*Je voudrais*	bridge	*pont*

OTHER NEEDS

doctor	*médecin*	chemist	*pharmacie*
I don't feel well	*Je ne me sens pas bien*	bakery	*boulangerie*
		food shop	*alimentation*
medicines	*médicaments*	supermarket	*supermarché*
prescription	*ordonnance*	to eat	*manger*
I feel sick	*Je suis malade*	to drink	*boire*
headache	*J'ai mal à la tête*	bank	*banque*
stomach ache	*mal à l'estomac*	money	*argent*
period	*règles*	with	*avec*
pain	*douleur*	without	*sans*
it hurts	*ça fait mal*		

QUESTIONS AND REQUESTS

The simplest way of asking a question is to start with *s'il vous plaît* (please), then name the thing you want in an interrogative tone of voice. For example:

Where is there a bakery ?	*S'il vous plaît, la boulangerie ?*	Can I have a kilo of oranges	*S'il vous plaît, un kilo d'oranges*
Which way is it to Bobo ?	*S'il vous plaît, la route pour Bobo ?*	**Question words**	
		Where ?	*où ?*
Similarly with requests:		How ?	*comment ?*
We'd like a room for two	*S'il vous plaît, une chambre pour deux*	How many/how much ?	*combien ?*
		When ?	*quand ?*
		Why ?	*pourquoi ?*
		At what time ?	*à quelle heure ?*
		What is/which is ?	*quel est ?*

ACCOMMODATION

a room for one/two people	*une chambre pour une/deux personnes*	second floor	*deuxième étage*
		with a view	*avec vue*
		key	*clef*
a double bed	*un lit double*	to iron	*repasser*
a room with a shower	*une chambre avec douche*	do laundry	*faire la lessive*
		sheets	*draps*
Can I see it ?	*Je peux la voir ?*	quiet	*calme*
a room on the courtyard	*une chambre sur la cour*	noisy	*bruyant*
		hot water	*eau chaude*
a room over the street	*une chambre sur la rue*	cold water	*eau froide*
		breakfast	*le petit déjeuner*
first floor	*premier étage*		

DAYS AND DATES

January	*janvier*	Wednesday	*mercredi*
February	*février*	Thursday	*jeudi*
March	*mars*	Friday	*vendredi*
April	*avril*	Saturday	*samedi*
May	*mai*		
June	*juin*	August 1	*le premier août*
July	*juillet*	March 2	*le deux mars*
August	*août*	July 14	*le quatorze juillet*
September	*septembre*	November 23	*le vingt-trois novembre*
October	*octobre*		
November	*novembre*		
December	*décembre*	1991	*dix-neuf-cent-quatre-vingt-onze*
Sunday	*dimanche*		
Monday	*lundi*	1992	*dix-neuf-cent-quatre-vingt-douze*
Tuesday	*mardi*		

NUMBERS

1	*un*	12	*douze*	30	*trente*	101	*cent-et-un*
2	*deux*	13	*treize*	40	*quarante*	200	*deux cents*
3	*trois*	14	*quatorze*	50	*cinquante*	300	*trois cents*
4	*quatre*	15	*quinze*	60	*soixante*	500	*cinq cents*
5	*cinq*	16	*seize*	70	*soixante-dix*	1000	*mille*
6	*six*	17	*dix-sept*	75	*soixante-quinze*	2000	*deux milles*
7	*sept*	18	*dix-huit*	80	*quatre-vingts*		
8	*huit*	19	*dix-neuf*	90	*quatre-vingt-dix*	5000	*cinq milles*
9	*neuf*	20	*vingt*	95	*quatre-vingt-quinze*	1,000,000	*un million*
10	*dix*	21	*vingt-et-un*				
11	*onze*	22	*vingt-deux*	100	*cent*		

TRAVELLERS WITH DISABILITIES

Although by no means easy, travelling around West Africa does not pose insurmountable problems for people with disabilities. For wheelchair or frame users, facilities are non-existent (and wheelchairs virtually unknown), but most hotels are single storey or have ground-floor rooms. Access ramps are rare, however, and travel within and between cities requires even more time and determination than usual. You'll at least have no problems recruiting local help and you can expect overwhelming consideration.

When choosing a **flight**, there are a number of factors to consider and you end up, as usual, having to compromise. By preference go for a flight with KLM, Lufthansa or Swissair – the best airlines for disabled passengers with a wide choice of routes. If you want to travel overnight and avoid the hassle of arriving after dark, you'll probably end up flying with British Airways to Nigeria or Cameroon Airlines to Douala. Both flights have the added advantage of being direct, though unfortunately the airports at Lagos and Douala are far from hassle-free.

From New York, the only direct flights are Air Afrique's service to Dakar (continuing to Abidjan) and Ghana Airways' flight to Accra.

From North America to Europe, Virgin and Air Canada have good reputations for their service and arrangements. Many US carriers publish travel information for passengers with disabilities; call ☎1-800/358-3100 for a free copy of Northwest Airlines' *Air Travel For People With Disabilities.*

Once in West Africa, attitudes to disabled people are generally good, though government provision for disabled needs is almost completely absent. **Getting around** in a wheelchair on half-paved or unpaved roads, or over soft sandy streets, is extremely hard work, while cabs are typically European or Japanese compacts. Inter-city travel is even tougher, though in some countries (Côte d'Ivoire stands out), the quality of long-distance buses can be well up to international standards.

Visiting **game parks and historical sites** is problematic unless you have private transport. Historical and archeological sites are often barely maintained, or at least require some climbing of steps or hiking through a bit of bush. In the case of the parks, it's not only difficult to reach them, but hard to figure out how to get around them when you arrive. Guided tours in safari vehicles with good springs are rare: in Nigeria's Yankari Reserve, visitors are thrown in the back of a lorry with wooden benches for game-viewing. On a positive note, most game lodges are accessible for wheelchair users and safaris can be arranged in advance in the capital – at a price.

Despite the difficulties, the effort is worthwhile if you count yourself a very outgoing individual, and are prepared to be carried repeatedly. **The Gambia** and **Burkina Faso** are sufficiently low-key, accessible and accustomed to visitors to make the hassles bearable.

Campbell Irvine Ltd, 48 Earl's Court Rd, London W8 6EJ (☎0171/937 6981) is one company offering **insurance** for disabled travellers.

CONTACT ADDRESSES FOR DISABLED TRAVELLERS

Access-Able Travel Source PO Box 1796, Wheat Ridge, CO 80034, US (☎303/232-2979; Fax 303/239-8486; *www.access-able.com/*).

ACROD (Australian Council for Rehabilitation of the Disabled), 33 Thesiger Court, Deakin, ACT 2600 and PO Box 60, Curtin, ACT 2605 (☎02/6282 4333); 24 Cabarita Rd, Cabarita NSW 2137 (☎ & TTY 02/6282 4333; *acrodnat@acrod.org.au www.acrod.org.au*).

Barrier Free Travel, 36 Wheatley St, North Bellingen, NSW 2454, Australia (☎066/551 733).

Holiday Care Service, 2nd floor, Imperial Building, Victoria Rd, Horley, Surrey RH6 7PZ, UK (☎01293/774535; Minicom ☎01293/776943).

Kéroul, 4545 av Pierre de Coubertin, CP 1000, succ. M Montréal, PQ H1V 3R2, Canada (☎514/252-3104; *www.keroul.qc.ca*).

Mobility International USA, PO Box 3551, Eugene, OR 97403, US (☎503/343-1248; *www.miusa.org/*).

RADAR (Royal Association for Disability and Rehabilitation), 12 City Forum, 250 City Rd, London EC1V 8AF, UK (☎0171/250 3222; Minicom ☎0171/250-4119).

Society for the Advancement of Travel for the Handicapped 347 Fifth Ave, Suite 610, New York, NY 10016, US (☎212/447-0027; *www.sath.org/*).

TRIPSCOPE, The Courtyard, Evelyn Rd, London W4 5JL, UK (☎0181/994-9294).

WOMEN TRAVELLERS

Machismo, in its fully fledged Latin varieties, is rare in West Africa. Male egos are softened by reserves of humour and women travel widely on their own or with each other, without the major problems sometimes experienced in parts of Asia and Latin America. Women's groups flourish in some countries, occasionally under the aegis of a government ministry – though in several they've hardly taken off. Where they exist, they're concerned more with improvement of incomes, education, health and nutrition than with social or political emancipation.

TRAVELLING ALONE

Travelling on your own or with a woman companion is by turns frustrating and rewarding. You'll usually be welcomed with generous hospitality, though occasionally you'll seem to get a run of harassment and hassles because of your gender. It's well to know, if you're overlanding from Europe, that the biggest difficulties will occur in North Africa – especially Morocco – and that Muslim regions south of the Sahara are altogether different.

On **public transport** a single woman traveller causes quite a stir and fellow passengers don't want to see you badly treated. They'll speak up on your behalf and get you a good seat or argue with the driver over your baggage payments. You can speak your mind, be open and direct and nobody takes offence. Fellow male passengers always assume protective roles. This can be helpful but is sometimes annoyingly restrictive and occasionally leads to misunderstandings (see "Sexual Attitudes", p.71).

Women get offers of **accommodation** in people's homes more often than male travellers (and most of them without strings attached). And, if you're staying in less reputable hotels, there'll often be female company – employees, family, residents – to look after you.

The **clothes** you wear and the way you look and behave get noticed by everyone and they're more important if you don't appear to have a male escort. Your **head** and everything from **waist to ankles** are the sensitive zones, particularly in Islamic regions. Long, loose hair is seen as extraordinarily provocative; doubly so if blonde. Pay attention to these areas by keeping your hair fairly short or tied up (or by wearing a scarf) and wearing long skirts or, at a pinch, very baggy pants.

In the heat it can be hard to be that disciplined, however, so if you have to wear **shorts** try to make them long ones. If you find it's too hot to wear a **bra**, it's not going to interest anybody. Breasts aren't an important issue and topless bathing is rarely offensive. If you'll be travelling much on rough roads, however, you'll need a bra for support. Seriously.

Teresa Driver writes:

I relished the opportunity to be with women but they continually made me feel dowdy. While gara (indigo tie-dyed damask) is becoming more fashionable, traditional West African dresses are made from brilliantly colourful printed cloth, used in vast quantities.

Senegalese women have to be the best dressers in the world. Their clothes are amazing, off-the-shoulder creations tailored to accentuate slim waists and sexy bottoms, and to show off long necks and broad backs (working backs). With towering headdresses the whole ensemble has an impressive, swaying grace. Or else they wear flowing, embroidered boubous. At parties and on festive occasions the women look stunning – decked in jewellery and flower-scented gowns and often wearing high heels that just add to the total effect. Even in the villages, women change into their best clothes to go market-shopping. The importance of your "look" can't be over-emphasized. If you make the effort to dress up it won't go unappreciated.

I took earrings and necklaces as small presents to give away (every woman has pierced ears). Body Shop cosmetics in small containers make excellent gifts, too.

It's often very difficult **getting to know women** in West Africa. Most contact is mediated, at least initially, through their male relatives, with whom you'll take on the role of honorary man, at least in the way you're treated socially. In the small towns and villages women are usually less educated than men and rarely speak English or French. They don't hang out in bars and restaurants either and are much more often to be found in their compounds working hard. Their fortitude as **housewives** is something to behold – always in total control of the family's food and comfort, from chopping wood to selling home-made produce in order to make ends meet. Even school-educated professional women dominate their household affairs and make sure everything runs smoothly. The extended family and the use of the younger girls as helpers is a major contribution. Men are away a great deal of the time.

For their part, West African women will try to picture themselves in your position, traipsing around *your* homeland – a scenario that most find hard to imagine. Family obligations are everything. Conveying the fact that you, too, have a family and a home is a good way of reducing the barriers of incomprehension but, assuming you're over fifteen, explaining the absence of **husband and children** is normally impossible. You can either invent some or expect sympathy instead – and perhaps the offer of fertility medicine.

BROADER ISSUES

Despite widespread paper commitments to **women's rights**, West Africa remains a powerfully male-dominated part of the world. Women do the large proportion of productive labour and most subsistence agriculture is in their hands, though this varies among different ethnic groups. Women have the explicit support of government ministries (for what it's worth) in very few countries. In other countries there's often a non-governmental women's organization working to improve the lot of mothers, agricultural labourers and crafts workers. Professional market women usually run their own informal unions in the cities.

Matrilineal cultures, which once held sway over large parts of the region, are on the decline, under joint assault by paternalistic Islam and Christianity. Matrilineal inheritance doesn't, in any case, necessarily imply *matriarchal* social structures but simply inheritance by a man from his mother's brother rather than his own father.

Current major **women's issues** in West Africa are primarily concerned with rights over women's bodies – contraception, abortion and the practices of genital mutilation, known, in a classic bit of male "anthropologese" as "female circumcision".

Few West African countries have successful **family planning** programmes, though there may be substantial improvements in the near future. Men are unwilling to co-operate by using condoms and women are pushed out-of-date pills at market stalls (sold singly if they prefer...). **Abortion** is virtually a taboo subject in some parts, though abortions by traditional methods (and less traditional backstreet operations) are believed to be widely performed. Few governments permit abortion on demand.

Genital mutilation is widespread and occurs to some degree in every mainland West African country. It's traditionally carried out by female practitioners on the occasion of a girl's initiation into womanhood. Today, although on the decline, it's also performed under anaesthetic in hospital and often at an early age. It varies from clitoridectomy, to excision of the inner labia, to excision of most of the outer labia as well (a major operation known as infibulation nearly confined, in West Africa, to Mali).

All these issues are complex. Both contraception and abortion (especially as encouraged by Rich World development agencies) are topics which can incense women as well as men, so be wary of crashing into conversation. In the case of genital mutilation, women campaigning to eradicate the practices have met resistance from traditionalist women. And mutilations can't be analysed just in terms of male sexual demands (a tighter vagina, loss of sexual response and consequent presumed fidelity). Unfortunately, it's an issue that many governments would prefer not to address.

SEXUAL ATTITUDES

Don't make any assumptions about puritanism on the basis of Islamic society in West Africa. It's the church which has successfully repressed sexuality. Otherwise, sexual attitudes are liberal (though you'll rarely see open displays of affection between men and women) and sex is openly discussed except in the presence of children. It's rarely the subject of personal hang-ups either, though sexual violence is surely as prevalent in families as it is anywhere. You'll be treated as a sexual person wherever you go. If you travel with a companion of the opposite sex, you'll find the relationship tends to insulate you – but not completely.

WOMEN TRAVELLERS

Flirting is universal in West Africa and in order to avoid it you'd have to be perspicacious about where you go in towns. This is particularly true for white travellers; the fantasy inventory of black–white sexual relations tends to get played out whenever you find yourself in a bar, or on a dance floor. If a man asks you to "come and see where I live", he means you should come and see where he and you are going to sleep together. You'll have no shortage of offers. They're usually easy to turn down if you refuse as frankly as you're asked. Unwanted physical advances are rare. But it always helps to avoid offence and preserve a friendship if you make your intentions (or lack of them) clear from the outset. If you're not with a man, a fictitious husband in the background, much as you might prefer to avoid the ploy, is always useful; though it may well be met with such responses as "Tell your husband you have to go outside for some air"...

If you're in a certain mood, all this can be fun. There's no reason you can't spend an evening dancing and talking and still go back to your bed alone and unharassed.

MALE TRAVELLERS

Much of what applies to women travellers in West Africa applies equally to men, though of course questions of personal safety and intimidation don't arise in the same way. It's common enough for women, and especially unmarried girls, to flirt with strangers. And many town bars and hotels are patronized by women who more or less make a living from **prostitution**. This is not the secretive and exploitive transaction of the West and pimps are generally unknown.

Unfortunately, **sexually transmitted diseases**, and the AIDS virus, are rife. Attitudes in West Africa have woken up to this new reality, but you should be aware of the very real risks – and prepared for the occasion – if you accept one of the many propositions which, travelling alone, or with a male friend, you're likely to receive. Always carry, and use, condoms.

GAY LIFE

Beyond the big cities, **homosexuality** is more or less invisible. People from a more traditional African background almost always deny it exists, find the notion laughable or childish, or describe it as a phase or a harmless peculiarity. As for the legality of gay sex, it's not *illegal* in Burkina Faso. Most countries, however, including all the Anglophone ex-colonies, inherited the laws of 1950s Europe and have hardly

---

ADVICE FOR WOMEN TRAVELLERS

- Carry pictures of your family.
- Beware of big men in small towns. Don't accept an invitation to the disco from the local commandant unless you're on very firm ground.
- Never meet someone as arranged if you're uncomfortable about it.
- Always lock your door at night.

- Take a supply of condoms. Don't tell yourself it will never happen. Be prepared, because he will never have any.
- And three useful French phrases for persistent clingers: *J'en ai marre de toi* (I've just about had enough of you), *Laisse-moi tranquille!* (Leave me alone!), or, in a crisis, *Va te faire foutre!* (Go and fuck yourself!).

changed – though in practice prosecutions are almost unheard of.

For gay male visitors, the only parts of the region you'll find like-minded company are the big capital cities and the resort areas. Contacts, however, tend to be rather exploitive on both sides.

Gay women can't hope to find any hint of a lesbian community anywhere.

The expatriate community has a statistically high gay constituency, and the Lebanese community, too, has a visible proportion of gay men.

WORKING IN WEST AFRICA

Exceptions are noted in one or two places in the book, but in general there's no way you can work your way through West Africa. Bed and board in return for your help is sometimes available on development projects, in schools or through voluntary agencies, but such arrangements are entirely informal and word-of-mouth. Teachers and engineers have the best chances. Direct, personal approach to the appropriate ministry might open some doors. But under-employment is a serious problem and work permit regulations everywhere make your getting a wage nearly impossible without pulling strings. You usually sign a declaration that you won't seek work when you obtain the visa or fill in the arrival card.

Voluntary work is more likely. **Peace Corps** accepts applications from US citizens over the age of 18 for field work in some 60 areas of speciality. Most commonly, they recruit people with a background in agriculture, education, engineering or health care, but volunteers with diverse experience in other fields also serve. The organization tries to respect applicants' geographical preferences; however, in order to be sent to a specific country, you must have skills currently being requested by the country. If you are willing to serve only in one region of the world, such as West Africa, your chances of being accepted are limited. The length of service is two years, following a three-month orientation. Peace Corps currently has programmes either in operation or in development for most of West Africa, with the exception of Burkina Faso, Nigeria, Sierra Leone and Liberia. For more details, contact ☎1-800/424-8580, or write to Peace Corps, Room 9320, Washington, DC 20526.

In Britain, **VSO** (Voluntary Service Overseas) accepts applications from people with useful qualifications and, usually, who have appropriate work experience, to work on local salaries in The Gambia, Ghana, Nigeria and Cameroon. Teachers and health professionals are primarily in demand. You do get the opportunity to state your preferred country. VSO is at 317 Putney Bridge Rd, London SW1J 2PN (☎0181/780 7200).

WILDLIFE AND NATIONAL PARKS

West Africa doesn't have the game reserves and wildlife concentrations of East or southern Africa. But it offers a number of major national parks that are worth taking in if you're an enthusiastic naturalist. Outside them, too, it's possible to see a good variety of Africa's birds and mammals in habitats ranging from desert to swamp and floodland, savannah, dry woodland and dense, moist forest – both lowland and mountain. Travelling by public transport, it always pays to spend a little more on a seat in the front. That way you can reckon on seeing a lot more creatures, mostly crossing or flying over the road – or squashed upon it.

WILDLIFE

The large animals you'll see most often out on the road, or in the bush, are **monkeys** and **baboons**. **Gazelles** and other small antelope are also quite common, especially in the Sahel. Larger grazing animals are localized and unusual sights. Along the Niger north of Niamey there are **giraffes**, and **buffalo** inhabit pockets of forest and bush thicket in various parts.

Elephants hang on in dwindling numbers in a surprising number of countries – most in fact – but it is difficult to assess their status. The **black rhino** has never inhabited more than the far east of the region: you can still see a few of them in Cameroonian parks.

None of these animals, even outside the confines of the parks, poses any threat to you as a traveller, even if you choose to camp out and hike or cycle. More threatening wildlife – the big cats, crocodiles, hippos – are very localized. You're extremely unlikely to see any large predators outside the parks. And even in a national park, seeing a **lion**, **cheetah** or **leopard** in West Africa is cause for some celebration. **Crocodiles** are hard to spot and are mercilessly hunted where they live because they do occasionally grab people at the water's edge. Be somewhat cautious by rivers and lakes. **Hippos**, too, have a justified dangerous reputation, especially when accidentally trapped on dry land or panicked in the water while dozing. You're quite likely to see them from a boat on the Niger in Mali, along the upper Gambia, along the Comoé in Côte d'Ivoire, or in Cameroon.

Another supposedly dangerous animal – the **gorilla** – is really very timid. It lives in the remote, southeastern forests of Cameroon and across the border in Nigeria in the Cross River National Park (full details in those chapters). **Chimpanzees** also survive here, as well as much further to the west, in patches of remote forest from Senegal to Côte d'Ivoire, but their existence is threatened by deforestation and the pet and laboratory trade.

Spiders and scorpions and various other multi-legged invertebrates are less often encountered than you might expect, or fear. The **butterflies** – as many as a thousand different species in some districts – are extensive and colourful, especially in the lowland forests.

Lizards are common everywhere. You'll soon become familiar with the vigorous push-ups of the red-headed male **rock agama**. Some towns seem to be positively swarming with them, no doubt in proportion to the insect supply. Large lizards (all species are quite harmless) include the **monitors**, of which the grey and yellow Nile monitor grows to an impressive two metres. They live near water, but you can often see them dashing across the road. **Chameleons** too, are often seen making painfully slow progress across the road, or wafer-thin, squashed on the tarmac. In some areas, at night, little house **geckos** come out like translucent aliens from who knows where to scuttle usefully across the ceiling and walls in pursuit of moths and mosquitoes.

West Africa's **birdlife** is astonishingly diverse – nearly eleven hundred species ranging from the diminutive pygmy woodpecker to the ostrich. Characteristic sights are the urbanite pied crows

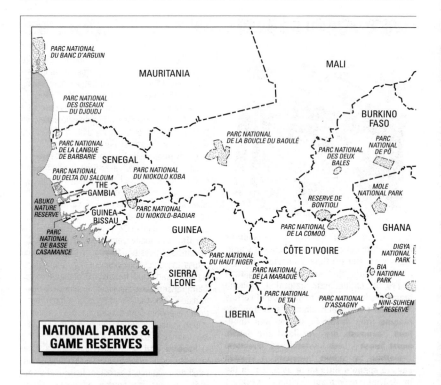

NATIONAL PARKS & GAME RESERVES

of the Sahel and savannah, electric blue Abyssinian rollers, perched on telephone wires in the grasslands, the marvellous, lurching flight of hornbills swooping across the road in forest areas, and quite unmistakeable flocks of grey parrots in dense bush along the coast.

NATIONAL PARKS

Most countries have some sort of national park network, though in several it consists of just the one park. The most important in the west are Mauritania's **Banc d'Arguin** (sea and migratory birds), Senegal's **Niokolo-Koba** (large mammals of savannah and forest) and Côte d'Ivoire's **Comoé** (savannah mammals).

In central West Africa there's Ghana's surprisingly good **Mole Game Reserve**, Benin's **Pendjari** (excellent game-viewing), and the **Parc National du "W" du Niger**, which extends across the borders of Benin, Burkina Faso and Niger.

Nigeria and Cameroon have probably the best parks in West Africa. Nigeria's prime savannah reserve, **Yankari National Park**, has well-organized game-viewing and quantities of animals, while the new **Cross River National Park** is a remote rainforest gorilla refuge. Across the border in Cameroon are **Takamanda Forest Reserve** and **Korup National Park**. Cameroon's other parks include **Waza National Park** in the floodlands near Lake Chad, which for faunal diversity and large herds of elephant is the best in West Africa.

Entrance fees, seasonality (many parks are closed during the rains) and **facilities** vary considerably. Of those included above, only Mole and Yankari are really accessible on a budget. Some of the smaller parks and reserves, however – in The Gambia and southern Senegal for example – are low-key enough to permit entrance on foot. Vital, if you're visiting parks, is a pair of good, light **binoculars**.

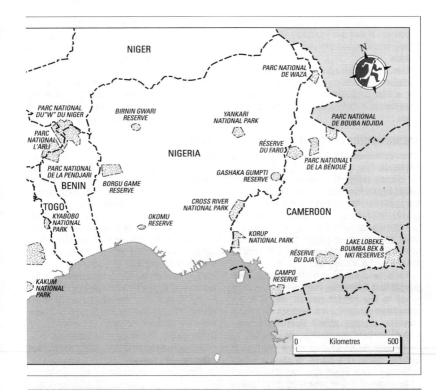

PHOTOGRAPHY

West Africa is immensely photogenic but to get good pictures takes skill and confidence, and a considerable amount of cultural sensitivity. While parts of the region have huge landscape potential at the right time of year, and there's obviously a wealth of opportunities for wildlife enthusiasts, you'll probably find people, villages and towns are your most compelling subjects – as well as being the trickiest. Except for wildlife photography, for which a telephoto is essential, you don't really need cumbersome equipment. It's often easier and less intrusive to take a small compact and keep your money for extra film.

Whatever you decide, if you take a camera, **insure it** and make sure you've a dust-proof bag to keep it in – film in the camera gets scratched otherwise. Take spare batteries, too – miniatures are hard to obtain.

Film tends to be very pricey so bring all you'll need. Try to keep it cool by stuffing it inside a sleeping bag. If you'll be away for some time, posting it home, or preferably sending it with someone flying back, is a good idea. Local **print processing** is available but tends to be hit and miss. The opportunity to process slides is rare.

CAMERAS, PEOPLE AND THE STATE

At the risk of generalizing, West Africa is hostile to the camera's probing eye. **Mistrust of your motives** comes from three main sectors. First, the people in markets, along the road and in the villages may, justifiably, resent you photographing them uninvited. Second, there are others, often teachers or civil servants, who may take it upon themselves to protect the state from your unwelcome inspection and ask you to stop taking pictures, or report you to the police. And third are the security forces themselves, who will often hassle you if they see you taking photographs – usually on the pretext that you are taking pictures of them.

None of this advice is intended to cause alarm, and plenty of travellers complete their trips with not a film confiscated or a camera opened. Nonetheless, disturbing encounters are not infrequent.

TAKING PHOTOS OF PEOPLE

There are two options if you want to get **photos of people**. First, you can adopt a gleefully robust (or blithely arrogant) approach, take pictures before anyone knows it's happened and deal with the problems after the event. But this is the kind of crass behaviour that will almost inevitably get you into trouble and spread bad feeling in your wake. Some travellers – few – seem to get away with it. Go to a busy market place at home and try the same thing. It's difficult.

Far better is a more interactive approach. **Ask people first**. Summoning the confidence and grace to ask to take people's portraits, and to accept refusal with equanimity, is at least half the affair. If they insist on posing, so be it. Try to come to terms with the reality of your position: you can't be a fly on the wall. As for shooting with a telephoto in crowded streets or a market, or using a sneaky right-angle fitting, they're almost always a failure.

Be prepared to **pay** something or to send a print if your subjects have addresses. If you're motivated to take a lot of pictures of people, you should seriously consider lugging along a **Polaroid** camera and as much film as you can muster, in order to offer a portrait on-the-spot. Very few people have a photo of themselves. Or you could have a lot of photos of you and your family printed up with your address on the back, which should raise a few laughs at least when you try the exchange. The exchange is what counts. A family you've

stayed with is unlikely to refuse a photo session and they may even ask for it. The same people might be furious if you jumped off the bus and immediately started taking photos. Or worse, if you stayed on the bus and did it through the window. Photos from Africa are full of examples of people who didn't want to be photographed. That you might have taken some of their soul is not an explanation, but it's a good metaphor.

SECURITY

You shouldn't take photos of anything that could be construed as **strategic** or **military** – including any kind of army or police building, police or military vehicles and uniforms, prisons, airports, harbours, ferries, bridges, broadcasting installations, national flags and, of course, presidents. Officially, this is seen as a "risk to state security", but some countries are specifically ill-disposed to tourists taking photographs of scenes reflecting poverty. With this kind of discretionary caveat, you can more or less rule out photography in the towns. It all depends on who sees you of course. Protesting your innocence won't appease small-minded officials. The Gambia, Senegal and Cape Verde are the least uptight about these subjects. Cameroon and Nigeria are notoriously touchy.

One or two countries still require you to have "**photography permits**". Details are given in the practical information section for each country.

TECHNICAL BUSINESS

Getting (slightly) **technical**, use skylight or UV filters to block haze and protect your lens. Take several speeds of film – don't let anyone tell you it's unnecessary to have fast film. Unless you intend to do some bird or game park photography (and you have to be quite determined about this, tracking and patiently setting up your prey) it's probably not worth taking a telephoto or zoom lens. Long lenses are very difficult to use in public places. But if you feel it's worth taking a camera bag of lenses for your SLR, then it really makes no sense not to take two camera bodies as well – less lens changing and two film speeds available. Or take two compact cameras.

Early morning and late afternoon are the **best times for photography**. At midday, with the sun almost directly overhead, the light is flat and everything is lost in a formless glare. In the morning and evening the contrast between light and shade can be huge, so be careful to expose for the subject and not the general scene. A flash is very

VIDEO CAMERAS

Everything that applies to still photography applies tenfold to **camcorders**. More and more people are wandering around with them, but it would be well worth asking permission in advance through the nearest embassy and trying hard to get something in writing from the country's Ministry of Information. Most of the laws allowing amateur filming apply to non-broadcast quality 8mm filming and haven't yet caught up with videos.

useful to fill in shade, even in bright sun. Remember too, as you frame your next master portrait, that dark skin needs extra exposure or you won't see people's faces: think of people as always back-lit – a half stop is normally enough.

The **rainy season** is perhaps the most rewarding time, especially when the first rains break. Months of dust are settled, greenery sprouts in a few hours, the countryside has a lush, bold sheen and the sky is magnificent.

PEOPLE AND LANGUAGE

Whether called peoples, ethnic groups, nations or tribes, West Africans have a multiplicity of racial and cultural origins. Distinctions would be simple if similarities in physical appearance were shared by those who speak the same language and share a common culture. The term "tribe" tends to imply this kind of banal stereotype. But "tribes" have never been closed units and appearance, speech and culture have always overlapped. Even in the past, families often contained members of different ethnic groups. Over the last fifty years or so, "tribal" identities have broken down still further in many parts, replaced by broader class, political and national ones.

The most enduring and meaningful ethnic distinction is **language**. A person's "mother tongue" is still important as an index of social identity. A *tribe*, if the word means anything, is best defined as a group of people sharing a common first language. But in the towns and among affluent families, even language is increasingly unimportant. Many people speak two or three languages (their own, French or English and sometimes a third or even fourth lingua franca like Hausa, Bamana or Krio). And for a few, the old metropolitan languages – French, English or Portuguese – have become a first language.

NAMES AND GROUPS

West Africa is the most linguistically complex region in the world. There are dozens of **major languages** and literally hundreds of less important languages and distinct dialects. Some four hundred of these are spoken in Nigeria alone. Most of West Africa's languages are viable and thriving and very few are in any danger of extinction.

For an outsider, the confusion is exacerbated by the fact that, until European colonization, almost none of these languages was written. Today, many are written, in the Roman alphabet, sometimes with additional phonetic symbols. But in the early days, even the language and ethnic names first recorded varied according to the nationality and ear of the researchers and the identity of the person asked. Often enough in West Africa the name of the language and of the people who speak it are genuinely distinct.

We have tried to be as consistent and simple as possible in this book, without sweeping distinctions away. Generally, we've used the **names** used locally (for example Mandingo in Liberia, Malinké in Guinea, Mandinka in The Gambia). On the other hand, varieties of names for the people and language often called *Fulani* are so diverse – *Peul, Peulh, Fulfulde, Fulbe, Foulah, Pulaar, Fula* – that we've gone for simple *Fula* throughout except in Nigeria, where "Fulani" is in common usage.

Some understanding of differences and relatedness is worth achieving in order, at the very least, to come to grips with what can otherwise

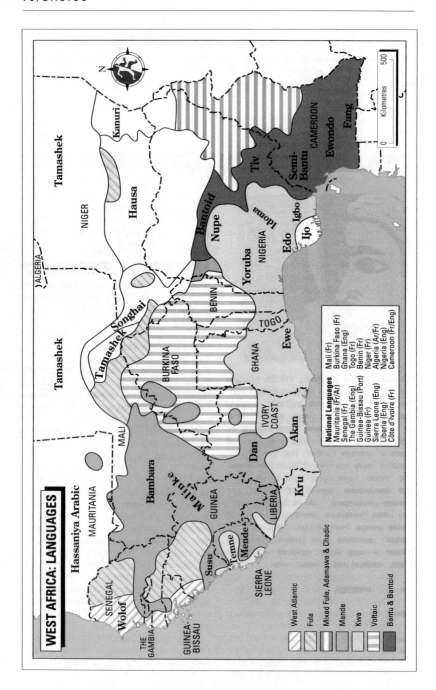

WEST AFRICA: LANGUAGES

National Languages
Mauritania (Fr/Ar)
Senegal (Fr)
The Gambia (Eng)
Guinea-Bissau (Port)
Guinea (Fr)
Sierra Leone (Eng)
Liberia (Eng)
Côte d'Ivoire (Fr)
Mali (Fr)
Burkina Faso (Fr)
Ghana (Eng)
Togo (Fr)
Benin (Fr)
Niger (Fr)
Algeria (Ar/Fr)
Nigeria (Eng)
Cameroon (Fr/Eng)

West Atlantic
Fula
Mixed Fula, Adamawa & Chadic
Mande
Kwa
Voltaic
Bantu & Bantoid

seem an incomprehensible and unfathomable cultural region. Most West Africans speak languages of one of **three great groups** – "Niger-Congo" (now renamed the Southern area of wider affinity – Sawa), "Afro-Asiatic" (the Northern area of wider affinity – Nawa) and Mande. African language classification (the attempt to assess the way the languages are presumed to have evolved from common ancestral languages) is immensely complicated and linguists have recently tried to get away from the notion of "families" of languages, in case it turns out they have things in common through long association rather than common ancestry.

In trying to work out where everyone fits in, it helps, especially when reading different sources, to keep a flexible attitude to **spellings** (try pronouncing the word in as many ways as possible). Two sets of much interchanged sounds are the p, b, v, f, w set and the d, gh, r, l set. And of course anything spelled "qu" might just as well be spelt "kw" or, for that matter, "cou" or "kou".

Likewise, "j" is commonly spelt "dy" or "di" in French transcription. The French are keen on apostrophes everywhere, too. They don't usually mean any more than that someone found the word hard to pronounce. Finally, look out for prefixes or suffixes that may mean "people" ("Ba-" in the Bantu languages for example, or "-nke" in the Mande languages).

THE "SOUTHERN AREA OF WIDER AFFINITY"

The **Sawa group** includes the 400 **Bantu** languages that are spoken all over Central and southern Africa. In West Africa, Bantu languages are only spoken in parts of southern Cameroon. Further west, the picture is much more complicated. The so-called **"West Atlantic"** languages, which include Wolof, Temne and Fula, are part of this grouping, though fairly distantly related to Bantu. Also part of the Sawa group is the **Kwa sub-family** of language clusters, which include the **Akan languages** (of which the Asante are the most famous speakers), the **Ewe languages** of Ghana and Togo and the **Yoruba** and **Igbo** language groups of Benin and Nigeria. To the north,

the **Voltaic sub-family** of language clusters includes the **Senoufo**, **More** and **Lobi** groups of Côte d'Ivoire, Ghana and Burkina Faso.

Many of the languages in the Sawa group have **class systems** (something like genders in French in that everything must agree) with up to 20 or more classes – Bantu languages are the classic examples. Many Sawa languages, too, are **tonal** – in which the pitch of a spoken word determines its meaning – and extra notations are often necessary when writing them properly.

THE "NORTHERN AREA OF WIDER AFFINITY"

The **Nawa group** includes most of the languages of North Africa, and the Middle East, including Hebrew, Arabic, Berber and Tamashek (the language of the Tuaregs). The most important languages in the area as far as West Africa is concerned are known as "Chadic", the biggest of which is **Hausa**, spoken by some twenty million people as a first language. Nawa languages are mostly non-tonal and classless, though many have masculine and feminine genders.

UNRELATED LANGUAGE GROUPS

The **Mande cluster of languages** doesn't belong to either area of wider affinity and, linguistically, it's on a classification level with both of them. The languages in this group are closely related and very old. Geographically, they're quite compact and appear to be centred in the Mali–Guinea border region – which, historically, was the heartland of the old Mande/Manding/Mali empire. From the linguistic point of view, the "nuclear Mande" family includes **Bamana, Malinke** (Mandinka), **Susu** and **Dyula**. This group is also known as "Mande-Tan" (after their word for "ten"). The languages of "Peripheral Mande" (or "Mande-Fu"), which deviate much more from the heartland languages, and from each other, include languages of Guinea, Sierra Leone and Liberia, such as **Mende**, **Dan-Gio** and **Vai**. Tones are important in this southern section, less so in the more mainstream Mande languages.

The **Songhai** of the middle Niger River are another old imperial people, with a language quite distinct from any other in Africa.

WEST AFRICAN LANGUAGES AND PEOPLES

The following loose classification is a broad and selective breakdown of West Africa's larger people and language groups into separate ethno-linguistic identities. Although listed together by languages, not all the names here are distinct languages. These lists are intended only to provide anchorages for the different names you'll encounter. Additional names are closely related dialects. Names in brackets are alternatives.

Southern Area of Wider Affinity – "Niger–Congo" Languages

WEST-ATLANTIC LANGUAGES

Fula (Fulani, Peul, Fulbe), Tukulor,	Sherbro, Bulom	Pepel, Manjak
Bororo	Kissi	Gola
Wolof	Limba	Baga
Temne	Jola (Diola), Fogny, Banjal	Tenda, Basari
Serer	Balante	Bijago (Bidyago)

VOLTAIC LANGUAGES

MORE/MOLE	*GRUSI*	*LOBI*
Mossi	Gourounsi, Kassena, Sissala	Loron
Dagomba	Dagara (Dagarti)	Nabe
Mamprusi	Lilse, Fulse (Kurumba)	Gan
Wala	Frafra	Koulango
	Builsa	
SENUFO	Wagala	*HABE*
Senoufo, Djimini, Karaboro		Bobo, Bwaba, Kos, Siby
Minianka	*TEM*	Dogon
	Kabré (Kabyé) Logba, Tamberma,	
GURMA	Lamba	*BARGU*
Gourmantché	Tem (Kotokoli, Cotocoli)	Somba (Betammaribe)
Bassari, Tchamba		Bargu (Bariba)
Moba		Yowa

KWA LANGUAGES

KRU	*EDO*	*YORUBA*	*IDOMA*
Bete	Edo	Yoruba, Oyo	Idoma
Dida	Bini	Egba	Igala
Grebo	Isoko, Urhobo (Sobo)	Ijebu	Egede
Krahn	Kukuruku	Ekiti	Iyala
Bakwe		Ife	
Bassa	*NUPE*	Bunu	*IGBO*
	Nupe	Itsekiri	Igbo (Ibo), Onitsha
	Igbira	Ana	
	Gwari, Koro		

TWI LANGUAGES

Akan	Ewe	Lagoon
Twi (Asante)	Fon, Adja, Xwala, Xuéda, Maxi	Abé
Baulé	Ewe, Ang-lo	Ajukru
Fante	Ga-Adangme	Abidji
Agni	Mina, Popo	Alladian
Abron	Gun, Tofinu	Assini, Nzima
Akwapim		Ebrie
Guang	**Central Togo**	
	Akposso	

IJO LANGUAGES

Ijo (Ijaw)	Brass	Kalabari

EASTERN NIGRITIC LANGUAGES
ADAMAWA

Fali	Mbum	Namshi	Longuda	Vere
Massa	Mundang	Chamba	Mumuye	Yungur

BANTOID LANGUAGES

Ibibio, Efik, Anang	Birom	Jerawa
Mada	Ekoi, Oban	Anyang
Katab	Orri, Ukelle	Basa-Kaduna
Boki	Korup	Yergum
Kamberi	Dukakari	Jukun

MACRO-BANTU

Tiv	Jarawa	Mambila

- -

North-Western Bantu	Batanga	Moun (Bamoum, Bamum)
Ewondo (Yaoundé)	Bakweri, Bimbia	Fia (Bafia)
Bulu, Fang, Eton		Nso (Bansaw)
Gbaya	*Cameroon Hlighlands Bantu*	Li (Bali)Ba-Fut
Sango-Ngbandi	*("Semi-Bantu")'*	Tikar
Bakundu	Ba-Miléké, -Djou, -Fang,	Widekum
Duala (Douala)	-Foussam, -Mendjou, -Ngangté	Fungom
Bassa, Bakoko	Ba-	Ndop

Northern Area of Wider Affinity – "Afro–Asiatic" Languages

ARABIC
HASSANIYA

Berabish	Kunta (Kounta)	Tajakant, Arosien	Zenaga, Chorfa, Tichit
Imragen	Regeibat, Rehian	Trarza	Choa (Shoa)

CHADIC LANGUAGES

Hausa, Adrawa, Tazarawa	Kapsiki (Margi)	Gude
Angas	Matakam (Mafa)	Gerawa
Bura	Mauri	Guizica, Mofou
Kotoko (Longone)	Wakura	Podoko
Tangale	Toupouri (Tuburi)	Bata
Mandara (Wandala)	Wajawa	Mousgoum (Musgu)

BERBER LANGUAGES	SAHARAN LANGUAGES
Tamashek (Tuareg, Touareg)	Kanouri (Kanuri, Beriberi)

Songhaic Languages

Songhai (Sonray)	Dendi	Djerma (Zerma)

Mande Languages

Nuclear Mande		**Peripheral Mande**	
Malinké (Mandinka,	Kuranko	Mende	Bussa (Busa)
Mandingo)	Diallonke (Yalunka)	Kpelle (Gerse)	Ngere (Guerze)
Bambara (Bamana)	Kasonke	Vai (Gallinas)	Kono
Soninke (Sarakolé)	Konyanke	Dan, Gio, Mano, Guro	Sia
Susu (Sousou)	Bozo	Loma (Toma), Buzi	Loko
Dyula (Dioula)	Kagoro	Samo	Gbande

DIRECTORY

ADDRESSES The postman never comes in West Africa. Mail is sorted into PO Boxes (BP in French, CP in Portuguese) or sometimes into Private Mail Bags (PMB). The lower the number, usually, the older the address – sometimes a useful indication of credentials when making bookings or enquiries. Street addresses are often buildings, or blocks – *Immeuble*, often abbreviated to *Imm.* in French. *Your* address is likely to be much in demand – a stack of small address labels is very useful.

BEGGARS Beggars are part of town life, though not as much as you might realistically expect. Most are visibly destitute and many are blind, or victims of polio or accidents, or lepers or homeless mothers and children. Some have established pitches, others keep on the move. They are harassed by the police and often rounded up. Many people give to the same beggar on a regular basis and, of course, alms-giving is a requirement of Islam supposed to benefit the donor. Keep small change handy all the time – it will hardly dent your expenses.

There's no question of confusing real beggars with the incessant demands – in the more touristy parts of several of the Francophone countries – for "*cadeaux*", usually from children. These you simply have to devise strategies to deal with. Like heat and mosquitoes, they seem to trouble new arrivals most.

CLOTHES Cotton is obviously the best material. Dirty-looking colours are best and clothes should be tough enough to stand repeated hand washing. Mostly you'll want to wear the minimum, but pack at least one warm jacket or sweater. Though

you can buy clothes as you go, they'll rarely be less expensive than at home. Even "junk clothes" – "deadmen's clothes" shipped in bulk from Europe and the US – which you'll find in every town, may be less pricey bought nearer to source. If you fancy kitting yourself up in local style, both cloth and tailoring are inexpensive.

People are generally very clothes-conscious. Ragged clothes and long hair on men don't go down well. Avoid absolutely any military-style, or army surplus, gear. Camouflage prints are out. And, however you dress, pack a set of "smart" clothes for difficult embassies and other important occasions.

Take the lightest, toughest, airiest footwear you can afford. Forget about waterproofs: all that plastic and nylon is too hot. You won't go out in the rain, and if you do, you'll get wet anyway.

ELECTRICITY When there is some, it is usually 220V AC 50Hz. Only top hotels have shaver points or outlets in the rooms.

GIFTS It's very useful to have some tokens to give to people. Postcards of sights from home are appreciated by people who have little or no chance of possessing colour pictures. Pictures of you and your family are of tremendous value, too, while school kids are also delighted with ball-point pens. However, you might consider visiting a school more formally, rather than just handing them out.

IVORY The elephants of West Africa are in such a dire predicament that little international effort is being made to save those isolated pockets still hanging on in remote bush against the poachers. Park boundaries aren't always much safeguard. Ivory is for sale in many West African cities, much of it carved in Hong Kong, and bracelets and bangles are widely touted. Tragically, it seems it's still a viable way to earn a living and will likely remain so as long as ivory itself remains unstigmatized. Although the following estimate of elephant numbers is now ten years old, it's a frightening indication of the situation. Mauritania – 30, Guinea – 50, Senegal – 54, Sierra Leone – 100, Liberia – 100, Mali – 1000, Niger – 400, Benin – 500, Ghana – 600, Nigeria – 1500, Burkina Faso – 1500, Côte d'Ivoire – 1600, Cameroon 17,000.

LAUNDRY Washing is always done by hand, in a stream with flat rocks by preference. You won't find laundromats, but there are plenty of people willing to do the job. Even the smallest hotel can

WHAT TO TAKE: A FEW FINAL SUGGESTIONS

- A **pocket French dictionary** or phrasebook is extremely useful. Try the *Rough Guide to French* (£3/$5).
- **Binoculars** (the small, fold-up ones) are invaluable for game- and bird-watching.
- A multipurpose **penknife** is essential, but avoid ones with blades longer than a palm-width which are sometimes confiscated.
- A **torch**.
- A **padlock** – vital in cheap hotels where doors don't lock properly.
- **Plastic bags** are invaluable – bin liners to keep dust off clothes, small sealable ones to protect cameras and film.
- If driving or hiking in remote areas, take a **compass**.
- **Camping gas stoves** are light and useful even if you're not camping. The cylinders are sold somewhere in every capital city.

- You might want to take your own pair of **flip flops** for hotel bathrooms and generally padding about, but these can be bought cheaply locally.
- A **sheet sleeping bag** (sew up a sheet) is essential for budget travel.
- A **mosquito net** – but don't spend a fortune: they're cheap to buy locally.
- A **sleeping bag** isn't much use since you'll sleep on top of it nine times out of ten anyway. If you do take one, get the best, most compressible bag you can afford – very useful for keeping film cool.
- If you shave, bring **disposable razors** (available only at import supermarkets) or preferably an old fashioned razor blade holder.
- **Tampons** are expensive and only available in big cities. Bring as many as you can be bothered with.

arrange it. If you have any choice, dry your clothes indoors. Avoid spreading them on the ground if you can – they may be infested by the Tumbu fly which lays its eggs on wet clothes. Ironing kills the eggs.

POWER CUTS It's common for electricity supplies to be restricted in West Africa, especially where hydroelectric power stations are responsible for providing power. The Akosombo Dam, in Ghana, for example, supplies power across a wide region but recent years of drought have reduced its generating capacity and power cuts are the order of the day, especially at the end of the dry season which is the very time when air conditioning and cold drinks are most welcome.

STUDENT CARDS If you're 32 or under, do what you can to obtain an International Student Identity Card (ISIC) before you go. Student unions and a number of student-minded travel agents sell them. They're valid from the start of the autumn term until December 31 the following year. They're no guarantee of cheap deals, but are worth waving for many payments (airlines, railways, museum entrance fees) you may make. If you are a student it's useful also to have a rubber-stamped letter substantiating the fact.

TOILET PAPER This is usually provided by the user of the facilities rather than the owner. Never run out – using a jug of water and your hand takes more time to get used to than most people have.

PART TWO

THE

GUIDE

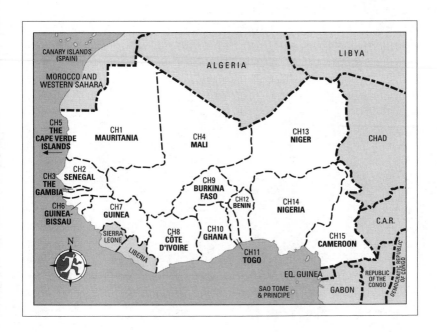

MAURITANIA

MAURITANIA

Scanning a map of West Africa, it's easy to see the vast obscurity of **Mauritania** as nothing but sand. Simple, too, to turn scraps of information on the country into pre-conceptions – of an austere, almost medieval nation, powered by Islam, riven by racial hatred and flayed by drought. These stark images certainly have some foundation in reality, yet Mauritania comes as a revelation to most travellers: pleasantly laid-back, spacious and physically comfortable because of its dry climate, scenically dramatic in several regions and culturally complex, with its rock paintings, thousand-year-old mosques and deep-rooted class structure.

Although the southernmost region of the country – made up of the **Chemama** flood plain along the river and the hilly savannah triangle of **Gorgol-Guidimaka** – extends south to the same latitude as Dakar, this anomalous "green" region covers less than five percent of the territory and is progressively being nibbled away by the advancing desert. Apart from the rocky uplands of the north and centre – the **Adrar**, **Tagant** and **Assaba** massifs – the rest of Mauritania is indeed largely sand, and harsh, challenging territory in which to travel.

People

The country's name comes from its dominant ethnic group, the traditionally nomadic **Moors**, who speak the **Hassaniya** dialect of Arabic. The Moors are broadly divided into "white" **Bidan**, who claim ancestors from north of the Sahara, and "black" **Haratin**, whose physical ancestry lies in Saharan and sub-Saharan Africa and who were subjugated and "Arabized" by the Bidan. Traditionally, the Haratin were vassals to the noble classes, but some Haratin elevated themselves into an independent caste which owed no tribute. The formal abolition of slavery in 1980 decreed that all "ex-slaves" (usually called Abid) were henceforth to be known as "Haratin" – a source of offence to "real Haratin" and of confusion to outsiders.

This characterization oversimplifies the make-up of a very diverse and multifaceted population. **Social status** in Mauritania is considerably more than a question of skin colour. The white Moor community is divided broadly into Hassanes (noble families), Zouaya (or Tolba, the pious maraboutic caste) and Zenaga vassals (herders and culti-vators). Status among black Moor families tends to be determined by their length of association and degree of intermarriage with white Moors. Within Hassaniya-speaking

---

FACTS AND FIGURES

The **République Islamique de Mauritanie** (often shortened to R.I.M.) covers over a million square kilometres, more than four times the size of Britain and nearly as big as California and Texas combined. The **population** of around 2.4 million gives it the lowest density in the world, but the eastern third of Mauritania is designated as *zone vide* (empty quarter) and there's heavy migration to the towns, to the south, and abroad. Mauritania's **foreign debt** is currently some £1.5 billion ($2.5 billion) – more than four times the value of its annual earnings from the export of goods and services but a relatively minor figure in global terms. The **government** is led by President Maawiya Ould Taya and his Parti Républicain Démocratique et Social (PRDS), last elected in 1997 and controlling 71 of the 79 seats in the National Assembly.

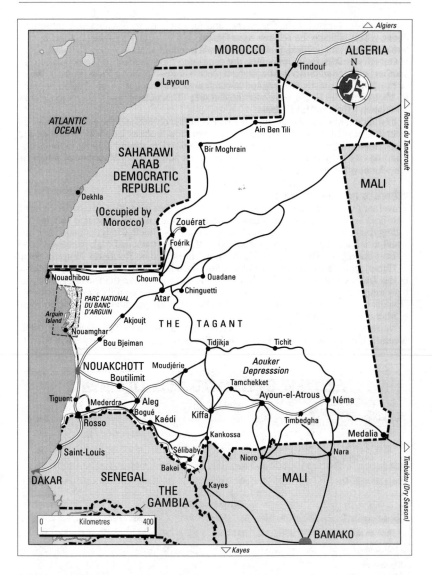

Moorish society, intermarriage has blurred racial distinctions and skin colour is ignored in many social contexts anyway.

You can get an initial fix on the social complexities of Moorish society from the **position of women**, which is less rigidly defined than in most Arabic-speaking countries. Women may travel alone, drink tea with men, take an active part in male-dominated conversations and breast-feed their children in public; they rarely cover their faces, though they always cover their hair. The Berber and African heritage is apparent in these free-doms, which indicate the relative superficiality of the country's Arabic culture. In matters economic and political, however, women's freedom to act is widely curtailed.

Outside the Moorish community, the remaining forty percent of the population are southerners – *Soudaniens* in Mauritanian phraseology – speaking **Fula** (Pulaar), **Wolof** or **Soninke** and mostly farming and herding near the Senegalese and Malian borders. In Mauritania, the Fula-speakers of the Tukulor (Toucouleur) and Fula ethnic groups are known jointly as **Hal-Pulaar**.

In addition, Mauritania had, until the racial conflict of 1989 and the early 1990s, a considerable population of African **immigrant workers**, from as far afield as Guinea and Niger, many of them working in the iron-mining districts around Zouérat in the north. The majority of them fled the country, along with some 70,000 Mauritanian southerners who now live as refugees in Senegal.

Where to go – and climate

Travel targets in Mauritania are easily pinpointed. Two roads cut across the country. The first leads to the central **Adrar region**, where a rugged landscape softened by rolling dunes shelters some ancient towns and oases – Oujeft, Chinguetti and Ouadane – and a rich archeological past, embodied in the stone tools and rock paintings found all over the region. The other road is the desperate-sounding **Route de l'Espoir** (Road of Hope), which runs out towards other **old cities** in Mauritania's inventory: Tidjikja, in the **Tagant region**, and Tichit and Oualata, further east on the fringe of the country's empty quarter. Dotted with ragged, newer, settlements on its way, the Route de l'Espoir is tarred its full eleven hundred kilometres, and provides an alternative route to Mali if you're driving from Senegal.

Nouakchott, the capital, is a nearly inevitable but unremarkable transit point, while **Nouadhibou**, the second largest town, is finding new significance as the point of entry to

AVERAGE TEMPERATURES AND RAINFALL

NOUAKCHOTT

Temperatures °C	Jan	Feb	Mar	Apr	May	June	July	Aug	Sept	Oct	Nov	Dec
Min (night)	14	15	17	18	21	23	23	24	24	22	18	13
Max (day)	29	31	32	32	34	33	32	32	34	33	32	28
Rainfall mm	0	3	0	0	0	3	13	104	23	10	3	0
Days with rainfall	0	1	0	0	0	1	1	3	3	1	1	0

NOUADHIBOU

Temperatures °C	Jan	Feb	Mar	Apr	May	June	July	Aug	Sept	Oct	Nov	Dec
Min (night)	12	13	14	14	15	16	18	20	20	19	16	14
Max (day)	26	28	27	27	28	30	27	30	33	30	28	25
Rainfall mm	0	0	0	0	0	0	0	0	8	12	3	10

ATAR

Temperatures °C	Jan	Feb	Mar	Apr	May	June	July	Aug	Sept	Oct	Nov	Dec
Min (night)	12	13	17	19	22	27	25	26	26	23	17	13
Max (day)	31	33	34	39	40	42	43	42	42	38	33	29
Rainfall mm	3	0	0	0	0	3	8	30	28	3	3	0

West Africa for overland vehicles since the closure of the Algerian trans-Sahara routes. Flights between Nouadhibou and the **Canary Islands** are not excessively expensive, while the rail line linking Nouadhibou with central Mauritania makes for an unusual trip. Nouakchott and Nouadhibou, incidentally, both have **beaches** that seem to go on forever.

Wherever you go in Mauritania, you'll find a release from the freneticism of lands further south, and **travel conditions** generally more peaceful than elsewhere in West Africa. The worthwhile goals make travelling around attractive, and the desert journeys are a fair substitute for actually crossing the Sahara. Alcohol is effectively banned, though one or two hotels serve drinks. Throughout the country, other travellers are fairly rare.

When to visit is conditioned more by burning temperatures than disruptive rainfall. The coast is cooled by sea breezes, but you'd probably want to avoid the interior between April and October – see the climate table for Atar, and remember these daytime figures are averages: the thermometer often pips 50°C in the shade. The **southwest** gets oppressive humidity and occasional cloudbursts between July and October. At this time of year dirt roads can be cut – especially near the Senegal River – and transport off the paved highway can be very difficult. Nouadhibou and the **north** get an occasional shower during the European winter, and very occasionally a summer torrent if the clouds drift far enough north. Otherwise rain is a very scarce commodity.

Arrivals

The land route from Morocco, which for many years was closed because of the war in Western Sahara, has recently reopened and is now the only viable way of entering West Africa overland from North Africa.

■ Flights from Africa

Flights between Nouakchott and **Banjul** are run by Air Mauritanie (MR) weekly. **Dakar** is linked daily via Air Senegal (DS), MR and Air Afrique (RK). RK also fly once a week from **Niamey, Abidjan, Ouagadougou** and **Bamako**.

Air Algérie (AH) flies each week from Algiers via **Casablanca** to Nouakchott and back. Also weekly from Casablanca is a flight on Royal Air Maroc (AT), and another via Nouadhibou on MR.

■ Overland

You'll generally find Mauritanian **border officials** straight dealing, if occasionally pedantic, but not often ostentatiously corrupt. There's a gauntlet of police and customs checks along the Rosso–Nouakchott highway who expect "*cadeaux*", while across the rest of the country, *postes de contrôle* will thoroughly check foreign drivers' paperwork.

From Morocco

Since late 1992, the Moroccan authorities have been allowing convoys of overland vehicles to continue south of Dakhla to the Mauritanian border (see "Red Tape" opposite for details). At least twice a week (currently Tues and Fri) a convoy of anything up to sixty vehicles makes the trip south along the **Atlantic route** with a soldier to escort them. Mauritania's official line on this is that the area immediately north of their frontier is too dangerous for travel because of unexploded land mines. They therefore allow entry to anyone arriving from Morocco, rather than sending them back across the "minefield"; by the same token, travel in the other direction, north into Morocco, is illegal, though it can (just) be done.

The southbound route itself is straightforward – you'll even see confident-looking distance signs for "Dakar". There's a regular overlander truck's camping spot 28km north of Dakhla, but most private vehicles will pull up in *Camping Moussaffir,* 500m before the first checkpoint to the north of town – far and away the best place to try for a lift.

In **Dakhla** itself, *Hôtel Doubs,* on the left as you arrive, has put its prices up since becoming guidebook favourite; try newly-established hotels on either side.

From Dakhla, the first ninety percent of the 450-kilometre road south to **Nouadhibou** is in reasonable condition, much of it hard-surfaced. At the Moroccan frontier itself, you enter the "minefield" with some bad sand – though there are plenty of people to push – and rough bitumen. After exit formalities there's more or less a day's travel to negotiate just 35km of sandy *piste,* dotted with Mauritanian border posts and various sand traps; the last of these is cleared a few kilometres north of Nouadhibou.

From Mali

From Mali, routes into Mauritania are only from **the south**: there are no official border crossings on Mauritania's long eastern frontier. The principal crossing is Bamako–Nioro–Ayoun, with a less-used route running Bamako–Nara–Néma (or Timbedgha). Few travellers use these, and you'll find little preparedness for nationals of countries other than Mali and Mauritania. You should therefore hasten to a police *commissariat* at Néma, Timbedgha or Ayoun and make sure you get the stamp you need. The Tuareg conflict (see p.310) has affected the southeast of Mauritania to some degree and there have been clashes and raids. Keep your ears open and don't proceed without being sure the route is safe. The lack of banks in eastern Mauritania makes it hard to operate the closed economy, so you will have to change money unofficially one way or another (see "Money and Costs", opposite) – carry undeclared cash French francs.

From Senegal

The main crossing point **from Senegal** is Rosso, near the mouth of the Senegal river. The car ferry makes the five-minute crossing throughout the day, except between noon and 3pm, when the crew take a lunch break – as does the small currency exchange booth on the Mauritanian side. If

---

The details in these practical information pages are essentially for use on the ground in West Africa and in Mauritania itself: for full practical coverage on preparing for a trip, getting here from outside the region, paperwork, health, information sources and more, see Basics pp.3–83.

you're on foot, you can take a *pirogue* at any time of the day. Other possible border crossings from Senegal are covered in that chapter.

Red Tape

Visas to enter Mauritania are required by most nationalities except West Africans, French and Italians – and even Italians will be required to obtain a visa before being allowed to drive south from Morocco. In countries without Mauritanian representation (such as the UK), it is generally possible to obtain your visa at the French Consulate – almost always easier than applying for one after you've left your own country.

To obtain a visa outside your country of residence, you'll probably have to provide a letter of introduction from your local embassy and an international air ticket before one will be issued. Some Mauritanian embassies will direct you to get a visa from the "country of embarkation" (in other words the one you'll be leaving immediately before entering Mauritania); if this happens to be Morocco, getting a visa will be expensive and can be difficult (see below).

Visa prices and durations vary considerably from embassy to embassy and even from one applicant to the next, but they are generally valid from the date of issue for a limited period only. Ask the price, get a receipt, and check what you've paid against the fiscal stamps stuck into your passport. In several embassies, a little discussion about Mauritania's historic sites can break the ice.

For **onward travel** from Mauritania, the **French embassy** in Nouakchott issues visas painlessly – but not cheaply – on behalf of a number of other Francophone countries, and there's also a Senegal embassy. If you're heading straight for Mali from Mauritania, there's a new **Malian Embassy** in Nouakchott. Without a visa, it's probably worth trying the border anyway – which is unsophisticated – with the intention of sorting things out when you get to Bamako.

Mauritanian officials can be quite keen on health certificates and may ask you to show your **yellow fever certificate** at checkpoints or borders.

■ Mauritanian paperwork in Morocco

If you're planning to travel south along the Atlantic coast of Morocco and enter Mauritania at Nouadhibou, you're best advised to obtain your visa *before* arriving in Morocco. In **Rabat**, Mauritanian visas are only issued to travellers who can show a return flight ticket, which can be an expensive charade.

First you have to buy an air ticket, checking carefully how much the cancellation fee will be. It should be about £50/$80 per person but is often twenty percent of the ticket price: £80/$120. Travel agents that "participate" change frequently, and you will have to tramp the streets until you find one that will help. Ticket in hand, take your passport, two photos and your visa fee, before noon, to the Mauritanian embassy (☎07/65.66.80), which is off Avenue Kennedy on Ave General Abdenbi Britel. A helpful official will ask whether you are travelling by land or air; on no account say land, or your visa will be refused. All being well, you can take your ticket back to the agent, pay the cancellation fee, and pick up your passport again in the afternoon. The visa may say "Valid for Air Travel Only" but this doesn't matter.

Tread carefully: policy on issuing visas varies, and you might instead be directed to their embassy in **Algiers**, which is scarcely feasible at present. A letter of recommendation from your embassy in Rabat (Australians should get these from the Canadian embassy) can help applications.

You also need to **check in** at the Moroccan police, customs and army posts in Dakhla before travelling south by convoy to the Mauritanian border. Allow plenty of time the day before the convoy leaves to complete these formalities.

Money and Costs

Mauritania's currency is the Ouguiya (or Uguiya) Mauritanien (UM, Oug, Ug), divided into 5 khoums (which you never see). It gradually lost value against the CFA franc, on which it was originally based (1 khoum to 1 franc CFA), but with the 1994 devaluation of the CFA it's now virtually back to the old parity again: UM300 = £1; UM180 = $1. Although the economy is closed, prohibiting the export and import of Ouguiya, there's only a limited black market, more useful for convenience than profit. Notes come in denominations of UM100, UM200 and UM1000, with coins of UM1, UM5, UM10 and UM20.

At the airports and main land entry points you'll be given a **currency declaration form** to complete, which usually has to be handed in on departure. At minor borders you may not be given one, and it's best to straighten your affairs at the first large town rather than risk a potential problem on departure. These forms are rarely examined, but in anycase, as long as you can provide several official exchange receipts it is not usual to have your remaining money counted and tallied. It does happen though and fines can be substantial.

Notionally, there is also a UM4000 **minimum daily expenditure** requirement: a sign at the airport bank in Nouakchott stipulates that any shortfall in expenditure may be forfeited on departure. This seems to be hardly ever enforced.

Outside of Nouakchott, **banks** are few and very far between. Nouadhibou, Rosso, Bogué, Kaédi, Kiffa, Ayoun el Atrous and Néma all have banks that might – or might not – be open. The biggest network, with six branches, is the Banque Internationale pour la Mauritanie (BIMA), the Mauritanian division of the West African BIAO. Banks are free to set their own exchange rates, so it's worth shopping around: BIMA tends to give the best. **Bureaux de change** and even black market street traders can also give official receipts for changed money, and although the rate is much the same (generally a bit lower for bureaux de change), they are far quicker.

American Express representation is relatively recent (see "Listings" on p.116 & p.137). **Credit cards** are accepted by a few airlines and hotels in the capital, but will be written out in US$ and calculated at unfavourable rates. Credit card cash advances can be arranged through certain travel agencies.

Note that the **CFA franc** is no longer a convertible currency and is not accepted by banks or hotels, though you may still be able to change CFA unofficially.

■ Costs

Daily living costs are somewhat higher than in Senegal or Mali. With distances long, travel can be costly, but as more travellers start to come through on their way overland from Morocco, cheap **hotels** are starting to appear. If you're prepared to accept lavish local hospitality with its concomitant obligations, you'll find costs plummet, though a Western "*cadeau*" is likely to be appreciated in return. For more on accommodation, see p.48.

There's no avoiding high **transport costs**, though these may fluctuate with the cycle of date

harvests and pastoral migration (prices generally escalate if you travel *away* from the attraction). You can quite easily spend £20/$32 on a day's travel. As a broad guide, expect to pay around UM300 per 100km on tarred roads and up to two to three times as much on dirt roads and desert *pistes*. Prices are fixed on what could be considered "scheduled runs", and you won't be overcharged; baggage, as usual, is another matter. If you want to get to out-of-the-way sites and towns, transport costs can quickly become exorbitant. The cheapest option is to wait for a vehicle that's going anyway.

Start **drinking** in Mauritania and kiss your travel budget goodbye; small cans of beer, when they're available, cost at least UM600.

Health

The most critical feature of travel in Mauritania from a health aspect, however, is the size of the country and the isolation of most towns and villages. You'll often be very far off the beaten track, and here, more than anywhere else in West Africa, you should have repatriation insurance in case of accident or sudden illness.

Beware of **dangerous vehicles** being used for relatively rough desert and mountain passages. In the north and east, spare parts for vehicles are very hard to obtain and the scarcity of vehicles keeps many in use long after their safe life.

Treat **water** with suspicion – reserves are usually low, and domestic animals depend on them too. It's good practice to carry a five-litre container and refill it at every opportunity.

Fresh camel or goat's **milk** (*zrig*) is often offered to guests and it's probably best to limit your consumption: although tuberculosis is a very minor risk (even in the case of fresh Zebu cow's milk), brucellosis and hepatitis A can be contracted from infected milk. Your hosts' health is probably the best criterion for deciding.

The **malaria** risk is generally thought to be slight, except along the Senegal river, where it's as high as anywhere in West Africa. Roughly north of a line from Nouakchott to Tidjikja it's not reckoned to occur at all, but there are still plenty of mosquitoes about and it would be stupid to break your course of anti-malarial pills for just a short stay in the country.

Hospitals and treatment facilities outside Nouakchott are strapped. The north, apart from

Atar and Nouadhibou, has almost no public health provision, and although some of the southern towns have regional hospitals/health centres, these should be seen as a last resort.

Pharmacies, however, are a major growth industry in Nouakchott and in the interior. These days they're often well stocked with a range of items, including medicines that most European doctors would hesitate to prescribe. Sanitary towels and disposable nappies are on sale in Nouakchott and upcountry.

Maps and Information

The IGN 1:2,500,000 (1993) map of Mauritania is too small a scale to be useful for serious exploration, and not really much better than the Michelin 953. However, the IGN 1:1,000,000 topographical surveys published in the 1960s are still available from their French headquarters (107 rue La-Boétie, Paris; ☎01.43.98.85.00) and might be obtained, or ordered, through one of the map suppliers listed in Basics on p.39.

There are no Mauritanian tourist offices, but the Direction du Tourisme (BP 246 Nouakchott; ☎253337) at the Ministry of Commerce, Small Industries and Tourism offers a "guide touristique" with perfunctory paragraphs in English. There's also a *Mauritanie* guide in the full-colour *Aujourd'hui* series from Editions Jeune Afrique – more mouthwatering than practical.

Getting Around

Most transport in Mauritania is by 4WD, though *taxis brousse* operate on the few main highways. Otherwise, air travel is not prohibitively expensive. The railway system – a single line for the iron ore train in the far north – is more of an adventure than an ordinary form of transport, but still a useful link between Nouadhibou and the rest of the country.

■ Road transport

The main **public transport** – between Rosso and Nouakchott, along the Route de l'Espoir to Néma, and north to Atar – is **Peugeot 504**, carrying nine passengers (six to Rosso). Be prepared for long, dust-blown journeys, frequent breakdowns, lack of water, and no toilet stops. Riding in the back of

trucks, along these same routes, is slower and less comfortable, but a good deal cheaper. Fares are normally paid in advance, so if there's a breakdown you have to stick with the vehicle until it's fixed or the driver buys a place for you in another.

Between Nouakchott and Nouadhibou, trucks and Land Rovers run along the shore to Nouamghar, then turn inland to follow the railway line for the last 100km.

South of the paved Route de l'Espoir, in the far south, a conventional *taxi brousse* network operates on most roads for most of the year. The vehicles are generally *404 bâchés*, but Peugeot 504 drivers work on some routes, especially between Rosso and Kaédi. The recent tarred road from Aleg to Bogué is transforming that part of the river's flood plain.

Road journeys **off the main routes** are arduous, with soft sand the recurring problem. Conditions are detailed in the main guide section. If you're driving yourself, you should treat Mauritania north of the Route de l'Espoir exactly as you would a trans-Saharan *piste*. In many respects, because of the scarcity of other travellers, the routes are tougher and more dangerous. The *piste* between the Tagant plateau and the Adrar (connecting Tidjikja with Atar), and the myriad tracks along the coast, are notorious. If you've no room to carry local people to guide you (never a problem to find), don't set off on little-trodden trails into the desert. The Mauritanians are not used to tourists' follies and nobody may think to prevent you from going – or search for you if you don't arrive.

Car rental, available only in Nouakchott, is as expensive as you'd expect. Since there's pressure to take a driver at little extra cost, it's often indistinguishable from a personalized "safari" arrangement. Keep your fuel tanks and spare jerry cans full. Off the main routes, **fuel**,

---

PUBLIC TRANSPORT ROUTES

Nouakchott–Rosso: frequent, 3–5hr

Nouakchott–Atar: up to 12 daily, 6–12hr

Atar–Choum: 3–6 daily, 4–5hr

Atar–Chinguetti (4WD and trucks only): 3–6 weekly, 4–7hr

Nouakchott–Kaédi: several daily, 7–8hr

Nouakchott–Ayoun el Atrous: 1 or more daily, 16–20hr

Nouakchott–Nouadhibou (4WD and trucks only): 2–6 weekly, 30–50hr

when available, is around European prices, at about UM100 per litre (UM400 per US gallon) or more.

■ Rail and air

Alternatives to road travel are worth using if the opportunity arises. If your point of arrival in Mauritania is Nouadhibou, the **train** from there to Zouérat is a good way into the country, and you can hop off in Choum, only 100km short of the Adrar plateau and a further day's travel down to Nouakchott. You can take vehicles on this train at reasonable rates (details on p.136), but be prepared to lose days in transit.

Air travel makes sense if time is short (the longest flight is under 2hr), and fares are surprisingly reasonable. Air Mauritanie's current domestic schedule, using the same two Fokker F-28 jets that are used on its international services, includes either one or two round-trip flights every day between Nouakchott (NKC) to Nouadhibou (NDB), plus:

Mon: NKC–**Atar**–NDB–**Atar**–NKC
      NKC–**Kiffa**–NKC
Tues: NKC–**Tidjikja**–NKC
      NKC–NDB–**Zouérat**–NDB–NKC
Wed: NKC–**Sélibaby**–NKC
      NKC–**Néma**–NKC
Thurs: NKC–**Atar**–**Zouérat**–**Atar**–NKC
Sat: NKC–NDB–**Atar**–NKC
      NKC–**Ayoun el Atrous**–NKC
Sun: NKC–**Sélibaby**–NKC

Examples of **fares** from Nouakchott are: Atar UM8500, Ayoun el Atrous UM11,000, Kiffa

UM8500, Néma UM12,950, Nouadhibou UM10,800, Sélibaby UM8600, Tidjikja UM8500, Zouérat UM11,700.

Accommodation

Mauritania's higher-class hotels generally resemble Moroccan or Middle Eastern establishments, while cheaper lodgings offer shared rooms, generally designed for three people. The minimum price you can expect to pay for a room is about UM1500, but less if you opt for a mattress only and sleep on the roof. Nouakchott has about a dozen hotels, and there's a handful in Nouadhibou, but most other large towns have just two or three, if that.

Travellers tend to rely on the **hospitality** of Mauritanians or expatriate residents. Moorish hospitality is legendary and you'll be well looked after by taxi drivers and other casual acquaintances across the country. Money will rarely be accepted as a gift, so you may want to carry cigarettes and lighters, pens and watches, tea and instant coffee.

Several Catholic **missions** have, in the past, been exceptionally helpful to travellers, and one or two are still generous, but many are pulling out of the country. The American **Peace Corps** may also put you up. Several of their *Maisons de Passage* are open to outsiders, at slightly higher prices than to volunteers (but still extremely cheap), on the understanding that they aren't hotels and volunteers always have preference.

ACCOMMODATION PRICE CODES

Accommodation prices in this chapter are coded according to the following scales – the same scales in terms of their pound/dollar equivalents as are used throughout the book. Prices refer to the rate you can expect to pay for a room with two beds. Single rooms, or single occupancy, will normally cost at least two-thirds of the twin-occupancy rate. For further details see Basics, p.48.

① **Under UM1000 (under £5/$8).** Likely to be a couple of mattresses in, or near, the open air.
② **UM1000–2000 (£5–10/$8–16).** Rudimentary lodging, perhaps with some rooms self-contained (S/C: private shower, or bath, and toilet).
③ **UM2000–4000 (£10–20/$16–32).** Basic lodging, usually offering S/C rooms, maybe some with AC (air conditioning); breakfast included.
④ **UM4000–6000 (£20–30/$32–48).** Mod-est, but adequate hotel with S/C, AC rooms, breakfast included.

⑤ **UM6000–8000 (£30–40/$48–64).** Tourist or business-class establishment.
⑥ **UM8000–10,000 (£40–50/$64–80).** Up-market, with close to international standards and facilities.
⑦ **Over UM10,000 (over £50/$80).** Luxury, cosmopolitan establishment.

Camping out, as long as you have access to water, is always a fine option; a tent can be useful to keep off the desert wind.

Eating and Drinking

Mauritania doesn't come up with much food that's memorable, but food is much more widely available than a few years ago. A number of small supermarkets are well stocked with a range of consumables and household commodities, even in regional centres in the interior – although the choice there is much more limited. There's no need to worry about stocking up with food supplies before a trip to Mauritania, but within the country, you'd certainly want to take in some provisions for longer trips off the beaten track.

Restaurants don't exist much outside Nouakchott and Nouadhibou, though there are chop-house eateries in most towns, sometimes run by immigrants from other parts of West Africa.

Bread (French style) is usually in good supply. Main meals are invariably **rice-** or **couscous**-based. Towns with flourishing gardens often have potatoes, carrots and onions. **Mutton, camel meat** and **chicken** are standard fare, as too is **fish**, usually dried and recooked. Lebanese-style grilled *chawarma* (pressed mutton slices) is quite common. More expensive eating houses tend towards Moroccan *couscous* dishes and *tajine* stews. If you eat with Mauritanians, **milk** (fresh, known as *zrig* – often diluted and sweetened – or curdled) often figures prominently.

As for fruit, **dates** are cheapest after the August and September harvest; Middle Eastern imports are generally better quality, and more expensive. Other fruit is limited to what comes over the border from Senegal or Mali (seasonal shipments of mangoes and more frequent truckloads of oranges) and what's grown in the far south of Mauritania itself – the whole range of tropical fruit from bananas to papaya and sugar cane. Nouakchott now has many fruit stalls with a good selection of local and European fruit, though you'll pay around UM250/kg for the former and perhaps UM600/kg for the latter.

Vegetarian travellers in Mauritania have quite a hard time of it – quantities of **eggs** are served to non-flesh-eaters in homes and restaurants.

Drinking is a serious business – not alcohol, which has ceased to be sold in public places out-

Mauritania's IDD code is ☎222.

side the major cities, but **tea**. Moors take their green tea often and seriously. Even more than in Mali or Niger, a few small glasses of scalding, bitter-sweet yellow froth are part of the daily round. There's invariably a shortage of glasses: throw yours back to the tea-maker as soon as you've drained it. Despite the insistence of the tourist literature, it's only rarely taken with mint. Travelling by taxi, the driver will usually foot the small tea bill for his passengers at rest-stops.

Communications – Post, Phones, Language & Media

The main PTTs are in Nouakchott and Nouadhibou (Nouakchott's PTT is open every day), and there's not much of a telecommunications service outside these towns – Zouérat, Atar and Kaédi are passable exceptions. Poste restante is reliable but slow.

Phoning or faxing abroad is reasonably efficient, and there is now IDD to the whole world. But communication is expensive even by Francophone standards, and you'll have to bargain with the plethora of public telephone and fax shops that have sprung up over the last two years. Britain and the USA may be difficult to contact for long periods from inside Mauritania but there is no trouble getting through to Mauritania from abroad. Rates are roughly UM300/minute to Francophone West Africa and the USA and UM600/minute to Europe.

■ Languages

Mauritania's most widespread language is Hassaniya Arabic, and although many people speak French, it is less popular – and slightly less widely acceptable – than formerly. Other languages are mostly concentrated in the non-Moorish regions of the far south and include Fula or Fulfulde, Wolof and the old Mande tongue known as Soninke or Sarakole. Few people speak English.

■ The media

Less than a decade ago, the *Bulletin of the Chamber of Commerce* was listed as one of the

HASSANIYA – SOME BASICS

Hassaniya, the language of the Hassanes and the sole language of the Moors, is a strongly Berberized form of Arabic. In 1991 it become, controversially, the official language of the country, usurping less divisive French for many purposes.

Moorish Mauritanians have an elaborate greeting ritual which they go through with resignation or enthusiasm depending on their mood. Farewells, on the other hand, are brief and free of sentiment.

GREETINGS

Lyak la bas – Hope you have no bad.
La bas – I have no bad, usually followed by numerous *lyak*s, eg *Lyak mo a vin* – Hope you have no sickness. If you want to end the *lyak* sequence try:
Mar Abah – So be it.
Mah Salaam – Goodbye.
Sh'halak is an informal "How are you?" that doesn't lead to anything much.

Il hum did illai – Praise be to God. (Stick it on the end of sentences – something like *Insh Allah* when talking about the future. *Il hum did illai* rolls off the tongue. You'll hear it a lot if you listen out.)
Salaam Alaikum – Peace be with you.
Alaikum Salaam – And also with you.
Sho'kran – Thank you (hardly used).
A phrase for "Please" is never used.

OTHER PHRASES

Where is?	*Mynayn?*	I am English	*Ana min Ingletra*
What time is it?	*Waqt shin hoo?*	Hotel	*Vondeg*
That's OK/enough	*Kavi*	Do you have?	*An dak?*
(if someone's serving		Is there?	*Halig?*
you something for example)		Water	*Ilma*
In the name of God	*Bismalai*	Food	*Lukil*
(said before eating or		White person	*Nasrani*
starting something)		Good	*Zaiyn*
Yes	*Ahey*	Very good	*Hutt zaiyn*
No	*Abdei*	Not good	*Mal zaiyn*
No, by God!	*Walahi!* or *Man Allah!*	How much is?	*Kem?*
Come here	*Wahai*	A little less? (to knock down the price)	*Ingus shwei?*
Tomorrow	*Subh*		
Yesterday	*Yemes*	A little (or slowly)	*Shwei shwei*
Today	*Ilyom*	I am full	*Ana stuk fai*
I am going to Nouakchott	*Ana nymshee shawr Nouakchott*	I am tired (male)	*Ana v'tran*
		I am tired (female)	*Ana v'trana*
		Take it easy	*Beshar*

If you're very displeased with something or someone, try *Gassa Ramarak* ("May God shorten your life"); use carefully, it's used a lot with disobedient kids.
Ski (with a short "i") is an expression of satisfaction, usually followed by a hand slap.

NUMBERS

1	*Wahid*	5	*Hamsa*	9	*Tesa'a*		
2	*Athlath*	6	*Setta*	10	*Ashara*		
3	*Ethnayn*	7	*Seb'a*				
4	*Arba'a*	8	*Thimayna*				

four main national periodicals and *Chaab*, the only daily paper, was eight pages of dull African and world news and rambling articles about Mauritanian development. Since free elections in 1992 the press has been liberalized and there are now a good dozen **daily papers**. Most still tend to serve up the same bland mix of news and articles about drought and the doings of the elite, but

A MAURITANIAN GLOSSARY

Aftout Seasonal water course or flood zone
Aklé Zone of jumbled, live dunes
Barkane Moving, crescent-shaped dune with characteristic "crest"
Barrad Teapot
Boubou Loose cotton shirt or cloak
Chemama Flood plain of the Senegal River
Dahr/dhar Fault line (cliffs or escarpment)
Darrah Boubou (see above)
Erg District of shifting ("live") sand dunes
Girba Goatskin waterbag
Guelb Isolated mountain or peak
Guetna Date harvest
Hal-Pulaar Fula-speaking people, including Fula and Tukulor

Houli Man's headscarf, turban
Kas Drinking glass
Kedia Long tableland, mesa
L'msal Prayer ground
Mehlafa Women's long upper wrap/headscarf
Nsara Nazarene/Christian: white person (pl. *Nsarani*)
Reg Flat gravel, windblown sand plain
Rifi Hot wind from the north
Sebkha Dry, salt plain
Sirwal Loose, cotton pantaloons
Tabel Tea tray
Tell Hill covering the ruins of a former settlement
Tishtar Dried meat, usually gazelle
Zrig Sweet, diluted milk

one or two are startlingly anti-establishment. Titles change with bewildering frequency and most are in Arabic.

You'll find French newspapers and magazines around Nouakchott and Nouadhibou, but only secondhand copies of English-language ones. The *Monotel* hotel in Nouakchott may carry them.

The state-run Radio Mauritanie and TV Mauritanie network broadcasts in French and Hassaniya with some programmes in Fula, Wolof and Sarakole/Soninke. **Television** has exploded in recent years, and even the current-starved *bidonvilles* around Nouakchott have battery-driven sets. The news and "cultural" programmes you'd expect are interrupted by the occasional French soccer match. Most hotels, even downmarket ones, have a satellite dish, though blurred Canal France International – hour-long interviews with the French prime minister and puerile game shows – isn't likely to occupy you for long.

Arts and Culture

Independent artistic expression is rather rare in Mauritania, in part a reflection of the Nomadic culture, where crafts were generally the preserve of specific castes. Poetry was the only widespread artistic activity, and even then rarely written down.

Cinema has a beacon in the shape of exiled director **Med Hondo**. His 1969 film *Soleil Ô* was a bleak and somewhat plodding mix of *cinema verité* and weird set pieces, dealing with African immigrants in France; more recently, with Burkinabe

backing, he made the impressive historical epic *Sarraounia*, about a queen who resisted both the colonialists and the Muslims.

Theatre is non-existent, as is any accessible **literature** (certainly none in English translation). There's a little more hope for **musical culture**, though at present it's not a lively scene. At best, it combines soulful, Arab singing with complicated picking and rapid clapping that makes the Berber antecedents of flamenco music clear. One of the best-known groups is headed by **Dimi Mint Abba** and **Khalifa Ould Eide** – they've made several foreign tours – but you'd have to be unusually lucky to catch a show in Mauritania itself. **Malouma** is another famous woman singer – she supported Ahmed Ould Daddah in his failed presidential bid in 1992.

Directory

AIRPORT DEPARTURE TAX None.
CRAFTS AND MARKETS Mauritania is famous for stylishly refined carpets, woven in Nouakchott. Sadly these are impractical purchases for most travellers, as are the brass-fitted, dark stained wooden chests and camel saddles. But there's quite a desirable selection of jewellery in silver (cheap) and amber (not so), tobacco pipes and pouches, sandals and printed cotton cloth (good value). In the Adrar and Tagant, children and market sellers hawk neolithic stone arrow heads and tools. You can turn up medieval glass trading beads as well, though these are becoming internationally sought after and increasingly rare. Be

prepared to find bargaining hard work: jocularity doesn't always hit the right mark.

HOLIDAYS Apart from those decreed by the Islamic lunar calendar, which are followed everywhere, Mauritania's public holidays are: January 1, February 26 (National Reunification day), May 1 (Labour day), May 25 (African Liberation day), July 10 (Army day), November 28 (National day) and December 12 (anniversary of the 1984 coup). December 25 is an office holiday, but you'll find most commercial doors open. Don't forget the week starts on Sunday, with Friday and Saturday the weekend.

NAMES You'll quickly notice almost all Moors retain traditional names. *Ould* and *Mint* mean "son of" and "daughter of" in Hassaniya: hence Mokhtar Ould Daddah, Dimi Mint Abba.

OPENING HOURS The office day is usually 7.30/8am–1.30/2pm. Banks are open for changing money Sunday to Thursday only until 12.30pm. Other businesses close at 2.30pm. Shops close for a long break at lunchtime and open again in the late afternoon, until about 7.30pm.

PHOTOGRAPHY There is no photography permit. People tend to be suspicious of cameras and prefer not to have their pictures taken, but the reaction is not normally heavy. Be especially careful in Nouakchott, check before snapping and avoid all broad, street scenes – there's often an upset. Film in Nouakchott is expensive and unreliably stored.

POLICE AND TROUBLE Mauritania is report-to-the-police territory. Large towns have control posts on the entrance roads where your particulars will be recorded. Smaller places don't, and it's up to you to find the man on duty and proffer your *pièce*. If you fail to do so, you could have an uncomfortable dressing down when they apprehend you. If you're driving, you may have your vehicle very thoroughly searched; searches are otherwise rare. If you're travelling in the far south, bear in mind that nobody seems to have told the posts on the Senegal River road that the troubles between Mauritania and Senegal are over – getting past these posts can still be trying and time-consuming. Alcohol is theoretically illegal, except in controlled upmarket bars and hotels. Drugs aren't much of an issue, though some expensive grass finds its way in from Mali.

SEXUAL ATTITUDES In the Moorish community, there is more openness than you might at first expect. Younger women are rapidly shaking off old values, if not always traditional costume.

Urban men, too, are beginning to accept a realignment of sexual attitudes. Affairs, "love-marriages" and divorces are increasingly common in Nouakchott, and the bride price (paid to the woman or her family) is less often stipulated. Clitoridectomy is still practised, though more in the far south. Male travellers aren't very likely to be hustled by prostitutes.

WILDLIFE AND NATIONAL PARKS Mauritania's wildlife has been depleted by hunting and the spread of the desert. Formerly, the south had a good cross-section of West African savannah animals, including elephants, giraffes, cheetahs, leopards, lions, and several species of antelope. The giraffes, cheetahs and lions have gone, but there are still a few leopards and there are said to be small numbers of elephants (small in stature too), hiding out in the hilly bush country between Kaédi and Ayoun el Atrous.

The uninhabited eastern desert is one of the last refuges of the endangered addax antelope, an extraordinary survivor – which, with careful husbandry, could become a source of domestic protein in an otherwise empty environment. Other species include mouflon (wild sheep) in the Adrar, and gazelles and oryx antelope scattered through the north; the occasional family of ostriches in the southeast; and very rare monk seals at Nouadhibou. You'll see plenty of camels, but these, like all of Africa's dromedaries, are domesticated.

For naturalists, the country's biggest potential attraction is the migratory birdlife of the isolated sandbanks and seashore in the country's only national park – the Parc National du Banc d'Arguin (see p.137), south of Nouadhibou. The park is administered from Nouadhibou where there's a permit-issuing office for the suitably equipped.

WOMEN TRAVELLERS Women travellers can expect a combination of chivalry and pestering, though not too much of the latter. Covering your hair is an effective way of cooling ardour: Moorish women never let their scarves slip. Fatness in women is considered desirable by older men, though younger men insist it's no longer important to them. Sex is openly discussed among women; if you find yourself among French-speaking Moorish women, or you speak a little Hassaniya yourself, the conversation can take remarkable turns.

It's natural that you'll spend a fair amount of time, like everyone else in Mauritania, lying on mattresses on the ground. Useful to know, then, that lying either on your back or your stomach is considered highly suggestive: Moor women, you'll notice, invariably lie on their sides, supporting their head with a hand. There's reportedly a high incidence of arthritis of the elbow.

A Brief History of Mauritania

Contemporary Mauritania doesn't coincide with the ancient "Mauretania Tingitana", a region confined to present-day Morocco and Western Algeria, and annexed to the Roman Empire by Claudius in 42 AD. The events and processes that led to the creation of the République Islamique de Mauritanie are taken up below in the fifteenth century with the arrival of the first mercantile Europeans. Accounts of some of the little-known early history of the region are scattered throughout this chapter.

■ European contact

Direct contact with Europeans began in 1445, when **Portuguese traders** set up a small *factoria* – a trading base – at the raised, southern tip of Arguin Island.

At about the same time, the **Hassane Arabs** from upper Egypt were moving into the northern parts of the territory, subjugating the largely Berber-speaking population, spreading the use of the Hassaniya language, and creating the cultural complex that became **Moorish society**.

Early Portuguese efforts to conduct a trade in slaves and gold were not hugely successful. Instead, acacia tree gum used in the manufacture of food and drugs (called "gum arabic" because it was originally exported to Europe by Red Sea Arabs) soon became the main item of commerce, most of it coming from the southwest region, near the mouth of the Senegal River.

When Portuguese commercial influence waned in the seventeenth century, the **gum trade** fuelled intense rivalry between French, Dutch and English trading houses. The Dutch pulled out in 1727, but Anglo-French competition (and war) continued until 1857, when the British withdrew from the region in exchange for the French ceding them Albreda Island in the Gambia River. Even alone, the **French** had forcibly to impress their control over the gum trade on the Moors in order to hold a profit.

Throughout the seventeenth and eighteenth centuries, the French had also been more successful than the Portuguese in whipping up the slave trade. From their main base at **St-Louis** at the mouth of the Senegal River, they sent foreign goods upriver, ensuring a supply of slaves from the feuding and rigidly class-stratified societies of the interior. Mauritania's involvement in this trade was heavy, and the class structure of the southern agricultural districts was set in aspic by the culling of non-Arabic-speaking peoples, who were sold down the river by their captors in exchange for firearms, cloth and sugar.

But the slave trade didn't account for the slow **decline in trans-Saharan commerce**. This came about through the increasing imposition of Arab (later Arab-Berber) rule throughout the territory during the seventeenth century. By 1800, most of today's Mauritania was divided into competing **"Emirates"** – Trarza, Brakna, Adrar and Tagant – highly organized internally, but with little in the way of constructive foreign relations, and inimical to commercial links between their domains. The French at St-Louis were thus able to take advantage of the divisions, and actively promoted **civil war** in order to divert ordinary trade, as well as the slave victims of battle, in their direction.

French expansion up the Senegal River (the fort at Bakel in Senegal was built in 1818) and gathering French interest in Morocco and Algeria led, towards the end of the nineteenth century, to the strategic penetration of the Mauritanian interior, with "protection" and "pacification" sounded as the keynotes to local people. The **assassination of Xavier Coppolani**, a French commander and Arabist, at Tidjikja in 1905, ended a period of relatively peaceful expansion and brought down a five-year reign of terror in the territory. The Adrar was occupied in 1908, the Hodh (in the southeast) in 1911. The next year, France reached an agreement with Spain over respective spheres of influence in the western Saharan region, and in 1920 **la Mauritanie** became a colony of French West Africa. "Police actions" against nomadic guerilla resistance continued throughout the north up until 1933, when complete "pacification" was finally achieved.

■ The path to independence

Mauritania was used by the French as a **buffer zone** protecting their more valuable assets in Senegal and Soudan (Mali), and as a place of internal exile for political agitators from their other colonies. Since the end of commercial slavery in 1820, only gum arabic and potential mineral wealth had provided any economic justification for occupying the territory. The French invested almost nothing in Mauritania's future, administering it as a part of Senegal and counting on nomadic conservatism to look after the population in traditional ways.

As late as 1946 there was still no political party in Mauritania. In that year, administrative apathy seems to have allowed **Horma Ould Babana**, a socialist, to become the first Mauritanian deputy to the National Assembly in Paris. In the view of the French administration, he was a dangerous radical whose presence on the National Assembly was intolerable.

Blatant interference in the 1951 National Assembly elections duly secured support for the pro-French nomadic chiefs from the 26 percent of the population who were registered to vote (one polling station controller declared "if a dog had come before me with a voter's card I'd have made him vote"). **Sidi el Mokhtar**, a member of the Gaullist Rassemblement du Peuple Français, and a puppet candidate of the white Moors, was duly appointed deputy.

In the Territorial Assembly elections of 1952, the Mauritanian representatives were still not seeking independence from France. Indeed Mauritania, still party-less, had no effective branch of the Rassemblement Démocratique Africaine – the affiliation of French West African parties led by Houphouët-Boigny of Côte d'Ivoire which was in the forefront of nationalist demands.

Although the 1956 National Assembly elections were free of administrative interference, and many French territories elected nationalist deputies, Mauritania again elected Sidi el Mokhtar, who stood with Gaullist support but then transferred his allegiance to the Mouvement Républicaine Populaire, a French Christian Democrat party.

In the same year, significantly, **Morocco** achieved independence. King Hassan V's ruling group was opposed in Morocco principally by Istiqlal, a party of conservative expansionists who wanted to see the reconstruction of a "greater Morocco" that included much of Mauritania. The king outflanked Istiqlal by taking up the expansionist cause himself. The claims naturally had repercussions in Mauritania, where an extreme, Moorish, irredentist movement took shape, fighting to hive off part, if not all, of Mauritania to Morocco which it believed was the true homeland of all Moors.

In the 1957 Territorial Assembly elections (the first with universal suffrage), the unaffiliated Union Progressiste Mauritanienne, Mauritania's first indigenous political party, won 33 out of 34 seats. **Mokhtar Ould Daddah**, a young, white Moor lawyer with considerable French support (he was de Gaulle's son-in-law), was elected vice-president of Mauritania's first governing council (the French governor was president). Ould Daddah, too, was territorially ambitious, calling on the people of the **Spanish Sahara** to unite with his own in a "great economic and spiritual Mauritania".

On November 28, 1958, Mauritania became an autonomous republic within the French community and the **République Islamique de Mauritanie** (the R.I.M.) was proclaimed. A national election held in 1959 gave Ould Daddah the post of prime minister, after his party (the Parti du Regroupement Mauritanien) won every seat in the new National Assembly, and on November 28, 1960, Mauritania became an independent nation state, with Ould Daddah as president. Its entry into the United Nations, however, was vetoed by the Soviet Union, because Morocco (which at the time had a pro-Communist foreign policy) still claimed Mauritania as its own.

■ Ould Daddah's presidency

With the founding of the new capital of Nouakchott, the development of the Fdérik iron ore mines and the completion of the railway to Nouadhibou in 1963, Mauritania's economic future looked fairly bright. But at the same time Ould Daddah set about eliminating **political opponents**. In December 1961, the four main political parties became one, the Parti du Peuple Mauritanien (**PPM**). Within three years, the de facto one-party state had been enshrined in law.

In the south and among the **black, non-Arabic-speaking population**, expectations raised by independence from France gave way to resentment and indignation. In 1966, Arabic was made the compulsory teaching medium in schools. Ensuing **riots in Nouakchott** were summarily suppressed and laws swiftly enacted to ban all discussion of racial conflict. The country had come close to civil war, but Arabization continued, with a 1968 law putting **Hassaniya** on a co-footing with French as dual official languages.

The government was intent on integrating the trade union movement into the PPM, a move which angered **teachers** and **miners** particularly, and led to strikes and demonstrations in 1968, 1969 and 1971. For two months in 1971 there was a complete shut-down of iron ore production. The force of government repression, and the determination of the ruling party to silence the opposition led to the creation of clandestine political movements and a simmering groundswell of anti-government feeling. Through much of this first decade of independence, however, foreign affairs issues served to dampen the opposition.

Through the 1960s, support from the **other Arab states** for Morocco's claim over Mauritania had resulted in very few of them recognizing the R.I.M. Ould Daddah's hope that the country would be seen as a bridge between Africa and the Arab world failed to materialize as his dependency on French military and economic support increased. Thus, with the isolation of Mauritania from the Arab world, the southerners' deepest fears had been partly abated during the first decade of independence.

But in 1969 came **Morocco's formal recognition of Mauritania**. Increasing Islamic radicalization, a slackening of ties with France coupled with growing Algerian support, and a clear state socialist programme were the natural consequences. The huge MIFERMA (Mines de Fer de Mauritanie) iron ore complex at Fdérik/Zouérat was nationalized and the country withdrew from the CFA franc zone to bring in its own currency, supported by the Arab banks, the Ouguiya. There was wide backing for these moves in the Arabic-speaking community and, by 1975, broad government confidence. Although the **drought** of the early 1970s had left the country reeling, the worst affected people were the Arabic-speaking nomads of the north and centre. Now, with trade unions and students in Nouakchott appeased, the problem of the disenfranchised southerners, who had found some voice through these groups, was less urgent.

Spain's decision to withdraw its garrisons from the Western Sahara plunged Mauritania into a **war with the Polisario** (Popular Front for the Liberation of Sagia el Hamra and Rio de Oro; see box p.104–105). The war, over the small and economically worthless piece of territory ceded to Mauritania by Spain, proved the downfall of Ould Daddah. Even with a massive increase in military spending, accompanied by a tenfold expansion of the army, popular support for the war was so low in Mauritania that it was clearly unwinnable.

■ The Lieutenant-Colonels

On the night of July 9, 1978, a quiet and bloodless **coup** ousted Mokhtar Ould Daddah. The coup's leaders dissolved the PPM party and announced the formation of a **Comité Militaire de Redressement National (CMRN)** – "to save the country from ruin and dismemberment" – under the chairmanship of Chief of Staff Lt-Col **Moustapha Ould Salek**.

Ould Salek tried to bring Polisario and Morocco together for a negotiated settlement, but the terms suited neither party. When Polisario's kidnapping of a Mauritanian prefect pushed Mauritania into a **peace treaty** with Polisario in August 1979, Morocco immediately moved into the territory vacated by Mauritanian troops. Morocco and Mauritania have had an uneasy relationship ever since as a consequence. Meanwhile, at home, Ould Salek was confronted by outbreaks of racial conflict, student agitation, and factional strife in the CMRN – upgraded, desperately, in April 1979, to the Military Committee for National Salvation (CMSN). Ould Salek resigned and was replaced as president by Lt-Col **Mohammed Louly**, whose prime minister, Lt-Col **Mohamed Khouna Haidalla**, in turn staged another palace coup in January 1980, to take control of government.

Haidalla's five years as head of state saw an overall improvement in foreign relations, but a deterioration in the domestic situation. The continuing war between Polisario and Morocco repeatedly spilled onto Mauritanian soil, hindering *rapprochement* with Morocco and delaying Mauritania's recognition of the state of the Sahrawi Arab Democratic Republic.

Internally, Mauritania's most dramatic event – as far as the rest of the world was concerned – was the formal **abolition of slavery** in 1980. This may have been intended to forestall links between the Dakar-based black opposition and supporters of exiled white Moor groups in Paris, and also to divert attention away from the increasingly blatant racial discrimination against the Soudanien southerners, but the effect of the pronouncement was to focus world attention on a brutal military dictatorship. Mauritania's law did indeed guarantee freedom from chatteldom, but not freedom from hunger, dispossession or political repression.

For a short time in 1980–81, President Haidalla experimented with **political relaxation**. He formed a civilian government led by prime minister

WESTERN SAHARA AND THE POLISARIO WAR

The colony of Spanish Sahara was acquired by Spain in a succession of Franco-Spanish conventions between 1886 and 1912. The motivation for coveting this 266,000-square-kilometre wedge of gravel plains and low hills (about the size of Britain) sprang from a desire to join in the "scramble for Africa", a sense of wounded imperialist pride at the loss of the South American colonies, and the proximity of the Spanish Canary Islands.

Villa Cisneros (Dakhla) and La Guera were the only Spanish bases until 1934, when the first foothold was established in the interior. **Smara**, an abandoned Arab town, was reoccupied, at France's behest, to help control nomadic anti-colonial resistance still swirling around the region at the time.

Africa Occidental Española had no apparent economic potential and **General Franco** didn't waste money on it. By 1952 there were only 216 civilian employees, 24 telephones and 366 schoolchildren in the entire territory. Until Franco's death, the **Provincia de Sahara** (as it became) with its capital El Ayoun (built in 1940), was ruled as a military colony where, as in Spain, independent political expression was ruthlessly crushed.

In 1966, the UN insisted on the right to self-determination for the colony. But a survey of Spanish Sahara's **phosphate reserves** in the early 1960s had indicated vast deposits of up to ten billion tonnes, and Spain was soon digging in.

Although there had been armed resistance to Spanish occupation in the late 1950s in the wake of Morocco's independence, urban **anti-colonial demonstrations** began only in June 1970, when troops fired on marchers in El Ayoun and hundreds more were arrested – and subsequently disappeared.

THE POLISARIO

The **Polisario Front** was born in Zouérat in Mauritania, on May 10, 1973, spurred into existence not just by Spain's continued occupation, but also by the threats posed by competing claims from Mauritania and Morocco. For two years Polisario acted as self-sufficient guerillas, with no outside support, but then in May 1975 thousands of Polisario supporters emerged in the Sahara to meet the UN mission of inquiry.

Meanwhile, as the world witnessed the break-up of Portugal's African empire in 1974, Spain was planning a process of decolonization and independence to thwart Polisario's growing influence, with blueprints for limited self-rule, a referendum, and a state-sponsored Sahrawi National Unity Party of Sahrawi moderates. But King Hassan put pressure on Spain to reconsider, came to an agreement with Mauritania over partitioning the territory, and then managed to persuade the International Court of Justice to consider some rather arcane questions of nine-teenth-century Saharan history. This last plea was turned down and the ICJ upheld the right to self-determination. Within three weeks, 350,000 Moroccans were marching, Korans in hand, into the Western Sahara, to claim their country's historical right to the territory.

After Franco's death, Spain agreed to **pull out of Western Sahara**, leaving the territory to Morocco, Mauritania and the Spanish-installed **Djemaa** council – a body of conservative, urban Sahrawis through whom they had ruled. Although the UN continued to uphold the resolutions on Western Sahara, a UN visit in early 1976 decided that the scale of upheaval was so great that there was no way the Sahrawis could be properly consulted. The guerrilla war now began in earnest, and more than half the population fled the country – old people, women and children to Algerian refugee camps around Tindouf, and men to join Polisario. The **Sahrawi Arab Democratic Republic** (SADR) was proclaimed – in exile in Tindouf – on February 27, 1976.

MAURITANIA AT WAR

Mauritania was never an enthusiastic ruler of the desert plain it called **Tiris el Gharbia**, nor was it prepared for a long and costly war. From the beginning Polisario concentrated on knocking Mauritania out of the picture, thus breaking the Morocco-Mauritania alliance. Mauritania's army was never sufficient to look after the new terri-tory, let alone defend the bulk of the country from highly motivated Polisario incursions. There were repeated, humiliating losses: the iron ore railway was under constant threat; foreigners working at the mines were kidnapped; and twice, in June 1976 and July 1977, Polisario mounted daring **raids on the outskirts of Nouakchott** itself, and shelled the presidential palace. In 1978 a desperate President Ould Daddah agreed to the stationing of 9000 **Moroccan troops** in the Saharan territory, and they were soon routinely skirmishing with Polisario in Mauritanian terrain. France too was heavily involved in defending Mauritania, President Giscard d'Estaing sending Jaguar bombers to blitz Polisario encampments and a steady stream of personnel to shore up Mauritania's flagging army. Mauritania was crippled by debt, doubt and drought, and its war was an undignified fiasco. For President Ould Daddah, the situation had become untenable, and he was relieved of his post in July 1978. The **new regime** sued for peace with Polisario the following year.

STALEMATE

The war between Morocco and Polisario has now lasted more than 25 years. Arms-dealing nations (including France, Britain and the USA) continue to supply Morocco, while maintaining token support for the UN resolutions on the Sahrawis' rights to self-determination. Despite this military support, Morocco has been increasingly stretched and, since the early 1980s, has pulled back its front line to **Dakhla** and the **northwest area** of Western Sahara (the so-called "useful triangle" containing the phosphate fields), while building immensely long, defensive, earthworks that now enclose almost ninety percent of the territory. Polisario chips away, but a **stalemate** has now dragged on since 1986.

Meanwhile, the **Tindouf refugee zone** has grown into a state-in-exile, a stable and, at first, relatively prosperous mini-republic which, though heavily dependent on international donations, managed to build a reputation for its agricultural efforts and welfare services.

After the resumption of diplomatic relations between **Algeria and Morocco** in 1988, King Hassan is no longer calling the Polisario "Algerian puppet terrorists" and there still seems a possibility of a **referendum** on the question of independence for the people of the territory (including the 200,000 refugees living in the four Tindouf camps). But the UN-monitored process of identifying who is eligible to vote has been lengthy and inconclusive. Moreover, Morocco has "West Banked" the sectors of the Western Sahara it holds, pumping resources – and 150,000 **Moroccan settlers** – into the region, in order to try to outwit a democratic solution for the indigenous people. Meanwhile, the three hundred **UN peacekeepers** in the MINURSO force (deployed at a cost of £50 million/$80 million per year) have noted dozens of ceasefire violations by Morocco and just a handful by the Sahrawis.

Not only are the Sahrawis very low in UN priorities, but King Hassan's stance on Western Sahara has widespread support in Morocco itself. The UN security council is loathe to do anything to upset the stability of the kingdom, fearing the potential for Algeria-style civil war between the state and the fundamentalist supporters of an Islamic greater Morocco. In response to the lack of progress, the Sahrawis have repeatedly threatened a resumption of full-scale hostilities, as much to draw the world's attention as to achieve any tangible advantage on the ground. They argue that there is a real possibility that without war, their plight might slip into obscurity as the second generation of camp-dwellers grows up and the Moroccan settlers become increasingly established. There have already been several high-level defections from the SADR government-in-waiting to the Moroccan side.

In 1995, the referendum was again delayed, partly as a result of the chaotic conditions in Western Sahara following serious floods. Finally, in 1997, Morocco was forced by a combination of US and UN pressure to accept **face-to-face meetings** with Polisario, brokered by UN Secretary General Kofi Annan and his personal envoy, the former US Secretary of State James Baker. As a result, an agreement was signed at the end of 1997 laying out the rules for registration to vote in the referendum, rescheduled for December 1998. The process soon broke down, however, as thousands made fraudulent claims of indigenous Sahrawi status, coached by Moroccan local government officials, and encouraged by the Moroccan Interior Minister, Driss Basri. The Polisario estimate of 75,000 eligible voters was less than half Morocco's suggested figure.

As the December 1998 date came and went, Polisario were still hoping to force a referendum. By mid-1999, the 120,000 long-suffering inhabitants of the Tindouf camps were still suffering terrible conditions, and King Hassan was looking forward to a day when the UN troops might wearily depart – a *fait accompli* for his colonial policy.

Ahmed Ould Bneijara, and drew up a draft constitution recommending a democratic multiparty
system. But rumours of a **Libyan-backed plot**
(part of the ripple of Libyan-inspired insecurity
that passed through West Africa at that time),
and then a genuine **coup attempt** by the **Parti
Islamique** of former government ministers operating from Morocco, shook the democracy idea
apart. Having executed the coup leaders, the
CMSN appointed a new prime minister, Lt-Col
Maawiya Sid'Ahmed Ould Taya, and remilita-
rized the government.

Despite this clampdown, another **military
coup** was foiled in February 1982, involving Ould
Salek and the just-deposed Ould Bneijara. In a
surprise display of clemency, the instigators were
given ten-year jail sentences.

Through the early 1980s, Mauritania's
prospects failed to improve. Severe drought in
1983 brought tens of thousands of famine-struck
nomads virtually to the door of the Presidential
Palace in Nouakchott; opposition groups continued to fight a war of words in France, Morocco
and Senegal; and Haidalla's recognition of the
Sahrawi Arab Democratic Republic early in 1984
brought further insecurity to the country as
Morocco seemed more than ever determined to
oppose any referendum in the Western Sahara –
increasing the tension between Morocco and
Mauritania. In August, Morocco entered a bizarre
pact of union with Libya, unsettling the
Mauritanians. The prime minister, Ould Taya, who
was already concerned about government corruption and inaction, deposed President Haidalla on
December 12, 1984, in yet another gentlemanly
palace coup.

■ Ould Taya: progress and reaction

President Ould Taya wasted no time. With
World Bank and IMF support he adopted a programme of economic recovery with heavy emphasis on fishing and agriculture. Targets were set,
and reached, and creditors were evidently
impressed by Ould Taya's abandonment of some of
the capital-intensive industrial schemes set up by
Haidalla to the detriment of basic infrastucture and
rural development. Iron ore is still a major source of
foreign exchange (reserves have been variously
estimated at between 500 and 2000 million
tonnes, which at the present rate of extraction
would last up to 200 years), but in the late 1980s
fish came to be seen as a more flexible resource,
and was briefly the country's biggest earner.

But the government's agenda was being set by
political concerns, rather than economic ones. In
1986, a tract in French entitled *Manifesto of the
Oppressed Black Mauritanian: From Civil War to
National Liberation Struggle, 1966–86* made the
rounds among students and staff at the National
Language Institute. It was the work of the Dakar-
based **African Liberation Forces of
Mauritania** (FLAM). Twenty prominent southerners were arrested and jailed on charges of
"undermining national unity". Widespread rioting
and destruction subsequently took place in
Nouakchott and Nouadhibou, and thirteen of
those involved were also jailed, in March 1987.
Strict **Islamic law** was subsequently introduced.

In October 1987, 51 Fula-speaking Tukulor officers were arrested on charges of insurrection.
According to the Interior Minister, "this plot was
more than an attempt to overthrow the government, it was a crime against the whole nation".
Three officers were executed (the first death sentences imposed by Ould Taya's regime) and 41
more were given long prison terms. This blow
against the southerners was followed by a **purge
of Tukulor army officers**, with over five hundred
dismissals. Tension continued through 1988, with
racial killings in Nouakchott. In connection, FLAM
pointed out that the "sensitization programme"
being carried out by the government in the
Senegal River flood plain region wasn't
appeasing local people, who bitterly resented the
new influx of Moorish and Arab land-buyers and
the pressures on them to make way for alien
development projects.

Towards the end of 1988, a number of southerners serving terms for political crimes, including
the author of the "Black Manifesto", died in
Oualata prison, an allegation denied by the government, who sent the Mauritanian League of
Human Rights to investigate. The league found
several Oualata inmates were, indeed, still alive.

■ The 1990 race riots

Events finally boiled over in April 1989, triggered by a minor incident on an island in the
Senegal River, near Bakel, in which Mauritanian
cows were supposed to have plundered
Senegalese vegetable gardens – the sort of dispute that would normally be settled by compensation. During an argument, Mauritanian border
guards opened fire on Senegalese onlookers,
killing two people. Thirteen Senegalese were
then captured and taken to Sélibaby in

Mauritania, where they were effectively kept hostage, which led to attacks on Mauritanian shops in Bakel on the Senegalese side.

Within days, violence had spread to other Senegalese towns, resulting in the deaths of dozens of Mauritanians, while thousands more were driven out as their shops and homes were ransacked. In Dakar, the entire Mauritanian community sheltered in the Grande Mosquée and the Mauritanian embassy. In Mauritania there were even more savage attacks on Senegalese and other black Africans as security forces and lynch mobs of Haratins hunted for southerners. Both governments were quick to condemn killings by the other side, but neither took decisive action to control the violence.

A massive dual **evacuation by air**, with international assistance, began, as it emerged that up to two hundred Senegalese had died in Nouakchott. In Senegal, the army remained on the streets of Dakar and President Ould Taya was accused of declaring war on Senegal and of supplying arms to the Casamance rebels in southern Senegal.

As the exodus from Mauritania went on (in the event, there was only a limited flight of Mauritanians from Senegal), it became clear that among those leaving Mauritania was a large proportion of indigenous southern Mauritanians – whom the regime now routinely refers to as "Senegalese" but who are largely **Hal-Pulaar** (Fula-speakers) – many of whom were being forcibly expelled. The government was taking the opportunity to banish up to twenty thousand potential opponents, to reduce the impact of the returning Moors and to lessen the numbers of non-Moorish Mauritanians, who had been claiming for several years that they were in the majority. The climax of this period came in November 1990, when the government announced there had been a coup attempt, fostered by Senegal. Over three hundred southerners were picked up by the authorities, and never seen again. Most southerners remaining in any positions of responsibility in the civil service were sacked over the next few months.

The 1990–91 **Gulf War** drew the world's attention away from the horrors of Mauritania's human rights record. But Mauritania's military rulers had long been allies of Iraq (Iraqi military advisors are believed to have helped organize the pogroms against Fula villages in the south), and the government stood behind Saddam Hussein throughout the conflict. This alliance put severe strains on Mauritania's relations with Morocco and, of more immediate economic consequence, France. Thus Ould Taya's pragmatic move to adopt a democratic constitution, when faced with the possibility of complete isolation, was hardly questioned: every other Francophone state in West Africa was undergoing the same process.

■ The multiparty era

Southerner political groups (and Muslim fundamentalists) boycotted the **referendum** on a multiparty constitution, arguing they hadn't been consulted in drawing up the document which in practice banned political parties based on religion. But, despite only a twenty percent turnout, the "yes" vote was carried into practice, and Mauritania became a multiparty state on July 20, 1991, with a president as head of state and a prime minister running the country's affairs for him.

In 1992, the country's first "free" **presidential election** since 1960 was marred by fraud. The post of president was won by the uninspiring former military leader, Ould Taya, despite the best efforts of his main rival, Ahmed Ould Daddah (half-brother of the country's first president, Mokhtar Ould Daddah) to have the results annulled by the supreme court. The general elections, later in the year, were boycotted by the opposition parties, and there was widespread vote-rigging, including the effective ruse of leaving candidates' names off electoral lists.

The flavour of the present political configuration is very much business as usual – a civilian incarnation of the military dictatorships of 1978–91. There is a large number of registered political parties, either allied with the ruling Parti Républicain Démocratique et Social (PRDS) or in opposition to it. The two main opposition groupings – the **Union pour la Démocratie et le Progrès** (UDP) led by Hamdi Ould Mouknass and the **Union des Forces Démocratiques** (UFD) led by Ahmed Ould Daddah – have found it hard to form a united front to challenge the PRDS. President Ould Taya's main rival, leader Ahmed Ould Daddah has lost much of his shine since the dawn of the "democratic" era, and while he certainly appears a preferable figure to the international community, and claims to support the wronged masses of the country, especially the southerners, few Mauritanians any longer believe he has any true agenda other than the pursuit of power – like his brother the late dictator – and discontent with his leadership is rife in the party.

On the streets, life is as hard as ever, though punctuated frequently enough by **demonstrations** in the otherwise somnolent city of Nouakchott. In January 1990, the government stage-managed protests against American attacks on Iraq. In June 1991, there were demonstrations by the wives and mothers of men who had "disappeared" after the November 1990 coup attempt. In October 1992, the city was hit by riots over price increases and the falling value of the Ouguiya. Bread price riots in January 1995 led to the arrest of Ould Daddah and Ould Mouknass, accused of organizing unrest.

Meanwhile, Mauritania has mended relations with **Senegal** and **Mali** and the three countries are attempting to co-operate in their border areas to crack down on banditry and smuggling. More than 40,000 Tuareg refugees who fled Mali during the Tuareg rebellion left their refugee camp in Mauritania to return home in 1997. Officially, all 70,000-odd **Mauritanian refugees** in Senegal are also encouraged to return home, though in practice, few have any papers, job or land to return to. In 1993, the Nouakchott government declared an amnesty for perpetrators of the 1989–90 racial violence – hardly an inducement to the victims to return. In January 1996 there were demonstrations in northern Senegal about Nouakchott's repatriation policy which, for southern Mauritanians, does not include any guaranteed return of property or even legal status equal to that of Moors.

As for Mauritania's relations with **the rest of the Arab world**, these have been going through convulsions in recent years. After the isolation it experienced during the Gulf War, especially from Morocco, Mauritania began a process of distancing itself from **Baghdad**. This was completed when the Iraqi ambassador was booted out of the country in October 1995, and a number of high-ranking Mauritanians – including both government and opposition MPs, army officers and a police commissioner – were arrested after rumours of a foiled coup plot, supported by Iraq, started circulating. There were a number of convictions, but the short prison sentences were commuted. Meanwhile, Mauritania's decision to start diplomatic relations with **Israel** led to a breakdown of relations with **Libya**, formerly an important source of economic assistance, but always an uncomfortably overbearing ally for Mauritania.

After legislative **elections in October 1997**, the PRDS has 71 of the 79 seats in the Assembly. There is a handful of independent (non-aligned) legislators but only one opposition member of the Assembly, from Action pour Change (AC) a party formed mainly to lobby for the rights of the Haratin ex-slaves. **Slavery** remains a highly sensitive issue, and excites great international attention. In early 1998, several human rights activists were arrested after their participation in a French TV documentary on the subject, and AC demonstrations to protest their treatment were met with police violence and more detentions.

■ The future

On the surface a certain stability is apparent, but **the future** for Mauritania looks very difficult. Economically, Ould Taya's support for Saddam during the Gulf War lost the country much credibility with foreign lenders and investors, which was further strained during the three-year rift with Senegal. Income from fishing has declined markedly and iron ore output has dropped too as the world market for it shrinks. The bread riots of 1995, although sparked by VAT increases, reflect real concern about the ability of the country to feed itself – there's an annual cereal deficit of around 100,000 tonnes which amounts to nearly a kilo missing from each Mauritanian's weekly food requirements.

One quite likely result of the current reactionary racial policies is civil war, and perhaps attempted secession by the south. Hope over this issue can only lie in the sort of far-reaching government concessions to **southern opposition** demands which at present seem remote and unlikely. Southerner elements of the unofficial opposition face huge difficulties in getting their voices heard: the first ever Soudanien presidential candidate, Kane Amadou Mockhtar, took a tiny share of the votes in the 1997 election. And with the rest of the world focusing on a different aspect of Mauritania's complex racial set-up – the slavery issue affecting Haratin black Moors – the southerners appear sidelined in every respect.

The final and most alarming difficulty facing the country is **Islamic fundamentalism**. Mauritania does not possess a large, marginalized, urban constituency in which support for fundamentalism can breed (like the slum-dwellers of Egypt; the young and poor of Algeria, or the working class of Iran under the Shah), and recent visits by Taliban and Algerian fundamentalist orators were not a success. Despite the country's "Islamic Republic" label, and a legal system strongly influenced by the *sharia* (the body of Muslim doctrines), the government has been distancing itself from fundamentalism; in October 1994, the work of a number of Islamic groups in the country was curtailed and up to sixty Islamic leaders were arrested for belonging to "secret foreign organizations".

However, the mere threat posed by fundamentalist activists, combined with the legal opposition's frustration, power-hunger and disunity, might lead the opposition parties into unholy alliance with the PRDS government against the fundamentalists. In this way the present government's ungodly, undemocratic, corrupt apparatus could trundle on for years. On the other hand, if the fundamentalists prove they do indeed have widespread grassroots support – and present evidence suggests they're only likely to gather more as the years go by – the crisis they are bound to precipitate will make the current status quo seem admirable in comparison. The most promising scenario would be for the PRDS, while condemning fundamentalism, to initiate some dynamic social and economic policies of its own, and thus develop some healthy support. However, on present evidence, again, that seems very unlikely.

NOUAKCHOTT

Whipped by dust storms for nine months of the year, Mauritania's capital, **NOUAK-CHOTT**, seems to be drowning under a sea of sand. This is the biggest city in the Sahara, a modern, sprawling place of almost a million inhabitants – nearly a third of the country's population. Once you're settled in, it's hard to dislike; you can wander around more or less unhassled, and there's a certain ease in the wide, tree-lined streets half-obscured by drifts of sand. However, there's also something soulless about the place, with its brutally severe state buildings and dearth of things to do. For most people, a couple of nights here are enough before moving on.

A short history
The site of the new city of Nouakchott – whose name may mean "Place of Wind" or "Place of Floating Seashells" – was nominated by Bidan elders in 1957, who chose to raise it near a French military post on the **Piste Impériale**, the old imperial road. The buildings were constructed on fixed dunes, in an attempt to give protection from the flooding of the Aftout es-Saheli seasonal watercourse, which nearly surrounds it – the original Ksar ("fortified village") settlement having been seriously damaged by floods in 1950. With funds limited and formal independence pressing, the city was hastily planned and constructed – medina, residential blocks, schools, ministries – for an antic-ipated population of 15,000. It was already 20,000 by 1969, when the first great Sahel drought tipped the country into crisis. By 1980 the immigrant influx had pushed it past 150,000, and since then it has risen to over 900,000.

Arrival, information and orientation

Drivers arriving from the north along the beach *piste* are introduced to Nouakchott by the thatched cottages of *Tergit Camping*, five hundred metres north of the city's Plage de Pecheurs, and separated from the city itself by 4km of waste-scattered dunes. *Taxis brousse* arrive at the **gare routière**, 3km northeast of the centre on rue Ghary, while flights land at the **airport**, on the opposite side of rue Ghary. The airport's new inter-national terminal is a big improvement on the warehouse still used for domestic flights. Officially badged "welcome" personnel will politely guide you through immigration and currency formalities and get you a taxi (on the understanding they can expect a UM500 tip). There's a small bank, and car rental available, but few other facilities. Ordinary **taxis** from the airport charge around UM500–600 to the *centreville*, possibly less if you haggle. There's no airport bus; best is to share a taxi for UM50–150 or find a green and yellow Transports Urbaines minibus (UM20–30).

The *gare routière* and airport are in the old part of town, Le Ksar, a slightly scruffy, industrious area where most of the car dealers and service stations are located. Once in the real city centre, and assuming the dust has settled, impressions do improve: the main road, bd El Nasser, is lined with new travel agencies and bureaux de change, while off the main commercial streets, sandy roads are draped with bougainvillea and twittering with birdsong.

For **tourist information**, make enquiries direct with the Direction Artisanat et Tourisme, near the Présidence.

Orientation
The **layout** of Nouakchott can be confusing at first, and there are no heights from which to get your bearings. **Le Ksar** is on the east side of town, from where the slums spread north along the Atar highway and east along the Route de l'Espoir. From the paved roads, there's no indication of their vast extent.

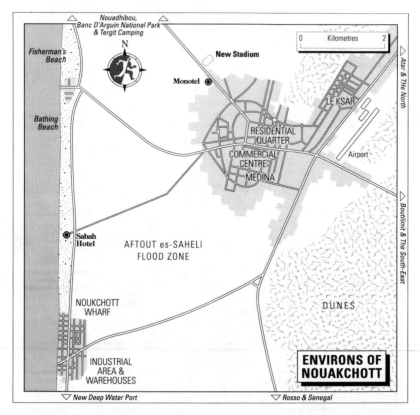

ENVIRONS OF NOUAKCHOTT

The city's main street, **Avenue Abd El Nasser**, runs east–west from just south of Le Ksar, through the new town, **La Capitale**, and out to the beach, 5km away. Cutting across it at right angles is **Avenue Kennedy**, which connects the affluent, ambassadorial and expat quarter of **Tavrak Zeina** on the northern edge of La Capitale to the **Medina** and the extensive commercial districts of the *cinquième arrondissement* in the south (Nouakchott is divided into numbered **arrondissements**, subdivided into alphabetical blocks called **îlots**).

Most hotels, restaurants and shops are within a short walking distance of the Kennedy–Nasser intersection and this district is likely to be the main focus for the time you're in town.

Accommodation

Nouakchott's new prominence on the overland route down through Africa has led to a greater choice of cheap **rooms**. Whatever the price bracket, however, determined haggling can produce discounts, especially for longer stays. All the lodgings listed below are in the Capitale apart from the *Sabah Hôtel*, though there are also a couple of basic places near the *gare routière* in Ksar. **Camping** by the seaside is another possibility.

Auberge de Jeunesse, rue Mamadou Konate, near *Phenicia* restaurant. Dirty but cheap and central. ②.

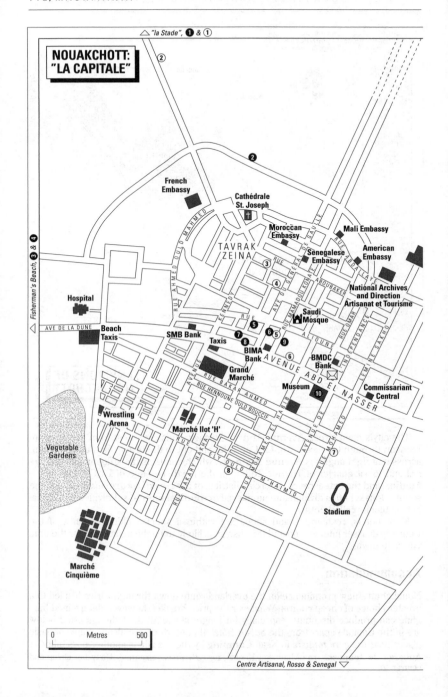

NOUAKCHOTT: "LA CAPITALE"

△ "la Stade", ❶ & ①

French Embassy

Cathédrale St. Joseph

Moroccan Embassy

Mali Embassy

Senegalese Embassy

American Embassy

TAVRAK ZEINA

National Archives and Direction Artisanat et Tourisme

Hospital

Saudi Mosque

AVE DE LA DUNE

Beach Taxis

SMB Bank

Taxis

BIMA Bank

BMDC Bank

Grand Marché

AVENUE ABD EL NASSER

Commissariat Central

Museum

Wrestling Arena

Marché Ilot 'H'

Vegetable Gardens

Stadium

Marché Cinquième

◁ Fisherman's Beach, 3 & 4

RUE AHMED OULD MAHMED

0   Metres   500

Centre Artisanal, Rosso & Senegal ▽

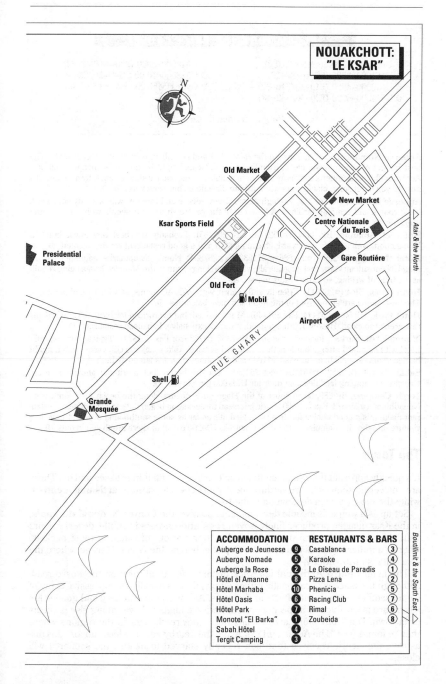

NOUAKCHOTT: "LE KSAR"

N

Old Market

New Market

Ksar Sports Field

Centre Nationale du Tapis

Presidential Palace

Gare Routiére

Old Fort

Mobil

Airport

RUE GHARY

Shell

Grande Mosquée

Atar & the North

Boutilimit & the South East

ACCOMMODATION

Auberge de Jeunesse	⑨
Auberge Nomade	⑤
Auberge la Rose	②
Hôtel el Amanne	⑧
Hôtel Marhaba	⑩
Hôtel Oasis	⑥
Hôtel Park	⑦
Monotel "El Barka"	①
Sabah Hôtel	④
Tergit Camping	③

RESTAURANTS & BARS

Casablanca	③
Karaoke	④
Le Oiseau de Paradis	①
Pizza Lena	②
Phenicia	⑤
Racing Club	⑦
Rimal	⑥
Zoubeida	⑧

ACCOMMODATION PRICE CODES

① Under UM1000 (under £5/$8)
② UM1000–2000 (£5–10/$8–16)
③ UM2000–4000 (£10–20/$16–32)
④ UM4000–6000 (£20–30/$32–48)

⑤ UM6000–8000 (£30–40/$48–64)
⑥ UM8000–10,000 (£40–50/$64–80)
⑦ Over UM10,000 (over £50/$80)

For further details see p.48.

Auberge Nomade, BP 7009, between the *Hôtel Park* and rue Alioune (☎291385; Fax 291386). The best budget choice in town: clean, friendly and well-located right by the city's cheapest eateries. Accommodation is under a canvas awning or in simple rooms, and parking is generally available. It's new so you'll get some blank looks when asking directions, but persevere. ①–②.

Auberge la Rose, No Zra 211, Tavragh Zeina. Quiet, secure and friendly, with a shady courtyard, basic rooms and camping facilities. A little out of the centre so best for people with cars; parking available. ②.

Hôtel el Amanne, BP 1147 (☎252178; Fax 253765). Probably the best downtown hotel in Nouakchott, with a pretty courtyard, charming staff and a good restaurant serving alcohol. ⑤.

Hôtel Marhaba, BP 2391 (☎251686 or 251838; Fax 257854). Nominally upmarket haunt of most visiting UN consultants now that expense allowances no longer run to the *Monotel*. It was being rebuilt at the time of writing, so expect rates to rise. ⑤.

Hôtel Oasis, BP 4 (☎252011). Friendly and central, with S/C, AC rooms, all with TV and hot water. The best rooms are at the front of the hotel and have balconies. ③.

Hôtel Park, BP 50 (☎251444; Fax 251446). Modest-sized, but overpriced for basic S/C, AC rooms that aren't too clean. However, it has a good, if rather expensive, Lebanese restaurant. ④.

Monotel "El Barka", formerly *Novotel*, BP 1366 (☎253526; Fax 251831). Typical purpose-built hotel with standard fittings but less than standard service. Takes major credit cards, which might be necessary: a small beer here is UM1000 and telephone charges famously high. ⑥.

Sabah Hôtel, BP 252 (☎251552; Fax 251564). On the beach, but moribund and uninspiring. Overpriced camping facilities next door for UM1000 per person. ④.

Tergit Camping, BP 689, 500m short of the Plage du Pecheurs along the beach *piste* south from Nouadhibou (☎256673; Fax 251684). Basic but clean three-person beach huts and an adequate restaurant make this a good choice for drivers; indeed, it's as far as some southbound overland travellers venture into the city. Camping is UM1000 (mattress UM200 extra) or there are thatched huts. ③.

The Town

It's quickly apparent that Nouakchott doesn't spill over with things to see and do. There are, however, some very rewarding local **markets** and various **artisanal centres**, while the most obvious destination is the **beach**.

Set up as a women's income development initiative, the **Centre National du Tapis**, in the Ksar quarter, produces finely woven **rugs and carpets** in subtle, desert colours with rigorous geometrical patterns – sadly, they are out of range of most pockets. There's another women's centre in the Capitale, behind the Grand Marché, where the speciality is **embroidery**.

The main **Centre Artisanal** is a walk or taxi ride out of town on the Rosso road. Although the place is occasionally rather empty, there's usually an impressive array of camel saddles, silver-inlaid chests and carpets. Although the jewellery and good-value silverware is worth close inspection, prices here are high, and everything else is cheaper in town. Don't buy stone arrowheads here: they're cheaper in the regions where they're found (see "The Adrar", p.125). Avoid the nearby **zoo**; the less support this disastrous menagerie receives (one lion recently starved to death), the sooner it will close.

The city's **general markets** are worth wandering around, though you'll not find much of note in the purpose-built Grand Marché/Marché Capitale, or in the Marché Ilot "H". Instead take a taxi or bus down to the **Marché Cinquième**, where you can shuffle down sandy lanes between tubs of home-made peanut butter, mirrors framed with drawing pins and fish in transition from fresh to dried, for as long as you can stand the heat. If you really dig through the reams of nylon and piles of plastic sandals you'll find a wealth of good fabrics down here, including exceptionally fine-weave lightweight muslin in attractive prints. A clutch of medicine and *gri-gri* sellers, with their displays of monkeys' and birds' feet and lizards' and turtles' heads, make for macabre browsing.

Across Avenue Kennedy from the Marché Cinquième, you'll find other **commercial districts** – a whole street devoted to dried dates for example. Ironically, they're almost as expensive here as in supermarkets at home, and the presence of imported dates from Saudi Arabia seems perverse, even by the standards of Mauritania's misshapen economy. If you fancy buying some dates anyway, go for the smooth, dry, pale brown quality; these should be hard but chewable, like toffee.

There's a **fish market** over to the west and, near it, the **wrestling arena**, which holds bouts on Saturday afternoons. The city **museum** (Sat–Thurs 8.30am–2.30pm; UM300), in the gaunt Maison du Parti du Peuple, contains ethnographical collections on the lifestyles of the Nomads.

The beach

The **beach** is the main event in Nouakchott. Once you've crossed the wasteland that separates the city from the sea, there's a solid phalanx of dunes, and then an impressively straight sweep of fine sand stretching north and south to the horizons. The **Plage des Pêcheurs** is crowded and atmospheric all the time, mostly with Senegalese fishermen, but the best time to visit is at around 5pm, when the boats come in against the setting sun, and there are cold drink kiosks and stalls selling freshly fried fish with hot sauce.

Five hundred metres south from here the beach is nearly deserted and perfectly clean, though there's no shade – come either early in the morning and have it to yourself, or late afternoon when there's a scattering of other people. Whether because of the strong currents, the occasional swarms of jellyfish or the stomach-sucking coldness of the water, you don't see many people swimming, though there are often young Bidan Moor couples strolling or making tea on the beach, especially at weekends (Friday and Saturday).

If you have to take a **taxi** by *déplacement* to the beach, you'll pay up to UM500. Coming back though, there's rarely any problem squeezing in a *bâché*.

Eating and drinking

Eating in Nouakchott is better than anywhere else in Mauritania. Several restaurants have been firmly established for many years, and even the odd new one opens occasionally. Many **cheap restaurants in the Grand Marché area** – the *Restaurant de l'Unité Maghrebien* is typical – provide a good basic plate of *couscous* or spaghetti and sauce for under UM300, with the food arriving on bare tables. Among the best of the **local restaurants** is the *El-Zourrah* on Avenue Kennedy heading towards *Pizza Lena* from Avenue Abd El Nasser, which has big sandwiches at UM150 and daily specials at UM400–500 for an adequate plate. The boom in **fast-food outlets** continues in the Capitale area, with *El Prince*, *Ali Baba's* and – best of all – *Snack Irak*, among others, serving *chawarma*, burgers, beans (*foul*), falafel and grilled chicken; most keep the TV on at maximum decibels. The **fancier places** listed overleaf are marked on our map. Some close on Fridays, either at lunchtime or all day.

Mauritania is officially dry, and **bars** don't advertise. The best places for a drink are the *Casablanca* and the *Karaoke* (see overleaf). Another option is the *Racing Club* on

Avenue de l'Independence, but this has a rather empty expat feel and is usually closed on Saturdays. For a distinctively Mauritanian tipple, ask a taxi driver to take you to the *Democratic Republic of Congo Consulate* (formerly known as the Zairian Consulate); rather disconcertingly for anyone in search of a visa, this has become a local code for "drinking club". The official *Congo Consulate* itself is the best-known, filled with local reprobates and the occasional prostitute, while any other house that can claim a diplomatic connection has also leapt into the act. Seats are worn-out metal beds, the drink of choice Pastis and the conversation often emotional.

Casablanca, off rue Kennedy, shaded by trees in a quiet suburban setting. Large open-air restaurant around a pool serving good food; bacon-burgers are the provocative speciality. The bar is equipped with pool table and serves reasonably priced beer – the only downside is that it doesn't open until 8pm.

Karaoke, facing a sandy square off rue Kennedy. French-run restaurant most notable for serving beer at any time of the day (in small and expensive glasses) but also serves delicious seafood. Be ready later on for soulful sing-alongs to French hits of the 1970s.

Le Oiseau de Paradis, near La Stade. Chinese cuisine.

Phenicia, rue Mamadou Konaté. Lebanese family atmosphere with good menu, most of which is available, and decent service. Main dishes around UM600, omelettes UM350–500.

Pizza Lena, av Kennedy. Established pizzeria popular with expats and trendy Mauritanians. Serves drink (but not during Ramadan), and has good ice cream.

Rimal, av Abd El Nasser. Lebanese and currently the restaurant of choice amongst gastronomes on a student budget. There's a supplement for the AC back room where you can escape the TV, but it's always quiet on the shady veranda out front. Excellent *steack cordon bleu*.

Zoubeida, rue Ely Ould M'haimid. Moroccan restaurant, hugely popular with less well-connected people, recommended for an evening out. The set-up here is piles of cushions and carpets, shoes off, TV in the corner, conversational opportunities – and endless food. Wonderful value.

Listings

Airlines Air Afrique, off av Abd El Nasser just west of the PTT (☎252081 or 252084); Air Algérie, av Abd El Nasser, west of the PTT (☎252059); Air France, Imm. SMAR, av Abd El Nasser, east of the PTT near the new Palais de Justice (☎253916) – may also sell tickets for Point Afrique's cheap charters out of Atar to Paris; Air Mauritanie, av Abd El Nasser east of the PTT (☎252211 or 52212; Fax 256470); Libyan Arab Airlines, near Air Algérie on av Abd El Nasser, east of the PTT (☎255390 or 255406); Royal Air Maroc, Imm. SMAR, av Abd El Nasser, east of the PTT near the new Palais de Justice (☎253648).

American Express Represented by SOPRAGE, av Abd El Nasser; note they charge a percentage.

Banc d'Arguin National Park To make a visit from Nouakchott, first visit the travel agents (see opposite). The park is most easily visited from Nouadhibou, where guides are available.

Banks The Société Mauritanienne de Banque (BP 614; ☎252602), the Union des Banques de Développement (BMDC; BP 219; ☎252061), and the Banque Internationale pour la Mauritanie (BP 210; ☎252363) seem the surest, but they can take ages to change money. All are open Sun–Thurs 7.30am–12.30pm; out of hours, your best bet is one of the many bureaux along av Abd El Nasser, the airport bank or the *Monotel*.

Bookshops Gralicoma, near the Grande Marché between av Kennedy and av de Gaulle, is the best bet in town, open Sun–Thurs 8am–noon & 3–6pm. Alternatively, check the *Monotel* shop's more tourist-oriented offerings.

Car parts and main dealers include Nosoco (☎252352) in the Ksar for Land Rover, and Peyrissac (☎252213) on av Abd El Nasser for Peugeot and Nissan. A good mechanic is Jules at TPA on the road leading away from the hospital.

Car rental Prices per day for the smallest town-car runabouts are around UM9000; 4WD twin-cab pick-ups and land cruisers go for around UM16,000 per day plus fuel, generally provided with drivers. Rival operators Gazelle du Desert (☎250669; Fax 258152) and Wefa (☎254901; Fax 255009) face each other across bd El Nasser; or check out Europcar (BP 791; ☎251136; Fax 252285) for self-drive: they have an office on av du General de Gaulle and a branch at the old airport terminal (☎252408). Naturally, you should bargain your mouth off.

Cinemas The Oasis and the El Mouna in La Capitale show Westerns, kung fu and occasional French and Egyptian movies. There's a couple more screens in the Ksar – the El Jouad and the Sahara.

Embassies and visas The UK consulate has lapsed, and Britain now has representation through an Honorary Consul, Mrs N Abeiderrahmane (BP 2069; ☎251756; Fax 257192); the nearest diplomatic help is the US embassy, or the British embassy in Dakar, though Britain's Mauritanian interests are looked after by the embassy in Rabat. Main embassies include France, rue Ahmed Ould Mahmed (BP 231; ☎251740); Mali, rue Abdalaye between the German and Spanish embassies (☎540218); Morocco, (BP 621; ☎251411); Senegal, av du General de Gaulle (BP 611; ☎252106); US, rue Abdallaye (BP 222; ☎252660). The visa service at the French embassy handles visas for Côte d'Ivoire, Burkina Faso, Togo and Centrafrique.

Emergencies Police ☎17, Hospital ☎252135. The national hospital is helpful, but you tend to come out with more illnesses than you went in with. Private clinics are expensive but preferable.

Internet The best Internet café is *Top Technology*, next to the *Hôtel el Amanne* on av Abd El Nasser. Connection speeds are slow, and keyboards are, of course, French (UM300/hour).

Post office The PTT on av Abd El Nasser is theoretically open daily 8am–12.30pm & 2–6.30pm. Air mail delivery times to and from Europe average seven to eight days. Collecting mail from poste restante depends on the availability of the bureau clerk but is otherwise efficient and costs UM24/item.

Swimming pools Largest at the *Monotel*, where brazen entry has the best chance of success, but there's also a pool at the *Racing Club*, where tact, good manners and a few words of French can get you in for free.

Telephoning Calls abroad are most easily made from the numerous "phone shops" around town, where you can also fax and photocopy. Don't use the *Monotel*; it's incredibly expensive.

Travel Agents Adrar Voyages (BP 926; ☎251717; Fax 253210) and ATV (BP 861; ☎251575 or 254749) are both recommended. Secutor (☎258081; Fax 257120), hidden in the back of the building next to *Rimal* restaurant, is also good for travel and general business transactions, and painlessly offers many useful services including cash advances on Visa cards.

Visas Visa "prolongation" is possible at the Commissariat Central, Lemine Sakho off av Abd El Nasser, east of the PTT. Check the amount you pay matches the stamps in your passport.

SOUTHERN MAURITANIA

Southern Mauritania is the most densely populated part of the country, its major settlements connected by the Brazilian-built **Route de l'Espoir**. The one thousand and ninety-nine kilometres of paved *transmauritanienne* highway have certainly opened up the isolated southeast, bringing the far-flung regional capital of **Néma** within three days' drive of Nouakchott. There's a grim irony to the name, though. Instead of spreading wealth to the provinces, the "Road of Hope" has sucked them dry, offering swift escape from the parched countryside to the even less hopeful Nouakchott shanties – where the nomads and impoverished farmers can only sit and wait. The road is good except for a deplorable stretch between Aleg and Kiffa which can take days; repair work is proceeding.

South of the Route de l'Espoir the population is largely non-Arabic-speaking and the land is dry savannah and bush, with irrigated rice and millet lands near the river. Shabby **Rosso** is a first glimpse of Mauritania for most travellers arriving from Senegal, but **Bogué** and **Kaédi**, further upriver, are more interesting towns. Along the Route de l'Espoir itself, **Boutilimit** is worth a stop, as are **Ayoun el Atrous**, **Timbedgha** and Néma itself. Off the road to the **north**, the Moorish citadels of **Tidjikja** and **Tichit** are spectacularly isolated and tough destinations – Tichit up to five days' travel from Nouakchott. **Oualata**, north of Néma, is also highly recommended if you have plenty of time.

Making for Bamako in **Mali**, various *pistes* drop down from the Route de l'Espoir: the one from Timbedgha to Nara passes near the site of **Koumbi Saleh**, probable capital of the ancient kingdom of Ghana.

Rosso and north to Nouakchott

Arriving on the north bank of the Senegal River, there's nothing to hold you in **ROSSO**, but if you need to stay the night, **rooms** are available at the *Hôtel Union* (☎569029; Fax 569139; AC, S/C rooms ④), the *Hôtel Negga* (⑥) and the *Restaurant de Fleuve* (②). Service and facilities in all three are fairly basic. Rarely will you be stuck for **transport to Nouakchott** however. Rosso's *gare routière* is 500m out of town, an arrangement that seems to have been designed to allow the *calèche* drivers the opportunity of giving you a ride in their horse-drawn buggies. Peugeots do the run up to Nouakchott in three to four hours along a coastal highway which for most of the year runs through dry dunes and sand hills with a scattering of trees. With rain, the dunes become gentle, grass-spiked hills, dotted with goats and camels and planted with the flapping white tents of nomads.

If you have your own 4WD, you could deviate from the highway some 20km north of Rosso to visit **Mederdra**, an old gum arabic centre at the heart of the defunct kingdom of Trarza, now renowned for wood and silver craftsmanship.

Boutilimit

A less than engrossing two-hour drive from Nouakchott, **BOUTILIMIT** is the first major settlement along the Route de l'Espoir, a Moorish caravanserai and also the site of one of the earliest French military bases in the country, with a large, permanent **market**. Perhaps it's major claim to fame is as the birthplace of Mokhtar Ould Daddah, Mauritania's first president. The religious capital of the country, Boutilimit is renowned for the literary collection of its *medrassa* (Islamic college), and for its crafts – goat- and camel-hair rugs, and silverware. Nowadays the town is very much under economic thrall to Nouakchott.

To Kaédi

From the anonymous town of **Aleg**, a brand new paved road leads 60km down to the river and the Chemama (flood plain) town of **Bogué**. You can get across the river by *pirogue* to the Isle à Morfil in Senegal from here, but the car ferry may no longer be operating.

The tarmac extends from Aleg via Bogué all the way to **KAÉDI**, Mauritania's third largest town, and a major market centre – it's a good place to buy cloth. In the late 1970s a meat-freezing plant was built here, with the intention of culling some of the over-grazing herds of the south and air-freighting the meat to Europe. But the land immediately around Kaédi is barren, and offers no grazing at all to cattle driven there, so the herders continue to drive their cattle for slaughter down to the coast. The meat plant has gone the way of many such in Africa and is slowly crumbling to dust. But Kaédi is progressing in other ways; it was the first regional capital to be equipped with electricity and is an important fabric centre. A high percentage of Kaédi's people are settled, or semi-settled, Tukulor, whose white, long-horn zebu cattle can be seen roaming everywhere in the Gorgol and Guidimaka districts, to the southeast.

For somewhere **to stay** in Kaédi, try the Base des Nations Unies way out on the eastern edge of town. It's officially intended for UN personnel, but if rooms are available (AC, S/C with hot water; ④), they're worth arguing for. The cooking is excellent and they have a swimming pool. The *case de passage* of SONADER (Societé National pour le Développement Rural) is nearer to the centre of town and cheaper (AC; ③), but you have to share facilities with the rest of the crowd.

Getting east from Kaédi towards **Sélibaby**, Mauritania's southernmost and least typical town, is difficult in the dry season and usually impossible if it rains, although several *taxis brousse* try to maintain stages between one flooded river tributary and another. The journey is not made any easier by the impressive number of checkpoints along this "border" road.

The Tagant

The **Tagant** is a region of sear, stony plateaux, the remote location of some of Mauritania's oldest towns and notoriously hard of access. By 4WD it takes between a day and a half and two days from Nouakchott to reach **Tidjikja**, geographically almost the dead centre of Mauritania. The final 200km of *piste* is very variable, and petrol supplies north of the *transmauritanienne* are unreliable, so fill your tank and jerry cans at every opportunity. Coming by **public transport**, you should fix up a vehicle for the whole journey in Nouakchott. Hop by *taxi brousse* if you like, but distances are long, junctions often deserted and scorching, and local transport (from Aleg or Magta Lahja, for example) is very uncertain. Many local people prefer to fly to Tidjikja: there's a flight from Nouakchott every Tuesday with a fare of about UM8500.

Tidjikja

A three-hundred-year-old bastion of conservative Bidan ideology, **TIDJIKJA** was founded by Moorish exiles from the Adrar, who planted the *palmeraies* for which it's still famous. In common with several other towns in this area, the sprawling mess of Tidjikja is split by a sizeable **wadi**, which runs wet for a few days at most each year. On the southwest side of the town, where you arrive, are most of the modern administrative blocks. After something of a tourist "boom" in the 1970s (dozens every year, before the banning of alcohol), Tidjikja doesn't expect many *Nsarani* visitors any more.

The interest, though, lies up the slope on the northeast bank of the wadi, a fifteen-minute walk away, where the **old city** surrounds the Friday mosque, with palm groves and a jumble of houses spreading on either side. The **architecture** of the Tagant region is clear to see here, even if many of the houses appear unoccupied and are falling apart (most are in fact owned by somebody). The houses, massively constructed out of dressed stone, cemented with and sometimes clad in clay, with flat roofs and palm-trunk waterspouts to drain storm water, display the ornamental *kefya* – triangular niches – that can be seen in various forms right across the Sahelian belt. Rooms are narrow, owing to the lack of long, strong beams, and focus inwards on interior courtyards.

As for **accommodation**, you will have to rely on the help of drivers and police until the construction of the *Centre d'Accueil de Tidjikja* is completed. There's a bank of sorts, a PTT, market, shops, a hospital and fuel.

North from Tidjikja

The caravan route **from the Tagant to the Adrar** – a journey of 470km from Tidjikja to Atar – is still viable but best undertaken with high-clearance vehicles (two in preference). Guides are absolutely essential: on no account set off without local expertise on board. It's easier to go in this direction than the reverse, because you're travelling "with the sand".

RACHID you can visit more easily – it's only 35km north of Tidjikja. 4WD vehicles can be rented in Tidjikja for about UM8000 a day, and it might even be possible to rent a camel. Rachid, perched high on the west side of the wadi, is an eighteenth-century Kounta Bedouin citadel, from where piratical tradesmen would prey on the caravans wending their way south from the Adrar massif to Tidjikja. It still has a magnificent, dense *palmeraie* and is referred to as Tidjikja's "beauty spot".

Tichit

TICHIT, too, is radically unprepared for tourism, which doesn't prevent them having piles of gear ready to sell, just in case. Such is the consuming nature of the dunes that

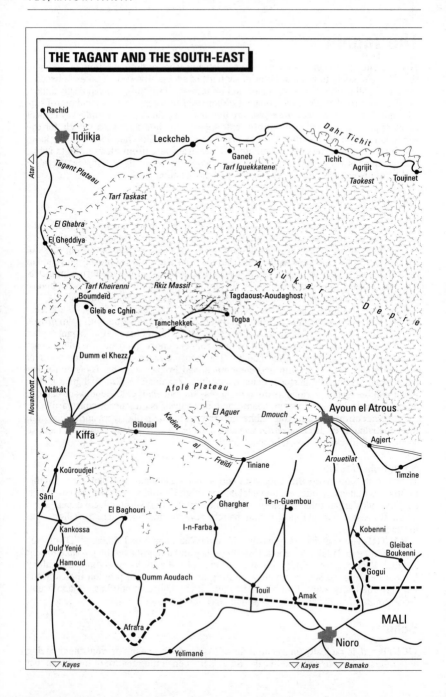

THE TAGANT AND THE SOUTH-EAST

Rachid

Tidjikja Leckcheb *Dahr Tichit*

Tagant Plateau Ganeb Tichit Agrijit
Tarf Iguekkatene *Taokest* Toujinet

Tarf Taskast

El Ghabra *A o u k a r* *D è p r e*
El Gheddiya

Tarf Kheirenni *Rkiz Massif* Tagdaoust-Aoudaghost
Boumdeïd
Gleib ec Cghin Togba
Tamchekket

Dumm el Khezz

Afolé Plateau

Ntâkât *El Aguer* *Dmouch* Ayoun el Atrous

Kiffa Billoual *Kediet* Agjert

el *Freïdi* Tiniane *Arouetilat*
Timzine

Koûroudjel

Sâni Gharghar Te-n-Guembou

El Baghouri I-n-Farba Kobenni

Kankossa Gleibat
Boukenni

Ould Yenjé Gogui
Hamoud Oumm Aoudach
Touil Amak **MALI**

Afrara

Nioro

Yelimané

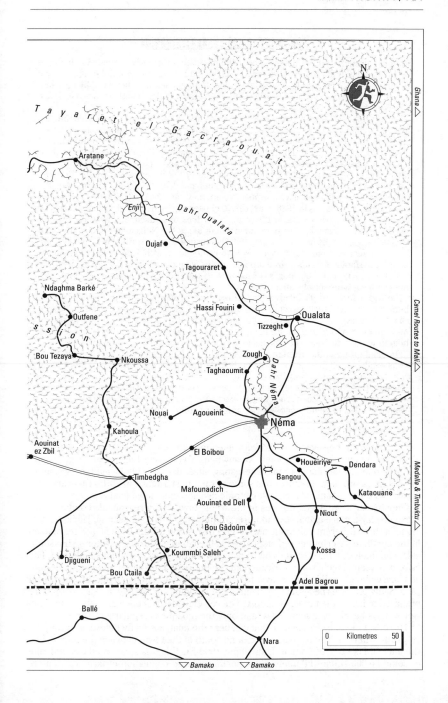

PEOPLE OF TICHIT

Founded around 1150 AD, Tichit once had a population variously estimated at between six thousand and one hundred thousand. Tichit's inhabitants now number around five hundred, as more families leave each year, and more houses are smothered by the sand. But the basic ethnic divisions are still visible, and encapsulate, though in an atypical way, the complexity of Mauritania.

The biggest and most economically active group, who call themselves **Masena**, are concentrated on the south side of the town, towards the modern administrative quarter. The Masena traditionally speak Aser, a Mande language closely related to the Soninke spoken in eastern Senegal. They're probably descendants of the black peoples who lived all over the Sahara in earlier, more prosperous times, and who were pushed south into oases like Tichit (and Oualata) by the expansion of the desert – and by the Berbers. Masena society has absorbed Berber immigrants and, like the Berber Tuareg, wealthy Masena families still keep slaves (*captifs*), whom they call **Abid** or **Bella**. Despite the formal freeing of the slaves in 1980, most *captifs* chose to hang on to their traditional way of life, working six days a week in the owner's gardens or household, in return for their basic needs. In comparison with an independent life in the Nouakchott slums, this kind of captivity seems less onerous. Today the Abid form a separate group in Tichit, living in their own quarter. Many Abid have mixed to some extent with Tichit's **Haratin** Moors, though the Haratins' status as free black ex-slaves is much longer established. Their reputation for piety and their long association with the Bidan Moors continues to endow them with superior social status.

The **Bidan** Moors in Tichit are called **Chorfa** – from *Sharif*, those families who believe themselves to be direct descendants of the prophet. Arabized Berbers who had established themselves in these parts by the ninth century, the Chorfa were originally part of the **Zenaga** group of Berber-speaking peoples from whose name the word Senegal is thought to have derived. The Chorfa are concentrated on the north side of Tichit.

The final group is the **Rehian**, nomadic Bedouin Arabs who pass through the town occasionally, to sell meat or take part in the date harvest. They move their tents around with the grazing, as much as 200km either way along the escarpment.

Despite this ethno-linguistic complexity, census returns from Tichit record 99 percent of the population as "Moor", meaning Hassaniya-speaking – a reflection, perhaps, of the assumption that to identify oneself with any other ethnic group is politically suspect.

swamp the town, however, there's every likelihood the old part will cease to exist as a viable community before too long. Meanwhile, if you have the means to get there, Tichit is one of Mauritania's most interesting sites: dramatically located at the foot of the Tichit escarpment, the town has some of the finest **Tagant architecture**, and also preserves the remnants of a complex ethnic division in its town plan.

Only two or three dozen **houses** in the whole town are in reasonable condition, but these display a more elaborate and purer architecture than that seen in Tidjikja. Local stone of three different colours is used – greenish stone for the Chorfa quarter of town in the north; more crumbly, red stone used in the ruinous Masena quarter on the south side; and finely cut, hard, white stone, used only for the most prestigious buildings. The *kefya* ornamental niches are intricate, and the doors of a few of the old residences are still marvellously solid, with heavy, hob-nailed bolts and latches made of wood from Mali. Sadly the skills necessary to maintain the buildings are fading, and few people are prepared to invest the time and energy. The red clay that was once used to plaster interior walls is hardly ever seen today, and only the mosque is regularly repaired.

The best time to be in Tichit, if you can bear the heat, is shortly before or during the July **date harvest**. The palm groves extend south of the town, between the houses and the ancient lake bed of Aoukar. Until about 1000 BC this was a vast reed-covered lake of some 50,000 square kilometres, supporting a large population of farmers, hunters and fishers on its shores. Today, the surface near the town is encrusted with **salt** which blows into the palm groves and coats the dates, making them inedible – and so the people of Tichit spend the last two months of the ripening season painstakingly washing the crop with well-water. The consequent joy and relief of the actual harvest make Tichit one of the best places to be at that time.

Travel practicalities

If you're **driving to Tichit**, you must take a **guide**. Heading out of Tidjikja, the route is clear enough to the Rehian stronghold of **Leckcheb** (a few windblown huts, some tents and a military post), but then the *piste* deteriorates. To the west of Tichit, the line of cliffs fades away and there's a waste of dunes in which to get stuck and lost. Eventually the track descends to the prehistoric lake floor of the **Aoukar depression**, where it winds along the base of the scarp.

Alternatives to your own 4WD vehicle are chancy. Getting a lift from Tidjikja isn't likely, except possibly after the plane from Nouakchott arrives on a Tuesday, and renting a vehicle for this expedition is an expensive business, even in a group – allow up to UM25,000, but bargain furiously. Air Mauritanie has ceased operating scheduled flights to Tichit, but at the prices you're liable to pay for surface transport, it would be worth enquiring about a chartered continuation of the Nouakchott–Tidjikja flight on a Tuesday. Obviously, you've every chance of getting stranded in Tichit, unless you go there by 4WD vehicle. You couldn't ask for much more adventure.

Unless, that is, you're determined to go further and make a full circle by taking on the three days and 400km of *piste*-driving **from Tichit to Oualata** (see p.124). This represents a major desert crossing, and the police in Tichit will make sure you take a guide. The *piste* follows the old caravan route around the Tichit and Oualata escarpments, with good wells at fairly regular intervals – Toujinet, Aratâne, Oujaf, Tagourâret, Hâssi Fouîni. The *piste* is mostly sandy, occasionally ascending the scarp to a kind of "Lost World" scene on top. You're unlikely to see other vehicles along the way and there are barely any wrecks to indicate much traffic in the past.

A less daunting forty-kilometre run east of Tichit leads to the nearly deserted and sand-swamped ruins of **Agrijit** – showing what Tichit itself is doomed to become.

The far southeast

East of the Route de l'Espoir's high point on the Tagant plateau – the Passe de Djouk – is the scrappy administrative town of **KIFFA**. The worn sign in the town centre for the *Hôtel de l'Amitié* (③) claims it has electricity and water; in fact it's unfriendly and often has neither, and its rooms are just simple cubicles with thin floor mattresses. At the prices they charge, try to get in instead at the Peace Corps' *Maison de Passage* or else endure the echoing luxury of the newly-built and empty *Hotel el Hemel* (☎632637; Fax 632638; ⑤). If you're desperate to escape, flights head back to Nouakchott on Monday and Saturday.

Deviating northeastwards from Kiffa, there's 120km of *piste* to another post, **Tamchekket** (transport most days), enticing only if archeological dedication drives you to find the ruins of **Aoudaghost** (see box, overleaf), poking from the rocky ground in the **Massif du Rkiz**, some 40km further east. This is one for motorized travellers only.

Ayoun el Atrous

Little **AYOUN EL ATROUS** is a more interesting town than most others along the road, but its economy is dead and even the caravanserai at the western town limits has had to shut down. Still, the buildings of red, dressed sandstone make it an attractive place to stop. And if you're into collecting old trade beads, you'll enjoy the **market**. If

---

AOUDAGHOST AND GHANA

Aoudaghost (modern name Tegdaoust) was once a great trans-Saharan trade city on the edge of what was then grassland. Its inhabitants were probably speakers of a Mande language like Soninke. From perhaps 500 BC, caravans of horses and bullocks used to arrive from Marrakech and the Roman Empire's Mediterranean shores. By the third century AD, the domestication of the camel had improved the viability of the trans-Saharan trade and Aoudaghost flourished on the commerce through most of the first millennium AD, in later years repulsing Berber Almoravid attempts to subjugate and convert it to Islam. The rapidly expanding empire of Ghana – focused on Oualata and Koumbi Saleh – captured the town around 1050, but within a decade Ghana's Muslim western neighbour, **Tekrur**, had helped the Berber Almoravids to invade and convert Ghana. By early in the twelfth century, the Berbers were leaving again, and over the next century both Tekrur and Ghana were swallowed by the mightier empire of Mali to the east. Aoudaghost was rebuilt in the sixteenth and seventeenth centuries, and then finally deserted. Today, it's only as interesting as the most recent excavations, and not easily visited (being so hard to find), unless a dig is in progress.

the sand-sweepers on the highway have been doing their stuff – and if the deplorable stretch of highway between Aleg and Kiffa has been repaired – **getting there** with your own transport (800km) from Nouakchott might be possible in one long, dawn-till-late day; public transport takes two days. If the highway is still bad, allow up to three full days of travel. The first of the three principal *pistes* to **Mali** starts at Ayoun, a two-day trip to Bamako by *taxi brousse*.

The *Aioun Hôtel* (☎631462; ④) doesn't get much business for its overpriced AC, S/C rooms. Food is available out of cans, but expensive, and takes a long time to come. Ayoun's bank should be able to change money but may not have a clear idea of the current exchange rate and will charge you for their call to Nouakchott.

Timbedgha and Koumbi Saleh

If you're bent on visiting the ruins of Koumbi Saleh, and can find someone who knows exactly where they are, press on to **Timbedgha** (Timbedra) and then aim for the Malian town of Nara from there. The site is some 65km southeast of Timbedgha, close to the main route to Nara, and there's a chance of getting there by ordinary *taxi brousse* bound for the border, as long as you're prepared to pay a little extra for the diversion.

KOUMBI SALEH, the putative capital of the Ghana empire, is the most important medieval site in West Africa. Archeologists have barely scratched its huge extent, which unfortunately means that unless you've got a shovel there's not much to see. The town is estimated to have had a population of about 30,000, which would have made it one of the largest cities in the world at the time. The Arab geographer Al-Bakri, writing in 1067, described a conurbation of two towns, a northern one with twelve mosques, and, 10km to the south, the royal town of **al-Ghala**, with huts arranged concentrically around a palace. Between the two, along the royal road, was a continuous "suburb" of houses. Curiously, although traces of the royal part of Koumbi Saleh have been found, the royal quarter doesn't appear to have been constructed in stone. The main part of town is more impressive, successive excavations having uncovered massive stone houses, an enormous mosque and flagstone floors covering a more ancient layer of buildings.

Néma and Oualata

The *transmauritanienne* ends with a whimper at **NÉMA**, where the architecture – stone clad with clay – intimates that of Oualata, 90km north. Vegetable gardens, like

Ayoun's, prettify Néma at the end of the brief rainy season, but for some reason hospitality here tends to be perfunctory. If you have your own 4WD vehicle, a guide can be hired for the deep desert drive from Néma to Tidjikja (4–5 days), and right up to Chinguetti (10 days) for a fee of around UM25,000–30,000, plus UM3000–4000 for his travel costs home again. A quarter of the fee is payable up front to his family. Your own 4WD can also take you along the *piste* from Néma down to Nara in Mali, but this route should really only be attempted in convoy.

There are fairly frequent vehicles from Néma to **OUALATA**, though not every day. The best chance of transport is on a Wednesday when there's a flight from Nouakchott to Néma; if you're in Néma by 8am, you may strike lucky with vehicles collecting plane passengers for Oualata. The plane returns to Nouakchott the same day.

Oualata's superficial glamour comes from the amazingly beautiful bas-relief **ornamentation** of its house walls. The decorations, of gypsum, white and red clay, and indigo, are designed and applied by the women, and although they're all unique, personal works, they share certain motifs and a thoroughgoing exuberance. The old town is partly abandoned and fewer and fewer households bother with decorating outside. Inside the houses, if you get the opportunity to look, the effects created can be stunning. Oualata's **doors** are highly stylized as well – the best ones studded with copper and silver.

Oualata's past is a fairly glorious one, and its present momentum as a viable community rests on its worldwide eminence as a centre of **Islamic scholarship**, the basis of long-term rivalry with Timbuktu. There are only twenty places in its Koranic school, creating a permanent waiting list of anything up to ten years. Less illustriously, Oualata, like Tichit, is also known as a place of internal exile, where outspoken political dissidents are detained.

You don't just show up in Oualata and wander around. Much as you'll have come to expect, a **visit to the police** is important, more so here than elsewhere. The Oualatans don't take kindly to Land-Rovies using their town as a photo backdrop, but allow some time for introductions and tea-drinking, and a day or two here can be rewarding. Such formalities are necessary, in any case, if you want somewhere to stay.

THE ADRAR

Breaking through the sands of the Sahara, the **Adrar Plateau** is Mauritania's most outstanding region. Though nowhere higher than 1000m, the gaunt, multi-brown scenery is strikingly clawed into deep **gorges** and sheer, cliff-edged mesas. In the southern parts, wind-carried **live dunes** stream ceaselessly across the landscape. The town of **Atar**, plus a handful of villages, and the ancient settlements of **Chinguetti** and **Ouadane**, account for almost all the population; camels and oases of date palms determine the economy.

Although the options are fairly limited unless you devote considerable time, the wildness of the desert, the isolation of the towns and the somewhat precarious feasibility of getting to them, make it a rewarding area to explore. The ubiquity of **neolithic stone tools** – some of them remarkably small and beautiful – adds further, acquisitive interest.

From Nouakchott to Atar

There are direct **flights** from Nouakchott to Atar for UM8400 on Thursdays and flights via Nouadhibou on Mondays and Saturdays. If you're taking a Peugeot **taxi** to Atar from Nouakchott's *autogare*, get to the Ksar early in the morning to secure a seat, preferably before dawn; you could otherwise be forced to wait until much later, even until the following day.

The tarmac road **from Nouakchott** as far as **Akjoujt** is smooth and fast, and taxis take about two hours to complete the journey plus time for prayer stops. After 250km

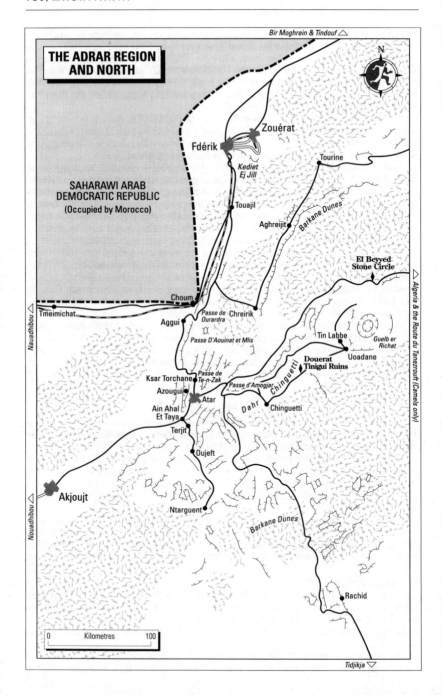

THE ADRAR REGION AND NORTH

of empty desert, **AKJOUJT** is a frightful place. Constructed in 1949, this artificial town is even more desolate now that it has ceased to be a copper-mining centre, which at least gave it a veneer of prosperity during the 1970s. The "technical reasons" blustered for the failure turned out to be simply the depletion of what little ore was worth digging. Old mud-brick buildings mix with newer, but dilapidated miners' housing in desert-utilitarian style. Akjoujt was given a shallow new breath of life with the start of **gold-mining** in 1992: a bunch of tough Australians struggled for a while to get a few dozen kilos every month but have now left. Around the town's main *place* you'll find a scattering of barely awake shops and eating houses which service a few dozen people a day and a barrack-like hotel, the *Hotel de Inchiri* (☎761607; ④) which provides decent-value rooms, if you bargain. At least the town always has fuel.

Beyond Akjoujt, the tarmac is gradually extending – with Chinese help – towards Atar, though there still remains 70km of swervy sand and a final 40kms of corrugated *piste* that makes Atar a welcome sight when you finally arrive. If you become lost, the low relief to the north, from where the wind usually prevails, can make for more excitement than you really want as other wheel marks are quickly erased under the blowing dust.

If you are driving yourself, you could check out the reasonably accessible **springs** at **TERJIT**, 12km from the main route, signposted about 5km before Ain Ahel Et Taya. A hot spring and several cool ones water a tight little oasis of exceptional beauty, crouching like moss between the cliffs. Three campsites offer basic accommodation at UM700 per night.

Continue a tough 35km further south and you come to **Oujeft** – another very lush oasis. Like many localities in the Adrar, Oujeft harbours archeological and paleontological relics: there's a gigantic human footprint impressed in a mudstone rock nearby (local people can tell you where it is). It's difficult, however, to get down this route without your own 4WD; occasional vehicles make the trip from Atar.

Atar and around

From the edge of the plateau the road commences a winding ascent through rocky hills to **ATAR**, the largest settlement in the northern interior. Modern buildings and offices are fairly few, but this is a surprisingly large and energetic place, drawing business from the deepest parts of the desert and, more recently, from a surge of visitors arriving on cheap charter flights from France (see Basics, p.5, for details). With lively markets and a fringe of *palmeraies* and irrigated gardens, it's a town that many travellers quickly come to like, and it can be a pleasant base for looking around the Adrar region. Heavy rains and severe floods in the early 1990s brought about the collapse of a number of the older mud-built quarters, which have been replaced by concrete hulks. It's a situation which, combined with Mauritania's other difficulties, has brought considerable hardship to the town's poor. Begging, unfortunately, is on the increase.

There's a fair number of shops and *boutiques*, all focusing on the market area, but only one specialist leather-working shop. A whole *quartier* of smiths (the Maalemine caste) make everything from jewellery to saddle fittings. Atar's reputation for handicrafts at first seems exaggerated, but you can find a fair amount of interesting stuff if you nose around. Much of it – Moorish clothing, camel saddles, pipe holders, belts and sandals – is designed and manufactured for local use. Apart from browsing, the standard thing to do is take a walk before sunset along the dike that separates the town from the gardens and *palmeraie* and holds back the rushing waters of the Séguélil wadi, which flow once a year at most.

The recent influx of visitors from France has resulted in an increasing number of **places to stay**, many of which also offer tours of Atar's surrounding attractions. The cheapest accommodation in town is at the *Auberge Azougi* (☎764371; ①), on the edge of the market near the town centre, around 100 metres from the roundabout. It's a characteristically Mauritanian hotel (communal rooms, mats on floor and not wonderfully clean), but has a friendly and helpful owner, and is just a short walk from the *taxi brousse* park. More comfortable is the friendly *Auberge Dar Slam* (☎764368; ①–②) on the Choum/Chinguetti road at the edge of town, which has pleasant rooms, thatched *tichits* and an airy restaurant/lounge in a quiet courtyard; take a mattress on the roof to save costs. The thatched *guetouns* of the *Auberge Salima* (☎764347; ①–②), in downtown Atar close to the big roundabout (take the Chinguetti road for about 100m), is the only place in town where you'll find hot showers, but is rather expensive for what you get; the owner, Salima Ould Sleiman, also offers excursions around Atar and has a fleet of Toyota 4WD's with which he chases the richer tourists. The "best" hotel in town is *Hôtel Mauribatine* (☎764383; ③), in the rather characterless administrative area, with AC, S/C rooms but no hot water and an air of decrepit gloom. **Camping** is often possible on the roofs of some restaurants.

In the **food** line, you'll find a number of cheap eateries in the older part of town where a bowl of rice and dried fish comes for around UM150, and camel meat and chips for under UM300. The best food can be had in the shady courtyard of the *Auberge Casablanca* on Atar's main street.

Excursions around Atar

There are various good excursions out of Atar, most requiring transport – 4WD, camel or at least a donkey. Top dog operator is Salima Ould Sleimane with a fleet of new Toyotas, but most of the auberges in Atar also offer tours and are often cheaper. Prices are usually UM18,000/day for a Land Rover taking four to six passengers, with fuel charged extra. It's best to combine road travel with a few days trekking with a camel; this will give a feel for the country and put some money back into the local community.

Ten kilometres east of Atar there are **stone circles**, and 20km north of the town, on the road to Choum, is Ksar Torchane, an attractive **oasis**. But the best local trip is up to the ruins of **Azougui**, the old Almoravid capital of the Adrar, about 11km northwest of Atar beyond the Tarazi pass, in the Tayaret wadi. Take the smallest of the three roads from the town's main roundabout; at the base of the tarmaced *piste* down the cliff, turn right. In winter, it's not too far to walk in a day and it's usually possible to hitch back. Otherwise, any car can make the journey.

Azougui (the "Azokka" of medieval Arab writers) was the eleventh-century Berber base from which the Almoravid holy warriors launched raids on the Ghana empire satellite of Aoudaghost, and the Ghana cities of Oualata and Koumbi Saleh. Having swept through the southern fringes of the desert, they turned north for their second great invasion, into Morocco and decadent Andalucian Iberia.

The remains of the main stronghold are still visible today, a relatively small **citadel** (about fifty metres square) within whose walls the social framework of medieval southern Europe and North Africa was, in large part, determined. A couple of hundred metres to the west of the fort is the **necropolis** of Imam Hadrami, one of the eleventh-century holy warriors. Imam Hadrami's mausoleum, surrounded by tombstones, continues to be venerated by many Mauritanians.

Chinguetti and Ouadane

Chinguetti, probably the single most visited site in the country, has started to charge UM1000 per group visitor's tax, though tourists in the broadest sense are still counted in handfuls each month. In itself, the town's mosque and jealously guarded library hardly add up to a compelling draw, yet the town does have picturesque qualities and the journey, through a landscape stripped to essentials, is emphatically worthwhile.

Ouadane, which is possibly more interesting, bears comparison with Tichit in its remoteness. Neither is particularly easy to get to, and the upper *piste* to Ouadane reportedly still harbours Polisario mines.

From Atar to Chinguetti

It's about 120km from Atar to Chinguetti and the trip takes anything from three to seven hours, depending on your vehicle and any stops along the way. Occasional **supply trucks** trudge through the sand and up the passes, but their departures are barely advertised and by no means regular. More likely, a lift will come in the shape of one of the battered **Land Rovers** that whirl around Atar. If you join a vehicle that's making the trip, the fare will be around UM1500; if you rent a vehicle to get you there and back, allow up to UM20,000, returning the next day. You're best advised to take along someone who knows the route, as several sections are hard to follow – there'll be no shortage of demand for a free lift.

There are two alternatives, with the new "road" following a less scenic but safer and more direct course. The **old route** runs first through flat, grey rock and sand; then for several kilometres past steep, yellow dunes above a *palmeraie* tucked into a wadi; then between high, dry mesas and finally, in a steeply twisting series of hairpins, to the head of the Amogjar wadi, a gorge which gives out to a further incline and the **Amogjar Pass**. In the interest of safety, it's common practice to get out and walk the steepest ascents and descents: don't hesitate to ask the driver to stop. Among the sandstone massifs you can see gun emplacements and the remains of military posts from the Polisario war. Up at the top squats the incongruous shell of the fake "Fort Sagane", built for the movie of that name in 1985.

Up at around 800m, a couple of kilometres after the final climb, you pass a conical rock stack on the left, fifty metres or so in height. Under an overhang near the top of the stack there are some intriguing **rock paintings** (ask for the *gravures rupestres* or *les dessins*), which are not hard to find, even unguided. While they're not up to Algerian or southern African standards in terms of size or confidence of execution, and give little more than hints about the people who sketched them, they're worth stopping for. There are several red-coloured lanky figures, though it's not possible to make out the animals that some books refer to. The curious circular design on the left, with its four inner circles and radiating strokes, looks like Von Daniken spaceship material – but the Paris–Dakar rally has passed this way, so it's perhaps unwise to assume authenticity.

More figures are to be found on rocks directly by the road, on the right, about 6km further on, but these have been disfigured by Arabic graffiti. The figures are different from those on the hill: the frog-like heads (or headdresses) and massive thighs, could mean anything, though several resemble pygmies most of all. Thousands of examples of such rock art exist in the Adrar: only those near the roads have been seen, or disturbed, by outsiders.

The road now levels out and ploughs once again through soft sand. Look out for the heavily built, tortoise-headed, half-metre-long black Dhub (or Dhab) **lizards**, which scamper into their holes and crevices as you pass. Harmless vegetarians, they subsist between rainfalls by drawing on reserves of fat in their spiky, club-like tails, which they use to guard their tunnels. If you find yourself with an hour or so in the desert, they adore the colour yellow, and bananas send them into a frenzy.

Chinguetti

The route passes the turning for the upper route to Ouadane, 10km before entering the "modern quarter" of **CHINGUETTI**. On this side of the town, the main building – in fact Chinguetti's most striking – is the abandoned Foreign Legion **fortress**, used in the movie *Fort Sagane*, starring Gérard Dépardieu, about the Legion's exploits in Algeria. The fort doubled as set and film crew accommodation, and the air conditioning and other facilities they installed made it the best hotel outside Nouakchott for a while. All is now deserted, but you can still climb onto the ramparts for fine views across the town (beware some very fragile sections). Other notable buildings on this side of town are the Gendarmerie, where you should check in on arrival, a Polisario-shot-up generator house hard by and a defunct solar water pump.

The *Auberge des Caravanes* is on this side of town, offering the choice of sleeping either in rooms, or out in tents, Mauritanian-style, for UM2000/person, but recent reports suggest standards have slipped. In the oldest parts of the town across the broad football-kicked and goat-trailed wadi to the south, and to the west, you'll find other, better-value, options: the basic *Maison de Bien Être* (UM1000/person), the *El Amein* and the *Terre Jaune* (both UM700/person). All these do some **food**, as do some perfunctory shops and stalls at the market, and a few cold Cokes are available at some *boutiques*.

Chinguetti's most venerable quarter, on the west side, dates from at least as far back as the thirteenth century. The town was established rather quickly, by exiles from the oasis of Abweir, just 4km down the wadi. Most of the buildings are made of stone, including the fine old **mosque**, off-limits to Nazarenes. Fortunately you can still get good views of it – complete with the five ostrich eggs atop its squat minaret and much of the interior courtyard – from surrounding dunes and piles of rubble. The "donnez-moi un cadeau" brigade are out in some force in the neighbourhood, and will show you to the *Maison de Bien Être* and the main **Koranic library**. The latter has been the object of some conservation work, and the most prized manuscripts are now contained in filing cabinets, opened only on payment of rather large sums UM1000 for up to three people; UM3–400 per person thereafter. Families round about may have kept some of their own documentary heirlooms, and it's worth asking if you're interested. Chinguetti is the most venerated city in Mauritania, and was once rated as one of Islam's holiest cities, along with Jerusalem, Mecca and Medina.

Relics of a much more ancient history can be bought in the **market**. Extraordinarily fine, small **flint arrowheads** seem to be two a penny, as do the **barbs** that may have been used for fishing in a long-ago Adrar of forests and streams. They are collected by children in the dunes. Weightier implements – beautifully shaped and much-worn cleavers and scrapers, for butchering meat and preparing skins – also appear occasionally. But they too are curiously small, and must have been used by small hands.

To Ouadane

The main route to **OUADANE** branches off the Atar–Chinguetti road, 10km outside Chinguetti; most transport between Atar and Ouadane calls at Chinguetti. Vehicles to and from Ouadane are few, so unless you have loads of time you're best advised to get a lift that's coming back again. The southern route to Ouadane, marked on the IGN map of Mauritania, is a sandy, wadi-course for high-clearance 4WDs only, but recently favoured after the discovery of land mines on the other route. If you're driving, neither route should be undertaken without a local guide.

Ouadane is a town of stones camouflaged in a landscape of stones. The place is quite extraordinary, collapsing in ruins amid the jumble of rocks from which it was constructed eight hundred years ago. So complete is the chaos that, arriving in the middle of the day, with no shadows to define the buildings, you don't even notice them stacked along the steep scarp until you're almost among them. Modern Ouadane – not a lot of it – perches above, on the plateau's edge. The rest house *Guelb Richat* offers accommodation at UM3000/room (sleeping four), while the *Hotel Ouadane* has slightly more basic lodgings at UM1000/room (sleeping three). Alternatively, rely on local hospitality, or camp in the *palmeraie* beneath the town.

Ouadane was founded in the twelfth century by **Berbers** of the Ida-u-el-Hadj tribe, and some of the present-day inhabitants still speak Berber rather than Hassaniya Arabic. Its huge reputation – secure beyond the limits of the West African empires – as a **caravan crossroads** and trading centre for gold, salt and dates lasted nearly four hundred years. There was even a **Portuguese trading post** here at the end of the fifteenth century, busily intercepting the trade for the main Portuguese base on the coast at Arguin Island. Ouadane's fortunes waned, unevenly, as first it succumbed to the onslaught of the sixteenth-century Saadian prince, Ahmed el Mansour of Morocco, who took control of the trans-Saharan trade and diluted much of the town's influence, and then lost its remaining economic power when the Alaouites invaded, also from the north, two centuries later.

Tin Labbé

Only 7km northwest of Ouadane, on the *piste* that curls round the mountain of Guelb er Richat, lies the semi-troglodyte village of **TIN LABBÉ**, where natural rock shelters and crevices have been incorporated into the cluster of stone and mud houses. If you've made it all the way to Ouadane, it would seem a shame not to walk up the wadi to see it. Among the tumble of huge boulders down by the vegetable gardens you can find rock paintings, and writing too, both in Arabic script and in the archaic Tifinar script of the Tuareg, a writing that traces its roots to a Libyan alphabet of the fourth century BC.

THE NORTH

For travellers flying in from Europe or the Canary Isles, or arriving by land from Morocco, **Nouadhibou**, Mauritania's second city, comes as an unlikely first taste of West Africa, and it's not a place on which to base any firm ideas of the region. Isolated north and south by desert, and with no road connections with the rest of the country, it is far removed not just from Africa, but from the rest of Mauritania too.

Coming from the south, only plans to fly on to Morocco or the Canaries would really provide motivation for heading so far out of the way (overland travel to Morocco is currently prohibited, though just about possible using a local guide). The immensely long **iron ore trains** do at least offer a straightforward way of getting to Nouadhibou from inland. If you're in the Adrar region, with a few days in hand before returning to Nouakchott, you can make a satisfyingly complete circuit by catching the train to Nouadhibou, and then either flying to Nouakchott, or taking the *piste* south, travelling either by 4WD *taxi brousse* or truck convoy; after crossing 400km of desert, the last third of the route takes to the beach to follow the sandy Atlantic shore.

Choum and Zouérat

The main draw of this region for travellers is the **iron ore railway** from Zouérat via Choum, which provides the best transport link to Nouadhibou. Taxis run daily from Atar to Choum in four or five hours, a rough trip with beautiful scenery much of the way. The Choum taxi drivers in Atar keep abreast of the news and will get you to the train on time. Before setting off from Atar, buy food for the journey, and take as much fresh water as you can – supplies on the train vary from limited to non-existent and the water at Choum itself is unpalatably salty. There's a habitual tea stop – a cool and friendly place of massive rocky outcroppings where camels are watered – halfway between Atar and Choum.

THE ORE TRAINS

The **iron ore trains** carry thousands of tons of crushed rock in a chain of wagons up to three kilometres long. Their schedules and frequencies depend partly on the speed of extraction at the mines, and on unpredictable hold-ups – damaged rails, engine failure and even, in the past, attacks by Polisario guerillas from over the border in Western Sahara – and travellers should realize that ore is the priority, not passengers.

Three trains a day go from Zouérat to Nouadhibou, but the only one with a passenger carriage passes through Choum at about 5.30–6pm. The usual journey time from Choum to Nouadhibou is around twelve hours. Two others may come through late at night, or early in the morning, but on these foot passengers have to huddle in the ore trucks.

The **fare** in the passenger wagon is UM650 Choum–Nouadhibou, and UM800 Zouérat–Nouadhibou, or UM1600 Choum–Nouadhibou for a fold-down bunk. Riding on the ore wagons is free – and you'll discover why, as the dust works its way into your soul. If you do go for this option, buy flour-sacks from a local patisserie to protect your baggage, take a *houli* to wrap round your head, and have something warm for later in the night, when it can get remarkably cool. Travellers with cars sit in their vehicles – in marginally more comfort – rocking on open platforms held together with wire (around UM6000 Choum–Nouadhibou).

The journey generally passes without incident these days, and there are no police checks. Restful dune scenery accompanies the trip for the last hour or two of daylight. There's generally one stop at Tmeimichatt (or *trois cents dix neuf* – kilometre post 319), to allow the empty train going the other way to pass. If you pick the right compartment you can find yourself sharing endless cups of tea and learning Hassaniya. At this point the interest outside the carriage, even on a clear moonlit night, is nil, and daylight brings no improvement, except hints of the sea as you approach the Nouadhibou peninsula. For information about taking the train **from Nouadhibou**, see p.136.

CHOUM, on the border of Western Sahara, consists of a string of restaurants and crash-out houses where Nouadhibou-bound passengers snooze through the afternoon, waiting for the train's arrival. When you arrive in Choum, leave your bags in the taxi: when the train arrives, you'll be driven alongside to meet the passenger wagon (usually attached at the end of the first train of the day). As the train may be over 2km long and often sets off within minutes, this is a taxi fare worth paying. If you're travelling with your own vehicle, there is the possibility of loading it aboard the train, but this is not easily done in Choum unless you have advised the SNIM (mining and railway office) in Zouérat of your requirement; local officials at Choum should be able to do this by radio.

Driving to Nouadhibou along the sandy *piste* which runs alongside the tracks is not recommended, as half-buried cast-off lengths of track can cause terminal damage.

Zouérat

The *route impériale* continues north from Choum to what is now the purely military town of Fdérik. East of Fdérik it's tarmac to **ZOUÉRAT**, the economic and political heart of the far north. If you're driving, drive on the left on this section of road until the town boundary, then change again to the right. There are two round-trip flights a week between Nouakchott and Zouérat – on Tuesdays via Nouadhibou and on Thursdays via Atar (Zouérat to Atar is UM3500). Apart from the usual small shops, the SOMASERT supermarket is virtually the only place to buy anything in Zouérat. Tours of the spectacular mining operations can be arranged relatively easily from the *Hôtel Oasian*, which is essentially a company rest house, with all the food in the restaurant imported from the Canary Isles (BP 42; ☎749042; Fax 749043; AC, S/C rooms with kitchen; ④).

Nouadhibou

Set on the eastern side of the Cap Blanc peninsula, a finger of desert pointing into the sea, **NOUADHIBOU** ("Jackal's Well") has become the first point of entry for overland travellers from Europe, since the problems on the Algerian trans-Saharan routes. It is a pale, flat, industrial city-satellite of Mauritania, where bars are permitted (or rather, alcohol is blind-eyed), and the mix on the streets adds European, Mediterranean and Oriental traces to the predominant blue flowing robes of locals and of rural immigrants. In French colonial times, this was Port Etienne ("Port Stephen") and many locals still think of themselves as "Stephanois".

The most obvious visit in Nouadhibou itself is to the **central market**, open until 10pm daily, which teems with cloth sellers, tailors and silversmiths. You may find that you can get most of the artisanal works cheaper in Nouakchott, but the laid-back, provincial atmosphere makes this a good place to browse and buy. Close to the town centre, the wind-sculpted **table remarquable**, just east of the main airport runway, is a geological formation worth investigation. Down towards the sea from the fresh fish market, you can wander through what's left of the *village canarien*, once the Canary islanders' settlement of **Tcherka** or **Thiarka**, while to the south of the town is an atmospheric ship's graveyard of abandoned fishing hulks.

Arrival and orientation

Arriving by train, the passenger wagon stops at the "station" (an old shipping container) on the way south out of downtown Nouadhibou. The *gendarmes* can be difficult, so be prepared for a hostile reception. They're closed from noon to 3pm, but don't let them keep your passport: tell them you'll return in the afternoon. The **airport** is 700m from the *Hôtel Sabah*; it's a twenty-minute walk or a UM600 taxi ride to the town centre – no shared taxis ply this route. There is a bank at the airport, probably never open, although the airport telephone office does work. Three or four wooden shacks sell stale biscuits and imported sardines: best to head into town.

Arriving **overland from Morocco**, it is necessary to report to the police to register your presence with a UM1000 fee. **Car owners** have rather more formalities to undergo: these require some Mauritanian cash and should be started as soon as possible after arrival in case any of the various offices decide to close early. First report to the **customs** (*douanes*) opposite the railway station to retrieve the car's *"carte grise"* registration document which will have been retained by the border guards the previous night. To show a carnet here is the exception rather than the rule; most drivers sign a

---

FISHING RIGHTS

Mauritanian fishing communities have been jolted by recent bans on the pursuit of their livelihood. Mauritania, whose fish stocks in the rich cold seas off its shores have long been a magnet for fleets from Russia, Korea and Japan, has entered into an agreement with the European Union, under which the country receives some $100m each year in licenses to allow unlimited fishing. The bizarre irony of the arrangement (crucial as far as the Ministry of Finance, with an eye on the country's $2.4 billion debt, is concerned) is that Mauritania, along with other West African countries, is a big market for the sardines that form the bulk of the catch. Processed in the Canary Islands, the canned sardines end up for sale, at high prices, in the same communities that once caught the fish themselves. In this way, Mauritanians, with an average annual income of around $400, help pay the wages of the men of the EU fishing fleets, who earn at least a hundred times as much.

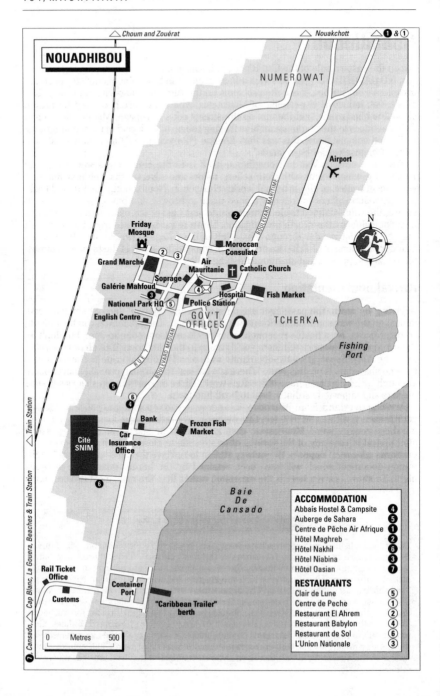

bit of paper promising not to sell their car, have its details entered into their passport, and pay the UM1000 fee. Next, take a photocopy of your *carte grise* to the **insurance office** approaching the centre of town, which is on the first floor above the Banque Al Barkae Mauritaniee Islamique (near *Abba's Hostel*). If the photocopy booth opposite is shut, turn right to the Elf station which has copying facilities. The minimum insurance period is five days, with the rate depending on the engine capacity; expect to pay about UM4000 for five days. Don't scrimp on dates: your insurance will be frequently checked south of Nouakchott. Finally, drive to the middle of town to report to the **police**. At this point any passengers will have to appear in person and a further UM1000/person is charged: officials will look at your passports for an hour before giving them back and – finally – you're legally in Mauritania.

Orientation

Nouadhibou, like many desert cities, is immodestly large, and it comes in three parts. The first is the new quarter of **Numerowat** in the north, with its mess of construction sites, fading into shantytown on the north side. This is where the majority of people now live. The various quarters of Numerowat are identified by *robinets* ("Premier Robinet", "Deuxième Robinet", etc) according to the nearest public water standpipe, which come at 500-metre intervals along the tarmac road to downtown Nouadhibou. Downtown is **ville**, with all the usual services and shops and the city's main market. On the south side of town, a full 10km from the city centre, is the iron ore company's dormitory town of **Cansado** ("Sleepy" in Spanish). Since nationalization, this area is almost entirely occupied by Mauritanians.

It is common to travel around town by shared taxi and prices are fixed. Fares are UM25 for any journey in the downtown area or up the tarmac to Numerowat; UM40 in the same areas, but leaving the tarmac; UM30 town to port or vice versa; and UM50 to anywhere in Cansado.

Accommodation

Nouadhibou is not well served for accommodation, and what little there is can be filled by the flood of overlanders arriving in convoy from the north. Since the overland route from Morocco reopened, **campsites** have become something of a growth industry, with any patch of enclosed waste ground in the centre boasting a campsite sign: the price should be about UM300/person but is often higher. Overland trucks often camp out on the beach, where it tends to be windy at night and baking hot by day. You can also camp near the station, waiting for the train to Choum, where a derelict building provides shelter from the wind, but you may get parties of gawping sightseers from town – not a bother but irritating.

Abba's Hostel & Campsite, bd Median (no telephone at hostel; Abba's wife's telephone number is ☎745877). Recommended hostel offering double and triple rooms around a comfortable and sociable lounge area. Secure parking and a good atmosphere amongst overlanders outweigh often overstretched facilities and only occasional hot water. Home-cooked Senegalese food prepared on request. Camping possible in guarded compound at the rear. Rooms UM1000/person, camping UM300/car or tent.

Auberge de Sahara, BP568 (☎ & Fax 746500). Perhaps the best of the budget options, with quiet and clean shared rooms, plenty of hot water, and access to the kitchen and a roof-terrace barbeque. There's a useful notice board giving local information and advice on onward travel, while the owner, Hamid Lellou, is friendly, helpful, and very well-informed. Large garages and secure parking make this a favourite with overlanders. Turn off bd Median by the *Sol* restaurant and take the third right to find it: it isn't well signposted. ②.

Centre de Pêche Air Afrique, 14km north of Nouadhibou at the Baie de L'Etoile (☎746415; Fax 746155). Surf-casting is the big affair here, and you won't feel one of the boys if fishing is not your bag. Although good value, it's hard to find, so call or fax ahead to get picked up from the airport. Cheaper if you camp nearby. ③.

MOVING ON FROM NOUADHIBOU

Leaving Nouadhibou by land, the **train for Choum** (taxi connection on to Atar) and Zouérat is detailed on p.132. For further information, contact SNIM, Nouadhibou BP 42 (☎745174 ext1700; Fax 745396), the state organization that runs the iron ore mines and the railway. Departure from Nouadhibou on the passenger train is generally about 2–3pm, arriving at Choum about midnight and at Zouérat about 6am. Motorists who are heading for Atar can load their cars onto open platforms, although this can take days: start waiting at the railway station opposite the *douanes* at 9am to stand a chance of getting loaded onto the 6pm freight train. The fee depends on vehicle length but is about UM6000. Note that if Nouakchott is your final destination and by taking the train you are hoping to avoid the risks of the coast *piste*, the route from Choum to the start of the tarmac well south of Atar is just as hard on vehicles.

There are no roads heading south of Nouadhibou, and the land route to Nouakchott is a demanding **desert drive by convoy**. With your own vehicle, you can link up with this – normal 2WD cars can normally get through, but 4WD is better – and if you're travelling by public transport, you can buy a ride for the trip. Land Rovers and trucks make the journey each day, departing from Garage Nouakchott next to the market, and cost about UM5000 depending on the vehicle. If you're driving yourself, it's possible to follow one of these *chauffeurs*, who will certainly try to charge a fat fee. Negotiate hard, and leave it that you will pay on safe arrival and that you'll be charging them if they break down and require your help. A better option is to club together with a group of other overlanders and hire a guide, preferably one that has been vouched for: expect to pay him about UM50,000 for the trip. Travellers without vehicles who want to travel cheaply could always get a lift: hang around long enough – speaking French – at *Abba's Hostel*, and if travelling light you're sure to get a ride with a Eurobanger vendor who hopes you can push, dig, and position sand ladders. The journey normally takes about 36 hours on the move, and the route is never quite the same twice in a row. The last third at least is along the shoreline. By driving day and night, it's not uncommon to complete this trip inside 24 hours, but it makes much more sense to allow two to three days. Be aware that you should have police permission to do this journey, and you will almost certainly have to pay entry fees for the Banc d'Arguin National Park, whether you plan to stop and "visit" or simply drive through unavoidably (see p.138 for details).

There are one or two **flights** each day to and from Nouakchott UM 10,400; 35mins; flights every Monday to and from Casablanca (about £200/$320); and twice-weekly flights (Sun & Thurs) to and from Las Palmas (about £120/$200 with Air Mauritanie, £100/$160 with Air Atlantique), even less if you can find an Antonov fish flight leaving from the airport; enquire there for details.

GOING NORTH TO MOROCCO

Driving north from the Nouadhibou region into Moroccan-occupied Western Sahara is difficult and somewhat risky, but frequently done by local and overland vehicles. The crossing is prohibited by the Mauritanians, so the key to success is avoiding Mauritanian officialdom. By far the best plan is to hire a good guide well in advance (in Nouadhibou for example, where guides are cheaper than in Nouakchott) and have him show you a safe route, avoiding both officials and landmines; your official story will need to be that you're returning to Nouakchott. The price will be at least UM50,000, best paid in two payments. If you find yourself in Mauritanian hands when obviously trying to cross, you will have some explaining to do.

Even if you do get across the border, you'll be in trouble when you hit the first Moroccan checkpoint: expect to be locked up for a day or two. Unless you have a valid Green Card you will then be sent on a two-day bus journey to Layoune to buy third-party insurance for Morocco before there's any question of getting back into your car and driving it north.

Hôtel Maghreb, in between bd Maritime and Median, BP 212 (☎745544). Respectable quiet hotel with garage and parking facilities. No restaurant at present but a bar that can get lively (by local standards) at night. ③.

Hôtel Nakhil, (formerly *Sharaf*) 300m south of the town centre towards the main port (☎746502; Fax 746526). Usually bursting with fishermen. Good facilities and clean rooms with TV. Credit cards accepted. ⑤.

Hôtel Niabina, town centre, BP 146 (☎745983; Fax 745835). Small, friendly and in a colourful part of town. The only problem is finding the place: ask first for the nearby Gallery Mafoud. ③.

Hôtel Oasian, 10km south of town at Cansado, overlooking the bay, BP 42 (☎749029; Fax 749053). Satellite TV, AC and mini-bars in the rooms, plus a bar and restaurant. This state-run establishment is the best hotel in Nouadhibou, but is far from the action. If you reserve ahead, a courtesy bus will meet you at the airport. ⑥.

Eating and nightlife

There are several quite good **supermarkets** along the main tarmac road, Boulevard Médian, and you can buy fish in the old fishing port area behind the stadium. There's a fair number of cheap **restaurants** near the central market. Standard lunchtime fare is rice and fish, with perhaps *couscous* and camel meat in the evening. The only "**nightlife**" that merits the term is *La Sirène* disco, in the traditional fishing port by the beach, which serves alcohol, but only to foreigners.

Centre de Pàche, Baie d'Étoile. Fixed menu, always fish, and never less than expensive.

Clair de Lune, off bd Médian. Pleasant tea-room retreat with snack meals and inexpensive ice cream.

Restaurant El Ahrem, town centre, next to the Grand Marché. Egyptian-run restaurant popular with locals and visitors alike. Serves great fish and chips.

Restaurant Babylon, in the town centre by the police station. Currently the most popular in town with Western visitors. French-run with good cuisine.

Restaurant Miade, next to Galérie Mahfoud. A little cramped, but a pleasant atmosphere.

Restaurant de Sol, bd Médian, near *Abba's Hostel*. Very clean place with good service, improved considerably by a wine list. Korean and global cuisine.

Restaurant L'Union Nationale, town centre, near the Grand Marché. One of a number of places that do chicken and chips and Mauritanian staples.

Listings

Airline offices Air Mauritanie, bd Médian (☎745011 or 745450); Air Atlantique (☎ & Fax 746000). **Airport flight info** ☎745147.

American Express Try the SOPRAGE travel agency, bd Médian (BP 307; ☎745280).

Banks BMCI (BP 324; ☎745106; Fax 745628); BNM, bd Médian (BP 228; ☎745045; Fax 745573), usually gives the best rates.

Consulates Spanish, bd Médian (☎745371); Moroccan, off bd Médian, towards *Hôtel Maghreb* (☎745084); French honorary (☎745571).

Emergencies Police ☎745072; hospital ☎745288.

Around Nouadhibou, and the Banc d'Arguin National Park

The area's wonderful **beaches** and extraordinary wave- and wind-formed **scenery**, on both sides of the peninsula, are the most obvious attractions **around Nouadhibou**. Thirteen kilometres north of town, on the east side of the peninsula, there's delightful, sheltered swimming in the almost enclosed **Baie de l'Étoile**. The game fishing lodge *Centre de Pêche* is here, and you can get a drink or a meal.

On the western side of the peninsula, **La Gouera** (Laguéra, La Guera), a run-down Spanish fishing town almost swamped by sand, is technically part of Moroccan-occupied Western Sahara, but is now administered by Mauritania – a head-scratching arrangement that applies to the whole west side of the peninsula. There's good swimming in the sheltered bay behind **Faux Cap Blanc** but no entry to La Gouera itself.

The Nouadhibou area is the home of a colony of very rare Mediterranean **monk seals** (*phoques moines*), the lone males of which you're likely to see if you go down to the lighthouse at Cap Blanc. In appearance they resemble young elephant seals, growing to over two-and-a-half metres in length. Their valuable oil and skin has led to widespread extermination, but hunting them is now forbidden.

Intrepid birders should call at the head office of the **Banc d'Arguin National Park**, on Boulevard Médian near the PTT, in Nouadhibou (☎745085). The only national park in the country, Banc d'Arguin is one of the world's great bird breeding sites, with millions of water birds nesting and raising their chicks here from April to July and October to January. The migrants include greater (and, uncommonly, lesser) flamingos, both grey and white pelicans, white-breasted cormorants, several species of heron and egret, European spoonbills, grey-headed and unusual slender-billed gulls, Caspian, royal and gull-billed terns and several species of waders. Turnstones come here in winter to scavenge the eggs of tropical birds. Fortunately for the birds (regrettably for birders) the park is highly inaccessible and requires a major outlay in funds for the 4WD vehicles, boats and guides necessary to visit it. The entry fee is UM800 per person per day, and trips can be arranged or guides provided if you

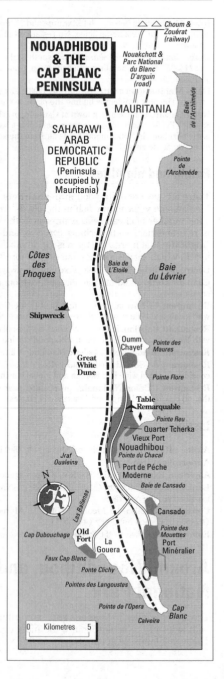

NOUADHIBOU & THE CAP BLANC PENINSULA

Nouakchott & Parc National du Blanc D'arguin (road)

△ △ *Choum & Zouérat (railway)*

MAURITANIA

Baie de l'Archimède

SAHARAWI ARAB DEMOCRATIC REPUBLIC (Peninsula occupied by Mauritania)

Pointe de l'Archimède

Côtes des Phoques

Baie de l'Etoile

Baie du Lévrier

Shipwreck

Oumm Chayef

Pointe des Maures

Great White Dune

Pointe Flore

Table Remarquable

Pointe Reu

Quarter Tcherka

Vieux Port

Nouadhibou

Pointe du Chacal

Jraf Oualeina

Port de Péche Moderne

Baie de Cansado

N

Las Ballenas

Cansado

Cap Dubouchage

Old Fort

La Gouera

Pointe des Mouettes

Port Minéralier

Faux Cap Blanc

Ponte Clichy

Pointes des Langoustes

Pointe de l'Opera

Cap Blanc

Calveire

0 Kilometres 5

have your own 4WD vehicle. This will only get you to the right area, however – the main Imragen villages of **Iouîk**, 200km south, or **Nouamghar**, about 250km south of Nouadhibou. To do some bird-watching you'll need to rent a boat and go out among the shallow seas and sand shoals.

THE IMRAGEN – LIFE IN THE DESERT WITH DOLPHINS

The Banc d'Arguin National Park contains the seven villages of the **Imragen**, an isolated group of five hundred **fishing people**. Their traditional harvest of yellow mullet is caught in November – the period when huge shoals of fish spawn amid the sea grass in the warm shallows. By what appears to be a remarkable feat of co-operation between humans and animals, the catch is brought to shore with the assistance of dolphins. Summoned by the Imragen beating the water surface from the shore, the dolphins drive the fish to the beach, where the mullet provide a feast for them and a tremendous haul for the villagers. Recent research suggests that yellow mullet may actually *like* swimming underneath pods of dolphins, so that the only human intervention is to signal to the dolphins the fish trap that is at their disposal. In any event, it's an extraordinary occasion, a spectacular chaos of leaping fish, thrashing cetaceans and ducking fishermen. Other Imragen fishing methods are less successful: they aren't skilled boatbuilders and they only have a few small vessels. Their survival on this barren shore is entirely dependent on an extractive economy, and even water has to be trucked into the villages from Nouakchott or Nouadhibou. The best windfalls are provided by ships scuppered offshore for insurance purposes. There are literally hundreds of these, providing fuel, building materials and occasionally more interesting bounty for the Imragen.

SENEGAL

SENEGAL

S enegal is the most French-influenced of all West Africa's Francophone countries. In 1658 the island of St-Louis became the first part of the continent to be colonized by the French, and there's an enduring relationship between the two countries. Partly as a result of this pervasive Europeanism – and in recent years a growing American cultural influence – you could breeze through Senegal and hardly notice anything distinctive about it. It is one of West Africa's biggest holiday destinations, with a fair number of beach hotels and holiday clubs, and until the Casamance conflict of the 1990s slowed the growth, attracted 200,000 visitors a year.

As soon as you start scraping away the French skin, however, a far more fascinating creature is revealed. The **Muslim marabouts** wield exceptional power in Senegal, commanding block votes at elections and even directing the course of the economy by their injunctions to followers. Although Islam in Senegal is quite different from its North African counterpart, the idea of a future Islamic state doesn't seem wholly fanciful. The name of **Touba**, the holy city of one of the most powerful Muslim brotherhoods, is one you'll see all over the country, incorporated into numerous names and signs.

French style and deeply felt Islam coexist with extraordinary success, though both elements are relatively recent introductions to most of Senegal. Islam did not have a wide reach until the end of the nineteenth century, while the French, although long-established in key towns on the coast, finally subdued parts of the interior as recently as the 1920s.

People

The people of Senegal are dominated by the biggest language group, the **Wolof**, who figure prominently in government and business and control the Mouride brotherhood. A clutch of Wolof kingdoms used to cover the heart of Senegal – an area now largely under fields of all-important **groundnuts** – in a highly stratified society based on class and caste differences. The first Muslims were the **Tukulor** and closely related **Fula** – people whose kingdom was in the northeast, which is still their heartland. The **Mandinka**, too, were widely converted to Islam before the Wolof. In the southwest, the

---

FACTS AND FIGURES

The Wolof have an apocryphal account of the derivation of the **name** *Senegal*, in which a witless explorer gestures across the Senegal River and asks some fishermen what it's called. "That? That's our boat" they reply – *li suñu gal le*. In fact the name probably derives from the **Sanhaja** Berbers who frequently raided the river region and were known by the early Portuguese explorers as *Azanaga*.

Today **La République du Sénégal** has a **population** of nearly nine million in an **area** of 196,000 square kilometres – roughly the size of England and Scotland combined, or half as big as California. The country's **foreign debt** totals more than £2 billion ($3.2 billion), a colossal figure in the West African context, and more than five times the annual value of its exports, but, to put it in a global context, Senegal's **political system**, a presidential democracy, is the longest practising multiparty democracy in West Africa (since 1981), though the ruling moderate Parti Socialiste has yet to be defeated at the much disputed polls.

Serer (Sérère) and **Jola** resisted Islam until the twentieth century – in parts they still do, preferring their indigenous religions – and they maintained more egalitarian, clan-based societies than the Wolof or the Muslim peoples. Christian missions have had a limited impact.

Today, most language groups are increasingly subject to **"Wolofization"** and a national Senegalese identity is emerging as people move to Dakar and other towns. More resilient have been the people of the south – the Jola (or Diola) of Casamance, and other scattered, largely non-Muslim, communities of Bassari, Bainuk, Konyagi and Jalonke.

Where to go

Senegal is one of the **flattest** countries in West Africa, rising to barely 500 metres in the Fouta Djalon foothills in the far southeast. Two main rivers, the Senegal and the Casamance, roughly mark the country's north and south limits, and the southern region is sliced through by The Gambia – the result of an asinine colonial carve-up in the 1890s.

From the travel and tourism perspective, Senegal is better organized than its neighbours: it's a country that's easy to get around, and one that's familiar with, and officially supportive of, independent travel. Since the devaluation of the CFA franc in 1994, it is one of West Africa's less expensive countries for visitors. It is also one of the freest countries with one of the region's best human rights records. But a land of contrasts it is not – flat and pale isn't unfair – and while there's some scenic variety to be sure, the country is most interesting at the cultural level.

The south, effectively screened from Dakar by The Gambia, provides the biggest attraction for travellers. The forests and mangrove creeks of the **Basse Casamance**, and the exceptional **beaches** of the short southern coastline, are the biggest pull – these combined with the largely non-Muslim culture of the Jola. The conflict between Casamance separatists and the government did not pose a major threat to travellers until the mid-1990s, but mines have been planted on many smaller roads and tracks in recent years and the dangers are now significant: intending travellers to the region should keep abreast of the situation. In the southeast, the **Niokolo-Koba National Park** is one of the best game reserves in West Africa, and from here it is well worth the effort to push on into the remote southeast corner of the country.

The attractions further **north** are round the edges: along the coast or up the Senegal River. **Dakar** – probably unavoidable, definitely two-faced – is a place to enter with some degree of caution. Yet for all its tough character, there are rewards in the city itself, and a number of good trips in the Dakar area. **St-Louis** is another ambiguous case, charged with atmosphere or depressingly run-down, as it strikes you. The upriver towns, small outposts along the Mauritanian border, are stopovers rather than ends in themselves.

Climate

Senegal's **climate** is one of the best in West Africa, with a short rainy season (*l'hiver-nage*) between June and September – or October in the south – and a dry period between December and April. The winds turn with the seasons, tending to blow warm and humid from the southwest during the rainy season, then hot, dry and dusty from the northeast and the Sahara (a wind known as the *Harmattan*) during the dry season. Early in the dry season, in December and January, Dakar and St-Louis can be surprisingly cool, especially at night. Through the rains, however, Dakar's combination of high humidity and city pollution can be pretty oppressive.

The weather needn't alter your travel plans as a rule, but you'll find some of the **national parks** closed during the wet season until tracks become passable again.

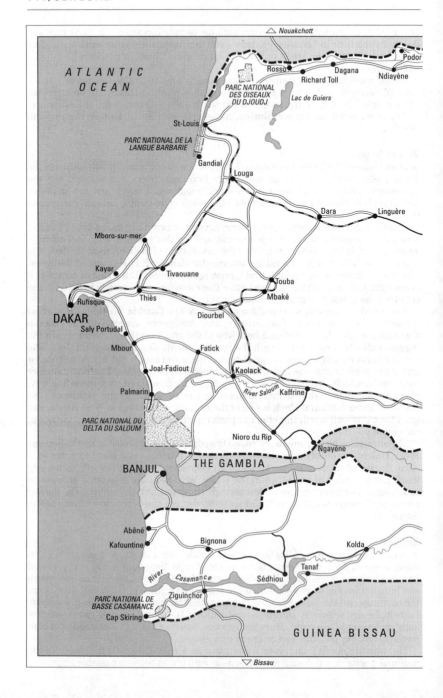

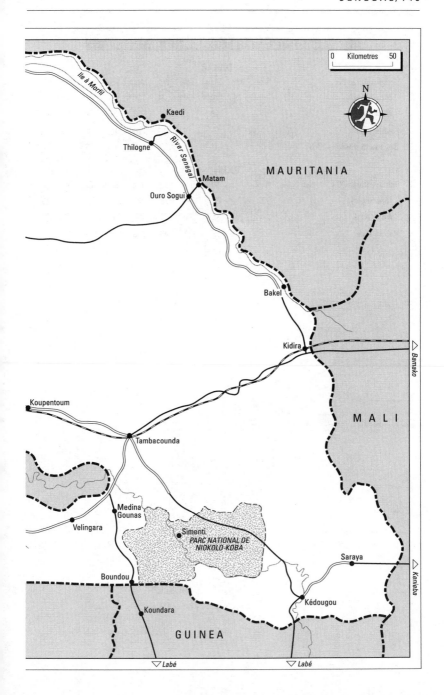

AVERAGE TEMPERATURES AND RAINFALL

DAKAR

Temperatures °C	Jan	Feb	Mar	Apr	May	June	July	Aug	Sept	Oct	Nov	Dec
Min (night)	18	17	18	18	20	23	24	24	24	24	23	19
Max (day)	26	27	27	27	29	31	31	31	32	32	30	27
Rainfall mm	0	0	0	0	0	18	89	254	132	38	3	8
Days with rainfall	0	0	0	0	0	2	7	13	11	3	0	1

ZIGUINCHOR

Temperatures °C	Jan	Feb	Mar	Apr	May	June	July	Aug	Sept	Oct	Nov	Dec
Min (night)	17	17	19	20	22	24	23	23	23	23	21	18
Max (day)	33	34	35	35	35	33	31	30	31	31	32	31
Rainfall mm	0	3	0	0	12	142	406	559	338	160	8	0

Arrivals

Dakar is a common starting and finishing post for overland travels, and in many ways the city feels like a stepping stone between Europe/America and Africa.

The details in these practical information pages are essentially for use on the ground in West Africa and in Senegal itself: for full practical coverage on preparing for a trip, getting here from outside the region, paperwork, health, information sources and more, see Basics pp.3–83.

■ Flights from Africa

The most useful flights from **North Africa** are direct flights from Tunis on Tunis Air (TU) via Casablanca, and from Casablanca via Nouakchott on Royal Air Maroc (AT).

There are direct flights to Dakar from every capital city in **West Africa**, with most of the few non-stop ones on Air Afrique (RK): daily or almost daily from Abidjan, Banjul and Conakry; and at least weekly from the other cities, including Praia on the Cape Verde Islands, which has four flights a week.

There are also good weekly connections from Nairobi and Johannesburg, both via Abidjan.

■ Overland

Senegal has for a number of years been a major overland terminus and departure point. These days, with the opening of the Atlantic route it is more of a crossroads.

The Atlantic Route via Mauritania

Since the early 1990s the **Atlantic Route** across the Sahara via the Moroccan-held Western Sahara to Mauritania has been open to all traffic. Military convoys depart twice a week (Tues & Fri) from **Dakhla** (1400km south of Rabat) escorting all vehicles through the sandy minefields just north of the Mauritanian port of **Nouadhibou**. From here an ore train can carry cars and passengers inland to the highway (14hr), or guides can lead suitable vehicles along the beach to the capital, **Nouakchott** (1–2 days). From Nouakchott it's just over 200km of reasonable tarmac to the Senegalese border at **Rosso** where a motor barge transports vehicles across the Senegal River. Other, less formal *pirogue*-crossings are possible upriver at Kaédi or Sélibaby.

From Mali by train

Most overland travellers arrive **from Mali** on the Océan-Niger **train**. Departures from Bamako are scheduled for **10am Wed & Sat**. It's a gruelling 30–36hr journey. Scheduled arrival time into Dakar is 4pm the following day, but the usual delays mean you're likely to arrive after dark.

Beware that **Muslim holidays**, and particularly the *Magal* (see the Islamic calendar on p.59), can alter train timetables.

An alternative is to take the train from Bamako only as far as **Tambacounda** (where it should arrive at around 7am), from where it's a hot, uninteresting, but quicker journey **by road** to Dakar.

Fares to Dakar range from around CFA23,000 2nd class, CFA31,000 1st class, to CFA47,500 sleeper. The Wed train from Bamako is air-conditioned, for which passengers pay a CFA4000 supplement. There are small **student reductions** in second class: it's worth paying the difference only if you want more leg-room and fewer companions. Once you're on the train, it's possible to upgrade to **sleeper class** assuming there are berths available (double cabins only), but the protracted border formalities take place during the night and require you to disembark, so you don't get much sleep in any case. There's a buffet car, serving snacks and drinks, and you can buy **street food** and drink from station vendors day and night.

From Mali by road

Driving from Bamako to Dakar is a feat of skill and endurance: the section from Bamako to Kayes via **Nioro** is notoriously sandy and the "direct route" via **Kita** requires a high-clearance vehicle. You can put your vehicle on the **train** to Dakar, but the hassle and expense makes the *piste* a far more interesting proposition for suitably prepared vehicles. There's a bridge, now, over the Faléme River on the Mali–Senegal border, where formerly the ford was regularly deeply flooded.

From Guinea-Bissau and Guinea

The principle route, now fully sealed, crosses into Senegal **from Guinea-Bissau** at **São Domingos**, direction Ziguinchor. Lesser crossings include Farim to Tanaf and Bafatá to Kolda.

Entering Senegal **from Guinea**, Koundara to Tambacounda is the usual route. A couple of spidery routes further east make the Labé to Kédougou crossing increasingly viable for suitable vehicles. You can expect daily transport except in the rainy season, when road problems will cause lengthy delays.

From The Gambia

Through traffic from Banjul **to Dakar** has increased over the last few years with a variety of buses and bush taxis making the trip from Barra on the north side of the Gambia River, facing Banjul. These are described in more detail in The Gambia chapter on p.235.

If the Basse Casamance is once again safe to visit, there are a variety of bush taxis from The Gambia **to Ziguinchor**, which leave from the main taxi park in Serrekunda market – 4hr by Peugeot 504, with border formalities at **Séléti** where there's usually little hassle. Make sure the Gambian officials stamp you in the right direction though – *Arrival* or *Departure*. If you're trying to visit the Casamance in a day-trip from a Gambian hotel, most taxi drivers will oblige – the fares to Ziguinchor and Cap Skiring are posted up. But Cap Skiring is really too far to do in a day: you'd be driving most of the time.

Red Tape

US citizens and British, Irish, French, Italian and German passport holders do not need visas to visit Senegal. Other EU passport holders too, should be exempt, but some officials may not be aware of this, and may try to insist you have a visa – in which case buy one at the airport or border.

Non-EU passport holders definitely need visas, but they're usually for multiple entry (ask) and can be issued quickly. Visa requirements are normally minimal and they can be obtained from Senegalese embassies or consulates in virtually every country in West Africa (see map on p.24).

For visas for **onward travel**, Dakar has embassies for most West African countries. Addresses and visa information are given on p.19.

A yellow fever **health certificate** is obligatory, even if you're flying in direct from Europe, though there's sometimes a negotiable line between what's stipulated by the Ministry of Health and

what's demanded by the official at the arrivals desk.

Money and Costs

Senegal's currency is the CFA franc (CFA100 always equals 1 French franc; approx CFA900 = £1; approx CFA560 = US$1. As in other CFA countries, carrying your money in French franc travellers' cheques makes most sense, but changing money in Senegal can be very difficult, so be sure to have French francs on you outside of Dakar, where banks are scarce and clerks unfamiliar with most other foreign currencies. Since devaluation, even French francs are commissionable when changed at some banks. There should be fewer problems in Dakar, as the city is one of the region's main financial centres.

If you're staying in Senegal for some time, or basing yourself in Dakar, opening a **bank account** with one of the main banks is effective, though not simple. It's better to have your bank open an account for you in advance – then you can take your account number to the bank in Senegal on their letter.

Banks tend to be closed from 11.30am until 2.30 or 3pm. The only out-of-hours exchange facilities are the normally exploitive hotel desks. There are 24hr **auto-tellers** at the BICIS banks in Dakar, St Louis, Mbour and Thiès.

Credit cards are of more use than in other countries, with Visa and MasterCard/Access leading the field for tourist services, car rental, fancy restaurants and flashier shops. **Cash advances** on Visa can be arranged through the SGBS and BICIS banks; travellers' cheques may be bought using **Amex** through Senegal Tours in Dakar (see p.189).

■ Costs

Fortunately for visitors, since devaluation in 1994, the country is no longer expensive. **Hotels** will cost you from around CFA10,000/day in Dakar (about £11/US$18), and even less outside the capital. A further boon for travellers in Casamance is the region's system of *campements touristiques rurals integrés* (CTRI), for more on which see p.152. Camping is also feasible in many places. **Travelling costs**, when you've taken baggage into account, are usually around

CFA1500 per100km. An ISIC student card is useful for reduced entry fees to sites and museums and worth trying for possible **discounts** on trains and planes.

Health

One of the most comfortable countries in West Africa, Senegal doesn't pose too many health problems. It's mostly dry, seasonally mild (at least along the coast), and has a relatively well-developed healthcare infrastructure.

Dakar used to be the place to convalesce from the diseases of the interior. Nowadays, however, if you're getting over something, perhaps you should find a resting-up spot away from the city. Many Dakarois have year-round colds and the city has the country's highest typhoid levels – attributed to exhaust fumes, industrial air pollution and the 1400 tonnes of garbage produced every day.

If you're basing yourself – or staying some time – in the Dakar area, especially during the cool, dry season from December to March, you may prefer to forget about **malaria** prophylaxis. Local doctors often insist it's more harmful than beneficial, and many expat residents don't bother – certainly the mosquito problem is minimal at this time of year. However, as soon as you move on, heading into the backcountry, especially in forested or watered areas, you expose yourself to risk again, a risk that is higher if you've broken your course.

Town **water** from taps is normally fine, though the Senegalese have taken to Evian and their own Montrolland bottled water with enthusiasm. From shops it's not too expensive; from hotels and bars usually much more. As in the other Sahel countries, seasonal drought means insufficient washing water. Away from large towns try to check on the provenance of the water used (if any) to wash your plate and glass in eating houses.

Water-borne schistosomiasis (**bilharzia**) poses no threat in the brackish tidal waters of the lower Casamance, Saloum and Senegal rivers (though the lower reaches of the Senegal are much less brackish, and thus more dangerous, since dams came into operation upstream). Make sure, nevertheless, that you're sufficiently downriver for it to be salty before plunging in.

Senegal has a higher than usual incidence of **diphtheria**. If you're not sure whether you were immunized as a child (possibly not if you were born after 1970), check with your doctor before leaving home.

In the north along the river, especially around Rosso, there are occasional outbreaks of **"arbovirus"** diseases – similar to yellow fever but with no antivirus available. Check locally. All you can do is try to avoid being bitten by insects.

Like much of West Africa, Senegal has become fully aware of the threat of **AIDS** and there's a massive anti-SIDA campaign. Needless to say, use prudence, and never have unprotected sex.

Maps and Information

Before you go, you can collect maps and information from your nearest Senegalese embassy; the Paris office is the big one. As well as a variety of tourist brochures, they may also have copies of the free monthly listings and adverts pamphlet "Le Dakarois", also available in Dakar itself.

You're best advised to stock up on **maps** before you arrive in Senegal, where they're hard to find and expensive. The IGN **Senegal** map at 1cm:10km is useful, and its companion 1cm:100m **Dakar** is invaluable in the city. There are also some moderately useful **regional survey maps** that you'll only find in specialist shops.

Getting Around

Compared with many parts of West Africa, Senegal is easy to get around: bush taxis will get you nearly everywhere; plane, train and even boat are all viable options, and hitching is possible in some areas. With over 4000km of blacktop, Senegal has one of West Africa's better tarred road networks. For the rest, flat landscapes make for lots of passable, if monotonous and dusty, pistes.

■ Bush taxis and buses

Most **public transport** is by bush taxi (**taxi brousse**). This may be (in descending order of price) a 7-seat Peugeot 504, a *car* (a white, ageing Saviem or Mercedes minibus), a *camion bâché* (covered pick-up van) or a *car rapide* (blue and yellow minibus). You'll travel fastest and most comfortably in a 504, as long as you're not too tall or squashed in the back. Minibuses are better for shorter journeys and give more opportunity to soak up Senegalese life.

Autogares, or **gares routières** are usually well organized, and the drivers (or their assistants) will always find you before you find them. Most of the motorable roads on the IGN map of Senegal get at least one vehicle of some description every day.

Real 40-plus-seater **buses** operate on a few routes but, apart from in Dakar, where there's an excellent bus system, they are not likely to figure much in your travels.

Fares, routes and frequencies

What follows is a **summary** of transport availability out of the capital and around Senegal.

The busiest road in the country is the **Dakar–Kaolack–Ziguinchor** route, part of which forms the *transgambienne* highway. For years this has been bedevilled with chronically unreliable **ferries** over the Gambia River between Farafenni and Soma, but now there are two new ferries and the crossing is effected in five minutes. Droves of *taxis brousse* use this route (departure is before noon, journey time 7hr plus).

The old route to **Ziguinchor via Barra and Banjul** (around 5 ferries daily each way between 8am and 7pm; 30min) is much less important as a transit route.

Thiès is an important transport hub, with a constant stream of vehicles running up from

Dakar (1hr) until late in the day. With a morning departure from Dakar you can also go straight through to **St-Louis** (3hr plus) and **Rosso** (5hr plus).

St-Louis is the transport focus of the north. There are departures all day for **Rosso**, **Richard Toll** and **Dakar**, but destinations further upriver are served only by a few early morning departures and require vehicle changes in each major town.

Eastwards, a good number of vehicles make a living on the **Tambacounda** road, despite the train. You can easily make it there in a day if you get down to the Dakar *autogare* early. Continuing to the **Kédougou** district in far southeastern Senegal, you'll be relying mostly on Tambacounda-based vehicles, which are few and far between.

The **Tambacounda–Ziguinchor** road is mostly quiet – and on this route too you'll need to make an early start.

■ Car rental

Spectacularly expensive for leisure travel, **car rental** in Senegal is really only worth considering for special targets which might otherwise be inaccessible (national parks, for example), and even then most realistically as a group of three or four travellers. The **main agents** for Avis (the biggest), Hertz and Europcar (one or more in Dakar, Ziguinchor, Cap Skiring and St-Louis) provide the guarantee of a reputable name and the chance to pay by plastic, but the all-in cost for a Renault 5 or something similar, assuming 1000km and including fuel, will work out around **£500 ($800) per week** and isn't negotiable. Daily rates are fractionally more than pro rata, a weekend's rental costs slightly less. There's a ban on driving off the sealed highways and a minimum age of 25. National driving licences held for one year are sufficient, but don't be surprised if an **international drivers' licence** is specifically demanded if you're stopped.

If you're not concerned about going with a big-name firm, it's worth checking out some of the **local car rental places** which are usually willing to negotiate, can be persuaded to give you unlimited mileage and aren't so fussy about off-road driving. They may work out less than half the price of the big agencies. A weekend is frequently the best deal, and a convenient length of time for many trips. Don't forget possible extras (*frais non-inclus*),

---

FARES

Current Peugeot fares from Dakar:
Karang (for Banjul) CFA3100; Kédougou CFA10,100; Kolda CFA6000; Mbour CFA900; St-Louis CFA2900; Tambacounda CFA6300; Thiès CFA800; Touba CFA2200; Ziguinchor CFA5400.

From Ziguinchor:
Séléti (for Serrekunda) CFA1400.

12-seater **minibuses** are about fifteen percent cheaper; 25-seater minibuses about thirty percent cheaper.

In Senegal it's usual to pay the bush taxi before the journey has finished, and often before it's even started. Don't pay, however, unless it's at least half full and other passengers have done so. It's also better to find out what the fare should be ahead of time as anyone who looks like a stranger is often a target for overcharging. Baggage supplements, which should be haggled over vigorously, can add about ten percent per large item.

such as collision damage waiver and twenty percent tax.

■ Trains

There's now only one main railway line: the **eastern Océan-Niger service** via Thiès, Diourbel and Tambacounda (see p.147 for details). The **northern service**, which used to run daily between Dakar and St-Louis, has been indefinately suspended, although it will still operate in heavy traffic times such as Christmas, and perhaps St-Louis' annual Jazz festival.

Dakar itself has its own Mon–Sat commuter service (**le petit train bleu**) running to and from **Tiaroye** and **Rufisque** several times during morning and evening rush hours (30min).

■ Hitching

Because of the number of private vehicles and expats in Senegal, and a relatively high volume of tourist traffic, **hitching** on some of the main routes is an option worth trying. Moreover, if you're stuck on a minor turn-off, trying to wave down passing vehicles is less frustrating than simply waiting for the day's bush taxi service. However, you do need to be clear that you're hitching, as some drivers may be offering their services for payments at much higher rates than you would pay for any type of public transport.

In decreasing order of feasibility, there are fair chances of lifts around the Dakar suburbs, to destinations on the coasts south and north of Dakar; and from Tambacounda to Dakar and into the Niokolo-Koba National Park. Before the unrest began, there were also reasonable hitching opportunities in the Basse Casamance.

■ Internal flights

Air Sénégal operates a few flights round the country from Dakar, but it's not a frequent enough service to be much competition for bush travel. Services include daily flights to **Ziguinchor** (returning on Tues, Wed and Thurs, sometimes via Banjul), and flights four times a week to **Cap Skiring** via Ziguinchor. Flights to **St-Louis** operate on Mon and Fri, and every Sat, there's a flight to **Tambacounda** and **Kédougou** which sometimes calls at **Simenti** in the Niokolo-Koba National Park.

Rough round-trip **fares** are CFA50,000 to Ziguinchor and CFA99,000 to Cap Skiring (during the season). Air Sénégal offers a whole range of discounts for students, groups and so on.

■ Other options

The MV *Joola* **steamer** operates twice a week between Dakar and Ziguinchor (17hr), while the new *Kassoumay* **catamaran** does the journey in just six hours, three days a week (see p.188). Smaller and more exclusive pleasure boats ply the waters of the Saloum and Senegal deltas; if you're interested, staying in the right hotels in those areas will give you rapid access. There's no steamer service higher up the Senegal or the Casamance rivers, though you can usually cross by *pirogue* and there's ample opportunity to arrange your own **river transport** locally. The Senegal is navigable all year by small boats as far as Kidira; the Casamance beyond Sédhiou.

A characteristically Senegalese form of transport is the horse- or mule-drawn two-wheel buggy called a **calèche**, which you'll see all over the north and centre but not south of The Gambia (because of tsetse fly). They're often used as town taxis in smaller places, ferrying goods and people from the *autogare*.

At several *campements* in Basse Casamance you can rent **bicycles** – not very rideable ones, admittedly, and most don't have refinements such as gears, but they make a welcome change of pace. Buying the commonly seen blue single-speed bicycles, complete with dynamo lights, mudguards, side stand, a chunky steel rack and a huge sprung saddle, will cost the equivalent of around £130 ($200). You can also rent (or buy) **mobylettes** in some towns in Casamance.

Accommodation

For the most part, accommodation in Senegal is sophisticated and wide-ranging. With the exception of youth hostels, most overnight options are available.

■ Hotels

Most large towns have several decent **hotels**. Coming overland from one of its neighbours, Senegalese establishments seem, on the whole, plush and heavily Europeanized. In the higher price brackets, if they're not actually part of a chain, they're very often French- or Lebanese-owned or managed. And a surprising number of quite modest places turn out to have French hands behind the scenes.

CFA8000 is about the bottom line for the most basic lodging (CFA5000 is possible but most likely to be a brothel too), while CFA15,000 is a more typical price for often unremarkable amenities. There is a **tourist tax** too, of CFA600 per person per night, sometimes included in the room charge, more often added to the bill afterwards.

■ Campements Touristiques Rurals Integrés

An important and gratifying exception to the ordinary hotels is the Senegalese network of **campements touristiques rurals integrés** (CTRIs) established by the Ministry of Tourism over the last 25 years to cater for smaller budgets and less mainstream requirements. Built by villagers with loans from central funds, often in a traditional architectural style, the *campements* theoretically bring tourist money into parts of the rural economy that don't usually benefit.

Facilities at the CTRIs, though basic, are adequate, and include European plumbing, cold running water, kerosene lighting, three-course meals, and cold drinks from a gas fridge. They provide mosquito nets and foam mattresses and sheets. For the same charge you can always camp outside. **Prices** are the same at all CTRIs and you can pay for accommodation only, or as many meals as you want. At the time of writing, costs are as follows: FB at CFA9800; bed only CFA3000; breakfast CFA1800; each meal CFA2500. Many CTRIs fill up over the Nov–Feb

peak season, so it's well worth **booking** in advance. Contact the Service Regional du Tourism, Ziguinchor (☎991 12 68) or Ministère du Tourisme des Transports Aeriens, Dakar (☎821 11 26; Fax 822 94 13; *mtta@primature.sn*). In recent years the laudable aims and popularity of the CTRI system have taken a beating from near-identical *campements* set up by private (and often more motivated) owners. These *campements* offer similar or often better facilities, sometimes at a slightly lower price.

■ Other accommodation

Camping out in the bush is normally feasible in Senegal, where there's a fairly indulgent attitude to the eccentricities of foreigners: the French community has been doing it for years. Be sure, though, that you're out of any urban "zone of influence" where you might conceivably be putting yourself at risk of robbery. The Dakar region, and the towns in the groundnut basin – Thiès, Diourbel and Kaolack – are areas to avoid, as are the beaches. Senegal has no formal camp-sites.

Staying with people frequently comes out of efforts to camp on their land – even if it's not demarcated. Rewarding areas for such contacts lie throughout southern Senegal east of Ziguinchor – a region which, except for the Niokolo-Koba park, gets very few visitors, and virtually none who stay.

ACCOMMODATION PRICE CODES

All accommodation prices in this chapter – the same scales in terms of their pound/dollar equivalents as used throughout the book – are coded according to the following scales. Prices refer to the rate you can expect to pay for a room with two beds. Single rooms, or single occupancy, will normally cost at least two-thirds of the twin-occupancy rate. For further details see p.48.

① **Under CFA4500 (under £5/$8)**. Simplest private *campement* accommodation, or rudimentary, small-town hotel.

② **CFA4500–9000 (£5–10/$8–16)**. CTRI *campements*, basic town hotel, or better quality provincial hotel. Some self-contained rooms (S/C) and possibly some with AC.

③ **CFA9000–18,000 (£10–20/$16–32)**. Decent hotel, usually with S/C rooms, some with AC.

④ **CFA18,000–27,000 (£20–30/$32–48)**. Good business or tourist-class hotel with better than adequate facilities, including a restaurant.

⑤ **CFA27,000–36,000 (£30–40/$48–64)**. S/C, AC rooms are the norm, with extra facilities such as a pool and restaurant likely.

⑥ **CFA36,000–45,000 (£40–50/$64–80)**. First-class hotel, with good range of facilities.

⑦ **Over CFA45,000 (over £50/$80)**. Luxury establishment (prices up to £150/$240 in some cases).

Some resort hotels have two rates – high season from November to Easter, and low season roughly from May to October. Price codes are for the higher rate.

Eating and Drinking

Senegal has some of West Africa's best food, giving opportunities for everything from serious dining to snacking on street food. Restaurants in the larger towns and main hotels incline towards French style, offering a menu (three courses or more, and usually a choice) and a *plat du jour* (main dish only). Predictably there's lots of tough steak and chips, heavy sauces and imported canned food. For a menu expect to pay CFA4500–6000, and upward of CFA3500 for the *plat*. There are some decent French restaurants, and a few other exotic eating houses as well, but with a few exceptions they're an unmemorable lot. The better value venues are covered in the chapter.

■ Dishes

Indigenous Senegalese food is the most interesting: you can often eat best – certainly in Dakar – by going to one of the cheapest places, and simply eating what's offered. Most of what you'll find has heavy North African and Middle Eastern influence, with lots of seafood, mutton and Lebanese snacks. If you've been travelling elsewhere in West Africa you'll notice the near absence of plantains and root crops, and palm oil is used much less than in the southern coastal countries. The **basics**, though, as everywhere, are starch – usually rice – and spicy sauces, though the key word is aroma rather than pungency.

The national dish, eaten every day by millions of Senegalese, is **chep-bu-jen** (spelled variously as *cep-bou-dien* and *tiéboudienne*), Wolof for "rice-with-fish". This can be anything from plain rice with boiled fish and a few carrots to a glorious kind of paella with spiced rice and half a dozen vegetables. There's no fixed recipe, but it's virtually the only common meal that usually comes with vegetables.

Stuffed fish (**poisson farci**), which is an ingredient of the best *chep-bu-jen*, is associated with St-Louis and sometimes denoted *à la saint-louisienne*. Done properly, the result can be delicious. The mullet (the variety usually used) is filleted and flayed, leaving the skin whole: the flesh is then chopped finely, spiced and herbed, sewn up inside the skin and the whole package baked.

Varieties of **yassa** – a Casamançais dish – are characteristic of most menus too. Traditionally it uses **chicken**, but any animal ingredient qualifies so long as it is marinated at length in lemon juice, pepper and onions.

Riz Jollof – a mound of vegetables and meat in an oily tomato sauce on rice, named after the old Wolof kingdom – is common here, as it is all over West Africa.

Other sauces include **Mafé** and **Domodah** based loosely around tomatoes and groundnuts. The latter, so peanutty in The Gambia, is sometimes nut-less in Senegal. Both are best with beef or fish. **Soupe kanje** is a sauce made from okra (gumbo, ladies' fingers) with fish and palm oil.

You'll come across lots of places serving **couscous** (or *basi-salete*), though this is traditionally considered a festive meal and eaten at the Muslim New Year. Comprising steamed grains of millet flour with a smothering of vegetables, mutton and gravy, it's best by far when you're very hungry.

Méchoui, a whole roast sheep, is one for *Tabaski* – the *Fête des moutons*.

Away from the main growing areas in the south, **fruit** tends to be expensive: oranges imported from Morocco, Ivoirian pineapples and French apples. The best stuff is found in the Casamance, where you should look for unusual wild fruits.

■ Breakfast and snacks

The great French bequest, as always, is their **bread**, consumed in vast quantities. *Pain beurre* and *café au lait* is the ubiquitous **breakfast** and roadside snack, often with real butter. Be warned, though, in some places the Nescafé is often unrelated to what you'll find in, say, Mali, Burkina or Niger, as it's made with an infusion like weak tea, from a shrub called **kenkeliba** (or *quinceliba*). Mild and indifferently nutty when mixed with sweet milk or just on its own, *kenkeliba* acquires a revolting flavour when mixed with Nescafé. Specify "made with water" if you want Nescafé proper. *Kenkeliba* bars are known as **tangana** – which literally means "it's hot".

For **snacks** in towns you'll often end up in a **chawarma bar**. *Chawarma*, like doner kebabs, are shreds of barbecued compressed mutton cut from a roll, wrapped in a pitta bread. They're normally a dependable standby, and very cheap. Alternatives include *merguez* (spicy sausage), *kofta* (meat balls), *fataya* (mince and onion pies), *nems* (like a pancake roll made of vermicelli pastry) and of course **brochettes** of grilled meat.

In the suburbs and countryside the **dibiterie** takes over. Roadside or market stalls, *dibiteries* are

WOLOF FOOD TERMS

The list below will help you ask for and identify food in out-of-the-way places. For more Wolof, see p.156.

bey/sikket	goat	*mburu*	bread
chep/maalo	rice	*meew*	fresh milk
chere	couscous/millet	*nag*	beef
chwi	stew	*ndox*	water
dom/garap	fruit	*nen*	egg
dugub	millet	*nex-na*	good (referring to food)
gejj	dried fish	*nyam dunde*	food
genar	chicken	*nyebe*	beans
gerte	groundnuts	*sangara*	alcohol, spirits
jen	fish	*soble*	onions
jernat	sorghum millet	*soow*	sour milk
kaani	hot pepper	*suukar*	sugar
lem	honey	*suuna*	bulrush millet
lemnad	soft drink	*tomate*	tomato
makka	corn	*xiif*	hunger
mar	thirst	*xorom*	salt
mbaam	pork	*yappa*	meat
mbum	boiled leaves	*yappi xar*	mutton

There are various **wild fruits**, sold seasonally in the markets:

ditak	oval, pebble-like fruit, with thin, dry skin and aromatic, acid green flesh surrounding a fibrous seed, some times made into a drink: very common in Casamance	*solon*	brown, pea-sized berry, with furry (edible) skin and a black seed
		cerise	tart, green "cherry"
		nuul	fruit from oil nut palm tree
		dimbu	medium size, green, soft fruit with a vegetable taste

really butcher's shops, where you can choose your flank of flesh which is then chopped and barbecued on the spot and served with a few slithers of raw onion. It's said that flies are attracted to the best cuts, so take their choice as a recommendation.

■ Drinking

Flag is Senegal's **beer**, and not at all bad. It comes in two-thirds and third-litre bottles, and the price depends on where you buy it – any bar that sells only the small size is going to be expensive. A quite acceptable alternative, assuming you're in need of refreshment rather than intoxication, is the far less alcoholic Gazelle (large size only), which tends to be one of the cheapest bottled drinks you can buy.

Wine is available in groceries in most town centres, and tends to be about twice the French price. **Palm wine** costs next to nothing but you need to be in Casamance and friendly with the owner of a tree.

Non-alcoholic alternatives to bottled sodas and mineral water are plastic bags of **iced fruit drinks**: hibiscus syrup (*bisap*), ginger water, **bouille** (sherbety baobab juice) or tamarind juice. If you're interested in unusual tastes, seek out *njamban* – a concoction of tamarind juice, smoked fish, salt and cayenne pepper. Mellower are **thiacry**, a mixture of *couscous*, sour milk and sugar that's closer to a dessert than a drink, and **lakh** – millet, sour milk, sugar and orange water. In many parts Sahelian **tea** – tongue-liftingly strong and sweet – is a much loved refreshment.

Communications – Post, Phones, Language and Media

Post offices (PTTs), normally open Mon–Fri **7.30am–4pm** plus Sat morning, operate with

Senegal's IDD code is ☎221.

grinding, morose efficiency. Senegalese mail is expensive, and overseas delivery from Dakar (where the central PTT has long hours) is slow.

Getting mail at **poste restante** may require infinite patience: letters commonly take two to three weeks to find their box in the Dakar poste restante, and are then only held for a month.

Phoning home costs around CFA750/minute to both Britain and the US. Shop around – some of the *télécentres* are much cheaper than others. Americans, in common with several other nation-alities, can make collect calls (PCV) – a service not available to Britain.

Centres téléphoniques – where you make your call from a metered booth and pay for it at the end – are now found in even the smallest towns. **Fax machines** are also often available for receipt and transmission at the same *centres*.

Internet cafés are springing up in Dakar, charging around CFA1500–2000/hour (see p.188). One has also opened in Thiès.

■ Languages

Though only twenty percent of the population has any fluency in the colonial tongue, communication will rarely be a problem if you speak French to

---

SENEGALESE TERMS – A GLOSSARY

Common words and expressions, French and Wolof.

Bana Bana wandering street vendor

Baye Fall zealous disciples of Mouridism, dressed in brilliantly coloured patchwork cloaks, often seen collecting money for their marabout

Bolon(g) mangrove creek (Casamance)

Borom *patron*, chief, owner

Boubou long gown worn by men and women

Ceddo traditional Wolof warrior caste

Clando clandestine bar for Muslim hypocrites

Damel pre-Islamic Wolof kings

Dara pioneering settlements of Mouride disciples

Dibiterie roadside butcher and barbecue artist

Djigeen woman

Fatou somewhat derogatory as it's a woman's name: means domestic servant or "girl"

Filao casuarina tree; a kind of weeping fir

La Fleuve "The River" – the Senegal River

Fromager silk-cotton tree or kapok

Gewel griot; praise singer, musician storyteller

Goor man/male

Gue ford, river crossing

Hajj/El Hajj the pilgrimage to Mecca/one who has been on the pilgrimage

Herbe Qui Tu grass, cannabis

HLM "Habitations à Loyer Modérés" – council flats, housing projects

Jeu de Dames draughts, checkers; a more com-petitive game than *wure*

Keur/kerr/ker place, home

Magal annual mass pilgrimage to Touba on the occasion of Cheikh Amadou Bamba's birthday

Maquis cheap place to eat

Marabout enormously powerful religious leader accredited with magical powers

Mbalax music – modern expression of tradi-tional roots rhythms

Mouridiya one of the two most powerful Islamic orders; headquarters near Touba

PDS Parti Démocratique Sénégalais, the main opposition party

Planton orderly, watchman, dogsbody

PS Parti Socialiste, the ruling party, though it has no socialist agenda

Radio Kankan public rumour

Sandarma *gendarme*

Sayisayi playboy

Sopi "Change", the slogan of the main political opposition alliance

Talibe disciple of a marabout

Teranga hospitality, generosity; sums up the Wolof code of behaviour to strangers

Tijaniya numerically the largest Islamic broth-erhood divided into dynasties, some of which are fundamentalist in nature; headquarters at Tivaouane

Touba the holy city east of Dakar; also means "happiness"

Toubab foreigner, usually white; from the Wolof "to convert"; you'll hear it a lot from kids.

Wure game of pebbles/seeds and holes

Yamba cannabis

ELEMENTARY WOLOF

Wolof (sometimes *Ouolof* or *Volof* to the French) is understood by an estimated fifty percent of Senegalese. Perhaps two-thirds of these are ethnic Wolof, the rest are mother tongue speakers of other languages, all of which are losing ground. Wolof is growing in importance all the time and there are regular calls for it to be adopted as the official national language. Wolof is classified as a "West Atlantic" language, in the same large basket of "class languages" as Fula and Serer, quite different from the "non-class" Mande languages like Mandinka, Bambara and Dyula. The main criterion for this classification is the grammatical system of Wolof, which groups nouns into fairly arbitrary classes something like genders. There's the usual confusion over **spellings** created by British and French transcribers using their own norms, but the following selection should be quite pronounceable. The letter "x" denotes a throaty "h" sound like the ch in loch. A double vowel simply lengthens the same sound, while a double consonant makes it harder.

GREETINGS

All purpose greeting...	*Salaam malekum*	How are you all?	*Naka waa keur ga?*
...and response	*Malekum salaam*		(formal)
How are you?	*Nanga def?*	How are your family	*Ana sa wa ker?*
I'm fine (lit. I'm here only)	*Mangi fii rek*	/home/people?	
How are you? (lit.	*Jama ngaam?*	(very informal)	
Do you have peace?)		They're fine	*Nyung fa*
I'm fine (lit. Peace only)	*Jama rek* (can be	Thank you	*Jerejef*
	used as the	What's your name?	*Naka nga tudd?*
	response to any	My name is Dave	*Mangi tudd Dave*
	greeting)	What is your surname?	*Naka nga santa?*
Thank God	*Alhamdoulila*	My surname is Warne	*Mangi santa Warne*
Good morning	*Jamanga fanaan?*	Goodbye (I'm off)	*Mangi dem*
(lit. did you sleep well?)			

GENERAL PRACTICALITIES

I don't understand Wolof/	*Man deguma*	Right	*Ndeyjoor*
French	*Wolof/Faranse*	Left	*Chamong*
Please repeat	*Wahat ko*	Far	*Sori*
Yes	*Waaw*	Slowly	*Ndanka*
No	*Deedeet*	Please (lit. If you want)	*Su la nexe*
Perhaps	*Xey na*	I don't mind/I don't care	*Ana sema yon*
Where is . . .?	*Ana. . .?*	When?	*Kan?*
Where are you going?	*Fan nga dem nii?*	No problem	*Anul sono*
Where is the road to Dakar?	*Yoni Dakar fan*	Wife	*Djabar/sohna*
	la?	Husband	*Jeker*

PLACES

Market	*Marse*	Bed	*Lall*
Village	*Deuke ko*	Field	*Toll*
House/Family compound	*Keur*	Forest/bush	*All*
Room	*Neeg*		

DAYS

Today	*Tey*	Monday	*Altine*	Thursday	*Alxemes*
Saturday	*Aseer*	Tuesday	*Telata*	Friday	*Ajuma*
Sunday	*Dibeer*	Wednesday	*Alarba*		

NUMBERS

1	*bena*	4	*nyenent*	7	*jerom nyar*	10	*fuka*
2	*nyar*	5	*jerom*	8	*jerom nyeta*	11	*fuka bena* (etc)
3	*nyeta*	6	*jerom bena*	9	*jerom nyenent*	20	*nyar fuka/nit*

21	*nyar fuka bena*	40	*nyenent fuka*	70	*jerom nyar fuka*	100	*temer*
	(etc)	50	*jerom fuka*	80	*jerom nyeta fuka*	1000	*june*
30	*nyet fuka/fanver*	60	*jerom bena fuka*	90	*jerom nyenent fuka*		

BUYING

Give me/sell me...	*Mai ma/jai ma...*	It's much too expensive	*Dafa ser torop*
I want /I don't want...	*Bognaa/boguma ...*	Cheap	*Yombe na*
Enough	*Doi na*	Expensive	*Ser*
More, again	*Dolili*	Not expensive	*Serut*
A little	*Tutti*	Money	*Xalis*
Lots of	*Yu bare*	Lower the price (a little)	*Wanil ko (tutti)*
Full	*Fes*	You're killing me!	*Hey! Yangi ma rey!*
That's all	*Bah na*	Leave me alone, I'm	*Baye ma, dama sona*
How much is that?	*Bi nyata le?*	fed up/tired	
It's too expensive	*Dafa ser*	Gift	*Ndimbal*

OTHER NEEDS

Please give me some water	*Mai man ndox bu la nexe*	I've got a stomach ache	*Suma biir day metti*
I'm hungry	*Dama xiif*	Show me the way to the post office	*Won ma yonu post bi*
What would you like to eat?	*Loo buga leka?*	What would you like?	*Lan nga bugg?*
I'm sleepy	*Dama neleew*	Do you have a little bit of aspirin?	*Amuloo tutti aspirin?*
I'm going to sleep	*Mangi neleew*		
I'm going to sleep now! (and leave me alone!)	*Mangi neleew waay!*	Do you smoke?	*Ndax dingay toox?*
		Do you drink palm wine?	*Ndax dingay naan sung?*
Where are you going?	*Fooy dem?*		
Are you going to the market?	*Ndax marse ngay dem?*	I don't have any money	*Amuma xalis*
		Someone's waiting for me	*Am naa ku may xaar*
I feel ill	*Dama feebar*		

EMERGENCIES

Thief!	*Sachee!*	Call the police/ a doctor quickly!	*Woo wall police/medecin gewal legi legi!*
S/he's ill!	*Dafa feebar!*		

TREES

Baobab	*Gouigi*	Mandingo	*Jorut*
Silk-cotton (kapok)	*Bentenki*	Kola Oil	*Netetu*
Raffia palm	*Bari*	Palm	*Tabu*
Locust bean	*Tir*		

ANIMALS

Horse	*Fas*	Lion	*Gawnde/daba*	Hyena	*Buki*	Monitor lizard	*Mbeutt*
Camel	*Guelem*	Leopard	*Tenev*	Porcupine	*Sav*	Gecko	*Onka*
Goat	*Bei*	Monkey	*Golo*	Ostrich	*Baa*	Snake	*Jan*
Pig	*Mbam*	Elephant	*Nye*	Pelican	*Jagabar*	Tortoise	*Mbonat*
Cow	*Nak*	Hippopotamus	*Leber*	Crocodile	*Jasik*		
Bull	*Yek*	Large antelope	*Koba*	Chameleon	*Kakatar*		

SIMPLE SERER

Hello	*Nafio*	Yes, they have peace	*Wamaha*	No	*Ha a*
I'm fine	*Miheme*			Coconut	*Koko*
Does your family live in peace?	*Fambina?*	Goodbye	*Mereta*	Rice	*Tju*
		Thank you	*Dkoka djal*		
		Yes	*Lo*		

some degree. (English alone won't get you far.) You'll have a far better time, however, if you know some **Wolof**. It's not an easy language, but making the effort to say even a few simple greetings will gratify people out of all proportion to your ability.

Wolof is not the whole story. Important minority vernaculars include: **Fula** (Pulaar), spoken by the Tukulor and Fula (or Peul); **Serer**, spoken by the partly Christianized people of the same name; **Kriyol**, a Portuguese creole spoken by up to 50,000 people along the coast south of Dakar; **Jola**, spoken in various dialects in the Casamance region; the **Mande** languages (Mandinka/Malinké, Bamana and Sarakolé/Soninké), spoken in scattered communities across the south and east; and the languages of the **Tenda** group – Konyagi, Bedik, Bassari. All are a major component of ethnic identity, especially so in the case of Jola (for a **Jola glossary** see p.219).

■ The media

Language politics are reflected in Senegalese government **radio**. French is the official language but programmes, more or less, reflect the ethnolinguistic diversity of the country with broadcasting in Wolof, Fula, Serer, Mandinka, Jola and Sarakolé/Soninké. The number of stations has increased considerably over recent years. Radio Sénégal (750m MW) carries Dakar information and, on Friday afternoons, news about music and shows, and you can also pick up FM92 (a Radio France/Radio Sénégal station), Sud-FM (98.5FM), Dakar FM (94FM), Radio Dunyaa FM, Nostalgie (playing French and African music from the 1970s and 1980s) and Walf FM (99.00FM), the newest addition and the most popular station. BBC Afrique relays Network Africa and Focus on Africa in English, daily at 6.30am and 6.30pm respectively.

TV, predominantly in French, is available all over the country – though watched mostly in Dakar – and, apart from the government station, RTS, there are also pay-TV channels such as the local Canal Horizons, the French satellite channel TV5, CNN, C-Span and a host of Arabic channels.

The Senegalese **press** is developing quickly now with a number of daily papers. *Le Soleil* – the "independent" paper of the Parti Socialiste but effectively the voice of government – has plenty of local news but not much international, while other dailies include *Walf*, *Sud*, *Le Matin* and *L'Info 7*. Since papers are still all published in French – which many of the population can't read – newspaper reading remains very much city based.

Most of the dozen or more political parties publish their own sheets more or less regularly, but they tend towards the turgid. For something oppositional, look out for the weekly *Sopi*, published by the PDS. If your French is up to it, *Le Politicien* is a monthly breath of fresher air, nicknamed *Le Cafard Liberé* after the Parisian satirical mag. Paris-based weeklies available include: *Le Temoin, Nouvelle Horizon, Jeun Afrique, L'Autre Afrique* and *La Nouvelle Afrique-Asie*.

Entertainment

Unlike a number of countries where organized entertainments can be somewhat inaccessible to outsiders, Senegal has plenty of spectator sport, in addition to musical performers, theatre and cinema.

■ Sport

Although **soccer** is big in Senegal, **la lutte** – wrestling – is the most popular sport countrywide, and consists of furious jostling of oiled and charm-laden poseurs trying to get each other down in the dust: fun to watch, but best at a small venue. Casamançais style is less violent than the Wolof brawls.

■ Music

Senegalese **music** is a revelation after the foreign imports heard in other countries. While traditional **griots** are less and less to be seen, many Senegalese musicians are internationally known. **Youssou N'dour**, for the complex **mbalax** style he developed with his band **Super Etoile de Dakar**, and for his singular presence in the world music firmament, is the biggest name, but he's just one of many. **Baaba Maal**, a conservatoire-trained Tukulor singer from Podor, is also internationally renowned. Major stadium **gigs** are held in Dakar, Ziguinchor and elsewhere, and you can pick up on even the big names in the Dakar clubs. There's much more in the music article in Contexts at the back of the book.

■ Cinema

Cinema is mostly imported. Senegal's own directors, notably Ousmane Sembène, Pape B. Seck,

Djibril Diop Mambety and Safi Faye, struggle for funds despite – in Sembène's, and to a lesser extent Faye's case – international critical acclaim.

■ Theatre

Theatre doesn't make much impression outside Dakar, where there is a small, active theatre community based around the Senegal National Theatre Company and the institutional Théâtre Daniel Sorano. Foreign cultural centres in Dakar, St-Louis and Ziguinchor may have something worth a look; where appropriate we've listed them in the chapter.

Holidays and Festivals

Apart from international Christian and Islamic holidays, during which all official and most business doors will be closed (see p.58), Senegal also has holidays on April 4 (National day, when independence as part of the Mali Federation was declared), May 5 (Labour day) and June 20 (Independence day).

There's also considerable unofficial disruption to normal hours and services at the time of **Magal** – the annual Mouride pilgrimage to Touba, which falls on the 18th of Safar, 48 days after the Islamic new year – ie on approximately May 25, 2000,

May 15, 2001 and May 5, 2002 (these dates are estimated on the early side: check the Muslim calendar closer to the time). Public transport all over Senegal is severely affected in the days before and after *Magal* with many drivers preferring to do pilgrim business only.

The popular weekend-long **St-Louis International Jazz Festival** (see p.204) is held around May or June each year.

■ Traditional festivals

One St-Louis and Gorée institution is the **Fanals** parade, featuring the decorated lanterns (*fanals*) that slaves used to carry in front of wealthy mixed-race women (*signares*) on their way to Christmas Mass. Competition developed between *quartiers* to produce the most elaborate lamp, the rivalry becoming so intense that the parades were banned in 1953 after violence between the teams. But they were revived in St-Louis in 1970, and you should be able to see them around Christmas. Impressive **pirogue races** also take place from time to time, notably in St-Louis.

In **the south**, in Basse Casamance and in the Bassari country beyond Niokolo-Koba park, a **seasonal cycle of festivals** and ritual events still dominates the cultural sphere, though to a

---

TRADITIONAL FESTIVALS

Olugu March: jubilant entry of Bassari initiates who underwent *Nit* the previous year, signifying their reintegration as adults.

Fityay March–April: ritual appeasement of the spirit Beliba, supplicated to look after the people of Essil (the region around Enampore) through the dry months.

Nit end of April: ritual battle in the Bassari villages of Ebarak, Etiolo and Kote, with masked attackers (*lukuta*) of boys undergoing initiation.

Ufulung Dyendena May: throughout the kingdom of Essil this ritual propitiation of rain spirits takes place before and after rice planting.

Synaaka May: "circumcision" of Jola girls, during which the initiates are instructed in retreat for a week; widespread partying.

Zulane May–June: festival of the royal priest of Oussouye.

Futampaf May–June: initiation of adolescent Jola boys into adulthood; lasts two to three weeks, commencing and concluding with major celebrations.

Kunyalen May–June: three days of ritual performed to ensure Jola female fertility and the protection of newborn infants.

Ekonkon June: traditional dances in Oussouye.

Bukut June: takes place in each Jola village roughly every twenty years.

Wrestling June–July: takes place all year, but the start of the rains is a traditional time in Essil.

Homebel October: after the rains, girls' wrestling bouts around Oussouye.

Beweng or **Epit** November–December: a two-day harvest festival in Basse Casamance when the spirits are asked to sanction the transfer of the rice crop to the granaries. Each head of household donates a sheaf.

Ebunay every two years: a festival in the Oussouye district involving all the women of the village; female (*Bugureb*) dances in the first week, followed by the enthronement of a ritual priestess.

diminishing extent. The events in the box overleaf are all worth checking out if you can; most take place towards the end of the dry season.

Directory

AIRPORT DEPARTURE TAX Usually included in ticket price.

OPENING HOURS Shop opening hours are Mon–Fri 8am–noon & 2.30/3–6pm, Sat 8–11am/noon. Banks usually follow the same hours. Most other offices are now open Mon–Fri 7.30am–4pm without a break, but closed on Sat. Many establishments, including some restaurants, close one day a week – museums usually Mon all day & Wed morning. The long lunch break is popular.

PARIS–DAKAR RALLY Since the late 1970s the annual Paris–Dakar Rally has torn across the Sahara and West Africa, covering up to 10,000km in around three weeks. The Rally, which usually sets off from the Champs Élysées on a New Year's dawn, was once hugely popular, but this has been tempered by frequent deaths among participants and onlookers and the questionable ethics of a multi-million-pound spectacle hurtling through the poverty stricken Sahel. Although still followed nightly on French TV, the inevitable loss of the Rally's early amateur spirit and the necessary elimination of the politically insecure central Saharan sections, where the Rally earned its reputation as the world's toughest trial for bikes, cars and trucks, have removed some of the Dakar's sex-appeal. These days it follows a less demanding route through Morocco and Mauritania, to Senegal, though in 1995 it added a circuit through Guinea's Fouta Djalon highlands. If you're in Dakar at the right time, don't expect to see much more than huge crowds and champagne-soaked desert racers parading through the Place de l'Indépendance. The Rally does, however, bring enormous accommodation problems to every town on the route, and Dakar especially.

PHOTOGRAPHY Officially there are few problems: you can even take pictures of the presidential guards and palace, though you should ask first. But you'll certainly hurt people's feelings if you take their pictures without permission, and in many areas, high prices will be demanded.

POLICE AND TROUBLE Law enforcers are of two main types – machine-gun-toting, brown-uniformed *gendarmes* and blue-togged *agents de police* who operate the occasional countryside road blocks. The latter, though generally not into bothering tourists, will pull you in if you're not carrying any identification. You can be held for 24 hours and fined – it happens, often. If you're out at night and would rather not take your passport, keep a photocopy and another piece of ID with you. ☎17 seems to be the best bet if you require the police in a hurry.

Be **security-conscious** on first arriving in Dakar. It can't be over-stressed that this is a city where too many new arrivals are robbed – usually in a snatch and run attack. (The rest of the country is as safe as anywhere.) Don't aggravate street pedlars by looking at their gear if you're really not interested, or by bargaining for fun when you've no intention of buying. In Dakar this can give rise to serious offence. *Always* ignore the guy who gets an item out of his pocket to sell you; this is a set-up for a mugging. On a wider front, despite some political detentions, Senegal prides itself on **freedom of speech**: domestic politics aren't taboo and you can converse openly without fear of offending or unnerving anyone.

SEXUAL ATTITUDES The Wolof tend to be exceptionally beautiful people, and unafraid of marrying out of their own communities, which tends to strengthen their already dominant position. **Prostitution** has a rather lower profile than, for example, in The Gambia. **Gay attitudes** seem relaxed, in Dakar at least: av Georges Pompidou and Ngor beach to the north are well-known cruising areas for *gor-digen*.

SHOPS AND CRAFTS Senegal doesn't stand out as a country to buy handicrafts, but you'll find a number of hole-in-the-wall **curio shops** in Dakar, where some musty old relics can be unearthed and argued over. Officially sanctioned **centres artisanals** tend to be touristic set-ups, where you can see the stuff being made (carved statues and masks, model *pirogues*, paintings on glass, sand paintings) but where you might not want to buy it. **Cloth** *pagnes* are generally cheaper than in The Gambia, with Dakar's suburban markets being the best places for a good deal – watch out for Sotiba's superb range of designs. Jewellery, in variety and notably in silver, is usually a good buy. There's detailed advice on shopping in Dakar in the account of the city.

WILDLIFE AND NATIONAL PARKS Senegal isn't well endowed with **large animals**. In **Basse Casamance National Park** you're not likely to see anything bigger than a monkey. In the

north, however, there may still be elephants along remoter parts of the river, and large numbers of camels. In **Niokolo-Koba National Park** you can see elephants, lions, buffaloes and western giant elands, plus several troupes of chimpanzees at the northernmost point of their range, and quantities of crocs and hippos. Senegalese **birdlife** is satisfying: the coast boasts some of the best spots in the world for watching palearctic migrants in the winter. For further information contact the Department of National Parks (BP 5135, Dakar; ☎825 05 40; Fax 825 23 99; *dpn@telecomplus.sn*).

WOMEN'S MOVEMENT Long-standing and continued French influence has been superficially helpful to women in terms of career opportunities. Dakar's fairly active **movement** is co-ordinated through the Fédération Sénégalaise des Groupements Féminins. The central issue of institutional female genital mutilation – still performed in some communities – is being tackled by a pan-African organization who have their headquarters in Dakar – the Commission Internationale pour l'abolition des mutilations sexuelles, Villa 811, SICAP Baobabs, Dakar.

WORK Although it's getting harder by the month, Dakar is one place in West Africa where you'll quite possibly find a job if you're prepared to settle in for a while. The most likely openings are English **teaching** (approach the British-Senegalese Institute, see p.188) and – if you have very good French – secretarial and other office jobs, or working in upmarket stores. All are strictly unofficial – making friends with the expat communities will help.

A Brief History of Senegal

The earliest deducible history of Senegal, from about 1300 AD, comes from the oral accounts of the aristocracy of the Wolof kingdom of Jolof, in the centre of the country. Jolof fragmented into a number of small Wolof kingdoms which, together with Casamance, had frequent contacts with Portuguese traders after 1500. In 1658, the French settled on an island at the mouth of the Senegal River, which they named St-Louis, after Louis XIV. This account picks up the story from there. For the history of Islam in Senegal, see the feature box on the Muslim brotherhoods on p.167.

■ French inroads

By 1659 the trading fort of **St-Louis** was properly established, buying in **slaves** and **gum arabic** – the first a product of upriver raids, the second a valuable extract from acacia trees, used in medicine and textile manufacture.

The permanent French presence at St-Louis stimulated the slave trade to a level at which it began to dominate the Senegal valley's economy, prompting a frenzy of warfare for profit in the region's indigenous states. Wolof rulers (the *damel*) and their warriors (the *ceddo*) were spurred to raid their own peasantry for slaves. In the 1670s a popular **jihad** by Muslim marabouts, rebelling against the social cannibalism of the traditionalist Wolof elite, was suppressed with the help of French soldiers and guns. Henceforth Wolof of all classes found themselves trapped between Islamic reformers and mercenary Europeans.

St-Louis in the eighteenth century

Throughout the eighteenth century St-Louis thrived and increasingly absorbed the Wolof people of Walo state, which occupied the area between Richard Toll and the coast. The Wolof had not been converted to Islam: on the contrary, the intermarriage of Wolof women and French Catholics created an exclusive miniature society, to a large extent run by the mixed race matriarchs known as **signares**.

By the time of the French Revolution, St-Louis had a population of 7000, of whom a large proportion, including the mayor, were *métis* (mixed race). In deference to French blood, but also to post-revolutionary notions of the rights of man, the people of St-Louis and Gorée, the island near Dakar, were accorded most of the privileges of **French citizenship**, including, after 1848, the right to elect a deputy to the National Assembly in Paris – a right later extended to the mainland *communes* of Rufisque and Dakar.

Futa Toro and Omar Tall

In the interior, developments were underway that would shape the future of the modern state. In 1776 a league of **Tukulor marabouts** from north of the Senegal River overthrew the Fula dynasty of Denianke in **Futa Toro** on the south bank, a region the dynasty had ruled for more than 250 years. They were replaced by a reforming government of Muslim clerics (known as *almamys*) who, with fundamentalist zeal, dispatched warrior-missionaries to spread Islam across the western part of the subcontinent.

The greatest of these expansionists was **Omar Tall**. On his way to Mecca in the 1820s, Tall was initiated into the **Tijaniya brotherhood**, which was founded in Morocco in the late eighteenth century. He was appointed the Tijani chief khalif for the region and travelled extensively, gathering a huge following. By the early 1850s Tall had carved out a vast **empire** centred on **Ségou** in present-day Mali and stretching as far east as Timbuktu. Westwards, his ambitions to expand to the coast were soon thwarted by the French.

■ French conquest

In the 1820s, after the abolition of slavery, Governor Baron Roger had tried unsuccessfully to develop agriculture upriver at Richard Toll with a view to French settlement. **Louis Faidherbe**, appointed governor in 1854, saw no mileage in that approach to imperialism. Instead he annexed the Wolof kingdom of **Walo**, and brutally subjugated the Mauritanians of Trarza, who had long frustrated French ambitions to control the gum trade. To pay for the military campaigns, the first harvests of **groundnuts** were shipped to French soap and oil factories. In 1857 a deal was struck with the head man of the Lebu village of **Daxar** (Dakar) – which became the administrative capital of French West Africa for the next hundred years – and further settlements were established along the coast at Rufisque and elsewhere. Faidherbe founded the Tirailleurs sénégalais (West African Infantry), who became the firepower of France's "civilizing mission" across West Africa and as far afield as Madagascar. He also strengthened the forts along the river at **Podor**, **Matam** and **Bakel**, which repulsed El Hadj Omar Tall's repeated attacks and provided bases for the French expansion across the Sahel.

Omar Tall was killed in 1864, besieged in the Bandiagara escarpment in present day Dogon country, his empire still landlocked. His son **Amadu Sefu** continued his reign.

Muslim conquest

After Omar Tall's death, **Ma Ba** – a senior disciple – carried on the work of the Tijaniya with a clutch of Soninké (Sarakole) followers. They led and sponsored *jihads* against non-Muslim Mandinka along the river Gambia (see **"The Soninke-Marabout Wars"**, p.250), and also converted most of the Wolof kings to Islam, goading them into individual armed resistance against the French. But a united front of Wolof states proved impossible to achieve. In 1867 Ma Ba died in a battle with the **Serer**-speaking state of Sine, marking a temporary halt in the advance of Islam and leaving the Serer to a different evangelical fate with the Christian missions.

As Wolof leaders were converted, however, pushing their people – or sometimes pushed by them – into accepting Islam, so **conflict with the French** became, with increasing clarity, a conflict between Muslims and infidels. Humiliated by their 1871 defeat in the Franco-Prussian war, the French found new reserves of aggression. And despite the marabouts' powers of mobilization, the French grip on the territory grew tighter every year through the 1880s. The Wolof armies were defeated one by one, and the old authority structures – already weakened by the imposition of Islam – were dismantled as each kingdom was annexed to France.

Wolof collapse

By now the French were irreversibly committed to making Senegal pay for itself and to directly administering the whole of their West African territory. When **Lat Dior**, the ruler of **Kayor**, appealed to the French not to build the Dakar to St-Louis railway through his kingdom, he was ignored, and the railway was opened in 1885, despite sabotage by Lat Dior and his *ceddo*. The same year the **Berlin congress** divided the African spoils among the European powers, splitting Senegal by the creation of The Gambia and formally ratifying France's sovereignty over her possessions. Lat Dior was killed at Dekhlé the following year, and became one of the country's folk heroes.

Another Wolof *damel*, **Alboury Ndiaye** (Alboury of Jolof), at first allied himself with the French at St-Louis against Amadu Sefu's empire to the east, even undertaking to facilitate the building of the ambitious, and never-completed, railway to Bakel. But, along with his distant cousin Lat Dior, Alboury had been converted to Islam in 1864, and he was secretly in contact with Amadu Sefu. He later became violently opposed to French expansion, allying his kingdom with the Ségou empire, leading fanatical attacks and trying to expand Ségou even farther to the east. His own kingdom, whose capital was Yang Yang, was formally annexed by the French in 1889 – the last

Wolof kingdom to lose its independence; Ségou fell in 1892, and Alboury died in exile in Dosso, Niger in 1902.

■ French administration

As everywhere in the early years of Afrique Occidentale Française (AOF) the French stressed their **mission civilatrice** – their peaceful aim to bring French civilization to black Africa. It was only in Senegal that this was accompanied by any real manifestation of assimilationist ideals. And even here, it was only in the four *communes* that French citizenship was available. Through the rest of Senegal and AOF, most people had the status of *sujet* – subject – and were at the mercy of the hated **indigénat** "native justice" code, under which they were ruled by the local *commandant* – the equivalent of a district commissioner – who could impose summary fines and imprisonment. The *indigénat* and a mass of oppressive legislation, including tax provisions, compulsory labour and restrictions on movement, were mostly operated through *chefs de canton* ("district chiefs") nominated by, and answerable to, the *commandant*. The chiefs were frequently corrupt and almost always regarded as collaborators. The only legitimate leadership in the countryside came from the **marabouts** (see p.166).

Blaise Diagne and the Marabouts

In marked contrast, Dakar, Gorée, Rufisque and St-Louis elected a territorial assembly – the **conseil général**, which controlled the budget for the whole of Senegal – and a deputy to the Paris National Assembly. In 1914 **Blaise Diagne**, a customs official from Gorée, became the first black deputy (previous deputies had been mixed race), a post he was to hold until his death in 1934.

The tone of Diagne's career was set early on when he offered to recruit Senegalese soldiers for the French war effort in exchange for legislation guaranteeing the political rights of the black *commune* residents – rights which the colonial administration was keen to erode. Laws were passed confirming that they were in fact full citizens of France. As far as Diagne was concerned, only further **assimilation** could better the lot of the Africans. He saw Senegal's fate as inextricably linked to that of France.

Outside the *communes* the Senegalese still had hopes of redemption through their marabouts, but the warrior evangelists of the nineteenth century were gone. In their place, men like **Amadou Bamba** – founder of the Mouride brotherhood – and **Malick Sy** – leader of the biggest Wolof dynasty of the Tijaniya – bought their religious independence by co-opting their followers in the colonial process, organizing recruitment drives and providing support to Senegalese politicians in the *communes*: Blaise Diagne's election owed much to support from the Mouride brotherhood, who counted on him to raise his voice on their behalf. The marabouts also encouraged the **cultivation of groundnuts**, a crop that quickly exhausted the soil, was totally dependent on the rains, forced farmers to buy food they would otherwise have grown for themselves and – as groundnut prices fell while others rose – led to falling living standards. In return the marabouts were given the administration's support in their land disputes with Fula cattle herders. By the end of the 1930s a system of **reciprocal patronage** between marabouts and government was established, and two out of three *sujets* were growing groundnuts.

Political developments

Diagne was succeeded as deputy by Galandou Diouf, a less enthusiastic assimilationist. His main rival was **Amadou Lamine Guèye**, Africa's first black lawyer, who came to prominence by demanding the extension of citizenhood to the *sujets*. Already elected mayor of St-Louis in 1925, he forged strong links with the French Socialist party and, in 1936, founded the Senegalese branch of the Section Française de l'Internationale Ouvrière (SFIO), Africa's first modern political party. When the French Socialists came to power and conceded some limited rights to non-citizens – the right to form trade unions for example – he began organizing among *sujets* in the backcountry towns.

■ World War II

With the outbreak of **World War II**, political life virtually ceased as the citizens' rights in the *communes* were abrogated, the country was scoured for supplies and the social advances of the prewar government were swiftly negated. The Allies blockaded Vichy-ruled Dakar as Churchill and de Gaulle's **"Operation Menace"** attempted to rally the AOF to the war. Senegal was starved of imports, causing enormous suffering in the groundnut regions. Peasants were forced to switch to subsistence crops, and for the first time were encouraged by the colonial administration to do so.

After two years of Vichy control, the colonial administration did turn to the Allies and for the rest of the war the country was an important logistical base for the Free French – though political rights were not restored until 1945. During the Allied occupation, an agricultural campaign – **"Battle for Groundnuts"** – was launched, which extracted more from the country, economically, than Vichy had.

Promises and blunders

The **Brazzaville Conference** of 1944 prepared the ground for major changes in France's relations with its colonies. A fairer deal for Africans, allowing them more administrative involvement, was the main theme, partly in recognition of the part played by them during the war, partly because France's credibility as a great and munificent nation was in question. The underlying aim was the reconstruction of postwar France and the incorporation of all its territories as integral parts of the Republic. The possibility of independence was explicitly ruled out.

Yet there was a clear call for "Equal Rights for Equal Sacrifices", a reference to the 200,000 Africans who were recruited to the war, the 100,000 who fought and the 25,000 who died.

Events in Senegal brought citizens and *sujets* closer together. At the end of 1944 at **Camp Thiaroye**, outside Dakar, demobilized West African soldiers just returned from Europe refused to be transported to Bamako without their back pay. When a general was taken hostage, French soldiers were ordered to open fire. Forty Senegalese were killed, many more were injured and a number of survivors sentenced to long jail terms.

Then, in 1945, the **vote for women** was finally won in France, but in the four *communes* only white women were enfranchised, a discrimination that under Blaise Diagne's 1915 guarantee should have been impossible.

Although the woman's vote decision was shortly repealed, both these events sullied relations with France and added fuel to growing demands for radical reforms.

■ The rise of Senghor

To speak of independence is to reason with the head on the ground and the feet in the air; it is not to reason at all. It is to advance a false problem.

L.S.Senghor, Strasbourg, 1950.

Early in 1945 a commission was set up to look into ways of organizing a new Constituent Assembly for the French colonies. One of the two black Africans to sit on it was a 38-year-old Catholic Senegalese, **Leopold Sédar Senghor**, who was chosen because, despite having lived almost continuously in France since 1928, he was the first African to achieve the rank of *agrégé* (the highest teaching qualification), and was in addition a war veteran and a *sujet*. Moreover, he was a Christian Serer rather than a Wolof and had close contacts with the French administration.

In October 1945 **elections** were held to two electoral colleges of the Assembly, one for citizens and one for *sujets*. **Lamine Guèye**, now mayor of Dakar and seen as the most experienced black politician in AOF, successfully rallied various political groups to form a popular front and was elected to the first electoral college. **Senghor**, fresh back from France, was easily voted to the second college – even though few Senegalese knew who he was.

Reforms and advances

Though not without hindrance, **reforms** were rapidly pushed through: the *indigénat* was abolished, as was forced labour. Even more significant, Lamine Guèye succeeded in raising the status of all *sujets* to that of citizen.

Senghor meanwhile was emerging from Lamine Guèye's political tutelage within the SFIO, campaigning to extend the role of the peasants in the interior, for increased financial credits and improvements in health and education in the overseas territories, and supporting the 1947–48 **railway workers' strike** for non-racial pay differentials on the Dakar–Bamako line. In 1948 Senghor formed his own party, the **Bloc democratique sénégalais** (BDS), and became leader of an association of African deputies – the Indépendents d'Outre-Mer.

The postwar reforms and the rise to power of the BDS in the early 1950s soon transformed Senegalese **politics**, even if the economy remained heavily dependent on the fickleness of the groundnut harvest. Senghor's party capitalized greatly on its leader's ex-*sujet* status and the credibility this brought him with the newly politicized peasantry. Senghor also took advantage of maraboutic favour to impress on business interests his influence over the groundnut economy. The **marabouts**, formerly an important behind-the-scenes factor, were becoming political focal points themselves. Lamine Guèye's SFIO meanwhile struggled for support in the urban centres beyond the four *communes* and continued to ignore the countryside, to his party's cost.

The third political grouping, a loose association of **Marxist intellectuals**, trade unionists and students, tended to see the established politicians as too closely wedded to Paris. Their calls for independence were drowned by the clamour for fairer assimilation.

The **Loi Cadre** ("Blueprint law") of 1956 was a step in both directions. Self-government was instituted for each of the overseas territories. But there was not to be the widely desired **federation** of territories with a capital in Dakar. And defence, higher education and currency would still be issues debated in Paris.

This was transparently an attempt to **balkanize** French Africa. It's been argued, and was at the time, that it gave more Africans the chance to participate in government than would have been the case had they been answerable to Dakar instead of their own capitals. In that sense it was a device to cloud over the real issue – independence.

The UPS and the 1958 referendum

Senghor continued to build a power base, drawing his support from the marabouts, the business community and **Mamadou Dia**'s socialist movement. He also attempted to make an alliance with Felix Houphouët-Boigny's Rassemblement Démocratique Africain in Côte d'Ivoire, arguing the need for federation. When this was blocked by Houphouët, the BDS moved left and changed its name to Bloc populaire sénégalais, taking with it the Mouvement autonome de Casamance – the regional independence movement for Casamance which had grown out of the final "pacification" in the region little more than a decade earlier. Mamadou Dia became prime minister in the new territorial government of 1957 after the defeat of Lamine Guèye's SFIO. His party subsequently merged with the BPS and the Union Progressiste Sénégalaise (UPS) was born.

The UPS was soon split by **de Gaulle's coming to power** in 1958 and his intransigent offer of either immediate independence and severance from the French Union or continued self-government within the French Union. It was a critical choice and one that Senghor was unwilling to make. Mindful of French economic clout as well

as his support among the marabouts and their mistrust of the party left wing, he ultimately sacrificed a section of young UPS radicals (who immediately formed their own party) and made sure that Senegal's vote to continue the Union was **Yes**. With this Lamine Guèye and even Mamadou Dia were in accord. But trade unionists, intellectuals and Casamance separatists were mostly alienated and disappointed at the submission to de Gaulle. Modern opposition politics have their roots in the 1958 referendum.

Independence

Senghor still favoured an independent, Dakar-led federation of states. Working with the ex-territory of Soudan (now Mali) and others, the **Mali Federation** was formed to further this end; but by the time it was constituted in April 1959, the federation's members were reduced to Mali and Senegal – an unworkable alliance given the influence of Dakar. But it was pursued nonetheless.

Lamine Guèye was now elected president of the new territorial assembly. Modibo Keita of Mali was elected president of the Federal Government and Mamadou Dia vice-president. In September, inspired by Guinea's secession, the Mali Federation lobbied France for independence. And in a *volte-face* that amazed most observers, de Gaulle conceded that total independence should not, after all, deny a country the right to remain within the French Union. On April 4, 1960 (now "National Day") the principle of independence for the Mali Federation was declared, and on June 20, 1960 **independence** was proclaimed.

On August 20, 1960, the Mali Federation suddenly broke down over the election of a president. The Senegalese had insisted on Senghor for this role, having begun to distrust Bamako's rigorous Marxist policies. Senegal proclaimed its **independence from Mali** the same day, arresting Modibo Keita and sending him back to Bamako in a sealed train wagon. Mali refused to recognize the new **Republic of Senegal** and for three years the Dakar–Bamako railway was unused.

■ The Senghor years

Senghor took the presidency of the new republic, keeping Mamadou Dia as his prime minister. Senghor's formulation of **négritude**, Senegal's nationalism, blended with his motto "Assimiler, pas être assimilés", urging Africans to assimilate European culture, not be assimilated by it. On this

ISLAM IN SENEGAL

Ligey si top, yala la bok – "Work is part of religion"
Amadou Bamba, founder of Mouridism

Any insight into modern Senegal requires an understanding of the country's extraordinarily influential **Muslim brotherhoods**. You won't stay here long without noticing – in the names on the bush taxis, the signs on the village shops and the flocks of multicoloured Hare Krishna-like disciples – that something very unusual lies in the dusty heart of Senegalese society.

ORIGINS

The Muslim **brotherhoods** are in conflict with original, Arabian Islam, which says everyone has a direct relationship with God. They resulted from the religion's spread to the Berber peoples of northwest Africa, the brotherhoods flourishing in these class-based societies, where it was natural to think that certain men should be gifted with divine insight, able to perform miracles and bestow blessings.

One of the earliest dynasties of Moroccan Muslims to make permanent contact with the people south of the desert was the **Almoravid** (whence marabout: holy leader/saint) who, in the twelfth century, made conversions in the kingdom of **Tekrur** in northeast Senegal. In the fifteenth century, the **Qadiriya** brotherhood was introduced south of the Sahara and, by the end of the eighteenth century, was firmly based near Timbuktu. Stressing **charity, humility** and

piety, Qadirism made no exclusive demands of its followers and recruited from all ethnic groups. A local Qadiri offshoot, the **Layen** brotherhood, was founded in the late nineteenth century as an exclusively Lebu-speaking order in the Cap Vert district near Dakar.

Another order, the **Tijaniya**, crossed the desert early in the nineteenth century and was spread over Senegal by the proselytizing warlord Omar Tall. Tijaniya laid less stress on humility than earlier orders. Indeed, its Moroccan founder Al-Tijani had claimed direct contact with the Prophet Muhammad and, as a consequence, his followers were forbidden allegiance to any other orders. The brotherhood rapidly recruited the mass of Tukulor speakers in northeast Senegal. Tukulor marabouts – notably the forefathers of the hugely influential **Sy** and **Mbacke** families – were largely responsible for the later conversion of the Wolof.

MARABOUTS AND THE FRENCH

The interplay between **the brotherhoods and the French** was complicated. Allegiances often cut through ties of birth and language, so that, typically, peasants found themselves in alliance with the marabouts against their own, traditional rulers who tended to conspire with the French. Moreover, "pacification" by the French often resulted in more fertile ground for the spread of Islam. By the early 1900s, with the conversion to Islam of even the

most resistant traditional rulers, a new establishment of **vested interests** had been founded, uniting the French and the marabouts. Although the Tijaniya traditionally had a core of fundamentalist, anti-French sentiment, the order soon adjusted to the material realities of colonialism. The latest and greatest brotherhood, the **Mouridiya** – exclusively rural and Senegalese – came, in practice, to be a bastion of the status quo.

MOURIDISM

The Mouridiya was founded in 1887 by **Amadou Bamba**, nephew of the Wolof king Lat Dior, and a member of the influential Mbacke family. An offshoot of the Qadiriya brotherhood, Mouridiya initially attracted many former anti-colonial fighters inspired by its discipline and dynamism, and by the charisma of Bamba.

Rumours of an armed insurrection from his court at Touba terrified the French ("We cannot tolerate a state within a state") and Bamba was twice exiled by the authorities – though these banish-

ments served only to increase his standing at home.

Mouride folk history places great emphasis on Bamba's anti-colonial credentials, but soon after his return to Senegal in 1907 (a return celebrated in the annual *Magal* pilgrimage), he was striking deals with the authorities and trusting in the slow wheels of political reform. He was also amassing a personal fortune.

One of Bamba's early disciples, **Ibra Fall**, was personally devoted to the marabout, but he was a poor

Koranic student. Bamba gave him an axe and told him to work for God with that. Sheikh Ibra Fall went on to found the fanatically slavish **Baye Fall**. Today, these dreadlocked devotees in patchwork robes now have their own khalif but are exempt from study and even from fasting at Ramadan.

The founding of Baye Fall signalled a radical shift in religious thought, making **labour** a virtue and bringing Mouridism into the very heart of contemporary life. Among Mourides (whose name means "the hopeful") there's a universal belief that hard work is the key to paradise. Bamba is credited with announcing "If you work for me I shall pray for you" and even the five daily prayers are less important than toiling in the groundnut fields. The colonial authorities and the Mouride marabouts – mostly from wealthy, landed families – soon found areas of agreement.

THE BROTHERHOODS TODAY

Many senior and middle-ranking Mouride disciples today form a **new business class**. Even French-educated businessmen would rather become disciples of respected marabouts than short-cut the system. Over a dozen Mourides are multi-billionaires in CFA francs (worth up to £100 million/$160million) and Lebanese entrepreneurs find that business is increasingly out of their hands.

Illegal traffic has been profitable too, not least in the Mouride capital **Touba** itself, where the absence of government agents brought **racketeering** on a grand scale. All the hardware of Western consumerism, and even alcohol and arms, was widely available until the chief khalif, under pressure from Dakar, admitted that Mouridism was in danger of losing its soul, and allowed *gendarmes* into the holy city. The black market is clandestine again, but still funnels huge quantities of money and goods between Senegal and The Gambia.

Co-operation between the government and the brotherhoods – and more pointedly between the ruling Parti socialiste and the Mourides – has continued into the independent era. Yet the relationship remains one of latent mistrust, and even if many of those involved profit through it, the potential for a reactionary and anti-secular revolt against the government has always been there, as the Mouride brotherhood is conservative and rigorously hierarchical.

The **Magal** pilgrimage to Touba has become the traditional occasion when the state president reiterates his support for the Mourides and his appreciation of the benefits they have brought Senegal. In turn, the chief khalif is expected to emphasize to his two million followers the sanctity of the groundnut harvest, the importance of not rocking the boat and their duty to support stable government. The implicit message is that a vote against the Parti socialiste would be a vote against the khalif, and therefore against God. The Tijaniya **Gamou** gatherings in Tivaouane and Kaolack are smaller-scale versions of the *Magal*, and similar back-slapping is the order of the day.

The **succession** to the position of chief khalif is a time of crisis in every brotherhood, since the relationship between the voters and the elected government hangs very heavily on the words of the marabouts. The current Mouride chief khalif, **Serigne Saliou Mbacke**, is considered to be less interested in worldly matters than his predecessor, and therefore less likely to throw his weight behind the government's posturing and campaigning. Since the death of the last Tijaniya chief khalif, Abdoul Aziz Sy, in 1997, there have been dynastic quarrels within that brotherhood, and the new Tijaniya chief khalif, **Serigne Mansour Sy**, has a reputation for independent thinking. These facts are worrying for the government, which remains concerned about the rise of a more **fundamentalist** strand of Islam in Senegal.

Economically, the Mouride-groundnut connection remains on the whole solid, with the **religious elite** supported by the harvest and the boundless offerings of their followers. With a few exceptions, the brotherhoods have rooted firmly in the safest political ground. The government, while insisting that the state and political process is strictly secular, lavishes publicity and patronage on the marabouts for delivering votes. In 1968 the chief khalif instructed Mouride university students to disobey the strike call. Twenty years later, the **general election** was won overwhelmingly by Diouf after the usual maraboutic injunctions.

It has long been an irony of Senegalese politics – and frustrating for the country's opposition movers and shakers – that Senegal, with its highly developed democratic structures, should find true democracy repeatedly brushed aside by the mass of its people in exchange for the grace of God. However, at the 1993 and 1996 elections, the influence of the ruling party over the brotherhoods was less brazenly evident, and as the country enters its fifth decade of independence, there are signs that the old order may at last be breaking down.

foundation, Senghor and the UPS built the ideology of **African socialism**, which amounted to a tacit defence of the status quo in its emphasis on consensus. Dia, whose own politics remained to the left of Senghor, failed to find a balance between the business community and the radical left, and succeeded only in irritating the French. In 1962, Senghor had him arrested (he was sentenced to life imprisonment after an alleged coup attempt in which the army came to Senghor's rescue), and relations with France began to prosper.

The one party state

The rest of the decade saw the government growing increasingly right-wing. In 1963 a **revised constitution** was approved, strengthening the role of the president and effectively forcing radical opposition underground. Cheikh Anta Diop's Bloc des masses sénégalaises (BMS) was the most powerful group the opposition could legally muster and this was smashed by a massive and disputed UPS victory in the elections of that year. **Riots** in their aftermath were put down by troops, with many deaths – the first serious smear on Senegal's hitherto spotless reputation. The BMS was banned; the remaining opposition had by 1966 been forced into the UPS or harassed out of existence.

Farmers were badly hit by the abolition of French subsidies for groundnut prices in 1967, while most town dwellers were no better off than they had been before independence. In May 1968 **trade unionists** and **students protested** at the government's complacency, confronting it with the charge of neo-imperialism. Senghor confronted the protesters with the **army**. Further strikes were followed by some concessions, then the government tried to force the unions into its own muzzled national confederation of workers (the CNTS). Some, like the teachers, resisted.

Repeated crises slackened off at the end of the decade when Senghor revived the post of prime minister – given to Abdou Diouf in 1970 – and, after further university unrest in 1973, banned the teacher's union and jailed some of the activists. The party was renamed the Parti socialiste (PS), a cosmetic alteration that convinced few.

Democratic reforms

In 1974, a cautious new liberalism was initiated with the release of ex-PM Mamadou Dia from twelve years in detention. Soon after, the **Parti démocratique sénégalais** (PDS) led by lawyer **Maître Abdoulaye Wade** was allowed to register and by 1976 various brands of liberal and social democracy were on offer, as well as a legal Marxist-Leninist party, which attracted a small number of radicals. A flood of political handouts and news sheets hit the streets. Anta Diop and Mamadou Dia were banned from forming parties, but not excluded from discussion.

By 1978, Senghor – now in his late sixties – was spending more time on poetry and the Académie française than running Senegal, and he began to groom his vice-president, **Abdou Diouf**, for leadership. Diouf was already taking responsibility for executive decisions and his status grew as he gained support from the major aid institutions for his austere management of the economy.

A sideshow in the late 1970s was the **militant Tijaniya dynasty** of Ahmet Khalif Niasse. Niasse went into exile in Libya allegedly intending to organize for an Islamic state in Senegal, which led to the cutting of diplomatic relations. The Libyan connection resurfaced across the border in The Gambia, where the "coup attempt" of October 1980 reportedly had the same roots. President Jawara invoked the two countries' historic relationship, and Senegalese troops were sent in.

■ Diouf in power

Senghor, the first African president to retire voluntarily, passed the presidency to Diouf on January 1, 1981. At first it was feared that Diouf's uncharismatic style would be insufficient to carry him, but **opposition groups** were hopeful he would lift remaining restrictions on political activities and their hopes were soon fulfilled. Cheikh Anta Diop's Rassemblement national démocratique (RND) was legalized, Dia founded the Mouvement démocratique populaire (MDP), and there were several others. Wade's PDS relinquished its role as the focal point of opposition and actually lost a few members in a purge of pro-Libyan sympathizers.

Diouf increased his popularity by launching an **anti-corruption drive** focusing on his own cabinet and firing Senghor's "barons". And traditional supporters of the government – the moderate Muslim masses – were gratified to have a president at last who spoke Wolof as his mother tongue and peppered his speeches with Koranic references.

The July 1981 coup in **The Gambia** was more serious than the effort of the previous year and served as the most severe test of Diouf's nerve in his first year in office. President Jawara called him from London to ask Senegal to restore him to power, which the Senegalese army accomplished with considerable bloodshed. A detachment stayed in The Gambia until the late 1980s.

However, the spectre of an unfriendly and destabilizing power taking control in The Gambia galvanized Diouf to do something about the dormant **Senegambia confederation**. In December 1981 an agreement was ratified and a Senegambian parliament met for its first session in 1983. The Gambia, with no army and little to offer Senegal except a headache and its river, was always likely to be the passive partner in a relationship that finally collapsed in 1989.

The **economy**, meanwhile, continued to decline. Although the state groundnut-buying monopoly was dissolved in 1980 after years of corruption and inefficiency, low prices and disastrous harvests that year and in 1984 meant no perceptible improvement for the peasant farmers. **Fishing** was pushed into first place as a foreign exchange earner, with **tourism** second and groundnuts third. Agricultural diversification is still desperately needed: as subsidies on fertilizer and seed are phased out, soil exhaustion and poor harvests are the prospect for the future.

The **1988 election** saw the first display of really serious political and social unrest during Diouf's presidency: an ominously quiet polling day was followed by the most violent riots in Dakar since the "Mamadou Dia affair" in 1963. Diouf declared a **state of emergency**; tanks and tear gas came onto the streets; a dusk to dawn curfew was in force for three weeks, and **Abdoulaye Wade**, who claimed to have been defeated by a rigged poll, was arrested. His trial and conviction on charges of incitement to subvert the state triggered further unrest, which was later quelled by his own, characteristically conciliatory, remarks.

Diouf, however, later withdrew any inference of a pact between him and Wade and set about making **changes to the electoral system**, ostensibly to guarantee fairer elections. In practice these adjustments delayed local elections and enraged Wade and the main opposition alliance, **Sopi** ("Change"), who accused Diouf of perpetuating the distortion of the democratic process by vested interests and vote-buying.

Even the intense dissatisfaction with the political scene was overshadowed during the **Senegal–Mauritania crisis** of April 1989 to October 1990. Triggered by a land dispute on the border, local fighting flared into racial conflict as Mauritanian shopkeepers (the 300,000-strong mainstay of Senegal's retail trade) were hounded out of Senegal, hundreds killed and their stores looted. An international operation assisted refugees to return to Nouakchott, while Senegalese immigrants in Mauritania (who were even more violently, and systematically, attacked) returned to Senegal, along with tens of thousands of Fula-speaking indigenous Mauritanians ("southerners" in Mauritanian parlance), whom the Nouakchott government had taken the opportunity to expel at the same time (see p.107). The borders closed and a cloud of deep mutual mistrust hung over the two governments, fuelled by their opposed positions during the Gulf conflict: Mauritania remained a guarded ally of Iraq, while Senegalese troops were sent to Saudi Arabia to assist in "Operation Desert Storm".

By the end of the 1990s, Mauritania was attempting a long-term reconciliation with its southern neighbour, though 70,000 Mauritanian "southerners" were still living in refugee camps in northern Senegal and unwilling to return home to a future with no clear guarantees.

■ The 1990s

Despite its troubles, Senegal is generally viewed as one of the most stable and democratic countries in West Africa. On the political front, the dominant theme of the 1990s – viewed from Dakar, at least, if not from Ziguinchor (see box, p.171) – has been a low-level, grumbling discontent with the inertia of the Parti socialiste, which has several times boiled up into riots.

Like those of 1988, the **elections of February 1993** were again the subject of condemnation by Abdoulaye Wade over alleged photocopied registration papers, multiple voting and other ploys. In the presidential ballot, Wade came out in front in the main urban areas of Dakar and Thiès but Diouf won overall. Three months later in the national assembly elections, Wade's PDS obtained less than a quarter of the 120 seats, while the PS won more than two-thirds, on a turnout of well under half the electorate. Wade claimed that if the election had been conducted fairly, the results would have put the PDS in the lead. Days after announcing the results the vice-chief of the electoral commission, **Babacar Sèye**, was assassinated. The perpetrators remain unknown (a previously unheard of "Armée du Peuple" claimed responsibility) but it was Abdoulaye Wade and three associates who were arrested without charge. One of them, **Mody Sy**, was kept in jail for more than a year.

The **devaluation of the CFA franc** in February 1994 – supported by Diouf, and partly engineered by him – was particularly hard on the poor. Later that year, in a mass rally for democracy in Dakar, led by the **Tijaniya brotherhood**'s fundamentalist-leaning youth organization Daira al Moustarchidines wal Moustarchidates, militant protestors precipitated a riot and then rounded on the security forces, killing six policemen in a frenzied attack that left the country stunned.

Wade and six senior opposition figures on the march were among a group of 177 people arrested for incitement to violence, though most were eventually released. As a result, a new opposition alliance, Bokk Sopi Sénégal ("Uniting to Change Senegal"), was formed in September 1994 from Wade's PDS, **Landing Savané**'s communist And-Jëf–Parti Africaine pour la Démocratie et le Socialisme (AJ–PADS), and Mamadou Dia's Mouvement pour le Socialisme et l'Unité (MSU).

Despite their opposition status, in 1995 Wade and six PDS colleagues took **cabinet posts** in the national government on the invitation of Abdou Diouf – better for Diouf to deal with the charismatic and outspoken Wade behind closed doors than across the barricades. This was not the first time that Wade had accepted a cabinet post, and his credentials as a man of the people – resigning from government to campaign against Diouf at each election, then returning to the cabinet on Diouf's invitation after losing the poll – are beginning to wear thin.

■ Prospects and threats

If Abdou Diouf wins the February **2000 presidential election**, he has just one more seven-year term in office (the rule allowing only two terms was written into the electoral code in 1991, after Diouf had already been president for ten years). Until 2007, jockeying for position as Diouf's successor will be an ongoing aspect of Dakar's political scene, both in the opposition alliance and within the ruling party, too. Diouf's own right-hand man, PS party secretary **Ousmane Tanor Dieng**, is a tough, dynamic figure in his early 50s, and widely believed to be the president's chosen successor.

PS defectors, under the banner of the Renouveau Démocratique, led by **Djibo Laity Ka** (who quit the ruling party in 1995) are probably too tarnished by association with government to drum up support in opposition hotbeds, while on the alliance side, **Maître Abdoulaye Wade**, now in his mid-70s, is possibly looking too old to lead the country. Moreover, after his trusted associate, **Ousmane Ngom**, stormed out of the PDS in 1998 criticizing Wade's egotistical manner, and setting up the Parti Libéral Sénégalais, Wade's star has clearly begun to wane.

A dark horse of the established opposition alliance is **Landing Savané**, who may yet emerge as a popular contender if he sheds some of his leftist ideological baggage. A Casamançais who believes in greater autonomy for the region and who has never soiled his reputation by accepting a job in government, Savané's party, AJ–PADS, may have enough appeal in the Wolof north as well as the Jola south, both in the towns and in the countryside, to push him to the front of the race.

Meanwhile, Senegal's **industry** is in steep decline, relying, as it does so heavily, on imported raw materials. **Education** is in a shambles after years of class boycotts, strikes and abrogated school years. Senegalese **society** is increasingly divided into those who have access to a state salary from a family member and those who rely on the private sector and the informal and subsistence economy. The average state employee's salary is ten times the national average income.

The polarization is easily exploited, and the most enthusiastic fishers in this river of discontent – at least in the northern part of Senegal – are **Muslim fundamentalists**. The government, acutely aware of the dangers, deports known foreign agitators while juggling the less dangerous demands of secular radicals like Wade, and its conservative marabout supporters and their followers in the countryside – the PS's loyal troops. The rift with Mauritania was an uncomfortable period, since that country too is the subject of fundamentalist pressures and, for a while, it appeared Nouakchott was acting to destabilize Senegal by arming the Casamance rebels. A pragmatic patching up of differences has taken place, shoring up central government against rebellion in both countries.

Casamance remains Senegal's biggest problem (see box, opposite), and at the start of the twenty-first century, it shows every likelihood of becoming a major regional flashpoint.

THE CASAMANCE CONFLICT

Demonstrations in **Casamance** in December 1982 signalled the reawakening of the Casamance separatist movement and resulted in a number of detentions without trial. The region is poorly developed and substantially non-Muslim: the charge that it's ignored because it produces less groundnuts than the north and can't muster heavyweight marabouts is not baseless. The Casamançais resent the snub, because it is Casamance rice that goes a substantial way towards feeding the country. Elections won by Abdou Diouf's Parti Socialiste have left in fragmented disarray the opposition parties with power bases in Casamance.

Violently suppressed **separatist demonstrations** in Casamance in December 1983 left over a hundred people dead and hundreds more in detention. Similar incidents continued sporadically in the Casamance through the 1980s, but it was only in 1990 that the violence erupted into serious armed conflict as the military wing of the Mouvement des Froces Démocratiques de la Casamance (MFDC) went into action. The government in Dakar believed the separatists were getting arms from Mauritania, channelled through Jola sympathizers in Guinea-Bissau. By 1993, in advance of the presidential and legislative elections (boycotted by the MFDC), there were five thousand troops in the Casamance and the region was under military control.

The MFDC claim that Casamance existed as a separate territory before the French colonial era, and a large part of its membership wants independence from Senegal. The movement is split into the *Front nord*, based around Baila and Bignona, and the more extreme *Front sud*, focused on Oussouye and the villages to the south along the Guinea-Bissau border. The movement's political leadership is provided by brothers Augustine and Bertrand **Diamacouné Senghor**, while its military wing is headquartered in France, under **Mamadou Nkrumah Sané**.

After a ceasefire agreement and the release of many prisoners by the government in 1993, there was an eighteen-month lull in fighting. But hostilities flared up again in the southern districts at the end of 1994 and, despite the establishment of a Commission National du Paix, the army and airforce retaliated with bombing raids and manhunts through the forest, in a sporadic, tit-for-tat war which has continued ever since.

The violence in Casamance puts at risk the **tourist industry** on which the region is heavily dependent for foreign exchange: the coastal resort area of Cap Skiring is traditionally one of France's most popular winter sun destinations. However, even after Nkrumah Sané explicitly warned tourists to stay away, many Cap Skiring hotels have often remained full throughout the season – though guests have been warned not to stray inland.

As it emerges that control of the local **cannabis** crop (worth $400 million each year by one estimate) is perhaps as important in military calculations as the political principles at stake, so the MFDC is beginning to turn in on itself. In the late 1990s, retired or disenchanted MFDC guerillas were murdered by active units; **mines** (smuggled in from Guinea-Bissau and laid on minor roads and farm tracks, particularly between Ziguinchor and Cap Skiring), have killed and maimed hundreds; and Amnesty International has accused both sides of terrorizing local people. The Diamacouné Senghor brothers have publically denounced the laying of mines and seem able and willing to negotiate a settlement that would satisfy the need for autonomy and greater recognition for Casamance without insisting on its outright independence.

President Diouf, meanwhile, fearful of leaving his southern border exposed to a flood of MFDC support from **Guinea-Bissau**, attempted to stave off the collapse of the corrupt Vieira government in Bissau by sending in 3000 Senegalese troops in the summer of 1998. The eventual collapse of the Bissau govenment in May 1999 was a serious blow to Dakar's belief that it can win in Casamance. There is a long history of mutual assistance between the Casamance liberationists, resentful of Dakar, and the old-school revolutionaries of Portuguese Guinea, who won their country's freedom and whose ostensible heirs now form the rebel government in Bissau. Culturally, too, the peoples of the two regions have much in common.

DAKAR, CAP VERT AND CENTRAL SENEGAL

West Africa's westernmost point and one of its most westernized capital cities, **Dakar** wields a powerful influence. Its pull extends well beyond Senegal's borders, drawing in migrants from across the Sahel and expatriates from overseas – especially, still, France. The city swarms with newcomers caught up in the neocolonial whirlpool, and its attractions are tempered by all this hustle and by the sheer size of the place. But the physical setting is striking, and the city has undeniable style, epitomizing the residue of French colonialism in Africa.

Out of Dakar, **Ile de Gorée** is a major draw, while the peninsula of **Cap Vert** offers beaches and out-of-town amusements. A more sheltered coast is **La Petite Côte** to the south of the city, which, beyond the dubious tourist magnet of **Joal-Fadiout**, merges into the bird-flocked creeks and islands of the **Sine-Saloum** region, adjoining the Gambian border.

Inland, the travel options from Dakar are harsher and the attractions scarcer, the focal points being the shady rail network hub of **Thiès** and the much more distant Islamic hothouse of **Touba**. If you're interested in the culture of the **Islamic brotherhoods**, some suggestions are made towards the end of this section, along with details on the Sine-Saloum **stone circles** complex.

Dakar

A giant of a city in African terms, with over a million inhabitants, **DAKAR** is hard work. The shock of arriving can be intense: it's incredibly dynamic, sophisticated and wretched in equal measure, and a test of will if your budget is tight. **French** influence is everywhere, especially in the downtown **Plateau** area, where the architecture and the whole feel of the place is more evocative of southern France than Africa. The results can be quite beautiful, without question. Between sprouting skyscrapers, the terracotta rooftops and shady, tree-lined avenues of the older quarters give Dakar an elegant maturity shared by few other African capitals.

Unfortunately some of the most attractive parts of the centre swarm with vendors, hustlers and hostile, hooting traffic, though this frenetic pace thankfully subsides on Saturdays, and on Sundays disappears altogether. At this time people hang out on shady shopfronts, kids play football in the streets and even the *colons* forsake their cars and taxis for a stroll out to Sunday lunch. During the week the **Ile de Gorée, Hann Park**, and the beaches at **Ngor** and **Yof** all provide degrees of space and seclusion, and if, rather than retreat, you'd prefer a more human participation, most of Dakar's teeming **suburbs** are a lot more open and easy-going than experiences in the city centre might lead you to imagine.

Some history

Ile de Gorée was first settled by European merchant adventurers in the fifteenth century, though the fortress-like peninsula of **Dakar** – the oldest European city in West Africa – was not established until 1857. The name Dakar was first used in the eighteenth century and is supposed to derive from the Wolof for tamarind tree – *daxar* – or refuge – *dekraw*.

The town's development really began towards the end of the last century, with the decline of St-Louis as a port, and the opening of the Dakar to St-Louis **railway** in 1885 (the first in West Africa), which gave a boost to groundnut farmers along its route. By

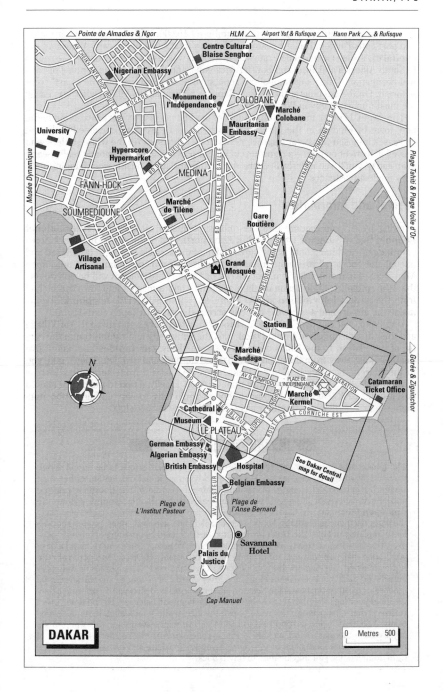

Pointe de Almadies & Ngor   HLM   Airport Yof & Rufisque   Hann Park   & Rufisque

Centre Cultural
Blaise Senghor

Nigerian Embassy

Monument de
l'Indépendance   COLOBANE

Marché
Colobane

Mauritanian
Embassy

University

Hyperscore
Hypermarket

MEDINA

FANN-HOCK

SOUMBEDIOUNE

Marché
de Tilène

Gare
Routière

Village
Artisanal

Grand
Mosquée

Station

Marché
Sandaga

PLACE DE
L'INDÉPENDANCE

Marché
Kermel

Catamaran
Ticket Office

Cathedral

Museum

LE PLATEAU

German Embassy
Algerian Embassy

British Embassy   Hospital

Belgian Embassy

Plage de
L'Institut Pasteur

Plage de
l'Anse Bernard

See Dakar Central
map for detail

N

Savannah
Hotel

Palais du
Justice

Cap Manuel

Musée Dynamique

Plage Tahiti & Plage Voile d'Or

Gorée & Ziguinchor

DAKAR

0   Metres   500

the turn of the century the population numbered 15,000. With considerable dredging and port construction, Dakar became a **French naval base** in the early 1900s and the **capital** of Afrique Occidentale Française in 1904. It was also a calling port on the routes to South America and West and South Africa runs, and throughout the century of colonial occupation, Dakar's cosmopolitan reputation as the first call on "the Coast" went before it. On the opening of the Dakar–Bamako railway line in 1923, Dakar was easily the most important city in West Africa.

The original Lebu and Wolof inhabitants of the Plateau district were forced out to the new town of Medina in the early 1930s, when the Depression coincided with rent increases imposed to pay for improvements to their houses. Yet the white settlers who moved in were often poor – a rigorous colour bar prevailing over economic reality – and even today you'll see elderly French, some running small businesses, hanging onto very modest existences.

Arrival and information

Arriving by air, you emerge into the milling confusion of **Aeroport International Leopold Sedar Senghor** (☎820 07 80), 12km northwest of the city in Yof. Track down your luggage and hang onto it: the supervision of the arrivals hall is pretty relaxed and not all the "porters" are honourable men. The **bureau de change** is only open Mon–Fri 8–11am and 4.30–8pm, but Cirrus or MasterCard holders will be able to use the 24hr autoteller. Information on flights, car hire and transport into town can be had from the airport **information desk**. There are some SONATEL **telephone** booths inside the airport and a *télécentre* directly across the car park (open 8am–11pm).

Until 9pm, you can take a SOTRAC **bus** (#8), which takes you through Yof Village and then the mishmash of Grand Dakar, past the University and right through the centre of the Plateau to the Palais de Justice. Alternatively, **car rapides** pass about five minutes' walk away from the airport – cross the car park and turn left. They'll take you to the Marché Sandaga in Central Dakar for CFA100, and from here, a taxi across downtown Dakar shouldn't cost more than CFA500. Finally, a **taxi** to the centre should cost around CFA3000 in the daytime, although you'll have to bargain hard. After midnight the price officially – though rarely – doubles; try for CFA4000.

SECURITY IN DAKAR

The question of **personal safety in Dakar** is one you can't afford to be casual about, particularly when you first arrive. Decide quickly on an initial destination rather than wandering in hope. A few gangs of organized **thieves** operate with extraordinary daring and, burdened with luggage, you're an easy and valuable trophy. **Place de l'Indépendance** and **av Georges Pompidou** are notorious trouble-spots, especially the *place* itself during banking hours – remain alert and keep valuables, purses and wallets completely out of sight. Don't be deflected or distracted by anything or anyone, however friendly – keep a steady pace and get where you're going. Once you've found a base you'll soon make up your own mind about the relative safety of Dakar. As a **general rule** however, avoid carrying anything you'd hate to lose and *never* keep purses or wallets in outside or back pockets. Distractions, be they words or a touch, should always be ignored or treated with suspicion. One group **technique** is to stop you by offering a bangle, hold your legs together from behind and grab your shirt sleeves. By the time you've realized what's happening, they're off down the street with your wallet. If you lose anything of personal value (as opposed to just money or expensive items), it's worth making a visit to the market in Colobane – the so-called *marché aux voleurs* – 500m east of the Monument de l'Indépendance, where, if you keep asking and manage to make the right connections, you may be able to buy it back.

Dakar is unusual in having just one main **gare routière**, Pompier, at the head of the autoroute that funnels suburban traffic into the city. It's fairly together, though not any less intimidating for that if you're not used to shouting in French at four people simultaneously while beggars pull at your clothing and the fumes from a hundred idling engines fill the air. From here it's a two-kilometre walk to the centre: much easier to take a taxi (CFA500–800) or a bus.

Trains come in at the old Art Deco station, north of the centre and just ten minutes from the closest budget hotels. The train from Bamako usually gets in after dark, so make sure you've looked at the map and know exactly where you're heading.

For **tourist information**, visit the Ministere du Tourisme des Transports Aeriens on rue du Docteur Calmette, just off bd de la Republique (BP 4049; ☎821 11 26; Fax 822 94 13; *mtta@primature.sn*); they have various leaflets and some English-speaking staff.

Orientation and city transport

Dakar is built on the twin-pronged **Cap Vert peninsula**. The southern spur contains the city's heart, with cliffs and coves along the ocean side and Cap Manuel, and the main port area along the sheltered eastern flank. The suburbs spread north and west towards the **airport** and the other prong of **Pointe des Almadies**, Africa's most westerly point.

Despite Dakar's size, the **city centre** is a relatively manageable two square kilometres of tightly gridded streets, with the **train station** to the north, the **museum** to the south, **Avenue Jean Jaurès** on the west and the **Kermel market** and **PTT** to the east. In the middle of it all stands the big, sloping centrepiece of **Place de l'Indépendance**, from where **Avenue Georges Pompidou** cuts the district into a northern, heavily commercial quarter and a southern, more affluent, residential one – the **Plateau**. Most of the grand buildings of state and several important embassies are south of this central district, where the street pattern breaks into graciously radiating avenues and looping clifftop corniches.

City transport

One of Dakar's great pluses is its excellent **bus system**. The Société des Transports en Commun du Cap Vert (SOTRAC) runs fast, frequent and cheap buses from dawn till late evening. They're numbered and carry destination signs, and charge between CFA140 and CFA180. You can get anywhere by bus, though during rush hours the squeeze – and the heat – are sapping. For long stays you'd do well to obtain a copy of the SOTRAC route map from the small **SOTRAC information office** (☎824 02 42) at the bus station at the north end of Avenue Jean Jaurès.

Cars rapides – boxy Saviem or Mercedes buses, usually sporting marabout monikers ("Touba") – are a poorer, and mostly private, version. Destinations are shouted by the fare collector (CFA85–120), and although they're more erratic than the buses and confusing to newcomers, you're guaranteed an insight into the street life of Dakar. Big white ones leave from Avenue André Peytavin, near Marché Sandaga, for the route de Ouakam, Yof and Ngor, while slightly smaller yellow and blue ones jostle together up the nearby Avenue Emile Badiane for Grand Dakar, HLM and Colobane.

As for **taxis**, supply is ahead of demand so you can always argue about the fare. In theory most operate meters, but nobody uses or trusts them any more, so agree the price up front. Daytime journeys in the town centre should cost no more than CFA500 and trips to the suburbs roughly CFA300/km; after dark (from midnight to 4am) the tariff officially doubles, but more usually just increases by about twenty percent. Keep some change and small notes handy for drivers, who often deny having any.

The **train** isn't a very functional way of getting in or out of the city, although it is at least comprehensible. There's a commuter service to the suburbs of Tiaroye and Rufisque

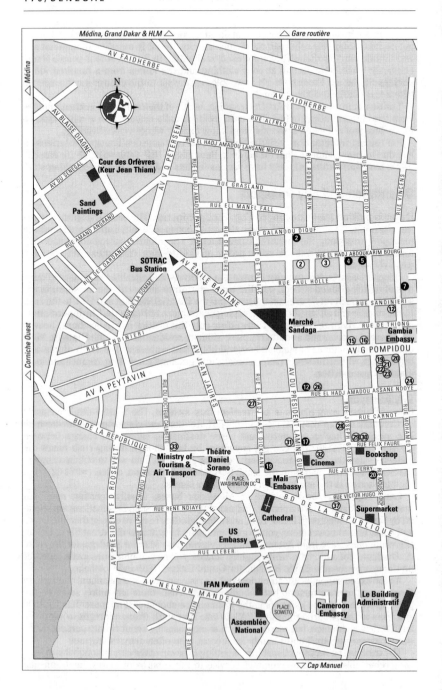

AV FAIDHERBE

△ Médina

AV BLAISE DIAGNE

N

AV DU SENEGAL

RUE AMAND ANGRAND

Cour des Orfèvres
(Keur Jean Thiam)

Sand
Paintings

RUE DES DARDANELLES

SOTRAC
Bus Station

RUE DE LA SOMME

△ Corniche Ouest

RUE SANDINIERI

AV A PEYTAVIN

AV FAIDHERBE

RUE ALFRED GOUX

RUE Q PETERSEN

RUE EL HADJ AMADOU LAHSANE NDOYE

RUE EL HADJ AMADOU PAYE ASSANE

RUE GRASLAND

RUE ELI MANEL FALL

RUE DE FLEURS

RUE GALANDOU DIOUF ②

RUE DE TOBIAC

RUE EL HADJ ABDOUKARIM BOURGI

② ③ ④ ⑤

RUE PAUL HOLLE

RUE ROBER BRUN

RUE RAFFENEL

RUE MOUSSE DIOP

RUE VINCENS

⑦

RUE SANDINIERI

⑫

AV EMILE BADIANE

Marché
Sandaga

RUE DE THIONG

⑮ ⑯

Gambia
Embassy

AV G POMPIDOU

AV JEAN JAURES

RUE DU DOCTEUR CALMETTE

BD DE LA REPUBLIQUE

RUE DU PRESIDENT LAMINE GUEYE

RUE EL HADJ MASS DIOKHANE

⑫ ㉖

㉗

㉛ ⑰

⑲

RUE EL HADJ AMADOU ASSANE NDOYE

⑲㉑
㉒㉓

㉔

RUE CARNOT

㉘

RUE JOSEPH GOMIS

㉙㉚

RUE FELIX FAURE

Bookshop

RUE MOHAMED V

㉟

Ministry of
Tourism &
Air Transport

AV ACHIMOU TALL

RUE ALPHA

AV PRESIDENT F ROOSEVELT

Théâtre
Daniel
Sorano

PLACE
WASHINGTON DC

Mali
Embassy

㉜
Cinema

RUE JULES FERRY

BD DE LA REPUBLIQUE

㉚

RUE VICTOR HUGO

RUE MOUSSE DIOP

㊲
Supermarket

RUE RENE NDIAYE

AV CARDE

AV JEAN XXIII

Cathedral

US
Embassy

RUE KLEBER

RUE DU BUIN

AV NELSON MANDELA

IFAN Museum

PLACE
SOWETO

Assemblée
National

Cameroon
Embassy

Le Building
Administratif

▽ Cap Manuel

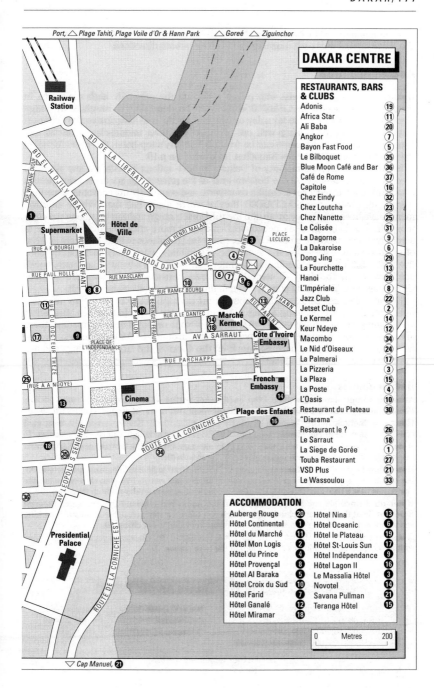

Port, △ Plage Tahiti, Plage Voile d'Or & Hann Park   △ Goreé   △ Ziguinchor

DAKAR CENTRE

RESTAURANTS, BARS & CLUBS

Adonis	⑲
Africa Star	⑪
Ali Baba	⑳
Angkor	⑦
Bayon Fast Food	⑤
Le Bilboquet	㉟
Blue Moon Café and Bar	㊱
Café de Rome	㊲
Capitole	⑯
Chez Eindy	㉜
Chez Loutcha	㉓
Chez Nanette	㉕
Le Colisée	㉛
La Dagorne	⑨
La Dakaroise	⑥
Dong Jing	㉙
La Fourchette	⑬
Hanoi	㉘
L'Impériale	⑧
Jazz Club	㉒
Jetset Club	②
Le Kermel	⑭
Keur Ndeye	⑫
Macombo	㉞
Le Nid d'Oiseaux	㉔
La Palmerai	⑰
La Pizzeria	③
La Plaza	⑮
La Poste	④
L'Oasis	⑩
Restaurant du Plateau "Diarama"	㉚
Restaurant le ?	㉖
Le Sarraut	⑱
La Siege de Gorée	①
Touba Restaurant	㉗
VSD Plus	㉑
Le Wassoulou	㉝

ACCOMMODATION

Auberge Rouge	⑳	Hôtel Nina	⑬
Hôtel Continental	①	Hôtel Oceanic	⑥
Hôtel du Marché	⑪	Hôtel le Plateau	⑲
Hôtel Mon Logis	②	Hôtel St-Louis Sun	⑰
Hôtel du Prince	④	Hôtel Indépendance	⑨
Hôtel Provençal	⑧	Hôtel Lagon II	⑯
Hôtel Al Baraka	⑤	Le Massalia Hôtel	③
Hôtel Croix du Sud	⑩	Novotel	⑭
Hôtel Farid	⑦	Savana Pullman	㉑
Hôtel Ganalé	⑫	Teranga Hôtel	⑮
Hôtel Miramar	⑱		

0   Metres   200

Railway Station

Supermarket
Hôtel de Ville
BD DE LA LIBERATION
RUE WAGANE DIOUF
BD EL H DJILY MBAYE
ALLEES R. DELMAS
RUE HENRI MALAN
RUE CALLE
RUE DAGORNE
PLACE LECLERC
RUE A K BOURGI
RUE MALENFANT
BD EL HADJ DJILY MBAYE
RUE PAUL HOLLE
RUE MASCLARY
RUE RAMEZ BOURGI
RUE DE HANN
RUE P MILLON
RUE BERANGER FERAUD
RUE A LE DANTEC
Marché Kermel
RUE PARENT
AV A SARRAUT
Côte d'Ivoire Embassy
RUE DU DOCTEUR THEZE
PLACE DE L'INDEPENDANCE
RUE PARCHAPPE
RUE MAGE
RUE SALVA
RUE A A NDOYE
French Embassy
Cinema
Plage des Enfants
ROUTE DE LA CORNICHE EST
AV LEOPOLD S SENGHOR
Presidential Palace
ROUTE DE LA CORNICHE EST

▽ Cap Manuel, ㉑

both sometimes used by travellers as bases. Called *les petits trains bleus*, these trains run about five or six times each morning and evening in both directions.

Accommodation

Dakar has dozens of **hotels**, with prices reflecting the generally high standards. In town, anything less than CFA6000 is likely to be depressingly rough, with dodgy plumbing and only bearable for a day or two, and for the real bargains you're better off staying on Gorée or looking well out of the city centre: middle-class suburbs like Dieupeul, Castors and Liberté can be fruitful. The city's top hotel, the *Hôtel Méridien Présidential*, out at Pointe des Almadies, is covered on p.19.

In the city centre, the majority of Dakar's budget options lie within a few blocks of Place de l'Indépendance. At the **bottom end** of the price range are a few grim, prewar establishments, usually set around a courtyard, and seemingly unrenovated since they were built. Costing around CFA5000, they're worth about half that. Where improvements have been made they move into the **mid-price** range and can be among the city's most pleasant lodgings, their neocolonial charm far more attractive than the range of similarly priced anodyne modern blocks. Many budget places twin as **brothels** and can offer good value – we've listed a few of the possibilities, where only particularly sensitive visitors will find the seediness uncomfortable. With the advent of fax many hotels are now easily **booked** – something worth considering around the popular Christmas/New Year/Rally period, when finding a room at all can be difficult.

Dakar makes few concessions to **apartment** hunters. Some hotels below offer this option, or if you are planning a long stay you could try Regie Immobilier Mugnièr et Compagnie, 11 rue Mohamed V (☎823 23 76). If your requirements are modest, there are always unfurnished rooms available for around CFA20,000/month in the Medina/Gueule Tapée quarters: knock on the doors of the larger buildings and ask "Vous avez des chambres à louer?"

Budget options

Auberge Rouge, 116 rue Mousse Diop ex-Blanchot/corner of rue Jules Ferry (☎823 86 61). Popular hotel with budget travellers, offering basic rooms with fans set around a courtyard. ②–③.

Hôtel Continental, 10 rue Galandou Diouf (BP 2324; ☎822 10 83). Below average with basic mod cons. The annexe at 57 rue Mousse Diop (☎822 03 71) is better; airy, light rooms with balconies. ③.

Hôtel du Marché, 3 rue Parent (☎821 57 71). An old stand-by (albeit a brothel) near Kermel market with large, unventilated and inexpensive S/C rooms. ②–③.

Hôtel Mon Logis, 67 rue Galandou Diouf (☎821 85 25). Hard to find and depressing when you do, but one of the cheapest hotels in town, and adequate as a last resort. Down an alley on av Lamine Gueye just past a blue-tiled mosque, left down a couple of steps and then right up the stairs. ②.

Hôtel du Prince, 49 rue Raffenel. Unmarked but numbered – behind the iron gate. *Midnight Express* without the bars, and plumbing to match, but there's a slim possibility of off-street parking and a laid-back owner who's open to long-stay deals. Very dingy, but cheap. ②.

Hôtel Provençal, 17 rue Malenfant (BP 1375; ☎ & Fax 822 10 69). Cheap and popular hotel/brothel with a nice garden, five minutes' walk south of the train station. ③.

ACCOMMODATION PRICE CODES

① Under CFA4500 (under £5/$8)	⑤ CFA27,000–36,000 (£30–40/$48–64)
② CFA4500–9000 (£5–10/$8–16)	⑥ CFA36,000–45,000 (£40–50/$64–80)
③ CFA9000–18,000 (£10–20/$16–32)	⑦ Over CFA45,000 (over £50/$80)
④ CFA18,000–27,000 (£20–30/$32–48)	

For further details see p.48.

Le Massalia Hôtel, 10 bd El Hadj Djily Mbaye (☎822 97 47). Clean and comfortable S/C rooms with AC or fans, plus a bar and restaurant. ③.

Moderate options

Hôtel Al Baraka, 35 rue El Hadj Abdoukarim Bourgi (BP 578; ☎822 55 32; Fax 821 75 41). Central place offering modern and clean rooms with TVs and telephones. All credit cards. ⑤.

Hôtel Croix du Sud, 20 av Albert Sarraut (BP 232; ☎823 29 47; Fax 823 26 55). Renovated 1950s hotel, centrally located but with little character. ⑤.

Hôtel Farid, 51 rue de Vincens (BP 1514; ☎821 61 27; Fax 821 08 94). Great-value modern, clean rooms, with TV, fridge and showroom-like bathrooms and balconies. There's an excellent Lebanese restaurant downstairs. Credit cards accepted. ④.

Hôtel Ganalé, 38 rue El Hadj AA Ndoye (☎821 58 54; Fax 822 34 30). One of central Dakar's newer refurbishments offering spotless motel-like rooms with TV, some apartments and a popular disco bar and restaurant. Breakfast CFA2000. Credit cards accepted. ④–⑤.

Hôtel Miramar, 25–27 rue Felix Faure (BP 973; ☎823 55 98; Fax 823 35 05). Slightly ageing S/C, AC rooms with TV. Afro-kitsch spaceship decor in communal areas and the *Soninké Bar* downstairs add eccentric character. Good breakfast served. ④.

Hôtel Nina, 43 rue de Docteur Thèze (☎821 41 81; Fax 823 81 56). Central hotel with all mod cons, though pricey and a bit bland. All credit cards. ④.

Hôtel Oceanic, 9 rue du Thann (BP 219; ☎822 20 44; Fax 821 52 28). Very pleasant old-style hotel, with clued-up owners and clean AC, S/C rooms, plus four-bed apartments. ③–④.

Hôtel le Plateau, 62 rue Jules Ferry (BP 2906; ☎823 44 20; Fax 822 50 24). Unprepossessing block situated right behind the Malian embassy with reasonable-value rooms and a good place to drink, the *Bar Americaine*. ④.

Hôtel St-Louis Sun, 68 rue Felix Faure (☎822 25 75; Fax 821 17 21). A charismatic choice, renovated in the *Louisienne*-style with an attractive patio and restaurant and tidy AC, S/C rooms. MasterCard accepted. ④.

Expensive options

Hôtel Indépendance, Place de l'Indépendance (BP 221; ☎823 10 19; Fax 822 11 17). Dakar's earliest modern four-star flagship tower block is overpriced but does have a great view from the rooftop pool. Breakfast extra. ⑦.

Hôtel Lagon II, rte de la Corniche Est (BP 3115; ☎823 74 42; Fax 823 77 27). Popular, French-run hotel right on the shore looking towards Gorée. No pool but has a private beach. ⑦.

Novotel, av Abdoulaye Fadiga (BP 2073; ☎823 88 49; Fax 823 89 29). Bland four-star high-rise with possible sea views from renovated rooms with modern facilities. ⑦.

Savana Pullman, rte de la Corniche Est (BP 1015; ☎823 60 23; Fax 823 73 06). Luxuriously landscaped tourist hotel – the best place in Dakar to spend gratuitously in genuine comfort. ⑦.

Teranga Hôtel, Place de l'Indépendance (BP 3380; ☎823 10 44; Fax 823 50 01). Dakar's priciest hotel – the preferred abode of visiting statesmen. Well into the top price scale. ⑦.

The Town

Dakar is every inch a capitalist capital with **consumption** as conspicuous and contradictory as you'd expect. Lepers, polio victims and various other beggars are a common sight, and you may find the contrasts repugnant. Unless you're going to do your necessary business as fast as possible and get out, you might as well resign yourself to participation and expenditure. Once you've learnt to deal with the inevitable hassle, the two central markets of **Sandaga** and **Kermel** are worth a visit, and you'll find the irrepressible *commerçants* spilling out onto any traffic-free surface in the surrounding area. Of interest too are the superb and highly buyable offerings of the artisans at **Keur Jean Thiam,** a few minutes north of Sandaga.

There's more to do in Dakar than shop, from visiting the IFAN **museum** to merely walking the avenues and exploring the backstreets, especially during the comfortable winter months. For a wonderful **bird's-eye view** of the city, go up to the seventeenth-floor swimming pool and roof terrace of the *Hôtel Indépendance* – just buy a soft drink to get access. From this height the old red-tiled quarters and the main avenues of dark green foliage stand out clearly.

The central markets

Down towards the port you'll find the **Marché Kermel**, rebuilt after it burned down in 1993 – a fate which, oddly enough, has befallen several metropolitan West African markets. The smart new market building houses a mass of stalls selling fish, fruit and vegetables, with flower sellers on the surrounding pavements. To the west, around the area of rue de le Dantec, market stands line the streets where offerings include stacks of basketry, faddish fashions, carvings and other **souvenirs**, plus a cornucopia of expensive produce for the old-style *colons* still living in the quarter. Beware of dastardly sales psychology – don't accept "gifts" or, if you do, insist on paying. Repeated visits improve the atmosphere as the pushers get used to your face, but it takes courage to leave without buying something – if you do, you may hear "*libanais*" hissed after you in contempt. You should experience less aggressive merchandising, and far less interesting merchandise, below Kermel, along the portside **boulevard de la Libération**, where a grubby street market has operated for some years. Don't come down here after dark though, as it's dodgy territory.

At the end of av Georges Pompidou is the **Marché Sandaga**, Dakar's big *centreville* market, an unpretentious two-storey emporium with a tremendous variety of fruit, vegetables and dry foods, and lots of wonderful fish in the morning. Today, Sandaga has

---

SHOPPING IN DAKAR

You can buy nearly anything at any time in Dakar from a haircut to bootleg cassettes. The following list gives some pointers.

Barbers Men can get their hair cut cheaply at the outdoor stalls on av Jean Jaurès (corner of av André Peytavin), though the barbers aren't too familiar with straight hair.

Books Librairie aux Quatre Vents (Tues–Sat 8.30am–12.30pm and 3–6.30pm) on rue Felix Faure, between rue Mousse Diop and rue Joseph Gomez, is probably the best bookshop in West Africa. They also sell a few books in English, a surprisingly rare commodity. Also try Clairafrique, 2 rue Sandiniéri, Place de l'Indépendance, next to the Chamber of Commerce.

Cassettes Stacks of bootlegs at stalls around Sandaga market and from street sellers in the vicinity. Beware of buying from the pavement cruisers down av Georges Pompidou. Prices should be close to CFA1000 – if you buy for CFA500 the quality will be dreadful. For "legitimate" recordings expect to pay up to CFA2000. For browsing and listening in a more controlled and relaxing atmosphere, head out to a suburban market such as Castors.

Curios For the real thing, visit El Hadj Traoré, rue Mohamed V, between rue Carnot and rue Felix Faure – a fine musty collection. There are more further north on Mohamed V, on the left before av Pompidou. Avoid flashy "galleries" – unreasonably expensive and not special.

Supermarkets Hyperscore, the city's biggest hypermarket (closed Mon), is out on av Cheikh Anta Diop/bd de la Gueule Tapée. More convenient are Bon Prix on bd de la République/rue Mousse Diop; Le Supermarché Soleil just north of the Place de l'Indépendance; and Leader Price next to Marché Kermel. Many supermarket exits have notice boards for buying or selling – cameras, cars, whatever.

Tailoring Good, reasonably priced tailors abound all over the centre and suburbs. The best bargains are at Marché HLM, where they will often run something up for you while you wait.

been almost completely taken over by Mouride traders. You can buy just about anything here and in the surrounding streets, from avocados to bootleg cassettes and attaché cases made of beer cans. The hassle can be intense, with the politest rejection of over-zealous salesmanship provoking accusations of racism; go in a patient and forgiving mood. The enormous crush also encourages pickpockets so you should take care around the fringes of the building.

The former Mauritanian silversmiths' yard, the *cour des orfèvres,* now renamed **Keur Jean Thiam** (after an early and renowned Senegalese artisan), has long been located at 69 av Blaise Diagne, 500m downhill from Sandaga. Mauritanian artisans are steadily returning to Dakar following the conflict of the early 1990s, and their superb **silver jewellery** and **wooden chests** (the latter are "authentic copies" no matter what story they spin you) are worth bargaining for; they can now also be seen all over the downtown areas, especially along rue Felix Faure. Senegalese carved **wooden masks** and figures are also made and sold at Keur Jean Thiam – if you're serious about making a purchase, be prepared to discuss the matter over a couple of hours or, better still, a couple of visits.

Nearly next door, at no. 65, there's a **sand painters' yard** where various grades and tones of sand are artfully used to depict some rather tacky tropical images of the "pouting silhouette" genre.

Medina, Bène Tali and Castors

You can't miss the **Grande Mosquée**, over to the northwest of Sandaga (bus #9 or #13). Finished in 1964 and built after the style of the Mohamed V mosque in Casablanca, it's truly impressive, with seventy-metre minarets standing out above the low rooftops of the **Medina** quarter. Non-believers are strictly barred most of the time, so your only option is to peer in through the windows. One day they'll put in the lawn that's crying out to be sown around it. The **Marché de Tilène**, a short distance north, brings you down to earth with its football-pitch-sized food market serving a massive array of **produce**. This is the place to come to absorb ordinary Dakar life.

Going a good deal further north, there's a vast array of **cloth** at the best possible prices in the market in the old African quarter of **Bène Tali** (bus #13 from Place de l'Indépendance), and more textiles at the less traditional **HLM V** (pronounced "ash-el-em-cinq" meaning "Council Flats 5") market in the middle-class suburbs out between Grand Dakar and the autoroute (bus #13 again).

Lastly, if you go out further to the suburb of **Castors**, there's a humdrum general market (buses #13, #18, #20) where you can wander in complete tranquillity. A place to buy food, spices, traditional remedies, cheap cassettes, secondhand clothes and so on, it's somewhat cheaper than the central markets and easier to bargain.

The IFAN Museum and the Plateau

In truth, Dakar's cultural showpiece, the **IFAN (Institut Fondamental d'Afrique Noir) Museum** (Tues–Sun 9am–12.30pm & 3–6.30pm; CFA2200), does not make a great first impression. The collection is basically thousands of objects from all over West Africa, many of them visibly decaying, pinned to the walls or lying in glass cases with little in the way of background information. You can happily spend an hour here however, longer if you're intrigued. If you don't speak French, there's an English-speaking guide who can help you to understand the displays.

On the **ground floor** look out for the **white man mask**, obviously modelled on a moustachioed colonial officer with a wrinkly neck. **Circumcision instruments**, the giant thighbone of an unidentified but hopefully prehistoric animal, and a large assortment of **Senoufo** (Côte d'Ivoire) initiation and ancestor ethnographia compete for attention, along with games of pebbles-and-holes (called here *Dodoi* and *Aji*), hundreds of **ancestor figures** and some fine **cattle and hippo masks** from Guinea-Bissau.

There's a fascinating account too, presented through a collection of printing blocks, of the development of a kind of African swastika, a stylized lizard or crocodile motif.

The **first floor** collections are slightly easier to distinguish, though there are **masks** everywhere. In the three central halls you'll see examples of **bark cloth** and the instruments used to beat it out, dyed and woven **strip cloth**, an entire case of spindles, whorls and looms, and the **costumes** of kings and lesser mortals. One especially striking outfit is the Guerzé mask-wearer's costume from southeastern Guinea, with its all-in-one gloves and feet: notice how worn and red-mudded the feet are. The Fula (*Peul*) **circumcision costume** also stands out: it's virtually identical to the white "Phrygian caps" worn by newly circumcised boys on the streets of Dakar, especially in July.

Dogon headdresses from Mali, now a commonplace image of West African art, are on show at the far right-hand end. Their remarkable geometric appearance, as if constructed from set squares, looks like the result of a stylistic evolution when compared with the more representational masks from Mali in the middle hall (first entry on the right as you come upstairs). The latter look much more like four-legged animals and the common "swastika" motif is clear.

Chairs and tableaux from the **Benin courts** (Nigeria) and illustrations of the arrival of the Europeans fill the central hall. Over in the big room on the right, notice the **sewn canoes**, and play the lovely **balafons** – they make a glorious sound.

Outside, you can see all the main state buildings of the **Plateau** – if you want to – in an hour or so, by wandering around the Parisian quarter centering on Place Soweto. On the *place* itself, across from the museum, is the **Assemblée Nationale**; along avenue Courbet stands the appalling **"Building Administratif"** a megablock of ministries crowned with scores of vultures; and then on the right, down avenue Leopold S. Senghor is the high-profile **Presidential Palace**, with its befezzed and unfazed presidential guards.

The beaches, corniches and Hann Park

There are plenty of opportunities for physical pursuits around Dakar. The best town **beaches** are **Tahiti** and **Voile d'Or** on the sheltered Pointe de Bel-Air, on the east side of the city; buses #18 and #20 pass the sign to *Tahiti plage*, from where it's a five-minute walk to the entrance gates. Unfortunately the whole of Bel-Air is a French military base, the only saving grace being that it makes the beaches as safe as you could wish (CFA500 entry fee). With the *militaires* on one side and chemical and groundnut plants fuming on the other, the scene could be prettier, but the sand and sea are clean enough, and palms and sunshades provide additional compensation. You can rent windsurfers, too, for around CFA5000 per hour. Tahiti is the nearer and smaller of the two beaches; the adjoining Voile d'Or is definitely the better, stretching out to rocks at the point. Both beaches get crowded at weekends so come early, and bring a bite to eat and water – the bars here are expensive. The *Tahiti Plage* club of old is now the *Monaco Plage* (reasonable entrance and drinks prices) – a faintly pretentious and restrained set-up, but with an unbeatable "chill-out area" under the palms. It's possible to **stay** on Voile d'Or: beach cabins cost around CFA10,000 per day (S/C with electricity), or there's the more upmarket *Voile d'Or Hôtel* (☎832 86 48; Fax 832 47 33; S/C ④).

Other possible beaches are south of the port along the corniches (see below) – the pretty **Plage des enfants**; the deep cove at **Anse Bernard** (crowded with local kids at weekends); and the **Plage de l'Institut Pasteur**, on the rougher Atlantic side of Cap Manuel. All of these are to some extent unsafe, but if you have no valuables on you there's little to worry about.

The corniches

Walking the corniches carries some risk, as both have reputations for bag snatching and various kinds of assault. Violent attacks are in fact rare, but you shouldn't go alone and under no circumstances carry valuables. Both the Corniche Est, from the end of Boulevard de la Libération to Cap Manuel, and the Corniche Ouest, from Avenue André Peytavin right up to Mermoz, are fine walks, mostly on the clifftop, with some stunning views.

The **Corniche Est** (4km) runs through dense vegetation, past the back gardens of various embassies and diplomatic residences and the front gate of the German ambassador's bizarre house, a kind of Sudanic-Teutonic construction. It then climbs to **Cap Manuel** via Dakar's most picture-postcard viewpoints over the city and Gorée. You pass the self-consciously tropical *Hôtel Savanna* – a good place for a break and a drink – and from the forbidding yellow slab of the nearby **Palais du Justice** you can bus back into town. As you go, look out for the beautiful **Aristide le Dantec maternity hospital** – Sudanic architectural influences in two shades of baby pink.

The eight-kilometre-long **Corniche Ouest** has a far less intimate feel – windswept, wave-ripped and racing with traffic and joggers. There's free use of jogging trails and weight-training equipment, courtesy of the Commune de Dakar. City tours come out here for the **Village Artisanal** on Soumbedioune bay, but it's frankly not up to much, with high prices and loads of pressure. However, as long as you're not carrying anything of value it's fun to go down on the ant's-nest-busy **beach** to watch the world go by in **Lebu** style. From mid-afternoon it's full of returning Lebu fishermen and women selling a fascinatingly diverse catch. The Lebu are related to the Wolof, from whom they broke away at the end of the eighteenth century. Most belong to the Tijaniya brotherhood rather than the Mourides, but a few are Layen, a largely Lebu fraternity.

The **Musée Dynamique**, on the far side of the bay, is not especially dynamic but occasionally hosts art exhibitions. Beyond, you come to the suburb of **Fann**: more diplomatic and expat residences with guard dogs and iron gates, and armies of Dakarois youth working out on the skyline – the **University** is nearby, and physical fitness is a big thing these days. Any time you get tired of walking, bus #10 follows this whole route back to the centre.

Hann Park

One part of the city that doesn't yet appear to suffer the problems of the corniches – though you should be cautious nonetheless – is **Hann Park** (daily 8am–noon & 3–6pm; bus #6), eighty hectares of woodland and swamp with a **zoo** and a network of paths. It's a pleasant place for a stroll, again full of joggers and keep-fit fanatics in the hour before dark, and a good complement to the beaches at Bel-Air. It's quite attractive to ornithologists, too, who can find several different habitats here. The **Parc Zoologique** (Tues–Sun 8am–noon & 3–6pm; CFA350), on the other hand, is not a happy place, a small collection of listless mammals and a large one of birds – not counting the vultures perching ominously on the trees outside. If you want to do it the Dakar way, go armed with sweets and groundnuts and feed everything; but it's probably best avoided.

Eating and drinking

Dakar has a blaze of restaurants, and some that are even affordable. If you're really short of cash, you could *survive* on streetside snacks and fruit for under CFA1000 a day. At the top of Sandaga market you'll find a very basic food hall selling the kind of nourishing breakfast foods sold around the suburbs of Dakar, like sour milk *thiacry* (*chagry*), with millet grains and sugar, or millet porridge *fondé*, all at about CFA50–100 a bowl.

The cheapest sit-down meals are found in the distinctly functional **hole-in-the-wall cafés**, or *gargotes*, sometimes unsigned, but distinguishable behind the multicoloured ribbons over the doorways. These offer a daily Senegalese staple or an omelette, served with bread and water, for less than CFA700. For about the same price you can get a *chawarma* or other Lebanese snacks from any of the **takeaway bars** found along

Avenue Pompidou. Pay twice that and you'll get a tablecloth, less austere surroundings, service with a smile and a genuine choice; in the exotic or better African **restaurants** a meal costs from around CFA2000.

Under CFA2000

Adonis, av G. Pompidou. Lebanese eat-in or takeaway. Fast service with great hummus and *baba ghanouge*.

Ali Baba, av G. Pompidou. Good-value Lebanese fast food.

Bayon Fast Food, rue Thann. Not exactly *McDonalds* but a selection of sandwiches and snacks such as *crevettes pekinoise*, as well as Flags beer. Mon–Sat 9am–10pm.

Capitole, av G. Pompidou. Mostly Lebanese fast food, and big mugs of coffee.

Chez Eindy, 63 rue Felix Faure. Small and friendly "tablecloth" café down an alley, offering Euro-Senegalese dishes with a smile. Mon–Fri 7am–11pm, Sat 7am–lunchtime.

Cité Claudelle, out past Soumbedioune, near the University. A row of five or six good-value restaurants offering specialities from various African countries. Frequented by a good mix of mostly African diners.

Le Nid d'Oiseaux, rue El Hadj AA Ndoye. Run by the same family as *Restaurant le ?*, offering a similar, excellent range of Senegalese meals.

Restaurant du Plateau "Diarama", 56 rue Felix Faure. Cheap, popular and with a moderately smart interior offering full African and European meals. Daily 8am–10.30pm.

Restaurant le ? ("*Le Point de Interogation*"), rue El Hadj AA Ndoye. Long menus of Senegalese food at outstanding value. Usually open.

Touba Restaurant, corner of rue de Denain/rue El Hadj AA Ndoye. Busy, clean lunchtime eatery with generous helpings of Senegalese staples. Highly recommended *mafé*. CFA600.

Le Wassoulou, 18 rue Felix Faure/bd de la Republique. Senegalese menu, and particularly tasty brochettes.

VSD Plus, rue Mousse Diop, near av G. Pompidou. Various good-value African dishes.

CFA2000–4500

Angkor, rue Dagorne, opposite *La Dagorne*. Pleasant Chinese restaurant just north of the Marché Kermel, specializing in Szechuan dishes. Daily noon–2pm & 6–11pm.

Le Bilboquet, 19 av Leopold S. Senghor (☎821 45 91). Bar and pizzeria. Eat in or takeaway.

Chez Loutcha, 100 rue Mousse-Diop (☎821 03 02). An exceptional Cape Verdean restaurant. Typically enormous meals; wonderful tuna salad and insurmountable three-course *menu*, including vegetarian options. Good breakfasts too. Closed Sun.

Chez Nanette, rue Wagane Diouf, near rue El Hadj AA Ndoye. Portuguese-run bar with upstairs restaurant featuring a shaded terrace at the back and a garrulous mynah bird.

Dong Jing, 58 rue Felix Faure. Reasonably priced Chinese place.

Farid, at the *Hôtel Farid*, 51 rue de Vincens. Dakar's best Lebanese restaurant with dishes from CFA3000 and daily non-Lebanese specials for a little less. Daily noon–10pm.

Les Gourmandises Africaines, rue A, Point E (☎824 87 05) Recommended for its Senegalese and other African food. Eat inside or in the leafy garden.

Hanoi, corner of rue Carnot/rue Joseph Gomis. Vietnamese food at good prices. Daily noon–late.

L'Impériale (aka "*Robert's Bar*"), Place de l'Indépendance, corner of Allée R Delmas. Pleasant restaurant/bar retreat, away from *place* hustlers, serving pizza and fish dishes and a good-value *menu*.

Le Kermel, opposite Marché Kermel. French and continental food and a very French atmosphere on Sun mornings.

Keur Ndeye, corner of rue Sandinieri/rue de Vincens (☎821 49 73). Upmarket Senegalese with *kora* minstrels; meals (including vegetarian and a wine list) are nicely served but contents much the same as in a *gargote*, for twice the price.

Le Matonge, rue A, Point E (☎824 31 64). Excellent food from Congo.

L'Oasis, 8 rue Ramez Bourgi. Inexpensive restaurant-bar right by the Marché Kermel, offering *plats* such as *boudin* and chips, plus three-course meals and Flag beer. Mon–Sat 9am–10.30pm.

La Palmeraie, av G. Pompidou. Good-sized portions of tasty sandwiches and snacks, but noted for its wonderful cakes, coffee and hot chocolate. Newspapers and magazines available to read, including English-language ones.

La Pizzeria, 47 rue A.K. Bourgi (☎821 09 26). Franco-Italian pizza restaurant. Clientele mainly expats and tourists.

Over CFA4500

Café de Rome, bd de la République. Tasty international menu with daily specials. Comfortable AC restaurant or a shaded terrace.

La Dagorne, 11 rue Dagorne. Ever-popular mid-range French restaurant that has been drawing them in for years with a great *menu*. Tues–Sun 7am–7.30pm.

La Fourchette, rue Parent (☎821 88 87). French and Mexican menu, close to the *Hôtel du Marché*, with an adjoining piano bar.

Lagon I, at *Le Lagon Hôtel*, rte de la Corniche Est. Great location, set on a small pier looking out to sea and popular with the French expat crowd. Seafood dishes pricey, but the *menu* is always good value. Daily noon–late.

Macombo, Corniche Ouest, behind the *Novotel*. French cuisine and beautiful views – on the best tables you're sitting over the waves.

La Plaza, 14 rue Raffenel (☎822 27 68). Varied menu including pizza and pasta.

Le Sarraut, av Albert Sarraut. Classy French restaurant a couple of minutes' walk east of the Place de l'Indépendance and popular with the expat community. An alfresco terrace cordoned by a thick herbaceous wall makes for a relaxing meal with *plats* and a *menu*. Daily 7am–11pm.

Nightlife

Despite the city's impeccably cosmopolitan credentials, Dakar's **nightlife** is less exotic than one might expect. If you want a fairly unpredictable night out, most of the bars and clubs we've listed will do the business. Most places tend to be pick-up joints for soldiers and all are pricey. The music played is generally a cosmopolitan mix of high and low energy Senegalese, Central African, Cuban and Western. For real action at a price, try one of the **big discos** or **music clubs**, which warm up around midnight (the "soirée"), but may also have an earlier session, from 7 to 11pm (the "matinée") that can be just as hot. If you're going to check out several places and move by taxi, anticipate spending at least CFA30,000 between two, and that's without many drinks – which may be as much as CFA2000–3000 after your first drink, included in the cover of CFA2000–5000. Going in a group works out cheaper and is more fun. Take IDs but leave all valuables behind.

For **theatre**, Théatre Daniel Sorano on Boulevard de la République is the place, though shows – which sometimes feature big name music stars – are not held nightly.

Bars

Blue Moon Café and Bar, corner rue Victor Hugo/rue Mohamed V. Pricey, stylish bar where you can also play chess.

La Bodega av Cheikh Anta Diop, near the University. Chic bar-resto and *tapas* joint.

Le Colisée, av Lamine Guèye. Quiet, French family-style bar. Fairly expensive, but a regular setting-off point. A nice, informal gathering of chess players meets here around 10pm on Tuesdays.

La Dakaroise, rue de Thann, near the PTT and Marché Kermel. Always thronging with sailors and prostitutes, this does good French and continental food, with African nights at weekends.

Le Hadong, behind the cinema in Gueule Tapée, corner of rue 6/bd de la Gueule Tapée. Try the courtyard here for a cheap drink in a relaxed African bar.

Jazz Bar Tamango, bd de l'Est, Point E. Could be in Paris: clean in all senses, with occasional live jazz but otherwise discreet background piping and civilized ambience. Rarely any cover, and the beer is not expensive.

Jazz Club, rue Mousse Diop. Laid-back, late-night hangout next door to *VSD Plus* restaurant.

La Poste, rue Dagorne, opposite the main PTT. Sleazy drinking hole with cheap beer and a pool table.

Le Soninké, at the *Hôtel Miramar*, 25–27 rue Felix Faure. Colourful, cosy, happy-hour type of bar.

Clubs and discos

Africa Star, 42 rue Docteur Thèze. Good *dancing* but very much a pick-up joint. Expensive.

Broadway, at the *Méridien Présidentiel* hotel, Almadies. One of Dakar's hottest clubs, though less lively on Mon or Tues. Expensive.

Jet Set, corner rue A.K. Bourgi/rue Robert Brun. Busy all week, great dancing and not too much hassle.

Le Ngalam, bd de l'Est, Point E. Recorded music and expensive drinks.

La Siege de Gorée, corner of allée R. Delmas/bd de la Libération, behind the Dakar Hôtel de Ville. A massive open-air dance floor with mixed Western/African music. Free entrance, cheap beer, packed with people. Go early – by 10pm – as the place quietens down at 1am and closes at 2am.

Le Sunset Sahel, av Cheikh Anta Diop/bd de la Gueule Tapée. A flashy place, used for fashion shows and pop video recordings.

Timi's, Ngor, just behind the *Hôtel Diarama*. Caters more for a tourist crowd, with more Western music. If you're in the vicinity, well worth calling in on, otherwise the town clubs are better.

Live music venues

These are the places to hit at weekends – or even around which to plan a stay in Dakar.

Liberté Bar, near av Bourguiba. Adjoining the right side of the Liberté Theatre in the heart of the SICAP Baobabs suburb, this is the regular Fri night venue for the re-formed Orchestre Baobab. Balla Sidibé, the host, mixes a mellow and friendly atmosphere to match a less pretentious crowd than most of the competition, reflected in relatively low prices.

L T Horoscope, av Bourguiba. A cracking place, though at first inspection not very promising. Four "venues" consist of a fast-food outlet at street level, an upstairs bar-restaurant with "traditional" *balafon* serenades, a sleazy *American Bar* video lounge, and a tiny but red-hot nightclub with a formidable twelve-piece house band who play every night from midnight till 4am.

Relais, av Cheikh Anta Diop, near the University. A student venue with cheap drinks and an open-air dance area. Small outside stage (check press for gigs) and good sound system encourage a lively young crowd paying more attention to moves than clothes. Not to miss if there's a band playing.

Stade Demba Diop, Liberté. If there's a concert at Dakar's big venue, the posters all over town will be pretty obvious. Get there on time, but be prepared for it to start two hours late and for gangs of robbers inside and out (take no valuables and get a taxi when you leave). But go!

Thiossane, rue E.H.D. Coulibaly, ex Dial Diop (☎824 60 46). Run by Youssou N'dour, who usually plays late on Sat and Sun.

Listings

Airlines Air Afrique, Place de l'Indépendance (☎823 10 22); Air Algérie, 2 Place de l'Indépendance (☎823 80 81); Air France, 47 av Albert Sarraut (☎822 49 49 or 823 29 41); Air Gabon, 5 av Georges Pompidou (☎822 24 05); Air Guinea, 71 av André Peytavin (☎821 44 22); Air Mauritania, 2 Place de l'Indépendance (☎822 81 88); Air Sénégal, 45 av Albert Sarraut (☎823 62 29); Alitalia, 5 av Georges Pompidou (☎823 31 29); American Airlines, office in av André Peytavin; Ethiopian Airlines, 16 av Leopold S. Senghor (☎821 32 98); Ghana Airways, rue Ramez Bourgi (☎822 28 20); Iberia, 2 Place de l'Indépendance (☎823 34 77); Nigeria Airways, 27 av Leopold S. Senghor (☎823 60 68); Royal Air Maroc, 1 Place de l'Indépendance (☎821 37 20); Sabena, 2 Place de l'Indépendance (☎823 27 73); Saudiair, 12 av Georges Pompidou (☎823 86 12); Swissair, 3 Place de l'Indépendance (☎823 48 48); TACV (Cape Verde), 105 rue Mousse Diop (☎821 39 68); TAP Air Portugal, 3 rue El Hadj AA Ndoye (☎821 01 13); Tunis Air, 24 av Leopold S. Senghor (☎823 14 35).

American Express Agents include: Senegal Tours, Place de l'Indépendance (☎823 40 40), who will sell you up to US$1000 travellers' cheques each week on your Amex card (which can be cashed in all banks except CBAO).

Banks Most head offices are on Place de l'Indépendance west: BICIS is efficient, but has poor rates; CBAO charges 2 percent commission on FF travellers' cheques, none on US$ travellers' cheques;

EMBASSIES IN DAKAR

Cameroon, 157–159 rue Joseph Gomis (BP 4165) ☎823 21 95; Fax 823 33 96

Canada, 45 bd de la République (BP 3373) ☎823 92 90; Fax 823 87 49

Cape Verde, 3 av El Hadj Djily Mbaye ☎821 39 36
You should be able to get a visa (CFA6600–8500) in a matter of hours, with one passport photo. Be sure to check when you're supposed to come back, as the office (in theory Mon–Fri 8am–noon & 3–5pm) keeps slightly irregular hours.

Côte d'Ivoire, 2 av Albert Sarraut (BP 359) ☎821 01 63; Fax 822 38 07
Allow 48hr to clear visa for up to 3 months' stay; CFA3000 single entry. Mon–Fri 8.30am–noon & 3–6pm.

France, 1 rue El Hadj AA Ndoye (BP 4035) ☎823 43 71; Fax 822 18 05

The Gambia, 11 rue de Thiong (BP 3248) ☎821 72 30; Fax 821 62 79
Immediate processing of visas; ask for multiple entry. They are valid for up to 6 months' stay and cost CFA10,000. Mon–Thurs 8am–3pm, Fri & Sat 8am–1pm.

Guinea, rue 7, Point E ☎824 86 06; Fax 825 59 46
Getting a visa is no longer a problem, though you need a letter of introduction from your own diplomatic representative in Dakar. CFA20,000 for 1 month, CFA40,000 for 2 months. Mon–Fri 9am–3pm.

Guinea-Bissau, rue 6, Point E (BP 2319) ☎ & Fax 825 29 46

24hr to process; CFA10,000 single entry (cheaper and less fuss in Banjul, or Ziguinchor). Mon–Thurs 8am–noon.

Israel, 3 Place de l'Independance (BP 2096) ☎823 35 61; Fax 823 64 90

Mali, 46 bd de la République (BP 478) ☎823 48 93
48hr wait for visas; valid for 1 month stay; CFA7500. Mon–Fri 8–11am.

Mauritania, 37 bd Général De Gaulle ☎821 43 43
Introductory letter required from your own embassy for a visa; 24–48hr to process; prices vary with status and length of projected visit, and should be negotiated. Mon–Thurs 8.30am–12.30pm & 3.30–6.30pm, Sat 8.30am–12.30pm.

Morocco, Av Cheikh Anta Diop ☎824 38 36

Nigeria, rue 1, Point E (BP 3129) ☎824 43 97; Fax 825 81 36
"Issue of visas all depends on circumstances"; 2 weeks to process; prices vary according to nationality; up to 3 months stay. Mon–Fri 9am–noon.

South Africa, 12 av Albert Saurrat ☎823 65 81

United Kingdom, 20 rue du Dr Gillet (BP 6025) ☎823 73 92; Fax 823 27 66
Letter of recommendation for certain visas costs CFA5000. Mon–Thurs 8am–4.30pm, Fri 8am–12.30pm.

USA, av Jean XXIII (BP 49) ☎823 42 96; Fax 822 29 91

Citibank offers good rates; SGBS, on av Leopold S. Senghor, is a Thomas Cook agent. There's also a bit of currency black market around rue Raffenel and rue Sandiniéri (ten percent mark-up).

Car rental Main agents are: Avis, 71 KM 2.5 bd du Centenaire de la Commune de Dakar (☎823 63 40); Europcar, bd Libération (☎821 38 49); Hertz, 64 rue Felix Faure (☎821 56 23; airport ☎820 11 74). Best value for money is Teranga Location de Voitures, 47 rue Felix Faure (☎822 59 99): a Peugeot 205 costs CFA88,200/week plus CFA140/km; a Suzuki 4WD costs CFA170,000/week plus CFA270/km; all credit cards accepted.

Cinemas The Paris on Place de l'Indépendance, the ABC on av du President Lamine Guèye and Plaza on av Georges Pompidou show familiar American or European movies either *v.o.* (*version originale* with subtitles if not in French) or *v.f.* (*version française* with French soundtrack).

Cultural Centres The **American cultural centre**, av Abdoulaye Fadiga (☎823 58 80) is no longer the retreat it used to be. Bring a letter explaining why you want to make use of the centre and your application will be considered. The library has now moved out to The West African Research Centre

MOVING ON FROM DAKAR

Moving on from Dakar, the obvious choices are **bus or taxi**, for which you need the main *gare routière*, or **train**, with the latest details available at the station. If you're going **to Banjul** by public transport your first choice should be one of the Gambian GPTC buses which leave from Place le Clerc early each morning at 7–8am; the next best option is a seven-seat Peugeot 504 from the *gare routière*. Train tickets from Dakar **to Bamako** go on sale at 3pm the day before departure – though first-class reservations theoretically can be made from 8am two days before. Second-class is always crowded. For full details see p.297.

For a summary of **flight connections**, check the practical information at the beginning of this chapter. If you're flying from Dakar to Europe, check out Aeroflot (cheap tickets; with a few nights at their expense in Moscow, but expect a few days' wait for the visa). For African destinations, Air Afrique offer good discounts. The main airlines are listed on p.186.

If travel is once again safe in the Basse Casamance region, you can take one of the **boats to Ziguinchor**, which are operated by COSENAM, 1 rue Galandou Diouf (☎822 54 43; Fax 821 84 85), or ask at the office down at Gorée wharf. The MV *Joola* leaves Dakar on Tues and Fri at 8.30pm, arriving at Ziguinchor the next day between 11am and 2pm, depending on the tides. Hard seats cost CFA3500; comfortable seats CFA6000; four-berth cabins CFA12,000/person; twin share cabins CFA15,000/person; and a cabin to yourself CFA18,000. Cars cost CFA15,000. The new *Kassoumay* catamaran (☎821 07 07) now operates a six-hour service to Ziguinchor, departing at 10am on Mon, Wed, Fri and Sun, stopping at Karabane Island on the way. Economy class costs CFA18,000, first class CFA30,000.

in Fan Residence (☎824 20 62). The **British Council** is at Immeuble Sonatel, 34/36 bd de la République (☎822 20 15). The **British-Senegalese Institute**, 18 rue de 18 Juin, off av Courbet (Mon–Fri 9am–noon & 3.30–6.30pm; Sat 10am–noon; closed Mon am; ☎822 28 70), caters to the small British community, and has a library and free film shows. The **Centre Culturel Blaise Senghor**, rue 10, Place de l'ONU, Cerf Volante (☎824 66 00; bus #9), hosts arty events and shows movies; closed in the summer vacation. The **French Cultural Centre**, 36 rue El Hadj A.A. Ndoye (☎821 18 21) has a library, cinema and concerts, all in French, and a relaxing café in the garden. The **Goethe Institute** (and German Cultural Centre – ☎822 34 82) is at 2 av Albert Sarraut (☎822 50 04).

Doctors If you need an emergency consultation try one of the following practitioners: Dr Chignara (gynaecologist), 5 rue Parchappe (☎822 15 66); Dr F Coulibaly (Mme), 69 rue Mousse Diop (☎822 19 78); Dr M Kaouk, 144 rue Joseph Gomis, (☎823 46 79; English speaker); or Dr Djoneidi, Point E, rue A/rue 1 (☎825 75 03; English speaker). For accidents, the Hôpital Principal is at the corner of av Nelson Mandela/Leopold S. Senghor (☎839 50 50), or try SOS Médecin, the private emergencies organization (☎821 32 13).

Internet *Metissacana Cybercafé*, 30 rue de Thiong (☎822 20 43; *metissacana@metissacana.sn*; CFA1500/hour; open 24hr); *Le Ponty Cybercafé*, av G Pompidou (CFA1000/half-hour).

Language courses Private and group courses in French and Wolof (100hr; CFA70,000) at the Alliance Franco-Senegalaise, 3 rue Parchappe (BP 1777; ☎821 08 22), or Africa Consultants International, Baobab Training Center, 509 SICAP Baobab (BP 5270 Dakar-Fan Residence; ☎825 36 37; Fax 824 07 41; *aci@enda.sn*).

Maps The best and cheapest large maps of Dakar and Senegal can be bought at Directeur des Traveaux Géographique et Cartographique, Hann (BP 740; ☎822 11 82). Up the autoroute to the Hann exit, turn right after 1km and look for the sign for the nearby "Le Soleil".

Newspapers The *Herald Tribune*, *Time* or *Newsweek* are available from newsstands along av Georges Pompidou and the Place de l'Indépendance end of Albert Sarraut. *West Africa* magazine is usually in by Friday. Also try the British-Senegalese Institute (see "Cultural centres", above).

Pharmacies Pharmacie Nelson Mandela, corner of rue Gomia/av Nelson Mandela (☎821 21 72) is open 24hr; or look in *Le Soleil* for the listing of after-hours pharmacies.

Police Commissariat Central, rue de Docteur Thèze/rue Sandinièri (☎822 23 33).

Post Main PTT, corner of bd El Hadj Djily Mbaye (Mon–Fri 7am–6.30pm and Sat 8am–3pm). Large parcels can be sent from Colis Postaux office at Place d'Oran, at the junction of av El Hadj Malick Sy/av Blaise Diagne.

Swimming pools Roof terrace at *Hôtel Indépendance*; Olympic-size and thoroughly tropical at the *Savana*, Cap Manuel (CFA2000); chic but slightly cheaper at the *Afritel*, av Faidherbe/rue Raffenel; CFA3500 at the *Teranga Hôtel*.

Telephones To make international calls you'll need to go to one of the numerous *télécentres* located all over town (don't use the one at Place de l'Indépendance, which has a vastly inflated tariff). Private *télécentres* are mostly reasonably priced. You can also call internationally at the PTT (8.30am–5pm daily) and can collect faxes for CFA1000 per fax (Fax 823 62 42).

Travel agents Try the good Senegal Tours, Place de l'Indépendance (☎823 40 40 or 823 31 81; Fax 823 26 44), or any any of the following: SDV Voyages, 47 rue Albert Sarraut (☎839 00 00); Sénégambie Voyages, 42 rue Victor Hugo (☎821 68 31), who can organize *piroguing* in the Saloum delta; or the established Nouvelles Frontières, 1 bd de la République (☎823 34 34).

Wrestling *La lutte* can be seen all over the city, with regular Sun evening shows at the Stade Demba Diop attracting the big stars. Wandering around Medina and Grand Dakar at weekends you can find amateur – and kids' – bouts; around the Monument de l'Indépendance seems a popular venue. Wrestling is also televised on RTS every Sat afternoon.

Ile de Gorée

Just twenty minutes by *chaloupe* from Dakar lies the tiny **Ile de Gorée**, a mere 800m end to end and 300m across at its widest point. Its **slave-trading** history makes it more or less a required visit, and UNESCO has declared the island one of its World Heritage Sites, but it's a compelling retreat in any case, and many people come back repeatedly. The island bristles with old buildings. Apart from the famous **House of Slaves**, there's the excellent **IFAN Historical Museum of the Diaspora** in the horseshoe-shaped Fort d'Estrées, and the less impressive **Maritime Museum**, a new **Women's museum**, the old **church** of St Charles Barromée and, at the southern end, the **castle** topping a warren of bunkers and underground passages from where there are colourful views over the island and across to Dakar.

Some history

The first Europeans on Gorée were the **Portuguese**, who used the island as a trading base in the mid-fifteenth century. **Dutch** adventurers captured it in 1588 – naming it *Goede reede* (good roadstead) – but the Portuguese regained control, before again losing the island, this time to the **French**, in 1678. This date marked the beginning of the golden age of the **signares**. Daughters of white colonists and slave women, the *signares* of Gorée wielded extraordinary power in a largely matriarchal, slave-worked society.

Gorée was fought over by the French and the **English**, who repeatedly captured and recaptured Gorée from each other – the score for the eighteenth century being France 5, England 4. The island prospered despite the changes of ownership: by the 1850s there was a population of 6000 – ten times the present figure. The first fortifications of Dakar in 1857 signalled the start of Gorée's slow, graceful demise.

Around the island

For a day-trip from Dakar, it's best to take an early *chaloupe* to beat the crowds, and you should try to avoid weekends, especially in the high season; Mondays are quiet, but the museums are closed. Early in the morning – when the pastel colours of the old buildings and the bougainvillea draped through the narrow alleys make it particularly beautiful – you may be the only visitor. Perhaps inevitably, pushy "guides" have found their way onto the island – their services are barely necessary but if you stay over, they'll probably leave you alone.

The **Maison des Esclaves**, or **House of Slaves** (Tues–Sat 10.30am–noon & 2.30–6pm; CFA200) is the sole survivor of a number of buildings once used to store "pieces of ebony" before they were shipped to the New World. A visit could be anticlimactic, though – especially if you've ever seen film of weeping black Americans visiting it. Until recently, the walls were smothered with the impressions of various showbiz and political luminaries (not to mention the director) felt-penned onto pieces of paper. Fortunately, the festoon of posters has been removed, allowing the walls, dark chambers and slit windows to speak for themselves once again; there's little interpretation, so it's all left to your own imagination. The building is a mournful and numbing reminder of the first major phase in the European exploitation of Africa. Scarcely believable though it seems, the white traders lived in some style above the warehouse, where there are well-proportioned rooms, a balcony and a reconstructed eighteenth-century Dutch kitchen.

Opposite, the **Musée de la Femme** (Tues–Sat 10am–3pm & 4–5.30pm, Sun 10am–5pm; CFA350) was opened in 1994 as a celebration of Senegalese women's role in the material and spiritual well-being of the family. Exhibits – the best of which are housed upstairs – include textiles and traditional dress. Some of the information is also in English.

The cleverly designed **IFAN Historical Museum of the Diaspora** (Tues–Sat 10am–1pm & 2.30–5pm; CFA200) takes you on an instructive tour through Senegal's history to the present day, while the **Marine Museum** (same hours and price) makes a more singular contribution, being in large part devoted to the life cycle of the dogfish – note the human foot in a preserved fish stomach. Note that in both museums, explanations are in French only. Gorée's oldest building is the seventeenth-century **police station**, believed to be built on the site of a Portuguese church dating from 1482.

In the town, dozens of flaking **houses** are virtually concealed from the street behind high walls and wrought iron: the president and the Aga Khan both have villas here. There's a cluster of fine and more easily viewed Gorée houses at the northern end. The sheltered harbour **beach**, backed by a row of low-key **restaurants** and bars, is a draw in itself, but the real pleasure of the island is just wandering the sandy, quiet lanes and soaking the place up.

Practicalities

The *chaloupe* makes up to a dozen journeys daily from Dakar's Embarcadère de Gorée, off Boulevard de la Libération; with very few exceptions, the return departure time from Gorée is thirty minutes later than departure from Dakar. The boat runs from

6.15am to 11pm with a quiet period between noon and 2pm; a return ticket (valid overnight) costs CFA3000.

Commercial **accommodation** options on Gorée are increasing. The often heavily booked *Hostellerie du Chevalier de Boufflers* (☎822 53 64; ④) is the classiest, has rooms with fan and breakfast, and a good but expensive seafood menu. The new and modern *Keur Beer Auberge* (☎ & Fax 821 38 01; ④) offers cool, comfortable rooms with fridge, while slightly cheaper is *Ani Sow's* (☎821 81 95; ③–④), above the crafts shop Gallerie 3A, where you could rent one of three nicely furnished and comfortable rooms set around a leafy courtyard. An alternative is to ask around town or at the many restaurants facing the jetty about the possibility of **private rooms** – the friendly *Tramina Eric* (☎821 19 31; ②–③) has three available – or accept one of the many offers of assistance you'll receive from the moment you step off the ferry.

The **restaurants** are all pleasant, alfresco affairs with meals around CFA2000–3000. *Restaurant St Germaine* offers a particularly warm welcome, a menu from CFA2000 and seven twin rooms (②).

Iles des Madeleines

Thirty minutes by motor *pirogue* from Soumbedioune Bay, the trip to the uninhabited **Iles des Madeleines** is highly recommended for naturalists. Now designated a national park, the Madeleines are the habitat of a number of interesting **plants** – including a dwarf baobab and American wild coffee – and many species of indigenous and migratory **birds**: the tropic bird (*Phaëton aethereus*), recognized by its bright red bill and immensely long pointed tail, is found only here. There's little in the way of coral to be found in the surrounding seas, but the clear waters harbour a rich variety of **fish**.

Sarpan

The island of **Sarpan** – the only one at which a boat can anchor – is best visited between September and November, before the seas become too rough and the anchoring point in the cove inaccessible. It's necessary to obtain a park permit (CFA1000) from the office on the Corniche Ouest past the Musée Dynamique. **Pirogue rental**, best done in a group, can be sorted out on Soumbedioune beach. You should get them down to below CFA20,000. Occasionally the British-Senegalese Institute arranges a trip and it's worth contacting them first (see p.188). Take food and drink as well as binoculars and a snorkel and mask if possible.

You'll almost certainly have the Gorée-sized island to yourselves. It slopes from thirty-metre cliffs at its northern end to a gentler southern shore where the boats moor. Although no one lives here, it hasn't always been completely deserted, as occasional finds of **stone tools** indicate. More recently however it's acquired a malevolent reputation, and "L'îlot Sarpan" (named after a French soldier banished here) was soon corrupted to "L'île aux Serpents", of which it has none. The Lebu traditionally believe that sea spirits live on the island; their own efforts to settle on it several centuries ago were met with odd weather and violent seismic effects and they chose Gorée instead.

North and east of Dakar

An easy and much-hyped trip out of town is the ride to the beaches of **Ngor** and **Yof**. From Dakar, white *car rapides* leave from near Marché Sandaga to take you up to Ngor past the two rounded hills of **Les Mamelles** and the turn-off to **Pointe des Almadies** – Africa's Land's End – which manages not to be totally smothered by its *Club Med* holiday camp. The *Hôtel Méridien Présidentiel* here is about twice as expensive as any

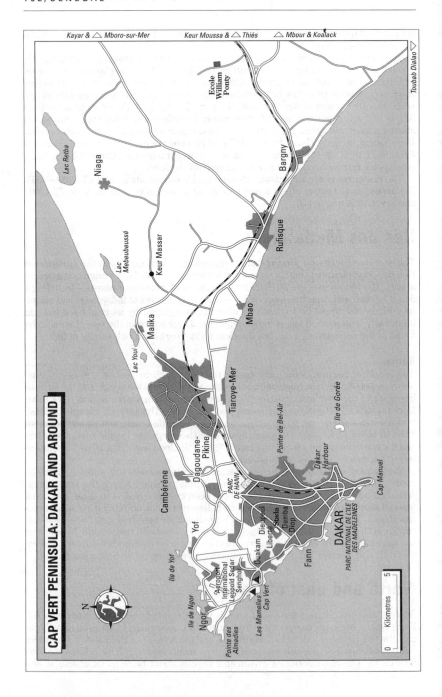

CAP VERT PENINSULA: DAKAR AND AROUND

Kayar & △ Mboro-sur-Mer   Keur Moussa & △ Thiés   △ Mbour & Koalack

Toubab Dialao ▷

Ecole William Ponty

Lac Retba

Niaga

Bargny

Lac Mebeubeussé

Rufisque

Keur Massar

Malika

Mbao

Lac Youi

Tiaroye-Mer

Ile de Gorée

Pointe de Bel-Air

Dagoudane-Pikine

Cambéréne

Dakar Harbour

PARC DE HANN

Cap Manuel

Yof

Dieuppeul

Liberté

Demba Diop

Stade

Ouakam

DAKAR

Ile de Yof

Fann

PARC NATIONAL DE L'ILE DES MADELEINES

Aéroport International Leopold Sedar Senghor

Cap Vert

Ile de Ngor

Ngor

Les Mamelles

Pointe des Almadies

N

0   Kilometres   5

other hotel in the country (☎820 21 22; Fax 820 30 30; ⑦) and is one of Africa's most important conference centres, with impressive facilities and standards if you can afford the CFA150,000 rooms. From Ngor, the *car rapides* continue on to Yof; if you want to bypass Ngor, bus #8 heads direct to Yof up the autoroute.

Public transport to **Lac Retba** and **Keur Moussa** can be unpredictable, and in truth neither place need come high on your list. At the bottom of the list is **Kayar**, further up the coast; once a fishing village, it's now a tourist-trap of the most oppressive kind, where groups are brought to see the fishermen coming in. You can see the same thing, less intrusively, all along the West African coast.

Ngor

NGOR has lost any charm it may once have had, with the hideous *Ngor Diarama Hôtel* (☎820 10 05; Fax 820 27 23; ⑥) invading the skyline, and a rash of beach clubs, restaurants and sporting facilities between here and Yof airport. The hassles are obvious and tedious, and the only escape is to take a *pirogue* (CFA100) out to the **Ile du Ngor**, which is probably the best reason to come here.

The **island** is mostly divided into small plots for private beach houses, pretty enough retreats between the casuarina trees, but hardly idyllic. An old military assault course adds nothing to the clifftops on the island's northern side. There's a couple of small beaches on the landward shore, but not much space when the tide comes in. **Accommodation** is sparse, but there are a few rooms at the *Hôtel Italienne* (☎820 27 48; ③) and at *Campement Seck* (☎820 44 49; ③).

Yof

The village of **YOF** – a maze of houses, boats on the beach, children everywhere – has a sense of community that Ngor has lost. The beach is the start of a continuous strand that reaches to the mouth of the Senegal River. There's also a tiny island just offshore, given over mostly to goats but yours for the exploring: a *pirogue* will take you over, though at low tide you can almost wade across. *Campement Touristique Le Poulagon* (☎820 23 47; ③), right on the fishing beach, is a great place to stay.

Yof is also a focus for the **Layen** brotherhood, a Lebu fraternity whose most venerated shrine is the **mausoleum** of the founder Saidi Limamou Laye and his son Mandione Laye. For members of the brotherhood, this temple-like building is the holiest of sites, and it attracts vast crowds at the end of Ramadan; if the festoon of vultures perched on its roof doesn't put you off climbing the steps, respect should. A nearby grotto contains perfumed sands and is believed to be where Muhammad's spirit dwelt for a thousand years before being reincarnated as the sect's founder.

If you want to participate in something unusual – you won't be the only tourist on the scene – come to Yof on a Thursday afternoon when **spirit possession dances** (*ndeup*) are organized by traditional psychiatrists with the mentally ill, who come with their relatives from all over Senegal.

Lac Retba

The popular Dakarois picnic spot of **Lac Retba** – also known as Lac Rose, "Pink Lake" – is certainly a remarkable spectacle, but a trip out here is worthwhile as much for the opportunity to get right out of Dakar and look at the Côte Sauvage as for the lake itself. The pinkness of the soda lake is caused by the action of bacteria that excrete red iron oxide; for maximum effect, watch the water as the sun goes down, when it turns from coral to mauve and violet. Women collect salt from the lake – almost as salty as the Dead Sea and just as hard to swim in – which is then packed into sacks by men at the far end. The shore is a beach of bleached shells, with banana plots and casuarina trees greening up an otherwise harsh landscape. Over the soft **dunes** to the north is the Atlantic, rough and swirling and definitely only for strong swimmers. Unfortunately the whole tourist area tends to be swarming with pickpockets and troublemakers. Be on your guard!

Getting to the lake, about 40km from Dakar, take a bush taxi to Keur Massar (not to be confused with Keur Moussa, see below) and then another to **Niaga**. The *campement* here – the *Keur Kanni* – has concrete thatched huts and a nice, local atmosphere (☎826 55 17; S/C, B&B ③). It's then a twenty-minute walk to the lakeside and another, more expensive, *campement*.

Keur Moussa

The Benedictine monastery of **Keur Moussa** (☎836 33 09), up in the hills off the Thiès road 50km from Dakar, has acquired a reputation for its touristy *messes africaines* – African masses – with koras, balafons and tam-tams, and plenty of stuff for sale afterwards, including rather good goat's cheese. Sunday morning Mass at 10am is the best. **Getting here** without your own car, you'll need early transport towards Thiès (hitchable) and a drop-off at the junction 5km past Sebhikotane, from where it's another 5km to the monastery.

South of Dakar

Beyond the city centre, on the busy **coast road** heading southeast, there's still forty or more kilometres before the edges of the capital finally give way to open, baobab-dotted countryside. Road and railway go through the agglomeration of Dagoudane-Pikine/Guediyawe, a huge spill-over of city workers and refugees from the interior: already larger in area than the rest of greater Dakar, the sprawl is fast encroaching on the shifting dunes of the north Cap Vert coast. At **THIAROYE-MER**, 14km from Dakar, there's a pleasant small hotel just a kilometre from the beach on the Route de Rufisque: *Chez Charlie* (☎834 07 42; ②–③) offers S/C twin rooms, some with AC.

RUFISQUE – the Portuguese fifteenth-century Rio Fresco – is the last Dakar suburb, and already provincial in feel. A scruffy seafront town with a couple of hotels, it's more human in scale than anything closer to the city (you'll see *calèches* here, for example). Several wholesalers of **exotic birds** line the road – middlemen between the poverty-stricken peasants and a market in the west which will pay the equivalent of a year's labour for a parrot.

If you're beach-hunting, there's little difficulty in travelling down this way by bush taxi, and it's one area you might **hitch** successfully. It's worth making the slight extra effort to get to **Palmarin**'s near deserted shore – especially if **Fadiout** leaves a sour taste in your mouth. Before reaching Mbour, check out the "Serer pyramids" in the **Bandia Reserve** , 63km from Dakar just off the main highway south to Kaolack.

La Petite Côte

At the small resort of Bargny, an hour or so from Dakar, the **Petite Côte** begins and both road and railway turn inland to the junction for Thiès, Touba and St-Louis. You'll notice a Portuguese influence in some of the region's architecture, and a strong Catholic presence, not unlike parts of the Casamance. Pope John Paul visited both districts during his hugely popular 1992 Senegalese tour – watch out for wonderful outfits made from the material designed to commemorate the visit, adorned with the benign papal countenance.

Popenguine, Sali-Portudal and the Bandia Reserve

Turning southeast onto the N1, 12km beyond Bargny, you pass several minor roads leading to **resort beaches** along the sandy, palm-fringed coastline. **Toubab Dialao** and **POPENGUINE** are both around 10km off the N1 and reachable by bush taxis or hitching: the former is popular with relaxing Peace Corp volunteers and has a few low-

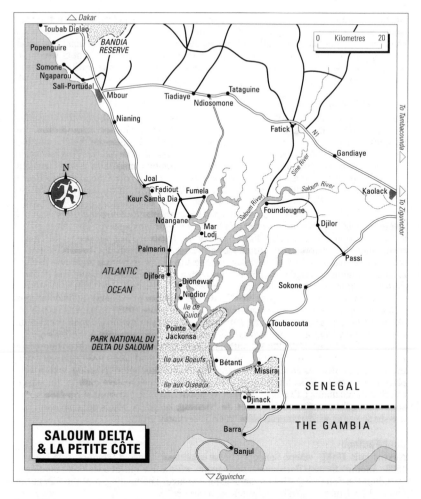

Saloum Delta map with labels: Dakar, Toubab Dialao, Popenguire, Somone, Ngaparou, Sali-Portudal, BANDIA RESERVE, Mbour, Tiadiaye, Tataguine, Ndiosomone, Nianing, Fatick, N1, Gandiaye, To Tambacounda, Sine River, Joal, Fadiout, Fumela, Keur Samba Dia, Saloum River, Kaolack, To Ziguinchor, Ndangane, Mar, Lodj, Foundiougne, Djilor, Palmarin, Passi, ATLANTIC OCEAN, Djifere, Dionewar, Niodior, Sokone, Ile de Guior, PARK NATIONAL DU DELTA DU SALOUM, Pointe Jackonsa, Toubacouta, Ile aux Boeufs, Bétanti, Missira, Ile aux Oiseaux, SENEGAL, Djinack, THE GAMBIA, Barra, Banjul, Ziguinchor

SALOUM DELTA & LA PETITE CÔTE

0 Kilometres 20

N

key places to stay; at the latter the only commercial lodging in the village is *Chez Ginette's* (☎957 71 10), right on the beach, which has a couple of roughly built rooms sleeping up to ten (CFA10,000 per room), and a choice between self-catering or home cooking. There's a fine restaurant, *L'Écho Côtier*, on the southern part of the beach, with a *plat du jour* for CFA3800. Back on the N1, at the village of Nguekokh, a road leads southwest to the sea and the resorts of **Somone** and **Ngaparou**, which have similar accommodation options. **SALI-PORTUDAL**, known as Saly, is a buzzing resort village with mostly extravagant lodgings, such as *Savana* (☎957 11 13; Fax 957 10 45; ⑦), *Palm Beach* (☎957 11 37; Fax 975 13 64; ⑦) and *Hôtel Espadon Club* (☎957 19 49; Fax 957 20 00; ⑦). For less expensive accommodation, restaurants and activities you'd be better off in the small villages along the coast.

Away from this coastal swing, the scrub-and-baobab **Bandia Reserve** (CFA5000), to the east of the main highway to Kaolack (1km south of Sindia, 23km from the Thiès junction), contains an interesting archeological site: the **burial mounds** of the vanished Serer village of Tay, and a **burial baobab**, where Serer griots were once entombed. A collection of skulls and bones still lie at the baobab's small entrance. Guided tours may be available; don't miss the **replicas** of the burial huts which lie beneath the hardened earth mounds. The reserve also harbours various animals, including ostriches and lions.

Mbour and Nianing

The dusty fishing town of **MBOUR**, 83km southeast of Dakar, is the obvious base for this part of the coast, though maybe not the most attractive. For **accommodation**, the most affordable place is *Les Citronniers* (☎957 24 57; S/C ③), opposite the church, and also known as both *Chez Marie* and the *Centre de Accueil at de Séjour*. This has basic but clean rooms and friendly, helpful owners; ask them for a map of the town. The main alternative in town is the touristy *Centre Touristique de la Petite Côte and Coco Beach Club* (BP 91, Mbour; ☎957 10 04; Fax 957 10 77; ⑤), right on the shore next to the Préfecture, with a pool, tennis court, boules bar … the lot.

Mbour has a fair number of bars and small **restaurants**: *Restaurant d'Islam* is an old favourite, while *Le Djembe* and *Kuer d'Janil* are good for inexpensive Senegalese plates as well as varied menus at night. For a treat try *Le Massai* or *The Calabash* on the Dakar road. Since the town depends foremost on fishing, not tourism, the **beach** is littered with fishy remains and associated odours, and the sea is uninviting anyway – usually calm and tending to weediness. Mbour has both a PTT and a BICIS bank, and it's *gare routière* is on the northeastern edge of the centre.

The road continues south past **NIANING** and a couple of exclusive holiday villages – *Domaine de Nianing* for the French on the landward side (☎957 15 03; Fax 957 15 04; ⑦), and *Club Aldiana* (☎957 15 49; ⑦) on the sands, catering for German packagers. Closer to the village itself are two far less expensive **campements** – the *Auberge des Coquillages* (☎ & fax 957 14 28; ④), with a pool and a wonderful beachside position, and *Le Ben'tenier* (☎ and Fax 957 29 74; ③), which has great food, and a lovely garden – and the simpler *Le Warang Hôtel* (☎ & Fax 957 20 10; ③), 2km before Nianing, with a well-placed restaurant overlooking the sea. There's also an inexpensive **café** in the village offering meals under CFA600 and beers for about half that. Substantial **birdlife**, to be seen among the remains of the **Forêt de Nianing**, keeps the whole area pleasant, and the shore scene, with scattered palm trees, is certainly pretty.

Joal-Fadiout

Next stop is **JOAL**, where Senegal's great statesman, Léopold Senghor, was born in 1906. Another former Portuguese settlement, with a few old houses still standing – including the Senghors' – it is today a fishing village. The hauling-in of the fish at the end of the day is as enjoyable to watch as anywhere.

But apart from a visit to Chez Senghor and a pat delivery of its history from the *gardien*, the big draw is a wander over to **FADIOUT**, the fishing village on the shell-bank **island** in the estuary facing Joal. By virtue of a wicked combination of attractive features – proximity to the tourist camps up the coast, houses built of crushed shells, granary huts on stilts like a field of mushrooms, and a fishermen's cemetery on a neighbouring island – Fadiout is one of the most aggressive hustler haunts in Senegal, though an association has recently been created to reduce the hassle. Down at the bridge to the island, there's a gauntlet of obnoxious teenage "guides" to be overcome, offering sea and turtle shells for sale, *pirogue* trips and uninviting offers of cheap *logements*. If you would actually like to do a **pirogue trip**, get into top bargaining gear and make sure you know how long you're going to get. Note, too, that the grain store island, a few hundred metres to the southeast of Fadiout, is virtually empty and not very impressive before the harvest.

All this notwithstanding, Fadiout is a fascinating place, a **"shell midden"** entirely composed of the refuse from centuries of shellfish consumption – it takes about an hour to trail around the houses and Serer cemetery.

For **food and accommodation**, look to Joal. You'll probably want to avoid the tour-group oriented *Hôtel le Finnio* (☎957 61 12; ③–④), but the new and nearby *Le Sénégaulois* (☎ & Fax 957 62 41; ③), right by the bridge, has some neat S/C rooms and a pleasantly located restaurant overlooking the island. Leave the Catholic mission alone, even if you're broke: they have absolutely no interest in putting you up. Instead, make for the centre of town and check out the well-signposted *Relais 114* (☎957 16 78; ②), run by a Guinean family who insist on having nothing to do with "guides". They offer clean non-S/C doubles and a pleasant balcony with hammocks. The *Relais* makes a big thing of its lobster; for cheaper eating, head for the many omelette and *chawarma* bars around town. If you want to stay in Fadiout, try *Le Paletuvier* (☎ & Fax 957 62 05; ②), a simple place on the waters' edge at the far side of the island.

Beaches in this area are all too crowded and hustly for abandonment to the sun, sea and sand. On the fishing beach near the town centre you can mingle with the masses at the end of the day and normally be ignored, but about the only place you might consider for a peaceful **swim** is the sandy, casuarina-covered bar to the south, past the school and football pitch.

The Saloum delta

Situated between Dakar and The Gambia, the delta of Senegal's third river – the **Saloum** – is growing in popularity as a weekend destination from Dakar and a bird-watching and fishing district for foreign visitors. Visiting the maze of islands and creeks by *pirogue* from the landward side – the usual way – can work out expensive, but there are lots of choices, including organized tours by Sénégambie Voyages (see p.189). The less expensive option is to organize your own *balade;* get a vehicle down from Joal to **PALMARIN**, 20km to the south – but be prepared to wait several hours and possibly to change vehicles at Keur Samba Dia. Going back again is harder, but there's always space when a vehicle comes, and if rains have washed the road out completely, you'll hear of it.

Palmarin has a good, if basic **campement** (☎949 96 05 at the *télécentre*; ②), right on the beach, a short distance from the village itself. An outpost of Casamance's system of CTRIs, it offers thatched, twin-bed huts among the palms, with electricity and shared ablutions. You can arrange to have all your meals cooked for you, and the owner can also give advice on *pirogue* rental (see overleaf).

Another departure point for the delta is **FOUNDIOUGNE**, west of Kaolack, 33km from the main highway at Passi, also accessible by road from Fatick and then a ferry. Here you'll find one of the least expensive places to stay, *Le Baobab*, also known as *Chez Marie* (☎948 11 08; Fax 948 11 76; some S/C; ③), a friendly Senegalese-run place which can get busy at times, so you're best to phone ahead. *Auberge les Bolongs* (☎ & Fax 948 11 10; S/C ④) offers African-style European comfort in a tranquil setting on the outskirts of town, while for a bit of luxury there's *Les Piroguiers* (☎948 12 12; Fax 948 12 10; S/C, AC ⑦). The ferry from Foundiougne operates every couple of hours from 7.30am until mid-afternoon; the first ferry meets a minibus going straight to Dakar. At **NDANGANE**, reachable from Joal or from the main highway east of Tiadiaye, you can take a *pirogue* to the island of **Mar-Lothie** which has a pleasant low-key hotel-*campement*, the *Limboko* (BP167, Mbour; ☎957 14 41; ③), good for bird-watching. A convenient, but more expensive, departure point is **TOUBACOUTA**, just 2km from the highway and 25km from the Gambian border. Toubacouta has two resort camps with pools, bars, restaurants and nightclubs: *Village Hôtel Keur Saloum* (☎ & Fax 948 77 16; ⑤) and *Les Paletuviers* (☎948 77 76, Fax 948 77 77; ⑥). Both organize expensive excursions, but you could try arranging cheaper ones through the souvenir stands outside the hotels. To the south of Toubacouta in the more remote **MISSIRAH** is the *Gîte Touristique du Bandia* (☎948 77 35; ⑤), while over the water is the exclusive *Ile Paradis* (bookable through *Les Paletuviers*, see above; ⑦).

Around the delta

Renting a *pirogue* for the day is most easily done at **Djifere**, south of Palmarin – but getting here by *bâché* will involve a wait. Prices for the day need serious discussion, but you shouldn't pay more than about CFA20,000 for six hours' worth of boat and crew.

Dionewar and **Niodior** on the **Ile de Guior** are laid-back villages, little affected by the gradual advance of tourism. Niodior, in particular, is very alluring under its coconut trees, with really welcoming people. Nearer the Gambian border and inside the **Parc National du Delta du Saloum**, the **Ile aux Oiseaux** has variably interesting birdlife – early evening tends to yield better bird-watching, and palearctic migrants swell numbers from October to March. Turtles are common, too, and you might even see a dolphin.

From Djifere it may be possible to take a trading *pirogue* down to **Banjul**, which is the closest large town by boat; they go several times a week (daily, some claim), and cost CFA2000 per person. The voyage – 60km along the shore – takes around six hours. Alternatively, if you're on haggling form and unwilling to wait, you could be *pirogued* to Toubacouta (4hr) and take a bush taxi to the border – expect to pay at least CFA15,000.

Thiès and onward

The great garrison town and rail hub of colonial days, and now Senegal's second largest town, **Thiès** is close enough to Dakar (70km) to be an easy visit, and also lies en route if you're journeying by train to other parts of the country. If you're interested in local crafts, the **tapestry factory** here is an essential stop; the workmanship is the very finest, and few weaving centres – if any – in West Africa match Thiès for sheer impact.

Moving north, you might visit **Tivaouane** if you're gripped by the fascination of the Islamic brotherhoods. Or, heading south, you could go to **Kaolack** via **Diourbel**, from where you might strike out to **Touba**, the big Mouride stronghold with the country's most impressive mosque. From Touba there's the option of following the dusty N3 highway northeast, onwards via **Linguère** to **Matam** on the Senegal River. Lastly, if you're heading through the **Sine-Saloum region**, either south on the *transgambienne* or east on the N1 to Tambacounda, you might take time out to look at some of the Iron Age **stone circles**. Independent transport is the best way to visit these places, though with the possible exception of the stone circles and Touba during *Magal*, you'll normally find public transport to the towns.

Thiès

THIÈS retains much of the character of a French town, with parks and wide shady avenues, solid brick and tiles, a remarkable old Sudanic-style cinema, and even the odd rampart from an earlier period of "pacification". Its history, even in recent times, has been punctuated by violent episodes, notably the 1947 strike by railway workers – "God's Bits of Wood" of Sembène Ousmane's novel, *Les Bouts de Bois de Dieu*.

The **Manufactures Sénégalaises des Arts Decoratifs** (☎951 11 31; Mon–Fri 8am–1.30pm & 2.30–6pm, Sat 10am–noon & 4–6pm), focuses the output of many of Senegal's artists and has an enormous influence on younger painters. Having work painstakingly redrawn and fabricated into glowing tapestries – many for exhibition and sale abroad – is an accolade providing a rare incentive.

Since its foundation in 1966, the Thiès school has produced fewer than five hundred pieces: its annual output works out at around three hundred square metres, each tapestry produced in an exclusive edition of eight. Prices are accordingly high – around £500 ($800) per square metre. Common themes are village life, nature, history and myth, executed in dazzling, graphic style. Look out for the stunning *Rendezvous au Soleil* by Jacob Yacouba, a giant ten-metre version of which was purchased by Atlanta airport. However, a lot of the designs suggest some fresh ideas are needed, and as more commercially oriented foreign painters begin commissioning the Thiès workshops to weave their own work for them, there's a danger the centre will lose its creative edge.

It's interesting to see all the stages of work, from drawing up the original paintings to dyeing the wool and the rapid but careful process of weaving itself. However, you may only be allowed into the exhibition hall if you turn up unannounced, so it's best to phone ahead to try to arrange a visit to the factory. You should be allowed to take photos in the workshops, but not in the exhibition hall.

Around the corner is the **museum** (Mon–Fri 9am–1pm & 3–6pm; CFA500), housed in the fort, first built in 1879. Aside from a number of interesting photos and a good deal of commentary on Senegalese history, there's a special concentration on the role of the marabouts. Opposite the museum is a small public library where a number of artists sell their paintings and sculptures.

Practicalities

Arriving in Thiès by bus or taxi you'll almost certainly be left at the *gare routière*, 3km out of town (CFA325 to get into the centre); if you come by train, you'll be delivered straight to the *centreville*. The railway is still the pivot of much of the town's life, its rhythms adjusted to the comings and goings on the track. The best **place to stay** is the centrally located *Hôtel Rex* (☎951 10 81; ②), which offers good AC and fanned rooms for about as cheap as they get in Thiès; otherwise, the *Hôtel du Rail* (☎951 23 13; ③), 2km from the centre in Cité Balabé Thiès, has comfortable AC, S/C rooms, or there's the *Hôtel du Thiès "Man Gan"* (☎951 15 26; Fax 951 25 32; ③), where the rooms are adequate and the garden offers a quiet retreat. Thiès's **restaurants** are mostly found along avenue Leopold Senghor south of the tracks, in the town centre north of the station, or in the town's hotels. Try *Restaurant Le Kien An* for French and Vietnamese fare (open lunchtime and from 8pm), or *Les Délices* for pastries and pizza – both on Avenue Leopold Senghor. A good place to sit and watch the world go by is *Restaurant Le Cailcédrat* on Avenue General de Gaulle, opposite Thiès' new Internet café; meat, fish and Lebanese dishes cost around CFA2000–4000.

Tivaouane, Mboro and the Grande Côte

Tivaouane, 5km off the main N2 to St-Louis, is the seat of the **Sy** dynasty of the **Tijaniya** brotherhood, the largest in Senegal. The grand North African-style mosque is best seen during *Gamou*, the Tijani pilgrimage, or *Maulidi*, the prophet's birthday, when thousands of believers pour into the town. Accommodation, which seems pretty minimal at the best of times, is impossible to find during these periods.

Just north of Tivaouane, on the N2 highway, a road leads northwest 28km to the fishing village of **Mboro-sur-mer** on what is known as the **Grande Côte**, a 150-kilometre unbroken sweep of sand linking St-Louis to Dakar, along which the Paris–Dakar Rally traditionally hurtles towards the capital. Despite the reforestation along this coastline, the *côte*'s exposure makes it a far less popular holiday destination than the Petite Côte south of Dakar, which may be all the reason you need to come here. *Le Gîte de la Licorne* (☎955 77 88; HB ⑤), 5km out of Mboro on the beach, offers great food and accommodation for up to twelve people in three huts; it's best to book ahead.

Diourbel and Touba

Diourbel, with its beautiful huge domed mosque, is one of the principal saintly towns of the Mourides, and capital of the region of the same name, the heart of the groundnut basin. Fifty kilometres east, following the Sine valley, lies **TOUBA**, the burial place of the founder of Mouridism, **Cheikh Amadou Bamba Mbacke** (1850–1927), and thus the high holy place of the brotherhood. The extraordinary 87-metre-high mosque – built over the family tomb in 1963 and visible for miles across the flat plain – is the largest and one of the finest in West Africa, and the most important religious shrine in Senegal.

Amadou Bamba's triumphal return home in 1907, after years of detention by the French, is celebrated annually in the festival of **Magal** (see the Muslim calendar on p.59 for dates). Up to half a million pilgrims flock here from all over Senegal and The Gambia, and public transport is virtually suspended on routes to and from Touba. *Magal* is the manifestation of a religious fervour whose only equal in Africa is found in northern Nigeria.

Senegalese authority is minimal here: the **maraboutic militia** is responsible for law and order, which includes absolute bans on tobacco and alcohol anywhere in the town precincts. Searches – especially of *toubabs* – aren't uncommon, and you will be fined and your drugs confiscated if found. Photography, too, isn't likely to please many. Despite this, Touba can be an irresistible challenge. If you're going there for *Magal*, expect to spend the night awake with the crowd of disciples: you'll almost certainly have found companions on the journey.

Be warned, though, that **accommodation** is impossible to find in Touba if you don't get invited to stay at someone's house. There's a *campement* 10km away in **Mbacke**, a kind of secular counterpoint to Touba, where the maraboutic laws don't apply. You could get stranded there for the big night anyway, as Mbacke goes into partying hyperdrive, diverting attention from the devotions at Touba and increasingly reducing *Magal* to a Christmas-style commercialism.

If you're driving into Touba, you may end up jammed in pedestrian traffic or directed to leave your vehicle in a designated zone and walk. However you manage it, don't confuse piety with honesty; a nimble army of hustlers and pickpockets filters the crowds, particularly during *Magal*. You'll also need to be aware of cultural sensitivities: shorts are not acceptable round here and heads will need to be covered if entering the mosque. You're best off adopting a "local guide" to help with all the niceties.

To Linguère

With stamina you could continue by road from Touba or Mbacke, to Linguère and from there on to Ouro Sogui/Matam. This route, the N3, goes right through the heart of the Fula **Réserves Sylvo-Pastorales** (wild grazing reserves), a fragmented cluster of bad-lands (virtually tribal reserves), glumly conceded to the pastoralists and always under threat from the expanding Mouride groundnut enterprises. With improved irrigation and increases in population, agriculture encroaches on all sides except the east, where the Réserves de Faune du Ferlo-Nord and Ferlo-Sud – areas in which no grazing is per-mitted – create a barrier between the cattle herds and the potentially rich Senegal River valley.

LINGUÈRE is the main town of this region. Surrounded by the reserves and no longer accessible by train, it's a bit of a dead-end rarely used by travellers. **Accommodation** is limited to the *campement*-style *Hôtel Touristique* (☎968 10 30 to leave messages; ④); informal enquires may elicit less expensive lodgings. If you've transport, or a dogged persistence coupled with a devotion to obscure archeological sites, you might move down the Ferlo river course from Linguère to the ruined **fortress** of Alboury Ndiaye – the last independent ruler of the Wolof kingdom of Jolof. The site is north of the road before the village of Yang-Yang.

From Linguère a rough track to the Senegal River near Ouro Sogui follows the nor-mally dry upper course of the Ferlo, between the faunal reserves. Transport is limited and vehicles depart early – you'll almost certainly be the only tourist on board.

Kaolack

A big, noisy interchange town, hub of five road routes (but no longer accessible by train), **KAOLACK** is not likely to be a place you'll want to linger. The **mosque** is the main sight of interest, a splendid creation paid for partly by Saddam Hussein. The Niasse dynasty of the Tijaniya brotherhood – based here – is bent on founding an Islamic republic, a movement which is also reportedly funded by Libya. Kaolack also has a venerable and bustling **market**, one of the biggest covered markets in West Africa, and a craft market on the northern edge of town. **Places to stay** include the decent *Hôtel de Paris* (BP 334, Kaolack; ☎941 24 70; Fax 941 10 17; S/C, AC ④), south-west of the market; the basic *Auberge Etoile du Sine* (☎941 44 58; non-S/C, some AC; ③), on Avenue Senghor, the main road out of town towards Tambacounda; and, along the same road, the older *Hôtel and Restaurant Adama Cire* (☎941 11 66; S/C ③). You may also be able to find a bed at the *Mission Catholique* (☎941 25 26; room ②, dorm ①). Inexpensive street **food** is available around the market and *gare routières*, while for a more varied menu, including pizza, fish, meat and salads, try *La Terrasse* (*Chez Anouar*) on rue des Ecoles, or *Le Brasero* (*Chez Anouar*) on Avenue Senghor – both busy in the evenings. Around the corner from *Le Brasero* on Avenue de Bugeaud is the buzzing *Blue Bird Nightclub*. The **gare routière** for Dakar and all northern destinations is 1.5km out of town to the north; for southern destinations, including The Gambia, *garage Nioro* is on the southern corner of the town centre. The *gare routière ville* for bush taxis around town is next to the market.

Sine-Saloum stone circles

Part of the same cultural complex as the circles in The Gambia (see p.287), the **mega-liths** scattered across the plain between Nioro du Rip on the *transgambienne* N4 and Tambacounda are vestiges of a prehistoric society about which virtually nothing is known. Including some unimpressive circles that you'd not glance twice at, they num-ber approximately a thousand in this region. Associated with them are burial sites which have yielded a number of skeletons and a certain amount of weaponry, pots and copper ornaments. Seeming to date from before the twelfth century, they bear no sign of any Islamic impact.

Most impressive is the site known as **Djalloumbéré**, at **Ngayène**, hard against the Gambian border. Over eleven hundred individual pillars here make up 52 stone circles – some of them the sites of mass burials. It's virtually impossible to get here without your own transport – turn left 9km south of Nioro du Rip to Kaymor (17km) on a decent track, then continue southeast another 15km via Tène Peul and Keur Bakari to Ngayène. From here you can head straight back to the main road at Medina Sabak, 28km from Nioro. In the middle of this "circuit", 10km due south of Kaymor, is the village of **Payoma**, where stones from the local circles have been uprooted to support the buildings – including the mosque. Numerous other circles are visible at various points along these tracks.

Assuming you've got transport or you're using a *taxi brousse*, there are more sites along the Tambacounda highway, at **Malème Hodar** (right by the road) and **Keur Albé** and **Sali**, respectively 9km and 20km southwest of Kongheul on a minor road to The Gambia. This road crosses the border just north of Wassu: if you're enraptured by the circles and your papers are in order, you could cross over for further observations and stay in Kuntaur or Georgetown.

THE NORTH AND EAST

Northern Senegal is the least populated part of the country, with few large towns and a landscape whose main interest derives from its harsh marginality. Northeast of Dakar stretches the **Sahel**, where the desert's southward advance is ever apparent. But there are two conspicuous attractions in the north: the **Senegal River**, forming the border with Mauritania and feeding a flood plain up to 30km wide; and the old French colonial capital of **St-Louis**, tucked behind the bar at the mouth of the river. Two **national parks** – the Djoudj and the Langue de Barbarie – are mainly visited by keen bird-watchers.

Should you be **heading north** to Mauritania and the Atlantic route across the Sahara, St-Louis is a natural break in the journey, a few hours by *taxi brousse* from Dakar. To **follow the river**, however, you have to be a little more determined and transport-hop your way inland to **Richard Toll**, **Ouro Sogui/Matam** and **Bakel**. Continuing south through the hills, you'll intercept the Dakar–Bamako train at **Kidira**, on the border, where there'll be a crush to find space on board. Coming in the other direction, into Senegal from Mali, the river course is a marginally preferable route towards the coast: the alternative, following the direct line of the railway has very little to detain you.

St-Louis

The oldest French settlement in West Africa and capital of Senegal and Mauritania until 1958, **ST-LOUIS** is something of a world apart. In later colonial times its *commune* status – shared with Gorée, Rufisque and Dakar – meant its inhabitants were considered citizens of France; today the town's crumbling eighteenth- and nineteenth-century European architecture and its white- and blue-draped Wolof and Moorish inhabitants maintain the culture clash. Like Gorée too, St-Louis is a UNESCO-protected World Heritage Site. If decay, abandonment and the ghosts of slaves and fishermen attract you then you'll enjoy this town. Taking advantage of the Casamance's recent woes, beachside *campements* have sprung up along the Langue

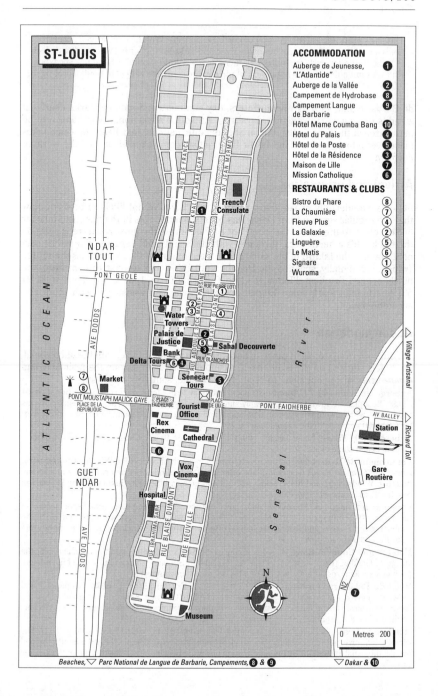

ST-LOUIS

ACCOMMODATION

Auberge de Jeunesse, "L'Atlantide" ❶
Auberge de la Vallée ❷
Campement de Hydrobase ❽
Campement Langue de Barbarie ❾
Hôtel Mame Coumba Bang ❿
Hôtel du Palais ❹
Hôtel de la Poste ❺
Hôtel de la Résidence ❸
Maison de Lille ❼
Mission Catholique ❻

RESTAURANTS & CLUBS

Bistro du Phare ⑧
La Chaumière ⑦
Fleuve Plus ④
La Galaxie ②
Linguère ⑤
Le Matis ⑥
Signare ①
Wuroma ③

French Consulate

NDAR TOUT

PONT GEOLE

RUE DE FRANCE
RUE KHALFA ABABACAR SY
AV JEAN MERMOZ

RUE PIERRE LOTI

Water Towers
Palais de Justice
Bank
Delta Tours
Sahal Decouverte
RUE BLANCHOT
Senecar Tours

Market
Pont MOUSTAPH MALICK GAYE
PLACE DE LA REPUBLIQUE
PLACE FAIDHERBE
PLACE DE LILLE
PONT FAIDHERBE

Tourist Office
Rex Cinema
Cathedral

Vox Cinema

Hospital

RUE IBRAHIMA SARR
RUE BLAISE DUMONT
RUE NEUVILLE

ATLANTIC OCEAN

AVE DODDS

GUET NDAR

AVE DODDS

Senegal River

Museum

N

▷ Village Artisanal
AV BALLEY
▷ Richard Toll
Station
Gare Routière
N2 ❼

0 Metres 200

Beaches, ▽ *Parc National de Langue de Barbarie, Campements,* ❽ & ❾   ▽ *Dakar &* ❿

The main **ethno-linguistic groups** of north Senegal are **Wolof**, concentrated around St-Louis and along the lower reaches of the river, and **Tukulor** higher up, who speak a dialect of Fula. In the far east, around Bakel, there are **Sarakolé** (Soninké/Serahuli) speakers, while communities of semi-nomadic **Fula** live in the scorched region of Fouta Toro.

de Barbarie and, with its warm winters, dry summers and national parks nearby, it all adds up to a worthwhile few days' stay. An added attraction, if you happen to be in the area at the time, is the annual St-Louis International Jazz Festival, which takes place over a long weekend in May or June; artists come from all around the world to perform.

Arrival and orientation

St-Louis' wonderfully ornate **train station**, which you're not likely to be using now that the regular service from Dakar has been suspended, is in the mainland quarter of **Sor**, close to the end of the iron Pont de Faidherbe; the **gare routière** is right by the tracks. It's a hectic area, thronged with stalls and child beggars. The oldest part of St-Louis is the **island** of the same name, a ten-minute walk away across the bridge (which, incidentally, spanned the Danube until 1897). For **tourist information**, the newly opened Syndicat d'Initiative et de Tourisme (9am–1pm & 3–6.45pm; ☎961 24 55) has helpful staff, some English-speaking, who can assist you with tours and accommodation.

Accommodation

St-Louis offers an excellent range of **accommodation** for its size, with the old colonial-era hotels situated on the island itself, a couple of places to stay on the mainland, and *campements* strung out along the spit of the Langue, south of Guet Ndar.

Auberge de Jeunesse, "L'Atlantide", north end of av Jean Mermoz, corner of rue Bouet (☎961 24 09). Best place in town to lodge cheaply and commune with other travellers. Segregated dorms and twins – with mosquito nets, shared ablutions and a modest breakfast included. Also offers *plats* for CFA1500 and trips to the national parks. ②.

Auberge de la Vallée, Blaise Diagne (☎961 47 22; Fax 964 10 92). Clean bright dorms with mosquito nets and some twins. ②.

Campement de Hydrobase, on the beach/river 9km south of Guet Ndar. Windblown *campement* run by the *Hôtel du Palais* (see below; lifts offered). Basic palm huts, shady *paillotes,* and a restaurant/bar. Windsurfers and horse riding extra; if you fancy a little more luxury, go for FB with all beach activities thrown in. ②–④.

Campement Langue de Barbarie, 20km down the spit. Plusher and more established version of the above (4WD only), run by the *Hôtel de la Poste* who will drive you down there (and on to the national park). *Pirogue* and fishing excursions offered. Lowest rates include breakfast, higher rate is for FB and all beach toys. ④–⑤.

Hôtel Mame Coumba Bang, Bois des Amoureux, 6.5km south of town on the mainland near the village of Gandiol (BP 214; ☎961 18 50; Fax 961 19 02). St-Louis' luxury tourist hotel including a pool, an excellent restaurant and trips into the surrounding countryside. ④.

Hôtel du Palais, rue Ababacar Sy (BP 92; ☎961 17 72; Fax 961 31 00). Friendly, co-operative and least expensive of the old-style hotels, offering clean AC, S/C rooms. Adjacent restaurant/patisserie has good croissants and coffee. Inexpensive excursions organized to regional attractions. Accepts credit cards – at a premium. ④.

Hôtel de la Poste, by Pont Faidherbe, on the waterfront (BP 48; ☎961 11 18; Fax 961 23 13). The island's definitive, authentic colonial-era hotel. Splendid rooms and ambience and a hunter-themed bar. All the usual excursions including day runs down the beach to their *campement* on the Langue (see above). ④.

Hôtel de la Résidence, av Blaise Diagne (BP 254; ☎961 12 60; Fax 961 12 59). One of the town's most comfortable hotels, with clever colonial details. Bicycles available for hire. ④.

Maison de Lille, bd Lamine Guèye (BP 457; ☎961 11 35; Fax 961 13 02). Fifteen minutes' walk south of the *gare routière*. Plain place with little to offer other than the cheapest bed in town and a working mens' hostel feel. ②.

Mission Catholique, unmarked wooden door (no. 8) at the west end of rue Duret (☎961 10 04). Possibly still taking travellers but will more likely direct you to the *Atlantide*. ①.

The Town

There's an excellent bird's-eye view **sketch map** (CFA3000) of St-Louis and its environs available from some hotels and bookshops which makes an informative companion for your wandering in and around town as well as making a great memento when you leave. *Hôtel de la Poste*, as the longest established tourist venue in town, offers **tours** all around St-Louis. They'll also take you down to the beach in the morning and pick you up at the end of the day – at a price. You can make cheaper arrangements through the *Hôtel du Palais*.

The island

You can walk round the **island** – *Ndar* in Wolof – in about an hour and a half. Shuttered windows, occasional balconies and flaking yellow paint are the abiding impressions. Some of the best houses – which, as in Gorée, tend to conceal their interiors from snooping strangers – are around and just north of the hotels, especially along rue Blanchot and rue Pierre Loti. Maurel et Prom was a slave market, and the *Hôtel de la Poste* started as a gum arabic warehouse. The old houses characteristically have interior courtyards, warehouses on the ground floor (mostly now converted) and first-floor, inward-facing living quarters.

At the Place de Lille, named after St-Louis's twin city, notice the plaque commemorating the town's most celebrated citizen, Mbarick Fall, who as **Battling Siki** became the first world professional boxing champion in 1925. Heading south round the corner from here, beneath a wonderful old silk-cotton tree, you come to the **Place Faidherbe**, centering on a bust of the eponymous French governor, and surrounded by government and military buildings.

At the southern tip of the island, the **museum** is worth a look (in theory, daily 9am–noon & 3–6pm; CFA500). The first floor has displays on the great marabouts and politicians of Senegal and the historic personalities of St-Louis, together with local ethnographia from neolithic times to the coming of the *colons*. Temporary exhibitions are held on the second floor; ask at the Syndicat d'Initiative et de Tourisme for details.

From the museum, if you head up the eastern side of the island, you pass the **Maison des Signares**, a particularly impressive example of St-Louisienne architecture. Back at the **north end** of the island, don't miss the **Palais de Justice** on rue Brière de l'Ile, with its massive staircase.

Ndar Tout and Guet Ndar

Across the other arm of the river on the spit of the Langue de Barbarie, the scene is much more animated. Turn right across either of the bridges and you're strolling on avenue Dodds, main drag of the **Ndar Tout** quarter. With its tall, gracious houses rising behind the pavement palm trees, it is easy to picture this as the Champs Élysées of the local *signares* set, at a time when there were four thousand French *colons* and military based in St-Louis. At the far north end, ruination sets in – skeletal buff and red remains of French army buildings and then a marker pillar designating the **Mauritanian frontier** (no official border crossing).

Action in Ndar Tout focuses on the **market** and sandy **Place de la République**, which gives out straight onto the Atlantic down avenue Servatius, itself ankle deep in sand. From here you can walk south along the shore into the fishing quarter of **Guet Ndar** – rewarding, if odoriferous in the late afternoon – and down as far as the Islamic fishermen's cemetery, a net-and-stake graveyard with the familiar and disquieting vulture retinue.

Sor

The **mainland** area of St-Louis – **Sor** – is the part of town whose population swells with every downward cycle of drought in the interior. On the whole it's an anonymous district, though there are some old buildings, and there's a lively African feel by night which the weary island can't match. On the route de Corniche at Sor's northern end is the **Village Artisanal** where you might pick up a wider and less expensive range of Senegalese and Mauritanian artefacts than those you'll be offered outside the island's better hotels.

Eating, drinking and nightlife

St-Louis has a few reliable and economical **places to eat** around the main centre on the island. A good spot for cheap street food is by the monument on Ndar Tout; for greater expense and quality take your pick from the better hotels such as the *Poste*'s or *Résidence*'s restaurants.

The hotels are probably your best bet for **drinking**, too, though there's also a classy **nightclub**, *La Chaumière*, in Ndar Tout, owned by the *Hôtel de la Poste* (free to all guests). Charging around CFA2000 at the door and with ordinary bar prices, it only gets into gear after midnight. Alternatively, simply cut east across the Servatius bridge to the mainland and let your ears track down the action: community events are easily located.

Restaurants and snack bars

Bistro du Phare, by the lighthouse on Ndar Tout. Great, well-prepared food and wonderful views over the Atlantic.

Fleuve Plus, rue Blaise Diagne. Popular restaurant with an extensive Senegalese menu; main courses for CFA1500–2200 and tasty juices – try the tamarind.

La Galaxie, rue Briere de l'Isle. About the best deal in town: friendly service and, for once, a pleasant interior plus entrees for CFA800. Daily 11am–3pm & 7–11pm.

Linguère, next to *Hôtel de la Résidence*. Good food at around the CFA1000 mark. Closed Thurs.

Le Matis, rue Khalifa Ababacar Sy, opposite *Hôtel du Palais*. *Chawarma* for CFA650 and everything with chips for CFA1500. Open 24hr.

Signare, rue Blaise Diagne. A plush non-hotel French option – when it's open.

Wuroma, also known as *Ker Gaye*, rue Khalifa Ababacar Sy. Basic daily specials of fish and chicken for CFA700–1500.

Listings

Bank BICIS, on rue de France/rue Blanchot (Mon–Thurs 7.30am–12.15pm & 1.40–3.45pm, Fri 7.45am–1pm & 2.40–3.45pm), are able to change cash and travellers' cheques, if the right staff are on duty. There's a 24hr automatic teller outside for those with Visa cards.

Car rental Ask at your hotel, or try Senecartours, rue Blaise Diagne (☎822 42 86); plan ahead as the vehicles are transferred from Dakar on request.

Cinemas Kung fu and Indian epics dubbed into French are shown at the open-air Rex. The Vox is more comfortable, has a roof and shows mostly US action films, also dubbed into French.

Travel agents Try Sahel Decouverte, rue Blaise Diagne (☎961 62 63), or Delta Tours, corner rue Blanchôt/rue Khalifa Ababacar Sy (☎961 17 72).

MOVING ON FROM ST-LOUIS

Trains to Dakar only operate during potentially busy times such as Christmas, and possibly the May jazz festival in St-Louis. **Bush taxis** leave from the *gare routière* on the mainland for Dakar (CFA2800; 4hr) and inland destinations along the Senegal River, including Rosso (CFA1450; 2hr), for the border crossing into Mauritania.

The Langue de Barbarie and its Parc National

With 4WD you can drive the entire length of the **Langue de Barbarie**, dodging the waves and hundreds of thousands of crabs as you go. The trip starts in Guet Ndar, passing the remains of the **Hydrobase**, the seaplane centre used as a staging post by the early airmail service between Europe and South America. The first South Atlantic crossing took off from here in 1930; the *Hôtel de la Poste* in town is full of mementos.

Many of the casuarina trees planted here by Governor Faidherbe when the Langue was called La Piste des Cavaliers, have since perished, and it's an often melancholy beachscape populated by new *campements* in various stages of completion. At the tip of the spit you look across the estuary to the area protected by the national park, where there's a good chance of seeing cormorants, pelicans and turtles.

The **Parc National de la Langue de Barbarie** (daily 7am–6pm; CFA2000) covers twenty square kilometres of estuarine islands and waterways around the southern end of the Langue. Its main entrance is on the landward side, after the village of Gandiol, which is accessible by bush taxi from the Sor *autogare* at St-Louis or through **tours** organized by the main hotels in town. The quantity of birds depends on the time of year – from November to August the park is a breeding site for terns, gulls and egrets – and on an element of luck: flamingos and pelicans are the obvious species, but rarer ones require more patience. On firmer ground you can see warthogs and, in a fenced enclosure, a pair of giant tortoises and a herd of deer – gift of King Juan Carlos of Spain.

Parc National des Oiseaux du Djoudj

Situated in the heart of the Walo delta of the Senegal River, and considerably bigger than the Langue de Barbarie park, the **Parc National des Oiseaux du Djoudj** (Nov 15–May 15 daily 7am–7pm, closed May 16–Nov 14; CFA2000, cars CFA5000) is Senegal's ornithological showcase, rated the third most important **bird reserve** in the world. If you're at all into birds and are here during the palearctic migrants' season between October and April, you should make the effort to get in. The track into the park is signposted to the left off the Rosso/Richard Toll road near the village of Ndiol; once in the park, however, restricting yourself to the tracks gives only half the picture. Try to get a good price for a **pirogue trip** (aim for CFA2000 per person per hour) across the shallow expanses, for it's here that you'll get close enough to the wildlife to take good pictures.

The Djoudj is West Africa's best bird reserve, its estimated 100,000 **flamingos** and 10,000 **white pelicans** among the world's largest concentrations. January is probably the ideal time to visit, with the migrants in residence but the water levels already receding. Flamingos prefer the high alkalinity – and the reduced water surface tends to concentrate the birds, making them easier to spot. Crowned cranes are among the park's more ostentatious inhabitants. You should also keep a lookout on the water surface for the eyes and snouts of **crocodiles**, especially visible in the dry season.

Those without their own transport can arrange **trips to the Djoudj** with *Hôtel de la Poste* (around CFA25,000 each for the day, minimum four people; cheaper en masse), or with the owners of the *Hôtel du Palais*, who do a similar trip for around CFA15,000 per person, which includes entrance fees, a two- or three-hour *pirogue* ride and unlimited stops en route. Taxis can also be persuaded to spend the day taking you there and back, but you'll pay at least CFA20,000 per taxi (plus fuel and entrance fees) and you've little room to protest if the trip is cut short. At the park entrance, the *Campement du Djoudj* (☎923 85 43; Fax 923 88 33; ④) offers overpriced S/C huts.

Along the Senegal River

From St-Louis there is frequent **transport upriver** to **Rosso** (for Mauritania) and Richard Toll. Thereafter, vehicles from St-Louis are scarcer, so you'll have to hop your way along the highway from town to town, and as the heat rises noticeably inland it can be a long slog in the back of a crowded *bâche* to Kidira, two long days and nearly 600km from St-Louis. There's little of interest to see along this route other than glimpses of the Senegal River and rural, upcountry communities getting on with life, although you'll find the former trading outpost of **Bakel**, just north of Kidira, a charismatic stopover. Once you've passed Richard Toll, the only banks along this route are the shores of the Senegal River, so make sure you have enough CFA, or at least French francs, to get you to Tambacounda or Kayes in Mali.

The Lower River

Between St-Louis and Richard Toll, the scene varies sharply with the time of year: in the dry season from November to May, you'll see the oblong, wicker huts of migrant Fula herders who've moved from the higher, drier lands of the interior. Signs of human habitation include the practice of planting old car tyres in the mud to stake a land claim – common all over West Africa.

Around the turn-off to Rosso, and all along the 6km causeway road to it, you see thousands of hectares of rice, along with **sugar cane**, intended not only to feed Senegal's considerable sugar consumption but also, eventually, to produce fuel alcohol to offset the high cost of oil imports. In the irrigation ditches, **Nile monitor lizards** abound, growing enormous – up to two metres long – on a diet of insects, frogs and rodents.

Rosso

On the frontier with Mauritania, **ROSSO** (about 90min from St-Louis by minibus) is bustling, with black marketeers trading Ouguiya, the Mauritanian currency, and a minor **smuggling** industry – not from relatively thriving Senegal into drought-stricken Mauritania, but the reverse, from aid-saturated Mauritania into IMF-austere Senegal. If you're heading for Mauritania you're likely to be offered Ouguiya at about ten percent above the going rate.

As you approach the town the road curls through desperate shacks and official buildings to a tongue of land from where a barge regularly crosses the brown flow to **Rosso-Mauritania**. If you're **crossing the river** – and there's little point in coming up here if you're not (there's even a local "Taxe sur les personnes Etrangères" of CFA300) – ask the driver to drop you at the first flagpoled white building on the left, where your passport gets stamped out of Senegal. If you're on foot you can get across the river easily enough using *pirogues* for about CFA500 per person. Between noon and 2 or 3pm this is the only way to cross – it's lunchtime for the barge crew. The border closes at 6pm.

Richard Toll

Meaning "Richard's Field", the dreary **RICHARD TOLL** is named after the ambitious regional development planned by the French planter Claude Richard in the 1820s. The town's only notable building is Baron Jaques Roger's **colonial mansion**, built on an island in the River Taouey – which flows into the Senegal on the east side of town. It's surrounded by the remains of his ornamental park – now a dusty and overgrown jungle and nothing special. For **accommodation** you've one or two options: directly north of the *gare routière* is the *Gîte d'Etape* (✆ & Fax 963 32 40; ④), a great spot to rest up if you've had a tiring few days, with its lovely riverside setting, restaurant, Saturday-night disco and, most usefully, a swimming pool (CFA2500 for non-residents). Otherwise, there's the less luxurious *Hôtel La Taouey* (✆963 34 31; ③), on the river behind the Shell station. Along the town's long main drag you'll spot plenty of **street food** snack bars. If you're moving on east and there's nothing remotely full in the *gare routière*, you might prefer to take a *calèche* the couple of kilometres to the edge of town (CFA150), and wait there for a passing vehicle.

Lac de Guiers

The **Lac de Guiers**, some 30km southwest of Richard Toll, has a more attractive scene. This is a wild area, and swarms with most of the birds present in the Djoudj, with the exception of flamingos. Warthogs are common and if you find a way to get out on the water you might even see **manatees** – strange, aquatic mammals which hold onto a precarious existence here. **People** of the area include Tukulor and Black Moor fishermen, and Fula herders at certain times of year. Protected from the Senegal River's brackish contamination by a dam in the River Taouey at Richard Toll, the lake supplies much of Dakar's drinking water, which is purified at Gnit on the western shore and piped 300km to the capital. You can't get right round the lake – it's best seen from the village of Mbane, on the eastern shore. The reedy western shore is accessible only from the St-Louis–Dakar road or a track which leads off south from the N2, 10km west of the Rosso junction – both unsignposted.

The Middle River

Beyond Richard Toll, the road rises out of the valley bypassing the town of **Dagana** – an old gum arabic entrepôt on the Senegal, with colonial buildings and semi-intact nineteenth-century fort. Just east of town you get a tempting flash of the river (a good spot for lunch, but stay out of the water) and from here you leave traditional Wolof country. East of here most of the people you'll see are **Tukulor** or **Fula**, and the atmosphere is more laid-back, with commerce no longer quite such a feature.

Moving upriver you pass various villages – some traditional mud and grass affairs, others agglomerations of concrete blocks. At the spartan settlement of **Ndiayène** you can change into a clapped-out Peugeot 504 for the 24km run north (CFA350) to **PODOR**, Senegal's northernmost town right by the river, passing twin-towered mosques along the way. Despite the town's notable history – the name comes from its gold (*or*)-trading past and there's the remains of an 1854 French fort – and the fact that it's singing star Baaba Maal's home town, there is little to recommend a diversion off the highway. If you end up **staying**, there are two simple choices, both within a few metres of the *gare routière*: *Auberge Eaux et Forets* (✆965 12 29; ②) and *Gite de'Etape "Le Douwara"* (✆965 12 71; ③).

Podor is situated on the western tip of the **Ile à Morfil** (Island of Ivory), a long slug of floodlands (120km by 10km) between the main course of the river and the meandering Doué. At one time the island had a large population of **elephants**, supported by the covering of dense, silt-fed woodland. It's still a good wildlife district, with monkeys,

---

THE STATE OF TEKRUR

The Ile à Morfil lay at the heart of the **state of Tekrur** (whence *Tukulor* and the misleading French spelling *Toucouleur*), which was at its most powerful in the eleventh century, when it became a major sub-Saharan trading partner with the Almoravid Arabs of North Africa. The Tukulor claim, as a result, that they were the first West Africans to adopt Islam, and went on to evangelize, among others, the Fula – with whom they share a common language and much else. Their own state was annexed by ancient Ghana, with its power base to the east at Koumbi Saleh, in present-day Mauritania. When the Almoravids attacked Ghana, Tekrur helped the invaders, only to fall shortly afterwards to the Mali empire.

There's a fair number of villages with Sudanic-style **mosques** scattered along the island's one main track as far as **Salde**, the furthest east, where you can ferry back to the main road 90km short of Matam. If you can find transport the length of the island, it's a far preferable alternative to following the main N2, which is unremittingly dull.

---

crocodiles and a proliferation of birdlife, but elephants haven't been regularly seen since the 1960s and it's doubtful if any survive.

The Upper River

Further inland, the next town of note is **Ouro Sogui**, the biggest settlement along the *haute fleuve* and around 280km and a hot and dusty seven hours by bush taxi from Ndiayène, shorter if you can catch a Peugeot 504. If you're coming from St-Louis you'll need to make a dawn start as you'll have to make a couple of vehicle changes. Along the way various routes to the river give access **into Mauritania** at Kaédi; branching north at **Thilogne**, 51km before Ouro Sogui, is the best bet. From Kaédi, there's regular transport around southeast Mauritania, and up to Nouakchott. Travellers frequently mistake the large highway town of Ouro Sogui with the former Tukulor **slave trading** station of Matam, a fading town 10km northeast of the highway, and still featured as the larger settlement on most maps.

At **OURO SOGUI**, turning south from the Elf station leads 1km along the main street to the town centre and market, passing cheap *dibiteries* such as *Chez Oussan* and the *Dibiterie d'Islam* next door. If you're being driven to the *gare routière* on the south side of town, keep an eye out for the two-storey *Auberge Sogui* (☎966 11 98; ③) on the right, the town's only regular **accommodation**, with large fanned or AC rooms, some S/C, and *plats* in the restaurant for CFA2500, if it's open. There's a rooftop terrace on which to rest when the *Harmattan* isn't tearing in from Mauritania. You might also be offered a less expensive bed, along with cheap platefuls of whatever's in the pot, at the friendly unnamed restaurant a few minutes beyond the *auberge*. The **gare routière** is the customary spot for basic nourishment and the place you want to get to early the next day for the run on to Bakel and Kidira.

Bakel and Kidira

Moving south from Ouro Sogui, the roads are much improved, and you can now expect a fairly smooth ride all the way to Tambacounda.

Tucked in a bend in the river among a knot of hills, **BAKEL**'s narrow streets and colonial architectural relics make it perhaps the only place to linger a couple of days in the northeast, while possibly waiting to intercept the twice weekly Dakar–Bamako train at Kidira. The hills around evoke a sense of isolation similar to the dunes surrounding Timbuktu – indeed René Caillié stayed here and later took the post as prefect of Bakel on his return from the legendary city. The old French **fort**, regrettably still a military emplacement and out of bounds to visitors (though a Centre René Caillié exists in theory in one of its towers), overlooks the river where *piroguiers* ply for fish, onto an uncharacteristically verdant corner of Mauritania.

Bakel's *gare routière* is a few minutes' walk from the town centre, where the cheapest **place to stay** is the rather crumby but very friendly *Hôtel d'Islam* (☎983 90 29; ①), across from the *boulangerie*, with a few fanned rooms, or mat space on the roof terrace. There's a **restaurant** here too, when there are enough guests; otherwise you could try the various fast-food places along the main street. For more comfort, check out the AC rooms in the *Hôtel de Macomba* (☎983 52 80; ③), on the river bank a little north of town. There's also the *Campement d'Apt* (Bakel's twin city; ☎983 90 52; ②), with ordinary little huts, some with fans, and a lively weekend dancing scene in the *Jikke* nightclub in the grounds.

Twin-town projects are common in the area and the whole district is surprisingly full of émigré money: many of the Soninké villagers in the district live in France, remitting savings which in turn become impressive houses. If you want to visit the villages, ideally if you have transport, **Golmy**, **Kongany** and **Ballor** are all to the north. You can also cross to the Mauritanian village of **Gouray**, or to the Malian village of **Guthurbé**. Most of the Soninké villages organize *journées culturelles* every couple of years, during which traditional Soninké ways are dusted off and presented to the community – occasions well worth planning around.

Minibuses leave daily from the *gare routière* for the 63-kilometre run to Tambacounda (5hr) via **KIDIRA** (2hr). On arrival in Kidira the bus delivers passengers to the *surête* at the west end of town, where you should get stamped out of Senegal if heading for Mali. Whatever time you arrive, you'll have to spend some time here, as both the east- and west-bound **trains** come through on Wednesday and Saturday evenings around midnight. Unfortunately the town has little to offer the visitor apart from some street food by the Kidira railway crossing, but the Falémé River (follow the tracks 1km east) is a good place to pass the time and maybe catch up on your washing.

Those passing through Kidira **by road** will find a new bridge spanning the Falémé River just south of the rail bridge, while a newly sealed road leads southwest 180km to Tambacounda. The road on the Malian side passes through light baobab woodlands to Kayes, just over 100km to the east, and may prove impassable in the wet season.

NIOKOLO-KOBA AND THE SOUTHEAST

Senegal's number one **national park** and the flag-bearer for the country's conservation policies, **Niokolo-Koba** covers 8000 square kilometres – a little smaller than the area of The Gambia – of savannah, forest and swamp. It's an undulating wilderness, straddling the Gambia River and two major tributaries in the gentle uplands of **Sénégal Oriental**.

Aside from the park, which is visited by around five thousand people a year, **southeast Senegal** is on the whole little affected by tourism. You'll find strongly traditional ways enduring, although hunting as a livelihood took a severe blow when the park opened, displacing a large, scattered population of Mandinka, Bassari and Fula. Tourist excursions to **Bassari country**, beyond the park, have been running in a small way from Tambacounda for some years and more recently from Kédougou, but to reap the high rewards of this part of the country, you must be prepared to hike or make your own informal arrangements.

Tambacounda

Getting to Niokolo-Koba can be difficult, feasible without your own transport only if you're prepared to put in considerable time waiting for a ride, probably at **TAMBACOUNDA**, 80km from the park entrance. The town is eastern Senegal's major transport hub, the big station on the Dakar–Bamako railway after Kayes in Mali. Situated in the flat, dreary scrub, a rough 180km from the Malian border and 460km from Dakar, the town has little of interest to detain you, but if you're using public transport you will almost inevitably have to spend time here.

Practicalities

The centre of Tamba is bunched around the station, where **trains** from Bamako are due around 7am on Thursdays and Sundays, and those from Dakar around 7pm on Wednesdays and Saturdays – although they are invariably extremely late. Trains are usually packed by this stage, whichever way you're going, so don't expect a seat or bearable toilets. In theory, there are fourteen seats reserved for passengers embarking in Tamba: book ahead the day before if possible.

Accommodation choices have increased over recent years. A kilometre or so down the main street you'll find the *Hôtel Niji* (☎981 12 50; Fax 981 17 44; ③), which offers an adequate selection of fanned, AC and S/C options, as well as organizing *soirées folkloriques* (CFA50,000, mini-

Mamacounda Nightlub
Market
Pharmacie
BNDS Bank
Police
BOULEVARD DEMBA DIOP
Keur Khoudia
Restaurant de la Gare
Railway Station
Restaurant Riko Kiss
Film shop
Gare Routiére Cotiari (for Kidira, Mali & NE Senegal)
BOULEVARD KANDIOURA NOBA
SGBS Bank
Darou Salam
Seasonal River
Main Gare Routière
Elf Station
N
Hôtel Niji
AV LEOPOLD SENGHOR
0   Metres   200
Hôtel Asta Kebé
TAMBACOUNDA
Chez Dessert
Airport, Kolda and Basse Casamance, Niokolo Koba National Park, The Gambia and Guinea ▽
Mali; National Parks Office & Complexe Leggaal Point ▷
Bamako ▷

mum 5 people) and *piroguing* along the Gambia River (same price). The very comfortable *Hôtel Asta Kebé* (☎981 10 28; Fax 981 12 15; ③–④), signed another 200m down the main road, gives you the works, including a pool; while the charmingly off-the-wall and unmarked *Chez Dessert* (②), next door to the carpenters opposite the *Hôtel Asta Kebé* sign, has bed or floor space and even meals with advance notice. Two recently opened *campement*-style places are the *Complexe Leggaal Pont*, 1km out of town (☎981 17 56; Fax 981 17 52; S/C, some AC; ②–③), with bar, restaurant and nightclub, and *Keur Khoudia* (☎981 11 02; Fax 981 90 49; ③), an annexe of the *Simenti Hôtel* at Niokola-Koba (see p.216), which can be found past the Total fuel station on the way out of town in the opposite direction.

You can **eat** cheaply at *Darou Salam*, north of the Elf station, or at the marginally more pleasant terrace at the back of *Restaurant Riko Kiss* up the road on the left. The *Niji* does a *menu* for CFA4000 or at the *Asta Kebé* you'll pay CFA5000.

If you're heading for the park, stock up on **supplies** in Tamba, as there's really nothing but a handful of restaurants in the park itself. There's a couple of well-stocked *épiceries* along Avenue Leopold Senghor and a shop selling camera film. The SGBS **bank** (Mon–Fri 8.15–11.30am & 3.15–5.15pm) should just be able to cough up a Visa or MasterCard cash advance. The BNDS bank, **PTT**, **pharmacy** and a market are grouped around Boulevard Demba Diop, near the station. The **national park office** (Mon–Fri 7.30am–5pm; ☎981 10 97 or 981 19 64; Fax 981 19 63), 1km out of town on the Mali road, has informative booklets with maps (in French) for CFA5000 and can also organize your accommodation for you, and book transport (CFA30,000 per vehicle per day; excluding fuel, entrance fees and guide hire). You can also buy park entry permits here in advance.

Moving on from Tamba, the **train** takes 20 hours to Bamako or 13 hours to Dakar, the latter journey quicker and cheaper **by road.** The main **gare routière** – for services to Dakar (daily), Kédougou, Ziguinchor (see below for details), Guinea and Guinea-Bissau – is located in the town's southwestern corner. There is also a daily bus to Dakar from opposite the train station. There's a second *gare routière* – for services to Kidira, Mali and northeast Senegal – along the Boulevard Kandioura Noba.

Onwards to the Casamance and Guinea-Bissau

Heading from Tamba by public transport for the full-day's ride (CFA4500) to Ziguinchor – safety conditions in the Basse Casamance permitting – you want to be sure you catch a pre-8am minibus or you'll be waiting till noon. Few people slow down on their southwesterly way through the increasingly luxuriant **Haute** and **Moyenne Casamance**, and to be honest the small town of **Velingara** has little to offer other than a *campement*.

Accommodation in the regional centre of **KOLDA** is limited to the *Hôtel Moya* (BP 14; ☎996 11 75; Fax 996 13 57; ②–③), a cosy nest of en-suite chalets with huge beds, located by the riverside 400m south of the *gare routière* and Elf station, and the *Hôtel Hobb* (☎ & Fax 996 10 39; ③–④), with a little more comfort but less character. For something to **eat**, there's a cheaper alternative to the *Moya*'s restaurant: two blocks west of the hotel the *Restaurant Moussa Molo* serves a heap of *tiéboudienne* for CFA700 at lunchtime, and meat in the evenings for CFA1250. The **bar** at the *Moya* is a centre for socializing in the evenings.

From Kolda a daily minibus takes a minor *piste* to Bafatá in Guinea-Bissau, a four-hour journey which includes border formalities – expect to have your baggage turned inside out by the Bissau customs – and a walk across a rickety bridge spanning the Rio Gêba. There's also a more direct bush taxi option to Bissau (via Farim) from Tanaf, 70km west of Kolda. At Tanaf you can also take a ferry from Sandenièr, 10km northwest of town, across the River Casamance to **Sedhiou** (*campement*) in the Haute Casamance region. Note that at the time of writing, travel in Guinea-Bissau was not advisable.

Parc National de Niokolo-Koba

Niokolo-Koba is officially open only during the **December to June** dry season (exact dates fixed according to the weather), when animals gather along the watercourses, and if you check in the right places – detailed below and on the map – you've a chance

ROUTES INTO GUINEA AND MALI

The main route from Tambacounda into **Guinea** parts from the Tambacounda–Ziguinchor road where it scrapes the Gambian border. From here the route goes via Medina-Gounas (a devout community of the Tijaniya brotherhood, where the women are veiled) to the Senegalese post at Boundou, whence an extremely rough *piste* leads 55km to Koundara on the Guinean side.

Getting transport via Niokolo-Koba into Guinea is fairly hit and miss. You should try hard in Tambacounda to find something going the whole way (keep an eye out for the all-terrain Russian lorries heading for Mali, a small town in northern Guinea, 120km south of Kédougou) rather than setting off on a series of bush taxi hops. The first of two possible minor routes passes 11km to the west of Kédougou, and heads up into the Fouta Djalon highlands, a ride you won't forget in a hurry and from which even experienced 4WD drivers have turned back. Another route, 11km east of Kédougou, winds for over 200km to the major town of **Labé**, right in the heart of the Fouta Djalon. You might be lucky with transport on the first route, which is also by far the most scenic. On the second, the Gambia River crossing in Guinea is particularly uncertain. Both are supposed to have Guinean entrance formalities on the border itself, but expect to have to check in again at Mali or Labé. In your own vehicle you might prefer the less arduous crossing to the Guinea town of Youkounkoun, 100km west of Kédougou.

From Kédougou, Land Rovers serve Saraya, 60km to the northeast, and occasionally continue another 70km along a maze of minor bush tracks to Kéniéba in the Republic of **Mali** (a rough half-day to two days' drive). This is not a regular route and is dependent on demand as well as the depth of the Faléme River which denotes the unmanned frontier – it's usually fordable from January until the rains come. Expect to pay CFA8000 each – if the car is full – for this unusual and rarely-used back route into Mali.

of seeing most of the larger species. The park's tracks are mostly well maintained, and good signposting ensures you won't have much trouble getting around; the only area where you might need a 4WD is around Mont Assirik. **Where to go** is a matter of hunches and good luck. It's useful to have some French names: where they differ markedly from the English, they are given below. The park fee per day is CFA2000 per person, plus CFA5000 per car. Note that if you're travelling in your own vehicle, you must also hire a guide (CFA600 per day) at the entrance to the park; all of these speak French, but are unlikely to speak English.

Commonest large species include buffalo, hartebeeste (*bubale*; uniquely ugly with their long faces and hooked horns), shaggy Defassa waterbuck (*cobe defassa*), timid and fast-moving bushbuck (*antilope harnaché* or *guib*; beautifully white-marked on russet coat), warthogs (*phacochère*), of course, and crocodiles in the rivers. **Hippos** are sometimes visible from the authorized halts along the Gambia River, and you can see them in many areas where the water is deep enough all year round. Don't ignore the commoner species, which quickly become part of the background, but look out for the large, maned **roan antelope**, (*hippotrague*) and especially for the huge and very uncommon **western giant eland** which stands a couple of metres at the shoulder. Baboons and other monkeys, notably vervet and red patas, are also common. The park's **chimpanzees** are exceedingly rare, numbering around 150; they can be seen east of Assirik, the most northerly chimpanzee outpost in Africa.

Sighting **lions** is rare; with patience, though, you might see them in pockets of deep shade at the base of trees, or in hollows, especially around the confluence of tracks known as Patte d'Oie – "Crow's foot". **Elephants** are said to gather in a broad zone around Mont Assirik, and in the months before the rains (March–May) are often found in the south of this area – a drive between Bangaré ford and Worouli could be suc-

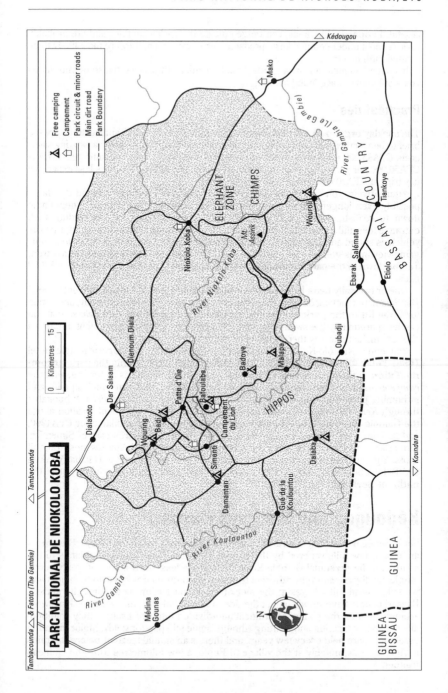

PARC NATIONAL DE NIOKOLO KOBA

cessful. **Leopards,** like lions, can range outside the park's confines and are probably Africa's most under-counted large predator; very rarely seen, they are most likely to be spotted high in a tree.

It's not a bad idea to **rent a guide** from Simenti, as they can often show you things you would never have found alone.

Practicalities

The one-day **organized excursions** from the *Hôtel Asta Kebé* in Tambacounda are too brief to be worthwhile. Cost is the main drawback of their other deals: a two-day safari costs CFA35,000 each for a minimum group of ten, while a day's chauffered 4WD is CFA50,000 per person plus fuel and entrance fees. The *Hôtel Niji* offers less expensive day-trips at CFA70,000 between six people.

Alternatively, you can always find a **taxi** driver who's willing to spend the day – possibly even longer – driving you round. The advantage is the price – negotiable down to realistic levels of CFA25,000–30,000 per taxi per day (excluding fuel, entrance fees and guide hire). But be sure the driver knows what he's about, that the vehicle is sound and has spares, and that you pay for fuel separately, otherwise your game-viewing is going to be limited indeed. Four people simply sharing a taxi from Tamba down to the park headquarters at Simenti can expect to pay around CFA5000 each.

One or two daily **taxis brousse** serve villages down the road to the park entrance at Dar Salam, but moving on from there can prove virtually impossible. Finally, one option for a **free lift to the park** from Tamba is to invest in a meal at the *Asta Kebé* so that you can hang around by the swimming pool, where there's usually a contingent of tourists about to make their way there whom you could ask.

You enter Niokolo-Koba at Dar Salam, where there's a *campement*-style hotel (☎981 17 00; ②). Note that driving isn't allowed after dark. Within the park, **accommodation** at the main centres of **Simenti** and **Niokolo-Koba** is expensive, with the *campements* almost indistinguishable from hotels, with restaurants, fuel supplies and swimming pools (non-guests can pay a fee for a swim). *Simenti Hôtel* (③; bookable through *Keur Khoudia* in Tambacounda, see p.212) has an excellent location above the Gambia River and a good game-viewing **hide**; meals are available for CFA4200, and half-day game drives for CFA6000/person. Eight kilometres east of Simenti is *Campement du Lion* (②), a much more basic set-up in one of the park's most tranquil spots. You can **camp** for free at Badi, Malapa, Damantan, Badoye, Dalaba, Wouroli and Bafoulabé. For up-to-date information and assistance with bookings contact the **national park office** (see p.161).

Kédougou and the Pays Bassari

Set in Senegal's verdant and rarely visited southeastern corner, the **Pays Bassari** is an area of low hills watered by the run-off from the Fouta Djalon highlands to the south and the perennial Gambia River. This is the least known part of the country, ethnically diverse and very different from the Wolof-Franco Senegal to the north and west. Living in hill villages at the foot of the Fouta Djalon mountains, the ancient Bassari people have stood against the tide of Islam that over the centuries has swept around them on the plains. Matrilineal and divided into age groups, they traditionally subsist on farming and hunting (though some still pan for gold). Major initiation ceremonies are held every few years, and there's an annual **festival** before the rains in April or May, notably at the village of Etiolo, a few kilometres from the Guinean frontier.

KÉDOUGOU is the only major settlement, a bit of a dead-end to all but the very few pushing on to Guinea or Mali, or for those using it as an alternative base for the Niokolo-Koba park. The town's *campements* offer a range of **excursions** to Bassari, Beduk and Peul villages in the region, along with the waterfall near Didefelo and visits to traditional gold mines – but not tours to Niokola-Koba. Kédougou has a post office, pharmacies and fuel as well as three **accommodation** options, all with annexes. *Le Relais* by the river at the west end of town (☎985 10 62; Fax 985 11 26; ④) and its annexe, *Hippo Safari Lodge* 4km to the east, are popular with tour groups (and offer several excursions). A better choice is *Chez Diao*'s *campement* (☎985 11 24; Fax 985 10 07; ②–③), 100m east of the *gare routière* in the town centre, and its annexe on the other side of the road, with all the same services for half the price. A new addition is *Chez Moise campement* (☎985 11 39; ②–③), north of the *gare routière* and very similar to *Chez Diao*, with an annexe out of town next to the river. The *campements* are the best places for **food**; the only other options are the fast-food restaurants around the *gare routière*.

If you've just turned up from Mali or Guinea, get your passport stamped at the **police** post, 500m up the Tamba road just past the phone box. The road from Kédougou to Tambacounda is now surfaced the entire way.

BASSE CASAMANCE

Basse Casamance – the lower reaches of the Casamance River – is the most seductive part of Senegal. Wonderfully tropical, with dense forest, winding creeks, rice fields and quiet backroads shaded by massive silk-cottons, the district seems to have little in common with the Senegal of Islamic brotherhoods, groundnuts, cattle and dust.

For centuries the mostly **Jola**-speaking population of Basse Casamance resisted the push of Islam (most successfully on the south bank of the river), while the Portuguese maintained a typically torpid presence. The ceding of the region to the French in 1886 didn't precipitate any great social shifts. Changes are underway, despite an isolation in which villages and language groups are cut off even from each other, but there's a resolve to maintain some degree of self-determination. Since independence, the **Casamance question** and the apparent threat to Wolof-speaking, French-abetted metropolitan Senegal, has been a prickly one. Casamance provides the bulk of the country's rice harvest and, furthermore, without its full participation in national affairs, the issue of *rapprochement* with The Gambia – an even more troublesome thorn in Senegal's side – will never be resolved.

WARNING

At the time of writing in mid-1999, sporadic **conflict** was continuing in the Basse Casamance between the Senegalese government and the various, disunified factions of the MFDC separatist movement. Both the British Foreign Office and the US State Department were advising visitors against all travel to the region. Although tourists have not directly been targeted, some violent incidents have taken place very close to tourist centres, and many earth roads and minor tracks were mined by the MFDC in 1998 and 1999. As the situation is fluid and might improve, we haven't deleted Basse Casamance from this edition, but the following accounts should not be read as a recommendation to go. Note also that because of the unrest it has not been possible during the research of this new edition to fully update all the practical information given in this section. Keep your ear to the ground and stay tuned to the travellers' grapevine.

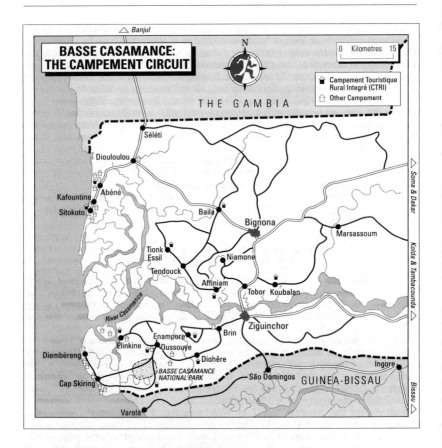

Getting to and around Basse Casamance

There are three **main roads** to Basse Casamance: from **Banjul**; from **Dakar** on the faster *transgambienne* route; and from far-off **Tambacounda** in the east. If you're coming from Mali on the train, this third route makes a much better introduction to Senegal than an after-dark arrival in Dakar. Two, or maybe three, minibuses depart daily from Tambacounda for Ziguinchor, all leaving early; a late start will mean changing in **Kolda**, making a full day on the road.

Getting around Basse Casamance is generally simple. You can **rent bikes** in Ziguinchor, Oussouye, Cap Skiring and a number of other places, making cycling around the popular southern part of Basse Casamance a practical option. Unless you have lots of time, it's perhaps best to rent in Oussouye or Cap Skiring, rather than Ziguinchor, as you'll probably spend your first day cycling straight to Oussouye anyway, and it's not the most exciting bike ride in the area. Ziguinchor is the main transport hub with daily transport to most sites of interest.

Because Basse Casamance is so affected by tides, no two **maps** of it ever look the same: much of what appears to be virtually underwater on some maps is actually firm ground most of the time.

THE JOLA

The people of Basse Casamance are predominantly **Jola** (or Diola; no relation to the Diola/Dyula of Côte d'Ivoire) – broadly divided by the river into Buluf and Fonyi on the north bank and Huluf (or Fulup) on the south. From around the sixteenth century they gradually displaced earlier Casamance inhabitants called the Banyun, who used to be great traders and still live among them. Where the Jola came from nobody seems to know, but their dialects are closely related to the Manjak spoken in Guinea-Bissau, and indeed the Jola generally claim to come from the south. They never developed a unified state, and their fragmentation has resulted in some **Jola** dialects being mutually unintelligible. In fact the idea of a Jola "tribe" is mostly a colonial one: only contact with outsiders has given the term any meaning for the people themselves. The word is supposed to derive from the Manding *jor la* – "he who avenges himself".

A distinctive style of **wet rice farming** has been practised for at least six hundred years in the reclaimed land between the creeks. **Dikes** are built around new fields so that the rains will flood them and leach out the sea salt, which runs away through hollow tree trunks in the dikes while the fields lie fallow. Once the field is flooded, the drains are blocked and the rice plants brought out from the nurseries and planted, one by one, in the mud. After three or four months of weeding and dike care by the men, the women gather the **harvest** in November or December. For the first half of the year, though, there's little work in the rice fields and increasingly this is a time when young people drift away to Ziguinchor, The Gambia or Dakar. Many don't return for the next season. Later in the year, you'll see villagers walking to the fields early in the morning with the amazingly long, iron-tipped hoes called **kayendos**. Traditionally, rice was never sold. Having huge numbers of granaries full of it, often for years, brought the kind of **prestige** every Jola man wanted. Consequently, conflicts over **land rights** have always been close to the surface and still occasionally erupt.

Islam has made little headway among the Jola, but an erosion of traditional values has been brought about by **groundnuts**. Introduced to the region in the early nineteenth century, the crop provided a commercial alternative to rice that could earn ready money, with relatively little labour, on land that had hitherto been unplanted bush. Now grown on raised ground all over the region, the groundnut crop has resulted in deforestation, soil degradation and reliance on imported food. "He who wears a *boubou* can't work in the rice fields" goes the Jola saying, ironically excusing the way things increasingly are in terms of Islam's stress on the individual.

JOLA WORDLIST

Jola is a diverse language, comprising several dialects: the following words and phrases could be helpful in Basse Casamance, but may not all provoke immediate recognition.

Kassoumay?	Hello, welcome	*Ounomom*	Sell me
Kassoumaykep	Universal response to kassaoumay (peace only)	*Ie dadat*	This is good
		Ie diacoutte	This is not good
		Katenom	Stop (leave me alone)
Aow	Yes	*Joom*	Stop (in a car)
Oolat	No	*Sinangas*	Rice
Safi	Bonjour, hello	*Siwolassou*	Fish
Oukatora	Goodbye	*Bunuk*	Palm wine
Karessy boo?	What is your name?	*Bulago bara ...?*	Which way to ...?
Karessom...	My name is...	*Boussana*	Pirogue
Oubonkatom	Please	*Sibeurassou*	Trees
Emitakati	Thank you	*Karambak*	Forest
Bunu kani?	How is it? Ça va?	*Falafou*	River
Iman jut	I don't understand		

Ziguinchor

Something of **ZIGUINCHOR**'s appeal comes through in its exotic name, pronounced "Sigichor" by most Jola. There's a luxuriant sense of repose here, found in no other Senegalese town of its size and life here is a good deal cheaper than in Dakar or The Gambia. Surprisingly, you need reminding that Ziguinchor is on the river: its colonial trading houses don't stand out, and the river port isn't likely to figure prominently in your meanderings. It's a town of trees and avenues, roosting birds, orchestral crickets and fluttering bats at dusk, with a strong flavour of the Guineas. Less pleasant is the attention lavished by local mosquitoes from March to October – and sporadically by highly persistent hustlers, vendors and hangers-on.

Arrival and orientation

Coming into Ziguinchor **up the river** on the MV *Joola* is the best approach; the ship deposits you at the heart of the town, a few minutes from the main hotels. Arriving **by road** from the north or from Tambacounda, you'll be dropped at the *gare routière*, 1km east of town, just south of the bridge. If you've come up from Guinea-Bissau, you may be dropped off on the new, wide, sealed road, just east of the Marché St-Maur and close to a few cheap accommodation options.

The old part of town is a comprehensible one-by-half-a-kilometre grid of streets extending south of the river to **Avenue du Docteur Gabriel** on which is situated the **rond-point** (roundabout). Within this area you'll find the banks, post office, main hotels and other services as well as the small portside market, good for fresh fruit, vegetables and early morning fish. South of the *rond-point*, Avenue Ibou Diallo leads past the cathedral a kilometre or two to the more animated quarter of town around the **Marché St-Maur**. If you arrive by air you're a kilometre further south on the same road.

Accommodation

Ziguinchor offers an excellent and inexpensive range of **accommodation** – basic, central rooms, *campement*-style set-ups, and a few plusher alternatives. This last category has suffered badly from the recent drop in tourist numbers, though the better establishments have remained popular – always a good sign.

Budget lodgings and mid-range hotels

Auberge Keur Clara, off av Ibou Diallo. Set in a quiet side-street with a great restaurant/bar upstairs (a weekly jazz venue) and basic singles or S/C twins. ②–③.

Hôtel Le Bel Kady, just south of Marché St Maur (☎991 11 22). Popular budget option run by a friendly bunch of youths. Faintly bordelloish with non-S/C rooms (some with AC) and dubious ablutions but a good-value restaurant. Also offers inexpensive *pirogue* trips. ②.

Hôtel Le Bombolong II (☎991 14 75; Fax 991 11 46). Surprisingly good-value S/C, AC rooms but lacking much ambience. Home of the *Bar Americaine* and, on a good night, the town's best nightclub (free to guests). ③.

Hôtel le Kadiandoumagne, rue de Commerce (☎991 16 75; Fax 991 11 46). Recommended colonial-style hotel and restaurant on the river front, with a beautiful garden. ③–④.

Hôtel Mapala, opposite *Le Bel Kady*. Decent, fanned S/C doubles plus a cheap restaurant and bar. ③.

Hôtel du Tourisme, rue de France (☎991 22 23; Fax 991 22 22). Old colonial-era favourite, offering the best value mid-range S/C rooms in town, an excellent restaurant and a level of service rare elsewhere. ③.

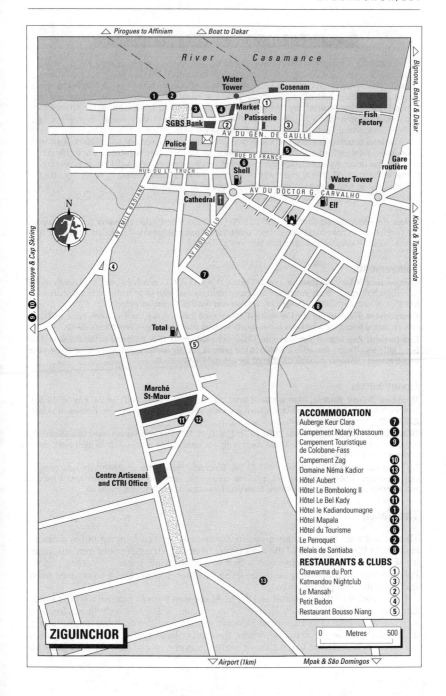

△ Pirogues to Affiniam   △ Boat to Dakar

River ~ Casamance

Bignona, Banjul & Dakar

Water Tower
Cosenam
SGBS Bank
Market
Patisserie
Fish Factory
AV DU GEN. DE GAULLE
Police
RUE DE FRANCE
RUE DU LT. TRUCH
Shell
Gare routière
Cathedral
AV DU DOCTOR G. CARVALHO
Water Tower
Elf
AV EMILE BADIANE
AV IBOU DIALLO
N
9, 10, Oussouye & Cap Skiring
Kolda & Tambacounda
Total
Marché St-Maur
Centre Artisenal and CTRI Office

ZIGUINCHOR

0   Metres   500

ACCOMMODATION
Auberge Keur Clara — ⑦
Campement Ndary Khassoum — ⑤
Campement Touristique de Colobane-Fass — ⑨
Campement Zag — ⑩
Domaine Néma Kadior — ⑬
Hôtel Aubert — ③
Hôtel Le Bombolong II — ④
Hôtel Le Bel Kady — ⑪
Hôtel le Kadiandoumagne — ①
Hôtel Mapala — ⑫
Hôtel du Tourisme — ⑥
Le Perroquet — ②
Relais de Santiaba — ⑧

RESTAURANTS & CLUBS
Chawarma du Port — ①
Katmandou Nightclub — ③
Le Mansah — ②
Petit Bedon — ④
Restaurant Bousso Niang — ⑤

▽ Airport (1km)   Mpak & São Domingos ▽

RIVER TRIPS AND RIVER CROSSINGS

You can take a *pirogue* to the **Ile aux Oiseaux**, across the river to **Dilapao** and continue up the serpentine Marigot de Bignona to **Affiniam**. At Dilapao you'll see two-storey mud-brick houses and can taste palm wine, while Affiniam's large **case à impluvium** is one of the oldest and nicest *campements* in the *rural integré* circuit. Just about every hotel offers this popular day-trip; prices start around CFA10,000 for a motor *pirogue* to yourself, supposedly less per person with a group, but can vary wildly from place to place. Ask around at the cheaper *campements* or hotels.

For **less touristy** travels, there's a cheap, regular *pirogue* service to Affiniam, leaving on Mon, Wed and Fri at 9.30am from the jetty by *Le Perroquet*; it returns from Affiniam at around noon. At other times you can try to reach an agreement with the *piroguiers* on the waterfront. This is a good way of starting a tour round the north bank region of **Buluf**, as an alternative to taxi-ing straight out of Ziguinchor.

Relais de Santiaba, qtr Santiaba (☎991 11 99). The town's best value *chambres de passage* up on the roof; plain but not rough, with decent, shared ablutions and breakfast included. Also some S/C rooms, a bar/restaurant and mountain bike rental. ①–③.

Campements

Campement Ndary Khassoum, rue de France (☎991 11 89). Centrally located, a bit rough round the edges but with a shady courtyard and large plain rooms, with huge bathrooms but shared toilets (S/C options available). *Pirogue* excursions and notably cheap beers too. ②.

Campement Touristique de Colobane-Fass, signed 2.5km down the Oussouye road (☎991 12 68). Standard prices for a bed or FB but poorly located and in need of a few guests. ①–②.

Campement Zag, signed 3km down the Oussouye road (☎991 15 57). Similar to the *Colobane-Fass* but a little less dingy; also adds CFA400 to the price in tax. An inexpensive option if you have your own transport. *Pirogue* excursions offered for around CFA7000. ③.

Luxury hotels

Domaine Néma Kadior, 3km south of town on the airport road (☎91 18 24; Fax 91 10 55). Luxury hotel-reserve in its own landscaped grounds, popular with tour groups. Pool open to non-guests. ⑤.

Hôtel Aubert, off av de Boucotte (☎91 13 79; Fax 91 10 15). The only luxury hotel to successfully survive the tourism crash of 1993, and deservedly so. Immaculate rooms with all mod cons, and a pool open to non-residents. ⑤.

Le Perroquet, rue de Commerce (☎91 23 29). Riverside French-run establishment very popular with jet-setters. Doesn't claim to be a hotel but offers neat, small S/C, AC rooms around a garden and a bar/restaurant with a great view from which to regard your bobbing yacht. ④.

The Town

There's not a great deal to keep you in Ziguinchor, but just hanging out is pleasure enough. In the old quarter of the town centre, there's a string of public gardens, heavily shaded, with park benches and – sign of a non-Islamic region – rootling piglets. Pelicans and storks congregate in the trees, however, making this a sometimes noisy and unpredictable place to relax.

Both **markets** – the **artisanal** and the **St-Maur-des-Fossés** (named after the southeast Paris suburb with which Ziguinchor is twinned) – are relatively hassle-free and well worth visiting. The municipal St-Maur, divided into merchandise zones, heaves with activity, while the *artisanal*, where the stall holders really are working at their crafts, is a relaxing place to get all your souvenirs in one go and offers real bargains for hardened hagglers. The **CTRI office** is here too, where you can make *campement* reservations (☎991 13 74 or 991 12 68).

Eating

With a few exceptions noted below, food in Ziguinchor is unremarkable. **Street food** is generally limited to fruit and nuts (cashews make a pleasingly inexpensive treat) or portside bread and coffee stalls. You'll find numerous nondescript **restaurants**, offering a low-priced daily *plat*, on the way to Marché St-Maur along Avenue Lycée Guignabo, south of the Total station; there's more sophisticated eating in town, especially at the hotels. For sweet neo-cream **pastries** check out the *patisserie* on Avenue du Général de Gaulle, and for ice creams, head for *Fast Food Mamy,* just south of the *rond-point.*

Chawarma du Port, down by the port. Wonderful Lebanese snacks for CFA750 or less. Daily 7am–10pm.

Hôtel Le Bel Kady, one block south of the Marché St-Maur. Ziguinchor's best place for an inexpensive meal, offering a fair selection for under CFA1250 as well as drinks and beers.

Hôtel du Tourisme, rue de France. Charming restaurant offering excellent Franco-Senegalese three-course menus and pricier à la carte options.

Le Mansah, rue de Capitaine Javelier. Right in the town centre and well worth a visit for great value three-course meals. Check out the huge carved masks up on the walls too – they're the real thing.

Le Perroquet, rue de Commerce. Franco-Senegalese meals for around CFA5000. Great location, but bring some mosquito spray.

Petit Bedon, av Emile Badiane. Serves delicious fish and European/French cuisine for CFA3000–5000 for a main dish.

Restaurant Bousso Niang, down a side road just southeast of the Total station. No tablecloths, napkins or drinks other than water, just dirt-cheap heapfuls of staple-based stodge that you couldn't finish if you tried, although their interpretation of *viande* errs towards offaldom.

Nightlife

After dark, Ziguinchor smoulders. *Le Bambolong* and *Katmandou* have been *the* places to visit for a number of years, both repaying the entrance fee with hot music – lots of *zouk* – and as many chance encounters as you want. *Le Bambolong* is pretty exclusive and scores highly with the French community, as well as passing *toubabs,* while *Katmandou* has a greater head of steam and a largely local crowd; the patio behind is a vital cooling-off area. Expect the drinks at *Le Bambolong* to be pricier than those at *Katmandou.*

Listings

Banks There are five banks in town but the CBAO (Mon–Fri 7.30am–noon & 1.15–2.30pm) and the SGBS (Mon–Thurs 8–11.15am & 2.30–4.30pm, Fri 8–11am & 3.15–5pm) are your best bets for foreign exchange. The latter provides Visa or MasterCard cash advances (with ID) on the spot, but charges twenty percent commission on travellers' cheques.

Bicycles One-speed bikes available for **rent** from the *Hôtel du Tourisme* and *Relais de Santiaba* for CFA2500 a day. The *Relais* also has some bearable 12-speed MTBs (VTTs), and at least one lightweight 21-speed jewel; these are the bikes for getting out to the countryside *campements*. Try to arrange a weekly rate. Blue Peugeots with mudguards, dynamo lighting, sprung saddles, a rack and a sidestand are **for sale** at several locations.

Doctor Dr Simon Tendang (Mon–Fri 8am–2pm & 4.30–6pm; CFA4500; ☎991 13 85, emergency ☎991 17 75); a minute north of the *rond-point* on rue de Capitaine Javelier.

Police ☎17.

There's an **Air Sénégal** (☎991 10 81) flight to Dakar (Mon–Wed 9.45am; CFA35,000), as well as flights to Bissau (Mon & Fri 8.30am), although these are suspended at the time of writing.

You can get on a **boat** from Ziguinchor **to Dakar**: the MV *Joola* leaves promptly on Thurs and Sun at 1pm for the seventeen-hour voyage. Prices are CFA3500 for a hard seat, CFA6000 for a comfy one, and CFA18,000 for a cabin to yourself. Meals cost around CFA4500. Book tickets at the COSENAM office, on rue de Commerce in the port area (☎991 22 01). There is also a new *Kassoumay* **catamaran** service (☎991 32 20) to Dakar, which takes just six hours and departs at 10am on Tues, Thurs and Sat, stopping at Karabane Island on the way. Economy class costs CFA18,000, first class CFA30,000.

For **Guinea-Bissau**, the Senegalese border post is at Mpak (18km); the Guinea-Bissau post is at São Domingos (25km). Plan for an early start from the *gare routière*. You can get Guinea-Bissau **visas** from the consulate, next to *Hôtel du Tourisme* (Mon–Fri 8/9am–noon & 2/4–6pm; ☎991 10 46). Three-month multiple entry visas are delivered in 24hr; photographs cost CFA5000. Due to strained relations between Senegal and Guinea-Bissau visas are sometimes unobtainable, and the *sûreté* in Ziguinchor may refuse to extend Senegalese visas. Note that at the time of writing, travel in Guinea-Bissau was not advisable.

Local transport for destinations in rural Casamance includes: a daily or twice daily bus to Enampore (large green vehicle leaving early morning and sometimes also 3pm; 90min); a daily afternoon bus to Mlomp and Elinkine; and frequent transport to Oussouye and Cap Skiring.

Northern Basse Casamance

Coming over **the border from The Gambia** at Séléti is a straightforward business – many tourists visiting The Gambia take the plunge into Casamance for a few days and are rewarded by a more leisurely pace of life, reasonable transport, and some idyllic and inexpensive lodgings.

It's a short taxi ride from Séléti to **DIOULOULOU**, the first Senegalese town, where you swap vehicles to head for the as yet unspoilt resorts of Abéné and Kafountine. Diouloulou has a good *campement* in the shape of *Relais Myriam* (②), a short way north of the main roundabout on the Gambia road, with helpful management.

The potholed N5 continues southeast across the tidal mudflats to Ziguinchor 80km away, passing through the underwhelming regional centre of **BIGNONA**, a two-kilometre string of roadside stalls at which point the N5 joins the *transgambienne* N4. In this area various tracks lead southwest into the often overlooked **Buluf** district of the northern Basse Casamance, served by a couple of CTRIs. Still less visited is the **Yassine** region to the east, sandwiched between the Soungrougrou and Casamance rivers.

The coast: Abéné and Kafountine

Southwest of Diouloulou a road heads seaward to unbroken beaches running down to the spit of the **Presque Ile aux Oiseaux** at which point the coastline breaks up into mangrove inlets and the mouth of the Casamance. The sealed road passes a turn-off to the village of Abéné (18km) and ends at the small town of Kafountine (24km) where a track continues to nowhere in particular. Waiting at the roundabout in Diouloulou for

For advice on security in the region, see p.217.

transport may take an hour or two, less in the high season.

From the main road a sandy track leads 2km to **ABÉNÉ**, hard work on a bike but passable in a car. The sandy-laned village is 1km from the sea and has a charmingly isolated and relaxed feel as well as a number of places to stay. In the village are two **campements**: *La Belle Danielle* (②) down a side track and the *Bantan Waro* (②) on the main road. Both are similar, offering inexpensive restaurants, excursions and bike rental; the *Belle Danielle*'s tap-operated showers and pleasant garden gives it the edge even though it's a little further to the beach. Continuing to the sea the track leads left to the *Samaba CTRI* (②) while a right turn ends at the delightful *Le Kossey*, a superior, dunebound *campement* offering S/C huts set in a lovely garden with HB or FB options (③). This is the place to head if you're looking for beachside seclusion rather than company. There are a few places to eat in the village, but most people take full board at the *campements*. Up the coast, 2km from Abéné village, the altogether different *Hôtel Village Kalissai* (⑤), run by the *Aubert* in Ziguinchor, is beautifully sited right by the beach with a landscaped mangrove creek. Even at the price, this beats much of what's on offer in the fast lane at Cap Skiring, but it's not exactly *integré*.

Continuing south down the sealed road another 6km brings you to the small fishing village of **KAFOUNTINE**, served by daily buses to and from Ziguinchor via Diouloulou. More animated than sleepy Abéné, Kafountine has a market, shops, a car rental outfit and a couple of **restaurants**: the *Africa* and, opposite, *Chez Mama Kendo*, both offer inexpensive and wholesome Senegalese dishes using local fish.

All **accommodation** is at least 1km south of town. On the inland side you'll see the *Campement Africa*, with shared toilets and the rest en suite

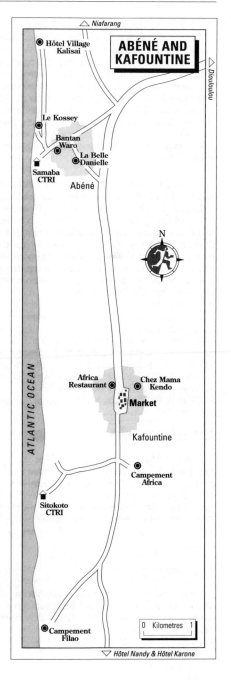

(HB minimum; ②). Right opposite is a turning to the *Sitokoto CTRI* (②) which, despite its beachside location, lacks the charm of Abéné's *campements*. A very pleasant, privately run *campement* is *Kunja*, which offers simple, comfortably furnished rooms (②) and good home cooking. The larger, long-established *Campement Filao* (②), set in a grove of casuarinas a couple of kilometres further south, offers a large restaurant/bar and good value S/C huts as well as beachside access and the usual excursions. Also recommended is the English-run *Mama Karamba* (☎994 55 28; ①–②). Beyond here are two newer developments as the resort area extends further south: *Hôtel Nandy* (③) is a selection of scattered upmarket chalets based around the usual bar/restaurant, and *Hôtel Karone* (BP 85; ☎994 55 25; FB ⑤), where the road ends, is Kafountine's most luxurious *campement* – secluded huts in landscaped grounds, beachside *paillotes* and a plush restaurant/bar.

South of Diouloulou: Affiniam and Koubalan

South of Diouloulou the potholed road continues across a *marigot* or two to the village of **BAILA** with its welcoming CTRI (②) set in a grove of mango trees at the village's northern end. Between here and Bignona several tracks lead southwest into the **Buluf district**, a wooded region of mango groves as well as orange and palm trees and rice fields. Passable tracks, as well as several minor, cycleable routes, lead to all the villages, with a new CTRI (②) at the southern end of the unremarkable settlement of **TIONK ESSIL**. Southeast of Tionk, along a rough track, the peaceful village of **AFFINIAM** is regularly visited by *pirogue* excursions from Ziguinchor. Spread out among the silk-cotton trees among webs of sandy tracks, the village has a strong Catholic presence and is one of the most appealing CTRIs in the network. Situated south of the village, this large-diameter, galvanized *case à impluvium* is one of the best spots in the region to rest up for a few days.

Ten kilometres south of Bignona (or 3km north of Tobor) on the N5, a large sign marks the sometimes sandy track leading to the CTRI at **KOUBALAN**. While not situated in an especially scenic spot, overlooking a cleared mangrove swamp, the *campement*'s cave-like interior is cool, the welcome warm and the food excellent (②). South of Tobor the woodlands end as the N5 crosses the dreary tidal expanse of Casamance to the river itself and the bridge leading into Ziguinchor.

Southern Basse Casamance

Between Ziguinchor and the coast lies the boxing-glove-shaped heart of the **southern Basse Casamance**: a district of tall hardwood forest and rice fields cut by three major creeks and their fringes of mangrove flats. As the longest distance between significant places is just 34km, this is an ideal region for **cycling**;. You can rent bikes, or mobylettes, at **Oussouye** or **Cap Skiring** if you haven't already done so in Ziguinchor. Apart from having a water bottle (minimum capacity 2 litres) and devising a way to carry your gear, there are no special practical problems in cycling around.

To Enampore

Climbing the gentle valley out of Ziguinchor, the road passes through the remains of the **forest** that once covered the entire area. The magnificent thirty- or forty-metre trees, strung with vines, are inhabited by large numbers of birds and small animals – though you'll only see monkeys where the trees are close enough together to form arboreal highways. Examples of the region's wildlife can be observed at the signposted **farm/orchard** (Mon–Sat 9.30am–6.30pm; CFA1000) about 4km out of town at **DJI-**

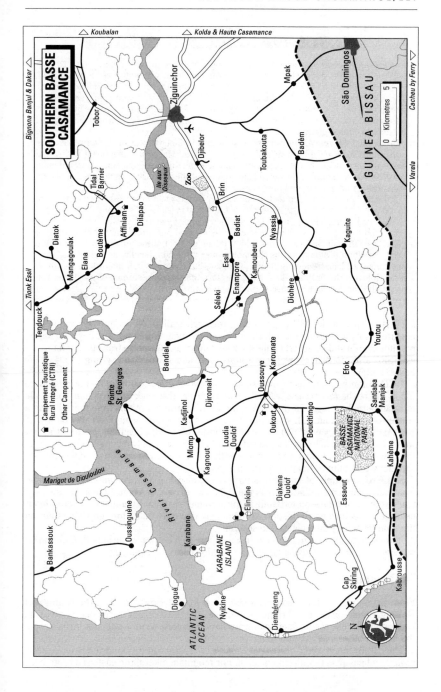

CASES À IMPLUVIUM AND FETISH SHRINES

Case à impluvium translates as "rain reservoir hut", a somewhat demeaning term that tells only half the story. The design is doughnut-shaped, with entrances into a shared, circular courtyard and internal doors into private rooms that are built as individual units. There's a stunning quality to the light reflected off the clean-swept courtyard floor to illuminate the living space. The thatched, saddleback roof circling above the living quarters is built like a funnel to allow rain to drain into a central reservoir, from where it runs outside through a drain.

In the past the *impluvium* was good insurance in times of war or drought, but since pure water wells have been dug all over, few *impluvium* houses are being built these days. Yet they make wonderful homes, and undoubtedly more Jola families would build new *cases à impluvium* if they could afford to – but the increasing nuclearization of families means that few can find the necessary money or labour.

Although it's often written that the only other examples of *impluvium* architecture are found in New Guinea, similar houses were traditional in Guinea-Bissau and parts of southwest Côte d'Ivoire, and also in parts of southern Nigeria, where they were square in plan.

In the bush around, you'll also come across isolated miniature huts in the briefest of clearings. Often just a forked stick under a thatched roof, these are **fetish shrines**, the earthly visiting rooms of spirits that hold power over rain, fertility and illnesses. They are consulted less frequently than in the past, but there are still matters about which many Jola feel the traditional spirits know more than modern science or medicine. You should be careful not to disturb them or take photos.

BELOR, opposite the ISRA agricultural research station. Near the river are several hectares of fruit trees and a collection of animals including lions, monkeys, tortoises, monitor lizards and dwarf crocodiles. Located down an 800-metre track through the forest, ISRA also offers a few workers' rooms in a tranquil woodland setting (☎991 12 05; Fax 991 12 93; AC, S/C ③).

BRIN, 6km further, has its own small *Campement Filao* (①) right by the Enampore track, where the *taxi brousse* will drop you off. It's a thirteen-kilometre, four-hour walk to Enampore, best done in the cool of the early morning – at this time there is also a chance of getting a lift with some village-bound transport – passing Essil at km6. The **ENAMPORE** *campement* (②) is one of the best preserved, a beautiful *case à impluvium* wonderfully constructed and a pleasure just to be in, especially during the hot hours of the day. However familiar you become with the region's *impluvium* architecture, the simplicity and calm of Enampore are memorable.

SÉLÉKI, a couple of kilometres further on, also has its own *campement* (①) and from here you can continue across the **dykes and rice fields** to Etama and then – if you've plenty of time – on to Bandial (15km round trip from Enampore). There's interesting architecture en route, and as the people don't get many foreign visitors out on the mud flats, they'll be pleased to see you.

It's also possible to rent a *pirogue* in Enampore to take you to the superb *Campement aux Bolongs* (③), in an idyllic creek-side location east of Oussouye.

To Oussouye

From Brin, the road turns south, looping away from the river to cross the **Kamobeul Bolong** creek on a new bridge. Oussouye, the next major focus, is 34km from Ziguinchor, across scrub, open mangrove flats and more scrub – good for birds west of the bridge, otherwise unenthralling.

The rurally integrated *Campement Diohère* (②), signposted 14km from Brin, is rarely visited and so appears rather neglected. For mountain-bikers, the eastward route back to Ziguinchor from Diohère through farms and forest to the Ziguinchor–Guinea-Bissau road is idyllic, but you'll have to ask around to locate the right turn-off.

Another 10km down the main road to Oussouye you come to the **Case à Impluvium chez Theodore Balousa** (①), signposted left a little after a sign for "Niambalang"; go 800m along the track and it's just after the well. A *case à impluvium* built in 1980, it has a lived-in feel – although the interior is now decorated with locally made dolls and other souvenirs – and the family charge less than the going rate for the two rooms offered, although they'll need advance warning if you want a meal. Busy with children and scuttling chickens, the house itself is a lot livelier than Enampore's, for example, and it's well worth a passing look.

Just before Oussouye you'll pass the small village of **EDIOUNGOU** with a winding track leading to its *Campement de Bolong* (☎993 10 01; ②), offering creek-side views from its bar as well as the customary excursions. Another kilometre brings you to **OUSSOUYE**, sitting on the largest patch of dry land around. Once the seat of a line of Jola **priest-kings**, royalty is no longer much in evidence, but the town is still an important and growing place and has several times been on the frontline in MFDC skirmishes with the Senegalese army. Although the market here is pretty dull, there are one or two good shops, the usual colourful plasticware emporia, and an intriguing **wooden church** on the road out to Cap Skiring, a good example of Jola architectural innovation.

The road leading to the roundabout has a couple of inexpensive **restaurants** should you choose to turn down the full-board options of the town's *campements*. Check out the sprightly *Chez Mata–Restaurant 2000*; there may be an impressive chalkboard menu but you eat what's in the pot, always good value.

A track from the roundabout leads to a couple of **campements**, the first of which is the small and exceptionally friendly *Auberge de Routard* (①), run by Goula Diallo – his wife prepares great food and a vat of palm wine is passed around afterwards. Continuing another 600m up the track you may see men hanging beneath the crowns of the palm trees tapping the wine for the day. Oussouye's unusual two-storey mudbrick CTRI (②) is on the left, the biggest in the network and popular with tour groups.

Moving on from Oussouye, there's a daily minibus from Ziguinchor to Mlomp and Elinkine which passes through Oussouye around 4pm, while Cap Skiring-bound vehicles pass through town every couple of hours. If you're biking into the surrounding countryside (notably the park), you might want to make use of the **bike rental** and repair shop in Oussouye right by the roundabout, close to the small market.

Mlomp and Pointe St-Georges

From Oussouye the road swoops through the forest to **MLOMP**, often crowded with tourists, come for the most part to see the pair of two-storey *banco* **cottages** with their amazing grove of silk-cotton trees. Two-storey buildings are uncommon in traditional African architecture, and nobody knows why Mlomp should have them: they're reminiscent of Ashanti houses from Ghana and it's possible that the earlier Banyun traders of Casamance brought the innovation back from their travels. The *patron* will show you round one of them, and a postcard from home is much appreciated: pictures of the Empire State Building, Windsor Castle and the Arc de Triomphe adorn the walls.

From the village a sandy footpath leads directly north to **Pointe St-Georges,** the Casamance River's last elbow before it reaches the sea. There's not much to the place – it's just a flat, densely wooded stretch of land, and the upmarket *Village-Hôtel* was burned down by the MFDC in 1992 – but the Pointe is reportedly getting its own *campement*. Access will remain a problem as the only driveable track (and 4WD at that) starts from the village of Kagnout, 5km west of Mlomp.

Elinkine and Karabane Island

Beyond Kagnout, the turning to Pointe St-Georges, several stands of huge silk-cottons give way to monotonous, open country as a flat, straight route leads to the fishing village of **ELINKINE**, 10km from Mlomp. Little more than a tiny naval base and a collection of creek-side buildings, Elinkine makes an enjoyable stopover, with two great *campements,* both of which provide bike or canoe rental and *pirogue* excursions up and down the *bolongs.*

The more secluded **accommodation** is the CTRI (②) 700m to the right as you enter the village from the east. A spacious *campement* by a sandy beach, this place has a tropical postcard view through the palms across the creek. Alternatively, the daily bus from Ziguinchor stops right outside the *Fromager* (②) in the town centre, a smaller and more animated *case à impluvium* with energetic hosts. Styling themselves as the village's *centre nautique,* they offer *pirogue* trips to Karabane, fishing, and so forth. A small **café** nearby provides budget food.

Karabane Island

At Elinkine the done thing is to take a trip to the history-laden island of **Karabane** in the river mouth. Expect to pay around CFA7000 for a *pirogue* for a small group, for the thirty-minute voyage; you might also be able to negotiate a motorized boat to yourself. Karabane, or rather its headland, was an early offshore trading base with the interior, and the first French toehold in the Kasa Mansa – the kingdom of the Kasa, one of the ancestral Jola peoples. Slaves, ivory, gum and hides were exported from here, paid for with cloth, alcohol and iron bars. There's a large Breton-style church, partly in ruins, dating back to the earliest days of the Holy Ghost Fathers, and a number of crumbling merchant houses. The beach is beautiful, with 10km of salty Casamance River in front and coconuts behind, but in truth, on a short visit, the whole place can feel slack with isolation and irrelevance.

Staying the night, the trip becomes more worthwhile. Once everyone else has left and you can walk along the beach in peace, Karabane quickly becomes a place that's hard to leave. The *campements* of *Chez Amathe* (②) in the village or *Chez Badji* (②) out towards the beach and owned by a painter, are both preferable to the *Hôtel Karabane* (③), a dull mission money-earner.

Cap Skiring and around

Despite its status as Senegal's foremost holiday resort – with The Gambia and the coast of Côte d'Ivoire, one of the top three in West Africa – the straggling and undistinguished village of **CAP SKIRING** has little to recommend it: a minimal market, a few small shops, a couple of snack bars. There's a *Club Med* here, too, with high barbed wire and soldiers guarding its *plage privé,* discouraging anyone from roving outside the tourist reserve. The sands, however, are undeniably pretty – spectacular, even, along the more deserted stretches – and the sea is warm and safe. This is hedonistic territory and lacks much of deeper interest. Find a room, peel off your clothes and get down to the beach.

Orientation

Arriving from Oussouye at the T-junction, the village itself is to the north, *La Paillote* hotel is directly ahead and the cheaper accommodation opportunities are 1km to the

For advice on security in the region, see p.217.

south. Right on the junction is *La Pirogue* bar/restaurant, which also offers the region's only **car rental** service (☎993 51 76; Fax 991 13 76); economical runabouts cost from around CFA20,000 a day (with unlimited mileage) and they'll provide you with a chauffeur virtually for free.

Accommodation

Accommodation options are plentiful. You won't be faced with gleaming white high-rises, either; Cap Skiring's luxury hotels are modest constructions, while budget lodgings are low-key affairs, and variations to a greater or lesser extent on the CTRI theme.

Auberge de la Paix, just south of the T-junction (☎993 51 45). Offering the same great views and beach as its neighbours on either side for far less money. Good food and a choice of plain rooms or some with shower and basin en suite. ①–②.

Les Cocotiers (☎993 51 51; Fax 993 51 17). Set in its own grounds and similar to *La Paillote* (of which it seems to be part) but offering better value in the mid-range. ⑤.

Hôtel Savana, 3km north of Cap Skiring village (☎993 15 52; Fax 993 14 92). The Cap's beautifully landscaped five-star jewel offers it all – at a cost. ⑦.

La Kabrousse, 2km south of the T-junction (☎993 51 26). Plush hotel with cabins set in landscaped greenery, similar to *La Paillote*, and with a pool, giant chess and the beach just a stone's throw away. ⑥.

Le Mussuwam (☎993 51 84; Fax 993 51 25). Established *campement* owned by Ziguinchor's *Bel Kady* with a good range of AC, S/C rooms. Also has a small collection of captive wildlife, evening music sessions, bike rental and land and sea excursions. ②.

La Paillote, opposite the Oussouye road junction (☎993 51 51; Fax 993 51 17). Virtually identical to the less expensive *Cocotiers* next door. Very comfortable beachside huts, plus a private golf course, fine restaurant and souvenir shop. ⑦.

Le Paradis. Lower mid-range *campement* with a *case à impluvium* alternative to the *Auberge*. ②–③.

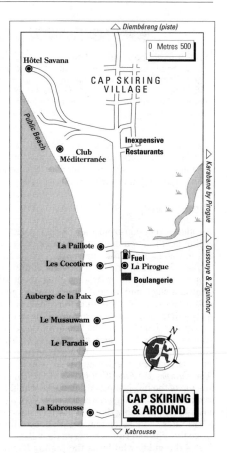

The beach

Bronzing and bathing are the main daytime occupations in Cap Skiring, and you can rent **windsurfers** from the more expensive hotels – there's almost always a good breeze. Just about everywhere rents out **bicycles** for a few thousand CFA francs per day, better value than a car or a 4WD.

By **bike** you can easily get up to Diembéreng in an hour or two along the beach at low tide when the sand is firm; the main motorable track through the bush is a sandy 8km (allow 1hr). Be careful not to venture onto the *Club Med*'s stretch: though it is ostensibly a public right of way, there are armed *militaires* at each end where the fence goes into the sea. Most people follow the fence down to the beach on its northern side

---

DAY-TRIPS TO KARABANE ISLAND

Day-trips to **Karabane Island** (see p.230), arranged by most hotels in Cap Skiring, leave from the creek behind the village (9am–5.30pm) – around CFA7000 from *Le Paradis* or *Mussuwam* and maybe twice as much from *La Paillote*. Trips normally take in Elinkine, Karabane, the Ile des Feticheurs, and an Ile aux Oiseaux or two. That's a lot of messing around on the river among low mangroves, which cast little shade, so make sure you wear a hat. It's not a bad way, incidentally, of getting to Elinkine.

then cycle from there, passing through the sunbed obstacle course in front of the *Savana* (dirty looks but no force of arms), and then climbing over a jumble of low rocks for a magnificent sweep of sand. Shortly after this point there's what looks like an open-air mosque built into the cliffside.

Diembéreng

An ideal excursion from Cap Skiring, **DIEMBÉRENG** lies deep behind the dunes, 8.5km north. If you don't want to walk or cycle, there's a daily bus, about 6pm, returning to Cap Skiring in the morning. It's a traditional village, its economy based on fishing and livestock, and by no means entirely dependent on its three privately owned *campements*. The most striking thing about Diembéreng is the hill that rises from its centre, a steep and ancient dune crowned and stabilized by a grove of venerable silk-cotton trees. It's no more than thirty metres high, but in Basse Casamance it looks like a mountain, and there's no escaping the strong and mysterious sense of place.

On your left as you come into town along the *piste* from Cap Skiring is the first **place to stay**; the *Asseb campement* (☎993 31 06; ②), which is nothing special but the only one that's accessible by car. You'll need the help of the boys who hang out under the mother of all *fromagers* (silk-cottons) to search out the other two accommodation options. The *Campement Aten-Elou* (☎993 31 05; ②), named after a local priestess, is situated at the top of the hill, just past a fallen tree trunk. Closer to the beach along a maze of fence-bound footpaths is *Albert's campement* (①), a *case à impluvium* set on the far side of the village, and probably the best place to stay (albeit with basic ablutions), undercutting CTRI rates and just ten minutes' walk over the dunes to the sea. You'll do well to memorize the lefts and rights between the village and the *campement* or you're bound to get lost – the guide who leads the nightly lamplit procession through the village to the evening meal at *Albert*'s **restaurant** is indispensable.

If you're craving true isolation, you could walk or cycle – again, preferably at low tide – up to **Nyikine**, a village at the very mouth of the Casamance. It's a place of coconuts and seclusion, recommended by some of the boys hanging around in Diembéreng, and possibly worth visiting in their company.

South of Cap Skiring

South of Cap Skiring, the road turns through the village of **KABROUSSE**, a scattered community of farmers. There's one last tourist hotel here (*La Kabrousse*; see overleaf), and nothing in the way of *campements* until you get to the Basse Casamance National Park (see opposite). It was here that a major anti-colonial rebellion was instigated during World War II under the leadership of Alinsitoé, a famous Jola visionary from Kabrousse. Aged only twenty, she spearheaded a revolt provoked by the tax burden placed on the Jola peasantry by the government. After a vicious battle at Efok, Alinsitoé was arrested and exiled to St-Louis, then to Timbuktu, where she died. Her name is evoked whenever the question is raised of Casamance secession from northern Senegal.

The forest path from Kabrousse to the Basse Casamance National Park

The tarmac goes into Kabrousse but fails to come out again, so make sure you pick the right path. It's rare for a motor vehicle to head out across these fields, understandably when you get to the creek, 6km on, and see the remains of the car ferry. But a bike can make it easily. A mobylette is less suitable, because you may have to load it onto a *pirogue* for the creek crossing, and take it through patches of deep sand later.

On the eastern side of the creek the path continues along the Guinea-Bissau border, clear enough but frequently bicycle-width only, and sometimes degenerating into sandy oblivion, where you'll have to push. Although the total distance to the Basse Casamance National Park gate is only some 22km from Kabrousse, it can feel longer. Not that it's a pain, as long as you allow a full half-day, because the entire route is blissfully peaceful, passing through family hamlets where frank stares of astonishment meet you. Much of the way is heavily overgrown, with thickets of bamboo and forest filling the gaps between farm plots and compounds.

Santiaba Manjak is the largest village you pass through before the park gate; 2km further, a right turning leads off to the Alinsitoé battle village of **Efok** (5km) and equally isolated **Youtou** (10km). Efok's main public place has a huge war drum, confiscated during the World War II rebellion, while at Youtou similar drums are apparently still being made.

Parc National de Basse Casamance

The **Parc National de Basse Casamance**, closed since 1993 due to rebel activity, comprises forty square kilometres of streams, marshy savannah, and partly untouched primary forest. Large mammals such as forest buffalo, leopard, hippo and bushbuck are rarely seen here, but there's wonderful **monkey-spotting** from several of the paths and lookout towers (*miradors*), **crocs** in the creeks, and the deep forest harbours species of **birds and insects** you're unlikely to come across anywhere else in Senegal. The best time to visit is well into the dry season, when, even in this relatively moist part of the country, waterholes dry up and sources become good spots to watch animals.

Park practicalities

Getting to the park by public transport is difficult at the best of times. Unless you make your own way there on foot or bicycle, the only other possibility is an organized trip from the Oussouye CTRI, but this generally means a bit of a rush.

The park (CFA2000) is not a place to visit in a single day: in order to get anything from it you'll need to stay for at least one dusk and dawn. The only **accommodation**, currently trashed, was a formerly very pleasant *case à impluvium* (②) near the entrance; it's not a CTRI, but used to charge similar rates and did excellent meals. You could also camp here if you wished.

Around the park

To maximize your chances of seeing animals, get out on the forest paths by about 6am. For animal-watching at the end of the day, come out at 4pm, install yourself somewhere comfortable, and wait. You can also look around at night, preferably in a vehicle or using a powerful torch. The hot, middle part of the day is quiet and often unrewarding.

The **Mirador du Buffle**, one of six observation platforms scattered through the park, is the best spot in the dry season, but only if you get there early. The 2.5km of the Circuit Houssiou, which runs past it, meanders into tall grass and near its end reaches the Mirador des Oiseaux, on the main track; this circuit is only negotiable by bike (just) or on foot.

Monkeys are everywhere, especially in certain trees during their fruiting seasons – they adore the tart *ditak* fruits. Lined with high trees, the Circuit Djiban Epor, which terminates in a rangers' encampment, is a good path for monkey-spotting.

Assuming the park has reopened and is safe, you need not be alarmed by noises in the undergrowth – they're most often caused by small **duiker antelope** and occasionally by **bushbuck**. Noisier – and heavier – movements are forest buffalo, relatively small and not dangerous; you're more likely to see their dung. **Leopards** are exceedingly shy and silent, and you would be fortunate indeed to see one; there are no records of any attacks. **Crocodiles**, particularly the dwarf (one-metre) species, are common enough if you're patient at the waterfront *miradors*. The Mirador des Crocodiles is easily reached off the main track, which terminates about 7km from the park entrance on the creek shore – with a jetty and picnic site.

The **Republic of Mali** was known as **Soudan Français** – the French Sudan – during the colonial period. The name Mali was chosen for its historical resonance and significance for the Mande (or Malinké) speaking people of the region. The largest country in West Africa, it spreads across nearly 1,240,000 square kilometres, an **area** five times the size of the UK and three times as big as California, but with a **population** of around twelve million. President Alpha Oumar Konaré leads the Adema party (Alliance pour la démocratie au Mali) which holds ninety percent of the seats in the multiparty National Assembly. Mali's crippling **foreign debt** stands in excess of £1.9 billion (US$3 billion), more than six times the value of its annual exports of goods and services. Looked at from a global perspective, however, this is just about one-eighth of the cost of building the cross-channel tunnel between Britain and France.

Despite the presence of the **Niger River**, which runs through Mali's heartlands, and the headwaters of the **Senegal River** which flow through the western tip of the country, much of Mali lies in the **Sahara**. The extreme north is desert, empty except for a few stranded oases and Tuareg camps. Between the desert and the river stretches the **Sahel zone**, mostly flat plains with scruffy bush and thin trees that are especially resistant to the arid climate.

Only a few ripples interrupt the overall impression of flatness across the country. West of Bamako, the **Manding Highlands** provide a rare hilly spectacle as they rise to heights of 500–1000m, and the **Bandiagara escarpment**, which winds across the landscape east of Mopti for some 200km, is striking for the sheer cliffs that drop some 500–600m to the plain. Other formations include the gaunt outcrops of the **Hombori Hills** a little further east, towering sheer to heights of nearly 1200m, and north of Gao, the inaccessible **Adrar des Iforhas** mountains astride the trans-Saharan chariot route of classical times.

region of Bamako and Ségou, their influence spreads much further, due in large part to their language, which is one of the most widely spoken in West Africa. To the west, the **Malinké** are closely related and share a similar language and customs. Living from the Manding Highlands to the Senegal River, many Malinké have retained traditional religions, despite Islam's early penetration in the region and repeated jihads. The **Senoufo** live near the Côte d'Ivoire border in the region of Sikasso. In the sixteenth century, they formed small kingdoms at Kong, Korhogo and Odienné (now in Côte d'Ivoire), and when the Songhai Empire collapsed they began expanding northward. Their social structure is strongly influenced by the *poro* – an initiation rite that lasts 21 years, during which time the men learn the secrets of Senoufo religion and philosophy.

The **Dogon** occupy the Bandiagara escarpment east of Mopti. There's reason to believe these people may have originated from the Nile Valley, but migrated to the isolated cliffs near the Burkina Faso border in the twelfth century. Here, they kept at bay the waves of Muslim invasions that swept through Mali over the centuries and, thanks to their tight social and religious organization, have been remarkably successful at maintaining ancient traditions. They speak a Voltaic language related to Senoufo.

Several peoples live in the north. The **Songhai** concentrate in the region of Gao where they migrated in waves after the seventh century, probably from northern Benin. **Fula**-speaking herders – after the Bamana, one of the most populous groups in Mali – traverse the country but are concentrated in the delta region between the Niger and the northwestern border with Mauritania – a historical region known as Masina (Massina is the contemporary town). The **Tuareg**, of Berber origin, were pushed southward into present-day Mali after the Arabs came to North Africa from Arabia. The Tuareg mixed with sub-Saharan peoples and formed numerous independent, and often warring, clans. They still cling to their nomadic traditions, though recent droughts and conflict with the state (not just in Mali, but also in Niger and southern

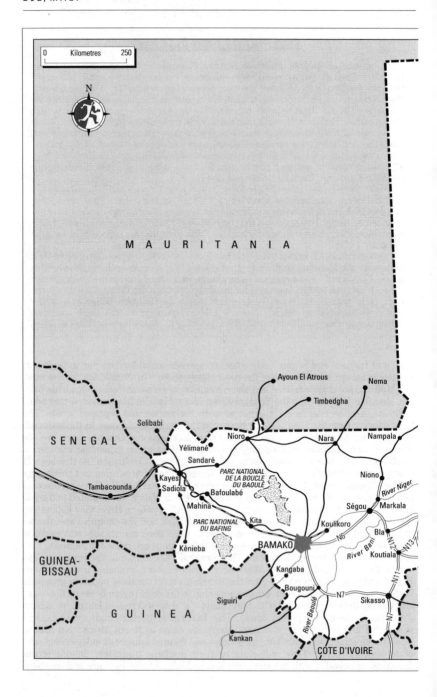

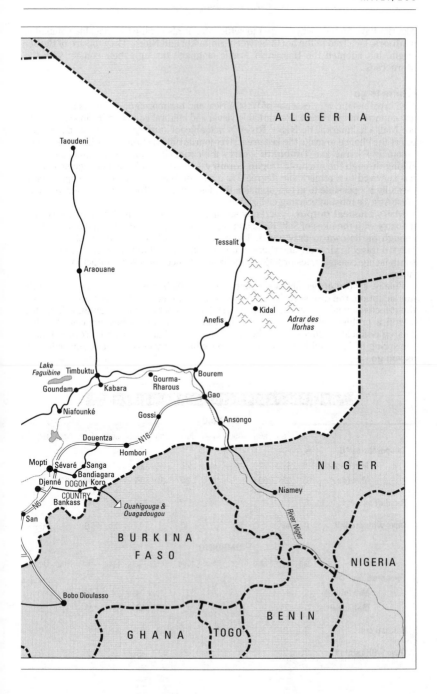

Algeria) have forced many Tuareg to settle. Mali is also home to a sizeable population of **Moors**, localized in the north between Timbuktu and Nioro. They too are of Berber origin, but adopted the Hassaniya Arabic language through their contact with the Moroccans.

Where to go

Mali breathes the very essence of West Africa, and has more good reasons to visit than any country in the region. Remarkable visual and cultural contrasts in close proximity are Mali's hallmark. The **Niger River** is magnificent (unforgettably so at dawn) and offers the chance to make the last great river journey in West Africa, while the old cities – notably **Djenné** and **Timbuktu** – carry their ragged history with immense grace. Hiking through the fractured **Dogon country** – where traditional, non-Islamic culture has survived to a remarkable degree – is a goal of most travellers. If you approach it carefully it's possible to get right inside this fascinating district and experience one of West Africa's most interesting civilizations.

Mali's **musical output** – currently stoking the pistons of the international record industry with the likes of Salif Keita and Ali Farka Touré – is another major attraction, enough on its own to draw music lovers. Mali is also the country best placed for onward travel to virtually anywhere in the region – by rail to Dakar, or by road to the south-facing coastal states or to Mauritania and thence, with some difficulty, to North Africa.

Finally, a word or two about **security**: the trans-Saharan route to Gao is currently not an option, the dire security situation in Algeria (see p.15) having brought about the effective closure of a track already made perilous by Tuareg banditry. Banditry is still a problem in the northern and eastern extremities beyond Gao, but the Tuareg political conflict was resolved in 1996. This chapter was fully researched in the spring of 1999 and is as up-to-date as possible, but you should ask advice locally as you go.

AVERAGE TEMPERATURES AND RAINFALL

BAMAKO

	Jan	Feb	Mar	Apr	May	June	July	Aug	Sept	Oct	Nov	Dec
Temperatures °C												
Min (night)	16	19	22	24	24	23	22	22	22	22	18	17
Max (day)	33	36	39	39	39	34	31	30	32	34	34	33
Rainfall mm	0	0	3	15	74	137	279	348	206	43	15	0
Days with rainfall	0	0	1	2	5	10	16	17	12	6	1	0

TIMBUKTU

	Jan	Feb	Mar	Apr	May	June	July	Aug	Sept	Oct	Nov	Dec
Temperatures °C												
Min (night)	13	14	19	22	26	27	25	24	24	23	18	13
Max (day)	31	34	38	42	43	43	39	36	39	40	37	32
Rainfall mm	0	0	3	0	5	23	79	81	38	3	0	0
Days with rainfall	0	0	1	0	2	5	9	9	5	2	0	0

Climate

Without taking into account seasonal variations, it's tempting to sum up Mali's climate in two words – gaspingly hot. Rains generally last from June to September in the south-west. In the northeast, they may arrive at any time during that period, either for a pro-longed wet season or in a few unpredictable cloudbursts. The dry season takes over the rest of the year. Between October and February the *Harmattan* can blow for days at a time causing temperatures to drop quite low in the evenings. Climate-wise, this is prob-ably the best time to plan a trip, and it's also the period when the Niger is most easily navigable.

Arrivals

Despite being positioned at the heart of the region, Mali's surface links with other parts of West Africa aren't brilliant: from Senegal, a twice-weekly rail link or a rough *piste*; from Burkina and Niger more rough *pistes*; and only from Côte d'Ivoire a good highway.

■ Flights from Africa

Air Afrique (RK) handles most of the traffic from other West African cities, much of it routed through Abidjan. Its regional services to Bamako are as follows:

From Abidjan: direct five times a week.
From Conakry: direct weekly.
From Cotonou: direct weekly; via Abidjan twice a week.
From Dakar: direct five times a week; via Conakry weekly.
From Lagos: via Abidjan weekly.
From Lomé: direct weekly; via Abidjan twice a week; via Abidjan and Libreville weekly.
From Niamey: direct weekly; via Abidjan twice a week; via Ouagadougou weekly.
From Ouagadougou: direct five times a week.

Air Ivoire (VU) flies non-stop from **Abidjan** to Bamako twice a week and via **Bouaké** weekly. Ghana Airways (GH) flies non-stop from **Accra** to Bamako twice weekly, and also weekly from **Banjul** to **Dakar**, where you can pick up a connection to Bamako with Air Afrique. Air Burkina (2J) has one flight a week from **Ouaga** to Bamako direct, plus another weekly flight via **Bobo-Dioulasso**, **Ouagadougou**, **Lomé** and **Cotonou**. Air Guinée (GI) flies weekly from **Conakry** to Bamako via **Lagos**. Air Gabon (GN) flies in from **Libreville** and **Douala** via **Lomé** once a week.

As for **flights from other parts of Africa**, Royal Air Maroc (AT) has a weekly non-stop flight from **Casablanca** to Bamako; Air Algérie (AH) has three flights a week (direct, via Niamey and via Ouaga) into Bamako from **Algiers**; Ethiopian Airlines (ET) flies in from **Addis Ababa** via **N'Djamena** (Chad) and Niamey twice a week; GI flies from **Kinshasa** to Bamako via Lagos weekly; and finally South African Airways (SA) covers the direct route from **Johannesburg** to Abidjan twice a week, from where you can pick up an RK flight on to Bamako.

> The details in these practical information pages are essentially for use on the ground in West Africa and in Mali itself: for full details on preparing for a trip, getting here from outside the region, paperwork, health, information sources and more, see Basics pp.3–83.

■ Overland

Coming from the north, the trans-Saharan **Tanezrouft route from southern Algeria** ends in eastern Mali at Gao on the Niger River, from where a paved road leads all the way to Bamako. Unfortunately a combination of civil strife in Algeria and attacks by Tuareg rebels has seen this desolate 1500-kilometre *piste* closed since the early 1990s.

From Niger

From **Niamey** the main route to Mali follows the Niger River to Tillabéri (where the tarmac ends) and continues through numerous villages and increasingly frequent patches of soft sand to Gao. SNTN in Niger and Askia Transport in Mali both provide a bus service between Niamey and Gao; SNTN buses leave Niamey on Monday morning and the one-way fare is CFA10,400. The wait for enough passengers to gather before departure is a standard delay. Bush taxis are available as far as the respective national borders.

The alternative is to travel through Burkina Faso, via Fada N' Gourma and Ouagadougou.

From Burkina Faso

The quickest routes **linking Burkina and Mali** originate in **Bobo-Dioulasso**. From here, you can travel either to **Sikasso** (tracks are extremely rough on the Burkinabe side, especially during the rains) or to **Ségou** via Mahou and Koutiala on a paved road. You can also get direct transport from **Bobo-Dioulasso to Mopti via San**.

Burkinabe border posts close at 6pm. Malian formalities should present no special problem, but the *agents* seem particularly keen on checking your health documents, so make sure you're up-to-date on yellow fever.

In the dry season it's possible to go directly into the **Dogon country** from Burkina – setting out from **Ouahigouya** and passing through Tiou and then Koro. This is one of the most rewarding ways of entering the Dogon country through one of the few corners not fairly saturated with tourists. Scheduled STMB buses depart from Ouahigouya on Saturday and Thursday at 6am, but other vehicles rarely pass along this stretch, so you may face long waits for the occasional goods truck or tourist.

From Côte d'Ivoire

The main point of entry from Côte d'Ivoire is along the road from **Ferkessédougou** to Sikasso, linked by daily buses. The stretch of sealed highway from the Pogo/Zégoua border to Sikasso has been resurfaced and is in good condition. Traffic between **Odienné** and Bougouni (from where a good paved road continues to Bamako) is far less frequent and you may make better time from that side of the country first heading east to join the main artery north.

From Guinea

After the Niger has swelled with seasonal rains (roughly August to December) it's theoretically possible to travel down the Milo – a tributary of the Niger – by **barge from Kankan** to Bamako, although this service is currently suspended due to falling water levels (see box, p.520). If the boat is running, the 385-kilometre trip will take you past Niandakoro, where the Milo joins the Niger, and Siguiri, before terminating some five days later at Bamako. This is an adventure, but it's no pleasure cruise: you sleep on mats and share mediocre toilets; food is provided. The boats leave weekly at most and reservations can be made through the CMN in Kankan. Another possibility is the **ferry from Kouroussa** to Bamako, though this too is currently suspended (see p.512).

The main alternatives are by **bush taxi** from Kankan or **Kouroussa**, the latter an especially pretty route. Malian formalities are less of a hassle than Guinean.

From Senegal and The Gambia

Most overland travellers arrive from Senegal on the Océan-Niger **train from Dakar**. Departures are scheduled for 10am Wednesday and Saturday, though it's wise to be there by 8am. You should reserve seats two days before. The Wednesday train is the Senegalese one – more comfortable, with AC, and more expensive. However, it's a gruelling 30- to 36-hour journey whichever train you choose. Scheduled arrival time into Bamako is 4pm the following day, but the usual delays mean you're likely to arrive after dark.

Fares to Bamako range from around CFA23,000 2nd class, CFA31,000 1st class to CFA47,500 sleeper (*wagon lit*). Second class is

not very dissimilar from first, and it's worth paying the difference only if you want more leg-room and fewer companions. Once you're on the train, it's possible to upgrade to sleeper class assuming there are berths available (double cabins only), but the protracted border formalities take place during the night and you have to disembark, so you don't get much sleep in any case. There's a limited buffet car for snacks and drinks (the best part of the train to watch the scenery incidentally), and you can buy street food from station vendors around the clock. There are small student reductions in second class at the beginning and end of term.

As an alternative to taking the train the whole way from Dakar, you could travel by road as far as **Tambacounda**, picking up the train to Bamako from there. Don't expect a seat or other comforts by this stage in its journey, however.

Finally, if you have your own vehicle, you *can* transport it by the train, though after all the complexities involved, not to mention the time – allow a full week altogether – and the expense – no less than CFA150,000 – you will wish you had driven instead. Unless your vehicle cannot be driven, forget it.

From Mauritania

The main overland route from Mauritania to Bamako starts at **Néma** (sealed road all the way from Nouakchott) and passes through Nara and Kolokani. The tracks between Néma and Nara may be impassable during the rainy season. It's best to get up-to-date information from other travellers before heading out.

From **Ayoun el Atrous**, you may also be able to get transport to Nioro from which point you can continue to Bamako, or to Kayes along difficult *pistes*. Again, rains can make this route impassable and even in other seasons the frequency of vehicles may not add up to much. Another option is to get down to **Sélibabi**, just 60km from the Mali border, from where you can try to make your way to Kayes.

Red Tape

Basically, everyone needs a visa for Mali except the French. You will need to show your yellow fever certificate when you apply. There's no embassy in London, the closest being Paris or Brussels. Embassy addresses, including those in the US are given in Basics, pp.20–21.

Mali was once notorious for its red tape, and tourists were subject to the scrutiny and control of the dramatically named SMERT tourist organization – now defunct. However, although official hassles such as photography permits and tourist cards have been abolished for some time now, the area north and east of Mopti is still a **zone securité** where officially you should report to the police and get your passport stamped in every town on arrival.

If you're **driving**, you'll need to get Malian insurance and a "tourist visa" (*carnet de passage* or *laissez-passer*) for your vehicle, on arrival, without which you may find your car threatened with being impounded. You will need to get this extended, too, at customs in Bamako, unless you're driving straight through the country.

Coming overland, travellers without **visas** are often let into the country anyhow and allowed to obtain them upon arrival in the nearest *préfecture* (this most likely means Sikasso, Kayes or Bamako). But it's a risk – although a bribe of some kind is the most likely hurdle, you never know when you'll happen on an unbending immigration officer. Unless you're flying into Bamako from outside Africa, it's advisable to pick up your visa en route in one of the neighbouring West African countries (there are Malian embassies or consulates in Dakar, Conakry, Freetown, Abidjan, Accra, Niamey, Banjul and Ouagadougou) as they're usually issued with less fuss and are much less expensive than visas issued outside the continent.

Visas for onward travel

You can get visas in Bamako for Burkina, Côte d'Ivoire, Guinea, Mauritania, Morocco, Nigeria and Senegal; Togo entry permits are available at the French embassy. Niger is a problem since there's no representation.

Money and Costs

Mali's currency is the CFA franc (CFA100 always equals 1 French franc; approx CFA900 = £1; approx CFA560 = US$1. The country is one of the region's more expensive destinations for travellers. Foreign status in Mali more often than not assures price hikes, especially for transportation on less-travelled roads, while if you're booking luxury hotels, tours, or car rental – items largely consumed by those with access to foreign currency – you'll find prices high.

Banks are rare throughout the country so you have to plan ahead. The Banque de Développement du Mali (BDM) has the most branches – in Bamako, Kayes, Sikasso, Ségou, Nioro, Mopti, Timbuktu and Gao – but its rates of commission and service charges for foreign exchange are notoriously high, especially outside Bamako. Others are more reasonable, charging a commission of 2–3 percent or a flat fee of around CFA3500–5000 when you change travellers cheques. Except in major towns, you can't expect to change money other than French francs, which are easily converted on the street at the fixed rate of CFA100:1FF.

Health

The only vaccination certificate normally required to enter Mali is yellow fever. Outbreaks of cholera occur from time to time, in which case this certificate is necessary too, even though the cholera vaccine has been acknowledged as ineffective by the WHO for many years.

Bilharzia is another disease that remains all too common, especially in rural areas with slow streams and brackish water. Don't swim in such areas, especially if they're bordered by grass. Even stretches of the Niger can be dubious, notably in the dry season when the low waters become stagnant in many places. Along the entire course of the river, you'll see people bathing, doing their washing and bringing their animals to drink. Swimming in the river is, in fact, usually safe, and you'll probably find yourself doing it at some point, but if you come to a place where no one from the area goes into the water, stop and ask yourself why.

Tap **water** is heavily chlorinated and drinkable in Bamako and other big towns. In distant villages, wells and river water are commonly used for drinking and the purity may be suspect. Bottled water is available in the large towns. In places like the Dogon country, which receive a lot of foreign visitors, you can also find it, though the price of a 1.2-litre bottle is usually high. Iodine tincture, purifying tablets or filters are a cheaper alternative.

Hospitals tend to be underequipped and overcrowded. For a serious problem, your best bet is either the Hôpital du Point G (☎22.50.02 or 22.50.03) or the Hôpital Gabriel Touré (☎22.27.12), both in Bamako. Anything requiring

surgery or setting may prompt ideas of repatriation. Consult your embassy (or the American
embassy) for advice.

Maps and Information

**There's little information about Mali avail-
able abroad and no tourist offices, apart
from the Espace Mali at the Malian embassy
in Paris (see Basics, p.20), a small resource
centre whose main mission is to provide
information for those planning to develop
business interests in Mali. The office manager is very helpful and will answer queries
over the telephone, but much of the information in the centre is out of date.**

In Bamako, the most useful function of the
recently established **Office du Tourisme et de
l'Hôtellerie** (see p.313) seems to be the policing
of local guides. Over recent years a number of
independent travel agencies have also sprung
up in Bamako and Mopti, principally concerned
with offering excursions along the Niger River,
into the Manding Highlands northwest of the capital and to the country's primary tourist attractions: the Dogon country and Timbuktu. They can
usually provide a few leaflets.

The best **map** of the country is IGN's 1:2 million "3165" series map of Mali, published in 1993.
Still rare in the country, save for the capital, it's a
covetable item to some border guards – keep it
out of sight. More detailed information is available
from the IGN 1:200,000 maps, which are difficult to
get hold of, but indispensible when travelling in the
desert.

Getting Around

**The longest navigable stretch of the Niger
flows through Mali, and it's possible to travel
by boat virtually from one end of the country
to the other, stopping along the way at historic towns like Ségou, Mopti, Timbuktu and
Gao. It's an exciting – if at times tiring and
uncomfortable – way to see the country, and
the regular steamer service is almost unique
in West Africa. To take advantage of the
boats, however, it's crucial to time your trip
with the rains (see below). If you can't
schedule it, Mali does have alternatives to
get you around the country, including a regular train service from Bamako to Dakar,**
**flights linking the main towns and, of
course, bush taxis. Car rental is available
from Bamako's more expensive hotels, but is
very costly.**

■ Bush taxis and buses

Most Malians rely on **taxis brousse** (over short
distances) and **buses** (over long distances) to get
around the country. If you're without your own
transport you will too, especially in the dry season
when the river boats don't operate. Bush taxis
aren't quite as plush as in some neighbouring
countries and prices are relatively high. In addition, drivers tend to charge quite steeply for baggage and you'll have to bargain hard. Foreigners
with limited linguistic skills will find themselves
at a definite disadvantage; check with locals, as
certain routes have fixed rates.

Mali's network of privately-run **buses** provides
a reasonably comfortable and practical means of
travelling between major towns. Most companies
run a one-person-one-seat system (including an
extra row sitting on stools down the aisle) and
reservations are required. These can be made on
the spot at the *autogare*, but it's always a good
idea to reserve in advance. The fare should
include one piece of luggage in the boot. SOMA-
TRA, COMATRA and Kénédougou Voyages all run
a decent service, though its worth checking
around the smaller companies too to compare
schedules and costs.

A final note of warning: on some imported
airconditioned buses the windows are not
designed to be opened. If the AC doesn't work,
you're in for an uncomfortable ride to say the
least: get a seat at the front.

■ Trains

The Régie du Chemin de Fer du Mali (☎22.59.67;
Fax 22.54.33) provides the **rail link from Dakar
to Bamako**, described in "Arrivals", p.297. There
are also trains from Bamako to Kita, Mahina and
Kayes, and to Koulikoro, the upper terminus of the
Niger River boats (for details see p.321).

Student reductions apply on train fares at
the beginning and end of term.

■ River travel

It's possible to travel over 1300km along the Niger
River, between Koulikoro (60km from Bamako) and
Gao. Such a trip can only be made, however, in the
period during and just after the rains – roughly

from August to November between Koulikoro and Gao, or from August to January/February downstream between Mopti and Gao – when waters are high enough for the steamers. The exact dates vary each year with the timing and volume of the rains. Aim for months in the middle if you want to be sure of travelling by boat.

Three boats, in theory, ply the waters: the *Kankou Moussa* (the youngest vessel, operative since 1982) is reportedly the most comfortable, followed by the *Tombouctou* and the *Général A Soumaré*. Reservations for the trip can be made through the Compagnie Malienne de Navigation (CMN) in each of the port towns.

Boat schedules

According to the schedule, one boat leaves weekly in each direction, from Koulikoro on Friday evening and from Gao Thursday evening. In practice this only happens if at least two out of the three vessels are operable, which is not often. The only fairly predictable elements of the service are the **approximate journey times** between ports if there are no delays. The entire stretch takes five days from Koulikoro to Gao (downstream) and six days back again. Services from Mopti to Korioumé (the actual port for the now high-and-dry port town of Kabara, and Timbuktu's nearest port) should depart Sunday evening and arrive Tuesday morning. In the other direction, boats should leave Korioumé Saturday evening and reach Mopti Monday morning; but these are indications only, not to be planned around.

Fares and facilities

There's a choice of **four classes** of accommodation: *Luxe*, a single or double cabin with (sometimes non-functioning) extras like a fridge, AC and hot showers; 1st class, a double cabin with AC, and WC located just outside the cabin; 2nd class, four people to a cabin with two bunks, washing facilities require a stroll; 3rd class, rather cramped cabins with eight to twelve people, according to the vessel, and no frills.

Approximate 3rd class **fares** from Koulikoro are CFA24,000 to Mopti, CFA28,000 to Timbuktu and CFA41,000 to Gao. 1st class fares are CFA62,000 to Mopti, CFA66,000 to Timbuktu and CFA96,000 to Gao.

Food, of different qualities in different dining rooms is served three times a day and included in 1st, 2nd and – hardly any worse – 3rd class. 3rd class is probably the best option if you're budget-

ing, and some cabins have fans. You can generally use the 2nd class showers and toilets, which is a big plus. On board each boat, a bar serves cold drinks. **Drinking water** is a problem: only in the 1st and 2nd class dining rooms is there any alternative to river water.

Smaller vessels

Anywhere along the Niger, and virtually year-round, you can find local **pirogues** to get you from A to B. These are rowed – or poled much of the time – and sometimes venture quite long distances with large consignments of rock salt or other goods. Details are given throughout the chapter, but after protracted negotiations you can expect to pay from CFA2000 per person per day (50–100km) with shared food. They provide the most rewarding, if basic, means of seeing the Niger – from a few inches above its surface.

It's also possible to get **pinasses** along certain stretches of the river. These are large handmade motorized boats covered with a type of matted overhang. They operate mostly in the area around **Mopti** and you can get them from here to **Djenné** and sometimes as far as **Gao**.

Although comfort is rudimentary, there's a nostalgic sort of attraction to this type of transport which has been operating for centuries along the Niger. Some people even arrange to travel along the river in **barges** used to carry goods (especially grain) and pile their vehicle on board. This last option is spur of the moment, however, and can't be counted on.

■ Internal flights

For domestic air travel, **Air Mali** operates flights from Bamako to: **Mopti** and **Timbuktu** (three flights weekly), **Kayes** (four weekly) and **Gao** via Mopti and Timbuktu (weekly), plus **Goundam** (three weekly), **Yélimané** (two weekly), **Kénieba** and **Nioro**. Schedules are frequently interrupted by delayed or cancelled flights, and it can take Herculean efforts to get seats. One-way **fares** from Bamako are approximately: CFA40,000 to Mopti, CFA69,000 to Timbuktu, CFA100,000 to Gao, and CFA45,000 to Kayes.

Accommodation

Mali has few luxury lodgings, and, while most towns will have at least one place with hot water, air conditioning and television,

ACCOMMODATION PRICE CODES

Accommodation prices in this chapter are coded according to the following scales – the same scales in terms of their pound/dollar equivalents as used throughout the book. Prices refer to the rate you can expect to pay for a room with two beds. Single rooms, or single occupancy, will normally cost at least two-thirds of the twin-occupancy rate; for further details see p.48. Note that all rooms are subject to a CFA500 per person and per night tourist tax included in our prices.

① **Under CFA4500 (under £5/$8).** Very rudimentary lodgings, with primitive facilities.

② **CFA4500–9000 (£5–10/$8–16).** Basic hotel with few frills. Some self-contained rooms (S/C) and possibly some with AC.

③ **CFA9000–18,000 (£10–20/$16–32).** Modest hotel, usually with S/C rooms and a choice of rooms with fans, or a premium for AC.

④ **CFA18,000–27,000 (£20–30/$32–48).** Reasonable business or tourist-class hotel with S/C, AC rooms and a restaurant.

⑤ **CFA27,000–36,000 (£30–40/$48–64).** Similar to the previous code band, but extra facilities such as a pool are likely.

⑥ **CFA36,000–45,000 (£40–50/$64–80).** Comfortable, first-class hotel, with good facilities.

⑦ **Over CFA45,000 (over £50/$80).** Luxury establishment – top prices around CFA60,000.

travellers on a budget will find their choice is usually limited to simple *campements*. All hotels charge a CFA500 per person and per night tourist tax, included in our prices.

Private *pensions* do exist in some of the small towns, but it's rare to find anything for much under CFA5000. Some towns have *campings* (not to be confused with *campements*) where you can sleep quite cheaply on mats in the courtyard or in simple rooms.

Note that the "Rail" hotels in railway towns tend to be sold on half-board (HB) basis, including dinner and breakfast.

Eating and Drinking

Mali's main staple is rice, often eaten with a thin beef broth mixed with tomatoes – *riz gras*. There are numerous regional variations on this common standby.

In the Dogon country, **millet**, or *petit mil*, provides the basis of nearly every meal and is prepared in hundreds of ways. Most commonly, it's served in a boiled mush called **tô**, and eaten with sauce, often made from local onions. For breakfast it's fried in small round patties known as *beignets de mil*.

The Senoufo tend more towards tubers (**yams** and **cassava**), supplementing the rice and millet dishes which they eat less frequently than other peoples.

Food in Djenné has retained a strong Moroccan flavour. A type of **couscous** is eaten

here, as is a noodle-like dish, known as **kata**, which is accompanied by meat. **Nempti** is a type of *beignet* mixed with hot peppers, while **fitati** is a kind of thin pancake. During special celebrations the people make a pastry called **tsnein-achra** from rice flour and honey. The Tuareg, too, make a variant of *couscous* from a wild grain known as *fonio* or "hungry rice".

All along the river, of course, the people eat **fish**. One of the most common varieties is *capitaine* (Nile perch) – a boney little creature that's quite good when deep fried in oil or grilled over coals. In the northern regions of the Fula herders, **beef**, **mutton** and **goat** outsell fish, although for many people red meat is still a luxury. Just about everywhere in Mali, *gargotes* and street food sellers grill marinaded meat **brochettes** (kebabs) over charcoal, to serve with French bread.

■ Drinking

The main **Malian beer** is Castel, expensive relative to other countries at CFA650 for a large bottle or CFA350 for a small one. Beer and soft drinks – called *sucreries* – are worth a small fortune in the remoter parts of the north and east. **Home-brewed beer**, made from corn or millet, is common to many different peoples – especially non-Muslims like many Dogon and Senoufo – and is known variously as *konjo*, *dolo* or *chapalo*. Lastly, sweet, yellow China **tea** is drunk all over the country, but with particular devotion in the north, and above all by the Tuareg.

Communications – Post, Phones, Language & Media

Contact with Europe and the rest of the world can be slow even out of Bamako. Though letters are inexpensive to send, they usually take their time arriving: estimate two weeks from the capital, and as much as a month from the provinces. The Office Nationale des Postes (ONP) in Bamako has a poste restante service which seems to work relatively well.

Although Mali is connected to the IDD **phone** system, only in Bamako can you guarantee international direct dialling. From the rest of the country you can make calls from the *télécentres* that, as elsewhere in West Africa, are reasonably common in commercial centres: you make your call from a private, metered booth and pay afterwards for the units used. It takes a while to get through, and it's often easier to call from the big hotels rather than small offices, where queues tend to be long and obstructions many.

■ Languages

Though a very small percentage of the population speaks it fluently, **French** is the official language in Mali and the one you'll have to deal with for all administrative preoccupations.

BASIC BAMANA

Compare these with the "Minimal Mandinka" words and phrases in "The Gambia" chapter p.245

GREETINGS

Hello	*Anitié/N-bifo*	They're fine	*Toro tei*
Good morning	*Ani so goma*	How's it going?	*I ka kéné wa?/Hera*
Man's response	*M-ba*		*bé?*
Woman's response	*Oun sé*	Everything's fine	*Toro si té*
Good afternoon	*Ani woula*	See you later	*An bé*
Good evening	*Ani sou*		*sogoma/Kanbé*
How's the family?	*Somo go bédi?*		

NUMBERS

1	*kélén*	40	*bi nani*	75 francs	*dormé tan ne*
2	*fila*	50	*bi douru*		*dourou*
3	*saaba*	100	*kémé*	100 francs	*dormé muga*
4	*naani*	120	*kémé ni*	200 francs	*dormé bi nani*
5	*douru*		*mugan*	300 francs	*dormé bi woro*
6	*wooro*	150	*kémé ni bi*	400 francs	*dormé bi segui*
7	*wolonwula*		*dourou*	500 francs	*dormé kémé*
8	*seguin*	200	*kémé fila*	700 francs	*dormé kémé ni*
9	*kononton*	5 franc piece	*dorem*		*bi nani*
10	*tan*	10 francs	*dormé fila*	1000 francs	*dormé kémé*
20	*mugan*	25 francs	*dormé*		*fla*
25	*mugan ni douru*		*dourou*	2000 francs	*dormé kémé*
30	*bi sabi*	50 francs	*dormé ta*		*nani*

USEFUL EXPRESSIONS

How much?	*Jeli/joli?*	Where are you going?	*I bi taa min?*
It's lovely	*A kaï*	I don't know	*N'ta lou*
I'll take it (give it to me)	*A di yan*	I don't understand	*N'ma fahamuya*
It's too expensive	*A songo ka gbélé*	Excuse me/Sorry	*Ya fan ma*
Do you know of a cheap restaurant?	*I bi resitoran da duman don wa?*	What did you say? (please repeat)	*Aw kodi*
		Yes/No	*Awo/Aï*
Where's the bank?	*Bank bé min fan?*	Thank you (very much)	*I ni tié (kosébé)*
Show me the way	*Sila jira kan na*		

Mali's IDD code is ☎223.

The most widely spoken national language is **Bamana** (more commonly, also called **Bambara**), which is similar to Malinké and used throughout the country, but especially in the region around Bamako. Other languages include Pulaar (Fula), Senoufo, Songrai and Dogon.

■ **The media**

The Malian **press** is improving. There's a rash of daily French-language tabloid newspapers of which *L'Essor* is the most respected; other widely-read titles include *L'Indépendant, Les Echos, Le Soir de Bamako* and the outspoken *Nouvel Horizon*. *Nyéléni* magazine, published monthly, covers environmental, developmental and women's issues, and there are a few music magazines, including the bimonthly *Starflash* with features on both new and traditional music. You might come across several dozen other occasional magazines, any of which is worth supporting to get a feel for what's going on in the country.

National TV (ORTM) is broadcast from about 5pm to midnight on weekdays and from 10am to midnight on Fri and Sat; **satellite TV** is becoming increasingly common. Government-controlled **radio** goes out in nine languages. The big development, as everywhere in the region, is a plethora of small **FM stations** operating from various *quartiers* in Bamako and other towns: Bamakan, for example is pro-government. Radio France Internationale (98.5FM) and Africa No. 1 (the Libreville-based station, 102.0FM) are both also available.

Directory

AIRPORT DEPARTURE TAX CFA2500 domestic, CFA8000 African and CFA10,000 inter-continental.

BARGAINING The first price on tourist items in Mali is invariably huge. If you make a dismissive offer expecting it to be turned down, you can be caught out. Beware: it's easy to cause offence if, in the end, you refuse to buy the item.

ENTERTAINMENT Mali is world-famous for its **music** – the names of singer Salif Keita and guitarist/bluesy phenomenon Ali Farka Touré stand out, but other musicians such as Oumou Sangaré and Habib Koité are also now enjoying huge international success – and a major part of the Contexts section on music is devoted to it. There's a wealth of live music and dance on offer

MALIAN TERMS: A GLOSSARY

ADEMA Alliance pour la démocratie au Mali. The leading political party.

AEEM Association des Élèves et Étudiants du Mali. The national students' union.

Azalaï Desert caravans that formerly dominated Saharan trade. They continue today in small numbers, notably between the salt mines of Taoudenni and Timbuktu.

Cadeauter Transformation of the French word *cadeau* meaning "gift", into a verb. Sometimes used by children in the expression: *il faut me cadeauter*, meaning "give me something".

Dourou-dourouni *Camion bâché*, pick-up or bush taxi.

Ghana In the historical context, usually refers to Ancient Ghana, the earliest Mande-speaking kingdom (precursor of Mali), the ruined capital of which, Koumbi Saleh, is located in southeast Mauritania. The name "Ghana" was the title used by its Soninké rulers.

Hogon Dogon priests who live in isolation. These elderly men represent the highest spiritual authority in the Dogon country.

Mali An old empire (based southwest of Bamako) as well as the modern state, "Mali" is synonymous with "Manding" just as the language Malinké is basically the same one as Mandinka. Mali in Malinké means "hippo".

Oued Pronounced "wed"; French version of Arabic word designating a rocky riverbed, dry except in the rainy season. The English equivalent is "wadi".

Pinasse Large wooden boat originally invented in Djenné to carry cargo. Though the basic covered design hasn't changed over the centuries, motors are added today.

Sudan/Soudan Former colonial name for the territory encompassing Senegal, Mali and Burkina Faso. Sometimes used today to refer to the same basic area. Sudanic architecture refers to the style that originated in Djenné and has nothing to do with the modern state of Sudan.

in Bamako; elsewhere your best chance of hearing traditional music is to happen to be around for a festival. Two villages which are particularly famous for their musical tradition are Kita and Kela; both have an unusually high population of *jalis* (or griots) who may be willing to give lessons or private performances. Malian **cinema** is also thriving and, likewise, takes up a large proportion of the article on film, also in Contexts. Two of the most famous names in Malian cinema are Souleymane Cissé, who made his international name with the memorable *Yeelen* (1986), and Cheick Oumar Sissoko, whose *La Génèse* opened the 1999 Panafrican Film Festival in Ouagadougou.

GUIDES In Mali, far more than in most other West African countries, it is common for young men to work full time as **tourist guides**. A guide who's touting for work will do his best to convince you that it's essential to be accompanied by a guide when travelling in Mali; this is certainly not the case (with the exception of the Dogon country), but a good guide can smooth your path and open your eyes to a lot of things that you would otherwise miss. The usual rules apply: don't take on the first guide to approach you (wait until you can gather some personal recommendations; Bamako's Office Malienne du Tourisme et de l'Hôtellerie may be able to help), trust your instincts, ask searching questions, and bargain hard.

When engaging a guide for more than a day or so, make sure it's clearly understood for what length of time you will need them, where you want to go during this time, and who will be responsible for what expenses; then draw up a contract in writing (the Office Malienne du Tourisme et de l'Hôtellerie can approve these). As a rule of thumb, the farther your guide is from home, the less likely they are to know much about a place, so if you're planning extensive travels it's well worth considering employing a series of guides as you go along.

HOLIDAYS AND FESTIVALS Muslim holidays are celebrated with fervour in Mali, and during the month of Ramadan virtually everything closes down during the daytime – though night-time feasts redress the balance. See p.59 for approximate dates. Christian celebrations – Christmas Day and Easter – are also public holidays as are New Year's Day and Labour Day (May 1). During Christmas and New Year it's on the nights of *la veille* (Dec 24) and *le trente-et-un* (Dec 31) that

Malians really let their hair down. National holidays include Jan 20, the *Fête de l'Armée*; Africa Day on May 25 and Independence Day on Sept 22.

NAMES The same ones crop up all the time and it doesn't mean everyone is related; these are great, clan branches incorporating many strands and complex class and caste-like hierarchies. Classic Manding names are **Diabaté/Jobarteh** and **Traoré** (which are historically related); **Keïta** (with its royal associations); **Kanté/Konté/Kondé**; and **Kouyaté**. Fula names include **Bari/Barry**, **Diallo/Jalo** and **Cissé**. Many people have at least one Arabic name – Fatima, Moussa, Ali, etc.

OPENING HOURS Businesses tend to open Mon–Fri 8am–noon & 2–6/7pm. Many are closed on Friday afternoons, most on Saturday afternoons. Government offices are open Mon–Fri 7am–2pm & Sat 7am–noon.

PHOTOGRAPHY Permits are not required to take photographs in Mali, but as elsewhere discretion and good sense should be used before snapping away. In certain areas, such as the Dogon country, there are still many taboos associated with taking pictures.

WILDLIFE Mali's vast expanses of bush and swamp provide a major sanctuary for West African wildlife, with large predators and many other mammals present in significant numbers. Hippos are still relatively common all along the course of the Niger. Mali's elephants appear to be surviving, even increasing in numbers; apart from the Baoulé elephants, a herd of 600 or more lives near Gossi, between Gao and Mopti, protected in part by the presence of the Tuareg who traditionally don't hunt them. Sadly, both the Parc National du Bafing and the Parc National de la Boucle du Baoulé suffer from inaccessibility and a lack of infrastructure and are rarely visited.

WOMEN'S ISSUES Women travellers don't find Mali a special hassle. In the West African context, there's a good deal of proud, feminine freedom in the country, coupled paradoxically with the highest incidence of initiatory **genital mutilation**, including the brutal practice of infibulation. Ninety percent of women are affected, and although healthcare organizations, such as PLAN International, run community education projects to increase awareness, progress is arduous. Other statistics are equally depressing: twenty percent of deaths among Malian women of childbearing age are pregnancy related, and one in seven women die during **childbirth** or as a result of an unsafe abortion. Mali has the highest birth rate in the world, and the highest infant mortality rate. Only 22 percent of girls receive more than four years of **schooling** in their lives and it's normal for girls to be married by the age of sixteen. Fifty percent are mothers by the age of eighteen.

Recent History of Mali

The outstanding features of Mali's history are the old empires. Much of the modern country was part of the ancient Mali (or Manding) empire during its maximum extent in the thirteenth and fourteenth centuries. When the Moroccans crushed the Askia dynasty of the Songhai Empire in 1591, they left Mali with a political vacuum, partially filled from time to time by the rapid rise and fall of mini-empires. The first was the kingdom of Ségou (written "Segu" in many histories), founded in the early eighteenth century and almost immediately eclipsed by the Fula jihad that spread from Masina (Macina). This kingdom was founded in 1818 by Cheikou Ahmadou Hammadi Lobbo – a religious zealot inspired by Dan Fodio's religious war that had spread from Sokoto in present-day Nigeria. And from Senegal, the Tukulor marabout El Hadj Omar Tall launched his own holy war, setting out in 1852 to conquer animist Mandinka districts to the east.

■ Arrival of the French

The Tukulor cavalry spread across the Niger belt with lightning speed, carving out an empire headquartered at **Ségou** that extended from Masina to Bandiagara. Increasingly, it came to be seen as a threatening obstacle to the designs of French colonials in St-Louis, Senegal, bent on commercial and military penetration into the Soudanese interior.

The governor of Senegal, **General Louis Faidherbe**, opted in the first instance for a diplomatic response to Tukulor expansion and sent an expeditionary mission to Ségou. Arriving in 1868, the French signed a treaty with the new ruler **Ahmadou**, son of Omar who had been killed in battle in 1864. By 1880, the French were back to renew the treaty, but, although Ahmadou was increasingly suspicious of their motives and this

time had the emissary locked up, it was too little too late. **French forces** had now advanced as far east as Kita and brought with them the parts of an armed gunboat which they assembled and launched at Koulikoro. They thus managed to control the river as far down as Mopti. But the Tukulor Empire based at Ségou refused to cede. Finally, the capital fell in 1890 and the other towns in the interior toppled like dominos in their turn – Djenné and Bandiagara in 1893, and, after fierce Tuareg resistance, Timbuktu in 1894.

Tieba and Samory

Meanwhile, resistance was fomenting in the Senoufo country around Sikasso. The Malinké chief **Samory Touré** had been carving out his own small empire since 1861 and had taken the Senoufo strongholds of Kong, Korhogo and Ferkessédougou. He ran into conflict with **Tieba**, king of Sikasso. Samory attacked Sikasso in 1887 and beseiged it for fifteen months, but the town resisted. The French, under Lieutenant Binger, watched the rivalry with close attention and eventually allied themselves with Tieba, helping him reinforce his regional power. Tieba died in battle in 1893 and was replaced by his son **Ba Bemba**. The new king, however, mistrusted the French and refused to follow through on the kingdom's commitment to help the colonials destroy Samory's influence. In May 1898 the French attacked and took Sikasso, and the king committed suicide, escaping the fate of Samory, who was captured in September as he dashed southwest towards Liberia, hoping to get more weapons from the British. The same year, El Hadj Omar's son Ahmadou died in exile in Sokoto. France was now the sole power in the region.

■ The French Soudan

Confident of eventual victory, the French had already declared the **Soudan** an autonomous colony in 1890. Later it was incorporated into the colony of **Haut Sénégal-Niger**, of which **Bamako** was made the capital in 1908. The railway had been extended from Dakar to Koulikoro in 1904 and, with the creation of the Office du Niger – a national agricultural agency based in Ségou – the French hoped to turn Mali into the bread-basket of West Africa and even make the colony turn a profit through the production of cash crops like groundnuts and cotton. *Pistes* were traced through the interior to facilitate the transportation of crops and, in

1932, a dam was built near Ségou in the hope of turning hundreds of thousands of square kilometres into irrigable land.

From the beginning, however, the ambitious designs were frustrated. In the first place, the colonial authorities soon ran into a shortage of labour which they solved by forcibly recruiting volunteers from neighbouring countries, notably the region of the Upper Volta (Burkina Faso). In addition, much of the soil in the Soudan turned out to be too poor to support cotton production and rice was substituted. Finally, the Office du Niger had restrictive financial limitations. As a result, only a small fraction of the territory destined to become an agricultural miracle was ever exploited. Not that it made much difference to Malians at the time, since the production was almost exclusively destined for export to France.

World Wars I and II – African participation

Of all the colonies in the AOF (Afrique Occidentale Française), Mali paid the highest price with the outbreak of World War I. The Bambara, especially, were recruited in large numbers to fill the ranks of the famous Tirailleurs Sénégalais – the **Senegalese Infantry**. These troops had already experienced European war as early as 1908 when they had been used by France to "pacify" Morocco. After 1914, tens of thousands of Africans were sent to Verdun where one in three died in the muddy war of attrition. Back in the Soudan, uprisings that sprouted to protest the draft of native soliders for a foreign war were brutally suppressed by the French authorities.

As if the price wasn't high enough, when war was over, the new colonial governor, Just Van Vollenhoven, began mobilizing civilians in the Soudan to develop agricultural production and the regional infrastructure. It was a move he deemed necessary to make the colony profitable after the stagnant period during the war.

Parallel to this, the French made minimal concessions to give Africans an extended role in the **politics** of their countries. By 1925, Africans could be elected to sit on the governor's advisory councils, although this of course gave them no direct political power. From the 1930s, laws were made to facilitate access to **French nationality** – a status considered by the government to be a great honour despite the sacrifices Africans had made during the war. But by 1937 only some 70,000 people in the entire AOF had been granted French cit-

izenship and the vast majority of these were Senegalese. World War II had the effect of nipping political and social development in the bud.

Postwar political developments

World War II acted as a catalyst that gave rise to a new political consciousness in Africa and a determination to achieve political rights. Independence was still only envisaged by a very few, and de Gaulle himself ruled out this possibility at the 1944 **Brazzaville conference**, although he did say France was willing to make concessions, including greater African involvement in the respective governments.

In the aftermath of Brazzaville, three **political parties** were formed in Mali: the Parti Soudanais du Progres (PSP) headed by **Fily Dabo Cissoko**; a Soudanese affiliate of the Section Française de l'Internationale Ouvrière (SFIO) with **Mamadou Konaté** at the helm; and the Parti Démocratique du Soudan (PDS) founded by French Communists living in Mali. Though Cissoko came out ahead in elections to a constituent assembly in 1945, the first year of government was characterized by infighting among the parties – notably the PSP and the SFIO. In 1946, Bamako hosted the **Rassemblement Démocratique Africain** (RDA) – a vast political convention that brought together over 800 delegates from Senegal, Côte d'Ivoire, Guinea, Benin, Togo, Cameroon, Chad and Mali. The main theme was **union**: so that West Africa could speak with one voice, it was imperative the Soudan have a single voice within the RDA. To the surprise of everyone, the three parties agreed to form a single Union Soudanaise within the RDA (USRDA). But within a couple of days, Cissoko announced that a bloc with what he called "unrepentant communists" was impossible and he reformed the PSP.

The Soudan swings left

The next decade saw an intense **rivalry** between the PSP and the USRDA but, by 1957, the latter had clearly won the upper hand. This was in large part because the USRDA had more effectively distanced itself from Paris and had better grassroots organization in Mali. After the elections of 1959, in which the PSP had fared so badly, they were constrained to join forces with the USRDA. On the eve of independence, there was no effective opposition to this party.

Changes had occurred within the USRDA when Konaté died in 1956. A moderate voice on the left,

Konaté had advocated union of all the peoples of Mali. The void he left in the party ranks was quickly filled by more radical elements headed by **Modibo Keita**.

In the same year, the **Loi Cadre** drafted in Paris had opened the door to semi-autonomous governments in each of the territories of AOF. This led to divisions in the formerly united RDA as a cleavage arose between leaders like Sekou Touré and Leopold Senghor – who advocated the maintenance of a federal government in Dakar – and those such as Houphouët-Boigny, who advocated the maximum autonomy for each of the territories.

Federalists and federation

Modibo Keita stood firmly in the camp of the Federalists, mainly because, as a poor country, the Soudan had a lot to gain from uniting itself with other territories (many of the country's colonial projects had been financed by AOF funds that originated outside Mali). Senghor's motives were more ideological, and he pleaded for a politically united West Africa that would maintain good relations with France. It became more pressing to decide on the pros and cons of a federation after the **1958 referendum** where AOF nations voted to continue self-government within the French Union.

Sekou Touré was the only African leader who, for better or worse, had the courage to storm out of the French Union. Guinea was therefore excluded from any West African federation as well. Côte d'Ivoire was also out since Houphouët-Boigny had already stated loud and clear that he wouldn't have his country become "the milk cow" to feed the mouths of hungry neighbours.

In January 1959, the four remaining members of the former AOF – Soudan, Senegal, Upper Volta and Dahomey – met in Dakar and drew up the constitution of their territories. Under pressure from Côte d'Ivoire, Upper Volta eventually backed out of its commitment and Dahomey followed suit. Hopes for a broad-based political union in the region had been pared down to two nations, but it was still an important step for pan-African ideals. The **Mali Federation** of Mali and Senegal was born.

Unhappy union with Senegal

From the beginning, the alliance was uneasy. Keita was eager that Mali be granted independence. Senghor was more methodical, less hurried. De Gaulle himself helped sort out this prob-

lem by recognizing in 1959 that it was possible for the federation to be granted **independence** while staying in the French Community. The Mali Federation did, in fact, become independent – on April 4, 1960 – but the honeymoon between Senghor and Keita lasted barely two months.

Although numerous social and economic inequalities existed between the two former territories (which without doubt had an adverse effect on the union), the most glaring divergences were political and symbolized by the **clash of personalities** of the two leaders. Keita championed a Marxist approach to "African socialism". He was a man of (often admirable) principles who liked decisive action and who was unused to compromise. Senghor's approach was more measured and tended to favour dialogue and diplomatic action. He was especially cautious and pragmatic in his attitude to France which he hoped to keep as a friend and ally.

The stand-off between the two men – and as a consequence the territories they presided over – came to a head during the 1960 elections for President of the Federation, a powerful office that the Soudanese were wary of Senghor occupying. Senegal ruled out any alternative nominee and the brief federal arrangement collapsed.

■ Birth of the Mali Republic

After the failure of the Federation, Keita set about creating the basis of the independent Malian state – a task of Promethean proportions at such short notice. He was helped, however, by the wave of **nationalist pride** and unity that swept the country, now destined to stand alone. Even Keita's former opponent, Cissoko, threw his support behind the USRDA in the name of the national cause. In September 1960, a special congress of the USRDA announced the implementation of a **planned socialist economy**. Shortly afterwards, Keita closed French military bases in Mali. He then set up state enterprises, starting with SOMIEX. This company had a monopoly on all imports and exports of primary products – an advantage French companies operating in the country hardly appreciated. In 1962, Keita pushed his country further into **isolation** by taking it out of the franc zone and creating a national currency, the Franc Malien. In the same year, a **Tuareg revolt** in the Adrar des Iforhas mountains northeast of Gao was savagely repressed by the army.

It was a difficult start, made even worse by the fact that Senegal stopped trains to Bamako for three years after the rupture and closed its borders with Mali. As Keita continued down his radical path (and he was sincere in his belief that Mali could be the spearhead of a new brand of "African socialism", though his conception of what this meant differed from that of other regional leaders) he distanced himself from other African nations. And the West, too, turned an icy shoulder as, in the middle of the Cold War, he chose to ally his country with the Soviet Union. Opposition mounted grimly at home as the business community saw their economic privileges being eroded into state assets.

By the **mid-1960s**, Keita had created a heavy state machinery that dragged mercilessly on the nation's already fragile economy. The situation was characterized by numerous national enterprises (almost all of them running a deficit), a plethora of civil servants clogging the administrative machinery, a soaring balance of trade deficit and foreign debt, and a rapid weakening of the currency. Inflation soared and wages were frozen – a combination that wasn't calculated to enthuse Malians. By 1967, taking his cue from Peking, Keita was engaged in a **"cultural revolution"** to purge the nation of enemies within. He was supported in this by radical students, some of the unions, and by some lower grades in the civil service who resented the corruption of senior officials and business profiteers. But in the same year, Keita was obliged to devalue the Malian franc by fifty percent. The public outcry was immediate; the government's entire direction came under attack from all sides.

The coup

Keita seemed not to notice that opposition was sprouting up all around him. Believing the monumental role he'd played in his country's development absolved him from criticism by a populace faced with a deepening economic crisis, he was apparently surprised and aggrieved when a group of young military officers staged a **bloodless coup** in 1968.

The **Comité Militaire de Libération Nationale** (CMLN) was quickly formed, headed by a 32-year-old lieutenant, **Moussa Traoré**. Keita and senior members of his government were arrested and the former president died in prison ten years later.

Initially the military didn't challenge the nation's socialist orientation. The officers did, however, recognize the need to correct certain

errors committed by the previous regime, to bring new order to the management of the economy and to boost production. To this end, Traoré continued to rely on Soviet and Chinese technical aid.

■ The Traoré years

The first years of military rule brought little relief to the country. Overnight revival of the economy was impracticable, and the **drought** that ravaged the nation in 1973 and 1974 had a disastrous effect on agriculture. Industrial development didn't fare much better and the 1974 **border war** with Burkina Faso put an extra drain on human and financial resources. Despite discouraging signs in the political and economic spheres, the military drew up a new constitution in 1974 that was approved in a plebiscite by what the government claimed was 99.7 percent of the population.

The new constitution, however, didn't go into effect until 1979 when a single party, the **Union Démocratique du Peuple Malien** (UDPM), was charged with running the country. Traoré remained at the head of government.

This symbolic transformation to civilian rule (cosmetic as it may be) was accompanied by a softening of the rigid socialist philosophy. This trend was accelerated after a second drought devastated the country from 1983 to 1985. In an effort to assure continued foreign aid, Traoré worked hard to improve relations with the West, notably with France. Most of the state organizations and companies that were a tremendous financial burden were privatized in an effort to dynamize the economy. Additionally, Traoré brought Mali into the CFA fold in 1985 which encouraged investment.

■ Democracy and the Third Republic

Through such steps Traoré thought he could bring his country out of the quarter-century of political and economic isolation into which it had retreated after the so-called Balkanization of French West Africa on the eve of independence, and especially after the final rupture with Senegal. But, intentionally or otherwise, he also opened Mali to the **pressure for democratic reform** which was sweeping the region by 1990 and which was increasingly a condition of foreign aid.

At first, Traoré tried to contain the pressure within the party framework. Opposition leaders from the Alliance pour la Démocratie au Mali (Adema) wanted more, and published an article in one of the new newspapers, *Les Echos*, calling for a national conference to draft a new constitution and lead the **transition to multiparty politics**. Soon after, a series of independent parties came into being, including the Comité National d'Initiative Démocratique (CNID) which has large support from the legal profession, and the Union Soudanaise–Rassemblement Démocratique Africain (US-RDA), the re-formed pre-independence party.

By December 1990, dissent was trickling down to the streets: the government tried to evict street vendors from downtown Bamako, provoking a **mass demonstration** that coincided with the anniversary of the Universal Declaration of Human Rights. On New Year's Eve, another pro-democracy demonstration attracted 15,000 marchers and, on January 8, 1991, a **general strike** for better wages was called – the first in Mali since independence 30 years before. **Student protestors** jumped into the fray, organizing a demonstration that was brutally suppressed by the police and resulted in a number of deaths, the first in the pro-democracy movement.

The government wasted no time in demanding that political parties and student organizations cease all activity. It closed the country's schools, and deployed heavy weapons on the streets of Bamako. In the **mass arrests** which followed, Amnesty International reported widespread torture in the prisons, sometimes of schoolchildren as young as twelve.

Malians barely had time to recover from these incidents when a more concerted round of **rioting** broke out in March. In three days of intense fighting, police and *gendarmes* had killed some 150 people, and injured nearly a thousand. Wave after wave of protestors swelled through the city, however, failing to be intimidated by the government's show of strength. In the face of a failed policy of violent suppression, coupled with international disapproval and complete disruption of the economy, Traoré made plans to flee, but promised elections, and said shortly after that he would not resign and that his troops were loyal.

The new era

The military responded by arresting Traoré. The **coup** leader, Lt-Col Amadou Toumani Touré dissolved the government, suspended the constitution and abolished the ruling party – the UDPM – saying it would work with the pro-democracy movement. Within days, a multiparty committee

had been formed to oversee the democratization of Mali. **Soumana Sacko**, a former finance minister sacked by Traoré when he tried a little too diligently to crack down on corruption, was appointed interim prime minister. More arrests followed, with ex-government ministers charged with corruption and murder. An unsuccessful **counter-coup attempt** was mounted by officers loyal to the ex-president but was easily quashed and a jubilant crowd swarmed through the streets of Bamako when it was learned the putsch had failed.

The people seemed less enthusiastic at voting time, however. The hero of the democratic revolution, Amadou Toumani Touré, or "ATT" to his millions of admirers, did not seek a permanent role in power and, in the first free municipal and presidential elections in 1992, barely 20 percent of eligible Malians bothered to vote. The Adema party secured a large majority, however, and their man, the academic **Alpha Oumar Konaré**, was sworn in as president of the Third Republic on June 8, 1992.

Traoré and several members of his disgraced government were convicted of murder and sentenced to death, but the sentences were later commuted to life imprisonment (Mali has had no judicial executions since 1980).

As Mali enters the twenty-first century, political life remains dominated by the issue of the Adema party's firm grip on power. Konaré is not an instinctive politician, and although his self-effacement has earned him broad respect, it also made his first term in office somewhat difficult and unproductive. It was only in 1994 that he established a proper working relationship with the brusque and effective **Ibrahim Boubacar Keita**, who became (and at the time of writing in mid-1999 remains) his prime minister. The Adema leadership is more willing to drive democracy forward than many party supporters in the rank and file, and has frequently been cited as being in the vanguard of democratic reform in Africa, but the plethora of opposition parties, many of them prone to internal division, has undermined any chance of a breakthrough by the loose Coordination des Partis Politiques de l'Opposition (Coppo).

Meanwhile, the potential of the **student population** to provoke unrest is rarely far below the surface. The students, not surprisingly, quickly switched from backing the democrats to opposing the government that was formed, and the new

ANATOMY OF A REBELLION

The roots of the Tuareg rebellion were put in place after France's abortive attempt to form a Tuareg state – "Azaouad" – in 1958, on the eve of independence. The revolt began in 1990 with an attack on a military post at Ménaka, 300km east of Gao, followed up by a much bigger attack in September on Bouressa, which left at least 300 dead on both sides. Gao was placed under curfew. The rebellion coincided with the return from Algeria of **drought refugees** who were unhappy with their reception in Mali, and was framed in terms of overthrowing Moussa Traoré and improving development aid to their regions. But as the democracy movement in Bamako took hold and Traoré was deposed, the Tuareg rebellion made more specific demands for, at the very least, greater autonomy for the desert regions. Ultimately the issues boiled down to one: **race**. The Tuareg viewed themselves, and were viewed as, "whites" and former lords (or oppressors), while the sedentary population considered themselves "blacks", newly enfranchised by democratic reforms.

A ceasefire agreement was signed in Tamanrasset in Algeria in January 1991. The rebels' signatory was **Iyad Ag Galli**, leader of the Azouad Popular Movement (MPA) whose agenda listed a better deal for the Tuareg above greater autonomy and specifically excluded the ideal of independence for a Tuareg state.

The accord was rejected by other Tuareg militia, which continued a campaign of armed attacks, usually by small groups of rebels, on police stations and government buildings. The rebels had Libyan support, and many of their military leaders had fought in various conflicts in the Middle East, including the Iran–Iraq war, Lebanon and Afghanistan. Rebel attacks were invariably followed by brutal military reprisals on the most obvious Tuareg target in the district. Tens of thousands of refugees, mostly Tuareg, fled the affected areas to southern Algeria and Mauritania.

Despite what appeared to be a fragmentation of any co-ordination between the different groups, a second peace agreement – the **national pact** – was signed in April 1992, with a new umbrella organization of the Tuareg in Mali, the Unified Fronts and Movements of the Azouad (MFUA), claiming to represent at least four of the groups. During the course of the year, 600 ex-rebels were integrated into the Malian army, 300 were given civil service posts and joint Tuareg-army patrols were instituted.

But the MFUA began to disintegrate, with several factions at war with each other and the MPA, with its demands for full Tuareg integration into Malian national life, was accused of a sell-out. There were also clashes between regular soldiers of the Malian army and "integrated" Tuareg troops.

Resentment at the Tuaregs' comparative success at achieving their aims through violence, led to the formation of various ethnic vigilante groups. The most menacing was a Songhai resistance militia, **Ganda Koi** ("Owners of the Land"), which launched vicious attacks on Tuareg camps; others included the **Alert des Bella** ("Bella Awakening": a reprisal force formed by the Tuaregs' former slaves, the Bella) and **Lafia**, a Fula group.

Despite the widespread violence, the Bamako government remained committed to a peaceful solution and, encouraged by positive talks in January 1995 between the Tuareg and Ganda Koi representatives in Bourem, a series of community meetings was launched, followed by a lengthy tour of northern Mali and Tuareg refugee camps in Algeria and Mauritania. The government's programme – to reinstall civilian local government and to improve education and healthcare provision in the conflict areas – boosted confidence, giving the predominantly young Tuareg fighters reasons to engage in civilian life, and led rapidly to the reintegration and disarmament of rebel fighters.

A **repatriation scheme** to bring back tens of thousands of Tuareg refugees from Algeria, Mauritania, Burkina and Niger was launched in October 1995, and a final **peace agreement** was signed in 1996. There was a symbolic burning of weapons in Timbuktu in March 1996, which marked the end of the six-year rebellion.

order has provoked rather than satisfied their demands. There were violent protests in Bamako over the devaluation of the CFA franc, a policy popularly interpreted as neocolonial. Konaré's government has been condemned by Amnesty for its frequently heavy-handed response to ordinary criticism from leading lights in the opposition – ad hoc imprisonment, harassment and detention remain regular occurrences – and for not doing enough to eradicate the use of torture in prisons. And the president has many detractors in the armed forces, although the usually benevolent background support of "ATT", now a general and an international emissary, should help to keep them in barracks.

In the country's **second elections**, which rolled for several tedious months through the rainy season of 1997, President Konaré got nearly 96 percent of the vote in the presidential election, while his Adema party took 130 seats out of parliament's total of 147 in the national assembly elections. In both cases, however, there was a widespread opposition boycott and a very low turnout (twenty percent across the country, but down to twelve percent in Bamako). The opposition claimed rigging; international observers recognized a chaotic lack of organization, but no direct evidence of fraud. The opposition had done more than accuse Adema of cheating; they accused the electoral commission itself of malpractice and demanded the entire electoral process be rescheduled. In the event both elections were simply rerun. To the dismay of many in his Adema party, Konaré's response to the landslide result was typically conciliatory, and he offered concessions to the opposition, including a fairer distribution of public money to opposition campaign funds.

■ Mali at the turn of the century

Behind the steady turmoil of Bamako party politics, the legacy of the old order continues to haunt the new Mali. The country's first success in recovering **looted public money** came in 1997, when several Swiss banks agreed to repay to Konaré's government more than £1.5million (US$2.4million) of state funds stolen by the former head of the national tobacco and match company. However, the return of two billion dollars (equivalent to three-quarters of Mali's current national debt) estimated to have been stolen by former

dictator Moussa Traoré, may take longer. The economic crimes committed by Traoré and his cronies were not brought before the courts until 1998, and, to the disgust of many Malians, the sums he was then accused of embezzling amounted to only fifteen percent of his estimated total scoop. He received another death sentence, which, like his first, is unlikely to be carried out.

The biggest single issue faced by Konaré's government in the 1990s was the **Tuareg rebellion** (see box, opposite). At the conflict's peak, an estimated 160,000 people had fled to refugee camps in Algeria, Mauritania and Burkina Faso. Two-thirds of the country – everywhere north and east of the Bamako–Mopti road – was too dangerous to travel through and the region's towns were transformed into besieged garrisons in the wilderness. The Tuareg fighters pursuing the war probably numbered no more than several hundred. But every new atrocity dug each side into a deeper hatred of the other. The fact that Konaré's government and the Tuareg faction leaders resolved this bitter and bloody dispute with little third-party assistance is one of the better chapters in post-colonial African history.

Mali's president and the country's *éminence grise*, "ATT", are men whom the international community respect and can do business with. While not all Malians would accept that democracy has brought significant benefits, the prospects for the economy and for inward investment are better now than they have been since independence, and better here than in most of Mali's neighbours. The run-up to the next elections, due in May 2002 – a bumper year for Mali as it also holds the African Nations football cup that year – will draw some serious contenders for the presidential succession out of the woodwork.

BAMAKO

Although **BAMAKO** has grown quickly since independence, evidence of modernization is only slowly penetrating the dusty city centre. Here, the mix of day-long crowds,
hostile traffic and sludge-filled sewers add up to an oppressive combination for visitors
just in from the *brousse*, although arrivals from Dakar welcome Bamako's less aggressive hustlers – debilitated, no doubt, by the perennial heat. At dusk the dust settles
down like a pink fog as the centre expels its torrid activity into the suburbs where the
conspicuous aid community reposes in air-conditioned comfort.

Architecturally, ostentatious modern developments like the Saudi-built **Pont du Roi
Fahd** and nearby, the neo-Sudanic **Tour BCEAO** – the city's stunning showpiece –
emerge from amid the medieval sanitation and dreary Soviet-funded blocks of the early
1960s. Compared with Mali's undeniable rural attractions, the capital is just too hot,
dirty and crowded to be immediately appealing, and for most the few days taken to
obtain the next visa, go to the supermarket, write a few letters or wait for the train will
be long enough.

Some history

As rock paintings (notably at the **Point G caves**) attest, Bamako is the site of ancient
settlements, peopled as early as the African Paleolithic and Neolithic ages. Oral history
traces the roots of the present town back to **Seribadian Niaré**, who sought refuge in
the Bamana empire after being chased from the region of Nioro du Sahel in the seventeenth century. Upon arrival in the capital town of **Ségou**, Niaré married the sister of
the king, **Soumba Coulibaly**. The couple had a son, **Diamoussadian Niaré**, and
moved to the region around the present capital of Mali. A hunter of heroic dimensions,
the son eventually killed a giant crocodile that had long terrorized the people of the
area, thus fulfilling a prophecy and laying the basis for the establishment of a dynasty
(also prophesied) that would grow up on the site. The Niarés thereby became rulers of
the chiefdom at Bama-ko (crocodile-river).

The alternative opening recounts how a hunter from Kong in Côte d'Ivoire, Bamba
Sanogo, killed an elephant here on the north bank of the Niger and received permission from the local lord to found a town, which he named Bamba-Kong after himself
and his city of origin. Leaving no heirs on his death, the town's chieftaincy went to
Diamoussadian Niaré.

Whichever its origin, Bamako grew to be a prosperous trading centre. By the time
the Scots explorer **Mungo Park** arrived in the early nineteenth century the population
had grown to about 6000. By 1883 the French had built a fort here and soon afterwards
colonized the region. In 1904 the railway line was pushed through from Kayes and in
1908 the town was made capital of the colony of **Haut Sénégal-Niger**. When independence was returned to the country in 1960, Bamako became the Malian capital. At the
time, the town's population was some 160,000, but in the following years of rapid
growth that figure has risen nearly sevenfold.

Arrival, information and orientation

Note that if you're coming from Mopti or beyond by **river boat** you'll get only as far as
Koulikoro, the port 60km east of Bamako, which has a rail link to the capital as well as
road traffic. If you arrive by **bush taxi** chances are you'll be let off at the **gare routière
de Sogoniko**, about 7km from the centre on the south side of the Niger River. You can
either take a taxi from here to town, catch a northbound BAMABUS for a fraction of
the cost, or hop on a Peugeot *bâché*. Whichever way, you'll cross the overworked **Pont**

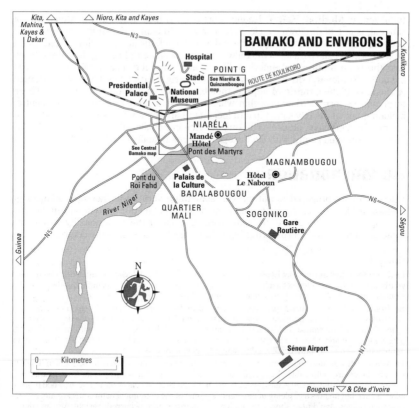

Kita, △   △ Nioro, Kita and Kayes
Mahina,
Kayes &
Dakar
                                                            ▷ Koulikoro
N3

BAMAKO AND ENVIRONS

Hospital

POINT G
ROUTE DE KOULIKORO
Presidential   Stade   See Niaréla &
Palace   Quinzambougou
                         map
         National
         Museum

NIARÉLA
Mandé ◉
Hôtel
See Central
Bamako map   Pont des Martyrs
                                    MAGNAMBOUGOU
                          Hôtel ◉
Pont du   Palais de   Le Naboun
Roi Fahd   la Culture
             BADALABOUGOU   N6
River Niger QUARTIER
N5   MALI   SOGONIKO
                          Gare
                          Routière   ▷ Ségou

◁ Guinea

N

0   Kilometres   4

Sénou Airport

N7

Bougouni ▽ & Côte d'Ivoire

des Martyrs which spans the Niger. Once over the bridge and in the centre, either walk to a hotel or take another taxi if you want to lodge in the outskirts. Arriving by **train**, the station is walking distance from many accommodation options.

Bamako's **airport** is 15km south of town at **Sénou**. If you have a booking with one of the city's top hotels, there should be a minibus waiting to take you straight there; if not, you'll have to catch a taxi to town as no bus service exists: it shouldn't exceed CFA7000, except after midnight.

For **tourist information**, the Office Malien du Tourisme et de l'Hotellerie is on rue Mohamed V, just north of Square Lumumba (Mon–Sat 7.30am–4.30pm; ☎22.56.73, Fax 22.55.41); it rarely has any maps to give away and can only offer limited advice, but will recommend guides, and, if you decide to hire a guide for a trip, approve the contract.

Orientation

Although Bamako's compact centre makes it an easy town to walk around, orientation can be difficult as one market-thronged street can look very much like another, especially at night. To get your bearings, the prominent *Hôtel de l'Amitié* and bat-eared **Tour BCEAO** serve as useful reference points: they are by the river and either side of the main thoroughfare which leads from the **Pont des Martyrs** to **Square Lumumba**, with the large French embassy and airline offices alongside. The **Avenue du Fleuve** (or **Avenue Modibo Keïta**), leading north from this square to the **Place de la Liberté**, is one of the town's main streets, lined with banks, restaurants and stores. If you follow this street all the way to the end, you'll reach the junction with the **rue Baba Diarra**, which runs parallel to the railway tracks. Turning right along this street, you'll pass the **train station** and American library and cultural centre (**USIS**) before arriving at the **Boulevard du Peuple**, where another right turn takes you past the **Centre Artisanal** and the **Grande Mosquée**, then back down to the Square Lumumba. These three streets form a triangle within which you'll find Bamako's commercial centre, including one of the city's principal (if incidental) attractions, the **street market**.

There's an efficient, privately run **bus service** in Bamako, TABA buses (☎22.23.87). They run on fixed routes with fixed stops and fares (usually CFA100 per hop).

Accommodation

Unless you are prepared to put up with something very basic, **accommodation** in Bamako is likely to carve a large chunk out of your budget during your stay in the city. Although many options are centrally located, most of the better-quality hotels are located in the relatively prosperous **Niaréla district**, 3km east of the centre.

Budget

Le Carrefour des Jeunes, av Kasse Keïta (☎22.43.11). The small, basic rooms in this community youth/arts centre are often set aside for visiting groups of students or performers but there's occasionally space for other travellers. The atmosphere can sometimes be rough. ②.

Le Centre d'Accueil Catholique des Soeurs Blanches, corner of rue 130 (El Hadj Ousmane Bagayoko) and rue 133. Bamako's best low-cost option. The nuns here take travellers if there is space (being a lone woman helps) and offer commendably clean S/C rooms with mosquito nets, peace and quiet and a key to the gate. New arrivals need to turn up before nightfall to gain entry; at busy times you may only be allowed to stay for a couple of nights. ②.

La Maison des Jeunes, blue three-storey complex near the Pont des Martyrs (☎22.23.20). Lowest rates in the centre, with a dirt cheap café/bar. Friendly enough, but security is far from guaranteed – the compound is not locked at any time. Choose between large dorms or basic 1-, 2- or 3-bed rooms, all with fans, but no nets and plenty of mosquitoes. Some of the communal bathrooms are more bearable than others. Avoid unlit short cuts at night – muggings have occurred. Various African educational groups often stay here and it could be a place to meet students. Camping is permitted. ①.

Inexpensive

Hôtel Le Naboun, a few minutes' drive from the *gare routière*, 200m past the *Hexagone* nightclub, Magnambougou (BP 8023; ☎77.38.01). Very good value, with S/C, AC rooms, all with balconies. There's a decent bar-resto and friendly, efficient management. Only possible drawback is its south bank location. ②–③.

Mission Libanaise (*Mission Père Francis*), rue Poincaré, 200m west of av du Fleuve. Secure haven with off-street parking, a few rather stuffy fanned and netted twin bedrooms and a shared bathroom/toilet. ③.

ACCOMMODATION PRICE CODES

① Under CFA4500 (under £5/$8)
② CFA4500–9000 (£5–10/$8–16)
③ CFA9000–18,000 (£10–20/$16–32)
④ CFA18,000–27,000 (£20–30/$32–48)
⑤ CFA27,000–36,000 (£30–40/$48–64)
⑥ CFA36,000–45,000 (£40–50/$64–80)
⑦ Over CFA45,000 (over £50/$80)

For further details see p.48.

CENTRAL BAMAKO

△ Zoo, National Museum & Point G   Koulikoro △

Kayes ◁

AV DE LA LIBERTÉ
AV VAN VOLLENHOVEN
Train Station
RUE BABA DIARRA
USIS
US Embassy
PLACE DE LA RÉPUBLIQUE
Fetish Market
AV KASSE KEITA
Sabena
Mairie
PL DE LA LIBERTÉ
RUE MOHAMED V
RUE TESTARD/ROCHESTER
RUE DU 18 JUIN
BD DE LA PAIX
Bank of Africa
RUE ARCHINARD
Centre Artisanal
Grande Mosquée
AV MODIBO KEITA
AV DE LA RÉPUBLIQUE
RUE KARAMOKO DIABY
BD DU PEUPLE
Niaréla ▷
AV DE LOJAKO
Cinema Vox
Cathedral
BMCD Bank
RUE FAMOLO
PLACE DU SOUVENIR
Marché Rose
Street Market
RUE GOURAUD
AV MAMADOU KONATÉ
AV DU FLEUVE
RUE MOHAMED V
RUE LYAUTEY
RUE LAPPERINE

ACCOMMODATION
Le Centre d'Accueil **④**
Catholique des Soeurs
Blanches
Le Carrefour des Jeunes **③**
Grand Hôtel **①**
Hôtel de l'Amitié **⑦**
Hôtel Buffet de la Gare **②**
Hôtel Le Fleuve **⑧**
Hôtel Lac Debo **⑤**
La Maison des Jeunes **⑨**
Mission Libanaise **⑥**

Sûreté
AV DE LA NATION
RUE PROSPER
RUE POINCARÉ
Tourist Office
RUE PASTEUR
BD DU PEUPLE
Centre Cultural Français
BDM Bank
AV DE LA MARNE
BIM Bank
AV RUAULT
AV DE L'YSER
SQUARE LUMUMBA
AV DE VERDUN
French Embassy

RESTAURANTS, BARS & CLUBS
Bar Bozo **⑩**
Le Bol de Jade **⑪**
Calao **③**
La Caverne d'Ali Baba **①**
Disco Colombo **⑨**
L'Escale de Jumeaux **④**
L'Evasion **⑥**
Patisserie Les Delices **⑥**
Patisserie Phoenicia **⑦**
Restaurant Central **⑤**
Restaurant La Pizzeria **②**
Le Tempo **⑫**

Guinean Embassy
Air France & Air Mali
AV MOUSSA TRAVALY
PONT DES MARTYRS
Airport & Gare Routière ▷
Tour BCEAO
River Niger
BD DU 22 OCTOBRE 1946
CMN Ferry Office

0 Metres 200

Hôtel Maxim & Musée Muso Kunda △

NIARÉLA AND QUINZAMBOUGOU

Burkina Faso Embassy

Stade Omnisports △

Hippodrome

ROUTE DE KOULIKORO

L'Express
L'Akwaba

Le Fourni &
Azar Libre Service
Supermarkets
Restaurant
Dienne
Restaurant
Restaurant
La Relax
San Toro
Restaurant
Rive Gauche

Station △

Hôtel
Le Rabelais

ROUTE DE SOTUBA (RUE TITI NIARE)

Restaurant
Asia
Restaurant
Coeur d'Afrique
Hôtel
Jamana/Metropolis

Grand Marché △

Metro Supermarket

Hôtel
Dakan

Hôtel
Tennessee

0   Metres   300

N

Russian Embassy

Moderate

Hôtel Buffet de la Gare, next to the train station (BP 466; ☎23.19.10). Fanned or AC rooms, some S/C. *The* place to stay for committed Rail Band fans. Live music on Sat nights and plenty of shunting and hooting at other times. Rates are HB. ③–④.

Hôtel Dakan, Niaréla district (BP 1385; ☎21.91.96). This pleasant and old-fashioned hotel offers a cluster of S/C, AC rooms with TV around shady gardens. It also has its own bar/restaurant. ③–④.

Hôtel Le Fleuve, 211 rue 311, off av de l'Yser (BP 2963; ☎22.65.03; Fax 22.65.13). Pleasant hotel in a quiet area with clean S/C rooms and a recommended restaurant/pizzeria. The lower priced rooms are very small; higher priced rooms have AC and TV. ③–④.

Hôtel Jamana, rte de Sotuba, next to the *Métropolis* nightclub, Niaréla (BP 1686; ☎21.10.50). Very clean S/C, AC rooms. Discounts available for stays of more than a night or two. ④.

Hôtel Lac Debo, av du Fleuve, corner of av de la Nation (BP 2742; ☎22.96.35). A little overpriced but handy for its very central position. Gloomy but sizeable and decent S/C rooms with fan or AC (but no nets), some with balconies. Small restaurant/bar. ④.

Hôtel Maxim, 1545 rue 224, qtr Hippodrome (☎ & Fax 23.98.56). Small, friendly hotel in a quiet location. Business facilities (phone, fax, email) are available, meals can be arranged, and there is satellite TV and a small pool. ④.

Expensive

Grand Hôtel, av Van Vollenhoven (BP 104; ☎22.24.92; Fax 22.26.01). Unexceptional international class hotel just north of the station with two pools, tennis courts and a business centre. ⑥–⑦.

Hôtel de l'Amitié, av de la Marne (BP 1720; ☎21.43.21; Fax 21.43.85). Ugly Soviet-built landmark offering service with a sneer unless you turn up with gold cards. Pool, golf course, business centre, fine restaurant and pricey rooms: for many NGO workers this is home. ⑥.

Hôtel Le Rabelais, rte de Sotuba, 3km east of station (BP 2126; ☎21.52.98; Fax 21.27.86). A warm welcome at this cosy and very popular French-run hotel, the best choice in this category for genuine comfort and hospitality. ⑥.

Hôtel Tennessee, Niaréla district (BP 771; ☎21.36.77; Fax 21.61.26). Modern hotel with a pool, garden, French restuarant and other comforts, patronized by aid workers. ⑥.

Mandé Hôtel, Cité du Niger (BP 2236; ☎21.19.93, Fax 21.19.96). Rather beautiful riverside hotel, well off the beaten track, offering accommodation in little rondavels, a pristine pool (open to non-residents during the Sunday buffet), and a recommended restaurant, *Le Toit de Bamako*, which often has live music and dancing. ⑤–⑥.

The Town

Bamako's bustle, filth and especially its heat make it a tiring place to enjoy at a leisurely walking pace unless, of course, you happen to thrive in sub-Saharan urban settings. In that case the **street market** around the new **Marché Rose** is the place for you. North of the **Centre Artisanal** along the Boulevard du Peuple, you'll find a good selection of **fetish stalls** with an impressive array of decomposing animal parts. And to the north of the railway tracks, the other main north–south avenue – Avenue de la Liberté – leads through the diplomatic district past the **Musée National**: if you do nothing else in Bamako, be sure to spend some time here.

The Centre Artisanal and Grande Mosquée

Built by the French in the 1930s in the Sudanic style, the **Centre Artisanal** or **Maison des Artisans** (at the corner of boulevard du Peuple and rue Karamoko Diaby) was designed to promote traditional Malian art. Today it houses an abundance of shops and stalls selling **crafts and curios** of variable quality – leatherwork, fabric, silverware, masks, carvings, bronze figurines and musical instruments – as well as artisans' **workshops** where you can watch woodcarvers, silversmiths, drum makers and other craftspeople at work. Prices are reasonable.

A little to the east of the crafts market, the **Grande Mosquée** was a gift to Bamako from Saudi Arabia. It's not one they can have been too enthralled by – an imposing twin-minareted dome lacking the grace of the country's indigenous Sudanic architecture.

The museums

Bamako's **Musée National**, rte de Koulouba (Tues–Sun 9am–6pm; CFA500 including tour; easily visited in a couple of hours), is housed in a low-rise building inspired by the smooth lines of Djenné's architecture and contains some remarkable masterpieces of African art. Inside, objects are beautifully displayed, with photographs discreetly lining the walls, putting the exhibits in a broader context. Lighting is subtle and the museum comfortably air-conditioned – in short, it's more than you might expect.

Something of a pioneering institution, the museum is engaged in efforts to repatriate some of the vast treasure-store of artefacts taken abroad in colonial times. They conduct research here and perodically round up materials from different parts of the country. Part of the museum concentrates on domestic objects, including those used in **forging** and **weaving** – and a large, particularly strong, section is dedicated to the techniques involved in making some of the many types of **cloth** for which the region has a wide reputation. A separate section displays religious objects from Mali's various ethnic groups. Highlights include the stylized antelope **tyiwara** (chiwara) masks of the Bamana; various **Senoufo statuary**; and, of course, the world-renowned antique **Dogon sculptures**.

Bamako's newest museum, the small but interesting **Musée Muso Kunda**, or Musée de la Femme, in Quartier Korofina on the northeast side of town (Tues–Sun 9am–6pm), is devoted to the traditional customs and dress of women from the various ethnic groups that make up Mali's population. There are displays on clothing, jewellery, hairstyles and marriage trousseaux, as well as some artisans' workshops with quality *bogolans* and crafts for sale, and a good restaurant.

Early in the twenty-first century, Bamako should also have a new **regional museum**: the building is currently under construction near the Place de la Liberté.

The zoo and botanical gardens

Bamako's **zoo** was a good idea whose time has passed. In theory, the cages and enclosures are designed to resemble closely the animals' natural habitats, but the whole place is so neglected and run-down that the best the keeper can normally do is identify cages whose inhabitants have long since expired. The surrounding **botanical gardens** are vast and, with a little attention, could provide a beautiful retreat from the city. But these too are suffering from neglect.

Point G

From the National Museum and zoo, you can walk up to the **north of the city** and to the hill known as **Point G**, the location of the main hospital. There are wonderful views from here, and some abandoned cliff dwellings featuring old **rock paintings**.

Eating and drinking

Street food is abundant in central Bamako but it's nice to get to know the locations of roadside stalls or *cafémen* who serve Nescafé and baguette breakfasts as well as meat-based snacks at other times of day. Most of the town's better **restaurants** – almost all French – are in the hotels (the *Rabelais*, *Mandé* and *Grand* have good reputations, as do *l'Amitié's* three restaurants).

Snacks and budget food

La Caverne d'Ali Baba, opposite US embassy on rue Mohammed V. Dim and uninspiring but popular breakfast/snack bar, serving drinks and light meals.

Coeur d'Afrique, rte de Sotuba opposite Shell station, Quinzambougou (☎22.69.42). Cheap meals in a courtyard; very popular with Peace Corps volunteers.

L'Escale de Jumeaux, rue 133, opposite the Catholic hostel. Cheap and friendly little shack whose affable owner offers good breakfasts and *riz gras* at rock-bottom prices.

L'Express, rte de Koulikoro, in the quartier Hippodrome. Upmarket French and Lebanese snacks. Daily till late.

Patisserie Les Delices de Bamako, rue Famolo Coulibaly. Welcoming new patisserie/restaurant with an irresistible display of cakes and pastries, plus ice cream, drinks and a long menu of light meals including omelettes, pizzas and salads. Choose between the sun-shaded terrace or the air-conditioned interior. Open 7am–midnight in the week and till 1am at weekends.

Patisserie Phoenicia, rue Mohammed V. Lebanese-owned *salon de thé* and snack bar. Fresh croissants and other pastries as well as drinks, snacks and meals. Daily 6am–midnight.

Restaurant Central, rue Loveran. Well-established formica-and-vinyl place with a small terrace outside and reasonably priced daily *plats*. Open late in the evening for meals or drinks.

Restaurant Le Relax, rte de Koulikoro near the Hippodrome (☎22.79.18). Airy patisserie/restaurant with a bright terrace; popular with the expat community. Fresh croissants and juice for breakfast, snacks and good, simple meals at any time of day. Recommended.

Restaurants

L'Akwaba, rte de Koulikoro, qtr Hippodrome. Reliably good African food, with live traditional music at weekends.

Le Bol de Jade, av Ruault. Well-established restaurant just west of Square Lumumba offering good-value Chinese and Vietnamese dishes.

Restaurant Asia, rte de Sotuba, Quinzambougou (☎22.22.48). High-quality Vietnamese cooking in plush surroundings (with prices to match).

Restaurant Djenné, off rte de Koulikoro, qtr Missira (☎22.30.82). Classy restaurant with an excellent reputation for Sahelian cuisine. There's often live traditional music (kora, balafon) in the evenings. No alcohol.

Restaurant La Pizzeria, rue Mohammed V, in front of the American embassy. Good selection of pizzas and other Italian dishes from about CFA4000. Carry-out and delivery available.

Restaurant Rive Gauche, rte de Koulikoro, opposite the *San Toro*. Affordable French and African food. Live music on Fri evenings.

San Toro, rte de Koulikoro. Slightly less expensive but no less agreeable Malian cuisine from the owners of the *Djenné*. The interior is decorated with authentic Malian artefacts and there's a pleasant garden; musicians often play live. No alcohol.

Nightlife

Bamako has a satisfying nightlife, though the action only really gets going late. The town's most famous nightspot used to be the *Hôtel Buffet de la Gare*, an early showcase for the **Rail Band**, a government-sponsored group that went on to massive stardom and launched Mali's first international superstar, **Salif Keïta**; the band still play there from time to time (generally on Saturdays). You're more or less guaranteed live music any night of the week at the *Kanaga Jazz Club* at the *Carrefour des Jeunes* on Avenue Kasse Keïta. Here there's an upstairs terrace bar where you can enjoy a beer under the stars while listening to Malian blues, Afro-Cuban dance music or reggae. Nearby is *Calao*, which advertises itself as a yuppie nightclub, but its door staff don't take this too literally.

In the centre near the cathedral, the *Black and White* packs them in almost every night, and just off Avenue du Fleuve is an upmarket disco, *L'Evasion*, a crowded weekend venue for hard-core zouk. Sleazier but much more fun, especially in the early hours, are the *Bar Bozo* and *Disco Colombo* along Avenue de la Nation. They have Malian bands on Friday and Saturday nights and there's street food and taxis outside – the latter is a good option as muggers around here prey on the inebriated and, increasingly, on the wide awake. More salubrious is *Le Tempo*, which has a garden bar and an indoor dance floor and bar/restaurant. Like everywhere else, it's busiest on Fridays and Saturdays, but the music is different every night of the week: regular sessions include a good choice of Senegalese, Cuban and Malian music, and there's also a monthly salsa night. Among the **hotel discos**, *Le Village* at the *Grand Hôtel* draws the largest crowds and features a good mix of music. East of the centre in the Niaréla district, the laser-lit *Métropolis* disco near the Métro supermarket is a favoured hangout for young Bamakois and French volunteers.

Listings

Airline offices Air Afrique, bd du 22 Octobre 1946 (☎22.58.02); Air Algérie, av Modibo Keïta/rue 324 (☎22.84.05); Air Burkina, at the *Hôtel de l'Amitié* (☎22.01.78); Air France, Immeuble SCIF, Square Lumumba (☎22.22.12); Air Guinée, at the *Hôtel de l'Amitié* (☎22.31.50); Air Ivoire, at the *Hôtel de l'Amitié* (☎22.73.84); Air Mali, Immeuble SCIF, Square Lumumba (☎22.94.00 or 22.93.94); Ethiopian Airlines, Immeuble SCIF, Square Lumumba (☎22.60.36); Ghana Airways, Square Lumumba (☎23.92.10); Sabena, 6 av Kasse Keïta (BP 2056; ☎22.71.01).

Airport Bamako-Sénou (☎22.27.04).

American Express Afric Trans Services, av Modibo Keïta (BP 2917; ☎22.44.35; *ats@malinet.ml*).

Banks Hours are typically Mon–Thurs 8am–3pm, Fri 8–11.30am. Major city centre branches include: BCEAO, qtr du Fleuve (☎22.37.57; Fax 22.47.88); BDM, av du Fleuve (☎22.20.50; Fax 22.50.85; also open Sat 8.30am–noon); BMCD, av Modibo Keïta, opposite the cathedral (☎22.53.36; Fax 22.79.50; accepts VISA cards for cash withdrawals mornings only); BIM, bd de l'Indépendance/av de la Nation (☎22.50.66; Fax 22.45.66). You can also change money at the major hotels; most don't charge commission when changing French francs cash and charge a commission similar to those of the banks on French franc travellers' cheques. It's also possible to change money in shops or on the street, which can be quick and convenient, but don't expect to save money this way.

Bookshops At the *Grand Hôtel* and the *Hôtel de l'Amitié*, each with a decent stock of books, newspapers and magazines in French and English.

Car rental Djenné Location at the *Grand Hôtel* (☎22.24.92) and Location Falaye Keïta at the *Hôtel de l'Amitié* (☎21.43.21). Expect to pay dearly.

Cinemas The nicest cinemas are at the *Hôtel de l'Amitié* and the Palais de la Culture (on the south side of the Niger). Apart from being the most comfortable, they also have screenings of recent releases.

Cultural centres The Centre Cultural Français, bd de l'Indépendance, has a café/bar and a good library including French newspapers and magazines: temporary membership is available. They also organize exhibitions, movies, concerts and events. Similar activities are arranged at USIS – the American cultural centre opposite the embassy.

Embassies and consulates Algeria, rte Aéroport, Daoudabougou (BP 02; ☎20.51.76; Fax 22.93.74); **Burkina Faso**, rue 224, north of the rte de Koulikoro, Hippodrome (BP 9022; ☎22.31.71; Fax 21.92.66); **Canada**, rte de Koulikoro (BP 198; ☎21.22.36; Fax 22.43.62); **Côte d'Ivoire**, Square Lumumba (BP 3644; ☎22.03.89; Fax 21.13.76); **European Union**, av OUA, Badalabougou-Est (BP 115; ☎22.20.65; Fax 22.36.70); **France**, Square Lumumba (BP 17; ☎22.29.51 or 22.30.48; Fax 22.31.36); **Guinea**, Immeuble Saidou Maiga, Quartier du Fleuve (BP 118; ☎22.29.75); **Mauritania**, rte de Koulikoro, Hippodrome (BP 135; ☎22.48.15; Fax 22.49.08); **Morocco**, av OUA, Badalabougou-Est (BP 2013; ☎22.21.23; Fax 22.77.87); **Nigeria**, south of the Pont des Martyrs, Badalabougou-Est (BP 57; ☎22.57.71; Fax 22.52.84); **Senegal**, 341 rue 287, av Nelson Mandela, Hippodrome (☎21.82.74; Fax 21.17.80); **UK Honorary Consul**, J. Chaloner, American School of Bamako (BP 34; ☎22.47.38; Fax 22.08.53); **USA**, rue de Rochester/rue Mohammed V (BP 34; ☎22.56.63 or 22.54.70; Fax 22.37.12).

Internet *Spider Cybercafé*, bureau A8/A9, behind Elf station, rue 247, off rte de Koulikoro (BP E1693; ☎21.23.02; *cybercafe@spider.toolnet.org*).

Maps The Direction Nationale de Cartographie, av de la Nation, is the place to go for 1:200,000 survey maps.

Post and telephones The *poste centrale* (Mon–Fri 7.30am–5.30pm, Sat 8am–noon) is on rue Karamoko Diaby, not far from the market. There's a reliable poste restante service here. Dotted around town are payphones which take phonecards. Alternatively, calls can be made (at higher rates) from one of the telephone offices where you make your call in a booth and pay afterwards for the units used.

Supermarkets At the eastern end of the city, where most of the expat community live. The Metro is 2.5km along rte de Sotuba, in Niaréla, next to the Shell station, and the *Fourni* and *Azar Libre Service* are an agonizingly similar distance from the centre along the rte de Koulikoro, near *Le Relax* restaurant.

Swimming pools In the centre of town, *l'Amitié* has a decent pool: non-residents can swim here for CFA2000. The pools at the *Grand* are small, but okay for cooling off; the one at the *Mandé* has the best setting.

Overlanders' convoy, Mauritania

Shipwreck, Nouadhibou, Mauritania

Road sign, Mauritania

Great Mosque, Touba, Senegal

Fula herder, Senegal

Beach scene, Banjul, The Gambia

Albert market, Banjul, The Gambia

Crossing the River Bani near Djenné, Mali

Masked dancers, Tirelli, Dogon Country, Mali

Sanga village, Dogon Country, Mali

MOVING ON FROM BAMAKO

By road
Bush taxis (covering short distances) and **long-distance buses** run by Kénédougou Voyages (for Sikasso; ☎62.07.19) and COMATRA (for Sikasso, Mopti and Bandiagara; ☎22.03.48), leave from Bamako's **gare routière**, south of the river. SOMATRA buses (☎22.38.96) leave from their own well-organized terminal on the opposite side of the same main road to: San (daily); Djenné (Sat); Mopti (daily); Gao (Mon–Thurs); Sikasso (several daily); Ségou (several daily); Koutiala (daily); and Bobo-Dioulasso (Tues–Thurs). There are also **two smaller autogares** in Bamako: one, serving Nara, behind the Grande Mosquée, and another, for Nioro, at the Nouveau Marché by the Stade Omnisport.

By train
The **train to Dakar** leaves Bamako on Wednesday and Saturday mornings at 9.15am, though it's wise to be there at 7am having reserved the day before. Wednesdays are preferable, since this is when the marginally more comfortable Senegalese train runs. The trip takes 36hr. You can get sleeping berths, but it's barely worth it due to disturbances at the border in the dead of night. It's also possible to put cars on a goods train to avoid the *pistes* that link Mali and Senegal but this is an expensive and complicated way to go about things.

Daily trains also leave for **Kayes** in the west (11hr by the international express, 12hr "local" service; departs 7.15am Mon, Tues, Thurs, Fri & Sun), which stops at many stations en route including **Kita** and **Mahina**. Kita is also served by a slow train which leaves at 3.30pm daily (5hr). Another line runs to **Koulikoro** to the east of Bamako (daily, 2hr) – the main embarkation point for the Niger River ferries.

Approximate first and second class **fares** from Bamako are: to Dakar, CFA29,000 (1st)/CFA22,000 (2nd); to Kayes, CFA10,000 (1st)/CFA6000 (2nd); to Mahina, CFA8000 (1st)/CFA6000 (2nd); to Kita, CFA4000 (1st)/CFA2500 (2nd). For the latest schedules and price information stop by the station, or contact the Régie du Chemin de Fer du Mali (RCFM), rue Kasse Keïta (BP 260; ☎22.59.67; Fax 22.54.33).

By boat
Ferries to Gao depart from **Koulikoro**, 60km from Bamako. Rapids between the two towns make it impossible to travel directly by water from the capital and you must take the train or a taxi to get around them. Boats from Koulikoro operate when the rains swell the river to a suitable level, roughly from late July or early August until November (for further details). For reservations (get them early, especially for 2nd and 3rd class) and up-to-date information on departures, contact the office of the Compagnie Malienne de Navigation (CMN; BP 150; ☎22.38.02; Mon–Thurs 7.30am–2.30pm, Sat 7.30am–12.30pm), bd du 22 Octobre 1946, on the riverbank across from the Tour BCEAO. You could also try calling the head office in Koulikoro on ☎26.20.34.

CMN can also give you information on **barges to Guinea**, which theoretically operate between August and December (or when the water level permits), although the service is currently suspended (see p.520). If you do manage to make the trip, the 385-kilometre journey to Kankan lasts about five days – a period entirely devoid of creature comforts since the boats were designed to transport cargo, not people. If you can put yourself in the right frame of mind, however, it's a cheap and exciting way to travel.

By plane
Theoretically, Mopti, Goundam, Timbuktu and Gao (in the north and east) and Kayes, Yelimané and Nioro (in the west) are served by at least one Air Mali **flight** a week, though these are frequently delayed or cancelled, and schedules should be taken with a pinch of salt. Departures for **Timbuktu** are currently timetabled for Tues, Thurs and Sat, returning the next day (CFA69,000 one-way); for **Kayes**, Mon, Thurs, Sat and Sun, returning the same day (CFA45,000 one-way); and for **Gao**, Tues, returning the next day (CFA100,000 one-way). The departure tax for internal flights is CFA2500. For more details contact Air Mali (see opposite).

Travel agents Agents are useful if you're looking to rent a 4WD vehicle and driver, or to join an organized tour. Common tour destinations are Djenné, Mopti, Timbuktu and the Dogon country, though some companies will also offer visits to Ségou and the Manding Highlands, and cruises on the Niger. Try ATS, av Modibo Keïta (☎22.44.35; Fax 22.94.50; *ats@malinet.ml*), Bani Voyages, av Modibo Keïta, near the *Hôtel Lac Debo* (☎23.26.03; Fax 23.44.74), or TAM Voyages, Square Lumumba (BP 932; ☎21.92.10; Fax 21.05.47; *tamvoyages@cefib.com*).

Visa extensions These are available at the Sûreté Nationale on the av de la Nation (Mon–Thurs 8am–2pm, Fri & Sat 7.30am–12.30pm).

KAYES AND THE WEST

Often ignored by travellers due to its poor transport connections, rough roads and inaccessibility during the rainy season, **western Mali** contains some of the country's most beautiful scenery and easily rewards travellers with their own robust vehicles or footloose adventurers with time and patience on their hands. It's a region of remote villages, wooded escarpments and rivers where the Baoulé, Bakoye and Bafing rivers rush from the **Manding Highlands** through the hilly landscapes of the **Malinké country** before joining forces to form the **Senegal River**. It's also the best place to encounter some of Mali's **wildlife**: warthogs, baboons and iridescent-blue kingfishers prosper in this isolated but prolific district. The region is also historically significant, for it was the heartland of the thirteenth-century **Mali kingdom** which expanded into a vast empire incorporating Djenné, Timbuktu and distant Gao.

The Senegal flows through the realm of the Fula-speaking **Tukulor** people, which extends west from **Kayes** – the regional capital and an isolated commercial centre of 50,000 people serving the region's mining ventures. The more commonly used *piste* from Kayes to Bamako passes through the town of **Nioro du Sahel** close to the Mauritanian border, after which it deteriorates still further.

South of Kayes, **Keniéba** is a remote outpost serving local gold mining activities and a dead end unless you plan to undertake the infrequently used backcountry crossings into Guinea or Senegal.

Kayes

KAYES is an agreeable riverside town and western Mali's principal administrative centre, which until the early part of this century served as capital of the Haut Sénégal-Niger colony, until the seat was transferred to Bamako when the train line pushed through from Dakar. Today it has the dubious honour of being Africa's hottest town, with afternoon temperatures between March and May crackling into the high forties Celsius.

Kayes is of most use as a transportation hub, with a **daily train** link to Bamako which slowly crosses the scenic west Manding Highlands in daylight. It is also the best place to seek out transport into parts of the region not served by the train.

Practicalities

The train station is on a rise southeast of the town centre. If you have arrived on the train from Dakar, you should head straight for the **Commissariat Special** next to the station to get your passport stamped. Several taxis greet the train's 3am arrival, but unless you're planning to catch the 7.15am slow train to Bamako (in which case bed down on the platform with the rest) you've only a few **accommodation** options. The *Hôtel du Rail* (☎52.12.33; ④) directly opposite the station, may have long passed its colonial-era heyday but still offers a certain faded splendour with spacious S/C rooms and suites, a restaurant/bar and another bar set in the garden out front. The rooms at

---

MOVING ON FROM KAYES

The obvious form of transport out of Kayes is the **train to Bamako** (daily express and local trains take 11 or 12 hours; CFA6000–11,500; advance booking advisable) or **Dakar**. If heading towards **Senegal**, you may consider taking the train only as far as **Tambacounda** (6hr), from where travel to the coast by bush taxi is quicker and cheaper. If you're **driving**, it's just over 100km through light baobab woodlands to the border post at **Diboli** where a new road bridge spans the Faléme River and leads straight into the flyblown Senegalese town of **Kidira**. If **Mauritania** is your destination, ask around in Kayes Ndi market (on the north side of the river) for vehicles heading for **Sélibabi**, just 160km to the northwest, or **Kiffa** on the Nouakchott highway.

In theory at least, four weekly Air Mali **flights** serve Kayes: on Thursday mornings, there's a flight from Bamako to Kayes which then returns to Bamako via Yélimané, and on Saturday mornings there's a flight from Bamako via Kéniéba to Kayes, then back to Bamako direct.

Because of the lamentable state of the "main road" between Kayes and **Bamako via Nioro du Sahel**, few people make the journey in a bush taxi. The rarely used track following the railway line **direct to Bamako** is occasionally rocky rather than sandy. Both routes are occasionally tackled by adventurous travellers on mountain bikes or motorbikes.

---

the newer *Hôtel Calderon* (②), also right by the station, aren't bad. At the adequate *L'Amical* (②), a few blocks from the market in the town centre and about 2km from the station, rooms have nets and a fan, and there's a shared bathroom, a shaded garden and a food stall across the road. Cheaper is the *Centre d'Accueil de la Jeunesse* (☎52.12.54; ②), a short 300m walk from the station (head towards town and turn left), where you can take a basic room or camp outside.

Except for the *Hôtel du Rail*'s mediocre restaurant, budget restaurants are thin on the ground – **street food** is the easiest alternative to feeding yourself at the large **market**. Kayes has a post office, airstrip, several pharmacies and three banks: the BMCD (Mon–Thurs 8am–3pm, Fri–Sat 8–11am) changes currency and accepts Visa.

Kéniéba

South of Kayes, a corrugated *piste* follows the **Falaise de Tambaoura** for 240km to the small town of **Kéniéba**, caught in a suntrap by a bend in the Tambaoura's towering cliffs. As this is the jumping-off point for the joint Russo-Malian **mining ventures** nearby, the kids here are more likely to greet a white face with a cry of "Russe!" than the usual "toubab!"

The women in this region have collected **gold** from the bush for centuries – local legends tell of their ostensibly destitute husbands having amassed several kilos of gold during a lifetime, preferring to hoard their cache rather than convert it into tangible wealth. These days Russian technicians stop at Kéniéba to purchase booze and other services available at the town's bar before heading out to the mining camps near Dombia. Kéniéba's frontier-town isolation and proximity to the Senegalese and Guinean borders make it something of a smuggling entrepôt for duty free cigarettes and alcohol coming in from Guinea, just 60km away.

Practicalities

Air Mali operates – in theory at least – a Saturday morning **flight** from Bamako to Kéniéba, which then continues on to Kayes and back to Bamako. Coming from Kayes by **road** may take a bit of perseverance. The section from Kayes to Sadiola isn't too bad, but south of here it's very rough *piste*. Your best bet is to ask around in Kayes for any Russian trucks which make the bumpy, six-hour journey every few days. You'll have to pay, but if you're lucky enough to be offered a front seat rather than a sack in the back, you'll enjoy some fine views on the way down.

The friendly and informal Ghanaian-run *Bar Mandela* (①) on the town's main street provides inexpensive, *campement*-style accommodation with "draw-your-own" well water, lanterns at night and not-so-cheap meals, depending on what's available at the small **market** at the end of the road. Down here you'll find a post office, some small stores and another, unmarked, hotel. The town also has a regional hospital and a couple of petrol stations.

Ask at the Total station, or the Land Rover garage around the back, if you're interested in lifts to **Guinea and Senegal**. Every Tuesday a truck is said to leave from the *centre transportique* opposite the post office for some illicit trading at Kali on the Guinea border, returning on Friday. If you head this way expect the unexpected on the Guinean side and have money, *cadeaux* and time to spare.

Rides to **Kédougou** in Senegal are dependent on enough passengers to fill up a Land Rover and the depth of the Falémé River (usually crossable from January till the rains resume) which marks the unstaffed frontier. If nothing turns up after a couple of days' wait in Kéniéba and you don't want to head back to Kayes, consider renting a **motorbike** (plus rider; ask for the mechanics near the market). Although twice the price of a shared 4WD, it's a memorable if no less uncomfortable six-hour ride along winding bush tracks into Senegal's Pays Bassari region.

Between Kayes and Bamako

In the dry season, the route to Bamako via **Nioro**, close to the Mauritanian border, is more travelled than the direct route via Kita, but both routes, and particularly the one via Nioro, are frequently impassable in the rainy season.

To Bamako via Nioro du Sahel

Between Kayes and Nioro lies a great region for exploration in your own suitably equipped vehicle. The whole district is beautiful, with impressive baobabs, roamed through by Fula herders. But the rough bush tracks are in a state of advanced disrepair and any kind of transport and facilities almost non-existent.

In recent years, there has been an emerald rush in the area of **Sandaré** (144km east of Kayes on the main *piste*), with hundreds of hopeful miners flocking to the area of Angoulá, living in improvised camps near the mines. You are certain to be offered emeralds for sale here. The most worthwhile diversion, however, is to **Yélimané**, turning left off the main *piste* 83km east of Kayes, and driving 68km north. Twenty kilometres or so before reaching Yélimané, there's a marshy area called **Goumbogo** that is highly recommended if you're interested in wildlife. From Yélimané you can make a 45-kilometre trip to the **Mare de Toya**, a spectacular geological rift and lake forming part of the Mauritanian frontier. There are twice-weekly flights (Mon and Thurs) from Yélimané to Bamako if you need civilization quickly (the Monday flight stops at Nioro).

From Yélimané, enquire about the condition of the 134-kilometre direct route from there to Nioro. Back on the main Kayes–Nioro *piste*, it's 168km from the Yélimané junction to Nioro, via Sandaré.

NIORO DU SAHEL is a seventeenth-century town built on a plateau and is famed for its **mosque**, one of the most important in Mali. Nioro has a police and customs post, petrol stations, a bank, a pharmacy, a hospital and an airstrip (flights to and from Bamako on Mon and Thurs) but **accommodation** is limited to a frugal *campement* (①). Nioro is a common departure point for **Mauritania**, but traffic along the 212-kilometre *piste* to Ayoun el Atrous is thin at the best of times and can dwindle to nothing in the rainy season between July and October. Check for trucks around the marketplace.

If you're driving to Bamako, you can bypass Nioro and save nearly 100km by forking east at Sandaré for Diéma, but ask at Sandaré about road conditions before taking this deviation.

There is a significant deterioration in the road for the last 430km from Nioro to the capital and if you are in a low clearance vehicle expect plenty of deviations and some digging. Just after Diéma the *piste* passes through the **Vallée du Serpent** named for the **Baoulé River**'s tortuous course as it snakes down from the Manding Highlands. The route marked on the Michelin map from Diéma to Didiéni can be very difficult, and you may need to go via Dioumara, 50km to the east of Diéma.

The route of the Baoulé River forms the northern borders of the **Parc National de la Boucle du Baoulé** – 3300 square kilometres of wooded savannah and forest, which once harboured a significant animal population, including antelope, buffalo, warthogs, giraffe and even lions. Today, however, practically all of the wildlife has been hunted out of the park, and the dearth of animals, combined with the fact that the park has virtually no infrastructure, have resulted in the park no longer being worth a visit.

To Bamako via Kita

The railway line **between Kayes and Bamako** passes through a scenic area of hills and wooded escarpments – a welcome change from the bleak Senegalese plains. The west-flowing **Bakoye** and **Senegal rivers** run parallel to the tracks for a good part of the journey, thrashing into rough rapids at several points along their courses. The lowest of these rapids are the **Chutes de Felou**, just 10km east of Kayes, but slightly disappointing since a hydroelectric dam was built by the French further upriver. The more spectacular **Chutes de Gouina** are 65km further upstream, towards Bamako, but even with a 4WD can be hard to get to.

The Bafing and Bakoye rivers converge to form the Senegal at **BAFOULABÉ**, about 130km east of Kayes. The town, 3km north of **Mahina** where the train stops, has a small market and a *campement* (②). An interesting detour eighty kilometres to the south is **MANANTALI**, perched on the northern point of a vast lake formed by the damming of the Bafing (you can still see the remains of submerged trees and buildings beneath the surface). It's a scenic spot favoured by development workers as a place to swim and hippo-watch. There's good cooking and accommodation in well-kept AC cabins available at *La Cité des Cadres* (③).

Leaving Bafoulabé, drivers share the long rail bridge across the Bafing river and continue 200km east to Kita. Just east of Bafoulabé are the **Chutes de Kale**, followed in turn by the **Chutes de Billy**, 270km short of Bamako. Unfortunately, none of these rapids is visible from the train, and you do need your own transport to get off the road that crisscrosses the railway line to get near them. If you're on the train, you'll welcome the extended lunch stop at **Toukoto**, 67km short of Kita, where plenty of cooked and fresh food is brought to the train.

Roughly midway between Kayes and Bamako, **KITA** is one of the former capitals of Sundiata Keïta's medieval Mali empire, and if you're into Malian **music** it's a good place to stop over a night or two as many traditional griots hail from around here. The *Hôtel Le Relais Touristique* (☎57.30.94; ③–④) is a clean and comfortable place with S/C rooms (some with AC and satellite TV) in a pleasant garden compound that includes a restaurant, a small bar-nightclub, and a pool (filled March–June); from the station, walk straight ahead down the station road to the main road, and it's signposted from there. Kita's other **accommodation** options are more basic: *chambres de passage* (①) are available at the station, and there's also a *campement* outside the centre (BP 43; ☎57.30.45; ②). For good inexpensive food you could try *L'Oasis* (*Chez Issa*), in the centre, which offers basic meals on the terrace, or *Restaurant Appia*, on the station road, which serves excellent rice and sauce. *Restaurant Mandela*, a flyblown *gargote* in the centre, is open all hours but is particularly good for breakfast.

Mont Kita Kourou, with caves decorated with rock paintings, rises impressively west of Kita. For the adventurous and independently mobile, a deteriorating track leads 140km southwest to the rarely visited **Bafing National Park**, close to the Guinean border. Wildlife is scarce here, due to intensive hunting, but there are a few chimpanzees and other primates.

The **train** for Bamako passes through Kita every afternoon; there's also a local train which starts its journey here at 5am and arrives in Bamako anything between five and eight hours later. If you're **driving** from Kita to Bamako, expect some confusion in correctly locating the main *piste*, especially when entering and leaving small villages with their various secondary tracks.

SÉGOU AND AROUND

Between Bamako and the Delta Region lies a broad expanse of territory where numerous kingdoms rose to power after the demise of the Songhai Empire. Most important were the **Bamana Empire** of Ségou and the **Kénédougou Empire** in the **Senoufo country**, with **Sikasso** its capital. Although they were eclipsed almost as quickly as they sprang up, these towns have remained commercially important thanks to their positions on well-travelled routes, and all are interlinked with daily bus or bush taxi services.

Ségou

The second largest town in Mali, **SÉGOU**, 240km northeast of Bamako, makes a very pleasant stopover between Bamako and Mopti. It was capital of a vast empire in the eighteenth century, and more recently became an important French outpost and headquarters of the Office du Niger – an irrigation scheme originally planned for the exploitation of cotton. Reminders of the colonial period still stand out in graceful administrative buildings in the neo-Sudanic style, especially at the west end of town. Traditional Bamana architecture has also held its own against more modern and easily maintained cement buildings, and today whole districts of this quiet tree-lined town are filled with rust-coloured *banco* houses. Away from the busy **market** (the main day is Monday), much of the modern activity focuses on the banks of the **Niger**, with its *pirogues* and crowds. The town also has a thriving community of artisans, including cotton weavers, *bogolan* artists, rug makers and potters.

Some history
The **kingdom of Ségou** had its roots in the seventeenth century, when a Bamana chief, Kaladian Coulibaly, brought his people to settle in the area. In 1620 his son established the village of Ségou-Koro (old Ségou, also known by the Bambara name of Sékoro), about 10km from the present town. In 1712 the able and despotic **Biton Mamary Coulibaly**, widely considered the true founder of the kingdom, became *fama* (king). The army he formed carved out a huge kingdom stretching from Timbuktu to the banks of the Senegal River, and the enemy soldiers captured during the conquests were marched to ports in Senegal and Ghana where they were traded with slavers for firearms. Along with the Songhai to the north, the Ségou Empire was one of the earliest in the Sahara to obtain guns, which were used effectively to subdue rival powers.

The Ségou rulers developed a **nationalist policy** where all rights were accorded to loyal Bamana subjects but the conquered peoples were excluded from the system altogether. It was a tenuous situation based purely on force of arms, and when the Fula empire of Masina arose in the northeast, disgruntled elements in the Bamana country rallied to it, assuring the demise of Ségou. In 1861, El Hadj Omar conquered Ségou and

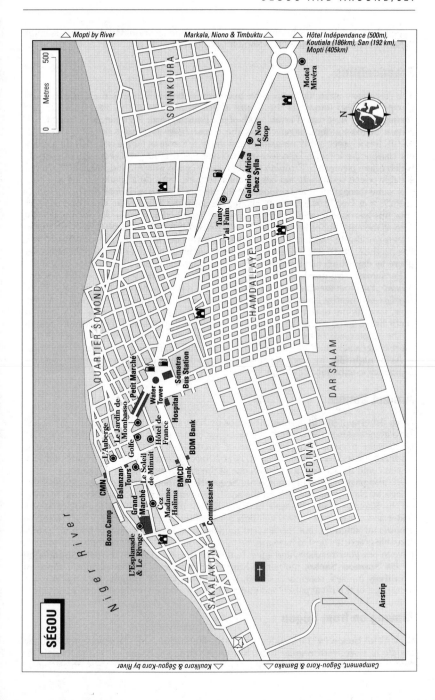

SÉGOU

Niger River

△ Mopti by River

Markala, Niono & Timbuktu △

△ Hôtel Indépendance (500m),
Koutiala (186km), San (192 km),
Mopti (405km)

Motel
Mivéra

Le Non
Stop

Galerie Africa
Chez Sylla

Tanty
J'ai Faim

SONNKOURA

QUARTIER SOMOND

HAMDALLAYE

DAR SALAM

MEDINA

SAKALAKONO

Bozo Camp

CMN

Balanzan
Tours

Grand
Marché

Le Soleil
de Minuit

Cez
Madame
Halima

L'Esplanade
& Le Rivage

L'Auberge

Le Jardin de
Mombasso

Golfe

Hôtel de
France

Petit Marché

Water
Tower

Somatra
Bus Station

Hospital

BDM Bank

BMCD
Bank

Commissariat

Airstrip

Metres
0   500

N

▽ Kouilikoro & Ségou-Koro by River

▽ Koulikoro, Ségou-Koro & Bamako

Campement, Ségou-Koro & Bamako

forced the inhabitants – who had remained one of the few **non-Muslim** groups in the Sahel – to convert to **Islam**. The French took the city in 1892.

Practicalities

The customary place for inexpensive **accommodation** in Ségou is the *Office du Niger Campement*, also known as the *Centre d'Accueil* (☎32.03.92; ②), 3km from the *gare routière* at the west end of town, south of the Bamako road. It's quiet, with fanned, S/C rooms. Ségou's other budget choice, the *Grand Hôtel de France* (BP 207; ☎32.03.15; ②–③), has a rather seedy reputation, and thirty S/C rooms (some with AC). In a different class is the friendly, Lebanese-owned *L'Auberge* (BP 400; ☎ & Fax 32.01.45; ③–④), which offers pleasant S/C rooms with hot water (some with AC and satellite TV), a reasonably priced restaurant and bar (popular with expats), and a shady garden and pool. The same management are responsible for the newly renovated *Hôtel de l'Indépendance* (BP 27; ☎ & Fax 32.04.62; ③–④), about 5km down the Mopti road. Quiet and comfortable, this has good-size S/C rooms and suites, again with hot water, AC and satellite TV. Also at the east end of town is the *Motel Mivéra* (32.03.31; ④) with all the charisma of motels worldwide. Back in the centre, the new riverside *Hôtel de l'Esplanade* (BP 27; ☎ & Fax 32.01.27; ③–④) has rooms to suit a variety of budgets, though a rather bleak atmosphere by day, which turns rowdy at weekends when the nightclub hots up downstairs.

For inexpensive **meals** fresh from a spotless kitchen, the best choice is *Le Soleil du Minuit* (it's sometimes possible to lodge here, too, if there's room). The food at the *Snack-Bar Le Golfe*, nearby, isn't outstanding, but it's a popular place nonetheless. A little further west, towards the mosque, is *Cez* (sic) *Madame Halima*, a small *gargote* with down-to-earth dishes for next to nothing, and table football while you wait. There are more options on the Mopti road: *Tanty J'ai Faim* is a reasonable bet for hefty servings of basic stodge; more congenial is the *Non Stop* with fine pizzas, plus *capitaine* and the usual standards.

As for **nightlife**, the *Jardin de Mombasso*, a garden bar/grill, hosts live music, and the *Esplanade*'s nightclub, *Le Rivage*, packs in the crowds at weekends.

Around Ségou

Bozo fishermen live in permanent camps on both sides of the Niger near Ségou, and have done so since the seventh century, long before the town was founded. It's possible to take a guided trip by *pirogue* or *pinasse* to visit their **riverbank villages**; Balanzan Tours (BP 402; ☎32.02.57), near *L'Auberge*, can make arrangements for you, or you could try striking a deal with one of the *piroguiers* down on the shore.

It's also possible to cruise upriver to **Ségou-Koro**, though it's more usual to visit this village by car or *mobylette*; it's on the south bank of the river about 10km out of town, off the Bamako road. The scale of Ségou-Koro – it's small enough to explore in well under an hour on foot – gives you little sense of the fact that this was once the seat of a powerful kingdom, but the ancient mud-brick and *banco* buildings have an unmistakeable grace. It's best to have a guide to show you round the village (in any case you'll have to pay your respects, and a fee, to the chief); sights include the delicate **mosque of Ba Sounou Sacko**, mother of King Biton Mamary Coulibaly, and the **tomb of Coulibaly** himself, recently restored. Look out too for the **ancient tree** that was the focal point of the royal palace and under which the council of elders sat.

Moving on from Ségou

SOMATRA **buses** (☎32.02.66) leave from the bus station behind the water tower in the middle of town, with regular departures westwards for **Bamako**, and eastwards for **Mopti** via San and Sévaré. Buses from Bamako to **Djenné** pass through Ségou on

Saturday evenings and you can get on if there's space, but a much more reliable way to get to Djenné is to charter a vehicle. Buses also head from Ségou to **Sikasso** in the south. If you're leaving the country, there is a weekly bus to Bobo-Dioulasso in **Burkina Faso**; an alternative route is to take a bus to San or Koutiala and pick up a connection there. For **Côte d'Ivoire**, make for Sikasso.

In the rainy season, you can of course travel **by boat to Koulikoro** (port of call for Bamako) or all the way up to **Gao**. The CMN ferry office (BP 13; ☎32.02.04) overlooks the jetty in Ségou. For more information on the river boats, see p.299.

If you're en route from Ségou south or east in your own vehicle, you might want to stop overnight some 40km from Ségou at **ZINZANA**, where the excellent *campement* (②–③) at the agricultural research station is a haven of peace and tranquillity – spotless sheets, vine-shaded terrace, cold beer and good food.

To Timbuktu by road

During the dry season, it's possible to zigzag all the way across the Niger delta **to Timbuktu** by a network of tracks. Although this involves tackling long stretches of tortuous *piste* and occasional muddy river crossings, it allows you to take in fascinating scenery along a little-travelled route. This short account assumes you'll be using your own 4WD vehicle, though given time you could achieve this with available local transport.

From Ségou, take the northern road to Markala, and then follow the road to Massina, 105km further. This route passes through the old city of **Sansanding**, "the great marketplace of the Western Sudan" according to the nineteenth-century scholar, Heinrich Barth. From Massina, you can make an interesting side trip, 44km to **Diafarabé**, a small village located on one of the narrowest points of the Niger (see box, below).

From Massina, tracks lead north towards Nampala, also accessible directly from Ségou via Niono passing lush green fields of **irrigated rice**. It's 90km from Nampala to Léré, a small village with a Friday **livestock market** that unites herders from all over the region – and another 136km across mud-cracked lagoons to the town of Niafounké, whose most famous resident is virtuoso musician Ali Farka Touré. Accommodation is available at Niafounké's small *campement*. A ferry crosses the river here, making it possible to connect with the road leading to Korientze and back south to Mopti. Alternatively, you can continue 90km northeast to the Songhai town of Goundam. An increasingly sandy track requiring 4WD then leads over the remaining 100km to the dunes surrounding **Timbuktu**.

Bla, San and Koutiala

Southeast of Ségou, the main road divides at the junction town of **BLA**, with the N6 continuing northeast to San and Mopti and the N12 heading south to Koutiala and Sikasso.

THE DIAFARABÉ CATTLE CROSSING

In December, **Fula herders** descend en masse on the village of Diafarabé – and several others at narrow crossing points in the vicinity – as they lead their cattle from the northern Sahel grazing grounds to the southern banks of the Niger to await the return of the rains in May or June. The spectacle of thousands of **cattle** crashing into the water and swimming to the other side as herders prod them along is memorable indeed. Music and festivities accompany the event, but there's no set date. Ask around in Ségou if you think you might be there about the right time.

Diafarabé is190km northeast of Ségou on the north bank. There's a very small ferry here. The town has an interesting old quarter between the market and the river, with an attractive, modern, Sudanic-style mosque. You can stay at the basic *campement* (①).

Drivers often make a stop at Bla to eat at one of the roadside *gargotes*, and there's basic accommodation here at *Le Refuge* (②).

SAN is an important commercial crossroads on the main road to Burkina Faso and Côte d'Ivoire, and a chief departure point for both places. The town **market**, best on Monday, is the largest in the region, trading in everything from livestock to agricultural produce and imported goods. There's no real reason to spend time here on any other day, but if you need to **stay**, try the rooms at the *Campement Teriya* (②). Basic **food** can be had at the *Snack-Bar Le Golfe*, just outside town on the road to Mopti.

KOUTIALA, like San, is an exit point for travellers to Bobo-Dioulasso, and is also a staging post between Sikasso and Ségou or Mopti. There's a bank here, and if you overnight it, you can stay comfortably at *Le Cotonnier* (②).

Sikasso and around

SIKASSO, Mali's southernmost town, was the last capital of the **Kénédougou Empire**, a kingdom founded by Dioula traders in the seventeenth century. Sikasso itself wasn't founded until the nineteenth century, and is traditionally a largely Senoufo town. A warrior named **Tieba** became ruler of the mini-empire in 1876, and he transformed Sikasso – his mother's birthplace – from a tiny agricultural village into a fortified capital, expanding his empire and developing trade. During the same period, the Malinké warlord **Samory Touré** was expanding his influence in the region, and thus came into conflict with the Senoufo, destroying the town of Kong and Senoufo strongholds in present-day Côte d'Ivoire, like Korhogo and Ferkessédougou. Samory laid siege to Sikasso in 1887 but fifteen months later the city had not fallen, and soon after Tieba received support from a new invasion force, the French, under Binger. Tieba died in battle in 1893, leaving his son, Babemba, as ruler. But Babemba fell out with the French and they attacked and routed Sikasso in 1898. Babemba committed suicide; his erstwhile enemy, Samory Touré, was captured by the French and sent into captivity in Gabon where he died.

The town grew to become a colonial outpost, as the decaying administrative buildings from that era attest. Few reminders are left of the bloodier history, but you can still see remnants of the fortifications – known as *tata* – that, despite their impressive size, couldn't hold out against the onslaught of the French.

Today this evergreen town drips with a humid tropical languor in which cotton and market produce flourish. Its proximity to Côte d'Ivoire assures a good deal of international activity, centred around the **market**, impressive on any day of the week but enormous on Sundays, and outstanding for its fresh fruit and vegetables. The market aside, the town has few obvious "sights"; it is, rather, Sikasso's gentle, welcoming atmosphere and verdant surroundings that make it so appealing. One place worth a visit is the **Galerie Kéné Arts** (daily except Thurs 8am–noon & 2–6pm), an artisans' co-operative selling jewellery, fabrics, leatherwork, masks and carvings; it's behind the Bank of Africa.

Practicalities

Sikasso's **autogare** is 1500m south of the town centre on the road to Ferkessédougou. For travellers who are just changing vehicles at Sikasso there are *chambres de passage* (①) available here or over the road at the *Solo Khan Hôtel* (☎62.00.52; ②), both of which are just about bearable if desperate.

The best **hotel** in Sikasso is the recently opened *Hôtel Panier de la Ménagère* (☎ & Fax 62.05.34; ③–④), on the north side of town on the old Koutiala road (signposted from the centre), which has secure, comfortable rooms, mostly S/C with AC and satel-

ONWARDS FROM SIKASSO

The best buses to Bamako or Mopti are operated by Kénédougou Voyages (☎60.07.19). The journey to **Bamako** via Bougouni takes around five hours (several daily; CFA3000); for **Mopti** via Koutiala, San and Sévaré, allow 10–11 hours (one daily). For **Ségou**, it's best to take the direct bus (one daily at 8.30am; CFA3000) operated by Somatri. Heading south, there are departures for **Ferkessédougou** and **Abidjan** in Côte d'Ivoire (daily). If you're heading for **Bobo-Dioulasso**, the Somatri bus leaves Sikasso each day at 10am and costs CFA3500 for the 4–5hr journey.
  Bus tickets can be bought the day before departure.

lite TV. More central is the *Hôtel Mamelon* (☎62.00.44; Fax 62.04.40; ③), which has plain S/C, AC rooms with TV, and a good restaurant. Less expensive options, both on the Bamako road, are the *Hôtel Tata* (☎62.04.11; ③), with decent rooms but a noisy location, and the *Hôtel Lotio* (②), a grubby, slightly seedy bar, but friendly enough, with fanned rooms and shared facilities.

For French and Malian **food** served in a pleasant garden setting, *Le Wassoulou*, on the new Koutiala road, is highly recommended; arrange a return taxi if you plan on making the trip out. Less upmarket and also a good bet is the *Bar-Restaurant Chez Les Amis*, a quiet, friendly place, serving excellent standards such as *couscous*, *capitaine*, and *poulet kédgénou* in a garden shaded with trees; it's off the old Koutiala road, about 200m from the *Hôtel Panier de la Ménagère*. There are a number of basic eating places near the *autogare* and on the Bamako road, but best of all is the central, small and friendly *Restaurant Kassonke*, which serves rice and sauce for CFA200–250 and grilled meat for CFA300.

Sikasso has a **post office** and two **banks** – Bank of Africa and BNDA, with a new branch of BCEAO under construction at the time of writing. There is 24-hour fuel at the Total garage on the Bamako road.

Around Sikasso

About 16km south of Sikasso, inside a cathedral-like limestone outcrop jutting up from the plain, are the **Grottes de Missirikoro**, home to colonies of bats, some tribal relics, and a latter-day cave-dweller. You can clamber up the outcrop itself by means of ladders and chains for a 360-degree view of the surrounding wooded plains. A taxi to the caves and back should cost around CFA6000 including waiting time. Take a torch to illuminate the gloomy recesses, and some kola nuts to offer to the caves' lone resident.

The **Chutes de Farako**, 30km east of Sikasso (take the N10 towards the Burkina border), are particularly impressive in the rainy season and can be visited in a day. There are smaller but equally picturesque waterfalls some 15km south of town, which are a favourite retreat of Sikasso's Peace Corps volunteers; the pool here is deep enough to swim in.

MOPTI AND THE DELTA REGION

The Niger's extraordinary **inland delta** is one of the most compelling places in West Africa, and bound to leave a lasting impression. As the Niger slows and spreads into hundreds of channels and lagoons it passes near medieval towns like **Djenné** and **Timbuktu** – once renowned as centres of commercial prosperity and Islamic piety. Today their economic importance has been overshadowed by the more accessible and frequently visited **Mopti**, with its bustling port. If you are prepared to explore away

---

By far the most fascinating way to travel through the region is by steamer, an option that requires a bit of planning. Ferries operate only after the rains – roughly from August to January/February between Mopti and Gao.

Along the river, the *gares routières* are replaced as the centres of trade by **steamer ports**, and wherever you arrive it will be amid a rush of activity as merchants from throughout the country scramble to buy whatever goods are available before the boat pulls out and continues its ponderous journey.

Small towns and villages dot the riverbank, ground-hugging mud buildings towered over by the traditional Sudanic-style mosques. Occasionally, fields of rice and other cereals can be seen from the decks of the boat – evidence of government attempts to irrigate large portions of the delta before they are irretrievably claimed by the advancing Sahara. Although Fula and Tuareg nomads still lead their flocks and herds through the region, vegetation is relatively sparse and the landscapes often flat and barren.

---

from these three towns by chartered *pirogue* or *pinasse*, you'll find the experience very worthwhile. There are several other towns with superb **architecture** between Ségou and Mopti that are hardly known to outsiders: try **Toa**, about 100km upstream from Mopti (two huge mosques), or **Kouakourou**, 45km upstream from Mopti (a busy Monday market and some stunning facades and interiors).

Mopti

MOPTI isn't immediately gripping. Its **Old Town** lacks aesthetic harmony, the **New Town** is neither modern nor impressive, and the hustlers are legion. However, the more time you spend wandering through Mopti – built on three islands connected by dykes – the more the place grows on you, and the port and canals, busy with the traffic of wooden *pinasses* and smaller canoe-like *pirogues*, begin to work their magic.

As a consequence of its setting on the water, Mopti has become the country's major route intersection, pulling together all the peoples of Mali – Bamana, Songhai, Fula, Tuareg, Moor, Bozo and Dogon. The mix of cultures and the town's buoyant pace add to the charm, making this one of the more interesting and popular stopovers anywhere in Mali. If you can, aim to be here on market day – Thursday.

Some history

Originally a cluster of islands inhabited by **Bozo fishing people**, Mopti became an important site early in the nineteenth century when, with the jihad proclaimed by the Fula scholar and ascetic **Cheikou Ahmadou Lobbo**, it gained strategic significance as an outpost of his Masina Empire, centred on Djenné and the Fula pasturelands around. Mopti was later captured by the Tukulor warmonger **El Hadj Omar** who turned the settlement into his principal military base, from where he launched attacks against his Fula rivals. A small town grew up around the site, but Mopti remained largely overshadowed by Djenné.

It wasn't until the beginning of the twentieth century that the town found commercial importance – at first with the export of white egret feathers to the *belle époque* couturiers of Paris. Indeed, economic development was largely due to the French, who exploited Mopti's position at the confluence of the Bani and the Niger and its accessibility from the main overland routes. When the railway line connecting Bamako to Dakar was built, Mopti became the largest river port in the **French Sudan**. Its popu-

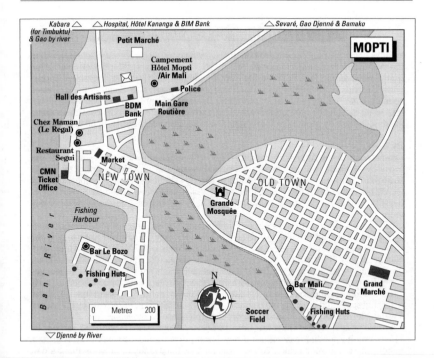

Kabara △ (for Timbuktu) & Gao by river — △ Hospital, Hôtel Kananga & BIM Bank — △ Sevaré, Gao Djenné & Bamako

MOPTI

Petit Marché
Campement Hôtel Mopti /Air Mali
Police
Hall des Artisans
BDM Bank
Main Gare Routière
Chez Maman (Le Regal)
Restaurant Segui
Market
CMN Ticket Office
NEW TOWN
OLD TOWN
Grande Mosquée
Fishing Harbour
Bar Le Bozo
Fishing Huts
Bani River
0 Metres 200
N
Bar Mali
Grand Marché
Soccer Field
Fishing Huts

▽ Djenné by River

lation has grown steadily and today, with around 70,000 people, it rivals Ségou as Mali's second town.

Police formalities and other headaches

Assuming you plan to spend the night in Mopti, one of the first orders of business is to stop by the **police headquarters** near the *campement* to get your passport stamped. Some people skip this formality with no apparent consequence, but if you stay long in town, the police will catch up with you sooner or later (surprisingly, they *can* be helpful and even friendly).

Mopti's heavy tourist influx has also resulted in another headache – that of pestering kids who try to earn a living **guiding** people through town. Mopti is straightforward enough not to need that kind of assistance, but you need to be firm with the persistent and sometimes aggressive candidates: having made your views clear, they won't usually waste their time with you.

One piece of positive practical information: the **post office** in Mopti is open 24 hours a day except for national holidays, and international calls are easily made.

Accommodation

Mopti offers surprisingly little choice when it comes to **accommodation** and in many ways, **Sévaré**, 12km from Mopti on the main Bamako–Gao road and easily accessible by collective taxi (15min; CFA350), is a preferable base; handy for the airport, Sévaré is also a main pick-up point for travel in any direction. If you are visiting Mopti for only a night or

MOVING ON FROM MOPTI

Besides being the major port of call on the Niger River route (tickets and schedules from the Compagnie Malienne de Navigation – CMN – near the port), Mopti is also just 12km from Sévaré on the Bamako–Gao highway. In addition, it's the most convenient spring-board for trips to Djenné (via river or road) and Bandiagara or Bankass in the Dogon country. Note that for both Bandiagara and Bankass, Mopti transport will normally go only as far as Somadougou on the tarmac: after that you take your chance with anything passing, though on Monday you might find vehicles going through to Bankass's market.

By boat

Downstream, from August to January/February (depending on the rains), you can travel by **steamer** to Gao. During this period, boats also provide the quickest link to **Korioumé**, the port of call for **Timbuktu**. Mopti–Timbuktu fares are approximately CFA12,000 3rd, CFA21,000 2nd, CFA29,000 1st class and CFA48,000 *luxe*. Upstream, to **Koulikoro** (port of call for **Bamako**), they usually stop running in mid-November due to the low waters.

You may also be able to get a **pinasse** to Korioumé. When enquiring at the port, spec-ify that you want a place on a goods boat, otherwise they'll think you want to rent the whole *pinasse* to yourself, a rather pricey alternative (say CFA300,000 to Timbuktu). Non-motorized *pinasses* or *pirogues* to Timbuktu should charge around CFA10,000 for the four-day voyage, but even these don't operate much after February. The journey varies from spellbinding (when you push off at dawn) to alarmingly uncomfortable (early afternoon out on the river), and it's fair to say the romance can wear thin given the restricted space and unpredictable nature of the whole trip. But, in retrospect at least, it's a wonderful adventure, and birdlife is prolific and hippos easily seen.

It's also possible to travel **up the Bani to Djenné**. *Pinasses* leave from the harbour on Friday evening for the overnight journey (local price around CFA4000). Chartering a motor *pinasse* for your group, count on about CFA100,000 for the trip of about a day, using a boat with *two* engines (an important point, if you're not going to end up spend-ing the night on board); non-motorized charters go for as little as CFA40,000, but it can take up to three days to pole and paddle to Djenné. Motor *pinasses* also operate up the Niger to **Ségou** – a three-day journey. You can usually arrange to have your food pre-pared for you on these wooden boats – otherwise bring your own provisions.

By road

Bush taxis to Djenné leave from the station across from the *Campement Hôtel Mopti*, pass through Sévaré and take about 3hr for the 130-kilometre trip. Your best chance of finding taxis is on Sunday and early Monday morning – Djenné's market day. Other times there may be nothing at all, or transport only as far as the Djenné turn-off, where you'll have to find another bush taxi in which to complete the remaining 35km of your

two, you could also consider **staying with people** on a mat on a rooftop terrace; though the practice is officially forbidden, the prices (negotiable) are usually very reasonable.

Mopti

Bar Mali, next to the swamp in the Old Town. The cheapest option in town, but one that should be avoided if possible – a grubby brothel with a reputation for theft. ②.

Campement Hôtel Mopti, near the *autogare*. Attractive, simple colonial-style accommodation, though a little overpriced. The restaurant serves good European food. Rooms and prices vary – the most expensive with mosquito nets and showers – but if you have transport or a tent, you can camp on the grounds for up to one-fifth the price. The Air Mali office is based here. ③.

Hôtel Restaurant Kananga (BP 224; ☎43.05.00; Fax 43.00.26), near the waterfront in the New Town. Comfortable, recently refurbished AC rooms with showers. Cable TV, thatched-roof open bar and a pool under construction. ⑤.

journey – a matter of both luck and patience. During the rains the overland route may be out altogether.

The main motor park for buses to **Gao, San, Ségou** and **Bamako** can be found on the stretch of road between *Bar Buffet Venise* and the CMN office, and in the surrounding side streets. Bus operators include Bittar Transport, Binke Transport and N'ga. The motor park for **Timbuktu** is behind the Palais de Justice, at the Place de Syndicat, also known as the Place de Timbuktu. Land-cruisers and bush taxis depart from here on Fridays from September to January when travel by *pinasse* is not possible. Cars will not make the trip (14hr) unless there are a minimum of seven to eight passengers. Note that the route north to Timbuktu is considered risky due to Tuareg bandit attacks.

By plane

From the **airport** in Sévaré, Air Mali operates flights three times a week to Goundam, Timbuktu, Gao and Bamako on the return leg. If you're in town during the late dry season, this may be your only hope of getting to Timbuktu. Note, however, that flights out of Timbuktu are rare and you could find yourself stranded for several days. Get full details of schedules – including those out of Timbuktu – from the Air Mali office in Mopti at the *Campement Hôtel Mopti* (☎43.00.32).

Travel agents and tours

A crop of new **travel agents** have recently sprung up in Mopti's New Town near the BDM bank, all offering tours of the main tourist circuits. Many can also arrange landcruiser rentals. Agencies include: Asselar Travel (BP 86; ☎ & Fax 43.05.56); Ashraf Voyages (BP 63; ☎ & Fax 43.02.79; *Ashraf.Voyages@malinet.ml*; English, French, Dutch, German and Bambara spoken); Le Bani Agence de Voyages (BP 55; ☎ & Fax 43.00.26); Bambara African Tours (BP 123; ☎ & Fax 43.00.80; *bambara@bambara.com*; English, French and Spanish spoken); Djoliba Travel (BP 232; ☎ & Fax 43.01.28; English, French and Bambara spoken). In Sévaré, Tellem Voyages is located about 500m from the electric power station.

Countless young kids in Mopti, Bandiagara and Bankass also lead **guided tours** through the Dogon country, all claiming to be from there. If you select a guide, you normally pay his transport to and from Mopti and a negotiable daily fee. Although most of the youngsters turn out to be quite informative and work hard, leading you on foot through the villages and down the escarpment, there are no guarantees, and when you get there, you may discover your guide knows little about the area, or that he can't arrange to get you to places he promised. Either way, it will cost you a fraction of organized excursions. It's often wise to agree a payment for your trip fully-inclusive before setting out to include transport, accommodation, food and the guide's fee. Pay part before leaving and the rest when you return.

Sévaré

Hôtel Le Bozo (reservations through *Bar Le Bozo* in Mopti on ☎43.02.46), near the *autogare* in Sévaré. Recently opened, with clean, spacious rooms – some S/C with AC – and English-speaking staff. A shuttle taxi service operates from 4–8pm between the hotel and *Bar Le Bozo* in Mopti. Jazz club purportedly forthcoming. ③.

Hôtel Oasis (☎42.04.98), 150m from the Mobil station on the Mopti–Sévaré road. No frills, but very tidy, with 24hr check-in. Five rooms only, with shared shower. ②.

Motel Sévaré (BP 45; ☎ & Fax 42.00.82; *sibyhotel@spider.toolnet.org*), on the airport road. Forty S/C rooms, all well-sized and tastefully decorated. Huge inner courtyard, and a restaurant serving a varied menu. ③–④.

Sévaré Hôtel Debo (BP 72; ☎ & Fax 42.01.24), on the airport road. The closest accommodation to the airport, this all-purpose utilitarian construction offers AC, TV and even bathtubs in all its rooms. ③–④.

Terenga Auberge Restaurant, 200m south of the Sévaré–Mopti road. Meals are served in the shady courtyard. The four available rooms – non-S/C – fill up quickly. ③.

The Town

Most of the sights in Mopti centre around the **harbour**, from where you can rent *pirogues* to take you to various Bozo or Tuareg camps. **Markets** in Mopti are colourful and famous for a wide range of crafts, including hand-woven Sahelian blankets.

The harbour

Mopti's *raison d'être*, the harbour, built by the French in the early part of the century, is always the centre of life in town. Large wooden *pinasses* with their canvas covers and colourful flags waving in the breeze tie up regularly to unload cargo and passengers, while *pirogues* taxi people back and forth from different points on the islands that make up the town. *Bar Le Bozo*'s terrace provides an excellent and breezy vantage point from which to take in all the activity in the harbour.

A **fish market** occupies the southern edge of the port near *Bar Le Bozo*. Behind it is a large open-air **"factory"** where craftsmen build the traditional *pinasses* from large planks imported from the south. On the northern edge of the harbour, Moorish traders mill around stacks of marble-like **salt slabs**, brought by camel caravan from the desert to Timbuktu and then transported by boat to Mopti. Formerly one of the desert's great riches, salt is still a precious commodity for herders who need it for their livestock.

The harbour is the place to get boats to take you along the river to see the **Bozo and Tuareg "camps"**. Kids will find you and propose the trip (just hang around the *Bar Le Bozo*); their brothers or uncles are inevitably **boatmen** who will give you a "special rate" – the going rate is CFA1000 per hour per boat, and no more, though the first price will be many times this. Although interesting, these trips are ultimately rather voyeuristic and artificial experiences, but the boat ride is enjoyable and gives an interesting perspective of the town.

The **Bozo** are a fishing people who build circular thatched huts, clustered in small *campements*, around Mopti during the rainy season when the catch is most prolific. If you take a *pirogue* to one of these communities, you'll see them repairing their boats and nets and engaged in other piscatorial activities. The **Tuareg camp** is nothing more than a few huts where women sell **crafts** – bracelets, necklaces and leather goods – at elevated prices.

The Old Town and markets

From the harbour, the **Grande Mosquée** is easily visible to the east. As you cross over the dyke leading to it, you enter the **Old Town** with its narrow pedestrian streets and grey *banco* houses. The mosque itself is a relatively recent construction, but faithful to the regional style that originated in nearby Djenné. Unfortunately, the interior is off limits to non-Muslims.

Also in the Old Town is the **grand marché**, southeast of the mosque in the Komuguel district. There's also a large covered **fish market**. More intimate is the **petit marché** in the New Town near the bank. You'll find more food here, plus various household items like **pottery** or **calabash** utensils.

The best place for **crafts** is the Hall des Artisans near the *petit marché*. Blankets are a regional speciality and Mopti has a wide selection at relatively low prices – costs vary according to the quality of the wool or cotton threads. Here you'll find weaves of local peoples including the Dogon, the Fula and the Songhai. Each of these peoples also has characteristic jewellery handcrafted in gold, silver, copper and bronze. Also worth a visit is the **cloth** market on the outer limits of the Hall des Artisans.

Eating

Street food is plentiful in Mopti, especially near the harbour and the motor parks. **Tea stalls** are open mornings and evenings for omelettes and bread with Nescafé or tea. A popular and low-priced **eating place** is *Le Regal*, also known as *Chez Mama*, which serves a limited but balanced selection of rice, fish and dairy dishes, while *Restaurant Segui* down the road provides more upscale fare – European, African and Asiatic dishes – in its cosy indoor and outdoor settings. The *Bar Le Bozo*, an outdoor terrace restaurant on the harbour, is a favourite haunt; there's nothing particularly fancy about the rice and fish dishes, but it's good value, and if you don't want to eat, you can come just for a beer and watch the *pirogues* slopping between the port and surrounding islands. Finally, *Tam Tam Africa*, next to the *Campement Hôtel Mopti*, serves grilled chicken, brochettes and fish under thatched umbrellas in the court-yard, and *Hôtel Kanaga*'s *Restaurant Le "Doun Ka Fa"* gives you the option to splurge with your credit card on carefully prepared African specialities and a wine list.

Over in **Sévaré**, *Motel Sévaré* has a generous menu for both visitors and guests. The latter may prefer dining in the large, square inner courtyard. *Teranga Auberge Restaurant* serves *riz senegalais*, *ragôut* and *capitaine* outside on its well-shaded patio.

Djenné and around

DJENNÉ is unquestionably the most beautiful town in the Sahel and, despite the inces-sant attention of unnecessary "guides", a superb place to visit. On an island for most of the year, the buildings are shaped in the smooth lines of the Sudanic style, moulded from the grey clay of the surrounding flood plains. In the main square, the famous **Grande Mosquée** dominates the townscape. People from throughout the region gather in town for the festive market day on Monday – the best time to plan a trip (transport to or from Djenné on other days is difficult). In Djenné you can easily imag-ine what life in the Sahel must have been like a century or more ago.

Originally a **Bozo settlement**, the town was founded around 800 AD, according to the *Tarikh es-Soudain* – one of the earliest written records of the Sahel. The orig-inal site was at a place called Djoboro, but it may have moved to the present location as early as 1043 (other sources put the date two centuries later). In the reign of the Soninké king **Koï Kounboro**, Djenné converted to Islam: the king himself dutifully raised his palace to make room for the town's first mosque in the thirteenth cent-ury. The town became a way-station for gold, ivory, lead, wool, kola nuts and other precious items from the south. Merchants had their depots in Djenné, and sold from outlets they operated throughout the region, notably in Timbuktu. They developed a large flotilla of boats – some up to twenty metres long – capable of transporting tens of tonnes of these goods to Timbuktu from where they made their way to the north.

In 1325, Djenné was incorporated into the **Mali Empire** under which it enjoyed a period of stability and continued prosperity. In 1473 – after a seige that purportedly lasted seven years, seven months and seven days – it was conquered by the **Songhai Empire**. The intellectual and commercial exchanges with Timbuktu were reinforced during this period until, in 1591, Djenné fell to the Moroccans, under whose domina-tion it remained until the nineteenth century. The town went into a slow decline that successive invasions were powerless to stop. **Cheikou Ahmadou** – a religious zealot from Masina – ousted the Moroccans in 1810, and destroyed Djenné's famous mosque. The **Tukulor Empire** briefly swallowed up the town in 1862, but held it only until 1893 when **French troops** arrived and took control.

The Town

Arriving by road, you'll see Djenné's **Grande Mosquée** from some distance as you travel over the dyke leading to town. This architectural masterpiece only dates from 1905, but was built in the style of the original mosque constructed in the reign of the Soninké king Kounboro. The rounded lines of the facade are dominated by three towers, each eleven metres high and topped with an ostrich egg. Protruding from the edifice, the beams serve more than an aesthetic function; like scaffolding they are essential for the upkeep of the building. Each year rains wash away the building's smooth *banco* outer layer and the people from town work to restore it in the dry season. Inside is a forest of pillars connected by sturdy arches. The mosque is said to hold up to 5000 worshippers – not bad when you consider that Djenné's total population is barely double that number. Regrettably, due to abuses of the site by insensitive visitors, the fascinating interior and rooftop are now off limits to non-Muslims. You can get a fairly good exterior view from the roof of the market (climb up the left-hand corner wall; as you walk into the market it's the wall nearest the mosque).

The weekly **market** is the other main sight, and it's worth making every effort to time your trip for a Monday when traders from throughout the region make a commercial pilgrimage to town. They spread their wares on the main square in front of the mosque in much the same way that French explorer **René Caillié** described in the nineteenth century in his *Travels through Central Africa to Timbuktu*. There are few if any markets as animated, as colourful and as *rich* – those colossal swaying earrings are solid gold – as Djenné on a Monday morning. After you've finished at the market it's satisfying to leave the crowds and wander through the dusty streets on your own, looking at the architecture and soaking up the way of life.

Practicalities

It is usually still necessary to **register with the police** in Djenné. **Guides** are not necessary to get around town, but CFA1000–2000 will give you a companion with some knowledge for a few hours, allow you to explore unhesitatingly, and keep the others away.

Accommodation is limited. *Chez Baba* (①–②), on a side street east of the Palais de Justice, has basic rooms, *camping* on the terrace and an overpriced restaurant which later turns into a bar and dance hall. Alternative lodgings can be found at the small *Kita-Kourou* (①–②), near the Gendarmerie, which also dishes up pancakes and *tiaom-tiaom* – a local speciality made with ground and dried onions and fish sauce. Behind the post office and through the village gate, the recently transformed *Hôtel Campement* (☎42.00.90; ②–④) has S/C, AC rooms, terrace *camping*, and an outdoor restaurant serving Malian favourites such as *sauce d'arachide, fonio* and *riz au gras*. Kids may also offer to put you up on the terrace of their homes. Some try to charge as much, or more than the going rate, so check the price.

Around Djenné

A number of **villages** surround Djenné, built on small elevations in the flood plains. One of the most interesting is **Sennissa** – peopled mainly by Fula and just 4km from Djenné as the crow flies (ask a kid to take you there). The village boasts two beautiful **mosques** and an abundance of artisans working along the small streets lined with single-storey *banco* homes. You're likely to see women here wearing the huge gold heirloom earrings that were once common in the region. The biggest ones may be the size of a rugby ball and hang down to the woman's breasts; some are so heavy they have to be strung from a cord that passes over the woman's head.

MOVING ON FROM DJENNÉ

There's now a hard-surfaced road from the landing stage on the other side of the Bani River to the *route national*. **Taxis** run from Djenné to Mopti on Monday afternoons when the market closes down. Alternatively, you can take one of the motor *pinasses* which leave early Tuesday morning and arrive in Mopti in the evening, transporting goods in time for Mopti's market day on Thursdays. Any kid in town can take you to the water's edge from where the boat departs. The *piroguier* will sell you a ticket (even a couple of days in advance if you like) that includes the price of transport plus food if you specify. The low-lying boats hug the water's edge, passing numerous villages on the river. The landscape, however, is remarkably flat and unvaried. Outside these two possibilities, there's no guaranteed transport out of Djenné. And it's a full, long day's hike along the dyke to the main road.

In 1977, a team of American archeologists discovered an ancient village 2km from town at a spot now called **Djenné-Djeno** (old Djenné). The foundations of buildings they uncovered here, along with terracotta statues, utensils and jewellery, date back as far as the third century BC and prick holes in a blanket of ignorance about archaic Africa – a highly developed, commercial society (the town counted over 10,000 inhabitants) that existed long before the arrival of Islam. For reasons still unclear, the town went into decline in the early Middle Ages and was abandoned by the fourteenth century. You're supposed to get permission from the police to visit the site, although kids will sometimes agree to take you there. In practice you can just go: keep your eyes on the ground and you'll see the pottery sherds everywhere.

Farther afield lies **Kouakourou**, a Bozo village about 45km northeast of Djenné on the banks of the Niger. Its original architectural style, known as *Saou*, is unique to the Djenné region. Of special interest are the dwellings for unmarried men whose walls are decorated with geometric forms. Market day is Saturday. Even better maintained is the river village of **Koulenze**, 40km northwest of Djenné, also an architectural gem and reachable by *pinasse* or by land in the dry season.

Timbuktu (Tombouctou)

> *If I told you why it is mysterious then it would not be mysterious*
>   Minister of Sports, Art and Culture
>
> *Is that it?*
>   Bob Geldof, after looking around

Long associated with mysterious beauty, learning and above all wealth, **TIMBUKTU**, "the forbidden city", has always fascinated outsiders. From the time of the crusades, it was one of the main entrepôts through which came the West African **gold** on which European finance relied. From the fourteenth century, when Mansa Musa, Emperor of Mali, passed through Cairo on his way to Mecca (stunning the city with his fabulous entourage and selling so much gold that its price slumped for decades), to the sixteenth, when Leo Africanus from Granada in Spain visited and described Timbuktu's opulent royal court, to as late as the eighteenth century when a lemming-like "explorers' rush" broke out to settle the enigma of the city roofed with gold, Timbuktu has achieved a near-legendary reputation. "Going to Timbuctoo" is still synonymous with going to the ends of the earth – or to hell – and only in the last few years has a more prosaic recognition forced itself into popular awareness.

Of course the town couldn't live up to the myths which disguised it so long and any illusions of grandeur you harbour are bound to be frustrated. As long ago as 1828, René Caillié wrote:

I found it neither as big nor as populated as I had expected. Commerce was much less active than it was famed to be . . . Everything was enveloped in a great sadness. I was amazed by the lack of energy, by the inertia that hung over the town . . . a jumble of badly built houses . . . ruled over by a heavy silence.

This frank assessment rings true today and, walking through the sandy streets, lined with pale grey stucco-covered mud-brick houses, you're more likely to be struck by the poverty and sense of despair than by the historical monuments evoking a prouder past.

A long and turbulent history

Towards the end of the eleventh century, a group of **Tuareg** who came to the Niger to graze their herds discovered a small oasis on the north bank where they set up a permanent camp. When they went off to pasture their animals, they left the settlement in the care of an old woman named Tomboutou – "the woman with the large belly button". Other versions have it that the woman's name was Buktu (or alternatively *bouctou* may derive from the Arabic for "dune") while *tim* in Berber signifies "place of".

The camp quickly developed into an important commercial centre where merchants from Djenné set up as middlemen between the salt caravans coming down from the north (and general dealers from across the Sahara) and the river traffic bringing goods downriver from the south. Although the Tuareg herders didn't live permanently in the town, they continued to control it, levying heavy and arbitrary taxes from the increasingly wealthy traders. Eventually, in response, the inhabitants invited the great Mali ruler **Mansa Musa** to liberate the town from Tuareg domination and he annexed it in 1330. To commemorate the occasion, the king visited Timbuktu and built a palace and the **Djinguereber mosque**.

Under the hegemony of the **Mali Empire**, Timbuktu enjoyed a period of stability and prosperity, but as the kingdom declined in the fifteenth century, the town again slipped into Tuareg control. Extortions began again, and by the sixteenth century the merchants turned to the Songhai ruler **Sonni Ali** who chased the Tuaregs west to the desert post of Oualata. Ali laid the foundations of the **Songhai Empire** which grew under the impetus of **Askia Mohammed**. Timbuktu reached its zenith at this point and became one of the Sahel's principal centres of commerce and learning. Reports of unimaginable wealth trickled back to Europe. The **Moroccan invasion** of 1591, however, when firearms were used in the Sahel for the first time, was a catastrophe for Timbuktu. The expedition's Andalucian leader, Djouder Pasha, had a number of senior scholars executed, exiled most of the others to Fez, and caravanned out the bulk of the city's wealth. Under the descendants of marriages between the invaders (some of whom were conscripted Scots, Irish and Spanish soldiers) and Songhai women – a group who came to be known as the **Arma**, after their guns – Timbuktu went into a steady decline that lasted throughout the seventeenth and eighteenth centuries. At different times it was attacked by the Mossi, the Fula, the Tukulor and the Tuareg. Subjected to pillage and oppression, the townspeople retreated behind the heavy, metal-studded wooden doors characteristic of Timbuktu houses. These were one of the few symbols of the city's former wealth that endured until the final arrival of the Europeans in the nineteenth century.

The European explorers
On the strength of a few translated books and a skein of rumours, Europeans set about uncovering Timbuktu's fabled riches. Between the late sixteenth century (by which time the city was, unknown to them, already nearly destitute) and 1853, at least 43 travellers attempted to reach it, of whom just four succeeded.

THE RACE BEGINS
The race really began in 1824, when the Geographical Society of Paris offered a prize of 10,000 francs for the first explorer to return with a verifiable account of the city. The earliest first-hand account by a non-Muslim, however, had already been given, not by an explorer, but by an illiterate American sailor, **Robert Adams**, who had been sold into slavery after his ship was wrecked off Mauritania, and who almost certainly spent several months in Timbuktu in 1811. But the story he related to the British Consul in Morocco in 1813 wasn't given much credibility, as Adams wasn't aware of the mystique surrounding the city and his dreary description was too flat to be believed – except by Moroccan Muslims who themselves had been there. Whether or not Adams did get to Timbuktu is still a matter of some argument.

GORDON LAING
The first explorer to succeed conclusively – a prudish Scot named **Gordon Laing** – reached Timbuktu on August 13, 1826, after a hazardous desert crossing from Tripoli in which he was almost slashed to death by Tuareg robbers. The squalid slaving town was a bitter disappointment, but Laing was apparently greeted warmly by the sheikh of Timbuktu and by the townspeople. On hearing of the arrival of a Christian, however, the Fula sultan who claimed authority over the town ordered Laing to either get out or be killed. Worried for his guest's safety, the sheikh sent Laing off towards Ségou (he was hoping to reach Sierra Leone) with an armed guide. Unfortunately, the latter turned out to be in the service of the sultan, and Laing and most of his servants were killed one night, 50km out of Timbuktu. One trailed back to Tripoli with Laing's notes and letters, two years later.

RENÉ CAILLIÉ
The first European to return from Timbuktu to write about the adventure himself was a Frenchman named **René Caillié** whose fantastic journey started on the West Coast on the Rio Nunez (now in northwest Guinea). Prior to taking off for Timbuktu, Caillié had lived in a Moorish village further north, learning Arabic and immersing himself in Muslim culture. Amazingly, he was sponsored by no government or association, and set off alone to the unexplored interior, disguised as an Egyptian. After making his way through the Fouta Djalon hills, he reached the Niger at Kouroussa, then continued to Tiémé (Côte d'Ivoire), where he fell gravely ill. After recovering, he pushed on to Tangrela and then to the devoutly Muslim town of Djenné where he made a deep and favourable impression on the sheikh – who would have had him instantly executed had his disguise been discovered. Caillié arrived in Timbuktu on April 20, 1828 and was received by Sidi Abdallahi Chebir. Two weeks later, the adventurer joined a camel caravan and headed across the Sahara to Tangiers. In eighteen months, he had crossed 4500km alone.

HEINRICH BARTH
Caillié's book wasn't considered the last word on Timbuktu, however, and in Britain, especially, it was judged to be bogus. The person who finally convinced the world was the German polyglot and explorer **Heinrich Barth**, who left Tripoli in 1850 on an expedition financed by the British government. He survived the desert crossing to Agadez,

then worked his way down to the Hausa country, his two companions dying en route. With delays and long residences in various towns, including diversions into Dogon country, he finally made it into Timbuktu on September 7, 1853. Like Caillié, he originally disguised himself as an Arab, but it didn't take long for the townspeople to discover he was Christian, after which his life was in danger. Barth, phlegmatic and undeterred, stayed eight months under the protection of Sheikh El Backay and collected the most detailed information known at the time. El Backay was virtually beseiged by his Fula overlords and only after long negotiations was Barth at last able to escape, following the river back east to Gao before continuing to Sokoto, Kano and on to Lake Chad. From here, he again set out across the Sahara, arriving in Tripoli in 1855. His explorations had lasted nearly six years and had taken him over 16,000km: the five-volume book he published at last overturned some of the myths.

RECENT TIMES
Apart from a lucky young German, **Oskar Lenz**, who skipped through Timbuktu in 1880 and apparently had a wonderful time, the next European visitors were French: they came through the 1890s, little doubting success, to conquer and colonize.

Recently Timbuktu has yet again suffered the traditional depredations of the Tuareg who, threatened by the continuing suppression of their nomadic lifestyle, and increasingly supportive of a movement to create their own state from parts of Mali, Niger and Algeria, rebelled against the agents of Bamako in the early 1990s. At one point history repeated itself as the Tuareg held the town in a state of virtual siege; it was their disruption which contributed to the dictator Moussa Traoré's fall and to subsequent reforms. For Timbuktu, however, the conflict continues, and these events have forced the moribund city still further into decline.

The Town

The oldest and most famous mosque in Timbuktu is the Friday **Djinguereber mosque**. It was first built in 1327 by El Saheli – an Andalucian architect whom Mansa Musa met in Cairo during his pilgrimage to Mecca – who is credited with the invention of mud bricks. Before bricks, all building was done using mud and straw, slapped on a wooden framework. Appropriately covered up and respectful, you may be able to climb the minaret here – but permission isn't always granted. The **Sankore** mosque dates from the fifteenth century. During Timbuktu's golden era, this mosque doubled as a **university**, renowned throughout the Muslim world, that specialized in law and theology. Up to 25,000 students were studying here in the sixteenth century. The **Sidi Yahya** mosque was first constructed in 1400 by a marabout named El-Moktar Hamalla and was intended to serve a saint whose imminent arrival had been prophesied. Four decades later, Sherif Sidi Yahya crossed the desert and asked for the keys to the mosque. He was declared imam, and is today one of the most revered of the town's **333 saints**.

Though the mosques are today the main sights, it's really more rewarding to spend some time walking through the confusion of narrow streets to take in the unique **architecture**. The finest homes – usually owned by Moorish merchants – are made of carved limestone brought from a desert quarry. Again, the basic design of these homes may date to El Saheli; the columns of square pilasters that decorate the facades are reminiscent of those in Egyptian temples, an element he may have picked up in Cairo. The small shuttered windows and heavy wooden doors with geometric ironwork designs also bear an Arabic stamp, though they seem to hark back to the Moroccan invasion of the late sixteenth century. Plaques still mark the homes where **Laing**, **Caillié** and **Barth** stayed during their exploits in Timbuktu. The first two were on the same street in the **Sankore district**; and any kid can point them out to you. Heavy rains occasionally reduce one or other of the houses to rubble, but they're regularly repaired

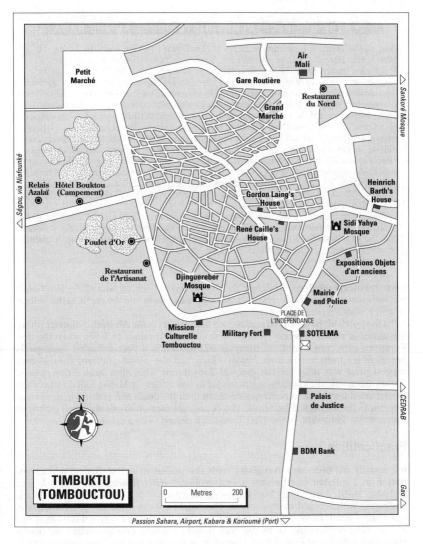

Petit Marché

Gare Routière

Air Mali

Restaurant du Nord

Grand Marché

Relais Azalaï

Hôtel Bouktou (Campement)

Gordon Laing's House

Heinrich Barth's House

Poulet d'Or

René Caille's House

Sidi Yahya Mosque

Restaurant de l'Artisanat

Expositions Objets d'art anciens

Djinguereber Mosque

Mairie and Police

PLACE DE L'INDÉPENDANCE

Mission Culturelle Tombouctou

Military Fort

SOTELMA

N

Palais de Justice

BDM Bank

△ Ségou, via Niafounké

Sankoré Mosque ▷

CEDRAB ▷

Gao ▷

TIMBUKTU (TOMBOUCTOU)

0 Metres 200

Passion Sahara, Airport, Kabara & Korioumé (Port) ▽

again for the sake of Timbuktu's precarious tourist industry – building in mud guarantees an authentic, weathered, historical look.

More modest houses are made of *banco* in a style that originated in Djenné. Along the streets you'll also notice dome-shaped **clay ovens** where women bake round loaves of bread – a speciality of the town, traditionally made from wheat grown near Lake Faguibine. The outskirts of Timbuktu are bordered by circular straw huts – the domain of Tuareg, Bella and Fula nomads. Walk out past the *Relais Hôtel Azalaï* in the west to see them, or climb one of the **dunes** at dawn to watch the sun rising above the town: the city looks best in silhouette. Also near the *Relais Hôtel Azalaï* on the west side of

CENTRE DES RECHERCHES HISTORIQUES AHMED BABA

One of the greatest remaining legacies of Timbuktu's former glory is the wealth of Islamic literature that was produced here. Traditionally, families wrote their histories in chronicles known as *tarikh* – one of the most important of which was the *Tarikh es-Soudan*, written by El Sadi in the seventeenth century. These and other related writings have provided invaluable information about the scientific, legal and social practices of the seventeenth, eighteenth and nineteenth centuries throughout the region, and indeed the entire Muslim world. In addition, they've helped trace Mali's history back to the empire of ancient Ghana. Countless volumes remain in private family collections, where, exposed to damp, dust and insects, the works (some of which may be four hundred years old or more) could soon be lost for ever. Timbuktu's **Centre des Recherches Historiques Ahmed Baba** (CEDRAB) is trying to persuade reluctant families to part with these priceless documents – at least long enough for them to be restored and copied on microfilm. To date, over 2500 volumes have been collected and copies have been made of 600 others. About eighty percent of these are written in Arabic, most of the rest in Songhai and a few in unknown scripts.

The centre is on the south side of town, down the airport road and left after the post office. It's very much worth a visit. You can leave a donation against an official receipt. Ask the staff to show you some of the older, handwritten documents, the most beautiful of which contain geometric artwork and gold lettering.

town, **terraced gardens** challenge the intense heat. Looking something like Greek amphitheatres, they're built around large craters dug deep into the earth, at the bottom of which stands a pond of brackish water.

To the north of the CEDRAB centre (see box, above) is the **Abaradio district** where the *azalaï* or camel caravans formerly arrived in great numbers (even when the first European explorers arrived, as many as 60,000 camels a year unloaded their goods here). Apart from goods from North Africa and the Mediterranean, the Sahara's biggest prize was salt from the oasis of **Taoudenni**. This ultra-remote desert post, 700km due north of Timbuktu, is famous for its salt mines – a Malian Siberia where the former president Modibo Keita was detained until his death and political undesirables were, until the 1980s, still banished. The occasional caravan of salt slabs still makes its way down to Timbuktu, but in 1989 Taoudenni ceased to be a prison camp.

Practicalities

It is usually still necessary to **register with the police** on arrival. Budget **accommodation** in Timbuktu has become a real problem. *Hôtel Bouctou* (BP 49; ☎ & Fax 92.10.12; ③–④), a traditional Moroccan-style structure with a good view of the dunes, has rooms with WC and mosquito nets. The hotel's annexe is the old government-run *campement*. *Relais Hôtel Azalaï* (QP 64; ☎ 92.11.63; ⑤) is the best option if you can afford it. They offer comfortable AC rooms (with power from their own generator) and have a restaurant with decent French food. *Passion Sahara* (③), a new hotel and expat hangout, is located on the Avenue de la Paix not far from the Shell station. For CFA7500, there is limited space for *camping* at the *Poulet d'Or*, which doubles as a restaurant. Otherwise, **staying with people** can be risky. There's no longer any law in Mali about staying with *indigènes*, but there *was* a law, formerly, and it proved a lucrative one for its "enforcers" in towns like Timbuktu. Most people are therefore reluctant to put up visitors.

There's surprisingly little in the way of **eating-houses** or bars. *Restaurant de l'Artisanat*, within the Maison d'Artisans, serves African and simple Western dishes. Prices at the *Poulet d'Or*, around the corner, are slightly lower and tables are set outside. *Restaurant du Nord* in the corner of the *grand marché*, is the cheapest option – and it shows. The market doesn't offer a great deal either, but as you'll either be staying in one of the hotels, or unofficially with a family who will provide meals in any case, it's not a big problem.

For **desert excursions** by camel or 4WD, contact Seydou Baba Kounta at *Hôtel Bouctou* (see opposite); note however, that price quotes will be double their actual worth.

Around Timbuktu: Lake Faguibine and Goundam

One hundred kilometres west of Timbuktu is **Lake Faguibine**, the size of which varies greatly with the seasons. It can swell to 120km long by 25km wide, making it one of the largest natural lakes in West Africa, but since the late 1980s, the lake has been completely dry. The approach is via **GOUNDAM**, an important agricultural town in the middle of a region considered to be the breadbasket of Mali (there are weekly flights connecting it with Timbuktu and Bamako). Rice, millet, corn and, remarkably, wheat, are all grown in the area. Situated on the much smaller **Lake Télé**, Goundam has a *campement* (②) and is linked to the river by a 34-kilometre road from Diré, a sizeable port on the Niger, 100km upstream from Timbuktu. From Goundam, continue to Lake Faguibine via the *piste* that passes through the village of Bintagoungou.

To get to these places using local transport you'd need luck or money to make much headway.

MOVING ON FROM TIMBUKTU

If you weren't impressed by Timbuktu's isolation during your stay, you will be when you try to leave. Unless you're travelling with your own vehicle, the options for **onward travel** are pretty much limited to river craft or the plane. The **river journey** from Timbuktu (Korioumé port) to Gao is beautiful – the Niger snakes between high yellow dunes – and hippos are often seen along the way. The current **flight schedule** consists, on paper, of a Tuesday flight to Gao and flights on Tuesday back to Mopti and Bamako and on Saturday back to Mopti, Goundam and Bamako. For up-to-date information, check at Air Mali (☎92.11.09) near the *grand marché*.

Note that a *bâché* from Timbuktu to the port, or vice versa, should be no more than CFA500, even with luggage – about half of what you'll be asked.

The piste to Gao

A demanding – and risky, due to bandit attacks – *piste* follows the Niger's north bank 420km to Gao. Along the route, deep sandy ruts winding through acacia bush make a 4WD or manageable trail bike essential. As unofficial cargo, merchants travelling overland will take passengers who are willing to sit atop baggage, be exposed to the desert winds and tolerate the general precariousness of the trip, all for a negotiated fee. It's 195km to **Bamba**, one of the first major villages along the route – a difficult stretch with deep soft sand. Sandwiched between the road and the river, the town is said to have been founded by the Moroccan invaders of the 1590s. It has been particularly vulnerable in the Tuareg conflict of recent years. Another 135km brings you to **Bourem** on the Niger River, a Songhai village with characteristic *banco* homes and a large market – and also the southern terminus of the trans-Saharan Tanezrouft route. From here, the road continues along the river to Gao, 95km away.

It's worth noting that a feasible route exists from Gourma-Rharous (about 100km east of Timbuktu on the south bank), to the new, paved, Gao–Bamako road. There's a basic car ferry across the river at Gourma-Rharous, though unless you're driving you won't need to worry much about the crossing as *pirogues* cross on demand.

THE DOGON COUNTRY

Until the end of the colonial era, the **Dogon** were one of the African peoples who had most successfully retained their culture and traditional way of life. This was in large part due to the isolation of their territory in the remarkable and picturesque **cliff-side villages** they built along the **Bandiagara escarpment** (the *falaise*) east of Mopti – a 200-kilometre-long wedge of sandstone, pushed up by movements of the earth's plates in prehistoric times.

They're still dogged defenders of their customs, religion and art, but in more recent years they have become the object of an intense **touristic exploitation**. Although much of the Dogon country can only be visited on foot or at best with a donkey cart – the area you can cover with a 4WD is limited – the place can be swarming with travellers, especially over Christmas. Off the main circuit you can often pay kids to take you around the villages, but you'll have to fork out a lot of cash even for this alternative. With patience and a lot of time, you can still manage to get completely **off the beaten track**, but only the most intrepid and persistent travellers can today hope to discover the real beauty of the Dogon people's outstanding civilization.

Some history

Recent **archeological research** has uncovered caves dug into the cliffs around the Dogon town of **Sanga** that date to around the third century BC. The Dutch scientists who discovered these caves called the people who made them the **Toloy**, but there seems to be a rather large gap between this culture and the next known inhabitants of the escarpment, the **Tellem**, who arrived in the eleventh century. The Tellem were small people, often said to have been "pygmies", although they probably weren't related to the contemporary Central African people of small stature. They're generally thought to have shared the escarpment for a couple of centuries with the **Dogon**, who arrived in the fifteenth century. Some time around the seventeenth century, the Tellem were pushed out of the Dogon country and migrated to Burkina Faso.

The Dogon may originally have come from the region of the Nile, but before moving to the Bandiagara escarpment they lived in the Mande country to the west. Determined to preserve their traditional religion in the face of Muslim expansionism and religious jihads, they migrated to the safety of the *falaise* in the fifteenth century. Even with this natural shelter as a homeland, they had to fight off numerous aggressors over the centuries. In the 1470s the country was invaded by the **Songhai**, and in the early eighteenth century it was attacked by the **Ségou kingdom**. Much later, in 1830, the Fula from **Massina** marched on the region and, in 1860, the Tukulor ruler **El Hadj Omar** brought his holy war to the escarpment, making Bandiagara his capital; he died in Deguembere near Bandiagara. The **French** occupied the region of Sanga in 1893, but it wasn't until the battle of Tabi in 1920 that the colonial army finally "pacified" the Dogon people.

In the 1930s Reverend Francis McKinney, an American, established the first Christian mission in Sanga. Several years later **Marcel Griaule**, a French anthropologist, came to the same town to study traditional Dogon religion and customs. He spent a quarter of a century living in Dogon country and helped them to set up dams for irrigation and introduced the onion crop that's now one of the only exports of the region to the rest of Mali and Burkina. Respected by the Dogon, he also helped open the eyes of the rest of the world to the complexity and integrity of a civilization that had long been regarded by Muslim and Christian invaders as merely primitive.

SEX, SPEECH AND WEAVING: DOGON COSMOLOGY

The Dogon believe in a single God, **Amma**, who created the sun, moon and stars. Afterwards, he created the earth by throwing a ball of clay into space. The ball spread to the four points of the horizon and took on the shape of a woman with an anthole for her vagina and a termite mound for her clitoris. Alone in the universe, Amma attempted to make love to the earth, but the termite mound blocked his path and he tore it out. Because of this violence, the earth could not bear the twins that would have resulted from a happy union and instead gave birth to a jackal.

Amma again had intercourse with the earth, and a pair of twins resulted, known as **nommo**. They were born of divine semen, the precious water found in everything in the universe. Green in colour, their upper bodies were human and their lower bodies like snakes. The *nommo* are present in all water. Living in the heavens with their father, the *nommo* looked down on their mother and, seeing her naked, made a **skirt** into which they wove the **first language**. Thus the earth was the first to possess speech.

Meanwhile, the jackal was running loose. His mother was the only woman, and he raped her. The earth bled and became impure in the sight of Amma. It's for this reason that today, menstruating women are considered impure in Dogon society – as they are in nearly all African cultures. When he forced himself upon the earth, the jackal also touched her skirt and thus stole language.

Having turned from his wife, Amma decided to create a human couple from clay. The couple had elements of both sexes – the foreskin being the feminine part of the man, and the clitoris the masculine part of the woman. Foreseeing that problems would arise from this ambiguity, the *nommo* circumcised the male and later an invisible hand removed the clitoris from the woman (circumcision of men and clitoridectomy of women is still an important step into adulthood for the Dogon). The couple was thus free to procreate and produced eight children, the original **Dogon ancestors**. After creating **eight descendants** of their own, the ancestors were purified and transformed into *nommo*, then went to join Amma in the sky. But before his ascension, the seventh ancestor was charged with giving the **second language** to humans. Using his mouth as a loom, he spat out a cotton strip from which the new speech was transmitted to humanity.

The eight ancestors didn't get along with Amma and the *nommo* and were eventually sent back to earth. On the way, the eighth ancestor came down before the seventh, who was angry as a result. He turned himself into a snake and set about disturbing the work of the other ancestors. They told the people to kill the snake – which they did. But this seventh ancestor – whose name was Lebe – held the **third language**, needed for mankind, since the second wasn't adequate. The oldest of the eight original descendants thus had to be sacrificed and was buried with the head of Lebe the snake. Humans then received the third language in the form of a drum.

Symbolism from the story of creation carries over to this day into **Dogon dances**. **Masks** are an important element of the dances and the Dogon use over eighty different varieties according to the celebration. The biggest ceremony is the **Sigui**, celebrated every sixty years to commemorate the passing of a generation. The frequency of Sigui is calculated by the periodicity of an invisible satellite of the "dog star", Sirius. Sirius itself appears brightly between mountain peaks exactly when expected, suggesting a level of astronomical knowledge which has long baffled outsiders. The event serves to venerate the Big Mask, made in the shape of a serpent in reference to **Lebe**, who is credited with leading the Dogon to the Bandiagara escarpment as well as bringing them speech and, simultaneously, death. The last Sigui festival was held in the 1960s; the next – without undue optimism – should be in the 2020s.

Traditional religion has a profound effect on Dogon art, architecture and symbolism, and is incorporated into the smallest item. Skin markings are charged with meaning. Even the baskets used by the Dogon are symbolic, the square bases representing the four cardinal points and the round top the celestial dome of the sky. It was formerly common to file the teeth in the shape of a weaver's comb, since speech is an action that weaves the world and should thus pass through a worthy loom.

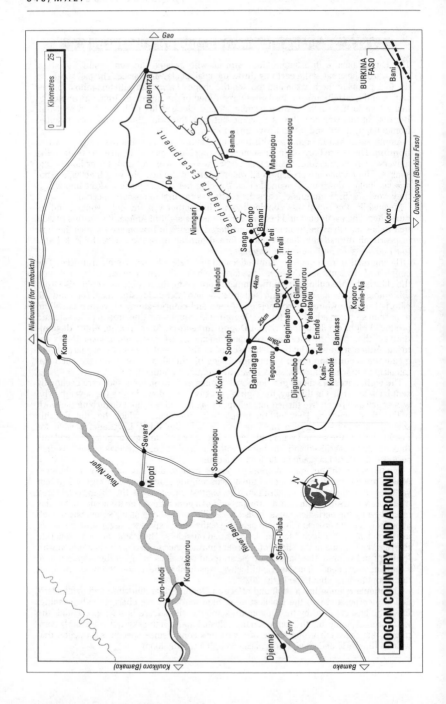

DOGON COUNTRY AND AROUND

Travelling around Dogon country

Dogon villages are scattered over three distinct areas: the Plateau Dogon, to the north-west of the Falaise de Bandiagara; the *falaise* or escarpment itself; and the Plaine de Gondo-Seno which stretches out to the southeast from the foot of the cliffs. A trip to the Dogon country can involve hours of **trekking** in the sweltering sun, and is likely to entail climbing up and down the 300-metre escarpment and walking over rocky terrain. You'll want to travel as light as possible, and you're recommended to leave all but the essentials behind before making the trip. Many people use Mopti (see p.332) or Sévaré as their **base** for exploring Dogon country: for a small daily fee various lodgings will guard your baggage while you're away. Alternatively you could make Bandiagara or Sanga your jumping-off point. Although the terrain is rough, you won't need any special walking shoes. Tennis shoes or even sandals should be fine, but you'll probably want some form of headwear.

Bring a **water bottle** or canteen for the long hot stretches between villages. Dogon villages have no running water, and you'll be drinking from local wells. Guinea worm is no longer a severe problem so it's not essential to filter your water but it's a good idea to try to boil or purify it. An expensive alternative is to buy bottled mineral water and *sucreries*; you'll find these, at a price, in many villages, particularly those with *campements*. You might want to take some fruit or light snacks with you, but most of your **food** will be bought in Dogon villages.

Your choice of **transport** will depend on how much time you have and how much ground you'd like to cover. A leisurely way to see the region is on **foot** (with or without a porter or *charette* – donkey cart – to carry your stuff); depending on the inclinations of your guide, you're likely to pass through about three villages a day this way. For greater flexibility and a speedier pace, you could travel by **mobylette** (moped), **moto** (motorbike), or **4WD**, though you should bear in mind that once you're off the paved road the routes are extremely challenging. Travelling by *mobylette* or *moto* is an invigorating way to discover the region, but few rented bikes go really well even in the best conditions. Around here you'll spend all your time fixing your bike, and then, when you return it, arguing about who should pay for the necessary parts. If you have your own vehicle and its not 4WD, you're best off leaving it behind.

Notwithstanding your experiences in Mali's other towns, **guides** are essential in Dogon country, and you'll be expected to have a local escort in all but the most remote communities. Without a guide, you'll have real problems just communicating: few of the people here speak French and, even more so than elsewhere in Mali, the manner in which people greet each other is elaborate, and a very important element of any social exchange. There are also a great many **taboos**, often specific to certain villages, and without the assistance of a clued-up guide you risk making cultural faux pas during your visit. Guides are also useful for locating villages and the quickest footpaths between them, for figuring out **market days** (every five days in most villages) and harvest **fetes** (many around mid-December), and making arrangements for sleeping and eating in isolated places. Finally, a good guide should also be able to fill you in on the history of the places you visit, and the significance of the various elements that make up each village.

As a rough indication, you should expect guides to **charge** a minimum of CFA5000 per day. Many Dogon villages now charge a flat **entry fee** for visitors, payable to the chief – usually CFA500 or CFA1000, rarely more. You generally then pay the same rate again for a meal and place to sleep the night (at the *campement*, if there is one, or on the roof of the chief's house), and half the rate again for breakfast. Some guides will quote you an all-in guiding fee to include transport, food, lodging, and village fees for an agreed number of days; others will fix a fee for their time and leave the other expenses up to you. A word of warning: an unfortunate by-product of the Dogon country's popularity as a tourist

ANATOMY OF A DOGON VILLAGE

Dogon villages are frequently divided into **twin parts** – as in Sanga which incorporates Ogol-du-haut and Ogol-du-bas – that signify the original twin ancestors. Many villages are further divided into distinct **quartiers** according to the religion of the inhabitants. The Christian quarter may include a simple church, while the Muslim quarter is, naturally, marked by its mosque (the mosque at Kani-Kombolé is particularly impressive). The Dogon resisted Islam for many years but now that it's the dominant religion, the Muslim quarters of Dogon villages tend to be large. However, Muslim practices are generally grafted onto animist practices rather than adopted to the exclusion of traditional rites. In the animist *quartier*, the external walls of houses contain niches for fetishes that allude to primitive ancestors, and you will see small rocks, mounds or clay pilasters that serve as altars.

A Dogon village is in theory laid out to a symbolic plan in which different areas represent different parts of a **human body**, with the forge and the *togu-na*, or elders' meeting place, at the head (the northernmost point), the house of the *ginna bana*, or chief, in the chest area (the centre), one or two *maisons des règles*, where women stay during menstruation, representing the hands (at east and/or west), and sacrificial altars at the feet (south). In reality this pattern isn't always strictly followed, but there is nonetheless a symbolic purpose in the positioning and layout of every structure in every village.

Village walls and buildings are collectively built, using dry stones or sun-fired mud bricks plastered with *banco*, which the Dogon make by hand from a sludge of straw, rice husks and clay. Walls often have graceful geometric patterns pressed into them. The roofs of the granaries and the *togu-na* are thatched with millet stalks and waterproofed with *banco* mixed with karité oil. Everything has to be rebuilt, or at least repaired, at the end of each rainy season.

Togu-na or case à palabres This open-sided, low-roofed construction is the meeting place where village elders (strictly men only) gather to discuss village affairs, or to socialize and swap stories. The Dogon have an extremely rich oral tradition (reading and writing is not widespread), so the village *togu-na* is effectively a cultural treasure-house. The *togu-na* is built according to strict rules. The thick millet-thatched roof is supported by eight wooden pillars, which represent the eight Dogon ancestors and are often decorated with carvings; there are particularly beautiful examples at the villages of Dombossougou and Madougou. The roof is low both to give maximum shade and also to help defuse any arguments before they get out of hand, the idea being that if the elders can't stand up, they can't come to blows.

House of the ginna bana The *ginna* (pronounced "gheena") *bana* is the head of a *ginna*, that is, an extended family or lineage. A *ginna bana*'s house tends to be more impressive than an average dwelling, and contains an altar where the founders of the village are honoured. On the outside of the front wall of the house there may be ten rows of eight niches representing the eight Dogon ancestors.

Family compounds A compound is shared by a family unit made up of adults and young children: at the age of 7–9 years, children leave home to live communally in a *maison des jeunes*. The family compound consists of a courtyard, rooms and granaries, linked by stone walls. Rooms are normally square with flat roofs on which millet and other produce is left out to dry in the sun. Inside, whatever the region, houses are constructed according to a standard layout (symbolizing a seated man). There are specific guidelines as to

destination is the problem of rogue guides, who are often inexperienced and unreliable, and who may not even be Dogon (Bamako and Mopti have their fair share of these). As usual, the best way to choose a guide is through a personal recommendation; if this isn't possible, make sure you quiz your guide carefully before agreeing to an itinerary.

One final point: it cannot be overemphasised that as a visitor to the Pays Dogon, you are a guest in a fragile community. As long as tourists continue to respect the Dogon people's culture and environment, and their right to privacy, there is no reason for rela-

which domestic duties take place where in the interior, and the system even runs as far as specifying where and in what position a couple should make love.

Granaries It is the pepperpot-shaped Dogon granaries that give the villages their distinctive fairy-tale quality. Tall and thin, they stand on stone legs to protect them from vermin. The interior of each granary is divided into compartments according to a pattern that represents the cosmos; these are used to store grain, obviously, but women also use their own granary to store their private possessions (jewellery, cloth, money).

Maison des règles While they are menstruating, women (referred to as "women who want a baby") are excused their domestic duties, and are isolated together in a round hut, overseen by a wise woman who offers them natural remedies for any ailments. The Dogon are renowned for their medical skills and their practices have recently become the subject of Western medical research.

Sanctuaire du binou This temple-like building, decorated with *boummon* (ritual painting) in animal blood and *bouillie de mil* (millet porridge), is a place where the *hogon* (spiritual leader of the village) conducts sacred ceremonies dedicated to the *binou*, an ancestral spirit. It's often a rectangular house with rounded corners and towers and a low door blocked by rocks. Over the door is a forked iron hook which symbolizes the mythical ram's horns on which clouds are caught to bring rain. Only the *hogon* knows the meaning of the symbols and totemic objects inside the sanctuary.

Altars Sacrificial altars are sometimes no more than small earth mounds or pilasters marked with traces of animal blood and *bouillie de mil*. It is thought that when the rain washes the blood and *bouillie* away, the *nyama* (vital power) that these carry is transferred to the fields to restore the equilibrium of the earth and ensure a good harvest. Chickens and goats are the usual sacrificial victims but special occasions may call for the sacrifice of a more valuable animal.

Tellem houses The Tellem pygmies built cave-like dwellings high up in the cliff face. It's a mystery how these diminutive people managed to scale the *falaise* but it's thought that they did so either by weaving rope ladders out of baobab bark or other vegetation, or by climbing the large trees that used to grow right up to the foot of the cliff until the Dogon cleared the plain to grow millet. Some Tellem houses still contain ritual objects. Many are now used by the Dogon to keep livestock, store belongings, or bury dead.

Hogon house The isolated dwelling near the village ritual sites is where the *hogon* lives, either temporarily or permanently, guarding the village's sacred bones and relics. The walls of this dwelling are painted in totemic symbols in the ritual colours of red, black and white: red for sacrificial blood (a sign of peace) and the blood of the *hogon*; white for purity of heart and for the light of day; black for the skin of the *hogon* and for the night.

Ritual sites The most important ritual sites of a Dogon village are often outside the village itself; in the *falaise* villages they are generally situated on an isolated platform or ledge high up on the cliff face. It is here that circumcision ceremonies take place, once every three years. The act of circumcision is performed on a designated blood-blackened rock, and the walls of the site are decorated with paintings in red, black and white. Each initiate adds his own personal symbol to those of his predecessors, and while older symbols follow traditional stylized patterns, more recent additions may reflect modern interests (a car, a plane). The cave paintings at Songo are particularly fine. The walls of some ritual sites (notably at Teli and Yabatalou) are hung with monkey skulls, totems in the Dogon farmers' war against the pests that steal their crops.

tions to become strained. In the more visited villages you will doubtless run into children demanding *bonbons*; if you want to give presents to anybody, far better to carry a small supply of kola nuts which are much appreciated by the village elders. You have a responsibility too, to resist buying any artefact that looks remotely old. The Dogon are rightly celebrated for their **artistic heritage** but, tragically, much of their art has been sold overseas. There are plenty of artefacts for sale that have been made expressly as souvenirs and the quality of workmanship is often extremely good.

Bandiagara and around

Although commercial tours are convenient if you want a perfunctory overview of Dogon territory, you may prefer less organization and the flexibility of following your own plans and pace. In that case it's usually best to head directly to **BANDIAGARA**, on the banks of the river Yamé, a seventy-kilometre taxi ride (1hr 30min–2hr) on a decent road from Mopti. A sizeable administrative town, Bandiagara is nothing like more traditional villages in the region (as the large mosque testifies) although the population is sixty percent Dogon. There's a good deal of commerce by Dogon standards, with a lively market on Mondays and Fridays, plus a hospital, mission and police headquarters. It's a convenient point of entry to the Dogon region, and a pleasant enough town, but brace yourself for kids swarming around you from the minute you arrive, offering their services as **guides**.

Practicalities

If you hire a guide in Bandiagara, he may be able to offer you **accommodation** and meals in his family compound. Otherwise, try *L'Auberge du Vieux Kansaye* (②), near the bridge over the river, a basic but popular place with a shady garden; or the *Hôtel Le Village* on the Sévaré road (BP 35; ☎42.03.31; ②), which has decent, clean rooms with shared facilities, and a slightly neglected garden which at weekends becomes the town's liveliest nightspot. More upmarket, and well-signposted off the Sévaré road, is the recently opened and Swiss-run *Le Kambary Hôtel/Restaurant-Bar Le Cheval Blanc* (BP 13; ☎ & Fax 42.03.88; ④), a strikingly atmospheric complex of dome-shaped stone buildings; even if you end up staying elsewhere it's well worth visiting for a drink or a meal to soak up the calming ambience. The *Italian Medical Centre* (②) on the east side of town can also sometimes put people up.

Inexpensive basic **meals** plus cold beer, mineral water and *sucreries* are available at *Restaurant Le Petit Coin* ("*Chez Moustique*").

Around Bandiagara

Once you've reached Bandiagara, you can choose between making the town your base while you make short trips to visit other villages (Songho, Sanga, Dourou and Djiguibombo can each be visited in a half-day round trip by car or motorbike from Bandiagara), or setting off on a longer itinerary, spending the night in villages as you go.

The village of **Songho** is spectacularly situated on the plateau, some distance from the *falaise*, between two craggy rock formations, and can easily be seen in a couple of hours (a guide can be found at the *campement* on the way in to the village). To get there from Bandiagara, take the five-kilometre sandy track that turns off to the north side of the Sévaré road, about 10km outside town. Although Songho is a Muslim village, the villagers keep their animist traditions very much alive, as testified by the freshness of the cave paintings at the village **circumcision site** – a large ledge a hundred metres up the crag. A circumcision ceremony takes place every three years and your guide will point out the rocks where the participants sit, and the painted targets which are the winning posts for the running race which takes place immediately after the ceremony. The newly circumcised have to complete a three-kilometre circuit and the winner is presented with a sack of millet and the wife of his choice. You may also be shown the vertiginous platform where dances take place, and the cave in which ceremonial musical instruments are stored.

From Bandiagara to Djiguibombo

Twenty-five kilometres of walkable or motorable track separate Bandiagara from **Djiguibombo** at the edge of the *falaise*. This relatively flat road over the plateau passes through sparse vegetation of bush savannah with the occasional baobab rising up to dominate the rocky landscape. After about 12km you pass the village of **Tegourou**. Nearby is a dammed stream and the terraced fields of the Dogon's famous onions. Before continuing the trip down the escarpment most guides will stop at Djiguibombo, the last village on the plateau and a charming and friendly place. It stands in an extremely rocky area near the cliff: a stone wall surrounds it and many of the houses use stone in their construction.

Along the plain from Kani-Kombolé to Teli

A couple of kilometres south of Djiguibombo, you finally arrive at the cliff: from the edge of the plateau, there's a sweeping vista over the plains below. At the time of writing, a new motorable road was being built from Djiguibombo down to the plain; for those on foot, although the cliff drops suddenly, your guide will lead you along walkable paths down it, and the 300-metre descent poses no special problem. Once on the plain, **Kani-Kombolé** – with a beautiful mosque, a Thursday market, a reasonable little *bar-resto* and somewhere to stay if you need it – isn't too far off.

Following the *falaise* eastwards, you come next to **Teli**, a four-kilometre walk over a flat, sandy stretch bordered by millet fields. If you don't manage to get to Sanga (see overleaf), Teli is a satisfying substitute that is still a lot less visited, with some of the most spectacular **cliffside houses** along this part of the escarpment and, in the rainy season, waterfalls nearby. If you take this route, it's worth coming at least this far. Some guides are better than others at getting you permission to climb up to the cliff-dwellings. An old lady used to live among the remains of Tellem ancestors in caves on the rock face, but she died in 1992 and latest reports suggest nobody has replaced her as *hogon*.

Enndé to Bandiagara via Dourou

Having reached Teli, you can consider you've had a pretty good overview of the Dogon country and will have seen villages on the plateau, in the cliffs and on the plains. At this point, you could either return to Bandiagara retracing the route described above, or continue east to **Enndé**. Here, you can spend the night on the roof of the house of the village chief's son, who's quite accustomed to putting up travellers. You can also pay to have meals of chicken and rice prepared and wash it down with home-brewed millet beer. There's a market every Sunday, and in the rainy season you can swim in the waterfall pool near the village.

After Enndé, the road continues through a number of villages. One of the more picturesque is **Doundouru**, known for the spectacular homes carved in the cliff. Still following the escarpment to the east, you next come to **Konsagou**, and finally **Gimini**. After this village, you can climb back up the *falaise* and walk along the edge of the plateau to **Dourou**, which has one of the most important **markets** so near the escarpment, and a **motorable** road from Bandiagara. Every five days, vehicles arrive here from Bandiagara and Mopti bringing traders and goods to the heart of Dogon country. In addition to ubiquitous Dogon onions, grown nearby and sold in large quantities, you'll find cereals, Fula milk and rough cotton weaves of indigo-dyed material, a common element in Dogon dress. If you time your visit to coincide with **market day**, you can hope to get a ride back to Bandiagara, 25km to the north.

A possible diversion from Dourou is to **Begnimato**, spectacularly situated under castle-like rock formations up on the plateau. The chief and his wife here are particularly welcoming to visitors who wish to stay.

A FEW WORDS OF DOGON

Many Dogon speak little or no French, so a few words in the Dogon language are bound to help comunication. The words and phrases below are intended as a guide but there are differences in dialect (sometimes major ones) between villages.

Yes/No	*Aha/Eye-ee*	God	*Amma*	7	*So*
Thank you	*Gana*	1	*Ti*	8	*Sira*
Village chief	*Emiru/*	2	*Loy*	9	*Tuwa*
	Amiru	3	*Tahnu*	10	*Peo*
Chief's wife	*Emeri Ana*	4	*Nay*	And, of	
Boy	*Ah*	5	*Noonay*	course,	
Girl	*Ñe*	6	*Kuray*	millet beer	*Konjo*

Standard greetings (often people will run through the entire sequence)

Hello/how's the work going?	*Po*
Good morning as above but addressing a group	*Poiye*
Good morning/evening (north village)	*Agapoyeh/Ey Wahna*
Good morning/evening (south village)	*Agayamwe/Eli Waleh*
How are you?	*Seyoma?*
– Fine	*Seyo*
How's the family?	*Gineh Seyom?*
– Fine	*Seyo*
How's your father?	*Deh Seyom?*
How's your mother?	*Na Seyom?*
How are the children?	*Ulumo Seyom?*
Everything's OK/Thanks	*Awa/Popo*
See you later	*Yemeh Ehso/Bolanee Jeh/Pinan Segeramo*

Sanga and around

Much has been written about **SANGA**, a striking example of a classic Dogon village with traditional homes and granaries, sited on the plateau above the escarpment. This is where Reverend McKinney set up the first mission in the Dogon country in the 1930s and where, soon after, Marcel Griaule lived and studied. Overflowing down the cliffs of the Bandiagara escarpment, the town was too picturesque to go unnoticed for long and some of the best and most popular **walking tours** through Dogon country start here.

Practicalities

If you don't sign up for an organized excursion in Mopti, you can get to Sanga by taking a bush taxi to Bandiagara. From here, it's possible to get transport to Sanga, notably on its market day (every five days).

Sanga is actually a conglomeration of small villages, the most useful of which is **Ogol-du-haut**, where you'll find the Gendarmerie and the *campement* (☎42.00.92; ③), one of Mali's best, with its own bar/restaurant. The alternative is the *Hôtel Monobeme de la Femme Dogon* (③), which is more basic but has clean rooms and decent food. Sanga is a good place to find a **guide** if you've arrived without one – the people at the *campement* will offer advice – and also to hunt out **souvenirs**.

Tours around Sanga

You may be offered three different **day-trips** from Sanga, ranging from seven to fifteen kilometres in length. The first includes a tour of Sanga and a **seven-kilometre** round-trip trek to Gogoli. A **ten-kilometre** tour continues from these villages to Banani, located partly on the *falaise* and partly on the plain below. The descent from the plateau takes you through a strange tunnel carved into the cliff near the village of Bongo. All along the escarpment, you see caves – originally used by the Tellem as granaries or for defence in case of attack – cut into the rocky face. The **fifteen-kilometre** tour extends the loop to include Tirelli, another particularly pretty village located both on the cliff and the plain. These treks last roughly between three and ten hours, and you can also arrange longer walking trips that last anything up to a week.

Bankass

An alternative route into Dogon country from Mopti and Sévaré bypasses Bandiagara altogether, entering the Dogon region via **BANKASS**, reached from the road that passes through Somadougou. This way you start the trek from down on the plains, and approach the escarpment from below. Bankass is a large market village with a mixed population, and although it is less centrally placed than Bandiagara for visits to the traditional villages, it makes for a pleasantly tranquil point of departure. Hiking access to the *falaise* is more difficult from here, but in the dry season it's possible to go by 4WD (or to rent a horse and cart) to Kani-Kombolé, Enndé and Teli. Although this is easier, the visit from Bandiagara is really more interesting and, approaching the scarp edge from above, certainly more impressive.

Practicalities

Accommodation in Bankass covers a range of budgets. *Campement Hogon* (②) offers rooms equipped with fans and mosquito nets, while on the road leading out of town, *Camping Hogon* (②), run by the same owner, merits a visit if only to appreciate the *togona* (a low stone structure where conflicts in the village are resolved) on the premises. Accommodation here is in roundhouses with traditional outside showers. The *Togona* (③), next to the water tower, has clean rooms with shared outdoor facilities, an interior garden, and a hallway decorated by the owner's private collection of masks and Dogon art. *Hôtel Les Arbres* (☎ & Fax 28.66.42; ⑤), behind the Centre des Impôts, offers overpriced, unventilated S/C rooms with mosquito nets. *Camping* is available at *Hôtel Les Arbres*, and on the terraces of both the *Togona* and *Campement Hogon*.

Both *Togona* and *Hogon* organize **excursions** to the Dogon country: a trip to the Bandiagara escarpment for two costs CFA17,500 per person per day (less in a larger group). If you're without transport, ask around about the possibility of renting a **mobylette** or **calèche** to Kani-Kombolé. Once there, you can visit other villages along the escarpment by following the routes described on p.353.

Koro

Coming from **Burkina Faso**, you can also enter the Dogon country by taking the road from Ouahigouya to the border post at Tiou. From here a very bad *piste* (often impassable during the rains) leads some 55km to **KORO**, where you go through Malian police and **customs formalities**. The STMB bus from Ouahigouya to Koro departs Saturday and Thursday at 6.45am and 10am, and costs CFA2000.

MOVING ON FROM BANKASS AND KORO

Transport out of Bankass towards Burkina is most likely on a Monday, market day in Bankass. Koro is somewhat problematic. Check with STMB and SOGEBAF transport companies. Taxis head fairly frequently to Bankass (at least daily), but are extremely rare to the border at Tiou and into Burkina Faso. Even in the dry season you may be stranded several days in Koro waiting for the occasional goods truck or tourist heading south. During the rains, the road may be impassable for weeks on end.

Koro has a large **market** and beautiful **mosque**, but is probably too far from the heart of the Dogon country to be a useful springboard for a trip there. To visit the *falaise*, you could head up to **Bankass** – *bâchés* generally make the trip at least once or twice a day (2hr; CFA1000) – and follow the routes outlined overleaf. Koro's lone and rather sad-looking *campement* (①) serves as a liaison for tours setting out from Bankass. Alternatively, you could make for **Douentza** in the northeast (see p.356). This last route passes through the Dogon villages of **Madougou** and **Bamba** and a wild, duney area. You will receive very genuine hospitality, with none of the commercialism of the villages further west. **Everi**, a seven-kilometre hike from Douentza, is built on a high mesa at the end of the escarpment. Infrequent vehicles link these villages on market days.

If you're heading to **Gao** with your own vehicle, the Douentza *piste* provides a kind of "rear view" of the Dogon country. The tracks, however, are very difficult (with taxing stretches of soft sand and boulders) and it's hard to follow their endless branches. Peugeot 404 taxis do ply between Douentza and Madougou for the market, so you should be able to go by normal car, although a 4WD is obviously preferable. It would probably prove just as quick though to follow the longer but more obvious route via Somadougou and the main Bamako–Gao highway.

GAO AND THE NORTHEAST

Arid and inhospitable, northeastern Mali is only habitable at all thanks to the Niger River, along which life in the area concentrates. The riverside town of **Gao**, formerly the capital of a great kingdom, is now the administrative and commercial centre for the region. From here you can follow the river south to **Niamey** (in Niger) along a difficult but scenic *piste* leading through small fishing villages; head upstream, along even more difficult tracks, to **Timbuktu** in the west; or go west the easy way, on the paved road **to Mopti and Bamako**. Alternatively **the river** itself can serve as your highway, certainly a more memorable way to travel – providing you time your travels to coincide with the rains.

Gao

In the repertoire of campfire travel talk, **GAO** was always one of the most romantic cities. As you arrived from the void of the Sahara, it seemed like a small miracle of civilization emerging from the wasteland. Passing the last stretch of soft sand thrown up by the desert around the town, and entering its dusty tree-lined avenues of mud-brick buildings, thronging with crowds, stirred certain exhilaration. Traditionally, desert-crossers would celebrate their arrival in West Africa by heading straight to the *Hôtel Atlantide* – a tatty colonial pile that might as well be the Ritz out here – and downing a few cold beers. Behind the hotel lies the source of all the vigour, the **Niger River**.

If you've come up from the south you get a rather different view of the place. The river, which from this direction is neither new nor unusual, is unlikely to stir much excitement, while the town itself resembles any other Sahelian city, bigger than most but neither especially beautiful nor unusually dynamic. All is relative.

Some history

The original founders of Gao, known in its early days as Kawkaw, were **Sorko fishermen** who migrated from Benin between the sixth and eleventh centuries. They mingled with the rural Gabili peoples living along the banks of the Niger, and eventually this mixture evolved into a people known as the Songhai. The first **Songhai** monarch at Gao was Kanda, who founded the **Za (or Dia) dynasty** in the seventh century. He quickly opened the town to trans-Saharan trade and to Berbers who wanted to settle there for commercial reasons.

The fifteenth king of Songhai, Za Kossoi, converted to **Islam** in 1009. The town prospered to the point where it rivalled all the great regional trading centres in power and wealth, even surpassing the capitals of Ancient Ghana and later Mali. Rulers of the Mali Empire coveted Gao's success and potential and annexed the town in 1325, although the Songhai princes managed to flee from their clutches. One of them, **Ali Golon**, went on to found the **Sonni dynasty** still based at Gao. The greatest of the Sonni rulers was the despotic Sonni Ali Ber, or **Ali the Great**. It was he who, towards the end of the fifteenth century, expanded the kingdom at Gao to the dimensions of an empire (see box overleaf). The capital continued to flourish under the reign of the **Askias**, founders of a new dynasty that lasted throughout the sixteenth century. At the time, Gao had 70,000 inhabitants and in the busy harbour were crowded over a thousand war boats from the Askias' flotilla, four hundred barges and thousands of *pirogues*.

With the **Moroccan invasion** of Songhai in 1591, the empire collapsed and Gao was virtually razed. The town never recovered and when the German explorer **Heinrich Barth** arrived in 1854, he described the once ostentatious city as "a desolate abode with a small and miserable population". Much of the town's present look dates to the beginning of this century. The **French** built up the port, traced new streets (which explains the rather uniform grid layout) and established an administrative district with characteristic colonial buildings still used by the present government. With a population of some 20,000, Gao still hasn't returned to its former grandeur and in its current economic and political predicament it is struggling.

The Town

Considering the centuries of history through which Gao has played a leading role, the **Musée du Sahel** (Tues–Fri & Sun 4–6pm; CFA1000) on the north side of town is disappointingly small, dedicated to the different **peoples of the Sahel**, with displays of their art and domestic implements. You'll see farming and fishing tools (some rather impressive harpoons), musical instruments, and household items used by the **Tuareg, Fula, Chamba** and **Arma** (descendants of Moroccan-Songhai marriages). Guided tours cost a little extra: the guides are extremely enthusiastic and their personal comments make it worthwhile, but if you want to go it alone you'll find that most of the exhibits are explained relatively well.

In the town centre, Gao boasts two outstanding **markets**. The *grand marché*, just opposite the *Hôtel Atlantide*, has an entire section devoted to **crafts**, for which the region is well known. The most common items are Tuareg **leather boxes**, knives and swords; on sale too are numerous examples of **Sahelian sandals** – flat and wide to facilitate walking on the sands. Some pairs incorporate intricate weaving and green-or red-dyed leather in the design. Fula and Tuareg **jewellery** can also be a

THE SONGHAI EMPIRE

Towards the end of the fourteenth century, Mali's influence and power had diminished greatly and the stage was set for **Sonni Ali Ber** – nineteenth ruler in the Sonni dynasty and the effective founder of Songhai as an empire – to embark on his great conquests. A shrewd administrator, Ali was also a brilliant and ruthless strategist and it is said he never lost a battle. A half-hearted Muslim, Ali quickly set about terrorizing the Fula and Tuareg nomads – his bitter enemies in the region. His expansionist designs were greatly facilitated in 1468 when he was invited by the governor of **Timbuktu** to liberate that town from Tuareg domination.

Historians of the period reported that Ali's conquest of Timbuktu was brutal, and many townspeople who had longed for the Songhai "liberation" fled west to Oualata for fear of persecution. After an initial period of purging religious leaders who stood in his path, however, Ali brought stability to the town which once again prospered under his rule. At the same time, he managed to neutralize the **religious influence** of Timbuktu's powerful marabouts who exercised considerable political power over the entire region.

Ali next turned his sights on **Djenné**, which proved a harder target. The Sonnis besieged the town for seven years, seven months and seven days before it finally fell in 1473. Rather than wreaking vengeance on the ruling class as he had in Timbuktu, Ali married his fortunes with those of Djenné by taking the queen mother to be his wife. **Masina** was his next objective, and he conquered this Fula stronghold shortly afterwards.

All the chief strategic points of the Niger and the delta region were now in Songhai control. The nation's military strength was founded in its **navy** and Ali depended so heavily on his flotilla that, at one point, he envisaged digging a canal from the port town of Ras al-Ma to the desert oasis of Oualata in order to attack the Tuareg there. Although work started, the plan was eventually abandoned as Ali extended his control southwards to the villages of Bandiagara, Bariba and Gourma.

After he died, Sonni Ali was succeeded by his son Bakari, but the new king followed his father's example of keeping a distance from the faith and thus incited religious disapproval. He was overthrown by Mohammed Torodo, the governor of Hombori, who formed a new dynasty known as the **Askia** or "usurper".

Though he had no hereditary claim to the throne, Askia Mohammed legitimized his rule through religious channels, soliciting the backing of powerful **marabouts**. He received the ultimate benediction to his rule after making the pilgrimage to Mecca with 500 horsemen and 1000 footsoldiers. There he was granted the title of Khalif for the entire Sudan. Returning to Mali, he set about expanding his empire into Mossi country, then pushed eastward to Hausaland and into the Aïr as far as Agadez.

While away on a campaign, Mohammed was forced out of power in 1528. Internal intrigue followed and a number of Askias succeeded one another until the reign of **Ishak I** who ruled from 1539 to 1549 – a decade which marked the Songhai Empire's apogee. The country now extended from Senegal to the Aïr mountains and from the Taghaza salt mines in the desert to the Hausaland in what is today Nigeria.

Meanwhile **Morocco** far to the north was in a period of crisis. Ejected from Andalucía and hemmed in to the east by the Turks, the Moroccan sultan turned his sights towards the south, where he sought to gain control of the salt and gold trade. In 1591 he sent an army to wrest the Sudan from Songhai control. Thanks to a combination of Moroccan firearms and the disarray of the Askia rulers, the Sultan's army won a decisive battle at **Tondibi**, 60km north of Gao: Gao, Djenné and Timbuktu all fell soon afterwards.

El Sadi, writing in the *Tarikh es-Soudan*, described the invasion in these terms: "Everything changed after the Moroccan conquest. It signalled the beginning of anarchy, theft, pillage and general disorganization". And indeed the entire Sahelian region suffered a blow from which it never recovered.

good buy here, but vendors generally set astronomically high starting prices: bargaining tends to be more of a headache than the good-humoured exchange you're hopefully used to.

Behind the crafts section, women bunch around desert wares – anonymous spices, dollops of peanut butter, sour milk, fish and meat, pyramids of miniature tomatoes, onions, peppers and lettuces carefully washed (in the river) – and, in season if you're lucky, the full range of tropical fruits and vegetables. The *petit marché*, next to the police station, specializes in **cloth**. Dozens of tailors – all men of course – treadle ancient sewing machines and will take orders if you want to have loose-fitting Sahelian clothes made to measure.

In physical terms, Gao has few reminders of its glorious past. The **mosque** in the centre of town near the police station was initially built by Kankan Moussa after he annexed the town in the fourteenth century but, its origins apart, it's unimpressive compared even with those in Timbuktu and certainly in comparison with the mosque at Djenné.

Following the Boulevard des Askias to the northeast brings you to the **Askia tomb** – a fifteen-minute walk from the centre. Now used as a mosque, you can visit this strange fifteenth-century mud structure (CFA1000) and climb to the top of the odd-shaped pyramid with wild wooden crossbeams sticking out porcupine style from the facade: from the top, you get a good view of the town and of the river. You should tip the guardian something for the visit.

Practicalities

You must **register with the police** and have your passport stamped on arrival. Their office is next to the market and central mosque. Note that people arriving with vehicles on the Bamako road after nightfall will not be able to cross the river (7km south of the town) into Gao and must camp out along the riverbank until the following morning, when the **ferry** resumes its service.

Accommodation within the city limits include the *Atlantide* (BP 29; ☎82.01.30; ③–⑤), which exudes an air of unmistakeable decay, for all its past grandeur, and *Camping Bongo* (②), with no electricity in the rooms. The newly opened *Passion Sahara* (③) has rooms with shower and fan, friendly owners and an excellent restaurant; it also organizes excursions in the region. Out of the centre, there are a few more options. About 4km down the Niamey road in *chateau secteur 2* (a local can walk you there for a small fee), *Tizi-Mizi Camping* (②–③) is the best option in Gao, with nice small huts, an outdoor bar and restaurant as well as a disco. The long-established *Camping Restaurant Yarga* (①) is also about 4km from the centre in the *8e quartier*, off the paved road leading to the Mopti road ferry, with traditional mud-brick buildings and a large central courtyard. You can have meals prepared here, and prices are slightly lower than those at *Tizi-Mizi*, but the rooms are less comfortable. *Yarga* is also close to good swimming beaches along the Niger, and can arrange excursions by *pirogue* or *pinasse*. Finally, the run-down *Hôtel Le Bel Air* (BP 154; ③), in *chateau secteur 4*, has S/C terrace rooms. *Camping* is available in all of the places mentioned above.

Gao doesn't boast very classy **restaurants** except, with a stretch of imagination, the *Atlantide*'s where you can sit down to French-style *steack frites* or *poulet* and vegetables – unexciting and rather pricey. *Sahara Passion*'s restaurant is probably the best in town, serving up good quality food in a nice garden setting. *Restaurant Koundji do, Saneye secteur 6*, has local cuisine including *halabadja, fakouhye* and the regional *ragoût d'igname*. Branching out from the motor park away from the city's centre, *Restaurant de l'Amitié* (BP 65; ☎82.04.32), 40m from the Musée du Sahel, has everything from *tô de maïs avec sauce gombo* to *poulet rôti*, except on Sunday when the ubiquitous *riz avec sauce* is the only dish available. Cheaper still is a string of **chop houses** on the road

MOVING ON FROM GAO

Now that the road has been paved from **Gao to Bamako**, getting out of town is much easier. During and after the rains, you can also take advantage of the **steamers** that pass along one of the most interesting stretches of the **Niger** between here (their terminus) and Mopti.

By river
In addition to the main August–November steamer services, most of the year it's possible to use smaller river craft for transport. Upstream, poled *pirogues* set off for **Bourem** (all day and half the next), **Bamba** (3–4 days), **Gourma-Rharous** (4–5 days) and Timbuktu (one week). Downstream, *pirogues* rarely go much beyond **Gargouna** (one day away; Tuesday market) or **Ansongo** (two days away; splendid Thursday market). This latter trip, below Gao, is especially rewarding from a natural history viewpoint, as the boats crush through marvellous deep reedbeds harbouring a wealth of **birdlife**, and then break onto open water where they regularly pass several herds of snorting **hippos**. *Pirogue* fares have increased enormously in recent years, but a place on an ordinary transport vessel shouldn't cost you more than CFA3000 per day, including communal rice and fish.

By air
Air Mali operates one **flight** a week from Gao airfield (7km from the centre) to Timbuktu (CFA34,000), Mopti (CFA45,000) and Bamako (CFA100,000). For more details, check out the Air Mali office which is in the centre of town next to the *Hôtel Atlantide*.

By road
Regular buses leave Gao for Mopti and **Bamako**.The Nigérien SNTN bus leaves Gao for **Niamey** once a week, usually on Tuesday morning. It's wise to book the day before as it's often full. The bus leaves Gao sometime after 7am and gets into Niamey early evening the following day. The one-way fare is CFA10,400. Askia Transport, a transport cooperative at the *grand parkage*, may also have scheduled departures. **Bush taxis** will go as far as the border for CFA6000.

To track down the exceedingly rare vehicles heading to **Timbuktu**, check at hotels, with children – who can be a help finding out about transport if you give them a small *cadeau* – and at the *grand parkage*. This destination involves the longest wait from Gao and at times there's nothing at all heading in that direction. If you get fed up, take a vehicle to Bourem and try waiting there. Some traffic crosses the desert and turns right to Timbuktu. Be aware that bandit attacks have occured on the Timbuktu–Gao *piste* and remain a risk.

At the time of writing in mid-1999, the route **north across the Sahara** is effectively closed due to Tuareg banditry and the poor security situation in Algeria, and travel in the region north of Gao is not advised. It's reportedly possible to travel north in relative safety as far as Kidal, but from there an armed guard convoy is required.

running parallel to the principal Boulevard des Askias – two blocks east as you walk away from the river. And be sure to sample Gao's delicious, long spicy sausages – always a reliable evening street food fallback.

International calls can be made 24 hours a day from SOTELMA or nearby at the **post office** (Mon–Fri 8am–noon & 2.30–4pm); the poste restante is notorious for its delays. The system at the BDM **bank** hasn't changed for years and involves repeated visits to various *guichets* for different signatures. The place is always stacked full of money and full of backcountry people trying to perform once-yearly transactions before it closes at noon.

Along the Mopti road

The early stages of the Mopti road are dull, with long stretches of monotonous Sahelian landscape. After 90km you arrive at **Doro**, a small town in a region where lions are said to exist. If these reports are true, you'd have to follow tracks a good 40km south of town to have any hope of seeing them. Ask in Doro if any have been spotted recently and enquire about the possibility of taking someone along as a guide.

Gossi is the next large Songhai village along the road, 160km from Gao. It's on the shore of a muddy lake and is the site of a sizeable reforestation and agricultural project headed by a Norwegian church fund. It also has a wildlife claim, one spectacularly authenticated by the BBC in a film documentary made in 1994. A herd of some six hundred **elephants** lives in the district, protected partly by the traditional **Tuareg** resistance to hunting these animals. Many Tuareg are making the uneasy transition to a sedentary lifestyle in this area, however, and their crops are threatened by the *elouan*. Gossi has no accommodation but it's a pleasant place to stop off for a lukewarm drink and bite to eat. Reasonably priced grilled meat is sold in large quantities at the market.

After Gossi, the scenery shifts from neutral into top gear, with unexpectedly large **rock formations** in the vicinity of Hombori, 250km from Gao. A strikingly situated village, Hombori is built partially on the rocky slopes of **Hombori Tondo** – a flat-topped mountain that rises to 1150m. Many of the homes here are built of stone, a rarity in West Africa, and there are a couple of small **restaurants** and bars. Then, 11km out of Hombori, the road passes the dramatic formation known as **La Main de Fatima**, since it resembles the symbolic hand – with outstretched thumb and finger – of the prophet's daughter.

Just under 400km from Gao, Douentza is a town with an important market and an impressive **mosque**, poised at the northeastern periphery of the **Bandiagara escarpment** which stretches some 200km south through the Dogon country. Just before arriving at Douentza, a signboard marks the turning for Koro. If you have transport, this *piste* provides an excellent means of getting to the Dogon villages of Amba, Bamba and Madougou. From here you can head back up to Bandiagara, and will have visited a good chunk of the Dogon country without ever running into police or tourist guides. Few people take this route, however, and with good reason. The tracks can be hard work in a low-slung car, though battered Peugeot 404 bush taxis do make the trip out from Douentza.

Back on the main paved road to Mopti, **Boré** (458km from Gao) boasts an unusually large and beautiful **mosque** for such a small place. A further 56km and you arrive at **Konna**, a market town on the junction of the road to Niafounké and Timbuktu. From here, it's a quick jog to Sévaré – the highway junction for Mopti.

South to Niamey

Although only 443km separate Gao and Niamey, the trip involves a very long day's drive – longer in the rains or if you take it easy and stop off at the numerous fishing villages. The road hugs the banks of the **Niger** through some exceptionally beautiful scenery. It's a well-travelled route, but full of sandy pitfalls and thorn trees whose spines work their way through hot, soft rubber.

The initial 95km presents few problems until you arrive at Ansongo – a picturesque village with an important **market** on Thursdays. The town is essentially Songhai, but you'll also see numerous Tuareg who make their way through the entire region. After Ansongo, the road becomes progressively worse, with stretches of treacherous sand that may become impassable during the rains. Despite the difficulties, it's a beautiful stretch that the government has officially classified as a protected natural area. Your chances are good of seeing **hippos** at some point along the river: in many instances they come quite close to the villages and the areas where people swim. **Giraffes** and numerous varieties of **gazelle** also roam through the region, though you're unlikely to spot them from the *piste*.

The road continues tortuously until you arrive at Labbenzanga, 191km from Gao, the Mali–Niger **border post** where you'll be subjected to protracted formalities. There's a bar and **restaurant** near the customs post. It's another 44km to Ayorou, a large market town where you pass through Niger customs, and 132km to Tillabéri where the **surfaced road** picks up the rest of the way to Niamey.

THE CAPE VERDE ISLANDS

THE CAPE VERDE ISLANDS

From a traveller's viewpoint, and indeed a West African one, the **Cape Verde Islands** are barely on the map. If you ever hear of the archipelago, it's usually as an offshore supplement to the grim process of desertification on the African mainland, 500km away. An Atlantic world apart, the Cape Verdes fall in more neatly with the Azores, or even the Canary Islands. They consist of nine main islands in two groups, the **Barlaventos** (Windwards) and the **Sotaventos** (Leewards). Six of them – **Santiago**, **Fogo**, **Brava**, **São Nicolau**, **São Vicente** and **Santo Antão** – are volcanic and inspiringly scenic, while the three to the east – **Maio**, **Boa Vista** and **Sal** – are flat and sandy. Although the islands are isolated, once you've arrived, they are not difficult to get around, using the good ferries and internal air service. There's usually somewhere to stay, a small hotel or *pensão*, and prices are reasonable. Despite the **cost** of flights to the Cape Verdes, the islands are, emphatically, worth the hassle.

The Cape Verdes were uninhabited until first colonized by the **Portuguese** in 1462. The first Portuguese immigrants, who in the sixteenth century made the islands an Atlantic victualling station and entrepôt for the trade in African produce and **slaves**, were a mixed population of landless peasants, banished malefactors, adventurers and exiles. The islands were soon being cultivated by the slaves and freed slaves who rapidly made up the bulk of the population. But while the mixed race population that emerged was considered "assimilated" – accepted as Portuguese by Lisbon – the islanders suffered in various degrees from oppressive and racist policies. In Cape Verdean society there was great emphasis on skin colour, the criterion by which "real Portugueseness" was measured.

Commercial planting was mostly of cotton, woven into the *panos* prized along the Guinea coastlands. But catastrophic **droughts** brought despair and neglect; for nearly the whole of their colonial period the islands remained a largely ignored backwater of the Portuguese empire. Over the last 150 years, tens of thousands of Cape Verdeans

---

FACTS AND FIGURES

The islands' name – **Cabo Verde** in Portuguese – is derived from their geographical position off Cap Vert, the Dakar peninsula of Senegal. Their total **land area**, just 4000 square kilometres, is about the same size as Kent or a little larger than Rhode Island. Less than 400,000 Cape Verdeans (under half the total) now live on the islands, with the remainder living or working abroad. In January 1991, Cape Verde was one of the first countries in the region to see democratic elections, with a peaceful transition from the PAICV single party regime to the Movimento para a Democracia (MPD). The MPD's politics are right of centre. Cape Verde's **foreign debt** is a severe test of its resources, yet at about £100 million ($160 million) – incidentally the annual sum spent on services and amenities in Kingston-upon-Thames, England (population 150,000) – is only half its annual gross domestic product of about £200 million ($320 million).

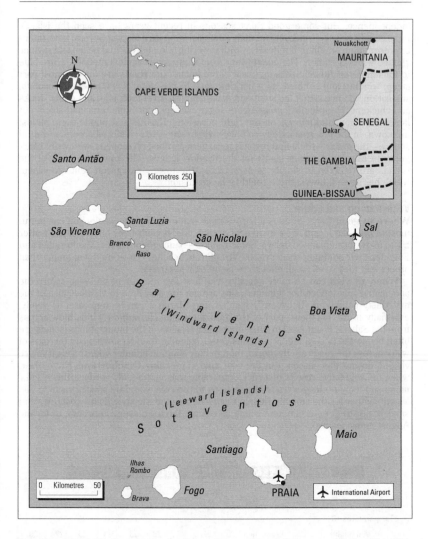

have left the islands for São Tome, Guinea-Bissau, Senegal, Europe and the USA. The **New England connection** is especially strong, with *americanos* remitting the hard currency which the island families need.

Visiting the islands

The **feel** of the Cape Verde Islands is unplaceable – not quite African, scarcely European, but Portuguese mannered and Kriolu-speaking (an African/Portuguese creole). The islands are no tropical paradise: banish any Caribbean associations. The most recent **drought**, which lasted from the early 1970s to 1985, brought malnutrition and hardships which only worsened the country's economic plight in the first decade of independence. But some good rainy seasons in recent years have seen the islands increasingly green – especially on their northern windward slopes. Several have interiors resembling anything but deserts, with towering, cloud-drenched peaks and ravines choked with vegetation. The **coasts** vary from white sands against metallic, azure blue to full-tempered Atlantic seas on black cliffs. Inland, the **roads** are for the most part steep, winding and cobbled, as if harking back to pre-motor days; **trees** are baobab, silk-cotton and breadfruit, coconut and date palm; the **livestock** pigs and goats, ducks and chickens. **People** distil *grogue* from sugar cane, fish for huge tuna, and strum out laments in mournful *mornas* on the right occasions. Rip-offs and hustle seem almost unknown. In the few small, tidily colonial-style **towns**, each clustered around a central square – the *praça* – you'll find restless teenagers perched on mopeds, widows in black going to Mass and potted plants on the window ledges. The towns on most of the islands are referred to simply as *povoação* – "the town". Except on Santiago island, which has several towns, there could be no confusion.

Where to go and when

Where to go in Cape Verde is a fairly simple matter – in a few weeks you can get to most of the islands and see a good deal of each one. If you've any choice in the matter try to allow for unplanned delays. Some islands – Santiago for its size, Santo Antão and Fogo for their stunning scenery, Boa Vista for its beaches – may hold you longer than others; but they're all small enough to be quickly graspable.

When to visit can be more specific. The first five months of the year before the anticipated July to October summer rains are not the best time to visit because of the dry, dusty conditions. Between December and March it can be unpleasantly windy, especially in the northeast part of the archipelago, as *Harmattan* winds blow across from the Sahara. From April to June, the higher reaches of the mountainous islands are often blanketed in cold fog. If the rains come, splendid thunderstorms and torrents of water across the roads are the norm, though they shouldn't hinder your travels if you're visiting during this season. But the best time is probably **October and November**, when the vegetative results of a successful rainy season are truly verdant, the islands' name suddenly no longer ironic. Exceptions to the rule would be special visits to São Vicente either for the annual Mindelo *Carnaval*, a riot of Rio-style floats, costumes and small-scale street entertainment which takes over the town every February, or for the August music festival.

AVERAGE TEMPERATURES AND RAINFALL											
PRAIA											
Jan	Feb	Mar	Apr	May	June	July	Aug	Sept	Oct	Nov	Dec
Temperatures °C											
Min (night)											
20	19	19	20	21	22	23	23	24	23	22	20
Max (day)											
27	28	29	29	30	30	30	30	31	31	30	27
Rainfall mm											
2	0	0	0	0	1	8	76	102	30	10	2

Arrivals

The Cape Verde Islands are remote. Apart from a sporadic ferry service from Dakar, flying to the islands is the only way of reaching them – unless you have an ocean-going yacht.

■ Flights from Africa

The only flights from the African mainland are to the capital, Praia, on Santiago island (all other international flights land in Sal). The fifty-seater flights from **Dakar to Praia** are usually full and routinely overbooked. Operated by Air Sénégal (DS) and the Cape Verdean airline TACV (VR), they fly in both directions three times a week. The cheapest official round-trip fare is CFA154,700 (£170/US$275), though students and over-65s can get thirty and forty percent discounts respectively. Make a reservation as soon as you can and be sure to reconfirm your seat a couple of days before – or to make a strong impression in the office in Dakar. If you're not confirmed, you'll have to hustle hard at the airport on the day of the flight. Note that because of an unreliable reservations system for these flights, "confirmed" seats on a ticket purchased in Europe are no guarantee. Check again when you get to Dakar.

The operation of flights from **Bissau** and **Banjul** has been patchy. There is still a weekly flight to Sal from **Las Palmas**, in the Canary Islands.

■ By sea

The Companhia Nacional de Navegação Arca Verde runs (in theory) a **monthly ferry service** from **Dakar** to Praia. Departures are normally on the first Saturday of the month: tickets from 18 rue Rafenel, Dakar. They also run a service from **Las Palmas** in the Canary Islands. Both are often out of commission for months at a time.

> The details in these practical information pages are essentially for use on the ground in West Africa and on the Cape Verde Islands themselves: for full practical coverage on preparing for a trip, getting here from outside the region, paperwork, health, information sources and more, see Basics, pp.3–83.

There are further possibilities (though fairly remote ones) of getting a berth on board a merchant vessel out of Europe. There's at least one merchant vessel a month from **Las Palmas**, **Lisbon** and **Rotterdam** to Mindelo. If you're interested in the latter two, try: Joaquim Pio & Martins Lda, Rua da Vitoria 7–0, 1100 Lisbon (☎ +351 (1) 877181 or 877182); or Viagens Cabo Verde B.V., Rochussenstraat 395, 3023 DK Rotterdam (☎ +31 (10) 258054).

Finally, if you're in Las Palmas, you might check around the **yachts** for anyone headed to the Cape Verdes. During the east–west transatlantic crossing season, roughly from October to March, hundreds make the journey and they invariably call at the "Verdes". Even without experience, it's possible to get a berth in exchange for some basic crewing and boat chores. Expect to pay the skipper around $10 per day for your keep.

Red Tape

All nationalities require visas. There are few Cape Verdean consulates and no diplomatic representation in Britain (see below). The easiest place in Europe to get a visa is Lisbon. In West Africa the only consulate is in Senegal, at 1 rue de Denain, Dakar (☎21 18 73).

Once you've found a consulate, visas are no problem. In Dakar, you should be able to get one in a matter of hours, with three passport photos. Be sure to check when you're supposed to come back, as the rue de Denain office keeps slightly irregular hours. If you arrive on the islands without a visa, experience suggests you're unlikely to be turned away as your immediate point of departure probably had no Cape Verde consulate in any case (airlines in cities with consulates will normally ask to see your visa before issuing a ticket). If you fly in on an unusual route, or arrive by sea, you can invariably obtain a visa quickly and simply at the immigration desk.

The easiest solution for UK residents is to contact the extremely helpful and well-informed specialist Cape Verde Travel, 10 Market St, Hornsea, East Yorkshire HU18 1AW (☎01964/536191; Fax 536192; *www.eastgate-travel.co.uk*. If you use their services, they will fax your details ahead to Sal to simplify the issue of a visa on arrival. In practice, the immigration authorities in Sal will normally issue a visa in any case, introduction or no introduction.

On **duty-free allowances** of alcohol and tobacco, there's a simple rule: none. But the principle is not adhered to and, in practice, reasonable personal quantities are fine. There's rarely much of a customs check anyway.

Money and Costs

Cape Verde is not a cheap destination and if you travel widely, you'll find you can spend alarmingly fast. Cape Verde's currency is the Cape Verdean escudo (CV$), which on the islands you'll normally see written thus – 500$00, meaning 500 escudos. Centavos account for the zeros but you're not likely to see any coins smaller than a 1 escudo piece. The exchange rate is fairly stable, currently about CV$160 = £1, CV$100 = $1.

A *conto* is 1000 escudos. Escudos are not convertible outside Cape Verde. Arriving at Praia there's no bank at the airport; Sal airport has one. The Banco Comercial do Atlântico is the most useful bank and most towns – and all island capitals – have a branch. They normally take travellers' cheques in all major currencies and service is efficient. Larger hotels also accept travellers' cheques, and you don't lose much in commission. The limited **black market** isn't worth bothering yourself (or Cape Verde's balance of payments) over; at most you'll add a few percent to your spending power as the rates are normally exactly the same as the bank's.

You won't save much by **bargaining** either; the practice is considered a little unworthy and most people prefer to stick by their starting price even if it means losing the sale. This is hard to accept at first, if you've grown accustomed to West Africa's noisy exchanges of mock outrage, but it makes life more relaxed and seems entirely appropriate in Cape Verde's almost hassle-free environment.

Credit cards don't help much on the islands. The big tourist hotels in Santa Maria, on Sal, take Amex, but they're about the only establishments that will.

■ Costs

Your **outlay** will very much depend on how and how much you travel between islands. The flight network is not inexpensive (£30–60, or roughly $50–100, for most of the short hops between islands) and travel costs can quickly break into

even fairly generous budgets. Buying air passes is a good idea (see opposite). Ferries are cheaper but they don't offer the same flexibility. Road travel is inexpensive; but the cost of exploring those islands which don't have much public transport can soon mount up unless you have time to do a lot of walking. A basic room in the very cheapest type of *pensão* will cost upwards of £6 ($10) and a straightforward three-course meal goes from about £3 ($5), with individual dishes in fancier establishments costing about the same.

In three weeks, visiting half a dozen islands and keeping flights to a minimum, staying in the cheapest *pensões* and restricting yourself to one restaurant meal a day, a rough estimate of spending would be around £700 ($1140), somewhat less if you're sharing and much less if you spend any time hiking and camping. **Prices** vary slightly from island to island and of course are much lower outside the few main towns; reading through you'll get a good idea of where is most expensive. Prices tend to be lower where much food is locally produced (Santiago, Santo Antão), and higher where there are international connections or a whiff of tourism (Sal, Praia itself, São Vicente, Fogo, Boa Vista).

Health

Arriving direct from outside Africa, you don't need any inoculations. Coming from the mainland, cholera and yellow fever certificates are routinely demanded, though you may get away without a yellow fever certificate if you're connecting straight through to São Vicente, Sal, Maio or Boa Vista.

One of the health successes of Cape Verde has been the virtual elimination of **malaria**. Until the nineteenth century a posting to the islands from Portugal was viewed as one step short of a death sentence. Now, all planes arriving from Africa get insect-sprayed before any passengers are allowed off and all visitors are issued with a health card asking them to report any fever they get on the islands. Only parts of Santiago have a malaria risk and few people use anti-malaria pills. If you're on Cape Verde for a short time only, however, and planning to return to the mainland, you shouldn't break your course.

Water from the tap is almost always good but water shortages mean that you'll sometimes be drinking water that's been stored or sold, so beware (80 people died of **cholera** in Mindelo in

1995). And be sparing too: islanders pay for tap water, which is metered, and big price increases are common during droughts. Bottled brands are widely available.

Health care on the islands isn't bad and while infant mortality is still high, life expectancy, at 63, is impressive. **Leprosy** is still a big problem on Fogo, but not one that will affect your own health. Surprisingly few people **smoke** – though it's a habit enjoyed in pipes by elderly ladies in rural Santiago. Litter bins and enjoinments to social responsibility are features of urban life and Praia is a refreshingly clean capital.

There are **hospitals** in Praia and Mindelo with adequate facilities for ordinary problems. Dispensaries, cottage hospitals and pharmacies (*farmácia*) in most towns or, failing these, *postos venda medicamentos* (health posts), should fulfil basic needs. If, on your travels, you had the misfortune to get ill, Cape Verde would be a good place to **convalesce**. Low humidity, sea breezes and clear skies are the norm.

Information and Maps

Cape Verde has no tourist offices abroad and the few embassies and consulates have either nothing or the most limited leaflets. To cover every angle, contact the national tourism institute INATUR (☎61.44.73; Fax 61.44.75), and ask them to send you what they have.

As for **maps**, there's a good general travel sheet of the whole archipelago – which you may come across on office walls in Cape Verde, but is only rarely available for sale. A British Admiralty naval chart based on nineteenth-century soundings (available from Stanfords in London; see p.39) shows quite a lot of topographical detail but is hopelessly out of date – despite twentieth-century updating – on roads and villages.

INATUR publishes aerial photo maps, which are better than nothing, but don't show much detail. They're available from the tourist info kiosks in Praia and Mindelo. Much more helpful are the island maps of Santiago and São Vicente, and the very detailed town plans, of Praia, Mindelo and the towns on Sal, also distributed through the Promex kiosks or direct from Tectoplaca, 14 rua do Tejo, Mindelo (☎ & Fax 32.22.18)

Getting Around

The most important inter-island connections are by plane, with ferries providing a good alternative if you have more time. Except on Santiago, road transport on the islands is very limited.

■ Domestic flights

All the inhabited islands are linked by **internal flights** run by Transportes Aereos de Cabo Verde. Fares range from CV$4000–9000 (£40–60 or $64–96). If you're reading this before arrival in Cape Verde, you can buy a Cabo Verde Air Pass (must be purchased abroad in conjunction with a ticket to the islands), of anything from two flight coupons (valid 15 days; £107/$172), to ten flight coupons (valid 22 days; £236/$378), with normal child (67 percent) and infant (10 percent) rates.

It's important to reserve seats as far ahead as possible, as flights are usually full (though sometimes cancelled); always reconfirm your seat if it's been booked for more than 24 hours. It's often possible, even when there's no direct flight, to get where you want to on the same day with a little island hopping. Note however that international arrivals delayed into Sal airport can sometimes knock the whole domestic service out of joint, as domestic planes are delayed for connections.

■ Ferries

Two German-built **ferries**, *Barlavento* and *Sotavento*, run weekly schedules through the islands on a roughly four-week cycle. The home port is Mindelo, on São Vicente, and the itinerary is either from Mindelo to São Nicolau, Sal, Praia, Fogo and back to Mindelo or, in the other direction, from Mindelo to Fogo, Praia, Sal, São Nicolau and Mindelo. On this latter route, the ferries also call at either Brava or Boa Vista, on alternate voyages.

In theory, the voyages start in Mindelo on Mondays and terminate there on a Friday or Saturday, but exact timings always depend on cargo requirements (the vessels are primarily supply ships) and, of course, on the weather. The big question is which itinerary is operating in any given week. If you want to plan ahead before arriving in Cape Verde, the Companhia Nacional de Navegação Arca Verde (see Praia "Listings", p.394, for address) can provide the latest details, but even they may not know which itinerary will be in force more than a month in advance.

OTHER PRINCIPLE FERRIES

The **Ribeira de Paúl** and **Mar Azul** sail at least daily between Mindelo (São Vicente) and Porto Novo (Santo Antão), the crossing taking about one hour; at any given time one is likely to be out of service, so check which ferry is operating.

The **Furna** operates a rather impenetrable timetable between Praia, Porto de Vale (Fogo) and Furna (Brava). The **Porto Novo** sails from Praia to Maio more or less every week, usually every Thursday or Friday.

FERRY: *RIBEIRA DE PAÚL*

From Mindelo		**From Porto Novo**	
Mon	noon	Mon	5pm
Tues	8am	Tues	11am
Wed	noon	Wed	5pm
Thurs	8am	Thurs	11am
Fri	noon	Fri	5pm
Sat	8am	Sat	11am
Sun	no voyage	Sun	no voyage

FERRY: *MAR AZUL*

From Mindelo		**From Porto Novo**	
Mon	8am	Mon	10.30am
Tues	no voyage	Tues	no voyage
Wed	8am	Wed	10.30am
Thurs	3pm	Thurs	5pm
Fri	8am	Fri	10.30am
Sat	3pm	Sat	5pm
Sun	9am	Sun	6pm

FERRY: *FURNA*

Mon	dep. Brava noon	Thurs	arr. Praia 6am
	arr. Fogo 1pm		dep. Praia 9.30pm
	dep. Fogo 6pm		
		Fri	arr. Brava 6am
Tues	arr. Praia 2am		dep. Brava noon
	dep. Praia 9.30pm		arr. Fogo 1pm
			dep. Fogo 5pm
Wed	arr. Fogo 6am		arr. Brava 6pm.
	dep. Fogo 5pm		
	arr. Brava 6pm		

Practicalities

Deck berths are cheap and insalubrious. Cape Verdeans are surprisingly poor sailors and the seas usually rough, leading to results which keep the crew occupied with mops and buckets. For a small supplement, there are comfortable four-berth **cabins** with basins and secure lockers. You'll find that cabin berths are often left unsold, giving you a private cabin and, in effect, a budget cruise. With a little planning you can spend the days visiting islands and nights aboard the pitching, rolling vessel. This kind of travel doesn't give you much time ashore but its great advantage is cheapness and – assuming you can handle the seas – an unexpected degree of luxury.

A few considerations: there's not much **food** for sale on board the ferries (though you can usually buy cold beers from the crew), no recommended **drinking water** (make provision) and **no showers**, so be inventive with the hand basins.

■ Buses and taxis – and hitching

Compared with getting between them, **getting around each island** is relatively straightforward: the longest land journey is less than 100km, on Santiago, and in practice most trips take under an hour. On some islands, however, transport is infrequent to and from outlying villages.

Minibuses called **carrinhos** (but usually known simply as "Hiace," after the popular Japanese make) have replaced nearly all the large buses that used to cover the islands. The minibuses operate wherever there's sufficient demand and usually carry a sign in red marked **aluguer** – "for hire". Prices tend to be fixed at fifty percent or more above the bus fare.

Particular ("private") taxis or cars are expensive, but the drivers are usually willing to bargain. For inaccessible places on the smaller islands they can be a viable option. The charter is often referred to as a **deslocação**.

Hitching, when there are any vehicles, is easy and drivers *simpatico* – though habitually reckless. The lack of traffic gives some drivers a vivid sense of immortality, but the combination of tortuous bends and precipices with cobbled roads is perilous. Be confident in saying "devagar" ("slow down") if you start shaking with fear. It's normal to pay for lifts when hitching, though it won't always be expected – agree in advance.

■ Car rental – and bringing a bike

The one or two local **car rental** places in Cape Verde are not very impressive, but at least they're not overpriced; the international companies haven't yet heard of the country. The largest choice of outlets is in Praia and Mindelo, but most islands have something. Deposits range from CV$6000 to CV$10,000 in cash. Credit card guarantees aren't required.

It's possible to **bring your own bike** by ferry from Dakar, a recommended option if you have one with you on the mainland. Local ferries are used to loading and unloading motorbikes. Lastly, Cape Verde is wonderful **cycling** territory for the fit and fanatical and, in view of the gradients, not to mention the cobblestone roads, obviously suited to mountain bikes.

Fuel costs are standardized at CV$75/litre for petrol (gasoline) and CV$40/litre for diesel fuel.

Accommodation

Putting your head down for the night is a simple business. You will usually find a Portuguese-style "pension" or *pensão* (*pensões* in the plural) offering clean, down-to-earth accommodation – often with a fan – for CV$1000–1500 for a room.

Ask to see several rooms and perhaps ask "*Tem um quarto mais barato?*" (which slips off the tongue and means "Do you have a cheaper room?"). Full-scale **hotels** – with hot water, private bath, air conditioning and restaurants – are less common,

---

ACCOMMODATION PRICE CODES

Accommodation prices in this chapter are coded according to the following scales – the same scales in terms of their pound/dollar equivalents as used throughout the book. Prices refer to the rate you can expect to pay for a room with two beds. Single rooms, or single occupancy, will normally cost at least two-thirds of the twin-occupancy rate. For further details see p.48.

① **Under CV$800 (under £5/$8)**. In practice, you will rarely find anything as cheap as this in Cape Verde, except perhaps the odd municipal resthouse.

② **CV$800–1600 (£5–10/$8–16)**. Rudimentary lodging, perhaps with some rooms S/C.

③ **CV$1600–3200 (£10–20/$16–32)**. Basic lodging, often offering S/C rooms, and breakfast included.

④ **CV$3200–4800 (£20–30/$32–48)**. Decent, better than adequate hotel with S/C rooms and breakfast included.

⑤ **CV$4800–6400 (£30–40/$48–64)**. Tourist/business-class establishment with good facilities.

⑥ **CV$6400–8000 (£40–50/$64–80)**. Up market, with close to international standards and facilities, including AC.

⑦ **Over CV$8000 (over £50/$80)**. Luxury, cosmopolitan establishment.

with rooms starting from around CV$2500 and rising to CV$8000 or more in a few establishments.

It is often assumed that you'll know about the **twelve o'clock checkout rule**, sometimes applied quite ruthlessly. Hotels, especially, will try hard to make you pay an extra half-or whole day if you haven't vacated on time.

In smaller towns you may have to ask to locate your accommodation: tourism is still of such minor importance that everyone knows where the lodgings are, and elementary signs are often missing. This may apply particularly in the case of the local **pousada municipal** – the town resthouse – where you may need to track down the landlord for the key. Such places are usually very basic and cheap.

If you want to spend a while in one place, there should be little difficulty in arranging **private accommodation**. Just ask around.

Cape Verde has no youth hostels or camping sites. Surprisingly perhaps, truly wild country suitable for **camping** – as opposed to marginal agricultural land – isn't plentiful. Still, as an eccentric foreigner you'll be happily tolerated if you camp in the neighbourhood. You're likely, anyway, to have an opportunity to ask permission when you collect water.

Eating and Drinking

It would be surprising if Cape Verde had an extensive and flourishing cuisine: with severe malnutrition and famines that killed thousands in living memory, the question of food has tended to concentrate on the number of calories – and in respect of variety most mainland countries can do a lot better than the islands. Still, the dishes on offer are a wholesome and always filling selection, probably little changed since the sixteenth century.

Apart from the big hotels in Sal, Praia and Mindelo, and a handful of restaurants where you'll get a decent variety of unremarkable international fare as well as local dishes, the choice is always strictly limited. In smaller towns the *pensões* usually serve meals somewhere in the building, but a **casa de pasto** (dining room/diner) is the standard, and often unmarked, place to eat. You eat what they have, the *prato do dia* (dish of the day), which as often as not will be *cachupa* (see box, opposite), the national dish, the name of which is believed to derive

from the same African term that resulted in "catsup" and "ketchup".

Staples include rice, potatoes (ordinary and sweet), beans, maize, squash, pork and – inevitably – tuna. Meals often start with a solid vegetable broth and finish with fruit, occasionally *pudim* (crème caramel).

■ Drinking

When it comes to drinking, Cape Verdeans usually think first of **grog** or *canna* (sugar cane distillates known collectively with other spirits as *aguardente*), which get consumed – and apparently made at home – in large quantities. A cautious approach is recommended when trying a *copa* (glass): liquor often comes from anonymous bottles and sacking-wrapped jars and you're never quite sure what the effect will be. There are "new" (*novo*) and "old" (*velho*) varieties and different degrees of smoothness. It's usually clean, but even so can be quite deadly, gasping stuff. "Punch" (*ponche, panche*) – a concoction of dark rum, honey and lemonade – is, like *aguardente*, often on sale over the counter in rural shops. It's not an ideal midday quencher.

Beer (*cerveja*) is still largely imported from Portugal – Sagres and Superbock – but Praia has its first brewery and bottles of very malty Ceris are now available in the bars and cafés. Some establishments serve draught Ceris – ask for a *cleps* (a glass of beer). Ceris also makes soft drinks. For juices ask for **sumo** – *de laranja, limão*, etc.

Wine has some potential on the islands as a significant industry, but the remarkably heavy, spicy, red product of Fogo's volcanic slopes doesn't inspire much enthusiasm just yet. Reasonably inexpensive **imports** of Portugal's favourites can be found in most bars and groceries.

Coffee, when it's not instant, is usually terrible, either utterly tasteless or swimming with over-roasted grounds. Angola once supplied a lot, but Fogo's own more recent contribution isn't that great; it's often stale or mixed with chicory.

Communications – Post, Phones, Language & Media

The day-to-day language of Cape Verde is Kriolu ("Creole"), quite distinct in structure and in much of its vocabulary from Portuguese (Cape Verde's official language): the two are not mutually intelligible. Kriolu

PORTUGESE AND KRIOLU FOOD TERMS

English	Portuguese/Kriolu	English	Portuguese/Kriolu	English	Portuguese/Kriolu
Beans	*Feijões*	Jam/marmalade	*Marmelade*	Shellfish	*Mariscos*
Bread	*Pão*	Maize/corn	*Milho*	Soup/broth	*Sopa*
Bread roll	*Bolho*	Meat	*Carne*	Squash	*Abóbora*
Butter	*Manteiga*	Menu	*Ementa*	Sugar	*Açúcar*
Cheese		Milk	*Leite*	Tea	*Chá*
(always goat)	*Queijo*	Pork	*Carne de*	Tuna	*Atum*
Coffee	*Café*		*Porco*	Vegetables	*Legumes*
Eggs	*Ovos*	Potatoes	*Batatas*	Water	*Agua*
Fish	*Peixe*	Rice	*Arroz*	Yams	*Inhames*
Food	*Comida*	Salt	*Sal*		

DISHES

Cachupa	A mash of beans and maize, sometimes with bacon and sausage, eaten at breakfast.	*Feijoada/Feijão Congo*	Beans and salt pork
		Frango	Chicken
		Langosta	"Lobster"; strictly cray fish
Cachupinha	Similar to *cachupa*, with green bits	*Lapas*	Tiny mussels, usually in a spicy sauce
Caldeirada de Peixe	Fish stew	*Licuda/linguiça*	Sausage
Carne de Vaca	Beef	*Linguado*	Sole
Coelho	Rabbit	*Polvo*	Octopus
Espadarte	Swordfish	*Prato do Dia*	Dish of the day
		Tubarão	Shark

TERMS

Assado	Roasted	*Frito*	Fried
Bife	Steak or cutlet, as in	*Molho*	Sauce
	Bife de Atum	*Piri piri*	Hot sauce
Cozido	Boiled		

FRUIT AND SNACKS

English	Port/Kriolu	English	Port/Kriolu	English	Port/Kriolu
Banana	*Banana*	Pawpaw	*Papaya*	Ice cream	*Gelado*
Guava	*Goyaba*	Dates	*Tāmaras*	Yogurt	*Iorgurte/*
Orange	*Laranja*	Grapefruit	*Toranja*		*Yaourt*
Mango	*Manga*	Breadfruit	*Frutapāo*	Pies	*Pasteles*
Watermelon	*Melancia*	Fish cakes	*Croquetes*	savoury	usually
Melon	*Melão*	Dessert/sweet	*Doce*		

contains many elements of Fula and Mandinka and a wide range of adopted vocabulary from archaic seafaring Portuguese and other European languages including English.

If you speak **Portuguese** – and it's one of the easiest languages to pick up, particularly if you're familiar with Spanish or Italian – you'll find you can get by easily everywhere. Even in rural areas everyone speaks some: papers, signs and radio are all in Portuguese and education is largely conducted in it. Learning Kriolu is another matter: Cape Verdeans tend to slip in and out of Kriolu and Portuguese, and Kriolu takes some time to tune into.

While a little Portuguese goes a long way, if you don't have any you'll be falling back on **French** and **English**, neither of which is spoken very widely outside the main towns. In most places, though, you'll run into younger people who've learned them at school as well as returnee emigrants from Europe, Senegal or the USA who speak them fluently.

■ The media

Radio and TV are important in Cape Verdean culture, and while you're not likely to see much of the latter (an eclectic mix of Brazilian soap

A BEGINNER'S GUIDE TO KRIOLU

BASICS

Hello	*Bon dia*	God go with you	*Deus ta kunpaño-lo*
How are you?	*Kuma ño sta?*	Please	*pur fabor*
I'm fine	*N sta ben*	Thank you	*brigod*
What's your name?	*Kali e bo nómi?*	Today	*oshi*
[or more formally]		Tomorrow	*mañan*
What is your		Yesterday	*ónti*
(masc./fem.) name?	*Kal e nómi di?*	Before	*ántis*
My name is Caroline	*Ña nómi é Caroline*	After	*dipos*
Do you have...?	*Ño ten...?*	Near	*pértu*
Is there any...?	*ño/di ña...?*	Far	*lonzi*
Goodbye	*Bon dia/te lóg*	Here	*li*
See you soon/sometime	*Te lóg/te dipos di mañan*	There	*la*

TRAVELLING

I'd like some water	*N kre agu*	I'd like a room for	*N kreba kuartu pa*
How do I get to Tarrafal?	*Kma N pode bai pa Tarrafal?*	one person/two people	*un psoa/dos psoa*
Is this the bus stop for Tarrafal?	*Undi e paraza di otukaru pa Tarrafal?*	Is there a toilet/	*Ten kasa di bañu li?*
What time does the plane leave/arrive?	*Ki óra avion ta sai/tchga?*	bathroom?	
		What is it?	*Kuse e es?*
		I don't know	*N ka sabe*
Where are you (masc./fem.) going?	*Undi ño/ña ta bai?*	We don't speak Kriolu	*Nu ka ta papia kriolu*
We're going to Praia	*Nu ta bai pa Praia*	Open	*abert*
How much is it?	*Kal e presu?*	Closed	*fetchod*
Change (money)	*Troco*	Where?	*undi?*
Is there a cheap hotel near here?	*Ten penson li pértu?*		

NUMBERS AND DAYS

1	*un*	15	*kinzi*	100	*sén*
2	*dos*	16	*dizasais*	101	*sén-t y un*
3	*tres*	17	*dizaséti*	200	*duzéntus*
4	*kuatu*	18	*dizóitu*	500	*kiñéntus*
5	*sinku*	19	*dizanóvi*	1000	*mil*
6	*sais*	20	*vinti*	Monday	*segunda-feira (2ªF)*
7	*séti*	21	*vinti y un*		
8	*oitu*	30	*trinta*	Tuesday	*terça-feira (3ªF)*
9	*nóvi*	40	*korenta*	Wednesday	*quarta-feira (4ªF)*
10	*dés*	50	*sinkuenta*	Thursday	*quinta-feira (5ªF)*
11	*ónzi*	60	*sasenta*	Friday	*sexta-feira (6ªF)*
12	*dozi*	70	*satenta*	Saturday	*sábado (S)*
13	*trezi*	80	*oitenta*	Sunday	*domingo (D)*
14	*katorzi*	90	*novénta*		

operas and right-on documentaries broadcasting for a few hours each day), Radio Nacional de Cabo Verde is a good FM station, with an enlightened play list. There's also a government-run Voz de São Vicente. The BBC World Service is hard to get hold of in mid-Atlantic and signals wander.

A GLOSSARY OF CAPE VERDEAN TERMS

Aluguer	shared taxi-van or pick-up truck (the public transport of the islands)	**Morabeza**	kindness, gentleness, considered to be a peculiarly Cape Verdean quality
Americano	Cape Verdean living in America	**Morna**	the heavy-hearted music of the islands, sweet-sounding, nostalgic and very characteristic
Badiu	peasant from rural Santiago descended, according to tradition, from runaway slaves		
		MPD	Movement for Democracy
Bairro	suburb, outskirts of town	**PAICV**	African Party for the Independence of Cape Verde
Branco	white – or wealthy – person		
Camâra	town hall	**Pano**	cloth, *pagne*
Cidade	city, town	**Paragem**	bus stop
Conto	one thousand escudos	**Pelourinho**	pillory, the slave auction post
Criança	child	**Povoação**	"town", the local town
Crise	drought, community crisis	**Praça**	square, *place*
Deslocação	private taxi trip	**Praia**	beach
Festa	feast, festival, party	**Quinta**	estate, owned by a landlord; rare today
Funco	round, stone, thatched house		
Grog, Grogo, Grogue	sugar-cane firewater, *aguardente*	**Quintal**	courtyard of a house
		Ribeira	stream, river or rivercourse
		Seca	drought
Igreja	church	**Sodade**	a defining term of Cape Verdean identity, signifying longing for homeland, yearning
Lenço	traditional headscarf worn differently by women of each island		
Liceu	secondary school	**Vila**	town

The **press** consists of two weekly newspapers: *A Semana*, a privately owned paper, and *Semanario Horizonte*, a newspaper with close government links. Portuguese is easier to read than to speak, which is just as well, as foreign papers are virtually unobtainable.

■ Post, phones and email

Both post and telephones in Cape Verde are run by the **CTT**, or simply Correio, now privatized as two companies – Correios de Cabo Verde and Telecomunicações de Cabo Verde. There's at least one CTT on each island, open Monday to Friday 8am to noon and 2.30 to 5.30pm, and sometimes on Saturday and even Sunday mornings. **Post**, both outgoing and incoming, is generally efficient and honest though not especially swift. For poste restante have your mail marked "Lista da Correios".

If you have **urgent mail** for home to post from one of the more isolated islands, try taking it to the local airstrip for the next flight to Sal, or even ask at the local TACV office if someone could give

Cape Verde's IDD code is ☎238.

it to the pilot – people are usually understanding.

Telephoning locally has become much more significant now that there are solar-powered phone boxes in every town and village. **Phoning abroad**, the IDD automatic system is now available to most countries; dial ☎0 then the country code. Phone cards are available from certain shops, bars and restaurants in values of CV$1000 and CV$2000; use the cardphone booths usually located conveniently nearby. Off-peak rates (8pm to 7am and all weekend) are CV$180 per minute to the US and Canada, CV$240 per minute to Europe and CV$400 per minute to most other countries. The international operator is on ☎111. You can't normally make reverse charges/collect calls. For AT&T, dial ☎112.

Mobile phones from Europe and North America cannot be used in Cape Verde, though this is likely to change in the near future. There is a local network. **Online services** have yet to take off in a big way. There is a new cybercafé in Praia, the country's first.

Entertainment

There's little in the way of an organized leisure industry – less than a handful of cinemas in Praia and Mindelo and no theatre to speak of. Portuguese bullfighting was never established. The game of *orzil* or *oril* (the hole and pebble mindbender common all over Africa in different versions, see p.59) is popular everywhere, as is draughts or chequers.

The commonest entertainments are homespun – births, baptisms, confirmations, marriages and funerals providing occasions for gathering together. In the evenings it's quite the thing for young people to meet in the town square (*praça*) with a guitar or two.

■ Music

There are a number of nightclubs (*boites*), and a clutch of them are regular venues for **live music** (*musica ao vivo*). The best-known Cape Verdean forms are guitar and fiddle songs – the **morna**, a mournful lament reminiscent of Portuguese *fado*, and the more upbeat and very danceable **coladeira**, music with a wonderful muscular rhythm. Many songs are love songs – addressed to the islands – and powerfully sentimental. **Cesaria Evora**, who has released a number of superb CDs, is the foremost musical emissary of the isles, now based in Paris. CDs by Cesaria and other artists are widely available and cost around CV$1500.

In the past, in smaller towns and rural areas, you might have heard someone playing the *cimbó* or the *berimbau*, old **one-stringed instruments** of African origin producing plangent, ancient sounds – either with a bow on the *cimbó*, or plucked and resonating in a sound box, or the mouth, with a *berimbau*. Both have virtually fallen into the realm of folklore, though in parts of Santiago you might still be lucky.

Directory

AIRPORT DEPARTURE TAX Included in the ticket price.

CONTRACEPTIVES You can get condoms (*preservativas* or, more colourfully, *camisas de vênus*) from most pharmacies and *postos venda medicamentos*.

EMERGENCIES These are fortunately rare in Cape Verde. If you can find a phone you can call the police on ☎132. Medical emergencies require a hospital: ☎130.

OPENING HOURS Most shops and businesses are open from about 8am to noon and again from

3 to 7 or 8pm. Lunch hours are long and lazy and *everything* closes, even – curiously and frustratingly – many bars and cafés.

PHOTOGRAPHY doesn't usually pose any problems. There are very few subjects which would get you in trouble and most people are uninterested where you choose to point your camera, or VCR except of course near obvious military installations or subjects of strategic interest. When taking pictures of Cape Verdeans, ordinary courtesy is your only restraint: you'll rarely be asked for payment.

PLACE NAMES AND RIVALRIES On the islands, Cape Verde is called Cabo Verde – or Cáu Berde in Kriolu – the people Cauberdianos. It's not uncommon on Santiago, however, to hear people referring to "Cabo Verde" when they mean Santiago, as if it was the mainland, while referring somewhat dismissively to the other Cape Verdes as "as Ilhas" – the islands. There's a good deal of **rivalry** between the islands, with competition between the people of the Barlaventos – who see themselves as more urbane and metropolitan – and the Sotaventos where, in Santiago particularly, a larger proportion of the population are descended from slaves. There are subtle cultural variations from island to island too, with differences in the local form of Kriolu. Look out too, as you travel, for the characteristic women's headscarf style – tied differently on each island.

Many towns and villages are called Ribeira something, which just means River – understandable where fresh water is so important. Tarrafal is another common name. Every island seems to have its Tarrafal – which makes it useful to know which one's being referred to.

PUBLIC HOLIDAYS Cape Verde follows the main **Christian holidays** (Dec 8, Immaculate Conception; Jan 1, Circumcision of Our Lord; Aug 15, Assumption; Nov 1, All Saints' Day), with some exotic additions: Jan 20, National Heroes' Day; May 1, Labour Day; July 5, Independence Day. There's a whole host of other days off – including any number of saints' days and a major **Carnaval** every February in Mindelo, emulated in the same month by Praia.

In addition, **annual festivals** take place on many islands, with horse and mule races, discos, bands and more than the usual grog consumption. They generally last about a week, and include:
Boa Vista: June 24

Brava: June 24
Fogo: April 20
Maio: early May
Sal: Sept 15
Santo Antão: early June
São Vicente: May 3, June 13 and August (music festival)

RELIGION Mostly Catholic, although American Protestant churches have made some headway since independence. There's probably quite a lot to be learned about the process of Islam's arrival and spread in West Africa from the fact that it's completely unknown in the Cape Verdes. It's likely that Islam hadn't made much impression in the African peasant communities from which slaves were commonly taken between the fifteenth and eighteenth centuries.

TAMPONS Usually available from larger general stores, but not easily outside the main towns.

TROUBLE It's hard to imagine getting into any in Cape Verde. Cape Verde is a tolerant country and etiquette has grown out of the combination of Latin manners and West African social convention that you'd expect. Drug use, in the close-knit island communities, carries a strong stigma and doesn't go unnoticed. While quite a few youngish men smoke home-grown weed, you could expect a barrel-load of trouble if seen by the wrong people. Nudity and topless bathing are pretty well out of the question and particularly ill-advised for unaccompanied women. You're just as unlikely to be a victim of trouble. While theft is not unknown, the islands are one of the safest places in the world for absent-minded travellers. Even long-term expatriates agree on this, which must say something – though they tend to single out Praia as an exception.

WATER SPORTS There's some good **snorkelling** in places and exciting **diving** in a number of wreck-strewn shallows, notably off Boa Vista and Sal. Cape Verde's **windsurfing** is some of the ocean's most challenging. The big centre (though not, in fact, big at all) is Santa Maria on Sal island (see p.420). Sal Rei on Boa Vista is now growing in importance.

WILDLIFE Cape Verde's native fauna is a meagre show, with no large mammals and few outstanding birds. There are monkeys on Santiago and Brava. Herpetologists are excited by *Tarentola giganta* (the giant gecko) and the Cape Verde Island skink (another relative giant) but disappointed at the total absence of snakes. Bird-watchers might want to go out of their way to

spot the Razo Island lark but it's fairly uninteresting for non-specialists. The seas are more rewarding, with good chances of seeing dolphins, whales, turtles and amazing flying fish.

WOMEN TRAVELLERS AND THE WOMEN'S MOVEMENT Women travellers will find the Cape Verde Islands relaxed after mainland West Africa. While **sexual attitudes** do contain an element of machismo, it's normally expressed as nothing much stronger than winks, whistles, stares and strong expectations that you *will* dance. It can also come across as almostly innocent: heavy sexual pestering is unusual. Younger women, travelling without men, may find that their "unmarried condition" gives them almost adolescent social status, which can be frustrating. But, with the possible exception of Praia, the towns are too small for problems to last long.

As for the lives of **Cape Verdean women**, little seems to have changed despite the government's on-paper commitments to reducing sex discrimination and promoting their rights and welfare. Yet there are good reasons why change is needed: the continued emigration involves mostly men, and there are now 108 women for every 100 men, leaving many rural women de facto household heads. The Organização das Mulheres de Cabo Verde (Rua Unidade Guiné-Cabo Verde, Praia; ☎61.24.55) is quite active and the main contact-making body; otherwise, it's quite difficult for women visitors to meet Cape Verdean women.

A Brief History of the Cape Verde Islands

The Cape Verde Islands blew out of the Atlantic in a series of volcanic eruptions during the Miocene period some 60 million years ago – though Maio, Sal and Boa Vista may be a geological extension of the African mainland. The islands were uninhabited (so far as is known) until 1462, making the country unique in West Africa. In the gloriously clumsy eloquence of Adriano Moreira, Portugal's Overseas Minister from 1961–2, the Cape Verdes were "islands asleep since the eve of time, waiting to be able to be Portugal". After five centuries of such paternalism, the turn of recent events has been remarkably peaceful.

THE CAPE VERDEAN SLAVE TRADE

As the New World opened across the Atlantic in the sixteenth century, the **trade in slaves** gathered momentum and the islands – now important stepping stones to Brazil and the Caribbean – became an emporium for their trans-shipment and taxation.

Although they were more expensive, slaves at **Ribeira Grande** (the main entrepôt) were better value than those bought directly on the Guinea coast: they tended to be healthier, as the sick had already perished; they spoke some Portuguese and some had even been baptized (the Portuguese were keen on finding religious justifications for their slave-trading, safeguarding the captives from purgatory). And for the slave ships, buying at Ribeira Grande was a much safer option than sailing directly into the creeks of Guinea to barter for slaves.

Roughly between 1600 and 1760 (the peak years) anything from a few dozen to several thousand slaves were sold annually through Ribeira Grande, most of them exported to the Spanish West Indies and Colombia. Large numbers were shipped off in years of bad drought on Santiago, when planters would sell their farm slaves to traders when they couldn't afford to feed them. This was prohibited in law: the only slaves supposed to be exported from Cape Verde were those just imported from the coast under licence.

From the earliest years of the colony, Lisbon had passed a succession of **trade laws**, ruling that the resale of slaves and foreign trade partnerships were illegal. In 1497 the sale of iron to Africans was banned, and between 1512 and 1519 further crushing edicts – equally unenforceable – were issued: outlawing the much-in-demand Indian and Dutch cloth from the islands; banning the commissioning of *lançado* adventurers to trade on the mainland; and ruling that all legally contracted slave ships bound for the Americas should first detour to Lisbon because Ribeira Grande could not be trusted to extract duty honestly.

The people involved as **trading partners** in the complex mesh of buying, selling and bartering were a mix of European merchant adventurers (sometimes merely pirates) and various mixed race labourers and entrepreneurs (see below) as well as bona fide licensed contractors waving charters from Lisbon or Madrid. But the trading networks rarely operated in a free market. For most of the time, Portugal tried to ensure that as many profits and tariffs as possible accrued to the crown, even if that meant making ordinary trade illegal and relegating much business to the status of **smuggling** – from which the crown received nothing.

Successive **governors** of the islands, who generally viewed their postings with misgivings if not actual horror, succumbed to the inevitability of **corruption** (if they survived malaria and other diseases long enough to care). Some succumbed too enthusiastically for the likes of the islands' clergy, aldermen, court and treasury officials – whose own commercial interests they threatened – but most governors managed to amass reasonable wealth while leaving space for smaller operators to do business.

The banes of Lisbon – the **lançados** – eventually became totally estranged from Portugal and even at times from Santiago. Once fully acculturated in Guinea, and unable to return to Portugal (on pain of death), they had no need to worry about the rules, as the contract holders were obliged to, and could trade with the Dutch, English and French boats which sailed around the Atlantic in growing numbers. In this way they kept a good selection of merchandise for purchasing slaves and other African goods, while contract holders were obliged to buy the limited range of goods for resale and barter offered by the state supply monopoly.

LANÇADOS, TANGOMAUS, GRUMETES AND LADINOS

A number of distinctly defined groupings were involved in the slave trade:

- **Tangomaus** (dragomans): cosmopolitan Africans who traded in the Guinea interior and did much of the initial negotiating for slaves but who were familiar with Portuguese ways.
- **Lançados** ("sent outs"): originally white or part-white Cape Verdeans who had familiarized themselves with African ways on the mainland and had settled in African communities to trade and transport goods along the coast. They eventually became indistinguishable from *tangomaus*.
- **Grumetes**: African or mixed race deckhands and carriers working for the traders.
- **Ladinos**: slaves or other Africans who could speak Portuguese or Kriolu.

■ Discovery and colonization

Although African sailors may have visited the islands in earlier centuries, it was a Genoese navigator, **Antonio da Noli**, working for Prince Henry of Portugal, who discovered and first documented Santiago (which he called São Tiago – St James) and four other islands, some 500km off Africa's Cap Vert, in 1455. Three more in the northwest (Santo Antão, São Nicolau and São Vicente) were reached by Diogo Afonso in 1461. Santiago, by far the biggest prize, was split between the two navigators, who were granted a captaincy each: da Noli set himself up at **Ribeira Grande** in the south and Afonso made his headquarters in the northwest. Slaves were brought from the African mainland to work the parcels of land allotted the handful of immigrants and in the capital, Ribeira Grande, work began on a cathedral. The Portuguese crown viewed the new extension of empire – 2500km from Lisbon – with indifference; but the archipelago could serve as a stepping stone to exotic riches, and it would certainly do as a penal colony.

Fogo was settled in the 1480s and its western region was singled out as one of the most likely productive areas on the islands – rolling, partly wooded country, with substantial rainfall in most years. But Fogo islanders were forbidden to trade with foreign ships – a right reserved by Santiago – and the island was considered a hardship post for the Portuguese officials sent there. By the end of the sixteenth century its population had barely reached 2000 and there were appeals to Lisbon for more settlers – petitions which were met with the arrival of convicts and political undesirables (*degredados*) from Portugal and the internal banishment, from nearby Santiago, of certain offenders.

The tiny volcanic pimple of **Brava** attracted its first colonists in the early 1540s. They kept much to themselves: climatically the island was one of the easiest to survive on, yet it was very remote. It was only when large numbers of families escaped here from Fogo in 1680, after volcanic eruptions and an earthquake, that Brava became heavily populated. It has had the densest population of the islands ever since.

The big island of the far northwest, **Santo Antão**, got its first inhabitants in 1548 but its large size, with remote and rugged interior valleys and craters, and its distance from the main shipping lanes, kept it very isolated and little known for at least 200 years. Among its settlers were Jewish families fleeing the Inquisition and subse-

quent European persecutions. The village of Sinagoga is a reminder.

São Nicolau offered fewer opportunities to adventurous migrants and only its northwest valleys – even these with uncertain rainfall – made colonization viable in the middle of the sixteenth century. The town of Ribeira Brava became an important literary and ecclesiastical centre and was the seat of the Cape Verdean bishopric from the end of the eighteenth century until the beginning of the twentieth.

São Vicente, one of the driest islands, was virtually uninhabited until the start of the nineteenth century, when the sheltered bay at Porto Grande (the best harbour in the islands) was chosen as the site of a British coal bunkering station for steamships on the Brazil and East Indies runs.

The "flat islands", **Boa Vista**, **Maio** and **Sal**, were also late in being fully colonized. Maio and Boa Vista had small numbers of herders and poor farmers, most of them freed or escaped slaves, and Maio eventually became the virtual private fiefdom of a freed slave family, the Evoras.

An early plan, conceived by Genoese merchant adventurers, was to create a major **sugar** industry on Santiago, following its success in Madeira. With the conquest and colonization of tropical lands, Europe could begin to grow the crop for itself instead of relying on expensive imports. But the Cape Verdean climate proved unsuitably dry and, although the **rum** which normally came as a by-product of sugar production was found to be useful for **slave trading** along the Guinea coast, the sugar farms at Ribeira Grande never really took off and by the late sixteenth century were already eclipsed by the vast quantities being produced in Brazil.

Instead, the Cape Verde Islands found themselves in the middle of a growing network of **trade routes** – between Europe and India, between West Africa and the Spanish American colonies and between Portugal and Brazil. They took on the function of **victualling stations** for the trading vessels, supplying fresh water, fruit, salted and dried meat, and carrying on a trade of their own in commercial goods – salt, hides, cotton *pagnes* and slaves.

■ 1640–1775: cloth and the crown monopolies

With the **break-up of the union between Portugal and Spain** in 1640, business went into the doldrums for a number of years. Several governors were denounced to Lisbon after they monopolized what trade there was or even started applying the rule of law in order to confiscate and penalize foreign trading ships for their own gain. The islands were at a severe disadvantage because international demand for slaves had saturated the Guinea coastlands with **iron bars**, the principal currency, causing huge increases in the price of slaves. Portugal, which produced very little iron and forbade its export, was unable to compete.

Cotton, though, had become Cape Verde's main commercial crop, grown especially on the estates of Fogo. Slave women spun it; men wove it into strip cloth, dyed it with cultivated indigo and native *orchilla*, and sewed the strips together into *pagnes*. Some of the material found its way to Brazil but most was traded – generally for more slaves – on the Guinea coast. Throughout the sixteenth and seventeenth century and for much of the eighteenth – until slave trading began to be threatened by abolitionists – Cape Verdean cotton **panos**, in a multiplicity of inventive designs, were the prized dress material of the West African coast, traded as far east as Accra and as valuable as iron bars in many districts. The value of Cape Verde cloth became so universal in the region that it was also the usual currency of the archipelago: administrative officials were commonly paid with it and accumulated vast hoards of the stuff, a soft currency which only had real value locally, not in Portugal.

In the **second half of the seventeenth century**, after the split with Spain, the private contracts system fell out of use. Portugal's African territory and trade routes were seriously depleted and for some years only the most recklessly optimistic merchants had been willing to purchase the expensive rights on slaving in those parts. With wily Cape Verdeans stealing the trade from under their noses and the price of slaves going up all the time it was difficult to make contracts pay.

Instead, in 1675, the first of the **Crown Monopolies** – the **Companhia de Cacheu** – was set up, reserving for itself sole rights to trade in foreign goods with the coast and outlawing (again) the trans-shipment of slaves through Santiago. Cape Verdeans were only allowed to export their own produce. Bitter feelings were aroused in Santiago. When a new company, **The Company of the Islands of Cape Verde and Guinea**, was formed, and bought a fat contract to supply 4000 slaves a year to the Spanish West

Indies, the governor of the islands was placed on the company payroll. His salary was doubled and he was expressly forbidden from engaging in any commercial activities. With their governor now effectively playing for the opposition, the islanders were more disgruntled than usual. And true to form, the new company did nothing for their prosperity, stockpiling goods to inflate prices, undersupplying vital commodities and levying high freight charges for their meagre exports.

With the **War of the Spanish Succession** (1701–13), which Portugal was pulled into against Spain and France, the company's valuable slaving contract was lost and in 1712, Ribeira Grande itself was comprehensively sacked and plundered by a French force. The **cathedral**, a century and a half in the building, had only been completed nineteen years earlier. About this time, serious attention began to be given to creating a new and better fortified capital at Praia. Ribeira Grande was in steep decline from the middle of the eighteenth century and **Praia** was eventually dedicated as the seat of island government in 1774.

The first half of the eighteenth century had witnessed a great **relaxation of trade embargoes**. But Lisbon's persistent and neurotic attempts to prevent the trans-shipment of slaves and the sale to non-Portuguese of Cape Verdean cloth (which in the economic climate amounted to much the same thing) mystified foreign traders, especially English and Americans, who broke the laws without compunction. Apart from its triumphant (but peaking) textiles industry, the archipelago was in a state of **economic ruin** and the population too poor and too isolated to worry much about Lisbon's laws, even if some did carry the death penalty.

With the foundation in 1757 of the **Companhia de Grão Para e Marnahão**, which had the sole purpose of providing slave labour to the states of the new Brazilian empire, a twenty-year era of unparalleled cruelty and hardship began for the islands. The annexation of political control which had begun with the last company was taken to its logical conclusion, so that the Company now effectively *owned* the islands; while in Lisbon, a clique of English gentlemen maintained discreet but weighty capital interest in its enterprises.

Apart from the utter destitution which the enforced **bypassing of trade** brought to the archipelago, a severe **drought** struck from 1772 to 1775. By this point in the islands' history the population had grown too big to be able to survive

CAPE VERDEAN SOCIETY TO 1950: THE POTENTIAL FOR REVOLT

The **slave estates** had varied in size from small landholdings run on paternalistic lines, where landlord and slave led similar lives, to extensive plantations (especially on Santiago) where wealth differences were extreme. The traditional *morgadio* system of land tenure, in which inheritance was strictly by *primogeniture* (inheritance by the eldest son), produced a growing population of landless aristocrats and tenant farmers on marginal land. Under the system, land could not be bought or sold. The **estate slaves** were often tied closely to the landlord's family, occasionally by blood. Over the centuries, intermarriage blurred the distinction between slaves and sharecropping peasants, the only practical difference being that the share-croppers were always in debt to the landlords, a life in many ways as arduous as slavery. Freedom for slaves – an act of "charity" periodically undertaken by some landlords, or else an economic necessity when food supplies were exhausted in a famine – was no release from the cycle. If they ran into debt as share-croppers, freed slaves lived on the sufferance of the landlord.

This, together with the fact that the islands are too small to offer much refuge, meant that **slave rebellions** were rare and provoked only by the most savage treatment. Among the landed families there were real fears, principally because they themselves were divided (the *morgadio* system created bitter feuds) and sometimes engaged in fierce vendettas with their rivals. At one time many slaves were armed by their masters, and gangs of pistol-toting slaves are known to have clashed on occasions, even in Praia. There was a certain insecurity about what might happen if the arms were turned against the elite. In the Santiago interior there was a large underclass of freed and escaped slaves, the **badius**, partly independent of the estates. And on Santiago, relations were less paternalistic and the estates often owned by absentee landlords. A group of slaves did organize a stand against their particularly oppressive landlord in 1822 and there was an

aborted general **slave revolt** in Santiago in 1835 (given passive encouragement by the administration's ragged armed forces). But that was about the extent of resistance, and it was largely brought about by anticipation in the run-up to the abolition of slavery.

As for **political resistance** which might eventually culminate in an independence movement, there isn't a great deal of early evidence for that either. Conditions on the estates in the **twentieth century** became worse. With the old *morgadio* system discredited and abandoned, and the landlords themselves in debt to the National Overseas Bank, much of the land was bought up by a new class of absentee landlords, often returned United States emigrants. Coaling labourers mounted **strikes** for increased pay at Mindelo in 1910, and again in 1911, but they were defeated.

Opportunities for **dissent** on the islands in the fascist "**New State**" of Portugal's prime minister Salazar (1932–68) were limited to the private publication and distribution, among a small intellectual circle, of poetry and subtly nationalistic Kriolu **literature**. Organized demonstrations of opposition were impossible, and even further ruled out by the chronic plight of the islands during the famine years of World War II and the labour migrations of the early Fifties. Debtor peasants were treated as criminals and could claim nothing from the state until their debts had been repaid. **Political dissidents** found themselves imprisoned in the notorious detention centre at Tarrafal, alongside victims ejected from Portugal, and interrogated by the Gestapo-modelled **PIDE** political police.

To make the possibility of grass roots resistance even less likely, Cape Verde has an **alcoholism** problem going back to the earliest years of the sugar industry. Never viable as a major export, cane was still grown in vast quantities for distilling *grogue*, on land that could otherwise have provided food crops. The national addiction to *grogue* was such that in the drought years of the 1960s sugar was imported to satisfy demand.

---

such disasters on whatever came to hand – as they had during the famine of 1689 in Santiago when they ate horses and dogs. In the face of **starvation** throughout the islands, the Company was implacable – it held back food supplies, pushed up prices and milked the islanders of every last resource. In return for food, hundreds were abducted abroad and forced into slavery by English and French traders. Smuggling, of course,

had never been so essential nor so profitable. The famine left an estimated 22,000 dead – out of a total population of less than 60,000.

■ Into the nineteenth century: famine and emigration

By the time the rains returned in 1777, the Company's charter had expired and it went into merciful liquidation. At the beginning of the **nineteenth century** the Cape Verdes faced a quite different future. The harsh Company regime had battered the textile industry with enforced low prices while drought had extinguished the cotton crop as well as many of the field slaves and textile workers. The emergence of the newly independent **USA** as a major economic power began to be more important than the distant historical links which tied the islands to Portugal. Lisbon, in any case, was too distracted by Napoleonic strife at home, and tail-and-dog upsets with Brazil about who ruled who, to be much concerned with the insignificant islands and their irrepressible flouting of trade laws. Moreover, Angola and Mozambique held far more promise.

New England whalers began calling at the Cape Verdes from the end of the eighteenth century, to take on supplies and crew and to do a little trading. Goatskins were a profitable sideline back in the States and, once the practice had become established, the Americans arrived each year with holds full of merchandise. Brava, Fogo and São Vicente were the main islands of contact and from these a steady trickle of impoverished Cape Verdeans escaped to New England through the closing decades of the nineteenth century.

Slavery in the nineteenth century was contained by the British and (ironically) by the American presence. While the trade in slaves from the Guinea coast was forbidden from 1815, slaves were still sold, by weight, well into the 1840s. Only with the end of the American Civil War and with pressure from Britain (to whom Portugal owed a debt going back to the Napoleonic era) was an abolition process set up on the islands. Slaves were not formally emancipated until 1869 and even then they had to work for their ex-owners as indentured labourers for a further ten years.

Drought and the Cape Verdean diaspora

A series of disastrous **famines** hit the islands during the nineteenth century. In the first of these, from 1830–33, an estimated 30,000 people died. No relief of any kind came from Lisbon, but America, on this and several other occasions, sent large consignments of relief aid, though towards the end of the century it was generally wealthy émigré Cape Verdeans who organized it.

While the dispossessed of the Sotaventos moved to Praia or tried to emigrate, the poor of the Barlaventos headed to the new "city" of

Porto Grande (Mindelo) on São Vicente to find work at the British-run **coaling station** or in the shops, bars and bordellos.

At the peak of its importance at the end of the nineteenth century the port of Mindelo was servicing over 1300 ships every year – and tens of thousands of sailors. The latter industry had a far-reaching effect on the culture of the islands, introducing even more of a racial mixture and enriching Kriolu with words like *ariope* (hurry up), *fulope* (full up) and *troba* (trouble).

Meanwhile, Portugal's first efforts at "humanitarian relief" took place during the drought of 1863–65 (with a death toll of 30,000). It seemed an ideal time to profit from the availability of labour eager for food by engaging the people in civil engineering projects. The islands' first **cobbled roads** date from this famine, when peasants were rounded up to work for starvation wages. A more sinister method of dealing with famine was **enforced migration** to the "Cacao Islands" of São Tomé and Principe. For a number of reasons, the abolition of slavery in São Tomé and Principe led to serious labour shortages. In the Cape Verdes the shortages were of land. Offered apparently huge bonuses by the recruiting agencies when (and if) they returned, thousands of poverty-stricken Cape Verdeans were persuaded to "go south" over the next ninety years to a system of equatorial plantation labour that was little better than ordinary chattel slavery. Like before, the monopoly companies of a century before, Portugal's **cocoa industry** found drought on the Cape Verdes was easily turned to its advantage.

Right from the first use of this system, measures were taken to limit the number of Cape Verdeans emigrating to a life of relative security in the USA: a heavy departure tax was imposed, beyond the means of those who desperately needed to go, and travel permits and passports were made almost impossible to obtain. Nevertheless, the trickle of emigrants to New England became a flood between 1910 and 1930 when an estimated 34,000 people left the islands. This mass exodus was to become enormously significant after World War II, when the emigrants were able to send back substantial **remittances** to the islands, and after independence, when the economy became largely dependent on them. The USA, however, began to make literacy a condition for emigration from 1913 and, after 1922, the door to new immigrants was progressively closed.

Drought in the twentieth century has continued to be the single most important factor shaping
the lives of Cape Verdeans. Only following the
drought of 1959–61 were genuinely compassionate
measures taken to alleviate the suffering and these
seem likely to have been initiated mostly by international outrage at the colonial labour migration
policies. Earlier, there were four big crises; 1902–4
(15,000 dead); 1920–22 (17,000); 1940–43 (25,000);
and 1947–48 (21,000 lives lost). The drought of II
World War was probably the worst catastrophe in
Cape Verde's history. Brava and Fogo suffered
appallingly when they had to cope with a surge of
re-emigrants returning from the American depression, because the "rainy" years of the Thirties had
lulled islanders into a false sense of security. And
during the war years remittances from American
relatives dried up completely. Older people of Furna
and São Filipe remember walking into town and
finding corpses fallen at the roadside.

When the last major wave of **emigration** took
place as a result of these famines, the authorities
were ruthless in their efforts to prevent flight to
the USA. As a result, sixty percent of applicants
ended up in São Tomé and Angola. There was a
small number, however, who emigrated to
Guinea-Bissau, not out of destitution, but with
ambitions. Since the opening of *liceus* (the colleges of São Nicolau in 1866 and São Vicente in
1917), about two-thirds of mainland Portuguese
Guinea's teachers and civil servants were Cape
Verdeans. It was principally from their ranks that
organized **agitation and resistance** to
Portuguese rule first germinated.

■ Organized resistance and the Portuguese revolution

In response to what they described as a "wall of
silence" around the islands, a group of mostly
Cape Verdean intellectuals led by **Amilcar
Cabral** – and including Luiz Cabral and **Aristides
Pereira** – met secretly in Bissau in 1956 to form
the **PAIGC** (Partido Africana da Independencia da
Guine e Cabo Verde). When peaceful representations to the colonial government were met with
indifference and more repression (culminating in
the massacre of striking dockers in Bissau – see
p.440), the PAIGC began planning for a **guerilla
war on the mainland**, with the declared aim of
liberating both Guinea-Bissau and Cape Verde.
After four years of preparation and fairly continuous efforts to negotiate a peaceful alternative,

war began in 1963. The Cape Verdes became a
massive Portuguese military base, swarming with
Portuguese troops drafted to the front in Guinea-
Bissau – and in Angola and Mozambique, where
wars of independence had also begun.

On the Cape Verdes themselves, the question
of a violent uprising was purely academic. The
small, barren and isolated islands are unpromising
ground for guerilla warfare. Yet the island government and police force (with help from the military
and the PIDE) were acutely sensitive to the possibility of open revolt: every subversive indication
was examined and squashed, and activists sent to
Tarrafal, on the island of Santiago, or worse places
in Angola. On Santiago, a *badiu* religious cult
movement, known as the **rebelados**, was
labelled communist for criticizing the corrupt,
state-run Catholic church, advocating the hands-
together system of community help (the *jun-
tamão*) and resisting outside interference, especially the anti-malaria campaign, which tried to
spray members' homes. The movement virtually
deified Amilcar Cabral. Its leaders were brutally
interrogated and deported to other islands. But
their threat was no more politically co-ordinated or
potentially subversive than that posed by the
Nazarene church, whose American-led, puritan-
inspired clergy were also subject to repression for
their denunciations of the Salazarist church.
Cultural opposition was the only kind available
and cultural repression the inevitable response.
Kriolu, virtually unintelligible to ordinary
Portuguese-speakers, was considered subversive
in itself and its use banned from state property.

Thousands of **women** emigrated in the early
1970s to find work as domestics in Portugal,
France and Italy. But the sex ratio on the islands
remained unbalanced, with women far outnumbering men.

On the mainland, **the war** was drawn-out but
successful. Only the **assassination of Amilcar
Cabral** at his headquarters in Conakry on January
20, 1973 (partly inspired by jealousy of the Cape
Verdean role in Guinea-Bissau's revolution)
deflected it from a well-planned and predictable
course. In September 1973, with most of
Portuguese Guinea controlled by the PAIGC, the
party proclaimed de facto independence. Portugal
withdrew from Bissau the following year after the
MFA's (Armed Forces Movement) **overthrow of
the dictatorship** in Lisbon on April 25, 1974. On
the islands, the pre-coup government continued in
office, even after the MFA had swept away the

basis of their power. But the tide was coming in fast. In less than a week, the clandestine fragments of Cape Verde's own PAIGC cells had coalesced, and a **public meeting** was held in Praia on May 1. The Tarrafal detainees were released and the PAIGC took its message around the islands, agitating semi-legally for the independence that was almost at hand. The "wall of silence" had caved in. There were other parties, hatched and nurtured by the administration, which tried to promote the idea of some kind of "shared independence" between the islands and Portugal. They were maintained by small groups of wealthy activists and had supporters in Senegal, who mistrusted the aims of the PAIGC. None of them convinced many islanders.

Lisbon sent a new governor in August 1974, charged with asserting **Portuguese continuity** in Cape Verde. He was shouted out of Praia and back to Lisbon within a month. Another arrived with a heavier hand. His troops shot into a demonstration in Mindelo in September. But with Guinea-Bissau already independent, the **demonstrations** only grew larger. By October, with "continuity" sounding increasingly hollow, the Portuguese were negotiating with PAIGC leaders. In December, a meeting in Lisbon agreed on a transitional government consisting of three PAIGC members and two from the MFA. The Portuguese capitulated by allowing a general election the following June. With a landslide of votes, **Aristides Pereira** took office on **July 5, 1975** as president of the new republic.

■ Independence and the split with Guinea-Bissau

Cape Verde and Guinea-Bissau were united by a common colonial experience. The war which began in Bissau culminated in the **liberation** of all Portugal's colonies and the emergence of democracy in Portugal itself. Amilcar Cabral had been obsessive about the importance of **Cape Verde–Guinea unity** and Aristides Pereira continued to emphasize it. But the most significant political event in the first twenty years of Cape Verdean independence has been the 1980 coup in Bissau which overthrew **President Luiz Cabral**, Amilcar's half-brother, and led to the formal separation of the two countries.

After the liberation war there was a lingering unease within the PAIGC in Guinea-Bissau. Luiz Cabral, though a close friend of party leader

Aristides Pereira, was not a statesman of the same rank, and he became an increasingly isolated figure, mistrustful of his own ministers and – it seemed to them – unwilling to discuss economic and social questions outside a clique in which Pereira figured too prominently. Suspicions grew that policy in Guinea-Bissau was being constructed by the two presidents in secret and that Cape Verde, which had achieved independence relatively painlessly – though at the cost of Guinean lives – was seeking to dominate the union. Furthermore, while Cape Verdeans had been instrumental in starting the independence movement, they had also formed a large proportion of the colonial civil service in Guinea-Bissau, most of whom had passively collaborated with the Portuguese. The charge of **neo-colonialism** didn't have to be made explicit.

Against Pereira's advice, Cabral modified the Guinea-Bissauan constitution to give himself more power and his nationalistic prime minister, **Nino Vieira**, less. It was Vieira who subsequently led the coup of November 14, 1980, putting himself in the Bissau presidency. Pereira, in condemning the coup, pointed out that the party constitution provided the means for dealing with factional problems. On January 20, 1981 (the eighth anniversary of the assassination of Amilcar Cabral) the Cape Verdean arm of the party renamed itself the **PAICV** and, at a summit in Maputo in 1982, a formal division of the two countries' assets ratified the split. A vague ideological union of the two countries still exists, but *rapprochement* has tended to come from the Cape Verdean corner.

One immediate effect of the events of 1980 was the fright it gave to **international aid donors** and partners. Since the early 1960s, support for the independence struggles against Portugal in the international community had been broad-based and confident. The high-profile style and actions of the PAIGC leadership were applauded and, after independence, both countries quickly came to rely on aid to rebuild their wrecked economies. After the 1980 coup, Pereira moved fast to allay fears about the region, successfully pursuing a diplomatic course to maintain international support not just for the islands, but for Guinea-Bissau – efforts which showed surprising good grace under the circumstances.

■ The PAICV era

After 1981, with the union of the two countries a fast fading dream, Cape Verde at least had a chance to address purely **national problems**. The question of the very habitability of the islands was raised, but the **economy** was made viable, a result of careful and sensitive development and a remarkable absence of corruption.

The PAICV government answered OAU demands that it apply the **sanctions policy on South Africa** and refuse refuelling rights to South African Airways with the response that it could not afford to commit suicide by solidarity. It also increased the level of **aid** coming into the country and used it on local projects of direct utility. Non-governmental aid, channelled through the National Development Fund, matched foreign interests to Cape Verdean requirements. By leaving the door open for *americanos* to return, it encouraged **private investment** and maintained a high level of goodwill amongst the vast majority of the Cape Verdean diaspora whose remittances continued to be the number one economic pillar.

Agrarian reform was patient, seeking to avoid alienating landlords, to persuade and cajole them rather than to force change and always to avoid damaging the country's overseas image of independence and openness. The worst effects of **drought** and flash floods were combated with tree-planting programmes on all the islands, and further measures like dyke building and better terracing.

Health was a priority for the PAICV government, which reckoned to spend three times as much per person as the average developing country. Mother and Child Protection and Family Planning programmes had a high profile, and were operated by the PAICV at a community level, with theatre shows and public demonstrations organized to mobilize people on the issues – including breast-feeding, contraception and nutrition. The off-loading of unwanted First World drugs, so common in underdeveloped countries, was avoided by setting up a national pharmaceuticals industry.

One hundred percent **adult literacy** as well as free and compulsory **primary education** are goals that the PAICV pretty well achieved (though adult literacy rates tend to improve naturally with the demise of illiterate senior citizens).

Even under one-party rule, the **legal system** in Cape Verde was one of the most progressive in Africa. There were no political prisoners – indeed there are still few of any kind – and there is no death sentence. The country has an almost spotless record on **human rights**: since independence there has been only one seriously violent incident involving the military, when a soldier accompanying the Agrarian Reform Commission lost his nerve in a noisy crowd on Santo Antão and opened fire, killing a man in the ensuing panic.

Respect abroad for the development of the Cape Verdean republic found a new dimension with the country's hosting of multilateral talks on Angola. Cape Verde's location and relative insignificance look likely to encourage this role as provider of neutral territory for delicate meetings.

Despite the successes, there remained several lurking problems which would not fade away. **Alcoholism**, especially in the rural areas, has been an ongoing problem for centuries. At root a strictly male issue, it is triply destructive where it not only wastes productive land on sugar cane but hard earnings as well, and reduces the workforce.

A more pointed issue in the late 1980s was the battle between church and state over the issue of **abortion** on demand which the PAICV supported. Although 80 percent of children are brought up in mother-only families, the position of **women** in Cape Verdean society has never had as much attention focused on it as the male-formulated charter of the Organization of Cape Verdean Women – OMCV – would suggest. The division of views was by no means straightforward: there were OMCV members among those taking part in the anti-abortion campaign. Violent anti-abortion demonstrations were led by church activists and the Catholic journal *Terra Nova* was, as a result of its anti-government stance on the issue, labelled an "opposition newspaper" by the foreign press.

Good **rainy seasons** in the late 1980s broke a drought that had persisted on some islands virtually throughout the years of independence. But the PAICV was not equipped to ride out the inevitable wave of rising expectations that came with better harvests and the end of the Cold War. It never properly examined its own renewal mechanisms, thus allowing the ex-guerillas of the party to grow old and stagnant together.

■ All change: the democratic era

At the PAICV party congress in 1988, there were discussions led by younger members about ending its status as the country's sole political party. The new **Movimento para a Democracia**

(MPD), led by lawyer Carlos Veiga, held its first meeting in June 1990 and demands were made for sweeping reforms to Cape Verde's "revolutionary" constitution and the established political culture in which the PAICV held such sway.

Under a tide of mounting pressure, especially from the church, the prime minister Pedro Pires took over as PAICV party secretary from Aristides Pereira (who saw himself as state president, outside politics), in preparation for the introduction of a **multiparty system**.

In Portuguese-speaking Africa's first ever multiparty legislative elections, held in January 1991, the MPD swept to power, taking more than two-thirds of National Assembly seats. They had the support of the US émigrés' biggest party, the UCID, formerly the party of the opposition in exile (long-term émigrés, however, were prevented at the last minute from voting). **Carlos Veiga** was subsequently elected prime minister – though not without opposition from within his own ranks – and former supreme court judge **António Mascarenhas** won the presidential election, soundly defeating ex-president Pereira. The MPD also won most of the seats in local council elections held later in the year, with PAICV wins only on the home islands of PAICV dignitaries. The loss of support for the veterans of the liberation struggle indicated the large proportion of the population too young to remember it.

Economically, the MPD government has put great efforts into making the country **investor-friendly**, with emphases on its tourism and fishing potential. The scrapping of the PAICV's last major initiative, the agrarian reform laws, was a popular move at home, and was judged to have signalled the right messages to overseas investors. The civil service payroll was reduced by half and investigations were carried out on embezzlement of state funds by former PAICV officials.

Yet despite the peaceful and widely approved transition to multiparty politics, there remains widespread **dissatisfaction** with lack of progress and the slow rate of economic improvement on the islands. The MPD has been torn by splits, resignations and defections. One ex-MPD official, Eurico Monteiro, has formed a new party, the Partido da Convergência Democrática, and gained a seat in the 1995 elections.

In terms of economic development, **tourism** is a promising avenue which is already beginning to yield results, with around 50,000 mostly Portuguese, French, Italian and German visitors each year. The islands are surrounded by massive **fishing** stocks, but there is little basic infrastructure to exploit them on a commercial scale – less than one hundred commercial fishing boats in the whole country, and many of these unseaworthy. The MPD government has made efforts to substitute the plantations of sugar cane – a crop which covers more than half of the country's irrigated land – with food and cash crops, encouraging a move away from the massive emphasis on local *grogue* production and the problems associated with alcoholism. But the cane-and-rum culture is deeply ingrained and the cash-economy alternatives not altogether convincing to poor landowners and tenants. **Unemployment** is running at around twenty-five percent, and for those families with no relatives in Europe or the USA, life is still desperately hard.

The next **elections**, expected in December 2000, are not likely to see major changes in parliament. The MPD, though widely criticized in the poorer communities, where peoples' lives have been hit hardest by the **economic adjustment policies** demanded by the World Bank and the IMF, is not likely to lose its huge majority (it currently holds 50 of the 72 legislative assembly seats, with Pedro Pires' PAICV holding 21). Assuming the occasional good rainy season and continued overseas investment, prospects for the future look reasonably healthy, at least in West African terms. The danger for the government is that people's expectations in the poor, rural heartlands of the most heavily populated islands of Santiago, Santo Antão and Fogo will outstrip its ability – some would say willingness – to tackle their basic needs.

THE SOTAVENTOS

Santiago, **Fogo**, **Brava** and **Maio** make up the **Sotaventos**, the leeward group of islands, with two-thirds of the population, more of the rainfall (which arrives from the south) and a good deal of the wealth.

If you're coming from Dakar, your first port of call on the islands will be **Praia** on **Santiago island**, Cape Verde's capital and the nation's largest town. It's a pleasant enough place but there are no gripping reasons to spend time here: if you're stuck for a few days, your time is better spent enjoying one of the easy and satisfying short **trips out of town**. The rest of Santiago offers more enticing attractions in the mountainous **central region** and the beaches in the northwest. But although it has a sizeable mountainous interior, Santiago's scenery doesn't compare with that of the Barlavento islands of São Nicolau and, outstandingly, Santo Antão.

Fogo island is a vast, semi-active volcano, rising to nearly 3000m above sea level, whose last eruption was in 1995. There's a magnificent road tracking along the lava-covered eastern slopes, fine walking country in the gentler western parts, and fascinating and very feasible hiking up in the old crater itself, now a domain of citrus orchards and vineyards.

The smallest of the inhabited islands is **Brava**. Cape Verdeans often rate it the most beautiful island and it's still somewhat hard to visit as, despite having a small airport, there are no scheduled flights and the sea journey is rough and unpredictable. Brava is certainly the most cultivated island, with a relatively benign climate – and it's long been a sanctuary for those families who could afford to flee the droughts on other islands.

Maio, one of the *ilhas rasas* or "flat islands", is duller and drier. Locally famous for its cattle, which provide the country's limited milk supply, other attempts to drum up interest seem a little desperate. As one Portuguese brochure of 1970 put it: "The desolation of its landscape contrasts with the warm welcome of its people and the fine flavour of its fresh lobsters". So there you have it.

Santiago

With half the cultivable land and half the population, **SANTIAGO** is the **agricultural backbone** of Cape Verde. Unusual among the islands, it takes a few hours to get from one end to the other, switchbacking through the mountains or along the jagged eastern coast. Santiago's main focus is the capital, **Praia**, at the southern tip. The village of Ribeira Grande (Cidade Velha), west of Praia, was the first settlement on the islands and remained the effective administrative centre until early in the eighteenth century. Praia then took over the role of capital, growing from village to town through the nineteenth century. From Praia, one main road snakes through the interior, sending secondary roads like suckers down to the coast; another forks off it to the northeast to link up the east coast fishing villages before meeting with the main route again at **Tarrafal** in the northwest – site of the best beaches. There are dozens of hamlets and villages scattered across the island, and any number of hidden coves and *ribeiras*. A few of the travel possibilities are covered in the next few pages, but Santiago, in common with all the islands, is still little explored by outsiders. Most of your discoveries will be very much your own.

Praia and around

The best way to arrive at **PRAIA** – and by far the most likely – is by plane. If you fly in from Dakar, the clean air, bright sunlight and wind are constant reminders of the

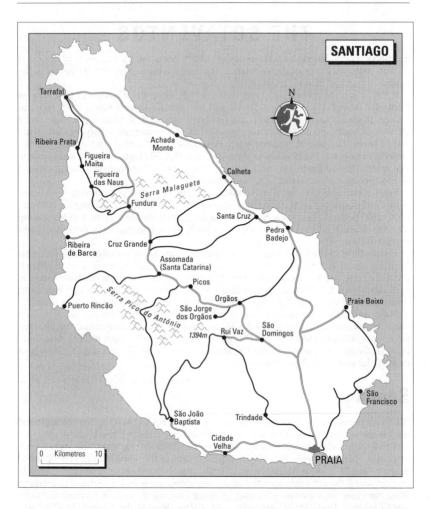

Atlantic. The presence of a couple of power-generating windmills rotating on the brown hills across the *ribeira*, the extraordinary tranquillity of the little town on its small proud plateau, everything about Cape Verde, you can see, is going to be quite different. Cape Verdeans – and foreign residents too – tend to complain that Praia is soulless, thinks of nothing but money and has no *joie de vivre*. If you're already tuned to Cape Verde's gentle sensibilities this may be relatively true. But after Dakar it all comes as a welcome drop in tension and the nicest possible culture shock.

Arrival, orientation and information

Arrival, by sea or air, and orientation, on foot, couldn't be simpler. **Gago Coutinho airport** at Praia is small and has basic facilities: a small terminal building with a small café-bar (not always open) and toilets. There are no money-changing facilities. You walk from the arrivals room to the front gate and out onto the forecourt. Below is the manageable muddle of the capital, five minutes away by taxi – about CV$300 to the plateau (Platô) and CV$500 to Prainha, at the southern end of town. The taxi-drivers are very laid-back, but, arriving from Senegal, you may find it hard to persuade your driver to accept CFA francs; dollars, deutschmarks or French francs would almost certainly be acceptable, or just ask him to wait till you've changed some at the end of your trip. Drivers often don't have change, so it's worth being prepared. Many people head for one of the more modest *pensões*, but unless you're loaded down with luggage you might just ask for the main *praça* in Platô – Praça Alberquerque – and hop out when you get there – it tends to be cheaper than naming a specific destination.

Arriving by sea you dock at the pier roughly beneath the end of the airport runway. Again, it's a five-minute taxi ride to town, barely two kilometres if you walk.

The downtown part of Praia is all concentrated on the fortress-like slab of the **Platô**, a neat grid of streets 800m long and 300m wide, which overlooks the expanding suburbs and is simplicity itself to get around. Off the Platô to the northwest is the Fazenda district; to the southwest is Várzea, with the impressive new ministries' building, the Palácio do Governo; beyond is Achada do Santo António (Achada Sto António) where many international organizations have their headquarters; while further south, facing the islet of Santa-Maria, is the embassy and smart hotels district of Prainha. Taxis between Prainha and Platô take five mintues and cost around CV$120–150.

The only real **tourist information** on offer in Praia is from the tiny Promex kiosk on the northeast side of the *praça* on the plateau. They have lists, maps, postcards and one or two friendly staff.

Accommodation

If your budget is limited, the best advice is to track down a **room** in one of Praia's few *pensões* as soon as possible and not to keep looking if you find one that seems OK. When planes and boats come in, the limited number of budget beds go pretty quickly and there are no vast differences in standards.

Hotel América, in Achada Sto António, opposite the offices of the EC and next to the Felicidade supermarket (☎62.14.31; Fax 61.14.32). Rooms with AC, TV and fridge. One of the newer hotels in Praia, with local amenities. Recommended. B&B from ④.

Hotel Felicidade, rua Serpa Pinto, Platô (CP 154; ☎61.55.84; Fax 61.12.89). A popular budget first choice. The S/C streetfront rooms are good value and have balconies and AC, while the non-S/C rooms at the back are stuffier, but quite a lot cheaper and more often available. Same price for one or two people. B&B. ③.

Hotel Marisol, Chã de Areia district (CP 129; ☎61.34.60; Fax 61.25.35). Slightly faded, upmarket place. Now somewhat gloomy and overpriced, but the seafront rooms are brighter and it's mostly well maintained. ⑤.

Hotel Praia-Mar, Prainha district (CP 75; ☎61.37.77; Fax 61.29.72). Reasonable tourist-class place, though not at all fancy, its reputation somewhat inflated by its airy, seafront position. Large saltwater pool and a reasonable dining room. Seasonal rates. ⑤–⑦.

Hotel Trópico, Prainha district (CP 413; ☎61.42.00; Fax 61.52.25; *hoteltropico@mail.cvtelecom.cv*). Praia's best hotel, with very spacious rooms and a large saltwater pool. ⑦.

ACCOMMODATION PRICE CODES	
① Under CV$800 (under £5/$8)	⑤ CV$4800–6400 (£30–40/$48–64)
② CV$800–1600 (£5–10/$8–16)	⑥ CV$6400–8000 (£40–50/$64–80)
③ CV$1600–3200 (£10–20/$16–32)	⑦ Over CV$8000 (over £50/$80)
④ CV$3200–4800 (£20–30/$32–48)	

For further details, see p.48.

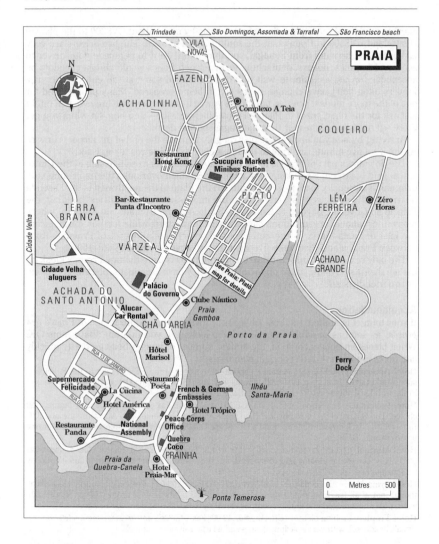

Pensão Paraiso, rua Serpa Pinto, at the north end of Platô (☎61.35.39). Clean, and better than adequate, especially in the balcony rooms (#3 and #9). ③, but more with TV.

Residêncial Adega, formerly the *Solmar*, av Amílcar Cabral, Platô (CP 154A; ☎61.59.24; Fax 61.59.02). Pricier than the nearby *Felicidade*, but clean and spacious, with a local atmosphere, and good breakfasts included. The rooms with a view over the square are #14, #15, #16 and #17. ④.

Residêncial Anjos, rua Serpa Pinto, Platô (CP 307; ☎61.41.78). Very presentable B&B; some rooms with balconies. ③.

Residêncial Sol Atlantico, unmarked entrance at 24 av Amílcar Cabral (☎61.28.72). Offers some of the cheapest rooms in Platô, though water and power problems continue to plague them. Room 1, despite being hot and noisy, is recommended for its window overlooking the square. ③.

Around the Platô

It takes about twenty minutes to realize that Praia has almost nothing to offer in terms of sights or entertainment. Not that this is an alarming revelation – this is a capital where just being here is enjoyable: the streets are friendly; the *praça* has benches and a bandstand where visiting naval bands sometimes play on Sundays; and there are good views from the edge of the Platô, particularly from one or two *pensões* on the western side.

Such action as there is on the plateau tends to focus around the **market**, refurbished in 1999, which, despite its small size, brings in country women from all over Santiago and, in a good harvest year, can pack surprising variety and colour: papayas, bananas, watermelons, potatoes and cassava, goat cheeses, piglets trussed in baskets, dried beans, slabs of red tuna, even potted palms. **Sugar** products are much in evidence. For the Portuguese in the sixteenth and seventeenth centuries, the islands were strategic in their efforts to dominate Atlantic trade routes: rum in particular – distilled from cane sugar – was enormously useful in the **slave trade**, commanding high prices along the Guinea coast. Cane, which grew well enough in lusher valleys on several islands, was never produced in the kind of quantities that would have led to huge commercial success. But Cape Verdeans continue to distil plenty of *grogue*, *canna* and *aguardente* (all variants on the same theme), and to make irresistible sweets. Various kinds of sickly fudge, often made with coconut, and cup-like moulds of brown molasses crystal are always on sale in Praia.

The few large public buildings around town hold no special interest, though the **Catholic Cathedral** is quite an imposing block of a place with its potted plants and figurines. Formerly, if you wanted a glimpse of the interior courtyard and gardens of the then Office of the Prime Minister, now the **Praia Municipal Council headquarters**, you needed the excuse of visiting to see if they were holding any unwanted seats on flights. With the advent of democracy, you can nowadays walk freely around the council building's pretty grounds and the perimeter of the presidential palace itself, the **Palácio da República**, which overlooks the beach. The **statue of Diogo Gomes**, the Portuguese explorer who was one of the first to visit the islands, has been reinstated here. While several dilapidated colonial buildings on the Platô are being renovated, much of Praia is new and drab, the scrawny suburbs crawling up boulder-strewn gulches away from the centre.

Despite the name Praia – which means **beach** – the one or two small coves near the town are none too great. The grey strip beneath where the road snakes off the end of the Platô – Praia Gamboa – is a possibility (and the site of a music festival in May – worth checking out if you're in Praia at the right time), but it tends to be used by exercising soldiers, and the pair of small crescents on either side of the *Hotel Praia-Mar*'s peninsula are nothing special. You'll do much better, if you can find transport, going out to São Francisco, 13km east of Praia (see p.395).

Eating and drinking

Praia has a decent variety of **restaurants** ranging from workaday eating house *casas de pasto* (CV$400–600) to more upmarket places (from CV$1000). The cheapest places are mostly away from the Platô area. If you want to save money, use the market or one of the supermarkets and put together your own picnics. Note that many places close on Sunday.

Bar-Restaurante Punta d'Incontro, av Cidade de Lisboa, west of the Platô. Lively meeting place.

Cachito, av Amílcar Cabral, Platô. Good café, right by the *praça*.

Cafe Pastelaria Lee, rua Andrade Corvo. Cute little café with a daily *prato do dia*.

Cafeteria Cap'Sul, Centro Cultural Francês (French Cultural Centre), rua Andrade Corvo, Platô. Pleasant retreat. Mon–Fri 9am–noon & 2.30–7.30pm, Sat 10am–1pm.

Casa de Pasto Amelia, av Amílcar Cabral, Platô. Long-established and justly popular with townspeople and a scattering of foreign workers and volunteers for its solid set meals (for around CV$300–400) and generous glasses of wine. Open Mon–Sat 7.30–8am, 12.30–2pm & 7.30–9pm.

Casa de Pasto Antonia, rua Dr Miguel Bombarda, Platô. Basic, Kriolu-speaking place with one dish a day. Cheap, friendly, filling.

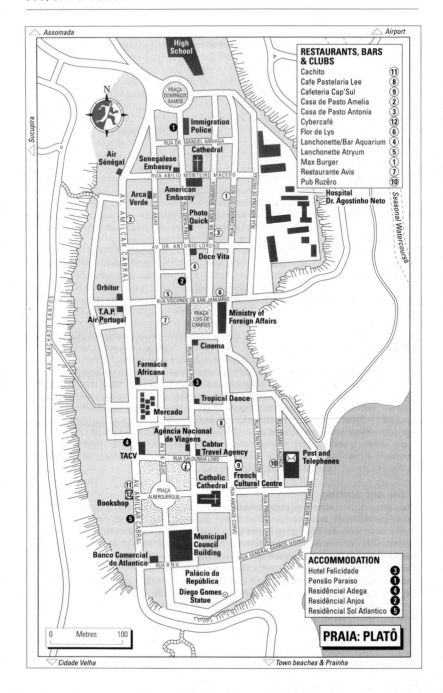

△ Assomada   △ Airport

RESTAURANTS, BARS & CLUBS

Cachito	⑪
Cafe Pastelaria Lee	⑧
Cafeteria Cap'Sul	⑨
Casa de Pasto Amelia	②
Casa de Pasto Antonia	③
Cybercafé	⑫
Flor de Lys	⑥
Lanchonette/Bar Aquarium	④
Lanchonette Atryum	⑤
Max Burger	①
Restaurante Avis	⑦
Pub Ruzêro	⑩

High School

PRAÇA DOMINGOS RAMOS

Immigration Police ❶

Air Sénégal

Senegalese Embassy

Cathedral

RUA DR. MANUEL ARRIAGA

RUA ABILIO MONTEIRO MACEDO

Arca Verde

American Embassy

Photo Quick

Hospital Dr. Agostinho Neto

AV. DR. ANTONIO LORENO

Doce Vita ④

Orbitur

❷

RUA VISCONDE DE SAN JANUARIO ⑥

⑤

T.A.P. Air Portugal

⑦

PRAÇA LUIS DE CAMÕES

Ministry of Foreign Affairs

Cinema

Farmácia Africana

❸

Mercado

Tropical Dance

⑧

Agência Nacional de Viagens

Cabtur Travel Agency

❹

TACV

RUA SALDUNHA LOBO

⑨

French Cultural Centre

⑩

Post and Telephones

Catholic Cathedral

⑪

⑫

Bookshop

PRAÇA ALBERQUERQUE

❺

Banco Comercial do Atlantico

RUA B.N.U.

Municipal Council Building

Palácio da República

Diego Gomes Statue

RUA GENERAL BARROS (closed)

ACCOMMODATION

Hotel Felicidade	❸
Pensão Paraiso	❶
Residêncial Adega	❹
Residêncial Anjos	❷
Residêncial Sol Atlantico	❺

PRAIA: PLATÔ

▽ Cidade Velha   ▽ Town beaches & Prainha

0   Metres   100

AV. AMILCAR CABRAL

AV. MACHADO SANTOS

AV. 5 DE JULHO

RUA SERPA PINTO

RUA DR. MIGUEL BOMBARDA

RUA CANDIDO DOS REIS

RUA BORJONA DE FREITAS

RUA TENENTE VALADIM

RUA CESARIO LACERDA

RUA ANDRADE CORVO

RUA PINHEIRO CHAGAS

RUA NEVES FERREIRA

Seasonal Watercourse

△ Sucupira

La Cucina, Achada Sto António (☎62.14.37), near the *Hotel América*. Pricey, with most main dishes – Italian, international – around CV$1000, but worth it.

Cybercafé, av Amílcar Cabral, Platô (daily 8am–8pm). Internet access, sodas and good, cheap espresso.

Flor de Lys, rua Visconde de San Januário, Platô. Large helpings of freshly prepared food from a limited menu. Good value in the CV$500–600 range.

Hotel Marisol, Chã de Areia district (☎61.34.60). Has a deserved reputation – order the rabbit if they have it – but it's rather expensive and not exactly overflowing with atmosphere.

Lanchonette Aquarium, rua Serpa Pinto, Platô, opposite the *Residência Anjos* (☎61.32.28). Very pleasant and lively place to eat and drink, with tropical fish on display and *Cleps* on tap. Mon–Sat 7am–11pm.

Lanchonette Atryum, rua Visconde de San Januário, Platô. Decent eatery and bar.

Max Burger, rua Cándido dos Reis, Platô. Cheeseburgers for CV$170. Open 8am–midnight.

Restaurante Avis, av 5 de Julho, Platô (☎61.30.79). Long-established and reliable café-bar, with snacks and one or two dishes. Great on a Sunday when other restaurants tend to be closed. Daily 7.30am–11pm.

Restaurante Hong Kong, av Cidade Lisboa, Achadinha (☎61.29.49). Reasonable Chinese meals.

Restaurante Panda, Prainha district, near the *Hotel Praia-Mar*, and a positive alternative if you're staying in the hotel. Chinese food.

Restaurante Panorama, rua Serpa Pinto, Platô, on the *Hotel Felicidade* rooftop (☎61.41.00). Though its rooftop position is perhaps the main attraction, this does passable food, and also runs a couple of excellent caravan snack bars – in the main *praça* and down by the *Hotel Marisol*.

Restaurante Poeta, Achada Sto António (☎61.38.00). Bland establishment, with reasonable international-style food, but rather a good sea view.

Nightlife

Evening is when the Platô is at its most delightfully unhurried. Plenty of people – whole families it seems – spend an entire evening lounging in the *praça*, playing with their children or strolling past the few shops, all of which stay open late (the café-bar in the *praça* is open until 10.30pm). The offerings at the Platô **cinema** are rarely very interesting and the **nightclub** scene is limited: none have opened in the restrictive streets of the Platô, though there are a number of friendly **bars** here. Clubs are mostly scattered across the suburbs and never get going until around midnight. Music is generally a sweaty mixture of chart-topping European and American sounds and Cape Verdean *coladeira* and *funana* dance styles.

CLUBS

Clube Náutico, Chã de Areia, by the beach (☎61.11.81).

Complexo A Teia, rua Che-Guevara, Fazenda district (☎61.66.11). Grand and flashy: you'll need to dress up a bit. CV$1000.

Discoteca Dallas, Pensamento district, on the road out towards Trindade. A broad mix of music; highly recommended.

Doce Vita, rua Serpa Pinto (☎61.25.60). Looks like, and mostly is, a shop and snack bar, with music at weekends – the only place on the Platô for a dance.

Pub Ruzêro, rua Cesário Lacerda. Platô, opposite the post office. Local bands sometimes play downstairs. Recommended.

Quebra Coco, at the *Hotel Praia-Mar*. Hotel club, but not bad for that.

Tabu Open-air disco in Lém Ferreira, along the *ribeira* off the road to the airport.

Zéro Horas, Achada Grande (☎61.00.00), between the port and the airport. Probably the most cosmopolitan musical mix of any of Praia's big clubs. CV$500–1000.

BARS

Bar Aquárium, rua Serpa Pinto, Platô (Mon–Sat 7am–11pm). Friendly atmosphere, beer on tap and English-speaking boss.

Casa de Pasto Amelia, av Amílcar Cabral, Platô. You'll usually find a good atmosphere here – if you're simply into knocking back a few *copas*.

Flor de Lys, rua Visconde de San Januário, Platô. Like the *Amelia*, a popular local hangout.

Hotel Marisol, Chã de Areia district. Attractive outdoor bar.

Restaurante Poeta, Achada Sto António. A better place to drink than eat, with a pleasant bar.

Listings

Airlines TACV, av Amílcar Cabral, Platô (☎61.58.13; Mon–Fri 8am–noon & 2.30–6pm, Sat 8–11.30am; airport office ☎63.30.82). Air Sénégal , av Amílcar Cabral, Platô (☎61.54.83), is open irregular hours (in theory Mon–Fri 8am–12.30pm & 2.30–6pm, Sat 9–11am) and tends to be closed while the Dakar plane is on the runway and the staff are at the airport hustling seats. TAP Air Portugal, av Amílcar Cabral, Platô (☎61.58.26) is open Mon–Fri 8am–noon and 2–4.30pm. There's no official airport **information** service, but the TACV office in town knows as much as anyone.

Bank The Banco Comercial do Atlântico, rua B.N.U., Platô (☎61.30.93) is open Mon–Fri, 8am–2.30pm.

Bookshop The best – nearly the only one – is the Instituto de Promoção Cultural, av Amílcar Cabral, Platô, under the *Cybercafé*, which has a limited stock of books in Portuguese, together with a few imported publications.

Buses Private Hiace minibuses run from a depot next to the main Sucupira market just west of the Platô. Cidade Velha *aluguers* go from a parking area in Terra Branca, southwest of the Platô.

Car rental Try Alucar, in Chã de'Areia, south of the plateau (☎61.73.24; Fax 61.49.00); Classic Auto Rental, av Cidade Lisboa, in Fazenda, just off the plateau to the northwest (☎63.22.22; Fax 63.22.25); or Sociarpa, rua Andrade Corvo, Platô (☎61.57.90; Fax 61.37.66). They all offer reasonable Japanese saloons for between CV\$3500 and CV\$5000 per day, inclusive of 100km, though none of them has a large fleet (reserve ahead) and only Alucar is normally prepared to rent for a single day (others insist on a minimum three days). Taxis can be rented by the hour for around CV\$1000.

CDs There are several shops in town where you can buy Cape Verdean music, apart from the Prainha hotels, which also sell CDs. Try the Instituto de Promoção Cultural, on av Amílcar Cabral under the *Cybercafé*, or Tropical Dance on rua Serpa Pinto, which has a good selection.

Email *Cybercafé*, on av Amílcar Cabral (daily 8am–8pm), offers good-value online time.

Embassies and visas Angola, Brazil, China, Cuba, France, Germany, Portugal, Russia, Senegal and the USA are the only countries with embassies in Cape Verde. There's an Italian consul in Fazenda (☎61.32.80), but most consuls, including Britain's, reside in Mindelo. The long-established American embassy on rua Abilio Monteiro Macedo, Platô (☎61.56.16; Fax 61.13.55), is generally helpful to Anglophone travellers. The German Embassy in Prainha (☎61.12.85) is open Mon–Fri, 8.30am–noon. The Senegalese embassy is on rua Abilio Monteiro Macedo, Platô (☎61.56.21; Mon–Fri 8.30am–12.30pm & 2.30–4.30pm; one-month visas CFA3000, three-month visas CFA7000). The French embassy in Prainha (☎61.55.89; Mon–Fri 8.30am–12.30pm & 2.30–6pm) has a visa service for a number of Francophone states including Burkina, Côte d'Ivoire, Mauritania and Togo. Most 6–30 day visas cost CV\$2805 and 31–90 days cost CV\$3305.

Ferries Arca Verde (Companhia Nacional de Navegação Arca Verde), at the top of av 5 de Julho, Platô (CP 41, Praia; ☎61.54.97; Fax 61.54.96), is the main ferry ticket office. The Agencia Nacional de Viagens, rua Serpa Pinto, Platô, can also assist (☎61.36.80; Fax 61.21.62).

Film and developing Photo Quick, rua Serpa Pinto, is a busy place, but no cheaper than anywhere else. To develop and print a 24-roll costs CV\$1150.

French Cultural Centre, rua Andrade Corvo (☎61.11.96; Fax 61.12.60; *ccf.praia@milton. cvtelecom.cv*) is open Mon–Fri 9am–noon & 2.30–7.30pm, Sat 10am–1pm. Does the things which all Centres Culturels Français do, offering a French library, videos and news broadcasts and French cultural programmes. There's also a pleasant café (see above).

Hospitals and emergencies If you need treatment the Agostinho Neto Hospital on the plateau (☎61.24.62) is adequately equipped and able to perform tests for malaria, amoebas and so on. It's worth trying to see a medically qualified person via one of the embassies first.

Immigration If you need to extend your visa, visit the police station on rua Serpa Pinto, near the high school at the north end of the plateau.

Pharmacy Farmácia Africana, av Amílcar Cabral, Platô (☎61.27.76), is one of the best stocked.

Post and telephones (CTT) The post office is open Mon–Fri 8am–5pm, Sat 8am–noon. For fast mail overseas, use the express service, with collections on Mon, Wed and Fri at 10.30am; poste restante is available. The telephone office, in the same building, is open Mon–Fri 8am–noon & 3–5.30pm, Sat 9–11am.

Supermarkets The Supermercado Felicidade, in Achada Sto António, is the biggest shop in Cape Verde, with a reasonable selection of groceries.

Tourist offices and travel agents Try Cabetur, rua Serpa Pinto, Platô (☎61.55.51; Fax 61.37.54; Mon–Fri 8am–noon & 2–6pm), or Orbitur, corner of av Amílcar Cabral and rua Visconde de San Januário, Platô (CP 161; ☎61.57.37; Fax 61.38.88), which caters mostly to Cape Verdean travellers. Flights and accommodation can be arranged.

Out of Praia – Southern Santiago

All the following trips from Praia are feasible within a day, or even half a day if necessary. The São Francisco area has been earmarked as a tourism development zone and, once Praia's new international airport is opened, it's likely to change substantially. Cidade Velha is less likely to alter much in the near future, while developments in the Assomada district are more likely to be to do with agriculture and forestry than tourism.

São Francisco beaches

Although there are a couple of half-decent beaches near the *Hotel Praia-Mar* , the string of coves at **SÃO FRANCISCO**, about 13km from Praia, is worth the effort required to get there, to escape the odd bit of pollution and occasional hassles at the town beaches. There's no public transport, but you could go by taxi: a three-hour trip, allowing you two hours at the beach, will cost around CV\$2000–3000. Otherwise, head in the direction of the airport, turn left just over the bridge, walk through the *bairro* and try hitching. This is most likely to be successful on a Saturday or Sunday morning. Take food and drink, as there's nothing at the beach. The track from Praia has been scraped across the island's steep and rocky southern corner, and tips you out onto a flat sandy plain by the sea. There are several **beaches** to choose from. The first you reach on the track is the biggest, dotted with palms and a couple of villas built further back, but the furthest to the south is the best, with steps for the arthritic ex-President Pereira to climb down for his swims. There's clean sand, good waves and ten thousand kilometres of South Atlantic to gaze across.

Cidade Velha

Heading out of town for 10km in the opposite direction brings you to the old capital – **Ribeira Grande** – now known simply as **CIDADE VELHA**, "Old City". *Aluguers* leave regularly from Sucupira and from the parking area in Terra Branca, southwest of the Platô.

Cidade Velha is just about Cape Verde's only ancient site and in truth, while the landscape around is magnificent, the ruins aren't wildly interesting. After the hot, dry

THE SACK OF RIBEIRA GRANDE

A relatively good anchorage – there was nothing any safer in Madeira or the Azores – **Ribeira Grande** rapidly became the main mid-Atlantic victualling point for European merchant vessels in the sixteenth century. The *ribeira* almost never dried up and was dammed at its mouth to provide a permanent pool of **fresh water**. The town became a "city" in 1533 when a papal bull made it the seat of a diocese extending along half the West African coast.

In Atlantic trading circles Ribeira Grande's reputation soon spread. The English sea dog **Sir Francis Drake** caught the scent in 1585 and attacked the settlement with a force of 1000. The assault was more than just piracy – the union of Spain and Portugal meant that Cape Verde was considered enemy territory by the English – and it was well-planned. Drake landed at Praia to sneak overland and attack Ribeira Grande from behind, only to find the town deserted: the inhabitants had sensibly fled inland. Drake's crew stayed a fortnight, plundering what little there was and foraying into the interior without reward. One of the force was killed and mutilated by African slaves and Drake torched Ribeira Grande in reprisal, sparing only the hospital – the Casa Misericorde – whose ruins are still visible to the right as you descend into the centre of the present-day village.

moors on the way from Praia, you round the last bend and the village is down below. The setting is everything – a living, moving sea, awash with foam, thundering against the black crags. If you think you'd like to stay, investigate the new *Baía do Coral* restaurant (☎61.28.60; Fax 63.14.86), which should have rooms by now.

Ribeira Grande was the site of the **first Portuguese base** in Africa, founded to create a slave-trading entrepôt, selling labour to the Spanish West Indies. The most notable building today is the **Cathedral**, finished in 1693, a century and a half after the foundation of the diocese. For a few years Ribeira Grande reached a peak of prestige, until its eventual defeat by a French force in 1712 led to a rethink on the part of the Portuguese and the more considered development of the new capital of Praia. The cathedral at Ribeira Grande was already falling apart by 1735 and, when a new bishop was appointed in 1754, he quickly left Santiago and spent the rest of his life on Santo Antão.

Nowadays Cidade Velha is badly neglected, a village of fishing people and farmers living among the ruins of sixteenth- and seventeenth-century Portugal. As one bit of local tourist literature points out: "Birthplace of our nationality, one can find valuable patrimonial witnesses still in ruins, thus deserving restoration, good keeping and consolidation". Deserving or not, it seems that in sad reality what Drake started (see box, above) will be finished off within twenty years if nothing is done to prevent further collapse: pigs and goats forage amid the fallen masonry of the cathedral and you're quite free to wander with them between the massive, roofless walls. Fortunately a team of UNESCO archeologists and restorers are currently working on the ruins at Cidade Velha and a museum is planned.

It's worth going down to the *ribeira* and up the other side, through cane and corn and under mango trees, to further, less explored ruins – the church of **Nossa Senhora do Rosário** which served as a cathedral in miniature when the diocese was first created, and the Capuchin **Monastery of São Francisco** higher up the valley. Once up there, you can admire the palm-filled valley and muse on what five centuries of Portuguese rule have brought, and taken from, the islands. When the first buildings were put up the treeless scene must have had much the barren cast of a tropical Iona: all the trees have been established since that time. Today, you're likely to come across sugar cane presses and *grogue* stills as you climb through the jungly allotments – the aroma is unmissable.

Down in the town *praça* stands Cidade Velha's most famous relic, the **pelourinho** or pillory, where captives were shackled on display. Today the village is mostly populated by grizzled old rustics: there are one or two general shops but no signs of anything to do with *turismo*. Though the large fleet of red fishing boats on the beach indicates more activity than you'd at first think, most of the young have moved to the mini-metropolis of Praia only twenty minutes away.

Getting back yourself can be a little problematic if you don't feel like waiting for the next *aluguer*. But you can easily fill the time drinking *grogue* with the elders down in one of the village stores or, if you manage to avoid that, hiking back up the rather magnificent descent into town and cutting back to the left, to look over the extensive remains of the **Fortaleza Real de São Filipe** which dominates the whole of Cidade Velha from on high. A vast empty shell, but in surprisingly good condition, it offers stunning views of the *ribeira* and, behind, of the Serra do Pico de Santo António.

São Domingos

There's no great reason to visit **SÃO DOMINGOS**, but it's worth it for the pretty **journey** – only half an hour from Praia by Hiace – which takes you rapidly from the trashy outskirts of the capital into the heartland of rural Santiago. The minibus plunges into deep valleys where straight-backed women grind corn with a boulder against a flat rock (a *pilão*), pigs root at the roadside, and be-satchelled children walk home from school. São Domingos itself is one of the earliest settlements on the island, over 450 years old; its church has a famous boat-shaped pulpit. Drake ventured this far inland in 1585 and, finding the settlement abandoned like Ribeira Grande, thought better of continuing into the wild interior. On the way into town from Praia, there's a craft sales cooperative on the right – a limited selection of pottery, weaving and ornaments, at sensible prices. If you want to stay in São Domingos, there's a *pousada* here – the somewhat imposing cream and orange *Bela Vista* (③) – which might open for your visit, on demand. It's a delightful place to stay, in the floor of the valley and surrounded by irrigated cultivation. Check out also the *Restaurante Morena*.

North and east Santiago

The main reason to go north is to visit **Tarrafal**, a beautiful fishing village that makes an ideal spot to rest up for a few days. It's right at the opposite end of Santiago from Praia, and there are two different minibus routes that go there – one over the rugged spine of the island, the other along the indented east coast. The journey can make a very satisfying round trip.

The mountain route

The mountain route goes straight across an unexpectedly fairy-tale interior – peaks and rocky needles, soaring valleys, narrow terraces and ridges – a fine journey, especially during or after the rains. There are steep climbs and some great views before Assomada, then higher passes in the Malagueta range, rising to over 1300m.

The highest point of the island, the 1394-metre Pico de Santo António – with some of the few monkeys in Cape Verde on its slopes – rises above the town of **São Jorge dos Orgãos**, a few kilometres south of the main road. **Picos**, a few kilometres further north, is the site of the INIDA, the National Institute of Agrarian Research and Development, which has a *miradouro* (panoramic viewpoint) overlooking the year-round-green plantations, and a flourishing Botanical Garden (☎71.11.47) where you can see Cape Verdean flora and birdlife.

Shortly before you reach Assomada, you come to the small town of **Picos** perched on a crag on the right next to a huge basaltic outcrop looking out over a wide, deep valley. In season, the blooms of jacaranda and frangipani bubble around the small *praça* and church.

ASSOMADA
En route to Tarrafal, if you've time and inclination, you can break your journey at **ASSOMADA**. The town, also known as Vila de Santa Catarina, is the second largest on the island – an interesting, lively place with a fine market and some quaint old architecture – and there should be no problem finding a place for the night here if you decide to stay – try *Cretcheu* (☎65.10.14; ②) or *Asa Branca* (☎65.23.72; ②). If you have only an hour or two, take a short walk out of town (north) and a turning right, then a steep path down into the *ribeira* to see what must be a contender for the biggest **silk-cotton tree** in the world – though it's always referred to locally as a "baobab". Ask for **Boa Entrada**, the neighbouring village, tucked in the *ribeira*. You can't fail to see the tree standing on the slope across the valley: it's a monster. The trunk – over fifty metres round at the base – is a maze of contorted buttresses, and it would stand out anywhere, but in Cape Verde, land of limited leafiness, it's a fantastic sight. The tree must be as old as the first generation of settlers. In 1855, according to a Rev. Thomas, chaplain to the African Squadron of the US Navy, it was "forty feet in circumference" and had been "standing where it now stands when the island was first discovered".

The east coast route
Heading north by the **east coast route** you follow the same road out of Praia as the mountain route, then cut right at the Ribeirão Chiqueiro junction, with the village of **Praia Baixo** 7km away on the coast. There is direct transport to Praia Baixo from Praia's Sucupira transport park but unless you come at the weekend you're likely to be the only visitor. The village is reached down a long, low *ribeira* of partially deserted smallholdings, the road to it passing over concrete flood crossings. The beach is safe, in a deep, sheltered bay, with beach shades on the sands, one or two holiday villas behind, and at least one functioning beach bar. Men do some fishing by boat, but it's very quiet and, with the graffitied evidence of frustration with the government (Nunca Mais MPD – Bandidos e Ladrões – A Baixa MPD ("Never Again – Bandits & Thieves – Down with MPD") it all has a rather depressing air.

The first village you come to on the main road is **PEDRA BADEJO**, with a magnificent **coconut** grove marking the entrance to the settlement and gigantic bananas on sale – if you're lucky. You can see *pedreiros* making cobbles here, each shaded under a banana leaf on the clifftop. It's all very floral and pleasant, with good beaches and caves, but there are no *pensões*. If you want to stay, make first for one of the bar-restaurants – *Joyce* (☎69.12.20; Fax 69.15.21), *Sereia* or *Falucho* – and take it from there; they should be able to organize a room.

Calheta de São Miguel, the next stop, has a big old church on the hilltop. The dependence on rainfall in the Cape Verdes comes home to you as the road repeatedly drops to cross stony *ribeiras* where women wash clothes in the narrow streams: when water is about, the flanks of the gulches are dense with crops – bananas, papayas, cane and cassava – and heavy rains can also bring floods that smash the cobbles in many places.

Tarrafal
TARRAFAL doesn't look much at first. You have to go right through the small town to discover the wonderful, clean white **beach** below its gentle cliffs. Once the site of a political prison under the Portuguese, Tarrafal's main claim to fame is now this **beach**. There are palms and discreet beach houses to one side and a working, fishing-beach atmosphere on the other. Once installed in Tarrafal it's easy to pass a few days – or even much longer – swimming and lounging, drinking cold beers, eating slabs of fresh tuna and watching the fishing boats coming in and the children playing.

Accommodation is easily fixed. The best-value **beach** option is the *Solmarina* (☎66.12.19; ②). The well kitted-out, but somewhat overpriced *Baia Verde* (☎66.11.28; Fax 66.14.14; ④) has chalets on the beach. *Hotel Tarrafal*, also on the beach (☎66.17.85;

Fax 66.17.87; ④–⑤), with its own pool, is better value. A more recent, recommended hotel is the *Marazul* (CP 33; ☎ & Fax 66.12.89; ③). **In the town** itself, among a number of *pensão* alternatives, you might try the *Chave d'Ouro* (☎66.11.78).

The town has an attractive hibiscus-filled *praça* with church and marketplace (and a bank, Mon–Fri 8am–noon) set around. There are one or two bars where you can drink *grogue* and play *oril*. With the mountainous interior of the island looming behind, Tarrafal can seem incredibly isolated; yet a boy shooting down the cobbled hill on his shiny new American mountain bike is a reminder of close and important ties with the outside world. Except at weekends, when Cape Verdean tourists and expatriate beach hunters zone in, it's marvellously peaceful. Walk south and you come to **further beaches** – of black sand – and more coconuts. Head north and a fine **coastal path** leads up over the cliffs above the crashing surf for as far as you like, with terrific views. There are some tiny coves along here, with great, natural swimming pools.

Fogo

The first impression of **FOGO** is of its tremendous mass – a brooding volcanic cone rising forbiddingly 2829m out of the sea, its steep peaks rising above the clouds. Flying from Praia, remember to sit on the right of the plane for the best views. The arrival at São Filipe, on the west coast, feels precarious, as the plane dips low over the rough ground to touch the runway, perched high on the dunnish cliffs. Below the airport, a striking beach of baking black-sand drops straight into an ultramarine sea. Mosteiros airstrip, on the dark northeast coast, is equally dramatic. The plane lands here like a fly picking a spot on a black wall: the airstrip, about the size of two football pitches joined end to end, seems to occupy almost the only flattish space between the thrashing sea and sheer lava walls rising through clouds to the peaks of the island. If you arrive by ferry, you dock at the tiny port of Vale da Cavaleiros, 3km north of São Filipe.

Although all the islands have their own distinguishing marks, it's Fogo which stands out as the great character of the Cape Verdes. It's impossible to forget you're on a **volcano**. Fogo – which means "fire" – last had an eruption in 1995, when deluges of molten lava streamed into the main caldera, and 4000 people were evacuated. On the west side of the island, the land is gentler, with better soil, low trees, farms and plantations. The old volcanic base in this district is undisturbed by fresh explosions and after rain it's often cloaked beneath a pastoral blanket of wild flowers. **People** on Fogo are often startlingly kind, accommodating hikers, showing you directions miles out of their way and doing everything possible to help. **Transport** on Fogo depends on *aluguers* and the odd private vehicle. The southern road between São Filipe and Mosteiros is the only one on which there's any real traffic.

São Filipe and around

SÃO FILIPE, Fogo's capital, has an orderly civility which sits oddly with its steeply sloping clifftop location, high above the black beach. The streets link a number of small squares and gardens and a promenade along the cliffs. All São Filipe seems to lack to be one of Cape Verde's most attractive towns is sufficient population. It is deathly quiet, the streets often almost deserted even on an ordinary weekday morning. After dark everyone's inside, apparently watching TV: through every open doorway there's a blue glow and a stack of silhouetted backs. At least this is an improvement on the 1930s when an English visitor, Archibald Lyall, reported a community in the grip of diabolical poverty, isolated from Praia, let alone Lisbon, and totally without electricity or transport – small, shaggy horses were the only way to get about.

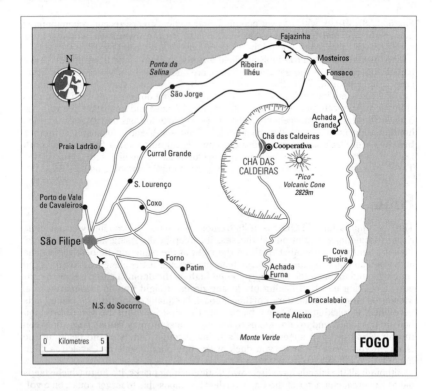

Accommodation

The lack of hotels and eating houses that Lyall suffered hasn't altogether been put to rights though the situation is improving.

Hotel Xaguate (☎81.12.22; Fax 81.12.03). Very run-down and basic for what purports to be the best hotel on the island, with dark rooms, intermittent (cold) water and very basic restaurant facilities. The swimming pool, when full, is too dirty to be useable. Good location, though, with fine views across the channel to Brava. ④.

Pensão Fatima (☎81.13.59). Nice place, with a roof garden. ③

Pensão Las Vegas (☎ & Fax 81.12.81). Pleasant, light and airy, with a roof terrace, good restaurant and ice-cream parlour. The S/C rooms have AC, TV and fridge – very good value. ③.

Pousada Bela Vista (☎81.12.20). Reasonable value for money, and often full. ③.

Restaurante Vulçao (☎81.18.96). Limited Cape Verdean fare in the dining room (order ahead) and basic rooms if you're on a low budget. ②.

Around town

The atmosphere in São Filipe is always easy-going, though there are usually scuffles of excitement when a big tuna is hauled up to be portioned and sold off in the street. There's little to do around town, but strolling through the near-deserted streets has its own quiet satisfaction: there are some fine old nineteenth-century houses and several small *praças* to sit in. The tiny **market**, with an all-purpose selection, is worth a visit.

Three kilometres north of São Filipe is **Porto de Vale de Cavaleiros**, where the boats come in. The walk down there is unremarkable and the "port" consists of little more than a cove with a jetty. Slightly superior, for recreation, is a walk up the airport road a couple of kilometres south of town and then a scramble down the cliffs past the ruins of a tiny church, to a *ribeira*, where you can join a path to the beach and some fish processing works. The **beach** itself is great if you're in the mood: a steep shelf of black sand – ferociously hot – with big waves breaking, seemingly without any fetch, directly onto it. You dive into them from the shore.

Heading back to town, take the fishermen's path and look out for the building with arms hanging out between bars – São Filipe's **prison**, on the cliff's very edge. You'll be scolded by the guards if you engage in shouted exchanges of greetings with the prisoners across the gully. It's a mournfully picturesque spot to be jailed, gazing out across the channel to Brava and the Atlantic.

Eating, drinking and nightlife

Boite Hexagonal/Café Katen Tadju, opposite the *Pensão Las Vegas*. Open Saturday nights or on special occasions.

Casa de Pasto Copacabana, in the south side of the block below the market. Basic, but filling.

Esplanada Tex. Snack bar overlooking the *ribeira* that separates the *Xaguate* from the rest of town, this is a fine spot for a sunset drink, with cheap *Cleps*.

Restaurante Leila (☎81.12.14). São Filipe's best meals and deservedly popular though unfortunately directly opposite the din of the town generator. Reserve a table and order ahead; reckon on CV$1500 each, with wine.

Listings

Aluguers From a small, mercifully shady *praça* in the centre of town, by the market.

Annual festival April 20, with processions and horse racing.

Bank Banco Comercial do Atlântico, Mon–Fri 8am–noon & 2.30–4pm.

Car rental Try Discount Auto Rent Car (☎81.14.80) or enlist the help of Ecotour (see below).

Electricity and water 24hr supplies aren't guaranteed; electricity is usually off from 5–6am.

Ferry details Information from Agenamar (☎81.10.12; Fax 81.13.12).

Hospital Basic treatment only (☎81.11.30).

Police ☎81.11.32.

Post office (Correio) Similar hours to the bank.

TACV The office is not always open (☎81.12.28).

Travel Agent/Guides Ecotour, directly below the market (☎81.22.55; Fax 83.10.04), offers useful services, including volcano trips, accommodation bookings, car rental and travel arrangements.

Exploring the volcano

The **volcano** is a dominant and potentially time-filling lure, but it can be hard to reach the crater if you try to set off at the wrong time of day. You can take a vehicle to **Chã das Caldeiras**, the huge, inhabited crater that was formed by the island's original, formative eruption. There are **aluguers** most mornings from São Filipe (2hr, about CV$400) but they are not super-abundant. If you ask taxi drivers about hiring a *particular* you'll usually get quoted fairly high figures – expect to pay at least CV$4000 and as much as CV$6000 for the one-hour-plus trip – because they genuinely aren't keen to do the trip: it's tremendously steep.

If you've got the time, an alternative plan would be simply to set off with water and supplies and **walk up**. The main staging post in this case is the straggling village of **Achada Furna** on the south side of the crater. From here, the crater rim is about 6km as the crow flies, but it's a steep climb and a good four hours' hike. Before you set off from São Filipe, make sure you have suitable snacks and drinking water. And if you plan to climb the peak itself, it's best to have hiking boots.

At the rim you may be lucky and have the whole eight-kilometre-wide bowl of the caldera spread clearly before you, or it may be blotted out by thick cloud. It's an extraordinary, unearthly, black-lava landscape, though the scanty vineyards and other cultivation soften it a little. The cobbled road winds through it like a causeway. The small, oblong houses are built of lava stone and crouch low against the hot ground. It's hard to imagine what keeps people here, or how they make ends meet in this inhospitable environment, but you'll see a variety of livestock, and the vineyards are relatively successful. Many families in this district trace their descent from a Duc de Montrond who is said to have fled France in the nineteenth century after a duel – and thoughtfully brought some vines with him.

This moonscape of lava and scattered mini-craters is dramatically surmounted by the main cone, the **Pico de Fogo**, which rises in a cindery, pyramid-shaped heap on the east side, about a thousand metres above the caldera floor. This cone has been dormant since the eighteenth century, but volcanic activity continues in a big way deep below the surface and new "mini-cones" are blown up within the giant caldera, once in every few decades. You may be reassured to know that vulcanologists monitor the activity and local people now get good warning of impending eruptions.

To **climb the Pico**, you should aim to make an early start. If you set off much after 7am, you'll find you're still out there in the midday sun, instead of back down in the village having a celebratory drink. It's an exhausting three-to-four hour scramble to the summit, up a two-steps-forward-one-step-back slope of fine volcanic scree. There are several guides in the village who will happily accompany you, and without one of them you won't easily find the best route, which in 1999 led up the north face. Companions are a good idea, anyway, as a fall in a remote place like this can be dangerous. When you reach the top, don't be tempted to try to ascend to the very highest point – it's an unstable and tricky little climb which has resulted in accidents in the past. There are routes down into the deep, red and yellow, egg-cup-shaped crater of the peak itself. But few people feel like tackling them at this stage in the day – it's much more tempting just to sit and absorb the views, especially down towards the eastern side of the island. Here, tens of thousands of years ago, during a heightened period of seismic activity, a cataclysmic landslide removed a huge part of the eastern side of the island, taking the original crater edge with it into the Atlantic and leaving the Chã das Caldeiras exposed on its eastern flank.

Coming down, in contrast to the climb, is like a free funfair ride, as you simply gallop down through the scree of the 40-degree slope in big bounds, and reach the floor of the caldera in little over an hour.

Practicalities

When arriving in Chã das Caldeiras, arrange to be dropped at the house of a guide in the first part of the village; most *aluguer* and taxi drivers will do this anyway. The standard rate for a guide to the peak is CV$1500. There's no formal **accommodation** in the village, but the going rate for dinner, bed and breakfast in a private house is CV$1000. You can also pick a spot anywhere on the black cinders and camp, but you should count on bringing your **food** requirements with you – there are no real shops in the caldera. At some point during your visit, you should go to the **Cooperativa**, the community's principal social venue, where you can buy bottles of the fearsomely robust local red and basic provisions. It's surprising how often the *Cooperativa* band sets up for a Cape Verdean jam – guitar, violin, cavaquinho, keyboard, scraper – behind the bar.

It's hard to get **public transport** back to São Filipe after finishing the climb. Most vehicles leave around 6am, so you're likely to have to stay in Chã das Caldeiras a second night. If you have to get back for a flight, you're at the mercy of whatever a vehicle-owner wants to charge you. Alternatively, you could hike out down to Achada Furna (14km), where you should have more luck with transport, or hitching.

If you aren't pressed for time, it's a beautiful descent – on foot or in a vehicle – from Chã das Caldeiras down the exposed eastern side of the volcanic massif to Mosteiros.

From Mosteiros to São Filipe

As an alternative to flying in and out of São Filipe, you could use Mosteiros as an entry or exit point for Fogo. From **Mosteiros** ("Monastery"), transport on to São Filipe normally awaits the plane. Otherwise, you'll probably have to walk a couple of kilometres to **Igreja** ("Church") which is the nearest thing to a town centre in this part of the island. The fare to São Filipe shouldn't be more than CV$700, but a *particular* could cost ten times as much.

Heading **anticlockwise** out of Mosteiros, there's a breathtaking road up to the hamlet of **Ribeira Ilheu**, terrifyingly steep if you're in a vehicle. Scarcity of lifts aside, this is really worth a walk – allow a day to climb the 15km – which rewards you with stunning views, sheltered and overgrown little valleys, and a village where your arrival will cause a minor sensation. Once committed, you'll probably have to continue on foot, covering the worst portion of the round-island road, another 10km or so, as far as São Jorge, where you should find transport on to São Filipe, some 17km further south. There's a good beach at Ponta da Salina, a short walk from São Jorge.

Travelling clockwise, you climb quickly from Mosteiros and skirt beneath the crater walls over a battlefield of strewn lava. The road runs high in places and, with a fast driver, it's not a journey you'll ever forget: the cobbled highway traverses the cinder slopes in an unnerving series of undefended loops hundreds of metres above the waves. The isolated **settlements** of lava block houses have a temporary look about them – there's a menacing slag-heap darkness here. It's high up on this eastern side that most of Fogo's famous **coffee** is grown.

Once the road curves **west**, the countryside opens out to more relaxing dimensions; a mellow, rolling landscape of maize and agave takes over and there's a surprising amount of tree cover, mostly acacias. In the pockets of fertile volcanic soil that haven't been rainwashed there are beans growing around the maize stalks, with squash, sweet potatoes and cucumbers between. Bananas (a Santiago speciality) are much scarcer.

Brava

BRAVA, the smallest inhabited island, has always been the most isolated of the Cape Verdes, only properly settled at the end of the seventeenth century after a major eruption on Fogo, in 1675. Its capital, **Vila Nova Sintra** (Vila) – named after the royal resort of Sintra outside Lisbon – is one of the archipelago's loveliest towns, sedately arranged in a long-extinct crater high above the coast. The island's stone walls overflow with lobelia and vines, and clouds drift through even when the rest of the archipelago is parched with drought. Although its name means "wild", the island has long enjoyed a remarkable degree of domestication, with virtually all the land under neatly tended cultivation, supporting the archipelago's highest population density. Bravans have a long seafaring tradition: the American **whalers** called at this island more than any other, and the largest contingent of *americanos* comes from Brava. Sadly, much of Brava's infrastructure was destroyed in 1982 by Hurricane Beryl, and not all has been rebuilt.

Small enough to walk all over, but precipitous too, Brava is worth the few days' visit you'll have to devote to it between ferry or plane connections. Flights from Praia are currently suspended (the airstrip on the west coast is so short, and so often very windy, that pilots were having to return to Praia without having landed), but check at any TACV office. The **ferry** connections are inconvenient: the *Furna* (a plucky little tug of a ship) leaves Praia twice a week for an overnight voyage either direct to Furna, or via São Filipe. Tickets are CV$440, plus CV$200 payable at each end for the five-minute trip in the lighter. Although the *Furna* doesn't usually sail during the weekend, its predictability can be disrupted at the drop of a hat.

The channel between Fogo and Brava is notoriously rough: you may well need seasickness pills and the voyage, even in "normal" conditions, can be quite frightening; there are moments when you seriously have to hang on. On most trips, everyone and everything gets drenched. The boat docks at the tiny port of **Furna**, five winding kilometres below Vila.

Vila Nova de Sintra

Vila is tiny – a five-minute walk from one side to the other – but the necessary offices are here. There's a Banco Comercial do Atlântico, Agencia Nacional de Viagens office for tickets on the *Furna* (☎85.12.70); and a TACV office (☎85.11.92). **Accommodation** is easy. Stay at the clean and quiet little state-run *Pousada Municipal* (☎85.16.97; if

---

TAVARES, WRITER OF MORNAS

Eugénio Tavares was a native of Brava, born in 1867. Tavares, a romanticized figure in Cape Verdean lore, was the country's best-known writer of the *morna* song form, the distinctive Cape Verdean music. Like Portugal's *fado*, the *morna* has a minor-key melody and both may have originated in the Portuguese slave islands of São Tomé. But the heart of a *morna* is its lyric. *Mornas* evoke an unmistakeably Cape Verdean feeling of *sodade* – yearning, longing, homesickness – and the classic examples are all by Eugénio Tavares. Tavares worked most of his life as a journalist and civil servant, achieving his huge popularity through his use of the Kriolu language, rather than colonial Portuguese. Tavares' *mornas* deal with the pain of love and loss. One of his best-known is "O Mar Eterno", inspired by his affair with an American woman visiting Brava by yacht. Her disapproving father set sail one night and the two never met again. Another famous composition, "Hora di Bai" ("The Hour of Leaving") was traditionally sung on the dock at Furna as relatives boarded America-bound ships. Tavares died in 1930. You can hear a set of his songs on a CD by the singer Saozinha, *Saozinha Canta Eugenio Tavares*, on the American label, MB Records.

there's nobody about, ask for keys in the Camara Municipal; ②). Alternatively, see how the similarly priced *Pensão Paulo Sena* (☎85.13.12; ②), is doing. Despite a good reputation and the owner's effusive welcome, the place is run-down and seriously in need of refurbishment (a large survey map of Brava on the wall is one reason you might call in). The food is variable and very slow, but that's a feature of Brava.

There's little to do in town: the market has nothing to offer, and there's no real sightseeing or shopping to do (the late-opening Shell station shop on the east side of town probably has the best selection of groceries). A nightclub, *Kananga*, fires up at weekends. Otherwise, a quiet coke at the *Ponto de Encontro* bar in the main *praça* is about as wild as it gets.

Fajã d'Agua and the west coast

Fajã d'Agua, on the west coast, is a more interesting prospect. You can walk here, two hours down an incredible switchback of a road, or take an *aluguer* (one or two drivers make the trip regularly enough) for CV$200 in a *collectivo* (locals pay only CV$50: a rare example of tourist profiteering) or CV$800 if you charter the vehicle.

Faja is simply an extremely pretty hamlet strung out along the shoreline, dotted with palm trees, hemmed in by mountains and backed by a steep, lush *ribeira*. It makes a good impression; people here are friendly; and it has possibly the best budget **hotel** in Cape Verde, *Burgo's Pensão* (☎85.13.21; ②), or, to give it its full name, *Bar Dos Amigos Campo Ocean Front Motel and Bar Restaurant*. Three pretty S/C double rooms with a shared balcony, perch above the family's own accommodation and the little bar-restaurant below. At night, the generator is fired up for a few hours (otherwise *Burgo's* has no electricity) and *Burgo's* becomes the Fajã cinema, with a couple of dozen people squeezed into the bar to watch a video at CV$30 each. There's nothing really much to do here – it's utterly peaceful – but you can always work up an appetite for the hearty meals (breakfast CV$200; dinner CV$400–800, to order) by hiking up the terraced *ribeira* or out to the wind-whipped, deserted airstrip, a couple of kilometres to the south.

If you want to swim, go beyond the airport to the neat little black-sand beach at **Portete**, about an hour's walk in total from Fajã. You should take a companion from Fajã the first time you go, to get on the right path. At Portete you'll meet a lone fisherman, and sometimes a couple of children, but it's otherwise deserted. Bring water and food and, if possible, something to shade yourself with.

Hiking

As for the rest of Brava, it's small enough to explore simply by **walking**: there are fine hikes and strolls everywhere, and even from coast to coast won't take more than a day. Be aware, however, that distances on the winding roads are always longer than they look on the map. There's a superb 3–4km walk from Vila Nova Sintra down to Santa Barbara and the fountain at Vinagre and another beautiful short walk from Nossa Senhora do Monte to nearby Cova Joana. There's also a good one-hour trail from Campo Baixo down to the beach at Tantum, 2km south of Portete; and a fine, easy walk from Vila Nova to the impressively sited village of Mato Grande, perched out on a promontory high above the east coast.

Maio

MAIO was first sighted on May 1, 1460 – hence its name – but there's really nothing very spring-like about it. Early on, slaves were taken there to look after the livestock surplus of landowners on Santiago, but historically, Maio was important as a **salt collect-**

INTER-ISLAND FLIGHTS FROM MAIO

Praia (5 weekly; 20min); Sal (Sat; 35min).
TACV in Maio: ☎55.12.56.

ing island. Vast quantities of evaporated sea salt – "huge heaps like drifts of snow" by Francis Drake's account – were available for the cost of the labour needed to load it on board ship. As that was often paid in old clothes or other unwanted items, the trade was a lucrative one. The English were largely in control of it and for a period Maio, by Portuguese default, was in English hands.

Today, Maio is a godforsaken place, poor in agriculture, a neglected neighbour of weighty Santiago – where most of its young people soon migrate – and touristically a dead loss. It's not likely to be high on your list, but if you do take the **flight** from Praia (five a week: a twenty-minute hop) or the weekly *Porto Novo* **ferry**, also from Praia, you're likely to be fêted as the first traveller they've seen for a while, and you'll find a place with a very distinct flavour. It's perhaps the least European of the Cape Verdes, with a relatively wooded, savannah esque interior and long, white, desolate beaches. It's surprising to find that the limited **accommodation** options in Vila do Maio are so good: try the excellent, business-like *Residêncial Bom Sossego* (☎55.13.65; Fax 55.13.27; ③) and the almost as good *Hotel Marilú* (☎55.11.98; Fax 55.13.47; ③).

THE BARLAVENTOS

Internationally – at least in the English-speaking world – it's the **Barlaventos** that have drawn most attention to the Cape Verde Islands. Among them, **São Vicente** stands out, the location of a British coal supply depot for over 100 years. Its capital, **Mindelo**, is now the travel hub of the Barlaventos and focus of much of what's happening culturally in the Cape Verdes. While the interior of the island is relentlessly barren, the town has a self-contained appeal that draws a good deal on its evident cosmopolitanism, and its rivalry with Praia for civic pre-eminence.

To see the Cape Verde Islands at their most naturally glorious, hop across the channel from Mindelo to **Santo Antão**, the most northerly isle, for restorative **hiking** among the magnificent canyons (*ribeiras*). Santo Antão is a splendid massif, comparable to Fogo but no longer volcanically active, with an awesomely rugged interior.

São Nicolau is like a poor relation of Antão. Its 400 years of human habitation seem to have been a dirge of destitution and fruitless toil and yet its town has the oldest educational and literary tradition in the country. It also offers breathtaking scenery, as well as opportunities similar to Santo Antão's for determined walkers.

Sal, the aptly named "Salt" Island, is now the site of Cape Verde's main international airport, and the focus of ninety percent of the country's tourist industry, all located along one glorious beach, Santa Maria. The last of the windward islands is **Boa Vista**, a large and flat island in the east of the archipelago that's beginning to vie with Sal as a target for water sports enthusiasts. It also has exhilarating desert travel opportunities.

São Vicente

It's hard to avoid identifying **SÃO VICENTE** with its main town and, indeed, there's not a lot on the island that matters outside **Mindelo**. The one or two unexceptional things to do are best achieved by striking out from the town – there are no other significant centres of population on this small hunk of moonscape.

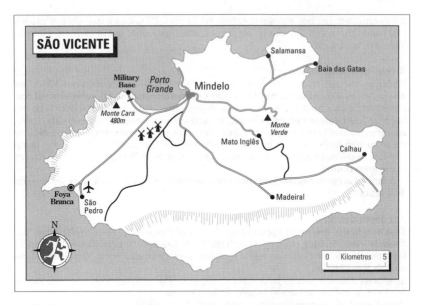

The **British**, as the operators of the **coaling station** at Mindelo, had a long and influential connection with the town. From 1838 until the 1950s, Mindelo – or rather Porto Grande as the town was then called – grew from nothing to a major supply depot on the East Indies and South America shipping runs. With the opening of the Suez Canal in 1869, the eastbound shipping diminished and diesel eventually took over from coal. But by the end of World War II, the hundred years of British presence had made some impact on the cultural life of the island. A number of English words were adopted into São Vicente Kriolu, including *blaqyefela* (blackfellow), *trôsa, ovacôte* (trousers and overcoat), *boi* (boy), *ariup* (hurry up), *djob* (job), *ovataime* (overtime) and, under American influence, *sanababiche*. English influence is still discernible in the architecture of some of the larger mansions. The British also introduced **cricket**, and though the game no longer figures very prominently, a team still plays occasionally.

Mindelo

A sense of identity has never been a problem for **MINDELO**. "Taken as a whole," thought Major A B Ellis of the 1st West India Regiment in 1873, "it is, perhaps, the most wretched and immoral town that I have ever seen." He stayed in the *Hotel Brasiliero* where a notice over the door proclaimed "Ici on parl Frances, Man spreucht Deutsch, Man spiks Ingleesh, Aqui se habla Español, Sabe American"; and where his room was invaded by a French farce of characters during the night. By the second half of the nineteenth century, Mindelo's importance as a coaling and victualling station was at its peak, and less reputable ancillary industries were in top gear.

Today, while only the faintest traces of the bawdiness remain, this is the liveliest town in the Cape Verdes – and no longer especially wretched. Relatively well-provided with hotels, restaurants and bars, it buzzes contentedly after dark, its *praça* a noisy hang out zone, its streets cheerfully animated. Although it's a small town, don't be surprised to find the atmosphere here tainted with hustle around the edges: yachts and cruise ships are intermittent and not infrequent callers (even the QE2 makes a stop once or twice a year) and the boys on the waterfront are still making escudos out of naive travellers in time-honoured ways.

Arrival and information

Flying in, the airstrip is 11km from town on a bleak flat at São Pedro. For CV$600, an *aluguer* gets you to Mindelo past brave acres of **reafforestation** where windswept acacias struggle for a foothold. With a stand of windmills – stark, whirling sentinels on the hillside, generating the island's electricity – and a strong ambience of desert and trash, appearances aren't encouraging, but these first impressions soon recede as you get into the town with its Portuguese buildings, restored pink Governor's residence and palm-tree-lined esplanade. Arriving **by boat**, it's a ten-minute walk south along the seafront to the town centre.

A limited array of **tourist information** is available from the small kiosk on avenida de 5 Julho.

Accommodation

Two new hotels are set to open during the life of this edition, the *Bay/Baía* and the *Mindelo* – both looking to compete with the *Porto Grande*. If you're staying in Mindelo for more than a few days, you might look into renting an apartment; try Holiday Lets on ☎ & Fax 32.60.76.

Aparthotel Avenida, av 5 de Julho (CP 120; ☎32.34.35; Fax 32.23.33). Soulless apartment-style hotel with AC and TV. Also acts as an agent for local lets. ④.

Hotel Porto Grande, praça Nova (☎32.31.90; Fax 32.31.93). Mindelo's best hotel, renovated in the late 1990s to international standards. Front rooms have a great view over the *praça*, but can be very noisy, especially at weekends. Good-size (freshwater) pool. No credit cards; seasonal rates; ⑥–⑦.

Pensão Atlantida, on the corner of rua de Santo António (☎31.39.18), up from the Agencia Nacional de Viagens. Pretty basic but reasonable value. ②.

Pensão Chave d'Ouro, av 5 de Julho (☎31.10.50). The "Golden Key" is a long-established budget focus, but its much appreciated ambience – lots of dark wood and musty furniture – is now beginning to feel more run-down than antique. There are tiny, inexpensive top floor rooms and big airy rooms on the first floor, all with shared facilities. ②.

Pensão Chez Loutcha, rua de Coco (CP 303; ☎31.16.36; Fax 32.16.89). High standards and good staff, with a popular restaurant and regular live music. The best of the less expensive places. ③–④.

Residêncial Maravilha, bottom of rua de Angola, near the seafront (☎32.22.03; Fax 32.22.17). Very pleasant, smaller place, with four airy rooms and two large, but semi-basement, suites. ⑤.

Residêncial Novo Horizonte, 62 rua Senador Vera Cruz (☎32.39.15). Adequate guesthouse with fanned rooms, but somewhat dark and stuffy given its location. Very reasonably priced for B&B. ②.

Residêncial Sôdade, rua Franz Fanon (☎31.35.56). Good-quality lodging house. ③–④.

The Town

Mindelo is the town that Cape Verdeans resident abroad always go on about – perhaps because so many Cape Verde expatriates come from here – and compared with Praia it does have a more animated, less official feel. Helped along by the bay with its twin headlands, its esplanade and its clutter of backstreets, Mindelo feels like a holiday. The **carnaval** in February tends to infect the town for the entire year, so it never entirely stops partying.

Exploring it for yourself is the main daytime pursuit and the seafront provides an obvious anchor point. The unusual eagle-topped **monument** commemorates the first Lisbon–Rio air crossing, in 1922, by aviators Cabral and Coutinho, who spent a number of days recuperating in Mindelo after their 80mph leg from the Canaries in the flying boat *Lusitania*. Nearby, the curious ornate little castle is the **Torre de Belem**, a copy of the tower of the same name outside Lisbon; the latter was built in the early sixteenth

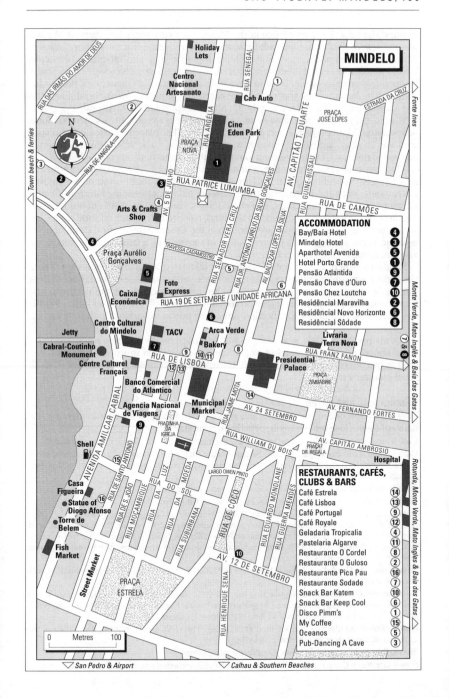

MINDELO

Holiday Lets

Centro Nacional Artesanato

Cab Auto

Cine Eden Park

PRAÇA NOVA

❶

PRAÇA JOSÉ LOPES

ESTRADA DA CRUZ

RUA DAS IRMÃS DO AMOR DE DEUS

RUA DE ANGOLA

RUA SENEGAL

RUA ARGÉLIA

AV. CAPITÃO T. DUARTE

RUA GUINÉ-BISSAU

Fonte Ines

Town beach & ferries

RUA PATRICE LUMUMBA

AV. 5 DE JULHO

RUA DE CAMÕES

Arts & Crafts Shop

Praça Aurélio Gonçalves

TRAVESSA CADAMOSTO

RUA SENADOR VERA CRUZ

RUA DR. ANTÓNIO AURÉLIO DA SILVA

AV. BALTAZAR LOPES DA SILVA

ACCOMMODATION

Bay/Baía Hotel	❹
Mindelo Hotel	❸
Aparthotel Avenida	❺
Hotel Porto Grande	❶
Pensão Atlantida	❾
Pensão Chave d'Ouro	❼
Pensão Chez Loutcha	❿
Residêncial Maravilha	❷
Residêncial Novo Horizonte	❻
Residêncial Sôdade	❽

Caixa Económica

Foto Express

RUA 19 DE SETEMBRE / UNIDADE AFRICANA

Centro Cultural do Mindelo

TACV

Arca Verde

Bakery

Jetty

Cabral-Coutinho Monument

Centre Culturel Français

RUA DE LISBOA

Banco Comercial do Atlantico

Municipal Market

RUA JAIME MOTA

AV. 24 SETEMBRO

Presidential Palace

PRAÇA ZIMBABWE

Livraria Terra Nova

RUA FRANZ FANON

AV. FERNANDO FORTES

Monte Verde, Mato Inglês & Baía das Gatas

Agencia Nacional de Viagens

PRACINHA DA IGREJA

RUA WILLIAM DU BOIS

AV. CAPITÃO AMBROSIO

PRAÇA DR. REGALA

Shell

AVENIDA AMILCAR CABRAL

RUA DE SANTO ANTÓNIO

RUA DA LUZ

RUA DA MOEDA

LARGO OWEN PINTO

RUA EDUARDO MONDLANE

RUA GUERRA MENDES

Hospital

Rotunda, Monte Verde, Mato Inglês & Baía das Gatas

Casa Figueira

Statue of Diogo Afonso

Torre de Belem

Fish Market

Street Market

RUA DE S. JOÃO

RUA MOÇAMBIQUE

RUA DA SOL

RUA SUBURBANA

RUA DE COCO

PRAÇA ESTRELA

AV. 12 DE SETEMBRO

RUA HENRIQUE SENA

RESTAURANTS, CAFÉS, CLUBS & BARS

Café Estrela	⑭
Café Lisboa	⑬
Café Portugal	⑨
Café Royale	⑫
Geladaria Tropicalia	④
Pastelaria Algarve	⑪
Restaurante O Cordel	⑧
Restaurante O Guloso	②
Restaurante Pica Pau	⑯
Restaurante Sodade	⑦
Snack Bar Katem	⑩
Snack Bar Keep Cool	⑥
Disco Pimm's	①
My Coffee	⑮
Oceanos	⑤
Pub-Dancing A Cave	③

0 Metres 100

N

▽ San Pedro & Airport   ▽ Calhau & Southern Beaches

century, the Cape Verdean replica in the 1920s. For many years the Torre at Mindelo was the seat of the Portuguese administrator of São Vicente, but even before independence it had been abandoned. For decades, the shored-up and rat-infested structure looked as if it had been deliberately ignored; it was renovated some years back, but is beginning to crumble again. Back in town a short way, the old **Governor's palace** has been well looked after and was recently restored in pale pink. Now the headquarters of São Vicente island council, it's clearly the object of considerable civic pride.

The closest you'll come to a museum in Cape Verde is a visit to the **Centro Nacional Artesanato** (Mon–Fri 8am–noon & 2–6pm; CV$50). The place is divided into a display area and a shop, and there's also a workshop at the back where you're generally allowed to nose around the weaving looms: doubtless this depends on the behaviour of the last batch of cruise passengers or shore-leave sailors. The knick-knacks on sale aren't hugely appealing, but the items on display, particularly some of the musical instruments, rugs and homemade toys, do seem old and of genuine interest. If you're drawn to **crafts and paintings**, you should pay a visit to a couple of other addresses. The arts and crafts shop on avenida 5 de Julho, close to the French cultural centre has some good ceramics and prices are lower than the Centro Artesanato's. Casa Figueira, near the Torre de Belem, is a private gallery of canvases by a father and son team, who also run a café on the ground floor.

Mindelo's **beach**, the Praia da Laginha, is a kilometre out of town on the north side. Backed by a rumbling industrial plant, the dark yellow sands are clean, nonetheless, the sea is warm and clear, and there's an animated beach bar at the northern end. Continuing northwards in the same direction, you can walk or drive up to the **Fortim del Rei**, a deserted hilltop fortification – one-time prison – overlooking the city and the bay.

For shoppers, Mindelo is at least as well-equipped as Praia. There's a scattering of small **shops**, a lively **fish market**, and a fine, newly restored **municipal market**, running to two floors, bang in the centre of town, which contains a good number of small, retail enterprises.

Restaurants and cafés

There are a few decent restaurants and snack bars – though it's well to remember that many of them close once a week, usually on a Sunday.

Café Estrela, av Fernando Fortes, by the palace. Limited range of top-value meals and snacks.

Café Lisboa, **Café Portugal** and **Café Royale**, facing each other on rua de Lisboa. Establishment, downtown cafés – unfussy, fast places where business types read *A Semana*, and much coffee, beer and *aguardente* is consumed.

Geladaria Tropicalia, av 5 de Julho. Good ice cream and snacks.

Pastelaria Algarve, rua de Lisboa. Snacks and cakes, with a bar.

Pica Pau, rua de Santo António (☎31.55.07). The "Woodpecker" is something of a Mindelo institution, a tiny restaurant, unchanged for fifteen years, and now festooned with the multilingual testimonials of happy eaters. Great-value seafood, especially the piping hot and tasty *arroz mariscos* (CV$700) or lobster (CV$1200), with wine and beer from the even tinier bar to wash it down. Reserve ahead: it's usually full.

Restaurante O Cordel, av Baltazar L da Silva (☎32.29.62). One of Mindelo's best restaurants, with dishes from about CV$700.

Restaurante O Guloso, rua Angola: ring the bell (☎31.70.66). Engagingly eccentric place where you definitely need to reserve ahead to get any food at all. English-speaking owner guarantees to provide food fit for the "gourmand" of her establishment's name.

Restaurante Sodade, rua Franz Fanon (☎31.35.56). The rooftop restaurant of the *pensão* of the same name. Great view, but the food isn't cheap.

Snack Bar Katem, rua de Lisboa. Good breakfast address.

Snack Bar Keep Cool, rua 19 de Setembro. Popular café, sometimes known as the *Unidade Africana*.

Nightlife

After dark, social gravity sooner or later draws most people down to **Praça Nova** (formerly Amílcar Cabral) where there's always some excitement and a lot of rather Mediterranean courting and flirting going on, accompanied by huge volumes of noise. Although the town's youth are steadily deserting the town for Praia and further, Mindelo still holds a racy and sophisticated reputation for the young people of the Barlavento country hamlets. Sitting in the square is really fun: you'll quickly find yourself in some kind of conversation, tuning in to the evening grapevine.

Mindelo has a number of **boites** (down-to-earth nightclubs), though they're generally discos rather than live music venues. Apart from Cape Verdean *morna*, *coladeira* and *funana*, you're most likely to come across variants of zouk, often with Senegalese influences. Not surprisingly, successful singers and bands don't wait long before flying out to Lisbon, Paris, Holland or New England, where Cape Verdean audiences (and certainly the market for CDs) can be larger than in Mindelo itself.

CLUBS AND BARS

Argentina, rua 5 de Julho, beneath the *Chave d'Ouro*. Earthy watering hole.

Boite Je t'Aime, Pedra Rolada, in Bela Vista (☎32.15.91), southeast of the 24hr Shell station at Rotunda. Popular and established venue.

Chez Loutcha, rua de Coco, in the *pensão* of the same name (☎31.16.36). Regular singers and bands, usually at weekends.

Disco Pimm's, rua Senador Vera Cruz (☎31.45.97). Always hot and crowded.

Discoteca Histep, just off Estrada da Cruz, in Fonte Inês, east of the town centre (☎31.35.81). Busy disco.

My Coffee, rua de Santo António. Bar and café.

Oceanos, travessa Cadamostro. New, sophisticated bar.

Pub-Dancing A Cave, Alto São Nicolau (☎31.16.81 or 32.74.81).

Listings

Bakery One of the best is the nameless place just off rua de Lisboa, at 4 rua Senador Vera Cruz.

Banks There are two: for changing money you want the Banco Comercial do Atlântico in the old building on rua de Santo António, south of rua de Lisboa.

Bookshops You could try the Livraria Terra Nova on rua 19 de Setembro, but it rarely has anything but a limited range of mostly evangelical works in Portuguese. Otherwise try the Centro Cultural do Mindelo (see below).

Car rental São Vicente is a good place to explore for a day by car. Half-daily or daily rates are around CV$2000 or CV$4000. One of the best is Cab Auto, Largo Medina Boé, behind the *Hotel Porto Grande* (CP 117; ☎32.28.00; Fax 32.28.12). A CV$10,000 deposit is required.

CDs There's quite a good music shop in the *Hotel Porto Grande* building, on rua Argélia.

Centre Culturel Français/Alliance Française, rua de Lisboa (☎32.11.49). The French do work hard at their culture, even with no consulate. Worth visiting for books, mags, movies and events.

Centro Cultural do Mindelo Good bookshop (Portuguese), gallery and lively theatre, always in use.

Consulates The British honorary consul is Mr Antônio Canuto, at *Shell Cabo Verde* on av Amílcar Cabral (☎31.41.32; Fax 31.47.55). Otherwise, the team from Europe includes: Denmark, Cais Acostavel near the port (☎32.15.60); Netherlands in rua Senador Vera Cruz (☎32.14.61); and Switzerland on av Dr. Alberto Leite/Che Guevara on the north side of town (☎32.35.22).

Ferries The main office for the ferries *Barlavento* and *Sotavento* is Arca Verde, 153 av de 5 Julho (CP 41; ☎61.54.97; Fax 61.54.96). Somatrans, 95 rua S. João (☎32.40.67), runs the Mindelo–Porto Novo ferry that links São Vicente with Santo Antão once or twice a day. For the full timetable, see p.370.

Film/processing Foto Express, 14 av 5 de Julho.

Post office (Correio) Mon–Fri 8am–noon & 2.30–5pm, Sat 8–11am & 3–5pm, Sun 9–11am.

TACV A busy office on av 5 de Julho (☎32.15.24). Availability on flights to Sal and Praia, notably

INTER-ISLAND FLIGHTS FROM SÃO VICENTE (MINDELO)

Praia: 1 or more flights daily; 50–75min.
Sal: 2 or more flights daily; 50min.
Santo Antão (Ponta do Sol): Mon, Tues, Fri & Sat; 25min.
São Nicolau: Tues, Wed, Fri & Sat; 25min.
TACV in Mindelo: ☎32.15.24.

those connecting with international departures, is often very tight. Plan ahead and remember to reconfirm everything.

Taxis Main ranks are in the obvious centre of town near the church (*igreja*). Town rates are reasonable (CV$50–100 in the centre; CV$150–200 to the suburbs), but island trips come much more expensive, though still not utterly unrealistic.

Travel Agents Cabetur, 57 rua Senador, Vera Cruz (☎32.38.47; Fax 32.38.42); Agencia Nacional de Viagens, off rua de Santo António (☎32.11.15; Fax 32.14.45).

Out of town trips

If you don't venture **beyond Mindelo** you'll not be in a minority. Away from Mindelo, the rest of the island is desperately arid, for the most part treeless, and largely uninhabited – all but a couple of thousand of the island's 50,000 inhabitants live in the *povoação*. There's virtually no public transport: no regular *aluguer* runs except to San Pedro, and if you don't hire a car, you'll have to rely on taxis to get around the island, which won't work out much cheaper.

Baia das Gatas

For a break, and really quite a nice **beach**, the twenty-minute drive to **Baia das Gatas** is a good trip. Transport is limited on São Vicente and you'll almost certainly have to rent a taxi unless you strike lucky, perhaps at the weekend, with a lift (walk out the length of av 12 de Setembro and wait where it bends). The cost of a taxi to Baia will depend on waiting time, as little as CV$1500 if you just want a quick dip, the best part of CV$3000 for a prolonged lounge that keeps the driver out of town for half a day. On Sundays, too, there's usually a bus that leaves at 9.30am and returns at 5.30pm. Baia, as it's commonly known (the reason for the *gatas* – cats – is unknown), is protected by a concrete mole and black boulders to break the thrashing surf. In the **lagoon**, the water is calm and delightfully transparent, though even with a mask there's not a lot to see. Beyond the lagoon's confines, the sea is more challenging and the combination of urchin-covered rocks and the threat of sharks should be enough to put you off. There's a Sunday beach bar, weekend bungalows and, in August, an annual international **music festival**, which includes artists from West Africa, as well as other lusophone countries, with a party atmosphere and plenty of side shows.

Monte Verde

The road to Baia climbs steeply past the junction for **Monte Verde**, the dark mass commonly wreathed in clouds that rears up behind Mindelo, and the island's highest point. This too is worth an outing but it'll cost more because of the strain on the taxi: you'll need to set aside a full morning or afternoon of your time. The last section on the Mato Ingles branch gets right to the summit. It is, truly, a "green mountain", covered in the once commercially important *orchil* lichen, used to produce brilliant scarlet and purple dyes. There can be stunning views down over Mindelo and Baia, but they're not to be counted on as the summit area is often wreathed in cloud.

Southern beaches

A difficult road leads southeast to **Calhau** (the direct route from Mindelo is easier than the one via Monte Verde), where there's a good beach and a restaurant – a branch of *Chez Loutcha* – open weekends only (sometimes only on Sundays). Another road heads south to Madeiral and the island's most dramatic and isolated region, a fifteen-kilometre ridge (altitude 500–700m) paralleling the southern coast at a distance of just two or three kilometres, from which *ribeiras* plunge down to the sea.

Another worthwhile beach, somewhat easier to get to (by taxi), lies just beyond the airport at **Praia de São Pedro**. This is the location of the island's only tourist development, *Foya Branca* (☎32.43.69), an oddly bleak but upmarket villa-style set-up that was very closed when last visited in April 1999. Across the bay, the scruffy, but colourful little village of San Pedro has a certain charm but offers nothing beyond an excuse for a walk along the shore.

Santo Antão

SANTO ANTÃO, the second largest of the Cape Verdes, is rugged and exciting – a tortoise shape cut into deep, arcing **ribeiras**, with the savage grandeur of a much bigger landmass. The island is also the last to suffer whenever a prolonged drought ravages the country, the northern slopes and valleys retaining a perennial verdure which is hard to believe after the desolation of Santiago and São Vicente.

However, communications have always been difficult. The story goes that Bishop Jacinto Valente visited Santo Antão from Santiago in 1755, and set off to cross the island on foot. Having been hauled up several precipices dangling from a rope, he eventually lost his nerve and had to stay put between a cliff and a chasm. The islanders went ahead, sent him back a tent and supplies, and began to construct a road for his rescue. A single **highway** now snakes up over the barren south face to edge between the peaks and abysses to the island's capital, Ribeira Grande on the north coast. Even as late as 1869, three

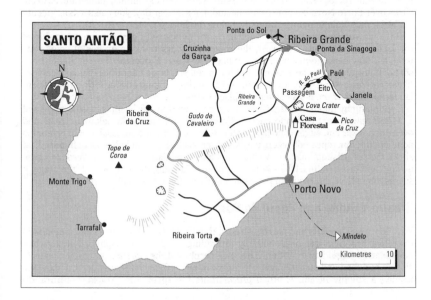

hundred years after it was first colonized, the Portuguese minister of colonies remarked that Santo Antão had "the appearance of an island that had only been discovered months ago".

Getting here today, you can fly from Praia and Mindelo to the airport at Ponta do Sol, near Ribeira Grande. Much cheaper are the ferries – the *Ribeira de Paúl* and the *Mare Azul* – across the deep, shark-infested channel from Mindelo to Porto Novo. As the crossing between the islands can be surprisingly rough, you'd be wise to take sea-sickness tablets if you've ever suffered.

From Porto Novo to Ribeira Grande

Porto Novo itself used to be an uneventful place subsisting on the daily contact with Mindelo across the channel, but in recent years, development funds have seen considerable growth. A crowd is always down on the quay to welcome the boat. In times not so long past, Mindelo got almost all its drinking water from Santo Antão – a lucrative trade that dried up with the withering of the coaling industry on São Vicente and the opening there of a water desalination plant.

If you need **rooms** in Porto Novo, the best place is the *Residêncial Antilhas* (☎22.11.93; ②), right above the port, with fresh S/C rooms and a separately run bar-restaurant on the ground floor. Just as nice, and at the same price (but less conveniently located, a couple of minutes walk inland from the clifftop) is the English-speaking *Gira-Sol* (☎22.13.83; Fax 22.18.91; ②), where the rooms are non-S/C, but include breakfast. You can **eat** quite well, and catch up with European football on the TV, at the *Sereia*, on the clifftop, quite a popular rendezvous, just two minutes walk towards the town centre from the *Antilhas*. There are one or two small eateries and bars in the town.

A fleet of **minibuses** meets the ferry; most head over the island's back to Ribeira Grande (CV\$300; 60–90min); try to get a front seat on the right for the most heart-stopping views. Leaving Porto Novo (and, it appears, almost the only trees on this side of Santo Antão), the haul up the south slope of the island presents a bleak picture to begin with: the neat, cobbled road snakes steeply through a lifeless mountain desert of tumbled volcanic rocks, bleached pale in the sun. As the vehicle climbs, temperatures drop, views over Porto Novo become dramatic and, if it's a clear day, you can see São Vicente – a black mountain hanging, strangely, below the horizon.

But save your enthusiasm and your film for the descent down the northern side of the island. Approaching the crest, the road's contours relax as groves of coniferous trees and low herbage make an appearance. The **Casa Florestal** (Forest Station) is a sort of halfway house where people will try to sell you large quantities of goat's cheese. If you intend getting straight on with some serious hiking through the magnificent landscape further on, it's a convenient place to hop out.

Continuing by minibus to the *povoação*, you sweep over the island's twisted spine and skirt the magnificent circumference of **Cova crater**. Clouds drift below the road, and over the houses and sugar cane plots patched into the crater's colossal scoop. From this point on, the bus repeatedly veers past steep terraced slopes and chasms of hundreds of sheer metres. Bishop Valente's vertigo was understandable: even Cape Verdeans gaze down – and cross themselves – at the hairpins. Glimpsing the sea through the crags, it seems impossible the road can get down to Ribeira Grande in such a short distance.

Ribeira Grande and Ponta do Sol

With fortress-like cliffs and narrow streets, **RIBEIRA GRANDE** feels like a mountain town lost in a huge range, its slightly forbidding, singular atmosphere quickly compelling and not quickly forgotten. The town perches at the *ribeira*'s mouth, a cluster of closely bunched and shady houses, hemmed in by cliffs rising behind and the dark sea lashing a shingly beach. A broad *praça* fronts the **Igreja de Nossa Senhora do**

Rosário, the formidable church intended, at one time in the eighteenth century, to be the cathedral of Cape Verde. There's a scattering of *pensões*, one or two restaurants, as well as a post office, a bank and even a disco.

Finding a **place to stay** is simple enough, even if none of the trio of inexpensive *pensões*, is particularly inviting. The options, none of them S/C, are the gloomy *Residêncial 5 de Julho* (☎21.13.45; ②), the cheap, charmless and rather untended *Residêncial Aliança* (☎21.12.46; ②) and the good-value, carefully looked-after rooms let out by Dona Bibi (②), down an alley opposite the *5 de Julho,* which are easily the best of a mediocre bunch. You can find Dona Bibi working in a little grocery, the *Mercearia Nascimento*, in the same alley. For **food**, the town has very little to offer. The *5 de Julho,* serves breakfast and basic meals in an unattractive little dining room, or, for something better, check out the *Restaurante Tropical*, which has a very solicitous owner and a nice patio dining area. It's a minute's walk from Dona Bibi's place: keep asking and look out for the huge rubber tree outside. Meals there are CV$600–1000.

As an alternative to staying in Ribeira Grande – and even an alternative place for a semi-decent meal, you could take an *aluguer* ten minutes up the coast (a fairly continuous stream of vehicles makes the 4km journey; CV$50) to **PONTA DO SOL**, a more spacious little town with the island's tiny airport, where the *Bar-Restaurante Lela Leite* (☎25.10.56; ②) offers good food and cold drinks in a pleasant atmosphere (call ahead from Ribeira Grande to order a meal), and good-value rooms.

Hiking the ribeiras

The most compelling activity on the island is **hiking**. With several days to spare, you'll have the chance to explore the three big **ribeiras** of eastern Santo Antão – Grande, Paúl and Janela ("Big", "Swamp" and "Window"). It's very helpful to have a decent **map**; a good map is sometimes available in *ribeira* Grande town (published in Germany by AB Karen Verlag, Sophienstr.152, Karlsruhe D-76135). Even better, though somewhat out of date, is the huge, 1cm:250m island map on the wall of a small, nameless bar on the south side of Ribeira Grande's main street.

The **hike up the** *ribeira* **Grande**, a solid morning's work, requires an early start and a good supply of drinking water. If you're heading back to Porto Novo for the same day's ferry, then in the dry season you should take an *aluguer* up the *ribeira* for a few kilometres: the route has to be rebuilt nearly every year after the rains. If you get a *particular* to meet you at the head of the Ribeira, expect to pay upwards of CV$3000. You might also want to hire a guide for the day – CV$1500 is a fair price. If you're lucky you will see the *ribeira* cloaked in green, but unfortunately it can't be guaranteed.

Ribeira do Paúl is the most beautiful and densely planted of the three canyons. Get there by *aluguer*, 10km along the coast road – again, a busy enough route (CV$50). There is currently no accommodation in the village of Paúl, at the bottom of the *ribeira*, but a steep kilometre or so inland, through the first tresses of deep, sugar-plantation verdure, you come to the hamlet of **Eito**, where the *Casa Familial Sabine* (☎23.12.13 or 23.11.75; ③), behind the radio repair shop (50m south of the road from the two-storey orange house: turn left if walking inland), offers slightly eccentric, beautifully located, accommodation. There's not much transport up the *ribeira*, but the cobbled road climbs far inland, snaking through a fantastic riot of vegetation and, some 4km from Paúl, at Passagem, fetching up at a kind of tropical garden with a swimming pool and café open at weekends. As an alternative to climbing, you can walk down the Ribeira do Paúl by getting dropped off on the main trans-island road above the Cova crater, then, with guidance, heading northeast.

There are possible hiking routes all over Santo Antão. One, a particularly dramatic route in its later stages, heads from Ribeira Grande to Ponta do Sol, thence to the precarious village of **Fontainas** and on to **Cruzinha da Garça** via a cliff-face footpath that is at times barely half a metre wide.

INTER-ISLAND FLIGHTS FROM SANTO ANTÃO (PONTA DO SOL)

Sal: Monday afternoon; 50min
São Vicente: daily except Wed & Sun; 25min.
TACV in Ponta do Sol: ☎21.18.14.

Deserted islets: Santa Luzia, Ilhéu Branco and Ilhéu Razo

Three desert islands line up in the lee of São Vicente. The biggest, **Santa Luzia**, had a bit of a population towards the end of the eighteenth century – mostly destitute farmers from São Nicolau – but successive droughts and an impossibly harsh terrain expelled them. A more recent inhabitant was the "Governor of Santa Luzia", Francisco Antonio da Cruz, who fled there from his wife and eighteen offspring and lived as a hermit for a number of years. It's now deserted again and, unless you make special efforts by boat, out of reach. Charles Darwin called here in *the Beagle*; herpetologists know Santa Luzia as the only habitat of a large, herbivorous lizard – though it seems likely that it's extinct.

Ilhéu Branco is more of a rock than an island, white (hence the name) from the guano deposits of generations of seabirds, and rising sheer from the sea in a shape supposed to resemble a ship at anchor. Ships stay well clear of its dangerous approaches. If you're sailing between Mindelo and São Nicolau, you're likely to get a good view of the **dolphins** which frequent this leg. **Flying fish** are common too – skittering things the size of a seagull which streak above the surface for several seconds at amazingly high speed.

By the time you reach **Ilhéu Razo**, you can see the jagged, cloud-protected silhouette of São Nicolau. Razo is famous – among ornithologists and conservationists – for the **Razo Island Lark**, a dun, ordinary-looking lark that, perversely, nests only on this barren slab, making it an exceedingly rare species. The Razo lark has an extra strong beak for digging up the drought-resistant grubs it feeds on. It should survive until population pressure and a solution to the problem of drought bring the first human colonists to the island.

São Nicolau

Like the peaks of a submerged mountain, **SÃO NICOLAU** rises from the ocean between São Vicente and Sal. There's no doubt about its **beauty** – an elegant, hatchet-shaped trio of ridges meeting in spectacular summits above the hidden capital of **Ribeira Brava**. But the cruelly desolate slopes (this is the driest of the "agricultural" islands) testify to a history of extraordinary hardship – eternal isolation, migration and desertion. The problem, as ever, is water, or chronic lack of it. In recent years, efforts have been made to tap the deep underground water table – notably with the help of French *cooperants* (paid "volunteers") – and a number of dams are planned, but the legacy of centuries of neglect lives on, and the drift away from the island is continuous. However there have been a few good rainy seasons in the last decade; corn, planted every year, actually grows to maturity some seasons, and water has flowed again from village pumps.

São Nicolau is a good place to have **transport** of your own. If, as is likely enough, you haven't – and don't have unlimited time on the island either – you should make

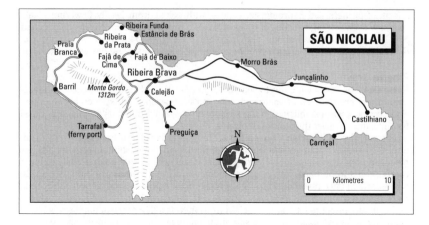

efforts to fix something up straight away; there's very little public transport. **Arriving by ship** at Tarrafal, the island's main port, you should aim to get the first transport up to Ribeira Brava. Shared *carrinhos* charge about CV$300, chartered taxis about CV$2500, and the journey time is about an hour. **Flying in**, the airstrip is just 4km from Ribeira Brava (midway between the town and the minor port of Preguiça), and you're likely to be able to find a taxi into town (CV$500).

Tarrafal

At **Tarrafal**, straggling along the southwest coast, none of the island's meld of destitution and scenic splendour is immediately obvious. The shallow bay gives on to the largest region of relatively gentle terrain on São Nicolau, from where the spectacle of the interior isn't apparent. Tarrafal's main activity is **tuna fishing**, supplying an important canning plant. While you'll see the great beasts hauled up on many a Cape Verdean beach, the evening business at Tarrafal seems to yield some particularly spectacular specimens, many as big as a person, and people are quite happy to have you watching as the fish are wheeled into the co-op on wagons. You can also join the kids on the **swimming beach** – the hot, grey sands of which are said to be good for rheumatism. A few kilometres further north, towards Barril, there are much better beaches, safe and good for snorkelling, among them the little white-sand cove of Praia das Francêses.

If you get stuck at Tarrafal, you'll soon locate the good *casa de pasto* at *Pensão Alice*, along the shore to the north, where the welcome is warm and the meals generous. **Rooms** are also available (②).

Over the island spine

The 26km of nearly deserted cobblestone between Tarrafal and Ribeira Brava is another of Cape Verde's scenically outstanding routes. After a steady and satisfying pull away from the broad, southwest bay and up to around 800m, the road takes a sudden and breathtaking swing to the left and within seconds is skating above the fractured bowl of the island's north side. Going by foot from here is a good plan: there's a steep track down to the town, an hour or two's knee-wobbling on foot or, with the day before you, take the gentler descent along the main road, incised into the cliff, with the soaring needle peaks of **Monte Gordo** dominating the skyline to the southwest. During the late summer months this – the *Fajãs* – can be a fabulously beautiful valley, spilling with green from the concerted efforts of farmers and hydrologists, dashed with colour from briefly flowering plants, spiked with the strange shapes of **dragon trees** – drought-resistant Nicolauan peculiarities. The enchanting road, about 15km from the peaks down to the town, winds down past the hamlets and farm plots via a swerving series of deep rents along the north coast.

Ribeira Brava

RIBEIRA BRAVA, facing out to sea on the north side, is firmly Portuguese in feel. A delightfully pretty mesh of narrow streets and whitewash, nestled deep between towering crags, it was established in the seventeenth century, about as far inland as possible, in order to resist the attacks of pirates.

The big, sky-blue **parish church** here, the Igreja Matriz, was the Cape Verdean see until the twentieth century. It's supposed to hold a small museum of religious bits and pieces, among them a valuable and unusual sixteenth-century golden chalice, but it rarely seems to be open. You've a better chance at the **seminary**, a little way up the *ribeira*, which once provided a classical education for students from all over the islands. Here there's a library and reliquary attached to the chapel, and you should be able to persuade the priest to let you in. Back in town there's a fine *praça* and a town hall with neatly tended gardens in front, the site of the birthplace in 1872 of José Lopes da Silva, a leading Cape Verdean poet. Down on the bank of the *ribeira* a shady, second *praça* hides a café and tables for serious draughts-playing and *grogue*-imbibing.

All rather obscure attractions perhaps, but they're central to the town's appeal: Ribeira Brava, once the flourishing centre of academic and literary life in Cape Verde, quickly establishes its remote, insular identity and is a rewarding place to **stay** for a few days. If you're counting the escudos, check out the large but rather scruffy *Pensão da Cruz* (☎35.12.82; ②) or the disappointingly rock-bottom but dirt-cheap *Residêncial Jumbo* (☎35.13.15; ②). The third alternative, if you want a clean, comfortable room, is the beautifully located *Pensão Residêncial Jardim* (☎35.11.17; ②–③). Ribeira Brava has several small *casas de pasto* (best is the *Bela Sombra Dalila*) plus a bank, post office, a small *mercado* and two or three basic general stores. You may even stumble across a workshop manufacturing cups and utensils – functional and miniature – out of bamboo; a tiny part of a tiny souvenir industry. It's not enough to keep many younger people here and the drift to Mindelo, Praia and abroad is unceasing.

The rest of the island

To get to the **rest of the island** you'll need to find someone who's driving. One of the few available Land Rovers is sometimes rented out (with owner) for around CV$5000 per day: it's almost worth the expense for the pleasure of being able to offer lifts to dozens of foot-weary Nicolauans as you go. The communities of the northwest – **Barril**, **Praia Branca** and **Ribeira da Prata** – are only accessible by road from Tarrafal. Looking east, the long axis of the island stretches 30km, narrowing at one point to less than three kilometres across. There are two principal tracks – a "ridgeway" and a north coast path – which meet high above the harbour of **Carriçal**. You'll need to be fit and determined to hike out here – supplies are very few and far between.

INTER-ISLAND FLIGHTS FROM SÃO NICOLAU

Praia: Tues & Sat; 40–45min.
Sal: Tues, Wed, Fri & Sun; 40min.
São Vicente: Mon, Wed & Fri; 30min.
TACV in Ribeira Brava: ☎35.11.61.

Sal

SAL, the "island of salt" – a piece of Sahara in the middle of the ocean – is the least invit-ing of the archipelago. Relentlessly windy and mostly flat, it's a good location for Cape Verde's main international **airport**. The majority of islanders seem to be involved with this in some way – or in the military base nearby – and the old salt-based economy looks pretty defunct. Whether you fly in from Europe or just pass through during a boat or plane connection, there's a high chance you'll sample Sal sooner or later. Attractions are simple to list – one beautiful white **beach**, and burgeoning associated water sports, which you're recommended to aim for without delay. There's almost nothing else worth a pause. On a positive note, if Sal is your first stop in Cape Verde, you can at least be sure that everywhere else you go will be more interesting.

Sal was one of the last islands to be colonized, early in the nineteenth century, when the Portuguese began to exploit its **salt** ponds properly and introduced purification tech-niques. In earlier centuries, vast heaps of salt could be loaded onto ships for the cost of the labour alone, though since it was full of donkey dung it was considered low-grade even then. Sal's salt was picked up by trawlers from England on their way to North Atlantic fishing grounds, and exported to the Newfoundland fishing towns, and later to Brazil for beef preservation.

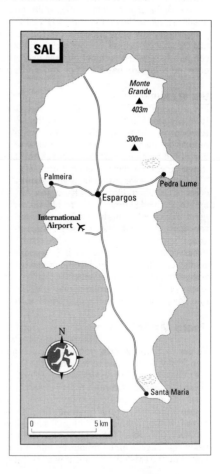

The tourist hotels and water sports – especially wind surfing, for which the island has a first-class reputation – are down at the beach at **Santa Maria**, at the southern tip of the island. **Espargos**, the capital, is the business end of things, with all the island's low-budget accommodation. Surprisingly modern as the **airport** is, it only bursts into life when an international flight is in. Airline offices – South African Airlines (☎41.22.83), TAP Air Portugal (☎41.11.95) and TACV (☎41.13.10) – are scattered around the tarmac. **Car rental** is available from Alucar in Santa Maria (☎42.11.87).

Arrival in Cape Verde

Most visitors arrive in the Cape Verdes at Sal and the introduction is relatively relaxed, if not without a cer-tain level of confusion. **Bags** normally clear customs here, so you will have to check in again if you're connecting to another island. If your **visa** has been arranged in advance, you'll need to pay for it (CV$200) in Cape Verdean escudos. If there's more than one of you, one person should queue at the **bureau de change** while the others waits at the police counter for the passports to be returned. There's an efficient and helpful **baggage store** where you can leave bulky items (CV$100 per 24 hours), if you want to spend a few hours unencumbered down at Santa Maria.

Espargos

If you fly into Sal, **ESPARGOS**, the main urbanization (town sounds too characterful) on the island, is less than 2km north up the road from the **airport** – you could probably walk there in twenty minutes. Taxis charge CV$150 into town, with a thirty percent surcharge at night. Arriving by boat you enter a drab grey bay – **Palmeira harbour** – 4km away, and have to wait for a lift, which shouldn't be too long in coming. Little Espargos is uninspiring – a post office in an unmarked pink mansion in the middle of town, a small market, a few groceries and a couple of bar/cafés. Sand whistles across the half-dozen nameless streets.

There are also a few **accommodation** options. The plain and simple rooms at the *Pensão Doña Angela* (☎41.13.27; ③) are your best target and there are decent evening meals. The *Residêncial Central* (☎41.11.13; ③) is another decent place with fairly priced food. Bigger and more modern, the *Hotel Atlantico* (CP 74; ☎41.12.10; Fax 41.15.22; ④) has the sort of ho-hum, airport-style facilities you'd expect; TACV sometimes lodge passengers here when connections are overbooked. For **eating**, the *Restaurante Arcada*, near the *Atlantico*, has a terrace and a surprisingly lively atmosphere.

Out of town

For whatever reason you're here, it's nice to get out of the town. You can do this quickly (and perhaps illicitly, so don't stop to ask anyone) by climbing to the summit of the **telecommunications hill** just five minutes' walk from the *praça*. From up there behind the dishes you have a good view of the entire, drab island; to the north a number of old volcanic hills; southwards the bleak brown wastelands fading away to the fringe of white beach at Santa Maria.

If you have several hours on your hands, go further, to **Pedra da Lume**, on the east coast of Sal, about 6km from Espargos. Any vehicle that passes is almost certain to stop for you. Pedra da Lume itself is an old salt port, comprising an apologetic set of bleak apartment blocks, a tiny harbour too shallow for any but the smallest vessels, and mounds of rock-hard, dirty salt. The ship repair yard still functions and the harbour is also home to a bizarre ship runway used to haul out small boats for loading and a set of rickety nineteenth-century pulleys and loading equipment. It resembles nothing so much as the mine set in a cowboy movie. Follow the creaking overhead pulley system uphill for a kilometre and you reach the rim of a gigantic, shallow, crater, vast in extent. It seems to lie below sea level – perfect for salt production as the sea water is simply allowed to flood in and evaporate. People will tell you it's all still in use, but it certainly doesn't look that way.

Santa Maria

To **get to Santa Maria**, you might catch an *aluguer* from Espargos, or likely as not a free lift if you take time to walk down to the turn-off for the **airport**. Taxis from the airport charge CV$700 *deslocação* to get to the resort. The short trip down to the south coast is a journey through a real desert. Goats are about the only animals you'll see: their introduction in the seventeenth century, before any significant human settlement, began a process of **soil destruction** which is now virtually complete. Nothing really grows, wild or cultivated. It all looks as if it was scoured by bulldozers earlier today.

SANTA MARIA DAS DORES (St Mary of Sorrows) was practically a ghost town only a few years ago. Ruined timber buildings in ornate style were scattered across the flats, linked by the twisted remains of narrow gauge rail track which once shifted tuna for the

INTER-ISLAND FLIGHTS FROM SAL

Boa Vista; daily (except Wed); 20min.
Praia: several daily; 45min.
São Nicolau: Mon, Thurs, Fri, Sat; 35min.
São Vicente: 1 or more daily; 45min.

Portuguese and ran out to the end of the thoroughly unsafe jetty. As Santa Maria enters the new millennium however, it has its sights set on a big revival. It's simple draw is the stunning flex of white sand dipping into blue-green waves of scintillatingly clear water, and the heady shade of the hotels by the beach. The old town, still ragged and poverty-stricken around the edges, is beginning to feel like a proper little resort, with a main drag, various restaurants with different themes, and enough bona fide, vacationing Europeans – a hard core of them globetrotting windsurfers – to give the place a gentle buzz. Happily, that rickety jetty is still there, now tastefully fortified, but still wobbly enough to make it fun. And the local boys still leap from the end of it into three fathoms of transparent water.

Accommodation and eating

There's a variety of **places to stay**, from the very affordable to the super-expensive. All have one or more **restaurants**. In addition to the facilities at your hotel, you can wander the main drag, rua Amílcar Cabral, and check out the following, from west to east: *Calema* (bar with plenty of action); *Esplanada Solel Mateus* (animated patio bar with live music); *Vulcao de Fogo* (pleasant little restaurant); *Pastelaria Relax* (café, pastries); the *Sport Clube Santa Maria* (local hangout, and very sporty); and the *Restaurante Lomba Branca*.

Djadsal Holiday Club, on the beach at the western end (☎42.11.70; Fax 42.10.70). Gargantuan Italian resort, defended by towering walls, in the style that Italians tend to expect – glamorous and sensation-seeking, with thumping music prevalent and a mass of activities to defer boredom. Very expensive (Cape Verde's priciest establishment). ⑦.

Hotel Albatros, on the beach at the eastern end (CP 49; ☎42.13.01; Fax 42.13.02). Normally known by its old name, *Hotel Aeroflot*, this is the most affordable of the four "international" hotels on Sal and comes with a saltwater swimming pool, cable TV and a gym. Forget the restaurant. ⑥.

Hotel Belorizonte, on the beach (☎42.10.45; Fax 42.12.10). Considering the price, this has a disappointingly holiday-camp atmosphere. European tour operators use it, and it's comfortable enough, but the rooms are none too big and many face inland. ⑦.

Hotel Morabeza, on the beach (CP 33; ☎42.11.11; Fax 42.10.05). Not a cheap place to stay but this is the best resort unless you're in a the *Djadsal* league. Rooms vary greatly in size: the best value are the sea-facing 300s. Good restaurant, popular disco. Visa accepted. ⑦.

Nha Terra Chico (☎42.11.09). Lively restaurant at what passes for Santa Maria's busiest intersection at the western end of town. Long menu with a large proportion of dishes available, mostly under CV$1000. Also has economical rooms. ③.

Pousada da Luz, northeast of the town centre (☎42.11.38; Fax 42.10.88). A really good place to stay, with an excellent restaurant, if somewhat away from the action. ④.

Residêncial Alternativa, (☎42.12.16; Fax 42.11.65). Perhaps the cheapest option in Santa Maria, and good value, at the back of the town centre. ③.

Boa Vista

Boa Vista is said to have been productive at one time; at present it is almost a desert. Its people, of whom there are four thousand, are almost always hungry, and the lean cattle, with sad faces and tears in their eyes, walk solemnly in cudless rumination over grassless fields. In the valleys there is some vegetation. Fishing, salt-making and going to funerals are the chief amusements and employments of the people.

Life was not easy when the Rev. Charles Thomas went to **BOA VISTA** in the 1850s, but things have improved a little, at least for the cattle. The rains of recent years have made the hillocky pancake of an island greener than in living memory, though it still retains large areas of spectacular shifting **sand dunes**, notably in the west.

The island's struggling economy long depended on salt, but that industry has died out and now date farming – there are large palm groves near the airstrip – supplemented by fishing and some livestock grazing, provide the main alternatives to emigration. Tourism is beginning to have an impact, too, with the more adventurous windsurfing aficionados barely pausing at Santa Maria these days before heading straight to Boa Vista. Italian visitors are by far the most prominent. Boavistans themselves seem to have made best use of the island's famous **shipwrecks** which frequently took place in the treacherous rocky shallows on the north and northeast coasts – and still occasionally do, since navigation charts for the seas around Boa Vista are still inaccurate, in some cases by several hundred metres. There are judged to be about a hundred wrecks, some of them quite old. **Turtles** were grist to the Boavistan mill as well, and unfortunately still are. There are precious egg-laying sites on many beaches.

Although a latecomer, even to Cape Verde's slightly esoteric tourist industry, more and more travellers are making the effort of somewhat patchy air service and rather sporadic ferries to visit an island that is best described as a slab of Sahara surrounded by sea. Boa Vista has a captivatingly desolate interior, and a necklace of spectacular white **beaches** all around (the one at Santa Monica is the most beautiful). It's a great island to explore in a rented Suzuki, with a clear enough route right round the island, though *aluguers* tend to be very scarce – less than 5000 people live on the island, eight out of ten of them in Sal Rei. If you make the effort to get into the parched and peaceful countryside, you'll find the few people graciously welcoming, with a high proportion of English-speakers who've spent years at sea. The traditional *mornas* (folksongs) of the island are rated the most cheerful and upbeat in Cape Verde. Boa Vista's annual festival takes place on June 24.

Sal Rei

Flights arrive at the **airport**, 5km south of Boa Vista's capital, Sal Rei, near the old village of Rabil. The fare into town depends on the number of passengers and the mood of the driver – CV$200–300. **Ferries** come close to the port, in the heart of the little town, and passengers come ashore by lighter.

SAL REI is remarkably quiet: the huge central square, mid-morning, might contain one parked car and a dog. The town beach is a little more lively at weekends, and if your visit coincides with a football match at the Sal Rei "stadium" you'll see most of the male population in one go. If you can find a boat, a trip out to the **Ilhéu de Sal Rei**, an islet opposite the town, is interesting: it holds the ruins of an old **fort** (Fortaleza Duque de Braganza) and the waters are good for snorkelling. Around the month of August you may even see turtles here.

If you want to be active, Sal Rei can offer a number of diversions, including **mountain biking**, **diving**, **whale-watching** (or, more precisely, whale-seeking) and, of course, **windsurfing**. Ask any hotel, or just visit the centre of all this activity, Boa Vista Water Sport System, on avenida Amílcar Cabral, the street running parallel to the seafront. Mountain biking (expect to pay about CV$500 a half-day) is more fun than it might at first appear: head south out of town, turning immediately left opposite the Enacal petrol station to join the cobbles of the old road down to the airport and Rabil, the so-called **Via Pittoresca**. It undulates through a veritable forest of palm trees for several pretty kilometres before rejoining the main road.

If you have a 4WD vehicle, it's possible to get right down to the wreck of the **Cabo de Santa Maria**, 8km northeast of Sal Rei. The Spanish freighter has been rusting off the beach since 1968, when its cargo of car parts, garlic, rosemary and pornographic magazines was seized and rapidly traded across the island – items can still be found in many Boavistan homes. From Sal Rei, drive out towards the Marine Club, then leave the road before the hotel entrance and head across country to the right, following the tracks for a few hundred metres until you reach a little church in a large, white-walled plot. From here, continue generally uphill and over the crests until you emerge above the island's northern coast with a clear view of the wreck a couple of kilometres away. A driveable track goes down to the beach and tyre marks lead you the whole way there.

Accommodation and eating

As for a **place to stay**, the small *Residêncial Boa Esperança* (☎51.11.70; ②) is your only option for a really cheap bed; some rooms are S/C. *Pensão Bom Sossego* (☎51.11.55; ②) is presentable if somewhat gloomy. Moving upmarket, the rooms at the *Pousada Boa Vista* (☎51.11.45; Fax 51.14.23; ④) are bright and clean and, if you're on the island to windsurf, you'll find like-minded company there – it's used by several smaller European tour operators – but it's a few minutes walk from the seafront. The pleasantly informal and welcoming *Hotel Dunas*, directly on the seafront (☎51.12.25; Fax 51.13.84; *bws@mail.cvtelecom.cv*; ④) has fine, large rooms and the unusual luxury of hot water. Their restaurant is good, too. In the top-spending bracket, the Italian-run *Estoril Beach Resort*, on the south side of town, near the most popular windsurfing area, is a nice enough place, but not sufficiently busy to be attractive (☎51.10.82; Fax 51.10.46; *casitalia@mail.cvtelecom.cv*; ⑤). Finally, another Italian establishment, the *Marine Club* (☎561.10.82; Fax 51.10.46; *marineclub@mail.cvtelecom.cv*; ⑦), a couple of kilometres out of town, along their own highway – paved with artificial cobbles – is where you go if you don't want to experience the subtle excitements of the capital. There's a cute little beach here, a fine swimming pool (visitors appear to be welcome to use it) and the club's villas are well appointed, but if you're not Italian it simply doesn't feel quite right.

Aside from the hotels, there are few places to eat, drink or shop in Sal Rei. The lively patio **bar** – usually called the *Esplanada* – behind the jetty, a stone's throw from the *Hotel Dunas*, is, by default, the obvious target. *Cleps* and seafood are the main standbys, but it's always best to order ahead. A number of more or less private houses in Sal Rei offer **dinner**, given enough warning. You might also make arrangements to eat in Rabil, at the *Sodade di Nha Terra* – a to-order-only restaurant run by an excellent cook.

Driving round the island

A highly recommended day can be spent **circumnavigating Boa Vista**. Any of the main hotels will arrange for a Suzuki to be parked outside ready for you first thing (CV$5000 for 24 hours; CV$10,000 deposit; Cab Auto is the usual outfit). Ensure you have sufficient drinking water and a good spare. The road south of Sal Rei goes through the wiry little village of Rabil, then descends to a seasonal watercourse to cross through palm trees onto the desolate open road across the central and northern part of the island.

After 45 minutes you reach **João Galego**, the first of three tiny hamlets comprising the small, inhabited district known as "Norte" (pretty much the only populated part of the island apart from Sal Rei and Rabil and a small town in the southwest, Povoação Velha). A couple of kilometres further is **Fundo de Figueiras**, with a little surrounding farmland, whence a 6km off-road diversion down a gentle shelving valley takes you to the splendidly wild and remote beach of **Baia das Gatas**. You'll find turtle bones and even the occasional dolphin skeleton here. Returning to the "main road", the southernmost Norte settlement is **Cabeça de Tarafes**, and at this point the cobbled surface ceases abruptly and the real adventure begins. The track (easy to follow even though you're now unlikely to see another human being for a couple of hours) scales the gentle, brown rocky slopes of the depopulated eastern part of the island, crawling across the little ravines of seasonal watercourses, and speeding up over the hilltops. As you finally descend to reach the **southern coast**, near a deserted palm tree oasis, and turn right to follow the shore, you'll need that four-wheel-drive as the track meets soft sand, and at the right time of year, even mud. You can drive straight down to a a marvellously empty strand from here.

Curral Velho, an abandoned settlement at Boa Vista's southern extremity, is 28km beyond Cabeça (about two hours). Don't try to continue direct to Santa Monica from Curral Velho – the rough track deteriorates as you leave the old settlement behind and rapidly becomes impossible. Instead, as you arrive in Curral Velho from the east, turn right at the first large wall leading off inland and start to follow it north, and you can pick up a clear track which leads across the great, bare back of the island, more or less north or northwest, to rejoin the Rabil to Norte road after about an hour. This track is mostly firm going, with some soft sand: keep the distinctive cone of Mount Santo Antóino in view to your left and you can't really go wrong. But drive carefully. If you have an accident out here (and Suzukis have been prone to roll), you may have a long wait for the first *aluguer* to come by.

INTER-ISLAND FLIGHTS FROM BOA VISTA

Maio: Sat; 40min.
Praia: Mon, Tues & Fri; 35–45min.
Sal: 1 or more daily from Thurs–Mon; 20–25min.
TACV in Sal Rei: ☎51.11.86.

GUINEA-BISSAU

GUINEA-BISSAU

O ne of the smallest and least-known countries in West Africa, **Guinea-Bissau** was also the last on the mainland to regain its independence – from Portugal, in 1974 – and it entered the world's consciousness as a highly charged symbol of colonial repression. Guinea-Bissau's revolutionary **war of liberation** helped overthrow the dictatorship in Portugal and its revolution persisted after independence. Until the end of the 1970s, the country's struggle for national survival inspired progressive movements in Europe and North America, as Nicaragua did in the 1980s. But political rigidity set in with economic failure, and enthusiasm for the revolution waned both in Guinea-Bissau and overseas. The military takeover in 1980 and subsequent lurch into a flawed democratic system brought little improvement, and long-standing rifts within the armed forces, fuelled by economic desperation, were the cause of the 1998/99 **military uprising** which finally ousted the elected government.

Geographically, Guinea-Bissau is spread across a region of low-lying jungle and grassland, meandering rivers, mangrove forest, estuarine flats and offshore islands. To the north lies the Casamance region of Senegal, and to the east and south the Republic of Guinea.

The country's **economic situation** improved a good deal in the 1980s and early 90s – gone are the days of unobtainable food supplies and bananas being exchanged for unearthly sums. Before the current crisis, the indigenous Fula community was in the vanguard of the commercial renaissance and Mauritanian traders had also moved in.

The **Guinea-Bissauans** are renowned for being very laid-back company. Before the fighting, gentle manners (men spend much time with their children for example) and a sense of personal security featured in your travels wherever you went. The agreeable atmosphere could be explained partly by the country's unusual history: although colonial rule was repressive and the war of liberation took a heavy toll, the relationship between the peoples of Guinea-Bissau and Portugal had already lasted nearly 500 years, since the mid-fifteenth century, and was generally good. From the earliest contact, Portuguese settlers married local women and the result has been a widespread creolization of culture in mainland Guinea-Bissau – outward looking, self-confident and somewhat cosmopolitan. The islands, as you'll discover if you visit them, are no less friendly, but very different.

Where to go

Travelling would be incredibly difficult were the country not so small: most journeys require at least one ferry ride, often more, and the tides determine when the ferries operate. The most worthwhile destinations are the admirably languid, dream-like

---

WARNING

At the time of writing (mid-1999) travellers were being discouraged from visiting Guinea-Bissau by the British Foreign Office advice notice and the US State Department travel advisory on the country. Air links are tenuous and mines are a particular danger. If you want to go, check the Internet for the latest news and stay alert to news on the travellers' grapevine. Rough Guides has been unable to confirm the validity of all the information in this chapter.

FACTS AND FIGURES

La Republica da Guiné-Bissau covers 36,000 square kilometres, barely half the size of Scotland or Maine. The population is about 1.1 million, but the rate of growth is slower than in most African countries. The country's **foreign debt** amounts to some £600 million ($960 million), which seems a massive figure until compared with the cost of building London's Millennium Dome – some fifty percent more. Yet the debt amounts to nearly twenty times the value of the country's annual exports of goods and services (this is analogous to living on the breadline and having debts amounting to twenty times your annual income). At the time of going to press (mid-1999), Guinea-Bissau was under the military control of General Ansumane Manè, the former chief of staff who deposed President Nino Vieira in May 1999 and installed Malam Bacai Sanka as acting president, pending elections due in November 1999.

Bijagós islands. Getting to them isn't that easily accomplished, however, and you need to allow for some discomfort and inconvenience, especially if you want to see more than the two most frequently visited islands – Bolama and Bubaque.

For the present, with the exception of one or two special, local attractions and a lovely absence of hustle, it's perhaps unfair to recommend the **mainland** very highly. What stands out is the poverty and inadequacy of most communities – including Bissau, the capital – despite a super-abundance of greenery and unexploited agricultural potential. Parts of the country still have an atmosphere of decay and abandon: the liberation war's toll accounts for much, even twenty years on, and it's now been exacerbated by the 1998 fighting. Yet despite the downside, visitors have rarely reported bad experiences over the years and, assuming the current tensions soothe enough to make it safe once again, you may well find you like Guinea-Bissau immensely.

The people

The biggest of Guinea-Bissau's two dozen ethnic groups is the **Balante**, people of the southern coastal creeks and forests. Much of the area under rice cultivation has been cleared by them over the centuries. In the northwest, the smaller population of **Fulup** (part of the Jola group from southern Senegal) are also great rice farmers. **Pepel** and **Manjak** farmers from the Bissau region are heavily dependent on the city as a market, and operate a more diverse economy. In contrast, the **Bijagó** people, on the islands, are mostly self-sufficient (principally through fishing and palm nut-gathering), though men increasingly find work on the mainland or abroad. The Bijagó (a population of less than 40,000) have been under little pressure to change over the last 200 years. They've easily resisted Islam and Christianity, and remain very attached to traditional ways. Women have relatively greater economic power than is usually the case, as they are the traditional owners of houses.

In the mainland interior, the biggest contingents are **Fula**- and **Mandinka**-speaking, and there's greater mixing and wider social horizons in the mostly Muslim towns and villages of the east and north. The Fula (the country's second largest language group) are, as ever, powerful players in local politics: their conservative, feudal roots can't be ignored by whoever governs the country.

A noticeable proportion of Guinea-Bissauans are mixed-race **Kriolu**-speakers; mostly from the Cape Verde Islands (much of whose population was composed originally of slaves from Portuguese Guinea), but also descendants of the small number of settlers and traders who came direct from Portugal. A fragmented Portuguese settler community still existed until 1998, bolstered by expat arrivals from Lisbon encouraged by the former government. Nearly all were evacuated as soon as the fighting started and it's too early to say how many may return.

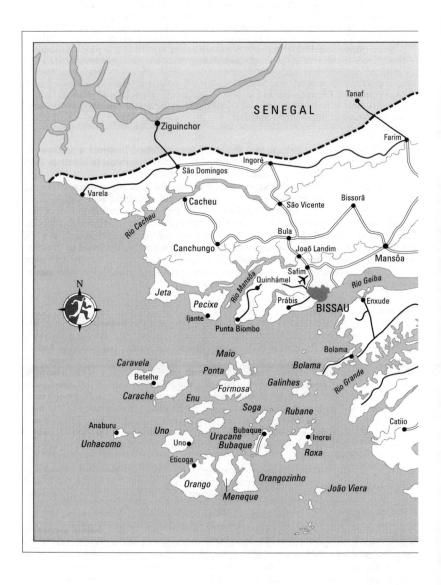

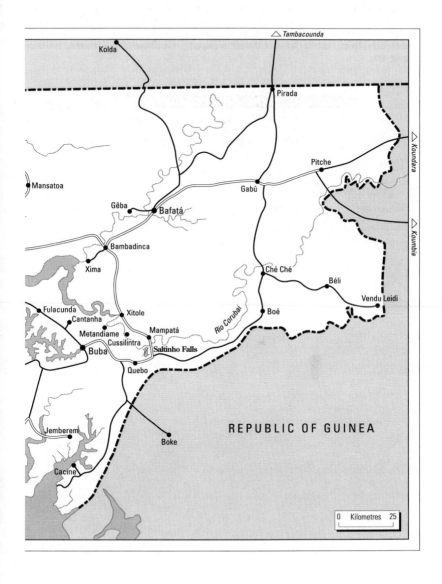

When to go

The **best time to visit** is December and January. During these months, the islands are really pleasant. The *carnaval* season in Bissau (February) is a good time to be in the capital. **Bad times**, particularly in Bissau itself, are the nerve-fraying run-up to the rains in April and May when breathing seems an impossibility, and the end of the rains in November, when the sun evaporates the moisture into the leaden air. In the five very wet months, from June to October, the air is dripping wet all the time – whether it's raining or not.

AVERAGE TEMPERATURES AND RAINFALL

BISSAU

	Jan	Feb	Mar	Apr	May	June	July	Aug	Sept	Oct	Nov	Dec
Temperatures °C												
Min (night)	18	19	20	21	22	23	23	23	23	23	22	19
Max (day)	32	33	34	34	33	31	30	29	30	31	32	30
Rainfall mm	2	2	7	1	45	200	850	900	390	180	40	5

Arrivals

Most visitors to Guinea-Bissau either fly in or cross the border from Senegal, though a few European yachts make it down here from the Canaries.

■ Flights from Africa

At the time of writing, Guinea-Bissau was in a state of unrest, the airport was closed, and many flights into the country indefinitely suspended. Even before the fighting of 1998/99 started, flights into Bissau were extremely limited, with Senegal, The Gambia, Guinea and Cape Verde the only countries linked by direct services.

Check the latest situation with Air Sénégal, Air Mauritanie, Air Afrique and TAVC – all of which have operated flights to Bissau in the past.

■ Overland from Senegal or The Gambia

Because of limitations on flights from Europe, many visitors fly into Dakar or Banjul and then travel **overland by public transport**, a journey which is straightforward despite its complicated appearance on the map (but see warning on p.217 about travel in the Basse Casamance region). Peugeot 504s go direct from Dakar to Ziguinchor in southern Senegal. You'll have to accept an obligatory night in Ziguinchor, and take another bush taxi on to Bissau in the morning. Alternatively, both the *Kassoumay* catamaran (2 weekly; 6hr) or the *MV Joola* (2 weekly) make the journey from Dakar to Ziguinchor; the latter is an overnight journey arriving in time to meet an early morning bus to Bissau. See p.188 for full ferry details.

The border crossing into Guinea-Bissau is at **São Domingos**. (closed at the time of writing). If the border has reopened, you'll travel to Bissau on the new sealed route via Ingoré and Bula, which involves a short ferry crossing at São Vincente. From Bula, bush taxis take the route east along the newly tarred road to Bissora, then on to Mansôa and Bissau. The alternative route from Bula – directly south – is shorter but involves a foot-passenger-only ferry crossing at Joaõ Landim. A bridge is being built here, but don't expect it to have been completed before at least 2002.

Less commonly used routes from Senegal into the country exist from Tanaf to **Farim**, from Velingara to **Gabú** and from Kolda, 70km east of Tanaf, to **Bafatá** in central Guinea-Bissau; Farim, Gabú and Bafatá all have regular connections to Bissau.

From The Gambia, via Ziguinchor, you can make the trip to Bissau in one long day, though you may prefer to plan for an overnight stop in Ziguinchor and continue the next day.

■ Overland from Guinea

Driving **from Guinea** in your own vehicle, you have a choice between two main routes. The first takes the tarmac road to **Labé** via Mamou, battles up to **Koundara** (a stretch that can be reasonable during the dry season), then crosses the border at Kandika, and follows the bush track to Gabú, from where it's smooth tarmac all the way to Bissau. This is a two- or three-day trip.

The second route goes from Conakry north to Boké, through **Koumbia and Foula-Mori**, then takes the ferry crossing at the border and joins the main road to Bissau at Pitche. Normal driving time between the capitals in the dry season is not much less than 22 hours on this route. With a dawn start from Conakry in a tough vehicle you might just make it to the border in time to catch the ferryman at dusk, and so be in Gabú or Bafatá late at night; but planning on a two-day journey is much more feasible.

On **public transport**, the route via Labé and Koundara is the only one with regular connections, allowing three long days for the journey. On the route via Koumbia and Foula-Mori, you'll be delayed waiting for vehicles in the border area.

The third, more obvious-looking route **following the coast** is an arduous trek, not recommended unless you have bags of time. From Boké it goes via a bridge and Sansalé to Buba in Guinea-Bissau, thence to Enxude and by *pirogue* to Bissau.

The details in these practical information pages are essentially for use on the ground in West Africa and in Guinea-Bissau itself: for full practical coverage on preparing for a trip, getting here from outside the region, paperwork, health, information sources and more, see Basics. pp.3–83.

Red Tape

Visas, generally easy to obtain, are required by nearly all nationalities apart from West Africans. Some, but not all Guinea-Bissau consulates in Europe issue visas for over-land entry. At the consulates in Banjul and Ziguinchor, they're cheap and normally issued while you wait. The embassies in Dakar, Abidjan and Conakry are more formal.

The consulate in Ziguinchor, Senegal, issues thirty-day **single entry visas** on the spot. These are useful if you're in doubt about whether you'll subsequently be allowed into the Republic of Guinea for, if there's any question, Guinea-Bissau border guards won't let you leave their country without a visa allowing you to re-enter.

If you're flying into Bissau from one of the many countries with no Guinea-Bissau embassy or consulate, you can get a visa at the airport in Bissau, though you're strongly advised to try to get one beforehand.

Extending your visa, once in the country, is not difficult, but allowing it to expire and over-staying can lead to surprisingly serious problems if detected.

For onward travel, don't count on getting many stamps in Bissau. **Nigeria**, **Senegal**, **Mauritania** and **Guinea** are the only West African states with diplomatic missions here and the French embassy can help with several others. There's no Cape Verde embassy. Full details are given on p.23.

Money and Costs

Guinea-Bissau joined the majority of the Francophone countries in West Africa in May 1997 and changed over from the Guinea-Bissau peso (GB$) to the CFA franc. Since the changeover, annual inflation has dropped from 50–100 percent down to 6–8 percent.

Changing money in **banks** – the main commercial bank is the Banco Internacional da Guiné Bissau – is a generally inefficient process that can take all morning. The **forex bureaux** in Bissau are much faster as well as offering better rates. Outside of Bissau, the only banks with exchange facilities are in **Canchungo**, **Bafatá** and **Gabú** and on the Senegalese border at **Pirada**.

Credit cards are virtually useless except in Bissau – and then only for guests in Bissau's top hotel. The BIGB bank can arrange credit card **cash advances**, but this will be difficult and expensive.

■ Costs

Costs aren't easily reckoned in advance and we give the best current estimates. Outside of Bissau, there's very little to spend your money on, so the cost of a stay in the country is generally low, and can be minimal. Hotels are clearly the main expense; a cheap room costs CFA5000–10,000 in Bissau but less on Bubaque or upcountry. Meals are usually excellent value and transport costs are low.

Health

Unless you fly straight in from Europe, you must show your yellow fever certificate on arrival. You should take extra care to avoid catching malaria – easily done here – and be aware of the potential hazards of going down with the disease in some isolated corner of the country, especially on a remote island. There was a moderately serious epidemic of cholera in the country in 1994/95.

The only **hospitals** are in Bissau (which has 80 of the country's 150 doctors), Bafatá, Canchungo and Bolama. Bubaque has some medical infra-structure. Out on the other islands and in the south, your health problems are largely your own to deal with.

Bilharzia is a menace on sluggish inland waters, but the rivers are tidal far into the interior (the Rio Gêba as far upstream as Bafatá, the Cacheu past Farim and the Corubal as far as the Saltinho Falls) and the schistosome worms can't survive in brackish water.

Unofficial reports suggest that the country has one of the worst **Aids** problems in the region; many people are infected with the long incubation HIV II virus.

Maps and Information

Tourist information on Guinea-Bissau in English is almost non-existent. There are no official tourist offices, nor much of an organized government department dealing with this minor industry.

If you want to exhaust all possibilities, write (preferably in Portuguese, or at least French) to the Centro do Informacão e Turismo, CP 294, Bissau, Guinea-Bissau.

The 1:500,000, 3615 series IGN **map** of the country, updated in 1993, is reasonable – and the only one available.

Getting Around

Most travel in Guinea-Bissau is ruled by the tides. On the coast there's a tidal range of over five metres, more than twice the world average. Many communities are cut off except at high tide when ferries can reach them. Departure times are therefore unpredictable, unless you've got local tide tables. Add in frequent breakdowns and the potential for delay is almost unlimited.

■ Ferries

The main ferry operator is the state line Rodofluvial. Their office in Bissau supplies monthly lists of dates and estimated departure times for the various routes. Approximate frequencies and journey times (one-way) are:

Bissau–Bolama–Bissau: out Fri/Sat, back Sun (3hr).
Bissau–Bolama–Catió–Bolama–Bissau: out Tues, back Fri (9hr).
Bissau–Bubaque–Bissau: out Fri, back Sun (4–5hr).
Bissau–Biombo–Pecixe–Biombo–Bissau: out Sat, back Sun (4–5hr).

Other destinations with at least twice-monthly service include **Empada**, **Xime** and **Cacine**.

Departures can be any time from 5am to 7pm (or the middle of the night for Pecixe), though the first daylight high tide is the usual one.

Tickets, which are quoted at two rates ("ticket office" and "on board"), are usually charged at the lower rate anyway; but if you have the chance, get them in advance. Bolama is around CFA2000 one-way, and Bubaque CFA3000. Argue like crazy about paying for your bags: as usual, they're negotiable. Bicycles are charged at a fixed rate around two-thirds of the full fare. Note that none of these regular diesel ferries are built to transport cars.

In addition to the Rodofluvial ferries, there are dozens of small hand-hauled ferry bridges and *pirogue* services around the country.

■ Road transport

The **bush taxi** network is improving all the time, but you generally have to be out and about first thing in the morning to get anywhere as there are relatively few vehicles. Conversely, later departures can take forever to fill up. Bush taxis are known as **kandongas** and sometimes marked **"aluguer"** ("for rent").

Car rental possibilities do exist in Bissau but not with any official car hire companies. Ask at hotels about private arrangements and they will usually come with a driver. Expect to pay at least US$60 a day, plus fuel.

If you are riding a **motorbike** or **mobylette**, note that, unlike in neighbouring countries, helmets must be worn.

Hitching around might seem a hopeless task, but unless you devote your days to arranging the next bush taxi trip, you'll find you often end up walking out of the town or village and waiting for a passing vehicle as a preferable alternative to waiting in the taxi park. In normal times, aid worker and volunteer vehicles comprise a high proportion of traffic.

Cycling through Guinea-Bissau, so long as you choose your season, is an attractive option. The 500-odd kilometres of sealed road are pleasantly quiet, flat or gently undulating, and often flanked by dense foliage and grass pouring over the road. With a week or two to spare you could explore the south and east, well off the beaten track, quite extensively. If you don't have your own bike, renting one privately in Bissau isn't too difficult. You should also try to do this if you're visiting the islands as, with the exception of Bubaque, transport is hard to come by.

■ Planes

In normal times, there are regular flights to **Bubaque** (usually Mon at 7.30am and Fri at 5pm) and, if there is enough demand, to **Gabú** and **Catió**. Try Guiné Tours in Bissau (see p.452) for the latest information.

Accommodation

There are very few hotels in Guinea-Bissau and the difficulty of getting an inexpensive room, especially in Bissau itself, is a routine feature of travel here. During *carnaval* in February and possibly also during football's Amílcar Cabral Cup Final in May, you'll have

---

ACCOMMODATION PRICE CODES

Accommodation prices in this chapter are coded according to the following scales – the same scales in terms of their pound/dollar equivalents as are used throughout the book. Prices refer to the rate you can expect to pay for a room with two beds. Single rooms, or single occupancy, will normally cost at least two-thirds of the twin-occupancy rate. In Guinea-Bissau there are not enough hotels to make any more than the simplest generalizations about the facilities you can expect in each price bracket.

① **Under CFA4500 (under £5/$8).** Rudimentary lodgings, with primitive facilities.

② **CFA4500–9000 (£5–10/$8–16).** Basic hotel.

③ **CFA9000–18,000 (£10–20/$16–32).** Modest hotel, usually with S/C rooms and sometimes AC.

④ **CFA18,000–27,000 (£20–30/$32–48).** Reasonable business or tourist-class *pensão*, with S/C, AC rooms and a restaurant.

⑤ **CFA27,000–36,000 (£30–40/$48–64).** Similar to ④.

⑥ **CFA36,000–45,000 (£40–50/$64–80).** Comfortable, first-class hotel.

⑦ **Over CFA45,000 (over £50/$80).** Luxury establishment with pool and other special features.

---

extra trouble. Your best bet is a *pensão* (plural *pensões*) – a family-run establishment along Portuguese lines. In most of the older, Portuguese-built towns – Canchungo, Bafatá, Gabú – you'll find one or two, but in more out-of-the-way places there is not much call for hotel accommodation and basic, sleazy, bar-restaurant establishments with a few rooms are the norm.

Camping is a tolerated and useful alternative: a tent is particularly helpful on the islands. But getting food and water supplies if you're in a good camping spot is always something of a problem. There are no campsites.

It's not uncommon for travellers to find **private lodging** with Guinea-Bissauans met travelling on public transport. This can be rewarding and illuminating, but most people are very poor and will appreciate your contributions to the evening meal.

Eating and Drinking

In a small country as poor and battered as this, it's no surprise to find little attention paid to gastronomy. White rice is the staple diet of nearly everyone and, for the majority, something to accompany it once or twice a week is the best they can expect.

This is unlikely to be your diet, at least not in Bissau itself. Restaurants in the capital (virtually the only town to have them) make the most of **seafood** and whatever else is available, and hotel dining rooms usually manage to produce enormous four-course meals in rustic **Portuguese style**. Rice soup, fish, chicken,

tough beef or pork and potatoes are standard fare with, invariably, a banana to finish.

If you're used to eating **bananas** all day, then Guinea-Bissau will be less of a shock to your system. They, together with oranges, cashew nuts and small loaves, are obtainable just about everywhere. Although small supermarkets and corner shops exist, they carry less range than you'd find in, say, Ziguinchor or Conakry, and you'll turn to the markets for basic food requirements. Incidentally, if you are given unshelled cashew nuts, do not try to crack them open with your teeth: the shell contains an intense irritant that will inflame your mouth for days.

There are few Guinea-Bissauan **specialities** but some dishes to try are: *kalde de manjara*, a peanut stew; *kalde de Chebeng*, crushed palm nut stew; *kalde branco*, fish in white sauce; and *galinha cafriella*, a chicken dish. *Cachupa*, a beans, corn and pork dish characteristic of the Cape Verde Islands, is a meal for special occasions. **Monkey meat** (*carne de mono*) is common everywhere and very variable: Bissau is one of the few West African capitals where it's regularly served, though be certain it's well-cooked to avoid the possibility of catching a dangerous virus. Seafood is good in Bissau. Delicious **gambas** – king prawns – are the stock in trade of the European-style restaurants. **Oysters** and other shellfish are often on Bissau menus too.

Locally made Pampa **beer** is the national brew. There are also a few imported beers – including Sagres from Portugal – and soft

Guinea-Bissau's IDD code is ☎245.

drinks. Local plastic bag juices – lime and lemon juice and wonderful **cashew juice** – can all be found for about CFA50–100 a bottle. Cashews are very widespread (something like forty percent of export earnings comes from cashew nuts), and a lethal **hooch** – *canna de cajeu* – is made from the cashew apples. The nuts themselves, as well as magnificent mangoes and a tart but not unpleasant little plum unfairly called *miseria*, help to make the end of the dry season bearable.

Communications – Post, Phones, Language and Media

Guinea-Bissau's mail, in and out, is not particularly efficient or reliable, although prices are in line with neighbouring countries. It is recommended that you don't send or receive parcels, as many get tampered with or simply don't arrive. For poste restante, letters should be marked Lista da Correios, CTT, Bissau. The main post office is in Bissau. There are functioning branches in provincial towns, but you should be prepared for considerable delays.

Faxing and **telephoning** are pricey, except to Portugal. The telephone system is generally good: you can phone Guinea-Bissau direct from abroad, and IDD dialling out of the country is no longer difficult. Note that reverse charge (collect) calls cannot be made except to Portugal. Phone boxes and *télécentres* have sprung up in the capital in recent years.

■ Language

Although the official language of Guinea-Bissau is **Portuguese**, the widely used, street-friendly vernacular is **Kriolu** (or **Crioulo**). An old amalgam of seafarers' Portuguese with various African languages, this is very similar to Cape Verdean Kriolu (see p.374), but significantly different from Portuguese. If you speak some Portuguese, Kriolu becomes semi-intelligible. Other important languages include **Bijagó**, on the islands of the same name, **Balante**, the related **Manjak** and **Pepel**, **Mandinka** and **Fula**.

■ The media

Broadcasting is mainly **radio**, which is generally in Portuguese – although Radio Mavegro transmits the World Service news in English most hours. **Television** broadcasting was introduced in 1989, and the national station shows programmes every evening from 7pm. The Portuguese channel RTP International can be received in the evenings but only near the capital, and there are still very few TV sets outside of Bissau.

Looking to **the press** for news, you'll not find the range of papers which used to be available. *Diario de Bissau* is the paper sold on the streets. There are a few **foreign papers** on sale around Bissau: popular tabloids from Lisbon are sometimes available, and if you're desperate, the two luxury hotels should have the *Herald Tribune*, *Time* and *Newsweek*.

Directory

AIRPORT DEPARTURE TAX For international departures US$12, but this is somewhat flexible in application.

ART AND ENTERTAINMENT Main artistic event of the year is the *carnaval* in February.

GLOSSARY

Assimilado In colonial times, an indigenous Guinean who, through education and connections had achieved the status of Portuguese citizen.

Bairro Suburb.

Feitoria "Factory" in the historical sense of a trading post.

Fermanza Local name for the dry, dusty *Harmattan* wind from the north.

Kana Sugar cane alcohol.

Kandonga Bush taxi.

Kirintim A fence of woven brushwood (like wattle) often surrounding and identifying a bar.

Navetanes Seasonal migrant workers.

Ponta Small land concession or trading post in Portuguese Guinea.

Tabanka Rural village.

Indigenous theatre is dormant. Music (see below) shows a little more promise. Before the 1998/99 war, The French Cultural Centre in Bissau had some exhibitions and events worth seeing.

BARGAINING Haggling over purchases is a brief business: few market traders will discuss for long. The last price is the last price, and quickly reached.

CRAFTS AND OTHER PURCHASES A couple of spots in Bissau sell woodcarvings: the main one, the Centro Artistico Juvenil (see p.450) is rather good. Because of the lazy-sell attitude of most craft-sellers, you can mull over a fair range without being hassled. Animal skins – crocodile, python, even leopard and serval – are openly displayed too. The government applies no effective sanctions, though the problem is a small one at present.

FUEL Fuel is a lot more readily available than it used to be, and every major town now has a petrol station. The price is around CFA225/litre diesel and CFA500 for petrol.

HOLIDAYS New Year's Day is a big event; **January 20** Heroes' Day (assassination of Amílcar Cabral); **February** (the weekend before Shrove Tuesday) Bissau *carnaval*; **March 8** International Women's Day; **August 3** National Day (Pidjiguiti Massacre); **September 24** Independence Day (the proclamation of the republic in the liberated zone of Boé in 1973); **November 14** Redemption Day of the Republic (1980 coup that brought PAIGC to power); **Christmas Day and December 26** (a family occasion in Bissau).

Throughout the northeast, the **Islamic calendar** is observed, but a few closures and holidays aren't likely to have much noticeable effect on your travels.

MUSIC Guinea-Bissau's special music is **gumbe**, which combines a contemporary sound with the country's ten or more musical traditions. A bit like a polyrhythmic samba it is usually acoustic (though sometimes from necessity rather than choice), and always sung in Kriolu. In Bissau there were several working groups before the war, who played the clubs. **Tabanka Jazz** stayed in Bissau, but just about every other band disintegrated and most artists fled to a fairly generous welcome in Lisbon. Names you'll hear spoken of with affection include the band of the moment (or at least the late 1990s), **Gumbezarte**, singers **Justino Delgado** and **Dulce Neves** – just about the only female professional musician in the country – **Rui**

Sangará, **Janota di Nha Sperança** and **Tino Trimo**. On the international stage, **Kabá Mané** and **Ramiro Naka** have both done what successful African artists tend to do and left the country for the big venues of Europe years ago, and they only return once every year or two. Upbeat kora-player Kabá Mané sings in a variety of languages, but often in the *kussundé* style of the Balante people, close to his Beafada roots. Guitarist Ramiro Naka puts on a flamboyant stage show. His songs are in Kriolu, with rhythms derived from traditional gumbe drumming – the sound that accompanies big occasions like weddings and funerals.

OPENING HOURS There is very little consistency. Few offices and businesses have more than one location, and that's usually in Bissau. A long lunch break is common, however, usually from 11.30am or noon to 3pm.

PHOTOGRAPHY Officialdom is very suspicious of cameras. A permit is required, in theory, but nobody can tell you where to obtain it nor do they seem especially bothered whether or not you have it, except during *carnaval* time when you will be asked. In Bissau, avoid the port, presidential palace and most other places with your camera. In country areas, people aren't much concerned and may even ask you to take pictures of them. Photography on the islands is relaxed. Video, and photography in general, is much easier if you're part of an aid project, or connected to one, rather than a "tourist".

SPORT The big sport is soccer, encouraged by the cultural ties with soccer-mad Portugal and Brazil. There are even two women's teams. Village football is often played at dusk, but the most exciting games take place at the impressive stadium outside Bissau, especially recommended if it's an international match. The Amílcar Cabral Cup Final in May is the major national sporting event.

TROUBLE Before the war of 1998/99, Guinea-Bissau was one of the least uptight countries in the region. There were few roadblocks and you could easily spend several weeks here without crossing the path of a uniformed official.

The laws on **drug possession** are very tough: possession of a few joints normally leads to deportation, but quite often only after a spell in jail. The maximum sentence for this offence is 25 years.

If you're out on the street at 8am or 6pm, remember that the official flag-raising and lowering, accompanied by a bugle, requires you to stand still in silence. The same rule applies when VIP convoys pass you on the road, or when a funeral procession goes by.

WILDLIFE Much of the indigenous wildlife was hunted out during the war years of the 1960s and early 1970s, or lost its habitat to defoliants or subsequent land clearance. Still, for such a small country, the fauna can be rewarding and it's likely that thorough investigations would turn up a few species unsuspected in this part of the continent. The best areas to look are the hilly southeast, parts of the forested centre, and the outer islands. The large terrestrial mammals are no longer found anywhere, but many species of monkeys and antelopes and some unusual coast dwellers – **manatees**, saltwater-dwelling **hippos** in the Bijagós islands (a UNESCO Reserve), and large **sea turtles** – compensate for this. Reptile life is prolific. Guinea-Bissau has no national parks, although before the war of 1998/99, there were plans to create one in the south of the country

WOMEN TRAVELLERS AND THE WOMEN'S MOVEMENT Men and women can mix freely in Guinea-Bissau, without their association carrying implicit sexual connotations. For women travellers, this makes the country one of the most relaxed in West Africa. Guinean women fought in the war of independance and their presence in the ranks of the revolutionary cadres made a lasting impression in the traditionally conservative and Islamic parts of the country. In these areas, the issues of female emancipation are still fairly hot ones. But the signals received by the rest of the world – that a sexual revolution was taking place in the country – have never been convincingly borne out in the communities and the movement's momentum slowed down in the 1980s, though the structures remain. Contact the União Democrática das Mulheres (UDEMU) if you're interested (☎21 40 81 or 21 27 40).

A Brief History Of Guinea-Bissau

Guinea-Bissau was first visited by Europeans in 1456, when Cadamosto, an Italian navigator working for the Portuguese crown, sailed as far as the Rio Mansôa and the Bijagós islands looking for the gold which figured so hugely in the trans-Saharan trade. Other sailors settled on the uninhabited Cape Verde Islands over the following decades. By 1500, these communities had sprouted subcolonies on the Guinean mainland: groups of Portuguese or mixed-race immigrants, partly absorbed into African society, trading with the interior and looking to the ocean. More about this early history of European contact is detailed in the Cape Verde chapter. The emphasis here is on the period of Portuguese colonialism and the brief era of independence since its demise. The story of the region's more ancient past, before 1400 – and of influences from within West Africa – is virtually unknown, except that it didn't result in powerful states or dynasties.

■ Kriolu society

Through the first half of the sixteenth century, the region traded out to Europe an average of over 200,000 grammes of West African **gold** every year. But with the opening up of the "New World", from the later years of the sixteenth century onwards, much of the region which is now Guinea-Bissau, was drawn into the Atlantic **slave-trading network** which linked West Africa with Europe, the Caribbean, South and North America through the Cape Verde archipelago.

Cacheu was the headquarters: by 1600 it had as many as 1000 Kriolu (mixed-race) slave traders and employees. Portugal established a military garrison in 1616 in order to guarantee the maximum revenue to the crown, charging duty on exported slaves and sending cargoes on to the Cape Verdes where they paid further duty. Other towns were established at Farim, Ziguinchor and, later, Bissau and Bolama. But despite Portugal's efforts, the benefits of trade tended to bypass Lisbon. French and English ships could offer better trade goods and more choice. Repeated efforts by the Portuguese government to enforce **trading monopolies** in their area of influence simply pushed traders into illegal commerce. The state administrators charged with extracting taxes and levies invariably exploited their positions, so that **corruption, smuggling** and **state control** became inextricably tangled.

The **slaves** tended to come from the least stratified ethnic groups of farmers, fishers and hunters; Fulup and Jola, Manjak and Pepel. The main **slavers** were Mandinka and, later, Fula. The Bijagó were notorious slave-hunters too, launching lethal canoe raids against the mainland. It was a circular business, however. Who was slave and who slaver depended much more on economic strength or vulnerability and on family contacts and position, than on "tribal identity". It wasn't unusual for a king or headman to sell off people under his own rule, such was the attraction of cloth and other imported goods. **Firearms** were available from the early eighteenth century to those who could afford them.

With the general **abolition of slavery** in the early nineteenth century, the slave trade from Guinea continued illicitly, given new life by the needs of Cuba's plantations. Domestic slavery (which was not abolished) was commonly used as a cover. The last big shipments, however, crossed the Atlantic in the 1840s.

Meanwhile, using labour locally, rather than selling it off unproductively, became significant with the introduction of **groundnuts**, first grown along the Gambia River at the end of the eighteenth century. Philip Beaver's attempt to start an English colony of groundnut planters on Bolama had been a disaster (see box on p.455), but local Kriolu landowners had more success. Agreements were made with Bijagó elders on Galinhas and Bolama, from where the crop was spread to the shores of the Rio Grande on the mainland. On the islands, the plantations used slaves. On the shores of the Rio Grande they called them contract labourers, with tools, transport, food, clothes and accommodation charged to the plantation workers out of their share of the crop, usually leaving nothing for wages. Portugal, however, even more than before, benefited little from the exploitation of its colonies. As much as eighty percent of the crop was sold to French trading concerns.

In 1879, Portugal's Guinean territory was separated from Cape Verde administration. The French had occupied Ziguinchor and, following a brief British occupation, **Bolama** became the **first capital** of "Portuguese Guinea".

■ The Portuguese province

The emptiness of Portugal's pride in its "colonial empire" – at least in the case of Guinea – continued through the end of the nineteenth century, and the formal carving-up of the continent. The **partition of Africa** after 1885 left Portugal with a scattering of territories, of which Guinea-Bissau was perhaps the least promising. Portuguese set-

tlers weren't interested in going there for fear of the climate; and there appeared to be no attractive natural resources. Then, **Fula aggression** – jihads against non-Muslim plantation workers and raids on the foreign-run *feitoria* groundnut stations along the Rio Grande – soon led to a slump in the country's only viable export. With the region now formally annexed to Portugal, only Bolama (the capital from 1890), and the fort-towns of Bissau, Cacheu, Farim and Gêba, were in any sense under colonial rule.

Military campaigns of "pacification" took fifty years to subdue the state of general **revolt** which ensued in the 1890s. And in that time there was precious little thought in Lisbon about the administration of Guinea or the other African territories. It was somehow understood that they had always been a part of Portugal, so there was no specific colonial service, and no consideration of the purposes of colonialism, beyond furthering the greatness of Portugal and extending its benefits to those Africans who could demonstrate their "civilization". The republican government in Portugal, wracked as it was by one military intervention after another, and by costly involvement in World War I, continued virtually to ignore Guinea.

Hut taxes were imposed and labour conscripted to help maintain the colony with as little support from Portugal as possible. Almost the entire African population was classified as **indígena** – disenfranchised, second-class non-citizens. Opportunities for education were very limited, and in practice most urbanites with prospects were Cape Verdeans, or the descendants of Cape Verdean marriages. They, together with mixed race Kriolus and a tiny proportion of **assimilado** mainlanders (less than one in 300, often Fula), formed the bulk of the civil service, as government agents and tax collectors. Cape Verdeans held many professional posts as well.

It was from this small middle class that the first calls were heard for political reform. Before World War I, a political group called the **Liga Guineense** campaigned for the interests of small traders and landowners, highlighting the abuse of powers by government agents and calling for a change in the laws favouring the big commercial enterprises. The Liga was outlawed in 1915 without making much impact, but it provided a background – the only indigenous political example – for the radical demands of the PAIGC that emerged forty years later.

The **groundnut trade** began to pick up after about 1910, though it crashed again in 1918 when a law came into force prohibiting peasant farmers from trading their crop to foreign buyers. The law was repealed, and by the 1920s, the central parts of the country, particularly around Bafatá, had become the groundnut heartland. The pressure to sell all surpluses to agents of Portugal, however, only tended to stifle production.

Despite the heavy exploitation and inequalities, there was a looseness in governing the overseas territories that failed to suppress the freedom of expression completely. The paternalistic idea of **"colonial trusteeship"** was taken seriously by some: Portuguese culture allowed a vague and distant respect for Africans stemming partly from its own infusion of African culture during the medieval Moorish occupation. But these sentiments were smothered after 1926.

Guinea under the Portuguese "New State"

The military intervention in Lisbon in 1926 was unexpectedly different from previous ones. Instead of installing a new government and withdrawing, **General Carmona** presided over the installation of a military dictatorship which was to last until 1974, holding Portugal back and crippling her overseas territories. **António de Salazar**, a monetarist economics professor, was prime minister from 1932 until 1968. He promulgated the Estado Novo, or **"New State"**, and ran Portugal on strictly authoritarian lines. The "Province of Guinea", along with the other parts of "Overseas Portugal" were brought to heel. The last pockets of resistance to the colonial invasion were finally "pacified" in 1936 and any chinks of progressive light from republican days were blacked out by the quasi-fascist curtain now drawn across the country.

Guinea was forced into becoming one giant groundnut and oil palm plantation with **compulsory planting and purchases**. Small traders were banned from dealing in cloth and alcohol, while Portuguese commercial agents tried vainly to interest the people in Portuguese wine and cotton clothing.

With economic repression, passbook laws and a continuation of forced labour (reduced to only five days a year after World War II) came an unwieldy and over-staffed **bureaucracy**. All potential sources of opposition were organized into officially sanctioned associations, from within which their members could be scrutinized by the PIDE – Salazar's political police force. For over four decades, there was an almost total suspension of political life.

In the 1950s, **Amílcar Cabral**, an agronomist of mixed Cape Verdean and Guinean parentage, was working in the colonial service, conducting agricultural censuses across the country. He analysed his remarkably detailed land use surveys in Marxist terms of modes of production. His conclusions convinced him that mechanization, collectivization, a rejection of the groundnut mono-culture and a return to mixed farming could transform Guinean society and set the country on a path to socialism. His reputation as a subversive assured, he quit the service and left the country.

■ The war of liberation

In Bissau, the capital since 1941, a small coterie of African tradesmen and Lisbon-educated civil servants began gently agitating for independence from Portugal. On September 12, 1956 Cabral (briefly back from work in Angola) and five others met secretly and formed the Partido Africano da Independência da Guiné e Cabo Verde (**PAIGC**). With painstaking discretion and patience they recruited people to their ranks. Within three years they had about fifty members.

The spark for armed conflict came with a **dockworkers' strike** for a living wage in 1959. On August 3, police confronted the strikers on the **Pidjiguiti** waterfront in Bissau (see box overleaf). When they refused to go back to work the police opened fire at point-blank range, killing fifty men and wounding more than a hundred. The massacre and subsequent police interrogations, convinced Cabral and the party leadership that peaceful attempts in the towns to bring about independence would be fruitless. Cabral, his half-brother Luiz, and Aristides Pereira went to Conakry (newly independent from France) to set up a party headquarters and training school. In Guinea-Bissau, others began organizing, clandestinely, in the countryside, for **social revolution** and a **war of liberation** against the Portuguese.

Other nationalist groups were forming at the time, both inside Bissau and in Senegal. Their ideologies tended to be less well-honed than PAIGC's. They were prepared to accept a transfer of political power without a transformation in the economy, and they didn't work on behalf of the Cape Verde Islands. Nor did they approve of the

"SINCE PIDJIGUITI WE NEVER LOOKED BACK"

Jose Emilio Costa worked for the Bissau Port Administration when this report was first published. In 1959 he took part in the Bissau dockworkers' strike that ended in a bloody massacre at the small Pidjiguiti pier. Fifty workers were killed and over a hundred wounded.

When I started working at the docks in 1949, conditions in Guinea were difficult. Many people were without work and food was always short. Our wages were almost nothing and the work hard, but we were glad not to be starving and accepted it, more or less.

This began to change after several years. More and more Africans became aware of what colonialism was doing to our country and tried to improve the situation. At the dock we formed a club to collect money and send youngsters to study in Portugal. But the Portuguese didn't like it and one administrator, Augusto Lima, tried to stop our activities. There was also an African worker by the name of João Vaz who always spoke against what we were doing. Some people in the club weren't dockers; Rafael Barbosa, for instance, was a construction worker and Jose Francisco a sugar cane worker. They were both active in the Party and so were Caesare Fernandes, Jose de Pina and Paulo Fernandes who worked with me. But this was something very few people knew at the time.

Most of us worked for the big Casa Gouvea company [part of the giant Companhia União Fabril's empire], either on the dock or on boats taking goods to and from company shops all over the country. But with our low wages, life was becoming more and more difficult. The basic wage was only ten escudos [approximately 15 pence/23 US cents] a day. In 1959, after much discussion in the club and at work, we finally decided to ask for higher wages.

The manager was Antonio Carreia who had just left his post as colonial administrator to work with Gouvea. Well, he refused even to listen. Of course, this was the first time in Guinea's history that workers united to confront their boss. So, Barbosa and Augusto Laserde said that we had to go on strike and show them we were serious.

On 3 August we all gathered at Pidjiguiti, about 500 men. Nobody worked, neither on the dock nor on the boats. Carreia came down and shouted and swore, but we just looked at him without moving. At about 4.30 in the afternoon several trucks of armed police arrived. First they sealed off the gate to the street, then they ordered us back to work. When no one obeyed, they began moving slowly down the pier, now packed with striking workers.

This old captain friend of mine, Ocante Atobo, was leaning against the wall of the office shed. When the line of police reached the spot where he was, an officer suddenly raised his gun and

Cape Verdean intellectuals who characterized PAIGC's executive. These other groups coalesced into the Front for the Liberation and Independence of Portuguese Guinea (FLING), based in Dakar under Leopold Senghor's sponsorship.

Morocco was the first country to supply the PAIGC, based in Dakar, with arms. There had been scattered attacks by the PAIGC from 1961, but military action began in earnest in January 1963. Senghor and Touré reluctantly allowed the guerillas to launch operations from Senegal and the Republic of Guinea. In Europe, the Scandinavian countries voiced their solidarity. Internally, the most enthusiastic insurgents were the brutally exploited, rice-planting **Balante** of the southwest, around Catió. But co-ordination of their sabotage attacks with PAIGC strategy was often tenuous. At the other extreme, many **Fula** communities in the north and east – long established in a feudal framework which had Islamic sanction, and posi-

tively supported by the Portuguese – resisted subversion, or tried to prevent their peasants from being politicized.

As large stretches of bush and countryside became liberated, and then the first few towns, the guerillas of the PAIGC became consolidated into an effective, mobile army, clearing the way for a network of **"people's stores"**, **new schools**, **medical services** and **political institutions**. Portugal attacked their bases with weaponry purchased from **NATO**: West Germany played a key role in supporting the airforce. Napalm was used and the fighting, at times, was as intense as in Vietnam. In retaliation, the guerilla army – the People's Revolutionary Armed Forces (FARP) – persuaded the Soviet Union to deliver arms on a regular basis.

While the war continued with relentless success for the liberationists, the first **internal cracks** were being felt in their upper ranks. All

shot him point-blank in the chest. Ocante collapsed in a pool of blood. For a split second everyone froze – it was as if time stood still. Then hell broke loose. The police moved down the pier, shooting like crazy into the crowd. Men were screaming and running in all directions. I was over by my cousin Augusto Fernandes' boat, the *Alio Sulemane*. Augusto, who was standing next to me, had his chest shot wide open; it was like his whole inside was coming out. He was crying: "Oh God, João kill me, please". But it wasn't necessary; when I lifted his head from the ground he was already dead.

Now all the men were running for the end of the pier. The tide was out so all the boats and *pirogues* were resting on the beach. To hide there, however, was impossible since the police, standing high up on the dock, were shooting right into them. One officer was kneeling on the edge firing at those trying to get away in the water. All around me people were shouting "Run, run!", but I stayed beside my dead cousin. "No, if they want to kill me, let them do it right here".

I don't know how long this lasted when a PIDE inspector named Emmanuel Correia arrived and ordered the firing to stop. The last one to die was a boatman hiding in the mud under his *pirogue*, out of sight of the police. A Portuguese merchant, however, spotted him from his apartment window and shot him in the back with his hunting rifle just after Correia had arrived. One Portuguese, Romeo Martins, always a friend of the Africans, had been trying to keep the police from shooting, but all by himself he couldn't do much.

When the massacre finally ended I saw dead and wounded men all over: on the dock, on the beach, in the boats, in the water – everywhere. Among the dead were Caesare Fernandes and Jose de Pina who had worked for the Party. Afterwards we were taken to the police for interrogation. For three straight days I had to report to the administrator, Guerra Ribeiro, who wanted to know who had organized the strike. My answer was always the same: "We all organized it; our wages were so bad we had no choice". Later, when Ribeiro had finished his enquiry, the wage went up to 14 escudos a day.

Soon after the massacre a message from Amílcar Cabral was secretly circulated among us. It said that August 3 would never be forgotten and that now we had to organize to win our independence from Portuguese colonialism. Since then we never looked back. Many other workers and I joined the Party and started the difficult work of political mobilization here in Bissau. With experience of Pidjiguiti behind us, we knew that we had to accept the risks and sacrifices of an armed revolution to win freedom for our people.

Reprinted from *Sowing the First Harvest: National Reconstruction in Guinea-Bissau* (1978), LSM Press, California.

PAIGC decisions were now being taken in Conakry by the Cape Verdean leadership. Increasingly the need to co-ordinate a national policy came into conflict with democratic imperatives. Although Cabral enjoyed enormous support and trust, his growing stature as a world leader physically distanced him from his half-million followers. In many liberated areas, there were very few democratically elected representatives between the top leadership and the people. Only at the village level were local committees elected, and then only to discuss how to implement party strategy, not to consider the strategy itself. Beyond the villages, the exigencies of war stalled and diverted elections. Party cadres with regional responsibilities were often unaccountable.

Cabral was conscious of these difficulties. In 1970, the war could have been won in a few months as heavy armaments had just been delivered from Eastern Europe. But Cabral decided to hold off the final assault on Bissau because the weapons were only useable by Soviet-trained Cape Verdeans. He thought it would only reinforce the unpopular high profile of Cape Verdean power-holders. After seven years of fighting, however, all the indications were that the mass of the people were fed up with the war and popularity would have been more likely to follow a swift end to it.

External factors intervened. In November 1970, an **invasion force of Portuguese troops** and African collaborators set off from Soga island in the Bijagós to attack Conakry, in the Republic of Guinea, with the intention of assassinating President Sekou Touré and Amílcar Cabral. They failed, and retreated in chaos (see p.482). But two years later, a more carefully planned action in Conakry, involving PAIGC traitors who sought a deal with the Portuguese dictatorship, led to the **assassination of Amílcar Cabral** on January

20, 1973. This was only partially successful because the party, nurtured for so long by one of Africa's most radical and humane political thinkers, did not disintegrate. Portugal's plan to install a puppet "liberation government" in Guinea-Bissau had no chance of success. Nonetheless, the damage to morale was serious and the leadership vacuum plain to see. Aristides Pereira took over as party chief and Luiz Cabral as president-in-waiting.

Major weaponry (heat-seeking SAM–7 missiles) came straight into play after Cabral's assassination. One aircraft after another was shot down. The Portuguese, in a hundred or so military camps across the country, were increasingly besieged by a confident People's Army under the general command of **João "Nino" Vieira** (later to succeed Luiz Cabral as president). In four months, through the end of the dry season of 1973, the Portuguese lost the war. With their airforce demoralized and growing discontent among their conscripted troops, rumbles of revolution began in Portugal itself.

On September 24, 1973, in the liberated village of Lugajole in the southeast, the People's National Assembly (elected the previous year in ballots held throughout the liberated zones) declared the **independence** of Guinea-Bissau. It only remained to kick out the enemy. Around the world, dozens of countries recognized the new republic and the United Nations passed a resolution demanding Portuguese withdrawal. The **coup in Lisbon** on April 25, 1974, by army officers of the Armed Forces Movement (MFA), made withdrawal inevitable. Despite a summer of political crises in Portugal, and repeated efforts by the right wing to find a way of hanging on, Portugal and the PAIGC signed a treaty on September 10 and the last Portuguese troops were gone within a month. **Luiz Cabral** became the new head of state, while the party leader and senior ideologue, Aristides Pereira, became president of the new sister republic of Cape Verde.

The colonial bequest to the newly independent country was dismal. Guinea-Bissau had only a handful of graduates and doctors, and only two percent of its population, at most, were literate. It's industrial base consisted of one brewery – there was no other manufacturing plant – and there was almost no energy production. Earnings from exports barely covered a tenth of the cost of imports, and the Portuguese had left a colossal national debt.

■ Independence: the first six years

The PAIGC took over a centralized and autocratic administration. Far from Amílcar Cabral's optimistic ideas of a decentralized state – of ministries scattered across a nation devoid of the usual top-heavy capital city – the party's preoccupations were almost all in **Bissau**. Realistically, with a population of 90,000 (many of whom had worked with the Portuguese to the end) the domination of Bissau city was inevitable. The urgency of the takeover, the shortage of resources (material and human) and the refugee problem in the capital, all led to government by crisis-management. The peasants of the liberated zones, who had supported the party and the war for so long and at such cost, were hardly consulted: nor were the minor-ranking party cadres who now expected to receive the fruits of independence.

Apart from national reconstruction, there was **political work** to do in Bissau. Compared with the peasants of the liberated zones, some of whom had lived under PAIGC government for ten years, not only were the Bissauans the least influenced by the war's ravages, they also tended to be the most cosmopolitan, the most educated and the most cynical. Now that the PAIGC was in control, they had to come to terms with it, but not necessarily support it down the line.

There were national **"elections"** in 1976, with voting consisting of a "for" or "against" to candidates nominated to the Regional Councils (who themselves elected the members of the National Assembly). There were no alternative candidates. Results showed the widest dissent in the traditionally suspicious and anti-PAIGC northern and eastern regions, a fifteen percent opposition in Bissau, but over ninety percent support everywhere else.

The broad approval seems surprising in light of the **difficulties** the party was having in delivering on its independence promises to build a new society. Bissau city, for example, received over half the country's resources – justified by Luiz Cabral in terms of attracting foreign aid agencies (who poured funds into the country between 1976 and 1979) and investors. **Drought** damaged the prospects of new agricultural projects and efforts to become self-sufficient in food made no progress. A joint fisheries enterprise with Algeria was a flop. The ludicrous N'Haye car assembly plant was a grotesque waste of money, as was the over-massive and never finished agricultural processing plant at Cumeré near Bissau. Salaries in the wallowing state sector were eating away (in fact *exceeded*) the national budget. The currency was kept overvalued, and inflation soared while in real terms agricultural production and exports declined. In a remarkable echo of the fascist "New State" policy, the government tried to control the marketing of produce, setting prices at levels too low to be worth selling at and perforce encouraging a black market economy. People in the rural areas could no longer afford basic imported goods like soap and matches.

The persistent street rumour was that all this was the fault of the Guinea-Bissauans of Cape Verdean origin who, in many cases, had kept civil service positions since Portuguese times. Many of the "People's Stores" were run by them, too, and often corruptly. But it was their visibility, as part of the self-interested and irrepressible middle class, that made them popular scapegoats for a **failing economy**.

In November 1980, an "Extraordinary Session of the National Assembly" had discussed the unification of Guinea-Bissau and the Cape Verde Islands. Luiz Cabral, having increasingly isolated himself, refused to budge on the issue, or on the misallocation of state funds to Bissau city and prestige projects. Four days later, came the largely bloodless **coup of November 14**, which toppled his government.

■ Guinea-Bissau in the 1980s

The Commissioner for the Armed Forces, **Nino Vieira**, revoked the constitution and took control of the country. Luiz Cabral was detained on Bubaque, then allowed to fly to Cuba. Guinea-Bissau remained in the charge of the military for four years. Despite popular anti-Cape Verdean sentiment, the new "Provisional Government", formed in 1981, looked much like a rearranged version of Luiz Cabral's. Several of Cabral's Cape Verdean ministers had fled, but Vieira was adamant in his speeches that Cape Verdeans were welcome in Guinea-Bissau, and that the two countries' destinies remained linked.

One of the first announcements of the new government, was the disclosure of a series of **mass graves**, containing up to five hundred bodies, in the Oio region northeast of Bissau. The story was taken up by the foreign press. Vieira's intention was to point out the summary justice meted out by his predecessor's government to dissidents and those who had collaborated with the Portuguese. But counter-claims by a furious **Aristides Pereira** (the president of Cape Verde) who believed Vieira had sabotaged any chance of unification, said that Vieira had known about the murders and was even implicated. Cape Verde set up its own party, and broke relations.

As it entered its second decade of independence, prospects for Guinea-Bissau had hardly improved. And by 1982 Vieira was already repeating history, closing himself off in a tight cabal of close advisers and shuffling his cabinet according to the dictates of his personal security. **Coup attempts**, allegations of plans for coup attempts and widespread repression characterized the early 1980s. In 1984, however, there was a shift to a freer climate with new elections (of the same type as before), a rewritten constitution and a return to civilian power. But still the plots continued. Despite international appeals (by Amnesty International and the pope among others), **Paulo Correia** (vice-president) and five co-accused, were executed in July 1986 after a trial of over fifty people, mostly Balante, for an attempted coup the year before. Six more of the accused were said to have died in prison.

None of this, of course, helped the government to run the country effectively. Although the **IMF** and the **World Bank** had given loans, the **austerity measures** on which they were conditional were hardly followed through and, despite debt rescheduling, the country's economic plight continued to worsen. The heady years of progress in the liberated times of the 1960s seemed light years away.

In August 1986, however, the government finally agreed to the **abolition of trade laws** that had reserved all import and export licences for state monopolies. The *peso* was massively devalued, knocking the life out of the black market and encouraging potential investors. Support for Vieira's government was suddenly stronger as exports rose impressively and the domestic economy began to revive. Within a year, Guinea-Bissau was entering into long-term agreements with the IMF and World Bank to **restructure the economy**, prune the state payroll by a third, reduce fuel subsidies and boost agriculture, fisheries and technical training. Although the countryside still lagged behind Bissau, the economic future began to look a little brighter. **Cashew nuts** continued to be the most valuable export, and many farmers were paid for their cashew crop in rice. The negative side-effect of this policy was a serious alcohol problem from the widespread distillation of cashew juice from the fruits, which have no other use.

■ The democratic era

In the late 1980s and into the early 1990s, political opposition to the one-party state increased. The banned **Movimento Bafatá**, with offices abroad, upped the pressure in 1990 with demands that the PAIGC should hold talks with it or face unspecified consequences. At the same time, and in common with other African partners of the World Bank and IMF, Guinea-Bissau was asked to reform its political institutions as a condition of further aid.

By the beginning of 1991, Vieira had set a schedule for **multiparty elections**. He also cut the link between the PAIGC and the **military**, which had supported the party in its early years (and which had, in turn, been mollified by kickbacks). The army had long felt betrayed by the years of independence from which it had received so little benefit, but this event marked the start of the slow crisis of relations between the government and the military, which culminated in the war of 1998/99. Increasingly, soldiers turned to making a living from regional cannabis smuggling and arms trading to the MFDC rebels in Casamance.

Over a dozen small **new political parties** were formed and recognized between 1991 and 1994. Among the most important were the Partido para a Renovação Social (PRS), headed by Dr Kumba Iala; FLING, the old Frente da Luta para a Libertação da Guiné (banned for 30 years and exiled in Senegal until 1992); and the Resistência da Guiné-Bissau–Movimento Bah-Fatah (RGB-MB), formed from the previously outlawed Bafatá movement.

Safeguards in the registration process ensured that none of the new parties had an entirely ethnic or regional basis, though as preparations for democratic elections got underway, the special interests of each group became clear. The PRS, for example, was dominated by the Balante, while the RGB-MB began as a vaguely right-wing movement of business interests with Mandinka and Fula support, opposed to the Marxist rhetoric of the PAIGC in the 1980s. However, once the PAIGC had shed every vestige of socialism from its agenda, it was hard to see how it differed from a party like RGB-MB, except in the ethnic allegiance of its membership.

While there were efforts on all sides to preserve the ethnic harmony which has traditionally characterized Guinea-Bissau, the brief campaigns mounted by the parties before the elections were mostly personality-led and ignored the big issues facing the country. At least Kumba Iala's PRS campaigned for the restoration of state property held in private hands – an open threat to the PAIGC elite about which they were remarkably phlegmatic. Meanwhile, **coup rumours** continued, with at least one attempt reported nearly every year.

The **elections**, when they were finally held in July 1994, were surprisingly trouble-free. Despite the torrential rain, power cuts and general muddle – with ballot boxes and papers arriving late due to lack of transport – the turnout was high, the mood good-humoured and the results widely judged to reflect a fair poll. The PAIGC won just under half the votes for seats in the national assembly (which, however, gave it 64 of the 100 seats), while Nino Vieira, the incumbent president and leader of the PAIGC, won a similar proportion of votes for president. To win, Vieira needed an outright majority, which he obtained a month later in a run-off against his closest rival, leader of the PRS, **Kumba Iala**, winning 52 percent of the vote against Iala's 48 percent.

Iala, Guinea-Bissau's most charismatic and trenchantly outspoken politician, complained, not unreasonably, that the PAIGC had been able to use the resources of the state, particularly in the remotest areas, to weigh the dice in Vieira's favour. Tactics included heavy-handed campaigning among largely illiterate communities and the denial of seats to Iala's poll-observers on the only helicopter flying to outlying islands. In fact, in the capital the votes were 53 percent to 47 in favour of Iala. Nevertheless, Iala's acceptance of his defeat seemed to bode well for the future stability of the country.

Guinea-Bissau's **economic plight** continued to worsen, however. The PAIGC government seemed powerless to halt the slide (and was, in the view of many observers, complicit in it) and appeared immune too to the scathing reproaches of the opposition and the majority of the electorate, whose only viable course of action was **mass protest** – strikes, street demonstrations and opposition censure of government incompetence. Entering the CFA franc zone in April 1997 added further to the miserable lot of most Guineans, as inflation spiralled.

■ The civil war

But it was the deteriorating situation in Senegal's Casamance region, on Guinea-Bissau's northern border (see p.217), which finally tipped the country into civil war. A Casamance-bound arms cache was discovered at a military barracks and the chief of staff, Brigadier **Ansumane Manè** (a Jola, born and raised in The Gambia, and with close connections to the Casamançais), was sacked. He then dragged President Vieira into the imbroglio by claiming, persuasively, that support for the Casamance separatists was long-established in Bissau military circles and Vieira had been fully aware of it.

When news emerged in June 1998 that Vieira was planning to halve the strength of the army from 20,000 men to 10,000, a group of **rebel troops**, led by Manè, seized strategic locations around the capital, including the airport, and demanded Vieira's resignation and immediate elections. Dakar and Conakry sent troop reinforcements to shore up the Vieira regime, and **war** broke out in and around Bissau city. Diplomats and expats were evacuated, a quarter of a million Bissau residents fled the capital into the countryside and towards the Senegalese border, which was promptly closed, and virtually the entire army joined Manè's forces. Efforts by President Jammeh of The Gambia to bring the sides together came to nothing, as his partiality in the conflict is widely suspected.

Talks between the government and Manè's side, brokered by Cape Verde, were held on the island of Sal, and a grudging **stalemate** held until December 1998, when Manè and Vieira agreed to a power-sharing arrangement. The Senegalese troops were eventually caught up in renewed fighting in early 1999 and had to withdraw, while the contingent from Guinea Conakry and smaller forces from other West African nations, sustained serious losses before also pulling out.

Finally, in May 1999, remaining loyalist troops surrendered to Ansumane Manè after fierce fighting in Bissau, and Vieira was granted political asylum by Portugal. Ansumane (now General)

Manè installed the former leader of the national assembly, **Malam Bacai Sanka**, as acting president, and elections were announced for November 1999.

A luta continua

There is an **international dimension** to the Bissau war. Since Guinea-Bissau's adoption of the CFA franc, it had been clear that Vieira was aiming for closer co-operation with Francophone West Africa (an admittedly rather mistrustful Dakar in particular) and Paris – trends viewed with great unease by Kumba Iala and many others in the opposition, who have traditionally looked for support from the Casamance and The Gambia and who have had sympathetic coverage from the Portuguese media.

Manè's mutiny evidently goes back to independence war days, when Amílcar Cabral was assassinated by PAIGC traitors who hoped to do a "liberation" deal with the Portuguese fascists. Nino Vieira, in many eyes, has turned out to be part of that legacy – the victorious army commander who went on to depose the revolutionary leader's brother (President Luiz Cabral) in 1980, promising true socialism but delivering only impoverishment while he enriched himself and his cronies.

As this book goes to press, in mid-1999, the **future prospects** for Guinea-Bissau – and for Casamance, with which it is now inextricably linked – are deeply uncertain. The new government may temporarily have the support of the opposition, and of the population at large, but it seems likely that President Abdou Diouf in Dakar, and his ally Lansana Conté, in Guinea, will redouble their efforts to establish a regional settlement that denies both independence for Casamance and the economic and tactical support from that region on which Manè's troops have come to depend. At the start of the new millennium, there seems tragically little prospect that any of Amílcar Cabral's message to the people of Guinea-Bissau "to live better and in peace, to see their lives go forward" will quickly come to be realized.

BISSAU AND THE NORTHWEST

In times of peace, the majority of overland travellers approach the relaxed capital, **Bissau**, from the north, using one of several overland routes from southern Senegal to travel for a day or so through **northwest Guinea-Bissau**. These routes aside, the northwestern region has little to offer apart from the vast beach along the coast at **Varela** – one of the best reasons to come to the country.

Bissau

BISSAU itself isn't a sightseeing city, but there are one or two visits worth making and the city is not without architectural interest in its narrow nineteenth-century houses with their wrought-iron balustrades. More memorable, however, is the city's absence of tension and clamour, which comes as quite a surprise if you've just arrived from one of the adjacent Francophone countries. Things have degenerated a little in recent years, however, and you'll have to be careful in the markets and at night, as there are occasional muggings.

Every year in November, after the rains, when the ground is steaming off its last sops and the sun begins to burn through, Bissau is struck by a swarm of flying crickets (*grilos*). At night they zoom into lights and batter against the walls as a handful of municipal sweepers come out with hoses and brooms. In the morning they litter the pavements and float in their millions down the gutters. After decades of neglect, Bissau is still one of the most impoverished of West African capitals, but it's on the move again: imported cars dodge the rusting shells of abandoned vehicles and new offices sprout between derelict buildings. The annual plague of *grilos* seems like a hideous goad in the right direction.

Arrival, information and city transport

There's one main road into Bissau. If your **arrival** is by bush taxi, you should normally be deposited at the **Mercado Bandim**, a busy market in a low-rent commercial quarter of the same name. Since the recent fighting however, the drop-off site has been moved out of town beyond the embassies. A taxi into the centre from here will cost around CFA200–500. The **airport** at Bissalanca – closed at the time of writing – is only 11km from the centre, but too insignificant to have much in the way of facilities. In normal times, private charter taxis meet all flights, but you can get shared transport too, or walk down to the main Safim–Bissau road and pick up a ride there: it's not far.

For **tourist information**, visit the Ministério do Comércio e Turismo (☎21 32 82) on avenida do 3 de Agosto near the fort. Ask to see the Secretaria de Estado do Turismo – Secretary of State for Tourism – who may be helpful.

Bissau's municipal **public transport system** consists of a fleet of small, green and white buses – most numerous along the avenida do 14 de Novembro – and a network of bus stops (marked *Paragem* – "bus stop"). Bus routes may not be clear to newcomers but most of Bissau's needs are within walking range. In any case there are masses of blue and white **taxis** and fares are low: expect to pay around CFA150 a ride.

Accommodation

The choice of **accommodation** in Bissau offers little of good value, even if you can find a hotel that's not full, and if you're travelling on a budget, you'll find you spend more on lodgings here than you're accustomed to. You could try hanging out at the *Imperio* where one or two friendly, multilingual hustlers are usually helpful with cheap, private rooms.

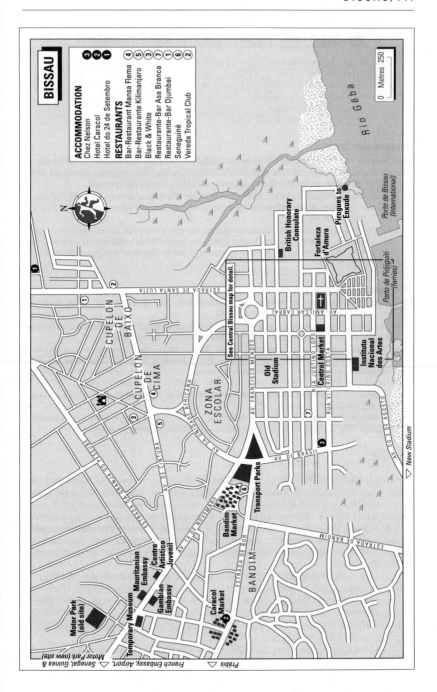

BISSAU

ACCOMMODATION
Chez Nelson — ❸
Hotel Caracol — ❷
Hotel do 24 de Setembro — ❶

RESTAURANTS
Bar-Restaurant Mansa Flema — ④
Bar-Restaurante Kilimanjaro — ⑤
Black & White — ③
Restaurante-Bar Asa Branca — ⑦
Restaurante-Bar Djumbai — ①
Seneguiné — ⑥
Vereda Tropical Club — ②

0 — Metres — 250

Rio Gêba

Porto de Bissau (International)

British Honorary Consulate

Pirogues to Enxude

Fortaleza d'Amura

Porto de Pidjiguiti (ferries)

See Central Bissau map for detail.

ESTRADA DE SANTA LUZIA

CUPELON DE BAIXO

CUPELON DE CIMA

AV AMILCAR CABRAL

Instituto Nacional des Artes

RUA JUSTINO LOPES

RUA VITORINO COSTA

Old Stadium

Central Market

AV FRANCISCO MENDES

ZONA ESCOLAR

AV DA UNIDADE AFRICANA

AV DE CINTURA

AV DO BRASIL

AV DO 3 DE AGOSTO

New Stadium

Transport Parks

Bandim Market

AV 14 DE NOVEMBRO

ESTRADA DE BOR

BANDIM

ESTRADA DE BANDIM

Caracol Market

Centro Artistico Juvenil

Mauritanian Embassy

Temporary Museum

Gambian Embassy

Motor Park (old site)

ESTRADA DE PESSUBE

Motor Park (new site)
Temporary Museum
French Embassy, Airport,
Senegal, Guinea &
Prábis

Inexpensive lodgings

Chez Nelson, rua Justino Lopes. Private accommodation – some of the cheapest in Bissau. ①.

Grande Hotel, av Pansau Na Isna (☎21 34 57). A long-standing, but run-down alternative to the *Pensão Centrale* but more likely to have a vacancy – mostly AC, non-S/C twins. ④.

Hotel Caracol, near Caracol market, about 2km from the city centre. Secure, stiflingly hot rooms, with portable fan (but no guarantee their generator will be on) and basic shared facilities. The cheapest hotel in town. ②–③.

Pensão Centrale, av Amílcar Cabral (up the blue stairs; ☎20 12 32). S/C rooms rented on strictly FB basis, often to long-stayers – so you'll need to win the heart of the Portuguese matron who runs it to have any chance of getting in. The place is not very secure however, and has a reputation for things going missing. ③.

Mid-range and luxury hotels

Hotel Aparthotel Jordani, tucked in a quiet street near the *Grande Hotel* (☎20 17 19). Well-managed, mid-range hotel, with pleasant rooms. ⑤–⑥.

Hotel do 24 de Setembro, Estrada de Santa Luzia (☎21 52 22; Fax 21 19 55). Established and spacious luxury complex 2km north of the centre, with a pool and car rental agency. ⑥–⑦.

Hotel Hotti Bissau, av 14 de Novembro (CP 107; ☎21 12 24). Located near the airport, this hotel was traditionally the place where contracts were signed between flights – a focal point for everything happening in the country. Unfortunately it was bombed during the fighting in 1998 and left in a pretty bad state; check to see if it's reopened. Amex and Visa cards accepted. ⑦.

Hotel Tamar, corner of rua 12 and av 12 de Setembro (☎21 48 76). Pleasant S/C rooms, renovated to quite a high standard. ④–⑤.

Pensão Sergio Centeio, 16 rua Antonio Mbana (☎21 29 66). Poorly advertised, and also known as *Pensão Lunar*, this has secure rooms around a courtyard and relatively good prices. ④.

The City

If you're in Bissau at the time of the **carnaval** – February – you'll get a lopsided view of the city's entertainment value as an endless stream of floats and elaborate papier-mâché masks is paraded through the streets. You can see the best creations (there's usually a theme, and winners) all year at the Instituto Nacional des Artes, on avenida do 3 de Agosto. Otherwise, there's little to see in Bissau. The covered **central market** is an obvious attraction, but its range of produce and other goods isn't huge and bargaining less of a custom here than you may be used to, which can keep prices frustratingly high.

There's no museum at present but the national collections, including modern ethnic artefacts from around the country, can be seen out on the avenida do 14 de Novembro in a large school near the *Hotel Hotti Bissau* – though in practice this is often closed. The building marked on the IGN map as the museum is in fact the UNTG (National Workers' Union) building which does, at least, have some gloriously lurid and intense paintings in the entrance hall and up the stairs.

Down by the port, you won't miss the impressive **Pidjiguiti Memorial** to the striking dockers massacred here on August 3, 1959 (see p.439); and on a wall at the bottom

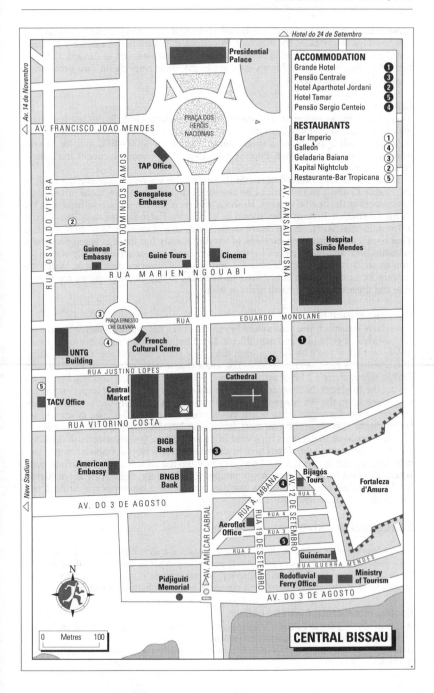

△ Hotel do 24 de Setembro

ACCOMMODATION
Grande Hotel ❶
Pensão Centrale ❸
Hotel Aparthotel Jordani ❷
Hotel Tamar ❺
Pensão Sergio Centeio ❹

RESTAURANTS
Bar Imperio ①
Galleon ④
Geladaria Baiana ③
Kapital Nightclub ②
Restaurante-Bar Tropicana ⑤

Presidential Palace

PRAÇA DOS HERÓIS NACIONAIS

AV. FRANCISCO JOAO MENDES

TAP Office

Senegalese Embassy ①

AV. DOMINGOS RAMOS

RUA OSVALDO VIEIRA

AV. PANSAU NA ISNA

Hospital Simão Mendes

Guinean Embassy

Guiné Tours

Cinema

RUA MARIEN NGOUABI

②

PRAÇA ERNESTO CHE GUEVARA

RUA

EDUARDO MONDLANE

❶

③

French Cultural Centre

④

UNTG Building

RUA JUSTINO LOPES

Cathedral

❷

TACV Office

⑤

Central Market

RUA VITORINO COSTA

BIGB Bank

❸

American Embassy

BNGB Bank

❹ Bijagós Tours

Fortaleza d'Amura

AV. DO 3 DE AGOSTO

AV. AMÍLCAR CABRAL

RUA A. MBANA

AV. 12 DE SETEMBRO

RUA 5

RUA 4

RUA 3

RUA 2

Aeroflot Office

RUA 19 DE SETEMBRO

⑤

Guinémar

RUA GUERRA MENDES

△ New Stadium

N

Pidjiguiti Memorial

Rodofluvial Ferry Office

Ministry of Tourism

AV. DO 3 DE AGOSTO

0 Metres 100

CENTRAL BISSAU

of avenida Pansau Na Isna you'll easily find a beautiful and unprotected tiled mural from colonial days. Regrettably, the imposing **Fortaleza d'Amura** is still a military barracks and there's no way you'll get in to look around. The **mausoleum** of Amílcar Cabral is located within, but even Guineans only get to pay their respects on rare occasions – reportedly on September 24.

Crafts

There has been an enormous resurgence of **strip-woven cloth** in the last few years, with Pepel- and Manjak-speakers the main weavers. You'll find a decent selection at the Mercado Bandim, prices for a single *pagne* around CFA3000–4000 and for heavier weaves perhaps twice as much. Popular patterns include *kassave* (a check) and *volta de Bissau* (bands).

You'll usually find a spread of **carvings** and similar souvenirs opposite the bank by the *Pensão Centrale* and on Praça Che Guevara, and there are always one or two stalls of artefacts at the central market. However the recommended place to browse is the **Centro Artistico Juvenil** (also known as the Centro Padre Batista; daily 9am–1pm & 3–7pm), located 3km from the centre on the north side of avenida do 14 de Novembro. This boys' centre produces carvings of varying quality but there is some fine craftsmanship here and many pieces have real flair. Look out for telling family statuary – woman supporting kids and husband – and beautiful, cowrie-inlaid stools. Watch the carvers for as long as you like: there's no pressure to buy although prices are reasonable and there's a mass of small items as well.

Beaches around Bissau

If you have transport, you can explore beyond Bissau – but renting a bicycle from a private owner is a good plan and not difficult. Don't bother struggling to get to the beach unless you know you'll be there at **high tide**. Tide tables are available from the offices of Guinémar, 4 rua Guerra Mendes. The nearest **sea swimming** is at **Perfilis**, near Prabis, where there's a bit of artificial beach – 18km from Bissau and reached by following the road past the new stadium. **Quinhámel** (39km; follow the airport road) has a fine beach, on the Rio Mansôa creek shore, and quite possibly the best food in the country at the Portuguese-run beach **restaurant**, 1km from the town down a shady track. **Punta Biombo** (22km further), has a nice, but tiny beach on the open sea.

Heading out on these short trips west of the city centre you pass through the intensively farmed lands of the **Pepel** people, the road winding like an English country lane in a deep trough between fenced and carefully tended raised fields – a curious landscape. The Pepel (one of the country's smaller ethnic groups, numbering about 60,000) used to take slain enemies' heads as trophies, but are more famous now as brilliant artisans, doing fine iron- and leatherwork.

Eating and drinking

Street food is poor in Bissau, limited to ubiquitous oranges, bananas and groundnuts, with doughnuts a treat at CFA50 a go. If you're in search of cafés with no names and basic meals, head for the Bandim quarter, where avenida de Cintura meets the main airport road. In the centre there are a couple of well-established **restaurants**.

Central restaurants, bars and cafés

Bar Imperio, av Amílcar Cabral. For watching the world go by, putting it to rights, and playing draughts, this can't be beaten. Snacks are available.

Geladaria Baiana, Praça Che Guevara. An ostentatious place to write postcards over croissants and coffee.

Grande Hotel, av Pansau Na Isna. The *Grande*'s terrace is one of Bissau's few rendezvous and there's generally fresh lemon juice and sandwiches worth patronizing (the *Grande*'s restaurant proper is something of a joke).

Pensão Centrale, av Amílcar Cabral (1–3pm & 8–10pm). A reliable lunch and dinner spot, dishing out three courses and a banana in a style that can't have changed in thirty years. They still apply the beer-only-with-food rule. CFA3000.

Restaurante-Bar Tropicana, av Osvaldo do Vieira. Moderately upmarket meat and fish dishes.

Restaurants and cafés away from the centre

Restaurante-Bar Asa Branca, rua Justino Lopes. Upmarket Portuguese and African fare.

Restaurante-Bar Djumbai, north of the centre near the *Hotel do 24 de Setembro*. A modestly priced alternative to guests of that establishment and anyone else who's longing for a Guinness.

Seneguiné, Estrada de Bor. Busy both at lunch and in the evenings, and serving up inexpensive local food.

Entertainment and nightlife

Before the war of 1998/99, the UDIB – a kind of sports club next to the cinema on avenida Amílcar Cabral – occasionally put on **theatrical performances**. The Instituto Nacional des Artes had a performance venue for infrequent output by the Ballet Nacional, while the French cultural centre often sponsored worthwhile events.

Entry to local **clubs** is normally reasonable at around CFA500. A taxi is worth renting for the evening but don't leave finding one too late, and be prepared to risk some of the fare on the driver's knowledge: Bissau has plenty of action under the surface. For a popular, unpretentious and very youthful disco check out the *Vereda Tropical Club* which occasionally hosts live sounds. *Kapital Nightclub* is plush and expensive.

You can **drink** after dark in the centre, with no danger of disturbance by sweaty bodies, at the nameless *kirintim* bar across from the *Imperio* at Praça dos Hérois Nacionais. Alternatively, the flamboyant *Galleon* is open very late and keeps its AC high and its vibes as sophisticated as possible. During *carnaval* bars crop up all over the place.

There are also some worthwhile nightspots out of the town centre. In the lively district of **Cupelon de Cima**, you can follow your ears, or try the *Black & White* or the nearby *Bar-Restaurante Kilimanjaro*, unpretentious *bairro* dance clubs along avenida de Cintura. Local artists perform occasionally at the *Bar-Restaurant Mansa Flema*.

Listings

Airlines Air Sénégal, at the airport; Air Afrique, at the airport and on av Amílcar Cabral, underneath *Pensão Centrale Hotel*; Aeroflot, 6a rua 19 de Setembro (☎20 13 10); Air Mauritanie, Pilon district; TACV (Transportes Aereas Cape Verde), corner of rua Vitorino Costa and av Osvaldo Vieira (☎20 12 77); TAP (Air Portugal), 14 Praça dos Hérois Nacionais (☎20 13 59).

American Express No proper agent in town. The *Hotel Hotti Bissau* is most likely to offer help.

Banks and exchange The Banco Internacional da Guiné-Bissau, on av Amílcar Cabral, will change your travellers' cheques and cash, after considerable delay. It is possible to get an advance on your credit card but this will be difficult and expensive. You can also change money at the forex bureau by the *Pensão Centrale* or with street changers outside the main post office or in the market.

Bookshops Pama Papeleria, at the south end of av Domingos Ramos, sells books and magazines in Portuguese, French and English, plus maps, postcards and an excellent range of stationery. You can also get newspapers and books at the cabin on Praça Ernesto Che Guevara.

MOVING ON FROM BISSAU

Bissau is the centre of all transport activity in the country. **By road**, most public transport normally leaves from the motor park off avenida. do 14 de Novembro. However, during the recent fighting of 1998/99, this site was moved out of town on the way to the airport. The location may move again, so check out the latest situation locally.

Ferry details and tickets are available from Rodofluvial on avenida do 3 de Agosto. Their office is on the left-hand side of the entrance to the port. Approximate frequencies and journey times (one-way) are:

Bissau–Bolama–Bissau: out Fri/Sat, back Sun (3hr).

Bissau–Bolama–Catió–Bolama–Bissau: out Tues, back Fri (9hr).

Bissau–Bubaque–Bissau: out Fri, back Sun (4–5hr).

Bissau–Biombo–Pecixe–Biombo–Bissau: out Sat, back Sun (4–5hr).

Other destinations with at least twice-monthly service include Empada, Xime and Cacine.

For information about **international shipping** check out Guinémar on rua Guerra Mendes. Bissau is a port where you might, with time and luck, find a passage: Conakry two days, Lisbon six days, Hamburg eight days.

Car rental Try Tupi Car Rental at the *Hotel do 24 de Setembro*, or talk to Guiné Tours on av Amílcar Cabral, who can help you find a private car with driver to hire.

Cultural centres The French cultural centre, on av Domingos Ramos, is worth checking out if you're in town for any length of time. The Portuguese equivalent up in the Zona Escolar has a good library – all Portuguese.

Doctors Ask your embassy or consulate. Cuban doctors, resident at the *Grande Hotel*, have in the past been helpful to travellers with routine stomach and malaria problems. Socomed, north of Praça Ernesto Che Guevara, also have some good doctors.

Embassies and consulates include: France, av do 14 de Novembro, near *Hotel Hotti Bissau* (☎25 10 31); The Gambia, av do 14 de Novembro; Guinea, Ua Marien Ngouabi (CP 396; ☎21 26 81; $45 for a one-month visa); Mauritania, near the Centro Artistico Juvenil in Chapa; Portugal, 6 rua de Lisboa (☎21 12 61; Fax 20 12 69); Senegal, near the Presidência do Conselho de Estado (☎21 26 36); UK, Jan van Maanen, Honorary Consul, Mavegro; USA, av do 14 de Novembro (CP 297; ☎ & Fax 20 11 59). Note that although a Cape Verdean ambassador is accredited to Guinea-Bissau, there's no trace of a Cape Verde embassy: see if the Portuguese embassy can help with visas.

Hospital Hospital Simão Mendes, av Pansau na Isna, just north of the *Grande Hotel*.

Travel agents Guiné Tours, on av Amílcar Cabral, can help with general information and car rental (see above).

Visa extensions If you need to renew your visa, you do so at the immigration office at the airport at Bissalanca, 11km from the city centre.

The Northwest

With the exception of the beautiful beach at **Varela**, the northwest of the country is little visited except by travellers passing through on their way from Senegal to Bissau; **São Domingos** (closed at the time of writing) is the country's principal entry point from its northern neighbour. Now that the ferry from São Domingos to **Cacheu** has stopped operating, the old route south to Bissau – via **Canchungo** – is rarely used; most travellers instead take the tarred road via Ingoré and Bula (see p.431 for further information). Note that this whole northwest region is jammed between the troubles in Casamance and refugees from further south, so the practical details that follow may be only of historical interest.

Canchungo and Cacheu

CANCHUNGO has a reputation as a happening place. The fine avenue of trees running into town gives a favourable first impression, and the central *praça* is alive with people waiting for transport – a renascent market area with sellers of boiled starch and oranges. Just off the square are a few places where beer, meals and rooms are available.

CACHEU, 100km from Bissau, has nothing much to offer. There are no restaurants, little in the way of shops or food, and just one hotel, currently closed; your only other accommodation options are camping somewhere in the town or finding an accommodating local. A traditional "fair" or market is held every eight days. Cacheu is the site of a sixteenth-century fort, the whitewashed substance of which (only twenty metres square) is still in place, along with its guns, and more ruins to the right, down on the shore. Notice the unusual material used on the roads in Cacheu: broken oil-palm kernel pits which are very hard-wearing, like vegetable gravel.

São Domingos and Varela

If you're stuck in **SÃO DOMINGOS**, there's a **restaurant** where they'll always rustle up a solid meal and, just opposite, a dirt-cheap **pensão**, the *São Felipe* (②), as well as a small market offering imported delicacies from Senegal.

The beach at **VARELA**, a wonderful place with gorgeous swimming, pine trees and low cliffs, is better than those across the border in the tourist ghettos of Cap Skiring, and largely empty but for local people. As a place to come for the weekend, Varela is a favourite among Guinea-Bissau's small expatriate community.

Accommodation is available at the *Jordani Hotel*, which offers pleasantly tiled AC, S/C rooms on the stepped cliffside, and good, though not inexpensive, food (enquiries through the *Jordani* in Bissau on ☎20 17 19; HB ⑥). The same hotelier also has a house with small annexed huts, which is pretty basic with shared facilities (②). More competitively priced than the *Jordani* is a new Portuguese-run hotel in Varela village, which also has a good restaurant.

Getting to Varela can be difficult, necessitating a fifty-kilometre earth-road journey west of São Domingos. This road can be very muddy after rain, but it's a beautiful route and very unaffected by tourism. Monkeys are a common prey here, their bodies slung from sticks over the hunters' shoulders.

THE BIJAGÓS ISLANDS

The **Bijagós archipelago** is the largest along the West African coast; at least sixteen inhabited islands in the main cluster – principal of which is **Bubaque** – plus the inshore islands of **Bolama**, **Pecixe** and **Jeta** and dozens of smaller islets.

The islands are mostly covered in dense forest, with large stands of oil palm and cashew groves, less impressive patches of cultivation and necklaces of white sand or mangroves along the seashore. The islanders – predominantly Bijagó-speakers who've lived surrounded by these calm, warm waters for centuries – are remarkably autonomous: you'll see women in palm fibre skirts (*saiya*), who've never left their own island. Many of the more remote islands felt little effect from the centuries of Portuguese presence in the region (several were never, officially, "pacified" at the end of the last century when the rest of the country was being shot into line). And several still have only the most tenuous of links with whoever happens to be in government in Bissau, or with the outside world.

Paradise the islands are, in a way – there are even snakes in some abundance to fit – but the cost in practical terms is inconvenient **ferry connections** and an almost complete lack of facilities outside the two very small towns of Bubaque and Bolama. To these two islands come 99 percent of the few travellers who make it out here. Bolama, so close to the coast, is relatively straightforward to visit, though as ex-capital, the existence of just one hotel is mystifying. Bubaque has the distinction of being the country's only "tourist resort" – don't be misled by that – and its range of accommodation has increased in recent years.

Bolama

A warped sliver of jungle and farm plots, 25km long by 5km wide, pressed in on most sides by dense mangroves, **BOLAMA** is the easiest island to visit. In the past it exercised the imaginations of the British as well as the Portuguese, and was the subject of a protracted colonial dispute in the nineteenth century. Today, where the jungle has been cleared, cashew trees for the export crop sprout between scattered termite mounds. The town of Bolama, although becoming more built up, is still a pleasant, quiet place facing the mainland and there are several super beaches on the south coast.

Some history

Curiously, the first colonial adventure attempted on Bolama was conducted by the **British** in 1792 (see box, opposite) and they tried again in 1814. But the agreements with local **Bijagó** elders on which these incursions were based were no more binding than the treaties the Bijagó had also signed with the **Portuguese**. And it was the latter – particularly the mixed-race Cape Verde islanders – who survived both Bolama's fevers and the Bijagó warriors long enough to establish a real community. Throughout the nineteenth century the British returned periodically to claim sovereignty by pulling up the Portuguese flagpoles, shouting at the settlers and shipping their domestic slaves off to liberation in the colony of Sierra Leone. But they made no serious efforts to settle permanently, or to take charge of the island, until 1860, when Bolama was annexed

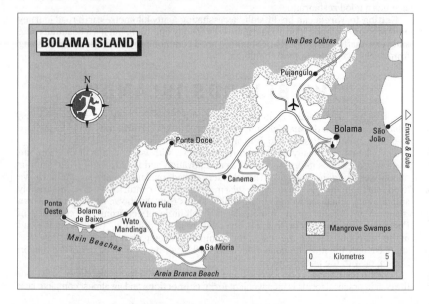

BEAVER'S COLONY

If the **British expedition to Bolama** had resulted in a successful colony, the map of West Africa might today be radically different. **Phillip Beaver**, 26, set sail from Gravesend on April 4, 1792 with 274 prospective settlers. Included among them were a ready-made Legislative Council and Governor, chosen in the Globe Tavern, London.

The first deaths occurred through smallpox before they had reached the Isle of Wight, and by the time the two ships, *Hankey* and *Calypso*, were nosing through the Bijagós islands six weeks later, half the passengers had malarial fever. Bolama, at first, seemed perfect and uninhabited, and those colonists who were well enough went ashore to chase elephants and butterflies, lie in the sun and collect oysters. Beaver was irritated at their lack of industry. They saw a Bijagó war canoe but Beaver insisted "the inhabitants were thought to be of peaceable disposition, well-inclined towards the English culture". A week later the warriors attacked, surprisingly well-armed with muskets and Solingen swords, killing and wounding a dozen people and kidnapping several women and children. The settlers' cannons had never even been unpacked.

The colony looked doomed from then on. Although the captives were released when Bolama was "bought" for £77 worth of iron bars from a pair of local headmen, over half the emigrants chose to continue to Sierra Leone in the *Calypso* in July. As the rains set in, the remaining 91 died of malaria at a remarkably even rate until by the end of the year there were only thirteen survivors. A typically laconic entry in Beavers' journal reads:

Sun 2nd Dec. Killed a bullock for the colony. Died and was buried Mr. Webster. Thermometer 92. Three men well.

Beaver and five others survived the rains of the following year and he and a companion sailed back to England in May 1794. "An ill-contrived and badly executed, though well intended expedition", he mused. The timing, arriving at the start of the rains, could not have been worse. His book was entitled "African Memoranda: Relative to an Attempt to Establish a British Settlement on the Island of Bulama on the Western Coast of Africa in the year 1792, with a Brief Notice of the Neighbouring Tribes, Soils, Productions Etc., and some Observations on the Facility of Colonising that part of Africa with a View to Cultivation; and the Introduction of Letters and Religion to its Inhabitants but more particularly as the means of gradually Abolishing Slavery". Published in 1805, and hugely readable, it's worth scanning the antiquarian bookshops for.

to Sierra Leone, hundreds of miles to the south. The Portuguese, desperate to preserve their stake in the slave trade which the British were busy trying to abolish, had formally lodged their own claim in 1830 and by the time the British annexed the island, there were 700 loyal Portuguese subjects living there. The dispute wasn't settled until 1870, when a commission headed by United States President Ulysses S. Grant found in favour of Portugal. Grant's efforts were rewarded with a statue in the town square.

Bolama town

The town of **Bolama** is on the landward side of the island, facing the mainland barely two kilometres away. Hollow, and partly deserted, it echoes with the past grandeurs of the Portuguese empire. Solid mansions attest a century of trading in ivory and forest products and the opening up of the West African groundnut industry, but since the capital of Portuguese Guinea was transferred to Bissau in 1941, Bolama has been steadily crumbling away. The town is still the seat of government of Bolama Region, however, which includes most of the islands and a little chunk of mainland. It has its own regional president, a hospital, a nurses' school and a teacher training college.

Walking around the town will take you all of forty minutes. Down by the port you'll not miss the ugly **sculpture** bestowed on the island by Mussolini after an Italian seaplane crashed here in 1931 (Bolama used to be a "hydrobase" on the Rome to Rio de Janeiro seaplane route). The solid construction of the monument means it hasn't fallen victim to the tide of nationalism which knocked Ulysses Grant off his pedestal near the bandstand in the overgrown main *praça*, a few minutes' walk from the seafront. The grandest buildings in town surround this main *praça*, and include the colonnaded **Governor's Palace**, the **post office** and the abandoned, Manueline-style **Hotel de Turismo**. This upper part of town reeks of post-colonial decay, though in fact most of the buildings are still in use. The only reminder of Britain's ephemeral presence on Bolama is down to the left behind the church: the reddish two-storey ruin almost throttled by rank undergrowth is the **Casa Inglesa**, a monstrous edifice built entirely of corrugated iron. Architecturally, at any rate, the Portuguese deserved to win the island.

There's a pleasant evening stroll out of town past the secondary school and down an attractive, sandy avenue of trees, with compounds set back on both sides – surely a colonial conception, but one that's endured. Out this way too, at the start of the avenue on the left, there's a rather Gothic graveyard which is worth a look: a curious assembly of souls, including a number of middle Europeans and even one or two Britons. Rapid brown snakes shimmer out of the way as you walk.

Around the island

Fork right at the end of the avenue out of the town and you soon find yourself on a delightful, narrow lane, twisting through cashew groves. There are no beaches down here, but you do pass a **cashew jam factory** which is open a few days every year – they make more deadly cashew wine than jam (out of the fruits, not the nuts) – and a cloth manufacturing plant that evidently hasn't been open from the day the looms were delivered. Passing through the hamlet of Pujangulo, the path becomes a muddy track through the mangroves at low tide, at which time it joins the main island to the **Ilha das Cobras** – an uninhabited islet. Exciting stuff, but watch out for snakes on the other side and don't get stranded by the tide. The walk is about 15km there and back.

There are other, shorter walks you could do in the peninsula immediately south of Bolama town. But the main interest lies **further south across the island**. Down here, unless you're prepared to set off early with food and water sufficient for a couple of days, you're really going to need transport. The dirt road cuts through pretty forest, farm and plantation lands, following the central ridge of the island (maximum elevation just 26m), never far from the sea. The people you'll meet are mostly Bijagó, though it's the women who stand out (many men are away labouring) and whose apparel is so distinctive. Although bras and cotton *pagnes* have arrived, the traditional costume of palm fibre kilt (*saya*) is still the standard wear for most women, though officially banned from the town and frowned on by missionaries. For rural Bijagó, tourists are a sensational novelty and you'll occasionally find children for whom such a meeting is a first.

Hamlets and clusters of compounds are, in many cases, named after ethnic groups. Some 17km from Bolama you turn left at Wato Fula and plunge into a tunnel of cashews. **Areia Branca beach** is a further 7km down here, a narrow lip of white sand dipping beneath the coconuts into a milky blue sea. It's said to be the best spot, and you're unlikely to find it anything but deserted, but there are other beaches along the southern coast. This corner of the island is very sparsely populated and you can nose around for hours completely alone. Remember, however, if you're tempted to knock off a few coconuts for their milk and flesh, all the trees are individually owned.

Practicalities

The **ferry from Bissau** to Bolama has been awaiting repair for some time now; check with the Rodofluvial office in the main port to see if it is operational again and to confirm the timetable. *Pirogues* operate on the weekends (Fri–Mon); the rest of the week you may be able to persuade one of the fishing boats to transport you. Otherwise, you can take the long route to the island via **Enxude**, which faces Bissau on the mainland: to get there, take a *pirogue* (Mon–Sat 1 daily between 7–8am; CFA1000) from Limpar port near the port official's building (*Al fandigo*) in Bissau. Once at Enxude, catch a Buba-bound bush taxi and get off at the junction to hitch the final 20–25km to São João, from where *pirogues* ply the short journey across the channel to Bolama.

Facilities for visitors on the island are very limited. There's one **hotel** (fan and shared bathroom; ②), run by the helpful Rucas – who may also act as your tour guide – and a **restaurant** by the harbour, although you have to order in the morning for your meal in the evening. You can normally spend a night or two here under a *paillote*, on the understanding you buy the odd meal. A local woman runs another, cheaper, restaurant in her house; ask anyone around town where to find her. Should you have problems finding somewhere to stay, you may come across aid workers or missionaries willing to put you up. A good idea is to bring your own **tent**, and a better plan still is to bring some wheels of your own. It's really worth tracking down **bicycles** to rent in Bissau and bringing them with you. Exploring the island otherwise means a lot of foot work, which is feasible but more difficult. There's no more than a handful of vehicles.

On the question of **food**, the only shops are in Bolama itself, and they don't amount to much at all. There's a limited market (in a large, walled marketplace) where a small selection of fruit and vegetables, fish, peanut butter and bread is usually available. Bring with you what you can from Bissau. What you don't use will find eager recipients.

Bubaque

In Guinea-Bissau, tourism begins and ends in **BUBAQUE**. In colonial days the island was a Portuguese favourite, and after independence Swedish aid provided a hotel (to which excursionists from The Gambia were flown for several seasons in the late 1970s) and a tarmac road to the beach. The trips from The Gambia ceased, to be later replaced by regular visits from French tourists, flying in for the renowned game fishing of the waters nearby.

Getting there

If you are not flying to Bubaque (check the latest situation with Guiné Tours in Bissau, see p.452), the alternative is the weekly Rodofluvial **ferry**, which leaves on Friday, returning Sunday (4–5hr; approximately CFA3500) – barely enough time for a flying visit. There are also less formal possibilities such as the *Vitoria*, a vessel belonging to the Estrela do Mar fisheries department, or small motorized **pirogues** operated by aid agencies and missions, although these latter craft are notoriously unstable in the frequently choppy channel and are not recommended. Prices should be the same as, or less than, ordinary ferry services, but comfort may be even more rudimentary. Take your own food, water and headwear for the hot and exhausting voyage.

On the outward voyage from Bissau, until you have cleared the **Ilha das Galinhas** (a midway stop where disembarking passengers are offloaded to a lighter), a dirty, spume-laden sea as flat as a millpond is the normal view in the dry season. But as you approach the isle of Rubane, the mood improves. The intense tropicality of the green, horizontal islands leaves a strong sense of place, reinforced as you enter the channel between Bubaque and Rubane and see the red tin roofs of Bubaque with its high pier. By this stage of the voyage, it will be low tide. The scene – children picking in the mud, the viridescent foliage of the two islands tumbling to the water, the tranquillity after the racket of the diesel and what seems like bustle in Bissau – is all a bit magic.

Bubaque town

Over the last decade Bubaque's popularity with overseas visitors has increased substantially and the town now offers a number of **places to stay**. The *Pensão Cadjoco*, run by a friendly Franco-Italian couple, has rooms with fans or inexpensive tents, both with full board options and excellent cooking (room only ①–②); they can also direct you to locals happy to **rent bikes** (about CFA2500 per day). Other budget bases include *Chez Paulino Cruzponte* (②), *Campini* ("Chez Nattie la Cubanne"; ②), which is getting an excellent reputation for its atmosphere and management, and *Chez Titi* (①–②), run by a friendly young Senegalese management and with an excellent cook. There are also a couple of more expensive *campements* which offer a good degree of comfort – *La Maina* and *Le Dauphin* (both ⑤). The renovated, but much older *Hotel Bijagós*, formerly the *Estancia Balnear* of the Swedish tourist years, is a 25-minute walk from the town near the airstrip and offers simple, S/C AC rooms of two different standards (☎82 11 44; ③–④).

As for **something to eat**, a good alternative to the expensive *Hotel Bijagós* and the *Cadjoco*, which caters for vegetarians and features local sauces and garnishes, is *L'Escale*, a French restaurant by the jetty which offers a warm welcome and specialities based on locally caught seafood. You should also try the inexpensive and friendly *Chez Raoul*.

Looking around Bubaque village is nice in the early morning and late afternoon. Immensely picturesque seascapes flicker through the mango boughs; oil palms in massive stands, many around the hotel, are covered in the nit-like nests of weaver birds, and resound with their chatter; lizards and butterflies dart everywhere; and mambas are occasionally seen. In the village a **produce market** sets up every morning and a growing number of **shops** sell all sorts of things. The **post office**'s reliability is uncertain but you can make international phone calls easily enough.

Praia da Bruce

It's certainly worth getting down to **PRAIA DA BRUCE**, 15km away on the south coast, for at least one day as it's practically deserted and very appealing. The beach offers shady cashew trees, as much clean sand as you could wish for and an isolation that's palpable – one or two fishermen may come by, stationing themselves in the waves with their throwing nets for hours on end to provide a garnish for the evening rice. All that's left of the *Bijagós* hotel's former annexe on the beach are rotting stools around a derelict bar, half-bald *paillotes*, ruined toilet blocks and evidence of bygone picnics. There's also a beautiful pond of lilies with intriguing rustles and plenty of birdlife. Try to be here when the tide is high, and bring drinking water – lots of it.

Some of the more expensive places to stay in Bubaque can arrange **transport** to Praia da Bruce, although this is pricey. You could alternatively try to fix something up with one of the village's few drivers or, ideally, bring a bike from Bissau or rent or borrow one on the island. The heavily overgrown tarred road to the beach is dead flat; a one-hour cycle ride. There are some tall stands of wild forest still to be seen and signs, too, of old Portuguese estates and villas. The only other road users seem to be women and naked children.

Before the fighting of 1998/99, a plush-looking hotel was under construction at the beach, which may be worth checking out to see if it's finished.

Other islands

Visiting the **other islands** is very much a trip into the unknown. Information is hard to obtain in Bissau; there are only regular Rodofluvial ferries to the inshore isle of **Pecixe** (out Sat, back Sun; 4–5hr), which has a long coastline of beaches facing the open Atlantic, usefully close to its main village, Ijante. Getting to the other islands in the main Bijagós group, Bubaque is the best place to look for **local fishing boats**, and getting from one island to another is often fastest via the hub of Bubaque, rather than direct. Wherever you go, be aware of the fact that the price you pay to get out – and the ease with which you do so – may not be the same on the return trip. The straightforward alternative is to book up a trip with one of the **French outfits** in Bubaque, who charge around £20/$32, on the basis of a four-person group, for a day-trip, and around £25/$40 per 24 hours (all inclusive). You can go as far as time and money permit.

Recognized **accommodation on other islands** consists of two extremely expensive French *campements* on Rubane (*Club Ajaca* and another; both ⑦), a highly recommended Guinean bungalow development on Galinhas (*Hotel Ambancana*; reservations ☎21 55 55 in Bissau; ②–③) and an Italian resort on Maio (⑥). Apart from these possibilities, you're at the mercy of Bijagó hospitality – usually profound – and your own ability to join in without offending people. The question of money is unlikely to be raised, except of course when travelling by boat, but you should be prepared with gifts of food and other small items when occasion demands some reciprocity. There is little experience of tourism out here and any generosity you show is unlikely to be exploited. The Bijagó have very severe sanctions in cases of stealing.

Central and northern isles

Rubane and **Soga** (the latter is the island from which the 1970 Portuguese invasion of the Republic of Guinea was launched) are close to Bubaque and not hard to get to. **Punta Biombo**, 60km west of Bissau, is a reasonable place to get a *pirogue* passage the thirty kilometres to relatively populated and forested **Formosa** island (CFA500–1000). Ask to be dropped at **Nago** in the creek between **Maio** island and Formosa.

On the archipelago's northwest periphery the string of stunning beaches and crystal-clear water surrounding **Caravela** are said to be the jewel in the Bijagós' crown: the island is a traditional stop-off point for cruises from Senegal and The Gambia. If you're in a group, the presence of an airstrip at Caravela suggests it might be worth enquiring about chartering a plane in Bissau: the distance from Bissau is only 80km.

Southern and western isles

The wilder islands are on the archipelago's seaward, southwestern edge and will take a concerted effort to reach with the probability of several days' wait for a return passage. All make Bubaque look cosmopolitan by comparison and offer tremendous rewards to adventurous and flexible travellers. You'll find no shops, police or *pensões*, almost no motor vehicles and negligible outside influence. The tenuous **missionary presence** succeeds only superficially in subduing the islanders' traditional values: clandestine **initiation ceremonies** incorporating the use of *irãn* (fetishes), combine freely with Christian beliefs and practices. You're almost certain to witness the rich cultural life of the islanders, expressed through drumming and dancing.

The marine and terrestrial **wildlife** on these remoter islands is extraordinarily prolific. Exploratory walks through the bush will reveal hornbills, monkeys and even green mambas; sharks and stringrays patrol the shallows. While the mamba's bite has no remedy (just don't get bitten), a ray's excruciating sting is soothed by the islanders with a slice of fresh papaya and a few cow-hornfuls of *canna*.

Eticoga, the principal settlement on **Ilha de Orango**, has an unusual population of saltwater-dwelling **hippos** in the creek east of town (ask if any have been seen recently). The hippos are able to swim between the islands, and are held in some fear by the islanders owing to their penchant for ruining crops and exhibiting menacing behaviour in defence of their young. Local legends on Orango refer to an ancient Queen Pampa: artefacts dating back centuries have been found here.

The islands of **Uracane** (with its colony of flamingos outnumbering the residents a hundredfold), **Uno** and **Unhocomo** take some getting to – and the seas become rough Atlantic swell on the other side of the furthest island, Unhocomo, which is the sea route that must be followed to reach the main settlement, Anaburu. It is therefore even more important to be sure your boat is safe.

THE SOUTH AND EAST

Reserves of enthusiasm for the **Bissau interior** – a patchwork of low ridges, divided by the country's creeks and rivers – run pretty low once you've visited the capital and the islands. From the travel perspective, the rest of the country divides into two: **the south**, a relatively inaccessible and little-known region, fronting up against the Republic of Guinea; and the **east**, hardly explored by travellers either, but Guinea-Bissau's main road runs out this way, with a number of large towns and villages along the line of travel.

The south

Before the 1998/99 war, the south – with its impressive areas of rainforest – was just beginning to open up, with considerable improvements in both roads and public transport. The gateway to the region is **Enxude**, across the Rio Gêba from Bissau and accessible by *pirogue* (see p.44) or by bush taxi. From Enxude, there are always bush taxis waiting to take you to Tite, Fulacunda and Buba. Banana wagons are a popular form of transport around the region.

The main town and transport hub of the south, **BUBA** is situated around a pretty natural port. It has a small hotel (*Buba Hotel*; ③–④), a less expensive Dutch guesthouse (①), two restaurants and a sprinkling of eating houses. Nearby there are swimming beaches and waterfalls along the Rio Corubal, which separates the south from the rest of Guinea-Bissau, but these are most easily reached from the northern part of the country via **Bambadinca** (117km east of Bissau) and the tarmac road down from there to Buba (111km). The falls (mere rapids in the dry season) are at **Saltinho**, near **Mampatá**, the only bridge over the Corubal. A French-run *campement*, *Samba Loba* (③), is located on the north bank of the Corubal, 5km from Mampatá (signposted), down a track. Beautifully situated, it's usually packed to the gills at weekends and school holidays, but it's a fair bet you'd have it to yourself at other times. The only potential drawback is the fact that you are more or less obliged to eat there too (generous and excellent French cooking, but the FB rate puts it into the ⑤ bracket). **Cussilintra**, a dozen kilometres downstream and closer to Xitole, was a colonial beauty spot, like Saltinho, and is still a popular weekend excursion with good swimming nearby. A hotel and restaurant are being built there; alternatively, take a tent and plenty of food. Before the troubles began in 1998, there were plans to set up a **National Park** in the Buba area; ask around to see if it's been designated.

To the south of Buba is the pretty village of **Cacine**, connected to Bissau by ferry (at least twice monthly), but there's not a lot to it. Nearby is another small village, **Jemberem**, where you'll find an area of unspoilt tropical rainforest and the chance to see monkeys, and maybe even chimps and elephants. To get there from Bissau, take a ferry (out Tues, back Fri; 9hr) or bush taxi as far as Catió, then hitch. Alternatively, banana wagons can take you directly there (ask at the banana wagon station near the airstrip).

Northeast of Buba, along a track which skims the Guinean border, is the town of **Boé**, famous as the first place to be liberated from the Portuguese by the PAIGC back in 1967. It's a false reputation, though, as the first town to be liberated was in fact in Boé *district*, a place called **Lugajole** in the deep southeast. A small plaque and hut there commemorate the occasion. Strange, hilly landscapes around Lugajole – the outliers of the Fouta Djalon – are a change from the maze of mangroves and mud nearer the coast.

The east

The two main towns of the interior, **Bafatá** and **Gabú**, are located along Guinea-Bissau's one main highway. You'll find **transport** fairly easily along here with several daily bus and *aluguer* departures between both towns and Bissau, and even reasonable hitching prospects.

It's a good road most of the way, with unremarkable scenery of tall grass and charcoal-burning villages. Before Mansôa, the road forks: right for the east, and left (north) over the Rio Mansôa for the town. **Mansôa**, at the centre of fighting in 1998, has no hotels, but you should be able to find rooms for rent and there are a couple of restaurants, one of which – a circular, thatched affair where you can drink beer, eat monkey and meet locals – is bang in the town centre by the bush taxi stop, and run by a helpful Cape Verdean. Mansôa also has a lively nightclub. The road on to **Farim** and the Senegalese border town of **Tanaf**, is a decent one, with two bush taxis making the journey each day. Plenty more bush taxis operate between Farim and Bissau. There's no ferry operating at Farim at the moment, although one is planned; in the meantime you can make the crossing by small *pirogue*. If you want to stay there's a hotel by the river (*Hotel Kandé*; ②), a Gambian-run restaurant in the centre of town, a video cinema showing English-language action films with Portuguese subtitles and a nightclub, *Altona*, serving cold beer.

Bafatá and around
Continuing east over the old trading river, the Rio Gêba, **Bambadinca** marks the start of the road south to Xitole. The nearby port of **Xime** is the furthest into the interior that regular ferries (at least twice monthly) run from Bissau.

BAFATÁ comes as a surprise, its street lights offering an optimistic welcome, its brick factory apparently turning the red dust that smothers everything into the neat, tiled houses you see all round. It's an orderly, appealing town, perched on a low rise, with an atmosphere as placid as the river which, laced with fishing lines and teeming with fish, winds its graceful course below the town to the west. If you're **staying**, there are two very basic *pensões* to be found in the maze of compounds east of the main road from Bissau: *Apartamentos Gloria* (①) which is attached to a lively nightspot; and *Pensão Fa*, which is cleaner, quieter and even cheaper (①). For **food**, the town has two flourishing markets – the one to the east of town is best – and there are a couple of restaurants, or you could ask around in the compound area for someone willing to prepare you a meal.

The most thriving upcountry trading post of the Portuguese province of Guinea in the late nineteenth century was **Gêba**, 12km west of Bafatá down a side road off the highway on the Bissau side of town. Now virtually a ghost town, Gêba's overgrown **ruins** are worth a look if you're drawn to such places.

Northeast of Bafatá, there's a well-maintained dirt road to the **Senegalese border** at **Pirada**, while a fork crosses a rickety bridge and continues along a deteriorating track to the frontier at Cambaju and on to **Kolda** on the Ziguinchor–Tambacounda road. From Bafatá to Gabú, unusual tall stands of bamboo flank the road.

Gabú
The country's eastern capital, **GABÚ**, is the Fula and Muslim capital too, an animated commercial centre prospering from its triangular trade with nearby Senegal and Guinea. The town itself has little of interest to offer visitors, but it's a convenient stopping place en route to or from Basse, Tambacounda or Koundara and it's used as a base for French-run hunting expeditions into the nearby bush.

USEFUL BIJAGÓ

Bijagó dialects don't vary much. These phrases are from Orango. Some of them are recognizably Kriolu in derivation. Accented letters are stressed syllables.

How are you?	*Ména?*	Water	*Ño*
I am fine	*Ñekagobo*	Good, beautiful	*Ngoséney*
Thank you/		Bad, ugly	*Odéyney*
expression of		1	*Mudíge*
agreement	*Eséyta*	2	*Asóge*
Yes	*Eng*	3	*Oñyóko*
No	*Ñidóku*	4	*Ngoyagáne*
What is your name?	*Amenáwe?*	5	*Modevokóko*
My name is John	*Aynáme John*	6	*Modevokóko na mudíge*
White person	*Ororá*	7	*Modevokóko na asóge*
Black person	*Utúngko*	8	*Modevokóko na oñyóko*
Where are you going?	*Mindánewe?*	9	*Modevokóko*
See you later	*Ñibóy*		*na ngoyagáne*
Rice	*Omán*	10	*Muranáko*
Fish	*Ngokáto*		(with a handclap)

Numbers after 10 are expressed with a combination of claps and the numbers 1 to 9.

There are four **places to stay**: *Mariama Sadje Djaló's*, an unmarked *pensão* with a bar-restaurant, not far from the market (①); *Oasis Hotel*, on the southwestern edge of town (there's a sign on the main road and it's ten minutes' walk from there), which has pleasant, S/C accommodation in small thatched rondavels (②); *Jomav Hotel* (②), which boasts 24-hour electricity, a restaurant and a good nightclub (noisy at weekends); and *Djarama Hotel* (②), conveniently located in the middle of town. Near the market are a bank, a telephone office, a handful of chop houses, and several butchers, where you can choose a piece of meat and have it chargrilled on the spot.

Gabú has good **transport** connections with all points along the road to Bissau, and vehicles heading for Senegal, The Gambia and Guinea pass through with some regularity. The northern route out of Gabú to Pirada and Senegal is a reasonable, maintained track, where you may even have luck hitching.

Into Guinea

The surfaced highway continues east to **Pitche**, and from here the **main road into Guinea** is a rough earth track which winds and bumps its way through the bush – chokingly dusty in the dry season, barely passable in the rains. Direct bush taxis bound for **Koundara** via Pitche, Kandika and Sareboïdo leave Gabú two or three times a week (around CFA5000), and Sareboïdo's Sunday market generates commercial traffic. It's best to expect the unexpected on this route (east of Pitche the road is truly appalling) and bear in mind that the Guinea-Bissauan frontier at Buruntuma closes for lunch. If you stop in the tiny village of Pitche, or if you have your own transport, you should certainly check out the **route south into Guinea** via **Foula-Mori**. On a Monday (market day in Pitche) you should find transport down this narrow track. At the river border, there's a hand-hauled ferry large enough for a small truck. The route is not marked on the maps, but it's a recognized border frontier (further details on p.468) and a journey you won't forget in a hurry.

GUINEA

GUINEA

Between 1958, when it reclaimed its total independence and effectively cut itself off from France, and 1984 on the death of dictator Sekou Touré, the **Republic of Guinea** was an isolated and secretive country. Only in the late 1980s did it begin, hesitantly, to open its borders to tourists.

Today, Guinea holds massive appeal as a place to **travel**. It sprawls in a great arc of mountains and plains from the creeks and mudbanks of the mangrove coast to the savannah of the Niger source-lands and the montane forests on the border with Côte d'Ivoire. The great rivers of West Africa – the Gambia, the Senegal and the Niger – all rise in Guinea. The Michelin map shows more green-bordered roads (*parcours pittoresques*) in Guinea than any other country – always a promising indication.

Guinea's best-known attraction is the **Fouta Djalon** highlands, populated by settled, largely Muslim, Fula herders and farmers; a plateau region dramatically dissected into myriad hills and valleys, spouting waterfalls like a colossal rock garden. The length of time needed to explore the area is the only negative consideration.

Further to the east, on **the plains** where the streams flow away from the sea, and where you feel the cultural resonances of the Niger valley's medieval empires, scattered **historical reminders** – and towns, rather than the sparse countryside – are the focus. To the south, another great highland region, **Guinée forestière**, fronts up against the coastal states in a zone of wet forest and remote peoples, where liana bridges cross the rivers and pre-Islamic tradition survives. One of the biggest weekly markets in West Africa is held up here, at **Guéckédou**.

Guinea's people share a wide cultural diversity. No single language predominates and there's considerable regional variation. **Susu**, the main language of the coastal region, is currently in ascendance and is the language of most of President Lansana Conté's government. Susu, as a Mande language, is related to **Kouranko** and **Malinké** (Sekou Touré's mother tongue, widely spoken in the northeast), as well as to **Kpelle** and **Loma** – minority languages of the highland forests – and to the market lingua franca known as **Dyula**.

Fula, the predominant language of the Fouta Djalon, continues to be under-represented in national life, as it was – maliciously – under the repressive regime of Sekou Touré. There's still deep bitterness among the Fula-speaking community who, with forty percent of the population, are the largest single ethnic group.

Overall, Guinea has extraordinary vitality and newly unleashed confidence – an energy debased only in the capital, **Conakry**, about which it's sometimes hard to be positive.

FACTS AND FIGURES

The **République de Guinée** is often called Guinea-Conakry, to distinguish it from other Guineas – reflection too of the colonial preoccupation with capitals. The population is just under eight million, around ten percent of whom live in Conakry. Guinea's land area (246,000 square kilometres) is about the same as Great Britain or Oregon. Guinea has a colossal foreign debt, estimated to be more than £2 billion ($3.2 billion), which is more than four times its annual earnings from the export of goods and services, yet roughly equivalent to only a month's expenditure by the British Ministry of Defence. The ruling party of President Lansana Conté (who has been in power since 1984) is the Parti de l'Unité et du Progrès, which currently holds 71 of the 114 seats in the national assembly. There are around a dozen other significant political parties.

AVERAGE TEMPERATURES AND RAINFALL

CONAKRY (COAST)

	Jan	Feb	Mar	April	May	June	July	Aug	Sept	Oct	Nov	Dec
Temperatures °C												
Min (night)	22	23	23	23	24	23	22	22	23	23	24	23
Max (day)	31	31	32	32	32	30	28	28	29	31	31	31
Rainfall mm	3	3	10	23	158	559	1298	1054	683	371	122	10
Days with rainfall	0	0	1	2	11	22	29	27	24	19	8	1

KOUROUSSA (MALINKÉ PLAINS)

	Jan	Feb	Mar	April	May	June	July	Aug	Sept	Oct	Nov	Dec
Temperatures °C												
Min (night)	14	17	22	23	23	22	21	21	21	21	19	15
Max (day)	33	36	37	37	35	32	30	30	31	32	33	33
Rainfall mm	10	8	22	7	135	246	297	345	340	168	33	10

MAMOU (FOUTA DJAOLON)

	Jan	Feb	Mar	April	May	June	July	Aug	Sept	Oct	Nov	Dec
Temperatures °C												
Min (night)	13	15	18	19	20	18	19	19	19	18	17	13
Max (day)	33	34	35	34	31	29	27	25	28	29	30	31
Rainfall mm	8	10	46	127	203	257	335	401	340	203	6	8

The years of dictatorship were harrowing, yet they've resulted in a strong political consciousness. And outside the capital, the veneer of European culture which frequently obscures the other ex-colonies is hardly noticeable: Africa shines through very brightly.

Climate

When you visit Guinea – and where you go – is likely to be determined largely by the **seasons**. Off the limited runs of main, surfaced highway, most of the countryside is isolated during the rains which are concentrated between June and October. Many minor routes are completely impassable for days or weeks on end, due to flooding. Be prepared for plans to go awry, though you may find that the spectacular storms, gushing waterfalls and brilliant abundance of greenery are more than adequate compensation.

In the weeks following the rainy season, which is shorter and lighter as you head north to Labé, the Fouta Djalon can be truly delightful. The southeast highlands, too, have a good spell of fine weather, though conditions vary greatly. Away from the coast, and especially in the mountains, temperatures can plummet at night: you need some warm clothes and perhaps a sleeping bag.

As the dry season progresses, travel in the Fouta Djalon and the Malinké plains becomes increasingly dusty and hot. The *Harmattan* winds from the north can bring haze and dust as early as December and by January photographers are likely to be disappointed by the flatness of the light, but poor visibility doesn't always affect regions outside the northeast.

Overall, the easiest time to travel in Guinea is from late November to March. Conakry, at the best of times, has an insupportable climate, with relative humidity rarely below eighty percent and July delivering the heaviest month's rainfall anywhere in West Africa, much of which, fortunately, torrents down at night.

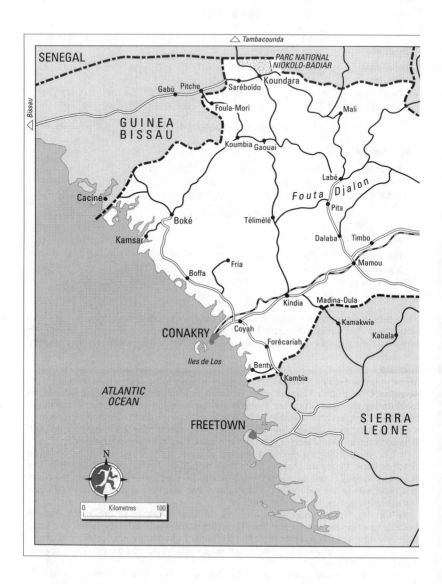

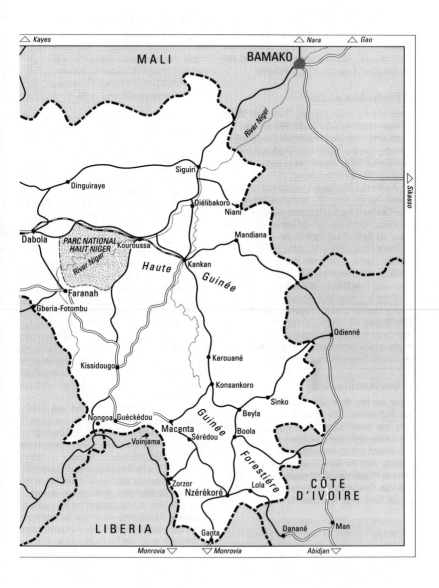

Arrivals

If you're not planning to fly in, there are overland routes into Guinea from all the surrounding countries. Most of these are
endurance tests of one sort or another, but
most also provide fine scenery and wild, little-travelled districts along the way.

■ Flights from Africa

There are flights to Conakry from most **West
African capitals**. Air Afrique (RK) provides the
widest-ranging service with flights from **Abidjan**
non-stop twice a week; from **Bamako** weekly;
from **Dakar** direct three times weekly, and from
Dakar via **Bissau** once a week.

Air Guinée (GI) itself operates the following
weekly flights: from **Monrovia** via **Freetown**;
from **Cotonou** via Abidjan; from **Abidjan** direct;
from **Bamako** direct; from **Dakar** non-stop; from
Dakar via **Banjul**; and from Banjul via **Labé**.

Ghana Airways (GH) is useful too, with twice
weekly flights from both **Accra** – one via
Abidjan and **Freetown**, the other via Abidjan
only – and from **Dakar** via **Banjul**.

Of the less important airlines, Air Gabon (GN)
flies in weekly from both **Lagos** via **Abidjan** and
from **Dakar**; Air France (AF) flies from **Bamako**
four times a week; and **Sabena** (SN) has three
flights into Conakry each week: one via **Banjul**,
another via **Lagos** and the third via **Bamako**.

■ Overland from Mali

There are two main possibilities from Bamako.
The first involves taking a **bush taxi** to Kankan (a
long day, even assuming nothing goes wrong).
The border itself seems usually to be hassle-free.
The second option, when the Niger River is high
enough, and the boat is working order, is the
ferry to Siguiri and Kouroussa, and sometimes
Kankan. This service (weekly at most) is operated
by the Compagnie Malienne de Navigation and

The details in these practical information
pages are essentially for use on the ground in
West Africa and in Guinea itself; for full
details on preparing for a trip, getting here
from outside the region, paperwork, health,
information sources and more, see Basics,
pp.3–83.

usually runs from August to January, although
services are currently suspended (see box, p.520).

■ Overland from Guinea-Bissau

Bissau to Conakry is one of the region's toughest international journeys, liable to be cut by
floods and mud pools during the rains. Public
transport along the various routes, especially in
the border region, is tenuous. If you can arrange a
ride in advance you'll save a lot of waiting en
route.

The "direct" coastal route to Conakry, over the
creeks **from Buba and Cacine to Boké**, is really
not a viable option except at the end of the dry
season – and in any case the places along the way
constitute little incentive to make the attempt.
There is, at least, now a bridge over the Kogon
River, east of Sansalé (20km inside Guinea after
crossing the border from Cacine) where formerly
there was often a long delay for the ferry.

The usual route follows the tarmac through
Guinea-Bissau via **Gabú** and **Pitche** (in Guinea);
thence via **Koundara** and back onto tarmac at
Labé. Bush taxis for Koundara leave Gabú two or
three times a week; the road between Pitche and
the border (which closes for lunch on the Guinea-
Bissau side) is little more than a bush track and
can be empty of passing transport as far as
Saréboido (in Guinea), though Saréboido's Sunday
market generates commercial traffic. From
Koundara there are daily departures for Labé,
through the beautiful northern Fouta Djalon. Note
that officials at Koundara will try to persuade you
to change money with them, but their rates are
poor. Change a note or two only.

You can also cross the border into Guinea
between Pitche and Foula-Mori, connected in
the dry season by a driveable 30km track and a
hauled ferry over the Koliba River. There's some
transport along the way on Monday – Pitche's
market day. You go through Guinea-Bissau (in)for-
malities at the ferry and Guinea formalities at the
friendly Foula-Mori post. Although not marked on
the maps, this is a recognized border crossing.
Koumbia, 80km further on, is then the first town
of any size and from here there's limited transport
to the coast or up into the Fouta Djalon. If you're
heading to Conakry, the road from Koumbia to
Boké is gradually being improved, though it
remains dire in many parts. The coastal forest is
heady compensation and, if you have the means,
a deviation out to the beaches at **Cap Verga** is
well worthwhile.

Driving yourself, in good conditions – and coinciding with the ferry across the wide Fatala River at Boffa – you can do the trip from Koumbia to Conakry in under twelve hours. By **public transport** – in these parts, mostly overstacked bush taxi wagons – allow a couple of days.

■ Overland from The Gambia and Senegal

The choice is between two main routes: firstly the fairly straightforward bush taxi route through **Medina-Gounas** (see p.214) to **Koundara** (see opposite); if you're coming from **Basse** in The Gambia or **Tambacounda** in Senegal, this makes the most sense. Second, there's the more interesting but very tough route from **Kédougou** in Senegal up into the Fouta Djalon to the village of **Mali** and on to **Labé** (for route details see p.214). The large trucks which ply this route take up to three days to cover the 120km of boulder-strewn *piste*. It's not really one for your average off-road Land Rover-type vehicle.

■ Overland from Sierra Leone

In ordinary times, (fighting and insecurity in Sierra Leone may render the following information obsolete) the relatively busy main route via Kambia and Pamelap connects **Freetown** with **Conakry** in a day's travel. As this book goes to press, there is little traffic, but in theory there are one or more buses to the border every day and no shortage of Peugeots and other vehicles to take you on to the pretty town of **Forécariah** and Conakry. There are numerous checkpoints along the way and while the border is normally fairly hassle-free for foreign travellers, lengthy searches and questioning are not unknown. Local people often have a hard time of it and you can expect delays on the buses.

If you've had enough travel by the time you get into Guinea along this route, you might be intrigued to make a side trip down to **Benti** – the country's old banana port and a colonial settlement predating Conakry.

A second important route connects the highland region in eastern Sierra Leone with **Guéckédou**, part of the fastest overland route between Freetown and Bamako (normally four days by public transport, ferries permitting). The point to make for in Sierra Leone is **Koindu**, two days out from Freetown, from where you cross to **Nongoa** in Guinea and get transport to the tarmac at Guéckédou. The *pirogues* on this river

border take bicycles and motorbikes; other vehicles have to pass through Liberia. Note that Guéckédou has no bank.

A third route from Sierra Leone to Guinea is the northern road via **Kabala** to **Faranah**. You might walk this border gap – about 12km from Gberia Fotombu on the Sierra Leonean side to Hérèmakono, the first village in Guinea – and it's attractive, breezy country, but you'll be lucky to find transport until you hit the main road 15km west of Faranah, which might mean a walk of 60km in total. Like Guéckédou, Faranah has no bank.

A fourth possibility is to find transport heading north from **Kamakwie** to **Madina-Oula**, and from here to Kindia or Mamou.

There's also the possibility of a **ferry service from Freetown** to Conakry, although this is currently suspended (see box, p.498).

■ Overland from Liberia

There's a spread of crossing points along the watershed frontier between Liberia and Guinea. But with the amount of smuggling that goes on and the legacy of the two countries' historic mutual distrust, not to mention the more recent refugee problem resulting from the Liberian civil war, it's no surprise to find these borders troublesome. **Main frontiers** are at Foya–Guéckédou (ferry), Voinjama–Macenta, Ganta–Diécké, and Yekepa–Yalézou/Bossou (for Nzérékoré).

There's also the possibility of a **ferry service from Monrovia** to Conakry.

■ Overland from Côte d'Ivoire

There are three main routes from Côte d'Ivoire. The first from **Odienné** to **Kankan** is better than it looks on most maps, but it's still an extremely tough drive and customs checks at the border are rigorous. TARMCI runs a weekly bus service between Abidjan and Kankan, departing Friday, going via Bouaké and Odienné, and arriving Sunday or Monday morning (around CFA20,000).

The second route – handy if you can't catch the bus – is from **Odienné to Sinko** and Beyla. There's a huge market in Sinko (Guinea) on Friday, for which vehicles leave Odienné early Thursday morning.

The third important route is the lovely forest road from **Danané** to **Nzérékoré**. Sometimes you'll find taxis along here and there's always transport on a Tuesday for Nzérékoré's big weekly market. The road is normally passable throughout the year, but it can be surprisingly difficult to find transport to **Gbapleu** – where Ivoirian formalities are conducted – and from there to the Guinean frontier near **Nzo**. You might, with reason, give up a day to walk through the forest: it's magnificent.

Red Tape

Guinean visas – required by all – used to be notoriously difficult to obtain. The situation has changed completely in recent years, with visas obtainable in a number of African cities and officials in Guinea genuinely welcoming to tourists.

Depending on where you apply for a visa, you may simply be required to present your passport with a photocopy of the ID pages, photos and a fee of around CFA20,000. However, some embassies still ask for a letter from a resident inviting you, or a **letter of accreditation** from your own embassy. The embassies at **Accra, Banjul, Bissau, Bamako, Dakar** and **Freetown** have lately been fairly easy. Three-month single-entry visas are the norm, but you can get an extension in Conakry. There are also embassies in **Monrovia** and **Lagos**.

There's a consulate in **London** which issues visas in 24hrs, while the embassy in **Bonn** reportedly issues visas without demur, and not only to people with return air tickets. Enlist the services of a visa agent if you want to get your visa in advance.

For visas for onward travel, apart from the embassies of the six **neighbouring countries**, other useful African embassies in Conakry include **Ghana, Morocco, Nigeria, Togo** and **Cape Verde**. The **French embassy** routinely handles visas for **Mauritania** and **Burkina Faso**. There's a full list of addresses on p.497.

■ Other bureaucratic business

The only **health certificate** formally required is yellow fever but it's best, as usual, to have a cholera certificate too. However, you'll rarely be asked for either.

If you're flying in, you may well be given a **currency declaration form**, though you may not be asked to complete one if you declare less than £2000/$3200; it is unlikely that you will be given one at land borders. If you'll be leaving the country by air you may be required to hand the form in, in which case it must indicate bank transactions.

You no longer need a **photography permit**, but you should still be very discreet.

Other official business in Guinea has been much reduced: the security police in provincial towns generally expect you to present yourself and your passport to them on arrival, but otherwise you'll be left alone most of the time. However, some hotels will still try to hold your passport until you check out, even if you pay first; it's best not to allow this.

Money and Costs

Guinea uses its own Franc Guinéen (FG), a soft currency intended to lead the way to the country's eventual inclusion in the CFA zone. With the abolition of Sekou Touré's syli currency, the Guinean franc was reintroduced at the same value as the CFA franc. It has slipped to a free market rate of FG12,000 to CFA5000. In mid-1999, the official exchange rate for the US dollar was approximately FG1250, so for the pound sterling you could expect about FG2000.

Information about currency declaration forms is given in "Red Tape" above. Although exchange controls have been relaxed, there is still a low-level **black market** – generally ignored by the police – in CFA, FF and US$, which offers around ten percent better rates than the banks. If you have CFA or FF you'll often be able to use them for accommodation and transport.

The lack of **banks** may force you to change money unofficially. The Banque Internationale pour le Commerce et l'Industrie de la Guinée (BICIGUI) is the main, and generally efficient, bank, with branches in **Conakry, Boké, Fria, Kankan, Kamsar, Kissidougou, Labé, Macenta** and **Nzérékoré** (though only in Conakry does it cash travellers' cheques). Don't count on finding banks anywhere else. If you don't have FF or CFA francs in cash you need to plan ahead.

Plan ahead with your FG cash too, once you've got it. Guinean franc coins are practically redundant, their values too small. It's the notes that are used, from filthy, damp twenty-five-franc bills to FG10,000 notes which are almost unuseable except in large towns – change them down to FG5000 and FG1000. Convert only as much as you'll need: you can buy CFA or other currencies with your remaining FG, in border towns – though usually at marked-up prices. Any remaining FG will be confiscated when you leave the country.

The utility of **credit cards**, even in Conakry, is strictly limited to a few of the larger hotels and car rental and air ticket payments.

■ Costs

Guinean **prices** generally compare favourably with those of neighbouring countries. Cheap hotels in most towns will be from FG4000–10,000 a room, rice and sauce doesn't normally cost over FG500, and you can readily get several of most kinds of fruit for FG50 or FG100. Conakry, however, is very much more expensive than the provinces, particularly for accommodation.

Transport costs are also high and can push up expenditure enormously. Seat prices are fixed on the main routes but depend on road conditions and vehicle – expect FG25–30 per kilometre on tarred roads in the west and anything up to FG80 per kilometre on rough roads in the east and northwest, especially those leading to borders.

Health

Guinea provides some of West Africa's roughest travelling and it's this, rather than any intrinsic unhealthiness, which can lead to problems. Out in the wilds, the basic health infrastructure is too limited to be a safety net.

Guinea is largely mountainous, and **temperatures** drop quickly after dark in the higher parts. Travelling by public transport, it makes good sense to keep something warm close at hand: your vehicle may roll for hours into the night with your luggage stowed in some inaccessible corner.

Water, as usual, is a major consideration. Although bottled Coyah water is increasingly available in the provinces, much of what you drink, outside a few main towns, will originate from pumped boreholes, which provide clean drinking water. The huge number of rivers and streams in Guinea means you'll likely end up wading through some of them. But try to limit this and particularly avoid slow-flowing waters and dry-season pools: there's a high incidence of **bilharzia**. There was a significant outbreak

of **cholera** in Conakry during the 1994/95 dry season.

Maps and Information

There are now a few small tourist offices dotted around the country, though most of them do not have any useful or up-to-date information. As for maps, the IGN map of Guinea at 1cm:10km (new edition published 1992) is definitely worth obtaining before you go, and vital if you intend doing any hiking or trail beating.

There are some colonial survey maps around (1cm:1km), but you're only likely to track them down in university libraries. For long stays in Conakry, the IGN map of the capital, although published in 1982, is also worth getting in advance; it's only occasionally available at the *Novotel* and other large hotels in the city.

Getting Around

Most travellers find Guinea the toughest country to get around in West Africa: journeys are frequently long and often follow equally long waits while seats are being filled. Surfaced roads account for only 1700km or so and alternative means of surface transport – the remains of the railway system and the odd river boat – don't add up to much.

There is, however, a **domestic air service**, offering several flights a week between Conakry and provincial towns, although this has cut back recently, with the closure of two airlines leaving just Air Guinée in operation.

■ Bush taxis, trucks and buses

Transport on Guinea's main routes is ordinarily by **Peugeot 504** with between eight and ten passengers. In the hills, they're a lot faster than the clapped-out *cars* and *bâchés* (with up to twenty passengers), but there are also some newer **minibuses** appearing on the roads.

504s tend to stick to surfaced and well-maintained earth roads. Travelling along the country's less comfortable byways is down to valiant and incredibly slow open-backed **goods lorries** – *gros camions* – and, to a lesser extent, elderly jeeps and Land Rovers. You should take some notice of the vehicle's condition and opt for the one least likely to break down or kill you. Price can

SAMPLE ROAD TRANSPORT FARES

Conakry–Kindia (135km) FG2500 by bus.
Conakry–Mamou (285km) FG8000 by 504, FG6000 by bus.
Conakry–Télimélé (265km) FG6000 by *bâché*.
Conakry–Labé (437km) FG12,000 by minibus.
Conakry–Faranah (475km) FG14,000 by 504.
Conakry–Kankan (804km) FG30,000 by 504, FG20,000 by bus.
Mamou–Dalaba (59km) FG2000 by 504.
Dalaba–Pita (53km) FG3000 by 504.

Pita–Labé (40km) FG1500 by 504.
Mamou–Labé (152km) FG6000 by 504.
Labé–Koundara (244km) FG13,000 by 504.
Koundara–Gaoual (111km) FG7000 by Land Rover.
Kissidougou–Kankan (190km) FG5000 by 504.
Kankan–Kérouané (175km) FG7500 by 504.
Kankan–Nzérékoré (383km) FG15,000 by lorry.
Kankan–Malian border (217km) FG16,000 by 504.
Kankan–Côte d'Ivoire border (250km) FG10,000 by 504.

be an uncanny indicator of speed and reliability.

The "head" price – the **fare** – is payable at the end of the trip – or often just before arrival. Be certain of your fare, especially if you're setting down en route when it can be very hard to argue if you feel you're being robbed. The price of baggage is normally discussed in advance of departure and paid then.

The Société Générale des Transports de Guinée (SOGETRAG) no longer runs **bus services** out of Conakry, although you may see one or two of its buses being used by private companies. Most of these private bus services are restricted to the Fouta Djalon and towns along the Conakry–Nzérékoré road, and all services originate in Conakry. For other parts of the country you'll have to use Peugeot 504s.

Routes and frequencies

The busiest route is from **Conakry to Mamou** with departures until early afternoon (5hr); the Conakry–Kindia section (3hr) is now smooth and regraded and too fast for comfort. **Mamou to Labé** (3hr) is another relatively busy and newly resurfaced road: much of the transport is local to the Fouta Djalon. **Mamou to Faranah** is fairly quiet with few local vehicles. **Conakry to Kankan** or **Guéckédou** (14hr plus) tends to be an all-night trip but it's perfectly possible to make a late arrival if you start early enough. **Conakry to Nzérékoré** though (20hr or more, until the tarmac road is finished), is best contemplated with a night stop somewhere en route.

In the eastern and northwestern fringes of the country, most transport is long distance. You can wait days for a vehicle away from the main routes, especially during the rains.

■ Trains

The **Conakry–Kankan line** has not operated as a regular passenger service for many years – a pity, as the scenery along the way reputedly makes the road look dull by comparison. Technically the service is merely "suspended", but there are no immediate prospects of it being revived. In theory, freight trains still run once or twice a month. Lines also go from Conakry to the bauxite works at Fria, and from Kamsar on the northwest coast to **Boké** and **Sangaredi** – all freight only.

■ Planes

There has been a recent cutback in domestic air services with the closure of Guinée Air Service and the indefinite suspension of Guinée Inter Air flights. Air Guinée is now the sole domestic carrier, making some cross-border hops as well. Towns linked with Conakry (and in some cases with each other) include: Kankan, Kissidougou, Labé, Nzérékoré, Sambailo (for Koundara) and Siguiri. Details are given on p.498 and in "Moving On" boxes throughout the chapter.

■ Other forms of transport

Car rental rates are extortionate. There are some outlets in Conakry, at the airport and the *Novotel*, but none upcountry. You're unlikely to find it worthwhile except for specific targets, and there still seem to be some niggling security doubts over driving rented cars beyond the 36km city limits. Whether you like it or not, you might find it impossible to rent a car without being obliged to hire a driver as well. From pumps, *essence* (petrol/gasoline) costs around FG850/litre, while *gasoil* (diesel) is FG450/litre. Both are cheaper by the jerry can from market traders.

A **ferry-barge** theoretically runs occasionally at high water times (roughly mid- to late July to the end of November) from Kankan, down a tributary of the Niger, to Siguiri and Bamako. There's usually another boat – currently broken down – from Kouroussa, that also makes a regular voyage via Siguiri to Bamako and back during the high water season. At the time of writing, however, both services are suspended, and future services will depend upon whether water levels continue to drop as they have in recent years.

Guinea has several possible **canoeing** rivers, including the upper Niger which is probably the best. Full details on obtaining a boat and paddling downstream are given on p.514.

The country is wonderful territory for **hiking, cycling** and **motorbiking**. During the French occupation, Guinea supported an enthusiastic fraternity of hunting and outdoor-pursuit fans with an infrastructure of *campements* and guides. Today there's little back-up and, as with canoeing, you need to be self-sufficient if you want to make the most of the wild country. Main requirements are a tent and cooking equipment, water bottles, spares if you're cycling (even locally bought bikes are poorly serviced), and as much time as possible.

Accommodation

Guinea's recovery from economic coma has so far precipitated a boom in hotel building
only in Conakry, and in the provinces there are just a few hotels above the level of bordellos and basic lodgings. There are no hostels or campsites.

Cheap places (from FG4000–10,000 in the provinces; generally much more in Conakry) are usually primitive – electricity sporadic, and water generally in buckets, though sometimes warmed for you. There is, however, a scattering of hotels and guesthouses in the Fouta Djalon and the east with a certain idiosyncratic appeal, all detailed in the town-by-town coverage.

In smaller towns and villages you can always ask to see the *sous-préfet* (the district officer) with a view to a night at the **villa** – accommodation for visiting government employees. Some larger towns, prefectoral capitals, also have *villas*. These places are often good, though they may need an airing and a broom, and you may, or may not, be asked for payment. Always leave something for the caretaker.

On the question of **private accommodation**, Guineans are most hospitable, aware to the point of angst of the country's shortcomings. But they may assume your needs can't be met and not think to offer an ordinary room. Once it's understood you need a roof, you'll repeatedly be offered places to stay in people's compounds; the only difficulty is in moving on without causing offence.

Camping, in the bush, shouldn't be a problem. Doing so near large towns is bound to cause suspicion, and the law against it could be reawakened by zealous police.

ACCOMMODATION PRICE CODES

All Accommodation prices in this chapter are coded according to the following scales, and throughout the book in the equivalent in UK£ and US$. Prices refer to the rate you can expect to pay for a room with two beds. Single rooms, or single occupancy, will normally cost at least two-thirds of the twin-occupancy rate. For further details see p.48.

① **Under FG10,000 (under £5/$8).** Rudimentary lodgings, with primitive facilities. No guarantees of electricity or hot water.

② **FG10,000–20,000 (£5–10/$8–16).** Basic hotel with few frills. Some S/C.

③ **FG20,000–40,000 (£10–20/$16–32).** Modest hotel, usually with S/C rooms and a choice of rooms with fans, or a premium for AC.

④ **FG40,000–60,000 (£20–30/$32–48).** Reasonable business or tourist-class hotel with S/C, AC rooms and a restaurant.

⑤ **FG60,000–80,000 (£30–40/$48–64).** As for the previous bracket but smarter. Usually a new hotel.

⑥ **FG80,000–100,000 (£40–50/$64–80).** Comfortable, first-class hotel, with good facilities.

⑦ **Over FG100,000 (over £50/$80).** Luxury establishment with pool and other special features, but not necessarily excellent in international terms.

Eating and Drinking

Guinean food is based overwhelmingly on three ingredients – rice, leaves and groundnuts – but there's a terrific variety of tastes and much that's delicious. Very strongly spiced food isn't common.

International or French restaurant fare is almost restricted to Conakry, which does have a few excellent and costly establishments. For the rest of the country, although you will find simple restaurants, it's street food that prevails. **Mafé** is the standard term for groundnut sauce; **atieké** or **tô** is steamed, grated cassava stodge, a less common alternative to rice as a staple.

Street food is a serious business, with big pots of rice, sauces, chipped yams, potatoes and bananas hiding under an awning where you squat on a bench to eat. Choose what you want and, if you're not alone, order for one person at a time and share – servings are on the gigantic side. Beware of going to eat too late. The main meal of the day usually comes around 11am and by midday most street eats are finished.

Consistently delicious – and usually meatless – is **sauce de feuilles**, best made with the finely chopped young cassava or sweet potato leaves you see being cut in the markets. If you order **riz-sauce**, it comes with chunks of meat and gristle. Order the rice only (usually home-grown and tasty) and it will be doused with thin sauce anyway. **Bouillon** is usually a beef or mutton stew made with offal. **Brochettes** (little kebabs) are common everywhere. **Bush meat** of various kinds is mostly found in off-the-road villages: if it's monkey you should be certain it has been very well cooked before eating it.

Avocados are surprisingly popular in the southeast highlands. **Taro** (cocoyams), **salads** of lettuce and tomato (something of a health risk – go by first impressions), **beans** and other garden produce are common in some parts of the country. **Oranges** are the biggest fruit crop; in the Fouta Djalon from November to April they're abundant and cheap enough to buy all day as a drink. **Bananas** in various shapes and sizes are everywhere much in evidence, especially around Kindia. Many towns have streets luxuriantly shaded by **mango** trees.

Beer drinkers can choose between locally brewed Skol (FG1000 for a half-litre) and Guiluxe, Guinea's "national beer". **Palm wine** is common in small villages, especially in non-Muslim areas. There are all the usual bottled **soft drinks**.

White **coffee** (Nescafé/*café au lait*) is served as a rule with *pain beurre*, not drunk on its own. Unless Nescafé is specified, however, you may, if you order *café*, be served *lait concentré sucré* with weak *lipton* poured on top – sweet tea, in other words, not coffee at all. *Café fort*, on the other hand, is exactly what it says and is even occasionally made with ground coffee beans rather than instant powder. Guinea's *kinkeliba* infusion is better tasting than Senegal's. **Sour milk**, laced with sugar and usually bulked out with starchy cassava flour, is more of a meal than a drink.

Communications-Post, Phones, Language & Media

Guinea's telecommunications network isn't one of the best in the region. Conakry's PTT leaves the worst impression of all. Forget about poste restante there: Kankan's is probably safer. If you must use facilities in Conakry, you're probably best off visiting the *Novotel* (for phones and fax) and using your embassy or consulate for mail-holding. Telephone calls to Europe cost FG15,000 for three minutes.

PTT hours vary (Mon–Sat 8am–2pm in **Conakry**, 7.30/8am–4pm in **Kankan** and **Nzérékoré**). Other main post offices are at **Boké**, **Kindia**, **Labé** and **Faranah**. From any of these provincial capitals you can theoretically phone or fax abroad.

■ Languages

The most important languages are the Mande tongue, **Susu** (mostly spoken in the west), **Fula** (spoken in the densely populated Fouta Djalon), and **Malinké** (spoken in the eastern plains). **English** is becoming increasingly important in the Fouta Djalon, where many refugees from Sierra Leone and Liberia have sought refuge.

■ The media

Radios are prized possessions in Guinea and, more than most countries, a **short-wave radio** is really worth having here in order to keep up with the BBC, VOA or frequency of your choice. Radiodiffusion-

---

Guinea's IDD code is ☎224.

SIMPLE SUSU

Susu is more straightforward in many respects, than Fula, but somewhat tonal, so that (like Chinese) the meaning of what you say depends on the tone of your voice when you say it. It bears comparison with Bamana (see p.302) and Mandinka (see p.249).

GREETINGS

Hello	*Inwali* (to one person)	Good afternoon/evening	*Tana mogegné*
	Wo inwali (two or more	How's the family?	*Tanamodinbayama?*
	people)	See you later/good bye	*Won je segué*
Good day	*Wo mamabé*		
Good morning	*Tana mokhi* (literally, "did		
	nothing bad		
	happen in the night?")		

NUMBERS

1	*keren*	10	*fu*
2	*firin*	20	*mokhein*
3	*sakhan*	25	*mokhein nu suli*
4	*nani*	30	*tongosakhan*
5	*suli*	40	*tongonani*
6	*senné*	50	*tongosuli*
7	*soloferé*	60	*tongosenné*
8	*solomasakham*	100	*kémé*
9	*solomanani*	200	*kémé firin*

USEFUL EXPRESSIONS

How much?	*Yéri?*	I don't understand	*M'ma fahamukhi*
I'll take it (give it to me)	*A sun nyi*	Excuse me	*Diyema*
It's too expensive	*Asaré khorokho*	Please repeat it	*Nakhadi*
Show me the way	*Kira ma sembé*	Where's the bank?	*Banque na mindé?*
I don't know	*M'ma kolon*		

These words and phrases are intended only as a way into further communication. Guinean women, especially, rarely speak French. For Malinké look at the Bamana language section on p.302.

Télévision Guinéenne (RTG) broadcasts **radio** in French, English, Portuguese, Kriolu, Susu, Malinké and Fula and puts out evening **TV** in French with news in six Guinean languages. Cultural programming (most shows made in Guinea) is a priority. Recently **local radio** stations have been introduced in Kankan, Kindia, Labé and Nzérékoré. All Guinean TV and radio is state-controlled – no Abidjan-style proliferation of FM fluff here.

The national **press** used to consist only of *Horoya* ("Dignity") – a weekly rag of inspired awfulness carrying limited African news. These days there are several other newspapers but the press still hasn't taken off, in large measure due to the attentions of Guinea's paranoid state security machine which regularly closes or busts up independent operations and arrests journalists or deports foreign correspondents. Among the struggling independents are the monthly

L'Evenement de Guinée, *L'Observateur*, *l'Indépendant* and *Le Lynx* – the latter a satirical weekly that is equally scornful of the government and the opposition. If you're famished for *actualités*, foreign papers and magazines are becoming increasingly available in Conakry.

Although **French** is the country's official language, Sekou Touré virtually eliminated its teaching so that a broad generation of people either speak it very badly or not at all. Since 1984 French lessons have been reintroduced into primary education.

Arts and Entertainment

In 1969, Guinea won the Grand Prix at the first Pan-African Cultural Festival (FESPAC), held in Algiers. It looks like the new regime is trying to build on the reservoir of talent

FUNDAMENTAL FULA

Fula (technically *Fulfulde*, and sometimes called *Pulaar*) is a **class language** with 21 classes, implying the usual agreement between nouns, demonstratives, adjectives and so on. There's no tonal system. A little problematically the class agreements "mutate"; the class suffix can actually change in sound within the same class depending on the noun's root. It's all a rather complicated jump from European languages and unless you've tried learning a relatively easy class language like Swahili, probably too much trouble. There's little instructional material in English. Note that the following is based on the Fula of Fouta Djalon and the language spoken in other parts of West Africa – the Fouta Toro in Senegal, Massina in Mali or in Nigeria or Cameroon for example, can differ markedly, especially in respect of greetings.

GREETINGS

How are you?	*On djarama?*	How's the work?	*Gollednen?*
Are you fine?	*Tanalaton?*	[response– fine]	*Gollednen*
[response– fine]	*Djamtum*		*no marsude*
How's the family?	*Bengure mandin?*	Sorry	*A tjana khake*
[response– fine]	*Bengure nden*	Please	*A tju hake*
	no djam		

CONVERSATION

Do you speak Fula?	*A volaj Fula?*	Nice to meet you	*Minko sadjo minete*
Yes	*Hiji*	What's your name?	*Kohono vjeteda?*
No	*Oo*	My name is Michael	*Kohono mi vjete*
I don't know	*Mi anda*		*Michael*
I don't understand	*Mi famali*	Where are you from?	*Kvonto ole kamo?*
Please repeat it	*Hondu buiyu da*	I'm from Guinea	*Govena mjuri*
Welcome!	*On njuti edjam!*		

TRAVEL

Where are you going?	*Konto jato?*	Village	*Hodho*
Where is Dalaba?	*Konto ole Dalaba?*	Big	*Non djardi*
Straight ahead	*Jee so mara*	Small	*No fandi*
Right	*Sengo njamo*	Hill	*Fello*
Left	*Sengo nano*	Waterfall	*Djurnde*
Far away	*Uwanto diri*	Mosque	*Djulirde*

SHOPPING AND FOOD

It's too expensive	*No sati*	Meat	*Deo*
Where's the bank?	*Hon to bank?*	Milk	*Birada*
How much?	*Jelu?*	Water	*Dija*
Food	*Njamete*	Tea	*Dute*
Rice	*Maro*	It's excellent (food)!	*No mo i!*
Potatoes	*Pute*		

NUMBERS

1	*goo*	6	*jegoo*	11	*sappo e goo*
2	*didi*	7	*jedidi*	20	*no gayi*
3	*tati*	8	*jetati*	25	*no gayi joyi*
4	*nayi*	9	*jenayi*	100	*témédéré*
5	*joyi*	10	*saapo*	200	*témédéré didi*

with its cultural season (October to June); details at the museum in Conakry.

■ Music

Travelling by Peugeot 504 across the country, you're accompanied most of the time by **music**. Driver and passengers take turns with the cassette deck and much of what you hear is Guinean – though Antillean *zouk* is increasingly popular even if only poor-quality recordings are made locally.

Guinea has nurtured some of Africa's most talented and original musicians and singers. Many are now based abroad, in Côte d'Ivoire or France. There are more details and background in the article on music in Contexts at the back of the book.

Mory Kante in particular has expanded into international stardom – arguably dishing his music for the sake of Europe's high-street record shops – but his audience at home is still huge. Enthusiasm for some of the names that became legends in Guinea and abroad before 1984 – **Bembeya Jazz**, **Les Amazones** – is less noticeable now. Tastes in Guinea are often quite local: put on a cassette by the Fula musician **Dourah Barry** in Malinké country and you risk offending all the passengers. Music is a good way into Guinea's cultural complexities.

Live music on stage is mostly a pleasure of Conakry's clubs. Upcountry, local bands play occasionally, but the big national *orchestres* with overseas recording contracts don't play much at home.

The **griots** retain a major role as entertainers in the countryside, and koras and guitars and a few beers are a common evening combination. In Guinea you can still have your praises sung for small change.

■ Other entertainments

For other cultural affairs, the best place to check what might be going on is the National Museum in Conakry which houses the "Office of National Heritage". **Theatre** is getting some encouragement with the formation of a Théâtre National d'Enfants and promotion of the Théâtre National and the Ballet National, but there's a lack of decent venues, even in Conakry. **Cinema** seems to be absolutely defunct, though as a creative force it never really began, and is totally disabled through lack of film stock, equipment and, perhaps, nerve. Those who wanted to create cinema – as opposed to those content with making ideologically sound documentaries – left the country long ago. Imported movies today are predictable – French, the occasional Hollywood blockbuster, and lots of cheap, cheerful violence.

In sport, African wrestling is less important than in the countries further north. **Soccer** is hugely popular and Guinea's national team is moderately distinguished.

Directory

AIRPORT DEPARTURE TAX FG3000 domestic, FG5000 Africa and FG20,000 inter-continental. Only Guinean francs are accepted.

CASSETTES Guinea's street and market vendors offer the best music deal in West Africa – about FG1000 each for copies.

GREETINGS Taken even more seriously in Guinea than in the rest of West Africa, traditional forms of greeting have been little diluted by European abruptness. Even in French you're expected to rattle off a few polite enquiries

---

GUINEAN GLOSSARY

Alfa King (Fula).

Bowe Eroded Fouta Djalon hill (pl. Bowal).

CTRN Transitional Committee for National Redress.

Dougou Place (Mande languages).

FLING The anti-Touré Front for the National Liberation of Guinea.

Foté White person (corruption of "Portuguese").

Fouta Place (Fula).

Gara Indigo (and indigo cloth).**Koro** Old (as in Dabolakoro – old Dabola).

Lumo Market held weekly or sometimes every four or five days.

PDG Democratic Party of Guinea, the party of the old regime.

PUP Unity and Progress Party, the ruling party of Lansana Conté.

Sofa Malinké chief (nineteenth century).

Syli Elephant (and defunct Guinean currency).

Woro Kola (Mande languages).

about family and life in general – particularly on official business. These phrases may pepper the whole conversation.

KOLA Kola nuts are a big crop in the southeast and very popular all over. Guinea is a country in which it's worth acquiring the taste. On long journeys a pocketful of white nuts (sweeter and speedier) keeps you from nodding off and is good to share.

MUSEUMS There's a residual national structure, with museums in Conakry, Boké, Kissidougou and Nzérékoré. There have been plans to build other new regional museums for several years.

PHOTOGRAPHY Most of the pictures you take in Guinea will be of people you know and their families, or of unpopulated landscapes when no-one is looking. Don't assume you can get out your camera as you might in neighbouring countries and snap away. You will cause a scene and you're quite likely to have your camera confiscated, for which a large *amende* will be payable. In Conakry you should be very careful with your camera. The *permis de photo*, while no such thing actually exists any longer, may still be demanded.

POLITICS Not completely taboo, but Guineans are often sensitive about the fact that Sekou Touré was tolerated so long, and at the same time quick to denounce neocolonialism in any form.

PUBLIC HOLIDAYS Aside from New Year's Day, May 1 (Labour Day) and the usual shifting Islamic calendar, the principal Guinean holidays are April 3 (anniversary of the 1984 coup), October 2 (Independence Day), and November 22 ("Victory Day"; anniversary of the repulsed 1970 Portuguese invasion). Christian holidays are observed more haphazardly – in the main by large businesses and government offices.

The commemoration of other landmarks in Guinea's history is dependent on more ephemeral political considerations: May 14, the anniversary of the founding of the PDG party; September 28, the anniversary of the "No" vote; February 9, National Women's Day; and August 27, the day in 1977 when the market women revolted and forced Sekou Touré to change tack.

Regional and local **non-Islamic festivals** were attacked as sectarian and unproductive during the Touré dictatorship and for many the generation-long repression destroyed their viability. You can still come across them if you're well-placed and well-timed – January to March is the most propitious season.

RELIGION As usual, the pig is a fair indication of the boundaries of **Islam**. You won't see many between the jungles of the northwest and the hilly forests in the southeast. Islam continues to consolidate and displace the indigenous religions, and its international dimension is increasingly important in shaping Guinean society. The vast majority of practising Muslims (about three-quarters of the population) are members of the Tijaniya brotherhood. Christianity is a minority religion, only significant locally around Conakry and in the southeast.

SEXUAL ATTITUDES Guinea under the old regime was moralistic and prying. Prostitution was brutally suppressed and polygamy outlawed – both in the cause of social justice. Things have changed, and prostitution is now as widespread as anywhere in West Africa. Homosexuality is presumably a crime; discretion is advised.

TOILET PAPER Hard to obtain except in major towns.

TROUBLE Much of the pre-1984 security fabric is still, doggedly, in place and trumped-up accusations and suspicions can only be resolved in the traditional ways. Driving in your own vehicle, you will experience repeated efforts at extortion from the police and military, ranging from mildly humorous (and irritating) to hysterical (and contemptible). Even if you're in a taxi or other public transport, these can affect you, though in theory the driver himself is meant to soothe thirsty tempers and meet the incessant roadblock demands for a few hundred francs. The current state of affairs – especially in and around Conakry and as far up the highway as Mamou – is greatly resented, not so much because money is taken, but because the demands are deemed excessive. Most transport drivers lose a full fare on every trip.

If you genuinely break the law, you can ordinarily buy yourself out. Treat the police with caution, force out some humour, defuse them with cigarettes.

WILDLIFE Guinea has two new **national parks**: the Parc National Haut Niger (see p.514), near Kouroussa, and Parc National Noikolo Badiar (see p.510) along the Guinea-Bissau border at Koundara. There are also a large number of gazetted **forêts classées** which help to preserve the environment – in theory. Guinea is one of the few West African countries which has preserved, largely intact, a diverse indigenous fauna. Most large species – including chimpanzees, hippos, elephants, lions and buffalo – hang on, unprotected and rarely seen. It's been forty years since any field surveys were carried out and the current position is hazy. Hunting appears to be as much of a threat as environmental destruction. Regionally, the best wildlife zones are the hilly acacia savannah in the northeast, between the Tinkisso River and the Malian border; the undulating bush and grassland between Mamou and Faranah where the Fouta Djalon slopes down to Sierra Leone; and the southeast highlands, particularly east of the Macenta–Nzérékoré road.

WOMEN TRAVELLERS AND THE WOMEN'S MOVEMENT Women travellers have a reasonably easy time in Guinea, sheltered from some of the hassles of Mali, Senegal or Côte d'Ivoire by the lack of tourists, and frequently escorted along the way. So long as your French is adequate you'll find quick access to people's homes and lives wherever you go. Be prepared for – normally low-key – sexual harassment. You might prefer to describe yourself as something other than a tourist, which carries slightly pejorative connotations.

Progressive women's organizations in Guinea suffered a setback though their association with Sekou Touré's deformed "socialism". Genital mutilation is still practised in many districts.

A Brief History of Guinea

The first French expeditions into the hinterland of the Guinea coast took place from Boké, a creek-head base in contact with Europeans since the fifteenth century. Following the expansion initiated by Colonel Faidherbe across the Sahel – and to prevent the British linking The Gambia with Sierra Leone – the French commanders in "the rivers of the south" (as the Guinea region was known) forced protection treaties with dozens of small rulers through the middle of the nineteenth century. In the 1880s they came up against the first serious resistance to their invasion in the shape of the guerilla army of the Almamy Samory Touré, a man who won headlines in the French press for two decades and became Guinea's national hero. This account follows the country's history from his defeat to the present day. Some earlier historical background can be found throughout the guide and on p.510 and p.516.

■ The French occupation

Once Samory had been deported to Gabon in 1898, there was only relatively minor resistance to the French incursion. The **forest communities** put up a fight, and were aided by the hilly jungle in which the French couldn't use cavalry, but their political organization was weak and the villages submitted one after another in the years leading up to World War I.

In the early days, wild **rubber** was Guinea's main crop. By 1905 the commerce was supporting a 700-strong Lebanese community in Conakry. But the export declined after 1913 as plantation markets opened in Southeast Asia.

By 1914, the French had driven a **railway** over 600km through mountain terrain to the river port of Kankan, thus linking Conakry with Bamako. This, however, was a strategic railway rather than a commercial one. Apart from limited gold and diamonds, upper Guinea didn't appear to offer much return. Better prospects lay in the forest regions to the south where **coffee** and other tropical crops were developed on French-owned plantations, and near the coast and southern foothills of the Fouta Djalon, where **bananas** – increasingly popular as an exotic fruit – flourished.

Guinea's biggest prize, though, was **bauxite** – aluminium ore – of which its vast high-grade deposits form nearly a third of the world's reserves. But the French only began to exploit them systematically in the 1950s and for most of their occupation the necessary investment wasn't attracted.

French rule in Guinea followed standard patterns except that, more so than elsewhere, the opportunities to become a privileged **evolué** were desperately few: until 1935 there was no secondary education in Guinea and, on the eve of independence, only 1.3 percent of Guinean children were receiving even primary schooling. With one singular exception, almost all the prominent Guineans before independence came from wealthy families who had sent them to the Ecole Normale William Ponty near Dakar.

■ The rise of nationalism

Ahmed Sekou Touré, a Malinké speaker from Faranah, first came to attention as a disruptive and perspicacious schoolboy in the late 1930s and then as founder of Guinea's first union – the Post and Telecommunications Workers – in 1946. In 1947 Touré and others formed the Guinean section of the Rassemblement Démocratique Africain (the broad alliance of French West African political groupings) and named it the **Parti Démocratique de Guinée** (PDG).

In the election for deputies to the new Constituent Assembly in 1945, the Guinean "subject" elected was **Yacine Diallo** – a Fula-speaker with the support of the Islamic old guard in the Fouta Djalon.

Guinea made huge strides after the war with major investment in the bauxite industry at last and a rapidly urbanizing workforce. Touré meanwhile was making his name as a politician and unionist. He was a delegate to the 1947 Communist French Trade Unions (CGT) Congress in Dakar and, with support from the French Communist party, he backed several **strikes** in the early 1950s and produced a labour newspaper – *L'Ouvrier*.

The most trenchant strike was the ten-week action in 1953 over the demand for a **twenty percent wage rise** to accompany a reform in the labour laws stipulating a 40-hour instead of a 48-hour week. During the strike, telegrams of instructions from Paris and Dakar to the Governor of Guinea were intercepted by radical telecommunications workers, and the strike resulted in a victory which made a lasting impression on the Guinean public and across French West Africa.

Sekou Touré's rise to power

By the time of the strike, Sekou Touré was the territorial assembly member for Beyla. From this platform, he and other trade unionists began a campaign to disaffiliate and Africanize the Guinean sections from the parent French unions.

Touré's career took a knock in 1954 when his Guinean **deputyship to the French assembly** came up on the death of Yacine Diallo. Convinced of his outright popularity, Touré was equally convinced that the election had been rigged when he was heavily beaten by a Fula candidate, Barry Diawadou (the Fouta Djalon was inimical territory for a Marxist Malinké). There had indeed been gross tampering by the French, and voters had even been struck off the register in areas of strong PDG support. The Minister for Overseas Territories came to Conakry to assure Guineans it wouldn't happen again. It was a debacle which many Fula had cause to regret after independence.

Instead, Touré became **mayor of Conakry** in 1955. He was just thirty-three. By 1956, with over 40,000 members in the CGT-Guinée, the break

with the French unions was achieved and a new, African federation of labour unions created – the Union Générale des Travailleurs d'Afrique Noire (UGTAN) with Touré its first secretary general. Uniquely in West Africa, Touré now succeeded in marrying the PDG party with the labour federation – an amalgam that was ratified in March 1958.

Touré's **second bid for deputy** was successful in 1956 in an election apparently free of abuses: his vote was up 200 percent on 1954 while Diawadou's was almost identical. Sekou Touré became **vice-president** of the new Territorial Council of Government in 1957, effectively prime minister of Guinea under the low-profile Governor Jean Ramadier. Touré firmly advocated an independent West African federation of states and denounced Senghor of Senegal and Houphouët-Boigny of Côte d'Ivoire as puppets for wanting to consolidate the French connection.

One of Touré's first major acts was the **abolition of chiefs** and their replacement by party cadres. The move was particularly resented in the Fouta Djalon, where chiefdoms had some traditional legitimacy. It was accompanied by some bloody settling of scores: the groundwork for the Guinean state security network was being prepared.

With **de Gaulle's return to power** in France Sekou Touré was soon given the chance to wield full power. The new constitution of the French Fifth Republic was unacceptable to him, and the idea of a free federation of completely independent states wasn't acceptable to de Gaulle – who insisted on their giving up some of their sovereignty to the federal government.

De Gaulle's visit to Conakry to put his case was a waste of time. He would "raise no obstacles" in Guinea's path if the country chose to "secede" from the community of French states – but he would "draw conclusions". Sekou Touré replied **"We prefer poverty in freedom to riches in slavery"** and the two leaders snubbed each other at every opportunity for the rest of the visit. "Good Luck to Guinea" sneered de Gaulle on his departure.

■ Guinea under Sekou Touré

While other Francophone leaders thought at first he was bluffing, Sekou Touré prepared his country to go it alone. On September 28, 1958 there was a 95 percent **"No"** vote to the referendum on staying in the French community. And on October 2, **independence** was declared.

The example of Ghana under Nkrumah was an inspiration while the swift **reaction of the French** in Guinea – flight with the booty, sabotage of the infrastructure, burning of files and cancellation of all co-operation and investment – was made to seem like good riddance by the party, though the severity of the withdrawal was a vindictive blow.

The country had virtually no technical expertise and a total of six graduates. It started work from scratch, with aid from **Czechoslovakia**, the **Soviet Union** and seven other Eastern-bloc countries, and solid support from the European and Third World left. Morale was high and the PDG organization initially effective.

France excluded Guinea from the CFA franc zone of the newly independent Francophone nations. Guinea adopted its own franc (and later the *syli*) which isolated it further from neighbouring states, and hindered what little (non-French) trade remained, but at least stemmed the drain of capital to France.

Despite Nato fears that Guinea might become a West African Cuba, United States **President Eisenhower** waited six months before even sending an ambassador to Conakry, for fear of offending de Gaulle. In 1962, a substantial American aid package was finally worked out and the Peace Corps went in. Revolution aside, **American aid and investment**, particularly in the bauxite industry, has been firm ever since.

The Teachers' Plot

The **Soviet Union** quickly fell out with Sekou Touré at the time of the Cuban missile crisis. Misjudging his prevailing ideology – which was more committedly anti-capitalist than pro-communist – the Soviet mission was accused of "interference" when left-wing students demonstrated for a firm espousal of socialism and the dumping of Touré's "positive neutrality" (a refusal to be anyone's puppet). As a result of this **"Teachers' Plot"**, the Soviet ambassador was expelled. Diplomatic ties continued, however, and aid and expertise from the Soviet Union was never turned away – even if its usefulness was sometimes in doubt, such as in the case of the submarine base planned for the Los islands or the famous import of snow ploughs (possibly a malicious rumour as they're not much different from earth graders).

Poverty in slavery

As the first few years of independence unrolled, Sekou Touré, the **Pan-African** ideologue and co-author of the **OAU** charter, began to be seen in a less glamorous light as his extreme policies started to bite, and the popular enthusiasm of 1959–60 sloughed away. A planned economy without planners was taking shape (or rather not), state enterprises were extended, private business curtailed and a small but growing **middle class** was reaping illicit benefits from mismanagement and fraud.

The results of the first **three-year plan** weren't encouraging. Critics in the PDG complained the party was out of its depth in trying to control the market economy, and mistaken in extending power to the illiterate masses. Sekou Touré scolded them in a twelve-hour speech designed to weed out the party faithful from the conspirators. He wrote later "Everything became rotten, the elite enjoyed riding in cars and building villas."

There was a massive **market crackdown** in November 1964, with widespread harassment of traders and confiscation of assets. Limits were set on the number of traders allowed outside the state sphere and arrests, interrogations and arbitrary punishments grew in frequency. The party was moulded in Touré's image and political life stagnated. The very freedoms which lay at the heart of party policy (on paper anyway) were savagely suppressed. To many, it was clear the government was at war with the people; thousands fled the country.

In 1965 a group of opposition exiles – the Front pour la Libération de Guinée (FLING) – began to organize outside the country with tacit support from Senegal and Côte d'Ivoire and less discreet help from France. The **"traders' plot"** of 1966 – an apparent attempt to install a liberal government with capitalist leanings – resulted in the complete rupture of diplomatic relations with Paris.

But denouncing conspiracies – imagined or otherwise – couldn't improve the economy. There were chronic **shortages** and production and distribution methods failed. As American aid continued to pour in, world opinion began to see Guinea as an American stooge and – perversely – relations with the United States turned sour.

■ The Terror

Guinea now entered a dark period of isolationism and widespread **terror**. At the end of 1967 the eighth party congress had **radicalization of the**

revolution at the top of the agenda. To shore up its bankrupt ideology, the party formally adopted a path of "Socialism". Local revolutionary authorities (the Pouvoirs Révolutionnaires Locals, PRLs) were set up in every village – ostensibly to allow power to flow from the base up; in reality to extend the security blanket to every corner of the country. In the leadership, the picture suddenly became hazier, with the inauguration of a seven-member Politburo – the Bureau Politique National – in place of Sekou Touré alone. And as China was promulgating its bloody Cultural Revolution, Guinea – one of China's biggest African aid recipients – started its own campaign against "degenerate intellectuals".

Remarkably, in view of his political agility, the inflexible ideology which Sekou Touré carried before him wasn't abandoned for another ten years. And the elaborate and cruelly anti-human **security apparatus** that continued its triffid-like growth lost any trace of even Kafkaesque rationale. Touré was not totally insulated from the misery of his people. Huge sums were certainly creamed off by the Touré family's **"Faranah clan"** (see box, below), but ostentatious displays of wealth were avoided. The funds – and particularly hoards of **diamonds** – were siphoned abroad, while the party hierarchy lived in relatively modest style.

The **army** was kept under constant surveillance by a network of junior officers. Early in 1969 came the first big **purge** of figures close to the party leadership. Chief of Staff Kamara Diaby and the soldier-poet Fodeba Keita were the two most senior victims. Keita met his death in the prison camp he himself had built. There was an assassination attempt on Touré and more arrests in Labé

the following year. As a result, the army was radically reorganized: each soldier was made a civil servant, effectively militarizing a civilian regime.

The invasion

Although Sekou Touré had been predicting an "aggression" with more than customary conviction, the country was unprepared for the **invasion** of November 22, 1970. Four hundred troops landed from ships at night and attacked Conakry and the peninsula. This was supposed to trigger a general uprising of Guinean dissidents and the overthrow of Sekou Touré. But although three hundred defenders were killed, and a number of prisoners released by the attackers, none of the key targets (the presidential palace, radio station or airport) was taken. When the landing ships moved away 48 hours later they left behind large numbers of stranded troops who were rounded up and subjected to people's justice.

Reactions to the invasion proved a crucial test of party loyalty and provided the **military victory** over the forces of imperialism that Sekou Touré had always craved. It was, he wrote, "one of those sublime moments of exaltation and patriotism: the affirmation of collective dignity."

The **United Nations** sent a fact-finding mission. They ascertained that most of the force had been composed of Guinean exiles of FLING and loyalist African soldiers from Portuguese Guinea, commanded by Portuguese officers from the Caetano fascist regime, with West German logistical support. The real aim of the invasion was to destroy the base in Guinea of the PAIGC guerillas fighting for independence from Portugal. It was to the lasting humiliation of the Guinea-Conakry opposition that their alliance with Caetano's fascist forces failed.

THE FARANAH CLAN

Sekou Touré's quarter-century in power witnessed flagrant **favouritism** to members of his own **Malinké**-speaking ethnic group. Yet this was more a case of **nepotism** than chauvinist tribalism – indeed his wife was half Fula. The family clung jealously to their privileges. Threats from those connected to the clan by marriage were sometimes dealt with internally, but outsiders who interfered were condemned to the Boiro death camp, or simply disappeared. Sekou Touré encouraged the clan to intermarry and foresaw a long dynasty. But the paranoia that eventually touched even the president was such that the clan split into two opposing factions – the **Tourés** and the **Keitas** – each practising its own nepotism. Ismael Touré, leader of the first faction, was Sekou's half-brother and a descendant of the warlord Samory Touré (a claim also made, but vainly, by Sekou Touré himself). The Keitas were led by Mamadi Keita, the president's brother-in-law. Despite the name, the Keitas seem to have won the battle for influence with the president in his last years. The clan's reach was legendary, and supporters and beneficiaries have not all been eliminated by the new regime.

The **purge** which followed was predictably brutal. In truth, there was grass roots opposition to the NATO-backed invaders – though considerably more support for the internal rebels. Ninety-one people were sentenced to death and hundreds of others imprisoned and tortured. The hundred-strong German technical mission was expelled and dozens of Europeans spent time in jail in the aftermath.

But the popular rage whipped up by the party against imperialist aggression clouded the question of how much positive support the government still had, and obscured the **mass violations of human rights** – torture, disappearances, summary executions and detention without trial – that ravaged Guinea through the early 1970s. An Amnesty International report in 1978 estimated there were between 500 and 1500 political prisoners in fifteen prison camps. In six months in 1974, however, over 250 people are believed to have been executed in Conakry's Camp Boiro alone. Tens of thousands of Guineans, particularly Fula-speakers, continued to flee the country every year.

Hanging on

As the pressures – internal and external – mounted against his regime, Sekou Touré resorted to increasingly desperate measures. **Food short-ages** were worsened by the effect of the security network in hampering the normal functioning of lines of supply and communication. There was nothing to encourage farmers. Obstinately, Touré authorized the local revolutionary authorities to handle all the production and marketing of commodities. Then early in 1975 came the **banning of all private trade** and at the same time the setting up of agricultural production brigades. The borders were closed and Touré declared a **"holy war"** against smugglers who were shot if caught. In the north of the country, the **Sahel drought** added to deteriorating prospects.

Guinea struggled for two-and-a-half years, going through another purge in 1976 in response to the **"Fula Plot"** (see box above). **Relations with France** (broken for a decade) were patched up through the new president Giscard d'Estaing, who agreed to ban Guinean dissident propaganda there. But the exodus from Guinea continued and by the end of the 1970s as many as a million Guineans were believed to be living abroad.

■ The turnaround

The country's commercial paralysis, supervised by – and unashamedly for the benefit of – the **"economic police"** couldn't be maintained. In August

---

1977 **market women** in Conakry and other towns spontaneously rose up against the intolerable market situation, which made it impossible for them to afford the produce of their own harvests. It was a turning point. **Riots** flared across the country and several provincial governors were killed. Sekou Touré's resolve collapsed. He began a slow process of **economic liberalization**. This coincided with a more pragmatic approach to government, a reduction of revolutionary rhetoric and – in response to outspoken criticism abroad – cosmetic improvements in democratic practices and human rights.

In his last few years, Touré left the running of the party and state more and more to a leading clique of ministers while devoting himself to the cultivation of an image as the grand old man of Pan-Africanism. 1982 saw the grotesque spectacle of Touré in Washington hailed by President Reagan as "a champion of human rights".

Progressive ideas were forgotten, however, as he forged close links with King Hassan of **Morocco** – whose side he took in the dispute over Western Sahara – and other bastions of the rigid right. Hassan provided money needed desperately by Touré to tide him over after the collapse of IMF negotiations in 1983, and arranged with conservative Arab states for Guinea to be the largest recipient of petro-dollar aid in sub-Saharan Africa. Touré was set to take his seat as 21st OAU chairman and had a special OAU village built (by Saudi Arabia) in Conakry, when, for administrative reasons, the summit was postponed to 1984.

In January and February of that year, groups of **soldiers** were arrested near the Senegalese border and accused of plotting against the government. At the time of **Sekou Touré's death** on March 26, 1984 in a private clinic in Cleveland (whence he'd been flown in Hassan's jet), it appears that sections of the army had indeed been planning a coup d'état.

■ The new regime

Colonels **Lansana Conté** (president) and **Diara Traoré** (prime minister) waited several days after the lavish funeral before announcing, after an almost peaceful takeover, the **dissolution of the constitution and the party**, the freeing of political prisoners, the unbanning of trade unions and the **reopening of Guinea** to private investment. Judicial reforms began and French was reintroduced as the main language of education. Most of the old party structures swiftly disintegrated. Asked why the military hadn't acted years earlier, Conté said "the spirit of the Guinean was such that he would not think. Some Guineans behaved like imbeciles. They were remote-controlled."

The Comité Militaire de Redressement National was given an enthusiastic welcome and ministers went on foreign tours to introduce the new Guinea and cultivate aid donors. But apart from a general liberalization, it was hard to pinpoint the direction of the new government. There was soon a split with prime minister Traoré however, and his post was abolished. Predictably, perhaps, in July 1985 Traoré and fellow Malinké officers attempted a **coup** against Conté.

In 1987, almost two years later, it was announced that those involved, together with a number of detainees from Sekou Touré's government – sixty people in all – had been given **secret trials** and were to be executed. It was widely presumed, however, that most of them had died extra-judicially long before and Conté was merely setting the record straight – a presumption that hinted how close a return to state terrorism might be and, perhaps, how little Conté might be able to do to prevent it.

On the economic front, Conakry was soon full of French technical advisors and business people. One of the **IMF**'s structural adjustment programmes was put in operation which, coupled with general **austerity**, state sector **job losses** and widespread civil service **corruption** and ostentation, was not warmly received. Conakry boiled over in January 1988 with **street riots** over **price rises** – which, yet again, had outstripped huge wage increases designed to control the black market. The riots forced the government to back down, and commodity prices were reduced.

■ Politics in the 1990s

Politically, the initiative Conté lost after abolishing the post of prime minister, and the subsequent coup attempt, was recovered when he increased **civilian representation** in the government – though some of his rivals were banished from Conakry in the process. **Malinké** speakers have been particularly under-represented since the demise of the old regime and they, together with thousands of returned **Fula** exiles, are regarded as the unofficial opposition to Conté's – predominantly **Susu** – leadership.

By the end of 1990, serious protests were emerging from schools and the university in Conakry, in protest at conditions, educational standards, and the slowness with which democratic reforms were to be instituted. A number of students were killed by police or army gunfire during demonstrations.

Conté maintained his slow pace, setting up the Comité Transitoire de Redressement National (the CTRN; the "Transitional Commitee for National Redress"), which he ensured had some recently departed members of his own cabinet sitting on it. Meanwhile, the demonstrations, and then strikes too, continued.

In 1991, **Alpha Condé**, long-exiled Malinké opposition leader and Secretary General of the Rassemblement du Peuple Guinéen (RPG), considered the time right to return home, but his plan to stay had to be aborted when the security forces fired on a crowd of his supporters. He took refuge in the Senegalese ambassador's home, before fleeing the country again. Within less than a year, it looked as if Lansana Conté's government was

becoming used to the idea of a democratic opposition, as more or less required by international donors: Alpha Condé's RPG was formally registered in April 1992 and Condé returned to Guinea.

Lansana Conté himself formed a puppet party as a front for the CTRN. Called the Parti de l'Unité et du Progrès (PUP), it focused on the parts of the country where the CTRN was providing development funds. Despite intimidating the opposition and operating with state support and government money, Conté's PUP was insufficiently confident of its electoral strengths to keep to the election dates scheduled for the end of 1992. The CTRN deferred the presidential and legislative elections for another year, during which Guinea saw some of the most savage **political violence** of the post-Touré era, with dozens of deaths from security forces' gunfire, and hundreds of injuries in two separate mass demonstrations in Conakry.

In the run-up to the **presidential election**, finally held in December 1993, the PUP held public meetings unhindered (despite the CTRN's banning of them and the fact that no other party was able to flout the "law") and every tool at the government's disposal was put into service to pump up votes for the party.

As a result, Conté, standing for the PUP, polled just over 51 percent. The votes from two massively anti-Conté (pro-Condé) prefectures, Kankan and Siguiri, were disallowed for reasons of the RPG's "malpractice", and Alpha Condé's RPG thus received barely 20 percent of the votes for president, with the other main opposition leaders, both Fula – **Mamadou Bâ** (Union pour la Nouvelle République, the UNR), and a former journalist on *Jeune Afrique* magazine, **Siradiou Diallo** (Parti pour le Renouveau et le Progrès, the PRP) – getting twelve and thirteen percent of the vote respectively. As it became clear that the opposition had been cheated, there were chaotic scenes at polling stations. Several Guinean embassies, acting as polling stations for Guinean émigrés in other parts of West Africa, were ransacked.

As "democratic" presidential elections in West Africa go, Guinea's first effort was one of the most dishonest and unimpressive. Foreign observers were all but excluded. In its wake, Condé's RPG and Diallo's PRP formed an alliance to contest the legislative elections. In response to this and other signs of opposition strength, the government disenfranchised Guineans overseas, thus excluding some three million potential voters from future elections.

Meanwhile, 1994 saw senior military officers getting increasingly agitated by the prospect of their gradual forced withdrawal from public life, as it became clear that civilian rule could not be permanently forestalled. There were rumours of a coup attempt and arrests in May 1994.

The multiparty **general elections** to the legislative assembly were finally held on June 11, 1995. In the run-up to them, opposition rallies throughout Guinea were disrupted by the security forces on the orders of the powerful interior minister, **René Aseny Gomez**. Condé and Diallo, having earlier said they would not boycott the elections despite the PUP's flagrant rigging, ultimately pulled out on the day. Although the coalition won about a quarter of the seats (28 out of 114 seats to the PUP's 71) they boycotted the national assembly.

Late pay increases was the provocation that led part of the army to **mutiny** in February 1996. The incident – which came close to toppling Conté, when various units seized the airport, radio and TV stations and shelled the city centre – was defused when Conté, banged up in his palace, offered an immediate 100 percent pay increase and no prosecutions, in exchange for his freedom. True to form, he reneged on the deal soon afterwards and a ragged series of trials and hearings ran for the next two years.

President Conté has **unfriendly neighbours** to the south (Charles Taylor in Liberia, and the Liberian-backed RUF terror gangs in Sierra Leone) and to the north, in the shape of the victorious rebels of Guinea-Bissau. His support for the legitimate government of Sierra Leone has cost him little, but the communities of the upland border region near Faranah are paying the price, and are now targeted by RUF gangs, while all the reward given to the army for its peacekeeping troop missions to Sierra Leone, Liberia and Guinea-Bissau is a rumour mill running at full power about its mutinous intents against Conté's government.

In the (once again, openly rigged) **elections of December 1998**, which had no independent Guinean or international oversight, Conté's PUP scored 56 percent, against the divided opposition consisting largely of the PRP (now merged with Mamadou Bâ's UNR, and led by him) which got 25 percent, and Alpha Condé's RPG (17 percent). Condé, the country's most high-profile opposition leader, had bided his time in exile in Paris – his

personal safety in Guinea always in doubt – until days before the election, arriving finally to a hero's welcome in Conakry. Soon after his arrival, he was arrested, accused of being a threat to state security.

■ Prospects

Guinea is itching to flex its muscles. With almost limitless agricultural potential, plus its bauxite, iron and other mineral reserves, the country has the potential to become the most prosperous state in West Africa and the region's dominant Francophone nation.

President Conté evidently believes he has a mandate to rule and his PUP national assembly members the right to govern. The Guinean people, in large part, do not. And, as during his last five-year term, the wait for the next presidential and legislative elections, not due until the end of 2003, implies a degree of patience that most Guineans may not be prepared to display. Daily, they face mass unemployment, low and late salaries and the economic pressures brought about by the influx of refugees from Sierra Leone and Liberia (more than half a million, mostly in the Guinée Forestière region). And the army is more restive and unhappy than ever.

Guinea is going badly wrong, once again. Violence, intimidation, media censorship, a cowed judiciary and heavy-duty corruption are the very hallmarks stamped on the country three decades ago by Sekou Touré's destructive regime and said to have been wiped away by Conté's fresh start. Conté himself is now being widely compared with Sekou Touré, and receives the support of the PDG-RDA, the party of the late dictator.

But the opposition is far less fragmented than has often been the case in similar circumstances in Africa. The **CODEM** alliance, an umbrella group formed in 1995 to bring together, among others, Diallo's PRP, Bâ's UNR and Alpha Condé's RPG, has frequently fought common causes against the government and has gone so far as to threaten the formation of a militia to protect its members against illegal detentions. If Lansana Conté was right in declaring that the generation of Guineans under Touré behaved like "remote-controlled imbeciles" he may well find their children less unthinking in the new millennium.

CONAKRY

CONAKRY, once "the Paris of Africa", is today a city of few graces. A continuous sprawl of urbanization claws its way off the peninsula and up into the hills behind the city centre. Away from the downtown districts, the elongated conurbation is animated, but morbidly dirty – with refuse, mud, dust and slicks of motor oil – and heavy with the raw noise and choking exhaust fumes of endless lines of jammed traffic trying to get from one end of town to another. Vehicle carcasses rot on the verges: a scrap metal business would make a fortune. Conakry has matured into one of West Africa's least user-friendly capitals – expensive and palpably soulless – and you may spend much of your time here planning your escape to the sweet fabled hills and grasslands of the Guinea interior.

On the positive side, downtown Conakry is a lot more pleasant now than a decade ago, and is easily walked around, with offices and businesses not far apart. The main **market**, the Marché du Niger, is bountiful and growing all the time; **restaurants and cafés** – so thin on the ground in the early 1990s – are now plentiful; and the **nightlife**, in this most climatically exhausting of cities by day, is still first-rate. Finally, the nearby **Iles de Los** are strikingly pretty and easily accessible.

Some history

Conakry was itself an **island** – as you can still see from the narrow causeway between the Palais du Peuple and the motorway bridge. For many years known as **Tumbo**, the island was the closest to the shore of the archipelago that provided safe haven for slavers and merchant vessels trading along the Guinea coasts.

The Portuguese adventurer, Pedro da Sintra, first set foot here around 1460 and named it Cap de Sagres, after Prince Henry the Navigator's residence in Portugal (until then the furthest point in the known world). At this time the inhabitants of Conakry were idol-worshipping, skin-wearing farmers, cultivating indigenous African dry-land rice and millet.

Early in the sixteenth century, the Portuguese began to anchor in the deep water on the southeast side of the island, but over succeeding centuries they and the Dutch, English and French all took turns to occupy the site and trade in slaves. By the end of the eighteenth century the Los islands were equipped as entrepôts for the transfer of slaves from the smaller coastal vessels to ocean-going merchant ships.

Yet by the time Britain, the principal contender, ceded rights over the fledgling colony to France in 1887, Tumbo island still only had four tiny settlements – Bulbinay and Konakiri and the non-native African toeholds of Krootown and Tumbo – with a total of just a few hundred inhabitants. A road into the interior was started and the channel between Tumbo and the Kaloum peninsula on the mainland was filled in. By the time Britain handed over the Los islands in 1904, Conakry – the new capital of Guinée française – had its present grid pattern and a population of 10,000. The **railway** to Kankan was completed in 1914 and bananas from Kindia became the biggest export. Major developments came in the brief postwar colonial period, and concentrated on improving the port for the shipping of newly discovered iron ore and bauxite. The last fifteen years have seen massive growth and a major transformation into a consumer economy. The city – whose population numbers well over a million – will soon cover the entire peninsula.

Arrival, transport and accommodation

Conakry is built twenty kilometres out to sea on a **promontory**. Most of what you'll want in the way of banks, embassies, post office, hotels and restaurants is right at the end, on the two square kilometres of **city centre** where all the old parts of the town are

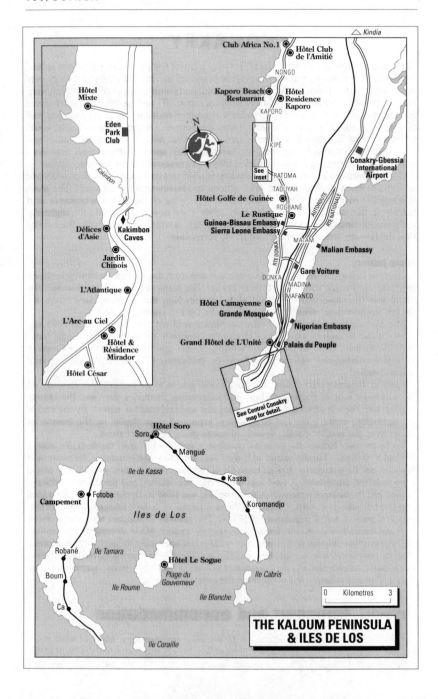

△ *Kindia*

Club Africa No.1 ●
Hôtel Club
de l'Amitié ●

NONGO

Kaporo Beach ●
Restaurant
Hôtel ●
Residence
Kaporo

KAPORO

Hôtel
Mixte ●

Eden
Park
Club

KIPÉ

See
inset

KALOUM

FRATOMA

Conakry-Gbessia
International
Airport

Hôtel Golfe de Guinée ●

TAOUYAH

ROGBANÉ

Le Rustique ●
Guinea-Bissau Embassy ●
Sierra Leone Embassy ●

Délices ●
d'Asie
Kakimbon ◆
Caves

RTE DONKA

MATAM

Malian Embassy ■

Jardin
Chinois ●

AUTOROUTE

RTE NATIONALE

L'Atlantique ●

DONKA

Gare Voiture ■

MADINA
MAFANCO

L'Arc-au Ciel ●

Hôtel Camayenne ●
Grande Mosquée ●

Hôtel &
Résidence
Mirador ●

Nigerian Embassy ◆

Grand Hôtel de L'Unité ●
Palais du Peuple ●

Hôtel César ●

See Central Conakry
map for detail.

Hôtel Soro ●
Soro ●

● Mangué

Ile de Kassa

● Kassa

● Fotoba
Campement

● Koromandjo

Iles de Los

Robané ●
Ile Tamara

Boum

Hôtel Le Sogue ●

Plage du
Gouverneur

Ile Cabris

Ca ●
Ile Roume
Ile Blanche

| 0 | Kilometres | 3 |

THE KALOUM PENINSULA
& ILES DE LOS

Ile Coraille

STREET NAMES

In the centre, the street grid is numbered, with avenues running east to west and boulevards running north to south; "1ère av" and "4ème bd" are the common local abbreviations we've used, but in English-language publications you may see 1st Avenue and 4th Boulevard. Note that 10ème av is also known as av de la Gare, 8ème av as av Tubman, 6ème av as av de la République (which leads into Route du Niger and the Autoroute), 6ème bd as bd Telly Diallo and 3ème bd as bd du Commerce. There are also two important "bis" avenues: 9ème av bis and 7ème av bis, not to be confused with 9ème av and 7ème av which run next to them.

Note that the street names have officially been altered to "KA" numbers – the old boulevards becoming odd-numbered KA numbers (eg: "1ère bd" changes to "KA 001") and the old avenues becoming even-numbered KA numbers (eg: "1ère av" changes to "KA 004") – but locals still generally refer to the old system. We give both the old and new street names on our map of Central Conakry.

located. Here, the grid pattern, divided into closely bunched districts, is easy once you have oriented yourself. The northern *quartiers* of the centre – Almamya and Kaloum – are the focus of business and bureaucracy while the southern districts – Manquépas, Boulbinet, Sandervalia – are mostly made up of tight-packed single-storey city compounds and still have a villagey atmosphere of brush-swept yards and open-fire cooking.

Landwards, past the huge **Palais du Peuple** and over the strategically narrow causeway onto the mainland, you hit the **Autoroute** (not a motorway or freeway in the usual sense, because all vehicles, and pedestrians, use it) and pass under the notorious bridge at Place du 8 Novembre from which so many of Sekou Touré's condemned prisoners were publicly hanged. The **Grande Mosquée** and then, behind the Donka Hospital, **Camp Boiro** (the main Touré-era prison camp) are over on the left. The *gare voiture*, in the Madina quarter, is further out, and stretching above the shore to the north, you hit the rapidly expanding and more affluent districts of Rogbané, Taouyah, Ratoma, Kipé, Kaporo and Nongo, where a number of Conakry's best hotels, clubs and restaurants are now to be found.

Arrival and public transport

If you arrive at Conakry **by air**, you'll find the open-plan airport is fairly well organized, though the introduction to Guinea is getting worse, with plentiful attempts to solicit bribes. It's worth noting that some airlines give out currency declaration forms: if you'll be flying out again it's advisable to obtain one in any case, to avoid hassles on departure.

Getting into town direct from outside the arrivals hall, take a taxi (FG5000 for the *déplacement* – private hire). There are no airport buses, though city buses run past the airport entrance on the Autoroute, from where you can also wave down a *taxi brousse* (FG200–500 depending on the time of day and how much luggage you have).

SECURITY

Elsewhere, people may tell you that Conakry is a den of thieves (and certainly you should be on your guard, in the ordinary way, for pickpockets and the like). But in comparison with, say, Dakar, it's relatively peaceful in that respect and the real hassles come from the police who can be quite inventive in trying to extract a bribe. Carry some ID, if not your passport, at all times.

If your flight arrives early enough in the day, you may be able to leave Conakry and head upcountry immediately. In that case, take a taxi towards town only as far as the *gare voiture* in Madina, which should cost you half the full fare to the centre.

Arriving at Conakry **by road**, the Madina *gare voiture*, 6km from the city centre, is as close to the centre as you're likely to fetch up. Find a bus or taxi into the town centre, along the Autoroute, or walk across the railway tracks and a few hundred metres further to the junction with Route Donka where you can try hitching a lift: a surprising number of expatriates, most of whom live on the north side of the peninsula, will oblige.

Public transport

Conakry has reasonable **bus services** – basically running the length of the peninsula – but at peak hours (7–11am and 4–8pm) it can take literally hours to get from one end of the city to the other. The main city centre terminus is the roundabout in the port area; the big depot is 6km up the peninsula at the Madina *gare voiture*. State-owned SOGETRAG buses have been replaced with UNTRG (Union Nationale de Transporteurs Routiere de Guinee) ones, and by more limited private lines such as Melia. Minimum fares are FG100 (per route sector) and only rise to FG250 to get out as far as Ratoma.

Taxis (allow one hour between city centre and airport) are exasperatingly hard to find off the main thoroughfares, from which they only occasionally deviate. The main routes for shared taxis are "Route Donka" (north side of the peninsula), "Autoroute" (Autoroute bridge to airport) and "Route du Niger" (joining with "Autoroute"). Taxis are unmetered, but are at least not too expensive, charging FG200 for short, shared journeys in town, and FG200–300 per kilometre for a private *déplacement*.

Accommodation

Conakry has an increasing number of mid-range and expensive **hotels**, but if you're on a tight budget, you'll find the options very limited. You might even prefer to stay out of town, in Coyah (see p.499), on the way to Kindia, and commute into the city. There are no hostels or travellers' haunts in Conakry and anything under FG20,000, even for a single room, is likely to be a basic brothel. Electricity and water are both unreliable and the really cheap places are usually in a disgusting state: we've selected just three – one of which, the *Djoliba*, is recommended. Climate has a lot to do with the tendency for all of Conakry's hotels to decline rapidly; only the places that can afford regular refurbishing survive more than a few years before going into a period of dormancy, or just closing for good.

There are a few church and aid organization guesthouses which have, in the past, been very welcoming to unexpected guests. There have been gentle complaints that directing readers to them in travel guides is exploiting the hospitality. Hence, they're not included here.

City centre

Bar-Restaurant Djoliba, 9ème av (☎44.15.60). *Chambres de passage* with bucket showers and shared toilets. It's a friendly, relaxed place, and good value too. Animated bar, good restaurant, and sometimes very busy club. ②.

Hôtel Galaxie (☎45.10.01). Brand new, no-frills hotel. The completely bare lobby contrasts with cosy, well-furnished rooms and satellite TV. All the comfort you need in an excellent location for a comparatively low price. No credit cards. ⑤.

Hôtel du Niger, rte du Niger close to the market (BP 14; ☎44.41.30; Fax 44.12.36). Fairly clean, secure and in a good position for downtown, this is always a safe bet. Slightly overpriced rooms with fan or AC. ③–④.

Motel du Port, av du Port (☎41.26.24). Why waste a good Portakabin? Approached through a court-yard thronged with children, this former German port engineers' housing offers a complex of double-decker cabins, with a pool, video room, bar and restaurant. AC, S/C rooms equipped with fridges. ④.

Novotel Grand Hôtel de l'Indépendance (BP 287; ☎41.50.21). Stylish example of the genre, insulated from Conakry's fickle utility cuts, with everything you could possibly need and much you probably don't. Amex, Visa, MasterCard, and crumpled FG all accepted. ⑦.

Pension Doherty, 5ème av (BP 3671; ☎ & Fax 44.38.75). Although central, this is in a residential quarter, full of kids and ordinary streetlife. Good pavement area. Various rooms and variable standards. ③–④.

Out of the centre

Hôtel Camayenne (BP 2818; ☎41.40.89; Fax 44.29.95). Conakry's most expensive hotel, fully refurbished and managed by Sabena. Rooms with satellite TV and every other facility. Right by the sea. All cards. ⑦.

Hôtel César, Taouyah. Take the rte de Donka past Rogbané, turn left at the *Mariador* hotels sign, and then left again. Italian, family-run, with a restaurant and swimming pool, big among the expat community. The AC, S/C rooms, with mosquito-netted beds, are good value. ④.

Hôtel Club de l'Amitié, about 13km from the centre, in Nongo. Take the left fork after Kaporo Port for about 1500m; there's a sign on the right. Clean sheets, fans, bucket shower in your room. Pleasant bar and simple restaurant. ②.

Hôtel Golfe de Guinée, rte de Donka, qtr Minière, Rogbané (☎46.43.10). Somewhat sterile place, with reasonable-value AC, S/C rooms, some with sea view. ④.

Hôtel Mariador, Rogbané, massively signposted (☎43.11.42). High-quality, immaculate rooms equipped with fridge and satellite TV. Swimming pool. Shares facilities with the *Résidence Mariador*. ⑥–⑦.

Hôtel Mixte, Kipé district. Turn left down a dirt track just after the *Eden Park* nightclub, directly opposite a mosque; then 500m on the right. A *maquis* and *maison de passage*, popular with civil servants. Dirty walls, clean sheets, fans or AC. ②.

Hôtel Residence Kaporo, rte de Donka, Kaporo, just after the Elf station. New family-run hotel with fresh, spotless rooms (some with shared baths) and a choice of fan or A/C. Decent restaurant, too. Excellent value. ③.

Résidence Mariador, adjoining the *Hôtel Mariador* (☎43.11.32). Larger and right above the rocky shore, with tennis facilities. All cards. ⑤–⑦.

The City and around

There are many more interesting West African capitals to fill the days while you wait for friends, visas, money or whatever. If you find yourself laden with spare time, you'll do best to visit the Iles de Los, or to get out of Conakry altogether and explore inland.

ACCOMMODATION PRICE CODES

① Under FG10,000 (under £5/$8)
② FG10,000–20,000 (£5–10/$8–16)
③ FG20,000–40,000 (£10–20/$16–32)
④ FG40,000–60,000 (£20–30/$32–48)

⑤ FG60,000–80,000 (£30–40/$48–64)
⑥ FG80,000–100,000 (£40–50/$64–80)
⑦ Over FG100,000 (over £50/$80)

For full details, see p.48.

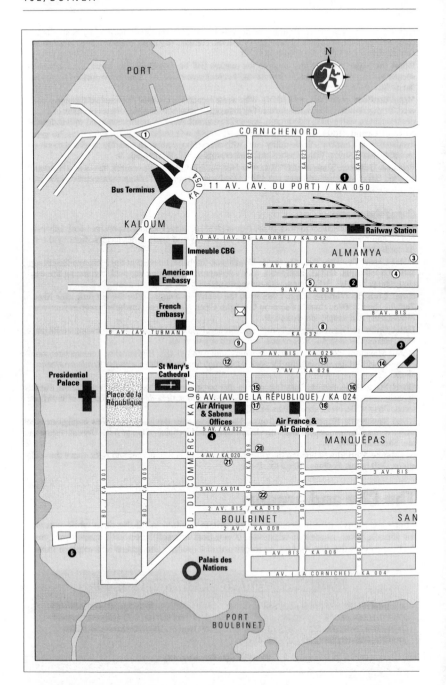

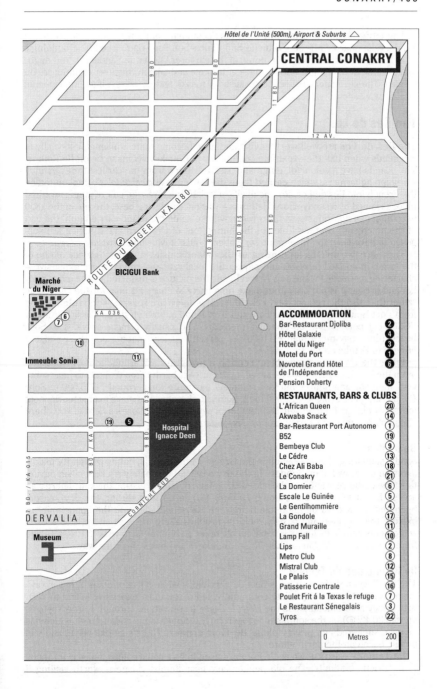

Hôtel de l'Unité (500m), Airport & Suburbs △

CENTRAL CONAKRY

9 BD
10 BD
11 BD
12 AV

ROUTE DU NIGER / KA 080

Marché du Niger

BICIGUI Bank ②

KA 036

Immeuble Sonia

KA 03

KA 031

8 BD / KA 015

7 BD

DERVALIA

Museum

Hospital Ignace Deen

CORNICHE SUD

⑲ ❺

⑥ ⑦ ⑩ ⑪

ACCOMMODATION
Bar-Restaurant Djoliba ❷
Hôtel Galaxie ❹
Hôtel du Niger ❸
Motel du Port ❶
Novotel Grand Hôtel
de l'Indépendance ❻
Pension Doherty ❺

RESTAURANTS, BARS & CLUBS
L'African Queen ⑳
Akwaba Snack ⑭
Bar-Restaurant Port Autonome ①
B52 ⑲
Bembeya Club ⑨
Le Cédre ⑬
Chez Ali Baba ⑱
Le Conakry ㉑
La Domier ⑥
Escale Le Guinée ⑤
Le Gentilhommiére ④
La Gondole ⑰
Grand Muraille ⑪
Lamp Fall ⑩
Lips ②
Metro Club ⑧
Mistral Club ⑫
Le Palais ⑮
Patisserie Centrale ⑯
Poulet Frit á la Texas le refuge ⑦
Le Restaurant Sénegalais ③
Tyros ㉒

0   Metres   200

The city's **National Museum** – an unexceptional hour's worth – is down in the Sandervalia quarter off the Corniche Sud (Tues–Sun 9am–6pm; free). The buildings, or at least part of them, were the home of the explorer Olivier de Sanderval. You might aim to come here at midday for a snack at the café and take in whatever exhibits are on display. The permanent collection consists of masks and other carvings, instruments and a few weapons.

The Iles de Los

The **Iles de Los** are well worth a visit and have become quite a magnet, especially at weekends when half the expatriate community of Conakry seems to be on Ile Roume. The islands have a colourful, enigmatic past, inhabited from the earliest times by idol-worshipping farmers, which earned them the Portuguese label "*idolos*", transmuted by the French into Iles de Los. Roume itself – a lavishly picturesque pair of jungle-swathed hillocks joined by a sandy-shored isthmus – was once a slaving base, the site of the 1850 execution of a notorious slaver, Crawford, whose name the island carried until the end of the nineteenth century. Tales of the buried loot of Crawford and his men are supposed to have been the inspiration for Robert Louis Stevenson's *Treasure Island*.

There are two options for **getting to the islands**: using a regular service of one of the large, motorized *pirogues* and paying the local rate, or – much more expensive – chartering a *pirogue* for the day. At weekends the picture is distorted by the expat market and pressure is put on you to make up a party to charter a boat for the whole day rather than use the regular services. Most days there are several "**scheduled" runs** from Port Boulbinet to Kassa village and Koromandjo, both on Ile de Kassa, for about FG300 per person, and on Sundays there are also usually *pirogue* services to Soro beach (don't pay more than FG1000 per person). At least once a day there's also a *pirogue* to Fotoba on Ile Tamara.

While there's never any problem **renting a pirogue** – ask around in Port Boulbinet or on the beach by the *Novotel* – agreeing the price is harder. You're likely to hear some very high starting figures but you shouldn't pay more than around FG15,000 to Soro (Ile de Kassa) or FG20000–25,000 to Ile Roume or Fotoba. And that's to charter the boat for the whole day for a reasonable number of people: unless there's a herd of you, there shouldn't be any extra surcharge for passengers.

Ile de Kassa

Sandy, palm-fringed **Soro beach** is the largest on the islands, but its popularity makes it extremely crowded on Sundays in the dry season. Fortunately it's kept clean during this time of the year and has the added advantage of huts to escape the sun. There's an access fee of FG1000 and a hotel, *Le Soro* (③), open only during the dry season. Spending a few days on eight-kilometre long Kassa will give you the opportunity to explore the secluded and largely rockless beaches along the west shore, and several settlements among its lovely forests. It only takes an hour or so to walk to Kassa village from Soro beach and you're likely to see monkeys and birds along the way.

Ile Roume and Ile Tamara

The small, central **Ile Roume** is best on a weekday when it's very quiet. It has always been favoured by the expatriate community and is the most expensive island to visit, with pricey accommodation in the *Hôtel le Sogue* (reservations through Karou Voyages on ☎45.20.42; ⑤) on the south shore (open early October to the end of June), which has its own, sheltered and private **plage du Gouverneur**. There's an extensive, and still public, beach on the north shore.

Ile Tamara – also known as Ile Fotoba – used to be a penal colony and was for many years strictly off-limits. The old penitentiary near Fotoba village is worth visiting if you're on the island, but as on Roume and Kassa, the main attractions are the forests and seashore. There's a *campement* (②), run by the Sylla Fotoba family, if you wish to spend the night.

Eating, drinking and nightlife

Eating in Conakry used to be either expensive and mediocre or just poor value for money. These days, there are dozens of restaurants – the best, admittedly, still very expensive – while street food, after years of savage austerity ("we have no potatoes, we have no rice . . ."), is once again great. Fast-food joints, specializing in *chawarma*, burgers and chicken, are opening all the time, while rice dishes at FG300 and grilled meat sandwiches at FG400 can be had on many street corners or in the markets.

Basic meals and snacks

Akwaba Snack, qtr Almamya. Reasonable-value Lebanese–American "specialities": burgers, *chawarma*, falafel, etc. From FG2000.

Bar-restaurant Port Autonome, at the port across from the bus terminus. Excellent breakfasts and lunches until about 3pm, cold beer until dusk.

Chez Ali Baba, ave de République, near Air France. Cheap burgers, fries and *chawarmas* in a sit-down area, adjoining the more expensive part of this well-liked Lebanese restaurant.

Le Damier, opposite Marché du Niger (also at Super-V supermarket in Ratoma). Good cakes and pastries, coffee, snacks. Open Mon–Sat until dusk.

La Gondole, av de la République, opposite the La Palace leisure complex. Expensive patisserie, but with excellent ice cream.

Lamp Fall, 7ème av. Very popular Senegalese *gargote*, easily recognized by the blue canopy outside. Huge portions of nutritious, tasty food from about FG2500.

Patisserie Centrale, av de la République, opposite the KLM building. Good place for ice cream, snacks, patisserie and coffee.

Poulet Frit à la Texas, Immeuble Sonia, rte du Niger, opposite the *Hôtel du Niger*. Lebanese/Greek international fast food: pizzas, roast chicken, burgers, all for around FG3000.

Le Restaurant Sénégalais, corner of 10av and 7bd. You won't find better rice and fish in Dakar, and they also have *mafé, poulet yassa* and *steak frites*. Around FG1500.

Restaurants

L'African Queen, 4ème av, Manquépas. Good reputation, but expensive, with pizza and pasta specialities from FG6000–10,000 and a FG9000 *menu*. Open Mon–Sat lunchtimes only.

L'Arc-en-Ciel, rue RA 370, Kipé. Excellent African specialities and some European dishes. Live music and dancing too. Open daily.

L'Atlantique, rte de Donka, Ratoma (☎42.10.03). Long-established and excellent seafood restaurant on the clifftop. Expensive. Open Tues–Sat evenings & Sun lunch.

Bar-Restaurant Djoliba, 9ème av. An affordable retreat with steak or *riz gras* for under FG2000 and *sauce de feuilles* or *sauce d'arachides* for FG1000.

Le Cedre, Almamaya. Small, intimate Moroccan restaurant, currently a lunchtime favourite amongst the expats.

Le Cesar, Corniche Nord, Taouyah. Appetizing Italian specialities – around FG12,000 – in this hotel restaurant.

Comme Chez Soi, Taouyah, near the *Mariador* hotels. French cooking. Pricey.

Le Conakry, 4ème av, by the Ministry of Finance (☎44.26.82). Solid, Guinean business-class restaurant, with a French chef, a lunchtime *menu* (FG8000), and a *carte* (dishes FG6000 plus). Closed Sun.

Délices d'Asie, rte de Donka, opposite the *commissariat* in Ratoma. Reasonable food, but a superb terrace. Dishes at FG10,000 from the *carte*. Closed Mon & Tues.

Escale de Guinée, corner of 5ème bd and 9ème av. Looks like it's been doing a quiet lunch trade on the same corner since the 1930s. As worthwhile for the company of the folks who run it as for the home-style French cooking. FG5000–7000 for the *menu*.

Le Gentilhommière, 9ème av bis, Almamya (☎44.26.24). Bamboo everywhere suggests Chinese, but this serves mostly French and Antillean food. *Menu* at FG7000, with *carte* dishes from FG5000. Closed Sun.

Jardin Chinois, rte de Donka, Ratoma. Good Chinese food, and relatively good prices. Open Tues–Sun evenings & Sun lunch.

Kaporo Beach, overlooking the sea at Kaporo, well signposted. Miles out of town, but a favourite weekend haunt of expats, with a good reputation for French, especially Niçoise, food and pizzas, and a pool.

Le Morocco, next to the *Hotel Camayenne* (☎44.67.79). Moroccan and international specialities. Pricey, but worth it.

Le Natraj, qtr Coléah, Matam, behind the "54 logements" (☎44.36.46). The only full-blown Indian restaurant in Guinea. Closed Sun lunch.

Le Refuge, Corniche Sud, Boulbinet, near the museum. Senegalese-owned, but strictly French cuisine. Sea views.

Restaurant des Iles, 1ère av, Boulbinet (☎44.27.64). French and African cuisine, with a deservedly good reputation and not unreasonably priced. Closed Mon evening.

Le Rustique, qtr Minière. European, and particularly German, cooking. Very expensive and always busy. Dishes from the *carte* FG8000–10,000. Open evenings only (closed Mon).

Tyros, 3ème av, between 4ème and 5ème bd. Classy Lebanese with a good selection of dishes from FG5000–7000.

Le Wonkefun, rte de Donka, Ratoma. The best choice among Conakry's Asian restaurants.

Nightlife

Conakry **nightlife** is an enjoyable scene, and an ever-changing one. The testing climate means that many clubs are in a poor state of repair by the end of the rainy season and don't always survive the consequent decline in business through the next dry season. The following selection, therefore, is likely to include one or two which have already gone for good and others temporarily *hors de combat*.

City centre clubs

B52, 5ème av, a couple of doors from *Pension Doherty*. Recommended watering hole.

Bembeya Club, av Tubman/4ème bd. Refurbished old-timer which has seen its glory days, but is holding up well.

Djoliba, 9ème av. A lively bar which has blossomed into a regular, if a little downmarket club.

Grand Muraille, 7ème av bis. Popular karaoke club, even on Sat, when entrance is FG4000. Closed Mon.

Lips, opposite the BICIGUI bank on rte du Niger. Great, young atmosphere if you like to dance. Usually offers two sessions: 5–10pm and 11pm–dawn.

Metro Club, 7ème av bis, Almamya. Approachable, middle-class club full of Guinean townies and their girlfriends. Cosy atmosphere, which livens up at weekends. Small cover charge.

Mistral Club, 7ème av. Cheap and seedy, but enjoyable.

Le Palais, av de la République. A flashy disco, mostly patronized by sailors, its atmosphere depending on the ships in port. Entrance FG3000 (free on weekdays). Upstairs bar is inexpensive, dark and full of women.

Zambezi, rte Nationale (all the taxi drivers know it). Very popular club with an eclectic mix of people and music. FG4000 cover.

Clubs along the peninsula

In recent years, many new clubs have sprung up in Conakry's burgeoning north-peninsula development. Rogbané, Taouyah, Ratoma and Kipé are the main suburbs to head for: in many cases the clubs in these districts are livelier than the older places in town.

Africa No.1, after the sign for *Hôtel Club de l'Amitié*, in Nongo. A little overshadowed by newer clubs, but still quite popular.

Eden Park, Kipé. FG8000 cover.

Evasion Club, along the Autoroute just after qtr Matam.

King's Club, Taouyah, near Cinéma Rogbané. FG3000 cover.

Safari Club, Autoroute, near the 8 Novembre bridge. FG3000 cover.

Wendys, Autoroute, near the airport. Very popular with Sierra Leonians, this small, but exciting club plays mainly American music.

Listings

Airline offices Unless otherwise noted, the following are all clustered along av de la République: Aeroflot, Imm. Banque Islamique (☎44.41.43); Air Afrique (☎44.47.70 or 44.47.72); Air Bissau (TAGB); Air France (☎44.36.57; Fax 41.47.27); Air Guinée (☎44.46.14); Air Ivoire (☎41.30.69); Gambia Airways, opposite Imm. CBG, bd du Commerce(☎44.30.00); Ghana Airways (☎44.48.13); Royal Air Maroc, Imm. Banque Islamique (☎41.38.96); Sabena (☎41.34.40; Fax 41.42.94).

American Express No representative. The *Novotel* may help.

Banks and money-changing BICIGUI on av de la République (☎41.45.15; Fax 44.39.62; Mon–Thurs 8.30am–12.30pm & 2.30–4.30pm, Fri 8.30am–12.45pm) is the main branch for foreign exchange in Conakry, and quite efficient. The black market money traders are mostly to be found outside the airport, around the port area and near the PTT. Rates are at least ten percent better than the bank, and police seem unfussed.

Car rental The rate for a small saloon car, assuming 100km per day and including obligatory, expensive insurance starts at around FG40,000/day or FG200,000/week. There's a sixteen percent tax on top. For a capable, off-road vehicle, you'd be looking at three times these figures. One of the cheaper outlets is Locadem (☎45.19.80) at the *Novotel*. Also try Locagui, by the Cité Douanes, rte du Niger, qtr Coléah, Matam (☎41.35.24) which rents out Toyotas, with or without driver. Local franchisees of the international companies have offices at the airport and *Novotel*, but they insist on you hiring a driver (around FG10,000/day) for trips inland from Conakry.

Cassettes Some of the cheapest in West Africa are available from the Marché du Niger. Make up a job lot and bargain your heart out: around FG1000 each for old titles, FG1500 for new releases, about half what you'd pay in Dakar or Abidjan.

Cinemas Of the ten or more in the city, the Rogbané in Taouyah – a fairly upmarket district – is the best, with the newish Liberté, by the Autoroute bridge, also quite good.

Crafts and curios A listless selection on the whole. The expensive hotels have a selection in their shops or on the forecourt, but they're expensive. Visit the market, and check out 4ème bd between av de la République and av de la Gare, near the post office.

Cultural centres Americans and others can visit the American Cultural Centre on the Corniche Sud, near the Autoroute bridge, for its library, periodicals, English- and French-language movies and American satellite TV (Mon, Tues & Thurs–Fri 9am–12.30pm & 2–6pm; Wed 2–6pm; Sat 9am–12.30pm).

Embassies, consulates and honorary consuls include: Canada, near Cité Douanes, Corniche Sud, Matam (BP 99; ☎46.23.95); Cape Verde, Com. de Ratoma, qtr Miniere (BP 1248; ☎22.17.44); Cote d'Ivoire, Com. de Kaloum, Boulbinet bd du Commerce (BP 5258; ☎45.10.82); France, bd du Commerce, entry on 8ème av (BP 570; ☎ 41.16.05; issues visas for Burkina and Mauritania); Ghana, Com. de Matam, Coléah (BP 732; ☎44.15.10); Guinea-Bissau, Com. de Dixinn, qtr Bellevue (BP 298; ☎46.21.36); Mali, Com. de Matam, between the Autoroute and rte de Niger, after the Total station (BP 299; ☎46.14.18); Morocco, Com. de Kaloum, Boulbinet, Cité des Nations Villa 12, Cité des Nations (BP 193); Nigeria, Com. de Matam, Corniche du Sud, Coléah (BP 54; ☎41.43.75); Senegal, Com. de Matam, Corniche Sud, Coléah (BP 842; ☎46.28.34); Togo, Com. de Matam, Madina (BP 3633; ☎46.24.08); UK Honorary. Consul Mrs Val Treitlein, Com. de Dixinn, Corniche du Nord, Donka, Cite Ministerielle (BP 834; ☎44.69.82; Fax 46.16.80); USA, opposite Imm. FRIGUIA, 2ème bd (BP 603; ☎41.15.21).

Film processing For one-hour developing and printing, try Amina Photo, Imm. Sonia, rte du Niger, next to the *Texas Poulet Frit*.

MOVING ON FROM CONAKRY

Flights to the interior are now handled solely by Air Guinée, since the other two domestic carriers (Guinee Inter Air and Guinee Air Service) have closed down indefinitely. Air Guinée flies to Kissidougou on Thurs; Nzérékoré on Thurs and Sat; Kankan on Wed and Sat; Labé on Mon and Fri; Sambailo (for Koundara) on Fri; and Siguiri on Wed and Sat.

There are limited possibilities for **sea travel** to other parts of West Africa: contact SOGUICOM, the main shipping agents (10ème av, BP 3115; ☎41.32.84). A service called Sierra Link connected Freetown with Conakry in the early 1990s (about FG40,000) but is still suspended. *The MV Remvi's* regular service to Monrovia is in operation, but not particularly useful for most travellers.

All upcountry **road transport** leaves from the Madina *gare voiture* which, unless you flew in, is almost certainly where you first arrived in the city. SOGETRAG **buses** are no longer running, and upcountry services are now provided by various private companies to a number of towns, including frequent runs to Dubreka, Coyah and Kindia, and daily services to Pita, Labé, Kissidougou and Kankan. There are also services to Guéckédou and Nzérékoré (20hrs); for these and the other less frequent services, you should ideally reserve seats the day before. The buses are much more comfortable and no more expensive than the principal alternative, **Peugeot 504s.** For the latter, you simply need to be at the *gare voiture* early to secure a place for practically anywhere in the country. Peugeot 504s offer more flexibility in price than the buses if you're getting out before the eventual destination.

Medical/dental attention For emergencies, go to Hôpital Ignace Deen (☎44.20.53) or Hôpital Donka (☎44.19.33). For private consultations, Dr Sureau in Taouyah is recommended by many expat clients. The French dentist at the university's *centre medicaire* is good.

Pharmacies Check a copy of *Djeli* or *Tam Tam* for *pharmacies de garde* (out-of-hours pharmacy rota).

Photo permits These are more a theoretical than a mandatory requirement. If you're feeling frivolous enough to want to take on Guinean bureaucracy, check them out at ONACIG, by the Cinéma Liberté at Place du 8 Novembre. Otherwise, keep your lenses capped in Conakry.

Post and telephones The main PTT is open Mon–Sat 8am–2pm. The telephone section stays open until 10pm, with stamps for sale. Poste restante is neither stunningly secure nor organized. The public fax number is 41.32.18.

Supermarkets The big ones are Superbobo on rte de Donka in Camayenne (English-speaking publications available) and Super-V in qtr Coléah, Matam.

Travel agents The airlines often act as general agents. Independent travel agents include Karou Voyages, on av de la République (☎45.20.42) and at the *Novotel* (☎44.32.65), and SDV Guinée (☎41.43.99).

Visa extensions Available from the immigration office at the Ministry of the Interior, corner of 8ème av and 1ère bd, at a cost of FG40,000 for three months.

THE FOUTA DJALON

Raising some spectacular cliffs just a short journey inland from Conakry and covering the greater part of the western interior, the **Fouta Djalon highlands** are Guinea's major attraction. Cut into innumerable, chocolate-bar plateaux – some denuded to mesa-like outcrops – the sandstone massif is the source of hundreds of **rivers**, including the Gambia and Senegal, major tributaries of the Niger and a lattice of streams running down to the Guinea coast. After the rains, **waterfalls** spume everywhere.

Populated by **Fula** (Peul) herders and the remnants of the indigenous agricultural groups whose territory they invaded, the region has a fascinating ethnic history and an extraordinary variety of landscape. Lushly cultivated or **jungle-filled valleys** rise – sometimes with **sheer cliffs** – to scrubby high ground, bare and rocky waste-lands or lightly wooded **plateaux**. Wherever the contours are gentle enough to retain the soil, swaths of **grassland** roll in the wind. It's fabulous country and needs only time, and average determination, to explore – wanderings which can be immensely satisfying.

The approach: Kindia and Mamou

You can get to the major Fouta Djalon centres – Dalaba, Pita and Labé – in a day's travel from Conakry on a good, surfaced road, but you will have to be at Conakry's Madina *gare voiture* early. If you're in no hurry, start the trip with the short journey up to **COYAH** (50km). Leaving Conakry, you follow the smog-laden fast lane, and the oily squalor and vitality of the city immigrants' highway-side *ateliers*, manufacturing every conceivable kind of item. You pass also through a string of tedious **checkpoints**, the last of which, Kilometre 36, at the Kindia–Dubreka junction, is an outlandish scene of strut-ting and loafing khaki where delays, particularly heading into the city, are commonplace.

Coyah (Guinea's source of bottled water) is surrounded by dense green forest and plantation, and innumerable food stalls throng its main street. There's a nice hotel here if you're in need – the *Mariani* (②–③), signposted off the main road, with good facili-ties, including S/C rooms.

Out of Coyah, pale dramatic **cliffs** rise to the south from a broken plain of bush and palms. Crowned with bubbling greenery, these isolated tablelands – more or less sep-arated from the plains by rock faces on all sides, and apparently uninhabited on top – would likely repay investigation by fairly intrepid naturalists. If you're interested and

HIKING, BIKING AND RELATED PRACTICALITIES

The Fouta Djalon is one of the best regions in West Africa for serious, stimulating **off-the-beaten-track travel**. Assuming you're armed with at least the IGN map of the country (the Michelin 953 isn't enough), there are hundreds of kilometres of, sometimes opti-mistically labelled, "motorable tracks" and footpaths throughout the region (see p.505 for an account of cycling along one of them). **Mountain bikes** are ideal, and on the main routes you'll have little trouble loading them onto vehicles whenever your enthusiasm for pedalling wanes. **Motorbikes**, preferably trail bikes, would also be fine. **Cars and off-road vehicles** however – even 4WD ones – will run into repeated difficulties on steep and rugged terrain and you'd need the most agile and powerful machine to negotiate more than the most often-used of the minor routes. The option open to all is **footing it** and the only consideration then is whether your visa allows you the time.

You should ensure minimal levels of **survivability** in the event of a breakdown or an accident. If you're cycling, or on a motorbike, take obsessive care: roads which seem rel-atively good can turn a bend and disappear without warning into a river, or lose them-selves in a jumble of rocks and gullies. Have purifying tablets for water – which often comes straight from the local stream – and carry some back-up rations for emergencies.

This is the most densely populated part of the country. The **people** of the Fouta Djalon are, in general, wonderfully kind and show a disinterested concern for the welfare of wayward *porto* (white people). There's a growing population of English-speaking refugees from the wars in Liberia and Sierra Leone, too. People will nearly always get water for you when you need it. The highlands, moreover, are a major citrus-growing area and during the early dry season you'll be able to rely on oranges in their hundreds as a cheap source of fluid. Remember of course to stock up on **essentials** like toilet paper and batteries which don't grow on trees, and also bear in mind that temperatures at night can drop below 10°C and you'll need something warm.

ready for a hike, stop at the village of **Tabili** and follow the left bank of the Badi upstream between the cliffs. It rises on top of the plateau.

Kindia

Born on the railway line in the early 1900s, **KINDIA** (135km from Conakry) is now a bustling, workaday place dramatically located beneath the hulk of Mont Gangan. The railway barely functions any more and there aren't any obvious attractions in town apart from the huge **market** – a large section of which is devoted to local cloth, where the vendors shout to be heard over the whirring of sewing machines. Shaded by innumerable **mango trees** (Kindia is a wonderful place to fetch up the mango in season, boasting many different varieties – *chocolat, fini pas*, etc), the town has a number of decent eateries along the main road and several places to stay if you arrive late in the day.

Practicalities

If you have to stop over in Kindia (the hotel at La Voile de la Mariée falls (see opposite), 18km further east, is much nicer), the best **accommodation** is probably the *Buffet de la Gare* (②), which has enthusiastic staff, several nearby cafés and large S/C rooms around a pleasant courtyard. It incorporates the *La Paillotte* nightclub, the noise potential of which you should consider when choosing a room. The most central hotel is the adequate, if grubby, *3 Avril* (①). Otherwise, choose between the hotel/dance bar, *Phare de Guinée* (②), 2km out of town on the road to Coyah on the left-hand side, or the neighbouring Vietnamese-run boarding house (①).

The few **eating** options in Kindia are quite diverse. *Le Mont Gagan* is pleasant, with African dishes and a surprisingly extensive French menu, and you can get *atieké* on the street, always served with fish. For a broadly international menu (chicken, fish, steak) the *Buffet de la Gare* or *Le Bananier* will provide, though it's wise to go in advance to be sure of getting what you want. *Le Bananier* is also one of Kindia's main **nightspots**, particularly good on Thursday and Saturday nights, when they charge a FG2000 entrance. At weekends, the *Buffet* can also be lively, and *King Kindy* is good for drinks.

There are good purchases to be made in Kindia, especially in **cloth** (*tissus*). A pair of batik *pagnes* (two-metre lengths of printed cloth) goes for FG5000–6000, indigo dyed cloth (*gara*) for not much more and beaten damask (*lepi*) for around FG15,000 a pair.

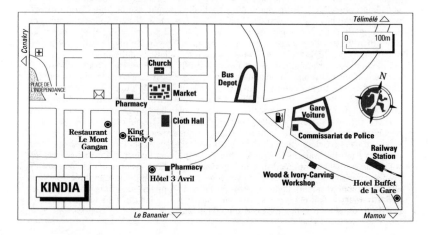

There's a large covered area devoted to cloth – the *marché aux tissus* – in the main market. Various beads and leatherwork are on offer across the street from it. You might also visit the woodworkers near the old station: expect to be offered ivory as well as woodcarvings. Kindia has a **post office**, but no bank.

Around Kindia

There are several worthwhile day-trips in the Kindia area: **Mont Gangan**, rising above the town 10km to the north; **Pastoria**, the birthplace of TB immunization; and the **Voile de la Mariée falls**, where you might even be tempted to stay a few days.

Mont Gangan

The massif of **Mont Gangan** is one of the highest peaks (1117m) in the southern Fouta Djalon and relatively easily climbed. The big plateau halfway up offers brilliant views over Kindia, especially after the rains. Just be careful not to stroll through the military camp on the way.

Pastoria

If you'd like to have a look at **Pastoria** – the "Institut Pasteur" – which is 6km up the road to Télimélé from Kindia, you'll probably have to *déplace* a town taxi for the trip, or take a long walk in hope. The institute was founded in 1925 as a primate research centre, principally with the aim of developing various vaccines for human use. We have their consumptive chimps to thank for the BCG (Bacillus Calmette-Guerin) anti-tuberculosis jab. The Pasteur Institute in Paris later charged Pastoria with the collection of snake venom for anti-venene preparations. It's still open for visits if you call first on the director. They have a large collection of primates and snakes.

La Voile de la Mariée

The best known of Kindia's local excursions is to **La Voile de la Mariée**, the "Bridal Veil" falls, a five-kilometre diversion off the road to Mamou, 13km from Kindia. Here, the Santa River leaps from a black and yellow cliff in two streams to crash against the rockface and break into a broad fan, a total drop of some sixty metres. It's a year-round phenomenon, but most impressive during and shortly after the rains. The area is looked after by a hotelier who manages fifteen spacious concrete huts (built by order of Sekou Touré for his weekly visits), now converted into a pleasant **campement**, set amid the jungle (S/C twin rooms in huts of two or three rooms; ②). You can also camp here. Meals are available, but you do need to order well in advance. If you stay several days, the hotel manager will be pleased to escort you into the nearby hills for a jungle trek and bird's-eye views of the district.

If you just visit for the day out of Kindia, you'll pay an entrance fee of FG1000, a FG2500 parking fee and whatever you agree with your taxi driver (FG7000 round-trip

---

MOVING ON FROM KINDIA

A minor route into the Fouta Djalon winds out of Kindia to **Télimélé**, with onward possibilities to Pita and the far north. There's a handful of vehicles each day and the road condition is kept up fairly well. There's a continuous flow of transport shuttling between Kindia and **Mamou**. For travellers heading for **Sierra Leone**, Kindia has occasional bush taxi departures for Madina Oula, from where it's possible to reach the Outamba-Kilimi National Park and Kamakwie, as well as direct buses to the border town of Pamelap. But, for current advice about travel in Sierra Leone, see box pp.14–15.

is about right). An alternative means of getting here would be to take a minibus *taxi brousse* as far as Segueya (FG400) and then walk the final couple of kilometres down the track to the falls.

Mamou

From Kindia, the steep, hairpinning 130-kilometre climb up to Mamou offers a sweeping panorama back over the broad tributary basins of the Kolente (or Great Scarcies) River, the border with Sierra Leone. Twenty or thirty kilometres before Mamou you'll find a couple of hamlets which have developed into sizeable "service stations" for the passing bush taxi trade, providing roadside food and prayer stalls day and night. **Madine** is the first; **Hafiya** the second and more important one.

If you're in the mood for more waterfalls – and have your own vehicle – take a side trip, 5km to the right, to the village and falls of **Konkouré**, some 25km before Mamou. There's an old sacred wood here, containing remnant examples of trees from the ancient forest which once covered large parts of the Fouta Djalon.

MAMOU, piled on the hillside, strikes a surprisingly low-key note with its sprawl of houses and compounds. Before the building of the railway, the religious and political centre of the Fouta Djalon *almamys* (Islamic leaders) was **Timbo** – now just a village 50km northeast of Mamou (see p.510). Despite considerable local opposition, the French decided to bypass Timbo and set up a new railway halt and fuel depot at the hamlet of Mamou. The Fula chieftaincy was transferred and, up until the end of World War II, Mamou was the chief administrative centre for much of the highlands. Today this unappetizing crossroads town has an agricultural college and a meat-processing industry. It also has perhaps the worst reputation for crime of any town in Guinea – though it's by no means evident and Mamouans will insist that Conakry is worse.

Accommodation options in the centre are limited to just one hotel: *Hôtel Luna* (②) has thirty nominally S/C rooms around a large courtyard – mobilize the patron to organize water if you find none in your shower/toilet. The *Luna*'s terrace, in the older part of the hotel across the street, is popular among local teachers and *fonctionnaires*,

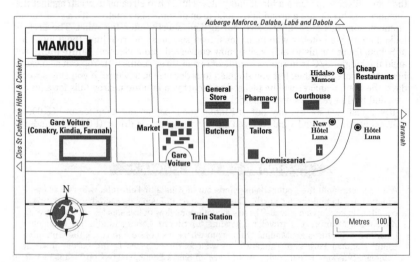

MOVING ON FROM MAMOU

Mamou is such a major transport hub that moving on is rarely a problem. The town's three taxi and bus parks, each surrounded by cheap little eateries, are hives of activity from dawn to dusk. The two in the town centre handle the Conakry–Faranah axis; the one on the road out of town towards Labé handles Fouta Djalon traffic and transport on the less busy routes to Timbo, Dabola and Dinguiraye.

and can be quite a scene. Musicians and griots come here and compete against the radio in the bar – pay them FG100–200 to sing someone's praises and you'll go down a treat. Out of the centre, the new *Auberge Maforce* on the Route de Labé has clean, dark rooms with fan (future renovations should rectify the state of the shared baths) and a pleasantly shaded open-air restaurant. A more attractive option is the *Clos St Cathérine* (③), a few kilometres out on the Conakry road, which also has a restaurant. There's plenty of street food in Mamou, and a good number of basic *gargotes*: try the *Hidalso Mamou*.

Mamou to Faranah

For some distance out of town, the rough road from **Mamou to Faranah** (see p.513) drops through forest and hilly bush with views to pass the time. Then the highlands are shed, the road flattens and the scenery breaks into quickly monotonous elephant grass and **bush savannah** for the rest of the journey to Faranah. The road, built after independence, arrows and loops determinedly through the flat wilderness, at times just a dozen kilometres from the Sierra Leone border. With time, Kouranko compounds and hamlets may gradually gather along it but for now it is still largely empty land. At night, this is one of the country's most soporific journeys, with little to enliven it but the cassettes on the driver's stereo. It's worth knowing, however, that the district is one of the richest faunal areas in Guinea and your chances of seeing exciting large wild **animals** quite high.

Mamou to Dabola

The hard-surfaced road from **Mamou to Dabola** (see p.512) cuts through impressive scenery: sheer rocky outcrops and forest populated by chimpanzees and other primates.

Timbo, 50km along the road, is the old capital of the Fula *almamys*. Timbo still has an eighteenth-century mosque – much restored – and there's a European cemetery dating back to the end of the last century when a French administrative *résident* was installed here to breathe down rebellious Fula necks. You'll also come across traditional Fouta Djalon houses out here; senior figures construct fine conical beehive affairs, with solid tiers of thatching to exclude the cold.

The central Fouta Djalon

The central Fouta Djalon – including the ancient settlements of **Dalaba**, **Pita** and **Télimélé** – offers some of Guinea's most beautiful countryside. The main road north from Mamou has fairly recently been resurfaced which is on the whole a dangerously speedy improvement. About 15km out of Mamou, the eastward-flowing stream you cross is the Bafing, first headwater of the Senegal; its source is in the hills a few kilometres off the road to the west. The road steepens after Bouliwel (which has a Saturday *lumo*), then drops to enter Dalaba, hidden in a conifer carpeted valley.

Dalaba

DALABA has a beautiful setting in the hills at 1200m (though why it's called Dalaba – "big pond" in Malinké – is a mystery), and the French considered the site so therapeutic that they built a sixty-room sanatorium, now in ruins. The South African jazz singer, Miriam Makeba, spent time in Dalaba, in the large white house with the strange roof (near the ruined sanatorium) during her period of exile from the USA in the 1970s.

Dalaba's layout is easy to grasp. The limited **market** – greatly enlarged on Sunday, when it hosts the district *lumo* – and a couple of streets around comprise the town centre, with a row of cheap eating and drinking places on the street along the bottom of the market. Market produce includes, from the end of December to March, cultivated strawberries – a colonial bequest. For **drinks** or **food**, try the *Renaissance Bar*, tiny but absurdly well stocked, or the *Bar Silence*, which sometimes converts to a *dancing*. There's a **post office** but no bank.

Away across the valley and behind the hill to the west (a thirty-minute walk) is the administrative quarter of Etaconval – rural in feel and spread among the woods – and the three best **places to stay**. The smart, new *SIB Hotel* (☎68.06.26; ③–④) boasts luxury bedrooms and stunning, panoramic views – best enjoyed from the huge windows in the dining room. Similarly good is the *Hôtel Tangama* (BP 26 Dalaba; ☎ c/o PTT, Dalaba, 68.04.00; ①–③), run by a French-Guinean couple and one of the best upcountry hotels in Guinea, with an excellent restaurant (more like a French family dining room) and hot showers in some rooms – some of which also have electricity. Dalaba's *villa* (②) is run-down these days – a cluster of bare houses on the hillside, with the main compensation being the infinite views. Occasionally it's booked for a conference, but you can always **camp** under the pines and use the limited facilities and a lock-up storage room. The caretaker's wife will cook for you if you order in advance – it's all pretty informal. Back towards the town centre is the *Etoile de Fouta* – a restaurant and sometime *boîte* which also has rooms to let (②). Unless they're busy, however, it's a mournful barn of a place (ex-French officers' club) with underwhelming appeal.

Whether you're staying in Etaconval or not, have a look out on the hillside at the remarkable Fula chiefs' **assembly hall** – *case de palabre* – built in the 1930s, with an inscribed floor and exceptional carving on its interior walls.

Dalaba to Pita

Moving on to Pita from Dalaba by public transport can sometimes prove difficult: most vehicles are either coming full from Mamou and going on to Labé, or vice versa. An early start might get you a ride without having to pay the fare the whole way to Labé.

While it's not inconceivable as a **walk** – and worth it for the stunning **scenery** which at last really opens up – fifty-two kilometres is a long way for unadjusted muscles. The first half of the route from Dalaba to Pita plunges down through various stages of gorgeous forest – conifer, broad leaf jungle, more open bush – and this section you might consider walking in the realistic hope of getting a lift further along the way.

If you have your own transport, consider a diversion down the steep grade to Tinka, 5km outside Dalaba on the right. The colonial, ornamental garden here – **Le Jardin de Professeur Chevallier** – is still just about kept up, and worth a visit. The **Chutes de Ditinn**, some 30km further at the village of Ditinn, are also accessible and you can swim here in the plunge pool. When there's sufficient flow, the eighty-metre falls, dropping from a perfectly vertical cliff, are very impressive.

Back on the main highway about 15km from Dalaba, look out for the **Chutes de Piké**, hard by the road on the left, just after the bridge over the stream of the same name. The falls are easily accessible down a couple of short paths, one of which leads to the pool at the top where you can stand at the precipice, the other to the ledges at the bottom where you can see the cascade, a pretty ten-metre drop, though unimpressive in the dry season.

The Fouta Djalon spurts pandemically with waterfalls, but some are more easily seen from a distance than reached: **Bomboli**'s chutes, for example, are very difficult to get to, but clearly visible about 15km before Pita, several kilometres over on the right.

Pita and around

As a place of beauty and repose, **PITA** can't match Dalaba. But they share the same zesty atmosphere and you'll quickly grow to like it. Market day is Thursday. Pita figures in most travel plans as a place to get the necessary permission (usually free, but not always) to visit the **Kinkon falls** – a simple matter of calling at the *commissariat* on the north side of town.

Most people who want to **stay** get directed to a fading hotel, the *Hôtel Kinkon* (①), in a quiet area near the school on the northwestern edge of town. It's very basic but just about adequate and quite *sympa*. Warm water can be ordered for the self-contained washing cubicles. It's also possible to stay at the *Centre d'Acceuil*, the imposing complex near the *commissariat*, which has spotless, very reasonably priced rooms (①).

In town there are various eating places, of which the *Café/Restaurant Montréal* is probably the best, and streetside bars, including the *Buenos Aires*, good for *café noir*. For added entertainment, there's a nightclub, *Le Koubi*, and big-screen action at the Cinéma Rex, with twice-daily showings of American movies.

If you're heading straight to **Conakry** from Pita, there is a scheduled private bus service three times a week.

The Chutes de Kinkon
The **Chutes de Kinkon** are the Fouta Djalon's best falls, a fairly easy cycle ride but a longish walk – 11km from Pita (you might be lucky and get a lift with a vehicle going to Dongol-Touma, leaving you just a kilometre to walk). A sign two or three kilometres along the road out to Labé sends you left (direction "Touma and Télimélé") and after a mostly downhill 7km you arrive at a control post where you hand in your *laissez-passer*. Here you'll be told it's 500m down to the right if you desire to inspect the dam (an unimpressive bridge across the lake; the reason for the piece of paper) and about a kilometre left for the main falls.

You can stand directly on the **rock platform** above the falls which – before the dam was built – would have surged with water, and possibly does still during the rains. There's evidence of colonial safety measures in the broken stumps of cliff-edge railings, but nothing to stop present-day visitors plunging dramatically to their deaths – take care, as the flow is powerful. Behind, on the cliffs, is a scrappy but just about legible list of various heads of state, with the dates of their visits.

Pita to Télimélé

Exceptionally beautiful in parts, the Pita–Télimélé "road" was formerly a tough route, with some very challenging sections. Since the surface was regraded in the early 1990s it's now a relatively straightforward drive and ideal for **motorbikes** or **4WD vehicles** (eight hours plus), **mountain bikes** (two days) or **hiking** (four to six days). The Paris–Dakar rally came this way in January 1995, but it's still little used by public transport. The route in reverse is considerably less attractive as the rewards are mostly westwards (eastbound you face a continuous thirty-kilometre climb from Léi-Mîro to Dongol-Touma).

If you're cycling or hiking, you may want to deviate from the road to take the short cuts in the company of local people. A walking route follows, roughly, the course of the

Fétoré River, which flows westwards, a few kilometres north of the road. Alternatively, you might try to get a lift as far as **Dongol-Touma**, where the thrills begin. There's at least daily transport from Pita to Dongol, though you'll probably have less of a wait if you go to the junction 3km north of Pita, where vehicles from Labé, as well as Pita or Mamou, turn off westwards towards Télimélé.

The people of the area, who live in immaculate mud-moulded compounds, are happy – once they've got over their disbelief and exchanged greetings – to bring water from their wells or the local stream, and will just as soon give you handfuls of oranges and bananas as sell them. Children in this isolated region may be just a little scared of white people.

Over the bowe

A signpost 3km up the Pita–Labé road marks the turn-off to Télimélé, which at first brings you to a confusion of tracks. Bear right where another sign points left to the Chutes de Kinkon (see overleaf), which, given an early start, could be easily appended to this route. The correct **track** soon starts bucking and twisting unmistakeably, with many descents to narrow streams and many wearing climbs to short, level ridges. There's a fair number of Fula people about, invariably surprised to see any strangers, let alone foreign travellers. The track heads northwest, southwest, east and south before establishing a more or less westerly course on a barren hogsback of rocky land discernible on the IGN map. In truth, this part of the journey, across the **bowe** – the Fula name for these high, sear plateaux – isn't scenically enthralling. In December smoke from burning grass obscures any views and the hazy dust brought by the *Harmattan* wind normally fogs the horizon between January and April. The path runs over unrelenting bare rock in places, and then begins a gentle descent, with occasional wooded intervals. The village of **Tulal** has an enormous mosque and, an hour's walk further west you reach **Combouroh**, where a remarkable country market takes place every Tuesday. Hundreds of Fula women converge to buy and sell a little, but mainly to share news and find men. The miracle of hairstyles and print patterns is stunning and happily typical. At the end of the *bowe*, you reach the strung-out village of **Dongol-Touma**, 55km from the Pita junction, and site of a Wednesday *lumo*. If you see the *sous-préfet* you'll likely be able to **stay the night** in Dongol's *villa*, superbly sited on a high bluff with 270 degrees of panorama. The *villa* is rarely needed for official purposes and you may receive a royal welcome and repeated donations of food and drink (something in return is appreciated the next morning). It's strange to think that dictator Sekou Touré stayed in these rooms – and may well have slept in these very beds if their condition gives any indication of age.

Downhill to the Kakrima River

The road snakes out of Dongol-Touma and starts a **steep descent**, with inspiring sweeps of Fouta Djalon visible through the trees now shading it. If you're cycling or motorbiking, the only effort for 26km is in keeping the brakes on. Driving a car or truck, exercise extreme caution: parts of the route are likely to have succumbed to erosion and you could turn a bend and run into a jumble of boulders and bedrock. When you're not watching the surface ahead, however, this is a breathtaking ride, zigzagging down a long spine and throwing up striking views of the bush country to the south, the fortress-like hills – Télimélé among them – rising in a ridge to the west, and plunging valleys right below. Streams, flecked with butterflies and overshot by parrots and hornbills, cut across the road and are quickly left behind hundreds of metres above. Giant leaves litter the ground and lianas strew overhead. Occasionally a hunter or a woodcutter emerges – usually to stand still, nonplussed, on seeing you. Monkeys, the hunters' main targets, are common.

At last the gradients relax and the road unwinds, through more cultivated country, towards the Kakrima River. The village of **Djounkoun** leaves little impression, but **Léi-Mîro**, 4km east of the river, is the second large settlement along the route. You'll find rice and other street food if you turn up early enough, or bread and sandwich ingredients if not. Léi-Mîro's *lumo* takes place every Thursday.

The winch-ferry across the **Kakrima River** has an engine, but it's not far across (either hauling the ferry's line or renting a *pirogue*) in the event of breakdown. **Koussi** is just beyond, where people know a good short cut, useful if you're walking to Télimélé. The main route beyond Koussi is hard work on a bicycle, mostly flat – and sandy in parts – with tall elephant grass jamming any view.

Sixty-one kilometres after Dongol-Touma the route hits the broad, red sweep of the Kindia–Télimélé road where you'll find a lift easily enough. The final gruelling fifteen kilometres to Télimélé up the soaring flank of **Mont Louba** is noted for gut-churning accidents on the hairpins.

Télimélé

A pleasing, well-kept town, perched as if to admire its grand views, **TÉLIMÉLÉ** sees very few visitors. In the area lies **Gueme Sangan**, the ruined **fortress** of Koli Tengela, the fifteenth-century Fula warlord who laid the foundations of the kingdom of Fouta Djalon. Télimélé – "the place where the *téli* grows" – is a town of pine trees, citrus orchards and fresh air, surrounded by imposing mountain flanks and trench-like valleys. If you're staying, there's an adequate **hotel** (②), up near the administrative quarter at the Kindia end of town, which has a formidable vista over the town from its terrace.

When you're ready to leave Télimélé there are two or three jeep or Land Rover departures per week to **Gaoual**, 130km along a beautiful route to the north. The road down to **Kindia** isn't too bad and transport is reasonably frequent, but it's worth investing a little extra for a place in a Peugeot rather than one of the minibuses. Stay awake for the last half-hour before Kindia; there are some outstanding tabular massifs, rearing like lost worlds across the valley.

Labé and the northern Fouta Djalon

Heading north from Pita, the **road to Labé**, 38km away, loops across a mellow, pastoral landscape of undulating grass, scattered with boulders and copses of oak-like *koura* trees, and fringed with lines of forest along the watercourses. The district, one of the highest in the Fouta Djalon, is a watershed between the streams that flow west and the Gambia and Senegal tributaries pouring off northwards.

Labé

LABÉ, the historic Fula stronghold and capital of the Fouta Djalon, is, by contrast with the surrounding landscape, a disappointment. Strategically situated in the middle of the highlands, it's a misshapen and unappealing, though evidently prosperous, town. Sizeable, and ranged confusingly over a number of hills, Labé is a growing centre, absorbing people from the regions of Guinea and not a few from neighbouring countries. All of which delivers a rather metropolitan jolt after the surrounding horizons and makes Labé a somewhat unsatisfactory place to stay.

Labé's pretty limited appeal arises from its status as the Fouta Djalon's largest market town and the area's main *artisanal* centre. If you venture a kilometre or so into the streets that lie to the right of the airport road – a district known as Taba – you'll come

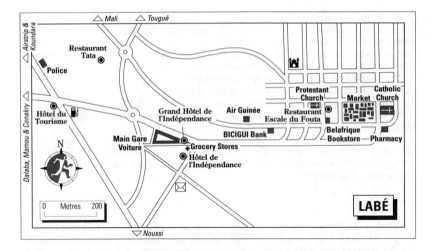

to the yards of a couple of **weaving** guilds. You might do well to enlist someone to guide you to the *tisserands* if you're interested in seeing the weaving in progress. Also on the way to the airport, you pass the National Apiculture Centre, with local potted **honey** for sale.

For something a little more substantial in the way of food, the **market** in the town centre – huge, vibrant and teeming – is one of Labé's strong points, though even more of a tight squeeze to walk around than usual. There's a remarkable variety of ground-nut pastes on offer, and all the usual Fouta Djalon profusion of produce. Look out for exquisite **gara** cloth, which is made from Czechoslovakian damask, tie-dyed with local indigo and beaten with clubs to a shine; it's sold, as usual, only in pairs of *pagnes*.

If you're in Labé long enough to want to do a day out, fix up with a taxi to visit the **Chutes de la Sala**, near the road to Lélouma. These falls, some 37km from Labé, are some of the most impressive in Guinea – a series of small cascades tumbling above one enormous waterfall.

Practicalities

Arriving from Pita, you enter Labé past the dominating hulk of the *Hôtel de Tourisme* – clearly a once grand place in vaguely Swiss-chalet style, but now, despite its newly painted exterior, somewhat decrepit. There's no running water, but the **rooms** (②) are very reasonably priced, the large bar-resto serves meals all day and the *Tinkisso* club downstairs comes alive at weekends. A good, and cheaper, alternative is the clean and very friendly *Hôtel de l'Indépendance* (①) at the lower end of the *gare voiture*. Across the road, the jointly owned *Grand Hôtel de l'Indépendance* (②), offers clean, modern rooms and a reasonable restaurant.

A good bar/café is the *Café Mamadou Oury Ly* which you'll find opposite the bookshop. The Italian *Restaurant Tata*, signposted in town, does recommended home-made pizzas and pasta (closed on Tues). Another on Labé's short eating-out list is the family-run *Escale du Fouta* in the centre of town; it offers various dishes including tasty *riz gras*, Nicoise salads and crepes.

Miscellaneous *renseignements* in the centre include the only **bank** in the Fouta Djalon, BICIGUI (open Mon–Fri 8.30am–12.30pm & 2.30–4pm; ☎51.09.47); the **PTT** (Mon–Sat 7.30am–4pm); and the Bel Afrique **bookshop** – owned by *Jeune Afrique* magazine, but no stronger in reading matter for that.

MOVING ON FROM LABÉ

Air Guinée operates **flights** to Conakry and to Banjul in The Gambia – both at least twice a week. The fare to Conakry is around FG40,000, to Banjul FG80,000.

Labé is something of a cul-de-sac as far as regular **taxi brousse and bus transport** goes. There are plenty of transport options down the Fouta Djalon spine to Pita, Dalaba and Mamou, and in theory, thrice-weekly buses to Conakry (Mon, Wed and Sat), as well as a good handful of Peugeot 504s to Conakry every morning. All these destinations are served from the main *gare voiture*. For a less steady stream of bush taxis and trucks to the north, including the town of Mali and Kédougou in Senegal, you should also use this *autogare*, though you may find some Mali-bound vehicles along the road out of Labé. A second main *gare voiture* – the gare Dakar – to the right of the road out to the airport, handles *taxi brousse* and truck traffic for Koundara and Senegal (note that taxis to Dakar take a full day and night).

The northern Fouta Djalon

If you've come up to Labé from the south, the most obvious onward option is to continue, off-tarmac, to the town of **Mali** and then to Kédougou in Senegal, though on average there's only one vehicle per day on this route, even in the dry season; the least obvious option is to head eastwards towards Kankan (see p.517).

Alternatives include the direct route from Labé to **Koundara** – much easier than the Mali–Koundara road, but still a full day's worth by bush taxi, even in the dry season. Don't be deceived by the tarmac leading out of Labé on this route – it only extends a few kilometres.

The fabulously picturesque route from **Labé to Gaoual** is an alternative for people heading for Guinea-Bissau and Senegal's Basse Casamance region. On this route you're almost certain to have to take a Koundara vehicle and change at Kounsitel to local vehicles for Gaoual, Koumbia and north to Guinea-Bissau. **GAOUAL** is a friendly little town, with a wide avenue of trees and an old colonial PTT. The only hotel in town, off the same avenue, is overpriced (②–③) and doubles as Gaoual's disco.

Mali

The route from Labé to the small town of Mali switchbacks through the Fouta's loftiest parts, with a number of fair-size villages on the way. Fourteen kilometres north of Labé, **Tountouroun** may still have its beautiful Fula houses and might be worth an exploratory excursion, even as a special trip out of Labé. Just a kilometre or so further, the small stream running east, which the road crosses, is the Gambia River – its source is nearby to the west. Further villages include Sarékali at 35km; the pretty hamlet of Pellal off to the left at 65km; and Yambéring, the largest, at 74km.

MALI has a small, primitive hotel, *La Dame de Mali* (①), and the slightly better *Villa/Centre d'Accueil* (①) a few minutes away on an outcrop of rock. At 1460m, the town is the highest Fouta Djalon settlement, renowned for low temperatures (down to 3°C) and views at the end of the rains. These are particularly good from the summit of **Mont Loura** (1538m), the highest peak in the Fouta Djalon, 7km northeast of the village. The local *curiosité* – not necessarily worth a major effort to get to – is **La Dame de Mali**, a cliff eroded into "a well-proportioned feminine profile", on Mont Loura's eastern flank.

If you're trying to get **from Mali to Koundara**, Mali's market day, Sunday, offers the best opportunities. Otherwise, you might have to wait days for a vehicle. When you finally get one, be prepared for a diabolical road with one-in-four gradients, some dangerous hairpins and several skeletal bridges.

LOCAL HISTORY: THE RISE OF THE JIHAD STATE

The original inhabitants of the highlands were Jalonke, Baga, Nalo and **Puli** (sedentary, animist, Fula speakers). They all coexisted in relative harmony, herding on the hills and farming the valleys. The region was known then as **Jalonkadougou**, after its dominant inhabitants, and was subject to the Mali empire.

The first ripples of tension through this rural idyll were felt during the thirteenth century, when **Fula immigrants** – the superficially Muslim clans of Ba, Sow, Diallo and Bari – arrived piecemeal, in search of pasture, from Tekrur on the Senegal River and Djenné on the Niger River. By the fifteenth century, they were sufficiently established for one of their kings, **Koli Tengela**, to shake off Mali's rule and raid widely to expand the Fula zone of influence. He later withdrew north to found the Denianke dynasty back in Tekrur.

This early Fula Muslim rule in the highlands wasn't especially zealous in its promulgation of Islam. With the demise of the Tengela dynasty, however, the increasingly fervent **Diallos** came up the Bafing and Tinkisso valleys and moved into the Labé region, spreading the faith among the Puli animists and quasi-Muslims who held local political power. Further migrations from outside the region quickened resentment of the incumbent infidel overlords. By the early eighteenth century, there was enough support for King **Karamoko Alfa Bari** to declare a jihad against the non-believers. He won a breakthrough military victory against them at Talansan in 1730.

The **Muslim Kingdom of Fouta Djalon** emerged, with Karamoko Alfa Bari as its *almamy* and its capital at **Timbo**. Karamoko's nephew, Ibrahima Sory, took power when his uncle went insane in 1767 and thereafter the **jihad state** was rapidly consolidated. The kingdom was divided into nine provinces, one of which, **Labé**, became a noted centre of learning. Labé was also a hotbed of *Alfaya* (supporters of Alfa Bari), unhappy with the rule of the nephew's line.

There were **conversions** among the animists, but many fled to less intense pastures, mostly coastwards. Those who stayed were either "**bush Fula**", employed as herders by the Muslim aristos, or **slaves** of non-Fula origin who worked partly for their landlords and partly on their own account.

Throughout the nineteenth century, Labé drew apart from Timbo. Labé's ruler, **Alfa Yaya**, the great-grandson of Karamoko Alfa Bari, achieved his position through ruthless assassinations of his opponents. By the 1890s, with his territory extended over most of northwest Guinea, Labé constituted as powerful a state as the Timbo-based kingdom of Fouta Djalon itself. With the arrival of the French, separate treaties were entered into with both realms. Today Alfa Yaya – or Alfa Labé as he's known – is a folk hero; his tomb lies behind the mosque near the airport.

In the 1970s, the Fula population suffered heavy **repression** at the hands of Sekou Touré's terrorist dictatorship. He labelled ethnic Fula "enemies of socialism", and many thousands were killed or fled into exile.

Koundara and the Parc National Niokolo Badiar

Most people tend to pass straight through **KOUNDARA**, 50km from the Senegalese border, on their way to or from Senegal and Guinea-Bissau. However, the newly opened **Parc National Niokolo Badiar**, which lies on the border adjoining Senegal's Parc National Niokolo-Koba, provides a good reason to linger. The park is one of two EU-funded conservation projects set up in Guinea in 1995 – the other is the Parc National Haut Niger (see p.514) – and although neither have yet attained a particularly high profile and funding is pretty thin on the ground, they appear to be surviving for the meantime. Although the facilities in Projet Niokolo Badiar are not quite as developed as those at Haut Niger, the chances of seeing big exciting animals – including lions and leopards – are better.

You can **stay** in the park itself in a tourist *campement* (①), or else base yourself in nearby Koundara, from where you can arrange organized tours of the park. For places to stay in Koundara, try the reasonable *Hôtel du Gangan* (①), or the *Mamadou Boiro* (①), which is no worse, and hosts Saturday night parties free for residents, with great music.

East of Labé

If you're heading **eastwards** for the Republic of Mali or Côte d'Ivoire, and feeling very expeditionary, then seek out transport to Tougué and work your way off the Fouta Djalon into the Malinké savannah region and Kankan. Generally the hills east of the main Labé–Mamou axis are more sparsely populated and even tougher travelling than those to the west, though for the most part not as steep.

THE MALINKÉ PLAINS

The great plains of the northeast – **Haute Guinée** – stretch, immensely vast and flat, over more than a hundred thousand square kilometres, big enough to swallow The Gambia ten times over. In this huge expanse, the few towns – Kankan the biggest, Kouroussa, Faranah, Siguiri – seem lost amid yellow grass, thorn trees and termite spires. In contrast to the Fouta Djalon to the west and the highlands further south, the population is sparse: most people live along the meandering **tributaries of the Niger** which pull together in a fan in the most populous part of the region around Kankan and Kouroussa.

Getting around

Without your own means of transport you're mostly restricted to a clutch of main routes tracking through the territory. If you leave them on foot or bicycle, distances between habitations with supplies are often too long for comfort – you can go miles without seeing a soul, even on the main roads. An option, for the more adventurous is to buy a boat and paddle down the Niger River, but for this you need to be completely self-sufficient (see p.514).

Dabola and Kouroussa

Dabola and **Kouroussa** are essentially **railway towns** whose appeal lies in a certain just-past nostalgia. Dabola, in particular, was a major centre during the French occupation and carried the Conakry–Kankan road, until the Mamou–Faranah link was built. Kouroussa, at a rail bridge over the Niger, was also once an important centre but is now somewhat cut off. It was the birthplace of Guinea's best-known author, Camara Laye.

THE MANDE PEOPLES

The agricultural and trading **Mande**-speaking peoples are cultural heirs to the medieval empire of **Mali**, whose capital from the thirteenth to the fourteenth century was Niani, northeast of Kankan. More recently, the self-styled *almamy*, **Samory Touré**, founded and burned out two "Dyula empires" at the end of the nineteenth century and caused the French considerable grief with his determined jihad against their invasion.

The traditional Mande **names**, Touré, Traoré, Camara, Konté, Keita and Kouyaté are still the most common. Various Mande **languages** are spoken – including Bamana, Dyula and Koranko – as well as mainstream Mandinka/Malinké.

Dabola

DABOLA grew up after 1910 as a staging post, and it retains a slightly Wild-West feel, hemmed in by gaunt plateaux rising directly behind the town and keeping those passing through well fed and entertained. It's not an unattractive place: in Dabolakoro ("old Dabola") neat compounds surround the small commercial centre. A couple of very decent **hotels** have recently been built here. The upmarket (and overpriced) *Hotel Tinkisso* (③), set in large grounds, has comfortable S/C rooms with showers and a large bar/restaurant with satellite TV. Equally comfortable, but cheaper, is the more intimate *Hotel Mont Sincery* (②), whose lobby doubles as a TV lounge bar.

The **Tinkisso Falls** are well worth a short detour. A gentle six-kilometre climb on the road to Mamou brings you to a track on your left, which drops over the railway line through a teak plantation – with drifts of huge, crunching leaves underfoot – and, forking right, to the top of the **dam** and a mass of birdlife (an alternative route just follows the power lines from town straight to the falls). The **falls** themselves – which must have been impressive indeed before the dam was built – cascade over rocky shelves below (except at the end of the dry season, when there's no flow). The path descends steeply to the power station and its Chinese retinue, with views back to the falls. Continue on the same footpath downstream and you reach an immaculate Fula village and, eventually, the Dabola–Faranah road. Persistent hikers will want to do the circle – it makes a good day, whether or not the falls are falling, for the landscape and birdlife.

Koroussa

KOUROUSSA is in a beautiful area, and is easy – though expensive – to reach, thanks to the new road from Dabola. The house of **Camara Laye**'s family, near the station, is quite well known and you'll have no difficulty tracking it down if you want to pay homage. The town is pleasant and leafy, and lodgings are available at *Bar La Baobab* (①), the *Hôtel Chateau D'eau* (①) near the *gare voiture*, and the *Sabari* (①) – all very basic. *Café Savane*, near the market, is friendly.

René Caillié, the indomitable French traveller who by disguising himself and mumbling in Arabic became the first European to return from Timbuktu, arrived in Kouroussa with a bout of malaria in June 1827:

> *We crossed the river in canoes… A great number of people were going across, and they were all disputing, some about the fare that was demanded, some about who should go first. They all talked at once and made a most terrible uproar.*

The ferry crossing on the Kankan road, 26km east of the town, has apparently changed little. When the ferry breaks down in the dry season, some truckers risk fording the shallows but most Peugeot drivers won't.

An alternative means of transport, in the right season (usually from mid-July until about November or December), is a weekly **ferry from Kouroussa to Bamako** in

---

MOVING ON FROM DABOLA

Dabola has daily transport connections to Mamou, Faranah and Kankan via Kouroussa. The 110-kilometre earth road to Faranah, which descends gradually from Dabola before running past irrigated rice fields and along the stripling Niger valley into Faranah, is in rough condition. The newly-constructed road from Dabola to Kouroussa has shortened the journey to less than three hours, but the Kouroussa–Kankan stretch is still tough-going – an uncomfortable five hours by 504.

Mali – although at the time of writing the ferry had broken down and the service was indefinitely suspended.

Faranah and around

After the long, nearly uninhabited void beyond Mamou – of which a hot, breezy yellowness is the enduring recollection – arrival at **FARANAH** makes some impact. A parade of mighty street lights lines up to greet you on the highway into town, and the **Niger River**, which flows beneath a rattling iron bridge, looks impressive already, with 4000km of meandering still to go before it reaches the sea. The Tinkisso dam at Dabola provides electricity; a Chinese team has been improving the system to give some juice in the dry season too.

Until independence in 1958, Faranah was an unimportant village on the old road from Dabola to Kissidougou. **Sekou Touré** pumped money into his native village, building a large mosque, as well as the Cité du Niger conference centre in 1981 and a massive block of a villa for himself, which, unfortunately, is now closed. Today, Faranah seems to be steadily slipping back towards it's original state as a sleepy village, suffering an ever-increasing paucity of restaurants and hotels. It's a town you're bound to pass through, and although it's still adequate for most practical needs (it lacks a bank) – there's little of interest to hold you.

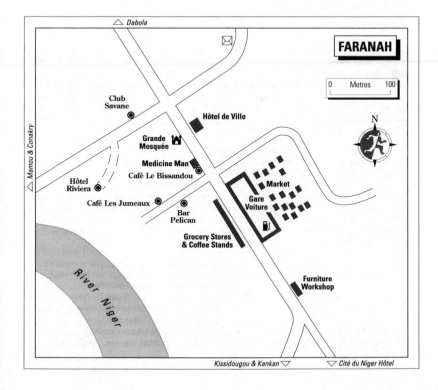

Practicalities

Since the closure of Touré's mansion, **accommodation** is limited to two hotels. For spacious, if rather neglected, S/C, AC rondavels with fabulous views over the river valley, head up the hill to the southeast of the town to the *Cité du Niger* (③). On the other side of town just off the Conakry road is the *Hotel Riviera* (☎82.08.74; ①), which has small, reasonably clean rooms with bucket showers. The hotel doubles as a nightclub and has one of the town's few restaurants.

Back in the town centre, cheap **eateries** compete at one end of the main *gare voiture*, serving high-quality street food all day, and – at least some of them – at night too. For more extended meals the *Café Le Bissandou* has a varying menu including *poulet yassa*. When satisfied, try the *Club Savane* nightclub, or the *Bar Pelican*. The *Café les Jumeaux* is good for breakfast. Finally, if you need to phone or fax abroad, Faranah has an "external telecommunications centre" which makes it relatively easy to do so.

Parc National Haut Niger

The **Parc National Haut Niger** is the second of Guinea's national parks to open in recent years (see p.510 for information about the Parc National Niokolo Badiar in Koundara). The

---

CANOEING DOWN THE RIVER

If you're looking for high adventure, and have a full life-support system (tent and cooking equipment essential), Faranah is a good place to acquire a boat and **canoe down the Niger**, either as far as Kouroussa, or all the way to Bamako, Mali. A four-metre plank boat, adequate for one, can be made to order for about FG60,000. A six- or seven-metre boat, big enough for two, will cost up to FG220,000. The wood is the main expense, and while a plank boat is slightly more expensive than a dugout, it is lighter, faster and more manoeuvreable.

It's not necessary to be an experienced canoeist for the trip. You need to take sufficient **food** (rice and canned food) to last the whole journey if necessary, as you cannot rely on the occasional fishing camps having food for sale (there are no villages in the Faranah to Kouroussa section). Money and precious items need to be protected in waterproof bags as you're almost certain to capsize sooner or later.

From Faranah to Kouroussa, a 350-kilometre trip which should take between ten and fourteen days, the river winds through **forest** which looms out from the banks. There are several sections of **rapids** along the way, but only at two points are they hard – any fisherman will give you advice. **Wildlife** is abundant and interesting: you'll see beautiful birds, monkeys and baboons, antelope, warthogs, snakes, small crocodiles and several groups of hippos. Because they are hunted, hippos tend to stay well clear of boats but you should give them a wide berth anyway as they can be dangerous. There are some larger crocodiles (up to four metres) but you are very unlikely to see them and are safe in a boat. Bilharzia is not a problem and the swimming, hippos permitting, is fine nearly everywhere.

Downstream from Kouroussa, the riverscape opens out. The channel is well over a kilometre wide in places and the scenery is farmland and savannah. There are plenty of villages to restock your supplies, but the journey is less interesting, with no rapids, no crocs and few hippos. From Kouroussa to Bamako by river is about 400km.

The **best time** to do this trip is after the rains (they usually finish in October) and before the end of the dry season (March–April). At the end of the dry season, parts of the river are very shallow indeed, making progress slow, and the rainy season is a bad time because the water level fluctuates and camping on the banks is unsafe. But note also that you're more likely to encounter fishermen during the rainy season, should you need assistance.

MOVING ON FROM FARANAH

Mamou- and Kissidougou-bound vehicles cluster at the main *gare voiture* below the market. It's easy to reach Conakry, Labé, Kankan or Nzérékoré in a day, though it's worth noting that the highway from Faranah to Kissidougou is in bad shape. The *gare voiture* for Dabola and Kouroussa is at the opposite end of town, its only landmark being a blue house.

Some 15km west of Faranah, a big sign on the left says "Direction Sierra Leone", and that's the way across the border to Kabala. Although vehicles for Kabala currently depart on Tues, Sat and Sun, there is reported rebel activity on the Sierra Leonean border, and you are strongly advised not to use this route.

park's **headquarters** – which offer **excursions** into the park – are in the village of Sidakoro, 45km from Faranah. For FG5000 a day you can hire a car and guide for a tour of the park where, hopefully, you can spot buffaloes, chimpanzees, waterbucks, hippos and elephants, among others. The animals tend to scatter after the rains, but quite what you will see even in the dry season is uncertain. An alternative tour of the park can be had from the waters of the River Niger; hiring a *pirogue* and guide for the day will cost FG10,000.

If you want to **stay** in the park, there's a tourist *campement* (①). Note that there is no public transport to Sidakoro, and you will need your own vehicle to reach it.

Kissidougou

KISSIDOUGOU ("Kissi") is composed of three no longer easily distinguishable villages. **Kenéma Pompo** is the oldest, a Kissi village which goes back to the eighteenth century, when it was tucked in its sacred forest, the head of a small federation of Kissi settlements. The second, **Hérèmakono** (which means roughly "Home Sweet Home"), is the administrative and commercial district built away from the forest. And the third **Dioulabou** – the "Dyula town" established by Samory's vanquished lieutenants in

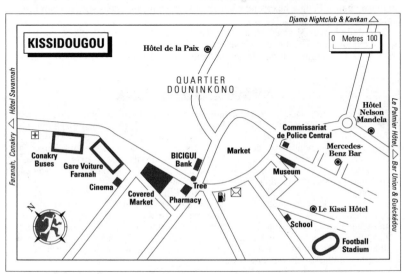

THE SOURCE OF THE NIGER

If you're curious about the **source of the Niger**, it's not difficult to get to, given a couple of days out of Kissidougou or Faranah. It rises at 9° 5' 0" North, 10° 47' 14" West, at an altitude of 74 metres. This puts it 93 metres northnortheast of a frontier marker post on the border between Guinea and Sierra Leone. First base is the village of **Bambaya**, northwest of Kissidougou, accessible up a road signposted "Kobikoro", off the Kissi–Faranah highway; you'll need to *deplace* a taxi to reach Bambaya. There's a Friday market at Baleya, 3km from Bambaya. Second base is **Kobikoro**, 12km further up, where the *chef* and *sous-préfet* are both welcoming and you should leave your luggage if it's heavy. In theory you need the *sous-préfet*'s permission to visit the source. From there on the route gets tough for walkers and the scenery interesting as you head up to third base, **Forokonia**, 20km from Kobikoro. There are magnificent forest trees up here, though cutting is going on all over. Forokonia has a Thursday market. You need a guide (quite often this will be a soldier) on reaching Forokonia, to show you the actual source, a three- or four-hour walk. The source itself is not impressive but the surrounding scenery is beautiful.

The best chance of **a lift from Faranah or Kissidougou** is on a Thursday or Friday to Baleya market; or from Kissidougou on a Tuesday, when two trucks go to Forokonia's Thursday market, returning to Baleya on Thursday afternoon for the Friday market there.

1893 – lies on the east side. Kissi Kaba Keita, the ruler of the town at the time of French penetration, put up a notional resistance. Today, this may seem just another fairly unremarkable town, but it borders the largest zone of **forest** in West Africa and the sense of transition is apparent in the patches of tropical woodland around the town. Kissidougou is also notable as the centre of Guinea's main coffee-growing area.

Spacious and unusually flat, the town isn't a bad place at all to be dumped after one of Upper Guinea's arduous taxi rides. A tiny **museum** (free), opposite the Commissariat de Police Centrale, contains two or three dozen local objects of some interest, including a young elephant's and a repulsive hippo's skull – both bereft of their ivory – various bits of Kissi and Kouranko ethnographia and some contemporary domestic items. Fading black-and-white photos show meaningless scenes from French colonial days.

The daily, **covered market**, in the quarter behind the central silk-cotton tree, is worth exploration. You'll find a fair selection, at fair prices, of the kind of imported stuff (Sierra Leone country cloth, Malian blankets, printed *pagnes*) that's found in greater

---

THE KISSI

The **Kissi** are the long-established indigenous people who live across the wide swath of territory from the southern Niger headwaters to the foothills of the southeast highlands. Adroit farmers (it's their swamp rice which you'll see along the Kissidougou–Guéckédou road), they traditionally worship their ancestors, on whose benevolence they depend for the success of their crops, and maintain strong beliefs in witchcraft. Until recently, nearly all Kissi villages had their own witch-hunters (the *wulumo*) whose skills were called upon to divine the evil-minded whenever misfortune struck.

Kissi people still venerate small stone figures, each imbued with the spirit of an ancestor. These sculptures, usually in soapstone and called **pomdo** ("the dead"), are dug up in the fields, or found in the forest, but never carved today. The Kissi traditionally believe the sculptures are the physical essence of their ancestors, but their origin is an enigma. Like the *nomoli* of Sierra Leone, they were certainly carved by an ancient culture, probably before the fifteenth century, but it's not certain that they were produced by the ancestors of the people who now revere them.

MOVING ON FROM KISSIDOUGOU

The road surface from Kissi to **Faranah** has recently been hugely improved, reducing the journey time to a couple of hours. Reasonably surfaced roads to **Kankan** and **Guéckédou** mean you should also be able to make time on these journeys – though the latter sometimes snarls up at **Yende-Milimou** when the village beneath the giant granite mound (great views from the top) has its Thursday *lumo*. A scenic place to stop on the way to Kankan is **Tokounou**, crowded beneath a mountain escarpment. There's a hotel here, eating places and a *balafon* workshop, where you can buy the instruments and watch them being made.

There is a **bus** operating from Kissidougou back to Conakry on Wednesdays. **Flights** from Kissidougou to Conakry are operated by Air Guinée on Thursdays (FG47,000 fare).

quantities at the international markets of Guéckédou, Nzérékoré and Kankan. Goods from Mali for example, often inflated in markets there, are offered at knockdown prices. Kissidougou's **football stadium** is near the *Kissi Hôtel*; national league matches are played here and watched by hundreds of spectators, some of whom stand on lorries and buildings to catch a glimpse of the action.

There's an interesting local visit you can make, to Kissidougou's **pont artisanal**, a liana bridge (well, not entirely lianas) about 2km east of the town centre off the road to Kankan. Take the second turning on the right after the roundabout and keep walking towards the water supply building, often to be seen emitting smoke.

Practicalities

Central options for a **place to stay** include the large, dingy and long-established *Le Kissi Hôtel* (①), which is frequented by prostitutes and truck drivers but is at least cheap enough for a basic non-S/C room. The *Hôtel de la Paix* (①), a few hundred metres round the road to the north, offers almost decent S/C rooms and good food. The best hotel in the town centre, however, is the new *Hôtel Nelson Mandela* (②), just off the roundabout near the road to Guéckédou. Rooms are large, with spotless baths and hot showers, and are arranged around a pleasant garden; a terraced restaurant serves cold beers, steaks, omelettes, chips and the like. Well out of Kissidougou on the Faranah road is the surprisingly good *Hôtel Savannah* (③), with well-appointed AC rooms and others with fans. Lastly – again if you have your own transport, or don't mind a walk – go and check out the quite fancy *Le Palmier* (③–④) nearly 2km from the centre on the Guéckédou road.

Strolling out on the Faranah road you'll find the largest selection of *gargotes* for street **food**. There are few proper restaurants in town – although you could try the *Escale Cosmos* near the banks – but plenty of enjoyable bars: *Bar Palmier*, at *Le Palmier*, *Bar Union* (on the Guéckédou road) and *Mercedes-Benz* (aka *Chez Madame Sow*), behind the *Kissi Hôtel* all have food as well as booze. There's a good number of clubs, too, including *Djamo*, on the Kankan road, *Africana*, close behind the *Kissi Hôtel*, and *Katouba* in the courtyard of the *Hôtel Savannah*.

Kissidougou has both a **post office** and BICIGUI **bank** (☎98.11.03), which face each other across the curve of the main street, as well as a **hospital** – a reassuring place to fall ill if the care lavished on the immaculate gardens extends to the patients.

Kankan

Its name alone is enough to make you want to come here: **KANKAN** sounds remarkably exotic and, although the town is mostly very ordinary, the notion doesn't dissolve once you've arrived. There's a sense of place here, a depth of history that knocks spots off every other town in the country, making it by far the most alluring in Guinea.

The spell it casts arises largely from the fact that Kankan was originally a **Malinké town**, one of the oldest and probably the biggest in the Mande region. Kankan is, in fact, composed of a loose federation of villages which have grown into each other over time – a fact which goes some way to explaining its very laid-back and open atmosphere.

It was Muslim warrior-traders, the "Soninké", speaking Sarakolé (a northern Mande tongue from the upper Senegal), who are credited with the foundation of a mini-empire centred on Kankan. They arrived at the end of the seventeenth century and set themselves up in a dozen villages stretched out along the banks of the Milo River, including the embryonic – and at that time non-Muslim – Kankan. This trading empire, which was also a hub of Muslim propaganda under the rule of marabouts, was known as **Baté** (Baté Nafadj, 40km north of Kankan, is a reminder). Kankan grew to become its capital and by 1850 had been walled and was already sizeable: its fleets of *pirogues* were plying the Milo and Niger rivers as far as Gao in Mali. Caravans arrived from the Sahel and the desert, and from the highland forests in the south, which it largely controlled, came kola nuts, palm oil and slaves. Another reason for Kankan's ascendancy was gold, from the Bure goldfields, which extended from north of Siguiri to far up the Milo.

Kankan's apogee didn't last long: Samory smashed the hegemony of the city in 1879 after a ten-month siege, and twelve years later the French were in occupation.

The Town

Kankan has a beguiling ambience. Its generous plan and long, mango-shaded avenues cast a different light; a woman on a bicycle is a rare sight in most of West Africa, common enough here. There's a university and *lycées* and lots of students, two hospitals and a considerable, scholarly, Islamic presence. The presidential villa no longer has hippos in the swimming pool, but the building itself is still there and, just across the avenue, so is the fountain where crocodiles once disported themselves.

The **markets** are well worthwhile, for the traders at least as much as for the goods on offer. The covered *marché central* sells mostly clothes: a lot of trashy imports and "dead men's" but also brilliantly coloured local confections that look great but would require lots of guts to wear; plus myriad selections of *pagnes*, and items imported from Mali and Niger, mostly rugs and blankets. There are also a couple of stalls specializing in old bits of carving, *gri-gris*, amulets and mystical substances. If you're interested, by the way, in receiving some supernatural aid, then Kankan is the place to ask: **marabouts** here are considered some of the most powerful in West Africa and inscriptions and potions can be obtained easily, for a fee – you don't have to be a Muslim.

The other, larger market sells mostly spices, vegetables and fruit. If you're in Kankan in the mango season (March to April) you're in for a real treat – the town is full of mango trees.

Practicalities

The main **gare voiture** is a shady patch of dust down by the river at the edge of town, but you may well find yourself dropped off at one of the minor taxi parks near the town's access roads.

Opposite the railway station, you'll find the dark and unappetizing hulk of the *Hôtel Buffet de la Gare* (①). They have a lousy reputation here – bucket water, intermittent power and sprouting vegetation in the courtyard – and apparent neglect has left the rooms in a sorry state. The main budget-level competition is *Chez Madame Marie*, also known as *Le Refuge* (②) – an interesting guesthouse about a kilometre from the centre off the Kissidougou road, roughly opposite the barracks and on the right as you come into town. It's not obvious, but ask and you'll find it. *Marie*'s has occasional discos – join

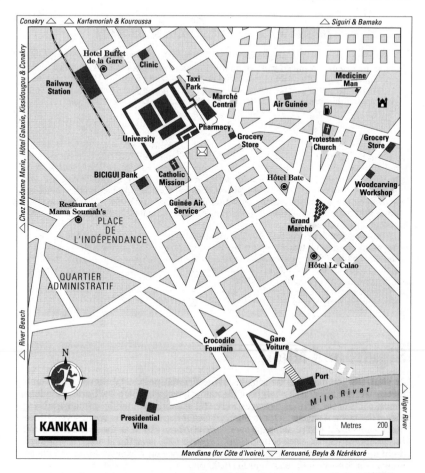

Conakry △ △ Karfamoriah & Kouroussa △ Siguiri & Bamako

Chez Madame Marie, Hôtel Galaxie, Kissidougou & Conakry

Hotel Buffet de la Gare
Clinic
Railway Station
Taxi Park
Marché Central
Medicine Man
Air Guinée
University
Pharmacy
Grocery Store
Protestant Church
Grocery Store
BICIGUI Bank
Catholic Mission
Hôtel Bate
Woodcarving Workshop
Restaurant Mama Soumah's
Guinée Air Service
PLACE DE L'INDÉPENDANCE
Grand Marché
Hôtel Le Calao
QUARTIER ADMINISTRATIF

◁ River Beach

N
Crocodile Fountain
Gare Voiture
Port
Milo River
▷ Niger River
KANKAN
Presidential Villa
0 Metres 200

Mandiana (for Côte d'Ivoire), ▽ Kerouané, Beyla & Nzérékoré

in or move out – good meals (FG2000–4000; but order hours in advance) and wine and beer in the fridge. The marginally more expensive *Hôtel Galaxie* (②), in the southwest of town beyond the Quartier Administratif, has good, clean S/C rooms and decent meals on request. *Hôtel Bate* (③) is the usual option for well-heeled tourists and business travellers; it has a good restaurant and bar, and, although the S/C rooms aren't inexpensive, you get a decent place to stay for your money, and you may even be able to negotiate a deal on the rate. An even better option for the same price is the new *Hôtel Le Calao* (③), right next to the market, which has spotless carpeted rooms with TV, plus a good restaurant in a quiet gravel courtyard.

There's a host of little **cafés and bars** around the centre – give *Mama Soumah's* courtyard restaurant a try – and also a couple of thinly stocked supermarkets where you can splash out on luxuries like marmalade and soft toilet paper. Breakfast in Kankan, as if by some magic Malian influence, is delivered with a flourish.

The **PTT** which handles poste restante, is open Mon–Sat 7.30am–4pm; the BICIGUI **bank** (☎71.24.89) is open 8.30am–12.30pm and 2–4pm.

From the time when the rains have begun in earnest (usually mid- to late July) until about the end of November, you can, in theory, take a **ferry** out of Kankan, down to the confluence of the Milo with the Niger and on to Siguiri and Bamako. However, the vessel is currently not in use due to falling water levels in recent years (down at the harbour you can see the remarkable effects of desertification – a new, lower landing has been built and a series of steps shows the progress of the drought).

If you're planning on travelling **by road** from **Kankan to Bamako** in one journey, be sure you know what you're paying for when you set off: many vehicles bound for "Bamako" turn out to be going as far as the border only, from where you're forced to pay for another ride to the capital. Kankan to Bamako should be FG28,000. A ride to the border only should cost slightly more than half this; a seat to Siguiri just under half. As this book goes to press, there is no car ferry across the Niger at Diélibakoro on the Kankan–Siguiri route. While large *pirogues* lashed together do carry some vehicles across, most Kankan taxis currently shuttle passengers only as far as Diélibakoro, for around FG3000. The alternative route from Kankan to Bamako – via Kouroussa – will cost around FG35,000.

For **Côte d'Ivoire** there's a TARMCI country bus service to Abidjan via Bouaké, leaving whenever it is full (usually on the weekend) costing FG45,000. Ask at the *gare voiture* the day before – the bus should be in by early Sunday morning. If you're not going to Bouaké, you should find the *taxis brousse* that run the rough road to the border once or twice a week a better bet at FG10,000.

There is a weekly **bus** service to **Conakry**, as well as **flights** on Wednesday and Saturday via Siguiri, with Air Guinée for about FG70,000.

Siguiri and Niani

At **SIGUIRI** you may find the remains of the **French post**, established in 1888 on the hilltop over the river, at the height of the campaign against Samory Touré. At independence, parts of the original defences were still standing around the administrative district of the town. A strong factor in Siguiri's favour lies in the presence of several decent **places to stay** if you're stopping over – *Hôtel Niani* (①) near the *gare voiture*; *Hôtel Indépendance* (②) or, even better, *Hôtel Tamtam* (②), near the airstrip. If you need a **flight** to Conakry, Air Guinée operates a direct service on Wednesdays, and another via Kankan on Saturdays (fare around FG70,000).

NIANI is a village on the Sankarani River (which forms the border with Mali), 80km on a very rough track southeast of Siguiri. It was here, as excavations among the baobabs have proved, that **Sundiata Keita**, the legendary founding king of the Mali Empire (aka, most probably, Mansa Mari-Djata, *c.* 1205–55), installed his capital. Sites of foundries and cemeteries are dotted around the town wall alignments. If you're motivated by this kind of historical charge – and more basically if you have your own transport, plenty of time and some imagination – it's unmissable.

Towards Nzérékoré: Kérouané, Beyla and Boola

Out of Kankan, Kérouané is the main town on the route southwards, which runs alongside the gaunt whaleback of the **Chaîne du Going** ridge and up into the remote and rugged region beyond Beyla.

This is a richly historical route. On the way down to Kérouané you pass by **Bissandougou**, the recruiting point and eventual capital of **Almamy Samory Touré**'s first empire; people in your vehicle will point it out to you. Whether the small cemetery with its *banco* wall surround is still there, is hard to tell, but the nineteenth-century fort has definitely returned to the soil.

Samory signed a treaty with the French at Bissandougou in 1887, hoping to keep them to the left bank of the Niger, but new French commanders swept the agreements aside and moved on Kankan and Bissandougou in 1890. Samory adopted scorched-earth tactics and retreated south, burning villages in his path. At Kérouané he had a fort constructed on the hilltop and from here his forces harassed the French while the holy warrior planned his next move. Samory was probably the most important indigenous figure of nineteenth-century West Africa: other fragments of his story (which ended with capture in Côte d'Ivoire and exile to Gabon where he died in 1900) can be found on p.305 and in the Côte d'Ivoire chapter.

Kérouané

Today, the small prefecture of **KÉROUANÉ** barely hints at its place in history. The remains (and very little remains) of the **Tata de Samory fortress** on a low hill are now the site of the "Villa" – the administrative quarter. Archeologically the interest is thin: a huge block of laterite bricks – part of the massive old wall of the fort which measured 170 metres across – and what looks like a gate house – a hollow hut like a honey pot near the entrance. Alongside, on the new wall, there's a faded portrait of Samory. The French **conquest cemetery** – final resting place of a number of troops of the Third Republic – is hard to find; it may have succumbed after independence.

With table-top hills rising around and the steep, bluish ridge of Going soaring to over 1300m, it's a fine setting. Kérouané is surprisingly lively and, although the attractions are hard to pinpoint, it does have appeal. Because of the transport situation, you may well end up **staying** a night here, at the so-called *caravanserai* or *chambres de passage*: at one time a rather cute little *gîte* called *La Chaumière* with open-air restaurant and courtyard, it's now a primitive and dingy night stop, with terrible security (①). There's an outside toilet and shower (watch the world go by as you scrub off the dust); staff will warm water only on request.

For **meals and food**, there's a large market and some good rice and sauce for the street leading away from the police station. Nice *café fort* and *thé vert* can be had at a couple of licensed cafés up here on the left, with pleasant patios to loaf and meet people. From here, through the dry season, you can watch the progress of bushfires on Mont Going – a sombre spectacle on December and January nights as giant orange tongues leap from its flanks.

MOVING ON FROM KÉROUANÉ

There's normally a truck or two out of Kérouané to **Nzérékoré** early each morning – and perhaps something a great deal more comfortable if you make eager enquiries. Open-back lorries, as long as they're loaded, aren't the worst travelling, but on this voyage it's important to have warm clothes and anticipate a very slow trip – fifteen to twenty hours – and late arrival.

From Konsankoro, south of Kérouané, there's a highly rated hundred-kilometre track over the ranges to Macenta through rarely visited **diamond-mining country**. You could wait a long time for a ride, but there's usually a vehicle out of Kérouané on Thursday. It's reputedly a beautiful route – massive granite sugarloaf mountains and mesas pushing from the bush – which later enters the forest.

After dark, try *Djigbe's Night Club*, where special dancing *soirées* on Wednesday and Saturday bring in a fair crowd, or one of the several video clubs.

Beyla and Boola

From Kérouané the route south winds up over a col and into **BEYLA**, founded in the thirteenth century by Mande-speaking kola traders, and favoured by the French in colonial times. If you've a tough vehicle of your own, the Beyla region is unquestionably one of Guinea's most worthwhile – a number of tracks run through the Kourandou mountains, just northeast of town. For **accommodation**, the grubby *Hôtel Simadou* (①) is about your only option.

If you're heading from **Beyla to Côte d'Ivoire**, make for **Sinko** on a Friday – its market day – and stay at the *Soumanso* (①) or the preferable *Hôtel du Nord* (①). Early Saturday is about the only day to find transport onwards for the long, rough journey to Odienné, the big town over the border.

South of Beyla the road roughens considerably. **BOOLA** lies at the foot of a bosky mountain and seems to be a regular truck stop with lots of street food. The route on to Nzérékoré passes patches of thickening forest and numerous streams – a couple of hours by car, four or five by goods lorry.

THE SOUTHEAST HIGHLANDS

The highland chains of the southeast, piling into the fractured border region where Guinea meets Sierra Leone, Liberia and Côte d'Ivoire, provide inducements to match the Fouta Djalon. Against their absence of towering cliffs and waterfalls, and their generally lower altitudes, the highlands of **Guinée forestière** – the common name – weigh in with **ridges** still partly covered by evergreen **rainforest**, routes which are just as tough as the Fouta's – and remarkably muddy outside the dry seasons – and a largely non-Islamic ethnic configuration.

Climatically this is perhaps the most appealing part of the country, even if travel can be stubbornly difficult between April and November. Altitude and clouds keep it mild or warm most of the year, and while the rains are torrential, storms are accompanied by impressive electrical phenomena. There also tends to be a drier spell in the rainy season, between the end of April and mid-June. The forest harbours significant numbers of **wild animals**, if you've the energy and resources to go looking; chimpanzees, leopards, forest elephant and buffalo, and hippos and crocs in the rivers.

Sadly the pleasures of being in the region are overshadowed by the all too obvious effects of the civil wars in Liberia and Sierra Leone on a large proportion of the people here – the half million or so, often English-speaking, **refugees** who have fled the fighting. In the Guinea highlands, they scrape together a precarious, semi-nomadic existence against the confusing and terrifying background of murder, reprisal and social disintegration in their homelands. Guinea has so far absorbed the shock with little protest on the international scene. The refugees' arrival is broadly tolerated and there have been relatively few violent incidents as a result of the turmoil. But you should be aware of the potential dangers as you travel in this region and alert to any news on the grapevine.

The cultural background

Ethnically, this is singular territory. The region's predominant **Kissi**, **Toma** and **Guerzé** inhabitants are linguistically diverse and resolutely independent. Ancestor worship, totemism and *forêts sacrés* ("sacred forests": usually a clearing within the forest where ritual is performed) are all important cultural elements. Islamic influences are far less pronounced than elsewhere and the stamp of colonialism lightly impressed. Colonial subjugation – a gruelling village-by-village war of invasion – wasn't complete until 1920, having persisted bloodily since Samory's demise in 1898.

Most of the **towns** in the forest region are recent creations, dating back no further than the first French post at a suitable source of food, water and labour. Once victorious, the French maintained a thin and rather miserable presence. During the reign of Sekou Touré, many Guineans sought refuge in the relatively unpoliticized highlands, and tens of thousands more fled the country from here, especially to Côte d'Ivoire.

Guéckédou

Large but somewhat ignored, **GUÉCKÉDOU** sprawls between jungle-tufted hills. A short walk from the Liberian border and only slightly further from Sierra Leone, this proximity provides most of the town's livelihood and ninety percent of its character. The vast **market** which floods the town every Wednesday is famous throughout Guinea, as the biggest in the country and one of West Africa's great commercial exchanges.

Main participants in the sales jamboree spilling along every street are Guineans, Sierra Leoneans, Liberians and Ivoirians, but you'll also come across Malians, Senegalese and Gambians as well as a few Mauritanians. It's not surprising – but still a disappointment – to find how little of the merchandise is in any way traditional or locally made. Apart from the agricultural produce and some domestic ware, most of the rest consists of cheap imports – Filippino clothing, Taiwanese toys, Korean radios, Greek cigarettes, Japanese cloth and Chinese tools. Despite the throng, hustlers and thieves seem uncommon, though ordinary tricksters, like the card shark with his *cherchez la dame*, clean up.

For a **view** of the townscape – which at times of clear visibility is quite attractive – head up to a vantage point near the hilltop mosque, by crossing the Boya River on the Kissidougou road at the edge of town.

Down on the north bank of the Moa (Makona) River, whose left – south – bank forms the frontier, the **Plage de Keno** is an attractive beach with safe swimming (at least in terms of bilharzia – security is another matter so talk to people before going).

Practicalities

The best day to visit Guéckédou for the market is Wednesday, but if you can manage it, go ahead of the crowds and find a room on Monday or, possibly, Tuesday morning. For real comfort, you can **stay** at the new *Auberge Tomandou* (☎97.13.05; ③), next to the Gendarmerie. Its fresh, immaculate rooms and decent meals are popular with UN personnel and other expats. There are several other likely lodgings: the *Hôtel Stadium* (①–②), near the bamboo-walled football ground on the road leading out to Kissidougou; the *Terminus* (①–②) on the same road; and the marginally preferable *Escale de Makona* (in the same quarter Sandia, but more central, behind some prefectural offices), which has a few S/C rooms (②) and a terrace where you can flop out with a cold beer. There's also a more upmarket hotel, the *Hibiscus* (②), with a good restaurant. The best budget accommodation, albeit a little out of town, is the clean *Hôtel Mafissa* (①), on the hillside overlooking Guéckédou near the road to Sierra Leone.

The town is full of **food**. Try the coffee house at the lorry park – good *café au lait* and espresso and excellent evening meals of steak, salad and potatoes. In the same vicinity you may still find a couple of excellent, cheap **cassette** booths. Guéckédou has a **post office** but no BICIGUI bank: on market days you're likely to find *commerçants* willing to change money, but the nearest BICIGUI banks are at Macenta and Kissidougou.

The easiest way into Sierra Leone from here is via **Nongoa**, from where *pirogues* large enough to carry motorbikes or bicycles ply the Moa River. At the time of writing, however, this border was unsafe. Cars and trucks have to go either via **Foya** in Liberia, or – an altogether easier crossing – from Macenta to **Voinjama**. Because of civil war in both countries, none of these crossings is advisable at the time of writing.

There is a **bus service** to **Conakry** on Wednesday.

Via Macenta to Nzérékoré

The route southeast from Guéckédou to Nzérékoré is rough and exciting, though expensive. The orange ribbon of the road buckles and falters for much of the way, and sometimes tunnels through towering green **jungle**.

Over the years parts of the road have been improved, but the latest development is a new, tarred **highway** being raised through the felled forest to link Guéckédou with Nzérékoré in three or four hours instead of the current eight to twenty. The project – slashing through the jungle, cutting villages and, bizarrely, houses in half, bulldozing massive earthworks to canopy level – is pursued by the rains which destroy so much of the foundations each year. By 1998 they had reached a little beyond Sérédou. When it's completed the voyage through the forest will have lost most of its romance.

Up to Macenta

Once out of Guéckédou, the serious forest starts with the climb on the new road from the bridge over the Makona, just beyond **Bofosso** – a large village and military post dating back to 1905. It's a steep haul up what's known, somewhat mysteriously, as the *descente des cochons*. Whether pigs or nefarious humans are being referred to, you do indeed begin to see small hairy swine poking around at the roadside – signs of a strong non-Muslim presence.

Around 44km from Guéckédou the new tarmac road passes through **Niagézazou**, tucked in the forest near a liana bridge over the Makona. Then, some 5km beyond the road bridge over the Makona River, you might check out the village of **Niogbozou** up a side track shortly after the old mission centre of Balouma. Niogbozou, built on a rocky platform and apparently encircled with lianas, used to have a famous troupe of acrobats, dancers and stilt walkers who toured Europe several times before independence.

Passing from Kissi country into the lands of the Toma you arrive in **MACENTA**. This used to be the most important town in the highlands, chosen for its central position as a supply base for the "pacification columns" sent to the remote areas. Free Liberian troops attacked Macenta in 1906 but were fended off, and it was only in 1908 that the limits of the two territories were set. The French tried to grow tea in Macenta, not very successfully. They had much more luck with **coffee**, which remains important, though much of the crop is smuggled out of the country. The biggest indigenous cash crop is **kola**.

Today, Macenta is only a moderate-size place and is quite dwarfed by Guéckédou and Nzérékoré. It's a pleasing town, set amid a tumble of hills with fine views all around, and still composed of hundreds of thatched, roundhouse compounds. If you find yourself **staying** in town, there's a lovely *villa* (①), or try the nicely reburished *Palm Hôtel* (①–②) in the centre, or the very basic *Hôtel Magnetic* (②) near the *gare voiture*. There are several decent **eateries** and a branch of the BICIGUI bank (☎91.06.28).

Out of Macenta through the Malinké quarter, there's a wild and wonderful **route to Kérouané** (see box, p.521) and, ultimately, Kankan. During the rainy season it's

---

THE TOMA

The oldest inhabitants of the Macenta district, the **Toma**, earned respect from the French "pacification" troops for their resilience against raid upon raid on their isolated villages. Of all the highland peoples, it was the Toma who most harried the French invaders. Their last stronghold, the fortified village of Boussedou, was attacked by two French expeditions and numerous cannon before it finally succumbed in 1907.

Once battered into submission, the Toma found favour with the French for being good scouts and solid soldiers, utterly at home in the forest. They're fairly small people and they may have distant pygmy ancestors: oral history in the forest regions recounts stories of ancient inhabitants of small stature who were decimated by the taller invaders from the north. What's certain is that the Toma lost ground to the Malinké and ultimately mixed with Dyula Malinké to form the Toma-Manian. Today, their language – **Loma** – is a Mande tongue, related to Malinké.

You should look out for highly impressive **dancing** while you're in the Toma region, but you'll be lucky indeed to have the opportunity to witness one of the major life-cycle **celebrations**. Traditionally at circumcisions, female mutilations, marriages, births and funerals, "bird men" – the *onilégagi* – danced, dressed in feathers and painted with kaolin; *lanebogué* pranced and hopped on their stilts; and *akorogi* swirled and bounded in their raffia-leaf costumes and haunted masks. Similar dances take place in Côte d'Ivoire, but generally with your attendance and money in mind.

---

extremely difficult to pass through, but this needn't stop you trying with your own vehicle or pestering drivers at the *gare voiture* in Macenta for information about transport – or even just setting off in comfortable shoes with three days' supplies on your back.

Through the forest to Nzérékoré

As you burrow through the jungle and over the ridges, there's a string of minor but interesting stop-offs if you have your own transport. Unfortunately, unless you pull off a ride with a very sympathetic driver, most of you won't catch these by truck or Peugeot.

One place where trucks and Peugeots often stop to stock up on palm wine or food, is **Sérédou**. At 800m it straddles a col through the moist, jungly Ziama hills and most vehicles need the rest. Church bells are heard ringing here: it's an old mission and quinine research station. At the time of writing, the new highway ends 10km beyond Sérédou.

The stretch of road from Sérédou to Irié is renowned for its lepidoptera, including the giant swallowtail *Papillio antimachus*, Africa's largest **butterfly**, with a wingspan of up to 23cm. The males are occasionally seen around the treetops and, very rarely, sipping moisture at muddy puddles; female giant swallowtails, however, are elusive in the extreme.

Irié itself isn't much, but the side road that heads off southwest from here 100km to the border takes you to **Koyama**, the biggest kola market in Guinea and the frontier town for **Zorzor** in Liberia.

Nzébéla is a traditional music centre, though whether you've much chance of hearing *divogi* drums and *pouvogi* trumpets it's hard to tell. Immediately down the road, however, if you can just stop awhile at the ferry across the Diani, there's a really enormous *pont de lianes* – a **liana bridge** – some 70m long. During the dry season, local men spend a lot of time mending this construction – when it was the only means of crossing, repairing it was a focal event of the year. The bridge retains a grudging mystery, and women are not allowed to witness the repairs (once even cows were banned), but the dramatic dusk-to-dawn communal effort that used to see the bridge serviceable after one night's work (thus proving the industry of the forest spirits) has been replaced with a slower and more alcoholic routine which takes some days. You'll have to make a generous contribution to the bridge fund if you want to take photos at this time.

Shortly after the village of **Samoé**, a path leads left to a small hamlet where a group of sacred tortoises are kept by the community. Different groups of people throughout the forest region identify with a wide range of animals; the tortoise is a simple and popular totem. If you can't find them, you could try asking the White Fathers in Samoé.

Nzérékoré

With a very large Wednesday market and an atmosphere of thriving commerce, **NZÉRÉKORÉ** is the big town of *Guinée forestière*. Set amid the forest and traced through by tributary streams which feed the Mani river border with Liberia, the town's shack-lined dirt streets straggle stylelessly over hillocky ground. Yet for a backwoods agglomeration with no discernible centre, so far from anywhere (it's closer to Monrovia and even Abidjan than to Conakry) and so dependent on smuggling as a way of life, Nzérékoré is really rather an enjoyable place to be, making a good-natured exit or entrance to Guinea. Despite its size there's a more open, less cluttered feel than in Guéckédou – though there are lots of UN diplomats and NGO officials here now, involved in trying to control the **refugee** crises from neighbouring Sierra Leone and Liberia.

Nzérékoré just has to be visited on **market day**, in which case it's a tough choice between here and Guéckédou. From the permanent market, stalls overflow onto the main street and the activity stretches from the hospital to the roundabout. Liberians and Ivoirians are prominent; women show off their best wraps and the atmosphere vibrates with the racket of trade – everything from multifarious qualities of palm oil and a riot of local produce, to clothes (some cotton shirt bargains), Liberian plastic trinkets, prints and indigo *gara*. Crafts, unless you count fabrics, are fewer, but there are good lines in leather sandals, wallets and some beautifully worked and relatively inexpensive silver. And of course you can add to your cassette collection. Lastly, and by no means unique to Nzérékoré, but unmissable if you've not seen them before, are the traditional **pharmacists** who set up on market day with a festoon of graphic boards, illustrating their range of treatments for complaints ranging from worms to impotence.

Practicalities

Much of the impression of the town depends on where you find **lodgings**. The *Bakuli Annexe* (①–②), on the road out to Yomou, is a popular truck drivers' haunt run by a

SOME LOCAL HISTORY

The people of the Nzérékoré district and eastwards are **Kpelle** or **Guerzé** – related by language and some cultural elements to the Toma, and distantly to the other Mande-speaking ethnic groups. They are profoundly animist by tradition and rather resistant to Islamic influence; their mythic ancestor descended from the sky, married a local woman and settled east of Nzérékoré. Tradition relates that a man called Yegu, with a number of followers, populated the Nzérékoré district late in the nineteenth century, and these headmen were the ones in power at the time of the French arrival. It's hard to unravel the veracity of stories like these – they can easily be read as apologetics for subsequent French actions – but it seems more likely that the Guerzé had been around for rather longer than the French wanted to believe, and that colonial chiefs were not often pre-invasion notables.

There's no doubt about the Guerzé revolt in 1911 – abetted by free Guerzé forces from Liberia – which was put down by a Captain Hecquet. His life was abruptly ended during the campaign by a poisoned arrow.

MOVING ON FROM NZÉRÉKORÉ

The main route out of Guinea from Nzérékoré is east via **Lola** and the foot of the Monts Nimba to the **Côte d'Ivoire border** and **Danané**. Make an early start or you'll get stuck in Lola (excellent Monday market and several hotels). Note that the traffic through Nzérékoré comes close to a standstill on Wednesday, though there's no shortage of transport onwards after market day.

Assuming peace prevails when you're in the area, there are several **routes to Liberia**. You can go southwest towards Yomou and turn off for Diécké and Ganta on the border. East of Nzérékoré you can make a right turn on the reasonably fast Lola road, 6km out of Nzérékoré (signposted), which a number of taxis use to Yekepa and Sanniquellie; and there's a third option – the track from Bossou to Yekepa.

Flights to Conakry with Air Guinée leave on Thursday and Saturday. The fare is about FG80,000.

Vietnamese family, with all the noise and distractions you'd expect. It also has a set of much cleaner S/C rooms further down the street. *Bar Hanoi* (②) is further out on the same street, and more recommendable: it's clean, safe, with both well and generator, and again Vietnamese-run. Otherwise, out of town on the Guéckédou road, try the *Hôtel Orly* (①), a quiet, bucket-shower sort of place, or the livelier *Case Idéale* (②) with a bar-resto and **dancing**. The new *Pension Boheme* (turn left off the Macenta road) has comfortable, excellent-value rooms (②) and a restaurant, while the *Mission Catholique* (②) on the northern fringes of town has huge rooms with large, refreshing balconies outside, plus good breakfasts. A fair number of **eating houses** are scattered around town; it's worth mentioning *Gargote Chez Mohammed Djouldé Baldé* at the Yomou *gare voiture* in the Quartier Goniah, where the patron puts together wonderful avocado salads with inimitable style.

The BICIGUI **bank** (☎91.06.07) is open Mon–Fri 8.30am–12.30pm and 2.30–4pm, but does not change travellers' cheques. The **PTT** opens Mon–Sat 8am–4pm.

The Monts Nimba and around

East of Nzérékoré, the scenery along the way is nothing special until you reach **Nzo**, from where you start to get good views of the **Monts Nimba** – the highest peak of which, at 1752m, is Guinea's highest point. The road tunnels through impressive thickets of **giant bamboo** and tracks over precarious wooden bridges in the forest.

If you have time, or your own transport, you might be interested in visiting the village of **Bossou** (turn right 5km east of Lola at Gogota, then continue 15km south), where "sacred chimpanzees" are under research by Japanese and Guinean primatologists. Ask around in Lola if you'd like to visit.

Lola is also the place to get permission to visit the **Monts Nimba Reserve**, which you should be able to get without much hassle from the *préfecture*. The reserve entrance is at **Gbakoré**, some 15km from Lola on the way to Côte d'Ivoire, where your *permis* is stamped by the *chef du village*. There's a **research project** based halfway up, between the reserve entrance and the peaks area, that can sometimes offer transport from Gbakoré, but if you don't find any vehicles, you may have to hike there (a two-hour walk). You can sleep at the research station (small apartment with kitchen; ②). From here, the ridge formed by the Monts Nimba peaks – all above 1600m, which is above the tree line – can be reached in a further two hours. There are some fine views from up here on a clear day. The summit, straddling the Ivoirian border 8km to the south, is a further two- to three-hour hike.

CÔTE D'IVOIRE

CÔTE D'IVOIRE

Surrounded by countries whose economic circumstances have ranged from hopeful to desperate, Côte d'Ivoire long stood out as an example of **pragmatic capitalism** at work in independent Africa. Politically, too, it was viewed as a close ally of the West, maintaining "stability" without the kind of outright repression the word usually implies. Côte d'Ivoire had, until recently, a generous press in Europe and America, where it was called everything from the "African Miracle" to the "Land of Welcome". Most of this impression hung on a single factor – **Houphouët-Boigny**. The diminutive and soberly engaging president's word and work determined much of the course of Côte d'Ivoire's thirty-year independent history. He never passed up an opportunity to profile his country as a place where new meets old and Western economic principles got along famously with African values. It's easy to apply scorn to this *National Geographic* approach to foreign relations – the coupling of images of **skyscrapers** with shots of local **folklore** such as Dan dancers or Akan kings – but glitzy development has encouraged investors, and the three decades of Houphouët's reign were marked by widespread prosperity and no coups or major ethnic conflicts. Under his tutelage, Côte d'Ivoire was close to becoming an emergent industrial nation, comparable, in its atmosphere of feverish transformation, to Brazil.

Much of the country's optimism faded in 1993 when Houphouët died and a new era of uncertainty set in. Many of the forty thousand **French** people who formerly lived in Abidjan (running businesses, hotels, restaurants, and even taking positions of high office in the government and civil service) abandoned ship. Thousands of others who worked on French government overseas salaries across the country also left. What appeared to be formal integration suddenly looked more like an overextended vacation, and when check-out time came, Ivoirians were left to tackle serious economic and political problems on their own.

The widespread prosperity never had deep roots and, as successful at generating wealth as the country has been – largely on the principle that if you allow virtually unlimited foreign exploitation without closing any doors, a proportion of the cash will stay behind and multiply – some of the very worst **malnutrition** in West Africa still affects parts of northern Côte d'Ivoire, while contrasts between rich and poor in Abidjan are as stark as can be found anywhere in the world.

Viewed from the villages, **Abidjan** is still the glittering capital, though the tarnish is very evident to new arrivals from Europe. Its highly developed service infrastructure, most of which works, still persuades rural Ivoirians to take the bus there in search of jobs and dreams. But well-off Abidjanis who once considered Paris to be the country's real capital have been spurned by the "metropolis" and France's desire to relinquish the responsibility of its "special relationship" with Côte d'Ivoire.

For these slightly voyeuristic reasons, Côte d'Ivoire is an interesting place to visit – a stage on which you can see the traditional and the modern clashing in a drama intensified by heavy capital investment and industrialization. **Tourism** here is probably the most developed in West Africa. The government actively encourages the industry through advertising campaigns emphasizing the exotic and mysterious aspects of traditional culture – images Ivoirians themselves tend to eschew. The cultural heritage is undeniably rich, but Senoufo initiation dances or funeral ceremonies are best witnessed in the bush, as an invited guest, rather than after dinner on a hotel patio.

People

There are more than sixty different peoples (or *ethnies*, in French) living in Côte d'Ivoire. Though their languages, customs and religious practices differ locally – and of course there's been wide intermarriage and blurring of difference – it's easier to come to terms with the diversity if they're considered as four major groups with distinct historical origins. Probably the largest is the **Akan**, to which the Asante in neighbouring Ghana belong. The **Baoulé** (centered around Bouaké), **Agni** (Indénié) and **Abron** (in the east) are all Akan-speaking, though the languages are only mutually intelligible in part. They're also related to peoples who settled around the lagoons – including the **Abé** (in Agboville), **Akies** (in Adzopé) and **Ebrié** (in Abidjan).

Another large group is the **Mande**, who migrated from the north in large-scale waves from around the fourteenth century onwards. Peoples of this group include the **Bamana**, the **Malinké** (around Odienné), and the **Dyula** or Dioula (around Kong). Southern Mande-speaking groups like the **Dan** (near Man) and **Gouro** (around Bouaflé) also belong in this ethnic configuration. **Voltaic**-speaking peoples –

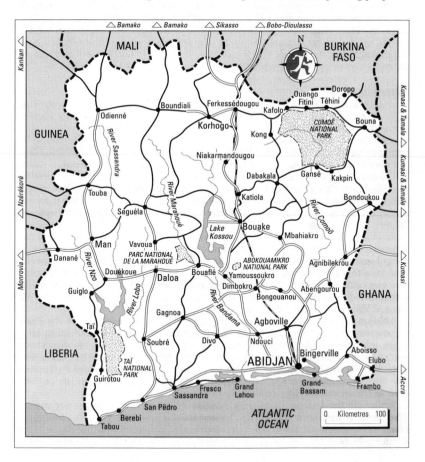

the **Senoufo** (focused around Korhogo), the **Lobi** (Bouna), and **Koulango** (Bondoukou) – were already living in the north by the time the Mande-speakers arrived.

In the southwest and west, the **Krou** (or Kru, or even Krumen) migrated from Liberia and Guinea from some time in the seventeenth century onwards. The name is supposed to derive from the common occupation of crewman on sixteenth- and seventeenth-century English ships. The **Bété** (Gagnoa), **Krou** (Bereby, Tabou), and **Dida** (Lakota) are part of this family of languages.

Côte d'Ivoire has a very large **immigrant population**, most of whom come from Burkina Faso, Mali and Guinea. These immigrants are frequently blamed for urban problems such as unemployment and crime. In addition to these African "strange workers", the **French** and around 120,000 **Lebanese** (traditionally Maronite Christians but including an increasingly high proportion of Shia Muslims) are especially conspicuous minorities because of their economic clout.

Roughly half the population practises traditional African **religions**, though many people – not just the other half – profess Christian or Islamic beliefs. As you'd expect, Muslims predominate in the north while smaller concentrations of various Christian sects live mainly in the south. **Harrism** – founded by William Wade Harris, a Liberian born at the turn of the century – is the oldest of these, and most developed in the Bingerville district. Other indigenous churches have also started to flourish on the basis of the preaching of a number of coastal prophets.

Where to go

Despite being publicized as a holiday paradise, most of Côte d'Ivoire is disappointingly monotonous – a uniform plateau with few variations in altitude. The highest peak, **Mont Tonkoui**, rises to a modest 1189m in the country's most mountainous region, the far west. Waterfalls and streams in the district make for some of the country's most scenic hikes and drives.

Côte d'Ivoire's **forests**, which fifty years ago covered most of the southern half of the country, are now hugely reduced – as a result of logging, shifting agriculture and road building which opens up remote jungle to settlement. If you're looking for adventure, the far **southwest** still contains vast districts of primary forest. Anywhere between Guiglo and San-Pédro can yield barely explored valleys and ridges.

An obvious target is the **coast**, where a major system of **lagoons** around Abidjan is separated from the ocean by long chains of sandbanks. But swimming tends to be dangerous: when the French say *Attention à la barre!* they're warning about a strong tidal race that claims many lives. For the best beaches, some with safe swimming, too, you really have to make for the **west coast**, where West Africa's most idyllic palm-rustled strands and coves are still almost untouched. Sassandra isn't too far from Abidjan and makes a good base.

Abidjan is itself part of the lagoon system. The snaking fingers of the Ebrié lagoon wind through the heart of the city, dividing a Manhattanesque urban landscape into manageable districts. If you're flying in from overseas, the only shock you're likely to face upon this first encounter with Africa is how familiar it all seems. Côte d'Ivoire, as showcased by Abidjan's glass and concrete, seems the least culturally disorientating country in West Africa. Even passing through the city on long African travels can feel like a quick trip to Europe.

While still the Ivoirian metropolis, Abidjan is technically no longer the capital. That mantle has been passed to **Yamoussoukro** which, virtually overnight, changed from a colourless village to a colourless administrative centre. Home of the former president, this burgeoning city with its monstrous **Catholic Basilica** lies in

FACTS AND FIGURES

The **République de Côte d'Ivoire** (often shortened there to RCI) is a sizeable country of 323,000 square kilometres – more than twice the area of England and Wales combined, or about the same size as New Mexico. Although long called Ivory Coast in English, Elfenbeinküste in German, Costa de Marfil in Spanish, and so on, the French name is now the official one in all languages. The **population** is estimated at nearly 15 million, of whom roughly a quarter are migrants from neighbouring states. Many Ivoirians live in urban centres – Côte d'Ivoire has at least ten towns with populations of more than 100,000.

Despite its image as a wealthy, progressive country, Côte d'Ivoire's **national debt** is one of the biggest in Africa, currently amounting to some £12.5 billion ($20 billion) – though, to put this in perspective, it's a somewhat smaller figure than the final cost of building the Anglo-French Channel Tunnel. The debt represents nearly £1000 ($1600) for every Ivoirian citizen, which is far and away the heaviest per capita debt burden on any African country. Moreover, Côte d'Ivoire's debt is equivalent to six times its annual export earnings, making the prospects for paying off the debt, or even a small fraction of it, negligible. Around one billion dollars is spent each year just servicing it.

the heart of Côte d'Ivoire. This is the **Baoulé country**, settled in the eighteenth century by refugees from the Asante Empire. Their customs and art – in which gold plays an important symbolic role – still resemble those of their neighbours in Ghana.

The **north**, despite the heat and the endless flat grasslands, has its share of interesting sites. There's a number of moderately old Islamic centres, which relate culturally to the medieval empires of the Niger River region. Towns are fewer and further apart up here and the pace slower, while the French influence, so pervasive on the coast, is much less entrenched. This is the home of some of the country's longest-settled ethnic groups; people like the **Senoufo**, whose elaborate system of education and initiation – the **poro** – served as the social glue that held them together in the face of colonialism, and more recently has preserved their identity against the onslaught of tourism.

Also in the north is West Africa's biggest game reserve, the **Comoé National Park**, where you stand a good chance of seeing some of Côte d'Ivoire's remaining ivory.

Climate

Côte d'Ivoire has **two climatic zones**, a fact which complicates any efforts to time your travels to miss the rains. In the **south**, a **long rainy season** from late April to July is followed by **short rains** in October and November, separated by a **long dry season** from December to late April, and a **short dry** in August and September. Dividing the seasons into months like this only gives an approximate idea of when to expect dry weather; "dry" seasons in the south include days of rain and dense clouds blowing in off the coast. Temperature-wise, the coast varies little through the year, neither does it cool down much at night.

The **north** has only two seasons. Rains usually last from late May to early November. Because of the mountains, the northwest receives more rain and is generally cooler than the northeast.

The **best time** to visit, especially the north, is probably between February and April, late enough in the season to avoid the *Harmattan* winds that may adversely affect travel (and dust that makes photos drearily flat). Remember, too, if you're intent on visiting the **game parks**, that they close during the rains, though the dates of closure vary from year to year.

AVERAGE TEMPERATURES AND RAINFALL

ABIDJAN

	Jan	Feb	Mar	Apr	May	June	July	Aug	Sept	Oct	Nov	Dec
Temperatures °C												
Min (night)	23	23	24	25	24	23	23	21	22	23	24	24
Max (day)	30	31	31	32	31	29	28	27	28	29	31	31
Rainfall mm	41	53	99	125	361	495	213	53	71	168	201	79
Days with rainfall	3	4	6	9	16	18	8	7	8	13	13	6

FERKESSÉDOUGOU

	Jan	Feb	Mar	Apr	May	June	July	Aug	Sept	Oct	Nov	Dec
Temperatures °C												
Min (night)	16	19	22	23	23	22	21	21	21	21	20	25
Max (day)	35	36	36	36	34	32	30	30	31	33	34	34

MAN

	Jan	Feb	Mar	Apr	May	June	July	Aug	Sept	Oct	Nov	Dec
Temperatures °C												
Min (night)	19	20	21	21	21	21	20	20	20	20	20	19
Max (day)	32	33	33	32	31	29	27	27	29	30	31	31

Arrivals

Abidjan, as the economic capital of Côte d'Ivoire, plays a pivotal role in the region, and is consequently well connected to the rest of Africa. Flights in are easy, and land connections excellent – relatively speaking.

■ Flights from Africa

Abidjan, the home of Air Afrique, is one of the region's busiest air hubs, with direct connections from almost every capital city in West Africa, many links with East and Central Africa and regular flights from Johannesburg.

From West Africa

Air Afrique (RK) handles most of the traffic **from other West African cities**. Its regional services to Abidjan are:

From Accra: non-stop daily.

From Bamako: non-stop five times a week; via Ougadougou twice weekly; via Ougadougou and Niamey weekly; via Cotonou weekly.

From Conakry: non-stop three times a week; via Bamako weekly.

From Cotonou: non-stop daily; via Lomé twice weekly.

From Dakar: non-stop six times a week; via Bamako three times weekly; via Bamako and Conakry weekly; via Accra weekly; via Conakry twice weekly; via Bissau and Bamako weekly; via Bamako and Ouagadougou weekly; via Banjul and Monrovia weekly.

From Douala: via Cotonou twice a week; via Lomé weekly.

From Lagos: non-stop four times a week; via Accra twice weekly.

From Lomé: non-stop daily; via Accra weekly.

From Niamey: non-stop twice a week; via Bamako weekly; via Ouagadougou and Bamako weekly; via Ouagadougou and Cotonou weekly.

From Nouackchott: via Niamey weekly.

From Ouagadougou: non-stop once a week; via Cotonou weekly; via Niamey twice weekly; via Bamako weekly.

Cameroon Airlines (UY) flies to **Douala** via Lagos three times a week; and via Cotonou and Lagos (in that order) weekly.

Air Guinée (GI) has two non-stop flights a week from **Conakry**.

Ghana Airways (GH) flies non-stop from **Accra** four times a week and from **Freetown**

weekly; it also has two flights a week from **Dakar**, one via Banjul and Freetown, the other via Banjul, Freetown and Conakry.

Nigeria Airways (WT) flies from **Lagos** non-stop once a week; and also has two flights a week via Cotonou, three via Lomé, two via Accra and one via Banjul and Conakry.

Air Ivoire (VU) flies non-stop from **Accra** twice a week; from **Bamako** four times a week – twice direct, once via Ouagadougou and once via Man, Korhogo and Bouaké; non-stop from **Ouagadougou** twice weekly; non-stop from **Conakry** weekly; and from **Freetown** twice a week – via Monrovia and Conakry respectively.

Air Burkina (VH) flies from **Ouagadougou** non-stop weekly; and via Bobo-Dioulasso four times a week.

Lastly, Air Gabon (GN) flies weekly non-stop from both **Conakry** and **Cotonou**, and has five flights a week from **Libreville** – two non-stop, two via Lagos and the final one via Cotonou.

From the rest of Africa

Ethiopian Airlines (ET) operates the following weekly flights from **Addis Ababa**: via Lagos and Lomé; via Nairobi, Kinshasa and Accra; via Lagos and Accra; via Nairobi, Kinshasa and Lomé; via Nairobi, Brazzaville and Lagos; and via Nairobi and Lagos.Royal Air Maroc (AT) flies from **Casablanca** non-stop twice a week.

Egyptair (MS) flies weekly from **Cairo** via Kano, Lagos and Accra. South African Airways (SA) shares the route from **Johannesburg** with RK, with two non-stop flights a week, plus another via Brazzaville.

■ Overland

Overland routes are good from Mali and Burkina – with the option of the train service from Ouagadougou to Abidjan – and from Ghana. Coming overland from Guinea, conditions are rougher, while travelling by land from Liberia – which always was slow-going – is not likely to be on your itinerary.

The details in these practical information pages are essentially for use on the ground in West Africa and in Côte d'Ivoire itself: for full practical coverage on preparing for a trip, getting here from outside the region, paperwork, health, information sources and more, see Basics pp.3–83.

DRIVING INTO CÔTE D'IVOIRE

If you're arriving with your own vehicle, you'll usually be given a fifteen-day *vignette de passage* by customs, which has to be extended in Abidjan. Don't ignore this if you're not going to Abidjan; be sure to sort the matter out before you leave the border.

From Burkina Faso

From Burkina, a main highway runs **from Ouagadougou** to Abidjan and is in pretty good shape. The border post stays open 24 hours a day. Backcountry *pistes* through the **Lobi country** are in bad condition. Very little traffic connects the towns of **Gaoua** and **Bouna**.

The **train** from Ouagadougou or Bobo-Dioulasso to Abidjan is still relatively popular (see pp.642 & 665).

From Ghana

The principal route **from Accra** is paved through the border town of Elubo, meaning you no longer have to catch a ferry across the Ehi Lagoon dividing the two countries. Besides the normal formalities, there are no special difficulties at this border and the crossing is generally quick. The road **from Kumasi** is also frequently travelled and in decent condition, except for the border stretch between Takikroum in Ghana and Agnibilékrou in Côte d'Ivoire.

From Guinea

Travelling from Guinea is somewhat problematic, owing to the bad condition of the roads. Rains and ferry breakdowns may bring traffic to a standstill. Two common routes head from **Kankan** and **Beyla** to **Odienné**, from where regular buses head through to Bouaké and Abidjan. There is also a regular Ivoirian bus that services Abidjan–Kankan–Bouaké–Abidjan. The short **Nzérékoré to Man** has become the most established and popular route. Though it skirts uncomfortably close to the Liberian border, customs formalities are trouble-free, and no reports have been received of travellers having problems related to the Liberian civil war.

From Liberia

The road is paved between Monrovia and Ganta, leaving about 90km of tracks until you arrive at Danané, in Côte d'Ivoire. An alternative, along the coast via Harper and Tabou, may take days if the weather is bad, but once you're at Tabou the road is tarred all the way to Abidjan.

From Mali

The easiest way into the country **from Mali** is via Sikasso, crossing the border at Pogo. The road has recently been resurfaced, and this gives you the possibility of joining Côte d'Ivoire's main north–south road at Ouangolodougou.

From Bamako, heading for western Côte d'Ivoire, you can cut down to Bougouni, at which point a *piste* leads directly to Odienné, although public transport along this stretch is unreliable and especially bad during the rains.

Red Tape

Visas for Côte d'Ivoire are required by everyone except US citizens – who only need a visa if their stay is more than ninety days – and nationals of ECOWAS countries. Visas are generally easy to obtain and are often issued at French consulates in those countries where Côte d'Ivoire lacks representation; they are not available at the border or the airport.

An international **vaccination card** proving you have an up-to-date yellow fever inoculation is required at the border. Be sure your arrival formalities are completed. At some borders you're expected to complete things at the first main police station, but you may not be told this – if in doubt, ask, because it may save you having to make a long trip back to the relevant police station later on. Ivoirian bureaucracy has a reputation for being extremely officious.

For **visas for onward travel**, all neighbouring countries – Guinea, Liberia, Mali, Burkina Faso and Ghana – are represented in Abidjan. Malian and Ghanaian visas are easily obtained, although the latter take up to 48 hours to be issued. Embassies' addresses are listed on p.562.

Money and Costs

Ivoirian currency is the CFA franc (CFA100 always equals 1 French franc; approx. CFA900 = £1; approx. CFA560 = US$1). If you are travelling cheaply, you will get the most benefit from the fifty percent devaluation of 1994: prices of goods and services consumed locally have risen only moderately since then. If you're booking expensive hotels and tours, or car rental, however, you'll find prices very high.

In towns across the country there are branches of the Société Générale de Banques en Côte d'Ivoire (SGBCI), Banque Internationale pour le Commerce et l'Industrie de Côte d'Ivoire (BICICI), the Afribail/Banque Internationale de l'Afrique Occidentale (BIAO) and Société Ivoirienne de Banques (SIB). Be aware, however, that they are often unwilling to change UK£, US$ or DM, especially in travellers' cheques issued by a company with whom they do not have arrangements. The only place you can routinely change non-franc currencies is Abidjan, where Citibank has branches and many banks work in conjunction with European banks.

French franc travellers' cheques are the easiest and safest form of money. The exception might be if you come into the country from Ghana, Guinea or Liberia and think you may have trouble changing money straight away at the border. In that case, French **notes** could come in handy and are usually accepted by taxi drivers, hotel operators and merchants in lieu of CFA. If you arrive by plane, the bureau de change at the airport opens for incoming flights.

Credit cards have made some headway, and are more use here than in any other West African country. Most big hotels now take Amex and often Visa, as do car rental and travel agencies. In Abidjan, they can be used in some of the fancier restaurants and supermarkets and in banks for cash advances. Access/MasterCard is uncommon.

■ Costs

A sluggish economy has brought **costs** in Côte d'Ivoire in line with other West African countries. Prices in Abidjan are certainly high, but other towns no longer seem prohibitively expensive.

Your major expense will be **accommodation**. Staying in the cheapest places, you should plan on averaging CFA5000–8000 per day on twin rooms in hotels, slightly less if you're travelling on your own. Decent hotels tend to be more in the CFA12,000–20,000 range. **Transport** also adds up, though the bus system is no more expensive and a lot more comfortable than the battered bush taxis of other countries. The average trip costs around CFA15/km. Car rental is unbelievably expensive. **Food** is still affordable; a meal in a market or *gare routière* comes to only a few hundred CFA, though sit-down *maquis* are slightly more expensive – CFA1000–2000. Ordinary meals in mid-range hotel restaurants cost a little less than what you'd pay for *le menu* in an average hotel in France – in other words about CFA5000–6000. Indulging at a foreign restaurant in Abidjan or Yamoussoukro, however, could easily set you back CFA30,000 per person.

Health

Notwithstanding some shocking malnutrition, Côte d'Ivoire has the best record in the region in terms of percentages of people affected by disease. You'll generally find adequately treated water supplies, Ivoirian bottled water everywhere, and soda water stocked in shop fridges.

Health care facilities, in the main towns at least, are pretty much up to international standards and, for long-term residents, there's not much that could befall you that would require evacuation abroad.

AIDS figures, however, are alarming; some estimates of HIV carriers run as high as twelve percent of the population and eighty percent of prostitutes. While the Ministry of Health figures are lower, the problem is undeniable and a huge AIDS prevention programme is now under way. Blood screening facilities have been introduced, condoms are readily available and billboards in town promote safe sex: *Confiance d'accord, mais prudence d'abord.*

Maps and Information

Despite its high profile in the French-speaking world, Côte d'Ivoire is little known in Anglophone countries. It's worth contacting their tourist offices abroad, which put out some very attractive material, though sometimes lacking in detail.

For **tourist information in Europe** contact the Délégation du Tourisme de Côte d'Ivoire, 24 bd Suchet, 75016 Paris (☎45.24.43.28); **in the USA**, DTCI, 117 E 55th St, New York, NY 10022 (☎212/355-6975).

As for **maps**, the best one currently available, regularly updated to take account of an active road-building programme, is the *Michelin 975 Côte d'Ivoire* which shows the country in satisfying detail at 1cm:8km and gives all Michelin's usual supplementary information.

Getting Around

Côte d'Ivoire is one of the easiest West African countries to travel around, thanks to good internal road and air connections and the Abidjan–Ouagadougou railway. Off the beaten track you can still get stuck, but rarely for long, even during the rains. There's no serious river transport.

■ Bush taxis and buses

Every city or town has its lorry park, or *gare routière*. 22-seater *"mille kilos"* minibuses and Peugeot taxis have almost been made obsolete by air-conditioned buses, which are more comfortable and cheaper, and run to regular schedules. There's not much need to consider Peugeots an option, unless you're in a *piste*-ridden area where buses don't run, or you're in a hurry and have missed the scheduled departure.

You may occasionally run into problems in the bush trying to pick up between "fare stages". Transport syndicates force vehicles to keep to set routes – no overlapping is allowed – and only vehicles in the syndicate are allowed to carry passengers.

■ By car

Côte d'Ivoire boasts eight-lane super highways – rarely seen in this part of the world. If you stick to the motorway linking Abidjan with Yamoussoukro, or the big highway running near the coastal lagoons to Ghana, you'll have a very favourable impression of the road network. In all, however, there are barely 5000km of paved roads, and in the north and southwest, dirt tracks are the rule.

■ Hitching

There's a lot of private traffic on the roads in Côte d'Ivoire and you've a reasonable chance of success in **hitching** on the main routes: Abidjan–Man, Abidjan–Ferkessédougou or along the coast. You *might* strike lucky on the approach roads to the game parks, but your timing needs to be impeccable (public holidays, weekends) to really make it worth a try. In any case, with such good public transport, hitching in Côte d'Ivoire may well take more time than it's worth.

■ Trains

The Société Ivoirienne des Chemins de Fer (**SICF**) runs 1173km of track between Abidjan and Ouagadougou, 655km of which are in Côte d'Ivoire. With a daily train in both directions (in theory), this would be a convenient way to cover the country, were it not for the fact that the whole service has been going downhill for years. It's common for the nominally thirty-hour journey to take forty hours or more, which means two nights on board. The first-class carriages are in reasonable condition while second is rather trashed, but not too bad considering the volume of passengers. Prices are higher than road transport – even second class is more expensive than going by bus.

For more information see box, p.563.

■ Internal flights

Air Ivoire links Abidjan to major towns in the interior, including Bouaké, Bouna, Korhogo, Man, Odienné, San-Pédro, Touba and Yamoussoukro. Most of these places are served by several flights a week, with fares generally falling in the CFA21,000–27,000 range. Note that there are some student and youth reductions on Air Ivoire; you have to be under 32, and you need an ISIC card if you're over 26.

Accommodation

Hotels in Côte d'Ivoire are generally very good and in most sizeable towns you'll find something affordable with airconditioning and self-contained rooms.

Unsurprisingly, **Abidjan** is the most expensive place to stay, though prices are better in

---

ACCOMMODATION PRICE CODES

All accommodation prices in this chapter and throughout the book are coded according to the following scales, in the equivalent in UK£ and US$. Prices refer to the rate you can expect to pay for a room with two beds. Single rooms, or single occupancy, will normally cost at least two-thirds of the twin-occupancy rate, for further details see p.48.

① **Under CFA4500 (under £5/$8).** Very rudimentary hotel with no frills at all – often a *chambre de passage* rented to the average guest by the hour.

② **CFA4500–9000 (£5–10/$8–16).** Basic hotel with simple amenities and some S/C rooms.

③ **CFA9000–18,000 (£10–20/$16–32).** Modest hotel, usually with S/C rooms and a choice of rooms with fans, or a premium for AC.

④ **CFA18,000–27,000 (£20–30/$32–48).** Reasonable business or tourist-class hotel with

S/C, AC rooms and often a good restaurant.

⑤ **CFA27,000–36,000 (£30–40/$48–64).** Similar standards to the previous code band, but extra facilities such as a pool are usual.

⑥ **CFA36,000–45,000 (£40–50/$64–80).** Comfortable, first-class hotel, with good facilities.

⑦ **Over CFA45,000 (over £50/$80).** Luxury establishment – top prices around CFA80,000–100,000.

---

other major towns. In the extreme north prices are generally lower than in the rest of the country, and at least comparable to those in neighbouring countries.

Côte d'Ivoire has a star-classified **rating system** for hotels. Five stars, the maximum, are given to luxurious places like the *Ivoire* in Abidjan or the *Président* in Yamoussoukro – both of which have state-of-the-art gadgets in the rooms and splendid facilities. A night in one of these places starts in the neighbourhood of CFA60,000. At the other end of the scale, one-star hotels usually have S/C rooms with AC and not a lot more for around CFA8000 per night for a double.

Unclassified hotels are the least expensive option. You'll find many throughout the country, their prices varying according to the region. The less respectable of these are known as *chambres de passage*, and although they're often rented out by the hour and not really intended for travellers, you can stay in them, usually quite cheaply, for the night. Some take their social responsibilities quite seriously and provide clients with clean bathrooms and towels.

Staying with people is perfectly feasible. However, Ivoirians see a lot of travellers and tourists, most of whom appear to be in a hurry, and you're not likely to get a lot of spontaneous invitations. This shouldn't be mistaken for a lack of hospitality.

Camping out is possible in many areas, particularly in the more open and sparsely populated

north. If you're anywhere near the big highways, or in the vicinity of one of the country's large towns, however, security may be a problem.

Eating and Drinking

Côte d'Ivoire has a variety of more or less unique dishes. In the south, you'll find the usual varieties of tubers – yams, cassava (manioc) – which, along with plantains, make up a large part of the diet. They are often pounded into *foutou* and eaten with a clear sauce.

Around Abidjan, cassava or manioc is commonly dried, grated and steamed. The result, called **atieké** (occasionally spelled here and in other countries *achéké*), is often compared to *couscous*, although the steam makes the manioc grains stick together in a large lump. It's a heavy meal served with **poisson braisé** and, for some reason, it seems to induce sleep. You can buy *atieké* ready-made in the markets – all wrapped in large leaves. Another staple is **aloko**, the local name for sliced, deep-fried plantains. In other countries this is more of a snack, but in the RCI it's the basis of a meal served with a bit of *piment* and fish.

Rice is grown in the northwest and is the main staple there, although you now find it throughout the country. In the northeast, millet and increasingly corn make up the basis of the diet. **Kedjenou**, which originates in the north, has caught on throughout the country and is commonly served in the _maquis_ of Abidjan. It's made from chicken, steamed together with vegetables – aubergines, tomatoes and onions – and served on rice.

Foreign restaurants catering to the big expat community are commonplace in Côte d'Ivoire, and this is where you'll find some of the best European eating in West Africa. In Abidjan, dining in a French restaurant costs substantially more than in Paris, but the quality compares well.

■ Drinking

Local **liquid refreshments** include palm wine – _banqui/bangi_ – commonly found in the south. _Chapalo_ (or _tchapalo_) is the millet beer favoured by northerners; Ivoirians usually drink it _pimenté_, adding hot peppers to give it an extra kick. _Mouroudji_, a non-alcoholic drink based on lemon and ginger, is sold throughout the country, notably in town markets and _gares routières_. Staple internationals – Coke and other soft drinks, notably soda water – are supplemented by Ivoirian **beer**. The thought of a giant, litre bottle of ice-cold Bock (_grand modèle_) has encouraged many a dusty traveller. Other popular brands are Flag and Mamba and locally brewed Stella Artois and Tuborg. A small, 33cl beer is known as a "Flagette".

Communications – Post, Phones, Language and Media

Côte d'Ivoire has a well-developed telephone system and good mail service, though you pay a lot for both. Poste restante tends to be held for a limited period only – better to use a private box number or the Amex representative in Abidjan. If you're travelling widely in West Africa, don't count on the Abidjan PTT as a major mail and telephone point: it's an exasperating place to deal with.

Internal, let alone international, **phone calls** can be fiendishly expensive. Cardphones have been established in various towns – cards cost CFA1000–15,000. Also common throughout the country, and handy after hours are _cabines téléphoniques_ – not public booths, but private phones in small stores. Rates are determined by impulses, and compare well with the PTT.

International calls go through quickly; if your funds are limited, say how much you want to pay and you'll be cut off at the appropriate point.

The AT&T access number is ☎00 111 11, though you need coins or a phoncard first.

■ Languages

The official **language** of Côte d'Ivoire (and God forbid you should call it Ivory Coast) is French. In addition there are numerous national languages, the most widespread of which is **Dyula** (often spelled _Dioula_), a Mande language of commerce very closely related to Bamana and Malinké (in fact the three are virtually dialects, to a large extent mutually intelligible). The Akan language **Baoulé** is also widespread; Baoulé people (Houphouët-Boigny's community) account for a large chunk of the total population (about fifteen percent) and are well represented in the administration. The Kru language, **Bété**, is the most widely spoken language in the southwest, while the Voltaic tongue **Senoufo** is spoken in a number of dialects across a substantial region in the north.

■ The media

Two major daily **newspapers**, the news sheet _Fraternité Matin_ (commonly referred to as "Frat-Mat") and sports and entertainments organ _Ivoir'Soir_ keep Ivoirians abreast of national and regional news, but neither has extensive international coverage and both are owned by the ruling conservative political party, the PDCI. The main opposition party, FPI, puts out the daily _La Voie_, although their weekly _Nouvel Horizon_ has a better reputation as a non-government paper. _Le Jour_ is a good independent paper and _Ivoire Dimanche_ a weekly magazine with in-depth articles and popular comic strips. _La Patrie_ takes an oppositional stance and was briefly banned in 1995 for writing "defamatory articles" about President Bédié.

Côte d'Ivoire has one of the most together and user-friendly **TV** and **radio** services in West Africa. Colour transmissions in French on Télévision Ivoirienne go out eleven hours daily on two channels. Radiodiffusion Ivoirienne broadcasts mostly in French, plus English and several Ivoirian languages. There are several FM radio

Côte d'Ivoire's IDD code is ☎225.

A SHORT GLOSSARY OF IVOIRIAN TERMS

A mix of French and Ivoirian language words.

Akwaba Welcome in Baoulé, and the name of numerous hotels, restaurants and bars.

Apatam Men's meeting shelter, palava house.

Barre The surf barrier; on the landward side, the tidal race is often too much to swim against.

Bia The thrones of the Akan-speaking kingdoms.

Deguerpi Meaning "he who had to get out", it refers to people displaced by development projects, notably those forced to move when the Kossou Dam flooded the region west of Yamoussoukro.

Maquis A French word meaning scrub or bush, and hence the French underground resistance in World War II. Formerly, local drinking places couldn't operate without authorization so they

moved to hidden courtyards, gaining the name *maquis*. Today it refers to small restaurants – now legal – that serve drinks with inexpensive Ivoirian food.

Mille kilos 22-seater, one tonne minibuses, generally the type of vehicle to avoid at a motor park.

Papo Palm fronds woven into roofs or fences, common along the coast.

Yacouba Name commonly given to the Dan people. A misnomer, it supposedly stuck when one of the first Europeans asked what the people were called and someone responded with a sentence that started "*yacouba*", meaning "he says". Frequently the area around Man is referred to as the Yacouba country.

---

stations, of which the most innovative is BBC Afrique, the British corporation's first venture into FM broadcasting in Africa.

Entertainment

Soccer is Côte d'Ivoire's national sport, and seeing a match in the Abidjan stadium is recommended. Considering the fairly elaborate recording facilities and relative availability of instruments, the Abidjan music scene is none too exciting.

■ Sport

Half a dozen Ivoirian footballers play for French clubs – and in 1998 Ibrahima Bakayoko was signed by Everton in the UK – but the domestic game is well worth a look, especially if you have the chance to see either of the two pre-eminent sides – **ASEC** and **Africa Sports** – in action. In 1999 ASEC won the African version of the European Champion's League, making them the best club on the continent. The **national team** has had a quiet spell since they won the African Nation's Cup in 1992 and then finished third in 1994.

■ Music

Live gigs are infrequent. Reggae superstar **Alpha Blondy** has lost some of his more politically

aware fans abroad and opted for comfortable sellout; crooner **Daouda** continues his gush of bilious sweet-soukous tunes; and **Ismaela Isaac et les Frères Keita** provide Blondy esque wallpapermusic. **Aïcha Koné** also records and tours overseas, but has preserved a fine style of her own.

Look and listen out for **Frederick Meiway**, who plays a dance beat called *zouglou* or *dance des jeunes*; **Gnaoré Djimi**, whose fourteen-member band play the amazingly fast *polihet* sound, which is a variation on the traditional *ziglibithy* rhythm; and **Zagazougou**, a percussion and accordions group who play at a rare lick.

Holidays and Festivals

The usual Christian holidays are official, while moveable Muslim feasts affect local services only. Beyond these are New Year's Day, Labour Day (May 2), Ascension Day and Assumption Day (both variable), All Saints Day (November 1), and Independence Day (December 7).

■ Festivals

Numerous **regional festivals** include:
January: Ancestral festival in **Tiagba**; harvest festival in **Dabou**; yam festival in **Abengourou**.
March: Carnival in **Bouaké** – Mardi Gras-like celebration.

April: Dipre festival of the sacrifice in **Gomon**, north of Abidjan (self-mutilation and trances); mask festival in **Behoua**.

June: Lagoon festival in **Yassap** near Dabou.

July: Circumcision festival in **Man**.

August: Generation festival in **Blokosso**; yam festival in **Sikensi**.

November: Abissa festival of the dead in **Grand Bassam**; Prophet Atcho festival in **Bregbo** (Harrist celebration); yam festival in **Bondoukou**; mask festival in **Man**.

Directory

AIRPORT DERARTURE TAX None.

OPENING HOURS Banks open Mon–Fri 8–11.30am & 2.30–4.30pm. **Government offices** operate Mon–Fri 8am–noon & 2.30–6pm, Sat 8am–noon.

PHOTOGRAPHY No permit is required and people are generally unperturbed by picture taking. In some areas where tourism is popular, artists, dancers or local chiefs may ask for money before being photographed. Either comply or don't take the shot. Other than that, the only real restriction concerns pictures of military installations, airports, bridges and the like.

TROUBLE You're less likely than usual to get into misunderstandings in Côte d'Ivoire. The manners and customs of tourists – especially young ones – are well recognized. That said, police and customs officers can be surprisingly prickly and in the roadside encounters you'll have with extraordinary frequency (especially in the east towards the Ghana border) they can be hostile and humourless – though not especially corrupt. It's as well to know that the official line on **illegal drugs** (in response to the threat of heroin and cocaine trans-shipments) is severe.

Situations where you're clearly a victim occur most often in **Abidjan**, only rarely elsewhere, and some advice is given in that section. The worst pickpocketing goes on at the end of the month, when Ivoirians are carrying their salaries home. Beware, too, in this very mobile society, of being robbed as you get off a night bus half asleep.

WILDLIFE AND NATIONAL PARKS You'd be forgiven for thinking Côte d'Ivoire has little to offer in terms of natural history; much of the countryside is dedicated to plantations or subsistence farming and it's fairly rare to see wild animals from the road. But the three main national parks – **Comoé** in the north, **Maraoué** in the central region and **Abokouamikro** nearby – harbour good numbers of animals, including buffalo, hippos, lions, elephants and many species of antelope. In the far southwest, the **Parc National de Taï** is a little-visited rainforest reserve which protects chimps and pygmy hippos and a wealth of other forest species in a region with a relatively low human population.

A Brief History of Côte d'Ivoire

The early history of Côte d'Ivoire is perhaps better known than that of many other West African countries because its northern fringes were part of the vast, literate, Mande cultural domain. Several towns are estimated to have been founded as far back as the twelfth or thirteenth centuries – including Kong, Bouna and Bondoukou – though not by Mande speakers, who arrived later. By the sixteenth century, the early European presence was being felt along the coast, but trading posts were strictly temporary affairs, dependent on the supplies of ivory, hides, gold and slaves that could be extracted from the people of the interior. Early slaving "factories" – but not stone forts – were set up at São Andreas (Sassandra), Grand Lahou, Jaqueville and Assinie. During the eighteenth century, the interior was transformed with the arrival and establishment of an Akan-speaking offshoot, the Baoulé, who set up a successful planting and trading economy in the forest and savannah lands of central Côte d'Ivoire, and became the country's most important people.

■ Arrival of the French

Apart from a brief contact at Assinie around 1700, the **French** only became interested in the coast after the Napoleonic wars, when they began to buy "treaties" with local kings and chiefs along the coast. In the 1840s, they built **forts at Assinie, Bassam and Dabou**, which during the 1860s and again in 1875 the French government tried to exchange with Britain for the Gambia colony. But the French "resident" at Bassam, **Arthur Verdier**, had his own plans for the future of the settlements and resisted the idea, a rela-

SAMORY TOURÉ

Pressured by the French advance from the west in the 1880s, the Malinké warmonger, jihadist and empire-builder **Almamy Samory Touré** organized a systematic scorched-earth retreat to the northern part of Côte d'Ivoire, where he set up a temporary second Dyula Empire stretching from Séguéla to the Upper Volta. In the process, Kong was largely destroyed (in 1897) and Bondoukou sacked. Thousands of people, especially Senoufo farmers, fled their homes, and several seasons' worth of crops were lost. Samory was planning to hold a heavily defended mini-empire based at Katiola, against the French on one side and the British on the other. But he altered strategy on learning of the defeat by the French in a single day of the well-fortified town of Sikasso (now in Mali) and the death of his ally there, Ba Bemba. He fled west again, only to be captured at Guéoulé, near Man, on September 29, 1898. He was exiled to Gabon, where he died of pneumonia on June 21, 1900.

tively minor obstinacy that did much to set the shape of West Africa. Verdier had already established *la Compagnie de Kong*, trading French goods far into the interior, via Bondoukou. A young director of the French school at Assinie, **Marcel Treich-Laplène**, was persuaded by the governor of Senegal to make an expedition to the northeast to consolidate the districts threatened by British expansion from the Gold Coast. Treich-Laplène's, and then Louis Binger's, expeditions effectively laid claim to most of the area of today's Côte d'Ivoire. It became a colony of France in 1893, with Grand-Bassam its capital.

■ "Pacification" and anti-colonial resistance

After the **1885 Berlin conference**, France had aggressive competitors for African territory in Britain, Belgium and Germany. With the commencement of the Abidjan–Niger railway and the building (after Grand-Bassam's yellow fever epidemic) of the new capital, **Bingerville**, the French adopted a vigorous imperialism which stressed their "mission to civilize". The exploits of Samory against the French had featured off and on in the French headlines for some years and "pacification" now became a violent series of repressions against poorly armed insurgents. Governor **Angoulvant**, whose name is still remembered in an Abidjan street name, had a reputation for using strong-arm tactics, and he made a deeper impression on colonized Ivoirians than any other Frenchman.

There were uprisings all over the country; the Agni kingdom revolted from 1895–96, sections of the Baoulé in 1899 and the Dida and Wobe groups of Kru-speakers in 1913. But the **Abé revolt** of January 8, 1910 was one of the most violent and well organized.

The Abé, from the area around Agboville, were directly in the line of the railway. Traditionally chauvinistic, the Abé were independent to the point of hostility; but, forced to pay taxes, intimidated into labouring on the railway construction, and press-ganged from their families and villages to walk for days through the forest carrying iron rails and sleepers, they prepared secret plans for an uprising. On the chosen day, the line to the coast was destroyed in several places and every non-Abé whom the rebels encountered was killed, including a number of French settlers and engineers.

Angoulvant reacted with characteristic swift brutality, bringing in troop reinforcements and organizing **manhunts** through the forest. But the Abé's guerilla war against the railway line – and against the creeping usurpation of Abé dominance in their homeland by other groups, some of whom actively collaborated with the French – continued for several years.

■ The Côte d'Ivoire Colony

Because of Angoulvant's energetic methods, the people of southern Côte d'Ivoire had to contend, in the early colonial years, with even worse treatment than was common in West Africa. Not unconnected with this, their country was also viewed as the most economically promising in French West Africa. Trade routes deep into the interior were well-established, the railway gradually drew more wealth to the coast and, most important, two crops of massive significance on the world markets – **coffee and cocoa** – flourished. Although their cultivation was at first forced on farmers, the value of coffee and cocoa wasn't lost on them and they soon began to devote most of their land to cash crops. By the 1920s, families with large holdings on coffee or cocoa land had become an incipient middle class. Côte d'Ivoire also exported rubber, palm oil, timber and fruit crops.

Meanwhile, Bingerville had been dismissed as a permanent economic capital and surveying and initial work at the site of Abidjan had begun in 1903, the same year the railway started its journey north. De facto capital and economic linchpin since the early 1920s, Abidjan finally became official capital in 1934.

Côte d'Ivoire was governed by decree, from Paris and Dakar. Its very attractiveness brought hardships for those who found themselves "Ivoirians" under colonial rule. Forced labour, "for the development of the country", was extracted through chiefs as part payment of dues and taxes. But subjects (the status of nearly all Ivoirians) were also forced to work on private plantations where corporal punishment and privation were normal practice. Such forced labour wasn't always a local matter, either; thousands of labourers were rounded up in the Upper Volta region and trucked south.

Chiefs were co-opted into the lower ranks of French administration, doing the dirty work of recruitment, tax collection, crop and livestock requisition (common during both World Wars) and enforcing compulsory cultivation. In large measure, too, the chiefs increased their customary **judicial power**, now with higher authority. Where districts were quiet and taxes and harvests flowed in, the French senior administrators did little to interfere with the running, smooth or otherwise, of colonized society. The corrupting effects of the system were almost immediately apparent.

■ Nationalist stirrings

It was injustice at a level above the grass roots that led to the earliest clear signs of nationalist aspirations. **French plantation-owners** benefited from both a cheap labour supply and the market rate for their coffee and cocoa. **African farmers** had to rely on their own kin and community networks for labour and were forced to accept low prices for their harvests, even though the differences in quality, compared with French produce, were negligible.

Nevertheless, African unions and associations were permitted and flourished, though at this stage (the 1930s) calls for more equality and faster assimilation were heard considerably more often than demands for self-government or independence. **Felix Houphouët-Boigny**, a Baoulé doctor, trained in Dakar, became involved in the question of cocoa prices in 1932, when he first lobbied on behalf of farmers in Abengourou.

World War II delayed political progress, and also marked a threshold. De Gaulle's appearance on the scene, and the 1944 Brazzaville declaration that ended forced labour and accepted the need to overhaul administrative methods, utterly transformed future possibilities in Côte d'Ivoire. Houphouët-Boigny had been given the job of *chef du canton* for Akoué in 1939. Now he set up, with several other wealthy farmers, the Syndicat Agricole Africain (African Farmers' Union), which had the support of the progressive French governor. The planters persuaded northern chiefs, including the Moro Naba in Upper Volta, to send labourers for their own plantations, to be paid four times the rate paid by French planters *and* to receive a share of the crop. In the climate of conflict between settlers and *indigènes*, this was a serious, political step; it also put the white tribe of Côte d'Ivoire on the defensive, and pitted them against their own liberal governor, **André Latrille**.

Postwar politics

In the **1946 elections** to the French Constituent Assembly, Houphouët-Boigny was elected as people's deputy for Côte d'Ivoire. He won by a narrow margin: there were other important candidates, one of whom received support from settlers trying to keep the African planters out of power. Houphouët's first act was to ensure that the Brazzaville recommendation on forced labour was followed through. The law that abolished forced labour was quickly coined the **loi Houphouët-Boigny** and the reputation of the planter from Yamoussoukro reached a new peak.

In response to clear messages of antagonism from postwar France, however, and especially to the French Socialist and Christian Democrat parties' failure to support the African cause, Houphouët, and several other African deputies (including those from Senegal and Soudan – later Mali), formed the Rassemblement Démocratique Africaine (RDA) in October 1946 to act as an umbrella negotiating body for local political parties in French West and Equatorial Africa – in Côte d'Ivoire, for the Parti Démocratique de la Côte d'Ivoire (PDCI). The settlers in Côte d'Ivoire finally succeeded in getting rid of the pro-Houphouët governor Latrille, whom they distrusted intensely. And, spreading the belief that the RDA was a hotbed of Soviet-backed agitators, the next colonial administration in Abidjan managed to break the ties between the Mossi chiefs in Upper Volta and Houphouët's new political power base.

Reactionary responses to political developments continued, however. During 1949 and 1950 a series of **"incidents"** across the country involved quarrels started by anti-RDA *provocateurs*, which provided the colonial government with pretexts to bully and arrest Houphouët's followers. In many of the disturbances dozens of people died, most of them innocent villagers killed when troops opened fire. And in several cases, cold-blooded extra-judicial executions took place. Most leaders of the RDA except Houphouët were arrested and imprisoned in Grand Bassam. A year of ferment ended when troops in Dimbokro shot thirteen people on January 30, 1950. A decree banning all RDA activity was issued two days later.

But the momentum for change couldn't be held back. Despite the predictable formation, under colonial auspices, of parties like the Parti Progressiste de Côte d'Ivoire and the Bloc Démocratique Eburnéen, vehemently opposed to the relatively mild and reformist goals of the PDCI-RDA, the movement made progress. Through the "dark years" of 1948–50, when over 3000 supporters were arrested, they staged **strikes and protests**, culminating in a 1950 boycott of European goods. To drive home the message of the PDCI's independence to anyone who still believed its actions were being orchestrated in Moscow, Houphouët-Boigny broke off his party's alliance with the French Communists which had given his critics so much political ammunition. Houphouët the Marxist had never sounded very credible.

■ Independence

The constitution of the PDCI declared its "struggle for the unity of the native people of Côte d'Ivoire with the French people, for political, economic and social progress following a programme of democratic claims". It didn't sound revolutionary, and when moves **towards independence** came after the 1956 *Loi cadre* (blueprint law) established local government for each of the French colonies (but expressly headed off calls for federalism), it was clear that Houphouët favoured

close ties with France over the kind of West or pan-African federation that Nkrumah (of newly independent Ghana), Senghor of Senegal and Sekou Touré of Guinea each envisaged in his own way.

When, in 1958, **de Gaulle** returned to power, established the "French Community", and made his famous Yes or No offer to the colonies (self-government within the French union or complete independence outside it), there was never much doubt that Houphouët wanted the country to plump for the first option. The idea of a French West African federation with its capital in Dakar had never appealed to the Ivoirians, whose country, already the richest in the group, stood to gain little. On the other hand, Houphouët would certainly have countenanced a federation of states which included France on equal terms.

By 1960, with de Gaulle suddenly prepared to see independence (which really meant control over currency and defence) *within* the French union, a scramble began in some territories to salvage the federal ideal. Houphouët prevented Côte d'Ivoire's involvement by unilaterally declaring **independence** on August 7, 1960. At the same time he formed the Conseil de l'Entente, consisting of Côte d'Ivoire, Niger, Haute Volta (now Burkina) and Dahomey (now Benin), to loosely pull together those economies which relied upon Abidjan, and further to hinder any West African federation which might seek to draw them away.

■ Independent Côte d'Ivoire: "Economic Miracle" – and crisis

The **first twenty years** of independence bore out the hyperbole pretty well; in comparison with every other West African country, Côte d'Ivoire made staggering progress. Economic growth rates were remarkably high, though everything depended on coffee and cocoa. There were strong developments in manufacturing, too, and the country moved into the "middle bracket" of underdeveloped nations.

By the late 1970s, however, Côte d'Ivoire's long and complacent record of success began to erode, and cutbacks in public expenditure were necessary as the country slid into serious debt. For nearly every year since the early 1980s the country has been the world's largest cocoa producer, but a glut on the world market forced cocoa and coffee prices down. At first Houphouët tried to hold up the producer price paid to the farmers, and stockpile the crop in an attempt to raise world market prices. But the ploy was unsuccessful and, ultimately, Côte d'Ivoire had to agree to World Bank and IMF adjustment plans in 1988 as the country was unable to service its foreign debts. As a result, cocoa farmers were paid in the early 1990s roughly half what they received in 1989.

On the **political scene**, events – or the lack of them – in the 1960s and 1970s seemed to mirror the stability of the republic. Houphouët-Boigny took personal control of the country's transformation from colony to regional power, directing the French-dominated economy and avoiding confrontation with political opponents by a skilful mix of stick and carrot.

As the country slipped into economic crisis, criticism of the president or of government policies was rarely tolerated and strikes often resulted in the temporary banning of the union involved. Denunciation of the top-heavy role of **French expatriates** in administration and senior management, on the other hand, was an escape valve generally sanctioned. Periodic reductions of their numbers, in drives for **Ivoirianization**, were greeted with applause.

The earliest clear opposition came in the 1960s, when Kragbe Gnagbe tried to set up an alternative party with support from his Bété ethnic community around Gagnoa. This led to **mass arrests** of alleged coup plotters in 1963 – and the death in detention of one of them, **Ernest Boka**, a former head of the supreme court. The perceived threat to the government led inexorably to the bloody **Bété revolt** in 1970 in which Gnagbe was banished to his village and several hundred people died in clashes with troops.

Côte d'Ivoire's relationship with its four neighbours and their leaders have sometimes been strained. Relations with **Liberia** and **Ghana** have long been soured by the presence in Côte d'Ivoire of political exiles and the country's relations with Blaise Compaoré of **Burkina** (who is married to Houphouët's niece) were not helped by an article in *Jeune Afrique* magazine which suggested that Côte d'Ivoire had played a role in overthrowing Thomas Sankara.

■ The growth of opposition

There's no number two, three or four in Côte d'Ivoire; there's only number one . . . and that's me.

Felix Houphouët-Boigny, July 1987

From the outside, Houphouët-Boigny seemed to signal dependable neocolonialism – at least until 1990 – with enough wealth trickling down and enough progress being made to keep the pot from boiling over. But **opposition** to the president's espousal of pro-Western, capitalist values – mostly from students and teachers' unions – resulted in several of the one-on-one *dialogues* for which the old man was famous, and which temporarily served to defuse the issues – or at least defer them – with large dollops of Houphouët charisma.

As long ago as 1975, with Houphouët-Boigny starting his fourth unchallenged term in office and already at least seventy years old, Ivoirians were beginning to wonder when (or if) he might step down, and who might replace him. The names of several senior figures were trailed before the public. By the early 1980s, however, the post of vice-president was vacant – and abolished in 1985 – and public debate on the question of **succession** was considered almost treasonable.

In 1987, another in the growing tradition of Bété critics of the government, **Robert Gbai Tagro**, took on the establishment in his own Parti Républicain de la Côte d'Ivoire by apparently pitting himself as a future president against Houphouët. His party was never banned, but nor would Houphouët recognize it. Its first major attempt to rally support – at the proposed first congress of the party in April 1987 – was crushed and its leaders detained.

A more outspoken thorn in Houphouët's side was **Laurent Gbagbo** (another Bété from Gagnoa). Long self-exiled to France and leader of the Front Populaire Ivoirien (FPI), he insisted he wouldn't return until a framework for multi party democracy was established. Houphouët managed to woo him back in September 1988 and, although the president was supposed to have offered him a ministerial post to absorb his political ambitions, he turned it down.

■ The 1990s

By the early 1990s the country was in the grip of **austerity measures** under an imposed "structural adjustment programme" of the kind which most of Côte d'Ivoire's neighbours had had to put up with for some years. Power worker strikes led to blackouts in February 1990. These in turn pushed **students** into marching on Abidjan city centre and finally led to the violent arrest of 150 students who had barricaded themselves in the Abidjan cathedral. They were demanding **Houphouët's resignation**, an **end to one-party rule** and better grants and conditions on campus. **Marcel Ette** of the lecturers' union SYNARES (which has always been vocal in support of democratic reforms) spoke out eloquently and with some courage against the "deep malaise afflicting Ivoirian society".

National turmoil

Houphouët's oft-repeated claim that "not a single drop of blood has been spilled in this country since I've been President" was conclusively sunk in April 1990, when a schoolboy was shot dead as police tried to disperse a crowd of demonstrators in Adzopé, north of Abidjan. Amid rumours that Houphouët was shortly to resign, **protests** flared in a number of towns and doctors went on strike.

Under siege, the government dropped the massive **tax increases** (effectively pay cuts) due to be implemented in 1990. Although peace was restored for a few weeks, there was an unprecedented **army rebellion** in May of that year, led by hundreds of young conscripts demanding improved conditions. They took over a radio station in Abidjan, and were soon emulated by air force personnel who staged an **occupation of Abidjan airport**. There was a further army uprising the next day, and a state of general panic and confusion reigned in the Plateau district of Abidjan as soldiers tore through the streets in commandeered cars. Dozens of other disturbances occurred in garrison towns around the country, most of them contained by the police, who remained loyal throughout. The 1000-strong contingent of **French troops**, based at Port Bouet, was placed on alert by Paris, but not deployed.

During this period of instability, Houphouët appeared to backtrack. He agreed to **legalize opposition** parties and scheduled legislative and **presidential elections** for 1990. Still, he refused to implement a transitional government or to convene a national conference of the type sweeping reform into other West African countries.

The campaign was kept short and the president was accused of adeptly wielding government powers to stymie the opposition. Access to the state-owned media was jealously guarded, particularly for the most serious threat, **Laurent Gbagbo**, running on the FPI ticket. The president

won a seventh term in the country's first contested elections, though the FPI was quick to point out voting irregularities and tried unsuccessfully to have the Supreme Court annul the results.

Despite the political jockeying, calm prevailed and significant constitutional changes were implemented. The first allowed for the president of the national assembly, **Jean Henri Konan Bédié**, to assume the presidency should the office become vacant, an indication that the ageing president was planning his own succession. The second allowed for the appointment of a prime minister, a post assigned to **Allasane Ouattara**, the former governor of the Banque Centrale de l'Afrique de l'Ouest, who had implemented the nation's economic reforms.

The post-election quiet broke down in May, 1991. As students and teachers began a campaign to protest poor conditions in the education system, security forces violently disrupted a meeting at Abidjan university. Troops swept through residency halls to round up ringleaders and killed four students, injuring and raping dozens of others. Though 180 people were arrested, the government denied deaths had occurred and expelled the bureau chief of Agence France Presse for reporting otherwise.

The incident carried over into 1992 when the commission set up to investigate it implicated high-ranking military officials. Although the army chief of staff was found to be directly responsible for the violence, the president refused to take disciplinary action, saying it would be bad for military morale.

Violent **demonstrations** immediately erupted as students and teacher's unions took to the street. They were soon joined by the FPI which organized a march that attracted 20,000 supporters who demanded the government step down. A hundred people were arrested as the protest turned violent; among them, Gbagbo and the president of the national human rights organization.

Despite the gravity of the situation, Houphouët never saw fit (or was physically unable) to leave the serenity of his mansions in France and Switzerland where he remained for five months. He only returned to Côte d'Ivoire in June 1992, and soon after, granted amnesty to opposition leaders who had been detained during his absence. Gbagbo was released in August and received a hero's welcome from thousands of supporters.

The tumultuous final years of Houphouët-Boigny's fifty-year political career ended on

December 7, 1993, when the president died and an entire era of West African politics ended. Bédié assumed the presidency as prescribed by the constitution, but was soon challenged by Ouattara, who was forced to resign as prime minister. He was replaced by **Daniel Kablan Duncan**, the former finance minister.

The **succession crisis** thus fizzled out fairly quickly, yet the battle to win the hearts and minds of the nation was just beginning. As the country finally faced the problems of debt, poverty and ethnic tensions that its neighbours had been grappling with for years, it did so on a very shaky political foundation.

A new and still uncertain era

The new mandate for leadership was staged to emerge in the local, legislative and presidential elections of 1995. Prospects for Bédié didn't look promising when a wing of his ruling PDCI joined Ouattara – who had traded his premiership for a post as deputy managing director of the IMF – to form a new party, the **Rassemblement des Républicains** (RDR). But Bédié deftly used his position as head of state to isolate opponents, introducing a new "parenthood" clause in the electoral code, which barred candidates who were not of direct Ivoirian descent or who had not lived in the country continuously for five years prior to the elections. Ouatarra's work in Washington D C for the IMF seemed to make him ineligible, as did reports that his father was Burkinabe.

In protest, the RDR, FPI and Union des Forces Démocratiques organized several mass **demonstrations**. Bédié responded with a ban on political rallies, and arrested opposition supporters who defied it. He also freely enforced far-reaching laws governing the press – a legacy of the media-sensitive Houphouët-Boigny regime – to prosecute journalists critical of the PDCI.

The RDR and FDI refused to put forward candidates as long as election conditions were not "clear and open". and in an atmosphere of distrust, major opposition parties called for a boycott. With a low voter turn-out preceded by weeks of violent demonstrations, Bédié, who ran virtually uncontested, could claim a technical victory, but not a popular one.

Legislative-elections later that year pointed to **ethnic and religious divisions** that had rarely surfaced since independence. The PDCI captured a majority of seats in the assembly, winning in the

Central, West and Southwest regions. The RDR carved out a niche for itself in the Muslim north, while the FPI staked its claim in Gbagbo's native Centre-Ouest. The new political landscape appeared divided, and fragile too, as in May 1996 reports emerged of an aborted coup attempt by disaffected members of the armed forces. That same month, Amnesty International alleged that opposition members were the target of systematic repression and detention, and almost two years after the presidential elections, Gbagbo asserted that of the 450 opposition activists who had been arrested in the protests, 70 remained behind bars.

In 1998, Bédié took to the grim task of reforming the economy and launched the **Enhanced Structural Adjustment Programme** (ESAP). The agenda demanded paying off the massive foreign debt, privatizing state-managed businesses, and bringing government spending in line. It was a formula that threatened the traditional support of those who had gained from the PDCI's system of political patronage – the cocoa and coffee farmers.

Privatization went forward quickly, but the president was accused of favouring buyers that included friends, family and political supporters. News reports that the president's son Patrick (whose company Cogeco had bought out the government rights to the local rice trade) earned CFA30 billion annually hardly endeared Bédié to a populace that was feeling the squeeze of rising prices. Also damaging were charges from a South African court, investigating illegal financial activities of the former apartheid regime, that Bédié had stood to gain $1.5 million from his involvement in an oil deal aimed at breaking sanctions. Another embarrassment occurred late in 1998 when a Lebanese businessman on trial for defrauding the government of $1.5 million testified that the money he received illegally from the government was destined for the PDCI's 1995 political campaign.

Bédié refuted the allegations, but none of the reports helped the growing perception that his government's focus was more on preserving political and economic privilege than on the public well-being. Protests erupted in April 1999, when the country's main student union – the Federation Estudiante et Scolaire de Cote d'Ivoire (FESCI) – called a **national strike** over grants, study conditions and health benefits. Bédié swiftly banned student meetings and sit-ins, dispatched security forces to trouble spots throughout the country, and finally resorted to shutting primary and secondary schools down. Weeks of **clashes between police and students** led to injuries on both sides, hundreds of arrests, and damages running in the CFA millions. After a month-long stand-off, the students called off their strike and the schools reopened shortly afterwards, though the situation remains tense.

At the height of the disturbances, Ouatarra declared his intentions to return home to Côte d'Ivoire and face Bédié in the **year 2000 elections**. His announcement was made as the president sat down for crucial talks with the IMF, which once again berated the government for its lack of discipline in the public financial sector and its inability to make headway on curbing the $19 billion debt. It was a bad omen, and left many to wonder if the government had disqualified itself from hundreds of millions of dollars in adjustment aid.

■ Future prospects

The 2000 elections promise to reveal much about the direction the country will take and could finally present a post-Houphouët mandate. Bédié still enjoys a strong party network and can count on France for help; Chirac has been a useful arbiter in relations between Côte d'Ivoire and Washington-based financial institutions. As the elections approach Bédié has tried to smooth things over with the bitter opposition, and in December 1998, he worked out an accord with Laurent Gbagbo of the FPI in which he agreed to the release of opposition activists sentenced to life imprisonment for inciting unrest during the 1995 campaign. Also significant was the pair's agreement on a policy for the funding of political parties and the establishment of a national electoral commission to organize the elections. Similar talks were scheduled with the RDR.

Ouattara appears to have momentum, but he has to be cautious. His connections to the IMF could work against him if people associate his candidacy with reforms they don't like. He has a good reputation as a technocrat, however, and the kind of connections with US financial institutions that could smooth the country's difficult relations with lenders.

Loan agreements and structural adjustment have been promising to kick Côte d'Ivoire into a new phase – the "second Ivoirian miracle" – for a long time now. The average person is today less concerned about high growth or privatization than about achieving a sustainable development that can produce benefits throughout the population. So far, not much has been trickling down.

ABIDJAN AND AROUND

ABIDJAN's wide **avenues** have names like de Gaulle, Marseille and République; **pavement cafés** and **billboards** push Orangina and L'Express – it is all one big monumental tribute to the heady days when it appeared the honeymoon between France and Côte d'Ivoire would never end. Downtown Abidjan looks like the work of a mad urban planner who dropped the Little Manhattan quarter of Paris' 15th arrondissement onto the set of the *Blue Lagoon*. But even if the coconut trees, red flamboyants and frangipanis lining the city's financial centre lend an exotic air to its supermarkets, **skyscrapers** and **traffic jams**, they barely camouflage the increasing signs of urban paranoia.

Now the second largest city in West Africa, Abidjan has grown from nothing in less than sixty-five years, and at an astounding pace since independence. Considering the number of **rural migrants and foreign workers** who've come in hope of easy money, the city has done a fair job of absorbing the influx – certainly much better than its nearest rival, Lagos. On first glance, this is a well laid-out and aesthetically appealing city. For many, it's the very model of what **prosperity** can bring to Africa. But you don't have to go far outside the centre to find shocking examples of poverty and **overcrowding**. In a scenario that has played itself out repeatedly around the world, the jobless and displaced turn to illicit survival tactics. Violent crime, prostitution and drug trafficking now taint the image of the "pearl of the lagoon". Ten years ago, you could have spent a good deal of time in the city without encountering its dark side. That's hard to imagine today.

Some history

The French abandoned their first capital, Grand-Bassam, in 1900 because of disease. The hilly location of the new capital, Bingerville, away from the sea, posed transport problems that limited its economic future. In 1934, the governor moved to a new mansion 17km to the southwest, in a spot then known as **Abidjan**.

The **European district** thus grew up on the Plateau peninsula, where administrative buildings sprang up beside trading depots, shops and villas. It was surrounded by two African suburbs – Adjamé to the north and Treichville across the lagoon to the south – although in the early days the collective population of these three districts was barely 20,000.

After 1950, however, Abidjan began to grow apace, and quickly took on the dimensions of a capital city. The catalyst was the **Vridi canal** which opened the Ebrié lagoon to the Atlantic and gave Abidjan the capacity to become an international port. Five years later, the railway line was extended from Treichville all the way to Ouagadougou, 1156km to the north. People started flocking to the town as new commercial possibilities developed. The population has jumped from 60,000 in the early 1950s to somewhere in the neighbourhood of two million today, and although Yamoussoukro became the country's administrative capital in the mid-1980s, Abidjan remains the undisputed economic nerve centre.

Arrival, orientation and information

Abidjan's most striking physical feature is the **Ebrié lagoon**, which divides the city into distinct landmasses, quarters which have evolved into large distinct neighbourhoods, each with its own flavour. Although there are officially ten such districts, only four are likely to figure prominently in your plans – Plateau, Treichville, Cocody and Adjamé.

Plateau, the futuristic financial district, is the showcase of Côte d'Ivoire's economic capital, and home to the stunning Cathédrale St-Paul and the National Museum. Two bridges, Houphouët-Boigny and de Gaulle, lead from the Plateau to **Treichville**, the city

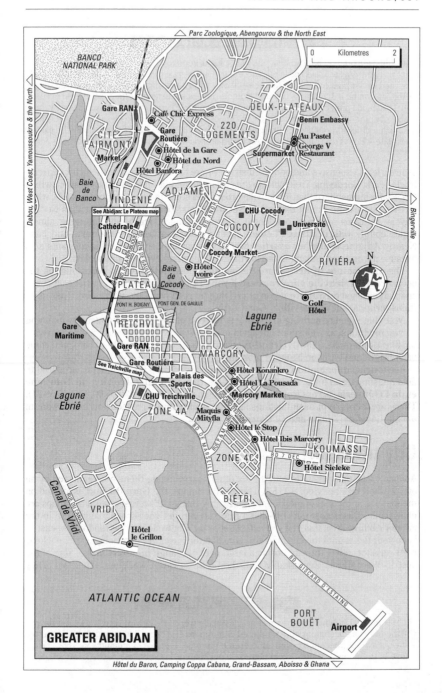

△ *Parc Zoologique, Abengourou & the North East*

BANCO NATIONAL PARK

Gare RAN
Café Chic Express

DEUX-PLATEAUX

Benin Embassy

220 LOGEMENTS

CITÉ FAIRMONT

Gare Routière
Hôtel de la Gare
Hôtel du Nord
Hôtel Banfora

Market

Au Pastel
George V Restaurant
Supermarket

Baie de Banco

INDENIÉ

ADJAMÉ

CHU Cocody

COCODY
Université

Cathédrale

Cocody Market

RIVIÉRA

Baie de Cocody

Hôtel Ivoire

PLATEAU

See Abidjan: Le Plateau map

PONT H. BOIGNY   **PONT GEN. DE GAULLE**

Golf Hôtel

Lagune Ebrié

Gare Maritime

TREICHVILLE

Gare RAN

MARCORY

Gare Routière

See Treichville map

Palais des Sports

Hôtel Konankro
Hôtel La Pousada
Marcory Market

CHU Treichville

Lagune Ebrié

ZONE 4A

Maquis Mityfla

Hôtel lé Stop
Hôtel Ibis Marcory

ZONE 4C

KOUMASSI

Hôtel Sieleke

Canal de Vridi

VRIDI

BIÉTRI

Hôtel le Grillon

ATLANTIC OCEAN

PORT BOUËT

Airport

GREATER ABIDJAN

◁ *Dabou, West Coast, Yamoussoukro & the North*

▷ *Bingerville*

0   Kilometres   2

N

△ *Hôtel du Baron, Camping Coppa Cabana, Grand-Bassam, Aboisso & Ghana* ▽

SECURITY IN ABIDJAN

It's not a surprise to find Abidjan one of the **least secure cities** in West Africa. As usual, stories get repeated and recycled, and the true incidence of attacks on tourists has to be related to the high number of tourists and expatriates passing through. Having said that, Abidjan can be a dangerous city and violent robberies – usually at knife point – do occur, in Treichville and, especially, Adjamé, but also on the Plateau. Simply leave all your valuables behind when going out and you'll feel less threatened and be less intimidated. The notorious **blackspots** are the bridges from Treichville to the Plateau, especially the eastern one – Pont Général de Gaulle. An emphatic warning: do not cross on foot.

---

centre's least expensive and poorest district, where life moves at a frenzied clip, especially after dark. Bordering Treichville to the east is the middle-class **Marcory** district, which has a safer atmosphere than Treichville proper and some moderately priced hotels, while further east are the similar districts of **Koumassi** and **Zone 4C**. To the north of Cocody Bay is Abidjan's foremost residential neighbourhood, **Cocody** and, merging almost imperceptibly with it, **Deux-Plateaux**, with a good number of restaurants and bars. Nearby **Adjamé** is another *quartier populaire*, swarming with recent immigrants and, because it's on the mainland in the north, expanding and evolving unchecked.

The main **points of arrival** are the **airport**, close to the city at Port Bouët on the ocean-front, **Treichville gare routière** if you're coming from Ghana or the east coast, and **Adjamé gare routière** if you're arriving by road from anywhere else. Passenger trains terminate at **Treichville's Gare RAN**.

Note that if you're arriving in the city at the end of the week with business to attend to, you might just as well shoot out again to somewhere less expensive and more relaxing like **Bingerville** (p.564), **Grand-Bassam** (p.574) or **Jacqueville** (p.566), and come back bright and early on Monday morning.

For **tourist information**, the travel agencies listed on p.563, are better prepared to field questions, and make travel arrangements, than the **Office Ivoirien du Tourisme et de l'Hôtelerie**, across from the post office on the Plateau (☎20 65 00; Fax 22 59 24). There are a couple of useful listings and entertainment magazines you might want to obtain – *Abidjan 7 Jours* and *Le Guido*.

City transport

Abidjan's four main districts, and the six others surrounding them, are connected by an overworked **bus service**, SOTRA. The main terminus, the **Gare du Sud**, is located on the Plateau, at the foot of the Houphouët-Boigny Bridge. It's a vast system and maps are unavailable. Buses cost CFA100–300 a ride and can get you virtually anywhere in the greater Abidjan area; that is if you can squeeze on. Controllers make random checks, so keep your ticket until the end, and also note that the buses are notorious for pickpockets.

As an alternative, the city boasts a large fleet of orange **metered taxis** – one of the best in West Africa. Remarkably fast, they can, however, work out expensive. They

---

STREET NAMES

Throughout 1998 the street names in Treichville were officially altered to "B" numbers – the old rues becoming odd-numbered B numbers (eg: "rue 7" changes to "B13") and the old avenues becoming even-numbered B numbers (eg: "ave 3" changes to "B92"). We give both the old and new street names on our map of Treichville.

ABIDJAN PLATEAU BUS ROUTES

A large number of bus routes run through the Plateau. The following selection is useful:

#05 Gare du Sud–Treichville–Koumassi

#06 Aeroport–Gare du Sud (daily 6am–9.20pm; every 10–15min)

#10 Gare du Sud–Cathédrale St-Paul

#12 Gare du Sud–Cathédrale St-Paul

#15 Gare du Sud–Gare Abobo

#18 Gare du Sud–Treichville *gare routière* – Vridi Plage

#20 Gare du Sud–Banco National Park (Cité Fairmont)

#28 Gare du Sud–Cocody market–*Golf Hôtel*

#75 or #76 Gare du Sud–Zoo

#86 Gare du Sud–Musée National–Adjamé *gare routière*–Blokosso (Cocody)

---

operate on meters with a daytime tariff (*Tarif 1*; CFA150 plus CFA100 per km) from 6am to midnight, and a higher night-time tariff after midnight – check you're on the right tariff. Fares from the airport to anywhere in Treichville or the southern half of the city shouldn't exceed CFA1200, to Plateau no more than CFA1600, to Cocody maximum CFA2300. You can also catch yellow, **shared "woro-woro" taxis** which operate within each district – each ride costs CFA125 – although these are generally old heaps from Europe and can be hazardous.

SOTRA also operates a **ferry service**, *bateaux bus*, to various points around the lagoon. The main *gare lagunaire* (☎22 56 94) is on the southern tip of the Plateau, near the Gare du Sud bus station and Houphouët-Boigny Bridge.

Accommodation

Abidjan boasts a good choice of comfortable **accommodation** in the middle-to-upmarket price range, but budget lodgings are extremely hard to come by. Not surprisingly, the closer you are to the centre, the more expensive things are – places on the Plateau are geared mainly to business travellers and wealthy tourists. At the very bottom of the scale, the campsites are preferable to *chambres de passage*. In the budget hotels, be sure to ask for the best room: you'll often be fobbed off with some fleapit in the hope they can keep the nicer accommodation for choosier guests.

Plateau

Grand Hôtel, off the av du Général de Gaulle/rue Montigny (01 BP 1785; ☎21 12 00). Near the lagoon, looking out onto Treichville. Newer and showier hotels have forced the *Grand* to keep its prices low in order to remain competitive. ④.

Hôtel Ibis Plateau, 7 bd Roume (☎21 01 57; Fax 21 78 75). Affordable luxury and one of the better bargains among the international-class options. Rooms with TV, video and phone. ⑤–⑥.

Hôtel des Sports, av du Général de Gaulle (☎32 71 37 or 32 71 97). The only hotel in the Plateau that approaches the inexpensive range, the *Sports* has dingy but acceptable AC or fan rooms. ②–③.

ACCOMMODATION PRICE CODES

① Under CFA4500 (under £5/$8).

② CFA4500–9000 (£5–10/$8–16).

③ CFA9000–18,000 (£10–20/$16–32).

④ CFA18,000–27,000 (£20–30/$32–48).

⑤ CFA27,000–36,000 (£30–40/$48–64).

⑥ CFA36,000–45,000 (£40–50/$64–80).

⑦ Over CFA45,000 (over £50/$80).

For further information see p.48.

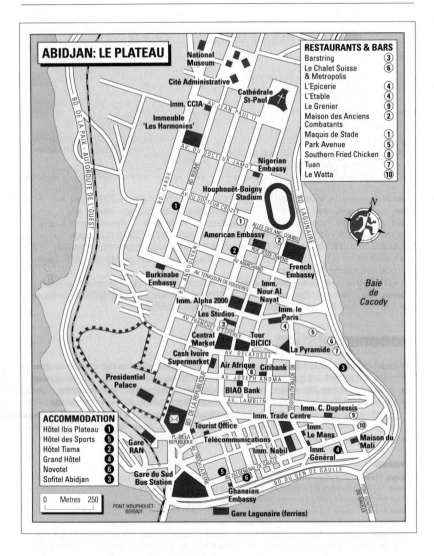

ABIDJAN: LE PLATEAU

National Museum
Cité Administrative
Imm. CCIA
Immeuble 'Les Harmonies'
Cathédrale St-Paul
AV. JEAN-PAUL II
BD. DE LA PAIX / AUTOROUTE DE L'OUEST
BD. CARDE
BD. RUXME
AV. DU DOCTEUR JAMOT
Nigerian Embassy
Houphouët-Boigny Stadium
AV. DU DOCTEUR CROZET
ALLEE DES ANC. COMBS.
BD. LAGUNAIRE
American Embassy
RUE JESSE OWENS
AV. MARCHAND
French Embassy
Burkinabe Embassy
AV. TERASSON DE FOUGERES
AV. ANOULIVAN
Imm. Nour Al Nayat
Imm. Alpha 2000
Les Studios
AV. FRANCHET D'ESPREY
Imm. le Paris
Central Market
Cash Ivoire Supermarket
Tour BICICI
AV. DELAFOSSE
La Pyramide
Air Afrique
Citibank
BD. BOTREAU ROUSSEL
Presidential Palace
AV. JOSEPH ANOMA
BIAO Bank
AV. LAMBLIN
Imm. C. Duplessis
Imm. Trade Centre
AV. DE LA REPUBLIQUE
Tourist Office
Imm. Le Mans
Maison du Mali
Télécommunications
PL. DE LA REPUBLIQUE
Gare RAN
Imm. Nabil
Imm. Général
AV. DU GENERAL DE GAULLE
BD. DU GEN DE GAULLE
Gare du Sud Bus Station
Ghanaian Embassy
PONT HOUPHOUËT-BOIGNY
Gare Lagunaire (ferries)
PONT GENERAL DE GAULLE
Baie de Cacody

RESTAURANTS & BARS

Barstring	③
Le Chalet Suisse & Metropolis	⑥
L'Epicerie	④
L'Etable	④
Le Grenier	⑨
Maison des Anciens Combattants	②
Maquis de Stade	①
Park Avenue	⑤
Southern Fried Chicken	⑧
Tuan	⑦
Le Watta	⑩

ACCOMMODATION

Hôtel Ibis Plateau	❶
Hôtel des Sports	❺
Hôtel Tiama	❷
Grand Hôtel	❹
Novotel	❻
Sofitel Abidjan	❸

0   Metres   250

Hôtel Tiama, 22 bd de la République (04 BP 643; ☎21 08 22; Fax 21 64 60). Located in the ministerial district and favoured by journalists and business people. Rooms on the upper floors look out onto the lagoon. Restaurant, brasserie, shops and car rental. ⑥.

Novotel, av du Général de Gaulle (01 BP 3718; ☎21 23 23; Fax 33 26 36). An imposing hotel and a great location. Rooms with all the amenities, and a pool. ⑦.

Sofitel Abidjan, av Delafosse (01 BP 2185; ☎22 11 22; Fax 33 22 18). Posh hotel with lagoon views. Very convenient for the city centre and much more personal than you might expect. Pool, sauna and massage parlour count among the perks. ⑦.

Treichville

Hôtel Argiegeois, bd de Marseille. Virtually next door to the *France* and not bad for the price. ②.

Hôtel Atlanta, corner av 15 and rue 15 (☎33 24 69). Fairly unrefined and somewhat overpriced. ③.

Hôtel de France, bd de Marseille (☎25 25 00). An older hotel that has some charm and is reasonably well maintained. ③.

Hôtel Fraternité, behind the Cinéma l'Entente. Musty rooms, though not too bad for a brothel. ①.

Hôtel le Prince, corner av 20 and rue 19 (☎24 17 38). Good-value clean, S/C rooms: those without AC are suitable for budget travellers. Take bus #3 from Plateau. ②.

Hôtel de Succès, corner av 14 and rue 25 (☎32 18 39). Basic but reasonable and quite friendly. Top-floor front rooms with AC are good value; *rez de chaussée* (ground-floor) rooms on the wrong side are dismal, mostly used for *passages*. ①–②.

Hôtel Terminus, bd Jean Delafosse (01 BP 790; ☎24 15 77 or 24 07 58). Large rooms, each with fan and corner kitchen. Located across from the train station, this one's convenient if you get into town late. ③.

Hôtel Tourbouroux, corner rue 8 and av 13 (☎32 64 48). Unmarked and sleazy. A last resort. ①.

Treichotel, 45 av de la Reine Pokou (☎24 05 59). This tall hotel is well situated and not too pricey, with S/C, AC rooms, mod cons and safe parking. ③.

Marcory

Hôtel Konankro, av de la TSF (BP 4237; ☎35 61 86). Small S/C rooms with AC in a busy part of the district, near the Église Sainte Thérèse. ②–③.

Hôtel La Pousada, behind the *Konankro* off Boulevard du Cameroun. This brothel has simple, clean rooms with shower and fan at very reasonable prices. ①–②.

Ibis Marcory, bd Giscard d'Estaing 15 (BP 594; ☎24 92 55; Fax 35 89 10). Comfortable AC rooms convenient for the airport. Pleasant garden restaurant under *paillotes*, and a swimming pool. ⑥.

Koumassi and Zone 4C

Hôtel Sieleke, bd 7 Dec Koumassi. A nice, no-nonsense hotel in a quieter part of town, not far from the airport. Clean S/C, AC rooms. ②–③.

Hôtel le Stop, 38 rue Pierre et Marie Curie, Zone 4C (01 BP 1947; ☎35 43 45). Smartish place with S/C, AC rooms in an upmarket neighbourhood, convenient for the airport. ③.

Cocody

Golf Hôtel, Riviera (08 BP 18; ☎43 10 44; Fax 43 05 44). Just east of Cocody near the golf course and lagoon. More intimate than the *Ivoire* but almost as classy. An attractive residential setting; well-cropped lawns sweep down to meet the clear pool. Garden *terrasse-bar*, restaurant, Internet facilities and waterskiing in the lagoon. ⑦.

Hôtel Ivoire, bd de la Corniche (08 BP 8001; ☎44 10 45; Fax 44 00 50). Abidjan's pride and joy, this Intercontinental hotel is really a city within the city, with everything from a bowling alley and car rental to West Africa's only ice rink. Cinema, sauna, casino, nightclub, swimming pool and tennis courts add to the razzle-dazzle, but jaded business travellers find it all a bit much. Numerous restaurants include the *Toit d'Abidjan* (☎44 10 45) on top of the tower – elegant and expensive French dining with the city's best view. ⑦.

Adjamé

Hôtel Banfora, off av 13 (☎37 02 52). Friendly hotel near the *gare routière* and Adjamé market – popular with merchants. ③.

Hôtel de la Gare, off rue 13, across from Gare UTB (the Union des Transports de Bouaké bus station). Convenient location and reasonably clean rooms, some with AC. ①–②.

Hôtel du Nord, 220 Logements area of Adjamé (09 BP 230; ☎37 04 63). Conveniently situated just north of the Plateau. Good-value, well-maintained AC rooms. ②–③.

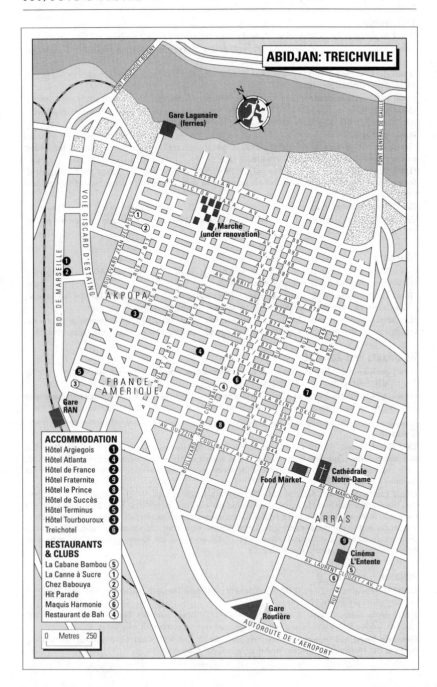

ABIDJAN: TREICHVILLE

Gare Lagunaire
(ferries)

AV. CRISTIAN/

AV. VICTOR BIAKA

Marché
(under renovation)

AV. GABRIEL DADIE / AV.

AKPOPA

FRANCE-
AMÉRIQUE

Gare
RAN

AV. DE LA REINE POKOU

AV. QUEZZIN

Food Market

Cathédrale
Notre-Dame

AV. DE MARCHORY

ARRAS

Cinéma
L'Entente

Gare
Routière

AUTOROUTE DE L'AEROPORT

AV. LAURENT CLOUZET / AV. 27

ACCOMMODATION

Hôtel Argiegois	❶
Hôtel Atlanta	❹
Hôtel de France	❷
Hôtel Fraternite	❾
Hôtel le Prince	❽
Hôtel de Succès	❼
Hôtel Terminus	❺
Hôtel Tourbouroux	❸
Treichotel	❻

**RESTAURANTS
& CLUBS**

La Cabane Bambou	⑤
La Canne à Sucre	①
Chez Babouya	②
Hit Parade	③
Maquis Harmonie	⑥
Restaurant de Bah	④

0   Metres   250

PONT HOUPHOS EBOGNY

PONT GENERAL DE GAULLE

VOIE GISCARD D'ESTAING

BD. DE MARSEILLE

BOULEVARD JEAN DE LAFOSSE

BOULEVARD GBON COULIBALY / AV.

Vridi Plage

Beach Camping, rue de l'Ocean, near the *Palm Beach* (☎24 84 50). Popular spot for overlanders; clean and without frills (rooms available for those without tents), not too far from the centre. Take buses #07, #17 or #18. ①–②.

Hôtel Le Grillon, Vridi Plage, near the SIR refinery (01 BP 2393; ☎ 27 52 60). Clean, quiet and convenient for the airport, but a long way from town. S/C, AC rooms on the beach. ③.

Palm Beach, rue de l'Ocean, Vridi (01 BP 2704; ☎27 42 16; Fax 27 30 16). Beachfront hotel with AC bungalows and rooms. One of Abidjan's older establishments, with a certain charm. Substantial savings on upstairs rooms with showers instead of baths. Saltwater pool, excellent restaurant, and a satellite dish to hook you up with CNN. ③–⑤.

Out of town

Camping Coppa Cabana, rte de Grand-Bassam, 15km from Abidjan. A bit far from the centre, but accessible from Treichville; take bus #17 or a collective taxi from the *gare routière*. Reasonable value, it also has a restaurant serving meals for CFA2000. Next door, *Camping Les Cocotiers* (☎07 01 20) provides stiff competition. ①.

Hôtel du Baron, rte de Grand-Bassam, 7km from Adidjan. A popular haunt of expats and affluent Abidjanis. Camping includes use of the pool. ①.

The Town

There's not a lot of **sightseeing** to do in Abidjan. You may be satisfied simply to absorb the energy of one of West Africa's busiest urban centres and, if your heart is gladdened by concrete and glass, to contemplate the merits of some of the city's more daring highrises on the Plateau.

One of the first of these was the **Nour al Hayat** building, built in 1966 on Avenue Chardy. A landmark of sorts, the modest tower has since been humbled by more recent skyscrapers, like the **Alpha 2000** building, whose 21 floors filled with shopping galleries, offices and the headquarters of the **Société Ivoirienne de Banque**, made it the largest commercial centre in West Africa when it opened in 1977. Other additions include the **BICICI Tower** with its fifteen storeys of tinted glass and, of course, **La Pyramide**, on the corner of Franchet d'Espérey and Botreau-Roussel avenues. Designed by Italian architect Olivieri, this building caused some stir when it opened in 1973; today it is more of an embarrassment with its broken windows, aged curtains and lack of activity inside. The modernist trend continues in the form of the **Cathédrale St-Paul**, erected in the north of the Plateau in 1985 with the futuristic towers of the **Cité Administrative** serving as a backdrop.

Abidjani cosmopolitanism hasn't obliterated one or two other distractions. The **National Museum** houses a fine collection of Ivoirian art, and the district **markets** make for interesting shopping. You could even get back to nature with a quick trip to the **Banco National Park** or the **Parc Zoologique** (see p.564), both of which are just a short distance from the city centre, north of Adjamé.

The National Museum

Set in the shadows of Abidjan's sparkling ministerial towers, the **National Museum** (daily except Mon 9am–noon & 3–6pm; free, donations anticipated) holds a fantastic collection of Ivoirian art containing several thousand pieces, shown off with careful lighting in thoughtfully organized displays.

Many of the works in the museum are **woodcarvings**, including religious statuary, Senoufo sculpted doors, and the symbolic sceptres of the Agni chiefs. An impressive

---

CIRE PERDUE

The **cire perdue** ("lost wax") process used in the artisans' co-operative at Grand-Bassam for metal-casting is one of West Africa's oldest craft techniques. Everything from the intricately ornate to the mundanely obscene starts as a model in wax. This is dipped repeatedly in washes of clay-water, each allowed to dry, and then finally wrapped with a thick coat of clay and fired, in which process the wax exits through a hole. Through this same hole, molten metal is poured and the clay "wrapping" is later chipped off to reveal the cast.

---

group of **masks** spreads over the walls, representing the ritualistic art of nearly every ethnic group in the country. **Musical instruments** from throughout Côte d'Ivoire make up a sizeable portion of the collection, along with sacred objects used in various ancestral cults and **pottery**, including vases, water containers and Agni figurines. Also on display are beautiful **bronze weights** used for measuring gold and other bronze objects made by the Akan-speaking peoples (especially the Baoulé) using the *cire perdue* or lost wax method (see box, above).

For those interested in **national dress**, there's a good variety of current Ivoirian attire, as well as genuinely old and handmade bark and raffia cloth, painted Senoufo cloths, and several serious hunters' outfits bedecked with *gri-gris*. The Yacouba, Malinké, Senoufo and Baoulé costumes are mostly *pagnes* in variations of blue, grey and black, sometimes made from broad strips.

On the walls, old **photos** of Côte d'Ivoire reveal life in the country in colonial times, including scenes of suavely reclining moustachioed young officers with their boots up, surrounded by crowds of bemused *indigènes*. There are pictures, too, of the Abidjan–Niger railway in construction; the Abé revolt prevented it from reaching Bouaké until 1912.

The markets

The **Central Market** on Boulevard de la République provides a burst of traditional colour in the heart of the Plateau high-rises. It's a great place to visit, not only for food shopping, but also to take a break in one of the bars or restaurants housed in the market building – a relaxing vantage point from which to watch the lively commerce. Nearby, the **Marché Artisanal** (also called *marché sénégalais*) targets tourists and is expensive. This doesn't mean you can't find well-made sculptures, bronze objects or cloth, but you'll have to brave the aggressive salesmen. Ultimately, however, towns such as Man, Bouaké or Korhogo offer the best buys and the most interesting selection when it comes to Ivoirian crafts.

Much bigger than the Central Market was the excellent **Treichville Market**, which burned down in March 1997. The market is being rebuilt in its original location, and is expected to reopen at the end of 1999; in the meantime, a temporary market can be found spread around the Treichville Gare Lagunaire.

The **Adjamé Market** spreads over several blocks near the train station. **Cocody** has a good **food and handicrafts market**, which is located near the intersection of Boulevard de France and Boulevard Latrille.

The Cathédrale St-Paul

When the **Cathédrale St-Paul** (Mass: Mon–Thurs 7pm, Fri 12.15pm & 7pm, Sun 8am, 9.30am, 11.15am & 7pm) was inaugurated on August 10, 1985 by Pope JohnPaul II, nearly 100,000 Ivoirians turned up for the event. At the time, it was one of the largest cathedrals in the world (though now there's also the Basilica in Yamoussoukro…). You really need to be standing over on the waterfront in Cocody to grasp the significance of its extraordinary design: it's a human figure, presumably representing St Paul himself, arms outstretched to the north, his robe trailing lavishly behind to accommodate 3500 seated worshippers and another 1500 standing.

If its construction endures, the Italian architect Aldo Spirito's cathedral will one day rate as classic twentieth-century church architecture. You enter under the back of the robe and it would be hard not to be impressed; the ceiling cleaves away and upwards with stunning grace. The lines pull you into the heart of the building, soaring 50m or more above the altar. Breathtaking **stained-glass tableaux** depict Paul's conversion on the road to Damascus, black slaves in his retinue, and, on the right, the arrival of the paddle steamer *Dahomey* with its contingent of French fathers come to spread the gospels in Africa. The picture is glorious, if naive, portraying unrealistically enthusiastic pagans rushing to the shore with welcoming smiles and baskets of fruit. If it is functioning, you can take an elevator up the towers for more views of the town.

Eating, drinking and nightlife

Abidjan has carved out a deserved reputation for good eating, and you can find cuisine from just about any corner of the world: the following **restaurants** are just a small selection. Some of the classier Asian, European and African restaurants are prohibitively expensive; to save money, eat the **street food** at the markets of Treichville, Adjamé, Cocody and even on the Plateau – Senegalese rice with a thick vegetable sauce is good. Also inexpensive are the many **maquis** scattered about town. The chain of *Opéra* croissanteries is recommended too.

Budget food

Abidjan's expensive reputation obscures a lot of reasonable places to fill up, where the competition helps keep prices down.

Bache Bleue, bd Giscard d'Estaing, Marcory. Very popular and easy-going *maquis* in a rowdy setting. All the taxi drivers know it.

Chic Café Express, north of Adjamé *gare routière*. Sidewalk café covered by large green canopy where you'll find petit pois with steak in the afternoons, *café complet* in the mornings. Espresso made with real coffee and excellent *lait caillé* (sweetened curds); a favourite of drivers from the *gare routière*.

George V, opposite Cash Centre supermarket, Deux-Plateaux. Inexpensive hummus and tabbouleh; a popular Peace Corps hangout.

L'Impeccable, off bd de Marseille, Vridi. *Maquis* near the port featuring excellent and inexpensive prawns.

Khadim Rassoul, av de la Reine Pokou, Treichville. Small, Senegalese restaurant serving cheap, tasty rice dishes.

Maquis Harmonie, av Laurent Clouzet, Treichville. One of a whole clutch of inexpensive places to eat surrounding the *Whiskey A-Go-Go*. The grilled fish is good. Down the street, you can order a drink at the popular *Café des Arts* and have it with street food prepared by women at the front.

Maquis du Stade, av du Docteur Crozet, Plateau. Excellent lunchtime *maquis*, shady and convenient. The service is slow, but when the food finally arrives it's delicious, from the plantain *foutou*, rice, meat and fish to the quite excellent *kedjenou*.

Restaurant de Bah, av de la Reine Pokou, Treichville, opposite the *Treichotel*. One of a string of inexpensive restos on the same street: clean, tasty and unpretentious.

Snackorama, adjoining the bowling alley of the *Hôtel Ivoire*, Cocody. Burgers, milkshakes and sundaes served to the sounds of crashing pins. Inexpensive Americana.

Southern Fried Chicken, av Anoma, Plateau. Colonel Sanders meets Ronald McDonald – real fast food ranging from chicken to burgers.

Moderate restaurants

In addition to the many moderately priced African restaurants representing cooking from across the continent, you can also eat international-style snack food without breaking the bank. Though mid-range restaurants are scattered all over the city, there's a concentration of them around Cocody market.

Chez Babouya, corner av 6 and rue 7, Treichville (☎32 39 28). Thoroughly enjoyable experience with Mauritanian specialities. Set-price dinner might be *pigeon aux dattes* or excellent *couscous*. Babouya's incomparable self is the extra attraction. Around CFA10,000.

Dolce Vita, Cocody market. Possibly the best pizza in West Africa.

Espace 331, Cocody, opposite Lycee Mermoz. Very popular *maquis* in an open-air terrace serving traditional Ivoirian dishes.

Maison des Anciens Combatants, allée des Anciens Combatants, off rue Jesse Owens, near the Stadium, Plateau (☎22 77 24). Very popular four-course set lunches – healthy servings of French and African dishes and nice service and atmosphere.

Le Mechoui, Cocody market. Diverse selection of Lebanese specialities.

Au Pastel, av des Jardins, Deux-Plateaux (☎41 35 80). French and Italian specialities, and home deliveries for pizza orders.

Pizza di Sorrento, bd de Marseille, Km 6, Zone 4 (☎35 57 75). Popular pizza place that's been around for thirty years.

Reine de Saba, bd Latrille, Cocody. Ethiopian eating experience with tea ceremonies taken at round tables from undersize chairs.

Shanghai, Cocody market. Good Chinese specialities; try the Beef Shanghai.

Le Vatican, near Eglise Ste Thérèse, Marcory (☎35 71 14). Very well-known *maquis* on upper level with views on the street. Grilled fish and chicken, *atieké* and the like.

Le Watta, rue du Commerce, Plateau. Airy terrace overlooking the lagoon. *Pintade*, or *agouti* served with style.

Expensive restaurants

At the expense-account end of the scale, Abidjan tends to lay on the style very thick. The best of these restaurants are usually excellent by any measure, but it's always wise to hear the latest reports on the grapevine before risking any of them for an important occasion – especially in view of the fact that a meal for two is not likely to cost less than CFA40,000.

Le Chalet Suisse, bd Lagunaire, Plateau (☎21 54 80). Popular spot for fondue or interesting French and Swiss specialities. Less expensive than many upmarket restaurants; book a table.

Chez Cakpo, rue du Canal, Vridi (☎35 29 78). African specialities served by the waterfront. Excellent lobster and grilled prawns.

L'Epicerie, just off av Chardy, Plateau. Charming restaurant serving French bistro-style cuisine.

L'Etable, av Botreau-Roussel, Plateau (☎22 23 93). Very upmarket steakhouse, currently quite in.

Le Grenier, av Crosson Duplessis, Plateau (☎32 34 94). Refined French cuisine, like *riz de veau bordelaise* and seasoned *escargot*. Closed Sun.

Maquis Mityfla, bd Giscard d'Estaing, at rue P & M Curie, near Zone 4 (☎24 93 34). Huge *paillote* entrance and fancy African specialities plus a piano bar.

Park Avenue, bd de la République, just before av Chardy. Fancy new eaterie with beautifully presented French cuisine. A current favourite among the middle-classes.

Tuan, bd Lagunaire, Plateau (☎21 63 80). Posh lacquered interior with fancy napkins and hovering waiters; considered one of the town's better Vietnamese restaurants.

Nightlife

Dinner over, there's the nightlife to look forward to. Abidjan has a busy scene, though as you might expect, most places only get lively towards the end of the week and closure from Sunday to Tuesday is common. Be safety conscious: you need to look after yourself, especially in Treichville, so be sure that at least one of your group stays fairly sober (less of a problem when you start counting the bills). Go out on the town with only as much cash as you need, no jewellery and no watch. You can get around easily by **taxi**, and you may even be lucky with a well-informed driver, but don't try to go clubbing on foot. The cover charge usually includes a drink and should be around CFA3000–5000. Drinks thereafter cost about CFA1000–3000.

The **Plateau clubs** are good if you need softening up. Currently, one of the most popular is the *Barstring* on Boulevard de la République, near Les Studios cinema, where African yuppies create a safe but satisfying ambience (it is possible). Near the *Sofitel*, the *Metropolis* attracts a more middle-aged clientele, while the young and restless head for the *Blue Note* – probably the Plateau's liveliest club with good music and loose dancing. You're now ready for **Treichville**. Try any of those in the following listing, or, for something a little cheaper and rather unstructured, ask the driver to suggest a club along **rue 12** – the famously sleazy Treichville street. *Jannick* is the best known.

Treichville clubs

La Cabane Bambou, av Laurent Clouzet, qtr Arras. A popular spot for years, still packing in the crowds.

La Canne à Sucre, corner of bd Delafosse and av 6, qtr Akpopa. Another long-established club. Flashy and expensive, though it only warms up after midnight. Open Thurs–Sun.

Djams, bd de Marseille. One of the hottest clubs, where the Central African DJs play an eclectic mix of music with all the latest light technology. Expensive, but no-one minds.

Hit Parade, bd Delafosse, near the *Hôtel Terminus*, qtr France-Amerique. Newly refurbished and likened by people of the neighbourhood to an American disco. Recommended – showy and fun, though pricey. Also doubles as a restaurant during the day.

Midnight Express. Another popular Treichville club in the qtr France-Amerique.

Listings

Air freight DHL are efficient, whether you're shipping in or shipping out. Main office is on av Marchand and bd de la République (☎24 99 99). Open Mon–Fri 8am–6.30pm, Sat 8am–noon.

Airlines Air Afrique, 3 av Joseph Anoma (☎20 30 00 or 20 33 89); Air Burkina (☎32 89 19); Air France, av Joseph Anoma (☎21 90 93; Fax 21 12 94); Air Gabon, Imm. Nabil, av Noguès (☎21 55 06 or 21 74 29); Air Guinée, Imm. Général, bd Botreau Roussel (☎33 14 64); Air Ivoire, Imm. SIDAM, av Houdaille (☎20 66 66); Air Mali, Imm. Maison du Mali, av du Général de Gaulle (☎32 19 62); American Airlines (☎22 13 15); British Airways, Tour BICICI, rue Gourgas (04 BP 827; ☎32 11 40); Cameroon Airlines, Imm. Pyramide, av Franchet d'Espérey (☎21 19 19); Cathay Pacific (☎22 62 43 or 22 62 46); Egyptair, av du Général de Gaulle, next to Nigerian Airways (☎32 57 13); Ethiopian Airlines, av Chardy (☎21 93 32); Ghana Airways, Imm. Général, av du Général de Gaulle (☎32 42 21); Iberia, av Delafosse, rue Alphonse Daudet (☎33 19 91); Nigerian Airways, 28/40, av du Général de Gaulle (☎22 35 65); Royal Air Maroc (☎21 20 38); Sabena, Imm. No ur al Hayat, av Chardy (☎21 29 36); Swissair, Imm. F d'Espérey, av Franchet d'Espérey (☎21 55 72); TAP Air Portugal, Imm. Botreau Roussel, 25 bd Botreau Roussel (☎21 57 26).

Airport information ☎23 40 76.

American Express Main agents are SOCOPAO Voyages, bd de Marseille, Km 1 (☎24 13 14).

Banks The Plateau is the main banking district where you'll find, all on av Joseph Anoma: Banque Africaine de Développement (☎20 07 44); BIAO (01 BP 1274; ☎20 07 20; MasterCard cash advances); Citibank, Imm. Amci (☎21 46 10); SGBCI (01 BP 1355; ☎20 12 34); SIB (☎20 00 00; Visa cash advances). Elsewhere on the Plateau are COBACI, Imm. Alpha 2000, bd de la République (☎21 29 10), which gives some of the best rates for non-franc currencies, and BICICI, av Franchet d'Espérey (01 BP 1298; ☎20 16 00).

Beaches On the south side of the city, Vridi Plage is the closest beach to the centre. Bus #18 runs here from the Plateau Gare du Sud.

Books Libraire de France, Imm. Alpha 2000, av Chardy, is the city's biggest bookshop. They also have a branch in the *Hôtel Ivoire*.

Car rental Avis (☎27 72 73) at the airport and the *Hôtel Ivoire*; Budget (☎25 60 11; Fax 25 45 09) at the airport and rue Dr Blanchard; Europcar, rue Dr Colmette (☎25 12 27), agencies at *Sofitel*, *Golf* and *Sebroko* hotels and airport; Hertz, bd Giscard d'Estaing (☎25 77 47; Fax 25 82 52), *Hôtel Tiama* and airport.

Cinemas There's usually something worth watching, though not always in "v.o." (*version originale*, undubbed). The big ones on the Plateau are Le Paris with two screens in Imm. Le Paris on av Chardy (☎32 64 96); the huge five-screen Les Studios on bd de la République (☎32 38 97); and Le Sphinx on rue du Commerce. Cocody's Ivoire (☎44 10 45) and Treichville's Plaza (☎22 20 21) are worth a try, too.

Cultural centres In Cocody on the bd de la Corniche, the American Cultural Center (☎44 05 97) has an AC reading library featuring US newspapers and magazines. The expansive Centre Culturel Français (☎21 15 99) is on the Plateau, next to La Pyramide. There's a strong flavour of Paris' Beaubourg about its high-tech interior design and sunken front courtyard. Relax amid shade and plants and simply sit. There's a library, conference centre and cinema, and the centre is a live performance venue with plenty going on.

Emergencies Police ☎170; Fire Service ☎180; Ambulance ☎185.

Hospitals University Hospital Cocody ("CHU Cocody"; ☎43 90 24); University Hospital Treichville ("CHU Treichville"; ☎24 91 52). Best place to be ill is the Polyclinique Internationale Ste Anne-Marie ("La Pisam") on av J Blohorn near *Hôtel Ivoire*, Deux-Plateaux district (BP 1453; ☎44 51 32; outpatients' clinic ☎44 62 83 or 44 62 84), which has a near-legendary reputation among sick expats in West Africa – though it can be rather expensive. The Clinique Avicènnes in Marcory is a highly recommended alternative.

Internet There's a cybercafé on the 1st floor, Imm. CCIA (☎21 78 42). You can send emails and browse the Internet for CFA2000/hour.

Lagoon trips The Promenade excursion gives you ninety minutes on the lagoons with a stop on l'Ile Boulay (departs from Plateau Gare Laguinaire Wed 3pm, Thurs 9am & 3pm, Sat, Sun and holidays 11am & 3pm; CFA2000).

Newspapers and magazines There are various outlets for foreign journals and papers, including the large hotels. On the Plateau, head to the Librarie de France (see "Books", opposite).

EMBASSIES IN ABIDJAN

Benin, rue des Jardins, Deux-Plateaux (09 BP 238; ☎41 44 13).

Burkina Faso, 2 av Terrasson de Fougères (01 BP 908; ☎21 15 01).

Cameroon, Imm. Général, bd Botreau Roussel (01 BP 2886; ☎21 33 31).

Canada, Imm. Trade Center, av Noguès (01 BP 4104; ☎21 20 09).

Central African Republic, rue des Combatants (01 BP 3387; ☎44 86 29).

France, rue Lecoeur/rue Jesse Owens (17 BP 175; ☎20 04 04).Visas available for Togo and Chad among others.

Gabon, Imm. Les Hévéas, bd Carde (01 BP 3765; ☎44 51 54).

Ghana, Résidence de la Corniche, bd du Général de Gaulle (01 BP 1871; ☎33 11 24).
Apply 8.30am–noon, Tues–Fri, collect 1–2pm two days later (closed Mon).

Guinea, Imm. C Duplesis, av Crosson Duplesis (08 BP 2280; ☎22 25 20). Allow two days for visas.

Mali, Imm. Maison du Mali, rue du Commerce (01 BP 2746; ☎32 31 47).

Mauritania, rue Pierre et Marie Curie, Zone 4C (01 BP 2275; ☎41 16 43).

Niger, 23 bd Angoulvant (01 BP 2743; ☎26 28 14).

Nigeria, 35 bd de la République (01 BP 1906; ☎21 19 82).

Senegal, Résidence Nabil, av du Général de Gaulle (08 BP 2165; ☎33 28 76).

South Africa, Villa Marc André, rue Monseigneur Réné Kouassi, Cocody Président 08 (☎44 59 63; Fax 44 74 50).

UK, 3rd floor, Imm. Les Harmonies, av Dr Jamot/bd Carde (01 BP 2581; ☎22 68 50 or 22 68 51; Fax 22 32 21).

USA, 5 rue Jesse Owens (01 BP 1712; ☎21 09 79).

MOVING ON FROM ABIDJAN

by road

The **main gare routière** is in Adjamé at the junction of the roads to Dabou, Abobo and Bingerville on the northern edge of the Plateau. **Buses** here service the entire interior of the country – Abengourou, Bouaké, Yamoussoukro, San-Pédro, Korhogo – and through to Mali and Burkina Faso. Those heading to towns along the railway line are generally cheaper than the trains and much quicker. Owing to the labyrinthine nature of the Adjamé *gare* and the alarmingly robust approach of some ticket touts, you're best advised to get a taxi directly to the part of the *gare* from where buses to your destination depart. The **gare routière** in **Treichville** handles eastbound traffic to Grand-Bassam, Assinié, Aboisso and coastal towns in Ghana.

by train

The SICF railway company (☎32 02 45; schedule and booking information ☎21 02 45) runs a daily **train** from Abidjan to Ouagadougou, calling at Dimbokro, Bouaké, Ferkessédougou, Ouangolodougou, Niangoloko, Banfora, Bobo-Dioulasso and Koudougou. In theory it leaves Treichville at 10.30am and arrives the next day in Ouaga at 1.30pm; in practice you may spend a second night on board. Prices to Ouaga are CFA21,000 first class, CFA17,500 second class. First-class ticket holders can pay a supplement for a couchette. Student discounts are no longer offered.

by air

Air Ivoire, Imm. SIDAM, av Houdaille (☎21 36 36) connects Abidjan to major cities in the interior, including Bouaké (daily flights), Korhogo, Man, Odienné and Yamoussoukro.

by boat

SITRAM (Société Ivoirienne de Transports Maritimes), rue des Pétroliers, Vridi (☎27 00 26; Fax 27 23 93) offers berths on **freighters** to Europe via West African ports.

Post and telephones The post office is on the Place de la République in Plateau. A trip here won't be your most pleasant as the *fonctionaires* are generally obnoxious. Poste restante costs CFA600 per letter and those not collected within three weeks are returned or destroyed. The Telecom office is around the corner on av Houdaille, where you'll find booths for local or international calling; or you can go through the operator. They sell phonecards here.

Swimming pools The big hotels all have pools, including the *Ivoire*, the *Sofitel*, the *Novotel*, and the *Palm Beach*; the *Golf*'s is probably the most alluring. Most of them charge about CFA2500 for non-residents.

Travel Agents For trips within Côte d'Ivoire, try Afric-Voyages, Imm. Le Paris, av Chardy (01 BP 3984; ☎21 21 11; Fax 21 28 88); Expace Voyages, av Houdaille (☎21 26 46; Fax 21 29 44); Haury Tours, Imm. Le Chardy, 23 av Chardy (☎22 16 94; Fax 22 17 68) and SAGA-CI Voyages, rue de Senateur Lagarosse (01 BP 1727; ☎32 75 03; Fax 32 38 42).

Around Abidjan

You don't need to spend much time in Abidjan to feel like getting **out of the city** – a little goes a long way. The **zoo** isn't exactly a big escape, but **Banco National Park** can be a good breather. Getting further out of town, **Bingerville**, on the shore of the Ebrié lagoon, 17km east of Adjamé, makes a pleasant break. A former colonial town now settled into comfortable obscurity, it's an interesting place for a slow-paced day-trip and, whether you have your own transport or not, can lead to an easy weekend round trip if you include Grand-Bassam on the way back.

The Parc Zoologique

Just north of town on the Williamsville road is Abidjan's **Parc Zoologique** (daily 8am–6.30pm; small entrance fee). Though now quite extensive, the town zoo was started many years ago by a French animal lover who raised chimpanzees in his backyard and crocodiles in his bathtub. Gradually his collection of beasts grew and was taken over by the state's National Park Service. Today you'll find hippos, crocodiles and tortoises, as well as lions, buffaloes, elephants, monkeys and various birds. This is one of Africa's better zoos and some attempt has been made to create a natural environment for the luckier animals. Others sit in bare cages. Take bus #75 or #76 from the Plateau.

Parc National du Banco

Just 3km from the noise and traffic of the city, the **Parc National du Banco** comprises thirty square kilometres of dense forest which have been set aside as a natural reserve. Though it's said that a wide variety of animals still lives in the park, they stay well hidden in the woodlands and you're likely to see no more than perhaps a monkey or two skirting along the main paved road leading to the lake in the middle.

Despite this, Banco's **towering trees**, oversize **ferns** and **hanging vines** make for a satisfying day-trip – a reminder of the thick rainforests that once spread along the entire coast. The best way to visit the park is by car; to get there, take the road towards Dabou from Adjamé. Or you can catch a #03 bus to Cité Fairmont and walk the last few hundred metres to the entrance. The main road crisscrosses the river as it leads to the lake in the heart of the park. From here various **foot trails** lead through the forest, passing through small villages which survive in the park interior.

Early morning at the park entrance there are unlimited opportunities for photographing one of Abidjan's classic scenes, the *fanicos*, or **Banco washer men** (if you're taking a taxi, ask for "Banco lavage"). The small Banco River runs by the park entrance, and along it hundreds of immigrant workers squeak out a living thrashing clothes against their rocks jammed in truck tyres in the stream. There's a lot of competition for this work. If you want to take photos, you're likely to find large members of the "syndicate" blocking your way and demanding CFA1000 for each visitor and each camera. It's best not to refuse.

Bingerville

Set in the hills that rise between the Ebrié and Aguien lagoons, **BINGERVILLE** is today a quiet town in a rich agricultural region (bananas, pineapple, oil palms). This was an early capital of the French colony, but you'll find surprisingly few vestiges of that era.

BINGERVILLE'S HISTORY

Bingerville – named after Côte d'Ivoire's first colonial governor, Louis-Gustave Binger – was known as Adjamé-Santey when it was an **Ebrié settlement** in the early part of the nineteenth century. Around 1850, the villagers first came into contact with Europeans, and by the end of the century they had signed a treaty with the French which paved the way for the creation of a colonial post. The first government buildings went up in 1901, after disease drove the French out of Grand-Bassam.

Bingerville thus became the colony's second political capital, but due to its hilly inland setting it never attained the economic importance of Grand-Bassam. In 1931, a new wharf was built at Port Bouët and, from then on, Abidjan grew to become Côte d'Ivoire's major town. The capital was transferred in 1934.

Today, the town has been utterly eclipsed by Abidjan (a mere twenty-minute drive away) and, with its *lycée*, military academy, psychiatric hospital and Catholic seminary, almost has the feeling of a distant suburb. It's an appealing, intriguing place, lapsed and restful.

One of Bingerville's most striking old buildings is the beautifully restored **Governor's Palace**, which now serves as an orphanage. Near the palace is the *jardin d'essaie* – a vast **botanical garden** where the French carried out agricultural experiments. Entering through a walk with giant bamboos forming a natural archway, you discover a wide variety of regional plants, trees and spices in the gardens, though the original layout today is rather overgrown and unkempt.

At the bottom of the steep grade that shelves to the lagoon (following the Eloka road) is the small **Musée Charles-Combes**. Combes was a French merchant who founded the Ecole d'Art Moderne Africain in Bingerville, where he taught until his death in 1968. The giant **sculptures** he left behind consist mainly of idealized busts of Ivoirian women from various ethnic groups. They're a bit much really and not very African, suggesting rather more about the artist than his subjects. There's no charge to visit the museum, but donations are appreciated. In the grounds, students chisel out copies of Combes' works as well as more original creations.

Practicalities

Frequent shared taxis to Bingerville leave from the Adjamé *gare routière*. To continue by transport to Grand-Bassam you need a ride, 15km further, to the **Eloka ferry** where you cross the Ebrié lagoon, with another 10km to Grand-Bassam on the other side.

There's not much here in the way of **accommodation**. The main place to stay is the *Bakona Hôtel* (②), a short distance from the *gare routière* as you walk towards the botanical gardens. It has simply furnished rooms, some with AC, and a restaurant that serves French and African food. The new and very pleasant *Prive 2 Hôtel* (①–③) has clean S/C rooms with fan for the same price, as well as AC rooms and suites. You can find it by turning right on a dirt track just after the Catholic Seminary.

Women prepare *foutou*, rice and other local dishes in small **restaurants** grouped around the *gare routière*. You'll also find stalls for **bangi** (palm wine) here, tapped freshly in the district. There's a string of good *maquis* in the **Quartier Sans Loi**, along the "rue 12" – not the street's real name, but coined, because of its lively reputation, in imitation of rue 12 in Treichville, Abidjan.

THE WEST COAST

Côte d'Ivoire's longest and most unexploited stretches of coast reach **westward from Abidjan**, and curve south to the remote Liberian border at Cape Palmas. Along the way, the string of **lagoons and sand bars**, scattered with the vestiges of old trading stations, gives out to a solid, forest-backed strand. Here, **Sassandra** is the first of the accessible towns; **San-Pédro** and **Tabou** lie beyond, offering some of West Africa's very best beaches if you're prepared to make a little effort.

Inland, in the far west, lies the country's remotest region and one of West Africa's most secure zones of primary **tropical forest**.

West of Abidjan: the lagoon coast

West of Abidjan, the coast shatters into a string of **lagoons and canals** for nearly 200km. You can find *pétrolettes* (boats holding thirty to fifty passengers and odoriferous fish baskets) in Treichville to take you along to **Tiegba** and **Grand Lahou**. The departure point is next to the *bateaux bus* station on the northern shore of Treichville. A less

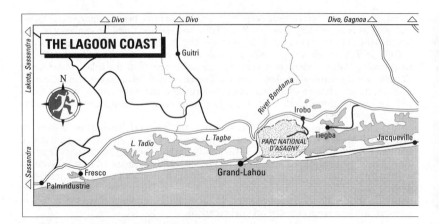

romantic option is to go by road; both these towns and **Jacqueville** are easily reached by the coastal highway, as is **Fresco**, further along the coast and inaccessible by boat.

Jacqueville

Something of a resort in the style of Grand-Bassam, **JACQUEVILLE** (once "Grand Jack" – an English slaving port) is out on the oceanfront sand bar which encloses the Ebrié lagoon, some 50km west of Abidjan. You can get here by taking a bush taxi or the 3A Express bus (several a day) from Adjamé and then a ferry for the last 500m from the mainland.

There's little sense of history in the modern town. Old buildings have been left to collapse. The *Hôtel M'koa* (BP 4375, Abidjan; ☎31 54 59; ③) is nice enough and not overpriced, set on the shore of a small, pretty lagoon now sealed off behind the town on the sand bar. The next best option is the English-run *Campement de Jacqueville* (☎57 71 25; ③), with comfortable bungalows scattered about the coconut trees (they allow camping, too) and a seafood restaurant; beware that prices double on the weekend though. Close to the *gare routière*, the *Hôtel Relax* (②) has less expensive, basic lodgings which, along with those at the *Beausejour* (②), are among the town's cheapest. **Toukouzou**, 44km west along the beach, is the headquarters of one of the coast's most famous **Harrist** bible prophets – Papa Novo. Ask if anything by way of celebration is going on while you're in Jacqueville; a visit is quite something.

Tiegba

On an island in the northwest corner of the Ebrié lagoon, **TIEGBA** is a **stilt village** – or used to be, many people having moved to the mainland. As with similar places, like Fadiout in Senegal or Ganvié in Benin, you're likely to be so overcome by pestering children that any appreciation of the village is flattened in the effort to survive without losing your temper. Go in an organized group and you might as well forget the whole point of the visit; try an individual approach and things seem a lot different. Tiegba is accessible by *pétrolette* from Treichville, and by *taxisbrousse* from Dabou. On the mainland, *Aux Pilotis de l'Ébrié* has **rooms** (①), near where the *pirogues* take you over the hundred-metre channel.

Grand Lahou and Parc National d'Assagny

Like other places on the lagoon, **GRAND LAHOU**'s old town is on the narrow strip of a sandbank, a short ferry ride from the new and developing modern town on the main-

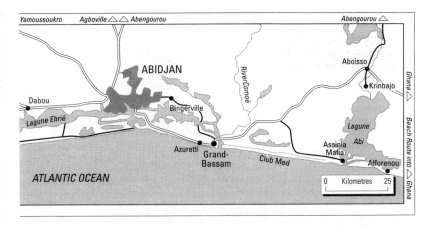

land proper. Grand Lahou is similar in many ways to Grand-Bassam (both were trading stations at the mouths of major rivers), but the old seafront buildings here, in a variety of styles according to the nationality of the owners – Dutch, English, German and only later French – are almost completely abandoned.

There's a fairly expensive and long-established *campement* (③) on the eastern tip of the old town sandbank, some kilometres from the centre, or in town you can stay in the very basic *Chez l'Habitat* (①). In season, the *campement* offers *pirogue* rides all over the place, especially to the **Parc National d'Assagny**, a few kilometres up the Bandama River. The park is renowned for buffalo and elephants, ideally observed from tree-house viewing platforms, but as it's only recently been opened to visitors, there's no network of roads. Another entrance is from the mainland side at **Irobo**, where you might get a lift with rangers into the park, if not around it.

Fresco

Another former trading "factory", old **FRESCO** is completely deserted, under the high **cliffs** (rich in fossils) across the lagoon from the new town. Since the road from Abidjan to San-Pédro was paved, this once isolated enclave is easily accessible by bus from both Abidjan and Sassandra.

Sassandra and around

SASSANDRA has really beautiful **beaches** nearby – the best, if not quite the only, reason for coming here. Unusually for the West African coast, there's also some topographical relief in the form of low cliffs that extend most of the way to the Liberian border.

The town itself is built at the mouth of the Sassandra River, so what with rivermouth islands and lagoons there's lots of water about and pretty views in every direction. The **best beaches** are out west, the first – Batelébré I, II and III – about 2km from town, further ones – Yeseko, Grand-Dréwin, Lateko, Poli-Plage and Niega – requiring transport and defined only by the roads and tracks that lead to them. One desirable option is to make Sassandra a base and spend a few days beach-hopping. Sleeping out on the sand is quite viable and for sustenance there are always coconuts . . .

Getting to the town from Abidjan takes only a few hours. A handful of daily buses (*cars*) leave Adjamé as well as 22-place Renaults and more expensive 504s.

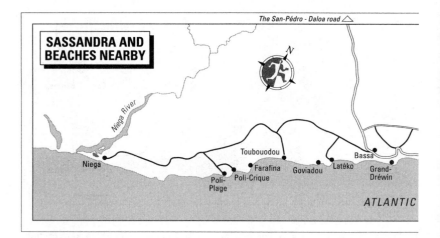

Accommodation

Accommodation in Sassandra is reasonably priced, if basic; many places have superb tropical settings.

La Cachette du Warf, 50m from the *gare routière* next to the old wharf. The least expensive accommodation in town, in palm-frond huts with cement floors and fans. Coconut trees, fishing boats and the sound of waves make for budget paradise. ①.

Chez Tanty Youyou, at the mouth of the Sassandra. Clean bungalows in a range of categories. Budget non-S/C rooms available, though most accommodation has AC and private toilets. Idyllic location. ②–③.

Hôtel Campement, on the seashore near the river's embouchure (BP 341; ☎72 05 15). Colonial hotel, fixed up and not lacking charm, though it doesn't see a lot of guests these days, perhaps due to the relatively steep prices for its S/C, AC rooms. ③.

Hôtel Eden, rte de San-Pédro, 1200m from centre (BP 349; ☎72 04 64). Rooms verging on the clean with shower and occasional water. ②.

Hôtel Grau, rte de San-Pédro (BP 168; ☎72 05 20). Clean, fanned or AC rooms and one of the town's best restaurants. ②–③.

La Terrasse du Phare, up the hill, 50m from the lighthouse (☎72 02 00). German-run hotel with very clean, comfortable double or three-share rooms and an excellent restaurant. Breathtaking views on the fishing port, ocean and mouth of the river. ②–③.

The Town

The **Portuguese** named the site of **São Andrea** at the mouth of the same-named river and there was a permanent French settlement here after 1730. The town only became really important, though, in the years leading up to independence, when it was the main port used by Soudan Français (later Mali) and a timber port for the forests of the Ivoirian southwest.

A relaxed stroll around Sassandra is a pleasant enough way to pass an hour or two. You can't miss the tall yellow **waterfront monument** to the British victims of the *SS Oumana*, sunk by a German submarine on Christmas Day 1943. A visit to the hospital, high above the river mouth, is recommended for the **view** – especially really early in the morning to watch local Neyo and migrant Fante fishermen pushing out to sea. To get there, go up the hill past the Ghanaian fish-smokers.

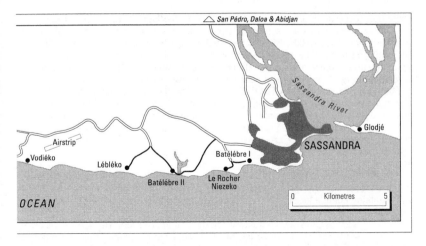

Numerous **pirogue trips** ply the Sassandra and can be arranged through any of the guides that hang out at all the hotels. Longer rides (3hr plus) usually include spottings of hippos and monkeys, though they can be quite expensive. If you are interested in seeing hippos, try to take a motor *pirogue*, as boatmen will not approach closer than a hundred metres in rowing boats. More affordable **taxi-bateaux** leave from behind *Tanty Youyou* and ferry townspeople across the river to the Neyo fishing village of **Glodjé**. The trip takes only a couple of minutes and upon arrival, you'll find there's absolutely nothing to do except watch the fishermen reel in their nets.

Eating

Unsurprisingly, the focus in Sassandra is on seafood, although most places expect you to order your lobster, swordfish or sole in advance. The row of *maquis* behind the market is the place for budget food, where you can fill up on *foutou* or rice with sauce.

La Croisière. Popular *maquis* with grilled fish and *atieké*. Also a good place for night-time drinking; the dance floor can get busy.

Maquis Tanty Jeanne, next to Garage Henri Kéké, near the cultural centre. Grilled fish or chicken *kedjenou*; reputed by those in the neighbourhood to be one of the town's best *maquis*.

Le Safari, (aka *Chez Francis*), directly behind the *gare routière*. One of the town's best addresses for moderately priced African and European dishes. The upstairs terrace overlooks the busy motorpark and the ocean, and the Nigerian owner is happy to take orders in English.

Beaches around Sassandra

You can sleep out along the beach near the village of **NIEZEKO**, about forty minutes' walk west from the centre along the coast. Here, a Robinson Crusoe affair of basic huts and shelters costs about CFA1000 per person (you'll need to be suitably equipped). The beach is pretty and the sea safe, so it's an ideal spot. Though it's popular at the weekend, on other nights you'll have the beach to yourself. Check the latest situation regarding water supplies and staff at the site. Nearby, the **lac au caïmans** is a sacred lake of sorts where the crocodiles apparently don't harm the townspeople – outsiders, though, need beware.

If you're mobile, opportunities for beach-hunting are limitless. If you're not, you can fix up a trip anywhere along the coast with the taxi drivers in Sassandra. If you have to make this (necessarily expensive) choice, then **Poli-Plage**, 16km from Sassandra, is the one to go for. Fares are settled by agreement, not meter; out and back shouldn't cost more than CFA10,000. Most drivers will return to town and come back for you later, but you need to be specific – and very firm – about your return time. For substantially less money and more effort, you can catch a collective taxi from the Sassandra *autogare* to Bassa and walk the remaining 6km.

There's a village at **POLI-CRIQUE**, and rustic, well-managed bungalows to sleep in (①) at the popular *Farafina* restaurant at the beach. This place seems to be more permanent than other beach accommodation that pops up from time to time, but it's still best to check in town before heading out – any kid can update you. If you're self-sufficient, then nearby beaches are heaven to camp out at – beautiful sand and coconut palms; hot rocks and a clear blue sea; tropical vegetation, dugout canoe-makers, total peace.

Niega, some 3 or 4km beyond Poli, is as far as the rough road from Sassandra goes. If you start getting into private *déplacements* to points much further down the coast you're talking about a lot of money. Instead, arrange a **daily rate**, pay for the fuel yourself, and try and get a group together. One popular destination is the stunning, sheltered cove at **MONOGAGA**, 65km away via the San-Pédro road, where the *Langouste d'Or* (☎24 84 80; Fax 24 81 97; ③) has fifteen beachfront bungalows that fill up fast at the weekend. Reserve in advance.

San-Pédro and beyond

Until twenty years or so ago, **SAN-PÉDRO** was earmarked for serious development as a timber exporting port. Thousands of immigrant farmers moved here to a vast shanty area called **Le Village** on the north side of the town. These days, San-Pédro is just about ticking over, and much of the energy devoted to its expansion remains fixed on the ground among the unfinished building sites and semi-deserted timber yards. Despite the sprawl it's still a relatively attractive place, with hills and a good bit of forest pressing in all around. Yet for a town of such grandiose proportions, San-Pédro seems strangely empty. Although it has a lot of good infrastructure, there's not much to do here but hang out and listen to stories of dashed hopes. On the plus side, the **beaches** are very underrated and often passed up by travellers who prefer the more tranquil coastal oases near Sassandra.

Some history

Forty years ago there was little in the region around the mouth of the San Pédro River save scattered Krou villages in a dense and otherwise uninhabited rainforest. The promise of something more significant, however, already began taking shape in 1959, when the government started to buy huge chunks of land amounting to some three thousand square kilometres. The river mouth was the natural site for a port, and, when Abidjan became too busy to handle increasing sea freight, the new port, with its hinterland of timber forests, seemed the ideal way of launching the far-western economy on the back of the timber industry. In 1969, with German, French and Italian loans, the state-operated Société pour l'Aménagement de la Region Sud-Ouest (ARSO) began construction of the port and town layout. Within two years, the first ship had pulled out with a full cargo and for fifteen years, San-Pédro experienced an economic boom in its isolated corner. By the end of the 1980s, however, the forests were already being overlogged, and the drop in price of cocoa pushed the region into recession.

San-Pédro was initially settled in large part by people displaced by another massive construction project, the Kossou Dam (see p.584), which flooded a good portion of

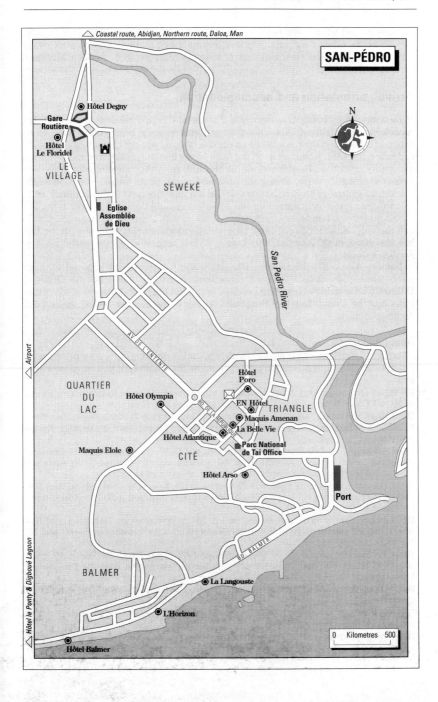

Coastal route, Abidjan, Northern route, Daloa, Man

SAN-PÉDRO

N

Hôtel Degny

Gare Routière

Hôtel Le Floridel

LE VILLAGE

SÉWÉKÉ

Eglise Assemblée de Dieu

San Pedro River

Airport

BD DE L'ENTENTE

QUARTIER DU LAC

Hôtel Olympia

Hôtel Poro

EN Hôtel

TRIANGLE

Maquis Amenan

La Belle Vie

BD DE LA RÉPUBLIQUE

Hôtel Atlantique

Maquis Elole

CITÉ

Parc National de Tai Office

Hôtel Arso

Port

Hôtel le Ponty & Digboué Lagoon

BALMER

BD BALMER

La Langouste

L'Horizon

0   Kilometres   500

Hôtel Balmer

the interior and left 100,000 homeless. San-Pédro's population grew steadily through the 1980s, as other rural migrants and foreigners came in search of work; more recently, the town has seen an influx of Liberian refugees from wartorn Maryland County.

Arrival, orientation and accommodation

If you come in by public transport, you'll arrive at the *gare routière* in the northern **Séwéké** quarter, almost 5km from the town centre. It's a pretty bleak place to be dropped off, though the town livens up considerably as you get closer to the commercial heart, the **Cité**. Branches of all the main banks line the main paved road – known along this stretch as **Boulevard de la République** – but none change travellers' cheques. Along the strip, among the pharmacies and photo shops, is a good supermarket, La Côtière. The Parc National de Tai has an office next to the landmark *Hôtel Atlantic*, and gives out information and advice on visiting the park. Nearby is the animated **quartier triangle**, a neighbourhood packed with inexpensive *maquis* and clubs and the only sensible place to head for evening entertainment, while west of the Cité lies the residential **Quartier du Lac**, a stylish area with all the pretensions of Abidjan's Cocody.

Boulevard de la République terminates in the south of town at the impressively large **port**, where the cargo ships and containers completely obliterate the **Quartier Balmer** whose string of tempting beaches, upmarket hotels and fancy seafood restaurants hug the strand. North of Boulevard Balmer is the **airport**, which sees regular flights to Abidjan.

Accommodation

There's no shortage of hotels in San-Pédro, and something for every price range. Some of the beachfront restaurants even allow for camping if you have your own gear.

EN Hôtel, qtr Triangle (☎71 22 83). Multistorey hotel in the qtr Triangle. Spotless rooms with fan or AC and TV. ②–③.

Hôtel Arso, off bd de la République, just south of Cité (☎71 24 74 or 71 20 26). One of the centre's nicer hotels with AC bungalows and rooms around an expansive courtyard, a swimming pool and restaurant. ④.

Hôtel Atlantique, bd de la République, Cité (BP 375; ☎71 18 50). Older and well-established venue dominating the city's main commercial street. AC rooms throughout – those on the top floors have views of downtown and the surrounding hills. Restaurants and nightclub. ②–③.

Hôtel Balmer, qtr Balmer (BP 652; ☎71 22 75 or 71 25 03). Resort-like hotel with AC bungalows built on the rocks jutting out over the beach. Excellent restaurant, and at 3km from the centre, a good place for quiet isolation. ④.

Hôtel Degny, directly on the *gare routière* (☎71 22 53). A depressing exterior belies a small flowering courtyard with impressively carved doors leading to attractive furnished rooms. AC available, or fans for the budget-minded. ②.

Hôtel Le Floridel, behind rue du Marche, Séwéké (☎71 29 70). Small, dark but exceptionally clean S/C rooms with fan, situated in a residential area not too far from the *gare routière*. Excellent value. ①.

Hôtel Olympia, qtr du Lac (BP 325; ☎71 10 10). Pleasant, well-run hotel with S/C, AC rooms and a restaurant. ③.

Hôtel le Ponty, qtr Balmer (☎71 23 46). Popular beach retreat, French-run with tidy bungalows, a good restaurant and camping facilities. ③.

Hôtel Poro, qtr Triangle (☎71 22 60). In the heart of one of the town's liveliest neighbourhoods, an attractive and quiet hotel with clean S/C rooms that have fans or AC. ②.

AN IVOIRIAN MYSTERY – THE RED HAIRY DWARVES

The huge area of almost uninhabited forest south of the road from Guiglo to Toulépleu (northwest of Taï National Park) is the most frequently mentioned haunt of mysterious, half-legendary **ape-men** creatures inhabiting the twilight zone between animals unknown to science and mythical human ancestors. As recently as the 1940s, there were reports of "little men with reddish fur", rarely seen in the daytime. The Ngere (or Guere) people of the district used to call these beings **Séhité**, and told how they had a system of barter with them, in which they left cultivated food and manufactured goods in the forest and received forest fruits in exchange. The Ngere claimed hardly to know who the Séhité were themselves. Anthropologists have suggested the stories may be part of a folklore about the pygmy people who are presumed to have lived throughout West Africa several thousand years ago. And the cultural memory may have been mixed with the existence until quite recently (possibly still) of a large, sometime bipedal primate with a superficially human appearance. This was not a chimpanzee mistaken for something else, but it may have been an animal that died out before it was ever given a formal zoological identification.

Eating

San-Pédro is bursting with restaurants and bars. The *gare routière* and markets are the obvious targets for inexpensive stalls serving *riz sauce* or pounded plantains. Inexpensive *maquis* line the main street from the *gare routière* almost to the port, and in certain areas, such as Triangle, restaurants are literally wall to wall. The fancier seafood and European restaurants are concentrated in the Balmer and Cité districts.

La Belle Vie, qtr Triangle. One of the countless *maquis* in the neighbourhood serving up inexpensive *atieké* and grilled fish smothered in a sauce of chopped tomatoes, onions, cucumbers and spices.

Le Caulally, qtr Nitoro, Cité. French-style *salon de thé* serving sandwiches, salads and ice cream.

L'Horizon, qtr Balmer. Popular beachfront restaurant specializing in moderately priced Vietnamese and African dishes.

La Langouste, qtr Balmer (☎711900). Pricey seafood served on the terrace overlooking the ocean.

Maquis Amenan, Cité, near the police station. A good address in the centre for inexpensive dishes of rice or *foutou* and grilled chicken.

Super Maquis Elole, qtr du Lac. Slightly upmarket *maquis* with grilled chicken and fish heading the menu.

Tabou, Boubélé and Grand-Bérébi

Now joined to San-Pédro – and thus to Abidjan – by tarmac, **TABOU** is reachable in a day from the capital (and there are two or three flights a week). The *Hôtel Campement* on the beach has plain S/C rooms (①), but the water supply can be problematic. More upmarket accommodation is found in the village of **BOUBÉLÉ**, 18km west of Tabou, where the *Hôtel Village de Boubélé* (reservations from Abidjan on ☎43 01 74; ④) has stylish AC bungalows overlooking the ocean and a club-like ambience. Beaches round about are good, of course, but rough and dangerous for swimming. Safer is **GRAND-BÉRÉBI**, midway between Tabou and San-Pédro – a wonderful east-facing beach with an expensive expat-favoured hotel and restaurant, *La Baie des Sirènes* (☎71 29 94 or 71 15 20; ④).

The Parc National de Taï

The **Parc National de Taï**, previously a conservation area, has recently been converted into a wildlife park as part of a government initiative to promote ecotourism in the country, and visitors no longer require an entry permit. The best way into the park is to hire a vehicle in San-Pédro and drive 100km to the village of Guirotou, from where the **Centre Ecotouristique** (on the southwest outskirts of the park) is a short drive east. The tourist **campement** by the Centre provides meals and accommodation for CFA20,000 per person per night which also includes – providing you have your own transport – a two-day guided excursion around the park.

The Taï forest is rated highly as a natural heritage site: human pressures on it are relatively light – although poaching is a problem – and it contains all the essentials to be West Africa's most important rainforest reserve. Unfortunately, the many animals here – forest elephants, leopards, pygmy hippos and buffalo – are notoriously difficult to spot. Even researchers living at the station rarely see more than duikers and various monkeys. The famous monkey-hunting chimps that featured in David Attenborough's BBC documentary series *The Trials of Life* live in the Taï reserve, but they're an uncommon sight.

The Réserve de faune de N'Zo

Bordering the Taï reserve to the north is the **Réserve de faune de N'Zo**, which, although it isn't a pristine reserve like Taï, is still pretty exciting country for the average visitor. Virtually all the mammals and birds found in Taï are found here – and can often be seen more easily. You'll need your own transport: access is quickest from Daloa, taking the road from Zakué (near Buyo) to Zro. Near Zakué, the **barrage de Buyo** provides a good vantage point for spotting some of the numerous species of birds inhabiting the area, including jacanas, egrets, palm nut vultures and different types of heron – though it also gives a plain view of the savage habitat destruction wreaked by the dam.

THE EAST COAST

East of Abidjan, the coastal highway runs through fine coconut plantations broken by the occasional fishing village. Craft stalls and *maquis* dot this touristy stretch of road and become particularly dense just before **Grand-Bassam** – a picturesque weekend retreat popular with Abidjanis. Further east, towards the Ghanaian border, **Assini** lies in another resort area renowned for its **beaches** and exclusive holiday clubs. **Crossing into Ghana** is straightforward if you use the obvious route: more adventurous travellers can experiment with shoreline hikes and obscure lagoons.

Grand-Bassam

Easily the most attractive settlement on the Ivoirian coast, **GRAND-BASSAM** is a simple day-trip from Abidjan, and makes an excellent excuse to get out of town. And if you're leaving Abidjan for Ghana, or you've just arrived from there, it's a great place to spend the night. Some travellers, too, find Abidjan's pace so frenetic that they use Grand-Bassam as a base, and go into the city as they need or want to.

Founded in the early nineteenth century by the Nzima people, the original village derived its name from the word **bassam**, meaning "coastal settlement". Grand-Bassam is one of the oldest settlements of the European era and was the **first capital** of the colony of Côte d'Ivoire from 1893 to 1900. Yellow fever decimated the town in 1898–99; the French evacuated, almost overnight, and the capital was transferred to Bingerville, considered healthier. For three more decades, Grand-Bassam survived and developed as an active commercial centre and the country's number one port. But the cutting of the Vridi canal opened Port Bouët and Abidjan in 1950, and the old centre of Grand-Bassam has been in decline ever since. Many of the town's graceful administrative buildings remain, however, and the hotels and seafood restaurants bask in the derelict elegance of their surroundings. In contrast, the mainland part of the town gets livelier every year.

Arrival: the Route de Bassam

From Abidjan, there's a good paved road to Grand-Bassam. Taxis leave frequently from the Treichville *gare routière*; the journey takes little more than thirty minutes. Less frequent buses also make the trip from Adjamé. The route also makes a great half-day **bike ride** – with the exception of Togo, the only strip of main highway actually **on the shore** along the entire West African coast.

The **Route de Bassam** is a seemingly endless coconut *bidonville* jammed with **artisans' stalls**, "motels", bars and hotels (some offering "room service"). Stalls sell a wonderful variety of useful and useless crafts – toys, ships, gaudy model motorbikes,

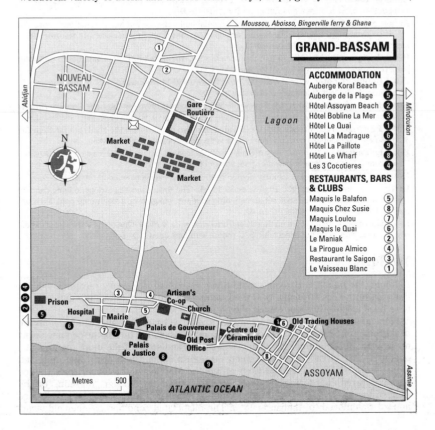

GRAND-BASSAM

Moussou, Aboisso, Bingerville ferry & Ghana

NOUVEAU BASSAM

Gare Routière

Lagoon

Market

Market

ACCOMMODATION
Auberge Koral Beach ⑦
Auberge de la Plage ⑤
Hôtel Assoyam Beach ②
Hôtel Bobline La Mer ③
Hôtel Le Quai ①
Hôtel La Madrague ⑥
Hôtel La Paillote ⑨
Hôtel Le Wharf ⑧
Les 3 Cocotieres ④

RESTAURANTS, BARS & CLUBS
Maquis le Balafon ⑤
Maquis Chez Susie ⑧
Maquis Loulou ⑦
Maquis le Quai ⑥
Le Maniak ②
La Pirogue Almico ④
Restaurant le Saigon ③
Le Vaisseau Blanc ①

Prison
Hospital
Mairie
Artisan's Co-op
Church
Palais de Gouverneur
Old Post Office
Palais de Justice
Centre de Céramique
Old Trading Houses

ASSOYAM

0 Metres 500

ATLANTIC OCEAN

basketwork, in fact everything from table mats to double beds. Further on, the shacks fade and the coconut trees begin to rustle in earnest. Between them concessions of *guérisseurs traditionnels* (healers) offer guaranteed cures, long-distance witchcraft and divine inspiration and support: "*La Maison du Tout Puissant*" (the House of the All Mighty) is a popular epithet.

You enter Grand-Bassam down a gauntlet of souvenir and craft shops. Arriving by taxi, you'll be let down at the *gare routière* in Grand-Bassam's modern district, **Nouveau Bassam**. The market is down on the right. From here, follow the bridge that spans the lagoon to the **old town**, and the **Quartier France**.

Accommodation

Most people come to Bassam to lie on the beach, and the majority of the **hotels** face the seafront. Generally accommodation is clean and comfortable, often European-run and catering to European tastes, with obligatory HB in the high season. The budget possibilities are limited (search out *Le Village*, on the beach, for basic camping), but some of the town's *maquis*, notably *Le Quai, Lou Lou* and *Balafon*, also have an odd room or two for little money (see "Eating", opposite).

Auberge Koral Beach (☎30 16 26; Fax 30 12 63). Fancy beachfront hotel with pool (CFA1000 for non-guests), bar, restaurant and rather posh rooms. ③–④.

Auberge de la Plage (☎30 14 40). Restored colonial building with wooden porches and courtyard full of archways and balustrades. Rooms are spacious but drab. Still, it's one of the town's least expensive lodgings and good value. ②–③.

Hôtel Assoyam Beach (☎30 15 57). Comfortable S/C rooms with AC, a private beach, saltwater pool, restaurant, and horses to rent for a seaside trot. ④.

Hôtel Bobline La Mer, west of *Hôtel Assoyam Beach* (☎30 14 18). Inexpensive rooms (fan or AC), with young friendly staff and a decent restaurant. ③.

Hôtel La Madrague (☎30 15 64; Fax 30 14 59). Stiff competition for the better-known *Taverne Bassamoise*, with twelve AC bungalows, a private beach and pool. Excellent seaside restaurant. ④.

Hotel Le Quai, in the French quarter. Divided into two parts across the road, not far from the *Maquis Le Quai*. Spotless new S/C rooms at a very modest price. Excellent value. ③.

Hôtel La Paillote (☎30 10 76). Very ordinary S/C, AC rooms, but one of the least expensive on the beachfront. They also have a saltwater pool and good restaurant. ③.

Hôtel Le Wharf (☎30 15 33). Chintzy double rooms and an excellent seafood restaurant. ④.

La Taverne Bassamoise (☎30 10 62; Fax 30 12 96). The town's most luxurious lodgings and an Ivoirian institution. Colonial-style set-up including gardens, bungalows, a swimming pool and a terrace restaurant overlooking the ocean. ⑥.

Les 3 Cocotieres, about 300m further west from *Auberge de la Plage*. One of the town's least expensive choices, with basic but acceptable S/C rooms with fans or AC. ②–③.

The Town

Although the **beach** is Bassam's main draw, swimming isn't really recommended on this part of the coast (people who think otherwise are swept out all the time) so the town itself is likely to occupy most of your active hours.

Some of the hotels (try *La Taverne Bassamoise*) sell a useful leaflet which details the background of Grand-Bassam's **old buildings**. Most of the turn-of-the-century structures were inhabited until the tidal wave of 1965 and some of the more monumental buildings have already been renovated through a combination of private funds and money from UNESCO. The **old post office**, the **Mairie** and the **Governor's Palace** have recovered their former grandeur. Don't be misled by the sign "museum" on the front of the last-mentioned – the collection of national costumes and history it once housed was moved to Abidjan in 1993. The dilapidated condition of other old structures, such as the **Palais de Justice**, the old bank and the early trading depots projects a haunting sense of the march of time, and it's questionable whether future restoration will happen soon enough to save those about to collapse.

Other reminders of the colonial period include the melancholic **Monument des Morts** (a weary white France holding her dead), the **old cemetery** (where many victims of the yellow fever epidemic were buried) and the **prison**. Following rioting on February 6, 1949, the French arbitrarily arrested leaders of the Parti Démocratique de Côte d'Ivoire and held them in this prison. In protest, the women of Abidjan marched here to demand the end of the incarceration and of political oppression.

Much better than you might expect is the **Artisans' Co-op** (Mon–Fri 8am–5pm, Sat & Sun 8am–6pm) on the lagoon side of the town – a huge warehouse selling a vast selection of carvings, fabrics and other crafts. Prices are fixed and not outrageous. Around the hall and outside you can watch dozens of co-op members fashioning their merchandise. Nearby, there's a **memorial pillar** to Marcel Treich-Laplène (1860–90), founder of the colony of Côte d'Ivoire. Treich-Laplène was also first explorateur of Indenié in 1887 and of Abron and Bondoukou in 1888 – an active young fellow in his short lifetime.

The **Centre de Céramique** co-operative (Mon–Sat 8am–6pm, Sun 9am–6pm) offers an uninteresting selection of pots and plates. Unfortunately they've got the measure of the ceramics market with their globby little pottery fishes. To get out of colonial (or neocolonial) France and find Africa again, strike off east of this quarter, through the heart of the old commercial district with its rambling trading houses, and you'll enter **Assoyam**, a fairly traditional fishing quarter.

Before leaving Bassam, take a look at an old Ivoirian quarter of the town – **Moosou** – once a village and 4km inland from the France quarter. There are a few budget places to eat here, and as for sights, an elaborate, angel-topped mausoleum in the main street. If you're on foot, you don't have to walk all the way back: climb up onto the highway and wave down a vehicle.

Eating

Dining is an extravaganza in Bassam and generally expensive. Low-budget *maquis* are pretty much limited to Nouveau Bassam, especially around the market and *gare routière*. The following are all in the old town.

Maquis le Balafon, near the bridge. Grilled *capitaine* or barracuda served in a quiet garden.

Maquis Chez Suzie. One of the few places in the old district where you can eat for about CFA1000. Grilled chicken and fish or pepper soup.

Maquis Loulou, opposite *Auberge Koral Beach*. A slightly pricey restaurant specializing in seafood and superb breakfasts. Highly recommended.

Maquis le Quai, opposite *Auberge Treich-Laplène*. French-style *maquis* with tomato and cream sauces to accompany calamari or *crevettes*. Popular expat meeting place and a good source of information for further travels.

La Pirogue Almico, near the Artisans' Co-op. Lobster and *crevettes* under a *paillote* overlooking the lagoon.

Restaurant le Saigon, near the bridge. Eclectic selection ranging from Vietnamese to pizza.

Nightlife

Nightlife in Bassam is low-key, but among places worth checking in the new town, *Le Maniak* is run by a former Ivoirian DJ who kept an extensive collection of records from his radio days and now boasts the best stock of oldies in all Côte d'Ivoire. A more classic nightclub, *Le Vaisseau Blanc*, is also popular (cover CFA1500 at weekends).

MOVING ON FROM GRAND-BASSAM

If returning to **Abidjan**, you can make your way (9km north) to the ferry across the Ebrié lagoon for the track to **Bingerville** (18km on the other side), and return that way, rather than using the coast highway; you should find transport every morning. Taxis and other transport leave town all the time for **Aboisso**, the last main town before **Ghana**.

On to Assini

East from Grand-Bassam, it's all **pineapples** and **coconuts**, pockets of secondary forest, a few old trees still standing, plantations of wispy, temperate-looking **rubber trees**, punctilious police and rather more military *gendarmes*.

At the town of **Abrobakro**, a secondary road leads down to the Assini canal, which stretches along the coast to connect the Ebrié and Abi lagoons. On the other side of the canal, **ASSINI** has gained fame for its **unspoiled beaches**.

The coast here tends to be exclusive. Many wealthy Abidjanis own private bungalows along the seafront for use as weekend getaways. This is package-tour country, too, with a number of **resorts** as luxurious as they're antiseptic. *Club Méditerranée* (☎30 07 17; ⑤) has a "village" in a coconut grove, with 200 AC rooms, the usual combination of sports facilities, a disco, boutiques and organized excursions. *Les Palétuviers* (BP 4375; ☎30 08 48; ⑤) is even more ambitious, a club complex with 338 luxury AC rooms and facilities from water-skiing to horse riding; open from October to April, it's mostly filled with tour groups flown in direct from Europe. Should you want to, you can only stay at the *Club Méditerranée* or *Palétuviers* by booking in advance via the above reservation numbers in Abidjan.

Into Ghana

Most travellers and nearly all vehicles enter Ghana via **Aboisso** and **Elubo**. For the sake of a more interesting route, turn off the main *route nationale* to **Frambo**, down a beautiful road in pitiful condition; then check out of Côte d'Ivoire in the customs and immigration shed by the wharf, before picking up a launch across the lagoon to **Jewi-Wharf** in Ghana.

It's also feasible to take a small ferry-*pirogue* across **from Assini-Mafia** on the Abri lagoon (22km east of Assini-Terminal) to a huge sand bar which, although part of Côte d'Ivoire, is connected by land only to Ghana. There's fairly frequent transport from Abrobakro to Assini-Mafia via Assini-Terminal (where the *Club Med* crowd cross the lagoon to their private paradise). Once on the sand bar, you can find transport east into Ghana. It's possible, however, that you'll be picked up by Ghanaian officials from **Newtown Post** (not, as marked on maps, a village as such), politely searched, escorted to Jewi-Wharf and sent on the launch to Frambo to complete Ivoirian exit formalities properly.

THE BAOULÉ COUNTRY

The **Baoulé** live in the centre of Côte d'Ivoire, where the northern savannahs meet the southern forests. Related by language and culture to the other Akan-speaking peoples of the east and Ghana, their prosperity formerly derived from trade in **gold**. Ancient mines can still be seen at **Orumbo Boka** (south of Toumodi) – the Baoulé's **sacred mountain**.

In the south of the Baoulé country, **Yamoussoukro** recently became the nation's administrative capital, a slice of architectural artifice that now just needs a couple of hundred thousand more inhabitants to lend it a real sense of city. Further north, the country's second largest town, **Bouaké**, is a bustling centre of trade and industry that attracts a diverse mix of people from throughout the country.

In addition to these **urban centres**, the Baoulé region also contains much unspoilt countryside. Though flat and unvaried landscapes are normally not cause for excitement, they lend themselves well to **game viewing**. The **Parc National de la Maraoué** near the town of Bouaflé could be a chance to take in wildlife ranging from elephant to antelope. Better still, Houphouët-Boigny's safari land, **Abokouamikro National Park**, within limo distance of Yamoussoukro, provides the surest chance of spotting animals imported at huge cost from South Africa; you can organize tours from the *Ivoire Hôtel* in Abidjan.

Yamoussoukro

In the 1950s, few people had heard of the small village of **Ngokro** except for the five hundred or so who lived there. One of those residents was Nana Yamoussou, whose son Felix became the president of Côte d'Ivoire. That fact permanently altered the hamlet's history, since Houphouët-Boigny tirelessly used his influence to turn his birthplace into a present for his family and descendants. In honour of his mother, he changed its name to **YAMOUSSOUKRO** and devised a plan to transform the town into a glittering metropolis. Many of the **monumental buildings** now dotting the cityscape are indeed impressive. Besides the imposing **Hôtel Président**, Yamoussoukro boasts modern college campuses, government buildings like the **Maison du Parti**, the **Hôtel de Ville** and, completed in 1990, a colossal **basilica** – a virtual replica of Saint Peter's in Rome and just a fraction smaller.

But in between these isolated pockets of pomp are vast stretches of nothingness – large open fields and vacant lots waiting for people to breathe some life into them. The vast layout is confusing and impersonal and the splendid dimensions of the futuristic buildings further diminish the human scale. The place is worth visiting as a phenomenon, but don't expect warmth or spontaneity, and don't expect to want to stick around.

Orientation

With a population now estimated at 150,000, Yamoussoukro comprises four main neighbourhoods. In the southeast part of town, **la Résidence** was the private domain of the former president. The town's main **market** is held in **l'Habitat** – the one part of town that feels really lived in – alive with the activity of merchants, restaurants and clubs. South of here, beyond the town's lake, lies **Dioulakro**, a residential *quartier populaire*, while **N'Zuessy**, to the northeast, is a slightly upmarket neighbourhood. The banks, PTT and the *gare routière* are on **Boulevard Houphouët-Boigny**, the major road dividing these two districts.

Accommodation

Yamoussoukro has a reasonably good choice of **rooms**. For a long time, much of the budget accommodation was grubby and unenticing – hole-in-the-wall hotels or *chambres de passage* – but it's becoming increasingly possible to find inexpensive, respectable places to stay, especially in the Habitat district.

Hôtel Agip (BP 9; ☎64 00 39). One of the plainest of the mid-priced hotels surrounding the *gare routière*, though S/C rooms are clean and have AC. The restaurant looks curiously like a Norman Rockwell painting of an American diner. ②.

Hôtel Akraya (☎64 11 31). If you have your own transport this multistorey hotel provides high-class, though somewhat stale, accommodation at a relatively low price. ③.

Hôtel Akwaba, Habitat, facing the lake (☎64 95 24). Good location a short walk from the *gare routière* and surrounded by *maquis*. Clean rooms with fan or AC and amiable staff. ①–②.

Hôtel Bonheure I, opposite the *gare routière* (BP 89; ☎64 00 61). Basic place, recently restored and good value. Bar and restaurant. ③.

Hôtel Bonheure II, opposite the *gare routière* (BP 89; ☎64 00 31; Fax 64 09 42). Same ownership as *Hôtel Bonheure I*. Revamped hotel with furnished AC rooms and, if you like, minibars and TV. Some suites available. Pool, bar, pizzeria and *salon de thé*. ④.

Hôtel la Découverte, opposite the *gare routière*. Dingy, but bearable rooms, with shower but no WC. Some AC available. ①–②.

Hôtel de la Paix, directly behind the *gare routière*. Inexpensive squalor. A lot of hourly rentals, but you can't find much cheaper. ①.

Hôtel Las Palmas, Habitat, opposite *Maquis le Jardin* (☎64 02 73). Very popular with overlanders and in a good location near Habitat's market, *maquis* and clubs. Inexpensive rooms with shower and fan; AC costs a bit more. Very friendly management. ①–②.

Hôtel Président (BP 1024; ☎64 01 58; Fax 64 05 77). Part of the Sofitel chain, this is one of Côte d'Ivoire's poshest hotels – 284 rooms (including 18 suites), all with colour TV and telephone. Here you can get a sauna, play squash and tennis, and cool off in one of the two pools. The 18-hole golf course adjoining the hotel is rated one of the best in West Africa. There are 3 restaurants and 4 bars, including one on the top floor with striking panoramic views of the city. All this, plus the disco, cinema and shops, just for you and the management (or so it may seem). ⑦.

Motel Shell (☎64 11 27). Newish hotel with clean rooms, a decent restaurant and, bizarrely, a small zoo at the back. Slightly overpriced compared to the *Hôtel Agip* next door. ③.

The Town

As early as the 1960s, Houphouët-Boigny already planned to convert Yamoussoukro into the nation's capital, moving ahead cautiously, however, so as not to incite criticism. One of the first moves was to build a system of roads capable of handling traffic for a vast metropolis. Wide **paved avenues** were traced through the empty countryside and **multi-laned highways** laid out, linking the village to Abidjan, Bouaké and Man. By the mid-1970s, the incandescence of 10,500 streetlights flooded the quiet nights of the burgeoning town whose population was still only around 30,000.

Prestige projects followed. The lavish *Hôtel Président*, a brash combination of reinforced concrete and marble, shot up and was surrounded by what must be the continent's most-watered **golf course**. Dominating a nearby hill, the gilded **Maison du Parti** became a showy symbol representing the power and grandeur of what was at the time the nation's only political party. (For a tip, you can be shown around the various assembly rooms.) Houphouët-Boigny then set out to create in Yamoussoukro the nation's **educational centre**. No expense was spared on the town's three outstanding **écoles superieures** – the INSET, ENSTP and the ENSA – blessed with beautiful **campuses** of inspired architecture and state-of-the-art facilities (permission to visit obtainable at the Hôtel de Ville). A Moroccan-style mosque established a sense of religious legitimacy as did the Neoclassical Saint Augustine church – built in honour of one of the president's brothers. By 1983, Yamoussoukro had sufficient trappings to back up its international pretensions. The president's private dream became a public reality when the National Assembly voted to transfer the political capital here from Abidjan and it became Côte d'Ivoire's fourth capital.

The crowning glory is the granite and marble **Basilique de Notre Dame de la Paix**, planned to be the largest cathedral in the world and entirely financed out of the president's own pocket – a claim far from politic, even were it true, in a country as poor as this. It can be visited (daily 9am–5pm; free) if you're suitably attired and preferably if you're prepared to buy some of the knickknacks offered by the nuns in charge of guiding visitors. To visit the cupola by escalator there's a nominal charge. Public Mass is held on Sundays at 10.30am.

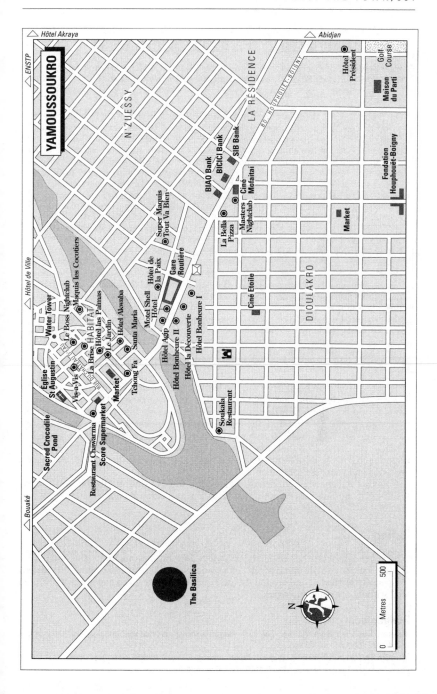

YAMOUSSOUKRO

△ Hôtel Akraya   △ Abidjan

◁ ENSTP

N'ZUÈSSY

LA RÉSIDENCE

BD. HOUPHOUËT-BOIGNY

● Hôtel Président

Golf Course

Maison du Parti

◁ Hôtel de Ville

Fondation Houphouët-Boigny

BIAO Bank
BICICI Bank
SIB Bank

Super Marquis
Tout Va Bien

Ciné Mofaitai

Masters Nightclub

● La Bella Pizza

Market

Le Boss Nightclub
Marquis les Cocotiers
Water Tower

Hôtel de la Paix

Hôtel Shell Hôtel

Gare Routière

DIOULAKRO

Ciné Etoile

HABITAT
Hôtel las Palmas
La Brise
Le Jardin
Hôtel Akwaba
Santa Maria
Motel Shell Hôtel
Hôtel Agip
Hôtel Bonheure II
Hôtel la Découverte
Hôtel Bonheure I

Église St Augustin
Vis-à-Vis
Tchong Fa
Market

◁ Bouaké

Sacred Crocodile Pond
Restaurant Chawarma
Score Supermarket

● Soukala Restaurant

The Basilica

N

Metres
0   500

THE BASILICA: H-B'S "DEAL WITH GOD"

When they built St Peter's, were there no hungry people in Rome? When England after the Great Fire built itself St Paul's, were there no poor or homeless in London?

Ivoirian craftsman, quoted in the UK's *Sunday Times*, December 2, 1989

On a clear day, the **Basilique de Notre Dame de la Paix** stands out from miles away on every approach road to Yamoussoukro. It was built between September 1986 and January 1990, in conditions of immense secrecy, by a labour force of **1500 men**, working continuously in two shifts a day between 7am and 2am. It cost an estimated **£100 million** ($150 million). Among other barely comprehensible statistics, the basilica required the equivalent of an entire year's output of French white cement; each of its 7000 seats has individual airconditioning; it can hold another 12,000 people standing; and on its "piazza" and surrounding areas of Italian marble, there's space, in theory, for 300,000 more – a theory that's unlikely ever to be tested as the figure surely exceeds the country's Catholic population. There are 36 **stained-glass windows**, in 4000 shades, each 30m high, covering an acreage of glass greater than that at Chartres cathedral. And, although the dome is a little lower than St Peter's in Rome – which the whole enterprise has so slavishly imitated – it is surmounted by an immense cross of gold soaring to **168m** above the savannah, which makes the whole edifice 23 metres taller than St Peter's.

In September 1990, **Pope John Paul II** finally consecrated the basilica – though with evident unease, and only after receiving assurances (hollow ones, it would now appear) that a new hospital would be built too. Far from being a resounding success, the pope's visit triggered a wave of protest and only served to increase Côte d'Ivoire's domestic political crisis and foment rumours of financial scandal. Houphouët claimed the basilica was inspired and made possible because "I did a deal with God, and you wouldn't expect me to discuss God's business in public, would you?"

While spending on his hometown, the late president didn't neglect his own fancies. The large **presidential palace** imposes itself on the city centre, but is enclosed and off-limits to visitors. Bordering the palace are the man-made **sacred crocodile ponds** filled with snappers – a gift from the former president of Niger. You can watch the reptiles being fed each evening. Behind the palace, the president's private plantation spreads out over 2000 hectares, making it one of the largest in West Africa. Experimental methods of farming national crops like rubber, coffee, cocoa, pineapples, avocados and yams are carried out here.

A further enhancement to personal glory was the **Fondation Houphouët-Boigny** (Thurs, Sat and Sun 7am–6pm), a vast historical and cultural complex in the south of town not far from the Maison du Parti.

Eating

While Yamoussoukro has its share of stylish **African restaurants** (and some very average European-style ones, which you should avoid) there are also numerous *maquis* – especially in Habitat and around the *gare routière* – where you can get tasty Ivoirian food without spending too much.

Budget food

Maquis Les Cocotiers, Habitat. Lakeside *maquis* serving *riz gras*, traditional grilled chicken and fish dishes. Simple and cheap.

Maquis le Ravin, Dioulakro. A good choice among a whole clutch of *maquis* opposite the *gare routière*. Grilled chicken with *atiéké* on the menu or *agouti*.

MOVING ON FROM YAMOUSSOUKRO

Frequent transport from the **gare routière** heads to Abidjan (266km), Kossou (43km) and Man (233km) – all accessible on paved roads. Taxis and *cars* also head regularly to Bouaké and Korhogo in the north.

Yamoussoukro's **airport** was designed to be large enough to receive any visiting heads of state who might need to fly in urgently by Concorde. More mundane traffic goes via Air Ivoire which has flights to Abidjan and Bouaké.

Restaurant Chawarma, Habitat, opposite the crocodile pond. Reasonably priced salads, sandwiches and *chawarma*.

Santa Maria, Habitat. Excellent Ivoirian food served in the evenings along the street overlooking the lake. Grilled chicken and fish head the menu.

Tchong Fa, Habitat. Small Chinese restaurant with very moderate prices and an eclectic menu.

Vis-a-Vis, Habitat. One of a string of restaurants along the rue du Chateau d'eau, where you can try popular local dishes like *tête de mouton* or *pied de boeuf*.

Moderate to pricey

La Bella Pizza, Dioulakro. The town's longest-running pizzeria with red-and-white checked tablecloths and heavy wooden furniture, just like the old country. The pizza's authentic too.

La Belle Epoche, Habitat (☎64 07 76). Brasserie, bar and restaurant featuring the town's finest French cooking. Prime beef and seafood and a good wine list.

La Brise, Habitat (☎64 15 62). Italian and French specialities. Good pizza and pasta and a couple of African dishes.

Maquis le Jardin, Habitat (☎64 14 22). Magnificent *paillote* for a very chic *maquis*. Along with European food, serves unusual African dishes such as *biche aubergines*. Recommended and reckoned the best in town.

Soukala Restaurant, Dioulakro (☎64 00 73). Relatively upmarket restaurant serving French and African cooking. Stunning lakeshore views of the Basilica.

Super Maquis Tout Va Bien, N'Zuessy (☎64 20 96). Fine French cooking including killer shrimp and thick brochettes. Some African dishes thrown in for good measure.

Nightlife

Yamoussoukro's two **clubs** to be seen at are the *Masters*, near the Ciné Mofetai, and *Circus* in the *Hôtel Bonheure II*. Both have a cover of around CFA1000 and draw large crowds out to enjoy a good selection of music. Less expensive nightlife is concentrated in Habitat around the **rue du Chateau d'eau**, where the *Boss* has a lively bar where a very young crowd flocks nightly for energetic dancing and no cover. Nearby, *Le Marco Polo* is equally young and enthusiastic, but has a CFA2000 entrance fee. On the stiffer side, the *Hôtel Président*'s disco – the *Kokou* – is where moneyed hopefuls pay a CFA2000 cover only to find that few other people had the same idea. At weekends there's usually more of a crowd.

The Parc National de la Maraoué and Kossou Dam

Set aside in 1968 to preserve wildlife in the relatively populated area of the Baoulé country, the **Parc National de la Maraoué** spreads across a thousand square kilometres. In environmental terms, that's really not much (a fraction of the size of the Comoé Park further north) and the variety of animals you can see here isn't overwhelming.

Bordered by the namesake **Maraoué River**, the park does, nonetheless, harbour various **antelope** species and different kinds of **monkeys**. The main _piste_ leading off towards **Mont Saninlego** leads through a valley where you can sometimes spot **elephant** or **buffalo**. **Hippos** still live in the rivers.

The **park entrance** is at the village of Goazra, near **BOUAFLÉ**, 59km west of Yamoussoukro. The park has no accommodation, but you can sleep in Bouaflé at the _Campement Hôtel_ (④), which has hot showers in the AC rooms and a good restaurant. For eating, the _Maquis du Centre_ does good grilled fish. While in town, you can pick up an authorization to camp in the park at the Eaux et Forêts office, where you might also be able to arrange a guide.

The road to the park from Yamoussoukro passes just south of the **Kossou Dam**, built where the White Bandama River joins the Maraoué (or Red Bandama). The hydroelectric dam created the nation's largest **lake**, which spreads, indented like an insect-eaten leaf, over 1700 shallow square kilometres, and which doubled the country's production of electricity when it opened in 1972. It also flooded numerous villages and displaced an estimated 100,000 people, most of whom were resettled in new towns. The paved road to Bouaflé passes near many of the sad concrete and aluminium villages which were built to replace the traditional settlements of local Baoulé fisherpeople and farmers by the AVB – the Bandama Valley Development Authority. In **KOSSOU**, you can stay at the **guesthouse** (②) of the national electrical company, the EECI, which has comfortable AC, S/C rooms, and a cantina.

Bouaké

The antithesis of Yamoussoukro, **BOUAKÉ** lacks glamour and a sense of overall planning. It has grown dramatically in the last fifty years, to become Côte d'Ivoire's **second largest city**, with a population not far short of a million. As workers and traders from throughout the country flocked to this commercial crossroads on the major north–south route, neighbourhoods grew up willy-nilly, attaching themselves loosely to the districts laid out by the colonials. The diversity and dynamism of the peoples who've come together here make it an exciting place to visit, although the town is visually unappealing and there's admittedly not much to see. The highlight of any trip here is a visit to the **market** – one of the biggest and most colourful in the country.

Some history

Sometimes called the capital of the Baoulé country (a title which more accurately belongs to **Sakasso**, 42km southeast near the lake, where the successors to Baoulé **Queen Pokou** still reside), Bouaké was already an important commercial centre at the end of the nineteenth century when the French established a **military base**. It was used to launch attacks against the armies of **Almamy Samory Touré**, then sweeping into the region from the northwest. When Samory Touré finally surrendered at Guéoulé, the colonials once again sought to open up trade routes to the north. Bouaké soon regained prominence as a **centre for trade** in cloth, gold powder, indigo and tobacco.

An added boost was given to commerce when the French brought the **railway** line up from Abidjan in 1912, eventually extending it all the way to Ouagadougou. That same year, **industry** was launched in the interior when a cotton seeding plant was opened in Bouaké. In 1919, Robert Gonfreville, a French agriculturalist, opened a textile factory – the first in Afrique Occidentale Française.

As maritime trade dwindled during World War II, the railway line took on added importance and Bouaké found itself in the centre of a wartime trade boom. The country's food supply rolled into this town – beef cattle from the Upper Volta, dried fish from Mali, rice from the western territories, peanuts and sheep from the north – from where it was redistributed to the regions. By the end of the war, the population had swelled beyond 25,000.

Since 1945, rural immigrants have continued to pour into Bouaké in search of work. Part of the influx was spurred by chronic rural dislocation caused by the building of the **Kossou Dam** in 1972. Though many people were resettled in villages specially created along the lake, many migrated to the towns. Today, Bouaké's wide **mix of people** includes Malinké and Sarakolé, Dyula (Dioula), Bamana, Senoufo and large numbers of Burkinabe. The original Baoulé inhabitants today only account for about a quarter of the total population.

Accommodation

Though Bouaké doesn't offer much in the luxury range, it has an excellent selection of moderately priced **hotels**. Overlanders will be pleased to find a **youth hostel** here (a real rarity in West Africa) and a couple of missions that sometimes take in travellers.

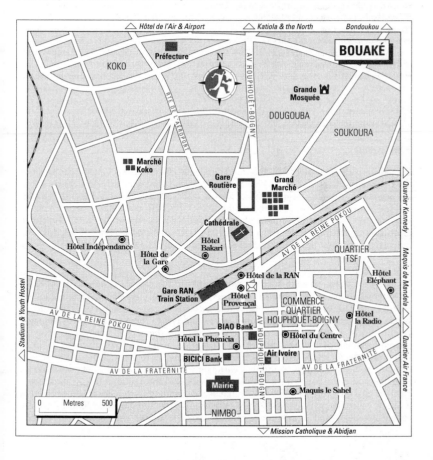

Budget accommodation

Auberge de la Jeunesse, near the stadium. Soft-sprung beds in communal rooms for four; showers and fans included. Recommended. Taxis to the centre are CFA125. ①.

Hôtel Bakari, Koko district, behind cathedral. Relatively cheap for the centre and not too run-down. Basic rooms with fan. ①.

Hôtel Eléphant, on the outskirts of the residential Air France district (BP 285; ☎63 25 24). Not bad value for AC rooms near the market. ②–③.

Hôtel de la Gare, near the train station. Great central location guarantees a lot of animation. S/C rooms not overly depressing. ①.

Hôtel Indépendance, Koko district. Basic accommodation, but friendly and good value. ①.

Hôtel La Radio, qtr Houphouët Boigny, near *Hôtel Eléphant* (☎63 34 81). Huge, clean S/C rooms with fan or AC, a restaurant and young, friendly staff make this by far the best value budget accommodation near the centre. ①.

Mission Catholique, Nimbo district on the Abidjan road. A very limited number of clean rooms in the *centre d'accueil*. ①.

Mid-range hotels

Hôtel de l'Aïr, rte de l'Aeroport (☎63 28 15). Twenty-two clean, comfortably furnished rooms with AC and bath. There's a good restaurant, too, but it's a taxi ride from the centre. ③.

Hôtel du Centre, Commerce (☎63 32 78). Rooms here come with AC and bath. The hotel has its own restaurant and nightclub, plus a crafts *boutique*. ③.

Hôtel Phenicia, rue du Commerce (☎63 48 34). A large, fully AC place in the heart of town with comfortable S/C rooms, some with TV. Popular terrace restaurant. ③.

Hôtel Provençal, Commerce, behind the PTT (☎63 34 91). Fifties-style hotel run by Belgians and conveniently located. Spacious and clean rooms with AC. The restaurant here is very good and the outdoor *terrasse* a nice place to come for a drink. ③.

RAN Hôtel, next to the train station (BP 566; ☎63 20 16). The town's classiest accommodation with sixty furnished rooms (TV, video, mini-bars), a popular restaurant and bar and Bouaké's best pool. ④.

The Town

Bouaké spreads confusingly in a thousand directions. The undisputed centre, however, is the **Commerce Quartier**, today known as the Quartier Houphouët-Boigny. This is one of the oldest neighbourhoods in the modern town, which grew up between the **train station** and the **Mairie**. Here you'll find the **banks** (BIAO, BICICI), **post office** and administrative buildings. North of Commerce, the **gare routière** is located in the **Koko District**, a principally Baoulé quarter. Near the *gare routière* is one of the town's few buildings of monumental proportions, the **Saint-Michel Cathédrale**, built in a heavy modern style.

The market

Bouaké's expansive **market** spreads over three separate neighbourhoods east of Koko – **Dougouba** (site of the **Grande Mosquée**), **Soukoura** (also known as the Quartier Dioula) and **TSF** (a residential area with large villas and shaded streets). This market is one of the most fascinating in Côte d'Ivoire and brings together over four thousand vendors from all parts of the country, guaranteeing the widest imaginable array of goods. A panoply of fruit, vegetables, cereals and spices from across the country comes together here: in season you'll find mangos from the north as available as pineapples from the south; palm oil as plentiful as *karité* butter; yams and other tubers as abundant as millet and corn. More intriguing than all this, and the sections full of hardware – everything from plastic wash bowls to handmade farming tools – are those devoted to a variety of locally made **crafts**. The Baoulé have a reputation for their **leather goods**, especially snake- and lizard-skin bags and wallets (consider your conscience and be

MOVING ON FROM BOUAKÉ

Bouaké's **gare routière** is in the Koko district across from the market. UTB **coaches** and **taxis** head from here in all directions – Man, Abidjan, Korhogo, Odienné. For **Guinea**, TARMCI runs a weekly bus service between Abidjan and Kankan, passing through Bouaké on Sunday and arriving Tuesday morning (around CFA20,000).

You can also go by **train**, daily, to Abidjan or Ferkessédougou (continuing to Ouagadougou).

Air Ivoire operates regular **flights** to Abidjan and other urban centres. If you're in a hurry – or suddenly get sick of the whole Ivoirian scene – weekly flights also link the town, at some considerable expense, with Ouagadougou, Bamako and Conakry. For flight information, contact Centre Voyages (☎63 75 67).

aware of import restrictions in Europe and elsewhere), but you'll also find a large selection of **jewellery** if you'd prefer to leave the reptiles in the bush. Also good value in Bouaké market are the intricate, hand-woven **blankets**, principally of Baoulé manufacture, but also in the distinctive styles of Agni and even Fula weavers.

Eating

Bouaké's *maquis* are some of the best and least expensive in the country, while the Koko district is probably the best place in town for great African food served in lively venues.

Maquis Le Mandela, just outside qtr Air France near *Hôtel Eléphant*. Large *maquis* with an extensive French and African menu.

Maquis Le Sahel, off av Houphouët-Boigny, qtr Nimbo. One of the centre's most popular places to eat with selections of "bush meat" (antelope or *agouti*), grilled chicken and fish, in an outdoor courtyard.

Le Poulet Show, down the street from the *Sahel*. The best chicken in town, marinated and grilled to perfection.

La Terrace, av Houphouët-Boigny. Lebanese food including salads and *chawarma*.

Katiola

Although small, **KATIOLA**, 50km north of Bouaké, enjoys fame throughout Côte d'Ivoire for its **pottery** – though it's a puzzle why the jugs and **canaries** made here should attract such attention when no one pays much mind to those produced elsewhere in the country. Chalk it up to a strange quirk of fate, but it's one that has drawn a lucrative **tourist trade** to the town – or at any rate capitalized on the traffic passing through.

The traditional jugs the women here turn out are, in truth, rather nice. They're almost perfectly symmetrical, but shaped without a wheel. The women smooth the surfaces with their hands and use a special tool to cut out ornamental motifs. If you want to watch them work these days, you're probably going to have to pay for it. Photos are extra and the price of the real thing – mainly sold through a co-operative – is downright expensive.

You can **stay** at the *Hôtel Hambol* (BP 144; ☎65 05 25; ③), a modern place with African-style archways lining the facade. Rooms have AC, and there's a restaurant and nightclub. Less expensive accommodation can be found at the *Hôtel l'Amitié* (①), an affordable place in the town centre, or at the *Hôtel la Paillote* (①), with round bungalows in a quiet setting 2km outside town.

WESTERN CÔTE D'IVOIRE

The big attractions of **western Côte d'Ivoire** are high forest-strewn ridges and valleys, and the relatively intact traditional culture of the Dan (or Yacouba) speaking people. **Man** is the main town, while **Danané** – close to both Guinea and Liberia – comes a close second. **Touba** marks the northernmost fringes of the mountainous west before the road winds away from the last remaining peaks into the drier savannah lands that are the cultural domain of the Malinké.

Although the main centres of the west are accessible enough at any time, the **rains** fall heavily in the region from March to October, and getting to some of the more out-of-the-way sites can be difficult. Lulls between showers provide fantastic conditions for photography, however; this is an area that needs clear air to be appreciated.

Daloa

The first western town you hit along the great central highway, **DALOA** is a good place to break your trip to Man. This is a coffee-growing area – which brings the district substantial wealth – and, although it doesn't figure much on the tour itineraries, Daloa is one of the country's oldest and most important towns, solid, well-planned and industrious.

Of the various **accommodation** options, *Les Ambassadeurs* (BP 754; ☎78 62 18; ③) is the most upmarket, while right on the *gare routière*, the comfortable and clean *Auberge de l'Ouest* (☎78 36 24; ③) has some AC rooms. Cheaper is the refurbished *Hôtel C12* (②) with a nice restaurant-bar, the *Collège Protestant* (①) near the *centre artisanal*, and the *Mission Catholique* (①) across the street.

Man and around

MAN, a large commercial centre of some 140,000 people, is rather hideous – most of the appeal derives from its spectacular geographical setting. Often called the "town of eighteen peaks", it spreads over a valley with mountains rising up on all sides and from the end of its wide streets. There's something of an American feel here; there are places in Colorado like Man and though the horizons inspire, the town itself is a muddled confusion of districts that leaves little impression. Still, it's lively enough, with much activity focusing around the market and adjoining *gare routière*.

It's best to use the town simply as a base for exploring the surrounding area; it consists of numerous districts, most of which you probably won't get the time to visit. The centre is occupied by the **quartier commercial**, where you'll find the large town **market** and the **gare routière**.

If you're interested in buying **masks** from the region, there's a wide selection sold around the market, along with numerous other crafts and a mass of musty fetish material. Nearby are countless shops and small businesses, and branches of the major **banks**, among which the SGBCI has in recent years been willing to change non-franc currencies.

On arrival in Man you're likely to be besieged by children offering their services as "guides", especially if you're driving. Although the children charge a lot (around CFA15,000 a day), they can be helpful, although bear in mind that many of the sites around town take a dim view of street children and may make life difficult for you if you are accompanied by one.

Accommodation

Man has a decent choice of **lodgings**, most of which are in the budget range, but there are also upmarket places with TV and pools.

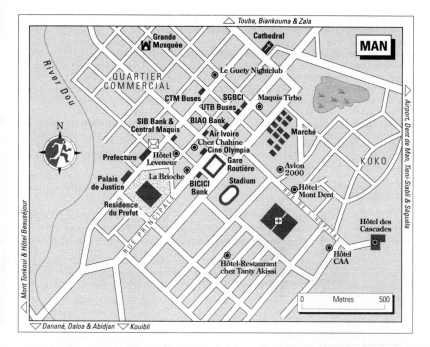

Hôtel Beauséjour "Les Masques", rte de Mont Tonkoui, 3km from centre (BP 1031; ☎79 08 55). Upmarket, popular place with bungalows (AC and TV) around an attractive courtyard. Smaller non-AC rooms and camping available for budget travellers. Recommended, especially if you're driving. ④.

Hôtel CAA, off rue de l'Hôpital. Excellent location on top of a hill with views of the town and surrounding mountains. From this vantage point, Man looks almost attractive. Large cavern-like bar downstairs with cool stone walls and a maze of arches. High standards of cleanliness in S/C rooms with fan or AC. Great value and highly recommended. ②.

Hôtel des Cascades (BP 485; ☎79 02 52). Another hotel in a hilltop location, this three-star – Man's best – also commands a brilliant view of town and mountains. AC rooms overlook the swimming pool, gardens and tennis courts. ③.

Hôtel Leveneur, qtr commercial (☎79 14 81). Good mid-range hotel with clean fan or AC rooms with TV. The French restaurant here is rated one of the town's best. Good value. ②–③.

Hôtel Mont Dent, rue de l'Hôpital. One of the town's least expensive places, near the market. Non-S/C rooms are very good value, and for just a bit more you'll get a fan and your own toilet. Attractive courtyard, lively bar and relatively clean. ①.

Hôtel-Restaurant Chez Tanty Akissi, behind the stadium (☎79 04 78). Feels more like sharing a room in the Akissi family home than staying in a hotel, with cooking, washing and tressing in the courtyard. The restaurant is well known in town. ①.

Eating, drinking and nightlife

Lots of places near the market serve inexpensive food – there's not much in the way of upmarket African or European restaurants, but you'll find excellent cooking nonetheless.

La Brioche, rue Principale across from the *gare routière*. Tasty cakes, brioches and ice cream on an outdoor terrace. A good place for breakfast.

Central Maquis, qtr commercial, near the PTT. Drinks and excellent *poisson braise* served in an outdoor courtyard. There's also dancing on Thursdays and Saturdays.

Chez Chahine, qtr commercial. Reasonably priced pizzas, pasta, hamburgers and salads. Everything from the mundane (sandwiches) to the unexpected (*lapin aux olives*).

Le Guety. One of the most popular nightspots in town, playing a mix of American and African music. Jam-packed on most nights.

Maquis Avion 2000, off rue de l'Hôpital. *Maquis* with mud-brick oven easily seen from the street. One dish only, roast pork with *atieké*, but they do it right. Numerous other inexpensive places line the same street.

Maquis Tirbo, qtr commercial. One of the better-known inexpensive *maquis* featuring grilled fish smothered with cucumbers, tomatoes and onions. Beer, wine and a pleasant atmosphere. Across the street, the *Maquis Univers* is a bit pricier.

La Paillote, qtr commercial (☎79 08 82). Upmarket *maquis* run by the owner of the *Leveneur*. Fine French dining under a *paillote* of monumental proportions.

Around Man

The bold, green mountain scenery around Man lends itself well to **day-trips**. For some of the longer destinations, you'll need to go by car or taxi, but if you're feeling in shape, there are rewarding outings within hiking distance. Some of the most popular excur-

---

THE MAN DISTRICT IN HISTORY

Hidden in the forests of the western mountains, the **Dan** (also known as Yacouba), lived in almost complete isolation after the beginning of their migration from the Guinea and Liberian regions in the fourteenth century. Other peoples of Côte d'Ivoire – the Akan, Senoufo and Malinké – had little contact with them, while the Europeans, who had been along the coast since the early 1700s, only made it to Man in 1897. It was largely the military victories of **Samory Touré** that drew the French to the region; they finally tracked down the most serious threat to their colonialist ambitions in 1898, capturing him in the village of Guéoulé, northwest of Man. They built a military post at Man in 1908 and used the town for regional administration.

DAN CULTURE

The Dan base their traditions and religion on a single God, **Zran**. Creator of the universe, Zran contains elements of both good and evil. Part of traditional education involves **secret societies**. After passing a first initiation, boys and girls enter these societies where they gain more profound religious instruction and learn to assume their adult roles. Members of the *gor*, for example, are charged with administering justice. They ultimately gain the power of turning themselves into animals, notably the leopard, in order to pass unnoticed as they survey the forces of good and evil at work in the community. **Masks** are important symbols in initiations and other ceremonies. Dan masks, unlike many others, characteristically have smooth, delicate lines and gentle, even sensual, human features. They're easily recognized and well known throughout the entire country.

Dance is another important element of Dan culture, and the region is famous for it. One of the most unusual is the **stilt dance** (Zekre Touli). Dressed in grass skirts and covered with cowrie shells, the masked performers make beguiling, inexplicable movements on stilts up to six metres high. Also impressive is the Menon or **juggling dance**. Young girls, about four years old, are specifically chosen for this dance and undergo a special two-year initiation. They live with the dance troupes and have no contact with their families until puberty. Their death-defying acrobatics include being tossed into the air to land on knife blades held by their adult partners. Such dances are performed in slightly sanitized form throughout the country and versions are frequently staged in large hotels.

MOVING ON FROM MAN

Several companies run buses to **Abidjan**, assuring several daily departures via either Bouaké or Yamoussoukro. They are UTB, near the cathedral, Fandasso Transport by the Shell station, and CTM in the commercial district. Prices are competitive at around CFA3500. The bus for **Odienné** on the route to Bamako has been discontinued, so taxis are now the only option; enquire at the *gare routière*. CTHK buses leave for **Korhogo** every Monday from their station on rue de l'Hôpital.

Peugeot 504s run from the *gare routière* north to **Touba** and south to **San-Pédro** (CFA5000), though the latter town is also covered by UTB buses. Heading west to **Guinea**, 504s go to Danané, from where a few taxis a day drive to Gbapleu (no shops or facilities). Going into Liberia from Man and Danané is not recommended.

If you want more information, or are interested in organized [...] contact the Délégation Régionale du Tourisme, BP 613 Man (☎79 06 90).

The cascade

One of the easiest trips, and one you won't regret taking, is to the **cascade**, only 5km from the centre of Man along the road to Mont Tonkoui. You can drive almost the entire distance (you'll have to park nearby and walk down a steep footpath to the base of the falls), and it's perfectly feasible to hike. Depending on the mud levels, it won't take much over an hour, and the road winds its way through beautiful mountain scenery. The last stretch passes through a thick bamboo grove where the rush of the stream in the valley below can be heard but not seen through the greenery. Walk towards the top of the waterfall and continue until you see a painted sign (where you'll be charged a small entrance fee) indicating where you scale down the cliffs to the bottom of the falls. In full view for the first time, they're magnificent, with the white water crashing down a stair-like rock formation. It's best to come during the week if you can to avoid the huge weekend crowd.

At the base of the falls is a **hanging bridge** – a copy of those for which the region is famous. Although real vines are woven into it, this one is supported by thick metal cables put in place by the French. From a distance it looks authentic enough for atmospheric photos, with the falls tumbling in the background. Nearby is a **restaurant**, closed for refurbishment at the time of writing.

Mont Tonkoui

Its name deriving from the Dan word *tonkpi*, meaning big mountain, **Mont Tonkoui** is the tallest mountain in Côte d'Ivoire. You can see it clearly from Man, its summit marked by an unsightly television transmitter. A *piste* leads northwest from town (the same tracks that pass the cascade) and continues about 20km to the mountain. The road winding its way up to the peak adds another 12km to the total distance. About two-thirds of the way to the top, tracks lead off to a guesthouse – formerly the *villa du gouverneur* – used occasionally by visiting dignitaries. From here you get a magnificent panoramic view of the mountain chains and thick forests of the region. On a clear day, it's said you can see for 150km, beyond the Nimba Mountains on the Guinean border.

La Dent de Man

The bald rock formation of **La Dent de Man** rises, incisor-like, 12km northeast of Man. Aptly named, the "Tooth" is the most distinctive of the mountains visible from Man and is practically a town totem. Some say it has special protective powers – a spiritual sentinel watching over the townspeople. If you're without transport, take a taxi from town to the village of Glongouin, at the foot of the mountain. Here you can find a kid to lead you up the *dent*, guiding you through the maze of footpaths and, hopefully, finding the easiest way up the steep parts. It's a hard climb in areas – you'll get hot – but you don't have to be in spectacular shape to make it. The view from the top is worth the effort.

Tieni – Siabli and Fakobli

The village of TIENI-SIABLI, 14km east of Man, has become a common target for travellers, though there's nothing of essential interest. Tieni was the original settlement, built atop a cliff. Few of the old huts left on the hill are still lived in, and most of the inhabitants live low in the uninspiring new town of Siabli. To visit the dwellings on the hill, ask permission from the town chief. Authorization will cost.

Ten kilometres further down the same road, you arrive in FAKOBLI, a quiet town that lies at the foot of numerous mountains. A branch of the Sassandra River runs a couple of kilometres, keeping the surrounding countryside green. It's best known as home of the *tematé* dance, performed by young girls around harvest time.

Biankouma, Gouéssésso and Touba

A paved road leads north of Man, cutting its way between the Dan and Toura mountain ranges and some of the region's most striking scenery. On first impressions, BIANKOUMA (47km from Man) is an unenticing *préfecture*, but away from the highway, the old town is an attractive collectivity of fifteen neighbourhoods, each with its protective *case à masques*, shrines and traditional round huts (CFA2000 is commonly demanded by the "village guide"). You can stay at the *Hôtel du Mont Sangbé* (①), which has modest S/C rooms and a good restaurant. Five kilometres west is the village of GOUÉSSÉSSO where the owner of Man's *Hôtel Leveneur* has another of his string of regional hotels and restaurants, *Les Lianes de Guéssesso* (☎79 12 85; ③), a Club-Med type resort; S/C, AC bungalows are built in a traditional fashion barely distinguishable from the village huts, with beautiful gardens around a lavish swimming pool and stunning views across the surrounding valley.

Further north, Touba was originally a Malinké town, founded in the 1870s by immigrants from Timbuktu. But the country here was Toura (people related to the Dan) before that, and the Toura, whose reputation as sorcerers has stayed with them, today live southeast of Touba, especially around the steep village of Zala. The tracks off the main highway stop abruptly at the village, and to climb Mount Zala you'll have to continue on foot, perhaps picking up a guide before proceeding. The pay-off is some of the best views in the entire country.

TOUBA is larger than Biankouma and has good accommodation along with other facilities like pharmacies, banks (no change), even a cinema. The most central **place to stay** is *L'Escale du Port* (☎70 71 30; ②), with comfortable AC rooms near the *petit marché*. Across the street is the more modest *Hôtel Savanne* (①), while closer to the *gare routière* on the rue de la Paix is another simple hotel, the *Belle Étoile* (①).

Danané and around

If you arrive in Côte d'Ivoire from southeastern Guinea, DANANÉ, sprawling across a great valley, is likely to be your first stop; entry formalities are completed at the police checkpoint on the edge of town. The **gare routière** for arrivals from the west is on the western side of town. Vehicles to Man, and on to other main towns in Côte d'Ivoire, leave from the other *gare* in the eastern *quartier* of Danané.

The best-value of the few **places to stay** in town is the *Hôtel Tia Etienne* (①) – well out on the east side of town, but on the Man road, and only 500m from the *gare routière est*. It's a nice enough place, with simple S/C rooms (choice of AC or fan) and quite good

São Pedro, São Vicente, Cape Verde

Chã das Caldeiras, Fogo, CV

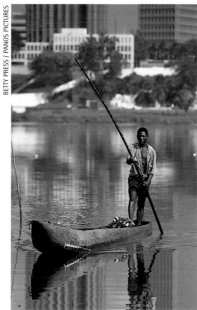

Abidjan, Côte d'Ivoire

JAMES McCORMICK

Riding a cow, Bubaque, Guinea-Bissau

JAMES McCORMICK

JAMES McCORMICK

Bijagós Islands, Guinea-Bissau

Bafatà market, Guinea-Bissau

Griot playing kora

Monts Nimba, Guinea

Old Mosque, Bobo-Dioulasso, Burkina Faso

Bella nomads near Gorom-Gorom, Burkina Faso

meals for around CFA1500; arriving from either of Côte d'Ivoire's western neighbours, the prospect of so much comfort (including wine, and TV in the bar) seems positively over the top. The *Maquis La Frontière* (①), on the road to the border, has clean rooms with AC or fan and a good bar and restaurant, or you could try the pricier *Hôtel des Lianes* (②) in the west of town, which offers very clean and decently priced A/C rooms.

The liana bridges

So long as you have your own transport to get around, Danané's **liana bridges** are worth the trip: authentic old swinging constructions that span the Cavally River south of town at Drongouineau (15km), Lieupleu (26km) and Vatouo (30km), all off the main road to Toulépleu. Like those in Guinea and Liberia, considerable mystique attaches to these bridges (which also makes them paying attractions) and they're supposed to be reconstructed when necessary in a single night – something that women and outsiders are not allowed to witness. The bridges at **Lieupleu** and **Vatouo** are the easiest to visit by Peugeot 504 from Danané (you'll have to walk 4–5km from the main dirt road).

THE NORTH AND EAST

Northwestern Côte d'Ivoire is sparse, mostly flat country, yellow and dusty for eight months of the year. While Odienné may figure only as a night stop en route to or from Mali, it offers an unusual and beautiful route into Guinea via Beyla. More central, **Korhogo** is certainly worth a detour if you're heading up the country's main transport axis. You can jump train or bus at Ferkessédougou and spend a rewarding two or three days in the Senoufo country.

The **northeast's** great attraction is the **Comoé National Park** – the largest in West Africa. For most travellers this is a fairly inaccessible reserve and doesn't always repay the expense and effort of getting there, though at the northwest corner there are opportunities for worthwhile, and just about affordable, **game-viewing trips** out of Kafolo. If you're travelling south from Burkina (or north from Abidjan), and you've some spare days, it's worth making a big loop through the northeast, calling in at the old Dyula capital of **Kong**, following the boundary of the park around its eastern side, and using an unusual backcountry route through the Akan centres of **Bondoukou** and **Abengourou** – nice untouristy towns the pair of them. Or else you can cut across the border to Ghana at one of several frontier posts and make for Kumasi.

The far northeast is **Lobi country** and you'll see Lobi hunters, tracking in the bush with bows and hunting tackle. But the **Koulango**, whose language is close to Lobi, have long had a more settled farming lifestyle and are the de facto land-holders in the region.

Eastern Côte d'Ivoire is the least touristy part of the country. The hilly central east, close to the Ghana border, is the heartland of the **Agni** and **Abron**, which, culturally and linguistically, have much in common with the Ashanti in Ghana.

Odienné

ODIENNÉ, an agricultural town of some 47,000 people, is the focus of the most scenic district in the northern grasslands. To the west, the **Dienguélé range** ripples over to the Guinean border. Another set of hills follows the road to Boundiali, peaking near Tiemé with **Mont Tougoukoli** which rises to over 800m. Although it's a historic town, Odienné has few reminders of the days when it was capital of the **Kabadougou Empire**, founded by the local hero Vakaba Touré, whose modest grave can still be seen on one of the town's main streets near the post office. In the 1970s Odienné was scheduled for radical urbanization, but the scheme only went far enough to give it an anonymous could-be-anywhere feeling. Though the old quarters were knocked down, the new city never came, and the former charm of the traditional houses and shady streets has long since been forgotten.

Despite the town's impressive **grande mosquée** – and the lively **market** with Dyula, Malinké and Bamana merchants from northern Côte d'Ivoire, Mali and Guinea – there's not much of interest in Odienné. But many travellers (and traders) on their way to or from Mali find it a good place to break the journey.

Some history

A Muslim fief, Odienné was originally founded by the Senoufo. But as early as the sixteenth century, Mande migrations had pushed all the way to Touba, and over the next two centuries their movements slowly displaced the Senoufo. Odienné remained in Senoufo control until the mid-eighteenth century, but eventually the native people were overwhelmed by the newcomers and made peace with the Malinké.

Soon after, the townships of **Samatiegla** and **Tiéma** became important Muslim centres along with Odienné. By the mid-nineteenth century, the town had also become a commercial stop on the **caravan routes** linking Bougouni (Mali) to Touba and Seguéla. Salt and horses from the north were traded here against gold and kola nuts from the south. And, as the town prospered, it grew to become the capital of a sizeable kingdom led by **Vakaba Touré**, who expanded his empire east to Boundiali. Vakaba's son, **Maagbé Mandou**, was later to marry one of the daughters of **Samory Touré**. Odienné thus became an important ally of Samory, whose hegemony extended over the town until it was captured by the French in 1893.

Practicalities

There's little choice when it comes to **places to stay** in Odienné; one of the best is the *Hôtel Les Frontières* (BP 135; ☎80 02 03; ③), a three-star hotel arranged in attractive S/C bungalows around a swimming pool and featuring one of the town's better restaurants. Two options for those on a limited budget are the *Hôtel le Refuge* (②), off Route d'Abidjan, which, although a little outside the centre, is clean and does at least have running water, and the *Hôtel Touristel* (next door to the *Hôtel Les Frontières*) which has large, cleanish rooms with fan or AC, and a *maquis* next door.

As for **food**, the *Yankadi*, near the police station, does a good chicken *kedjenou*. You could run into northern-based expats here. Opposite the market, *La Bonne Auberge* is another popular *maquis* with rice and manioc dishes served with grilled beef or chicken. A little further afield, *La Villa* dishes up inexpensive food and salads, and more unusually for the region, ice cream.

If you're heading north, Odienné is a springboard to **Mali**, and taxis run to Bougouni, though the tracks are often bad. *Pistes* are well-maintained east as far as **Korhogo** where the tarmac to Abidjan begins. Heading south, the road to **Man** is paved.

Boundiali

The short drive east from Odienné to **BOUNDIALI** passes through a hilly agricultural region before entering the flat plains of the **Senoufo country**. The town, whose name means "drum dried in the sun", was founded around the twelfth century by a Senoufo ancestor, a hunter named Nambaga Ganon. Eventually, it was incorporated into Vakaba Touré's empire, and it's said that René Caillié, the first explorer to be recognized for reaching Timbuktu and returning again to recount the tale, stayed here on his way to the "mysterious city".

The town has an attractive **hotel**, the *Dala* (BP 90; ☎82 00 54; ③), run collectively by a community association and laid out like a small village with comfortable S/C accommodation in round, thatched huts. The venture has been quite successful at attracting tourism, with the villagers organizing events like dancing (troupes from throughout the region come to perform) and excursions. Less expensive accommodation is found in town at the *Hôtel Record* (①).

Korhogo

KORHOGO is capital of the Senoufo country, and the most touristy of Côte d'Ivoire's northern towns. It's famous for its rough, unusual, painted *toiles*, examples of which seem to hang in every hotel and expat home in the country. Fortunately there's more to the town and its district than this pretty, but somewhat debased, art form. **Senoufo culture** finds its firmest expression in the district and there's every possibility, if you make some effort to meet people, of witnessing some of the frequent ceremonial events that take place – worlds apart from what you might be served as after-dinner entertainment in some of the hotel lounges.

The Town
The **centre artisanal** (daily 8am–6.30pm) exhibits some of the best examples of Korhogo's crafts. To get there, head for the roundabout near the Préfecture and walk

---

THE PORO

Senoufo society is regulated by a process of **training** (sometimes called initiation) that may last an entire lifetime. Young men normally go through three phases of this training, known as *poro* (the same name as a similar institution found far to the west, especially in Sierra Leone), each of which lasts seven years. Girls go through an initial phase that ends when they get their first period. After their menopause, women are considered asexual and may begin the training again. If they live long enough, they become fully initiated.

Traditionally, the *poro* served as the basis of Senoufo government. Communities were led by elders who had reached the highest level of the training. These elders themselves chose the members of their ranks from the brightest and most talented initiates, thus ensuring that the governing body was composed of the most able leaders. Though effective, this system of ruling broke down somewhat when Malinké invasions sparked the need for village elders to relinquish some of their authority to a central chief – the most famous of which was **Gbon Coulibaly**.

But the initiation lived on and is today still practised throughout Senoufo country. Exactly what is learned during the seven-year cycles is unknown by outsiders, since it is a highly guarded secret considered vital to the survival of *poro* and thus to Senoufo society. In very general terms, initiates receive religious and professional education and learn about social obligations. Among other things, they learn to communicate in a special language. Part of the training takes place in the **sacred forest** in **Korhogo**.

Various stages in the initiation are marked by festivals – a sort of graduation ceremony. One of the better known is the **dance of the leopard-men**, celebrated after a group of initiates returns from the sacred forest having learned to master religious forces. Similar celebrations may mark a birth or a death, and since the whole community participates, the whole community takes part symbolically in the important stages of an individual's life. Many of these dances are now acted out in major regional hotels (the **Mont Korhogo** or, in Boundiali, at **Le Dala**). This may be your best shot at experiencing such an event (or at least a commercially staged version thereof), but if you stay any time in the region and get to know some people, it's not unrealistically difficult to accompany them to one of the celebrations. They leave a lasting impression.

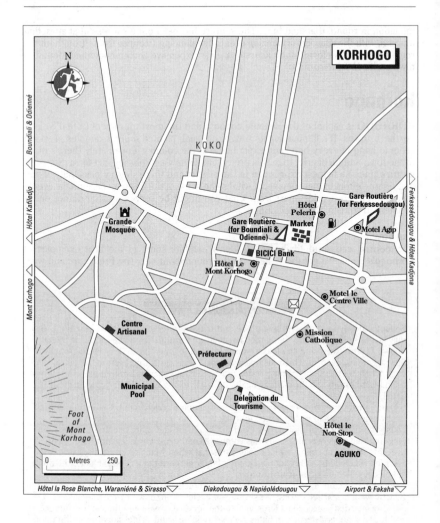

towards the **municipal pool**, from where you can already see the large conical thatching of the centre's rooftop. Inside, the wide selection of local artwork includes weaving, carving and basketry. The quality is strictly controlled and artists receive a take of the (non-negotiable) selling price.

You can get better buys, though, in the **Koko district**, where many craftsmen have workshops. Here you have to bargain the price of sculpted masks and wooden objects and must be your own judge of the workmanship; it varies from good to shoddy. This district borders the fenced-off **fôret sacrée** – where *poro* initiates go through secret training (see box, overleaf).

South of Koko, you'll see the **Grande Mosquée**, built in 1980 in a style similar to the mosque at Yamoussoukro. On Fridays, men turn out in large numbers for the afternoon prayer. And in the distance, the mountain looming up with its **sacrificial rocks** recalls a different religious tradition: in former days, when a chief died, his slaves were sacrificed on these rocks and he was buried on a bed of their skulls.

Practicalities

Due to the large number of visitors, Korhogo has many services. You can **change money** at the Société Générale, the BICICI or the Société Ivoirienne de Banques, all located in the town centre. Sometimes, however, they have trouble getting current rates from Abidjan in which case they only change French francs.

If you haven't got transport, but want to visit some of the **surrounding villages** described below, it's possible to do so by arranging an excursion through the **Délégation du Tourisme** (☎86 05 84), just off the same roundabout as the Préfecture, who can arrange **car rental** or organized tours of the region. Private **tourist agencies** providing similar services are AGUIKO (Association des Guides de Tourisme de Korhogo; ☎86 22 43), next door to *Hôtel Le Non-Stop*, and Agence du Nord, next to the *Hôtel Kadjona*.

Accommodation

There's a wide accommodation choice in Korhogo, with hotels capable of handling large organized tours and individual backpackers on a budget.

Hôtel Kadjona, rte de Ferké (BP 117; ☎86 20 87). Quiet garden setting for comfortable AC accommodation with pool. Popular *maquis* and *boîte*. ③.

Hôtel Le Mont Korhogo (BP 263; ☎86 04 07). The town's plushest, ideally located near the market – to which you may be dragged by one of the crafts vendors who sell their wares at the hotel entrance. S/C rooms with AC throughout. The hotel has a pool, restaurant and bar. ④.

Hôtel Le Non-Stop, rte de l'Aeroport (BP 142; ☎88 01 85). New hotel with spotless, carpeted S/C rooms with fan or AC and TV, plus a good restaurant. Suitable for all budgets, and by far the best choice in Korhogo. ①–③.

Hôtel le Palmier, near the market. Popular with budget travellers due to the good location, friendly management and high standards of cleanliness. ①.

Hôtel Pelerin, near the market. A good central location and rock-bottom price make up for dirty, noisy rooms. ①.

Hôtel La Rose Blanche, qtr Residentiel, near the Préfecture (BP 64; ☎86 06 13). This quiet, upmarket hotel is set in a pretty compound with pleasant AC rooms, and a restaurant, all for a very reasonable price. ②–③.

Mission Catholique. A limited number of well-kept rooms, with collective showers. Simple, but about the town's cheapest. ①.

Motel Agip, near the market, next to *Le Palmier* (☎86 01 13). One of the better bets in the medium price bracket and centrally located. It's a small place, with spotlessly clean rooms. The French restaurant here is one of the town's better eating places. ②.

Motel Le Centre Ville (☎86 13 35). Respectable S/C rooms with choice of fan or AC and a restaurant serving *chawarma*. ①.

Around Korhogo

Many of the crafts you see in town – at the *Mont Korhogo* hotel or the *centre artisanal* – are made in the surrounding villages, which make easy **day-trips**. However, because it's a lot more interesting to see the artisans at work and was once less expensive to buy from them directly, in recent years the neighbouring villages have become suspiciously touristy and prices have risen to the point where you can probably find better buys in Korhogo itself from sellers undercutting each other.

One of the easiest villages to get to – and therefore one of the most visited – is **WARANIÉNÉ**, noted for its weavers (*tisserands*). Now, in addition to the rough handwoven cloth, you can buy embroidered tablecloths with matching napkins – one suspects tourism has affected local production. Waraniéné lies only 6km southwest of town on the road to Sirasso, close enough to take a taxi or even to try hitching if you've no other means of transport. You can **camp** in the gravel pit on the right just before you enter the village from Korhogo.

Other villages lie along the southern road which leads to Dikodougou. At Tioroniaradougou, turn left towards **Fakaha** (35km from Korhogo), where the *toiles peintes* seen all over Korhogo and, indeed, in markets throughout West Africa are produced. Originally these fabrics were made for costumes used in *poro* ceremonies and had geometric patterns – if you get the chance to go to a funeral or initiation, you'll still see dancers wearing them. Now, however, they're mostly made into wall hangings for tourists, and designs represent scenes from folklore and local legends; the colours are made from mud and vegetable dyes. Note that those in black and white retain their colours fairly well, but the multi-toned patterns fade almost immediately and the slightest moisture causes the dyes to run. Because of the demand, prices are steep. Taxis head here from Korhogo's market. The nearby town of **Napiéolédougou** (Napié) also produces the same fabric.

Ferkessédougou

Whatever you do in **northeast Côte d'Ivoire**, you're likely to pass through **FERKESSÉDOUGOU**, an unexceptional road town, but nice enough. Ferké, as it's known, stretches a couple of dust-blown kilometres along the highway, with turnings west towards Korhogo and east to Comoé Park and Kong. The best time to come is for the **market on Thursday**, when all morning the lorries rumble in loaded with tomatoes, yams, hot peppers and whatever's in season. If you've come up by public transport from Abidjan, Ferké is about as far as you'll get in one day, and it's likely you'll have to stay the night.

Incidentally, if you're **heading north** and have your own transport, it's worth mentioning here the lovely ancient little mosque at Kauara, 60km beyond Ferké. It's beyond **Ouangolodougou**, just off the road to the left and deserves a look.

Practicalities

Branches of the major **banks** line Route de Bobo, but none will change travellers' cheques and even French franc notes could be difficult. The **post office**, on Route de Bobo, is useful for reliable but expensive international calling and faxing. On the same street, across from the BICICI bank, is the Pharmacie de Ferké and for serious medical problems, the Hôpital Baptiste has a good reputation.

If you arrive in Ferké by **train**, note that taxis don't serve the station after dark.

Accommodation

Auberge de la Réserve, rte de Bouaké, 2km south of the centre (BP 142; ☎88 01 85). A very comfortable S/C, AC place with an interesting menu if you want to splurge. A shame the pool is such an unappetizing lurid green. ①–②.

Hôtel Koffikro, off rte de Bobo, near BICICI bank. Down a small street bathed in the shade of mango trees, this place has simple S/C rooms around a courtyard. Friendly and good value. ①.

Hôtel de la Muraille, off the rte de Bouna. Inexpensive S/C rooms that are good value if unexceptional. Right next to the *gare routière est*. ①.

Hôtel La Paillote, off rte de Bobo. Curious outcropping of traditional-style round huts (fully AC) with thatched roofs. Pleasant garden and calm setting. ③.

Hôtel La Pivoine, off rte de Bouaké (☎86 83 90). Converted house with a small number of clean, comfortable AC rooms with TV. A bit far out of town, but very good value nevertheless. ②.

Hôtel Refuge, off rte de Bobo, behind Shell. A satellite dish dominates the otherwise plain courtyard. Very reasonable AC, S/C rooms with round beds and TV. The best option in the centre. ①–②.

Relais de Senoufo, directly behind Shell (BP 104; ☎88 03 23). The entrance looks posh, with bright cushions on the armchairs and Korhogo prints on the wall, but the tidy S/C rooms (choice of AC or fan) are good value. Friendly staff can give information on visiting Comoé National Park and the surrounding region, and you may even hook up with a guide. ③.

Eating and drinking

L'Arc au Ciel, in the market, just off rte de Bobo. Large, shaded *maquis* serving all the traditional Ivoirian dishes at a stiff price.

Maquis Agroville (*Chez Germain*), rte de Bouaké. A straw screen fences off this backyard restaurant where chickens scratch around the outdoor *paillotes*. Wild boar and rabbit smoked on the premises and grilled to taste.

La Primature, off rte de Bobo, opposite the *Relais de Senoufo*. Rather spiffy tables in a large shaded courtyard. Popular watering hole, and they serve meals too.

Super Maquis "The New Pergola", just off rte de Bobo, near Elf. Chicken with *foutou* or rice in courtyard with *paillote*. Good grilled fish.

Nightlife

Of the few **clubs** worth mentioning, *Le Metro*, which adjoins the *Primature* restaurant, is the most popular. Stiff competition is provided by the newer *Le Village* off the main road near the market. Both places have a cover of about CFA1000. Less expensive entertainment can be had at the *Maquis Excellence*, one of a few *maquis* in an open clearing behind *La Primature*, which is busy most nights and at the weekend (no cover).

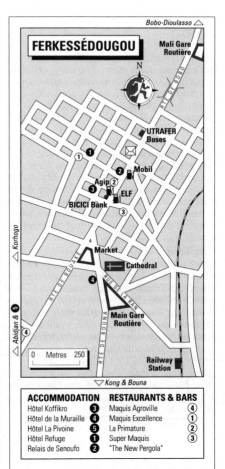

FERKESSÉDOUGOU

ACCOMMODATION		RESTAURANTS & BARS	
Hôtel Koffikro	❸	Maquis Agroville	④
Hôtel de la Muraille	❹	Maquis Excellence	①
Hôtel La Pivoine	❺	La Primature	②
Hôtel Refuge	❶	Super Maquis	③
Relais de Senoufo	❷	"The New Pergola"	

MOVING ON FROM FERKESSÉDOUGOU

On the Route de Bobo, UTRAFER has clean and reliable **buses** to Abidjan (CFA3500) and Bouaké (CFA2500) with twice daily departures at 8am and 7.30pm. Departing from the Mali *gare routière* north of the post office, there are also **Peugeot 504s** to Bobo (CFA4000) and Ouaga (CFA8000), as well as **minibuses** to Sikosso (CFA4500) via Ouangolodougou.

The **train** is less expensive (at least the one heading north), with a departure in each direction every other day at around 8.30pm – though it's often late.

The **gare routière est et Abidjan** is on the rue de la RAN near the cathedral (look for the spires). Here you'll find taxis to Abidjan, Ouaga and Bobo in addition to daily transport to Kong (CFA1500) and Kafolo/Bouna (CFA2500/5000).

Kong

Known and visited for its old Sudanic mosques – sloping *banco* walls on a wooden frame with characteristic protruding joists – **KONG** is worth a side trip from Ferkessédougou especially if you've not seen the much more impressive architecture in Mali. It's not on the way to anywhere else; occasional vehicles come up from some of the Djimini Senoufo villages to the south (from Dabakala, for example), but this means a diversion in any case; and several times a week something goes from Kong to Kafolo, up on the main Ferké–Bouna northeast axis.

Otherwise you're pretty much limited to one or two vehicles a day from Ferké, and the same back again. This isn't a bad trip (3hr), with a foretaste of Kong's architecture at Nafana, 22km before it. But you'll see some of the poorest villages in Côte d'Ivoire around here and, at the end of the dry season, when the granaries, like giant egg-cups, are empty, you come face to face with the awful downside of the country's economic "miracle" – serious malnourishment. The people here are suffering partly as a result of wildlife conservation policies which have ignored their needs – they depend upon hunting to survive, and much of the local game is now protected in the Comoé park.

The Town

Once prevalent, **"guides"** nowadays rarely approach the few visitors who make it to Kong. They're hardly needed in any case, as all there is to see is standing before you. The large **Friday mosque** dates from the seventeenth century (though most of it was rebuilt in 1905 after its destruction by Samory Touré) and the smaller one to the south, behind the houses on the main square, from the fourteenth. This latter has white painted coconuts on its turrets which you'll be told are ostrich eggs from Mecca. Both are impressive enough relics in an environment largely devoid of monuments, but neither is accessible to non-Muslims.

The other sites are really hardly worth bothering about. There's the rubbish-strewn grave of a certain **Voyageur Moskowitz** who succumbed here in 1894 while on Marchand's expedition, and the **Maison du Binger**, of dubious authenticity, which stands in ruin some way off as memorial to the French expansionist who based himself in Kong for a while in 1889.

If you end up **spending the night**, there are basic S/C chalet rooms at the *campement* (①), which is straight down the road through town about 800m and then up on the left. Food and drink is concentrated up by the town centre.

THE KINGDOM OF KONG

The town of **Kong** was founded, probably in the twelfth or thirteenth century, by Voltaic-speaking ancestors of the Senoufo, but was relatively unimportant until its commercial invasion by Muslim Mande-speaking **Dyula merchants** at the end of the seventeenth century. Islamic scholarship followed in the footsteps of mercantile success, and the town became the capital of a **trading empire** that stretched south and east to the Baoulé- and Akan-speaking farmers of the hills and north to the edge of Ségou's domain near the Niger River, while the **mosques and Koranic institute** extended its reputation. But, although the Dyula exerted a powerful influence in Kong, it was another hundred years before **Sekou Ouattara**, chief of one of the most influential Dyula families, seized power in a bloody coup directed against the ruling **Falafala-Senoufo** incumbents. The new kings of Kong were constantly in dispute with the Bamana of Ségou and the peoples of the south. As a political entity, Kong ceased to have much cohesion by the early nineteenth century. But it was still a prestigious centre as late as 1897, when Samory Touré swept in – and then moved on having all but destroyed the town in his scorched-earth flight from the French.

Parc National de la Comoé

The **Parc National de la Comoé** is the largest in West Africa – 11,500 square kilometres of rolling, tsetse-plagued savannah and bush with patches of forest in the south. As late as the 1950s colonial maps marked the region "uninhabited", and while this wasn't quite true (the Lobi and Koulango hunted and planted there, and continue to do so despite the rangers), it's basically wild animal territory. And the animals know it.

The main feature of the park (which is also known as the **Réserve de Bouna**) is the broad and twisting **Comoé River**, flanked by stretches of riverine forest. Seasonal streams flow in from the north and the generous scattering of lakes and pools across the park provides animal-viewing targets in the dry season. The zones to concentrate on are westwards; the eastern borders of the park are included more as a buffer against human encroachment than as recommended game country.

Visiting the park

The park is generally **open** from December to the end of May (but check in Ferké, Katiola or Bondoukou before setting off, just in case). Entry (CFA2000 per person per day) in the north is through Kafolo or Ouango Fitini, in the south Gansé or Kakpin, and in the east Bania.

The most enjoyable way to see Comoé is from a **private car**, with a ranger on board to navigate and scan for wildlife. There are no facilities inside the park, so you need to plan ahead to avoid retracing your route, or else aim to cross the park, most rewardingly north to south (or south to north). While the east may be worth exploring at the beginning of the park season, when the animals are dispersed, if you're here after the end of January you're best advised to stay fairly close to the main river.

If you've **no transport**, Kafolo is the place to head for, though the visit is still likely to cost you dear.

Kafolo

KAFOLO is hard by the Comoé bridge right on the park boundary. You can **stay** at the *Comoé Safari Lodge* (Dec–May only; ④); pretty good, with cool, pyramid-shaped rooms, a fine swimming pool and some imaginative, if expensive, cooking (including homemade bread). The construction of the lodge disturbed some old middens: you can find pots and other scraps of domestic Lobi life all around the perimeter. There might be less expensive accommodation at the *Maquis Chez M le Maire* (①), which has been known to put up travellers in rustic *chambres de passage*-type rooms. Kafolo has a few **snack and chop sellers** where your food may well come wrapped in the chits you signed at the lodge.

Subject to four or more takers, **game-drives** round the northwestern corner of the park run from Kafolo every morning (CFA10,000). What you see is very dependent on luck, but on a good run you should see buffalo and elephants and possibly lions. Hippos are nearly guaranteed (afternoon *pirogue* rides, also arranged in the lodge, afford the best opportunities to get close up). At the very least there'll be antelope (great numbers of hartebeest), warthogs and monkeys. Persuade the driver to make a diversion to **Lake Dalandjougou** – a major dry season watering place. You'll be out from 6am until at least 11am, so take fluids and something to eat.

If you're travelling without a car, you may well strike lucky anyway and get a free lift into the park. They don't see many backpackers out here, and there's at least a good chance of a ride out again with tourists or a tour group.

Gansé and Kakpin

On the southwest perimeter of the park, **GANSÉ** and nearby **KAKPIN** are not at all easy to get to without your own vehicle. Access from the southeast is from Bondoukou (see p.603), some 170km away, and from the southwest from Bouaké (180km; see p.584) or, with less *piste*, Katiola (160km; see p.587).

The big draw in the 150 square kilometres of bush and forest between Kakpin, Gansé and the river (known as **"Kakpin triangle"**), is the singular presence of lions. There's a good network of tracks here, too. You need sharp eyes, binoculars and patience. Keep stopping to scan around (remember to look behind you) and take notice of the behaviour of prey animals like hartebeest and warthog.

Kakpin's **accommodation** is a simple *campement* (①), with S/C huts and a sometime bar-restaurant. Gansé has the *Comoé Sogetel* (④), an all-in lodge along the same lines as *Comoé Safari Lodge* and similarly priced, but styled, with cubist abandon, on local architecture.

The Lobi country and Bouna

In Côte d'Ivoire, **traditional Lobi territory** begins somewhere along the road from Ferkessédougou towards the Parc National de la Comoé (the people and their culture are covered in more depth in the Burkina Faso chapter). Until you reach Kafolo, however, you won't see any Lobi compounds, as the whole area is part of the Muslim domain of Kong. The easiest way to get an impression of Lobi life is to take an excursion from *Comoé Safari Lodge* in Kafolo (see p.601) up the road to **Bolé** village. The market here (on a five-day cycle) is a gathering place for a wonderful diversity of people (mostly women) who come to buy and sell. Among the Dyula, Koulango and Senoufo, you'll even meet a few Fula women – though perhaps not all year round.

But the chief purpose of the *Safari Lodge*'s four-hour "Tour Lobi" (CFA8000) is a visit to a compound – a *soukala* – on the way to Bolé, usually one where the guide has friends or family; the chance to look around the organically sculpted, rectangular, mud-built houses around a central courtyard; and the opportunity to meet some Lobi people – including elderly ladies who dutifully arrive, lip plugs in place, to sit and be photographed. You get to poke around in private homes and climb up notched tree trunks onto the roof terraces. The whole event reeks of forced welcomes, and the impression of smiling tourists hurling sweets at the naked children through the windows of the minibus (an established ritual) is hard to stomach. Nevertheless, if you're not set up for independent travel well off the beaten track between Kafolo and Bouna (the Lobi heartland), then the tour is probably worthwhile. Take a Polaroid camera if you can.

The **heartland of the Lobi region** in Côte d'Ivoire (their main districts are in Burkina) lies to the north of the Bouna road. At the park ranger post at **Téhini** (where there's a Monday market), try for a vehicle on a Wednesday, or early Thursday morning up to **DOROPO**, whose Thursday market and location on a crossroads close to the Burkinabe border make it a major rural centre. It's a surprisingly active town, especially at weekends when the open-air bar on the main street jumps to the sounds of highlife. At the opposite end of the street, the *Restaurant Sénégalais* serves decent food and has *chambres de passage* (①).

The time to get the most out of a trip up here would be during the **Djoro** – the moveable initiation of boys to men which takes place every six to ten years for all the uninitiated boys who are big enough to stand the rigours. The rites of passage are fairly secret, but there's no mystery about the celebration that concludes them, when the boys return home decked in cowrie-covered costumes.

Bouna and beyond

Originally a Lobi town, **BOUNA** is nowadays a workaday mixture of Koulango, Dyula and administrators from the south. It lacks a strong ethnic or religious identity: the Eglise Baptiste is a stone's throw from the mosque and fetishes of the market; rows of cinderblock houses topped with corrugated metal bear the stamp of an anonymous crossroads. Bouna suffers and benefits from being the country's remotest outpost. Chokingly dusty in the dry season and so muddy in the wet it's almost cut off, it has never quite recovered from the savagery of Samory Touré's full frontal assault in 1892.

Today it's a garrison town and capital of the country's biggest *département*. Bush taxis pull into the central square surrounded by single-storey shops and **gargotes** such as *Au Sable*, which serves beer until the last vehicle of the night pulls in from Ferké. For **accommodation**, the inexpensive *Hôtel Eléphant* (①–②), 100m from the *gare routière*, has clean and fresh rooms with optional AC and S/C. Slightly upmarket, the *Hôtel La Réserve* (②) is over by the market, and easily distinguished by its pseudo-Sudanic tower. Rooms are clean and comfortable with AC throughout, and the hotel also houses the town's only **nightclub** (open Saturdays and holidays) and a *maquis* that will prepare food if given advance warning. Bouna's permanent **market** is busy and interesting, spilling over with unusual trinketry and magical paraphernalia as well as the usual pots and pans and a rather limited selection of fruit and vegetables (seasonal commodities this far north).

If you're staying for a day, there are some particularly good examples of Lobi architecture at **Pouon**, 18km northeast of Bouna. You should be able to get transport there several times a week, or charter a taxi. But you won't make it across the Koulda River (a tributary of the Volta Noire) in the rainy season – and even if you do, you might not get back again.

South from Bouna, the road along the eastern boundary of the Comoé park (transport to Bondoukou mornings and afternoons for around CFA3000) passes through desolate regions cleared of human inhabitants. Run-down and abandoned Lobi *soukalas* seem to indicate mass migration or expulsion – or maybe, in the dry season, simply that people are away on Lobi business. Traditionally the Lobi were quite nomadic, returning to their homesteads only periodically. Between the park ranger posts at Bania and Kotouba, however, the road tracks dustily through wild bush, with never a compound.

Continuing south, the desolation of the far northeast is left behind. Beyond the village of Saleye, the land begins to rise and the road passes through fine, hilly forest and dense cultivation on the approach to Bondoukou. On the east side of the road, some 10km beyond **Yézimala**, a group of impressive **Abron tombs**, inhabited by life-size plaster figures, signals the start of a new cultural zone. If you're coming in by public transport, Bondoukou's northside *gare routière* is just a few minutes beyond here.

Bondoukou and around

Set amid rising hills which hint at the forests further south, **BONDOUKOU** has a distinctive flavour, a long-established centre of Islamic studies with an old Koranic university and now some forty mosques. The town also has a heavy Ghanaian population, who, along with the culturally related Abron community, help to knock off some of the Ivoirian brashness and also provide strong alternative religious counterpoints to the town's Islam. Despite its dust (or mud) and a real shortage of decent places to stay, it's a likeable town and worth a day or two, especially as a base for making several worthwhile **short excursions** to the surrounding countryside.

The Town

Architecturally, Bondoukou's most striking attribute is the exotically pink **Ancien Marché** building, in the centre of town and visible all the way up the approach road from Abidjan. Its appearance belies its history, however; built in the colonial style *soudanais* by the French in 1952, it served briefly as a civic museum, before the collection was moved to Abidjan, and now no one seems to know what to do with the building. They do have dance performances here periodically.

More authentic is the **Maison de Samory** (yet another) – not actually one of the leader's abodes, but once inhabited by a fellow Touré. It has a massive, fortress-like appearance and a flat, increasingly decrepit, roof, reached up a flight of steep stairs (watch your step). Below, in the street, **metalworkers** turn out bracelets and rings for local consumption – painstaking and surprisingly earnest labour.

Another surviving historical fragment is the hut of **Goudougou** or Boutougou, the Lobi or Loron-Koulango hunter and semi-mythical founder of Bondoukou. The hut, according to Bondoukou civic tradition, has been preserved to this day; a curious mud case in an open compound down below the Abidjan *gare routière*.

The market

The best day to visit Bondoukou's **Grand Marché** is Sunday, when people come from the dozens of farming villages in the hills around. For the rest of the week the market, though imposing in its purpose-built two-storey hall, is like any other, except that, unusually for West Africa, it's full of the most amazing selection of secondhand clothes.

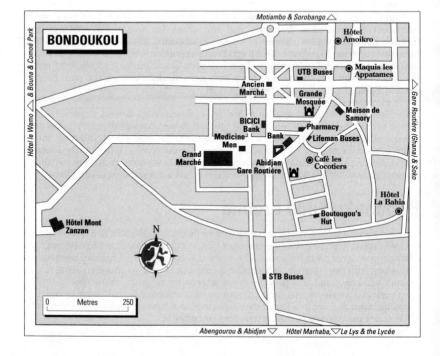

BONDOUKOU IN HISTORY

Whatever the real date of the first settlement in Bondoukou (probably in the fifteenth century), the **mosques** began to be built quite a lot later with the arrival in the 1800s of Mande-speaking Dyula from the north. Few of those you see today were built before the turn of this century and many have gone up since World War II, as the town's **old quarters**, each with its own **gate** and built entirely in the style of the Touré house, have been progressively replaced by concrete and *tôle* (at one time, there was even a cloth-dyers' quarter, with dye pits and all). The oldest surviving mosque in town has a square minaret, a portion of which stands behind its modern-day descendant in a slumped lateritic pyramid, like a termite hill. This relic goes back to the nineteenth century and may be the last of the mosques of the Dyula era.

Also in the nineteenth century, Akan-speaking people – the **Abron** – began arriving from the east. With some administrative and military efficiency they succeeded in establishing themselves as the region's overlords. Unusually, however, many families adopted **Islam** and the language of the Koulango inhabitants and, today, the Abron kingdom is one of the most Islamicized and deracinated of all the Akan societies.

By the end of the nineteenth century, **King Ardjoumani** of the Abron was in contact with the rulers of the British Gold Coast (flushed with their victory over the Asante – see p.734). But the French, as usual, were quicker to take the initiative, and they entered into agreement with the Abron and later annexed the kingdom for France. Meanwhile, **Samory Touré**'s gale-force transit through Bondoukou in 1895 largely wrecked the district's economic stability; thousands of families fled east and south out of his way. Bondoukou never fully recovered its pre-eminent position, and was left in the economic wilderness by its proximity to the British frontier and by the new **railway**, which had reached as far as Bouaké by 1912 and which sucked trade away.

Nearby, traditional "pharmacists" (**medicine men** is probably a fair term) stand at stalls overflowing with a cornucopia of python skins, baby crocodile and viper heads, dried chameleons, baboons' feet, shrivelled bats, hyenas' genitals, skins of countless small mammals, turtle shells, bones, tails, tufts, feathers and beaks; and then leather *gri-gris*, amulets, bracelets, beads, bark, fibres, stones, crystals and powders. They even have old British coins (Victorian shillings, for example) from Gold Coast days. These traders rarely speak French, and bargaining with tourists isn't their strong point.

Practicalities

Gares routières for the north and for Ghana are several kilometres out of the town centre; take an orange taxi. Vehicles coming in from Abidjan and the south, however, will stop at the *gare routière* or the Lifeman bus station right in the middle of town.

Accommodation options are rather limited, especially at budget level. In town, the budget choice is *La Bahia* (①), an almost respectable *chambres de passage*, but note that the AC rooms are scruffier than the simple ventilated ones and the place is a real thrash at weekends. Out of town on Route de Bouna, you can stay at the *Hotel Le Wamo* (☎92 55 68; ①) which, though a long way out, has clean, well-furnished S/C rooms only marginally costlier than those at *La Bahia*. The *Hôtel Amoikro* (BP 184; ☎92 53 80; ①–②), out of town on the Route Sorobango, is a decent place with S/C, AC rooms, bar and restaurant, while more luxurious accommodation can be found near the *lycée* at the *Hôtel Marhaba* (☎92 55 09; ③–④), which has modern, carpeted AC rooms and suites plus a swimming pool, restaurant and bar.

As for **eating**, Bondoukou offers plenty of street food, but nothing more sophisticated for a sit-down meal than a clutch of *maquis*. The best of the bunch are *Les*

Appatames, set in a large garden with excellent grilled chicken and *kedjenou*, and, a bit further out, *Le Lys*, on Route d'Abidjan, opposite the *lycée*. At breakfast time, the *Café Les Cocotiers* near the Abidjan *gare routière* does bread and generous bowls of coffee.

Around Bondoukou

Most famous of the many sights clustered around Bondoukou is the village of **SOKO**, right on the Ghanaian border, 8km from town. Soko is a **monkey village**, where the local vervets are especially tame and demanding; harmed – let alone eaten – by nobody. The story goes that in 1895, with Samory's forces ransacking the district, the people of Soko turned to their fetish priest for help. He transformed them into monkeys but he himself was killed by the invaders and the monkeys were powerless to become humans again. Tradition requires that the people of Soko now treat the monkeys as their relatives. It's interesting to guess at how such a story came to be invented: the likeliest explanation is that most of the inhabitants fled the village, or were killed or sold into slavery, and the pride of survivors demanded an alternative explanation.

Take your passport to Soko, as you have to pass through a police checkpoint. Take some food for the monkeys, too, and try to come early in the morning, before the monkeys retreat to the forest to hide through the heat of the day. The whole place has become a bit gimmicky of late, and the monkeys tend to stay in the centre of the village where they've come to expect food from visitors. You'll be asked to pay CFA6000 to see them, but this can be avoided if you don't come in a large tourist group.

Northeast from Bondoukou, **MOTIAMBO** (8km on the Sorobango road, turn right at the "lion house") is a good village to visit if you're after local pottery. The technique is the great thing; work is done by hand, not on a wheel, and they **dance** around the work to fashion it. Potting is generally done on Wednesday and Thursday and firing on Friday in time for Bondoukou's Sunday market. If you go on to **SOROBANGO** (29km from Bondoukou), you'll find more potters, Koulango weavers, an old mosque and (somewhere) plates embedded in the walls – an Islamic style rarely found in this part of Africa.

Akan country: Abengourou and beyond

The route from Bondoukou to Abengourou is along a brilliant, twisting forest road studded with the amazing figurative **Akan tombs**. There's a fine set down on the left of the road (beyond a cemetery on the right) as you leave the village of **Aprompronou**, 25km south of Agnibilekrou.

Abengourou

ABENGOUROU is solidly Akan – both culturally and linguistically. Royal capital of the **Agni** kingdom of **Indénié**, it's of the south, firmly engaged with metropolitan Côte d'Ivoire, and, if you've come from sparser northern regions, offers a first taste of a big Ivoirian town.

The Agni left the Akan homeland around Kumasi in the eighteenth century and moved west to set up a new community with its capital at Zaranou, 40km to the south of the present site. Abengourou seems to have been established by a part of the royal family about a hundred years ago in a zone of good hunting country they named

N'pekro ("I don't like chatter") for its tranquillity, from which the present name was Frenchified.

Orientation
The town spreads widely, though its heart is compact, with many of the restaurants and most other commerce on the main paved street, **rue Principale**, which runs from the water tower to the market. **Banks** are on the east end of this street; only BICICI and BIAO change non-franc currencies, and even then you can't be certain that they'll have the current rates.

Accommodation
Hôtel Forêt, rue Principale (☎91 34 88). Central location and very decent standards, some rooms with balconies overlooking the action, and one room with AC. ①–②.

Hôtel Goma, rte de Bondoukou by the *gare routière* (BP 1187; ☎91 34 76). New and upmarket with AC rooms including TV and video. Good restaurant. ③.

Hôtel Relais Agni, rte d'Abidjan (BP 322; ☎91 35 75). The town's best value, with very friendly staff and large AC rooms. ②.

Hôtel le Relief, 200m south of rue Principale, Dioulokro (☎91 36 32). Actually respectable, though very cheap S/C rooms with fan or AC. ①–②.

The Town
Abengourou's recently relocated **market** is great, a (never threatening) warren of packed stalls and dark alleys and masses of possibilities if you're looking for crafts and locally manufactured items – from the smallest size of **daba** (digging hoe) forged virtually before your eyes to children's play-kitchen sets made of old tuna cans, and very inexpensive leatherwork.

Nearby, the **royal palace** (built 1883, restored 1988), a big oblong villa with wooden balconies running right round, isn't a remarkable sight. The large courtyard in front, however, is the scene of serious ritual and festivity each year in December or January, when the **Yam Festival** (*la fête des ignames*) takes place and astonishing quantities of gold and finery are on display. It may be possible to arrange an audience with the recently appointed king. Make an appointment with local officials, dress as smartly as possible, and take something as a gift: postcards of other royal families seem appropriate and welcome, but a bottle of Scotch goes down just as well. The best time for an audience is usually between noon and 3pm.

Another site of interest is the **museum/art gallery** (Mon–Sat 8am–noon & 3–6pm, Sun 8am–2pm; free), which has ambitions to be a regional showcase. However, the banality of putting masks and statues around a room strikes forcibly. Out of context they lose most of their meaning, and many of the pieces are in urgent need of woodworm treatment. Most interesting of the ethnographia are the Senoufo crime-detection statuettes with headdresses and swivelling arms for seeking out culprits, though it's not quite clear how they worked.

Eating
The best option for good street **food** is the endless string of *maquis* behind the water tower. Take your pick from the array of stalls for *foutou*, *atieké* or rice. You can find moderately cheap fare, including *agouti*, at the *Maquis Desiree* near the *Hôtel Relais Agni*. For something fancier, head to the *Maquis Elogne* on rue Principale where they serve sandwiches and salads or more substantial meals with chicken. Another step up is the highly recommended *Cave des Rois* on rue Principale (☎91 37 28), a large *maquis* with colourful wall murals and indoor or outdoor eating. The *poisson braisé* is great, and the **nightclub** among the town's best.

South from Abengourou

Several companies have scheduled bus departures **to Abidjan** (4hr) all day from rue Principale in Abengourou. Having bought your ticket, you can sit in a waiting room with a television for the next departure.

Since the road was tarmacked, the alternative route, via Aboisso, is no longer much used except by local traffic. But if you make an early start from Abengourou, this dirt road, which stays on the east side of the Comoé close to the Ghanaian border, features some exciting jungle scenery. You could stop off at the old Indénié capital of **Zaranou**, where there's a small museum originally conceived as a memorial to Binger, who spent a total of three years here. The nice little town of **Aboisso** itself – site of France's earliest (late seventeenth century) base in the country – is also worth a stay.

BURKINA FASO

BURKINA FASO

There are few such unlucky countries as **Burkina Faso**. But for a twist of administrative fate in colonial times, it would never have existed. It is desperately, and famously, poor, with an almost total lack of raw materials or natural resources. Although it shares its landlocked predicament with Niger and Mali, unlike them it lacks direct access to the important trans-Saharan routes. And its experiments with radical forms of government, under young and ideological leadership, have unfortunately cost it dear in terms of foreign relations and investment.

Added to these national difficulties are several superficial disadvantages from the traveller's point of view: the country is unremittingly flat, and offers little of the natural spectacle and traditional cultural colour of its neighbours; it has a bare minimum of places to stay and roads to travel on; and it suffers from an image problem in the foreign press which acts as an unreasonable deterrent.

Despite all this, however, most visitors really enjoy Burkina. Although there are endless military checkpoints throughout the country, soldiers and customs agents treat you with respect, and even familiarity, as they venture a "Bonne arrivée, ça va?" while verifying your passport. For all the slogging poverty, there's a climate of youthful **optimism**, and you'll encounter a refreshing lack of complexes and a vital popular culture. Getting business done is perhaps no easier than anywhere else, but as a place to travel, or simply hang out, Burkina leaves a good taste with most visitors.

People

With some sixty different language groups, Burkina has the usual West African ethno-linguistic mosaic. But most Burkinabe (Burkinabè is also used, but not Burkinabé) speak languages of the large Voltaic group, and the country is unusual in having an

---

FACTS AND FIGURES

The country's official name, **Burkina Faso** is a hybrid of a More word meaning dignity-nobility-integrity and a Dioula word meaning homeland. The name, changed in 1984 from Haute Volta (Upper Volta), and commonly abbreviated to Burkina, thus means roughly "Land of the Honourable".

With an **area** of 275,000 square kilometres, the country is slightly larger than Great Britain and slightly smaller than the state of Nevada. Nearly all flat, most of it is swathed in semi-arid **grasslands**. The further north you go, the drier things become until you arrive at the denuded **Sahelian landscapes** of the extreme north. Only in the southern regions of Banfora and the Lobi country will you find much greenery. Around Banfora, the forests are run through by streams that fall in striking waterfalls from the cliffs. Although the Volta Blanche, Volta Rouge and Volta Noire rivers all rise in Burkina, only the Volta Noire flows in the dry season. The three meet up much further south in Ghana where they form a navigable river the Portuguese called *Rio da Volta*, or "River of Return".

Burkina's **population** numbers perhaps ten million people, around 500,000 of whom live in the capital, Ouagadougou. Since 1991 it has had a constitutional democracy (though political participation has not always appeared too free), which replaced the military regime. On the economic front, Burkina's **foreign debts** total above £800 million ($1.3 billion), which is nearly double the value of its annual exports of goods and services – but it's still a piffling amount in international terms, less than the cost of an aircraft carrier for example.

	Jan	Feb	Mar	April	May	June	July	Aug	Sept	Oct	Nov	Dec
AVERAGE TEMPERATURES AND RAINFALL												
					OUAGADOUGOU							
Temperatures °C												
Min (night)	16	20	23	26	26	24	23	22	23	23	22	17
Max (day)	33	37	40	39	38	36	33	31	32	35	36	35
Rainfall mm	0	3	13	15	84	122	203	277	145	33	0	0
Days with rainfall	0	1	1	2	6	9	12	14	11	3	0	0
					BOBO-DIOULASSO							
Temperatures °C												
Min (night)	18	21	23	24	24	22	21	21	21	21	20	18
Max (day)	33	34	35	35	34	31	30	29	31	32	34	32
Rainfall mm	3	5	28	54	119	124	253	310	219	65	18	0
					GOROM-GOROM							
Temperatures °C												
Min (night)	12	17	22	26	28	26	25	23	25	25	18	15
Max (day)	32	35	38	42	41	38	36	33	38	38	35	32

overwhelming majority of a single people, the More-speaking **Mossi**, who live in the central plains around Ouagadougou, and make up over half the population. They are related to the **Gourmantché,** who live in the east around Fada-Ngourma, and less closely to the Grusi or Gourounsi from around Pô and Léo.

Main peoples of the north include the **Fula**, the **Hausa** and the **Bella**. Near the northwestern border with Mali, live small enclaves of **Dogon, Samos** and **Pana**. In the south, different **Bobo** peoples – Bwaba, Kos and Siby – populate the area around Bobo-Dioulasso. The **Senoufo** occupy the southwestern tip near Côte d'Ivoire and Mali, while the **Lobi**, towards the border with Ghana, remain one of the most isolated peoples in the country.

Burkina's population has suffered greatly over the last two or three generations. It was from the region of the Upper Volta that the French recruited much of the **labour** to work plantations in their Côte d'Ivoire colony, and the Burkinabe continue to look south for work in relatively prosperous Côte d'Ivoire as the land at home becomes impoverished. Burkina has been one of the countries most blighted by the recurrent Sahel droughts and it remains a main focus of many aid and development agencies.

Where to go

Specific targets for travel include **Bobo-Dioulasso** ("Bobo"), which is unquestionably one of the most attractive cities in West Africa; the hilly and prettily wooded **Banfora region** in the southwest; and the remote and fascinating **Lobi country** in the south with its mysterious stone ruins. The appeal of the capital, **Ouagadougou** ("Ouaga"), isn't especially strong, but a visit here benefits from some background knowledge of the venerable **Mossi kingdoms**, of which Ouagadougou was formerly one of several in the central region. Ouagadougou also has a major attraction in the FESPACO festival of African film held every odd-numbered year in February.

Climate

Burkina's climate is characterized by two main seasons. The **rains** last from June to October, with violent storms gathering quickly, inundating everything and blowing

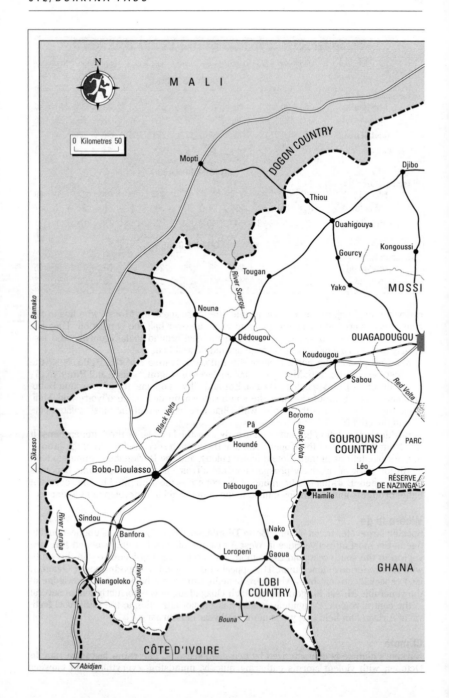

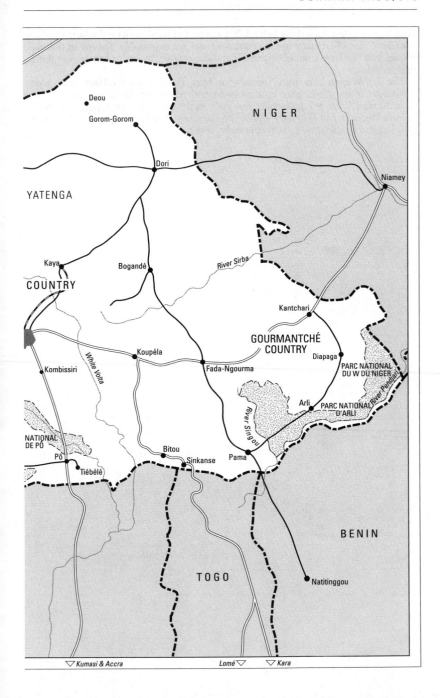

away to leave clear blue skies behind. It's a period of hard work on the farms and, for travellers, one when many of the country's *pistes* are impassable. Except on the main routes, you can have trouble getting around the country by car or *taxi brousse* during this period.

The **dry season** lasts from November to May. This is when the **Harmattan** blows across the country, whipping up dust and smothering everything in a dreary ochre haze. At night it can get quite chilly, especially in the north. The **best period to travel** is from December to February – after the rains have finished, but before the ground gets hot and temperatures reach oppressive levels.

Arrivals

Burkina is a great West African travel cross-roads, with main highways from Niger, Benin, Togo and Ghana converging on Ouagadougou, and roads from Mali and Côte d'Ivoire meeting at Bobo-Dioulasso. Transport on these axes is relatively good. Air links, apart from the regular services from Abidjan, are weaker.

■ Flights from Africa

There are flights almost daily to **Ouagadougou** from Abidjan, but other West African capitals have flights only two or three times a week at most. Air Burkina (VH) flights usually stop at **Bobo-Dioulasso** before going on to Ouagadougou.

Air Afrique (RK) has direct flights once a week from **Bamako**, **Dakar**, **Abidjan** and **Cotonou**, as well as weekly flights from **Libreville** via **Lomé** and Abidjan; from Bamako via Abidjan; and from Dakar via Bamako. It also flies direct from **Niamey** twice a week, and from Niamey via Abidjan weekly.

Air Burkina (VH) flies from Abidjan to Ouagadougou via **Bobo-Dioulasso** three times a week; from **Lomé** non-stop weekly; and once a week from **Bamako**, from **Cotonou** and from **Lomé** – all via Bobo.

Lastly, Air Ivoire (VU) flies non-stop from **Abidjan** to Ouagadougou three times a week.

There are no direct flights to Ouagadougou from Banjul, Bissau or Conakry: in most cases Abidjan offers the best connection.

There are no direct flights from **east and southern Africa**: again, the best connections are via Abidjan.

■ Overland

Burkinabe borders, with the exception of the Côte d'Ivoire border, often close from 6pm to 7am. Otherwise these border crossings are some of the most travelled and straightforward in the region.

The details in these practical information pages are essentially for use on the ground in West Africa and in Burkina itself: for full details on preparing for a trip, getting here from outside the region, paperwork, health, information sources and more, see Basics, p.3–83.

From Niger

A 499-kilometre surfaced road links **Niamey** with Ouagadougou via Fada-Ngourma. *Taxis brousse* and buses regularly make the trip in about 12 hours. Fares range from around CFA6000–12,000, depending on the vehicle.

From Mali

The usual routes from Mali are from **Bamako** to Bobo-Dioulasso via Sikasso, or from **Mopti** to Bobo (via San). Once a week there's a reasonably comfortable bus from Bamako to Bobo, but taxis run along each of these routes regularly and take about 12 hours in good conditions. The latter route is all surfaced; but Sikasso to Bobo (168km) is very rough *piste* in parts, and periodically washed out during the rains, when it's necessary to do a big detour north via Koutiala (345km). Fares range from around CFA5000–10,000, depending on the vehicle.

It's also possible to come down through the **Dogon country** via Koro. There's no regular *taxi brousse* service on this route, and it's often well-nigh impassable during the rains. If you don't have your own vehicle, you will be dependent on passing tourists or goods trucks. You can't rush this approach, but it gives an interesting first perspective on Burkina through Ouahigouya and the historic Yatenga region.

From Côte d'Ivoire

The privately owned Société des Chemins de Fer du Burkina (SCFB) and the Société Ivoirienne des Chemins de Fer (SICF), created out of the old consortium, the Régie du Chemin de Fer Abidjan-Niger (RAN), run the daily train from **Abidjan** to Ouagadougou via Bobo-Dioulasso. The trip is scheduled to take about 30 hours and sleeping cabins are available. With departure from Abidjan around 10.30am, you cross the border in the middle of the night to arrive in Bobo in the early morning and Ouagadougou, in theory, early afternoon.

The bus and bush taxi alternatives to the train are generally a little faster and competitive on price, and the 1224-kilometre road is in reasonable condition. Note that the routes through the Lobi country in the northeast are very lightly trafficked and transport there mostly depends on markets on five-day cycles.

From Ghana

Taxis and Ghana State Transport Corporation (STC) buses run to Ouagadougou from **Kumasi** via **Tamale**. From **Accra**, you can take a "direct" bus to Ouaga, spending the night at the Bolgatanga bus station, as the border closes at 6pm, and continuing the next morning around 7am. Otherwise, you can change buses in Kumasi to Bolgatanga, and find transport from there across the border. The 977-kilometre road between Accra and Ouagadougou is good on the (short) Burkina stretch, but poor in Ghana. Allow 24–26 hours.

If you are crossing at the Hamile border, note that transport to Ouaga becomes scarce on the Burkina side, just one *taxi brousse* leaving early in the morning each day for the ten-hour plus journey (CFA9000).

From Togo

Bush taxis ply regularly between **Lomé** and Ouagadougou. They take about 20 hours to cover the 967 kilometres and cost around CFA16,000. As usual, you'll save money by changing vehicles between countries (in this case about CFA5000), but you'll have to spend the night in Dapaong. The surfaced road is in general good as far as the Burkina border where it is in a deteriorated condition as far as Koupéla.

From Benin

The usual route from **Cotonou** is via Lomé. If you're coming from northern Benin, vehicles link Natitingou with Fada-Ngourma where you can change for Ouagadougou.

Red Tape

Visas for Burkina are required by everyone except nationals of ECOWAS countries. Burkinabe embassies are few and far between, but in many countries where Burkina lacks representation, the French embassy can process the visa.

■ Visas for onward travel

Although there are relatively few diplomatic missions in Ouagadougou, the **French embassy** handles visas for several West and Central African countries (see p.641). Note that they don't take care of visas for Benin, Niger, Cameroon or Guinea, none of which have representation in Ouagadougou. The consulate in the Canadian embassy handles the affairs of Commonwealth citizens and may be able to issue visas for The Gambia.

Money and Costs

Burkina Faso is part of the CFA zone (CFA100 = 1 French franc; approx CFA900 = £1; approx CFA560 = US$1). In Ouagadougou and Bobo-Dioulasso, you'll have little trouble changing travellers' cheques or cash (French francs are best) although banks can be fussy in other towns, for example refusing to change travellers' cheques without the original receipt.

Banks in small towns in the extreme north of the country may refuse to change even cash, including FF, although if you're in a fix, you can usually pay for transport and commodities with French currency. The major banks in towns throughout the country are the Banque Internationale pour le Commerce, l'Industrie et l'Agriculture (BICIA) and the Banque Internationale du Burkina (BIB).

Credit cards are not widely accepted. You will find Visa and Amex of some use for expensive hotels and travel services in Ouagadougou and, to an even more limited extent, in Bobo-Dioulasso. If you're taking a Visa card, it's worth knowing that to get a cash advance on it in Burkina can be very difficult (try BICIA). With Access/MasterCard you will have an even harder time getting a cash advance as most banks, even in the larger cities, no longer accept MasterCard. If you get in a fix, try the major hotels.

■ Costs

Prices in Burkina are reasonable and even Ouagadougou is inexpensive. Rooms in budget hotels around the country will cost you from CFA3000–6000. Eating street food, you can fill up on *riz sauce* or *tô* for as little as CFA300. Transport costs are also reasonable, ranging from CFA7–20 per kilometre (rarely more), depending on whether the road is paved or *piste* and the type of vehicle.

Health

You'll need a yellow fever vaccination certificate in Burkina as elsewhere in West Africa. During outbreaks of cholera, you may (unpredictably) need that certificate too.

Tap water is treated in Bobo-Dioulasso and Ouagadougou. It smells of chlorine, but otherwise is drinkable. In the bush, progress has been made on water purity, but some supplies are still dubious. If you have any doubts, use purifying tablets. The only other real worry is **bilharzia**. Except around Bobo, where a number of bodies of water are clean, you should be careful of swimming, especially where the water is stagnant or grassy.

Note that Burkina has one of the world's highest incidences of onchocerciasis and whole villages have been evacuated where this **river blindness** has run its course (notably near streams where the *simulium* blackflies breed). A giant WHO project is wiping out the disease and allowing the resettlement of these areas. Oncho rarely affects short-stay visitors.

Maps and Information

In recent years, the government has promoted Burkina Faso in quite a big way. However, there are no overseas tourist offices as such. The best map of the country is that published by the Institut Géographique du Burkina, after the style of the French IGN maps. It's available anywhere that stocks IGN.

In Ouagadougou, the Institut Géographique du Burkina has good city maps of Ouaga and Bobo. For tourist information, branches of the Office National du Tourisme Burkinabe (ONTB) in Ouagadougou and Bobo-Dioulasso can be helpful. An IGN National Parks map, covering Burkina, Niger and Benin, is also useful.

Getting Around

With the exception of the Lobi country near the Ghanaian border, a decent road system connects Ouaga with most places in the south of Burkina. The north is still a problem area, however, and many towns are virtually impossible to get to during the rainy season.

■ Bush taxis, trucks and buses

Bush taxis are usually 504 *breaks* (estate cars/station wagons) or 404 *bâchés* with boarded-up back ends. The latter are cheaper and, given the level of comfort, rightly so. You won't see much of the countryside in them unless you arrange to have a seat in the cab – a possibility that a small supplement usually fixes.

A far better option are the numerous **private bus companies** which have been springing up in Burkina Faso over the past few years. Competitive prices, less hassle at highway checkpoints and greater comfort (some even have AC) make these the preferred choice. The ones you will come across most frequently are STMB, SOGEBAF, TRANSMIF, Rakieta, STWS, Sans Frontières and SOTRAO – each usually with their separate bus stations and all fairly reliable. The Régie X9, formerly the largest bus company in Burkina, is also present in some locations, but quickly being phased out.

Routes, frequencies and sample fares

There's plenty of traffic along the main *route nationale* axis Banfora–Bobo–Ouagadou –Fada–Ngourma, and frequent enough vehicles north to Ouahigouya and Dori and south to Pô. It's only when trying to get to more remote northern towns – or to other isolated areas such as the Lobi country – that you might experience long waits for vehicles (several days in some cases).

Ouaga–Bobo, 360km, CFA4000, many daily (5hr);

Ouaga–Fada-Ngourma, 234km, CFA3000, three times a week (4hr);

Ouaga–Gaoua, 385km paved to Pâ (halfway), CFA5000, three times a week (8–9hr);

Ouaga–Gorom-Gorom, 300km paved as far as Dori, CFA4000, three times a week (8–9hr);

Ouaga–Ouahigouya, 182km, CFA2000, daily (3–4hr);

Ouaga–Pô, 142km, CFA2000, daily (3hr).

■ Car and bike rental

You'll find **car rental** agencies in Ouagadougou and Bobo-Dioulasso (see the "Listings" for those towns), and they are not excessively expensive.

But it's more economical, and potentially much more satisfying, to rent a **bicycle**, **mobylette** (**moped**) or **motorbike**. This is an excellent way to see the sights around Ouagadougou, Bobo-Dioulasso and Banfora: you'll find people around the market places who rent out machines. You can even transport these rentals on the roofs of *taxis brousse* – an extra cost, but worth it for mobility in the more remote areas.

■ Trains

The Ouagadougou–Abidjan Express train runs, in theory, daily via Koudougou, Bobo-Dioulasso, Banfora and Niangoloko – the Burkinabe border post. Check prices and arrival/departure times by calling the SCFB (in Ouagadougou ☎30.60.47 or 30.60.48) or visiting the *gare chemin de fer* in

Ouaga. Another line runs north from Ouaga as far as Kaya (weekly service on Saturday).

■ Internal flights

On its outward and return flights to/from Abidjan, Bamako, Cotonou and Lomé, Air Burkina flies most days between **Ouagadougou** and **Bobo**.

Accommodation

Ouagadougou and Bobo-Dioulasso have their fair share of international class hotels, invariably full during the big festivals (see p.621). But in any town smaller than Koudougou, the country's third largest, accommodation is much more basic. In smaller towns, especially in the extreme north, electricity and running water are luxuries. Hotel rates carry VAT of ten percent, included in our prices.

A network of **auberges populaires** has been set up by the Ministry of the Environment and Tourism, which has put at least a basic hotel in each of Burkina's thirty main towns.

Off the few beaten tracks, **staying with people** is a viable and recommended option. In the bush, so too is **camping**: much of the country is ideal.

Eating and Drinking

The staples in Burkina are rice and millet. After grinding, the rice or millet is boiled and made into a mush known as *tô*. One of the most common sauces to accompany *tô* is made from cassava (manioc) leaves with palm oil, fresh fish and seasonings. Gumbo (okra) is another common sauce base.

Despite its drought-land reputation, most towns in Burkina have an array of **street food** and throughout the country, you'll find women selling bean or banana fritters, yam chips, fried fish and brochettes.

■ Drinking

Nationally brewed **beers** include SOBRA, Brakina and Flag. You may be offered the unopened bottle to see if it's cold enough.

Different **home-made drinks** are enjoyed in the various regions. A national favourite is *chapalo*, locally made millet beer, also known as *pit* or *dolo*. The deadly African gin, known in Burkina as *patasi* or *"qui me pousse"*, is cheap.

Around Banfora, you'll find a lot of palm wine, *banji*, which you can order by the (beer) bottle in most small bars (*cabarets*). Sweet and frothy, it goes down easily and has the added advantage of being cheap.

The usual foreign soft drinks compete against hideously coloured Spark (in lemon, orange and banana flavours). Savanna is a non-gassy bottled fruit drink in exotic flavours like mango — far too sugary. Throughout the country (especially in motor parks), you'll run into *Lemburgui*, thirst-quenching home-made ginger beer frozen in small plastic bags.

ACCOMMODATION PRICE CODES

Accommodation prices in this chapter are coded according to the following scales – the same scales in terms of their pound/dollar equivalents as are used throughout the book. Prices refer to the rate you can expect to pay for a room with two beds. Single rooms, or single occupancy, will normally cost at least two-thirds of the twin-occupancy rate. For further details see p.48.

① **Under CFA4500 (under £5/$8).** Very rudimentary hotel with no frills at all - often a *chambre de passage* rented to the average guest by the hour.

② **CFA4500–9000 (£5–10/$8–16).** Basic hotel with simple amenities. S/C rooms with fans are the norm, and possibly some with AC for slightly higher rates.

③ **CFA9000–18,000 (£10–20/$16–32).** Modest hotel, with S/C rooms the norm, and a choice of fans or, for a premium, AC.

④ **CFA18,000–27,000 (£20–30/$32–48).** Reasonable business or tourist-class hotel with S/C, AC rooms, and often a good restaurant.

⑤ **CFA27,000–36,000 (£30–40/$48–64).** Similar standards to the previous code band but extra facilities such as a pool are usual.

⑥ **CFA36,000–45,000 (£40–50/$64–80).** Comfortable, first-class hotel, with good facilities.

⑦ **Over CFA45,000 (over £50/$80).** Luxury establishment – top prices around CFA60,000–80,000.

Communications – Post, Phones, Language and Media

You can make direct-dial international phone calls from Burkina to the UK, North America and most of Europe. Ouagadougou's poste restante works well, although you should be careful to have your letters addressed with the exact name that appears in your passport – which you have to produce.

Burkina Faso's IDD code is ☎226.

towns. The most widely spoken African language is **More**, mother tongue of the Mossi and spoken by over half the population. Other widely spoken languages are **Pulaar**, spoken by the Fula herders of the north, and **Dioula** (Dyula), which has become the major commercial lingua franca spanning most of the borders in this part of West Africa.

■ Languages

French is the official language of Burkina, although it's estimated that only fifteen percent of the population speak it with any degree of fluency. That percentage is noticeably higher in the large

■ The media

The national **press** consists of a government French-language daily, *Sidwaya* ("Truth"), and the independent dailies *Le Pays* and *L'Observateur*.

The weekly magazine *Carrefour Africain* is another mouthpiece of the information ministry

---

A LITTLE MORE

GREETINGS

Good morning (early)	*Neyibeogo*		*Lafi beeme?/*
Response	*Yibeoog soab*		*Laafi bala?*
	yeaala	Response	*Lafi bala*
Further response (men)	*Naaba*	Goodbye	*Wend na tasse*
Further response (women)	*Eyn*	See you later	*Wend na kodnin*
Good day	*Neywindaga*		*daare*
Response	*Windg soab*	See you tomorrow	*Wend na kodbeo*
	yeaala		*go*
Good evening	*Neywungo*	Response	*Wend na kod-*
Response	*Yung soab*	*beo*	*go/Ammi*
How are you?	*Yibeoog yaa?*		
	laafi?/		

LIMITED CONVERSATION

Excuse me	*Ysugri*	Yes	*Nye*	I have no money	*Ligidi kabay*
Sorry	*Ykabre*	No	*Ayo*	Water	*Koom*
Thank you	*Barka*	How much?	*Wanwana?*		

DAYS

Today	*Dunna*	Monday	*Fene*	Friday	*Arzuma*
Tomorrow	*Beoogo*	Tuesday	*Falato*	Saturday	*Sibri*
Yesterday	*Zaame*	Wednesday	*Arba*	Sunday	*Hado*
This evening	*Zaabre*	Thursday	*Lamusa*		

NUMBERS

1	*Aye*	5	*Anu*	9	*Awe*
2	*Ayiibu*	6	*Ayoobe*	10	*Piiga*
3	*Ataabo*	7	*Yopoe*	100	*Koabga*
4	*Anaase*	8	*Anii*	1000	*Tusri*

BURKINABE GLOSSARY

Américain General term for a missionary regardless of nationality or religious affiliation. Early missionaries in the region were anglophone Protestants.

Brousse Common West African term for bush or countryside, but to the Mossi, it means anywhere outside the Mossi country, especially outside the purlieu of Ouagadougou. Thus someone who has gone to study in Côte d'Ivoire or France is said to be *en brousse*.

Burkinabe (or Burkinabè). Man or woman from Burkina Faso; there is no masculine or feminine form.

Cabaret A rural bar (especially in Lobi country).

CDR (Comités pour la défense de la Révolution) – first established by Sankara to implement government policy and organize local affairs on a regional level.

Ghanéenne A popular term for a prostitute, equally insulting to Ghanaian women and barmaids (since most are Ghanaian).

Koure Mossi funeral ceremony.

Kwara Gourounsi chief's sacred insignia, equivalent of a staff of office.

Marabout Muslim holy man who may use his spiritual powers for divination.

Mogho Naba Also spelled *Moro Naba*; traditional leader of the Mossi people who resides in Ouagadougou. *Mogho* signifies the traditional cultural realm of Ouagadougou.

Naba King of a Mossi state, and also village chief.

Nassara Common appellation for white people and other foreigners.

Ouédraogo The most common surname in Burkina, it's derived from the More *ouefo* (horse) and *raogo* (male). It is the Mogho Naba's name and that of other important political and cultural leaders.

Zaka Round house in the countryside with *banco* walls and thatched conical roof. The plural is *zaksé*.

but the weeklies *Journal du Jeudi* and *L'Intrus* attempt a satirical treatment of current events and are worth a look. Among other weeklies that have sprung up in the "democratic" era, are *Le Clef, Regard, Zoom* and *Le Républicain*. Look out, also, for the sports and culture magazine, *Big Z*.

Listening to **Radio Burkina** government radio (in sixteen Burkinabe languages, on 705 AM) or watching TV (one channel, with very limited transmission and audience) aren't likely to be major leisure activities. **Canal Arc-en-ciel** (96.6 FM), **Radio Energie** (103.4 FM), **Horizon FM** (104.4 FM, in Ouaga and Bobo) and **Radio Bobo-Dioulasso** are commercial stations with more promise.

Entertainment

There's a thriving, though severely underfunded, popular culture in Burkina. In Ouaga and Bobo live music is a nightly occurrence and even isolated villages come alive with the sounds of impromptu *balafon* bands. During the major festivals, Burkina's international stars can be counted on to make appearances. But Burkina is best known as the capital of African cine-ma: you have a better chance of catching an African movie here than in any other country in the region.**

■ Music

Despite the ease with which you can hear local **music** in Burkina Faso, very few artists have reached a wide African or international audience. A couple of good albums of traditional music are available, including *Haute Volta* – a compilation of Mossi, Peul (Fula), Bambara, Lobi and Gan music – put out by the Agence de Coopération Culturelle et Technique (ACCT).

In a more popular vein, **Hamidou Ouédraogo** – the self-proclaimed *Vedette Voltaïque* – is one of the nation's better-known stars. A Fula-speaker from the region of Dori, he moved to Ouagadougou in the 1970s and formed the group **l'Orchestre Super Volta**. Popular albums from the period include *Le Vedette Voltaïque* and *Le Chanteur Voltaïque* both on Sonodisc. The best-known artists outside the country are the brilliantly watchable percussion group **Farafina**, and the very exciting **Coulibaly Twins**.

All are based, when at home, in Bobo-Dioulasso, the town to head for if you want to get to grips with Burkinabe music. The big **Semaine** de la Culture festival held each even-numbered year in February or March offers a tremendous opportunity for dance and percussion enthusiasts. It's attracting increasing interest from drummers around West Africa.

■ Theatre

Burkinabe drama has received a boost in recent years and the major towns (Ouagadougou, Bobo-Dioulasso, Koudougou) all have well-equipped theatres. The country has over a dozen drama troupes that give regular performances. Check out what's going on by calling in at the French cultural centres in Ouagadougou or Bobo, and if you're really keen, be sure to catch the Festival du Théâtre (see overleaf).

Holidays and Festivals

Burkina has a growing reputation for major arts festivals, of which the best known is the big African filmfest, FESPACO. It's well worth timing a trip around one of these.

Office holidays include all the usual Muslim and Christian celebrations. Additional Christian holidays include Ascension Thursday, Pentecost and Assumption. New Year's Day is also a bank holiday. The principal national holidays are January 3 (1966 Revolution), May 1 (Labour Day), August 4 (Revolution Day), August 5 (Independence Day) and December 11 (Proclamation of the Republic).

■ FESPACO

The Festival Panafricain du Cinéma is held in Ouagadougou every odd-numbered year at the end of February. FESPACO was founded in 1969 and is dedicated to promoting African film-makers throughout the world. Thrusting Burkina to the forefront of African cinema, the festival now attracts tens of thousands of people. If you happen to be here at the time, you won't find a hotel room unless you've booked in advance, as the city fills with an international crowd of film-makers and movie hacks flocking to the ten-day extravaganza. Rooms in private homes help mop up the overflow; enquire at the festival's headquarters or at the information centre in the *Hôtel Indépendance*.

In theory, the event is open to all, and CFA20,000 buys you a badge that allows access to the myriad of films showing simultaneously in the capital's many theatres – a good deal, but a steep price for locals. You can also purchase individual tickets at the respective cinemas (CFA200–1000, depending on the cinema). If you have the stamina, you could easily take in thirty or more African films in the course of the event – substantially more than most people see in a lifetime. The badge also allows access to: the opening and closing ceremonies (the president inevitably speaks); debates with the directors (including headphones for simultaneous translation); press conferences; and the Film Market at the French cultural centre, where you can view films in competition on video monitors.

This is undoubtedly the most star-studded event you'll see in Africa (besides a whole host of *vedettes* from the continent, celebrities from throughout the African diaspora, such as actor Danny Glover, or film-makers Sembene Ousmane, Djibril Diop Mambety, Idrissa Ouedrago and Zairean Balafu Bakupa-Kanyinda, increasingly make the pilgrimage) and the energy is absolutely electric. Local bands play everywhere, as people crowd the streets stopping for a drink or to browse at the countless booths for traditional crafts and FESPACO merchandise. Organization is excellent: schedules are posted throughout town; a free daily festival paper lists each day's events; and hotels provide free shuttles. For more information, contact FESPACO (01 BP 2505, Ouagadougou; ☎30.75.38; Fax 31.25.09; *sg@fespaco.bf*, *www.fespaco.bf*).

■ SIAO

Another biennial event (held in October in even-numbered years), the Salon International de l'Artisanat de Ouagadougou is touted as the largest crafts meeting on the African continent. The SIAO attracts over 300 artisans from across Africa and over 100,000 visitors, including buyers from throughout the world. Focused around the Maison du Peuple, the entire city centre fills with exhibitors' booths and stalls – some laid out under the traditional architecture of a specially created village. While the objectives – to promote African crafts as cultural expression while stimulating the industry – is serious, the atmosphere is festive, with music, food, fashion shows and performances of dance and theatre on every street corner. For information, contact the Secrétariat Permanent, SIAO (01 BP 3414, Ouagadougou; ☎30.20.25; Fax 30.61.16).

■ Festival du Théâtre

Ouagadougou's biennial **Festival du Théâtre** (late November in even-numbered years) gives the chance to catch national troupes performing works as diverse as Greek tragedy and modern African comedies. For information, contact the Secrétariat du Festival (☎30.73.89).

■ Semaine de la Culture

The **Semaine de la Culture** is another biennial event (February/March), this time held in Bobo-Dioulasso. The town turns into a fair for the event with **dance and percussion troupes** from throughout the country performing non-stop. You can also catch demonstrations of traditional **wrestling** and **archery**; booths everywhere display national crafts and regional cooking and music spreads throughout the town.

Directory

AIRPORT DEPARTURE TAX None.

CRAFTS Crafts are an important industry in Burkina, ranging from those intended for everyday use (pottery, basketwork, wooden utensils) to those used in ceremonies (masks, statues) or as tourist fodder/decoration. Bronze statues, cast using the lost wax method, were traditionally made for the royal court, but are now widely available in Ouagadougou. Pottery is the most widespread craft in Burkina and is used everywhere. Look out for leatherwork, too, an offshoot of the country's large livestock industry. Traditional sandals, bags and pouches are sold in village markets, and in Ouagadougou, you can see new uses for old materials at the Société Burkinabe de Manufacture de Cuir – check out the leather-covered chessboards.

OPENING HOURS Businesses open 8am–12.30pm and 3–6pm on weekdays. Many are open Saturday mornings too. Government offices operate 7am–12.30pm and 3–5.30pm on weekdays only.

PHOTOGRAPHY In theory, before taking any pictures in Burkina you need to obtain a photo permit at the Ministère de l'Environnement et du Tourisme in Ouagadougou (see p.644). Obtaining the permit is definitely advised if you want to use your camera in the city, but you will rarely be checked for the permit except in Ouagadougou. The ONTB tourist office has a long list of scenes and places of which photos are prohibited.

WILDLIFE AND NATIONAL PARKS Burkina's flat, overgrazed, relatively overpopulated lands offer poor refuge for the country's natural savannah fauna. A conscientious conservation programme does exist (with controlled tourist hunting part of its policy), though its best chances of success lie with the Burkinabe ethic stressing community before individual. Hippo and crocodile "pools" are recognized tourist assets. Encouraging reports indicate a relatively large elephant population in the Burkina sector of the Parc National du W, in the Parc National d'Arli (both in the remote southeast) and in the little-visited Pô and Nazinga reserves south of Ouagadougou. For information on the game reserves contact the ONTB tourist office in Ouagadougou (☎31.19.59 or 31.19.69; Fax 31.44.34).

Recent History of Burkina

The Mossi empires dominated the Volta region's politics until the French usurped the independence of their states in the 1890s. For two decades the colonials simply merged their new territory with the Colonie du Haut-Sénégal Niger, and it wasn't until 1919 that they divided this huge mass into two separate colonies – Soudan Français and Haute Volta (Upper Volta) – the latter comprising present-day Burkina Faso. In 1932, commercial considerations (primarily a need for manual labour in neighbouring colonies) led the French to divide Upper Volta again, annexing half the colony to Côte d'Ivoire and dividing the rest between the French Sudan and Niger. It wasn't until September 4, 1947, that Upper Volta re-emerged as an entity.

■ Independence

Maurice Yaméogo, the prominent figure in pre-independence politics, founded the **Union Démocratique Voltaïque** – the UDV, a local section of Félix Houphouët-Boigny's Rassemblement Démocratique Africain – shortly after World War II. By 1958, Upper Volta had become an autonomous territory, and Yaméogo was its prime minister. When full independence was granted on August 5, 1960, he was elected the country's first president.

The French did little to upgrade the Upper Volta, or give it an infrastructure capable of spurring economic development. Admittedly, Yaméogo had inherited a desperate situation, but he did little to reverse the trend, and outside of Ouagadougou the country had few roads or communications systems. As the economic situation deteriorated, Yaméogo introduced austerity measures unpopular with increasingly disgruntled workers and civil servants. In the face of rising opposition, he banned political parties outside the UDV and adopted an autocratic style. He was ousted, on January 3, 1966, in a coup led by the army chief of staff, **Sangoulé Lamizana**.

■ The 1970s

The army, with Lamizana at its head, ruled the country during a four-year period in which the nation was ostensibly being prepared for a **return to civilian rule**. Parties were formed and a new constitution was drafted. In 1970, a semi-civilian government was elected with the UDV winning a majority of the seats in parliament.

But the UDV's leadership was split, with a rivalry developing between **Joseph Ouédraogo** and **Gérard Ouédraogo** – both of Mossi origin though unrelated. After a period of political infighting, it was agreed that Gérard would serve as prime minister and Joseph as president of the assembly. Lamizana remained in office as head of state and the army retained real power.

By the early 1970s, drought had struck the country and the economic outlook was bleaker than ever. As parts of the north were struck with the prospect of starvation, a scandal erupted with the discovery of **food aid embezzlement** by members of the government distribution committee – confirming rumours of widespread administrative corruption. The government suffered a further crisis in 1973, when conflict developed between civilian leaders and the militant teacher's union and a **general strike** swept through the public sector. As the situation deteriorated, the national assembly refused to pass further legislation until the prime minister stepped down. Gérard Ouédraogo refused to do so and on February 8, 1974, the army took control of the country once again, dissolving the parliament and suspending the 1970 constitution.

A new crisis hit Upper Volta in 1975, when **war** broke out with Mali over the **Agacher Strip**. Their rival claims to this 150-kilometre-wide border strip in the desolate northern regions of the · Sahel – believed to be rich in mineral deposits – were based on legal documents dating back to

when Upper Volta had been divided and redivided between Côte d'Ivoire, the French Sudan (Mali) and Niger. Before the dispute was settled with OAU mediation, a new generation of popular military heroes had arisen, including a young officer, **Thomas Sankara**.

■ The rise of Sankara

Under pressure from the labour unions, **elections** were once again held in 1978, and on May 28 of that year, the Third Republic was proclaimed. Lamizana was elected president, but his UDV party didn't have an overall majority in parliament and his tenure was habitually challenged by the trade unions (at the time, an unusually powerful force since half of all wage earners belonged to one of the four national unions) and students. He was overthrown in a quiet palace coup on November 25, 1980, by **Colonel Saye Zerbo** who became head of the new "Military Committee for Recovery and National Progress" (CMRPN).

The coup was initially supported by the unions, but they quickly became disgruntled after the CMRPN's **banning of political activity**. Relations deteriorated utterly when the Military Committee withdrew the right to strike in 1981. Serious cleavages began to become apparent within the Military Committee, and in 1982 Sankara – whose popular appeal was growing – was removed from his influential position in the Ministry of Information.

Unrest quickened, and a **coup d'état** followed. On November 7, 1982, a group of military officers forced out Zerbo and set up the "Provisional People's Salvation Council" (CSP) with an army doctor named **Jean-Baptiste Ouédraogo** at its head. The new regime let fire a volley of denunciation at Zerbo's corrupt and repressive government and took a radical pro-union position, championing the right to strike. In January 1983, Sankara was named prime minister.

By early 1983, it was clear that the new government was divided between **traditionalists** – led by the army chief of staff, Colonel Gabriel Somé – and **radicals**, headed by Sankara. The two factions came into open conflict when Sankara invited Colonel Gaddafi to Upper Volta in May 1983. The day after the Libyan leader's departure, Ouédraogo ordered Sankara's arrest on the grounds that he had dangerously threatened national unity.

The arrest of the prime minister triggered a rebellion in Sankara's commando unit at Pô, a small town near the Ghanaian border. The commandos, led by **Captain Blaise Compaoré** believed the move to have been instigated by Somé and encouraged by France. They took control of Pô and refused orders from the capital until Sankara was unconditionally released. But Ouédraogo refused to dismiss Somé and gradually the rebellion spread to other commando units in the country. On the eve of the 23rd anniversary of independence – August 4, 1983 – Sankara seized power. Ouédraogo had lasted less than a year as head of state.

■ Changes: Burkina Faso

Sankara settled in as president of the new governing body, the Conseil National de la Révolution (CNR), and as head of state. Compaoré was nominated minister of state to the president. The country was renamed Burkina Faso. With the logistic help of the previously underground **"Patriotic Development League"** (LIPAD), the CNR quickly set about reorganizing the administrative regions of the country and ousting **traditional rulers** from their positions of power and influence. Revolutionary **"people's courts"** were established to try former public officials charged with political crimes and corruption. One of the first to be tried was Lamizana, who was acquitted. But several former ministers were convicted and sentenced to prison, as were ex-president Zerbo (who was also ordered to repay US$200,000 in public funds) and Gérard Ouédraogo, former UDV leader.

The style of Thomas Sankara

Only 34 years old when he came to power, **Sankara** symbolized a new generation of leaders with innovative ideas, but his popularity went beyond his ability to compose revolutionary music on his guitar or eloquent denunciations of capitalism and imperialism. Sankara may have had a penchant for facile rhetoric, but he could also transform words into **action**. He waged war on desertification, women's inequality and children's diseases (creating a "vaccination-commando"). When foreign investors refused to finance a railway line to magnesium deposits in the north of the country, he launched the *bataille du rail* – encouraging peasants to build the tracks themselves. (Although critics said his recruitment methods were hauntingly reminiscent of French *travaux forcé*, Sankara was too young to remember that.) But perhaps his greatest achieve-

ment was the virtual elimination of **corruption** and government waste, proving his commitment to the cause by having himself chauffeured around in the back of a Renault 4, rather than the customary black Mercedes.

In another popular move, Sankara early in his term announced free housing for all Burkinabe and called a moratorium on rents (an incautious decision from which he later had to retreat). But even though the young president seemed to prove himself as a capable, if unpredictable leader, he was gaining a long list of enemies.

Detractors – at home and abroad

By early 1984, there was growing **opposition** to Sankara's radical style, and in May of that year a plot to overthrow the government was uncovered. The leaders were hastily arrested and tried. Unlike the people's courts, these proceedings took place in secrecy and the penalties were severe. Seven of the alleged plotters were executed and five others sentenced to hard labour.

In light of these events, **relations with France** soured, and Sankara accused the French government of supporting exiled political rivals. Other Western nations also viewed the new regime with scepticism, though the fact that Sankara made efforts to distance his government from Libya and the Soviet Union was interpreted as an encouraging sign. Gradually, the "revolution" came to be identified less with Marxist ideology, and was seen more as a means of unifying a wide cross-section of society. The success of the CNR and the genuine popularity of the movement hinged primarily on the dynamic personality of its founder.

War with Mali flared up again in late 1985. Over fifty people were killed and better-armed Mali did major damage in Burkina. In December 1986, the International Court of Justice in The Hague divided the disputed Agacher Strip between the two countries and peace was restored.

But relations were also deteriorating with other West African neighbours – especially **Côte d'Ivoire** and **Togo**. Close ties between Sankara and Jerry Rawlings of Ghana were regarded suspiciously by these conservative nations – especially after 1986 when the two socialist neighbours decided to work towards political integration by the late 1990s. Relations with Togo were nearly broken off after an attempted coup in Lomé shook President Eyadema's regime in September 1986.

Both Ghana and Burkina were accused of involvement and of harbouring Togolese dissidents. Despite a 1987 visit to Ouagadougou by François Mitterrand, **France** continued to treat Burkina with reserve – a wait-and-see attitude generally shared by Western powers.

At home, Sankara was frequently criticized by intellectuals, labour unions and business leaders, though he had a charismatic knack for diffusing enmity from all these groups. In January 1985, opposition to the austerity measures Sankara introduced led unions to wage a "leaflet war", but the tumult quickly died down and no major dissent ensued. Even salary cuts for civil servants and the military were accepted on the grounds that they were necessary to raise the level of social services among the poor. In the absence of serious opposition from **traditional political forces**, it was a growing lack of consensus within the governing CNR and resulting rifts that ultimately proved Sankara's downfall.

■ The new regime

Thomas Sankara was killed in a botched and bloody coup on October 15, 1987. It was precipitated by a group of soldiers loyal to **Blaise Compaoré** (Sankara's companion in arms and partner in the government), who opened fire on Sankara after arresting him. The precise nature of the overthrow is still shrouded in mystery. It did not, at any rate, take a planned course and it doesn't seem likely that Compaoré intended to come out of it looking like a murderer. He later said "Thomas confiscated the revolution and brought untold suffering to the people", and it's clear at least that Sankara had allowed himself to become fatally isolated. But Compaoré's image as a West African leader with the blood of a brother on his hands won't easily be erased.

Sankara's death sent shock waves through the region and chilled progressive movements round the world. For even if his methods were often open to question (something he never denied), he had demonstrated sincerity in his aims and proved himself a credible friend of the people. Most importantly he had managed to instil **national pride** and create a realistic **sense of hope** in one of West Africa's most brutalized countries. Most West African, and not a few Western governments seemed relieved with the change, but the Burkinabe people's response varied from mournful to muted – not a good sign for the new president.

The basis of the revolutionary system Sankara set in place remained intact, although Compaoré quickly announced that "rectification" would be made, signalling a willingness to conform to the inevitable pressure of World Bank and IMF loan negotiations.

However, the early years of the new regime were characterized by the almost continuous rumble of **rumour and incident** within the Front Populaire (high-level disagreements, coup attempts and a number of subsequent executions). Though by 1990 the party had been purged, by death or desertion of all members of the original 1983 revolution, events suggested considerable latent support of Sankara and serious threats to the survival of the new leadership, which could hardly have been forgiven. Compaoré therefore sought to bring disenfranchized political groupings into the fold and to achieve peace with the powerful unions.

Towards this end, a new constitution was drafted in 1990, which called for a multiparty **electoral system**. Political parties mushroomed, and a transitional government was set up with Compaoré as head of a council of ministers that contained a smattering of opposition leaders. But conflict arose quickly at a conference to discuss the constitution's implementation. The new parties decried the fact that their input was merely consultative and there was to be no sovereign national conference such as those taking place elsewhere in West Africa. Soon after, opposition leaders resigned their government posts to protest Compaoré's intransigence on the issue.

■ The Fourth Republic

As the **presidential elections** approached, opposition parties united under the banner of the **Coordination des Forces Démocratiques** (CFD) and collectively pushed for a sovereign national council. Popular demonstrations in support of opposition demands occurred throughout the second half of 1991 and, as the outcomes tended increasingly towards violence, the government banned political rallies. By the end of the year, it was clear there would be no council and no opposition: "opposition" candidates withdrew from the presidential race and called for an election boycott.

Compaoré was left as the only candidate and, naturally enough, won the election, although three out of four voters stayed away from the polls. He was sworn in as president of the **"Fourth Republic"** on December 24, 1991, but was probably no closer to having obtained wide public support than he was after the unpopular coup of 1987.

Even as the president called for **national reconciliation** following the elections, he became increasingly mistrusted when opposition leaders were attacked. One, Clément Oumarou Ouédraogo, was assassinated just outside the *Hôtel Indépendance* as he left a CFD meeting. Although Compaoré condemned the murder, there was general public cynicism, and angry crowds stoned the minister of defence when he showed up at Ouédraogo's funeral. Still, with some deft political manoeuvring, the president managed to persuade much of the opposition to participate in the upcoming **legislative elections**. By May 24, 1992, the polling date, almost half of the nation's 62 political parties had decided to contest.

Although Compaoré's party, the Organisation pour la Démocratie Populaire/Mouvement du Travail (ODP-MT) won a majority of the parliamentary seats, the president's image suffered as a result of the popular belief that the elections had been rigged. **Youssouf Ouédraogo** – a young economist from the ruling party – was appointed prime minister and formed a cabinet that, in keeping with the theme of reconciliation, contained some opposition leaders, mostly relegated to the least important posts. Ouédraogo resigned in 1994 after failed union negotiations in the aftermath of the crippling devaluation of the CFA franc. His successor was **Roch March Christian Kaboré**.

In the early years of the Fourth Republic, Burkina Faso was most often in the headlines as a sponsor of several rebel forces in West Africa and as a mediator of regional conflicts. Most notably, Compaoré actively supported **Charles Taylor's** military effort to win the civil war in **Liberia**, supplying troops and arms to assist in military operations – to the disgust of the Nigerian-led ECOMOG peacekeeping force of West African troops – although following a 1995 Liberian peace agreement, Compaoré agreed to commit Burkinabe troops to the ECOMOG force in preparation for Liberia's 1997 elections. Compaoré also played a key role in negotiating a settlement to the **Tuareg crisis** that gripped **Mali** and **Niger** – partly because Burkina was one of the countries most affected, with 50,000 refugees sheltering there at the height of the conflict – and he participated too in talks to resolve the political crisis in the **Central African Republic** in 1996. Burkina's relationship with **France** grew warmer following the election of Jacques Chirac in 1995.

At home, Burkina's **economy** experienced the fastest growth of any country in West Africa at the end of the 1990s – a performance that bolstered Compaoré's chances to keep his seat as his first term drew to a close. More importantly, there was no real alternative to his candidacy. As the **1998 elections** neared, the main opposition parties again called for a boycott, but this time voters seemed weary of complaints about the electoral process, and the boycott gathered only a lacklustre following. More than 50 percent of the voters participated in the elections and gave Compaoré a resounding victory, making him the first president since independence to survive a first term and be re-elected.

Trouble at home and abroad

Compaoré barely had time to bask in the glow of his victory, however, when a scandal erupted that had far-reaching political implications. In December 1998, four charred bodies were found in a vehicle that had apparently crashed near the village of Sapouy. One of the victims was **Norbert Zongo**, editor of the *L'Independant* newspaper and president of the Private Press Association in Burkina. Zongo had been investigating the suspicious circumstances surrounding the death of the chauffeur of Compoare's brother Francois, and alleged that he had been tortured to death by the Regiment de Sécurité Presidentielle, the president's own security forces. **Demonstrations** in Ouagadougou called for an investigation into Zongo's death, which the public widely believed to be murder, and Compaoré set up an independent commission to look into the matter.

The commission's report, returned in May 1999, was damning to the presidency: "Norbert Zongo was assassinated for purely political motives because he practiced investigative journalism. He defended a democratic ideal and had chosen to become involved, with his newspaper, in the struggle for the respect of human rights and justice, and against the poor management of the public sector and impunity."

Protestors flooded the streets of Ouagadougou, setting up barricades and burning tyres as they marched to the Ministry of Justice. Security forces met with tear gas and as unrest spread to the University, police raided dormitories and arrested students. The rest of the country was not spared from the violence. In

Koudougo – the birthplace of Zongo – rioters burned private residences and destroyed public property. The key opposition leader and MP, Herman Yameogo, was accused of inciting the rioters and arrested.

Although Compaoré denounced the commission's findings, the damage was already done. It was a huge blow to his attempts to reinvent himself as a legitimately elected democratic leader.

The domestic unrest completely overshadowed other serious **developments outside Burkina**. In April 1999, the commander of ECO-MOG, Major-General Felix Mujakperuo, accused the Burkinabe government of supplying arms to the **Sierra Leone** resistance and announced that his forces would not tolerate countries in the region supporting rebel forces. It was the first hint that the ongoing war could spread beyond Sierra Leone's borders, and the chastisement was an embarrassment for Compaoré. That same month, the president lost a friend and political ally in the region when Niger's head of state, **Ibrahim Mainassara**, was assassinated in Niamey.

■ Prospects

Compaoré has done much to consolidate his position as head of state, relying on a shrewd mix of carrot and stick. He has established a ruthless **security network** and remains intransigent to any opposition he cannot co-opt. But he has also formed a wide, if at times shaky, **coalition of political support** ranging from ambitious right-wing professionals to heads of the influential socialist and communist parties. Leaders from all these groups have been rewarded with ministerial posts and top-level participation in national politics. In return, they have kept criticism of the government to a minimum.

Though Compaoré can be expected to ride out the scandals that plague him at the end of the millennium – he is recognized as perhaps the only figure who can hold the army at bay – he unquestionably suffers from lingering Brutus syndrome. Despite his country's status as an outstanding example of IMF/World Bank-imposed economic restructuring, Compaoré now faces an even tougher time obtaining the genuine respect accorded to his former friend, whom most Burkinabe still credit for any positive social developments in their country.

CENTRAL AND NORTHERN BURKINA

Lying in the centre of Burkina, **Ouagadougou** is an inevitable stopping point and a pleasant place to rest up for a few days before heading off to some of the country's more isolated outposts. Though relatively small for a capital city, it generates a satisfying amount of commercial and cultural activity.

Main roads head from here to all major national and international destinations. West of Ouaga, the route to Bobo-Dioulasso is lined with small Mossi towns and villages such as **Sabou**, famed for its sacred crocodile pond, while a branch road leads off to **Koudougou** – the nation's third-largest town and a centre of Burkina's textile industry. The eastern route to Niamey passes through the **Gourmantché country** and the important market town of **Fada-Ngourma**. Another busy junction along this route is **Koupéla**, where the highway to Dapaong in neighbouring Togo starts its southern course.

Possible trips to **northern Burkina** include the impressive market town of **Gorom-Gorom**, near the point where Burkina, Mali and Niger meet, and through the old **Yatenga state** to the historic town of **Ouahigouya** – an obvious overnight stop if you're heading for the Dogon country in Mali.

Ouagadougou

On the surface, **OUAGADOUGOU** – routinely abbreviated to "Ouaga" – has little to offer. Capital of one of the world's poorest countries, it seems more like a shambling provincial town. The heat is oppressive; the flat, dirt streets are filled with choking red dust in the dry season and muddy morasses during the rains; and overhead, vultures wheel on the lookout for scraps, and bats flutter from roosting sites.

Yet despite its unpromising appearance Ouaga turns out to be exceptionally animated – and there is more to attest to this than simply the clouds of exhaust that sputter from the thousands of *mobylettes* crushing into traffic jams at rush hour. Over the last twenty years, drastic measures have been taken to try to improve the city's image. New roads have been paved, more efficient sewerage systems are being laid and the government has encouraged people to clear the streets of garbage and goats, both of which had come to be permanent fixtures. As the town modernizes, building projects have included the striking Grand Marché – an attractive and spacious brick complex in the city centre – and the enormous BCEAO Bank, a tower distinctive enough that a locally modernist haircut has been named after it – though on the whole there's a notable absence of the strutting skyscraper architecture so popular in many other West African capitals.

Ouaga is the traditional capital of the **Mossi empire**, but all the country's major ethnic groups, religions and languages coexist here with remarkable harmony. A good number of international organizations, and the nation's only university, are also based in Ouaga. Life moves at a brisk pace, but as a visitor, you'll find that contact with the people is much more immediate than in other West African cities.

Some history

Mossi oral literature traces the beginning of the **Mogho** or **Moro** (the Mossi empire: *Mogho* literally means "the world") to the thirteenth century and a chief named Gbewa or Nédéga who ruled over Pusiga in present-day Ghana (see p.758). In the course of a battle, Gbewa's daughter, a horsewoman named **Yennenga**, was separated from the clan when her horse took fright and fled into the Bitou woods. She chanced upon the forest's one inhabitant, an elephant hunter named **Rialé** (a corruption of the More

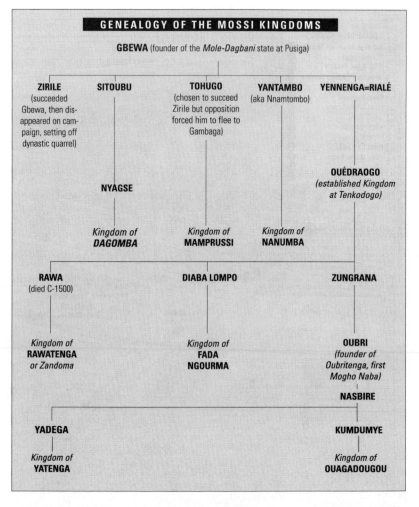

GENEALOGY OF THE MOSSI KINGDOMS

GBEWA (founder of the *Mole-Dagbani* state at Pusiga)

ZIRILE (succeeded Gbewa, then disappeared on campaign, setting off dynastic quarrel)

SITOUBU

TOHUGO (chosen to succeed Zirile but opposition forced him to flee to Gambaga)

YANTAMBO (aka Nnamtombo)

YENNENGA=RIALÉ

OUÉDRAOGO (established Kingdom at Tenkodogo)

NYAGSE

Kingdom of **DAGOMBA**

Kingdom of **MAMPRUSSI**

Kingdom of **NANUMBA**

RAWA (died C-1500)

DIABA LOMPO

ZUNGRANA

Kingdom of **RAWATENGA** or Zandoma

Kingdom of **FADA NGOURMA**

OUBRI (founder of Oubritenga, first Mogho Naba)

NASBIRE

YADEGA

Kingdom of **YATENGA**

KUMDUMYE

Kingdom of **OUAGADOUGOU**

words *ri*, "to eat", and *yaré*, "anything", since bush-dwellers ate anything they found). The couple eventually returned to Gambaga and had a baby, which they named **Ouédraogo**, after Yennenga's steed – from *ouefo*, "horse", and *raogo*, "male".

But the territory of Pusiga became overpopulated and Ouédraogo set off with a company of his father's cavalry to conquer the northern territories. He established a kingdom at **Na Ten Kudugo** (Tenkodogo). Much later, Ouédraogo's grandson **Oubri** sought to conquer new territories and founded the statelet of **Oubritenga**, later known as Wogodogo or Ouagadougou. A grandson of Oubri broke off to form another small state, **Yatenga**, with Ouahigouya as its capital.

The autonomous Mossi states or kingdoms (see box above for genealogy) remained remarkably stable for over four centuries, but by the end of the nineteenth century, the French, Germans and British were pressing in on the region. In 1898, the French

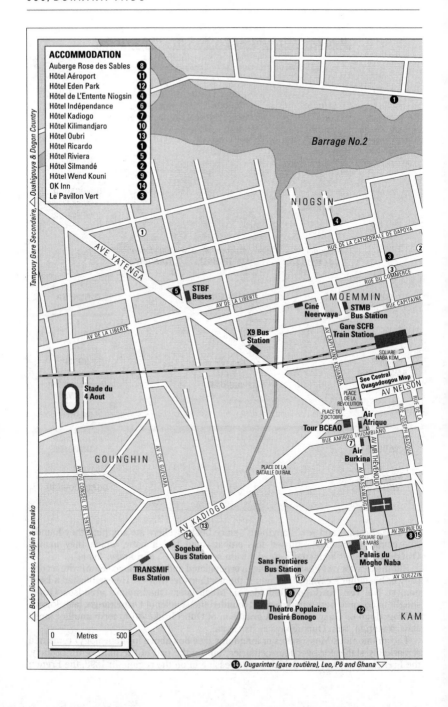

ACCOMMODATION

Auberge Rose des Sables	**8**
Hôtel Aéroport	**11**
Hôtel Eden Park	**12**
Hôtel de L'Entente Niogsin	**4**
Hôtel Indépendance	**6**
Hôtel Kadiogo	**7**
Hôtel Kilimandjaro	**10**
Hôtel Oubri	**13**
Hôtel Ricardo	**1**
Hôtel Riviera	**5**
Hôtel Silmandé	**2**
Hôtel Wend Kouni	**9**
OK Inn	**14**
Le Pavillon Vert	**3**

Tampouy Gare Secondaire, △ Ouahigouya & Dogon Country

△ *Bobo Dioulasso, Abidjan & Bamako*

Barrage No.2

NIOGSIN

RUE DE LA CATHÉDRALE DE DAPOYA

AVE YATENGA

STBF Buses

AV DE LA LIBERTÉ

RUE DU COMMERCE

MOEMMIN

Ciné Neerwaya

RUE CAPITAINE

STMB Bus Station

AV DE LA LIBERTÉ

X9 Bus Station

Gare SCFB Train Station

SQUARE NABA KÔM

See Central Ouagadougou Map

AV NELSON

Stade du 4 Aout

PLACE DE LA RÉVOLUTION

PLACE DU 2 OCTOBRE

Air Afrique

GOUNGHIN

Tour BCEAO

RUE AMIROU THIOMBIANO

Air Burkina

PLACE DE LA BATAILLE DU RAIL

RUE JOSEPH BADOUA

AV CHE GUEVARA

AV DU CONSEIL DE L'ENTENTE

AV KADIOGO

AV BASSAWARGA

AV 260 (RUE DU

AV MR THEVENOUD

SQUARE DU 8 MARS

Sogebaf Bus Station

AV 258

Palais du Mogho Naba

AV QUEZZIN

TRANSMIF Bus Station

Sans Frontières Bus Station

Théatre Populaire Desiré Bonogo

KAM

0   Metres   500

Ougarinter (gare routière), Leo, Pô and Ghana ▽

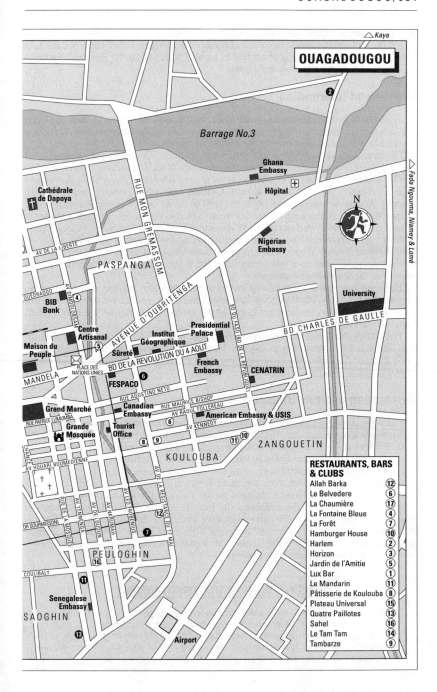

OUAGADOUGOU

Barrage No.3

Ghana Embassy

Hôpital

Cathédrale de Dapoya

Nigerian Embassy

AV DE LA LIBERTÉ

PASPANGA

University

OUEDRAOGO
BIB Bank

BD CHARLES DE GAULLE

AVENUE D'OUBRITENGA

Presidential Palace

Centre Artisanal
Institut Géographique

Maison du Peuple

Sûreté
BD DE LA REVOLUTION DU 4 AOUT

French Embassy

CENATRIN

MANDELA

PLACE DES NATIONS UNIES

FESPACO

RUE AGOSTINO NETO

Grand Marché
Canadian Embassy

RUE MAURICE BISHOP

RUE PATRICE LUMUMBA

AV RAOUL FOLLEREAU
American Embassy & USIS

Grande Mosquée

Tourist Office

AV KENNEDY

ZANGOUETIN

AV HOUARI BOUMEDIENNE

KOULOUBA

RUE DE LA MOSQUEE
DR GOURMISSON

PEULOGHIN

COULIBALY

Senegalese Embassy

SAOGHIN

Airport

RESTAURANTS, BARS & CLUBS

Allah Barka	12
Le Belvedere	6
La Chaumière	17
La Fontaine Bleue	4
La Forêt	7
Hamburger House	10
Harlem	2
Horizon	3
Jardin de l'Amitie	5
Lux Bar	1
Le Mandarin	11
Pâtisserie de Koulouba	8
Plateau Universal	15
Quatre Paillotes	13
Sahel	16
Le Tam Tam	14
Tambarze	9

△ Kaya

△ Fada Ngourma, Niamey & Lomé

occupied Ouagadougou, and within a short time subjugated the surrounding empires which they integrated into their colony of Haut-Sénégal Niger. Today, there are still four Mossi kings, whose authority is applied in parallel with that of the Burkinabe state in the kingdoms over which they hold sway.

Arrival and information

Ouagadougou spreads across a considerable area, though the centre is fairly compact. It's officially divided into thirty *secteurs* (like the *arrondissements* of Paris), though you're likely to spend time only in the few at the centre.

The **international airport** is well within the city limits. Collecting your baggage and going through **customs and immigration** is normally an untraumatic experience, but you'll be asked your place of residence; just say the *RAN Hôtel* or any other that comes to mind. There's no bank at the airport. **Getting into town** is easy. Taxi prices are marked up outside the airport (check, and tell the driver before setting off what you're prepared to pay). A quick zip up Avenue Yennenga gets you to the centre in a matter of minutes. Alternatively you can take a #6 bus and disembark at Place des Nations Unies.

Arriving **by train** is even more straightforward as the **station** is just a stone's throw from Avenue Nelson Mandela and the *zone commerciale* in the heart of the city. You could reasonably walk to a hotel from here, but if you've got a lot of luggage bear in mind that the taxis aren't expensive.

The main *gare routière*, commonly known as **Ouagarinter**, is some 6km south of the city on the Route de Pô. If you get into town after dark, you'll have to rely on urban taxis. In the daytime, you can get buses to the centre: they stop on the Route de Pô across from the *gare routière*.

The **Office National du Tourisme Burkinabe** (ONTB) is on Avenue Frobenius, one and a half blocks north of Avenue Boumedienne, near the *Hôtel Indépendance* (☎31.19.59 or 31.19.69; Fax 31.44.34).They have a variety of brochures, but are more useful for game reserves information and bookings.

Orientation and city transport

The precise centre of Ouaga could be considered the **Place des Nations Unies**, with its ironwork globe sculpture. All the major roads seem to start from this square. To the east, Boulevard de la Révolution leads through the **administrative quarter** down to the *style coloniale* **Palais Présidentiel**. The Avenue d'Oubritenga leads off to the northeast, past the **hospital** and on to the **Zone du Bois** (formerly the Bois de Boulogne). This road then joins the main route to Niamey. West of the Place des Nations Unies, Avenue Nelson Mandela passes through the **zone commerciale** and continues to the semi-modern **Maison du Peuple** and the **Place de la Révolution** where speeches and political gatherings take place. To the south, Avenue Kwame Nkrumah runs parallel to Avenue Yennenga. This latter is one of the most animated streets in town, running past the **Grande Mosquée** in a neighbourhood of small *commerçants* before ending near the **airport**.

SECURITY IN OUAGADOUGOU

Ouagadougou is generally very **safe**, but incidents do happen, the most common of which is bag-snatching by thieves riding on the back of *mobylettes* (mopeds). If you need to have all your valuables in one bag, make sure you've a good grip on it and walk on the left-hand side of the road against the traffic. If you pay modest attention, it's very unlikely that anything will befall you.

The town also has distinctive *quartiers* each with its own flavour. Behind the train station, **Moemmin** is the traditional Muslim neighbourhood. Home of Ouaga's grand imam, it was also the site of the town's first mosque. Further north, **Niogsin** is a residential area known for its metalworkers, many of whom still work here in small *atel-iers*. Nearby **Paspanga** has a reputation for having the best *dolotières* – women who make millet beer (*dolo*). Bars and small *cabarets* are common here. In the centre, the Avenue Yennenga passes through **Tiendpalogo** ("the newly arrived"), **Zangouetin**, and **Peuloghin**. The latter two are respectively the Hausa and Fula neighbourhoods with Muslim-style homes and Koranic schools.

City transport

Although you can walk around much of the town centre, you may want to take **buses** to some of the further extremities (Ouagarinter *gare routière*, the *Hôtel Silmandé*'s pool). Ouagadougou has a reasonably good system that will get you almost anywhere for CFA150. In the centre, most buses depart from the Place des Nations Unies, or from in front of the nearby post office.

The alternative is to share a **taxi** – in Ouaga, that's likely to mean a battered Renault 4L. Flag it down on the road and shout your destination. If the other passengers on board are headed the same way, the driver will pick you up. Prices are fixed within the centre, so find out beforehand what they are (usually not more than CFA250). To certain destinations (the airport, train station, luxury hotels and outer suburbs) a higher tariff is normal, and after midnight, the price doubles. But fares are never very high.

Accommodation

From camping sites to four-star hotels, Ouagadougou has a wide range of **places to stay** and backpackers are as well served as business travellers. Beware, however, of arriving in town with no room reservation during the biennial FESPACO film festival fortnight (February 2001, February 2003), as everywhere will be full.

Budget

Auberge Rose des Sables, qtr Saint Leon (BP 2338; ☎30.31.14). Very clean rooms, fans or AC, next door to a garden bar and restaurant. ②–③.

Fondation Charles Dufour, rue de la Chance (BP 2855). From av Yennenga, head west on av Houari Boumedienne and turn left on the third street, the extension of rue de la Chance. A block and a half down to your right you'll find the cheapest accommodation in town, along with a very appealing courtyard. Although there are only three basic, non-S/C rooms, there's a fully equipped communal kitchen. ①.

Hôtel Kadiogo, one block west of av de la Résistance and a block north of av Coulibaly (BP 716; ☎30.69.44). Simple accommodation, but pretty cheap S/C ventilated double rooms (though if you happen to be two women or two men, you'll pay a slight surcharge to share a room). ②.

Hôtel Kilimandjaro, av Coulibaly next to the Théâtre Populaire (01 BP 3407; ☎30.64.74). Hotel with a reputation for cleanliness and friendly service. Budget travellers won't be overstretched by the cost of the tidy S/C rooms with fan, although AC is more expensive. ②.

Hôtel Oubri, rue de la Mosquée, near Place Yennenga and the airport (BP 1689; ☎30.64.89). Clean AC rooms and a bar loaded with ambience – maybe more than you'd want. There's a nice airy terrace and something for every budget – from a bed in a dorm to private rooms with TV for three times the price. ①–③.

Hôtel de la Paix, av Yennenga, three blocks south of the Grande Mosquée (BP 882; ☎33.52.93). This hotel boasts some of the cleanest and most comfortable S/C budget rooms – with AC or fans – and friendly staff. ②.

Hôtel Riviera, av Yatenga beyond Place de la Revolution (BP 410; ☎30.65.99). Decent rooms with fan, a pleasant coutyard, and nice management. Also serves basic meals. ②.

Hôtel Wend Kouni, off av Bassawarga in the Kamasaoghin district (BP 6356; ☎30.80.79). Basic cheap hotel that's beginning to look a little worn. Non-S/C rooms with fans count among the town's best value for money. ②.

Les Lauriers, in the gardens of the Catholic cathedral (BP 387; ☎30.64.90). From av Yennenga, go west on av Houari Boumedienne about 600m and turn left from the concrete roundabout into the cathedral grounds. The *centre d'accueil* for the mission offers spotless accommodation with starched sheets and mosquito nets. Mostly women-only, though four rooms in the women's building are reserved for couples. ①.

Le Pavillon Vert, av de la Liberté, 500m from av Kouanda (01 BP 4715; ☎31.06.11). A popular place with pleasant courtyard that appeals to travellers on a budget as well as those in search of comfort and basic amenities. A range from non-S/C rooms to AC apartments with private WC. The congenial atmosphere and setting tend to make up for the distance from the centre. ②.

Pension Guigsème, av Yennenga, south of the Grande Mosquée (BP 1135; ☎33.46.98). Nothing fancy – non-S/C rooms grouped around a pleasant courtyard – but the price is the centre's cheapest. Cleanish rooms and a decent shower and toilet area make this good value. ①.

Mid-range and expensive

Hôtel Aéroport, av Yennenga, one block south of av Coulibaly (BP 3407; ☎31.39.20). Fairly new hotel with comfortable S/C rooms – most with balconies – and fully AC. ③.

Hôtel Belle Vue, av Nkrumah, one block south of BICIA bank (BP 71; ☎30.84.98; Fax 31.10.32). Clean, comfortable and centrally located hotel with furnished S/C, AC rooms with TV. Also a rooftop terrace where you can look over central Ouaga as you drink or dine. ③.

Hôtel Central, rue de la Chance at northwest corner of Grande Marché (BP 56; ☎30.89.24; Fax 30.89.27). A colonial-style hotel with a great location, and a range of rooms. The popular bar-restaurant (great pizzas) is always full of action. ③–④.

Hôtel Continental, av Loudun across from Ciné Burkina (BP 3593; ☎30.86.36). Clean AC rooms, many with balconies that look onto the bustling commercial centre. Great location, and a popular dining room. There are TVs in the rooms, though these cost extra to watch. Ask about their **annexe**, which is a little cheaper, though in a slightly less convenient area. ③.

Hôtel Delwendé, rue Lumumba, half block west of Grande Marché and BIB bank (BP 570; ☎30.87.57). S/C rooms within the reach of budget travellers in an excellent location. Streetside rooms have balconies from where you can take in the busy life around the market. The balcony restaurant is a popular place for salads and grilled meat. AC rooms available. ③.

Hôtel Eden Park, av Bassawarga, three blocks south of the Mogha Naba palace (01 BP 2027; ☎31.14.86 or 31.14.90; Fax 31.14.88). Luxury high-rise with extras such as swimming pool, nightclub and restaurants, including a rooftop terrace. Comfortable furnishings (colour TV, video, minibars) and some good views from the upper floors. ⑥.

Hôtel de L'Entente Niogsin, one block east of av Kouanda and two blocks north of av de la Liberté (BP 558; ☎31.14.37). A little shabby, but in an interesting neighbourhood of bronze-workers. Cheaper fanned rooms, or AC rooms with private WCs. ②–③.

Hôtel Indépendance, av Coulibaly (BP 5397; ☎30.60.60; Fax 30.67.67). Top hotel in the centre, with good-value rooms and bungalows and a popular poolside bar. ⑥.

Hôtel Relax, av Nelson Mandela across from Maison du Peuple (BP 567; ☎31.32.31 or 31.32.33; Fax 30.89.08). Quite posh hotel with swimming pool. Central location and very good value. ⑥.

Hôtel Ricardo, north of *barrage* no. 2 (BP 439; ☎30.70.72). It's a shame this hotel is so far from the centre, because the comfort and friendly reception are worth the effort. Near a fishing reservoir to the north of town. Good disco, restaurant, and pool. ④–⑤.

Hôtel Silmandé, 3km from the centre, near the reservoir and the Bois de Boulogne (BP 4733; ☎30.01.76; Fax 30.09.71). One of the few high-rises in town, the *Silmandé* is Ouaga's luxury base with total comfort and facilities to unwind – tennis courts, pool, disco and the rest – at prices far in excess of anywhere else. Great views and photo opportunities from the roof. ⑦.

Hôtel Tropicale, av Frobenius in the Tiendpalogo district (BP 1758; ☎31.27.38; Fax 31.08.75). Clean and comfortable, this place is in a busy neighbourhood near the centre. Brace yourself for 5am prayer calls from the nearby mosque. ④.

Hôtel Yibi, av Kwame Nkrumah (BP 1014; ☎30.73.23 or 30.73.70; Fax 30.59.00). New upmarket hotel in the heart of things, with immaculate rooms and a nice pool in a courtyard setting. ⑦.

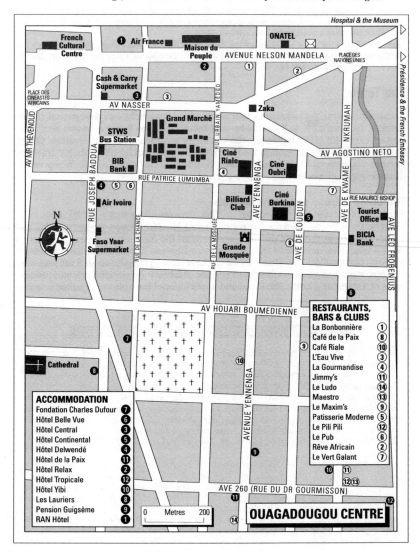

OUAGADOUGOU CENTRE

OK Inn, bd Circulaire, near Ouagarinter and Route de Pô (BP 5397; ☎30.40.61; Fax 30.48.11). Spacious grounds with attractive rooms and bungalows around the pool and gardens. About 6km from the centre, but with free transport to the centre and to the airport. Complete comfort (AC, colour TV, even 12-hole mini-golf) in a relaxing environment. ④–⑤.

RAN Hôtel, av Nelson Mandela (BP 62; ☎30.61.06 or 30.61.07). The colonial era's best, the old station hotel has aged with a certain grace. No longer the swankiest, it still offers good service and facilities, with a pool (CFA1500 for non-guests), French restaurant and bars. ④.

Camping

Ouaga Camping, on Route de Pô, 500m from Ouagarinter; signs mark the way from the *gare routière* (☎30.48.51). Quiet setting with inexpensive bungalows and plenty of space to pitch your tent. They also have a good restaurant and bar. ①.

Le Poko Club, 15km west of Ouaga on the Bobo road (BP 275; ☎30.24.06). The rooms here are slightly more expensive than at the *Ouaga*, and it's only accessible with your own transport, but the camping's cheaper, and nicer too. ①.

The Town

A satisfying way to get to know Ouaga is to settle at a favourite *café terrasse* and simply observe the town's life as it passes by your table. Once you become known you'll find contact easy with other habitués, who are never too rushed for conversation. Ouaga has few sights to take in, though the lure of the **Grand Marché** will probably draw you to more than one visit. The small **Musée National** is also worth a look. When you're through with sightseeing, the shopping possibilities are endless.

The Grand Marché and crafts markets

After Sankara razed the old market in 1985, Ouagadougou had a gaping hole in its heart for three years. Then the **Nouveau Grand Marché "Rood Woko"** opened, and Ouaga now boasts the most modern (and perhaps the most attractive) marketplace in West Africa. The variety of stock ranges from Chinese bicycles to American beauty products and local *gri-gris*. This is by far the best place to shop for fresh **fruit and vegetables**, meat and poultry (live), and cereals. Basketry (of which Burkina produces some of the region's best), like the round multicoloured **baskets** with leather-wrapped

---

THE NABAYIUS GOU – OR FALSE CEREMONY

Ouagadougou's answer to the changing of the guard, the **Nabayius Gou** is a re-enactment, every Friday at 7am by the western side of the Mogho Naba's palace, of events that took place in the early eighteenth century, in the reign of Ouarga, the twentieth Mogho Naba, when the kingdom's frontiers were under threat by raids from Yako.

The Mogho Naba's favourite wife had obtained his permission to visit her family, but she hadn't returned on the agreed date. Heartbroken, he prepared to set out and find her, but his courtiers, fearing war, begged him to stay. With a heavy heart, the king concurred that his duty to his subjects came before personal concerns and, dismounting from his horse, he returned to his palace. The ceremony reaffirms this commitment to his people.

The present-day Mogho Naba comes out of his palace dressed in red for war. His courtiers surround him, begging him to stay, and eventually he heeds their pleas and returns to the palace, to re-emerge in white. This rather solemn affair isn't a spectacle put on for tourists, and needs to be approached with some respect. Nonetheless it's a fascinating ceremony, well worth getting up early for. Photographs aren't usually allowed, but you may be able to get special permission by applying (in advance, with a normal photo permit) to the Naba's secretariat.

handles, are sold beside Asian-made enamel bowls, commonly used for eating throughout Africa. Much of the market is reserved for **fabric sellers**, who sit by stacks of much-prized Holland wax prints, made in the Netherlands, and the slightly less revered "Manchesters," made in England. They also sell quite decent, and substantially cheaper, prints made down the road in Koudougou and Côte d'Ivoire plus a good selection of indigo tie-dyed cloth from Guinea and Mali. Tailors work inside the market to the hum of lovingly tended, foot-operated sewing machines, and will make clothes to order. They're adept at European styles (shirts, trousers, dresses) if you don't think you'll get much wear out of more African designs. But the best way to get what you want, as always, is to take along a garment to be copied.

A good place to start shopping for **crafts** is at the state-operated **Centre Artisanal**, 3 av Dimdolobsom (BP 544; Mon–Fri 8am–noon & 3–6pm), near the post office. The quality of the bronze castings, carvings and weavings is quite good, and prices are fixed, while Burkinabe artists have mastered the exotic **batik** form better than any others in the region, mixing beautiful colours with striking village scenes. Come to get an idea of how much items should be before heading off to bargain in the **Grand Marché** or at the **antiquaires de l'Hôtel RAN**. These latter operators sell from tables set up along the av Nelson Mandela in front of the hotel. Despite their name, they don't deal in antiques, but do offer one of the widest selection of **bronzes** in town as well as many other crafts. **Masks**, imported from the Côte d'Ivoire and Mali, may be treated in workshops in Laglin or Dapoya to give them an ancient look, which is often aesthetically effective if nothing else. Other wooden objects include **Senoufo chairs** and **Dogon carvings**. You'll also find jewellery – desert crosses and terracotta beads from Niger for example, and the ubiquitous old glass trade beads. Vendors can also be found in front of the Cobodium supermarket, across from the Maison du Peuple, where there tends to be more of an emphasis on **Tuareg leather boxes**.

Try too, the **Centre de Formation Féminine et Artisanale** at the exit of town on the Bobo road (Gounghin district). This is a religious-sponsored organization, where the women make a variety of crafts such as Tuareg-inspired **woollen rugs**, and less compelling tablecloths and napkins embroidered with African motifs. For **leather goods**, there's the **Centre du Tannage** on the Fada road opposite the prison. Finally, the Galerie Art et Emballage, 51 av Yennenga, offers a good selection of **masks** and **wooden statues**; a bigger selection, including paintings, carved tables, jewellery and antiques can be found at the Galerie des Arts, 4 av Oubritenga.

The Musée National

Ouaga's **Musée National** (Tues–Sat 7.30am–12.30pm & 3–5.30pm) is currently situated in the Maison du Peuple on Avenue Nelson Mandela until the contruction of its new building on Avenue Charles de Gaulle is completed – planned for 2001/2002. Primarily an **ethnographic collection**, it holds various Burkinabe household utensils, tools and weapons. Numerous **clay pots** are on display, including ones made specifically to store clothing, jewellery or grain. Among the most interesting are the magic pots used for keeping medicines. Their potency was protected with sacrifices. **Basketmaking** and **weaving exhibits** from around Burkina are complemented by **regional costumes**, including a Mossi **chief's regalia** – compare it with what the Mogho Naba wears on a Friday morning at the *Nabayius Gou* ceremony. A good part of the display is dedicated to sculptures in wood, including **ancestral statues** of the Bobo, Mossi, Lobi and Gourounsi. These are accompanied by carved stools and sceptres (*kwara*) symbolizing the authority of chiefs, and a fantastic collection of **masks** showing the different regional styles: abstract and geometric in the north; exaggerated animal shapes in the Senoufo country; cylindrical helmets used by the Mossi; and horizontally shaped *masques papillon* ("butterfly masks") common among the Bobo-Bwa.

Sankara's grave

After Sankara's assassination (see p.625), his body was relegated to an **unmarked grave** outside the centre. Martyrdom made the leader an international symbol of hope, and people from throughout the continent still make the pilgrimage to his burial site. The route to the grave follows much the same path that the body took – from the presidential palace, head east along Boulevard Charles de Gaulle for 2.5km, turn right at the Tagui petrol station and head straight on for 1km. To the left, you'll see a large tree behind a row of *banco* houses. Fifty metres east of the tree is a row of whitewashed tombs, bearing only the name and rank of those killed in the 1987 coup – among them, Thomas Sankara. Despite the isolation of the site, it's not uncommon to find mourners paying their respects, or leaving scribbled notes on the grave. An elderly woman living nearby daily fills a clay pot with fresh water – her personal homage to the man who lashed out against the system, and provided her with low-cost housing.

Eating

Finding good, reasonably priced **places to eat** is no problem in Ouaga. The town is full of small **café terrasses** separated from the dusty streets by brightly painted fences. A host of such places along Avenue Yennenga all serve similar food – spaghetti, rice and meat sauce, *couscous*, potato stew. Most of them also do large bowls of home-made **yogurt** – delicious, especially at breakfast when it's freshly made.

The more upmarket restaurants – and there are some very good ones, serving a range of international cuisines – are rarely overpriced, but where the city really excels is at **street food**. In the evenings, the streets fill with **brochette vendors** gathered around the glow of their charcoal fires. You can get beef and lamb, beautifully cooked, but if you want to savour the smoky flavour, be sure to ask for *sans piment*. Kerosene lamps light the tables of *les cafémans* who also emerge in the morning to whip up omelettes and sticky Nescafé concoctions. Finally, Ouaga's **patisseries** are wonderfully lively places to sit eating fattening cakes while watching the world go by.

Patisseries

La Bonbonnière, av Nelson Mandela across from the Maison du Peuple. Still the most popular (and pricey) pastry shop in Ouaga and a great breakfast address. Fresh and flakey croissants to go with juices and yoghurt. The apple turnovers and meat pies are also excellent. Magazines on the tables for browsing.

Boulangerie/Pâtisserie de Koulouba, av de la Résistance, one block north of av Houari Boumedienne. Second only to *La Bonbonnière* in popularity. Great pastries, sandwiches and omelettes. Ice cream served until 8pm.

Boulangerie/Patisserie Moderne, rue Lumumba, half a block south of rue de la Chance. Well-known bakery and a *de rigueur* breakfast joint if you're staying at the *Delwendé* upstairs.

La Gourmandise, southeast corner of the Grand Marché. Upstairs café with terrace overlooking the market. Popular spot for expats to wind down after the rigours of shopping. Hamburgers, hot dogs and Lebanese sandwiches to chase with juice, ice cream and pastries.

Budget

Café de la Paix, av Loudun near Ciné Burkina. Mostly African food; baked chicken a speciality (CFA1000 and up).

Café Riale, av Yennenga, one and a half blocks south of the Grande Mosquée. The best of the countless *café terrasses* in the area with a more extensive menu, including fish, than most.

Jazz Temple, av Loudun, near av Houari Boumedienne. Small African place with courtyard where you can hear live music Fri and Sat nights.

Les Lauriers, unmarked restaurant in the grounds of the Catholic cathedral. Run by the sisters, this restaurant serves home-style meals with soup, veg, meat, bread and fruit plus a dessert. Only one menu each day, and you have to sign up ninety minutes in advance. Be punctual or you will miss the noon–12.15pm and 7–7.15pm serving times. Solid meals for under CFA1000.

Resto/Maquis Le Coin, corner of av Yennenga and av Houari Boumedienne. This small restaurant has a long and varied menu, mostly of French food. Meals for about CFA2000 and the best murals in town.

La Rose des Sables, near the Mogho Naba palace. A signboard on av Bassawarga (two blocks north of av Coulibaly) points the way to this popular restaurant. Good and inexpensive African food in a protected courtyard.

Moderate to expensive
AFRICAN

Akwaba, av Kwame Nkrumah, Cite an IV (☎31.23.76). Excellent African dishes prepared by a Ghanaian cook; slightly on the pricey side, but worth it.

Allah Barka, av de la Résistance. Moderately priced African and European specialities served in an AC dining room or in the shaded outdoor eating area.

La Forêt, av Bassawarga (BP 1363; ☎30.72.96). Where well-heeled Ouagalais head for lunch, this restaurant has its own swimming pool beside which you can snack on sandwiches or order the *menu du jour*.

Horizon, near *Pavillon Vert*. Good local dishes including *riz gras, couscous* and great salads.

Quatre Paillotes, av Kadiogo (☎34.04.05). Situated in an attractive courtyard with shady trees and flowering shrubs. Extensive choice of African and European dishes ranging from *agouti* to pigeon or rabbit. Around CFA2000.

Rêve Africain, 100m southwest of Place des Nations Unies. Disco which doubles as a popular restaurant with West African specialities. Pleasant courtyard and friendly service.

Tambarze, av de la Résistance. Well known by the expat community, this reasonably priced restaurant features excellent salads and a fine beef fondue. Desserts are recommended too.

Le Walemb, off av Coulibaly, behind *Hôtel Aéroport* (☎33.24.52). Large walled courtyard with some of the best African food in town. Try the *yassa au poulet* or *atieké au poisson*. Well worth a visit.

EUROPEAN AND ASIAN

Le Belvedere, av Raoul Follereau (☎33.64.21). One of Ouaga's fancier restaurants with pizza and other *cucina Italiana* complemented by African and Lebanese dishes. Shaded terrace and AC dining room.

Central Pizzeria, *Hôtel Central*. The only place in town where you can get pizza at lunchtime.

La Chaumière, 106 av Coulibaly, two blocks east of the Théâtre Populaire (☎33.43.23). Cuisine from the south of France with a special accent on salads, fish and prime cuts of meat. Attractive setting on a terrace shaded with *paillotes*.

Chinois Restaurant, av Lumumba, west of rue de la Chance. Ouaga's foremost Chinese restaurant with a wide selection of à la carte dishes.

L'Eau Vive, rue du Marche (☎30.63.03). Most famous restaurant in Ouaga, this is an appealing place where the sister-waitresses pause mid-service to belt out *Ave Maria*. More international than French, the daily rotating menu shifts between African, European and American specialities (from CFA5000). Closed Sun.

La Fontaine Bleue, 12 av Dimdolobsom (☎30.70.83). Excellent French dishes in a charming garden setting.

Hamburger House, av Houari Boumedienne (☎30.80.92). American fast-food staples served with more unusual, slightly pricier, dishes like . . . Japanese crepes? Try that with a milkshake.

Hôtel Ricardo, north of *barrage* no.1. Hotel restaurant which concocts its pizzas in a wood-burning oven and offers a variety of *grillades* on the side.

Le Mandarin, off av Houari Boumedienne (☎33.23.75). Vietnamese food including *nem* and excellent pork ribs. Good service if a little pricey. Look for the sign near *L'Escapade*.

Ougarit, av Houari Boumedienne (☎31.18.60) Classy pizzeria also serving well-prepared French and Middle Eastern cooking.

La Pizzeria, *Hôtel Indépendance*. In the evenings, good pizza which you can eat poolside.

Le Pub, rue Lumumba next to *Hôtel Delwendé* (☎31.25.25). Intimate restaurant with small wooden booths and a terrace in front. Excellent and reasonably priced European menu (salads, *fruits de mer*). The proprietor is a jazz aficionado, hence the good music and American jazz photos gracing the walls.

Le Safari, av de la Résistance. Pleasant French restaurant where you can eat in the AC dining room or outdoor courtyard.

Le Tam Tam, av Kadioga at av Che Guevara near SOGEBAF station (☎30.28.04). Sauerkraut, sausages, breaded veal and cordon bleu – a range of Austrian specialities you never dreamed of seeing here. Well-prepared and not overly pricey. Occasional live performances in the outdoor courtyard.

Le Vert Galant, rue Amirou Thiombiano (☎30.69.80). This French restaurant features fish and meat dishes accompanied by salads and soups, crepes and sorbets and a small wine list. Around CFA5000 and up.

Nightlife

One of the few Sahelian towns that's predominantly non-Muslim, Ouagadougou lives for the night. Energy suppressed by the day's heavy heat is ecstatically released when the sun sets. The streets fill with thousands of Ouagalais walking to the cinema, checking out the clubs or just looking for conversation and a breath of night air (staying inside, of course, is mostly too hot). Ouaga's **bars and discos** pack out nightly and often feature live music and dancing. As an extra bonus, they're cheap (cover charges and drink prices are fixed by law and covers are never more than CFA4000). All this adds up to a good time – and some credit to the revolution.

Host city to the FESPACO (see p.621), Ouaga is full of cinephiles and, in addition to a town square (the Place des Cineastes) dedicated to the seventh art, boasts some great movie theatres, showing some of the very best in new African **cinema**. For **theatre**, it's worth checking out the Théâtre Populaire Desiré Bonogo on Avenue Coulibaly in the southwest of town (☎30.88.09 or 30.88.06), which also hosts a biannual theatre **festival** in late November. You might also catch a show at the French Cultural Centre (see p.643) or the Atelier Théâtre Burkinabe ATB (☎33.50.84). It's worth picking up the *Burkina A Faire* weekly announcement of events, including film and live acts; ask at any hotel. You can also find out what's happening in town from the notice board outside Zaka Cultural Center on Avenue Yennenga.

Clubs and bars

Burkina Bar, av de la Résistance, one and a half blocks north of av Houari Boumedienne. Loudspeakers blast African and Western pop over the courtyard dance area every night from 9pm. Food served. Modest cover at weekends.

Harlem, Dapoya Secteur, north of av de la Liberté and east of *Hôtel Pavillon Vert*. Outside courtyard with *paillotes*. Nightly live performances and disco sounds. No cover.

Jardin de l'Amitie, near Place des Nations Unies. Very popular garden bar, especially during FESPACO. Occasional live music.

Jimmy's, av Kwame Nkrumah, corner of av 260. One of the most popular indoor discos in Ouaga and usually packed out on weekends. Cover Fri and Sat (free entrance during the week) and pricey drinks thereafter. Open from 10.30pm.

Le Ludo, half block south of *Hôtel de la Paix*. Also known as *Lido*, this is an outdoor *resto-dancing* with excellent *coq au vin* and loud music.

Lux Bar, Kologo Naba Secteur, off av Yatenga. Loud pop music nightly and occasional dance competitions. You'll need to take a taxi from the centre to get there. No cover.

Maestro, near *Jimmy's*. Piano bar like no other, featuring live bands in a red and black loungy decor. No cover.

Le Maxim's, av Loudun, half a block south of av Houari Boumedienne. Plush indoor disco with music from 10pm. Wed to Sun; weekend cover includes drink.

Le Pili Pili, av Kwame Nkrumah next to *Jimmy's*. Live music nightly. Beers are reasonably priced, and they serve pizza. No cover.

Plateau Universal, near *Rose des Sables*. Local drinking bar, with a friendly terrace atmosphere which picks up at night. Simple cheap meals also available.

Sahel, av Loudun. Vibrant new hot spot for live music and dancing; crowded nightly. Popular with expats.

Le Waguess, Cité An III, av Capt Kouanda (☎31.36.33). Pricey but popular outdoor disco shaded by *paillotes*. Thurs–Sun from 11pm. High cover.

Zaka Cultural Centre, av Yennenga (☎31.53.12 or 31.42.41). Live traditional music nightly, and both open-air and indoor restaurants plus a bar.

Cinemas

Ciné Burkina, near the Grande Mosquée. Modern AC theatre with bar and the newest films.

Ciné Oubri, rue Lumumba near the Grand Marché. Outdoor theatre, low prices and, generally, older films.

Kadiogo, Gounghin Nord near the Lycée St Jean. Enclosed, but no AC. Foreign or "B" films.

Neerwaya, Cité An III off av Capt Kouanda. The newest AC theatre with big screen and some African films.

Rialé, rue Lumumba near the Grand Marché. Another inexpensive open-air theatre.

Listings

Aid agencies If you want to contact any of the agencies, there's a central bureau for all the NGOs in Burkina, the Secrétariat Permanent des ONG, on ☎30.01.75.

Airlines Aeroflot, av de la Résistance at rue Neto (☎30.71.29); Air Afrique, av Bassawarga (☎30.18.29 or 30.65.18); Air Algérie, av Kwame Nkrumah (☎31.23.01 or 31.23.02); Air Burkina, off av Bassawarga, (☎31.47.05 or 30.76.76); Air France, 12 av Nelson Mandela (☎30.63.65 or 33.40.61); Air Ivoire, rue Badoua at rue Lumumba (☎30.62.07 or 30.11.95); Sabena, av de la Résistance at av Raoul Follereau (☎30.58.80, 30.58.81 or 36.15.72).

American Express There's no official representation. The BICIA Bank on av Kwame Nkrumah will replace lost or stolen cheques if you present receipts.

Banks Bank hours may vary. Typically they are Mon & Thurs 7.30–11am & 3–4pm, Tues, Wed & Fri 7.30–11am & 3.30–5pm. Note that there's no bank at the airport. In town, the fastest service tends to be at the BICIA, av Kwame Nkrumah, a block east of Ciné Burkina, who give Visa cash advances and accept travellers' cheques at their separate first-floor change counter. To change money, enter by the door to the right of the main entrance. You can also try the BIB on av

---

EMBASSIES AND CONSULATES IN OUAGADOUGOU

Canada, av Agostino Neto, west of av de la Résistance (☎31.18.94 or 31.18.95). Handles the affairs of nationals of Commonwealth states in Burkina.

Côte d'Ivoire, av Raoul Follereau, opposite the American Embassy (☎30.66.37 or 31.36.20).

France, bd de la Révolution (☎31.32.73 or 31.32.74; Fax 31.32.81; Consulate: ☎30.67.70). Visas issued for Togo and Mauritania. Two photos required, prices vary.

Ghana, av Bassawarga (☎30.76.35 or 34.37.77).

Mali (☎38.19.22 or 30.05.35).

Nigeria, av d'Oubritenga (☎30.66.67 or 36.10.87).

Senegal, off av Yennenga (☎31.28.11). At Hôtel Aéroport , go south; turn right at the first street, and it's one-and-a-half blocks on the left.

UK, Honorary Consulate, Tobacco Marketing Consultants Ltd, 306 rue 13, 04 av Oubritenga heading east past the hospital (☎31.11.37).

USA, av Raoul Follereau, 3 blocks east of av de la Résistance (☎30.67.23 or 31.63.60; Fax 31.23.68; Consulate: ☎30.75.41).

Dimdolobsom off Place des Nations Unies, but you will have to show receipts or proof of purchase. If you want to change cash when the banks are closed, and are willing to accept a lower rate, try the counter at the Marina Market on av Yennenga. Try to get the smallest denominations possible when changing money, as change is hard to find in town.

Bicycles and mobylettes The best place to try is the bicycle/moped market next to the cemetery on av Houari Boumedienne, two blocks west of av Yennenga. A new bike costs about CFA100,000, or you can get one secondhand for perhaps half that. You can rent too – rates are open to discussion, but range between CFA3000–6000 per day.

Books and magazines The premier place for books is the Diacfa Librarie on the rue du Marché at the northwest corner of the market. They have a large selection of French titles and a good sampling of the foreign press. Some maps and tour guides also available. Also check out the bookshop at the *Hôtel Indépendance*. Used books, including a few English-language titles, are sold on av de la Résistance, across from Aeroflot. Finally, try the bookshop at the *Silmandé* or the racks of the *Patisserie Koulouba*.

Car rental In Ouaga, typical rates are CFA7000–10,000 per day for a small car, plus a distance charge of around CFA100/km and a 22 percent road tax. It adds up to about CFA25,000/day if you drive 100km or so. You usually won't need to get a chauffeur, but you may have to pay insurance (CFA3000/day) if you don't. A driver costs about CFA3000. The two main rental agencies are: Burkina Auto Location at the *Hôtel Indépendance* (BP 147; ☎30.68.11 or 30.64.61), and at the *Hôtel Silmandé* (☎30.02.03); and Express Auto Location, *Hôtel RAN* (☎30.61.06 or 30.61.07). Other agencies include DEZ Auto Location on av Yennenga (BP 4222; ☎30.46.56); Ets Derme Abdoulaye (☎30.66.56); EABIEF (☎38.22.90); Proneval (☎31.71.83); and STE Auto Location Services (☎33.56.69). Alternatively, **taxis** can be rented in town for about CFA15,000 per eight-hour shift.

Cultural Centres The American Cultural Centre (USIS) is on av Kennedy near av Houari Boumedienne (Mon–Fri 7.30am–noon & 1–4.30pm; ☎30.17.13). They have an exhibition space here

---

MOVING ON FROM OUAGA

Buses
Many bus companies provide services from Ouaga to every conceivable national and international destination – except Lomé, which is currently serviced only by *taxi brousse*. Major bus companies are:

Sans Frontières (☎31.30.41), av Coulibaly across from the Théâtre Populaire in Bilbalogho district. Two buses daily to Abidjan via Yamassoukro. Quicker than the train, unless you don't manage to clear customs by midnight and have to sleep in your seat at the border (not unheard of). They also have two daily buses to Bobo, and a daily service to Ouahigouya, Kaya, Djibo and Kantchari, from where you can continue to Niamey.

SOGEBAF (☎30.36.27), av Kadiogo at av Che Guevara in Gounghin district near *Le Tam Tam*. Eight buses a day to Bobo-Dioulasso and a daily departure to Ouahigouya.

STC, av Houari Boumedienne (☎30.87.50). The Ghanaian State Transport Corporation provides six coaches a month to Accra with stops at Pô, Bolgatanga, Tamale and Kumasi. Departure days alternate between Mon and Fri (on certain weeks buses leave on both days); call in advance. Buses depart from Ouagarinter.

STMB, between rue de Commerce and av Cpt. Niande Ouedraogo (☎31.44.72 or 31.13.63). Reported as the most reliable bus service. Daily afternoon buses – some AC – to Bobo (CFA4000–6000). Also buses to Ouahigouya, Djibo, Gorom-Gorom, Kaya, Banfora, Fada and other locations. There are also STMB taxis which are metered, but more expensive (call for one on ☎31.89.75).

TRANSMIF, on av Kadiogo, near SOGEBAF (☎87.00.10). Four weekly buses to Gaoua via Diébougou. Also buses to Banfora and Ouahigouya.

Other useful bus companies include: **La Societe Colombe du Faso** (☎31.61.53) for buses to Pô and Leo; **SOTRAO**, av Charles de Gaulle (☎30.42.96) for buses to Bobo-Dioulasso and Gaoua; and **STBF** (☎31.27.95) for buses to Bobo (3 daily; CFA4000) and Ouahigouya (2 daily).

and show videos of last week's ABC and CBS news along with various films and events. Pick up a schedule here or at the library (major newspapers, weeks out of date) located across the street from the embassy on av Raoul Follereau (Mon–Fri 9am–noon & 3.30–7pm). The French Cultural Centre (Centre Culturel George Méliès) is on av Nelson Mandela (Tues–Sat 9am–noon & 3.30–7pm; ☎30.60.97; *ccf@fasonet.bf*). With a vast library, exhibition space, open-air theatre, indoor cinema and shaded café featuring direct broadcasts of French television, this is the most active cultural centre in Ouaga and an excellent source of information. Get the month's programme when you arrive in town. Finally, the Zaka Cultural Centre, av Yennenga (☎31.53.12 or 31.42.41), has live traditional music nightly, and both open-air and indoor restaurants plus a bar.

Film and developing Many places in the centre develop black-and-white or colour film – some with same- day service. One such place is Photo Olympia on av Loudun, across from Ciné Burkina. To buy film, try Photo Vision across from the *Hôtel Central*; Photo Optique off av Loudun one block west of Ciné Burkina; and Photo Lux on av Lumumba across from the Ciné Oubri.

Horse riding Conyougo Polo Club, 12km south of Ouaga on the Pô road. No membership necessary to ride. Around CFA5000 an hour, and an interesting way to see some of the countryside. Polo matches Sun at 4pm. Also try Cheval Mandingue on ☎34.04.04.

Hospital and medical treatment Hôpital Yalgado Ouédraogo, av d'Oubritenga (☎30.66.43; ambulance: ☎30.65.44). For a simple consultation, contact Dr Bernard André (☎33.67.79) at the Belgian embassy.

Internet The best place in town is CENATRIN (Centre National de Traitement de l'Information) at 876 Boulevard du Faso (☎31.26.74 or 31.26.75; *www.cenatrin.bf*).

Maps The Institut Géographique du Burkina, 21 bd de la Révolution (☎32.48.23 or 32.48.24) has decent city maps of Ouaga and Bobo (CFA1500 each), plus a good national map with routes

Official Taxi Brousse Stations

Taxis from the **Ouagarinter gare routière** leave for: Lomé, Niamey, Abidjan, and Hamalé and Bolgatanga in Ghana. Ouagarinter also serves most destinations in Burkina.

Northern towns like Djibo and Ouahigouya are served by the **Tampouy gare secondaire** on Avenue Yatenga, just north of the railway tracks and 4km from the city centre. You can even get to Bobo, Kaya and Dori from here.

Uuofficial Taxi Brousse Stations

There are also several **unofficial stations** in town, which are subject to closure by the police (not that the vehicles themselves are in any way illegal). Fairly established is the station at the Total station near the Zaka Cultural Centre, southwest of Place des Nations Unies. Taxis collect fares here for Lomé and to the eastern towns on the road to Fada. For some unknown reason, Lomé taxis are about thirty percent cheaper from this station than those leaving from Ouagarinter. Also check at the service station across the road for other destinations.

If you're heading to Bobo, Diebougou, Gaoua and Léo it's worth checking the station on Avenue Kadiogo at Avenue de l'Entente (across from the Elf).

Trains

The Société des Chemins de Fer Burkinabe runs a daily train via Koudougou, Bobo, Banfora to Abidjan in Côte d'Ivoire. Trains are comfortable, but often late. There is also a service to Kaya, departing once a week on Saturday around 8am. Since schedules do change, you should check them at the station, or call ☎30.60.47, 30.60.48 or 30.60.49). At certain times of the year, for example at the beginning and end of school terms, national holidays and vacation periods, you can get a thirty percent student discount for one-way travel and fifty percent off a round-trip ticket by showing an ISIC card.

Planes

Air Burkina operates flights to Bobo most days of the week.

(CFA3250), and detailed topographic maps (CFA3250) which are useful if you're heading off the beaten track.

Pharmacies Two central pharmacies are Pharmacie du Sud on av Yennenga (☎30.65.37 or 33.36.31) and Pharmacie Keneya across from the market.

Photography permits Obtainable from the Ministère de l'Environnement et du Tourisme, rue Cpt. Niande Ouedraogo (☎30.63.99; Fax 32.00.29) – a process which normally takes no more than five minutes and which costs nothing.

Post office The main PTT is open Mon–Fri 7am–12.15pm and 3–5.15pm, Sat 8–11.45am.

Supermarkets Near the Grande Marché you'll find: Self Service, the town's best-stocked store, a half block west of av Yennenga and a block north of rue Lumumba; Cobodium, on av Nelson Mandela across from the Maison du Peuple; and Cash and Carry, on rue du Marché at rue Badoua. The Marina Market, on av Yennenga across from the Grande Mosquée, is open daily until at least 10pm.

Swimming pools One of the cheapest pools is at *La Forêt* restaurant on av Bassawarga (CFA1000 Mon–Fri, 9am–6pm; weekends it can get a little crowded and the price goes up). Of the hotels, the *RAN*'s pool is inexpensive, central and never crowded (CFA1500 Mon–Fri; CFA2000 on weekends).

Telephones Go to the ONATEL–Agence building three doors down from the main post office on av Nelson Mandela (daily 7am–10pm). They sell a magnetic *télécarte*, which can be used in booths outside the building, as well as in the *Hôtel Indépendance* and Ciné Burkina. You can also send telexes and faxes from the ONATEL (Mon–Fri 7am–12.30pm & 3–5.30pm, Sat 8am–noon).

Travel agents Besides national excursions to places like the Lobi country, the southern Sahel and the reserves, larger operators arrange interesting treks to the Dogon country and Timbuktu in Mali, to Togo, Côte d'Ivoire, Ghana and Benin. The major ones are: Globe Voyages, av Loudun next to BICIAB (☎30.58.98; Fax 30.87.94); Kenedia Travel, 1029 av Kwame Nkrumah (BP 1908; ☎31.59.69; Fax 31.59.70); Sahel Voyages, 608 av de la Résistance in the RDC building (06 BP 9186; ☎31.53.45; Fax 31.35.04); Savanna Tour, at *Hôtel Indépendance* (BP 0457; ☎30.60.61; Fax 30.67.67); Vacances OK Raid, at the *OK Inn* (01 BP 5397; ☎31.70.42 or 30.40.61; Fax 30.48.11).

Visa extensions Processed at the *Sûreté*, on the corner of bd de la Révolution and av de la Résistance.

Western Union Money transfers possible at Residence Aziz on av Kwame Nkrumah (☎30.85.48 or 30.85.49) or Sonapost (☎30.64.20).

From Ouaga to Koudougou

West of Ouaga, the **road to Koudougou** passes through a number of villages where you could reasonably stop if you've got your own transport and aren't pressed for time. Barely out of the city, you arrive in the small town of **Tanguin-Dassouri** which has a lively market every three days. From here a *piste* leads 6km north to a friendly village renowned for its sacred crocodiles – **Besoulé**. When you arrive here, teenage boys collect a small fee for your visit and the cost of a chicken and will show you where the *caïmans* live. After sacrificing a chicken, you can touch and photograph the reptiles (the oldest male is the most docile). There's no public transport from Tanguin-Dassouri to Besoulé, and the place is much less visited than **SABOU** – about 90km down the main road to Bobo – where the crocodile pool (CFA1500) is a staple destination for tour operators. Sabou has become a ghastly trap, although at least it's in a pleasant setting and has a modest *campement* (BP 1311; ☎44.55.01; ②).

Koudougou

Before reaching Sabou, the main road to Bobo branches in the direction of **KOUDOUGOU**, Burkina Faso's third-largest town. It's a quiet place with wide tree-lined avenues, but a certain level of activity is assured by the country's largest textile factory, **Faso Fani**, and no less than three secondary schools (*collèges*). Koudougou is also the hometown of the first president of Upper Volta, Maurice Yaméogo.

During the day, wander around the **market**, which is especially good for its fruit – mangos, pineapples, avocados, bananas – vegetables and cereals. There's also a reasonable selection of **handicrafts** too; woven goods (hats and baskets), leather (handbags, wallets and shoes) and pottery (jugs and bowls of all sizes). You'll find ready-to-wear outfits made from locally handwoven and embroidered cloth. There's a superb bronze maker in Koudougou – seek out Gandema Mamadou's shop in Secteur 7 if you're interested in buying.

Practicalities

Koudougou boasts a variety of **places to stay**: nothing very luxurious, but several comfortable places with AC and a number of more inexpensive options. Cheapest is the *Auberge Boulkiemde* (①), a local hangout with a restaurant, lively bar and slightly depressing non-S/C rooms. The *Relais de la Gare* (BP 250; 44.01.38; ②), 100m from the train station, houses a spacious bar and a *dancing*, while the friendly *Hôtel Yelba Centrale* (☎44.00.91; ②–③), on the same street as the old mosque, has clean, non-S/C rooms, some with AC, and a nice bar. *Hôtel Toulourou*, in the centre near the motor park (BP 100; ☎44.01.70; ②–③) is convenient and comfortable with S/C rooms, some AC, and also has a European-style restaurant serving good, reasonably priced African and continental meals. Probably the nicest hotel in town, though a bit far from the centre, is the *Hôtel Photo-Luxe*, on the junction of the old and new roads to Ouaga (BP 47; ☎44.00.87; ③). Clean and friendly, with many S/C, AC rooms, it also has an excellent bar, nightclub, and small pool (fee for non-guests).

Apart from the hotel restaurants, plenty of **street food** is sold near the market or at the train station. A Koudougou speciality is *pintade* (guinea fowl) which you see being grilled on roadside braziers in the evening.

Evening diversions include a couple of **cinemas** – the Nelson Mandela on the main road to Ouaga, and a second one north of the market near the mosque. The town also boasts an impressive new **théâtre populaire** in the west beyond the Palais de Justice. Koudougou has its own troupe that puts on periodic performances (mostly in More), worth seeing if you're in town at the right moment. On other nights, the theatre doubles as an open-air cinema. Good **discos** in town include the *Boulgou* on the Old Ouaga Road which also serves African food, *Au Joie du Peuple* in the north of town and, the newest addition, *Lambada*. For a daytime or evening drink, try the *Auxi-Détente* bar across from the *taxi brousse* station, at the entrance to the Cine Yam.

Changing money is far easier in Bobo or Ouaga. The Koudougou BICIA changes cash (FF) only and the BIB wants to see receipts before changing even major travellers' cheques.

Moving on, a daily **train** leaves Koudougou in each direction. The **autogare** for Bobo and Côte d'Ivoire is next to the train station, while vehicles leave for Ouaga (frequent buses operated by STWS; CFA1000) and the north from near the market.

From Ouaga east to Fada-Ngourma

The route to Niamey runs from Ouagadougou through the **Gourmantché country**. The first town of any size on this road is **Koupéla**, which, on the main road to Togo, is one large and very busy intersection.

Koupéla

The flow of traffic through **KOUPÉLA** makes for a lively scene. The town has a large daily **market** renowned for its pottery, concentrated around the southern end. There's also a small *centre artisanal* on the junction of the Ouaga and Togo roads, with a very limited selection of leather and weaving by artisans with disabilities. Across from the *centre artisanal* is a BICIA **bank**, though there's no guarantee you can change travellers' cheques here. If you want to take in a movie, the Buuru Cinema is right next to the *Hôtel Calypso* on the main road; they don't show recent releases.

Practicalities

If you want to **stay the night** in Koupéla, there are several options. The *campement* (BP 62; ☎70.01.33; ①) on the main Ouaga road has a bar, restaurant and basic, non-S/C rooms; for twice the standard price they throw in a "shower" – for which read bucket, as there isn't any running water. Better value is the *Hôtel Calypso* next door (BP 31; ☎70.03.50; ①), which has very clean S/C rooms – if you can stand the noise from the adjoining bar. If both places are full, you can try the friendly *Bon Séjour* behind the post office (BP 10; ①), though their rooms – non-S/C – tend to be dirty.

Food is no problem in town as countless vendors line the streets waiting for taxis and buses to roll in, many after the slog of the appalling road from the Togolese border. Buy a grilled *pintade*, take it to the *Amicale Bar* on the eastern edge of the market, and wash it down with a cold Brakina, or buy good grilled fish from just outside the *campement* and eat it in the bar there. On the same road, there's a couple of bar/restaurants right next to each other – *Neeb Nooma* and *Welcome* – both serving local dishes, or try *Le Routiere*, off the main road. Right next to *Routiere* is *Numero One*, a lively drinking bar.

Fada-Ngourma and beyond

Midway between Niamey and Ouagadougou, **Fada-Ngourma** is another of Burkina's junction towns, the eighth largest in the country. It was founded by Diaba Lompo, who is variously claimed to be the son, maternal uncle or cousin of Ouédraogo (see the Mossi genealogy, p.629). The town was originally called Bingo, meaning a slave settlement, but Fada-Ngourma is a Hausa appellation, mysteriously meaning "The place where you don't pay tax". It happens to be twinned with Epernay, the champagne capital of France, where the prosperous burghers certainly do pay tax. A more unlikely match is hard to imagine.

Fada is a pleasant, tranquil place, and hosts a colourful **market** with a wealth of goods from across the Sahel region. The beautifully woven **blankets** and **rugs** on sale are invariably better buys here than in Ouagadougou.

Practicalities

For **places to stay**, *Hôtel de la Liberte*, conveniently located not far from the STMB bus station, has cheap, though slightly grubby, non-S/C rooms (BP 10; ①). A bit further out, the *Hôtel l'Avenir* is the best value in town, with extremely clean and comfortable S/C rooms, and an elegant courtyard bar and restaurant (BP 92; ☎77.04.09; ②). The *Auberge Yemmamma* (BP 62; ☎77.00.39; ②), at the eastern end of the market, is also popular, though its plain rooms (with fan or AC) are a bit on the dirty side and it's rather pricey for what you get. They do have a good **restaurant** however, serving grilled chicken and chips and the like. Next door, the *Restaurant de la Paix* has a peaceful courtyard eating area, and you can also eat at *Restaurant du Gourma*, north of the market.

The BIB **bank** in town won't change travellers' cheques unless you can show receipts; they will exchange cash. You'll find the **autogare** on the main road near the modern, particularly strange-looking cathedral. There are direct, frequent departures for Ouagadougou and Niamey.

From Fada to Benin and the Parc National d'Arli

Besides the main, paved Ouaga–Niger highway, an important *piste* to Natitingou and northern Benin leads out from Fada and past the **Parc National d'Arli** (open mid-December to mid-May), home to a variety of wildlife including lions, monkeys, hippos and elephants, and definitely worth a visit. You can **stay** at the village of **Pama** at the western end, where there's the budget *Campement Yentangou* (☎77.01.45; ③–④), a more expensive hotel, the *Burkina Peche* (BP 5081; ☎33.24.11; ②–③), and the upmarket *Hôtel de La Brousse Kompienga* (BP 8; ☎31.84.44; ⑤), with its own pool and tennis courts. There are fairly infrequent taxis down here. If you're driving – and there's really no other way of looking around the park independently – you might do better to continue on the Ouaga–Niamey road to Kantchari and then skirt south through **Diapaga** (where there's a *campement de chasse*) to **Arli** village and the district's pretty lodge, the *Safari Hôtel* (BP 14, Diapaga; ☎79.15.79; FB ⑤), which is the base for game-viewing trips around the park.

Northeast from Ouaga to Gorom-Gorom

Until recently the 300 kilometres of dirt roads and tracks separating Ouaga from the remote outpost of **Gorom-Gorom** in the **Sahel** took considerable time to cover, even in the dry season. Now the road is paved as far as Dori, making it a relatively easy journey from the capital. Along the way you'll notice a change in the peoples as Mossi-speakers give way to northerners – principally Fula, Tuareg and Bella – and the Muslim influence becomes more predominant. The vast majority of the people of the north are farmers and herders, whose livelihoods are especially sensitive to the drought conditions that continue to threaten the country.

From Ouagadougou to Kaya

The route to Kaya passes a couple of villages with important roles in Mossi tradition. Whenever the Mogho Naba dies, a **blacksmith** is sent to the Muslim fief of **Loumbila**, and confined there for three years in order to cast a bronze effigy of the deceased ruler. Since the death of Ouédraogo, thirty-six sets of five statues (each representing the Mogho Naba, one of his wives, a servant and two musicians) have been cast, and are carefully guarded in the chief's compound. The other village, nearby **Guilongou**, marks the spot where, according to Mossi legend, pottery was first invented. It's still an important industry here.

Kaya
KAYA, 98km from Ouaga, is the last major Mossi town on this route. Kaya's flourishing **market** sells many of the **crafts** for which the region is widely reputed; there are weavers and tanners in town and more pour in from neighbouring villages to sell their wares. This is the place to buy leatherwork.

From Kaya there's a weekly **train** to Ouagadougou, and STMB (☎66.03.32) also operates regular **buses** to the capital.

MARKET DAYS IN THE BURKINABE SAHEL

Market days north of the Djibo–Dori road follow a predictable weekly pattern – useful to know about whether you're interested in coinciding with a market or simply want to use bush taxis which are usually only available on market days.

Mon – Markoye, Tongomayél	Fri – Dori
Wed – Djibo, Ti-n-Akof	Sat – Aribinda, Déou, Falagountou
Thurs – Gorom-Gorom	Sun – Oursi, Assakana

From Kaya to Dori – and Djibo

Sixty-eight kilometres beyond Kaya, Tougouri marks the northern limits of the Mossi country. A short distance further, **Yalogo** is a Fula village with a large Tuesday market. Another 60km brings you to the Islamic stronghold of **Bani** with its solid, large mud-brick *mosquée* standing out among the numerous other minarets that push against the side of a hill, and an important regional market held every Tuesday.

Dori and Djibo

Despite its small size, **DORI** is an important administrative centre. There's a **bank** (though they don't change travellers' cheques, only French francs), numerous bars, and a few **accommodation** options – the most inspiring of which is *Chantier Jeune* (BP 98; ☎66.00.68; Fax 66.02.80; ①), a friendly youth cultural centre, home to the internationally acclaimed dance and theatre troupe, Fomtugol. The centre has a few rooms for visitors, a (non-alcoholic) bar and restaurant serving tasty, inexpensive local dishes (*riz gras* CFA250) and, in the courtyard area, nightly live performances and practices by Fomtugol and other groups. The centre also sponsors cultural tourism, organizing traditional homestays with Peul families and excursions to nearby Sahelian villages. Similarly priced (all ①), but less interesting, places to stay are: *Action Sociale*, 2km southeast of town with dormitory-style rooms; *Sahel Hebergement*, offering both S/C and non-S/C rooms with fan; and *Auberge Populaire*, which has non-S/C rooms and lies north of the market. The upmarket choice is *Hôtel Oasis* (☎66.03.29; ②–④).

Dori's **market day** is Friday and, just as reported by the German explorer, Heinrich Barth – who passed through in July 1853 – it's really good for blankets. They have a variety of styles and prices, those woven from camel hair being the most expensive.

From Dori, there's a rough, but pretty route through hilly bush to **DJIBO**. Founded in the sixteenth century, the town became capital of the Peulh (Fula) kingdom of Djilgodji, and, in the nineteenth century, came under the control of the Muslim state of Masina, in present-day Mali. Little evidence of that remains, however, outside the handed-down memories of a few old men and women. Djibo today is a livestock market, at the mercy of the encroaching desert. It has an *Auberge Populaire* (①) and a small, not so clean hotel, *Le Massa* (①), where you can eat basic local dishes. You can also eat inexpensively at *La Callisette* and *215* – the latter with a thatched interior patio with a bar up front, serving nice fish dishes.

Getting to Djibo from Dori may be problematic if you don't have your own transport. Djibo's only really accessible by public means from Ouahigouya (daily STMB bus; CFA1500) and from Ouaga (at least daily STMB bus) – the latter route via a newly improved *piste* that passes through **KONGOUSSI**, a town that is just about capable of handling visitors. There's a hotel, the *Pouiwende* (①), but no electricity.

Gorom-Gorom

Fifty-three kilometres of lousy earth road separate Dori from **GOROM-GOROM**, a large Sahelian village with a **market** – one of the biggest in the north – that draws a vast array of northern peoples. Tuareg, Fula and Bella nomads trek into the mostly Songhai-run market on Thursday, the main trading day. In addition to the foodstuffs, you'll find a variety of leather goods, jewellery and textiles, all produced locally. A short distance away, camels, goats, sheep and donkeys are bought and sold at the **animal**

market. The town itself is a picturesque blend of *banco* houses and narrow dusty streets dotted with numerous mosques.

Practicalities

An interesting **place to stay** in Gorom-Gorom is the *Campement Hotelier*, built by the now defunct airline Le Point as "the cornerstone of a different kind of tourism based on dialogue and exchange." Today the villagers run the *campement* themselves (BP 1311; ☎66.01.44; ②). Contacts here are direct and motivated by the people's genuine desire to open their town to you. The complex is modelled after a Sahelian village, with houses and thatched lean-tos surrounded by a large mud wall. House interiors match the local style. There's a **bar** on the premises and a **restaurant**, though, admittedly, meals, like the accommodation, are slightly more expensive than you would normally expect to pay in these parts. To get there, follow the signs to the "Le Relais Touristique du Gorom-Gorom". Alternatively, you could stay at the *Auberge Populaire* – not as clean, and slightly overpriced but still good (①). You can also eat inexpensively there. The *Mission Catholique*, opposite the church behind the square (☎66.02.57), also takes in visitors for CFA2500 per person.

The *campement* also offers **excursions**, including a 12km camel trek to a nearby village (CFA7500), where it's also possible to spend the night for an extra charge. Emphasis is placed on getting to know regional lifestyles and the relationship between the people and the Sahel's fragile ecosystem. With the continuous threat of desertification, the **agro-ecological centre** opened in conjunction with the *campement* is designed to provide local farmers with information and technical advice with the aim of self-sufficiency in food production.

If you've got your own 4WD transport, it's very worthwhile getting to the sand dunes at **Oursi**, a two-hour drive from Gorom – or you could rent a 4WD vehicle and driver for the day for CFA45,000, including a guide and fuel. *Taxis brousse* heading out of Gorom-Gorom may also stop briefly at Oursi on their way south. The *mare d'Oursi* is a vast watering hole that attracts herders and livestock from throughout the region – an amazing sight. The dunes themselves offer a picturesque foretaste of the Sahara. Ask any of the small kids from Oursi village to direct you there.

If you're continuing **into Niger** from this corner of Burkina, further details can be found on p.894.

Ouahigouya and the Yatenga state

Sparse and mostly bone dry, but historically important, **Ouahigouya** is the capital of northern Burkina. It was founded in the eighteenth century as capital of **Yatenga**, the northernmost Mossi kingdom, which had broken away from Ouagadougou some three hundred years before. It's a relaxed and pleasant place to mooch around, perhaps dallying in its large market, or taking in some of the 37 picturesque mosques. Most of Yatenga's sights, however, lie outside the city in the villages: its former capitals at **La** and **Gourcy** in the south; the burial sites of many of its *nabas* at **Somniaga**; and the region's most impressive mosques at **Ramatoulaye** to the west, and **Yako** to the south. All these places are worth a look, but you'll be back in Ouahigouya by sunset if you value cold beer and music.

The Yatenga region is an arid, undulating **plateau**, barren for most of the year. The rains in May lay a green carpet on the earth that lasts until October, during which time the region's main crops, particularly millet and sorghum, but also maize, cotton, groundnuts and indigo, are sown and harvested. Outside this season, Yatenga reverts to a scrubby savannah of tree-dotted thornbush – shea-nut, *neré* (carob) and false mahogany trees – with tamarind and types of plum (*nobega*) and fig (*kankanga*) among the wild fruits.

HISTORY OF YATENGA

The first great Mossi conqueror, **Naba Rawa**, eldest son of Ouédraogo, founded the kingdom of **Zandoma** or Rawatenga, maybe around 1470. His great nephew Ouemtanango, son of Oubri, perhaps jealous of Rawa's success, expanded his father's Oubritenga kingdom (later Ouagadougou) to the north, moving its capital from Tenkodogo to **La**.

The kingdom of Yatenga was probably founded around 1540 on the death of the fourth Mogho Naba, **Nasbire**. It happened thus. Nasbire's son and heir, **Yadega**, who was away, heard about his father's death and rode straight to La to claim the kingdom. He arrived, however, to find that his brother Kumdumye had taken power, kept the news from reaching him and moved south to Ouagadougou. Yadega followed but found Kumdumye's authority already well established. He returned angrily to La, where he was soon followed by his sister Pabre, who'd managed to seize the **royal amulets** embodying the Mogho Naba's power. With these, Yadega declared a new kingdom and had himself enthroned at La. His new state was known after him as **Yatenga** (from *Yadega tenga*, "Yadega's land"). A legacy of the dispute is the continued mutual avoidance of the holders of the offices of Mogho Naba and Yatenga Naba who to this day refuse to set eyes on each other.

Oral history is a bit confused on some of these points. Ouagadougou tradition inserts a fifth Mogho Naba between Nasbire and Kumdumye, making the latter the sixth Naba, and also claims that the royal amulets were recovered from Pabre – though Yatenga tradition says they got nothing more than her horse's droppings. It's possible that Nasbire had named Kumdumye his heir in any case. But why Yadega was away from La, and where he was, are also disputed, as is his relationship to Kumdumye, who may have been his cousin. The date of Yatenga's foundation could have been as much as four hundred years earlier.

The Rise Of Yatenga

At first the Yatenga statelet was the runt of the Mossi litter. Consisting of the towns of **La**, its first capital and **Gourcy**, its second, plus a few surrounding villages, it lay sandwiched between Zandoma to the north and Oubritenga to the south. When Yadega's brother Kouda jumped on the bandwagon and set up his own kingdom of Risiam, to the southeast (independent until the nineteenth century), it was bigger than Yatenga. What changed this balance was a tradition of conquest and expansion that commenced with the activities of the ninth Yatenga Naba, **Vanteberegum**. He moved the Yatenga capital to **Somniaga**, extending the kingdom to do so, and his son set out on a campaign of aggrandisement that gobbled up most of Zandoma and established Yatenga as the second most powerful Mossi kingdom. However, it was the twenty-fifth *naba*, **Naba Kango**, famous for his cruelty as much as his conquests, who really fixed Yatenga in the oral histories.

Deposed almost as soon as he took power in 1754, Naba Kango returned after three years, aided by the formidable advantage of **firearms**, to retake power with an army of mercenaries. He then built a new capital at **Ouahigouya**, with an enormous **palace**, and summoned all Yatenga's chiefs (including the *naba* of Zandoma) to pay homage to him there. Those who failed to do so received a visit from his troops, who then went on to invade neighbouring territories, leading to a vast expansion of Kango's kingdom. Within it, he maintained an impressive unity, largely by burning down any villages that defied his authority. He had criminals publicly burnt to death

The animal life is unimpressive (there was still the odd lion in the region fifty years ago, but you'd be lucky to see as much as a gazelle today) but **birds** are much in evidence – especially vultures, which seem even more overbearing here than in

and even massacred his own Bamana troops when they misbehaved. He was succeeded in 1787 by his nephew, **Naba Sagha**, but the large kingdom was growing unwieldy and, within forty years, Yatenga had plunged into the series of civil wars that were to destroy it.

Civil War And Dissolution

The wars concerned the succession of Sagha's 133 sons, the first of whom, **Tougouri**, managed to succeed him in 1806. Following his death in 1825, war broke out between those of Sagha's sons who were next in line. Only after 1834 was there a lull in the strife. On the death of Naba Yende, in 1877, however, the dynastic conflicts flared up once more.

This time the dispute was between Sagha's grandsons. The sons of his first-born and successor, Tougouri, claimed that they alone were entitled to rule. The sons of Tougouri's brothers and successors disagreed, pointing out that the intended *naba*'s mother had been a concubine, and that in any case, each branch of Sagha's family should take a turn. The two groups formed opposing parties called **Sons of Tougouri** and **Sons of Sagha**.

When two Sons of Sagha were successively enthroned as *nabas*, the Sons of Tougouri went to war against them. Baogo, the incumbent *naba*, turned to the **French** – who, although new on the scene, had just taken Bandiagara, and were hovering on Yatenga's borders. **Desteneves**, the leader of the French expeditionary force, offered only to mediate. Undeterred, Baogo went into battle against the Sons of Tougouri in 1894 and was killed.

All other eligible branches of Sagha's family having had their turn, the kingdom now returned to Tougouri's family. His senior son, Naba Boulli, took the throne but predictably the Sons of Sagha refused to accept him and set up a rival *naba* in **Sissamba**. Boulli turned to the French, who this time seized the opportunity and, on May 18, 1895, declared Yatenga a protectorate, thus usurping its independence.

The French sacked Sissamba, but the Sons of Sagha successfully recaptured Ouahigouya as soon as they had left. The French bailed out Boulli and put him back on the throne twice more, by which time half Ouahigouya was in ruins. The rebellion of the Sons of Sagha wasn't put down until 1902, and violent incidents in connection with it continued as late as 1911.

Modern Yatenga

French military occupation ended in 1909 when Yatenga passed to civilian colonial rule, and the region was generally quiet during the 1916 anti-conscription rebellion. With the 1932 division of Upper Volta, Yatenga became part of the French Sudan until the re-creation of Upper Volta in 1947. The 1930s and 1940s saw the rise of **Hammalism**, a reformist Muslim cult which the French considered anti-colonial (it was). The movement was largely responsible for the spread of Islam in Yatenga (hitherto strongly resisted because of its association with hostile empires, especially Songhai to the north). This in turn became the base for opposition to the traditionalist, chief-led Union Voltaïque in the region. A UV breakaway, the MDV (Mouvement Démocratique Voltaïque), carried Yatenga in the 1957 election with a base of Muslim support.

Since independence, Yatenga has been a *département* of Burkina, divided into four *cercles*: Ouahigouya, Gourcy, Séguénéga and Titao. Yako lies outside it in the *département* of Koudougou.

the rest of Burkina. A good deal more agreeable are the electric blue **Abyssinian roller birds**, perched on telegraph wires in the barren landscape, like travellers' heralds.

Ethnography

The main ethnic group in Yatenga is the Mossi, who were living around here by the end of the 1330s, when they sacked Timbuktu. They took political power probably in the second half of the fifteenth century (some claim several centuries earlier). The Dogon, then living in the north of the region, fled up to the Bandiagara escarpment in Mali, while the Samos, based in the east, stayed on and have now more or less assimilated with the Mossi.

The principal state was run by the **Kurumba** or Fulse, who claim to have come from the region of Say and Niamey some two hundred years before the Mossi, to set up the Kingdom of Lurum, with its last capital at Mengao, now in Djibo district. Just as the Dogon hadn't resisted the Kurumba invasion, so the Kurumba hardly opposed the Mossi, and the two communities have merged into the dual sociopolitical system largely still existent today, in which the **Mossi** hold political power (as "masters of the sky") while the Kurumba have authority over agriculture and the land (the "masters of the earth"). Each village has a Kurumba "earth chief", whose functions complement those of the Mossi *naba*. There's a third element in this system, the **blacksmiths** (*saaba*), who never marry out, usually live in their own wards (*zaka*) inside Mossi villages (though they have one or two villages of their own, like Séguénéga) and have special ceremonial duties such as performing circumcisions. Only the men are smiths; women are generally potters.

Within this same system are the captives (*Yemse*). Descendants of prisoners of war, and loyal to the Yatenga Naba, they live in their own section of town called the *bingo*. Ouahigouya's *bingo* consists of half the city and captives form more than half its population. Village chiefs and court dignitaries are often captives by descent.

The **Peulh** (Fula) are the region's other main group. Although based in Djibo and outside the Mossi-Kurumba system, they've played an often major role in Yatenga's history. The **Silmi-Mossi**, descendants of a union, considered somewhat disreputable, of Fula and Mossi, live in their own villages, mainly isolated in the south and southeast of the region. Lastly, members of three Islamic trading nations, the **Songhai**, **Bamana** and Mande-speaking **Yarse**, also live in Yatenga. The Mossi themselves, despite having resisted the advances of Islam for so long, are nowadays mostly Muslim here too.

Ouahigouya

OUAHIGOUYA's wide streets and low buildings give a lazy feeling of space, especially after the dust and shimmering heat of day. The market sprawls, the *autogare* sprawls, the main square sprawls: you can't rush about here.

The town's lack of specific "sights" belies its significant **history**. Most important buildings were destroyed in the nineteenth-century **Yatenga civil wars**. Ouahigouya was founded in 1757 – the last of Yatenga's capitals – and marked the northern limit of the state's expansion. King Kango's summons to the chiefs of Yatenga to pay him homage gives the town its name (from *Waka yuguya!* – "Come and greet"). Unfortunately, the great palace where this took place was destroyed in 1825 during one of the struggles for the throne, in which the city was razed to the ground.

Kango may originally have built Ouahigouya as a salt depot; he certainly had his eye on trans-Saharan commodities (gold and kola for example) and hoped to make money by channelling more of their trade through Yatenga. Another motive in building the town could have been to escape from the power of the Mossi aristocracy which had always resented his rule and may well have been responsible for usurping him in the first place. At any rate, Kango populated the new city with captives and ethnic minorities, from whose number he chose many of his officials.

As well as the dynastic struggles of the 1820s and 30s, Ouahigouya suffered serious damage in the later wars between Sons of Sagha and Sons of Tougouri. By the time the French managed to secure their stooge Boulli on the throne at the end of 1896, it was

Koumbri, Bani & Douentza (Mali) — Djibo, Dori & Gorom-Gorom

Hôtel Dunia

Hospital

Yatanga Naba's Compound

Tomb of Naba Kango

Séguénéga & Kaya

TRANSMIF Bus Station

Restaurant Faso Benie

Mairie

Boulangerie

STMB Buses

Ciné Restaurant & Restaurant du Centre

Market

Auberge Populaire

Cinema

BICIA Bank

Police Station

Hôtel de l'Amitié

BICI Bank

BND Bank

Autogare/ SOGEBAF Buses

Sports Ground

Gendarmerie

Yako & Ouagadougou

Dogon Country & Mopti (Mali)

OUAHIGOUYA

Tougan & Bobo Dioulasso

0 Metres 200

half in ruins again, but they needed a base for eastward conquest and "pacification" of Yatenga, and so constructed a fort and rebuilt the town as the regional capital.

Accommodation

Ouahigouya's **hotels** range from dirt cheap and seedy to French-style de luxe.

Auberge Populaire, along the main road near the *quartier administrative*. Simple rooms with fans, showers and nets. ②.

Hôtel de l'Amitié, 500m down the Mopti road (BP 112; ☎55.05.21). More polished than the above with large, airy rooms, some S/C and AC. ②.

Hôtel Bamb-Yam, out of the centre off the main road (☎55.00.88). Clean, non-fussy S/C rooms with fans or AC – worth the long trek. ②.

Hôtel Dunia, off the Kaya road, east of the hospital (BP 145; ☎55.05.95). AC luxury and even a pool: excellent value for money. ③.

Hôtel de la Liberte, Pied de Terre – follow the signs from the main road (BP 03; ☎55.07.69). Both S/C and non-S/C rooms, some with AC and TV. Food upon request. ①–③.

The Town

By day, Ouahigouya lends itself to gentle meanderings. The only sight as such is **Naba Kango's tomb**, an imposing white edifice between the Mairie and the present Naba's compound. According to popular legend, anyone who walks all the way round it will die. The **Yatenga Naba's compound** lies on the old site of Kango's palace. With luck, you

MOVING ON FROM OUAHIGOUYA

If you're **heading for Ouaga**, you have plenty of choice of vehicles, including the STMB bus which leaves three times a day. The road is now paved the whole way to Ouaga; allow three hours for the trip. You should also be able to find transport to **Djibo** (STMB; twice daily), and **Bobo-Dioulasso**, weather permitting (STMB; twice daily), and even the odd **Abidjan**-bound truck. **Into Mali**, however, transport is scarcer and there's no through service to Mopti, just a vehicle (STMB; daily) to **Koro**, where you'll have to change. The *piste* to Koro is passable in the dry season, but be prepared for tough travelling conditions.

Taxis brousse leave from Ouahigouya's main square, but if you end up waiting for days, try the lorries that head out on Saturday to Koro.

may even get to meet the Naba, who's said to be an expert on Yatenga history – as well he would need to be to justify his position. On the way back, you could check out the **market**, always worth a wander. Ouahigouya also boasts no less than 37 **mosques**, built in a pretty and distinctive style. Not to be overlooked either is the attractive lake formed by the **barrage** just 100m west of *L'Amitié*; the desert is in bloom around here and you can stroll across the *barrage*.

Eating and other practicalities

Hotel food in Ouahigouya is good; the *Amitié* serves up satisfying meals, and the *Dunia*'s excellent French-Middle Eastern food makes it the first choice of local expats. Smaller places, where you pay for the food and not the service, include the *Ciné Restaurant*, the *Restaurant du Centre* and the *Faso Benie* – rice, yam, pasta, soup, chicken, liver, beans and salad. For **picnic supplies**, there are two small supermarkets just off the market square. The BICIA bank in Ouahigouya will change FF travellers' cheques.

In the evenings, **cold beer and hot music** at the *Nord* and the *Populaire* take you through to midnight – and you can keep going beyond that if you move on to the *Amitié*'s disco – the main nightspot in Ouahigouya and a bit of a thrash.

Around the Yatenga district

Most of Yatenga's **sites of interest** are spread around the villages. Its first capital, and the Mossi capital before Yatenga's secession, was La, now called **La-Todin**, beyond the borders of modern Yatenga, 22km west of Yako.

The fourth Yatenga Naba, Guéda, moved his capital north to **Gourcy**, where you can see the **sacred hill** on which his successors are still enthroned. Here, too, are the royal amulets stolen by Pabre on behalf of her brother Yadega. In the civil wars of the 1890s, the Sons of Sagha kidnapped the amulets, thus preventing the French from crowning Naba Boulli until they were returned at the end of 1897. Gourcy is on the main Ouagadougou–Ouahigouya road, 42km south of Ouahigouya.

The kingdom's third and penultimate capital, **Somniaga** was seized from the kingdom of Zandoma by Naba Vanteberegum as part of his campaign to enlarge Yatenga. Seven kilometres south of Ouahigouya on the Ouaga road, it makes an easy walk first thing in the morning (don't forget to carry a few litres of water), or you can hitch. Most of Yatenga's *nabas* are buried here in the **royal cemetery** (*nayaado*) and looked after by the Yaogo Naba, the man to find if you want to see it. One quaint little Yatenga burial custom was the interment of the *nabas*' court jesters – alive – with their dead king.

Of the capitals of neighbouring traditional states, **Yako** is the easiest to visit. Some 70km south of Ouahigouya, it is now accessible by paved road. The most striking first impression is of its **mosque**, but its main claim to local fame goes further. Capital of a kingdom founded by Naba Yelkone – son of the same Kumdumye who split with Yadega over the question of the Mossi throne – it was a perpetual object of Yatenga–Ouagadougou rivalry, generally a fief of the latter. Naba Kango managed to force its submission and the flight of its *naba*, who was only allowed to stay on condition that he planted a sacred grove of thorn bushes (*kango* in More) outside the town. The French also found Yako a tough nut to crack. More recently, **Thomas Sankara** was born here; with some discretion, you may be able to get someone to show you exactly where.

Zandoma, the region's very first Mossi capital, is now a tiny village some 40km southwest of Ouahigouya, northwest of Gourcy. The chief still claims descent from **Naba Rawa**, whose tomb can be seen close to his compound.

Other places of interest in and around Yatenga include: **Ramatoulaye**, 25km east of Ouahigouya on the road to Rollo, with another impressive **mosque**, a major centre of Hammalism in colonial days; **Lago**, some 30km south of Ouahigouya (but 41km by road from Zogoré), **burial site** of the first Yatenga *nabas*; **Sissamba**, 11km southwest of Ouahigouya and en route to Lago, where the Sons of Sagha installed their pretender to the throne on Naba Boulli's accession in 1894 and which the French sacked the following year; and **Mengao**, 82km northeast of Ouahigouya on the road to Djibo (27km further), which was the last capital of the kingdom of Lurum and is still the home of the **Kurumba paramount "earth chief"**, the counterpart of the Yatenga Naba – the Mossi paramount sky chief.

THE GOUROUNSI COUNTRY

The area **around Pô** on the Ghanaian border **south of Ouagadougou** is dominated by the Grusi or **Gourounsi**, which usually includes the **Kassena**, the **Nouna** and the **Sissala** from around Léo. Their distinctive **architecture** provides the region's main attraction. Gourounsi country also boasts a couple of **national parks** – difficult to get to without your own transport – and some interesting archeological remains near Léo.

The Gourounsi build their **houses** from mud in smooth, sandcastle shapes, often painted with striking diamond patterns. Larger compounds may consist of whole labyrinths of submerged rooms and doorways through which people weave and duck.

THE GOUROUNSI

How long the people known as **Gourounsi** (originally a Mossi term of denigration) have lived in this region isn't clear, but Mossi tradition claims they were pushed back across the Red Volta River by the thirteenth Mogho Naba, Nakiem, at the end of the seventeenth century. Never united, the various strands of Gourounsi-speakers have long existed in a state of near-permanent village war. Their lack of central government has always made them vulnerable to attack from more organized groups, especially the Mossi who often made kidnapping raids for slaves. Many Mossi dissidents set themselves up as chiefs in Gourounsi-land, and their families continue to live here. Gourounsi chiefs possess sacred objects called *kwara* – insignia of office – which are handed down from generation to generation.

At the end of the nineteenth century, the Gourounsi were the targets of Djerma Muslim zealots from the Niamey region, who stormed down on horseback and engaged in heavy slave-raiding under a *jihad* banner. They converted the son of the chief of Sati and set up shop there, almost decimating the lands of the Sissala, Nouna and Kassena, before being defeated by a Gourounsi–French alliance in 1895.

THE GOUROUNSI LANGUAGE

If you learn no other Gourounsi, at least learn to say *Din le*, the all-purpose greeting, which means "Thank you". The following sampler comes from "Kassem", the main dialect of Gourounsi, spoken by the *Kassena*.

| Good morning | *Tim paga* |
| Good evening | *Tim dadan* |

1	*Kalo*	6	*Trodo*	20	*Finle*
2	*Inle*	7	*Tirpai*	50	Finnu
3	*Nto*	8	*Nana*	100	*Bi*
4	*Nna*	9	*Nogo*	500	*Bi yennu*
5	*Unu*	10	*Fuga*	1000	*Moro*

Buildings are not expected to last more than a few seasons and new houses are built around the foundations of older dwellings, resulting in a characteristic organic appearance. Also typical are the forked and notched logs, leant against the walls as ladders to the **flat roofs** where grain is commonly dried, out of goat-reach. Women gather here to chat and smoke during the day, the whole family often sleeps here, and all sorts of stuff is stored. Village chiefs usually have the largest and most impressive compounds – though not necessarily the prettiest. You can often tell the status of a family from the height of its walls.

On the way to **Pô**, the region's main town, from Ouagadougou, you pass through **Kombissiri**, 40km south of the capital. This town became a Muslim centre following the settlement here of a community of **Yarse** (Mande-speaking traders) in the eighteenth century. Its religious status was developed by the pro-Muslim 25th Mogho Naba, Sawadogho, who ruled from 1825–42 and had the mosque built. It's 4km east of the town: follow the *piste* from the police checkpoint at the northern end of Kombissiri.

Pô

PÔ lacks traditional architecture, but has plenty of fountains with revolutionary names – "Nelson Mandela", "Enver Hoxha", "Les Trois Luttes". If this is your last town in Francophone Africa, make the most of the plentiful cold beer and relative lack of petty corruption. Coming the other way, it's a gentle introduction to some of French Africa's more tiresome aspects – high prices and an obsession with *papiers*. The Pô police are fond of asking for these and you can expect a fair number of spot checks, but like most of the townspeople they're friendly enough and there's no big hassle. Pô is also a garrison town with a chequered recent history – though the soldiers don't obtrude.

Some history

According to legend, Pô was founded around 1500, by a Mossi man, **Nablogo**, son of Mogho Naba Oubri. He started cultivating a field (*pô*) but got into a land rights dispute with Kassena neighbours. About this time, a certain **Gonkwora** from Kasana near Léo turned up here, having left his village after being disinherited of his rightful chiefship. He brought three magic bracelets with him (still looked after by his descendants in Pô) and fell in with Nablogo, who helped him, and in whose dispute with the Kassena he interceded. Gonkwora's brother – the ancestor of Pô's present chief – then arrived from their home village with the village *kwara*. Gonkwora meanwhile married Nablogo's daughter and they all lived happily ever after. Gonkwora's tomb is supposed to be under a sacred baobab in the Kasno quarter of town.

More recent and less halcyon history has also been made in Pô. In 1976, **Thomas Sankara** set up the Centre Nationale d'Entrainement here, taken over by Blaise Compaoré in 1982. The following year the Ouédraogo regime arrested Sankara and fellow officers. Pô became a radical focus for students, young workers and academics, who came to join the commandos. In August 1983, the coup that toppled Ouédraogo, fired the revolution and put Sankara in power, was launched here. And it was from Pô that Compaoré planned a second takeover in 1987, that led to Sankara's untimely death and put Compaoré in power.

Practicalities

Accommodation in Pô is pretty basic, but as a frontier town, there is at least some choice. Your most economical option is the *Auberge Populaire* (①), not far from the lorry station, which has no electricity, and bucket showers. A step up is the friendly and brightly painted *Auberge Agoabem* (☎39.01.42; ①), with running water, clean non-S/C rooms, and a decent restaurant in the grounds. For a little more luxury, you could check out the *Hôtel Mantoro* (BP 19; ☎39.00.25; ③), behind the *cité* (housing development) north of the town; the 24 aid workers' houses here, built by Sankara, are looked after by an elusive caretaker, and the rooms (some S/C) are the cleanest and most modern in town.

For street **food**, try near the market and around the cinema. Every evening, there's good fried fish from the Black Volta, brochettes, guinea fowl, roast mutton and plenty more. There's a variety of sit-down places, too, dishing up *couscous*, sandwiches, omelettes, rice, spaghetti, *tô* and brochettes. Pô bursts into life in the **evenings**, despite the fact that electricity is mainly confined to the north end of town; the *Commando Woro* down near the customs post (look for the "Honte a l'Imperialisme" sign) is worth braving despite its military atmosphere (it's an army club) for the ice cold beer, music till midnight and edible food. The *Consolatrice Bar Restaurant*, opposite the *cité*, plays music till 11.30pm, and *Sounoogo*, next door to the *Auberge Agoabem*, is a popular drinking spot.

There is a BICIA **bank** in Pô, and people in the market or around the *autogare* will change Ghana cedis, FF and dollars (but not sterling) for CFA francs.

Around Pô

The best of the Gourounsi country is to be found outside the modern city of Pô and in the smaller villages along the roads parallel with the frontier on both sides. The Gourounsi traditional capital, **Tiébélé**, has the finest architecture, and the highest volume of visitors. The **Pô National Park** lies across the road from Ouaga to Pô

MOVING ON FROM PÔ

Frequent *taxis brousse* to **Ouagadougou** (anything from 2–7hr) leave from the *autogare* in front of the police station. South **into Ghana**, there are taxis to Paga and even as far as Bolgatanga, especially on Friday (market day in Bolga). Alternatively you could reasonably expect to hitch from the customs post just south of town. The STC Ouaga–Accra bus also halts in Pô and is scheduled to churn into town on Monday or Friday morning.

Vehicles to **Tiébélé** only operate on market days there (Tues, Wed, Thurs) and to **Léo** likewise (Sun). On other days, and to other destinations such as the wildlife reserves, you'll have to make private arrangements with taxi drivers or car or moped owners, though taxis are expensive if you want to do a *déplacement*. To rent, ask around the *autogare* or market, or see if your hotel proprietor knows anyone.

and, south of **Nobéré**, you may see representatives of the district's elephant herd – one of the few places in West Africa where "Elephants on Road" is a delightful possibility. Finally, if you can find transport from Pô (tricky except on Sunday, market day), you could make the 126-kilometre trip to the Djerma-Gourounsi ruins near **Léo**.

Tiébélé
TIÉBÉLÉ, the traditional Gourounsi capital, 31km east of Pô, is something of a tourist attraction, and worth the visit. The chief here is the most important *chef de canton* in Gourounsi country and you should go and see him on first arriving: his compound is, in any case, the town's main attraction. Tiébélé's houses are better built and decorated than others in Kassena country and the Tiébélé chief's is a magnificent maze of mud-pie huts. For a good view of the whole compound, scale the refuse heap behind it.

Coming into town from Pô, you'll find yourself travelling down an avenue of large trees that unexpectedly cleaves off from the road, leaving you on a much more recent road. To find the chief, you want to leave the road and follow the original avenue of trees, which will take you to his compound. You have to sign the visitor's book and pay a steep fee for a guide and authorization to take photos.

Tiakané
TIAKANÉ, 7km west of Pô, is more laid-back. Its houses aren't as striking as those in Tiébélé but you'll feel more like a visitor and less like a punter. The Cave de Binger in the chief's compound is a mini underground labyrinth where the villagers hid the nineteenth-century French explorer from a party of Mossi who were out to kill him. Binger went on to become governor of Côte d'Ivoire. His family have evidently not forgotten Tiakané: recently they sent funds from France to build a village school. The chief provides a guide to show you round Binger's hide-out and both will expect a reasonable tip. Tiakané makes a nice early morning walk from Pô, especially after it's rained.

Parc National de Pô and Nazinga reserve
Without your own transport, you'll have to make private arrangements to get to the two **reserves** near Pô. Cycling down from Ouagadougou isn't a bad idea. To visit the **Parc National de Pô** (main gate 31km north of Pô, 5km south of the bridge over the Volta Rouge; open Nov–May), you first need a permit from the rangers' office by the PTT in Pô town, behind the police station. The park *pistes* aren't currently in good shape and rangers have been advising moped riders against using them. The sector **east of the main road** does have a feasible circuit of about 35km however, which you could ride around, preferably in the early morning from the unstaffed south gate – some 9km north of Pô – to the north gate. Baboons and antelope are the most obvious inhabitants but the elephants are there if you keep looking, and there are buffalo and warthog too. Tracks are mostly rather sandy, the vegetation tall rank grasses, thick bush, stands of dense forest near the watercourses and occasional clearings of more open country savaged by fire. Going round the park alone may be an exciting business, but if you try it by bicycle, be sure to take at least ten litres of water per person and leave word of your plans in Pô.

The **Nazinga Reserve** (open December to July) south of the Léo road (its north boundary runs along the road from about 15km to about 40km west of Pô) is an easier target, and you may have better luck spotting game there. Set up by the Canadians to study wildlife resource management, the place is (comparatively) bursting at the seams with **elephants**, and also harbours several species of monkeys, baboons, antelopes, gazelles and warthogs and, rather surprisingly, **lions**. You'll have to get a ranger to accompany you from the office; he'll know where you're likely to find animals. It's even possible to do a tour on foot, though entirely at your own risk. **Accommodation** is available but it's rudimentary and you'll need a mosquito net and mattress or sleeping bag.

Léo and the Djerma-Gourounsi ruins
A small border town with a couple of hotels, **LÉO**'s main attraction is the nearby **ruins** in the villages of Satí and Yoro. They date from the period of the **Djerma invasions** at the end of the nineteenth century, when the Djerma made alliances with Gourounsi Muslim chiefs. Satí became the capital of a Djerma mini-state and Yoro was fortified as a warehouse for slaves and booty acquired in raids on the local "infidel" Gourounsi. Later, the Gourounsi Muslim leaders had a change of mind about their Djerma business partners and revolted – a resistance which eventually involved collusion with a Djerma renegade called Hamaria who successfully enlisted French support to defeat the Djerma. French involvement led, as everywhere, to a colonial sell-out and the formal "protection" of the Gourounsi.

Satí, 22km northwest of Léo, should still have the remains of fortifications and battlements, especially on the eastern side, while a kilometre to the south, the chief's personal mosque and compound may still be visible. Seven kilometres back down the road to Léo are the ruins of more fortifications – including triangular loopholes and a well, used by the Djerma while besieging Satí. **Yoro**, 32km west of Léo on the way to Diébougou, still preserves a long stretch of wall, part of the Djerma treasure house.

None of this amounts to very impressive archeology, but the search for the ruins makes a good hook from which to hang idle wanderings. And if you have your own transport, Léo is a reasonable night stop en route from Gourounsi to **Lobi country** (see p.668); try the *Cosmopolis* (☎41.30.19).

BOBO, BANFORA AND THE SOUTHWEST

Fed by the **Comoé** and other lesser rivers, the southwest is the most densely forested, and hilliest, region in Burkina and a pleasant change from the relentless grasslands covering most of the rest of the country. Rich vegetation camouflages a wealth of natural sites, ranging from **waterfalls** and lakes to striking cliff formations. But the southwest also contains important urban centres – **Bobo-Dioulasso** and **Banfora** – that grew up on the Abidjan train line in a productive agricultural region.

Bobo-Dioulasso and around

Burkina's second city, with around 350,000 inhabitants, **BOBO-DIOULASSO** ("Home of the Bobo and the Dioula") was long the country's economic capital, a position which has only in recent years been convincingly usurped by Ouagadougou. Yet life moves at a slow pace here, and Bobo has style and a great atmosphere. Sweeping avenues roofed by the foliage of cool mango trees, colonial buildings in the *style soudanais* and a rich mixture of peoples give it a unique character that makes it one of the most inviting places to unwind anywhere in West Africa. It's also a traditional music centre, with *balafon* orchestras and electric bands adding night-time action to the town's many bars.

Some history
Bobo was founded in the fifteenth century, when it was known as **Sya**, or "island". According to oral history, a man named Molo Oumarou came here and, after founding villages in Timina and Sakabi, built a house in a clearing of the woods by a stream called

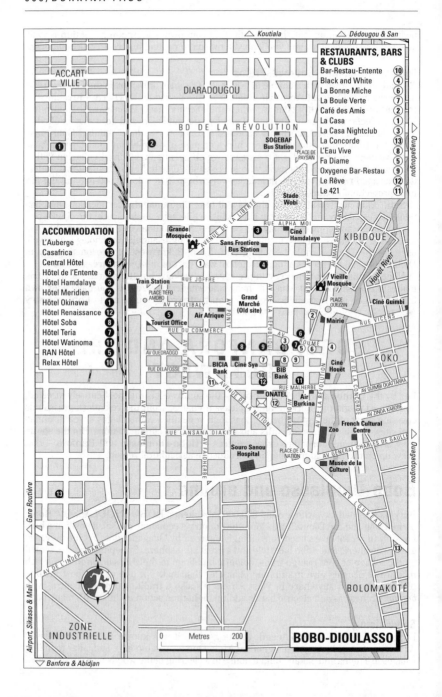

BOBO-DIOULASSO

RESTAURANTS, BARS & CLUBS
Bar-Restau-Entente	⑩
Black and White	④
La Bonne Miche	⑥
La Boule Verte	⑦
Café des Amis	②
La Casa	①
La Casa Nightclub	③
La Concorde	⑬
L'Eau Vive	⑧
Fa Diame	⑤
Oxygene Bar-Restau	⑨
Le Rêve	⑫
Le 421	⑪

ACCOMMODATION
L'Auberge	⑨
Casafrica	⑬
Central Hôtel	④
Hôtel de l'Entente	⑥
Hôtel Hamdalaye	③
Hôtel Meridien	②
Hôtel Okinawa	①
Hôtel Renaissance	⑫
Hôtel Soba	⑧
Hôtel Teria	⑦
Hôtel Watinoma	⑪
RAN Hôtel	⑤
Relax Hôtel	⑩

the Houët. A village of Bobo-Fing and Bobo-Dioula people grew up around this original home. The French arrived in the late nineteenth century, and set up their first administrative headquarters here in 1897. In 1928, Pépin Malherbe broadened the town limits as Bobo awaited the arrival of the **railway line** from Abidjan. The RAN pushed through in 1934, two decades before the line was extended to Ouaga, and a large colonial town grew up around the station, a short distance from the original settlement (the graceful Sudanic-inspired architecture of the *gare routière*, market and Palais de Justice dates from this period). Thus Bobo gained a large economic jump on the present capital, which helps to explain its commercial importance today. On the main routes to Mali and the Côte d'Ivoire, too, the town has acquired an international flavour with numerous foreign workers and students.

Information and accommodation

For tourist information, contact the Office National du Tourisme Burkinabe (OTNB; ☎97.19.86; Fax 97.19.87), on Avenue de l'Unite across from *RAN Hôtel*. The staff can answer questions about nearby excursions and provide some useful brochures. **Lodgings** in Bobo range from dormitory beds to AC hotels with pools. In between there's a good number of inexpensive *auberges*, lacking in luxury but usually well maintained.

Accommodation

L'Auberge, av de la République (☎99.14.26; Fax 97.21.37). Centrally located, this restaurant (French cooking at a good price) also has nice, S/C, AC rooms, a clean pool in the shaded courtyard and billiards in the bar. The hotel also has a newer wing with thirty additional rooms. The *terrasse* is a popular place for drinks. ④–⑤.

Casafrica, off av de l'Indépendance near the Brakina brewery (☎98.01.57). Best budget place in town, French-owned, with clean rooms ranged around a delightful shady courtyard, where you can also camp for a very low rate. ①–②.

Central Hôtel, cnr rue Crozat and av de la République (BP 986; ☎97.01.47). Clean and quiet S/C and non-S/C rooms, some with AC, in a central location. ②–③.

Hôtel de l'Entente, corner of rue du Commerce and av Binger (BP 1346; ☎98.12.05). Large non-S/C rooms with fans and nets or AC. Well-maintained and attractive courtyard. Also rents out Land Rovers. ②–③.

Hôtel Hamdalaye, rue Alpha Moi, Dienepo, near SOGEBAF (BP 2170; ☎98.22.87). Nice management and very clean, S/C, AC rooms in terraces. Only possible disadvantage is the very loud disco right next door (the music stops at 11.30pm Mon–Fri). Otherwise, top-of-the-line Bobo budget boarding. Bike rental too. ②.

Hôtel Meridien, av de l'Unité (☎98.08.42). Good-value, clean and friendly accommodation in SC and non-S/C rooms with fans. ①–③.

Hôtel Okinawa, Accart Ville district, Secteur 9, on the way to the stadium (BP 800; ☎98.06.34). Simple rooms without fan but clean and friendly. The attractive courtyard hosts a (noisy) nightly disco (no cover) and there's a restaurant, serving reasonably priced meals. ①–③.

Hôtel Renaissance, av de la République (BP 1092; ☎98.23.31). Popular restaurant and *dancing*, brilliantly located in the very heart of town, with clean, adjoining rooms with fans or mosquito nets, grouped around an attractive courtyard. ②.

Hôtel Soba, av Ouédraogo (BP 185; ☎97.10.12). Colonial-style place, with good rooms, some with AC and TV, and a pleasant patio-garden. ③.

Hôtel Teria, 2129 rue Alwata Diawara (BP 3307; ☎97.19.72). Comfortable and calm with an ideal location near the market, a very nice courtyard, and friendly staff. ②.

Hôtel Watinoma, corner of rue Malherbe and av Binger (BP 1219; ☎98.21.62). Clean AC rooms. They also have an excellent restaurant with European food. ④.

RAN Hôtel, near the train station (BP 50; ☎98.18.45; Fax 98.18.45). This three-star place is the best in town. S/C, AC rooms and a pool. ⑤.

Relax Hôtel, av Ouédraogo (BP 115; ☎97.22.27; Fax 97.13.07). Well-located hotel with pool (CFA1500 for non-guests) and S/C rooms with AC. ③–④.

The Town

Once situated in the heart of Bobo, the **grand marché** has been torn down by the City Council and replaced by a new market – currently just a series of scattered shacks and vendors – at the edge of town on the way to the airport.

The **Vieille Mosquée** – a *banco* construction originally built in 1880 – is located in Bobo's **old town** in the **Kibidoué** district. Except during prayers, it's possible to visit; ask the guardian and leave him a small tip after the tour, but beware of taking photographs. From here, kids will doubtless pick you up and want to show you around the historic core of town. First on their list of worthy sites is the "Konsa", the **oldest house** in town, said to date from the fifteenth century. As you follow them through the narrow streets of the ancient neighbourhoods, they'll point out **traditional artisans** – mostly blacksmiths and weavers – and finish the tour with a stop at the **sacred fish pond** – the murky backwaters of the Houët stream where oversize mudfish peer up for food. There's no telling what makes them sacred: fishy totems are a Bobo speciality.

In the midst of your meanderings, don't miss the **Marché de Poterie**, two blocks north of the mosque, where demand is still high for earthenware vessels from remote villages like Dalgan, Tcheriba and Sikiana. Pots vary in size and shape depending on their function, but they're all quite reasonably priced, and there are striking examples of unusual water jugs painted in bright colours and bold designs.

Lastly, do take time to see the **Musée de la Culture**, on the Place de la Nation (9am–noon & 3.30–6pm; closed Mon). Small, but pleasant to wander through, the museum boasts an interesting collection of **ethnographic artefacts** such as Bobo wooden statues and Senoufo funeral masks as well as regional clothing as worn by the Fula, Senoufo and other nationals. Outside, stroll through examples of Burkinabe housing styles – Bobo, Fula and Senoufo – beautifully decorated and furnished.

Incidentally, Bobo's **zoo**, on Avenue de la Révolution, is a pretty sad collection of half a dozen beasts, none faring too well in captivity. Don't bother with it.

Eating

Quite apart from the consistently good hotel restaurants, Bobo has plenty of fine **places to eat,** many of them serving up the especially delicious local **beef.** The best street snacks in town are to be had from a group of women opposite the cinema south of the market, who serve huge, tasty **avocado salad submarines** for next to nothing.

La Bonne Miche, av Binger at av Ouédraogo. Popular *patisserie* and a likely place to bump into other travellers in search of the country's best *pain au raisin*.

La Boule Verte, av Ouédraogo at av de la République (☎99.02.79). Counts among Bobo's better French restaurants.

Café des Amis, av Binger. Fresh yogurt daily and a really nice place to sit and eat.

La Casa, near the cathedral on av du Gouverneur Faidherbe, one street north of the old market site. A narrow leafy entrance leads into one of Bobo's hidden delights. The food is excellent (inexpensive too) and the music and ambience enjoyable in this shaded courtyard retreat.

La Concorde, av Louveau (☎98.12.59). Classic French cuisine, with a lively atmosphere. Courtyard tables grouped around a dance floor – a favourite local haunt.

L'Eau Vive, rue Delafosse across from the *Relax Hôtel* (☎97.20.86). Sister restaurant (literally) to the *Eau Vive* in Ouaga, with similar international specialities and waitressing nuns.

Fa Diame, across from *Bonne Miche* on av Binger. African and European specialities in an ideal location.

Restaurant La Beninoise (aka *Chez Dominique*), across from the Pharmacie du Levant (☎98.02.02). Meat and fish with spicy vegetable sauces. Great cooking, friendly service and affordable prices.

Restaurant Delwenee, opposite the *Relax Hôtel*. Inexpensive local dishes with great fish soup, rice sauce, and salads.

Sidawaya Bar/restaurant in the gardens near the train station.

La Sirene, Place Ouezzin. Inexpensive local dishes with great *couscous arabe*.

Le Transfo, zone des Ecoles (☎98.17.05). Out of the centre, but well known by taxi drivers. Energetic bar/*dancing* where you can eat moderately priced European dishes including salads and a variety of grilled meats.

Yan Kady, av de l'Unité. A good place for inexpensive and well-prepared African food.

Nightlife

Like the Ouagalais, the people of Bobo are great night-timers. The percussionist **Coulibaly Twins** and **Mahama Konaté**, the founder of Farafina, are from Bobo and regularly play the town clubs when home from Paris. Some restaurants are worth a visit – including *La Concorde* and *Le Transfo*, see above. In the excitement of the urban clubs, don't overlook the wealth of **traditional music** that vibrates from balafons and calabash drums at *dolo* bars in the Bon Makote district just south of the city centre – by far the lowest priced entertainment in town.

Le 421, rue Malherbe at av du Gouverneur Faidherbe. Dark indoors bar, very frenetic and usually full despite the high cover charge.

Bar-Restau-Entente, av de la République at rue Delafosse. Open-air bar-*dancing* with attractive *paillotes* in the courtyard and live bands almost nightly. A lot of people, and hustlers can be a hassle.

Black and White, av Binger at rue du Commerce. The restaurant is bad (limited menu, dreadful service), but the disco's fine. Good music and plenty of sweaty bodies.

Bonmaso, av de la Révolution across from the Mairie. Bar-restaurant-disco with good food and frequent live music.

La Casa Nightclub, rue Alwata Diawara. Happening club across from *Hôtel Teria*; busy at weekends.

Club Diguya, rue de la Mairie Centrale. Traditional West African music spot.

Le Daffra, rue Alpha Moi, next to *Hôtel Hamdalaye* (☎98.20.55). Inexpensive bar/*dancing* and notorious pick-up joint.

Oxygene Bar-Restau, rue Alwata Diawara. Lively place on weekends with music and dancing.

Le Rêve, opposite the PTT (☎98.04.19). A little touristy, but with good music during the week and live bands at the weekends. Popular restaurant too.

Around Bobo

Some rewarding **side-trips** are within easy distance of Bobo. If you haven't got a car, perhaps the best way to see them is by renting a bicycle or moped (see "Listings", overleaf).

Top on the list of Bobo excursions is a swimming hole called **La Guinguette**, 18km west of town in the **Kou Forest**. You can splash around in bilharzia-free waters, though it's sometimes crowded, especially at weekends. Some 15km further, the Sikasso (Mali) road takes you to the village of **Koumi**, with characteristic, pseudo-fortified, Bobo architecture. This is a popular spot, and your presence will surprise no one; check with the chief if you want to take pictures (whether you've a permit or not).

Dafra, 8km southeast of Bobo, boasts a **pool of sacred fish**, in beautiful surroundings, much more important than the underwhelming mud hole in Bobo. Chickens are sacrificed to the enormous catfish – some even wearing earrings ("a miracle") – who are the symbol of Bobo and reproduced on the Mairie wall in town. To get there, take a taxi most of the way, or walk along the **path** from the junction of the Ouaga road and Avenue du Gouverneur Général Eboué, right on the edge of town. It's a tricky route to follow and you'll probably need a guide (kids en route will no doubt oblige for the customary *cadeau*) but it's worth it for the scenery. Set off early and take water. Unfortunately, there have been some recent muggings, so take no valuables. Remember, too, to wear nothing red – it's prohibited at this sacred place.

Another popular attraction, the **hippo lake** (*mare aux hippopotames*), is located some 60km from Bobo, near Satiri on the Dédougou/Ouahigouya road. It's a little far for a moped and the difficult tracks (even in the dry season) just about rule it out, so take a Dédougou-bound taxi from the main *gare routière*, or head to the *gare de Satiri* on the intersection of Boulevard de la Paix and Avenue Général Merlin. The Satiri taxi stops in small villages along the way – many of them featuring picturesque **Sahelian-style mosques** – and takes up to three hours (as opposed to less than two for the Dédougou-bound taxi) to cover the scenic route. To get to the lake from Satiri, you could hope to hitch with passing tourists at weekends, or, if you're alone, you could probably find someone to take you on the back of a bike (fix an arranged price for the return trip). Fishermen at the lakeside will take you out by *pirogues* for as close an inspection of the hippos as you're likely to want. Again, fix the fee in advance – they appreciate aspirins and cigarettes as a tip. If you're extremely lucky, they say, you may even spot elephants.

Bobo listings

Airlines Air Afrique is on av Ponty (☎98.19.23). The office is useful for information and flight bookings only; there are no Air Afrique flights to/from Bobo. Air Burkina is on rue Malherbe at av de la République (☎98.18.87).

Banks Both BIB and BICIA have branches near the centre. Changing travellers' cheques is usually no problem.

Bike/mobylette rental Easy to find, around the old market site, especially at the west end towards the train station. CFA3000–6000 per day.

Books, newspapers and maps International press, mostly French, available at *L'Auberge*. *Librairies* in the market area include Diafca near the site of the old market, where you can also buy city maps.

Car rental Auto-Location has an office on the av de la Nation.

Cinemas In addition to the new and comfortable AC, Cine Sanon on rue Alpha Moi across from the stadium, are less state-of-the-art neighbourhood theatres: Ciné Sya, av Ouédraogo; Ciné Houet, av de la Révolution; and Ciné Guimbi, off rue Vicens.

French Cultural Centre Junction of av Géneral Charles de Gaulle and av de la Concorde, just east of the river. Good library and outdoor reading area, with magazines and newspapers. African, European and American films, several nights a week.

Hospital Hôpital Sourou Sanou, av Lansana Diakité at av Ponty (☎98.00.79 or 98.00.82).

Internet CENATRIN (BP 2454; ☎97.10.14; Fax 97.05.00).

Post office av de la Nation at av de la République. Functioning poste restante. International calls from the ONATEL office. Open 7.30–11.30am and 3–4.45pm.

Supermarkets Faso Yaar, off av Ouédraogo; Socibe, av de la République; and best of the lot is the well-plenished Self Service across the street.

Swimming The *Auberge*'s pool is not open to non-residents: try the pools at the *Rélax* or the *RAN*, which are likely to be less fussy about it.

Theatre Check the schedule at the Théâtre Amitié, on av Géneral Charles de Gaulle. Also ask at the French Cultural Centre.

Western Union Money transfers possible at Sonapost (☎98.25.41).

MOVING ON FROM BOBO

In addition to domestic destinations, Bobo is a springboard for Mali (Mopti, Bamako) and Côte d'Ivoire. You can get fuller details on buses and flights from Bobo's travel agents: try Egi Voyages on rue Delafosse.

Trains
There is currently a daily train to Abidjan, a possible means of reaching **Banfora**, and another in the opposite direction to Ouagadougou. Call the SCFB (☎98.29.50, 98.29.22 or 98.23.91) for schedule changes or check at the station – and buy your tickets in advance.

Bush Taxis and Buses
The main *gare routière* for *taxis brousse* is on the west side of town. This is the quickest means to points in **Mali** (punishing *piste* as far as Sikasso if you go that way, reasonable tarmac to Ségou if you go that) and **Côte d'Ivoire** (good sealed road) as well as to Ouagadougou and Dédougou, Banfora and Boromo. Bobo is also a possible departure point for the **Lobi country** via a difficult *piste* to Diébougou.

There are several private bus stations coveniently located in the city's centre, all fairly reliable: **SOTRAO**, av Géneral Charles de Gaulle (☎97.02.43), has buses to Ouaga, Gaoua, Ouessa and Hamile (for Ghana) and Dédougou (for Ouahigouya and the north); **Rakieta**, av Guillaume Ouédraogo (☎97.18.91), has buses to Ouaga, Banfora (six daily; CFA800), Niangoloko and Gaoua (two daily); both **STMB** (☎97.08.78) and **SOGEBAF** (☎97.15.35 or 98.24.58) on bd de la Révolucion operate daily buses to Ouaga, Banfora and Côte d'Ivoire; **STBF** (☎97.00.65 or 97.23.13), on the same road, also runs services to Ouaga and Abidjan; and **Sans Frontières** (☎98.23.22) has daily services to Ouaga, Bamako and Abidjan.

Flights
Airport information from Bobo airport on ☎98.03.68.
There are currently flights most days from Bobo to **Ouagadougou** on Air Burkina (☎98.18.87). The flight takes 40–50min. There are also flights from Bobo to **Abidjan**, also on Air Burkina (3 weekly; 1hr 10min).

Banfora and around

Although the town of **Banfora** lacks the spark of Ouaga and Bobo, it lies in a beautiful region of cliffs and forests. Today, the economic importance of the region springs from the vast **sugar cane** projects that have made Burkina a net exporter of manufactured sugar. On the approach from Bobo by train or taxi, you see streams and **waterfalls** from the roadside and notice the vegetation getting denser.

MARKET DAYS IN WESTERN BURKINA

Market days west of Bobo follow a predictable weekly pattern which can be useful in itself and for ensuring you don't get stranded somewhere remote without transport: most small villages only have *taxi brousse* connections with main towns on market days.

Mon – Koloko, Kotoura, Samorogouah, Sindou, Soukouraba
Thurs – Mahon

Fri – Kangala
Sat – Oroda
Sun – Banfora

Banfora

With a population of some 17,000, **BANFORA** is Burkina's fifth-largest town, developed during colonial times due to its position on the railway line. Banfora's only paved road is its main street – centre of the limited commerce in town. There are few distractions in town and wandering about won't turn up much apart from the **traditional drinking places** scattered about the backstreets, where you can guzzle *banji* (palm wine) and *chapalo*. To kill an hour or two in the afternoon, a ten-minute walk along the Sindou road takes you across the tracks to the **palm wine sellers**. Join the old men and women under the mango trees for a calabash or two.

In the **evening**, you could take in a film at the Paysan Noir cinema or head to one of the many open-air nightclubs with garden seating and large dance areas. Banfora has two **banks** – BICIAB and BIB.

Accommodation

Since the area around Banfora has become a major attraction in Burkinabe terms, enterprising young people have started **renting rooms** in their homes (you may be asked at the motor park upon arrival). A bed and bucket shower at these places usually costs less than CFA2000. There are a few reasonable official places too.

Hôtel la Canne à Sucre, near the train station (BP 104; ☎88.01.07). Banfora's top hotel, with clean and comfortable AC rooms, a nice pool and beautiful breezy gardens. The restaurant dishes up excellent international cuisine – a good place for a splurge. Popular with expats. ③.

Hôtel Comoé (BP 68; ☎88.01.51). No-frills budget accommodation with rooms (some with private bath) around a shaded courtyard that serves as restaurant, bar and nightclub. Some AC rooms. ②–③.

Hôtel Fara (BP 112; ☎88.01.17). Conveniently located near the train station, with clean S/C rooms with fan and its own restaurant and bar. ②.

Eating and drinking

Calypso. Popular local drinking spot.

Chez Djana. Well-known place on the Bobo road frequented by travellers and townspeople alike. Reasonable prices and a menu that's a bit more varied than most. Friendly service.

Le Creuset du Militant, near the police station. Popular café serving cold drinks and inexpensive food.

Le Flamboyant, just north of the market. *Restaurant-terrasse* with inexpensive meals and night-time dancing.

L'Harmattan, behind the market. This busy place specializes in *grillades* including excellent fish, chicken and kebabs.

Maison des Femmes. An unusually large *paillote* under which you can eat cheap *riz-sauce*, salads and *couscous*. The restaurant was built by the townspeople and is run by an organization of women.

Around Banfora

To see the region west of Banfora – quite richly endowed with sites of scenic beauty – it's best to rent a *mobylette* at the market, which can be rather pricey (starting from CFA6000 for a half-day). The **Lac de Tengréla** and **Chutes de Karfiguéla** are surprisingly difficult to find (numerous tracks lead through a tall growth of sugar cane most of the year), so you might consider taking someone from town along with you.

Lac de Tengréla

Some 7km from Banfora, Tengréla lake makes a great excursion. Take the Banfora–Sindou road west out of town. A sign about 5km from town points to the left of the lake, from where a two-kilometre-long track passes through the hamlet of Tengréla

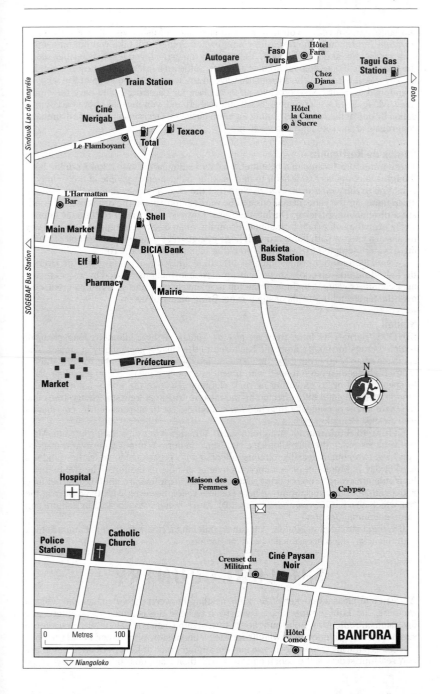

BANFORA

(no supplies). En route, you may want to stop and refresh yourself at the thatched *Farafina Buvette* near the lake; the young owner, Souley, will take you out on a small boat across the lake for CFA1000. Alternatively, on arrival, you'll see fishermen along the shore who'll take you out in their *pirogues*. Settle on a price before heading out. It's usually possible to spot the **hippos** that live in the waters. At the edge of the lake, an abandoned cement house provides an ideal place for **camping** if you have the equipment. Mosquitoes are a problem, but if you wait around, you may be offered accommodation by one of the *piroguiers* touting for extra business. Occasionally, *djembe* drummers congregate at the lake for a jam session.

Chutes de Karfiguéla

These waterfalls, located in a beautiful, verdant setting, are about 12km from the lake, though again, the way is difficult to find (ask the fishermen or people in the vicinity to point you to the *chutes* or *cascades*). Note that the river has been dammed as a source of irrigation for the cane plantations and be warned, too, that in the dry season, the falls are a disappointing trickle. During the rains, however, they swell to thunder impressively over the solid rock formations. From the main track, you approach the falls by means of a narrow path bordered with huge mango trees, requiring a small bit of climbing. If you're tempted to swim, take note that bilharzia is a risk here.

Around 3km from the falls (and also difficult to find without a guide) are the **Domes de Febedougou** – an oddly-shaped cluster of rock formations created by water erosion over countless years. Climbing to the top is relatively easy and gives you a great view over the far-stretching fields of sugar cane. Bring plenty of water.

Sindou

SINDOU derives its fame from *les pics de Sindou*, a three-kilometre-long chain of sculpted crags forming a dramatic backdrop to the village, particularly at sunset. The sandstone has been eroded by the elements into spectacular pancake **towers** and 50-metre-high needles often topped with precarious rocky crowns. It's an excellent place to spend a day or so exploring or rock climbing. Despite the area's natural beauty, Sindou has remained little affected by the meagre trickle of tourists. Mango trees line the main street of conically thatched *banco* houses, yet to be replaced by corrugated iron shacks. Bring lots of film.

Getting to Sindou is not straightforward. Although it lies on a back route into Mali, few vehicles make the fifty-kilometre run from Banfora. Without your own transport, you have two equally feasible options: hitching with occasional local traffic (Sindou's market day is Monday), or renting a mobylette or bike in Banfora. The two-to-three-hour ride on a rough road is tiring, but rewarding. **Supplies** are limited to street food and a couple of tiny restaurants. There is some relief, however, with tepid beer at the **bar** which also has *chambres de passage* (①). Much better is to stock up in Banfora and camp out among *les pics*.

If you get stranded in Sindou, you can try hitching a ride with the enormous Sofitex cotton trucks which occasionally head for Banfora.

THE LOBI COUNTRY

A green and pleasant corner of Burkina, nestling between the Ghanaian and Ivoirian frontiers, the **Lobi country** is a favourite travellers' destination and an interesting diversion en route from Bobo and the southwest into Ghana. It's all hilly, tree-scattered savannah, and rich enough in wildlife for the elephant stories to be just about credible.

Although the lively town of **Gaoua** and the strange ruins of **Loropeni** are the region's only real tourist draws, the Lobi themselves, with their traditions and their *cabaret* drink-

LOBI TRADITIONS

The Lobi believe in maintaining their **traditions**. Lobi men, for example, still hunt with bow and arrows for hares, guinea fowl and gazelles, and it's common to see men carrying these weapons – traditionally poison-tipped – as they walk along the road. Another notable aspect of Lobi culture is the cutlery embedded in gravestones: the Lobi are buried with their fork, spoon, plate and saucepan. Every seven years, too, the new generation of young people still take part in the **djoro** initiation ceremony. Some customs, however, are disappearing. Few Lobi women nowadays wear the disc plugs through their lips which used to be so admired. And the old-fashioned, all-in-one method of house building is giving way to easier mud-brick construction.

The traditions the Lobi maintain best are the ones with widest appeal – booze, music and markets. No Lobi town or village would be complete without its **cabarets** – not nightclubs but places where *chapalo* and *qui-me-pousse* or *patasi* (home-brewed firewater) are consumed in serious quantities and **traditional music** is often played. Many *cabarets* brew their own *chapalo*, a process that thankfully only takes three days. And it's so much cheaper than bottled beer that you could afford to shout the whole place a drink for the same price as a bottle of Brakina in a bar. Many *cabarets* keep a drum and a balafon handy in case anyone feels like playing, which they often do. Even in the unlikely event you don't acquire a taste for *chapalo* and Lobi music, *cabarets* are the best places to go and be sociable with the locals – there's never any shortage of welcome. The **markets** are traditionally held on a five-day cycle, though now increasingly on the same day every week. In more remote ones, you can still use cowries if you have any (you could buy some).

ing bars, not to mention their friendliness, make their corner of the country one of the best to visit, in spite of the fact that transport in the region is often difficult.

Food in the Lobi country is generally of the rice and sauce variety though there are other staples, such as fish and guinea fowl, if you look for them. More typically Lobi is millet *tô* with a sauce of baobab leaves, shea nuts or *néré* fruit.

Gaoua and around

Though the principal reasons for coming to Lobi country are to see the **ruins** and bustling **market** at **Loropeni**, the region's main town is **Gaoua** – absolutely shaking with *cabarets* – and it's here that you'll probably want to base yourself.

Gaoua

GAOUA is almost certainly the best place to get thoroughly acquainted both with *chapalo* and traditional roots music, though obviously the sounds in Bobo-Dioulasso are more refined. The main draw in town though, apart from the *cabarets*, is the magnificent Sunday **market**, a maelstrom of colour and activity. Look out for the leatherworkers just north of the market, spread out under a tree in front of the mosque.

On the west side of the hill, you can visit the **escarpment** with its sacred grotto, easily identified by the masses of plucked feathers from sacrificed chickens. You're supposed to have permission, and a guide (any kid in the town can take you), who will tell you spine-tingling tales of the pythons living in the caves.

Up the hill in the administrative quarter, the Centre Sociale has opened a **museum** (CFA2000 including guided tour) in an old, colonial-style house with exhibits of traditional art, Lobi lifestyles and homes typical of local ethnic groups, together with interesting photographs from the colonial period. An Action Sociale welfare centre, library and crafts centre is worth a visit.

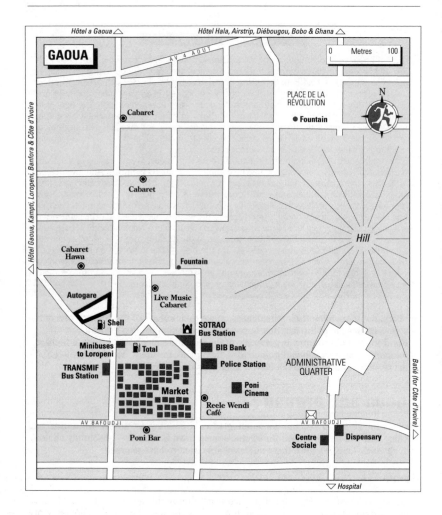

Hôtel a Gaoua △   Hôtel Hala, Airstrip, Diébougou, Bobo & Ghana △

GAOUA

AV 4 AOUT

◁ Hôtel Gaoua, Kampti, Loropeni, Banfora & Côte d'Ivoire

0   Metres   100

PLACE DE LA
RÉVOLUTION

● Fountain

N

◉ Cabaret

◉ Cabaret

Cabaret
Hawa
◉

● Fountain

Hill

Autogare

◉ Live Music
Cabaret

🏠 Shell

⌂

🏛 SOTRAO
Bus Station

Minibuses
to Loropeni

🏠 Total

■ BIB Bank

TRANSMIF
Bus Station

■ Police Station

ADMINISTRATIVE
QUARTER

Batié (for Côte d'Ivoire) ▷

Market

■ Poni
Cinema

◉ Reele Wendi
Café

AV BAFOUDJI

AV BAFOUDJI

✉

◉
Poni Bar

■ Centre
Sociale

Dispensary

▽ Hospital

Practicalities

Gaoua has a few **hotels**. The *Poni Bar* (☎87.02.00; ①), in the centre by the market, has
moderately priced S/C rooms – reasonably comfortable either with or without fans but
with no choice about the reggae and *soukous* sounds till midnight. Out of the centre, the
Hôtel a Gaoua, Base Canadienne, (①) about 400m from the market, offers very basic
rooms, some with AC; you may have to enquire in town to arrange a stay. The *Hôtel
Hala*, a pleasant 1.6km walk out on the Diébougou road (☎87.01.21; ③), offers a little
high living in its ultra-clean, super comfortable, AC rooms with sit-down toilets, and has
a laundry service if you want to make a fresh start.

Food-wise you'll find plenty of stalls doing roast meat and fried fish, especially
around the mosque, and there are several **restaurants**, including two on the road
to Diébougou; the first of these, a shack selling rice in a rather salty sauce, is on the

LIMITED LOBI

The simplest Lobi greeting is *Me foaré* ("Hello") to which the normal response is *Monicho?* ("How are you?") and the reply to that *Michor* ("Fine thanks"). "Thank you" is *Ferehina foaré*.

FOOD

Water	*Ñyoñi*
Chicken	*Yolo*
Egg yolk	*Pala*
Meat	*Nuni*
Maize	*Wologyo*
Millet	*Gyo/di*
Yam	*Puri*

TIMES

Today	*Ni*
Tomorrow	*Kyo*
Day after tomorrow	*Gye ale*
Yesterday	*Daoule*

NUMBERS

1	*Biel*	6	*Maado*	20	*Kpuele*
2	*Yenyo*	7	*Makonyo*	50	*Kpalanyo nuor*
3	*Yetter*	8	*Makotter*	100	*Tama*
4	*Yena*	9	*Nuor biri pero*	1000	*Bulani*
5	*Yamoi*	10	*Nuor*		

right just as you leave the market square. Another place to try is the *Reele Wende Café* in front of the Poni Cinema and across from the market. The frozen yogurt here is more of a draw than the plates of kidney, liver or heart, and the owners are exceptionally friendly to travellers. For a splurge, make for the extravagant selection of Lebanese, African and French cuisine on offer at the *Hôtel Hala*; they also offer a *petit dejeuner* for CFA1500.

Drinking is mainly a *cabaret* sport – the *Cabaret Pastis* and the *Cabaret Hawa* both stay open until late, or until the *chapalo* runs out, and both have sporadic live music. There are dozens of others, located by ear.

For **telephone** calls, it is cheapest to use the ONATEL, on the hill. There is a BIB **bank** in the centre of town, but note that you can only change French francs there, not dollars.

MOVING ON FROM GAOUA

Sunday is the best day for transport into or out of Gaoua, though **Nako** is best reached on its own market day, when vehicles usually leave early in the morning and return in the evening. To reach **Loropeni**, take one of the minibuses which leave regularly (in theory every fifteen minutes) from opposite the TRANSMIF office; the ride only takes about half an hour, but you might have to wait at least an hour until a car fills up, especially on Sundays.

There's usually something to **Doropo** in Côte d'Ivoire, especially on its market day, Thursday, where you'll probably have to change for other Ivoirian destinations. Often there's also a vehicle or two to **Diébougou**, where you may have to change for Bobo and Hamile.

TRANSMIF (☎87.00.10) has a service to **Ouaga** four times a week (Mon, Wed, Sat & Sun; CFA4000), via Diébougou, a ten-hour or more ride along a road that is in very bad condition up to Diébougou. Alternatively, SOTRAO operates a service to Ouaga via **Bobo** three times a week (Tues, Thurs & Sun). Rakieta (☎87.02.18) runs a daily bus to **Banfora** (CFA2500).

If all else fails, try **hitching** from the police post 2km out of town on the Diébougou road.

Around Gaoua

Better known for its market than its ruins, **Loropeni** is an easy excursion from Gaoua on trading day, when transport is certain – although you can get there, and back, on other days too, if you're lucky. To the north of Gaoua, **Nako** is the jumping-off point for a slow short cut into Ghana.

Loropeni

LOROPENI's market, held every five days, is a bustling throng of colour. You can buy fruit, hot food, chillies, multicoloured ground spices and peanut paste, and watch flip-flops being made out of old tyres, and enamel bowls being re-bottomed with bits of vegetable oil tins ("furnished by the people of the USA"). You might meet Ghanaians selling worming tablets (armed with lurid photographic displays), or Gan women, from the west, often wearing brown string mourning bands on their heads, arms, necks and ankles. You can change, and use, **cowries** here.

The only **accommodation** is in the basic places around the *autogare*. Ask around and you'll come up with something for about CFA1000. Apart from the *riz-sauce* **restaurant** in the middle of the market, there are plenty of *tabliers* along the main road doing grilled meat and soup, though tea and coffee become a scarce commodity after breakfast. Across from the car park is a *cabaret* of thatched *paillotes* shading wooden log benches and drinkers waiting for the balafon bands to start up again. Bottled drinks are available at the *buvette* behind the *autogare*, though they are no cooler than the inside temperature of the bar.

THE RUINS

To get to Loropeni's enigmatic **ruins**, head out of town on the Banfora road. After 3.5km you come to a small hill, at the top of which a track leads off to the right. Follow it for 500m to the ruins. Though not massively impressive, the Loropeni ruins are among West Africa's very few stone remains, rising up out of the scrub like some lost temple in a Hollywood movie. Unlike the great stone ruins of East Africa and Zimbabwe, they don't get many visitors, and since their origin and the identity of their builders are still viable mysteries, your ideas about them are as good as anyone else's. The ruins are more or less rectangular, some 50m long, by 40m wide, by (originally) 6–7m high, and noticeably lack any doors or windows. Inside, like other rectangular Lobi ruins, they're divided into two enclosures, one large and one small, connected by a door and each divided into chambers.

If you don't have transport, head to the *buvette* behind Loropeni's *autogare*. The owner has a mobylette and for a couple of litres of petrol, he'll take you out to the ruins and throw in a trip to the Gan village of **Obiré**, 8km northwest of Loropeni. The latter has no mysterious walls, but is remarkable for its round thatched huts (a thatching style very different from Lobi houses) and for the **life-size mud statues** representing ancestral kings. The chief requests CFA500 to visit.

The **Gan country** a few kilometres north and west of Loropeni harbours more archeological oddities if you can get the transport. There are ruins near **Yerifoula**, others near **Oyono** and **Lokosso**, and some large relics at **Loghi**.

Nako

NAKO has its market always the day after Loropeni's. You may find yourself here if taking the short cut **into Ghana via Lawra**: from Nako you'll need a lift 11km to **Boukéro** and then a *pirogue* ride across the Black Volta, which forms the border here. It's straightforward enough to do this, and fun, but quite time-consuming, especially when you add in the fairly long walk from the Ghanaian bank of the river to the main road, and the likelihood that you will be asked to go 50km north to Hamile to be officially received into Ghana. Be sure to go to **immigration in Nako** to get stamped out of Burkina in the first place or the Ghanaians will send you back.

Diébougou and Hamile

Lying outside the Lobi country proper, **DIÉBOUGOU**'s people are mostly Lobi-Gan and Dagara (Dagarti). The place doesn't hold a lot of interest in itself, but it's friendly, full of kids and has better transport connections than Gaoua (but note that no banks change money).

There are two **hotels**, both near the *taxi brousse* and bus stops. The *Campement Danabone* has rooms in not too bad a state, some with fans (①), and it's also a bar, disco and pick-up joint with generator electricity in the evenings. There's a rather mucky shower and sink for each pair of rooms. The nearby *Relais la Bougouriba* is slightly smarter with a shower in every room and fans too; rooms are cleaner and the extra price is worth it (☎86.02.88; ②). The *Bougouriba* also has a generator, a bar and plenty of atmosphere. The only **restaurants** are at the hotels, with rice, guinea fowl, steak and the usual solid stuff. Outside there's a run of food stalls around the market and lots of *cabarets* to slake your thirst. Deserving of a mention is the *Flambeau Café*, a breakfast joint with real coffee, tea, omelettes and so forth. Passing an evening in Diébougou you'll likely gravitate to the hotel discos or possibly the cinema.

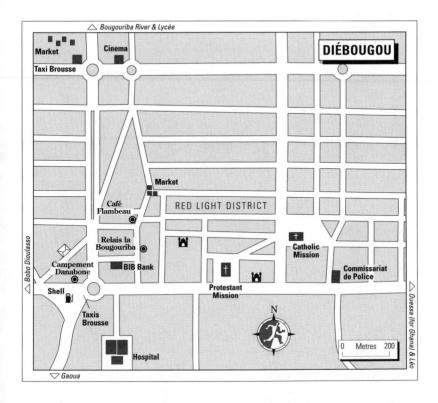

During the wet season **crocodiles** (though not, it's important to point out, sacred ones) collect in the swamp that forms at the eastern end of town. They're best observed around dawn, if you can manage it, when coolness keeps them calm and visible. Older folk can be overheard complaining that they don't have swamps like they used to; needless to say, the crocodiles are diminishing in number.

For **transport** out of Diébougou, TRANSMIF buses run to Gaoua and Ouaga. Other transport east to Hamile often comes in late at night from Bobo.

Hamile and into Ghana

A busy border town and the main crossing point into Ghana from Bobo-Dioulasso, **HAMILE** rarely has much to offer – at least when beer supplies in Ghana are satisfying demand. When Ghana goes dry, periodically, Ghanaians, including police in uniform, pop across the border for a drink at the *Zodo Bar*. You can stay at the *Zodo*, but you might as well spend a cheaper night in Ghana.

Burkinabe border formalities take place at Ouessa, where you visit police and customs, and probably the Gendarmerie too, just to be sure. Cedis are available at the ordinary (poor) border rate, a rate beaten just about everywhere else. **Transport on the Ghanaian side** almost all goes to Lawra and Wa, including the twice daily STC bus.

GHANA

GHANA

Ghana was the first modern African country to retrieve its independence, in 1957. At the time it was one of the richest nations on the continent – the world's leading **cocoa** exporter and producer of a tenth of the world's **gold**. But after Kwame Nkrumah's optimistic start it suffered a hornet's nest of setbacks. Repeated coups, food shortages and sapping corruption for years combined to make Ghana a place to be avoided.

No longer. Conditions have improved almost out of recognition since the terminal bottoming-out in 1979 and the country is back on its feet and pursuing a course of IMF rehabilitation, with great success as far as the international development agencies are concerned. Ghanaians complain, justifiably, about continued inefficiency and corruption but, from a traveller's point of view, Ghana now has an excellent reputation in the region. Compared with the other Anglophone countries in West Africa, Ghana offers a **transport and accommodation** infrastructure that's second to none; a **cultural mix**, inevitably stressing the **Asante** nation's rich and vibrant lifestyle, that's every bit as rewarding as Nigeria's (without that country's immense size or intimidating reputation); and better **beaches** than The Gambia. The Ghana government has, moreover, an enthusiastic commitment to tourism, with a number of regional tourist offices set up and plenty to engage visitors.

The country has a distinctive personality and perhaps more claim to a **national character** than any other in the region. On the other hand, Ghana has had long contact with European cultural forms. School education has had a major impact, going back four generations now, and there's a high level of literacy and an inventiveness with language – both written, on signs and in the press, and spoken, in repartee – that hints at a creativity as yet barely unleashed in Africa. Ghanaians are hospitable and generous to a fault and there's more warmth to be experienced in Ghana than in either of its coastal neighbours.

The country

Ghana is compact and mostly flat. With the exception of the striking **scarp system** that curves through the country from the Gambaga escarpment in the northeast, round to the Wenchi scarp west of Lake Volta, and southeast as the Mampong scarp through the forest, there are few striking highland regions. But there are some attractive rolling

---

FACTS AND FIGURES

Known as the **Gold Coast** during the colonial era, **Ghana** took its present name from the former West African empire (with which it has no historical connection) located in present-day southeast Mauritania. With a **population** of around 18 million and an **area** of 240,000 square kilometres – about the same size as Britain or Oregon – Ghana is one of the region's most densely populated states. The fast-growing **foreign debt** stands at around £3.9 billion ($6.2 billion), which, for some sense of scale, is not much more than half of Britain's annual armaments research budget, or, seen from another perspective, less than a third of the value of the Chrysler corporation. It is also, however, more than four times the country's annual earnings from the export of goods and services.

Since 1981, Ghana has been led by Flight-Lieutenant Jerry Rawlings who ruled dictatorially through the Provisional National Defence Council, until he was elected president by universal suffrage in 1993 and again in 1996. The next elections are due in the year 2000.

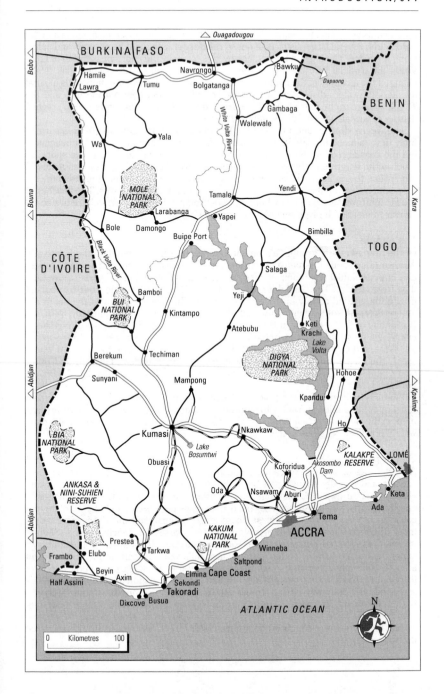

green landscapes and, in the central regions, away from the **cocoa** plantations and the **goldfields**, several large districts of dense **rainforest** with giant hardwoods and palms vying for space. The biggest impact, however, is made by the enormous stretch of **Lake Volta**, an artificial lake created in the wooded savannah in 1966, which has totally changed the anatomy of the country – not to mention the lives of the thousands of rural dwellers its waters displaced. In the eastern Volta region, between the lake and the Togolese border, the hills of the **Akwapim range** roll across the landscape to create a district of verdant green valleys and gentle peaks.

The **Accra district** and much of the surrounding bushy, **coastal plain** is surprisingly dry – almost desolate in places, partly the result of an unusual local subclimate – but the coastal road to the west runs at least within striking distance of the shore for much of its length and the beaches themselves are alluring. The coast has a special dimension, too, in its European **forts and castles**, some dating from the fifteenth century, which were built as trading posts for gold, ivory and, later, slaves. The beaches of the far southwest are backed by lowland forest and patchy jungle agriculture in a scene similar to most of the Ivoirian coastline over the border.

The people

Of the myriad ethnic groups that people Ghana, the **Akan** – including the **Fante** and **Asante** (also spelled Ashanti) – predominate. The Asante occupy the central forest, and in pre-colonial days their empire stretched into the regions of present-day Côte d'Ivoire and Togo. The **Ga-Adangme** and **Ewe**, who probably came from Yorubaland in Nigeria, settled mainly in the east and south. The major peoples of the north are all speakers of Voltaic languages and share much in common, culturally, with the Burkinabe over the border in Burkina Faso. They include the More-speaking southern Mossi kingdoms of **Mamprusi** and **Dagomba** in the northeast, the More-speaking **Wala** and Grusi-speaking **Dagarti** in the northwest, the **Gonja** (some of whom speak the Grusi tongue, Wagala, and others the Akan dialect, Guang), and other Grusi peoples – **Kassena**, **Frafra**, **Sissala**, **Builsa** and **Talensi** – near the Burkinabe border.

Islam is widespread among the northerners, some of whom migrated south from Muslim communities in Mali. **Christianity**, of course, spread with European involvement in the Gold Coast, but pantheistic beliefs and ancestor veneration remain the most widely practised religions in the country.

Where to go

After decades of neglect, **Accra** has made a strong comeback in recent years. It's manageable and friendly enough and beginning to look the part of a capital once again. Unless you're drawn to the nightlife, however, and your visit coincides with some weekend live shows, you'll only want to spend a few days here before getting out along the coast or into the interior. The **west coast** is exceptional, and the European **castles**, most of which can be visited, provide excellent focuses for beach-hopping. Slightly inland, the protected rainforest of the **Kakum National Park** is one of the country's major natural attractions. To the east, the lush hills and waterfalls of the **Volta region** are also currently generating great interest among travellers. **Kumasi**, in the centre of the country, has a strong sense of identity, and the forest region of which it is capital is scenically and culturally Ghana's most appealing area. The **north** is quite different, both in landscape and people, but its climate is more tolerable and, if there's not a lot that demands to be seen as you pass through – apart from **Mole Game Reserve** – there's plenty of interest in its ethnographic history if you have more time or are based in the area.

Climate

Ghana has a lot more **climatic variation** than most of West Africa. Central and southern Ghana – south of Tamale – is unusual in having **two distinct rainy seasons**, the first lasting roughly from March to June and the second from September to October. The far southwest gets heavy rains, but in Accra they tend to be light and it's uncommon to experience day after day of torrential downpour. The central rainforest regions tend to be wetter and (although you wouldn't know it because of the high humidity) slightly cooler. The north is basically hot and dry most of the year, with a climate much like that of Ouagadougou in Burkina, and a single rainy period from June to October.

AVERAGE TEMPERATURES AND RAINFALL												
ACCRA												
	Jan	Feb	Mar	Apr	May	June	July	Aug	Sept	Oct	Nov	Dec
Temperatures °C												
Min (night)	23	24	24	24	24	23	23	22	23	23	24	24
Max (day)	31	31	31	31	31	29	27	27	27	29	31	31
Rainfall mm	15	33	56	81	142	178	46	15	36	64	36	23
Days with rainfall	1	2	4	6	9	10	4	3	4	6	3	2
TAMALE												
Temperatures °C												
Min (night)	21	23	24	24	24	22	22	22	22	22	22	20
Max (day)	36	37	37	36	33	31	29	29	30	32	34	35
Rainfall mm	3	3	53	69	104	142	135	196	226	99	10	5
Days with rainfall	1	1	1	6	10	12	14	16	19	13	1	1

Arrivals

Ghana is one of the most popular countries for independent travel in West Africa and its good connections and central location make it an excellent starting point for longer travels.

■ Flights from Africa

Accra has good links to **Abidjan**, a one-hour hop with flights most days: Ghana Airways (GH) and British Airways (BA) operate four flights weekly, while both Air Afrique (RK) and Air Ivoire (VU) have three services a week.

Other flights in the region mostly emanate from further west. RK flies **Dakar** to Accra weekly. GH makes two long treks up the coast each week, calling at **Banjul**, **Conakry**, and Dakar twice a week before returning to Accra.

From the other direction, there are non-stop flights from **Cotonou** three times a week (two with GH, one with RK), and non-stop flights from **Lagos** once or twice daily on both GH and Nigeria Airways (WT), plus services most days of the week with BA. **Lomé** is connected by twice-weekly flights with GH and BA.

With the exception of Air Burkina's (2J) daily flights from **Ouagadougou**, flights from other cities in West Africa require a plane change, usually in Abidjan. **Bamako** has reasonable twice-weekly connections using VU and GH. If you're flying from **Douala**, the best connections are through Lagos. There are no good connections from Nouakchott, Bissau, the Cape Verde Islands or Niamey.

Ethiopian Airlines (ET) provides the link from **East Africa** with a flight from **Addis Ababa** four times a week, and from **Nairobi** twice weekly. From **North Africa**, Egyptair (MS) has flights from **Cairo** to Accra twice a week.

From **Southern Africa**, GH and South African Airlines (SA) both fly twice a week from **Johannesburg**, and GH also operates a twice-weekly flight from **Harare**.

The details in these practical information pages are essentially for use on the ground in West Africa and in Ghana itself: for full details on preparing a trip, getting here from outside the region, paperwork, health, information sources and more, see Basics, p.3–83.

ORGANIZED STAYS IN GHANA

For details of organized stays in Ghana with Insight Travel of England and the Suntaa-Nuntaa project based in Wa, Upper West Region, see p.8. The American Council on Educational Exchange, 205 E 42nd St, New York (☎212/661-1414) also arrange trips to Ghana, as part of their International Workcamps programme.

■ Overland from Burkina Faso

Coming from Ouagadougou, you have several possibilities: taking a **bush taxi** or **bus** to the border at Paga, or getting transport through to Navrongo, Bolgatanga or Accra. Going by bush taxi you'll make better time on the road but the buses are more comfortable and generally get through the border and various checkpoints more quickly. If you're lucky with connections, it can sometimes work out cheapest and fastest to change transport at the border, which is generally amicable – though note that it closes at 6pm. The direct STC bus leaves Ouaga for Accra twice a week, and is by far the most comfortable of all the options (around ₵40,000).

Other crossings include the one between Léo and Tumu and the one at Hamile. Transport is patchy on both sides of the border, and there's no direct through transport to speak of in either case – your prospects are best by far on market days.

The **fast route to Accra** goes via Tamale, Kintampo and Kumasi; the more easterly route, involving a Lake Volta ferry or canoe crossing between Makongo and Yeji, is extremely rough.

■ Overland from Togo

The road from Lomé to Accra is surfaced. The quickest way between the two capitals is by **bush taxi** but you'll save some hassle if you first get yourself to the border on the west side of the city of Lomé, cross on foot to Aflao, and then continue by bush taxi or bus – a journey of about three hours. You can also take the Ghanaian STC buses which depart twice daily to Accra, and which are always more comfortable than bush taxis, but take slightly longer. The border – open 6am to 6pm – was closed frequently in the early 1990s due to historically strained relations between the two countries, but is today generally reliable.

■ Overland from Côte d'Ivoire

The coastal stretch between Abidjan and Accra is in good condition, and Ghanaian STC, STIF and TEE **buses** – not to mention fleets of **bush taxis** – connect the two capitals in a day (around 14 hours). Buses leave from the Treichville *gare routière* in Abidjan. There's also a fast route direct to Kumasi via Abengourou – also a day's journey – from Abidjan's Adjamé *gare routière*.

Red Tape

Visas, which tend to be expensive, are required by all non-Commonwealth nationals. Commonwealth citizens need an entry permit, which amounts to the same thing. Multiple-entry visas valid for three months are also available.

Entering the country, you will be asked how long you plan on staying and your reply is noted in your passport. If you say a week, that's your limit, even if you have a one-month visa. It's wise to get the longest possible stay, since extensions are in practice only delivered in Accra and are difficult to obtain (see p.716). You'll also be asked at the border for a Ghanaian address, so have a hotel in mind.

The form that you fill out on arrival may still indicate that you should present yourself with passport photos to the **Immigration Department** of the Ministry of the Interior in Accra within 48 hours of arrival. In fact this has not been necessary for several years (staff at the airport may tell you it's "optional", as if there might be some advantage in it for the traveller), but until they get round to printing new forms, the uncertainty will continue.

Yellow fever certificates are required for overland entry, and are closely checked at the borders.

■ Visas for onward travel

Ghana's three neighbours (Côte d'Ivoire, Burkina and Togo) issue **visas in Accra** as do most West African countries. **Nigeria** has become somewhat sticky, at times insisting you need a residency permit for Ghana in order to be issued a visa at the embassy in Accra. **Benin** visas are quick and inexpensive. For addresses and further details see p.19.

Money and Costs

Ghana's currency is the cedi (₵). Formerly, one cedi was divided into 100 pesewas, but inflation long ago rose well past the point at which pesewas had any value. The biggest note is ₵5000, which is worth just over £1 (roughly $2). Notes of ₵50 and ₵100 are being withdrawn. There are ₵20, ₵50 and ₵100 coins.

The official **exchange rate** is currently around ₵4300 = £1; ₵2700 = $1, and inflation runs at around ten percent a year. There is no black market.

In other countries market women tie up their money in their skirts, but in Ghana they keep it in huge plastic bags. You'll find yourself walking around with **wads of money** that don't add up to much. But don't destroy any – a tourist was once fined ₵200,000 and jailed for a month for lighting a cigarette with a ₵100 note. Small notes and coins are worth hanging on to – it's always hard to get change.

For changing money you'll find **foreign exchange (forex) bureaux** in Accra, Kumasi and other major towns, and new ones springing up all over the country, including Aflao on the Togo border. Shop around for the best rates which are always to be had for large denominations such as US$100 bills. Forex bureaux offer rates slightly higher than the banks, not all of which change money anyway.

Cash US dollars are the prime medium of exchange, with other currencies, including pounds sterling, and all travellers' cheques, worth relatively less. (Note that it can be difficult to change travellers' cheques at forex bureaux and Thomas Cook cheques are particularly unwelcome on account of their perceived forgeability.) You can also buy hard currency from forex bureaux.

If you're stuck for a forex bureau the most likely banks are the Ghana Commercial Bank (which has over 100 branches throughout the country), Barclays, Standard Chartered and the Agricultural Development Bank, all of which have several dozen branches, covering all the main towns. **Banking hours** are Monday to Thursday 8.30am to 2pm, Friday until 3pm.

Credit cards are accepted in major hotels in Accra and Kumasi and at some travel agencies. Outside the main cities they won't get you far.

Barclays handles Visa cash advances at a reasonable exchange rate, but subject to a two percent fee. When banks are closed, you can obtain cash advances through Barclays automatic teller machines, mainly found in Accra or Kumasi, with credit cards or Visa cheque/debit cards.

You can have **money sent to you** easily enough at the Bank of Ghana, Thorpe Road, Accra (PO Box 264; ☎021/66.69.02). In the UK you can do this through the Ghana Commercial Bank, 69 Cheapside, London EC2P 2BB, or HSBC International, 110–114 Cannon St, London EC4N 6AA. You can also use Western Union through select Agricultural Development Banks, found mainly in Accra.

■ **Costs**

Cedi devaluations make it difficult to gauge **costs** but in terms of foreign exchange value – even in Accra – they are dropping all the time.

Accommodation in Accra runs as low as ₵16,000 (£3.70/$6) for a twin room, and can be cheaper still upcountry. Businesses which rely heavily on customers wielding foreign currency (which of course includes the more expensive hotels and restaurants, imported goods outlets and so on) tend to keep a close eye on the exchange rate and adjust their prices accordingly. Hence they often quote prices in hard currency and accept payment at prevailing rates – often skewed in their favour – in any currency. Note that a fifteen percent **value added tax** has recently been introduced and will be added to your bill at hotels and restaurants.

Although Ghanaians find even street **food** expensive on their wages, it will seem cheap enough to you, as you can usually eat heartily for under ₵1500 (£0.30/$0.50).

The other major cost, **transport**, is also cheaper in Ghana than surrounding countries – roughly half the cost of travel in Burkina or Côte d'Ivoire – especially if you travel by State Transport Corporation (STC) buses.

Health

Yellow fever vaccinations are required before entering Ghana. Cholera epidemics occur, especially in isolated regions with limited sources of clean water. Bilharzia is another concern; stay away from stagnant ponds or slow-running streams – especially in savannah areas. Lake Volta is notorious.

In large towns, **tap water** is always drinkable. In smaller places, and villages, the well or stored rainwater isn't always the purest and you may want to try some combination of boiling (not always practical), filtering or adding purifying tablets. Except in the remotest areas, bottled water is available though expensive.

The main **hospitals** are in Accra and Kumasi. Smaller hospitals and clinics can be found in towns throughout the country, but for a major medical problem you may prefer a private clinic. For a reference, consult an embassy.

Ghana has a surging **AIDS** problem, as much as any other country in the region, with thousands of cases reported and hundreds of thousands of HIV carriers. Fortunately, there is a growing acknowledgement of the problem, as demonstrated by emerging radio and television broadcasts and several recent health awareness campaigns.

Maps and Information

Virtually no official tourist information is supplied outside the country. You can get to know Ghana quite well, however, through the detailed coverage provided by *Ghana Review International* (700 High Rd, Tottenham, London N17, UK; ☎0181/808 5655; Fax 0181/808 9889; *www.ghanareview.com*) and the weekly *West Africa* magazine. On the Internet, try *www.ghanaweb.com* for general information and *www.ghanaclassifieds.com* for current events.

Map availability is improving, although you will not find any decent, up-to-date single sheets of the whole country. In Accra, the best place to find detailed regional and basic national maps is at the Survey Office (Cantonments, PO Box 191, Accra; ☎021/77.73.31) on Giffard Road near the airport – the only place in the country with a dependable supply, though many admittedly are out-of-date. They sell **town maps** for a number of places outside the capital, as well as an **Accra city map**, the latter also available at the KLM office in town on Ring Road, or Shell stations. A more recent map of Accra (1997) can be found in the *No Worries* guide, produced by Mobil and the North American Women's Association and available at any Mobil station. The Ghana

Wildlife Department (PO Box M.329, Accra; 021/66.46.54 or 66.23.60) has a recent and useful map of Ghana's national parks.

The **Ghana Tourist Board** has offices, in theory, in Accra and all the regional capitals throughout the country (Cape Coast, Takoradi, Kumasi, Tamale, Wa, Bolgatanga, Ho, Koforidua, Sunyani), as mandated by the newly implemented fifteen-year **Tourist Development Plan** (1996–2010). Some offices, however, are easier to locate than others and continue to shift locations. Services are as yet uneven across regions, with little communication between them; they are most useful in tourist areas such as Cape Coast.

Getting Around

The government has made real improvements to the transportation system. They have resurfaced roads, bought new rolling stock for the railway system and expanded the country's now highly efficient bus service. Buses, in fact, are the most convenient means of travelling around the country and you'll find them a real luxury after the battered bush taxis you may have grown accustomed to using elsewhere.

■ Buses

The State Transport Corporation's **bus service** provides a cheap and hassle-free way to get around the country with a minimum of waiting at roadside checkpoints. The buses run on fixed schedules to all towns of any size and are safe and comfortable. It's always a good idea when possible to book seats in advance with STC, especially if you're heading for popular destinations like Accra, Kumasi or Tamale. The STC yard in each town usually adjoins the main motor park. You will need a luggage ticket too in order to get your gear into the hold, unless you're prepared to carry it on your lap. In some parts you'll also find Omnibus Services Authority (OSA), TEE, STIF and Bluebird (City Express) buses. They are all now non-smoking.

■ Bush taxis and tro-tros

Minibuses (*tro-tros*) and **Peugeot 504s** ("caravans") are less comfortable than the coaches, but they leave more frequently and travel faster.

ROAD TRANSPORT:
SAMPLE FARES AND TIMES

Accra–Kumasi, 253km, ₵7000 (STC bus), 4hr.
Accra–Cape Coast, 165km, ₵4500 (STC bus), 3hr.
Accra–Tamale, 611km, ₵16,000 (STC bus), 10hr.
Accra–Hohoe, 235km, ₵7000 (STC bus), 4hr.
Accra–Takoradi, 237km, ₵7000 (STC bus), 3hr.
Tamale–Bolgatanga, 191km, ₵5000 (OSA & City Express buses), 3hr.
Hamile–Wa, 115km, ₵4000 (*tro-tro*, rough track), 3hr.
Wa–Kumasi, 454km, ₵7000 (OSA bus, mostly bad road), 7hr.

They're notoriously overloaded and, if you're out to enjoy the ride, should be used only if you're not going far or can't get on a bus. Worse than the bush taxis are the **lorries**, or mammy wagons, which you'll only want to consider as a last resort. These squeeze as many people as can possibly fit onto wooden planks in a boarded-up truck. You'll see nothing on the way and collect lots of bruises to boot.

■ Trains

Trains are the cheapest way of travelling and, since the government bought new rolling stock in the 1980s, they're actually quite comfortable, though there is still a tendency for them to derail – not that derailment usually causes a disaster, as they travel so slowly. Of the three main lines, the most useful is the stretch linking **Kumasi to Takoradi** (about eight hours) which is a better alternative than the beaten-up roads that run through the forest and connect the Asante country to the coast. There are two trains daily, one in the morning and an overnight sleeper. The other two lines connect **Accra to Kumasi** (2 daily, one of which is overnight; also about eight hours) and **Accra to Takoradi** (1 daily train overnight); the Accra–Takoradi line unfortunately skirts inland, well away from the coast, and in terms of scenery, therefore, the road is better along this stretch.

■ Planes

Flights within Ghana are provided by two airlines: Ghana Air Force runs **AirLink**, which has three flights a week to both Tamale and Kumasi; and **Fan Airways** has two daily flights to Kumasi, and a daily flight to both Tamale and Bolgatanga. Less regularly, Fan Airways also provides services between Bolga and Tamale.

Details can be obtained in Ghana directly at the airports or from M&J Travel in Accra (see p.716). One-way **fares** from Accra are around ₡95,000 to Kumasi, ₡150,000 to Tamale, and ₡200,000 to Bolgatanga.

■ Volta ferries

You can cover part of the country by boat, as a Lake Volta **ferry service** links the southern town of Akosombo (100km north of Accra) with Kpandu (213km from Accra) and Kete Krachi (520km from Accra) once a week, taking 12hr. Apart from this "scheduled" passenger service, vessels also ply this route and venture further north – as far as Yapei, just 32km east of Tamale (except at the end of the dry season), a voyage which can take up to three days, depending on stops en route. The scenery is not as exciting as you might expect – long stretches of dead tree trunks sticking up through flooded landscapes, but it is a peaceful alternative to *tro-tro* travel.

One-way **fares** from Akosombo to Kete Krachi are around ₡30,000 (first class), ₡13,500 (second class), and ₡11,000 (third class). First class offers a very limited number of overrated sleepers. For current information, check at the Volta Lake Transport Service (in Akosombo ☎0251/686 ext 204; in Accra ☎021/66.53.00) or, as a last resort, the Tourist Board in Ho (see p.744), the regional capital.

■ Driving and cycling

Outlets for **car rental** are still limited, though Accra has a number of possibilities, including some licensed outlets for the big international groups. Rental normally includes a driver. **Fuel** is relatively cheap at about ₡820 per litre.

Lastly, outside of Accra, Ghana is a good country for **cycling**, covering a manageable area (two to three weeks from north to south) and offering immense scenic variety. You don't need to be super-fit: the hilly zones are fairly restricted. You can tour along the coast, slog up to Kumasi, then take the switchback route back to Accra – again a perfect trip for two to three weeks.

Accommodation

Although luxury accommodation is rare in Ghana, major towns have decent hotels which are in general comfortable if lacking in conveniences. Running water and AC can be had in most places, but may only work sporadically. Since the Tourist Development Plan started up in 1996, most former state-owned hotels have been privatized, and many new middle-range hotels have been

---

ACCOMMODATION PRICE CODES

Accommodation prices in this chapter are coded according to the following scales – the same scales in terms of their pound/dollar equivalents as are used throughout the book. Prices refer to the rate you can expect to pay for a room with two beds. Single rooms, or single occupancy, will normally cost at least two-thirds of the twin-occupancy rate. VAT of 15 percent will be added to your bill, included in our price codes. For further details, see p.48.

① **Under ₡21,500 (under £5/$8).** Anything from very rudimentary lodgings to an adequate, simple hotel with S/C rooms with fans, and possibly some with AC for slightly higher rates.

② **₡21,500–43,000 (£5–10/$8–16).** Modest hotel or guesthouse, usually with S/C rooms and a choice of fan ventilation, or AC for a premium. Often the best place in a small town.

③ **₡43,000–86,000 (£10–20/$16–32).** Usually a reasonable business or tourist-class hotel with S/C, AC rooms and often a good restaurant.

④ **₡86,000–129,000 (£20–30/$32–48).** Comfortable, first-class hotel, with good facilities, including phones in rooms and full AC (though some city hotels in this price bracket offer poor value for money).

⑤ **₡129,000–172,000 (£30–40/$48–64).** Luxury establishment.

⑥ **₡172,000–215,000 (£40–50/$64–80).** Luxury establishment, primarily found in Accra.

⑦ **Over ₡215,000 (over £50/$80).** Accra-only luxury.

built, mostly in Accra. There has also been an effort to develop more four- and five-star outfits in major tourist cities. Added to your bill is a fifteen percent state hotel tax, which has been included in our calculations of room price codes.

Special mention should be made of the handful of **forts** along the coast which have been converted to rest houses. They offer exceptionally cheap and characterful accommodation, though they have limited space so are often full in high season. The museum at Cape Coast may help with bookings.

■ Staying with people

Ghanaians are generally curious to meet travellers, and if you're on your own, you may be surprised how many offers you get to **stay with people**. It can be rewarding, but you should be extremely conscious, when accepting such offers, of the expense your stay imposes, and be aware that even for salaried government workers a bottle of beer may be a luxury in which they rarely indulge. Be as generous as your host; pay at the cinema, bars or discos and, if you go to the market together, pay for the food. Ghana's cost of living is incredibly high relative to local wages and most people are barely scraping by, and generally doing so outside the money economy.

For details of organized home stays with UK-based Insight Travel, see p.8. You can also try Friendly Homes of Ghana (FHOG), an organization of Ghanaian families and individuals who open their homes to visitors for an arranged fee (PO Box 0621, Osu, Accra; ☎027/54.47.05; Fax 021/23.23.07).

■ Camping

If you have your own transport, you have the freedom to get off the beaten tracks and visit many small towns and villages which don't have accommodation. **Camping** is feasible in the bush, though in practice it's most pleasant in the north, beyond the damp forest zone. If you arrive in a village you can ask the chief if and where you can spend the night, and he'll make the arrangements. **Camping gas** is very hard to find in Ghana; stock up in Francophone countries where it's readily available.

Eating and Drinking

In southern Ghana, the most common staple is *kenkey* – fermented maize flour balls,

steamed and wrapped in maize leaves. You'll see it in markets everywhere. The sour taste takes a while to acquire, and you don't often get much sauce to help it down – just a splash of ground tomatoes, onions and peppers and deep-fried fish. But it does, eventually, taste good. In the north, *tozafi* (or *TZ*) takes over – a mush made from millet (occasionally maize) flour, and commonly eaten with palm nut or okra soup.

Plantains are used a lot in Ghanaian cooking and, together with **beans**, **groundnuts**, **rice**, fresh and dried **fish**, **guinea fowl** (especially in the north) and **grasscutter** (the large, tasty rodent, also known as bush rat, hunted mainly in the south), supply the basis of one of West Africa's best national cuisines.

If you're adventurous, there are other flavours, including clay-baked **lizard** (in Dagomba country; the skin comes off with the clay) and giant forest **snails** – even bat, rat, cat and dog in various parts of the country.

Bread, as you would expect, reflects the taste and style of the British former rulers and is usually soft, white and plastic bagged, available in "tea", "sugar", or "brown" varieties. Baguette-style bread sticks and loaves made of wholemeal flour are becoming more widely available.

Ghana has a lot of good **chocolate**, available everywhere and not expensive, but it's not popular with Ghanaians.

The country's outstanding fruit is the **pineapple** – notably along the coast – cheaper in Ghana than anywhere else in West Africa. **Coconuts**, too, are incredibly cheap and surprisingly good for you.

■ Drinking

Ghana was the first West African country to possess a brewery and it now has a wide range of **beers**. One of the most popular, perhaps because it's got the highest alcohol content, is Gulder. Other brands include Star, ABC, Club and bottled Guinness. **Minerals** include the usual Coke and Fanta varieties. Refresh comes in orange, mango and pineapple and, with 25 percent juice, it's not bad. A more acquired taste is Malta Guinness, dark and sugary with a burnt caramel flavour. Home-made drinks include Taka Beer (a ginger drink) and Ice Kenkey – sweetened, fermented maize flour in water, a taste you may not acquire.

GHANAIAN FOOD TERMS AND DISHES

Abenkwan	Palm nut soup (Akan)	Koko	Corn or millet porridge
Aduane	Food (Akan)		with milk and sugar
Akawadu	Banana (Akan)	Kokonte	Cassava meal (Akan)
Akokoh	Chicken (Akan)	Kontumbre	Cocoyam leaves
Amadaa	Fried, ripe plantain	Kyinkyinga	Beef with vegetable
	(Ga)		sauce (Hausa)
Ampesi	Plantain and yam	Momone	Sun-dried fish (Akan)
Banku	Corndough, good with	Nsuomnam	Fish (Akan)
	groundnut soup	Nuhuu	Cocoyam porridge
Bodie (kokoo)	(Ripe) plantain (Akan)		(Akan)
Boflot	Doughnut (north)	Ode	Yam (Akan)
Borodo/Panu	Bread (Akan)	Omo tuo	Mashed rice balls
Ekwei bemi	Boiled, sweetened		with soup or stew,
	corn kernels		usually served
Enam	Meat (Akan)		Sundays only (also
Fufu	Yam mash		written Emo or
Gari	Cassava grated and		Amo tuo)
	dried	Rice water	Rice pudding, often
Gari foto	Gari dish, mixed with		for breakfast
	palm oil and other	Shito	Pepper soup (Ga)
	ingredients	Suya	Small shish kebab
Kelewele	Spicy fried ripe	Tatare	Ripe plantain,
	plantain with stew		pounded and fried
Khosay	Bean cakes (north)	TZ (Tozafi)	Millet mush (north)
Klaklo	Ripe plantain dough,	Waachi	Rice and red beans
	deep-fried		

Pito is the millet-based beer commonly drunk, from shared bowls, in the north; it varies greatly but is quite likeable. In the south, the favourite local brews are naturally fermented **palm wine** (known in Akan as *ntunkum* when it's fresh and low in alcohol and *nsa* when it's winey) and **akpeteshie**, a potent firewater distilled from palm wine, also called "VC10" or "Kill-me-quick".

Communications – Post, Phones, Language & Media

Ghana's postal services are inexpensive and relatively efficient to Europe and America. Letters take a week to ten days to Britain and slightly longer to North America, although to neighbouring West African countries they can take up to two months. Accra's poste restante service is free and reliable.

Telephones are improving all the time and card-operated public phones in Accra provide international direct dialling. AT&T's World Connect service can be accessed on ☎0191. Collect (reverse charge) calls are expensive from a hotel or even communication center, and your best bet is to use a private telephone.

Ghana has phone numbers of three to six digits, and area codes which are three or four digits always commencing with 0 (which you omit if calling from abroad). In this chapter, the full area code and number are given, except for manual exchanges, where just the number is given.

Ghana's IDD code is ☎233.

■ Languages

Ghana's official language is English and you can use it without much trouble throughout the country, although you'll likely need a period of adjustment before completely understanding the broader **pidgin** accents. If English is not your first language, you might be misunderstood.

The two main language "families" into which Ghanaian languages fall are Kwa in the south and Voltaic in the north (see p.80).

The great **Twi group** of Kwa languages and dialects includes the **Akan languages** like **Asante-Twi**, spoken by the Asante and Fante, **Ewe** and its associate dialects (spoken in the southeast – see p.80), and **Ga**, or Ga-Adangme, the traditional language of the Accra region.

Important **Voltaic languages** include the big **More** (or Mole) cluster – including **Dagomba** and **Mamprusi** – and various **Grusi** tongues, among them **Frafra** and **Nunumba**.

A number of Ghanaian languages have long been written with unfamiliar **orthography** and you'll see satisfyingly exotic-looking spellings used in many hand-painted signs: c (pronounced "o" as in "cost"); 3 (pronounced "e" as in "men"); n (pronounced "ng" as in "sing"); and Y (pronounced as a very soft "h").

■ **The media**

Ghana has an established and respected press, with an enthusiastic readership. Press freedom is

---

TWI PHRASE LIST

Twi, pronounced somewhere between "Twee" and "Chooi", is the name commonly given to the language of the Asante and Fante people. It's a difficult tongue to master, with a complex tonal system – and anyway most people you meet will have some English – but a few words and phrases in Twi always go down well. Note that it's usually written with the somewhat impenetrable orthography mentioned above, but we've gone for a simple transliteration that should sound OK.

GREETINGS

Hello, you are welcome	*A kwaaba*	Good evening	*Mma adjo*
Response	*Yaa*	Response	*Ye muu*
Good morning	*Mma ache*	Anyone home?	*Ebi wo fie?*
Good afternoon	*Mma aha*		

BASIC CONVERSATION

How are you?	*Wo o te sen?*	Thank you	*Meda ase*
I'm fine	*Me ho ye*	Response (you're welcome)	*Mme enna*
Come here (to children)	*Bra*		*ase*
Go away (to children)	*Koh*	Do you speak English	*Wote Borofo*
Yes	*Aan*	(lit. "white language")?	*anna?*
No	*Dabe*	I don't understand	*Mnta se*
Please (lit. "I beg you")	*Me pawocheo*	I'm married	*Ma ware*
		(Please) give me water	*Ma me nsuo*
What's your name?	*Ye ferew sen?*	I want/like . . .	*Me pe . . .*
My name is . . .	*Ye fere me . .*	I'm not well	*Me nti apoh*
Where do you come from?	*Wo fri he?*	I'm hungry	*E komdeme*
I come from . . .	*Me fri . . .*		

TRAVEL

I'm going	*Me ko*	Tonight	*Annajoh*
We're going	*Ye ko*	Lorry	*Lore*
Today	*Enne*	Bus stop	*Bossogy*
Tomorrow	*Echina*		*inabea*
Yesterday	*Enrah*		

NUMBERS

1	Biako	7	Asong	30	Aduasa	500	Ahannum
2	Abieng	8	Awotwe	40	Aduanang	600	Ahansia
3	Abiesa	9	Akrong	100	Oha	700	Ahansong
4	Anang	10	Du	200	Ahannu	800	Ahangwotwe
5	Anum	11	Dubiako	300	Ahasa	900	Ahangkron
6	Asia	20	Aduonu	400	Ahannang	1000	Apem

GHANAIAN TERMS – A GLOSSARY

Adinkra Cotton, funeral cloth with printed black symbols worn by Akan mourners.

Agbada Large embroidered robe, usually white, worn on special occasions.

Akan The language that includes dialects spoken by the Fante and the Asante.

Asafo Military-style "company" of the Fante.

Asante Standard spelling of the Kumasi-based ethnic group.

Ashanti Popular European spelling and name of the administrative region.

Burglar Means rip-off artist in general, including con-merchant.

Chop Food, or "to eat".

Colo Ingratiating, "colonial" behaviour.

Concert party Popular entertainment that started in the villages. When people couldn't afford to go to clubs, they began "concert parties" with a theatrical performance – usually humorous – and highlife music.

Dash From Portuguese for "to give", it means a gift or bribe. It can also function as a verb as in "How much you dash me?"

Durbar Not the horse rally of northern Nigeria, this is the occasion that climaxes traditional festivals when chiefs receive distinguished guests.

Ghana Ancient Ghana was based in what's now southeast Mauritania. It never reached the borders of modern Ghana.

Highlife "Big Band Highlife" is Ghana's best-known dance music form, but Ghanaians use the term to refer to a much broader range of music which is no more homogenous than, say, rock.

How be? Common greeting meaning "How are you?"

Kalabule Corruption and palm greasing.

Kente Multicoloured, woven strip fabric, sometimes silk, made by the Akan and Ewe.

Kotoko Porcupine, symbol of the Asante. The animal's countless sharp quills stand for boundless Asante bravery, reflected in the saying "Kill a thousand porcupines and a thousand more will come" (*Kotoko wokum apem, apem beba*).

Obroni wawu Imported secondhand clothes (lit. "A white man has died").

Oware The game of pebbles and holes (see p.59).

Paa "Very", for example "It's expensive, paa", very expensive.

Posuban Shrines made by Asafo companies.

Silly Pejorative term implying an insult to one's intelligence – stronger term than in US or Britain.

Stool The royal throne of Akan-speaking peoples. "Stooling" means enthronement.

Wee Marijuana.

Weeding, or Weeding-off, is the collective grave-tending ceremony that takes place some time after a funeral.

---

a fact of everyday Ghanaian life and there are dozens of weekly papers and regular magazines.

The main **newspapers** are the *People's Daily Graphic*, the *Ghanaian Times* and the more critical Kumasi-based *Pioneer*. They stick fairly close to the government line (*Graphic* and *Times* are both state-owned), but often have interesting coverage of national and regional events. International news is barely scratched by them, but the *Graphic's* "Tit Bits" column is a bizarre collection of snippets from around the world – worth the price of the paper alone.

Other papers, mainly serving as mouthpieces for different political parties include *The Ghanaian Voice*, *New Nation*, the *Weekly Spectator* and the *Statesman*, which together have a circulation of over 800,000 a week. Most are unsophisticated in their layout and tend more towards editorializing than hard journalism.

As for **foreign press**, there's normally a reasonable selection of British and American papers available at Accra airport and the posher hotels, as well as in expatriate areas such as the kiosks and shops along the main Osu road in Accra. *West Africa* magazine, which provides probably the most detailed regular coverage of the country in English, is always on sale.

There's colour **TV** broadcasting on three channels: Metro TV, TV 3, and the government-owned GTV which transmits CNN. These are all competitive and constantly improving in their programming. M-Net is a subscriber channel which includes international programming. Ghana also has several **radio** stations, the most popular of which are Gold FM (90.5), Choice FM (102.3), Atlantic FM (the only jazz station), Vibe FM (91.9), Groove FM (106.3) and Joy FM (99.7). Of these, Joy FM is the most highly respected, and it broadcasts *Focus on Africa* at 3pm daily. The state-owned GAR FM (95.7) covers news and the social scene and plays current pop. Radio Canada and Radio France are also available on FM.

Holidays and Festivals

The main Christian and Muslim holidays are celebrated in Ghana, but the impact of Islam is strongest in the northwest. Shops and businesses also close down for Fourth Republic Day (January 7), Independence Day (March 6), Revolution Day (June 4), Republic Day (July 1) and Farmers' Day (first Friday in December). While the Anniversary of the Second Revolution (December 31) is not a public holiday, it is celebrated on New Year's Eve, which is.

See box, p.690 for details of **regional festivals**.

Entertainment

Ghana has a satisfying cultural life, with theatre, cinema and especially music accessible. If you're in Accra in June, you'll catch notice of the annual Entertainment Critics and Reviewers Association of Ghana awards. Every two years or so (1992, 1994, 1997, 1999), somewhere between the end of July and November, you will find the Panafest music and arts festival in progress, which is now coupled with the newly created Emancipation Day, instituted to commemorate slavery and the diasporic heritage, and celebrated annually.

■ Theatre

Accra's fine, new, Chinese-built **National Theatre** and the **Greater Accra Centre for National Culture** are the capital's two main theatre venues. The **School of Performing Arts** at Legon University also stages occasional productions in Accra. In the country as a whole,

"Concert Party", a traditional type of lightly satirical musical-comedy-drama, is the theatrical form you're most likely to come across. *Akpeteshie* is the drink and the party typically goes on all night. Many itinerant bands cover the village and small town circuit. You might get a taste, if you can't attend a show, by tracking down a Concert Party cassette, like the one by the stand-up comic "Waterproof" (on the local "Q" Production label).

■ Cinema

Ghanaian **cinema** has a wealth of unexplored potential (there's talent in the wings, held back by financial constraints), but you're still more likely to get a helping of Bond or Stallone than something from top Ghanaian director **Kwaw Ansah**. In Accra, the Ghana Film Institute is beginning to show more regularly Ghanaian and African films along with the usual European and American blockbusters. Video shows, in any case, are fast taking over from fleapit cinemas. There's more background in the "Cinema" piece in Contexts at the back of the book.

■ Music

While Ghana is famous for the urban goodtime dance music known as **highlife**, the country has an active tradition of **rural music and dance** that continues to influence urban sounds. Look out for folkloric gigs and events.

Although "big band highlife" declined in the 1970s with the frequency of coups, curfews and power cuts, these technical problems didn't really affect guitar highlife, which can still be heard all over. Concert parties and **gospel highlife** took off in the 1970s and are still thriving. With the advent of the Charismatic Christian Church, gospel has boomed tremendously, with artists such as **Daughters of Glorious Jesus**, **Tagoe Sister** and **Stella Dugan** benefiting from the trend. So popular is the music now that even secular musicians record gospel albums to appeal to the emerging market.

Following the 1970's, many "name" stars migrated to Europe, and more went to Nigeria, where they've kept the highlife flame burning. Those currently based in Ghana include **Kwame Ampadu and the African Brothers**, still one of the nation's top electric guitar bands after nearly three decades and the irrepressible **Alex Konadu**. New artists

THE GHANAIAN FESTIVAL YEAR

In addition to the official public holidays, many **regional celebrations** or festivals (*afahye* in Twi) animate the country throughout the year. Dates often vary. This **selective listing** covers most of the country but there are very many more. Note that dates are approximate in most cases and, in some, the local name of the occasion just means "festival".

FESTIVAL (DATE)	LOCALITY
JANUARY	
Kwafie (early)	Berekum
Ntoa Fokuokese (10th)	Nkoranza, west of Ejura, Asante Region
Kpini-Kyiu (22nd)	Wa, Upper West Region
Danso Abaim Afahye (end)	Techiman, 130km north of Kumasi
Tengbana	Tongo, Upper East Region
Jimbenti A period of purification and pacification of the gods. An all-day festival, *Jimbenti* ends at sunset when burning sticks are thrown into the eastern sky to scare away unknown demons.	Tumu (Sissala people)
Adae Kese Asante festival culminating in the purification of the ancestral stools.	Kumasi and other Asante towns
FEBRUARY	
Damba	Wa, Upper West Region
Amu Harvest festival including ritual *Asafo* dances and other cultural displays.	Vane Avatime near Ho, Volta Region
MARCH	
Kotokyikyi (first Fri)	Senya Beraku, west of Accra
Kyiu Sung (7th)	Throughout Upper West and Upper East
Golgu (around Easter)	Bolgatanga
Lalue Kpledo (10th)	Prampram, east of Accra
Ogyapa (end March, early April)	Senya Beraku
Sigi Sheep and chickens are slaughtered and *pito* offered to God through the ancestors in a thanksgiving and harvest celebration that includes drumming and dancing.	Navrongo
APRIL	
Dam and *Bugum* festivals	Tamale and around
Godigbeza Celebrations to commemorate migration from the Ewe ancestral lands at Notse (Togo) include drumming, dancing, ceremonial costumes.	Aflao
Aboakyer **antelope-hunt** (late April/early May) More commonly known as the Deer-Hunting Festival, this famous event involves two hunting groups competing to bring back a live antelope. The first to present it to the chief and elders is proclaimed champion.	Winneba, Central Region
MAY	
Don (14th)	Wa, Bawku and Bolgatanga
Sallah	Tamale and Tumu
Chimisi	Bawku, Upper East Region
JUNE	
Dzimbenti or *Bugum* (11th)	Throughout Upper West and Upper East Region

Apiba	Senya Beraku, west of Accra
Fire festival	Tamale and Bawku
Dongu	Wa, Upper West Region

JULY

Bakatue Festival (first Fri)	Elmina, coast
Damba (last week of July or early Aug)	Dagomba people, Northern Region
Yam Festival	Tamale
Edjodi	Senya Beraku, west of Accra
Bugumlobre	Bongo, Upper East Region
Jimbanti	Tumu, Upper West Region
Dzumbanti	Wa, Upper West Region

AUGUST

Asafotufiiam (first week)	Ada, coast east of Accra
Akumasi (second week)	Senya Beraku, coast west of Accra
Damba (Aug/Sept)	Tamale and surrounding region
Bontungu Five days of drumming and dancing in which villagers clear all superfluous or undesirable objects from their homes and ask God for good health and prosperity in the coming year.	Anomabu, near Saltpond, west of Accra
Homowo (Aug/Sept) Traditional festival of the Ga people including street processions of twins and offerings of ceremonial *kpokpoi* food to the gods.	Accra, Prampram and surrounding districts

SEPTEMBER

Odwira Thanksgiving festival held any time in September.	Held throughout the Asante country and by most Akan people
Yam Festival (all month)	Volta Region
Oguaa Fetu Afahye (first Sat) A big, dressy occasion lasting several days.	Cape Coast
Black Stool Festival (25th)	Seikwa, north of Berekum
Yam Festival (last week or early October)	Effiduasi, Asante Region

OCTOBER

Daa (1st–12th)	Tongo, Upper East Region
Sabre dance (9th)	Lawra, Upper West Region
Akonedi (9th–13th)	Larteh, 56km north of Accra
Kobina (15th)	Lawra, Upper West Region
Boaram (28th)	Tongo, Upper East Region
Yam Festival	Ejura and Effiduasi, Asante Region
Fijyiiyna/Monomene Bayere Afahye	Nkoranza, west of Ejura

NOVEMBER

Atweaban (second week)	Ntonso, northeast of Kumasi
Yam Festival	Ejura, northeast of Kumasi
Afahye	Agogo, 100km east of Kumasi
Yango	Bawku, Upper East Region
Boaram	Tongo, Upper Region
Hotbetsotso Commemoration of the Anlos' migration from a tyrannical kingdom to their homeland.	Anloga, on the Atlantic shore southwest of Keta

DECEMBER

Fao (1st)	Navrongo, Upper East Region
Kwafie (over the New Year)	Berekum
Kpini guinea fowl festival	Dagomba and Gonja people

like **Kojo Antwi, Nana Achampong**, and **Charles Kojo Fosu (Daddy Lumba)** – the threesome formerly known as the **Lumba Brothers** – have focused on their solo careers, once in a while recruiting session musicians for live performances.

Musicians playing traditional African music include the great traditionalist **Mustapha Tetteh Addy** who, with his **Obunu drummers**, incorporates African drums and xylophones into his music, and **Nana Danso Abeam and his Pan African Orchestra**. Rather than using Western-style batons to conduct his orchestra, Nana uses castanets, traditional African percussive instruments.

For concert dates in Accra, get hold of a copy of the listings mag *Ghanascope* and see the *Daily Graphic*'s "Entertainments" page every Saturday.

Wildlife and National Parks

Ghana's native fauna is not in as desperate a position as you might expect. The current wave of interest in new national parks and the attraction they hold for travellers and tourists are positive signs for the future of Ghana's flora and fauna. On the downside, much of the rainforest was felled decades ago, never to return.

Along the coast, the British RSPB and the Ghana Wildlife Department have been effective in helping to curb the killing of **sea birds** for sport and food – especially the very rare and now protected **roseate tern**, which migrates to these shores every winter from northern Europe. RSPB can be contacted at the Environmental Protection Agency (☎021/66.46.97). Ghana **Friends of the Earth** (PO Box 3794, Accra; ☎021/22.59.63; Fax 021/22.79.93) is an active group, one of the few such in Africa.

The Ghana Wildlife Department (☎021/66.46.54 or 66.23.60) is currently in the process of opening up several of its parks to exploration. However, while Ghana's largest and longest-established park, **Mole National Park**, is a functioning and well-stocked park with the full complement of bush-savannah mammals, most of the newer parks don't yet provide facilities and some tracks are not maintained. This means you are limited to what you can see on foot, but the park rangers are typically very enthusiastic and helpful in organizing excursions.

Listen on the travellers' grapevine to find out if there have been any developments in the **Digya**

National Park. Bordering the western edge of Lake Volta, this is one of Ghana's larger parks, harbouring elephants, various antelopes, hippo, waterbuck and a wide range of other species. It's also worth checking whether facilities have been added to the **Bia National Park** in the rainforests of the west near the Côte d'Ivoire border. Further north, the **Bui National Park** straddles tributaries of the Black Volta in a protected woodland, and has very basic chalet accommodation and camping facilities.

In the Western region, the twin reserves of **Ankasa** and **Nini-Suhien** near the Ivoirian border are relatively unexplored with no tourist facilities as of yet, but open to independent travellers.

In the Volta region, **Shai Hills Reserve** is a popular day excursion from Accra, home to over 160 bird species, a few primate bands, and a bat colony; the scenic **Kyabobo Resource Reserve** is home to several large animals including various elephant, lion, leopard, buffalo and antelope species; and the **Kalakpe Resource Reserve**, 15km southwest of Ho, has a proliferation of birdlife, along with buffalo, antelope and many varieties of monkeys.

Finally, the **Kakum National Park** in the south of the country, just 35km from Cape Coast, is easily accessible, and the infrastructure is improving month by month.

Directory

AIRPORT TAX $20. Also payable in cedis (around ₵48,000).

CRAFTS AND OTHER PURCHASES Ghana has a huge variety of arts and crafts, still widely made for local consumption. Accra is good for imported printed cloth. The Asante region is a prolific producer and well known for its *kente* and *adinkra* cloths. These can be bought in villages around Kumasi or at the town's cultural centre. The region is also famed for its carvings – especially of stools made in Ahwiaa. The north specializes more in leather goods, rough cotton weaves and basketry, all of which are found at the Bolgatanga market. Perhaps the best place for selection is in Accra where art from all over the country – and from throughout West Africa – comes together at the crafts market.

If you buy antiques, or anything in substantial quantities, you may have to obtain an **export**

permit from the Ghana Museum and Monuments Board declaring the item has no historical value. Take your pieces to their office in the Centre for National Culture or the National Museum and they'll sell you a certificate on the spot. This ensures your purchases won't be confiscated when you leave Ghana.

DRUGS *Wee* (**marijuana**) is illegal, though widely available. The main areas of production are around Ejura in the Asante region and Nsawam north of Accra. Generally looked upon more as a bad habit than a dangerous drug, consumers aren't likely to run into big trouble, though discretion is always advisable.

EDUCATION Ghana has traditionally been known for a relatively high level of education. The country has four universities – the University of Ghana, near Accra; the University of Science and Technology, Kumasi; the University of Cape Coast; and the University of Development Studies, Tamale. Primary school is compulsory.

FOOTBALL Soccer is the most popular sport in Ghana and a number of Ghanaians play overseas, including Tony Yeboah and Abedi Pele. Since the mid-1980s, the most consistently top-quality team has been Kumasi Asante Kotoko: the Kotokos have won the Africa Cup three times. The oldest team is Accra Hearts of Gold.

GOLD This is the country all right, but you'll be hard pressed to find much sign of the precious metal (except during major festivals, notably the *Ogua Fetu Afahye* in Cape Coast) away from the big goldfields around Tarkwa and Obuasi, southwest of Kumasi. Visits take some advance preparation (see p.739).

OPENING HOURS Government offices are open Monday to Friday 8am–12.30pm and 1.30–5pm. Most businesses operate Monday to Friday 8am or 9am–noon and 2–5.30pm. Many shops also open on Saturday, from around 8am to 1pm. Shops are closed on public holidays, without exception – it's the law.

PHOTOGRAPHY You don't need a **permit** to take pictures in Ghana, though the usual regulations against snapping military installations and strategic points are rigorously enforced. Especially sensitive is Osu Castle in Accra – the seat of government. Taking pictures anywhere in the vicinity could lead to the confiscation of camera and film, if not arrest, though this has not happened for a while.

STUDENT CARDS ISIC cards may entitle you to discounts on STC buses if you get a letter of certification from a Ghanaian educational institution, or possibly produce a letter from your college.

TROUBLE Muggings aren't too much of a problem in Ghana, not even in Accra – though there have been reports of muggings in Black Star Square. Ordinary pickpocketing is probably worst in Kumasi market, while theft is a problem on the Accra beaches. Police sometimes stop travellers (and Ghanaians) and pretend to be really angry about a minor infraction (such as jaywalking, which is illegal at certain places including Kwame Nkrumah Circle in Accra). Customs and immigration officers employ similar tactics. They are almost certainly angling for "dash" (a present or bribe), and you may have to pay up, but large amounts aren't necessary and politeness and smiles will help.

WOMEN TRAVELLERS AND THE WOMEN'S MOVEMENT Most travellers experience great kindness and there are few special problems for women – indeed, many rate Ghana one of the most hassle-free countries in West Africa. However, even more than in other parts, Ghanaian men and boys are likely to respond with unrestrained lewdness to what may be seen as provocative clothing or inappropriate behaviour in a woman.

As for women in Ghanaian society, the Akan-speaking people (but not all other groups) are mostly **matrilineal** – a system in which men inherit from their maternal uncles, rather than their fathers – but the impact on women's status is, if anything, reduced as a result and there is firm government pressure against this form of inheritance.

On a more positive note, however, Ghana is further advanced than other African countries in actively encouraging women to become more involved in business and other areas of public life, and many women's organizations have sprung up in recent years. The 31 December Women's Movement (DWM), for example, led by the First Lady, Nana Konadu Agyemang, has made considerable advancements – such as providing day care centres for children throughout the country. If you're interested in making contact with women's groups, write to the Ghana Assembly of Women (PO Box 459, Accra) or the Federation of Ghanaian Women (PO Box 6326, Accra).

A Brief History of Ghana

Though the present country has been peopled for well over two thousand years, some of the earliest migrations to the region that are known about in any detail occurred after the Ghana Empire was sacked in the eleventh century. At this time, the Ntafo, early ancestors of the Akan people, moved south to the parkland west of Gonja, in northern Ghana. About 700 years ago, they began moving further south in three waves consisting of the Guan, Fante and Asante peoples. Early trading relations existed with much of West Africa, particularly with the western Sudan. Gold and kola nuts were important products which poured out of the region, across the Sahara and into North Africa. Mande peoples from the Niger bend greatly influenced the economy and culture of the north as they established numerous trading centres alongside existing townships.

By the early nineteenth century the Gold Coast interior had developed a complicated network of northern states – Gonja, Dagomba, Mamprusi and Nanumba – and, in the south, smaller confederations (the Fante for example) and statelets (Ga, Ewe, Nzima). In the central region, the Asante confederation was rapidly mushrooming. Given time, the Asante empire might have conquered and assimilated most of the smaller political units in the surrounding territories which were later to come under French rule. Such a scenario, however, was thwarted by the colonial experience which began in earnest in the nineteenth century. European involvement in the region had begun, on a smaller scale, much earlier and provoked a shift in the emphasis of trade away from the northern routes to the southern ports.

■ European arrival

Searching out new trade routes and a way to obtain the gold of the trans-Saharan caravans closer to source, the first **Portuguese** ships came to Ghana in 1471. By 1482 they had returned to build a fort at **Elmina** ("the mine"), using a mixture of persuasion and threats to gain the consent of the local ruler. The region turned out to be rich in gold, ivory, timber and skins, and other Europeans followed the Portuguese. Over the next four hundred years, sea powers like the Dutch, Danes and British competed heavily for the trade. With the European colonization of America, this expanded to include **slaves**, in exchange for which the Europeans brought hard liquor and manufactured goods like **clothing** and **weaponry**. Guns eventually helped the **Asante** – the principal traders with the foreigners – to expand their influence over the region's interior and to apply pressure to the **Fante** middlemen through whom they'd been dealing with the British since the 1600s.

■ The British colony

By the early nineteenth century, the British had emerged as the strongest foreign power on the "Gold Coast". In 1807, they abolished the slave trade in the region and began looking for other exploitable resources. Over the next hundred years, palm oil, cocoa, rubber, gold and timber were developed as exports. These products drew the British – hitherto content to remain in their coastal forts – increasingly into the hinterland.

The stage was set for the outright **conquest** of the interior when the Asante invaded the Fante confederation in 1806. The Fante had long been able to resist the attempts of their powerful northern neighbours to dominate them, thanks in large part to their role as preferential trading partners with the Europeans. Now the British rallied to the aid of their Fante "allies", even offering them protection in one of their coastal forts.

Hostilities flared and **tenuous treaties** were reached between the two Akan factions throughout the first half of the century. But, as competition increased for the control of trade, the British decided there could be only one victor. They ultimately found the excuse they needed to invade the interior when war again broke out between the Fante and Asante in the 1870s. The British sacked the Asante capital, Kumasi, in 1874. Subsequent **Asante wars** followed in 1896 and 1900, when the ruling Asanthene was finally exiled (see p.734).

By that time Germany, France and Britain had already agreed on borders for the areas they would control. The British introduced elements of **indirect rule** in their new colony, even allowing the Asante confederation to be re-established under the Ashanti Confederacy Council – a government agency – in 1935. After World War I, part of German Togoland was integrated into the British colony.

The rise of nationalism

Nationalist movements were created early in the colonial period, with one – the Aborigines' Rights Protection Society – dating as far back as 1897. Other parties sprang up during the 1920s and 1930s and, by 1946, concessions to African demands for representation had led to an African majority in Ghana's Legislative Council, although the executive branch – and effective rule – was still in the hands of the British Governor. In 1947, **JB Danquah** formed the United Gold Coast Convention (UGCC), a party which favoured the principle of a gradual shift to self-government and independence. The same year, the party invited **Kwame Nkrumah** to join its ranks as party secretary in an effort to broaden a base that consisted mainly of the educated elite – civil servants, lawyers, businessmen and doctors.

In the aftermath of the 1948 **Accra riots** (see p.702) Nkrumah lost patience with conservatives in the UGCC and split from it to form his own party, the **Convention People's Party** (CPP) – campaigning slogan, "Self-government now". He gained prominence among the masses as a result and the British detained him when he called for a national strike in 1950. The CPP, meanwhile, won the Legislative Assembly election of 1951, and the governor, Sir Charles Arden-Clarke, prudently released Nkrumah and invited him to help form a government. Thus, in 1952, Nkrumah became the first African prime minister in the Commonwealth. He went on to win the elections of 1954 and 1956 – a period during which his CPP party shared power with the British. On August 3, 1956 the Legislative Assembly passed a unanimous motion calling for complete independence.

■ Independence: heady days . . .

When **independence** was ultimately returned on March 6, 1957, the future looked bright for the first African country to break colonial bonds. Ghana was then the world's leading cocoa exporter and produced a tenth of all the world's gold. Other valuable resources, of which the country had many, included bauxite, manganese, diamonds and timber. Perhaps Ghana's greatest asset was a high percentage of educated citizens who seemed well qualified to run the new nation (25 percent of the population was literate, compared, for example, to an estimated 1 percent in Portugal's colonies).

Nkrumah became a larger than life figure, respected throughout Africa and the African diaspora and highly regarded in the West. He was an eloquent advocate of **pan-Africanism** and the **non-aligned movement**. His economic principles looked sound, too, as he sought to create an industrial base that would reduce dependence on foreign powers while improving social services throughout the country (hospitals and clinics, universities and schools were part of his legacy). The port city of **Tema**, with its smelting and other industrial plants, was constructed at this time as was the ambitious **Akosombo Dam**, built to supply hydroelectric power.

. . . and disaster

Nkrumah's economic strategy was, however, extremely costly, and with four decades of hindsight it seems painfully clear that his biggest mistake was to overemphasize **prestige projects** at the expense of a solid agricultural base. Worse still, many of the projects held no prospect of any economic return: Accra's showy conference centre – designed to be the headquarters of the Organization of African Unity, which based itself instead in Addis Ababa – and symbolic monuments like Black Star Square and the vainglorious State House were the dizzy results of a belief in the invincible rightness of Nkrumah's ideals. Foreign currency reserves dwindled at a frightening rate and the country accumulated a debt running to hundreds of millions of pounds.

As the economic situation turned suddenly bleak, political discontent rose. Despite concern for his international reputation, Nkrumah responded with increasing repression at home where his support was dwindling. Government suppression of a 1961 workers' strike had already seriously alienated Nkrumah from the working class and the educated elite had long been disillusioned with his expensive brand of scientific socialism. When the world price of cocoa plummeted in the mid-1960s, Ghana's hopes for economic self-sufficiency – and long-term stability – were dashed.

By 1964, Ghana was legally a **one-party state.** As the CPP tried measures to stamp out opposition, the government increasingly arrested those it feared under the Preventive Detention Act which allowed for "enemies" of the regime to be held for up to five years without trial. Public gatherings were strictly controlled, press censorship became commonplace and an extensive network of informants was developed by the party central committee. Such measures were effective in crushing opposition, or at least in driving it deeply underground, but Nkrumah still had to contend with the military. Suspicious of the army's loyalty, he lost his nerve and made policy decisions that were bound to antagonize officers – placing limits on recruitment and hedging military procurement procedures with elaborate safeguards. Isolating himself still further from the support of the military, he formed an independent **presidential guard**, accountable only to him.

In the light of such developments, Western nations increasingly criticized **governmental corruption** and recognized a **personality cult** surrounding Nkrumah, where previously they'd seen a charismatic figure. Nkrumah was forced to abandon his non-alignment and turn to the Soviet bloc for support. By then he had totally lost the backing of the military and almost every other element of society. Only a blind sense of impunity could have allowed him to travel abroad. On February 24, 1966, while on a visit to Peking, he was overthrown in a bloodless coup by British-trained officers. He died in exile in Conakry in 1972.

■ Coups and "kleptocrats"

Following Nkrumah's flight, Lieutenant-General **Joseph Ankrah** was appointed head of the National Liberation Council (NLC) that ruled until 1969. The conservative junta went on a witch-hunt, arresting left-wing ideologues, banning the CPP and harassing its leaders. The junta's **economic direction** seemed promising to the West, however, as they privatized many state enterprises and broke off relations with the Soviet Union and its allies. But for all the promises made to better the economy, life for most people without special connections grew steadily worse.

From its inception, the NLC viewed itself as a provisional government and much of its period of rule was spent preparing for a return to civilian democracy. A bill of rights was drawn up, and safeguards implemented to ensure the independence of the judiciary – measures intended to stop the reconstitution of an autocratic one-party state. In May 1969, political parties were legalized. The **Progress Party**, headed by Kofi Busia – an Akan who represented the traditional middle-class opposition to Nkrumah's rule – was counterbalanced by the **National Alliance of Liberals** led by Komla Gbedemah, an Ewe and one-time associate of Nkrumah who had broken with the leader and gone into exile.

In September 1969, Ghanaians gave democracy another try, and elected **Dr Kofi Busia** prime min-

ister. But the new leader struggled to wade through the economic mess. Cocoa prices dropped again in 1971, sparking a new crisis and, at the same time, mismanagement and racketeering led to shortages in food production, supplies and foreign exchange. Under mounting pressure, Busia took the necessary but politically dangerous step of **devaluing the cedi**. Massive price increases followed and the public enthusiasm that had ushered in the new regime faded almost immediately. Busia was overthrown on January 13, 1972.

General corruption

From 1972 to 1979, Ghana was led by a series of juntas with remarkably **corrupt generals** at the helm. One of the most flagrant offenders was **General I Acheampong**, who headed the National Redemption Council (NRC) from 1972 to 1975 and then the Supreme Military Council until 1978. During his period in office, Ghanaians coined the term "kleptocracy" – rule by thieves – as the official economy moved closer and closer to complete collapse. The **black market** thrived, meanwhile, as basic goods like bread and eggs became unattainable for the poor. Production declined even further and what few agricultural goods emerged onto the market were smuggled abroad to Togo and Côte d'Ivoire, where they fetched higher, hard currency prices. The educated elite – doctors, teachers, lawyers – led a brain drain to Nigeria and overseas where they had some chance of supporting themselves.

The basis of Acheampong's economic policy was **"self-reliance"**, symbolized by programmes such as "Operation Feed Yourself", launched in 1972. Moderate successes were achieved in the early years of the NRC, but by the mid-1970s the economic outlook was so grim that the professional middle class, and especially the Ghana Bar Association, demanded a return to party politics. Acheampong sought a compromise by proposing a **"union government"** where power would be shared between civilians, the armed forces and – radically – the police. The opposition viewed UNIGOV as a mechanism to keep the military in power and reacted cynically when Acheampong pushed his idea through on the back of a trumped-up referendum held in 1978.

As criticism grew, so did **repression**, and hundreds of opposition leaders were jailed without trial. Viewed increasingly as a tyrant, Acheampong withdrew into isolation. He was quietly deposed in a coup led by **General William Akuffo** on July 5,

1978. Akuffo established the "Supreme Military Council II" and eventually set a date for elections in June 1979, but little else changed and widespread discontent in the country now spread to the ranks of the military.

■ A new age: Rawlings Mark I

There can be no peace where there is no justice – and there will be no justice unless everyone can be made to answer for his conduct.

Jerry Rawlings, 1979

On May 15, 1979, there was a bungled uprising of junior ranks in the army, led by a 32-year-old flight lieutenant of mixed Scottish–Ghanaian parentage – **Jerry Rawlings**. He was captured and imprisoned but freed by fellow soldiers and they made a second, successful, attempt to take power on **June 4, 1979**.

Rawlings made it clear that his coup would be different, that he was out to eliminate corruption and restore national pride to an economic order neglected in fifteen years of waste. The title of his governing **Armed Forces Revolutionary Council** (AFRC) set the tone – Rawlings envisaged a "moral revolution" based implicitly on socialist principles of an economy for need rather than profit. He took a hard line, sending high-ranking officers to the firing squad (including Acheampong and Akuffo) and approving a purge of public figures under suspicion of fraud. At the same time he pledged that the AFRC would work quickly to restore order and return the reins of power to a civilian government.

The world community noted little more than another coup d'état in Ghana, but, in a remarkable departure (no African military ruler had ever voluntarily relinquished power before, except arguably, Eyadéma in neighbouring Togo), the promise was kept. Following elections held on June 18, 1979, the newly elected president, **Dr Hilla Limann** took office in September and the soldiers returned to their barracks barely three months after leaving them.

Limann rode in on a wave of popularity at home and in the West where his conservative politics won respect. But despite his best intentions, the economy continued to slide – production dropped further, the cedi remained overvalued (fearing unpopularity, the president refused to devalue the currency and thereby cost his country a major IMF loan) and the country's infrastructure became hopelessly eroded. And despite the moral high ground captured by the Rawlings clique, and Rawlings' own shadowy behind-the-scenes presence, **corrupt practices** had been re-established by the end of 1980 in virtually every sphere of public life.

■ Rawlings' second coming

On December 31, 1981, Rawlings led a **second successful coup**, toppling the Limann government, abolishing the entire "democratic" framework, and placing the government in the hands of a **Provisional National Defence Council** (PNDC). As before, he justified the action by the urgent need to halt corruption and put Ghana's wrecked and abused economy in order. This time, however, no plans were made to restore the country to civilian rule. Rather, the PNDC decided to put into practice the leftist populist principles of the original coup.

Early moves were made to democratize the decision-making process and to decentralize political power. This was done through **People's Defence Committees** (PDCs), which replaced district councils and which were intended to increase local participation in the revolution while raising political consciousness at the grass-roots level.

The political orientation of the second revolution proved too much for large sections of the army, particularly northerners, and there were several **coup attempts** in 1982 and 1983, including a nearly disastrous attempt mounted from Togo (see "Foreign Affairs", overleaf). Meanwhile, the revolution itself provided excuse enough for a few hard-line radicals to undertake terrorist attacks under the guise of "popular justice". There were calls from several quarters for a complete overhaul (even abolition) of the judiciary and there was worse in June 1982 with the kidnap and **murder of three senior judges**. Unfortunately for Rawlings, the trial and conviction of the two murderers wasn't sufficient to clear all elements of the PNDC of any involvement and it was forced into a public position of greater moderation.

Like Thomas Sankara, who arrived on the scene in Burkina Faso two years later, Rawlings initially enjoyed huge popularity among the masses fed up with government lies and excesses. With his battle cry of **"accountability"**, he proved sincere in the **war against corruption** and, although the economy continued to slide during his first years, he soon managed to produce a **turnaround** (by

1984, the economy was showing a five percent growth rate, the first upswing in ten years).

Despite Rawlings' penchant for revolutionary rhetoric, his early friendship with the Libyan leader Colonel Gaddafi and his ties with Cuba and Eastern Europe, his pragmatic economic approach – including taking the risky political step of drastically devaluing the cedi – earned him high marks with the IMF, which started once again to provide sizeable loans to the country.

Foreign affairs

Relations with **Burkina Faso** were extremely close while Sankara was alive, and at one point the countries even envisaged a common currency. Plans were also made to co-ordinate their energy, trade, transportation and education programmes which shared many similarities of emphasis.

Predictably, more conservative regimes were less receptive to Rawlings' style of government. Relations with **Britain**, **Côte d'Ivoire**, and especially **Togo** have been, at best, cool. All three countries have harboured Ghanaian exiles, some of whom have maintained links with **dissident opposition** groups in Ghana. In 1983 this secret opposition came dangerously close to toppling the government as they infiltrated Accra from Togo and took over the GBC broadcasting station before being apprehended. The January 1994 coup attempt against Togo's President Eyadéma triggered new tension between the two countries (the rebels were said to have entered Lomé from Ghana), and the border was frequently closed throughout the early and mid-1990s.

Rawlings has been an eloquent critic of the world's **commodity markets**, pointing out, for example, that the tyranny of cocoa price-setting in determining Ghana's earning power (and thus the living standards of its people) quite overshadowed what he viewed as the necessary curtailments on personal freedom in a society effectively under siege.

■ The coming of the Fourth Republic

By the end of the 1980s, after a decade in power, Rawlings had made much of what seemed a hopeless situation. But he had not always had an easy time straddling diverse elements in society. Although most rural dwellers and many wage earners remained loyal, he had suffered scrapes with the ambitious middle class, who loathed his

socialist rhetoric and raised the banner of human rights. Many students and academics, on the other hand, charged him with selling out to the IMF, saying he presided over a neocolonialist state. Still, the performance of the economy (Ghana recorded the highest consistent rates of economic growth in Africa throughout much of the 1980s) seemed to shield the president from pressure to liberalize the government, whether it came from disgruntled nationals, or Western donors.

Ghana entered the 1990s against the background rumble of the **Quarshigah Affair** – apparently yet another attempt to murder Chairman Rawlings and overthrow the PNDC. Major Courage Quarshigah and six other officers were sentenced for their connection with the alleged plot. One of them was found hanged in his cell, and Amnesty International adopted the others, denouncing what they claimed was imprisonment for political dissension. Ghanaians rallied around the affair, demanding the abolition of a number of laws, particularly those allowing detention, and an end to the ban on political parties. Foreign pressure to democratize also increased.

Rather than entrenching, Rawlings surprised many when, in July 1990, he formed a **National Commission for Democracy** to review decentralization and consider Ghana's political future. Though opponents criticized the commission for being too close to the ruling party to instigate reform, changes took place quickly. By 1991 the commission was recommending a new constitution and presidential and legislative elections – recommendations approved by the PNDC which, contrary to all expectations, endorsed the restoration of a **multiparty system.**

Rawlings remained on the defensive, however, and in June 1991, had to reiterate denials that political prisoners remained behind bars. He invited Amnesty International to see for themselves, but was soon back in trouble with them when **John Ndebugre**, leader of the Movement for Freedom and Justice (MFJ) and an outspoken government critic, was jailed because he failed to stand for the national anthem.

Despite what appeared a questionable commitment to democracy, reforms continued apace. In addition to the completion of the new constitution and the unbanning of political parties, 1992 saw the emergence of a **free press** and three new human rights organizations plus the release of remaining political detainees.

KONKOMBAS AND NUNUMBAS

A setback for Ghana that was not widely foreseen was the outbreak of an **ethnic war** in the northeast in 1994. The conflict between **Konkomba** and **Nunumba** people, in the region of Bimbilla, flared from a marketplace brawl over a chicken to widespread carnage in the space of a few days, costing the lives of over 2000 people, leaving another 150,000 homeless in refugee camps, destroying or badly damaging as many as sixty villages and small towns and paralyzing much of northern Ghana for months.

The roots of the conflict lie in the tensions between the Konkomba, who have no traditional system of chiefhood, and the chieftancy-organized Nunumba. The Nunumba have always assumed a dominant stance in areas where both groups live, claiming that the Konkomba are "newcomers" from Togo who pay them tribute in the form of work, crops and livestock, in return for the use of Nunumba land. The Konkomba, for their part, retort that this is just an arrogant take on the facts of the matter – that the Nunumba invaded their lands from the north centuries ago and have never had any rights over it. The oral histories of most ethnic groups in the region tend to support the view that the Konkomba are the "indigenous" local people.

In 1995, the government created a **Permanent Peace Negotiating Team** (PPNT) made up of religious leaders, NGO representatives and Council of State members, to help resolve the continuing tensions. In 1996 the PPNT held highly publicized "peacemaking" ceremonies, with leaders on both sides pledging to solve their differences through negotiations.

The focus of the dispute shifted from land to the issue of **chieftancy**. While Nunumba chiefs have traditionally held sway in the Northern Region House of Chiefs and have some key figures in government, there has been no equivalent role for Konkomba leaders. The Konkomba have thus been marginalized when government spending plans are put into effect and have missed out on local and national decision-making. They are therefore now seeking the creation of a Konkomba paramount chieftancy.

In 1997, the PPNT supervised a peace accord among all parties to the conflict, but clashes between the Konkomba and Bimoba people in 1998 led the government to send reinforcements to the forces monitoring the region. At the time of writing, there is a continued ban on firearms in the Northern region and northern part of the Volta region.

As the November **presidential election** drew near, opposition parties – especially the **New Patriotic Party** (NPP), an Asante-based group in the Danquah-Busia tradition, headed by **Professor Albert Adu-Boahen** – seemed confident of success in the polls against Rawlings' National Democratic Congress (NDC – the party formed from the PNDC). **Dr Hilla Limann**, who had been overthrown in Rawlings' second coup, returned to the political arena as candidate for the **People's National Convention** (PNC).

The opposition euphoria faded fast after the elections: Rawlings took 58 percent of the vote (compared with 30 percent for Adu-Boahen), and a stunned opposition protested that the government must have rigged the vote. Some **voting irregularities** undoubtedly did take place, though the margin of victory was large enough to have ensured a win even under perfectly fair conditions. In the eyes of many Ghanaians, however, Rawlings had held onto power without a clear popular mandate. The subsequent **opposition boycott** of the ensuing

legislative elections assured victory to the NDC and its affiliates, the NCP and the EGLE party, and denied the new Fourth Republic (based on the constitution devised by the National Commission for Democracy) the legitimacy it might otherwise have had. As a result, the post-democracy government looked oddly like the military dictatorship that had preceded it, and rather than usher in a new era of optimism, the elections poisoned the political atmosphere which had seemed so promising at the beginning of the 1990s.

But there were encouraging signals. In his first address to Parliament, Rawlings offered an olive branch to opposition parties, inviting them to dialogue with the legislature from which they had excluded themselves. Soon after, the NPP stated it was ready to "do business", a spokesperson adding, "we should start settling some of the crucial, outstanding issues that can only be resolved sitting down with the government, not sitting in a corner sulking." The deadlock between the president and his opponents seemed to be loosening.

Also encouraging was the role of **the press** in providing a platform for opposition. Before and during the elections, Rawlings was generally credited with exercising restraint towards the slew of publications that emerged when the press ban was lifted, especially since many bolstered sales with the type of president-bashing articles still considered treasonous throughout much of Africa. Although the "Culture of Silence" appeared to have ended for newspapers, soon after the elections, the NPP charged the state with **television censorship**. The complaint arose after *Talking Point*, a current affairs programme, abruptly went off the air just as an NPP spokesman was launching into an attack on Rawlings' economic policy. The Supreme Court agreed the government acted unconstitutionally and ordered it to share the airwaves. That ruling was in itself reassuring: a sign **the judiciary** would not be a rubber stamp.

A new era of prosperity?

Important as political issues were, however, success or failure for Rawlings' government was dependant ultimately on **the economy**, as it tried to juggle policies that maintained foreign approval while not further alienating Ghanaians at home. The IMF talked about Ghana in glowing terms, and in a report, *Ghana in the Year 2000*, recommended an Asian-style **Accelerated Growth Strategy**.

Despite the economic growth, partly measurable by the rapid expansion of the country's new **stock market**, and by populist programmes including rural electrification and road-building, the poor and the wage-earners paid a heavy price for economic reform. Equally troublesome was the fact that much of the expansion had been fuelled by a boom in the **gold-mining industry**, with gold surpassing cocoa as the most lucrative export of the 1990s. But local businesses complained about unfavourable policies and tight money supply: high lending rates stunted the development of local manufacturing.

The first signs that the population at large had reached breaking point came in May 1995, when parliament approved a **Value Added Tax** rate of 17 percent. With a rallying cry of **Kume Preko** ("Why not just kill me?"), tens of thousands of protestors demonstrated on the streets of Accra. Five people died in the melee, including at least two who were killed by unidentified gunmen. It was the most serious display of popular opposition to date and was seized upon by detractors – many in exile overseas – who deplored Ghana's human rights record and insisted that politically inspired murders and deaths in detention were commonplace.

With **elections** on the horizon in 1996, the government was forced to rescind the tax. Against its defensive posturing, a group of opposition parties found room for agreement. The NPP, PCP (People's Convention Party) and NDM (New Democratic Movement) formed the **Alliance for Change**, with NPP member **John Kufuor** – a Danquah Busiaist lawyer from Kumasi – as its candidate. This initially provided Rawlings with a serious challenge, but Kufuor let the momentum of the VAT resistance slip away, and couldn't compete with Rawlings on the level of personal charisma or party organization. Rawlings won 57 percent of the vote at the December elections.

Renewed from his election victory, Rawlings once again was hailed in the west as a champion of constitutional democracy with a wise free trade policy. Ghana was feted in a BBC special report titled "Rays of Light In Africa", and in a *Time* cover story called "Africa Rising". But economic prospects seemed less fortuitous from within the country itself, where the years right after the election were characterized by budget deficits, debt servicing burdens and slow aid disbursements. The percentage of people living below the **poverty line** had barely decreased since the preceding decade; social services were all but non-existent; there were fees to attend state-run primary schools; and in many areas the only available health care was from mission-run clinics. Poor rains in the late 1990s led to lower than expected agricultural production, and just as importantly, reduced the Akosombo Dam's capacity to keep pace with the country's need for energy. Resultant rationing of water and electricity was hard on the populace and precipitated a slowdown in industrial growth. The same period saw the world price of gold plummet, and with it much of Ghana's foreign earnings. With prices already rising, the government once again took the unpopular move to introduce VAT.

■ The present and the outlook

The economic situation at the beginning of the twenty-first century compares favourably with the bottoming out period of the 1980s, and even with most of Ghana's neighbours. But performance has fallen far short of expectations and, increasingly, the people have placed blame on the NDC leadership, which by the end of the decade has cultivated a reputation of mismanagement, corruption and intimidation.

Opposition charges of a lack of accountability (in 1998, NPP leader Kwame Pianim called the government the most corrupt in the country's history) have gained credibility at the grass roots and even within the NDC. Early echoes of a **rift within the ruling party** first came in July 1998, when several members – including long-time friend and political ally of Rawlings, **Augustus "Goosie" Tanoh** – published a full-page advertisment in local newspapers challenging the president's willingness to investigate corruption within his government, and criticizing his commitment to democratization within the NDC. Many were suspicious that Rawlings' style of top-down decision-making would continue into the post-Rawlings era, and pointed as evidence to the way that **John Atta-Mills** had been thrust into the number two seat by Rawlings, who seemed to be grooming him to take over the reins of government.

Throughout, however, Rawlings has remained personally popular and largely unscathed by the attacks on the NDC. He has not been untouched by charges of corruption (in 1998 he was accused of having accepted $5 million from the Abacha regime to bolster his election campaign two years earlier – charges he strongly denied), but he at least is seen to represent stability and he has brought stature to Ghana in regional and international politics.

With the sinking of the NDC's popularity, the field now seems wide open for the **year 2000 presidential elections**, which Rawlings cannot contest (he has already served the maximum two terms allowed by the constitution). But even as he prepares to step out of the limelight, the president has positioned himself to play a continuing role in government. At its December 1998 convention, the NDC established a **Consultative Committee** as the party's top decision-making body and appointed Rawlings Chairman for life. That move dashed any hope among party rebels that the NDC was open to increased democratization, and in January 1999, Goosie Tanoh and allies announced that they were formally breaking away to create the **Reform Movement** (RM). The RM has widespread political organization throughout the country, and could rob the NDC of much of its traditional base in the countryside.

Whatever the results of the upcoming elections, Rawlings will leave the government on much better footing than when he arrived. Despite the country's reputation for corruption, the **World Bank** announced in March 1999 that it would provide $100 million to fund Ghana's **public sector reform programme**, expected to run for eleven years. Parts of that programme will be painful – many will lose jobs in government agencies that depend on national subsidies – but the assistance should help restore the confidence of investors. In fact, the ink was hardly dry on the agreement, when **Coca Cola** announced plans to invest $12 million in Ghana for bottling and production facilities. Another boost could come in the form of the **West African Gas Line Project**, a 1000-kilometre pipeline connecting gas supplies in Nigeria's delta region with Benin, Togo and Ghana. If the project goes forward as scheduled, it would create many new jobs and help the nation towards its goals of growth and greater self-sufficiency. But the prospect of prosperity just around the corner has tantalized Ghanaians for so long that many have become cynical about it. The people will be demanding big results from whoever leads the country into the next century.

ACCRA AND AROUND

Flat, sprawling and for the most part aesthetically nondescript, the cityscape of **ACCRA** is still blighted by heavy concrete stacks harking back to the Soviet-inspired early years of independence. But belying first impressions, Accra is an exciting city making a rapid comeback. Renewed prosperity is evidenced by a flurry of new building ranging from the Nkrumah mausoleum to the International Conference Centre, a stylish building opposite State House. Such structures symbolize a vibrancy matched by the energy of the people, including a good number of foreigners attracted to one West African capital that can look ahead with some confidence.

With a population of 1.7 million – and unofficial estimates of almost double that – Accra is one of Africa's biggest cities and hasn't been spared the urban problems of traffic, noise and overcrowding, especially now that the economy is on a steady rise. Despite some uninspiring images – including open drains and sewers that hark back to the malodorous era of decay – the city's trees make it exceptionally green. Rush hours are dynamic and the streets thronged with a racket of vehicles and people, while after dark, Accra's club scene is one of the liveliest in West Africa.

Some history

Accra's **Ga founders** arrived in the region some time before 1500, setting up their capital at Ayawaso ("Great Accra") some 15km inland, and building a "Small Accra" on the coast for trade with the **Portuguese**, who put up a fort here in the sixteenth century. Trade – of slaves, gold and palm oil for guns – increased over the next hundred years with the building of the Dutch **Fort Ussher**, Danish **Christiansborg** and the British **Fort James**.

Accra originally consisted of **seven quarters** – the Ga quarters of Asere, Abola, Gbese, Sempe and Akunmadzei; Otublohu, the Akwamu quarter; and Alata, which later became the core of the British-protected area of Jamestown. Other quarters placed themselves under Dutch protection and became Usshertown. Much later, in 1840, the chief of Abola was chosen as the military leader (*Ga Mantse*) for the whole city, and treated by the British as the Ga king. Nowadays he is considered the Ga paramount chief.

Akwamu expansion from the north led to victory over the Ga in 1660 (Chief Okai Koi, defeated by treachery, put a curse on Accra that it should remain disunited against its enemies ever after) and to the destruction of Ayawaso, now just a tiny village. But the Ga regained much of their independence in 1730, when Akwamu fell to the Akim state of Akwapim, which now took over control of the **"notes"** (documents issued by African rulers giving Europeans the right to trade) for the Accra forts. These "notes" later passed to the Asante, who gained control at the beginning of the nineteenth century, but gradually lost it in a series of wars with the British. Battle was averted in 1863 when British and Asante armies were both struck by dysentery and too ill to fight, but a decisive victory in 1874 led to the British taking over and setting up the Gold Coast Colony with its capital at Accra after 1877.

Since then the city has expanded considerably, despite serious earthquakes in 1862 and 1939. After the introduction of **cocoa**, Accra became a major export port, also shipping out gold, palm oil and rubber and, from 1933, boasting West Africa's first brewery (Club). The municipality, set up in 1896, was expanded east to include Christiansborg and, in 1943, to bring in the ancient, walled, farming and salt-producing village of Labadi.

On February 28, 1948, major **anti-colonial riots** in the city centre followed British police shootings at a demonstration at the junction of Rowe, Castle and Christiansborg roads. Twenty-nine protestors died and 237 were wounded in an outburst that caused £2 million worth of damage.

Arrival, orientation and information

At **Kotoka International Airport** there's generally a crowd of KIA porters in boiler-suits (inscribed "Porter", with a number), trying to handle your luggage and earn a "dash". Keep cool and nominate one, or make it clear you'll do it yourself. Customs procedures tend to be slow and the currency declaration form delays matters further. You can **change money** with the officials – legally – but their rates are even worse than those at the forex bureau in the arrivals hall, which in turn are worse than at places downtown.

There's no airport bus into town and **taxi drivers** converge on you as soon as you leave the terminal building. They can be quite heavy and stories circulate about menacing demands. It's all bark: stay cool and do nothing until someone calms down enough for you to go with them. The fare into the city centre should be clearly agreed before you go, and although it's easy to be pressurized into paying ₵10,000 or more, the fare to virtually anywhere should be no more than ₵7000, even at night. The city centre is only about 8km away – a ten-minute ride. Alternatively, you can walk out of the airport zone to the main road, and pick up a **shared taxi** for around ₵500 to Kwame Nkrumah Circle, or other points around the Ring Road.

If you're **arriving by road**, entering Accra can be a confusing business, with little in the way of landmarks to indicate where you are and a generally chaotic cityscape of dust (or mud) on the outskirts. If you're arriving by public transport, it's possible you will want to hop out before reaching the terminus. Check our map for likely arrival points for your vehicle.

The **train station** is in the heart of the city, a short taxi ride from just about anywhere.

Orientation

Despite the urban sprawl, downtown Accra is neatly contained by the **Ring Road**, in relation to which points of interest in the city are usually located. Lined by shops and commercial and business premises, two main thoroughfares – Nkrumah Avenue and Kojo Thompson Road – run through the city centre south to north from the old **Jamestown** district to **Kwame Nkrumah Circle** (known to taxi drivers simply as "Circle"). Shady **Independence Avenue**, sprinkled with embassies and business headquarters, also leads from the south of town, past East Ridge and North Ridge and

---

PUBLIC TRANSPORT IN ACCRA

The main group of **parking stations** in town is at the junction of Barnes and Kinbu roads.

Taxis in Accra can be rented outright for the journey, in which case they're **"dropping"** (₵2500–6000 in town and ₵7000 for the outskirts, depending on the distance, but confirm the price before setting off; fares may increase at night and during the rains), or by the hour (the current rate is ₵8000 per hour, although this is not automatically enforced and you may have to argue for it). Alternatively, you can share the collective **"line taxis"** for around ₵300–750 per hop. Line taxis roll along fixed routes, often from circle (roundabout) to circle, servicing virtually the whole city. For these, only flag down a taxi and state your destination if there is already one passenger inside. Note that "Circle" always refers to Nkrumah Circle, never Sankara or Danquah, and a circling motion of the finger means that's where you're going.

Tro-tros (uncomfortable vans) are slower and about thirty percent less expensive than saloon car line taxis. Tourists are generally assumed to be chartering, so make it clear if you're not.

Ringway Estate to **Sankara Circle** in the northeast and on out to the airport. **Cantonments Road** runs from the coast near **The Castle** (the seat of government) northeast through the district of **Osu** to **Danquah Circle**, and then on through the Cantonments district to the airport. Cutting east to west through the city centre are the main arteries of Castle Road, Liberia Road and Kinbu Road.

The core of Accra stretches from the banking district of **High Street** near the water-front to the **Makola market** – a colourful hive of activity that overflows into the sur-rounding streets. In between, the ample proportions of the stately colonial **Old Parliament House** and **Supreme Court** give an idea of the importance the British placed on their Gold Coast Colony.

It's worth noting – in case you were wondering – that Accra's **port** is at the separate town of **Tema**, some 30km east of the capital.

Tourist information

If you want to make the trek to Taesano, you can visit the **Ghana Tourist Board** on Barnes Road (PO Box 3106, Accra; ☎021/23.18.17 or 22.21.53; Fax 021 24.46.11; *gtb@africaonline.com.gh*), but most of the information they provide – including a directory of hotels, restaurants, travel and car rental agencies (₡12,000) and a helpful tourist newslet-ter, *Okwantumi* – can be found within the city centre in various hotels and bookshops. The **Ministry of Tourism** is located more centrally (PO Box 4386, Accra; ☎021/66.63.14 or 66.64.26; Fax 021/66.23.75) and should have Tourist Board publications to hand, as well as a variety of other literature and local guides. If you will be spending a lot of time venturing into national parks, it is worth visiting the **Wildlife Department**, near Independence Square (☎021/66.46.54) for maps and information. Finally, The **Ghana Tourist Development Company**, on Sanchi Road in the Airport Residential Area (PO Box 8710; ☎021/77.20.84 or 77.61.09; Fax 77.20.93), may be worth a visit.

It's also worth getting a copy of the Accra listings magazine, *Ghanascope*.

Accommodation

Accommodation in Accra is relatively cheap and varies from absolutely basic dorm space for those counting every penny to luxury hotel rooms. Problems with power cuts and water shortages are diminishing. The nearest **campsite** is at Coco Beach, about 10km east of the centre on the Tema road (around ₡2500). Beware of theft in the area.

Hostels and student rooms

Accra Polytechnic, Barnes Rd opposite *Novotel* (☎021/66.29.39). Basic and very inexpensive rooms during the holiday season. ①.

Teacher's Hostel, Castle Rd, near the National Museum. Budget accommodation open to all if they have space, which they often don't. ①.

YMCA and **YWCA**, both located on Castle Rd near the National Museum (PO Box 738; ☎021/22.47.00). Central and some of the cheapest dormitory rooms in town. Good places to meet Ghanaians. ①.

Cheap hotels

There's a great deal of variation in the standards of the following places. Check care-fully before settling on a room and always ask first for the best room they have.

ADABRAKA

Bellview Hotel, Tudu Crescent, off Kojo Thompson Rd, behind the Accra Polytechnic (PO Box 10, TUC; ☎021/66.77.30; Fax 021/22.58.38). Good budget hotel, with S/C, fanned rooms in a conve-nient location and a well-liked restaurant. ③.

Crown Prince Hotel, Kojo Thompson Rd (PO Box 4005; ☎021/22.53.81). The AC rooms with shared facilities aren't expensive, but the noise here never stops. Water is often off. ②–③.

The Date Hotel, Adami St (PO Box 3401; ☎021/22.82.00). One of the best-value places, with a good bar area and open space and a great restaurant for *fufu* and groundnut soup. ①–②.

Hotel de California, Kojo Thompson Rd at Castle Rd (PO Box 7337; ☎021/22.61.99). Long a popular haunt with travellers, but now only a good prospect for that reason. The fanned rooms (shared facilities) are dirty and the whole place needs an overhaul. ①.

Nkrumah Memorial Hotel, Kojo Thompson Rd (PO Box 10528; ☎021/57.88.59). Walls are thin, but the place is kept clean and the location is great. Very good food, including *omo tuo* in the restaurant. ①–②.

Station View Hotel, Kinbu Rd, 25m east of Kojo Thompson Rd, opposite lorry park. Nice for the location; but rooms with fans are very basic. Bar and restaurant with rice and *fufu* type dishes. ①.

ASYLUM DOWN

Korkdam Hotel, 18 2nd Crescent, off Mango Tree Ave, Asylum Down (PO Box 4605; ☎021/22.32.21; Fax 021/22.34.24). Range of rooms from S/C singles with hot water and fridges to "executive suites" with the works (phones, TV, AC). ③. (Note that there's a more expensive *Korkdam* in New Achimota, several kilometres north of the centre off the Kumasi road.)

Lemon Lodge, 2 Crescent Rd off Mango Tree Ave (PO Box 76, Kanda; ☎021/22.78.57). In a quiet, leafy neighbourhood, this offers good value and is usually full. Clean rooms with fan. ①–②.

KOKOMLEMLE

C'est Si Bon Hotel, near Challenge bookshop (PO Box 1389; ☎021/22.03.79). Reasonable singles and doubles, clean and airy with fan or AC and private bath. ②.

Hotel Britannia, Nsawam Rd opposite Accra North P&T (PO Box 6043; ☎021/22.42.14). Very good value with decent S/C rooms and a robust atmosphere at the in-house bar featuring slot machines and Jack Daniels. ③.

Kokomlemle Guesthouse, Oroko St near ATTC (☎021/22.45.81). Excellent value, with clean S/C rooms, friendly staff and a relaxed atmosphere in the lively bar and restaurant. Well known and liked by visiting NGO workers and travellers. ①.

New Haven Hotel, east of Nkrumah Circle and north of the Ring Rd Central behind Paloma (PO Box 651, Tema). Good value for clean S/C rooms with fan. ①–②.

Mid-range hotels

Adeshi Hotel, Ring Rd Central, 1km east of Nkrumah Circle (PO Box 11386; ☎021/22.13.07). Rooms are small and none too clean, but with all the amenities. Friendly staff. Breakfast included. ④.

Beachcomber Guesthouse, Teshie-Nungua. Five small, modern, circular thatched huts overlooking the sea away from the city bustle. Worth being fifteen minutes outside the city centre for the picturesque view and proximity to Coco Beach. A pleasant alternative to the luxury beach resorts. ③.

King David's Hotel, near Nkrumah Circle, Kokomlemle (PO Box 10323; ☎021/22.52.80). Small, very clean hotel with friendly staff and large rooms, used by transiting Ghana Airways' passengers. Good restaurant too. ⑥.

Penta Hotel, Cantonments Rd near Danquah Circle (PO Box 7354; ☎021/77.45.29; Fax 021/77.34.18). Great location for clubbing and eating out and you can nearly always get a taxi from outside at just about any hour of the day or night, but rooms with mediocre facilities are somewhat overpriced. ⑥.

ACCOMMODATION PRICE CODES

① Under ¢21,500 (under £5/$8).	⑤ ¢129,000–172,000(£30–40/$48–64).
② ¢21,500–43,000 (£5–10/$8–16).	⑥ ¢172,000–215,000 (£40–50/$64–80).
③ ¢43,000–86,000 (£10–20/$16–32).	⑦ Over ¢215,000 (over £50/$80).
④ ¢86,000–129,000 (£20–30/$32–48).	

For further details see p.48.

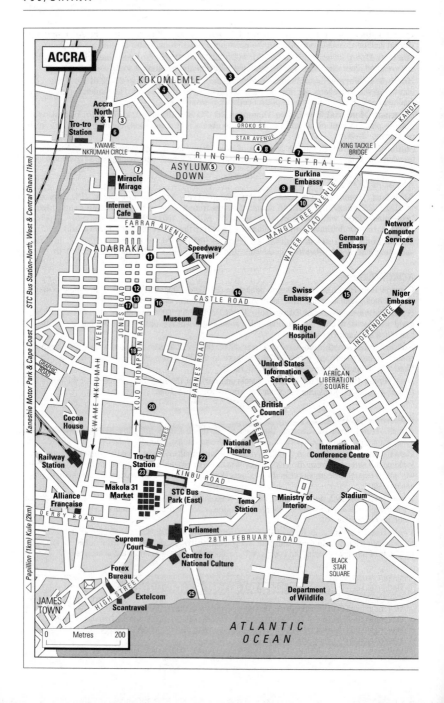

ACCRA

KOKOMLEMLE

❸
❹

Accra
North
P & T
❸

Tro-tro
Station
❻

OROKO ST
❺

STAR AVENUE

KWAME
NKRUMAH CIRCLE

❹ ❽

RING ROAD CENTRAL ❼

KING TACKLE
BRIDGE

ASYLUM ❺ ❻
DOWN

❼
Miracle
Mirage

Burkina
Embassy

❾

❿

Network
Computer
Services

Internet
Cafe

FARRAR AVENUE

German
Embassy

ADABRAKA

Speedway
Travel

❶❶

JONES ROAD

Swiss
Embassy

❶❺

Niger
Embassy

❶❷
❶❸

❶❼
❶❻

CASTLE ROAD

❶❹

Museum

Ridge
Hospital

❶❽

United States
Information
Service

AFRICAN
LIBERATION
SQUARE

KOJO THOMPSON ROAD

British
Council

KWAME NKRUMAH AVENUE

GRAPHIC
ROAD

❷❾

Cocoa
House

TUDU CRES

National
Theatre

International
Conference Centre

Railway
Station

Tro-tro
Station
❷❸

❷❷

KINBU ROAD

Makola 31
Market

STC Bus
Park (East)

Tema
Station

Ministry of
Interior

Stadium

Alliance
Française

DERBY ROAD

Parliament

28TH FEBRUARY ROAD

Supreme
Court

BLACK
STAR
SQUARE

Forex
Bureau

Centre for
National Culture

HIGH STREET

Extelcom

❷❺

JAMES
TOWN

Scantravel

Department
of Wildlife

ATLANTIC
OCEAN

0   Metres   200

STC Bus Station-North, West & Central Ghana (1km) △

Kaneshie Motor Park & Cape Coast △

Papillon (1km) Kule (2km) △

WATER ROAD

MANGO TREE AVENUE

INDEPENDENCE

KANDA

BARNES ROAD

SERIA ROAD

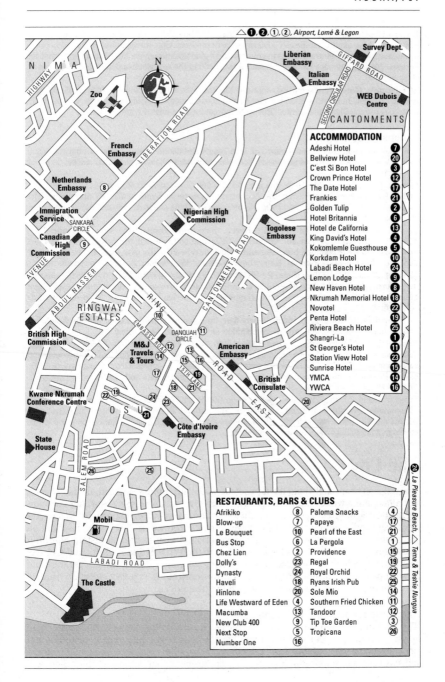

△ ❶, ❷, ①, ②, Airport, Lomé & Legon

N I M A

HIGHWAY

Zoo

Liberian
Embassy

Italian
Embassy

GIFFARD ROAD

Survey Dept.

WEB Dubois
Centre

CANTONMENTS

SECOND CIRCULAR ROAD

LIBERATION ROAD

French
Embassy

Netherlands
Embassy

Immigration
Service

SANKARA
CIRCLE

Canadian
High
Commission

AVENUE

ABDUL NASSER

Nigerian High
Commission

Togolese
Embassy

RINGWAY
ESTATES

RING

EMBASSY ROAD

CANTONMEN'S ROAD

DANQUAH
CIRCLE

British High
Commission

M&J
Travels
& Tours

American
Embassy

British
Consulate

ROAD

EAST

Kwame Nkrumah
Conference Centre

O S U

Côte d'Ivoire
Embassy

State
House

SALEM ROAD

Mobil

LABADI ROAD

The Castle

ACCOMMODATION

Adeshi Hotel	❼
Bellview Hotel	⑳
C'est Si Bon Hotel	❸
Crown Prince Hotel	⑫
The Date Hotel	⑰
Frankies	㉑
Golden Tulip	❷
Hotel Britannia	❻
Hotel de California	⑬
King David's Hotel	❹
Kokomlemle Guesthouse	❺
Korkdam Hotel	❿
Labadi Beach Hotel	㉔
Lemon Lodge	❾
New Haven Hotel	❽
Nkrumah Memorial Hotel	⑱
Novotel	㉒
Penta Hotel	⑲
Riviera Beach Hotel	㉕
Shangri-La	❶
St George's Hotel	⑪
Station View Hotel	㉓
Sunrise Hotel	⑮
YMCA	⑭
YWCA	⑯

㉔ La Pleasure Beach, △ Tema & Teshie Nungua

RESTAURANTS, BARS & CLUBS

Afrikiko	⑧	Paloma Snacks	④
Blow-up	⑦	Papaye	⑰
Le Bouquet	⑩	Pearl of the East	㉑
Bus Stop	⑥	La Pergola	①
Chez Lien	②	Providence	⑮
Dolly's	㉓	Regal	⑲
Dynasty	㉔	Royal Orchid	㉒
Haveli	⑱	Ryans Irish Pub	㉕
Hinlone	⑳	Sole Mio	⑭
Life Westward of Eden	④	Southern Fried Chicken	⑪
Macumba	⑬	Tandoor	⑫
New Club 400	⑨	Tip Toe Garden	③
Next Stop	⑤	Tropicana	㉖
Number One	⑯		

Riviera Beach Hotel, Marine Drive, Victoriaborg (PO Box 4226; ☎021/66.29.90). The name suggests something exotic, but the S/C, AC rooms are run-down. Still, the beautiful views of the coastline help make up for shortcomings in comfort and a giant swimming pool that hasn't had water for decades. Excellent terrace bar and restaurant overlooking the sea; worth a detour even if you don't sleep here. ③.

St George's Hotel, Amusudai Rd, opposite Methodist School, Adabraka (☎021/22.46.99). In a restored colonial home, this hotel has charm plus conveniences like fridges, phones, TV and AC in posh S/C rooms. Clean and comfortable, with a great location near the museum. ④.

Expensive hotels

Frankies, Cantonments Rd and Oxford St, Osu. Single and double rooms – with AC, hot water and cable TV – newly added to this popular and conveniently located bakery, snack bar and second-floor restaurant. ⑦.

Golden Tulip, Airport Rd, Cantonements (PO Box 16033; ☎021/77.53.60; Fax 021/77.53.61). Run by KLM, this luxury hotel has central AC, lots of hot water and rooms with TV and phone. The swimming pool is an added draw. *Tulips* nightclub sees a little action at the weekend. Happy hour in the bar Thurs 7–8pm. ⑦.

Labadi Beach Hotel, La (Labadi) Beach, 5km from centre (PO Box 1, Trade Fair; ☎021/77.25.01; Fax 021/77.25.20). Opened in 1991, right on the beach, this is by far Ghana's most expensive and well-appointed hotel. Amenities include a health club, gym, pool and beautiful garden, and a huge breakfast buffet. Happy hour in the bar Wed 6–7pm. Accepts most cards. ⑦.

Novotel, Barnes Rd, north of Kinbu Rd (PO Box 12720; ☎021/66.75.46; Fax 021/66.75.33). Accra's first international establishment still has an antiseptic feel. Free airport shuttle for guests. Great buffet breakfast – non-guests welcome. Happy hour in the bar Tues 5–6pm. Major credit cards accepted. ⑦.

La Palm Beach Hotel, La (Labadi) Beach, 5km from centre. Ghana's second five-star hotel, due to open in the year 2000, will provide competition for the *Labadi Beach Hotel*. ⑦.

Shangri-La, 1500m from the airport (PO Box 9201; ☎021/77.75.00; Fax 021/77.48.73). More intimate than the *Novotel* and somewhat cheaper, though not lacking in facilities like tennis courts and swimming pool. The local feel makes it deservedly popular with expats. Great pizzas at reasonable prices. *Harmattan* nightclub attracts a lively crowd of young expats and rich kids on Fri nights. Accepts all major credit cards. ⑦.

Sunrise Hotel, 7th Ave Extension, North Ridge (PO Box 2287; ☎021/22.45.75; Fax 021/22.22.01). Five minutes from the centre and in a quiet neighbourhood. Emphasis on business travellers with fax and other services available. Stylish AC rooms with fridges and TVs. Swimming pool and tennis courts in a pleasant garden. Amex accepted. ⑦.

The City

Accra doesn't especially lend itself to scenic walks and sightseeing and, by day, there's not much in the way of things to see. The main diversion is simply absorbing the energy of an African urban centre. Even the coast and lagoons aren't shown off to any real advantage and, from most places in town, you're barely aware that Accra lies right on the seafront – though Jamestown is an exception. A visit to the interesting **National Museum** is recommended, as is a quick trip to the **WEB Dubois Memorial Centre**, and perhaps a look at the gradually improving **zoo**, on Kanda Avenue, past the Ring Road (open daily 9.30am–5.30pm). The **crafts market** offers a vast selection from all over the region, though not necessarily at the best prices.

The National Museum of Ghana

The **National Museum of Ghana**, on Barnes Road near the junction with Castle Road (daily 9am–6pm; ₵2000), houses one of West Africa's best ethnographic, historical and art collections, with exhibits from Ghana and across the continent. You could conceivably visit the entire museum in a morning or afternoon, but because of the variety and eclecticism of the exhibits, it's perhaps best to pop in several times to avoid cultural fatigue. The exhibits are well displayed, though poorly explained – and in some cases in need of a dusting. It's worth investing in the **museum handbook**, which contains numerous black-and-white photos and detailed descriptions.

The museum is dedicated in large measure to still-thriving **local crafts**. There are numerous examples of clay water-coolers, bowls and lamps, calabash drums, iron clappers and wooden zithers, ornamental brass pots and implements, while complementary exhibits show the **technology** of the cottage industries. You can see how iron is forged (still common in the north), how brass weights, once used for weighing gold, are cast, and how glass beads are manufactured.

Interesting, too, are the **ceremonial objects** so common among the Akan and other peoples of the country. Gilded umbrella tops, carved royal stools, metal swords of state and intricate *kente* cloth are charged with a social and religious significance that the displays help illuminate. Artefacts from further afield in Africa (Congo, South Africa, Angola) are interspersed among the national exhibits. Upstairs, dusty **archeological relics** trace the country's history back to the late Stone Age.

The National Theatre and the Greater Accra Centre for National Culture

The **National Theatre**, on the corner of Liberia Road and Independence Avenue, diagonally opposite the British Council, houses a permanent, specially commissioned exhibition of Ghanaian musical instruments, sculpture, carvings and other items. It's free and well worth a look.

Downtown on 28th February Road, near the *Riviera Beach Hotel*, the **Greater Accra Centre for National Culture** is a new concrete showpiece dedicated to promoting the arts. Inside is a large gallery for exhibitions by national painters and sculptors. The building also contains theatres to showcase national dance and theatre troupes and periodic live music shows. A schedule of activities is posted outside, or check the listings magazine, *Ghanascope*.

Monuments and other central sights

Jamestown, a bustling centre of small commerce at the heart of the colonial town, is worth a wander, though **Fort James** itself (see p.718) is to be avoided – it's a prison. You can, however, visit the nearby colonial-era **lighthouse** for scenic town views.

Opposite the Parliament building on High Street, the new **Nkrumah Mausoleum** at last pays homage to the pan-African pioneer and nation builder. The architecture is a throwback to 1960s triumphalism, but the surrounding gardens provide a peaceful refuge from the mayhem of the city.

Osu Castle, the former Danish Christiansborg (see p.718), is today the seat of government, and called simply "The Castle". All surrounding streets are somewhat barricaded, so you can't get too near to this historical curiosity.

A wander around **Independence Square** (also known as Black Star Square) is worthwhile, but be aware of possible muggings and theft. Here, the **Triumphal Arch**, a Nkrumah-era monument of heroic dimensions, built to herald African liberation, looms behind The Castle – no photos allowed. The square itself is a giant parade ground, site of the Eternal Flame of African Liberation, lit by Nkrumah. Nearby are the ministries and **National Stadium**. A few hundred metres to the east stands the first president's proudest legacy, the monumental **State House** and adjoining **Kwame Nkrumah Conference Centre**, built in 1965 to serve as headquarters of the Organization of African Unity. Across the street is the impressive new **International Conference Centre**, built in record time to house the 1991 conference of non-aligned nations.

The WEB Dubois Memorial Centre for Pan-African Culture

The home – House no. 22, 1st Circular Rd, Cantonments (near the airport) – where **WEB Dubois**, the black American champion of pan-Africanism, died in 1963 and is buried has been turned into a cultural centre with a research library and gallery full of manuscripts and other Dubois memorabilia (Mon–Fri 8am–12.30pm & 1.30–5pm). Photographs and brief biographies of other black world leaders line the walls of his living room and study. The centre contains facilities for lectures – keep an eye out for these if you're around in the summer – and other educational and cultural programmes. It's not ostentatious, but a highly informative and inspiring monument to pan-Africanism and its vanguard. Surrounding Dubois' tomb, you will see commemorative wreaths from devotees including reggae dancehall greats Shabba Ranks and Buju Banton.

Markets and crafts shops

Vast **Makola market** is where you feel the city centre's retail pulse most strongly. These days it contains just about everything in the food and domestic line, including cheap glass beads. The **Kaneshi market** by the motor park on Weija Road is also huge and an excellent place for rummaging.

Spreading out around the Centre for National Culture on 28th February Road is the **crafts market**, a huge depot for works from throughout West Africa. On the whole, buying here isn't as satisfying or cheap as searching out such goods in the regions where they're manufactured, but if you've got no time or just like one-stop shopping, this is the place. You'll find everything from **Asante sandals** and **kente cloth** to **leatherwork** from the north, woven cotton fabric and glass beads, any of which can easily be bought more cheaply elsewhere. The wood crafts – **masks**, **carvings** and **boxes** – and the **brasswork** are somewhat harder to find. Expect heavy pressure to buy; bargaining tends to be a battle of wits here and not a great deal of fun. If you buy anything, even if it doesn't look like an antique, you might have to obtain an export permit, proving it has no historical value (see p.692).

The Ark crafts shop, just past the *Golden Tulip Hotel* on the way to the airport (Mon–Fri 8.30am–4pm, Sat 8.30am–1pm), is less overwhelming if you're not up to speed with your bargaining skills. The Loom gallery, at the top end of Kwame Nkrumah Avenue, also has a good selection of crafts and jewellery.

Finally, in Nungua, some fifteen minutes' drive east of central Accra on the coast road to Tema, you'll find the Artists' Alliance, an art gallery/shop selling artefacts, modern art, cloth, pottery and jewellery. All the goods are high quality, and there's a relaxed buying atmosphere, but most prices differ little from what you'd expect to pay for Africana in a shop at home. The most compelling items are the samples of old *kente* cloth (see p.739), which surpass anything else you're likely to come across. This is cloth with soul, and very dear – ₵200,000–500,000 a piece – and you can't help wondering how it came to be here.

For **batik cloth**, try Betdove Batik Factory on the La road (☎021/77.23.89), a five-minute drive from Danquah Circle. Fabrics here run from ₵3000–6000 a yard, and you can also watch the fascinating dyeing and waxing process in the open-air factory. The fabrics are also less likely to fade and are better priced than those you find on the roadside as you wander around Osu. For batik designs of superb quality, try Mercy Asi Ocansey and Sons Dyeing Enterprise in Osu (☎021/77.78.35), just off the main road on 4th Lane opposite the police hospital – though the fabrics here are much more expensive (around ₵10,000 a yard).

Beaches

The best area for sea swimming in Accra is **La Pleasure Beach** (formerly Labadi, with a small entrance fee), directly below the International Trade Fair site. There are lifeguards at La, occasionally called upon to rescue swimmers swept out by the strong undertow. This is *the* place to be on weekends when Accra's young people turn out for beach parties – and just to see and be seen. Taxis and *tro-tros* run here from Nkrumah Circle. You can also take a dip below the *Riviera Beach Hotel*, but take nothing of value (and be seen to have nothing of value).

Eating

In addition to the places listed below, cheap **street eats** are available in the motor parks, markets and in certain districts. Adabraka, for example, has many cheap eateries and, if you're staying in one of the neighbourhood's inexpensive hotels, you'll find numerous *kenkey* and fish vendors in backstreets running between *The Date* and the *Hotel de California*.

Inexpensive
In most of the following establishments you can eat heartily for ₵3000–8000–standard international fast food in most of them, with salads and some Ghanaian dishes also featuring.

Bus Stop, Ring Rd Central, near the Agricultural Development Bank. Pavement tables and a varied menu of snacks (sandwiches, kebabs), European specialities, ice cream and cheap beer.

Dolly's, Danquah Circle near the *Penta Hotel*, Osu. Basic fast-food place (one of a chain) featuring tasty burgers and chips.

Ghana National Museum Café (aka Edvy Restaurant), at the museum gate, Barnes Rd, West Ridge. Excellent Ghanaian food served at lunchtime only; liable to unpredictable closure. Nice buffet on Wednesdays.

Kule, Eduardo Mondlana Rd, Larte Biokorshi, west of the Korle lagoon (on the west side of Korle-Bu Hospital). Ghanaian-style fast-food joint, with "palava" huts outside. Inexpensive, and owes nothing to tourist or expat expectations. About ₵7700 a plate.

Maison Afrique, Adabraka, not far from *Hotel de California*. Very clean local chop bar with excellent *fufu* and *banku*.

Papaye, Cantonments Rd, Osu (PO Box 10505, Accra-North; ☎021/77.37.54). *Dolly's*-style but better – good chicken, burgers (₵3000) or fish and chips. Grilled chicken with rice is ₵7000. The epitome of Accra's growing fast-food culture.

Papillon, Guggisberg Ave, Mamprobi, on the south side of Korle-Bu Hospital (over the Korle Lagoon bridge, 1km west of Jamestown). Ghanaian home cooking and live music at weekends. Goat meat, chicken, soup, *fufu*, *banku*, and rice dishes are about ₵7700.

Providence, Cantonments Rd, just off Danquah Circle. Very good, reasonably priced Ghanaian food (lunch only, open to 5pm).

Southern Fried Chicken, Danquah Circle. Fast food. Fried, flamed, and charcoal-grilled chicken by the bucket. Also serves Indian and Lebanese food and vegetarian pizzas. Open 11am–11pm.

Western Fried Chicken, near American embassy annexe. Very good southern fried chicken with coleslaw and chips. A little pricey, but worth it.

Moderate and expensive
In a moderately priced league, the options are more varied, with a good variety of Asian restaurants and several high-quality Middle Eastern and European-style establishments, as well as a number of very classy African places. Prices at the most expensive eating houses, which include hotel restaurants not mentioned here, run to about ₵20,000 a head.

AFRICAN
Afrikiko, Liberation Rd, near Sankara Circle. A very popular expat hangout, known for cheap beer and moderately priced African dishes in a garden bar setting. Good chicken and salads. There's often live music and dance at weekends, but it's worth knowing that the place has some notoriety as a pick-up joint. Open noon–midnight. Next door the *Afrikiko Leisure Centre* serves up ice cream and the usual snacks.

Fikodar, near Obetsebi-Lamptey Circle, Kaneshi. Expensive, but a good reputation for well-prepared national specialities including "grasscutter marengo" (very fancy bush rat). Some European dishes as well.

Kikiriki, Basel St, Osu. It's worth coming a little out of your way for excellent spicy chicken (the house speciality), beers and occasional live music.

La Pergola, on the Airport Rd, near *Golden Tulip Hotel*. Togolese restaurant serving Ghanaian and continental food in a pleasant, partial open-air atmosphere. Around ₡8000 a head. One of the best restuarants in town for the money with a friendly owner.

ASIAN FOOD

Chez Lien, Osu. Vietnamese restaurant with magnificent food.

Dynasty, Cantonments Rd near Danquah Circle. A newer Chinese restaurant providing stiff competition for the older venues. Clean surroundings and high-quality meals. Atmosphere tends to become smoke-filled. Open 11am–3pm & 6–11.30pm.

Haveli, Osu. Popular Indian restaurant with a large variety of Tandoor, rice, vegetable and curry dishes. Open noon–3pm & 7–10.30pm.

Hinlone, in Labone, off Ring Rd East, first left and left again 500m south of the American embassy. Wonderful fresh selections of premium quality vegetables, meat and seafood. Open noon–3pm.

Pearl of the East, 15th lane, off Cantonments Rd, behind *Penta Hotel*, south of Danquah Circle in Osu. Perhaps the best Chinese restaurant in Accra, with authentic dishes and great vegetables (daily except Sun, noon–3pm & 7–11pm).

Regal, off Cantonments Rd, Osu. Excellent Chinese restaurant. Moderate prices. Open noon 3.30pm & 6.30–10.30pm.

Royal Orchid, off Cantonments Rd, Osu. Reasonably priced Thai and Ghanaian food. Sometimes has live music on Fri.

Tandoor, Embassy Rd, just off Danquah Circle. Indian tandoori cooking. There's a no-smoking section – something of a novelty in Accra – and vegetarian options. Open 11am–3pm & 6–11pm.

LEBANESE

Le Bouquet, Ring Rd East, north of Danquah Circle. Varied menu of French dishes and Lebanese meze. Open noon–3pm & 6.30–11pm.

New Club 400, Ring Rd East, just south of Sankara Circle. Art gallery and restaurant with wide range of Lebanese food.

Tropicana, Salem Rd, Kuku Hill, Osu (☎021/77.66.31). Lunch and dinner service featuring Middle Eastern and European specialities.

EUROPEAN

Frankies, Cantonements Rd and Oxford St, Osu. Quickly becoming an Accra landmark, the family-owned complex includes a boulangerie with fresh baguettes and pastries and the best (Italian) ice cream in town, a snack shop selling great beef burgers, *chawarmas* and pizzas, and a newly-opened restaurant on the second floor. Extremely popular with expats and tourists. European prices. Open 6.30am–11pm.

Home Touch, Giffard Rd, near the Elwak stadium, just south of the airport. Stylish wining and dining, with European and Ghanaian dishes on the menu.

Le P'tit Paris Cafe, Ground Floor of Sedco House in Kanda. Expensive French bakery, selling fresh bread, pastries and sandwiches. One of the few places to serve brewed coffee. Very popular among expats.

Life Westward of Eden, Ring Rd Central in the Paloma Complex. Small, pleasant vegetarian restaurant with tofu, lentil burgers and pizzas. Open Sun–Thurs 9am–6pm, Fri & Sat 6pm–midnight.

Number One, Danquah Circle. Busy, noisy spot (loud music at night), with a wide choice of pizza, salads, ice cream, all fairly good. Cheap draught beer. Slow service. Sit outside on the terrace.

Paloma Snacks, Ring Rd Central, east of Kwame Nkrumah Circle. Europeanized Ghanaian food including decent *fufu*, excellent kebabs, pizza, salads and ices, and its famous burger. Live music at weekends. Lively atmosphere mix of tourists, locals and expats. Open 11am–midnight.

Sole Mio, Osu, opposite *Tandoor* restaurant. New Italian restaurant with antipasti, pasta, meat and fish dishes – and European prices. Hours are noon–3pm & 6.30–11pm.

Nightlife

Nightlife in Accra is an ever-evolving scene. Accra's clubs and dives change hands almost as often as shifts. Many of the following venues serve food and may even present themselves as restaurants some of the time, just as certain restaurants sometimes offer live music – anything to get the punters in. From Monday to Wednesday the action – if it happens at all – starts late, though there are one or two "ladies nights", usually Wednesday, when women get free admission. Thursday, Friday, Saturday and Sunday are the big nights out. Thursday night is La beach party night. At weekends you can party most of the daytime, too, in some venues. Covers are very moderate by international standards – ₡4000 is about the most you'll pay, if anything at all.

African Heroes Hotel, Nima, Accra Newtown, just north of Ring Rd Central. Similar to *Tip Toe* and the *Apollo*, but rougher; the African Brothers stronghold with some hardcore regulars and underworld vibes. "Now you're on the borderline of where angels fear to tread." Remember they warned you.

Aquarius, off Cantonments Rd, south of Danquah Circle. Supposedly a "German pub" (though feels anything but), with pool tables. Expensive, but a popular starting point for a night out.

Baseline, in Northridge, near *Le P'tit Paris Cafe*. The only jazz club in Accra plays live music all weekend.

Big Boss, in North Kaneshie not far from Awodome Roundabout. Very busy hangout spot on weekends, with good draught beer.

Blow-up, Kwame Nkrumah Circle. No longer *the* place to go, but still a place to go, early, before moving on somewhere hotter.

Chester's Place, Gbatsuna St, Nyaniba Estates, Osu (☎021/77.75.03). Well known and well liked by expats: wide selection of chilled cocktails and light snacks. Half-price drinks at happy hour, weekdays 5.30–7.30pm, but it gets crowded much later.

Fusion, Osu. Cocktail bar and restaurant (dishes run from ₡3000 to ₡25,000) with a lively atmosphere – very popular with expats.

Glenns, in Adabraka, off Kojo Thompson Rd. New happening disco playing mostly funk and reggae DJ music.

Macumba, Ring Rd East, near Danquah Circle. Elaborate disco establishment with good music. Still very popular.

Mr Rees, near *Golden Tulip Hotel*. Garden drinking bar popular with expats and travellers.

New Connection, Osu. Slick two-level New York-style nightclub, very popular at weekends.

Next Door, in Teshie-Nungua on road to Tema. Newly renovated weekend hot spot for live African music. Open-air and a cliffside setting – with spectacular views – on two levels, the lower one consisting of thatch-covered tables near the shore. Saturday nights are the most popular. One of the best places to hear African music, and highly recommended.

Next Stop, on Ring Rd, above *Bus Stop*. Very small and crowded drinking and dancing spot, especially on weekends. Sometimes a queue to get in.

Oops, in North Kaneshie, at Bubuashie Roundabout. Popular new nightclub, where the DJ plays lots of highlife and rhythm and blues.

Red Onion, North Kaneshie. One of the best discos in Accra, popular with a mostly Ghanaian crowd. African and funk sounds. Reasonably priced drinks.

Ryans Irish Pub, off Cantonments Rd in Osu. New, popular hangout spot for expats. Jazz on Thursdays and live African and pop music on weekends in a tree-enclosed outdoor area, There's a sizeable indoor bar and restaurant area too. Happy hour Mon–Fri 5–8pm, and good Guinness.

Tip Toe Garden, north of Kwame Nkrumah Circle. Open-air, with stage and large dance floor. Changes hands often and is frequently at the mercy of Accra trend-setters. A good, well-mixed crowd of locals and foreigners enjoys plenty of live musical variety, including highlife and "copyright bands" (playing cover versions).

Listings

Air freight DHL, C913/3 North Ridge Crescent, near KLM (☎021/22.16.47).

Airline offices include: Aeroflot, 57 Kojo Thompson Rd (☎021/77.74.14); Air Afrique, Ring Rd Central, Provident Towers (☎021/22.83.28); Air Ivoire, Cocoa House (☎021/24.14.61); Air Mali, 23 CFC, Taesano (☎021/22.22.11); Alitalia, 08/03/326 Ring Rd Central (☎021/30.19.73) Balkan Bulgarian Airlines, Caledonian House, Kojo Thompson Rd (☎021/22.20.97); British Airways, Kojo Thompson Rd, corner of North Liberia Rd (☎021/24.03.86/7); Egyptair, Ring Rd East, just south of Danquah Circle, Osu (☎021/66.79.76); Ethiopian Airlines, Airport (☎021/77.51.68); Fan Airways, F.767/1 Osu Ave, Osu (☎021/76.31.46/7); Ghana Airways, White Ave, Airport Residential Area (☎021/77.33.21); KLM, 86 North Ridge, Ring Rd Central (☎021/22.40.20); Lufthansa, 34 North Ridge near the German embassy (☎021/23.17.54); Nigeria Airways, Danawi Building, D631/4 Kojo Thompson Rd (☎021/22.37.49 or 22.47.35); Swissair, E.45/3 Pegasus House, Independence Ave (☎021/23.19.18/9).

American Express Represented by Scantravel, High St (☎021/66.31.34 or 66.42.04).

Banks Major commercial banks are on High St near the intersection of Bank Lane and include: Barclays Bank (☎021/66.49.01; Fax 021/66.74.20); Ghana Commercial Bank (☎021/66.49.14; Fax 021/66.21.58); and Standard Chartered Bank (☎021/66.45.99; Fax 021/66.77.51). Remember the private forex bureaux offer better rates, though Barclays now offers a similar rate for travellers' cheques to those offered by the forex bureaux for cash. The High St, Circle, Osu, and Tema branches of Barclays Bank all have teller machines.

Books Try the southeast corner of Kinbu and Kojo Thompson roads (secondhand), the UTC bookshop on Kwame Nkrumah Ave, or Omari Books near Danquah Circle.

Car rental Avis through Speedway Travel and Tours, 5 Tackie Tawia St, Adabraka (☎021/22.87.60); Hertz, off Nima Highway (☎021/77.50.09). Also try Vanef in Sobukwe/Farrar Ave, Adabraka (☎21/22.23.74). The big hotels can usually help, too. Note that most companies only rent out cars with drivers.

EMBASSIES AND OTHER DIPLOMATIC MISSIONS

Working days are Monday to Friday, unless otherwise stated.

Australian affairs are handled by the Canadian High Commission.

Benin, 80 Volta St, corner of 2nd Close, Airport Residential Area (8am–3pm; PO Box 7871; ☎021/77.48.60; 15-day-stay visas, valid 3 months, issued overnight or in two days).

Burkina Faso, 772/3 Asylum Down, off Mango Tree Ave (7.30am–2pm; PO Box 651; ☎021/22.19.88).

Canada, 42 Independence Ave (8am–12.30pm and 1.30–4pm; PO Box 1639; ☎021/22.85.55/6).

Côte d'Ivoire, F.710/2 18 Lane, off Cantonments Rd, Osu (7.30am–2.30pm; PO Box 3445; ☎021/77.46.11).

Guinea, 11 Osu Badu St (8am–3pm; PO Box 5497; ☎021/77.79.21).

Mali, 8 Agostino Neto Rd, Airport Residential Area (7.30am–2pm; PO Box 1121; ☎021/77.51.60).

New Zealand affairs are handled by the British High Commission.

Niger, E 104/3 Independence Ave (PO Box 2685; ☎021/22.49.62).

Nigeria, 5 Josif Tito Ave (8am–3pm; PO Box 1548; ☎021/77.61.58; visas delivered Tues only and quite often hard to obtain here if you're travelling abroad).

South Africa, Plot 12, Airport Residential Area (PO Box 298, Trade Fair, La; ☎021/76.23.80).

Togo, Cantonments Circle (8.30am–2pm and 3–4.30pm; PO Box C120; ☎021/77.79.50).

UK High Commission at 1 Osu Link, off Abdul Nasser Ave (7.45am–3.45pm; PO Box 296; ☎021/22.16.65; Fax 021/66.46.52). Consulate on Ring Rd East.

USA, Ring Rd East near Danquah Circle, Osu (7.30am–12.30pm and 1.30–4.30pm; PO Box 194; ☎021/77.53.48; Fax 021/77.60.08).

MOVING ON FROM ACCRA

BUSES
STC buses for the west and north depart from the STC station (☎021/22.19.42), on the Ring Road north of Kaneshie Roundabout (Lamptey Circle). **Kumasi**-bound STC buses (some of which are AC) leave roughly hourly, from dawn until 4–5pm, taking 4hr. Air-conditioned STC buses also run direct to **Abidjan** once daily, and "direct" to **Ouagadougou** once a week (₵ 42,000) – but be prepared to spend the night at the Bolga bus station since you will arrive slightly after the Burkina border closes at 6pm. Alternative routes to Ouaga are either to change in Kumasi and spend the night there, or to take an STC bus to Bolga (two weekly) and find a car heading across the border. STC runs a twice-weekly direct service to **Wa**, and a weekly service to **Hamile** (departs Wed at 4pm) in the far northwest on the Burkinabe border. STC buses for the **east** go from the transport park along Kinbu Road, between Tudu Crescent and Barnes Road.

Ordinary bus lines to all destinations follow roughly the same division, with north- and westbound buses operating out of a transport park just to the west of Nkrumah Circle and eastbound buses departing from Kinbu Road.

TRO-TROS
Tro-tros pretty much follow the bus pattern – with less organization. Greater Accra and the coast are their main areas of operation. For the northern and eastern suburbs, get a seat at the transport park along Kinbu Road, between Tudu Crescent and Barnes Road. For the western suburbs go to Nkrumah Circle, and for the western coast, at least as far as Takoradi (though you really have to want to save money to go so far by *tro-tro*), go to Kaneshie.

TRAINS
Very slow passenger **train** services are available from Accra to Kumasi (2 daily, one of which is overnight) and Takoradi (1 daily, overnight). Check the latest schedules and information in person at the train station.

PLANES
AirLink operates three **flights** a week to Tamale (1hr 15min) and Kumasi (40min), and also offers occasional services to Sunyani. Bookings can be made through M&J Travels and Tours (☎021/77.34.98 or 70.60.81). Fan Airways (☎021/76.31.46/7) has two daily flights to Kumasi, and a daily flight to both Tamale and Bolgatanga. One-way **fares** are around ₵150,000 to Tamale, ₵95,000 to Kumasi and ₵200,000 to Bolgatanga.

Cinemas The best place to see newish European and American films, plus Ghanaian hits, is the Ghana Film Institute north of Sankara Circle. Other theatres include the AC Film Corporation Theatre, off Independence Ave (near the French embassy); Orion Cinema on Liberation Circle; the Globe on Adjaben Rd; and the Rex, behind Parliament House.

Cultural centres Among the foreign cultural centres is the British Council, Liberia Rd, just off Independence Ave (Mon–Wed 9am–5pm, Thurs & Fri 9am–2.30pm, Sat 9am–noon; ☎021/66.34.14; Fax 021/66.39.79), which has an excellent library and British papers and regularly hosts musical and theatrical events; the Alliance Française, on Derby Ave, down in the town centre, just off Kwame Nkrumah Rd, does the same in French. The USIS (American cultural centre) on Independence Ave and the German Goethe-Institut on Ring Rd also run active programmes.

Foreign exchange bureaux Numerous and widespread. Several on Kojo Thompson Rd have good rates.

Horse riding Bookable through the *Shangri-La Hotel*, at about ₵5000 per hour (☎021/77.21.78 ext 269; no riding Sat pm or Wed).

Internet The least expensive place is Network Computer Services' (NCS) "Cyber Café" near Immigration Services and KLM on 7 6th av. They charge ₵10,000 per hour. Arrive early (opens 9am). *Internet Cafe* at the overland bridge at Kojo Thompson Rd also has competitive prices.

Newspapers Overseas newspapers, mostly British, can be bought at the *Novotel*, the *Labadi Beach Hotel*, the *Golden Tulip* and the *Penta Hotel*.

Phones Main hotels are the best bet, or use the Extelcom, on the seaward side of High St or at the North Accra PO. Phonecards can be purchased at telecommunication centres or fuel stations, and there are public phone booths everywhere.

Photos If you want decent quality passport photos, head to a studio (there's a 24hr one on the corner of Kojo Thompson and South Liberia roads and another at Danquah Circle). Otherwise, you can get fuzzy wooden-box photos done more cheaply in five minutes on Kinbu Rd, across from the lorry park.

Post office Post restante is available free of charge at the GPO. Open Mon–Fri 8am–4.30pm.

Shipping agents If you want to try getting a berth on a ship, Umarco Ghana Ltd, PO Box 215, Harbour Area, Tema (☎021/40.31 or 40.35), are the port agents for Grimaldi Lines.

Supermarkets Many have sprung up to the south and west of Danquah Circle near the *Penta Hotel*. Kwatsons is expat heaven, with fresh cheese, meat and French bread. Others nearby include Quick Pick and Afridom. Kingsway on Kwame Nkrumah Ave often has wholemeal bread. UTC, also on Nkrumah Ave, is an extensive store, with just about everything, including inexpensive books. The Lebanese supermarkets along Cantonments Rd in Osu have a big range of imported goods. Shellshops have become very popular for bottled water, bread, cheese and ice cream.

Swimming pools The best pool is the one at the *Shangri-La* which non-guests can use for a small fee. The swimming pool at the *Labadi Beach Hotel* is extremely expensive. Canadian nationals can use the bar and pool at their High Commission.

Travel agents Very helpful for a range of organized tours in the country is Starline Travel & Tours, Ring Rd Central (☎021/22.96.46; Fax 021/22.29.17). Another agent worth checking out is Silicon Travel & Tours, Coplan House, Adabraka, 231 Kojo Thompson Rd, near the corner of Castle Rd (☎021/22.85.20; Fax 021/22.55.00). M&J Travels and Tours in Osu (☎021/77.34.98 or 70.60.81) are helpful for booking internal flights with AirLink.

Visa extensions are arranged at the Immigration Office on Independence Ave near Sankara Circle (Mon–Fri 8am–1pm). They expect two photos and a typed letter explaining why you need the extension (typists can be found in front of the GPO). They may retain your passport for up to two weeks; change money first.

Western Union At four branches of Agricultural Development Bank, the most central of which is in Adabraka on Kojo Thompson Rd.

North and east of Accra: short excursions

Getting out of the city for a while, especially at the hottest and most humid times of the year, from January to June, can be a relief. To the north, **Aburi**, a former hill station whose large gardens are still well maintained, offers the best escape from the heat. The **beaches** to the east, and the inland **Shai Hills Reserve**, are less often visited than the coast west of Accra.

Legon, Aburi and Shai Hills

LEGON, 14km north of Accra, is the headquarters of the **University of Ghana**, described by the tourist board as "a showpiece of Japanese architecture" – judge for yourself! There's a good bookshop but less opportunity to meet students than you might wish.

You can visit the university's botanical garden in the grounds, but there are older, more interesting and extensive gardens at **ABURI**, on Akwapim Ridge, 23km further north, with potentially magnificent views north over the forest and south to the city when the air is clear. Aburi, several hundred metres above the plain, was a colonial hill station and site of a sanatorium (now a hotel), and the gardens still bear the well-tended hallmarks of landscaped colonial taste, with hundreds of tree specimens from all over the tropical and subtropical regions. There's a pleasant restaurant in the gardens as well as a snack bar. The *Aburi Gardens Rest House*'s S/C bungalows (☎081/23.00.55 ext 22; ②–③) are frequently full, but an excellent alternative is the *Olyande Guesthouse*, which has very nice rooms, with tea and toast for breakfast included in the price, and a pleasant family atmosphere (②). Popular too is the little English-run place in Aburi village called *May Lodge & Restaurant* (PO Box 25; ☎081/25) with fine views from its S/C rooms (②).

Tro-tros from the Tudu Crescent/Barnes Road station run frequently to Legon, taking half an hour or so, and **buses** from the same area take about an hour to Aburi (the last one back to Accra leaves at about 6.30pm, not at 6pm as taxi drivers may tell you). If you're driving to Aburi, you continue past the airport to Tetteh Quarshie Circle, then take the Akosombo road until it forks right; you take the left-hand fork and start climbing.

Some 60km to the northwest of Accra is the **Shai Hills Reserve**. You can **stay** at an old office block/camp near the rangers' office here and guards are available to take you around the reserve (horse riding may still be available). Troops of baboons and parrots are the most likely sights, though kob antelope and ground hornbills can also be seen. There are some extensive bat-filled caves that can also be visited, which were formerly used as sites of worship by the Shai people, until they were moved out by the British in colonial times. They return annually, to perform ceremonies.

East of Accra

Looking east of Accra towards Togo, the quiet beach at **Prampram** (40km from Accra), distinguished by the French **Fort Vernon**, is reputed to be Ghana's best. Beyond Prampram, water sports resorts at Ada (120km from Accra), at the mouth of the Volta River, and Keta, out on the Volta delta (175km from Accra), are popular with Ghanaians. Both locations provide first-class bird-watching; you can rent a motorboat for around ₵20,000 an hour.

Accommodation at **ADA FOAH** village includes *Seaview Cottage* (②; food prepared on request), a collection of very basic wood and thatch huts on the beach which, like much of the village, is constantly under threat of being washed away by the sea. The *Manet Paradise Hotel*, a German-run water sports hotel (④–⑤) is the soulless upmarket alternative. For local Ghanaian dishes (₵7000) in a cheerful garden bar setting, try the *Brightest Spot*, off the main road. Ada's **tourist centre** (daily 8am–6pm; ☎0968/212) on the main road, can give information on excursions, and ferry rides up the Volta. To reach Ada Foah from Accra, take a bush taxi from the Tudu station (₵5000) to the last stop. If you have private transport, follow the main Accra–Lomé road and branch off at the Kasseh–Ada junction.

KETA's serene golden sands and unbelieveably blue shores are amongst the nicest in Ghana. Unfortunately, a lot of the village, built on sand, has been destroyed by the sea and much is in ruins, including many people's homes – replaced by "temporary" tents on the beach – and what is left of the fort. Despite these misfortunes, the fishing village is still inviting, and the *Keta Beach Hotel* (PO Box 377; ☎0966/288), off the main road, is a pleasant surprise, with excellent-value clean, quaint rooms (②–③), and a garden restaurant.

To reach the Togolese border from Keta, take a shared landrover from the Keta lorry station (₵1000; 40min).

THE COAST WEST OF ACCRA

The scenic coastline stretching from Accra to the Côte d'Ivoire border is one of the most obvious tourist targets in West Africa. The big attractions are the densest concentration of European **forts and castles** anywhere on the continent – twenty-nine of them, some over five hundred years old – and innumerable, unspoiled Fante **fishing villages** tucked between links of sandy, coconut-backed beaches. It's an irresistible combination, and not one you'll be alone in discovering. Tourism has increased dramatically since the late

1980s, and this trend is set to continue. You'll have to come on a weekday or out of season to have much hope of finding your own isolated paradise. Nevertheless, few places are ever more than quietly humming with tourist business.

From Accra to Cape Coast

Leaving Accra, the highway at first stays well inland, running through scrubby bush and farming country, hot and unyielding. Just 30km west of Accra is the first break, at **KOKROBITE**, a beach resort with a dance and music school (Academy of African Music and Arts Ltd, PO Box 2923, Accra; ☎021/66.59.87 or 027/55.40.42) which doubles as a hotel and bar – look out for the "AAMAL" sign on the main road. The Ga master drummer Mustapha Tettey Addy, an internationally renowned percussionist with several CDs on general release, is the leader of the group and joint owner of the establishment. There are wonderfully dynamic drumming and dance displays on weekend afternoons between 2pm and 6pm, and the school offers courses in African dance and drumming. The **hotel**, though quite swanky in a Ghanaian way, isn't too expensive (②–③). They also allow **camping** and have an excellent **restaurant** – a foretaste of the grilled seafood that abounds further along the coast. Another good place to stay is *Big Milly's Backyard Home* (PO Box 11167; ②), an English-owned establishment with some very reasonably priced mud-thatched cottages and rooms. The vegetarian bar and restaurant here is excellent and always lively. Nearby, you can enjoy pizza and pasta at the Italian-run restaurant *Kokrobite Garden*, or try the fabulous new Ghanaian restaurant near the beach.

THE FORTS

Soon after the Portuguese found the maritime routes to the Gulf of Guinea in the fifteenth century, they began setting up trading posts. Rumours of the vast wealth of the region filtered back to Europe and it wasn't long before other nations established themselves on the coast, building sturdy fortresses to protect their interests in the trade of gold, ivory and, later, slaves. By the end of the eighteenth century, thirty-seven such forts dotted the coastline, eight of which have since been completely destroyed. After independence several forts started taking in travellers – it's now theoretically possible to sleep at the rest houses (marked "RH" below) in at least four of them.

Recent restoration work – including the whitewashing of slave cells – has enraged African-American visitors, who argue they have a right to a say in how these relics of their history are to be preserved. They complain that the Ghanaian Ministry of Tourism is trampling on their history for profits, sanitizing the crumbling slave forts at the behest of grant-making bodies like the "white" Smithsonian Institution and USAID. Limited catering facilities at one or two forts have had to close after vigorous protests.

Along the coast from east to west, the **major forts** include:
• **Prampram** Fort Vernon was built in 1756 by the French and taken by the British in 1806.
• **Accra** Christiansborg was built by the Danish in 1659. Earlier a Swedish fortress, which at one time had probably belonged to the Portuguese, stood on the same spot. Ussher Fort was built by the Dutch in 1642. Ten years later it was taken by the French and named "Fort Crevecoeur", then passed through the hands of the Dutch and finally the British who rebuilt it in 1868. James Fort was built by the Portuguese in the mid-sixteenth century, taken by the English, and rebuilt in 1673.
• **Senya Beraku (RH)** The last fort built by the Dutch, Fort Good Hope was erected in 1702 and extended in 1715.
• **Apam (RH)** Fort Leydsaemheyt was built in 1698 by the Dutch. Occupied by the British (who named it Fort Patience) in 1782 and retaken by the Dutch three years later, it was abandoned around 1800.

Kokrobite has become a popular weekend retreat, despite the difficulty of getting here, partly because the beach – and for an hour's walk west and east – is not the public toilet that many other beaches only too obviously are. Take a *tro-tro* from the Kaneshie motor park in Accra (about ₵ 800) and get dropped at the "AAMAL" sign; from there, you may find continuing transport down the minor road to Kokrobite, or else you'll have to walk the remaining 8km. You have a better chance of getting transport down this stretch if you get off at the village just west of the AAMAL sign.

The first fort along this coast is **Fort Good Hope** at **SENYA BERAKU**. To get here from Accra, take a bush taxi to Awutu junction (not Senya junction, from where you won't easily get onward transport). From there, you can get another taxi down to the coastal village, 8km away. The village is dull, but the setting is scenic, and the trip interesting mainly for the fishing activities of the Fante inhabitants (remember, the Fante don't fish on Tuesdays). You get sweeping panoramic views from the fort which hangs over the sea, and you can **stay** the night – bucket showers included (①–②). Senya Beraku is the site of a number of **festivals** throughout the year (see p.690).

WINNEBA, the main town in these parts, perched on raised ground between the Muni and Oyibi lagoons, is reached from Swedru junction on the main coast highway. Although it is beginning to acquire a reputation for its **pottery**, Winneba is most famous in Ghana as the site of the *Aboakyer* or **"deer-hunting festival"** which takes place at the end of April or early May (see p.690). At other times of year, there's little to do in the town itself apart from watching canoes at work and fish being smoked, and enjoying the noise and bustle of dusk. You can **stay** right on the beach on the far west side of the

- **Anomabu** A Dutch lodge was founded here in the seventeenth century and taken by the British in 1665. Fort Charles was built on its site in 1674, expanded in the 1730s and renamed Fort William.
- **Mouri (Moree)** Fort Nassau was built by the Dutch in 1598. It went back and forth between the British and Dutch until it was finally abandoned in 1815. It is now in ruins.
- **Cape Coast** The original castle was founded by the Swedish then taken by the Danes and passed to the hands of the Dutch before finally being taken by the English in 1662. After a French bombardment in 1757, it was entirely reconstructed in 1760 when it lost its original design.
- **Elmina** Saint George's Castle, the oldest European monument in sub-Saharan Africa, was built by the Portuguese in 1482 with dressed stones brought from Europe. The original castle was expanded by the Dutch in 1637. Fort São Iago **(RH)**, which faces it, dates from the seventeenth century and was taken by the Dutch in 1683.
- **Komenda** Fort Vredenburg was built by the Dutch in 1688, taken by the English in 1782 and abandoned three years later. Fort English, in the same town, was founded by the English in 1663. Both forts are now in ruins.
- **Shama** Fort Sebastian was founded by the Portuguese around 1560 and occupied by the Dutch in 1640.
- **Sekondi** Fort Orange was built by the Dutch in 1640; it became British after 1872.
- **Dixcove (RH)** Fort Metal Cross was built by the English in 1691, and occupied by the Dutch from 1868 to 1872.
- **Princestown (RH)** Grossfriedrichsburg was built in 1683 by the German Brandenburgers and taken by the Dutch and later British. In ruins at independence, the fort has since been restored.
- **Axim** Fort Santa Antonia (Fort St Anthony), built in the fifteenth century, was the second Portuguese fort on the coast. Taken by the Dutch in 1642 it was rebuilt on several occasions.
- **Beyin (RH)** Fort Apollonia was built by the English Committee of Merchants in 1756.

town, at the *Sir Charles Tourist Centre*, which offers run-down bungalows with no fans (①–②), and good food – there's a saltwater pool for swimmers who don't want to struggle with the dangerous sea, and a very clean beach. You can also try *Labone Lodge* (①), *Yes Motel* (①) at the junction en route to the beach or the modest *Winneba Rest House* with airy rooms looking out to the sea (①). Out on the (almost shit-free) beach you can watch **drag fishing**, with music and singing, and fifty men hauling the net rope. Between the beach and the town an amazing **posuban shrine** is watched over by a genial priest who'll go out of his way to explain his job (see box, below). For meals, *Hut D'Eric* off the Accra road serves continental and Ghanaian dishes for around ₵7000.

Some 20km west of Winneba you can stay at **Fort Patience** in **APAM** (see p.718). Getting to Apam requires taking a taxi or *tro-tro* to the Apam junction and changing. Near the junction, you can eat cheap chop at *The Hut* (along the road to the east a little) while you wait for a vehicle. It's about 8km down to Apam – too far to walk in the heat of the day. At the entrance to town is another imposing *posuban* shrine: colourful statues of Africans mounted on horseback decorate the three-storey affair which is topped by a white Jesus. Fort Patience is beautifully sited above the town and has well water for washing (①). Food is limited pretty much to the market.

The next town is **SALTPOND**, 42km west of Apam junction (you may have to change buses at Mankessim, 35km west of Apam junction), which offers precious little reason to call in (a bypass skirts the town) though it vies with Winneba for importance. If you fetch up here for the night, try the *Palm Beach* (☎101; ③).

A better plan is to go another six kilometres west to **ANOMABU** where the *Adaano Hotel* is recommended unreservedly, especially on a Friday when it becomes the musi-

---

THE ASAFO COMPANIES AND POSUBANS

Like other Akan states, the Fante maintain a highly formalized military institution known as **Asafo** (from *sa*, "war", and *fo*, "people"). The original function of the *Asafo* was defence of the Fante state. Although that role largely disappeared after the colonial invasion, *Asafo* companies still thrive and exercise considerable political influence. They enstool chiefs – and can destool them in certain instances – and act as royal advisors.

The companies put on at least one major festival each year and also provide community entertainment in the form of singing, dancing and drumming.

A Fante town typically has between two and twelve *Asafo* companies, each identified in a military fashion by number, name and location (for example No. 5 Company, Brofumba, Cape Coast), with members in ranks, easily identifiable as general, senior commander, divisional captain and so on. *Asafo* membership is patrilineal (in contrast to the chieftaincy, which is matrilineal, passing to the next man through the line of his maternal uncle).

As well as their military-ceremonial duties, the *Asafo* are active in the arts. In every Fante town there are painted cement **Asafo shrines**, known as **posuban**, for each of the town's companies. Rich with symbolism, the *posuban* evoke proverbs proclaiming one company's' superiority over its rivals. The shrine of No. 3 Company, Anomabu, for example, is guarded by two life-size cement lions, recalling the saying "A dead lion is greater than a live leopard". The rival No. 6 Company boasts a warship-shaped shrine, symbolic of its military prowess.

Similar symbolism carries over into the vibrantly coloured, appliqué **Asafo flags** made and paraded by each company. These can be seen flying over shrines or, more often, displayed throughout a company's area during town festivities. They have recently acquired serious value in European and American galleries and private collections – a phenomenon that, more than anything else, threatens to unravel the social fabric of the *Asafo* companies.

cal focus of the village (②). Slightly cheaper and equally pleasant is *Ebenezer Rest Stop* (①). Buses between Cape Coast and Accra can be hailed outside the *Adaano*. Anomabu's fort, Fort William, is a prison, so no photos allowed – and in any case there is little to admire (see p.719).

The last place of note on this stretch is the idyllic crescent of sand and coconuts at **BIRIWA**, 3km west of Anomabu. It's right beneath the main highway, which makes it both accessible and a little too popular at weekends. Time was it sheltered various semi-resident hippies in wooden shacks at the village end of the beach, but those days have passed and there's now a fair-size crowd on the beach at weekends. There's also an excellent, if somewhat pricey restaurant at the German-run *Biriwa Beach Hotel,* on the hill behind the strand. If the comfortable S/C chalets, or more modest non-S/C rooms are beyond your budget (room 201 is the nicest by far; ⑤–⑥), they allow camping for a small charge. Supplies are available in the village above the rocky bluff.

Cape Coast

British capital of the Gold Coast until 1876, **CAPE COAST** is a relatively large town with a solid infrastructure. The site of the nation's first university and major secondary schools, your chances of running into Ghanaian students here are good. The major attraction is the seventeenth-century **Cape Coast Castle** and museum. There are no recommendable beaches nearby. Note that through traffic doesn't go via the town, but round its north side on a **bypass**, off the frame of our map.

The Cape Coast **Tourist Board** (☎042/32062) is located in the SIC (State Insurance Cooperative) building off the Cape Coast–Takoradi highway on the outskirts of town. Closer and equally helpful is the **Tourist Information Office** (daily 8.30am–5pm; ☎042/3344); this is currently located on Jackson Street, but is in the process of moving into what will be called the "Heritage House", the former governor's house.

Accommodation
Several of Cape Coast's recommended hotels are out of town, in particular in the village of **Pedu**, just north of the bypass on the road to Kakum National Park, about 5km from the centre of Cape Coast. If you're on a budget, it's worth trying Cape Coast's university hostels (①).

Fairville Guesthouse, off the main Accra–Takoradi highway on North Ola (PO Box 1039; ☎042/33322). New higher-priced hotel with all the amenities – TV, refrigerator and AC. ④.

Hotel Mudek, 5km from the centre in Pedu (take a shared taxi) (PO Box A9; ☎042/32787). Very modest hotel, but you get a large bed and it's much cheaper than anything in town. ②.

Nama Bema Lodge, Sam's Hill off Sarbah Rd (PO Box 1420; ☎042/32103). Down-to-earth choice in this price range, with a cozy bed-and-breakfast feel in a quiet, elevated location – with a fabulous 360-degree view of Cape Coast. Restaurant serves meals for ₵5000–10,000. ⑤.

Palace Hotel, Aboom Rd (PO Box 658; ☎042/33.55.66). One of the cheapest lodgings in town with acceptable non-S/C rooms. ②.

Sammo Guest House (PO Box 1312; ☎042/33242). Newer budget hotel near *tro-tro* station with restaurant and bar. A step above *Palace Hotel*, with larger rooms and friendly staff. ②–③.

Sanaa Lodge, off the Elmina Rd (PO Box 504; ☎042/32570). Comfortable accommodation with AC and minibar in the stylish, S/C rooms. The town's best. ⑤–⑦.

Savoy Hotel, Sam Rd and Ashanti (PO Box 646; ☎042/28.66). Best value in town. Clean rooms with fan. Centrally located near the beachfront on the east side of town, and often full. Restaurant serves average food. ③.

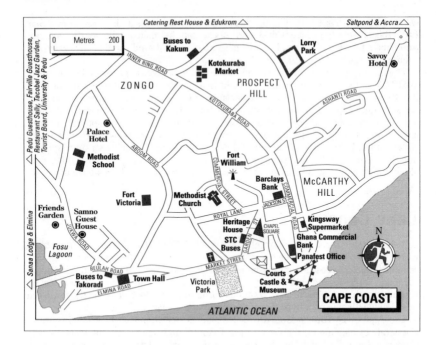

CAPE COAST

The Town

Perched on a rocky ledge that juts out over the ocean, **Cape Coast Castle** is today a classified monument open to the public. Originally a Swedish and then a Danish fort, it was taken in 1662 by the British who made it their Gold Coast headquarters until 1876. In the nineteenth century, the building was enlarged to its present dimensions (see p.719). A guided tour (₵10,000; half-price for self-guided tours) takes you

THE OGUAA FETU HARVEST FESTIVAL

Of many harvest festivals held in the region, one of the biggest is Cape Coast's **Oguaa Fetu Afahye**, which takes place on the first Saturday in September. Traditional chiefs from throughout the surrounding districts parade in sumptuous *kente*-cloth togas bedecked with gold crowns and medallions. The most important rulers are carried in canoe-like stretchers balanced on the heads of four manservants and shaded by huge parasols. They're accompanied by the queen mothers, wearing bracelets, necklaces and rings of solid gold, with more gold ornaments in their beehive coiffures. Fetish priests dance through the procession dispensing good fortune and collecting payment; palm wine flows freely. The parade lasts most of the day, terminating in **Victoria Park** for speeches by the chiefs and government representatives. Later, the streets fill up again and the party continues through the night with orchestras and dancing. This carnival atmosphere reigns for a couple of days and if you can time your trip right, it's worth making a detour. Come early and try and book a hotel in advance – most are crammed solid for the duration.

EMANCIPATION DAY

Emancipation Day was celebrated for the first time in July 1998 – its aim to commemorate slavery and the diasporic heritage.

Throughout the day, a series of elaborate ceremonies took place in Accra, Cape Coast, and Assin Manso, whereby the bodies of diasporic citizens transported to Ghana, were received at Independence Square in Accra and then transferred to Cape Coast Castle. Here, they were carried in reverse back through the "door of no return" to be welcomed by *Asafo* companies and shipped to their final resting place at Assin Manso in the Central Region.

The response to this first Emancipation Day was overwhelmingly positive, and the commemoration has now become an annual event.

through the maze of damp, suffocating **dungeons** where slaves were held before being shipped to Europe through the "door of no return". The tour also includes a visit to the small adjoining **museum**, which contains scattered examples of Ghanaian pottery, carvings and other artistry mixed with historical exhibits documenting the slave trade – don't leave without seeing the Governor's wardrobe. Displays on local religion give a few clues about the fascinating *posuban* architecture and symbolism.

The new Centre for National Culture on the road to the University is worth seeking out – it houses a **Gramophone Records Museum** (₵4000) that is a must for serious devotees of mid-1960s and early 1970s highlife music and students of early West African recordings – the collection includes 15,000–20,000 recordings representing 700 artists. Also worth a visit is the **Ecumenical Women's Centre** (Mon–Fri 9am–5pm) in Kumasi House, Awendaze, about fifteen minutes' walk away from the castle. Dedicated to the education and development of women in the area, the centre runs a batik vocational training school, in which the seamstresses make a wide range of batik cloths and clothing which are sold at the adjoining shop. Custom-made orders are accepted at no extra cost, and all proceeds go to funding the centre. The school also gives daily demonstrations of the dyeing process.

You might also want to visit the **Panafest Office** on the third floor of the SNIT House on Commercial Street near the castle (☎042/33085; Fax 042/33086; *panafest@africaonline.com.gh*), if you are interested in the roughly biannual arts and culture festival, which generally runs between the end of July and early September. The Panafest Office has now also taken over responsibility for **Emancipation Day** (see box, above).

Food and other practicalities

Though there are plenty of cheap chop houses and bars, very few **restaurants** stand out in Cape Coast apart from those in the hotels. One central and unusual place to grab a bite is in the Law Court's canteen which is open to all (₵ 2000). *Restaurant Sally* at the Mobil filling station near the Pedu junction offers reasonably priced Ghanaian and continental dishes (₵ 3000–5000), while *Tacobell Jazz Garden*, near the Centre for National Culture, sells cheap snacks (₵5000) and is a drinking spot too. For evening drinking, try the *Friends Gardens* bar, a popular hangout spot near the lagoon.

When it's time to **move on**, the lorry park and STC yard near the castle can connect you with Accra, Takoradi or Kumasi. Peugeot pick-ups and station wagons also depart regularly for the fourteen-kilometre trip to Elmina, the nicest stretch of the coastal highway, where it runs directly above the beach through endless swaying coconut trees.

Kakum National Park

If you don't manage to get to the north and the Mole National Park, you could do a lit-tle safari-ing at the superb **KAKUM NATIONAL PARK** (entry ₡500), 35km north of Cape Coast. The park consists of 360 square kilometres of protected forest, harbouring monkeys, elephants and antelopes. Park facilities are as yet quite limited, though there's a good-value restaurant at the park entrance, where the views and even the ani-mal watching are excellent. The park's infrastructure is improving month by month, and there's now a helpful **visitor's centre** at the park HQ in the village of **Abrafo** (☎042/32583). Also recently opened is a hugely popular 300-metre **aerial walkway** high through the rainforest canopy, 30m above the forest floor. Although the price is steep (₡22,000 for the first hour, ₡2500 for each subsequent hour), it's still a must, just to mingle with the birds, butterflies and squirrels amongst the towering trees and glimpses of sunshine you would miss out on at the dense forest's base. Get there early morning or late afternoon to avoid the rush.

Down on the forest floor, **trail hikes** to see the animals, medicinal plants and variety of butterflies cost ₡6000 for the first hour (₡2500 for each subsequent hour) with a mandatory guide. The best times for these walking tours are the very early morning or late afternoon; if you arrive at midday, they'll take you on a shorter trek to point out the wide range of flora, explaining the names and various medicinal and domestic uses of the different trees and shrubs. A **two-day tour** of Kakum, including a night out on a tree platform, costs around ₡40,000 per person in a group of two or more. It's at night that you are most likely to see wildlife, though the chances of coming across large mammals are very slender. **Camping** at the park is ₡20,000, and an extra ₡5000 if you need a tent, plus a fee for the guide to take you to the site.

For more information, contact the visitor's centre (see above) or the Senior Game Warden (PO Box 895, Cape Coast; ☎042/23.96 or 22.88; Fax 042/28.29).

Tro-tros are fairly frequent from the Kotokuraba Market in Cape Coast to the visi-tor's centre in Abrafo (Jukwa, or Dwokwa, the only village in the vicinity that is marked on the Michelin 953 map, is about two-thirds of the way there). Five kilometres south of the park in the direction of Cape Coast, you can **stay** in the oddly named *Hans Cottage Botel* (③), which boasts a terrace on piles over a crocodile pool. The crocs are usually invisible except at feeding time, but the bird-watching is good. It's a great place for a late breakfast after an early morning park trip, or for a late-night drink in the dou-ble-decker thatched restaurant bar overlooking the pond. Camping is also allowed.

Elmina and around

ELMINA, now a small but active fishing town, was one of the first European toeholds on the West African coast – its name is Portuguese, and means "The Mine". The prin-cipal attractions remain the **Portuguese castle and fort**, although the slow pace makes Elmina a rewarding place to relax and absorb the rhythms of a coastal town. But it's not all calm – when the fishing boats come in, Elmina can be spectacularly vibrant – and the town's unusual layout is arresting, counterposing the ocean against the lagoon and the two castles against each other. There are also a number of interesting *posuban* shrines, and this is one of the most rewarding places for photographers along the coast.

The castle and fort
One of the oldest buildings still standing in West Africa, the castle of **St George El Mina** was built by the Portuguese in 1482 – ten years before Columbus discovered

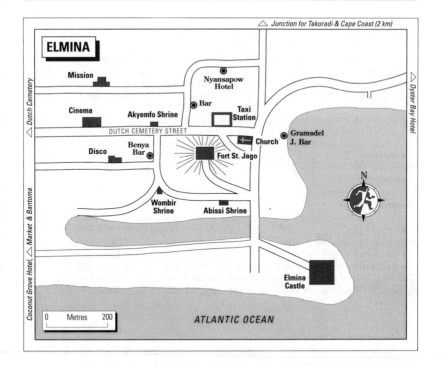

America – although the original stockade was barely half the size of the present structure. It served as the **Portuguese headquarters** in West Africa for over 150 years until it was captured by soldiers of the Dutch West Indies Company in 1637. By that time, Saint George had grown roughly to its present size. In the courtyard, you'll notice a **Catholic church** built by the Portuguese. The Protestant Dutch transformed this place of worship into a mess hall and **slave market** – an onerous image that poignantly drives home the barbarity of the trade. In 1872, the British bought Elmina castle, along with Holland's other possessions on the Gold Coast.

Given its age, the castle has held up well, but parts are beginning to deteriorate rapidly, notably the **Governor's kitchens** and the **officer's mess**, whose beautiful arched facade dates from the eighteenth century. Restoration work under UNESCO supervision is under way. Extremely good tours of the castle cost ₵10,000, but you can gain entry and simply walk around on your own, communing with the baffling past, for half the price.

Across from the castle atop a steep, partly artificial hill, **Fort St Jago** (São Iago) dates from the seventeenth century. Built to protect Elmina, it was taken by the Dutch in 1683. Formerly a resthouse and one of the best places to stay in Ghana – if only on account of its dramatic position – it has been under renovation for several years, but should soon be open again.

Accommodation and practicalities

Fort St Jago, if they *ever* finish the "renovations" which have been under way for at least fifteen years will eventually house a high-class guesthouse. Until then, you've a limited choice of **places to stay**: try the good *Nyansapow Hotel*, a family-run establishment with S/C rooms with electricity around a lovely courtyard (①–②) or, at the town entrance as you come from Cape Coast, the *Oyster Bay Hotel* (PO Box 277; 042/33605; ④), which has fairly high-standard AC accommodation with a terrace restaurant, and sometimes live music on weekends. The posh *Coconut Grove* (⑤–⑥) is situated on a nice stretch of beach, and worth stopping by for a drink, if not to stay. In general, it's probably better to stay in Cape Coast and make the short day-trip to Elmina.

For **eating**, you generally have to rely on the streetside chop stands or hotel restaurants: *Oyster Bay's* meals and setting are fine if you can afford it (₡5000–15,000 a head). Or try the good *Gramsdel J Bar* along the beachfront, which has a big selection of Ghanaian and European dishes (₡5000–6000). A good place to unwind is the Shell station close to *Oyster Bay Hotel*, where there are tables outside and music playing nightly.

Brenu-Akyinim

Ten kilometres west of Elmina, accessible by foot along the coastal track, **BRENU-AKYINIM** has one of the most spectacularly perfect beaches on the Ghana coast, a long strip of palm-laden white sand with swimmable breakers, though with a strong current. Part of the beach has been taken over on a private basis quite recently, where the sand is kept clean and loungers and other facilities are available (entry fee ₡2500). Most of the time there's almost nobody here. In the village itself, built like Elmina, between the sea and a lagoon, there are basic, clean **rooms** to be had at the *Celiamen's Hotel* (①). The cook there, Aggie, does wonderful meals of crayfish, plantain and rice.

If, rather than walk along the coast from Elmina (for which you'll need to allow a good three hours), you use **public transport**, you'll almost certainly be dropped off at the Brenu-Akyinim junction on the main highway, approximately 12km west of Elmina and 4km from Brenu and the beach. Aggie keeps a shack at the junction, *Ocean Style Restaurant*, where you can sample her cooking if you decide to wait for a lift down to the coast (₡5000–18,000).

Takoradi

If you're just in from the glitter of Côte d'Ivoire and **TAKORADI** is your first Ghanaian town, take heart – it's probably the least inviting. By no stretch of the imagination is this another scenic coastal stop. Primarily an industrial centre, the ungainly sprawl has few redeeming features but, as home of the nation's second **port**, the town has a certain vitality and it's a convenient springboard for places as far afield as Abidjan, or as near as Dixcove. Takoradi is often referred to as Sekondi-Takoradi, **Sekondi** being the naval base 10km to the east which existed before the neighbouring harbour was built.

Practicalities

The **main market**, completely encircled by an enormous roundabout, is Takoradi's nerve centre. Liberation Road leads from Market Circle south to Sekondi Road, which continues down to Takoradi harbour. All the major **banks** are on Liberation Road, as is the **Tourist Board** (☎031/22357; Fax 031/23601), where you can pick up a city map and information on travel in the Western Region. **Forex bureaux** are on John Sabah Road on either side of the market: none of them change travellers' cheques. Minibuses ply between the market and the harbour district where the **GPO**, hospital and **railway**

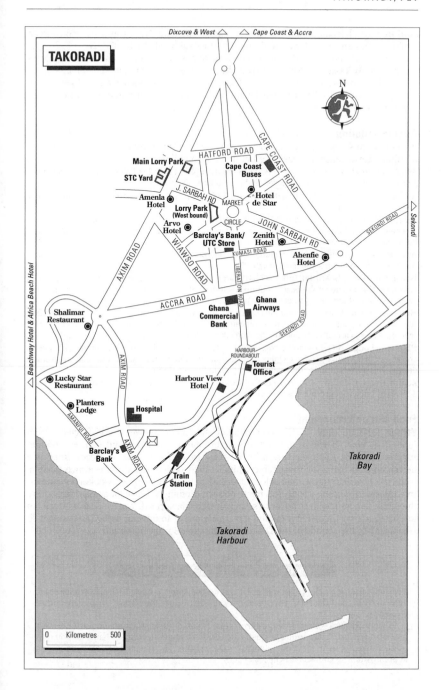

station are all located. Central **travel agents** include Nita Tours on PWD Road (☎031/24732) and Pine Travel and Tours on Bekwai Road (☎031/22201).

As you push out towards the Ivoirian border, you encounter the twin rainforest reserves of **Ankasa** and **Nini-Suhien**. The reserves – home to forest elephants, monkeys, chimpanzees and an abundance of parrots – are seldom visited and not yet tourist-ready, but Takoradi's Tourist Board can give you further information should you wish to make the effort.

Accommodation

If you have to spend the night, there are several convenient **places to stay** around the triangular town centre, all passable but none outstanding.

Africa Beach Hotel, Beach Rd (PO Box 648; ☎031/25148). Upmarket hotel with all the amenities, a nice circular pool (¢7000 non-guests) and a good view. ⑥.

Ahenfie Hotel, Axim Rd (PO Box 0608; ☎031/29.66). Large AC rooms, a video lounge, plus a very good restaurant and disco. ③.

Amenla Hotel, John Sabah Rd (PO Box 0208; ☎031/22435 or 22542). Well-kept and highly recommended hotel in the heart of Takoradi; very clean non-S/C and S/C options with fans or AC. Get there early, because the four S/C rooms fill up fast. ②.

Arvo Hotel, on Colins Ave near the motor park (PO Box 0269; ☎031/21530). Very basic clean S/C rooms with fresh linen; some have AC. ①–②.

Beachway Hotel, Beach Rd (☎031/47.34). Large and well-scrubbed non-S/C rooms, many with balconies. Good-value on the beachfront makes it the VSO choice when staying in Takoradi. First-level restaurant/bar where you can easily meet other travellers. ②–③.

Hotel de Star, on Market Circle at the corner of Califf Ave and No 2 Rd (PO Box 825; ☎031/22625). A well-run hotel, and recommended, if you can put up with the high-volume cassette stall opposite (choose a room carefully). Simple rooms with shared facilities. ①–②.

Planters Lodge (PO Box 1096; ☎031/22233). Ghanaian-owned high-priced outfit with twelve chalets set in attractive grounds. Open-air restaurant, the *Palava Hut*, serves fast food and tropical drinks. The owners promise the opening of a pool in the near future. ⑦.

Zenith Hotel, Califf Ave. Circus decor that looks like something out of a Fellini film. It's plain and a bit dirty, but a room with fan is very cheap. ①.

Food and entertainment

Street food abounds in the area around the *Zenith* between Califf Avenue and Liberation Road, if you're in need of a night-time fix of *kenkey* and fish. For budget African food, try *Effe's* restaurant in the *Arvo Hotel*. *Lucky Star* on Beach Road is a newer popular place for reasonable Chinese food (¢4000–6000) with a nice garden, while the *Shalimar* has a good selection of Indian food. The current weekend venue for **live music** is *Westline*, about 1km north of town (definitely a case for a taxi ride), where the music and atmosphere attract a smartish Ghanaian crowd. You can also venture out to *The House* on Chapel Hill (again, a taxi ride away) to unwind with young smartish Ghanaians to the sounds of the DJ in either the outdoor or indoor bar.

MOVING ON FROM TAKORADI

The main **motor park** is within Market Circle (transport to Cape Coast, Accra, Dixcove and Abidjan), and the **STC yard** is nearby on Axim Road (transport to Accra will cost ¢7000).

To get to **Busua**, you can take *tro-tros* from Takoradi to Agona junction for ¢1000 and pick-up a line taxi from Agona to Busua for ¢1500. If you're heading to **Kumasi** you may want to take the **train**: daytime departures are at 6am and noon, and there's a night train at 8pm with first- and second-class sleepers.

Dixcove and Busua

Sheltering behind Ghana's southernmost headland, Cape Three Points, the twin villages of **DIXCOVE** and **BUSUA** have long been a favourite overlanders' hideaway. There are two principal attractions: first, the cute, whitewashed hilltop **Fort Metal Cross** at Dixcove, overlooking the exceptionally animated fishing village and its deep, forest-bound, circular bay; and second, the long strand of **Busua beach,** (watch the strong current). Dixcove and Busua are no longer isolated retreats, though. Since the new highway was completed between Ghana and Côte d'Ivoire, it's easy to make the small diversion en route, and the area draws people from Abidjan as well as Accra.

If Busua does get a little crowded at weekends, and particularly in season from December to February, it doesn't detract much from the area's intrinsic appeal – the quintessential Ghana **beach scene**. It's hard to feel anything less than equable about a place where you can be met on arrival with the words "Hi friend, welcome to Busua, my name is Possible". More disappointing is the dying coconut forest all around, attacked by a morbid blight that has reduced it to a miserable cemetery – there are plans, however, to replace the trees with resistant varieties at some stage.

Dixcove and Busua are about 13km from **Agona junction** on the main highway and there's little direct **transport** from east or west going down there. Change vehicles at Agona: collective transport is about ₵1500 to Dixcove, or you can charter a cab for substantially more. If you're independently mobile, there's a fork 6km down the road to the coast: left to Busua or right to Dixcove. It doesn't matter greatly which you decide to take, as the two are connected by a twenty-minute walk through the coastal bush.

Dixcove

Fort Metal Cross was serving as a rest house for a little while under the ownership of a Dutch company for its expatriate employees until 1998, but has now been taken over by the Ghana Museums and Monuments Board who have plans of renovating it – there's yet a slim hope that the four rooms with erratic water supplies and electricity will one day be operational. The fort's site, otherwise eminent, is regrettably marred by a monolithic block of flats of surpassing ugliness right in front of it. A fee of ₵ 2000 allows you gate entry and a brief informative tour.

If you want to stay in Dixcove, an engaging fishing community with an intimate feel, strongly focused on the waterfront, the *Quiet Storm* is the only hotel (PO Box 331; ②). If you're more intent on lying in the sun and swimming, however, you'll need to be on Busua beach.

Busua

To reach **Busua** from Dixcove, you have to walk via the bush-farm footpath that leads off, northeasterly, from behind the fort. Once you get up the rise, you can practically see Busua and it would be difficult at this point to get lost. In the rainy season, you'll have to ford the shallow Busua River on the Busua side and walk past the fishing beach and right through the village. During the day, the short walk is a pleasant outing, but after dark, the path is dodgy and the walk best not attempted.

The beautiful sands and equally clean, surfy sea of Busua are together a very big plus, but watch out for the strong current. **Camping** is allowed but, because of thieving, not encouraged. The *Busua Beach Resort* monstrosity (PO Box 80; ☎031/21857; ⑥) is unfortunately unmissable on the sands. For a cozier feel, try the welcoming *Dadson's Lodge* (②), just a three-minute walk from the beach, and run by the extremely friendly Mr Dadson. The comfortable and airy rooms here are mostly non-S/C (no running water), and there's also a great restaurant off the lodge courtyard. Another seaside option is the *Alaska Beach Club* (②) – thatched rounded huts with mosquito nets, bucket showers, and no electricity; a nice place for the backpacking crowd. The newest and cheapest spot in town is the grapevine-strewn, bright yellow *Djembe Backpack Hostel* (①), run by Richard, a Rastafarian artist and musician who also offers drum and traditional Volta and Asante region dance lessons (₡5000 per hour).

If these places are full or if you're determined to avoid the inevitable overlanders' "scene" around the chalets, there are rooms available in the village of Busua. Ask anyone to direct you to *Sister Elizabeth's, Peter's, Sabina's* or *Aunt Mary's*, which, like other places, provide a bare room in a family compound (①). Reasonably priced meals are available at *Frank's Restaurant* and at *Dan the Pancake Man*. You can also eat very cheaply at the village street stalls, or have *fufu* and palmnut soup at the *Don't Mind Your Wife* chop bar.

A multitude of short **walks** are possible in the area, either west to Cape Three Points, 5km beyond Dixcove, or east along Busua Beach, cutting over the headland and down to **Butre**, just a kilometre beyond the beach, which used to have a fort of its own – Fort Batenstein – now completely in ruins.

Princestown and west to the Ivoirian border

The principal attractions on this stretch of coast are **Princestown** and **Axim,** the latter served by most buses along the main road towards Côte d'Ivoire. Both have fine castles and magnificent views, but neither can compete with the charms of Dixcove and Busua. Off the coast from **Beyin**, you will also find the traditional stilt village of **Nzulezo** on Lake Tadane.

Princestown

In 1681, Prince Friedrich Wilhelm of Brandenburg sent an expedition to the area of what is now **PRINCESTOWN** (aka Prince's Town) in an effort to break the seventeenth-century Portuguese, British and Dutch hold over West African trade. This led to the founding of **Fort Grossfriedrichsburg** (see p.719), within whose walls the Brandenburgers soon fell victim to malaria and repeated attacks by the Dutch and British. They abandoned the citadel in 1708, turning it over to the Ahanta-Pokoso chief **Johnny Konny**, who earned the dubious title "Last Prussian Negro Prince". The Dutch stormed the fort in 1748 and renamed it Hollandia. It was finally abandoned around 1800.

Restored since independence, the fort has spectacular views and is open to visitors. You can also spend the night here (①); the caretaker is very helpful. The nearby beaches are beautiful, and for real isolation you can take a canoe trip across the river.

Axim, Beyin and Nzulezo

Now in the small town of **AXIM**, **Fort San Antonio** was built by the Portuguese, probably in the fifteenth century, and taken by the Dutch in 1642 (see p.719). Today the fort houses government offices, but if you ask politely you should be allowed to visit. There's a very basic hotel on the edge of town (*Monte Carlo*; ①) with no running water or electricity. *Frankfaus Guesthouse* (②–③) is more expensive and a lot nicer with clean rooms, running water and an excellent restaurant.

Near Axim is the **Ankobra Beach resort** (PO Box 79; ☎031/21349; ④), a combined cultural centre and hotel which, if you can't afford to stay there, is worth visiting just for a drink on the spectacular palm-lined beach. The hotel and centre, created and run by a forestry expert, a civil engineer and an art historian, is built and run on environmentally conscious lines, with beautifully designed accommodation modelled on the round huts of northern Ghana, with semi-modern stone interiors, mosquito nets, and electricity only during designated hours. *Ankobra* arranges a variety of cultural excursions to nearby villages such as Nzulezo, and environmental sites such as the Ankasa and Nini Suhien reserves. Keep an eye out for African music, dance, and craft workshops and performances which the centre hosts.

By the village of **BEYIN**, Fort Apollonia (see p.719) is the last of the forts along the Ghana coastline and has rudimentary accommodation (①). Head by *tro-tro* to Mpataba, then to Bonyeri down the road towards Half Assini, and finally eastwards along the shore to Beyin (36km from Mpataba) or, alternatively, take a bush taxi from Axim to Aniyanzer and pick up another from there to Beyin.

Beyin is the most likely departure point for the stilt village of **NZULEZO**. Tradition has it that the inhabitants of the village originally came from Mali and moved to the lagoon for protection from enemies, led by a snail to their current place. Guided **canoe trips** to Nzulezo (¢12,000) can be arranged at Beyin's Fort Apollonia, which during the dry season can take at least two hours each way. On arrival, the elders of the village will have you sign a mandatory guest book and pay a fee of ¢4000. The chief of Nzulezo, a professor at Cape Coast University, is not around when the university is in session, but in his absence another elder should be able to tell you the history of the village. A donation of a local drink in exchange is expected, so don't come empty-handed. Visitors are welcome every day but Thursday, the village's sacred day.

Into Côte d'Ivoire

Onward travel into Côte d'Ivoire is simple from Axim. There are daily buses through to the border at **ELUBO**, where, if you don't cross directly, you can find accommodation with the friendly people at the *Hotel Cocoville* (☎031/0345; ③), near the motor park. It's a comfortable place with AC, S/C rooms, and its staff organize a number of excursions in the area, including canoe trips on the Tano River or the Juen Lagoon. Travellers who change at **Mpataba** junction to tackle the seashore route into Côte d'Ivoire report numerous problems and are often turned back. If you still want to try it, some details of this route in reverse are given on p.578. Last (or first) money-changing facilities in Ghana are at a big new branch of the Ghana Commercial Bank in Half Assini.

KUMASI AND CENTRAL GHANA

The **central part of Ghana** is one of the country's most attractive regions. The road from Accra, skirting past the northeast fringe of the old **Asante heartland**, is scenic and hilly. Around the great hub of **Kumasi** itself, a clutch of different routes radiate through steep scarp and forest country. Much of this has long been under cultivation – especially **cocoa**, which brings a dark, gloomy silence to the woods – but plenty is still jungle-swathed, stacked with impressive, buttress-rooted forest giants, and scattered with hillside villages. These settlements, misty grey-green in the chilly mornings, sticky and brilliantly coloured in the afternoons, are the key elements in an area to savour. Travel is easy, and the cultural heritage as rich as anywhere.

Kumasi

In the main Asante city of **KUMASI**, history weighs heavily. You feel it walking through the streets where monumental **colonial buildings** – a reminder of half a century of British domination – have become worn with time and covered in water-stained layers of ochre-red dust. Foreign edifices have taken on an African look in a town that oozes with the traditions and customs of the **Asante** – one of the most powerful nations in

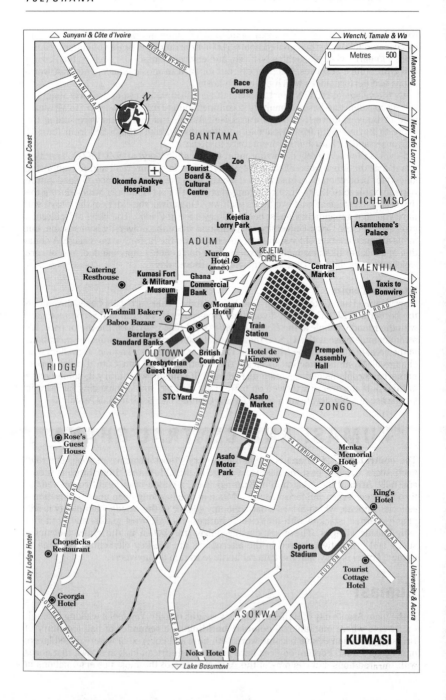

West Africa at the end of the nineteenth century. A combination of the old order and hectic modernity makes this extremely active commercial centre one of Ghana's most satisfying cities.

Orientation and information

Even in its early days, Kumasi was an imposing capital. Today it spreads widely over the hills, and is home to close on a million people. The heart of the downtown district is marked roughly by **Kejetia Circle**, a large roundabout with a wonderfully kitsch replica of the Golden Stool (see box, p.734) rising from its centre. Nearby, the **central market** – the largest in Ghana and one of the very biggest in Africa – spills over the railway tracks to fill a hollow in the city centre.

Just west of the market, the **Adum district** is the commercial centre where you'll find major **banks**, supermarkets, department stores and the post office. Most **forex bureaux** are here too, though the Sweet Money Forex, between Kejetia Circle and the Asantehene's palace, consistently offers the best rates. Up the hill northwest of Adum, **Bantama district**, site of the expansive **Ghana National Cultural Centre**, takes over.

The **Ghana Tourist Board** (PO Box 3085; ☎051/26243), adjacent to the museum in the Ghana National Cultural Centre, has friendly and enthusiastic staff, and complete guides to hotels, restaurants and sights in the Asante Region, plus large-scale Kumasi city maps. If you want to access the **Internet**, try the CEDEP Library in Adum, CPC Services in Asafo, or Africa Online on the Santase Road at the south junction.

Accommodation

Although Kumasi lacks any really luxurious **accommodation**, inexpensive lodgings abound, getting cheaper the further you move from the centre. In vacations, the university halls of residence are often open to volunteers and travellers: the pleasant **Unity Hall**, for example, has a pool, gardens and no lack of company.

Inexpensive

Ayigya Hotel, 24th February Rd, near the university junction (PO Box 3515). Clean rooms with common or private baths and fans. Restaurant, bar and car park. ②.

Hotel de Kingsway, Prempeh II Rd, Adum district (PO Box 178; ☎051/26228). Handily situated in the commercial centre, this is a big favourite. The restaurant, bar and occasional nightclub ensure a lot of activity; rooms with fans. Live high-life music on Saturday night. ③.

Menka Memorial Hotel, 24th February Rd, Amakom district (PO Box 3371; ☎051/64.32). Large, and very dilapidated, hotel about 2km from centre; S/C and non-S/C rooms with fans. Lively bar and restaurant. Rooms at front are noisy. ①.

Montana Hotel, Adum district (PO Box 1416; ☎051/23.66). Central location, within easy walking distance of points of interest downtown. Rooms with fans – or AC for a small premium – and shared facilities. The place is a bit run-down but cheap. ①.

Presbyterian Guest House, Mission Rd near the STC yard and British Council. Comfortable twin rooms in an imposing colonial building once used as the missionary's residence. The best budget place in town – a good place to meet fellow travellers – "the presby" has a low-key atmosphere that's hard to tear yourself away from. Communal cooking and eating are the norm. Camping is available if the rooms are full. ①.

Tourist Cottage Hotel, in Asokwa, not far from the stadium (PO Box 4649; ☎051/25219). A bit hidden away, but worth the search. Pleasant good-value rooms in a quiet setting. Highly recommended. ②–③.

Moderate and expensive

Catering Resthouse, Ridge district (PO Box 3179; ☎051/23635). Unpretentious and good value for money: furnished rooms, some with phone and AC. Convenient for downtown. ③.

THE ASANTE

The Asante trace their **origins** to the northern regions of the savannah belt. Along with other Akan peoples, they came to this region around the eleventh century and settled in the area of **Lake Bosumtwi**, carving farms from the wild rainforest. These districts contained rich gold fields and trade in the metal gradually developed, at first to the north, supplying the Saharan caravans. By the fifteenth century, however, the Akan also had commercial links with the Portuguese and, by the seventeenth century, they were organized into dozens of small states, each vying for control of the mines and the slave-supplying districts in the far interior where European merchants hadn't ventured.

THE FOUNDING OF THE ASANTE NATION

In the 1690s, **Osei Tutu** – the first great **Asante king**, or *Asantehene* – brought together a loose confederation of states into a single nation under his rule. **Kumasi** was chosen as the site of the new capital on the advice of Osei Tutu's most trusted adviser, **Okomfo Anokye**, an extremely powerful fetish priest. Okomfo planted the seeds of two *kum* trees in separate locations, one of which sprouted, indicating where the Asante seat was to be established (*kum asi* means "under the *kum* tree"). Having received this sign, the priest evoked the **Golden Stool** from the heavens. This "throne" descended from the clouds to alight upon Osei Tutu, and thereby became the single most important symbol of national unity and the authority of the king. The Asante nation was born.

EXPANSION AND CONSOLIDATION

Osei Tutu set about expanding his empire. One of his most important early victories was against the Denkyira king, **Ntim Gyakar**, under whom the Asante had traditionally lived as vassals. They captured, tried and killed Ntim Gyakar in 1699. Other rival powers fell in their turn, each conquered state left intact, but owing allegiance and taxes in goods and labour to the Asante. Gradually the kingdom grew to include most of present-day Ghana and Côte d'Ivoire, with only the **Fante** states of the coast putting up realistic resistance, using European allies to their advantage.

The sheer size of the Asante kingdom spawned a royal **bureaucracy** and **judicial system**. Administrative functions were transferred from the hereditary nobility to a new class of appointed functionaries controlled by the king. Even **commoners** could fill lower court offices which included linguists and commissioners or governors sent to oversee vassal states. The Asantehene himself was chosen by the queen mother, who

Cozy Lodge Guesthouse, in Nhyiaeso (PO Box 3028; ☎051/27030). Ghanaian-owned hotel away from the city centre in a quiet garden setting, with a newly-opened 24hr fast-food restaurant – also serving Ghanaian dishes for ₵4000–7000 – and bar on its grounds. ⑥–⑦.

Georgia Hotel, Harper Rd, Adiebieba (PO Box 2240; ☎051/24154). Stylish hotel with a pleasant bar in the gardens and well-furnished rooms with TV and AC. Friendly management, and a pool. Used to be one of Kumasi's best, but is now somewhat on the decline. ⑦.

King's Hotel, Ahodwo district (PO Box 8803; ☎051/24490). Small garden hotel in a quiet residential neighbourhood. S/C rooms have AC and phones and there's a car park and a bar and restaurant that "welcomes you with finger-licking meals". ③.

Noks Hotel, Asokwa district (PO Box 8556; ☎051/24162). One of the better hotels, with comfortable S/C rooms and efficient service. Some of the rooms have AC and carpets. Restaurant, bar and car park. ④–⑤.

Nurom Hotel, Suame district (PO Box 140; ☎051/40.00). Wins the prize for best design, from the colourful statue of the chief in front, to the Asante symbols on the modern facade. S/C rooms with fan or AC. The *Nurom* also has a cheaper **annexe** in the Adum district. ③, annexe ①–②.

Rose's Guest House, Ridge district (PO Box 4176; ☎051/24072). An intimate place with very comfortable and tidy S/C, AC rooms, complete with satellite TV, in a pleasant garden setting. *Rose's* restaurant is well known. ⑤.

consulted with advisers before making her decision (in the matrilineal system, successors were chosen from the king's brothers or his sisters' offspring). Though his power was nearly absolute, an unworthy Asantehene could be "destooled" – removed from the throne – by the royal family.

WAR WITH THE BRITISH

The Asante empire had reached its apogee by the year 1800 when **Osei Bonsu** ascended to the throne. The borders of the country now extended well beyond the present-day borders of Ghana, and Kumasi was a capital with a population of 700,000. In the vast market in the heart of town, trade was so healthy that the king's servants periodically sifted the sand to collect loose gold dust. Despite the prosperity, **rebellion** was fomenting among Asante refugees who took shelter in the Fante confederation of the coast. In 1806, Osei Bonsu launched a full-scale attack against the Fante and invaded their lands. The attack marked the beginning of the last phase of the great conquests.

The coastal **Fante** had traditionally traded directly with the British, and Osei Bonsu's invasion thus led to direct **conflict between the British and the Asante**. In 1824, on the death of Osei Bonsu, the British were anxious to squash this main obstacle to the control of Gold Coast trade. Hostilities, which were to simmer throughout the nineteenth century, erupted in the **First Anglo-Asante War**. War broke out again in 1826 when the Asante were heavily defeated and Britain assumed the role of "Protector" along the coast and as far as 130km inland. A third war, in 1863, was inconclusive, though Asante history relates it as a victory, with a strong invasion force from Kumasi holding the British back for a few years. After some preparation, the British marched on Kumasi in the **Fourth Anglo-Asante War** (1874), but found the palace empty since the Asantehene and his retinue had fled to the forest. The British troops took whatever treasure they could find in the palace (most of which was later auctioned in London) and then blew it up. The rest of the city was razed to the ground.

By the end of the nineteenth century, the British had annexed the Asante country as part of their Gold Coast colony. They sought to humiliate and demoralize the nation by publicly arresting the young Asantehene, **Prempeh**, and exiling him to the Seychelles. The final slap in the face came in 1900 when the new colonial governor, Sir Frederick Hodgson, demanded the Golden Stool be handed over for him to sit on. Having foreseen such a scenario, astute royal court members had made a fake golden stool and concealed the real one, which was only discovered by accident much later, in the 1920s. Nobody, not even the Asantehene, had ever sat on it. To do so would have violated national unity.

The Town

Kumasi is one of the rare West African towns where you can go **sightseeing** in the formal sense. In addition to the **museums**, other historic points of interest, like the **palace** of the Asante king, dot the cityscape, and you could easily spend a few days just checking them out. The large **central market** alone merits a couple of trips to search hidden corners for unusual finds. There's a terrible "**zoo**", north of Kejetia Circle. Be kind to yourself – and potential future captives – and avoid it like the plague.

The central market

Despite the tumbledown appearance of rambling, rusty, corrugated-iron-clad stalls, the **central market** is a fantastic place to explore, and the largest market (certainly in terms of acreage) in West Africa. Traders come from all the surrounding countries, and beyond, to buy and sell here. You can while away hours just wandering by the stalls of fruit and vegetables, provisions, plastic imports and spare car parts (if you need the latter, incidentally, "Magazine", in the north of the city, is a separate, vast district entirely devoted to spare parts). You can also search out the "zones" filled with every kind of **Asante craft** (beads, sandals, leather goods, pottery) and, most importantly, **cloth**.

This is probably the best place in Ghana to buy *kente* cloth and it's worth paying a child to take you to the row of stalls where it's actually stored – a dedicated lane in the northwest of the market, near Kejetia lorry park – as they're easily missed otherwise. Prices are high and depend on whether you're buying single- or more expensive double-weave *kente*. To add a further complication, there's *kente* woven from imported rayon and real silk. You can sometimes buy just a small piece, or even a souvenir strip.

Prempeh II Jubilee Museum and the National Cultural Centre

In the grounds of the **Ghana National Cultural Centre**, the small **Prempeh II Jubilee Museum** (Tues–Sun 9am–6pm; nominal entrance fee) holds a rich collection of Asante artefacts housed in a reproduction of a traditional Asante regalia house, few examples of which remain since the nineteenth-century wars with the British. Such buildings served both as palaces and **shrines**; note the characteristic mural decorations on the lower walls. The designs, like those found on the **adinkra cloth** for which the region is famous, symbolize proverbs commenting on Akan moral and social values.

Among the many historical articles inside the museum is the **silver-plated stool** that the Denkyira chief Nana Ntim Gyakari was supposedly sitting on when captured in a surprise attack by the Asante in 1699. This victory marked the expansion of the Asante empire and the stool, with its intricate carving and design, became an important symbol of liberation and power. Also on display is the fake **golden stool**. The real one remains guarded in the Manhyia palace, and is only brought out for special occasions. The replica was designed at the beginning of the century to deceive the British, who demanded that the most sacred of all Asante symbols be handed over to them.

Notice, too, a **treasure bag** on display that was presented to the Agona king by the fetish priest Okomfo Anokye. No one knows what the leather sack contains, for according to tradition to open it would bring about the downfall of the Asante nation. Other articles include examples of traditional dress, jewellery, furniture and musical instruments.

In addition to the museum, the grounds of the cultural centre contain a model Asante village, a cocoa farm, a palm wine "factory", performance facilities for music and dance, and a **crafts centre** where you can see how **kente** and **adinkra fabrics**, traditional sandals, brass weights and pottery are produced. Prices are fixed and seem fair. Don't miss the centre's small **library** with numerous works dedicated to Asante civilization.

Fort Kumasi and the military museum

Housed in a British-built fort dating from around 1900, the **military museum**'s collections have a heavy emphasis on modern **weaponry** captured by Ghanaian troops in World War II's East Africa and Asia campaigns. Far more interesting, but less extensive, are the exhibits documenting the **Anglo-Asante wars**, with period photographs and mementos. **Fort Kumasi** itself is an intriguing structure where, as part of the obligatory guided tour, you'll be locked in a dark dungeon, to experience briefly the manner in which the British dealt with rabble-rousers. Those who went in rarely came out alive, and a few seconds is plenty to impart a sense of the terror the condemned must have felt.

Manhyia: the Asantehene's palace

The traditional **Asantehene's palace** was sacked by the British, and the present royal residence (Mon–Fri 9am–5pm), where the Asantehene and his family live, has a curiously colonial look to it. Completed in 1926, it first served as the residence of Nana Prempeh I when he returned from exile. Until 1956, the palace also served as the **Asantehene's court**, where criminal, civil and constitutional cases were heard. Even today a traditional council presides over customary and constitutional matters

AKAN NAMES

People are named according to the day of the week on which they are born.

	GIRLS' NAMES	BOYS' NAMES
Monday	Ajoa	Kojo
Tuesday	Abena, Aba	Kwabena, Kobina
Wednesday	Akua	Kweku
Thursday	Yaa	Yao, Ekow
Friday	Efua	Kofi
Saturday	Ama	Kwame, Kwamena
Sunday	Esi	Kwesi

here: the Prempeh dispenses judgements on land disputes and chieftaincy matters every Monday and Thursday at the unusual hours of noon–2pm. Every sixth Sunday at noon, the chief receives visitors and welcomes a bottle of schnapps from the many nationals and foreigners who show up to pay their respects. If you sit out the lengthy speechifying, he will shake your hand as you leave. The museum can give further details.

The Okomfo Anokye sword

Across the street from the National Cultural Centre, the **Okomfo Anokye Teaching Hospital** contains another sacred Asante symbol in its grounds. This is the **Okomfo Anokye sword** that Osei Tutu's fetish priest planted on the spot shortly after choosing Kumasi as the Asante capital in around 1700. According to the legend, the day this sword is pulled from the ground, the Asante nation will collapse. The deteriorating state of the heavy metal blade seems an ominous portent, but locals swear that bulldozers have tried and failed to budge it – though they don't explain why.

The University of Science and Technology

When it first opened in 1952, this university was one of the largest and most sophisticated in Africa. The beautifully landscaped grounds are still impressive even if many of the buildings and facilities are beginning to show their age. A self-contained "city of technology", the university has its own hospital, sports facilities (including an Olympiclength pool, open to the public), banks, library and a limited bookshop. *Tro-tros* to "Tech" leave from Asafo market or Kejetia lorry park.

Eating

Kumasi is a fine place for **street food**, which you'll find throughout town, notably in the motor parks and markets where numerous **chop bars** serve rice dishes, *fufu* or plantains with sauce. Streetside coffee men whip up two-egg omelettes with Nescafé and sweet Ghana bread at breakfast time.

Baboo Bazaar Cafeteria (Vic Baboo's Café), Prempeh II Rd opposite *Hotel de Kingsway* in Adum. Good pizza, falafel, spring rolls and burgers. Chicken and chips for ₵8000. Extremely popular with travellers.

BB Spot, Asafo market. Clean, smart establishment on the second floor, serving up Ghanaian and continental dishes. Chicken or fish and chips ₵8000–10,000.

The Beat Club, opposite Edward Nassar St. Fast-food restaurant where you can sit outside and watch passersby. Tasty meals for ₵5000. Also a lively nightspot for drinks.

Chopsticks, Nyiaeso district, near the golf club. Chinese, and one of the best restaurants in town – usually crowded. Relatively high prices reflect the popularity (closed Mon).

Jofel Restaurant, on Airport Rd in Asokwa. Two-level establishment with a pleasant rooftop. Variety of Ghanaian and continental dishes. Live music on Saturdays.

Kentish Kitchen, at the Cultural Centre. Tasty, moderately priced Ghanaian dishes.

Moti Mahal, Nyiaeso district. Very good Indian dishes.

Nsuase, Adum. Popular local chop bar.

Royal Garden Chinese Restaurant, *Georgia Hotel*. Another good choice for Chinese cooking or a chance to try frog's legs. More refined though no more expensive than *Chopsticks*.

Windmill Bakery and Snack Bar, opposite Barclays Bank in Adum. Inexpensive Ghanaian and European fare including excellent toasted cheese sandwiches, real wholemeal bread and great almond cake.

Nightlife and entertainment

Keep your eyes and ears open for **live music** in Kumasi; shows take place irregularly at the main hotels. The best bet for a musical night out in Kumasi is the *Old Timer's Club* at the *Kingsway* (☎051/24.41). The Cultural Centre hosts programmes of music, dance, poetry and drama, as well as occasional **live concerts** – often of highlife – and less recreational **choral evenings** with church choirs. Check the centre's schedule of events.

Drinking spots are numerous, but popular ones include the lively open-air *Timber Gardens*; *Goil Rest Spot* at the Santase Roundabout, for the over 30s crowd; and the slick *Moves Pub*, near *Chopsticks*, for the smarter Kumasi crowd. On Friday nights, *Royal Basin Resort* claims to have live jazz around the poolside.

Among the **clubs**, *Berkeley's* across from the railway station (the sign can be seen from the road, but you enter from a small street in back) is currently popular and they have a good restaurant where you can eat before dancing. Other popular spots include *Kiravi*, a spacious disco in Nyiaesco district; *Foxtrap* in Bompata, which has pool tables, a big screen and dancing; *Black Panther* in Asokwa near the *Tourist Cottage Hotel*, with a rooftop setting and an underground dance floor – very popular but in the process of being renovated; and the newest slick disco, *Tsar*. Bear in mind though that clubs in Kumasi open up and close down as often as in Accra.

MOVING ON FROM KUMASI

Several major **lorry parks** service Kumasi if you're heading out by **bush taxi** or **tro-tro**. They include New Tafo park, in the north, for vehicles to Tamale, Bolgatanga, Navrongo and Yendi; Asafo park, by the Asafo market, for Lake Bosumtwi, Konongo, Koforidua, Accra and Takoradi; and Kejetia park for Mampong, Sunyani, Berekum, Wenchi, Wa and Abidjan.

The new bus station on Prempeh Road, a few hundred metres south of the railway station, is the departure point for **STC buses** to Accra (4–5hr), Tamale, Wa and Bolgatanga. Most of these destinations have twice-daily service, though runs are commonly cancelled at the last minute. Less frequent are the buses to Ouagadougou and Abidjan. Check the boards – in theory, departure for Ouagadougou is at 9am, with a stop from midnight to 6am in Tamale.

There's a daily City Express TATA bus to Mole National Park departing mid-afternoon from Kejetia Circle (be there by 2pm). Departure is usually about 4pm, arriving at Mole 2am.

The passenger **train** to Accra is runs twice a day (one service overnight), and there are also two trains a day down through the forest to Takoradi, leaving at around 6am and 8pm – a twelve-hour trip.

Fan Air (☎051/20087 or 30197) and AirLink have regular **flights** to Tamale and Accra; call M&J Travels & Tours (☎051/62.34 or 41.32) or D.J. Travel and Tours (☎051/25.37) for bookings.

On Sunday afternoons it's worth checking if there's a **soccer match** at the Sports Stadium. When the home team (**Kotoko**, meaning porcupine, the Asante symbol) plays it's wild: tickets are very inexpensive.

The best **cinema** is the Rex near the Prempeh Assembly Hall. Others include the Roxy in Manhyia; the Rivoli in Bantama; the Royal in Asawasi; and the Romeo in New Tafo. The British Council is on Bank Road (☎051/34.62).

Around Kumasi

Venturing into the rainforest hills around Kumasi, numerous villages offer a less urbanized glimpse of Asante lifestyles. Many villages – **Bonwire** to the northwest, and **Pankronu**, **Ahwiaa** and **Ntonso** along the road to Mampong – are known for the **traditional crafts** industries for which the entire region is famous, and best treated as day-trips. You may want to spend a night in the resthouse at the **Boabeng–Fiema Monkey Sanctuary** to the north, a hundred kilometres or so from Kumasi. **Lake Bosumtwi**, too, has a well-cared-for resthouse on the top of the hill overlooking the pretty shore, and makes a good retreat. If you have your own transport, even a bicycle, **the road past Mampong** to the shore of Lake Volta – once the main route through Ghana, but now very much a backroad – offers some exciting travel. A more obvious excursion, though one that is seldom embarked on, is a visit to the **gold fields**.

Kumasi is also a good base for the Bia, Bua and Digya **national parks**, the last of which is one of the country's largest, with elephants, antelopes and hippos amongst its animal population. Since the parks are not yet tourist ready, however, they are really only suitable for independent travellers; check with the Wildlife Department in Accra (☎021/66.46.54) for the latest on evolving accommodation and transport.

Obuasi gold mines

The gold mines at **OBUASI**, 50km southwest of Kumasi, are a relatively easy trip from the city. The Obuasi district is interesting but not a scenic place to visit: the whole area is scarred into a lunar landscape by the open mining pits, while the toxic drainage ponds add an alarming note to what's already a rather depressing landscape.

On Thursdays and Fridays it is possible to see gold being smelted and on Sundays and Tuesdays you can go underground and witness the mining itself. Tours of the surface works, conducted at present free of charge, are enjoyably informative (call the head of public relations on ☎0582/494 to arrange one). Only those who can

---

KENTE CLOTH

Kente dates from the early days of the Asante empire. The dazzling patterns are intended to enhance their owners' status as kings, queens and nobles. Court designs took on the name of the clan or individuals by which they were commissioned (a common pattern known as *mamponhema*, for example, derives its name from the Queen of Mampong). *Asasia* designates a pattern and type of cloth worn only by the Asantehene. *Kente*, like most African cloth, is woven in narrow strips, later sewn together. The highest quality pieces are made entirely of silk threads, which in former times were unavailable to the Asante. To satisfy the demands of royalty, the craftsmen therefore unravelled imported silk fabric and rewove the threads into *kente* patterns. In addition to the name denoting their owner, the most valuable cloths bore another name – *adweneasa* – a technical term indicating that the already complicated pattern contained an additional inlaid design. The word means "my skill is exhausted", indicating that the weaver had made his supreme effort.

demonstrate commercial or technical interest will be escorted underground, however. Obuasi is full of English and Italian expat technicians and managers who may be able to advise on accommodation if you want to stay; there are several budget **hotels**.

Bonwire

A frequent target for tourists, **BONWIRE** is a traditional Asante village and principal home of the famous **kente cloth**. Along the streets in town you can still see weavers working hand-operated looms to turn out the long strips of intricately patterned material. *Kente* is still the usual dress of Asante people on special occasions and great significance is placed on the cloth which, because of its importance and its complex design, is very expensive – especially here. Bonwire is just over 20km northeast of Kumasi, southeast of Ntonso on the road to Effiduasi. **Taxis** go to the town regularly from the Kejetia motor park. The quickest route if you're getting there under your own steam is down the Accra road, then turn left near Kumasi airstrip.

Boabeng-Fiema Monkey Sanctuary

An increasingly popular target, about 100km north of Kumasi, 22km north of Nkoransa off the Wa road, is the **Boabeng-Fiema Monkey Sanctuary** – a remarkably successful experiment in community conservation. The villagers of Boabeng and Fiema have a traditional veneration for the large numbers of monkeys living in the small patch of forest nearby. The **sacred grove**, just 4.5 square kilometres, complete with a monkey cemetery, has been set aside under their guardianship and they run the guesthouse (②) as well as keeping an eye on the primates. The forest has one of the highest densities of monkeys of any forest in West Africa and inhabitants include **Lowe's mona monkey** and the strikingly beautiful **black and white colobus**. There's a threat hanging over the reserve, however, from the rapidly increasing human population and the ravages of dry season bushfires. It all comes down to the number of visitors coming: if it makes economic sense to local people (a trust fund for entrance fees and overnight charges has recently been set up), they'll continue to support it. To get to Boabeng from Kumasi (about 40km), take a bush taxi to Techiman, a shared taxi from there to Nkoransa, and a final *car* from Nkoransa for the remaining 12km to Boabeng. There are a few places to stay in Techiman if you get stranded waiting for a *car* to fill up. Try the *Agyewiaah Hotel* (①–②) or *Emmanuel Inn* (①).

Lake Bosumtwi

Only 35km south of Kumasi, **Lake Bosumtwi** fills a crater surrounded by steep hills that rise nearly 400m above sea level. With a diameter of 8km, this is the largest natural lake in Ghana. You can get here by taking a Benz **bus** or **tro-tro** from the Asafo lorry park to the town of Kuntansi (a half-hour drive that costs almost nothing); from there you can either catch another vehicle (expect a long wait) or walk the remaining 5km to the village of Abono on the lakeshore, via the resthouse which overlooks it. You may also be able to get a direct *car* at Asafo to Abono, but these are very infrequent; ask for the "Abono/Lake" *car*.

The lake itself lies in the midst of lush greenery, a superbly relaxing scene in which to unwind. Traditional boats are still used to fish the lake, propelled by fishermen with calabashes cupped in their hands to serve as paddles. Formerly, the spirit of the lake forbade other forms of transport but, as one villager commented, "people used to be scared, but we don't believe in that nowadays." Clearly not, because expats and rich kids from Kumasi come to waterski and there are now motorboats buzzing over the lake. Government-run boat trips for thirty minutes or so cost a very pricey ¢50,000, or you may be able to find some locals to take you out on a motorboat for a cheaper price. Swimming, in the bilharzia-free waters, is fine.

The government **resthouse** on the hill (③) offers fantastic views of the natural setting. To stay here, you have to book beforehand at the regional tourist office in Kumasi (☎051/20146 or 20147). Alternatively, a woman in the village nearby rents out two overpriced rooms (no running water) for around ₡15,000–20,000.

Along the Mampong road

Within a short distance of Kumasi, the small towns along the Mampong road – which is in excellent condition – have developed reputations for artwork and handicrafts. Because these villages are almost a straight shot, it might be worthwhile arranging a taxi to take you to all three villages. The first you come to is **PANKRONU** (5km from Kumasi), a village known for its **pottery**, traditionally produced by the women. All kinds of clay objects, from water jugs to characteristic Asante *fufu* bowls, are piled high in front of the homes and sold at prices that are rather inflated compared with those in Kumasi. The women will do a demonstration for a small donation.

The next stop along the road is the town of **AHWIAA**, which specializes in **wood carvings**. Numerous shops along the main road sell tables, statues and games, but the **carved stools** you'll see craftsmen sculpting in open-air workshops along the street stand out among the wares. Throughout Ghana, such stools were not merely for decoration, but were considered prime necessities. Commonly the first gift a father would give to his child was a stool, which his soul was believed to occupy until death. To this day, stools still represent one of the most important elements of a chief's regalia and symbolize his office. When he dies, a good chief's stool is blackened with ash and smeared with the yolk of an egg, and this **black stool** is preserved in a special house in memory of the late owner. "Enstoolment" and "destooling" are terms often seen in Ghanaian newspapers.

The stools carved in Ahwiaa today are mostly made with an eye for tourism, and you may not admire the lacquers and shoe-polish dyes that give them a tawdry finish. Nonetheless, they contain many intricate **traditional symbols** (the carvers can explain what they mean), and there's no cause for complaint about the quality of craftsmanship. They're expensive, a result of the time involved in making them and the high demand from tourists, among whom they're extremely popular despite their weight. Ask about the types of wood used. It's worth avoiding the more expensive hardwoods – not just for the sake of the forests, but because softer wood is lighter, cheaper and more authentic.

Further down the Mampong road, **NTONSO** is the famed home of **adinkra cloth**. Not quite as prestigious as *kente*, it's made of cotton material (often a deep red colour) covered with black patterns. These are produced with stamps carved from bits of calabash and dipped in a tree-bark dye. Craftsmen use a variety of such stamps, some with geometric patterns, others with stylized representations of plants or animals, but most with symbols reflecting an Asante saying (see box, below). A cloth incorporating all

---

NTONSO DYE STAMPS

Nyame biribi wo soro na ma embeka mensa: "God, there is something in the sky, let me reach it"

Gye Nyame: "God must be part of everything we do," or "Alone we can do nothing unless God helps us"

Dwonnin ye asise a ode n'akorana na ennye ne mben: "The heart, not the horns, leads a ram to bully"

such symbols in its pattern was known as the **Adinkrahene** and was reserved for the Asante king, but it wasn't uncommon for the ruler to wear a cloth marked by a single symbol that reflected a specific message he wanted to convey to the people. Today, you still see these cloths being worn toga-fashion throughout the Asante country, notably at funerals and on other important occasions. Unfortunately you'll be pestered to death in Ntonso. Weavers will speed up their work as you approach to give a better impression and teenagers hassle you to buy cloth at enormous prices.

Mampong and northeast to Lake Volta

MAMPONG itself is surprisingly large and busy, perched on the lip of the impressive **Mampong escarpment**. There's a number of places to stay, but a good choice is the *Midway Hotel*, a welcoming place with basic but clean non-S/C rooms on the outskirts of town (①). Beyond Mampong, the road north curls down through formidable forest to the deep valley of the Afram River and then steeply, in a series of hairpins, up the other side to **Ejura**. The scenic beauty of this road is matched by the pleasure of being relatively off the beaten track. **Atebubu**, the next settlement, is a small, smoky town at the savannah's edge. Beyond, there's only the villages of **Prang** – which on this road, once tarred, now ragged asphalt and dirt, could hardly have a more appropriate name – and then **Yeji**, on the bleak Volta shore, where unpredictable small boats make the crossing to **Makongo**, 150km short of Tamale.

THE SOUTHEAST: AKOSOMBO, HO AND HOHOE

Southeastern Ghana is home of the **Ewe**, who have traditionally been farming and fishing people. Formerly part of German Togoland, the region has periodically provided a bone of contention between the governments of Ghana and Togo and those who favour the reunification of the Ewe, who also live in Togo. The **Ewe people** are primarily involved in maize and yam farming, with cocoa plantations adding a further cash crop stimulus to the region. The administrative capital is at **Ho**, a large town in the middle of an agricultural area rich with cocoa plantations. The mountains add to the beauty of the fertile landscapes, but the outstanding geographical feature of these parts is artificial – the vast body of **Lake Volta**, created when the dam and hydroelectric plant was built at **Akosombo** in the mid-1960s.

This region provides an interesting alternative **route to northern Ghana**, either through the remote eastern border region via **Hohoe** or straight across the great lake to Tamale Port by ferry. The forest and hills – Ghana's highest – are rapidly becoming a major draw for travellers, though transport and facilities are limited.

Akosombo

Nkrumah's pet hydroelectric project – the giant **Akosombo Dam** – once provided electricity for the greater part of Ghana, with some left over for export to neighbouring countries, but today Ghana's economy has grown beyond its capacity and the dam no longer provides surplus power. Indeed, during 1997, the diminishing levels of Lake Volta – the largest artificial lake in the world – prompted power rationing throughout the country. Amid the landscape of hills and water, the general interest of the once insignificant village of **AKOSOMBO** lies more in the **scenic beauty** – and it is beautiful – than in the traditional lifestyle of the people here, who are a broadly cosmopolitan mix of employees from all over Ghana.

Note that both the Akosombo Dam and the Atimpoku Bridge are considered strategic installations and it is therefore technically illegal to photograph them. Now that tours are available of the site, so many people have done so, however, that few officials seem concerned any more.

Atimpoku district

Akosombo's **lorry park** is 5km south of the town in the district of **Atimpoku**, a quiet locality on the main Accra road in the shadow of the large bridge spanning the **Volta River**. Taxis run regularly from here (or walk up the road to the fire station and get a lift) to the lower part of Akosombo town proper. Most of the **cheap accommodation**, however, is here in Atimpoku. Near the motor park, the *Benkum* (PO Box 36; ①) is a basic hotel with the town's least expensive accommodation. The *Lakeside Motel* (PO Box 84; ☎0251/310; ②–③), an out-of-the-way though pleasant and slightly upmarket place, is just south of Atimpoku, while not far from the centre of town, *Zito Guesthouse* (PO Box 77; ☎0251/747; ②–③) is pleasant and quiet and also serves decent food. **Street food** abounds: oyster kebabs and smoked shrimp to go with *abolo*, the slightly sugary, but not unpleasant, dumpling commonly eaten in the region. Across from the motor park, the *Royal Spot* chop bar and the *Delta Queen* serve inexpensive *fufu* and palm nut soup along with cold drinks. Finally, *Aylos Bay Leisure Spot* serves tasty Ghanaian and continental dishes (₡7,000) in a beautiful garden setting near the river. Camping is also permitted here.

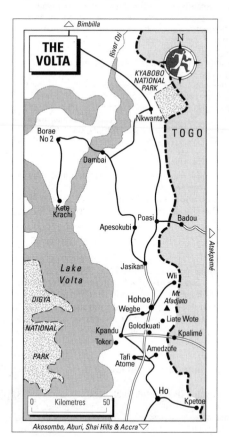

Akosombo, Aburi, Shai Hills & Accra ▽

Akosombo town

Akosombo proper consists of two communities, both of which emerged in the 1960s when workers flooded here to fill demand for labour. The first perches on a hillside, whence it commands a magnificent **view of Lake Volta** and the mountains around. The spot was too scenic to resist putting in a tourist hotel, yacht club and public **swimming pool** among the luxurious expat and executive villas. The second community, in the valley below, is a working-class neighbourhood for employees of the Volta Power Authority – no hotel, but there is a **community centre** with library, bar and the Dam Video Theatre. Buses run between the two districts during daylight hours.

The *Volta Hotel* (PO Box 25; ☎0251/66.26.39; Fax 0251/66.37.91) is ideally situated on the hill with a bird's-eye view of the lake and dam. Following recent renovations, it is now quite showy and expensive,

---

CROSSING LAKE VOLTA

Lake transport has been unpredictable for years. This deters many travellers, but while it's true that transport is erratic and timetables unreliable (there are generally less options than theoretically available), it's also true that the trip is highly enjoyable. If you're setting out from Akosombo, there'll usually be some kind of vessel in a day or two.

The official **ferry** is the *Akosombo Queen*, which plies betwen **Akosombo** and **Kete Krachi** once a week. Departures from Akosombo have in recent years been Tuesday mornings, with arrival at Kete Krachi around twelve hours later; meals are available on board. Ferries return from Kete Krachi to Akosombo on Wednesday evening, arriving Thursday morning. First-class fares with cabins are about ₵30,000, while both second class (₵13,000) and third class (₵11,000) provide a limited number of benches on which to spend the journey. Midweek, the vessel runs a shuttle between **Kete Krachi** and **Kpandu**. Unfortunately, it's often out of commission. Note that the ferry dock in Kete Krachi is a ten-to-fifteen-minute walk from the centre of this isolated town: there is nothing at the dock itself in the way of services or food. If you must spend a night or two in Kete Krachi for the ferry to arrive, you can stay at the well-hidden *Administration Guesthouse* overlooking the lake (①–②), but you'll need to find a vehicle to take you there.

When the passenger ferry isn't running, **cargo barges** – the *Yapei Queen*, *Yeji Queen*, the excellent *Volta Queen*, and the even more modern *Buipe Queen* – also make the trip, but rarely run on fixed schedules. They sometimes go as far upriver as **Yapei** (Tamale Port) on the White Volta's course to the north, but this port is sometimes out of reach at the end of the dry season, in which case the port of **Buipe**, on the course of the Black Volta further to the west, is used as the northern terminus. En route there are usually stops at **Kpandu**, **Kete Krachi** and **Yeji**. The voyage to Yapei or Buipe takes between one and two days (and nights) and you sleep on the deck. You should stock up on **food** for the trip: water and cooking facilities are provided.

For all details, enquire at the *Volta Hotel* in Akosombo on arrival or make advance contact with the Volta Lake Transport Company in the Ghana Commercial Bank building in Akosombo (PO Box 75, Akosombo; ☎0251/686 ext 204 or in Accra ☎021/66.53.00).

---

with modern and comfortable AC rooms (⑦). At least have a drink in the terrace **restaurant** overlooking the lake – the views are terrific.

If you want to visit **the dam** itself, for which you need authorization, you're only likely to get a lift at weekends. Hang around at the site office down the road from the hotel.

Ho and around

Despite its prestigious designation as the Volta Region's capital, **HO**, 50km northeast of Akosombo, remains a quiet, rural community. Set in a green valley dominated by **Mount Adaklu**, Ho is graced with a tidy tracing of narrow paved roads winding through the trees, a large hospital and banks, and even an interesting **regional museum** – some surprise in a rather remote corner like this. The **Ghana Tourist Board** can be found in the SIC building and offers helpful information for the entire Volta Region (☎0756/22431).

Accommodation

Ho has a good choice of inexpensive **accommodation**, though little to tempt you upmarket.

Akpenamawu Hotel, off main road near lorry station (PO Box 76; ☎091/81.56). Decent non-S/C rooms in a central location. ①.

Alinda Guesthouse, near the museum and directly across from *Pleasure Garden Bar and Restaurant*. Basic inexpensive accommodation, with a bar and restuarant. A bit run-down. ①–②.

EP Church Social Centre, 1km from the centre at the church headquarters (PO Box 224; ☎091/670). Very clean and inexpensive S/C rooms, or dormitory space for next to nothing. ①.

Fiave Lodge, near the central market (PO Box 352; ☎091/412). Clean and quiet, an intimate retreat with friendly management. ①.

Freedom Hotel, near the road bordering the lorry station (PO Box 739; ☎091/81.58). Newer hotel with good facilities, and an average restaurant. Something of a social focus, so often noisy, but clean and well located. ②–③.

Tarso Hotel, up the main street from the Ghana Commercial Bank (PO Box 6; ☎091/80.72). Pleasant and relatively inexpensive hotel with S/C rooms and a nice large courtyard. ①–②.

Woezor Hotel, west of the town centre (PO Box 339; ☎091/83.39). The town's most expensive accommodation with bar and restaurant. New "chalets" or less expensive rooms in the older and shabbier main block, all somewhat overpriced. ③–④.

YMCA, in the town centre, just north of the cathedral. The cheapest singles in town. ①.

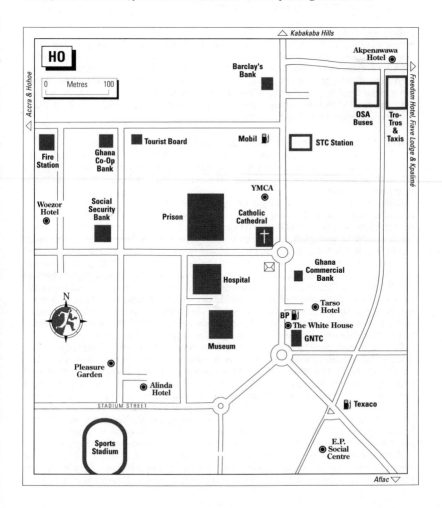

The Town

The road leading from Aflao, on the coastal border with Togo, constitutes the main street in town. It heads from the Texaco and BP filling stations in the south, past the regional police office, on to the **central market** and out to the main **lorry park** on the north side of town. Main **banks** are on this street but there are no forex bureaux. Changing cash or travellers' cheques is possible here but it takes ages while they phone to Accra for current rates.

Along this same road, you'll find a large roundabout near the **post office**. The road leading off west from here runs down to the hospital, behind which are the grounds of the **Volta Regional Museum** (daily except Mon 8am–6pm). Well presented and little frequented, the museum is worth a visit to see exhibits of ceremonial objects (Akan "spokesmen" staffs and swords), traditional **musical instruments**, and carved **stools** from various regions. **Colonial relics** complement the ethnic displays, including some dating to the district's German Togoland period.

Eating and entertainment

Street food is readily available near the main lorry park: a traditional Ewe dish is cat, often advertised rather graphically. Not far from the museum, the newly opened *Pleasure Garden* is a popular bar-restaurant in a garden setting; the restaurant serves up African dishes, and there's a stage too, which occasionally hosts live music. *Nelike* is a popular local drinking spot and the *White House* attracts a lot of travellers, serving food and drinks. In the evenings several places show **videos**, notably Foxtrot Video Theatre along the main drag.

North of Ho: Amedzofe, Tafi Atome and Liati Wote

In addition to the verdant slopes of some of Ghana's highest hills, the road north towards Hohoe passes traditional Ewe cemeteries shaded by groves of white, pink and yellow frangipani. However, explorations off the main road are limited if you don't have your own transport.

Relatively easy to get to by public transport is the village of **Amedzofe**, 30km north of Ho and just east of the road at the base of **Mount Gemi**. The staff at the newly opened visitor's center (☎0931/22007) can fix you up with a guide to seek out the village's namesake **waterfall**, difficult to find on your own and accessible by an almost vertical leaf-strewn path. At the summit of Mount Gemi you'll find a tall iron cross erected as a transmitter by German missionaries in the 1930s, but more striking are the vistas stretching in every direction. From up here, the Volta stands out shimmering beyond the Biakpa hills. There's a modest **government resthouse** in Amedzofe with sporadic electricity and water provided by an outside tap. The bungalows have large bedrooms and living rooms, a lush setting and wonderful views from the terraces (①–②). Another option is to stay at a private home near the tourist centre: Matilda's is very welcoming and comfortable (no electricity or running water; ①). Ask at the tourist centre.

From the main road, you could alternatively branch westward, 25km north of Ho, towards **Tafi Atome**, a town known as a refuge for various species of **monkeys**, including the Mona. Early in the morning, they romp unhindered through the streets and courtyards looking for scraps. Later in the day, they retreat to the surrounding bush and you'll have to rely on a guide to find them. With the help of Peace Corps efforts towards eco-tourism and community-based tourism, the villagers have set up a visitor's centre, from where you can arrange both **guides** to see the monkeys (¢3000) and **homestays** with a local family (mosquito nets included, meals upon request) – the total cost for the "village live-in" is ¢20,000, which funds local development projects.

Further north, a branch road at the Golokuati police post leads to the village of **Liati Wote** near the base of Ghana's highest peak, **Mount Afadjato** (968m), a few kilometres east of Hohoe. Residents in town will find you a guide to seek out the main village attraction, the **Tagbo Falls** (¢3500 for both waterfalls and mountain visit). It's an easy one-hour walk through dense bush full of bright flowers and butterflies, and fields of cocoa and coffee. The falls themselves appear without warning as they flow off an almost circular cliff formation covered with moss and ferns into a pool. The resthouse in Liati Wote is now a private residence, but **accommodation** is easy to arrange with the villagers and there's always the possibility of a warm beer at *Stella's Inn*.

South of Ho: Kalakpe Resource Reserve
About 15km south of Ho at Abutia Kloe, you may want to explore the **Kalakpe Resource Reserve**, with its proliferation of birdlife, monkeys and antelope. It is not quite yet developed for tourism, but there are plans underway. Check with the Tourist Board in Ho (☎0756/22431).

Hohoe and around

A town of few sights of specific interest, **HOHOE** is busier than Ho and has a number of hotels and banks, as well as a forex bureau near the post office. As a base for treks to nearby waterfalls, or as a stopping point on the eastern route to the north, it is both convenient and restful.

Accommodation
Hohoe has a number of reasonable places to stay, and your main consideration is simply one of expense.

African Unity Hotel, near the post office. Central yet quietly situated with inexpensive if slightly dingy accommodation. ①.

Grand Hotel, on the main street, opposite the Bank of Ghana (PO Box 38; ☎0935/20.53). Very central with bright rooms and a courtyard bar. ①–②.

Matvin Hotel, Jasikan Rd, fifteen minutes' walk from the post office (PO Box 397; ☎0935/21.34). Upmarket place with rooms in various categories ranging from AC chalets equipped with fridges and TV to rooms with fans and shared facilities. The good restaurant and bar have some fine views over the Danyi River. ②.

Pacific Guest House, on the south side of town, signposted off the Ho road 300m south of the post office. A nice place to stay in Hohoe, quiet and clean with restaurant and bar. ②–③.

Taste Lodge, near *Pacific Guest House* (PO Box 299; ☎0935/80.72). A better choice than the *Pacific*, though slightly more expensive. Very clean rooms with private porches in a relatively quiet garden setting. Excellent restaurant with reasonable prices. ③–④.

Eating
For cheap **eating**, the area around the post office abounds with street stalls. Near the *Grand Hotel*, the *Eagle Canteen* does good and inexpensive Ghanaian dishes like *fufu* with palm nut soup. Also good is the *Winatrip* bar, a few minutes' walk from the post office, near the Glamow department store. Slightly upscale is the *Maryland Restaurant*, past the *Grand* as you head towards the *Matvin*. In the evening, try the ultraviolet lights and grassy lawn at the *Prestige Terrace Bar*, or seek out the *Tanoa Gardens*, off the

---

MOVING ON FROM HOHOE

The main motor park is south of the centre on the Ho road. Vehicles leave daily for points north (Kadjebi, Nkwanta and **Bimbilla**) as well as for **Ho** and **Accra**. Bush taxis also go direct to Kpalimé in **Togo**. Besides the STC bus that leaves daily at 4am **to Accra**, there is a private bus that leaves from a point near the Mobil station at 9am.

main road near Ghana Commercial Bank, which has music and better food. For a sit-down meal, the restaurant at *Taste Lodge* is outstanding for Ghanaian dishes.

Wli Falls and on to Togo

The most obvious target for sightseeing around Hohoe are the **Wli Falls**, 20km to the east. *Tro-tros* are relatively frequent from the Hohoe motor park to the village of Wli which nestles at the foot of the hills forming the Togolese border. You'll be shown to the Game & Wildlife office to pay a ₵500 fee and be assigned a largely unnecessary guide. The path to the falls crosses and recrosses a winding brook over eleven log bridges. Set in a coomb among thousands of nesting bats, the cascade plunges thirty metres into a pool just deep enough for swimming.

If you've got the gear, you can **camp** by the falls, where the tranquillity will only be disturbed by kids shooting the bats with home-made flintlocks and locally manufac-tured shot. If you want to try the local bat, they'll gladly sell you their catch, and even cook it up for you.

To continue **to Togo**, Ghana border formalities are casually carried out at the east-ern end of Wli. From there, you must walk the half-kilometre to **Yipa-Dafo** for the Togo crossing. Transport onwards from here heads either to Dzobégan or Kpalimé, both routes tracing the scenic curves of the Danyi plateau.

West of Hohoe

Off the Kpandu road, 10km west of Hohoe, the "seven-stepped cascade" **Tsatsudo Falls** provide another opportunity for exploration. Stop at the village of Alavanyo Abehenease and pick up a guide there. **Ferries** theoretically leave **Kpandu** Wednesdays and Fridays at 3pm to arrive in Kete Krachi six hours later. Check sched-ules as they are notoriously unreliable (see p.744).

The route north and Bimbilla

As the route towards Tamale continues north, cultivation declines and the road nar-rows noticeably. Between Jasikan and Poasi, it deteriorates into deep ruts and channels dug out by the overloaded yam lorries that ply the route. Arriving at Nkwanta, you can branch left towards **Dambai** to catch a fifteen-minute ferry or canoe across the lake (boats leave several times daily) or you can continue north over the flat open land-scapes that lead directly to Bimbilla. En route is the **Kyabobo National Park**, home to several large animals including lions, leopards and elephants, but as yet undeveloped and therefore only accessible to independent travellers. Check at the Tourist Board in Ho (☎0756/22431) for the latest information on the park's facilities.

BIMBILLA provides a convenient place to break up the long trip from Hohoe to Tamale. **Accommodation** can be found here at the basic *31st December Women's Movement Guest House* on Salaga Road in the town centre (①). Though there's no elec-tricity, it's a comfortable and welcoming place. If it's full, they'll direct you to the *Teacher's Hostel* on the Yendi road (①). For **food**, the *Kotoko Bar* near the old market is a good place to head for filling rice and meat dishes during the day, or grab a bite with the regulars at the *Pito Bar* near the clinic. The town's best address for a cold drink is the *Work and Happiness Bar*.

It was in a nearby village to Bimbilla that the **Konkomba-Nunumba "war"** started in 1994, sparked by an argument over a guinea fowl and breaking out into ethnic vio-lence between local Nunumbas and Konkombas over land rights. The clashes took the lives of several thousand people, orphaned hundreds of children and cost billions of cedis in homes and businesses destroyed (see p.699). Because of these troubles, it is not a bad idea to report in to the District Chief Executive when you arrive; he can help with accommodation and other practicalities too.

MOVING ON FROM BIMBILLA

Buses leave for **Kete Krachi** (linked by ferry to Akosombo) Monday, Wednesday and Friday between noon and 3pm. Daily buses to **Tamale** leave between 5 and 6am or you can try to catch a seat on the Wulensi bus which passes through Bimbilla around 9am. The daily bus to **Accra** via Hohoe leaves at 11am and arrives in the late evening.

NORTHERN GHANA

Coming either from the coast and Kumasi, or up the country's eastern fringe, you'll be struck by the changing landscape, as the central forests give way to arid, low-lying **grasslands**. Due to the harsher, unpredictable climate and the effects, to this day, of the slave trade (from which the inhabitants of the open plains and plateaux lacked natural protection), the region is sparsely populated, characterized by traditional **compound agriculture**. The few urban centres like **Tamale** or **Bolgatanga** seem more subdued than their counterparts to the south.

The main peoples of the north include the More-speaking **Dagomba**, with their capital at Yendi, and the **Mamprusi** people, based around Nalerigu. The **Gonja**, with their capital at Damongo, are an interesting ethnic group, formed partly of the remnants of sixteenth- and seventeenth-century Mande-speaking migrant invaders from Songhai in the north, and partly of local Voltaic-speaking peoples. As a result, the Gonja, who are mostly Muslim, speak different languages according to their class – the nobles using a dialect of Akan known as Guang, and the commoners speaking Wagala. **Sudanic influences** have been important in this region, reflected in architecture, customs and dress – *boubous* for the men and long veils for women, draped over their heads. In short, the north is a completely different world and, with the exception of the popular **Mole National Park** – easily visited and well set up for inexpensive stays – a region where you're unlikely to run into throngs of fellow travellers.

Tamale

Capital of the **Northern Region**, **TAMALE** is a large commercial town and junction of the main roads leading from Burkina Faso in the north, Togo in the east and Accra and Kumasi in the south. Despite its size and importance, it lacks the slightest cosmopolitan spark, and you're not going to want to spend an inordinate amount of time here. Still, if you are stopping over en route to other destinations, you'll find a reasonable number of hotels and diversions. Note that the water is a constant problem in Tamale, with the taps often dry.

The **Ghana Tourist Board** has now opened a regional office in Tamale, in the Labour Building on the same road as the *Tohazie Hotel*. Although the office is not always open, it's probably worth a visit to see if there have been any developments in their plans for excursions to the Mole National Park and around the region.

Accommodation

Accommodation in Tamale tends to be basic. Some places run to S/C rooms with AC, but problems with running water are perennial.

Al Hassan Hotel, across from Ghana Commercial Bank (PO Box 73; ☎071/22834). Balconied rooms, with or without showers, around a central courtyard. None too clean (especially in the shared showers) and rarely quiet. Its proximity to the motor park, plus the restaurant and video theatre, make it a bit of a caravanserai where you might run into other travellers. ②.

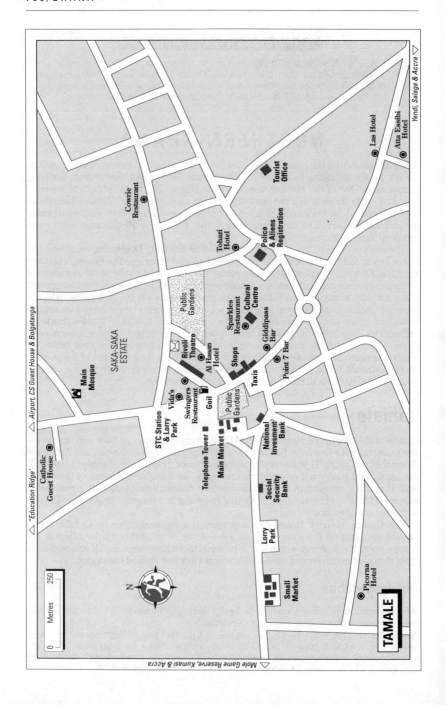

Atta Essibi Hotel, St Charles Seminary Rd (PO Box 233; ☎071/25.64). Reasonable if dingy rooms, some S/C, on the southern fringes of town. ②–③.

Catholic Guest House, Bolgatanga road near the Agricultural Turning Point (PO Box 18; ☎071/22267). Breakfast is included in the price of the S/C rooms in a garden setting. Very popular and often full. ①–②.

Christian Services Guest House, near the Agricultural Turning Point. Doubles with fans are more basic than at the *Catholic Guest House*, but it's cheaper here and the staff are friendly. ①–②.

Las Hotel, Hospital Rd (☎071/22.17). Comfortable S/C rooms with fans, plus a very popular bar and nightclub. A lively town meeting place worth a visit even if you don't stay here. ③–④.

Picorna Hotel, Kaladan Park (PO Box 1212; ☎071/26.72 or 20.70). Perhaps the best of the lot with S/C, AC rooms, hot water and a nice garden. Reasonable bar and restaurant on grounds with very large outdoor movie theatre and performance stage area. ③.

Tohazie Hotel, 1km from the centre (☎071/23610). Several muraled round huts – S/C, some with AC – in a quiet off-the-road setting with a decent restaurant. ②–③.

The Town

The centre of town wraps around the **motor park** and STC station, easily recognized by the towering telephone transmitter which juts up next to it and can be seen from almost anywhere in town. The **central market** (good for locally woven cloth) and major **banks** are an easy walk away. Next to the market is a shaded **public garden** that makes a good place to read the *Daily Graphic* (usually a day or so late in these northern parts) or watch the adept draughts players who gather here daily for lightning-quick tournaments. A paved road leading out from the west of the market heads down past the Social Security Bank and a small market before arriving at a large **classified forest** – a rather unusual thing to find in the middle of an important administrative town. The shade of the teak trees makes for an excellent place to retreat from the afternoon heat, which reaches oppressive levels on the exposed avenues downtown.

The **National Cultural Centre**, near the central market, off the Yeji road, is in a horrific state of repair, but holds sporadic performances of **regional music and dance**; in the afternoons, you can sometimes catch a rehearsal. If nothing's going on, there are good leather stalls opposite. Don't confuse the centre with the Tamale Institute for Cross Cultural Studies (TICC) – where the man in charge is a mine of information on northern culture and society. You can watch some excellent **soccer** on Sunday afternoons, when major Ghanaian teams play at the main stadium.

It's possible to rent a **bicycle** in town (hotels seem able to help) and take it up to Education Ridge, off the northwesterly road out of town. There's a fine ride commencing behind the Polytechnic and running for about 8km through lovely villages, coming back the same way. If you need to cool down afterwards, check out the **swimming pool** at Kamina barracks (small entrance fee), about 3km out of town on the Bolgatanga road.

Eating and nightlife

There are plenty of **places to eat** in Tamale, including the hotel restaurants. All around the Goil fuel station after about 6pm there's a mass of street food, especially guinea fowl. For something a little more formal, *Sparkles Restaurant* does a good chicken curry with rice and has really good salads. The *Cowrie Restaurant* (Kalpuni Estates) is another popular and straightforward spot for European and Ghanaian food, while *Vida's* and, especially, *Swingers* both do good chop. But the best place at the moment is the *Picorna Hotel* which serves great kebabs and has a popular **disco**. *Las Hotel*'s *Sweet Gardens Chinese Restaurant* is also popular.

The *Giddipass* **bar** is a large set-up with rooftop seating – a good place to come for an evening drink with views out on the town. Across the street, *Point 7* (with music) is

MOVING ON FROM TAMALE

As the north's major city, Tamale is the springboard for **Burkina Faso** via **Bolgatanga**, and the road north is in excellent shape. Heading south, the road is paved to **Kumasi and Accra**, and passes through **Yapei** where you cross Lake Volta. On the west side of the lake the Accra highway splits from the road going west to **Sawla** in **western Ghana** via **Damongo**, which is the point of entry to **Mole National Park**. STC and OSA **buses** head in all these directions as do *tro-tros* and taxis. There are also two daily buses from Tamale southeast to **Bimbilla** where you can continue to Accra via eastern Ghana and **Hohoe**.

Tamale also has a **ferry** link with Akosombo and the south. The boat leaves from Tamale Port (Yapei), to which there are buses from Tamale motor park. Full ferry details are given on p.744.

There are regular AirLink **flights** to Accra, bookable in town through M&J Travel & Tours (☎071/24.26 or 24.35).

reasonable for a cold beer and you can while away a pleasant few hours on Education Ridge (ask for Tamasco, the Tamale Secondary School) in the *Drop In* bar, or in any of the *pito* bars around town. In the evenings, the Rivoli Theatre attracts a big crush to see dated **movies** (Hindi, kung fu, Rambo). It competes with a rash of **video** theatres throughout town – look out for the street-corner blackboard announcements.

Mole National Park

Set in the savannah country west of Tamale, the 5000-square-kilometre **MOLE NATIONAL PARK** (open throughout the year, entrance fee ¢4000) protects a wide variety of fauna – including elephants, lions, leopards, buffalo and numerous species of antelope, monkeys and birds – in an environment little differentiated but for the Konkori escarpment, which runs northeast to southwest. Although the concentration of animals is not as high as in some other West African parks, Mole's striking advantage, if you don't have your own transport, is **ease of access**. Christmas is the best time to visit, when animals are most visible and the mosquitoes least oppressive (at other times it's vital to have repellent). From the lodgings inside the park, armed rangers run inexpensive foot safaris to track the game. A network of tracks crisscross the park, and in the dry season you can also cover a lot in an ordinary car.

Getting to the park couldn't be less complicated, since an OSA bus leaves regularly from the transport yard in **Tamale** (2pm daily except sometimes Sunday, but check at the station to be sure; the four-hour ride costs ¢4000) and takes passengers all the way into the park, dropping them off at the motel (the last stop). Be sure to purchase tickets early in the morning to ensure a space as the bus is popular and always crowded. Reservations for the return bus to Tamale must be made the night before departure at the *Mole Motel*. There's also a daily City Express bus **from Kumasi** (see p.738). If you're coming from any other direction, most obviously Bouna in Côte d'Ivoire or Wa, you can connect with one of these buses at **Damongo** (other transport is extremely rare), where they stop before continuing into the reserve, although be warned that they are very often full. Drivers and buses stay the night in the reserve, and depart again for Tamale and Kumasi at 5–6am, so you will really need to stay at least two days in the park in order to see any animals.

Accommodation and other park practicalities

At the park's entrance, the *Mole Motel* perches on a bit of a hill dominating two artificial water holes where animals gather to drink in the dry season. **Accommodation** ranges from rooms in a bunkhouse to twin-bed spacious chalets with large bathrooms and screened verandahs overlooking the water hole (②–③). Electricity and water are fairly reliable and there's also a swimming pool and **restaurant** – though you have to order in advance for meals and there's little choice. If you're arriving by bus in the evening, eat before leaving or bring your own food: you won't get anything much until next morning's breakfast. The motel turns its electricity off from 11pm to 6am. If you have a tent, you can **camp** for next to nothing near the motel buildings, using the pool's toilet block and showers.

In addition to the motel, two **camps** may still be open (no provisions; bring your own bedding and food). **Lovi** is in the centre of the park about 30km from the motel and **Konkori** is in the northeast, near the scarp (both ①). You need your own vehicle to get to the outlying camps, although park vehicles can occasionally be used for a fee. The only vehicles that can be easily rented at the park are the rangers' **bicycles** (₡1000 per day).

Reservations can be made through the Senior Warden, Mole National Park, PO Box 8, Damongo, Northern Region (☎071/25.63), or through the Chief Wildlife Officer, Dept of Wildlife, PO Box M.239, Accra; ☎021/66.46.54). In the dry season – especially during weekends or holidays – you should be sure to reserve in advance as accommodation is often booked out. During the rains, this doesn't seem to be much of a problem. It's always worth telephoning to see if it has recently rained: if it has you're not going to see many animals.

Game viewing

When you check in at the motel, book a ranger to wake you in the morning for a **walking safari**. An official hourly fee of ₡2500 is required, but worth it, because the guides are generally quite helpful and know where to find what's around. Your chances of seeing **elephant**, **antelope** and **buffalo**, at dawn near the motel water hole, are relatively good.

To have any real chance of seeing other large animals, like **lions**, you'll need a vehicle. The motel claims to offer Land Rover rental, at reasonable rates, but they're normally broken down. In the absence of other transport, you might therefore try your luck with other park visitors. Even with your own transport, for safety reasons you're obliged to take a ranger to help in the quest for animals.

Wa and the Upper West Region

Capital of the Upper West Region, **WA** is predominantly Muslim as the many **mosques** dotting the townscape attest. Although noticeably poorer than towns in the south, shortages of food and other goods no longer pose the problems they did fifteen years ago. The **market** near the lorry park is large and well supplied.

Wa is home of the **Wala** people who migrated from Mali. Upon arrival in Ghana, they chased the resident Lobi population to the west and converted the Dagarti inhabitants to Islam. The **traditional chief**, the Wa Na, still lives in a large white **palace** built in the Sudanese style. You can visit the palace (located behind the government transport yard), but if you do so you're expected to greet the Wa Na. Courtiers outside will arrange this; ask permission before taking photos. Apart from his ceremonial role, the Wa Na still adjudicates disputes between his subjects. The small Wa museum would be worth visiting if there was anything in it: it's just a shell.

Besides local people, a number of office workers have come from outside to work in local administrative posts. Even so Wa feels remote from Accra, and even Tamale seems positively metropolitan in comparison.

The **Ghana Tourist Board** is located in the Ministry of Trade and Industry (PO Box 289; ☎0756/22431), and can offer information on nearby sites.

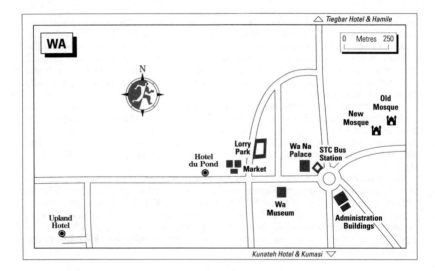

△ *Tiegbar Hotel & Hamile*

WA

0   Metres   250

N

Old Mosque

New Mosque

Lorry Park

Hotel du Pond

Market

Wa Na Palace

STC Bus Station

Wa Museum

Upland Hotel

Administration Buildings

Kunateh Hotel & Kumasi ▽

Wa practicalities

The *Kunateh Hotel*, a ten-minute walk from the OSA station, has the best-value accommodation in town, with clean comfortable rooms and an upbeat atmosphere, but get there early since it fills up fast (①). A fallback budget option is the clean *Hotel du Pond* at the west end of town, past the motor park on the road to Dorimon (①). The *Tiegber* (meaning "stretch your leg") *Catholic Diocesan Guest House* is on the outskirts of town, but has extremely clean rooms, a garden drinking bar, and a good restaurant run by the friendly nuns (②–③). The upmarket option in Wa is the *Upland Hotel* (PO Box 308; ☎0756/22180; ③–④), with a garden bar and restaurant, but it's also a bit out of town.

The restaurant at *Tiegber* is probably the best choice for Ghanaian and continental dishes, but you will have to take a taxi to get there. You can also try the slightly more expensive restaurant at the *Upland*. Other than that, meals are pretty much limited to the many **chop bars** located around the market and transport park. Cold beers can be had at the *Meet Me There*.

If you are interested in working and staying in a development context, then contact the **Suntaa-Nuntaa project**. Located near the *Upland Hotel*, this is a tree-planting initiative, aiming to provide local women with the means to obtain regular supplies of fruit and fuel wood. Up to half a dozen overseas volunteers stay each year to help out and involve themselves in local life: you'll be expected to make a modest contribution to your keep.

STC **buses** leave for Tamale twice daily, Kumasi daily, Tumu daily, Hamile via Lawra twice daily, and three times a week for Bolgatanga.

Around Wa

Lawra, 80km north of Wa on the road to Hamile, is well known locally for its **musical instruments**, notably balafons. Lawra also hosts the culmination of the important northern harvest festival of **Kobine**, now a nationally televised event, which usually takes place in mid-October. Dancing and percussion teams come from throughout the north to take part. **Accommodation** is available at the *Catering Guest House* (①–②) or the *District Assembly Guest House* which is rarely used despite the running water in the bathrooms and periodic electricity (①–②).

Hamile, in Ghana's far northwest corner, 35km north of Lawra, is a regular crossing point for Burkina and has a couple of places to stay. The one near the petrol station offers occasional highlife bands. Hamile's market is held on the second day of the six-day cycle. It's easy to visit Burkina briefly, whether you have your passport or not (much less your visa): Ghanaian and Burkinabe officials are unlikely to mind if you want to pop across the border for a few hours. There's a direct STC bus from Hamile to Accra on Fridays at 4.30pm.

On the Kumasi road **south of Wa**, there are interesting mosques at **Sawla**, **Maluwe**, and especially at **Bole** and **Banda Nkwanta** (one of the oldest in the district). They all date from the sixteenth-century Gonja conquest.

Navrongo and around

Coming south from Ouagadougou on the main highway, **NAVRONGO** is the first Ghanaian town. In the middle of a vast but undeveloped **agricultural region** (where crops include rice, millet and yams), it has a distinctive rural flavour. This is the second town of the Upper East region (Bolgatanga being the first). The people here are mostly **Kassena** farmers, part of the Gourounsi group of closely related language speakers.

Navrongo enjoys a reputation in the north as a centre of education because of its large secondary school. It was also one of the first towns in the region to have a church built, in around 1920. This, now a **cathedral**, was done in the traditional style with *banco*, and the interior decorations reflect regional art and cultural values. Today it's one of the few "sights" in town and definitely worth a visit, Sundays especially.

Navrongo practicalities

Navrongo still has very limited facilities, which make it less convenient as a stopping point than Bolgatanga, but the *Catholic Social Centre* does have good clean **rooms**. It's about 300m behind the market and any kid can show you the way (②). *Hotel Mayaga* is a slightly better option, with some AC rooms (①–②).

Numerous **chop houses** and bars crowd around the market and adjoining motor park. *Pito* bars are also plentiful. Evenings you have your choice of several **video theatres** showing "action" and "brutal" films.

Daily STC **buses** link Navrongo to Bolgatanga and Tamale (buy your ticket in advance as these are often full), and there are also services to Burkina's capital, Ouagadougou, several times a week, although **taxis** are more frequent and faster. Heading west, the buses stop at Tumu, from which point you can get onward transport to Wa and Côte d'Ivoire.

Around Navrongo

Some 6km from Navrongo, down a turning off the Tumu road, is the *Tono Guest House*, built on the edge of **Tono Lake**. Sometimes referred to as the "Akosombo of the Upper Region", the lake resulted from a dam designed to create a massive irrigation project for sugar, rice and tomato production. There's a pool, sports facilities and first-class bird-watching on the dam lake. The **guesthouse** is one of the best in the north, though there's no guarantee you'll be offered a room, especially not if it's already busy (①–②).

Twenty kilometres further west, beyond **Chuchiliga**, are the **Chiana-Katiu caves**, 1km out of Chiana village. They feature natural rock formations that appear, eerily, to be of human construction – though no one seems to know much about them.

Five kilometres north of Navrongo on the Burkina border, the **sacred crocodile pool** at **PAGA** has become a popular destination and something of a fleecing operation. When you approach the lake, a hustler brandishing **chickens** runs up to prevent you from getting too close without paying. He'll demand at least ₵5000 for the chicken, and, money in hand, will ask for another ₵2000 for your right to take pictures. After you've paid, the crocs are summoned and you pose for snaps holding their tails or squatting lightly on their backs. Finally the chicken is fed to them. Expect to feel ripped off – it's not so much the amount you pay, but the way they grab it. Pick-ups run regularly up to Paga from Navrongo.

Bolgatanga and villages of the Upper East

As capital of the Upper East Region and of the Grusi-speaking **Frafra** people, **BOL-GATANGA** is much larger and faster-growing than Navrongo. Growing too fast, perhaps, for it's own good – it looks a real mess. However, if you're entering the country from Burkina it's a good place – far better than Navrongo – to take care of business, change money or find decent accommodation. The large town **market** is a good place to hunt for local **handicrafts**, especially leather, and there are a number of interesting sites nearby.

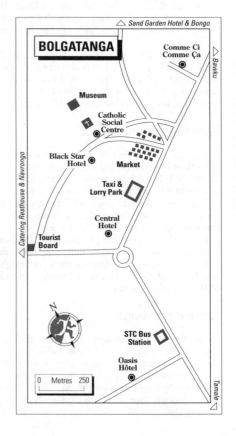

Accommodation

Most accommodation in Bolga (with the exception of the excellent *Catering Rest House*) is at the budget end of the scale, but there's plenty to choose from – and new lodgings pop up all the time.

Black Star Hotel, Tamale road (PO Box 40; ☎072/23.46). A reasonable stand-by, with surprisingly clean shared bathrooms, loads of good atmosphere and occasional disco nights. ③.

Catering Rest House, in the Bukere quarter (PO Box 50; ☎072/23.99). Expensive bungalow-type rooms – and a fifty-metre swimming pool. ③.

Catholic Social Centre, Tamale road (PO Box 5). Clean and secure individual non-S/C rooms, plus a welcoming management. Only slightly more expensive than the dive hotels. Dorm space also available although they often don't say so. ①.

Central Hotel, Community St opposite the market (PO Box 44; ☎072/22.98). Ideally located as the name suggests and a little nicer than the average, with clean S/C rooms and a very friendly management. ②.

Oasis Hotel, Kumasi road (PO Box 297; ☎072/30.08). In a quiet area a couple of hundred metres from the STC station this reasonable hotel offers clean, S/C and non-S/C rooms. ①–②.

Sand-Garden Hotel, Daportindongo (PO Box 47; ☎072/34.64). In a decent location with very clean S/C and non-S/C options. Good value. ①–②.

The Town

The main feature downtown is the **central market**, walled in around large boulder formations. Many goods are still handmade in the market itself. **Leather items** (a local speciality), superb **basketwork** and clothes are all produced here and have their own sections. Beautiful examples of handmade smocks – sewn from locally woven material and commonly worn by men throughout the region – are still sold more for local consumption than for the tourist market. The main market day is on a three-day cycle.

Bolgatanga has a **museum** in the administrative block behind the *Catholic Social Centre*, which exhibits the region's cultural, historic and ethnographic heritage in two small rooms (small entrance charge). It's not a big draw, but an interesting way to spend an hour or two, with displays of stools, pots and musical instruments.

The **Ghana Tourist Board** has a regional office near the *Catholic Social Centre*, where the staff are extremely receptive to enquiries (PO Box 395; ☎072/34.16). They are beginning to compile information about little-known regional sights, and eventually plan to organize excursions in the north.

Eating

A pleasant garden **restaurant** is the *Comme Çi Comme Ça* where dishes like guinea-fowl with rice and salad go for around ₵4000 – a price most locals find expensive. *Top in Town* is a smaller version of *Comme Çi Comme Ça* at the edge of town on the Navrongo road, while *Sand Garden*, in a similar vein but cheaper, is behind the fire station. If you want really inexpensive eating, an alley of cheap **chop stands** and **pito bars** runs behind the *Black Star*, near the Catholic social centre. The favourite local dish is *TZ*, often eaten with *kino* sauce made from bitter green leaves. A more specialized Bolga taste is hot **dog**, available as very spicy kebabs from stalls at the Tamale taxi station, and only appreciated by strong constitutions.

MOVING ON FROM BOLGATANGA

Lots of **taxis and tro-tros** leave Bolgatanga daily for Ouagadougou, Kumasi and Accra from the main taxi and lorry park. Smaller villages in the vicinity (see below) are also served. Vehicles for Tamale leave from a separate motor park near the police station. STC **coaches** have regular departures for Accra, Kumasi, Sunyani, Tamale and Wa from their own depot.

Around Bolgatanga and the Upper East Region

Bolgatanga has quite a hoard of local interest if you're here for a few days. If you don't have transport of your own, it's worth enquiring in town about **renting a bicycle** to get you around the closer sites. The following destinations are ordered clockwise.

North of Bolgatanga

Sambrungo, 8km out of town on the Navrongo road, has a **night market**, offering an atmospheric – romantic even – stroll through the lanterns in the cool, evening air. Trouble is that it's not easily accessible by public transport so you may have to walk, hitch or cycle there and back.

Heading out of town to the northeast, the turning to the left (which takes you to the *Sand Garden* restaurant) runs out towards the Burkinabe border via the village of **Bongo**, 15km away. Two drinking spots on the outskirts of Bolga, *Meet Me There* and *Monkey No Fine*, are worth a pause en route. The goal at Bongo is the Bongo Hills and notably **Bongo Rock**, which, when thumped, makes an appropriately resounding boom that can be heard all over the district.

Eastwards to Bawku

The road **east from Bolga** takes you through the villages of Nangodi, with sacred fish and a disused gold mine, Zebilla, with beautifully decorated houses (try to get invited in, as the hospitality is superb), and on to the (black) market town of **Bawku**, right on the Burkinabe border and only 30km from Togo. Apart from smuggling, now on the wane, Bawku is a centre for the manufacture of *fugu* shirts, the north's characteristic costume. Look out for the **Naba's palace** and geometric designs on the houses.

Tongo and around

Southeast of Bolga, the hills around the Talensi village of **Tongo** are interesting, though not that easy to get to. Apart from their natural beauty, they're the site of **Tenzugu**, a famous religious shrine in a rocky cavern. The British destroyed it in 1911 and again in 1915, but couldn't prevent people from going there. Tongo is two **bus** rides away from Bolga – either 6km along the Bawku road to Zwarungu then 10km south, or 10km along the Tamale road, then 6km east – and has its market day on a Friday. The people are very friendly in Tongo, including the chief, who can arrange for someone to guide you on the hefty hike through the hills to Tenzugu. If you're doing this, you should take some *akpeteshie* with you.

Between Zwarungu and Tongo is the village of **Bare**, where the sacred **bat tree** makes a change from crocodile pools and holy fish ponds. The best time to visit the Tongo area would be for the **Sowing Festival** around Easter or the **Harvest Festival**, usually in September or October. Both reflect a curious blend of old and new – iron-bangled dancers shaking radios, tennis rackets and rubber dolls.

HISTORY IN THE UPPER EAST

The Upper East Region is the traditional domain of the More-speaking peoples. Their history goes back to a thirteenth-century chief named **Gbewa** who founded a kingdom at **Pusiga**, east of Bawku on the Togolese border (where his tomb can still be seen). His sons fought over their inheritance and founded a number of mini-states in the region which grew from the fourteenth century and remained essentially intact until the nineteenth – **Mamprusi**, founded at Gambaga, **Dagomba**, and the other "Mossi"kingdoms mentioned in the Burkina Faso chapter (genealogy on p.629). These nations are now the names of distinct ethnic groups speaking dialects of More. Dagomba's first *Ya Na*, or king, founded a capital at **Yendi Dabari** (Dipali), north of Tamale, where ruins were unearthed in 1962. That capital was abandoned for **Yendi** (100km east of Tamale) after the sixteenth-century Gonja invasions. The *Ya Na*'s palace is still there. At **Bagale**, in the remote country south of Gambaga, is the Dagomba kings' mausoleum. The house built over it is the abode of the spirits of all departed *Ya Nas*.

The road from Walewale to Nakpanduri

South of Bolga, **Walewale** is the site of a venerable mosque, the Nakora. **Gambaga**, 50km east of here, is famous for its scarp, stretching out towards the Togolese border and up to 300m high in places. The town is also the **ancient Mamprusi capital** and the site of current excavations investigating the origins of the Mamprusi kingdom (see the box, opposite). The modern Mamprusi capital is **Nalerigu**, 8km east of Gambaga, with administration offices and a highly regarded mission hospital. Here you can see the palace of the Mamprusi kings as well as remains of the defensive walls built around the town when it was founded in the seventeenth century.

NAKPANDURI, 30km further east, is an unspoilt village situated high on the scarp. The **government resthouse** here is superbly sited, with a magnificent view north and some inspiring hikes nearby through rocky outcrops (①). Vehicles run here from Bawku, and though traffic is slow outside the market day (a three-day cycle), the relaxed and scenic atmosphere is worth a detour.

TOGO

TOGO

Although still comparatively little known outside the region, **Togo** has been in the papers often in recent years. Once considered a safe bet and an island of stability, it has had a particularly difficult time moving beyond the post-colonial era of dictators and there have been several violent episodes led by the military – and at least two **coup attempts** in the late 1980s and early 1990s – involving days of shelling and shooting in the capital. Hundreds of Togolese died in these disturbances and hundreds of thousands have fled to Ghana or Benin over the years. The relaxed atmosphere, for which Togo was famous among overlanders and business travellers in the early 1980s, evaporated, leaving tension and uncertainty throughout the country. Even basic issues, such as who needs a visa, can sometimes seem open to question; police and military checkpoints occasionally turn even short trips into drawn-out nightmares; and as tourists head to more dependable spots in Ghana and Benin, a number of hotels and restaurants have closed indefinitely.

Years of strikes and disinvestment have left the economy in tatters and the formerly excellent roads and service infrastructure are returning to West African norms. The mood of despond is not so pervasive, however, that it completely overshadows Togo's attractions. The country packs satisfyingly diverse **scenery** into a small space and has a vigorous **culture** differentiated into over a dozen linguistic and ethnic groups.

Where to go

The country's small size makes **transport connections** relatively easy. The main *route nationale*, which shows off the country's **cultural and geographical variety**, runs from Lomé north to Dapaong, near the Burkinabe border, and even the most isolated villages lie within 100km of its path.

The capital, **Lomé**, while not without its modern districts, feels for the most part like a provincial town, tuned to the shuffling pace of crowded narrow streets, where goats and chickens share space with the occasional taxi. At the worst moments of the military madness, tens of thousands of people fled Lomé, leaving it like a ghost town. Although many refugees have returned, the 1980s spark has gone.

Once you leave Lomé, the **coast** is worth savouring, not just for the palmy villages rustling between the lagoons and the Atlantic, but also for **voodoo**. The fetishes, shrines and festivals of **Togoville**, **Aného** and **Glidji**, reveal a lot about a religion no less bizarre than the **Catholicism** with which it is strikingly interwoven. Followers are usually open about *vaudau* and willing to discuss it with interested travellers – surprising in view of

---

FACTS AND FIGURES

The République Togolaise is a strip of a country with a 56-kilometre coastline and an area of only 57,000 square kilometres – less than half the size of England or New York state. The name Togo means "By the water" in Ewe. The **population** is officially estimated at about 4.3 million, with some 500,000 living in the capital, Lomé; during the upheaval of the early 1990s, however, hundreds of thousands of refugees fled to Ghana and Benin. Togo has a **foreign debt** of about £950 million ($1.5 billion), a relatively small sum even by modest West African standards, yet still amounting to four times the annual value of its exports. The **government** is theoretically democratic, although President Gnassingbe Eyadéma has been in power for more than thirty years and was most recently re-elected in 1998 after elections of breathtaking iniquity.

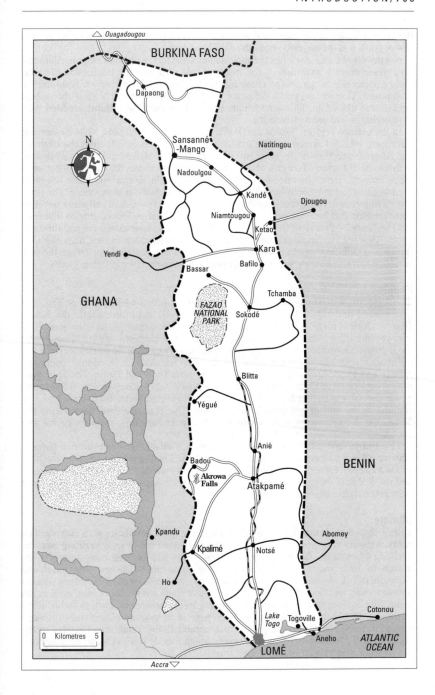

the secrecy under which traditional religions are often shrouded – and here is one area where you'll feel the unjaded strength of the continent.

Northwest of Lomé stretches the mountainous and fertile **plateau region**. Although they never exceed 1000 metres, the peaks of this area give the impression of being higher, especially when you're climbing the twisting roads to **Badou, Kpalimé** or **Atakpamé**. These three towns delineate the **coffee and cocoa** triangle – the richest agricultural district in the country, characterized by **thick woodland** studded with fruit orchards and palm plantations.

In the **central region**, Sokodé and Bafilo are Muslim strongholds, while Bassar and Kara have retained predominantly traditional religious beliefs (although the customs and religious practices in the latter two differ markedly). Mango and Dapaong, located in the semi-arid savannah region of the **far north**, already evoke the Sahel and the spectre of drought. Here, the once fine **Parc National de la Kéran**, straddling the main highway, has had most of its large mammal species poached out of existence. The president's hometown, **Kara**, has benefited from a number of industrial and other development projects that have catapulted it into "second city" status. The enormous influence of "The Guide" – President Gnassingbe Eyadéma – is unmistakeable here and throughout the country. His ample presence on photos in homes and businesses, on posters, on the TV and radio, is ubiquitous and overbearing. People are usually jumpy when the conversation turns to politics, which it rarely does, and almost never in public places.

People

The big groups in Togo are, in the south, the Ewe (often spelled Ewé or Evé, and pronounced midway between "Ehveh" and "Eyway"), and in the north, the Kabyé (Kabyié, Kabré, Kauré). The **Ewe**, who are divided into a multiplicity of local and district communities – the Mina-speakers are one of the biggest – are traditionally the most powerful ethnic constituency in the country. They have linguistic and cultural affiliations with other Twi-speaking peoples like the Akposo in central Togo, the Asante and Fante in Ghana and the Fon in eastern Togo and Benin. The Ewe diaspora – especially in France and Ghana – is a source of firm opposition to Eyadéma, while the Ghanaian border, which splits the Ewe traditional homeland into two regions, is the butt of considerable frustration. The Togolese Ewe, particularly the Mina, are the producers of much of Togo's export earnings, through coffee and cocoa.

The **Kabyé** and related **Tamberma** peoples are mostly poor subsistence farmers who have tended to unite behind the president's regional development plans (he himself is a Kabyé). Other Voltaic-speaking northerners include the Tchamba and Bassari, and the Kotokoli, one of the nation's most populous groups, whose people also count among the most influential traders.

Climate

Togo's pleasant **climate** has always been a factor in its popularity with visitors. The **rainy seasons** vary from north to south, but they need not be an overriding factor in deciding when to go. Lomé and the southern region has its "long rainy season" from March to June and a period of short rains some time between September and November. Sokodé and the north get a single, and less predictable, rainy season between April and September. Note, though, that there's not a lot of rain, even in the south (the baobab, that archetypal dry-country tree, grows right down to within 10km of the coast) and the table for Lomé given here is an average of wet and dry years. Except in small villages off the paved road, notably in the Tamberma Country or the areas around Bassar and Tchamba – where steep muddy tracks can be demanding – the weather won't greatly hamper your travels.

AVERAGE TEMPERATURES AND RAINFALL

LOMÉ

Temperatures °C	Jan	Feb	Mar	Apr	May	June	July	Aug	Sept	Oct	Nov	Dec
Min (night)	23	24	25	24	24	23	23	22	23	23	23	23
Max (day)	31	31	32	31	31	29	27	27	28	30	31	31
Rainfall mm	15	24	52	118	145	224	71	8	35	61	28	10

Arrivals

Since the trouble of the early 1990s, Togo has not been a common target for travel. The situation has improved considerably since then, but uncertainty remains about the stability of the country. On a more positive note, the border with Ghana – closed frequently in the early 1990s – is today generally reliable, and if you're entering Togo by road, you'll find the routes are mostly paved, and the frequency of public transport better than average.

■ Flights from Africa

Air Afrique (RK) and Nigeria Airways (WT) provide most of the direct flights from West African capitals to Lomé.

From **Abidjan** there are one or more flights most days on RK or WT, though note that some of RK's routings will have you doubling back via Lagos or Cotonou. Non-stop flights are mostly at weekends. There are also twice weekly flights with Air Ivoire (VU).

WT flies direct from **Banjul** once a week. RK has a direct weekly flight from **Dakar**, plus daily flights that route via Abidjan. RK also runs weekly non-stop services from both **Niamey** and **Ouagadougou**. Also from Ouaga, Air Burkina (2J) and Air France (AF) both fly non-stop four times a week. From **Cotonou**, RK, 2J and VU all run weekly flights.

There are several non-stop flights from **Lagos** to Lomé each week: four a week with RK; two a week with WT; and weekly with Air Gabon (GN). From **Bamako** there are non-stop weekly flights with RK. GN and RK both fly **Douala**–Lomé non-stop twice a week.

Lastly, although there are no longer any direct flights from **South Africa**, you can fly Ethiopian Airlines (ET) from Johannesburg to Addis Ababa on Thursday, and continue onto Lomé the next day.

■ Overland from Burkina Faso

The road from Ouagadougou is sealed all the way to Lomé (with minor exceptions in Togo where stretches are undergoing repairs). Border formalities pose no special problems on either side of this well-travelled route, and the posts are now open 24 hours. Coming from Ouaga by **bush taxi**, you can save money by going as far as Dapaong and changing vehicles there.

> The details in these practical information pages are essentially for use on the ground in West Africa and in Togo itself: for full practical details on preparing for a trip, getting here from outside the region, paperwork, health, information sources and more, see Basics, pp.3–83.

■ Overland from Ghana and Benin

The international highway along the coast is in good condition throughout the route from Abidjan to Lagos. There's a lot of traffic from both Accra and Cotonou and, in normal times, catching bush taxis from Cotonou or buses from Accra is no problem.

The **border with Ghana** was closed frequently and unexpectedly in the early 1990s due to strained relations with Ghana, but is today generally reliable. Just get transport to the Ghanaian border town of Aflao (post open 6am to 6pm) and walk into the centre of Lomé from there. The taxis that drive right into Lomé to deliver you at the *gare routière* charge a big premium for a few extra kilometres.

The Hilakondji border post between Togo and **Benin** is open 24 hours a day.

Red Tape

Visas for Togo are required by everyone except nationals of ECOWAS countries. Where Togo has no diplomatic representation, you can usually get one at the French consulate. Visas are issued at the border (CFA10,000, no photo required), but these are valid for one week only, and will need to be extended in Lomé (see p.790).

Whether you enter by air or overland, customs and immigration officials usually give you little grief and will certainly permit the maximum stay. Sometimes you may be asked how much money you're carrying, but the amount is rarely verified. The only other piece of paper you'll need is a **yellow fever certificate**.

For **visas for onward travel**, Lomé has only a limited number of West African embassies and consulates – addresses are given on p.790. Visas for some Francophone countries, including Burkina Faso, are issued from the French consulate. Nigerian visas are issued to Togo residents only, no exceptions. Benin has no embassy, but visas are issued at the Hilakondji border.

Ghana has embassies in Cotonou and Ouagadougou.

Money and Costs

Togo is part of the CFA zone (CFA100 = 1 French franc; approx CFA900 = £1; approx CFA560 = US$1). Coming overland, you're likely to have some CFA but, arriving by air from Europe, it's a good idea to bring some French francs in cash as they are generally acceptable for taxis, services and hotels. The airport banks close at 6pm: arrive later than this and you'll find it difficult to change money.

Changing other major **international currencies** (travellers' cheques or cash) is no problem in Lomé, Kara, Sokodé and Dapaong. In smaller towns, **banks** are likely to accept only francs or dollars, not pounds sterling or Deutschmarks. Banking hours are short and inconvenient: Monday to Friday 7.30–11.30am and 2.30–4pm. **Credit cards** are accepted in the major hotels, and in Lomé you can get Visa cash advances at the UTB or MasterCard cash advances at the BIAO.

■ The black market

Lomé has the biggest currency **black market** in West Africa, near the old Cotonou taxi station and Grand Marché, and all along the aptly named rue du Commerce. The quarter is notorious throughout the region and the free market operates here quite openly. You can buy Nigerian naira and Ghanaian cedis but also CFA (useful if you get caught without when the banks are closed) and other international currencies. Though you're not breaking any Togolese law, you should bear strongly in mind the fact that cedis and naira may not legally be exported or imported.

Streetwise **moneychangers** are very adept at sleight-of-hand tricks, so go with a friend, pay attention, and only carry the money you want to change. In general, it's advisable to avoid the sharks on the street who'll perform magic before your eyes, and deal with one of the bigger bosses at a shop front, doing the actual exchange inside the shop. Hand over nothing until you've verified your deal note by note. Much cooler exchanges are often to be had with resident expatriate money-dealers who have legal currency businesses and will give better-than-bank rates if you're buying CFA. Ask around.

■ Costs

The **cost of living** in Togo is substantially below that in other Francophone countries, but if you plan on living and eating *à l'européen*, you'll pay dearly for imported goods that would be cheap at home. **Hotel rooms** in Lomé run anywhere from CFA4000 to CFA100,000 but the interior of the country is less expensive and you can find good rooms for CFA5000–10,000 nearly everywhere. Ready-cooked **street food** and market produce is quite cheap, especially in the productive southwest. **Restaurants** serving European food generally do meals from about CFA2500. Beer and soft drinks are very inexpensive, although the big hotels and tourist hangouts knock the prices up as you'd expect. In a local bar, prices are the same from north to south (CFA350 for a beer, CFA130 for soft drinks). **Petrol** costs about CFA430 per litre for super but all over the south you often find it sold more cheaply in jerry cans along the roadside.

Health

In common with most of West Africa, a yellow fever vaccination certificate is compulsory – though rarely checked. Malaria tablets are essential. Chloroquine resistance has been reported, so extra care is needed.

Towns and large villages have either a hospital or – more likely – a **dispensary**, but these are characteristically overcrowded and lack adequate supplies. If you get seriously ill, it's best to get to your embassy (never very far in Togo) or one that speaks your language. They'll be able to refer you to a specialist or decide if you wouldn't be better off flying back home to get the help you need.

As in other countries, official reports invariably say that only a handful of AIDS cases have been registered in Togo and of course they're all prostitutes and foreigners; in fact, AIDS is now prevalent.

Maps and Information

The best travel map of Togo is the large 1cm:5km sheet produced by the French IGN, with its optimistic scattering of animal life (latest edition 1991). The tourist office in Lomé also sells large national maps, but the single fold of the Michelin 953 is more useful.

In Lomé, the Togolese survey office, the Direction de la Cartographie Nationale, is responsible for large-scale (1:200,000 and 1:50,000) mapping. Whether they will sell you any sheets is another matter.

North Americans can get preliminary information from the **Togo Information Service**, 1625 K St NW, #102, Washington DC, 20006 (☎202/569-4330). Europeans can try writing to the Office National Togolais du Tourisme, 23 rue François 1er, 75008 Paris.

Getting Around

Getting around Togo is most easily done by road. The railway in the south dates from the era of German occupation and its days are numbered. There's no domestic air service.

■ Bush taxis and car rental

There are few bus services in Togo and most of the time you'll be using privately run **taxis**. Every year Japanese vans gain ground on the traditional Peugeot 504s: the Nissans and Hiaces are new and comfortable. Laws against overloading are enforced more often than in the past – though the number of passengers a driver will take usually depends on how many policemen he thinks he'll meet on the road, and whether the fines he pays will cancel out the extra fares. You will often be asked by minibus drivers to pay extra for your luggage; never pay more than CFA100–300, according to distance.

In Lomé itself, **zemidjans** (moped taxis) are common and convenient.

Togo has good roads on the whole and you can drive on tarmac to all the neighbouring capitals. Lomé and Kara have **car rental** agencies, but prices are prohibitive.

■ Trains

The Germans built **railway lines** to Aného (for freighting out the coconuts), Kpalimé (for coffee and cocoa) and Blitta (for cotton), an antiquated system, which is enthused over by rail buffs. However, trains stopped running to Aného and Kpalimé some years ago, and the reduced service to Blitta has been frequently out of commission, and may also soon be discontinued. If the twice weekly train is still running and you're in no hurry, the wooden carriages with shutters and colonial styling are rather fine, and travel by train is the cheapest form of transport, albeit not the most comfortable. Schedules are given in appropriate sections of the guide.

Accommodation

Except in Lomé, Togo has little in the way of luxury accommodation. From north to south, however, it does have an adequate number of more modest lodgings, either privately owned or government-run. Accommodation is usually good value compared with neighbouring Francophone countries, although amenities like air conditioning, TV and phones are less common.

Togo has no youth hostels and little in the way of mission accommodation, though the **Affaires Sociales** government rest houses will

---

ACCOMMODATION PRICE CODES

Accommodation prices in this chapter are coded according to the following scales – the same scales in terms of their pound/dollar equivalents as are used throughout the book. Prices refer to the rate you can expect to pay for a room with two beds. Single rooms, or single occupancy, will normally cost at least two-thirds of the twin-occupancy rate. For further details see p.48.

① **Under CFA4500 (under £5/$8).** Basic hotel ranging from rudimentary *casa de passage* to decent S/C accommodation.
② **CFA4500–9000 (£5–10/$8–16).** S/C rooms, often with AC.
③ **CFA9000–18,000 (£10–20/$16–32).** Modest business or tourist-class hotel, often with a restaurant.

④ **CFA18,000–27,000 (£20–30/$32–48).** Comfortable hotel with good facilities.
⑤ **CFA27,000–36,000 (£30–40/$48–64).** First-class hotel.
⑥ **CFA36,000–45,000 (£40–50/$64–80).** Luxury accommodation.
⑦ **Over CFA45,000 (over £50/$80).** Luxury accommodation.

always put you up cheaply if they have a room free.

There's a handful of organized **camping** sites east of Lomé and a limited number of other sites throughout the country. It's also useful to know that some hotels allow campers to pitch on their grounds for CFA2000–3000 a night. If you have your own transport and are out in the bush, you can pull off the road discreetly and camp for the night; it's advisable though – not to mention polite – to let local people know who and where you are first.

Officially, **staying with people** is frowned upon unless you made a declaration at the town *préfecture*. However, Lomé is big enough for you to be able to skip this formality, and it seems that, even outside the capital, the authorities do not bother too much with it nowadays.

Eating and Drinking

Togo has a reputation in West Africa for some of the best cooking in the region. Small restaurants or street stands as far afield as Niamey, Bamako and Abidjan are often run by Togolese women. The secret of their success lies in their sauces, which tend to be less oily than usual and contain more vegetables. Not that you'll necessarily love Togolese food; some of it may seem unappealing at first (slimy gumbo, or okra, can be a real turnoff) and all of it is guaranteed to be heavily laced with hot peppers.

Staples vary across the country. In the south, **cassava** (manioc) predominates, along with **palm oil** and **maize**. Cassava is often grated and steamed as *atiéké*. In the plateau region, the diet contains more tubers – **yams, cocoyams** and **sweet potatoes** – boiled, grilled, steamed or fried. **Plantains** are another favourite staple, commonly pounded into **fufu** (which can also be made with cassava or yams). In the north, **sheanut oil** is commoner than palm oil. Likewise, **rice, millet** and **sorghum** (any of them can be ground, boiled and served as a mash) are eaten more frequently than towards the coast.

Vegetables include tomatoes, gumbo, aubergines (small and yellowish), squash and beans. These are used in **sauces** with cassava, baobab or taro leaves and mixed with fish, shellfish, meat or poultry. Common **spices** are ginger, peppers, anis, garlic, basil and mustard.

The south and plateau region have the most **fruit**, although even in the extreme north you'll find a good variety. **Pineapples, mangos, papayas**, all the **citrus fruits, avocados** and **guava** are plentiful in the markets (depending of course on the season) and downright cheap in the south.

Supplements to the basics include **agouti** (the large and tasty herbivorous rodent known in Ghana and Nigeria as "bush rat" or "grasscutter") and **koliko** (deep-fried yam chips). Togo's best-known dishes are **moutsella** (a spicy fish and vegetable dish), **adokouin** (shellfish with a prawn sauce known as *azidessi*), **djekoumé** (chilli chicken), and **gboma** (a spinach and seafood based dish). You're most likely to sample these at an important private gathering, or as part of the *Cuisine Togolaise* menu in one of the more expensive restaurants.

Togo has a great line in **street food** and, even in the smaller **village markets**, women sell exotic as well as fairly familiar food by the portion, from basins. The variety is huge.

If such a variety of dishes isn't already enough, the large towns all have restaurants serving **European food**, but these tend to be fairly expensive, especially if you want wine.

■ Drinking

Togo has its share of local drinks, similar to the other common intoxicants of West Africa. **Palm wine** is big in the south: the juice that flows from the trunks is already fermented and ready to drink, its frothiness indicating its freshness (if it's flat it will be high in alcohol). A hard liquor can be produced by distilling it. Though illegal, this highly potent "African gin", or **sodabi**, flows freely in the coastal region. Northern Togo specializes in millet beer, known locally as **choucoutou** – a taste somewhat reminiscent of dry cider. Filtering it produces **chacbalo**, which is clear and slightly sweeter than *choucoutou*.

Togo's brewery pumps out a wide selection of more familiar drinks. The **beer** here is excellent and cheap. Bière du Bénin (referred to as BB, "Bé-Bé") is the standard lager. Eku is more potent. Guinness is also available, served cold. There's a wide range of soft drinks, good Lion Killer lemonade, soda water, tonic and the rest – even a splendidly fruity, carbonated Cocktail de Fruits. They all come in large and small bottles and they're all refreshingly inexpensive.

Communications – Post, Phones, Language and Media

Post is not too expensive: CFA315 for letters to Europe, CFA335 to the US, and CFA370 to Australia. Postcards are slightly cheaper. Parcels are only sent air mail and are very expensive. Phoning home, reverse charge (collect) calls are only possible to France, and normal calls are pretty expensive (CFA1500 per minute to America and most of Europe, CFA1000 to France). There are now some phone boxes in Lomé where you can phone abroad on IDD using phonecards.

Togo's IDD code is ☎228.

■ Languages

The official language of Togo is **French**, which is widely spoken. Due to the commerce with Ghana and Nigeria, many traders also speak rudimentary **English**, especially in the area around Lomé.

There are some fifty African languages and dialects, the most widely spoken among them being **Mina**. Mina is spoken by thirty percent of the population in the coastal region and into Ghana. Government reports list President Eyadéma's mother tongue **Kabyé** (also known as Kabré or Kauré) as being the second most common language in the country. To arrive at this claim, they lump Kabyé together with a host of related **Tem** dialects from the Voltaic group, spoken in the Kara region. Linguistically, if not politically, **Kotokoli** – the language of Sokodé and environs; see box on p.805 – is certainly more prevalent than Kabyé. Other languages include **Bassari**, in the area around the town of Bassar, **Tchamba** in the east, **Moba** around Dapaong and scattered communities of **Hausa, Fula** and **Mossi** in the extreme north.

■ The media

Communications with Europe are relatively good, at least from Lomé. The local media is limited, but papers and magazines are imported, and in Lomé you won't feel out of touch with the news.

Radio Togo, the national station, broadcasts news in French, Ewe, Kabyé and English (endless reports of telegrams the president received that day followed by a wrap-up of West African events). Libreville's **Africa Numero Un** and **Radio France Inter** are better music stations with more comprehensive international news coverage, and there are some **private stations** (Tropique FM, Nostalgie, Radio Galaxie, Radio Evangile), although their political coverage is not of a very high standard.

National TV broadcasts every evening – news in French and local languages plus old movies.

The only readily available **newspaper**, the state-owned *Togo Presse*, in French, with Ewe and Kabyé pages, has sketchy international coverage, but local news items are often interesting. A vigorous free press sprouted in the early 1990s, but bombings and other intimidation has dampened the enthusiasm of most publishers. Look out for *Crocodile, Tribune Africaine* and *Combat du Peuple*.

You'll find international **English-language press** like *The Herald Tribune, Time* and *Newsweek* (as well as French and German magazines and papers) at the airport and the big hotels.

Holidays and Festivals

Both Muslim and Christian holidays – including Catholic festivals like Pentecost, Ascension and Assumption (the former two variable and the latter on August 15) – are celebrated in Togo, along with New Year's Day. National holidays are: January 13 (National Liberation); April 27 (Independence Day); May 1 (Labour Day); and a few days in July on the occasion of Evala (see below) which, with so many Kabyé employees granted leave, is increasingly a public holiday.

Traditional festivals take place in the regions, many with ancient ethnic roots and corresponding celebrations in Ghana and Benin. The following are the most notable among them.

July

Evala: initiation celebration in the Kabyé country with wrestling matches (*lutte traditionelle*). The tournaments in Kara are now televised nationally and attended by the president, said to be a former champion.

MINIMAL MINA AND ESSENTIAL EWE

Mina is spoken by about a third of the population in Togo, making it the most common language in the country. You'll run into it mostly along the coast, including in parts of Ghana and Benin. Unlike **Ewe**, to which it is closely related, Mina is not written. Both languages are tonal, so that meaning varies (as in Chinese for example) with the pitch of the voice. They're therefore rather hard languages for speakers of European tongues to come to grips with, and the following words and expressions can only be a very rough guide to pronunciation.

MINA GREETINGS AND BASICS

Good day	*Sobaydo*	Yes	*Aaaaa*
Reply	*Dosso*	No	*Ow*
How are you?	*O foihn?*	Come here (to a child)	*Va*
Reply ("fine")	*aaaaa* (as in cat)	See you later	*Sodé* or *Sodaylo*
Thank you	*Akpay*	Until we meet again	*Mia dogou/mia*
Thank you very (very) much	*Akpaykaka (kaka)*		*dogoulo*
Have a nice day	*Nkekay anenyo*	See you tomorrow	*Ayeee'soh*

MINA NUMBERS

1	*Dekaa*	5	*Ametón* (high tone)	9	*Amesidiké*		
2	*Amevé*	6	*Amadé*	10	*Amewo*		
3	*Ametòn* (low tone)	7	*Ameadrreh*				
4	*Amené*	8	*Ameni*				

EWE GREETINGS AND BASICS

Good morning	*Nngdi*	I don't understand	*Nye mese egome o*
Good afternoon	*Nngdo*	Goodbye	*Hede nyuie*
Good evening	*Fie*	I'm a stranger	*Amedzro menye*
Good night	*Do agbe*	Please	*Taflatse*
Welcome	*Woe zo*	What is your name?	*Nko wode?*
How are you?	*E foa?/ Ale nyuie?*	My name is . . .	*Nngkonyee nye . . .*
I'm fine	*Mefo/Meli nyuie*	I am leaving Ewe land	*Mele Evegbe srom*
Pleased to meet you	*Edzo dzi nam be*		
	medo go wo		

EWE NUMBERS

1	*Deka*	10	*Ewo*
2	*Uhve*	11	*Wedekee*
3	*Etoh*	12	*Weuhve*, etc
4	*Enah*	20	*Blave*
5	*Atoh*	30	*Blatòh* (low tone)
6	*Adee*	40	*Blana*
7	*Aderen*	50	*Blatóh* (high tone)
8	*Enyee*	60	*Bladee*, etc
9	*Asiekee*	100	*Alohfa deka*

A GLOSSARY OF TOGOLESE TERMS

Anasara In the northern parts, a white, derived from Nazarene, or Christian.

Authenticité Programme initiated by Eyadéma to instil pride in "authentic" roots, requiring French names to be exchanged for African and proficiency in Ewe, Mina or Kabyé for all school children.

Auto-suffisance alimentaire Food self-sufficiency – which, in non-drought years, Togo had nearly obtained before the unrest of the early 1990s.

Evala The annual wrestling matches in the president's hometown of Kara.

Soukala A compound of round huts connected by a wall, found in the north.

Vaudau/Vodu Generic names for the spirit children of God – *Mawu-Lisa* in Ewe.

Yovo White person (Mina).

Akpema: Kabyé young women's initiation ceremony.

August

Kpessosso: Gun harvest festival celebrated in the region of Aného and marked by traditional dances (Adjogbo and Gbékon).
Ayize: bean-harvest festival celebrated by the Ewe, particularly in the region of Tsévié.

September

Agbogbozan: festival of the Ewe diaspora celebrated on the first Thursday in September and especially colourful in Notsé.
Yékéyéké or *Yakamiakin*: week-long festival starting on the Thursday before the second Sunday in September, in Glidji near Aného.
Dipontre: yam festival celebrated around the first week of September in Bassam.

Directory

AIRPORT DEPARTURE TAX None.

CRAFTS There are numerous places throughout the country where crafts are plentiful. The principal mart in Lomé is the Passage des Arts – a small street near the market with nothing but art vendors selling sculptures, bronzes, jewellery and textiles from across West Africa. Near Kpalimé, the Centre Artisanal is a noble attempt to keep regional crafts alive: here, traditional forms of **pottery**, **calabash decoration** and **woodcarving** have taken on a modern, more commercial flavour. Kpalimé itself is a good place to buy **kente cloth** (see p.794) which is woven in the town streets. Traditional cloth is also woven in Bafilo and can be purchased directly from the Coopératives des Tisserands in the town centre. An unwelcome footnote is the presence of **ivory** in Lomé's craft shops and a flourishing ancillary trade in fake ivory bangles.

MUSIC In the world of pop music, Togo's sole international star has been **Bella Bellow**, who was "discovered" by Cameroon's Manu Dibango and who had a successful career before her death in a car accident. Some of her cassettes can be found in Lomé. More recent musicians who've made a name for themselves include **Itadi K. Bonney** and **Afia Mala**. But one of Togo's biggest stars is **Jimmy Hope**, a rock/blues musician with a huge following who often plays around Lomé.

OPENING HOURS Offices and most businesses are open from 7.30am–noon and from 2.30–4.30pm. Banking hours vary slightly from one institution to the next, but are roughly 7.30–11.30am and 2.30–4pm. The more modern "journée continue" hours (roughly 8am–2pm, with no closure) are increasingly common in all institutions.

PHOTOGRAPHY No photography permit is required in Togo, though the usual restrictions apply to taking pictures of military installations and strategic points. People generally tend to be less camera-shy than in some African countries.

SOCCER A popular sport, with particularly fierce competition between Semassi, the team from Sokodé, and Gomido from Kpalimé.

WILDLIFE PARKS None of the game reserves and national parks are faring too well. The **Parc National de la Kéran** that once straddled the northern highway has reverted to farmland as most of the game had been killed off. The other large park, the **Parc National du Fazao**, west of the main north–south highway near Sokodé, closed its gates for rehabilitation after much of its wildlife was also decimated, and although it has now reopened, chances of seeing wildlife are slim.

WOMEN Tradition, in rural areas especially, dictates a strict sexual division of labour, but women have considerable economic clout, particularly in the south where well-organized women merchants – known in Lomé as the *Nanas Benz* after their favourite cars – are a political force of consequence. The government recognizes and sanctions the Union Nationale des Femmes Togolaises. Women have access to all administrative functions and professions but the reality is that education, though compulsory in theory for all children, is less likely to be received by girls than boys and there are few women with high-level positions in government or business.

A Brief History of Togo

For centuries, Togo has been on the fringes of several empires – Mali, Asante, Benin, Mossi – but the centre of none. The country – which formed part of what was once called the Slave Coast – came into contact with Europeans in the fifteenth century as the Portuguese made their sweep of the African continent. Porto Seguro (Agbodrafo) and Petit Popo (Aného) evolved to become important trading posts where slaves were exchanged for European goods. By the end of the nineteenth century, trade had shifted to "legitimate" products – principally palm oil, used in soap manufacture in Europe. French and German companies competed along the coast in their dealings with the Mina people.

■ The colonial period

In 1884, **Gustav Nachtigal** sailed into Togo and signed a treaty with a village chief that made the country a **German protectorate**. In the following years, **Togoland** developed into the Reich's "model colony" as the Germans tried to force the country to produce economic miracles. Railways and roads were laid, and forests cleared for coffee and cocoa plantations. A direct radio link with Berlin was established and wharves were built.

The beginnings of an ill-defined educational system tried to create Christians and wage labourers out of reluctant farmers and fishermen. It took the Germans until 1902 to "pacify" the people of Togo, relying on forced labour and other repressive measures to push through their progress.

Despite the colony's economic importance, German military presence in Togoland was weak. When World War I broke out, the British and French easily overran the territory, forcing the Kaiser's soldiers to capitulate at **Kamina** on August 26, 1914. The tiny village was thus the site of the Entente Powers' very first victory. After the war, a **League of Nations mandate** placed a third of the territory under British administration and two-thirds (corresponding to the present country's borders) in the hands of the French.

The way to independence

Both **France and Britain** showed only half-hearted interest in their new acquisitions which technically were not colonies. The British quickly attached western Togo (today the Volta Region in Ghana) to the Gold Coast, but the French administered eastern Togo as an entity separate from its other holdings in West Africa. Thus several of Togo's peoples – the Adele, Konkomba and especially **Ewe** – suddenly found their communities divided by a border. Reunification was an early political theme, but one the European powers looked on unfavourably. A "pan-Ewe" vision, championed by early nationalist leaders like **Sylvanus Olympio**, was dealt a severe blow in 1956 when people of West Togo voted in a referendum to amalgamate with the Gold Coast, then preparing for independence.

At the same time, the French were grooming eastern Togo for independence. In 1956, Togo became an autonomous republic, with **Nicolas Grunitzky** as prime minister. Two years later, Olympio took over the role and, when Togo became fully independent on April 27, 1960, he was elected the nation's first president.

■ A shaky start

Olympio aspired to the ideals of early nationalists such as Nkrumah, Touré and Senghor, although he never achieved their stature. In any case, even as he ushered in a new era, the stage was set for his own demise. In a scenario all too common to the former colonies, the Germans and later French had groomed a class of coastal peoples to be civil servants and the educated elite. After independence, these peoples inherited political power and, as a consequence, economic advantages. It was a formula guaranteed to result in **ethnic tension** in countries where unity should have been of primary importance.

In the case of Togo, Olympio, an Ewe from Aného, represented the **elite minority**. He tended to put reunification with the Ewe in Ghana ahead of Togolese national unity and was openly contemptuous of the northern Togolese, whom he called *petits nordistes*. Increasing repression and disregard for the poor north didn't help to broaden his already narrow political base.

Meanwhile **Nkrumah of Ghana**, who had supported Olympio's efforts for Togo's independence, had apparently intended the territory to be integrated with Ghana and, that objective thwarted, actively harassed Olympio's new government with border closures and trade sanctions. But the worst blow to Olympio's prestige came in 1963, when **returning Togolese soldiers** who had fought for France in the Algerian war of independence, were refused permission by him to join Togo's national army, since in his eyes they had betrayed the African liberation movement. For the troops, in the main Kabyé men from the north, it was a humiliating snub, and seemed to be proof that Olympio was determined to exclude northerners from participation in the new nation.

On January 13, 1963, a group of disenfranchised soldiers, including a young Kabyé sergeant named **Etienne Eyadéma**, staged the first coup in independent Africa. They stormed the president's home and, according to the official version, shot and killed Olympio while he was trying to escape by scrambling up the wall from his residence and into the grounds of the American embassy where he had hoped to seek refuge.

The soldiers set up a civilian government and placed Grunitzky, who had returned from exile, at its head. The new president lasted four ineffectual years and, as the country's increasing problems outstripped his competence to deal with them, he was replaced in a bloodless coup by Eyadéma – staged in a symbolic style that became his hallmark, on January 13, 1967, four years to the day after Olympio's assassination.

■ The Eyadéma years

After his second coup Eyadéma seized power "at the insistence of the people", suspended the constitution, dissolved political opposition and set about, much after the style of the former Zaire's President Mobutu, protecting his political future through the powerful mechanism of the single party he himself controlled – the Rassemblement du Peuple Togolais (RPT). By 1972, he was secure enough to hold a referendum on his future as president, in which voters held up one colour card to indicate a "yes" vote and a different colour for "no" as soldiers guarded the booths. A landslide 99 percent of the population thus expressed its desire for Eyadéma to remain the national leader.

Two years later, the president profited from a bizarre series of events that seemed to give supernatural backing to the demonstration of popular support. It started in 1974 with what has gone down in Togolese political legend (actively encouraged by the president) as the **"Three Glorious Days"**. On **January 10**, Eyadéma announced that a 51 percent share of the French-operated phosphate mines (one of the country's principal resources) would be nationalized. Exactly two weeks later, **January 24**, the president's private plane crashed over **Sarakawa**, but Eyadéma walked away from the wreck virtually unmarked. An international plot was suspected, and, without any real proof, the world was led to believe this was a classic case of capitalist meddling – an assassination attempt on the man who had dared to liberate his country's economy.

After recovering, the president made a drawn-out journey from Kara to Lomé, and throngs of people came to look at the man who had become

a myth. On **February 2**, Eyadéma made his **triumphal return** to the capital and announced that the phosphate industry was henceforth one hundred percent in Togolese hands.

The incident turned into a political windfall that made Togo look like the mouse who roared. **Eyadéma's anti-imperialist record** was enshrined in myth. He began an **"authenticity"** campaign, again modelled closely on Mobutu's in the former Zaire, abolishing French names (and renaming himself Gnassingbe) and introducing Kabyé and – with a little shrewdness – Ewe into the schools as languages of instruction. Phosphate money helped build a few modern buildings in Lomé and Kara and ambitious projects like an oil refinery, steel plant (both now closed) and cement factory near Lomé. But rather than creating jobs, these simply lost money, forcing the country to bend to IMF pressure to denationalize as the economy slumped badly in the 1980s. The irony of Togo's position ever since Sarakawa is that it became one of the most pragmatically **pro-Western** countries of the Cold War era.

■ International affairs

Despite economic decline, Eyadéma managed to keep a high diplomatic profile and created a new larger-than-life image for himself as **West African peacemaker**. At one point he served as an intermediary between combatants in the Chadian war and helped smooth over relations between Nigeria and the Francophone countries that had backed Biafra. More recently he provided another African platform for **Israel**, with which Togo opened diplomatic relations in 1987.

On an economic level, Eyadéma has championed ECOWAS (the West African common market, known in French-speaking countries as the CEDEAO). Along with Nigeria, Togo was a major sponsor of the organization, established in 1975 when fifteen regional nations signed the Treaty of Lagos. But his proudest achievement was hosting the meeting that resulted in the signing of the **Lomé Convention**, giving Third World nations in Africa, the Caribbean and the Pacific preferential treatment from the EC and linking the name of Lomé with co-operation in development policy.

Cross-border relations

Relations with **Ghana** have traditionally been rocky, partly as a result of the pan-Ewe movement, which dates from the colonial era and continues in a more subtle form today. The ideological opposition of Rawlings' and Eyadéma's regimes has also led to serious tensions between the two neighbours. During Thomas Sankara's period in power, Togolese relations with **Burkina Faso** also chilled, but improved rapidly after Compaoré's assumption of power in 1987. Eyadéma was the first African head of state to recognize the new Burkinabe government, and he did so just hours after Sankara was overthrown.

Ideology has also been a source of conflict with **Benin** – a country periodically charged by Togo with giving refuge to politically active exiles. During the 1980s, the Togo–Benin border was frequently closed.

■ At home: increasing opposition

Eyadéma, who orchestrated two coups and has been witness to numbers of others in the states neighbouring his own, has been careful to nip **opposition** in the bud. Active underground dissent has long existed, and it rises to the surface in periodic **eruptions of violence**.

In 1984, when the papal visit focused international attention on Togo, a series of **bombings** rocked Lomé. A **coup attempt** occurred in a 1986 shoot-out with armed rebels who got perilously close to the presidential residence. The attempted takeover was blamed on an exiled movement led by Gilchrist Olympio (son of the former president) who was subsequently sentenced to death *in absentia*. The date of the aborted uprising – September 19 – is today celebrated as a national holiday.

In 1990, the government was again shaken when members of the **Convention Démocratique des Peuple Africains du Togo** (CDPA-T), an opposition group which had been based in Côte d'Ivoire until ousted by Houphouët-Boigny in 1989, were arrested for distributing anti-government literature. The ensuing trial led to massive demonstrations in Lomé which left many dead or injured.

Subsequent protests forced Eyadéma to **legalize political parties**, but student unrest again erupted in April 1991. Fatalities were reported in Lomé when security forces dispersed demonstrators who demanded Eyadéma's resignation. Afterwards, mutilated bodies began surfacing in Lomé's brackish Bé district lagoons. Twenty corpses were discovered, and the opposition

blamed the **brutality** on the military. Anxious to dispel the idea that army thugs now publicly perpetrated the types of **human rights abuses** they had long been suspected of carrying out behind prison walls, Eyadéma ordered an investigation. But the opposition persisted and called a **general strike**, again demanding Eyadéma's resignation. More protests followed, and in June 1991 the government was constrained to agree on the mandate for a **national conference**, similar to the one that had brought sweeping reform to Benin.

In July 1991, delegates of newly legal political parties and the government convened and, with lightning speed, the conference proclaimed itself sovereign and suspended the constitution. By August, Eyadéma had been stripped of most of his power and the RPT had been outlawed. In an act of defiance, the president suddenly changed course and suspended the conference.

Opposition leaders refused to disband and proclaimed a **provisional government** under the leadership of **Joseph Kokou Koffigoh**, a lawyer and leader of the Ligue Togolaise des Droits de l'Homme. To stave off further unrest, Eyadéma consented to recognize Koffigoh. But within weeks of being instated, the new prime minister woke up to find soldiers had seized his house, captured the radio and television stations, and surrounded his office with tanks. Troops returned to the barracks on Eyadéma's orders, but in the following months, repeated popular protests led to bloody clashes with security forces. In November, **the army arrested Koffigoh** and demanded the transitional government be disbanded.

In prison, Koffigoh "reconsidered" his stance and consented to Eyadéma's euphemistically titled **"government of national unity"** which paved the way for the RPT's re-entry into the political scene. Although he spared the transitional government and allowed Koffigoh to remain as head, Eyadéma padded the council of ministers with close associates. With a tight grip on the council, the president allowed the appearance of reform to continue and laid plans for **new elections**.

Early 1992 was marked by repeated delays in the transitional process and by resulting protests. Trouble intensified when Olympio was shot while campaigning in Eyadéma's northern stronghold. The security forces were implicated in the **assassination attempt** and evidence even pointed to the president's son, Captain Ernest Gnassingbé. While Olympio recovered in Paris, a massive two-day general strike paralyzed Lomé as demonstrators once more flooded the streets.

Undaunted, the president cautiously took back all the power he had ceded to the national council in 1991. The sham of democratization was further highlighted in October 1992 when security forces stormed the parliament and held forty MPs hostage until the speaker pushed through a bill returning frozen funds to the RPT. In November, another **general strike** was called as opposition parties and union members demanded the creation of a politically neutral security force, a new government and free and fair elections.

The promised elections still hadn't materialized by January 1993 and the strike dragged on. A French and German delegation arrived in Lomé to help mediate the crisis, but their efforts were thwarted when security forces fired on a crowd of opposition supporters, killing at least twenty according to the French minister of co-operation who witnessed the atrocity. After two security officers were found murdered on January 30, the army went on a retaliatory **shooting and looting spree** which left hundreds dead at the hands of the military.

The new wave of violence led to a **mass exodus**, adding to the tens of thousands who had previously fled (including the wife of the prime minister, Rosaline Koffigoh). Forty thousand refugees streamed over the borders to Ghana and Benin, straining Togo's already dismal international relations. President Jerry Rawlings of Ghana condemned Eyadéma's continued denial that security forces were responsible for the slaughter and seemed to advocate sending ECOWAS troops to Togo to prevent it from becoming "another Liberia". While both Ghana and Benin mobilized troops along their borders to protect the refugees, the United States, France and Germany suspended aid to Togo.

■ New elections and more of the same

Against such a troubling backdrop, Eyadéma announced **presidential elections** would be held in August. Opposition leaders objected, demanding a recomposition of the Supreme Court and a postponement of the election date as preconditions for participating. They also called for a revised voter register and the issuance of new voter's cards. Eyadéma rejected the requests and furthermore denied the candidacy of Gilchrist

Olympio on the grounds that his medical examination was invalid.

Even the team of international observers monitoring the elections denounced the polls as "undemocratic", and US and German observers withdrew from the process. Candidates **Edem Kodjo** (Union Togolaise pour la Démocratie, UTD) and **Yao Agboyibo** (Comité d'Action pour le Renouveau, CAR) pulled out of the race in protest and called for a **national boycott**. On a turnout of only 36 percent, Eyadéma garnered 96 percent of the vote and proclaimed himself victorious. The following day, fifteen CAR members who had been arrested for allegedly tampering with electoral material, died in prison.

On January 5, 1994 gunfire once again erupted near Lomé's Tokoin military base where President Eyadéma normally sleeps. Simultaneous **rocket fire** blasted a presidential motorcade, striking Eyadéma's bulletproof Mercedes and sending it skidding off the road. Soon after, the government issued a communiqué saying that the city was under a **commando attack**, but that the president and prime minister, who were in a private meeting far away from the motorcade at the time of the incident, were unscathed.

Fighting continued for four days as Loméans remained locked in their homes. When the dust had settled, Eyadéma announced that government forces had defeated the insurgents which he charged had infiltrated the capital from Ghana. Official reports put the death toll at 69 people, mostly members of the commando. Some estimates, however, ran as high as 300–500 victims, including many civilians.

The nation was shocked and demoralized as **legislative elections** were held in February. With the exception of Olympio's Union des Forces du Changement and a couple of lesser parties, most of the opposition decided to participate. In a tight race, Agboyibo's CAR won 36 seats in the 81 member parliament, while Kodjo's UTD won 7 and the RPT won 37. Though the RPT thus formed the minority in parliament, Eyadéma gained leverage by appointing Kodjo to the premiership – a move that gave the appearance of benevolence to the opposition, while effectively dividing it, since Agboyibo naturally felt he had claims to the post.

As a result, CAR members refused to sit on the cabinet of ministers, which was quickly padded with Eyadéma backers, and the party began a parliamentary boycott. This was called off in 1995 after Eyadéma offered guarantees for a fairer approach to future elections, and CAR resumed its representation in parliament. But even with a majority there, the opposition couldn't get a grip on governance, and Kodjo complained that he was increasingly left out of decision-making. Notably, he wasn't consulted as the president called **by-elections** in 1996 designed to pad out RPR seats in the assembly. Angered at the manouevering, and at the fact that the president refused to live up to his earlier promises and appoint an international monitoring committee to oversee the elections, CAR refused to participate. The RPT and allied parties gained enough seats to have a majority and Kodjo was swiftly replaced by **Kwassi Klutse**, a more conciliatory technocrat and former minister. The opposition was left out of the cabinet completely.

■ The continuing slide from democracy

In 1997, as he celebrated thirty years as head of state – and his survival through six years of political upheaval and the economic ruin of his country – Eyadéma was firmly back in control. Noticeably absent from the military parade and lavish government ceremonies marking the anniversary, were foreign dignitaries, both regional and international, who were reluctant to endorse the nation's slide from democratic rule. But **foreign money** was beginning to trickle back in to aid-dependent Togo. France first broke rank and the government received handy subsidies from international agreements that had been worked out during the happier days of the Lomé Conventions. But the EU, and especially Germany – which experienced first hand the tyranny of Togo's overzealous military when an embassy staffer was shot to death at a roadblock in May 1996 – remained highly critical of the regime and refused to renew aid.

There was reason for concern too. With control of the presidency, parliament and courts, Eyadéma was accused of wielding his power to repress genuine opposition and secure another five-year term in the elections scheduled for 1998. Reports of **human rights abuses** were legion by 1997, and the president's security forces were charged with extrajudicial killings, beatings and arbitrary arrests that the government neither investigated nor punished. Intimidation restricted freedom of speech and the press; police and RPT youth groups harassed streetside sellers of private publications like *Crocodile* and *Le Kpakpa*

désenchanté, seizing copies of critical newspapers, beating or arresting the vendors and smashing their stalls. A **student strike** to protest the non-payment of study grants ended abruptly in January 1998, when *gendarmes* raided Lomé's Université du Bénin. In the ensuing melee, the president of the Union Nationale des Étudiants Togolais – who had refused to sign a government communiqué ordering students to return to classes – "fell" from a second story dormitory window fracturing his spine. Eleven other students were arrested.

Trade unions fared no better. Despite the economic slump of the late 1990s and the fact that government salaries often went unpaid, the Union Nationale des Syndicats Indépendants (UNSI) could do little to improve working conditions, complaining that it operated under "extreme difficulty". The government promised reprisals for even modest strike action; in 1998, the deputy secretary of the UNSI was shot execution-style in his Lomé home. No one was charged in connection with the killing.

The mood was thus sombre as the **presidential elections of 1998** took place. Olympio and Agboyigbor, along with four other opposition candidates, courageously contested the elections, but it was really a no-win situation; if they had boycotted, as in 1993, they would only be assured of remaining outside of power. The establishment of a **National Election Commission** (NEC) to oversee the voting was a positive sign, but members were packed with supporters of the RTP and refused to act on recommendations of international observers, especially those that called for early issuance of voter registration cards. The government ban on political rallies, conveniently ignored by the RPT, was widely viewed as an attempt to limit the opposition's ability to recruit supporters. And the state-owned radio and television gave little coverage to opposition candidates, despite constitutional guarantees of equal access. In the months preceding the polling, Olympio (who, for obvious security reasons, still lived in Ghana) returned to Togo on brief visits only – to accept his party's nomination, submit to the mandatory medical examination and to campaign.

Voting proceeded without incident in June 1998, at least in pro-Eyadéma precincts. But stations in opposition strongholds, such as Lomé and Sokodé, opened late or not at all, and many voters were turned away because they hadn't been issued registration cards. Even more egregious, the army confiscated ballot boxes in many precincts and refused to let the NEC preside over the counting of votes; the chair of the commission resigned rather than declare Eyadéma the winner, stating that members of the NEC had been the victims of "pressure, intimidation and threats". That left the counting to the government, which interrupted television programming the following day to announce that Eyadéma had been re-elected, having received 52 percent of the vote and an outright majority. From Ghana, Olympio, who received 34 percent by official accounts, claimed that he had been robbed of the victory and many international observers believed he was right. Days of protests and strikes followed the elections, but the government would not budge on the results, which the Supreme Court dutifully rubber-stamped.

Completely demoralized, and with no hope of a better outcome for the **legislative elections** planned to follow in July 1999, the opposition called for a **boycott** of them. In its mind, the government was illegal anyhow. As the crowning acheivement of Eyadéma's return to absolute supremacy, the RPT took all the seats but one in the assembly.

■ Prospects

Western nations roundly criticized the outcomes of both elections and continue their reluctance to pursue dealings with the Eyadéma regime.

EU sanctions have been in effect since 1992 and most major bilateral donors have suspended aid to Togo due to its poor record of human rights. Having silenced the critics at home, Eyadéma decided in May 1999 to take on his international detractors, and hired a French lawyer to sue Amnesty International over allegations that large numbers of people were killed by security forces before the presidential elections of 1998. French president Jacques Chirac's visit in July 1999 coincided with confirmation from the Benin League for the Defence of Human Rights that **mass executions** of hundreds of people had taken place and their bodies had been dumped at sea. More than 100 bodies had been washed ashore in Benin's coastal villages.

After over three decades in power, Eyadéma appears as secure at the top as ever, but he has not emerged from events unscathed. Whatever the outcome of the case against Amnesty International, no one at home or abroad is likely to forget the catastrophic 1990s when he governed through intimidation and force. The popular image Eyadéma once fostered of himself as a peacemaker and protector has been permanently damaged. He stands little hope of restarting Togo's crippled economy before the next presidential elections, and even less of persuading the gaping pockets of resentment in Togolese society that he represents their best interests. Olympio still waits in the wings.

LOMÉ AND THE COAST

The pace of **Lomé** falls far short of the frenzied tempo you find in the other big cities of West Africa, with most of its activity centring around the bustling market and surrounding commercial district – a pleasantly archaic area laid out by the French. The mix of urban sophistication and rural informality once combined to make Lomé West Africa's most enticing capital: for overlanders a popular respite from the rigours of travel in the bush; for the large expat community working in finance, development or as volunteers, an important centre of operations. But the strikes and violence of the early 1990s hit Lomé badly, and it is only now that the city's spark is slowly beginning to return.

East of the city, there are just fifty kilometres of coastline, wedged between the Ghanaian and Benin borders. The surf is notoriously rough, even dangerous at times, yet the whole **Atlantic shorefront** is picture-postcard perfect, with its coconut groves, white-sand beaches and **fishing villages** – none more than an hour's journey from the capital. The towns of **Togoville**, **Aného** and **Glidji**, with their fetishes, shrines and festivals, offer the possibility of interesting insights into local voodoo customs.

These towns also served as the spearhead for the German colonial invasion which began in 1884 – the year when Gustav Nachtigal landed in Togoville and signed a treaty placing the chief under the Kaiser's "protection". Soon after, Aného became capital of German Togoland. Today, the coastal villages are full of colonial vestiges and, in varying states of dilapidation, they stand in sharp contrast to the dominant voodoo culture.

Lomé

Although **LOMÉ** spreads widely, the city's population (normally a manageable 500,000, though this number was nearly halved during the worst moments of unrest) is hardly enough to push it into the major metropolis category. The heart of the downtown district sweeps around the crowded, old **Grand Marché**. In the immediate vicinity, throngs of **shoppers and street vendors** press through a maze of narrow avenues and sandy streets lined with two-storey colonial buildings – the domain of Lebanese shopkeepers and small import-export businesses. The whole area is dominated by the **beach** and pervaded by an ocean breeze ambience. Only along **Boulevard Circulaire** (renamed but rarely referred to as the Boulevard 13 Janvier) do you encounter the broad streets and high-rises that attest to the city's one-time status as West Africa's financial capital. The city's factories are out of sight, about ten kilometres east beyond the port.

Some history

The settlement of Lomé was founded by Ewe people fleeing a tyrant ruler in their homeland of Notsé in the eighteenth century. By the end of the nineteenth century, the Germans had moved the **capital** of their newly declared colony from Aného to Lomé. Reminders of their rule, like the **neo-Gothic cathedral** or the **old wharf** near the Grand Marché, are still visible. Lomé remained the capital of the French protectorate after World War I, but Togo had lost its former importance, and development was minimal compared with other colonies.

Much of the infrastructure of the old part of town dates from the colonial period and has proved inadequate in coping with rapid growth. **Development** has been concentrated elsewhere. The first part of the city to be modernized was the **administrative centre** just west of the Grand Marché. Wide tree-lined avenues were traced here, and the capital's first skyscraper – the **Hôtel du 2 Février** – erected. Built in the middle of

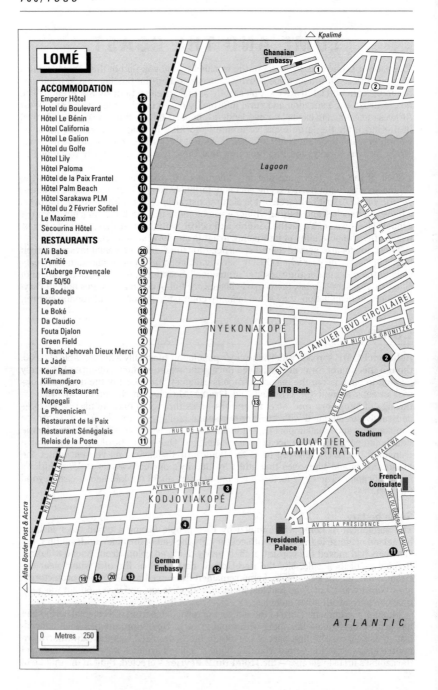

△ *Kpalimé*

LOMÉ

ACCOMMODATION
Emperor Hôtel	**13**
Hotel du Boulevard	**1**
Hôtel Le Bénin	**11**
Hôtel California	**4**
Hôtel Le Galion	**3**
Hôtel du Golfe	**7**
Hôtel Lily	**14**
Hôtel Paloma	**5**
Hôtel de la Paix Frantel	**9**
Hôtel Palm Beach	**10**
Hôtel Sarakawa PLM	**8**
Hôtel du 2 Février Sofitel	**2**
Le Maxime	**12**
Secourina Hôtel	**6**

RESTAURANTS
Ali Baba	**20**
L'Amitié	**5**
L'Auberge Provençale	**19**
Bar 50/50	**13**
La Bodega	**12**
Bopato	**15**
Le Boké	**18**
Da Claudio	**16**
Fouta Djalon	**10**
Green Field	**2**
I Thank Jehovah Dieux Merci	**3**
Le Jade	**1**
Keur Rama	**14**
Kilimandjaro	**4**
Marox Restaurant	**17**
Nopegali	**9**
Le Phoenicien	**8**
Restaurant de la Paix	**6**
Restaurant Sénégalais	**7**
Relais de la Poste	**11**

Ghanaian Embassy

Lagoon

NYEKONAKOPÉ

BLVD 13 JANVIER (BVD CIRCULAIRE)

AV NICOLAS GRUNITZKY

HÔTEL DE PALIMÉ

AV DES VINES

UTB Bank

RUE DE LA KOZAH

Stadium

QUARTIER ADMINISTRATIF

AV DE SARAKAWA

French Consulate

AVENUE DUISBURG

KODJOVIAKOPÉ

AV DE LA PRÉSIDENCE

Presidential Palace

AV DU GÉNÉRAL DE GAULLE

German Embassy

ROUTE CIRCULAIRE

△ Afiao Border Post & Accra

0 Metres 250

ATLANTIC

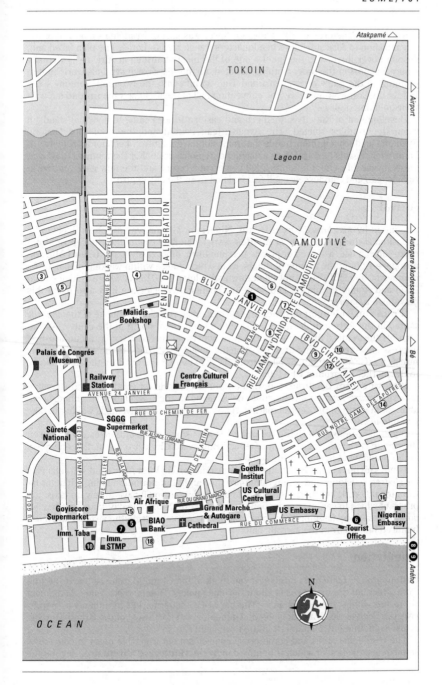

nowhere, this 37-storey marble-and-glass tower was part of Eyadéma's bid to have the Organization of African Unity's headquarters transferred to Lomé. The plan failed and, despite government PR, the hotel – one of the most luxurious in Africa – is virtually empty for most of the time. Nothing daunted, further expensive symbols were built to promulgate the glory of Eyadéma and Togo's entry into the twentieth century – the **Palais de Congrès** (formerly the convention hall of the RPT) and the **ministries** with their gold-tinted glass.

Development of the city's northern and eastern fringes came to a virtual standstill when the troubles started. The Avenue Jean Paul II and the Boulevard Général Eyadéma lead to neighbourhoods that may still have a future of economic activity – if Lomé ever regains its position as a magnet of regional trade. For the moment, however, the Nouveau Marché, the Lomé 2000 conference centre and the new *gare routière* at Agbalepedo and Akodessewa still feel isolated from the city centre.

Arrival

Coming in by *taxi brousse*, from **Benin**, **Nigeria** or **Ghana**, you are most likely to be deposited at the *gare routière* at **Akodessewa**, about 3km east of the city centre. From here, you can take a shared or private taxi into town, most easily to the **Grand Marché autogare** right in the middle of things, from which you're within walking distance of a number of hotels if you're not piled down with luggage. This is where vehicles from Aflao and Aného terminate, and some international vehicles are now also using this downtown *autogare*.

From Ouagadougou and northern Togo, most vehicles terminate at the *nouvelle station* in the **Agbalepedo** neighbourhood, a good 10km north of the centre. As you turn off the route d'Atakpamé, the lack of activity in the area tends to confirm first impressions – you're being dropped off in the boondocks. To get to the centre of Lomé, hire a cab (CFA500–1000), or pile into a collective taxi. These ply from the *gare routière* to the market for around CFA100.

If arriving **from Kpalimé**, you wind up (unless your driver continues to the centre) at a small *gare routière* on the route de Kpalimé in the Casablanca neighbourhood, about 5km north of the central market. Again, there are collective taxis waiting to take you into town.

If you happen to be **arriving by rail**, taxis are usually waiting to meet any trains, on the rue de la Gare between the market and Boulevard Circulaire. If not, flag one down at the roundabout in front of the station.

Lomé's **airport** is small, but one of the most modern in West Africa and still relatively hassle-free (customs and immigration are thorough, but not intimidating). It's not far from town (7km), but there's no airport bus service, so you'll have to rely on taxis, the prices of which to various destinations are posted up. During the day, you can often get collective taxis by flagging them down on the main road outside the airport, just a few hundred metres from the arrivals hall.

Orientation

Getting around Lomé isn't difficult if you think of the Grand Marché as being the hub from which all the major roads shoot out like spokes. Hotels, restaurants, banks and shops are within walking distance. The big SGGG supermarket (pronounced "S-trois-jay", the Societé Générale du Golfe du Guinée), 500m northwest of the Grand Marché, is also something of a landmark in the town centre.

The residential areas and commercial centres fan out from this heart in concentric semicircles, the first of which is hemmed in by the **Boulevard Circulaire**. Beyond the

STREET NAMES

Lomé has its fair share of street names surplus to requirements. Among the more important, the Boulevard 13 Janvier is almost always known as the Boulevard Circulaire; the route d'Amoutivé is also known as Avenue Mama N'Danida; and the main seafront avenue goes by the names Boulevard de la République, Boulevard de la Marina, route d'Aflao, route d'Aného and *route internationale*.

Quartier Administratif and west of this artery, the **Kodjoviakopé** neighbourhood was hardly more than a fishing village twenty years ago and still moves to a slower rhythm than the city centre. Many travellers opt for one of the beachfront hotels here.

To the north, the **Amoutivé** neighbourhood – the home of the traditional chief of Lomé, a descendant of the city's founder – is presently one of the most active quarters in town. Streets here are more crowded at night than in other neighbourhoods and the area throbs with commerce.

Bé, to the east, is another active neighbourhood that was formerly a village in its own right. Although it's still a stronghold of **voodooism**, the external signs of the religion are increasingly rare. Flagpoles bearing a white banner in certain homes in the area indicate the presence of a fetish priest.

North of **the lagoon**, another semicircle unfolds. Important institutions such as the CHU hospital, the Université du Benin and the Lycée are situated beyond this natural barrier among the unpaved streets and vacant lots of the essentially residential **Tokoin** district, accessible both by the Atakpamé and the Kpalimé roads.

Tourist information and city transport

The **tourist information office** on the rue du Commerce (☎21.43.13) has detailed city maps and very little else.

In the absence of a bus system, public transport in Lomé is down to **taxis** (either *taxis collectives* for about CFA100 per short hop, or chartered for a specific journey – about CFA500 is the average fare around town), collective **minibuses** (again, about CFA100 per short hop), or **zemidjan** "moped taxis", who will take you right to your destination for CFA100. These are especially useful at night, when they're easier to find than taxis, though not all the moped drivers are very good.

Gares for *collectives* are scattered around the vicinity of the Grand Marché: those for Kodjoviakopé, Tokoin, Casablanca and Agbalepedo are west of the market; for Amoutivé and Lomé 2000 they are to the north on Avenue Mama N'Danida; for Bé and Ablogamé to the east. The *collectives* run on fairly fixed routes – for example up and down the main radial thoroughfares from the Grand Marché to Boulevard Circulaire, or clockwise around Boulevard Circulaire to Bé and back again.

SECURITY

Lomé has become increasingly dangerous even in periods of calm. **Crime** is on the rise; many travellers have been robbed at knifepoint or been sprayed in the face with something in a mugging. Thieves are well aware of the tourist penchant for hotels along the western parts of the beach, and night-time robberies along the *route internationale*, especially in the area of *Le Maxime* are common. After dark, the area around the Grand Marché is also unsafe. Other areas may seem quite safe to wander around, but nothing should be taken for granted, and certainly walking anywhere at night with valuables is inadvisable.

Accommodation

Lomé has dozens of hotels, but most people head to the **beachfront** when seeking out places to stay. Along the *route internationale*, from the Ghana border to the eastern outskirts of town, you'll have no trouble finding a place to fit your taste and price range. The **camping sites**, beyond the port to the east of the centre all have rooms and/or bungalows, as well as tent pitches.

Budget and moderate options

Emperor Hôtel, bd de la Republique, not far from *Le Maxime*. Clean and comfortable rooms set in a fairly spacious compound. ②.

Hôtel Le Bénin, on the seafront, corner of av du Général de Gaulle (BP 128; ☎21.24.85). Actually a training hotel, which is not known for stunning service and is currently not very popular, despite the good atmosphere, location and competitive prices. ⑤.

Hôtel du Boulevard, bd Circulaire, one block from av Mama N'Danida (☎21.15.91). A bit run-down but still quite comfortable. Bar and restaurant. ①–②.

Hôtel California, behind the German embassy (☎21.18.75). The S/C rooms here are clean and have AC. Pleasant, well-stocked bar and restaurant. ②.

Hôtel Le Galion, rue Professeur Lassey, Kodjoviakopé, via rue Houndjagoh, the small street running next to *Le Maxime* (☎21.65.64). Immaculate rooms in a refurbished home with landscaped courtyard. Stylish design and attentive staff make this very popular with travellers and excellent value. ②–③.

Hôtel du Golfe, rue du Commerce (BP 36; ☎21.02.78). An older but well-kept establishment. Extremely central, with high standards of service. Rooms with AC and phones. ④.

Hôtel Lily, bd de la République, Kodjoviakopé, a stone's throw from the border and the beach. Spacious rooms and reasonable rates, but a bit far from the centre. ①.

Hôtel Paloma, rue du Grand Marché, corner of rue de la Gare. Scruffy and windowless cells with the merits of cheapness and a very central location. Bargain hard. ①.

Le Maxime, bd de la République, near bd Circulaire (BP 1909; ☎21.74.48). Formerly a magnet for younger travellers attracted by the outdoor bar and restaurant, and S/C, AC comforts, this is gradually becoming less appealing with the absence of the crowds. ①–②.

Secourina Hôtel, 63 route d'Aného with annexe 100m down the street (☎21.60.20). Comfortable AC rooms with phones and lots of hot water. Good value for creature comforts without chain-hotel sterility. ②–③.

Expensive options

Hôtel de la Paix Frantel, 3km east of the city centre, set back from the sea (BP 3452; ☎21.52.97; Fax 21.23.02). Badly run-down with chipped paint, water stains and a depressing atmosphere. Despite the attraction of its own beachfront, hard to recommend. ④–⑤.

Hôtel Palm Beach, bd de la Marina at rue Gallieni. Newer high-rise hotel with comfortable rooms overlooking the beach plus a pool, nightclub and casino. ⑥–⑦.

Hôtel Sarakawa PLM, 3km east of downtown (BP 2232; ☎27.65.90; Fax 21.71.80). A huge pool dominates the grounds and you'll find TV and phones in every room. But even this once irreproachable (if perfectly predictable) international hotel has become tatty of late. ⑥–⑦.

Hôtel du 2 Février Sofitel, place de l'Indépendance (BP 131; ☎21.00.03; Fax 21.62.66). Not the one you'd be likely to choose, as it's the most expensive of the lot – a mad folly with nearly 400

ACCOMMODATION PRICE CODES

① Under CFA4500 (under £5/$8).
② CFA4500–9000 (£5–10/$8–16).
③ CFA9000–18,000 (£10–20/$16–32).
④ CFA18,000–27,000 (£20–30/$32–48).

⑤ CFA27,000–36,000 (£30–40/$48–64).
⑥ CFA36,000–45,000 (£40–50/$64–80).
⑦ Over CFA45,000 (over £50/$80).

For further details see p.480

rooms and a handful of guests knocking around inside like seeds in a calabash. Somewhat spooky really, and the impeccable views are the most it has in its favour. ⑦.

Camping

If you don't have your own transport, collective taxis can get you out to the camping beaches for under CFA300. Camping **rates** are around CFA750–1000 per person at all three. Unfortunately, the immediate vicinities of the beach camping sites are now notorious for armed **robbery**. Take precautions if you're carrying valuables and be especially careful after dark.

Chez Alice, 14km east of the centre near the village of Baguida, a good 300m from the seashore (☎27.91.72). Something of a roadside holiday camp, with rooms and bungalows ranging from basic to moderate, as well as tent pitches. The good restaurant and bars make this a favourite overlanders' haunt. ①.

Ramatou Plage, 10km from the centre (BP 1256; ☎27.43.53). Places to camp or rooms (some with private bath). This place is OK, but nothing special, particularly considering it's barely out of range of the industrial zone (the air can be smelly round here). Fairly expensive restaurant. ①–②.

Robinson Plage, 10km from the centre, next to *Ramatou* (BP 9149; ☎27.58.14). The nicest of the lot with AC, S/C rooms around landscaped gardens on the seafront, or simpler bungalows with fan and mosquito nets. The seafood restaurant is very good, though expensive. ①.

The City

There's not really a lot in Lomé to go out of your way to see, but there's plenty to take in as you wander through town. At some stage in your stay, try and have a look at the **Hôtel du 2 Février**, built to commemorate the president's miraculous escape and "Triumphal Return" after his plane crashed near Sarakawa. On clear days, you get a splendid panoramic view of Lomé, Ghana and the coastline from the top-floor restaurant and bar. Even a small drink costs a packet.

The focal point of the city, the **Grand Marché**, takes up a full city block near the ocean and may occupy a lot of your time. Lomé has numerous other market districts specializing in everything from bicycle parts to fetish paraphernalia.

If you're looking for a **beach** to lie on, in town you're limited to stretches of shore in front of *Hôtel de la Paix* and the *Hôtel le Bénin*, the latter more popular, especially at weekends; however they're both dirty, prone to crime and the sea has a fearfully strong undertow. Out of town past the port, Robinson Plage draws a large weekend crowd and is a far better bet. The sand bar makes for safe swimming and the shipwreck adds a certain something.

The Grand Marché

Business in the **Grand Marché** has picked up considerably after the strikes, and though Lomé's market is not the regional draw it once was, there's again a wide range of goods. It's not an attractive building but it is about the only place you need to go for provisions, presents, in fact purchases of any kind. Commerce spills over into all the surrounding streets as traders (mostly women between the ages of 3 and 103) zigzag through the crowd to hawk everything from rat poison to greetings cards.

The **ground floor** of the building is filled with food – canned food, fruit and vegetables, meat, poultry, fish, and staples like yams, rice, cassava and pasta, spices and peanut butter. Sellers have a flare for display and fruit and vegetables are invariably arranged in eye-catching pyramids of colour. Quality is generally high, though if you're cooking it's best to buy meat first thing in the morning, for obvious reasons.

Up on the **first floor**, the celebrated, and extravagantly proportioned **"Nana Benz"** (which, roughly translated, means "Mercedes Mamas", a reference to the cars they often drive) lounge around fanning themselves in a decadent style befitting their reputation as some of the richest and most adept business people in Africa. They monopolize the sale of **cloth** and journey as far as Europe and Saudi Arabia to assure a stock that attracts buyers from the whole region. "Made in Holland" Dutch wax prints are their most expensive and prestigious wares, but you'll also find English and African prints, hand-woven *kente* cloth from Ghana, Ewe strip cloth, naturally dyed indigo wraps from Guinea and Mali and rough cotton weaves from the Sahel.

Generally you'll have to buy in relatively large quantities here (the rue du Commerce is the place for single cloths), though after recent lean years the Mamas have begun to make exceptions. Material is traditionally sold by *la pièce*, *une pièce* being six *pagnes*, and a *pagne* roughly equal to an arms-spread – or about 1.8m, the length of a wrap. The smallest length you can traditionally buy in the market is a *demi-pièce* or three pagnes' worth, the cost of which varies according to the method and place of manufacture. Prices are marked and, although you may be able to get the vendor to come down slightly, bargaining never gets you very far here.

The **second floor** at the top is a hodgepodge emporium of goods – everything from bicycle tyres to wigs, envelopes and Chinese enamel basins to plastic dolls (white as well as black). Mountains of cosmetics – lotions, shampoos, make-up – swamp an entire section. This is also where you can buy the cheapest cigarettes in town, by the carton.

Handicraft markets

Crafts from all over West Africa filter into Lomé and there are several locations in town to look for them. The main selling venue is the **Passage des Arts**, where you'll find a large selection of carvings, batiks, sculpture and other handicrafts, although the majority come from Nigeria, Cameroon, Ghana and even Kenya; there's little in the way of typically Togolese art. Beware of "antiques": they almost never are. Prices are steep and the pressure to buy can be unpleasant, but the urgency of the vendors gradually gives way to something more bearable if you hang on for a few minutes, especially if you make a purchase, even of something small.

Opposite the cathedral on the rue du Commerce, the handmade **sandals** sold on the streetside are comfortable and sturdy, qualities that have made them popular throughout West Africa. The kind with the cushioned soles and toe loop go for about CFA2000 and are worth every franc. On the same street, you'll also find **cloth**, and you can easily buy short lengths of one or two *pagnes* here.

On the rue de la Gare, next to the *Bopato* café, you'll find the biggest selection of **batiks** and some vaguely African-looking tie-dyed dresses and shirts mixed together with carvings and other bric-a-brac.

Over on the route d'Aného, near the tourist office, you'll find brilliantly patterned **blankets** – mainly from Mali and Niger. These are handmade and expensive, but patient bargaining gets results. Something big enough to cover a double bed or look huge and striking on a wall should ultimately cost somewhere between CFA20,000 and CFA30,000, though price is determined to some extent by the state of the market, the time of year and the number of profligate punters in town. Another regular treasure trove of blankets is laid out on the pavement across from the Goyi Score supermarket on rue Gallieni.

On the eastern end of the rue du Commerce, the tourist information office has a **showroom** for regional crafts, including batiks, carvings and brasswork, produced mainly for aesthetic appeal – the traditional function of the masks and other objects has pretty much ceded to the desire to please souvenir-hunters. Prices are marked here, so you can get a rough idea how much things are going for.

The museum

The **National History Museum** (Mon–Fri 8.30–11.30am & 1.30–4.30pm, Sat 9am–noon; donation appreciated) has been relegated to a small room in the Palais de

Congrès (formerly the party headquarters) for over a decade, and the pickings are decidedly slim. Musical instruments and religious objects (statues, masks and ceremonial dress) give the merest glimpse into the material cultures of various ethnic groups such as the Kabyé, Mina and Ewe. One room is dedicated to the colonial period, tracing it from Nachtigal's landing in 1884 through the division of Togoland between the French and British in 1914 and ploddingly on to independence, with a succession of pictures of moustachioed governors puffing their bemedalled chests.

The Bé and Amoutivé markets

The **Bé market**, on the rue Pa de Souza, lost much of its charm when walls went up around it in the early 1980s and the adjoining fetish market was moved to Akodessewa (see below). Now Bé is mainly a neighbourhood market with food items and a scattering of pottery, calabashes (rapidly losing ground to "Made in Nigeria" plastic ware) and other household items. The **Amoutivé market**, on the avenue Mama N'Danida, is similar.

Akodessewa fetish market

The **Marché des Féticheurs** at Akodessewa is a popular draw for visitors and Loméans alike, despite its distance some 8km from the city centre. Adjoining a small food market in this northeastern suburb, it is West Africa's largest fetish market – a myriad of stalls displaying animal skulls, rotting bird carcases, statues, bells, powders and all the imaginable and unimaginable ingredients of **traditional medicine and religion**.

Children are always pestering to show you around the stalls and explain some of the charms or **gri-gris** – as usual, explain what you'll give (CFA100–200) before setting off, and make the most of what they know. Mostly they'll try to interest you in a talisman for safe travel or success in love – disarmingly inexpensive items that it's easy to take an interest in. Scorpions and dead snakes, used to make potions for ailments such as arthritis and rheumatism, have a more ghoulish and less user-friendly appeal. Though fetishers won't hesitate to make a quick sell, at times giving the feeling of a fleecing operation, it's a serious profession, still handed down jealously from generation to generation. The reputation of the Togolese for their spiritual gifts is widespread. A little time spent here listening to tales of supernatural healing and therapy will sow seeds of doubt in the most rational mind.

The powers of the *féticheurs* are sought after by all classes. In Togo, the overwhelming majority still practises traditional ("animist") religions and even the Christian and Muslim minorities commonly incorporate traditional practices into their beliefs. But the reputation of Akodessewa also attracts people from all over West Africa, and from as far away as Gabon and Congo.

There are two ways of **getting to the market**. The first is to head out on the Nouvelle rue de Bé or the rue Notre Dame des Apôtres, which converge by the old **Fôret Sacré** ("Sacred Forest", on the left) and pass the former site of the fetish market at Bé. The forest is a remarkable little jungle, surrounded by buildings, but out of bounds to non-believers. Alternatively, you can go the more boring way, by taking the route d'Aného along the coast, past the *Hôtel Sarakawa*. At the rond-point du port, 6km from central Lomé, turn left and follow the paved road for a kilometre and a half. If you're getting to Akodessewa by private taxi, expect to pay over the odds for the distance. A *zemidjan* all the way there shouldn't cost you more than CFA300–350.

Eating

Cheap **street food** can be found – during the day only – mainly around the different markets in town. At the Grand Marché, women serve delicious salads from stands directly opposite the taxi park. They'll throw anything that strikes your fancy onto the bed of lettuce – tomatoes, macaroni, avocadoes, even grilled chicken or Guinea fowl – and top it off with a tangy vinegar sauce. It's an excellent meal, so long as your system is acclimatized to somewhat insanitary conditions. Behind these stalls, women sell *fufu*, or *akoumé* (fermented white corn mash) with different sauces and meat (beef, goat, chicken). Similar food can be found in the Amoutivé and Bé markets.

For cheap eating **after dark**, try in front of the popular *50/50 Bar-restaurant* (aka *Free Time*) on Boulevard Circulaire. At **breakfast** time, keep your eye out for *les café-man*. Scattered about town, they serve cheap omelettes with Nescafé and bread.

If you're looking to off-load some funds in an **upmarket restaurant**, Lomé can easily oblige. Note, however, that places have a tendency to open and close their doors erratically, and the following is an abbreviated list of the restaurants that seem to be the most stable.

Budget

L'Amitié, bd Circulaire. A pleasant place to sit, with a bar, simple, inexpensive food and no pretentions. Local musicians often drop by.

Le Boké, rue du Commerce, opposite the BIAO. Friendly, inexpensive and clean restaurant serving good Guinean food.

Bopato, rue de la Gare, across from the BIAO bank. Sandwiches and snacks in the outdoor café. The tourist custom assures a steady flow of hawkers. Tedious, but still a good place to meet people and one of Lomé's main rendezvous.

Fouta Djalon, 238 bd Circulaire. Good-value Guinean restaurant where you can eat for about CFA1500.

I Thank Jehovah Dieux Merci, bd 13 Janvier, near the Kpalimé road. A huge range of interesting bean dishes, yam stew, things fried and boiled – a diversity of tastes and incredibly inexpensive. You pay by the portion, average CFA200–300. It's not slick, but for real food, well cooked, it's one of West Africa's best eating houses.

Nopegali, 229 bd Circulaire. Simple, cheap African food served in a relaxed and friendly atmosphere.

Restaurant de la Paix, north of bd Circulaire, northeast, near the *Hôtel du Boulevard*. A third Guinean place and likewise excellent value – *steack-frites*, omelettes, *couscous*, *lait caillé*.

Restaurant Sénégalais, rue du Commerce. Reasonable meals on a pleasantly shaded street terrace.

Moderate

Kilimandjaro, bd Circulaire near rte de Kpalimé (☎22.04.67). Ethiopian restaurant (*njera* bread "plates" served with *wat* stew) with indoor or outdoor dining and currently popular with the expat crowd. The chinese food is also quite good, with an excellent buffet twice weekly.

Marox Restaurant, near the market, always pulls in a crowd, mainly expat and showy Togolese. It's run by Germans and does a big trade in sausages and meat dishes with fries and salads from around CFA2500.

Le Phoenicien, av Mama N'Danida, just south of av 24 Janvier. Good Lebanese food and salads.

Relais de la Poste, av de la Libération. Good French food at reasonable prices. Only fifty metres from the post office, it's also a fine place for breakfast while you read your mail.

Expensive

All the big hotels serve French cuisine at elevated prices. There are also several good, independent, French establishments, plus a number of other international restaurants worth trying.

Ali Baba, bd de la République. Good fresh fish dishes. Accommodating owner and reasonable prices: expect to pay around CFA4000.

L'Auberge Provençale, bd de la République, at the border (☎21.16.82). A flashy place to spend a lot of money, preferably someone else's. Wonderful bouillabaisse and other seafood, plus *couscous* and paella (specialities need advance ordering).

Le Belvedere, av Duisburg in the Kodjoviakopé neighbourhood. Good French cooking in the open air for around CFA3500.

La Bodega, bd Circulaire, near *Nopegali*. Pleasant interior, Spanish music and good food – with a *menu* at CFA4000.

Da Claudio, 298 bd Circulaire. Formal and expensive Italian food.

Le Galion, off bd de la République (see "Accommodation", p.784). This popular hotel also has the town's best Vietnamese restaurant with a superb selection of reasonably priced specialities and very friendly service.

Golden Crown, bd du Mono, around the corner of bd Circulaire and route d'Aného. A first-class Chinese/Vietnamese restaurant with wonderful dishes, and not overpriced, from CFA4000 a head.

Green Field, bd de Cebevito Tokoin-Hôpital, just east of the rte de Kpalimé. Very busy place where the chef slaps pizzas together behind the horseshoe bar and the overworked waitresses try to cope with 100 customers or more. Good atmosphere, but not the place if you're in a hurry.

Le Jade, route de Kpalimé. Superb class Chinese food – around CFA5000 per head.

Keur Rama, 290 bd Circulaire (☎21.54.62). Delicious fricassee of *agouti* and a long *carte* of other African specialities. Highly recommended and shouldn't cost more than CFA6000 a head.

Nightlife

Nightlife has picked up considerably since the early 1990s, when people tended to keep indoors after dark, but sections of town are still considered dangerous when the sun goes down, notably anywhere along the beach road or around the Grand Marché. There's a range of **discos**, running the gamut from popular spots where you pay no entrance and drinks are hardly more expensive than in daytime bars, to flashy joints with complicated light shows and DJs hyping up the crowds.

Among Lomé's workaday **bars**, *Le Pajar Bar* by the Goyi Score supermarket stands out – exceptionally cheap draught BB, served in an atmosphere of advanced mayhem. For a good bar to kick the evening off, the *Free Time* (still known as the *50/50 Bar*) is perennially popular and doesn't draw an especially touristy crowd.

Bars, clubs and discos

L'Abreuvoir, rue de la Gare, near SGGG (☎21.64.88). Lively bar, popular with travellers.

African Queen, rte d'Atakpamé, Tokoin. Low prices and the ambience of a youthful *boîte populaire* have helped this one hang on as other clubs have closed.

Byblos, just near *Da Claudio* on bd Circulaire. Good atmosphere – if a bit pricey – playing mainly African music.

The Circus, 8 av de Calais (☎21.75.55). Popular European-style dance house, previously known as *Maquina Loca*. Full sound and light show plus a heavy emphasis on Euro-American disco. Cover and drinks relatively expensive.

Domino, rue de la Gare, near SGGG. Popular nightspot but drinks are not cheap.

Privilège, *Hôtel Palm Beach*. The most "in" disco in town at the time of writing: throbbing, trendy and expensive.

Safari Club, route de Kpalimé, just north of the lagoon. Large dance area and low prices attract an exuberant crowd of young partiers.

Z, rue Kokéti near the *Abreuvoir* bar. Expensive club that attracts an upmarket crowd, with lights and the whole shebang.

Listings

Airline offices Aeroflot, 7 av 24 Janvier (☎21.04.80); Air Afrique, 12 rue du Commerce (☎21.20.42 or 21.20.44); Air France, Immeuble TABA, 1 rue du Commerce (☎21.05.73); Ghana Airways, 16 rue du Commerce (☎21.56.91 or 21.72.91); KLM, Immeuble TABA (☎21.63.30 or 21.63.31); Nigeria Airways, Immeuble John Holt (☎21.58.26); Sabena, Immeuble TABA (☎21.73.33 or 21.75.55); and Swissair, 9 rte d'Aného (☎21.31.57).

American Express The representative is in the Immeuble STMP, 2 rue du Commerce, (☎21.26.11).

Banks BIAO, on the corner of rue du Commerce and rue de la Gare (Mon–Fri 7.30–11.30am & 2.30–4pm; ☎21.32.86); UTB, 20 rue du Grand Marché (Mon–Fri 7.45–11.30am & 2.45–5pm); and BTCI, bd Circulaire near av de la Libération (Mon–Fri 7.30–11.30am & 12.30–4pm; ☎21.46.41; Fax 21.32.65).

Books and magazines Foreign newspapers (though no British ones) are sold at the airport. You'll sometimes find *Time, Newsweek* and even *West Africa* magazine hawked around town. Malidis bookshop, off bd de la Libération, has a good selection of books and foreign newspapers. Librairie Bon Pasteur, corner of rue du Commerce and av de la Libération, has a wide selection of French papers and mags plus fiction and non-fiction. For secondhand books in English, try the pedlars along the rue du Commerce.

Car rental Try Africom, 37 bd Circulaire (☎21.13.24); Avis, 252 bd du 13 Janvier (☎21.05.82) and at airport; Budget Rent-a-Car, Kodjoviakopé (☎21.09.31) and at airport; Hertz, rue du Commerce (☎21.44.79), with branches in *Hôtel du 2 Février, Hôtel Sarakawa* and at the airport; Loc-Auto, bd Circulaire (☎21.42.50); and Europcar (☎21.13.24).

Clinics and hospitals The Centre Hospitalier Universitaire (CHU) in the north of town in Tokoin is the main hospital. There's a good Chinese-run clinic, the Bon Secours, across from the American embassy on rue du Maréchal Foch. Also worth trying is the Clinique de L'Union in Nyekonakpoe.

Embassies and honorary consulates Democratic Republic of Congo, 325 bd Circulaire (BP 102; ☎21.51.55); France, 51 rue du Colonel de Roux (☎21.25.71; issues visas for Burkina Faso, Côte d'Ivoire, Mauritania and Senegal); Gabon, Tokoin Super-Taco (BP 9118; ☎21.47.76); Ghana, 8 rue Paulin-Eklou, Tokoin Ouest (BP 92; ☎21.31.94); Nigeria, 311 bd Circulaire (BP 1189; ☎21.34.25 or 21.34.55); UK, Honorary Consul Mrs J.A. Sawyer, British School, Cité du Benin (BP 20050; ☎26.46.06; Fax 21.49.89); USA, corner of rue Pelletier Caventou and rue Vauban (BP 852; ☎21.29.91; Fax 21.79.52).

Emergencies Police ☎17; ambulance ☎21.20.42; hospital, ☎21.25.01.

Immigration The Sûreté National on av Georges Pompidou handles requests for residency permits and visa extensions.

Libraries and cultural centres The American Cultural Centre at the corner of rue Caventou and rue Vauban has a free library with American magazines and papers (Mon–Fri 9am–12.30pm and 3–6pm, Sat 9am–noon), ABC TV news and free movies every Fri afternoon at 3pm and 6pm respectively. The Centre Culturel Français on rue 24 Janvier is the most active of the cultural centres with theatre, dance, music, library and videos. The German equivalent, the Goethe Institut, is worth visiting for shows and events.

Maps Direction de la Cartographie Nationale, inside the Ministère des Travaux Publiques (☎21.03.57). In theory, survey maps of the whole country at 1:50,000 and 1:200,000 are available.

Mechanics Professional and reliable service at Turbo Garage (☎21.16.28), rue Rhodes, Kodjoviakopé.

Pharmacies *Togo Presse* carries the changing list of pharmacies open out of hours (*pharmacies de garde*).

Phone Telephone and fax service behind the PTT. Calls can also be made from major hotels (more costly) and from an increasing number of phone boxes.

Photos and film Best-equipped place is Colorama, bd Circulaire, next to *La Bodega* restaurant. Magic Photo, rue du Commerce, offers more expensive one-hour development and on-the-spot passport photos. There's a photo booth on the rue du Commerce.

Post office The main PTT (Mon–Fri 8am–noon & 2.30–5.30pm, Sat 7.30am–12.30pm) is on av de la Libération, near bd Circulaire. Poste restante is helpful and reliable.

Supermarkets Goyi Score, rue Maréchal Gallieni, near the Grand Marché, and SGGG, which has several stores at the corner of rue Gallieni and rue de la Gare.

Swimming pools The nicest and most expensive are at the hotels *2 Février* and *Sarakawa* (CFA2000 for non-guests). The *Hôtel de la Paix* has the cheapest pool in town.

Travel agents Perhaps the best address for finding reasonable air tickets is STMP at 2 rue du Commerce (☎21.57.93). Compare prices here with nearby agencies such as Togo Palm Tours, 1 rue du Commerce (☎21.57.84), or Togo Tourisme, 9 rue du Commerce (☎21.09.32), who are also agents for Nouvelles Frontières.

The main **gare routière** is in **Agbalepedo** district 10km north of the centre, which handles northbound traffic to Atakpamé, Sokodé, Kara, Dapaong and Ouagadougou. For Kpalimé and towns along the Kpalimé road, there's a *gare routière* in the **Casablanca** neighbourhood, about 5km from the centre on the route de Kpalimé. Most taxis for Aflao, Aného, Cotonou and Lagos depart from the old **downtown** *gare routière* near the Grand Marché, but the *nouvel autogare* at **Akodessewa** also handles transport on the coastal routes, including direct taxis to Accra, Cotonou and Lagos.

The **train** schedules out of Lomé for **Blitta** are very unreliable and services may stop without warning – check at the station. In theory, the schedule is: depart Lomé 6.30am on Thursday and Saturday, arrive Blitta some twelve hours later (CFA1160).

East of Lomé

The short drive from Lomé to the Benin border passes along the coastal highway, with alternating views of the lagoon and the Atlantic. The villages along this stretch are peopled by Mina and Gun (or Guin), who migrated from Ghana at the beginning of the nineteenth century. Today, they make their living principally from fishing, coconut planting and small-scale cultivation. Main towns like **Togoville** and **Aného** are interesting combinations of colonial relics and fetish symbolism and move to a slower rhythm than the capital.

Agbodrafo and Togoville

Perched atop a hill on the north shore of Lake Togo, Togoville is most easily reached by *pirogue* from behind the main coast road. First step is a taxi from Lomé, 30km to **AGBODRAFO**. Formerly known by its Portuguese name, Porto Seguro, this village was the site of a small coastal fort similar to those in Ghana. Today it's ruled by one **Fio Adjete Sedo Assiakoley IV** who keeps the royal sceptres, thrones and weapons that have symbolized his family's authority in the region for 150 years.

Pirogues ply regularly between Agbodrafo and Togoville, leaving from a lagoon landing about 100 metres from the highway; any kid can point you there. You can rent a *pirogue* by paying the round-trip fare (at a price you negotiate) and arranging to be picked up in Togoville at a specified hour. Alternatively, you can simply wait for the boat to fill up with market women, though you will have a hard time convincing the *piroguier* to take you for the normal collective fare, and you may have a lot of hanging around on both shores.

Togoville town

Once you dock in **TOGOVILLE**, your itinerary will be pretty much determined by the boys who wait at the shorefront to be hired as semi-obligatory guides. You might as well go with the flow; they're nice enough and very adept at showing strangers the more interesting local curiosities. The first order of business, and one you can't refuse, is to **visit the chief** and advise him of your arrival. If he's in, the chief will greet you personally and show you his memorabilia, including photographs of his ancestors and copies of the famous document signed with the Germans. With great pomp you'll be asked to sign the **"Golden Book"** and a small gift is expected at this point.

The present ruler is a direct descendant of **Mlapa**, the village king who signed the treaty that made the Germans protectors of the region (at which time the town was known simply as Togo, meaning "beside the water"). The contract signed with this tiny village was the basis on which the colonial government laid claim to all of present-day Togo and much of Ghana.

Formalities completed, you can wander around Togoville at your leisure. The children take you first to the **Catholic cathedral**, built in the early part of the century by the Germans. Notice the interior murals of African martyrs being burned at the stake, and a shrine to the Virgin who was seen walking on the lake in the early 1980s. This miracle reportedly inspired the pope's 1986 visit to Togoville.

Despite the work of the Catholic church, Togoville remains essentially animist. Walking through the narrow backstreets, you'll be shown several fetishes, including two **fertility shrines** – one of a formidably endowed man and the other of a well-rounded woman with spikes protruding from her body. Photographs are permitted provided you leave a small offering. Beyond the small market, on the north side of town, a modern **statue** marks the centenary of the Germano-Togolese treaty, celebrated in 1984.

Practicalities

From the waterfront, the silhouette of the cathedral in Togoville stands out on the hill across the lake, while on the right, windsurfers, boaters, and swimmers disport themselves in the schistosome-free waters in front of **Agbodrafo**'s pleasant *Hôtel Suisse-Caste* (③) – closed for refurbishment at the time of writing. Other **accommodation** options in Agbodrafo are the *Hôtel Le Lac* (☎35.00.05; ③), with comfortable AC rooms and the *Auberge du Lac*, 4km west of town, which offers S/C bungalows with good food and an excellent setting on the lake (②–③).

In **Togoville**, modest accommodation can be had at both the small *Auberge de l'Arbre de Palabre* and the *Hôtel Nachtigal*, which offer basic non-S/C lodgings (①).

Aného

Of all Togo's towns, the colonial presence is most strongly and most eerily felt in **ANÉHO** (10km from Agbodrafo). The Portuguese were the first to come to the spot – a pleasing natural setting with sea and lagoon vistas – which soon developed as a major slave market. Current African family names like de Souza and the light skin of the people are surprising reminders of this "Brazilian" period, further reflected in the history and culture of Ouidah in Benin (see p.842).

Many buildings bear witness to the days when "Anecho" was the capital of Kaiser Wilhelm's prize African possession – among them, the **Peter and Paul Church** (1898), close to being washed by the ocean, the thick-walled **préfecture** near the bridge, the interesting **German cemetery**, and the finely restored **Protestant church** (1895) on the route de Lomé. Other buildings are reminders of the French presence, including a number of grandiose villas used by colonial administrators when Aného was capital of the protectorate.

Aného has been in a slow decline for decades. Walking the streets, there's a feeling that residents are too entrapped in their daily routines of farming, fishing and trade to have any illusions of grandeur – or much opportunity to bring the old town to life. It's a small community, completely overshadowed by Lomé and with no hope

---

THE VODU

For some background on "voodooism" and the *vodu*, see the next chapter, "Benin", and in particular, the box on p.844.

MOVING ON FROM ANÉHO

The main *gare routière* in Aného is across the lagoon in the east of town towards the Benin border at Hilakondji. **Taxis** run direct from here to Cotonou and Lomé. It's also possible to flag down taxis to Lomé if you stand on the main road near the market.

of reviving its former commercial importance. All of which is a source of frustration for the young, most of whom migrate to the capital to seek their fortunes. But they leave Aného a satisfyingly moody place for travellers. The main **market** is on Tuesday and has a small fetish selection: monkey heads, crabs dead and alive, various skulls . . .

In contrast to the crumbling reminders of European occupation, Aného's **voodoo culture** thrives. Fetish priests are highly respected members of the community and are often more trusted than doctors practising Western medicine. Sacrifices are offered to shrines guarding many of the homes, and regular festivals are dedicated to the cult.

Practicalities

It isn't hard to find your way around Aného since virtually the whole of the town stretches along the **route de Lomé/Cotonou**. The market, post office, bank, *préfecture* and most shops are along this street between the Protestant church and the bridge. A more residential neighbourhood, and the area where you'll find all the major hotels and restaurants, lies across the bridge.

The first **hotel** you come to as you cross the bridge towards Cotonou is the *Oasis*, which has the best views of the sea and lagoon in town, and S/C rooms, most with AC (BP 171; ☎31.01.25; ②–③). Even if you don't stay, have a drink at the thatched terrace restaurant and watch the fishermen cast their nets into the shallow lagoon waters. More upmarket is the *Hôtel Relais de l'Union* (☎31.02.38; ③), a stone's throw from the Benin border, with slightly overpriced S/C, AC rooms. The cheapest place to stay is the friendly and reasonably comfortable *Auberge Elmina* (①), on the seafront about 80m east of the Peter and Paul Church.

The market is the place for cheap **eating**; otherwise try one of the hotels listed above. For drinking, check out *La Paillotte* on the route de Lomé, which has an unremarkable bar, but good music and atmosphere. The *Jardin Mama N'Danida*, in front of the Protestant church, serves cold drinks and food during the day in its shady garden.

Glidji

On the surface, **GLIDJI**, 4km north of Aného, looks just like any other Mina village. You'll notice the same *banco* huts with thatched roofs and the same narrow sandy

THE YÉKÉYÉKÉ FESTIVAL

Because of its **historical and religious pre-eminence**, Glidji is the site of the **Yékéyéké festival**, celebrated annually on the Thursday before the second Sunday in September. Delegations arrive from all the major Mina and Gun centres to make offerings to the deities and to be blessed by the priests. Animals are sacrificed, but the climax of the ceremonies occurs when the colour of the **sacred stone** is revealed. This stone determines the fortune of the coming year. For example, a blue stone indicates abundant rain. If your stay in the area coincides with the festival, these are four days of celebrating not to be missed. Note that there's no **accommodation** in Glidji, so you have to stay in Aného. And, around *Yékéyéké* time, room availability is very tight.

streets found all along the coast. Yet the town is symbolically important since the present chief is a direct descendant of **Foli-Bebe** – the first ruler of the region and the man responsible for the political organization of the Gun and Mina into independent chiefdoms after these peoples migrated from the Accra area in the early seventeenth century. Before starting off through town, you should pay a **visit to the chief**. To do so, you have to fill out a request at the royal secretariat. If the chief is around, and not otherwise occupied, he will receive you.

Glidji is also important from a religious perspective, since all the major sanctuaries to the principal **voodoo deities** are found in this town. You won't have trouble finding a boy to take you around to visit the different **fetish shrines** and voodoo **meeting places**. Ask to see the **temple of Egou**, the deity who is traditional protector of the Mina people.

THE PLATEAU REGION

Some of the country's most beautiful and fertile rural backcountry is located in the **plateau region** in the southwest quadrant of the country along the Ghanaian border – Togo's most agriculturally significant district. With its mountain vistas, thick vine-strewn forests and streams leaping in cascades from ragged clifftops, this corresponds to a stereotype of the jungle – especially if you've been brought up on Tarzan-type images. The wild country is as much a part of the region's scenery as the lush plantations of coffee, cocoa and fruit crops that make it so important economically.

Just a few hours from Lomé, the whole area is wonderfully accessible too, ethnically diverse and full of opportunities for hiking and discovery. The **coffee and cocoa** triangle, hemmed in by the towns of **Kpalimé**, **Badou** and **Atakpamé**, is home to several ethnic groups who came here from Ghana and the coast. Kpalimé and surrounding villages retain essentially Ewe populations but Badou and Atakpamé are melting pots of agricultural peoples.

Kpalimé and around

Capital of the *pays cacao* – the **cocoa country** – and of the entire fruit-growing region, **KPALIMÉ's** unusually busy market is your first hint of its importance. Early on in their brief rule, the Germans recognized the agricultural potential of this mild and attractive district. Once the plantations were established, they wasted no time in driving a **railway** through the forested hills to the town, and since that time Kpalimé has never been long out of the news in Togo. It was a stronghold of Olympio support in the early days after

---

EWE NAMES

As in the Asante country in Ghana, Ewe people usually take at least one name after the day of the week on which they were born.

	GIRLS' NAMES	BOYS' NAMES
Monday	Adzo	Kodjo
Tuesday	Abla	Komla
Wednesday	Aku	Kokou
Thursday	Ayawa	Yao
Friday	Afi	Koffi
Saturday	Ami	Komi
Sunday	Kosiwa or Essi	Kossi

independence and even now is considered to be anti-Eyadéma.

There's enough to see and do around Kpalimé to keep you busy for a couple of days – and longer if you're into **trekking** in the nearby mountains. But the town is small and, if you have less time, you can still get a good feel of the place in a day.

Arrival and orientation

If you're **arriving by taxi**, you'll find the *autogare* is near the old market building, off the road leading to Klouto. The train station (now disused) is right on the **market square**, on a hilltop in the town centre. Standing here, mountains rise in all directions around you. To the east, a TV tower rockets up from a distant peak to interrupt the harmony of the setting but helps you spot Togo's

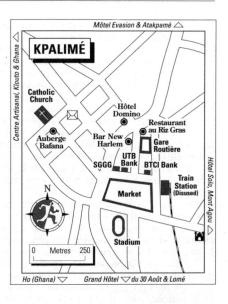

highest summit – Mont Agou (986m). Closer to hand, most immediate needs can be met in the area around the market. **Banks** (UTB and BTCI: Mon–Fri 7.30–11.30am & 2.30–4pm), **shops** (including an SGGG supermarket) and cheap **restaurants** line the streets that box in the market area. The **post office** is on the north side, towards the Catholic church.

Accommodation

Besides the **hotels** in Kpalimé, of which there's a good choice, you can also find accommodation around the pretty nearby town of Klouto (see p.796), but, despite the beautiful scenery, you're likely to feel stranded there if you don't have your own car. Places in Kpalimé include:

Grand Hôtel du 30 Août, at the entrance to town as you arrive from Lomé (BP 85; ☎41.00.95). Government-run hotel, with comfortable rooms, restaurant and a crafts centre, but far from the centre. ③.

Hôtel Bafana Bafana La Marquise, by the church (☎41.04.87). Brand new and very clean – the best deal in town. Rooms are S/C with fan. ①.

Hôtel Domino, close to the *gare routière*. One very inexpensive room with fan or moderate ones with AC. Also has a popular bar-restaurant. ①–②.

Hôtel Solo, ten minutes' walk (signposted) from the market towards Mont Agou. Very basic rooms with thatched roofs and no electricity. The family who run the hotel will cook for you and help you in any way. Kids pass by regularly and can show you around town if you want. ①.

Motel Evasion, rte d'Atakpamé, signposted 1km from centre (☎41.01.87). Comfortable place with thatched *banco* huts (some with AC) scattered around a compound which also sports a bar-restaurant and weekend nightclub. ②.

The Town

On the northeast side of town, the towering steeple of the **Eglise Catholique** dominates the skyline. Built by the Germans in 1913, this makes every effort to appear a *kirche* from the Bavarian countryside. The building imposes an incongruous beauty and calm of its own, and it's worth strolling up to have a closer look.

Kpalimé's **market** is the town's most compelling attraction. For produce, this is one of the best markets in the region. Among the **citrus fruit** you'll find beautiful oranges, grapefruit and mandarins – green-skinned, juicy and sweet. Avocadoes as big as boats sell for next to nothing and bananas, pineapples and lesser-known fruits are all available in abundance. Also on sale is woven **kente cloth** and other fabric. Kpalimé is known for its weavers and the quality of the material is very good – it's said Eyadéma's official ceremonial wrap was made here. The president made other news in Kpalimé when he announced in a speech here on August 30, 1971, the founding of what was then the nation's single party, the RPT. A giant **statue** of the president was erected to commemorate the event just south of the market, but was toppled in the riots that followed the 1991 coup attempt. Now a stronghold of anti-Eyadéma sentiment, thousands of refugees passed through the border here into Ghana during the upheaval of the early 1990s.

Down near the stadium, **weavers** work foot-operated looms at the roadside. They'll be happy to chat if you want to stop, never breaking the rhythm of their movements in the course of conversation. It's not hard to appreciate the time involved in making cloth and why it's so expensive. You can order directly from the weavers, but you have to be prepared to wait several days (or even weeks) for bespoke products.

The **Centre Artisanal de Kpalimé** (Mon–Fri 7am–noon & 2.30–5.30pm, Sat 8.30am–noon & 3–5pm, Sun 8.30am–1pm) on the route de Klouto, a couple of kilometres from the town centre, offers more immediate fulfilment. The work in this state-run crafts complex consists of modern interpretations of conventional forms – calabashes carved into delicate lampshades, pottery ashtrays, and decorative statues and batiks depicting ceremonial masks or village scenes. The excellent woodcarvings, such as the chairs and tables sculpted out of single tree trunks, represent a more traditional – though less portable – type of expression. *Kente* cloth is made at the centre too, but prices are well up on the market in town.

Eating and drinking

There are lots of good and cheap **food stalls** in the market. Alternatively, you could try *Restaurant au Riz Graz*, just north of the *gare routière*, which serves up the usual assortment of chicken and chips, omelette, *couscous* and *riz gras* for around CFA800–1200 a plate. *Bar New Harlem* nearby is a good place to relax, and also serves some food – all to the accompaniment of reggae.

Klouto and Mont Agou

Some 12km northwest of Kpalimé, **KLOUTO** (also spelled Kloto) is a mountain retreat and site of an old **German hospital** built before World War I. The road up here from Kpalimé is nothing short of spectacular. Carved out by the Germans, it snakes up steep slopes through cocoa plantations and burrows through the dense **Missahohé Forest** where tree branches form a complete tunnel over the road in certain areas.

MOVING ON FROM KPALIMÉ

From the *gare routière* in Kpalimé, **taxis** run to the **Ghana border**, **Lomé** (1hr 15min) and **Atakpamé** – the latter a pretty route skirting the Danyi plateau.

Should you be heading to – or just arrived from – Ghana **moneychangers** openly convert CFA to cedis and vice versa – but try to get an idea of the street rate in advance.

Collective taxis run pretty regularly from the Kpalimé *gare routière* (CFA200–250), but your best chances are on market days. In the village of Konda, which you pass on the way to Mont Klouto, the *Auberge des Papillons*, is managed by local celebrity, Prosper the butterfly collector. It offers basic **accommodation**, with no running water or electricity, arranged round a *paillote* and all set in fledgling jungle (①). Guided bushwalks are extra. Less rudimentary lodgings are to be found near the summit of Mont Klouto where, amid the rolling hills and forest, the old colonial buildings of the *campement* provide a rustic retreat with pretty views in every direction (③). Even if you don't sleep here, it's worth stopping at the large *paillote* where you can order food and drinks. As you follow the road leading up here, you'll see the entrance to the **Chateau Viale** – a stone fortress of medieval aspect built during World War II by a French lawyer, Francois-Raymond Viale. It became state property in 1971 and is now used by the president, so you can forget about visiting it. Photography is forbidden.

Once you've arrived at the *campement*, you'll notice a path bordered by huge mango trees that leads to the top of **Mont Klouto** (741m). Before you set off, there's a CFA1000 fee to pay to the *gardiens* who keep the paths clear. From the mountain, you can see across into Ghana and may even be able to make out the shining, artificial expanse of the dammed **Lake Volta** 35km away to the west. Numerous rural villages are hidden in the forest around the *campement*, and the kids will be happy to take you around to see any of them or other curiosities in the area, including streams, small waterfalls and palm-wine makers. Of course, you're expected to give them something, but for finding your way around the wilds, there's really no better way.

On market days, it's also possible to catch taxis from Kpalimé to villages on **Mont Agou** and to hike around its 1000-metre peaks. For more information, ask at the *Hôtel Solo* in Kpalimé. You'll have to plan on setting off at dawn and returning early, or risk missing the last taxi back to Kpalimé. If you have a car, a good road leads all the way to Mont Agou's 986-metre summit.

From Kpalimé to Atakpamé: the Danyi plateau

The road from Kpalimé to Atakpamé runs along the base of the sheer cliffs of the **Danyi plateau**, rising up to the west. About 10km out of Kpalimé, you can see the **Kpimé falls** from the roadside, a couple of kilometres up on the left (the driver or other passengers will point them out if you're in a taxi). The results of the hydroelectric dam built in the late 1970s haven't done much for the site's aesthetic appeal and in the dry season the falls are little more than a trickle, but during or after the rains, they tumble rewardingly a hundred metres off the cliffside.

It's a picturesque drive to Atakpamé, passing through numerous Akposso villages where you could easily stop and have a look around if you have your own transport. At **Dzogbégan** (turn off the road at Adeta, 30km from Kpalimé; then it's 20km further) no one will be surprised to see you as the **Benedictine monastery** a kilometre from the town has become a local attraction. Their chapel, built entirely of local materials – teak, iroko, mahogany, bamboo – is unusual, but the real interest is gastronomic. The monks run an orchard and produce jams from the exotic fruit as well as coffee, honey and other comestibles not so often found in these regions. The *soeurs bénédictines*, who run a convent closer to the village, sell some of the same items.

Atakpamé and around

Situated in the mountains, **ATAKPAMÉ** has historically been a place of refuge. The **Ewe** were the first to arrive, from Notsé, in the seventeenth century. They were followed

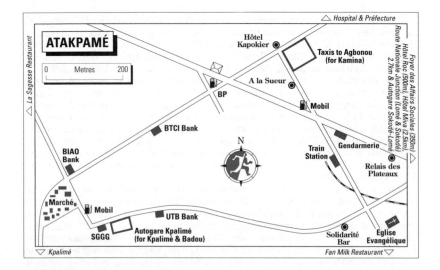

by the **Ana** – a people related to the Yoruba who came from the east in the nineteenth century – and then by the Akposso who came down from the surrounding mountains in the early part of this century to farm the **fertile plains**. Today, Atakpamé's road links with Lomé, Badou and Kpalimé and the measure of **industry** in the area – a nearby textile works, the new hydroelectric power station and a sugar refinery 20km to the north in Anié – have all helped it maintain its status as a regional hub and an ethnic melting pot.

Arrival and orientation

The most scenic approach to Atakpamé is from Kpalimé, via Hihéatro, a couple of kilometres west of the town. After this village, vehicles wind their way up one last steep hill and, before you were aware the town was anywhere nearby, turn a bend to pull into the *autogare Kpalimé* right by Atakpamé's marketplace. If you're coming from Lomé or Sokodé, you'll be dropped at the main *autogare Sokodé–Lomé* across the other side of town, about 1km west of the *route nationale* junction and 1km east of the town centre. If you're planning on staying the night, most of the **hotels** are just around the latter *autogare*. The hilly topography of the town and its scattered environs are confusing. The local neighbourhoods – sprouting in the hillocky valleys or on the rocky hillsides – have grown up wherever people found it possible to build.

The **route de Lomé**, which runs northwest–southeast to meet the *route nationale*, is the major thoroughfare in town. Main hotels and the PTT are along this street, while **banks** (BIAO and BTCI: Mon–Fri 7.30–11.30am & 2.30–4pm) and **shops** cluster around the market on the west side. The **market**, although located on the edge of town, is substantial enough to be the real town centre; on Friday – market day – the commotion is sensational. If you head left down the road on the other side of the market, towards the Eglise Evangelique – whose modern bell tower can be seen for some distance – then take another left after the *Solidarité Bar*, and pass the **train station**, you'll have seen pretty well the whole of Atakpamé town centre.

Accommodation

Of **places to stay**, the cheap *chambres de passage* at the *Le Retour* bar, located very near the main *gare routière* off the route de Lomé, offer the minimum of comfort and lots of late-night noise, but it's not fair to complain given the cost (①) and central location.

Foyer des Affaires Sociales, rte de Lomé near the main *gare routière*. Clean but spartan rooms typical of those run by the Affaires Sociales throughout the country. ①.

Hôtel de l'Amitié, on the Sokodé road, 200m from the *route nationale* junction (☎40.06.25). Clean rooms with fan, plus a bar and a good restaurant. ①–②.

Hôtel Kopokier, off the rte de Lomé on the hospital road (BP 42; ☎40.02.84). Comfortable S/C, AC rooms. ②.

Hôtel Miva, near the *route nationale* junction. Inexpensive, clean lodgings and friendly staff. ①.

Hôtel Oasis, a further 300m north of *Hôtel de l'Amitié* on the same road (☎40.04.31). More upmarket than *Hôtel de l'Amitié*, with some AC rooms. Food on order. ①–②.

Hôtel Roc, off the rte de Lomé, just north of the *gare routière* (BP 266; ☎40.02.37). Set on a hill overlooking the entire town, this government-operated hotel is the town's most expensive. The pleasant S/C, AC rooms have good views. Disco at weekends. ③.

Relais des Plateaux, rte de Lomé by the Commissariat de Police (☎40.02.31). Long a travellers' favourite with clean and comfortable S/C rooms with or without AC. ②.

Eating, drinking and nightlife

Atakpamé's **bars** and **restaurants** are mostly workaday places. *A la Sueur* – "By the sweat (of my brow)" – on the route de Lomé near the PTT, is a good stand-by, with Brasserie du Bénin drinks at normal prices and street food outside – cheap rice and spaghetti dishes, avocado, tomato and egg salads, kebabs and bread – which you can take into the bar. At weekends, the tables are removed to make room for dancing. The *Solidarité* near the Eglise Evangelique does African food at reasonable prices, and is recommended for evening drinking and music. For ice cream and yogurt, visit *Fan Milk*, just down the street. Near the market on the rue Djama, *La Sagesse* is a good place for solid meals including *couscous* and *poulet frites*. On the Sokodé road near the *Hôtel de l'Amitié*, just 100m from the junction, *La Camérounaise* offers tasty and inexpensive African and European food.

Kamina

KAMINA – a major German military post in the colonial era, complete with airstrip – is an easy excursion from Kpalimé. Today, a few buildings dating from the end of the nineteenth century are a reminder of the German occupation, one of which is now used to house a **boys' reform school**. The idea of such a school is quite revolutionary in this part of the world, and you might find it more interesting to visit than the town's historical remnants, which are hardly spectacular.

Assuming you don't have your own vehicle, the only way to get to Kamina is by collective taxi to **Agbonou** on the *route nationale*; from Agbonou you can take a local taxi for the four kilometres of dirt road to Kamina.

Along the route, you'll notice the chief military officer's headquarters. Now in a ruinous state, it's still called the "first house" by locals, since it was the first cement building to go up in the area. Across the street is the grave of a German soldier dating from 1914. Apart from the barracks which are now a school and some cement pylons that once hooked up to a giant wireless transmitter linking Togo direct with Berlin, these are all that's left of the German presence. Most of the pylons have been reclaimed by the bush, but if you take a closer look at the only one visible near the school you'll see a hole chiselled into its base. Local folk history relates how the French put dynamite inside when they captured the colony and tried to blow the thing up. When the dust settled, the pylon was still standing.

Badou and around

BADOU is the smallest, most isolated and most distinctly rural of the three towns of the coffee and cocoa triangle. Most of its people are cash crop farmers and, despite the small size of the average farm, cocoa and coffee have brought a measure of prosperity to the people of the region. In neighbouring Akrowa they've even managed to pay for all their streets to be paved. But there have been setbacks in recent years with the falling price of cocoa on the world market. Recent gluts of both crops have wreaked economic havoc in the quiet forest districts around Badou, and many young people are pinning their hopes on salaried jobs in the towns.

Practicalities

You'll get your bearings pretty quickly since Badou has only one proper hotel, one bank and one restaurant, all located near the market. Taxis let you off at the town entrance at the junction of the Atakpamé and Tomegbé roads. To get to the **market**, head down the road that leads to Ghana, across a small bridge and past the *Toyota Bar*. Further along this same thoroughfare, you'll come to another fork marked by the *Carrefour 2000 bar/dancing*, Badou's liveliest place at night, which also offers somewhat overpriced *chambres de passage* (☎43.00.47; ①). Turning left at this junction, you pass the post office on the way to Badou's fanciest **accommodation** – the government-run *Hôtel Abuta*, with a European-style restaurant and AC rooms costing little more than those at the *Carrefour 2000* (☎43.00.16; ①–②). You can also **camp** in the grounds here for CFA1800 per person. The **BTD bank** is right next door and they will change both cash and travellers' cheques. Badou's **pharmacy** is just behind the hotel.

Young boys like to earn a few francs showing visitors round their town and its surrounds. Although Badou itself doesn't merit this treatment, you might want someone to take you to nearby hamlets. They'll sometimes even offer lodgings *en famille*, a cheaper and more enjoyable option than staying in town.

Around Badou

One of the main attractions around Badou, and well worth taking the time to discover, is the **Akloa Falls**, 11km to the south. **Getting there**, you first need a taxi along the Tomegbé road to the village of Akloa (Akrowa on some maps). At its entrance, you'll see a hand-painted sign advertising the falls and a bar-restaurant. This is the official starting point for the falls hike up the mountain, and the place where you pay CFA500 for a ticket to proceed.

The **climb** to the falls is strenuous, but it requires determination rather than fitness. In any case, there's no rush; it's hard to resist dawdling through the cool, dark underbrush of the forest. After some thirty minutes of hiking through the dense vegetation, you arrive at the falls – a drop of over thirty metres from the granite cliff. You can swim in the pool at the base of the falls and it's said the waters are therapeutic. If you've come with people from the area, ask them to tell you about **Mamy Wada** – the spirit that guards the water – or about the numerous other supernatural forces in the forest. Two generations ago this whole area was sacred and off-limits to the uninitiated.

SOKODÉ AND THE CENTRAL REGION

In the semi-daze of a long and comfortless taxi ride, you could miss the many signs indicating the shifts in peoples and lifestyles as you move from the balmy south of Togo to the central and northern regions. Gradually, however, you take in the change from the traditional square buildings of the south to the round, thatch-roofed **banco huts** of the interior. Around these are fixed silos of baked earth, used to store millet and corn. North of the coffee and cocoa zone, **subsistence farming** is the major economic activity of the people, and, along the roadside, the earth is pushed up into small mounds planted with yams, groundnuts and cassava. Traditional **African religions** retain a tight hold on the inhabitants of **Bassar** and **Tchamba**, two major towns in the region. The place of the church in southern Togo, however, is increasingly taken by **Islam** as you head north. And by the time you reach **Sokodé**, a long day's travel from Lomé, the whole environment – natural, cultural, social – has changed.

The predominant ethnic group of the central region is the **Kotokoli**, a people who migrated south from Mali in the late eighteenth or early nineteenth century. They brought Islam with them and Sokodé is now the most devoutly Muslim town in the country. Numerous **mosques**, in faded pastel colours and crowned with the star and crescent moon, attest to their faith. So, too, does **dress style**, especially the flowing *boubous* (embroidered gowns) and skullcaps commonly worn by men. Women don't wear veils, but they do drape a long, transparent scarf over their heads, wrapping it around their necks and letting it fall over their backs to flap on the ground when they walk. In accordance with the strict code of manners, people bow to one another in greeting and children even go down on their knees when greeting parents or elders.

Sokodé

In terms of numbers, **SOKODÉ** is easily Togo's second largest town, with around 50,000 inhabitants. Development has been slow in coming, but several roads are now paved, including the Lomé–Dapaong *route nationale* and the road to Bassar, both of which run through the centre. Sokodé's position at the focus of the routes assures it a certain vitality despite an obvious lack of government interest in stimulating the local economy. A good number of homes in the heart of town are still made of *banco* and thatch and most of the people are involved in trade and subsistence routines.

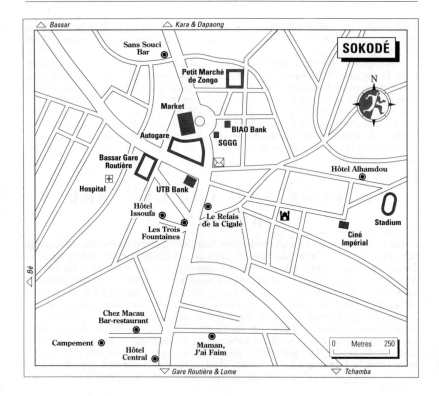

Accommodation

Sokodé has a number of possible **places to stay**, either to break a journey north or south, or if you're here for one of the festivals. If you are here during a festival, don't delay in finding a room – they can fill up quickly.

Le Campement, off rte de Lomé near the *préfet*'s residence. An old colonial building set on a wooded hill overlooking the town. The place hasn't been kept up (they have modest rooms, or you can camp on the grounds) but it has a pleasant bar and restaurant. ③.

Hôtel Alhamdou, near the stadium. Among the cheapest rooms in town – with shared facilities and nothing fancier than fans, but clean and friendly. If it seems far from the centre when you take a taxi there from the *gare routière*, it's an easy walk once you get your bearings. ①.

Hôtel Central, rte de Lomé (BP 37; ☎50.01.23) Fully S/C, AC rooms or bungalows, and formerly an expat favourite. Pleasant restaurant and bar. ③–④.

Hôtel Issoufa, on a side road by *Les Trois Fontaines* (☎50.09.89). Comfortable AC rooms with fan. Bar and restaurant. ①–②.

Le Relais de la Cigale, rte de Lomé. The AC rooms here are a cut above the rest, and those with fans are priced competitively with the town's budget hotels. Also a well-run restaurant and popular bar on a shady terrace, plus a boutique full of ethnic knickknacks. ①–②.

Les Trois Fontaines, off the rte de Kara. One of the town's busier restaurants and good accommodation with tidy double rooms and fans. ②.

The Town

The international highway that runs through Sokodé – known as the route de Lomé on the south side and the route de Kara on the north – is the main street. Numerous bars and restaurants jostle for custom along this two-kilometre thoroughfare through town. In the middle of it all Sokodé's centre of gravity is defined by a major roundabout and the large, two-storey **market building**. Despite official efforts to move the traffic bustle out of town, coming in by taxi you are still let off in the *autogare* just behind the market. Drivers have been reluctant to move to the new *gare routière*, on the route de Lomé near the customs post, despite the fact that the crowded market *autogare* is obviously too small to handle the traffic.

On the same roundabout – an independence monument at its centre and the SGGG supermarket to one side – is the filling station where every taxi passing through stops to refuel. Passengers with five minutes to spare mill around the market buying presents and provisions, and there's an incessant barking from hawkers desperate to sell their gear before the driver pays the filling station *pompiste*, yells his passengers back into the sweat-box and hits the road again.

The **Petit Marché de Zongo**, which is more traditional in flavour than the central market, is located northeast of the roundabout. Everything from charcoal to yams to used shoes and clothing is sold under thatched stalls winding their way through the narrow streets of the quarter.

One block south of the roundabout, the route de Lomé intersects with the route de Bassar/route de Tchamba, Sokodé's other important street. The UTB bank and the **PTT** (with a poste restante that works, incidentally, if you really reckon you'll be staying here) face each other at this junction. Turning to the right, the paved road leads to the Tchaoundja neighbourhood and passes by the police station, the hospital, *Les Affaires Sociales* and the modern-looking BTD bank (no foreign exchange facility). Turning left, the dirt road leads down to the town's main **mosques**, the **cinema** and the **stadium**. If you happen to be in town during a soccer match, be sure to get a ticket: **Semassi**, the home team, is one of the nation's best and, even if soccer isn't your bag, the enthusiasm of the crowd would give anyone a buzz.

FESTIVALS IN SOKODÉ

Sokodé is well known for its **festivals**, most of which revolve around Muslim religious holidays. During these occasions, the town breaks from its normal slow pace to become surprisingly animated – and even prospects of another bleak year for the economy don't seem to dampen people's spirits. One of the most important festivals is that marking the **end of Ramadan** (see p.59 for dates). The day this month-long fast ends, the entire male population of the city – decked out in embroidered *boubous* – gathers at the stadium for a collective prayer. Afterwards, the day dissolves into feasting and dancing.

The **Fête du Tabaski** – celebrating Abraham's sacrificing the lamb in place of his son – takes place two months later. Several days prior to this festival, the streets in town begin filling with sheep and goats, which on the day of *Tabaski* are slaughtered en masse, roasted and shared out among the community.

The **Knife Festival**, or *Adossa*, mixes Muslim elements with a custom that certainly predates the introduction of Islam into Kotokoli society and has many parallels in other West African societies. On this occasion – marking Muhammad's birthday about three months after *Tabaski* – the men drink a potion specially prepared by a marabout which supposedly renders their skin impenetrable. In public dances, they then proceed to cut one another with knives. It's even said that babies who have been administered the potion are rolled over broken bottles with no harm coming to them.

Near the stadium is the site of Sokodé's new **Grande Mosquée**. The old Grande Mosquée, located a couple of streets southwest of the post office, is beautiful for its simplicity. It's completely devoid of ornamentation – you could walk right by and not even see it – but the humble architecture has a tolerant and undogmatic appeal.

Eating, drinking and nightlife

For **food**, budget travellers naturally head for the market. **Local specialities** include *watche* (rice and beans boiled together with onions and hot peppers), *kadadia* (mash made from finely ground cassava mixed with millet or corn) and *wagassi* (locally made cheese either served plain or deep-fried). In the evening you can get lamb kebabs. For snacking, be sure to try *kosse* (bean batter deep-fried in peanut oil) or *koliko* (yam chips), both local favourites.

Besides the hotel **restaurants**, *Maman, J'ai Faim* dishes up good food outside under the mango trees, while for inside dining and European-style food, try *Chez Macau Bar-Restaurant*. *Sans Souci* is a popular **bar** up on the route de Kara and also serves some of the best kebabs in town. In the evenings, *Les Affaires Sociales* runs an outside **bar** in a courtyard giving onto the route de Bassar. There's a regular cluster of women on the street outside, serving salads and rice dishes.

Nightlife

The uncertainties of the early 1990s have left their mark on Sokodé, perhaps a consequence of the historical ill-feeling between the Kotokoli and the Kabyé. People in town speak of the dangers of going out **after dark**, citing a lack of security and increase in the crime rate. It's not likely that you'll notice any clear cause for alarm, although walking in the streets after 9pm, you will probably feel quite alone. One of the only places going that late is *Les Trois Fontaines*, but you might also see what's going on at the *Relais de la Cigale*.

North and west of Sokodé

The mountainous scenery and good roads around Sokodé provide opportunities for some easy excursions. The **Fazao National Park**, closed for rehabilitation after many of the animals within it were exterminated, has now reopened, though chances of seeing much wildlife remain slim. You might still, with a little luck and a helpful taxi driver, see an animal or two along the hilly and forested **road to Bassar**, which passes right along the game park boundary, offering glimpses of shy **monkeys** scampering as soon as they hear the car coming.

The road to **Bafilo** runs through equally striking scenery including the famous **Faille d'Aledjo** – a dramatic chasm, dynamited out of the cliff, through which the highway passes. Pictures of it help keep the Togolese postcard industry alive. Skull and crossbones warning signs line the twisting and looping road as it works its way over the

---

MOVING ON FROM SOKODÉ

Taxis brousse head in all directions from Sokodé and most leave from the town centre or from the main *gare routière* (on the route de Lomé). Taxis heading to **Bassar** have their own *autogare* on the route de Bassar. If you're making the long haul north, there are no direct taxis to **Ouagadougou**. Direct vehicles come up from Lomé and are already full. Get as far as Dapaong and change – or preferably stop over there for the night.

mountains: if you're driving, the wrecked vehicles strewn in the valleys below are evidence they should be taken seriously. If you're a bush taxi passenger, tell the driver *allez doucement!*

Bafilo and around

Surrounded by mountains, **BAFILO** is the Kotokoli's second largest town and another Muslim fief – you'll see the large white **mosque** some distance before arrival. Bigger than any of the mosques in Sokodé, this place of worship was built by the funds of a single **alhadji** (one who's been to Mecca), a wealthy merchant and native son. Bafilo is a small town, easily visited in a day and famous for its hand-weaving industry.

The route de Kara is the only paved road and village life centres around the *gare routière* and adjoining marketplace. The main dirt road leads from the *gare routière* down to the mosque. About halfway between these landmarks, a small road (little more than a path) leads down to the **weavers' yards**. You can spot them easily enough by the looms they operate in the middle of the street, and by the skeins of yarn stretched out along the roadside. If you don't see these tell-tale signs, ask someone to take you *chez les tisserands*. The quality of their work has brought them distinction throughout the country, and prices, depending on your bargaining skills, are as low here as you'll find anywhere. They sell either strips of woven cloth, complete *pagnes* or ready-made clothes direct from their shops near the looms.

Practicalities
The **accommodation** choice is simple since there's only one hotel, the *Maza Esso* ("I thank God"; ①–②). On the route de Kara, this extremely clean and well-managed establishment looks expensive, but the prices are wonderful, considering the quality (with fans and even AC available in higher-priced rooms).

Bafilo Falls
The **Bafilo Falls** are the main attraction near the town. Located about 4km from the centre, you can get to them easily enough by continuing down the main road past the mosque. After about a kilometre, turn right through the fields of corn, groundnuts and

---

A LITTLE KOTOKOLI

Welcome, bonne arrivée	*Nodé*	Yes	*Mmm*
		No	*Ay*
Bonjour (5–8am)	*Nyavinakozo* (pl. *Mivinekozo*)	How are you/ Ça va? (" in health?")	*Alafyaweh?*
Bonjour (8am–4pm)	*Nawsé* (pl. *Minawose*)	Fine/Ça va ("fit") Fine/Ça marche	*Mumumum*
Bonsoir (4–7pm)	*Neda nana* (pl. *Minadananga*)	("the work") How much?	*Kokani Ngyinidé?*
Good night (may God wake you well)	*Esofesi*	Money Five	*Lidé Byé*
See you tomorrow /later	*Blabtcheri* or *blabtesi*	Ten Twenty-five	*Byefu Tchente*
Thank you (for a gift), (for help or work completed)	*Eesobodi* *Natimaré*	One hundred Two hundred One thousand	*Alfa Alfa nolé Milé*

beans and head for the mountains. You'll see villagers out tending the fields at most times of year and you can ask them to point you to *la cascade*. Small kids may even offer to accompany you, in which case a modest dash at the end (value dependent on how old they are) will bring smiles and peals of laughter – they're not too mercenary here, yet. A concrete staircase leads to the top of the falls where a small dam assures a **swimming hole** filled with fresh spring water. It's a great escape and perfect for a break in the middle of your travels. If you wanted to stay longer, there are two other waterfalls located a bit further from town to which the kids, or the hotel, can give directions.

Bassar

Culturally, the **Bassari** (no relations of the people of southeast Senegal) are worlds apart from the Kotokoli – and linguistically they belong to another cluster of Voltaic languages, **Gurma**, while the Kotokoli speak **Tem**. Unlike the Muslim Kotokoli, they maintain traditional religious beliefs, and they are known for their many festivals and powerful fetishes. Traditionally the Bassari were the iron smelters for the region – in Africa, indication enough of their special status – and traces of their smelting furnaces can still be seen in some of the villages neighbouring the town of **BASSAR**. The Bassari **fire dance** is still celebrated in the town and surrounding villages. Staged versions are sometimes organized by the hotel in town, but only spirits can determine the dates for the real thing by speaking through a member of the community, who enters the arena in trance.

Practicalities

The paved road coming in from Sokodé runs right up to the town **marketplace** – where it suddenly stops. A dirt road runs in a ring round the market and functions as the high street. To the right where the tarmac ends is the *école centrale* and, just after, the BP station with, hard behind it, the **autogare** and PTT. Continuing, you pass Shell, the SGGG and the *Cascade* bar, before coming to a huge carbuncled **baobab**, revered by the Bassari, and thus tolerated bang in the middle of the street. Beyond it there's not a lot – unless you count a couple of small bars – until you get back to the paved road, having by now completed the circle. Note that there is no bank in town.

There's a **campement** – closed for refurbishment at the time of writing – off the paved road in the Kebedipou neighbourhood (near the *préfecture*) with basic, rather run-down rooms, some of them S/C with fans (①). The *Hôtel de Bassar* on the other hand is part of the state-run network, moderately expensive and somewhat dull, but nicely sited on the hilltop overlooking the town (③).

For cheap **eating**, the market provides the best sources of tasty calories. And for unwinding after dark, two **bars** not far from here – *Le Palmier* and the quieter *Le Bar Tchin Tchin* (aka *Centre Culturel de Bassar*) – usually run spirited discos at a small charge. The first is a hundred metres down the dirt road that runs out, left, from the market as you enter from the Sokodé direction; the second is by the *gare routière*.

KARA AND THE NORTH

Relatively harsh geography and climate make the north **Togo's poorest region** and one where you're not likely to spend much time. Much of the area is open savannah where the ochre grass of the dry season suggests the drought conditions of the Sahel, just a few hours' travel to the north. During the rains, however, green shoots quickly cover the hilly countryside, briefly lending a lush appearance to the region.

The north used to harbour Togo's highest densities of **wild animals**, but the former **Kéran National Park** doesn't even exist as a reserve anymore; the whole area is reclaimed farmland. Further north, the lions long ago left the classified **Forêt de la Fosse aux Lions** and the elephants that once congregated at its large waterhole have been killed or have moved to less hostile conditions in Benin and Burkina. Much of the former wildlife wound up as meat in local marketplaces when unrest cut off food supplies in the north, but papers in Ghana also reported massive military sweeps through the park, claiming that a "shoot to kill" policy was used to clear the region and that villages were bulldozed as helicopters fired on anything that moved, including many innocent villagers.

The people, mainly small farmers of the Voltaic language group, including Tamberma, Lamba, More and Kabyé, grow staple crops of millet and, in isolated areas, rice. Cotton – an important cash crop – is grown around **Dapaong**. But the only town of any size north of Sokodé is **Kara**, which is gradually becoming the nation's administrative centre. The **Kabyé country** spreads over a rocky, mountainous area where the people have acquired a reputation as renowned agriculturalists despite the hostile setting. This is the homeland of President Eyadéma – who, not unexpectedly, has made great efforts to develop his district and to transform its humble city, Kara, into the capital of the north. Other towns – **Sansanné-Mango** and **Niamtougou** – are extended villages with markets of local importance.

Despite a feeling of stagnation hanging heavy like a heat wave, the north offers a number of interesting sites. The **Tamberma country**, in the valleys around **Kandé**, is famous for its remarkable architecture, each home being built like a small fortress. Until very recently, this region remained quite isolated, and to this day certain Tamberma communities have little contact with the outside world. As a result, the traditional **folklore**, **festivals** and **customs** of the Tamberma people have changed little over time.

Kara

KARA doesn't impress as a major metropolis and, taking the town in for the first time, you start to realize why the hype about "Togo's second city" is so necessary. But even if the town retains a provincial, not to say rustic, flavour, it has come a long way in just over two decades, since its days as a rural village called Lama-Kara. Crucial political considerations – it was the nearest village of any size to Eyadéma's birthplace, and home-town of his most ardent supporters – have favoured Kara's development and in the space of a few years it has become the nation's second most important centre for **administration** and **manufacturing industries**. Today, incontestably the main town of the north, its infrastructure and continued growth look like helping it maintain that position for a long time to come. Some of the institutions here are worthy of a city of international pretensions, including the four-star *Hôtel Kara*, the imposing Banque Centrale, the sophisticated radio station and especially the grandiose **Maison du RPT** – the party headquarters. The town also boasts more paved roads than anywhere outside Lomé and flashy illuminated road signs just like those in Paris. But the biggest boost has come from new regional industries (the Brasserie du Bénin brewery, textile mill and shea nut oil refinery) which have been the driving force behind the expansion.

Kara is a town with a lively market and pleasant setting, and a lot going on. Every July, the **Evala** initiation celebrations and wrestling contests take over the town. Traditionally a strictly Kabyé affair, *Evala* is now a national event, televised across the country, and of huge importance to the town's economy. Competitions start as neighbourhood bouts, then move on to competitions within villages, and finally competitions between villages. Champions from the first, second and third year of initiation face each other for the supreme bouts. Greased with shea nut butter (to prevent their opponent

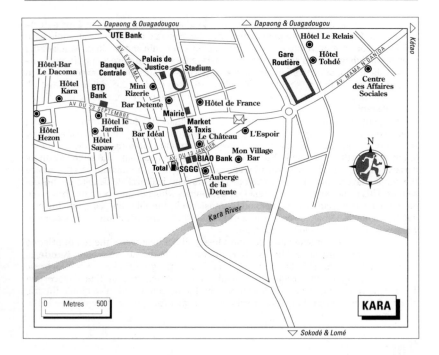

getting a firm grip), they try to grab their opponent's arms or legs to topple him over and pin him in the dust. Bouts rarely last longer than a minute or two but the atmosphere among the rival spectators is feverish.

The centre of town is marked by the **Marché Moderne** and the adjoining *gare routière* for town vehicles – the **main autogare** is to the east of town at the intersection of the main Lomé–Dapaong highway and the Kétao road. It's a chaotic area with a constant flow of passengers and traders swarming about frenetically, despite the heat. To escape this, most of your needs can be met in the immediate vicinity – banks, PTT, shops, bars and restaurants.

You can change money at the UTB **bank**, on the Dapaong road, and at BIAO, right beside the SGGG. At weekends use the *Hôtel Kara*'s reception desk; they usually don't ask for a receipt of purchase for travellers' cheques (as the banks often do) and the rates aren't too bad.

Accommodation

There's a good variety of **places to stay**, though they fill up quickly for *Evala* in July and when other important national festivities are taking place.

Auberge de la Détente, one block south of *Le Chateau* (☎60.14.92). Clean, secure rooms with fan or AC. ①–②.

Centre des Affaires Sociales, rte de Kétao. Inexpensive dorm rooms with clean showers and baths down the hall, or private rooms, some with AC. Their restaurant serves inexpensive European dishes and good continental breakfasts. ①–②.

Hôtel de France (☎60.03.43). Rooms with fan or AC, and an inexpensive restaurant. ①–②.

Hôtel Hezon. Basic but clean rooms with fan. ①.

Hôtel le Jardin, opposite the BTD bank (☎60.01.34). More popular as a French-style garden restaurant, this place has comfortable AC rooms in a relaxing environment. ②.

Hôtel Kara, west of the town centre (BP 5; ☎60.60.20 or 60.60.21). With its rough stone and beam facade vaguely reminiscent of a hunting lodge, this stands in strange contrast to the iron-roofed huts of local people in the vicinity. The hotel is as expensive as it looks, but it boasts many of the extras you'd expect – and its swimming pool (CFA2000 to visitors) is an obvious place to beat the heat. ⑤.

Hôtel Le Relais, off the rte de Kétao (signposted from the *autogare*; ☎60.62.98). Reasonably clean hotel built around a courtyard with *paillotes* and exotic plants. Good value S/C rooms with fan or AC. The restaurant has a long menu of African and European meals and is reasonably priced. ②.

Hôtel Sapaw, off rte de l'Hôtel Kara. Variety of good-value rooms with a popular neighbourhood bar-restaurant attached that lends a family atmosphere. ①–②.

Hôtel Tohdé, just before *Le Relais.* Clean rooms with fan. ①.

Hôtel-Bar Le Dacoma, off the rte de l'Hôtel Kara, past *Hôtel le Jardin* (look for signs). One of the cheapest hotels in town. The rooms with shared facilities are rather wretched, but the bar and restaurant are quite good. ①.

Eating, drinking and nightlife

Despite Kara's rapid modernization the town still has many traditional elements like the old **streetside restaurants**: you'll find the majority of these chop houses around the *gare routière* and market. At the northern end of the *gare routière*, stalls have been set aside as *fufu* bars and this is where you'll get the best calorie-to-money ratio in town. Nearby, women also sell tastier things – rice, beans, macaroni and so on – and you can drink *choucoutou* round the corner.

Besides the **hotel restaurants** – and if you try none of the others, *Le Jardin's* is especially recommended, if not for the excellent French and Chinese specialities, then at least for a drink on the garden terrace – there's a couple of other places worth mentioning. One of the most popular is the *Mini Rizerie*, which offers rare tastes like pizzas and burgers, as well as salads and sandwiches from around CFA2000. Next to the market, *Le Château* is at once casual and classy and clearly trying to up the town's reputation. The terrace dining, overlooking one of the liveliest streets, has well-prepared European dishes from CFA4000 up and excellent pizza.

After dark, your best chance of finding **entertainment** is at *L'Espoir*, a *dancing* west of the *gare routière*. Its central location and inexpensive prices have assured a long-running popularity. Nearby is the *Mon Village* bar, another lively place with cheap drinks and dancing. Also check for signs of life at the *Bar Idéal*, not far from the BTD, and the *Détente* bar, a stone's throw from the Total station and the market. More expensive and less youthful entertainment can be found at the Saturday disco of the *Hôtel Kara*.

MOVING ON FROM KARA

Kara's *autogare* is the largest in the north and you can get transportation to any point between Lomé and Dapaong. If you're heading to **Bassar**, there are direct taxis that go via a good *piste*, saving you the trouble of changing in Sokodé. For international destinations, the road is good in Togo as far as Kétao and the border of **Benin**, but deteriorates after that until you arrive in **Djougou** (regular taxis from Kara) where a well-kept *piste* connects with Parakou. The road to **Ghana** is also good on the Togo side.

North of Kara

The route north from Kara leads through the Kabyé country, dotted with characteristic *soukala* – round *banco* houses covered with conical thatched roofs, commonly called *tatas* by the French. The picturesque road, with its striking **mountain vistas**, continues as far as **Kandé**, the departure point for travel in the **Tamberma country**. After Kandé, it passes through the farmland that once was the **Kéran National Park** and the village of **Nouboulou**, former site of the reserve's lodgings, now abandoned. Finally the road stops at **Dapaong**, the last major town before Burkina Faso.

There's a deviation in the road that takes you around **Pya** – the president's birthplace just north of Kara. From the *piste* you've been relegated to, you can see an odd building on a distant hilltop, with monumental dimensions that might lead you to mistake it for a modern cathedral. That's the general's humble abode and the reason why you're making a detour.

Kandé and the Tamberma country

KANDÉ (also spelled Kanté) would surely have faded into obscurity had it not been on the nation's main *route nationale*. There's not much of anything in this tiny town of the Lamba people, where the surrounding countryside is hardly conducive to cultivating more than the bare staples of millet and yams. There's a small *gare routière* in the middle of town, with vehicles mostly to Kara, and one or two women selling food in the vicinity. On the north side there's also **accommodation** and a decent restaurant at the modest and good-value *campement* (②).

Kandé would be easily overlooked if it weren't the starting point for excursions into the **Tamberma country**. The region was settled by the Tamberma (closely related to the Somba across the border in Benin) in the seventeenth century, as they sought refuge from the king of Abomey on the coast, who raided far and wide in his quest for slaves to trade with the Portuguese. This explains the amazing fortress-like construction of Tamberma houses and their deep-rooted suspicion of outsiders.

Because these people have lived so long in isolation, their customs have remained largely unadulterated by outside influences. For that reason, if you get the chance to visit one of the villages, it can be a fascinating experience. On the other hand, this region is no longer a secret and the Tamberma country has long figured on the route of tour buses driving up from Lomé. This in turn has whetted the community's appetite for tourist money and reduced their fear of foreigners. You may be invited into a Tamberma home only to find, as soon as you enter, the women pulling off their tops, inserting bones through their lips, lighting up pipes and grinding millet. Meanwhile the men are rounding up bows and arrows, clay pipes, carvings and anything else that looks like something a tourist might buy. It's all about as spontaneous as a circus performance, and probably not as traditional, but you can take pictures – as long as you pay of course.

These reservations apart, however, the **homes** are indeed remarkable, self-sufficient settlements, both aesthetic and functional, built some distance from each other with millet fields planted around each one. Their large central entrances were originally designed to store animals in case of attack, while grain was stockpiled in the towers and everything necessary for preparing and cooking food kept inside the house. The roof doubled as a lookout post, with rooms for sleeping built into those towers not being used as silos. With **fetishes** dotted around the house and built into the walls, the Tamberma had everything necessary in their homes to allow them to withstand long sieges. While the threat that led to the creation of such fortresses no longer exists, their architectural style has remained unchanged.

In Kandé, there is no *gare routière* for **Sansanné-Mango** (also called Mango, or Nzara, and nothing to recommend it), **Dapaong** or other towns in the far north. To get there, you have to wait on the roadside by the customs post (the *douane*, where all traffic is obliged to stop) near Kandé's *campement*. The customs agents will find you a place in a vehicle if you ask. Usually, it's best to go in the early morning, because there are more cars and because this stretch is full of roadside inspections; a whole day of answering questions, showing your documents, and packing and unpacking your bags. If you're heading south, catch a taxi to **Kara** from the *place* in the centre of Kandé, and change there.

Transport in the Tamberma country

Unfortunately, if you're without your own car, **getting to the Tamberma country** can be mightily difficult, unless you **walk**. Since the first village is some 25km from Kandé that idea may not appeal – and remember this is raw bush and hotels and even *buvettes* are unheard of. The alternative is to find a **taxi** to take you in Kandé, but drivers will charge as much as they can get away with and are unlikely to take you at all for much under CFA25,000. Much cheaper are the collective taxis, which leave from Kandé's customs' post (see box, above) on Wednesdays and go as far as **Nadoba**, on the Benin border (CFA500). Another possibility is to hang around Kandé in the hopes of striking up a friendship with someone who'll invite you to a village – an idea that may seem implausible, but which is perfectly feasible. You'll probably end up walking anyhow, but at least you'll have a local companion and you'll know there's a place to sleep and eat when you arrive.

If you do have a vehicle of your own, the *piste* from Kandé leads all the way to **Natitingou** in Benin – although at times it's hard to tell if you're still on the road or in the middle of a millet field. If you see people walking along the road, don't hesitate to stop and give them a lift. It could lead to that first contact you've been waiting for. Kids flagging down cars along the roadside are invariably looking for tourists and, if you stop, they'll show you inside their homes and expect you to pay. It's a cringing notion, perhaps, but it's the easiest way to see inside a home and, as long as vast sums aren't laid out, doesn't do the Tamberma economy any harm.

Dapaong

Togo's last town in the north, **DAPAONG** (also spelled Dapaongo and Dapango) is home to a mixture of peoples of whom the **Gourma**, immigrants from the Burkina region, are the most numerous. This is a **farming district** where cotton and rice are important crops. **Cattle ranching** is also prevalent, owing to the presence of a sizeable Fula (Peulh) population, who came down from the Mossi Country in Burkina in the mid-nineteenth century. Not many travellers show up in these parts, which is a pity since Dapaong is a very pleasant town, a route focus and a reasonable enough stopover.

Arrival and orientation

The **autogare** is at the entrance to Dapaong, some 2km south of the centre. Normally, if you come in by taxi, you should be let off in town, but if you do get dropped at the *gare routière* either walk north along the paved road (it leads directly into town) or get a town taxi to the centre. *Taxis brousse* coming into town usually stop where the road forks around the *douane*, with the Hôtel de Ville and hospital off to the west. From here it's an easy walk to the hotels, most of which are within a 500-metre radius.

The **market** (main market days Wednesday & Saturday) is just east of the *douane*, down the dirt road opposite the Hôtel de Ville and past the *Relais des Savanes*. Besides the usual bric-a-brac, you'll find handmade farm tools, pottery and cheap woven gear like the broad-rimmed hats that are so common in the region. And there's no shortage of *choucoutou* bars where you can pause if the shopping gets too heavy. Around the market square are several small *boutiques* and the inevitable SGGG supermarket. On the hill behind the market, the UTB **bank** is the only place in town to change money.

Accommodation

There is nowhere luxurious to stay in Dapaong, but several pleasant and inexpensive hotels compete for custom.

Auberge des Passagers Sonu be La Manne, rte de Ouagadougou, near the *gare routière*. Nice, large, fanned rooms, friendly staff and cheap food. ①.

Auberge des Travailleurs, rte de Burkina (☎70.81.61). Upmarket lodgings used for conferences of the Confédération Nationale des Travailleurs Togolais and other groups, though it's more often used by travellers. Very clean AC rooms with private bathrooms, and a reasonable restaurant. ②.

Centre des Affaires Sociales, rte de Burkina. Typical of the *Affaires Sociales* throughout the country with clean dorm space available or private S/C rooms, some with AC. ②.

Hôtel Campement, on the hill overlooking Dapaong (☎70.81.59). The mundane name belies very pleasant accommodation in a colonial-style building. Clean rooms with fan or AC. The courtyard bar and restaurant, shaded by thatched arcades, serves excellent French food and *pression* beer. ②–③.

Hôtel Lafia, rte de Mango. Clean and friendly, and only five minutes' walk from the *autogare*, with comfortable AC rooms, or less expensive lodgings with shower and fan. Try for a room with a balcony. ①.

Hôtel le Ronier, behind the hospital (signs indicate the way from the *douane*). Basic lodging. ①.

Hôtel Le Sahelien, on the market square. S/C rooms with AC or fan. The restaurant prepares tasty food at reasonable prices. Central and excellent value. ①–②.

Hotel Le Verger, off rte du Burkina on the north side of town. New, clean rooms with fan or AC. ②.

Eating

There is plenty of the usual street food around the market, including coffee and omelettes in the morning, but a better **place to eat** is the popular *Relais des Savanes* bar, which has great food, including tossed salads and, if you arrive at the right moment, guinea fowl with groundnut sauce – dishes from CFA1500. The terrace bar of *La Flamboyante* is another good place and a big Dapaong meeting point, where you stand a good chance of running into any travellers passing through the region.

MOVING ON FROM DAPAONG

Heading south, you can get taxis to Kara, Sokodé and Lomé from the main *gare* on the Mango road. Note that if you want to get off before Kara (for example in Mango, Niamtougou or Kandé), you still have to pay the full fare to Kara. Many people up from Lomé heading for **Ouagadougou** change taxis in Dapaong because it's cheaper than going direct. In fact, you can save about thirty percent on your fare by changing vehicles here. You'll almost certainly wait several hours, however, for a Ouaga-bound vehicle – if not a day or two – which tends to cancel out any saving. There are periods when traffic is particularly slow at this depot, so even if you're planning to stay in town before moving on to Burkina Faso, check the transport forecast from time to time and be set to go if something looks ready.

It often works out faster to take a taxi from Dapaong to **Sinkanse**, the border town nominally in Burkina (though much of it spreads into Togo). Vehicles regularly ply the route to drop the market women, and from Sinkanse you have a better chance of finding transport to Ouagadougou. If you give the driver something, he'll find you onward transport quickly, but if you get stuck, there's a very basic hotel (①) in Sinkanse where you can put up. Whatever option you take, be sure to head out early, as this stretch is notorious for its many checkpoints, which often make the journey to Ouagadougou a ten- or twelve-hour affair.

BENIN

BENIN

The world's lack of awareness of **Benin** – the Gulf of Guinea's least-known nation – is partly the result of two reclusive decades of struggle through one of West Africa's least successful and most repressive revolutions. Then, in 1991, the revolutionary rhetoric was thrown out, and Benin adopted a multiparty democracy and a liberal economic system. For years the government had been wary of **tourism**, never especially encouraging visitors. This attitude has changed rapidly over the last decade and Benin is now a popular and pleasant place to travel, though the country still has a somewhat limited tourist infrastructure.

Benin's years of seclusion have left it an intriguing country, considerably more open than you might suspect, its people mostly warm and mild in their dealings with outsiders but quick to strike up conversations on real issues – especially now that freedom of expression is acceptable. Several factors distinguish the country. First, a number of sophisticated indigenous states developed here, the largest and most urbane of which was the Fon kingdom of **Dan-Homey**, whose capital, in the heartlands of the southern savannah, was **Abomey**. Second, this well-organized and prosperous kingdom was one of Africa's biggest centres of the slave trade from the sixteenth to the nineteenth century. The trade wasn't finally ended until 1885, when the last Portuguese slave cargo steamed out of Ouidah, bound for Brazil. Already by then, a considerable amount of imported wealth had been amassed in the country. Lastly, it was in the French colony of Dahomey – as Benin was known – that Catholic **mission schools** were most influential in the old empire of Afrique Occidentale Française. Thousands of highly qualified students graduated from its secondary schools, giving the country a dynamic intellectual reputation that has coloured its personality deeply.

Where to go

Benin is mostly thinly wooded savannah, part of the **open country** that penetrates south more or less to the coast between the rainforests of Nigeria and Ghana and which partly accounts for the different shifts of history that have taken place here – easier travel and trade, more successful armies and faster conquests.

A flat sandy plain runs the whole length of the **coast**, broken up by a string of picturesque **lakes and lagoons**. The coast offers little enticement in the sea (rough and

---

FACTS AND FIGURES

Known as **Dahomey** during the colonial period (after the Fon kingdom, Dan-Homey), the **République du Bénin** adopted the name of the ancient West African kingdom located in present-day southern Nigeria, after the 1972 coup led by northerner Mathieu Kérékou, the nation's most durable president. The **population** is around six million, a good tenth of whom live in Cotonou, the largest city and the de facto capital. The **official capital** remains Porto Novo, a much smaller coastal town that served as the colonial administrative centre. Benin's area is 113,000 square kilometres, approximately the size of Louisiana, or slightly smaller than England, and its **national debt** is around £1 billion ($1.6 billion), a figure roughly equivalent to France's annual state subsidy for the arts. In 1990 Mathieu Kérékou's dictatorship collapsed as the nation began converting to a **multiparty democracy**, a process completed in 1991 when democratic elections were held and Nicéphore Soglo became president. In 1996, Kérékou became president again, after disputed elections.

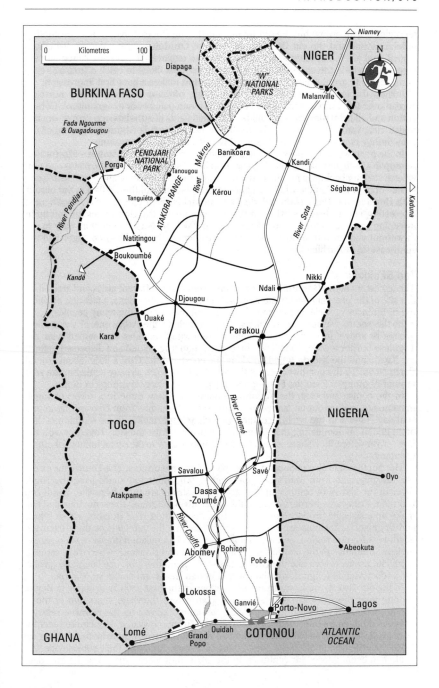

terrifyingly dangerous) but the **old towns** – including **Porto Novo**, Benin's crumbling official capital, and the old Brazilian quarters of **Ouidah** – have a certain flaked-out appeal, and are full of interest if you have time to explore. The over-exploited stilt village of **Ganvié** is the coastal site of which you're most likely to catch a (tourist's-eye) glimpse, while grubby, post-revolutionary **Cotonou** makes a poor first impression.

Inland, the improvement is rapid, as a gentle **plateau** slopes gradually north to spread over the entire centre of the country in a rich patchwork of agriculture. Coffee, cotton and oil palm **plantations** collide with small fields of **subsistence crops** – maize, millet, rice, yams and cassava. The most interesting town is **Abomey** – capital of the Dan-Homey empire and site of its surviving royal palaces and museum.

In the northwest, the sheer cliffs and abundant greenery of the **Atakora Mountains** rear up in a long, dramatic ridge that stands in impressive contrast to the plains and provides a striking backdrop for one of the country's most interesting and inaccessible cultures – that of the Somba, who lived in relative isolation until the 1970s. On the border with Burkina, the **Parc National de la Pendjari** is rated one of West Africa's most interesting faunal reserves; while in the extreme north, the Gourma plains roll up in sweeping grasslands to the **Parc National du "W" du Niger** – not at all easy to get to without your own transport – which spreads across the borders into Niger and the southeast tip of Burkina Faso.

The Béninois

The ancestors of the **Béninois** of today come from many different areas and arrived on the site of the present country after several centuries of migrations, a fact that explains the differences in social organization and cultural practices of the many peoples.

In the south, various Ewe-speaking peoples include the **Adja**, one of the earliest groups to arrive, formerly a community of renowned warriors that settled near the Togolese border town of Tado. Over time, the group fragmented and dispersed to form the **Xwala** and the **Xuéda** (Ouidah) along the coast and the **Gun** a little inland around Porto Novo. To the northwest, the Adja mixed with peoples already settled in the area around Abomey to form the **Fon** – presently one of the largest groups in Benin.

In the centre and east, the **Yoruba** predominate. They came in a series of vague movements, setting out on family and community migrations from Oyo and Ife in present-day Nigeria in the twelfth century. Founding important regional kingdoms, they often ended up dominating the commercial activities of the interior. Together with the Fon – with whom they share some cultural affinity – they make up an influential ethnic grouping.

The northeast is also populated by peoples of diverse origins. The **Dendi**, for example, are migrants from Mali's Songhai empire, who migrated south from the Niger River in the sixteenth century to the savannah districts around Malanville, Kandi and Djougou. **Fula** cattle herders crossed the Niger River at around the same time and still make up a sizeable proportion of the northern population. The **Bariba**, whose ethnic and linguistic affiliations are obscure, arrived before the fifteenth century from the northwest Nigeria region. Settling first around Nikki, population pressure soon spread their communities to the districts of Parakou, Kandi and Kouande, where they came to dominate predecessors like the **Bussa**, speakers of another obscure language (probably a relict Mande tongue), who had also migrated west from northern Nigeria.

In the northwest, the **Betammaribe** were one of the first peoples to arrive in Benin, settling near the Atakora range at an unknown date a thousand years ago or more. Living in relative isolation, these people, commonly known as the **Somba**, resisted changes inflicted by the spread of Islam and the French invasion. Until quite recently, they lived in the seclusion of their fortified *tatas* and farmed their lands, wearing no more than the traditional *cache sexe* of their ancestors. Although their subsistence way of life had been ignored for centuries, in the 1970s they were exposed to the raw glare of the French press – delighted to have located a rare example of "real Africa". Stung by the sensational reports of naked tribesmen, Kérékou's government ran a campaign to force the Somba to wear clothes. As a result of this humiliation and other insensitivities, the Somba remain a very private, reserved people, and outside of the main towns, such as Natitingou – where traditional ways are fast breaking down – it's difficult, and perhaps from no-one's point of view very desirable, to penetrate their tight-knit communities.

Most Béninois adhere to traditional African **religious beliefs**. Along the coast, **voodooism** is common, particularly among the Ewe-speakers. **Islam** was brought from the north by Arab, Hausa and Songhai-Dendi traders. It extended as far south as Djougou, and even into the Yoruba country. Perhaps as much as fifteen percent of the population are Muslim. **Christianity** came with the Europeans and spread principally along the coast – where it was soon integrated into voodoo – and over the central plateau.

When to go

Given the generally bad condition of roads in Benin, the weather can have a very adverse effect on travel and it's best to avoid the rainy seasons, which can be prolonged and oppressive. In the **south**, there are two **rainy seasons** (a long one from April to July and a short one from October to November) and two **dry seasons** (a short one from August to September and a long one from December to March). Temperatures fluctuate little throughout the year.

In the **north**, the year divides simply into the rainy season, which lasts from late May to October, and the dry season, which lasts from November to early May. In parts of the Atakora region – Natitingou, for example – the rain falls virtually unabated from April to November. Temperatures vary more dramatically than in the south. When the northerly *Harmattan* wind blows in December, nights can be quite cool.

AVERAGE TEMPERATURES AND RAINFALL

COTONOU

Temperatures °C	Jan	Feb	Mar	Apr	May	June	July	Aug	Sept	Oct	Nov	Dec
Min (night)	23	25	26	26	24	23	23	23	23	24	24	24
Max (day)	27	28	28	28	27	26	26	25	26	27	28	27
Rainfall mm	33	33	117	125	254	366	89	38	66	135	58	13
Days with rainfall	2	2	5	7	11	13	7	3	6	9	6	1

Arrivals

Despite being so centrally placed in the region, Benin is not a country to which many travellers make initial flights into West Africa. Entering overland is straightforward enough from Togo or Niger, but the routes down from Burkina Faso are little used, and the way in from Nigeria can sometimes be a hectic hassle.

■ Flights from Africa

Most **direct flights to Cotonou** from neighbouring countries in West Africa are handled by Air Afrique (RK), which flies from **Abidjan** to Cotonou at least once daily. Also from Abidjan, Cameroon Airlines (UY) and Nigeria Airways (WT) fly weekly and Air Ivoire (VU) flies twice a week.

Other West African cities have much less frequent links. From **Lomé**, Air Burkina (2J) and RK fly twice a week and VU flies weekly.

From **Ouagadougou** to Cotonou, RK flies weekly, Air France (AF) flies twice a week and 2J flies three times a week.

From **Lagos**, there are a number of direct, non-stop flights to Cotonou: RK, UY and WT fly twice a week; Ghana Airways (GH) has one weekly flight and Aeroflot (SU) flies twice a month.

From **Dakar**, there is an inconvenient weekly flight on Air Gabon (GN) via Abidjan and Lagos. RK has two direct services a week and indirect flights pretty well daily, all connecting in Abidjan. Similarly, the only flights from **Bamako** are indirect ones connecting in Abidjan, three times a week.

Other cities with links to Cotonou include: direct from **Accra**, on GH (2 weekly) and VU (weekly); **Conakry** via Abidjan, on WT (weekly) and RK (weekly); **Freetown** via Accra, on SU (2 monthly); **Douala**, on UY (direct; 2 weekly) and RK (via Lagos; 2 weekly); and **Niamey** via Lomé on RK (weekly).

There are no direct links or convenient connections to Cotonou from Nouakchott, Banjul or Bissau.

> The details in these practical information pages are essentially for use on the ground in West Africa and in Benin itself; for full practical details on preparing for a trip, getting here from outside the region, paperwork, health, information sources and more, see Basics, p.3–83.

■ Overland

Beninois customs and immigration rarely present any special problems, but at most border posts you must state where you plan on staying. Give the name of any hotel, whether you intend to stay there or not. Most border posts now operate around the clock, but visa sections are only open during business hours (Mon–Fri 8am–12.30pm & 3–6.30pm, Sat 8am–12.30pm).

From Nigeria

The commonest point of entry has traditionally been via the **Badagri** coastal road from Lagos to **Kraké** on the Benin side. When it's open, this frontier is always crowded and it may take some time to get through the formalities. Your bags will be given a perfunctory search, but it's not likely your Nigerian currency declaration form will even be checked. Previously, the Badagri route has been known to be closed, and travellers have used the border crossing from **Idiroko** in Nigeria to **Igolo** in Benin, 30km north of Porto Novo. Roads on both routes are surfaced and in reasonable shape.

From Niger

From Niamey to Cotonou, the road is tarred the whole way. At the Gaya border post, a bridge spans the Niger River and leads to the Benin customs at **Malanville** (open 24 hours). Transit visas are issued by the police in Malanville, not at the border post.

From Burkina Faso

Most people coming from Burkina take the sealed road through Togo and branch over to Benin either at Kara or Lomé, as described below. There's no regular public transport between Fada-Ngourma and Natitingou, but you may be able to find a share taxi; note that you may have to change vehicles at Pama, the last Burkinabe town of any size.

From Togo

Taxis speed along the coastal highway from **Lomé** to Cotonou all day long. Although there's no Béninois embassy in Togo, **visas** are issued on the spot at the border post of **Hila Kondji**.

From the north of Togo, a paved road leads from Kara to the border post at **Kétao**. Customs and immigration agents here are generally quite good-humoured and the *piste* leading on to Djougou in Benin is well maintained, if a bit slippery when wet. Alternatively, if you have your own vehicle, you could take a very minor and neglected *piste* that branches off the main road at Kandé and heads through the **Tamberma country**. Little traffic uses this route and you're not likely to be aware that you've crossed the border until you get to the main road to Natitingou. When you arrive at this latter town, go to the police and customs to get your passport stamped.

Red Tape

All nationalities, apart from ECOWAS member states, need a visa.

Visas are issued at all borders for a 48-hour period. You'll need two photos and the CFA4000 fee. This is not a major problem if you arrive in the south, since **extensions** are easily obtained at the immigration office in Cotonou. If you arrive by road from the north, however, you'll have to rush your trip to get to the coast within two days – an obvious headache if you'd planned on taking in sights along the way.

■ Visas for onward travel

Visas for **Nigeria** are only issued to residents of Benin, and no exceptions are made. The **Ghana** embassy issues visas within 48 hours, but if you're planning to do the journey by land, note that the Togo–Ghana border can be randomly closed, although this is unlikely at the moment. Ghanaian visas cost CFA12,000 for a month or CFA6000 for a 48-hour transit visa. **Niger** visas can be issued the same day and cost CFA22,500.

Money and Costs

Benin is part of the CFA zone (CFA100 = 1 French franc; approx. CFA900 = £1; approx. CFA600 = US$1). The major banks have branches in most towns, but often deal only in French franc notes. Bank opening hours are usually 8am–12.30pm & 3.30–7pm. The main bank, and the best for travellers' cheques, is the Banque Internationale du Bénin (BIB). The Bank of Africa gives the best rates for cash.

■ Costs

Costs are broadly similar to those in franc-zone neighbours Niger, Burkina and Togo – though the price of fuel is a little cheaper. Except in Cotonou

itself, there is little opportunity to spend much money. Public transport works out around CFA13 per kilometre. Outside Cotonou, accommodation is fairly inexpensive – budget travellers can usually find something very decent for under CFA4000.

Health

Yellow fever is currently the only vaccination required for travel to Benin. Malaria is widespread and, as in neighbouring Togo, increasingly resistant to the common chloroquine-based drugs.

Except in Cotonou, some sort of **water purification** is highly recommended. You should avoid swimming in streams and lakes in the lagoon regions of coastal Benin, and don't walk barefoot in the grass surrounding them. These areas are almost invariably infested by schistosome parasites which transmit **bilharzia**. **Hospital facilities** throughout the country are meagre, with drugs and equipment in short supply, but Cotonou has more reliable places.

Maps and Information

The best maps of Benin and Cotonou are published by IGN (1cm to 6km), which include detailed *pistes* and topographical material, and are especially useful in the confusing lagoon areas along the coast. If you're not planning on staying long or travelling much off the beaten track, however, the Michelin 953 map of West Africa is adequate. If you can't buy a map before you travel, the Institut National de Cartographie in Cotonou has reasonable maps – their Cotonou map is excellent.

Benin has no overseas tourist offices, but the embassy in Paris and the London honorary consulate have very limited supplies of leaflets. In Cotonou, the **Ministère du Commerce et du Tourisme** has very limited material and is of little practical help. Any *librairie* in the country stocks a hundred-page reader intended for school children called *Le Bénin*, which gives an overview of the nation.

Getting Around

Benin's road network has improved dramatically since the early 1990s and now

compares favourably with that of Togo. Police checks are refreshingly infrequent. The rail network, on the other hand, is down to one line between Parakou and Cotonou. There is no scheduled domestic air service.

■ Road transport

The main **national highway** runs for 742km from Cotonou to Malanville and is paved the entire distance. The other main road runs 114km across the country from the Nigerian border in the east to the Togolese border in the west.

The Béninois have remained faithful to the *taxi brousse*, the Peugeot **bush taxi**, which can be found at the *gare routière* (also known as the *autogare*) in every town. Peugeot 504 *familiales* – nine-seater estate cars – are the common mode of transport for most people, despite the influx of new Japanese vehicles.

Government-run **buses** are mostly old and battered, but they run on regular schedules and seats are cheaper than bush taxis. They usually leave from the same *autogare* as the bush taxis. Ask for times in advance and arrive early, as they tend to fill quickly. Buses stop at major towns between Malanville and Cotonou.

Public transport in large towns is the preserve of **share-taxis** and **zimi-djans**. *Zimi-djans* are *mobylette* drivers – usually identifiable by a coloured shirt – who rent out the back of their scooter seats to passengers. It's a cheap (and negotiable) means of transport, but you won't be protected by a helmet.

■ Trains

The national **railway** company, l'Organisation Commune Bénin-Niger des Chemins de fer et Transports, operates the only railway line still running in Benin. Built between 1900 and 1939, the **northern line** covers the 438km from **Cotonou to Parakou**, via Bohicon, Dassa and Savè. Despite the time involved, many Béninois still take the train over this stretch since the price is slightly less than bush taxis. The trip to Parakou takes over ten hours, but it's possible to reserve a *couchette* on a night train.

■ Planes

Domestic **air transport** is handled only by travel agents who occasionally charter planes from Cotonou to the country's three main airports – Parakou, Kandi and Natitingou.

Accommodation

The hotel network in Benin has improved considerably in recent years. Typical budget accommodation now offers quite pleasant rooms, almost invariably with electricity and running water, sometimes with a shower,

---

ACCOMMODATION PRICE CODES

Accommodation prices in this chapter are coded according to the following scales – the same scales in terms of their pound/dollar equivalents as are used throughout the book. Prices refer to the rate you can expect to pay for a room with two beds. Single rooms, or single occupancy, will normally cost at least two-thirds of the twin-occupancy rate. For further details see p.48.

① **Under CFA4500 (under £5/$8).** Rudimentary hotel with no frills – often a *chambre de passage* rented to the average guest by the hour.

② **CFA4500–9000 (£5–10/$8–16).** Reasonable hotel with simple amenities. S/C rooms with fans are the norm, but some rooms may have AC.

③ **CFA9000–18,000 (£10–20/$16–32).** Modest, but adequate hotel, with S/C rooms, many of which are AC.

④ **CFA18,000–27,000 (£20–30/$32–48).** Reasonable business or tourist-class hotel with S/C, AC rooms, and often a swimming pool.

⑤ **CFA27,000–36,000 (£30–40/$48–64).** Similar standards to the previous code band but extra facilities such as a pool are usual.

⑥ **CFA36,000–45,000 (£40–50/$64–80).** Comfortable, first-class hotel, with good facilities.

⑦ **Over CFA45,000 (over £50/$80).** Luxury establishment – top prices around CFA60,000–80,000.

and most often with outside toilet; fans are common, AC less so. Increasingly, and especially in well-travelled towns like Ouidah, Abomey and Natitingou, a few good mid-range hotels are opening, with S/C rooms and airconditioning. International-class establishments are limited to the Cotonou *Sheraton* and Natitingou's hotel in the PLM chain.

The Béninois are hospitable and may invite travellers for meals or to stay the night – activities which were forbidden until the advent of democracy. *Camping sauvage* (pitching your tent in the bush, or on the beach) has also been legalized beyond city limits.

Eating and Drinking

Food in Benin largely resembles that of neighbouring Togo: for background and details on local staples and popular dishes, refer to the food section in the previous chapter. Cotonou has no gastronomic reputation in West Africa, but there is a growing variety of restaurants, and well-prepared street food sauces can be very tasty. A number of hotels, even less expensive ones, have their own restaurant.

In the provinces, eating houses are usually small *buvettes* specializing in rice, *pâte* (the generic term for pounded starch based on cassava, yam or sweet potato), *moyo* (like wheat semolina) or macaroni served with sauce.

One of Benin's leading industries is the Societé Nationale des Boissons which produces the national beer, **La Béninoise**, and a variety of carbonated soft drinks. Along the coast, **palm wine** is plentiful, as is the lethal African firewater known as **sodabi**. In the north, **home-made beer** made from millet, known as *chapalo* or *tchacpalo*, is more common.

Communications – Post, Phones, Language and Media

If you're just passing through, Cotonou is the only reliable place to receive post. The main PTT is fairly efficient and the poste restante service good. Parcels are only sent air mail and are very expensive.

Benin's IDD code is ☎229.

International phone calls can be made either from the PTT in Cotonou, or from the *Sheraton* hotel, although the latter is twice as expensive and you've no way of knowing if the operator is adding an unofficial commission. A phone call costs CFA1825 per minute to France, CFA2440 to elsewhere in Europe, CFA1900 to the US and CFA3450 to Australia.

■ Languages

Benin's official language is **French**, and it's widely spoken. The fifty or so Béninois ethnic communities speak about as many different languages or distinct dialects, though some languages have become regional lingua francas. In the south, **Adja** and **Fon** – closely related to Ewe and Mina under the "Ewe group" umbrella – are widely spoken and are probably the most useful if you want to learn a few phrases. In the centre and east, **Yoruba** takes over (see p.927). **Bariba**, a Voltaic tongue, is the common language of Parakou and the northeast, while the old Songhaic language, **Dendi**, is spoken in the extreme north near the banks of the Niger. **Hausa** and **Fula** are also widely used in the north. Because of the proximity and influence of Nigeria and the importance of commerce, some Béninois speak a kind of trading **English**, though it's not likely to get you very far, even in Cotonou.

■ The media

Although not as visible as the press in other countries, there are two daily **newspapers** – *Le Matin* and *La Nation* (the government-owned paper) – and dozens of small weekly, fortnightly or monthly sheets. None of them have big circulations. The best for a political-economical analysis are *Point, Matinal* and the weekly *Gazette Du Golfe*, the main opposition paper under the Kérékou regime.

The state-run Office de Radiodiffusion et de Télévision du Bénin (ORTB) has **radio** broadcasts in French, English and eighteen national languages, and several hours of television from the afternoon onward. There are many privately owned radio stations and the only privately owned TV station in West Africa, LC2.

Directory

AIRPORT DEPARTURE TAX CFA5000, if not already included in the ticket.

BUSINESS HOURS Most businesses are open Mon–Fri 8am–12.30pm & 3.30–7pm; government offices open and close half an hour earlier in the afternoons.

HOLIDAYS Christian holidays and New Year's Day are public holidays. Muslim celebrations are less formally observed, though everything shuts down in the north for them. Ramadan, however, isn't conspicuously disruptive. In addition there are secular holidays on **May 1** (Labour Day), **August 1** (Independence Day), **October 26** (Armed Forces' Day), **November 30** (Benin Day) and **December 31** (Harvest Day).

MUSEUMS Benin has several museums. By far the best is housed in the former Dan-Homey palace in **Abomey**, which has undergone massive renovations with the help of UNICEF funds. **Porto Novo** also has two museums, one in the former residence of King Toffa. The museum in **Ouidah** is dedicated primarily to the voodoo religion.

MUSIC Angélique Kidjo is the one internationally known name from Benin – a hugely charismatic singing star based in Paris whose songs are heard on dance floors worldwide. In Benin itself, there's little thriving musical culture, though every indication that with economic liberalization, a less insecure government and relaxations on censorship, there'll be more musical instruments, better facilities and greater freedom of expression in the future. Listen out for the local cassette star **Stan Tohon**, whose *tchink system* percussion is interesting. See the "Music" section in Contexts.

PHOTOGRAPHY You need no official permit to take pictures in Benin, but photographing people can be a very sensitive issue, especially in Somba country. People in touristed areas like Ganvié and Ouidah are likely to demand money, and snapping away without permission can lead to problems.

VOODOO The religion of the coast, especially among Ewe-speakers. In many ways, Ewe practices are similar to those of the Yoruba and Fon: all believe in a single supreme God who created the universe (*Mawu* in Fon). On earth, lesser divinities are charged with power over thunder (*Xebioso* or *Shango*), iron and war (*Ogun* or *Gu*), land and disease (*Sakpata* or *Cankpana*), and so on. They possess and "mount" the bodies of their devotees and their help can be solicited through the work of fetish priests. See box on p.844 for more details.

WILDLIFE Although densely farmed and populated in their southern parts, Benin's northern regions spread into a broad zone of thinly populated savannah and uplands – one of West Africa's best game-viewing areas. There are significant concentrations of wildlife, especially in the Pendjari and "W" du Niger national parks, including several hundred – possibly a thousand – elephants.

WOMEN'S ISSUES The position of women in Benin has been little improved by the revolutionary 1970s and 1980s, or by democratization. In fact it appears they have even less involvement in politics and decision-making than elsewhere in West Africa. **Women travellers** report Béninois men generally pleasantly reserved and low-key and there's relatively little sexual harassment.

A Short History of Benin

The earliest history of the territory that is now Benin is obscure. The far north was under thrall to the Niger River's Songhai empire by the end of the fifteenth century. Meanwhile, in the south, having built the fort at El Mina in Ghana in 1482, the Portuguese continued along the coast and began trading

with local rulers from the 1520s. **Porto Novo and Ouidah developed through the sixteenth and seventeenth centuries into important commercial centres where slaves were traded for European cloth and guns. The British, Dutch and French, seeking labour for their American colonies, soon joined the Portuguese in the traffic, establishing their own coastal forts and commercial depots during the seventeenth century. By the 1690s, some 20,000 slaves were being shipped annually out of Ouidah and lesser ports.**

■ The Slave Coast

By as early as the beginning of the eighteenth century, the **Dan-Homey kingdom** (though itself effectively a vassal of the great Yoruba Oyo empire to the east) dominated the politics of the region. One of Dan-Homey's rulers, **Agadja** (in power 1708–40), subjugated the districts south of his capital Abomey, and finally took Ouidah itself. With access to the coast, his empire was now poised to control international trade – primarily in slaves. But he had exceeded the terms of his license with Oyo and a protracted conflict ensued which resulted in Oyo's definitive conquest of Dan-Homey. There followed a period of desperate slave-hunting as the Dan-Homey king **Tegbesu** tried to rebuild his country's war-shattered economy (more background on p.852).

After the French Revolution, however, a wave of **anti-slavery sentiment** began to sweep Europe. In France, the *Decret du 16 pluviôise an II* (February 4, 1794) abolished the trade, though it was later reinstated by Napoleon. In 1802, Denmark became the first European nation to abolish the slave trade permanently. Britain followed in 1807 and from 1819 to 1867, British ships patrolled the coast, arresting slave ships and resettling the captives in Freetown, Sierra Leone. France definitively outlawed the trade in 1818.

These moves coincided with a severe shortage of slaves in the region, in large part because of excessive human sacrifices in Abomey. A Brazilian mulatto, **Francisco Felix de Souza** entered into a blood pact with the young **Prince Ghezo** of Dan-Homey and supplied the guns for him to overthrow the incumbent of the stool (throne) in Abomey in 1818, in return for which he was granted a monopoly over the slave trade (and became the "Viceroy of Ouidah"; see "Books" in Contexts).

By the 1830s, however, the nature of most commerce in the region had fundamentally changed and **palm oil** became the primary export. The French soon gained the upper hand in the regional oil trade when representatives from Marseille soap-making companies arrived in Ouidah in 1843 and travelled to Abomey, where they signed a contract with the Dan-Homey king, the same Ghezo, granting them trading rights at Ouidah. In 1861, Lagos became a British colony. **King Toffa** of Porto Novo had claims on the town of Badagary which the British now controlled. Worried that their influence would spread westward, Toffa called on the French for support and, in 1863, Porto Novo became a **French protectorate**. In 1868, the new **King Glele** of Abomey ceded rights to Cotonou to the French who had by now established themselves as the most prominent European power along Benin's coast.

■ French conquest

Good relations between France and the Dan-Homey kingdom had soured by the end of the century. In December 1889, a new sovereign, **Behanzin**, was enstooled. He adopted a more combative attitude to the French, who were beginning to look less like trading partners and more like a force of occupation. He refused to recognize French rights over Cotonou and was angered that the foreigners had allied themselves with one of his bitterest enemies, King Toffa of Porto Novo. After funeral ceremonies for his father Glele, Behanzin ordered an **attack on Cotonou**. On March 4, 1890, some five to six thousand Dan-Homey warriors marched on the city and withdrew only after inflicting numerous casualties. A month later, the army surrounded Porto Novo and clashed with the French at Atchoukpa on the northern outskirts of the city.

Other skirmishes followed and in April 1892, Behanzin sent the following message to French authorities:

I warn you that if one of our villages is touched by the fire of your cannons, I will march directly to crush Porto Novo and all the villages belonging to Porto Novo. I would like to know how many independent French villages have been overtaken by me, King of Dan-Homey. I request you to keep calm and do your business in Porto Novo. That way, we can remain in peace as it was before. But if you want war, I am ready. I will not finish it. It will last a hundred years and will kill 20,000 of my men.

The threat was taken seriously by the French who knew that Behanzin possessed more than 5000 modern firearms and was still being supplied by the Germans and the British. The government in Paris sent a distinguished commander to handle the situation, **Colonel Dodds**, a mulatto from Saint Louis in Senegal.

In August 1892, Dodds began his northern march to conquer Abomey. Accompanied by Senegalese and Hausa infantry, the French went to the Oueme River and followed its course. Although the army was sporadically engaged by Dan-Homey troops, including divisions of Amazons – skilled female warriors specially trained to use the new Martini-Henry rifles – it was the Dan-Homey which received the heaviest casualties in the clashes. By November 1892, when the French arrived at Cana – the village where Dan-Homey kings were traditionally buried – Behanzin's army had lost 4000 dead and twice as many wounded.

The king prepared himself for a **last stand**. He recruited every warrior capable of carrying a gun, including the massed ranks of his Amazons – even those specialized in hunting, and got the nation's slaves to join the battle, promising them freedom in return. But the effort was in vain; the army was defeated and Behanzin was forced to retreat with meagre reserves. On November 16, 1892, Dodds marched on Abomey to find the city already in flames, torched by the retreating army. It took another two years for the French to track down and capture Behanzin (betrayed by the newly French-enstooled Fon king) and he was transported to exile in Martinique.

■ The colonial Era

Their main rival in the region at last conquered, the French went on to subdue the north of the country, which they now called **Dahomey**. Colonial frontiers were drawn up in agreement with Britain to the east and Germany (which held Togo) to the west. In 1901, the present borders were fixed and, in 1904, Dahomey became part of AOF (French West Africa).

French policy in Dahomey was partly shaped by the influence of Catholic missions, which sent large numbers of envoys into the territory in the 1920s and 1930s. Catholic seeds had been sown from a very early period, with the arrival in the eighteenth century of influential **Brazilian** families and Christian **freed slaves**. Moreover, the climate, open country and dominant voodoo religion of the south were not strongly antithetical to missionary activity. The result was that early in the colonial period, Dahomey acquired a reputation for mission-educated academics and administrators. By the 1950s, many middle-ranking posts in the French colonial service – right across West and Central Africa – were occupied by Dahomeyans, most of whom were Fon or Yoruba from the relatively prosperous south.

With few mineral resources – no gold or other precious metals – Dahomey's economy depended very heavily on its **oil palm plantations**. In addition, there were close commercial relations with Nigeria, both legal trade and illicit smuggling.

■ Independence

No single, national leader rose to pre-eminence during the fifteen-year postwar period on the road to independence. Instead, an ethnic and regional competition developed in which three prominent figures jockeyed for political prominence. They were **Hubert Maga**, representing the north, **Migan Apithy** of the southeast, and **Justin Ahomadegbe** from the southwest. On the eve of independence, the three managed to form a coalition, the Parti Progressiste Dahoméen, but unity was superficial. Each commanded the loyalties of about one-third of the country's population and distrusted the others. After some seventy years of French rule, the **Republic of Dahomey** became independent on August 1, 1960.

In December, 1960, **elections** were held in which Maga's Parti Dahoméen de l'Unité won. The northerner became the nation's first president. But an uneasy dissatisfaction prevailed in the south where supporters of Apithy and Ahomadegbe suspected the new leader was trying to consolidate his position and eliminate his two most formidable rivals. By 1963, unrest had led to **political riots**, as students and workers took to the streets of Cotonou. Truckloads of angry northerners descended on the town to confront the protestors.

■ Years of instability

The situation had got out of hand and it was clear that serious violence would ensue if Maga stayed in power. At the same time, it also seemed possible that the north would try to secede if either of Maga's rivals took over the presidency.

The impasse was resolved in October 1963 when Maga was deposed in a **military coup** led by **Colonel Christophe Soglo**. The takeover was not a sudden or unexpected event, however. For two days prior to the coup, Soglo met with Maga and Apithy (who was vice-president) and members of the trade unions and the army. His ascent to power seemed the only way to maintain order. Soglo never mobilized the army and no shots were ever fired. After taking over the leadership, he immediately set about restoring civilian rule. A new constitution was adopted and, in January 1964 transparently undemocratic **"elections"** took place.

During the period of military rule, **Apithy and Ahomadegbe** had formed a coalition party which received 99.8 percent of the vote. Maga had meanwhile been jailed on charges of conspiracy to assassinate the two southern leaders. Apithy thus became the new president and Ahomadegbe took on the job of prime minister. Under a false guise of unity, the two men worked against one another, each trying to consolidate his own position within the party. The **exclusion of the north** from the political process led to more riots and bloodshed in Parakou and there were more political detentions for conspiracy to overthrow the government. But what brought the two southern leaders to loggerheads was a law concerning the appointment of members to the Supreme Court – Maga happened to be on trial at the time – which placed the judiciary in conflict with the government. Ahomadegbe, with the party behind him, demanded President Apithy's resignation. The president refused. Chaos within the party was coupled with widespread public discontent from outside its ranks, which reached fever pitch with the announcement of a 25 percent salary cut for civil servants to try to reduce the country's burgeoning deficit. In its distress, the government was virtually unable to act and normal administration began to break down. The military again intervened, and Colonel Soglo forced both Apithy and Ahomadegbe to step down.

A provisional government, headed by **Tahirou Congacou**, who was president of the National Assembly, released Maga from prison and set about writing a new constitution with the joint consultation of all three leaders. Elections were to be held in January 1966, but campaigning never began as, still posturing for position, Maga and Apithy allied themselves against Ahomadegbe in a move which triggered trade union protest. On December 22, 1965, Soglo intervened for a third time, and on this occasion

assumed power as the head of a **military regime**. Maga, Apithy and Ahomadegbe exiled themselves in Paris.

Soglo remained head of state for two years, but his term soon met with criticism. He was accused of mishandling Dahomey's affairs and of presiding over a military structure that was rife with **corruption**. In 1967, workers went on strike to protest against intolerable economic conditions. The subsequent and predictable ban on union activity led to yet another, equally predictable **coup**, led by **Major Maurice Kouandété**, and supported by junior officers including one Captain Mathieu Kérékou.

■ Continuing coups

After protracted disputes and negotiations, the army chief of staff **Alphonse Alley** took over as head of state, with Kouandété his prime minister. The military government had a strongly northern cast. Kouandété drew up another constitution and scheduled new elections for May 1968. Many politicians were banned from participating, however, including the elder statesmen, Maga, Apithy and Ahomadegbe. The trio, reunited in their exclusion, called for a boycott, and on the day of the elections, only 26 percent of the eligible voters turned out. An unknown doctor, **Basil Akjou Moumuni**, won the presidency, but the elections were immediately annulled, and the military instead conferred the presidency on a low-profile former Foreign Minister, **Emil Derlin Zinsou**.

In December 1969, sixteen months into his term, Zinsou was himself overthrown by the same man who had put him in power, Kouandété. The newest coup was spurred by divisions within the military and seemed to have more to do with corruption and personality differences than with ethnic tensions. Though there was no special crisis to justify the military takeover, it was the first time force had been used. Zinsou's car was sprayed with bullets in downtown Cotonou, but the president escaped with his life.

Fellow officers prevented Kouandété taking power himself. Instead, a **Military Directorate** was established with Lieutenant-Colonel **Paul Emile de Souza** in charge. Once more, elections were set and this time the three old-guard politicians were allowed to participate. Maga was set to win in his loyal Atakora region, but not to receive a majority over Apithy and Ahomadegbe combined. De Souza cancelled the Atakora poll. Declaring that the north would secede if the

Military Directorate refused to accept his presidency, Maga pushed the country to the brink of civil war. Apithy upped the stakes by stating his region would attach itself to Nigeria if Maga was instated. In a last-ditch compromise to save Dahomey from self-destruction, a **Presidential Council** was formed in which the three men would rotate power every two years. Maga was the first to serve as president, replaced in 1972 by Ahomadegbe.

The system seemed to be working when, in 1972, internal rivalries within the army triggered two mutinies at the Ouidah military camp. Though they were put down, more than twenty high-ranking officers were arrested, and six of them, including Kouandété, sentenced to death. That move prompted one last coup, led by a man who, like Kouandété, was a northerner from Natitingou – **Major Mathieu Kérékou**.

■ Stability – and a step to the Left

At the time of Kérékou's takeover on **October 26, 1972**, Dahomey had suffered nine changes of government in twelve years. Administration had grown used to the notion of government by crisis control and the nation had struggled with no clear lead and almost continual uncertainty.

Although remarkable **stability** marked the next phase in the country's history, it seemed at first that the pattern of biennial coups might continue. In **1973**, the national radio, "The Voice of the Revolution" reported that top-ranking military officers had been arrested for trying to overthrow the government. Later that year, some 180 student organizations were banned following demonstrations and strikes.

1975 was another bleak year for the government. Finance Minister Janvier Assogba was arrested after it was disclosed he had documents allegedly linking the president and other important government members in a financial scandal. In March, former president Zinsou was sentenced to death *in absentia* (he had been living in Paris where he headed the outlawed Parti Démocratique Dahoméen) for allegedly planning to assassinate Kérékou. And in May, Captain Aikpe, the Minister of the Interior, was shot to death by a Kérékou bodyguard when the president allegedly caught him *in flagrante delicto* with Mme Kérékou.

In **1977** there was another dramatic **coup attempt** when a group of **mercenaries** landed at Cotonou airport and, after trying to shell the pres-

idential mansion, were forced to retreat (events on which some of Frederick Forsyth's thriller *The Dogs of War* are said to have been based). Most of the mercenaries, led by the notorious thug Bob Denard, were French and, afterwards, already dismal Franco-Béninois relations sank to a new low. Morocco, Gabon and the Mouvement de la Rénovation du Dahomey – an exiled political party based in Brussels – were all implicated. A personal experience of the events is described by Bruce Chatwin, in typically laconic fashion, in "A Coup" (*Granta 10: Travel Writing*, Penguin, 1984).

Kérékou's revolution

Kérékou weathered all the storms. Two years after his coup, the new leader announced that Dahomey would engage in a **popular revolution**, embarking on a socialist path based on Marxism-Leninism. The country established relations with the People's Republic of China, Libya and North Korea and received the blessing of Sekou Touré of Guinea. Benin also moved closer to the Soviet Union and its tributary states.

Also in 1975, Kérékou changed the country's name from Dahomey to the **République Populaire du Benin** and launched the single political party, the Parti de la Révolution Populaire du Benin (PRPB). The new course instigated significant changes. Schools were nationalized, the legal system was reorganized and committees were established round the country to stimulate participation in local government. In 1977, a *Loi Fondamentale* established new political structures including the Assemblée Nationale Révolutionnaire. In 1979, the assembly's 336 members were selected by the party and approved by 97 percent of the voters. Later in the year, the party selected Kérékou as the sole presidential candidate and the assembly unanimously elected him in February 1980.

It would be hard to assert that Kérékou was ever a committed Marxist. Certainly it was a late conversion which only became clear after he took power and which was only defined in 1974. While the **centralized economy** hardly produced miracles for the nation, the revolutionary stance was a major contributing factor in maintaining stability in the 1970s. In the first place, it significantly reduced the regional disputes that continuously brought down early governments, by shifting political argument from ethnic loyalties to issues of social and economic ideology. It also helped to appease Benin's radical intelligentsia. For a long time, Benin's dissatisfied intellectual elite (the French called the country the "West African Latin Quarter") were unable to find work in the stagnant economy. Their calls for radical reforms in the early days of independence were popular with unions and student groups and helped to topple more than one president.

Liberalization

While rhetorically supporting the revolution, Kérékou began gradually to embark on a path of **liberalization**. By 1982 the government was busy selling off or reforming its unproductive and corrupt state-run companies and *sociétés*. Under IMF and World Bank pressure, Cotonou also began retraining officials and adopting measures to encourage private investment. In 1985, the government asked the IMF for assistance – a policy, it said, designed to "exploit the positive factors of capitalism".

The former leaders, Maga, Apithy and Ahomadegbe had been released in 1981 and many other political prisoners were pardoned (though those implicated in the bitterly resented "mercenaries invasion" of 1977 remained behind bars). The country also began fostering **relations with the West**. The relationship with France improved after the Socialists came to power in 1981, especially following President Mitterrand's official visit to Benin in 1983. Three years later, Kérékou made a series of trips to West European nations urgently seeking more aid and better debt terms. He also moved closer to conservative African nations, repairing old rifts with Togo, Côte d'Ivoire, Cameroon and Gabon.

Most of the policy reforms of the early 1980s were prompted by the deteriorating state of the economy and a scramble to find new sources of foreign aid. **Oil**, discovered off the coast, began to be exploited in 1982. It provided some relief to the government as the country was able to produce sufficient for its own consumption and to export small quantities. Bright prospects, however, turned gloomy as the world price of oil dropped and ambitious plans for increased exploration and drilling were scrapped. With few other viable resources, the economy was still heavily reliant on the agricultural sector – cotton and, especially, palm oil.

Economic woes had already forced the government to devise extreme austerity measures, announcing in 1985 that it would no longer guarantee **jobs to graduates**. That decision sparked bloody rioting and widespread arrests. Kérékou

quickly removed the Minister of Education, who was a Fon, thereby isolating himself from that ethnic community. When the border with Nigeria closed that year and relations with Benin's powerful neighbour deteriorated, resentment also grew among the Yoruba-speaking communities in the southeast, diminishing still further Kérékou's political stock. His resignation from the army seems to have impressed no one.

■ The democratic era

Lénin n'aura plus de chance au Bénin

Slogan of revolting students in Cotonou, December 1989

There were **demonstrations** in **December 1989**, unprecedented since Kérékou's coup of 1972, as they involved public demands for his resignation, for the adoption of a multiparty system and for a complete purging of entrenched, corrupt economic practices. Students and civil servants hadn't received allowances or pay for months, absenteeism had reached epidemic proportions and the country was in a state of muddle, discontent and stagnation not witnessed since the 1960s. Because of the **fear of coups**, most of the armed forces were no longer armed and, for several days in December 1989, anti-riot police stood by in Porto Novo and Cotonou as tens of thousands of protesters roared for Kérékou's downfall. In the middle of all this, Kérékou decided to go on a walkabout in the poor quarters of Cotonou. He got a mixed response, state radio reporting his progress at one stage as taking place "amid ovations and stone-throwing".

The events were inevitably compared to similar scenes being played out in **Eastern Europe**, and certainly the Béninois were encouraged by the limited news from there that filtered through. But it had been abundantly clear for many years that Benin's wasteful command economy was not working and that the human resources at the country's disposal – some of the best-trained **administrators, teachers and intellectuals** in West Africa – were being squandered by a top-heavy and grossly inefficient bureaucracy.

After the events of December 1989 – which coincided with an agreement by the IMF and World Bank to bale out Kérékou one more time, and pay some of the salary backlog – the Marxist-Leninist ideology was dropped: this was a condition of French economic support. By March 1990, a **multipartite national conference** had been held to establish a framework for the country's future – and to decide what role Kérékou might play. Fifty-two different political groups were represented; the conference declared itself sovereign, reduced the powers of Kérékou to that of a figurehead, and appointed a new cabinet headed by **Nicéphore Soglo**, a former official of the World Bank.

So wide-reaching were the reforms and so effective was the transitional government in replacing members of the military regime with civilian administrators, that Benin was quickly dubbed the first country in West Africa to experience a "civilian coup". Independent newspapers flourished; Amnesty International commended Benin for releasing all its political prisoners. A giddy sense of renaissance swept the country. With the referendum of August 1990 overwhelmingly supporting the conference's draft multiparty constitution, the way forward seemed optimistic and when Soglo soundly beat Kérékou in the **presidential elections** of 1991, the nation's mood was ecstatic.

In the run-up to legislative elections in March 1995, Soglo formed, and became leader of, the **Parti de la Renaissance du Bénin** (RB), which soon merged with another new party, the Pan-African Union for Democracy and Solidarity. At the elections, 31 parties fielded over 5,000 candidates for just 83 deputies' seats. The majority went to the opposition alliance, with the Front de l'Action Pour le Renouveau et le Dévelopement (FARD) capturing a commanding 18 seats. Though FARD was led by Porto Novan barrister and long-time political activist **Adrien Houngbedji**, the job of speaker of the assembly went to the head of a smaller opposition party, **Bruno Amousso**, who was voted to the position with the help of ministers loyal to Soglo, apparently in an attempt to diminish Houngbedji's influence.

Despite the new lines of credit, Western-imposed structural adjustment hit wage earners especially hard, reducing Soglo's popularity. Labour unrest continued through the early years of his administration with strikes and demonstrations causing occasional havoc in Cotonou, and several coup attempts were reported in the early 1990s. Approval for Soglo had already begun to drop in 1994, after he accepted a regional agreement for the devaluation of the CFA, a move widely interpreted as bending to Western insistence on

painful **economic remedies**. He was accused of "duvalierism" because of the way he transformed the government into a family affair: his wife Rosine was a member of parliament; his brother-in-law Desiré Vieyra was minister of defence; and his son Liadi was in charge of military affairs at the presidency. But more troublesome to most were the rising prices and high levels of unemployment at a time when aid was arriving. There was a feeling that money was being squandered, and Soglo was blamed.

The late 1990s

At the same time, **Kérékou's** star was beginning to rise. He had managed to seem dignified in the way he accepted the results of the elections in 1991, and human in the way he conceded the failure of his rule. His post-leadership conversion to Christianity prompted speeches defending the poor and displaced. When he announced that he would run for the presidency in 1996, conventional wisdom was that he was the candidate Soglo needed to beat. When both Houngbedji and Assoum threw their party support behind Kérékou, it was enough to give the former president 52 percent of the vote.

Calling for national unity, Kérékou began setting up his government. He created the position of prime minister – the post was not stipulated in the constitution – to repay Houngbedji for his support. The fact that the two men had come together at all surprised many – in 1975, Kérékou had sentenced his new ally to death for plotting against the revolution. It was a measure of how much things had changed. Still remembered as a Marxist-Leninist Kérékou included privatization as part of his economic revival plan and continued the **austerity measures** that Soglo had initiated.

International relations had improved in the aftermath of democratization, particularly with Western nations such as the US and France, and the good will continued following Kérékou's return to power. Co-operation also improved with neighbouring **Nigeria** as negotiations took place over the demarcation of their common border and measures aimed at curbing smuggling. In 1998, Kérékou was elected chair of the Conseil de l'Entente, and worked to consolidate relations of countries in the group that included Benin, Cote d'Ivoire, Togo, Burkina and Niger.

As he got deeper into his term, Kérékou, like Soglo before him, began to feel the pull between the agencies that set up austerity programmes and the people who felt their sting. Some aspects of economic reforms were palatable, such as Kérékou's early **crackdown on corruption**. In 1997, he took his own cabinet to task for the mismanagement of funds allocated for development projects; later that year the heads of four large state-owned companies were sacked on charges of fraud and mismanagement. But the unveiling of the 1998 budget led to a series of **strikes** by civil servants who demanded an end to privatization, unpaid wage bonuses and the scrapping of the value added tax. As the strikes continued, Houngbedji resigned from his post as prime minister and withdrew the FARD's remaining ministers from the governing coalition.

That departure proved decisive in the legislative **elections of 1999**, when Houngbedji switched allegiance and aligned his Parti du Renouveau Democratique (PRD) with those parties opposing Kérékou, including Soglo's RB. Once again providing the swing vote, Houngbedji gave a one seat majority to the opposition and was elected president of the national assembly. The extremely close margin leaves the presidential elections scheduled for 2001 wide open. Both Kérékou and Soglo, who are likely to face each other once again, will require skilful manoeuvring to create a coalition that will assure their re-election.

For those in the country growing increasingly frustrated with the slow pace of trickle-down development, little distinguishes the economic differences between the ruling parties these days. Clearly, policy is being set by **foreign creditors**. Yet, while parliament and the president come in for criticism, the **democratic ideal** is rarely questioned. At a time when boycotts dominated the election news of neighbouring countries with stifled oppositions, Benin's participation in recent elections has ranged from 70 to 85 percent of eligible voters, and the country counts over 100 political parties. Though Nigeria now overshadows Benin as the barometer of democratic reform in the region, it doesn't have the track record. The fact that the European Union saw no need to send a monitoring commission to the last legislative elections is an encouraging sign and one unparalleled in West Africa.

COTONOU AND THE COAST

On the basis of physical appearances, **COTONOU** is one of West Africa's least enticing cities. Though the population is under half a million, it spreads over a considerable reach of monotonously flat landscape, dotted with lakes and clogged with residential, commercial and administrative *quartiers* that run chaotically into each another. At rush hour, the cratered, grubby grid of streets becomes a seemingly endless tide of rattling *mobylettes* kicking up clouds of dust and exhaust fumes. You might expect the **waterfront** to add a picturesque backdrop to this bleak environment, but the harbour view is unfortunately blocked by the **modern port** – located right in the heart of the city and redolent of export produce that's waited too long in the sun. To cap it all, with not a hill or geographical landmark in the whole of Cotonou, it's difficult to get your bearings on first arriving in the smoggy clamour.

But the city is something of an African melting pot, with a still intact intellectual reputation that has only grown more visible with the government's recent liberalization. Commercially, it has gained considerable importance due to the frequent closures of Lomé's duty-free port – most hotels here are more geared to regional traders than to tourists. Cotonou's saving grace is its fantastic **markets**. For want of other things to do by day, you could spend a good deal of your time in town shopping and browsing. Cotonou **nights** are thoroughly enjoyable by any standards, buzzing with people out to enjoy the cool air, and vendors crowding through the streets. There's a clutch of good **nightclubs** where you can hear music and dance till late.

Three of the country's best-known attractions are each less than an hour out of the city. **Ouidah** can strike a slightly hollow note in its "fetish tourism", and the stilt village of **Ganvié** is a thorough rip-off – though none the less striking for that – but the official capital of Benin, **Porto Novo**, has a proud gravity that no amount of superficial exploitation could conceal. Lastly, if you're heading to Lomé, or arriving from that direction, you might stop a night at the virtually derelict old trading town of **Grand Popo**, whose magnificently picturesque lagoons and coconut groves provide the backdrop for a lethargic day or two sunning on the beach.

Cotonou

Though Cotonou is a large city, you'll spend most of your time in the diamond-shaped **centre**, defined by three main thoroughfares – **Boulevard Saint Michel** in the northwest, **Boulevard Steinmetz** in the northeast and **Avenue Clozel** to the southeast. The **port** forms a natural barrier to the southwest, marking the centre's fourth boundary. Many of the hotels and restaurants listed below are within the confines of these streets, as are the major **businesses**, the **post office** and the **banks**.

East of the centre, Boulevard Saint Michel extends to the Nouveau Pont, and crosses the **lagoon** that cuts Cotonou in two, linking the downtown districts with the **Akpakpa district** on the east side of the city. At the bridge's western foot spreads the vast **Dan Tokpa Market**, one of the largest along the West African coast. About 1.5km down the lagoon towards the ocean, Avenue Clozel extends over the **Ancien Pont** and continues east to join the road to Porto Novo.

West of the centre, Boulevard de France follows the coast to the high-rent **Cocotiers district** near the airport. Along the way, it passes near the French and American embassies and the imposing Presidential Palace, or **Présidence**, a modern pile encircled by a seriously large fence with security cameras peering from every corner.

On the **north side of town**, Avenue de la République leads west from the Nouveau Pont up to the **Place de l'Etoile Rouge** – a monumental square (complete with torch-bearing cast-iron statue rising up from the giant red star at its centre) commemorating the country's now lapsed revolution.

Arrival, information and city transport

The **airport** (with a small **exchange bureau** that opens for the day's few incoming flights) is 5km from the centre and you'll need to take a taxi to get into town. Though the fare is officially fixed at around CFA2000, few drivers are keen to take you for this sum, so try to get an idea of the going rate, and bargain strenuously. If you don't have much luggage, **zimi-djans** (*mobylette* drivers wearing yellow shirts with numbers stencilled on the back; pronounced, more or less, "semi-john") wait in front of the airport and will take you to the centre for around CFA200–250.

Coming in by **bush taxi**, you're most likely to be let off in the city centre. Towns in Benin have their own *autogares* in Cotonou (see "Moving On" p.841), conveniently situated on or near one of the three main streets marking the centre – Boulevard St Michel, Avenue Steinmetz or Avenue Clozel. Arriving from Lomé, for example, you end up at the **Jonquet autogare** right in the heart of the downtown district. If you happen to arrive from the north by train, the **railway station** is also centrally located, near the port.

The Ministry of Commerce and **Tourism**, at the Carrefour des Trois Banques (☎31.54.02), is happy to hand out a slew of brochures, and maps. Otherwise, they won't be able to do much for you. To find out about renting a car or joining an organized excursion to somewhere like Ganvié or the Pendjari National Park, you're best off going to a travel agent (see Listings, p.840).

Within the city centre, **taxis** are shared and cost CFA200–300 for most destinations, though they are not as widely available as *zimi-djans* – by far the most frequent form of transport in the centre. These should only cost you CFA100–150, even for quite long rides in town; as you're the only passenger, rates are of course completely negotiable. There are no town buses.

Accommodation

From dirt-cheap *chambres de passage* to luxury money temples, Cotonou has **accommodation** for everyone. Unless you are penniless, avoid the low-budget places where levels of hygiene are about as low as the prices: there's a number of very decent midrange lodgings which aren't expensive. Most of the less expensive hotels are in or near the centre, while the more upmarket places are found east across the Ancien Pont, in Akpakpa, or west towards Cocotiers.

Campers are well provided for at the rustic but friendly *Camping Ma Campagne* (CFA1500 per person to camp; simple rooms ②) 12km west of the centre on the route de Lomé. Pitching your tent in an isolated spot along the beach, on the other hand, is unsafe.

ACCOMMODATION PRICE CODES

① Under CFA4500 (under £5/$8).
② CFA4500–9000 (£5–10/$8–16).
③ CFA9000–18,000 (£10–20/$16–32).
④ CFA18,000–27,000 (£20–30/$32–48).
⑤ CFA27,000–36,000 (£30–40/$48–64).
⑥ CFA36,000–45,000 (£40–50/$64–80).
⑦ Over CFA45,000 (over £50/$80).

For further details, see p.48.

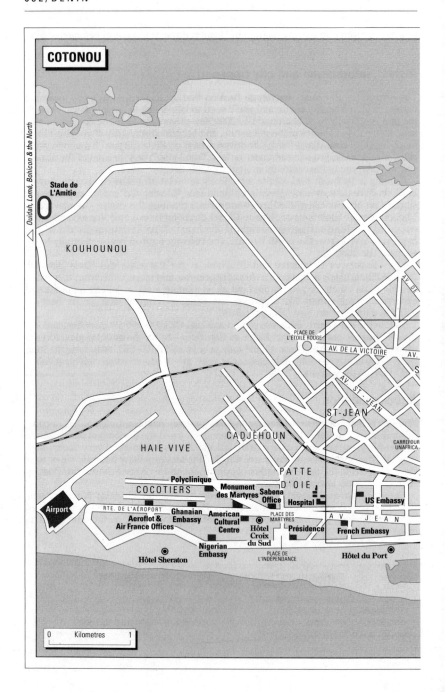

COTONOU

◁ Ouidah, Lomé, Bohicon & the North

Stade de
L'Amitie

KOUHOUNOU

PLACE DE
L'ÉTOILE ROUGE

AV. DE LA VICTOIRE

AV.

AV. ST - JEAN

ST-JEAN

CARREFOUR
UNAFRICA

CADJÉHOUN

HAIE VIVE

PATTE
D'OIE

Polyclinique

COCOTIERS

Monument
des Martyres

Sabena
Office

Hospital

US Embassy

Airport

RTE. DE L'AÉROPORT

Aeroflot &
Air France Offices

Ghanaian
Embassy

American
Cultural
Centre

PLACE DES
MARTYRES

Hôtel
Croix
du Sud

Présidence

A V   J E A N

French Embassy

Nigerian
Embassy

PLACE DE
L'INDÉPENDANCE

Hôtel Sheraton

Hôtel du Port

0   Kilometres   1

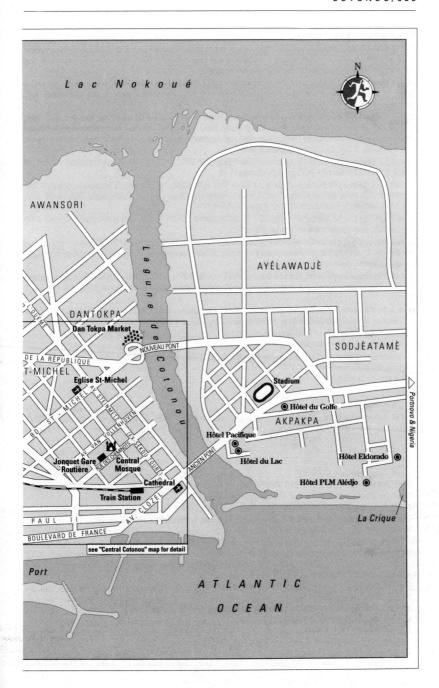

Lac Nokoué

N

AWANSORI

AYÉLAWADJÈ

DANTOKPA

Laguna de Cotonou

Dan Tokpa Market

NOUVEAU PONT

SODJÈATAMÈ

DE LA RÉPUBLIQUE

T-MICHEL

Eglise St-Michel

Stadium

AV. STEINMETZ

◎ Hôtel du Golfe

BD. ST-MICHEL

AKPAKPA

AV. VAN VOLLENHOVEN

Hôtel Pacifique

ANCIEN PONT

FX. TOURE

Jonquet Gare
Routière

Central
Mosque

RUE DES CHEMINOTS

◎

Hôtel Eldorado ◎

Hôtel du Lac

Cathedral

Train Station

Hôtel PLM Alédjo ◎

AV. CLOZEL

PAUL II

La Crique

BOULEVARD DE FRANCE

see "Central Cotonou" map for detail

Port

ATLANTIC

OCEAN

Portnovo & Nigeria

Inexpensive to moderate

Hôtel Babo, rue Agbeto Amadore (☎31.46.07). In shades of pastel green and cream, this is visible from bd St Michel (easy to spot as it's the tallest building around). Basic but tolerable rooms on the 4th and 5th floors, some with shower and balcony. ①.

Hôtel Bodega, av Proche, near the train station (☎31.29.74). Renovated S/C rooms with AC and a sense of spaciousness, but a bit expensive for what you get. Landscaped garden, bar and restaurant, with a *menu* at CFA4200. ③.

Hôtel la Colombe, PK 5, rte de Porto-Novo, Voie Sobetex, fourth block on the left (BP 156; ☎33.32.02). Although some way from the centre (5km), this is an obliging and recommended hotel and they'll pick-up free from the airport – a fifteen-minute drive at night. Share taxis into town cost only CFA200. Some S/C rooms, fanned or AC. ③.

Hôtel le Concorde, bd Steinmetz near Ciné Vog (BP 1557; ☎31.55.70). AC and fanned rooms, of which those with shared facilities are cheapest. ③.

Hôtel le Crillon, off bd Steinmetz near Ciné Vog (BP 1433; ☎31.51.58). The most central of the inexpensive hotels, and well cared for. Clean S/C rooms (floors swept, beds made daily) with fans and attentive staff – towel and bar of soap provided. ②–③.

Hotel le Crystal, bd Steinmetz, opposite Ciné Vog (☎31.22.08). Clean and comfortable rooms with fans or AC, and attractive wooden panelling. ③.

Hôtel Miva, PK 6, rte de Porto Novo, 6km from the centre (BP 9112; ☎33.12.08). A good place near the beach, if you want to get away from Cotonou, rather than explore it. Budget rooms with fans, or comfortable AC accommodation. ②–③.

Hôtel Pacifique, av Clozel, across the Ancien Pont (BP 423; ☎33.22.35). Good value, and not too far from the centre. Rooms of various standards, most quite spacious and some with lagoon views. ②–③.

Hôtel de l'Union, bd St Michel (BP 921; ☎31.27.49). Large rooms with fans or AC in a good location across from the Hall des Arts; reductions if you stay several days. ③.

Pension de l'Amitié, off av Proche (☎31.42.01). One of the cheapest in town, with reasonably clean rooms and shared facilities. ①–②.

Pension des Familles l'Amazone, av Proche (☎31.51.25). Simple accommodation, but central and very clean, with spacious S/C rooms and overhead fans. The Cameroonian owners can give travel tips if you're heading that way. ①–②.

Expensive

Hôtel Croix du Sud, facing the beach on the landward side of the bd de France (BP 280; ☎30.09.54). Creeping towards luxury class, but more informal. Rooms are divided between a main block and a complex of bungalows clustered round a 25-metre pool. ④.

Hôtel Eldorado, east side of Cotonou (☎33.09.23). Beach club next to the expensive *PLM Alédjo* with a pool and tennis courts, and large rooms with fans or AC. Good value for fun in the sun. ④–⑤.

Hôtel du Golfe, av Clozel, Akpakpa district (BP 37; ☎33.09.55). Clean and roomy quarters with AC. The hotel is near some of the city's better bits of beach – though far from the centre. Price includes breakfast. Restaurant, disco and even a gym. ④–⑤.

Hôtel de la Plage, near the fishing port (☎31.25.60). Central, colonial-style place with a good share of old-time charm, plus a pool and a private beach, nicely furnished with coconut palms. All rooms have AC. ④.

Hôtel PLM Alédjo, on the east side of town, 4km from the centre (BP 2292; ☎33.05.61). A dull modern hotel in a large tropical park, the *Alédjo* found a place in history as the venue of the March 1990 democracy conference. There's a pool and the hotel offers horse riding; it's also right next to a protected ocean bay ("La Crique") with windsurfing. ⑤.

Hôtel du Port, bd de France (BP 7067; ☎31.44.43). Not in the most attractive part of town, but the AC rooms and bungalows are spacious and well kept. Rooms around the courtyard come with balconies overlooking the clean, 25-metre pool. Garden restaurant. ⑤–⑥.

Hôtel Sheraton, bd de France, 4km from the centre, near the airport (BP 1901; ☎30.01.00 or 30.12.56; Fax 30.11.55) Two hundred luxury rooms and bungalows (some with hazy ocean views), all fitted out with colour TV, video and phone. The hotel is right on the beach with a popular poolside bar and a flourish of restaurants, including one with first-class breakfast buffets. There's also a disco, sauna, crafts shop, travel agency and bank. Generically international and sterile. ⑦.

Hôtel Vickenfel, off bd Steinmetz, near the Ciné Vog (☎31.38.14). Next door to the *Crillon*, but a little more upmarket and expensive. All rooms AC. ④.

The City

By way of **sights**, Cotonou is unexciting. On the western approach to the city, a striking example of revolutionary architecture, the Chinese-built **Stade de l'Amitié** ("Friendship Stadium"), dominates the district and flaunts an untypical **pagoda** at the entrance. In the city centre, there's a **cathedral** built in an Italian neo-Renaissance style. Making a special effort to see these buildings, however – or for that matter, the **central mosque** over by the Jonquet *autogare* – seems like scraping the bottom of a very small barrel. In the end, it's really only the **markets** that will leave a lasting impression, and Cotonou boasts some very good ones.

The Dan Tokpa Market

Every day, a steady stream of people can be seen skirting down the Boulevard Saint Michel or over the Pont Martin Luther King (the "Nouveau Pont") towards the **Dan Tokpa market**. From the bridge, you can sense the energy of commerce as you look down on the confusion of taxis, traders, stalls and merchandise spreading out in a thousand directions near the banks of the lagoon. In the middle of it all stands the heavy cement shoe-box structure of the **market building**, inside which are the cloth boutiques and stands of merchants.

The ground level of the market building is the food hall, devoted to everything from locally grown tubers and grain to boxes of Milo and Nescafé. Other floors have their own ranges of goods. One large section is filled with Nigerian-made cosmetics – skin lotion, shampoos and hair softeners. Piles of Savon de Marseille crush against Chinese enamel bowls and Nigerian plastics. **Cloth** is an especially important item. Colourful Parakou prints are quite reasonable, though less prestigious than the expensive Dutch wax designs. **Clothes** and **shoes** – flip-flops, plastic sandals, Bata-style loafers and imitation Italian dress shoes – also have their own specialist domains and dealers.

The Dan Tokpa **Fetish Market** is worth investigating: it's up along the lagoon shore, north of the main market building. After the big open square, the pole market, the wicker market and the empty bottle market, you come to the fetish market. The usual wide assortment of animal body parts and whole dried specimens is on offer – and the usual excessive demands for cash are made if you want to take photos.

Marché St Michel, the Village Artisanal and Marché Ganhi

The **Marché St Michel**, between the church and Dan Tokpa, is a small, pleasant area, on the edge of which you'll find people selling books – in English as well as French.

The **Village Artisanal** (crafts market) on Boulevard St Michel provides the best location in town to shop for Béninois handicrafts. A series of hut-like shops contain familiar specimens of traditional national art – for example, the colourful **patchwork cloths** originating from Abomey that were once used as the banners of that city's kings. Wooden carvings and **masks** from the various regions are also common, as are different varieties of drums – though the ones sold here are mainly decorative. The good collection of jewellery makes for easily portable gifts.

Marché Ganhi is a small produce market down near the port, essentially these days aimed at and used by expats and wealthy Béninois. There's a general selection of produce here, but it's also a good place to score cheap cassettes of the latest sounds. Tapes recorded for you or bought straight from the stalls should never cost more than CFA1200, except possibly those by Angélique Kidjo.

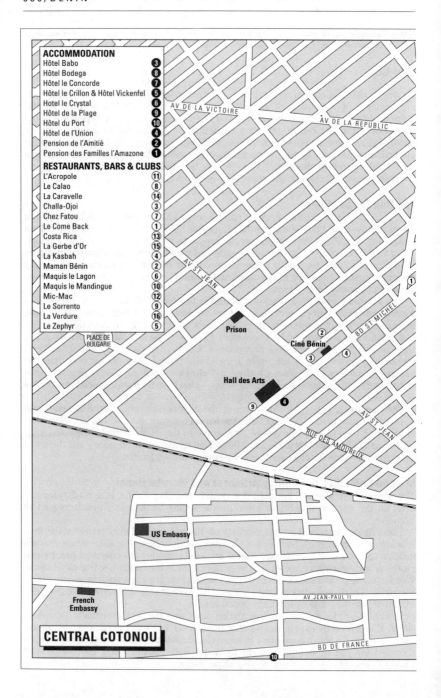

ACCOMMODATION
Hôtel Babo	③
Hôtel Bodega	⑧
Hôtel le Concorde	⑦
Hôtel le Crillon & Hôtel Vickenfel	⑤
Hotel le Crystal	⑥
Hôtel de la Plage	⑨
Hôtel du Port	⑩
Hôtel de l'Union	④
Pension de l'Amitié	②
Pension des Familles l'Amazone	①

RESTAURANTS, BARS & CLUBS
L'Acropole	⑪
Le Calao	⑧
La Caravelle	⑭
Challa-Ojoi	③
Chez Fatou	⑦
Le Come Back	①
Costa Rica	⑬
La Gerbe d'Or	⑮
La Kasbah	④
Maman Bénin	②
Maquis le Lagon	⑥
Maquis le Mandingue	⑩
Mic-Mac	⑫
Le Sorrento	⑨
La Verdure	⑯
Le Zephyr	⑤

AV DE LA VICTOIRE

ÀV DE LA REPUBLIC

AV ST JEAN

BD ST MICHEL

PLACE DE BULGARIE

Prison

Ciné Bénin

Hall des Arts

AV ST JEAN

RUE DES AMOUREUX

US Embassy

French Embassy

CENTRAL COTONOU

AV JEAN-PAUL II

BD DE FRANCE

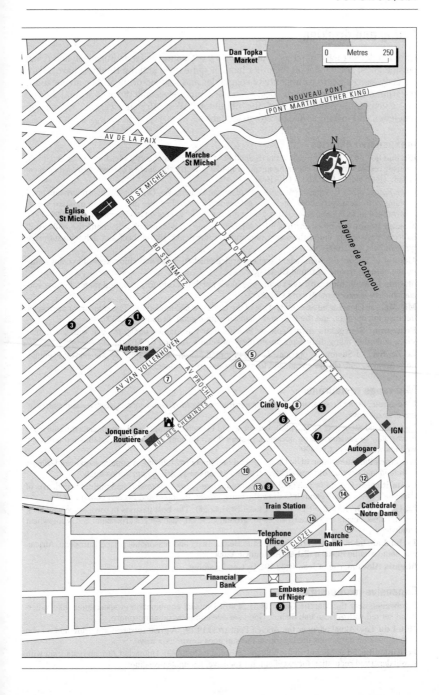

Dan Topka Market

NOUVEAU PONT
(PONT MARTIN LUTHER KING)

AV DE LA PAIX

Marche St Michel

BD ST MICHEL

Église St Michel

BD STEINMETZ

Lagune de Cotonou

N

0   Metres   250

3 **2** **1**

Autogare

5

6

AV VAN VOLLENHOVEN

AV PROCHE

7

RUE 312

Ciné Vog **8**   **5**

6

7

Jonquet Gare Routière

RUE DES CHEMINOTS

IGN

Autogare

10

12

13 **8**   **11**

14

Train Station

Cathédrale Notre Dame

15

Telephone Office

AV CLOZEL

Marche Ganki

16

Financial Bank

Embassy of Niger

9

Eating and drinking

Cotonou doesn't have much of a high culinary reputation as far as European and Asian cuisine goes. Local food, on the other hand, is quite good and the Béninois have a flare for tasty sauces made with plenty of vegetables and seafood or meat. For **street food**, try around the markets and *autogares*. In the centre, especially the area around the rue des Cheminots, you'll also find the ubiquitous West African *cafémen*, serving up omelettes and instant coffee on streetside tables.

Inexpensive eateries

Challa-Ojoi, av St Jean, one block north of bd St Michel. One of the city's best and least expensive open-air restaurants. Home cooking in cauldron-like pots; try the *purée d'igname* with *pied de boeuf* or fish. Good salads too. About CFA1500.

Chez Fatou, off av Proche, one block south of av Van Vollenhoven (☎31.49.78). Fair prices and good cooking, with local specialities like *sauce poisson* and Frenchified fare like rabbit in mustard sauce. Always packed, as it's also a popular watering hole, with cheap beer on tap (*pression*). CFA2000–3000.

Maman Bénin, one block north of bd St Michel. A good, well-known choice among the wall-to-wall informal restaurants lining the street behind the Ciné Bénin. Bits of beef and fish with different types of *pâte*. CFA1000–2000.

Maquis le Lagon, bd Steinmetz. Excellent grilled chicken, salad and chips, served evenings only on the outdoor *terrasse*. Around CFA1500.

Maquis le Mandingue, off av Proche, one block north of *Costa Rica*. Limited menu, but the special chicken is excellent. Around CFA2000.

Mic-Mac, av Clozel at bd Steinmetz. One of the city's few fast-food joints. The *chawarma* are a safer bet than the burgers, and the fries and salads are quite good. Around CFA2000.

Restaurant Sénégalais Awa Seck, av Proche, near the Jonquet *autogare*. Rice with groundnut sauce and other filling dishes in a small, pleasant setting. Around CFA1000.

Le Zephyr, bd Steinmetz, opposite *Le Lagon*. Small *buvette*, with various meals served evenings only. Always good, always cheap, and there's always great company.

Mid-range restaurants

L'Acropole, off av Proche, around the corner from *Costa Rica*. Good snacks, pastries and espresso, but it's expensive.

Le Calao, bd Steinmetz (☎31.24.26). Lebanese and French cooking with daily specials ranging from *boudin noir* to *couscous* or, on occasion, oysters flown in from France. Long established and very well known. *Menu* at CFA4000.

La Caravelle, intersection of av Clozel and bd Steinmetz (☎31.26.56). A popular expat rendezvous, with food and beer on the upstairs terrace, and expensive pastries. Sometimes dusty.

Costa Rica, av Proche (☎31.33.66). If the draught beer, *piste de pétanque* and nightly broadcasts of *Antenne 2* news wasn't enough to draw the expat crowd, the pizza and French cooking is.

La Gerbe d'Or, near the PTT on av Clozel (☎31.42.58). The best pastries in town since way back – rum babas, eclairs and custard slices for around CFA500. Also serves croissants and wholewheat sandwiches.

La Kasbah, bd St Michel, 50m east of Ciné Bénin. Tasty and reasonably priced European, African and some Middle Eastern dishes. Around CFA2000.

Maquis Akwaba, rue St Jean (☎32.19.21). Good standby.

Expensive restaurants

Edelweiss, near the Marché Ganhi (☎31.27.40). Unusual combination of specialities, like sauerkraut served with African fish dishes. Good service and pleasant atmosphere.

Hôtel du Lac, Akpakpa, near the Ancien Pont (☎33.19.19). A great terrace for a drink and maybe a meal, looking out across the lagoon as the sun goes down. Expensive.

Le Kinkeliba, bd St Michel, in the Village Artisanal (☎30.27.89). Upmarket African restaurant with a well-deserved reputation for excellent, if expensive, national specialities.

L'Oriental, Kadjehoun (☎30.18.27). Excellent Lebanese restaurant with a superb meze (titbits) dinner on Wed & Sun. About CFA7000.

Le Rufino's, Zone Residentielle, near the German embassy (☎31.33.38). Haute cuisine from China and Vietnam, served in the AC dining room or on the terrace.

Le Sorrento, bd St Michel near Ciné Bénin (☎30.37.79). Benin's best Italian restaurant, and one of the most popular dinner addresses in Cotonou. Excellent pizza and unusual pasta dishes.

La Terrasse, rue Goa (☎31.54.25). Large garden restaurant in the city centre, with a long list of Vietnamese specialities.

The Three Musketeers, off av Clozel (☎31.38.72). Colonial house converted into an English pub, featuring fish 'n' chips and shepherd's pie. Downstairs drinking area with darts and snooker and a pleasant outdoor beer garden.

La Verdure, off av Clozel (☎31.32.56). Casual bar-restaurant with lobster and seafood specialities. Something of a gathering point for expats and young people, with pinball and a small pool table.

Nightlife and entertainment

For a cheap night on the town, **rue des Cheminots**, down near the Jonquet *autogare*, is a lively introduction. Names and owners can change rapidly. In addition to the many restaurants and boutiques that stay open late, a couple of good **clubs**, listed below, have made this one of Cotonou's most active after-dark centres.

La Cabanne, av Proche (☎31.23.75). Nice club, though usually low-energy until Thursday when diverse bands come to kick off the weekend. No cover most nights.

La Case de la Musique, bd St Michel. No cover most nights, but the price of drinks – though not all that unreasonable – keeps the crowds away. Good venue for talented musicians, and livens up at weekends. Well worth checking out.

Le Come Back, off bd St Michel, 100m east of Ciné Bénin. A quiet, pleasant piano bar with live classic jazz. Drinks reasonably priced for a nightclub.

Le Golden's Club, out of the centre in the Kadjehoun district. Béninois bar and disco – lively after 10pm.

New York, New York, bd St Michel, inside the Hall des Arts. Currently the place to be seen among young trend-setters. CFA4500 cover, but offers a dependably good time, especially after midnight.

So What!, off av Clozel near the cathedral. One of the most popular live music clubs, with consistently good music. Musicians from Benin, Togo and Nigeria play an extraordinary range of styles from jazz to urban African pop. CFA1000 cover on big concert nights (Fri & Sat). No entry charge for jam sessions (Wed & Thurs).

Le 2001, rue des Cheminots. Extremely popular despite the relatively high price of drinks (CFA2000–3000) and the cover charge (CFA3000). Attracts a younger crowd looking for music and romantic encounters and can get rather sleazy.

Listings

Airline offices Aeroflot, rte de l'Aéroport (BP 032014; ☎30.15.74); Air Afrique, av Clozel (☎31.10.10; Fax 31.53.41); Air France, rte de l'Aéroport (☎30.18.15); Air Gabon, av Steinmetz, (☎31.20.67); Cameroon Airlines, 119 av Steinmetz (☎31.52.17); Ghana Airways, off av Clozel (☎31.42.83); Nigeria Airways, av du Gouveneur Ballot (BP 221; ☎31.58.24); Sabena, place des Martyrs (BP 2622; ☎30.03.55).

Banks In the centre, the best bank for changing money is the BIB, near Air Afrique (BP 03-2098; ☎31.55.49; Fax 31.27.07), which has good rates and takes no commission. The Financial Bank, off av Clozel by the PTT (BP 2700; ☎31.31.00; Fax 31.31.02), is slow and takes a three percent commission but they do give cash advances on Visa. Other possibilities include the Eco Bank, near the Ganhi market, and the Bank of Africa, on av Jean Paul II (BP 1280; ☎31.40.23; Fax 31.33. 85), both of which give Access/MasterCard cash advances for the same commission.

Beaches Most of those around the city are filthy and, in any case, often have a dangerous undertow. The best strands are in front of the hotels, notably the *Sheraton* and *Croix du Sud*, which are cleaner than that of the *Hôtel du Port*. Near the *Alédjo*, the protected cove known as La Crique is popular among expats and townspeople, since swimming is relatively safe. Don't take valuables on to any beach – La Crique, especially, is notorious for grab-and-runs.

Books and magazines SONAEC, av Clozel, has all the national papers as well as the best international selection, along with books in French – African and French literature, travel guides, etc. Also try the Librairie Notre Dame, near the junction of av Steinmetz and av Clozel, behind the cathedral, and La Plume d'Or, bd St Michel, near the US embassy.

Car rental Of the major companies, Hertz has a branch at the airport, represented by Loc Auto (☎31.27.85), which only opens up for incoming flights. Hertz is also represented at 157 av Steinmetz (BP 8128; ☎30.19.15) and at the *Sheraton*. Smaller firms often work out substantially cheaper, though their cars and conditions may not be as dependable. These include ONATHO (☎31.26.87), Locar Benin (BP 544; ☎31.38.37), Sonatrac (BP 870; ☎31.23.57), and Loc Auto (BP 117; ☎31.34.42).

Cinemas It's generally hard to see a decent film except on a small video screen or at the American or French cultural centres, but Ciné Bénin shows a range of films, mostly action movies in French.

Cultural Centres The dynamic Centre Culturel Français is on rte de l'Aéroport (☎30.08.56; Fax 30.11.51), next to the French embassy. Besides the library with books and newspapers (Tues & Thurs 9am–noon & 3–9pm, Wed 9am–7pm, Fri & Sat 9am–noon and 3–7pm, closed Sun & Mon), they have regular art exhibitions and theatrical performances by local artists.

Embassies and consulates France (embassy) rte de l'Aéroport, Cocotiers (BP 966; ☎30.08.24 or 30.08.25), (consulate) av du Général de Gaulle, just south of Air Afrique (☎31.26.80 or 31.26.38) – the consulate issues visas for Togo, Burkina Faso and a number of other Francophone countries; Ghana (BP 488; ☎30.07.46); Niger, one block behind PTT (BP 352; ☎31.40.30); Nigeria Lot 21, Patte d'Oie district (☎30.11.42); UK a consular officer from the British High Commission in Lagos is available every alternate Monday from 10am–2pm at the *Sheraton*; and USA, rue Caporal Anani (BP 2021; ☎30.06.50; Fax 30.19.74).

Hospitals The privately run Polyclinic (☎30.14.20), in Cocotiers, has the best reputation, though the most obvious place to head for with medical problems is the Centre National Hospitalier et Universitaire in the Patte d'Oie district. For emergencies, call ☎30.06.56.

Maps The Institut National de Cartographie, on rue des Libanais, close to the av Clozel junction, has reasonable survey maps of the country in 1:50,000 and 1:200,000 series. Many are out of print.

Pharmacies Of many, the main ones are: Pharmacie Jonquet, rue des Cheminots (☎31.20.80); Pharmacie Notre Dame, av Clozel (☎31.23.14); and Pharmacie Camp Ghezo, bd St Michel (☎31.35.55).

Photography Passport photos for your visa extension or onward visas are done quickly at Photo Minute, on av Clozel near the main PTT, and Zoom Service, av Steinmetz, near Ciné Vog. The price is around CFA2000, depending on speed (five minutes to two days). Across the street from Zoom Service is an anonymous place that does one-hour film developing. Royal Photo, by the Telephone Exchange on av Clozel, also does a good job at a reasonable price.

Post and phones The main PTT (post office) is off av Clozel, near the port. The poste restante service seems reliable here. International calls can be made easily from the telephone office on av Clozel (collect calls can be made only to France). Phonecards have been introduced, though there are few phones which accept them, other than at this PTT.

Supermarkets The three largest are all near the intersection of av Clozel and av Steinmetz. La Pointe is the best for imported European products, though it's now got stiff competition from the newer Prisunic, which carries some department store goods along with the groceries. Benin-Self has a more limited selection, though the hours are longer.

Swimming pools The cheapest and most central pool is at the *Hôtel du Port*, which non-guests can use for CFA1000. Though much nicer, the *Sheraton*'s pool costs a stiff CFA3000 (and it's circular, so hopeless for serious length-swimming). The *Alédjo* has a smaller but equally expensive pool.

Travel Agents One of the best organized is Savana Tours, on bd St Michel (☎31.46.26), which runs trips to national attractions like Ganvié and Pendjari. Also reputable are C & C Voyages, rte de Porto Novo, near the Ancien Pont (☎33.00.15; Fax 33.01.49) and Phimex Voyages, av Steinmetz (☎31.52.13; Fax 31.57.13). CBM Voyages, bd de France, by the *Hotel du Port*, has English-speaking staff and is extremely helpful (☎31.05.28).

Visa extensions From the Ministry of the Interior, av Jean Paul II (Mon–Fri 8am–noon). Extensions for a month cost CFA7000. Two photos are required and the process takes about 48 hours.

ROAD
The main international *autogare* for travel along the coast on the **Cotonou–Lomé axis** is the **Jonquet** *autogare*, on rue des Cheminots, near the central mosque. Vehicles depart regularly for Ouidah, Grand Popo and Lomé. The most common vehicles are Peugeot 504 saloon and estate cars, which fill quickly before leaving. The Itajara *autogare* is focused a block or so south of Jonquet on Avenue Proche, but in practice is almost indistinguishable from Jonquet. This is the place to get vehicles for **Parakou and the north**. For **Porto Novo, Lagos** and **Abidjan**, head to the *autogare* de Porto Novo, near the Ancien Pont, where, depending on the destination, you will find cars, buses and minibuses. Vehicles for Lagos also leave from the **Dan Tokpa** *autogare* near the Dan Tokpa market. **Abomey** is serviced from a separate *autogare* located near the Ciné Vog, between Avenue Steinmetz and the lagoon.

TRAIN
If you want to head north by train, you'll find the station downtown, near Avenue Clozel. One train leaves daily for **Parakou** at 9.56am and costs CFA3100 second class and CFA5100 first class. **Couchettes** (CFA6630) are available on the evening train, which leaves Cotonou on Tuesdays and Thursdays at 7.15pm. The whole journey takes about 12 hours.

Ganvié

GANVIÉ, said to be Africa's largest **lake village**, is an extraordinary sight. The entire town spreads across the shallow, grey-green waters on the northwest side of **Lac Nokoué**, opposite Cotonou, with wood and thatch houses built on tall stilts rising above the rippling surface. The lake is "grooved", as the tourist leaflet puts it, "not by gondolas like in Venice but by graceful *pirogues* or heavy boats loaded to the boards". The village is home to some 15,000 people who make their living primarily from **fishing**. In the shallow waters, they plant branches that form a network of underwater fences known as *akadja*. Fish trapped in this way can be eaten, sold or kept for breeding.

Ganvié is only accessible by boat, and all around the northwest part of the lake the water is crowded with bumping log jams of vessels – even the market is held on the water, women selling wares from their canoes. Not altogether surprisingly, the stilt village is overrun with tourists whose presence has encouraged a commercial free-for-all in the little town, destroying the initial impressions of a tranquil aquatic idyll. If you have a low tolerance for this sort of thing, it's best to avoid Ganvié altogether and make your way to the less-commercialized places around Porto Novo (see p.847).

Some history
As the **slave trade** expanded after the Portuguese arrival on the coast in the sixteenth century, armies of the Dan-Homey king swept the surrounding countryside, rounding up people to trade with the Europeans for exotic goods such as cloth, gin and guns. Insecurity led to the widespread migration of weaker communities, and it was in this manner that the ancestors of the **Tofinu people**, who now inhabit Ganvié, came to settle in the area around Lake Nokoué. The earliest may have arrived in the sixteenth century, although at the end of the seventeenth century, an exodus of peoples from Tado near the Togolese border is known to have settled at the site of the present village,

where they found sufficient space for grazing and farming. More importantly, the people were safe from invasion since, for religious reasons, the Dan-Homey were forbidden to extend their attacks over water. The name Ganvié probably derives from the Tofinu words *gan*, meaning "we are saved", and *vié*, "community".

Practicalities

The departure point for Ganvié is **Abomey-Calavi**, 18km north of Cotonou. From the Akpakpa market station in Cotonou, take one of the frequent collective **taxis** for around CFA200 per person. Once you've arrived in Abomey-Calavi, you can find motorized boats to take you on a two-hour tour of Ganvié. There is some sort of official price list at the jetty, but the actual cost will depend on the number of people and your ability to bargain; on average, a boat will work out at roughly CFA2000 per head. Some of the villagers also run *pirogue* trips through their own watery backyards, allowing people to take photos of kids standing on porches yelling *"cadeau!"*. If, instead of stopping at Abomey-Calavi, you continue 5km up the northern highway to **Akassato**, you can approach Ganvié from behind and at slightly less cost, avoiding the worst tourist excesses. *Pirogues* punt you south 4km or so through the creeks and marshes to the edge of the lake and the stilt village.

There is some cheap and basic **accommodation** on Ganvié itself, or you can stay right by the jetty at the comfortable *Auberge du Lac* (☎36.03.44; ②–③), with clean AC or fanned rooms and a bar-restaurant with good Western-style food.

Ouidah

Hauntingly quiet after centuries of dynamic history, **OUIDAH**, 30km west of Cotonou, and located on a backroad off the main Cotonou–Togo highway, works a wonderful spell. This is a **voodoo** stronghold and the religion's influence penetrates as deeply as the salt air blowing off the ocean, its power outliving that of the **Portuguese fort** (now a museum). There are streets of French **colonial architecture** – all cracked facades and sagging wooden porches and shutters, and now dwelt in by poor families. The **python temple** adds a kitsch touch, but the use of snakes is part of authentic fetish practice – never mind the fact that they get rather more of a workout than they did in the days before tourism. There are plenty of other altars and temples scattered about the town, keeping the faith alive without the touristic overtones.

Some history

Back in the days when the shore of the Gulf of Benin was known as the **Slave Coast**, some of the largest trading posts and slave markets were sited here. Grand Popo, Porto Novo and Ouidah were synonymous with the trade and thus have infamous origins. Ouidah was captured by the "Amazon" warriors of **King Agadja** of Abomey in the early eighteenth century (see p.852) and, in the following years, the town grew into one of the foremost trading posts between Europe and the Dan-Homey empire. The **Portuguese**, who arrived at the spot, then known as Ajuda ("Help"), in 1580, waited over a century to build the fort of **São João Batista**. Part of their story is told in Bruce Chatwin's *The Viceroy of Ouidah* (see "Books" in Contexts) and another version in Herzog's quirky film *Cobra Verde*. Nearby, the **Danes**, **English** and **French** also built forts as they tried to gain their share of the growing trade with Africa. The last Portuguese slave ship left for Brazil in 1885. The Danish and English bastions today house businesses, while the Place du Fort Français now features a small outdoor theatre. Ouidah remained an important coastal city while under French dominion, but in

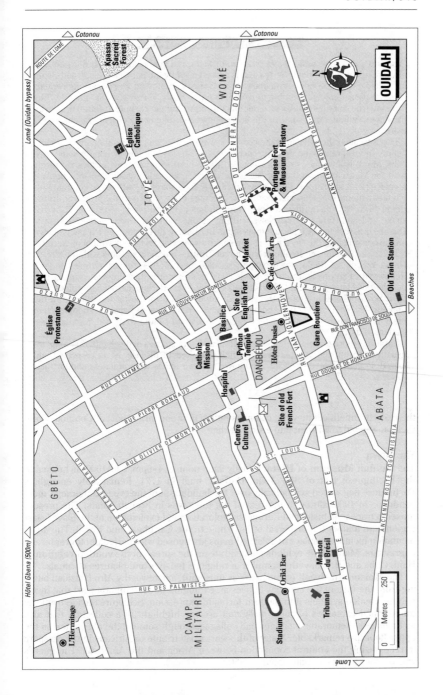

VOODOO

"Voodoo", also spelt *vodu, vodun, voudou,* or *vudu,* is a confusing term. It does not signify a religion, at least not in Africa, but is a word used by the peoples of Togo and Benin for a spirit, demigod or intermediary. *Vodu* "priests", male and female, are individuals who are particularly susceptible to *vodu* influence, easily "possessed" or "mounted" by the *vodu* who can thus display its emotions through a human channel. A **fetish** is an ordinary object imbued with some of this sacred power – a token *vodu* charm available at any market.

The **Ewe** and other people of the coast – as well as the Fon around Abomey in Benin – believe in a supreme God, **Mawu.** Their religious stories link him or her (in some societies, Mawu is a woman, or even a couple, Mawu-Lisa) with creation. Shrines are rarely built for Mawu, however, but for the *vodu,* many of whom are associated with **natural forces** or with **ancestors.** The benevolence of *vodu* is sought by offerings; communities often pay homage to a specific *vodu* who becomes their main spiritual protector. In the Benin town of Ouidah, for example, **Dangbe** has a special place. Represented by the snake and sometimes by rainbows, curling smoke, running water, or waving grass, Dangbe is associated with life and movement. In Abomey, he is known as **Da** and is shown on the bas reliefs of the royal palace as a snake swallowing its tail – a symbol of eternity.

Throughout Togo and Benin, people honor **Buku** – a *vodu* associated with the sky. At Dassa Zoumé in Benin, townspeople dedicate one of their oldest temples to her. Renowned as an oracle, Buku's name is evoked in proverbs, blessings and curses, and people travel long distances to her shrines to pray, give offerings or make sacrifices. The *vodu* So (Hebiosso in Fon) is the *vodu* of thunder. With the power to strike down the impious, he is depicted at the Abomey palace as a red ram with lightning shooting from his mouth and two axes at his side. Gu, the guardian of smithing and war, also has associations with the sky.

Sapata is more closely identified with the earth and shrines dedicated to this *vodu* are usually seen outside villages near the fields. Linked to disease, he is respected and feared. Priests devoted to Sapata are known for their ability to treat illness and for their

the early twentieth century the colonists built a new and larger port at Cotonou. From then on, the old town went into a slow decline.

The Town

The **Ouidah Museum of History** (daily 9am–noon & 4–6pm; CFA1000) is housed in the Portuguese fort of **São João Batista,** built in 1721. Remarkably enough, a Portuguese flag waved symbolically over the building until the eve of Dahomey's independence in 1960, although the rest of the town was in French hands. The present museum traces the history of European exploration and exploitation of the Slave Coast region, and follows the dispersal of its people to the Caribbean and Brazil. The documentation includes displays of enlarged maps juxtaposed with period photographs and engravings. Many of the exhibits concentrate on the spread of the **voodoo religion** to Haiti, Cuba and Brazil, with examples of religious fetishes and pictures of rituals.

The **Maison du Brésil** (same hours as museum), a noteworthy Afro-Brazilian building from the turn of the century, houses an exhibition of contemporary art that incorporates voodoo symbols into modern forms of expression. Sculptures made from the transformed carcasses of rusty *mobylettes* are the highlight of a collection that also includes less memorable paintings and collages, though some of the old photos on the upper floor are remarkable. Many of the works pay tribute to Africans in the diaspora in recognizing the cultural connection between Africa and the Americas. The guards will ask for money – donate about CFA500.

understanding of medicinal plants. **Hu** is connected with the ocean and water. His daughter, **Avlekete**, is honoured at the port of Cotonou and in nearby villages. **Legba**, the trickster, whose image is distinguished by an exaggerated phallus, contains elements of good and evil. Though Legba can bring bad luck on a house, he can also chase it away. His shrines can be seen everywhere – guarding the entrance to a community or compound, in a market, in fields, or at a crossroads.

Countless other *vodu* exist, and many occupy natural niches. **Iroko** trees, for example, are often inhabited by *vodu*. The creation stories of some societies in the region tell of men and women descending to earth from the branches of an iroko. They are associated with fertility or new life, and you will often see sacrifices among their roots.

There are many parallels between the *vodu* and the *orisa* of Yoruba religion in Nigeria, and also between *vodu* and elements of Akan religion further to the west in Ghana and Côte d'Ivoire – all the result of migrations and the wax and wane of empires. A further complexity was introduced by the return of Brazilians between the seventeenth and nineteenth centuries to the land of their (partial) ancestry. They reintroduced elements of Yoruba custom when they settled on this part of the coast.

Slaves sold across the Atlantic took their religious systems to North and South **America** and the Caribbean. Even metropolitan areas carry reminders: Legba statuaries made in the last fifty years can be found in New York City and Miami. But West African religions are more often identified with Brazil, Cuba and **Haiti**. Many Haitian slaves came from the Dahomey (Benin) coast and the names of numerous *vodu* are virtually unchanged to this day. Legba is known as Papa Legba, Sapata as Sabata, Avlekete as Aizan-Velekete. The iroko tree, known as *loko* in Fon, became Papa Loko. Only the supreme god, Mawu was given a completely new, French, name – Bondieu.

In the Americas, **Catholicism** and the *vodu* system were soon melded together. But even in West Africa, many elements of Catholic teaching found fertile soil in the local belief system: the pantheon of a supreme God, the Virgin Mary and saints who could be called upon for help was a similar enough structure to Mawa and the *vodu*. Saint Patrick, not surprisingly, was identified with the snake *vodu* Dangbe, while Saint Peter was considered to be the Catholic incarnation of Legba.

Ouidah's large **cathedral** is a formidable monument that was upgraded to the rank of basilica during the 1989 visit of Pope John Paul II, who also consecrated the new altar. Dating from the beginning of the century, it's recently been restored and fitted with new stained-glass windows.

The cathedral attracts nowhere near as many visitors as the nearby **python temple**, however, which guards the secrets of Ouidah's snake cult. The key to the secret of the fetish serpents of Ouidah lies in the strength of your donation to open the temple doors. The demand of visitors – coupled with the open encouragement of voodoo tradition by the new government – has led to a thorough restoration of the site (with UNESCO support) and the price of admission seems to have stabilized at CFA1000. For this, you get to pose with the tame pythons – wrap-around snakes believed to give vitality and protection over your person. But on days when the reptiles are, understandably, tired, your payment may get you no more than a peek into the room where they're kept. The whole performance is rather graceless.

An interesting walk through the town's residential streets leads to the **sacred forest of Kpasse**. Tradition holds this site to be where Kpasse, a fourteenth-century chief, transformed himself into a tree in order to hide from his enemies. The ancient iroko tree still marks the spot and believers leave offerings by its roots. Modernist bronze statues depicting voodoo divinities are scattered about the woods and are explained (in French) by the caretaker who meets you at the entrance. Photography is permitted and the tour is free – though a tip is appreciated. While not an extraordinary adventure, a visit here is a pleasant pretext for a tramp through some pretty woods, and the guide's enthusiastic explanations are vivid. In fact, the more questions you ask, the more insightful become the answers.

Practicalities

Budget **accommodation** can only be found in a *chambre de passage* at one of the town's *bar-dancings*: very basic rooms with shared facilities can be had at *l'Hermitage* (①). More official lodgings, all of which serve **food**, are listed below. *Le Bon Snack,* on a street around the corner from *Hôtel Gbena*, makes excellent salads, and *Le Café des Arts,* near the *Hôtel Oasis,* is good for breakfasts and coffee.

Hôtel Gbena, rte de Lomé (BP 36; ☎34.12.15). For a long time the only place in town, this government hotel is still probably the best accommodation, although a bit far from the centre (on the main road to Togo). Good food and excellent service. ③.

Hôtel Oasis, across from the *autogare* and an easy walk from the fort (BP 24; ☎34.10.91). Clean AC accommodation in the heart of town. Within the range of most budget travellers, it's excellent value for money and breakfast is included. The hotel restaurant is a classy place for *akassa, monyo* or *agouti* – or even foreign fare, including pizza. ②.

Oriki Bar, rue Marius Moutel (☎34.10.04). Very presentable, mostly AC rooms set around the flowering gardens. Good value and a homely atmosphere. ②.

Grand Popo and around

At the height of the slave trade, **GRAND POPO** rivalled Porto Novo, Ouidah and Aneho (in Togo) as a major port. With the demise of the trade, however, its importance declined more dramatically than the other towns and, today, even vestiges of the more recent colonial past have literally been washed away by the advancing ocean. Locals remember the large church, commercial depots, administrative buildings and colonial mansions that disappeared into the water as recently as the 1960s, and though a few **antiquated buildings** still dot the road that leads to town from the main highway, most of the old quarter is entirely submerged.

As a result, Grand Popo looks very much like any of the other small fishing villages that stretch between Lomé and Cotonou, tucked between the lagoon and the ocean and lost in a sea of coconut trees. Though **voodoo** thrives here, few visitors even notice the snake pit, fetishes or temples and confine themselves mainly to the idyllic **beach**. In fact, there is little else to do once you get here.

The lagoon provides the possibility for excursions, however (small boys will try to recruit you from the moment you arrive), and fishermen are happy to supplement their incomes ferrying guests of the *Auberge* in their *pirogues*. The most popular destination is the **Bouche du Roy** – a vast expanse of water where the Mono River empties into the ocean. Along the way, you pass through scenic island villages.

Practicalities

Taxis from Lomé or Cotonou let you off on the main highway. There's a small bar on the intersection of the road that heads down to the strand and this is your last chance of inexpensive food and refreshment. *Zimi-djans* and taxis wait at the junction and for CFA200 will take you to the town's only **accommodation**, the French-run *Auberge* (☎ & Fax 43.00.47; ②–③), 4km away. Housed in refurbished colonial buildings, the lodgings offer a refreshing combination of nostalgia and comfort; all rooms have private baths and fans, but there's no AC. It also offers camping facilities at CFA 1000 per head. The hotel's **restaurant** terrace sits right on the waterfront – spectacular scenery for European dishes. You can also try and find simple accommodation in a private home. By the beach in the nearby village of **Ewe Condji** is the excellent, new *Hotel Awalé Plage* (BP 29; ☎43.01.17; ②–③).

Lac Ahémé

The lagoon that extends for thirty kilometres inland from Grand Popo is **Lac Ahémé**. It's a highly picturesque area to visit and there's a pleasant **hotel-restaurant** on the west shore, *Village-Club Ahémé* (BP 2090, Cotonou; ☎43.02.21; ③) – a place for lazing away a few days, with plain, comfortable S/C, AC rooms and optional excursions on the lake and around the district. **Possotomè**, 87km from Cotonou, is the nearest village. To reach it, turn right at Comè, and then go 20km north on a bad road, in the direction of Bopa. There are occasional taxis and *mobylettes*.

Porto Novo and around

Capital of Benin, but only in name, **PORTO NOVO** has two attributes Cotonou lacks – a geographical setting of some presence and a place in **history**. Sprawling over the hills surrounding a sizeable lagoon, the town was formerly the centre of a large kingdom of the Gun people; their **palace** has now been restored. More recently it served as capital of the French colony of Dahomey – the **colonial buildings** are reminders of this period – and the town was, and remains, the centre of the country's intellectual life and something of a barometer of political opinion in Benin. For visitors, it's one of Benin's most interesting towns, with a strikingly good ethnographic museum.

Despite a population of around 150,000, Porto Novo seems much smaller. Perhaps this is because of its coherent layout, but the narrow streets and absence of modern structures also add to the provincial, passed-by feeling: most of the architecture in town harks back to the colonial and pre-colonial periods.

The Town

Porto Novo consists of four main parts. The **old town** in the centre is characterized by narrow dirt roads and *banco*-built houses. The old town runs into the **commercial centre**, with the **Grand Marché** and surrounding businesses that stretch down to the lagoon on the southern flanks of the town. In the east, the **administrative district** is the location of the former **Governor's Palace**, the Présidence, and a couple of ministries and office buildings. Scattered around the margins, the zone of new **residential quarters** is inhabited by those who've moved to the city in recent years.

Porto Novo's superb **museum of ethnography** (daily 9am–12.30pm and 3–6pm; CFA1000) contains a wealth of well-presented artefacts from all Benin's peoples, but concentrating on the southeastern Fon and Yoruba communities – each item accompanied by explanations and background. The visit kicks off at the entrance with a pair of beautifully **carved doors** from the palace of the king of Kétou, 100km north of Porto Novo. The rooms inside are each organized around cultural themes – one dedicated to **masks** and other carvings of religious significance, including fetishes used in the voodoo cult, another devoted to **local arms**, with examples of old rifles and poisoned spears, and another containing a large collection of Béninois **musical instruments**. A major part of the museum is dedicated to **regional history** and the treaties signed by local rulers that led to Porto Novo's transformation into a great slave-trading centre. A French and English speaking guide is included in the entrance fee.

East of the market, the **Palais du Roi Toffa** (or Palais Honmè) has been restored and costs CFA1000 for the obligatory guided tour. It's an impressive maze of baked mud and thatch divided between the private residences of **King Toffa** and his entourage, and the public assembly halls, but rather empty, except for a few rare mementos of the local kings. You have to rely on your imagination to bring to life the guide's detailed explanations of local history and court life.

The market is held every four days in Porto Novo's **Grand Marché**, in keeping with the traditional calendar. It's a colourful affair that spreads over a large central square, with stalls selling agricultural goods from the surrounding countryside and fish from the nearby lagoon. Dominating the scene, the curious Brazilian-style building painted in muted pastel colours was built in the nineteenth century as a church, but is today the central mosque.

Practicalities

Although this is Benin's capital, Cotonou is the centre of business and government. Porto Novo doesn't even benefit greatly from Lagos traffic and trade, as it's off the main coastal highway. There is a post office, a **hospital** (☎21.34.91) and pharmacies, but for banking (you can't change money here) and just about every other business, you'll find Porto Novo very limited indeed. Taxis and minibuses run frequently to both Cotonou and Lagos.

Accommodation
Porto Novo has a number of hotels, but for a town of its size, the options are fairly limited.
Casa Danza, av Victor Ballot (☎21.48.12). This popular eatery now offers the town's most central accommodation. Clean and comfortable S/C rooms are reasonably priced and come with choice of fan or AC. ③.

Hôtel Beaurivage, out of the centre on the bd Lagunaire (BP 387; ☎21.23.99). Old, but well-maintained hotel with a nicely planted terrace overlooking the lagoon. Extremely accommodating staff and comfortable S/C, AC rooms, but the food is of variable quality. ③.

Hôtel La Détente, off the bd Lagunaire. The cheapest place in town, and well located: there's a panorama of the lagoon and it's within walking distance of the palace and market. Spartan but clean rooms with fans or AC. ①.

Hôtel Dona, rue Catchi/bd Extérieur Nord, near the water tower (BP 95; ☎21.30.52). Modern hotel with twenty well-furnished S/C, AC rooms, a bar-restaurant and a nightclub. ③–④.

Hôtel Malabo, bd Lagunaire. Basic, low-budget accommodation that caters mainly to the guests of its lively bar-restaurant. Near the lagoon, but a bit far afield – take a *zimi-djan* to town. ①–②.

Eating

Apart from the street food in the markets and *autogare*, or the pricey hotel **restaurants** at the *Dona* and *Beaurivage*, there's a surprising dearth of places to eat. Off Boulevard Lagunaire, near the *Beaurivage, Aux Ventes de la Mer* is a good outdoor restaurant near the water. A safe choice in town is the slightly upmarket *Casa Danza*, which serves moderately priced European and African food in a well-manicured courtyard. More basic is the *Java Promo*, nearby on Avenue No. 6, where you can eat inexpensive meals like *moyo* with chicken or fish, in the shade of the expansive patio.

Around Porto Novo

Across the lagoon from Porto Novo are a number of stilt villages that are less of a hassle to visit than Ganvié. Nearby too, is the lively market centre of Adjarra.

Adjarra

An important market – held every fourth day like Porto Novo's – takes place in **ADJARRA**, 8km northeast of Porto Novo on the Kétou road. This small village has a reputation for its **drum-makers** and produces over fifty different types of *tam-tams* varying in construction, material (wood or clay) and colour. Their quality attracts many buyers from Nigeria. Alongside fruit and vegetables, the market also sells a selection of useful fetishes, medicinal herbs and *gri-gris* (lucky charms), as well as locally made pottery and hand-woven cloth.

The stilt villages

Porto Novo's surrounding lagoon contains a number of stilt villages not unlike Ganvié, but until recently, travellers never ventured to them. The outlying area has still not become a tourist trap, though the price of a *pirogue* has become steeper in recent years. The closest, and easiest to reach is **Aguégué**, 12km through the creeks. *Piroguiers* near the bridge in Porto Novo can easily be found to take you there. There is no accommodation in the village, but just gliding through and observing makes for an interesting excursion. You may be asked for money if you want to take pictures. The *Hôtel Beaurivage* in Porto Novo also organizes trips to the villages by motorboat, which doesn't work out vastly more expensive and avoids the hassle of negotiating with the *piroguiers*.

CENTRAL BENIN

Benin's interior is a relatively homogeneous series of **plains** dominated by low, sloping hills. This was the site of early kingdoms, most notably that of the **Fon** founded at **Abomey**. The **Yoruba** also established a number of chiefdoms in the area, while further north, the **Bariba** carved out a small territory – the **Borgou country** – in the region of **Parakou**. These are still the main peoples of central Benin, an area of intensive agricultural production and small industries.

Driving **north from Cotonou** to Abomey, the road passes through the **Lama depression**, a low-lying swampy region of clay soils, patches of rainforest and a designated forest reserve, the **Forêt de Ko** or **Lama**.

Abomey and Bohicon

Capital of one of the great West African kingdoms in pre-colonial times, **ABOMEY** boasts a fascinating history and counts as one of Benin's greatest attractions. Commercially the town is overshadowed by **BOHICON**, of which Abomey is essentially the ancient precursor, and which has benefited from its position on the rail line and main north–south highway (the French deliberately laid the railway to the east of Abomey to reduce the commercial power of the Abomey royal dynasties). Despite Bohicon's immense **market**, however, the town is a chaotic sprawl with little that could tempt you to stay for a prolonged period. If you do decide to stay, the *Hôtel Relais Sinnoutin*, on the main road at the south end of town (BP 27; ☎51.00.75; ②), has decent rooms with shared facilities. The Bank of Africa changes both cash and travellers' cheques. Most people skip Bohicon altogether and head straight out to Abomey, 9km from the highway, which is more manageable and, with the **royal palace and museum**, infinitely more interesting.

Abomey town

Abomey is fascinating to wander through; any path off the main roads leads through twisted alleyways with *banco* houses and colourfully painted **fetish temples**. Between the **royal palace** and the *préfecture*, overgrown plots with weather-worn mud ruins are vestiges of former royal palaces. It's also an excellent place to shop for local **crafts**.

The royal palace and museum

In the three hundred years of the Dan-Homey empire, the kings gradually constructed a magnificent **palace** in the centre of Abomey. In fact, it was a vast complex of many palaces, since the sovereign never occupied the residence of his predecessor, but built a new one next to the old. By the time the French attacked the city in 1892, there was thus a honeycomb of twelve **adjoining palaces**, ten of which were soon destroyed by the invading army. Today, only two – those belonging to Ghezo and his successor Glele – remain intact, but even these have suffered badly from the effects, ultimately no less brutal, of the climate. They are currently being restored with the help of funds from UNESCO. Work carried out so far shows up magnificently the pomp and grandeur of the royal court – and there's no doubt that this will be a spectacular site when restoration is completed, in around 2003. There are even plans to rebuild the ten ruined palaces – eventually – though this would seem to require decades of work.

In the meantime, you can visit the first two renovations (CFA1500 with compulsory guided tour) though it's disappointing to find rusty corrugated iron, rather than old-style thatch, used to cover the **animist temples** (where the kings communicated with their ancestors), the **throne room** and other ceremonial buildings. It's all impressive nonetheless, with the massive walls of the complex clad in brilliantly coloured symbolic bas-relief designs, and as you walk round, the history of this powerful, energetic, brutal society comes alive. All the stools of the kings are guarded in the throne room with their individual banners – including that of Ghezo, built on top of four human skulls, a symbol of his conquests and domination over weaker peoples. The banners, which are known as the **royal tapestries**, are remarkable, vivid patchworks, sewn with symbols and emblems relating the qualities of the various kings.

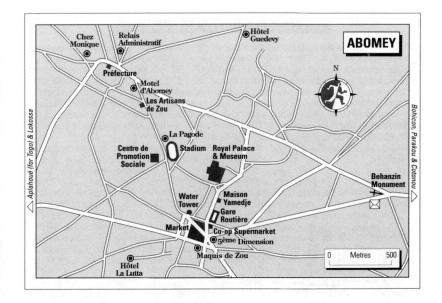

Part of the collection of the **museum** – housed in one of the palaces – is devoted to the **treasures of the kings**, including gifts they were offered by European royalty and merchants. Mixed in with examples of silver jewellery are wood and iron sculptures, though some of the pieces on exhibit are copies, the original works of art stored in French museums since colonial times.

Crafts outlets

Attached to the palace, the **centre artisanal** is an effort to keep alive the crafts-manship that was the pride of the Abomey kings. The artisans were formerly con-strained to produce their works for the royal court only. Crafts that were popular with the kings – brightly decorated tapestries, bronze statues made by the *cire per-due* (lost wax) method and jewellery – are still churned out, although the quality required by tourists is rather less than that demanded by royalty. This centre is the most obvious place to shop for crafts – although it may seem expensive, prices are wide open to discussion.

Along the road running in front of the palace, notice the house with the lion and inscription painted on front. This is the residence of the **Yamedje family** – the tradi-tional embroiderers for the king. Walking in the courtyard, you'll see members of the family still sewing the tapestries, their works strewn over the ground, all for sale. Next to the *préfecture*, a collective organization, the **artisans de Zou**, is an outlet for still more crafts. The tailors here can whip together quick African outfits.

Abomey practicalities

Despite its importance as a tourist centre, Abomey has few services beyond the town **post office**. To **change money** you have to go to neighbouring Bohicon, where the Bank of Africa will change both cash and travellers' cheques.

THE DAN-HOMEY KINGDOM

From as early as the sixteenth century, much of the present territory of Benin was coalescing into small, socially stratified **states** – a string of them along the coast (including Grand Popo and Ouidah) and a cluster of less clearly defined smaller states inland. A more powerful (though still very small) city-state had developed around the town of **Allada**, just 40km from the coast, which was renowned for its slave-trading. At the end of the sixteenth century, three princes were in dispute over the rule of this little empire. The first, Meidji, eventually wrested power from his father. Of his two brothers, Zozerigbe headed south to Porto Novo where he founded the **Hogbonou** kingdom while Do Aklin went north where he founded the kingdom at **Abomey** in the early seventeenth century.

In 1654, one of the descendants of Do Aklin, **Ouegbaja**, killed the sovereign of Abomey, a king named **Dan**. Ouegbaja then built his palace over the body of the deceased monarch and his kingdom came to be known as **Dan-Homey**, meaning "from the belly of Dan". In the succession of kings, one of the greatest was **Agadja** who ruled from 1708–1740. He conquered the surrounding mini-states of Allada, Savi and Ouidah and, in expanding his empire to the coast, earned the title *Dé Houito*, or "man of the sea". Having gained a gateway to the Atlantic, the empire embarked on a period of direct trade with Europe, a trade dependent above all on slaves. Meanwhile, however, the powerful Yoruba state of **Oyo** (to the east, in present-day Nigeria) was increasingly bent on retaining as much as possible of the trade for its own benefit, and through the middle of the eighteenth century, repeatedly intimidated and attacked Dan-Homey, which, after 1748, formally became a vassal state of Oyo.

The Dan-Homey state became a dictatorship under the reign of **Ghezo**, who overthrew the previous king in 1818 and ruled bloodily for forty years. He ceded his monopoly rights in the slave trade to his right-hand man in Ouidah – the Brazilian **Francisco Felix de Souza** (the "viceroy" depicted in Bruce Chatwin's biographical novella and by Klaus Kinski in Werner Herzog's movie *Cobra Verde*) – and increasingly preyed on his own subject peoples. His autonomy was only limited by the duty he owed to Oyo. He reorganized the army into a powerful unit comprising 10,000 soldiers and 6000 female "**Amazon**" warriors, who were better armed than their male counterparts. Trained to use rifles as well as bows, they were reputed to cut off one of their breasts if it impaired their ability to shoot – an apocryphal story that probably sprang from the reactions of European visitors to the sight of well-drilled women soldiers.

The Dan-Homey kings amassed a stockpile of weapons through trade with the Europeans. By the end of the nineteenth century, the royal arsenal was full of modern weaponry and the stage was set for an intense conflict as the French started out in conquest of the interior. Hostilities were high and fighting had already broken out between the French and the Fon when **King Behanzin** led an attack against the forces of **Colonel Dodds** as they advanced on Abomey. Behanzin lost the battle, and the capital of the Dan-Homey kingdom fell to the French on November 16, 1892. Abomey was already in flames as the colonial army marched into the city.

Accommodation

There's not a lot of choice of **hotels**, though there's something for every price range. Most accommodation is a stiff walk from the centre. *Zimi-djans* and taxis come in handy here.

Chez Monique, on a dirt side street, 200m west of the *préfecture* (☎50.01.68). Immensely popular with overlanders, *Monique's* is an exotic spread, with pet monkeys and antelopes in the yard. The simple, but clean S/C rooms with fans are comfortable. Success has pushed prices up, but don't be afraid to bargain. ②.

Hôtel Guedevy, 3km north of the centre (☎50.03.04). Brand-new, pleasant lodgings, with Abomey-style bas-reliefs on the walls as you enter. Choice of fan or AC in the clean S/C rooms, plus an inexpensive restaurant and even a *bar-dancing*. Good value. ②–③.

Hôtel La Lutta, 500m west of the centre (BP 2009; ☎50.01.41). From the centre, follow the signs to this pleasant African-style abode – Abomey's most central lodgings and a great find for bud-

MOVING ON FROM ABOMEY AND BOHICON

Abomey's small *autogare* has vehicles to surrounding villages and Cotonou, though for road transport to most other destinations, it's faster to take a *zimi-djan* or cab to the train station in Bohicon, from where there are two trains a day to Parakou and Cotonou.

get travellers. The twin rooms are plain but decent and have fans and showers. The management here is very friendly and will arrange for inexpensive guided tours of the town. Food available on order. ①.

Motel d'Abomey, 100m from the *préfecture* (BP 2168; ☎50.00.75). The town's best hotel. Well-heeled travellers can enjoy beautifully furnished private bungalows with TV, video and phones, while the smaller S/C rooms with AC are not out of reach of those on a budget. The restaurant is one of the town's best, and the new disco is an added draw. ③–⑥.

Relais Administratif, across from the *préfecture*. Run-down colonial lodgings offering the option of pretty miserable S/C rooms (no fan) if you're in a fix. ①.

Eating

Inexpensive **street food** is available all around the market, where small **buvettes** offer low-cost African meals; you can sit indoors or on the terrace. Among the many are the *Maquis de Zou*, the *5ème Dimension Bar* and, a little further out on the road to Bohicon, *Le 2 Fevrier*. At night, women set up tables under the awnings of the Co-op supermarket for the town's best cheap eats. Closer to the hotels around the *préfecture*, the tiny but tidy *La Pagode* is a good place for a breakfast omelette with coffee, or a lunch of rice and fish.

North from Abomey: Dassa and rough routes in the west

The most straightforward way north is via the **trans-Benin highway** to Parakou. Alternatively you could fork left at Dassa to follow the western *piste* leading directly to **Djougou** (see p.858), though public transport is slow and irregular. **DASSA** (or Dassa-Zoumé), a village tucked in a landscape of heavy boulder formations and thick greenery, has nothing of essential interest, with the possible exception of the **Grotte de Notre Dame de l'Arigbo** – a cave which has become a pilgrimage site for local Christians. If you want to explore more of the surrounding countryside, you can **stay** at the moderately priced *Auberge de Dassa*, just by the junction (☎53.00.98; ③). It has very comfortable, clean rooms with fans or AC, excellent food in the restaurant and deer and monkeys lurking in the gardens. In town, you can stay at *Les Trois Paillotes* (☎53.01.07; ①), about 500m out of town on the Route de Savalou, which offers clean rooms with outside toilets; just opposite, the restaurant *Au Paradis* is cheap and cheerful.

The western route beyond **Savalou**, 30km north of Dassa, is little travelled, and involves longer waits for transport. It's difficult going, too, especially the washboard-infested stretch up to **BASSILA**, 173km from Dassa, which is the first town along the way where you'll find **accommodation** and, perhaps more importantly, a *buvette* with the possibility of cold drinks. There's a small *chambre de passage* (①) next to the filling station, run by a very friendly family.

The **west** is an agricultural region hemmed in by the forests of the Mont Kouffé and Mont Agoua, and was the location of an early **Yoruba** kingdom, conquered in the eighteenth century by the **Maxi** (related to the Fon). These are still the main peoples of the area, although numerous smaller groups result in a variety of regional building styles and customs. Despite the relative difficulties in getting about along this stretch it can be rewarding to travel off the beaten track, and you're likely to find contacts with people warm and immediate.

THE NORTHERN UPLANDS AND PARKS

Parakou is the last big town on the main road. Beyond it, in the **northeast**, the only main centres of activity are **Kandi** and **Malanville**, small towns bolstered by agriculture and trade. The **northwest**, though harder to travel through, is a region of striking natural beauty dominated by the country's only serious highlands, the **Atakora Range**, and populated by a relatively ancient people, the **Somba**. Two towns of some size, **Natitingou** and **Djougou**, are the bases for discovering this outback region. Lastly, northern Benin has some of West Africa's best faunal areas in the **Pendjari National Park** and, in the extreme north, the **"W" du Niger National Park**, which spreads across the frontiers of Niger and Burkina Faso. Access to Pendjari is relatively straightforward and there are several places to stay, but the Benin sector of the "W" park is extremely inaccessible (the most promising access is via Kandi) and has abundant wildlife – probably as a result.

Parakou

Formerly a station on the caravan routes, **PARAKOU**, with a population of nearly 100,000, is today the largest northern town – and the first, as you go north. Its importance still derives from its position on the major roads and on the **railway** which terminates its snail-like trail here. The brewery, and peanut oil mill have brought about rapid growth in the last couple of decades and Parakou is now the undisputed commercial centre of the interior. It's a town of little enduring interest, but abuzz with the activity of hundreds of small businesses, bars and passing traders.

Practicalities

With the burgeoning business activity, there are branches of all the major **banks**; Eco-Bank gives the best rates for cash, while Bank of Africa is the best for changing travellers' cheques.

Accommodation
Parakou has nothing in the way of world-class **accommodation**, but there's plenty of small comfortable hotels that border on fancy, and one or two cheaper alternatives.

Auberge La Cigale, on the Malanville road. Run by young, English-speaking French people. Reasonably priced, clean rooms with fans, plus a bar and a restaurant with Moroccan, French and Mexican food. ①–②.

Auberge Le Paradis, on a side street not far from the railway station. Old-fashioned furnishings, but very spacious, reasonably clean S/C rooms with fans. ①.

Hôtel les Canaris, near the station (☎61.11.69). Two shady courtyards provide a pleasant backdrop for various rooms ranging from non-S/C, low-comfort quarters (among the cheapest in town) to fully furnished AC accommodation with private bath. ①–②.

Hôtel Central, near the station (☎61.01.24). A little far from the town centre, but arguably the best accommodation in town, in an imposing building hidden behind a walled garden where you'll find a bar and restaurant. Some of the AC rooms have TV and phone. ④–⑤.

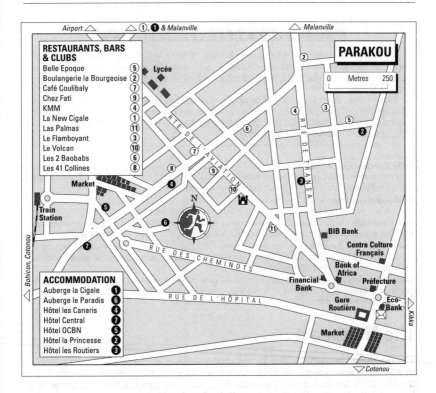

Airport △   △①, ❶ & Malanville   △ Malanville

RESTAURANTS, BARS & CLUBS
Belle Epoque ⑤
Boulangerie la Bourgeoise ②
Café Coulibaly ⑦
Chez Fati ⑨
KMM ④
La New Cigale ①
Las Palmas ⑪
Le Flamboyant ③
Le Volcan ⑩
Les 2 Baobabs ⑥
Les 41 Collines ⑧

Lycée

PARAKOU

0   Metres   250

RTE DE L'AVIATION

RTE DE TRANSA

Market

Train Station

Bohicon, Cotonou

RUE DES CHEMINOTS

BIB Bank
Centre Culture Français
Bank of Africa
Préfecture

ACCOMMODATION
Auberge la Cigale ❶
Auberge le Paradis ❻
Hôtel les Canaris ❹
Hôtel Central ❼
Hôtel OCBN ❺
Hôtel la Princesse ❷
Hôtel les Routiers ❸

RUE DE L'HÔPITAL

Financial Bank

Gare Routière

Market

Eco-Bank

Kikka

▽ Cotonou

Hôtel OCBN, next to the market by the train station (☎61.10.06). A crocodile in the courtyard watches over this well-managed, colonial-style hotel. Airy rooms, great bathrooms and a reasonable restaurant and bar. ②–③.

Hôtel La Princesse, *qtr* Ladjifarani, in the north of town (☎61.01.32). The rooms, surrounding a courtyard, are a little posher than the norm, with phones, TV and video among the extras. French and African food served in the *Nafi* restaurant, or snacks in the *Plantation* bar. ③–④.

Hôtel Les Routiers, rte de Transa (BP 81; ☎61.21.27 or 61.04.01). Centrally located, upmarket accommodation, popular with expats. Clean, comfortable AC rooms, plus tennis courts and a tiny pool. ④–⑤.

Eating and nightlife

Despite Parakou's status as second city, **nights** are low-key and street lights noticeable only by their absence. Instead, kerosene lamps light the darkness, indicating the stands of hundreds of night-time vendors. It's safe and satisfying to wander around the Route de l'Aviation, stopping for **street food** or a drink at one of the many *buvettes – Les 41 Collines, Le Volcan, les 2 Baobabs, Chez Fati...*

The best options for **nightlife** are *Le Miel*, at the *Boulangerie La Bourgeoise*, which gets rolling at weekends, and *La New Cigale*, with draught beer, live music on weekends, and there's no entry charge. Finally, you could try the *KMM* which draws a large crowd to its disco (small cover charge) and lively outdoor *buvette*, tucked in a clump of teak trees.

The prospects for good **eating** are actually better than the town's initial impression suggests, and you'll find a wide range of upmarket African and European cuisine.

MOVING ON FROM PARAKOU

One **train** a day chugs out of Parakou at 8.40am, arriving in Cotonou about twelve hours later. Second-class travel costs only CFA3100, making the drawn-out journey a lot cheaper than going by taxi. The night train, which leaves on Wed and Fri at 7pm, has *couchettes* for CFA6630.

Taxis leave from the main *autogare* by the market and head towards **Niger** via Malanville, or **Togo** via Djougou, as well as to domestic destinations. There is next to nothing direct to Natitingou and the Somba country so it's best to catch a vehicle to Djougou and continue north from there.

Belle Epoque, qtr Ladjifarani, near *Hôtel La Princesse*. French restaurant with specialities ranging from *charcuterie* to *filet de boeuf au roquefort*. Also Italian lasagne, ravioli and pizza. Tables under a *paillote* with unmistakeable lion statues at the garden entrance. From CFA5000.

Boulangerie-patisserie La Bourgeoise, rte de Malanville, in the north of town. *Salon de thé* with sandwiches, salads and ice cream, or a more filling *menu du jour*. Good rooftop bar.

Café Coulibaly, rte de l'Aviation. A modest affair that's just a small step up from the streetside *café-man*, but a good place for really cheap omelettes and Nescafé, or *riz sauce* in the evening.

Las Palmas Bar Jazz Club, on rte de l'Aviation. "Jazz Club" in this case just means they play pop music, but it's a lively place with a terrace overlooking the main street, and some good brochettes and other food available from vendors in front.

Super Maquis Le Flamboyant qtr, Ladjifarani, near *Hôtel La Princesse* (☎61.11.90). African dishes like rice with fish, or *couscous* with chicken, plus Ivoirian specials, including chicken *kedjenou*. Attractive gardens and friendly service. From under CFA1000.

The Northeast

The **northeast** is characterized by unvaried woodland and savannah scenery, broken by a series of small rivers (the Mékrou, Alibori and Sota) that descend gradually to join the Niger. It's the least densely populated region of the country, the principal peoples being the **Bariba**, the **Dendi** and the **Fula**. Despite the important highway running through the region, linking Cotonou with Niamey, the Niger Basin remains economically undeveloped. Cotton is a big cash crop, but industrialization hasn't penetrated much beyond a cotton-seed plant in Kandi and a rice-shelling factory in Malanville.

Kandi and around

Like Parakou, **KANDI** was formerly a stopping point on the caravan routes and grew to become a sizeable chiefdom – a vassal state of Bariba rulers in Nikki, to the southeast. A small town, it relies heavily on farming, a livelihood with which young people are becoming increasingly disenchanted. They've been deserting the countryside in numbers that are unsettling to the local economy, and heading east to Nigeria, which is linked to Kandi by a well-travelled *piste* that heads through Segbana. You may question the attractions of a place from which even the townspeople are engaged in a mass exodus and, true enough, there's not a lot of note. Still, it's a convenient highway stopover and, with its dusty mango-shaded streets, not entirely charmless.

Practicalities

As district headquarters, Kandi has a post office, supermarket and bank – which only changes cash. Formal **accommodation** is limited to the *Auberge La Rencontre*, about 200m south of the *autogare* (☎63.01.78; ②), which has clean rooms, with outside toilet, and a reasonably priced restaurant. Cheap *buvettes* for **eating and drinking** are scattered around the marketplace. Among them, the *Alibori Bar,* has inexpensive *chambres de passage* (①).

North of Kandi: Alfa Kouara
In the dry season, you can make simple arrangements at **Alfa Kouara**, about 40km north of Kandi, to walk to a nearby **waterhole**, where **wildlife** gathers; with luck, you'll even see elephants.

Malanville

Tucked in the northeast corner near the Nigerian and Nigérien borders, **MALANVILLE** is a trading town *par excellence* where you can run into people from all over West Africa. The **market** is Benin's largest after Cotonou and large-scale regional rice-planting attracts wage-hungry labourers from as far afield as Mali. The presence of many foreigners, mixed with the Fula and Songhai-speaking **Dendi** locals who form the base of the town's inhabitants, makes for an upbeat atmosphere, although the lack of notable sights means you're not likely to want to make an extended stay.

Practicalities
Border formalities usually present no problem here. If you're **entering the country at Malanville**, you have to state your destination and intended address. The immigration officers have a list of all hotels in the country – pick any one, there's no obligation.

Besides the rudimentary and inexpensive *campement* located near the police and customs post at the town entrance (①–②), there's **accommodation** with shared facilities at the comfortable, but slightly overpriced *Hôtel Rose des Sables* (☎67.01.25; ②). Numerous **street food** stands line the paved road near the *autogare*, churning out cheap meals for travellers. You'll also find a host of *buvettes* with cold drinks.

When **moving on**, remember that in addition to the many taxis waiting in the central *autogare*, cheaper state-run **buses** also head south to Kandi and Parakou, but they usually leave quite early in the morning. If you're heading north to **Niamey**, it's quicker and cheaper to catch a taxi to Gaya, on the other side of the river, and to find another vehicle there.

Parc National du "W" du Niger

The **"W" du Niger National Park** (open early December to late May) spreads over 10,000 square kilometres of wild bush in Niger, Burkina Faso and Benin – an area, virtually without human habitation. The "W" (pronounced *double-vé* in French) refers to the double U-bend in the course of the Niger River at the point where the three countries all meet. Though nearly half the park is in Benin, the only real viewing trails, and all the park lodgings and *campements*, are in Niger (see p.896) and Burkina.

Most of the big plains game is here, however, if you can find a way in. Although the **buffalo** herds are thinning out, **elephants** can still be spotted in the Béninois sector – notably in the Mékrou valley – while in the Mékrou's waters, unmistakeable herds of snorting **hippos** are fairly plentiful. All the cats are found in the "W" as well – **serval, caracal, leopard, cheetah** and **lion** – but you can visit repeatedly and never see a single specimen. Most commonly encountered are a good number of **antelope** species – bushbuck (*guibs harnachés* in French), cobs or waterbucks (*cob de buffon, cob defassa*), reedbuck (*redunca*) and the red-fronted gazelle – and, of course, **warthogs** (*phacochères*) and **baboons** (*babouins*). Aardvarks (*oryctéropes*) are around, too, but their strictly nocturnal habits ensure they're rarely spotted.

Practicalities

You need your own 4WD vehicle to visit this park, at least on the Benin side. Even with one, there are no reliably motorable *pistes* until you cross the borders. The most common way to get to the park is up from Kandi to **Banikoara** (69km from Kandi), a small town where you'll find the last **accommodation** (a small *campement*; ②) before entering the reserve. From here, it's a short drive to **Kérémou** – one of the main gateways to the park in Benin.

The only area that's normally visited is the 400-square-kilometre triangle formed by the Kérémou–Diapaga road, the Mékrou River (which the road crosses) and the Benin–Burkina Faso border. There's a *piste* along the left bank of the Mékrou that leads up to the **Koudou Falls**. A plan is apparently under consideration to build a bridge across the Mékrou at this point and to develop tracks that would follow the Benin side of the river all the way to Pekinga near the confluence with the Niger. In the meantime, you have to cross over to Burkina Faso near the falls to keep on motorable tracks.

The Somba Country

The **northwest** is home to some of the oldest **civilizations** to migrate to Benin – a number of which lived for long periods with virtually no interaction. The best known are the **Somba** (more accurately the Otammari, or Betammaribe), famous for the fortress-like houses known as *Tatas-Somba* that they built to protect themselves from the slave raids of Dan-Homey warriors. They still live in largely isolated villages scattered along the base of the **Atakora Mountains** (and don't, as a rule, take kindly to foreign visitors), though the young people are increasingly inclined to migrate to urban centres such as **Natitingou** – the Atakora provincial capital. Further south, Somba give way to the Yowa, part of the same cluster of Voltaic-speaking peoples, and the Songhai-speaking Dendi who live in the region of **Djougou**, a large commercial town on the main road to Togo.

Djougou

With a population of some 30,000, **DJOUGOU** is a large and busy town easily accessible by paved road. Its importance as a major regional market has been assured by its position on the main roads linking Natitingou to Savalou, and Parakou to the Togolese border and through to Kara.

Practicalities

Accommodation is pretty much limited to the *Motel du Djougou* (☎80.01.40; ②), a basic hotel that at least has fans in the rooms. You could also rent a *chambre de passage* in the *La Cachette* nightclub on the market square (①). Apart from the motel restaurant, the **market** is the obvious place for **eating** – besides the numerous vendors selling local staples, there's a number of small restaurants and bars surrounding the market square – *Le Papyrus* is one of the best.

Djougou's large **autogare** adjoins the market and you shouldn't have any problem finding transport to Natitingou and Parakou. Many vehicles also head to **Kara** in Togo, via the border post at Kétao.

Natitingou

Home town of the former president, Mathieu Kérékou, **NATITINGOU** never received the degree of patronage extended to Yamoussoukro in Côte d'Ivoire or Kara in Togo, but even if Kérékou didn't go so far as to turn his birthplace into the national capital, he didn't forget it either. Though it's only a small centre, Natitingou has received the beginnings of an industrial base with the siting here of a SONAFEL juice factory and rice- and peanut-husking factories. You're more likely to notice other manifestations of the president's munificence in the town's modern Financial Bank (changes travellers' cheques and cash) and beautiful luxury hotel. But despite these surprise perks, the real draw of the town lies in the countryside that surrounds it – a magnificent region of hills dotted with the *Tata-Somba* homes that have become as famous as anything in Benin. The small **museum** is not worth a visit.

Accommodation

Natitingou has a surprisingly good range of accommodation, from budget to business-class. You can often bargain. All hotels have a bar and restaurant unless otherwise indicated.

Auberge Taneka, rte de Djougou (☎82.15.52). Recently renovated and very clean, with a pleasant garden. Choice of fanned or AC rooms. ②–③.

Auberge le Vieux Cavalier (☎82.13.24). AC and fanned rooms with views onto the pretty garden, decorated with traditional-style bas-relief sculptures. *Menu* at CFA2500. ②.

Hôtel Bellevue, follow the sign on rte de Djougou about 200m north of the cinema. (☎82.13.36). Good location on top of a hill, with all S/C, AC rooms. Professional and very helpful manager. Good *menu* at CFA4000. ②–③.

Hôtel Nekima, signposted down on a side street in the town centre (☎82.10.46). Clean and pleasant fanned S/C rooms and bungalows; an excellent deal. ①–②.

Hôtel Tata Somba, BP 4 (☎82.11.24 or 21.65.90). A classy hotel in the French PLM chain with stylish AC rooms, a swimming pool and the town's swankiest restaurant. The same chain manages the *campements* in the Pendjari game park, so this is the best place for information on accommodation and vehicle rental if you're heading there. ④–⑤.

Eating and nightlife

In addition to the hotel **restaurants** and the market, *City Coffee*, on the main road heading out of town towards Parakou, is good for omelettes and fry-ups. It's also a place to meet young people from the region and possibly work out an arrangement to visit some of the Somba countryside. Other possibilities are *Chez Antony*, on the Route de Tanguiéta, where they serve up well-prepared and relatively inexpensive African dishes, and *Le Gourmet,* opposite *Hôtel Bourgogne,* which offers good simple meals at reasonable prices.

You'll find a couple of **discos** in town including one built into a "Somba-style" house at the *Hôtel Tata Somba.* Another popular place for dancing – and it's less expensive and more local in flavour – is the open-air *Le Village,* located in the centre of town.

Around Natitingou

Rather than forming large communities, the Somba built their homes about five hundred metres apart from one another; the distance a man could throw a spear, you'll be told – which would surprise the current javelin world-record-holder (under 100m). Whatever the brawn of their throwing arms (it seems more likely that 500m is the maximum dangerous range of an eighteenth-century musket), this defensive safeguard was adopted during slave-raiding days and the custom has carried over. Houses are still built like fortresses with round turrets for grain storage and internal animal pens. During slave raids, families could hole up in these houses for days on end until the marauding Dan-Homey armies went off in search of easier prey (see the "Tamberma Country" section in Chapter 11, "Togo").

The **Tata-Somba** still dot the countryside around the Atakora region and it's worth a trip through these parts to take in the unusual architecture. The people are rather friendly and not too camera-shy, provided you ask permission. Coming in by bush taxi from Djougou, you'll see some of the architecture from the roadside, notably along the stretch between Perma (56km from Djougou) and Natitingou. One of the highest concentrations of *Tata-Somba* is found further west, however, along the road from Natitingou to **Boukoumbé**, 43km west of Natitingou, near the Togolese border, which has a Wednesday **market** and a simple, but decent **hotel**, *Le Refuge* (☎83.00.29; ②). If you have your own vehicle, you could cross the nearby border and drive to **Kandé** in Togo, via a *piste* that leads through the region of the **Tamberma**, a people closely related to the Somba. Though difficult, it's one of the most beautiful drives in this part of West Africa.

Parc National de la Pendjari

The **Pendjari National Park**, one of the best game-viewing reserves in West Africa, spreads over 2750 square kilometres of woody savannah north of the Atakora Range, up against the Pendjari River, which runs along the Burkinabe border. Unlike the "W" National Park, access to Pendjari is relatively straightforward.

From Natitingou, the usual route goes north through **TANGUIÉTA**, a village at the edge of the reserve with a lively market on Mondays. There are three **hotels**: *A Petits Pas* (aka *Chez Basille*; ①), with mosquito nets and noisy dancing on Saturdays; the similar *Le Galaxie 2000* (☎83.02.07; ①); and the more upmarket *Le Baobab* (②), about 1.5km north-west on the Route de Porga, with comfortable S/C rooms. There are two **waterfalls** in the area, both on the road to Batia – the **cascades de Tanguiéta** near the village of Nanèbou, 6km northeast of Tanguiéta, and the larger **cascades de Tanougou**, near the village of the same name, 33km northeast of Tanguiéta. Swimming at the latter, with the falls pounding your back, is a memorable experience. *Le Relais de Tanougou* (③), by the waterfall, has six rooms you can book through the *Hôtel Tata Somba* in Natitingou.

At Tanguiéta, the road divides. You can aim northeast to **Batia**, where there's a park entrance, though no accommodation. However, most people continue northwest to the town of **PORGA**, on the Burkina border, which has **lodgings** and the main park entrance gate. The *Campement de Porga* (④–⑤) has bungalows and rooms – some with AC.

If you've made it this far without your own transport, you might hope to tag along with tourists heading into the park at Porga, though your chances would be just as good if you looked for a lift at the *Hôtel Tata Somba* in Natitingou, where you can also rent Land Rovers (ring in advance) and book the *campement*.

The south and northeast of the park are called **Zones Cynégétiques**, and are hunting areas which can be crossed even when the park is closed.

Lions still stalk these parts and your chances of seeing them are relatively good. Other large mammals you have a good chance of spotting include **elephants** (notably in the south of the park) and **buffalo**, which roam in large herds. **Hippos** and **crocodiles** (*caimans* in colloquial French) are widespread in the Pendjari River, while the same species of **antelope** as are found in the "W" park, plus **warthogs** and **monkeys**, are pretty sure bets. As usual, however, all the animals are most easily and abundantly seen at the end of the dry season, when their movements are restricted by the need to stay close to water.

Park practicalities

The park is only open from mid-December to the end of May. Permits to visit can be obtained from the *postes forestiers* in Porga, Batia, Kandi and Natitingou, but for compplete information, contact the Ministry of Tourism in Cotonou, or the *Hôtel Tata Somba* in Natitingou.

Inside the park, **accommodation** can be found at the *Campement de la Pendjari*, located near the river (③–④). They have smart bungalows and twin rooms, plus a restaurant, bar and, miraculously, a swimming pool. If it's full it's possible to **camp**. Camping, under the supervision of rangers, is also permitted at the **Mare Yangouali** and the **Pont d'Arli**, where you can cross the Pendjari River into Burkina Faso and the Pendjari's extension there – **Arli National Park**.

CHAPTER THIRTEEN

NIGER

NIGER

Vast expanses of **Niger**'s million-plus square kilometres are desert. But most visitors see only the south, where thriving commerce and relative prosperity characterize the towns and agricultural districts. The **Niger River**, flowing for over five hundred kilometres through the southwest, is one of the country's few bodies of water – an attraction in itself. The cosmopolitan capital, **Niamey**, straddling the banks of "Le Fleuve", draws a mix of local and regional traders and international aid and business visitors. Air-conditioned hotels and restaurants provide welcome relief

WARNING: SECURITY IN NIGER AND THE SAHARA

In the late 1980s, **Tuareg herders** fleeing drought in the deep Sahel in northern Niger and southern Algeria began returning *en masse* to central parts of Niger. Although the government had earmarked relief aid to ease resettlement, there was no actual assistance. In 1990, amid rumours that allocated funds had been embezzled by government officials, angry Tuareg – many of whom are scathing of their Nigérien citizenship – mounted a military attack against the remote Gendarmerie at Tchin-Tabaradene between Tahoua and Agadez. Government forces retaliated, killing around 100 Tuareg and arresting over 200 people, of whom some 40 were executed in jail. Tuareg resistance intensified as a united movement with an agenda to form a Tuareg homeland – the Front de Libération de l'Aïr et l'Azaouad (FLAA) – launched violent raids and took its own prisoners. By 1992, the government was admitting to a full-scale rebellion. Trans-Saharan traffic was cut as tourist vehicles were randomly commandeered by the FLAA. Outlying regions in the north were put off-limits to visitors and those overlanders who made it to the region reported **harassment** by the military and frequent delays due to searches and the confiscation of documents. The domestic situation in northern Niger improved after 1994, when the FLAA agreed to a truce, but the region remains extremely volatile.

Problems on the **Algerian side of the border** are even more severe. Since October 1993 when they declared all non-Algerians should leave the country under threat of death, the Groupe Islamique Armée (GIA) – extreme fundamentalist militia – have murdered nearly 100 foreigners, not to mention tens of thousands of Algerians (the precise figure is not known). Tourism in Algeria has entirely ceased and the trans-Saharan routes are effectively closed to foreigners (although the Algerian Sahara is not of much interest to the GIA, who have committed nearly all their atrocities in the far north). The spark for the present civil war was the secular government's cancellation of democratic elections in 1991 which would have brought the fundamentalist party, the Front Islamique du Salud (FIS) to power. The FIS claim not to control the GIA, who refuse all dialogue. At the time of writing, in mid-1999, after several quiet months, there were signs from Algiers that some kind of rapprochement was in the air.

Niger travel advisories are blunt. Americans on official business who intend travelling anywhere north of a line connecting Tillaberi, Tahoua, Tanout, and Nguigmi must have permission from their ambassador. In the wake of the April 1999 assassination of president Maïnassara, British visitors are simply advised not to visit Niger except on essential business. Neither position is very helpful, as overland traffic continues to move through Niamey and southern Niger with relative ease, and by the end of the 1990s, even the Aïr adventure tour operators were beginning to gear up again. But Niger remains highly unpredictable and the combination of unpopular military rule, unresolved Tuareg demands and the ever-present risk of banditry in the remote north and east make the local and travellers' grapevines important sources of information before your arrival, and indispensable when you're in Niger.

FACTS AND FIGURES

The **République du Niger** has a confusing name for English-speakers. Pronouncing it like an unfinished "Nigeria" means nothing to Nigériens – the people of the country – who pronounce it "Nee-zhé". It is a vast country on the map, spreading over 1,270,000 square kilometres – twice the size of Texas and five times as big as Britain. In reality, however, the Sahara covers most of the northern region, making a large proportion of the country uninhabitable. A population of some ten million people is concentrated at fairly high density, mainly along the borders with Nigeria, Mali and Benin. Nearly one million people are reckoned to live in Niamey.

Niger's foreign debt amounts to some £1 billion ($1.6 billion) and, with that being equivalent to nearly six times the value of its annual goods and services exports, the country faces bleak economic prospects. Ninety-eight percent of the population is employed in agriculture, livestock and informal trade; and mining and manufacturing continue to slump due to the unstable price of Niger's unhealthy principal export resource – uranium.

Coup-leader turned elected president, Ibrahim Maïnasarra, was assassinated in a putsch in 1999 and, at the time of writing, the army was once again in power.

---

from the Sahelian bush, but the city's modern high-rises coexist uneasily with its sprawling markets and slum neighbourhoods of mud-brick homes.

From the capital, you can travel by road along the east bank of the Niger towards the Malian border, visiting Songhai villages and the commercial centres of **Tillabéri** and **Ayorou**, which has a spectacular market that unites all the peoples of the region. South of Niamey, the Niger is navigable only in short sections as it closes in on the game reserve named after the bends in the river – the **Parc National du "W" du Niger**.

A second main line of travel lies along the southern border with Nigeria and the **Hausa** towns of **Birnin-Konni**, **Maradi** and **Zinder**. These historic centres lie in the country's green belt and have been bolstered by agriculture – the region's dominant feature. The road from Zinder is paved all the way to **Nguigmi**, a Kanouri settlement near **Lake Chad**.

Given the instability in the Sahara, few visitors make it to the third great travel axis, **the north**, where the government has long restricted all movement. Whether you will be allowed to travel north of **Tahoua** or Zinder, and then usually only in a military convoy, depends on the latest round of negotiations with the Tuareg rebel movement, or the latest battle (see box, opposite). **Agadez** is the region's main town, an ancient desert metropolis, seat of a powerful sultanate, and one of the most important centres in the southern Sahara. For several decades, it has also been the base for determined travellers to make, usually costly, visits to isolated oases in the **Erg du Ténéré** and the **Grand Erg du Bilma**, where occasional camel caravans still cross the shifting dunes to the salt mines of **Bilma**. Similarly, if you get permission from the local police and military in Agadez to visit the historic villages of the less remote **Aïr mountain region** – such as Timia, Iferouâne and Assodé – you will need to make fairly specialized advance preparations for desert travel in Agadez. Again, whether you sign up for some kind of tour, or take a guide or guides in your own vehicle, the whole expedition is likely to cost a small fortune.

People

Nearly half the population of Niger are **Hausa**-speaking. Engaged principally in agriculture and commerce, the Hausa are mostly based in the south, where they long ago established large urban centres such as Maradi and Zinder. The overwhelming majority of Hausa are Muslim, but small splinter groups have retained traditional religious beliefs, notably in the Birnin-Konni district. If you don't have a chance to get further

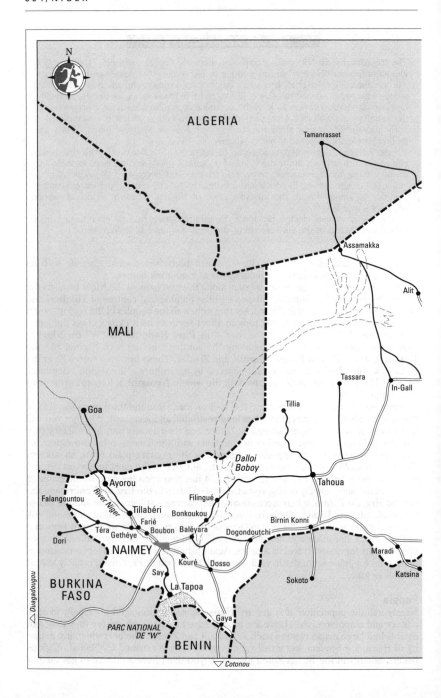

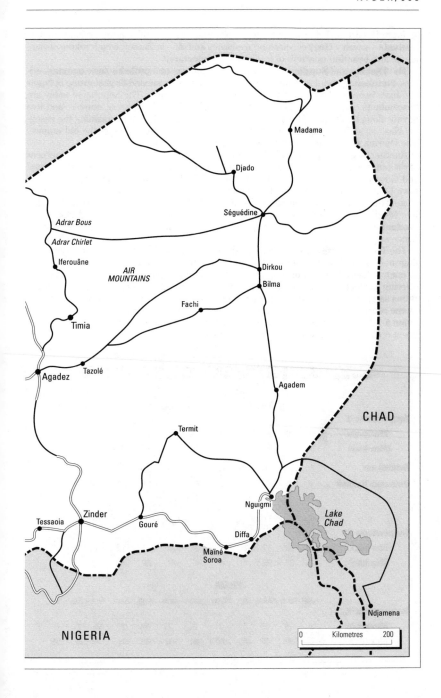

south to the original Hausa city states in Nigeria, you can still see the brilliant **durbar festivals** – cavalry charges, clashing costumes and all – in Zinder, which retains its sultanate and beautiful quarters of traditional architecture.

The **Djerma** and **Songhai** speak the same language and probably have common origins. Numbering about one and a half million, they're the second largest group in Niger and have been politically dominant in Niger for generations. The Songhai of today are descendants of those who fled the collapse of Gao's great Songhai empire, and live mostly along the banks of the Niger as far downstream as Tillabéri, retaining the essential class structure – nobles, commoners, slaves and craftspeople – of the old empire. The Djerma live further south in the regions of Niamey and Dosso.

Another large group, the **Fula** (Peul or Peulh in French), make up some ten percent of the population. Centuries ago they founded large kingdoms in what are now Senegal and Guinea, before spreading east. By the end of the nineteenth century, a group of town Fula (as opposed to nomads), led by Uthman Dan Fodio, had established a huge Islamic theocracy centred on Sokoto in Nigeria. In Niger today, the Fula are still divided into Muslim townspeople (Fulani) and nomadic herders, commonly called **Bororo** or **Wodaabe**, who largely follow traditional beliefs and maintain a colourful cultural life of dance and life cycle ritual.

The **Tuareg** represent less than a tenth of Niger's population. Of Berber origin, they migrated to the desert regions of the Aïr around the seventh century, when they came to control long stretches of the Saharan routes, either pillaging passing caravans, or offering protection to them, or both. Some Tuareg still take camel caravans to the Bilma salt mines, but an increasing number have been forced to seek jobs in the towns by the recent droughts and the rebellion. The Tuareg have a rather exaggerated reputation as sharp operators: they often work as guides and also produce some of Niger's finest crafts – especially leather – and silverwork.

AVERAGE TEMPERATURES AND RAINFALL

NIAMEY

	Jan	Feb	Mar	Apr	May	June	July	Aug	Sept	Oct	Nov	Dec
Temperatures °C												
Min (night)	14	18	22	26	27	25	24	22	23	23	19	15
Max (day)	34	37	41	42	41	38	34	32	34	38	38	34
Rainfall mm	0	0	5	8	33	81	132	188	94	13	0	0
Days with Rainfall	0	0	0	1	4	6	9	12	7	1	0	0

AGADEZ

	Jan	Feb	Mar	Apr	May	June	July	Aug	Sept	Oct	Nov	Dec
Temperatures °C												
Min (night)	10	13	17	21	25	24	24	23	23	20	15	12
Max (day)	29	33	38	41	44	43	41	38	40	39	35	32

BILMA

	Jan	Feb	Mar	Apr	May	June	July	Aug	Sept	Oct	Nov	Dec
Temperatures °C												
Min (night)	6	8	13	17	31	22	23	24	21	16	11	8
Max (day)	26	29	35	40	43	44	42	40	41	39	33	28

In the region of Lake Chad, the **Kanouri** are one of Niger's smaller groups. These people are part of the legacy of the great neighbouring empires of **Kanem** and **Bornu** which reached a peak in the sixteenth century. With the advent of colonialism, their territory was divided between Chad, Nigeria, Niger and Cameroon. Today, they're principally farmers and fishers, and in towns like Zinder they have mixed significantly with the Hausa. Descendants of marriages between the two groups are known as **Beriberi**.

Climate

Most of Niger is scorching hot all year round. The heat is least oppressive from about October or November through to March. If you're travelling on the rough overland route from Gao in Mali to Niamey, it's also worth trying to avoid the **rainy season**, which falls roughly between July and September, when heavy storms can knock out the *pistes* for days. In contrast, when the *Harmattan* wind blows down from the north in November, it can kick up blinding clouds of dust and sometimes cause morning temperatures to tumble near to freezing point, especially in the north around Agadez, and in the Aïr mountains.

Arrivals

Formerly West Africa's main overland entry point (from Algeria across the Sahara), the dire security situation in Algeria has placed Niger on the extreme fringe of West African travel routes. Meanwhile, flight connections with the rest of the region remain barely adequate.

■ Flights from Africa

Within **West Africa**, direct flights to Niamey are nearly all from **Abidjan**, Air Afrique (RK) or Air France (AF) providing most services. AF flies Abidjan–Niamey non-stop daily, en route to Paris. There are four RK flights a week, and two on Air Ivoire (VU).

RK flies Abidjan–Niamey daily, via **Bamako**, and there are non-stop RK flights from Bamako to Niamey twice a week.

RK also has four weekly flights from **Ouagadougou**, and flies Abidjan–**Cotonou** –**Lomé**–Niamey weekly. Ghana Airways (GH) and VU fly **Ouagadougou**–Niamey weekly, and there's a non-stop AF flight from **Cotonou** to Niamey (destination Paris) once a week.

There's nothing useful from **Lagos** – only a weekly round-the-capitals flight on RK (to Niamey via Lomé and Abidjan), or twice-weekly RK connections through Abidjan (arriving after midnight). These, however, are still probably more efficient than flying on a Nigerian domestic carrier to Sokoto and taking a taxi the last 500km.

There are no direct flights from **west coast cities** (Nouakchott, Dakar, Banjul, Bissau, Conakry), nor from Accra, but there are reasonable connections from **Conakry** twice a week via Abidjan.

From **the rest of Africa** (south of the Sahara), Abidjan is the obvious hub, although there is a weekly flight to Niamey on Ethiopian Airlines from **Addis** via **Ndjamena**.

There are also weekly flights from **Casablanca** on Royal Air Maroc (AH) via Bamako.

The details in these practical information pages are essentially for use on the ground in West Africa and in Niger itself: for full practical details on preparing for a trip, getting here from outside the region, paperwork, health, information sources and more, see Basics pp.3–83.

■ Overland

As this book goes to press, the overland route through the **Algerian Sahara** is effectively closed (see p.15).

From Mali

The route follows the Niger River between Gao and Niamey. It's a difficult stretch for drivers, awash with deep soft sand and the dreaded thorn trees (endless punctures), but motoring frustrations are more than compensated by Sahelian scenery at its best – dust-shrouded sunsets over the broad river and numerous fishing villages along the banks. SNTN in Niger and Askia Transport in Mali both provide a bus service between Niamey and Gao. Alternatively, bush taxis are available as far as the respective national borders.

From Burkina

The 500-kilometre paved road linking **Ouagadougou** with Niamey is a relatively busy and straightforward route. The border is now open 24 hours a day, and formalities are pretty routine, although at the border, or at some of the checkpoints before Niamey, the police may try to make some money by requesting all sorts of vaccination certificates (meningitis, measles, etc).

From Benin

The 1030-kilometre road **from Benin** is paved all the way from Cotonou. The offices on both sides of the border at Malanville are open 24 hours and present no special problems.

From Nigeria

Numerous paved roads feed into Niger **from Nigeria**, retaining a Hausa-land commercial unity despite the frontier dividing it. Main lines of entry are Sokoto to Birnin-Konni, Katsina to Maradi and Kano to Zinder. From the south, the best route is direct to Sokoto, then to the border at Birnin-Konni. If you're setting off from Kaduna or Kano, the best surfaced route is via Katsina to Maradi.

Red Tape

Niger cultivates one of the most irksome bureaucracies in the world. Although Nigériens are subject to much more scrutiny at police and customs checkpoints throughout the country than tourists, officials have a reputation for being painfully no-nonsense. Though the situation seems to be improving, don't expect jocular exchanges or upbeat conversation.

■ Visas and health certificates

Visas for Niger are required by all visitors except citizens of ECOWAS countries. They are not issued at the border, and are most easily obtained in neighbouring West African countries: Benin; Côte d'Ivoire; Ghana; and Nigeria (Lagos and Kano). Note that French embassies don't handle visas for Niger but some Ivoirian embassies do; and that Niger has no representation in Bamako. If you're arriving from Mali and need a visa, plan ahead. In general, Niger officials are literate and well-versed in the rules and regulations. Bluffing in any situation is rarely effective.

If you apply for a visa outside Africa, Nigérien embassies may ask for a return air ticket or, at the very least, the registration details of the vehicle you'll be travelling with. To avoid these headaches, you're better off getting the visa in Africa. In either case, the visa is expensive.

To enter Niger you need a **yellow fever certificate** (except infants under 12 months).

Visas for onward travel

In Niamey, you can get visas for most neighbouring countries with little problem. Burkina Faso, Togo and Chad have no representation, but the French consulate handles their visas. Nigerian visas, however, are only granted to residents of Niger, and no exceptions are made. Should overland travel through Algeria become a safe option again, there's an Algerian embassy in Niamey, and a consulate in Agadez.

■ Vehicle passes

If you're driving, the police require to see a **carnet**. If you don't have one, they'll issue you with a Temporary Importation document. You'll also be issued with a *laissez-passer*, a visa for your vehicle, with the same details as your Vehicle Registration Document (V5) or *Carte Grise* (French and West African equivalent), to be surrendered on exit. There's no charge.

Third party **insurance** is compulsory, and the police like to check it. It's not available at frontier posts, but the police allow travel without it to the nearest town. The large and efficient Société

Nigérienne d'Assurances et de Réassurances, av de la Mairie, Niamey (BP426; ☎73.55.26), has branches throughout the country and charges about CFA2000 a day.

■ Bureaucracy

Officially, you're no longer required to **report to the police station** in every town you visit. In Arlit and Agadez, however, they still like to put a stamp in your passport. If police in these towns seem keen to do so, let them, but if they ask for money, don't pay. And if they don't seem concerned about stamps, you shouldn't be either.

Money and Costs

Niger is in the CFA zone (CFA100 = 1 French franc; approx. CFA900 = £1; approx. CFA560 = US$1). It's essential, arriving either by air or from Nigeria, to have some US dollars or, preferably, French francs in cash to tide you over until you reach a bank where you can change travellers' cheques.

The two main **banks** in Niger are the BIAO and the SONI Bank. Outside Niamey, one or the other has branches in Zinder, Tahoua, Birnin-Konni, Maradi, Agadez and Arlit. SONI will often charge three percent commission even for changing cash, but often gives a better rate for US dollars. The BIAO doesn't generally charge for cash and the commission is lower for travellers' cheques.

Credit and charge cards are pretty much limited to use in Niamey, and even then only for major expenses such as car rental, luxury hotels and a handful of upmarket restaurants. Major ones that are accepted are American Express and Diner's Club (Visa and MasterCard to a lesser extent). No bank gives cash advances on credit cards.

As far as **costs** are concerned, Niger is **expensive** relative to other CFA countries, though still fairly cheap in real terms. You can always find street food and a basic room for the night, even if the choice is often limited. If your budget is less restricted, the biggest expenses are likely to be hotels and car rental, both of which can eat deeply into your pocket.

Health

In Niamey and other large towns, tap water is usually suitable for drinking; the borehole water of Arlit and Agadez is noted for its

purity. **Cholera epidemics, however, occur frequently along the Niger and in the bush you should use purifying tablets, or boil water. In case of an epidemic, even town water is suspect.**

Health care facilities are very limited. For minor ailments you can be treated at Niamey's **hospital**. If you have a medical problem, embassies will always recommend a **private clinic**. For anything serious – surgery for example – they're sure to suggest repatriation.

Maps and Information

Tourist information on Niger is virtually nonexistent outside the country: there are no tourist offices abroad. In Niamey, the tourist office has a good plan of the capital, with many of the city's restaurants and hotels indicated, and although it dates back to 1992, it's still largely reliable.

The IGN publishes maps in scales of 1:2,500,000, 1:1,000,000, 1:500,000, 1:200,000, and 1:50,000. You're not supposed to obtain the latter three series without authorization, which you can apply for at any Niger embassy – though in practice you'll only really need them for serious *piste* driving. In Niamey, maps are available at the Direction de la Topographie (see p.891).

Getting Around

Niger has some good roads, a decent bus service, plus some feasible hitching prospects at checkpoints. In the southwest of the country, you also have the limited possibility of using the Niger River.

■ Buses, bush taxis and trucks

Three main, surfaced routes cover the western parts of Niger: Niamey–Gaya, Niamey–Zinder and Birnin-Konni–Agadez. Furthermore, the Route de l'Uranium – from Niamey to Agadez and Arlit – and the Route de l'Unité – connecting Maradi, Zinder and Lake Chad in the southeast – are in reasonably good condition.

The state-run Société Nationale des Transports Nigériens (SNTN) operates a scheduled **bus network** between major towns. Because of their popularity, it's imperative to book a seat in advance at the local SNTN office. **Taxis brousse** soak up the excess passengers; they're slightly

less expensive and always overcrowded. It's best to avoid the bigger **private buses** as although they're less expensive, they're slow, uncomfortable and mechanically unreliable, as well as taking forever to fill up. Transport rates on main routes are about CFA12–13 per kilometre. **Trucks** also run between certain centres and often take travellers for a fee – a useful option for remote areas where transport is scarce.

■ Driving your own vehicle

On tarmac, experienced local drivers tank along at 150kph. If you're driving yourself you can keep up a good speed too; visibility is excellent and all bends and hazards are marked well in advance. Driving **off the paved roads** is still subject to police jurisdiction, though in practice they're rarely fussed about it.

Petrol (gasoline) and diesel are generally plentiful, but supplies can be far apart. **Fuel** can be bought from either a filling station – dependent on electricity – or from an entrepreneur with half a dozen fifty-gallon drums at the roadside. Maps aren't generally a good guide to fuel supplies, so ask regularly. Fuel is generally expensive, except along the southern border between Birnin Konni and Zinder, where there's a thriving black market in Nigerian petrol. North of Zinder, lubrication oils and transmission fluids can be hard to come by.

■ Hitching

Roadblocks and police checks at the entrance to every large town help to make **hitching** a possible alternative. Cars are obliged to stop at these controls and while the *gendarmes* are checking the papers you can ask drivers if they're headed your way. The police may help – or ask for a dash. Foreign aid workers often take hitchers for free; Nigérien drivers will almost invariably ask for money, in which case it pays to have an idea of the corresponding public transport fare, as drivers may try to overcharge you.

Hitching is fast. On the three main axes you can expect a vehicle going to one of the big towns or a neighbouring country at least once an hour, and most vehicles will stop. Lorry drivers sometimes turn off en route, so check the final destination and any detours to be made.

A hitch on a lorry usually means standing in the back for several hours under the blazing sun; hats and/or *cheches* are essential plus **at least two litres of water**. Lifts in the cab can be noisy and very hot, and get exhausting if you're also trying to make conversation in French.

■ River travel

Large steamers don't ply the Niger below Gao, in Mali, but motorized **pirogues** venture along the river between Ayorou (near Mali) and Gaya (near Benin). They operate only during and after the rainy season when the water level is high enough. Deals have to be struck on your own in the river towns. Between March and September, it may also be possible to canoe-hop downstream from Gaya to Port Harcourt in southern Nigeria but rapids and artificial barriers block the way at numerous points and prevent a continuous journey in the same vessel.

■ Internal flights

There are no scheduled domestic flights in Niger: your only recourse is to rent a light aircraft and pilot from the Transniger company (☎73.20.55) in Niamey.

Accommodation

Hotels tend to be relatively expensive in Niger, but at least you'll find comfortable places with toilets and air conditioning in all the major towns. Budget accommodation seems especially bad value: you'll often have to pay upwards of CFA4000, even for a room with just a fan and shared facilities.

Camping sites are an idea that's caught on in Niger and you'll find them scattered lightly throughout the country. They usually cost around CFA2000 per person plus extra for each vehicle. **Staying with people** is now officially sanctioned (it used to be banned).

Eating and Drinking

Though Niger has concentrated heavily on improving its agriculture, food shortages occur in years of bad harvest or drought. Staples tend to be less varied than in countries to the south, meals being usually based around millet, rice or *niebé* – a type of bean that has become an important crop. Along the river, these are usually eaten with sauces and fresh or smoked fish. Another traditional food, *foura*, is one of the most common dishes, and eaten throughout the country. It consists of small balls of ground and slightly fermented millet, crushed in a calabash with milk, sugar and spices added. Brochettes are sold everywhere on the streets: stuffed into a *demi-baguette* and doused with a bit of Maggi sauce, they make a quick, satisfying meal.

The Songhai often make a cornmeal stodge (or **pâte**) eaten with a baobab leaf sauce perked up with fish or meat. Beef and mutton is common in

---

ACCOMMODATION PRICE CODES

Accommodation prices in this chapter are coded according to the following scales – the same scales in terms of their pound/dollar equivalents as are used throughout the book. Prices refer to the rate you can expect to pay for a room with two beds. Single rooms, or single occupancy, will normally cost at least two-thirds of the twin-occupancy rate. For further details see p.48.

① **Under CFA4500 (under £5/$8).** Very rudimentary hotel with no frills at all – often a *chambre de passage* rented to the average guest by the hour.

② **CFA4500–9000 (£5–10/$8–16).** Basic hotel with simple amenities. S/C rooms with fans are the norm; some rooms may have AC for slightly higher rates.

③ **CFA9000–18,000 (£10–20/$16–32).** Modest, but adequate hotel, with S/C rooms, and a choice of rooms with fans, or for a premium AC.

④ **CFA18,000–27,000 (£20–30/$32–48).** Reasonable business-or tourist-class hotel with S/C, AC rooms, and often a restaurant.

⑤ **CFA27,000–36,000 (£30–40/$48–64).** Similar standards to the previous code band but extra facilities such as a pool are usual.

⑥ **CFA36,000–45,000 (£40–50/$64–80).** Comfortable, first-class hotel, with good facilities.

⑦ **Over CFA45,000 (over £50/$80).** Luxury establishment – top prices around CFA60,000–80,000.

BASIC HAUSA

Surpassing even French and English, **Hausa** is the most international language in West Africa, and is spoken by anything from 25 million to 100 million people. The language developed into a regional lingua franca in the fifteenth century, when Hausa traders led caravans to North Africa. Through their widespread commercial liaisons, Hausa became a trade language throughout northwest Africa and, in terms of the area over which it's spoken, Hausa is today second only to Swahili in sub-Saharan Africa. Though there are many dialects, the two most important are **Kano** and **Sokoto**. Differences are primarily phonetic and discrepancies don't prevent speakers of different dialects from understanding each other. The following words and phrases are based on the Kano dialect, which is generally considered to be "classical" Hausa.

NUMBERS

1	daya	10	goma	70	saba'in
2	biyu	11	goma sha daya	75	saba'in da biyar
3	uku	12	goma sha biyu	80	tamanin
4	hudu	20	ashirin	90	casa'in (or tamanin
5	biyar	25	ashirin da biyar		da goma)
6	shida	30	talatin	100	dari
7	bakwai	40	arba'in	200	dari biyu
8	takwas	50	hamsin	250	dari biyu da hamsin
9	tara	60	sittin	1000	dubu

In Niger, money is commonly counted in multiples of CFA5 (*dela*) – which can be difficult to calculate even if you're thinking in English.

CFA100	dela ashirin	CFA450	dela tamanin da	CFA1000	jikai
CFA150	dela talatin		goma		
CFA200	dela arba'in	CFA500	dela dar		

GREETINGS

If the following list seems long and trivial, it barely gives a taste of the extended formal exchange that's so important in Hausa, as in most African languages. Just learning the three words *sanu, lafiya* and *yauwa*, will permit you to carry on a surprisingly lengthy conversation.

All purpose greeting (men)	Salamu alaikum	Fine (general response)	Lafiya lau
(Response)	Alaika salamu	Are you tired? (how's the	
Greetings	Sanu	tiredness)	Ina gajiya?
(Response)	Yauwa, sanu kadai	No, I'm not tired	Ba gajiya
		What's the news?	Ina labari?
Are you in good health?	Kazo lafiya?	Everything's fine	Labari sai alheri
(Response)	Lafiya lau	Good afternoon	Barka da yamma
How's the household		(Response)	Barka kadai
/your family?	Ina gida?	See you tomorrow	Sai gobe
Good morning (how		Okay, see you tomorrow	To, sai gobe
was the night)?	Ina kwana?	See you later	Sai an juma
How are your children?	Yaya yara?	Okay, see you later	To, sai an juma

SHOPPING

How much?	Nawa nawa ne?	They're expensive!	Kai, suna da tsada!
Do you have oranges?	Akwai lemo?	I'll give you CFA100	Zan biya ka
Yes I do/no I don't have them	I, akwai/ah ah babu	dela	ashirin
		No deal (seller refusing)	Albarka
How much are your oranges?	Lemo, nawa nawa ne?	Give the money (offer accepted)	Kawo kudi

the Hausa country and the nomadic regions of the north.

Niamey has a reasonable selection of **foreign restaurants**, but outside the capital, eating places tend to be much more modest, the selection of dishes usually something like grilled chicken or *steack frites*. **Street food** is common with vendors selling omelettes, salads, *riz gras* and a variety of other cheap meals.

■ Drinking

As for **drinks**, Niger's great beverage – in common with other Sahel countries – is **tea**, drunk on most occasions, especially on the road whenever a little time is available to fix up a fire. You'll also find Flag **beer** in most towns, though it's rather expensive.

Communications – Post, Phones, Language and Media

The official language of Niger is French, but by far the most important lingua franca is Hausa. Niamey's PTT is quite modern and efficient, with a reliable poste restante. Phoning directly abroad with IDD is straightforward.

Niger's IDD code is ☎227.

If you want to make a reverse-charge (collect) call, known as PCV in French, you may be told that such calls are possible only to France, but ringing ☎16 from a payphone puts you through to the foreign operator, who should be able to connect a reverse-charge (collect) call anywhere. Persistence may be needed.

■ The media

There's nothing much in the way of **newspapers** in Niger: *Le Sahel*, a government-owned news sheet, is published daily in Niamey, but has a very small circulation and holds little of any interest. There are also various independent news magazines, including *Kakaki, Alternative, Haske, Kakaki, La Tribune du Peuple, Le Democrate* and *Le Républicain*. You can find French papers and news magazines in some of the bigger Niamey hotels and news and book stores, but little or nothing in English.

Nigérien **radio**, La Voix du Sahel, broadcasts in French, Hausa, Songhai-Djerma, Kanouri, Fulfuldé (Fula), Tamashek, Toubou, Gourmantché and Arabic. The **TV service**, Télé-Sahel, comes on air each evening for a few hours, but the quality of reception and programmes is extremely low.

Entertainment

Wrestling and one-armed boxing (fist wrapped in cloth) attract big crowds, but there's not a great deal going on in terms of national "culture" in Niger – no theatre except the odd event in Niamey, and little happening musically. The film tradition, brief as it is, shows more promise.

■ Cinema

Cinema in Niger has been dominated by three film-makers, none of whose work you're very likely to come across abroad. **Oumarou Ganda** began his career as an actor in a Jean Rouch film, *Moi,*

A SHORT NIGÉRIEN GLOSSARY

Azalai Camel caravans.

Baba Old man; a term of respect.

Birni Hausa word meaning a formerly fortified town.

Boro Bi Black person or people.

Canaris Large clay pots for storing water.

Djoliba Malinké name for the Niger. Literally "River of Blood", since the body of water was as vital to life as blood flowing in the veins.

Erg Shifting sand dunes common in the Ténéré.

Fech-fech Soft sand hidden beneath a hard crust.

Gravures Rupestres Rock paintings, common in the Aïr and Djado regions.

Kaya-kaya Wandering salesmen.

Kori Seasonal river course, or wadi (Hausa).

Razzia Slave raid.

Reg Stony wastes.

Wonki-wonki Launderers, common along the banks of the Niger in Niamey.

Zongo Section of a town or village where newly arrived strangers live.

un Noir, and went on to become a director in his own right and one of the great cultural archivists of African cinema. You're more likely to see his (largely autobiographical) works at Niamey's Centre Culturel Franco-Nigérien, or even abroad, than in any ordinary Nigérien cinema.

Jean Rouch also inspired another relatively well-known director, **Moustapha Alassane**, whose most famous feature film is *Femme, Villa, Voiture, Argent* (1972), a popular comedy dealing with the issue of cultural identity.

Another film-maker to gain international acclaim is **Djingary Maïga**, producer of *l'Etoile Noire* – in which he also starred – which deals with the clash between Western and traditional values.

◾ Music

In the realm of **music**, Niger remains rooted in tradition and the country has produced no international stars. In Niamey, look out for performances of the national music and dance troupe, **Karaka**. You might also catch a less worthy, mimed show that goes out on Télé-Sahel TV. For a taste of Nigérien music, the Agence de Cooperation Culturelle et Technique has put out two volumes of a record entitled *Festival de la Jeunesse Nigérienne*, while an international CD release from **Moussa Poussy** and **Saadou Bori** (*Niamey Twice*; Stern's) has put Niger on the musical map.

Directory

AIRPORT DEPARTURE TAX CFA3500 (if not included in ticket).

CONTRACEPTION Birth control was only legalized in Niger in 1988. There's now an active *planification familiale* programme, but contraception still isn't widely available.

CRAFTS AND MARKETS Niger has a wealth of mostly inexpensive and portable crafts. Agadez is well known for its **silversmiths**, who turn out some fine jewellery: popular items are the pendants known as desert crosses, particularly the Croix d'Agadez. The Hausa towns, notably Zinder, specialize in **leather goods,** including sandals, bags and boxes. Fula weavers (*tisserands*) are noted for their geometrically patterned **blankets**. To get a good overview, the National Museum in Niamey shows a wide range of the country's artisanal output. Best buys are in local markets,

though for guaranteed quality and variety you should also check out the official Centres Artisanales in Niamey.

HOLIDAYS As 85 percent of Niger's population is Muslim, **Islamic holidays** are of key importance (see p.59). The best place to be during festivities is Zinder. Other national holidays are: **January 1**, **April 15** (Anniversary of the 1974 coup), **August 3** (Independence Day) and **December 18** (Proclamation of the Republic). Christmas and Easter are also office holidays.

OPENING HOURS Due to the heat, business starts early in the morning and generally closes down for at least three hours in the afternoon. Banking hours vary from one institution to the next but they're approximately Mon–Fri 7.30–11.30am & 3.30–5.30pm. Government offices are open Mon–Fri 7.30am–12.30pm & 3.30–6.30pm. Most businesses are open Mon–Fri 8am–12.30pm & 3–6.30pm, plus Saturday mornings.

WILDLIFE AND NATIONAL PARKS Niger's harsh climate and terrain have preserved some rare species from the vicissitudes of habitat spoliation and hunting (which was outlawed in 1964). Even in the south, hippos can nearly always be seen in the Niger River and several herds of giraffe live in the vicinity of Tillabéri, Baleyara and Dosso (to the north, east and south of Niamey), where they're often to be seen from the road. The **Parc National du "W" du Niger** (which crosses borders into Burkina and Benin) has a good crosssection of savannah fauna, including several hundred elephants. Niger's portion of the park has the best visitor facilities.

WOMEN TRAVELLERS Though Niger is a Muslim country, women don't wear the veil and their public presence is strongly felt. Women travellers generally have few problems and female Western volunteers, for example, feel comfortable making trips across the country unaccompanied. Advances tend to be frequent but harmless and easily rebuffed.

A Brief History of Niger

After the demise of the Songhai empire, whose territory spread into western Niger, two spheres of influence predominated in the region. In the twelfth century, the Tuareg settled in the north around Agadez, and soon controlled regional trade. The Hausa spread

from the original seven city-states founded in Nigeria in the tenth century to settle southern towns like Zinder and Maradi. Unlike the western Sudan, where trans-Saharan trade focused mainly on gold, slavery was the mainstay of the eastern routes and the basis of local economies.

■ Explorers on the Niger River

For centuries, news of cities like Timbuktu, Gao and Djenné (all in present-day Mali) had circulated in Europe, but although the Portuguese had been trading along the West African coast since the fifteenth century, no Western power had penetrated the interior. It wasn't until the eighteenth century that expeditions were launched into a region notorious for its hostility to Christians. In 1796, **Mungo Park** reached the Niger near Ségou (again, in present-day Mali) and described its eastern course. Until that time, Europeans believed the river flowed west – as documented by Leo Africanus in the sixteenth century – or that it was a branch of the Nile.

It was another thirty years before the Europeans saw Timbuktu. In 1826, **Gordon Laing** became the first white man to reach it, though he didn't return from the legendary city alive. In 1850, **Heinrich Barth** led a new expedition into the interior, his route from Tripoli, in Libya, taking him south through Agadez, Zinder and the Hausa country as far as Kano. He thus became the first European to explore the region of present-day Niger – and to return to Europe.

■ Colonial conquest

The information gleaned by these expeditions opened the doors to colonial conquests. France, anxious to link colonial settlements in West and central Africa, was the most ambitious usurper of Sahelian territories. In 1854, General Louis Faidherbe became governor of Senegal and plotted the eastward expansion of France's West African empire. He sent troops up the Senegal River and east to the Niger. Following its course, they broke the resistance of such formidable adversaries as **Samory Touré** and **El Hadj Omar Tall**, who had founded the Tukulor empire of Ségou. By the end of the nineteenth century, the French had established a military presence at **Niamey**, which they quickly turned into the most important army post east of Bamako.

In 1898, spheres of influence were established between France and the United Kingdom, the prin-

cipal powers vying for control of the Niger. The following year, the French sent an expedition to Lake Chad to demarcate borders between Niger and Nigeria. Led by two generals, **Voulet and Chanoine**, it was to be one of the bloodiest of the colonial missions. As the two soldiers pushed east with troops of Senegalese infantry, they embarked on a series of massacres, torching villages in their path and slaughtering the people. Birnin-Konni was virtually razed to the ground. Reports of the brutality reached France and the government sent an expedition led by Colonel Klobb to investigate. Infuriated that their tactics should be questioned, the generals went over the edge, murdered Klobb, broke with France and apparently set about conquering the territories for themselves. Their madness was only stopped when they were killed by their own infantrymen. Replacements were sent out and Lake Chad was finally reached in 1900.

■ French rule

With the territory's southern borders established, Niger became part of French West Africa in the following year. But the nature of this territory differed from that of its West African neighbours: officially, it was an **autonomous military territory**, and its importance was strategic, rather than commercial. Outside the army, the French presence was minimal: there was no French settlement and development was barely considered.

"Pacification" was a difficult process in Niger, as resistance sprouted in pockets across the country. One of the most serious **uprisings** was that of the **Kel Gress Tuareg**, who occupied Agadez from 1916 to 1917 and controlled most of the Aïr highlands. In 1919, a rebellion broke out in the region of Tahoua, which was only quelled in 1921, the same year that Niger was finally upgraded to the status of a colony.

World War II was a turning point in West African politics, and following the Brazzaville Conference of 1944, reforms were enacted which provided African representation in the national assembly, the senate and the assembly of the French Union. In 1956, the famous *Loi Cadre* was passed, establishing local government for the French colonies.

In the wake of these reforms, two political movements developed in Niger, the more radical of which was embodied in the *Union Nigérienne Democratique* – also known as **Sawaba** – which dominated political life in the 1950s. Led by **Djibo Bakary**, the party fought vigorously against close ties with France and de Gaulle's proposed constitution, the main provision of which was for a Franco-African Community with limited autonomy for individual colonies, but continued economic dependence on Paris. For a while, it seemed probable that Niger would join Guinea in saying "No" to de Gaulle's proposal and in opting for immediate independence "with all its consequences".

In the event, the new constitution was approved in the landmark **1958 referendum** – a victory for the Parti Progressiste Nigérien of **Hamani Diori**, who had advocated the alternative of close links with France. It's generally believed the election results were falsified. According to the official count, 370,000 people voted for the union compared to 100,000 who voted against, leaving 750,000 people who ostensibly didn't exercise their voting rights.

Despite its wide support, the Sawaba party was banned in 1959, and Bakary forced into exile. With the implicit backing of the French, the PPN was thus poised to dominate post-independence politics and Diori was assured the presidency of the new nation, formed in 1960.

■ Independence

Conservative politics prevailed in the days after independence, as Diori aligned his country with France and developed close ties with moderate neighbours, notably Côte d'Ivoire. Diori ruled with a small Council of Ministers, carefully selected to maintain the status quo. Sawaba tried to operate from abroad (its foreign backers included Algeria, Ghana and China), but opposition to government policies was rigorously suppressed. Various plots to overthrow Diori's regime in the early 1960s led to mass arrests and violence. When Sawaba was accused of leading a series of guerilla attacks near the Nigerian border in 1964, seven of the presumed assailants were publicly executed in Niamey.

By the late 1960s, the PPN – by then the only political party – was in a state of disarray and the target of mounting criticism. Diori made an effort to reorganize it, but was careful to stack the party leadership with faithful pre-independence politicians – and ensured that it remained ineffective as a forum for the discussion of opposing views. Despite his tight control over the political reins, however, he began to lose his grip on power as the economic situation deteriorated drastically in the late 1960s.

Diori was given a political reprieve when the mining of **uranium**, discovered in 1968, gave new financial hope to a nation that had previously gained seventy percent of its export earnings from groundnuts. Eager to take advantage of the new source of revenue, Diori accepted a minimal seventeen percent share for the national mining company, Société des Mines de l'Aïr (SOMAÏR), which was controlled by the French Atomic Energy Commission. However, 1968 also saw the start of the first great **Sahel drought**. Lasting until 1974, the natural catastrophe brought Niger to its knees.

By the early 1970s, over a million head of livestock (nearly two-thirds of the national herd) had died, and the pasturelands of the northern nomads had disappeared. International organizations helped establish emergency refugee camps and sent food supplies, but rumours began circulating that government officials were hoarding food and selling it off at hefty profits, rather than distributing it to those facing starvation. These were quickly confirmed by the discovery of **emergency food aid**, stockpiled in the homes of several of Diori's ministers.

■ Kountché's coup

Disillusion with the government turned to anger. When Lieutenant-Colonel **Seyni Kountché** overthrew Diori in April 1974, there was widespread satisfaction, and even the French conceded they could do business with the new order. Kountché established a Conseil Militaire Suprême (CMS), which made a priority of dealing with corruption and reinvesting the government with credibility. In a conciliatory move, hundreds of political prisoners were released and Djibo Bakary, Sawaba's leader, returned home from exile. In 1975, Kountché pulled off an economic coup, when he managed to renegotiate the terms under which uranium was mined, raising SOMAÏR's share to 33 percent and making the national company the biggest single partner.

Fuelled by uranium revenues (prices for which soared following the oil crisis of the 1970s) and aided by the end of the drought, the economy began to pick up. Government workers received wage increases, roads were improved and prestigious building projects undertaken in Niamey. Even the agricultural sector improved dramatically. Niger, one of the countries hardest hit by the drought, was also one of the quickest to recover, and by the end of the decade, it could boast self-sufficiency in food production – no mean feat.

Niger had become something of an **economic oasis** in the middle of a poverty-stricken region, and that alone was enough to lend stability to Kountché's military regime. But policy and personality conflicts within the CMS threatened his authority, and he repeatedly reshuffled the ruling council and expelled critics. Following a new outbreak of political activity, Bakary was rearrested in 1975. A coup attempt the following year led to the execution of its alleged protagonists. Even as he tightened the screws, however, Kountché made a number of goodwill gestures. In 1980, Diori and Bakary were granted a degree of freedom, along with many of their supporters. And by 1982, the president appeared to be making plans for a return to a constitutional government.

■ Setbacks in the 1980s

A Conseil National de Développement was established in 1983 as a means of granting greater participation on a local level. But the CND had barely started functioning when another coup attempt, this time led by some of Kountché's closest aides, nearly toppled the government while he was abroad.

Reforms thereafter proceeded at a slower pace, though the president eventually announced that a **National Charter**, or draft constitution, would be drawn up and submitted to a referendum. Approved by the government in 1986, the charter was submitted to voters in May 1987 – the first time elections had been held in the country since independence – and received overwhelming approval.

But even as Kountché was setting about reorganizing the government, the **economy** took an unexpected dive. Already in 1980, a combination of the world recession and cuts in nuclear power programmes had led to a drop in the price of uranium. Production in Niger has since continued to fall off and plans to mine some of the country's unexploited reserves have been scrapped. Hopes that Niger would become one of the world's leading uranium producers faded rapidly. And as revenues dwindled and the national debt grew, another drought struck the country in the early 1980s. By 1984, the number of livestock had dropped by a half and, as cereal shortages climbed to nearly 500,000 tons, the country again found itself importing vast quantities of food, depending much on the USA. At about the same time, Nigeria closed its land borders and cut off some of Niger's important markets.

The downswing was accompanied by tensions with Niger's northern neighbour, **Libya**, which claims some 300 square kilometres of territory in northern Niger, an area with certified uranium deposits. After the Libyan army occupied northern Chad in 1980, Kountché's government had become wary of possible destabilization – with some justification after Gaddafi told reporters "We consider Niger second in line". Gaddafi accused the Niger government of persecuting its **Tuareg** population – an issue about which Niamey is acutely sensitive – and may have encouraged dissent among the nomads, who have generally been sold short since independence. Many observers suspected Gaddafi of behind-the-scenes support for the 1983 coup attempt and although relations have subsequently improved between the two countries, they remain strained. Relations with other Maghreb countries – Morocco, Algeria and Tunisia – were strengthened over this period, however, and Niger has developed close ties with Saudi Arabia, Kuwait and other Arab states in the Gulf, Muslim confrères who have proved reliable sources of aid.

■ Colonel Ali Saïbou

In 1986, Kountché travelled abroad to countries that had been traditional sources of political and financial support. He made his first official trip to France, during which he suffered a brain haemorrhage and subsequently died, in November 1987.

Kountché's chosen successor as head of state **Colonel Ali Saïbou**, the military Chief of Staff and a long-time supporter, followed the same orientation as his predecessor. In mid-1988 Saïbou announced the creation of a one-party state (the PPN and all the other parties were disbanded when Kountché came to power), a move which he said would "normalize" political expression and which was generally perceived as a step to further reforms started in the early 1980s. In 1989, the first congress was held of the military council's **National Movement for a Society of Development** (MNSD), a supra-political organization which promised great things, but within a party-state order that threatened to be elitist and almost exclusively urban-based. The government's fear of ethnic divisions in the country was so great that even acknowledging the plurality was viewed as a danger.

The IMF-ordered economy forced in austerity measures which hit poor urban dwellers very hard. Students, too, felt the full impact of rising prices and reductions in already strapped services. In 1990 the university in Niamey was the scene of large-scale **student demonstrations** that ended in a violent clash with security forces and the deaths of three students and many serious injuries. A week later a mass protest rally swept through the streets of the capital, while the Lagos-based opposition, the **Niger Movement of Revolutionary Committees** (MOUNCORE), issued statements demanding a popular uprising in Niger and the overthrow of the Saïbou clique.

Niger was put under the spotlight in June 1990, after *Le Monde* reported a **massacre** of about two hundred Tuareg civilians in reprisal for a Tuareg raid on Tchin-Tabaradene, near Tahoua. Amnesty International reported other atrocities near Tchin-Tabaradene and at In-Gal, in which dozens of people were summarily executed.

■ "Democracy" and Tuareg rebellion

As the national crisis deepened, Saïbou was compelled to speed up reforms. By the end of 1990, he had legalized opposition parties and formed a **national conference** to plot the country's future. Within a year, conference delegates had reduced the president's role to a ceremonial level and voted to suspend austerity measures imposed by the IMF and World Bank, an act which effectively made the country an outcast from the international financial community.

Despite two military mutinies (during which the army not only took over state broadcasting, but also detained Saïbou's prime minister before returning to the barracks when the government agreed to pay back-wages), plans for **elections** pressed on. A majority of seats in the national assembly was ultimately won by a new group of opposition parties – the Alliance des Forces du Changement (AFC) – whose candidate for president, **Mahamane Ousmane**, won the title in the presidential elections in March 1993. A Muslim and the first Hausa head of state in a traditionally Djerma political culture, the new leader of "democratic" Niger pledged to address the country's economic and social crises. He appointed another presidential contender, **Mahamadou Issoufou**, prime minister.

But student and labour unrest continued through 1992–93, and **Tuareg resistance** in the wake of Tchin-Tabaradene grew into a full-blown rebellion headed by the Front de Libération de l'Air et l'Azaouad. Martial law was imposed across the entire north as security forces launched a major offensive against the rebels. There were violent clashes and, by early 1993, two hundred Tuaregs were in prison and the FLAA was holding some 50 government troops.

Secret negotiations in France in 1993 led to a precarious truce whereby the north was to be demilitarized and talks were to open on the principal **Tuareg demands**: greater political autonomy; assistance for the return of refugees from Algeria; and a commitment to regional development. Though the truce held into 1994, the FLAA began to splinter into more militant groups that refused to support any agreement that didn't specifically address demands for a federal system of government.

Meanwhile, President Mahamane tried to rekindle talks with Western creditors in the hopes of securing new loans and much-needed debt relief. During a 1993 visit to France, he received emergency financial assistance, which allowed him to settle some pay arrears to public sector employees, but when he conceded the government could not afford the back-pay accumulated under the transitional administration, new **strikes and mutinies** broke out in Maradi, Agadez, Tahoua and Zinder. Though the government found the funds to pay an extra month's arrears, the weakened economy continued to make the situation extremely volatile.

By mid-1994, the country was in a state of continual upheaval. A campaign of civil disobedience seeking proportional representation was mounted by key opposition leader (ie opposition against the AFC) **Tandja Mamadou**, of the National Movement for the Society of Development–Nassara (MNSD–Nassara, which had been the sole party between 1988 and 1990). Meanwhile, trade union leaders called an indefinite strike over demands for back-pay. Although the strike soon withered, Prime Minister Issoufou resigned in September for party political reasons; then his successor **Souley Abdoulaye** was voted out of office on a no confidence ballot. President Mahamane, faced with the loss of two governments in a single month, shied away from nominating a third prime minister, and instead called a general election and announced the dissolution of the national assembly.

The election, held in January 1995, gave a majority to the opposition parties grouped under the banner of the MNSD, whose candidate for prime minister was **Hama Amadou**. Hama's cabinet was chosen entirely from the ranks of the opposition. Two women were among them – a new departure in Niger – but no associates of President Mahamane, the figurehead of the first wave of democratic reforms in the country. The political climate had come full circle.

Niger in 1995 seemed ready for **reconciliation**. The new government came to a back-pay agreement with the unions, and repealed anti-strike legislation. Most significantly, in Ouagadougou on April 15, the new government and the Tuareg rebels signed what was billed as a definitive and lasting peace accord – with Algerian, Burkinabe and French mediation (to many Nigériens the French are the least attractive partners in this as they have long been suspected of promoting Tuareg nationalist ideals with the aim of creating a Francophile Saharan state).

After a brief period of goodwill, however, political cohabitation in Niger turned sour, and the constitution – which hadn't anticipated that the president and prime minister would come from different parties–was vague on power sharing. Frequent disputes arose between Mahamane and Hama, who wrangled over everything, from who had the authority to sign amnesty agreements with the Tuaregs to the appointment of nationalized company executives. The rift wasn't helped by the fact that Mahamane was a Hausa and Hama a Djerma; new government appointees, therefore, represented an ethnic as well as a political shift in power. Mahamane frequently refused to convene the Council of Ministers or to sign legislation and the wheels of government were just barely turning by the end of 1995. In the midst of the **deadlock**, the USTN once again renewed strike actions to demand payment of arrears to civil servants. They were soon joined by miners and students, who formed a campaign of disobedience.

In January 1996, the military intervened through a **coup d'état** led by **Ibrahim Baré Maïnassara**. He formed a ruling military body, the Conseil de Salut national (CSN), suspended the constitution, placed Hama and Mahamane under house arrest and declared a state of emergency. Western Nations viewed it as an assault to democracy, even one that functioned poorly, and the IMF broke off loan negotiations. Maïnassara, however, seemed sincere in his desire to turn power back to the people, and within a few months set up a committee to draft a new constitution and scheduled elections for July. Apparently the taste of being on top agreed with

him, since he also soon announced his intention to run for the presidency as a civilian.

Mahamane, Hama and the last elected head of the assembly, Issoufou, all threw their hats in the ring as well. The polling took place in July, but candidates outside the CSN were not reassured when the electoral commission overseeing the voting was dissolved before the polls had closed, nor by the fact that the government put them all under house arrest on the day of the election. Under such dubious circumstances, Maïnassara claimed an outright majority, with 52 percent of the vote.

■ The Fourth Republic

In his inaugural address as first president of the Fourth Republic, Maïnassara called for national unity as a means of creating social and economic stability. But in its outrage against the manipulation of the presidential elections, the opposition was hardly in the mood to be charitable. As the legislative elections approached, major opposition parties grouped to form the Front pour la Restauration et la Défense de la Démocratie (FRDD), which demanded that the presidential election results be annulled and that an unbiased election committee be re-established as conditions for participation. They must have known there was no chance of either happening and were cornered into boycotting the elections. Pro-Maïnassara parties swept the seats in the national assembly.

Future attempts to form a government of "national unity" met with equal resistance, so Maïnassara set out to further exclude and silence the opposition. **Human rights** organizations bemoaned the worsening situation in the country, citing increased arrests and deportation to northern cities, the intimidation of journalists, and the harassment of opposition activists. On the anniversary of the coup, the FRDD organized a demonstration in Niamey, which degenerated into violence. Among those arrested (yet again) were Mahamane, Hama and Issoufou. It was only a precursor of protests that would continue throughout 1997–98, most notably in politically sensitive Maradi and Zinder.

The government enjoyed more co-operation from the unions, offering high-profile posts to leaders of the MSTN. But the privatization programme Maïnassara had committed the country to seemed to put him on a collision course with state workers too. Faced with a very narrow political base, Maïnassara based his presidency on the support of the **military**. In the regional and municipal elections of February 1999, the opposition swept polls throughout the country – excluding the government strongholds of Dosso and Agadez – but the results were annulled in their most powerful pockets of support, including Tillabéri, Tahoua, Maradi, Zinder and Diffa. Once again, the democratic process had been railroaded and the threat of unrest seemed imminent. Although that prospect didn't bode well for the president, worse were rumblings that he planned to reshuffle the military to exclude members who increasingly disapproved of his means.

Before he got the chance, Maïnassara was gunned down, in April 1999, as he prepared to board the presidential helicopter. Although his body had nearly been severed in two by the blast of gunfire that came from his own presidential guard, the military played down the incident as "an unfortunate accident". Junior officers **seized power** and quickly formed the Conseil de Reconciliation Nationale (CRN), headed by Major **Daouda Malam Wanké**, who dissolved the assembly and the supreme court and sacked all senior members of the army and the police. On a more positive note, he immediately thereafter held closed-door meetings with the leaders of Niger's five largest political parties to set up guidelines for an interim government and a possible calendar for the restoration of democracy.

Although the country remained remarkably calm following the putsch, **international opinion** came down hard on the new regime. West African leaders, from Blaise Compaore of Burkina Faso to newly elected Nigerian president Obasanjo, who called the action "a step backward for democracy and for the people of Niger", condemned the assassination. The EU suspended aid to the country, followed by the Organisation de la Francophonie, whose 30-year anniversary was scheduled to take place in Niamey in 1999.

■ Prospects

As this book goes to press, the implications of the coup are not clear. In mid-May 1999, Wanké began a diplomatic offensive to try and rally support from abroad and at home. He pledges a commitment to a return to **civilian rule** and promises legislative and presidential elections by December 1999. Mahamane appears willing to use his influence with Nigeria to bolster regional support. Help from national leaders who could never find their way to co-operating with Maïnassara could pave the road for some much-needed assistance. And Wanké looks willing to uphold the Enhanced Structural Adjustment Programme that his predecessor worked out with the IMF and World Bank, a move expected to calm the fears of other donor nations.

At home, the appointment of **Mohammed Anako**, leader of the Tuareg ex-rebellion's Patriotic Front for the Liberation of the Sahara, as a special advisor to Wanké and minister without portfolio in the transitional government was widely seen as a gesture to appease Tuaregs, who remained frustrated throughout the Maïnassara era at the slow pace of their reintegration into Niger society following the peace accords. But student clashes with police on the streets of Niamey in May 1999 were an early indication that the government could face a hard time trying to mend fences with other disgruntled sectors of society. It is hard to imagine how the government can appease the powerful **trade unions** and international lenders at the same time.

Economically, Niger remains a classic case of a country over-dependent on a **single resource** (uranium) and held hostage to fickle world market prices. The importance of improving agriculture is critical, as only three percent of the land is arable. In addition to the vast **irrigation projects** that have been undertaken in regions around Tillabéri, Birnin-Konni and Dosso, there has been a positive trend towards smaller-scale projects involving co-operatives for individual farmers. Cereal production was nonetheless down in the late 1990s and further economic sliding could easily translate to political unrest. With its huge **public debt** and limited possibilities for further credit, the new government will have to look increasingly to Niger's untapped resources to underwrite both future development and better prospects for stability.

Beach near Cape Coast, Ghana

Baking bread, Sokodé, Togo

Stilt village near Porto Novo, Benin

Voodoo shrine, Ouidah, Benin

Roumsiki mountains, Cameroon

"Durbar" cavalry display, Nigeria

Replacing a roof, Wukari, Nigeria

Sunset, Niger

Tuareg girl in front of her home, Niger

NIAMEY

As uranium money showered on Niger in the 1970s, **NIAMEY** changed almost overnight. Many of its dusty roads were paved, and a Voie Triomphale was traced through town, its bright streetlights blotting the Sahelian nights from memory. Avant-garde buildings such as the Palais des Congrès and, fittingly, the Office National de Recherches Minières were built, to be joined by futuristic hotels, banks and offices.

This development, however, was nowhere near as dramatic as in Abidjan or Lagos, and the juxtaposition between modernity and tradition – and between city and country – works remarkably well here. The sight of camel caravans crossing the Niger River on the Kennedy Bridge hardly seems incongruous, and neither does the spectacle of Fula, Hausa, Tuareg and Djerma traders gathering at the Petit Marché under the shadow of high-rise office blocks.

As a place to stay, or live, however, Niamey leaves plenty to be desired. It's bigger and more aggressive than other Sahel capitals – Bamako or Ouagadougou for example – and has developed some notoriety for muggings and other unpleasant encounters. In compensation, it offers an outstanding museum, good markets and some pleasant retreats within a short drive of the city.

Some history

Before the colonial era, Niamey was no more than a small village whose origins probably didn't predate the eighteenth century. When French troops swarmed into the desert in the 1890s, they recognized the strategic importance of this spot on the river and dug in their heels. By 1902, it had grown into one of the most important military and administrative posts east of Bamako. When Niger officially became a colony, the larger urban centre at Zinder was chosen as the new capital, but the French administrators preferred Niamey's climate, and in 1926 they transferred the capital back again.

Throughout the colonial era, Niamey never developed much beyond the **European quarter** built in the plateau district. The population in the 1930s was under two thousand, though by independence it had increased to around thirty thousand. Real growth only occurred in the 1970s, with the population surging to over a quarter of a million by 1980. A great deal of the influx was caused by the **drought** of the mid-1970s, which sparked a rural exodus of biblical proportions. Niamey, fattened on uranium income, flourished as immigrants from the devastated provinces poured into the city where they could hope to find food, housing and work. A second drought in the mid-1980s led to a new wave of immigration, forcing the city's population still higher. Today, it's estimated nearly 800,000 people live in Niamey, and virtually every ethnic group is represented here. This rapid growth, combined with the recent fall in the world price of uranium, has put huge strains on the city. Though Niamey provides comforts for travellers and expats with cash in their pockets, the benefits of modernization are now tempered by the spectre of shantytowns, mass unemployment and urban blight.

Arrival, city transport and information

Coming in by *taxi brousse* you're most likely to be let off at the **gare routière** in the Wadata district, about 4km from the centre. It's not difficult or expensive to get a taxi into town: **collective taxis** cost an average of CFA150 each, though at night drivers often ask twice that. If you take a cab for yourself it will cost around CFA1000 per short trip. During daylight hours, **city buses** also operate and work out a little cheaper than shared taxis, but there are no printed schedules or map routes, and even a trip to the SNTN office on the Corniche de Yantala (☎72.30.23) may not help you sort it out.

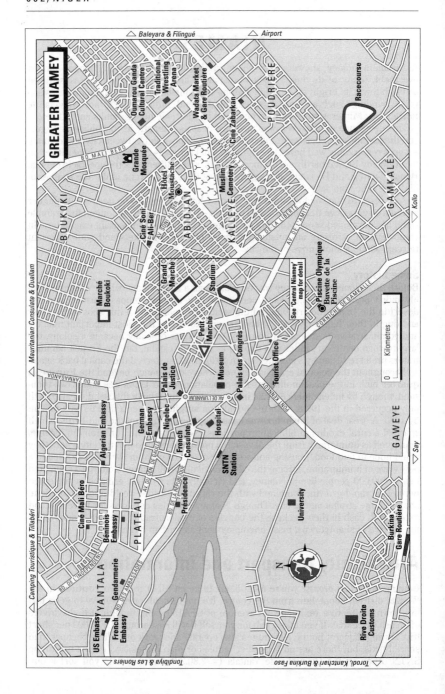

GREATER NIAMEY

Though you'll see signs marking bus stops scattered throughout the town, there's no way of knowing where the bus is going except by asking.

Niamey's **airport** (☎73.23.81) is 12km southeast of the city centre on the Boulevard de l'Amitié (which becomes the Boulevard du 15 Avril). Unfortunately, buses don't shuttle into the centre, so you'll have to take a cab. Expect to pay about CFA3000.

While the **tourist office** on rue Luebke (BP 612; ☎73.24.47; Fax 72.33.47) is not much help with enquiries about Niamey itself – apart from possibly being able to sell you a city map, and give you a few leaflets – it is useful for organizing excursions to places like the Parc National du "W" du Niger, their prices comparing favourably with those of travel agents.

Orientation

Niamey spreads along 7km of the Niger's left (north) bank, and has now expanded to the other side of the river. The size of the city makes it difficult to get an immediate grip on its layout – a problem compounded by the French-style planning, with numerous roundabouts and streets that rarely run parallel.

You'll spend virtually your whole time on the left bank. To define a centre, use the **Pont Kennedy** as a landmark. To the north of the bridge, rue de Gaweye leads straight up to the **Grand Marché**, bordered by Boulevard de la Liberté. The entire **commercial centre** lies between this new market and the river, and this is where you'll come to shop, eat, change money and visit sights such as the **Musée National**. A number of embassies and airline offices are located in two important commercial buildings along rue de Gaweye: **Immeuble Sonara II** and **Immeuble El Nasr**.

To the **west of Pont Kennedy**, Avenue F. Mitterrand runs past the impressive *Hôtel Gaweye* as it heads towards the tree-lined avenues of the **Plateau district**. This colonial-looking neighbourhood is where most government ministries are located, along with the Palais du Président and many of the embassies. Continuing west, you come to the underdeveloped **Yantala district**, which you'll become familiar with if you stay at the *camping* near the entrance to town on the Tillabéri road.

East of the bridge, the rue du Sahel leads to the residential neighbourhoods of Abidjan and Kalleye (known collectively as the **Niamey Bas** district). Streets are comfortably shady in this area, where you'll find a good number of hotels and restaurants. Further east, Niamey Bas gives onto the **Gamkalé district** and then to the capital's **industrial zone**.

SECURITY

Once a travellers' haven, Niamey has acquired a rough edge in recent years. The increase in crime is mainly due to Niger's dismal economy, which is even more severe since the drastic decline in trans-Saharan trade. **Petty theft** is commonplace, and the principal area to avoid is the **river bank on the north side**, especially the stretch along the Corniche between the *Grand Hôtel* in the east, past the Pont Kennedy, to the SNTN bus station in the west. Muggings at knife point, and in broad daylight, occur often here and anyone carrying a bag that seems to contain cameras, money or valuables is a target. The area around the **Petit Marché** can seem tense, though given the volume of people, the greatest danger here – and incidentally, in front of the banks – is posed by pickpockets. Apart from these areas, the town still feels quite safe even to walk at night, and by taking precautions (like leaving all bags at your hotel) you're not likely to feel, or be, threatened.

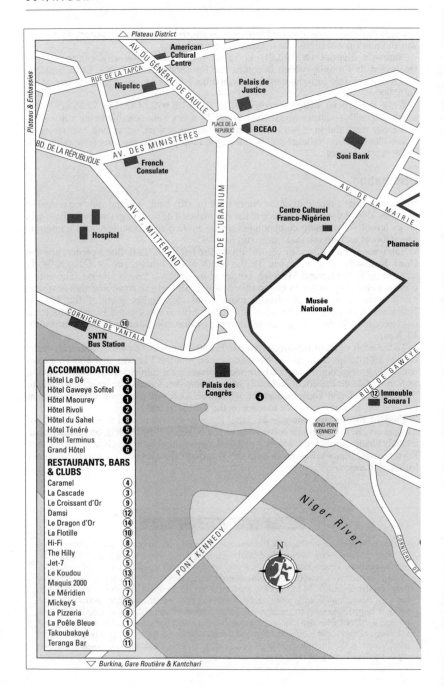

Plateau District

American Cultural Centre

AV. DU GENERAL DE GAULLE

RUE DE LA TAPCA

Nigelec

Palais de Justice

Plateau & Embassies

PLACE DE LA REPUBLIC

BCEAO

BD. DE LA RÉPUBLIQUE

AV. DES MINISTÈRES

French Consulate

Soni Bank

AV. DE LA MAIRIE

AV. F. MITTERAND

AV. DE L'URANIUM

Centre Culturel Franco-Nigérien

Hospital

Phamacie

CORNICHE DE YANTALA

Musée Nationale

⑩

SNTN Bus Station

ACCOMMODATION
Hôtel Le Dé	❸
Hôtel Gaweye Sofitel	❹
Hôtel Maourey	❶
Hôtel Rivoli	❷
Hôtel du Sahel	❽
Hôtel Ténéré	❺
Hôtel Terminus	❼
Grand Hôtel	❻

Palais des Congrès

④

RUE DE GAWEYE

⑫ Immeuble Sonara I

ROND-POINT KENNEDY

RESTAURANTS, BARS & CLUBS
Caramel	④
La Cascade	③
Le Croissant d'Or	⑨
Damsi	⑫
Le Dragon d'Or	⑭
La Flotille	⑩
Hi-Fi	⑧
The Hilly	②
Jet-7	⑤
Le Koudou	⑬
Maquis 2000	⑪
Le Méridien	⑦
Mickey's	⑮
La Pizzeria	⑧
La Poêle Bleue	①
Takoubakoyé	⑥
Teranga Bar	⑪

Niger River

PONT KENNEDY

CORNICHE DE

N

Burkina, Gare Routière & Kantchari

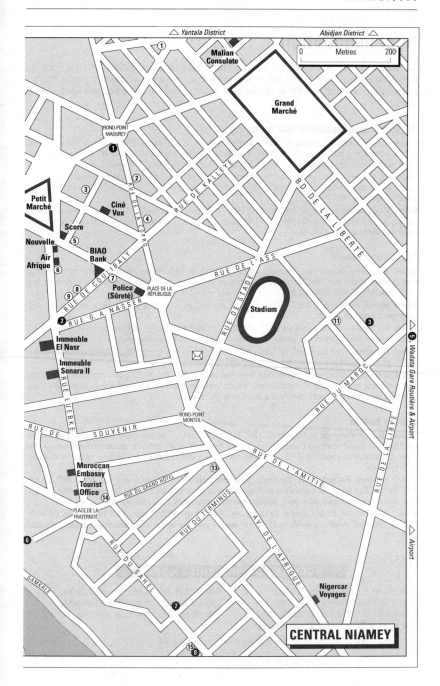

CENTRAL NIAMEY

Accommodation

Although Niamey has a number of mid-range and expensive **hotels**, there are few in the cheaper brackets. Some relief is provided by a couple of shabby places in the centre that can put you up at reasonable rates – and by the **campground** out of town.

Budget accommodation and camping

Camping Touristique, rte de Tillabéri, Yantala district. A well-run site with decent showers and toilets. Ideal if you have a car, but a little out of the way otherwise. The very noisy bar tends to stay open until late. A bus stops nearby every 10–15 minutes on its way to the centre. ①.

Hôtel Le Dé, off the bd de la Liberté and rue du Maroc. Niamey's cheapest rooms, and central enough, but the downstairs bar may keep you awake and you may have to ask them to clean the room in advance. ①.

Hôtel Moustache, av Soni Ali Ber, north of bd de la Liberté (☎73.33.78). Another inexpensive alternative, a bit farther from the centre. S/C rooms with AC; cheaper accommodation is usually reserved for hourly guests. ②.

Mid-range hotels

Hôtel Maourey, Rond-Point Maourey (☎73.28.50). A good location about halfway between the Grand Marché and the Petit Marché. Not nearly up to the standards of hotels like the *Terminus*, but its decent S/C rooms with AC are very reasonably priced. ④.

Hôtel Rivoli, rue Luebke (☎73.38.49). Once a popular place among overlanders, now dusty and somewhat decrepit. ②–③.

Hôtel du Sahel, rue du Sahel (BP 627; ☎73.24.31). Well-maintained and comfortable, with 35 AC rooms (some facing the river), restaurant, disco and various crafts *boutiques*. ④.

Hôtel Terminus, rue du Sahel, (BP 882; ☎73.26.92). Good value, with 38 AC bungalows around a well-kept garden, plus a swimming pool, bar and restaurant. ④.

Les Roniers, Tondibia road, about 7km from the centre (BP 795; ☎72.31.38). Far from the centre and suffering from a lack of overlanders, which perhaps explains its good value. Bungalows are grouped around a park with swimming pool, near the river. ③.

Luxury hotels

Grand Hôtel, Place de la Fraternité (BP 471; ☎73.26.41). Colonial-style hotel which holds its own against more modern competitors, partly because of its striking location overlooking the river. Comfortable rooms and 35 bungalows plus pool and restaurant. The best value in this category. ⑤–⑦.

Hôtel Gaweye Sofitel, Place Kennedy, near the Palais des Congrès and the river (BP 11008; ☎72.34.00). The most distinguished and luxurious of Niamey's hotels, but impersonal. 248 rooms, with river or town views, plus pool, tennis courts, restaurants, bars and nightclubs. ⑦.

Hôtel Ténéré, bd de la Liberté (☎73.20.20). Part of the PLM chain, the *Ténéré* has 55 very comfortable AC rooms, a pool, conference rooms and the usual abundance of restaurants and bars. ⑤.

ACCOMMODATION PRICE CODES

① Under CFA4500 (under £5/$8).
② CFA4500–9000 (£5–10/$8–16).
③ CFA9000–18,000 (£10–20/$16–32).
④ CFA18,000–27,000 (£20–30/$32–48).

⑤ CFA27,000–36,000 (£30–40/$48–64).
⑥ CFA36,000–45,000 (£40–50/$64–80).
⑦ Over CFA45,000 (over £50/$80).

For further information see p.48.

The Town

Niamey isn't exactly brimming with pleasures and pastimes, but it's not difficult to find ways of passing the day. The obvious place to start is the **National Museum** complex, which, apart from exhibits on national peoples and culture, incorporates extensive gardens, a zoo and shops. Niamey also boasts a couple of innovative cultural centres that regularly feature exhibitions, films and theatre and dance performances. The **markets**, too, each with its own character, provide active diversions – the Grand Marché is one of the biggest in the Sahel.

The Musée National

Inaugurated in 1959, the **Musée National** (Tues–Sun: Nov–March 9am–noon & 3.30–6pm; April–Oct 9am–noon & 4–6.30pm; CFA100) was a radical breakthrough at the time and is still out on its own among West African museums. Contained within the extensive grounds are the museum exhibition halls, a zoo, a working crafts centre and a village of Nigérien housing styles. The place feels alive and, especially at weekends, is crowded with an eclectic mix of young and old, foreign and local, scholarly and illiterate.

The main entrance to the grounds is from a side street off the Avenue de la Mairie. Before heading into one of the pavilions housing the exhibition spaces, take a stroll around the **zoo** – especially popular with the young kids from town. A big draw are the hippos in their artificial pond, but cages scattered around the grounds display the other fauna of Niger – lions, hyenas, various monkeys, crocodiles and tortoises, all in a reasonable state of health. Aviaries contain vultures and a variety of more colourful birds.

Each of the museum pavilions – of stylized Hausa architectural design – is dedicated to a theme: for example costumes and jewellery, weapons, handicrafts and musical instruments. The paleontology and botany pavilion contains **dinosaur skeletons** from Gadoufaoua, in the Agadez region. Discovered accidentally by geologists prospecting for uranium, these skeletons are around 100 million years old, and the remote district is today one of the world's most renowned dinosaur sites outside the western USA. In the same pavilion is the amazing **Arbre du Ténéré**, a tree that once stood alone in the Ténéré desert and became a famous overlanders' landmark, until it was knocked over by a truck driver. Formerly the only living thing for hundreds of miles around – and still marked on the Michelin map – the tree was transported to the museum and a sturdy steel replacement erected in the desert.

In a far corner of the park are examples of traditional Nigérien housing – a good opportunity to compare Fula thatched cones, Hausa mud-brick and plaster, Tuareg tents and other styles.

The Centre Artisanale

While at the museum, be sure to check out the Centre Artisanale, or **crafts centre**. Goods sold here are usually more expensive than on the streets (in certain cases substantially so), but part of the profits subsidizes the museum. Quality is controlled, so your silver jewellery won't turn green hours after you buy it or the camel-hide bag smell suspiciously of goat when it gets wet.

Cultural centres

Across from the museum's main entrance, the **Centre Culturel Franco-Nigérien** (Tues–Sat 9am–12.30pm & 4.30–7.30pm) has an active schedule that includes exhibits by local artists and craftsmen, dance and theatre performances, and regular film screenings. You can stop by and pick up their events programme, or check the pages of *Le Sahel*.

Also check the paper for the schedule of the **Centre Culturel Oumarou-Ganda**, named after the late, great Nigérien film-maker and right across on the other side of town on Boulevard Mali Béro, near the Grande Mosquée. The centre has an open-air amphitheatre where concerts of traditional music, ballet and theatre are often staged.

The **Centre Culturel Americain** also sponsors events and runs American news programmes and movies. It's located near Nigelec, the state electricity supplier; ask a taxi to drop you there, and then follow the dirt side street behind the Elf station.

The markets

Niamey's **Grand Marché** (daily until sunset) – also called the Nouveau Marché – makes a decidedly modern statement, with monumental entrance gates and a fountain or two for show, yet the smooth lines and earth tones still respect the more traditional styles of the Sahel. Inside, paved alleys lead through a maze of merchant stalls grouped into sections according to wares – clothing and fabrics; soaps, cosmetics and pharmaceuticals; hardware; ironmongery and utensils, and so forth. Along with the main market in Ouagadougou, this is one of West Africa's finest.

Further south in the **Zongo district**, where rue du Président Luebke and Avenue de la Mairie intersect, the **Petit Marché** has a more casual flavour. Merchants who can't secure a space in one of the Grand Marché stalls simply clear space on the ground and set up shop. It's primarily a **food** market, and you'll find a good selection of fruits and vegetables, meat, fish and grains. People from all over the country converge here to buy and sell – a wide mixture of Fula, Djerma, Tuareg and Hausa. Nearby streets give way to **crafts** stands, which are reasonable places to pick up jewellery, leather goods or blankets – but dealers tend to be aggressive and bargaining can turn into a battle.

There's another small market, devoted entirely to **pottery**, across from the tall SONI Bank down Avenue de la Mairie – look for the beautiful hand-painted water pots produced in the village of Tondibia, just outside Niamey.

Several communities have their own **neighbourhood markets**, usually specializing in everyday domestic goods. At the **Marché Boukoki**, north of Boulevard de l'Indépendance near the Lycée, vendors sell firewood, calabashes, mats, scrap metal and small livestock. In other districts, you'll find the **Marché Yantala** (along Boulevard de la République) and the **Marché Gamkalé** (on the Kollo road).

Eating and drinking

Niamey has a number of upmarket restaurants, and **street vendors** are very common. In the mornings there's a *caféman* on every busy corner, while evening stalls sell *fufu*, rice, macaroni or *tô* (cornmeal dough).

Inexpensive

During the day, you can get really cheap food at the Petit Marché, the Grand Marché or the *gare routière*. For street food after dark – notably beef brochettes or fried omelettes with onions, tomatoes and Maggi sauce – head for the places around rue de Kabekoira, especially in the general area of the Ciné Vox. You can eat at all the places listed below for under CFA1500.

Bar La Terrasse, av de l'Islam. Courtyard bar, open evenings only; rice and macaroni served with fish or mutton.

Buvette de la Piscine, behind the Piscine Olympique on rue du Sahel, near the *Hôtel du Sahel*. Hardly a soul in the day, when it offers cheap beer and a view not to be missed (as good as that from any of the expensive hotel *terrasses*), but at night this is a popular restaurant serving inexpensive grilled chicken, with occasional music and dancing. Take a cab; it's a bit dodgy to walk here after dark.

Caramel (Chez Michel), rue de la Copro. Pastry shop with decent, affordable croissants, brioches and sandwiches (home-made bread).

Chez Ali Houssein, at the main junction near *Hôtel Le Moustache*. Modest but clean and friendly, with a wide menu and pure (bottled) fruit juices.

La Fontaine Bleue, near the PTT. Outdoor restaurant under a roof shelter, with salads, meats and snacks.

The Hilly, rue de la Copro, near *Hôtel Maourey*. Typical outdoor bar where the Béninois chef cooks up, among other things, some of the tenderest brochettes you'll ever taste. Good music and quite lively at night. Recommended.

Le Méridien, rue Coulibaly next to BIAO bank. Fast-food stand serving burgers and *chawarma*.

La Poêle Bleue, Place Liberté, a few blocks from the Grand Marché. Extensive menu includes omelettes, steak sandwiches, freshly made yogurt. Very good prices.

Le Refuge, rue du Maroc, near *Hôtel Le Dé*. Courtyard African place, where the *plat du jour* will set you back little more than CFA1000.

Snack Bar La Cloche, near the corner of rue Luebke and rue du Coulibaly. Salads, sandwiches and *chawarma* just a stone's throw from the Petit Marché. An expat haunt.

Teranga Bar, one block north of rue du Maroc and two blocks south of bd de la Liberté. One of the best African restaurants in town. Meticulously maintained gardens with flowering bougainvillea. Rice, pasta or *couscous* with *capitain*, beef or tripe. Always crowded.

Moderate

From Italian pizza to Ivoirian *poisson braisé*, it's possible to treat yourself to something a little out of the ordinary without spending much more than CFA2500.

Le Croissant d'Or, rue de Coulibaly. Patisserie patronized by French expats – a good sign if you crave something sweet.

Damsi, Immeuble Sonara I (☎73.44.91). French, African and Asian food, all excellent quality. CFA2000–3500.

Maquis 2000, near *Hôtel le Dé* (☎73.55.56). Slightly upmarket Ivoirian food, featuring shellfish and *grillades*.

Marhaba, off rue de Kalleye, near the Grand Marché. "Discovered" by Peace Corps workers and other expats, the chop-house meals at around CFA3000 may seem pricey, but it's a good place to meet people.

Mickey's, rue du Sahel next to the *Hôtel du Sahel*. A big expat hangout (nice sunset views across the river) with beer on tap and very reasonably priced brochettes and fries.

La Pizzeria, rue du Coulibaly, next to *HiFi* (☎74.12.40). Niamey's best pizza, using real mozzarella and fresh vegetables.

Expensive

Niamey has a surprisingly good selection of upmarket places to eat, with the raw ingredients usually imported direct from France. You'll pay up to CFA5000, and even above.

La Cascade, near the Petit Marché (☎73.28.32). The best French restaurant in town, specializing in fish with a variety of interesting sauces. Good wine list, and reasonably priced.

Diamangou, Corniche de Gamkalé (☎73.51.43). French and African dishes served aboard a boat docked in the Niger – one of the town's more interesting venues.

Le Dragon d'Or, rue du Grand Hôtel (☎73.41.23). Wide variety of Chinese food including soups, spring rolls, sweet and sour pork and the like. Very popular.

La Flotille, Corniche de Yantala (☎72.32.54). Russian food cooked by a native. French specialities are also on the menu of this very good – and accordingly expensive – restaurant.

Hôtel Gaweye Sofitel, Place Kennedy. Lavish Sunday breakfast buffet (8–11am) for around CFA4000.

Ize-Gandy, Corniche de Gamkalé. Popular with expats for the French food and the lively disco ambience. Especially crowded at weekends when you can dance under the stars until the wee hours. For safety's sake, take a cab there and back.

Le Koudou, facing the police station near Rond-Point Monteil. Good-value European and African dishes, and good grilled meats.

Tabakady, near the PTT (☎73.58.18). Another well-known French restaurant whose traditional cooking gets high marks from the French community, offering exotic items such as oysters or salmon.

Nightlife

Niamey nights are very low-key, and eating is the principal after-dark pleasure. The bigger hotels have **discos** – the *Kakaki* at the *Gaweye* and the *Fofo* at the *Sahel* – with high covers and expensive drinks; the latter is the looser of the two, and on weekends can be quite fun. Of the **downtown clubs**, the *Takoubakoyé*, near the *Rivoli*, still draws an enthusiastic crowd, though its popularity is seriously challenged by the energetic – at weekends anyway – *Hi-Fi*, just a block away on rue du Coulibaly. *Jet-7*, just by the Score supermarket, offers good music and an informal atmosphere for a reasonable price.

Less expensive entertainment can be found at the *Niamey Club* on rue du Coulibaly near the *Rivoli*. For a small cover, it has good music and occasional live bands, though locally it's known as a bar that caters to Europeans – especially tourists – and is clogged with prostitutes after dark. The *Hilly* near the *Hôtel Maourey* is generally more satisfying, but although this outdoor bar often breaks into dance in the evening (especially Friday and Saturday), there's no guarantee of it.

Listings

Airlines Most are in the area of the Petit Marché, near the *Rivoli*: Air Afrique, Immeuble Air Afrique, rue Luebke (BP 11090; ☎73.30.11); Air Algérie, Immeuble Rivoli (BP 10818; ☎73.38.98); Air France, Immeuble Sonara I (BP 10935; ☎73.31.61); Ethiopian Airlines, Immeuble Sonara (BP 11051; ☎73.50.52 or 73.50.53); Royal Air Maroc, Immeuble El-Nasr (BP 10311; ☎73.28.85).

Banks Most are on, or near, av de la Mairie, most convenient of which are the BIAO and the SONI Bank. Citibank also has a branch in Niamey (☎73.36.20).

Books Try Camico, near the Score supermarket on av de la Mairie, or Papeterie Burama, on rue de la Copro, near the *Hôtel Maourey*.

Car rental Hertz is represented at the *Hôtel Gaweye* and has an office at the airport. Other options are Niger-Car Voyages, av de l'Afrique (☎72.23.31; Fax 73.64.83; on Sun call ☎74.01.67), or Sonauto at the *Hôtel Terminus*. The tourist office can also set you up with a rental agency.

Cinemas The Studio (☎73.37.69) – an AC place with perhaps the town's newest films – and the Vox (☎73.32.19) – an outdoor theatre where old action films often play – are downtown near the Petit Marché. In other districts, you'll find the Cinema Soni Ali-Ber (Haut Niamey), the Cinéma Zarbakan off the av de l'Entente (Poudrière), and the Cinema HD (Yantala).

Embassies and Consulates Algeria, off av de l'Imazer, Plateau district (BP 142; ☎72.35.83); Benin, Plateau district (BP 11544; ☎72.28.60); Canada, Immeuble Sonara II, rue Luebke (☎75.36.86); France, Embassy: bd des Ambassades, Yantala district (BP 10660; ☎72.24.31), Consulate: av des Ministères, by the hospital roundabout (BP 607; ☎72.27.22 or 72.27.33), visas issued for Côte d'Ivoire, Togo, Burkina Faso and Chad; Mali, just off bd de la Liberté, next to the Grand Marché (☎75.24.10); Mauritania, off bd Mali Béro, Yantala district (BP 12519; ☎72.38.43); Morocco, rue Luebke (BP 12403; ☎73.40.84); Nigeria, bd des Ambassades, 400m west of the US embassy (BP 617; ☎73.24.10); UK, Honorary Vice Consulate (BP 11168; ☎73.20.15 or 73.25.39; Fax 73.36.92); USA, bd des Ambassades, Yantala district (BP 12011; ☎72.26.21).

Maps The Direction de la Topographie off bd de la République in Yantala, near the French embassy, has 1:50,000 and 1:2,500,000 coverage of the country. Although there are restrictions on the availability of all survey maps, these are not always applied.

Newspapers and magazines A sprinkling of international papers (mostly French) and news magazines such as *Time* and *Newsweek* are sold in the *Hôtel Gaweye* bookshop. Check also the *tabac* in the *Rivoli* Arcade, the Camico Papeterie, av de la Mairie, near the Score supermarket, and the Papeterie Burama, between av Coulibaly and the *Hôtel Maourey*. For browsing, there's also the library of the American Cultural Centre.

Pharmacies Almost every *quartier* has a small neighbourhood pharmacy. Two of the most central and best stocked are: Pharmacie Kaocen on the rue du Coulibaly (☎73.54.54) and the Pharmacie Nouvelle on rue Luebke.

Post office The PTT is on rue de Kabekoira, down from the Sûreté National, with efficient poste restante (fee for every item collected) and phone services.

Supermarkets The best of the European-style supermarkets is Score on av de la Mairie. It's completely AC and a carbon copy of a Parisian *supermarché* – from the shopping trolleys down to the boxed Camembert. Vegetables and fruit are flown in directly from France – for which you'll pay prices two to three times higher than at source. Next door, Peyrissac is somewhere between a department store and discount hardware store. They may have hard-to-find camping supplies.

MOVING ON FROM NIAMEY

BUSH TAXI AND BUS TRANSPORT FROM WADATA

Peugeot 504s and Japanese minibuses head from the main **Wadata gare routière** north to Tillabéri, south to Dosso and Gaya, east to Birnin-Konni, Maradi and Zinder and northeast to Tahoua and Agadez. Private buses covering the same destinations also leave from this *autogare*. Likewise, taxis for most **international destinations** – Lomé, Kano or Cotonou, for example – leave from Wadata.

TO BURKINA AND SAY

Taxis to Burkina leave from the Rive Droite – across the river from town, near the Douane. This is also where you can catch a *taxi brousse* to Say and possibly on to Tamou (for the Parc National du "W"). To leave quickly, it's best to break up the trip, paying for a seat for anything heading in the direction of Kantchari, the Burkinabe border town. From here, you can catch another bush taxi or, if you arrive fortuitously, the more comfortable Burkinabe Sans Frontières bus that leaves daily for Ouagadougou. Arrive early in the morning as traffic on this stretch is far from dense and after midday, you could wait hours for a vehicle.

SNTN BUSES

The depot for the more comfortable and expensive **SNTN buses** is on the Corniche de Yantala (☎72.30.20), west of the *Hôtel Gaweye*. Take a taxi to the "station" as muggings are frequent along this stretch of the riverbank. There are three buses a week for Ouagadougou (Tues, Wed & Thurs) and a bus for Gao on Sundays. Buses for Arlit – calling at Tahoua and Agadez – leave Monday, Wednesday, and Friday afternoons. A further service heads to Zinder, with stops in Birnin-Konni and Maradi, on Monday. and Saturday. Check with SNTN to confirm times as schedules may vary and are never printed or posted in town. You'll need to buy tickets in advance to be sure of a seat.

FLIGHTS AND TRAVEL AGENTS

You can often get good deals on **flights to Europe** from Niamey, notably with Air Algérie, and Royal Air Maroc has recently had cheap one-way fares **to New York**, including an overnight in Casablanca. For the most current information, contact the airlines direct. Among the **travel agents**, Nigercar-Voyages, av de l'Afrique (☎73.23.31 or 74.01.67 on Sun; Fax 73.64.83), is reliable, and offers a comprehensive set of trips through Niger and surrounding countries. Other travel agents tend to go in and out of business unpredictably.

Swimming pools Non-guests may pay to use the pools of the three major hotels – the *Ténéré*, the *Grand* and the *Gaweye*. The last is the nicest, most central and priciest. Less expensive than any of the above is the Piscine Olympique on rue du Sahel, near the *Hôtel du Sahel*. On most days, you'll have the whole place to yourself.

Visa extensions Get your stay permit extended at the Sûreté, on the corner of rue Nasser and av de la Mairie.

Wrestling Just down from the Centre Culturel Oumarou-Ganda, on bd Mali Bero, the Arène des Jeux Traditionels is a good place to check out a *lutte traditionelle*, at which Niger excels. Scan the paper for announcements.

SOUTHWEST NIGER

Southwest Niger is the greenest and most densely populated part of the country. As well as being an important crossroads for travel between Nigeria, Benin and Burkina, there are some worthwhile destinations in the region, just a few hours' travel out of Niamey, including superb markets to the northeast, and pleasant riverside excursion areas just north of the city.

North of Niamey, the scenic road to Gao in Mali, via **Tillabéri** (the end of the tarmac) and **Ayorou**, hugs the river most of the way. A paved road runs the whole way **south** to the Niger–Nigeria–Benin border at **Gaya**, but it's less interesting scenically than the route north of Niamey. A second southbound route traces the west bank of the river on tarmac to **Say**, before reverting to *piste* en route to Niger's only game reserve, the **Parc National du "W" du Niger**.

Northeast of Niamey: market towns

For a change of pace and a taste of Nigérien rural life, make a trip a few hours out of the city to the northeast. Taxis head daily from Niamey along the scenic route to **Filingué**, passing through the market towns of **Baleyara** – itself worth a day-trip from the capital – and **Bonkoukou**. Considerable regional commerce derives from crop and livestock production, and the paved road runs along a water-worn valley – a vestige of a river that once flowed south from the Sahara into the Niger. It's inspiring scenery, with rugged cliffs and hills all 197 kilometres of the way to Filingué. If you're heading for Tahoua and Agadez, this route provides an alternative to the main highway via Birnin-Konni.

Baleyara

Although the name **BALEYARA** (97km from Niamey) roughly translates as "where Bellah come together", it is primarily a Djerma settlement, where Tuareg, Hausa and Fula people come to trade at the gigantic **Sunday market**. The animal market is well known throughout western Niger, and for days before the market caravans can be seen wending their way towards the village. This is also one of the best places to find hand-woven Fula and Djerma blankets, leather goods, and intricately carved calabashes. There's really nowhere to stay in Baleyara, but there are several bars and no shortage of street food.

Bonkoukou and Filingué

Beyond Baleyara, the road follows the **Dallol Bosso** – a rich valley cut out centuries ago by run-off waters from the Aïr Mountains. Another large depression, the **Dallol Boboy**, extends north of **BONKOUKOU** – a town of semi-sedentary Tuareg that holds an impressive Saturday market. You have to work hard to find crafts at Bonkoukou, but they are here.

A Hausa settlement and administrative town, with characteristic architecture (note the *chef du canton's* house), **FILINGUÉ** boasts another important regional market, though it's less impressive than the two described above. On Sundays, the town snaps into life as traders make their way from the countryside and converge on the market square. Herds of livestock file in and are sold beside millet and other regional produce, and you'll find good buys on crafts ranging from pottery to woven blankets and mats. Filingué is the only town along the route with **accommodation** – *La Villa Verte* (①), a substandard *campement* with bucket showers and kerosene lamps. There's a filling station in town, and a pharmacy, though little else in terms of services apart from a couple of small canned goods stores.

Transport to **Tahoua**, 225km beyond Filingué, depends on demand created by local market days; you may have to wait several hours. The main route – subject to deviations during the rains – passes through **Talcho** (where the tarred surface ends) then veers eastward through an agricultural region dotted with Hausa villages, the largest of which are **Sanam** (market on Tuesday), **Chéguénaron**, and **Tébaram**.

North of Niamey

A small village on the banks of the Niger, **BOUBON** has become a popular weekend rural getaway for Niamey's expatriates. The town is some 25km north of the capital, approached by a small *piste* leading west from the main paved road; **taxis from Niamey** leave from in front of the Petit Marché. The village is especially known for its handmade pottery, sold in vast quantities in Niamey's markets, and is also good for bird-watching. There used to be a government-run *campement* on **Boubon Island**, reached by *pirogue* from the mainland, but it's currently closed pending renovation. Ring the Niamey tourist office to check on progress (☎73.24.47).

Midway between Niamey and Tillabéri, the town of **FARIÉ** used to be an important crossroads, as the only point between Gao and Gaya where cars could cross the river. A **ferry** still links the Niger's banks, and at the end of the dry season there's usually a passable ford, but the Kennedy Bridge in Niamey has removed the crossing's main significance. Although there's nothing of specific interest here, Farié makes a base for scenic riverside meanderings.

A WALK ALONG THE NIGER

If you've missed out on seeing riverside village life from a *pirogue*, a viable, albeit arduous, alternative is to take the four-hour **hike from Farié to Gothèye**. The path takes you close to the Niger through a series of small villages surrounded by vegetable gardens and mango orchards. After the rains, rice is grown in the shallows, but a short distance inland, the verdure soon gives way to Sahelian savannah with cattle and goats getting meagre nourishment from the gleanings of the harvest. Occasional water holes provide some good **bird-watching** opportunities: golden orioles are common.

The Djerma-speakers who inhabit the villages are unused to tourists, especially those on foot, and are keen to communicate – even if "Ça ba?" is about the limit of the conversation. The general greeting in Djerma, *Fofo* (literally "Thank you"), goes a long way in breaking the ice.

There are plenty of opportunities to **camp** along the riverbank, but you'll need to bring everything with you. Supplies in the whole region are sparse. From the Niamey–Tillabéri road, it is 2km down to the vehicle ferry at Farié which crosses every hour during the day (10min). A **path** then leads upstream from the tiny market on the far side and stays roughly parallel to the road.

The route to Burkina: Gothèye and Téra

A viable, if slow, alternative to the direct Niamey–Ouagadougou route is to cross the river at Farié and continue 10km north towards **Gothèye**, which has basic food supplies and a bar/restaurant, but no fuel. The Sunday market boosts the otherwise limited traffic flow. Here, the road – now paved all the way to Téra – veers "inland", away from the river towards northern Burkina Faso. The route passes through occasional villages among the millet stubble and acacia, but as the road climbs away from the river, larger trees and more intensive cultivation take over. Some 40km further, **Dargol** only comes to life for the Friday market. The next stop along the route, **Bandio**, has a small Saturday market, but otherwise no facilities.

The largest town in the region, **TÉRA** is backed by an earth dam that forms a reservoir after the rains (July–Dec). Built in the early 1980s to irrigate rice and bean fields, the reservoir and the pools below are now the focus of village life. The only **accommodation** is in the rudimentary *campement* (①), which has no water or electricity. Their bar-restaurant is one of the only places to eat apart from streetside stalls.

SNTN leave Niamey for Téra on Wednesdays and Saturdays, returning the following days; minibuses go from the Wadata *gare routière*. If you're heading to Burkina Faso, leave your passport at the police checkpoint over the bridge on the way into town. They'll hold it until you leave, and stamp you out of Niger as this doubles as the border control. The *gare routière* and two filling stations are near the market on the opposite side of town to the *campement*.

Into Burkina

The most direct route to Burkina Faso from Téra is via Dori, but it may be quicker to take a back route to **Falangountou**, along a narrow track across open savannah dotted with acacia, baobab and occasional Fula villages. Burkinabe formalities are efficiently dealt with in Falangountou, and from there your route will depend on local market days. From Téra, vehicles leave either to Dori or towards Gorom-Gorom via Asakam (12km; Sunday market) and Gozé (13km further on).

Until a gold mining company moved into **Gozé** ten years ago, there was nothing in the village. Now, despite the company's departure, it is booming. Hundreds of ex-employees and hopeful immigrants prospect by hand, digging tunnels up to 20 metres deep and trading their gains along the dusty main street. There are few facilities in town, but it is only 25km on to Gorom-Gorom.

Tillabéri and Kokomani

A Djerma town, and an important agricultural centre surrounded by fields of rice and millet, **TILLABÉRI** was never very lively even in the days when it saw a steady stream of overlanders grateful for the paved road after enduring hundreds of miles of thundering desert *piste*. Moreover, since the drought of the 1980s, the **giraffe herds** that once roamed the wooded savannahs and provided a tourist attraction have migrated further south, and there's little to do in town besides take in the **market** – notably on the big trading days, Sunday and Wednesday.

Tillabéri is a good place for a roadside stop, however, as it has a number of small **restaurants** and **bars**, some with fridges. There are modest and affordable **rooms** at the *Relais Touristique* (②–③), which tries to bolster tourism by offering *pirogue* rides.

On a Wednesday, a better destination than Tillabéri is **KOKOMANI**, a small riverside village 24km downstream, which bursts into life for its weekly market. The water's edge is littered with *pirogues* as hundreds of people squeeze into interconnected courtyards resonating with the sound of braying donkeys and the calls of calabash carvers working under low wooden shelters.

Ayorou

AYOROU, 88km north of Tillabéri, is a quiet Songhai fishing village on weekdays. But on Sundays the population is swelled by a diversity of Sahelian peoples who, having crossed the river by *pirogue* or the savannah by mule, camel or on foot, converge for the weekly **market**. Famous throughout West Africa, it's an event well worth catching.

An important element is the **animal market**, the main draw for nomads – Fula cattle herders, Tuareg with their camels, and Bello with mules. Songhai, Djerma and Sorko people bring fruits and vegetables, various grains, fish, goats and chickens, while Moorish (Mauritanian) merchants, in distinctive light blue robes and white headscarves, run their typical general stores. Traders also sell traditional medicine and a variety of **regional crafts**, especially jewellery and leatherwork.

Though most of Ayorou crouches along the eastern bank of the river, the oldest part of town, with traditional *banco* houses, spreads over the island of **Ayorou Goungou**. You can rent a *pirogue* to visit it, or one of the surrounding islands, at the mooring point near the market square. Your chances of seeing **hippopotamus** along this stretch of the river are good, and exotic **birds** are common, especially near the island of **Firgoun**, 12km north of town.

Ayorou's sole **hotel** is the *Hôtel Amenokal* (⑥), which was closed for renovation at the time of writing.

If you have time for a jaunt downstream , you might want to take a **pirogue from Ayorou to Tillabéri** after the market closes – a one-day voyage, setting off Sunday evening or Monday morning. The trip involves plenty of weaving between the rapids and manoeuvring down narrow channels and there are some particularly exciting rapids just before you enter Tillabéri. There's no fixed price. During or shortly after the rainy season – when the river is high enough – you may even be able to rent a *pirogue* to take you as far as Niamey.

South of Niamey

South of Niamey towards the Benin border, the main road and river separate, joining up again only at Gaya. Near the town of **Kouré**, 60km down the road from the capital, the **giraffe herds** that once were the pride of Tillabéri, have found refuge from drought and poaching in the surrounding countryside. In the rainy season, this is an easy daytrip from Niamey: taxis to Kouré are no problem, and there's no shortage of local kids eager to take you to the giraffes. Expect to be mobbed, but choose a guide nonetheless, as they know where the herds are located. With luck, you may walk no more than a couple of kilometres before spotting two dozen of these extraordinary animals sailing by in their slow-motion canter; however a ten-kilometre trek is not uncommon. In either case the experience is well worth it, even more so given that these are some of the last giraffes left in West Africa. In the dry season the herds migrate again, well out of walking distance from the town.

Further south, the road passes through the important trading town of **DOSSO**, which occupies a crossroads position between Niamey, Benin, Maradi and Zinder. The *gare routière* is frenetic and there's a large market (though, importantly, no bank). Dosso still has its traditional Djerma chief who lives in the *Djermakoye* – a compound built in the Sudanic style. With permission you should be able to visit it. **Accommodation** is pretty much limited to the *Hôtel Djerma*, which charges science-fiction rates for some very average fanned rooms (☎65.02.06; ③), and the far preferable *Auberge du Carrefour*, on the Route de Niamey, which has simple rooms with a choice of fan or AC (☎65.00.17; ②). *Bar Koubeyni* (①), just around the corner, is the cheapest place in town; the rooms are very simple and have outside toilets. The town is teeming with bars and places to eat.

GAYA is the last town in Niger before crossing the river into Benin. If you decide to stay – the border post is now open 24 hours – you can choose between the cheap *Hôtel Dendi* (①), right by the *autogare*, offering simple, clean fanned rooms with water and electricity, or the upmarket *Hôtel Hamdallah* (③), about 1km from town, on the main road northeast, which has a bar and restaurant. You may notice people in your taxi heading to a house near the *gare routière*, where they get mats to sleep on the earth floor inside. People pay next to nothing for this privilege and there's no reason not to join them, though you'll elicit some embarrassed laughter.

Parc National du "W" du Niger

Part of the vast reserve that spreads across into Burkina Faso and Benin, the **Parc National du "W" du Niger** (pronounced *double-vé* and named after the double U-bend in the Niger River) covers 2200 square kilometres in Niger alone. It's one of West Africa's better game parks and relatively good for animal-watching, with herds of **elephant** concentrated in the Tapoa valley and **buffalo** (*buffle*) on the wooded savannahs. Reports still come in of **lions** and **leopards** roaming the park, but they stay very well hidden. Easier to spot are antelope – waterbuck (*cob de buffon* or *cob defassa*) and **duiker** especially, as well as the big roan antelope (*hippotrague*) and hartebeest (*bubale*) – and large troops of **baboons** (*babouins*) scampering through the bush, often near the camp (see opposite). **Warthogs** (*phacochères*) and **hippos** are also quite common. The park

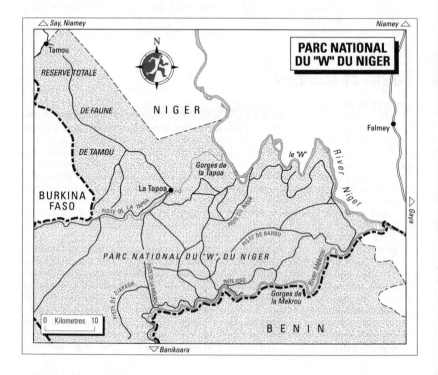

counts some 300 species of **birds**, with good showings of storks, herons and ibis. When the rainy season begins in June the park closes down, and doesn't usually reopen until early December, after the 400-odd kilometres of *piste* have been groomed.

The park entrance is 150km south of Niamey, via **Say** and **Tamou**. For the last 40 kilometres, after turning south at Tamou, the route runs through the **Réserve Totale de Faune de Tamou**, an appendage of the main park. If you're not driving or on an organized tour (and a visit to the park is hard to arrange otherwise), public transport from Niamey will get you as far as Say, where you may have to change to head on to Tamou. You're not likely to get down to La Tapoa without a lift from a park administration vehicle or from fellow travellers. At the park entrance you pay for a visitor's permit valid for the duration of your stay. You can also pick up a road map that is quite detailed and useful for orientation, though an accompanying guide is obligatory. The main **park accommodation** is the *Hôtel de la Tapoa* (HB; ⑤–⑥), at the village of **La Tapoa**, on the edge of the reserve. It has comfortable bungalows or AC rooms grouped around the swimming pool, and you can make reservations in Niamey at the **tourist office**, or through any travel agent. Nigercar Voyages (see p.891) has set up a safari-style *campement* (HB; ④), about 40km east of *Hôtel Tapoa*.

SOUTHERN NIGER

Southern Niger is the nation's richest agricultural belt. It also contains the bulk of the country's population and is home to the biggest ethnic group, the **Hausa**. Renowned traders and leatherworkers, with a long history of regional statehood, they are energetically commercial, the vigour of their towns enhanced today by the region's proximity to Nigeria.

From Dogondoutchi to Birnin-Konni

Two hundred and thirty kilometres east of Niamey, **DOGONDOUTCHI** (commonly shortened to "Doutchi") is a small town surrounded by sculpted red cliffs reminiscent of a cowboy movie backdrop. It's inhabited by the **Maouri**, a people of Hausa origin who consistently refused to adopt Islam, even in the nineteenth century when the Sokoto jihad led to the conversion of the entire region. Islam has made some inroads in recent years, but this is still a stronghold of traditional beliefs, and local fetishers – notably the old chief of the nearby village of Baoura Bawa – are respected and feared. They're said to have control even over the elements.

Doutchi's only **place to stay**, the new *Hôtel Magama* (☎282; ①–②), signposted about 200m from the bus park, has clean, comfortable bungalows and a friendly bar-restaurant.

Birnin-Konni

BIRNIN-KONNI is an attractive and soulful town, with traditional *banco* houses and characteristic dome-shaped granaries in the older neighbourhoods around the market. Its Hausa prosperity is owed to its position on the border. Some neighbourhoods actually spill into Nigeria, and a paved road pushes through the town to Sokoto, only 93km south. There's a lot of **trafficking** going on in these parts – most notably of cheap Nigerian fuel, which you can buy from jars on the streets for a fraction of the price you'd pay at the pumps. Birnin-Konni also lies in one of the country's most fertile regions – the main streets are shaded by towering trees which were planted during the colonial period, and the **market** has a range of goods and produce that are expensive and scarce further north (Wednesday is the main day of trading). The rows of moneychangers seated on grass mats along the main street surrounded by piles of Nigerian *naira* and CFA francs attest to the amount of cross-border trade. In fact, the street is the only place where you can change money – and, of course, it's cash only.

Accommodation

Birnin-Konni has a couple of comfortable and affordable **places to stay**. You'll find decent rooms and bungalows plus camping facilities at the *Relais Touristique* (☎338; ①–②). Their bar and restaurant are pretty good, and they sometimes pull the TV onto the terrace in the evenings – a chance to see Niger's tiny TV station (Télé-Sahel) at work. The more upmarket *Kado Hôtel* (☎364; ②–③) has S/C rooms (AC optional), some of which are upstairs and have interesting streetside views. If you're broke, the choice is between a simple *campement* (①), with showers and fans, just up the road from the *Kado*, or the *Hôtel Wadata* (①), just behind the *autogare*, which looks like an old caravanserai and is just as basic. The *Kado*'s restaurant does appetizing continental breakfasts and *poulet frites* at night, and across the street is a rather good **disco**.

Maradi

Sometimes dubbed Niger's "groundnut capital", as over half the country's crop is grown in the surrounding region, **MARADI** – Niger's third largest town – lies in an area of nascent industrialization. Formerly it was a province of Katsina, one of the original seven Hausa city-states, which lies over the Nigerian border, just 90km south. After the nineteenth-century Sokoto jihad, Hausa refugees fled to Maradi and eventually overthrew the Fula here. Sokoto and Maradi remained at odds for years afterwards.

Despite its historical links, Maradi has lost much of its traditional flavour (an anonymous-looking grid of streets was laid out in the 1950s) but it isn't devoid of interest. Foremost among the "sights" is the **Place Dan Kasswa**, bordered by the **Grande Mosquée** and the **Chief's Palace** – a colourful and typically Hausa confection. The **marketplace** is also impressive, spreading over a couple of blocks along the main Katsina road. You'll find a vast array of produce grown in the region or imported from Nigeria, at prices much lower than in Niamey (Monday and Friday are the main days). Over by the Hôtel de Ville there's a shady public garden, with gazebo-like bar in the middle and a church nearby.

Practicalities

The town's least expensive **accommodation** is at the *Campement Administrative* (①), which has decent rooms, but it's quite a way out of town. Other low-priced options include *Hôtel Liberté* (☎41.03.80; ①–②), which has some S/C rooms with AC. To find it, ask for the hotel's *BLB Bar*. For a little luxury, the four-star *Hôtel Jan Gorzo* (☎51.01.40; ④) on the Route de l'Aéroport, about 3km from town, has a nightclub, one of the town's better restaurants and a **pool** (open to non-guests for a fee, assuming it has water). In the same league is the *Guest House* (☎41.07.54; ⑤) reached by following the signs on the east side of the Katsina road, then turning right at the old water tower. The four AC rooms, two of them S/C, are the nicest in Maradi, and the European-style restaurant has a devoted following. The *Babylon Palace* (☎41.04.65; ④), by the Dan Kasswa mosque, has ten S/C rooms, all with AC, and a good bar and restaurant.

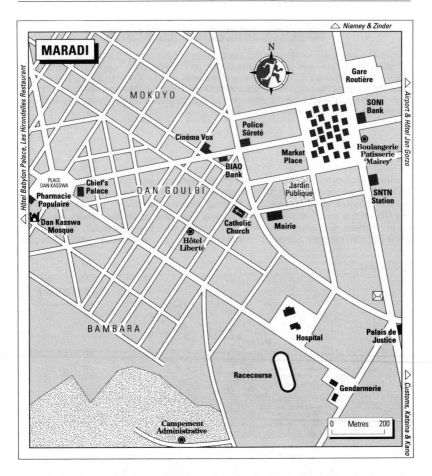

Map labels: Niamey & Zinder / MARADI / MOKOYO / Gare Routière / SONI Bank / Police Sûreté / Cinéma Vox / Market Place / Boulangerie Patisserie 'Mairey' / BIAO Bank / Jardin Publique / SNTN Station / PLACE DAN KASSWA / Chief's Palace / DAN GOULBI / Pharmacie Populaire / Dan Kasswa Mosque / Catholic Church / Mairie / Hôtel Liberté / BAMBARA / Hospital / Palais de Justice / Racecourse / Gendarmerie / Campement Administrative / Hôtel Babylon Palace, Les Hirondelles Restaurant / Airport & Hôtel Jan Gorzo / Customs, Katsina & Kano / 0 Metres 200

Look in and around the market for inexpensive Nigérien eating houses. *Le Yorumba*, just north of the *gare routière*, and the *Cercle de l'Amitié* are two good places for rice with beef scraps served in a soup, and other inexpensive regional dishes. In the evenings, the Jardin Publique is a popular spot for grilled chicken cooked and served in outdoor stands. *Les Hirondelles*, across from the Dan Kasswa cinema, is good for rice and meat dishes and local specialities like goat's head soup, served with a cold beer. The *Mairey* is the only ·patisserie in town, and good for snacks and cakes.

Maradi has a number of useful facilities. There are two **banks** – the BIAO, across from the Sûreté, and the SONI, on the Katsina road across from the market. The **post office** is also on the Katsina road, near the Palais de Justice. One street north of the Sûreté, you can get **car parts** at the SONIDA store, or try Auto Service near the SONI. For medical needs, head to the Pharmacie Populaire, on Place Dan Kasswa, or to the **hospital**, in the south of town.

Zinder

Formerly the largest town in Niger and briefly capital of the French colony, sleepy **ZIN-DER** has more recently seen its influence slide. It's still Niger's second city, but much of the commerce with Nigeria – long the main source of its wealth – now bypasses it via Maradi, on the faster Kano–Niamey highway. But even in decline, Zinder remains a centre of trade, as a quick stroll through the impressive Grand Marché confirms. Nor has it lost all its former glories: it retains some of the finest **traditional Hausa archi-**

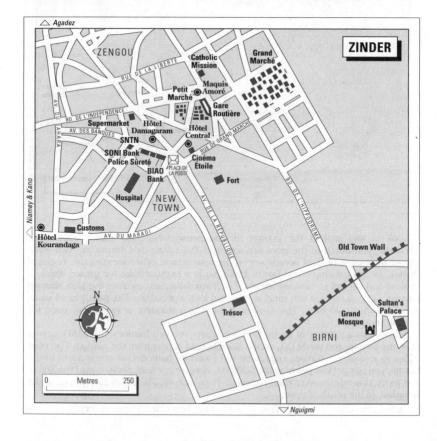

tecture anywhere, and the old town of **Birni** is even better preserved than its Nigerian counterparts in Kano, Zaria or Katsina.

Some history

The **sultanate** of Zinder was founded by the Kanouri, descendants of the Kanem Bornu empire of the Lake Chad region. They settled here after being chased from northern territories by Tuareg invaders, and mixed with the Hausa population which itself had fled the region of Sokoto under pressure from the Fulani. In the eighteenth and nineteenth centuries, the Kanouri and Hausa joined forces to found the powerful **Damagaram state**, of which Zinder was capital. The sultan is still Kanouri.

Zinder reached its apogee in the mid-nineteenth century under the reign of **Tamimoum**, who greatly enlarged the boundaries of Damagaram, introduced new crops and developed trade. Under his rule, a vast wall or *birni* was erected around the town. Originally ten metres high and fourteen deep, this wall has long since crumbled, but its ruins can still be seen around the old town. According to legend, the structure's invincibility was ensured by incorporating into the walls a number of Korans and several virgin girls. Under subsequent rulers, however, Zinder's fortunes were tied more to those of the slave trade than to magic. By the 1890s, one of the Sahel region's biggest **slave markets** was regularly held here. To support his empire, the sultan led frequent raids on vassal villages and captives were sold in town, taken to Kano and then force-marched down to the coast. The **French** captured Zinder in 1899. With a population well in excess of 20,000, it was by far the region's biggest metropolis at the time and remained the effective capital of Niger until 1927.

The Town

Zinder comprises three separate districts, so distinct they're almost individual towns. To the north, **Zengou** was the original Hausa settlement, formerly a stopping point for camel caravans. **Birni** – the old fortified town and site of the sultan's palace and Grande Mosquée – lies about a kilometre to the southeast. Between the two is the **new town**, with administrative buildings laid out in characteristic French colonial style.

The most obvious attraction in town is the old quarter of **Birni**, reached from the new town by following Avenue de la République south beyond the old French fort (still used by the Nigérien military). This will take you past the **Grande Mosquée**, the front of which gives onto a large public square facing the **Sultan's Palace**, a two-storey *banco* building set apart by its size. There are tombs of the former sultans in the grounds, which you should be able to visit with authorization from the Mairie. Another noteworthy residence is that of the Fulani chief, just east of the mosque; the facade is decorated with colourful raised motifs, a common feature of Hausa architecture. All of Birni's buildings have been left in the traditional style, and walking through the narrow streets you get a real sense of what life was like in Zinder's heyday a century ago.

Although **Zengou** has its fair share of modern cement buildings and corrugated iron roofs – elements that are completely absent in Birni – the **traditional flavour** is still strong. The oldest house in Zinder is in this quarter, and some of the town's showiest examples of Hausa architecture have been built here by the wealthier merchants. The pride in this style of decoration is by no means dead, and new, quite innovative, examples are commissioned all the time.

Zinder's **Grand Marché**, one of the country's biggest, has long been an important way-station between the Sahel and the regions to the south. Thursday is the main trading day. Salt pillars brought down from the Ténéré are sold next to the **animal market**, with its Tuareg, Fulani and Bousou traders. Hausa and other peoples from the south sell a variety of local and imported goods in and around the arcaded market building, which dates from the colonial period. This is perhaps the best place in the country to get low-price, quality **leather**, for which the Hausa have a long-standing reputation: sandals, bags, pouffes and pouches are sold around the market or by wandering merchants. Craftsmen also sell their wares direct from a number of workshops in the district.

Services are entirely concentrated in the **new town**. They include the hotels and better restaurants, three **banks** (BIAO, SONI and BCEAO), the **post office** and a couple of **supermarkets**. There's also an outdoor cinema, L'Etoile.

Practicalities

For such a large town, Zinder doesn't have an overabundance of **hotels**. The two main ones are both located off the central Place de la Poste. The *Hôtel Central* (☎51.20.13; ②–③) is the cheaper alternative, a colonial-style pile with average comfort – rooms with shower and fan. The outdoor bar-restaurant is a popular place in the evening; people often hook up here before going to the cinema or out on the town. Up the street, the *Hôtel Damagaram* (☎51.00.69; ③–④) is bigger, nicer and correspondingly more expensive. Its furnished AC rooms are considered the best in Zinder and the restaurant is excellent too.

The **least expensive places** in town are a number of small hotel-bar-restaurants clustered in Zengou, about twenty minutes' walk past the *Central* in the Agadez direction. The *Hôtel Kalkadamou*, also known as *Hadji Hata* (①), is the best of them, with clean, fanned rooms with shower. Heading out of the centre the other way, the Kano road leads past the customs building (where, if you're driving, you may or may not be stopped), and on to the *Hôtel Kourandaga* (☎51.07.42; ②–③). Spacious Hausa-style rooms surround a courtyard, and, built over a spring, it has its own reliable water supply – there's even hot water on tap. There are a couple of cheaper fanned rooms. This is where Zinder's middle classes go for a quiet drink; you might meet the chief of police or the mayor. The restaurant does good meals at slightly high prices.

Street **food** is easy to find in town, especially in the Place de la Poste, across from the *Hôtel Central*. For something a little upmarket, try *El Ali*, behind Nigelec, which serves good chicken and *steack frites* in an attractive garden of banana trees, papayas and formidable *paillotes*. The *Maquis Amore*, near the *gare routière*, has good, cheap local and European food. Watch the hygiene everywhere, as Zinder's **water** is considered suspect and usually needs purifying.

For **night-time** drinking, the *Scotch Bar*, near the market, is popular, and the *Damagaram* and the *Central* hotels both have nightclubs. Popular spots you could check out in town include the *Pacifique*, well known by expats, and the *La Cascade*. For something a little less local in flavour, you could – if feeling homesick, decadent, or a combination of the two – try the *Club Privé*. Besides a swimming pool, and sports facilities, it has a classy bar open until 2am on weekdays and 24 hours at weekends. Officially, you can only enter upon introduction by a member; some smooth talking may be in order. For dancing, the open air *Babylon Palace,* near the Catholic Church, has a friendly atmosphere.

MOVING ON FROM ZINDER

SNTN buses link Zinder to Niamey (departing Tues and Sun at dawn), Nguigmi (Mon and Fri) and Agadez (Sat). The *gare SNTN* is on the Avenue de la République across from *Hôtel Damagaram*. Private buses and bush taxis leave from the **gare routière** near the Petit Marché and connect with all major towns. **Taxis** also head regularly to Kano in Nigeria along a good road; it works out a little cheaper to take a vehicle to the border, where you can easily find a taxi continuing to Kano.

For advice on security in the region, see box, p.862.

Zinder to Agadez

The journey north **from Zinder to Agadez** (see p.904) can be accomplished comfortably in a day. If you're driving, it's worth taking your time on this stretch, as it's a relatively narrow band of the Sahel, with sights you won't get elsewhere. The **Kel Gress Tuareg** live in the region in their huts of fibre matting. There are tall **Sodom apple trees** as well as many smaller, sometimes colourful, plants, and you might see an **ostrich** or two. Be careful walking in what appear to be tufts of grass – the seeds have a casing like a small, horse chestnut, the spikes of which draw blood.

The small town of **Tanout**, 140km north of Zinder, is a good stopping point for a cold drink, and sometimes has petrol. Several wells beyond Tanout contain water – for which you'll need a forty-metre rope. At the little village of **Aderbissinat**, there's sometimes a cursory police check, and foreigners stopping here are regarded with interest and curiosity by traders in the market (leather, sweets and basic food). There's usually a fuel dump with diesel and petrol on the right of the road, as you leave the village. The road then passes near the **Falaise de Tiguidit**, an escarpment with a wonderful view back across the plain.

On to Lake Chad

This infrequently travelled route heads through a region that was part of the Kanem Bornu empire up to the nineteenth century, and today is peopled by Hausa, Kanouri, Dangara and Manga. The road is sealed all the way, albeit with numerous potholes, particularly around Gouré, occasional sand-drifts around Maïné-Soroa and the usual hazards of animals and large birds in your path. Just 22km east of Zinder you arrive at **MIRIA**, the first **oasis** in these arid parts. The gardens here harbour date palms and groves of mango and guava. Sunday is the main **market day**; look out for local pottery.

A further 144km brings you to the small *sous-préfecture* of **GOURÉ**, and its overpriced and rudimentary *campement* (②). It's another 330km to **Maïné-Soroa**, the next place of any size, where the people make a living drawing salt from the earth. The desert looms close to the east of town, and you can see large dunes from the roadside. **DIFFA**, an administrative town on the banks of the **Komadougou River** – which sometimes flows into Lake Chad – is 75km further and has the last reliable filling station for eastbound drivers. The *Hôtel Kanady* (☎54.03.32; ②–③), in front of the filling station, has clean and comfortable S/C, AC and fanned rooms and a reasonable bar-restaurant.

Finally you arrive at **NGUIGMI**, a full 1500km from Niamey and nearly 600km from Zinder. An important town during the days of the Kanem Bornu empire, when it was home to the semi-nomadic Kanouri princes, Nguigmi became wealthy from its position on the trade routes to the **Kaourar oases** (whence salt was brought by caravans) and, of course, from its site on the shores of **Lake Chad**. Today access to the lakeshore is difficult: it has shrunk much farther south and virtually disappears in periods of drought. Indeed, at times the closest standing water to the town is 100km to the south. Nguigmi is devoid of basic facilities (including filling stations), so stock up in Diffa. You can ask the local churches to put you up for the night. An SNTN bus leaves for Zinder (Wed and Sat). An extremely arduous *piste* leads north of here to Bilma. If you're heading **into Chad**, Nguigmi is where you take your official leave of Niger and drive, or find a ride, east, then south, around the lake zone to Ndjamena.

THE NIGÉRIEN SAHARA

To travel through the north of Niger takes some determination. It's a region with a stifling climate, great expanses of emptiness between the towns and very little water. From Niamey, a paved road leads the whole way to the boomtown of **Arlit** – the northernmost major settlement – passing through the commercial centre of **Tahoua** and the historic Tuareg stronghold of **Agadez**. Other interesting sites are extremely hard to reach and require preparation and a good guide.

The effort and expense is rewarded by beautiful **desert oases** which eke out a living from the **salt trade**, and the continued spectacle of **camel caravans**. Trips through the volcanic moonscapes of the **Aïr region**, or through the awesome dunes of the **Ténéré desert** also provide opportunities to visit a wealth of **prehistoric sites** – including the rock paintings near **Iferouâne** – and a number of **springs and waterfalls**.

> For advice on security in the region, see box, p.862.

Tahoua

Niger's fourth largest town, **TAHOUA** is a major stopping point on the main road between Niamey and Agadez. Despite a population of over 40,000 and a wide mix of peoples, the town hasn't really warmed up to travellers – indeed it was expressly closed to them until the mid-1980s. There's little to detain you here except the authorities – and even the rosy dunes that have settled permanently on the edge of town, while pretty examples of their kind, aren't worth a special detour.

Primarily a commercial centre, Tahoua does, however, boast a singularly animated **market** – the building is itself an attractive example of Sahel-inspired architecture. It's one of those places where everyone in Niger – Djerma, Hausa, Bororo, Fula, Tuareg, the odd tourist – comes together, notably on Sunday, the main trading day. The nomads bring salt pillars, dates, livestock and leather, which they sell to regional farmers who provide grain, cotton, spices, peanuts, tobacco and locally made indigo fabrics. Look out for the intermediaries called *dillali*, who bring together traders, help them strike a deal and even serve as translators.

Practicalities

Tahoua's most useful facilities are the two **banks**, in the town centre, SONI Bank and BIAO, which change travellers' cheques for a small commission. **Accommodation** is limited. On a budget, head to the shady and moderately hygienic *camping* (①) about 2km west of town, next to the *arènes des jeux traditionels* (wrestling arenas). In town, the cheapest place to stay is the run-down *Hôtel Galabie* (①–②). More expensive are the AC *Hôtel de l'Amitié* (☎61.00.61; ③), about 1km from the centre, and *Les Bungalows de la Mairie* (☎61.05.53; ③), across from the town hall and surrounded by pleasant gardens, with furnished AC bungalows and a recommended **restaurant**. Another good restaurant is *Les Délices*, just down the road from the *Bungalows*.

Agadez

AGADEZ has been a major stopping point on the trans-Saharan routes for hundreds of years. You can read its history through buildings like the **Grande Mosquée** – a monument known throughout West Africa – or the more prosaic **camel market**, which has been drawing the peoples of the Sahel here for generations. While the salt caravans still come from Bilma, they do so very rarely, and after the uprisings of the early 1990s, coupled with the trouble in Algeria, other once-common visitors, such as cross-Sahara travellers, tour groups and even film crews, have tapered off as well. The discovery of uranium to the north, and the roads linking Agadez to Niamey and Zinder still offer hope of future prosperity, but for now the town seems cut off in dusty isolation.

Some history

In the fourteenth century, Agadez was a small but expanding town, a **centre of commerce** where Arabs from Tripoli traded with the Hausa from Nigeria and the Songhai from Gao. By the fifteenth century it was on its way to becoming the **capital of the Tuareg** – as far as such a thing existed for the nomads – and in 1449, a **sultanate** was established under the leadership of **Ilissaouane**. Fifty years later, the town came to be controlled by the Songhai and throughout the sixteenth century, Agadez marked the northernmost point of their great empire, with a huge population, for the time, of perhaps 30,000.

After the Songhai were defeated by the Moroccans, the Tuareg regained the town, but like other trading posts in the region it was already entering a period of long decline. Agadez fared better than most, however, thanks in large measure to its location near the

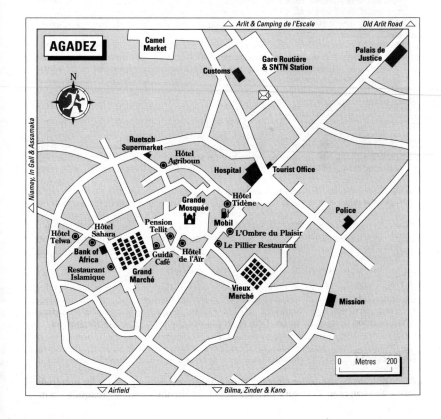

FESTIVALS IN THE AGADEZ REGION

The town of Agadez celebrates the Muslim holidays in style, especially the end of **Ramadan**, **Tabaski** and the **prophet's birthday**. Festivities marking these events begin with a morning prayer led by the *imam*, who then kills a lamb according to tradition. Families return to their homes for a feast, after which the entire town reassembles along the streets between the mosque and the sultan's palace, as drummers announce the recommencement of festivities. Men gather on horseback, among them the red-turbanned sultan's guards, ready for the **cavalcades**, the highlight of the celebrations that last until sundown and then pick up again the next day. When the signal is given, the riders race their horses at a frenzied pace, kicking up clouds of dust. Men, women and children all strain for a better look, pressing dangerously close to the horsemen, who halt their charge in front of the palace, where the sultan and dignitaries are gathered. The elaborate costumes, the music and the excitement of the races leave an indelible impression – you won't regret making an effort to be in town for the festivities.

THE CURE SALÉE

Along with the Muslim festivals, one of the more interesting celebrations of the nomadic Fula and Tuareg is the **Cure Salée**, a traditional homecoming that takes place some time after the rains, between July and September. Herders who have migrated to the far south in the dry season return to the region around **In-Gall**, west of Agadez, when the large salt flats fill with water. It's a period for fattening the animals and giving them the "salt cure", punctuated by festivities including music, dancing and, frequently, camel races.

During the month of September, the **Bororo** – a nomadic Fula people – stage a remarkable ceremony called the **Gerewol**, as part of their *Cure Salée* celebrations. Often likened to a beauty pageant, this is a party for unmarried men, who spend hours adorning themselves with jewellery and putting on make-up – red ochre on the face, white outlines for features like the nose and mouth, black on the lips and round the eyes. Elaborate hairpieces are also concocted with scarves, beads, braids and feathers. Having prepared themselves to emphasize Bororo ideals of male beauty – long slender bodies, bright white teeth and eyes, and straight hair – the bachelors line up in the festival arena to dance, roll their white eyes, flash their broad smiles and chant a droning melody. The young women, who also spend a considerable amount of time beautifying themselves, look on, and one by one come forward and take their choice of the most handsome man. According to custom, if a girl doesn't like the husband proposed for her by her parents, she can marry the man she desires, chosen at the *Gerewol*. A man who isn't happy with his new partner has some difficulty getting out of the social obligation to spend a night with her, but numerous weddings do take place over the course of the *Cure Salée*. Another Bororo *Cure Salée* event is the virility test known as the **Soro**. Here men stand in front of their girlfriends and allow other men to strike them several times across the chest. To show their courage to their loved one, they're expected to smile as they're beaten.

These elaborate demonstrations of manliness are part of an extensive and complex **codified social life**, which characterizes many pastoral peoples – it's similar in many respects, for example, to that of the Maasai, Samburu and Dinka in East Africa – and which finds expression in a mesh of taboos and ritual behaviour maintaining extraordinary social cohesion and group identity.

Although the events at the Bororo *Cure Salée* have been filmed and photographed often enough to make them relatively familiar images, the occasion is not a tourist spectacle and it's difficult to arrange to witness it. Increasingly, government bureaucrats are setting the agenda, however, so you might find that you can visit on an official tour. If you have time enough to be persistent, the best approach would be to make friends first in Agadez.

salt mines of Bilma; trade continued, especially with Hausa-land to the south. Nonetheless, by the time the German explorer **Heinrich Barth** arrived in 1850, the population had dwindled to about 7000 and many of the old buildings were in ruins.

Early in the twentieth century, Agadez was incorporated into French territory, but not without resistance. One of the most serious threats to colonial rule was led by the Tuareg reformer **Kaocen Ag Mohammed**, who swooped down from Djanet to take Agadez in 1916, aiming to reunite all Muslims of the region and to terminate foreign domination. Supported in his efforts by the Germans and the Turks, Kaocen held the town for three months before being ousted by the French, who sent up emergency reinforcements from Zinder. The rebellion quelled, the colonials killed over 300 suspected conspirators and guillotined many of the town's *marabouts*.

Since independence, the population of Agadez has rapidly increased, in part because of the discovery of uranium in Arlit, which provided an economic boost to the entire north, and partly due to the droughts of the 1970s and 1980s, which resulted in tens of thousands of Tuareg and Bororo herders converging on the town for food and water.

Arrival and information

The government-run **tourist office**, north of the Grand Mosquée, can set you up with tours of the town – if you're lucky – and do little else for you.

As the main administrative town in the north, Agadez has plenty of facilities: **service stations**, a **hospital** and a small **airfield**, plus a **PTT** with poste restante (Mon–Fri 8am–noon & 3–5pm). The Bank of Africa, just off the Grand Marché, changes cash and travellers' cheques (Mon–Fri 8–11.30am & 3.30–5pm).

Note that because of the scarcity of tourists, **travel agents** tend to go in and out of business erratically. For travel to the Ténéré desert and Aïr mountains, the most reliable seem to be: Dunes Voyages (☎44.03.72); Arakao (☎44.04.36); Hadrar Maded (☎44.03.81); Tekarek Voyages (☎44.05.97). Guides **must** have a professional guide card; check it.

Accommodation

Agadez has a number of **places to stay**, many of them good value, especially since the downturn in tourism. *Camping de l'Escale*, about 4km out, on the new (tarmac) Arlit road, is currently closed for improvements.

Hôtel Agriboun, town centre (☎44.03.07). A recommended cheaper place, with unsophisticated S/C rooms with fans and toilets outside; bargaining usually gets good results. They'll let you park inside the fenced courtyard. ②.

Hôtel de l'Aïr, town centre (☎44.02.47). Formerly the sultan's palace and still wonderfully quiet, cool and dignified. Except the bar, that is, which has a wide selection of booze and customers. Despite the architectural grandeur and the clientele, the *Aïr*'s rooms are not fancy, though some have AC. Rooms with inside toilet are more expensive, while budget travellers can sleep on the roof. ③–④.

Hôtel Sahara, west of the Grand Marché (☎44.04.80). Conveniently located, and a traditional haunt of overlanders, but overrated. Its rooms are looking shabby these days and the management has a frustrating *laisser-aller* attitude. You can sleep on the roof at great savings. ①–②.

Hôtel Telwa, west of the Grand Marché (☎44.01.64). Two buildings, one with the bar and restaurant (currently being renovated), the other with comfortable, S/C rooms with AC. ④.

Hôtel Tidène, not far from the mosque by the Mobil station on the old Arlit road (☎44.00.51). A new, *banco*-style building with a pleasant garden, clean AC rooms and a good-value restaurant. The manager speaks English, and breakfast – with fruit juice – is included. You can sleep on the terrace for next to nothing. ②–③.

Pension Tellit, across from *Hôtel de l'Aïr* (☎44.02.31). Attractively decorated and spotlessly clean S/C rooms with AC. Luxurious roof patio with an Italian restaurant and some good ice cream. ④–⑦.

The Town

Agadez is a sprawling town, so taking up the offers of a young guide may be invaluable. You might find yourself invited into houses (men should avoid looking at the women within the courtyard), and you'll see all the sights you ask about.

The Grande Mosquée and around

Spiring through the one-storey skyline to a height of 27 metres, the tower of the **Grande Mosquée** is a landmark whose fame has spread beyond West Africa. Built in 1515, the mosque is a classic example of medieval Sudanic, with the wooden support beams protruding from the minaret like quills from a porcupine. Over the years the structure has been much renovated and was completely rebuilt in 1844, following the original style. In former days, the tower doubled as a sentry post, and it's worth climbing today for views of the town and surrounding countryside. Though the mosque is normally off limits to non-believers, there's a guardian who, in exchange for a *cadeau*, will lead you to the top, providing you don't arrive at prayer time. He's recently become accustomed to hefty *cadeaux* from wealthy tourists, and you may not be let in for less than several thousand CFA francs.

The nearby *Hôtel de l'Air* served as the **Kaocen Palace** early this century. It's a beautiful building, and even if you don't stay here you should stop by for a look. The large dining hall is where the sultan formerly received his audiences and, it's said, where subversives were hanged after the 1916 Tuareg uprising. You can go upstairs to the rooftop terrace for an interesting perspective on the mosque and town.

Also in the centre, the massive *banco* structure of the **Sultan's Palace** is the current residence of the traditional city ruler. The Nigérien government has left the basic structure of the sultanate intact, but although he's often called upon to mediate in local disputes, the sultan has at best blunted powers at the state level. Agadez's main festivals always culminate at the informal public square in front of the palace.

SILVERSMITHS AND SADDLEMAKERS IN AGADEZ

The refined craftsmanship of the Agadez **silversmiths** has become a byword in West Africa and even in some international circles. Though these artists make a variety of innovative jewellery and other objects from precious metals, they're best known for the **desert cross** pendants, especially the renowned *Croix d'Agadez*. Other towns with their own unique crosses include Bilma, In-Gall, Iferouâne, Tahoua and Zinder.

The smiths still work out of small *ateliers*, which you won't have to seek out, as young boys make it a point to propose a **tour of the workshops** to every tourist passing through. They say there's no obligation to buy, but once you're in the shops, the pressure to do so is intense. If you're fairly certain you're not interested in making a purchase, perhaps you should decline the whole show. That said, watching the *forgerons* producing jewellery by the time-honoured **lost wax process** is genuinely interesting. A wax form of the intended object is used to make a clay mould, which is then baked in a charcoal fire until all the wax has trickled out of the holes made for that purpose; liquid silver is poured into the mould, which after cooling is broken to free the hardened metal. Detailed carving and polishing can then take place. The craftsmen are known not only for the quality of their work, but also for the honesty of their materials. Unlike the market vendors, they have a reputation for straight dealing – when they say something is pure silver, it usually is.

Other artisans specialize in the **leather work** for which Agadez is also famous. The workshops still produce *rahlas* (camel saddles), covering the wooden frames with treated hides that are then decorated. They also make colourful sandals, with red and green leather in the design, and Tuareg "wallets" – stylized pouches worn round the neck with compartments for money, tobacco and other necessities.

About ten minutes' walk east of the Mosque, the **Maison du Boulanger** is a beautifully decorated baker's house, with the old oven and other tools of trade still in place.

The markets

Not far from the mosque, the **Grand Marché**, often called the Marché Moderne, is the town's main commercial venue. Tumbledown corrugated iron sheds offer a variety of goods, loosely divided into food sections (expensive, as most fruit and vegetables have to be trucked in from the south), tools, fabrics and so on. Many traders sell **crafts** aimed at the tourist trade, and this is one of the cheapest places to get Tuareg and Fula **jewellery**. Quality is often wanting, however, since the shiny trinkets are often made from melted-down Algerian dinars or other alloys that quickly acquire a dull green patina. Leather goods – sandals, pouches and bags – also abound.

On the eastern side of the main north–south road that splits the town in two, the **Vieux Marché** is much less hectic, but worth visiting, since it lies in one of the town's oldest quarters. The dusty streets surrounding the market are tightly hemmed in by *banco* houses bearing the stamp of Sudanic and Hausa influence, with their smooth lines and decorated facades.

Most interesting, though, is the **camel market**, on the town's northwestern outskirts. In the mornings, camels, donkeys, sheep and goats are bought and sold in an open field bordered by stalls featuring nomadic goods – mostly salt pillars, rope, water containers and mats. If you've never sat on a camel, you can do so here by approaching one of the Tuareg traders. In exchange for a small tip, he'll help you into the saddle and let you circle the area – not exactly an adventure, but it gives you a taste.

Eating and nightlife

In addition to the hotel **restaurants**, Agadez has several small places dishing up inexpensive meals. Near the mosque, the *Tafadak* serves copious helpings of *couscous* and other regional specialities in a pleasant interior courtyard. The nearby *Restaurant Chez Nous* is also recommended – *riz sauce* and a full range of Niger dishes, along with cheap, help-yourself coffee. Behind the market near the bank, the *Restaurant Islamique* is popular for its friendly service, good salads and inexpensive main courses. For sandwich-type snacks and *gelati* there's an Italian ice-cream place – *Vittorio's/Guida* near the *Hôtel de l'Air*. A bit further out on the Route de l'Aéroport, *Le Pillier* (☎44.03.31) is a fancier restaurant run by the owner of the *Pension Tellit* and highly recommended for moderately priced Italian specialties served alongside more traditional Sahel food.

For **picnic supplies**, you can find European canned and dry goods plus a selection of wine at Ruetsch, across the main road from the *Hôtel Agriboun*. The main supermarket, though, is MiniPrix, on the main tarred road. They sell French cheese, British biscuits, Italian pasta and Mars bars – and it's not that expensive. Incidentally, the **water** in Agadez is perfectly drinkable straight from the tap.

MOVING ON FROM AGADEZ

The **gare routière** is on the asphalt road to Arlit (the old *piste* to Arlit is not used any longer), across from Customs. Most of the *taxis brousse* from here seem to be heading to Niamey via Tahoua, though with patience you can also find transport to other major towns. SNTN **buses** leave from nearby and can get you to Arlit (three times a week), Zinder (weekly), and Tahoua, Maradi and Niamey (three times a week).

Niamey in a day is just about possible on *taxis brousse*, with an early start and no delays – it's a little over 900km. The 430-kilometre journey from Agadez to Zinder can be accomplished comfortably in one day.

At **night**, you could check out the open-air Cinéma du Sahel, near the airfield: films are generally bad but the crowd reaction adds a little excitement to quiet Sahel nights. You could also have a drink at the *maquis L'Ombre du Plaisir*, opposite the Mobil station, and try Agadez's one and only *"night club"*, next door.

Arlit

Overland routes from Algeria have been effectively closed from 1993, and travellers today miss the spectacle of approaching **ARLIT** from the Algerian Hoggar and seeing the town appear from nowhere, like a vast aberration on the fringes of the Sahara. As little as thirty years ago there was virtually nothing here, but after the discovery of uranium in the mid-1960s a town burgeoned beside the vast complex built for the SOMAÏR company. Despite its recent origins, Arlit's prosperity has drawn a wide mix of people that formerly made it an attractive stopping point for desert-crossers, but it holds little appeal for travellers coming from the diverse commercial centres of the south and is today rarely visited.

Arlit is really **two towns**. The first, built entirely for the mining company and its employees, is well planned and exclusive, with villas for engineers and executives, supermarkets stocked directly from France, a well-equipped hospital, and the town's best restaurants. The obvious divisions between the African and European workers – unequal housing, salaries and living standards – make this a disturbing sight, and you won't really have access to the facilities unless you know or befriend someone working here. A more **traditional town** has grown in a chaotic fashion alongside the mining complex. The large **market** – a maze of tiny stalls covered by mats and corrugated iron – sells vegetables, fresh meat (cut before your eyes in the open-air abbatoir), and household items like decorated calabashes, pottery and basketware.

> For advice on security in the region, see box, p.862.

Practicalities

On arrival, you should pay your respects to the **police**. You don't have to pay any money, but they might want to stamp your passport. The police station is at the north end of the main street on the east side of the older, African part of town. For **banks**, the SONI and the BIAO both have branches in town.

Arlit has a pleasant **hotel**, the *Tamesna* (②), on the main street near the market; its rooms are nothing to write home about, but some of them have AC. You can also sleep on the terrace. The bar here is a popular place to hide from the heat (cold beer and soda with ice cubes – Arlit's **water** is perfectly pure), and the tables spill over into the shaded interior courtyard. At night this is the centre of town activity.

The town's two **campsites** are suffering badly from the dearth of overland traffic, and are not to be relied upon. The first, where facilities don't go much beyond showers, is about 3km out of town, along the road to Agadez, and is in rather bad shape. The second, some 3km to the north of town, is an equally basic set-up and is "temporarily" closed.

The **restaurant** at the *Tamesna* does reasonable European-style meals such as *poulet frites* with canned peas. Down the street the popular *Sahel* is good for inexpensive meals – *steack frites*, rice and sauce – and at night has a lively bar. Also on the main drag, the *Restaurant N'Wana* prepares good *couscous* and salads that go down well with a cold beer on the patio.

The Aïr Mountains and the Ténéré

Two classic journeys from Agadez lead through the volcanic **Aïr Mountains** and the rolling dunes of the **Ténéré Desert**. *Pistes* wend through both areas, but they are mostly demanding in the extreme and often get washed away during the rainy season, or obliterated from sight when unheralded winds kick up a desert sandstorm. Travel in this area requires experience, a good guide and equipment, none of which comes cheap.

The Route de l'Aïr

The **Route de l'Aïr**, accessible from the old, unsurfaced Arlit road northeast from Agadez, is relatively good *piste* apart from the jostling washboard surface and one or two other unexpected hazards. The road forks at Teloua (take a left), and about 15km later there's the possibility of a diversion left to **Tafadek**, a deep spring that's great for swimming and diving, and believed to possess curative properties. Back on the main *piste*, 77km out of Agadez, you branch off to the right from the Arlit road, and follow the sign to Elméki, 125km from Agadez.

Just outside Elméki, you'll notice a number of tracks leading off the main route – they head to the mines and nowhere else. Follow instead the large *piste* to the village of Kreb Kreb, 72km from Elméki. (About 15km before Kreb Kreb, an alternative route leads directly north to Assodé, a short cut that bypasses Timia.) Just after Kreb Kreb, the tracks lead through the beautiful **Agalak Range** – difficult driving, as the route crosses dry riverbeds (*kori*) and hidden stretches of sand.

Timia to Iferouâne

Roughly 220km from Arlit and a little more from Agadez, **TIMIA** is a large Tuareg-controlled village nestled between the Agalak mountains and a wide desert *kori*. The town itself is one of the most beautiful oases in the Aïr, with extensive gardens and palms. Away from the box-like *banco* houses that spread over the valley, **Fort Timia**, built by the French colonials in the 1950s, commands a striking view of the In-Sarek *oued* (riverbed) and mountains. On the outskirts of town the **Cascade de Timia** grows from a trickling waterfall into something quite spectacular during the rains.

North of Timia, the road continues some 30km to the **ruins** of **ASSODÉ**. Founded as long as 1000 years ago, Assodé preceded Agadez as **capital of the Tuareg** and was once the most important town in the Aïr. As trans-Saharan trade declined, so did its fortunes and Kaocen dealt the final blow to the struggling community when he sacked it in 1917. Today the site is a ghost town – its ruins lie east of the *piste* and you'll need sharp eyes to spot them. A maze of empty streets winds through abandoned houses and squares with many of the larger buildings – including the **grande mosquée** – remarkably well preserved.

For advice on security in the region, see box, p.862.

Beyond Assodé, the tracks are progressively easier. After 90km, they lead to Niger's northernmost settlement of any size, **IFEROUÂNE**, a marvellous oasis on the fringes of the striking **Tamgak Mountains**. The *kori* running through town breathes life into some of the most beautiful **gardens** in the Aïr, and there's a small *campement*, the only bona fide **accommodation** on this route.

Iferouâne is also the starting point for visiting the Aïr region's wealth of **prehistoric sites**. Just north of the town along the Zeline *kori*, neolithic rock paintings of giraffes, cattle and antelopes can be seen on a distinctive boulder outcrop. More such paintings are found in the valley of the Aouderer *kori* near Tezirek, 90km from Iferouâne.

The Ténéré

The route east from Agadez to Bilma leads through what's often described as the most beautiful desert in the Sahara – the **Ténéré**. This is strictly for the well-equipped; an arduous, 620-kilometre journey, with a great deal of very soft sand and hardly any supplies or water along the way. You must have a guide, and usually be in convoy, before the police will let you go. Markers along the route include the graves of victims of the crossing.

Leaving Agadez, take the Zinder road and, after a couple of kilometres, follow the eastern branch towards Bilma. The first 200-odd kilometres run through the southern Aïr, with alternating stretches of sand and rock-strewn *piste*. After 270km, you arrive at the site of the **Arbre du Ténéré**, formerly the only tree growing in a region the size of France. For over a century it served as a landmark for desert crossers, until it was knocked over by a truck driver in 1973. A scrap-metal sculpture now marks the spot.

After 500km, you arrive at **Fachi**, a small Toubou and Kanouri village with a few hundred inhabitants and cool groves of date palms. In the centre, the fortified palace (*ksar*) is built of salt blocks – you can visit the **salt mines** on the eastern outskirts of town. The road covering the remaining 110km to Bilma is the one used by the *azalai*, or camel caravans, that still ply the region. It's full of long stretches of soft sand, and can be tough going.

Bilma and the pillars of salt

With around a thousand Kanouri, Tuareg and Toubou inhabitants, the small fortified town of **BILMA** is nearly a miracle out here in the middle of nowhere. Set against the backdrop of the **Kaouar Cliffs** – and as picturesque and hospitable as you could wish – Bilma owes its existence to natural water sources, which support a sizeable *palmeraie* and gardens. People in Bilma often refer to themselves, distinctively, as **Beriberi** (or *Blibli*), a term which has various interpretations but usually implies Hausa-Kanouri. Many Beriberi are Hausa in all but name and some speak Hausa most of the time.

Bilma is best known for its **salt manufacture** (for animal, rather than human, consumption) which just about maintains the viability of one of the desert's last camel caravan routes. Perhaps twenty to forty caravans a year make the trek from Agadez, with altogether up to a thousand camels in train in each one – although in living memory the figure was sometimes 50,000 or more. In recent years, the demand for Bilma's commodity has slackened in the traditional Hausa markets of southern Niger and Nigeria, where drought has depleted so much livestock in recent years. Meanwhile Bilma is filled with unsold sixty-centimetre pillars of dirty brown, rock-hard salt. They continue to make them in moulds of saline mud, piling up vast reserves for a fatter future.

NIGERIA

NIGERIA

Listen to Nigerian leaders and you will frequently hear the phrase this great country of ours. *Nigeria is* not *a great country. It is one of the most disorderly nations in the world. It is one of the most corrupt, insensitive, inefficient places under the sun. It is dirty, callous, noisy, ostentatious, dishonest and vulgar. In short it is among the most unpleasant places on earth.*

Chinua Achebe

Nigeria is a country many people feel needs no introduction: corruption, military dictatorships and urban violence seem to be its very definition. And if Chinua Achebe – one of the country's most humane and respected writer-philosphers – can describe Nigeria thus, then seeking to defend it may seem perverse.

But in truth, Nigeria's notoriety is unduly influenced by its *de facto* capital, **Lagos** – a city of incalculable population and urban distress. If you can handle the Lagos tempo its one big compensation is fine musical opportunities – no other city in West Africa is blessed with such night energy. If not, then leave the city – for **Oyo**, **Oshogbo**, **Ife**, **Benin**, or even giant **Ibadan** – and Lagos soon seems an anomaly: other cities certainly have their share of blight and bluster, but none really compares. These hinterland towns, where growth has been less dizzying and local traditions not yet bulldozed into oblivion, still show you hints of the greatness of the old Yoruba and Benin kingdoms in their palaces and museums, festivals and sacred sites.

To the **east** – beyond the geographical and cultural dividing line of the **Niger River** – the forests and plantations of the **Igbo Country** stretch out behind the vast fan of the **river delta**. This region has made a remarkable recovery since the civil war of the late 1960s, caused by its attempted secession, and its creek and waterfront towns – **Onitsha**, **Warri**, **Port Harcourt** – have gained a new prosperity with their oil reserves. They're mostly busy, self-interested cities and faintly anonymous until you root around a little, but the engaging old trading base of **Calabar** is immediately attractive and probably the country's most easy-going city. There's a conservation focus, too, in this corner of the country, since the rediscovery in 1987 of **gorillas**, long thought to have been extinct, now protected in the wilds of the **Cross River National Park**.

Central Nigeria is a region of lower population, higher ground and some inspiring scenery, dotted with outcrops and massive stone inselbergs. It is one of the best parts of the country to travel around and its main city, **Jos**, is an old hill station with a rare line in museums. Two other **national parks** – **Kainji Lake** in the northwest, and the long-established **Yankari** with its remarkable natural swimming pool – are located in this central region. And the **eastern highlands** are some of the most beautiful and unexplored mountains in Africa, abutting Cameroon's much better known Rhumsiki region.

The north of the country is **Hausa-Fulani** territory, predominantly Islamic, like the neighbouring regions of the French-speaking Sahel. There's a more comfortable climate at these latitudes and the cities are manageable, but it's the region's history – embodied in the **walled old city** quarters of Zaria, Katsina and the big metropolis of Kano – that gives northern Nigeria a special slant. While they can't compare for flavour and historical atmosphere with the old cities of North Africa or the Middle East, these emirates do have their special character. In the afternoon crush of the **Kurmi market** in Kano, or wandering through Zaria's striking **architecture**, or witnessing any of the amazing *Sallah* **durbar** festivals at the end of Ramadan, a much bigger and more rewarding view of Nigeria begins to emerge than the one most visitors bring with them.

FACTS AND FIGURES

The **Federal Republic of Nigeria** is the most populous country in Africa, with an estimated 120 million people; its land area of 924,000 square kilometres is nearly four times as big as Britain and bigger than Texas and New Mexico combined. **Lagos**, the largest city (at least eight million inhabitants), is the country's economic and cultural hub; administration, however, is slowly being transferred to the Federal Capital Territory of **Abuja**, in central Nigeria, which became the country's capital in 1991. The principal **export** is oil, followed at some distance by cocoa, palm products, rubber, timber and tin. Nigeria's **foreign debt** is in the order of £20 billion ($32 billion) – two and a half times the value of its annual exports of goods and services and equivalent to $270 for every Nigerian – which puts the country in a major league when that's compared with the relatively small sums owed by most African nations. Even so, in global terms, it's not an unimaginable figure – merely equivalent to the annual public expenditure of the state of New Jersey (population eight million), or roughly what the British Ministry of Defence spends in a year. In 1999, Nigeria returned from years in the wilderness under the despotic regime of General Sani Abacha to a democratically elected government, with former general – now civilian head of state – **Olusegun Obasanjo** in the presidential palace in Abuja.

Nigeria is a federation, like the USA, divided into 36 states (plus the Federal Capital Territory of Abuja), each with its own capital and state government. The states are commonly divided into three groups, separated by the Niger River and its tributary, the Benue.

SOUTHWEST	SOUTHEAST	NORTH
Anambra (capital Awka)	Abia (capital Umuahia)	Bauchi (capital Bauchi)
Delta (capital Asaba)	Adamawa (capital Yola)	Borno (capital Maiduguri)
Edo (capital Benin City)	Akwa Ibom (capital Uyo)	Gombe (capital Gombe)
Ekiti (capital Ado-Ekiti)	Bayelsa (capital Yenagoa)	Jigawa (capital Dutse)
Kogi (capital Lokoja)	Benue (capital Makurdi)	Kaduna (capital Kaduna)
Kwara (capital Ilorin)	Cross River (capital Calabar)	Kano (capital Kano)
Lagos (capital Ikeja)	Ebonyi (capital Abakaliki)	Katsina (capital Katsina)
Ogun (capital Abeokuta)	Enugu (capital Enugu)	Kebbi (capital Birnin Kebbi)
Ondo (capital Akure)	Imo (capital Owerri)	Lafia (capital Lafia)
Osun (capital Oshogbo)	Rivers (capital Port Harcourt)	Niger (capital Minna)
Oyo (capital Ibadan)	Taraba (capital Jalingo)	Plateau (capital Jos)
		Sokoto (capital Sokoto)
		Yobe (capital Damaturu)
		Zamfora (capital Gusau)

The people

Geographically, Nigeria has been profoundly shaped by its two great rivers – the **Niger** and the **Benue** – which flow together in a Y-shape at the town of Lokoja. This isn't the centre of the country, but it exactly corresponds to the meeting place of the three great cultural spheres which dominate Nigerian life – the southwest (**Yorubaland**), southeast (**Igboland**) and north (**Hausaland**).

The **ethnic differentiaion** of these regions is a convenient way of coming to grips with exceptionally complex cultural and linguistic groupings, but it does the country's "minorities" – several of which number in the millions and could be in the majority elsewhere in West Africa – a profound injustice. Nigeria in fact has no fewer than 250 peoples, speaking nearly as many languages in perhaps a total of 400 dialects, making it linguistically one of the world's most complex regions.

In the central part of the **southwest**, the Nupe are a major group and are culturally somewhat assimilated to the Yoruba. Other non-Yoruba speakers include **Edo**, **Urhobo**, **Itsekeri** and **Ijaw**.

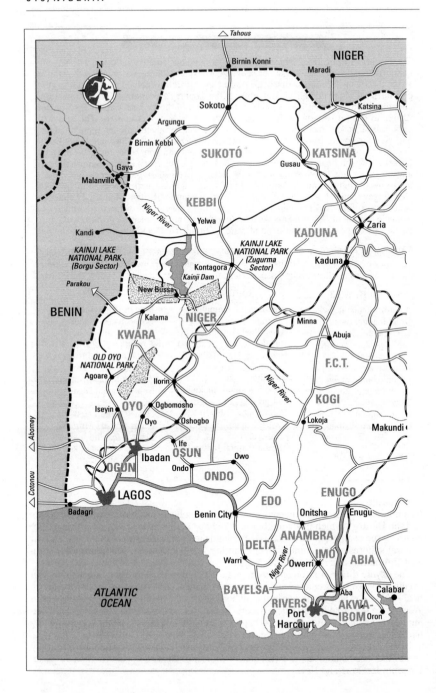

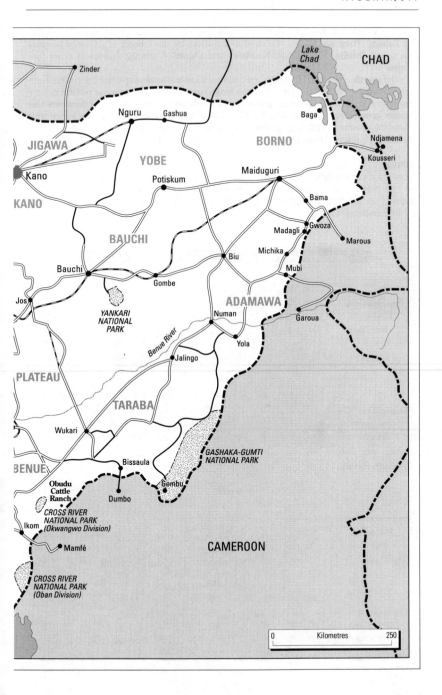

CHAD

Lake Chad

Zinder

Nguru Gashua Baga

JIGAWA YOBE BORNO Ndjamena
Kousseri

Kano Potiskum Maiduguri

KANO Bama

BAUCHI Madagli Gwoza
Michika Marous

Bauchi Biu Mubi

Gombe ADAMAWA

Jos Numan Garoua

YANKARI NATIONAL PARK

Benue River Yola

Jalingo

PLATEAU

TARABA

Wukari GASHAKA-GUMTI NATIONAL PARK

BENUE Bissaula
Obudu Cattle Ranch Gembu
Dumbo

CROSS RIVER NATIONAL PARK (Okwangwo Division)

Ikom CAMEROON

Mamfé

CROSS RIVER NATIONAL PARK (Oban Division)

0 Kilometres 250

In the **southeast**, the Igbo (formerly spelt Ibo) have cultural affiliations with the **Tiv** and **Jukun**. They are almost matched in numbers by the cluster of minority peoples who speak **Ibibio, Efik, Ekoi, Kalabari** and **Ogoni** – among dozens of other languages.

In the **north**, the great Hausa-Fulani configuration has tended to obscure groups such as the **Gwari**, as well as the **Bauchi area** languages. In the northeast the picture is very fragmented and, in the many mountain districts where languages of the **Adamawa** and **Chadic groups** are spoken, who speaks what and who claims common ancestry with whom are questions still largely unanswered. In the far northeast people speak mainly **Kanuri** – a Saharan language that is the legacy of an independent imperial past.

Climate

There's a clear climatic division between north and south and many variations within the two major zones. The most comfortable time to be in Lagos is December and January; on the Plateau, November to February; in Kano, November and December; and in Calabar, December.

AVERAGE TEMPERATURES AND RAINFALL

LAGOS

	Jan	Feb	Mar	Apr	May	June	July	Aug	Sept	Oct	Nov	Dec
Temperatures °C												
Min (night)	23	25	26	25	24	23	23	23	23	23	24	24
Max (day)	31	32	32	32	32	29	28	28	28	29	31	31
Rainfall mm	28	46	102	150	269	460	279	64	140	206	60	25
Days with rainfall	2	3	7	10	16	20	16	10	14	16	7	2

KANO

	Jan	Feb	Mar	Apr	May	June	July	Aug	Sept	Oct	Nov	Dec
Temperatures °C												
Min (night)	13	15	19	24	24	23	22	21	21	19	16	13
Max(day)	30	33	37	38	37	34	31	29	31	34	33	31
Rainfall mm	0	0	3	10	69	117	206	310	142	13	0	0
Days with rainfall	0	0	0	1	8	8	14	19	12	1	0	0

JOS

	Jan	Feb	Mar	Apr	May	June	July	Aug	Sept	Oct	Nov	Dec
Temperatures °C												
Min (night)	11	12	15	17	17	16	16	16	16	16	13	11
Max (day)	31	33	34	34	33	30	28	28	29	31	31	31
Rainfall mm	3	3	27	85	205	226	330	292	213	41	2	3

CALABAR

	Jan	Feb	Mar	Apr	May	June	July	Aug	Sept	Oct	Nov	Dec
Temperatures °C												
Min (night)	23	23	23	23	23	22	22	22	22	22	23	23
Max (day)	30	32	32	31	30	30	28	28	29	29	30	30
Rainfall mm	43	76	153	213	312	406	450	405	427	310	191	43

Rains in **the north** fall during a single season, roughly between May and September. Usually this amounts to no more than 500mm (20 inches), most of it falling in the months of July and August. Typically the hottest months are March and April, when the *Harmattan* winds have run their course and the rains not yet begun; at this time, midday temperatures often rise above 45°C (113°F) in the shade.

In the **southwest**, the long rains bucket down from March to July with the wettest months usually May and June. There's a short lull, usually sometime in August (the "little dry"), then further heavy rain from September to October. The yearly rainfall in the southwest averages around 1800mm (72 inches).

In the **southeast**, the total annual rainfall can exceed 4000mm (160 inches – about five times the annual average of London or Minneapolis) and there is a continuous and somewhat depressing rainy season from April to October, with a brief drying-off period in the middle which is not guaranteed every year. Temperatures in the south tend to be lower than in the north despite the region's proximity to the equator, but the humidity can be really oppressive.

Arrivals

Flying into Lagos hardly provides an easy introduction to the continent (it helps to be met on arrival), but flying to Kano is much less intimidating and can be convenient for starting your travels in West Africa. Overland routes from Niger are good and there are also fast connections to Nigeria along the coast from Togo and Benin. Road links with Cameroon are poorer.

■ Flights from West Africa

While Nigeria's intercontinental air links are well developed, links within **West Africa** have surprising gaps: there are no direct flights, for example, from Niamey, Nouakchott, Ouagadougou or Bissau. The only options are on Air Afrique, with connections in Abidjan, Lomé or Cotonou. Although several Nigerian airports have international facilities, all flights from other parts of West Africa currently arrive in Lagos. Nigeria Airways (WT) handles the largest share of the traffic (it occasionally suspends certain routes), followed by Air Afrique (RK).

WT flies once a week from **Banjul**, via **Conakry**, **Abidjan** and **Lomé**. Another weekly flight originates in **Dakar** before following the same route. Air Gabon (GN) follows a similar route (Dakar–Conakry–Abidjan–Cotonou–Lagos) twice a week.

Conakry also has a weekly service on Air Guinée (GI) via **Bamako** – which is Mali's only air link with Nigeria.

From **Abidjan**, there's an average of two non-stop and one or two stopping services every day. Any travel agent can fix you up with a seat.

Of the other nearby capitals, **Accra** has one or two flights daily to Lagos, all of them non-stop. **Lomé** has a flight most days of the week; and **Cotonou** at least one flight every day (though from Cotonou you should seriously consider going by land – it's only 120km and you'll probably get there quicker, airport delays taken into account).

The details in these practical information pages are essentially for use in West Africa and in Nigeria itself: for full practical coverage on preparing for a trip, getting here from outside the region, paperwork, health, information sources and more, see Basics pp.3–83.

Lastly, **Douala** has at least one flight each day to Lagos on RK, WT or Cameroon Airlines (UY). Flights with WT go via Port Harcourt on Saturday and Calabar on Monday.

■ Flights from elsewhere in Africa

From **Central Africa** there are several direct flights each week to Lagos from Kinshasa (Ethiopian Airlines and WT), Bangui (RK), Libreville (GN, RK, WT via Port Harcourt) and Brazzaville (WT), and weekly flights on UY from Malabo, Equatorial Guinea, via Douala.

From **East Africa**, Ethiopian Airlines (ET) flies five times a week from Addis Ababa. Kenya Airways (KQ) has two weekly direct flights from Nairobi to Lagos. UY also flies from Nairobi, but you have to transfer in Douala.

From **southern Africa**, South African Airways (SA) operates two direct flights a week from Johannesburg.

■ Overland from Cameroon and Chad

The main frontier crossing from Cameroon is **Mamfé to Ikom**, over the Cross River bridge. Customs and immigration for Cameroon are in **Ekok**, on the east bank of the Cross (open daily 8am–7pm), whence you walk over the bridge to **Mfum**, the Nigerian post. As Nigeria and Cameroon have been close to war at several times in the last decade, over disputed offshore territories, you would do well to assume this border will be a hassle. The heaviest traffic is at dusk and dawn, when it can take hours to get through (many drivers stay overnight in Ekok), but because of the geography on the Cameroonian side it's almost impossible to time your arrival during the day. There's a less often used, but viable and more direct route from Mamfé to Calabar, turning off south (left) from the "main" Ikom road at **Eyumajok**, 48km west of Mamfé. Note also that the Mamfe–Ikom road is frequently impassable on the Cameroonian side during the rainy season. For further details see box on p.991. From Mfum, catch another taxi to **Ikom** and onwards to **Calabar** or **Enugu**.

Further north, out of the Bamenda Highlands, you can cross on foot from **Dumbo to Bissaula** (see p. 1033), and there are minor crossings all the way along the mountainous border, though few see much traffic.

The rough route from Garoua to **Yola** is a little busier, as is the northern route from Mora to **Banki** – a village straddling the border. Customs and immigration at Banki are generally low-key, but the small post is poorly equipped and the waits can sometimes be long. Taxis are generally no problem from here to Maiduguri.

Finally, there's the northernmost crossing from **Kousseri** to **Fotokol** (Cameroon formalities) and **Gambaru** (Nigerian post). This is your likely way into Nigeria coming from Ndjamena in Chad. If you're transiting Cameroon like this, the Cameroon customs will issue you with a free one-day transit visa at the immigration post in Kousseri.

■ Overland from Niger

Coming from Niger, two main routes aim for **Kano**: one from **Maradi**, which would allow you to take in the old Nigerian emirate of **Katsina**, the other from **Zinder**, a beautiful Hausa town. You can also cross from **Birnin-Konni to Sokoto**, or, further west, from **Gaya to Kamba**, from where you can connect to Sokoto. All four routes have good bush taxi transport.

■ Overland from Ghana, Togo and Benin

The **coastal route** from **Accra** (476km) and **Lomé** (275km) to **Lagos** takes in some picturesque coastal scenery of palms, creeks and beaches. By private car, the trip takes a full day (about eight hours) but it may take half as long again or more if you're travelling by public transport, as the vehicle is repeatedly unloaded and reloaded at the three borders, each with customs and immigration posts on both sides.

You can get taxis direct to Lagos from Accra, Lomé or Cotonou. They're relatively cheap these days, but you can cut further on costs by taking the taxi to the **Kraké** frontier post and finding another vehicle on from there.

If you're intent on avoiding Lagos altogether, get yourself to **Porto Novo** in Benin, from where you can enter Nigeria 30km north at the Idioko frontier post, continuing from here on the A5-1 to meet the main A5 Lagos–Abeokuta road 10km north of Ikeja. If you're relying on public transport, however, you will end up at the Oshodi motor park in northern Lagos, where you can get onward transport without going into the city centre.

Red Tape

Visas are required by all except ECOWAS nationals. Nigerian officials are not usually **familiar with the idea of foreigners visiting the country for tourism and some border crossings can be heavy. You may well be asked to pay customs duty on some of your personal belongings – it's up to you to prove as cheerfully as possible that they are your personal belongings, and not dutiable merchandise.**

Nigeria has embassies or high commissions in most major capital cities. Most embassies will only issue visas to nationals (or long-term residents) of that country, so it is always recommended that you obtain visas in your country of residence, before travelling abroad, since it is much easier for foreign embassies to renew expired visas than to issue new ones.

For **visas for onward travel**, most West African countries have embassies in Lagos or Abuja. Visas for Niger can also be obtained from the consulate in Kano, and Cameroonian visas at the Calabar consulate (generally with less hassle than in Lagos where a letter of reference from your embassy is required). Cape Verde and Guinea Bissau have no representatives; for these, a visit to the Portuguese embassy, one of the few in West Africa, might be worthwhile.

■ Vehicle documents

Nigeria requires a **Carnet de Passage en Douane** issued by the AA or similar organization (see Basics, p.46). Be sure to get one before arriving here as the alternative is to pay 250 percent of the value of the car in hard currency at the border and receive it back in Naira when you leave. When leaving the country, be wary of giving up your carnet, as the authorities may neglect to return their copy of the document to your national motorists' association as required, thereby holding up the release of your funds from bond.

Local Nigerian **insurance** doesn't cost much at the frontier, so it seems foolhardy not to buy it. If you have already bought regional coverage in another ECOWAS member country, a Carte Brune (see Basics, p.16), it is valid in Nigeria.

■ Other red tape

It's illegal to export antique works of art, and there's full scope for anything that looks old to be confiscated when you come to leave, unless you have obtained a **certificate of export** from the National Museum in Lagos. Barring that, anything you buy that looks like art or an antique is best sent home through an air or sea freight agency.

Money and Costs

Nigeria's currency is the Naira (₦), divided into 100 kobo. There are coins of 50 kobo and ₦1 (though you rarely see coins in use), and notes of ₦5, ₦10, ₦20 and ₦50. Currently, the approximate official rate of exchange, pegged to the US dollar, is ₦80 = US$1 (₦130 = £1). Export and import of Naira is prohibited.

Changing money can take ages, but is rarely a problem in Lagos. In other towns, banks can be fussy about travellers' cheques, sometimes asking to see receipts from the place of issue. Privately operated forex bureaux (bureaux de change) are less of a hassle to deal with and give higher rates than banks for cash in £ or US$. Travellers' cheques and all other currencies in cash attract much lower rates.

As regards banks, you'll generally have best luck changing francs at branches of Afribank Nigeria. The other main banks – African Continental, UBA (United Bank for Africa), First Bank of Nigeria (FBN) and Union Bank of Nigeria (UBN; ex-Barclays) – have branches in large towns throughout the country. It's almost impossible to get a cash advance on any credit card in Nigeria.

The Black Market

You can still change hard currencies on the streets of Lagos and other cities close to the borders, but it hardly seems worth the risk and hassle as you'll get more or less the same deal from an authorized currency dealer in a forex bureau or hotel. Currency smuggling and illicit dealing are treated as a serious offence.

■ Costs

The Naira has fluctuated substantially over the last few years, and anything may happen in the future. You should generally find costs reasonable – even quite decent hotels can usually be found for under £10 ($16) a night, and long-distance travel can be a real bargain. Fuel should cost no more than ₦75 per gallon (₦20 per litre); the question is always whether to queue at filling stations to buy it at the official price, or to pick it up from roadside hawkers for two or three times the price.

Health

Vaccination certificates for yellow fever are mandatory. Immigration officials sometimes also demand cholera vaccination certificates. Malaria, however, should be your main health concern.

Water is good and drinkable from taps in most towns across the country. In isolated rural areas, it requires filtering or purification tablets. In the dry season, rural areas are often short of water and people have to make great efforts to keep supplied, so if you're travelling in the sticks in March or April don't be surprised if there's a certain reluctance to fill your water bottles, at least for free.

Hospitals are reasonably well equipped in comparison to neighbouring countries. In Lagos, the Eko Hospital is one of the better places.to go for treatment (see p.958). Also recommended is the Sacred Heart Hospital in Abeokuta, 100km north of Lagos. In a case of serious illness, contact your embassy.

Maps and information

Tourist offices and local branches of the Ministry of Information can be found throughout the country, and are listed throughout this chapter. There are now local tourism boards in most states, as well as six federal tourism boards.

As for maps, The Michelin #953 (1cm:40km) is largely accurate (make sure to get the latest edition). In Nigeria you'll find several larger scale national road maps – published by Spectrum, Peugeot, and the Nigeria Mapping Company – all at 1cm:15km. Recently published town plans of some cities are available in bookshops and stationery stores and/or at their respective tourist offices.

For a long stay in Lagos, get hold of a copy of one of the best Lagos guides, *Lagos Easy Access*, published in 1998 by the American Women's Club. The book is packed with some three hundred pages of information (including maps) – enough to manage several years in the commercial capital. John O. Olumide-Faoseke's *Travellers' Guide to Nigeria* (Photocare Travel, 1997) is also helpful.

Getting Around

Nigeria has some 70,000km of paved roads – a fairly remarkable figure for this part of the

DRIVING IN NIGERIA

Nigerian **petrol** (*gasoline*) is inexpensive, though filling stations often have long lines or low supplies and people often buy at the side of the road from jars or four-gallon "Sunflower" cans, although this is more expensive. Much of the petrol is smuggled out of the country to be sold on the roadside in Benin or Cameroon.

If you're on a long overland trip, it's worth **stocking up** with two or more complete fluid changes. You won't be taxed at the border and it'll be four times as expensive in the surrounding franc zone countries (and possibly unavailable for days or weeks in the Sahel). Beware of taking large quantities of fuel into Cameroon, where you may be accused of fuel-smuggling: there's a major trade in smuggled Nigerian petrol, which is sold, often watered down, by the roadside.

ROADS

Most Nigerian **main roads** were superb until the early 1990s, by which time they were beginning to need more maintenance than they were getting. Since then, the neglect of the network has become an increasing problem, causing serious accidents and millions of dollars' worth of damage in a society by now very mobile and car-oriented. The worst roads are found in the southeast. In theory, collapsed sections of road are flagged by signs with a skull and crossbones followed at 100m intervals by 60, 50, 40 and 30 "Slow Down" **signs**. But hundreds of kilometres of road surface are now in a very bad state and the warning system is becoming redundant, so drive with caution. Otherwise, few traffic signs are posted along the roads (outside the major cities), except regular roadside **marker stones** marked with the first three letters of the name of the next and previous major towns, and the distance in kilometres.

CAR RENTAL

The cost of **car rental** has gone down in recent years, but it's still quite pricey, as a **driver** often comes with the vehicle. Many Lagos outlets insist on this – and it's preferable if you're new to the city; elsewhere you may be able to drive yourself. The distinction between chauffeur-driven car rental and taking a taxi is blurred; make it clear who will pay for fuel.

See also "Trouble on the road", p.932.

---

world. Road transport is easily the fastest in West Africa – often dangerously so. A rail network connects the northern and southern extremities of the country. Domestic air services are relatively good and reasonably priced. River travel on the Niger and Benue isn't developed commercially.

■ Bush taxis and buses

Bush taxis are quick and comfortable – though any concerns you may have about speeding are justified: be prepared to shout at the driver to slow down if you fear for your life. Fortunately, overcrowding is the exception rather than the rule. There's usually a choice between a Peugeot 504 (estate or saloon) and a 16-seat Japanese minibus. There's rarely a long wait in the motor parks of major cities. **Buses** ("luxury buses" as the companies like to call them) also link major cities and usually run to fixed schedules.

■ Trains

The Nigeria Railway Corporation (NRC) operates services from **Lagos to Kano** (via Ibadan, Kaduna and Zaria), from **Port Harcourt to Kano** (via Enugu), and from **Port Harcourt to Maiduguri** (via Enugu and Bauchi). Services are erratic however, and you should check the latest schedules with the NRC headquarters in Abuja (☎09/523 7498).

■ Planes

Nigeria Airways links Lagos, Abuja, Calabar, Enugu, Jos, Kaduna, Kano, Maiduguri, Makurdi, Port Harcourt, Sokoto and Yola. Tickets are cheap and on some routes there are several flights a day to and from Lagos. Reservations normally aren't taken, so get to the airport early even though your plane is likely to leave late.

Several **private airlines**, including ADC (currently one of the largest), Triax Airlines, Belleview, Harka Airservices, Okada Air and Kabo Airlines operate out of the domestic airport at Ikeja, Lagos. They generally offer relatively inexpensive and professional service (though flying with Kabo is always an adventure) and are preferred by frequent-flyers over the premier Nigeria Airways. ADC, Harka and Belleview are probably the most reliable.

■ City Transport

Every Nigerian town has countless bust-up old **taxis** making the rounds. The usual distinction applies between those which are driving fixed routes and piling customers in for very modest fees per sector and those which hire out as private cabs and cost appreciably more for pre-agreed journeys. Whichever you choose, your progress may be extremely slow, especially at rush hours. To overcome the "go-slows" (traffic jams) a common phenomenon in most cities is that of **choba** – motorcycle taxis, also known as *akada* – which you hail at the roadside and are very cheap. They're mostly very competent, but not much use unless you're travelling alone and without luggage.

■ Other forms of transport

Hitching in Nigeria isn't especially difficult but you need to be confident of your abilities to tell a bad driver from a fast driver, and to act decisively on your conclusion – it's much better to be stranded on the highway than spread over it. Truck drivers are your best bet, and they'll often want payment.

The perspective you get on the country from a **bicycle** saddle is unlike any other. Everyone you meet will think you're mad, but the rewards of cycling in Nigeria are as big as the country itself, and the supposed dangers fade to a manageable scale. You will never be ignored on the road, so the chance of being hit is diminished. Nevertheless, you should keep off the main highways as much as possible.

River transport is mainly bulk goods traffic rather than passengers. Boats operate along some 6500km of waterways in Nigeria, half of which consists of the Niger and Benue rivers. During the rainy season, boats go up the Benue all the way to Garoua in Cameroon. Boats also operate along the **creeks and lagoons** of coastal towns, details of which can be found in the Lagos, Port Harcourt and Calabar sections.

Accommodation

In the 1970s and 1980s, international-style hotels started springing up everywhere from Lagos to Maiduguri, and Calabar to Sokoto. Although multinational chains are represented, some of the newer hotels, notably in the Arewa chain, are Nigerian owned and operated; these are cheap by the standards of neighbouring countries, and very comfortable. Two important, general points to note: all hotels levy a fifteen percent tax and require a deposit, usually at least equal to a night's lodging.

Upmarket hotels have every mod con in the rooms and some also have tennis courts and pools. Water and electricity can shut down frequently and unpredictably, but bigger places have generators to cope. Most hotels of standing have rates for residents and non-residents, the latter being substantially higher and often payable in foreign currency.

ACCOMMODATION PRICE CODES

Accommodation prices in this chapter are coded according to the following scales, as used throughout the book. Prices refer to the rate you can expect to pay for a room with two beds. Some hotels charge twice the normal rate for foreigners. Where they exist, such "non-residents" rates are the rates given in the guide. Single rooms, or single occupancy, will normally cost at least two-thirds of the twin-occupancy rate. For further details see p.48.

① **Under ₦650 (under £5/$8).** A range of possibilities, from the most rudimentary flophouse to a modest budget-priced hotel with good facilities.

② **₦650–1300 (£5–10/$8–16).** S/C rooms (usually with some sort of AC unit), and a reasonable restaurant.

③ **₦1300–2600 (£10–20/$16–32).** Adequate, business-class establishment, often with extras, such as phones or TV in rooms.

④ **₦2600–3900 (£20–30/$32–48).** Standard, business-class hotel, with full facilities, in which the AC generally works efficiently.

⑤ **₦3900–5200 (£30–40/$48–64).** Similar standard to the previous code band but extra facilities such as a pool.

⑥ **₦5200–6500 (£40–50/$64–80).** Comfortable, first-class hotel, with good facilities.

⑦ **Over ₦6500 (over £50/$80).** Luxury, international-class hotel.

NIGERIAN NOSH

THE BASICS

Àmàlà
Yams ground before boiling – the finished product has a brown colour of little initial appeal.

Eba
Moist ball of steamy *gari* (cassava flour), overwhelmingly the favourite national dish. Bland on its own, and extremely heavy, but always eaten with a hot sauce.

Fufu
Fermented pounded cassava.

Pounded yam
Boiled yam that's been pounded to a wonderful, glazey, aerated blob – which can be delicious when you're really hungry. Commonly eaten in the south, often with a palm oil or groundnut-based soup.

THE TASTY PART

Àkàrà
Cake made from beans (cow peas or Ogbono).

Begiri
Yoruba bean soup.

Bitter leaf
Not distant from spinach.

Bushmeat
Any kind of game meat, including antelope, but the most valued is grass-cutter (or cutting-grass), the giant herbivorous rodent also known as cane rat and, euphemistically in French, as *agouti* (an unrelated animal).

Cowleg
Prosaic local term for shin of beef.

Dodo
Fried plantains.

Draw Soup
Igbo soup which "draws" (ie it's viscous), made from ground Ogbono seeds.

Egusi
Oily soup based on pounded melon seeds, usually containing stock fish or meat, and green leaves (bitter leaf or pumpkin leaf).

Eja gbigbe
Yoruba smoked fish on a stick.

Ìgbín
Large forest snails; rubbery in texture and usually eaten with an extremely hot sauce.

Jollof rice
Rice cooked with palm oil, served with vegetables and meat.

Moin-moin
A delicious steamed bean-cake snack with a slightly gelatinous texture, found mainly in the south. Kause are the fried variety.

Okro
Gumbo, okra, ladies' fingers.

Soup
Any stew, often thick, often hot.

Stock fish
Air-dried fish, usually cod (from Iceland, Norway or Portugal) that's soaked and cooked.

Suya
Grilled kebabs of beef, mutton or occasionally camel, sold everywhere but especially in the north. In the Yoruba and Ibo countries you'll find a variation on these kebabs made from black-eye peas, or fried bean fritter.

Rooms in **budget hotels** (£2–20/$3–32) may range from a bed with four walls to gadget-filled abodes cluttered with TV, rattling AC units and leaking fridges. Note that some hotels, particularly the cheaper ones, double as **brothels**. In towns of any size, rooms without electricity and facilities are becoming rare. The term "**single**", incidentally, refers to the number of beds in the room. The price you pay is for the room, and you'll often find the single bed is nearly two metres wide.

If you're **driving**, it's essential to find a hotel with a **compound**, where the gates are locked and usually guarded through the night. There's no extra charge.

■ Missions

The Evangelical Church of West Africa (**ECWA**) runs a series of **mission guesthouses** throughout the country, often in association with the Sudan Inland Mission (**SIM**). They're very cheap – and VSOs and other volunteers get a discount. Rooms are generally tidy and spartan, but come quite well equipped in the better places.

■ Camping

If you have your own transport, **camping** can be a good option – but the further off the beaten track the better. You should be very wary of camping within 50km of the urban centres and it's wise to stay right away from the more congested parts of the south. Don't camp anywhere near busy roads with a car or other large vehicle, as the attention you'll attract spreads rapidly and isn't always welcome.

Eating and Drinking

European, Lebanese and Asian restaurants are found in almost any large town, and most hotels have their own restaurants for either Nigerian or European meals (often with two menus). Many hotels also serve English breakfasts of eggs, toast, marmalade, tea and juice. Beware: Nigerian food in the south is usually fiery hot.

There's a wide range of foods and dishes in **chop houses** (*buka* in Yoruba) and local restaurants (see box, overleaf). In addition, chicken and chips (fries), and omelette and chips are universally available; in cheaper places the price of an omelette includes bread and "Lipton's".

Vegetarians have a moderately difficult time in restaurants, as many apparently (even explicitly) "vegetarian" items on menus should be understood as "plus a bit of meat" – usually goat. But salad vegetables are often crisp and fresh, and delicious once you overcome any worries about them having been washed in unsterilized water. Good transport helps to provide fresh fruit and veg even to dry regions and parts of the country where they would otherwise be out of season.

If you're travelling cheaply it's easy enough to **live on the basics**. Bread (sweet, brick-shaped and often coloured yellow or pink), hard-boiled eggs, portions of deep-fried fish (with or without scalding chilli sauce), bananas, oranges and salted roast peanuts make for a reasonably balanced diet that's obtainable in the remotest parts of the country.

■ Drinking

Nigerians are great **beer** drinkers. Every state has its own breweries and their advertisement hoardings are one of the countries' most pervasive symbols. A widely available brand is **Star**. Among the other thirty-odd brands, Rock, Gulder, Harp and 33 are probably the most popular. Be cautious with Nigerian **Guinness** – an impressive eight percent alcohol by volume – and with cheaper brands,

which tend to provoke treacherous hangovers and, some maintain, diarrhoea.

Palm wine, tapped from oil palms, is drunk in the south. Pasteurized bottled versions are available, although their taste is a far cry from the frothy sweetness of the bush brews. Distilled, the wine becomes potent *ogogoro*, also common but usually more discreetly sold.

Coke, Sprite, Fanta and Crush figure prominently in a long list of minerals manufactured in Nigeria. You can find them cold from fridges – at a filling station if nowhere else – all over the country.

Communications – Post, Phones, Languages and Media

Mail is unpredictable and letters to and from Europe and North America can take anything from a couple of days to two weeks or more to arrive. The poste restantes in Lagos, Kano and Kaduna, however, work well enough. To send mail out, the post office's EMS Speedpost is quick, inexpensive and reliable.

Nigeria's IDD code is ☎234.

To **phone** abroad, you can dial directly from all cities and most towns. Connections are usually good, but you may be cut off in the middle of a conversation for no apparent reason. To make a reverse-charge (collect) call to an overseas number, dial the international operator (☎191).

■ Languages

Nigeria's official **language** is English and in the larger cities – especially those with universities – it's spoken widely and with accents you'll adapt to easily. Pidgin English, however, which is spoken as a lingua franca everywhere, especially in the smaller towns and rural areas, will initially throw you. Keep trying, though; ask people to repeat phrases, and before long most visitors find their own speech punctuated with pidgin expressions.

The three most widely spoken ethnic languages are **Hausa**, **Yoruba** and **Igbo** (see boxes

YORUBA

Yoruba is the name given to a cluster of close dialects in the Kwa grouping, and as a tonal language, it can be difficult for foreigners to master even the basics. Because tone carries so much meaning, it's possible to communicate with little or no vocalization: talking drums were (and still are) able to transmit messages, and you don't have to listen to much of Sunny Ade's music to realize how easily this is accomplished. The diacritics in the following words and phrases are not accents but indicate the tone of the sound – either rising (´), or falling (`). *E* is pronounced "Eh" or "Ey" and *O* is pronounced "Or" or "Oh". The prefix "E" indicates a plural or formal construction.

GREETINGS

Good morning	*E káàárò*	Greeting someone just	
Response	*E káàárò*	arriving or returning	*E káàbò*
Good afternoon	*E káàsán*	Greeting someone	
Response	*E káàsán*	who is working	*E kúushé*
Good evening	*E káalé*	Response (lit. thank you)	*Adúpé*
Response	*E káalé*	How are you?, How's life?	*Shé alaáfìa ni*
On entering a house	*E kúulé*	Response (lit. thank you)	*Adúpé*
Response	*E káàbò*	Goodbye	*Ó dàbò*

PERFUNCTORY CONVERSATION

I want	*Mo féé*	Please, reduce the price	*E dín owó lori e*
I don't want	*Mi ò féé*	Give me	*E fún mi*
Which one?	*È wo?*	All right. OK	*Ó dáa*
This is the one	*Eléyìí*	Please	*E jòó*
Take (it)	*E gbà*	Don't be annoyed	*E má bínú*
Water	*Omi*	What's your name?	*Kini oruko ré?*
Meat	*Eran*	My name is Dayo	*Dayo ni oruko mi*
Palm wine	*Emu*	Greetings/commiserations	*Pèlé*
Thank you (on receiving it)	*E sheé*	I don't understand	*Mi ò gbo*
How much is (it)?	*Èló ní?*	Yoruba	*Yoruba*
It's ten Naira	*Naira mewa ni*	No, (not) at all	*Rárá*
To pay	*Sanwó*	My friend	*Òré mi*
Money	*Owó*		

NUMBERS

1	*ookan*	12	*mejila*	25	*mèd ogbon*		
2	*méjì*	13	*metala*	26	*meridin logbon*		
3	*méta*	14	*merinla*	30	*ogbon*		
4	*merin*	15	*mèedogun*	40	*ogoji*		
5	*marun*	16	*meridlogun*	50	*adota*		
6	*mefa*	17	*metadinlogun*	60	*ogota*		
7	*meje*	18	*mejidinlogun*	70	*aadorin*		
8	*mejo*	19	*mokondinlogun*	80	*ogorin*		
9	*mesan*	20	*ogun*	90	*adorun*		
10	*mewa*	21	*mokan le logun*	100	*ogorun*		
11	*mokanla*	22	*meji le logun*				

on p.872, above and on p.928). Next to these, are some four hundred separate dialects representing twelve language families. The linguistic situation in central and southeast Nigeria is one of the most complicated in the world – on the islands of the Delta region there are villages a few kilometres apart with mutually incomprehensible tongues.

■ The media

Nigeria is a country where it's fun to read the **newspapers**, and some fifteen percent of the

IGBO

Igbo is also a tonal language and part of the great Kwa grouping – but it is not intelligible to Yoruba speakers. Again, be prepared to squeeze your mouth a little to get an intelligible vowel sound.

GREETINGS

Hi/How are you?	*Kèdú/Kèdú ka í mère?*	Welcome (to one who	
How are the children?	*Kèdú maka umú-*	has arrived)	*Nnòo*
	àka?	Keep up the good work	
I'm fine	*Ó dì nma*	/well done	*Jisie ike*
Good morning?	*Ututu òma?*	Thank you	*Daalu/Imèela*
Good night	*Ka chií fò*	Good bye	*Ka e mesia*

BASIC CHAT

Please	*Bìkó*	This one	*Nke á*
Sorry (commiserations)	*Ndó*	How much is this?	*Nka á bù olé?*
What's your name?	*Kèdú àha gí?*	How much?/How	
My name is Theodora	*Áhà m bu*	much money?	*Olé?/Egó olé?*
	Theodora	Give	*Nyé*
Where are you from?	*E béè ka ísì?*	Give me	*Nyé m*
I'm from Scotland	*E sim Scotland*	Come	*Byá*
Where are you going?	*E béè ka í na-*	Go	*Jé*
	ijè?	Come in	*Bhàta*
I'm going to Enugu	*Á na m èje*	Good	*Ézí*
	Enugu	This soup's tasty	*Ófé tòrò èto*
I want	*Á chorò m*	It's good	*Ó dè úmá*
I want to go to the market	*Á chorò m ije*	Meat	*Áné*
	ahia	Pepper	*Ose*
I want to buy	*Á chorò m ego*	Water	*Mmírí*

NUMBERS

1	*ótu*	12	*irí na abúo*	30	*irí àtó*
2	*abúo*	13	*irí na àtó*	40	*irí ànó*
3	*àtó*	14	*irí na ànó*	50	*irí ìsé*
4	*ànó*	15	*irí na ìsé*	60	*irí ìsí*
5	*isé*	16	*irí na ìsí*	70	*irí asáà*
6	*ìsí*	17	*irí na asáà*	80	*irí asáto*
7	*asáà*	18	*irí na asáto*	90	*irí itenanì*
8	*asáto*	19	*irí na itenanì*	100	*nari*
9	*itenanì*	20	*irí abúo*	1000	*puku*
10	*irí*	21	*irí abúo na ótu*		
11	*irí na ótu*	22	*irí abúo na abúo*		

population does so regularly. Most of the hundred or more titles are privately-owned, outspoken and informative, and there's a wide range of styles and opinions. Six national dailies dominate – *The Daily Times* (government-owned, with a circulation of nearly half a million), *The Guardian*, *The Punch*, *New Nigerian*, *Vanguard* and *National Concorde*. Of these, *The Guardian* and *National Concorde* provide the most complete economic and political analysis, but none of the papers is very strong on international news. The *Sunday Times* has a huge readership, and there are some twenty weekly news magazines.

Television

The first private **television** stations were licensed in 1993, when the government gave up its monopoly, and there are now more than thirty stations broadcasting to some five million TV sets. Programmes are in English and the national languages (Igbo, Yoruba, Hausa).

NIGERIAN TERMS – A GLOSSARY

Abule Hamlet or small village (Yoruba).

Agbada Yoruba cloak for men.

Alhaji One who has been to Mecca.

Amingo White person (from Portuguese), used in Cross River State.

Ariya Enjoyment, having a good time (Yoruba).

Babanriga Long Hausa tunic.

Batoure White person (Hausa).

Buba Yoruba shirt.

Buka Chop house (Yoruba).

Chiroma Traditional title of the far northeast.

Dash Bribe or payment for service rendered or simply a gift (verb and noun).

Durbar Staged horse gallops in which senior men pay homage to an emir in the Muslim regions.

FCT Federal Capital Territory (Abuja).

FESTAC Festival of Arts and Culture hosted in Lagos in 1977 at incredible cost. Legacies from this event include the National Theatre and the housing project of Festac Town.

Galadima Traditional title of the far northeast.

Go-slow Traffic jam.

GRA Government Reserved Area, civil servants' housing district.

Ileto Village (Yoruba).

Ilu Alade Big town (Yoruba).

Ilu Oloja Small market town (Yoruba).

Kabu kabu Commercial transport (Hausa).

Lappa Casual loin cloth (men and women).

Mai Traditional Kanuri ruler.

Moto Any car – a term you'll hear a lot if travelling by bush taxi.

NEPA Nigerian Electric Power Authority – also translated as *Never Electric Power Always*.

Oba Traditional Yoruba king. The Nigerian government has allowed traditional rulers to keep their titles and in some cases has even supported regional monarchies. Although the *obas* have less *de jure* power than they once did, they still enjoy considerable prestige and often mediate in local disputes. In some cases, they've taken on official government functions to complement traditional roles.

Off To turn/switch something off.

On To turn/switch something on.

Onyeocha White person (Igbo).

Oyinbo White person (Yoruba).

Sabi To know (pidgin, from Portuguese).

Sabon Gari Foreigners' town (Hausa).

SAP Economic Structural Adjustment Programme.

Shehu Chief, big man (Hausa).

Sokoto Yoruba trousers.

Touts Hyperactive youths who take it upon themselves to escort you through customs, health, immigration and currency declaration at airports or land borders, or onto vehicles in the motor parks. Much as they can be a pain, they're usually very hard to shake off. Use them, because if you let them hang on, they'll demand payment anyway.

Radio

Radio is organized under the **FRCN** (Federal Radio Corporation of Nigeria), which broadcasts three short-wave programmes in English and national languages nationwide. Individual stations for the different states also broadcast their own medium-wave programmes, and some private radio stations are emerging (Ray Power in Lagos is dominant).

You can also receive *Voice of Nigeria* transmissions – in English, French, German, Spanish, Hausa, Arabic and Swahili – abroad.

Holidays and Festivals

Nigeria's official public holidays include the major Christian and Muslim celebrations plus New Year's Day, May Day and Independence Day (October 1). Muslim holidays marking the end of Ramadan (*Sallah*), Abraham's sacrificing of the sheep (*tabaski*) and Muhammad's birthday are based on the lunar calendar (see p.59 for dates). In the north, notably in Kano and Katsina, these often climax with spectacular "durbar" cavalry displays.

■ Traditional Festivals

Ekpe festival January. Ritualistic three-day festival celebrated among the Oboro's in the area between Umuahia and Ikot Ekpene. Harvest festival and general thanksgiving for surviving the year.

Fishing festival February. Argungu, near Sokoto.

Pategi Regatta February–March. A regatta held every other year at Pategi, the big crossing point on the Niger, 100km downstream from Jebba (70km from Ilorin). This is one of the country's best-known events, and includes horse racing, swimming, dancing and music.

Egungun Usually April. A whole host of Yoruba ancestor festivals. Those at Ibadan, Badagry (near Lagos) and Okene (on the A2 between Benin City and Lokoja) draw huge crowds. Masquerades and sporting events accompanied by exhilarating dancing and drumming.

Ikeji Izuogu Usually April. A five-day yam festival celebrated by the Arondizuogu people in parts of Imo State, for religious worship, thanksgiving, census and family reunion.

Ogun Between June and August. Yoruba festival in honour of the god of iron, with singing, dancing and drumming. Held in numerous towns of the region.

Oshun August/September. Festival in honour of the river goddess and guardian spirit of the people of Oshogbo. Another well-known celebration, but much of the week-long event is considered too sacred to be shared with visitors.

Sekiapu October. Masquerades, regattas and a great deal of merriment in River and Cross River states.

Igue December. Procession of the Oba of Benin. The ensuing celebration lasts several days and includes traditional dancing and a lot of drinking and eating.

Ofala December. Festival in Onitsha and other towns along the Niger to honour the traditional ruler, who appears before his people.

Entertainment

Nigeria has a thriving and complex cultural scene. Music, of course, is a massive industry. Theatre is lively and inventive and now benefiting from cross-fertilization with TV. Cinema is blighted by financial incapacity (see Contexts). Nigerian literature is of world importance – there's a clutch of great writers, including Nobel prize winner Wole Soyinka (who spends much time in the USA) and the renowned and more accessible author and opinion-moulder Chinua Achebe (who's often in Britain). There's also a new generation of writers
who live abroad, the most well known being Ben Okri and Adewale Maja-Pearce (see "Books" in Contexts). In sports, soccer and athletics are the big crowd-pullers.

■ Music

Lagos feels the heartbeat of Nigerian music. You can hear all the styles here and stand a good chance of seeing international stars – **Femi Kuti**, son of the late **Fela Kuti**, **King Sunny Ade**, **Victor Uwaifo**, **Sonny Okosuns**, **Victor Olaiya** – at any of three dozen or so clubs and hotel dance floors. In other cities around the country, especially in the south (Ibadan, Benin, Enugu, Port Harcourt or Calabar) you can also be lucky enough to catch an international act. For further background and insights, see the "Music" section in Contexts.

■ Theatre

Nigeria has a 400-year-old theatrical tradition with the **Yoruba language** as its outstanding vehicle. The **Alarinjo Theatre** was the court entertainment of sixteenth-century Oyo. Once allowed by the rulers to become a popular form, it spread and travelled from city to city among the old kingdoms. By the nineteenth century, it was a major cultural influence, but it waned with the penetration of Christianity, only to resurge again in the 1940s, when players performed biblical scenes before church congregations.

Duro Lapido, **Kola Ogunmola** and **Hubert Ogunde** were the most famous names in the travelling theatre genre. They took plays from town to town, giving voice to the changing social and cultural scene in southern Nigeria, right through the pre-independence era and successive federal governments since. You may be lucky and catch one of the noisy, half-improvized productions. But these days many groups are more involved with making their own **films** (see Contexts), which are popular well beyond southwest Nigeria.

As for **English-language drama** groups, they're mostly attached to the universities, don't attract any state or federal support and inevitably don't have a mass audience. **Wole Soyinka**, **John Pepper Clark**, **Femi Osofisan**, **Ola Rotimi** and **Bode Osanyin** are some of Nigeria's best-known playwrights. In Lagos, check how the **Pec Repertory Group** is faring. They're the first full-time professional rep group, established by John Pepper Clark.

■ Football

With more than 100,000 licensed players, Nigeria's soccer skills are highly respected in Africa, and the national side – **Super Eagles** – has been riding high on a wave of victories in recent years. Current star players are the experienced strikers **Daniel Amokashi** and **Nwanko Kanu**, the maverick midfield player **Augustine Azuka Okocha**, and the defender and combative all-rounder **Ogorchukwu Sunday Oliseh**, as well as **Okechukwu Alozie Uche**, nicknamed the "Gentle Giant". Many of the star Nigerian players appear in European teams.

Successful regional teams include **Shooting Stars** of Ibadan and **Enugu Rangers**, whose matches are often attended by enormous crowds. Port Harcourt has the attacking **Sharks**, and women's team, the **River Angles** – Nigeria's female team won the African Championship in 1998. Most major cities have their own football stadium, including of course the arenas used during the 1999 World Youth Championship.

Trouble

Nigeria's dreadful reputation for trouble is exaggerated, but security is not something to take lightly in Lagos and other large cities. Lagos gangs are active and well organized. Even more disturbing is the huge number of handguns and other weapons in private possession and the implication of some police in criminal activities. Though outlaws may "control" entire neighbourhoods, you're most unlikely ever to see one, or anyone out of uniform carrying a gun. Leave valuables behind when you go out, and you're likely to be fine.

If you spend much time in expat circles in **Lagos**, you'll hear plenty of recycled gossip about the **security problems**. Despite mandatory death sentences for armed robbery, burglaries are extremely common and night-watchmen are often killed. But visitors, even long-term ones, are rarely at risk. Be alert, not paranoid.

You're unlikely to get yourself into real trouble in Nigeria unless you cross someone with serious influence. There are a lot of **drugs** floating around Lagos, however, and if you become involved you could easily find yourself in deep water. **Marijuana** is cultivated in the south and commonly smoked. It became popular in the army during the civil war but its use is officially considered a serious offence. The Indian Hemp Decree of 1966 provides for ten-year jail sentences for smokers and the death sentence for cultivation or import. Lorry drivers have long used amphetamines, but Lagos' pivotal position in the worldwide transportation of **hard drugs** is bringing heroin and cocaine onto the domestic market. Stay well clear.

If you're British, and considering doing business in Nigeria, you might want to check credentials with the Nigeria Desk of the Department of Trade and Industry (☎0171/215 4844).

Directory

AIRPORT DEPARTURE TAX US$20 on international departures. For non-residents it is only payable in dollars. Now usually included in the ticket price.

CRAFTS Nigeria has a fantastic wealth of things worth acquiring, both utilitarian and aesthetic. Jewellery (including the antique, multicoloured glass trading beads that are now getting expensive), leatherware, carved calabashes, bronze figures made with the lost wax method, handwoven cloth and woodcarvings are the most obvious. Regrettably, you're likely to be offered ivory from time to time and various other animal products – lizard-snake-and crocodile-skin bags and belts. Possibly the best value and longest-lasting interest is to be had from musical instruments, which you'll find if you look beyond the souvenir stands at the big hotels. Talking drums – the expressive *iyaalu* tension drums which so unerringly imitate the Yoruba voice – are particularly worth looking out for. See the "Music" section in Contexts.

EMERGENCIES If you run into trouble, the police emergency number is ☎199, but help doesn't always come in a hurry.

GAY LIFE Being gay in Nigeria is not easy, but there is a community, with its own advocacy group Gentlemen Alliance, that is attempting to overturn centuries of ignorance about gay issues. AIDS awareness campaigning is important, but their priority is to educate the public at large about the existence of gays in every walk of life in

TROUBLE ON THE ROAD

If you have **your own vehicle**, be careful where you leave it. Overlanders will encounter no special problems in northern Nigeria, but in the south some take a lesson from residents who carve their licence numbers on all windows and use crook locks. Never park in an unguarded area and leave nothing of value in your car at any time.

There are few **roadblocks** in central Nigeria, but they appear with increasing frequency towards the borders (seven, for example, in the last 21km before Ikom). Most have oil drums staggered across the road, or two nail-studded planks, and they're illuminated by torches at night. Very occasionally a roadblock will consist of just a piece of string. Although often privately on the make, the officials are there to maintain law and order and, sometimes only a few hundred yards apart, may be staffed 24 hours a day by police, army, customs, the Agriculture Ministry or detectives, each with their own particular interest in your documents, movements and motivations. Any of them may wave you through, but it's always advisable to slow down to be sure. When stopped, remain inside until told what to do, as half the officials will want you to stay put and the other half will want you to assemble outside: it's impossible to predict which.

The Nigerian **police and civil service** has its quota of thugs and morons but they themselves are respected occupations, and many officers, even in the lower ranks, are educated and well read. You'll meet senior officers who've been to university in the UK, US or Canada. Often posted far from their home town, they may welcome a chat about books or politics. They may also be waiting for a lift, and the minor inconvenience of an extra passenger is far outweighed by the ease with which one passes through subsequent roadblocks.

Nigerians' **sense of humour** varies greatly. Generally, officials in the north are restrained and courteous while in the south it seems to be a great joke for a soldier to storm up to a foreigner shouting about illegal parking, the wrong colour of numberplate or some other misdemeanour. When you've been adequately embarrassed or terrified, there's a hearty thump on the back, and an invitation to share the joke (try to be polite!). It's worth pointing out that the police – and others in uniform – keep abreast of the news and know full well that expatriates and other foreigners break the law and indulge in criminal activities from time to time. Rumours circulate fast among the police. Your behaviour may be impeccable, but they don't know that. In a country as big and hard to control as this, it's important you find every last ounce of tolerance.

Lastly, it's not unknown for enterprising traders, or even highway **bandits**, to pose as a roadblock by setting up their wares on a couple of oil drums. Sometimes it's hard to tell. Nigerian officials are sometimes in plain clothes, but they usually show their ID as soon as you pull up, or on request. Bandits really do exist – and their ingenious exploits are faithfully reported in all the tabloid newspapers – but the number of robberies, as a proportion of the number of journeys made, is negligible. The more you talk to locals, the more you'll hear, and the safer you'll be. Incidents are reported close to the Niger border, on long haul routes between the north and the south, and in and around cities during "go slows". Fortunately, the number of roadblocks in towns and on the roads has been officially reduced since the early 1990s, and armed robbery and road accidents have dropped significantly – surely some connection.

Nigeria, and to overcome the view that homosexuality is an imported phenomenon.

MUSEUMS Nigeria has more museums than anywhere in West Africa. The main ones are in **Lagos**, **Kano**, **Ife**, **Jos** and **Calabar**, but just about every town of any size has a museum of some sort. They tend to focus either on history, art or customs, though there's also an **oil museum** in Oloibiri (50km from Port Harcourt), a **mining museum** in Jos, and **military museums** in Zaria and Umuahia (former headquarters of Biafran military leaders).

OPENING HOURS Banks open Mon–Thurs 8am–3pm and Fri 8am–1pm. Shops usually open Mon–Sat 8am–5pm. Some goods are available almost 24 hours.

PHOTOGRAPHY Although no permit is required, photography is something the military, the police and security agents are extremely touchy about. Be particularly careful around public buildings, including mosques, palaces, offices and railway stations. Photographing people in traditional costume, at country markets and the like, is likely to incur wrath among interfering types who may report you. On the other hand, many Nigerians are flattered if they attract the attention of your lens – although some may expect a small reward for their co-operation. On departure, you may be quizzed by the police about photographs, although they may accept your word that you haven't taken any. Remove film from your camera, and repack it, as a precaution, before the border. If you fly out, there's no problem.

UNIVERSITIES Nigeria has far more universities and colleges than all the other countries in West Africa put together, including the **University of Lagos** (UNILAG) and the **University of Ibadan** (UI), the nation's first, founded in 1949. There are still some expat visiting scholars and teachers, but you'll more often find Nigerian "profs" who have spent some time abroad. Nigeria also has a number of **research institutes**, some of which have a world-wide reputation.

WILDLIFE There's still a fair bit of wildlife to be seen in Nigeria, though little in the big game league. The northern **Yankari** and **Kainji Lake National Parks** contain elephants, hippos and larger antelopes, and there's the remote possibility of glimpsing lions or other big cats. More exciting perhaps, is the discovery of gorillas in the thick forests of the southeast. The **Gashaka-Gumpti National Park** covers a huge area with terrain that varies from savannah grasslands to mountain forests. There are no elephants left here, but a variety of other wildlife, including chimpanzees. The **Nigerian Conservation Foundation** (NCF), 5 Moseley Rd, Ikoyi, Lagos (☎01/268 6163 or 268 7385) is making valiant efforts to rouse Nigerians from a complacent attitude to the wildlife heritage. One positive sign is the creation of the **Cross River National Park**, comprising rainforest and mountain forest reserves.

WOMEN Most foreign women working in Nigeria don't feel comfortable travelling alone in the Islamic-dominated north (pay special attention here to covering arms and legs) but the southern half of the country doesn't pose any gender-related problems: flirtatious sexual harassment may occur in clubs and at parties, but not on the street.

In a country where the change from traditional to urban-industrial values is taking place remarkably quickly, women have achieved larger real gains here than elsewhere in West Africa. But while they occupy positions in business, government and increasingly in the universities, there's still a lot of ground to cover. Two groups – the **National Committee for Women and Development**, formed in the early 1980s, and the **National Council of Women Societies**, twenty years

older – aim to fight for more equitable integration in all spheres. A radical alternative to NCWS, **Women in Nigeria** (WIN), was founded in 1985 in the male bastion of Zaria, and now has groups nationwide. Finally, the **Federation of Muslim Women** (FOMWAN) is a northern fundamentalist grouping.

A Brief History of Nigeria

Nigerian history is the most complex and also one of the most ancient in West Africa. The earliest indications of the use of iron in the region come from the Nok culture (named after the Jos plateau village where much of the evidence was found) and date back to 300 BC. For reasons unknown, this civilization faded, and the next discoveries date from over a millennium later. The development, by the ninth century, of mineral wealth in the Yoruba and Igbo regions of the south, led to long-lasting and sophisticated political structures. In the north, kingdoms arose at much the same time – first the Bornu empire in the ninth century, then, not long afterwards, the Hausa city states – and they became powerful stations on the trans-Saharan caravan routes, supplying many of the exotic requirements of medieval Europe.

The slave trade and, much later, colonial invasion, wreaked havoc on these indigenous states, as well as on the weaker, stateless communities living among them. Detailed coverage of pre-colonial history is included on a regional basis throughout the main guide section of this chapter.

Since the end of the nineteenth century, the colonial protectorates, and then the federation of modern Nigerian states, have been the setting for a panoply of events and characters set against a background of poverty, booming population and almost continual crisis. Unlike most smaller West African nations, a substantial and expanding literature exists on the history, sociology and political science of Nigeria (see "Books" in Contexts). The following summary is only the simplest historical framework, picking out the most salient features of Nigeria's history.

■ The arrival of Europeans

The **Portuguese** were the first Europeans to reach the Benin Gulf, in 1472, and within a short time they had made contact with the kingdom of **Benin**. Trade soon began, initially centred on pepper, ivory and other exotic goods. It was not until the second half of the seventeenth century, when the Americas had been widely colonized and plantations needed increasing supplies of labour, that the focus shifted to slaves.

The early Europeans had few permanent forts or settlements, basing themselves instead on off-shore "hulks" near the ports. By the 1660s, these permanently moored ships were highly developed, sparking off an explosion of competitive slave-trading at ports like **Lagos**, **Warri**, **Calabar** and **Bonny**. Much of the driving force behind the trade, which was exploited by local chiefs, came from the insecurity of a West African arms race for the latest European muskets and cannon. In exchange for weaponry, the French and British, who had supplanted the Portuguese and Brazilians by the eighteenth century, were scarcely interested in buying anything except slaves.

The colonial carve-up

At the beginning of the nineteenth century, things appeared to change, as the newly republican **French** sent warships to the southeast Nigerian coast to break up the slave trade. To French cries of *Liberté, Egalité, Fraternité*, the British added their own hollow "Christianity, Commerce and Civilization". In fact, slaves no longer made economic sense; instead, in the wake of the European industrial revolution, **markets** were needed for manufactured goods and there was a massive demand for supplies of raw materials – cotton, sugar and the rest.

In 1851, the British shelled Lagos, ostensibly to quicken the demise of the slave trade, in practice to impose a puppet regime and improve the newly important palm oil trade. The slave trade went underground, and slavers hid out in the lagoons around Lagos from where they would sneak out their cargo to Brazil, which was still an importer. Meanwhile the British seized Lagos Island in 1861 – which then became Lagos colony, the first particle of Nigeria.

After the European Powers' **Berlin Conference** of 1885, the London-based **Royal Niger Company** was granted exclusive trading rights in the Niger River basin. With the Germans expanding to the east, and the French to the north and west, the British government took over the RNC in 1899 and began pushing it in all directions.

By 1900, they'd succeeded in drawing borders around a vast region of diverse peoples, who found themselves under the ultimate authority of northern and southern protectorates. In 1914 a federation was formed – in preference to a united colony – and named **Nigeria**, a term coined by the wife of Lord Lugard, the British colonial commander in the region.

Indirect rule

From the beginning, Nigeria was an ill-matched association and it was clear that conflict would arise between the conservative, largely Muslim and feudal **north**, and the more outward-looking **south**, with its Christian missions and, in the southeast, lack of rigid social hierarchies. At the very least, problems would be caused by the new territory's southward-looking orientation, away from the old Saharan routes and towards the ports and European trade.

The British, however, pressed ahead with their system of "**indirect rule**", which in the **north** worked easily enough, to the benefit of both the Hausa-Fulani emirs (who carried on much as before) and the British administration. Lord Lugard simply took over the role of regional overlord from the Sultan of Sokoto, whose functions were perforce purely religious and ceremonial.

But indirect rule was a disaster in the **southeast**, where decisions and judicial processes were traditionally applied by consent among groups of senior men. In **Igboland**, the "Warrant Chiefs" commissioned by the British had no mandate for their authority, and on the contrary were usually independent-minded status-seekers who had acquired a mission education.

In **Yorubaland**, another variation was imposed. The British held Yoruba traditional rulers, with British "advisors", accountable for their decisions. But the British had failed to understand the fabric of Yoruba politics and perceived in their centralized **government of obas** and the traditional ceremonial-executive titles of the **Alafin of Oyo** and the **Oni of Ife**, simple dictatorships somewhat akin to the emirates of the north. Disregarding the fact that the Yoruba offices were posts given to selected senior men by others of high rank, Lugard tried to control the selection of pliant chiefs by men who, again, had no mandate to enforce his requirements. And he actively connived to empower those Yoruba elements who posed least threat to white prestige, to turn the clock back, as far as possible, to his own avowedly racist vision of an Africa untainted by progress.

While British rule led to internal schisms in Yorubaland, the region benefited from the fastest input of technology and **modern infrastructure**. There was electricity in Lagos by 1898, bridges between the islands and a rail link with Ibadan by 1900, all of which was to prove another source of division for north and south to deal with after independence.

■ The road to independence

Nigerians became involved in the political process relatively early, by the standards of other African colonies. In 1923, the first Africans, led by **Herbert Macaulay**, a Yoruba whose father had returned from slave captivity in Sierra Leone, were elected to a legislative advisory council in Lagos. But local parties really only developed after the experience of World War II, when Nigerians returned from fighting for European ideals like "self-determination" and "liberty".

In 1944, the **National Council for Nigeria and the Cameroons** was formed by Herbert Macaulay and **Dr Nnamdi Azikwe**, an Igbo. Four years later, **Chief Obafemi Awolowo**, a Yoruba, founded a second party, the **Action Group**. By the end of the decade, the northerners also had their own party, the **Northern People's Congress**, with **Tafawa Balewa** at its head.

Predictably, these three parties came to represent the **regional interests** – the NPC for the north, the NCNC for the east, and the AG for the west. As they jockeyed for position to rule an independent nation, the parties agreed on nothing, delaying the process of reform in the process. In a dispute over the date for self-rule, suspicious northerners walked out of the colonial assembly in 1953, and bloody **riots in Kano** followed. Members from each region felt sure the other two were conspiring to dominate, and there was talk of dividing the country into several smaller political units in an effort to relieve the tension. The British argued such a measure would only stall independence further, an argument in which they were supported by the northern region, which had to have a friendly route to the sea.

Finally, in 1957, it was decided the nation would be formed of the three rival regions. **Tafawa Balewa** became the head of the new central government and Nigeria gained independence on October 1, 1960.

■ Independence: the early years

The early 1960s were characterized by an **uneasy coalition** between the **north** and the **southeast** against the powerful **southwest** region dominated by the Yoruba. The latter thus saw its worst fears realized and its leaders panicked when a bogus census in 1963 suggested the north had four million more inhabitants than the rest of the nation combined. The threat of Muslim domination in the political arena now seemed very real.

The southeast eventually slipped out of the coalition and Chief Awolowo raised angry cries against government tinkering with the country's structure. He was tried for treason and jailed. **Early chaos** seemed to be gaining momentum and in January 1966 the army toppled the government – killing Tafawa Balewa in the process – and set about trying to restore order.

Military rule

The new **military government** was headed by **General J. Aguiyi-Ironsi**, an Igbo. Northerners rioted in reaction to the radical early reforms that abolished the federation and imposed a unitary government dominated by Igbos. Fighting broke out within the army and, after only six months, Ironsi was killed in another **coup**, this time led by northern officers. As many as 7000 Igbos living in the north were massacred in the aftermath and up to half a million fled to the east.

But the military's new leader was different from his predecessors. **Yakubu Gowon** was a Christian northerner, a young and charismatic figure, who restored the tripartite federation and released Awolowo and other Action Group leaders of the west. But the southeast region, led by the military governor, **Lieutenant-Colonel C. Odumegwu-Ojukwu**, who rejected Gowon's leadership, pushed instead for a loose confederation.

In September 1966, elements of the northern army began the systematic **killing of Igbos** who had remained in the north. Official reports placed the deaths at 5000, though Igbos claimed that as many as 30,000 were massacred. The pogrom was a decisive blow to the shaky federation. High-ranking Igbo civil servants began returning from Lagos to the regional capital at Enugu and pressuring Ojukwu to secede.

National politics in the early part of 1967 were completely dominated by the **question of the future of the Federal Republic**. The Ghanaian government attempted to mediate between the sides and, in January 1967, leaders of the federal government met with Ojukwu in Aburi. The meetings produced no acceptable compromise; nor did subsequent government moves to appease the east with conciliatory measures and guarantees.

At the last minute, Gowon announced the **division of the federation** into twelve separate states in an attempt to undermine the overweening north and disarm his critics from the ethnic minorities, especially in the southeast, who had long sought greater autonomy. It was too late. Fearing the Igbo constituency would be pushed permanently into the margins of national politics, Ojukwu unilaterally withdrew the Eastern Region from the federation and declared the independent **Republic of Biafra** on May 30, 1967.

The Biafran War

In July 1967, Biafran troops marched into the Western Region in an attempt to surround Lagos. Federal troops responded by blockading eastern ports and by attacking Biafra from the north and west. Despite a lack of manpower and resources, Biafra scored a number of military successes in the early days of the war, but by the end of 1967, the conflict had degenerated into a brutal **war of attrition**. Fighting was vicious and confused. Most of the major towns changed hands several times. Federal forces captured a number of coastal towns, reducing Biafra to an enclave in the Igbo heartland. Federal military atrocities, of which many were reported, further convinced the Igbos that they were engaged in an all-out war for survival.

Biafra gained considerable sympathy in the international press: for the first time, public opinion in the rich world was mobilized against Third World poverty. Yet few countries gave official recognition to Biafra, and French military and technical aid seemed suspiciously self-interested. The war dragged on for three years, claiming the lives of at least 100,000 soldiers, but many more Igbo civilians, of whom between half a million and two million are estimated to have perished as a result of the government's policy of **blockade and starvation**. Supported by British aid and Soviet arms, the Federal government finally captured the last rebel-held town of Owerri and quelled the rebellion in December 1969. Much of the southeast was ravaged.

■ Reconstruction

The gaping wounds of the war appeared to heal with remarkable speed. Gowon, who was still in power after four years, was careful not to humiliate the defeated and bereaved easterners or exclude them from the new federation. In fact, he offered an **amnesty** to all who had fought on the Biafran side, and vowed to rebuild the east while furthering the economic development of the entire country.

Reconstruction didn't take place overnight, but it is remarkable today how little evidence of the war remains, even in cities that were virtually destroyed. Gowon was aided in the early days of reconciliation by **oil revenues** that flooded into the coffers in the early 1970s, as Nigeria became one of the world's ten largest producers. But as blatant corruption became a national issue, and Gowon began dragging his feet on promises of a return to civilian rule and devoting most of his energies to international image-building, he was ousted, after nine years in power, in a bloodless coup led by **General Murtala Muhammed** in July 1975.

Murtala Muhammed

Of all Nigeria's leaders, Murtala Muhammed has been without doubt the most popular. Even today, his name is referred to with a reverence not normally reserved for politicians. Another northerner with considerable charisma, he structured all his policies around the return of power to an elected leadership and devoted himself to wiping out corruption.

Shortly after coming to power, Muhammed instigated "**Operation Deadwoods**" – a policy of forced dismissal or retirement of public officials on a whole range of charges from corruption to "infirmity". In all, more than 10,000 civil servants – police officials, senior diplomats, university professors, even military officers – were relieved of their posts. Swift action was taken against embezzlement of public funds. Assets were confiscated. Appointees were sacked for reasons as simple as a conflict of interests. It was a breath of fresh air in a stagnating and counter-productive bureaucracy and brought the government huge popularity.

By the end of 1975, Muhammed had concluded the purge and announced a four-year countdown to return the country to civilian rule. He had come to be regarded as a politician who made promises and kept them, and drew attention to the future and away from the divisive tragedy of the past. Nigerians felt they were leaders in a liberalizing movement that would sweep the continent and break the cycle of totalitarianism in Africa.

It's difficult to know if posterity would have been so kind to Muhammed had he lived to see his programmes carried out. After only six months of reshaping the country he was assassinated by disgruntled members of the military, shot while his car was in a Lagos traffic jam.

■ The Second Republic

The counter-coup was effective only in eliminating Muhammed, for the plotters were rounded up and with the help of Major General Ibrahim Babangida, was smoothly transferred to Muhammed's chief of staff, **Olusegun Obasanjo**, a Christian Yoruba. Obasanjo pledged to adhere to Muhammed's schedule for the return to civilian government and continued reshaping the civil service. A new constitution, based on that of the USA, was drawn up, and political parties were legalized in September 1978.

Five **political parties** were finally approved, but four were headed by familiar old names, had vague right-of-centre programmes and seemed to indicate the persistence of regional divisions. **Awolowo** and **Azikwe** (now in their seventies) headed parties largely representing the west and the east respectively, or at least their personal powerbases in those regions – the Unity Party of Nigeria and the Greater National People's Party. The National People's Party, from which the GNPP was a breakaway group, was led by a northern businessman, **Alhaji Waziri Ibrahim**. The National Party of Nigeria, based on Kaduna and led by **Alhaji Shehu Shagari**, claimed to cut across regional loyalties but was essentially the old NPC northern party, controlled as ever by the Fulani oligarchy. Shagari, himself a Fulani from a leading northern family, had been a member of the first civilian government and had served under Gowon's military regime. Lastly, in opposition to the NPN, another northern party had also been formed – the People's Redemption Party. Led by **Alhaji Aminu Kano**, it had radical socialist leanings and was explicitly committed to the cause of inter-ethnic co-operation.

In the complicated elections that spread over six weeks in 1979, all the parties achieved some representation, but **Shagari** won the all-important **presidential election**. He rode out his first term in Nigeria's new "Second Republic" on a wave of genuine popularity and public relief that the long period of military rule was over. But the new president didn't survive long untarnished. **Crackdowns on the press** – which had begun

reporting government corruption, and even daring to point fingers at Shagari and his Kaduna clique – clearly signalled his insecurity, and he faced serious challenges from other northern parties and eastern allies in his unstable coalition.

The **economy**, too, was slipping badly. The oil boom had peaked in 1980. In December of that year serious **riots** broke out in Kano, prompted by the popular "jihadist" teachings and calls for social justice of Mai Tatsine. As foreign currency reserves dwindled and the external debt skyrocketed, the standard of living for most Nigerians rapidly declined, while government officials, cabinet ministers and the president himself made fortunes, indulging in what came to be known as "squandermania". Further, serious **riots in Maiduguri**, in October 1982, were dismissed by Shagari as "religious agitation" and, in February 1983, some two million immigrant workers – from Ghana, Cameroon, Chad and Niger – were expelled as economic scapegoats.

Despite these various obstacles, Shagari managed to get elected to a second term in October 1983, a sounder win, in fact, than his first, though achieved with less than sound methods.

■ Another coup: a new military regime

The inevitable happened barely three months after the 1983 elections, when another northerner – **Major-General Mohammed Buhari** – staged a bloodless takeover of power and suspended the 1979 constitution. Explaining his actions, the new leader announced shortly after the takeover: "the economic mess, the corruption and unacceptable level of unemployment could not be excused on the grounds that Nigeria was a practising democracy."

Buhari announced the "voluntary retirement" of high-ranking military officers and the inspector general of the police, all of whom were implicated in financial mismanagement and corrupt practices on a gigantic scale. Prominent members of Shagari's party were arrested, as was the president. Through such moves, Buhari sought to associate his regime with the purist popularity of Muhammed. Important elder statesmen from the martyred president's administration were brought into the new government, including former head of state Obasanjo.

The attack on graft – the **"War Against Indiscipline"** – even crossed international borders. One of the most wanted offenders was the former transport minister **Alhaji Umaru Dikko**, who was living in luxurious exile in London, from where he openly criticized the new government. In one of the more bizarre instances of abuse of diplomatic privilege, Dikko was kidnapped, drugged and bundled into a crate, ready to be shipped off as diplomatic baggage from Gatwick airport. The plot was only aborted when British customs officials queried the contents of the crate. Buhari's government quickly denied any responsibility, although the Nigerian High Commission was strongly implicated in the abduction. Diplomatic relations between the UK and Nigeria nearly broke over the incident.

Buhari, however, seemed serious in his efforts to wipe out corruption, and as a result was initially quite popular with people fed up with government abuse. But it soon became apparent that members of Shagari's Kaduna clique were not prominent among those convicted on corruption charges. In addition to the accusation of partiality, it was not long before Buhari himself was gaining a reputation as an unbending **autocrat**. As those accused of corruption were given sentences of as much as 72 years, Buhari arrested many of his regime's critics and suppressed the Nigerian media in ways Shagari had not dared. On the discovery of an alleged coup plot in 1984, he swiftly executed a group of some forty soldiers. And two government decrees, reflecting the new hardline, proved extremely unpopular with the masses. The first, known as Decree 2, allowed for detention without trial of citizens regarded as a threat to the state. Decree 4 imposed press controls by insisting journalists verify the "truth" of their reporting.

Even more unpopular were **austerity measures** adopted by Buhari in 1984 as he sought to remedy the country's growing economic problems. Strong opposition to his rule grew as resulting price increases and shortages of consumer goods jolted the nation – especially its poorer citizens. Buhari tried to deflect criticism, as Shagari had done, by blaming the country's economic woes on foreign workers robbing Nigerians of jobs. **Mass expulsions of immigrants** were instigated and, in May 1985, up to a million foreigners – again many of them Ghanaian – were shipped out in chaotic conditions. Relations soured with Nigeria's neighbours which, facing economic crises of their own, suddenly found a flood of displaced and unemployed refugees on their doorsteps.

None of Buhari's drastic measures worked, partly because there was virtually no popular support

for the man behind them and principally because the Naira was overvalued and worthless. With the economy hardly performing any better after his two years at the top, and a foreign debt of some £12 billion ($18 billion) pulling the country down, a new coup was orchestrated, in August 1985, by close associates of Buhari in the Supreme Military Council, led by army chief of staff **Major-General Ibrahim Babangida**, born in Minna, in Niger State, but brought up in Kano.

■ The "Period of Transition": Ibrahim Babangida

Within a short time of taking office, **Babangida** and his new Armed Forces Ruling Council had released many of the political prisoners from Nigerian jails and a new sense of freedom began to be felt. Not without misgivings, though, for in December 1986, ten officers from Benue State, who, Babangida alleged, had been conspiring to overthrow him, were executed.

Babangida began preparing the country once again for national elections. Such political moves went down well at home, though his economic policies were tough and unyielding. Shortly after taking power, he declared an **economic state of emergency** and, in 1985, broke off loan negotiations with the IMF – a move that met with popular nationalistic support. But enthusiasm waned when the president imposed austerity measures of his own. He devalued the Naira fourfold, in the hope of attracting investors, and began privatizing unprofitable public enterprises and lifting government subsidies, notably on petrol.

Periodic **demonstrations and strikes** resulted, and, although conflict tended to be sparked by economic policies, **ethnic and religious tensions** were never far away. In 1986, Babangida announced that Nigeria had joined the Organization of the Islamic Conference. Despite stressing this had been done for cultural and religious reasons – and not political ones – non-Muslim southerners feared that the government and its northern powerbase were trying to impose Islamic rule on the whole country. There were **campus protests** and a number of deaths in northern universities in 1986 and, in 1987, **religious riots** broke out between Muslims and Christians in Kaduna State, leading to the deaths of dozens of people, the arrest of over a thousand and the banning of religious organizations at schools and universities.

Adding to the political frustration, Babangida postponed the elections three times between 1990 and 1992, leaving many to question if he ever intended to step down. In April 1990, a group of junior, Christian officers attempted a coup, which was quickly put down but resulted in 300 deaths. Over the next two years, ethnic-religious clashes intensified. In April 1991, Muslim demonstrations erupted in Katsina, leading to violence and many deaths. In Bauchi, 130 people were killed when Christians slaughtered pigs in a market shared by Muslims. Later in the year, 300 people died in Kano, following demonstrations provoked by a touring Christian minister.

Babangida's solution to the regional problem was to create **nine new states** in 1991, arguing they would stimulate stability and development while ensuring more equitable representation of ethnic minorities. Despite the measures, it seemed ethnic enmities remained the driving force of Nigerian politics. In February 1992, fighting broke out in Kaduna State between Hausa Muslims and Kataf Christians. In the east, a land dispute between the Tiv and Jukun peoples resulted in an estimated 5000 deaths.

The deteriorating economy put a further strain on Babangida's government. By mid-1992, **inflation** was already soaring at 50 percent and widespread rioting broke out in Lagos over a sharp increase in transport fares. There were a number of reported deaths as demonstrators, who demanded the government resign, were brutally dispersed by security forces. More protests ensued after prominent human rights activists, including Dr Beko Ransome-Kuti (brother of musician Fela Kuti) and Chief Fani Fawehinmi were arrested for accusing the government of instigating the riots so as to delay elections. In June, the Academic Staff of Nigerian Universities called a nationwide strike in a wage dispute. Despite his stated commitment to collective bargaining, Babangida banned the union and, with it, the National Association of Nigerian Students. Most of the nation's thirty universities closed as a result.

The mood of the country was therefore downbeat as Nigerians prepared for **National Assembly elections** in July 1992. Despite the vast sums of money spent on the campaign, the election sparked little excitement among voters. Babangida had insisted on a **two-party system** and created the Social Democratic Party and the National Republican Convention in order to pre-vent the rise of regional, ethnic or religious interest groups. But Nigerian commentators liked to call them a "Yes" party and a "Yes Sir" party. The fact that the increasingly unpopular military regime had created, funded and written the platforms of both SDP and NRC led to widespread **voter apathy**. Despite slick, state-financed media blitzes, neither party challenged the government's handling of issues such as inflation or ethnic tension. Serious opposition seemed only to come from the nation's human rights organizations, students and lawyers.

Although the SDP won majorities in both the House of Representatives and the Senate, the Armed Forces Ruling Council decided in mid-July that the legislature would not be inaugurated until after a new civilian president was sworn in.

■ Failed elections

When the **presidential elections** finally rolled around in June 1993, there were few signs of voter enthusiasm. The two candidates that emerged – **Moshood Abiola** of the SDP and **Bashir Tofa** of the NRC – stood out more for their abilities to amass huge fortunes than for any record of public service. Cynicism ran high among voters who found it hard to digest promises of prosperity in a country where yearly per capita income had fallen from $1000 to $290 in the ten years preceding the elections.

The results, however, surprised observers. Abiola – a Muslim from the mainly Christian Yoruba country of the southwest – won an apparently clear victory with 58 percent of the vote. Winning in several northern states, he appeared to seal a mandate that cut across ethnic lines. Marring this triumph was a deadlock created by legal wrangling over the election results. The judiciary's partisan colouration in giving judgments on the elections created an atmosphere of suspicion between the north and south. On June 23, Babangida stepped in and annulled the elections.

Human rights organizations immediately called for a campaign of civil disobedience. Mass **pro-democracy demonstrations** led to more violence and brought Lagos and much of the southwest to a standstill. Abiola declared himself winner on June 24, stating in a national broadcast, "From now on, the struggle in Nigeria is between the people and a small clique in the military determined to cling to power." But the standoff between civilians and the military also aroused old regional divisions: southerners remained convinced the military would never accept a southern president.

Babangida, who had started his presidential career as a liberal reformer, seemed, after the elections, ominously entrenched and intolerant of dissent. As troops put down anti-government riots in Lagos, the military threatened the death sentence for anyone whose words or deeds might undermine "the fabric of the nation" and shut down critical newspapers including the *Sketch*, *Observer*, *Punch* and *Concord*. Abiola fled the country.

But in August 1993, Babangida unexpectedly stepped aside as president and commander-in-chief of the armed forces. He insisted, however, that an **interim government** backed by decree would be the most favourable alternative to military rule and appointed **Ernest Shonekan** – former chairman of the United African Company, Nigeria's largest conglomerate – to lead the country until the next elections were held.

Abiola promptly returned from abroad, where he had been trying to rally foreign support for his claims to the presidency. But within weeks of taking over as head of state, Shonekan seemed to have swung public opinion behind himself. Former presidents **Nnamdi Azikwe** and **Olusegun Obasanjo** supported the interim government and the unions called off strikes. Meanwhile, Abiola isolated himself from the masses with his calls for an "economic blockade" of Nigeria and warnings of "a bloodbath" were he not sworn in. Preferring to stay in Lagos rather than tour the country to rally support, he increasingly became associated with a Yoruba, rather than a national cause.

But neither was Shonekan a credible figure. Ardent democrats labelled him a puppet of the military. Shonekan's ultimate downfall, however, was provoked when he tried to cut fuel subsidies in late 1993. As the price of petrol increased 600 percent, rioting again broke out in Lagos and a general strike threatened economic devastation. In November, **General Sani Abacha**, who was instrumental in the coups that toppled Shagari and Buhari, seized power, and, once again, the military stepped in "to save the nation from chaos".

■ Military rule: the Abacha government

Abacha quickly set about purging the military of officers loyal to Babangida, who remained in exile, and dissolved all political parties and

elected institutions. By then, politically numbed Nigerians didn't seem much worried that elected governors were replaced by military appointees and that the National Assembly ceded authority to a mainly military legislative council.

By mid-1994, Abacha was already being attacked from all sides. Civil liberties groups, students and unions, with the support of retired generals like Olusegun Obasanjo, publicly urged him to step down. Although political parties were banned, **political organizations** were formed and began turning up the heat. Abacha could only count on northerners for support, and even there he was losing ground. The Sultan of Sokoto, and other powerbrokers from Katsina and Maiduguri, criticized the military's policy, leaving the **Emir of Kano** as Abacha's only ardent supporter.

The **Campaign for Democracy** became influential, having gained credibility by organizing many of the demonstrations that led to Babangida's downfall. Meanwhile, the **National Democratic Coalition** (Nadeco) campaigned for a return to a civilian government headed by Abiola, and grew into a broad-based movement with support in the north as well as the south. On the first anniversary of the elections, Abiola was persuaded to declare himself president. He was promptly arrested.

Abacha never fared well in terms of **international relations**. Western nations deplored the banning of parties, arbitrary detention of opposition members and tight controls on the press. Officially, it was these policies that provoked **economic sanctions** against Nigeria, although the West was equally displeased with Abacha's resistance to IMF pressure to impose a tougher economic policy, the country's continued refusal to address the question of its £20 billion ($33 billion) debt and the new administration's tougher terms for drilling rights to Nigeria's oil reserves. London suspended Nigeria's membership to the Commonwealth, the US government "decertified" Nigeria, making the country ineligible for aid or for US support credits from the IMF, and Canada suspended it's diplomatic representation in Lagos. Some leaders – Nelson Mandela in particular – pushed for harder sanctions, including an oil blockade.

Amid the political turmoil, the economy provided no good news for Abacha. In early 1995, inflation was running at about 80 percent, exports had slumped badly and several banks looked set to collapse. Underlying this, a crisis in the oil industry had been triggered by a fall in world market prices, by repeated strikes and by gross corruption. Billions of dollars were stolen from the country's oil earnings between 1995 and 1998. Nigerians had few illusions about the level of **government theft**, but seemed more angered than during past regimes, when grand building projects and government spending at least had a trickle-down effect.

The Ogoni affair (see box, below) did not encourage **foreign investors**. During Abacha's tenure Nigeria was ranked the world's third riskiest location for business investment, after Iraq and Russia, with (to add to its unenviable human rights record) a well-established reputation for perpetrating fraud against unwary foreign investors – a notoriety of extreme concern to reputable Nigerian businesses.

Throughout Abacha's tenure, revelations of coup plots and reports of bombings near the army barracks in Abuja led to the arrest of numerous officers, including high-ranking generals whom Abacha had considered loyal. Hundreds of dis-

senters languished in jail – including the 24 men convicted of a supposed coup attempt in March 1995, one of whom was former head of state, Olusegun **Obasanjo**. Former secretary to Ibrahim Babangida, **Olu Falae**, joined him in jail two years later on charges of "conspiring to cause explosions".

Even mild critics described Abacha as unable to confront powerful economic interests at home or to make the tough choices needed to set his country on the right path. Cynics claimed that the general and his cronies had no other motive than self-enrichment, whatever the cost to Nigeria. Life, for the vast majority of people, was as bad as it had ever been – a slamming indictment of the failure of those in power to accomplish anything of value.

In response, in June 1995, the exiled Nobel laureate **Wole Soyinka** and others announced the formation of a **National Liberation Council** (NLC) of seventeen prominent opposition leaders. The NLC aimed to form a government in exile to campaign for the removal of the Abacha regime.

THE CASE OF THE OGONI

In recent years, a major focus of anti-government resentment has been the oilfields of the southeast, culminating in the 1995 murder trial over the deaths of four **Ogoni people** in the Ogoni district of Rivers State. The Ogoni, one of the southeast's minority ethnic groups, number half a million. The well-known TV writer, publisher and author, **Ken Saro-Wiwa**, who led the Movement for the Survival of the Ogoni People (**Mosop**), was charged in the affair, which escalated from a local incident to a national crisis, with international implications. Saro-Wiwa was sentenced to death and hanged in November 1995.

The Ogoni case has a history of army abuses and government apathy behind it, going back three decades. The 25km by 40km strip that comprises Ogoniland, to the southeast of Port Harcourt, now contains ten oilfields, over a hundred oil wells, a petrochemical complex, two oil refineries and seven flares burning off waste gas day and night. The land is scarred by pipelines and sludge-filled canals. When Shell Oil, which partly operates the Ogoni oilfields, was accused of neglecting its environmental responsibilities – oil pollution has damaged crops and farmlands and caused serious health problems – **Amnesty International** and **Greenpeace** took up the cause of Saro-Wiwa and the Ogoni and were joined by celebrities and opin-

ion-formers as diverse as British Labour MP Glenda Jackson, US presidential contender Jesse Jackson and Body Shop supremo Anita Roddick. Both Amnesty and Greenpeace have been banned from Ogoniland. As a British TV documentary showed, in 1990, in the single worst incident to date, a village was razed to the ground and 80 people massacred, when resentment among the Ogoni first exploded. Critics accuse Shell of standing by, while the government is accused of purposely stirring up ethnic tensions as a smoke screen, and of depleting the resources of the oilrich region, while returning almost nothing to the poorly developed local infrastructure.

The Ogoni were not all united behind Saro-Wiwa, but there is no disagreement that revenues from the oil drilled from their land (some £200 billion or $300 billion in thirty years of drilling, equivalent to 80 percent of all Nigeria's foreign currency earnings) are not being fairly shared. As local militants began sabotaging drilling facilities, the region was put under the charge of a tyrannical military commander – Major Paul Okuntimo – who publicly boasted of his murderous activities. The glare of bad publicity has more or less driven Shell out of business in Ogoniland, and has placed the company at the centre of violent skirmishes that continued in the Delta Region throughout the 1990s.

Like many before him, Soyinka was charged *in absentia* for treason and, more than ever, was forced to militate in exile. Shortly thereafter, **Kudirat Abiola**, the wife of the imprisoned victor of the last presidential election and an outspoken critic of the administration, was murdered by unidentified assailants. The nation saw the hand of the government behind the assault and rioting broke out, above all in Abiola's Yoruba homeland. Students were especially vociferous and the university of Ibadan was closed by government troops.

Nervous unrest was not limited to the south. In late 1996, the arrest of the local leader of Kaduna led to Muslim demonstrations that were violently quelled by the army. A year later, **Shehu Musa Yar Adua**, a respected northern politician who had been deputy head of state under Obasanjo, died mysteriously in jail, provoking thousands of supporters to riot in Katsina, calling for Abacha to step down. In the Delta Region, early 1997 saw an escalation of violence between the Ijaw and Itsekiri.

Disruption in petroleum production, along with gross mismanagement and the siphoning of billions of dollars into the pockets of the generals, led to a national **fuel shortage** that, by 1998, effectively suspended the transportation system in much of the country. To stave off a deepening crisis, Abacha, as head of the world's sixth largest crude oil producer, was forced to begin importing oil. As if that wasn't embarrassment enough, the country's poverty soared to its highest level since independence.

In 1996, Abacha made some gestures at **reform**, when he announced the creation of five new parties and a calendar for the return to civil rule by 1998. But most of the country's civilian opposition was already in jail, and the parties that had been granted official status by the national electoral commission were all seen as being loyal to Abacha. At the same time, the government talked of sweeping economic reforms that included the sale of state assets, even in the oil and gas sector, the elimination of the preferential exchange rate for government ministries and a campaign against corruption. These plans, intended for the ears of the IMF, the World Bank and foreign investors, were shot down by the military Provisional Ruling Council, who feared a short-term hike in unemployment and a long-term setback to their system of political patronage.

Just months before the scheduled elections, in June 1998, Abacha died from a **heart attack**; the news was greeted by a collective sigh of relief nationally and worldwide. When Nigeria radio announced the general's passing, critics and opponents of the regime poured into the streets of Lagos to celebrate. From abroad, Soyinka explained: "the people were sick of military dictatorship. So it's up to the military to recognize this – and up to the international community to say that we're sick and tired of the degeneration of a potentially great society."

■ Prospects

Most analysts, both nationals and foreigners, considered Abacha's government the most incompetent and brutal military regime ever to blight Nigeria, and there was hope that the **transitional government** that took over would bring some relief. Headed by **Abdulsalaam Abubakar**, the regime sent up encouraging early signals. Within weeks of taking office, he called for the establishment of new parties and elections to be held the following year and released hundreds of political prisoners, including Obasanjo. But just days later, Nigerians were shocked and sceptical when Moshood Abiola died of an apparent heart attack in his jail cell after four years of solitary confinement, and just one day before his scheduled release. Foul play was immediately suspected and news of the death brought hundreds of youths onto the streets of Lagos where they clashed with police.

As events pressed quickly forward, the mood changed to cautious optimism. Accompanying preparations for a return to **civil rule**, Abubakar began seeking economic reform to lift the country out of crisis. Negotiations began with the IMF for the implementation of a structural adjustment programme that included privatization and accountability – two essential ingredients for restoring the faith of creditors. At home, interest focused on the local elections of December 1998. Out of nine contesting parties, three gained more than five percent of the vote in 24 states, thereby gaining official status and the right to present candidates in the upcoming presidential elections. They were the People's Democratic Party (PDP), the Alliance for Democracy (AD) and the All People's Party (APP).

As head of the PDP, **Obasanjo** was the presidential candidate to beat from the start. From his time as head of state in the 1970s, he was remembered for being the only military leader ever to hand power back to civilians, and for governing during a time of economic prosperity. He enjoyed broad support throughout the country. In fact, northerners were more enthusiastic about his candidacy than people in his Yoruba homeland, and his choice of a northern running mate gave him extra impetus in the region. Well respected internationally, Obasanjo counts world leaders ranging from Jimmy Carter to Nelson Mandela as friends. Above all, it was widely believed that Obasanjo's military background could help him keep the military in line and bring about needed reforms.

Chief Olu Falae, an economist who represented the combined ticket of the AD and APP, struggled to keep pace with the political campaign machine run by the PDP. Also a Yoruba with a northern running mate, Falae had less money and only patchy support outside his southwest stronghold. When the polling took place in March 1999, Obasanjo captured nearly two-thirds of the votes.

The president elect didn't waste the momentum the elections had given to **foreign support**. One of his first visits after being elected was to Sierra Leone president Ahmad Tejan Kabbah, who asked for continued Nigerian backing. Obasanjo seemed to be re-evaluating the role of ECOMOG, or at least how it was funded, and his election remarks that troops "will not be in Sierra Leone a day longer than necessary" led to speculation about a withdrawal of monitoring forces. US president Bill Clinton sent the Reverend Jesse Jackson as a special envoy, and foreign secretary Robin Cook represented the British government for talks aimed at smoothing relations. In the time remaining before being sworn in, Obasanjo made a global trip that covered Asia, Europe, the United States and Africa, from the cape to Kenya. Overnight, Nigeria was an international player again.

Abubakar dutifully turned power over to the **elected government** in May 1999, and in his last official act banned Decree 2, the detention without trial law that had come to symbolize the tyranny and terror of successive military governments. In his inaugural address, Obasanjo said "I am determined to make significant changes within a year." It was a bold pledge and one he may have trouble keeping. He will have to step lightly as he works to clean corruption and put in place the kind of economic reforms the military has been resisting for years. World oil prices were still at record lows when he took office, a factor that forebodes recession, rising prices and a balance of payments crisis that may be worse than analysts anticipated. Balancing the regions will present the same challenge as it has for every administration before him – just days after he took office, armed youths sprayed gunfire through villages and burned down buildings in the Delta Region, causing oil companies to evacuate staff and the government to send in soldiers.

Despite the obvious challenges, there was real hope that a new era had arrived in 1999, and the country's mood was upbeat. Obasanjo can count on the backing he needs from the international community. In June 1999, as Nigeria's first elected parliament in over fifteen years convened, the EU lifted the last of the sanctions that had been in place since 1995, and resumed development aid. It was indicative of renewed co-operation and the desire to support efforts within Nigeria to rebuild a credible and stable government and return to more prosperous times.

LAGOS

If you're reading nervously, you wouldn't be the first traveller to approach **Lagos** with a sinking feeling of despair and trepidation, convinced you're going to hate the place – should you live through it. A city with somewhere above six million inhabitants, Lagos has grown too big too fast. Long ago, the city overflowed from the **islands** at its heart, and the urban sprawl on the mainland has mushroomed alarmingly. Of the infrastructure – housing, roads, public transport, water, electricity and sewerage – only the new expressways show any sign of keeping up. Pollution, squalid overcrowding, violent crime and a 24-hour din are the inevitable results of the shortfall. Although the crime rate has decreased over the last years because of tightened security, the underlying social problems have not been solved.

But you might just be surprised. It's the **international airport** – the business of arrival or connecting planes there – that is (or was until recently) to blame for much of the terrible first impression. On approaching the city itself, you may find rather less chaos – and more to excite. For Africa's foremost metropolis is, at the very least, a city of intense, voluble personality and breathtaking dynamism. Ships from around the globe berth at its **ports** of Apapa and Tin Can Island, and the **skyscrapers** that spike Lagos Island house a swarm of international firms. A more immediate sign of "success" is the commuter traffic packing the **flyovers**, regularly grinding to a halt in rush hour "go-slow" traffic jams, to be exploited by thousands of irrepressible **street vendors** trying to sell anything from imported apples to bathroom scales. And beyond the non-stop, unrestrained commercialism on the streets, universities, museums, galleries and the national theatre all attest to a thriving **intellectual and cultural life**.

While it would definitely be misleading to downplay its problems, Lagos is no more of a hell hole than any other gigantic, seething, impoverished city with an oppressive climate which was ruled by a military administration for many years. The risks of muggings and pickpocketing are high, but most people get through their stays safely. Travel…with as much confidence as you can muster and you may well have a good time…and debunking some myths and surviving the experience unscathed, as nearly everyone does, carry their own satisfaction.

Some history

The swampy mangrove zone around Lagos was originally inhabited by small hunting and fishing communities, but rainforest and marshes probably prevented large scale settlement. **Portuguese mariners** first arrived at the islands around Lagos in 1472 and named the place *Lago de Curamo*, but it wasn't until much later that the area became an important port of trade. In the sixteenth century, **Yoruba settlers** came to Iddo and later moved onto Lagos Island and beyond. The settlement was eventually incorporated into the **Benin kingdom** – which at the time extended all the way to the area of Cotonou – and renamed *Eko*, the Benin name for camp or war camp. In the early eighteenth century, the ruling Oba granted a trade monopoly to the Portuguese whose main export was, by then, **slaves**. A hundred years later, the French and British governments began sending warships to break up the slave trade, as Lagos was used as a hideout by profiteers who took advantage of the many creeks and rivers to conceal their human cargo. In 1851, the **British** shelled Lagos and eventually forced the Oba to abandon the slave trade. Soon after, they captured the islands and formed Lagos colony.

Early this century, Lagos grew into an important commercial centre thanks to the port and the **railway line**, begun in 1896 and opened through to Kano in 1912. It became the capital of the southern Nigerian protectorate and later of the entire

Federation, when north and south were merged. After independence, Lagos maintained its role as capital until 1991, when the seat of government moved to Abuja. The city is still the country's undisputed commercial, industrial, cultural and diplomatic centre, although more and more countries are moving their main embassies to the new capital.

Arrival, information and city transport

Lagos spreads over some 200 square kilometres and comprises myriad **neighbourhoods**. But the heart of the city, where you're likely to spend most of your time, is tucked onto **Lagos and Ikoyi islands** – now merged – and **Victoria Island**, to the south. If your stay is going to be any longer than a day or two, it's worth getting hold of a map or street atlas before you arrive, or as soon as possible afterwards.

By whatever means you come to Lagos, the **mainland** is your point of entry. Although there are bland neighbourhoods here (like the administrative district of **Ikeja**), most are populated by the city's working class and poor – and they can feel distinctly threatening. This is where many Lagos horror stories have their origins, but that's largely because most of the city's rich don't live there. As a temporary visitor you're no more likely to run into serious, violent trouble on the mainland than anywhere else in Lagos (perhaps, in truth, less).

Arrival

Arriving by plane at **Murtala Muhammed Airport** used to be the most harrowing experience you'd be likely to have in Lagos, with customs agents routinely aggressive and unsubtle ("What are you going to dash me?"). The situation is improving, however, and some travellers report no problems at all.

Only limited numbers of **taxis** are licensed to trade at the airport (ask to see the driver's ID card), and there are no buses out here. You could pay much more than the going price, but there are set rates posted in the airport and on the driver's tariff card, which you should insist on seeing. If it's after dark, your main concern, rather than worrying about saving a little money on the fare, should be to get out of the airport and into a hotel. If you're lucky enough to be flying in during daylight hours, you could, alternatively, walk down the airport road about 2km and pick up a shared taxi or a bus. The best option of all is to arrange to be **met from the airport** – all of the travel agents detailed on p.959 offer this service.

By **long-distance taxi**, you'll arrive at one of several points on the mainland – Mile Two, Yaba, Ojota, Iddo, Oju Elegba or Ebute Ero. From these places, battered yellow private buses drop you at Lagos Island, where you can get a cheap taxi to a hotel.

These days it's unusual to arrive by **ship**, though a number of cargo lines still offer berths. If you're interested in leaving this way, follow up the address in "Moving on from Lagos" on p.959. Ships berth at Apapa, opposite Lagos Island.

THE TAXI DRIVERS ACTUALLY SCREAM

"Well, it's true you have to fight to pay a normal taxi fare. For women, including Nigerian women, it's harder. The taxi drivers actually scream at you if you try to pay the regular price. But the regular price is the regular price and you can pay it after a fight (verbal) and all is well. This didn't bother me, but then I spent fourteen years living in New York City. By comparison Lagos is a gentle place."

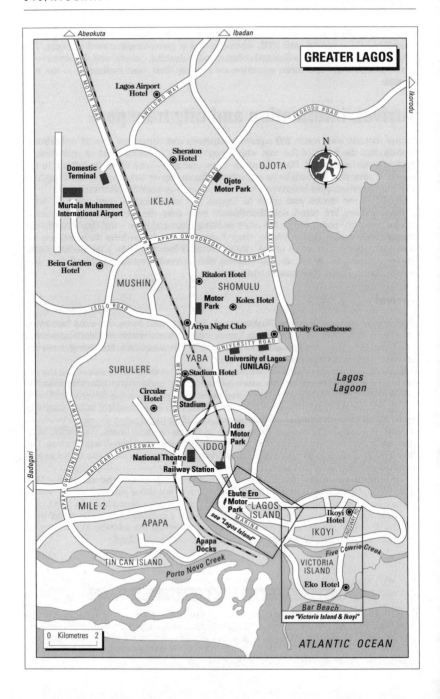

GREATER LAGOS

Information

The Nigerian Tourism Development Corporation's **tourist office** (Tourism Information Centre) is on the mainland, at 34 Kodesoh St, Ikeja (PO 14151; ☎01/493 0220), and can help with general tourist information and hiring guides. If you haven't got a **street map** already, the WABP's *Street Map of Lagos* is out of date but still useful, while the recent guidebook, *Lagos Easy Access*, available from Quintessence, at Falomo Shopping Centre, is big and expensive but an invaluable source of more detailed information if you plan to stay for a long time.

City Transport

Getting around Lagos can be a nightmare unless you have unlimited time or patience – or your own car and driver, like many expats. **Taxi** fares are expensive because of the scarcity of fuel, and the array of inexpensive **buses** and **minibuses** is potentially baffling (although manageable if you can learn the names of the bus stops). It's probably easiest to combine buses with **motorcycle** (*okada*, or *choba*) **taxis**.

A big, hundred-seater **ferry** runs across Lagos Harbour, from the south of Lagos Island (midway along Apongbon Street) to Apapa and Mile Two, on a canal west of the Apapa–Orowonsoki Expressway. Ferries also run from Victoria Island to the beaches (see p.955).

Taxis and minibuses

Lagos **taxis** are usually yellow Peugeot 504s with black stripes. The drivers like to "pick" people as they go, effectively running a **share-taxi** service, often on the route of their choice, and ignoring the regular fares (a table of which they're obliged to display) and the protests of passengers. You hail them by yelling out your destination. Use some discretion over where you say you're going (be prepared to get out and walk a hundred metres) as it can affect the fare, which you should discuss and agree on first. Stand in the door till you're sure the driver knows the price is agreed. Try also to have the notes ready (if possible wave them in the driver's face) to emphasize the fare you're prepared to pay. Change is a rare thing in any case. The kinds of fares you'll end up paying vary from ₦10–20 for district-to-district hops and ₦70–150 for lengthy cross-city trips. If you want to **charter**, rather than wait for a share, shout "Drop!" to hail a taxi. You'll pay much more – ₦100 for short hops, ₦200–400 for cross-city journeys. Be prepared to haggle.

In addition, Lagos swarms with motley **privately owned minibuses** – either VW or Japanese *kombis*, or local Mercedes or Bedford conversions known as *molue* (large, with aisles) or *danfo* (small, seat only). While these are cheap (maximum fares around ₦13), the discomfort and hair-pulling slowness of them can undermine the resolve of even the staunchest city survivor.

Accommodation

There's no shortage of **hotels** in Lagos, and most of them are on the mainland, which is, on the whole, less convenient than the islands. Although it has a reputation as a dangerous area, those who actually enjoy aspects of Lagos life aren't intimidated – most of the music clubs are there for example. Upmarket hotels are expensive if you're paying the non-resident tariff, but moderate places with AC and TV are good value. Budget travellers won't be disappointed, as plenty of cheap hotels and hostels are available.

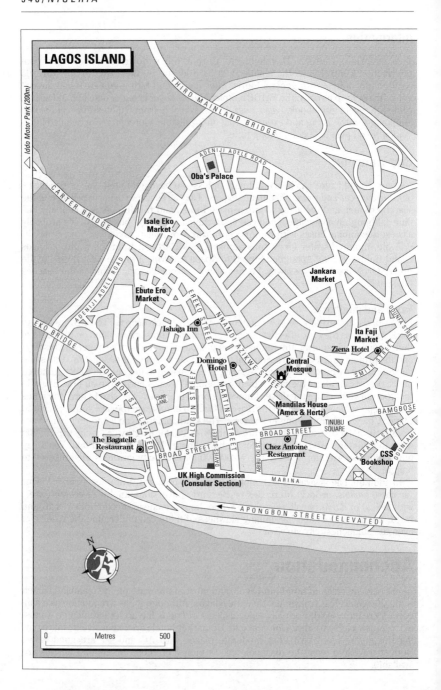

LAGOS ISLAND

Iddo Motor Park (200m)

THIRD MAINLAND BRIDGE

CARTER BRIDGE

ADENIJI ADELE ROAD

Oba's Palace

Isale Eko Market

ADENIJI ADELE ROAD

Jankara Market

EKO BRIDGE

Ebute Ero Market

EREKO STREET

NNAMDI AZIKWE STREET

ODUNTA STREET

Ishaga Inn

Ita Faji Market

Ziena Hotel

SMITH STREET

APONGBON ST (ELEVATED)

Domingo Hotel

Central Mosque

CARR LANE

BALOGUN STREET

MARTINS STREET

Mandilas House (Amex & Hertz)

BAMGBOSE

TINUBU SQUARE

AKAWA STREET

ODUWLAMI

The Bagatelle Restaurant

BROAD STREET

DAVIES STREET

ABIBU OKI ST

BROAD STREET

Chez Antoine Restaurant

CSS Bookshop

UK High Commission (Consular Section)

MARINA

APONGBON STREET (ELEVATED)

N

0   Metres   500

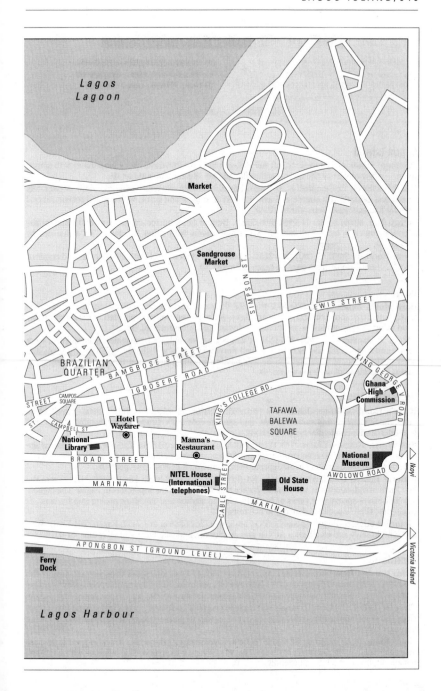

ACCOMMODATION PRICE CODES

① Under ₦650 (under £5/$8)
② ₦650–1300 (£5–10/$8–16)
③ ₦1300–2600 (£10–20/$16–32)
④ ₦2600–3900 (£20–30/$32–48)

⑤ ₦3900–5200 (£30–40/$48–64)
⑥ ₦5200–6500 (£40–50/$64–80)
⑦ Over ₦6500 (over £50/$80)

For further details see p.48.

Lagos Island

Domingo Hotel, 4/6 Oluwole St, off Alli Balogun St (☎01/266 6440). Very basic hotel with simple rooms – often rented by the hour – with toilet and fan. Restaurant and bar. ①.

Hotel Wayfarer, 52 Campbell St, by Lagos Island Maternity Hospital (☎01/263 0113). Moderately priced and central, with simple and safe S/C, AC rooms. Good value, with a small restaurant and friendly management. Book ahead. ②–③.

Ishaga Inn, 42/44 Ereko St (☎01/266 5397). Budget hotel on the colourful western side of the island, hemmed in by a cloth market. S/C single rooms with either AC, fan or TV, and a nearby annexe. ①.

Zeina Hotel, 11 Smith St (☎01/263 3254). Moderately priced hotel, with a folksy feel and comfortable AC rooms. Book in advance as space is limited. ②.

Ikoyi

Ikoyi Hotel, Kingsway Rd (PO 895; ☎01/269 0148 or 1522). Once a colonial institution and top-notch hotel, now somewhat frayed at the edges, although renovation is planned. It's still reasonably good value and the amenities are all there – including a pleasant pool. ⑤.

YMCA, 77 Awolowo Rd (☎01/268 0516 or 2680885). Men only, but conveniently equidistant from Lagos and Victoria islands. Scruffy four-bed dorms with fans and shared facilities. Nigerians and other Africans board here and can be a big help showing you around the city. With only eight rooms, it is often full, so book ahead. ①.

Victoria Island

B-Jay's Hotel, 24 Samuel Manuwa St (☎01/261 2391 or 262 2902; Fax 01/262 2903). Small, clean hotel; the S/C rooms and suites have AC and satellite colour TV. Friendly service-minded staff, and located in a safe residential neighbourhood. Continental breakfast included. ⑦.

Eko Hotel, Kuramo Waters (PO 12724; ☎01/262 4600; Fax 01/261 5205). The sparkling white tower – rising a short distance from the open Atlantic – is one of the best and most expensive hotels in Lagos. Complete comfort in all departments, including a crystal-clear pool. ⑦.

Federal Palace Hotel, Ahmadu Bello Rd (PO 1000; ☎01/262 3116; Fax 01/262 3912). From the first flush of independence, the *Federal Palace* has been one of the top hotels in Lagos. The lagoon-side bar offers spectacular views of the Lagos Island skyline and the ships nosing into harbour. At weekends, there's poolside dancing to live music. ⑦.

Victoria Lodge, 5 Ologun Agbaje St (PO 72615; ☎01/262 0885 or 261 7177; Fax 01/261 7131). Very pleasant, homely and clean, with AC bar and restaurant, and satellite TV in all rooms. ⑥–⑦.

Mainland

Beira Garden Residential Hotel, Ayao Estate, Plot 41 Olakunle Selesi Crescent, off Airport Rd, Ikeja (PO 5088; ☎01/523 858 or 470 1744). A well-kept hotel with all conveniences, good management, and a pleasant atmosphere. Conveniently near the airport. ⑤.

Circular Hotel, 136 Bode Thomas St, Surulere (☎01/835 061). AC rooms with TV and room service. The very helpful management goes out of its way to please guests, sometimes even showing them around town. ③.

Hotel Rialto, 6 Alhaji Amoo St, Ojota (PO 4963, Marina). Off the beaten track in a working class neighbourhood in the far north of the city, but offers very inexpensive S/C lodgings with TV. Small restaurant, bar, nightclub and friendly staff. ①.

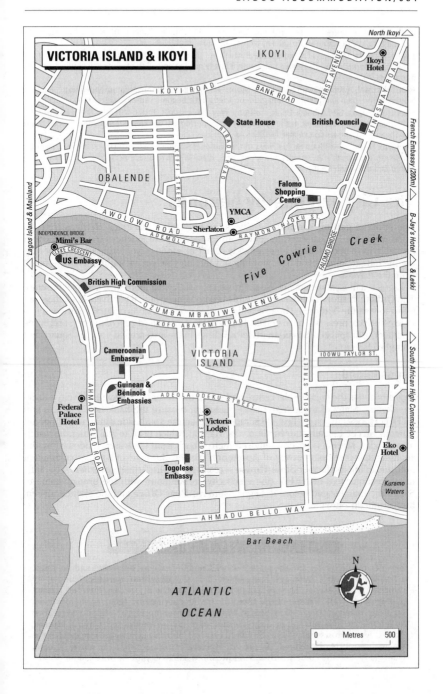

Kolex Hotel, 3 Olufeko Close, off Femi Adebule St, Fola Agoro, Yaba (☎01/820 174 or 822 532). Small, quiet, comfortable and modern, with an in-house nightclub. ③.

Lagos Airport Hotel, 111 Obafemi Awolowo Way, Ikeja (PO 21041; ☎01/497 8670; Fax 01/493 7573; *laph@rcl.nig.com*). Exclusive hotel with a lovely garden and all the facilities, including a swimming pool. ⑤.

Ritalori Hotel, Animashawun St, off Eric Moore Rd, Surulere. Highly recommended hotel in a lively area, with a pool and friendly management, though it's become rather expensive. ④.

Sheraton Lagos, 30 Mobolaji Bank, Anthony Way, Ikeja (PMB 21189; ☎01/497 8660; Fax 01/497 0321). Lagos' smartest hotel, right by the airport, catering for businesspeople with no need to go into the city. All the usual five-star facilities. ⑦.

Stadium Hotel, 27–33 Iyun St, just west of the National Stadium, Surulere (☎01/833 594). Popular hotel with comfortable AC rooms and an exciting disco with live music performances; always animated and often full. ②–③.

The City and nearby beaches

The effort of **getting around** the city is the only thing that really detracts from its worthwhile sites. It can literally take hours to accomplish journeys by car that could probably have been walked more quickly. Don't be afraid of venturing out on foot during the day: so long as you have nothing of value on you, you've nothing to fear – apart from the drivers.

Lagos is almost alone among West African cities in having more than a single museum. The **Onikan National Museum** is highly recommended and, if you have time, make an effort to visit the **National Theatre** and see what's on view at its cultural centre and galleries; the local press will have details. **Lagos Island**, the oldest part of the city, preserves a number of dilapidated **Brazilian-style buildings** in the area around Campos Square and Campbell Street.

Lagos Island

Lagos Island is the commercial centre and site of the towers that provide the city's striking skyline. Many of these high-rises – including most of the bank headquarters and **NITEL House**, Africa's tallest skyscraper – are on the south side of the island behind **Marina Street** (usually known simply as Marina), which used to run along the waterfront. Today, Marina is several hundred metres back from the water, shadowed by the zooming split-level expressway of **Apongbon Street**. But it retains some buildings of note, including the former **State House** – residence of the British governors – the infamous headquarters of **NEPA** (the electricity corporation), with the bronze statue of Sango the thunder god before it, Lagos' **General Post Office** and the eighteenth-century **Anglican church**.

BRAZILIAN–STYLE BUILDINGS

Between the high-rises and the market shacks, and the exhaust emissions and the rains, a few Brazilian-style buildings have survived in the **Brazilian quarter**, founded by returned former slaves. They're falling apart, however, and jealously guarded against photographers. The **Palace of the Oba** (the traditional ruler of Lagos), on the northern tip of the island on Upper King Street, is particularly unimpressive. Still, if you're keen on a hunt, the following, all on Lagos Island, may still be worthwhile: **Chief's House**, Ado St; **Ebun House**, 85 Odunfa St (300m east of Tinubu Square), a great pile of a place dating from 1914; **Brazilian House**, 29 Kakawa St, off Marina; **Da Silva House**, Odufege St; and the comely **Shitta Mosque** on Martins St, with its Brazilian tilework.

Broad Street, which runs parallel to Marina, is another well-known thoroughfare with more banks and markets and some fairly upmarket shops. It runs into **Tinubu Square**, a landscaped roundabout, with a perpetually defunct fountain, in one of the busiest parts of town. Nearby, the **markets** of **Jankara**, **Isale Eko**, **Ebute Ero** and **Balogun** all run into one another, filling the western part of the island with frenetic small-scale commerce.

The eastern end of Marina is dominated by the great scar of **Tafawa Balewa Square**, with its monumental equine statues rearing up at the entrance on the south side, in memory of the old racetrack that used to be here. The north side of the square is now where many of the major airlines and travel agencies have their offices; the south is mostly shops and cheap restaurants.

The Onikan National Museum

Just east of Tafawa Balewa Square, the **National Museum** (daily 9am–6pm), is Nigeria's foremost, and a required visit, especially if the travelling exhibition, "Treasures of Ancient Nigeria", happens to be home for a rest from world touring.

The "**Treasures**" exhibition traces 2800 years of Nigerian art from the earliest terracotta figures from **Nok** in the Jos Plateau, through extraordinarily intricate and sophisticated **Igbo Ukwe** bronze castings from southeast Nigeria, to the almost Hellenic realism of the later **Ife and Owo** brass and terracotta busts – which provide a glimpse into Yoruba court life from the twelfth to the fifteenth century. The famous **Benin bronzes** were made exclusively for the Oba by master craftsmen working for the court, and represent some of the greatest masterpieces of West African art.

In the permanent collection, the **Ethnographic Gallery** is designed to give an overview of the cultural materials of Nigeria's diverse ethnic groups. The display of **masquerades**, common to a range of peoples, shows off one of the oldest forms of cultural and artistic expression. In Nigeria, masquerades not only served to provide a link with the realm of the dead but were important in instigating other art forms like music, dance and drama. Other exhibits range from decorated pottery and calabashes from the different regions to shrines and household gods reflecting the importance of the supernatural in people's lives.

The **Benin Gallery** contains a selection of bronzes and ivory carvings, including the well-known waist mask that appears on the Naira note and was symbol of the FESTAC festival. Unfortunately, many masterpieces of Benin art are still held abroad, despite numerous requests for their return from the Nigerian government.

An additional permanent exhibition – **"Nigerian governments: Yesterday and Today"** – traces the political history of the country from the slave trade to the present. The post-independence section acts as a visual *aide-mémoire* in figuring out the rather complicated train of events since the days when Abubakar Tafawa Balewa became Nigeria's first prime minister. Amid the displays recounting the coups and governments that followed, President Murtala Muhammed's bullet-holed car pays menacing homage to one of Nigeria's most popular assassinated leaders.

If you're looking to buy woodcarvings, check out the **Komson Arts Gallery** in the museum's craft village, at least for an idea of how much you can expect to pay for works in Lagos – prices here are fixed. In fact, the chances are you won't find prices any cheaper outside the big hotels, where all the gear is often laid out. Lastly, you can take a break from all the culture in the very good **Museum Kitchen** (see p.956).

Ikoyi and Victoria Island

The swamps that used to divide **Ikoyi** from Lagos Island have been filled in, and today the two sections of town are separated only by a tangle of motorway flyovers, but Ikoyi

MARKETS

Wherever you fetch up in Lagos, you'll find a **market** close by: there are literally dozens on the mainland, notably Tejuoso in Surulere, and the market in Apapa, which is also close to a good range of ordinary shops and supermarkets. On Lagos Island, **Jankara market** is the prime site and one of the cheapest places for new clothes or secondhand garments, general hardware, **traditional musical instruments**, cassettes, **jewellery** and **trading beads**, magical materials (*juju*, skins, powders) and *aso-oke*, beautiful woven cloth which is used on special occasions. West of Jankara, between Adeniji Adele Road and Ebute Ero Street, **Isale Eko market** specializes in food, crocks and baskets; you can also find some ready-made clothes here. In the same area, near the old Carter Bridge, is an **Ogogoro market** with scorching local spirit for sale.

Focusing around the street of the same name on Lagos Island, **Balogun market** is the best place for **cloth**. In the rambling maze of alleys you'll find mostly imported material, including damasks, plus a wide range of African prints. A little to the east, around Nnamdi Azikiwe Street, you can find batiks and ready-made clothes, plus records and cassettes.

Between Lewis and Simpson streets at the eastern end of Lagos Island, **Sand Grouse market** is the best bet for **food** – fresh fish, shrimps and huge snails, as well as more conventional provisions.

Another food market, **Bar Beach market**, can be found towards the end of Ahmadu Bello Road on Victoria Island. In view of all the money and expats on the island, it's no surprise to find some **crafts** here too – including basketry, batiks and even Tuareg leather chests.

still retains its individual flavour. Its main artery, **Awolowo Road**, links Lagos Island with Victoria Island via the **Falomo Bridge**. Awolowo contains chic **boutiques** – many operating out of converted private homes – high-priced **restaurants**, a sprinkling of **embassies** and the **Polo Club**, a reminder of the days when Ikoyi was the posh colonial neighbourhood. The **Falomo shopping centre** crowns Awolowo Road at the junction with Kingsway Road, near the bridge.

The centre of Ikoyi, dominated by the **administrative district**, includes the former **State House**. Further west, **Obalende** is a vibrant working-class neighbourhood with a large market, numerous chop bars (good places for authentic pepper soup or *suya*) and watering holes where locals come to drink and dance. Although it's one of the safest low-income areas in town, it's still a good idea to go accompanied at night.

The principal modern residential area of Lagos, **Victoria Island** (V.I.) is divided into thousands of expensive plots, many of them taken up by foreign **embassies** and expatriate residences. Near the **Independence Bridge** to Lagos Island, **Eleke Crescent** has the highest concentration of diplomatic missions, including those of the UK and the USA. **Bar Beach**, the city's closest strand, runs along the island's southern flank.

The mainland

A vast reach of working-class districts, industrial zones and shanty towns heaves over the mainland for miles. Other than getting to and from the international airport, railway station or motor parks, there's little reason for visitors to spend much time here, although the residential **Surulere** district, 10km from Victoria Island, is home to the **National Stadium** and a vibrant **nightlife** quarter, and **Ebute Metta**, just short of Lagos Island, is the site of the **National Theatre** complex.

The National Theatre complex

Rising out of the low-rent district of Ebute Metta above the creeks, the **National Theatre**'s characteristic concave roof appears on your right-hand side as you leave the mainland. Built for the 1977 FESTAC cultural festival, the theatre is a classic example of high-prestige, low-reward development. It's more a cultural complex than simply a theatrical venue, which is actually a role it rarely has the chance to play. The main ancillary site is the **Centre for Black and African Arts and Civilization** (Mon–Sat 8am–5pm), which contains archives, a library and a museum with periodically changing exhibits. The original FESTAC 1977 exhibits should still be on show.

The **National Gallery of Modern Art**, at Entrance B of the theatre complex (Tues–Fri 10am–5pm, Sat & Sun noon–4pm) is an exhibition space for the work of young Nigerian talents. Entrance C leads to two cinema halls.

Across the street northwest of the theatre complex, the **National Gallery of Crafts and Design** (Mon–Fri 9am–5pm, Sat 10am–5pm), the red-brick building, displays and sells traditional Nigerian handicrafts. The drinks stalls nearby are a great place to hang out in the early evening with a cheap beer and a meat pie or *moin-moin*, and watch the actors and artistes.

Beaches

There are a number of beaches in and around Lagos, although the best of them are further out of town and you'll need transport to reach them. Many of the beaches conceal dangerous undersea currents; ask locals about possible risks, and never bathe alone.

Bar Beach, on Victoria Island, has always been unattractive and shadeless, but it's the closest spot to swim in the sea (and a meeting place for Christian sects). Since exceptional spring tides in 1990 and 1994 swept most of the sand away, the beach has been steeper and less enticing than ever. Still, people continue to come here because of the location – just off Ahmadu Bello Way, within walking distance of the homes on Victoria Island.

The most attractive beach near the city centre is **Tarkwa Bay**, sheltered within the harbour and safe for swimming. **Lighthouse Beach** is beyond Tarkwa, and also attractive, but dangerous because of its strong currents.

Lekki Beach, 10km east of town, off Lagos expressway along the Lekki Peninsula, is lined with coconut palms. Take a taxi to Gbara village and walk 2km down the sand road leading from the expressway to the beach, or arrange to be dropped directly at the beach. You can ride horses quite cheaply here, and food and drink are on sale. The Nigerian Conservation Foundation (NCF) has a fine **nature trail** at Lekki, with a well-marked route. It's a peaceful haven out of the city, and you can see monkeys and small crocodiles. The **market** at Lekki is also a good place for a wander, with a range of beads, cloth and crafts, and the usual fruit, herbs and commodities.

If you have your own transport, try the much quieter **Eleko beach**, 50km further east on the Epe Expressway. Many expats rent beach huts on a long-term basis, but empty ones can usually be rented by the hour. **Badagary**, 55km to the west of Lagos (along the highway towards the Benin Republic) is another good area with a lovely beach.

Boat trips

Most **boat trips** out to the beaches tend to be private affairs. Lagos is a place where it pays to have friends, or make friends quickly; a lot of boats take off every weekend from the Motor Boat Club at the west end of Awolowo Road on Five Cowrie Creek. Otherwise, **ferries** run from Victoria Island to **Tarkwa Bay** and other local beaches:

Tarzan Boats operate a service from Eleke Crescent (on the north side of Victoria Island).

Eating, drinking and nightlife

Lagos has thousands of cheap eating places, but is also geared up for splashing out a bit: flashy restaurants, bars, clubs and discos abound, as do more tacky establishments. None of these, however, will burn a big hole in your pocket. If you think you might go out on the town later, leave all but the necessary minimum of possessions in your hotel.

Cheap to moderate eateries

By day, numerous snack bars line the southern edge of Tafawa Balewa Square on **Lagos Island**. All serve similar fare of meat pies, sausage rolls and pizza – nothing fancy, but quick and inexpensive. Over on Marina Street, the supermarkets all have cafeterias for reasonable lunches. In **Ikoyi**, there's a favourite small restaurant near the *YMCA* (left down Raymond Njoku Road when coming from the Y, then 300m) marked only by two *7 Up* signs at the entrance. They do plain Nigerian food – *eba*, rice and beans, *dodo* and *àmàlà* – with cold beer and minerals: the best cheap eats in the neighbourhood. The **Obalende area**, on the west side of Ikoyi, is full of inexpensive restaurants and outdoor stands where you can buy fish, *suya* (kebabs), rice and so on. Don't miss the pepper soup, a speciality of this quarter, and the wonderfully flavoured chicken, charcoal grilled to order. On **Victoria Island**, street food is available from a small side street directly opposite the *Eko Hotel*: boiled yams, beans and rice, *fufu* with meat or fried fish. Eat here and then have a drink in the *Eko* for rapid culture contrast.

The Bagatelle, 208 Broad St, above 1st Bank, Lagos Island. Established fourth-floor eating house with Middle East-influenced menu, harbour view, bar and dancing. Open 8am–3pm only.

Delikisis, 4 Dipeolu St, off Obafemi Awolowo Way, Ikeja. Bar and restaurant, with a friendly atmosphere and music at weekends.

Josephine's Restaurant, Keffi St near the junction with Awolowo Rd, Ikoyi. Reasonable fish-and-rice type meals at rock-bottom prices.

Manna's Restaurant, Western House, first floor, 8/10 Broad St, Lagos Island. Highly recommended bar-restaurant, serving Nigerian and international cuisine at moderate prices.

Museum Kitchen, National Museum, Lagos Island. Extensive and excellent selection of reasonably priced stand-bys – *eba, moin-moin, fufu, dodo, egusi, ogbono* – plus a daily regional speciality dish.

Victory Restaurant, 31B Bishop Oluwole St, V.I. One of the most affordable restaurants on the island, serving Nigerian dishes only.

Upmarket restaurants

Most of Lagos' **pricier restaurants** are on Lagos Island and Ikoyi. A number of these are quite formal, and you'd do well to dress smartly and book ahead. On the mainland you're best off in the pricier hotels, all of which have restaurants of a reliable standard.

The Brasserie, 52 Adetokunbo Ademola St, near the *Eko Hotel*, V.I. (☎01/615 464). Complex of eateries including Indian, Chinese and European restaurants.

Calabash, Plot 8, Ozumba Mbadiwe Av, V.I. (☎01/262 4207). Very pleasant waterside place facing the "1004 Apartments" development, with Nigerian dishes and live music some nights.

Chez Antoine, 61 Broad St, Lagos Island (☎01/664 881). Popular restaurant with French and Lebanese cuisine and sandwiches at lunchtime. Cool and relaxing after the heat and bustle of the street.

Ciao!, 184 Awolowo Rd, Ikoyi (☎01/269 3763). Smart Italian restaurant with a comprehensive menu, plus a bar and nightclub for later in the evening.

Double Four, 44 Awolowo Rd, Ikoyi. Pizzas, Lebanese meze and a good range of other dishes. Tends to be crowded, with the TV blaring, but the food is tasty and not overpriced.

La Scala Restaurant, Muson Centre, 8/9 Marina, Lagos Island (☎01/264 6885). Exclusive and expensive restaurant in a commercial centre, with French and Italian dishes and wines.

The Light House, *Federal Palace Hotel*, Ahmadu Bello Rd, V.I. (☎01/262 3116, ext 541 or 775). The city's top restaurant, with a Chinese menu every Wednesday evening.

New Yorkers, 59 Raymond Njoku Rd, Ikoyi. US-diner-style place with high quality fast food and confident service.

Peninsula, 8 Ozumba Mbadiwe Ave, V.I. (☎01/616 911). Terrace restaurant right on the lagoon, serving good Chinese meals. Even if you're not hungry, you can come for a drink and the view.

The Sherlaton, 108 Awolowo Rd, Ikoyi (☎01/269 1275 or 1282). One of Lagos' best Indian restaurants and, despite its name, neither overpriced nor ostentatious.

Nightlife

Lagos is famous as a **music** centre, and the styles that have originated and evolved here – **Highlife**, **Juju**, **Fuji** and **Afrobeat** – are as legendary and international as any in Africa. Lagosians are proud of this and prefer listening to their own music than to the anodyne Anglo-American pop that's current over so much of West Africa. The daily *Evening Times* normally has details of what's on across a span of forty or fifty venues where you can dance till dawn and often see live performances. Several restaurants turn into nightclubs as the clock turns 11pm, while other nightclubs are just "gigs". The following clubs (mainly selected for their live show pedigrees) are mostly on the mainland. Don't be intimidated. Get a taxi and get on down.

Ariya Night Club, 12 Ikorodu Rd, at Jibowu St, Yaba. Belongs to Juju maestro King Sunny Ade, who plays here on Fridays – when he's not touring.

Avondale (Thristle Bar), 36 Marine Rd, Apapa. Restaurant and bar, with live music at weekends.

Faslak Nightclub, opposite NNPC, Apapa. Orlando "Dr Ganjah" Owoh, rebel granddad inventor of the Juju-Highlife hybrid he calls "toye", plays here every Thursday.

Jazzville, 21 Majaro St, Onike, near Yaba. Bar, restaurant serving local dishes and fish-and-chips (noon–10pm) and live jazz every Friday night from midnight till dawn. Friendly management and lively clientele.

Mimi's Bar, 3 Eleke Crescent, within the NAPEX Complex, V.I. 24hr bar, popular with both expats and locals.

Motherlan', 64 Opebi Rd, Ikeja. Popular nightclub in an outdoor amphitheatre, run by the equally popular Nigerian musician Lagbaja, playing Highlife music.

Neighbours, by the *Stadium Hotel*, Surulere. The place for weekend Makossa sounds.

Niteshift, 34 Salvation Rd, off Opebi Rd, Ikeja. Former Lagos celebrity hangout, now relocated to a dome-like building called The Coliseum, less than a ten-minute drive from the *Sheraton* and *Airport Hotel*.

Pinto's, 5 Allen Ave, Ikeja. Expensive, but very popular, this is one of the best international-style clubs, with a resident jazz band accompanying different singers. Open all night at weekends.

Stadium Hotel, 27 Iyun Rd, just west of the National Stadium, Surulere (☎01/833 593). Home of Highlife supremo Victor Olaiya and boasting a fantastic floorshow with dancers and contortionists.

Listings

Air freight DHL, 32 Awolowo Rd, Ikoyi (☎01/269 2231); UPS, Tinubu Square, Lagos Island (☎01/774 0452-3).

Airlines Most have their main office at Victoria Island, while some can still be found on Lagos Island, mainly on Tafawa Balewa Square. Opening hours are roughly Mon–Fri 8am–4pm. They include: ADC Airlines, Shop 5, Tafawa Balewa Square (☎01/263 1792 or 5023); Aeroflot, 36 Tafawa Balewa Square (☎01/263 7223); Air Afrique, 24 Amodu Tijani St, off Sanusi Fafunwa St, V.I.

(☎01/261 6443 or 2616 405); Air France, Danmole St, off Adeola Adeku St, V.I. (☎01/262 1456); Air Gabon, 28 Tafawa Balewa Square (☎01/263 2827 or 7104); Balkan Bulgarian Airlines, 39–41 Martins St (☎01/661 974 or 102); British Airways, C&C Towers, Plot 1684, Sanusi Fafunwa St, V.I. (☎01/261 3004 or 262 1225); Cameroon Airlines, 16A Oko-Awo Close, off Karimu Kotun St, V.I. (☎01/261 6270 or 4993); Ethiopian Airlines, 20A Tafawa Balewa Square (☎01/263 2690 or 7655); Ghana Airways, 128 Awolowo Rd, S.W. Ikoyi (PO 3749; ☎01/269 2363 or 1397); Kenya Airways, 1st floor, Okoi Arikpo House, 5 Idowu Taylor St, V.I. (☎01/261 9338); KLM, 5 Idowu Taylor St, V.I. (☎01/261 9423 or 9413); Lufthansa, 150 Broad St at Martins St (☎01/266 4430 or 4505); Nigeria Airways, Tafawa Balewa Square (☎01/263 3055 or 1002); Okada Air, Terminal Two, Domestic Airport, Ikeja (☎01/963 881); South African Airways, c/o Five Star Travel, 1st floor, Block B, Unit 11, Falomo Shopping Centre, Awolowo Rd (☎01/269 0184).

American Express Mandilas Travel Ltd, 33 Simpson St, Lagos Island (PO 35; ☎01/636 887).

Banks and exchange Bank opening hours are Mon–Thurs 8am–3pm, Fri 8am–1pm. Banks include: Afribank Nigeria, 94 Broad St (☎01/266 3608); African Continental Bank, 106–108 Broad St (☎01/266 0579); First Bank of Nigeria, 35 Marina (☎01/266 5900); Société Générale Bank (Nig), 113 Martins St (☎01/266 1881); Union Bank, 40 Marina (☎01/266 5439); United Bank for Africa Plc, 57 Marina (☎01/264 4651). There are also a number of bureaux de change, including Consolidated Bureau de Change, 94A Bode Thomas St, Surulere (☎01/585 1595) and Garun Malam Bureau de Change, *Federal Palace Hotel*, Ahmadu Bello Way, V.I. (☎01/261 3677).

Bookshops Lagos has the best English-language bookshops in West Africa. Besides the hotels (reasonable selections in the *Eko Hotel* and the *Federal Palace*), there are a number of places in the Falomo Shopping Centre, Awolowo Rd, in Ikoyi: try Glendora, The Bestseller and Quintessence. On Lagos Island, check out the bookshops on Broad St, particularly CSS Bookshop at 50/52 Broad St, or the New World Bookshop on Tafawa Balewa Square.

Car rental There are many agencies in Lagos, but nearly all insist on supplying a driver with the vehicle. Avis, 225 Apapa Rd, Iganmu (PMB 1155; ☎01/846 336) and at *Eko Hotel*, V.I. (☎01/262 4600 ext 6261); Europcar (PO 6569; ☎01/662 572); Hertz agents are Mandilas, 96–102 Broad St, Lagos Island (PMB 35; ☎01/663 514) and PAN (Peugeot Nig), Plot 19, Agoro Odiyan St, V.I. (☎01/261 3143). Hertz, Europcar and Budget have branches at the airport.

Cultural centres and libraries include: The British Council, 11 Kingsway Rd, Ikoyi (PO 3702; ☎01/269 2188–92; *bc.lagos@bc-lagos.bcouncil.org*); Alliance Francaise and the Centre Culturel et de Cooperation Linguistique (CCCL), 2 Aromire Rd, off Kingsway Rd, opposite *Ikoyi Hotel* (☎01/269 2035 or 2365; *cccl@linkserve.com.ng*). The National Library, 4 Wesley St (Mon–Fri 7.30am–3.30pm; ☎01/265 6590) is a good reference library with books and periodicals.

Embassies and consulates Most are on Victoria Island (V.I.) and are open Mon–Fri. They include: Australia, 2 Ozumba Mbadiwe Ave, V.I. (PO 2427; ☎01/261 8875 or 3124); Benin, 4 Abudu Smith St, V.I. (PO 5705; ☎01/614 411); Burkina Faso, 170 Moshood Olugbani St, V.I. Annex (PO 12605; ☎01/611 849 or 681 001); Cameroon, 5 Elsie Femi-Pearse St, V.I. (PMB 2476; ☎01/612 226 or 614 386); Canada, c/o US embassy (☎01/262 2513); Central African Republic, Plot 137, Ajao Estate, New Airport, Oshodi (☎01/682 820); Chad (see Abuja); Côte d'Ivoire, 3 Abudu Smith St, V.I. (PO 7786; ☎01/610 936); France, 1 Oyinkan Abayomi Drive, Ikoyi (PMB 12665; ☎01/269 3427; *ambfrancelagos@micro.com.ng*); Gabon, 8 Norman Williams St, S.W. Ikoyi (PO 5989; ☎01/684 566 or 673); Ghana, 21/23 King George V Rd, Onikan, Lagos Island (PO 889; ☎01/263 0015 or 0493); Ireland, 34 Kofo Abayomi St, V.I. (PO 2859; ☎01/261 7567); Niger (see Abuja); South Africa, 4 Maduike St, off Raymond Njoku St, S.W. Ikoyi (☎01/269 2174 or 2709); Togo, Plot 976, Oju-Olobun Close, V.I. (PO 1435; ☎01/617 449); UK (Deputy High Commissioner) 11 Eleke Crescent, V.I. (PO 12136; ☎01/261 9531 or 9541), UK Consular Section at Chellarams Building, 54 Marina (☎01/266 7061 or 6413); USA, 2 Eleke Crescent, V.I. (PO 554; ☎01/261 0050 or 0078), Consular Section *lagoscons@lagoswpoa.us-state.gov*.

Hospitals and emergencies The best hospital is undoubtedly the Eko Hospital in Mobalaji Bank Anthony Way, Ikeja, near the *Sheraton*. Akimbola Awoliyi Memorial Hospital, 183 Bamgbose St, Lagos Island (☎01/631 520 or 930 916), is also good, with a 24hr casualty service. Recommended general practitioners include: Dr Williams, 13 Airport Rd, Ikeja (☎01/933 482) and Dr M. Semaan and Dr D. Semaan, St Francis Clinic, Keffi St, Ikoyi (☎01/684 125). A recommended dentist is Dr E. Solarin, Flat 2, Block D, Eko Court, Kofo Abayomi Rd, V.I. (☎01/610 917).

MOVING ON FROM LAGOS

BY ROAD

Motor park

Ojota motor park, on Ikorodu Rd, near the junction with the airport road in the Ojota district.

Iddo motor park, on Murtala Muhammed Way near the train station.

Oju Elegba motor park, Oju Elegba junction in Surulere district.

Ebute Ero motor park, near Eko Bridge at the western tip of Lagos Island.

DESTINATIONS

The southwest, including Ibadan, Oshogbo, Ilorin, Ife and other towns in Yorubaland.

The north, including Kaduna and Jos, Zaria, Sokoto and Kano.

The east, including Benin City, Onitsha, Enugu, Aba, Port Harcourt and Calabar.

International destinations, including Lomé and Cotonou.

BY TRAIN

The **railway station** is on Murtala Muhammed Way, near the Carter Bridge in Iddo. There is an express train from Lagos to Kano, calling at Ibaden and Kaduna. For train times and frequencies, call the Nigerian Railway Corporation's Lagos headquarters at Ebute-Metta junction (☎01/833 377).

BY PLANE

Nigeria Airways and several private airlines – ADC (currently one of the largest), Chachangi, EAS, Harka, Kabo, Okada and Triax – fly from the Domestic Airport at Ikeja, to the east of Murtala Muhammed Airport. There are, in theory, flights on Nigeria Airways at least every day to Abuja, Jos, Kano, Maiduguri, Port Harcourt and Yola, plus several flights a week to Calabar, Enugu, Kaduna, Makurdi and Sokoto.

Pharmacies Nigerian Medicine Stores Ltd, 4 Tinubu Square, Lagos Island (☎01/263 2546).

Post and telephones The GPO (Mon–Fri 8am–noon & 2–4pm, Sat 8am–noon) is on Marina St, Lagos Island, with main branches on Awolowo Rd, Ikoyi and Adeola Odeku St, V.I.; both branches are closed Sat. Phone calls can be made from the NITEL Building on Marina, Lagos Island (24hr), at Falomo Shopping Centre, Ikoyi (daily 7am–8pm), or from cardphone booths around the city (cards available from NITEL offices).

Supermarkets While not comparable with Western supermarkets, Victoria Island hosts quite a number of well assorted shopping malls, including La Pointe Supermarket, at 74B Adetokunbo Ademola St and Park 'N' Shop at Guru Plaza, 47B Adeola Odeku St. In Ikoyi, there's Goodies Supermarket at 195 Awolowo Rd, and on the mainland you'll find Park 'N' Shop at 16 Mobolaji Bank Anthony Way.

Swimming pools The big hotels have pools, but those at the *Ikoyi* and *Federal Palace* (in theory open for a fee to non-guests) usually don't have water. The *Eko Hotel* has the cleanest water, but it's reserved for residents only.

Travel agents and tour operators Many agencies are grouped around the north side of Tafawa Balewa Square. Important firms include: Bitts Travels & Tours, E7 Falomo Shopping Centre (PO 54945; ☎01/269 6095), which organizes excursions for groups to various tourist destinations; Da Silva Travel Services (PO 6979, Marina; ☎01/583 1398; Fax 01/497 0907), which books hotels, runs sightseeing tours, and has an airport reception and shuttle service; Tours and Trade International, 4 Adeyemo Alakija St, V.I. (PMB 70047; ☎01/261 8665), which runs trips to the game parks, Obudu Cattle Ranch and other sites; and Transcap Travel, CFAO Building, 1 Davies St (PO 2326; ☎01/660 321 or 665 063).

Women's Groups Nigerwives (PO 54664, Falomo, Lagos), the association of foreign women married to Nigerians meets at 3pm at St Saviour's Church, Tafawa Balewa Square, on the last Saturday of the month.

THE SOUTHWEST

The towns and rural parts of the southwest, often referred to as **Yorubaland**, have an exceptional wealth of cultural interest and natural beauty. In pre-colonial times, the **Yoruba** created one of the most powerful empires on the West African coast – and the area is still charged with reminders. Most of the larger towns, for example, still have ruling **Obas**, or kings, who wield a good deal of political clout despite limitations imposed on them by the federal government system. The Obas continue to live in **royal palaces**, many of which can be visited, like the palace at **Oyo**, former capital of the Yoruba empire of the same name.

Some of what is now known about the area's more distant past is the result of excavations carried out in **Ife**. The brass and terracotta statues found here drew international attention and suggest a sophisticated civilization dating back to at least the ninth century. According to Yoruba legend, however, Ife is even older – the first place in the world to be created. It has naturally enjoyed a position as the holiest place in the Yoruba realm, a sort of Mecca of Yoruba religion. Here and throughout the region, the living wood of the **old religion** still breathes beneath a thick layer of Christian or occasionally Islamic belief. You'll see shrines and temples in almost all the towns. At **Oshogbo**, a whole **Sacred Forest** has been set aside as a reserve for worshippers, or "fetishers": the shrines here are vast and amazing and the worshippers only too eager to show visitors around – definitely a Nigerian highlight.

Once you cross over into **Edo State**, it's a short distance to **Benin City**, once a formidable kingdom, though already in decline by the time the British arrived. Faced with the modern town of the same name, you may be hard pressed to conjure up images of the former empire, but there are vestiges of the past, including ruins of the **great wall** that surrounded the city, and numerous bronze and ivory **sculptures** housed in the city's renowned museum. Some traditional skills have been preserved in the numerous workshops and galleries around town – excellent places to buy art- and craft-works, particularly in brass and bronze.

Abeokuta

ABEOKUTA, north of Lagos, on the old road to Ibadan, is "Ake" in Wole Soyinka's novel of the same name (the name of the royal district of the town where he grew up). The capital of Ogun State, Abeokuta was founded in the early 1800s as a site for freed Yoruba slaves, some of whom were liberated by the British Royal Navy, and some of whom had made their own way back to their homeland from Freetown and elsewhere. It's an attractive town, with a spectacular, and easily climbable, outcrop of gigantic granite boulders overlooking it – Abeokuta means "under the rock". At the summit, the **Oluma Rock Museum** traces the early settlement and history of Abeokuta, while at the base, the **Oluma Art Movement** has set up workshops and a gallery for traditional and modern art. The centre of the town is dominated by the **Oba's palace** and adjacent **Anglican church**, the oldest church building in Nigeria.

The town's top **hotel** is the *Gateway Hotel*, on Ibrahim Babangida Boulevard, Ibara (☎039/200 130–35; Fax 039/231 716; ④), with AC, satellite TV and olympic-size pool. A cheaper option is the hotel's annexe on Ademola Road, Ibara (☎039/240 004; ②) – a relaxing retreat in a pleasant park, with a good restaurant and very helpful management. Other budget options are the *Alafia Guest House,* in Oke Ilewo district, next to NITEL (☎039/240 788; ②), and the *Frontline*, on Oluwo Road, Onikolobo Ibara (②).

Ibadan

The south's second city, **IBADAN** (pronounced as in "pardon") is the modern capital of Oyo State – a vast metropolis that sprawls so far you think it's never going to stop.

The city's horizons are marked by few Lagos-style high-rises but instead by a plethora of two-storey, corrugated iron-roofed houses, spreading like an urban fungus over the low hills. People here assert Ibadan has the biggest population of any city in Africa – twenty million people, some say; the real figure is probably around five million.

Sometimes the crowds, congestion and noise are especially oppressive, and as the city lacks a real centre, a shambolic, unfocused tumult is about the only lasting impression. However, coming from Lagos, this is likely to be your first stop in Yorubaland and, with its numerous hotels, banks and other facilities, it's a convenient base for visiting other sites in the region.

Some history

Originally founded by Yoruba renegades, at the end of the eighteenth century, Ibadan occupies a strategic position between the forest and the plains, its name deriving from *Eba Odan*, meaning "field between the woods and the savannah". The settlement began to grow after 1829, when it became an important Yoruba military headquarters and a refuge for people dispossessed in Fulani raids on northern Oyo. By the time the British forced it into a treaty of protection in 1893, it was already extraordinarily large for its time, with an estimated population of 120,000.

In colonial times, Ibadan went on to become an important trading centre, which it remains. It is also a major academic city: the **University of Ibadan** (UI), founded in 1948, was the first in the country and is still considered one of West Africa's best.

Accommodation

Ibadan has dozens of hotels and lodging houses. The following selection includes some of the more pleasant and/or convenient among them:

Alma Guest House, 19 Oyo–Ibadan Ave, Bodija, near the customs post (☎02/810 0657). Small, quiet and clean, with a bar, and a restaurant serving Nigerian and continental dishes. All rooms S/C with satellite TV. ③.

Green Springs Hotel, Old Ife Rd (☎02/712 801). An older hotel with both AC, S/C bungalow-style rooms, and S/C suites with AC and satellite TV. Good bar, a pool, and a restaurant with live Highlife and Juju music every Sun evening. ②–③.

Hotel Influential, on Mokola Hill (☎02/241 4894). Reasonably priced and recently renovated hotel in a handy location next to *Premier Hotel*. ③–④.

International House, International Institute of Tropical Agriculture (IITA), Oyo Rd (☎02/241 2626; Fax 02/241 2221; *iita@cgnet.com*). Private guesthouse within the beautiful and secure compound of the Institute, with a vast range of facilities, including a sports centre, bar, snack bar and cafeteria. ⑦.

Kakanfo Inn, 1 Nihinlola St, off Adebiji St, leading from the Mobil Station on Ring Rd (☎02/231 1471–2; Fax 02/231 8909; *kakanfo@ibadan.skannet.com.ng*). Stylish hotel on the south side of town, with spacious AC doubles and an excellent restaurant. ⑤.

Lizzy Guest House, 40 Adenle Ave, Mokola Hill (☎02/241 3350). Comfortable guesthouse with cheap S/C rooms with AC and satellite TV. ②.

Pastoral Institute (PI) Guest House, UI-Secretariat Rd, near the University (☎02/810 3928). Clean S/C rooms with fans and mosquito nets; breakfast included. ②.

Premier Hotel, Mokola Hill (☎02/241 1234). Expensive-looking place that's not unreasonable for what it offers. You can relax in relative style here, with all the amenities, including a pool and Chinese restaurant. ④.

Trans Nigeria Motel, 1 Bale Oyewole Rd, Jericho Reservation (☎02/241 4680). Nice colonial-style building in a quiet neighbourhood, with reasonably priced AC, S/C rooms and a Nigerian-European restaurant. ①–②.

The City

Given the city's unwieldy dimensions, it's hard to pinpoint Ibadan's heart (note the very small scale of our map). By default, however, you'd have to say it beats around the **New**

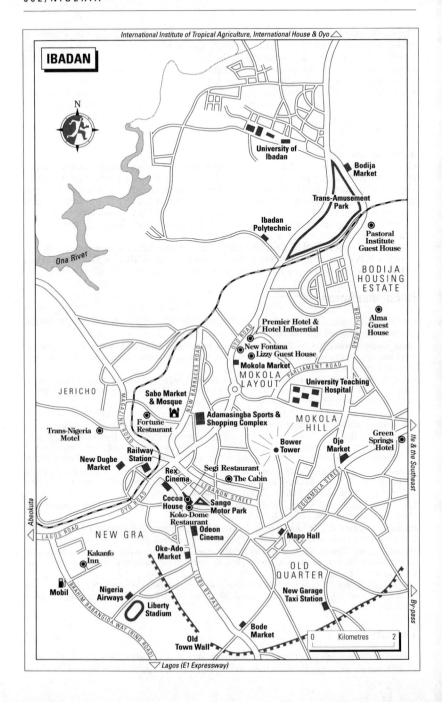

IBADAN

International Institute of Tropical Agriculture, International House & Oyo △

N

University of Ibadan

Bodija Market

Trans-Amusement Park

Ibadan Polytechnic

Pastoral Institute Guest House

Ona River

BODIJA HOUSING ESTATE

Premier Hotel & Hotel Influential

Alma Guest House

New Fontana
Lizzy Guest House

Mokola Market

MOKOLA LAYOUT

University Teaching Hospital

JERICHO

Sabo Market & Mosque

Fortune Restaurant

Adamasingba Sports & Shopping Complex

MOKOLA HILL

Trans-Nigeria Motel

Bower Tower

Oje Market

Green Springs Hotel

Railway Station

New Dugbe Market

Rex Cinema

Segi Restaurant

The Cabin

Cocoa House

Sango Motor Park

Koko-Dome Restaurant

Odeon Cinema

Mapo Hall

NEW GRA

Kakanfo Inn

Oke-Ado Market

OLD QUARTER

Mobil

Nigeria Airways

Liberty Stadium

New Garage Taxi Station

Old Town Wall

Bode Market

0 Kilometres 2

Abeokuta △

Ife & the Southeast ▷

By-pass ▷

△ Lagos (E1 Expressway)

Dugbe Market – one of Nigeria's largest. Ibadan's streets seem to wind at will, so your chances of getting lost while exploring are high. Should that happen, look for the strange **Bower Memorial Tower** on **Agala Hill** to the east, a good viewpoint to climb and a visible reference point from virtually anywhere in the city.

The tower of **Cocoa House** is another guide for the disoriented. One of the few sky-scrapers in town, Cocoa House is evidence of the regional importance of a vital export crop and marks Ibadan's commercial centre. You'll find **banks** in the area (Afribank, First Bank, Central Bank; all Mon–Thurs 8am–3pm, Fri 8am–1pm), and, of more relevance if you're changing money, several **bureaux de change** – a good place to change French francs is Hakasurs, along Lebanon Street. Leventis and UTC **supermarkets** are located nearby. A couple of hundred metres to the west of this area, on Abeokuta Road, is the already old-looking **New GPO** (Mon–Fri 8am–noon & 2–4pm). The **railway station** is directly across the street.

More good views are to be had in the **Old Quarter**, where the British established themselves on the city's highest hill. **Mapo Hall** was built on the summit of **Mapo Hill** in the 1920s and served as the colonial government house. Today, the stylish building is mostly used for wedding receptions, and if it hasn't been rented out, you're welcome to wander around.

On the north side of town, on Oyo Road, the campus of the **University of Ibadan** (UI) was designed for the most part by the distinguished British architect, Maxwell Fry, who also worked with Gropius and Le Corbusier. You can meet and mix with people here at the **cafeteria** or the **coffee shop** (open to all), or use the university **bookshop** (Mon–Fri 7.30am–4.30pm). The Institute of African Studies building houses a **museum** (open on special request) with bronze statues and carvings. The UI **Zoological Garden**, near the Zoological Department, has been neglected for years, but has recently got a face lift and some new animals. The **International Institute of Tropical Agriculture** (IITA) is 5km beyond the university campus on the Oyo road. If you can make friends with someone to get in, you'll find a crystal-clear pool, ice cream, hot dogs and guest chalets in the grounds.

On your way to these centres of academia, you'll pass the huge new **Transwonderland Amusement Park**, an attraction as close to Disneyland as you'll find anywhere in Africa. It's a somewhat surreal experience to sample the rides and Ferris wheel in the environment of Ibadan, but it's proving a big hit in the city and, at weekends and holidays, the place is packed.

For something less active, visit the **British Council**, at 54 Magazine Rd in Jericho (☎02/241 0678), or the **Alliance Francaise**, in the CFAO building, at 7 Lebanon St

---

IBADAN AREA MARKETS

Most of Ibadan's **markets** work on an eight-day cycle, which is fine as long as you know where you are in it: check local papers such as the weekly *Irohin Yoruba* for details.

Bode, near Molete bridge, specializing in beads.

Mokola, daily, 3km north of Cocoa House. Food, pots and baskets.

New Dugbe, daily, near the train station. A massive general market.

Oje, every sixteen days, near Mapo Hall, east of Bere Road. One of the biggest cloth marts in Africa, with over three million yards sold annually (watch out for the *Asooke* strip cloth made in Iseyin and locally produced tie-dyes), plus trade beads.

Ojoo, every eight days, 2km north of UI, west of the Oyo road.

Onidundu, every eight days, 14km north of IITA, west of the Oyo road, specializing in spices, herbs, mats and baskets.

Sabo, daily, near the Friday mosque. The big food and domestic market; this is *the* place to get a good food pounder.

University market, UI, a daily souvenir market.

MOVING ON FROM IBADAN

LONG-DISTANCE TAXIS

Vehicles heading to Oyo and further north leave from the **Sango motor park** near the Cocoa House. The **New Garage taxi station**, off Lagos Road in the southeast of town, is the departure point for Lagos, Ife and the southeast.

TRAINS

Trains leave for Lagos via Abeokuta, and Kano via Kaduna. Check at the station to get the latest schedules, or call NRC's Kaduna office (☎062/231 880 or 791).

FLIGHTS AND TRAVEL AGENTS

Nigeria Airways has offices at Lister House, Southwest Ring Rd (☎02/246 2550) but no scheduled flights out of Ibadan – the closest large airport is Lagos. A number of **travel agents** act as agents for the international airlines; Tess Travels, at Femi Johnson Broking House (the Glass House), 1 Alhaji Jimoh Odutola Rd (☎02/241 0942; Fax 02/241 0230), is an excellent place to make travel arrangements in Nigeria and beyond.

(☎02/241 4937): both have a good range of reading material and a full artistic and cultural programme.

Eating and drinking

For cheap, quick calories, **chop bars** – serving *eba*, *àmàlà* and pounded yam with the usual *egusi* and other soups and stews – line Magazine Street near the junction with Abeokuta Road close by the train station. Up on Mokola Hill, *bukas* serve *begiri* (traditional bean soup) and *amala*. If you're at the university, use the **student cafeteria** – bland but cheap food (and, of course, a good place to meet students).

The Cabin, Onireke St, off Lebanon St (☎02/241 4846). Lebanese and European specialities; great steaks and ice cream.

Fortune Restaurant, 27 Kudeti Ave, Onireke. A long and good Chinese menu.

Kakanfo Inn, 1 Nihinlola St (☎022/311 471). This upmarket hotel also features one of the town's best Indian restaurants, with a varied menu and friendly service.

Koko-Dome Restaurant, near Cocoa House (☎02/241 3384). Lebanese, European and American food, including cheeseburgers and fries. For a small fee, you can spend the day at the clean pool and have food brought to your patio table. Sit-down eating is upstairs and there's a good disco here at weekends (*Legend Nightclub*); there's no cover charge, but you have to eat at the restaurant to enter.

New Fontana, Mokola. Hotel restaurant, and one of the town's best places for European and Nigerian specialities.

Segi Lebanese Restaurant, the Glass House, 1 Alhaji Jimoh Odutola Rd (☎02/241 4838). Restaurant with excellent food, and a nightclub.

Oyo and around

OYO is a relatively small town by Nigerian standards, with only a quarter of a million inhabitants, and its characteristic rust-stained roofscape looks like an Ibadan that never quite took off. On its earlier site to the north, the town was the capital of a Yoruba-speaking empire that stretched as far as present-day Togo (including, in its hegemony, such vassal states as Dan-Homey). At its apogee in around 1700, Oyo was probably the most powerful state in West Africa.

Some history

Oyo was founded on the northern Yoruba savannah, some time between the eleventh and thirteenth centuries, according to legend by **Oranmiyan**, the youngest of the Ife princes (sons of Oduduwa). It was strategically located in a part of the savannah relatively free from tsetse flies, and so could use **horses** for transport and war.

From its old capital in **Oyo-Ile**, in the present-day Oyo-Ile National Park, Oyo began to expand southwards in the sixteenth century, using both its highly efficient cavalry and its infantry to extend its power to the coast. Until the end of the eighteenth century, most of its wealth came from control of the trade routes between the coast and the north. By the late eighteenth century, however, the courts of **Lisbon** and Oyo were increasingly involved as partners in the slave trade.

The name "Yoruba" is a corruption of "Yooba", meaning "the dialect of the Oyo people". The fact that missionaries applied the term to all the peoples of the region attests to the city's far-reaching power, but revolt by vassal states and war with the Muslim jihadists from the north spelt the end of the empire in the nineteenth century.

The present town of Oyo was founded in the 1820s, when Oyo-Ile fell to Muslim raiders. The *Alaafin* attempted to re-establish the grandeur of the old capital at **Ago**, a market town south of Oyo-Ile, which he named Oyo. Now, the only hint of its grand past is a sign welcoming visitors to "The City of Warriors".

The Town

Everything in Oyo centres around **Abiodun Atiba Hall** (also called Town Hall), perched high on a hilltop. If you're walking from one of the hotels, you can see this monumental building from a kilometre away. When you arrive at the Hall, you'll see the **market** spreading out before you on Palace Road. Besides the usual provisions and various household goods, you can find wonderful **leatherwork** and intricately **carved calabashes** – a local speciality, carved at the market in small *ateliers*. Another speciality are **"talking drums"** – *dundun* – and these too are made and sold in market workshops.

Oyo's main point of interest is the **Alaafin's Palace**, situated near the market on Palace Road. Townspeople will tell you that the present ruler is still head of all the Obas of Yorubaland, although the Oni of Ife is also considered to hold the title. In fact a raging dispute – going back to colonial times when the practice of rotating the Chair of the Council of Obas was upset – has occupied attention for years and the two leaders are effectively at daggers drawn. The Oni of Ife, as the descendant of Oduduwa, is more a spiritual leader, however, and in theory should not be open to challenge by earthly office-holders.

Whatever disputes there may be, the Alaafin of Oyo is one of the nation's most influential traditional rulers. His residence is a curious compound with numerous low buildings roofed in the ubiquitous rusty corrugated iron. Some of the buildings are decorated with traditional symbols and statues and carvings line the grounds. You'll have to get a guide at the gate before visiting the grounds – money is never discussed, but at the end of the tour you're expected to dash something. Put all thoughts of seeing inside the palace out of your head.

Practicalities

The **post office** is directly opposite the market. There are branches of First and National **banks** on Atiba Street, though you're advised to change money before arriving. If you're planning to visit Oyo-Ile National Park, contact the **park headquarters** off Iseyin Road, Isokun (☎038/230 125; Fax 038/230 699) before leaving Oyo.

The two best-known **hotels** are located at the entrance to town as you arrive from Ibadan, and both have moderate rates. The *Labamba Hotel* on Ibadan Road (☎038/230 443–4; ③–⑤) is the more charming and expensive of the two, but the *Adeshakin International Hotel*, Asaba, on Iwo Road (☎038/230 907; ①–③) is also good, with a bar and a restaurant serving Nigerian dishes. The cheaper *Oyo Merry Time* (☎038/230 344; ③) has clean S/C rooms at the junction of Iseyin Road and Ibadan Road, and a lively atmosphere after dark.

For cheap **eating** in Oyo, you can eat at the chop bars in the marketplace, and wash down the meal with frothy palm wine. Don't leave town without sampling **gbegiri** (bean soup) and **wara** (curd cheese), which you can buy in **Akesan market.**

Iseyin and Oyo-Ile National Park

West of Oyo, though best reached on the new highway from Ibadan, the small town of **ISEYIN** is famous locally for its wonderful **night market** and cashew trees. It's also one of the main centres for **Aso-oke** strip cloth – most of its weaves come from here. If you're staying, try the *Trans-Nigeria Hotels Resthouse*, on the way into Iseyin from the south. A good day-trip from Iseyin is to the **Ikere Gorge Dam**, where you can go fishing or boating on the lake.

Between Iseyin and the border of Benin, there's a wealth of beautiful countryside dotted with old Yoruba **hill forts.** If you've got your own transport, visit **Ado-Awaiye**, 26km south of Iseyin, and **Shaki** and **Ogboro**, respectively 87km and 105km to the north of Iseyin, both off the Agoare–Kaiama road that leads north through the Oyo and Kwara backcountry to Borgu Game Reserve (see p.994).

North of Iseyin, the road to **Oyo-Ile National Park** leads through **Sepeteri**, where you'll find park rangers, guides and chalet accommodation (②), but the nearest point of entrance from Oyo is in fact at **Igbeti**, also equipped with rangers. The park is not only important for its animals (including elephants, buffaloes, antelope, hartebeast and duikers), but also archeologically, as the northern part is the site of the ruined city of Oyo Ile.

North towards Jebba

Heading north from Oyo towards Jebba, you pass through **OGBOMOSHO**, a large and unpleasant industrial centre, and **ILORIN**, the capital of Kwara State, a workaday trading town with a strong Muslim flavour. Neither offer much to entice visitors, though accommodation can be found at both and Ogbomosho has an excellent Baptist hospital. If you're driving, note that the road between the two towns is a notorious accident blackspot.

Some 50km southeast of Ilorin, on the Lokoja road, turn off at the small town of **Oro** to the fascinating village of **Esie**, where over eight hundred carved soapstone images of humans and animals date from the twelfth century. Their origin is difficult to trace, but some features resemble findings from the Nok culture.

Ife

According to Yoruba legend, **IFE** (also known as **ILE-IFE**), was the first Yoruba city, and indeed, the first city in creation. Custom says it was at this spot that the supreme God **Olodumare** threw an iron chain from the heavens into the waters below. He then instructed his son **Oduduwa** to climb down the chain, carrying with him a calabash full of sand, a chicken and an oil palm nut. Oduduwa dumped the sand on the water and let the chicken loose. The bird began scratching in the sand, causing dry earth to appear, and meanwhile the palm nut produced a tree. The sixteen fronds of the palm tree represented the sixteen crowned rulers of Yorubaland and its sixteen cities. More prosaically, **excavations** indicate that Ife was probably founded as a Yoruba city in the ninth century. They have also revealed much about the lifestyle of the royal court: many of the brass and terracotta sculptures from the digs are today on display in the **Ife museum**.

Although Ife was already in political and economic decline by the early 1500s, the town remained a spiritual focus and is still an important symbol of Yoruba nationhood. In addition, it has had a post-independence renaissance as a modern cultural centre with Nigeria's most extensive university campus – the **Obafemi Awolowo University**. The thousands of students add energy to what would otherwise be a sleepy town and provide the opportunity for animated conversation.

Accommodation

Central Olympique Motel, Ondo Rd (PO 579; ☎036/231 591). Ife's budget option, with S/C single and double rooms in chalets, and some non-S/C single rooms. ①–②.

Hotel Diganga, Ibadan Rd, near the university (PO 1276; ☎036/231 791 or 233 200). S/C rooms with AC, fan and satellite TV. The bar-restaurant fills with students in the evening, (though *Folabab*, next door, serves cheaper Nigerian food). There are buses to the centre during the day but you'll have to rely on rare taxis at night. ②–③.

Mayfair Hotel Ltd, 22/26 Ife–Ibadan Rd (PO 153; ☎036/233 254 or 232 102). A good hotel in the moderate range with comfortable AC rooms – a reasonable distance from the centre. ②–④.

Motel Royal, Ede Rd (towards Oshogbo). Compensates for being slightly run-down by having a swimming pool and tennis courts. All rooms S/C with AC. ③.

University Conference Centre, on the campus (☎036/230 809; Fax 036/230 705). AC accommodation with TV in the rooms and access to facilities including a pool, tennis courts, bar and large restaurant. Good value, and not too far from the centre of the campus (there's a short cut through the gardens at the back that makes it a lot closer – if you can find it). ②–③.

The Town

Although you won't be able to visit the residence at the Oba's or **Ooni's Palace** in the Enuwa area of Ife, it's easy enough to walk around the courtyard, with its statues and dignitaries milling about. One of the Oba's messengers will take you around (with a translator) to show you the **meeting hall** where local criminal cases are tried under the Yoruba penal code, and the **shrine to Ogun**, where a dog or goat is sacrificed each September.

The National Museum

Adjacent to the royal palace, and not to be missed, is the **National Museum** (daily 8am–6pm; small fee). As much as a millennium ago, the Oni of Ife wielded great political and spiritual powers. He commanded a whole army of servants, including indentured artists who made brass castings for him and his retinue – staffs, chest ornaments, and miniature pieces in abstract designs or animal shapes. The museum also contains terracotta works dating from the tenth to the thirteenth centuries and more recent wooden carvings. But the most precious treasures are the magnificent **brass and bronze heads** of the Oni and other senior royal figures, made by the lost wax method (although some of the best examples are in the National Museum in Lagos). The sculptors of the heads worked pure copper and copper alloys of various composition – either with more tin (to make bronze) or more zinc (to make brass) – in a realistic mode of expression that is relatively uncommon in African art. They were clearly technical virtuosos of enormous skill, producing heads of rare grace, scored with the fine lines of scarification indicating royal rank. But there is an imperious, remote, vanity about these heads, and a sense of duty and proscribed creativity, indicating the sculptors' obsession with formal ways of doing things.

The Pottery Museum and the Oranmiyan Staff

Ife also has a small **Pottery Museum**, on More Street – two floors of dusty pottery works including musical jars (like skinless drums), coolers and cooking jugs. Entrance is free, but you're encouraged to make a contribution on departure. In an unmarked garden in the middle of town, the **Oranmiyan Staff** – a carved and decorated stone monolith about five metres high – symbolizes the sword of the first Alaafin of Oyo.

The university

Obafemi Awolowo University was established in the 1960s, and renamed after the first premier of the Western Region when he died in 1988 – a nametag that didn't meet with unanimous approval. The 1960s architecture looks very dated now, but the scope of the grounds and facilities (this is the third largest university campus in the world) is an impressive indication of the stress laid on higher education by the governments of the early independence era.

The university has its own **Museum of Natural History** (Mon–Fri 8am–6pm, Sat & Sun 11am–6pm) and a rather unspectacular **zoo** (daily 10am–5.30pm). To get there, take one of the frequent minibuses from the town centre to "Campus" which drops you in the heart of things. If the driver lets you down at the **campus gate**, you're only halfway to the university and must catch another bus or flag down students driving into college.

Eating and Drinking

The *Samtad*, by the Ondo junction, has a garden **restaurant and bar** and features Nigerian and continental food in a relaxed atmosphere; if you're not eating it's a good place for a few beers. Over on the Ondo road, the *Beacon Disco & Restaurant* does inexpensive Nigerian food – including great fish pepper soup – and has been known to get lively at night.

For **cheaper eating**, try the *Modern Food Centre* at 14 Aderemi Rd (behind *Prof. Ojulari's Pool Agency*) for *eba* and pounded yam with soup, or the host of eateries on or around the **campus**. Apart from whole areas of *bukas* doing hot food all day, the student union cafeteria offers a pretty good and inexpensive greasy spoon selection, and you can also get chicken and chips in Oduduwa Hall or eat in the more expensive staff club restaurant. *Banwill* is a "Chinese" restaurant on campus in the New Bukaria, two rows of largely African mini-restaurants flanking a concrete yard.

Oshogbo

Despite a population close on half a million and an important modern sheet metal plant, **OSHOGBO** seems somehow smaller and more traditional than either Ife or Oyo. **Traditional religion** is perhaps no more prevalent here than in other Yoruba towns, but it's more obvious, especially in the **Sacred Forest**, with its sculptures and temples. Ironically, the renaissance of the religion and art of the town was in part due to an influx of European artists and philosophers who moved here in the 1950s, the most notable of whom was **Suzanne Wenger**, an Austrian painter and sculptor. In 1991, Oshogbo became capital of the newly created Osun State. Its new status has brought a flurry of activity and pushed up rents, but doesn't yet seem to have translated into increased prosperity for the townspeople.

The Town

In Oshogbo town itself, try to visit the **Oba's Palace**, on the junction of Catholic Mission and Okeoshun streets. Besides the old and new palace buildings, the grounds

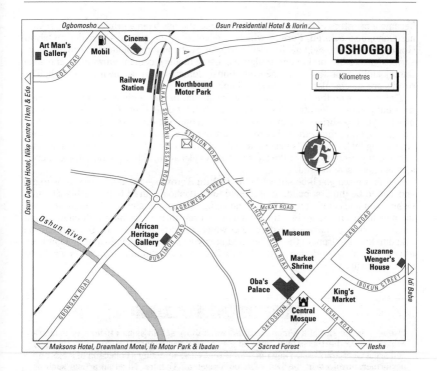

contain a temple to Oshun with traditional wall paintings and sculpted wooden pillars. Aged priestesses guard the inside of the temple and will say prayers for you in exchange for an offering. To see the Oba in person, you can write in advance to: Oba's Palace (Alaafin), Oshogbo, but it may also be possible to meet him on short notice.

Directly across from the palace is one of the most interesting buildings in town, the meeting place for elders and **"King Makers"**, decorated with carved wooden totems and abstract paintings at the front, and with a tree growing out of the back. Flamboyant **Brazilian houses** with wild ornamentation and bright colours line the whole length of Catholic Mission Street.

King's Market spreads out opposite the palace. Besides the wide selection of fruit and vegetables, which grow easily in this fertile part of the country, you'll notice a lot of *juju*, sacred pots and other ritual articles. **Suzanne Wenger's house** is nearby on Ibokun Street and it's worth having a look at from the outside for the imaginative architecture and ornamentation replete with traditional imagery and symbolism. If Adunni (Wenger's Yoruba name) is in, you may be able to meet her. She has a shop with artefacts for sale, and will gladly sell you a copy of her book, *The Sacred Groves of Oshogbo*. For a deeper understanding of Yoruba religion, it makes interesting reading, and the photographs are beautiful.

The Sacred Forest

Suzanne Wenger was interested in the beliefs and language of the Yoruba as inspiration for her painting, but she soon became a follower of **Obatala** – the Yoruba God of Creation – and, as local women came to appreciate her charismatic "artistic power", became a priestess of the religion in the 1960s. She has been a prime mover in restoring Oshogbo's **Sacred Forest**, which is devoted to the female water deity **Oshun Goddess**. With the help of Nigerian artists, she set about rebuilding the broken-down shrines, places of worship and sculptures, using modern cement on wooden and steel frames and a style that combined traditional elements with her own inspiration. The results are spectacular, mysterious and unique.

The forest is on the outskirts of town. It's not far to walk – about 2km from the centre – but you're better off taking a taxi there the first time. From the roadside, you can observe various shrines and an elaborate fence confining the retreat, before arriving at the gate. During the **Oshun Festival**, usually celebrated in August, you'll find followers waiting by the road. It's best to be accompanied during your visit, since it's difficult to make any meaning out of the sites without explanation, although the artistic expression is impressive in itself.

The first place you'll be shown is the **Oshun Temple** – the main place of worship and said to be the first building of the old town (Oshogbo used to be on this site until Oshun said she couldn't live with human beings any longer and sent them off to found the new town). If you go into the temple, you'll see shrines dripping with palm oil and might be asked to make a **sacrifice**, after which, prayers will be made. You may also be asked to kneel in front of the shrines and pray yourself: what you do at this point is up to you, though a rendering of the Lord's Prayer or any humble invocation would be quite adequate.

THE OSHOGBO SCHOOL

Oshogbo is the site of a famous **artists' workshop**, set up as an offshoot of Ibadan's Mbari Club in the 1960s, by writer Ulli Beier (previously married to Suzanne Wenger) and artist Georgina Beier. They ran it for three years, attracting a collection of locals and performers involved in the Duro Ladipo Travelling Theatre. Nigerian artists such as Twins Seven Seven, Muraina Oyelami, Jimoh Buraimoh, Rufus Ogundele, Adebisi Fabunmi and others learnt new techniques from Georgina Beier. Some of these artists are now world famous, and rich and influential at home.

You can meet the artists and buy their work (and batiks, a speciality of Oshogbo) at their open studios. **Twins Seven Seven** is a particularly entertaining, maverick character, who has determinedly made his art the most commercially successful (if you and he are talking money, talk hard!). **Jimoh Buraimoh** works with beaded collage, beads being traditionally a part of royal insignia on the Yoruba beaded crown, and his murals adorn public buildings all over Lagos.

Lastly, Nike Davies (a former wife of Twins Seven Seven) has set up the **Nike Centre** for young artists, on Iwo Road (take a taxi from the Oke Fia garage and if the driver doesn't know it ask for the Dada estate and look out for the signpost). Recently renovated and enlarged, it's booming with creativity, and heavily into batik, painting, carving and even quilt making.

For a look at the Oshogbo School's works in general, visit the **workshop** on Station Road (you can't miss the green-and-white sign), where there's a permanent collection.

Other arts

The favourable creative environment of Oshogbo has laid the basis for other arts and crafts. The **Onirese Arts Gallery**, at 58 Station Rd, is run by Ayanfemi Ayanbukola, who carves and engraves calabashes, works leather and makes batiks and talking drums. Okonfo Rao Kawawa, a musician, stages music and dance performances at his **Jungle Communication Centre**, on Eleyele Farm (☎ & Fax 035/232 381). To get there, take a taxi to Ogo Oluwa, drop just before Ogo Oluwa petrol station, and branch at the last road to the left before the station – a five-minute drive.

A GLOSSARY OF YORUBA RELIGION

Aje The malevolent and destructive aspects of womanhood.

Efe Male masks.

Egungun Masks to honour family ancestors, worn during the annual festival of the secret, male society of the same name. Some *egungun* are put on just for entertainment, to mock police, prostitutes, avaricious traders, people with deformities or anyone who unsettles the community. Many come from Abeokuta, and reflect that town's links with Sierra Leone.

Ekiti Masks of the eastern (*ekiti*) Yoruba kingdoms. Best known is the *ekiti epa* mask, a wooden helmet surmounted by a carved figure.

Eshu Messenger of the *orisha* (gods) and the divine trickster responsible for everything that goes wrong in the world. Every marketplace has a shrine to him, often a simple pillar of sun-baked mud, over which the priests pour daily libations to preserve harmony in the market and community. Devotees of Eshu keep wooden sculptures of him in their houses.

Gelede The Gelede society is found only in some of the western Yoruba kingdoms. Its job is to appease female witches by entertaining them.

Ibeji Twins. If a twin dies, an image is carved of the dead child.

Ifa (also known as Orunmila) A powerful and respected oracle, consulted by those afflicted by disease or madness, or by anyone with a problem to solve. A series of sacred texts – poetic sayings – are interpreted by the *babalawo* or "father of secrets" using the Ifa board and cowries, seeds or stones thrown in a pattern.

Ijebu masks The Ijebu kingdoms of southern Yoruba have imported some of the delta region societies – like Ekine, from the Ijo. Their masks tend toward the formalistic cubism of Ijo sculpture, quite distinct from the naturalistic lines of northern Yoruba sculpture.

Iyamapo Goddess of women's crafts, including weaving and dyeing.

Nanabuku Controller of the wind.

Obatala (or Orishanla) is responsible for the creation of each individual human form, to which Olodumare (or Olorun), the Supreme God, gives life and destiny. Obatala's devotees wear white beads and on ceremonial occasions dress in white cloth.

Ogboni The Ogboni society, to which all Yoruba chiefs, priests and senior men belong, is the cult of the earth. It also has a judicial role, being responsible for all cases of human bloodshed – which are an offence against the earth – and a political one, in providing a forum for discussion free of outside interference. Meetings take place in a cult house, where the society's rites and discussions are kept secret from non-members.

Ogun God of war and iron, traditionally worshipped at times of war to seek success in battle, and by hunters seeking successful hunting. More modern devotees include all those who use iron or steel to make a living, or who drive on roads or fly planes.

Olodumare (also known as Olorun) The Yoruba supreme deity and creator god.

Orisha Oko God of the farm.

Osanyin God of medicine, responsible for the magical therapeutic action of leaves, herbs and other ingredients. There's a fundamental relationship between Osanyin and all other cults: devotees use appropriate medicines in order to enter into a close relationship with their chosen *orisha* during their initiation and subsequent life in the cult.

Oshun (or Oya) Goddess of the river which flows through Oshogbo, the patron deity of the town and bringer of fertility to women.

Shango God of thunder and lightning, identified with one of the very earliest kings of Oyo. Has now been co-opted by NEPA, the national electricity company.

Next, you'll be taken down to the **river** – the sacred domain of Oshun, the water Goddess – where you may be handed a calabash full of murky river water. It makes a big impression if you drink it and you probably won't die if you do, but you know best how your body is likely to react. Either way, you're unlikely to cause offence.

Walking through the forest, you'll be shown shrines depicting a myriad of deities (see box, p.971), all of whom are represented by statues on the site of the market of the old town. The god of creation, **Obatala**, is portrayed riding on an elephant. Other temples in the forest include **Ohuntoto's Building**, a place of prayer to Ohuntoto, the son of Obatala. Designed by Wenger, the architecture forces you into the world of the fantastic – one of the rooms is in the shape of an ear so that those who pray will have their prayers heard.

Practicalities

The **post office** and NITEL telephone office are both on Station Road. The main **motor park** is Dugbe (old garage), but others are spread around at the entrances to the town – the motor park for Ilesha is outside town on the Ilesha road. If you're staying on in Oshogbo, there are several reasonable **hotels**, or for good **food**, *Lanby Restaurant* is the best in town.

Dreamland Motel, Gbongan Rd, near the Governor's office (☎035/232 700). Decent budget rooms for a price you can afford to dream about. ①.

Maksons Hotel. Woleola St, opposite Governor's office (PO 425; ☎035/230 902). Clean rooms with satellite TV, plus a restaurant, bar and nightclub. ②–③.

Osun Capital Hotel, Iwo–Ibadan Rd, Dada Estate (PO 1804; ☎035/230 396). Budget accommodation featuring S/C single rooms with fan, and doubles with AC, fan and TV. Restaurant and bar. ①–②.

Osun Presidential Hotel, Old Ikirun Rd (☎035/232 399). One of Oshogbo's top hotels, with comfortable AC rooms, plus a nightclub, cinema, car rental and a new swimming pool. ④.

Rofson Hotel, 51 Gbongan Rd (☎035/230 701). Inexpensive S/C rooms with AC, fan and satellite TV. Some single rooms are only S/C with fan. Restaurant, bar and VIP bar; Friday night gig. ①–②.

Terminus Hotel, Ajegunle St (PO 139; ☎035/230 423). Comfortable hotel with S/C double rooms and junior suites, all with AC, plus a restaurant, bar and disco. ①.

Benin City and around

Long before Europeans arrived on the West African coast, Benin, now the capital of Edo State, was capital of a powerful empire with a **divine king**. A direct descendant of this line, the **Oba**, still rules over his kingdom, even in the restrictive context of federal government. Today the city is as businesslike as any in Nigeria – feverish, dirty, noisy and crowded. It has a wretched climate, no coast, and little in the way of open spaces to escape to, yet its remarkable history, traced in the **Benin National Museum**, has made the town into something of a cultural centre.

Some history

> *When you go into it you enter a great broad street, which…seems to be seven or eight times broader than the Warmoes street in Amsterdam…and thought to be four miles long…The houses in this town stand in good order, one close and evenly spaced with its neighbour…They have square rooms, sheltered by a roof that is open in the middle, where the rain, wind and light come in…The king's court is very great…built around many square shaped yards…I went into the court far enough to pass through four great yards…and yet wherever I looked I could still see gate after gate which opened into other yards.*
>
> From O. Dapper, *Description of Africa*,
> recorded in 1602, published in Amsterdam 1668

Benin is west of the Igbo country, and mainly peopled by the **Edo** or **Bini** (hence "Benin") who according to their own oral history migrated from the east – perhaps, some would dare say, Egypt. This is a fairly common origin myth, until recently presumed biblical and mission-inspired, that may turn out to have a deeper and more ancient grain of truth as more is learnt about the black roots of pharaonic civilization. Whatever the case, the Edo settlement in West Africa was founded by **Ere**, a man credited with being the inventor of order and instigator of traditions.

Sometime in the late twelfth century or thereabouts, the chiefs impeached their king and for some years were governed by a democratically elected ruler. But this system also failed and the chiefs appealed to Ife to send over a capable monarch. The Yoruba prince **Oranmiyan** arrived and married a local woman. Their son **Eweka** became the first Oba and the royal palace was built during his reign.

From Oranmiyan's time onward, **bronze** achieved status as an important symbol. The very notion of kingship seemed to reside in this alloy of local tin and copper imported at great expense. When an Oba died, it was customary to send his head to Ife to have a portrait cast, but in the mid-fourteenth century, the Edo became bronze-workers themselves. This art form, however, was reserved strictly for the court. A smith foolish enough to waste his talent on anyone other than the Oba was quickly executed.

The kingdom enjoyed its **golden era** between the fifteenth and the seventeenth centuries, its warrior kings conquering and ruling a huge empire reaching from Porto Novo in the West to beyond the Niger River in the east. One of the greatest rulers was **Oba Ewuare** who ascended to the throne around 1440. He expanded the empire and brought new wealth – slaves, ivory, livestock – rolling into the city. Ewuare also greatly enlarged the capital, adding wide avenues and nine new gates each manned by a tax collector. When the **Portuguese** first arrived here, in 1485, they encountered a vast capital – the heart of a capable kingdom.

Other Europeans – English, Dutch, Florentines – quickly followed the Portuguese to the Bight of Benin. Their requirements were slaves, ivory, pepper, leather and handmade cloth. The Oba, **Ozula the Conqueror**, had plenty to offer from a string of fruitful conquests but he refused to sell slaves after 1516, after only a few seasons of trade. He willingly exchanged his stocks of pepper and ivory, however, for metals, silk and velvet cloth, mirrors and European horses – most of which quickly succumbed to sleeping sickness. Ambassadors were exchanged with several European nations in the sixteenth century and the Oba's court acquired a Portuguese cultural veneer.

The Oba became interested in **guns**, but the pope had forbidden traders to sell weapons to heathens. Oba Ozula sent a son to Portugal to be converted and promised to build churches in his kingdom. He never built any, but he got the guns: the Vatican looked the other way and trade flourished. Copper and copper alloys became plentiful and the Oba could afford to commission unlimited metal plaques to line his palace walls. Heady from the booming business, the trade partners even fought side by side, as when Portuguese mercenaries aided the Edo in their war against the neighbouring kingdom of Idah to the northeast, at the end of the sixteenth century. The Portuguese did very well out of the trade, even though they only succeeded in overturning the sanction against slave-trading out of Benin's dominions in the eighteenth century. Even then, the Obas placed strict limits on the numbers sold.

By the late nineteenth century, the **British Empire** had become the Benin kingdom's principal partner, and London was increasingly determined to develop new commodity sources and expand her markets for manufactured goods. The Oba's council increasingly perceived the calculating Europeans as a threat, while the Oba himself tried hard to find ways of negotiating a peaceful takeover that would allow him maximum power. His council sabotaged his plans and attacked and slaughtered a British negotiating team, though civil war was averted. Benin retreated behind the massive city walls to concentrate on metaphysical ways of dealing with the impending disaster of invasion.

Creating an image of savagery was in Britain's interest, since public opinion at home would accept relatively painless war and invasion as long as it was linked to a "civilizing mission". When the British Army launched a retaliatory "punitive expedition" to crush and seize Benin in 1897, they apparently found the Oba had made one last desperate effort to save the city in the only way he knew, and had ordered human sacrifices on a massive scale. The British reported corpses lying everywhere and the pervasive stench of death in the town. The king himself had escaped, but was captured in the forest and sent into exile. His palace was pillaged. The great art treasures were sent to England – where they remain to this day, many in the Museum of Mankind in London. Others were sold to private collections.

The stories of sacrifice undoubtedly had some basis in fact – the Oba's efforts to appease the spirits and ward off the encroaching white men were by no means extraordinary – but there was certainly sensationalist reporting too. Writing in the *Evening News* forty years after the event, Major James F. Ellison referred to a "14 hours running fight with the fleeing enemy" all around the city walls. Inside,

> *Benin ran with blood. Human sacrifices were everywhere. Some of the human beings who were in chains were still alive, speedily to be liberated. Around a huge tree in the centre of the city were erected poles on which were cross-pieces. On these were bodies, remains of those who had been sacrificed. In the Valley of the Skulls were hundreds of human heads and bones.*

After the campaign, the British press referred to Benin as the "City of Blood and Crucifixions". Whatever the magnitude of the barbarities carried out on the kingdom's own slaves and convicts, however, there was far more blood shed by the conquering British force.

Accommodation

As you would expect in a big city, there are plenty of hotels to choose from in Benin, from basic sleazy dives to attempts at international reputation-building. Several are conveniently located near "Ring Road", a roundabout off which runs Akpakpava Road.

Central Hotel, 76 Akpakpava Rd (☎052/200 780). A little run-down, but perfectly acceptable S/C rooms with AC, or cheaper ones with fans. Listen out for live music performances in the popular courtyard bar. ①.

Edo-Delta Hotel, 134 Akpakpava Rd (☎052/252 722). S/C rooms ranging from cheap singles to moderate suites, with a TV in every room, laundry service, bar-restaurant and constant water supply. ②.

Edo Hotel, George Idah Ave, GRA (☎052/258 984). Old-fashioned charm and competitive prices for S/C rooms with AC and satellite TV. AC restaurant and pleasant garden with a bar. ③–④.

Hotel Doris Dey, 35 Benin–Asaba Highway – the extension of Akpakpava Rd. Big, well-appointed modern hotel. All rooms S/C, with AC and satellite TV. ③.

Lixborr Hotel, 4 Sakponba Rd, Idubor Arts Gallery Building (☎052/256 699). Ideally situated near the museum and King's Square. Comfortable AC accommodation with private bath. ②–③.

Motel Benin Plaza, 1 Reservation Rd (☎052/254 779). In a quiet neighbourhood, with chalets – with AC and satellite TV – grouped around a swimming pool. Pleasant indoor bar and restaurant serving Nigerian and European dishes. ③.

Saidi Centre, 271 Murtala Muhammed Way, near Sapele Rd junction (☎052/252 125). Large, popular and somewhat upmarket hotel with AC rooms and suites with satellite TV. Good Chinese-European restaurant, swimming pool and bar. ④.

Splash Motel, 19 Uwangbo St, by Etete Rd, GRA. Small, fairly new motel, with S/C, AC rooms. ②–③.

University Palace Hotel, 4 Federal Government Girls College Rd, Ugbowo (☎052/600 361). The guest house of UNIBEN, but located outside campus. AC and non-AC rooms, plus a restaurant with assorted continental and Nigerian dishes. ②–③.

Victory Hotel, 2 Victory Rd, off Lagos Rd. AC, S/C rooms, friendly staff, and a car park. ①–②.

YWCA, 29 Airport Rd (☎052/252 186). Budget accommodation for women only. Central and friendly. ①.

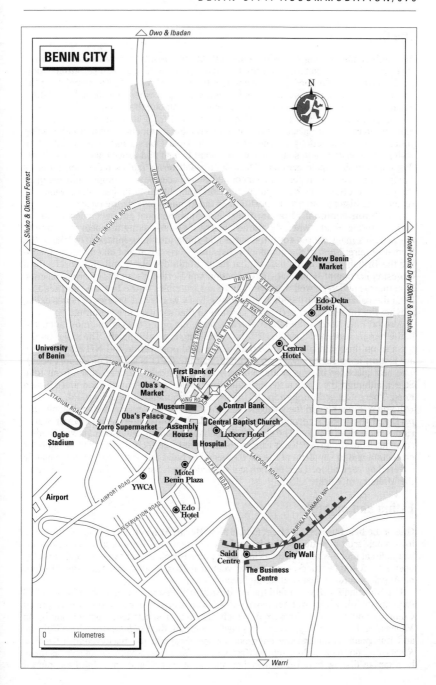

The City

Although Benin is a big city with some 300,000 inhabitants, it's well laid-out and not especially difficult to get to grips with. Everything centres around **King's Square** (popularly known as Ring Road), a roundabout at the heart of town. As the name, if not the square's various bronze statues, would suggest, this is where you'll find the **Oba's Palace**. You may have to ask someone to point it out among the various buildings along the square, because the bland exterior doesn't shout to be noticed. You can visit the modest interior of the palace but you have to write for an appointment first (addressing yourself most respectfully to The Secretary to Oba, Oba's Palace, Benin City, Edo State). Since you have to state the date you want to visit and provide a return address, this may be difficult to arrange. The Oba himself never makes public appearances except for festivals or important court or civil state occasions. By simply showing up at the palace, on the other hand, you're virtually guaranteed to find someone willing to recount the history and give a short tour of the grounds outside the palace.

The **Benin National Museum** (daily 9am–5pm; nominal entrance charge), in the middle of Ring Road – when the traffic's heavy, it's a life-risking manoeuvre getting to it – contains many sacred royal treasures and some of the legendary artworks of the former empire. Most of the kingdom's treasures were stolen and taken abroad following the British invasion of 1897, so that today Benin can claim only the world's third largest collection of Benin art – after London and Berlin. It's an impressive collection nonetheless and very well displayed: there are examples of the **bronze plaques** that lined the palace interior together with masks, ivory works and a series of heads exemplifying the three distinct periods of an art form that spanned five centuries.

Also on Ring Road is the **Oba's Market**, once one of the largest and most animated in the region. It burned down in 1983, but rebuilding is now complete. The major **banks** are also on this roundabout, while the most central **post office** and **NITEL** call office are just off it, on Akpakpava Road (but note that the **GPO** is located on Airport Road). The best place for buying **crafts**, naturally including replica bronze busts, is on Igun Street, although there are also workshops and galleries on Airport Road and Mission Road. There's a good **bookshop** at 34 Federal Government Girl's College Rd.

If you're interested in the vestiges of the **old City Wall** – once a 1000-mile-long rampart, and the world's second largest man-made structure after China's Great Wall – ruined morsels of it can still be seen on Sakpoba Road on the outskirts of town. Another remnant from the great Benin Empire, is the **Moat** – a ditch dug around Benin – for protection and to supplement the earth needed to build the walls. Although it's mainly covered by vegetation, it can be seen at it's junction with Sapele Road, immediately after the Ministry of Works.

Eating and nightlife

One of the best markets for street food is **New Benin Market**. You can get some of the town's best fruit here during the day and cheap finger food (*suya* or grilled chicken, for example) at night, when this turns into a very active area and many shops and bars stay open late. A smaller market in a similar vein near Ring Road is the **Agbadan Market**, on Akpakpava Road, just next to the *Central Hotel*.

For Nigerian **food**, you'll find the good *Estamatts Restaurant*, at 4 Eben Lane, off 73 Akpakpava Rd, while over on Sapele Road, you can get decent, moderately priced Chinese food at *Rima Restaurant*, which also has a snack bar. Further south, on Murtala Muhammed Way, is the city's best restaurant, the *Saidi Centre*, with a Chinese and European menu and the energetic owner always in the background. *Memories Restaurant*, on the first floor (above Karo Chemist's), at 29 Akpakpava Rd, serves mainly Nigerian dishes, but also sandwiches and hamburgers, and shouldn't be confused

MOVING ON FROM BENIN CITY

Vehicles to **Onitsha and the east** leave from the Abo motor park on Ikpoba Road out at the end of Akpakpava Road to the northeast. To **Lagos** and the west, head to the Uselu motor park on Lagos Road. **Buses** – cheaper and slower than taxis – leave from a row of service stations on Urubi Street in the Iyaro neighbourhood. Departure times and destinations need careful advance checking.

If you're **driving**, the main A232 goes east to Onitsha, from where you branch either to Enugu by the new expressway link, or south on the A6 to Owerri and Port Harcourt. You'll hear dire warnings about this route, as it holds something of a record for accidents in Nigeria – and that says a lot. If you're going directly to **Port Harcourt**, you might want to consider the A2 rainforest route via Sapele and **Warri**. Look for palm wine sellers along the roadside, but don't even inhale near the stuff if you're behind the wheel.

Domestic **flights** are covered mainly by Okada Airlines, with an office at Airport Road (☎052/244 942 or 241 504). The **travel agency** at 63 Akenzua St (☎052/222 806 or 244 724) handles Lagos bookings on BA, KLM and others.

with *Memories Nightclub*, 42 Ihema Rd, a bar and restaurant with a lively **nightclub** from 10pm till dawn on Wed, Fri & Sat.

Okumu Nature Sanctuary

The **Okumu Nature Sanctuary** is a patch of indigenous forest of the kind that blanketed southern Nigeria before the nineteenth-century European invasion and, as such, it's an important island of biodiversity (the endangered white throated monkey is found only here). At 35km west of Benin City, near the small town of **Udo**, it makes an easy day-trip from Benin City. You might make it to Okumu by taxi, but most visitors drive themselves. It's possible to **stay** in the forest reserve, at the somewhat disconcertingly named *African Timber & Plywood Guest House* actually a delightful old colonial cabin in a remote setting; you'll need to bring your own food for the nature trail. Despite encroaching development, a herd of **forest elephants** is hanging on at Okumu, as well as scattered bushcows and yellow-backed duikers, plus various species of monkeys, an array of birdlife and the usual startling variety of reptiles and invertebrates. An observation platform in the forest canopy provides good viewing possibilities and there's a river where you can swim.

THE SOUTHEAST

Most of the southeast is known as the **Igbo Country** (see box, overleaf), although numerous other peoples also live in the region. The whole southeastern area, from Enugu south to Port Harcourt, has also been called the "Taiwan" of Nigeria, due in part to its heavy industry and oil riches, but mostly because of its thriving smaller industries, capable of fixing and copying almost any product. There are a number of thriving commercial towns in the region which might provide a useful stopover on longer journeys, though none are worth going out of your way to see. The **Niger River** passes through one such town, **Onitsha**, which was heavily damaged in the Biafran war but has quickly regained its commercial buzz. **Enugu**, to the northeast, has survived the civil war largely unscathed, and is now a vital economic centre and home to many multinational firms.

As it approaches the coast, the Niger River fans out into the endless meandering channels of the **Delta Region**. The major town in the area, **Port Harcourt**, is another modern town that has grown quickly since independence. You'll understand why when you see **oil flares** belching black smoke and flames on the seaward horizon: this is the

THE IGBO

Igbo speakers have played an important role in the uncertain history of Nigeria. Unlike the Yoruba of the southwest, or the city-states of the centre and north, the people of the southeast forest country have traditionally maintained much more clan-based societies with fewer social hierarchies, centred around the village and its all-male council. The lack of evolution of a central kingdom among the Igbos can partly be explained by the difficulties of communication in their rainforest.

Largely spurning slavery in their own culture, these communities fell easy prey when it was imposed from outside from the sixteenth to the nineteenth centuries. Later, having few cumbersome political structures to set up barriers, they quickly adapted to the new ideas of colonial society – its stress on personal achievement, on virtue earned through work and self-advancement, on business acumen and the creation of wealth. By the time World War II was over, the Igbo were clearly dominating the roles allowed to native Nigerians by the colonial government. Their success was partly responsible for the bloody trauma of **Biafra** – the still-born Igbo republic declared in 1967 – which resulted in civil war and a federal blockade which brought widespread starvation. And their continued dynamism is still the source of frustration among other groups in Nigeria – in particular the Hausa and Fulani Muslims of the north. It has tended to earn southeast Nigerians a reputation as survivors. After all, they have the **oil**. But, having relatively poor representation in the Federal Republic's formal political structures (and those representatives often corrupt and rarely called to account) has meant an acknowledged deficit of infrastructure and social services in the southeastern states. The image of the Igbo in Nigeria is a cruelly contradictory one which has parallels with many commercially successful peoples around the world.

heart of Nigeria's oil country. But it's also a good place for exploring **creek villages** and island towns like nearby **Bonny**. **Calabar**, relaxing and scenic, spreads over a hill overlooking the Calabar River in the very far southeast. This town, once a big slave port and now devoted to the palm oil trade, is one of Nigeria's most enjoyable.

Calabar is the natural base for visits to one of Nigeria's most exciting natural history sites, the **Cross River National Park**, separated into the Okwangwo and Oban Divisions. Like the long-established **Obudu Cattle Ranch**, a little further north, gorillas live in these protected hill forests, and basic facilities are in place for visitors to see them.

Enugu

In sharp contrast to Benin City, **ENUGU**, capital of the newly formed Enugu State and the effective capital of Igbo-land, is a town without a long history. It was founded in 1909 when **coal deposits** were discovered in the area. Some time later iron ore was also found, and when the railway came through in 1916, the town's economic future was sealed. It became capital of the Eastern Region in the 1930s (which dates most of the large government buildings) and later was the headquarters of the secessionist republic of Biafra. Although the town was all but deserted during the Civil War, it has since rediscovered its old vitality. Industry has taken off and there's even a Mercedes assembly plant, which must be some crude indicator of local prosperity. Enugu displays a certain colonial charm and has the odd, shady open space, but with mines, railway tracks, smoky factories and a population pushing past half a million, you'll have to work hard to like it.

Accommodation

There's a decent selection of **hotels** in Enugu, making it a good stopping-off point between Calabar and the Cameroon border, or the centre and north of Nigeria.

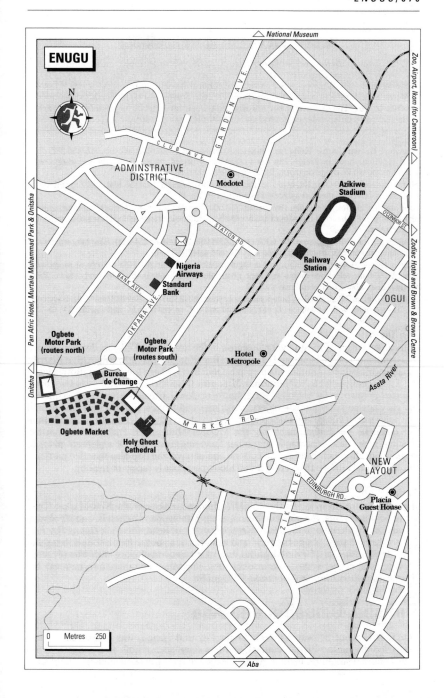

MOVING ON FROM ENUGU

Vehicles for **Onitsha and west** leave from the New Market motor park. Southbound vehicles for **Port Harcourt** via Aba and Umuahia, leave from near the Holy Ghost Cathedral at the Ogbete motor park. **Northbound** vehicles also leave from Ogbete motor park, but from opposite the prison. There are **train services** north to Kano and south to Port Harcourt, and several **flights** a week on Nigeria Airways to Lagos and Calabar, with independent carriers covering other major cities.

Brown & Brown Centre, Ezillo Ave, Independence Layout (☎042/458 993; Fax 042/455 287). The most luxurious hotel in Enugu, but not unreasonably priced, especially as cheaper rooms with access to the whole range of luxury facilities are available. ④.

Hotel Metropole, 19 Ogui Rd, near the train station (☎042/251 971 or 250 464). Flamboyant decor, moderately-priced rooms and a decent restaurant and bar. ③.

Modotel, 2 Club Rd, off Garden Ave (☎042/258 000; Fax 042/258 868). A sparkling international-class set-up in the heart of the administrative district, with a wide range of facilities and surprisingly moderate prices. ③–⑤.

Pan Afric Hotel, 6A Kingsway Rd, GRA (☎042/256 089, 255 248 or 251 844). Elegant gardens and reasonably priced S/C rooms equipped with AC and satellite TV. ③.

Placia Guest House, 25 Edinburgh Rd, Ogui (☎042/255 851 or 251 565). Choice of rooms with S/C, AC, TV and telephone in this well-kept, good-value guesthouse in the older part of town. Good restaurant and bar, and exceptional staff. ②.

Zodiac Hotel, 5/7 Rangers Ave, Independence Layout (☎042/457 900; Fax 042/457 758). Busy, well-established hotel, with a pool, excellent restaurant and S/C rooms with AC and satellite TV. ③–⑥.

The Town

You can take care of most of your business in the area around Okpara Avenue, where you'll find most of the banks and the **post office**. Enugu's vast **administrative district** straggles off behind. Another main strip is Ogui Road, where the **train station** is located. The recently-established **National Museum** (Mon–Fri 8am–4pm), is in the northern part of town, at 58 Abakaliki Rd. It houses cultural artefacts from the area, including carvings and masquerade objects, costumes and fabrics, musical instruments and weapons; a craft village and museum kitchen are currently under construction. A number of **parks** dot Enugu, including the Murtala Muhammed Park across from the bustling new market; jacaranda and other flowering trees make it a pleasant place to relax in the afternoon heat. At the eastern end of town, the **zoo** also has nice gardens, but the animals (those that remain) don't look particularly happy or healthy.

Eating

A good place for cheap food is the *MOWLT Canteen* across from the New Market. They serve pounded yams, *eba*, rice and beans, along with beer and minerals, and it's always full and noisy. Or, next to the *Hotel Metropole* on Ogui Road, there's a *Danny Boy Fast Food* with meat pies, "mega burgers" and samosas. It's not the freshest food, but quite OK. *Ideal Cuisine*, at 15 Edinburgh Rd, is a nicely decorated place with friendly staff, serving good pepper soup, *egusi* or okra soup. For something more international, try the pleasant *Raya Chinese Restaurant*, 77 Ogui Rd.

Onitsha, Umuahia and Aba

ONITSHA, about halfway between Benin City and Enugu, was almost completely destroyed during the Biafran conflict, and has since been rebuilt as a congested, frenetic commercial centre. Famous as the location of the earliest indigenously published literature in Nigeria (novels and tracts from 1949, under the label "Onitsha Market Literature"), it's still a highly energetic place – though the first impression of the city might be that there's no compelling reason to stay, except for a night stop. In that case, there's decent **accommodation** at the *Traveller's Palace Hotel*, conveniently located near the taxi park at 8 Agbu Ogbuefi St (☎046/211 013; ②); the excellent-value *People's Club Guest House*, off Owerri Rd (☎046/212 717; ①–③); and the more upmarket *Bolingo Hotels and Towers*, at 74 Zik Ave (☎046/210 943; ②–④), which has a pool and Chinese restaurant.

Midway along the expressway linking Enugu and Port Harcourt, **UMUAHIA's** large central market and quiet tree-lined streets belie the days when this town served as a strategic military headquarters in the Biafran conflict. The private **bunker**, at 15 Okpara Ave, GRA, from where Biafran leader, Colonel Ojukwu, commanded his troops, is being renovated to receive visitors, but the current focus is on the **National War Museum**, housed in the former Eastern Nigeria TV relaying station from where the *Voice of Biafra* was transmitted during the war. It's an interesting collection of memorabilia, with period photographs accompanying displays of guns, swords and uniforms. Outside you can wander among the "Red Devil" Biafran troop transporters, field guns and aircraft. A small **café** has been set up inside the carcass of a naval ship. Entrance is free, but the museum is on a dirt track that dead-ends half a kilometre from the main road. The *Abia Guest House*, at 11 Ekwuruke St (☎088/222 032; ①), and the *Banana Hotel*, at 37 Warri Rd (☎088/220 879; ②), provide reasonable **accommodation**.

Continuing south from Umuahia, the road bangs into the unprepossessing outskirts of **ABA**, an ugly commercial town and the capital of Abia State, with its vast **Ariara Market** spilling onto the expressway. If you choose, or are obliged, to stop here, the **Museum of Colonial History** (daily 9am–6pm; small entrance fee) is only a two-minute walk from the chaos of the main motor park, on the A342 Ikot Ekpene Road (leading east out of town). A small, orderly collection, housed in a wooden British administrative building, traces the history of Nigeria through well-presented and informative exhibits of photos from pre-colonial times to the 1960s. There's a cluster of crafts shops, chop bars and weaving huts in the museum compound. Among more inexpensive **hotels**, the *Ariss Plaza Hotel*, at 70B Ikot Ekpene Rd (☎082/221 731; ②–③), and the *Crystal Park Hotel*, Crystal Park Ave, off Port Harcourt Rd (☎082/221 588; ③), are fairly good value, while the modern *Binez Hotel*, at 5/7 Nwogu St, Umungasi (☎082/440 030; ④), is more upmarket.

Port Harcourt and around

Capital of Rivers State, **PORT HARCOURT** ("Po-ta-ko" in Pidgin) promotes itself as the **"Garden City"**. Given its location in the rainforest, it would be remarkable if it wasn't green. Port Harcourt first came to prominence during World War I, as a result of military operations mounted from here against German Kamerun. But the fortunes of the modern city are thanks primarily to the **oil wells** that have sprouted throughout the region since 1956, when commercial quantities were discovered in **Oloibiri**. The first shipload of Nigerian crude was exported from Port Harcourt in 1958 and the country was launched on a new economic course that promised rapid industrial development and prosperity. As a side benefit, Port Harcourt has acquired a strikingly **modern aspect**, with wide avenues, flyovers and high-rise blocks easily outshooting the last of the giant forest trees left standing in the city limits. Yet the **"Old Township"** (founded in 1913) has survived the rapid growth and if you were to limit your time to this corner of the city, you could come away believing that Port Harcourt is still a small town with a good deal of charm.

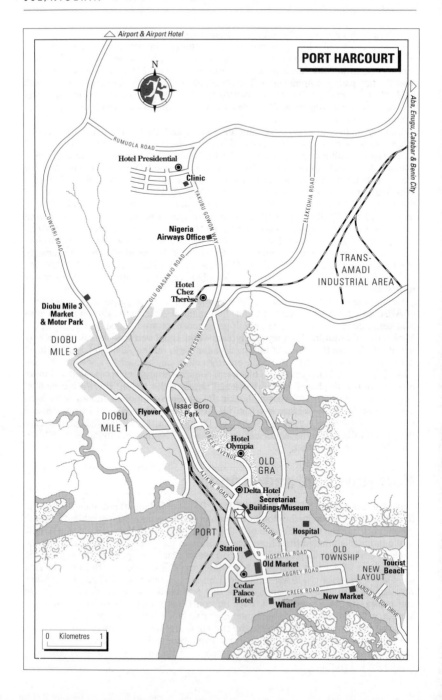

PORT HARCOURT

Airport & Airport Hotel

Aba, Enugu, Calabar & Benin City

RUMUOLA ROAD

Hotel Presidential

Clinic

OWERRI ROAD

YAKUBU GOWON WAY

ELEKEOHIA ROAD

Nigeria
Airways Office

OLU OBASANJO ROAD

Hotel
Chez
Thérèse

TRANS-
AMADI
INDUSTRIAL AREA

Diobu Mile 3
Market
& Motor Park

DIOBU
MILE 3

ABA EXPRESSWAY

DIOBU
MILE 1

Flyover

Issac Boro
Park

FORCES AVENUE

Hotel
Olympia

OLD
GRA

AZIKWE ROAD

Delta Hotel

Secretariat
Buildings/Museum

MOSCOW RD

Hospital

PORT

Station

HOSPITAL ROAD

OLD
TOWNSHIP

Old Market

AGGREY ROAD

NEW
LAYOUT

Tourist
Beach

Cedar
Palace
Hotel

CREEK ROAD

New Market

HAROLD WILSON DRIVE

Wharf

0   Kilometres   1

Arrival, orientation and information

If you're using public transport, the main problem in the city is its sheer size. You're likely to be dropped at either the Abali Motor Park on Aba Road, or at the Diobu Mile 3 Motor Park, which is a good 5km from the most appealing parts of town. If you have to get around a lot, taxi fares from one end of the city to the other will soon start to eat into your pocket.

Port Harcourt is divided by the **flyover** – a freeway overpass that's something of a symbol of the town's modernity – into two distinct zones: the new town to the north and the old town to the south. The **Aba Expressway** runs clean through the new part of town, from the air force base in the northern suburbs down to the flyover. "Expressway" is no exaggeration, since cars seem to be out to break speed records as they scream down it; pedestrian overpasses are few and far between. **Banks** and various governmental buildings line this artery, and just off it, the **Kaduna Street Public Market** is a good place for food, including the fresh fish which is so plentiful around here. Other markets are in **Diobu neighbourhood** at Mile 1 and Mile 3. **Azikiwe Road**, south of the flyover, is effectively the city centre, where you'll see the towering state headquarters of further **banks** and a fine showing of **supermarkets**.

In the **Old Township**, Aggrey Road runs through the heart and constitutes the high street. From here, in the crowded southern quarter of the city, you get striking views of the distant oil flares as you take in a wide variety of stalls, restaurants and shops lining the street. On the southern side of the township, down near the creek, you'll find two of Port Harcourt's main markets – the wonderfully chaotic **Creek Road Market**, excellent for fish, and **New Layout Market**.

The offices of the helpful **Rivers State Tourism Board** are at 35/37 Aba Expressway (PMB 6176; ☎084/334 901).

Accommodation

Port Harcourt has a good cross-section of places to stay, though some are a fair distance from the central area: this town is built for drivers.

Airport Hotel, Owerri Rd, 40min from the centre (☎084/331 513 or 332 309). Currently undergoing renovation to regain its premier position. Has all the facilities you might want, even a heliport. ③–⑦.

Cedar Palace Hotel, 11 Harbour Rd (☎084/333 668). Moderate hotel near the train station and port, with AC rooms. ③.

Delta Hotel, 1–3 Harley St (☎084/300 191). The old catering rest-house is now a renovated AC hotel, and the twin rooms offer good value. The restaurant is somewhat limited. ③.

Erijoy Hotel, Plot 5 Trans-Amadi Industrial Layout, Rumuobiakani (☎084/232 750). Moderate hotel with reasonable standards (all rooms are AC) and frequent live music performances. ④.

Hotel Chez Therese, 23 Udom St, off Aba Expressway (☎084/331 908 or 334 808; Fax 084/230 820). Inexpensive place with clean S/C rooms with AC and TV, plus a restaurant, bar and bookshop. ②.

Hotel Olympia, 45 Forces Ave, Old GRA (☎084/230 923–5; Fax 084/230 928). Smart hotel, conveniently located near the post office, banks and museum. ⑥.

Hotel Presidential, Aba Expressway (☎084/239 505; Fax 084/234 165). The international-class hideout, with three restaurants (Chinese, Lebanese and Nigerian), a huge pool and a gym. ⑥–⑦.

Hotel Sunnyville, 7 Olu Obasanjo Rd (☎084/333 169 or 238 286). Clean AC hotel near the Mile 3 motor park, with S/C rooms and an in-house nightclub. ④.

Ibani Castle Guest House, 31/33 Harold Wilson Drive. (☎084/333 244). Atmospheric guesthouse in the Old Township with reasonable standards and accommodating staff. ①–②.

The Town

The Secretariat Complex at the bottom of Azikiwe Road houses the city's small **ethnographic museum**. Its examples of regional art include outstanding examples of the colourful, often bizarre local **masks**, and there are also limited and poorly displayed scatterings of domestic utensils from major ethnic groups in the area – Ijaw, Ikwerre, Etche, Ogoni, Ekpeye and Ogba. Not far away, on Bonny Road, the **Cultural Centre** (Mon–Sat 7.30am–3.30pm, closed holidays) has various exhibits on handicrafts, which you can also buy here, and canoe building.

In the **Old Township**, a **"tourist beach"** was recently set aside down by Ndoki Street, and though the surrounding parks are quite pleasant, the site hasn't yet sparked much interest. In keeping with Port Harcourt's image as a garden city, the **Isaac Boro Park**, near the flyover, adds a bit of extra green to the city centre. The park is dedicated to Major Isaac Adaka Boro, a champion of the minority peoples of the southeast, who, in defending his cause against Governor Ojukwu's Igbo domination, was killed in 1968 fighting for the Federal forces during the civil war. In the north of town the **zoo park** contributes a wild touch to the otherwise relentless **Trans-Amadi Industrial Area.**

Eating and nightlife

For **inexpensive eating** head to "Suya Street" in the Old Township. Every taxi driver is familiar with this atmospheric road lined with food stalls and glowing with the warm light of charcoal fires in the evening. There's a wide range of chop here, more than the street's name suggests, though if *suya* is all you are interested in, it's available along with grilled corn on just about every street corner. For **foreign cuisine**, the *Eastern Garden Chinese Restaurant*, at 51 Aba Expressway is easily the best Chinese restaurant in town; for Lebanese food, the *Hotel Presidential* hosts the excellent *Why Not Restaurant*. Moving upmarket, *Charlie's Restaurant*, at 214 Aba Expressway, has a wide range of dishes, including salads and desserts, and plays live jazz on Wednesday and Sunday, while at 175B Aba Expressway, *Chez Alex Restaurant* has a menu of Lebanese, Chinese, Nigerian and continental dishes, and serves wine.

As you would expect in a town the size of Port Harcourt, there are numerous **night-clubs** catering to all (male) tastes, although the scene changes rapidly. Ask around to find out which place is currently popular or is likely to have a live band; the big nights are Thursday to Saturday. *Metro Garden Restaurant & Nightclub*, at 38B Aba Rd, is a current favourite, while further north, but still in the new part of town, *Heartbeat Nightclub*, 205 Aba Rd, next to the *Presidential*, has a flashy dance floor and adjacent snooker bar. In the old part of town, have a look at the *Ibani Castle Hotel*'s in-house *Orupolo Night Club* at 31 Harold Wilson Drive, or the *Tropicana* in the *Cedar Palace Hotel*. Of the numerous **cinemas** around town, the one in the *Hotel Presidential* is best.

Bonny and Brass islands

You can travel by irregular motorboat to **Bonny and Brass islands** (three and six hours respectively), or alternatively take the smaller boat "taxis" used by people of the creek villages. They depart from Bonny Waterside (at the bottom of Bonny Road by the Cultural Centre) and head to numerous destinations (Ke, Bekingkiri, etc). There are sheds for booking the ferries, but for the small boats just go to the jetty where people and cargo are loading. Expect to bargaining hard to get the regular price.

Bonny and Brass were the first fifteenth-century Portuguese toeholds in Nigeria, and later became missionary gateways (St Stephen's on Bonny is one of the oldest Anglican churches in the country), but are now devoted to the oil industry. There are still some wonderfully ornate Victorian tombstones and monuments and some great old houses. Local chiefs tend to wear Edwardian shirts with tucked fronts and top hats.

Accommodation can be found at a number of hotels on Bonny. The least expensive is the *Beach Hotel* (②), with shabby rooms with shared facilities that still cost more than anything on the mainland. The other town hotels are considerably more comfortable. Beware of zealous immigration officials, and be fully armed with your paperwork.

Port Harcourt has vehicles to almost everywhere – it's literally at the end of the road, or at least the Old Township is – and transport isn't hard to find. The **Mile 3 motor park** at Ikwerre Road caters mostly for intra-city buses, taxis and share taxis, although it's also possible to get from here to the nearer towns (Owerri and Onitsha), and to Ibadan and the Borikiri terminal in Lagos. The main motor park, for services to Calabar, Benin City and just about everywhere else is **Abali Park** (also known as **Leventis motor park**), located near the flyover on the Aba Expressway, Mile 1. To get a seat on the cheapest buses, you'll need to book a day in advance, or start very early.

As for **trains**, there's a service to Kano via Enugu, Makurdi, Kaduna and Zaria. Ask at the station on Odual Road, Old Township, or at the local NRC office on Old Market Road (☎084/301 060) to get the latest timetable.

Flights to **Lagos**, on Nigeria Airways, leave at noon daily (except Sat); they also run weekly services to **Libreville** and **Douala**. There are also numerous domestic airlines with frequent flights to Lagos and to most major cities in Nigeria: these include Okada, ADC, Triax, Kabo and Harka. Oriental Airlines has a daily flight to **Abuja**. Helicopter flights for oil industry personnel run to **Bonny** and **Brass**: check at the tourist office to see if it is possible to hitch a ride.

Calabar and around

It's not just its position perched high on the hills overlooking the river that makes **CALABAR** such a pleasant town to visit. There's a general good ambience created by its compact size and the outgoing nature of the Efik, Ibibio and Kalabari people. Calabar offers a fine introduction to the nicer facets of Nigerian life and, if you're heading east, it's a good place to prepare for in-your-face Cameroon and the rigours of Central Africa. The waterfront sums up its elegantly run-down, colonial feel: apart from Lagos, Calabar is the only Nigerian city near the coast, and the tension that crackles in so many other large towns is absent, as if whisked away on the ocean breeze. Calabar also has the best **culinary reputation** in the country, with lots of varied, traditional cooking. Nigerians say that if a Calabar woman cooks for you, you'll never leave the town.

If you've any choice about when you visit, opt for October, **masquerade month** in Calabar, the time when cultural values and traditional beliefs are most in evidence. The masquerades – **Sekiapu** – include not only continuous drumming and dancing, sculpted masks and elaborate and dazzlingly costumed performers, but regattas of huge, fabulously decked, competitive society canoes.

Some history

The **Qua** (or Ekoi), who came from the northern woodlands and were principally hunters and farmers, were the first people to settle in the Calabar area. Later migration brought the **Efik** and **Efut** – predominantly fishers and subsistence farmers. The Portuguese arrived in the closing years of the fifteenth century and the economic orientation of the local people slowly shifted to **trading**. By the seventeenth century, the Efik were in control of the lucrative export of **slaves**. Efik settlements on the estuary of the Calabar River developed into trading **city-states** that dealt with the Portuguese, Dutch, French, German and English. Rich and powerful, the rulers took European names to emphasize their importance – the Dukes, the Jameses, the Henshaws – and welcomed **missionaries**, despite their opposition to the slave trade. Calabar thus became a centre of education and religion, and local rulers gained further advantages with the European trading partners, as the Efik forbade missionaries

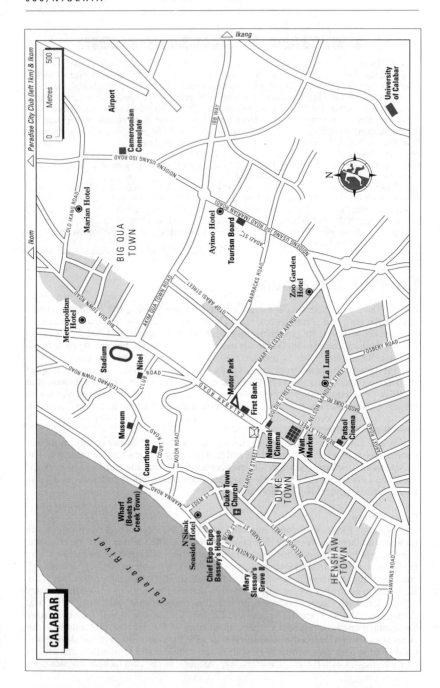

CALABAR

to come into contact with ethnic groups in the hinterland. With their understanding of the ways of the West, the Efik made the transition as smoothly as anyone could have expected when trade shifted from slaves to **palm oil** and, later, when Nigeria became a colony and the Efik were ruled "indirectly", through their chiefs. At the end of the nineteenth century, Calabar became the capital of Southern Nigeria and during the **Biafran War**, the town was recaptured from the secessionists and served as an important federal forces naval base.

Arrival and city transport

The busiest streets in town are the long-established and central **Calabar Road** and the newer commercial street called **Ndidem Usang Iso Road**. The **bus park**, where you're likely to arrive, is near Watt Market on Calabar Road. Calabar is an easy town to get around. **Taxis**, together with even cheaper buses and motorcycle taxis, provide nearly 24-hour mobility. City buses run on set routes but will usually stop if you wave them down. **Motorcycle taxis** – or "motor drops" – usually cost the same as a shared taxi for a single drop, though it may be double this for long transits across town. Like taxi fares, prices double after dark, though you may be able to negotiate a good price for two up on the bike.

Accommodation

There's a host of pleasant, small, family-run hotels, many of which have air conditioning and TV at affordable prices.

Achive Guesthouse, 3 Clifford Lane (unpaved alley that runs alongside the ITC supermarket), off Calabar Rd. S/C single or double rooms with fans near the market. Not exactly of good repute, but the people are very nice and they have a bar/TV room with snacks – try the snail kebabs, a local delicacy. ①.

Ayimo Hotel, 74 Ndidem Usang Iso Rd (☎087/221 770). An older place which has worn well, the *Ayimo*'s double rooms are quite reasonable for two, but slightly pricey if you're on your own. ②.

Marian Hotel, 125 Old Ikang Rd (☎087/230 233). Luxury hotel, challenging the older *Metropolitan*. Modern chalets in a quiet area away from the centre, with a garden. Excellent Nigerian and continental restaurant, plus parking space for cars. ③–④.

Metropolitan Hotel, Calabar Rd (☎087/220 911 or 222 257). Calabar's large, international-class place, with the usual amenities. The AC rooms *without* TV are very reasonable, and the restaurant, cocktail bar and nightclub are highly rated. ③–⑥.

Nelbee Executive Guest House, 5 Dan Achibong St, off Calabar Rd (☎087/222 684). Inexpensive lodging in S/C rooms with AC, and a good restaurant featuring garlic steak and fish pepper soup. ②–③.

Nsikak Sea-Side Hotel, 23 Edem St (☎087/228 443). On the waterfront, a modern-looking facade belies a faded interior with scruffy S/C or non-S/C rooms. The top floor bar is enclosed by huge bay windows for a beautiful view of the river and town. ①.

Zoo Garden Hotel, Mary Slessor Ave, opposite Target St (☎087/224 673). Good-value S/C double rooms with AC and satellite TV. No alcohol served in the restaurant or bar. ②.

TOURIST AND PARKS INFORMATION

Call in at the **tourist office**, 28 Marian Rd (PMB 1288; ☎087/230 988), to pick up the informative *Cross River State Tourist Guide*. If you're heading to the forest reserves, up-to-date information can be had at the **Parks Liaison Office**, at 8 Okon Inok Close, State Housing Estate.

The Town

At the centre of Calabar is **Watt Market**. Calabar Road runs through the middle of the market, dividing foodstuffs on one side from cloth and household goods on the other. Also on Calabar Road, between the market roundabout and the *Metropolitan Hotel*, you'll find the **post office** and major **banks**. For really spectacular views of the town, the river and the surrounding forest, climb to the top of the **Calabar University Library** – the largest library building in Africa. The **NITEL** call office is up towards the huge Calabar Stadium, at 2 Club Rd.

There's still a good deal of **colonial architecture** in the older parts of Calabar, especially around the Henshaw Town, Duke Town and waterfront districts. The **courthouse** is a characteristic piece of period design and many other buildings are still inhabited, or in use, despite their dilapidated condition. Another good example is the nineteenth-century **house of Chief Ekpo Ekpo Bassey** at 19 Boco St, now falling into extravagant disrepair. Nearby, the **Duke Town church** is one of the oldest in Nigeria, established in the nineteenth century by Presbyterian missionaries. Continuing uphill on Eyamba Street past the church takes you to the **old cemetery** – an enchanting, if neglected, spot, with stunning views over the town and river. The tomb of one of southern Nigeria's most influential missionaries, **Mary Slessor**, from Dundee, near Edinburgh, lies here, marked by a plaque.

Calabar Museum

On the hill overlooking the waterfront, **Calabar Museum** (daily 9am–6pm) is housed in the **Old Government House**, the former residence of the colonial governor. The building, designed and built in Glasgow and shipped over in pieces, has been beautifully restored. As a museum, it has few, if any, equals in the country.

The museum concentrates on the **history** of old Calabar, rather than on ethnography or art, and the collections are clearly documented and displayed. In fact, there's almost too much to contemplate here in one visit, with a mass of details on trading, missionary activities and colonial administration. It's a remarkable collection spanning pre-colonial days, the slave and palm oil eras, British invasion and anti-colonial resistance, ending with the path to independence. The museum also contains a **craft village** and shop and there's a good outdoor bar with wonderful views over the town. The small **bookshop** has interesting material on the history and culture of the region.

Eating, drinking and nightlife

A number of zesty **clubs** enliven Calabar nights and, since this is one of the southern Nigerian cities where you can feel relatively safe after dark, it's fun to wander around checking them out. *La Luna*, on Fosbery Road, has regular live music at weekends; *Paradise City*, at 87 Atekong Drive, off Ndidem Usang Iso Road is currently one of Calabar's flashiest and most popular clubs, with live music (reggae or Highlife) from Wednesday to Saturday; and *Tuxedo Junction*, at 39 Chambley St, has a different theme each evening, including a Makossa night on Friday – doors open around 8pm, but the real excitement is after midnight.

For **food**, try the nationally famous Calabar soup with periwinkles. Another local delicacy is dog meat; if you walk past houses with cages full of canines, they're not there as guards – these are restaurants.

Duchess Restaurant & Bar, 8 Mayna Ave, off Goldie St (☎087/220 205). Small, exclusive and not too expensive, with an à la carte menu.

Freddy's Restaurant, 90 Atekong Drive (☎087/232 821). Upmarket restaurant with continental and Lebanese dishes, and specialities like hummus, pepper steak and avocadoes stuffed with shrimp. A popular choice among expats.

High Quality Bakery, 34 9 Ndideng Usang Iso Rd (behind Unity Supermarket). Fresh bread and cakes or superb meat pies and pizza. Good ice cream too.

Restaurant Sans Tache, 19 9 Ndideng Usang Iso Rd. Inexpensive eatery and a great place to try local Efik specialities like *afang soup* and *gari* with *edikang ikong* (vegetable soup).

Union Group Restaurant, 9 Ndideng Usang Iso Rd. Simple Nigerian dishes like chicken, rice, *gari* and pounded yam for around ₦200.

Creek Town

From the waterfront (Marina), you can catch a "fly boat" (motor boat), or a rowing boat, to nearby **Creek Town** (also spelt Greek Town: even residents seem to have lost track of the correct name), a one-hour ride down the Calabar River, with dense mangrove greenery reminiscent of scenes from *The African Queen*. On arrival, there's little specifically to visit, but you can wander around and absorb the intimate creek-side village atmosphere. The people here are very proud of the **Creek Town church**, which is, indeed, a fine piece of colonial architecture, and, they claim, older than that in Duke Town. Some of the houses still have small "factories", where they produce **palm oil** using antiquated nineteenth-century mills from Britain. If you express interest, people are surprised but happy to show you their production methods. The town has a small

---

MOVING ON FROM CALABAR

BY ROAD

Most vehicles go from the **Watt Market motor park**, from where there's regular transport west to **Port Harcourt**, north to **Ekang** (the route you need for Oban Rainforest Reserve and Cameroon) and north to **Ikom** (for Cameroon and northern Cross River State). Crosslines has its own garage in Calabar Road, north of Watt Market and runs a daily bus to **Jos** (12–14hr), plus services north to **Ekang** (via Oban village) and **Obudu** (via Ikom), and west to **Aba**. There's also a motor park for **Oban** at the junctions of Akim Qua Town Road and Ndideng Usang Iso Road.

BY AIR

Nigeria Airways fly non-stop to **Lagos** three times a week, and to **Douala** (Cameroon) weekly. ADC domestic airlines provides two daily flights to Lagos. Airline agents' addresses (for information, bookings and ticket alterations – in theory) include British Airways, 164 Ndideng Usang Iso Rd (☎087/224 466); KLM, Tripton Travel Agency, 1 White House St (☎087/224 488); and Nigeria Airways, 45 Bedwell St (☎087/232 488 or 230 194).

INTO CAMEROON

Details on crossing into Cameroon by **land** are given on p.991. For **sea crossings**, there is a regular ferry service direct from Calabar to Limbé (3–4 weekly); alternatively, boats depart from Oron (see p.990), 25km away from Calabar, to the Cameroonian town of Idenao, 48km north of Limbé. Ferries from Calabar to Oron leave from near the *Nsikak Hotel*.

Even if your application for a **Cameroonian visa** was refused at the Lagos embassy, your chances of getting a visa at the Cameroonian Consulate, 21 Ndideng Usang Iso Rd (☎087/222 782) are good, though they are very expensive – CFA30,000 for single entry (CFA60,000 multiple entry). Bring three passport photos, and you can normally get the visa the same day.

market and numerous **palm wine bars** – look for the tell-tale phallic gourds that serve as cups, hung in front of the bars – where you'll find the beverage much fresher, and therefore much less alcoholic and more quaffable, than in Calabar town itself. It's often served with grilled **monkey meat** – not a bad accompaniment if you can get into the frame of mind the wine will ultimately induce anyway. Check it has been thoroughly cooked.

Oron

ORON is a departure point for **boats to Cameroon** (assuming the territorial dispute between Nigeria and Cameroon over the Bakassi peninsula has not arisen again). Boats ply regularly from Oron to the Cameroonian town of **Idenao**, 48km north of **Limbé** (Victoria). Motor boats are the quickest option (3–4hr) for the 150-kilometre sea voyage around the creeks and mangroves, though substantially more expensive than the fishing boats that take up to two days. The latter are commonly taken by local people, but you may be dropped on the coast almost anywhere and then run the risk of missing official entry procedures to Cameroon. Make sure your passport is stamped as soon as possible after arrival.

It's likely you'll have to spend the night in Oron in order to get an early boat to Cameroon, in which case, decent and affordable **accommodation** can be found at the *Maycom Guest House* (②). You'll find a brilliant collection of regional artwork at Oron's **National Museum**, located right next to the ferry dock and easily visited while waiting for a boat. The Oron region is famous for its woodcarvings, especially the Ekpo figures, used in ceremonies for communication with ancestors. There are some fine examples on display in the museum which is quite extensive, despite being greatly damaged in the Biafran conflict. You can pick up a copy of the *Guide to the Oron National Museum* which is full of information about the musical instruments, bronzes, pottery and carvings on display.

Cross River National Park and around

The natural vegetation of **Cross River State** is almost entirely **rainforest**, though large reaches have been cleared for oil palm plantations since the turn of the century. Some of the most exciting wildlife and conservation projects in Africa are currently under development in the two areas of the **Cross River National Park**: the **Oban Division** and the **Okwangwo Division** – the latter with its rediscovered **gorilla** denizens. It was thought the gorilla had disappeared from most of West Africa in the last century, and from Nigeria and western Cameroon several decades ago, but the WWF has located at least four separate gorilla populations, mostly around Mbe Mountain in the Okwangwo Division. It's thought there may be around four hundred individuals in the park. The park is one of the richest reserves in rainforest plant species in the whole of Africa, and also features some 1500 species of animals, including forest elephants, duikers, antelope and chimpanzees.

Oban Division

From Calabar, **public transport** to Oban (some 60km along the A4-2 to Ekang) is irregular, and a more reliable option, though much more costly, would be to **rent a vehicle** and obligatory driver at the *Metropolitan* hotel (see p.987). This allows you the flexibility to turn off the road near the village of Aningeje (about fifty minutes from Calabar, look for the sign indicating the Kwa Falls oil palm plantation) and have a wander around the

---

CROSSING INTO CAMEROON

The most direct crossing from Calabar is between **Ekang** and **Otu**, at the end of the Oban Division road. Cross River State's main crossing point, however, is southeast of Ikom, from **Mfum** to **Ekok**. Taxis from Ikom stop a few hundred metres before the Nigerian customs and immigration posts at Mfum. At the taxi park, "guides" will try to show you the way, which isn't really necessary.

You should allow a few hours for customs and immigration at **Mfum** (open 8am–7pm). In the past, officials here have been oppressive in the extreme – confiscating used film for example – and it may require full reserves of humour on your part to rescue the situation. "Yes sir" is important, and you'd better mean it. Once you've filled in your Nigerian exit forms and been questioned, searches are usually fairly limited. You can then be on your way across the bridge into Cameroon (see p.1082).

Ekok, the first small town in Cameroon, is a lively place to stay the night, with something of a Wild West feel about its bright lights, loud music, hotels and burger bars. There's no bank, however, for changing money into Central African CFA. Naira are acceptable currency for the short journey to **Mamfé** (see p.1081), which has banks, but the price will be a lot more than you're officially allowed to export from Nigeria. French francs are probably the best cash to have.

It's also possible to cross by **boat** from the seaside border town of **Ikang** over to **Ekondo beach** and **Bulo beach** in Cameroon, near the town of Mundemba, from where you can get transport through Ekondo Titi to Kumba (see p.1075).

---

dramatic **Kwa Falls**. The entire stretch to Oban is a rough one, though once you reach the village, the road improves towards the Cameroon border. Just outside Oban village, **accommodation** can be found at the *Jungle Club* (①), with simple S/C rooms.

Each village between Oban and the border has a Village Liaison Assistant (VLA), a resident employee of the Nigeria National Parks, easily tracked down by asking around town on arrival. Besides providing up-to-date information on the state of the conservation project and how it affects their local communities, VLAs can also arrange **guided treks** in the forest for a reasonable fee. The forest trail at **Mfaminyen** (the last village before the border) is the best organized.

You could also drive straight to the park's headquarters at **Akamkpa**, a 45-minute drive north from Calabar along the highway to Ikom, where there's a permanent camp with twenty well-equipped guest chalets, a restaurant and the **Information Centre** (PO 1028, Calabar; ☎087/222 261 or 221 694; Fax 087/221 695).

Ikom and around

The border town of **IKOM** is hardly a Cross River attraction but it's busy and tolerable enough. If you need to stay, the *Lisbon Hotel*, at 70 Calabar Rd (☎045/670 007; ①), is clean and has friendly staff, but it's somewhat tatty. The town has several banks (though you will not be able to buy Central African CFA, even if travellers newly arrived from Cameroon can exchange them for Naira) plus a number of shops, and the usual services. If you are making for Cameroon and arrive early enough in Ikom, it's preferable to move straight on to the border: there are regular taxis to Mfum, 26km away.

The surrounding countryside is famous for the **Ikom Monoliths**, curious stone steles intricately carved with abstract human figures. There are some three hundred of these statues spread throughout the area, but the easiest to reach are near the village of **Alok**, just off the A4, 50km north of Ikom. You can find a guide in the village. Though early estimates traced the monoliths to the sixteenth century, they are now believed to date as far back as 200 AD. Their origins and significance are unclear.

Okwangwo Division

Hidden in the bush between Ikom and Obudu, the **Okwangwo Division** consists of a breathtaking expanse of cloud-drenched mountain forest, home to a number of rare primates, including gorillas, chimpanzees and drills, as well as duikers, mountain foxes and porcupines. A trek along its trails (plan a couple of days at least) will see you crawling through thickets, forging streams, and grabbing at branches as you slip on mossy boulders. Expect to come out bruised, battered and blistered, and to have a brilliant time. There are two forest camps at the park, with **tents for hire** and camp catering facilities, but no electricity; bring your own provisions and sleeping gear.

One camp is situated near the small town of **Kanyang**, some 45 minutes from Ikom. If you're relying on public transport, ask to be dropped at Kanyang and follow the signs to the Kanyang forest camp. You may be able to get a local guide here to take you off through the forest to places with evocative names like **Gorilla Rock** and **Swimming Pool Camp** (a large splash pool formed by a waterfall cascading into a limestone gully). You camp out along the way, and you should be prepared for dampness and cold. Don't forget provisions and something to start a fire.

Half an hour further north is **Buatong**, where you'll find the **park headquarters** for the Okwangwo Division and another forest camp with tents for hire. Numerous trails for trekking and a botanical garden are available, as well as guided treks into the heart of the spectacular beauty of the area.

A third, less frequented means of entering is via the village of **Buanchor**, further north again on the road to Obudu. By public transport, ask to be dropped at the Olum junction. Irregular vehicles pass the junction on their way to Olum village (9km from the road), from where you can walk the remaining 6km to Buanchor. You'll be asked to pay the chief for permission to visit the forest and given a guide. Villagers seem amused by the few visitors that wander through these parts, offering a "you're welcome" at every turn. They'll arrange **accommodation** if you arrive late, and probably set you up with some palm wine, but once you set off through the forest, you'll be camping or sleeping in caves. The guides are good company in addition to being informative and are handy at rustling up forest snails and mushrooms to snack on. You may see gorilla tracks, gorilla nests, gorilla dung and even fruit half-eaten by gorillas, but very few people manage to see the gorillas themselves, or even many of the other monkeys that abound here. The splendid mountain scenery is compensation enough for the difficult hike, however, and any wildlife you see, an extra bonus.

For further **information**, contact the Cross River National Park liaison office in Calabar. You may be able to get a permit here which would exempt you from paying the local chief, though going over his head is not likely to put you in his good books.

Obudu Cattle Ranch

The best-known attraction in Cross River is **Obudu Cattle Ranch**, in the north of the state. This hill resort-cum-cattle station is spread across the north-facing slopes of Oshie Ridge in the folds of the beautiful **Sonkwala Mountains** (1500–1900m above sea level). Obudu Ranch used to be a fashionable place for oil industry expats to escape the rough climate of the delta oilfields, as it offered a virtually European climate and exotic fresh garden produce like strawberries and cauliflowers. Today, the *Ranch Hotel* (PO 87, Obudu, Cross River State; ②–⑤) still offers chalet **accommodation** ranging from moderate singles to executive suites, or you can rent a private lodge. You can buy basic provisions at the workers' village, or at the on-site shop, where there's a bar.

More interesting than the putting green or table tennis are the **hiking** opportunities in the district. Try to avoid the dusty *Harmattan* period, and visit at the end of the rainy season, when the air is clean and fresh, the views are fantastic and the nights almost cold. A path leads from the hotel to a striking waterfall about 7km away. Also in the area is a natural spring – "the grotto" – but most interesting is the **Gorilla Camp**, a thirteen-kilometre trek through dense bush, involving some arduous climbing over hills and valleys. A guide is necessary and even if you don't see gorillas (not really very likely), the lush mountain scenery is reward in itself.

The easiest way up here from Calabar is to head to Ikom (take the A4 if driving, not the A4-2). There are usually direct vehicles from Ikom to Obudu village (along the N40), or you can find transport for Ogoja, whence it's 66km to Obudu. In the village, you can rent a taxi or motorbike to the ranch. The road is good all the way and still improving; the final stretch – beset with hairpins as it snakes up to the ranch – is a wonderful climax to the trip. Getting away depends on the vagaries of taxis returning to Obudu after dropping other guests, or lorries heading into town. The ranch gets busy during holidays and **advance bookings** are always advisable – Obudu Cattle Ranch office, ADC Building, 2 Barracks Rd, Calabar. Alternatively, local travel agents can usually help, as can the Cross River National Park headquarters at Akamkpa (see p.990).

CENTRAL NIGERIA

The huge area that is **"Central Nigeria"** is an artificial division, and really consists of the middle margins of the country's more natural divisions into southwest, southeast and north. However, the centre has quite a concentration of places of interest. If the new federal capital of **Abuja** has little to offer, the same cannot be said of one of the country's most favoured towns, **Jos**, on its fine, high plateau of almost Mediterranean climate. **Bauchi** is less attractive, though pleasantly spacious, while **Yankari National Park**, not far away, is the country's best-organized park and its **Wikki Warm Springs** a pristine attraction in their own right. On the way north, you might consider striking out to the **Kainji Lake National Park** – something that's a lot easier to do with your own vehicle.

Kainji Lake National Park

Scenically and climatically, the **Kainji Lake National Park** feels more like a part of northern Nigeria, but it's remote and far to the west, and most commonly and easily approached from the south. The park is split into two sectors, **Zugurma** and **Borgu**, each with accommodation and a restaurant at the park entrances. The park is open from December to June, but the best time to visit is in the dry season, after the grass is burned, when you've a better chance of seeing the animals – waterbucks, lions, leopards, baboons, green and pates monkeys, crocodiles and hippos. For **information** about the park and its accommodation, contact the park offices in New Bussa (☎031/670 035–6) or Abuja (☎09/530 0429).

Jebba and Zugurma

North of Ilorin (see p.966) you leave Yorubaland and enter a drier and less monoethnic environment, populated by a mix of Nupe, Bussa, Borgu, Kamberi, Fulani and Hausa communities. After some 70km you reach **JEBBA** (off the road to the right) and cross the Niger on a fine, low bridge. There's nothing of particular interest to see in Jebba, other than the huge dam a couple of kilometres upstream, but if you decide to break the journey, there are several reasonable **places to stay**, including the excellent-value

Nigerian Paper Mill Guest House, (☎031/400 007; ①), on the hillside to the left of the northbound highway, and the decent *Goodwill Guest House and Canteen*, 2 Elder Etim St, off Paper Mill Road (☎031/400 114; ①).

From **Mokwa**, 38km north of Jebba, a good road sweeps off northwest to New Bussa and the national park. There are few towns up here amid the wild bush and dry patchy farmlands. **Zugurma** (24km from Mokwa) is a pretty halt, however, with a fine, jungly stream running past and, beyond, you're sure to see some wildlife – monkeys at least. Some 18km further up the road towards Kainji Dam, **Ibbi**, the gateway to the smaller **Zugurma sector** of the national park, has **accommodation** at the *Ibbi Tourist Camp* (①–④).

Kainji Dam and New Bussa

Kainji Dam is impressive, though you probably won't be allowed to go onto it – the road runs past it, below. It was just north of here, at Old Bussa, which has now been submerged by the artificial Kainji Lake, that the Scottish explorer Mungo Park was killed in 1805 by people on the bank – who apparently thought he and his expedition was a party of raiding Fulani jihadists. You can take a boat cruise on the lake, and even tour the hydroelectric complex.

The local town, **NEW BUSSA**, around 100km from Mokwa, is dull and scruffy. There are various basic hotels, but little of interest. The best place to stay is the well-appointed *Hotel Holy Year*, at Wawa Road (☎031/670 709; ②), although inexpensive beds can be had at the *Student Hostel* and the *NIFFR Guesthouse* (①–②). The chalet rooms and safari atmosphere at the *Niger Crescent* (☎031/670 032; ①–③), 3km out of town, make a pleasant alternative; it's popular with expats and makes a good first base for the Borgu sector, just 20km to the west.

Borgu sector

The **Borgu sector** of Kainji Lake National Park doesn't get a lot of visitors, and it's doubtful if it has a lot of big game wildlife – in fact it looks certain that much has been poached out. However it's uninhabited by humans, and its 4000-odd square kilometres do contain plentiful numbers of various **antelope** species and there are several families of **hippos** in the pools of the somewhat seasonal Oli River which flows through the reserve. Lions may still roam the bush too, but elephants have not been seen for years. The smaller animals are surely there, but harder to spot for visitors.

The roads through Borgu tend to be well maintained. Vehicles can be rented, as can rangers, compulsory companions to your game drive; they are to be found up at the guard post and headquarters at Kaiama Road, **Wawa**, where you pay your entrance fee (₦100), and where you'll find the *Wawa Tourist Camp* (①–④). Alternatively, you can stay inside the park at the *Oli River Tourist Camp* (①–④), 72km from Wawa, on the banks of the Oli River. Both camps offer chalets and hotel accommodation, with full catering facilities.

Bida

Heading east towards Abuja from Kainji Dam, you'll pass through the old Nupe capital of **BIDA**. Nupe was an early kingdom, contemporaneous with the Hausa emirates, that lasted from around 1400 until its submission to Fulani rule after the nineteenth-century jihads. The Nupe people (who speak a Kwa language related to Yoruba) are still renowned **crafts experts** and Bida has a reputation as a place to buy locally made metal jewellery, and cylindrical coloured glass "trading beads" whose style is supposed to have originally derived from the markets of medieval Venice.

Neither of the town markets particularly reflects Bida's reputation for crafts, but a quick walk along the **Sotamaku Road** brings you to a host of **metal workshops** heralded by a glittering array of brass and aluminium plates, bowls and ornaments. Inside the *ateliers*, school-age boys pump away at goatskin bellows while their elder brothers reshape old pans and scrap metal using gearbox housings, crankcases and steel rods as anvils. The same sweatshop approach is used in the **Masaga** area where **glass beads** are made from melted down beer and minerals bottles which lend an opaque lustre quite different from the trading beads found elsewhere. Steel rods are dipped into the glass and a single bead is formed as the rod is spun over a furnace. The panoply of patterned beads so formed is then strung on to necklaces or sold singly on roadside stands.

Harder to locate are the traditional Nupe **ten-legged stools** carved from a single piece of wood. Apart from their intricately patterned tops and unsurpassed stability, they are unusual because the seat is cut along the grain of the wood rather than across. Stools can still be bought in local villages, but dealers rapidly snap them up to sell in Lagos, where they fetch high prices. If you're keen to buy, start asking around a hundred metres south of the Total petrol station, and hopefully someone can lead you to an artisan with some unclaimed stock.

Practicalities

Arriving in Bida, you are likely to be dropped at the motor park on the Abuja–Ilorin road. Most points of interest are within walking distance of here but you may want a taxi to the **hotels**, which are mostly on the outskirts of town; the closest to the centre, but with little else to recommend it, is the *Nasara Guest Inn*, on Kontagora Road (①). The *Niger Motel* (☎066/641 025; ③) has good value S/C rooms with AC, but the best hotel in town is the *Dhiyafah Satellite Motel*, opposite the Emir's Palace in the centre of town, at Niger Street (☎066/462 179; ①), with a reasonable **restaurant** serving Nigerian and continental dishes. Otherwise, the scope for eating isn't great, but you'll find ordinary street food around the Total station junction.

Abuja

ABUJA has a beautiful setting, with a backdrop of stunning stone inselbergs and a good deal of greenery, but the landscaped boulevards with wonderful views across the savannah are gradually being filled with international hotels and office buildings. Abuja is developing into a real political capital, with increasing numbers of foreign **embassies** based here, but you'd have to be especially interested in urban planning or golf – Abuja has possibly the best course in Africa – to find any reason to want to stay. The city was designed with a population of three million in mind, but at the current rate of growth, it could soon be too small.

Don't expect to meet an "Abuja local". The indigenous **Gwari**, a semi-nomadic people, were unceremoniously evicted from their ancestral lands, and the capital is now populated by people from all parts of the country. Today, the Gwari have nearly disappeared as a distinct ethnic and linguistic (Kwa-speaking) community, although their remnants can be traced in Suleja.

Accommodation

Cheap lodging doesn't really exist in Abuja, though good-value weekend deals can be found at the international hotels. Many hotels are found in **Garki**, the southern district of Abuja, and if Abuja could be said to have a city centre, it's here.

Abuja Sheraton Hotel & Towers, Ladi Kwali Way, Maitama (PMB 143; ☎09/523 0225; Fax 09/523 1570). Over six hundred rooms, four restaurants, a nightclub and casino, pool and garden bar, health club, travel agency, business centre and banquet hall – this hotel has it all. ⑦.

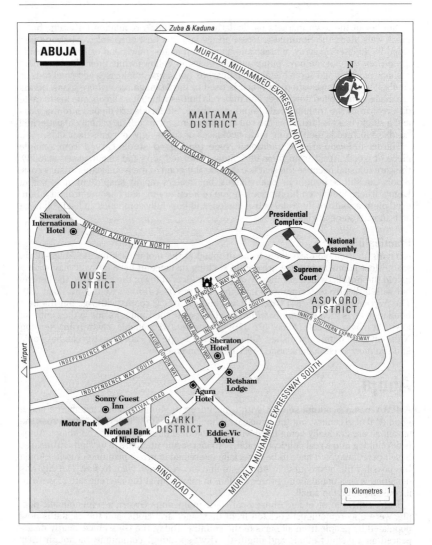

Agura Hotel, Festival Rd (PMB 40; ☎09/234 1753–60; Fax 09/234 2115 or 2750). All the perks and facilities of the big hotels, but much cheaper and less pretentious. ⑤–⑦.

Eddy-Vic Motel, Plot 466 Ahmadu Bello Way, Area 2, Garki (PO 308; ☎09/234 5576). Cheap lodge with S/C rooms, plus a restaurant and bar. ②–③.

Retsham Lodge, Plot 808 Uyo Crescent, Area 11, Garki (☎09/234 0805 or 4813; Fax 09/234 0806). Good-value lodging, with S/C rooms with AC, TV and fridge, as well as a laundry service and restaurant. ④–⑤.

Sharon Intl. Hotels Ltd, Plot 220, Wuse Zone 6 (☎09/523 3444; Fax 09/523 3447). Moderately priced hotel. All rooms with AC, fan, fridge, satellite TV, plus there's a restaurant and snack bar (no alcohol). ④–⑤.

Sunny Guest Inn, Plot 11 Benue Crescent, Area 1, Section 1, Garki (☎09/523 1881; Fax 09/523 1365). Inexpensive high quality hotel with clean and pleasant AC rooms. ②–③.

The City

The federal government's decision to create a new capital dates from 1976 when the experience of the civil war made it clear that Lagos, with a seventy-five percent Yoruba population, was not conducive to relieving ethnic tensions. Besides, Lagos had already outgrown its capacities. Work on the new capital began in 1981 and, almost overnight, the peaceful setting of this hitherto sparsely populated corner of the Niger State was transformed into Africa's biggest construction site. The enormous cost of creating a city from scratch, especially one with such ambitious designs and such opportunity for misappropriation, led to serious economic difficulties for the civilian presidency of Shehu Shagari. After the 1983 coup which deposed him, the project came to an abrupt standstill and the capital was officially transferred from Lagos in 1991. A distinctive Abuja pulse is only now beginning to emerge.

Although new high-rise buildings rise on all sides, the magnificent **Central Mosque**, with its large golden dome and fairytale minarets, is still a definite landmark. There's a **market** on Kashim Ibrahim Way, in Wuse Zone 4, and **Julie Useni Park**, in Garki Area 1 is a pleasant park with a small zoo, but in the continued absence of the projected National Museum, or any other worthy distraction, many travellers resign themselves to one of the air-conditioned cocktail lounges in the *Nicon Hilton* – the largest hotel in Africa – or the *Abuja Sheraton*.

Designed for motor **transport**, the city is too large to manage on foot, though it's a challenge to find the rare buses and shared taxis, or even the less expensive *okadas*.

Eating and nightlife

All the hotels have **restaurants**, most of which are fairly good and open to the public. Elsewhere in the city, the outdoor *African Kitchen*, Area 1 Shopping Centre, Garki, is the place to get your pounded yam with *egusi* soup, while the affordable *Halal Restaurant*, at the National Centre for Women Development, in the Central Area, serves Nigerian, continental and Lebanese dishes. *McDowals Restaurant*, 6 Addis Ababa Crescent, Wuse Zone 4, is popular among Abuja's expats for its delicious and affordable food, but doesn't serve alcohol.

The major hotels also have more or less functioning **nightclubs**: those at the *Agura*, *Hilton* and *Sheraton* hotels are among the best. The *Abuja Club*, Plot 62 Sunyani St, and the *Verdict*, Plot 1057 Adetokunbo Ademola St, are popular places, both found in Wuse Zone 1.

Listings

Banks and Exchange First Bank of Nigeria, Abuja (Main) Branch, Muhammedu Buhari Way, Central Business Area (☎09/234 6833–35). Bank of the North, First Bank of Nigeria, Union Bank of Nigeria and United Bank of Africa (UBA) all have branches off J.S. Tarkwa St, Area 3, Garki (near the junction with Tafawa Balewa Way). There's a bureau de change, AIA, at Suite E02, Abuja Shopping Complex, Plot 2161, Area 3, Garki.

Embassies Australia, A.L.D. Building, Plot 665 Nog Vall St, off IBB Way, Maitama (☎09/523 7380; Fax 09/523 7381); France, Europe House, Usuma St (☎09/523 3786; Fax 09/523 3147); Niger, 7 Sangha St, off Mississippi St, Maitama (PO 4251, Garki; ☎09/523 6206; Fax 09/523 6205; 8am–noon); UK (British High Commission), Dangote House, Aguyi Ironsi St, Maitama, (☎09/523 5460 or 4560; Fax 09/523 4565); USA, 9 Mambilla St, off Aso Drive, Maitama (PO 5760, ☎09/523 5857 or 0960–6; Fax 09/523 0353).

Post office The GPO (8am–4pm) is on Festival Rd, Garki Area 10.

Tourist Information Nigerian Tourism Development Corporation (NTDC), Block 2 Sefadu St, Wuse Zone 4 (PMB 167; ☎09/523 3191).

Travel agents Try Emerald Tours, Ali Akilu Crescent, off Usman dan Fodio Crescent, A.Y.A. Asokoro (09/234 979); they can arrange trips to Yankari, Obudu Cattle Ranch, Kano and Katsina.

Jos and around

Set 1200m above sea level, **JOS** enjoys a mild climate that has long attracted Europeans weary of the coastal humidity or the northern heat and dust. Laid out in a beautiful, rocky landscape, the hill resort grew up around **tin mines** exploited by the British at the turn of the century – and still partly managed by expatriates. Jos's history, though, can be traced back much further to the **Nok culture** (named after the Jos plateau village of the same name) which spread throughout central Nigeria between 2800 and 1800 years ago. Terracotta artefacts left behind by this civilization were discovered quite accidentally in the mines and are today housed in the **Jos Museum**.

This is only one of many sights around a town that seems to have been intentionally designed for visitors. Other diversions include the **zoo** (now slightly depressing) and the **Museum of Traditional Nigerian Architecture**, where lifesize replica buildings from Zaria, Kano, Katsina and other cities have been constructed. Here you can visit the gems of traditional architecture which have largely fallen into disrepair or disappeared altogether in their native cities.

Orientation and information

The **main market** is an unmistakeable landmark, covering a large area in the middle of town. It's a massive modern structure with a wild, colourful design, and well stocked to boot. From the market, **Ahmadu Bello Road**, one of the town's main thoroughfares, runs down towards the **post office** (with email service). Along this road, you'll find a number of **supermarkets** and several **banks**, although the major ones are behind the post office around Bank Road. For international **telephone calls**, Grakol, at 10 Ahmadu Bello Rd, is half the price of NITEL, on Zoo Garden Road. **Beach Road** ("The Beach") runs parallel to the railway tracks, across from the main goods yard. Vendors line this street selling a variety of local **crafts**, with a heavy emphasis on leather and basketwork. A pedestrian bridge leads over the tracks to **Murtala Muhammed Way**, another major thoroughfare, which runs from the redundant train

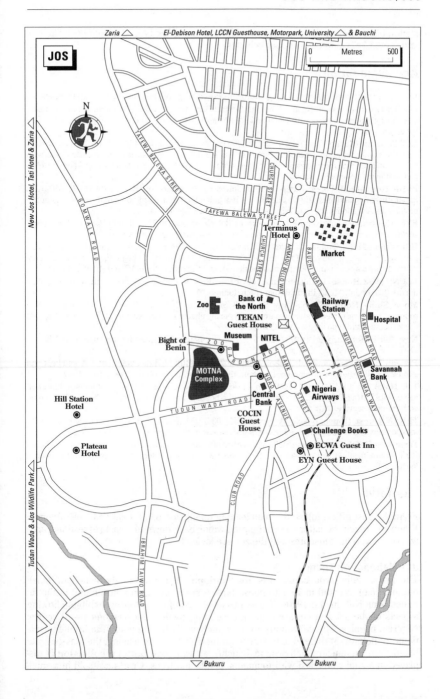

station back down to the main market. The **tourist office** is at 31 Yakubu Gowon Way (☎073/465 747), and can rent out vehicles.

Accommodation

Jos has a variety of places to stay, including several good mission-type guesthouses.

COCIN Guest House, 5 Noad Rd, behind Central Bank (☎073/453 679). One of the town's many missionary-oriented places with clean and comfortable S/C rooms where they'll put you up if they have space. ①.

ECWA Guest Inn, off Kano Rd – behind Challenge Books (☎073/454 482). Clean, inexpensive and safe, this is often used by travellers; rooms (including dorms) are at various prices, some S/C with hot water. The restaurant serves solid helpings of meals like "Irish stew and two veg" and there's a pleasant living room with satellite TV. ①.

El-Debison Motel, Forest Camp, behind University Staff Qtrs, off Bauchi Rd (☎073/610 519). Small, charming and inexpensive guesthouse in a quiet neighbourhood north of the centre, near the motor park. All rooms are S/C, with fans or AC, and satellite TV. ②.

EYN Guesthouse, off Kano Rd, opposite *ECWA Guest Inn* (☎073/454 482). Good-value budget accommodation with cooking facilities in the rooms (no meals are served). ①.

Hill Station Hotel, Tudun Wada Rd (☎073/455 300; Fax 073/454 817). An attractive building overlooking the hills and still one of the best hotels in town, even though it's beginning to feel a little run-down. There's a pool (small fee for non-residents), and the rooms have AC and satellite TV. ④.

LCCN Guest House, 14 Dogun Dutse Rd (☎073/612 810). Pleasant gardens with small bungalow dorms (five beds). Meals in the dining room/lounge. ①.

Moon Shine Hotel, 18 Igbo-Ukwe St (☎073/611 116 or 610 361). Good value for comfortable rooms – those with (clean) shared bath are especially cheap. Decent restaurant. The annexe across the street is slightly posher with S/C rooms. ①–②.

New Jos Hotel, Zaria Rd (☎073/610 381). Well-run hotel maintained by the state tourist board. ①–③.

Plateau Hotel, Resthouse Rd, Tudun Wada (☎073/455 740). Slightly expensive, but well-kept and good value. Pleasant swimming pool, restaurant and bar with occasional live music. ③–⑦.

Tati Hotel, Zaria Rd (☎073/455 897). In a pricier league than the mission guesthouses, but good value, with extras like AC, fan and phones, and a popular weekend nightclub. The comforts come with friendly service. ②.

TEKAN Guest House, 6 Noad Ave (☎073/453 036). Friendly and clean missionary centre with inexpensive S/C rooms, and even less expensive beds in the dorm. ①.

Terminus Hotel, E13 Ahmadu Bello Way (☎073/454 831). An attractive, timeworn colonial building overlooking the main market. The S/C rooms with fan are a decent bargain given the central location. ①.

The Town

From the post office, follow the road leading uphill past Bank Road and Noad Avenue. When you reach the latter street, the road winds back down to a vast recreational area where the various museums and the zoo are located.

Jos National Museum

The first building you come to is **Jos National Museum** (daily 8am–5pm; small entrance fee), created in 1952 to house **Nok terracotta figures** first found in the tin mines near Nok in the 1920s. These pieces are complemented by exhibits showing aspects of the art and culture – masks, weaving, medicine, ceremonies – of central Nigerian peoples. The collections are extremely well presented and the brief explanations are helpful. At the end of the museum (notice, as you're leaving, the massive gate taken from the ancient wall around Bauchi), an extensive **pottery collection** is displayed in a cool courtyard with fountains, ponds and trees. **Crafts** are sold in a small shop across from the museum and leatherwork, pottery and weaving is carried out in nearby workshops.

The zoo and Tin Mining Museum

The **zoo** (daily 7.30am–5pm) adjoins the National Museum, spread over a large park with trees and streams. The zoo has recovered from former neglect, but it is still less interesting than the wildlife park (see below). Near the zoo, several old locomotives and carriages from the **Bauchi Light Railway** (which closed in 1959) are on display. You can clamber over the antiquated steam engines and wander through the compartments of trains dating from around the early part of the century.

Also nearby, the **Tin Mining Museum** (daily 7.30am–6pm) is dedicated to the history and technology of mining in the area. If you're minded to find out more about how the metal is extracted – it's a wet and messy, open-cast business requiring considerable land rehabilitation – try contacting the Nigerian Tin Mining Company Ltd (PMB 2036, Jos; ☎073/280 632) for a **guided tour**.

Museum of Traditional Nigerian Architecture

Probably the most unusual museum, and one well worth spending some time to discover, is the **Museum of Traditional Nigerian Architecture** (MOTNA), which covers a vast area behind the zoo. Full-scale reproductions of the country's most impressive monuments have been built on the site. You get a better idea of the magnitude of the **Kano Wall** here than you do in its city of origin, especially if you climb the narrow staircase leading to the top. The **Zaria Friday Mosque** with its impressive vaulting reveals the highly sophisticated technical skills of the Hausa. There are also smaller copies of the **Katsina Palace** and the **Ilorin mosque**. Be sure to agree a price before entering.

Jos Wildlife Park

Not to be confused with the zoo, the **Jos Wildlife Park** (daily 10am–dusk; small charge), southwest of town, off the Jos–Bukuru road (Yakubu Gowon Way), is a more worthwhile encounter. The drive-through park, covering an area of about eight square kilometres, contains a large variety of animals, including antelopes and monkeys, lions in a large enclosure, some elephants, buffaloes and hippos, and various other species, some of which are in ordinary cages near the entrance, or in semi-natural large enclosures. If you're in a 4WD vehicle, you should be able to make it to the observation tower at the highest point in the park, where there's a good view of Jos and the plateau. Otherwise, rent a taxi in Jos for a three-hour visit, or take Bukuru-bound public transport, which can drop you at the junction for the road to Miango to the west. The park entrance is 4km down this road: if it's a weekend, you might get a lift with other visitors.

Eating

Eating out in Jos isn't a richly satisfying experience, but you should find something reasonable among the following.

Bevelyns, 2 Ahmadu Bello Way. A central place for African and European eating at fair prices.

Bight of Benin, Zoo Garden Rd, near the museum. Good cooking, in a replicated Benin noble's house. A cool place to take a break, with a limited menu of national specialities at reasonable prices.

Café Felak, Ahmadu Bello Way. Fast-food restaurant, good for breakfasts and snacks, with an attached shop where you can buy fresh farm products, including cheese.

Palace Restaurant. The Chinese restaurant at the *Hill Station Hotel*.

Sharazad, Yakubu Gowon Way, out of the centre towards Bukuru. Near the similar *Cedar Tree*, with a range of good, well-prepared Lebanese, European and Chinese dishes at reasonable prices (although it's one of the more expensive places in town). Popular with expats.

MOVING ON FROM JOS

The main motor park for the **east, northeast** and **southeast** is the Bauchi Road motor park, 3km north of the centre. Daily bus services to **Calabar** and **Port Harcourt** are operated by Crosslines and depart in the morning from here. Bus services to **Bauchi** and **Maiduguri** are run by Yankari Express, who park next to Crosslines. The main motor park for the northwest, including **Kano** and **Kaduna**, and for **Lagos**, is the Zaria Road motor park, out of the town centre to the northwest.

There have been no **train services** on the Jos branch line for several years.

Nigeria Airways **fly** daily to **Lagos**, via Abuja on Monday and Sunday, and via Kadun on Monday. They have offices at the airport (☎073/461 508) and at 6 Bank St (☎073/452 298).

Stabok, Bank Rd near Museum Rd. Toasted sandwiches and fish-and-chips-type meals complement Nigerian specialities.

Jos Plateau and south towards Cameroon

If you want to get into the **Jos Plateau** countryside, take a taxi or minibus out to **Bukuru** from the end of Tafawa Balewa Street, near the market. Get out somewhere en route and camp, or stay in the very nice *Yelwa Club* (the former Tin Miners' Club) in Bukuru, which has a pool and is surprisingly cheap. For **camping**, the Vom area to the southwest of Jos is pretty, with plenty of good grassy spots amid boulders and groves of gum trees. **Vom** itself has a mission and a dairy where, on weekdays, you can sample fresh Friesian milk at next to nothing a litre and wonderful cheese. Although they don't mind visitors, you should ring in advance to make an appointment (☎073/280 247).

Heading further south, the topography is complex and travel delightful. Forests of gum trees spread around **Panyam** and from here on the road (surfaced, whatever the maps may say) drops down a breathtaking escarpment through coniferous woods and Mediterranean landscapes to **Shendam** and **Yelwa**. It's fine cycling country; otherwise, apart from one or two exhausting through bus services to big cities in the southeast, travelling by road becomes chancy as you get into this eastern part of Central Nigeria. If you're travelling south on this road into **Taraba State**, you're in a position to make an unusual entry into the **North West Province of Cameroon** (see p.1033). The more direct route south from the Jos Plateau follows the A3 and A4 into **southern Cameroon**, a regular driving route bringing you to Mamfé and the highway for Douala.

Makurdi

MAKURDI, the capital of Benue State, lies roughly midway between Jos and Cameroon, on the south bank of the Benue River. Although on the fringes of Igboland, Makurdi is one of the original homelands of the farming Tiv people, Located in the fertile middle belt, where the forests of the south gradually turn into the savannah of the north, Benue State has been called "the food basket of Nigeria" and Makurdi has become a major agricultural trading centre.

Makurdi is a fair-size town with several small and medium **hotels**: the *Dolphin* – part of a complex of cinemas, restaurants and lodgings in Secretariat Road to the north of town – is clean, welcoming and inexpensive. A passenger service runs on the **railway** line between Kano and Port Harcourt; check at the train station for schedules.

Bauchi and Yankari National Park

Northeast from Jos, the road drops down from the cooler plateau in a spectacular curve, turns east and then runs across featureless plains to **BAUCHI**, capital of the state of the same name. Bauchi is a large seemingly impersonal place, with wide avenues and ranks of office buildings, though it gives a more exotic first impression from the north down the A3 Kano/Maiduguri route. This approach lines up a grand assembly of inselbergs known as the Belo Hills, shortly before you reach town.

After the Fulani jihad, in the 1840s, an emirate was established at Bauchi. But despite the **Emir's palace** and the **old mosque**, the town has little of enduring interest. Bauchi is the nearest big centre to **Yankari National Park** and if you don't have transport you'll very likely have to spend a night here before getting to the reserve.

If you're stuck waiting for transport, you could spend an interesting half-hour at the **Mausoleum of Tafawa Balewa** (daily 7am–6pm), celebrating Nigeria's first prime minister; on weekdays you may be able to see a video of his Independence speech. A tour of the complex takes you up a ramp through regions of dark and light symbolizing colonial repression and the hope of independence and leads to the roofless mausoleum. The concrete and stone are austere, but it remains a powerful monument to the fight for self-determination.

Bauchi practicalities

There are a dozen or more **inexpensive** hotels, all charging about the same price. The best of these are the *CFA Hotel*, Gombe Rd (☎077/543 563; ①–②), conveniently located if you're planning to catch an early taxi to the national park; the *Rendezvous Hotel*, Tudun Wada Dan'iya area, off Murtla Muhammed Way (①), which stands out because of its friendly management, but has no restaurant; and the *Sogiji Hotel*, Ran Gate (☎077/543 454; ①–②), slightly run-down but still fairly good. Of the more **upmarket** places: the *Awalah Hotel* (☎077/542 344; ④) has a swimming pool, and the similar *Zaranda Hotel* (☎077/542 377; ③–⑦), has a booking office (☎077/542 174) for Yankari National Park and Lodge, and can arrange transport.

For **flights** on Nigeria Airways, the closest airport is **Jos** – enquiries and bookings at 40 Kobi St, Bauchi (☎077/542 800).

Yankari National Park

Yankari National Park (Nov–June) was the first game reserve in Nigeria and it remains the most popular. It covers over 2200 square kilometres of protected bush, but despite the authorities' best efforts, poaching is still widespread and has taken its toll on the once abundant wildlife. You're likely to see herds of **gazelle and antelope**, and **elephants** with a little luck, but **lions**, which still hunt in the park (together with leopards), are getting increasingly shy and elusive. Other animals include warthogs, hippos, waterbuck, buffaloes, several species of duiker, hartebeest, various monkeys and crocodiles.

In addition to the animals, **Wikki Warm Springs** is reason to come to the park in itself. If you have any difficulty organizing game-viewing trips at the lodge, you probably won't be unhappy spending your time in its crystal-clear waters.

Getting there

There is no regular transport from Bauchi to *Wikki Warm Springs Lodge*, the main focus in Yankari. If you don't have a car you can take a **collective taxi** from the Gombe station on the east side of Bauchi. These vehicles can drop you at **Dindima** on the highway, where the Yankari road splits off south – or they sometimes go to villages along the latter road and will let you off right in front of the park gate en route. Either way, you still have to get a lift for the rest of the journey with incoming visitors (if you inform the guards at the gate you're looking for a ride into the park, they're usually pretty good about asking the cars on their way in). Note that in the middle of the week and on certain quiet weekends, the park may be devoid of visitors, in which case you could be really stuck. For that reason, avoid setting off from Bauchi in the late afternoon.

Another way of getting to the camp is to **charter a taxi** in Bauchi and arrange a price with the driver – you'd pay around £40 ($64). If you're **cycling**, the road from Bauchi highway to Wikki is a fine and exciting day's ride in the park, with no access problems, and no serious worries about animals.

Accommodation

If you're visiting the park on a weekend or any major holiday, it's a good idea to make advance **reservations**. The lodge gets very full, particularly at Easter. You can book at the *Zaranda Hotel* in Bauchi (☎077/542 174), or at the park headquarters – Yankari National Park, Maiduguri Bypass, Bauchi (PMB 006; ☎077/543 674), or by fixing things up several days beforehand with any local travel agency.

Arriving at the camp, a range of **accommodation** is available in chalets or *rondavels*, from double rooms to family chalets with kitchens. A double chalet costs a little more than a cheap hotel in Bauchi, though water and electricity are frequently off during the day (and routinely go off at a set time late each evening).

The **restaurant** near the lodge serves European meals at reasonable prices – and it could be a lot worse considering there's no alternative. To save money, bring provisions from Bauchi and do your own cooking. A pleasant **outdoor bar** overlooks the savannah, and the lodge has a small **natural history museum** (free) – well laid out and full of local tales.

Game-viewing

Morning and afternoon **game-runs** are organized at the lodge. If you don't have your own car, you can go on one of the camp vehicles (a lorry with benches in the back) for a fee, provided they get enough people together to form a worthwhile group. If you have your own vehicle, you must take one of the rangers – which isn't a bad idea anyway, as they're most likely to know where to see animals and can direct you to other sites like the **Marshall Caves**, believed to have once been inhabited, or the **Borkono Falls** (at their most spectacular in September). On any drive – assuming you go early in the morning, which is best, or late afternoon – you'll see antelope and gazelles of various species, and there's every likelihood you will see elephants. To see any predators at all, however, you'd need to be very lucky.

Wikki Warm Springs

Below the restaurant, a steep path leads down to **Wikki Warm Springs**. It's hard to imagine any site in West Africa more completely satisfying from a hedonistic point of view. Twelve million litres a day of perfectly clear, clean water at a steady ideal temperature of 31°C comes bubbling up from a dark hole at the bottom of a deep pool, at the base of a steep, sheltering cliff. Nothing, save perhaps the persistent hassles of monkeys and baboons, detracts from the site's beauty. From its source, the water flows out for a hundred metres or more past steep banks of overhanging foliage, over a bed of glistening sand. It's almost too pretty, especially at night when it's lit by floodlamps – like an elaborate bit of New Age interior design.

The access side of the stream is concreted over, which keeps it clean, and there are parts shallow enough for toddlers to enjoy, and deeper areas for bigger swimmers. Downstream, camp staff wash clothes and bathe. Access is free if you're staying at the camp but there's a charge if you're just here for the day – as, at weekends, rather a lot of people are. If you take food or valuables down there, watch out for those monkeys.

THE NORTH AND NORTHEAST

Formerly a conglomeration of disunited and often warring emirates, the **Hausa country** spreads over the arid **savannah** of the northern plateaux and comprises the largest geographical entity in Nigeria. In this vast region, Hausa makes sense as a linguistic grouping rather than an ethnic one, since there are many different northern peoples. The religious and in many respects political head of all the Hausa peoples is in fact a Fulani – the **Sultan of Sokoto** – and has been for over 180 years. Thanks to the common faith of **Islam** and the lingua franca of Hausa, however, a bond has been created among northerners that puts them politically at an advantage over the south.

The area near **Lake Chad** in the northeast of the country is peopled by the **Kanuri**, who, in around the ninth century, migrated from the northern, desert regions of Kanem to form the new empire of Bornu which grew rich on **trans-Saharan trade**. In the context of the current Federal Republic, this kingdom translates roughly into the **Borno State** with its capital in **Maiduguri**, the only major town in the rather depressed northeast. Further west, the **Hausa city states** (the *Hausa Bokwai*: Gobir, Katsina, Kano, Zaria, Daura, Rano and Biram) developed into powerful emirates from around the eleventh century and had partially converted to Islam by 1400. Old walled cities from this era still exist in **Katsina**, **Zaria** and **Kano**. Kano today is a major urban centre, with international airport and diverse industries. Development has come more slowly to the conservative Islamic stronghold of **Sokoto**, the spiritual capital of the north, while **Kaduna** is a much more anonymous, modern town neatly laid out by the British colonials as an uncontroversial administrative capital.

This section also includes the remote eastern reaches of Nigeria – the states of **Adamawa** and **Taraba** – where the mountain forests remain poorly mapped and very little travelled. Here, there are some fine opportunities for hiking and some unusual options for routes into Cameroon.

Birnin Gwari

If you're driving north towards Kaduna on the A1 and A125, you go through the town of **Birnin Gwari** (or Sabon Birnin Gwari). There's a **wildlife reserve** here (access on foot) with the basic *Birnin Gwari Hotel* (①) just outside. The reserve has a small herd of elephants and other savannah species along with a mass of birdlife.

Kaduna

With no palace (the town was formerly a fief of the Zaria Emirate), no city wall and no ancient mosque, **KADUNA** is essentially a **modern town** of broad avenues, with an oil refinery, a good smattering of industry and a bustling business environment. It's not the kind of place you'd want to spend weeks or even days discovering (indeed there's not much to find), but hitting upon this kind of cosmopolitan atmosphere, second only to Kano in the north, is not completely disagreeable either, especially if you've just arrived from the remote rural areas of Niger or Nigeria.

Coming up from southern Nigeria, Kaduna is usually looked on as the first town of the north. This is a slightly misleading assumption since it doesn't have much in common with the other towns in this section. It's a place, however, that on any major travels through Nigeria, you're unlikely to avoid.

A short history

Originally conceived as the capital of the Northern Region, and perhaps the entire federation, Kaduna represents one of the best examples of a town created to be the seat of

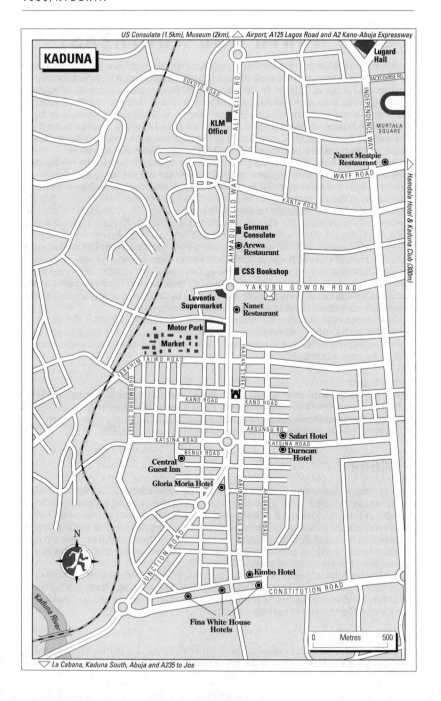

KADUNA

US Consulate (1.5km), Museum (2km), △ Airport, A125 Lagos Road and A2 Kano-Abuja Expressway

Lugard
Hall

RACECOURSE RD.

SOKOTO ROAD

ALI AKILU RD.

INDEPENDENCE WAY

KLM
Office

MURTALA
SQUARE

Nanet Meatpie
Restaurant ◉

△ Hamdala Hotel & Kaduna Club (300m)

WAFF ROAD

KANTA ROAD

AHMADU BELLO WAY

German
Consulate
◉ Arewa
Restaurant

CSS Bookshop

YAKUBU GOWON ROAD

Leventis
Supermarket

✉

◉ Nanet
Restaurant

Motor Park

Market

BRAHIM TAIWO ROAD

OGBOMOSHO STREET

BADA STREET

KANO ROAD

KANO ROAD

ARGUNGU RD.

◉ Safari Hotel

KATSINA ROAD

KATSINA ROAD

◉ Durncan
Hotel

BENUE ROAD

Central ◉
Guest Inn

ABUBAKAR KIGO ROAD

ABEOKUTA ROAD

Gloria Moria Hotel ◉

N

JUNCTION ROAD

◉ Kimbo Hotel

CONSTITUTION ROAD

Kaduna River

◉   ◉   ◉

Fina White House
Hotels

0   Metres   500

▽ La Cabana, Kaduna South, Abuja and A235 to Jos

HAUSA ORAL HISTORY: THE ORIGIN OF THE SEVEN STATES

The Hausa have a rich oral literature outside the overweening influence of more recent Islamic tales. In folk history, the origin of their states is traced to **Bayajida**, son of the king of Baghdad, who fled his homeland after a bitter dispute with his father. After years of wandering, he arrived in Bornu and was recognized as a natural leader by the *Mai* or king, who gave one of his daughters in marriage to the boy. Bayajida fell out with his father-in-law, and fled again, with his pregnant wife, to a place called Garun Gabas. He left his Bornu wife here, where she gave birth to a son, **Biram**, who later established the first of the *Hausa Bokwai*, named after him, in the area to the east of Kano. Meanwhile Bayajida had taken off again for the west and, in the middle of the night, fetched up at Daura, a place east of Katsina that was ruled at the time by a dynasty of queens. He stopped an old woman, Ayana, to ask for water and was told it was the wrong day of the week: the snake who owned the well only allowed people to draw water on a Friday. Nobody had been able to kill the snake. Bayajida, of course, went straight to the well, woke up the snake and chopped its head off. Then he drank his fill, pocketed the head and moved on. The next day was Friday and the queen wanted to know who had killed the snake. Ayana told her about the stranger and the queen sent messengers to catch up with the restless Bayajida, who agreed to return – and then asked her to marry him as a reward. They had a son, **Bawo**. Following the death of Bayajida, Bawo's own six sons went on to found the remaining towns of the *Hausa Bokwai* – Daura, Katsina, Kano, Rano, Gobir and Zaria.

government. The original **northern capital** was at Zungeru, on the Kaduna River 150km southwest of Kaduna, but when **Sir Frederick Lugard** became governor of the amalgamated colonial federation in 1912, he shifted the site to the small town of Kaduna which had the advantage of being near a good water supply and on the line of the newly constructed railway. Within easy striking range of all the former emirates, the spot was also strategically important. The West African Frontier Force moved here from Zaria in 1912, and in 1917 the civil administration was transferred from Zungeru.

Kaduna lost its role as capital of northern Nigeria when the states were created in 1967, but it has continued to thrive as a centre for the **army** (in 1965, 28 percent of the city's area was taken up by the armed forces) and **industry**. Near Nigeria's main cotton growing region, Kaduna contains several textile mills, a vast oil refinery under constant repair, a Peugeot assembly plant and numerous other industries.

Accommodation

Kaduna has a good range of hotels for all budgets, including one of the best in the north, and a clutch of decent cheap lodgings on Constitution Road.

Central Guest Inn, Benue Rd. One of the centre's cheaper options, if you can live with the basic single rooms (shared showers and toilets) and raucous atmosphere. ①.

Durncan Hotel, X6 Katsina Rd (PO 672; ☎062/240 947). Good-value, comfortable fan or AC double rooms, and delicious meals in the restaurant. ②.

ECWA Guest House, Alli Akilu Rd. Small guesthouse with dorm rooms. Although reserved for ECWA staff, they'll let you have a bed if one's available (ask at Challenge Books). ②.

Fina White House Hotels, NE20 Bonny Rd (☎062/240 979). Actually three establishments near each other, with rooms of varying degrees of comfort and sanitation. The better ones are S/C with AC (②–③).

Gloria Moria Hotel, ZZ2 Ahmadu Bello Rd (☎062/240 720). Clean S/C rooms with AC and TV. ②.

Hamdala Hotel, 20 Waff Rd (PO 311; ☎062/235 440-8). Upmarket hotel with TV and video in the newly renovated rooms, a good restaurant and a large, but somewhat cloudy, swimming pool. ④.

Kaduna Residential Hotel, 46 Gwari Ave (PO 6069; ☎062/233 007). Located across from the Abuja motor park, with reasonably priced AC, S/C rooms, plus a restaurant, pleasant garden bar and friendly staff. ②.

Kimbo Hotel, Constitution Rd. The decent AC rooms have recently been renovated, but are still reasonably priced. ②.

Safari Hotel, 10 Argungu St (☎062/241 754). Single and double rooms with shared facilities. A little grubby, but inexpensive and central. ①.

The Town

Kaduna's vast and purposeful layout reflects its former function as seat of government. One of the principal tree-lined avenues, Independence Way, is lined with **administrative buildings**, including, at the northern end, the monumental **Lugard Hall** with its impressive dome. The golf course and racecourse are nearby. The main commercial axis, **Ahmadu Bello Way**, runs in a north–south direction parallel to Independence Way. The major offices and businesses are along this street as are most of the banks, restaurants and hotels. In the extreme north of town, Ahmadu Bello Way becomes Alli Akilu Road.

> The **Tourist Information Centre** is near the KSBC Radio station, on Wurno Road, off Alli Akilu Road, at the northern end of town.

Past the State House on Alli Akilu Road, the **Kaduna National Museum** (daily 9am–6pm; free) houses a small collection of masks, musical instruments, leather-and brasswork and miscellaneous ethnographia. Its **Gallery of Nigerian Prehistory** traces the country's past back to Neolithic times (the New Stone Age ended in parts of Nigeria, as in many other parts of West Africa, within the last two thousand years), and exhibits Nok bronzes and terracotta work from Ife and Benin. It doesn't take very long to look round the museum, but the exhibits are well presented and documented. Behind, a **Hausa village** has been re-created, and **traditional crafts** – weaving, forging, leatherwork – are carried out in the different buildings. Just north of the museum, the **Arewa House** in Rabah Road, off Alli Akilu Road, was the residence of Sir Ahmadu Bello, the Sardauna of Sokoto, when he served as Regional Premier of Northern Nigeria. It now contains a library with archives and pleasant gardens.

Kaduna's large **market** is off Ahmadu Bello Way, in the centre of the commercial area. As in many northern cities, it's a good place to get leather goods and cloth, although most of the area is dedicated to plasticware, factory clothes and other modern goods. There's a good food section at the back of the market with a range of fruit and vegetables. Further south, Ahmadu Bello Way becomes Junction Road, then crosses the bridge spanning the **Kaduna River** to **Kaduna South** – the industrial side of town.

If you fancy getting out of town a little, the **riverbank** on the northeast side of town is a recommended area, though somewhat difficult to get to. Get a town taxi and ask for Malali village – or just "village" and get out near Malali "GTC" on Rabah Road. A walk parallel to the school, then over the hill through a housing estate, brings you down to the river. You can watch fishermen and lounge around on the rocks in relative peace and quiet; *kaduna* means crocodile in Hausa, but you're very unlikely to see one. There's a pleasant but modest restaurant, *Lesbora*, on the Rabah Road extension nearby.

Eating

If you're a *suya* fan, try some of the local **street food**. More upmarket alternatives are scattered around the centre; the *Jakaranda Farm and Pottery* is essentially a weekend excursion.

Arabian Sweets, 5B Yakubu Ave. Turkish coffee, fresh juices and real ice cream.

Arewa Chinese Restaurant, Plot 28 Ahmadu Bello Way (☎062/240 088). Generally considered to have the best Oriental food in Kaduna – if not the whole of Nigeria – and they do a splendid buffet on Sunday. Open evenings only Monday and Tuesday.

Bakers' Delight, D80 Ahmadu Bello Way, opposite African International Bank. Highly recommended bakers and confectioners, with everything from birthday cakes through yogurt to breads and meat pies.

Byblos Restaurant, D80 Ahmadu Bello Way (☎062/241 902). Stylish AC restaurant serving delicious Oriental and Nigerian food to musical accompaniment.

Chicken George, 16/17 Ahmadu Bello Way. Assorted local varieties of fast food, including chicken and hamburgers.

Jakaranda Farm and Pottery, KM20 Kachia Rd, Sabon Tasha, Kaduna South (☎062/212 399 or 211 346). Beautiful outdoor restaurant fifteen to twenty minutes' drive southeast of Kaduna, with a crocodile pool, landscaped water garden and fruit orchards. Excellent African and European food lunches only, and buffets at weekends. Right behind the restaurant, there's a complex of shops producing and selling quality clay pottery at good prices.

Kaduna Club Restaurant, Waff Rd, opposite *Hamdala Hotel* (PO 205; ☎062/241 681). Besides showing CNN, serves reasonably priced Nigerian and continental dishes.

Nanet Restaurant, 6 Ahmadu Bello Way. Solid, mostly African meals, neither overpriced nor overspiced, served in a large, fresh dining area. There's another branch – *Nanet Meatpie Restaurant* – on Waff Rd.

Listings

Banks The banking district is around the intersection of Ahmadu Bello Way and Yakubu Gowon Rd. You'll find main branches of the major banks along either of these roads, where you shouldn't have any trouble changing major international currencies (preferably US$ or £ sterling) either in cash or travellers' cheques. Otherwise there's the Al-Ameen Bureau de Change (☎062/238 474) at *Hamdala Hotel*.

Consulates British High Commission Liaison Office, 7 Alimi Rd (PMB 2096; ☎062/233 380; Fax 062/237 267); US Information Centre, 11 Maska Rd (PMB 2060; 062/235 990–2).

Post office The GPO is on Yakubu Gowon Rd in the heart of the banking district. The poste restante is reasonably reliable. Branches can be found across from the railway station, in Kaduna South, and at Bank Roundabout, Kaduna North. Note that they close early on Saturdays.

Supermarkets There's a large Chellarams and a Leventis Superstore on Ahmadu Bello Way near the intersection with Yakubu Gowon Rd. Also try the Kurfi Memorial Shopping Centre on Alkali Rd, north of the racecourse.

MOVING ON FROM KADUNA

The town's main **motor park** is adjacent to the market; but note that Kaduna is bypassed by the highway (A1/A125) between Lagos and the north. The motor park for **Lagos** is Mando motor park, while for **Zaria** and **Kano** it's New Kawo motor park; both are at the top of Alli Akilu Road. **Abuja** is served from the Kadung Yam motor park at Kachia Road, Kaduna South.

Kaduna Junction **train station** is just south of the river bridge. Kaduna grew up with the railway and is Nigeria's major railway town, with services to Kano, Port Harcourt and Lagos. Check at the station for train times, or ring the NRC direct (☎062/231 880 or 791).

According to the (not altogether reliable) schedules there are at least daily **flights** to Lagos on Nigeria Airways; the office is at 26 Ahmadu Bello Way (☎062/238 503). In addition, Kabo Airlines, 11 Alli Akilu Rd (☎062/242 248 or 249) and at the *Hamdala Hotel*, provides a domestic service to a number of cities. Satellite Travel Services, 22 Ahmadu Bello Way (☎062/240 232; fax 062/239 387), is an IATA accredited agent for a number of international airlines, and most Nigerian and African carriers. The KLM office is at Philips House, 4 Alli Akilu Rd (☎062/241 133).

Telephones The NITEL call office is on Golf Course Rd, with additional offices at Lafia Rd, GRA and in Kaduna South. Talaphone Payphone, 28B Alli Akilu Rd, has call booths with cardphones, and also offers a fax and email service.

Zaria

One of the seven *Hausa Bokwai*, the old town of **ZARIA** has withstood the tests of time rather better than most of the other emirates. The **ancient wall**, built by Queen Amina some 950 years ago, has largely crumbled away, but some of the old gates have been restored and are very impressive. The **Emir's Palace** is a beautiful example of traditional architecture. Nearby, the **Friday Mosque** was formerly one of the most magnificent in the region, though it's now enclosed by a plain-looking modern structure. Almost all the homes in old Zaria are built in the traditional style, and many display the detailed exterior decoration for which the town is famous.

After the British arrived, a new town – **Sabon Gari** – was built some 3km north of the walled city, across the **Kubani River**, and this is the quarter where you'll arrive if coming in from Sokoto or Kano. In the centre, the **train station** and the main **motor park** stand next to each other on Main Street. It was in this part of town that, early this century, Yoruba and Igbo traders settled near the tracks. The new town's **main market** is in the neighbourhood, with **banks** and major businesses nearby around Crescent Road and Park Road. Hospital Road leads south across the bridge to the **Tudan Wada** neighbourhood where most of the infrastructure is located – the hospital, schools and teacher training colleges. Zaria is noted for the radical student life of **Ahmadu Bello University**, to the north, which has been the scene of some violent clashes with security forces in the past, but things seems to have calmed down since the Vice Chancellor, a former army major, left office.

Accommodation

It's quite possible to arrive in Zaria in the morning, take a look around, and then head out of town again before evening. If you want to stay, however, you'll find a number of pleasant, inexpensive hotels and one that's a cut above what you might expect.

Hotel Kuta, 8 Aliyu Rd, off Hospital Rd, Tudun Wada. Dusty, but characterful non-S/C rooms, with balconies giving onto the courtyard. At present, the AC and water no longer work, but the hotel is undergoing renovation. ①.

Kongo Conference Hotel, Old Jos Rd (PO 1068; ☎069/32872). The town's nicest hotel, with a pool, restaurants and a bar – one of the few places in Zaria with reliable cold beer, even during Ramadan. ⑤.

Royal Guest Inn, 8 Park Rd. Conveniently located near the motor parks and market, and one of the most inexpensive options in town. Non-S/C singles and S/C doubles, all with fan. ①.

University Guest House, Ahmadu Bello University, Samara. Limited amount of rooms, but the twelve S/C rooms are more or less like suites, with small kitchens, cable TV and AC. Very good value, but far out in the north part of town. ①.

Zaria Hotel, Samaru/Sokoto Rd (PMB 1066; ☎069/32820 or 32829). Big hotel with clean AC rooms, restaurant, bar and nightclub in a quiet neighbourhood. Friendly staff and an excellent bookshop. Good value all round. Frequent buses to Zaria centre stop nearby. ②.

The Town

To explore the **old town**, the best plan is to rent a taxi for half a day with a clued-up driver or – failing that – to rent a taxi and find a guide at the same time. To visit the Emir's Palace you have to make a request at the secretary's office next door – normally granted if the Emir is at home.

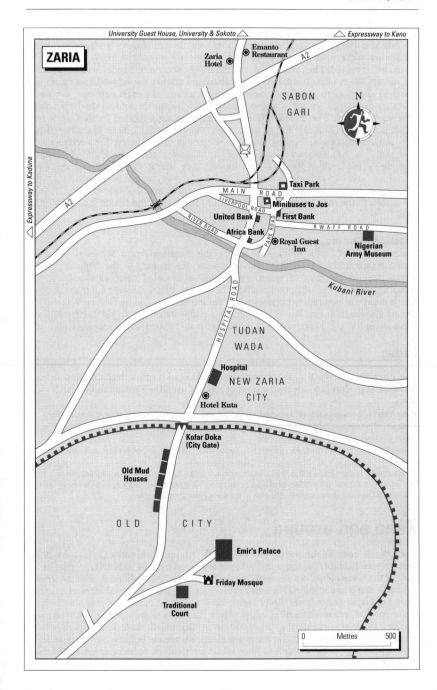

The main centres of activity in the old town are the **Emir's Palace** (Gidan Sarki) and the **market**. The houses and stores of traders and the craftsmen's workshops (including leatherworkers, tailors and dye pits) are scattered around the market and many of them can be visited. The palace, with its elaborately decorated facade, is to the south of the market (as in other northern cities, palace and market are set well apart from one another) and is surrounded by a high-walled enclosure. The main entrance, the **Kofar Fada**, faces a large square where ceremonies, including the annual **durbar** cavalry charges are held. The **Friday Mosque**, disappointingly hidden behind a modern facade, dominates one side of the square, surrounded by the offices of court counsellors and the homes of leading citizens. According to the story, the architect who designed it in 1834, Babban Gwani Mallam Mikaila, was later commissioned to build a mosque for the Emir of Birnin Gwari. Immediately after it was completed, this Emir seized him and had him put to death so he would never create a more beautiful building elsewhere. The architecture is outstanding, especially the inside vaulting, though the replica of the mosque in Jos gives a better idea of what the building actually looks like.

Nigerian Army museum

Located in the Chindit military barracks, the Nigerian Army Museum (Mon–Fri 8am–2.30pm) houses a small exhibition tracing the history of the Nigerian armed forces through displays of weaponry and other assorted memorabilia (uniforms, medals, maps and period photographs). The eras of military government are covered with a degree of comradely back-slapping, but the sections on the Biafran War and the Burma Campaign during World War II make a visit worthwhile. To get there, follow the signs along RWAFF Road, or take a motorbike from Sabon Gari (it's a long walk).

Eating

There are few noteworthy restaurants in Zaria. Alcohol is rarely available, and, outside of *Sallah* time (Muslim celebrations, especially at the end of Ramadan) it's a fairly quiet town.

Blue Velvet, 5 Gaskiya Rd, off Hospital Rd. A tiny and very cheap eatery with African dishes.

Emanto Restaurant, opposite the *Zaria Hotel*. A very good, rather stylish restaurant with avant-garde photos on the wood-panelled walls.

Hunger Clinic Restaurant, 3 Crescent Rd. Good-value Nigerian dishes served up by the Salvation Army.

Shagarikun, Kongo Rd, Tudun Wada. Formerly in a *banco* house, the restaurant is now in a modern "storey building" (ie with several floors), but they've thoughtfully kept a section where visitors can eat on the floor. Inexpensive, but one of the best restaurants in town.

Kano and around

The largest town in the north, and effectively Nigeria's second city (despite being smaller than Ibadan), the thousand-year-old Hausa metropolis of **KANO**, capital of the state of the same name, is a strange mixture of modern and traditional, with the former gaining ground and invading the latter every year. The **international airport** has daily flights to Lagos and several direct flights each week to Europe and the Middle East, while growing **industrialization** in the region continues to draw people from the countryside. The city currently has a population of two million, and continues to spread, apparently unchecked, over the dusty savannah. Its vehicle pollution, especially at the close of the dry season in April or May, has to be breathed to be believed. Like Lagos, Kano combines its commercialism with being an important **academic** centre.

Kano is a good place to start West African travels – reasonably lively but not so intolerably frenetic and intimidating as to put you right off – and well placed for Niger and Mali, or for Cameroon. **Aminu Kano International Airport** is only 8km from the central Sabon Gari quarter of the city, an inexpensive taxi ride. KLM now operate the only direct non-stop flight from Europe (from **Amsterdam** on Monday and Friday, arriving early evening), but other international airlines have served the airport in the past, and may do so again in the future. Egyptair flies from **London** via **Cairo** (Tuesday and Saturday, overnight in Cairo, arriving the following afternoon).

The other side of Kano is its history. The **Gidan Makama Museum** is a beautiful effort to protect its heritage, housing historical exhibits of the city and its environs in a former Makama chief's palace, completely restored to show off the intricacy and technical excellence of the ancient architecture; qualities which can also be admired at the **Emir's Palace** and the **Central Mosque** nearby. Other reminders of the past include the **old market** and the **dye pits** where, beside a busy multi-laned avenue, cloth is still soaked in indigo in the gloriously messy way it's been done for centuries. Yet everywhere there's a distinct feeling that much more could be done to preserve the ties with Kano's past, especially maintenance of the **old city wall**, which resisted British colonial invaders with greater success than it has the elements in recent years. Although a few of the great **gates** that once protected the emirate still stand, much of the wall has now become huge lumps of rain-smoothed mud, and people still dig away at it to make bricks for new homes.

Some history

Kano's history (its courtly history at any rate) has been preserved in the **Kano Chronicles**, which give the most detailed account of any Sudanic nation with the exception of Songhai. A compilation of brief histories of the region, the Chronicles originated in the mid-seventh century, shortly after the introduction of Arabic. The first settlement of Kano was founded on **Dala Hill**, where archeologists have uncovered furnaces and slag heaps indicating iron-working from as early as the sixth century; this settlement was later conquered by the descendants of **Bagauda** – one of the six sons of **Bawo** who founded the *Hausa Bokwai* – the seven legitimate Hausa states (see p.1007).

Kano was fortified at the beginning of the twelfth century during the reign of **Gijimasu**. Later, under **Yaji** (1349–85), it developed a powerful army that used new technology – quilted armour, iron helmets and chainmail – to overthrow its adversaries. The city became independent of its neighbours and gained control of the trans-Saharan trade in gold and salt. It thus acquired wealth and power to rival Timbuktu and Gao. Additions to the walled city were made in the fifteenth century under **Muhammed Rumfa**, who had converted to Islam and who transformed Kano from a local military chiefdom to an Islamic sultanate with close links across the Sahara and to Arabia.

Contact with Europe came in the mid-sixteenth century. **Portuguese** attempts to establish a trading centre were thwarted, but settlers from Ragusa (now Dubrovnik in Croatia) maintained a presence in Kano throughout the 1560s and 1570s, under the protection of the North African-based Turkish Ottoman sultan.

Over the next two centuries, Kano warred continuously with the neighbouring states of Borno and Katsina. At the same time, European maritime powers on the coast slowly undermined the trans-Saharan routes that were the basis of Kano's power and autonomy. Although the textile and leather **industries** kept the economy going (indigo-dyed cloth and soft red leather, known as "Moroccan", were exported as far afield as

ID AL-FITR IN KANO

In the cities of the north, the festival of **Id al-Fitr**, at the end of Ramadan (for dates, see Basics, p.59), is an important social as well as a religious occasion, allowing the emirs, their officers and their people to meet and reaffirm their mutual positions in society. Some festivals, particularly those in Kano and Katsina, draw sizeable tourist crowds to see the annual **durbars**, or cavalry parades.

Kano's *Id al-Fitr* festivities begin at 8am, when the emir leaves his palace through the **Fatalwa gate** and appears at the Id ground, where, after a prayer, the emir's ram is slaughtered, followed by other sacrifices. The emir leaves, but reappears at the **Kwaru Gate** at around 9.30am to address the crowds.

The following day, the **Hawan Daushe Durbar**, is the most dramatic, when no less than 50,000 heavily decorated riders parade through the streets of the old city to salute the emir. The durbar sets out from Kofar Arewa at 4pm and ends when the emir returns to his palace at around 6.30pm.

The third day of *Id al-Fitr* dates back to the colonial days when the emir used to pay homage to the resident administrator, followed by an exchange of addresses. This tradition (**Hawan Nassarawa**) is maintained, only with the colonial governor replaced by the head of the state government. On the fourth day, known as **Hawan Fanisau**, or the Dorayi Durbar, the emir treats his district heads to lunch at his palaces of Fanisau or Dorayi.

Europe), the state's political structure was fragile. When the Fulani, led by Usman dan Fodio, waged their religious war, or **jihad**, Kano was unable to resist: the city fell in 1807. A new era of hostilities followed, and it was during this period that **European explorers** reached Kano – Clapperton in 1824, Barth in 1853 and Monteil in 1891. By the end of the nineteenth century, **British imperial designs** posed a direct threat to the emirate. Kano refortified its walls and prepared to resist, but in 1903 the city fell to British troops.

Kano effectively became a laboratory for testing the theories of colonial rule. The British appointed a compliant emir in order to try out a system of **indirect rule** – successful in colonial terms, but a disastrous precursor to independence. The railway was opened in 1911 and the airport in 1937 and Kano's future as the dominant city of northern Nigeria, and the biggest in the Sahel, was sealed. After World War II, Kano became the centre of a renewed **Islamic nationalism** in Nigeria, intent on resisting the power of the southern regions of the country as much as, if not more than, the British who were clearly intent on pulling out. The rift with southern Nigeria, especially with the Igbo community in the southeast, continued after independence, through the Biafran War and into recent years. In 1980, a mad Kano prophet, **Maitatsine**, whipped up a frenzy among landless peasants and unemployed townspeople against Nigerian armed forces in the city, in an uprising that left dozens of casualties. And almost every year sees at least one major disturbance arising from ethnic tensions, usually an ordinary urban murder that leads to an ethnic riot.

Accommodation

Kano has a very wide range of places to stay, ranging from camping grounds or dorm beds to international-class hotels. Many inexpensive **small hotels** are concentrated in the Sabon Gari district.

Inexpensive to moderate

Baptist Guest House, 58 Abuja Rd, Sabon Gari (PO 196; ☎064/648 113). Twin rooms (if you're alone, you may end up with a roommate) with fans. Very simple, but clean and cheap. ①.

Criss Cross Hotel, 2 Ibadan Rd, by Church Rd, Sabon Gari (PO 742; ☎064/634 652). Basic accommodation in single or double rooms with fans and bucket showers, but very inexpensive. ①.

ECWA Guest House, Mission Compound between Mission Rd and Zaria Ave. Very clean rooms and friendly staff, but its "budget" prices are almost up to the small hotel range. Family atmosphere, but you have to be on your best behaviour. ①–②.

Hotel De France, 54 Tafawa Balewa Rd, Sabon Gari (PO 29; ☎064/646 416). A decent, central hotel with tiled floors and a range of well-equipped S/C rooms (AC, TV, phone). ③.

Kano Tourist Camp, 11A Bompai Rd (PMB 3528; ☎064/626 309). Camping places, dormitory space and private rooms with showers and fans, all at reasonable rates. Safe, friendly and central with the Kano State Tourist Board on site, as well as the sociable and high-quality *Gewi Restaurant*. ①.

Remco Motel, 61 New Rd, Sabon Gari (PO 1724; ☎064/648 600). Clean rooms with AC, and fridge. Friendly staff. ②.

Skyworld Hotel, 95 Niger Ave, Sabon Gari (☎064/647 622). One of the better options in Sabon, with a variety of rooms, a restaurant with African and continental dishes, a garden bar and a spacious car park. ②–③.

TYC Hotel, 44 Abuja Rd (☎064/647 491). Options range from singles to elaborate suites with colour TV and fridge. The restaurant serves full Nigerian meals – or just pepper soup or sandwiches – and the "roof garden" is nice for drinks while looking out on the lights of Sabon Gari at night. Good value and very friendly. ②.

University Guest House, Bayero University (BUK), Old Campus (PMB 3011; ☎064/661 480–1, ext 223; Fax 064/665 904). Pleasant lodge in a safe environment, with S/C, AC rooms with satellite TV. ②.

Upmarket hotels

Central Hotel, Bompai Rd (☎064/630 000–2; Fax 064/630 628). The main international-class hotel with swimming pool, tennis courts, bookshop and, most alluring of all, an air-conditioned bar – a popular expat rendezvous. ⑤.

Prince Hotel, Tamandu Rd, off Audu Bako Way (PO 356; ☎064/639 402 or 633 393; Fax 064/635 944). Highly recommended hotel, with a pleasant patio restaurant and a bar that's popular for an evening out, especially now with the new swimming pool. Efficiently run with all modern facilities; advance booking recommended. ⑤–⑦.

Royal Tropicana Hotel, 17/19 Niger St (PMB 2653; ☎064/639 352, or 647 496; Fax 064/639 358). New hotel in the huge, international-class category. High-quality restaurant and no less than three bars. ⑤.

The old city

Most of Kano's special appeal lies in the **old city**, down Kofar Mata Road from the modern centre. The fortified **town wall** has all but disappeared, but some of the original **city gates** (*kofar*) have been restored and are worth a look. The best-preserved gates are all on B.U.K. Road – Kofar Na Isa (literally, "I have arrived"), Kofar Dan Agundi and Kofar Sabwar.

As you walk round the old city, be on the lookout for examples of **traditional Hausa exterior decorations**. Particularly beautiful is the "masque" style of house facade, but if you have the chance to travel widely, you'll notice how much dirtier the Kano houses are than similar buildings in, say, Zinder in Niger, where the destructive combination of rain, exhaust fumes and industrial pollution is that much less. There's a fine "masque" house just past the dye pits on the left as you head into the old city.

The dye pits

Inside Kofar Mata, a modern gate into the old city (small hillocks indicate where the wall used to be), you'll see the **dye pits** on the right. They soak cloth here in natural indigo as they have for hundreds of years, using great basins of dye buried in the hard

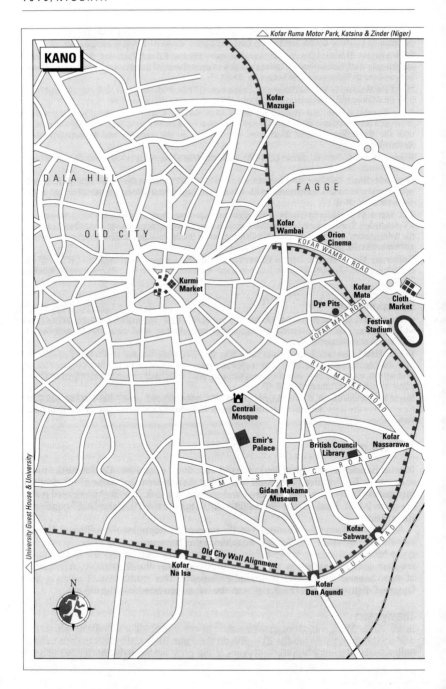

KANO

Kofar Ruma Motor Park, Katsina & Zinder (Niger)

Kofar
Mazugai

DALA HILL

FAGGE

OLD CITY

Kofar
Wambai

Orion
Cinema

KOFAR WAMBAI ROAD

Kurmi
Market

Kofar
Mata

Cloth
Market

Dye Pits

Festival
Stadium

KOFAR MATA ROAD

RIMT MARKET ROAD

Central
Mosque

Emir's
Palace

British Council
Library

Kofar
Nassarawa

Gidan Makama
Museum

EMIR'S PALACE ROAD

University Guest House & University

Kofar
Sabwar

B.U.K. ROAD

Old City Wall Alignment

Kofar
Na Isa

Kofar
Dan Agundi

N

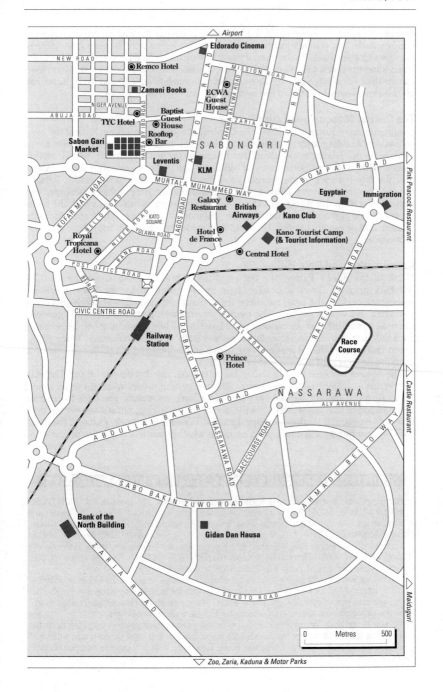

ground. Kano fabrics once clothed most of the people in the Sahara region and were highly valued. You can buy material or ready-made clothes here, or even have some of your own clothes dyed. But beware: if you take a picture, you'll be asked for a dash (the demanding upturned palms are plain to see on most snaps of the dye pits). More spectacular than Kano's dye pits are those in **Kura**, a small town 30km south of Kano, just off the expressway to Zaria, in the heart of a major cloth-dyeing area.

The Central Mosque and Emir's Palace

Continuing down Kofar Mata Road, the **Central Mosque** is imposing, but not the most noteworthy building architecturally. It has, however, been of enormous importance as a focus for the Islamic nationalism that has so bedevilled successive federal governments. With proper authorization you can climb one of its two minarets for fine views over the city (enquire at the secretary's office at the entrance to the Emir's Palace). Behind the mosque, the **Emir's Palace** spreads out over a huge acreage, and approaching from this direction its traditional architecture blends easily with the buildings of the old city, albeit on a rather larger and more stately scale. The front is far more modern and obviously palatial. Unfortunately, whichever way you approach, you can't visit inside.

Kurmi market and Dala Hill

North of the Emir's Palace, the ancient **Kurmi Market** (also known as the **City Market**) forms an almost impossibly tight maze of alleys and stalls. They're pressed together to exclude the heat, but there are so many people milling about, it gets claustrophobic and sweaty anyhow. The market swarms with petty hustlers and "**guides**". Come to terms with just one, accept you'll have to pay him something and be prepared for a little transparent salesmanship at certain stalls of his acquaintance. Once you've got to know each other, a guide is instructive and helpful and his presence saves you from the onslaught of other would-be assistants.

The busiest and best time to visit is the afternoon, any day except Friday. The market retains a strong traditional flavour, although certain sellers with an eye on tourist bucks turn out shoddy and not very traditional junk. As always, you have to confront the question of the "authenticity" of the goods you're buying, but it's not yet too common a dilemma, and **leather**, **textiles**, **brass-silver-and ironwork**, **pottery**, **calabash carving** and **beads** will continue to be made whether tourists buy them or not – and are still good value. Be sure to stop at the section for local riding tack, housed in the market's oldest structure, dating from the nineteenth century.

Dala Hill, site of the original settlement in Kano, rises up to the north of the Kurmi market, pretty well in the centre of the old city. You can walk up there – it involves finding your way through narrow alleys and backstreets – and can usually find a kid to take you for a dash, but remember to fix the price first.

The museums

Across the square in front of the Emir's Palace, the grandiose building is the **Gidan Makama Museum** (daily 10am–4pm; free). Formerly a palace itself, the building is as interesting for its superb, fifteenth-century Sudanic architecture as for the exhibits inside. Fittingly, the displays in the first room explain the technological and decorative aspects of traditional Hausa building styles. Rooms two to six trace the history of Kano and the other Hausa states through drawings, photographs, documents and reconstructions spanning a thousand years – a dense and informative chronology, not for the faint-hearted. The coming of Islam to Kano and the Muslim tenets are laid out in the seventh room. Finally, rooms eight and nine are dedicated to a less demanding selection of **traditional arts** – music, weaving, brasswork and so on. Set aside a couple of hours to visit, as it's well worth the time – you may want to come back.

A new museum, the **Kano State Museum**, is slated to open in the **Gida Dan Hausa** – the first British colonial residence in Kano. Built in 1909, it's a remarkable Hausa structure with beautiful gardens, and until the exhibits are ready, you can explore at will.

The new city

The intersection of Murtala Muhammed Way and Lagos/Airport Road is the centre of modern Kano, the heart of its main commercial district, at any rate. Continuing south on Lagos Road brings you to Post Office Road and the **GPO** (8am–5pm). The **train station** is nearby, on Fagge Road. Up on Club Road, the **Central Hotel** makes a good place to stop for a cold drink: even if you don't stay here, you can pay to use the pool, though the water is often murky. Across from the *Central*, vendors sell various **crafts**. The quality is not bad, and while prices start high, patient bargaining can reduce them to realistic levels.

North of Murtala Muhammed Way, the **Sabon Gari** ("New Town") neighbourhood is home to mainly Igbo and Yoruba workers and has a distinct southern Nigerian flavour, with flocks of cheap hotels and energetic bars – particularly animated after dark and something of a relief after the more austere "dry" areas of the old city. The recently rebuilt **Sabon Gari Market** always draws a lot of colour and crowds. Get your food and other odds and ends here, but for traditional crafts head to the old city.

Slightly out of town on the Zaria road, the **Audo Bako Zoo** has an exotic collection of animals, including a kangaroo – nothing to go out of your way for but a good excuse for a late afternoon stroll if you've nothing else to do. There's also a beer garden.

Eating, drinking and nightlife

If your travels have featured Kano as a significant goal for any length of time, you won't be disappointed with the variety of edible treats on offer. The whole gamut of West African food is available here, together with a full variety of imports in the supermarkets – Kano is, after all, only six hours from London.

Inexpensive eateries

Arabian Sweets, 4 Beirut Rd. Lebanese pastry shop – with deliciously sticky Middle Eastern sweets and Italian ice cream.

Benaroo International Restaurant, 1 Bompai Rd. Breakfast, salads or sandwiches for lunch and Nigerian or continental dishes for dinner, accompanied by soft drinks.

Choice Restaurant & Takeaway, 40A Niger St. Excellent simple meals – plantains, omelette and meat, for example – for a few Naira.

Galaxy Restaurant, 139 Murtala Muhammed Way, not far from the *Tourist Camp*. Good omelettes and chips for breakfast, and dishes like rice with chicken or beef stew later in the day. In an old cottage with an outdoor terrace for drinking at night.

Halal Meat Restaurant, 101 Inuwa Wada Lane, opposite Beirut Rd (☎064/647 205). Combination of Lebanese, continental and African dishes – eat well for a moderate sum.

Upmarket restaurants

Castle Restaurant, 20 Ahmadu Bello Way. Lebanese and European food. Adjoining nightclub.

Le Cercle Club, 9 Lagos Rd. Club with restaurant serving traditional Nigerian food, an inside bar and a larger garden restaurant outside. You have to become a member, but the fee amounts to little more than a cover charge abroad.

Jay's Restaurant, 2B Niger St. A wide range of European food, including pizza, and an upbeat atmosphere.

La Locanda, 40 Sultan Rd, off Ahmadu Bello Way. Superb Italian food in a lively ambience. Pizzas can be ordered to go.

Pink Peacock, 10A Dantale Rd, Bompai area (☎064/646 150). Popular Chinese restaurant; open 6.30–11pm.

Smart Tandoor, 3 Bompai Rd (☎064/645 089 or 647 879). A decent restaurant with real Indian dishes on the menu. Desserts include ice cream, Indian sweets and coffee.

Nightlife

The place to be is **Sabon Gari**, the old city being pretty quiet in the evening, and the new city south of Murtala Muhammed Way hardly sparkling. **Cinemas** – including the Plaza on Kofar Mata Road, the Orion on Kofar Wambai Road, the Eldorado on Lagos Road near Mission Road, and the Rex and Sheila along Murtala Muhammed Way – and **bars** are the main diversions, though there's the odd **disco** too. *Lilywhite*, next to the *Galaxy Restaurant* on Murtala Muhammed Way, at the bottom of Club Road, is a positively outrageous example. Otherwise, try the *Body 'N' Soul Nightclub*, at the *Universal Guest Inn*, 86 Church Rd. The bar of the *Central* hotel is usually quite animated too, but as you'd expect there are frequent and fickle shifts of favour among their regular customers. If you're looking for a calm evening, spend it drinking on the *Rooftop Bar*, opposite Sabon Gari market.

Listings

Airline offices Alitalia, c/o Italair, 16C Murtala Muhammed Way (☎064/637 290 or -281); British Airways, Hafsatu House, 7 Bompai Rd (☎064/626 040 or 624 834); Egyptair, 14C Murtala Muhammed Way (☎064/630 759); Kabo Air, 6775 Ashton Rd (☎064/625 291); KLM, 17 Airport Rd (☎064/600 240); Nigeria Airways, 3 Bank Rd (☎064/647 314), and at Kano International Airport (☎064/637 801); Sabena, *Central Hotel*, Bompai Rd (☎064/621 364).

Books Used books are sold in front of the post office. Zamani Books, at 84 Church Rd, Sabon Gari, has a broad spectrum of good, cheap books, including novels by African writers, and a *Kano Street Guide* (Mon–Fri 8am–12.30pm & 2–5pm, Sat 8am–1pm).

Consulates The British High Commission's Commercial Liaison Office on State Rd (Mon–Fri 8am–1pm), is a good place for business advice. The Niger Consulate is on Katsina Rd, near the army barracks. There are no consulates for Cameroon or Chad.

Banks and exchange Most of the banks – Afribank, First, Union and Bank of the North (Mon–Fri 8am–2pm, Sat 8am–noon) – are located around the intersection of Lagos and Bank roads. There are a number of forex bureaux, notably along Bompai Rd near the *Tourist Camp*; the one in the camp itself is as good as any other.

History and Culture Bureau, across from the Governor's mansion. A good place to find out about dance performances.

MOVING ON FROM KANO

Most long-distance taxis and minibuses leave either from the **Ngwa Uku motor park** (Lagos, Maiduguri, Enugu, Sokoto and Abuja) or the more distant **Nai Bawa motor park** (Jos, Kaduna, Zaria). Both are about 5km out on the Zaria road. Buses and minibuses towards the **Niger border**, and to Niger itself, go from the **Kofar Ruwa motor park**, north of the old city off the Katsina road. Vehicles heading, broadly, east – to northern parts of **Cameroon** and to **Maiduguri** and the Chad border – leave from **Murtala Muhammed Way**, near Sabon Gari market.

There are **train services** to Lagos and Port Harcourt. Check at the station, or call the NRC in Kaduna (☎062/231 880 or 791).

Nigeria Airways has at least a couple of **flights** a week to Maiduguri, Sokoto, Port Harcourt and Kaduna, and several daily flights to Lagos. Kabo Air covers other domestic destinations. See "Listings", opposite, for airline addresses.

Hospitals and emergencies For doctors, try Dr K. Khouri, Club Rd (Mon–Fri 8.30am–12.30pm & 3–6pm, Sat 8.30am–12.30pm) or the Bompai Rd Clinic (24hr); dentists include Dr J.P. Rossek, Kowa Specialist Clinic, Club Rd (Mon–Fri 8.30am–noon, Sat 9am–12.30pm), and Ahmadiya Clinic, Club Rd (Mon–Fri 8.30am–12.30pm, Sat 8am–1pm).

Pharmacies B. Olojo Pharmaceuticals, 110 Murtala Muhammed Way, is recommended, although relatively expensive.

Post Office The GPO, on Post Office Rd has a free, reliable and relatively swift poste restante.

Supermarkets Spring Time Supermarket, 11C Murtala Muhammed Way, is a Lebanese grocery store; Delight, 10C Murtala Muhammed Way also has a bakery and confectioners.

Telephones The new NITEL office at the end of Zoo Rd is reasonably modern and comfortable and long-distance connections are better than at the Lagos Rd centre (near the corner of Ibrahim Taiwa Rd). More convenient, although more expensive, are the *Central* and *Daula* hotels' services. Emcol Communication Services, at 30 Beirut Rd, has a fax and cardphone service.

Travel Agents African Wing Travels, Civic Centre; Habis Travels Ltd, 15/16B Post Office Rd (☎064/631 258 or 279), agents for KLM and BA.

The Hadejia-Nguru wetlands

Three hours' drive northeast from Kano is **NGURU**, in Yobe State, the gateway to the **Hadejia-Nguru Wetlands Conservation Project**, where there are excellent opportunities for **bird-watching**. The wetlands are unique both in their extent – encompassing eastern parts of Jigawa State and western parts of Yobe State – and in their location in the dry north (the rest of the region is attractively desert-like, with scattered camel caravans and several oases).

The project was started in the 1980s, to preserve the wetlands for agricultural purposes, and to create a sanctuary for migrating birds seeking refuge in Africa during the cold European winter – thousands seek shelter here during the dry *Harmattan* season. The **Dagona Wildfowl Sanctuary** is one of the best places to view the birdlife, including ibis, duck, geese, waders and pelicans.

You'll find the project headquarters in Nguru and some **accommodation**, though it's not the most attractive.

Katsina

Tucked in the extreme north, **KATSINA** flounders in the dry Sahelian badlands. During the *Harmattan* season, from December to May, it's easy to appreciate the value of the traditional clothing, protecting everything except the eyes from the blowing sand. Efforts to pump some modern development into the region, notably through the installation of a steel rolling plant in 1982, have so far brought few noticeable signs of change, other than the dual-laned highways that wrap around the outskirts of town.

Vestiges of the once powerful **Katsina Emirate** – one of the oldest of the seven Hausa states – have hardly fared better. One or two of the original city gates still stand in varying states of ruin, but the fortifications that once surrounded the town have been all but flattened. Reminders of the past remain in the **Emir's Palace** and the **Gobarau Tower** that once served as a sentry post. You can visit these, but the real pleasure of Katsina perhaps lies more in simply wandering the dusty streets, absorbing the atmosphere of a traditional Hausa city that shows few signs of modernity.

Katsina is strategically located along the highway linking Kano with Niamey, the capital of Niger. Besides the long-haul transport passing through, there's an important short-distance trade across the border, making for lively **markets** both in Katsina and in neighbouring Maradi.

The Town

"Downtown" Katsina spreads along IBB Way between the **Kofar Kaura**, a recent stone gate built to replace an older mud-brick one, and the **Central Mosque** with its onion domes. Along this road, you'll find the major **banks**, the **post office** and the big trading stores. Just beyond the mosque, IBB Way veers to the left and continues to the **Emir's Palace**. The entrance to this building looks more recent than you might expect, but this is in part because it's one of the few buildings that is well maintained. Inside, the large compound is a hodgepodge of old mud-brick and new concrete buildings. To visit the palace, enquire at the Ministry of Information building on IBB Way.

The huge **Kangiwa Square**, in front of the palace, is the site of the annual **Sallah Durbar**, the high point of the *Id al-Fitr* celebrations, when horsemen decked in their finest regalia parade through the town and stage a mini *durbar* in front of the Emir's Palace, and women perform traditional dances. Every Friday, the square is filled with the overspill from **Katsina Central Mosque**, just to the south.

Following the paved road to the west, the **Central Market** is a short way from the palace. You'll find a few fruits and vegetables here (mangos in season, oranges, tomatoes, onions and okra), decorated calabashes and pottery with a bronzey glaze, cereals (corn and different kinds of millet) and livestock including the occasional camel. Notice the open-air "butcher's shop" and Fulani women selling milk from calabashes.

To the north of the market, you can make out the **Gobarau Tower**. To reach this minaret follow the unmarked street (Gobarau Road) on the eastern edge of the market. Built in the seventeenth century as a lookout post, the tower later served as the muezzin's platform in pre-loudspeaker days. A guide will take you to the top and explain the history for a small dash. From the minaret, Hospital Road leads past a walled cemetery to the **Kofar Uku**. This gate "of the three doors" was formerly attached to Katsina Teacher Training College, the first institute of higher learning in town, and Alma Mater to Ahmadu Bello (the first premier of Northern Nigeria), Abubakar Tafawa Balewa (Nigeria's first prime minister), Alhaji Shehu Shagari (the first president) and General Yakubu Gowon, the former military head of state. According to locals, the gate – now falling into ruin – was built in the seventeenth century. Other gates of note include the **Kofar Guga** and, at the end of Nagogo Street, the **Kofar Durbi**, where you can still see part of the ancient wall called **Ganuwar Aminu** and supposed to originate from the reign of King Marabu about 900 years ago. Nowadays the old Katsina College has become **Katsina Museum**, which is well worth a visit.

Practicalities

From the new motor park on the outskirts of town, get a taxi or a motorbike (*"express"*) into the centre or to the serenely located *Katsina Motel*, 1 Mohammed Bashir Rd (☎065/30017; ②). Most of the central **hotels** are on Ibrahim Babangida (IBB) Way, outside the Kofar Kaura. The *Abuja Guest Inn*, off IBB Way (☎065/30319; ①–②) has S/C doubles with AC and fan and is reasonably priced. Right near the Kofar Kaura, *Katsina Royal Garden Hotel*, 15 Hassan Osman Rd (☎065/34812; ②), is very clean with pleasant staff and has a good AC restaurant serving Nigerian and European food, but no alcohol. For a spot of luxury, *Liyafa Palace Hotel* (④–⑥) is the best in town, although some distance outside the centre towards Kano. For **eating**, *Katsina City Restaurant*, at 115 IBB Way, serves local and continental dishes, but no alcohol – only water, juice and soft drinks.

Sokoto and around

Until the beginning of the nineteenth century, **SOKOTO** was a small town of little significance, surrounded by the Hausa city states. It only gained its present status as **reli-**

SOME SOKOTO HISTORY

The **Fulani** of Sokoto are thought to have migrated from Mali in the thirteenth century and to have settled in **Gobir**, then a powerful ancient kingdom. Known as *Fulanin Gida* (town Fulani as opposed to pastoral nomads), they were mainly traders and highly regarded Muslims. The most learned were welcomed into the Hausa emirs' courts as advisors, where some succumbed to lives of indolence; others kept on the move and preferred a more ascetic lifestyle, teaching and speaking on behalf of the poor.

Usman dan Fodio, from Gobir, was of the latter mould, preaching energetically against the corrupt influence of high office and the lax ways of the traditional non-Muslim (or quasi-Muslim) Hausa emirs. There was much support for his stand, which called for the retrenchment of the widely ignored or circumvented *Sharia* legal code. Naturally, there was also plenty of resentment of his politicking piety from traditionalists with an interest in maintaining the status quo. By 1804, the tension had led to the birth of a radical reform movement and to civil war in Gobir, where the traditionalist emir first used arms against the reformers. Dan Fodio was a reluctant warrior and, while he agreed to be appointed Amir al-Muminin (Commander of the Faithful), the military leadership of the **holy war**, or jihad, was handled by his brother Abdullah and son Muhammedu Bello.

Weakened from centuries of warring, the Hausa emirates fell quickly and, over the space of four years, with growing popular support, dan Fodio became the uncontested ruler of the entire north. Although often characterized as a war of pious Muslim Fulani against corrupt Hausa, the reality was considerably more complicated and very much determined by people's economic position – the jihad promised a more equitable distribution of wealth and the reduction of taxes and levies. In 1809, dan Fodio's son, **Bello**, who later became the first sultan, established Sokoto as the *Sarkin Musulmi*, the spiritual and political capital of the empire. By the time of Bello's death in 1835, Sokoto was effectively the capital of Islam for the whole of West Africa.

The **social consequences** of the jihad were many. Dan Fodio had created, for the first time in the region, a single state with a central government controlling the entire north (with the exception of Bornu) and extending deep into present-day Cameroon and south into the Yoruba country which up to then had resisted Islam. As a result, trade was facilitated throughout the region and the Arabic language and writing spread with the teachings of the Koran. When the **British** conquered Sokoto in 1903, they took advantage of the highly stratified and unified government system to implement their policy of indirect rule.

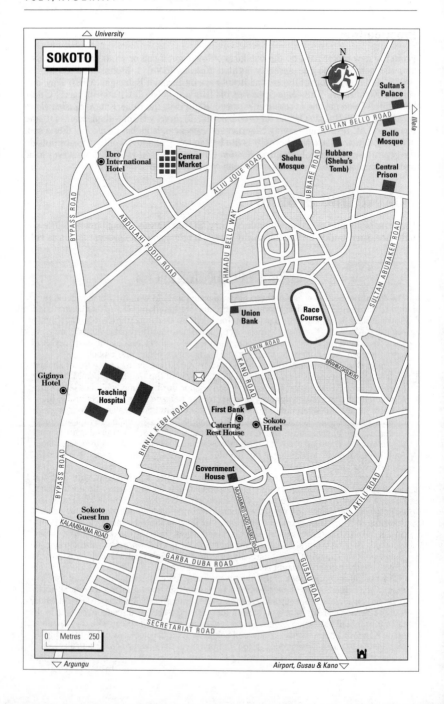

gious **capital** of the north after Usman dan Fodio's Islamic jihad led to the creation of the **Sokoto Khalifate** in 1807. The present emir is leader of all other Hausa emirates to this day, and effective spiritual leader of Muslim Nigeria. Modernization came slowly to this region as development goals conflicted with the khalif's own ideas about what "civilization" should entail. Thus, at the wish of the khalif, the railway line that pushed northwards as far as Kaura Namoda, in the 1920s, was never extended to Sokoto. The town's isolation from corrupting outside influences was thus preserved.

The Town

Despite Sokoto's rich history and its position as spiritual capital of the north, there's little in the way of sightseeing, unless you regard the city, with its calm self-esteem and well structured pattern of wide streets, as an attraction in its own right. The city's core is the **Sultan's Palace** and the nearby **Masallachin Shehu** (Shehu Mosque), on Sultan Bello Road. These buildings, with their Sudanic aura, are pleasant enough to look at, but you cannot go in. About halfway between the palace and the mosque is the **Hubbare**, the former home of Shehu Usman dan Fodio (located off Sultan Bello Road, it's a bit tricky to find, but if you're near the mosque, any kid will take you there). Take off your shoes before entering and be as respectful as possible. Inside the house is the **Shehu's Tomb**, where dan Fodio is buried with his companions. People from throughout the region still make pilgrimages to this spot to pay homage.

The **Sokoto Museum** exists only as the **Waziri Junaidu History and Culture Bureau**, on Alli Akilu Road. The few exhibits are poorly maintained and you're not likely to find much of interest – unless you count some damaged musical instruments, Arabic scripts and letters from members of the ruling family.

You won't be disappointed by Sokoto's **Central Market**, adjacent to the central motor park. It's one of the biggest and best stocked in the entire Sahel Region – an amazingly well-planned, clean, modern site with a startling abundance of flowering plants and trees. And for what seems like such an isolated city there's a remarkable variety of stuff here – if you're lucky, you could find a **produce** selection ranging from pineapples, coconuts and mangos to millet, sorghum, a mass of vegetables and all the usual proliferation of spices and condiments. There's a large **cloth emporium** with busy tailors who sew to order on the spot. Prices, especially for cloth, are cheap when compared with elsewhere in Nigeria and mostly fixed: there's little or no haggling here. When you're tired of drifting around, a pleasant and inexpensive **outdoor restaurant** has been set up round the large, green-and-white tower that dominates the whole area.

Practicalities

Sokoto's main commercial district runs along Kano Road, where you'll find the major **banks** and hotels. The **GPO** is on Birnin Kebbi Road, not far away. **Public transport** in Sokoto is based almost entirely on motorcycles (*kabuski* or *kabukabu*).

Accommodation
Sokoto doesn't have an overwhelming selection of hotels, especially in the lower price brackets, but there are a number of good-value places.

Catering Rest House, Shinkafi Rd (☎060/232 505). All rooms S/C, with AC suites and more spartan doubles. Not up to *Shukura* standards, but still good value. ①–②.

Giganya Hotel, By-Pass Rd (☎060/231 262; Fax 060/231 460). Big five-star hotel with AC, and satellite TV in the spacious double rooms. Excellent basement disco ("Nite club"), despite the lack of alcohol. ⑤.

Ibro International Hotel, Abdullahi Fodio Rd (☎060/232 510). Excellent location next to the central market and motor park, and offers luxuries like AC, satellite TV and hot water. There's a good restaurant in the hotel and a small supermarket across the street. The best bargain in town. ①–③.

Mabera Guest Inn, 15 Darge Rd (☎060/232 178). Inexpensive but decent S/C, AC accommodation in a lively part of town. ②.

Shukura Hotel (☎060/230 006; Fax 060/234 648). One of the town's best: efficient, with comfortable double rooms with AC, TV and telephones. The AC video bar and restaurant are also popular. ③–⑤.

Sokoto Guest Inn, Kalaimbaina Rd (☎060/233 205). Good-value accommodation, with a restaurant and pool. ①–③.

Sokoto Hotel, Kano Rd (☎060/232 126). Offers a range of good-value S/C rooms with or without AC. Other attractions are the restaurant, the bar (with beer), and the swimming pool. ②–④.

Argungu

Ninety-nine kilometres southwest of Sokoto by good paved roads, **ARGUNGU** makes for an interesting excursion. Well known for its annual fishing festival in February – photo library shots of which have been reproduced on countless occasions – the town also has the excellent **Kanta Museum** with historical relics and traditional artefacts, and an impressive **Emir's Palace**. You can **stay** at the *Government Catering Resthouse* or the *Grand Fishing Hotel* (☎060/550 547).

Some history

Argungu has an illustrious place in the annals of West African history. The **Kingdom of Kebbi**, which had formerly been an outlying province of the **Songhai empire**, was founded near here in the early sixteenth century by **Muhammedu Kanta**, a general in the army of the Songhai emperor Askia Muhammed. When the Songhai invaded the Hausa states between 1512 and 1517, Kanta revolted against his overlords, and established himself as an independent ruler of the area between the Niger and Sokoto rivers. The capital of his kingdom was Argungu or "Birnin Lelaba Dan Badan" as it was named at that time.

Later, Argungu was one of the pockets of traditionalist resistance to the Fulani jihad led by Usman dan Fodio, and was never successfully conquered by Sokoto. An apocryphal account even derives the town's name from the Fulani moan *Ar sunyi gungu* (Oh dear, they've regrouped), since their invasions were repeatedly repulsed. Another theory has it that the original name of the town was changed to Argungu from the Kebbi saying *Ar! Mu yi gungu*, a fishing expression meaning "Let us get together in one place".

The Kebbi emirate fell to the British at the beginning of the twentieth century and became part of the Northern Nigeria protectorate. Although historians date the fishing festival back to the era of the great Kunta in the sixteenth century, the festival as it exists today dates from 1934, when the Sultan of Sokoto made his first peaceful visit to Argungu.

The fishing festival

Most years, in late January or February (sometimes even as late as March), the **fishing festival** takes place on a stretch of the **Sokoto River** (the **Rima** to people who live here) known as *Matan Fada*, where it braids into a multitude of channels. Here, thousands of huge *giwan ruwa* fish (some weighing as much as 100kg) are penned in a confined, shallow lake. On the chosen day, the signal is given and hundreds of fishermen plunge into the waters watched by thousands of onlookers. Using only hand-held "butterfly" or clap nets called *homa*, and hollowed calabashes with an opening at the top, they thrash around among their prey. Fishing is banned for the rest of the year in this part of the river, and rituals are performed to try to ensure the biggest possible catches. The fishing show, however, is only the climax of a festival that spreads over three days, and includes a long list of other sporting activities and competitions (box-

MOVING ON FROM SOKOTO

The main **motor park** in the north of the city handles regular transport for **Kano** and **Illela**, the bordertown facing **Birnin-Konni** in Niger. Note that the shortest distance between Sokoto and Katsina is to head into Niger and follow the Niamey–Kano highway from Birnin-Konni through **Maradi** and back into Nigeria from the north, although this requires a visa for Niger and a multi-entry visa for Nigeria. Vehicles to **Argungu** (and on to the Nigeria–Niger–Benin border at Gaya/Malanville) are less frequent, as too are vehicles heading south down the A1 to **Yelwa** and **Kontagora**.

If you want to order or confirm a ticket on an airplane, Nigeria Airways is at 2 Sultan Ibrahim Dasuki Rd (☎060/233 139). For international travel arrangements, the *Sokoto Hotel* has an accredited travel agency that can make airline bookings.

ing, archery, camel and donkey races), punctuated with endless speeches by commissioners of Kebbi State government, local leaders and sponsors. Since 1970 a big agricultural fair has also been part of the festival, and in Mala, downstream from Argungu, the **Kabanci displays** are another side show, with canoe races and swimming and diving contests. If you want to see the festival, it's imperative to make room reservations in advance through the Ministry of Information, on Secretariat Road, Sokoto, since rooms at the available accommodation in Argungu get solidly booked. There are also several guesthouses in nearby Birnin Kebbi, the state capital.

Maiduguri

The north's closest major town to the Cameroon border, **MAIDUGURI** is the first (or last) stop in Nigeria for many overlanders. The town is incredibly flat and hot, and has that quiet, nothing-happening feeling characteristic of so many places in the arid Sahel regions. If it wasn't for the **neem trees** lining the neatly laid-out avenues and providing a bit of respite from the merciless sun, you might find it unbearable. But as capital of the **Borno State**, it has a good infrastructure and makes a reasonable resting point for further travels in the arid north. The people of Borno are largely **Kanuri**, and women, especially, are elegant dressers and hairstylists and often wear nose rings. If you spend a night here – or more – you may also come to appreciate a second level of life in Maiduguri, as experienced by the many students from all over Nigeria, who live on the Maiduguri university campus and probably feel almost as much strangers in this northwestern outpost as you do.

Accommodation

Maiduguri has all kinds of **accommodation** ranging from cheap lodgings to international-standard hotels.

Borno State Hotel, 1 Talba Rd, Old GRA (☎076/231 333). Heading out of town, turn right at the Eagle roundabout. S/C rooms with fan or AC. ②.

Deribe Hotel, Deribe St, off Kashim Ibrahim Rd (☎076/232 663; Fax 076/232 662). Pleasant rooms with AC and satellite TV and the town's best pool. Among the nicest of the international-standard hotels. ④.

Dujima International Hotel, off Shehu Laminu Way, opposite the Open Air Theatre, in the old GRA (☎076/233 297). Rooms range from single rooms to business suites with satellite TV. ③–⑦.

Lake Chad Hotel, Kashim Ibrahim Rd (☎076/232 746). Doubles and suites with AC and satellite TV. Looking slightly worn, despite extras like the pool and tennis courts. ③.

Maiduguri International Hotel, Stadium Rd (☎076/235 979 or 984; Fax 076/235 871). Huge hotel opened by the state government in the late 1990s, with all the usual five-star facilities. What with all

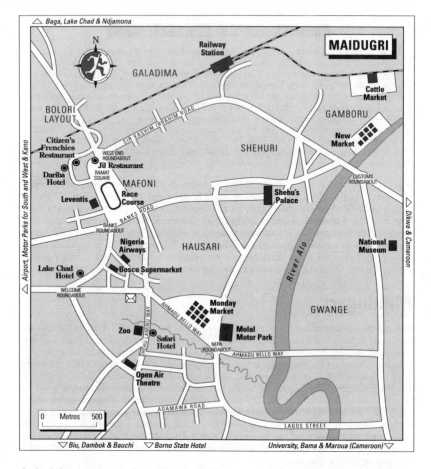

the bookshops, restaurants, hair salons and so on, it's almost a tourist attraction in itself, although perhaps a bit far from the city centre. ④–⑤.

Mairi Palace, Mairi Ward, off the Bama road (☎076/232 168). Recommended hotel in the south of town, not too far from the university, with comfortable rooms and a bar in the garden. ①–②.

Merry Joe Guest Inn, Bolori Layout (☎076/231 261). Clean and pleasant S/C rooms, with or without AC, starting at less than half the price of the upmarket places, plus a good bar and an inexpensive restaurant. The *Sefcon Hotel*, just behind, is similar. ①.

Safari Hotel, 21 Shehu Laminu Way (☎076/234 692). A range of AC rooms, plus a restaurant and a bar without alcohol. ①.

The Town

Thanks to its fairly modern origins, Maiduguri is a well-planned city and easy to get around. Its characteristic landmarks are the **roundabouts** which have come almost to designate neighbourhoods and are thus convenient markers for orientation. The major ones include **"West End"**, with three large cast-iron fish in the middle, **"Banks"**, a large

THE KANEM-BORNU EMPIRE

The rise of the **Kanem-Bornu empire** was a consequence of the spreading Sahara and the subsequent migration of nomadic peoples who concentrated in the **Lake Chad** basin, in districts that had been covered in lake water in earlier times. Conflicts flared between the newcomers and established communities. The **Kanuri** (a people of distinctively Saharan origins, with a language quite unrelated to Hausa, whose distant ancestors are presumed to have farmed and hunted in the era of Saharan fertility) eventually gained the upper hand in the struggles, out of which arose the **Sefawa dynasty** which ruled over **Kanem** – the concretion of mini-states northeast of Lake Chad – from about 850 AD.

Oral history claims that the founder of the dynasty was **Sayf Dhi Yazam**, and that he was of Arabic origin. It is possible, and more likely, that the first dynastic family had Berber connections rather than Arab. Whatever the truth, the authority of the *Mai* (as the kings of the dynasty were known – they converted to Islam in the eleventh century) gradually spread over nomadic peoples, and the *Mai* came to be accepted as a divine ruler. In Mecca, a special guesthouse was built for Kanem pilgrims and in Spain, the court of El Mansur (1190–1214) in Seville numbered renowned Kanem poets among the courtiers.

The Bornu empire functioned as a channel for trade and the **exchange of ideas** across the Sahara, connecting the three major camel caravan routes from Tripoli, Egypt and Sudan. It was through Bornu power that Islam entered Nigeria from the twelfth century onwards, spreading peacefully across the northern Hausaland during the fourteenth century, and reaching as far as Yorubaland in the same period.

A new series of conflicts arose in the thirteenth century that incited **Mai Umar bin Idris** to emigrate west to Bornu. The new empire – now effectively Bornu, rather than Kanem – remained unstable until the end of the fifteenth century when **Mai Ali Gaji** came to power, put an end to dynastic squabbles and established a new capital at Gazargamo, the first permanent residence in more than a century. A new golden era was thus launched that reached its peak under the best known of the Bornu rulers – **Idris Aloma** – who ruled until 1603. He was a zealous Muslim reformer under whose reign Islam became the basis of Bornu ideology and who also achieved military advances by importing Turkish mercenaries and military advisors to instruct his troops in the use of muskets. Although the empire was among the most severely affected by the decline in trans-Saharan trade, Bornu was the only northern power to repulse dan Fodio's invasion. The Fulani did manage to attack the capital city and sent the king into retreat, but a Bornu *malam* (teacher) named **Al-Kanemi** organized a counter-offensive that successfully drove out the enemy. Al-Kanemi took the title of Shehu and moved the capital to **Kukawa**, near Lake Chad. In a later power struggle with the Sefawa dynasty, the Mais were defeated and the dynasty abolished. As a result, Al-Kanemi became the Bornu ruler and his sons started a new dynasty, drawing to a close the dynasty of the Sefawa, which, with its origins in the ninth century and a final date of 1846, may have been the world's most enduring line of royal rulers. Kukawa on the other hand, still exists today, ruled by the Shehu ancestors of Al-Kanemi.

Maiduguri gained its importance as a regional capital only after 1907 when the British reinstated the Shehu in the new town where they had established a military base. It wasn't until after independence, however, that the town was linked to Kaduna by rail and thus gained a slight advantage for its beef, leather and groundnut exports.

spikey phallic symbol, **"Welcome"**, a green-and-white concrete statue, **"Post Office"** near the GPO, **"NEPA"** near the market, **"Customs"** near the museum, and **"Eagle"**, with a large eagle statue in the south of town. The easiest way to get around town is by collective taxi to one of these roundabouts, and walking from there to your destination.

Maiduguri doesn't have much in the way of sights, and any exploring, at almost any time of year, should be done in the early hours before the town gets intolerably hot. An obvious place to start is at the **Shehu's Palace**. A colonial-style building with a clock tower, the palace has no organized tours, but if you tell the guards in front that you're interested in visiting they usually try to arrange it. Inside, the emphasis is more on modern administration than Bornu history: after taking off your shoes, a guide trails you from one scorching patio to the next, making a point of showing you every room with a typewriter or a leatherette armchair.

Much better for a historical overview is the small **museum**, near the customs warehouse on Bama Road, which provides a useful introduction to the customs of different peoples living in Bornu State. Artefacts – pottery, jewellery, mats, utensils – are well displayed with accompanying texts. In the courtyard there's an interesting reproduction of an "Arab" tent with characteristic furnishings.

Maiduguri's colourful **Monday Market** now takes place in a covered cement building in the commercial centre of town. The **New Market** sprouted a few years back in the Gamboru district near Customs roundabout. Apart from all the usual gear, it's well known locally for its attractive hand-woven **mats** made of Lake Chad reeds.

The **zoo**, located across from the *Safari Hotel* at the end of Shehu Laminu Way (Mon–Fri 9am–noon & 3–6pm, Sat & Sun 9am–6pm), is actually not bad, whatever your feelings about zoos. Many of the animals are captives without cages, and are kept in place by large ditches surrounding reproductions of their habitats. Shaded in a forest of neem trees, the zoo and park are excellent places for a picnic, and the whole town seems to turn out here on Sundays.

When the afternoon sun begins to drum down, head to one of the town's two **swimming pools**. The best is at the *Deribe Hotel*, which has crystal-clear water, but unfortunately serves no beer. The more central *Lake Chad Hotel* has murkier water and more people, but there is a poolside bar. Some dilemma.

Eating, drinking and nightlife

Many **restaurants** are found near the main roundabouts. In the Galdima area, you'll get pounded yam or other Nigerian staples at the *Feel at Home Restaurant*, right at the Galadima junction. Nearby, *Pujo Snacks Bar & Restaurant*, opposite *Travellers Palace Hotel*, is an excellent large place serving both African and continental dishes. Between

---

MOVING ON FROM MAIDUGURI

WITHIN NIGERIA
There are several **motor parks** in Maiduguri. To **Kano** and Biu (the Calabar road), the motor park is just outside the town gates along Airport Road. To **Baga**, Geidam and Gashua, the park is just up from the West End, past the railway tracks. To **Bama** (the Cameroon road), the motor park is after the Customs roundabout on Ring Road.

   Trains run to Port Harcourt (change at Kafanchan junction for Lagos); check the latest schedules at the local station.

   There are 3 weekly **flights** on Nigeria Airways to **Lagos**, via **Yola** (Fri), via **Abuja** (Sun), and direct (Mon). Nigeria Airways is at 19 Hospital Rd (☎076/232 743), and at the airport. Chanchangi Airline operates a daily morning flight to **Kano**.

TO CAMEROON AND CHAD
If you're making the short crossing of Cameroon to **Ndjamena**, Chad, start off by taking a vehicle from the **Gamboru motor park** on the northeast side of Maiduguri (you won't need a Cameroon visa if you're simply passing through this narrow neck of the country en route to Chad). Four-and six-seater taxis shuttle to the village of Gamboru (Nigerian exit formalities). From **Fotokol** on the Cameroonian side (where you'll have to seek out the *douaniers* and *gendarmes*, 1km away, but they're pleasant enough) you take a much more expensive ride to **Kousseri**, 100km away. For Kousseri and onward details into **Chad**, see opposite.

the *Dujima* and *Safari* hotels, along Shehu Laminu Way, *Hanna's Restaurant* serves assorted African dishes. *Jil Restaurant* is a popular place near the West End round-about, with English and African dishes and fresh juices. Another popular place is *Citizen's Frenchies Restaurant*, behind Savannah Bank off Kashim Ibrahim Road, where you can wash down the Nigerian and European food with wine, beer and CNN.

Because of the strong Muslim influence, nights in Maiduguri tend to be tranquil. But the presence of the university, which has a large proportion of students from the less Islamic regions of the south, means there are a lot of young people out to drink and have a good time, and a few decent **clubs** to dance away the nights. One of the most popular is the *Chez Coan Nightclub* on Bama Road, near the West End roundabout in the Galadima area, which also offers lodging. It's young and lively and also features a half-decent restaurant. In addition, the *Alliance Française* at 3 Yerima Rd, Old GRA, has a regular *disco-soirée* with a good mix of music, that attracts expats and some of the university crowd.

The Far East

Although Maiduguri feels like the end of the road – and certainly most Nigerians consider the town is already at the back of beyond – it is still 100km further to the borders of Niger, Chad or Cameroon. If you're driving in far northeastern Nigeria, it's as well to know that it's an area of some political sensitivity where you should notify the authorities of your movements before setting off from each town or village.

To Lake Chad

Getting to **Lake Chad** is somewhat difficult, and police are suspicious of people who want to go to the region whether they've come by their own means or with public transport. An additional problem is the total retreat of the lake itself from Nigerian territory over the last few years. The place to go if you want to check out the situation is **Baga**. Taxis head here from Maiduguri. When you get into town, check in with the police, who won't take long anyhow to discover your arrival. There's a customs and immigration post at Baga and, if the water is high, foot travellers may be able to get a boat across into Chad: the village of Baga Sola is 76km away to the northwest, about three days by pole and paddle or a full day by outboard. If there's no water, there's **accommodation** at the *Baga State Hotel*.

Bama and around

BAMA, on the main road from Maiduguri to Cameroon (still in Borno State), is a Kanuri town with a large market – Saturday is the big day. There's a good *Guest House* on the southern side of town, which features occasional gatherings with dancing and *brukutu*, locally made Guinea-corn beer.

If you're driving a 4WD vehicle, and want to experience the **old route to Cameroon**, it starts with a left turn down a sandy, but motorable track, 38km down the A13 Bama to Gwoza road from Maiduguri. The track soon leads into a dry riverbed which you follow to **Ashigashiya** and then, out of the riverbed, along tracks to **Mora** in Cameroon – about 25km in all.

Adamawa State

The wedge of **Adamawa State** spreads from the Sahel near Maiduguri south along the mountainous Cameroon borderlands. It's a huge and very little travelled region but, if you can devote the necessary time, offers some of Nigeria's best rewards in terms of landscapes and traditional rural communities.

As you enter the state south of Gwoza, the scenery starts to become spectacularly spiky and volcanic. There are terrific hikes up into the **Mandara Mountains** east of the A13 Madagli–Mubi road. One route starts off from **Chambula**, about 12km southwest of Madagli, and goes some 10km southeast to **Mildo Market**. About 5km further you reach a school (keep asking, young people generally speak English and there's even hope of flagging down transport, especially during the market on Tuesday) from where you can expect (or hope) to be taken around the district. Bring food and flexibility.

The payoff for such remote meanderings is **SUKUR**, the seat of a once powerful mountain kingdom. There's a remarkable stone causeway – product of ancient civil engineering – from the school up to this village. Very few travellers make it this far and the people are refreshingly welcoming. They've set up a small "**guesthouse**", a traditional round hut with straw mats to sleep on, and have started a regional artefacts museum. Neither is exactly a reason for coming here, but the village itself is and people are more than willing to share their guinea corn and green leaf soup and show you around their unusually constructed compounds – round huts held together with stone, mud and thatch and surrounded by a protective wall. You can **visit the king** (*heedi*); slow clapping to greet him meets with enthusiastic approval. Though he doesn't speak English, he's remarkably hospitable, and – through translators – seems eager to recount the history of Sukur, from the early slave raids to the period when this village was part of Cameroon. People don't expect payment, even, as yet, for staying in the guesthouse, but given the level of generosity, you'll find it hard not to reciprocate with a gift. Photos seem appropriate (a Polaroid camera would come in handy here), as do hard-to-come-by pharmaceuticals. Even food makes a good gift – it's a long way to the market.

Further south along the A13, **Kamale** is a village with an amazing **volcanic plug** nearby – accessible from Michika, 20km south of Chambula. This whole area has everything in common with its Cameroonian counterpart and mountain people don't generally draw much of a boundary line (see p.1129).

Yola and Numan

The Adamawa State capital is **YOLA**, an unexceptional, flat, spacious town near the banks of the Benue. Yola is fairly accommodating, and the cheaper **hotels** tend to be a bit less expensive than elsewhere. The *Bekaji Guest Inn*, 21 Galadima Aminu Way (①), Jimeta, is centrally located, next to Lamido Cinema – showing evening movies. *Maiyaki Lodge*, in the Karewa GRA Ext. (☎075/624 289; ①) is a pleasant compound with decent S/C rooms. For something more upmarket, try the *Yola International Hotel*, on Kashim Ibrahim Road (☎075/625 739; Fax 075/624 538; ⑤), with high standards of comfort and efficiency. If you need to travel fast, there are daily **flights** out of Yola on Nigeria Airways to Lagos and Maiduguri: their office (☎075/624 713) is on Main Street in Jimeta, the new suburb on the riverbank 7km from the city centre.

If you're travelling on the **A345 Bauchi–Numan–Yola road** be sure to do so by day, and if you're going by public transport, get a window seat on the left. Gombe to Numan, however, is a superb stretch of scenery and, if you've got your own transport, there are some fantastic **hikes and climbs** in the Mouri mountains. Don't stay in **Numan**, 60km west of Yola and an older town somewhat left behind by the state capital's surging modernism: both its hotels are dreadful. **Tangale Hill** near Kaltungo, is a steep and stunning volcanic plug and a brisk three-hour climb, but you'll need permission from the emir of the little town and help from local men in guiding you up.

Gashaka-Gumpti National Park and Gembu

Dramatic highland regions span Adamawa and **Taraba** states – to the southeast of Yola the **Atlantika Mountain Range**, to the southwest the **Shebshi Mountains** (with

2042-metre Vogel Peak), and, in the far south, in the corner of Nigeria tucked into western Cameroon, the verdant **Mambila Plateau**. Although the region – a high grassland plateau with a pleasant climate and sparse cattle ranches and tea plantations – is similar to Obudu (see p.992), few travellers venture here. It comprises some of the least explored, most exciting and unknown territory in the whole of Africa.

An area of nearly 7000 square kilometres of mountain forests and savannah abutting the border – still harbouring a sizeable **chimpanzee** population and, after an absence of several decades, elephants – is now protected as the **Gashaka-Gumpti National Park**. This is the site of a major World Wildlife Fund project in collaboration with the Adamawa and Taraba state governments, responsible for the Gumti and Gashaka parts of the park respectively. Efforts to gear up the park for visitors are in progress at the park headquarters in **SERTI**, a village on the "main" road between Yola and Gembu, where there is some simple **accommodation** (①). The park entrance is 15km to the southeast. Besides the rich biodiversity and hydrological importance of the national park, it is thought that the park also harbours such rare species as leopards and lions, as well as giant forest hogs and hartebeests.

In **GEMBU**, the main town of the region, 137km south of Serti and 430km south of Yola (very hard and slow travel by occasional bush taxis or land rovers), or 220km southeast of Wukari (see below), there's a half-decent **hotel**, though it has only sporadic electricity and water (①). An hour's trek towards Cameroon from Gembu takes you to the red-clay valley of the **Donga River**, a superb sight as it snakes through the jungle. You can cross by canoe or raft, and climb a towering rocky peak on the other side for magnificent views (two hikes/4WD routes lead up into Cameroon near here, but ascertain driving viability locally). Another excursion from Gembu takes you to the **Highland Tea Plantation** and factory, beyond Kakara (a village 30km northwest of Gembu). You'll be the first traveller the management here has seen in a while, and they'll not only give you a tour of the place, but let you stay in the club (①), watch TV and videos, eat and drink beer, before sending you off with a kilo of produce.

Wukari to Cameroon – the Dumbo Trek

The bustling market town of **WUKARI** has a number of lodging options: try the good-value *Hospitality Motel*, IBB Road (☎041/20559; ①–②) or the central and very inexpensive *Isaku Hotel*, at the junction of Takum Road and Rafia Road (①). From here, head for **TAKUM**, where the highlands ahead begin to make their presence felt (the *Dadin Kowa Supper Inn*, on the Yola road, is a reasonable place to stay; ①). Takum is at the southern end of the paved road and beyond it, looping into the green hills, with bananas and fleshy jungle plants increasingly conspicuous, there is just an earth track, mostly in reasonable condition, passing over innumerable frog-filled streams up to the village of **Bissaula** (also spelled Bissuala). You'll be able to get transport as far as here, though don't miss any vehicles that are going, as they're not numerous.

The Michelin map used to mark as a "recognized track" the route that snakes from Bissaula to **Dumbo** on the Bamenda Highlands Ring Road: an optimistic gesture, as it consists only of the roughest footpath, the first few kilometres of which scale a steep, rocky, root-entangled, forest-smothered escarpment, inaccessible to any vehicle. If you are keen to do some **trekking**, though, it's a winner: a moderately tough two-day hike (about 40km) that takes in towering trees, squealing parrots, leaping monkeys, thatched-hut hamlets in smoky forest clearings, and lines of porters (mostly portering on their own accounts, beer, cigarettes and cloth). When you reach the top, it seems half of southern Nigeria is spread out below.

You shouldn't set off trekking on your own – orientation here is very difficult – but for about ₦3000 (or CFA20,500) you can hire the services of a **porter** to walk up to Dumbo with your luggage (the Nigerian immigration post will stamp you out and write

"Footing" in your passport). You can carry your own luggage, of course, but you should join with a group for the initial stages of the trek. You walk for about two hours through lush forest and farm plots, then start climbing the steep scarp, which takes a couple of hours to the top. People generally leave Bissaula late afternoon, and either spend the night in a village at the foot of the scarp and then set off at 4am, or reach the top of the scarp after dark and spend the night in the village there. With an early start on day two you can be in Dumbo by the evening, but it's less exhausting to arrive mid-morning on day three. You should be aware of the fact that the Cameroonian immigration and customs post at Dumbo isn't frequently blessed with tourists and may try hard to extract presents from you. If you take photos on the trek, try to be discreet – it's a slightly sensitive border area – and remove film before you get to Dumbo.

CAMEROON

CAMEROON

The **landscapes of Cameroon** are exceptional. The country stretches from the fringes of the Sahara in the north to the borders of Congo and Gabon in the south and takes in every African variation in between; from equatorial rainforest (some of the continent's most unexploited tracts) to moist, tree-scattered savannah; from dry grassy plains to bucking volcanic ranges flecked with crater lakes; from gaunt rocky massifs to the hot swampy basin of Lake Chad; and, to cap it all, the highest mountain on this side of the continent – the 4095 metres of Mount Cameroon – rising direct from the ocean shore to an impressive cloud-wreathed summit. For good measure, the country also has some entrancing beaches and several large parks, with rewarding quantities of wildlife, including species found nowhere else in the region. At the simple level of tourism, it's hard to oversell Cameroon – it's simply the most dramatic country in West Africa.

There's another side to Cameroon in its hugely stimulating cultural make-up, which exhibits some striking **ethnic distinctions**: the Muslim sultanates of the north are reminiscent of northern Nigeria and also have strong Arab connections, but exist alongside the avowedly non-Muslim people of the mountainous Rhumsiki district; in the forests of the far south, the so-called "Pygmies" – the original inhabitants – still live a hunting and gathering life largely untroubled by the concerns of the modern nation state; and in the mountains and pasturelands of the country's western "bulge", a remarkable complex of kingdoms has developed over the last four hundred years, speaking dozens of Bantoid languages (closely related to Bantu). This is the only country in West Africa with a large **Bantu-speaking** population (the Bantu languages, including Swahili and Zulu, are some of the most important in Africa), which gives the south much in common with the Central African region. Coupled with its natural diversity, it's a country that can claim to embody cultural elements of the entire continent.

Cameroon has a colonial past of German, French and British occupation. With the current division between Francophone and Anglophone in every aspect of national life, impressions of contrast and fragmentation are never far away. Recently the old Anglo-Francophone tensions have flared up fiercely, leading to calls for secession in the west. And as the economy began faltering in the 1990s, opposition has become more vocal in the northern regions as well. Wherever your travels take you, the prospects for political debate are good, though due to widespread police harassment, people are still wary whose ears their commentary may fall on.

The increasing importance of **tourism** as a source of foreign exchange has led to some improvement in official attitudes to foreign visitors. The searches and controls that once dogged visitors from the moment of arrival are no longer so aggressive. There are, however, still numerous roadblocks – little havens for police and custom officials to extract dash money – throughout the country. If you wander off the beaten tracks leading to selected, officially promoted sites, you may well attract suspicion. And the tourist industry has upmarket expectations: backpackers who sleep in D-class hotels and cram into bush taxis are still prone to be put down as *pauvres blancs,* and may experience the disdain of local law officers.

Where to go

Cameroon's main city, **Douala**, is a seething, sweltering metropolis that wins few accolades. Fortunately, an hour's drive from Douala, the black-sand beaches of Limbé, in **South West Province**, are a good, quick getaway. Between the strands, in the rich soil

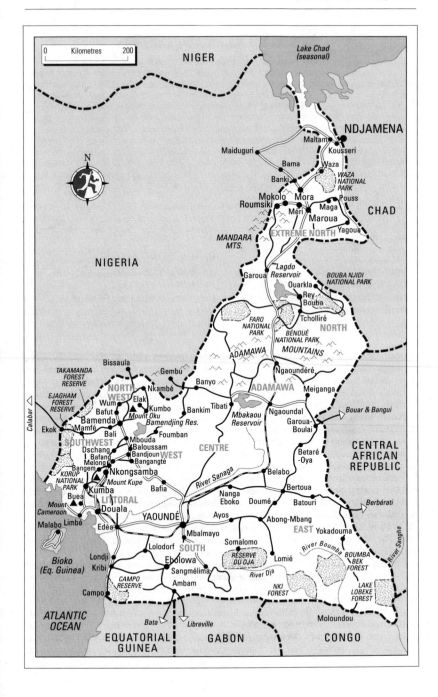

FACTS AND FIGURES

The **Republic of Cameroon** (or *République du Cameroun* to Francophones) covers 475,000 square kilometres, an area twice the size of Britain and somewhat larger than California, with a population estimated at more than fourteen million. The name derives from *camarões*, the Portuguese for prawns, which the first European visitors found in large quantities in the Wouri River. The common reference to **"Cameroons"** is a legacy of the colonial division into two Cameroons – French and British – a dual heritage preserved in the official bilingualism (easily dominated by French). The country has been ruled since 1982 by **Paul Biya**, long the head of the Rassemblement Démocratique du Peuple Camerounais (RDPC), the country's sole political party until opposition parties were legalized in 1990. The country's foreign debt, at £6 billion ($9.6 billion), stands at more than three times the value of its annual exports of goods and services – a huge figure for the country's relatively small population, equivalent to £425 ($680) for every Cameroonian, a sum few could expect to earn in a year.

Cameroon is divided into ten administrative **provinces**, with governors appointed by the president. You may find their names confusing at first, especially in western Cameroon, in that, for example South West Province extends further north than West Province. The provinces and their capitals are:

Centre/Centre (Yaoundé)	**North West/Nord Ouest** (Bamenda)
South/Sud (Ebolowa)	**Adamawa/Adamaoua** (Ngaoundéré)
East/Est (Bertoua)	**North/Nord** (Garoua)
Littoral/Littoral (Douala)	**Extreme North/Extrême Nord** (Maroua)
South West/Sud Ouest (Buéa)	
West/Ouest (Bafoussam)	

beneath Mount Cameroon, the dense vegetation pushes right to the water's edge, although it has increasingly been cleared to create plantations of coffee, bananas, rubber trees and oil palms. **Mount Cameroon**, a still active volcano, offers a challenging – but perfectly feasible – trekking ascent. To the north of the mountain, the country drops towards the Nigerian border and the **Korup rainforest**, now an accessible national park.

North West and **West** provinces (the former predominantly Anglophone, the latter mostly Francophone) are the most densely populated parts of Cameroon, and contain some of the country's most popular sites. West Province (the Province de l'Ouest) is relatively well-equipped for tourists, with a developed infrastructure of roads, hotels and other facilities, and even a quite cosmopolitan feel in the larger towns. Nevertheless, the landscapes are often rugged. Together, these provinces form probably the easiest part of Cameroon in which to strike out on your own; visiting the Bamiléké district and **Foumban**, with its Sultan's Palace and major crafts market; the **traditional chiefdoms** of the Bamoun Tikar and others around the 400-kilometre red-earth **Ring Road**; and the beautiful **Grassfields** area through which the Ring Road circles. The whole of this upland region is renowned for its thatched architecture and animated traditional life.

The capital, **Yaoundé**, is climatically a better city to live and work in than Douala, and a more relaxed place to rest up from travels. But it remains a fairly aggressive metropolis with its share of tension. The vast **plateau** that stretches to the east, covered with huge tracts of hardwood rainforest – sapele, mahogany, iroko and obiche – has been little logged (in either sense) and renders great expanses of the **Central**, **South** and **East** provinces impenetrable. A number of **"Pygmy"** bands, including the Baka, hunt and gather in the jungle, and this is also the domain of **gorillas**, which are quite prolific in certain areas. The Campo and Dja reserves are remote and have virtually no facilities.

North of Yaoundé, the northern sectors of Central and Eastern provinces are an immense, empty savannah, patched with forest. Together with the gaunt **Adamawa Range**, they effectively cut the country in two and hinder north–south overland travel. Further north you come into pre-Sahelian grasslands and dusty bushcountry. The upper tributaries of the **Bénoué** (Benue) flow through this region, where you'll find the **Bénoué National Park** and **Bouba Ndjida National Park** – home to herds of elephants and buffalo, lions and the only native rhinos in West Africa.

In the far north, **Waza National Park**, in the flat plains, is Cameroon's outstanding faunal reserve, with, at the end of the dry season, good conditions of visibility for its elephants, lions, giraffe, ostriches and a host of antelope species clustering at the waterholes. To the west, a few hours away, the other worldlyvolcanic plugs of the **Mandara Mountains** are a beautiful, unsettling backdrop to the stony homeland of the non-Muslim Kirdi "mountain people". The northernmost tip of the country, leading up to what's left of **Lake Chad**, is usually dry, but floods under the waters of the **Logone** and **Chari** rivers during the brief, annual rains.

The people

The oldest group of people to have lived in Cameroon are the **"Pygmies"** of the south and southeast forests. Although forced onto the defensive by the expansion of the various Bantu-speaking groups (many have settled in small villages, notably in the area around Kribi), most of these people have opted for the traditional independence of the impenetrable rainforest where they continue to live by hunting and gathering.

Although, over the best part of two thousand years, there had been a gradual southeasterly spread of **Bantu-speaking** populations through the Cameroon region into central Africa, Bantu-speaking communities migrated in strength from the Adamawa range and settled along the coast from about the fifteenth century. The first to migrate were the **Bassa** and **Bakoko**, followed by the **Douala**. In the nineteenth century, pushed in a chain reaction by migrations engendered after the Fula Sokoto invasions in Nigeria, the **Fang, Ewondo** and **Eton** came from the plateaux in the east to settle in the central southern region around Yaoundé.

In the west of the country, waves of northern immigration between the sixteenth and nineteenth centuries saw the installation of **"Semi-Bantu"** peoples. The first to arrive were the **Tikar**, who probably came from the area near Ngaoundéré and who today live in semi-autonomous chiefdoms throughout the Grassfields. In the eighteenth century a splinter group broke away from the Tikar country to form the powerful **Bamoun** empire a little to the east. The **Bamiléké** – a fusion of peoples from the north, east and southwest whose arrival spread over three centuries – settled in the plateau region south of the Noun River. Now the country's largest single ethnic group, the Bamiléké are also numerous in Douala where they have come to control a good deal of the national economy.

The predominant group in the north is the **Fula** (also known as Foulbé or Peul) who settled in principalities (*lamidats*) around the early nineteenth century, bringing Islam with them. But the mountains of the far northwest are inhabited by staunchly non-Muslim groups known collectively as **Kirdi** – which just means "infidels". Pushed to these desolate extremities by the Muslim invasions of dan Fodio, they comprise numerous Adamawa- and Chadic-speaking peoples: the **Podoko, Fali, Kapsiki, Mafa** and **Bata**. Principally farmers, they grow millet in terraced gardens on the rocky slopes of the mountains.

The northern plains near Lake Chad are home to the **Choa**, semi-nomadic peoples of Arab origin, who share these open spaces with the **Kotoko** – descendants of the ancient Sao culture – who live from fishing and growing a few cereals. Near the Logone River live the **Toupouri, Massa** and **Mousgoum**, people of pre-Islamic belief who are increasingly becoming Islamicized.

Climate

The region around Mount Cameroon and the western mountains has the dubious benefit of one of the highest levels of **rainfall** in the world: Debundscha, 30km west of Limbé, is the second wettest place on earth, after Cherrapungi in India. The general pattern here and in **the south** can be divided into three approximate seasons: a period of relatively light but persistent rains from March to June; the long rainy period from July to October; and the dry season from November to February. Travel can involve great waits during the rains, especially to or from towns accessible only by track, such as Mamfé. Roads around the Grassfields are often unmotorable during the rains when even four-wheel-drive vehicles can have problems. The savannahs further north choke towards the end of the dry season with fine red laterite dust, blown up by the northerly *Harmattan*. Plants and crops turn rusty red, while lungs – and cameras – seize up.

Northern Cameroon, north of the Adamawa Plateau, has a different weather pattern, characterized by a long rainy season from May to October. Although travel in the north doesn't present any special problem during this period, note that the national parks are closed, depending on the rains, roughly between May and December. Overall, the **ideal time to visit** the country, taking into account the different regional patterns, is December and January.

AVERAGE TEMPERATURES AND RAINFALL

YAOUNDÉ

	Jan	Feb	Mar	Apr	May	June	July	Aug	Sept	Oct	Nov	Dec
Temperatures °C												
Min (night)	19	19	19	19	19	19	19	18	19	18	19	19
Max (day)	29	29	29	29	28	27	27	27	27	27	28	28
Rainfall mm	23	66	147	170	196	152	74	79	213	295	117	23
Days with rainfall	3	5	13	15	18	17	11	10	20	24	14	4

DOUALA

	Jan	Feb	Mar	Apr	May	June	July	Aug	Sept	Oct	Nov	Dec
Temperatures °C												
Min (night)	23	23	23	23	23	22	22	22	22	22	23	23
Max (day)	30	30	30	30	30	28	27	27	27	27	29	29
Rainfall mm	46	94	203	231	300	539	742	693	531	429	155	64
Days with rainfall	4	6	12	12	16	19	24	24	21	20	10	6

KOUSSERI

	Jan	Feb	Mar	Apr	May	June	July	Aug	Sept	Oct	Nov	Dec
Temperatures °C												
Min (night)	14	16	21	23	25	24	22	22	22	21	17	14
Max (day)	34	37	40	42	40	38	33	31	33	36	36	33
Rainfall mm	0	0	0	3	31	66	170	320	119	36	0	0
Days with rainfall	0	0	0	1	6	10	15	22	13	4	0	0

Arrivals

Getting to Cameroon is facilitated by the fact that Cameroon Airlines is one of Africa's best. Flying in, however, suffers the disadvantage of arrival in the rather heavy city of Douala (unless you use one of the few direct flights to Yaoundé or Garoua). Arriving overland from the east, Cameroon feels like the threshold of a new region, which it is, as you leave the confines of the Central African rainforest and enter West Africa.

■ Flights from Africa

Cameroon has **international airports** at Yaoundé and Garoua, but most foreign flights still arrive in Douala. **Cameroon Airlines** (UY) has a good network connecting African cities with Douala. West African flights to Douala on UY include: from **Lagos** (weekly); from **Abidjan** via Lagos (3 weekly); from Abidjan via **Cotonou** and Lagos (weekly); and non-stop from Cotonou (2 weekly).

Air Afrique (RK) flies to Douala from **Dakar**, via **Bamako**, Abidjan and Cotonou (weekly); from Abidjan via Cotonou (weekly); and from Abidjan via **Lomé** (2 weekly).

Elsewhere within West Africa, Nigeria Airways (WT) flies weekly from **Lagos** via **Port Harcourt** (weekly). From the Sahel capitals of Ouagadougou and Niamey, the most likely reasonable connections to Douala are via Abidjan.

Close political and economic ties ensure that Cameroon has good air links with its neighbours in **Central Africa**. Between RK, UY and Air Gabon (GN), direct flights originate in **Bangui** (2 weekly); **Brazzaville** (4 weekly); and **Libreville** (4 weekly). Three flights a week leave from both **Ndjamena**, Chad (on either UY or RK) and **Malabo**, Equatorial Guinea (on UY or GB).

From East Africa, UY flies twice weekly from **Nairobi** (always heavily booked); one service flies via **Kigali**, the other via **Kinshasa**. Kenya

Airways (KQ) also has two weekly non-stop connections from Nairobi. From southern Africa, there's a weekly UY flight from **Johannesburg** via **Harare** and Kinshasa.

■ Overland from Nigeria

The two main overland routes from Nigeria lead to **Mamfé** in the west of Cameroon and to **Mora** in the north. Coming in via the north, if you don't already have a Cameroon visa, you may be forced to head south (see "Red Tape", overleaf).

The western route is straightforward and involves getting a bush taxi from **Calabar to Ikom**. From here small taxis leave regularly to the busy border, where the tarmac ends abruptly, and where, after completing Nigerian customs and immigration formalities, you walk over the bridge spanning the Cross River and up the hill to the Cameroonian post at **Ekok**. Taxis from Ekok to Mamfé rattle along bumpy tracks through a beautiful but tortuous mountain region. A couple of variations on this route involve travelling by *pirogue*: one leads from Ekok down the Cross River to Mamfé, the other passes through the creeks from Calabar via the Oban Rainforest National Park. You can also take the coastal ferry from Calabar to Limbé (see p.1071).

The main northern route leads from **Maiduguri to Bama** over a good flat paved road, where taxi drivers love to get up a bit of speed. Forty kilometres separate Bama from the border post at Banki. From here you can get taxis across the unpaved plains (look out for antelope) to **Mora** and on to Maroua or up to Waza National Park.

■ Overland from Central African Republic

A reasonable, graded road runs from **Bouar**, in the west of Central African Republic, to the Cameroonian border post at **Garoua Boulai**, and a rougher route leads from **Bébérati** in Central African Republic to **Batouri**. In each case, the road deteriorates in Cameroon to become a difficult, bone-shaking track. To minimize the *piste*, either head north from Garoua Boulai to Meiganga and find continuing transport to Ngaoundal (273km from Garoua Boulai), where you can take the **train** southwest to **Yaoundé** or north to **Ngaoundéré**; or take transport south to Bertoua (260km from Garoua Boulai and 90km from Batouri), from where a 45-minute taxi ride will deposit you at the train station at Bélabo. For

---

The details in these practical information pages are essentially for use on the ground in West Africa and in Cameroon itself: for full practical coverage on preparing for a trip, getting here from outside the region, paperwork, health, information sources and more, see Basics, pp.3–83.

schedule details, see the relevant "Moving On" sections.

■ Overland from Equatorial Guinea and Gabon

The main road from **Bata** in **Equatorial Guinea** heads far inland to **Ebebiyin**, at the point where Gabon, Cameroon and Equatorial Guinea all meet. From here, you travel via **Ambam** to **Ebolowa** where there's the choice of heading either direct to Yaoundé or taking the roundabout but more scenic coastal route via **Kribi**. From Bata there's also the option of travelling straight north on the *piste* to the border town of **Elende** on the **Ntem River**, where you can pick up motorized *pirogues* travelling downriver to **Ipono**, a few kilometres south of **Campo**. From Ipono there are share taxis to Kribi.

You'll use the Ambam arrival point if you come from **Gabon**, reached from **Libreville** by heading to **Oyem**, where you can pick up transport to Ambam.

■ Overland from Chad

There is now a bridge between **Ndjamena** – the capital of Chad – and **Kousseri** in Cameroon. Details of this border are given on p.1133.

Red Tape

All passport holders (other than certain African nationals) need visas to enter Cameroon. In the past these have been given only with reluctance at Cameroon embassies other than in the applicant's country of residence.

In West Africa, **Calabar, Abidjan, Lagos** and **Dakar** are the only places which have Cameroonian embassies or consulates, and of these, Abidjan and Lagos have been refusing visa issue to transient travellers. The consulate in Calabar is slightly more flexible and may reluctantly issue visas, but you should try to exhaust all other options before arriving this far. There are no embassies or consulates in the Sahel states.

Broadly, **visas** are expensive (about $50), valid for three months, and must be activated within one month of issue. The main requirements are either a return air ticket, a letter of invitation from a Cameroonian resident, or proof of your intended onward route – including any other relevant visas.

It's not hard to extend your stay in any of the provincial capitals, but it's just as pricey as getting a visa.

If you are travelling from Central or East Africa, Cameroonian embassies and consulates can be found in **Central African Republic** (BP 935, Bangui; ☎61.16.87; Fax 61.18.57); **Chad** (rue des Poids Lourds, Ndjamena; ☎52.28.94); **Equatorial Guinea** (19 calle Rey Boncoro, Malabo; ☎24.64 or 26.63; Fax 22.63); **Congo Brazzaville** (BP 2136, rue Bayardelle, Brazzaville; ☎83.34.04; Fax 83.67.99); **Democratic Republic of Congo** (BP 1988, 171 bd du 30 Juin, Kinshasa; ☎34787); and **Ethiopia** (Bole Rd, Addis Ababa; ☎44.81.16 or 15.04.58; Fax 51.03.50).

■ At the border

When you arrive in Cameroon – especially if you come in overland – immigration officers may well want to check that you have what they consider to be **sufficient funds** to stay in the country. If your visa is in order, you shouldn't have difficulties getting in.

Health certificates are rarely checked on the road, but must be presented at the border. A certificate for yellow fever is always obligatory, and for cholera when there are epidemics in Cameroon or neighbouring countries. It's a good idea to have this latter certificate, though the jab itself is not considered effective (see p.31).

Money and Costs

Cameroon is part of the Central African economic zone and uses the CFA franc (CFA100 for 1 French franc; approx. CFA900 = £1; approx. CFA560 = US$1). Although West African CFA are exactly equivalent in value, the bills for the two regions are different and they cannot be used on the street or exchanged in the banks; as with the Nigerian Naira, it is possible to change West African CFA on the black market.

The best way to carry your money is in **French francs**: banks are more likely to accept French franc travellers' cheques, and the fees (which vary enormously from bank to bank) are lower than for other currencies. The only banks that change **sterling** (cash and travellers' cheques) are Standard Chartered, Amity and the main branches of BICEC (Banque Internationale du Cameroun Pour l'Epargne et le Credit). These banks also change **dollars**, as do SGBC (Societe

General de Banques au Cameroun) and the main branches of Credit Lyonnais Cameroun. SGBC is linked up with Western Union and it is possible to have **money transferred** to Cameroon within weeks or less, at no cost to the recipient.

To avoid the high bank charges for buying and selling pounds and dollars, a **black market** has developed, and you may be able to get up to ten percent more for your cash. It shouldn't be too hard to find one of the many businessmen needing foreign currency to buy goods abroad (ie in Nigeria) – try asking in your hotel.

Outside the two major cities, banks frequently run out of money, especially around payday (at the end of the month). **Credit cards** have made advances in big city hotels and some shops and restaurants, but can only be used for cash advances in the hotels you stay at – it is not possible to withdraw cash on credit cards in any bank.

There is no limit on importation of cash in any currency. There's an **export limit** on CFA francs of CFA20,000, unless you're going to a Central African franc zone country, in which case there's no limit. Any CFA you have left over when leaving Cameroon can, in theory, be exchanged at the fixed rate – if you can find a bank that admits to having French francs.

■ Costs

Cameroon is one of the three or four most expensive countries in West Africa. Living cheaply, and travelling on your own, you can probably expect to average CFA3000–5000 daily for **accommodation** (maybe CFA4000–7000 for two). Douala is the country's most expensive city for lodging by far, and even budget accommodation here is no bargain. Fortunately, there are numerous missions throughout the country that take in travellers, especially in the Anglophone North West and South West provinces. The country's most expensive **luxury hotels** charge up to CFA150,000 per night.

The cost of **public road transport** varies widely, depending on the remoteness of the route and the condition of the road. A general guideline is CFA1000 for half an hours' travel; in the rainy season, when the roads are bad, you'll pay more for the same distance.

Health

Cameroon poses no exceptional health problems. Malaria prophylaxis is essential throughout the country and there are multi-drug resistant strains. It's not recommended to drink the tap water in major towns; you can find bottled water everywhere except in small villages, though it becomes increasingly expensive the further north you go.

Cameroon, like most countries in West Africa, has a serious **schistosomiasis** (bilharzia) problem, though it's usually safe enough to use free-flowing stream water in the highlands, especially after recent rain. A major regional initiative based in Cameroon and assisted by USAID has helped to eradicate the disease from large areas of the country.

Medicines, mostly well within their sell-by date, are available over the counter in most pharmacies. **Dental care** in Douala and Yaoundé is excellent. **Hospital care** is also very good in the capital, although the "polyclinics" in the rest of the country are generally poorly stocked with medicines and equipment, and often dirty. You're expected to supply your own food in hospital.

Information and Maps

Abroad, tourist leaflets and information are best obtained at the Cameroon Airlines offices in Europe, listed below. The embassies too, may have some information, though it's probably the same stuff (see p.20).

It's well worth getting hold of some **maps** before arriving in Cameroon. Much the best-looking is the Macmillan road map of Cameroon, which has excellent city maps for Douala and Yaoundé on the flip side, but was published in 1988. The 1994 Institut Géographique National map is more up-to-date on newly surfaced roads,

---

CAMEROON AIRLINES

UK 44 Conduit St, London W1 (☎0171/734 7778).

France 12 bd des Capucines, Paris 7500 (☎43.12.30.10); and 55 pl de la République, Lyons (☎78.92.87.89).

Germany Speicherstrasse 2, 60327 Frankfurt (☎69 23 20 62); and Im Taubengrund 23, 65451 Kelsterbach/Main (☎61 07 60 37).

Italy via Vittorio Veneto, 93, Rome (☎84.11.81).

Switzerland 12 quai Gi Gruisan, Geneva (☎20.28.44).

but inaccurate about the year-round viability of many others and less clearly designed. Both maps are at 1cm:15km. The Michelin #953 is good, though you need the #955 as well if you want coverage of the southernmost hundred kilometres of the country. Within Cameroon, some maps can be found at the bigger city bookshops.

Getting Around

The main choice for travelling around Cameroon is between road and rail. The roads can be OK, though the good-quality paved sections are often separated by endless kilometres of rough dirt track, while the trains only cover certain very limited routes – barely venturing into the north or west, for example. As for flying, Cameroon Airlines cover a good deal of the country, though at a price.

■ By road

Although 35,000km of roads crisscross Cameroon, only about 4300km are paved. Even those are often in decay, with sections washed out by floods or pitted with potholes. Less-used dirt roads in particular can also be blocked for several days by overturned vehicles or collapsed bridges.

That said, the roads around and between **Douala** and **Yaoundé** are always reliable, as are those from Douala and Yaoundé to **Bamenda** or **Foumban** via Bafoussam (though not via **Mamfé**, which some maps show as the main road).

Western Cameroon has a reasonable road network and there's a long-unrealized plan to surface the Bamenda highlands Ring Road. The north is

well served by the highway which runs between **Ngaoundéré** and **Maltam**, past five national parks.

The entire **centre** of the country, however, lacks a good system, the **Adamawa Plateau** providing a formidable obstacle. Between **Yaoundé** and **Ngaoundéré**, where the dirt roads are quite appalling, you'd be wiser taking the train – in fact you can even take a car on the train, though that option has become quite expensive (CFA95,000) and is sometimes unsafe for the car. In the east of the country, the dense forest is another barrier to overland travel, and there are no good paved roads.

Pretty well everywhere **south of Yaoundé** is held together by dirt roads and tracks through the forest, although there are paved roads to Ebolowa, Sangmélima and Kribi.

A couple of **dangers** are peculiar to road travel in Cameroon: first, the law that forbids motorists involved in an accident to move their cars until the police have inspected the site – meaning that all traffic may be held up for a couple of hours (quite apart from the implicit danger of hanging around if you are the party at fault); and second, the behaviour of Cameroonian hitchhikers, who often attempt to stop cars by standing in the middle of the road with both arms outstretched. Stopping is an implicit offer of a lift, so they tend to stand just round a blind corner where cars will be forced to screech to a halt to avoid killing them. Recent years have also seen an increasing number of *coupers de route* (road bandits) in action, especially in Adamawa Province and the north. They tend to operate in large gangs and are often armed, but generally cause no harm if there is no resistance. They simply stop the vehicle, take everybody's valuables and let you go. If you do

ROADBLOCKS

The one hazard even the most careful driver can't avoid in Cameroon is **police roadblocks**. These are usually on the outskirts of towns, often outside a bar or café. They're not easy to spot, as they may consist of no more than a policeman fast asleep in camouflage fatigues and a piece of string stretched across the road, or, more worryingly, the occasional nail-studded board.

Cameroonian police are less troublesome to foreigners than they were a few years ago, but can still be drunk, abusive, surly, and alarmingly casual about pointing a gun at your stomach.

The best precaution you can take is always to travel with a full clutch of **documents**, whatever current regulations may say – better to show an International Medical Certificate ("carte jaune") than to insist that you aren't required to carry it.

As a foreigner, you're permitted to move about with a certified photocopy of your passport, which avoids the fear of having it confiscated at a police check. Take the original and copies of the first five pages (as well as your visa) with a CFA500 fiscal stamp (available from the Ministry of Finance) to any main police station, where it will be stamped and signed.

resist, however, it can get quite nasty. The basic rules are: don't stop for anybody you don't know, and don't offer lifts to people in uniform – the bandits are more likely to shoot first if you are unlucky enough to be held up.

Taxis and buses
In the absence of a national transport system, most Cameroonians rely on **share taxis**, **clandos** or **agences de voyage** to get around. The *agences* (agencies) have sprung up during recent years, providing timetabled transport to most larger towns. Each agency runs certain routes, and finding out which goes where can be very time-consuming, especially as both agencies and routes change constantly. Even more confusingly, the agencies don't use official motor parks, but instead fill their vehicles outside their own ticket offices. Fortunately, booking offices for agencies going in the same general direction are often found in the same neighbourhood. Most agency vehicles are minibuses, but for connections between major towns and cities they run more comfortable buses. Both tend to pass police checkpoints with less trouble than share taxis and *clandos*.

Share taxis are government-registered minibuses or saloon cars travelling from motor park to motor park at a fixed rate, but often piling in extra passengers after leaving the motor park control. **Clandos** are similar vehicles, and operate as unregistered unofficial contestants to the agencies and share taxis. They tend to run on routes that none of the others cover, or snatch passengers from the share taxis outside the motor parks, piling people on top of each other and charging similar prices.

Within cities, **yellow taxis** are also shared and cost CFA140 for most short distances (a "drop" in English, *ramassage* in French) – one of the few real bargains in Cameroon. Taxi drivers generally don't attempt to overcharge – it's hard to imagine why not – but be sure to agree on a fare before you get in. In all smaller towns and most of the north – from Ngaoundéré and up – **motos** provide the easiest form of transport. For CFA100 these small motorcycles will take you anywhere you choose within the city limits and, for a bit more, outside the limits too.

Car rental
Car rental rates border on the outrageous. This is especially true of the main operators – such as **Hertz** and **Avis** – although they at least back up their high prices with reliable cars and services.

You'll find car rental agencies only in the larger towns (Douala, Yaoundé, Garoua, Maroua, Bafoussam and Ngaoundéré); their addresses are in the "Listings" or "Moving on" sections of the guide. Rental charges are higher in the north, and you'll be charged extra for any *piste* driving. If you rent on a daily basis, expect to pay about CFA46,000 per day for a small European or Japanese car, made up of a basic rate of around CFA22,500 per day, plus CFA220/km and extra charges for taxes and insurance. For a 4WD vehicle you should expect to pay around a basic rate of around CFA50,000, plus CFA300/km and charges.

■ By rail
The **Régiefercam** operates nearly 1200km of track, along two main routes. First is the western line from **Douala to Nkongsamba** (172km, up to eight hours' travelling time), although this route is quicker by road. The branch to **Kumba** from Mbanga is more useful, however, as the road can be very difficult, especially in the wet season.

The substantially longer Transcamerounais line links the country's two major cities with Ngaoundéré in the north. **Transcam I** covers the 308-kilometre stretch from **Douala to Yaoundé** with one service a day in each direction (about CFA6700 first class), leaving Douala at 7am and Yaoundé at 1pm. Given that this train takes over three hours, it's often more convenient to do the 233 kilometres by road. **Transcam II** forges on for 620km from **Yaoundé to Ngaoundéré** with a daily overnight service in each direction (about CFA15,000 first class). This is a fairly quick trip – roughly twelve hours assuming there are no delays. Certainly you couldn't expect to get through this part of the country any more quickly by road.

Carriages are relatively comfortable, with couchettes (linen, blankets and pillows provided), fans and sinks in first class. Second class (roughly two-thirds of the first-class fare) has seats only and is often crowded. Food is available from vendors in the stations, but you ought to take your own water for the trip. Reductions are possible with **student cards**.

The railway authorities are extremely sensitive about foreigners taking **photographs**, and it would be wise to pack your camera deep inside your bag during the journey. Due to the increased risk of **theft** it is also advisable to keep your bags far away from the windows. Thieves tend to sit on the roof of the train and poke their arms in through the windows to grab whatever they can get – personal stereos, sunglasses and shoes have been seen leaving the carriage in this fashion.

■ By air

Cameroon Airlines operates a reasonably efficient domestic service connecting **Douala** and **Yaoundé** with each other and with **Garoua**, **Maroua** and **Ngaoundéré**. Details are given in the relevant town sections in the guide. The northern towns are usually linked in series, which makes the flight up to Maroua very long. Note that Cameroon Airlines offers **student reductions** and **weekend excursions** (available to all, out Friday or Saturday, back Sunday or Monday).

One to two daily flights connect Yaoundé and Douala. Most other links have services varying from three to five times a week. Note that flights are often overbooked: arrive early and hope for the best.

To reach more inaccessible areas, such as isolated national parks and game reserves, it's possible to charter small planes through Air Affaire Afrique, but this is outrageously expensive.

Accommodation

Hotels of international standard in Cameroon are officially rated from one to five-stars. After the obvious five-star category, it's hard to discern how hotels are classified, but as long as a hotel has a star it should guarantee some degree of international standard.

The majority of hotels and auberges, however, are classified as "unclassified", which really gives you nothing to go by, and doesn't necessarily mean that the place is not worth staying at. You tend to get more for your money in the unclassified category. The **price** tends to be negotiable in all categories, with the more expensive places in particular prepared to reduce their rates if you give them a good reason – such as staying more than one night, or considering staying in the hotel across the road.

■ Camping and missions

If you have your own transport, **camping** away from the major urban centres is a fine alternative to hotel living. The game parks and natural reserves are sometimes restricted, but elsewhere, there are tens of thousands of square kilometres of wild country you can freely pitch in. See p.49 for advice.

The **missions** scattered throughout Cameroon may put up travellers, but they don't have to – and don't always want to. In Douala and Yaoundé, the religious institutions are a real godsend if you're travelling on your own and don't want to pay for a double room in a hotel. In face of the ever-increasing demand, however, many missions have started putting up their prices and are starting to turn away all who are not on church business. In recent years the government has tried to enforce this policy by decree.

■ Staying with people

There's a large Western presence in Cameroon, so you won't be thought special or exotic.

ACCOMMODATION PRICE CODES

Accommodation prices in this chapter are coded according to the following scales – the same scales in terms of their pound/dollar equivalents as are used throughout the book. Prices refer to the rate you can expect to pay for a room with two beds. Single rooms, or single occupancy, will normally cost at least two-thirds of the twin-occupancy rate. For further details see p.48.

① **Under CFA4500 (under £5/$8).** Rudimentary hotel or auberge with basic amenities – usually cold showers.

② **CFA4500–9000 (£5–10/$8–16).** Commonest budget-price bracket, S/C rooms with fans are the norm. Some rooms may have AC.

③ **CFA9000–18,000 (£10–20/$16–32).** Modest hotel with S/C, AC rooms, and often a restaurant.

④ **CFA18,000–27,000 (£20–30/$32–48).** Standard business or tourist-class hotel with S/C, AC rooms, and a restaurant.

⑤ **CFA27,000–36,000 (£30–40/$48–64).** Similar standards to the previous code band but extra facilities such as a pool are the norm.

⑥ **CFA36,000–45,000 (£40–50/$64–80).** Very comfortable hotel, with good facilities.

⑦ **Over CFA45,000 (over £50/$80).** Luxury establishment – top prices around CFA150,000.

Travellers are treated with nonchalance and you're unlikely to receive many offers to **stay with people**. You may find exceptions in the north, where the rocketing price of accommodation in out-of-the-way villages such as Mokolo has given enterprising young people the idea of "inviting" travellers to spend the night in their homes. If you stay a couple of days, they can earn a month's income, even for a contribution that is negligible compared to what you'd pay in a hotel. You may find this blend of commerce and camaraderie a little difficult to handle, but it's a solution that benefits both parties. Be clear about prices before agreeing to any such arrangements.

Eating and Drinking

Cameroon has a rich and varied cuisine, with a heavy emphasis in the north on maize, millet and groundnuts, and in the south on cassava, yams and plantains. These staples can be boiled, pounded or even grilled, but invariably turn out bland – a characteristic which may put you off at first, but that complements the fiercely peppered sauces quite nicely.

Fruit and vegetables are probably the best in the whole of West Africa and the variations in climate and altitude mean you can get nearly everything all year round – except the luscious and varied types of **mangos** in which Cameroon excels, which are in season from February to May. There is a healthy **salad** culture in Cameroon.

In **streetside cafés**, an item such as "omelette" (about CFA700–1000) is likely to include bread, a cup of tea or soft drink, chilled water, and perhaps chips or peas. In the south, a popular evening meal is **grilled fish**, served at street stalls with beer and *miondo* or fried plaintain. All over the country, but in the north especially, you'll find tasty little snack kebabs known as **soya**, exactly like the *suya* of Nigeria, which make a good meal with some French bread.

In common with much of Francophone West Africa, **French cuisine** dominates in the big hotels and expensive restaurants – though all the glitter is no guarantee of special food. When you're paying CFA10,000–20,000 (the price per head in many Douala and Yaoundé restaurants), you don't expect tough meat and soggy vegetables.

As for **Cameroonian cuisine**, although you're unlikely to find such specialized regional treats as fried termites, grasshoppers, dog, snake or cat in Yaoundé, you can taste a wide variety of national dishes without leaving the capital. But beware, upmarket restaurants serving *plats typiques* may be simply charging the earth for ordinary Cameroonian dishes.

■ Dishes

Bongo tchobi is a striking fish or meat dish, cooked in a black sauce made from various forest seeds and bark. **Bobolo**, from the south and central provinces, a heavy, nearly translucent, fermented cassava preparation, comes in a miniature baguette shape. **Miondo,** from Littoral province, is practically the same thing, but made with smaller strips wrapped in banana leaves. The most widely eaten southern dish is **ndolé**, made from a boiled, finely shredded, bitter leaf and groundnuts or agussi (melon seeds). Seasoned with hot oil and spices, cooked with fish or meat and eaten with one of the many starchy staples. The similar **kwem** is made from pounded cassava leaves and groundnuts cooked in a red, palm oil sauce. Such meals are served throughout the south in small restaurants known as *chantiers* ("worksites"), run by *veuves joyeuses* ("merry widows") or *tantes* ("aunties").

■ Buying your own food

A wide range of foods is available in the markets, and basic vegetables like potatoes, cereals, onions and yams are roughly the same price throughout the country, with reductions near the place of cultivation. Fruit and vegetables for export, such as pineapples and mangos, vary enormously in price depending on growing area and season. At harvest time in a growing area you can buy a sack of ten pineapples for CFA1500; you often see the roof rack of a minibus with half a dozen sacks on top, perhaps to be sold in a mango-growing district down the road.

Good **bread and pastries** are available throughout the country at fixed prices, and there's a good selection of **supermarkets** in most major towns. One final bargain, wherever you might be in Cameroon, is superb local **chocolate**.

■ Drinking

The **breweries** represent some of the country's most important industries. The Brasseries du Cameroun produce the most popular brand "**Le 33 Export**". Guinness Cameroon brew **Gold Harp**, slightly more expensive and considered the most prestigious of Cameroon's beers, hence the acronym "**G**overnment **O**fficers **L**ike **D**rinking **H**eavily **A**fter **R**eceiving **P**ayment".

You can also find international **soft drinks** everywhere, including Coke, Sprite and Fanta, or there are plenty of local, sweet, brightly coloured carbonates. Pamplemousse (grapefruit) and Djino Cocktail (mixed fruits) are tasty carbonated fruit juices. **Mineral water** can be had almost everywhere that sells drinks and from most grocery stores.

Of **traditional alcoholic** drinks, palm wine (*white mimbo*, *matango* or *mbu*) is available throughout the south and west, hence the many names. Try to buy any wine as close to source as possible and make local enquiries to be sure that it has not been diluted with bad water, or artificially sweetened with saccharin. The **distilled spirit** from palm wine is generally known as *afofo* (*arki* in the Francophone areas). This "African Gin" mixes well with a tonic. Other indigenous drinks include the millet beer of the north (*bilibili*) and *kwatcha* (or *sha*) a thick, opaque corn beer.

Communications – Post, Phones, Language and Media

Cameroon has a real mixture of facilities for communication, with sophisticated telecom systems in the metropolitan areas and virtually no communications, apart from post, in remote parts of the centre and far south. Linguistically it's very diverse – easily the most complex and interesting country in Africa. In the field of the media, there's much less to be proud of, through no fault of the journalists, who've endured well-documented harassment despite the liberalization of the press laws in the 1990s.

■ Post, phones and email

Post offices keep the same hours as most other offices, Mon–Fri 8am–3.30pm & Sat 8am–1pm. Letters to Europe take a week to fourteen days. The **poste restante** service seems to operate well enough in Yaoundé and Douala, and costs CFA200 per letter.

> Cameroon's IDD code is ☎237.

Douala and Yaoundé have a sophisticated, generally reliable **telephone** system, with IDD to Europe and America. First-try connections within or between the two cities are common, though phoning upcountry is considerably less reliable. Most towns have a multitude of fax/phone shops which can tell you the best times of day for connections to different areas.

Cybercafés are gradually spreading to the major towns around the country. The setup is generally quite relaxed – they tend to keep mail that hasn't been picked up for many months even though they don't know the person it's for.

■ Languages

Uniquely in Africa, Cameroon has **two official languages**, French and English, and a demanding but worthy policy of bilingualism in education and the civil service. In practice, French has always had the upper hand, as English is spoken only in the North West and South West provinces, these comprising only 22 percent of the population. This of course does not mean that most people speak one or the other language, although you might get that impression in the big towns. In North West and South West provinces, people in major towns usually speak **Pidgin English**, which is a different language, and doesn't come easily to an outsider – though you'll recognize a few words.

Of the four generally accepted groups of **African languages** (Afro-Asiatic, Nilo-Saharan, Niger-Congo, and Khoisan), all but Khoisan-related tongues are spoken in Cameroon. In all, some 160 different dialects are spoken, representing seventeen different language families. In the face of such diversity, some languages have become lingua francas. In the south, **Douala** and **Bassa** are often used as trading languages, while in the north, **Fulani** has taken on that role.

■ The media

The press is quite limited in Cameroon, especially if you've just come from print-mad Nigeria. *The Cameroon Tribune*, the only daily **newspaper**, is published in French and English editions and represents the (laconic) voice of the government – with so few lines to read between it's hard keeping informed. The independent press mushroomed in the early 1990s but has been the target of severe government harassment in the mid-1990s. *The Herald* is the thrice weekly Anglophone opposition party organ and almost as uninformative as

A CAMEROON GLOSSARY

Auberge Cheap hotel or *maison de passage*, most often with shared facilities.

Ba- Means "people of" in the Bantu and Semi-Bantu languages, widely extended (by European geographers) to indicate their towns and villages. Place names are a good deal easier to remember if this prefix is mentally dropped.

Boukarou In hotel jargon, bungalow-like huts with thatched roofs.

Chantier Literally a construction site. In Yaoundé's popular jargon "street food stands".

Circuit Northern appellation for *chantier*.

Fon In western Cameroon, a chief or king.

Kirdi Collective name for the mountain people of the Mandara range. It means pagan, since most of these people are non-Muslim and non-Christian.

Lamidat In the north, equivalent to a sultanate. The sultan is the Lamido.

Mayo In the north, a river or dried riverbed.

Ramassage "Collection" or "pick up". You take a taxi *en ramassage*, meaning you share it (and the fare) rather than rent it individually.

Saré Sudanic-style huts common in the north.

Sauvetteurs Wandering vendors, hawkers.

Stationnement Motor park.

The Cameroon Tribune. The Francophone opposition paper *Le Messager* and the *Cameroon Post*, the two most widely read weekly opposition papers are the best of the domestic press; they may or may not survive.

Cameroon Radio and Television Centre (CRTV) in Yaoundé broadcasts on one **television** channel across the country. The programme quality is not bad, and there are some English-language broadcasts, but **satellite** is becoming more and more common – hotel bars are more likely to show CNN (or TV5 in Francophone areas).

CRTV also run a national **radio** station in both English and French. Local news, often in local languages, is broadcast from its ten provincial stations between programmes of African music.

Arts and Entertainment

Cameroon has produced a number of highly regarded dramatists, film-makers and novelists, of whom the best known are *cinéaste* Jean Pierre Dikongue-Pipa and writers Mongo Beti and Ferdinand Oyono (see Contexts). But it's the country's musicians who have most successfully put Cameroon on the map for a world audience.

By repute and commitment, **Francis Bebey** – multitalented artist in the broadest sense – is Cameroon's honorary cultural ambassador to the world. But more familiar in the record shops is the tireless saxophonist, singer, pianist and arranger **Manu Dibango**, who helped popularize the Makossa style. Makossa – the name derives from *kosa*, to strip off – is Cameroon's biggest dance music, a sexy fast-paced rhythm, now increasingly underscored by thunderous bass and, with the influence of Paris, only a squeeze away from Zouk. Of the hundreds of musicians, **Sam Fan Thomas** and **Moni Bile** are the two other best-known exponents (more coverage in Contexts).

Less enduring stars of recent years were **Les Têtes Brulées**, who became internationally famous in 1989 with an album of the same name. Their music and wild cross-cultural appearance (day-glo "tribal paint", shaved and sculpted hair and the clumpiest trainers they could find) stirred up a whirlwind of excitement abroad, and confusion and controversy at home. If their success has now burnt itself out, their fast-paced musical style, **Bikutsi**, is still very popular, especially in Yaoundé.

Directory

AIRPORT DEPARTURE TAX CFA10,000.

ARTS AND CRAFTS It's illegal to take antiques and certain works of art out of the country without government authorization. That still leaves a wide variety of arts and crafts to choose from. The most famous region for art is the Bamoun-Bamiléké district of West and North West provinces, known for carved statues, masks and bas-reliefs. The long tobacco pipes used by the Tikar and others of the region have become popular tourist items and are widely available. Northern Cameroon is more renowned for leather and jewellery, fashioned primarily by the Fulani. Samples from all the regions can be found at the *marché artisinale* in Yaoundé.

Many antiques are smuggled down the Gamana and Donga rivers from Nigeria, which has strict views about the export of its heritage, and harsh penalties for smugglers. If you are continuing north from Cameroon, don't buy anything that even looks old; it will almost certainly be confiscated by Nigerian customs officers, whether antique or not.

There's not likely to be a problem exporting artworks through Douala airport, as export rules are loosely observed. If you want to check, contact the Délégation Provinciale du Tourisme in Douala (☎42.14.22 or 42.11.91) or Yaoundé (☎23.50.77) and they will direct you to the appropriate ministry, depending on the material the artefact is made of.

CRIME Douala and, increasingly, Yaoundé are especially dangerous after dark; stabbings are common, with money the main motive. It's safest not to carry anything of value in the street – preferably not even a bag – and to take local advice about which areas are dangerous seriously. Always try to look as if you know where you are going. Cameroonian justice is rough: the death penalty exists even for minor thefts, though few get as far as the courts. They may be dealt with by a roughing-up behind the police station or, if the cry of "*voleur!*" is heard, by a beating from an angry crowd.

DRESS AND APPEARANCE A strong streak of puritanism runs through Cameroon's official psyche, especially in the Anglophone regions. Western men will attract the disdain of officials and many locals if they go bare-chested, wear earrings, or have long hair – especially in dreadlocks. At best you may be regarded as a "bush man", at worst as the village idiot. Shorts are acceptable if you are engaged in some kind of sporting activity, like hiking or biking. In the Muslim areas of the north the dress code is even stricter – women especially should not show knees or shoulders. In general, Cameroon is cover-up country, unless you're prepared to put up with the sniggering or don't mind causing offence.

EDUCATION Relative to many of its neighbours, Cameroon performs relatively well in terms of education. In 1994, the last time a survey was carried out, nearly ninety percent of children were receiving primary education and, in 1995, UNESCO estimated an adult literacy rate of over sixty percent. The **University of Yaoundé** now has an enrolment of 20,000 students, and in the early 1990s, the specialist faculties at Douala,

Dschang, Buea and Ngaoundéré were upgraded to university campuses. Students from South West and North West provinces commonly head to Nigeria to pursue higher education.

EMERGENCIES Police ☎17; Fire ☎18.

HOLIDAYS AND FESTIVALS Shops and administrative services all shut down for the major Muslim and Christian holidays. The most important of the official holidays, the Fête Nationale, takes place every May 20. On this day, parades and speeches commemorate the 1972 approval of the referendum for a united Cameroon. Other national holidays include Labour Day (May 1) and Youth Day (February 11). Local festivals take place too, the most well-known of which are the *Lela* festival in Bali, taking place over three days in mid-December; the grass-gathering ceremony at the end of April and the End-of-Year festival in late December, both held in Bafut; the December *Ngoun* festival in Foumban; and the harvest festivals in the north, taking place at any time from January to March.

OPENING HOURS Most businesses, banks and offices now follow the practice of continuous weekday opening (Mon–Fri 7.30/8am–3pm, Sat 8am–1pm), but the old opening hours (Mon–Fri 8am–noon & 2.30–5.30pm) are also common.

PHOTOGRAPHY Although you're theoretically allowed to take pictures openly, photography is hedged about with restrictions. These go beyond the usual military and "national security" taboos to include anywhere the president is likely to stay when travelling, parades, festivals and anything "likely to cause a decline in morality and damage the country's reputation". The interpretation of this law is left to the person who decides to take you to task for breaking it. Taking pictures in Yaoundé, Douala and anywhere in the forest zone is likely to lead to trouble unless you're very discreet or very charming.

RELIGION Officially, Catholics, Protestants and Muslims number about a million each, but this estimate sounds too fortuitous to be true. Given that the country's population is now about twelve million, it seems clear at least that an overwhelming majority still practises traditional African religions.

SOCCER Always a wildly popular sport in Cameroon, the Indomitable Lions' mighty result in the 1990 World Cup (they reached the quarter-finals against odds of 100:1), lifted the status of soccer to almost a religion. Two contentious disallowed goals in the 1998 World Cup match against Chile lost Cameroon the game and took them out of the competition, leaving the nation feeling cheated. In Yaoundé and Douala, several violent incidents took place after the match. Some attacks were directed specifically at Europeans – particularly the French – but trouble lasted only a few days. Cameroon certainly has some of Africa's, and the world's, finest players, though regrettably for home games, many have given their careers to European clubs. The big teams are **Canon** and **Tonnerre** of Yaoundé, **Union**, **FC Rail** and **Dynamo** of Douala, **Kumbo Strikers** of the North West and **Cottonsport** of the North. Go to a match.

WILDLIFE Cameroon is blessed with a wonderful natural heritage, as Gerald Durrell discovered in the 1950s. Fortunately, it seems the government is fairly committed to saving some of it – even at the expense of lucrative logging contracts and difficult decisions over local development. The latest initiative, in league with the influential Worldwide Fund for Nature, is taking place in the extremely remote south eastern corner of the country, south of Yokadouma. Of the three areas of wildlife-rich rainforest in this area, Lake Lobeke Forest has been designated as a "Gift to the Earth", to be managed by WWF. It is hoped that the other two forests, Nki and Boumba Bek will soon follow suit.

Cameroon's **national parks** offer the closest thing to an East African safari to be found on this side of the continent, although it's an altogether different experience. There are greater opportunities for walking too. Cameroon has the last – dwindling – population of rhinos in West Africa. Along with most other African big game, including large numbers of elephants, these can be seen in several localities. Cameroon also actively encourages paid-up hunting, as part of its conservation strategy.

A Brief History of Cameroon

In the southern half of the Cameroon region, the first Bantoid-speaking peoples had moved in by 200–100 BC from the Nigerian plateau, displacing the original inhabitants (the people of small stature known as "Pygmies") and pushing them deep into the forests. But the earliest clearly defined presence in Cameroon is that of the materially advanced Sao culture, which developed around Lake Chad, and left archeological evidence in the form of works in bronze and terracotta – human and animal figures – coins, dishes, jewellery and funeral jars. From the eighth century, the Sao evidently began mixing with peoples pushed southward by the powerful empire then forming in Kanem (the Kotoko who live along the banks of Lake Chad and the Logone River are thought to be their descendants). Today, Cameroon is a complicated mixture of peoples, none of which is really predominant. As an archetypal example of an artificial state, its present configuration derives in large part from the imposed colonial history of the last hundred years, a legacy from which it is still struggling to break free.

■ The arrival of the Portuguese

In 1472, the Portuguese navigator **Fernando Po** led an expedition around the Bay of Biafra and was the first European to penetrate the estuary of the **Wouri River**, which he called Rio dos Camarões ("Prawn River"). From this time on, the coastal region gained influence, taking over from such northern powers as the **Bornu Empire** (which extended down to the Benoué in the sixteenth century). The centre of trade shifted to the regions around Douala, Limbé and Bonaberi, where local chiefs signed consecutive trade agreements with the Portuguese, Dutch, English, French and Germans. These chiefs rounded up slaves and ivory which they traded against cloth, metal and other European products.

Although commerce flourished over the ensuing four centuries, the Europeans didn't settle on the Cameroonian coast until the nineteenth century, when British missionaries began to protest against the **slave trade**. In 1845, an English pastor, **Alfred Saker**, founded the first European settlement in Cameroon at Douala. Although he set up churches and schools Saker was hardly a liberator. He recognized early on the strategic importance of **Douala** and **Victoria** and pushed for them to become crown colonies.

With the arrival of British, German and French **commercial houses**, trade shifted to "legitimate" exports of palm oil, ivory and gold. But the **Douala chiefs** became increasingly worried they would lose their role as middlemen between interior peoples and the Europeans and sought British guarantees that would have led to a protectorate. Queen Victoria hesitated. By the time she finally sent an envoy to make an arrangement, the

Germans had beaten her to it. On July 12, 1884, **Gustav Nachtigal** signed a treaty with the Douala chiefs **Bell**, **Deïdo** and **Akwa**, who willingly ceded their sovereignty to Kaiser Wilhelm in exchange for trade advantages.

■ The German, French and British occupations

In 1885, Baron von Soden became the first governor of Kamerun, and spent the next ten years trying to quell **rebellions** in the interior. He was replaced by **von Puttkamer** who relied on forced labour and brutality to carve out the colony's first **railway line** in 1907. But the promising economic results of the German activities, which included building some roads, hospitals and schools, came to an abrupt halt with the outbreak of **World War I**. In 1916, after a long, arduous and bloody campaign, the Allies wrested control of the territory from Germany and, in 1922, it was officially placed under French and British mandates – with only about one-fifth of the area ceded to Britain.

The **British Cameroons** were joined to Nigeria in an administrative union, but lay outside the framework of development plans for Nigeria, and received only minimal funding. Ironically, much of the growth in the region after World War I was spurred by the **Germans** who returned as private citizens to develop the plantations around the Victoria plains. (When, in the 1930s, many of them rallied to the call of Nazism, they were expelled and their private development efforts consolidated into the Cameroon Development Corporation, today the country's second biggest employer.) The **French** were more active in developing the infrastructure. Cultivation of the main export commodities of cocoa, palm oil and timber increased dramatically. French plans, however, relied heavily on exacting taxes and forced labour (in lieu of tax), to extend the road network, enlarge Douala's port and build up the vast plantations. Arising from such methods, well-founded grievances grew up over French rule.

■ The beginnings of nationalism

After World War II, the United Nations renewed the French and British mandates. The **British sector** continued – essentially – to be ruled from Nigeria. On the eve of independence, two camps emerged; the first pushing to become a state within the Nigerian federation, and the second calling for reunification with "the other" Cameroon.

In the **French territory** the call for reunification was also voiced. Political parties began to form, including the **Union des Populations Camerounaises** (UPC) and the less radical **Bloc Democratique Camerounais** of northerner **Ahmadou Ahidjo**.

The UPC was the first party to call both for unification of the two separate Cameroons and for **independence from France**. Prevented by force of opposition from attaining these demands legally, it organized a **revolt** in the larger towns of the French colonies in 1955. The uprising was put down, but at the cost of hundreds of lives and huge economic waste and destruction. The UPC, using increasingly extreme and violent liberation tactics, was banned in 1956 by the French government, but its influence barely diminished, especially in the **Bamiléké country** and **Sanaga region** where rebellion continued to foment and was brutally suppressed.

The UPC's actions acted as a catalyst to Cameroonian nationalism and focused the attention of more conservative parties on developing specific policy. Its influence was felt by leaders such as Ahidjo, who was still working within the political mechanism put in place by the French. In 1958 he founded a new party, **l'Union Camerounaise** and became the prime minister of the Assemblée Legislative du Cameroun. His platform called for reunification, total independence and national reconciliation.

■ Independence

Ahidjo met his first aim when he proclaimed **independence** on January 1, 1960. The following year, his goal of reunification was also partly satisfied. Following a United Nations plebiscite, the northern half of the former British territory voted to join Nigeria, while the southern British Cameroons voted to join the Francophone territory. But national reconciliation proved more difficult as the UPC problem dragged on and it took a further twelve years before Ahidjo (with continued French assistance) prevailed over the rebels when their last members were executed. In remarkably astute political manoeuvring, he then neutralized much of the internal opposition by integrating it into his government and the enlarged party, **l'Union Nationale Camerounaise**.

As the political wrinkles were being ironed out (symbolized through the adoption of a new constitution, the dissolution of the federal system and the formation of the **United Republic of Cameroon** in 1972), progress was also being made on the economic front. Like Houphouët-Boigny in Côte d'Ivoire, Ahidjo focused first on developing agriculture and then moved on to basic industry. Thanks in part to the discovery of oil, the country's GNP nearly doubled in the first twenty years of independence. By the end of the 1970s, Cameroon was thus shaping up as one of the rare stable countries in the region. If reports of **political prisoners** and repression trickled out of the country, and **Anglophone students** (to single out just one obvious group) were supremely dissatisfied with the way Cameroon was going, the West turned a blind eye to the autocratic excesses of a reliable friend.

■ A change of regime

Yet, as the years dragged on, it looked as though Ahidjo was settling into a pattern all too familiar in post-independence Africa – that of the powerful political leader who refuses to relinquish power or look to the future. He had been president for 22 years when he rather unexpectedly stepped down in 1982, citing ill-health as his reason. Just as Senghor had done in Senegal, he passed the sceptre to a young prime minister of his own grooming, from a different background – the 49-year-old bilingual southerner, **Paul Biya**. Recognized for his honesty and competence, Biya had barely been in office a year when his reputation, and that of Cameroon, took a beating in the international press.

Trouble started in 1983 when Biya fired the prime minister and several members of his cabinet, on the grounds that he had uncovered a **treasonous plot**. Ahidjo resigned as UNC party boss and, from his residence on the French Riviera, he openly criticized his heir, claiming that Biya was turning Cameroon into a police state, and asserting that he had been tricked into relinquishing power by faked health reports (it seems the former president was resentful that Biya would not allow him to transfer his vast fortune out of Cameroon, and was sensitive to Muslim worries that the balance of power had shifted to southern Christians). The showdown had begun, but Biya seemed to have all the cards. Ahidjo was sentenced to death *in absentia*.

Although Biya then pardoned his predecessor, things went from bad to worse in 1984, when units of the presidential guard formed by Ahidjo

(and still loyal to the ex-president) revolted in Yaoundé. They were only put down by the army after three days of **fighting in the streets** of the capital and an unknown death toll that has been estimated as at many as 1000. Ahidjo denied any involvement, but Biya cracked down on dissidents, and dozens of guard members were secretly tried and executed. Calm returned and Biya consolidated his position, but the incident showed the world that, even in Cameroon, stability is fragile.

■ Consolidation of power

For months after the coup attempt, Biya rarely left the presidential palace. Indeed, many observers expected a further attempt to overthrow him, and it was widely believed that an irreparable rift between the north and the rest of the country had been opened. But after a series of purges within the government, military and public sector, the president seemed to gain confidence.

As the nation prepared for the five-year congress of the UNC, in 1985, expectations ran high that Biya would announce sweeping reforms, including the revival of a multiparty system. Such hopes were disappointed when the president directed that no legal opposition to the ruling party would be allowed. Furthermore, he announced he was changing the UNC's name to the Rassemblement Démocratique du Peuple Camerounais (RDPC), apparently a move to distance the political body from its association with Ahidjo. At the same time, he moved towards a **cautious democratization** within the party, and in 1986, elections were held for members of RDPC bodies from the village level up to the *départements*, which saw the emergence of a lot of new blood.

On an **international level**, relations improved with the West, and in 1985 Biya made a much-publicized official visit to France. This was viewed as a conciliatory move, as the two countries had been on bad terms due to the widely believed suspicion of French complicity in the attempted coup of 1984. In 1986, Cameroon became the fourth African nation, after Zaire (Democratic Republic of Congo), Liberia and Côte d'Ivoire, to restore diplomatic relations with Israel, partly in response to the wishes of the American government, with whom Biya was seeking closer ties after the cooling of relations with France.

These events, however, were largely overshadowed by the worst **natural disaster** in the nation's history. In late 1986, an eruption of under-water volcanic gases escaped at Lake Nyos, a crater lake in the grassfields of North West Province. A cloud of deadly chemicals leaked into the atmosphere, suffocating at least 2000 people almost instantly and killing thousands of head of livestock. It caused great insecurity among local people who depend heavily on the crater lakes for fish and drinking water. Even some of the Anglophone intelligentsia persisted in the belief that a crude American or Israeli experiment in chemical warfare had been carried out at the lake site. Rumour aside, Lake Nyos served to bring Cameroon under the international spotlight once again.

At the end of 1986, Biya announced that **elections**, scheduled for early 1989, would be brought forward to April 24, 1988. The sole presidential candidate, he was "elected" to a new term by 98.75 percent of the votes, a bit of a dip since his 99.98 percent win in 1984.

■ The 1990s

At the end of the 1980s, Biya's great strength – apart from skill at political manoeuvre – lay in the relative stability of the economy. Cameroon moved to the middle-bracket status of under-developed nations, its gross national product per person much above West Africa's average. When coffee and cocoa prices dropped in the early 1980s, Cameroon was able to fall back on its rapidly growing oil exports, which actually pushed foreign trade into a surplus. But as the country entered its fourth decade of independence, economic and political stability were about to undergo serious challenges.

Pro-democracy – anti-people?

Not that the decade didn't start without optimism. In 1990, Biya indicated a willingness to go down the road to a multiparty system. However, **Amnesty International**'s much publicized concern on political detentions and torture, and steady pressure from Paris on reforms, explicitly tied to **debt relief**, made this announcement of measures to liberalize politics look like a response to unexpected events, rather than a planned programme of reform. Nonetheless, in anticipation of the changes, the newly formed, but unlicensed **Social Democratic Front** – the vanguard of the pro-democracy movement – proceeded, despite a government ban, with its inaugural rally in

Bamenda on May 26, 1990. The organizers managed to get over 30,000 people onto the streets. After a peaceful demonstration, attempts to disperse the crowd met with stone-throwing and, in the ensuing rout, troops shot into fleeing marchers, killing six people and injuring dozens more. On the same day in Yaoundé, the university campus was the scene of brutal attacks on **students** supporting the rally.

Leaders of the SDF, not all of them from the Anglophone region, claimed the Anglophone districts were being treated like a colony by the Francophone areas. As support withered for the government in the North West and South West provinces, the Bamiléké of West Province – powerful in Cameroon commerce – also lost enthusiasm after the slaying of a senior lawyer, **Pierre Bouobda**, at a Bafoussam roadblock. The ill will from the west, added to continued resentment from the north about the treatment of Ahidjo and his barons, amounted to a heavy show of support for the opposition.

As pressure mounted, the national assembly adopted a draft law in December 1990 for the introduction of a multiparty political system. By early 1991, over twenty opposition parties had registered and collectively – under the banner of the **National Coordination Committee of Opposition Parties** (NCCOP) – they began calling for a **national conference** to outline the country's political future.

Biya flatly refused and seemed taken aback that the opposition, with its disparate regional, ethnic, religious and political elements, had united so quickly against him. He placed seven of Cameroon's ten provinces under military rule, lashed out at the mushrooming **independent press**, and prohibited opposition gatherings. As security forces became increasingly violent in their crackdown on opposition rallies, the NCCOP tried a tougher tactic – a nationwide campaign of civil disobedience. **Operation Ghost Town** began in July 1991 as a highly effective strike that closed the ports and brought business and transport to a halt from Monday to Friday, allowing the public to buy food at weekends. The economic effect was crippling for the big towns and industries. Even in Douala, business slammed to a standstill.

The strikes dragged on through November 1991, when the government, opposition and civilian organizations agreed on the formation of a constitutional committee. Biya finally consented to release all political prisoners, lifted the ban on opposition meetings and set legislative elections for February 1992. Not everyone was happy, however. As Biya began tailoring the process to suit RDPC aims (he insisted on a single round of voting and forbade coalitions from participating), many opposition elements – including two of the four principal parties, the SDF and the Union Démocratique Camerounaise – called for an **election boycott**. The RDPC won 88 of 190 seats.

Biya's political support was clearly flagging and the president mounted an assiduous attempt to secure re-election. A secret committee was set up to control every aspect of the poll and was shameless in its bid to influence the National Vote Counting Commission and to skew the voter register. The domestic media were tightly controlled: the Douala-based printing house which published most of the independent newspapers was surrounded and closed, papers such as *Le Messager* and *Challenge Hebdo* were censored or banned and some opposition candidates were refused free access to public radio and television.

But the principal opposition contender – the SDF's **John Fru Ndi**, an Anglophone bookseller from Bamenda – was better organized than Biya expected and he gathered widespread support throughout the country. Internationally, he scored high marks as he travelled to Germany, Britain and the US, and Nigeria openly backed his candidacy.

The opposition's momentum, however, was no match for Biya's tight control over the election process. After the polls of October 11, 1992 the president claimed 39.9 percent of the vote to Fru Ndi's 35.9 percent. The United States' National Democratic Institute, which had monitored the elections, wrote a scathing report of wilful fraud and widespread irregularities. Predictably, demonstrations broke out, provoking the kind of repression reminiscent of Africa's pre-democratic dictatorships. Amnesty International reported mass arrests and related deaths as a **state of emergency** was declared in western Cameroon. Fru Ndi and other prominent leaders were placed under house arrest. Journalists were detained and tortured.

The bad press refocused international attention on Cameroon. South Africa's Nobel Prize-winning peacemaker **Desmond Tutu** tried to negotiate a settlement, but the government and opposition were too far apart to consider his proposals for a unity government. After his release, Fru Ndi, flew to Washington, where he had been invited for the January 1993 inauguration of President Clinton, who quickly imposed economic sanctions on the Biya government. For his part Biya flew to Paris and negotiated a loan of $115 million to help stave off IMF pressure to resolve the growing **national debt crisis**.

The current impasse

Biya, who had spent years cultivating the image of a humane and stable leader, came out of the fight bruised and battered. International papers described him as a degenerate autocrat – an epithet that had already been circulating inside the country for some time.

Nonetheless, Biya slowly gathered hesitant support from the international community. His first major breakthrough came at the end of 1995 when, after protracted discussions, Cameroon was admitted into the **Commonwealth**, despite opposition objections that the country did not respect stipulated standards of human rights and democracy. Improved ties with Britain piqued French interest in Biya, as did the fact that by the end of the 1990s, Cameroon was one of the few Central African countries that was not in complete crisis. Given the regional instability, foreign governments were reluctant to stir up divisions within Cameroon and resigned themselves to the status quo.

At home, the president was effective in dividing the opposition. Western Cameroonians increasingly called for a return to a federal system of government, and more radical members advocated **secession**. In 1995, the **Southern Cameroons National Council** (SCNC) emerged and called for an autonomous state. English speaking representatives in the government criticized the demands, which also alienated Bamiléké support within the SDF. By focusing on regional rather than national issues, the movement estranged northerners from an opposition coalition; their principal party, the Union Nationale pour la Démocratie et le Progrès (UNDP) had participated in the legislative elections and could therefore pursue regional aims in parliament.

There was little cohesion left within the opposition by the time of legislative elections in 1997, but Biya took no chances of an upset. His government apparatus tightly controlled the proceedings, refusing once again to institute an independent electoral commission. International observers substantiated opposition accusations of vote rigging and fraud, but there was little recourse. The RDPC claimed 109 of the 180 national assembly seats, the SDF took 43, and the UNDP saw its representation sink to 13 seats. Despite the setback, the opposition couldn't unite to back a single candidate for the presidential elections later that year. They decided instead to call a boycott, citing the country's history of corrupt elections and the lack of any meaningful reform. When both the United States and France criticized the boycott as "undemocratic", it was a signal that they had abandoned supporting change in Cameroon and had accepted the idea of seven more years of Biya.

Only the **threat of war** shifted the focus from the sphere of domestic politics when, throughout much of the 1990s, hostilities with Nigeria flared over the long disputed border at the Bakassi Peninsula. Though the conflict was originally limited to localized incidents, the military posturing on both sides led to clashes in 1996. Tensions eased in 1998, following an exchange of more than two hundred prisoners of war, but the situation remains unresolved and could degenerate again when the World Court in The Hague eventually rules on the sovereignty of the peninsula.

Addressing **the economy** is Biya's biggest task, and his first priority is to keep relations as smooth as possible with foreign creditors. By 1999, the IMF was financing its fifth structural adjustment agreement with Cameroon and, in a notable turnaround from ten years earlier, was lauding the country for its good implementation of the programme. As 2000 approached, economic growth was above 5.5 percent, with inflation held to 3 percent. But despite the good news, the German-based non-governmental organization Transparency International ranked Cameroon as the world's most corrupt country in 1998. Biya downplayed the report as "exaggerated", but still promised to crack down on those "who are well versed in cheating, fraud and even swindling". Though a few prominent managers of state-owned companies were sacked after the report, there still remains substantial room for improvement.

Despite the economic upswing, members of Biya's own cabinet acknowledged that the positive economic growth had not brought much in the way of improved development to the country. One hope to reverse the trend is the project to build a thousand-kilometre **pipeline** from the oilfields of southern Chad through Cameroon to the port at Kribi. The country stands to gain $500 million annually from the pipeline which will generate thousands of new jobs. The timing is fortuitous since Cameroon's own oil industry has declined and the country will soon be a net oil importer. Though work on the project is imminent, construction hadn't begun by the end of the 1990s due to objections by powerful international environmental lobbyists. Another boost could come from the EU's commitment to finish work on the proposed road linking Douala with Bangui, Central African Republic. In 1999, work began on the stretch between Bertoua and Garoua Boulai on the border.

With the opposition splintered and the economy – for the meantime – performing well, Biya is poised to lead the country well into the first decade of the new century. Secession and Bakassi loom before him, but the president has expressed confidence that these issues will be easier to work through with the new leadership in Nigeria than with the sabre rattling Abacha regime. But economic and social problems – unpaid back salaries, unemployment (coupled with cuts in the public sector), poor health and education services and rampant corruption – will not disappear, and are likely to be exacerbated by privatization, notwithstanding strong growth. Violent crime has risen dramatically, with arms easily available to a new category of desperate bandits. But, as the twentieth century came to a close, the volcanic eruptions of Mount Cameroon generated more media attention than the myriad social problems churning just beneath the country's political landscape, and the current generation of opposition leaders has almost certainly lost its chance to bring them to the surface. The next challenge to Biya's tenure is only likely to come from a new generation of leaders better equipped to loosen the RDPC control of entry into the political system and to unite the nation in tackling the challenges of the future.

DOUALA AND SOUTHWEST PROVINCE

As **economic capital** of Cameroon, **DOUALA** is a vast and energetic city. The driving force behind its growth has been the **port**, which handles ninety-five percent of the nation's maritime traffic and has stimulated regional development in trade and industry. But despite Douala's activity and relative prosperity, the cityscape is a relentless urban jungle distinguished neither by traditional flavour nor modern flashiness. Urban planners have concentrated their efforts on Yaoundé in the interior, with the result that Douala suffers from overpopulation and a worn-down and inadequate infrastructure. For **nightlife**, however, Douala cannot be contested. The multitude of **restaurants** include some of the best in West Africa and **live music** is always to be found somewhere around the corner.

Within easy reach of the metropolis, are a wide variety of natural highlights. For simple rest and recuperation, you can't beat the **black-sand beaches** around **Limbé**, a small town with a distinctly colonial flavour at the foot of **Mount Cameroon** – West Africa's highest peak. The colonial town of **Buea** is only 70km away, 1000m up the slopes of the mountain, and makes a good base for climbing expeditions. Continuing north, **Kumba**, a vibrant commercial town located near beautiful **Lake Barombi Mbo**, makes a good stopover on the way to **Korup National Park** and Nigeria. East of Kumba, and still only a few hours drive from Douala, **Mount Kupe** and the **Manengouba twin crater lakes** provide enjoyable hiking.

Douala

Despite its status as the nation's largest and wealthiest city, **DOUALA** is not its most attractive. The dreary architecture, relentless bustle and oppressive heat and humidity can be somewhat overwhelming, but if you can muster the energy to explore, the **market area** around the Lagos neighbourhood is the liveliest in Cameroon, the Akwa and Bonapriso quarters offer some of the best **nightlife** to be found and the German **colonial buildings** in the Joss district have recently been classified as a UNESCO World Heritage Site, although they are rapidly disintegrating. Douala's many different facets are apparent in its many quarters, and with a population that has skyrocketed in recent years to over a million, it has undergone some rapid changes. Although most of the city is fairly safe, crime is rampant in other areas. The area around the port is just plain dangerous, and bag snatching on the bridge linking Akwa and Bonanjo is common – don't walk around with anything visibly valuable and try to look as if you know where you are going.

Some history

Like so many settlements on the West African coast, the Douala area was once home to small fishing communities who first came into contact with Europe when the **Portuguese** made contact at the end of the fifteenth century. Although trade – especially in slaves – between local rulers and seafarers continued, Europeans only settled on the banks of the Wouri (or Cameroons) River in the nineteenth century. The first of these were **English missionaries** led by **Alfred Saker** who, in 1845, founded a small community at the site where the Église du Centenaire stands today. By that time, the **Douala people** (who probably arrived in the estuary at the beginning of the seventeenth century) were established into two groups united around the **Bell** and **Akwa** families.

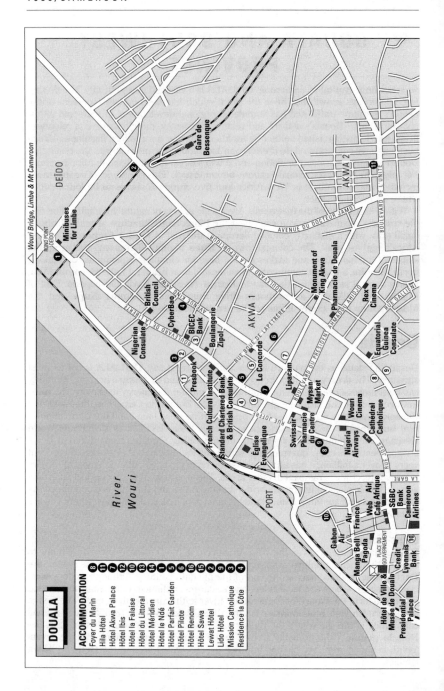

DOUALA

ACCOMMODATION

Foyer du Marin · **8**
Hila Hôtel · **11**
Hôtel Akwa Palace · **7**
Hôtel Ibis · **12**
Hôtel la Falaise · **10**
Hôtel du Littoral · **13**
Hôtel Méridien · **11**
Hôtel le Ndé · **1**
Hôtel Parfait Garden · **5**
Hôtel Pilote · **6**
Hôtel Renom · **16**
Hôtel Sawa · **15**
Lewat Hôtel · **2**
Lido Hôtel · **9**
Mission Catholique · **3**
Residence la Côte · **4**

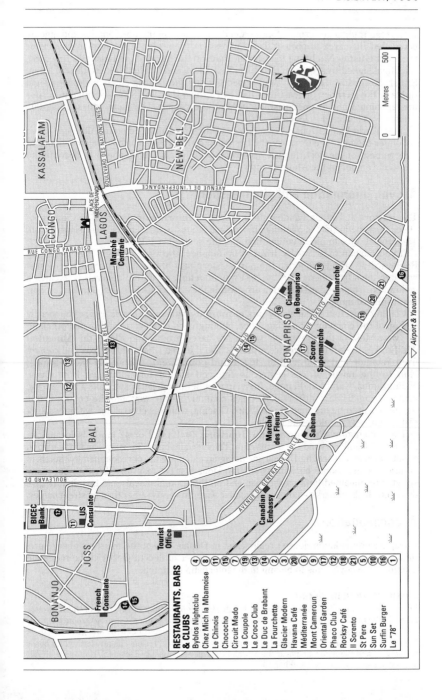

RESTAURANTS, BARS & CLUBS

Byblos Nightclub	④
Chez Mich la Mbamoise	⑧
Le Chinois	⑪
Chococho	⑮
Circuit Mado	⑦
La Coupole	⑲
Le Croco Club	⑬
Le Duc de Brabant	⑭
La Fourchette	②
Glacier Modern	③
Havana Café	⑳
Méditerranée	⑥
Mont Cameroun	⑨
Oriental Garden	⑰
Phaco Club	⑫
Rocksy Café	⑱
Il Sorento	㉑
St Pere	⑤
Sun Set	⑩
Surfin Burger	⑯
Le "78"	①

German trading companies followed in the footsteps of the missionaries and quickly persuaded Bismarck to protect their interests in the region. The German chancellor thus sent **Gustav Nachtigal** to claim the lands in the name of the Kaiser. In July 1884, Nachtigal signed treaties with the chiefs Bell, Akwa and Deïdo. With the flick of a pen, British designs in the region were wiped out and the Douala chiefs had ceded legal rights to the territory (at least they had by German law). In 1885, a German governor was appointed and **Kamerunstadt** became the capital. The name stuck until 1907 when it was changed to Douala.

After World War I, Douala became part of the French protectorate. Although it was no longer capital of the territory, the French began large-scale urban construction, and enlargement of the port. Industry followed and Douala forged ahead to become the economic engine of the whole country.

Arrival, information and city transport

The **airport** at Douala handles the majority of **international** flights to Cameroon. Older than the airport at Yaoundé, it's showing signs of age, and is surprisingly small. The official price to hire a **yellow taxi** into the centre is CFA2300.

If you happen to arrive **by train** from Yaoundé, the Gare de Bessenge is just off Boulevard de la République in the northeastern part of the city centre. The quickest way into town from here (and the best way of getting around in general) is to catch a yellow taxi. The standard fare for a drop within the city is CFA140, although longer journeys will cost more.

Coming into central Douala **by bus** or **minibus** with an *agence de voyage* you usually end up at the company's booking office, although you can ask to be dropped off along the way. Most of the *agences de voyage* are based around the **Place du Ahmadou Ahidjo**, 1.5km east of the centre, which is also the area where share taxis and *clandos* from Yaoundé and Kribi tend to stop. **Rond-point Deïdo** (or simply "Rond-point"), 2km to the north of the centre, is the end station for minibuses from Buea, Nkongsamba, Kumba and Limbé. Arriving at either place, it's best to take a cab into the centre. Long-distance drivers sometimes continue all the way into the centre. If this happens, ask to be dropped at the Wouri Cinema, which is central and within walking distance of several moderate hotels.

The **Délégation Provinciale du Tourisme** (☎42.14.22 or 42.11.91) is located on Avenue de Gaulle beyond the tennis club. They usually have **city maps** and information about travel in and around Douala, including an extensive list of recommended hotels in all price ranges. Some bookshops sell the Douala street map for CFA4000, but many streets are unnamed both on the map and on the ground. Locals and taxi drivers give directions by landmarks – hotels, nightclubs, water towers – rather than by street names.

Accommodation

Cheap accommodation doesn't really exist in Douala – even the missions charge premium rent on rooms. Although there are a number of decent places in the moderate category, the city seems to belong to the international hotels.

Inexpensive to moderate

Foyer du Marin, rue Galliéni, off bd de la Liberté (BP 5194; ☎42.27.94). One of the best-value places in the moderate range, although supposedly reserved for seamen. Clean S/C rooms with AC and a swimming pool on the premises. Popular with expats, perhaps due to the draught beer. ②–③.

Hila Hôtel, 515 bd de l'Unité (BP 17497; ☎42.15.86; Fax 42.33.27). Conveniently located for buses to Yaoundé and Bamenda, and near the Marché Central. Well-managed, clean S/C rooms with AC, and a good-value restaurant and bar. ②.

ACCOMMODATION PRICE CODES

① Under CFA4500 (under £5/$8).
② CFA4500–9000 (£5–10/$8–16).
③ CFA9000–18,000 (£10–20/$16–32).
④ CFA18,000–27,000 (£20–30/$32–48).
⑤ CFA27,000–36,000 (£30–40/$48–64).
⑥ CFA36,000–45,000 (£40–50/$64–80).
⑦ Over CFA45,000 (over £50/$80).

For further details, see p48.

Hôtel du Littoral, 38 av Douala Manga Bell, Bali (BP 2023; ☎42.24.84). Not the classiest place in town – it's slightly grubby – but decent value and near the Marché Central and the famous *Phaco* club. ②.

Hôtel Pilote, rue Castelnau (BP 1813; ☎ & Fax 42.14.65). In the centre of one of the most happening areas of town for nightlife, with simple, clean AC rooms. ③.

Hôtel Renom, (formerly *Hôtel de l'Air*) av de Gaulle (BP 17578; ☎43.34.52; Fax 43.06.23). Good-value S/C rooms with AC, but only cold water. Within walking distance of the restaurants and bars in the Bonapriso quarter. ②.

Lido Hôtel, rue Joffre, near the *Foyer du Marin* (☎42.04.45). In a quiet and therefore slightly dodgy area, this hotel has S/C rooms with AC, plus its own bar and restaurant. ②.

Procure Générale des Missions Catholiques, rue Franqueville, Akwa (BP 5280; ☎42.27.97). Very comfortable (AC in rooms, swimming pool) and reasonably priced, but missionaries get first priority, and it's often full. ③.

Residence la Côte, av King Akwa (BP 4014; ☎40.50.34). Small, box-like S/C rooms with AC, often rented out by the hour. ②.

International class

Hôtel Akwa Palace, 52 bd de la Liberté, Akwa, (BP 4007; ☎42.26.01; Fax 42.74.16). The oldest of the international hotels, still boasting an older wing in all its colonial pomp. Pleasant pool and gardens plus a casino and an excellent restaurant. Major credit cards. ⑤.

Hôtel la Falaise, rue Kitchener, Bonanjo (BP 5300; ☎42.46.46; Fax 42.68.91). Very good value for an established, well-maintained hotel. Perched on a hill with swimming pool, restaurant and AC rooms overlooking the Wouri River. In fact, this pleasant retreat isn't much more expensive than some moderate hotels. ③.

Hôtel Ibis, off av de Gaulle, Bonanjo (BP 12086; ☎42.58.00; Fax 42.36.05). Affordable luxury – though the rooms are a bit small – abuzz with the activity of the poolside terrace, restaurants and shops. ⑤.

Hôtel Méridien, av des Cocotiers (BP 3232; ☎42.46.29 or 42.90.44; Fax 42.35.07). The most expensive and classy hotel in town. Features an eighteen-hole golf course, a swimming pool and tennis courts as well as free massage in the fitness club (guests only). Major credit cards. ⑥.

Hôtel le Ndé, 105 bd de la Liberté (BP 12990; ☎42.70.34; Fax 42.76.04). Clean middle-of-the-range place with comfortable AC rooms, a small swimming pool and a good restaurant and bar. ③.

Hôtel Parfait Garden, 58 bd de la Liberté near *Hôtel Akwa Palace* (BP 5350; ☎42.63.57; Fax 43.02.65). All the services of a luxury hotel, but lacking charm. Major credit cards. ④.

Hôtel Sawa, av de Verdun, off av de Gaulle, in Bonanjo (BP 2345; ☎42.08.66 or 42.14.70; Fax 42.78.31). Complete comfort and extras like video, tennis, sauna, and poolside barbecue. Crafts, curios and some good jewellery are sold in the foyer. Major credit cards. ⑤.

Lewat Hôtel, 2699 bd de la République, not far from the railway station (BP 12563; ☎40.00.24; Fax 40.16.77) Comfortable rooms and a restaurant with a good cook who also prepares vegetarian dishes. ④.

The City

Douala sprawls in every direction. Much of its industry and many of its workers are housed on the far side of the Wouri Bridge, on the west bank of the river. Nonetheless, the various distinct quarters into which the town is divided – most of them named after local ruling families – aren't too difficult to figure out.

Akwa: the modern centre

As the main commercial area, the **Akwa neighbourhood** is more or less the centre of the modern city. Its lifeline is the Boulevard de la Liberté, with the **Cathédrale Catholique** something of a landmark at its southern end. Built in the 1930s, this is one of the few attractive edifices in town, even if its neo-romanesque style is a bit incongruous in this sweltering climate.

Continuing north, you pass the Akwa PTT (post office) and the Wouri Cinema before arriving at the wide tree-lined **Boulevard du Président Ahmadou Ahidjo**. Here, numerous department stores, supermarkets and boutiques provide an upmarket commercial backdrop for the street vendors selling clothes, shoes and accessories. Turning down the east side of the boulevard, toward the river and away from the shops, takes you past the **Église Évangelique** (or Temple du Centenaire, built to commemorate the 100th anniversary of Alfred Saker's arrival) and down the hill to the **port**. The surrounding area is run-down and has a very dangerous reputation, so it might be wise to skip this detour and continue north on Boulevard de la Liberté to the **Akwa Palace**. This old colonial hotel was Cameroon's ultimate in luxury accommodation for many years, and still retains a certain charm. Beyond the hotel, businesses become more sparse on Boulevard de la Liberté as it leads on to **Rond-point Deïdo**, where it turns west towards the **Wouri Bridge** and over to the industrial **Bonabéri** neighbourhood on the west bank of the Wouri River.

Bonanjo and the administrative district

Heading south from the cathedral, instead of north, the Boulevard de la Liberté curves to the west and crossing the bridge (reputedly a risky area for pedestrians) becomes rue Joss – a street that leads downhill to **Place du Gouvernement** where it turns into Avenue de Gaulle. This is the heart of the administrative quarter and the **Bonanjo** district. The **Poste Centrale**, with a large monument commemorating the World War II exploits of General Leclerc, dominates the square. On one corner, you'll see the pagoda-shaped colonial house which was once the **palace** of Prince Rudolf Manga Bell. The grandson of a Douala signatory of the German treaty, the prince was later killed by the Germans for treason. The pagoda is still owned by the Manga Bell family but it now houses a travel agency and an art museum (**Musée Doual'art**) with a small collection of modern African art. East of the square, the main branches of all the major **banks** congregate, and continuing further south on Avenue de Gaulle you reach the Joss neighbourhood with all its old **German colonial buildings**. Heading north again from *Hôtel Méridien*, Avenue des Cocotiers gives a good impression of German colonial architecture and city planning. Unfortunately, when you eventually reach the **Presidential Palace**, also from the German colonial era, you must not go anywhere near the impressive buildings, especially not with a camera. Horrible stories of unknowing tourists being beaten up by the security police are not unheard of.

The national museum

The rather forlorn **Musée de Douala** (Mon–Fri 8am–2pm, Sat 8am–noon; CFA1000) is housed in the **Hôtel de Ville** behind Place du Gouvernement. It's not marked anywhere, so don't worry about just walking into the City Hall and heading upstairs to find the museum on the first floor.

The museum consists of a dusty collection of poorly presented and inadequately explained national art, but if you're going to be travelling around the country, it gives a generous overview of regional art, and has one or two rare pieces. Visits start in a sort of entrance hall, framed by posts from the famous **Bandjoun chiefdom**. Here the whole **history** of the nation, from the Paleolithic Age (Old Stone Age) to the colonial era via the slave trade, is represented by a somewhat haphazard assortment of articles. Drawing the attention from the clutter are some clay **Bamoun statues** and one beautiful bronze cast.

The other four rooms of the museum are much more coherent. The **Salle du Sud** represents art from the forests of southern Cameroon. Wooden objects dominate, such as **Fang statues** and colourful sculpted Douala decorations for the bows of *pirogues*. A Basso cloak made of hammered tree bark is especially striking and there are also various musical instruments and games. The **Salle du Nord** is military, with an emphasis on Fulani arms such as a suit of mail together with spears, saddles and harnesses. In the **Salle Bamoun**, dedicated to the Bamoun culture, is a series of coloured drawings evoking the region's history up to the reign of the great innovator and statesman Sultan Njoya. Numerous sculptures adorn the room, including a magnificent **bas-relief** depicting the sultan returning from war. Lastly, the **Salle Bamiléké** contains a collection of thrones, and statues representing the chief and his servants. Notice the sculpted wooden posts – a traditional part of Bamiléké architecture used to decorate the house of a chief.

Markets

The districts of Lagos and Kassalafam are two of the liveliest neighbourhoods in town, and well worth visiting even if you don't want to buy anything from their bustling markets. From Bonanjo, Avenue Douala Manga Bell leads east through the Bali quarter and on to the **Lagos** quarter, where you'll find the **Marché Central** – the biggest market in the country. It spreads south of Avenue Douala Manga Bell and is hemmed in by the rue Congo Paraiso to the west. The northeast corner is marked by the busy Place de l'Indépendance and the adjacent **mosque**, in front of which assorted barks, seeds and powders – the essential ingredients of African pharmacy – are on sale. Nearby on rue Congo Paraiso, the **Marché Congo** specializes in African and imported fabrics. The market area continues past Place de l'Indépendance, stretching up Boulevard des Nations Unies where it merges with the **Marché de Kassalafam**, primarily a fruit and vegetable market.

Arts and **crafts** are sold at the **Marché des Fleurs** off Avenue de Gaulle in the Bonapriso quarter. Foumban (see p.1098) has a reputation for being the best place in Cameroon to buy authentic artefacts (and high-quality reproductions), but this market rates a good second. They sell good-quality jewellery as well as both real and fake antiques. The masks, both new and old (and it's pretty hard to tell which is which), are imported from all over West Africa, and are the same as those on sale in London or Paris at ten to twenty times the price.

Eating and drinking

Eating in Douala can be very expensive. Many of the upmarket restaurants are grouped in the **Bonapriso** quarter, the town's prime residential area. The town also flaunts a number of Paris-style **cafés**, where shoppers retire for a break and business people do their deals. You can relax in their air-conditioned comfort for as long as you like for the price of a coffee (about CFA1000). *Akwa Palace*, *Le Delice* and *Glacier Modern* take turns at being the in place of the moment. If you're feeling flush or homesick, splash out CFA1500 on one of their superb pastries.

Cheap to moderate

You'll pay at most CFA6000 a head (without drinks) to eat at these restaurants and bars, and considerably less at some of them.

Chez Mich la Mbamoise, bd de la République, Bali. An outdoor restaurant with a lively atmosphere, friendly staff and reasonably priced Cameroonian dishes. Estimate CFA5000 per head.

Chococho, rue Njo-njo, Bonapriso. A popular local bakery which has expanded its repertoire from producing the best chocolate croissants in Douala to making pizzas with serious toppings (around CFA1500 a slice) and sandwiches.

Circuit Mado, Akwa, near the *Hôtel Akwa Palace* (150m from Photo Prunet). Down-home Cameroonian cooking, featuring freshly grilled sole or *Poulet DG* – a mixture of chicken and plantains in a spicy sauce. Expect to pay CFA3000–4000 per head.

La Coupole, 115 av de Gaulle, Bonapriso (☎42.29.60). Good-value Italian-style food (including pizzas) as well as some Lebanese specialities. Expect to pay between CFA4000 and 6000 per person.

Le Croco Club, rue de l'Union Francaise, Bali (☎42.78.54). Easy-going bar-restaurant with live music, a pool table, draught "33" and friendly management. It also serves a good variety of reasonably priced Cameroonian dishes; the crocs laze in a small pool.

Foyer du Marin, Akwa (☎42.27.94). Tasty German sausages (CFA1200 each) and cool draught beer served in the relaxing poolside atmosphere of the German Seaman's Mission.

Il Sorrento, av de Gaulle, Bonapriso. A lively pizza place with music every night. Around CFA5000 per head, without drinks.

Méditerranée, bd de la Liberté, Akwa (☎42.30.69). Outdoor restaurant on one of the busiest streets in Douala, serving Greek dishes at reasonable prices – CFA3000 for moussaka. Popular with prostitutes.

Le Pacha, rue Njo-njo, Bonapriso. A popular Lebanese restaurant with salads and snacks – *chawarmas* at CFA1200 – and also more filling meals.

Surfin Burger, rue Monoprix, off rue Njo-njo, Bonapriso (BP 13012). Elected best burger joint in Cameroon by the US Peace Corps – the local experts. A cheeseburger and chips cost CFA2500.

Expensive

Le Chinois, av de Gaulle, Bonanjo (☎42.33.10). The oldest Chinese restaurant in Douala, so they must be doing something right. Allow CFA15,000 per person.

Le Duc de Brabant, rue SNEC, Bonapriso (☎30.72.40). Exclusive French restaurant with good cuisine and fine wines at around CFA20,000 per head.

La Fourchette, rue Franqueville, Akwa (☎42.14.88). One of the few good French restaurants in the Akwa quarter; comfortable and not too expensive.

Oriental Garden, 10 rue Afcodi, Bonapriso (☎42.69.38). Excellent Chinese restaurant with trained chefs imported from China. This is where the Chinese eat. Allow CFA15,000 per head for an evening out.

Phaco Club, just off av Douala Manga Bell, near the Sonel building (☎42.68.81) As rumbustious as the warthog it's named after – and much friendlier. Tasty African food, including chicken wrapped in banana leaves and exotic bush meats. Dancers or musicians entertain every night. Allow CFA10,000 per person, without drinks.

Le Tournebroche, next to the pool at *Hôtel Akwa Palace* (☎42.26.01 ext 5225). A top-class hotel restaurant with French cuisine of the highest standard, allow CFA15,000 per person without drinks.

Le Wouri, *Hôtel Méridien*, Bonanjo (☎42.46.29). Another exclusive hotel restaurant serving beautifully presented grand buffets. Prices are high but you get what you pay for. Allow CFA25,000 per head excluding drinks.

Nightlife

Douala's **clubs** open, close down and change hands quite frequently, but even if the name of a place changes it generally remains a club, and the taxi drivers tend to know both past and present names. Clubs usually open around 11pm or midnight and close when they get quiet, sometime between 3am and 5am.

Entry **prices** vary enormously for foreigners, locals, men and women, but once in, you rarely come under pressure to spend. Drinks cost anything from CFA3000–8000, or you can buy a bottle of whisky for about CFA20,000 to be kept for you behind the bar.

Byblos Nightclub, across from *Hôtel Beausejour*, Akwa. An upmarket local club featuring mostly African music. Cheap entrance fee at CFA3000.

L'Elysée, near Marché Deïdo. A popular locals' bar with local music – you're likely to be the only foreigner here.

Havana Café, av de Gaulle, Bonapriso. A classy mix of café, nightclub and bar, with a pool table.

Mount Cameroun, bd de la République. A lively dance bar conveniently opposite *Chez Mich la Mbamoise* restaurant.

Rocksy Café, rue Toyota, Bonapriso. The Cameroonian version of a *Hard Rock Café* with lots of dancing and new performers every night.

St Pere, rue Castelnau, behind *Hôtel Parfait Garden*. Popular among expats as a place to begin the night, with western pop; most head off to *Le "78"* later on.

Sun Set (formerly *Jet Set*), av de Gaulle, near Cameroon Airlines. Attracts a mainly young Cameroonian crowd to its good mix of African and Western music.

Le "78", rue Sylvani, Akwa. Popular venue for expats and prostitutes, with modern (imported) light and sound systems, and mainly up-to-date Western music.

Listings

Airfreight Parcels, precious and express items can be sent and received through DHL, 224 rue Joss, Bonanjo (☎42.98.82).

Airlines Most airline offices are in the Bonanjo neighbourhood or in Akwa along bd de la Liberté. They include: Aeroflot, 83 bd de la Liberté (☎42.79.91); Air Afrique, rue Joss (BP 4084; ☎42.42.22 or 42.93.02; Fax 42.45.75); Air France, 1 Place du Gouvernement (BP 4076; ☎42.28.78; Fax 42.99.52); Air Gabon, 5 rue Joss (BP 371; ☎42.49.43 or 42.70.07); Cameroon Airlines, 3 av de Gaulle (BP 4092; ☎42.25.25 or 42.32.22; Fax 42.49.99) and at *Hôtel Akwa Palace* (☎42.26.01); Kenya Airways, at Saga Voyages, rue de Trieste (☎42.96.91; Fax 42.01.37); Nigeria Airways, 17 bd de la Liberté (BP 1126; ☎42.73.21); Sabena, 60 av de Gaulle (BP 2074; ☎42.72.03/34; Fax 42.60.74); Swissair, 33 bd de la Liberté (BP 1283; ☎42.29.29; Fax 42.21.70).

Banks Major branches in the Bonanjo neighbourhood include: Banque Internationale du Cameroun Pour l'Epargne et le Credit (BICEC), av de Gaulle (☎42.84.31; Fax 42.60.47); Société Général de Banques au Cameroon (SGBC), rue Joss (☎42.70.10; Fax 42.87.72), which represents **Thomas Cook**; Société Commercial de Banque-Crédit Lyonnais (SCB-CLC), rue Joss (☎42.65.01; Fax 42.95.12); and Standard Chartered Bank Cameroon, 57 bd de la Liberté (☎42.36.12; Fax 42.27.89). Credit Lyonnais and SGBC only change French francs travellers' cheques and only US\$ and French francs cash. Standard Chartered changes all major European cash currencies at a fixed (high) commission.

Books Librairie Papeterie de Bonapriso, 10 rue Batibois, next to Cinema Bonapriso (BP 2301; ☎42.63.67; Fax 43.24.96) is one of the few places selling international magazines and books in English. Lipacam, 27 av Ahidjo (BP 5487; ☎ & Fax 42.04.69) sells mainly educational books, while Presbook, rue Joffre, behind Sho Plus (BP 5474) has a selection of books by African authors. Most of these sell IGN or Macmillan maps.

Car rental The major firms are at the airport and in the larger hotels: Avis at *Hôtel Akwa Palace* (☎42.03.47 or 42.70.56; Fax 42.66.56) and at Douala Airport (☎30.02.01); Auto Joss on rue Monoprix near the Score supermarket (☎ & Fax 42.86.19); Business H Center, at *Hôtel Méridien* (☎42.27.05); and Europcar (☎43.21.26; Fax 43.21.24).

Cinemas The three big air-conditioned cinemas are Le Concorde on rue Lapeyrère, Le Wouri on bd de la Liberté (☎42.02.52) and Cinema Bonapriso on rue Njo-njo. Smaller movie houses showing old re-runs include The Rex on bd Ahidjo and Le Toula on rue Kitchener.

Consulates Most main embassies are in Yaoundé, but a number of countries maintain consulates in Douala, including: Benin, Bepanda Collège Maturité (☎40.13.41); Canada, 1726 av de Gaulle (BP 2373; ☎43.31.03/05; Fax 42.31.09); Central African Republic, rue Castelnau (BP 175; ☎42.14.65; Fax 30.15.84); Democratic Republic of Congo, 70 rue Sylvanie (BP 690; ☎43.20.29; Fax 43.19.69); Equatorial Guinea, bd de la République (BP 5544; ☎42.27.29); France, av des Cocotiers (BP 869; ☎42.62.50; Fax 42.96.26); Nigeria, bd de la Liberté (BP 1553; ☎43.21.68); Togo, 490 rue Dicka Mpondo (BP 828; ☎42.11.87); UK, 3rd Floor, Standard Chartered Building, bd de la Liberté (BP 1016; ☎42.21.77; Fax 42.88.96); USA, Immeuble Flatters off av de Gaulle (BP 4006; ☎42.03.03; Fax 42.77.90).

Cultural centres British Council, av Drouot, off bd de la Liberté (☎42.51.45); Centre Culturel Français, bd de la Liberté (☎42.69.96); Centre Culturel Africain in Collège Liberman, rue des Écoles (☎42.28.90). The latter runs courses in African languages.

Internet *Cyberbao Café Internet*, 1482 bd de la Liberté (☎42.29.16; *cyberbao@cyberkoki.net*). CFA1500 for half an hour on the Internet, or you can buy your own private address for CFA2000; it then costs CFA250 for each message received and CFA500 for each mail sent. *Web Café* is on rue Joss next to Air Afrique (☎42.87.34; Fax 42.82.31; *technopole@camnet.cm*). Sending and receiving mail costs CFA1000 per message; half an hour on the Internet costs CFA3000.

National Parks For information on Korup National Park, contact the Worldwide Fund for Nature (BP 2417; ☎43.06.64; Fax 43.21.71).

Pharmacies The two main 24hr pharmacies are Pharmacie du Centre, 38 bd de la Liberté and Pharmacie de Douala, bd Ahidjo. Both are well stocked and central.

Photo processing Laboratorie Photo Prunet, 545 rue Pau (☎42.08.67) does high-quality but expensive processing; they also sell old photos of Douala.

Post office The Poste Centrale is on Place du Gouvernement, near the banks in Bonanjo. Branches include: Poste d'Akwa, bd de la Liberté; Poste de New Bell, av Douala Manga Bell; and Poste de Deïdo, rue Dibombé.

Supermarkets Score and Unimarché stock French delicacies flown in regularly from Paris – lobsters, caviar, champagne, pastries and fresh European vegetables are all available at something less than twice the Champs Elysées price. Mysan Market (a supermarket) is much cheaper and sometimes has American goodies.

Swimming pools Non-guests can use the pools at the *Akwa Palace* and the *Sawa* for a fee. They're both expensive, but worth it when the humidity gets too much.

Travel agencies Most business is made through domestic and international airline bookings. Most travel agents do, however, offer a small selection of tours within the country which are quite expensive, along the lines of CFA800,000 for a ten-day round trip, including domestic flights, but tend to be well organized. Agencies in Akwa include: Jully Voyages, on rue Boué de Lapeyrère behind Standard Chartered Bank (BP 1868; ☎42.32.09; Fax 42.84.38); and Jet Cam Tour, on the corner of bd de la Liberté and rue Galliéni (BP 5300; ☎ & Fax 42.30.78). Agencies in Bonanjo include: Cameroun Horizon, behind the Pagoda Manga Bell (BP 3237; ☎42.94.24; Fax 43.09.80); and Delmas Voyages, rue Kitchener (BP 263; ☎42.11.84; Fax 43.14.99).

MOVING ON FROM DOUALA

BY ROAD

Almost all of Douala's **agences de voyage** are based around Place de Ahidjo. The main companies for Yaoundé are Beauty Express (☎42.83.96); Centrale Voyages (☎42.03.16 or 42.26.69); Félicité Express; Super Voyages; and Garanti Express (☎42.61.91). Garanti Express also have buses to Bafoussam, Bamenda, Limbé and Buea. For Nkongsamba and the west, Linda Voyages (☎40.39.57 or 40.26.60), Margo Voyages and Tahiti Voyages (☎49.14.43) have regular connections. Use Transline for Kribi and Edéa. **Share taxis** to Limbé, Buea, Mbanga and Kumba leave from Rond-point Deïdo, near Wouri Bridge.

BY TRAIN

The **Gare de Bessenge** train station is in the northeastern part of the city centre, off Boulevard de la République. Enquiries should be made in advance to Régiefercam (BP 304, ☎42.91.20), since the schedules change frequently. You can buy tickets to Yaoundé, Nkongsamba and Kumba. There is only one daily train to Yaoundé, which leaves at 7am (4hr; CFA6700 first class, CFA2250 second). Trains to Nkongsamba and Kumba leave daily but are extremely slow: passengers don't use these trains. The preferred and quickest route to Kumba, especially in the wet season, when the roads are bad, is to take a share taxi on the good road to Mbanga and catch the afternoon train to Kumba (3 daily; 2–3hr) from there.

BY AIR

Cameroon Airlines, 3 av de Gaulle (☎42.32.22 or 42.25.25) has flights to Garoua (Mon, Weds, Thurs, Fri & Sun); Maroua (Mon, Tues, Thurs, Sat & Sun); Ngaoundéré (Tues, Thurs & Sat); and Yaoundé (daily).

Limbé

LIMBÉ is everything Douala isn't – small, scenic and restful – with the mass of Mount Cameroon looming to the north. This is the nearest town to Douala on the open ocean, and it owes its popularity primarily to the surrounding beaches along the shore of **Ambas Bay**. There's a holiday feel to it, with historical touches added in its well-preserved German and British **colonial buildings** and its shady **botanic garden**. Yet despite the influx of holidaying expats and weekenders, Limbé is not the expensive and overdone resort town you might expect. There's enough economic stimulus in the old **port** and the market, plus the nearby oil refinery and various agricultural projects, for the town not to rely wholly on its tourist industry, and it has retained an authentic provincial feel.

Some history

Limbé (called Victoria until 1983) was created by the **London Baptist Missionary Society**, after they were chased from Fernando Po by the Spanish in the mid-1850s. The missionaries turned to **Alfred Saker** – a former navy engineer converted to missionary work – and asked him to get them a foothold on the mainland. Saker bought the lands around the **Ambas Bay** from the Isubu king, **William of Bimbia**, and, in 1858, founded Victoria.

At first, Victoria was effectively an African Christian colony The first inhabitants of the town were mostly **freed slaves** from Jamaica, Ghana and Liberia, and converted Bakweri and Bimbia (indigenous peoples related to the Douala). From 1859, these townspeople were governed by their own tribunal, headed first by a Jamaican and then by a Sierra Leonean recaptive. At first, the town centred around the church, the school (established in 1860), and the missionary residences. But by the 1870s, English and German **commercial enterprises** – John Holt, the Ambas Bay Trading Co. and the Woermann Co. – had established their own businesses alongside the church. Contrary to Saker's wishes, the site was neither turned into a British naval base nor declared a colony of the British crown. It was left to the Baptists to administer.

British holdings in Cameroon were ceded to the Germans on May 7, 1875. Victoria posed a special problem, however, as it belonged technically to the missionaries and not the crown. The problem was solved in 1887 when Presbyterian missionaries from Basel purchased the land, and incorporated it into the Kaiser's colony. The town then became an important urban centre surrounded by the commercial plantations of the **West Afrikanische Pflanzung Victoria**. By the beginning of the twentieth century, the Victoria–Buea–Douala triangle had become the political and economic nerve centre of German *Kamerun*, and Victoria grew to become the colony's second port, exporting large quantities of cocoa and other agricultural products. Although the Victoria territory became part of the British protectorate in 1915, German companies swiftly regained economic control of the district by buying back their old concessions.

With the outbreak of World War II, the Germans' lands were once again confiscated. In 1947, the British founded the **Cameroon Development Corporation**, and the vast regional plantations – dense stands of cocoa, bananas, oil palms and rubber trees still to be seen as you drive through – spurred Victoria into a new period of expansion. After independence, the CDC was partly taken over by the government, although it is soon to face privatization; it remains the district's biggest employer. In recent years, Limbé has become an opposition stronghold, focusing Anglophone resentment at being treated in a colonial fashion by Yaoundé.

Accommodation

Most hotels are oriented to affluent Douala weekenders. However, given the standards of accommodation, prices seem reasonable if you've just come from the city.

Atlantic Beach Hotel (BP 63; ☎33.32.32 or 33.23.33; Fax 33.26.89). Originally the research laboratory for the Botanic Garden although converted into a military hospital used by the Kaiser's imperial army. It is now Limbé's most luxurious hotel with AC rooms, *boukarous* and a seaview restaurant that features a lunch buffet with masses of beautifully presented Cameroonian and French food. The reception changes money without commission. ③.

Bay Hotel, near the main roundabout. Co-managed by the *Atlantic Beach Hotel* (same BP and telephone) but not nearly as luxurious and slightly run-down. The restored colonial building has a good view of Ambas Bay and clean S/C rooms with fans. Guests can use the *Atlantic Beach* swimming pool for free. ②.

Botanic Garden Guest House, (BP 437; ☎43.18.83 ext 381). A scenically-located colonial building with small and large shared dorms, cooking facilities and a designated campsite (CFA1000 per person). Pay at the Botanic Garden Visitors' Centre. ②.

Holiday Inn Resort, at the end of the road off Church St (BP 126; ☎33.22.90). A promising, fairly large establishment with a range of S/C AC rooms suiting all tastes, suiting all pockets; the bar-restaurant is good value. ②.

Hôtel Mondial, just past the Gendarmerie, 1.5km west of the centre (BP 227; ☎33.26.35). Basic, good-value S/C rooms with fans or AC. Home to the popular *Negrita* nightclub and a pool. ②.

King William Square Hotel, off the main roundabout (☎33.27.29). Centrally located, with simple but clean AC rooms. The manager arranges "eco-touristic" treks and excursions in the Limbé area. ③.

Park Hôtel Miramare, about 2km west of the centre. Co-managed by the *Atlantic Beach* (same BP and telephone), but much cheaper. From its seaside position it has a beautiful view of Ambas Bay. Basic but clean *boukarous*, some with AC, and a pool with algal growth. ②.

Victoria Guest House, next to the *Bay Hotel* (BP 358; ☎ & Fax 33.24.46). A mixed bag of rooms with or without AC, most of them S/C, and always clean. Friendly staff and a homely atmosphere. ②.

The Town

The beachfront is the obvious place to start a visit. A main thoroughfare runs along the shoreline from **Down Beach** and the nearby **fish market** and German colonial-era **government school**, over to the *Atlantic Beach Hotel*. In between are most of the town's major **banks** (BICEC, Credit Lyonnais, Amity and SGBC), and the Presbook and Prescraft centres where you can buy books and regional **artwork**. Looking out over Ambas Bay from the Down Beach area, you can see a group of recently de-populated small islands. Some still have the foundations of buildings, still used for traditional rites and ceremonies. It is possible to visit the islands if you strike a deal with one of the fishermen at the port, but it's safer to arrange a trip through your hotel or through Seagrams Voyages, by the mouth of the river Limbé (BP 11; ☎33.21.41; Fax 33.23.76). West of the *Atlantic Beach*, a road winds between the sea and the hills of the **Botanic Garden** (CFA1000) to the *Miramare* and the garden's main entrance. The Botanic Garden was laid out by the Germans in the early nineteenth century for agricultural experimentation, and originally covered most of present day Limbé. Nowadays the garden is connected to the ecological Mount Cameroon Project, mainly as an educational resource emphasizing the diversity of plant and tree species growing on the mountain. With the hundreds of varieties of trees and the **Limbé River** flowing through the middle, it creates a relaxing spot for an afternoon stroll – stopping on the way for a meal or a cold drink at the *Hot Spot* bar-restaurant overlooking the bay.

Across Idenao Road you find the **post office**, oddly remote from the town centre. Further down this road is the **Limbé Zoological Garden** (also known as the Limbé Wildlife Centre – LWC), which is primarily a **primate sanctuary**, but also houses a

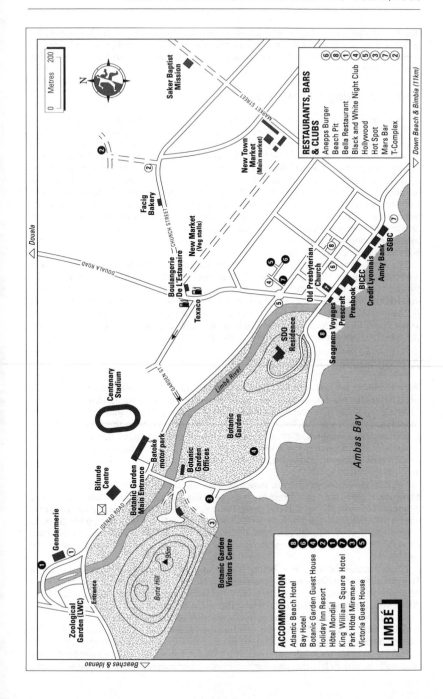

LIMBÉ

ACCOMMODATION

Atlantic Beach Hotel	⑧
Bay Hotel	⑥
Botanic Garden Guest House	④
Holiday Inn Resort	②
Hôtel Mondial	①
King William Square Hotel	⑦
Park Hôtel Miramare	③
Victoria Guest House	⑤

RESTAURANTS, BARS & CLUBS

Anepps Burger	⑥
Beach Pit	⑧
Bella Restaurant	①
Black and White Night Club	④
Hollywood	⑤
Hot Spot	③
Mars Bar	⑦
T-Complex	②

number of types of monkey as well as other animals. The orphans of mother apes killed as bush meat are often brought here, as are unwanted household pets. With international help, this former dilapidated zoo is becoming the focus of primate conservation work in Cameroon.

Eating, drinking and nightlife

Away from the more expensive European food in Limbé's hotel restaurants, there are quite a few good inexpensive places in town. Every evening **Garden Street** is lined with women preparing grilled fish served with your choice of *miondo* or grilled plantain in one of the many roadside bars. **Church Street** has many "off licence" bars and inexpensive restaurants. The *T-Complex* makes excellent salads and has the standard chicken and chips menu. The *Hollywood* restaurant by the main roundabout is a good spot for burgers, seafood and other dishes. *Anepps Burger*, off the Down Beach road, makes tasty Cameroonian dishes as well as burgers. The slightly pricier *Bella Restaurant*, behind the wildlife centre, offers excellent Cameroonian and European dishes. If you're into trying a local speciality, the *Beach Pit*, around the corner from *Anepps Burger*, make a delicious *eru and water fufu* – eru is a protein-rich forest vegetable exported to Nigeria in large quantities, *fufu* is pounded cassava.

The *Mars Bar* perches precariously on the sea wall at the beginning of Down Beach, a pleasant spot for sun-downers and slightly pricey seafood meals. Further along the Bimbia road, by the fish market, fresh fish are grilled and served at the *Red Cross* building, which doubles as a bar at night. For other **nightlife**, the *Limbé Palace* under *King William Square Hotel* is an AC bar with a games room in the back, while the *Black and White Night Club*, next door, offers the best **dancing** in town – its only serious competition is the *Negrita* nightclub at *Hôtel Mondial*.

Around Limbé

West of Limbé, a whole string of **beaches** awaits, all with fine **black sand** (actually, a deep bitter-chocolate colour) a result of the ocean's grinding of ancient **lava flows** from Mount Cameroon. The combination of lush tropical vegetation with the sea and the mountain produces a paradisiac landscape, often enriched with the brooding purple and yellow of an impending storm or the green-and-gold sheen left behind by a recent downpour. Furthermore, the waters around here are perfect for swimming – unlike most places along the West African coast. The beach scenes of the film *Chocolat* were shot here.

You can get **transport to the beaches** from the Batoké motor park in front of the **stadium**. Either hire a cab direct to your destination, or take a shared taxi with people heading to neighbouring villages along the coast. To get to the most popular beach, where you can also camp, ask to be dropped at **Mile 6**; a signboard points through 500m of palm groves to the sea. Mile 6 is a public beach with a guardian, so you have to pay CFA300 to use it. The nearby oil refinery is not nearly as distracting as might be expected.

If you'd rather be watching fishing boats, you might head two miles further on to **Batoké**, a fishing village with a stunning (free) beach surrounded by mountains that drip with vegetation. A sign on the main road leads down to *Etisah* (②), a small hotel 300m from the beach on the outskirts of Batoké, offering basic rooms with fans, and a restaurant serving exotic bush meat meals. Further along the coast road, you reach the popular **Mile 11** beach and the comfortable *Seme New Beach Resort* (BP 130; ☎33.22.26; ④), where you can see the 1999 lava flow close up, use the guarded beach for a fee and eat at a slightly overpriced restaurant. After Mile 11, the paved road continues all the way to **Idenao**, passing numerous other unspoiled beaches, as well as the

---

MOVING ON FROM LIMBÉ

The motor park for **Douala, Buea** and **Kumba** is at **Mile 4**, on the Douala road, from where there are frequent share taxi departures. The main *agences de voyage* in Limbé are Guarantee Express (for **Bamenda, Bafoussam**, Douala and Yaoundé, with booking offices at **Mile 2**), and Petit Papa (for Bafoussam and Bamenda, with booking offices near the New Market).

If you want to visit **Korup National Park**, it is possible to reach Mundemba – the village at the main entrance – **by boat** from Limbé, costing around CFA30,000 per person per day. Seagrams Voyages (see p.1068) arranges four-hour trips through creeks and up the Ndian River. Birds and monkeys are prolific in this area.

There are direct passenger **ferries** from Limbé to Calabar, in **Nigeria**, departing three or four times a week from the port, off Idenau Road. Departures are usually early evening, so make sure you know were you're going once you reach Calabar at around midnight. It's also possible to take a share taxi 48km up the coast to **Idenao** and continue to Nigeria by smaller boats from there. Avoid the cheaper cargo vessels which are laden with smuggled goods and apt to sink quite often (June 1995, for example, with the loss of 100 lives). They tend to make clandestine entries in remote areas, leaving you with the task of finding further transport. Much worse, you'll have no official stamp in your passport and will face serious problems with immigration officials somewhere down the road. Note that you'll be passing through waters which are at the centre of an intense border dispute, over the Bakassi Peninsula, between Cameroon and Nigeria. Navy boats patrol the area and the frontiers have closed for brief periods. Pick up the latest news in Limbé before heading out this way.

---

second wettest place on earth, **Debundscha**, 28km from Limbé (Mile 17). There's a crater lake at Cape Debundscha which is well worth exploring, and from Idenao you can trek through the dense forest to the **Bomana falls**; guides to both places can be arranged though the Visitors' Centre at the Botanic Garden, in Limbé.

Heading south from Limbé, after 10km you pass the army camp at Man O' War Bay (don't take any photos) before reaching the small village of **Bimbia**, the site of the original **Camp Saker**, where the missionary first landed. Today, Bimbia consists of a Baptist Church and a small holiday camping and chalet set-up overlooking the ocean (②). Bookings are made in Limbé through the Saker Baptist Mission just north of Market Street (BP 29; ☎33.23.23), which also arranges transport – cheaper than the share taxis from the fish market. Two kilometres past Bimbia, the **Bimbia-Bonadikombo Nature Trail** is a two-hour hike towards the sea, following the course of a river through mangroves and a variety of lowland forest types. Arrangements for a guide can be made through the Botanic Garden.

North of Limbé, heading inland from Bota, an enjoyable 5km trek uphill to **Bonjongo**, following the Bonjongo road, leads to the impressive old German Palatine Mission Church and a great view of Ambas Bay. Bonjongo is a departure point for a day-trek up **Small Mount Cameroon** (also known as Etinde). Again, you can arrange this through the Botanic Gardens: it's a hard days' trek up the steep slope, but you'll get a good impression of the montane forest.

Buea and Mount Cameroon

Briefly capital of *Kamerun*, **BUEA** is located on the slopes of **Mount Cameroon** some 70km west of Douala. Perched more than 1000m above the ocean, the town breathes in a relatively cool climate – something the Germans were always keen to seek out during their colonial days, but apart from being a base for climbing the mountain, Buea doesn't have a lot to offer.

In 1895, with the arrival of colonial governor **Jesco von Puttkamer**, the Germans began establishing military outposts in their new protectorate. Buea was one such spot, and was made capital in place of Douala from 1901 until 1909. It still has many reminders of its **colonial past**, including administrative buildings, an old school, numerous villas built on piles and a magnificent **palace** built as von Puttkamer's residence. Today, this German *schloss* is used by the president – you could be arrested for taking pictures.

During British rule, Buea was under the authority of the Lieutenant Governor of the Southern Provinces of Nigeria. On the eve of independence, the town had dwindled to 3000 inhabitants and was primarily a colonial resort. But Buea once again found its prestige as an administrative centre when it became capital of the English-speaking West Cameroon, in the post-independence federation. Over the next ten years, it received substantial public investment in the form of government buildings and the population grew rapidly. Since then, Buea has been demoted to capital of South West Province only, and expansion has once more given way to calm stagnation.

Mount Cameroon's most recent **eruption** was in March 1999, lasting roughly three weeks. Nobody was hurt, but a few lost their homes. Tourists flooded to the area to see the lava flow, which crossed the main road, but stopped 100m short of the sea, and to buy "very hot" beer.

Buea Practicalities

If you're heading on to Nigeria, there's a Nigerian consulate in town (☎32.25.28), where, with persistence, you may be able to get a visa, though they tend to refer non-residents to the High Commission in Yaoundé. To find the consulate, turn left at the police station roundabout as you're coming into town from Limbé, then it's around 200m past the *Mountain Hotel*, on the left. The **tourist office**, on the main drag, (Mon–Fri 8am–3.30pm, but best before 2.00pm; ☎32.25.34; Fax 32.26.56), organizes guided ascents of the mountain. Arranging practical matters for the climb invariably requires you to spend the night in Buea, before making an early start on the ascent; there are several reasonably comfortable places **to stay**:

Hôtel Mermoz, Long St – the old Limbé road (BP 13; ☎32.23.49). A recently renovated hotel in an oval-shaped stone building with a good-value restaurant and bar. Clean comfortable S/C rooms with hot water and TV. ②.

Mountain Hotel, (BP 71; ☎32.22.35). Cosily nostalgic and reminiscent of an old hunting lodge, with a fireplace in the trophied lobby, plus a pool. Slightly run-down these days and the garden restaurant seems a little overpriced. ③.

Parliamentarian Flats, 250m south of the police station roundabout (BP 20; ☎32.24.59). Government-owned hotel overlooking the slopes of Mount Cameroon. Clean and comfortable S/C rooms with hot water. Pleasant restaurant and bar. ②.

Presbyterian Mission, past the police station roundabout up the hill towards Upper Farm (BP 19). Basic double rooms, S/C or with access to cold water shower facilities and a well-equipped kitchen. ②.

Mount Cameroon

Buea is the usual starting point for the ascent of the occasionally-active volcano **Mount Cameroon**. At 4095m high, and rising directly from sea level, Mount Cameroon is easily the tallest mountain in West Africa. To get a sense of scale, it's on a par with the higher peaks in the Alps and just lower than Mount Whitney in California. Despite the equatorial latitude, the highest slopes get freezing rain and occasional snow mixed in with unusually high winds, and the climate at the summit is alpine – conditions which, in conjunction with the very steep, stony slopes, can make it an arduous climb. You'll need a guide.

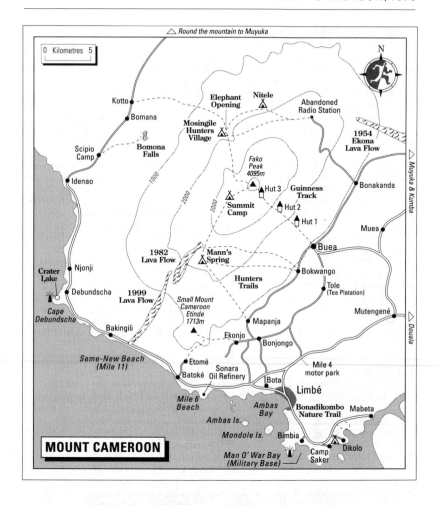

Determination, however, rather than super-fitness or technique, is the attribute that will get you to the top – as most people do. Ideally you should go during the "dry" season, roughly from mid-November to the end of April. With the arrival of eco-tourism a number of new **trails** have been opened and it is now possible to reach the summit via these routes as an alternative to the direct and steep old trail, known as the Guinness Track. All trails to the summit are up the mountain's southeast face, avoiding the extremely heavy rainfall of the western slopes and the thunderstorms of the east and northern slopes. The new descent trails follow an old elephant track on the northwestern slope.

The tourist office in Buea only organizes climbs up the Guinness Track (CFA9000 per person per day), but this has not been well maintained in recent years, and only offers a limited impression of the mountain's complexities. If you wish to support the conservation of the mountain's unique biodiversity, you should arrange your climb through the **Common Board of Eco-tourism** in the Mount Cameroon Region (☎40.73.99), currently based at the Mount Cameroon Project in Buea. They arrange tours up the new routes on old hunters' trails, using local guides (often ex-hunters). If you wish to start out from Limbé, you can seek advice from the Botanic Garden, where the Mount Cameroon Project also has an office (see p.1068).

Every climber with the eco-tourism board pays CFA2000/day towards a fund, a major proportion of which goes into village development projects. Every group must have a guide (CFA6000/day) and porters (CFA4000/day). For trips of two or more days, you need at least one porter to every climber, especially when climbing to the summit when they have to carry sufficient water for one and a half days of drinking and cooking.

Depending on the trail you choose to follow, the climb to the summit and down again can be done in between two and five days. It is possible, if you are very fit, to do the trek in one day, making a pre-dawn start to be on the summit by mid-afternoon, and down in Buea again shortly after dark. A major disadvantage of this high-speed approach is not having time to pause to absorb the mountain's moods and images.

Equipment requirements need not be daunting. Footwear is the most important item: ideally you should wear waterproof hiking boots with ankle support. Plenty of people tackle the mountain in running shoes, but only the sturdiest will cushion your feet from jabbing rocks. Good sleeping bags and warm, waterproof clothes are necessary if you're staying the night on the mountain and you'll also need to bring a tent if you're camping. These can possibly be hired in Buea or Limbé along with a few other items, but don't count on it. Depending on the food arrangements you make with the guide and porters, you can choose to bring a stove and cook your own food, or you can eat together with them by paying for the supplies. Take plenty of dried foods (nuts, raisins and chocolate are recommended), and water, which is only available at Hut 1 and Mann's Spring.

The climb

You can start the climb from several points – depending on how many days you have set aside to explore the mountain. The so-called **Guinness Track** takes a straight line from Buea to the summit, along which there are three basic (and rat-infested) **mountain huts**, with a bare minimum of furnishings.

Most people prefer to ascend by one of the old **hunters' trails**, where there are newly cleared basic **campsites**. From **Bokwango** or **Mapanja**, you ascend through farmland and village plantations, then into montane forest, until breaking out again to

---

THE GUINNESS MOUNTAIN MARATHON

Since its inception in 1973, the annual **Guinness Mountain Marathon** has achieved a reputation as one of the toughest athletic events in the world. On the last weekend in January, a field of about 350 runners slog 37km over tortuous terrain from the Buea sports stadium up the jungly lower slopes to the chilly summit and back. Although Cameroonians dominate the competition, they have been joined by an international array of athletes including Europeans and representatives of most African countries. Fifty thousand spectators watch the proceedings, with the men's winner usually completing the event in around four and a half hours and the women's winner in about five hours fifty minutes. Guinness no longer organizes the race, as this responsibility has been taken over by the Ministry of Youth and Sports. The race has officially been renamed "the Race of Hope", though many still refer to it by the old name. If you want to take part, you must be nominated by a sports club and complete the qualifying races. For more information contact the Provincial Delegation of Youth and Sports in Buea (☎32.21.52 or 32.26.47).

the open savannah after about four hours. On clear days there are wonderful views of Small Mount Cameroon (Etinde), the ocean and Malabo Island, the sister volcano to Mount Cameroon. The first camp is on the forest/savannah margin next to **Mann's Spring** (after German geographer Gustav Mann), which is also the destination of a shorter one-day trek up the mountain. If you're lucky you might find antelopes drinking at the spring. The ascent to the summit continues on the second day passing the lava flow from the 1999 eruption. From here on the climbing gets steeper as you move through colder **grasslands** to the Summit Camp about 450m from the top. By now you're likely to be noticing minor altitude effects – shortness of breath and lassitude. Before sunrise on the third day you make the final ascent to **Fako peak** at 4095m (13,435ft) and can sign the book to mark your triumph. Disappointingly, whatever the time of year or day it's rare to get a clear view from Fako, but early morning is the best bet.

The **descent** can be made into Buea down the Guinness Track in just five leg-dissolving hours – with occasional encouragement from a "Guinness Is Good For You" sign. With more time available you can descend on the opposite side of the mountain through a completely different microclimate. This descent starts down a deep lava valley into a savannah region where you may see antelopes. Close to the Bonakanda hunters' village you come across **Bat Cave** and, a little further on, the camp for the third night close to the Mosingile hunters' village.

Heading northwest from Mosingile takes you through forest towards Kotto, past the **elephant opening**, a clearing ploughed by forest elephants where they congregate to eat, drink and bathe. Forest elephants are extremely elusive, so it's very unlikely that you'll see the beasts themselves, but you may see their spoor. This route continues to meet the mountain ring road, where you can be collected by vehicle or walk east to Nitele hunters' village. From Nitele it's a 4–5-hour steep climb to an abandoned British Post and Telecommunications Radio Station, now classified as an **industrial monument**. You can prearrange for a good 4WD vehicle to collect you here, or camp again and trek back to Buea over a remarkable plateau and down a motorable road from Bonakanda.

An alternative route from Mosingile hunters' village follows the contours east direct to the radio station, avoiding the climb but also forfeiting the elephant opening.

Kumba and around

The first of the major towns of western Cameroon that you come to heading north from Buea or Douala is the agricultural and commercial centre of **KUMBA**. Although the town itself is large and uninspiring, with a population approaching 60,000, it's in the heart of a beautiful region. **Lake Barombi Mbo** – a picturesque crater lake just 5km out of town – is like another world.

Kumba's layout is disorienting: the town has no real centre – or rather it has too many – and single-storey wooden-plank houses spread in all directions. But there's a very big **market** here, specializing in goods imported from Nigeria (there's a large Igbo immigrant community in Kumba), and if, like most travellers, you're only passing through, you should head for the market. East of the market, you'll find the old main **motor park**, the **post office**, the **banks** (BICEC and Credit Lyonnais) and the *agences de voyage* with connections to Douala and Mamfé. The main **administrative quarter** is located a good 4km northwest of the market and yet another centre has grown up around the **train station**, at the terminus of a branch line from the Douala–Nkongsamba line.

For **share taxis** to Tombel, Bafoussam and Bamenda, the Three Corners motor park is 3km northeast of the stadium along a potholed road. The Buea motor park, on the

Buea road, caters for share taxis to Limbé, Foula and Buea, while the Mbanga road motor park, west of the town centre, on the Ekondo Titi road, has share taxis to Ekondo Titi (for Korup National Park) and Mundemba.

Accommodation and eating

As you'd expect in a busy market centre such as this, there's a host of reasonably cheap hotels, most with reasonable **restaurants**. *Classy Burger* serves decent fast food and beer.

Azi Motel Extension, on the Buea road (BP 304; ☎35.42.91). Conveniently located for arrivals by public transport from the south, this hotel has clean S/C rooms with fans or AC. It's the priciest but also the best hotel in town with friendly staff, a restaurant, two bars and Kumba's most reliable telephone for making long-distance calls. ②–③.

Bridge Inn, on the outskirts of town, on the Mundemba road (BP 385). Simple S/C rooms with AC or fans, and a restaurant serving inexpensive food. You can camp in the grounds for CFA2000 per person. ①.

Hotel Metropole, off the Mundemba road. A relatively new hotel featuring comfortable S/C rooms – some with hot water – AC or fans. Often full. ②.

Queens Inn, Endele St, near the market. Cheap basic rooms with or without shared facilities, in a central location. ①.

Tavern Cross Junction Hotel, on the Buea road, near the town centre. Simple, good-value rooms with fans and S/C or shared facilities. Inexpensive Cameroonian food is served in the lively street-front restaurant. ①.

Western Inn, Kramer Ave (☎ & Fax 35.41.48). Clean S/C rooms with AC or fans. Pleasant restaurant serving both European and African dishes. ②.

Lake Barombi Mbo

You can walk from Kumba to **Lake Barombi Mbo** in about an hour and a half but a newly constructed road makes it possible to get to the lakeshore by taxi (CFA500). The road goes off to the left just after the SDO's (Senior Divisional Officer's) office, about 3km from the town centre. An alternative is to take a taxi to this junction (CFA150) from where it's a pleasant 2km walk to the lake.

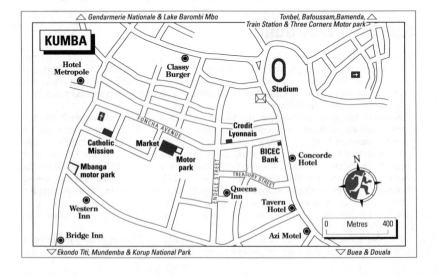

THE ECOLOGY OF BAROMBI MBO

The **Barombi** people of the lakeshores are completely dependent on the lake and seem to have lived in a harmonious symbiosis with it for hundreds of years. The **fish** they catch are an obscure series of small cichlid species (mouth-breeding fish) called *pundu*, *kululu*, *dikume* and *pingu* – and a single type of catfish. All of them live only here, some at depths scientists haven't been able to account for in terms of normal fishy physiology. Traditional hand-woven gill-nets and basket traps select only larger fish, ensuring their continued survival. Traditionally, the Barombi took further care to guarantee their livelihood by actively appeasing the lake at their Ndengo cult grove. More and more young people, though, are installing themselves down in Kumba or further afield and leaving the old ways behind. Kumba itself is now drawing not just people but the lake's very water, piped to the town system. The surrounding forest is also under increasing pressure as areas are cleared for farming and the wood taken for fuel. It now remains to be seen if the new road will improve the local economy or accelerate the destruction of the resource that locals have always depended upon.

The dense forest of the area crowds right down the inside of the crater to the lakeshore, providing an unbelievable green backdrop. The lake – 2.5km across and 110m deep – is crystal clear and perfect for swimming. You'll see a couple of fishing boats when you arrive, and if their owners are around, they'll paddle you around the lake, or take you across it to the small village of Barombi on the other side. The price of the trip is negotiable (around CFA500). Although the lake is basically safe for swimming, stay out of the water immediately around the village as bilharzia is quite prevalent here.

The Mamfé Depression

The Mamfé depression is a low-lying, thickly forested area bounded to the north, south and east by a semicircular range of mountains. **Mount Kupe**, with its unique flora and fauna, is in the southeast of this range approximately 45km east of Kumba. Following the volcanic rift north, taking the Bangem road, is the Manengouba Massif and the beautiful **Twin Crater Lakes**.

Passing through the depression is the southernmost of the two main overland routes from Cameroon to Nigeria. It runs through the somewhat isolated enclave of **Mamfé**, in the middle of dense forest about 65km short of the border. Only Nigeria-bound travellers are likely to visit Mamfé and generally only in the dry season. In the rainy season, the roads leading to Mamfé become some of the most difficult in Cameroon, even for four-wheel-drive vehicles, and despite the many extra kilometres, Mora, in the north, has now become the preferred crossing point into Nigeria (see p.1131).

Meanwhile, if you can cope with its difficulties, the direct route from Kumba to Mamfé is quite a trip. The road passes through dense rainforest, and occasionally yields spectacular views as it detours around mountains. This region has its own unique flora and fauna, and contains many forest reserves and protected areas such as **Korup National Park**. From **Mundemba**, the entrance to the park, it's relatively straightforward – depending on the status of the border dispute over the oil-rich Bakassi Peninsula – to continue by boat via the creeks to Ikang and Calabar in Nigeria.

Mount Kupe

Mount Kupe (2050m), revered by the local people as home to their ancestral and forest spirits, is approached from the small Bakossi village of **NYASOSO**, about 10km north of Tombel. Regular share taxis connect through from Kumba. The mountain is shrouded in a unique cloud forest which supports rich biodiversity, much of it endemic to the area. **Chimpanzees** and several species of globally threatened primates live on the mountain, but it's the vast **birdlife** that has given the mountain its international reputation – over 320 species have been recorded to date.

The Mount Kupe Forest Project have headquarters in Nyasoso and can arrange **accommodation** in private homes in the village at a fixed rate of CFA3000/person. If you arrive after office hours ask for either the *Women's Centre* or *Mrs Ekwoge's Guest House*. The project also has information about the unique ecology of the mountain and if you are a keen bird-watcher they may provide you with a species list. To climb the mountain each person has to pay a Community Forest Fee of CFA2000 and take a guide at CFA3500 for the day.

The **climb** to the summit is steep, and slippery when wet, but can be done in six hours if you are reasonably fit. There are two marked routes up to the summit, known as **Max's Trail** and **Shrike Trail**, which can be used to make a round trip. The trail leads you through a fascinating forest with fruits, flowers, soft green mosses, lichens and other epiphytes dangling from the trees. Once you have pushed your way up and out of the thicket onto the summit, you are rewarded with a spectacular view – if the weather is clear – and you may be lucky enough to hear chimpanzees calling in the misty forest below. You can also go out **at night**, and with the aid of a guide and a good torch, you are likely to see several species of bushbaby and loris. Camping is also possible on the mountain.

As an alternative to the demanding climb, the project has created an informative 2km self-guided **nature trail**. A printed guide is available free from the project office.

Manengouba twin crater lakes

BANGEM, approximately 40km north of Nyasoso, is a good base for some rewarding day-treks in the area, including the spectacular **twin crater lakes** nestled in the huge grassy bowl of the Manengouba caldera. These sacred lakes, **Man Lake** and **Woman Lake** are curiously different in colour – the larger "female" lake is blue and the smaller "male" lake is vivid green from algal growth.

Bangem, a small administrative centre, has several options for basic **accommodation**. In the town square, *Farmers Bar and Guest House* (①) has rooms with a shared toilet and bucket shower. About 100m from the town square, up 1st Street, *Pentagon* (①) has similar rooms, although less well-kept and behind the potentially noisy bar and disco. Heading out of town on the Melong road, the government guesthouse (CPDM *Party House*; ①) on the right-hand side, is slightly more expensive and has tidy rooms. The *Catholic Mission* (①), close to the town square, generally only accommodates missionaries.

The **walk to the lakes** is straightforward and can be done without a guide, but you must register and pay a fee of CFA1000 per person to the council clerk at the police station by CPDM *Party House*. Buy provisions and drinking water in the town, as there are no shops on the way. To reach the lakes, head southeast out of town on 2nd Street and stick to the main track. The walk takes about three hours and is a steady climb until the final approach to the summit, where the track switches back and forth up the steep crater rim over which the flat expanse of the caldera floor comes into view. The track continues into and across the crater but soon becomes indiscernible among the cattle tracks and grasses. Carry on in the same direction towards the peaks on the far side and the larger Woman Lake reveals itself. The male lake is a short climb to the right around a distinctive small steep hill. You can **camp** by, and fish and swim in, the female lake, but swimming is forbidden in the male lake. Attempts to do so would be pretty foolhardy anyway as the lake is surrounded by treacherously steep forested slopes.

Korup National Park

The **Korup National Park**, which adjoins Nigeria's Cross River National Park (see p.990) harbours one of the richest remaining equatorial ecosystems in Africa. The WWF-managed Korup project covers an area of about 3000 square kilometres, stretching across most of the area west of the Kumba–Mamfé road, but the core protected area, where no logging or agriculture is permitted, is just 1259 square kilometres. It contains forest elephants, 327 species of birds, 400 different kinds of tree and a quarter of all the primate species known in Africa, including chimpanzees. It was thought that gorillas lived in Korup, but it's now believed this was a misunderstanding over the Pidgin for chimpanzee (gorillas do live further north, just north of Eyumojok in the Takamanda Forest Reserve, contiguous with the Okwango division of the Cross River National Park, see p.990). In the fast-flowing rivers – the Ndian, the Bake, the Yafe, the Madie and the Munaya – many varieties of fish previously unknown to zoologists have been discovered, and new finds in natural pharmacological products are being made all the time.

Access

The *piste* leading from Kumba to the village of **Mundemba**, the main entrance to the park, is reasonable and clearly signposted and **share taxis** run regularly between the two towns. Count on a full day's travel from Douala to the park, via Kumba and Ekondo Titi. You can reach Mundemba **by boat** from Limbé (see p.1067) and if you're coming **from Nigeria**, it's possible to get here by boat from Ikang, a two- to three-hour trip along the Ndian River to arrive at Bula Beach near Mundemba. Customs and border controls are dealt with before proceeding into town, and are usually uncomplicated. Coming overland **from Mamfé**, the northernmost entrance to Korup is at **Baro**, which you reach via **Nguti** on the Mamfé–Kumba road. Transport is hard to find for the 30km from Nguti to Baro, but there are occasional share taxis and you may be able to get a ride with one of the project staff (anyone in Nguti can direct you to the WWF office). If you want to spend a night in Nguti, the *Green Castle* (①) has S/C rooms, running water, electricity in the evenings, and a common room where you can buy drinks and order food. Further from town, with smaller rooms and shared facilities, is the *Samba Inn* (①).

Mundemba

On arrival in **MUNDEMBA**, the **Korup Information Centre** (7.30am–noon & 2.30–5pm) is unmissable on the right-hand side of the road as you reach the middle of town. They collect a CFA5000 **park entrance fee** and assign an obligatory guide (CFA3500/day, plus CFA2000/day per porter as needed). An additional CFA500 is collected per person for each night of camping (including porters). The guides are excellent company and since they live in the forest, they know the terrain well and are enthusiastic in their explanations. Formalities out of the way, it's 8km from the Visitor's Centre to the park entrance, and you can either walk it with your guide, or take a Korup vehicle which charges CFA3500 for a return journey.

Modest **accommodation** is to be had at the *Iyas Hotel* (②) with clean S/C twin rooms with fans, and a bar-restaurant serving *steack frites* or fish and chips. The more basic *Vista Palace* (①) has neat and reasonably priced rooms with shared facilities.

If you want to make guide or accommodation arrangements before arriving at Korup, contact the WWF representatives in Douala (BP 2417; ☎43.06.64; Fax 43.21.71), or Yaoundé (BP 6776; ☎21.42.41; Fax 21.42.40).

The park

At the park entrance, an impressive **wooden suspension bridge** spans the Mana River, allowing year-round access to the park. If you only have time for a **day-trip**, fol-

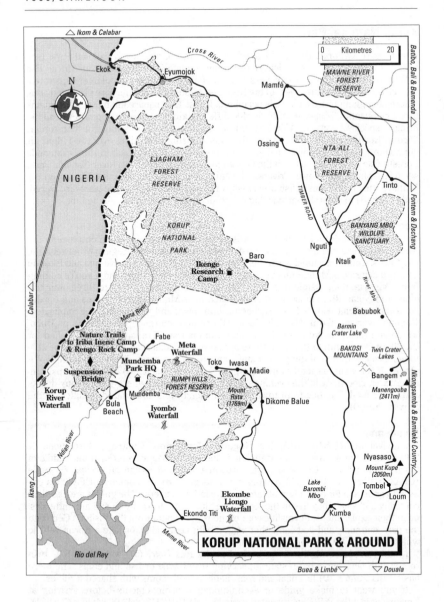

low the nature trail marked with indicator posts which points out the forest's interesting features – everything from termite mounds to an endless variety of plants and trees.

For longer visits, several **campsites** have been set up inside the park, with accommodation in insect-screened huts. The closest, *Iriba Inene Camp,* is only 1.5km from the park entrance, on the nature trail. There are kitchens with firewood, water for drinking and bathing and latrine-type toilets. Insect repellent is a good idea as tiny sweat bees sometimes swarm the camps during the day, and swimming in rivers during your hikes is likely to attract blackflies, known in French as *mout-mout* – nasty creatures with a stinging, itchy bite. Beware too of driver ants.

The possibilities for exploring are pretty well unlimited, and two or three days of hiking is not unreasonable. In the southern sector of the park, trails lead to the **Mana River Waterfall**, to the **Rengo Rock** camp (cave explorations in the area), and up to **Mount Yuhan** which peaks at 1079m. Ten kilometres from the entrance is **Chimpanzee camp**, where if you are lucky you may hear or even see chimpanzees. Hiking in the opposite direction (out of the park) leads to the **Meta Waterfall**, on the headwaters of the Mana River (half a day's trek from Mundemba), and on to the **Iyombo Waterfall**. Further east, **Mount Rata** rises to an elevation of 1769m, the highest peak in the **Rumpi Hills**. Despite the wealth of wildlife, your chances of seeing large animals are slim, though most people at least spot red colobus monkeys scampering through the canopy, and duiker antelope in the undergrowth.

If you enter the park's northern sector at the **Baro** subheadquarters, you penetrate the forest by crossing the **Bake River**. A suspension bridge once made this an all season access, but this is currently awaiting repairs. In Baro, the park staff are welcoming, but there are no guides and porters. There's a building to sleep in, but you'll need your own sleeping and cooking gear – it's possible to hire these in Nguti.

Mamfé and around

MAMFÉ is basically a stopover point for travellers or traders, many of whom use the town as a base to unload goods they have smuggled from Nigeria on small boats up the **Cross River**. The constant comings and goings add energy to the otherwise sleepy town, but make it rather anonymous as well: it could be almost anywhere in West Africa. Today the administrative headquarters of the Manyu district of South West Province, Mamfé (the name is a corruption of Mansfield, the settlement's first German district officer) was later part of the British Cameroons and subject to the policy of **"indirect rule"** expressed through the creation of Native Authorities. When it was administered as part of Nigeria, it was an important town. In 1959, the town hosted the **Mamfé Conference** which tried unsuccessfully to establish voting rules for the upcoming UN plebiscite. In 1961 its inhabitants voted for unification with the Cameroon Republic, since when its status has declined.

Practicalities

Considering its remoteness, Mamfé has a reasonable infrastructure – district buildings, hospital, filling station and missions. If you've just arrived from Nigeria, and have made it this far without CFA francs, you may be relieved to discover there's a BICEC bank here. In principle they should change travellers' cheques and cash (except, of course, for Naira and West African CFA) but as they usually don't have the current rates, you can only be certain of changing French francs without any problems. There's also an active black market in Mamfé for changing Naira, but the rate is better at the border, and even better in Nigeria.

Fresh in from Nigeria, Cameroonian prices are rather a shock. But **accommodation** seems pretty expensive in Mamfé even if you've come from the other direction, especially once you see what you actually get for your money.

Data Guest House, 15 minutes walk north of the town centre (BP 29; ☎34.13.99). The best value hotel in town, with clean S/C rooms and a striking view over the Cross River. Good eating and friendly staff. ②.

Great Aim Hotel, north of the motor park (BP 69). Good bar-restaurant and basic rooms with shared facilities and fans. ①.

MOVING ON FROM MAMFÉ

Regular share taxis and minibuses to **Ekok** and **Kumba** leave from the main motor park in the centre of town. Tonton Voyages and Tchatcho Voyages are the only *agences de voyage* with regular connections to Kumba; their offices are near the motor park. Motorized *pirogue*s heading up the **Cross River** to Ekok can be caught by the old German Bridge. To **Korup National Park** (see p.1079), take a taxi as far as Nguti for the northern entrance, or proceed to Kumba and change there for Mundemba, the main entrance.

The two mountain roads – to **Bamenda** and to **Dschang** – are difficult at any time of year and generally impassable during the rains. Enquire at the motor park to see if any transport is headed in the direction you wish to go, and in either case prepare yourself to be panic-stricken for much of the trip. Wrecked vehicles strewn down the cliffsides attest to the real danger of both routes. Going through this beautiful scenery by mountain bike, in the other direction – downhill – is a much better option.

Heritage Hotel, opposite the government high school on the Nguti road. One of the better places in town with a range of clean rooms with varying degrees of facilities, but you have to order food a day in advance. ②–③.

Ekok: the Nigerian border

Sixty-three kilometres west of Mamfé is the border town of **EKOK**. In the dry season it's possible to cover this stretch in two to three hours; in the wet season the road is practically impassable and the only viable alternative is to reach Ekok by motorized *pirogue*. The gates on the Nigerian side close at 8pm; clear Cameroonian customs with ten minutes to spare unless you're willing to camp in the muddy lorry park in no-man's-land. Otherwise, stay in Ekok – a brash, noisy place with an authentic, frontier-town feel. There are several **hotels**, almost always full of overnighters waiting for the border to open. Rock music blares from every stall, kerosene lamps dazzle and street sharks besiege you with all kinds of nefarious suggestions. Note that there's no bank in Ekok.

THE CENTRAL HIGHLANDS

The landscapes of Cameroon's mountainous west – the Central Highlands – are overwhelmingly beautiful, ranging from the **volcanic hills** of the **Grassfields** to sheer cliffs with **waterfalls** and **crater lakes** hidden behind dense vegetation. The area is also interesting from a cultural point of view, with many of its old chiefdoms surviving into an era when increasing agricultural prosperity has brought one of the fastest rates of development in the country. There's a wealth of sights and towns which you could spend weeks, or months, exploring.

The area divides up fairly clearly into the **Bamiléké country** in the south, the **Bamenda Grassfields** in the north and the **Bamoun country** in the east. The main town in Bamiléké country – and the capital of West Province – is the rapidly growing centre of **Bafoussam**. Its wealth was formerly based on coffee production, but in recent years industrialization has come fast and it's not a very soulful place. Situated on a junction of good paved roads, though, it's a convenient springboard for visiting other, more characterful regional towns. **Bandjoun**, for example, retains the traditional flavour of its old chiefdom, and boasts the best-preserved **palace** in the region. **Dschang**, situated in the mountains at an altitude of 1400m, has a mild, almost European climate, and its German colonial vacation resort attracts many visitors.

Bamenda is the capital of North West Province. From here, you can set out on the difficult **Ring Road** which dips and bends through the mountainous **Grassfields**, a district of hilly, moist savannah, passing through a number of **Tikar chiefdoms** and

Fulani settlements along the route. Recently it has become impossible to complete the ring, due to two collapsed bridges, but they may be restored.

In Bamoun country, the cultural and historical highpoint is **Foumban**, a town with a remarkable turn-of-the-century palace, notable museums and a thriving crafts industry. For all its rich past, however, Foumban takes an economic backseat to Bamenda.

Bafoussam

The **administrative capital** of the Western Province, **BAFOUSSAM** is a noisy and vibrant centre of commercial hyperactivity. In the last two decades, the population has mushroomed to over 150,000; if you thrive on the hustle and bustle of a Third World city, Bafoussam will have a strong appeal. Situated on the edge of the Francophone zone, the Gallic influence is fairly unmistakeable too, especially if you've just arrived from "Anglo" Bamenda.

The Bamiléké, who dominate the city, are notorious for their commercial energy and are renowned as traders throughout the country. However, they never sell their land, so newcomers rarely integrate and the city is culturally very homogenous. The traditional **chefferie** (chief's compound) – to the southeast, off the Route de Douala, may be worth a visit if you don't have time to visit the more impressive *chefferie* of Bandjoun, but in true Bamiléké style they tend to demand an extortionate entrance fee and you will have to haggle hard to be allowed in for the standard CFA1000 per head and CFA1500 for a camera.

Bafoussam owes its prosperity largely to **Arabica coffee**, which flourishes in the surrounding hills. **Industry**, spurred on by earnings from the coffee crop, has also made deep inroads in recent years. The Union des Coopératives du Café de l'Ouest (UCCAO) set up a coffee processing plant in the 1970s and since then, a Brasseries du Cameroun brewery, a cigarette factory and a printing press have all gone into operation.

Accommodation

Bafoussam has a surprisingly narrow range of inexpensive **accommodation** for a town of its size.

Hôtel le Continental, av de la République (BP 136; ☎44.14.58). Slightly run-down but quite comfortable. S/C rooms with balcony and TV. The once busy restaurant and bar is a bit too quiet for comfort these days. ②.

Hôtel Fédéral, near the Foumban *gare routière* on rte de Foumban (BP 136; ☎44.13.74). Completely renovated and the best-value hotel in town. Crispy clean sheets in S/C rooms with hot water. The hotel also runs a good restaurant and bar. ②.

Hôtel Le Président, rue Nguetti Michel, near the BICEC bank (BP 78; ☎44.11.36). Once Bafoussam's grand hotel but, sadly, can no longer be considered luxurious. The dark AC rooms are, however, available at a very reasonable price. ②.

Hôtel SN Palace Garden, rte de Bamenda, at the outskirts of town (BP 745; ☎44.16.96). The best hotel outside the town centre, with a swimming pool, tennis courts, bar and restaurant. ③.

Ramada Motel, near the Foumban *gare routière*. Simple S/C rooms with cold water and a comfortable TV bar. ①.

Résidence Saré, rte de Bamenda (☎44.25.99). Slightly run-down chalets, with hot showers and AC. ③.

Talotel, centrally located off the marché *rond-point* (☎44.41.85 or 44.61.81; Fax 44.43.46). The newest and most luxurious hotel in town. Tastefully decorated S/C rooms with carved furniture and the obligatory TV. Restaurant, nightclub and a lively outdoor bar. ③.

The Town

Bafoussam's dual administrative and commercial functions are reflected in its layout. The broad avenues of the administrative quarter, where you'll find the Résidence du

BAFOUSSAM

ACCOMMODATION

Hôtel le Continental	❶
Hôtel Fédéral	❹
Hôtel le Président	❼
Hôtel SN Palace Garden	❷
Ramada Motel	❺
Résidence Saré	❸
Talotel	❻

RESTAURANTS, BARS & CLUBS

Arcade	⑦
La Bauxite	③
Coffee Shop	⑤
Evasion Night-club	⑧
Express Café	①
Patisserie de la Paix	④
La Refuge	②
Rubis Club	⑥

Gouverneur, Préfecture, and Mairie, are neatly gathered on a hill in the **Tamdja neighbourhood**. From the roundabout where the Palais de Justice stands, the main **Avenue Wanko** heads downhill to the north towards the **market**. You'll find the major **banks**, including CBC and BICEC, either on or around Avenue Wanko, and Crédit Lyonnais at the *rond-point* by the Foumban *gare routière*. Don't bother to visit the unhelpful **Ministère du Tourisme** (☎44.77.82).

Bafoussam's **market**, which occupies a small hill, and is held every four days, is in the middle of the older commercial neighbourhoods known as Djeleng and Famla. A wide range of **crafts** can be bought in the market, although it's better to head to rue Nguetti Michel, the street in front of *Hôtel Le Président*. Here you'll find numerous workshops where artists carve decorative wood panels, furniture and sculptures, and it's possible to bargain directly with them.

MOVING ON FROM BAFOUSSAM

The main **gare routière** is right next to the market and has share taxis to most destinations south of Bafoussam, including Banjoun and Bafang. Taxis to **Foumban** leave from the *gare routière* in front of the Texaco station at the Foumban *rond-point*. Share taxis leave for **Dschang** and **Bamenda** from the Shell station en route de Bamenda. Further along this road, across from *Hôtel le Continental, agences de voyage* such as Savannah Enterprises have regular connections to Bamenda.

A number of other agencies run scheduled services to **Yaoundé, Douala, Bamenda** and **Dschang**. Garanti Express and Jeannot Express have booking offices off rue du Marché near the main *gare routière*.

To get around the region under your own steam, expensive **car rental** can be arranged through Avis (BP 1045; ☎44.13.71; Fax 44.20.71), located on the Route de Foumban on the east side of town. It may be difficult to find 4WD vehicles here.

Practicalities

There are a number of good, cheap **eating places** near the Foumban *gare routière* and *Hôtel Fédéral*. Try *La Refuge* for excellent African dishes, or *La Bauxite*, a snack bar selling salads and simple meals. Next to *La Bauxite*, the *Patisserie de la Paix* makes a good place to stop for fresh baked bread and pastries. The *Coffee Shop*, further along the same road, serves quality coffee with breakfast and healthy portions of rice, beans and vegetables during the day. For espresso, the *Express Café* is a good option, and further out along the Bamenda road, turning right after the Shell Station, a whole line of street stalls sell cheap, freshly made omelettes and salad. An excellent **bar** from which to watch the hectic street life is the *Rubis Club*, on rue du Marché, where food vendors pass by in a steady stream selling delicacies such as filled intestines and sausages, or you can be served whatever is on the day's menu from the nearby streetside chop shops.

For **nightlife**, the *Arcade,* off Avenue de la République across from the market, has live music every Wednesday and weekend nights. The newly renamed and redecorated *Evasion Nightclub* is also worth a weekend visit for the disco and live music – even though they don't sell beer and expect you to buy spirits by the bottle.

The Bamiléké Country

The **Bamiléké country** is roughly a triangle, delineated by the Noun River to the northeast and the Bamboutous mountains the west. The main roads in the area (all paved) pass through **Bafoussam, Bandjoun, Bangangté, Bafang, Dschang** and **Mbouda**, all accessible by public transport. The area has numerous **chefferies** (chiefdoms) and natural sites including **crater lakes** and **waterfalls**.

Bandjoun

Twenty kilometres south of Bafoussam, **BANDJOUN** is the largest and best preserved of the Bamiléké chiefdoms. The **chefferie** (chief's compound) is situated 3km south of Bandjoun on the Route de Bangangté and you can reach it by catching a share taxi from the *gare routière* for CFA125.

Bandjoun is the ideal place to admire traditional Bamiléké architecture at its best (see box, p.1087). Traditionally, the chief's compound was the largest in town, incorporating several huts encircled by a bamboo fence. Inside were rooms and granaries for the chief and each of his wives, who could be quite numerous. Larger public buildings used for assemblies, judicial gatherings and dispute settlements or meetings of secret societies also figured in the compound. Commonly, a large square preceded the entrance-way to the "palace" and served as a **market** (market day in the Bamiléké country traditionally falls every eight days).

The Bandjoun chieftaincy follows this basic pattern more faithfully than others in the region, where cement and corrugated metal sheeting are replacing traditional building materials. But even here, the chief lives in a modern palace, completed in 1994, and opposite is the colonial-style palace which houses the **treasury** – the chief's collection of carved thrones, arms, pipes and other memorabilia. You have to pay an **entrance fee** of CFA1000 to visit the grounds, and there's a further charge of CFA1500 to take photos. Included in this price is a visit to the treasury museum.

For **accommodation**, the *Hôtel de Bandjoun* (②), near the *gare routière*, has definitely seen better days. Better value is the *Hôtel Ino* (①), fifteen minutes walk from the *gare routière*, which has clean S/C rooms – sometimes with hot water – a good gym and an excellent bar-restaurant. *Concorde Restaurant*, near the market square, serves good food – the chicken DG is especially delicious.

From Bangangté to Bafang

There is a direct road from Bafoussam to Bafang, but the scenery along the newly paved road that heads south from Bandjoun via Bangangté provides a good reason for a detour. Though it makes a longer circuitous route to Bafang it passes one of the Bamiléké country's most spectacular stretches. West of Bangangté, the **Col de Bana** (the Bana Pass) offers grand panoramic views.

BANGANGTÉ is a fairly large town, with its share of administrative buildings and a wide, divided avenue that leads from the Préfecture down to the modern Maison du Parti. The **chefferie** has recently been renovated: modern buildings have been replaced with traditional Bamiléké structures, and the complex promises eventually to rival that of Bandjoun. You can **stay** in Bangangté at the *Hôtel le Paysan* (☎48.41.88; ②), with nice S/C rooms, conveniently located next to the *gare routière*. There is also the deceptively grotty-looking *Hotel le Bazar*, 200m up the main street east of the *gare routière* (BP 35; ☎48.91.66; ①); the large balcony in front of the clean S/C rooms provides a great vantage point from which to watch the busy Bangangté streetlife. The town also has a **post office**.

The road from Bangangté to Bafang is good (share taxis ply regularly between the two towns) and passes by another traditional chiefdom, the **Chefferie de Bana**, located off the main road.

Bafang

A line of small businesses at a major intersection on the Foumban–Douala road marks the centre of **BAFANG**. This could be a convenient stopping point, but there's no exceptional reason to spend a long time here, particularly as **accommodation** is limited and generally on the expensive side. The overpriced *Hôtel la Falaise* (BP 143; ☎48.63.11; ③), across from the Palais de Justice, is fully air-conditioned and has a bar and restaurant. Next to the Palais de Justice, the brand-new *Grand Lux Hotel* (BP 396; ☎48.61.58; ②) offers clean S/C rooms with a relaxing view of the surrounding hills from its balconies. There's no restaurant, but a café-bar serves espresso and delicious but pricey sandwiches. The least expensive option is the *Hotel le Samaritain* (BP 155; ①), with very basic S/C rooms.

The paved road continues directly south from Bafang to Douala, though if you're travelling by share taxi you may have to change vehicles in Nkongsamba. The two *agences de voyage*, for Yaoundé and southwards, are Gala Voyage and Nufi Voyage; their offices are near the *gare routière* and tickets can be booked in advance.

Around Bafang

The scenery around Bafang is striking, with numerous **waterfalls**. One of these, the **Chute de la Mouenkeu**, is only a kilometre outside the town (on the Nkongsamba road). A sign points to the falls, which you can see by walking a short way into the woods.

More spectacular (and more famous) are the **Chutes d'Ekom**, 30km further down the Nkongsamba road. Assuming you have your own car, you turn off the main road onto a dirt road heading southeast at a red sign indicating the *Chefferie de Bayong* and – in smaller writing – the *Chutes*. From here, it's about 10km to the falls, though you have to walk the last few kilometres. At weekends, there are plenty of villagers from Ekom Nkam around who will be keen to give you directions for a small fee; they'll know what you're looking for even before you tell them. In a beautiful forest setting, the **Nkam River** plunges eighty dramatic metres from the clifftop to the valley below. Unfortunately, the dirt road is almost impassable in the rainy season – you may wish to enquire about the status of the road before you head off.

Dschang and around

Three routes lead to the pleasant university town of **DSCHANG**: the paved road from Bafoussam, which takes less than an hour by share taxi; the 40km paved stretch from Mbouda passing the Bamboutous Mountains; and the German-built **route des Mbo**, a scenic but slow *piste* that starts in Melong and winds its way through coffee and cocoa plantations.

Dschang was founded by the Germans in 1903. In the 1940s, Europeans forced by the war to stay in Africa all year round built a **vacation colony** here, attracted by the mild climate. The resulting complex, the *Centre Climatique* (BP 40; ☎45.10.58; Fax

---

BAMILÉKÉ ARCHITECTURE

Characteristic Bamiléké houses consist of a square room topped with a conical roof covered with a thick layer of thatch. Although the principle seems simple enough, an elaborate framework is necessary to make the conical roof sit on square walls. These walls are built of palm fronds or bamboo filled in with mud. A circular platform is then made and set on top of the walls. Finally, a pyramid-shaped frame is constructed on top of the platform and the thatch added. The exteriors of the buildings are often decorated with bamboo and intricately carved wooden boards.

45.12.02; ③–⑤), still attracts numerous tourists with its landscaped gardens, first-class restaurant, swimming pool and tennis courts. The centre offers some of the best – although these days slightly run-down – accommodation in the region and consists of bungalows in various categories, some luxurious, with a fireplace and large veranda, and others more basic, with shared toilet facilities. It is possible to rent vehicles at the *Centre* for around CFA30,000.

The town also has smaller **hotels** that are reasonable value. A good choice is *Hôtel Escalier 90* (BP 138; ☎45.13.26; ②), a short *moto* trip from the town centre. Other reasonable small hotels are the *Hôtel Constellation* (BP 22; ☎45.10.61; ②), near the Bafoussam *gare routière*, and the *Hôtel Menoua Palace* (☎45.16.93; ①). A recommended place to eat is the *Phenix Restaurant*, which specializes in Cameroonian dishes such as hedgehog and partridge priced between CFA1000 and CFA4000. Of the **bars**, the *Jardin Gardens*, on the road opposite the entrance to the market, sells cool drinks from a bamboo shack in pleasant green surroundings, and on Saturdays there is traditional dancing at *La Maison Combatant de la Menua – Las d'Or*. After dark, *Club 53* is the nightclub to head for.

Unless you've been drawn here by the hill resort facilities, Dschang doesn't have much to offer apart from its colourful **market**, one of the biggest in the area, and the **arts and crafts shops** at the university entrance. The surrounding countryside, however, is well worth exploring if you have a car. From Place de l'Indépendance, the route to Fongo-Tongo leads through a series of hills and valleys, passing two waterfalls. The first, the **Cascade de Lingam**, 10km from Dschang, is signposted. The more impressive **Chute de la Mamy Wata** is roughly 10km past Fongo-Tongo and reached by a small side road that ends at the top of the falls. Towards the end of the dry season, however, both waterfalls are fairly unimpressive. Another excursion is to the **tea plantation** at **Dsjutittsa**, a beautiful and tranquil place 20km north of Dschang, where it's also possible to stay at the plantation lodge (①).

Bamenda and around

Apart from the glorious pines-and-bananas setting of the town, **BAMENDA** stands out as being at the centre of Cameroon's opposition movement. Home of the presidential candidate, bookseller **John Fru Ndi**, it was here that the initial riots leading to multi-partyism took place after police opened fire on the inaugural rally of the Social Democratic Front. Following the elections, security forces arrived en masse in the town, surrounding Fru Ndi's compound and arresting prominent party leaders. In 1995, members of the newly-emerged Anglophone organization, the Southern Cameroon National Council (SCNC) demanded the establishment of an **Anglophone republic** – Southern Cameroon – and throughout the early and mid-1990s Bamenda was the site of numerous violent confrontations, driving local businesses to despair. More recently, peace has been restored in Bamenda and it is now probably one of the safer large towns in Cameroon.

There are good excursions from Bamenda to the nearby Fondom of **Bali**, a major crafts centre, and to the swimmable **Awing Crater Lake**, near **Mount Lefo**.

The Town

Capital of North West Province and the heart of Anglophone Cameroon, Bamenda is really two towns – one administrative and the other commercial – separated by a steep scarp. The **government buildings** perch high on the clifftop in a neighbourhood known as **Upper Station** (or Supply Station). With its sweeping views and cooler air, this used to be a spot favoured by the wealthy Germans and British, and even today it remains a high-class **residential area**, the stomping ground of expats, civil servants

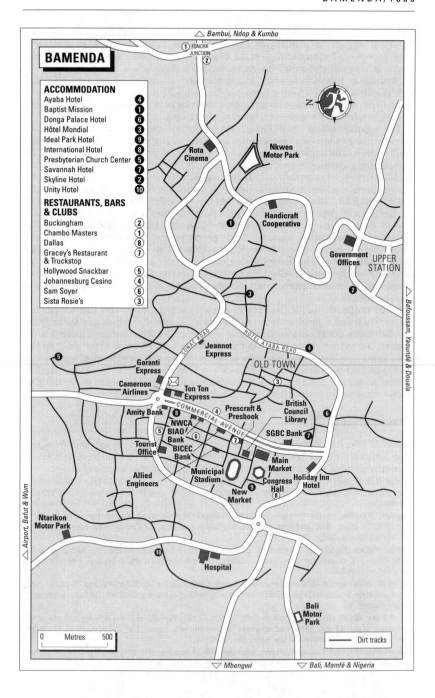

BAMENDA

ACCOMMODATION
Ayaba Hotel — ④
Baptist Mission — ①
Donga Palace Hotel — ⑥
Hôtel Mondial — ③
Ideal Park Hotel — ⑨
International Hotel — ⑧
Presbyterian Church Center — ⑤
Savannah Hotel — ⑦
Skyline Hotel — ②
Unity Hotel — ⑩

RESTAURANTS, BARS & CLUBS
Buckingham — ②
Chambo Masters — ①
Dallas — ⑧
Gracey's Restaurant & Truckstop — ⑦
Hollywood Snackbar — ⑤
Johannesburg Casino — ④
Sam Soyer — ⑥
Sista Rosie's — ③

and the local business elite. Arriving from the cities of the south to this part of town, Bamenda seems to be nodding off, almost suburban. From Upper Station, a tortuous road, carved out by the Germans at the beginning of the century, snakes its reluctant way to the hot valley and the **Nkwen motor park**, 300m below.

Downtown Bamenda is a vast conglomeration of small businesses and working neighbourhoods and it's here that most of the town's life happens. A mid-morning stroll down Commercial Avenue, with its dual carriageway of workshops and ghetto blasters, is as fit an introduction to the real heart of town as any.

The **tourist office** (☎36.13.95), 250m west of the northern roundabout on Commercial Avenue, has **maps** of the town and of NorthWest Province. It's also a good source of information about travel in the province, and has plenty of ideas for excursions, including to the Ring Road and the Fondoms of Bafut and Bali (see pp.1093 & 1091). Bamenda's only **travel agency**, ECO Travels & Tourism, providing worthwhile **tours**, is found in the NWCA building on Commercial Avenue (BP 4045; ☎36.16.16). All the major **banks** – Amity, BICEC, SGBC and BIAO – are found on Commercial Avenue and change travellers' cheques and cash. At the southern end of Commercial Avenue, the **British Council Library** (BP 622; ☎ & Fax 36.20.11; *bc-bamenda@camnet.cm*) has a good range of books and periodicals and some dated English newspapers; it also shows BBC World Service television throughout the day. The library is due to open a public **email** service, or you can send and receive mail at Allied Engineers Cameroon (BP 422; ☎ & Fax 36.21.11; *allied_engineers@compuserve.com*); it costs CFA2300 to send a page and CFA300 to receive one.

Local crafts are sold at the Prescraft Centre, next to the British Council Library, where you'll find a good selection of fixed-price bronzes, carvings and basketwork. Another crafts centre well worth visiting is the Handicraft Cooperative, located at the eastern end of town, along the road that climbs to Upper Station. Here you'll find an even larger stock of crafts – from extravagant masks and life-size tribal warriors, to woven baskets and dinkey bottle-openers – sold at fixed prices. The **Main Market**, behind *Ideal Park Hotel*, is one of the biggest in the west, and offers cheap deals on goods smuggled in from Nigeria, and on local crafts.

Practicalities

Bamenda offers **accommodation** of almost every imaginable description, from mission dorms and cheery brothels to comfortable hotels, so it's a good base for trips out to nearby districts. Whatever your budget, you'll find suitable sleeping quarters.

Ayaba Hotel, Hotel Ayaba Rd (BP 515; ☎36.13.56 or 36.13.92; Fax 36.30.75). A luxury hotel with all the mod cons you might wish for. The swimming pool can be used by non-guests at CFA1500 for a full day. ⑤.

Baptist Mission, at the foot of the road to Upper Station, near Nkwen motor park (BP 1; ☎36.12.85). A quiet, clean and friendly place; slightly pricier than the Presbyterian Mission, but bargaining sometimes helps. ②.

Donga Palace Hotel, Hotel Ayaba Rd, at the southern end of Commercial Ave. Inexpensive but quite dingy S/C rooms; the hotel bears a distinct resemblance to a cheap brothel. Friendly bar to hang out and chat. ①.

Hôtel Mondial, up the hill from the northern end of Hotel Ayaba Rd (BP 9; ☎ & Fax 36.18.32). Very clean and large rooms with peaceful balconies overlooking town. A path from the hotel leads up to Upper Station. ③.

Ideal Park Hotel, off Commercial Ave (BP 5; ☎36.11.66). The oldest hotel in town and one of the best-value places to stay. Clean and spacious S/C rooms with a good bar and restaurant. For safety reasons, take a taxi to and from the hotel after dark. ①.

International Hotel, Commercial Ave, near the NWCA building (BP 124; ☎36.25.27). Central, with spacious carpeted rooms, but showing signs of wear and tear. ②.

Presbyterian Church Center, 1km north from Commercial Ave (☎36.40.70). Tidy rooms with clean sheets, or camping at CFA1000 per tent. A bit far from the town centre, but well signposted. Couples wishing to share a room have to be "married". ①.

Savannah Hotel, off the southern end of Commercial Ave. Cheap, basic rooms, some S/C. Conveniently located for the town centre and for the Savannah *agence de voyage* (in the same building), which runs regular services to Bafoussam. ①.

Skyline Hotel, Upper Station (BP 11; ☎36.12.89). The tremendous cliff-edge perch overlooking downtown Bamenda makes it the favourite mid-range hotel. Offers very good deals for comfortable AC rooms and has a pool and an excellent restaurant. ③.

Unity Hotel, off the Wum road (BP 477; ☎36.37.82). Comfortable rooms with hot water, convenient for the Wum and Bafut motor park. The lively bar and restaurant downstairs can be quite noisy at night so you may wish to opt for the slightly more expensive upstairs rooms. ①.

Eating, drinking and nightlife

Street eating is good in Bamenda. Besides the **finger food** like *soya* and grilled corn cobs available all around town, more solid meals can be had at any of the numerous **roadside restaurants**. A good selection is found behind the *International Hotel*, among which *Sam Soyer* is a good choice. For good inexpensive food in lively surroundings, try the **bar-restaurants** around Foncha Junction, in the east of town, such as *Chambo Masters* and *Buckingham*.

Several informal sit-down restaurants offer Western and African fare at moderate rates. Beside the Prescraft Centre is one of the best places, *Gracey's Restaurant*, with filling dishes of omelette, salad and chips at very reasonable prices and, on the other side of the centre, the *Truckstop,* also known as *Cameroon Café,* a popular place for basic Cameroonian dishes. *Johannesburg Casino* on Commercial Avenue offers the standard chicken and chips menu in an upstairs bar overlooking the busiest street in town, as well as gambling in the downstairs backroom. The *Hollywood Snackbar and Restaurant* serves burgers, Cameroonian dishes and expensive Western food in rooms of different categories and price ranges; the most expensive features a pool table. Some of the town's best grilled fish is served at *Sista Rosie's,* east of Commercial Avenue, in the Old Town. The famous salad and stunning views at the *Handicraft Cooperative's* restaurant, on Station Road, are also well worth experiencing.

The **high-class restaurants** are in the big hotels, a notable exception being the newly renovated *Dallas* restaurant, where European dishes and excellent grilled chicken are served on the pleasant terrace. For atmosphere, you can't beat the *Skyline Hotel* in Upper Station, a taxi ride from downtown, which serves good European food in the garden restaurant.

The only **nightclubs** in Bamenda are connected to the bigger hotels. The *Njang* club in *Ayaba Hotel* is one of the best in town, and the nightclub at *International Hotel* is quite lively at weekends.

Bali

Of the region's main chiefdoms – Bafut, Bali and Nso – only **BALI** is not accessible by the Ring Road. A **Chamba** settlement (the Chamba are part of the Adamawa linguistic grouping), it was founded relatively late, around 1830. Its history has been a series of wars and conflicts, notably with the nearby kingdom of Bafut. Only 20km west of Bamenda, Bali is an interesting stopover on the rough road to Mamfé, and a satisfying day excursion from Bamenda, especially in the dry season when the *piste* is good. The beautiful **scenery** makes the trip well worthwhile.

Bali's main attraction is the town's **Prescraft centre** where they make most of the artefacts sold in the Prescraft shops in Bamenda and Limbé. If you arrive during the working week, you can see the skilled artists busy carving, weaving and calabash decorating. A shop at the centre sells a small selection of the results.

Another good reason to stop is for the **Fon's palace**, not so much for the modern palace, but more in the hope of having an audience with the Fon (chief) himself. He is a German-educated philosopher, and keen to meet visitors to his Fondom, especially for the sake of a good discussion. If you're lucky he might even pull out some of his palm wine – reputedly the best in the area. At the palace, you can get information and a guide for day-trips in the area such as to the sacred cave where you'll see the skulls of Bali's many warrior enemies. Also recommended is **Forthung's Tower of Babel**, an incomplete 72-room building, which would have outdone the Fon's palace, had witchcraft not been used to prevent this grand treason from happening. Forthung died before it was completed.

There are three **accommodation** options in Bali, each catering to a different taste and budget. *The Savanna Inn* (①), behind the old German church (built in 1903) in the centre of town, offers basic rooms, S/C or with shared facilities. At the *Prescraft Centre* (①–②), two rooms – with two and four beds – are available in one of the old mission houses. Book at Prescraft in Bamenda (☎36.12.81); the price is reduced if you bring your own bedding. A more luxurious option is the German run *Safari Lodge* (BP 19; bookings at *Atlantic Beach Hotel* in Limbé, ☎33.23.32; ③), 2km before town on the Bamenda road.

Awing Crater Lake and Mount Lefo

Another possible excursion from Bamenda is to the tranquil **Awing crater lake**, just north of Santa on the Douala–Yaoundé road. A signpost points to a road leading east to the Bafut Ngemba Forestry Reserve; the lake is just beyond the reserve. Many Bamenda expats come to swim at weekends, and Cameroonians come here to fish, although for superstitious reasons many prefer to steer clear of it altogether. If you ask the Fon of Awing for permission (a few kilometres further down the road) you can **camp** in the beautiful hills surrounding the lake. A major **tourist resort** is planned for the area – but may not take off for many years yet – with restaurants, bars, a fully equipped campsite, *boukarous* and souvenir shops.

The fourth highest mountain in Cameroon – and West Africa – is **Mount Lefo** (2250m), a day's demanding climb from Lake Awing; the Fon of Awing will provide you with a guide (around CFA2000–3000). On the lower slopes the climbing is easy, but the last few hundred metres to the peak are very steep, although not unmanageable. From the peak there are wonderful views of the Bamenda plateau, and of crater lakes in various stages of geological formation.

MOVING ON FROM BAMENDA

Bamenda is an excellent place for onward connections, with numerous *agences de voyage* such as Garanti Express on Sonac Road, for **Limbé, Douala, Yaoundé, Kumbo, Nkambé** and **Fundong**; Petit Papa for Limbé and **Buea**; Ton Ton Express, behind Cameroon Airlines, for Kumba; Savannah Enterprises, by *Savannah Hotel*, for **Bafoussam**; and Jeannot Express, on Hotel Ayaba Road, for Buea. There are no agencies direct to **Foumban,** you'll have to go via Bafoussam.

The three motor parks that serve Bamenda are the **Nkwen park**, for Yaoundé, Bafoussam and Douala; the **Ntarikon park**, in the north of town, for Mankon, Bafut and Wum on the **Ring Road**; and **Bali park** for vehicles to Bali, Batibo and Mamfé.

The Ring Road

The **Ring Road** comprises 360km of difficult red-earth road interspersed by a few paved sections. Despite the demanding road conditions, this is a highly recommended route, bucking and swerving through some of the finest scenery in Africa, the verdant pasturelands of the **Grassfields**. But don't expect rolling savannahs – for the most part the Grassfields are hilly meadows of rank herbage between stands of hardwood forest and patches of shifting agriculture. Natural sites in the region include the thundering **Menchum Falls**, a number of volcanoes such as **Mount Oku** (3011m), and nearly forty clear **crater lakes**, many of them sacred, and at least one of them (Nyos) potentially dangerous. Terraced farmlands defy the steep slopes; the mountain soils, ploughed along the contours, sustain crops like cocoyams, maize and plantains. Cash crops, such as coffee, grow at higher altitudes, and **Fulani herders** roam the pastures to graze their cattle.

The best way to tour the Ring Road is by **car**, which allows you the freedom to stop between the route's main centres, **Bamenda, Wum, Nkambé** and **Kumbo**. Unfortunately, at the time of writing, the northern stretch of the road – between Nkambé and Wum – has become completely **impassable** to vehicles since the bridges at Nyos and Weh collapsed. It should be possible to complete the route in a 4WD vehicle, however, and eventually the whole road should be surfaced and upgraded. Until the northern stretch is linked once more, the choice stands between doing the Ring Road as a "U" or following an increasingly popular alternative route – **the small ring road** – via Bamenda, Wum, Weh, Fundong, Belo and Bambui. The Bamenda tourist office (☎36.13.95) can update you on road conditions. With a good 4WD vehicle, and provided the bridges have been repaired, you could rush round the Ring Road in two days.

All towns on the two routes are accessible by **public transport** and offer basic accommodation. However, many of the most interesting sites outlined below are off the main road and you'll have to forgo them if you don't have your own transport unless you are willing to trek. Travelling by public transport also means it's very difficult to camp as you travel, and camping in the countryside – when you can find a flat space – is one of the Ring Road's greatest pleasures. Should you choose to **cycle** some or all of the way round, beware that any rain will stop your machine dead in its tracks, horribly clogged with mud. In dry conditions, though, this is outstanding mountain-bike territory; allow around a week for the circuit. Whichever way you go, try to have a larger scale **map** than the Michelin (try the tourist office in Bamenda); there's a certain frustration in trying to follow a twisting, village-spotted route at 40km to 1cm. It's also a good idea to bring some local whisky, available in most larger towns, to present to the Fons (chiefs), if you visit any of the palaces in the various chiefdoms.

Bafut

The first stop along the Ring Road, heading in a clockwise direction from Bamenda, is the chiefdom of **BAFUT**, which acquired international fame in the 1950s and 1960s as the site of two animal-collecting trips by the naturalist, Gerald Durrell. His account of the first, *The Bafut Beagles* (a reference to the team of hunters he assembled), makes amusing reading, though Bafut today feels a far cry from those slightly mythologized days of Assistant District Commissioners and pink gins.

Bafut is a **Tikar** community – people who migrated to Bafut from the northern regions of Lake Chad. It's the most powerful of the traditional kingdoms in the Grassfields, divided into 26 **wards** in a ten-kilometre stretch of the Ring Road that trails along a ridge above the Menchum valley. The current Fon of Bafut – **Abumbi II** – is a

Paramount Fon, titular overlord of a large number of lesser Fons in the region, and son of the Fon featuring in Gerald Durell's book. Still quite young, Abumbi was chosen from his father's 100-odd offspring to ascend to the throne when the aged Fon died in 1971. Although he was educated in Yaoundé, he was allowed to succeed his father – in theory, upon pain of death if he broke local tradition. In **religion**, although the Tikar have long been dominated by Fulani Muslims, and thus heavily Islamicized themselves, they've also (perhaps not coincidentally) been the subjects of intense Presbyterian missionary work, so you'll meet a fair few Christians too.

For **accommodation**, Gerald Durell's old residence overlooking the palace grounds is currently being refurbished as a guesthouse (②). You can book rooms through the palace (☎36.38.18; call early morning or late evening). Alternatively, you can stay at the *Savanna Botanic Gardens*, 5km down the Bamenda road (BP 2153; ☎36.38.70; ②). They have a few new S/C rooms and an excellent but pricey bar-restaurant. Camping is possible on the park-like grounds.

The Town

The main attraction in Bafut is the **Fon's Palace**, a large complex laid out in a quiet pattern of dark interiors and bright courtyards. The most sacred building in the complex is the **Achum**, the previous Fon's palace, with its striking, pyramidal thatched roof. Dedicated to the ancestors, only the Fon and other notables are allowed to enter this shrine. A visit to the royal compound and grounds costs CFA1000 per person and CFA1500 for a camera. The Fon's wives act as guides, and sell home-made souvenirs within the compound.

Bafut's **market** takes place every eight days and is very lively. People come from all over the region for its selection of fruits, vegetables, spices, meat and animals. Next to the market lives a local celebrity, Peter Shu, **King of the Snakes**, famous as one of Gerald Durrell's "beagles". A magician of sorts, Peter holds cobras and green mambas in his bare hands and maintains a large collection – in and out of cages – in his **exhibition room** (CFA1000). He's been bitten so many times (scars cover his arms and legs) that he claims he's now immune to the strongest venom. He is highly respected in the community for his power over the reptiles, and you're in for a memorable experience if you get to meet him.

The yearly **grass-cutting ceremony**, is still performed much as it was in the 1950s when described by Durrell. The entire community goes into the grasslands at the end of the dry season, usually in late April, to collect bundles for rethatching the Achum and other important buildings. They troop before the Fon with their offerings. It's a confirmation of community spirit and always ends with tremendous feasting and the consumption of huge quantities of palm wine. A second annual **festival** takes place a week or so before Christmas, with formal, dressy presentations and much discharging of old guns, followed by a noisy series of dances and musical shows.

Wum and around

Travelling towards **Wum**, the last important town along the west side of the Ring Road from Bafut, the vegetation grows increasingly dense as the road follows the course of the **Menchum**. This stretch of road has deteriorated drastically during the past years and is virtually impassable in the wet season (at present the easiest way of reaching Wum is via Fundong and Weh on the small ring road; see opposite). About 20km short of Wum, the **Menchum Falls** plunge spectacularly down a rocky cliffside, but they're set slightly off the road (on the west side) and you could easily pass right by without noticing them. If you have your own car, start looking out about 30km north of Bafut and listen for the thundering sound of falling water. At the exact spot, you'll probably see tyre marks where cars have pulled off the road. If you ask your taxi driver to pull off for a moment here, he's likely to oblige. There are no "tourist facilities" of any kind here, nor anything to stop you boulder-hopping across the river in the dry season – except common sense; a French woman was swept over the edge in the 1990s doing just this.

WUM is effectively a roadhead: beyond the town, public transport more or less fades out. The best **hotels** in town are the *Morning Star Hotel* (①), which has some S/C rooms and a restaurant, and the slightly better *Lake Nyos City Hotel* (①), which has no restaurant, but can usually arrange to have **food** prepared for you. Otherwise, try the *Peace, Unity and Hygienic* restaurant. The *New Deal* near Ambassador Books is a popular "off-licence" where you can also buy food.

Three kilometres northwest of the town centre, **Lake Wum** is a beautiful crater lake nestled in the patchily cultivated hills. Fulani herders graze their cattle in the open fields and bring them down to the lake to drink. The banks are a bit muddy but you can swim here; the cool, green waters are immensely deep. If you're equipped to **camp**, contact the SDO (Senior Divisional Officer) in Wum for permission. You should be aware of the justified paranoia of some locals about their crater lakes: see the advice about Lake Nyos on p.1095.

It is impossible to **move on** from Wum to Nkambé by collective transport now that the bridges have collapsed at Weh and Nyos. If these have been repaired, there is possibly a weekly vehicle to Nkambé. But when the rains start in April, even that will not run. At the motor park, however, you may be able to rent a truck and driver for a steep CFA40,000 to take you to Nkambé. When you see the condition of the road – it's not much more than a cattle track – you'll understand why the price is so expensive. Get ready for a very rough ride.

Wum to Bambui: the small ring road

Northeast of Wum, the Ring Road branches at **Weh**. If you head right (to the south), you get back to Bamenda via the **small ring road** (with infrequent public transport) and the town of **FUNDONG**, where you'll find the **Chimney waterfalls** and good basic **accommodation** at the *Tourist Home Hotel* (①). Further along this road is **BELO** village, the starting point for a three-hour hike into the **Ijim Forest** – bordering the Kilum forest and Mount Oku. In Belo you can **stay** at the quiet *Women's Farming Guest House* (①), or the livelier *Downtown Hotel* (①) and *City Hotel* (①).

Wum to Nkambé

Continuing east on the main Ring Road, Weh offers the last chance until Nkambé of pumped water, market produce and chop-house food. After Weh, the road becomes wilder and switchbacks into a broad valley where a **collapsed bridge** abruptly stops all further traffic. Once it's repaired you'll be able to continue on through an area where the population diminishes drastically. The **landscapes** are astonishingly beautiful, at their pristine best when the **rains** have started in April. At this time, when the region is so inaccessible, there are complex vistas of startling colour and dimension in every direction.

You won't notice many villages along this part, but will understand fully why the area has acquired the name Grassfields. Frequent burning on the slopes favours the growth of grass over shrubs and bushes. It makes for excellent grazing and you're likely to see Fulani and their cattle along this stretch.

Lake Nyos
The dead village of **Nyos** is on the Ring Road about 30km from Weh (not, as marked on some maps, south it). The notorious **Lake Nyos** is a couple of kilometres to the

south. The deep crater lake was the site of a mysterious natural **gas eruption** in 1986 which killed up to 3000 people when a cloud of suffocating gas, mainly carbon dioxide, billowed off its surface, and rolled northwards down the valley towards Su-bum. The cause is still not completely understood, although some scientists have postulated that a reaction between the warmer surface waters and the cold carbon dioxide saturated waters of the lake depths caused the huge release of gas, which could happen again at any of the deep lakes in the region. Many people still believe that Western scientific experimenting caused the event. The crater lakes are supposed to be the homes of the spirits of the Fons and foreigners are regarded suspiciously by some locals, who you may have to convince of your harmless intentions.

Su-Bum (Soumbon) – a scattering of houses and smoke-stained compounds looped along the valley about 30km from Weh – is now the only settlement of any size in the Nyos area. It too suffered a number of casualties from the gas disaster. More happily it boasts quite spectacular avocadoes.

Kimbi River Game Reserve
Some 50km from Weh, but currently only accessible from Nkambé in the east, you enter the **Kimbi River Game Reserve**, where the most abundant animals are said to be **waterbuck and buffalo**. There's a **rest house** (①) of doubtful standard in the reserve – ask at the tourist office in Bamenda (☎36.13.95) – but you have to have your own 4WD transport to head out in search of the fauna.

Dumbo: trekking into Nigeria
Seventy-four kilometres from Weh (21km from Nkambé) at **Misanje**, a pleasant market village with a small **hotel** (①), a branch road heads north to **DUMBO** (17km) and the start of an exceptional trekking route – strictly foot traffic only – into Nigeria, covered on p.1033. Customs and immigration are in Dumbo. Officials are generally friendly here, and may even help you find a guide-cum-porter to continue to Nigeria (about CFA5000). There's a small **hotel** in Dumbo (①), where you can rest up before starting off on the forty-kilometre hike. The first 10km of the trek is a gentle climb, which levels out for a few kilometres before reaching the edge of the escarpment and the steep, beautiful descent into Nigeria. The first small town you reach is **Bissaula**, where customs and immigration officials will be waiting. With an early start, the trek can even be done in one day, but there's no accommodation in Bissaula, so you may choose to spend a night in a mountain village before catching early morning transport out of Bissaula

Nkambé to Kumbo
NKAMBÉ, on the northeast side of the Ring Road, is a large town by Grassfield standards, signalling your return from remote regions with filling stations, a bank, numerous eating and drinking houses and *Central Hotel* (①) as your best overnight option. From Nkambé, you can catch a share taxi heading north to **Ako** and the Nigerian border. To the south, the route continues at an altitude of between 1500 and 2000m and soon becomes more densely populated. Among the settlements through which it passes is the chiefdom of **Mbot**, which has its own Fon and palace. **NDU**, a couple of kilometres further, is the site of Cameroon's largest tea plantation, an enterprise begun by the British in the 1950s. In Ndu, *Dalla Hotel* (①) is a clean and convenient stopover, with bucket showers and electricity. A road leads east from Ndu to **Sabongari**, where a motorable track connects with Gembu in Nigeria. South to Kumbo, about 10km before you reach the town, the region's largest cattle market takes place every Friday in the small village of **Takija**.

Kumbo

KUMBO stands on a plateau 2000m above sea level. One of the biggest towns in the Grassfields, it has no shortage of accommodation, banks and other facilities, including two of the best hospitals in the region. But it's also the seat of another powerful **chiefdom** – as important as those of Bali and Bafut – that of the **Nso** linguistic group (the Banso). The Fon lives here in a **palace** with both old and new sections (the latter with a decidedly Islamic flavour, as the last Fon was from the Muslim side of the family lineage). Though now predominantly a Catholic community, the Banso are traditionalists. Don't offer traditional office-holders your hand when greeting, nor cross your legs while seated, nor drink in their presence, nor pass the traditional policeman (the *Ngwerong*) on his left. The Banso were defeated by the Germans in 1906, and their Fon executed in Bamenda – bitter history to which they have never been completely reconciled.

There's a large **market** in Kumbo, every eight days, and every year Guinness sponsors a **horse race** at the Tobin Stadium. Fulani and Banso people from throughout the region assemble here for the event, which usually takes place in November. If you can plan it right, it's exhilarating to watch their daredevil bareback riding. You can get information about the actual date by contacting the Guinness Kumbo Depot (☎48.12.23) or the tourist office in Bamenda (☎36.13.95). On a slightly more offbeat note, there's a cave about half a kilometre east of Kumbo which is the resting place of a number of old skulls from long-ago traditional feuds. Find someone to take you.

As for **accommodation**, the bottom line is the *Central Inn Hotel* (BP 47; ☎48.10.15; ①), overlooking the central motor park. *Merry Land* (BP 89; ☎48.10.77; ②) is better and more expensive, but the most comfortable and best-value hotel in town is the *Fomo 92* (BP 46; ☎48.16.16; Fax 48.16.61; ②) off the Nkambé road just north of town. For **food**, the *Casablanca 2000* serves excellent chicken DG and cold beer at very reasonable prices. The recently opened **nightclub**, *Shady Grove,* is a good place to shake off the dust of the rugged Ring Road.

Elak

From Kumbo, you can deviate off the Ring Road to **ELAK**, the principal village of the Oku Fondom. The Oku people are renowned for their black magic and traditional medicines as well as their rich culture. The Oku cultural week, held at the **Fon's palace** around Easter, is a good opportunity to witness Oku masked dancing.

Elak is situated high on the northern slopes of **Mount Oku** which at 3011m is the second highest point in West Africa after Mount Cameroon. It is a pleasant climb to the summit, passing first through steep farmland and then into the **Kilum Forest** which together with the neighbouring **Ijim Forest** constitutes the largest remaining fragment of the montane forest that once covered much of the highlands. The forest has a diverse birdlife: you may see the very localized and unmistakeably red-headed **Bannerman's turaco** and the rare **banded wattle-eye**. At 2800m the forest gives way to subalpine grassland. From these cool heights you can reputedly see Mount Cameroon on exceptionally clear days. For more information about the ecology of the forests contact the **Kilum Mountain Forest Project** in Elak.

On the western slopes of the mountain, at 2200m, is **Lake Oku**, a spectacular deep green crater lake encircled by a splendid dark forest. Lake Oku is sacred and tradition forbids fishing and swimming, though exceptions are sometimes made for foreigners. However, for the sake of protocol, you should ask the Fon for permission before setting out to the lake or up the mountain. To do so, go to the **Fon's palace** at the far end of town equipped with the customary gift of a bottle of wine or local whisky. Here you will be given permission to climb the mountain or see the lake and someone will be assigned as your guide. Agree a price before setting off (CFA2000–3000).

The basic *Touristic Hotel* (①), just below the marketplace, has friendly service and a bar – usually playing loud music. There are also several private houses in Elak with rooms available to rent. While in Oku, don't miss the extremely tasty local honey.

Kumbo to Bamenda

The stretch from Kumbo to Bamenda is the most populated district along the Ring Road. South to **JAKIRI** it affords panoramic views of the **Ndop Plains** that stretch out to the east, forming a bed for the vast waters of the reservoir, **Lake Bamendjing**. Jakiri was the headquarters of British troops from 1958 to 1961 when Southern Cameroon was on the verge of independence. A spectacular range of hills rears up near the town. If you decide to **stay** in Jakiri, there's the *Hotel Trans Afrique* (①).

From Jakiri, you can branch off on a direct road to Foumban, 75km to the southeast. The main Ring Road continues on through ravishing scenery to **NDOP** and Bambui, whence it's a twelve-kilometre hop to Bamenda.

Foumban

Capital of the Bamoun people and seat of their **sultan**, the town of **FOUMBAN** is charged with history and culture. You're reminded of it at every turn as you pass monuments like the outstanding **Royal Palace**, built at the beginning of the century, the **Musée des Arts et des Traditions Bamoun** or the *ateliers* of the talented **craftsmen** who churn out works in bronze, ebony and a host of other materials. These elements have given Foumban the most touristy feel of any town in the west. You get endless offers from children who want to be your guide, shouting claims to be "sons of the sultan" (with such a prolific ruler, there may be an element of truth to many of them). There's definitely an unusual pressure to spend money at every turn – "come in to my shop, just for the pleasure of your eyes". Such an atmosphere, however, shouldn't deter you from visiting Foumban. Delving into its history and culture is a rewarding step towards an understanding of the whole region.

The Town

While the **administrative quarter** – with the town hall, post office, hospital and *préfecture* – clusters on the west of town, the sites more likely to draw your attention are all in the centre, within walking distance of the **Royal Palace**. Built in 1917 by King Njoya, the old palace (the present sultan lives in a new one) is a notable architectural achievement, unique in Africa. The townspeople may tell you the king conceived his design in a dream, but he must have done some studying to enable him to combine assorted elements of German Baroque with such pure Romanesque forms. He was greatly influenced by a visit to Buea, where he saw the German castle.

The Palace and Sultan's Museum

You approach the palace by means of a vast **courtyard** lined with *rônier* palms, tempering its blue tones with long shadows. Constructed entirely of locally-made bricks, the mass is supported by strong pillars, the walls are carried by arcades and the structure embellished with balconies worked with intricately carved wood. As you enter the building, you can't help but be impressed by the grandeur of the entrance hall, the armoury and the reception hall with its ceiling supported by four majestic columns. In the morning you can pass by to watch as the sultan holds court in the palace foyer. After prayers on Fridays, starting at around 1.30pm, you can also witness a colourful and

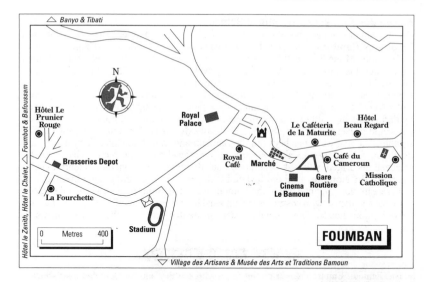

Village des Artisans & Musée des Arts et Traditions Bamoun

deeply traditional event take place. Court musicians play for the sultan while brilliantly dressed subjects pay their respects and seek the sultan's advice and good offices.

Tickets are on sale in the reception hall (CFA2000) to visit the **Sultan's Museum** upstairs, possibly one of the most interesting museums in Cameroon. A private collection of memorabilia from the long line of kings gives a very personal overview of Bamoun history. Among the eclectic assortment of objects there are thrones decorated with beadwork, masks, shields and weapons made from hides and woven raffia palms, and a large collection of **sculptures**. One room contains the personal possessions of Mbuémbué – his pipe, shields and dagger, and a calabash decorated with the jawbones of his enemies. Writings by Njoya are also on display – including the famous *History and Customs of the Bamouns* in the Shumom script he invented, still taught today. The museum has very knowledgeable bilingual guides who will show you around.

The Village des Artisans

Don't listen to the small boys in Foumban's main square, who insist that the handful of little artisan shops clustered round the palace entrance constitute the town's main craft market. In fact, the real **Village des Artisans**, a major distribution centre for crafts and antiques from all over Cameroon and neighbouring countries, is about 2km away. Go west for 500m down the Bafoussam road, and turn left before the post office. Take the left fork after the stadium, and you will find that each of the twenty or thirty houses lining the short road up to the village square contains a **workshop**. Here you can watch craftsmen from all over the country casting and beating metals, and carving kola wood, mahogany and, from time to time, ivory.

Some of the finished artefacts are bright and new-looking, some tarnished to suit European tastes for elusive "authenticity", but there's little attempt to fool you that you are buying a valuable antique when you can see identical items being manufactured alongside. Nevertheless, some shops do also sell genuine antiques, mainly smuggled from Nigeria, and you need some expertise or wit to tell the difference.

Musée des Arts et des Traditions Bamoun

On the square above the Village des Artisans is the **Musée des Arts et des Traditions Bamoun**. You enter through two ornate carved doors, and begin your visit in the **Salle Mosé Yeyap** (Mosé Yeyap was a patron of the arts at the time of Sultan Njoya, and this museum started off as his private collection). Along the walls, a series of intricately-carved wooden plaques portray important events in Bamoun history. Beside these are jugs for heating palm wine, clay masks, and samples of naturally dyed cloth. Notice the collection of clay and bronze pipes (some up to two metres long) used by dignitaries in traditional ceremonies, as well as the engraved gongs which the sultan would present to military heroes. The **Salle du Guerrier** contains military relics recalling the many clashes between the Bamoun and their Bamiléké, Tikar and Fulani neighbours. You'll see spears, *coupe-coupes* (engraved cups), protective charms and a calabash decorated with a skull and jawbones that was used in victory celebrations. In the **Salle du Notable**, a carved bed and table, weapons for fighting and hunting, and riding gear evoke the lifestyle of the Bamoun elite. The **Salle du Danseur** is dedicated to music and dance, with costumes and unusual instruments including a xylophone with carved snake heads. The Sultan's **court orchestra** still play these instruments to

---

THE BAMOUN EMPIRE

The Bamoun Empire dates from the fourteenth century and was founded by **Nshare Yen**, the first of seventeen kings in the present dynasty. Son of a Tikar chief, Nshare led a faction of rebels away from the main territory and settled in the eastern country known as Pa-Mben. Here he consolidated his power and proclaimed himself king, establishing **Mfom-Ben** (whence Foumban) as his capital. The subsequent history has been carefully recorded, and today the accomplishments of all Nshare's successors are known in detail.

One of the most remarkable was **Mbuémbué**, a giant of a leader (he is said to have been 2.6m tall) whose first words were, "I will make the borders of the kingdom with blood and black iron; borders made with words are inevitably erased." Speaking at a normal level, his voice carried 2km, but when he shouted, he could be heard for 15km away. Not surprisingly, people listened. He fortified his capital (ruins of the old walls can be seen today), withstood Fulbe (Fulani) invasions and pushed back his Tikar and Bamiléké rivals, thus expanding the empire.

Of all the kings, however, the greatest was the sixteenth in the dynasty, **Ibrahim Njoya** (who reigned from 1895–1924), under whose rule Bamoun culture had a golden age. A remarkable figure, he masterminded numerous inventions, not least of which was the **Bamoun alphabet** (one of only two in the whole West African region; the other was the Vai script in Liberia). Shumom, the language of the Bamoun, consists largely of monosyllabic roots, so Njoya's 510 original signs were easily converted, in 1909, into a syllabary and later refined into a true alphabet.

Once the alphabet was created, Njoya founded schools throughout the kingdom to teach the new writing. He also tried, less successfully, to design a printing press, and set about recording Bamoun tradition. It is thanks to his *History and Customs of the Bamouns* that so much is known about the empire (or, to be accurate, about his account of it, as related through oral tradition). Njoya also drew up a map of his kingdom, invented an electric mill and designed the outstanding **Royal Palace**.

Having converted to Islam he was proclaimed Sultan of Bamoun, but with the arrival of Christian missionaries, he attempted to create a **new religion** that fused Islam, Christianity and traditional beliefs. The secular state (first colonial, later independent) tended to restrain this development, but Bamoun **court music and theatre** still reflect it and Islam, especially, is a strong influence on Bamoun sculpture. Njoya was deposed by the French in 1924, and eventually exiled to Yaoundé where he died in 1933, his pro-German views still mistrusted by the French. The present sultan is Mboumbou Njoya Ibrahim.

MOVING ON FROM FOUMBAN

The only **motor park** is next to the market. Vehicles head to Kumbo (via Jakiri), Nkongsamba, Bafoussam and Bamenda. Although the route looks straightforward to **Ngaoundéré** and the north, there's no direct transport and you will have to count on two to three days of travel to get there, depending on the condition of the road. To do so, first take a taxi to **Banyo** where you can spend the night at one of the inexpensive hostels near the market: *Auberge le Saré* (①) or *Auberge Possada* (①). From here to **Tibati** takes half a day. From here, you can then get another taxi (along paved road) to **Ngaoundal** (1hr 30min), where you can catch the 3am train to Ngaoundéré – which means waiting at the famously thief-ridden railway station for many hours, especially as the train is usually delayed. Alternatively, you can take the completely jam-packed afternoon bus from Tibati, which stops in every small village on the way and arrives at Ngaoundéré around midnight.

---

accompany elaborate set theatrical pieces, and have toured abroad. The final room, the **Salle de la Cuisine Bamoun**, contains cooking utensils – pottery, baskets for smoking meat and mortars – used by Bamoun women.

The attendants are welcoming and helpful, not importunate but always ready to answer any questions; happily, you're positively encouraged to take photographs.

Practicalities

For **food**, apart from the few hotel restaurants, you might try the *Caféteria de la Maturité* close to the *gare routière,* they serve fresh salad and good helpings of rice, beans and meat for about CFA500. Nearby, the *Café du Cameroun* does good breakfasts of omelettes, bread and coffee. The *ETS Royal Café*, across from the mosque, is owned and run by one of the many princes of Foumban. From the terrace you get a great view of the Foumban valley, and the restaurant sells well-prepared though somewhat expensive Cameroonian dishes. *La Fourchette*, further along the Bafoussam road, makes hamburgers and pizza.

Due to a heavy tourist presence, **hotels** tend to be slightly expensive in Foumban.

Hôtel Beau Regard, on the main commercial street (☎48.21.82). Most rooms are S/C in this centrally-located, half-renovated haunt. Limited bar and restaurant. ②.

Hôtel le Chalet, off the rte de Bafoussam (☎48.62.67). Airy rooms in a quiet setting. Comfortable and good value despite the distance from the centre. For safety, take a taxi home at night. ②.

Hôtel le Prunier Rouge, near the Brasseries depot, within walking distance of the centre (BP 13; ☎48.23.52). An older place with some charm (though the namesake plum tree that grew through the roof of the restaurant is gone). Rooms are very basic but there is a picturesque view from upstairs. ②.

Hôtel le Zenith de Foumban, off the rte de Bafoussam on the edge of town (BP 122; ☎48.24.25). New hotel, with small but clean S/C rooms, and hot water. ②.

Mission Catholique, near the *gare routière*. Four rooms with dormitory beds – clean, friendly and set in a pleasant garden. There is no fixed price, you donate what you think reasonable. ①.

YAOUNDÉ AND THE SOUTH

As the capital of Cameroon, Yaoundé has been consciously developed as a showcase, but remains essentially a large town interspersed with prestige buildings, not all of them finished. Still, you'll find most of the facilities you need, many good restaurants, and a city that is relatively easy to get around.

Only a few hours away to the southwest, spectacular **beaches** dot the Atlantic coastline between the fishing village of **Londji** and **Campo**, on the border of Equatorial

Guinea. In between, the nation's second port, **Kribi**, has become something of a holiday centre where the well-to-do from the capital head for the weekend.

Thick rainforest covers the southern interior and there are few decent roads, making travel difficult. With determination and time, you could begin to explore the forests by using towns like **Ebolowa** or **Mbalmayo** as bases.

Yaoundé

Comparisons between the rival cities of **YAOUNDÉ** and Douala are inevitable; most visitors prefer the capital. It lies amid magnificent natural surroundings, heavy with green vegetation, and with a range of peaks, including **Mont Fébé**, as a backdrop. At an altitude of some 700m (over 2000ft), Yaoundé also enjoys a cooler climate. The city's architectural attributes add to the overall visual effect; new buildings, especially in the administrative quarter, give at least a superficial feeling of upward momentum lacking in Douala. But what Yaoundé has gained in credibility, it has perhaps lost in colour and spontaneity; somehow it all seems a bit stiff.

Some history

The name **Yaoundé** is a corruption of **Ewondo**, the name of the ethnic group living in the area when the Germans arrived, who, incidentally, still use the areas original name: *Ongola*. The Ewondo's history has them crossing the **Sanaga River** on the back of a giant snake before settling on the hilltops of the site of present-day Yaoundé. When the **Germans** crisscrossed the country at the end of the nineteenth century, setting up military posts to affirm their influence in the new protectorate, they established a small presence here. The first commercial enterprises followed in 1907. After World War I, the French chose the budding settlement as capital of what was now their territory; the British had claims to the former capital, Buea, so Yaoundé became the administrative centre more or less by default. It has continued in that role ever since (except for a brief period during World War II), although its population and industry remain far behind Douala's.

Arrival, information and city transport

The most likely place to arrive by **road** in Yaoundé, when travelling with one of the many *agences de voyage*, is at the company's booking office, in the **Mvan gare routière** area, about 15km south of Place Ahmadou Ahidjo (better known as the Score roundabout). You can catch a **yellow share taxi** into town for a standard price of CFA150 for a drop (more for longer distances). If you come in by **share taxi** from West or North West Province – Bafoussam, Foumban and Bamenda – you might be dropped off at Carrefour Obili near the University of Earth Sciences, west of the city.

The **airport** is roughly 18km south of Place Ahmadou Ahidjo down Boulevard de l'OCAM; a taxi into town costs CFA1700 (CFA3900 private hire). By train, you'll arrive at the **railway station** just off Place Elig-Essono, about a kilometre north of Place Ahmadou Ahidjo. Several of the cheaper accommodation options are located north of the station, away from the centre.

With its undulating hills spreading over an area of some eight kilometres by five, and with few straight streets, orientation can be difficult. Unless you have your own transport or a healthy budget, you'll probably find yourself dependent on the omnipresent yellow **share taxis** for the time you're in Yaoundé.

The **Ministère du Tourisme** on Boulevard Rudolf Manga Bell (BP 266; ☎23.50.77; Fax 22.12.95) should be able to help with information about the city, but they find it very difficult to comprehend the concept of travelling on a budget.

Accommodation

While Yaoundé has the luxury hotels you'd expect of a capital city, it's also got a reasonable network of moderate accommodation. Small hotels here are less expensive than those in Douala. If you're on a budget, but can't get a bed in a mission, you still have a pretty good selection of inexpensive lodgings to fall back on.

Inexpensive to moderate

Auberge de la Paix, off bd de l'OCAM (BP 106). Lacks basic comfort and wins no hygiene awards, but it's in a good location near Place Ahmadou Ahidjo, and is very affordable. The six rooms are often full. ①.

Le Caseba Catholic Missions Guesthouse, off rue Joseph Essono Balla (☎21.30.13; Fax 20.69.66; *casba@rctmail.net*). A relaxed and comfortable guesthouse with single and double rooms. Breakfast is included in the price. ③.

El Panaden, Place de l'Indépendance (BP 8457; ☎22.27.65). Near the Hôtel de Ville and ideally located for exploring the commercial district on foot. The modest AC rooms have hot showers and there's an excellent garden restaurant. ②.

Foyer Internationale de l'Église Presbytérienne, off rue Onembele Nkou by *rond-point* Nlongkak (walk up the hill behind the concrete water towers). A colonial-style guesthouse; clean and friendly with double rooms and dormitories. Missionaries get first crack and so the place is often full. ②.

Fraicheur Hôtel, on the road parallel to bd de l'OCAM (BP 4707; ☎22.86.05) Excellent-value hotel with everything you need: friendly staff, clean S/C rooms, a good restaurant, and a pleasant rooftop bar. ②.

Hôtel Grand Moulin, rue Joseph Essono Balla (BP 4336; ☎20.68.19; Fax 20.68.20). Within walking distance of the Gare Voyageurs; a friendly place with large S/C rooms. ③.

Hôtel Idéal, by *rond-point* Nlongkak (BP 20274; ☎20.98.52). A good-value hotel located conveniently for Bastos and the city centre. The S/C rooms are clean but have no AC. ②.

Hôtel de l'Indépendance, av Winston Churchill (BP 474; ☎23.47.71; Fax 22.97.26). Faded glory, but this once-luxurious hotel is now very affordable. AC rooms with hot water. ②.

Hôtel Prestige, av Charles Atangana (BP 2697; ☎22.60.55 or 22.60.39; Fax 22.60.40). A new marble-clad place with AC rooms, a good restaurant and bar, and a French-style café serving delicious espresso. ③.

Sim's 1 Hotel, off rue Joseph Mballa Eloumden in Bastos (BP 4293; ☎20.53.75; Fax 20.53.76). A new place, lacking in charm but very convenient for the Bastos nightlife. Small but very clean AC rooms. ③.

Expensive

Hilton Hotel, bd du 20 Mai (BP 11852; ☎23.36.46; Fax 22.32.10). This swanky hotel far outranks Yaoundé's other upmarket establishments, both in style and price. Lavish gardens with health club, pool, shops, restaurants, tennis, nightclub and casino. Major credit cards accepted; prices may be negotiable. ⑦.

Hôtel des Députés, in the administrative quarter near the lake (BP 24; ☎23.15.55 or 22.46.80; Fax 23.37.10). Bland modern hotel with AC rooms, pool, tennis courts, bar and a restaurant overlooking the lake. Only American Express credit cards accepted. ⑤.

The City

There are not that many specific targets to aim for in your explorations of Yaoundé, beyond the usual pleasures of terrace cafés and the main market. The small **Musée National** is worth a visit, and the city's two other collections could hardly be more different from each other: the jumble of clobber in the **Musée d'Art Nègre** (only really worth visiting for its **library of African history**) and the immaculately presented **Petit Musée d'Art Camerounais**, one of West Africa's most worthwhile museums.

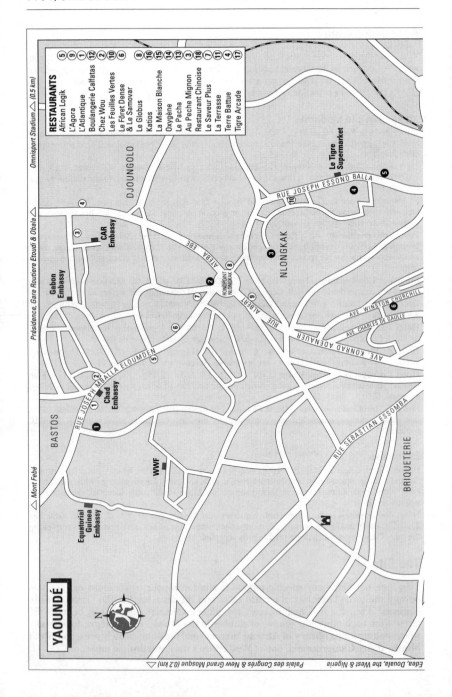

YAOUNDÉ

RESTAURANTS

African Logik	⑤
L'Agora	⑨
L'Atlantique	①
Boulangerie Calfatas	⑫
Chez Wou	②
Les Feuilles Vertes	⑩
Le Fôret Dense	⑥
& Le Samovar	
Le Globus	⑧
Katios	⑯
La Maison Blanche	⑮
Oxygène	⑭
Le Pacha	⑬
Au Peche Mignon	③
Restaurant Chinoise	⑱
Le Saveur Plus	⑦
La Terrasse	⑪
Terre Battue	④
Tigre Arcade	⑰

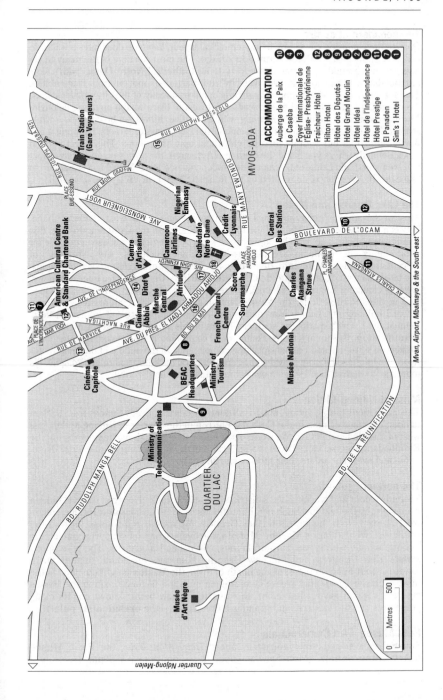

ACCOMMODATION

⑩	Auberge de la Paix
④	Le Caseba
③	Foyer Internationale de l'Église-Presbytérienne
⑫	Fraicheur Hôtel
⑧	Hilton Hotel
⑨	Hôtel des Députés
⑤	Hôtel Grand Moulin
②	Hôtel Idéal
⑥	Hôtel de l'Indépendance
⑪	Hôtel Prestige
⑦	El Panaden
①	Sim's 1 Hotel

The commercial centre

Despite the confusion caused by its asymmetrical layout, Yaoundé does have a walkable centre, with its heart at **Place Ahmadou Ahidjo**. The most startling of the many buildings grouped around this square is the very 1950s **Cathedral Notre Dame**, with a sloping roof that seems to go on forever. The city's main arteries shoot out from Place Ahidjo. To the east, Avenue Monseigneur Vogt runs uphill past many of the city's major banks. Avenue du Président El Hadj Ahidjo leads northwest of Place Ahidjo up to the colourful **Marché Central** – a building sprawling with innovative thieves, so be cautious – while Avenue Kennedy, off Avenue Ahidjo, is one of the city's classier streets, flaunting a distinctly French flavour with its **terrace cafés** and upmarket shops. This street ends in Place Kennedy where you'll find the **Centre d'Artisanat**, the town's biggest crafts depot and well worth checking out. Avenue de l'Indépendance leads from Place Kennedy to Place de l'Indépendance, dominated by the futuristic **Hôtel de Ville** – the town hall.

The Lake Quarter and Melen

Most of the administrative buildings in town congregate to the west of Place Ahidjo, between Boulevard du 20 Mai and the town lake. Known as the **Quartier du Lac**, this tranquil neighbourhood, with its imposing avenues, has long been a construction site for experiments in modern architecture. Buildings such as the Ministry of Telecommunications **Ministère des Postes et Télécommunications** or the imaginative headquarters of the **Banque des Etats de l'Afrique Centrale** have gone a long way towards changing Yaoundé's self-image in recent years. On Boulevard Rudolph Manga Bell, next to the High Court, the **Musée National** is housed in an impressively restored colonial building off Avenue Marchand, next to the High Court. On Boulevard de la Réunification, which marks the southern fringe of this *quartier*, the **Monument de la Réunification** rises up in a helter-skelter spiral commemorating the coming together of Cameroon's French- and English-speaking components. In the middle of this neighbourhood, the **lake** itself hardly provides the serene natural backdrop you might imagine. It's more like a stagnant pond – and a perfect mosquito breeding ground.

Mass at Ndjong-Melen

This is a famous tourist outing, but it isn't done for tourists. Every Sunday from 9.30am to noon the congregation in the **Catholic church** in the quarter of Ndjong-Melen, just west of the Musée d'Art Nègre, works itself into a state of high excitement during the Ewondo language service. There is wonderful music and dancing, high-energy drumming, and everyone wears their most colourful outfits.

The northern suburbs

Yaoundé's poor and working-class districts are mostly tucked away in valleys, hidden from sight by the hilltops. Such neighbourhoods include the **Briqueterie**, just northwest of town, with the town's former **Grande Mosquée**, and **Messa**, also in the northwest, which houses **Marché Mokolo**, the liveliest and most approachable market in Yaoundé where you can find fabrics, clothes and foodstuffs. The prestigious **Palais des Congres** and the new **Grande Mosquée** are found further north towards Mont Fébé. In the extreme north of town, the **Bastos** neighbourhood is the most exclusive residential area. Site of the nation's first factory (making the Bastos cigarettes which gave it its name), this quarter is now better known for its many embassies and the modern, and grandiose Présidence – the **presidential palace**.

Petit Musée d'Art Camerounais

Situated in a Benedictine monastery above *Hôtel Mont Fébé*, the **Petit Musée d'Art Camerounais** (Mon–Sat 8am–noon & 2–5pm, Sun 2–5.30pm; free, but a donation is expected) is way out of the centre and only accessible by taxi. A narrow flight of steps takes you up to the museum from the main road that continues to the hotel. Ring the bell when you arrive at the monastery and a monk will lead you to the exhibition.

Like a monument to minimalism, the museum's interior is completely stark, with clean whitewashed walls and appropriate lighting to draw your attention to the displays. Although the collection is small, it contains many masterpieces, notably from the western provinces. First of all is a display of pipes (in ivory, wood and terracotta) including some amazing **Bamoun bronze pipes**. Another room features **masks**, mainly from the Grassfields, and a fantastic wooden **bas-relief** depicting a market scene. Notice too a king's carved wooden bed, and intricate wooden panels showing scenes from a hunt. A third room contains **Tikar bronzes** and includes pipes, bells used to call the ancestors, and a king's throne.

Eating, drinking and nightlife

The surest way of guaranteeing yourself **cheap eating** is to go for the streetside food stalls. During working hours, there are lots of these around the administrative Lake Quarter, catering for government employees. If you're staying at the Presbyterian Mission or *Hôtel Idéal*, there are numerous **small eateries** nearby on rue Onembele Nkou and rue Joseph Essono Balla. They serve good breakfasts of omelettes and Nescafé in the morning, and filling rice and bean dishes in the afternoon and evening.

Inexpensive to moderate restaurants

Cheaper places are easy to stumble upon in the residential districts of Bastos, Messa and especially Briqueterie, though they are noticeably rarer in the centre. Many of these places also double as live music venues.

African Logik, rte de Bastos behind the designer-clothes boutique. Grilled food and chips accompanied by the in-house jazz band. An annual three-day Jazz Festival takes place here in February.

L'Atlantique, rte de Bastos. Good starters and excellent pizzas served in a pleasant courtyard. Reasonable prices (CFA3000–5000).

Boulangerie Calfatas, rue Nachtigal, just south of Place de l'Indépendance. The address for fresh pastries, croissants, *pain au chocolat* and other decadent snacks, including ice cream.

Le Globus, looking down on *rond-point* Nlongkak. Watch the city's bustle while drinking cold beer and tucking into dishes from a well-prepared menu.

La Maison Blanche, rue Rudolphe Abessolo. Lively outdoor nightspot for excellent grilled fish and streetlife.

Le Marseillais, av Foch. Very good value for the centre, with home-style French dishes such as *steack frites* with *haricots*. There are other branches of the *Marseillais*, one of them across from the Abbia Cinema.

Au Peche Mignon, off rue Albert Atebe Ebé, Bastos. Not at all fancy, but serves satisfying Cameroonian specialities in a pleasant atmosphere. Live music every Thursday, Friday and Saturday, starting at 9pm.

Le Saveur Plus, near *rond-point* Nlongkak. A small family-run restaurant with a good selection of inexpensive basic African and European meals.

La Terrasse, next door to hotel *El Panaden* by Place de l'Indépendance. A garden restaurant selling mainly Italian food but also some Cameroonian dishes. Pizzas between CFA2000 and CFA3400.

Terre Battue, off rte de Obala (rue Ebé). One of the best live music spots in Yaoundé, where musicians spend their evenings off, and sometimes even decide to give a helping hand. Good grilled food after 9pm; expensive beer.

Tigre Arcade, av John Kennedy. A central lunch spot frequented mainly by city workers, with well-made burgers, salads, chicken and chips, all at good prices.

Expensive restaurants

As in Douala, upmarket restaurants can be extremely expensive – up to CFA30,000 – but you can find well-prepared food at down-to-earth prices in some of the hotels and in many of the Asian restaurants.

L'Agora, off *rond-point* Nlongkak (☎22.35.96). Upmarket Cameroonian cuisine with unusual main dishes including crocodile, pangolin and porcupine. Less adventurous tastebuds will be tempted by the excellent fish and chicken dishes.

Chez Wou, rue Eloumden. This Chinese restaurant features authentic decor and terrace eating. A good place for a special dinner, but expensive.

Le Fébé, *Hôtel Mont Fébé* (☎22.43.24). One of the best restaurants in town for French cooking, and one of the most expensive. There is a cheaper coffee shop in the hotel and a poolside buffet.

Les Feuilles Vertes, rue Joseph Essono Balla. One of the most famous Cameroonian restaurants in Yaoundé; pricey, but definitely worth a visit.

Le Fôret Dense, rue Eloumden (BP 6552; ☎20.53.08). Excellent Cameroonian food like *ndole* and *folong*, as well as porcupine *ndombas* and other exotic dishes, served indoors or in pleasant outdoor *boukarous*. Popular with expats.

Restaurant Chinoise, on the corner of av Kennedy and av Ahidjo. Good-value Chinese food in a very central location.

Le Samovar, rue Eloumden (☎20.76.98). Run by a Russian couple, the *Samovar* features authentic dishes from the old country and some not-so-traditional pizza fired up in the outdoor oven.

Nightlife

Apart from the many restaurants doubling as music venues, Yaoundé has little of Douala's after-dark energy. There are a few well-known clubs and of course the hotel discos but, apart from these, a number of bars and a few small places in Briqueterie and Messa are about all the city can offer. Unfortunately, idle meanderings have become dangerous after dark. Take a taxi to get around or go in the company of someone who knows the terrain well. The places listed below are geared towards dancing.

Le Caveau, south of Place Ahidjo. An unpretentious *boîte populaire* that throbs with the latest Central African hits. Occasional live bands playing the local *bikutsi* music.

Katios, av Ahidjo at rue Goker. One of the most expensive places in town, with pulsating lights, good music and several dance areas. Good energy guaranteed.

Oxygène, by *Hôtel Royale*, off av de l'Indépendance. Popular club, with Western and African sounds and a middle-class clientele that includes a good number of expats.

Le Pacha, basement of Immeuble Hajal Massad, av Foch. A disco palace that's been around forever and still packs them in.

Super Paquita, east of Place Ahidjo, qtr Mvog-Ada. Dancing and high-powered music in an inexpensive neighbourhood club well-frequented by local youth. Good local bands are regularly invited to play here.

Listings

Airfreight DHL (☎23.13.58) and Jet Service (☎21.15.32).

Airlines Air France, 528 rue Nachtigal (BP 14335; ☎23.43.78; Fax 23.43.79); Cameroon Airlines, av Monseigneur Vogt (☎23.03.04 or 22.80.98); Sabena, 52 rue Nachtigal (BP 13812; ☎23.47.29/35; Fax 23.47.40); Swissair, *Hilton Hotel* (☎22.97.37; Fax 22.63.29). For additional flight information, including international carriers, call the airport (☎23.06.11).

Banks The main banks are near Place Ahidjo: BICEC (BP 5; ☎23.41.30); SGBC (BP 244; ☎23.10.60 or 22.04.15; Fax 22.04.92), the agent for Thomas Cook; Crédit Lyonnais (BP 700; ☎23.40.05; Fax 22.41.32). Standard Chartered is just south of Place de l'Indépendance (☎22.38.80 or 22.22.61).

Bookshops An interesting selection of books can be found in the street stalls by Place Ahidjo.

Car rental Reliable but expensive: Avis, *Hilton Hotel* (BP 1740; ☎23.17.10 or 23.36.46) and rte de Douala (☎30.22.85 or 30.20.88; Fax 30.30.10); Jully Voyages, av Mvog-Fouda Ada, near the train station (BP 6064; ☎22.39.47 or 22.14.48; Fax 22.27.17); and Sam Auto, *Hôtel Mont Fébé* (☎21.77.35; Fax 21.77.34).

Cinemas The best cinemas, with the most up-to-date films, are Le Capitole, av Marechal Foch (☎22.49.77), and l'Abbia, rue Nachtigal (☎22.31.66).

Cultural centres British Council, av Charles de Gaulle (BP 818; ☎21.16.96 or 20.31.72; Fax 21.56.91); Centre Culturel Français, av Ahidjo (☎22.09.44); Centre Culturel Camerounaise (☎20.47.99); American Cultural Centre, rue Nachtigal (☎23.16.33).

Dentists Adventist Clinic (☎22.11.10) and Polyclinic Fouda (☎22.66.12 or 22.93.67), rte de Ngousso, east of the railway tracks.

Doctors Polyclinic Fouda (see above); General Hospital (☎21.31.81 or 20.14.59).

Embassies and consulates Canada, Imm. Stamatiades, av de l'Indépendance (BP 572; ☎23.02.03 or 23.23.11); Central African Republic, off rue Albert Ateba Ebé (BP 396; ☎22.51.55); Chad, rue Joseph Mballa Eloumden, Bastos (BP 506; ☎22.06.24); Côte d'Ivoire, Bastos (BP 11357; ☎ & Fax 21.74.59); Democratic Republic of Congo (BP 632; ☎22.51.03); Equatorial Guinea, Bastos (BP 277; ☎22.41.49 or 21.14.04); France, Plateau Atémengué (BP 1631; ☎23.40.13 or 22.17.76; Fax 23.50.43); Gabon, off bd de l'URSS, Bastos (BP 4130; ☎22.29.66); Liberia, Bastos (BP 1185; ☎21.05.21); Nigeria, off av Monseigneur Vogt (BP 448; ☎23.34.55); UK, av Winston Churchill (BP 547; ☎22.07.96 or 22.05.45; Fax 22.01.48); USA, rue de Nachtigal (BP 817; ☎23.40.14 or 23.05.12; Fax 23.07.53).

Internet *Cyber Espace Ditof Internet*, av de l'Indépendance (☎23.40.86; *ditofem@ditof.org*) receives email for CFA300 per mail; *ICCnet*, *Hilton Hotel* (☎22.02.00; Fax 23.50.75; *iccnet@iccnet.cm*) also receives and send mail.

Maps The Centre Géographique National, av Monseigneur Vogt (☎22.34.65), has city, regional and national maps.

National Parks For information about Waza National Park and Dja Reserve, contact IUCN (International Union for Conservation of Nature and Natural Resources), rte de Mont Fébé, near the Nigerian High Commissioner's residence, Bastos (☎20.88.88). Worldwide Fund for Nature,

---

MOVING ON FROM YAOUNDÉ

BY ROAD

All of Youndé's *agences de voyage* are found in the area around the **Mvan gare routière**, 15km south of town on Boulevard de l'OCAM. A drop with a yellow taxi from the Score roundabout (Place Ahidjo) costs CFA150. The main *agences* are: Garanti Express (☎30.69.38), for Douala and Bamenda; Central Voyages (☎30.39.94), for Douala; Beauty Express (☎22.94.06), for Douala, Kribi and Mbalmayo; Ocean Voyages, for Kribi; Amour Voyages for Bamenda; Comfort Voyages and Binam Voyages for Bafoussam; Jeannot Express for Bamenda and Bueau; Relais Voyages for Bertoua. You can also find **share taxis** for Mbalmayo, Ebolowa, Bertoua and Abong Mbang at the *gare routière*.

For the **northwestern towns** of Bafoussam, Foumban and Bamenda, **share taxis** and **minibuses** leave from the *gare routière* Etoudi on the north side of the city, near the presidential palace.

BY TRAIN

The night train (daily; departs 6pm) to **Ngaoundéré** via Belabo and Ngaoundal (for road routes to the Central African Republic) leaves from the Gare Voyageurs, off Place Elig-Essono (enquiries ☎23.40.03). The daily **Douala** train leaves at 1.30pm, but the journey is much quicker by road.

BY PLANE

Flights leave from Nsimalen International Airport, 18km south of the centre (a CFA1700 share taxi drop). Cameroon Airlines runs **domestic** flights to Douala (daily); Garoua (Mon, Weds, Thurs & Fri); Maroua (Mon, Tues, Thurs, Sat & Sun); and Ngaoundéré (Tues, Thurs, Sat & Sun), plus a weekly service (Wed) to Ndjamena, Chad via Garoua. Most other **international** flights, including those to Europe, leave from Douala, although both Air France and Cameroon Airlines fly twice a week to Paris, and Swissair and Sabena fly weekly to Zurich.

Bastos (☎21.42.41 or 21.62.67; Fax 21.42.40) can help with information about the various WWF project sites in protected areas, and how to reach them.

Pharmacies Among the best stocked and most central is the Pharmacie Française (☎22.14.76) on the corner of av Kennedy and av Ahidjo.

Post offices The main post office (Mon–Fri 7.30am–3.30pm, Sat & Sun 7.30am–noon) is on Place Ahidjo and has an international (only) phone and fax service. Poste restante costs CFA200, but they don't hold letters very long.

Supermarkets The Fokou chain is one of the cheapest, their three stores are in Mvog-bi (south of the Score roundabout), Messa (western qtr) and Nlongkak. Score, on Place Ahmadou Ahidjo is well stocked, but Tigre, in the north of town on rue Essono Bella, is a mega-mart and considered the best place for one-stop shopping.

Travel Agencies Camvoyages, av de l'Indépendance (BP 606; ☎23.22.12); Intervoyages, Place Hôtel de Ville (BP 127; ☎22.03.61); Jully Voyages, av Mvog-Fouda Ada (BP 6064; ☎22.39.47 or 22.14.48; Fax 22.27.17); Transcap Voyages (BP 153; ☎23.12.96).

The Province du Sud

As an escape from Douala or Yaoundé, or from the rigours of overlanding, **Kribi** and the white-sand **beaches** of the "south coast" are hard to beat. The quickest route to Kribi **from Yaoundé** is via **Edea**. This attractive town, at the southernmost bridge over the broad **Sanaga River**, has a good range of basic accommodation, a market, a post office and banks, and makes a good living from the passing Douala–Yaoundé–Kribi trade. Two alternative routes from Yaoundé to Kribi run through the forests along tracks which, in the dry season at any rate, are usually passable in normal cars; in either case the first stage is to **Ebolowa**, then on either via **Lolodorf** or **Akom II**. Travel can be painfully slow along these stretches, but the roads take in lush scenery punctuated with the occasional waterfall, and skirt a number of **"Pygmy"** villages.

Mbalmayo and Sangmélima

Heading south through rich forests broken by plantations of coffee and cocoa, the N2 highway links the capital to Ebolowa, then continues to the borders of Gabon and Equatorial Guinea. The first major stop along the way is **MBALMAYO**, a prosperous town with a bank, post office and a choice of **accommodation**: *Jardin des Tropics* (☎28.16.10; ③) is well-appointed, with AC rooms, while the older *Hôtel de la Poste* (BP 226; ☎28.11.52; ②) is a good budget option. About 10km out of town, on the Ebolowa road, you can also stay at the *Ebogo Tourist Site* (②), located on the western edge of the Mbalmayo Forest Reserve, which arranges day-trips up the **River Nyong** by *pirogue*. You can actually get as far as Mbalmayo by train, but the road is so good (and so frequently served by **share taxis** and **minibuses**, as well as a regular service by Beauty Express) that there's little point.

From Mbalmayo, the N9 branches southeastward to **SANGMÉLIMA**, another large town in the forest region, centre of the president's Beti ethnic group. There's modest **accommodation** in Sangmélima at the *Hôtel Bel Air* (③), with simple S/C rooms. Slightly upmarket, the *Hotel Afamba* (③) has AC and TV in the rooms, but for atmosphere, you can't beat the *Jardin des Tropiques* on the Route de Mbalmayo (BP 537; ☎28.86.91; ③), where the AC bungalows press right up to the forest's edge. The **Gabonese border** at Nsak is 150km away to the south.

Ebolowa and around

To get to the coast or the borders, take the road that leads from Mbalmayo via Ngoulemakong to **EBOLOWA**, a lively provincial capital and important cocoa market-

MOVING ON FROM EBOLOWA

From the main *gare routière*, there are frequent share taxis to **Yaoundé**; Ebolowa's few *agences de voyage* are based nearby. Share taxis to **Kribi** are less frequent and depend very much on the status of the roads, but *clandos* are usually to be found close by. If you're continuing to **Gabon** or **Equatorial Guinea**, you need to get to **Ambam** (see p.1111), which has its own *gare routière* to the south of Ebolowa on the route d'Ambam.

ing centre. While there's not much in the way of sights – though you could stop by the **Hôpital Enongal** to contemplate the chair where Albert Schweitzer sat while having dental work done – it's a pleasant stopping point in the forest region, with a large market that spreads out near the town's artificial **lake**. With over 40,000 inhabitants, Ebolowa also has good services, including a **bank** (Credit Lyonnais), a **post office**, pharmacies and even a small supermarket.

Ebolowa practicalities
There are several small **hotels**, most with **restaurants** and **bar/dancings** that make for rather wild nights in the jungle. Water supplies are irregular in town, and even the best hotel can't guarantee enough pressure for a decent bath.

La Cabane Bambou, north of the *gare routière*, towards the market (BP 144; ☎28.44.44). Inexpensive hotel and restaurant, popular with overlanders. ②.

Hôtel le Ranch at the foot of Mount Ebolowa (BP 670; ☎28.35.32 or 28.63.68). Comfortable S/C rooms, some overlooking the mountain. ③.

Hôtel de la Santé, north of the market, opposite the lake (BP 216; ☎28.35.17). Spotless S/C rooms. ③.

Hôtel Sotha Ane Rouge, off the town's main roundabout and an easy walk from the *gare routière* (BP 315; ☎28.34.38). Clean, good-value S/C rooms with mosquito nets. ①.

Porte Jaune (BP 817; ☎28.39.29 or 28.49.39). The best hotel in town with a choice of S/C rooms with AC or fan. ③.

Ambam and on to Gabon and Equatorial Guinea
The paved road stops just south of Ebolowa, making for an adventurous trip through dense forest to **Ambam**, the last major town before the borders of Equatorial Guinea and Gabon. There's a large market here with an international array of traders, and **accommodation** at the rudimentary *Auberge du Petit Calao* (①) or the slightly better *Ambam Sejour* (BP 7; ②). But this is a transit town and like most people who pull in, your main objective will be to get on to somewhere else.

Share taxis **to Gabon** leave from Ambam's market and take little more than an hour to reach the border. On Saturdays, they stop at **Aban Minkoo** for the eventful weekly market. Once at the border, you can take a ferry across the Ntem River, or hire a *pirogue*. Taxis on the other side assure regular transport to **Bitam**. Share taxis **to Equatorial Guinea** leave from the motor park, across from the post office. Halfway to the border, your vehicle crosses the Ntem River on a regular ferry and then pushes on to the frontier town of **Ebebiyin**. You'll be dropped on Cameroonian territory, some 2km before reaching the town. After walking through customs, you can continue in a waiting taxi.

Lolodorf
From Ebolowa, it's 73km by decent *piste* to **LOLODORF** (its name about the only reminder of the German presence in the area – "Lolo's village" – as most towns were renamed by the French), where you can find accommodation at the *Auberge de Cantenaire* (②) and fill up with fuel. Only 110km separate Lolodorf from Kribi, but the

rough tracks that wind through the hilly tropical forest make for a long trip. As a pay-off, however, this route does pass by numerous "Pygmy" villages where, unlike in the extreme east of the country, the people have adopted a sedentary lifestyle. After 34km you reach the village of Bidjoka, from where you can walk to the **Bidjoka Falls**. Ten kilometres further on is the larger village of Bipindi, whence it's another 66km to Kribi.

Kribi

As a backdrop to the daily activity of commerce, fishing and forestry, colonial reminders abound in **KRIBI**, creating a quiet nostalgic feeling. The home-town of the Bassa, Kribi was a noted hotbed of UPC radicalism in the 1950s. The **port** at the centre of town was built by the Germans and is today too shallow for larger vessels to enter the harbour: from the nearby hillside, crowned with its colonial **cathedral**, you can see ships anchored a few kilometres offshore as their cargo is docked by lighter. The former **German administrative buildings** lining the beachfront in the northwest of town now house government offices such as the *préfecture* and the **tourist office** (BP 128; ☎46.10.80). Kribi's only **bank** (BICEC) is found on the Lolodorf road.

Kribi is Cameroon's second-largest port, but has long remained in relative isolation. Since the new highway linking the town to Yaoundé and Douala opened in 1991, how-ever, travelling time from Doula has been slashed from nine hours to less than three. The road has given a much needed economic boost to the region and opened the tourism floodgates. Fortunately, there are still numerous remote corners where you can escape from the weekend sunseekers.

Accommodation

Because of the relatively heavy tourist influx, **accommodation** tends to be expensive in Kribi, though a number of relatively inexpensive places still do good business. In the off season, on weekdays or if you're staying for an extended period, bargaining can shave ten to thirty percent off the regular room rate.

Auberge Annette II, south of the bridge, 1km from the centre (BP 35; ☎46.10.57). An ideal beach-front location that justifies the price; one of the cheaper places on the sea. ②–③.

Auberge de Kribi, two blocks east of the *gare routière* (BP 355; ☎46.13.15). Simple rooms with fans and shared facilities. ①.

Auberge du Phare, south of the bridge (BP 319; ☎46.11.08). Clean and well managed, with AC rooms and a few excellent-value non-AC rooms. Breezy beachfront vistas from the popular restau-rant. ③–⑤.

Hôtel Coco Beach, south of the bridge, on the beach (BP 302; ☎46.15.84; Fax 46.18.19). Well-scrubbed and luxurious AC rooms with showers and hot water. The ten rooms are often full, so book beforehand. ④.

THE KIRIDI

Kribi's name is said to come from the word *kiridi*, which roughly translated means "short men". It's a reminder that you're in **"Pygmy"** country – these were the original inhabi-tants of the district. Now, however, Bantu-speakers like the **Batanga** and **Bakoko** pre-dominate, and you might not see a single convincing "Pygmy". The "Pygmies", of course, don't call themselves by that term and every community is part of a small cluster of bands. They are traditionally nomadic, but increasingly sedentary these days, and more and more dependent on the larger economy of Cameroon, beyond the forest. All Africa's people of small stature have completely lost their original languages and now speak the local language of the dominant people – in this area Bassa.

△ *Douala &* ❶

KRIBI

NGOÉ

MFAW
MABÉ

N

**Alpha
Cinema**

❷ **Gare
Routiére**
Gendarmerie **Marché**

Présidence

RUE DE MARCHE

①

❸

BAS
ZAIRE

Lolodorf ▷

❹

②

Hospital **BICEC**

MOKOLO

ATLANTIC

**Tourist
Office**

③
④
⑤

Ebolowa ▷

OCEAN

PORT

Kienke River

Cathedral

TALLO

❺

❻

❼

0   Metres   200

▽ *Campo &* ❽

ACCOMMODATION

Auberge Annette II	❽
Auberge de Kribi	❸
Auberge du Phare	❺
Hôtel Coco Beach	❻
Hôtel Ni d'Or	❷
Hôtel de la Paix	❹
Hôtel Résidence Jully	❶
Palm Beach Plus Hotel	❼

**RESTAURANTS, BARS
& CLUBS**

Barracuda Restaurant	③
Big Ben	⑤
Liberty Bar	①
Restaurant le Marseillais	④
Village de la Paix	②

Hôtel Ni d'Or, close to the market and *gare routière* (BP 186; ☎46.14.35). Comfortable but slightly run-down S/C rooms. Good bar-restaurant. ②–③.

Hôtel de la Paix, near the tourist office. Excellent-value hotel with clean S/C rooms and friendly, informative staff. ①.

Hôtel Résidence Jully, by the seafront off the Douala road, just north of Kribi (BP 195; ☎46.15.62/64; Fax 46.19.62). Luxurious AC rooms with sports facilities and a beachfront restaurant. ④.

Palm Beach Plus Hotel, 750m south of the bridge, at the end of the paved road (BP 351; ☎46.14.47; *hotelpb@iccnet.cm*). Large new, hotel with comfortable sea-facing rooms and a good but pricey bar-restaurant. Email received (only) for guests, free of charge. ④.

Eating, drinking and nightlife

For moderate to expensive **dining**, you can hardly beat the beachfront seafood restaurants of the hotels, many of which are so busy at weekends, they run out of food midway through the dinner hour. Of the restaurants in town, the *Barracuda* (☎46.14.15) and *Restaurant le Marseillais* (☎46.18.63), both on Route de la Poste, are also well known for their seafood. The rue du Marché is the best place to go for more affordable meals.

Kribi has a number of good **clubs** that play late into the night at weekends. *Big Ben*, near the bridge, is the oldie-but-goodie of Kribi; the newer *Village de la Paix* nightclub, across from *Hotel de la Paix*, is another happening place. Up near the *gare routière*, the *Liberty Bar*, also known as *Maison Blanche*, is less expensive, but equally lively.

The coast around Kribi

The beaches along this southern stretch of the coast, north and south of Kribi, are, with their wild vegetation, white sand and calm waters, among the most beautiful anywhere in Africa. They stretch over 100km, from the small village at **Londji** to the town of **Campo** on the border of Equatorial Guinea. Beach bums will be in their element, though the paradise is far from being a well-kept secret.

Londji and the beaches to the north

North of Kribi, the road to Edéa hugs the coastline as it skirts some of the most picturesque strands. It passes the village of Mpalla and, after 15km, **Cocotier Plage** (a beautiful beach where there are rudimentary bungalows for rent) before arriving at **LONDJI**. Some 25km from Kribi, 500m before the Kribi tollgate, this small fishing village spreads round a large bay with calm, warm water, white sands and coconut trees. The comfortable *Auberge Jardinière* (BP 250, Kribi; ☎46.11.27; ③), with electricity and running water, nestles on the beach offering the best **accommodation** in the village and an excellent seafood restaurant. Though it fills with expats at weekends, on other days you'll have the place and the beach to yourself. If you're on a low budget, humbler *boukarous* (②) are rented out along the beach. **Camping** is also possible on the two beaches, Paris Plage and London Beach, for around CFA2500 per person, payable to the village chief, who has employed guards to keep the *voleurs* at bay. You can order fresh fish from the guards, or fill up in town on fish, snail kebabs and rice. A couple of local bars sell beer, minerals and freshly tapped palm wine.

After midnight, **fishermen** set out in wooden canoes across the bay, stirring up phosphorescence in the water as they paddle towards the deeper ocean. You can arrange with the beach guards to be taken along – for a price – though it's not always an eventful experience. Staying in Londji is as relaxing as the fishing technique, but despite its position on the main *piste* it does feel isolated. If you're missing nightlife and restaurants, you can catch share taxis to and from Kribi during most of the day. They stop running in the early evening, however, and it costs CFA2000–3000 to hire a taxi back to Londji.

The southern beaches to Campo

Another *piste* follows the coastline southwards from Kribi to the Ecuato-Guinean border, passing still more beaches, all exotically named – Marseilles, Océan Amerique, Azure. Seven kilometres from town, just before **Grand Batanga**, a small signpost points down to the **Chutes de la Lobé** where the river of the same name comes thrashing over a rocky descent as it plunges directly into the ocean. The force of these rapids stirs up an unappealing brownish foam in the bay, but the surrounding beaches are clean and have excellent swimming. You will find a couple of eating places at the foot of the falls selling grilled shrimp and fish specialities. There are also several good places to **stay**, such as *Tara Plage* about 1km before the waterfall (BP 103; ☎46.20.82; ②), with large S/C rooms, and the idyllically located *Hotel Ilomba* about 500m from the falls (BP 305; ☎46.17.44; Fax 46.21.44; ④), which offers luxurious *boukarous* and runs a good but expensive restaurant. You can walk to the *chutes* from Kribi, but be aware that thieves reputedly try their luck along this stretch of the beach.

You need transport to reach the fishing village of **Eboundja**, 20km south of Kribi, where the local chief authorizes camping on the beach, and will arrange meals and fishing boat excursions. The more complicated **trips** that you may be offered up the Lobé River, however, tend to be both expensive and disappointing, for while paddling upstream is not without interest, the "Pygmy" villages you've ostensibly come to visit are completely inauthentic and the "traditional" hunting trips – with people taller than you – really seem like something out of a second-rate theme park.

Some 25km further south, a rocky land formation, the **Rocher du Loup** – a photo of which is unfailingly included in all the tourism literature – rises dramatically, but not very wolf-like, from the water. South of here, you're getting into very remote districts: the road passes yet another fishing village, Ebodje, before petering out at the two-bit border town of **CAMPO**. You can expect customs and immigration checks in the vicinity, whether or not you're crossing. The big **Réserve du Campo**, 3000 square kilometres of gazetted but unmanaged rainforest, hasn't yet had much to offer visitors, but if you are interested in exploring, contact the tourist office in Kribi (☎46.10.80) for information about Campo's tracks and accommodation. The town beach stretches south out to the mouth of the **Ntem River**, which marks the border with Equatorial Guinea. In **Ipono**, 10km south of Campo, you can find basic accommodation at *Auberge Jardin des Princes* (①) and negotiate with a *piroguier* to take you 10km up the Ntem River to **Elende** in Equatorial Guinea. There's a frontier post here (make sure to get your passport stamped before continuing), and walkable tracks leading to the road to **Bata**.

The Province de l'Est

Three hundred kilometres of *piste* separate Yaoundé from **Bertoua**, the capital of East Province – a region which has changed dramatically due to gold prospecting and virtually unrestricted logging of the rainforest. In recent years, places like **Yokadouma** and **Lomié** were isolated villages surrounded by undisturbed forest havens. Now, they ooze with the atmosphere of the boom-town, spawning a multitude of newly opened bars, brothels and auberges.

The roads heading east from Yaoundé are maintained by the logging companies, but the heavy trucks often corrugate the roads badly and from time to time they become impassable to ordinary vehicles. Formerly, the main route to Bertoua followed the **Sanaga River** to **Nanga-Eboko** (accommodation at the *Etoile d'Or de Nanga*; ①), but a couple of broken bridges has made this route impassable at the time of writing. An alternative route, following the course of the **Nyong River** via **Abong Mbang** is now used; it's paved as far as **Ayos** (145km from Yaoundé). If you can distract your attention from the hundreds of logging trucks, these routes do provide a sense of being away from it all. **Lomié**, 127km to the south, is a good base for treks in the rarely visited **Réserve du Dja**, a large swath of pristine rainforest to the west.

Most travellers press eastwards towards **Bertoua**, passing through **Doumé**, formerly the capital of the eastern region and site of some remarkable colonial vestiges, including a French cathedral and an imposing German fortress. Moving on from Bertoua to the **Central African Republic**, the main road shudders northeast to **Garoua-Boulai**, a long journey through a great swath of jungle and grassland to a busy crossing point and marketplace on the savannah fringes of central Cameroon.

Heading directly east from Bertoua, you reach **Batouri**, a busy town en route to Berbérati in the Central African Republic, and to **Yokadouma**, the gateway to the southeastern corner of the country. The three **forest reserves** in this area, Lake Lobeke, Boumba Bek and Nki are gradually becoming more accessible to visitors and offer some of the most satisfying game viewing in West Africa.

Bertoua

Situated on the border of the savannah and the forest, Bertoua has grown rapidly in recent years, thanks to its economic base of logging. Some industry has grown up around this sector and there's an urgent sense of commerce about, but this town of some 30,000 is above all an **administrative centre**, seat of the East Province and of the Lom and Djérem *département*. Despite the **bank** (BICEC), cinemas and bars, however, it's an uninspiring place to visit. For overland travellers, the most salient feature is likely to be the well-stocked provisions shops and the good selection of **accommodation** which makes Bertoua an obvious stopping point on the roads to and from the Eastern Province and Central Africa.

Accommodation

Auberge Central, near the motor park (BP 278; ☎24.10.93). A good choice for budget travellers with very inexpensive rooms; private bath optional. ①.

Hôtel de l'Est, at the *rond-point* Poste Central (☎24.23.42). Slightly better than the budget hotels, with spacious AC rooms; shared bathroom facilities or S/C. ①–②.

Mansa Hôtel (BP 285; ☎24.15.50 or 24.15.88). A symbol of recent economic expansion and far and away the town's top hotel. Fully AC accommodation set on an artificial lake. ③.

Pheonix Hôtel, convenient for the motor park (BP 215; ☎24.25.01). A good-value friendly hotel with clean S/C rooms and a recommended bar-restaurant. ②.

Réserve du Dja

The **Réserve du Dja**, bounded in the north and south by the River Dja, is the largest intact area of primary rainforest in Cameroon, but rarely visited by tourists. The **forest wildlife** – which includes a large population of lowland gorillas, chimpanzee, mandrill, forest elephants, sitatunga and buffalo – is very difficult to see unless you are extremely dedicated. This is partly due to the nature of the forest where it's difficult to see more than a few metres, but also as a result of intense hunting. **Bird-watching**, however, can be rewarding, and the northwest of the reserve is especially good for hornbills. For information and guides, contact ECOFAC (Ecosystem Forestier d'Afrique Centrale) in Yaoundé (☎20.94.72).

The eastern part of the reserve is home to **Baka pygmies**, or *gens du forêt*, who live around the reserve boundary in relatively traditional camps. From Lomié, you can arrange to trek into the forest with Baka guides, and stay in their villages. The best place to **stay** in Lomié itself is the *Auberge de Raffia*, 2km out of the town (②), which is clean and helpful.

MOVING ON FROM BERTOUA

If you're travelling by **share taxi**, the *gare routière* is easy to locate in the town centre. From here vehicles leave for all the surrounding towns including **Belabo** in the west, **Batouri** to the east and **Garoua-Boulai** to the north. The main **agences de voyage** are located near the *gare routière*. Relais and Alliance Voyages have daily departures for **Yaoundé**, and there are also regular connections to Belabo, the closest town on the **Transcam railway** line. Unfortunately, trains heading both north and south reach Belabo late at night and as the trains are more often delayed than on time, you may end up waiting for many hours. The train station in Belabo has a reputation for being very unsafe, so if you choose this route beware of hands exploring your luggage.

Garoua-Boulai

The *piste* leading north of Bertoua to **GAROUA-BOULAI** tends to be tough going during the rainy season, but takes in some fine mountain scenery near Ndokayo with panoramic views over the valley of the **Lom River**. The Adamawa Mountains are not far to the north and many Fulani herders pass through Garoula-Boulai. Several small *auberges* provide inexpensive **accommodation** in town, including one right in the motor park (①). Another option is the *Mission Catholique*, with rooms or dormitory space a stone's throw from the border (②).

Garoua-Boulai's main motor park is at the border, the crossing of which is relatively uncomplicated on either side. After dealing with customs in Béloko, the frontier post in the **Central African Republic**, it's another 160km to Bouar on the main road to Bangui. If you're continuing to **northern Cameroon**, share taxis can be found to **Meiganga** where you can either branch westward to catch the train at **Ngaoundal**, or continue by road to **Ngaoundéré**.

Batouri

East of Bertoua, the forest yields to hilly savannah broken by rivers and woodlands. Travel is difficult along the poorly maintained *piste* leading to **BATOURI**, the last main town before the border with the Central African Republic. You can **stay** at the basic but pleasant *Cooperant Auberge* (①) near the motor park in the centre of town, or, a *moto* ride away, at the *Auberge au Bon Tabac* (BP 57; ☎26.21.57; ②), with presentable S/C accommodation and a good bar and restaurant. The cheapest option is the *Mission Catholique* (①).

With **Mount Niong** and **Mount Pandi** flanking the town, Batouri is also the base for some interesting expeditions. The southeast is famous for its **gold mines** which still attract prospectors from many parts of West and Central Africa; find a guide to take you to the makeshift mining village 6km from town. Seeing the river panners and the gold scales in the market (dominated by Hausa speculators), it's hard to avoid Wild West comparisons, but behind these images lies the real danger inherent in digging.

Share taxis usually leave from the *gare routière* before dawn to tackle the 102 kilometres of tortuous tracks leading to the frontier town of **Kentzou**. Border formalities are dealt with efficiently and connections by share taxi to **Berbérati**, 100km into the Central African Republic, are usually quick.

Yokadouma and around

YOKADOUMA is one of the fastest growing towns in Cameroon, abuzz with the activities of opportunist gold diggers, game hunters, loggers and environmentalists from all over west and central Africa.

Reaching Yokadouma can be a trying experience. The 200km *piste* from Batouri is maintained regularly by the logging companies, but it's wrecked as rapidly as it's repaired. Bridges often collapse and traffic jams of hundreds of trucks are not uncommon. Before you travel, enquire in the motor park in Batouri or Bertoua about the state of the road.

There are a number of good **places to stay** in Yokadouma. In the centre of town are *La Cachette* (☎24.28.63; ②), with clean S/C rooms, and *Hôtel Libeta* (①–②), slightly more dingy but a lot quieter. Basic but comfortable rooms with showers can be found at *Auberge de Commissair* (①), behind the commissioner's office – a convenient place to stay if you need exit visas to travel into the Central African Republic. For **food**, you can't beat the pleasant atmosphere at *La Falaise*, and for music, head for the nearby *Village de la Paix*, where local bands play every weekend.

The southeastern rainforests

The hilly southeastern corner of Cameroon is covered by dense, humid Congo Basin rainforest supporting a rich variety of **wildlife**, including forest elephants, buffalo, bongo, chimpanzees, gorillas, duiker and a multitude of monkeys. You'll need a reliable 4WD vehicle to reach the three **forest reserves** in the area, and once you're there the only infrastructure within the forests are research camps managed by WWF, who lead the conservation initiatives in the area. Its possible to stay at the camps, soon to become part of a larger eco-tourism scheme, for a fee. Bordering reserves in the neighbouring Central African Republic and Congo Brazzaville, **Lake Lobeke Forest** forms part of the largest area of protected tropical rainforest in Africa. Its rich fauna can be viewed from stilted platforms – *miradors* – constructed by WWF. **Boumba Bek** and **Nki forests** are pristine, protected by rivers. The westernmost reserve, Nki, is only accessible by boat up the Dja River. To enquire about the **practicalities** of a trip, contact WWF in Yokadouma (☎24.29.19; Fax 24.29.01).

NORTHERN CAMEROON

Northern Cameroon is remarkably detached from the rest of the country by a vast, almost trackless region in the centre. This huge expanse of rolling savannah and forests – as big as Scotland or Maine – is thinly populated and crossed by just three *pistes*, and the railway. On its northern edge, the **Adamawa Mountains** cut across the centre of Cameroon, and as you cross this barrier, it's striking how effectively it divides the country into two distinct parts. It's a tough journey by road from Yaoundé or Bamenda to the first town of northern Cameroon, **Ngaoundéré** – good enough reason to use the train. Beyond, a flat plateau stretches over much of the north, where light forests and grasslands replace the south's thick vegetation, indicating that the climate is harsher and nature less generous. But there's more variety to the scenery than you might detect from the mostly flat sealed highway, running from Ngaoundéré all the way to **Kousseri**, which makes the north one of the easiest regions to travel through.

No less than six **game parks** are situated in the north, ranging from the hilly **Bouba Ndjida National Park**, home to the almost extinct West African **black rhinoceros**, to the popular **Waza National Park**, where the flat savannah is ideal for seeing herds of giraffe and elephant, as well as lions and numerous other species.

In the extreme northwest, the volcanic **Mandara Mountains** have been scoured by thousands of years of *Harmattan* winds and the people of the region squeeze their livelihood out of the dry rocky slopes. Although this region has been "discovered" by travel operators, you can, if you're determined enough, work your way off the more beaten tracks and away from such overrun sites as **Roumsiki** to villages which may not be any more authentic but are at least less tainted by organized tourism.

While the mountain people of the northwest have retained traditional religious beliefs, the rest of the region bears the stamp of **Islam**, brought by Fulani migrants who established principalities called **lamidats** in the eighteenth century. The Muslim influence is especially noticeable in towns such as **Garoua** and **Maroua**, which seem unusually large and dynamic in a region where you might expect climate and geography to reduce energy to a minimum.

Ngaoundéré

Coming from the south, **NGAOUNDÉRÉ**, with its mango-shaded streets and mild climate resulting from its 1400-metre elevation, proves a satisfying introduction to the north. Though rapidly growing, the **old Fulani settlement** is well contained in the neighbourhood around the **Lamido's Palace**, where the architecture of the houses and mosques and the dress of the people bear witness to a Sudanic tradition that is very much alive.

Some history

The first people to settle around Ngaoundéré – which means "navel in the mountain" in their language – were the **Mboum**, whose claims to the area were lost to the **Fulani** after a military siege in the early 1830s. By 1835, **Ardo Ndjobdji** had established the Muslim **lamidat** and the Mboum became Fulani vassals. A large town of some 10,000 at the end of the last century, the city was surrounded by a protective wall in 1865; its influence extended over a vast territory to the south and east. Even during the colonial period, the traditional town changed little, and it wasn't until the **Trans-Cameroonian Railroad** was extended here in 1974 that a real boom occurred. In the early 1970s, the population paused briefly at around 20,000, but by 1983 it had rocketed to nearly 60,000 and may be close to 120,000 people by now. New *quartiers* have grown up all around the old centre, adding a sense of vitality to the traditional core. Improved transportation also facilitated economic activity that today includes an industrial slaughterhouse (livestock is a regional mainstay), a dairy and a tannery.

Accommodation

Auberge les Alizés, slightly out of town on the Plateau Mandock (BP 405; ☎25.16.89). Newly redecorated S/C balconied rooms with countryside views. Good bar and restaurant, and a pleasant garden. ②.

Auberge de Château d'Adamaoua, off rue du Petit Marché (☎25.20.42). No-frills rooms without fan or bath, but among the cheapest in the centre. ①.

Auberge de la Gare, near the train station (BP 203; ☎25.22.17). Friendly place with 24hr reception and well-maintained S/C rooms around the courtyard, where you can park safely. The restaurant serves good cheap food. ②.

Auberge Possada Style, off rue Ahidjo north of the cathedral (BP 518; ☎25.17.03). A new place featuring small but cheerful S/C rooms with hot water. ①.

Hôtel du Rail, rte de Garoua, a 10min walk from the train station (BP 319; ☎25.10.13). Clean and very comfortable S/C rooms, slightly more upmarket and expensive than *Le Relais*. ②.

Hôtel le Relais, behind the Cinéma le Nord (BP 47; ☎25.11.38). Spacious but slightly run-down AC rooms, convenient for the centre. ②.

Transcam Hôtel, off the rte de Garoua-Boulai (BP 179; ☎25.13.32; Fax 25.12.52). A showy place with TV and other perks in the AC rooms and *boukarous*. First-rate service, tennis courts, bar, restaurant and nightclub. Amex and Visa accepted (with cash back) if you're staying in the hotel. ③.

The Town

The **old town** centres around the **Lamido's Palace**, which is a *saré* – the Hausa word for this style of housing – made of *banco* huts with vast straw rooftops that swoop down nearly to the ground. A large wall surrounding the compound keeps the maze of courtyards, private dwellings and public rooms out of view from the street. For an **inside visit**, ask at the Lamido's Secretariat, a new concrete building at the palace entrance, or preferably go to the **tourist office** on rue Ahidjo, as touts tend to hang around by the entrance charging fees for their own pockets. The tourist office will make a booking for you. An entrance fee is optional, but CFA2000 is considered reasonable.

By far the best time to visit the palace is on Fridays in time for the **Friday prayer**. Dignitaries in brightly coloured *boubous* – magnificent accents of orange and red against the ochre tints of the town – come to pay their respects to the Lamido, who leads a procession to the mosque. Similar displays take place on Saturday and Sunday.

Ngaoundéré's **Grand Marché**, adjoined by the **gare routière**, is down the main avenue from the palace, and surrounded by an arcaded wall. Recently the **Petit**

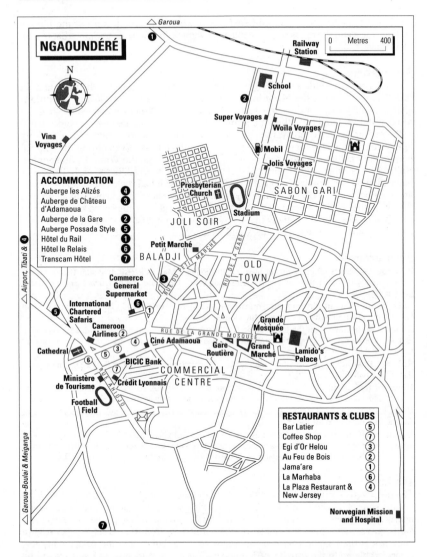

Marché, on the road of the same name, has become the main market, and is far more interesting to visit. The main avenue from both markets lead to the commercial centre, with its **banks** and **post office**.

The **Ministère du Tourisme** on rue Ahidjo (BP 527; ☎25.25.89) has enthusiastic staff and good regional travel tips. They can also recommend places to eat and sleep in town and aren't snooty about directing you to the cheaper *auberges* if you emphasize you're on a budget. It's a good idea to also check the events calendar of the Alliance Franco-Camerounais de l'Adamaoua at the tourist office while you're there; during the year they arrange various musical and cultural events that would be a shame to miss.

Eating, drinking and nightlife

You'll find numerous cheap eating places around the *gare routière*. For something a little fancier, there are lots of places to choose between in the commercial centre. *Au Feu de Bois* specializes in *ndolé* but also serves the standard chicken-and-chips menu. The *Bar Latier* not only serves six varieties of yogurt and milk, but also produces steaks, salads and coffee and cake at reasonable prices. For grilled fish, cold beer and dancing at weekends, *La Marhaba* is a good choice. In the *Coffee Shop*, near the BICEC bank, you can get well-made *steack frites* and good portions of salad. In the morning, hot croissants and *gateaux* are served with fresh coffee at the *Egi d'Or Helou*, which serves pizza, hamburgers and *chawarmas* later in the day. If you're feeling extravagant, *La Plaza Restaurant* serves good French cuisine at European prices and the neighbouring *New Jersey* nightclub offers similarly priced **nightlife** at weekends. The Alliance Franco-Camerounais de l'Adamaoua sometimes arranges live music events, and the *Jama'are* is a popular venue for live bands.

Listings

Banks BICEC is on the main avenue between the Lamido's Palace and the tourist office, but first try Crédit Lyonnais on av Ahidjo – the best (and sometimes only) place to change travellers' cheques.

Bookshops Adamaoua Loisiers, next to the Shell station by the tourist office, and Slipa-Sports, across from BICEC, carry a good selection of magazines and newspapers.

Car and moto rental If you want to rent a car, to visit the game reserves for example, it's very expensive after you figure in the daily rate, the insurance, the driver, the kilometre charge and of course fuel. Prices for more than a day are negotiable. Try International Chartered Safaris (☎25.16.60) by the cathedral junction, or Vina Voyages (BP 322; ☎25.25.25) on av Ahidjo. *Motos* can be hired for the day in front of *Hôtel le Relais*.

Cinemas The Cinéma Adamaoua (☎25.13.04) is in the centre of town.

Hospital If you need medical help, head for the Norwegian Mission hospital, to the southeast of town (☎25.11.95).

Supermarkets Wine, cheese and other imported goods are available at ETS Alisar Alimentation, close to *La Plaza Restaurant*, and at Commerce General, behind Hôtel le Relais.

Travel Agencies For excursions in and around Ngaoundéré, Alto-Tour Conceil (☎25.15.24) across from the motor park and right in front of the *litahi* tree, offers some interesting day-trips on horseback or mountain bike.

Around Ngaoundéré

If you have your own transport – or make yourself mobile by renting it – you're well positioned to take some easy side trips in the environs of Ngaoundéré. The nearest site of scenic interest is **Lac Tison**, just 10km from town. Take the Meiganga road south and after 6km a signpost points east to the crater lake, deep in the woods 3km further on. It's a pleasant ride along a *piste* bordered by awkward boulder formations, but forget swimming when you get there, as bilharzia is a real risk. Back on the Meiganga road, 15km from town just past the village of Wakwa, the well-known waterfall, **Chute de la Vina** tumbles 30m down onto a table of rock.

A popular weekend getaway is the **Ngaoundaba Ranch** (③), 40km towards Meiganga on a dry season road. Perched in the mountains by a beautiful **crater lake**, the main lodge recalls a Hemingwayesque vision of Africa from where the now-deceased founder once led guests on hunting safaris. The image lives on as visitors gather for meals at a long trestle table with animal trophies on the heavy stone and wood beam walls. Most of the bougainvillea-bedecked *boukarous* have panoramic views of the area, which is great for **bird-watching**. Other diversions include swimming, fishing and boat trips on the lake. The ranch is open from November to May; reservations BP 3, Ngaoundéré (Fax 25.19.05). **Camping** is also possible, at CFA1000 per person.

MOVING ON FROM NGAOUNDÉRÉ

Heading south, the best bet is the **train**. The modern railway station (enquiries ☎25.13.77) is 1km north of the commercial centre. Couchette trains leave every evening at 8pm for **Yaoundé**. If you're heading to **eastern Cameroon**, or on to the **Central African Republic**, take the train to Bélabo, from where taxis continue to Bertoua.

Several **agences de voyage** now operate daily connections to the north. Woïla Voyages (BP 630; ☎25.25.08) has two daily departures to Garoua and Maroua (one morning, one early afternoon) in comfortable buses, and Jolis Voyages (☎25.14.19) leaves three times a day to Garoua and Maroua; Amy Voyages and Super Voyages also head north.

The **gare routière** is next to the central market. **Share taxis** can take you from here to **Tibati**, on the long and rugged road to Foumban; to **Tcholliré**, between the Bénoué and Bouba Ndjida parks; to **Meiganga** on the main overland route to Yaoundé and Central Africa; and up the road 300km north to **Garoua**.

If you want to move on fast, Cameroon Airlines (☎25.12.95) has four **flights** a week to Yaoundé and Douala, although some of the departures take a time-consuming detour via Garoua or Maroua. You can confirm schedules by calling the airport (☎25.12.84).

Bénoué and Bouba Ndjida National Parks

Although overshadowed by the superb Waza National Park further north (see p.1132), some of the best **game viewing** in West Africa can be had at the **Bénoué** and the **Bouba Ndjida National Parks,** off the Ngaoundéré–Garoua road. The once prolific wildlife of Faro National Park has been severely depleted by poaching, so unless you wish to see the landscape (a mountain-dotted slab of bush) there is really no reason to go there. Unfortunately, you can't get around the parks if you don't have transport, so assuming you're not taking an air tour out of Douala or Yaoundé, you're left with the painfully expensive option of **renting a car** in one of the main towns (Ngaoundéré, Garoua or Maroua), or the uncertain option of hitching a lift in with mobile tourists. To stay at any of the *campements*, you should reserve in advance, especially for weekends or holidays when bed spaces fill up (contact the Délégation Provincial du Tourisme pour le Nord, BP 50, Garoua; ☎27.22.90; Fax 27.13.64). Note that Cameroonian conservation policy makes special provision for big game hunting, with macabre head prices on every species, from elephant down to monkey. Hunting blocks are well defined and the paths of camera- and gun-users don't cross.

Rey Bouba, west of Bouba Ndjida National Park, is one of the most influential and traditional of the Fulani *lamidats*. It's a worthwhile excursion to the village, where you can stay on the floor of a traditional resthouse (①), but you may have to wait days for an audience with the Lamido himself. Share taxis run from Ngaoundéré to Tcholliré, but you'll have to find a vehicle going north for the remaining 35km to Rey Bouba; your best chance is Friday – market day.

Bénoué National Park

Coming north from Ngaoundéré, you can enter the **Bénoué National Park** (Dec–May; entrance fee CFA5000; obligatory guide CFA3000/day; vehicle CFA2000/day) either at Mayo Alim or Banda. From both these towns, tracks lead through the park to the *Campement du Buffle Noir* (reservations through Délégation Provincial du Tourisme pour le Nord, BP 50, Garoua; ☎27.22.90; Fax 27.13.64; ④). Situated on the banks of the Bénoué River, this camp has S/C **rooms** grouped in simple and comfortable *boukarous*. With prior permission from the tourist office in Garoua, you can camp on the grounds, and if you take your meals in the **restaurant**, you get free access to a shower and toilet. Meals at the restaurant cost CFA5000–8000.

Antelopes such as **kob, waterbuck** and **hartebeeste** predominate in the park, but you may also see **buffalo** and **eland**. **Elephants** and **lions** are not as prolific as at Waza, but **hippos** and **crocodiles** are common in the river. Fishing is possible in the park, although at CFA70,000/day it's very expensive. A popular spot for fishing is at the *Campement du Grand Capitaine* (④), the park's second resthouse, which lies on the main road leading from Guidjiba to Tcholliré.

Bouba Ndjida National Park

The **Bouba Ndjida National Park** (Dec–May; entrance fee CFA5000; obligatory guide CFA3000/day) was created in 1968 to protect the now nearly extinct **black rhinoceros** and the increasingly rare **Derby eland**. The main access is via Koum, 40km east of Tcholliré; fees are paid to the conservator of Bouba Ndjida in Tcholliré, who also arranges vehicles into the park. The rugged landscape, with rivers and relatively thick vegetation, makes this one of the country's most beautiful parks, but the vast space (2200 square kilometres and 450km of track) and thick bush means that the animals are more dispersed and not as visible as in Waza, for example. A salt lick was created to attract the rhinos, but it's still almost impossible to spot them. There's more chance of seeing **elephants** and **buffaloes**, and, with luck, **lions** (which sometimes approach the resthouse) and **leopards**. The *Bouba Ndjida camp* (reservations as above; ④) is 40km inside the park and faces the Mayo (river) Lidi.

Garoua

Capital of Northern Province, **GAROUA** has grown rapidly since independence, and now has a population nearing 200,000. Surprisingly, for a town situated so far into the interior, it has the country's third largest port, on the banks of the **Bénoué (Benue) River**. This has helped smooth the way for local industrialization – though being former president Ahidjo's birthplace was no hindrance: he was always ready to invest in his home town. As the principal administrative and economic focus of the north, Garoua's more traditional aspects have been eclipsed to a large extent by its heterogeneous blend of northern Cameroonians, Nigerians and Chadians. Traditional *saré* buildings – quite common up to the 1960s – have given way to cement homes with tin roofs, and the centre of town is dotted with modern blocks. Growth has brought increased facilities – banks, hotels and tourist information – making Garoua a convenient springboard for the next destination.

Some history

Fali and Bata people were the first to settle along the banks of the Bénoué, in the eighteenth century. They were followed by **Kilba Fulani** – herders who came in the early nineteenth century. After dan Fodio's *jihad* (see p.1023), the Fulani built a fortification (*ribadou*) around the town they called Ribadou-Garoua, to stave off Fali invasions. Other Muslims – Hausa, Bornu and Shua Arabs – arrived in the second half of the nineteenth century, lending an early urbanism to the settlement. The present **Lamidat** dates from 1839.

The **Germans** colonized Garoua in 1901 and set up a small·port (British steamers from the Niger Company had been trading in ivory, salt and cloth since 1890). Enlarged in 1930, the port served as a vital link between Cameroon, Chad and Nigeria, even though it has only ever been able to function during the rainy season, from mid-July to mid-October. Garoua became an important international focus and has always had a large expatriate community. After independence, the roads were improved, and investment increased in cotton, the regional cash crop, and its related industries. In time, these were joined by a brewery and soapworks.

Accommodation

For a town the size of Garoua, there are surprisingly few hotels, but there is some accommodation in all price ranges, including a couple of very comfortable places in the international class.

Auberge Centrale, rue Adamou Amar, (BP 33; ☎27.33.49; Fax 27.29.55). New *auberge*, just behind the Marché Central, with clean AC rooms, some S/C. ②.

Auberge de la Cité, rue du Petit Marché (BP 14; ☎27.26.49). Somewhat in decline, but offers S/C rooms, some with AC, and a reasonable restaurant. ①–②.

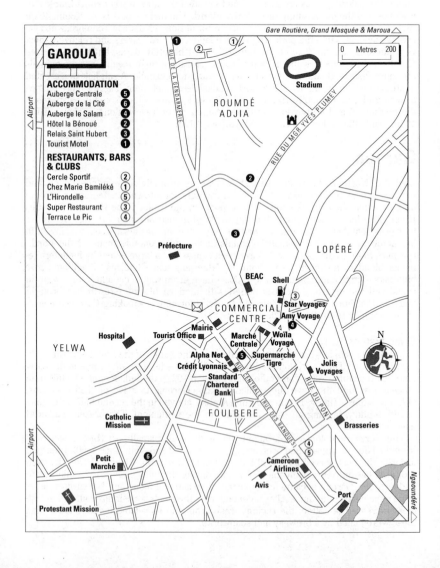

GAROUA

Gare Routière, Grand Mosquée & Maroua

0 Metres 200

ACCOMMODATION
Auberge Centrale ❺
Auberge de la Cité ❻
Auberge le Salam ❹
Hôtel la Bénoué ❷
Relais Saint Hubert ❸
Tourist Motel ❶

RESTAURANTS, BARS & CLUBS
Cercle Sportif ②
Chez Marie Bamiléké ①
L'Hirondelle ⑤
Super Restaurant ③
Terrace Le Pic ④

Airport

RUE DE LA GENDARMERIE

ROUMDÉ ADJIA

Stadium

RUE DU MGR YVES PLUMEY

LOPÉRÉ

Préfecture

BEAC Shell

COMMERCIAL CENTRE

Star Voyages
Amy Voyage

Mairie
Tourist Office
Hospital

YELWA

Marché Centrale
Woïla Voyage

Alpha Net
Crédit Lyonnais
Supermarché Tigre
Jolis Voyages

Standard Chartered Bank

CENTRAL, RUE DES BANQUES

RUE DU PONT

FOULBERE

Catholic Mission

Brasseries

Airport

Petit Marché ❻

Cameroon Airlines

Avis

Port

Protestant Mission

Ngaoundéré

N

Auberge le Salam, conveniently opposite the main *agences de voyage* and close to the Marché Central (BP 496; ☎27.24.26). A dingy exterior belies clean rooms, some S/C, around a small courtyard. The outdoor showers are perfect for the hot climate. ①.

Hôtel la Bénoué (BP 291; ☎27.12.04 or 27.15.58; Fax 27.15.53). Smart and comfortable, in shaded surroundings with a pool, tennis courts, good restaurant and a nightclub. Major credit cards accepted. ④.

Relais Saint Hubert, near the commercial centre (BP 445; ☎27.31.55 or 27.30.33). Very nice S/C, AC *boukarous* in an attractive garden setting. Decent restaurant and bar. ③.

Tourist Motel, rue de la Gendarmerie (BP 1169; ☎27.32.44; Fax 27.31.62). Despite its youth this hotel is already showing signs of wear. Rooms have phones, TV and AC and there's a very nice swimming pool (CFA1000 for non-guests). ④.

The Town

Aside from the monumental **Grande Mosquée** on the Route de Maroua – one of Cameroon's largest, but closed to non-Muslims – there's nothing around town worth going out of your way for, apart from the huge **Marché Central**, best at weekends. Just north of the market is the **centre artisanal**, though the name is somewhat overstated as it merely indicates a place under the neem trees where traders spread out their wares. The masks and statuettes tend towards airport art anonymity, but this is the most concentrated place for **crafts** and some of the leatherwork is tempting. Depending on the time of the year, you may well find other tourists in the area, so be prepared to bargain vigorously. Across the street, bookings for game park lodgings can be made at the **tourist office** (Delegation Provinciale du Tourisme pour le Nord, BP 50; ☎27.22.90; Fax 27.13.64).

The commercial centre encompasses **banks** (BICEC, SGBC, Crédit Lyonnais and Standard Chartered, all within 100m of the **post office**), and administrative buildings such as the Mairie, with the obligatory fountain in front. It's more interesting to wander through the Yelwa district where the **Petit Marché** keeps things lively and where there's a good concentration of bars and *circuits* (the northern name for a small eatery). The energy, which continues **after dark**, makes it a likeable place to seek out an evening's entertainment.

Eating, drinking and nightlife

There are a number of cheap restaurants grouped around the central cluster of *agences de voyage*, all serving omelette breakfasts, rice, plantains, yams or macaroni with beef sauce. The *Super Restaurant,* opposite the Shell garage, serves the same sort of hunger-stoppers with a Sudanese influence, and freshly blended fruit juices. Popular bar-restaurants are the *Cercle Sportif* and *Chez Marie Bamiléké* at the northern end of Roumdé Adjia *quartier.* The beer is very reasonably priced and both serve decent food for about CFA1500 a plate. *L'Hirondelle*, near the port, has a more varied menu for the same price and in the evening you might even see the local friendly hippo walk past. For something upmarket, *Le Nautic,* on the road towards the airport off Route Périphique, serves excellent French food and pizzas at a price.

If you're looking for somewhere to **dance**, head for *Terrace Le Pic* bar towards the port, or the more expensive nightclub at the *Hotel Benoué.*

Listings

Bookshops Reading is limited to books and newspapers in French, the best selection of which you'll find at the Librairie Nouvelle Moderne and Lipamaf, both near the Mairie.

Car rental Avis, in the port area (BP 336; ☎27.12.98; Fax 27.20.51); Auto Location de la Benoué, rue Ahmadou Ahidjo (BP 1323; ☎27.20.38); Lasal Voyages, in the Commercial Centre (BP 1617; ☎27.21.37; Fax 27.33.05); Norga Voyages, near Cameroon Airlines (BP 777; ☎27.26.17; Fax 27.22.61); Sawaba Safari, in *Auberge de la Cité* (BP 14; ☎27.24.93).

Hospitals Hôpital Centrale (☎27.14.14); and Southia Clinic (☎27.21.33).

MOVING ON FROM GAROUA

Transport out of Garoua is straightforward. The main *agences de voyage* are clustered close to the Marché Central. All of them run a service north to **Maroua** and south to **Ngaoundéré**. The larger agencies include Amy Voyages (☎27.33.05), Jolis Voyages (☎27.11.16), Star Voyages (☎27.14.85) and Woïla Voyage (☎27.30.82), the last of which is considered the most comfortable although they do charge a little more. For destinations such as Gaschiga (customs and immigration) and Demsa for Yola in **Nigeria** (a bad road), share taxi minibuses leave from the *gare routière*, 4km from the centre of town on the Route de Maroua.

Cameroon Airlines **flies** to Douala and Yaoundé (Mon, Wed, Thurs, Fri & Sun), Maroua (Sun & Mon) and Ndjamena, Chad (Wed). Precise information and reservations are available by calling Cameroon Airlines (☎27.10.55) or the airport (☎27.14.81).

Internet Alpha-Net, rue des Banques (BP 1532; ☎ & Fax 27.19.52; *alphanet@camnet.cm*) charges CFA1000 to send or receive a page.

Supermarkets Imported boxes, tins and produce are sold at the Supermarché Tigre near the Marché Central. Directly opposite is the smaller Supermarché Kandre.

Maroua

One of Cameroon's few pre-colonial cities, **MAROUA** already had a population of some 25,000 when French administrators took their first census in 1916, and four times that number lived within 20km of the town. Today it remains the largest northern city, and has retained a much more traditional flavour than its main rival Garoua. The old neighbourhoods of Maroua, spread out on both banks of the **Mayo Kaliao** – a dry expanse of sand for half of the year – are run through with streets shaded by sweet-smelling neem trees.

Accommodation

A popular town in its own right and convenient stopping point for northern adventures, Maroua has a good selection of accommodation for all budgets. Most of the inexpensive *auberges* can be found on the south side of the river near the stadium, though there is some choice near the *gare routière*. Upmarket lodgings are in the west, near the river and the Kaygama district.

Auberge le Diamaré east of the *gare routière*, (BP 519; ☎29.26.68). Convenient if arriving by share taxi. The well-kept ventilated rooms are very reasonable. ①.

Auberge Fety (☎29.29.13). A new place conveniently situated near the main *agences de voyage*, with a small bar and good-value restaurant. Fresh S/C, AC rooms with hot water. ②.

Auberge Maidjiguilao Domayo, south of the river, off bd de Renouveau (BP 705). Basic S/C rooms with fans. ①.

Campement Bossou, a quiet place south of the river, off bd de Diarenga. *Boukarous* with fans and shared (cold) showers. Clean and well known to budget travellers. ①.

Hôtel Maroua Palace, qtr Djoudandou (BP 381; ☎29.71.64; Fax 29.15.25). An international-class hotel rising from the base of the northern hills a good kilometre from the centre. AC rooms have TV and phones, plus there's a pool (CFA1400 for non-guests) and a good restaurant. American Express and Visa accepted. ③.

Hôtel Mizao (BP 205; ☎29.13.00; Fax 29.13.04). Lavishly furnished rooms, tennis courts, and a swimming pool (CFA1500 for non-guests) make up for what it lacks in character. The restaurant offers a *menu* at CFA5000, and there's a popular nightclub. American Express and Visa accepted. ④.

Motel Le Saré (BP 11; ☎29.12.94; Fax 29.18.04). As spacious as the *Mizao*, but far more likeable, in a large shaded garden with its own pool. American Express accepted. ④.

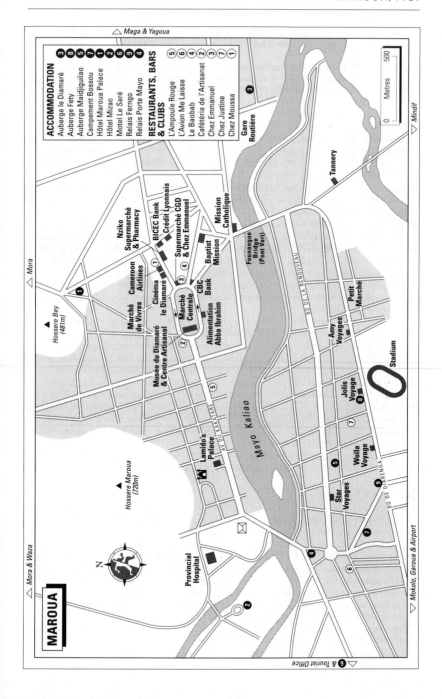

MAROUA

△ Mora & Waza
△ Mora
△ Maga & Yagoua
▽ Mindif
▽ Mokolo, Garoua & Airport
▽ **6** & Tourist Office

ACCOMMODATION
Auberge le Diamaré **3**
Auberge Fety **8**
Auberge Maidjiguilao **5**
Campement Bossou **7**
Hôtel Maroua Palace **1**
Hôtel Mizao **2**
Motel Le Saré **6**
Relais Ferngo **9**
Relais Porte Mayo **4**

RESTAURANTS, BARS & CLUBS
L'Ampoule Rouge **5**
L'Avion Me Laisse **6**
Le Baobab **4**
Cafétéria de l'Artisanat **2**
Chez Emmanuel **3**
Chez Justine **7**
Chez Moussa **1**

Gare Routière **3**

0   Metres   500

Hossere Bey (481m)

Hossere Maroua (720m)

N

Provincial Hospital

Lamido's Palace

Musée du Diamaré & Centre Artisanal

Marché de Vivres

Cinéma le Diamaré

Cameroon Airlines

Nziko Supermarché & Pharmacy

BICEC Bank

Crédit Lyonnais

Supermarché CGD & Chez Emmanuel

Baptist Mission

Mission Catholique

Marché Centrale

Alimentation Abba Ibrahim

CBC Bank

Fouanangue Bridge (Pont Vert)

BD DE LA RENOUVEAU

Tannery

Mayo Kaliao

AV DU KAKATARE

Stadium

Amy Voyages

Petit Marché

Jolis Voyage

Woila Voyage

Star Voyages

BD DE DJARENGA

Relais Ferngo (BP 112; ☎29.21.53). Budget satellite of the *Relais de la Porte Mayo* (below), with less classy S/C, AC *boukarous*, a quiet bar and a campsite (CFA1000 per person) with a shower and toilet. ②.

Le Relais de la Porte Mayo, near the river (BP 112; ☎29.26.92; Fax 29.29.92). Comfortable AC *boukarous* in a garden setting with a pleasant courtyard restaurant, shops and a steady stream of crafts vendors. It's a popular rendezvous for expats and a good place to seek information, hire vehicles or arrange tours (through Porte Mayo Voyages). The best in the moderate range. ③.

The Town

The **Musée du Diamaré**, near the market (Mon–Sat 8am–1.30pm & 3.30–5.30pm, open Sun on special request; free, but tip the guide), contains only a small collection of regional objects, but it's worth checking out nonetheless. They don't get many visitors, so the caretaker is usually very eager to provide thoughtful explanations of the assortment of objects from the **Sao civilization**, and artefacts collected from the Toupouri, Massa and Mousgoum peoples. The **Fulani** are represented by carved calabashes, jewellery and clothing, including a beautifully crafted *boubou* (large gown) worn by a *lamido* for special occasions. Notice the shield made from a dried and shaped elephant ear.

The **centre artisanal**, in the same building as the museum, is a large craft market with innumerable stands. The emphasis is on the locally made **leather goods** for which Maroua is famous (sandals, bags, round floor cushions) but there are goods from throughout Central and West Africa as well. Jewellery and hand-woven cloth can be good value here, but bargain astutely and take your time choosing; there's a vast selection. The photogenic **tannery**, to the southeast of town, on the road to Mindif, is another interesting place to visit.

Maroua's large **market** spreads out behind the museum. Although it's held daily, the main market day is Monday when **Kirdi** ("pagan") peoples come from all over the region to trade. Everything, from car parts and Japanese electrical goods to locally made cloth and traditional medicines, is sold here. Just north of the market, the *Marché de Vivres* sells fresh produce. From the main market, a broad avenue leads several hundred metres southeast, to the Founangué Bridge (*Pont Vert*), while Avenue du Kakataré stretches southwest nearly 2km to the very colonial **post office**. From the post office roundabout, the road heading uphill to the northwest leads to the **hospital**. The **tourist office** (☎29.11.65 or 29.22.98) is reached by crossing the bridge and heading on a further 2km southwest, but you are probably better off making arrangements through one of the larger hotels.

The main way of shuttling between sites is on the back of a **moto** (CFA100); they're quicker and easier to flag down than shared or private taxis.

Eating and Drinking

Maroua offers a good range of eating places, from the inexpensive *circuits* to the more formal restaurants of the big hotels. L'Avion Me Laisse, a street close to the western end of Boulevard de la Renouveau, has a collection of small lively bars, where you can eat grilled fish. The name was given by the first woman who started a business there – after her German boyfriend had left her. A number of the cheap restaurants cluster around the *centre artisanal*. The greatest concentration of **bars** and **clubs** are along Boulevard de la Renouveau; the better ones include the *Jupiter Club*, *Club 105*, *La Fermière* (which also has a good restaurant) and *Oxygène*, which has a smart little disco.

L'Ampoule Rouge, av du Kakataré. Easily spotted at night by the red lightbulb hanging outside. This small place serves excellent brochettes, but no beer.

Le Baobab, east of the market, across the street from CBC Bank (☎29.19.03). Good Cameroonian dishes, like chicken in groundnut sauce (CFA2000), served in thatched *boukarous*.

Cafétéria de l'Artisanat, directly opposite the *centre artisanal*. Good ready-made meals for around CFA700 a plate.

The **gare routière** east of the Founangué Bridge has regular transport to destinations across the extreme north. However for travel south to Garoua and Ngaoundéré it is more comfortable to use one of the *agences de voyage*: Woïla Voyage (BP 578; ☎29.17.57), Jolis Voyages (BP 4; ☎29.31.31) and Amy Voyages (BP 143; ☎29.16.99) are all situated on Boulevard de Diarenga across from the stadium, and Star Voyages (BP 96; ☎29.25.22), which also has services to Mokolo, Yagua, Kaele, Guidguis and Toloum, is on Boulevard de la Renouveau.

Cameroon Airlines **flies** to Yaoundé (5 weekly), Douala (5 weekly) and Ngaoundéré (weekly). Contact Cameroon Airlines (☎29.10.50) or call the airport (☎29.10.21) for flight information.

Chez Emmanuel, just east of the market (☎29.19.95). A very popular restaurant for a good mix of foods at moderate prices, and for drinking cold beer while watching the latest news on satellite TV.

Chez Justine, across from the stadium. Enjoy well-made, inexpensive Cameroonian dishes sitting on soft chairs in what appears to be somebody's home. Evening meals should be ordered earlier in the day.

Chez Moussa, east of the market, by Cameroon Airlines. A likeable place where you can sit outside on mats. Wash down the cheap side dishes or daily *menu* (CFA1000–1500) with excellent fresh juice.

Le Relais de la Porte Mayo. Fills nightly with an expat crowd chatting noisily in French, English and German to the clink of china and glass. They offer a good varied menu including Vietnamese specialities, but expect to pay between CFA4000–5000 a dish.

Listings

Banks BICEC, CBC and Crédit Lyonnais are in the immediate vicinity of the market.

Car rental You can rent 4WD vehicles with a driver from the *Relais de la Porte Mayo* at fair prices. Other options are: Socotren (☎29.10.89 or 29.15.25) at the Elf petrol station opposite CGD Supermarché; and Transcontinental Travels (☎ & Fax 29.24.49), north of the market, which also organizes tours.

Cinema The only choice is Diamaré, next door to Cameroon Airlines.

Hospitals Provincial Hospital (☎29.11.75); and Hospital Meskine, Centre Medical Afrique de l'Ouest (☎29.25.79).

Internet You can send and receive email at Transcontinental Travels and Services Agency, on the north side of the market (☎ & Fax 29.24.49; *ttsa@camnet.cm*).

Massage Florence Ngue Massage (☎29.29.89 after 3.30pm, or enquire at the *Relais de la Porte Mayo*). After a few tiring days walking in the Mandara Mountains or a dusty safari in Waza you can get what feels like the best massage in West Africa – complete relaxation for CFA5000.

National Parks For information about Waza National Park, contact IUCN, qtr Kaygama (☎29.22.68; Fax 29.22.69).

Supermarkets CGD Supermarché, east of the market, is large and well-stocked, but Nziko, opposite Cameroon Airlines, with a pharmacy, and Alimentation Abba Ibrahim are better value. The latter may also change money.

Swimming pools The closest pool to the centre is at *Hôtel Mizao*, which you can use for CFA1500, but for the same price the pool at *Le Saré* has a nicer setting; they may even light a barbecue by the pool in the evenings.

Mokolo, Mora and the Mandara Mountains

Beautiful and haunting, the denuded volcanic plugs of the **Mandara Mountains** rise up to the west of Maroua like stony brown fingers. They form the backdrop to some of the country's most fascinating, desolate scenery, and are home to communities who have come to be known as the "mountain people" – staunch non-Muslims who were pushed to the extremities of the inhabitable areas during the Muslim wars of the nineteenth century. Today, the region highlights Cameroon's most striking contrasts in the cultural clash of Kirdi, Fulani and Shua Arabs from the far north. In its ethno-linguistic complexity, highland setting and stone buildings – as well as the rise of organized adventure tourism – the Mokolo district bears superficial similarities to the Dogon country in Mali.

There is **no bank** in Mokolo nor in any of these villages and towns, so change money in Maroua. **Fuel** is usually sold along the roadside but this has to be transported from Maroua and is more expensive, so if you do have a vehicle it is better to set off with a full tank.

Mokolo and around

The main point of entry to the region, **MOKOLO** is the capital of the **Mafa** people (also called Matakam by the Fulani) – one of the most populous groups in the mountains. Mokolo, however, is a quiet town (perhaps "village" is more accurate) with round houses of stone with thatched roofs, a market (on Wednesdays), a motor park and not much else.

You can **stay** at the expensive *Campement de Flambouyant* (☎29.55.63; ③) which has AC *boukarous,* a restaurant and a bar, or there are the less expensive rooms at *Auberge Mecheme* (①). As an even cheaper solution, some people in town will put up travellers for a negotiated fee. The **centre artisanal** in the village of **Djingliya**, 15km from Mokolo, also puts up travellers for a small fee (①) and has a restaurant and bar.

Mokolo's small **museum** occupies a square off the motor park. Besides visiting the exhibition of **local crafts**, ask the guardian about the possibility of getting a **guide** to get you into the rugged countryside away from the tourist hot spots. There are numerous villages in the mountains where you can arrange to stay in people's homes for a small fee. Payment is not necessarily appreciated in cash, so discuss appropriate alternatives with your guide before leaving. A guide should cost about CFA3000 a day, and you can hire a donkey with driver to carry your luggage for another CFA3000. It's also possible to arrange to go on horseback. On the highest paths, you can cross undetected and unmolested into Nigerian territory (see p.1032) but you should be wary of going further into Nigeria without making a formal exit from Cameroon.

If you're heading on to Roumsiki, note that trucks from the **motor park** depart early in the morning. If you arrive after 8am, you are likely to have missed the day's transport.

Roumsiki

A brief visit to **ROUMSIKI**, 50km from Mokolo, is very much a standard item on Cameroon's tourist circuit. It's a small and fairly ordinary village in itself, but the setting is fairly spectacular. The appeal of the visit is largely to get a taste of the "real" Cameroon, and the built-in flaw is that the more people come, the more distorted and unreal life in the village becomes. However, there's one overwhelming reason why it is genuinely worth making the trip. Wherever you look, the scenery is breathtaking. Roumsiki lies deep in the mountains, surrounded by magnificent time-worn peaks, the highest of which is much-photographed **Kapsiki**. Houses built of local stone in the traditional style blend in with the gothic backdrop, changing shades of ochre and orange to umber and russet as the sun moves over the horizon.

You have no option when arriving at Roumsiki other than to allow the little kids who greet you to act as your guides (unless you brought a paid companion with you). They follow their own rigid programme in showing you what they imagine every tourist wants to see. There's no point resisting their help and trying to explore the village on your own; you'll just be made to feel like an unwelcome voyeur. So let the boys show you the **féticheur** who tells your future by watching the way a river crab moves pieces of wood; the **weavers** who make cloth by hand; the **potters** and the **blacksmiths**. They explain how the huts are made and tell you about local customs and history. The people of Roumsiki are called **Margui**, or often **Kapsikis** – "those who have grown tall". In the evening, your guides even accompany you to a nearby peak to get a better view of the sunset. Your every question, in fact, is answered before you ask it. It's all quite interesting on a superficial level, but it's about as personal as watching a television documentary. The bottom line is definitely money, and you'll just have to accept that (bring lots of small change).

You can **stay** in the village at the *Campement de Rhumsiki* (BP 27, Mokolo; ③) – a tastefully rustic cluster of AC *boukarous* with beautiful mountain views. Less expensive is *Village de l'Amité* (BP 43; ③) which has similar accommodation but without AC. Cheaper still is *Auberge Le Casserole* (②), with fans and shared facilities, plus a bar and restaurant. Alternatively you can arrange to sleep in people's homes. Ask the little kids, but do so before the last taxi heads back to Mokolo. Once they know you can't escape, prices rise.

Mora and around

On market days (Wednesday for Mokolo and Sunday for Mora) you can get a share taxi from Mokolo to **MORA** via **Koza** – a picturesque track road that cuts through the heart of the **Mafa country**. Even on these days, you will have to leave Mora very early in the afternoon to get back to Mokolo with the last taxi. On other days, you'll probably have to go by the less scenic route that passes through Maroua.

Capital of the **Wandala** (also called Mandara) – a people who accepted Islam in the late seventeenth century after their contact with the Bornu Empire – Mora is especially known for a **market** which attracts a wide range of peoples from throughout the region. Muslim Fulani, Wandala and Shua women sell their goods alongside the traditionalist mountain people – **Podoko, Guizica** and **Mofou** – who retain their own firm views on suitable dress and headgear. It's a colourful mixture of cultures, and the market produce ranges from goat's milk to mangos and millet. Donkeys and goats are sold in the **animal market**. You'll also find jewellery and carved calabashes.

The best option for budget **accommodation** is the *Auberge Mora Massif* (①), located just a couple of blocks east of the motor park. The rooms here are kept clean by the attentive staff and the bar-restaurant serves meals with inexpensive cold drinks that make their way in from Nigeria. Similar in price, the *Hotel Podoko* (①), off the main road to Maroua, also offers good value for its S/C *boukarous* with fans and good restaurant. The mid-range *Campement du Wandala* (③), at the northern entrance to town, has accommodation in *boukarous* but has had troubles keeping afloat.

Oudjilla

Mora is the departure point for the eleven-kilometre trip to the village of **OUDJILLA** in the mountains, a spot which, like Roumsiki, has become a magnet for tourism. You can barely set foot in Mora without a posse of gushing teenagers racing up to you on motorbikes and asking, "Mistah, tu vas où, à Oudjilla?"

Oudjilla is an authentic **Podoko village**, though once again your experience there may seem a bit contrived. You're led on arrival to the *saré* of the chief, who lives in a walled compound with over fifty wives and countless children. For an incredible price, you get to visit the chief's compound and see the hut that serves for public deliberations; another where the chief's father is buried and where jugs of millet beer are stored; and the sacrificial pen where the chosen cow awaits slaughter during the harvest festival. You're taken into the hut of one of the wives to see the kitchen and the utensils used for pounding millet, storing water and so on. At the end, you are "invited" to take pictures of the chief and some of his wives with shaved heads and bare chests. For just a little more money, the wives might even do a harvest dance. It makes for the kind of photographs that put postcards to shame, but, at the same time, is liable to leave you feeling rather empty. To get beyond the performance, however, would take more time and dedication than most people have. There's nothing to stop you putting your feelings back in balance by exploring some of the other roads in this region; or by trying, "Non, merci, Oudjilla ne m'intéresse pas, mais pourrais-tu me diriger à...?" (then picking a small name from the map).

Waza National Park

With a minimum of vegetation, **Waza National Park** (mid-Nov to mid-June; entrance fee CFA5000; obligatory guide CFA3000/day) spreads over 1700 square, and flat, kilometres, and is probably the best site for savannah game viewing in West Africa. The main park entrance, just outside the small town of Waza, is marked by two Mousgoum huts. Pay your fee here, before heading to the nearby *Campement de Waza* (BP 13, Maroua; ☎29.10.07 or 29.11.65; Fax 29.13.00; ③), which you should book in advance. It's an excellent camp set on a hill, with comfortable AC *boukarous* equipped with running water and electricity and grouped around a clean swimming pool (CFA1000 for non-guests). Expect to pay about CFA4500 for casual meals taken at the restaurant, which affords a splendid panorama of the surrounding park. If such accommodation is out of your range, the new *Centre d'Accueil* (☎29.22.07; ②) near the park entrance has *boukarous* with mosquito nets, fans and shared facilities. You can also camp here for CFA3000 a tent and there is a restaurant which prepares Cameroonian and standard tourist food (CFA2500). In Waza village itself, *Chez Suzanne*, a bar-restaurant, has a limited number of box-like rooms (①).

Since Waza is the most popular of the game parks, it's also the one you have the best chance hitching into. Enquiries at the *campement* invariably yield good results, but if your luck is down, vehicles are available to rent by the hour.

Giraffe are quite plentiful here, and congregate near the gate. There's a substantial **elephant** population too, which, with luck, you should have no problem seeing. Your chances of finding **lions** are also pretty good. **Ostriches** tend to be shy but **antelopes** such as waterbuck and roan antelope are often spotted. Waza is especially good for **bird-watching**.

Kousseri and the northern extremity

At the confluence of the **Logone** and **Chari** rivers, **KOUSSERI** lies directly opposite the capital of Chad – **Ndjamena**. The bridge and *pirogues* that link them are the main *raison d'être* for a town that otherwise would be right off the beaten track.

Principal sites in town include the **port** and **market** where, not surprisingly, fish is the mainstay (market day is Thursday). There are three **places to stay**, none of them cheap. Outside the centre, *Campement du Relais de Logone* (☎29.41.57; ②) has rooms overlooking the river. The *Hôtel Kousseri Moderne* (☎29.47.48; ②) is slightly less expensive, and the new *Auberge Le Confort* (☎29.46.36; ②) has a restaurant and bar. There are **no banks** in Kousseri. A good road links Kousseri to the south via Maroua. Boats still provide an important link with **Ndjamena** but the bridge downstream from the centre of Kousseri is an easier crossing.

Lake Chad and the Kalamaloué National Park

Accommodation facilities don't exist **north of Kousseri**. In the towns along the route to **Lake Chad**, you're therefore at the mercy of the local authorities (police or sultans). Problems you may have getting to the lake, however, generally have less to do with police than with the fact that the elusive waters have receded well to the north of the bigger towns.

From Kousseri, take a share taxi to **Makari**, which has a market on Wednesdays, when transport is easiest to arrange. It's a scenic route that hugs the banks of the **Chari River**, then veers westward through desert landscapes to **Maltam**, before heading north. In Makari, you can get a share taxi on to **Blangoua** on the river. Between July and October, the only months when the river isn't dry, you can charter a motorized *pirogue* for the hour-long journey to Lake Chad (around CFA5000). An alternative is to charter a taxi at great cost.

Just outside of Kousseri, you'll pass through the smallest and most recently created of Cameroon's northern reserves, the **Kalamaloué National Park**, which stretches along the road from Kousseri to Maltam. It's not much of a park, with very few animals remaining, but you can can take guided **walking tours** to see **crocodiles** and **hippos** in the Chari River that borders the park and separates it from the outskirts of Ndjamena on the opposite bank. The rudimentary *Campement de Kalamaloué* (①) allows free camping.

MOVING ON TO CHAD, NIGERIA OR NIGER

From Kousseri, you can enter **Chad** – directly into its capital, Ndjamena – across the new bridge. Taxis across are cheap and frequent. Since the situation in Chad has calmed down, there appears to be no more than the routine drama of border formalities you'd expect to encounter anywhere.

If you're continuing into **Nigeria**, Fotokol is your last destination in Cameroon: Gamboru, over the border in Nigeria, is 140km short of Maiduguri (see p.1027). If you happen to be travelling **direct from Ndjamena to Maiduguri** in Nigeria, you shouldn't need a visa to cross the 100km or so of Cameroonian territory from Kousseri to Fotokol.

Making for **Niger** circumventing Nigeria, you can cross the border into Chad at a number of places for the detour around the lake to **Nguigmi** (see p.903). If you're in Kousseri, cross here to Ndjamena, rather than risk going further north and finding yourself in a difficult position with nobody authorized to process your entry. If you're driving and intending heading the same way, Ndjamena is your most northerly reliable crossing point in any case.

BOOKS

While there's a substantial volume of reading material on West Africa, its subject matter and authorship is very unevenly distributed. By far the largest body of literature in English comes from Nigeria, with its hundreds of novelists and academics. By contrast, many of the Francophone nations have scant coverage other than in French. In the following listings, publisher details are in the form (UK publisher; US publisher), where both exist; if books are published in one country only, this follows the publisher's name (eg: Penguin, UK). University Press has been abbreviated as UP, and o/p means out of print. If a book is recently o/p you may still find copies in some bookshops. Otherwise, check libraries.

For pre-departure reading, probably the best foretaste is provided by West African fiction – much of which is available in paperback in Heinemann's **African Writers Series**.

The following recommendations are divided first by subject matter across the region, and then country-by-country. French works have been included only when there is little alternative in English. One-

off travel guides and similar publications are mostly covered in the "Maps and Information" section at the beginning of each chapter.

SERIES PUBLICATIONS

African Historical Dictionaries (Scarecrow Press, US). If you're seriously looking to find out about a country, the Scarecrow series is what you need. They have titles on many African countries, covering names, places and events in detail.

Heinemann African Writers Series. AWS books are the vanguard of African publishing in English and add regularly to their list – over 200 titles, though kept erratically in print. Catalogue from Heinemann, Halley Court, Jordan Hill, Oxford OX2 8EJ, UK (☎01865/310366).

Jeune Afrique and **Hachette** both do one- or two-country guides of a more practical nature, in French only, to most of the Francophone countries. Jeune Afrique also publishes an excellent and affordable series of thematic **atlases** on the Francophone countries.

World Bibliographical Series (Clio Press). Annotated coverage, mainly of social and natural sciences and humanities. To date, available for every country in West Africa. Catalogue from Clio Press, Old Clarendon Ironworks, 35A Great Clarendon St, Oxford OX2 6AT, UK (☎01865/311350).

TRAVEL BIBLIOGRAPHIES

Oona Strathern (ed), *Traveller's Literary Companion: Africa* (In Print Books, 1994; Passport Books, 1995). Brief selections of literature from – or about – virtually every African country, including passages from many of the books included in this bibliography.

BOOKSHOPS AND LIBRARIES

Useful **bookshops** and **libraries** for obtaining African (and out of print) books are detailed on pp.41. Any UK resident can make use of the **Inter-Library Loans** system to obtain even the most obscure titles – given time.

If you're seriously interested in keeping up with scholarly or literary African writing, the **African Books Collective** offers thousands of updated titles from over forty independent, state and university publishers in West Africa. Their biannual catalogues – available from African Books Collective Ltd, The Jam Factory, 27 Park End St, Oxford OX1 1HU, UK (☎01865/726686; Fax 01865/793298) – include annotated reviews of new and recent publications.

For **books in French**, La Page French bookshop (7 Harrington Rd, London SW7; ☎0171/589 5991) may be able to help. The best African bookshop in Europe, however, is L'Harmattan in Paris (16 rue des Ecoles, 5ᵉ).

Louis Taussig, *Resource Guide to Travel in Sub-Saharan Africa Vol. 1 East and West Africa* (Hans Zell, UK, 1994). The definitive guide to the guides and much more. Extraordinarily detailed country-by-country coverage of every published source of interest to travellers or expatriates, as well as bookshops, libraries, mapping institutes, children's resources and conservation societies, to list just a few. Libraries will obtain it for you.

TRAVELOGUES AND RELATED LITERATURE

Michael Asher, *Impossible Journey: Two Against the Sahara* (Viking Penguin, UK, 1987; o/p). Adventurous Mauritanian and Nigérien foretastes are to be gleaned from this account of a first-ever west to east Saharan crossing. Asher, an ex-SAS man, travelled with his wife, plus camels, from Chinguetti to the Nile. **Geoffrey Moorhouse**'s *Fearful Void* (Penguin, 1974; o/p) details his own, unsuccessful, earlier attempt.

Thomas A. Bass, *Camping with the Prince and Other Tales of Science in Africa* (Moyer Bell, 1997). An interesting slant for the travel genre. The author keeps a focus on African solutions to, for example, agricultural problems.

Peter Biddlecombe, *French Lessons in Africa* (Little, Brown & Co, 1995). Like an uninvited travelling companion, businessman Biddlecombe rattles out his observations on Francophone West Africa so fast, it seems, there's barely the time to notice the stream of contradictions and inconsistencies. Funny, warm and light, and a good book for lone travellers to argue with.

Dea Birkett, *Mary Kingsley: Imperial Adventuress* (Macmillan, UK, 1992). Finely worked and very readable biography written with relish. The same author's *Jella: A Woman at Sea* (Gollancz, UK, 1992; o/p) – the account of her return from West Africa as a member of crew on a cargo ship – is superbly funny and instructive.

Thomas Coraghassen Boyle, *Water Music* (Granta Books, 1998; Viking Penguin, 1983). Lengthy, meticulous, at times outrageously funny, fictionalized account of Mungo Park's explorations. T.C. Boyle's vision of the West Africa (and Britain) of two centuries ago is utterly captivating. Essential *in situ* reading for those long roadside waits: if you only take one book, take this.

Jens Finke, *Chasing the Lizard's Tale: By bicycle across the Sahara* (Impact Books, UK,

1996). Entertaining and insightful travelogue, recounting Finke's journey from Morocco to a sudden end in The Gambia.

Blaine Harden, *Africa: Dispatches from a Fragile Continent* (HarperCollins, 1992; Houghton Mifflin, 1991). The *Washington Post*'s former African bureau chief can't shake the arrogant pessimism American journalists seem to thrive on. Coverage of Ghana, Liberia and Nigeria.

Mark Hudson, *The Music in My Head* (Vintage, UK, 1999). A "World Music" novel for the new millennium: energetic, constantly amusing and inventive, and incorporating glowing passages of superb descriptive prose. If you're going to Senegal – sorry, Tekrur – this is the one for the beach.

Elspeth Huxley, *Four Guineas* (1954; o/p). This account of Huxley's trip through the four Anglophone colonies on the eve of independence is full of credible conversations – and the occasional lapse into racist angst.

Mark Jenkins, *To Timbuktu: A Journey down the Niger* (Robert Hale, 1998; Quill, 1998). Well-written and likeable – though admittedly macho – kayaking adventures.

Lieve Joris, *Mali Blues* (Lonely Planet, 1997). Four accounts of travel and conversation in Senegal, Mauritania and Mali. The main story, "Mali Blues", is a kind of extended on-the-road interview with the singer and guitarist Boubacar Traoré, exploring the pervasive and unsettling spiritual dimension of Africa – though never quite following through to confront or enter it. You hope one day Traoré will reply with his own account of his time with the author.

Mary Kingsley, *Travels in West Africa* (1897; Everyman, 1993; Adventure Library, 1997). The title is misleading these days, as Kingsley's dauntless travels in search of fetishes and fish took her – with a quick hike up Mount Cameroon – principally to the region of Gabon. But a terrific book: funny, intelligent and a worthy classic.

David Lamb, *The Africans* (Vintage Books, UK, 1987). *The Africans* was a bestseller, but Lamb's fly-in, fly-out technique is a statistical rant couched in Cold War rhetoric – and, even when ostensibly uncovering a pearl of wisdom, he can be rebarbatively offensive.

Sven Lundqvist, *"Exterminate all the Brutes"* (Granta Books, 1998; New Press, 1997). Taking its title from Kurtz's remark in Conrad's *Heart of*

Darkness, Lundqvist weaves his own trans-Saharan journey together with the story of how imperialism begat racism. A luminous, agonizing read.

Patrick Marnham, *Dispatches from Africa* (Penguin, UK, 1980; o/p). Although now dated, this journalism remains devastatingly sharp – especially on the aid industry. Notable essays on Senegal, Mali and The Gambia.

Mungo Park, *Travels into the Interior of Africa* (1799; Eland, 1983; Ayer, 1977, o/p). Absorbing and short-winded account of the then youthful Scottish traveller's two journeys – 1795–1797 and 1805 – along the Niger.

Pamela Watson, *Esprit de Battuta: Alone Across Africa on a Bicycle* (Aurum Press, UK, 1999). Muscular modern travelogue-diary, that takes the Australian author from Senegal to Cameroon and beyond – very strong on anecdotal highs and lows, and detailed documentation, less satisfying on insights.

HISTORY

Most histories cover the whole continent, and, inevitably, jump from place to place: Boahen, or Davidson, Buah & Ajayi are the easiest to follow, and are well complemented by various historical and cultural atlases.

THE AFRICAN CONTINENT

A.E. Afigbo, E.A. Ayandele, R.J. Gavin, J.D. Omer-Cooper and R. Palmer, *The Making of Modern Africa, Vol. 1 Nineteenth Century, Vol. 2 Twentieth Century* (Longman, 1986; Addison-Wesley, 1986). A detailed, illustrated guide, putting West Africa in the continental context up until the first big changes after independence.

Cheik Anta Diop, *Pre-Colonial Black Africa* (Africa World Press, US, 1990). First published in the 1950s, Diop asserts that the origins of Western civilization, as well as African, began in Africa. The work encouraged a whole generation to reinterpret the past from an African perspective.

Basil Davidson, *Africa in History* (Scribner, 1995). Lucidly argued and readable summary of Africa's dominant nineteenth- and twentieth-century events.

Christopher Hibbert, *Africa Explored: Europeans in the Dark Continent, 1769–1889* (1984; o/p). Entertaining read, devoted in large part to the "discovery" of West Africa.

UNESCO, *General History of Africa* (Heinemann, UNESCO, University of California Press & UNIPUB). For serious scholarship, this twelve-volume series recounts over three million years of Africa's past. Written by some of the continent's leading historians, it attempts to break from Western analysis to give a clearer picture of African peoples in the sociocultural context.

WEST AFRICA

Adu Boahen, *with J.F. Ade Ajayi and Michael Tidy, Topics in West African History* (Longman, 1987; Addison-Wesley, 1987). An excellent introduction to basic themes in West African history, written in a clear and concise fashion by one of Ghana's most respected historians.

Basil Davidson, F.K. Buah and J.F.A. Ajayi, *A History of West Africa 1000–1800* (Longman, US, 1977). Clear, wide-ranging and readable.

A.G. Hopkins, *An Economic History of West Africa* (Longman, UK, 1973). Well-written grounding, offering an invaluable economic perspective.

Patrick Manning, *Francophone sub-Saharan Africa 1880–1985* (1988; Cambridge UP, UK, 1999). A rare book on the subject in English.

J.B. Webster et a.l, *West Africa Since 1800: The Revolutionary Years* (Longman, 1980; Addison-Wesley, 1980). An excellent follow-up companion to Davidson *et al.* above.

Paul Tiyambe Zeleza, *History of Africa: Vol. 1, The Nineteenth Century* (African Books Collective, UK, 1993). Winner of the NOMA Award 1994.

HISTORICAL ATLASES

Brian Catchpole and L.A. Akinjogbin, *A History of West Africa in Maps and Diagrams* (Collins Educational, UK, 1984; o/p). A remarkable and highly recommended encapsulation of the region's history from ancient times to the 1980s. Its only flaw is an utterly inadequate index.

Colin McEvedy, *Penguin Atlas of African History* (Penguin, 1995; Penguin, 1980, o/p). Useful for placing West Africa, and the whole continent, in context, and for getting to grips with some of the names and themes. Fifty-nine maps of Africa with facing text.

Jocelyn Murray (ed), *Cultural Atlas of Africa* (Facts on File, 1988). An attractive, highly polished book, if also an inevitably oversimplified view of the continent.

LAND, PEOPLE AND SOCIETY

Thomas D. Blakely, Walter E.A. van Beek, Dennis L. Thomson (eds), *Religion in Africa: Experience & Expression* (Heinemann, US, 1994). Thorough examination of religion in Africa and the diaspora.

R.J. Harrison Church, *West Africa* (1979; o/p). Formerly the standard geography reference – traditional in approach but much updated from its 1957 original edition. Excellent and unexpectedly absorbing.

Donal Cruise O'Brien, *Contemporary West African States* (Cambridge UP, US, 1990). Survey of Burkina Faso, Cameroon, Chad, Côte d'Ivoire, Ghana, Liberia, Nigeria and Senegal.

Thomas A. Hale, *Griots and Griottes: Masters of Words and Music* (Indiana UP, US, 1998). A comprehensive look at griots – male and female – of Niger, Mali, Senegal and The Gambia and their roles as historians, genealogists, diplomats, musicians and advisors.

Betty Laduke, *Africa: Women's Art, Women's Lives* (Africa World Press, 1997). Laduke turns her worldwide focus on women's art to Africa to examine the pottery of Mali, Cameroon and Togo; bead making in Cameroon; wall painting in Tiébélé, Tiakane and Po in Burkina Faso; and textiles and leather-working in the Sahel.

Keletigui Mariko, *Les Touaregs Ouelleminden* (Karthala, France, 1984). French survey of the Tuareg nomads who live in Algeria, Niger and Mali.

Patrick R. McNaughton, *The Mande Blacksmiths: Knowledge, Power, and Art in West Africa* (Indiana UP, 1993). Accessible scholarship that deals both with the aesthetic qualities of ironworking and its social implications for Mande peoples.

Claire Robertson and Iris Berger (eds), *Women and Class in Africa* (Holmes & Meier; Africana, 1986). An assessment of gender, money, and socioeconomic power with case studies from across the continent, including Ghana and Nigeria.

Robert Farris Thompson, *Flash of the Spirit: African and Afro-American Art and Philosophy* (Random, US, 1984). "Art history to dance by" in the words of the *Philadelphia Inquirer's* reviewer, and this is a unique book, illuminating the art and philosophy that connects the black worlds on both sides of the Atlantic. Big on Yoruba and Dan-Homey roots. Lots of illustrations.

Stephen Wright, *African Foreign Policies* (Westview Press, 1998). A rare analysis of foreign policy in Africa that targets 11 countries across the continent. Interesting section on relations between Benin and Nigeria and the effects of changing domestic coalitions on their international strategies.

Claudia Zaslavsky, *Africa Counts: Number and Pattern in African Culture* (Lawrence Hill, 1998). A unique, extraordinary book, with a chapter on "Warri" games (see p.59).

LANGUAGE

There is little available on West African – or even African – languages in the sense of general background, but you will find various phrase books and some language-learning material.

Pierre Alexandre, *Languages and Language in Africa* (Heinemann, UK, 1972; o/p). Surprisingly entertaining tour of the arcane world of African linguistics, led by a magnificently enthusiastic French professor.

E.C. Rowlands, *Teach Yourself Yoruba* (Teach Yourself Books, 1993; McKay, 1979) and **Charles H. Kraft and H.M. Kirk-Greene** *Teach Yourself Hausa* (Teach Yourself Books, 1990; McKay, 1979). Serious application required.

US State Department Foreign Service Institute This department has developed a number of self-instructional language courses available through Audio-Forum, Suite LA30A, 96 Broad St, Guilford, Connecticut 06437 (☎1-800/243-1234; Fax 203/453-9774; *www.audioforum.com*). The average price is around $250 and each one comes with a textbook and cassettes. Languages available include the Senegambian dialect of Fula (20hr of cassettes); Hausa (15hr); Igbo (12hr); More (18hr); Twi (6hr); and Yoruba (36hr).

ARTS

Most works dealing with the arts cover the whole continent. For books on West African music, see the box on p.1185.

Stephen Belcher, *Epic Traditions in Africa*, (Indiana UP, 1999). Elements of epic poetry described, followed by colourful narratives from across the continent in translation. Includes texts from the Sunjata and literary traditions of the Mande and Fula.

Roy Braverman, *Islam and Tribal Art* (Cambridge UP, 1980). A useful if somewhat specialist paperback text.

Caren Caraway, *African Designs of the Congo, Nigeria, The Cameroons and the Guinea Coast* (Stemmer, 1986). Black-and-white designs from masks, fetishes and textiles.

Margaret Courtney-Clarke, *African Canvas* (Rizzoli, 1990). Sumptuous colour photos bring out vivid details of exterior and interior house painting by women in a number of countries.

Susan Denyer, *African Traditional Architecture* (Holmes & Meier, 1978). Rewarding study, featuring hundreds of photos (most of them old) and a wealth of detailed line drawings.

Werner Gillon, *A Short History of African Art* (Penguin, 1991; Viking Penguin, 1991). A substantial study despite the name, though inevitably still very selective.

Elian Girard, Brigitte Kernel and Eric Megret, *Colons: Statuettes Habillées d'Afrique de l'Ouest* (Syros Alternatives, France, 1993). Fascinating illustrations of a little-known genre of sculpture: statues of Africans dressed in European clothes.

Michael Huet, *The Dance, Art and Ritual of Africa* (Harry N. Abrams, US, 1996). Remarkable photos of ceremonies and costume, captured with an exceptional clarity and power.

David Kerr, *African Popular Theatre: From Pre-Colonial Times to the Present Day* (Heinemann, UK, 1995). Includes sections on masquerade and concert party.

Jean-Marie Lerat and Jean Seisser, *Ici, Bon Coiffeur* (Syros Alternatives, France, 1992). French text accompanies photos of the colourful barbershop boards displaying hairstyles, so characteristic of West African towns.

Labelle Prussin, *African Nomadic Architecture* (Smithsonian Institution Press, 1997). A specialist volume, but also a fine, richly illustrated book, thick with symbols, which includes accounts of Tuareg and Moorish architecture.

Esi Sagay, *African Hairstyles* (Heinemann, 1983). What they're called, and how to do them; a wonderful little book.

Jan Vansina, *Art History in Africa* (Longman, 1984; Addison-Wesley, 1984). Readable theorizing by an interesting French anthropologist.

Frank Willett, *African Art* (Thames and Hudson, 1994). A cheaper, more accessible and better illustrated volume.

Geoffrey Williams, *African Designs From Traditional Sources* (Dover, 1971). A designer's and enthusiast's sourcebook, from the copyright-free publishers.

FOOD

Daniel K. Abbiw, *Useful Plants of Ghana* (ITP, 1989). Unusual reference guide to plants, organized by use – as food, fuel, medicine. Highly recommended for impoverished volunteers.

Dorinda Hafner, *A Taste of Africa* (Ten Speed Press, US, 1995). Enthusiastically conveyed recipes, but not a very practical book outside the region – "take half a pound of lemon grass . . ."

Jessica B. Harris, *The Africa Cookbook: Tastes of a Continent* (Simon & Schuster, 1998). Africa-wide collection of recipes for streetside samplings (bean cakes and fried plantains) and full-course meals.

G.B. Masefield, M. Wallis, B.E. Nicholson and S.G. Harrison, *The Oxford Book of Food Plants* (Oxford UP, UK, 1976; o/p). A good, traditional guide, covering most of the fruit and veg that will come your way.

NATURAL HISTORY

The following field guides are invaluable.

B. Bousquet, *Guide des Parc Nationaux d'Afrique: Afrique de l'Ouest* (Delachaux, Lausanne, 1992). French coverage of the important national parks of Francophone West Africa.

T. Haltenorth and H. Diller, *A Field Guide to the Mammals of Africa* (Collins, 1981; o/p).

W. Serle and G. Morel, *A Field Guide to the Birds of West Africa* (HarperCollins, 1977).

John G. Williams, *A Field Guide to the Butter-flies of Africa* (Collins, 1969; o/p).

COUNTRY BY COUNTRY

MAURITANIA

Literature in English on Mauritania is minimal. There's a good account of the Adrar in Michael Asher's *Impossible Journey* (see p.1138).

Catherine Belvaude, *La Mauritanie* (Karthala, France, 1989). Describes peoples, the state, religion, economy, fishing, arts and society. The French reader's essential starting point.

Tony Hodges, *The Western Saharans* (Minority Rights Group, 1984). Trenchant background on the situation in Western Sahara. *Western Sahara: the Routes of a Desert War* (Croom Helm, o/p; Chicago Review, o/p) amplifies the analysis and brings the coverage more up to date.

Peter Hudson, *Travels in Mauritania* (1990; o/p). Tale of a two-month trek.

Odette du Puigaudeau, *Barefoot in Mauritania* (1937; o/p). The author and his female companion took camels across "the land of death" – an entertaining ramble through a Mauritania that hardly knew it existed.

SENEGAL

There are several books by Senegalese writers in the Heinemann and Longman series. Other, mostly academic, English-language works are only likely to be available in libraries. In French, there's a very wide range of literature – by both French and Senegalese – and a steady output of glossy tomes to whet travellers' appetites.

Lucy C. Behrman, *Muslim Brotherhoods and Politics in Senegal* (Harvard, 1970; o/p). Fascinating, though dated, study with interesting statistical information about the marabouts at the turn of the century.

Michael Crowder, *Senegal: A Study of French Assimilation Policy* (1962; o/p). Concise, fairly unacademic look at how the French colonized African minds.

Donal B. Cruise O'Brien, *Saints and Politicians: Essays in the Organization of a Senegalese Peasant Society* (1975; o/p); *The Murides of Senegal: The Political and Economic Organization of an Islamic Brotherhood* (1971; o/p). This latter work is the definitive text in English on the Mouride brotherhood.

Rita Cruise O'Brien, *White Society in Black Africa: the French of Senegal* (1972; o/p); *The Political Economy of Underdevelopment: Dependence in Senegal* (1979; o/p).

Sheldon Gellar, *Senegal: An African Nation Between Islam and the West* (Dartmouth, 1983; Westview, 1995). A condensed and very readable survey.

Maureen Mackintosh, *Gender, Class and Rural Transition* (Zed Books, 1989; Humanities,

1989). An alternative view of the effects of development, agribusiness and the food crisis.

Christian Saglio, *Sénégal* (Petite Planète, Editions Seuil, France, 1980). A good introduction to the country, if you read French, full of incisive commentary. Saglio was instrumental in setting up the *campement integré* network.

Robin Sharp, *Senegal: a State of Change* (Oxfam, UK, 1994). Basic primer, written for students or inquisitive visitors. Illustrated.

Janet G. Vailant, *Black, French and African* (Harvard UP, 1990). Biography of Léopold Senghor.

NOVELS AND POETRY

Mariama Bâ, *So Long a Letter* (Heinemann, 1981). Dedicated to "all women and to men of good will", this is the story of a woman's life shattered by her husband's sudden, second marriage to a younger woman. Bâ's second book, *The Scarlet Song* (Longman, UK, 1995), published posthumously, eloquently traces the relationship between a French woman and a poor, Senegalese man.

Nafissatou Diallo, *A Dakar Childhood* (1982; o/p). Short and sweet; a middle-class girl growing up in the postwar years. Illuminating on family life.

Birago Diop, *Tales of Amadou Koumba* (1966; o/p). A collection of short stories based on the tales of a griot, and rooted in Wolof tradition.

Cheikh Hamidou Kane, *Ambiguous Adventure* (Heinemann, 1963; Heinemann, 1972). The autobiographical tale of a man torn between Tukulor, Islam and the West. Recommended.

Sembène Ousmane (or Ousmane Sembène), *God's Bits of Wood* (1960), *Xala* (1973), *The Last of the Empire* (1981), and others; all since reprinted by Heinemann UK & US. A committed, political and very immediate writer (and filmmaker, see "Cinema" p.1155) who can also be very funny, as in *Xala*, the satirical tale of a wealthy Dakarois' loss of virility. The best of these, by far, is *God's Bits of Wood*, the story of the rail strike of 1947.

Leopold Sédhar Senghor, *Nocturnes and Prose and Poetry* (Okpaku Communications, US). Collections of poems and writings by the country's ex-president, and member of the Académie Française. *Leopold Senghor: Collected Poetry* (Virginia UP, US, 1998) gathers poems from the negritude era, including *Songs of Darkness and Nocturnes*.

THE GAMBIA

For general works on The Gambia, and fiction by Gambian writers, the in-print choice is limited.

Mark Hudson, *Our Grandmothers' Drums* (Mandarin, UK, 1990; o/p). Rich, absorbing story of Hudson's stay in the village of "Dulaba" (Keneba) in the Kiang National Park area.

Arnold Hughes and David Perfect, *A Political History of The Gambia, 1816–1994* (C. Hurst & Co, 1995). The most up-to-date history of the country.

Berkeley Rice, *Enter Gambia: The Birth of an Improbable Nation* (1967; o/p). A digestible work, but marred by an unpleasantly derisory tone.

Patience Sonko-Godwin, *Ethnic Groups of the Senegambia* (1985; o/p). A brief and graspable social history of the region.

Bamba Suso, Banna Kanute, Lucy Duran, Graham Furniss and Gordon Innes, *Sunjata* (Penguin, UK, 1999). In Mande culture "Sunjata" is the big one, the legend of the founder of the Mali empire. This new Penguin edition presents two strikingly different Gambian versions of the epic.

FICTION

William Conton is a writer from the colonial era, heavily influenced by his Sierra Leonean upbringing. *The African* (Heinemann, UK, 1965; o/p) is a classic rags-to-premiership story.

Ebou Dibba, *Chaff in the Wind* (Macmillan, UK, 1986; o/p). Highly accomplished author, now living in Britain, decribes lives and loves in the 1930s. *Fafa* (1989; o/p) tells of goings-on at a remote trading post on the Gambia River.

Alex Haley, *Roots!* (1976; reprinted by Vintage, 1994; Dell, 1980). Good honest "faction", and a reasonably entertaining American saga to read on the beach, though only the first few dozen pages are set in Kunta Kinte's semi-mythical Gambian homeland.

Lenrie Peters, *Selected Poetry* (Heinemann, UK, 1981; o/p). *The Second Round* (1966; o/p) is a readable, if somewhat downbeat, story.

MALI

There's **very little accessible writing in English** from, or about, Mali.

Ibn Battuta, *Travels in Asia and Africa* (Routledge, UK, 1983). Selections from the writings of the great fourteenth-century wanderer, including his travels along the Niger.

Brian Gardner, *The Quest for Timbuktoo* (1968; o/p). An easily digested, though old-fashioned and not altogether reliable, collection of explorers' biographies; can often be found in second-hand bookshops.

Jean Marie Gibbal, *Genii of the River Niger* (University of Chicago Press, 1992). The French author's personal account of travels by *pirogue* through eastern Mali. Some of the more interesting passages depict healing ceremonies, which revolve around the river.

Pascal James Imperato, *Mali: A Search for Direction* (Dartmouth, UK, 1989). The author of the *Historical Dictionary of Mali* (Scarecrow, 1996) here devotes himself even more extensively to the country's history, society, economy and politics.

Seydou Keïta, *Seydou Keïta: African Photographs* (Scalo, 1997). Keïta's flattering work is the photographic parallel of the *jeli* praise-singer: an extraordinary collection of black-and-white studio photos of Bamako people from the 1950s to 1970s – a stunning testament to the richness of African urban culture.

Stephen Pern and Bryan Alexander, *Masked Dancers of West Africa: The Dogon* (Time-Life Books, 1982; o/p). Fine photography and good text. Highly recommended pre-visit (or even carry-around) reading.

William Seabrook, *The White Monk of Timbuctoo* (1934; o/p). It's worth checking libraries and secondhand bookshops for this biography of Père Yakouba, a white priest who married a Timbuktu woman and changed his vocation.

Bettina Selby, *Frail Dream of Timbuktu* (Ulverscroft, 1993). Selby's account of her bicycle journey from Niamey to Bamako is beautifully written and covers much more than just the journey – with interest-filled deviations and asides.

Fa-Diga Sissoko, *The Epic of Son-Jara* (trans. John William Johnson; Indiana UP, 1992). A new translation – and a new spelling for Sundiata/Sunjata – of the 800-year-old story of the Mali empire's founder.

Richard Trench, *Forbidden Sands* (1978; o/p). Stodgy travelogue, but an unusual route: Tindouf–Taoudenni–Timbuktu.

FICTION

You'll be lucky to find much of the following in English translation but Malian literature in French repays the effort.

Seydou Badian, *Le Sang des Masques* (Laffont, France, 1976). Nightmarish vision of the city, in this follow-up to Badian's earlier novel *Sous l'Orage* (Présence Africaine, France, 1963), in which the young generation – moulded by Western education – criticize traditional practices of religion and authority.

Maryse Condé, *Segu* (Penguin, US, 1987). An epic historical novel – already a Francophone classic – by a Guadeloupan author of Bamana descent, that paints a mesmerizing and unsettlingly graphic portrait of the Segou empire from 1797 to the middle of the nineteenth century. Translated from the French by Barbara Bray.

Mandé-Alpha Diarra, *Sahel! Sanglante Sécheresse* (Présence Africaine, France, 1981). The story of a doomed village schoolboy's life during the drought – a kind of documentary fiction.

Amadou Hampate Ba, *Fortunes of Wangrin* (1987; Indiana UP, 1999). An administrative interpreter tells of the colonial period from 1900 to 1945, and his successful collusion with it. Hampate Ba, born in Bandiagara, was a Fula academic and transcriber of oral literature (he died in 1991). His *Kaïdara*, an esoteric Fula cosmological epic poem, has also been translated into English (Three Continents Press, US, 1988).

Mamadou Kouyaté, *Sundiata: An Epic of Old Mali*, transcribed into French and annotated by D.T. Niane (trans. by G.D. Pickett; Longman, 1995). Slim and fascinating transcription of a griot's history of Mali.

Yambo Ouologuem is Mali's only writer to have achieved international recognition. In *Bound to Violence* (trans. Ralph Manheim; 1971; Heinemann, 1975), his treatment of brutality and deceit in an invented African empire, Nakem, insists that West African society rests on foundations as bloody and self-destructive as any other and screams for a new, rehumanizing look at the liberal romantic version of black history – a position that upset the earnest negritude movement. Most of Ouologuem's works excite controversy – he specializes in unabashed plagiarism, pornography (*Les Mille et une Bibles du Sexe*, 1969) and cudgel-like satire – but he can also be very funny. He's been out of circulation for a number of years.

Fily-Dabo Sissoko was one of Mali's earliest contributors to written literature. *Crayons et Portraits* (Mulhouse, France, 1953) recounts his idyllic childhood in rural "Soudan"; *La Savane Rouge* (Presses Universelles, France, 1962) offers further reminiscences; *Sagesse Noire* (Editions de la Tour du Guet, France, 1955) is a collection of over 500 African proverbs and axioms.

CAPE VERDE

Cape Verde is one of the least documented countries in the world. Sources of information in English are few, and most are technical, research-based studies that you'll find only in university libraries.

Antonio Carreira, *The People of the Cape Verde Islands* (C. Hurst, 1982). An indigestible analysis of a very important subject – the forced labour policy of the Portuguese in Cape Verde.

Basil Davidson, *The Fortunate Isles – a Study in African Transformation* (African World Press, 1990). The most recent book on Cape Verde by one of its most ardent supporters, this is a positive and not unduly critical survey, mixing impression with historical accounts to the present.

A.B. Ellis, *West African Islands* (1885; o/p). Adventures from Madeira to Ascension with a couple of lively chapters on "St Vincent" and "San Antonio". Entertaining stuff.

Colm Foy, *Cape Verde: Politics, Economics and Society* (Pinter Publishers, 1988; St Martins Press, 1988). The first and only contemporary survey of Cape Verde – very comprehensive on politics and economics, sparser on society.

Anne Hammick and Nicholas Heath, *Atlantic Islands* (Imray, Laurie, Norie & Wilson, 1998). A comprehensive sailors' pilot, with a healthy chunk on the Cape Verdes and plenty of navigational charts and photos.

Archibald Lyall, *Black and White Make Brown: An Account of a Journey to the Cape Verde Islands and Portuguese Guinea* (1938; o/p). Very hard to obtain – but well worth trying.

Deidre Meintel, *Race, Culture and Portuguese Colonialism in Cabo Verde* (Maxwell School of Citizenship and Public Affairs, Syracuse University, NY, 1984; o/p). An expanded PhD thesis, this fascinating study of race and self-image gets right inside the psychological effects of Portuguese colonialism.

GUINEA-BISSAU

Again, works in English are extremely sparse – and there's no Guinea-Bissauan literature in translation.

Amílcar Cabral, *Unity and Struggle* (Heinemann, UK, 1980; o/p). Cabral speaks well. Such was his immense popularity, there seems little doubt his assassination marked a point of turning back for the country, and for the whole of Africa.

Basil Davidson, *No Fist is Big Enough to Hide the Sky: The Liberation of Guiné and Cape Verde* (Zed Books, UK, 1983). Enthusiastic, quirky account of the war of liberation and its aftermath. The late Davidson's close and sympathetic involvement with the liberation fighters, particularly Amílcar Cabral himself, gives a rosy picture, tarnished by subsequent events.

Joshua B. Forrest, *Guinea-Bissau: Power, Conflict and Renewal in a West African Nation* (Westview, US, 1992; o/p).

Rosemary E. Galli and Jocelyn Jones, *Guinea-Bissau: Politics, Economics and Society* (Pinter Publishers, UK, 1987). A well-researched, rather gloomy survey, which found parallels between the independent governments and the fascist New State regime in their alienation of the rural people.

Ole Gjorstad and Chantal Sarrazin, *Sowing the First Harvest: National Reconstruction in Guinea-Bissau* (LSM Press, US, 1978; o/p). Dated and rhetorical; but sounded good at the time.

Walter Rodney, *A History of the Upper Guinea Coast 1545–1800* (Monthly Review, US, 1981). An Afrocentric history covering the region from the Casamance to Sierra Leone, dealing in depth with the area the Portuguese moved into and providing a mass of fascinating material on its social complexity.

Stepanie Urdang, *Fighting Two Colonialisms: Women in Guinea-Bissau* (Monthly Review Press, UK, 1979; o/p). Journalistic essays on escorted travels through the liberated zones and after the war of independence. Detailed and interesting but with much wishful thinking.

GUINEA

There's little published in English, though libraries may reveal some of the following.

Politique Africaine, Guinée: L'après-Sékou Touré (Karthala, France, 1989). A useful collection of articles (in French) looking at political and economic change since the death of Sékou Touré in 1984.

Anonymous, *Sékou Touré* (Panaf Great Lives Series, 1978; Humanities, 1978). Read now, a naive tribute to an obsessive despot, yet interesting for putting the ruler's case better than he himself did. Clearly and readably delivered.

Manthia Diawara, *In Search of Africa* (Harvard UP, 1998). Diawara, best known for his books on film, returns to Guinea to shoot a documentary on Sékou Touré, and pens a moving analysis of the state of Africa forty years after the independence movement.

FICTION

Alioum Fantouré, *Tropical Circle* (1972; Virginia UP, 1989). A "novel" about Guinea between the end of World War II and the reign of terror. The build-up to independence is a muddle but the second half is illuminating, despite a dire, Anglicized translation.

Camara Laye, *The African Child* (1954; Fontana, UK, 1989; o/p). One of the best-known books by an African writer, these sweet-scented memoirs of a privileged rural childhood are a homage to the author's parents. Other translations of works by Laye include *The Radiance of the King* (1954; *reprinted* Random, US, 1989; o/p), *A Dream of Africa* (1966; o/p) and *The Guardian of the Word* (1978; o/p).

CÔTE D'IVOIRE

Books in English on – or deriving from – Côte d'Ivoire are few, though the French publishers Karthala (22–24 bd Arago, 75013 Paris) publish a number of titles.

Marcel Amdonji, *Félix Houphouët-Boigny: L'envers d'un légende* (Karthala, France, 1985). A hard look at the man.

Laurent Gbagbo, *Histoire d'un Retour* (L'Harmattan, France, 1989). Senior opposition figure putting the case for an alternative to the status quo.

V.S. Naipaul, *Finding the Centre: Two Narratives* (Penguin, UK, 1985). Includes a long, characteristically interesting and perceptive essay "The Crocodiles of Yamoussoukro".

Abdou Touré, *Les petits métiers d'Abidjan: L'imagination au secours de la "conjoncture"* (Karthala, France, 1985). A series of lucid interviews giving a remarkable inside view of survival strategies on the city's streets.

Susan M. Vogel, *Baule: African Art/Western Eyes* (Yale UP, 1997). A thorough yet highly readable questioning of art for art's sake, thankfully low on academic jargon in its analysis of the Baule world view – expressed through sacred objects and utilitarian items, ranging from divination spools to weaver's pulleys. Generous colour and black-and-white illustrations.

FICTION

Bernard Dadié, *Climbié* (1956; Holmes and Meier, 1971; o/p). A sedately elegant portrayal of growing up in colonial Côte d'Ivoire and Senegal, shot through with occasional flashes of bitterness against the colons. Dadié, who was for many years the Minister of Cultural Affairs, has also edited *The Black Cloth* (1968; o/p), a collection of tales from the oral tradition.

Ahmadou Kourouma, *The Suns of Independence* (Heinemann, 1981; o/p). A very African novel, full of imagery and suspended reality.

BURKINA FASO

There is next to nothing published in English on Burkina – and nothing very digestible in French either. A handful of locally published French-language novels are available in Burkina.

Politique Africaine: Retour au Burkina (Karthala, France, 1989). Survey of changes since the death of Sankara.

Thomas Sankara Speaks (Pathfinder Press, 1988). Collection of the revolutionary's speeches – worth dipping into to see where the revolution was supposed to be going.

Pierre Englebert, *La Révolution Burkinabé* (L'Harmattan, France, 1986). Thorough look at the country's modern history by a political scientist.

Ben O. Nnaji, *Blaise Compaoré: The Architect of the Burkina Faso Revolution* (African Books Collective, UK, 1991). Unashamedly propagandist offering, with some general information on the country.

Robin Sharp, *Burkina Faso: New Life for the Sahel* (Oxfam, 1990). Shows the depth of the country's difficulties without being patronizing.

GHANA

Ghana has an established literary tradition with a number of widely available works.

HISTORY, SOCIETY AND ART

Mike Adjei, *Death and Pain: Rawlings' Ghana, the Inside Story* (Black Line, UK, 1994; o/p). Highly critical of the Rawlings regime, cataloguing alleged political murders.

Peter Adler and Nicholas Barnard, *Asafo! African Flags of the Fante* (Thames & Hudson, UK, 1992). Affordable and striking photo collection of Asafo flags and details.

F.K. Buah, *History of Ghana* (Macmillan, UK, 1980). A basic text, with a fair amount of illustration.

Gracia Clark, *Onions Are My Husband: Survival and Accumulation by West African Market Women* (University of Chicago Press, 1994). Insightful portrait of Kumasi market women.

Jeff Crisp, *Story of an African Working Class: Ghanaian Miners' Struggle* (Zed Books, UK, 1984). Epic struggle retold.

Eboe Hutchful, *The IMF and Ghana* (Zed Books, UK, 1987). Collection of original IMF documents, displaying the Fund with its pants down.

Kwame Nkrumah, *Kwame Nkrumah: the Conakry Years*, ed. June Milne (Zed Books, UK, 1990). Fascinating and remarkably large collection of correspondence, both weighty and trivial, from the complex mind of the exiled ex-president.

Thierry Secretan, *Going into Darkness: Fantastic Coffins from Africa* (Thames & Hudson, 1995). A photo-documentary about a visually exciting artform – the model coffins (in the form of a boat for a fisherman, a Merc for market woman, etc) of the Ga in Ghana.

FICTION

Ama Ata Aidoo, *The Dilemma of a Ghost* and *Anowa* (Longman, UK, 1997). Aidoo, one of Africa's relatively few female writers, deals in *Dilemma* with the unusual theme of a black American girl married into a Ghanaian family and in *Anowa* with a Ghanaian legend about a girl who refuses her parents' chosen suitors. *No Sweetness Here* (Longman, 1995; NOK Pubs, 1979) is a collection of short stories, most of which handle the theme of conflict between traditional and urban life in Ghana. *Our Sister Killjoy* (Longman, 1988; Feminist Press, 1995), Aidoo's first novel, explores, in an experimental fashion, the thoughts and experience of a Ghanaian girl on a voyage of self-discovery in Germany. *Changes* (The Women's Press, 1991) is a love story, used to portray urban African women – and the social forces that combine to make them both powerful and vulnerable.

Maya Angelou, *All God's Children Need Travelling Shoes* (Virago, 1987; Random, 1997). The story of American black activist Angelou's emigration to newly independent Ghana and her growing sense of disillusion, picked out in dialogue.

Ayi Kwei Armah, *The Beautiful Ones Are Not Yet Born* (1968; Heinemann, 1988; Heinemann, 1989). Politics, greed and corruption in newly independent Africa, seen through the life of a railway clerk; Armah beautifully captures the sense of frustration and crisis that befell Ghana after the fall of Nkrumah. Armah's second novel, *Fragments* (Heinemann, UK, 1974), is the story of a young African who comes home to Ghana after five years in the USA. *The Healers* (Heinemann, UK, 1977), a compulsive historical novel set in the Asante empire at the time of its demise, retains an optimistic vision.

Joseph Casely-Hayford, *Ethiopia Unbound* (1911; F. Cass, UK, 1969). Generally considered the first West African novel, *Ethiopia Unbound* treats a theme that later became familiar in African literature: the student who goes to study in London, and returns home to find he's a stranger. Early suggestions of what later became "negritude".

Amma Darko, *Beyond the Horizon* (Heinemann, UK, 1995). Provocative story of a Ghanaian woman's prostitution in Germany.

Amu Djoleto, *Hurricane of Dust* (Longman, UK, 1987). A vital, rap-paced tale, set in a post-coup Accra.

TOGO

Very little devoted to Togo has ever been published in English.

Tete Michel Kpomassie, *An African in Greenland* (Ulverscroft, 1988). The narrative of a Togolese explorer on a whimsical journey among the Inuit. Never quite transcends the basic oddity of its theme, and begs a few questions along the way, but entertaining nonetheless.

George Packer, *The Village of Waiting* (Random, US, 1988; o/p). An informative book, recounting the experiences of a Peace Corps volunteer.

Comi M. Toulabor, *Le Togo sous Eyadema* (Karthala, France, 1986). A solid discussion of 1980s politics – and about the only one to appear.

FICTION

David Ananou, *Le Fils du Fétiche* (Nouvelle Editions Latine, France, 1955). Intended to combat the racism of its time by a portrayal of a typical Togolese family, the effort is confounded by Ananou's rejection of traditional beliefs for the "lofty" tenets of Christianity.

Yves-Emmanuel Dogbé, *La Victime* (Editions Akpagnon, France, 1979). A treatment of the interracial theme in West Africa: a white girl's parents come to recognize the error of their prejudice, but too late.

BENIN

With the exception of Chatwin, who also contributed a memorable piece to *The Best of Granta Travel* (1991) on the coup that installed Kérékou, there is little available from, or about Benin.

Bruce Chatwin, *The Viceroy of Ouidah* (Vintage, 1988; Viking Penguin, 1988). Without a doubt the first book to read on Benin – gripping, in Chatwin's inimitable style, from the prologue on.

Robert Cornevin, *La République Populaire du Bénin* (Editions G-P Maisonneuve et Larose, France, 1984). A complete, if dryly chronological, history, with a French nationalist slant.

Patrick Manning, *Slavery, Colonialism and Economic Growth in Dahomey 1640–1960* (o/p). Heavy scholarship, but well done.

FICTION

Olympe Bhêly-Quénum, *Snares Without End* (trans. Dorothy S. Blair; Longman, 1981; o/p). The only Béninois writer to have been translated into English.

Paul Hazoumé, *Doguicimi* (Larose, France 1938; o/p). The essence of the Dan-Homey kingdom is captured in this carefully documented work of realist-romantic fiction, unfortunately not yet translated from French.

Maximilian Quénum, *Légendes Africaines* (1946; o/p). One of the earliest African writers inspired by the doctrine of "negritude". The legends include an account of the founding of the Dan-Homey empire along with that of kingdoms in Côte d'Ivoire and the Soudan (Mali).

NIGER

Published material in English on Niger is really limited: if you want more than the handful of volumes devoted to the country, you'll need to read French.

The late **Boubou Hama** was one of Niger's most prolific writers, publishing numerous historical works on the empires of Gao, Gobir and Songhai. A former president of the National Assembly, he also wrote works on politics, philosophy and folklore.

Politique Africaine: Le Niger (Karthala, France 1990). Survey of Nigérien politics, aid and economics – and the Sahara.

Carol Beckwith and Mario Van Offelen, *Nomads of Niger* (Harvill Press, 1984; Abrams, 1993). Superbly illustrated essay on the Wodaabe Bororo.

Robert B. Charlick, *Niger: Personal Rule and Survival in the Sahel* (Westview, US, 1991; o/p). Profile of the nation.

Finn Fuglestad, *A History of Niger 1850–1960* (Cambridge UP, 1983; o/p). Somewhat inaccessible, but there's no English alternative.

Paul Stoller *Fusion of the Worlds: An Ethnography of Possession among the Songhay of Niger* (University of Chicago Press, 1989) and **Paul Stoller and Cheryl Olkes**, *In Sorcery's Shadow: a Memoir of Apprenticeship among the Songhay* (University of Chicago Press, 1997). Stoller is a kind of Nigérien answer to Carlos Castaneda – apprenticed to a sorcerer, taking drugs. All interesting stuff.

FICTION

Ibrahim Issa, *Grandes Eaux Noires*. The first Nigérien novel to be published (before independence), this manages to describe humorously the travails of second-century BC Mediterranean explorers south of the Sahara.

More recent writers include:

Idé Oumarou, *Gros Plan*. This won the Grand Prix de l'Afrique Noire award in 1978.

Halilou Sabbo Mahamadou, *Abokki ou l'Appel de la Côte, Les Caprices du Destin*.

Amadou Ousmane, *Quinze ans, ça suffit*. Aspects of contemporary Nigérien society illuminated. Kicks off with the food aid-hoarding scandal (see p.876).

NIGERIA

There's a vast body of books on and from Nigeria in print – and more being published all the time.

COUNTRY AND STATE

Nigeria, the Land, its Art and its People (Studio Vista, 1977; o/p). A brief, good-value anthology of prose, with photographs.

Chinua Achebe, *The Trouble with Nigeria* (Heinemann, 1984). A brief and immensely useful insight into the complexity of Nigerian society and politics.

Claude Ake (ed) *The Political Economy of Nigeria* (Longman, UK, 1985). A classic, uncompromising in its critique of political and economic conditions and the stranglehold on Nigeria of structures beyond its grasp. This book made the late Ake's reputation as one of Nigeria's most outspoken academics. With his later works like *How Politics Underdevelops Africa* and *Democratization of Disempowerment* he became one of the most brilliant observers of what went wrong.

William D. Graf, *Nigerian State: Political Economy, State, Class and Political System in the Post-Colonial Era* (James Currey, 1989; Heinemann, 1990). An overview analysing political, social and economic shifts over the last 25 years.

Peter Holmes, *Nigeria: Giant of Africa* (Oregon Press, 1985; o/p). Coffee-table format with nearly 200 photos. Detailed and interesting notes; nothing else on Nigeria of this type compares.

Richard A. Joseph, *Democracy and Prebendal Politics in Nigeria: The rise and fall of the Second Republic* (Cambridge UP, US, 1987). Still the reference work on the twisted Nigerian political economy. Joseph takes his reader down to the root causes, making the the distortions, if not acceptable, understandable.

Egohosa E. Osaghae, *The Crippled Giant*, (Indiana UP, 1999). Pessimism in the title and analysis relates to the book's publication during the crisis of the Abacha regime. Overall, a concise introduction to four decades of Nigerian political history.

Ken Saro-Wiwa, *A Month and a Day, A Detention Diary* (Penguin, UK, 1995). A living testimony from the leader of MOSOP (executed by the Abacha regime in 1995) against the atrocities meted out to the Ogoni people in Cross River State. His *Genocide in Nigeria: The Ogoni Tragedy* (African Books Collective, UK, 1992) set out the disastrous effects of government policy and the oil industry on a region in Cross River State.

Wole Soyinka, *The Open Sore of a Continent: A Personal Narrative of the Nigerian Crisis* (Oxford UP, US, 1996). Accessible diagnosis of one of Africa's biggest wounds from one of its most admired writers.

ART AND PEOPLE

Omofolabo S. Ajayi, *Yoruba Dance: The Semiotics of Movement and Body Attitude in a Nigerian Culture* (Africa World Press, 1997). An insightful introduction to themes of Yoruba dance and the philosophical, aesthetic and religious underpinnings of movement as a means of communication.

J.S. Boston, *Ikenga* (1977; o/p). Explores the symbolism of carvings amongst varied peoples of Nigeria.

T.J.H. Chappel, *Decorated Gourds in North Eastern Nigeria* (Ethnographica Press, 1977; o/p). A substantial survey of their use, decoration and symbolism.

Henry J. Drewal and John Pemberton III, *Yoruba: Nine Centuries of African Art and Thought* (Abrams, 1990). Sumptuous and terribly expensive – a majestic, detailed photo and essay documentary on various Yoruba states and their individual artistic traditions.

Edward Fox, *Obscure Kingdoms* (Ulverscroft, 1995). Excitingly written and brilliantly evocative accounts of journeys to the world's remoter royal corners, including a sizeable chapter on meetings in Nigeria with various *onis*, *obas* and emirs.

Bryan Freyer, *Royal Benin Art* (Smithsonian Institute, 1987; Prentice Hall & IBD, 1987). Illustrated and informative catalogue from a major exhibition of the art of the Benin Empire.

Berkare Gbadamosi and Ulli Beier, *Not Even God Is Ripe Enough* (Heinemann, 1968; o/p). Full of amusing stories.

Paula Girshick Ben-Amos, *The Art of Benin* (British Museum Press, 1995; Smithsonian Institution Press, 1995). Plenty of photos of bronzes and more.

Barry Hallen and J.O. Sodipo, *Knowledge, Belief and Witchcraft* (Stanford UP, 1997). A survey of Yoruba philosophical ideas.

G.I. Jones, *Ibo Art* (Shire, 1989; State Mutual, 1989). Well-illustrated survey of arts and their role in Ibo (Igbo) society.

A. D. Nzemeke and E. O. Erhage (eds) *Nigerian Peoples and Culture* (United City Press, Nigeria, 1997). A cultural history of Nigeria's ethnic groups. Highly recommended in-depth study of the history of Nigerian society.

Robert S. Smith, *Kingdoms of the Yoruba* (James Curry, UK, 1988). The classic historical work on pre-colonial Yoruba civilization.

FICTION

Nigeria's post-colonial literature has been the continent's most prolific and most outspoken, its writers enjoying a greater liberty than most of their African counterparts. Today, by far the most influential Nigerian writers are Chinua Achebe and the Nobel prize-winning novelist and playwright Wole Soyinka. One of the greatest impetuses to national writing, however, was Onitsha Market Literature, which emerged between 1947 and 1966. At the time, Onitsha was one of Nigeria's most important commercial centres, with a long history of mission education and cosmopolitan influence. Dozens of spare-time writers – teachers, office clerks and journalists – turned out some 200 books that were printed in the market itself.

Chinua Achebe, *Things Fall Apart* (1958), *No Longer at Ease* (1960), *The Arrow of God* (1964), *A Man of the People* (1966), *Anthills of the Savannah* (1987); all published (and in print) by Heinemann in the UK and Anchor in the US. One of Africa's best-known novelists, Achebe gained international fame with his classic first novel *Things Fall Apart*, which deals with the encounter, at the turn of the century, between missionaries, colonial officers and an Igbo village. Okwonkwo, a self-made man, rises to respected seniority, then falls, inexorably and tragically. It's a brilliant, moving book – universal in what it says on pride, and on fathers and sons. With it, the three following novels form part of a loose quartet: in *No Longer at Ease*, Okwonkwo's grandson, Obi, is a corrupt Lagos civil servant, trapped in his head between home and ambition; in *Arrow of God*, set in the 1920s, there's direct confrontation between an Igbo priest and a colonial officer; and in *A Man of the People*, Achebe adopts a more satirical approach, setting up an idealist against a rogue and showing how close their paths run. Achebe's characters bend and sweat with life and develop unexpected traits just as you thought you had the measure of them. His 1995 novel, a humanist fable, *Anthills of the Savannah*, was shortlisted for the Booker Prize.

Zainab Alkali, *A Virtuous Woman*, *The Stillborn* (Longman, 1984; o/p). Alkali is unusual in being a woman writer from the conservative north of the country. "I see myself as a typical Nigerian woman who wants to get married, raise a family and live according to the expected norms of the society . . . A woman can never be anything else but a woman."

T.M. Aluko, *One Man, One Wife* (Heinemann, 1967; o/p). Entertaining tale of Yoruba villagers' disillusionment with the missionaries' God and their return to traditional worship. *One Man, One Matchet* (Heinemann, 1965; o/p) is written in a similarly crafted and satirical style as it portrays conflict in a Western cocoa community. *Chief the Honourable Minister* (Heinemann, 1970; o/p) is the less amusing story of a schoolmaster appointed minister in a corrupt government. His latest book, *Conduct Unbecoming* (African Books Collective, UK, 1994), is a parable about corruption and sanctimoniousness.

Tafawa Balewa, *Shaihu Umar* (1968; Wiener, US, 1989; trans. from the Hausa). Portrayal of a Hausa family at the turn of the century by Nigeria's first prime minister.

Simi Bedford, *Yoruba Girl Dancing* (Viking, US, 1994). A British Nigerian's depiction of early life in Nigeria, adjustment to the UK, and the getting of wisdom.

John Pepper Clark Three of Clark's books, *A Reed in the Tide* (1965; o/p), *Casualties* (Longman, 1970; Holmes & Meier, 1970; a lament written during the civil war), and *A Decade of Tongues* (o/p) are poetry collections with which Clark first gained recognition. He is now better known as a playwright: for *Ozidi* (Harvard UP, US, 1991), a play based on an Ijaw saga; *State of the Nation*, a piece of social criticism written in 1985 (o/p); and *America, Their America* (o/p), a biting indictment of values in the United States where he studied in the early 1960s.

T. Obinkaram Echewa, *I Saw the Sky Catch Fire* (NAL-Dutton, US, 1993). Fictional accounts of the effects of war, especially as it touches the lives of women. Powerful and moving, from the author of *The Land's Lord*.

Cyprian Ekwensi, *Jagua Nana* (1961; Heinemann, 1987). Superbly captures the life and rhythm of 1950s Lagos using a style resembling that of the traditional storyteller. *Burning Grass* (1962; Heinemann, 1990) is set in the north among Fula herders (an unusual setting for Ekwensi). One of Nigeria's most popular novelists, Ekwensi started his writing career at Onitsha market. *Lokotown and other stories* (o/p) is a collection of short tales, again set in the city, while *Survive the Peace* (o/p) is his most political novel, set in the aftermath of the defeat of Biafra, a secession he had supported.

Buchi Emecheta, *Slave Girl, Second Class Citizen, In The Ditch, Head Above Water, Joys Of Motherhood, Double Yoke, The Bride Price, Destination Biafra, Gwendolen* and *Rape Of Shavi* (all in print, mostly in Ogwugwu or Heinemann, UK, and Brazillier, US). Emecheta writes, with a humour that refuses to be submerged, about the struggle to be a Nigerian woman and an independent person – in Nigeria and the UK.

Olaudah Equiano, *The Life of Olaudah Equiano* (1789; St Martin's Press, UK, 1997). Classic autobiography and one of the earliest West African books. Equiano was born in Igboland in 1745 and captured by slavers at the age of ten. Highly recommended reading.

Festus Ijayi, *Violence* (Longman, 1979; o/p), *Heroes* (Longman, 1986; o/p). A commitedly political writer, Ijayi was detained in 1988 for protesting against the government's human rights abuses. *Violence* is a howl of anguish at the inhumanity of urban survival in Africa. *Heroes* is set in the dark backyard of Nigeria's soul, the civil war of 1967–69.

Vincent Chukwuemeka Ike, *Toads for Supper* (o/p), *The Naked Gods* (o/p), *Chicken Chasers* (o/p) and *Sunset at Dawn* (o/p). A series of entertaining, critical novels by a brilliant comic writer. Recent works include *Our Children are Coming* (African Books Collective, UK, 1990).

Eddie Iroh, *Forty Eight Guns for the General* (Heinemann, 1976; o/p), *Toads of War* (Heinemann, US, 1979) and *The Sirens in the Night* (Heinemann, 1982; o/p). Three thrillers that rode in on the wave of writing following the Biafran War.

Karen King-Aribasala, *Kicking Tongues*, (Heinemann, 1998). A wonderful collection of perspectives shared by travel companions who meet up at the *Eko Holiday Inn* in Lagos before embarking on a trip to Abuja. The characters, who range from a prostitute to village chief, seem to have little in common but are united in their disaffection with corruption and other facets of Nigerian politics.

Adewale Maja Pearce, *Loyalties* (Longman, 1987; o/p). Evocative short stories and vignettes set in a society always on the brink of chaos (Nigeria) by a writer based in Britain.

Flora Nwapa, *Efuru* (Heinemann, 1966). The first African woman to publish a novel. As in the later *Idu* (Heinemann, 1970; o/p), Nwapa looks at women's roles – not always in a traditional way – in a society precariously balanced between the traditional and the new. *This is Lagos* (African World Press, 1992) is Nwapa's follow-up to her novels portraying women at odds with society – a collection of effective short stories on life in the metropolis. Flora Nwapa died in 1993.

Ben Okri, *Flowers and Shadows* (1980; Longman, UK, 1989; o/p). Okri's excellent first novel was published when he was only twenty. The angry, hallucinatory short story collections, *Incidents at the Shrine* (1986; Vintage, UK, 1993) and *Stars of the New Curfew* (1989; Vintage, 1999; Viking, 1990) propelled Nigerian literature into a new wide audience. Okri, based in Britain, provides razor-sharp dialogue and settings, fine evocations of character (male and female) and an angular wit. With his Booker Prize-winning *The Famished Road* (1991; Vintage, 1992; Anchor Books, 1993), he comes home to the themes of tradition and of Yoruba mythology. It was followed by a sequel, *Songs of Enchantment* (Vintage, 1994; Doubleday, 1994) and then by *Astonishing the Gods* (Phoenix House, UK, 1995), *Dangerous Love* (Phoenix House, UK, 1997) and *Infinite Riches* (Phoenix House, UK, 1999).

Niyi Osundare, *Moonsongs* (1988; African Books Collective, UK, 1991); *Songs of the Season* (African Books Collective, UK, 1990); *Waiting Laughters* (African Books Collective, UK, 1991); *Midlife* (African Books Collective, UK, 1993). One of Africa's best-known poets, committed to performance of poetry together with drumming and dancing, Osundare is a Commonwealth Prize winner, who received the NOMA Award in 1991 for *Waiting Laughters*. His most easily obtained collection is *Selected Poems* (Heinemann, UK).

Ken Saro-Wiwa, *Sozaboy* (1985; Longman, 1994; Addison-Wesley, 1994); A *Forest of Flowers* (1986; Longman, 1995; Addison-Wesley, 1997); *Basi & Company: A Modern African Folktale* (African Books Collective, UK, 1988); *The Prisoner of Jebs* (Saros, 1988); *Pita Dumbrok's Prison* (African Books Collective, UK, 1991). Saro-Wiwa was a major figure on the Nigerian literary and political scene who was jailed and executed for his campaigning work on behalf of his fellow Ogoni people. Saro-Wiwa fought on the Federal side in the Nigerian civil war and his maverick career spanned publishing, TV and political activism.

Wole Soyinka When Soyinka won the Nobel Prize for Literature in 1986, he not only gained international recognition for himself (becoming the first African to be so honoured), but for the writers of his continent. Known primarily as a playwright, his early works include *The Lion and the Jewel* (1963), *A Dance of the Forests* (1963) – an exercise in demythologizing Africa's historic idyll – and *Kongi's Harvest* (1967). Oxford UP publish UK and US editions of these plays. He later published poetry, sketching beautiful images in *Idanre, and Other Poems* (1967; Hill & Wang, US, 1987). He has also worked substantially as a novelist with *The Interpreters* (Heinemann, 1970) – in which a group of young intellectuals living in Lagos attempts to "interpret" their role in traditional and modern Nigeria – and the luminous, dream-like *Ake* (Vintage, 1983; Vintage, 1989) – an autobiographical account of his childhood in Abeokuta. *Isara* (Random House, 1991; Vintage, 1989) is a biographical account of Nigeria in the times of his father, the memorable schoolmaster "Essay" from Ake. The sequel to *Isara*, *Ibadan: the Penkelmes Years* (Minerva, UK, 1994), focuses on his fight against the everyday repression of early post-independence Nigeria. As a writer of even greater prominence than Achebe, Soyinka's work is denser and less easy-going. He is also politically more outspoken, and during the Abacha regime, he helped organize a major opposition group in exile.

Amos Tutuola, *Palm Wine Drinkard* (1952; Faber, 1995; Grove Press, 1994). This, the first West African novel, is heavily under the spell of Yoruba oral tradition as it recounts a journey into the "Dead Towns" of the supernatural. It was followed by *My Life in the Bush of Ghosts* (Faber, UK, 1954).

CAMEROON

A fair number of books dealing with Cameroon have been published, and the country has the advantage of a dual linguistic heritage which has inspired a relatively rich literature, though predominantly in French.

GENERAL/TRAVELOGUES

Nigel Barley, *Innocent Anthropologist: Notes from a Mud Hut* (Penguin, UK, 1986), *A Plague of Caterpillars* (Penguin, UK, 1986; o/p). The books that did for anthropology what Durrell did for animal collecting – and infuriated anthropologists.

Gerald Durrell, *The Overloaded Ark* (1953; Faber, 1995; Viking, 1995), *The Bafut Beagles* (1954; Penguin, UK, 1970), *A Zoo in my Luggage* (1960; Penguin, UK, 1970). Durrell's animal-collecting exploits in the British Cameroons – first freelance, and then for his Jersey Conservation Trust zoo – are delightfully recounted and still funny, with exceptions made for an unexceptionally colonial attitude to quaint native behaviour. But it's hard indeed to recognize the present town of Mamfé – even less Bafut – in his misty pictures.

Dervla Murphy, *In Cameroon with Egbert* (John Murray, 1989; Overlook Press, 1991). Murphy and daughter with a horse.

HISTORY/POLITICS/ART/SOCIETY

Mark DeLancey, *Cameroon: Dependence and Independence* (Dartmouth, UK, 1989; o/p). Survey of history, economics and politics.

Philippe Gaillard, *Le Cameroun* (L'Harmattan, France, 1989, two volumes). General political and economic survey in French from colonial times to the late 1980s.

Albert Mukong, *Prisoner without a Crime* (Nubia, 1989). The darker side of political life under Biya, this tells the story of six years of imprisonment with graphic details of arbitrary justice, brutality and torture. Leave at home.

Tamara Northern, *Art Of Cameroon* (University of Washington Press, 1986). Large-format, colour-illustrated survey of regions and their art.

Joseph Sheppherd, *Leaf of Honey* (Bahai, US, 1988). An American anthropologist's study of the Ntuumu people of Cameroon, laced with their proverbs and their views about life.

Colin Turnbull, *The Forest People* (1961; Pimlico, 1994; Touchstone Books, 1987). An account of the Ituri forest Bambuti ("Pygmies") in Congo; the best writing in English on the oldest African people. Essential, delightful reading for forest stays in Cameroon.

FICTION

Léon-Marie Ayissi, *Contes et Berceuses Béti* (1966). A satisfying collection of Beti folktales.

Francis Bebey, *Agatha Moudio's Son* (trans. from *Le fils d'Agatha Moudio*; Heinemann, 1971; o/p). Better known as a musician (see p.1182), this was Bebey's first novel, a tragicomic study of human relations in a traditional village society.

Mongo Beti, *The Poor Christ of Bomba* (trans; Heinemann, 1971). One of the senior figures of African literature – living in exile since 1959 – Beti's novels combine political satire with more basic human conflict. *Poor Christ*, the most cynical of his novels, deals with the perverse efforts of a French priest to convert the whole village, with disastrously ironic consequences. Later works, *Mission to Kala* (1957; trans; Heinemann, 1964) and *King Lazarus* (o/p) established his mastery of social satire. After independence, Beti embarked on a long period of silence until the publication of his critique of the Ahidjo regime – *Main basse sur le Cameroon* (F. Maspero, 1972), which he followed with *Remember Ruben* and *Perpetua and the Habit of Unhappiness* (trans. John Reed and Clive Wake; Heinemann, 1978; o/p).

Calixthe Beyala, *Your Name Shall be Tanga*, (trans; Heinemann, UK/US, 1996), *The Sun Hath Looked Upon Me* (trans; Heinemann, 1996). An emergent name in West African fiction, Beyala's heroes are women forced to act against poverty and the injustices of male-based societies.

Benjamin Matip, *Afrique nous t'ignorons* (1954). Matip contemplates the past from a young African's perspective – separated from tradition by Western education and World War II. The novel also hits out at the exploitation of Cameroonian planters: it contributed to an outpouring of anti-colonial literature in the 1950s. Matip's *A la Belle Etoile: Contes et nouvelles d'Afrique* (Présence Africaine, France, 1962) is a classic collection of folktales.

Ndeley Mokoso, *Man Pass Man!* (Addison Wesley, US, 1998). A string of darkly funny short stories. The subject of the title tale – maraboutic meddling on the football pitch – was rumoured as an explanation for Cameroon's success in the 1990 World Cup.

Jacques Mariel Nzouankeu, *Le Souffle des Ancêtres* (Editions CLE, France, 1965). Tales that illustrate the conflict between humans and the metaphysical forces that are believed to dominate their destinies.

Ferdinand Oyono, *Houseboy* (1956; trans. from *Une Vie de Boy*; Heinemann, 1990). Oyono was one of the first satirical writers of the anti-colonial period to break from an autobiographical form in this scathing satire about colonialism. *The Old Man and the Medal* (1967; trans. from *Le Vieux Negre et la Médaille*, Heinemann, 1982) is less caustic, but equally effective, both in its criticism of colonial insensitivity, and of blind adherence to tradition.

Guillaume Oyônô-Mbia, *Three Suitors, One Husband* and *Until Further Notice* (both in *Faces of African Independence: Three Plays*, Virginia UP, US, 1988). Comic masterpieces, written in English. His later play in French, *Notre Fille ne se mariera pas*, like *Three Suitors*, deals with the familiar theme of the brideprice in a changing African society. It was made into the 1980 film *Notre Fille* by Daniel Kamwa (see p.1161).

René Philombe, *Lettres de ma Cambuse* (Editions CLE, France, 1964). Life in the urban slums described – even on the basis of personal experience – with humour. Subsequent work includes an inspired collection of short stories *Histoires queue de chat: quelques scènes de la vie camerounaise* (Editions CLE, France, 1971).

SIERRA LEONE

Sierra Leone has never had as much literary or scholarly attention as its Anglophone neighbours, Ghana and Nigeria, though there are works to be found if you're prepared to scour libraries.

BACKGROUND AND TRAVELOGUES

Graham Greene, *The Heart of the Matter* (1948; Penguin, 1998). Set in Freetown during World War II, Greene's novel uses the town as a seedy web in which his protagonists struggle. No great insights on Sierra Leone, but it touches illuminatingly on the racism and repression then present in the colony. Enduring, and still worth reading as wry introduction or *in situ* mental scenery. *Journey without Maps* (1936; Penguin, 1991) includes several dozen atmospheric pages narrating Greene's progress towards the Liberian border in 1935.

F.W.H. Migeod, *View of Sierra Leone* (1926; o/p). Fascinating and readably scatty account of a six-month trek through the country, with interesting appendices on secret societies and Mende songs.

Christophe and Emmanuel Valentin, *Sierra Leone* (Editions Xavier Richer, France, 1986). The coffee-table book of Sierra Leone. Nice pictures, mostly of Freetown and the peninsula (some interesting older black-and-whites, too) but the feeble French/English text is at tour brochure level.

HISTORY AND SOCIETY

Joe A.D. Alie, *A New History of Sierra Leone* (Macmillan, UK, 1990). An accessible and copiously illustrated general history. Explores social and economic as well as political developments.

Sylvia Ardyn Boone, *Radiance from the Waters: Ideals of Feminine Beauty in Mende Art* (Yale UP, 1990). Circumspect account of the Mende women's Sande society by an art historian who promised not to reveal all.

Adelaide M. Cromwell, *An African Victorian Feminist – the Life and Times of Adelaide Smith Casely Hayford 1868–1960* (F. Cass, 1986; Howard UP, 1992). A remarkable, epoch-bridging biography on a figure from the Krio elite.

John W. Nunley, *Moving with the Face of the Devil* (University of Illinois Press, US, 1987). A sociology of Freetown's contemporary masquerade societies complemented by brilliant photos.

E. Frances White, *Sierra Leone's Settler Women Traders* (University of Michigan Press, US, 1987). A study of the central economic role of Freetown's "Big Market" women in the nineteenth century.

FICTION

Syl Cheney-Coker, *The Last Harmattan of Alusine Dunbar* (Heinemann, 1990). American-educated professor's first novel – a black comedy of life in a neocolonial state. Honesty versus Ali Baba and his forty thieves.

Yema Lucilda Hunter, *Road to Freedom* (African Universities Press, 1982; o/p). A historical novel about the early Krio settlements in Sierra Leone. Tracing the expedition of thirteen-year-old Deannie, who leaves Nova Scotia with her family to resettle in Sierra Leone, Hunter provides a vivid and elegant description of Freetown in the late eighteenth century.

Yulisa Amadu Maddy, *No Past, No Present, No Future* (Heinemann, 1973; o/p). Three Sierra Leonean boys in Europe make up for, and make the most of, their different backgrounds. Maddy's *Obasai and Other Plays* (Heinemann, 1971; o/p) is worth looking out for too.

Prince Dowu Palmer, *The Mocking Stones* (Longman, 1982; o/p). Palmer uses a mixed-race love affair as a backdrop for an examination of social and economic exploitation in this novel about the Kono diamond business.

People's Educational Association, *Fishing in Rivers of Sierra Leone* (1987; o/p). A work of the German-funded organization, this is a major collection of oral literature – stories and songs – from thirteen Sierra Leonean language groups with hundreds of colour and black-and-white photos of the performers in action. Highly recommended.

Robert Wellesley Cole, *Kossoh Town Boy* (Cambridge UP, 1960; o/p). Classic novel of a childhood in pre-World War I and early 1920s Freetown.

LIBERIA

Liberia does have a modest literature, but much of it is American sociopolitical and development analysis – and hardly screaming out to be read.

Liberia: a Promise Betrayed (Lawyers Committee for Human Rights, New York, 1986). Deeply disturbing background on the nature of the Liberian state under Samuel Doe, setting the present mess in its bloody context.

Anthony Daniels, *Monrovia Mon Amour* (John Murray, 1992; o/p). Interesting and surprisingly enjoyable account of the author's sojourn in the city in 1991.

Graham Greene, *Journey without Maps* (see overleaf, under "Sierra Leone"). Acid account of the author's walk in 1936 from Foya to Buchanan, via Ganta. He was accompanied by a cousin (hardly mentioned) and a line of porters.

Barbara Greene, *Too Late to Turn Back* (Settle Press, UK, 1981). Revenge of the above-mentioned cousin. "It sounded fun", she writes of her anticipation, but evidently it wasn't.

J.G. Liebenow, *Liberia: The Quest for Democracy* (Indiana UP, US, 1987). A detailed, if rather dry political history.

Alice Walker, *The Colour Purple* (The Women's Press, 1993; Pocket Books, 1990). Part of the story offers an oblique glance at the conditions that led to the creation of America's Liberian colony.

CINEMA

West African cinema provides a stimulating way into the complexities of the region's culture and concerns. This short introduction maps out its history and highlights some of the better-known films and film-makers.

THE BEGINNINGS

In 1963 a short film by the acclaimed novelist **Ousmane Sembène** – *Borom Sarret* – managed to get onto the screens of Africa and Europe. Well received by the critics, this work laid the foundations for what, by the end of the 1960s, had become a great cinematic movement south of the Sahara. In 1968, Sembène released *Mandabi* ("The Money Order"), the first movie by a Black African to reach a large audience; critics also hailed the film, which won the Silver Lion at the 1969 Venice Film Festival.

The success of *Mandabi* inspired a whole generation of West African film-makers, and the 1970s turned out to be the region's most prolific decade. Early directors, many of them trained in the Soviet Union, were aware of their power to reach the masses and of Lenin's assertion that "the most important of all the arts is cinema". From the beginning they perceived their craft as a functional art form, which could break down stereotypes by giving a realistic portrayal of Africa from an African perspective, and could take an active part in national development by adapting film to the needs and aspirations of their newly independent countries.

Though early West African films were the products of many different cultures and looked at the continent in various historical, political and social stages, they were remarkably similar in their **themes**. Most commonly, they dealt with the conflict that arose from traditional values and those imported from the West. Typically, the opposition between the old and the new is expressed by the opposition between **the city and the country** – the implication being that the process of rural migration has contributed to a loss of cultural identity. Among numerous examples of films of this type are *Kwami* by Quenum Do-Kokou from Togo (1974), *Sous le signe de Vaudou* by Pascal Abikanlou from Benin (1973), and *Le Bracelet du Bronze* by Tidiane Aw from Senegal (1974). Other topics include the **alienation** faced by African emigrants abroad, the **exploitation** of the masses by a corrupt and unscrupulous elite, the weight of **social traditions**, and the **injustices** of colonial or neocolonial systems.

African film-makers also struggled with the limitations imposed by a film language that has evolved in the West. Thematic inspiration that derived from **African tales and legends** necessitated a new style capable of breaking down a story, of using digression to accept the irrational within the logical structure of a tale. There has thus been a tendency to move away from the slow-paced linear narrative of early films in order to forge an authentic African aesthetic, based on the conventions of oral literature.

FESPACO

As the cinematic movement progressed, **Burkina Faso** (then called Upper Volta) emerged as the "capital" of African cinema. In 1969, Ouagadougou hosted the first **Festival Panafricain du Cinema** (FESPACO), a forum for African film-makers held every other February. Winners of the "Yenenga" – the African Oscar – have increasingly achieved international plaudits, and though participation in the main event is limited to Africans, an increasing number of entries from the diaspora – the United States, Latin America and the Caribbean – have gained recognition through presentation in a special category. Burkina Faso has produced its own notable directors too: **Samon Emmanuel**, who won acclaim for his 1985 film *Dessé Bagato*; **Idrissa Ouédraogo**, whose *Yaaba* earned a prize at the 1989 Cannes festival; and **Gaston Kaboré**, a two-time winner of the Grand Prix at FESPACO – once for *Wend Kuuni* ("The Gift of God") in 1985, and again for that film's sequel, *Buud Yam*, in 1997.

OUSMANE SEMBÈNE

Senegal's **Ousmane Sembène**, a Marxist whose films are explicitly political, remains the "papa" of West African cinema. Since his debut in 1963, he has made over a dozen films, of which several are considered classics. Besides *Borom Sarret* ("Cart-driver", 1963) and *Mandabi* ("The Money Order", 1968), his most famous works are **Xala** (1974) – a satire that gets darker and darker about a corrupt Dakar bureaucrat who loses touch with the people and thereby becomes impotent – and the less accessible **Ceddo**, which deals with the three-way conflict in the nineteenth century between the jihadists, the traditionalists and the French. The title character of Sembène's 1993 film, **Guelwaar**, is a political activist and baptized Catholic who through bureaucratic mix-up gets buried in a Muslim cemetery. Sembène uses the community's attempts to rectify the situation to expose the petty jealousies and divisive religious dogmatism that bely contemporary politics. Like many of Sembène's works, the film was banned in Senegal when it was released and remains difficult to see abroad.

RECENT SETBACKS

Throughout West Africa, the remarkable creativity that characterized the 1970s, began a **decline** by the end of the decade that continued into the 1980s and 1990s. A major reason for the stagnation can be found in the system of film production and distribution. With few exceptions, films are made with state subsidies, which limits creative possibilities in countries where the treasury doesn't give high priority to cinema. Most people in business consider film a risky investment. Moviegoing is popular in towns but the gate receipts are small, and imported **videos** are increasingly driving cinemas out of business. Adding to the frustration, most countries lack film industries of a technical level that would permit post-production control (laboratories, synchro, editing). Most post-production work for African-produced films is still carried out in Europe.

Distribution has proved a further stumbling block. Although mostly nationalized in West African countries, distribution companies still depend on larger European and American firms which control the African screens. Sadly, they exhibit minimal enthusiasm for national products, and films made in Africa have little or no chance of being shown in their countries of origin. Today, in fact, it is easier to see African films in Paris, London, Rome and New York than in Abidjan, Conakry, Lagos or Lomé.

THE NEW GENERATION

Despite these difficulties, independent film continues to progress, and the early pioneers are being followed by a hopeful new generation.

Recent FESPACO festivals have pointed to the growing diversity of African cinema and the emergence of a new generation of film-makers. They put their own spin on the **social realism** films of predecessors, drawing from local theatre (Yoruba theatre in Nigeria, or Koteba theatre in Mali and Côte d'Ivoire), oral tradition, and song and dance. Like Sembène, new film-makers treat issues of class, gender, tradition or religion, yet tend to be less didactic in the way they view oppressive forces. Often comedic, the youthful exuberance of films like *Quartier Mozart* (Jean-Pierre Bekolo, Cameroon, 1991), *Ça twiste à Poponguine* (Moussa Sene Absa, Senegal, 1993), or even *Finzan* (Cheikh Oumar Sissoko, Mali, 1989) have made them some of the most talked about films in recent festivals.

Increasingly too, films are replacing muted references to romance and desire with more **open images of sexuality**, identity and interpersonal relationships. The comedy *Taafe Fanga* ("Skirt Power", Draba Adama, Mali, 1997) draws on a traditional Dogon tale to investigate gender roles and the status of women, themes also picked up in *Monday's Girls* (Ngozi Onwurah, Nigeria/UK, 1993), the story of two friends who have very different views about initiation rites in the Niger Delta. Just as radical in terms of challenging common taboos is the honest portrayal of gay love in *Dakan* (Mohammed Camara, Guinea, 1997) and in the documentary *Woubi Cheri* (Laurent Bocahut, Côte d'Ivoire/France, 1998).

Contemporary, almost hip, new social realist films commonly incorporate **popular music stars** in the scoring or acting – *Les Guerrisseurs* (Sijiri Bakaba, Côte d'Ivoire, 1988), for example, featured performances by Alpha Blondy, Salif Keita and Nayanka Bell, while *You Africa!* (Ndiouga Moctar Ba, Senegal, 1993) covered the West African Tour of musical superstar Youssou N'Dour. Still, there is a commitment to addressing societal malaise and the heroes are workers, women, or children – those commonly marginalized by the elites of modernity and tradition.

Another trend is towards **"return to source"** films, which re-examine African rural life. **Souleyman Cissé**, whose early works were highly political, embarked on this course with *Yeelen* (Mali, 1987) – a young boy's initiation journey that reveals the oral cultures and traditions of the Bamana, Dogon and Fulani. More recently, Burkina Faso's Idrissa Ouédraogo has been the most prominent proponent with films like *Tilai* (1990). Critics sometimes charge these films with aesthetic excess and with romanticizing village life. But adherents defend efforts to reclaim local history, religion and humanism, and to explore African value systems on their own terms, disregarding Western ethnocentric understandings.

Anti-colonial films also remain popular, as witnessed by Sembène's *Camp de Thiaroye* (Senegal, 1988), or Kwaw Ansah's *Heritage Africa* (Ghana, 1987). These films position viewers to identify with national and personal resistance to European political domination and cultural imperialism and to reconsider **history from the African perspective**. Recent films in this tradition also focus on post-independence regimes, calling into question "official" versions of national histories. David Aschkar thus probes the injustices of Sékou Touré's Guinea in *Allah Tanto* (Guinea, 1991), while in *Clando* (Cameroon, 1996) – a feature and follow-up to his documentary *Afrique, Je te Plummerai* (Cameroon, 1992) – Jean-Marie Teno investigates exploitation and repression in contemporary dictatorships.

SENEGAL

Senegalese directors – notably Ousmane Sembène, **Pape B Seck** (*Afrique sur Rhin*, 1984), **Djibril Diop Mambety** (*Touki Bouki* – a groundbreaking anti-modernization film from 1973 – and *La petite vendeuse de Soleil*, released just after his death in 1999), and one of the continent's first women film-makers, **Safi Faye** (*Lettre Paysan*, 1975; *Mossane*, 1991) – have relied heavily on the state for funds.

But film-makers have also attempted to diversify the image of African cinema through Le Collectif l'Oeil Vert, an association that aims at increasing co-operation between African film-makers and decreasing dependency on the state. The collective was founded by **Cheikh N'Gaido Bah** who advocates a greater commercialization of film and who cast box office draws like Jean-Paul Belmondo from France and Isaak de Bankolé from Côte d'Ivoire in *La Vie en Spirale*. Bah's film *Xew Xew* (1983) dealt with the popular culture of Senegalese music and featured well-known artists like Xalam and Youssou N'Dour. **Moussa Bathily** partly financed his popular film *Petits Blancs au Mainioc et à la Sauce Gombo* (1989) with personal savings and profits from his earlier films.

Senegalese film-makers were highly visible throughout the 1990s. At the 1993 FESPACO, **Ahmed Diallo** won the category for best short for *Boxumaleen* (1991), and **Mansour Sora Wade** (*Picc Mi*, 1991), Djibril Diop Mambety (*Hyenes*, 1991) and **Clarence Delgado** (*Niiwan*, 1988) were all honoured with special prizes. One of the most entertaining films of the period was by **Moussa Sene Absa** whose coming of age film, *Ça twiste à Poponguine* (1993), is a breezy but insightful look at identity, dreams and the way cultures overlap. His *Tableau Ferraille* (1997) is more in the tradition of Sembène's *Xala* in its view of the ways that modernization erodes traditional culture and development. Another well-known member of the new generation is **Amadou Seck**; his *Saaraba* (1988) – an indictment of a corrupt older generation – is already something of a classic in the neo-realist tradition.

MALI

The most famous name in Malian cinema is **Souleymane Cissé**, who studied film in the Soviet Union, before returning to Mali and launching his career (see box, overleaf). His first full-length feature, *Baara*, was followed by *Finyé* ("The Wind", 1982). This was filmed entirely in the Bamana language, yet became an international success, and was presented at Cannes, Carthage and Ouagadougou, where it won first prize.

Two other early Malian film-makers also received their training in the USSR – **Djibral Kouyaté** and **Kalifa Dienta**. Kouyaté was the first Malian to make a fiction film, *Le Retour de Tiéman* (1970) – the story of a young agriculturalist who runs into the resistance of traditionalists when he tries to implement modern methods in his village. Dienta is best known for his feature *A Banna*, in which the main character, Yadji, takes his new bride from Bamako to meet his family in the village. The clash between urban and rural val-

SOULEYMANE CISSÉ

Souleymane Cissé, from Mali, was trained, like Ousmane Sembène, at the famous Moscow film school. Since the early 1970s, he has been as prolific as Sembène and has made a good number of films which have gone on to commercial and critical success in Africa and Europe. Unlike Sembène, however, his craft always leads his message, not the other way round.

In addition to well-known early works like *Cinqs jours d'une vie* (1972) and *Baara* ("The Porter", 1977) – a full-length look at the relationship between workers and patron in a textile factory – he has made perhaps the two best films to come from Africa. In the first, *Finyé* ("The Wind", 1982), about the overweening pressures of seniority on youth, the wind symbolizes a new generation of post-independence youth, struggling against the repression of the military government. The second, *Yeelen* ("Brightness" 1986), at last saw his recognition as a major film-maker. Through the conflict of the main character, Nianankoro – an initiate possessed of magical powers – with his father, *Yeleen* looks at the conflict of generations in Africa and gives non-African moviegoers a spine-tingling insight into traditional values. With its deft visual impact and atemporality – and a deliberate ambiguity about the level of reality at which the images operate – the metaphysical world of the old West Africa comes alive and is as real as any drought or slave trade. For this lyricism – which made the film an art-house hit in the West – Cissé inevitably ran into criticism from those who would prefer a more realist cinema talking about exploitation, colonialism and repression. *Yeelen* went on to win the Grand Prix du Jury at the 1987 Cannes Film Festival.

Cissé's latest film, *Waati* (Mali/South Africa, 1994), is the epic story of Nandi, a South African girl living under apartheid. In her quest for freedom, she leaves her homeland and heads on a quest that takes her to Namibia, Mali and Côte d'Ivoire. As she passes from childhood to adulthood she discovers a continent in search of an identity.

ues comes into focus as Yadji's wife has to contend with everything from the authority of the griot to old-fashioned divisions between men and women.

Alkaly Kaba was another pioneer, best known for films portraying the conflict between Western and African worlds. Early films (1970s) in this vein include *Wallanda* and *Wamba*.

Sega Coulibaly comes from a new generation of film-makers whose experiences are rooted in post-independence society. Born in 1950, he briefly studied film in Paris before returning to Mali where he helped Kaba shoot *Wamba*. Coulibaly's first feature, *Mogho Dakan* (1976) follows a city teacher stationed in a village, whose success with women (because of his status), backfires when one of them gets pregnant. Coulibaly's second feature, *Kasso Den*, is all-action, a prisoner wrongly jailed seeking vengeance on the men who framed him. **Issa Falaba Traoré** gained recognition for *An Be Nodo* (1980), the story of a promising student. Too poor to continue her studies, she brings shame on her family when she drops out of school and becomes pregnant.

Cheik Oumar Sissoko emerged in the late 1980s as a new film-maker in the social realist tradition. An early documentary, *Rural Exodus* (1984) considered the plight of peasants displaced by drought, while *Nyamanton* ("Garbage Boys", 1986) focused on the condition of urban children. Sissoko gained international recognition for *Finzan* (1989), a fictional piece that uses the theme of genital excision to address wider social issues of women's rights and the struggle for freedom. Titles at the beginning of the film remind the viewer that women do two-thirds of the world's work, receive only one-tenth of the reward and only one percent of the property. Sissoko won the best picture award at the 1995 FESPACO for *Guimba*, the tale of a chief whose obsession for power drives him to make a dangerous pact with the devil. Sissoko describes the film as an allegory about the downfall of Malian president Amadou Traoré.

Another name to emerge in recent years is **Draba Adama**, whose film *Ta Dona* (1991) fuses elements of ancient mysticism and modern corruption. More recently, his *Taafe Fanga* ("Skirt Power", 1997) used a Dogon folk tale as a vehicle to poke fun at gender roles while making a serious comment about the status of African women. Of the same generation, **Mahamadou Cissé** is a novelist who shot his latest feature, *Waati*, in 1994.

GUINEA

Even under Sekou Touré, when cinema took on a propagandist role, Guinea produced some fine films, most notably *Naitou* (1982) by **Diakité Moussa Kemoko**. Featuring the Ballet National de Guinée, the film recounts an African folk tale exclusively through music and dance – a radical, and universally comprehensible, attempt to deal with the issue of appropriate language for African cinema.

Among the newer film-makers, **Mohammed Camara**, who trained as an actor, made an impressive entry at the 1993 FESPACO with a short, *Denko*. Camara tackles his difficult subject with sensitivity: a mother commits incest to restore sight to her blind son and reveals the hypocrisy of society through her transgression. Diving deeper into controversy, Camara's *Dakan* (1997), will forever be famous as the first film in sub-Saharan Africa to treat the subject of male homosexuality; filming was often interrupted by protests. **David Aschkar** also created a stir with his 1991 experimental documentary *Allah Tanto* – the story of the director's father, Maroff Aschkar, who was Guinea's ambassador to the United Nations until his imprisonment and death in one of Sekou Touré's infamous political prisons.

In a totally different vein, film historian and critic **Manthia Diawara**'s documentary *Rouch in Reverse* (1995) is an interesting analysis of one of the most influential ethnographic film-makers ever, and provides a rare look at European anthropological studies from an African perspective.

BURKINA FASO

The government of Upper Volta/Burkina Faso, has long been active in promoting the cinema in West Africa. To gain more control over the film industry, the country nationalized movie theatres in 1979, the first nation besides Guinea to do so. In its early days, the national film company helped finance mainly educational films. It also produced **Djim Mamadou Kola's** *Le Sang de Parias* (1971), the first national feature. Kola is still an active film-maker; his award-winning *Etrangers* was released in 1993.

In 1981, a private businessman, Martial Ouédraogo, invested in **CINAFRIC** – a production company with 16mm and 35mm cameras. The only private film company of its kind in Africa, CINAFRIC has been criticized as "Hollywood on the Volta", yet despite its commercial intent, it has helped free local film-makers from dependence on the West. Within a year, CINAFRIC produced its first feature, *Paweogo* (1981), and thus launched one of the country's most prolific film-makers, **Sanou Kollo**.

Burkina Faso was thrust into the spotlight by **Gaston Kaboré**, who won a French César in 1985 for *Wend Kuuni* – a rural tale that demonstrates how traditional values can heal a modern African state. A prominent figure in Burkinabe, and indeed in pan-African cinema (he is currently director of the Pan-African Federation of Film-makers), Kaboré has gone on to make numerous features including *Zan Boko* (1988) – about the problems of urbanization, its impact on people and their relationship to the environment – and *Rabi* (1991). His film *Buud Yam* (1996), a sequel to *Wend Kuuni*, won the grand prize at the 1997 FESPACO.

Idrissa Ouédraogo is probably the country's best known film-maker in the West. *Yaaba* (1988), *Tilai* (1990) and *Samba Traoré* (1992) are strongly rooted in the African rural experience, while *Kini and Adam* (1997) was a co-production shot on location in Zimbabwe with the collaboration of Zimbabwean and South African crew and cast – a kind of cross-continental collaboration that is becoming increasingly common.

Today, the government continues to be supportive and new film-makers continue to emerge. **Drissa Touré** was widely acclaimed for his first feature *Laada* (1991), while **Pierre Yameogo**'s *Wendemi* (1992) received several awards at the 1993 FESPACO. The son of a griot, **Dani Kouyaté** weaves the epic adventure of Soundjata with the present-day education of a young boy in *Keita* ("The Heritage of the Griot", 1995).

CÔTE D'IVOIRE

Many Ivoirian film-makers got their start in television, since the country had facilities as early as 1963, a good deal sooner than most neighbours. In 1964, **Timoté Bassori** made a short film for television, *Sur la Lune de la Solitude*, an adaptation of the popular Mamy Wata folk tale about the spirit of the waters. In the same year, **George Keita** directed *Korogo*, based on the national heroine Queen Poku. Many film historians regard this two-hour epic as the most important television film made in Africa to date.

Gnoan M'Bala also got his start directing short films for television. He was one of the earliest African directors to use comedy and satire in films such as *La Biche* (1971) – in which a woman pretends to be a married man's sister so that she can have an affair with him while living in the same house with his wife – and *Amanié* (1972), the story of a peasant who moves to the city and cons people into believing he's a rich diplomat. Some of M'Bala's recent films deal with more serious issues. His latest work, *Au Nom du Christ* (1992), received the award for best picture at the 1993 FESPACO.

The national film industry, however, didn't begin picking up steam until the late 1960s when a new name in Ivoirian film emerged. **Henri Duparc** was one of the early directors to receive support from the Société Ivoirienne du Cinéma (SIC). His first films were mainly documentaries, but in 1969 he directed his debut feature *Mouna, ou Le Rêve d'un Artiste*. In *Abusuan* ("The Family", 1972), Duparc probes the parasitic relationships in a family where a successful member's resources are drained by those who depend on him. In Europe, Duparc is best known for *Bal Poussière* (1988), a comic look at the patriarchal excesses of polygamy.

A few Ivoirian film-makers have managed to make pictures with little or no government support. **Lanciné Kramo Fadika** produced his first feature, *Djeli* (1981), with personal finances and borrowed money. The film – which considers the inequalities of traditional social hierarchies in Côte d'Ivoire – went on to win the best picture award at FESPACO. **Jean-Louis Koula** and **Leo Kozoloa** began their own production company, Les Films de la Montagne, in the late 1970s, though it's been mainly an advertising firm. The two have also produced their own documentaries: Koula's, *Adjo Tio* (1980), on traditional inheritance, and Kozoloa's *Petangin* (1983), on corruption.

More recently, **Sijiri Bakaba**, a prominent actor who appeared in dozens of regional films including Sembène's *Camp de Thiaroye*, directed *Les Guerrisseurs* (1988), a highly popular venture that featured stars of television and music. **Kitia Touré** has won acclaim for his feature *Ça n'arrive qu'ux autres* (1991), a film on AIDS.

NIGER

Nigérien cinema has been dominated by three film-makers. **Oumarou Ganda** began his career as an actor in Jean Rouch's *Moi, un Noir*, after he was discovered by the noted French *cineaste* on the docks in Abidjan. After appearing in other Rouch films, notably *La pyramide humaine*, he went on to become a film-maker in his own right and one of the great cultural archivists of African cinema, with works such as the autobiographical *Cabascabo, Wazzou polygame* (1971), *Saitane* (1973) – which looks critically at the authority of the Muslim marabouts – and *L'Exilé*. In 1981, he died unexpectedly at the age of 46, while filming his last work, *Gani Kouré, le vainqueur de Gourma*. Reflecting a distribution problem faced by most contemporary African film-makers, you're more likely to see his works abroad or possibly at Niamey's Franco-Nigérien Cultural Centre than in any ordinary Nigérien movie theatre.

Jean Rouch also inspired another relatively well-known film-maker, **Moustapha Alassane**. After studying at the Institut Nigérien de Recherche en Sciences Humaines, Alassane made a number of shorts, including *Aouré* (1962), and *La Bague du Roi Koda* (1963). His most famous feature film is *Femme, Villa, Voiture, Argent* (1972), a popular comedy dealing with the issue of cultural identity.

The third director to gain international acclaim is **Djingary Maïga**, producer of *l'Etoile Noire*, in which he also starred. Like many early African film-makers, Djingary's movies deal with the clash between Western values and traditional wisdom.

GHANA

The wave of productivity that swept the Francophone countries generally bypassed the English-speaking states, only two of which – Ghana and Nigeria – have gone beyond government-sponsored documentaries to create an independent cinema. In Ghana, independent film-makers began producing features that combined comedy and melodrama.

Ghana is the best equipped of the West African states and the government branches of the film industry have left their mark on some of the country's top film-makers. The documentary style of the state-run Ghana Film Industry Corporation, for example, has influenced the style of such well-known directors as **Sam Aryete** (*No Tears for Ananse*, 1968), **King Ampaw** (*They Call It Love*, 1972; *Kukurantumi*, 1983; *Juju*, 1986), **Kwate Nee Owo** (*You Hide Me*, 1971; *Struggle for Zimbabwe*, 1974; *Angela Davis*,

1976), and **Kwaw Ansah** (*Love Brewed in the African Pot*, 1981).

Ghana's film industry does not rely on state funding and some of the best-known film-makers finance their projects through local and international backing. Kwaw Ansah, for example, produced his latest film, *Heritage Africa* – which won the grand prize at the 1989 FESPACO – with the backing of the Ghana Commercial Bank, the National Investment Bank and other financial institutions. The films of these more independent directors have produced a good box-office return both in and outside Ghana. *Love Brewed in the African Pot*, for example, conveys its narrative through musical performances, wedding ceremonies and sports events – all popular with African audiences – and drew record attendances not only in Ghana, but also in Sierra Leone, Liberia, Kenya and Nigeria.

NIGERIA

Francis Oladele was one of the producers of Nigeria's first film, *Kongi's Harvest*, based on the play by Wole Soyinka. He also co-produced *Bullfrog in the Sun*, adapted from Chinua Achebe's novels *Things Fall Apart* and *No Longer at Ease*. Because of the sensitive political subject matter, this latter film was never properly distributed in Nigeria.

The director **Eddie Ugbomah** also draws his inspiration from current political events but turns them into Hollywood-style popular movies. In *The Rise and Fall of Dr Oyenusi* (1977), he considers the true story of a Lagos gangster who was arrested and publicly executed in the early 1970s. *The Mask* (1979) follows the adventures of a Nigerian secret agent sent to Britain to take back a Benin mask stolen by the British and housed in a London museum. *The Death of a Black President* (1983) treated the events that led to the traumatizing assassination of the popular General Murtala Muhammed.

Other Nigerian directors include the late **Hubert Ogunde** whose films, such as *Aiye* (with Ola Balogun) and its sequel *Jaiyesinmi*, often deal with witchcraft or with the significance of tradition. Ogunde set up a "film village" at Ijebu Ososa near Lagos, to encourage Nigerian film-makers. And in the field of comedy, **Moses Olaiya** – better known as Baba-Sala – moved into film from Nigerian music and TV and made a name for himself with films like *Orun Mooru* ("It's not easy") and *Mosebolatan* ("I thought my wealth was finished").

The most prolific film-maker in West Africa is Nigeria's **Ola Balogun**, who has released a steady stream of documentaries and feature films since the early 1970s. His 1975 production of *Amadi* was the first film in the Igbo language, while the 1976 *Ajani Ogun* was the first in Yoruba.

Yoruba cinema emerged in the early 1970s out of the Yoruba theatre tradition (see p.930). Its success was partly due to the huge home market – over twenty million Yoruba-speaking Nigerians in the southwest of the country – though films in mother-tongue languages are still a novelty in Africa. In 1978, Balogun's film, *Black Goddess*, dealt with the African-Brazilians who returned to Nigeria after being freed from slavery. But some of Balogun's biggest hits in Nigeria draw their inspiration directly from Yoruba popular theatre. In 1976, *Ajani Ogun* starred one of the country's top theatre performers, **Ade Folayan**, in a story about a young man who runs up against a conniving rich buffoon as he struggles to keep both his fiancée and his inheritance. The popularity of *Ajani Ogun* led to *Ija Ominira* (1977), a tale of a tyrannical king in which Ade Folayan again starred. Outside Africa, films such as *Cry Freedom* (1981) and *Money Power* (1982) secured Balogun's international reputation.

CAMEROON

Jean-Paul Ngassa was one of the pioneers of Cameroonian cinema with his production of *Aventures en France* in 1962, followed by *La Grand Case Bamilékeé* in 1965. After *Une Nation est Née*, in 1970, Cameroonian production went into a lull until **Daniel Kamwa** brought a new spark with his 1972 prize-winning short *Boubou Cravatte*. The 1977 production of *Pousse Pousse* – a comical look at the conflict between traditional customs and modern urban lifestyles as expressed through the issue of bride price – established him as a producer with wide public appeal, even if the movie got a mediocre reception in Europe. *Pousse Pousse* was seen by some 700,000 moviegoers, making it one of the most popular African films of the period. The success was followed by *Notre Fille* in 1980.

During the same period **Jean Pierre Dikongue-Pipa** began making waves. *Muno Moto*, made in 1975, won encouraging reviews in France although it was hardly as popular at home as *Pousse Pousse*. Pipa's other productions include *Prix de la Liberté* (1978), *Badiaga* (1983) and *Music Music* (1983).

Although Kamwa and Dikongue-Pipa are still the best-known Cameroonian producer/directors, a new generation seems to be emerging. After studying at the Ecole Supérieure d'Etudes Cinématographiques in Paris, **Louis Balthazar Amadangoleda** made his first full-length film, *Les trois petits cireurs*, in 1985. Based on the novel of the same name by Francis Bebey, it looks at delinquency and its consequences.

A former professor of literature, **Arthur Si Bita** turned to film in 1978 and made a couple of shorts, including *No Time to Say Goodbye*, shot in Ouagadougou. His first feature-length film, *Les Cooperants*, traces the adventures of six youths from the city who decide to return to the village.

With his first feature-length film, *L'Appat du Gain* (1982), **Jules Takam** breaks away from common themes of bride price, marriage and traditional custom and offers instead a fast-paced political intrigue based in Paris.

Jean-Claude Tchuilen came out with a promising first feature film in 1984 – *Suicides* – a well-paced psycho-drama, also set in Paris. It was banned for being inflammatory when first released in Cameroon and never bounced back commercially after the ban was lifted.

Of the new generation, **Jean-Marie Teno** has emerged as the most internationally recognized. Early shorts – *Schubbah* (1984), *Hommage* (1985) and *La caresse et la gifle* (1987) – earned him acclaim, but his feature, *Afrique, Je te Plummerai* (1991), thrust him into the spotlight. His follow-up to that documentary on the abuses of the Biya government, *Clando* (1996), treats similar themes of corruption and chaos in modern Africa through the story of a black-market cab driver whose scrapes with the law lead him on a journey to Germany, and back.

Also well known is **Bassek ba Kobhio**, whose *Sango Malo* (1991) examines a rural teacher's struggle to replace a strict and inappropriate European curriculum with education that the villagers can use to build a self-reliant community and shape their own future. He takes a revisionist view of Albert Schweizer in *Le Grand Blanc de Lambarene* (1995), shot on location in Gabon, the site of the doctor's hospital.

Finally, **Jean-Pierre Bekolo** directed his first feature, *Quartier Mozart* (1992), at the age of 25. The imaginative story treats a young girl with magical gifts who transforms herself into a virile male, Mister Guy, and has a lot of fun with gender roles in the process. Bekolo's background in music video, producing and directing for the likes of Manu Dibango, is on show with his quick and unconventional camera work.

RECOMMENDED FILMS

The following filmography provides a good overview of the styles and interests of African film-makers over the last four decades.

Moussa Sene Absa *Ça twiste à Poponguine* (Senegal, 1993). Feel-good coming-of-age story set in a Senegalese fishing village. Compare with the sharp political criticism of his follow-up, *Tableau Ferraille* (1997).

Kwaw P. Ansah *Love Brewed in the African Pot* (Ghana, 1981). In English. Comedy, social satire and commercial success – a big hit across Anglophone Africa.

Ola Balogun *Ajani Ogun* (Nigeria, 1976). In Yoruba. A comedy, based on a man's struggle to keep both his inheritance and his fiancée, derived from Yoruba theatre.

Jean-Pierre Bekolo *Quartier Mozart* (Cameroon, 1992). New social realism, upbeat and hip, with a style influenced by both oral tradition and music video.

Ferid Boughedir *Camera d'Afrique: 20 Years of African Cinema* (Morocco, 1983). A valuable documentary and early evaluation of film on the continent. Contains interviews with Ola Balogun, Oumarou Ganda, Souleymane Cissé, Gaston Kaboré, Ousmane Sembène and others, along with extracts of important films.

Mohammed Camara *Dakan* ("Destiny", Guinea, 1997). In French with English subtitles. The first film to treat homosexuality in sub-Saharan Africa.

Souleymane Cissé *Yeelen* ("Brightness", Mali, 1987). In Bamana with English subtitles. A coming-of-age story rooted in oral tradition.

Henri Duparc *Bal Poussière* (Côte d'Ivoire, 1988). A comic investigation of polygamy's social consequences.

Gaston Kaboré *Wend Kuuni* (Burkina, 1982). In the More language with English subtitles. Portrays a boy's traumatic experiences after losing his family. *Zan Boko* ("Homeland", 1988), in More with English subtitles, shows how modern culture subverts traditional society.

Djibril Diop Mambety *Touki Bouki* ("The Hyena's Journey", Senegal, 1973). In Wolof with English subtitles. An avant-garde film that remains true to the narrative structure of traditional storytelling while breaking the conventions of film structure.

Idrissa Ouédraogo *Yaaba* (Burkina, 1988). In the More language. A classic of the "back to the roots" genre.

Ousmane Sembène *Mandabi* ("The Money Order", Senegal, 1968). The first West African film to be distributed commercially outside Africa, this film marks the beginning of an era. *Xala* (1974) in French and Wolof, is an allegorical tale of corruption that succinctly combines many important motifs of African film.

Cheik Oumar Sissoko *Finzan* ("A Dance for the Heroes", Mali, 1989). In Bamana with English subtitles. Socially engaged storytelling dedicated to the status of African women. *Guimba* (Mali, 1994) is an award-winning film about power and arrogance.

BOOKS AND JOURNALS

Ecrans d'Afrique (International Quarterly of African Film, COE, Communicazione & Media, via Lazaroni 8, 20124 Milan, Italy). The official publication of the Pan-African Federation of Film-makers, in French with full English translations.

Manthia Diawara *African Cinema: Politics and Culture* (Indiana UP, 1992). One of the leading voices in African film criticism outlines the key figures in African cinema, their works, and the complex relationship between politics, economics, and culture.

MUSIC IN WEST AFRICA: AN INTRODUCTION TO THE FEAST

Nowhere in the world can match the rhythm, melody and musical colour of West Africa. You can hardly fail to come back with at least one tune in your head, and probably a handful of tapes in your luggage. The question is: where to start?

You'll usually hear the cassette stalls when you arrive in any town, and if you want to meet local musicians you'll often find artists glad to play if you can pay something. Your interest may surprise people, so let them know.

Notices about dances and concerts are often posted up but they're most likely to take place around the end of the month – when people have some money in their pockets – and at public holidays, epecially Christmas and Muslim feasts.

This introduction to West African music kicks off with a section on **Manding** (or Mande) music, the sound of much of the western part of West Africa, particularly Mali and Guinea. This is followed by short pieces on **Tuareg**, **Hausa** and **Fula** music. These, like influential Manding, easily transcend national boundaries. There then follows a country-by-country roundup of national styles and artists, of Mauritania, Senegal and The Gambia, Guinea-Bissau, Côte d'Ivoire, Burkina Faso, Ghana, Togo, Benin, Niger, Nigeria, Cameroon, Sierra Leone and Liberia. For much fuller accounts, see the second edition of the *Rough Guide to World Music, Vol 1*, which has articles on all these countries and more.

The division in several of the country sections into "folk" (or "traditional") and "modern" categories is somewhat arbitrary – and much of what you might hear played by local musicians is likely to fall somewhere in between – but it serves as a useful cut-off point. "Folk", embedded in traditional society, whose artists don't as a rule have record deals or tour Europe, includes much that's disappearing; "modern" includes the whole gamut of recording artists, most with devoted local followings. But it also includes a number of styles and performers tearing away from their roots in the attempt to present music that stands alone.

THE REALM OF MANDING MUSIC

"Manding" music is about sweet melodies and hypnotic rhythms. You'll find this broad genre from The Gambia to Mali and down through Guinea – an area roughly corresponding to the spread of the Mande languages. The music of the Mande-speaking peoples (the Malinké, Mandinka and a number of others; see p.81) is largely untouched by Western influences and has a swingalong quality, to which you can either dance or daydream.

Manding musicians are easy enough to track down. Only certain families – notably Konté or Konteh, Kouyaté or Kuyateh and Diabaté or Jobarteh (note the French/English variations) carry the title of **jeli** or hereditary musician, often called a **griot** in French. They have been around since at least the thirteenth-century origins of the Mali empire, based in the northeast of what is now Guinea, under Emperor **Sundiata Keita**. Traditionally, the **kora** – a harp-lute – and most other instruments are restricted to them.

A jeli's reputation is built upon humility and correct behaviour as well as his (or her) knowledge of history and family genealogies. Originally, the job was to do with the preservation of oral history. Mostly, this meant singing the praises of the noble and wealthy (no occasion – a wedding or child-naming ceremony for example – would be complete without a jeli), but now they're just as likely to have business or civil service patrons. Jelis, moreover, are personalities who have the ears of the people and any corrupt politician or civil servant has to reckon with them.

Releases available on CD are marked ⓒ. Otherwise, the entry is only available on vinyl or, more commonly, cassette.

Jelis call on a great **repertoire of songs**. If you have the chance to hear a number of artists, however, you'll start to recognize lyrical variations on common melodic themes. Old classics like "Sundiata Faso", "Tutu Jara", "Lambang", "Koulanjan", "Duga", "Tara" and "Sori" are heard time and time again, interspersed with songs from this century, often with a regional flavour, such as "Alla I'aa ke" from The Gambia and "Kaira" from Mali. A jeli's skill lies in the improvised flourishes and ornamentation – the *birim-intingo* – that he brings to the recurrent theme or core melody, called the *donkili*.

In Mande-speaking society **men** always play the instruments. **Women artists** are considered the better singers and often receive extraordinary gifts, especially in Mali – even planes and houses aren't unknown. Even at "ordinary" live shows, women commonly receive gold. Moved by a particular song, people in the audience just shed their jewellery there and then.

Traditional Manding music is a lasting influence on the modern music of Mali and Guinea. **Mory Kanté**, **Salif Keita** and **Kasse Mady** all derive artistic sustenance from it, and popular bands like **Bembeya Jazz** and **Les Amazones** reinterpret Manding songs.

THE MANDING JELIS

Some of the great jelis of the Manding region are introduced below, though there are many other, almost equally famous, kora musicians and female singers.

Alhaji Bai Konteh

One of The Gambia's most revered jelis, an exponent of Casamance-style kora, with bluesy tuning and lightning-fast variations.

 ⓒ *Alhaji Bai Konteh* (Rounder, US). Atmospheric 1972 recordings made at the Konteh home in Brikama.

Dembo Konteh and Kausu Kouyaté

Although there are hundreds of wonderful jelis in the region, Alhaji Bai's son Dembo and his Casamançais brother-in-law, Kausu are, after numerous tours, probably the best known overseas.

 ⓒ *Kairaba Jabi* (Rogue, UK). Duets and songs in deep Casamance style. Highlights of two previous albums.

 ⓒ *Jeliology* (Rogue, UK). The duo meet up with Mawdo Suso on balafon. Sterling stuff.

Sidiki Diabaté

From Mali, Sidiki toured with his ensemble in 1987, when they recorded a beautiful LP, *Ba Togoma*, which features the talents of **Kandia Kouyaté, Djelimadi Sissoko, Mariama Kouyaté** and Sidiki's son, **Toumani** – who has also made a name for himself as a soloist.

Batourou Kouyaté

Probably the most famous of all Malian kora players, born in about 1920 in Kita. Entirely self-taught, he evolved a unique, highly staccato style and went on to make his reputation as the accompanist to the singer Fanta Damba.

 ⓒ *Cordes Anciennes* (Barenreiter Musicaphon, Germany). Classic 1970 recording of Sidiki Diabaté, Batourou Kouyaté and Djelimadi Sissoko, featuring rippling instrumentals by these legendary figures. A privileged view into the past.

Toumani Diabaté

Mali's brilliant young kora virtuoso. An ambitious and highly creative artist and probably the best young kora player around at the present time.

 ⓒ *Kaira* (Hannibal, UK). Instrumental solo kora music at its finest, including melodies like "Alla I'aa ke" and "Jarabi". Toumani has worked widely with non-African musicians, including the unconventional flamenco band, Ketama, and Danny Thompson on *Songhai* and *Songhai 2*.

 ⓒ *New Ancient Strings* (Hannibal, UK). With Ballaké Sissoko. Instrumental kora duets recorded in Mali on state-of-the-art equipment, showing the extraordinary artistry of these two young cousins following in their legendary fathers' footsteps.

Jali Musa Jawara

Mory Kanté's kora-playing half-brother leads an excellent, all-acoustic ensemble, who made one of the all-time classic African albums, repeatedly re-released under different titles.

 ⓒ *Yasimika* (Hannibal, UK). Superbly ethereal, flowing music on guitars, kora and balafon, with luscious choruses from Djanka Diabaté and Djenne Doumbia and soaring vocals from Jali Musa himself. Recorded in Abidjan in 1983, this is one of the classics of Manding acoustic music and nothing he's done since has matched it. Previously released as *Jali Musa Jawara* (Tangent, France), as *Fote Mogoban* (Oval, UK) and *Direct from West Africa* (Go Discs, UK).

Kandia Kouyaté

"La dangéreuse" has a stunning stage presence and has been Mali's top jelimuso for the past two decades. Her forceful voice and choral arrangements and her working of traditional social and court music has earned her huge wealth and a status unequalled by any other female artist from Mali.

⦿ *Kita Kan* (Stern's, UK). Kandia's first international release. The kora, ngoni, guitars and balafon xylophones just keep on rolling and there are enough lush studio effects – and even full orchestral backing – to qualify *Kita Kan* for any number of radio playlists.

Tata Bambo Kouyaté

One of Mali's leading female vocalists, Tata Bambo claims that everything she has – and she has a lot – came to her because of her voice. She's one of the new breed of jalis who travel between patrons with a portable PA system.

⦿ *Jatigui* (GlobeStyle, UK). Stunning praise-singing from 1985 by one of Mali's most accomplished female artists. Entirely acoustic accompaniment from the full range of instruments, plus Fulani flute.

MODERN MALIAN MUSIC

Mali's music is steeped in tradition. Even in the modern popular music there's very little influence from cultures outside Mali. The musics of the Mande-speaking Bamana and Malinké, the Fula, the Songhai and the Dogon have all helped to give today's Malian music its flavour and colour.

After **independence**, there was a renaissance of popular music in Mali. The bands, who had for many years been playing latin styles, became aware that people wanted to hear music from their own cultures. The government supported this search for roots and a number of groups received state sponsorship. Orchestras were at last able to afford modern instruments. "Janfa", a popular song of the time, recorded by the **Orchestre National Formation "A"**, made a plea to people not to betray their traditions.

One of the most famous venues in Mali is the **Buffet Hôtel de la Gare** in Bamako, a venue which emerged from the hotel's quest for financial salvation. The director of Mali's state railway in the 1960s, **Djibril Diallo**, was a big music fan, or *melomane*, and decided to create a station orchestra. The *Buffet Hôtel* soon became the hottest spot in Bamako and the **Rail Band**, as they

became known, rapidly acquired legendary status, mixing plaintive vocal styles over traditional Manding rhythms played with electric instruments.

Over the years the Rail Band – still going today – has provided a launch pad for many talented musicians, including **Salif Keita** and **Mory Kanté**.

Salif Keita

Now a major international star, his first album, *Soro*, has sold more than 200,000 copies in Europe alone. An albino, Salif Keita started out singing in bars for loose change, evidently to the disgrace of his family. In 1970 he joined the Rail Band, which gave him an opportunity to modernize traditional songs. After being ousted from the *Buffet Hôtel* by the then balafon (xylophone) player Mory Kanté, Salif joined the Ambassadeurs – who had immediate success with hits like "Primpin" – and recorded three albums for Safari Ambience. In 1978 he moved to Abidjan and, with Kanté Manfila, formed Ambassadeurs Internationaux, who recorded the wonderful song "Mandjou" – dedicated, ironically, to the despotic ruler of Guinea, Sekou Touré. Then he left for Paris and international stardom.

⦿ *Soro* (Stern's, UK; Mango, US). One of the biggest selling African recordings ever – outside the continent – and one of the greatest successes of world music. Breathtaking and seamless high-tech arrangements of Manding music with contributions from guitarist Ousmane Kouyaté and French keyboard player Jean-Philippe Rykiel, the perfect backdrop to some extraordinary vocals.

⦿ *Folon: The Past* (Mango, UK). More spontaneous and funky than anything he'd done since Ambassadeurs, this went back to Salif's roots in Manding culture with stunning melodies and vocals. Plus a new more jazzy version of "Mandjou".

⦿ *The Mansa of Mali... a Retrospective* (Mango, UK). Includes highlights from his three Mango releases, plus the all-time hit from 1978 with Les Ambassadeurs: "Mandjou". Worth getting the album just for this – one of the finest Manding praise songs ever, with remarkable guitar solos from Ousmane Kouyaté and soaring, passionate vocals from Salif.

⦿ *Papa* (Metro Blue/Blue Note, France). The 1999 album, recorded in Paris, New York and Keita's own Studio Wanda in Bamako, holds few surprises in its high-tech production values and diverse credits. A deep strand of melancholy runs through this album, even on the bright "Tolon Willy" (The Party's On), where Grace Jones adds a dark tone.

Habib Koité and Bamada

A fast-rising singer-songwriter, the jeli Koité goes well beyond Bamana praise songs to include traditions from across Mali.

ⓒ *Maya* (Putumayo, UK). Koité's first international release with his band puts his acoustic guitar to the fore and uses no synths, delivering a subtle and intriguing set of songs with a folkloric sensitivity to subject matter and roots. Fans of Senegal's Ismael Lô will like this a lot.

Kasse Mady Diabaté

Arguably the best contemporary Mande voice, Kasse Mady Diabaté rivals Salif Keita for beauty and lyricism, but is absolutely rooted in the jeli tradition. He made his name playing with National Badema for twelve years. Kela, where he was born, is a Malinké village in western Mali, almost entirely inhabited by jelis of the Diabaté family.

ⓒ *Kela Tradition* (Stern's, UK). An almost entirely acoustic studio-produced album, featuring ngoni and balafon as well as guitars and Jean-Philippe Rykiel on keyboards. Long, expansive and gorgeous versions of Mande classics like "Koulandjan" and "Kaira". Essential.

Super Biton de Ségou

Around since the early 1960s, when they were one of the state-payrolled regional bands under the leadership of trumpeter Amadu Ba, Super Biton de Ségou successfully pioneered the transfer of the Bamana variant of the Manding sound onto guitars and horns.

ⓒ *Afro-Jazz du Mali* (Bolibana, France). Hard-driving dance rhythms powerfully translated onto guitars and horns create an exciting departure from the more stately Maninka tradition of the likes of Salif Keita. Early 1980s recordings.

Ali Farka Touré

Not from one of the traditional families of hereditary musicians, Ali Farka Touré started playing purely for his own pleasure and doing so in a style which – although he had never heard the blues until he was already firmly established – resonates with American blues affinities. Deeply spiritual, he caused a sensation when he first came to Europe in the late 1980s.

ⓒ *Talking Timbuktu* (World Circuit, UK). A world music record out of left field that actually sounds like people (including Ry Cooder) playing together in a room – a miracle of 1994 and top of many of the indie charts within days of release.

ⓒ *Radio Mali* (World Circuit, UK). Beautifully produced compilation of radio recordings in Ali's swinging, bluesy style, made from 1970–78, a decade or more before he achieved international recognition, and at a time when, as he says, "I was an absolute fool for the guitar".

ⓒ *Niafunké* (World Circuit, UK). Recorded in AFT's home town, this is a determined return to roots in every sense, allowing the world to hear Ali doing his wonderful stuff in his own backyard. The relaxed, but impromptu nature of every track bursts out. "I don't feel as good anywhere else as I do at home" is Ali's explanation. The result is a formidable work.

GUINEA FOLK MUSIC

Traditional music in Guinea can be roughly divided into four areas. In the lowland coastal forest of the west the musics of the Mande-speaking Susu and Jalonke are related to the Manding tradition. The Fouta Djalon highlands of the centre and north are mainly inhabited by the Fula (see separate account). In the northern Fouta Djalon, near the frontier with Senegal, the Konyagi people play a variety of wind instruments, including long, bamboo flutes, short flutes (usually played in pairs), and a stick-zither, similar to a mouth bow.

The eastern savannah, towards the Niger River, is mainly occupied by the **Malinké**, whose cultural domain spreads into eastern Mali. But the Guinean Malinké use a number of instruments not usually associated with Manding tradition (though possibly more traditional, as this is the area where the Mali empire first emerged) including **slit-drums** (usually a hollowed log with a single longitudinal gash). **Ground bows** (in which a hollow in the earth acts as the soundbox, are now only used as child's toys.

In Guinea's southeast highland forest region the **Kissi**, **Toma**, **Guerze** and **Kono** use single- and double-headed drums, slit-drums and xylophone-drums. Xylophone-drums are made either from hollowed logs or from bamboo stems, slit to produce vibrating "keys" of different lengths.

MODERN GUINEAN MUSIC

With independence in 1958 and Sékou Touré's *authenticité* campaign, the government actively encouraged the development of modern musical styles, based on traditional music, but using electric instruments. Local radio was directed to play authentic Guinean music, and state-sponsored national festivals became a focus for the new Guinean sound.

Many new bands were formed, including **Bembeya Jazz**, **Les Balladins** and **Les Amazones**. The Guinean label, Syliphone, re-issued some of these albums in the late 1980s. Three well worth listening to are the **Tropical Djoli Band**, **Orchestre Nimba Jazz** and, especially, **Tele-Jazz de Télimélé**.

Balla et ses Balladins

One of Guinea's best ever bands, superbly modernizing deep Maninka songs.

⊙ *Reminiscin' in tempo with Balla et ses Balladins* (Popular African Music, Germany). Compilation of greats with the classic Guinea-rumba sound of the 1960s and 1970s, including two stunning versions of one of the greatest Mande love songs, "Sara".

Bembeya Jazz

Formed in 1961 by singer Aboubacar Demba Camera, Guinea's greatest band of the post-independence era mixed Malinké praise songs with Congolese musical threads and Islamic traditions with Cuban rumba. The death in 1973 of Aboubacar Camera robbed Africa of one of its greatest singers. The band is now led by lead guitarist, Sekou "diamond fingers" Diabaté. Still the country's defining musical export.

⊙ *Live – 10 Ans de Succès* (Bolibana, France). Atmospheric recording from 1971 of Guinea's most famous band at their finest hour.

TRADITIONAL INSTRUMENTS OF WESTERN WEST AFRICA

MANDING INSTRUMENTS

Kora 21- to 25-stringed harp-lute made with a large decorated half-gourd covered with a skin. The strings – which used to be twisted leather, but tend now to be various gauges of fishing line – are attached with leather thongs to a rosewood pole put through the gourd. The top of the body has a large sound hole that doubles as a collection point for money from the audience.

Balo Rosewood xylophone with between 17 and 20 keys, known to have been around since the fourteenth century.

Kontingo Small, oval lute with 5 strings.

Bolom (or *bolombato*) Lute with 3 or 4 strings and an arched neck that used to be played for warriors going into battle. It's now an instrument played by men who are not of a jeli family.

MAURITANIAN INSTRUMENTS

Tidinit Lute with 2 long strings on which the melody is played, and 2 short ones which give a fixed drone-like rhythm; played by men.

Ardin 10- to 14-stringed women's harp.

Tbol Large kettledrum.

Daghumma Slender, hollowed-out gourd with a necklace, which acts as a rattle.

SENEGAMBIAN INSTRUMENTS

The most widespread instruments are plucked **lutes**, known generically in Wolof as *khalem* or *xalam*.

Molo The most common variety, a single-string lute with a half-gourd, skin-covered soundbox.

Diassare 5-stringed, roughly boat-shaped, lute with a carved wooden soundbox.

Bappe and **ndere**, often played as a pair, are similar to the *diassare*.

Riti Single-stringed Wolof lute played with a bow.

Gnagnour The Tukulor *riti*.

Paly-yela Sets of gourds of different shapes and sizes, bumped on the ground to produce different notes and tones to accompany Tukulor women's songs.

Tama Small, hourglass-shaped talking drum, which produces an amazing series of tones.

Sabar Large, freestanding cylindrical drums.

Wild solos from Diabaté measure up to the unforgettable voice of Aboubacar Demba Camera.

ⓒ *Bembeya Jazz National* (Sonodisc/Esperance, France). Bembeya in the mid-1980s with their classic recording of "Lanaya", featuring the romantic voice of Sekouba Bambino.

Mory Kanté

Started playing music at the age of seven, later joining the Rail Band in Bamako before embarking on a hugely successful solo career playing what he describes as kora-funk. Loathed by purists, his music has a global village feel that makes him a star of the world stage. He still plays the occasional solo kora piece as part of his stage show and he played the instrument on Kanté Manfila's *Tradition*.

ⓒ *10 Cola Nuts* (Barclay, France). Heavy on the drum kit and synth, but this includes some fine material, including the beautiful "Teriya".

ⓒ *Akwaba Beach* (Barclays, France). Kanté's breakthrough album, with his worldwide hit "Yeke yeke". High-tech kora music for the dance floor.

ⓒ *Tatebola* (Arcade/Missliin, France). The latest from Mory is still driven by techno rhythms but in slightly more mellow mode, with a lovely version of the classic kora song "Alla l'aa ke".

Kanté Manfila (aka Manfila Kanté)

The guitar wizard of the Ambassadeurs, and one of Africa's most innovative guitarists.

ⓒ *Tradition* (Celluloid, France). Gorgeous rolling acoustic melodies from Kankan with guitars and balafon, and kora accompaniment by cousin Mory Kanté.

ⓒ *Diniya* (Celluloid, France). Some fine melodies buried underneath a full-blown, high-tech production.

ⓒ *Kankan Blues* (Popular African Music, Germany). Probably the best of the acoustic offerings on PAM.

TUAREG FOLK MUSIC

The Tuareg have put up with a somewhat embattled existence over the past decade. Drought in the early 1980s pushed them away from a nomadic lifestyle and towards the towns at the edge of the desert. And then in the early 1990s a simmering Tuareg uprising boiled over against the military regimes in Mali and Niger.

Although Tuareg men and women both make music, they have separate forms and styles.

Women's songs include **tinde nomnas** (praise songs), **tinde nguma** (songs of exorcism) and **ezele** (dance songs). The **tinde**, used to accompany women's songs, is a drum made from a goatskin stretched over a mortar.

Other instruments used by women include the **assakhalebo** water drum, made from a half-gourd floating upside down in a bowl of water, and the **tabl** – a kettledrum (traditionally a battle drum) with a broad camel-skin top.

The men's songs, or **tichiwe**, are, in striking contrast to the women's, essentially lyrical. They sing about the beauty of the women they love or celebrate some happy event. The songs are performed by soloists – whose virtuosity lies as ever in improvization – either with or without an accompaniment. This is usually provided by a single-stringed fiddle, the **inzad**, which consists of a half-gourd, goatskin-covered resonator and a horsehair string stretched over a bridge in the form of a small wooden cross.

The Tuareg also use an end-blown **flute**, called the *sarewa*, constructed from a sorghum stem in which four holes are made, with leather thongs tied round its body for ornamentation and protection.

HAUSA MUSIC

The Hausa, whose communities are concentrated in the cities of Niger and northern Nigeria, have spread right across West and Central Africa, setting up shops in the smallest towns, content to live among strangers. They have long been famous for their art and music which has flourished since the sixteenth century and the fall of the Songhai empire, with whose music Hausa has many parallels.

Hausa music splits into **urban music** of the court and state, and **rural music**. State ceremonial music – *rokon fada* – still plays a great part (though not a very musical one) in Hausa traditions, while court praise singers still play for the amusement of emirs and sultans, usually in private. The emirates of **Katsina** and **Kano** together with the sultanate of **Sokoto**, and to a lesser extent **Zaria** and **Bauchi** (all in Nigeria), are the major creative centres.

The instruments of **ceremonial music** are largely seen as prestige symbols of authority, and ceremonial musicians tend to be chosen for their family connections rather than any musical ability: they don't present the most dulcet of tones.

Court musicians, on the other hand, are always chosen for their musical skills. Exclusively dependent on a single wealthy patron, it's hardly surprising that the most talented players are rarely seen in public. The greatest praise singer was **Narambad**, who lived and worked in Sokoto in northwest Nigeria; he died in 1960 and it's doubtful if you can still get his recordings.

The most impressive of the state **instruments** is the elongated state trumpet called **kakakai**, which was originally used by the Songhai cavalry and was taken up by the rising Hausa states as a symbol of military power. Kakakai are usually accompanied by **tambura**, large state drums. Lesser instruments include the **farai**, a small double-reed woodwind instrument, the **kafo**, an animal horn, and the **ganga**, a small snare drum. Ceremonial music can always be heard at the **sara**, the weekly statement of authority which takes place outside the emir's palace on a Thursday evening.

The principal instruments accompanying praise songs are percussive – small kettledrums, **banga** and **tabshi**, and talking drums, **jauje** and **kotso**.

Traditional **rural music** appears to be dying out in favour of modern popular music which still draws inspiration from the traditional roots. The last expressions of rural music are to be found in traditional dances like the **asauwara**, for young girls, and the **bori**, the dance of the spirit possession cult, which dates back to a time before Islam became the accepted religion and continues to thrive parallel with the teachings of the Koran. Zaria is the main stronghold of the bori.

Popular music thrives in town and countryside and although very little seems to be of interest outside Hausaland, musicians can still make a good living satisfying local needs and, as ever, expressing, and sometimes moulding, public opinion. The leading Hausa singer, **Muhamman Shata**, is always accompanied by a troupe of virtuoso drummers who play **kalangu**, small talking drums. There's a fair number of other worthy artists such as **Dan Maraya**, leading exponent on the kontigi one-stringed lute, **Ibrahim Na Habu**, who popularized a type of small fiddle called the **kukkuma**, and **Audo Yaron Goge** who plays the goge or fiddle.

Saadou Bori and Moussa Pousy

Two singer-songwriters who worked together in the Nigérien national music school's house band, Takeda, in Niamey, Saadou Bori and Moussa

Pousy went on to bigger things in Abidjan. Both have spiritual backgrounds: Hausa-speaker Saadou Bori is a practitioner of *dango* (Hausa spirit music) and trance-dancing.

⊙ *Niamey Twice* (Stern's, UK). A double helping of modern Niger, recorded in Abidjan under the direction of Ibrahima Sylla. Six original compositions from each singer swing along happily. The music of Saadou "Bori" (his nickname acquired for his Nigérien hit of the same name, after the traditional Hausa spirit possession cult of Bori) is more interesting than Moussa Pousy's, for its rare presentation of Hausa influences, and on the more offbeat numbers – "Dango" and "Bori" itself – the spirit-loving polyrhythms bubble through frenetically.

FULA MUSIC

The Fula are commonly called Fulani in Nigeria where they form a large and powerful community. This name has tended to be used as the standard form in English. The same people, however, are Fullah in Sierra Leone, Peul or Peulh in Senegal and Mali, and Pulaar in Mauritania. Nomadic Fula-speaking groups in Niger include the Bororo and the Wodaabe, while in Senegal, the Tukulor are a Fula-speaking ethnic group who have been Muslims for nearly a thousand years.

With their wide geographical distribution and considerable cultural diversity (most fundamentally between the traditional cattle herders – the Fula stereotype – and the urban communities) it's hard to generalize about **Fula music**. There are, however, two distinct genres. The first is pure Fula music, composed and played by them or their recognized professional musicians; the second consists of the hymns and songs which, though mostly still in the Fula language, have been passed down and evolved from the Islamic tradition.

TRADITIONS AND INSTRUMENTS

There are three **classes of professional musician** in Fula society. The **wammbaabe** and the **maabube** were, and in some cases still are, court musicians, singing the praises of chiefs and wealthy patrons and telling tales of their ancestors and epic stories of the Fula past. The **awlube** are less closely associated with the court and more often found praising and entertaining the people in general, using a wider frame of reference and a wider range of **instruments**. The instrument used most by the *wammbaabe* and *maabube* is the **hoddu**, a three-stringed lute. The *wammbaabe* also play the **nyaanyooru**, a one-stringed fiddle. The *awlube* play everything, but their main instruments are drums.

In some areas – for example The Gambia, where Fula live in proximity to Mandinka – you also find a three- or four-stringed lute, the **bolon**, very similar to the Mandinka *bolombato*. At the other end of West Africa, in Cameroon, the instruments used in Fula court music are similar to those used by the Hausa court musicians of Nigeria.

Professional troupes – and the Fula are famous for their bands of entertainers, which play in all communities – nearly always use at least one **percussion** instrument. The most common is the **horde**, a half-gourd vessel with a rattling metal plate attached inside. The player holds the open end towards his chest and beats the outside with his hands or uses rings on his fingers. The *horde* player is usually the acrobat of the troupe. Another percussive instrument is the **lala**, a pair of L-shaped stick-rattles. Each one has three or four calabash discs which move up and down on the stick.

Lastly, the **instruments of the pastoral Fula** – flutes of wood, bamboo or corn stalks, two-stringed lutes, single-stringed fiddles and jew's harps – are mainly played for their own enjoyment. They have a range of songs for pleasure, similar to that of many other African peoples – work songs, lullabies, love songs and herders' songs (often in praise of cattle, sung at them as they graze).

MODERN FULA SOUNDS – WASSOULOU

Of modern Fula music, try to hear **Dourah Barry** from Guinea, and the stunning voice of **Sali Sidibé** from the **Wassoulou** region of southwest Mali. The people of Wassoulou do not have jelis, and their music is based on an ancient tradition of hunters' songs, with pentatonic (five-note) melodies. This tends to be viewed as music played by people in their teens: only a few decades ago such songs were regarded as slightly subversive, and forbidden by the elders. Sali Sidibe uses traditional instruments like the *nyaanyooru* and *bolon*, which create a hypnotic bass beat, together with what sounds like a Casio keyboard complete with drum machine.

◉ *The Wassoulou Sound: Women of Mali* and *The Wassoulou Sound: Vol. 2* (Stern's, UK). Excellent compilations featuring a range of female voices and Wassoulou styles, including the pioneers of "Wassoulou electric", Kagbe Sidibé and Coumba Sidibé. Buy the CDs as a set as the notes were written for both.

Sali Sidibé

Sali Sidibé, an influential Wassoulou singer and a former member of Mali's Ensemble National, has a wonderfully earthy and emotive voice and has created her own firmly traditional brand of Wassoulou. Her ensemble includes the large Senufo bala, the four-string bolon bass harp, and the single-string Fula horsehair fiddle, the soku.

◉ *Wassoulou Foli* (Stern's, UK). A medium-tech, but enjoyable outing.

Oumou Sangaré

The best-known exponent of the Wassoulou sound, whose passionate style ("I sing of love, not praises") has shaken up the musical status quo in Mali, still largely dominated by the fat-cat jelis and Paris-based elite.

◉ *Ko Sira* (World Circuit, UK). A breath of fresh air from a young woman singer whose impact on traditional musical culture could hardly have been greater, wielding her voice like a weapon, and deploring, as she puts it, the male-dominated status quo. Beautifully produced, this is Wassoulou music at its best.

◉ *Worotan* (World Circuit, UK). On her most ambitious album yet, Sangaré defies tradition with her lyrics ("Marry you? Why?!"), custom with her musical arrangements (Pee Wee Ellis and others adding funky horn grooves) and stereotyping with her range.

MAURITANIA

Until the ethnic conflict of 1989, it was easier to hear Mauritanian music in Senegal than in its homeland. This situation has now changed but it's still true that very little Mauritanian music is heard outside the region.

The professional musical caste in Mauritania are called **igaouen** or *iggiw*. In the past they depended, like the jelis, on the patronage of big men and nobles. The more flexible modern *igaouen* repertoire includes complex songs of Middle Eastern character and others simple enough to be taken up in chorus by the audience.

The music is based on a sophisticated modal system – known as the "black and white ways" – derived from Arab musical theory.

◉ *Mauritanie Vols 1 and 2 – Anthologie de la Musique Maure/Hodh Oriental* (Ocora, France). Concentrates on the black and white ways for solo instruments and voice.

◉ *Saharawis* (NubeNegra, Spain). Stunningly packaged 4-CD set of music and images (one of the CDs is a CD-ROM) from the people of the Western Sahara refugee camps in Algeria. Complete with colour booklet, detailed liner notes and recordings old and new, this is instructive, hauntingly beautiful – and even funky at times.

Khalifa Ould Eide and Dimi Mint Abba

Khalifa and Dimi, together with Dimi's two daughters, were the first Mauritanian group to tour in the English-speaking world, in the mid-1980s.

◉ *Moorish Music from Mauritania* (World Circuit, UK). A beautiful and evocative CD – if you haven't seen them on tour then this gives some insight into their special sound. Notice the flamenco-style hand-clapping.

Malouma

Malouma is in a league of her own, a hereditary *ardine*-playing griot and modern singer at the same time, who mixes the Senegalese *mbalax* style with her own Moorish traditions, and while singing exclusively in the Hassaniya dialect of Arabic, shows no obedience to Moorish musical strictures.

◉ *Desert of Eden* (Shanachie, US). Compared with the recordings of most of her compatriots, this jazz-inflected debut CD is highly accessible. The *ardin* shines through to distinctive effect.

Tahra

Born in Nema in southeastern Mauritania in 1959, Tahra Mint Hembara is a hereditary griot (her aunt was the famous Lekhdera Mint Ahmed Zeidane, who has been steeped in Moorish musical tradition since the age of ten.

◉ *Yamen Yamen* (EMI, France). Released in 1989, with Jean-Philippe Rykiel on synth, this tested the stretchability of classic musical traditions on the world stage. An intriguing album of Mooro-tech.

SENEGAL AND THE GAMBIA

Senegal and The Gambia share a common musical heritage and are heavily influenced by the traditions of the Mande heartland to the east. You're most likely to hear Wolof, Fula, Tukulor (Toucouleur) and Serer music north of the Gambia River, and Mandinka, Jola and Balanta music in The Gambia itself and the Casamance region of southern Senegal.

FOLK MUSIC OF SENEGAMBIA

In the south, listen out for the huge double xylophones or **balo** of the **Balanta**, played by two people facing each other. You may hear them, but you'll have difficulty seeing them, because they're invariably surrounded by a jostle of whooping and clapping women.

The best-known **drums** are the Wolof **tama** and **sabar** (both used to great effect by Youssou Ndour and his band). Drums of all shapes and sizes are in great abundance in the Senegambia region and are the only instruments that can be played by absolutely anyone. Wrestling matches are fine opportunities to hear some first-class drumming – in snatches. The wrestlers bring their own drummers to support them and the drum teams jog and pace around the arena, competing with each other with cacophonous dedication.

MODERN SENEGAMBIAN MUSIC

Modern music in the region is essentially Senegalese, largely because of the country's cultural domination of the tiny Gambia and the inevitable magnetism for musicians of Dakar's big audiences and serious money.

The scene has been dominated for some years by the soaring voice of **Youssou Ndour** backed by his band, the **Super Etoile de Dakar**. Youssou plays **mbalax**, a style rooted in the Wolof tradition, featuring frenetic rhythms with bursts of *tama* (battered by **Assane Thiam**) and complex time signatures.

◉ *Streets of Dakar – Génération Boul Falé* (Stern's, UK). Gutsy, invigorating overview of the current scene, showcasing a wealth of emerging artists, from the earthy neo-traditional sounds of Fatou Guewel and Gambian kora duo Tata and Salaam to rap and super-charged *nouveau mbalax* from Assane Ndiaye and Lemzo Diamono.

Youssou Ndour

One of the outstanding African music stars of his generation, yet when he's in Senegal, Youssou still plays at his club, the *Thiossane* in Dakar, at least once a week in order to keep in touch with his core audience. Youssou's huge body of work is patchy, varied and fascinating, continually reworked to cater to the separate demands of his markets at home, in France and in the English-speaking world.

ⓒ *Etoile de Dakar Vols 1–4* (Stern's, UK). The collected works of one of Senegal's seminal bands, featuring Youssou Ndour. Near-essential.

ⓒ *Immigrés* (Earthworks, UK). Homage to Senegalese migrant workers, this mid-period cassette, lovingly remastered for CD, has great warmth and an unusually open-ended feel. Mid-price and good value.

ⓒ *The Guide* (Sony/Columbia, US). Probably his most successful attempt at giving *mbalax* the big budget, international treatment. Containing many moods, it seems uncertain in places, but the single "7 Seconds" (with Neneh Cherry) certainly found an audience.

ⓒ *Gainde: Voices from the Heart of Africa* (World Network, Germany). With Yandé Codou Sène, the *grande dame* of Serer song (and her daughters) creating a a haunting polyphony, directed by Youssou and joined on several tracks by him. A unique CD.

Baaba Maal

The rising star of Senegalese music, who sings in the Tukulor language (a dialect of Fula), accompanied by guitarist Mansour Seck and electric band Dande Lenol (which means "The Voice of the People").

ⓒ *Firin' in Fouta* (Mango, UK). An exciting slab of Afro-modernism. British producer Simon Emmerson finds Celtic resonances and enlists salsa hornmen and Wolof ragga merchants. A highpoint of its kind.

ⓒ *Djam Leelii* (Palm Pictures, UK). Playing acoustic guitar and singing with childhood friend, Mansour Seck, Baaba Maal interprets the traditional tunes and themes of the Senegal River region where he was born. Music to be transported by.

ⓒ *Lam Toro* (Mango, UK) is the most personal of all Maal's albums, dedicated to his mother who died young but who remains the guiding spirit in all his art.

Orchestre Baobab

Formed in 1971 by saxophonist Issi Cissokho and vocalist Laye M'Boup, Baobab were one of the first groups to use Wolof and Mandinka songs as the basis for electric music. If you find any old Baobab tapes, buy them; you won't be disappointed.

ⓒ *Pirate's Choice* (World Circuit, UK). Blissfully good 1982 session from the best Senegalese band of the 1970s. How did they come up with these fantastic songs? The *On Verra Ça* collection (also World Circuit, UK) is almost as hot.

Thione Seck

The one-time singer with Baobab has been building a reputation in Europe for his rousing, up-tempo *mbalax*, with his band, Raam Daan.

UNESCO (local cassette, Senegal). Offering the bravest *mbalax* in the business with almost hysterically up-tempo rhythms against his robust, measured vocals, Seck is a musician's musician *par excellence*.

Super Diamono de Dakar

They call their style Afro-feeling music. Quite different from *mbalax*, Super Diamono go for a much harder sound with heavy bass and powerful kit drums. The "people's band" of Dakar's proletarian suburbs, Diamono mixed reggae militancy, jazz cool and hardcore traditional grooves. Their influential early incarnations await some enterprising archivist: try to hear the early album, *Ndaxona*, which features the wailing vocals of Omar Pene.

ⓒ *Fari* (Stern's, UK). Two cassettes of material on one CD from the early 1990s when main man Pene had reformed the band with top Dakar session men. A bit smooth for some tastes, but the overall feel is deeply Senegalese.

Cheikh Lô

One of the Baye Fall (one of the dreadlocked guardians of Touba) and a sometime drummer with the band Xalam, Lô had to wait years before finally finding a chance with Youssou Ndour's local studio.

ⓒ *Ne la Thiass* (World Circuit, UK). Strong songs and a warm organic feel make for joined-up pop with real international appeal. Deservedly a huge hit.

Ismael Lô

Harmonica-player and guitarist, Lô was a member of Super Diamono during their early days in the late 1970s. "Super Diamono's manager asked if I wanted to join them and go with them on tour and I stayed with them for four years. My pay was a packet of cigarettes a day, and if you wanted something like shoes, you asked the boss."

⊙ *Diawar* (Stern's, UK). Features one of Ismael Lô's best tracks, "Sophia", a 1989 interpretation of the song "On Verra Ça" previously recorded by Orchestra Baobab.

Ifang Bondi

Standard bearers for Gambian music since their 1960s incarnation as the Super Eagles.

⊙ *Gis gis* (MW, Holland). Their most recent and best album employs Fula and Mandinka sounds from young traditional musicians in a very modern context.

GUINEA-BISSAU

Guinea-Bissau's special music is *gumbe*. It combines a contemporary sound with the ten or more musical traditions that survive in the area. It has been compared to samba, though it's much more polyrhythmic.

Gumbe is a catchall word for music in Guinea-Bissau. But it's just one of several Kriolu mixtures of ethnic and modern culture. In Bissau city you also find *tina* and *tinga* – more acoustic than *gumbe*, with lots of spoons and calabashes. And there are other more ethnic styles like *kussundé* and *broxa* from the Balanta people; *djambadon* from the Mandinga people; and *kundere* from the remote Bijagos islands.

Gumbezarte

The most interesting new band to emerge from Bissau. Led by the witty and inventive Maio Coopé who is irresistible on stage, this multicultural group includes veterans from Cobiana Djazz and Mama Djombo (Miguelinho N'simba and Narciso Rosa) as well as young talents like Sanha N'Tamba on bass and Ernesto da Silva on drums.

⊙ *Gumbezarte Camba Mar* (Balkon Zuid, Guinea-Bissau; Lusafrica, France). A 1998 release, with *gumbe* in the name and is several of the songs, but the album is really an electrifying tour of lesser known music styles, including *kussundé* and *djambadon*. No synths or drum machines; the album was mixed as the group wanted it to be, with lovely shifting rhythms.

Kabá Mané

Born into the Beafada – a Mande people – Mané is master of a variety of ethnic styles. He learned the kora when young and plays electric guitar in kora style.

⊙ *Best of Kabá Mané* (Mélodie, France). This has good tracks from Mané's delightfully infectious *Chefo Mae Mae* album – in the *kussundé* rhythm of the Balanta people, this was the first to dent overseas charts – and its equally seductive follow-up, *Kunga Kungake*.

Ramiro Naka

Naka is an exuberant talent who makes *gumbe* rock without destroying its uniqueness. Though living in Paris, he remains very popular in Bissau.

⊙ *Salvador* (Mango, UK). Showcase album with material ranging from upfront rock on the title track to Kriolu/Cape Verdean inflection on "Tchon Tchoma" and "Rabo de Padja" and an appealingly offbeat roots sound on "Nha Indimigo".

CÔTE D'IVOIRE

Côte d'Ivoire, with Abidjan's high-quality studios, has long been a musical centre for the Francophone states, but has very few international stars of its own. But Ivoirians have no lack of traditions to call upon. In the north the Senoufo and Lobi people are famous for their xylophone music; while in the centre and east, the Akan peoples – Baoulé, Abron, Agni and Atié – together with the Bété of the southwest, have produced most of Côte d'Ivoire's popular musicians. All have strong, under-recognized, folk music heritages.

In the 1940s, there were **Akan street groups** who played a traditional dance called **akpombo**. Gradually they started introducing guitars and accordions to their line-up. After independence it was these street groups that became the first popular dance bands. In the 1960s these bands would play cover versions of European and American hits over traditional rhythms like the Bété **gbegbe**. The best-known groups of the day were **Agnebi Jazz, Souers Comoé, Anoma Barou Felix** and, much later, **Ernesto Djedjé**, who updated the Bété dance, the *ziglibithy*.

⊙ *Anthology of World Music: the Dan* (International Institute for Traditional Music/Rounder US). Rare insight into the music of one of the country's most culturally exciting ethnic groups. The detailed booklet documents their music culture as it was in the early 1960s. Songs, percussion and an amazing orchestra of six ivory trumpets.

⊙ *Côte d'Ivoire Compil* (Syllart, France). Highly danceable and recommended, including tracks by Meiway, François Lougha, Jimmy

Hyacinthe and an excellent Monique Seka number, "Missoumwa".

ⓒ *Maxi Ivoire* (Déclic, France). Two-CD compilation released in 1997 showing a wide panorama of Abidjan's productions. Moving from Afro-zouk star Monique Seka to king of *polihet* (a variation of *ziglibithy*) Gnaore Djimi, it also includes music from popular young *zouglou* band, Les Poussins Chocs.

ⓒ *Super Guitar Soukous* (Hemisphere EMI, UK). A fine album with a misleading title, as the best tracks are wild Ivoirian *polihet*. Just listen to Zoukunion's "N'Nanale"!

Alpha Blondy

Seydou Koné was struck by reggae in the early 1980s while living in New York. Back home, he took the name Alpha Blondy and the first song he ever recorded, "Brigadier Sabari", was an instant hit in 1983. After nearly two decades of stardom, he is still the leader of a powerful West African reggae stream.

ⓒ *Yitzhak Rabin* (Stern's, UK). Blondy's tuneful 1998 album is muddied slightly by dubious "agit-pop" themes, gently espoused in French, English and Dioula.

Angelo

Angelo is Côte d'Ivoire's main rap star – and presenter of the local hip-hop TV show.

ⓒ *Represent* (Showbiz, Côte d'Ivoire). Accomplished rap and ragga sung in English and French, plus some more interesting material in Adioukou using deep traditional percussion and singing styles.

Daouda

Singer and composer who mixes Congolese *soukous* with Cameroonian *makossa* and local rhythms.

ⓒ *Le Sentimental* (Stern's, UK). Slick slush from a superstar crooner. "La Femme de Mon Patron" (a massive hit all over West Africa, and later covered in English) is its one redeeming feature.

Aïcha Koné

Aïcha learned the tricks of her trade in the 1970s as a singer with the Orchestre Radio Television Ivoirienne. Influenced by Miriam Makeba, she is one of the first international female pop singers from Côte d'Ivoire.

ⓒ *Mandingo Live from Côte d'Ivoire* (Weltmusik, Germany). Very solid set of dance-floor grooves, featuring Miriam Makeba's famous paean to pan-Africanism, "Kilimanjaro".

Meiway

Originally from the colonial coastal town of Grand-Bassam, Frederic-Désiré Ehui, alias Meiway, created *zoblazo* in the early 1990s, borrowing dance rhythms from his Apolo people's traditions, but making abundant use of digital instruments. He has created a powerful stage act with his group Zo Gang.

ⓒ *200% Zoblazo* (Sonodisc, France). A club and radio hit all over West Africa when first released in 1991, it remains a classic dance-floor wake-up remedy.

Le Zagazougou

Zagazougou's style derives from a country, happy-go-lucky music invented during the first half of the century. In 1990, it was reintroduced, entirely refreshed, to modern audiences and was just as readily adopted once again.

ⓒ *Zagazougou Coup* (Piranha, Germany). Côte d'Ivoire unplugged: all accordions and percussion, and very, very fast.

BURKINA FASO

Very little Burkinabe music reaches the ears of other West Africans, let alone Europeans. Yet the country has a rich musical heritage and an annual percussion festival in Bobo-Dioulasso.

A few **traditional groups** have made tours of Europe. Dance is an important part of their acts so they tend to get booked at outdoor festivals.

Farafina

The musicians of Farafina have been touring Europe and America since the mid-1980s, driving the public to dance to their complex but clearly structured polyrhythms. Apart from the balafon they also use the *djembe*, *tama* (the Wolof hourglass drum), *bara* (calabash drums) and flutes.

ⓒ *Faso Denou* (Real World, UK). Feel the percussive power of the two balafons (xylophones), *bara*-skinned open calabash, *doumdou'ba* tall drums and voluble *djembe*.

Les Frères Coulibaly

The Coulibaly "griot" family belongs to the Bwa people living in the north of Burkina. Brothers Souleyman, Lassina and Ousséni lead a standard percussion orchestra with *djembe, bara, tama* and *kenkeni* drums, *barafile* rattle, balafon xylophone and *kamele ngoni* harp-lute.

CD *Musiques du Burkina Faso & du Mali* (Musiques du Monde/Buda, France). Features brother Lassina Coulibaly with his traditional acoustic group Yan Kadi Faso. Beautiful kora playing is the standout, but there's also a great balafon duet "Massoum pien".

GHANA

Ghana's "town music" is well known abroad but the country has a strong tradition of rural music still commonly performed, which continues to influence urban sounds.

GHANAIAN TRADITIONAL MUSIC

The main types of music you can hear are **court music** played for chiefs, **ceremonial music** and **work songs** – and of course music for its own sake. It's probably clearest to explain traditions region by region.

Northeastern Ghana is home to a cluster of Voltaic-speaking peoples – best known of whom are the **Dagomba, Mamprusi** and **Frafra**. In this area you find mostly fiddles, lutes and wonderful hourglass talking-drum ensembles. It's customary for musicians to perform frequently for the local chief – in the Dagomba country each Monday and Friday. In towns like **Tamale** and **Yendi** you might find something going on, because professional musicians, although attached to chiefs, regularly perform for the general public. Dagomba drummers are always a great spectacle, their flowing tunics fanning out as, hands flying, they dance the *takai*.

GHANAIAN INSTRUMENTS

NORTHEAST
Gonge One-stringed fiddle.
Kologo Two-stringed lute.
Donno Talking drums, in an ensemble.

EWE
Sogo and kidi Drums.
Atsimewu Master drum.
Axatse Rattles.
Gankogui Double bells.

ASANTE
Atumpane Sets of twin drums.
Ntahera Ensemble of ivory horns.

In the northwest, the main instrument of the **Lobi, Wala, Dagarti** and **Sissala** is the xylophone – either played alone or with a small group of drums and percussion instruments. Finger bells and ankle bells are often worn by the dancers.

The **Ewe** are the main people of eastern Ghana. Their music is closer to the traditions of Togo and Benin than to that of other Ghanaian peoples and with their enthusiasm for music associations and dance clubs they've developed many different kinds of recreational music.

In the southern part of central Ghana the **Akan** peoples, notably the **Asante** and **Fante**, have an elaborate court music using large drum ensembles and groups of horns. Another great spectacle is that of the huge log xylophones played in **asonko**, a form of recreational music.

PALM-WINE MUSIC

Palm-wine is the popular music of the Asante. Primarily solo guitar music, it originated in the palm-wine bars – usually under a big tree. A musician would turn up with his guitar and play for as long as people wanted to buy him drinks. This is very much good-time music and such palm-wineists tend to be comedians as well as parodists of the local scene.

Palm-wine guitar music is slowly dying out partly because musicians are being enticed into the guitar bands and concert party groups, and partly due to the lack of instruments in Ghana. In any town someone will be able to point you in the direction of a palm-wine player but you may have to find an instrument for him to play on. Buy the man a drink and you may well find your name included in the current song.

GHANAIAN HIGHLIFE

Highlife originated in Ghana and Sierra Leone and has proved to be one of the most popular and enduring African styles. Originally a fusion of traditional percussion and melodies, with European influences like brass bands, sea shanties and hymns, it started in the early 1920s with the growth of major ports along the West African coast. The term itself is no more than a reference to the kind of European-derived evening of dressing up and dancing (the "highlife") to which new immigrants to the towns of West Africa between the wars were quite unaccustomed – but which they soon made their own.

The first 78rpm records were released in the 1930s and highlife's international reputation started to grow. There are about a dozen **different styles of highlife** but the two main ones are the guitar band and dance band styles. Guitar band highlife is basically a more organized, less horizontal form of palm-wine music. It became known as concert party when exponents added other elements – dance routines and comic turns. "Dance band" highlife, in its extreme form, was all toppers and tails and as much brass as possible. There's a wonderful highlife variation in "Gospel Highlife" – do everything possible to hear something recorded by the **Genesis Gospel Singers**.

⊙ *Classic Highlife* (OsibiSounds, Germany). A veritable *tour de force* featuring the very best of late 1980s and early 1990s international highlife – Crentsil, Agyeman, Darko and, almost inevitably, Osibisa. Required listening for anyone who thought that highlife died in the 1970s.

⊙ *I've Found My Love* (Original Music, US). Guitar band highlife from the 1950s and 1960s. Relaxed shuffles based on the prototype highlife tune, "Yaa Amponsah".

E.T. Mensah

The "King of Highlife", Mensah had a musical childhood and developed his skills on the guitar, organ, sax and trumpet. During World War II he came into contact with British and American styles like calypso, swing and cha-cha, and in 1948 he formed the Tempos Band, then the only professional dance band in Ghana. After a string of hits, including "Donkey Calypso", "School Girl" and "All for You", the group went international with frequent tours of West Africa – a golden age of highlife. Soon there were hundreds of bands imitating their style and, in the 1950s and 1960s, a host of exciting groups including The Uhurus, Broadway and the Black Beats. Mensah's popularity declined during the 1970s, but he made a comeback towards the end of the decade.

⊙ *All For You* (RetroAfic, UK). All the classics from the 1950s are here, including the wacky "Inflation Calypso", "Sunday Mirror" and the title track. Never mind the crackles, everyone likes it.

African Brothers International Band

Formed in 1963 by Nana Kwame Ampadu, and still one of the country's most innovative and enduring guitar groups. They had their earliest and one of their best-loved hits in 1967 with "Ebi Tie Ye" – a plea for democracy in the dark days following the fall of Nkrumah – and had released over 100 discs

before 1970 and the release of their first LP. Since then they've released over twenty albums and countless singles. Always a group to mix street wisdom with thinly veiled political comment, they never let this interfere with good music, and are forever trying something new. During the 1970s they experimented with a variety of styles including reggae, rumba and what they called Afro-hili, a James Brown-inspired beat which was a challenge to Fela Kuti's Afrobeat.

⊙ *Agatha* (BNELP01, Ghana only). A West African hit in 1981, this was perhaps their best album – although their singles of the mid-1960s and late 1970s would give any band a run for their money.

King Bruce & the Black Beats

King Bruce (1922–77), was a major figure of the classic highlife era, a trumpeter who formed the Black Beats, the first of a string of successful dance bands in Accra, in the early 1950s.

⊙ *Golden Highlife Classics from the 1950s and 1960s* (RetroAfric, UK). Superb introduction to the sound of Ghana nearly half a century ago – all laid-back grooves and claves and slightly pear-shaped horns.

Koo Nimo (Daniel Amponsah)

Guitarist who has done as much as anyone to enrich and preserve Ghana's traditional guitar music. Now in his late fifties, he still performs regularly at concerts and festivals with his all-acoustic Adadam band and commands huge respect among Ghanaians at home and abroad.

⊙ *Osabarima* (Adasa/Stern's, UK). Now acknowledged as one of the masters of palm-wine music, Koo Nimo originally recorded this in 1976, his only commercial recording to date.

A.B. Crentsil's Sweet Talks

One of Ghana's most successful highlife bands in the 1970s. The group gained national popularity after a string of hit albums, the first of which was *Adam and Eve*. In 1978 they went to the US and recorded their classic *Hollywood Highlife Party*.

⊙ *The Lord's Prayer* (Stern's African Classics, UK). Classic reissue of 1970s gospel-style highlife and a serious lesson in sexy religiosity – the opening bars of the title track lift you straight onto your feet. Just great.

Osibisa

Formed in London by three Ghanaians: Teddy Osei, Mac Tontoh and Sol Amarfino. Their Afro-rock singles climbed the British charts in the 1970s with three of them, "Dance the Body Music", "Sunshine Day" and "Coffee Song", rising to the top ten. Perhaps they were five years too early, but by the time Sunny Ade was making headlines with undiluted juju, they had melted away.

ⓒ *Fire – Hot Flashback Vol 1* (Red Steel, UK). All the hits are here from "The Coffee Song" to "Sunshine Day". If you're too young to remember what all the fuss was about, move heaven and earth for this collection. Red Steel have also reissued all seven original LP recordings on CD.

Alex Konadu

Today the uncrowned king of guitar band highlife, Konadu plays music firmly rooted in Ghanaian traditions and has enjoyed massive sales all over West Africa. He claims to have played in every town and village in Ghana.

ⓒ *One Man Thousand Live in London* (World Circuit, UK). The master of sweaty, good-time music – infectious tunes that come back to you months later.

TOGO

Traditional music tends to split into two: Kabyé in the north, "Ghanaian Folk Music", and Ewe/Mina in the south.

The **Kabyé** have a rich musical culture. Some of the most interesting instruments are only used for special celebration, like the **picancala**, a xylophone-like instrument made of stones and rocks – a "lithophone" – and the unusual **water flutes**. There's music played on horns, flutes and whistles and even a trumpet – the **xokudu** – made from the fruit of the baobab tree.

Ocora has an album of Kabyé music. There's a less recherché selection on *Togo: Music from West Africa* on Rounder Records, released a few years back, which has a good mixture of traditional and modern styles and features some nice acoustic guitar songs from **Ali Bawa**.

Modern music in Togo has not thrown up any great stars and most of the few singers seem content to imitate external styles. Togo's urban music was greatly influenced by Congolese styles during the 1960s and 1970s and reggae, soul, highlife and Latin music have all dominated the local scene at some time or other.

Bella Bellow was the leading singer in the late 1960s. She toured Europe and America and made an album, with the help of **Manu Dibango**,

Album Souvenir which is on Safari Ambience. **Afia Mala** recorded an album in 1984 called Lonlon Viye.

King Mensah

Mensah Ayaovi Papavi has performed on stage since he was nine years old. A singer with Les Dauphins de la Capitale, he is also a storyteller, has been part of the Ki-Yi M'Bock Theatre in Abidjan, and is today the most popular musician in Togo.

ⓒ *Madjo* (Bolibana, France). Driven by powerful percussion deeply rooted in African traditions, King Mensah's music, moving from Afrobeat to reggae, is also strongly influenced by jazz and jazz-rock.

BENIN

Benin has a variety of cultures and a diverse musical tradition, with the Hausa, Kabyé and Bariba in the north, and the Yoruba, Gun and Fon people in the south. The music of the Fon played a crucial ceremonial role in the court at Abomey, capital of the country's major pre-colonial state Dan-Homey. The Gun people use a wide variety of instruments including a huge double log xylophone, percussion pots and raft zithers. Benin's best-known musical export, however, is the dynamic voice of Angélique Kidjo.

Modern music of Benin mixes indigenous rhythms and melodies with Congolese styles. During the 1970s Benin's popular music scene was severely impeded by government curfews, but orchestras carried on somehow, the most successful being **Orchestre Poly-Rythmo**, led by horn player **Ignace de Souza**, **Disc Afrique** and **Les Astronauts**.

Angélique Kidjo

A singer of extraordinary power and grace, Kidjo is the first African woman since Miriam Makeba to achieve real international stardom. An irrepressible figure, she hates artistic ghettoization ("world rock") and despises purists who would curtail her freedom to record as she likes.

ⓒ *Parakou* (Mango, UK). From 1989, the first and one of the best of her modern output, with stylish arrangements, intriguing percussion and vocals allowed full rein.

ⓒ *Oremi* (Island, UK). This is a remarkable disc for Kidjo, exploring the music of the African diaspora – and, in particular, American R&B. She covers Jimi Hendrix's "Voodoo Child", employs jazz saxophonist Branford Marsalis, and generally funks things up big-time. With South African backing vocals adding timbre and texture, her art has never been more mature and sweetly inspired.

Stan Tohon & the Tchink System

With his wild stage act, Stan has led his Tchink System to popularity all over West Africa, since the late 1970s.

ⓒ *Tchink Attack* (Donna Wana, France). This may lack some of the spontaneous power of the Tchink System's stage performances, but it's a vibrant disc, nonetheless, with some very interesting rhythms on the hit song "Dévaluation".

NIGER

Not much is heard in Europe about music from Niger. A few records of traditional music are available, but little of its modern music travels far.

Niger's major ethnic groups are the **Tuareg**, **Bororo**, **Songhai** and **Hausa**. The Bororo are nomads closely related to the Fula. They have no musical instruments and all their songs are for voices only.

Pop artists you may well hear include Hausa singers **Mahaman Garba** and **Yan Ouwa** – both use mostly percussive backing – and the reggae of **Amadou Hamza**. In Niamey, listen out for the female singer, **Madelle Iddari**, as well as Saadou Bori and Moussa Pousy (their CD is included in the "Hausa" section, on p.1169).

Mamar Kassey

Inspired by Fulani, Hausa, Songhai and Djerma traditional music, Mamar Kassey is the first group from Niger to take their music to an international audience and they can now compete with the best from Mali.

ⓒ *Denké-Denké* (Daqui, France). Flute, lute, percussion, electric guitars and vocals lead you through old legends and tales from the sixteenth century, when the Songhai empire was the leading power in West Africa.

NIGERIA

As far as the music industry is concerned, Nigeria is one of the two or three big hubs of African music. The industry is well developed here, with numerous recording studios and pressing plants and, in spite of reces-sion and poverty, a huge home market. Of more intrinsic interest, Nigeria also has a big enough population to sustain artists who sing in regional languages and experiment with indigenous styles. Drawing from traditional sources and outside influences, three main types of modern music have developed – juju, highlife and fuji. Both juju and fuji are almost entirely sung in local languages, principally Yoruba.

IGBO MUSIC

The Igbo people of the southeast have always been receptive to cultural change. This ease is reflected in their music and in the incredible variety of instruments played in Igboland. No local occasion would be complete without musicians and you should find them at any event associated with the *obi* (chief). The other major occasions would be seasonal festivals, wrestling matches, a visit by a high-ranking official or the funeral of a prominent citizen.

In more traditional communities, royal music is played every day, when the **ufie** slit drum is used to wake the chief and to tell him when meals are ready. A group, known as **egwu ota**, which consists of slit-drums, drums and bells, performs when the *obi* is leaving the palace and again when he returns.

One of the most pleasing Igbo instruments is the **obo**, a thirteen-stringed raft zither, which can be heard at many a nostalgic palm-wine drinking session.

YORUBA MUSIC

Yoruba instrumental traditions are mostly based on drumming. The most popular form of traditional music today is **dundun**, played on hourglass tension drums of the same name. The usual *dundun* ensemble consists of tension drums of various sizes together with small kettledrums called **gudugudu**. The leading drum of the group is the *iyaalu* ("mother of the drums"), which talks by imitating the tone patterns of Yoruba speech. It's used to play out praise poetry, proverbs and other oral texts. Another important part of Yoruba musical life is **music theatre**, which mixes traditional music with storytelling or live drama.

JUJU

The origins of *juju* music are not very clear, but it's said to have emerged as a Lagosian variation of palm-wine music. The word *juju* is thought to be a corruption of the **Yoruba** word *jo jo*, meaning "dance" – or may just be a dismissive epithet coined by colonial officers and retained, defensively, by its exponents. The first records of this dreamy style started coming out in the early 1930s but it really took off just after World War II with the introduction of amplified sound. The major stars of the prewar period were **Irewolede Denge** ("grandfather of *juju*") and **Tunde King**; and after the war, **Ayinde Bakara** and the **Jolly Orchestra**.

The **1960s** saw the emergence of a great number of new *juju* singers and bands. Three came to dominate the scene; **IK Dairo**, **Ebenezer Obey** and, in the later 1960s, **Sunny Ade**. During and after the Nigerian civil war (1967–70) *juju* thrived at home as highlife artists from the eastern region either went to Biafra or fled abroad, and highlife as a whole lost its popularity.

ⓒ *Juju Roots, 1930s–1950s* (Rounder, US). Excellent introduction to the early *juju* years, with comprehensive sleeve notes, featuring Irewolede Denge, Tunde King and Ojoge Daniel.

I.K. Dairo

Dairo had been playing in bands for a good part of his life when he formed the Morning Star Orchestra in 1957. By 1961, he had set up the popular Blue Spots and rose to become the best-known *juju* player in Nigeria.

ⓒ *Juju Master* (Original Music, USA). Singer, composer and band leader, Dairo was responsible for the consolidation of *juju* music among the Yoruba and introduced the accordion to the style. A classic round-up of Decca West Africa 45s.

ⓒ *Ashiko* (Xenophile/Green Linnet, US). Dairo in tune, at last. The talking drums are really speaking here.

Ebenezer Obey

Obey formed his first group, The International Brothers, in 1964. Since then the man-mountain has released over fifty LPs. The success of his blend of talking drums, percussion and guitar had already caught on by the time he renamed his group The InterReformers in 1970. With guaranteed advance sales of over 100,000 records, he went international in 1980. With over fifty albums to his credit and enjoying a new lease of life in his middle age, Obey maintains an immensely loyal following for his infectious, danceable *juju*.

ⓒ *Ju Ju Jubilation* (Hemisphere/EMI, UK). Satisfyingly bluesy, slightly offbeat *juju* music from the man who has released dozens of albums and, whose expansive features and rather right-wing, Christian image, are in contrast to rival *juju* artist Sunny Ade.

King Sunny Ade

Ade started his musical career playing with highlife bands in Lagos before making the transition to *juju*. He went solo in 1966 when he formed The Green Spots, and struck gold with Challenge Cup the following year. He changed the name of the group to the African Beats in 1974 and released hit albums including *The Late General Murtala Muhammed*, *Sound Vibration* and *The Royal Sound*. By the end of the decade, Ade was one of the most popular musicians in the country. In the 1980s he broke into the international scene with tours of Europe, Japan and the US, and signed to Island records, with whom he released three albums. Nearly two decades on, he's still flying high.

ⓒ *Juju Music* (Island, UK). The record that launched a million passions for African sounds. Still wonderful after all these years, *Juju Music* includes many of Ade's best songs, among them the sweet "365 is My Number". If the Velvet Underground had been African, this is how they might have sounded.

On Bobby (Sunny Alade, Nigeria). Probably the best *juju* album of all time – Ade runs through all the classic riffs in a flowing 1983 tribute to legendary band leader Bobby Benson.

Synchro System (Island, UK). Classic album, also from 1983, but a more measured approach to the western market. With Ade back on the international circuit, someone must surely bring this masterpiece into the CD age.

APALA AND FUJI

Though never knowing the international success of *juju* and highlife, the wall-of-percussion sound of *fuji* has been popular in Nigeria since the 1970s. It has its roots in the Yoruba styles of *apala* and *sakara*, themselves products of Muslim influence on older musical forms, such as there were, in northern Yorubaland.

One of Nigeria's greatest *apala* performers, **Haruna Ishola**'s music helped pave the way for *fuji*. Before he died in 1983, he had produced some 25 LPs and opened his own recording studio. It's still relatively easy to find many of his later records like *Apala Songs*.

Sikiru Ayinde "Barrister"

The leading Yoruba *fuji* singer, Barrister started singing *were*, the singing alarm clock songs performed for early breakfast and prayers during Ramadan, at the age of ten. After a brief army career, he turned back to music and, in the early 1970s, formed the Supreme Fuji Commander, a 25-piece outfit. They soon became one of Nigeria's top bands, firing off a battery of hit records. One time rival of Ayinla Kollington but now peacefully co-existing in a market big enough for both, Barrister started life as a *were* musician before poverty drove him into the army.

Ⓟ *New Fuji Garbage* (GlobeStyle, UK). A recording which is likely to define *fuji* for Western ears for years to come. Barrister's voice here is slightly mellower than usual and the band surround it with a pounding panoply.

Ayinla Kollington

Fuji's "Man of the People" – the source of social commentary in the Yoruba Muslim music scene – is ranked second in the *fuji* popularity stakes behind Barrister.

Ijoba Ti Tun (KRLPS, Nigeria). Challenging lyrics, driving percussion and a touch of Hawaiian guitar.

NIGERIAN HIGHLIFE

Highlife came to Nigeria from Ghana in the 1950s, but it was quickly moulded by indigenous styles and influences from Cameroon and the Congo so that it came to have a flavour that was unmistakeably Nigerian. Extra polish, and Western instruments – brass sections, electric keyboards and guitars – were added to home-grown rhythms and, by the 1960s, highlife was in the forefront of popular urban music. It lost its universal appeal during the civil war, when it retained mass popularity only in Igboland, and quite quickly lost ground to *juju* among the Yoruba.

Old albums from the early highlife stars are rarities these days although it is still possible to lay your hands on 1970s and 1980s material by the fabulous **Oriental Brothers** (and offshoots Dr Sir Warrior and Kabaka). Meanwhile a steady trickle of rereleases continues to refresh the style.

Oriental Brothers

Originally formed by three virtuoso brothers, Dan Satch, Godwin and Warrior, the Orientals then spawned three of the finest highlife bands ever, dominating the 1970s with hit after hit.

Ⓟ *Heavy on the Highlife: Original Music* (Original Music, US). After dozens of Nigeria-only releases, came this wonderful burn-up of a guitar-highlife album – relentless, sexy grooves.

Prince Nico Mbarga and Rocafil Jazz

It's reckoned Prince Nico sold some thirteen million copies of "Sweet Mother", making it the biggest-selling African song of all time. Hundreds of bands copied it; radio stations played it incessantly; vinyl copies could only be had at twenty times the normal price. If Ade carries the flag for *juju* and the Kutis' Afro-beat will, in time, become a global source sound, then the late Prince Nico will forever be Igbo highlife.

Ⓟ *Aki Special* (Rounder, US). A bumper CD with nearly two LPs' worth on it – including "Sweet Mother" – which makes as good a starting point as any for a collection of Nigerian music.

Sweet mother, I no go forget you,
For the suffer wey you suffer for me, yeah,
Sweet mother, I no go forget you,
For the suffer wey you suffer for me, yeah.

When I de cry, my mother go carry me.
She go say, "My pickin, wetin you de cry?, oh,
Stop, stop, stop, stop, stop, stop
Make you no go cry again, oh".

When I want sleep, my mother go bed me,
She go lie me well well for bed, oh.
She cover me clothes, say "Make you sleep,
Sleep, sleep, my pickin, oh".

AFRO-BEAT

Afro-beat was almost solely the creation of one extraordinary musician, **Fela Anikulapo-Kuti** (1938–97). The style has its own distinctive beats and rhythms which provided a flexible vehicle for Fela's political lyrics and call-and-response vocal style. He chose to sing in the lingua franca of pidgin English to avoid limiting his audience, and his eruptive performances and defiant lifestyle found him huge following and brought him into constant conflict with the Nigerian authorities. A steady stream of hit LPs included *Black President*, *Perambulator*, *Coffin for Head of State* and *Expensive Shit*. Two excellent retrospective collections are available, five CDs from Stern's (UK) and a true collector's edition 10-album boxed set from Barclay (France).

Stern's kicked off with the *69 Los Angeles Sessions* (some vintage numbers from Black Panther days – and ten tracks all under seven minutes make it unique in the Fela oeuvre) and Fela's *London Scene* from the very early days, followed by *Open and Close* (1971) and *He Miss Road* (1975) from the golden middle period, and completing the series with the effervescent *Underground System* (1992) – a combined paean of praise for Kwame Nkrumah, the ultimate African hero, and a renewed verbal assault on Babangida, Abiola and Obasanjo.

Barclay's boxed sets of a dozen classic original vinyl discs take Afro-beat appreciation to a higher level, pulling together key releases from the 1970s, his purplest period. Box 1 includes *Open and Close, Gentleman, Upside Down, Yellow Fever, J.J.D.* and *I.T.T.*, the last being Fela's original attack on Abiola, a reminder of his capacity to know a rogue when he saw one. Box 2 brings together the all-time classics *Shakara* and *Expensive Shit*, before completing the tribute with *Monkey Banana, Na Poi, Sorrow, Blood and Tears* and the lasting critique of dictatorship in Africa, *Authority Stealing*.

Femi Kuti

Fela Kuti's son has had an independent career since the late 1980s with his group, the Positive Force. But only since his father's death in 1997, has his stock really risen.

⊙ *Shoki Shoki* (Polygram, UK). First big internationally promoted release for the son of Fela. Recognisably a Kuti, both in his voice and in the subject matter and lyrics of the songs with their muscular arrangements, but infused with a fresh new dance-floor sensibility which old man Kuti's stoned diatribes never aimed to deliver. Still, from the sweatily explicit "Beng Beng Beng" to the affronted "Victim of Life" he's a chip off the old block.

CAMEROON

In Cameroon there are hundreds of ethnic groups, many of them with a distinctive musical culture and dances. More than two hundred different dances are still performed on a whole range of occasions and the majority are accompanied by instrumental ensembles.

FOLK MUSIC

In the south the **Bakweri, Bamiléké, Bamoun** and **Beti** have mostly xylophone or drum ensem-

bles and their masked dance dramas are well worth seeing. The Sultan of Bamoun's Musical Theatre (see p.1100) is a remarkable institution. Also in the south live the **Bulu, Fang, Eton** and **Mvele**, who play a wide diversity of musical instruments including the **ngkul**, a slit-drum formerly used to send messages but now only to accompany the **ozila** or initiation dance; the **mendzan**, a small xylophone; and the **mvet**, a long stick zither (*mvet* refers not only to the instrument but also the pantomime and dances associated with it). The **Baka** forest people have a range of fascinating instruments, including the earth bow, which uses the forest floor as a resonator.

⊙ *The Baka Forest People: Heart of the Forest* (Hannibal, UK/US). Showcase for the Baka pygmies' extraordinary singing, and their various instruments – inspiration for the group Baka Beyond (whose Martin Cradick recorded this). Seamlessly stringing together trancy instrumental grooves, sploshing water drum sessions, kids' campfire rhymes and, best of all, *yelli* songs that draw you deep into the forest, the selection gives a generous overview of the Bakas' music without descending into ethnomusicology. Everyone on it gets a cut of the royalties.

Francis Bebey

Africa's "Renaissance Man", Bebey has worked his way through jazz and most of his country's roots music. A multi-instrumentalist and musicologist, amongst other things, he defies categorization, singing in English, French and Douala, experimenting with styles ranging from classical guitar and traditional rhythms to makossa and regular pop. He has released some twenty albums since 1969 and you never know what you'll find on any of them.

⊙ *Nandolo/With Love – Works 1963–1994* (Original Music, US). A fine sampling of Bebey's talents, from skill on the bamboo flute to wonderful guitar and thumb piano pieces.

MAKOSSA AND OTHER POP MUSIC

Makossa, the pop music of Cameroon, was created in the 1950s but has its roots in the 1930s. Mission schools created their own bands to usher the pupils into assembly, using xylophones and percussion instruments. These bands performed at dances outside school hours, playing a mixture of Western and local styles. Guitars were introduced before the war and guitarists would perform accompanied by a bottle player. There were three main dance styles at the time: *asiko* – percussion and xylophone music; *ambasse bey* – a guitar-based dance with much faster rhythms; and the fledgling *makossa*, a popular folk dance, named after the word for "to strip off".

Although *makossa* endures, other styles are more ephemeral. The huge publicity given to **bikutsi** – the war rhythm of the Beti people zapped up for amps and guitars – in the early 1990s was at least partly due to the ethnic provenance of the president. For a few months it looked as if **Les Têtes Brulées** would make it big on the world stage.

Bend-skin is a new kind of street-credible percussion-led folk music, of which Kouchoum Mbada are the main protagonists. On their album *Bend Skin* (cassette only) they have Sam Fan Thomas on keyboards.

Manu Dibango

Sax-player, composer, singer, pianist and arranger, Dibango's inspirations are diverse. He has lived and recorded in Brussels, Paris, Zaire, the United States, Jamaica and Côte d'Ivoire. He started a whole wave of urban popular music with the release of his album *Soul Makossa* in 1973 (somewhat confusingly named, as it contains nothing that a Cameroonian musician would recognise as *makossa*). This record paved the way for a new generation of artists who now rely on a combination of traditional inspiration and high-tech recording facilities to produce the highly exportable dance music that has turned Douala into one of the dynamos of African music. Now in the superstar class – more than thirty years after his first single – Manu Dibango is one of the few African artists guaranteed to draw a full house anywhere in the world.

ⓒ *Live '91* (Stern's, UK). The catalogue of Africa's foremost jazz sax-player is so vast, it's hard to know where to begin. If you find nothing to please among the eclectic set on this old but representative CD you probably don't like him.

ⓒ *Homemade* (Celluloid/Melodie, France). Classic cuts from the 1970s when Manu was really blowing up his own kind of Afrofusion into a massive sound. Includes the often reprised "Ah Freak son fric".

ⓒ *CubAfrica* (Celluloid/Melodie, France). Mellow versions of Cuban classics, accompanied on acoustic instruments by Cuarteto Patria and Manu's eternal guitar partner, Jerry Malekani.

Sam Fan Thomas

Thomas recorded several albums with minor hits, but had to wait until 1984 and the release of *Makassi* to achieve a wider reputation. The album's single "African Typic Collection" ignited his reputation when it became an international dance hit.

ⓒ *The Best Of Sam Fan Thomas* (TJR, France). Thomas ran out a string of soundalike records following that first big hit and tried to trademark *makassi*. Here we have an hour and a quarter of bright, perky, singalong tunes.

ⓒ *African Typic Collection* (Virgin Earthworks, UK). Four Cameroonian songs (and one stray Cape Verdean number via Paris) packaged around the mega-hit title song. With Charlotte Mbango.

Moni Bilé

Suave but exciting, Bilé maximized the enjoyment potential of *makossa*. He was the most influential artist of the 1980s, and his high-tech productions outsold all others.

ⓒ *10th Anniversary: Best of Moni Bilé* (MAD Productions/Sonodisc, France). Enjoy the mellow growl and revisit those great, dance-floor stirrers, "Bijou" and "O Si Tapa Lambo Lam".

Anne-Marie Nzie

"La voix d'or du Cameroun" started singing at the age of eight and was a national star by the 1950s. Though no longer a chart-topper, she remains one of the most respected and popular female singers in the country, still pumping out robust music with her quavering Piaf-like voice.

ⓒ *Beza Ba Dzo* (Label Bleu, France). Produced by, and featuring, the drum motivation of Brice Wassy, Anne-Marie's second album renders her folklore-based material with power and energy. Her semi-acoustic amalgam of traditional and modern instrumentation, and the variety of rhythms and moods make a welcome change from *makossa*.

Lapiro de Mbanga

Master of Cameroonian rap – a tough blend of politics, rhythm and language: Cameroon's Fela Kuti perhaps, but comfortable with a range of styles from *makossa* to Congolese *soukous*.

ⓒ *Ndinga Man Contre-Attaque: na wou go pay?* (Label Bleu, France). With a hard mix of *makossa*, *zouk*, *soukous* and Afro-beat, Lapiro rebuts the criticism that he sold out to the powers that be.

Les Têtes Brulées

The Têtes Brulées came to Europe on a high note, just when the national football team was showing promise in the 1994 World Cup. Early shows had them playing football on stage. A flash of excitement that has since burnt out.

⊙ *Les Têtes Brulées* (Bleu Caraibes/France). The CD which Stern's licensed, by the band that broke *bikutsi* to the world, now available on French import only. Lots of energy but little depth.

SIERRA LEONE

Although relatively small, Sierra Leone has a rich variety of music and its influence, through the spread of people and ideas from Freetown over the last 200 years, has been large. Elements of early highlife can be traced back to the prewar Krio dance halls. Inland, a much less cosmopolitan scene still prevails: folk music is closely connected with dance, storytelling and drama. Praise songs are also widespread and one unusual characteristic is that male soloists tend to sing in a high register while women sing in low voices.

SIERRA LEONEAN FOLK MUSIC

To list the enormous number of Sierra Leonean **instruments** would take pages. **Thumb pianos** are common in the north, among the Temne, Limba and Loko. **Xylophones and lutes** are used in the north by the Susu, Mandingo, Yalunka, Temne and Koranko. A good selection of traditional music is available on the Ocora label.

MODERN MUSIC OF SIERRA LEONE

In popular music the two main styles, which developed during the 1950s, were acoustic guitar **palm-wine music** (music for drinking with) and **maringa**, a peculiarly Krio style. The *maringa* singer **Ebenezer Calender** was one of the most popular; he played guitar and trumpet and wrote all his own songs. While the Freetown recording industry died in the 1970s, a number of **dance bands** struggle on in concert parties and at public holidays and the odd hotel residence. Local percussive sounds are still popular, but conditions rarely allow for good performances and today the best music is heard abroad.

⊙ *Sierra Leone Music* (Zensor, Germany). Lovingly packaged compilation of Krio and up-country tracks, recorded for the radio in Freetown in the 1950s and early 1960s. A real collector's item with an excellent accompanying booklet.

S.E. Rogie

The doyen of Sierra Leonean musical entertainers picked up the trail led by two great guitarists, Ekundaio and Joboynor, and had hits in the 1960s all along the West African coast. He developed an effortlessly sensual style of palm-wine guitar playing and emigrated to the US in the early 1970s, where he taught and performed. He had sell-out gigs in Britain shortly before his death in 1994.

⊙ *The Palm Wine Sounds of SE Rogie* (Stern's, UK). Includes classics such as the original "Joe Joe Yalal Joe" and "Tourist Girl" – destress music based around guitar, percussion and vocals.

LIBERIA

Liberian music can be put into three rough and ready groups: music of the indigenous people, music from the freed slave tradition of repatriated Africans, and modern, more decultured, popular music. The "Congos" – people with connections with the freed slave heritage – sing a lot of religious music, which bears close comparison with American gospel.

Most indigenous Liberian peoples incorporate "music" within a broader term that describes an event involving music, dancing and celebration. The **Kpelle** call this the **pelee**, and its songs the **wule**. In traditional **Kpelle** and **Gio** culture, a wide variety of flutes, xylophones and drums are used. The coastal **Kru** people also play the guitar and may have been partly responsible for the creation of highlife guitar playing.

Liberian **pop music** was in a parlous state of disarray even before the war. It's hard to say what might be going on there now that a tense peace has been achieved.

Thanks to Dave Muddyman for the version of this article which appeared in the first edition, and to contributors to the 2nd edition of *The Rough Guide to World Music (Vol 1)* for selected passages.

MUSIC BOOKS

Francis Bebey, *African Music: A People's Art* (Lawrence Hill, 1997). First published in French in 1969, this is an excellent and well-illustrated ethnomusicological survey, concentrating on Francophone Africa.

Wolfgang Bender, *Sweet Mother: Modern African Music* (University of Chicago Press, 1991). A cultural history of African urban music. Includes an extensive bibliography and discography.

Simon Broughton, Mark Ellingham and Richard Trillo, eds, *The Rough Guide to World Music: Vol 1 Africa, Europe & the Middle East* (Rough Guides, 1999). Revised, updated and expanded 2nd edition. Detailed articles cover most West African countries individually, together with hundreds of potted artist biographies and CD reviews.

Jenny Cathcart, *Hey You!* (Fine Line Books, UK, 1989). A detailed biography of Youssou Ndour, with translations of many of his lyrics.

Samuel Charters, *The Roots of the Blues* (Da Capo Press, 1991). A bit of a classic, Charters' serendipitous journey (The Gambia, Senegal, Mali) aimed to find the blues' roots in West Africa. While he failed, his other discoveries make great reading.

John Miller Chernoff, *African Rhythm and African Sensibility* (University of Chicago Press, 1981). A travelogue and easy-to-read analysis of Ghanaian drumming, music's spiritual meaning and the place of art in African society. Beautifully written.

John Collins, *Music Makers of West Africa* (Lynne Rienner Publishers, UK; Passegiatta Press, US, first published 1985). A collection of articles and interviews, mostly on highlife and its offspring, by a committed veteran of the Ghana music scene.

Manu Dibango and Danielle Rouard, *Three Kilos of Coffee: An Autobiography* (University of Chicago Press, 1994). West Africa's most famous musician traces his own story from childhood outside Douala to international success.

Graeme Ewens, *Africa O-Yé!* (Da Capo Press, US). The best Africa-only music book published to date, with a mass of colour and black-and-white photos.

Ronnie Graham, *Stern's Guide to Contemporary African Music* (Pluto Press, UK, Vol 1 1988, Vol 2 1992). Invaluable, country-by-country survey of styles, artists and releases. Published in the US as the *Da Capo Guide to Contemporary African Music*.

Chris May and Chris Stapleton, *African Rock: The Pop Music of a Continent* (1989, o/p). A highly readable account of the development of African music's many and diverse strands.

Christopher Alan Waterman, *Juju: A Social History and Ethnography of an African Popular Music* (University of Chicago Press, 1990). A detailed account of the origins, evolution and social significance of *juju*, tracing the roots back more than fifty years.

INDEX

Stay in touch with us!

ROUGH*NEWS* **is Rough Guides' free newsletter. In four issues a year we give you news, travel issues, music reviews, readers' letters and the latest dispatches from authors on the road.**

ROUGH GUIDES: Travel

Amsterdam
Andalucia
Australia

Austria
Bali & Lombok
Barcelona
Belgium &
  Luxembourg
Belize
Berlin
Brazil
Britain
Brittany &
  Normandy
Bulgaria
California
Canada
Central America
Chile
China
Corfu & the
  Ionian Islands
Corsica
Costa Rica
Crete
Cuba
Cyprus
Czech & Slovak
  Republics

Dodecanese
Dominican
  Republic
Egypt
England
Europe
Florida
France
French Hotels &
  Restaurants 1999
Germany
Goa
Greece
Greek Islands
Guatemala
Hawaii
Holland
Hong Kong
  & Macau
Hungary
India
Indonesia
Ireland
Israel & the
  Palestinian
  Territories
Italy
Jamaica
Japan
Jordan

Kenya
Laos
London
London
  Restaurants
Los Angeles
Malaysia,
  Singapore &
  Brunei
Mallorca &
  Menorca
Maya World
Mexico
Morocco
Moscow
Nepal
New England
New York
New Zealand
Norway
Pacific Northwest
Paris
Peru
Poland
Portugal
Prague
Provence & the
  Côte d'Azur
The Pyrenees
Romania

St Petersburg
San Francisco
Sardinia
Scandinavia
Scotland
Scottish Highlands
  & Islands
Sicily
Singapore

South Africa
Southern India
Southwest USA
Spain
Sweden
Syria
Thailand
Trinidad & Tobago
Tunisia
Turkey
Tuscany & Umbria
USA
Venice
Vienna
Vietnam
Wales
Washington DC
West Africa
Zimbabwe &
  Botswana

AVAILABLE AT ALL GOOD BOOKSHOPS

ROUGH GUIDES: Mini Guides, Travel Specials and Phrasebooks

MINI GUIDES

Antigua
Bangkok
Barbados
Big Island of
  Hawaii
Boston
Brussels
Budapest

Dublin
Edinburgh
Florence
Honolulu
Jerusalem
Lisbon
London
  Restaurants
Madrid
Maui
Melbourne
New Orleans
Seattle
St Lucia

Sydney
Tokyo
Toronto

TRAVEL SPECIALS

First-Time Asia
First-Time
  Europe
Women Travel

PHRASEBOOKS

Czech
Dutch

Egyptian Arabic
European
French
German
Greek
Hindi & Urdu
Hungarian
Indonesian
Italian
Japanese

Mandarin
  Chinese
Mexican
  Spanish
Polish
Portuguese
Russian
Spanish
Swahili
Thai
Turkish
Vietnamese

AVAILABLE AT ALL GOOD BOOKSHOPS

ROUGH GUIDES:
Reference and Music CDs

REFERENCE
Classical Music
Classical:
  100 Essential CDs
Drum'n'bass
House Music
Jazz
Music USA

Internet
Millennium

ROUGH GUIDE MUSIC CDs
Music of the
  Andes
Australian
  Aboriginal
Brazilian Music
Cajun & Zydeco

Opera
Opera:
  100 Essential CDs
Reggae
Reggae:
  100 Essential CDs
Rock
Rock:
  100 Essential CDs
Techno
World Music
World Music:
  100 Essential CDs
English Football
European Football

Classic Jazz
Music of
  Colombia
Cuban Music
Eastern Europe

Music of Egypt
English Roots
  Music
Flamenco
India & Pakistan
Irish Music
Music of Japan
Kenya & Tanzania
Native American
North African
Music of Portugal

Reggae
Salsa
Scottish Music
South African
  Music
Music of Spain
Tango
Tex–Mex
West African
  Music
World Music
World Music Vol 2
Music of
  Zimbabwe

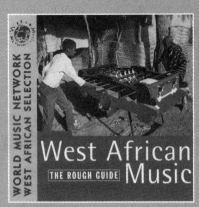

CAPE VERDE TRAVEL
and Eastgate Travel
Tour Operator and Retail Agent
Proprietor : Ron Hughes, P.Q.R.C.
**10 MARKET PLACE, HORNSEA, EAST
YORKSHIRE, HU18 1AW ENGLAND**

Allow us to co-ordinate your travel and business
arrangements, conventions and festivals.
We have a working knowledge of all islands.
Our resources are tried and tested.
Leisure opportunities are many and plentiful.
Appreciate the variety of experiences. Sunshine,
water sports, trekking, mountain walks, bird life,
sailing, diving and cultural understanding.

Entrust your business and leisure
management to us.

Air travel, Ground arrangements, Hotels and
Transport.

We connect world-wide, so from where ever you are
in the World, contact us and let your Cape Verde
experience begin.

E-Mail : eastgatetravel@btinternet.com
Web site : www.capeverdetravel.co.uk
Tel : 00-44(0)1964 - 536191
Fax : 00-44(0)1964 - 536192

ABTA
V9926

ATOL to ATOL UK Tour Operators

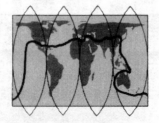